MAP PAGES

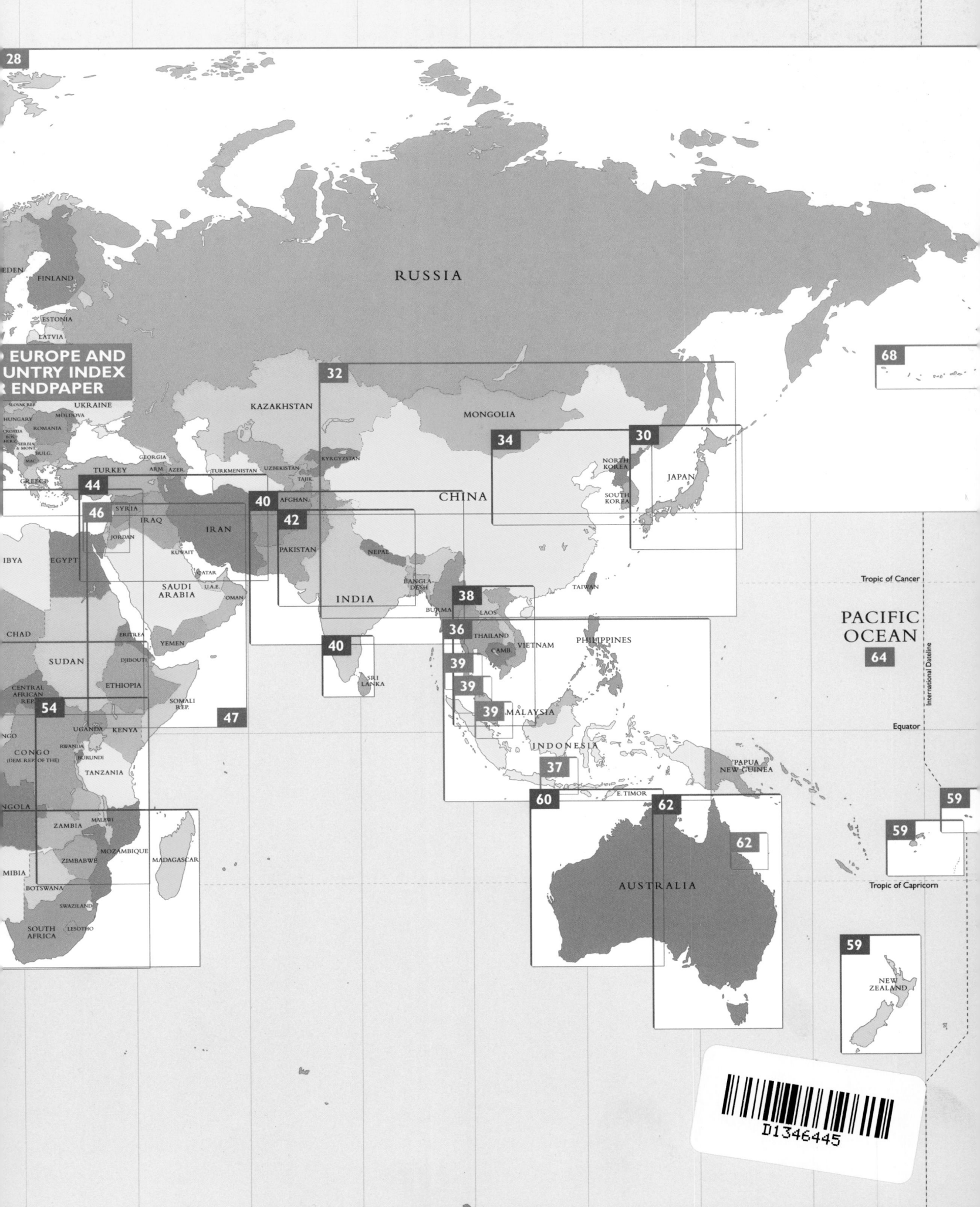

PHILIP'S

WORLD ATLAS

& GAZETTEER

31/3/04

Dear Elisabeth,

Happy Birthday for some time ago!
This is an Atlas published in Great Britain,
printed in Hong Kong & purchased in South
Africa. So it knows what it's talking about.
Happy travels — I'm sure I'll be there
on some of them. And if you ever
get lost — well then — here you are!

Love Simon

CONSULTANTS

Philip's are grateful to the following people for acting as specialist geography consultants on 'The World in Focus' front section:

Professor D. Brunsden, Kings College, University of London, UK
Dr C. Clarke, Oxford University, UK
Dr I. S. Evans, Durham University, UK
Professor P. Haggett, University of Bristol, UK
Professor K. McLachlan, University of London, UK
Professor M. Monmonier, Syracuse University, New York, USA
Professor M-L. Hsu, University of Minnesota, Minnesota, USA
Professor M. J. Tooley, University of St Andrews, UK
Dr T. Unwin, Royal Holloway, University of London, UK

THE GAZETTEER OF NATIONS
Text: Keith Lye

THE WORLD IN FOCUS
Cartography by Philip's

Picture Acknowledgements
NASA/GSFC page 14

Illustrations: Stefan Chabluk

WORLD CITIES
Cartography by Philip's

Page 11, Dublin: The town plan of Dublin is based on Ordnance Survey Ireland by permission of the Government Permit Number 7617. © Ordnance Survey Ireland and Government of Ireland.

Page 11, Edinburgh, and page 15, London: This product includes mapping data licensed from Ordnance Survey® with the permission of the Controller of Her Majesty's Stationery Office. © Crown copyright 2003. All rights reserved. Licence number 100011710.

Vector data: Courtesy of Gräfe and Unser Verlag GmbH, München, Germany
(city centre maps of Bangkok, Beijing, Cape Town, Jerusalem, Mexico City, Moscow, Singapore, Sydney, Tokyo and Washington D.C.)

All satellite images in this section courtesy of NPA Group Limited, Edenbridge, Kent (www.satmaps.com)

Published in Great Britain in 2003
by Philip's,
a division of Octopus Publishing Group Limited,
2–4 Heron Quays, London E14 4JP

Copyright © 2003 Philip's

Cartography by Philip's

ISBN 0–540–08407–7

A CIP catalogue record for this book is available from the British Library.

Printed in Hong Kong

Details of other Philip's titles and services can be found on our website at: www.philips-maps.co.uk

Philip's World Atlases are published in association with The Royal Geographical Society (with The Institute of British Geographers).

The Society was founded in 1830 and given a Royal Charter in 1859 for 'the advancement of geographical science'. It holds historical collections of national and international importance, many of which relate to the Society's association with and support for scientific exploration and research from the 19th century onwards. It was pivotal in establishing geography as a teaching and research discipline in British universities close to the turn of the century, and has played a key role in geographical and environmental education ever since.

Today the Society is a leading world centre for geographical learning – supporting education, teaching, research and expeditions, and promoting public understanding of the subject.

The Society welcomes those interested in geography as members. For further information, please visit the website at: www.rgs.org

PHILIP'S

WORLD
ATLAS
& GAZETTEER

IN ASSOCIATION WITH
THE ROYAL GEOGRAPHICAL SOCIETY
WITH THE INSTITUTE OF BRITISH GEOGRAPHERS

Contents

World Statistics

Countries | vi
Physical Dimensions | vii
Philip's World Maps | viii

The Gazetteer of Nations

An A–Z Gazetteer of Countries | 1–48

The World in Focus

Planet Earth | 2–3
Restless Earth | 4–5
Landforms | 6–7
Oceans | 8–9
Climate | 10–11
Water and Vegetation | 12–13
Environment | 14–15
Population | 16–17
The Human Family | 18–19
Wealth | 20–21
Quality of Life | 22–23
Energy | 24–25
Production | 26–27
Trade | 28–29
Travel and Tourism | 30–31
Index | 32

World Cities

Amsterdam | 2
Athens | 2
Atlanta | 3
Baghdad | 3
Bangkok | 3
Barcelona | 4
Beijing | 4
Berlin | 5
Boston | 6
Brussels | 6
Budapest | 7
Buenos Aires | 7
Cairo | 7
Calcutta (Kolkata) | 8
Canton (Guangzhou) | 8
Cape Town | 8
Chicago | 9
Copenhagen | 10
Delhi | 10
Dublin | 11
Edinburgh | 11
Helsinki | 12
Hong Kong | 12
Istanbul | 12
Jakarta | 13
Jerusalem | 13
Johannesburg | 13
Karachi | 14
Lagos | 14
Lisbon | 14
London | 15
Lima | 16
Los Angeles | 16
Madrid | 17
Manila | 17
Melbourne | 17
Mexico City | 18
Miami | 18
Milan | 18
Montréal | 19
Moscow | 19
Mumbai (Bombay) | 20
Munich | 20
New York | 21
Osaka | 22
Oslo | 22
Paris | 23
Prague | 24
Rio de Janeiro | 24
Rome | 25
San Francisco | 25
St Petersburg | 26
Santiago | 26
São Paulo | 26
Seoul | 26
Shanghai | 27
Singapore | 27
Stockholm | 28
Sydney | 28
Tokyo | 29
Tehran | 30
Tianjin | 30
Toronto | 30
Vienna | 31
Warsaw | 31
Washington | 32
Wellington | 32
Index to City Maps | 33–39
World Cities Satellite Images | 40–48

World Maps

Map Symbols | 1

The World: Political
1:95 000 000 | 2–3

Arctic Ocean
1:35 000 000 | 4

Antarctica
1:35 000 000 | 5

Europe

Europe: Physical
1:20 000 000 | 6

Europe: Political
1:20 000 000 | 7

Scandinavia 1:5 000 000
Iceland 1:5 000 000

| 8–9

Ireland 1:2 000 000

| 10

Scotland 1:2 000 000

| 11

England and Wales
1:2 000 000
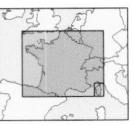
| 12–13

British Isles 1:5 000 000
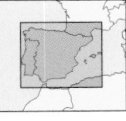
| 14

Netherlands, Belgium and
Luxembourg 1:2 500 000

| 15

Central Europe 1:5 000 000

| 16–17

Eastern Europe and Turkey
1:10 000 000
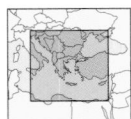
| 18–19

France 1:5 000 000
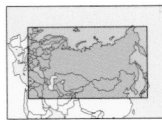
| 20

Spain and Portugal
1:5 000 000

| 21

Italy and the Balkan States
1:5 000 000

| 22–23

Balearics, Canaries and
Madeira 1:1 000 000 / 1:2 000 000
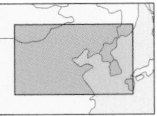
| 24

Malta, Crete, Corfu, Rhodes
and Cyprus
1:1 000 000 / 1:1 300 000
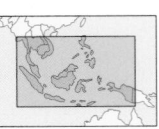
| 25

Asia

Asia: Physical 1:50 000 000 | 26

Asia: Political 1:50 000 000 | 27

Russia and Central Asia
1:20 000 000
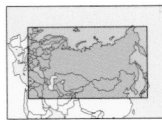
| 28–29

Japan 1:5 000 000

| 30–31

China and the Far East
1:15 000 000
Hong Kong and Macau 1:1 000 000

| 32–33

Northern China and Korea
1:6 000 000
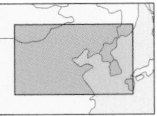
| 34–35

Indonesia and the Philippines
1:12 500 000
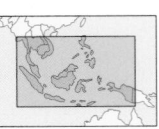
| 36–37

Mainland South-east Asia
1:6 000 000
Ko Phuket 1:1 000 000
Ko Samui 1:1 000 000
Pinang 1:1 000 000
Singapore 1:1 000 000

| 38–39

South Asia 1:10 000 000

| 40–41

Northern India and Nepal
1:6 000 000
Jammu and Kashmir 1:6 000 000

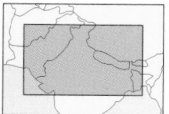

42–43

The Middle East
1:7 000 000

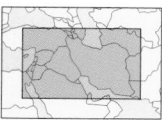

44–45

The Near East 1:2 500 000

46

Arabia and the Horn of Africa 1:15 000 000

47

Africa

Africa: Physical
1:42 000 000   48

Africa: Political
1:42 000 000   49

Northern Africa
1:15 000 000

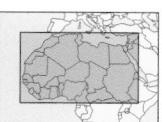

50–51

Central and Southern Africa
1:15 000 000

52–53

East Africa 1:8 000 000

54–55

Southern Africa
1:8 000 000
Madagascar 1:8 000 000

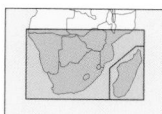

56–57

Australia and Oceania

**Australia and Oceania:
Physical and Political**
1:50 000 000   58

New Zealand 1:6 000 000
Samoan Islands 1:12 000 000
Fiji and Tonga 1:12 000 000

59

Western Australia
1:8 000 000

60–61

Eastern Australia
1:8 000 000
Whitsunday Islands 1:2 500 000

62–63

Pacific Ocean
1:54 000 000   64–65

North America

North America: Physical
1:35 000 000   66

North America: Political
1:35 000 000   67

Canada 1:15 000 000
Alaska 1:30 000 000

68–69

Western Canada 1:7 000 000

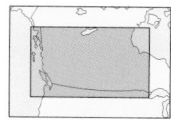

70–71

Eastern Canada 1:7 000 000

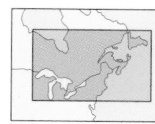

72–73

United States 1:12 000 000
Hawaii 1:10 000 000

74–75

Western United States
1:6 000 000

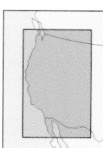

76–77

**Central and Southern
California and Washington**
1:2 500 000

78–79

Middle United States
1:6 000 000

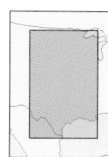

80–81

Eastern United States
1:6 000 000

82–83

North-eastern United States
1:2 500 000

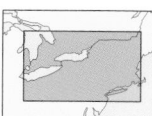

84–85

Mexico 1:8 000 000

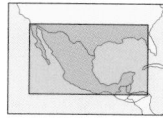

86–87

**Central America and the
West Indies** 1:8 000 000
Jamaica 1:3 000 000
Guadeloupe 1:2 000 000
Martinique 1:2 000 000
Puerto Rico 1:3 000 000
Virgin Islands 1:2 000 000
St Lucia 1:2 000 000
Barbados 1:2 000 000

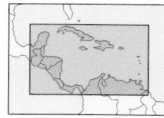

88–89

South America

South America: Physical
1:35 000 000   90

South America: Political
1:35 000 000   91

South America – North
1:16 000 000
Trinidad and Tobago 1:2 500 000

92–93

Central South America
1:8 000 000

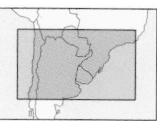

94–95

South America – South
1:16 000 000

96

Index to World Maps
97–176

World: Regions in the News   177

World Statistics: Countries

This alphabetical list includes all the countries and territories of the world. If a territory is not completely independent, the country it is associated with is named. The area figures give the total area of land, inland water and ice. The population figures are 2002 estimates. The annual income is the Gross Domestic Product per capita† in US dollars. The figures are the latest available, usually 2001 estimates.

Country/Territory	Area km^2 Thousands	Area $miles^2$ Thousands	Population Thousands	Capital	Annual Income US $
Afghanistan	652	252	27,756	Kabul	800
Albania	28.8	11.1	3,545	Tirana	3,800
Algeria	2,382	920	32,278	Algiers	5,600
American Samoa (US)	0.2	0.08	69	Pago Pago	8,000
Andorra	0.45	0.17	68	Andorra La Vella	19,000
Angola	1,247	481	10,593	Luanda	1,330
Anguilla (UK)	0.1	0.04	12	The Valley	8,600
Antigua & Barbuda	0.44	0.17	67	St John's	10,000
Argentina	2,767	1,068	37,813	Buenos Aires	12,000
Armenia	29.8	11.5	3,330	Yerevan	3,350
Aruba (Netherlands)	0.19	0.07	70	Oranjestad	28,000
Australia	7,687	2,968	19,547	Canberra	24,000
Austria	83.9	32.4	8,170	Vienna	27,000
Azerbaijan	86.6	33.4	7,798	Baku	3,100
Azores (Portugal)	2.2	0.87	234	Ponta Delgada	12,600
Bahamas	13.9	5.4	301	Nassau	16,800
Bahrain	0.68	0.26	656	Manama	13,000
Bangladesh	144	56	133,377	Dhaka	1,750
Barbados	0.43	0.17	277	Bridgetown	14,500
Belarus	207.6	80.1	10,335	Minsk	8,200
Belgium	30.5	11.8	10,275	Brussels	26,100
Belize	23	8.9	263	Belmopan	3,250
Benin	113	43	6,788	Porto-Novo	1,040
Bermuda (UK)	0.05	0.02	64	Hamilton	34,800
Bhutan	47	18.1	2,094	Thimphu	1,200
Bolivia	1,099	424	8,445	La Paz/Sucre	2,600
Bosnia-Herzegovina	51	20	3,964	Sarajevo	1,800
Botswana	582	225	1,591	Gaborone	7,800
Brazil	8,512	3,286	176,030	Brasília	7,400
Brunei	5.8	2.2	351	Bandar Seri Begawan	18,000
Bulgaria	111	43	7,621	Sofia	6,200
Burkina Faso	274	106	12,603	Ouagadougou	1,040
Burma (= Myanmar)	677	261	42,238	Rangoon	1,500
Burundi	27.8	10.7	6,373	Bujumbura	600
Cambodia	181	70	12,775	Phnom Penh	1,500
Cameroon	475	184	16,185	Yaoundé	1,700
Canada	9,976	3,852	31,902	Ottawa	27,700
Canary Is. (Spain)	7.3	2.8	1,694	Las Palmas/Santa Cruz	18,200
Cape Verde Is.	4	1.6	409	Praia	1,500
Cayman Is. (UK)	0.26	0.1	36	George Town	30,000
Central African Republic	623	241	3,643	Bangui	1,300
Chad	1,284	496	8,997	Ndjaména	1,030
Chile	757	292	15,499	Santiago	10,000
China	9,597	3,705	1,284,304	Beijing	4,300
Colombia	1,139	440	41,008	Bogotá	6,300
Comoros	2.2	0.86	614	Moroni	710
Congo	342	132	2,958	Brazzaville	900
Congo (Dem. Rep. of the)	2,345	905	55,225	Kinshasa	590
Cook Is. (NZ)	0.24	0.09	21	Avarua	5,000
Costa Rica	51.1	19.7	3,835	San José	8,500
Croatia	56.5	21.8	4,391	Zagreb	8,300
Cuba	111	43	11,224	Havana	2,300
Cyprus	9.3	3.6	767	Nicosia	11,500
Czech Republic	78.9	30.4	10,257	Prague	14,400
Denmark	43.1	16.6	5,369	Copenhagen	28,000
Djibouti	23.2	9	473	Djibouti	1,400
Dominica	0.75	0.29	70	Roseau	3,700
Dominican Republic	48.7	18.8	8,722	Santo Domingo	5,800
East Timor	14.9	5.7	953	Dili	500
Ecuador	284	109	13,447	Quito	3,000
Egypt	1,001	387	70,712	Cairo	3,700
El Salvador	21	8.1	6,354	San Salvador	4,600
Equatorial Guinea	28.1	10.8	498	Malabo	2,100
Eritrea	94	36	4,466	Asmara	740
Estonia	44.7	17.3	1,416	Tallinn	10,000
Ethiopia	1,128	436	67,673	Addis Ababa	700
Faroe Is. (Denmark)	1.4	0.54	46	Tórshavn	20,000
Fiji	18.3	7.1	856	Suva	5,200
Finland	338	131	5,184	Helsinki	25,800
France	552	213	59,766	Paris	25,400
French Guiana (France)	90	34.7	182	Cayenne	6,000
French Polynesia (France)	4	1.5	258	Papeete	5,000
Gabon	268	103	1,233	Libreville	5,500
Gambia, The	11.3	4.4	1,456	Banjul	1,770
Gaza Strip (OPT)*	0.36	0.14	1,226	–	630
Georgia	69.7	26.9	4,961	Tbilisi	3,100
Germany	357	138	83,252	Berlin	26,200
Ghana	239	92	20,244	Accra	1,980
Gibraltar (UK)	0.007	0.003	28	Gibraltar Town	17,500
Greece	132	51	10,645	Athens	17,900
Greenland (Denmark)	2,176	840	56	Nuuk (Godthåb)	20,000
Grenada	0.34	0.13	89	St George's	4,750
Guadeloupe (France)	1.7	0.66	436	Basse-Terre	9,000
Guam (US)	0.55	0.21	161	Agana	21,000
Guatemala	109	42	13,314	Guatemala City	3,700
Guinea	246	95	7,775	Conakry	1,970
Guinea-Bissau	36.1	13.9	1,345	Bissau	900
Guyana	215	83	698	Georgetown	3,600
Haiti	27.8	10.7	7,064	Port-au-Prince	1,700
Honduras	112	43	6,561	Tegucigalpa	2,600
Hong Kong (China)	1.1	0.4	7,303	–	25,000
Hungary	93	35.9	10,075	Budapest	12,000
Iceland	103	40	279	Reykjavik	24,800
India	3,288	1,269	1,045,845	New Delhi	2,500
Indonesia	1,890	730	231,328	Jakarta	3,000
Iran	1,648	636	66,623	Tehran	6,400
Iraq	438	169	24,002	Baghdad	2,500
Ireland	70.3	27.1	3,883	Dublin	27,300
Israel	20.6	7.96	6,030	Jerusalem	20,000
Italy	301	116	57,716	Rome	24,300
Ivory Coast (= Côte d'Ivoire)	322	125	16,805	Yamoussoukro	1,550
Jamaica	11	4.2	2,680	Kingston	3,700
Japan	378	146	126,975	Tokyo	27,200
Jordan	89.2	34.4	5,307	Amman	4,200
Kazakhstan	2,717	1,049	16,742	Astana	5,900
Kenya	580	224	31,139	Nairobi	1,000
Kiribati	0.72	0.28	96	Tarawa	840
Korea, North	121	47	22,224	Pyŏngyang	1,000
Korea, South	99	38.2	48,324	Seoul	18,000
Kuwait	17.8	6.9	2,112	Kuwait City	15,100
Kyrgyzstan	198.5	76.6	4,822	Bishkek	2,800
Laos	237	91	5,777	Vientiane	1,630
Latvia	65	25	2,367	Riga	7,800
Lebanon	10.4	4	3,678	Beirut	5,200
Lesotho	30.4	11.7	2,208	Maseru	2,450
Liberia	111	43	3,288	Monrovia	1,100
Libya	1,760	679	5,369	Tripoli	7,600
Liechtenstein	0.16	0.06	33	Vaduz	23,000
Lithuania	65.2	25.2	3,601	Vilnius	7,600
Luxembourg	2.6	1	449	Luxembourg	43,400
Macau (China)	0.02	0.006	462	–	17,600
Macedonia (FYROM)	25.7	9.9	2,055	Skopje	4,400
Madagascar	587	227	16,473	Antananarivo	870
Madeira (Portugal)	0.81	0.31	241	Funchal	16,800
Malawi	118	46	10,702	Lilongwe	660
Malaysia	330	127	22,662	Kuala Lumpur/Putrajaya	9,000
Maldives	0.3	0.12	320	Malé	3,870
Mali	1,240	479	11,340	Bamako	840
Malta	0.32	0.12	397	Valletta	15,000
Marshall Is.	0.18	0.07	74	Dalap-Uliga-Darrit	1,600
Martinique (France)	1.1	0.42	422	Fort-de-France	11,000
Mauritania	1,030	398	2,829	Nouakchott	1,800
Mauritius	2	0.72	1,200	Port Louis	10,800
Mayotte (France)	0.37	0.14	171	Mamoundzou	600
Mexico	1,958	756	103,400	Mexico City	9,000
Micronesia, Fed. States of	0.7	0.27	136	Palikir	2,000
Moldova	33.7	13	4,435	Chişinău	2,550
Monaco	0.002	0.001	32	Monaco	27,000
Mongolia	1,567	605	2,694	Ulan Bator	1,770
Montserrat (UK)	0.1	0.04	8	Plymouth	2,400
Morocco	447	172	31,168	Rabat	3,700
Mozambique	802	309	19,608	Maputo	900
Namibia	825	318	1,821	Windhoek	4,500
Nauru	0.02	0.008	12	Yaren District	5,000
Nepal	141	54	25,874	Katmandu	1,400
Netherlands	41.5	16	16,068	Amsterdam/The Hague	25,800
Netherlands Antilles (Neths)	0.99	0.38	214	Willemstad	11,400
New Caledonia (France)	18.6	7.2	208	Nouméa	15,000
New Zealand	269	104	3,908	Wellington	19,500
Nicaragua	130	50	5,024	Managua	2,500
Niger	1,267	489	10,640	Niamey	820
Nigeria	924	357	129,935	Abuja	840
Northern Mariana Is. (US)	0.48	0.18	77	Saipan	12,500
Norway	324	125	4,525	Oslo	30,800
Oman	212	82	2,713	Muscat	8,200
Pakistan	796	307	147,663	Islamabad	2,100
Palau	0.46	0.18	19	Koror	9,000
Panama	77.1	29.8	2,882	Panamá	5,900
Papua New Guinea	463	179	5,172	Port Moresby	2,400
Paraguay	407	157	5,884	Asunción	4,600
Peru	1,285	496	27,950	Lima	4,800
Philippines	300	116	84,526	Manila	4,000
Poland	313	121	38,625	Warsaw	8,800
Portugal	92.4	35.7	9,609	Lisbon	17,300
Puerto Rico (US)	9	3.5	3,958	San Juan	11,200
Qatar	11	4.2	793	Doha	21,200
Réunion (France)	2.5	0.97	744	St-Denis	4,800
Romania	238	92	22,318	Bucharest	6,800
Russia	17,075	6,592	144,979	Moscow	8,300
Rwanda	26.3	10.2	7,398	Kigali	1,000
St Kitts & Nevis	0.36	0.14	39	Basseterre	8,700
St Lucia	0.62	0.24	160	Castries	4,400
St Vincent & Grenadines	0.39	0.15	116	Kingstown	2,900
Samoa	2.8	1.1	179	Apia	3,500
San Marino	0.06	0.02	28	San Marino	34,600
São Tomé & Príncipe	0.96	0.37	170	São Tomé	1,200
Saudi Arabia	2,150	830	23,513	Riyadh	10,600
Senegal	197	76	10,590	Dakar	1,580
Serbia & Montenegro	102.3	39.5	10,657	Belgrade	2,250
Seychelles	0.46	0.18	80	Victoria	7,600
Sierra Leone	71.7	27.7	5,615	Freetown	500
Singapore	0.62	0.24	4,453	Singapore	24,700
Slovak Republic	49	18.9	5,422	Bratislava	11,500
Slovenia	20.3	7.8	1,933	Ljubljana	16,000
Solomon Is.	28.9	11.2	495	Honiara	1,700
Somalia	638	246	7,753	Mogadishu	550
South Africa	1,220	471	43,648	C. Town/Pretoria/Bloem.	9,400
Spain	505	195	38,383	Madrid	18,900
Sri Lanka	65.6	25.3	19,577	Colombo	3,250
Sudan	2,506	967	37,090	Khartoum	1,360
Suriname	163	63	436	Paramaribo	3,500
Swaziland	17.4	6.7	1,124	Mbabane	4,200
Sweden	450	174	8,877	Stockholm	24,700
Switzerland	41.3	15.9	7,302	Bern	31,100
Syria	185	71	17,156	Damascus	3,200
Taiwan	36	13.9	22,548	Taipei	17,200
Tajikistan	143.1	55.2	6,720	Dushanbe	1,140
Tanzania	945	365	37,188	Dodoma	610
Thailand	513	198	62,354	Bangkok	6,600
Togo	56.8	21.9	5,286	Lomé	1,500
Tonga	0.75	0.29	106	Nuku'alofa	2,200
Trinidad & Tobago	5.1	2	1,164	Port of Spain	9,000
Tunisia	164	63	9,816	Tunis	6,600
Turkey	779	301	67,309	Ankara	6,700
Turkmenistan	488.1	188.5	4,689	Ashkhabad	4,700
Turks & Caicos Is. (UK)	0.43	0.17	19	Cockburn Town	7,300
Tuvalu	0.03	0.01	11	Fongafale	1,100
Uganda	236	91	24,699	Kampala	1,200
Ukraine	603.7	233.1	48,396	Kiev	4,200
United Arab Emirates	83.6	32.3	2,446	Abu Dhabi	21,100
United Kingdom	243.3	94	59,778	London	24,700
United States of America	9,373	3,619	280,562	Washington, DC	36,300
Uruguay	177	68	3,387	Montevideo	9,200
Uzbekistan	447.4	172.7	25,563	Tashkent	2,500
Vanuatu	12.2	4.7	196	Port-Vila	1,300
Vatican City	0.0004	0.0002	1	Vatican City	N/A
Venezuela	912	352	24,288	Caracas	6,100
Vietnam	332	127	81,098	Hanoi	2,100
Virgin Is. (UK)	0.15	0.06	21	Road Town	16,000
Virgin Is. (US)	0.34	0.13	123	Charlotte Amalie	15,000
Wallis & Futuna Is. (France)	0.2	0.08	16	Mata-Utu	2,000
West Bank (OPT)*	5.86	2.26	2,164	–	1,000
Western Sahara	266	103	256	El Aaiún	N/A
Yemen	528	204	18,701	Sana	820
Zambia	753	291	9,959	Lusaka	870
Zimbabwe	391	151	11,377	Harare	2,450

*OPT = Occupied Palestinian Territory N/A = Not Available

† Gross Domestic Product per capita has been measured using the purchasing power parity method. This enables comparisons to be made between countries through their purchasing power (in US dollars), showing real price levels of goods and services.

World Statistics: Physical Dimensions

Each topic list is divided into continents and within a continent the items are listed in order of size. The bottom part of many of the lists is selective in order to give examples from as many different countries as possible. The order of the continents is the same as in the atlas, beginning with Europe and ending with South America. The figures are rounded as appropriate.

World, Continents, Oceans

	km²	miles²	%
The World	509,450,000	196,672,000	–
Land	149,450,000	57,688,000	29.3
Water	360,000,000	138,984,000	70.7
Asia	44,500,000	17,177,000	29.8
Africa	30,302,000	11,697,000	20.3
North America	24,241,000	9,357,000	16.2
South America	17,793,000	6,868,000	11.9
Antarctica	14,100,000	5,443,000	9.4
Europe	9,957,000	3,843,000	6.7
Australia & Oceania	8,557,000	3,303,000	5.7
Pacific Ocean	179,679,000	69,356,000	49.9
Atlantic Ocean	92,373,000	35,657,000	25.7
Indian Ocean	73,917,000	28,532,000	20.5
Arctic Ocean	14,090,000	5,439,000	3.9

Ocean Depths

Atlantic Ocean	m	ft
Puerto Rico (Milwaukee) Deep	9,220	30,249
Cayman Trench	7,680	25,197
Gulf of Mexico	5,203	17,070
Mediterranean Sea	5,121	16,801
Black Sea	2,211	7,254
North Sea	660	2,165

Indian Ocean	m	ft
Java Trench	7,450	24,442
Red Sea	2,635	8,454

Pacific Ocean	m	ft
Mariana Trench	11,022	36,161
Tonga Trench	10,882	35,702
Japan Trench	10,554	34,626
Kuril Trench	10,542	34,587

Arctic Ocean	m	ft
Molloy Deep	5,608	18,399

Mountains

Europe		m	ft
Elbrus	*Russia*	5,642	18,510
Mont Blanc	*France/Italy*	4,807	15,771
Monte Rosa	*Italy/Switzerland*	4,634	15,203
Dom	*Switzerland*	4,545	14,911
Liskamm	*Switzerland*	4,527	14,852
Weisshorn	*Switzerland*	4,505	14,780
Taschorn	*Switzerland*	4,490	14,730
Matterhorn/Cervino	*Italy/Switzerland*	4,478	14,691
Mont Maudit	*France/Italy*	4,465	14,649
Dent Blanche	*Switzerland*	4,356	14,291
Nadelhorn	*Switzerland*	4,327	14,196
Grandes Jorasses	*France/Italy*	4,208	13,806
Jungfrau	*Switzerland*	4,158	13,642
Grossglockner	*Austria*	3,797	12,457
Mulhacén	*Spain*	3,478	11,411
Zugspitze	*Germany*	2,962	9,718
Olympus	*Greece*	2,917	9,570
Triglav	*Slovenia*	2,863	9,393
Gerlachovka	*Slovak Republic*	2,655	8,711
Galdhöpiggen	*Norway*	2,468	8,100
Kebnekaise	*Sweden*	2,117	6,946
Ben Nevis	*UK*	1,343	4,406

Asia		m	ft
Everest	*China/Nepal*	8,850	29,035
K2 (Godwin Austen)	*China/Kashmir*	8,611	28,251
Kanchenjunga	*India/Nepal*	8,598	28,208
Lhotse	*China/Nepal*	8,516	27,939
Makalu	*China/Nepal*	8,481	27,824
Cho Oyu	*China/Nepal*	8,201	26,906
Dhaulagiri	*Nepal*	8,172	26,811
Manaslu	*Nepal*	8,156	26,758
Nanga Parbat	*Kashmir*	8,126	26,660
Annapurna	*Nepal*	8,078	26,502
Gasherbrum	*China/Kashmir*	8,068	26,469
Broad Peak	*China/Kashmir*	8,051	26,414
Xixabangma	*China*	8,012	26,286
Kangbachen	*India/Nepal*	7,902	25,925
Trivor	*Pakistan*	7,720	25,328
Pik Kommunizma	*Tajikistan*	7,495	24,590
Demavend	*Iran*	5,604	18,386
Ararat	*Turkey*	5,165	16,945
Gunong Kinabalu	*Malaysia (Borneo)*	4,101	13,455
Fuji-San	*Japan*	3,776	12,388

Africa		m	ft
Kilimanjaro	*Tanzania*	5,895	19,340
Mt Kenya	*Kenya*	5,199	17,057
Ruwenzori (Margherita)	*Ug./Congo (D.R.)*	5,109	16,762
Ras Dashan	*Ethiopia*	4,620	15,157
Meru	*Tanzania*	4,565	14,977
Karisimbi	*Rwanda/Congo (D.R.)*	4,507	14,787
Mt Elgon	*Kenya/Uganda*	4,321	14,176
Batu	*Ethiopia*	4,307	14,130
Toubkal	*Morocco*	4,165	13,665
Mt Cameroon	*Cameroon*	4,070	13,353

Oceania		m	ft
Puncak Jaya	*Indonesia*	5,030	16,503
Puncak Trikora	*Indonesia*	4,750	15,584
Puncak Mandala	*Indonesia*	4,702	15,427
Mt Wilhelm	*Papua New Guinea*	4,508	14,790
Mauna Kea	*USA (Hawaii)*	4,205	13,796
Mauna Loa	*USA (Hawaii)*	4,169	13,681
Mt Cook (Aoraki)	*New Zealand*	3,753	12,313
Mt Kosciuszko	*Australia*	2,237	7,339

North America		m	ft
Mt McKinley (Denali)	*USA (Alaska)*	6,194	20,321
Mt Logan	*Canada*	5,959	19,551
Pico de Orizaba	*Mexico*	5,610	18,405
Mt St Elias	*USA/Canada*	5,489	18,008
Popocatepetl	*Mexico*	5,452	17,887
Mt Foraker	*USA (Alaska)*	5,304	17,401
Ixtaccihuatl	*Mexico*	5,286	17,342
Lucania	*Canada*	5,227	17,149
Mt Steele	*Canada*	5,073	16,644
Mt Bona	*USA (Alaska)*	5,005	16,420
Mt Whitney	*USA*	4,418	14,495
Tajumulco	*Guatemala*	4,220	13,845
Chirripó Grande	*Costa Rica*	3,837	12,589
Pico Duarte	*Dominican Rep.*	3,175	10,417

South America		m	ft
Aconcagua	*Argentina*	6,962	22,841
Bonete	*Argentina*	6,872	22,546
Ojos del Salado	*Argentina/Chile*	6,863	22,516
Pissis	*Argentina*	6,779	22,241
Mercedario	*Argentina/Chile*	6,770	22,211
Huascaran	*Peru*	6,768	22,204
Llullaillaco	*Argentina/Chile*	6,723	22,057
Nudo de Cachi	*Argentina*	6,720	22,047
Yerupaja	*Peru*	6,632	21,758
Sajama	*Bolivia*	6,542	21,463
Chimborazo	*Ecuador*	6,267	20,561
Pico Colon	*Colombia*	5,800	19,029
Pico Bolivar	*Venezuela*	5,007	16,427

Antarctica		m	ft
Vinson Massif		4,897	16,066
Mt Kirkpatrick		4,528	14,855

Rivers

Europe		km	miles
Volga	*Caspian Sea*	3,700	2,300
Danube	*Black Sea*	2,850	1,770
Ural	*Caspian Sea*	2,535	1,575
Dnepr (Dnipro)	*Black Sea*	2,285	1,420
Kama	*Volga*	2,030	1,260
Don	*Black Sea*	1,990	1,240
Petchora	*Arctic Ocean*	1,790	1,110
Oka	*Volga*	1,480	920
Dnister (Dniester)	*Black Sea*	1,400	870
Vyatka	*Kama*	1,370	850
Rhine	*North Sea*	1,320	820
N. Dvina	*Arctic Ocean*	1,290	800
Elbe	*North Sea*	1,145	710

Asia		km	miles
Yangtze	*Pacific Ocean*	6,380	3,960
Yenisey–Angara	*Arctic Ocean*	5,550	3,445
Huang He	*Pacific Ocean*	5,464	3,395
Ob–Irtysh	*Arctic Ocean*	5,410	3,360
Mekong	*Pacific Ocean*	4,500	2,795
Amur	*Pacific Ocean*	4,400	2,730
Lena	*Arctic Ocean*	4,400	2,730
Irtysh	*Ob*	4,250	2,640
Yenisey	*Arctic Ocean*	4,090	2,540
Ob	*Arctic Ocean*	3,680	2,285
Indus	*Indian Ocean*	3,100	1,925
Brahmaputra	*Indian Ocean*	2,900	1,800
Syrdarya	*Aral Sea*	2,860	1,775
Salween	*Indian Ocean*	2,800	1,740
Euphrates	*Indian Ocean*	2,700	1,675
Amudarya	*Aral Sea*	2,540	1,575

Africa		km	miles
Nile	*Mediterranean*	6,670	4,140
Congo	*Atlantic Ocean*	4,670	2,900
Niger	*Atlantic Ocean*	4,180	2,595
Zambezi	*Indian Ocean*	3,540	2,200
Oubangi/Uele	*Congo (D.R.)*	2,250	1,400
Kasai	*Congo (D.R.)*	1,950	1,210
Shaballe	*Indian Ocean*	1,930	1,200
Orange	*Atlantic Ocean*	1,860	1,155
Cubango	*Okavango Delta*	1,800	1,120
Limpopo	*Indian Ocean*	1,600	995
Senegal	*Atlantic Ocean*	1,600	995

Australia		km	miles
Murray–Darling	*Indian Ocean*	3,750	2,330
Darling	*Murray*	3,070	1,905
Murray	*Indian Ocean*	2,575	1,600
Murrumbidgee	*Murray*	1,690	1,050

North America		km	miles
Mississippi–Missouri	*Gulf of Mexico*	6,020	3,740
Mackenzie	*Arctic Ocean*	4,240	2,630
Mississippi	*Gulf of Mexico*	3,780	2,350
Missouri	*Mississippi*	3,780	2,350
Yukon	*Pacific Ocean*	3,185	1,980
Rio Grande	*Gulf of Mexico*	3,030	1,880
Arkansas	*Mississippi*	2,340	1,450
Colorado	*Pacific Ocean*	2,330	1,445
Red	*Mississippi*	2,040	1,270
Columbia	*Pacific Ocean*	1,950	1,210
Saskatchewan	*Lake Winnipeg*	1,940	1,205

South America		km	miles
Amazon	*Atlantic Ocean*	6,450	4,010
Paraná–Plate	*Atlantic Ocean*	4,500	2,800
Purus	*Amazon*	3,350	2,080
Madeira	*Amazon*	3,200	1,990
São Francisco	*Atlantic Ocean*	2,900	1,800
Paraná	*Plate*	2,800	1,740
Tocantins	*Atlantic Ocean*	2,750	1,710
Paraguay	*Paraná*	2,550	1,580
Orinoco	*Atlantic Ocean*	2,500	1,550
Pilcomayo	*Paraná*	2,500	1,550
Araguaia	*Tocantins*	2,250	1,400

Lakes

Europe		km²	miles²
Lake Ladoga	*Russia*	17,700	6,800
Lake Onega	*Russia*	9,700	3,700
Saimaa system	*Finland*	8,000	3,100
Vänern	*Sweden*	5,500	2,100

Asia		km²	miles²
Caspian Sea	*Asia*	371,800	143,550
Lake Baykal	*Russia*	30,500	11,780
Aral Sea	*Kazakhstan/Uzbekistan*	28,687	11,086
Tonlé Sap	*Cambodia*	20,000	7,700
Lake Balqash	*Kazakhstan*	18,500	7,100

Africa		km²	miles²
Lake Victoria	*East Africa*	68,000	26,000
Lake Tanganyika	*Central Africa*	33,000	13,000
Lake Malawi/Nyasa	*East Africa*	29,600	11,430
Lake Chad	*Central Africa*	25,000	9,700
Lake Turkana	*Ethiopia/Kenya*	8,500	3,300
Lake Volta	*Ghana*	8,500	3,300

Australia		km²	miles²
Lake Eyre	*Australia*	8,900	3,400
Lake Torrens	*Australia*	5,800	2,200
Lake Gairdner	*Australia*	4,800	1,900

North America		km²	miles²
Lake Superior	*Canada/USA*	82,350	31,800
Lake Huron	*Canada/USA*	59,600	23,010
Lake Michigan	*USA*	58,000	22,400
Great Bear Lake	*Canada*	31,800	12,280
Great Slave Lake	*Canada*	28,500	11,000
Lake Erie	*Canada/USA*	25,700	9,900
Lake Winnipeg	*Canada*	24,400	9,400
Lake Ontario	*Canada/USA*	19,500	7,500
Lake Nicaragua	*Nicaragua*	8,200	3,200

South America		km²	miles²
Lake Titicaca	*Bolivia/Peru*	8,300	3,200
Lake Poopo	*Bolivia*	2,800	1,100

Islands

Europe		km²	miles²
Great Britain	*UK*	229,880	88,700
Iceland	*Atlantic Ocean*	103,000	39,800
Ireland	*Ireland/UK*	84,400	32,600
Novaya Zemlya (N.)	*Russia*	48,200	18,600
Sicily	*Italy*	25,500	9,800
Corsica	*France*	8,700	3,400

Asia		km²	miles²
Borneo	*South-east Asia*	744,360	287,400
Sumatra	*Indonesia*	473,600	182,860
Honshu	*Japan*	230,500	88,980
Sulawesi (Celebes)	*Indonesia*	189,000	73,000
Java	*Indonesia*	126,700	48,900
Luzon	*Philippines*	104,700	40,400
Hokkaido	*Japan*	78,400	30,300

Africa		km²	miles²
Madagascar	*Indian Ocean*	587,040	226,660
Socotra	*Indian Ocean*	3,600	1,400
Réunion	*Indian Ocean*	2,500	965

Oceania		km²	miles²
New Guinea	*Indonesia/Papua NG*	821,030	317,000
New Zealand (S.)	*Pacific Ocean*	150,500	58,100
New Zealand (N.)	*Pacific Ocean*	114,700	44,300
Tasmania	*Australia*	67,800	26,200
Hawaii	*Pacific Ocean*	10,450	4,000

North America		km²	miles²
Greenland	*Atlantic Ocean*	2,175,600	839,800
Baffin Is.	*Canada*	508,000	196,100
Victoria Is.	*Canada*	212,200	81,900
Ellesmere Is.	*Canada*	212,000	81,800
Cuba	*Caribbean Sea*	110,860	42,800
Hispaniola	*Dominican Rep./Haiti*	76,200	29,400
Jamaica	*Caribbean Sea*	11,400	4,400
Puerto Rico	*Atlantic Ocean*	8,900	3,400

South America		km²	miles²
Tierra del Fuego	*Argentina/Chile*	47,000	18,100
Falkland Is. (E.)	*Atlantic Ocean*	6,800	2,600

Philip's World Maps

The reference maps which form the main body of this atlas have been prepared in accordance with the highest standards of international cartography to provide an accurate and detailed representation of the Earth. The scales and projections used have been carefully chosen to give balanced coverage of the world, while emphasizing the most densely populated and economically significant regions. A hallmark of Philip's mapping is the use of hill shading and relief colouring to create a graphic impression of landforms: this makes the maps exceptionally easy to read. However, knowledge of the key features employed in the construction and presentation of the maps will enable the reader to derive the fullest benefit from the atlas.

Map sequence

The atlas covers the Earth continent by continent: first Europe; then its land neighbour Asia (mapped north before south, in a clockwise sequence), then Africa, Australia and Oceania, North America and South America. This is the classic arrangement adopted by most cartographers since the 16th century. For each continent, there are maps at a variety of scales. First, physical relief and political maps of the whole continent; then a series of larger-scale maps of the regions within the continent, each followed, where required, by still larger-scale maps of the most important or densely populated areas. The governing principle is that by turning the pages of the atlas, the reader moves steadily from north to south through each continent, with each map overlapping its neighbours.

Map presentation

With very few exceptions (e.g. for the Arctic and Antarctica), the maps are drawn with north at the top, regardless of whether they are presented upright or sideways on the page. In the borders will be found the map title; a locator diagram showing the area covered; continuation arrows showing the page numbers for maps of adjacent areas; the scale; the projection used; the degrees of latitude and longitude; and the letters and figures used in the index for locating place names and geographical features. Physical relief maps also have a height reference panel identifying the colours used for each layer of contouring.

Map symbols

Each map contains a vast amount of detail which can only be conveyed clearly and accurately by the use of symbols. Points and circles of varying sizes locate and identify the relative importance of towns and cities; different styles of type are employed for administrative, geographical and regional place names. A variety of pictorial symbols denote features such as glaciers and marshes, as well as man-made structures including roads, railways, airports and canals.

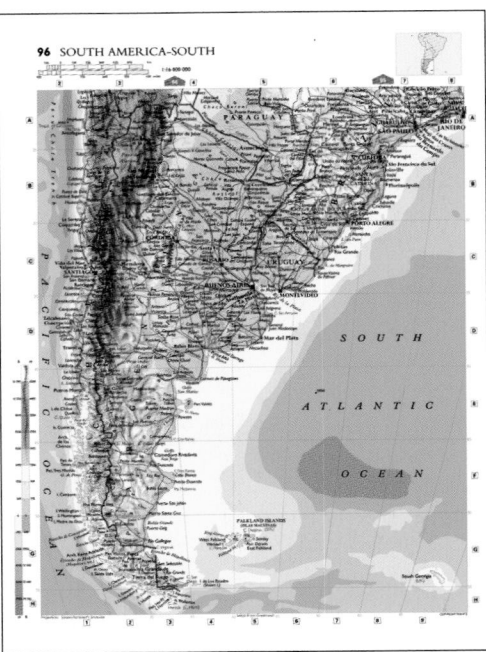

International borders are shown by red lines. Where neighbouring countries are in dispute, for example in the Middle East, the maps show the *de facto* boundary between nations, regardless of the legal or historical situation. The symbols are explained on the first page of the World Maps section of the atlas.

Map scales

The scale of each map is given in the numerical form known as the 'representative fraction'. The first figure is always one, signifying one unit of distance on the map; the second figure, usually in millions, is the number by which the map unit must be multiplied to give the equivalent distance on the Earth's surface. Calculations can easily be made in centimetres and kilometres, by dividing the Earth units figure by 100 000 (i.e. deleting the last five 0s). Thus 1:1 000 000 means 1 cm = 10 km. The calculation for inches and miles is more laborious, but 1 000 000 divided by 63 360 (the number of inches in a mile) shows that the ratio 1:1 000 000 means approximately 1 inch = 16 miles. The table below provides distance equivalents for scales down to 1:50 000 000.

LARGE SCALE		
1:1 000 000	1 cm = 10 km	1 inch = 16 miles
1:2 500 000	1 cm = 25 km	1 inch = 39.5 miles
1:5 000 000	1 cm = 50 km	1 inch = 79 miles
1:6 000 000	1 cm = 60 km	1 inch = 95 miles
1:8 000 000	1 cm = 80 km	1 inch = 126 miles
1:10 000 000	1 cm = 100 km	1 inch = 158 miles
1:15 000 000	1 cm = 150 km	1 inch = 237 miles
1:20 000 000	1 cm = 200 km	1 inch = 316 miles
1:50 000 000	1 cm = 500 km	1 inch = 790 miles
SMALL SCALE		

Measuring distances

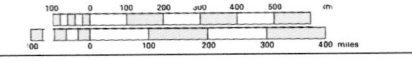

Although each map is accompanied by a scale bar, distances cannot always be measured with confidence because of the distortions involved in portraying the curved surface of the Earth on a flat page. As a general rule, the larger the map scale (i.e. the lower the number of Earth units in the representative fraction), the more accurate and reliable will be the distance measured. On small-scale maps such as those of the world and of entire continents, measurement may only be accurate along the 'standard parallels', or central axes, and should not be attempted without considering the map projection.

Latitude and longitude

Accurate positioning of individual points on the Earth's surface is made possible by reference to the geometrical system of latitude and longitude. Latitude *parallels* are drawn west–east around the Earth and numbered by degrees north and south of the Equator, which is designated 0° of latitude. Longitude *meridians* are drawn north–south and numbered by degrees east and west of the *prime meridian*, 0° of longitude, which passes through Greenwich in England. By referring to these co-ordinates and their subdivisions of minutes ($^{1}/_{60}$th of a degree) and seconds ($^{1}/_{60}$th of a minute), any place on Earth can be located to within a few hundred metres. Latitude and longitude are indicated by blue lines on the maps; they are straight or curved according to the projection employed. Reference to these lines is the easiest way of determining the relative positions of places on different maps, and for plotting compass directions.

Name forms

For ease of reference, both English and local name forms appear in the atlas. Oceans, seas and countries are shown in English throughout the atlas; country names may be abbreviated to their commonly accepted form (e.g. Germany, not The Federal Republic of Germany). Conventional English forms are also used for place names on the smaller-scale maps of the continents. However, local name forms are used on all large-scale and regional maps, with the English form given in brackets only for important cities – the large-scale map of Russia and Central Asia thus shows Moskva (Moscow). For countries which do not use a Roman script, place names have been transcribed according to the systems adopted by the British and US Geographic Names Authorities. For China, the Pin Yin system has been used, with some more widely known forms appearing in brackets, as with Beijing (Peking). Both English and local names appear in the index, the English form being cross-referenced to the local form.

THE GAZETTEER OF NATIONS

Index to Countries

A
Afghanistan 2
Albania 2
Algeria 2
American Samoa 2
Andorra 2
Angola 2
Anguilla 2
Antigua and Barbuda 3
Argentina 3
Armenia 3
Aruba 3
Australia 3
Austria 3
Azerbaijan 4

B
Bahamas 4
Bahrain 4
Bangladesh 4
Barbados 4
Belarus 4
Belgium 4
Belize 5
Benin 5
Bermuda 5
Bhutan 5
Bolivia 5
Bosnia-Herzegovina 6
Botswana 6
Brazil 6
Brunei 6
Bulgaria 7
Burkina Faso 7
Burma (Myanmar) 7
Burundi 7

C
Cambodia 8
Cameroon 8
Canada 8
Cape Verde 9
Cayman Islands 9
Central African
  Republic 9
Chad 9
Chile 9
China 10
Colombia 10
Comoros 10
Congo 10
Congo
  (Dem. Rep. of the) 11
Costa Rica 11
Croatia 11
Cuba 11

Cyprus 12
Czech Republic 12

D
Denmark 12
Djibouti 13
Dominica 13
Dominican Republic 13

E
East Timor 13
Ecuador 13
Egypt 13
El Salvador 14
Equatorial Guinea 14
Eritrea 14
Estonia 14
Ethiopia 15

F
Falkland Islands 15
Faroe Islands 15
Fiji 15
Finland 15
France 15
French Guiana 16
French Polynesia 16

G
Gabon 16
Gambia, The 16
Georgia 17
Germany 17
Ghana 17
Gibraltar 18
Greece 18
Greenland 18
Grenada 18
Guadeloupe 18
Guam 18
Guatemala 18
Guinea 18
Guinea-Bissau 19
Guyana 19

H
Haiti 19
Honduras 19
Hungary 20

I
Iceland 20
India 20
Indonesia 20
Iran 21
Iraq 21

Ireland 21
Israel 22
Italy 22
Ivory Coast 22

J
Jamaica 23
Japan 23
Jordan 23

K
Kazakhstan 23
Kenya 24
Kiribati 24
Korea, North 24
Korea, South 25
Kuwait 25
Kyrgyzstan 25

L
Laos 25
Latvia 25
Lebanon 26
Lesotho 26
Liberia 26
Libya 27
Liechtenstein 27
Lithuania 27
Luxembourg 27

M
Macedonia 27
Madagascar 28
Malawi 28
Malaysia 28
Maldives 29
Mali 29
Malta 29
Marshall Islands 29
Martinique 29
Mauritania 29
Mauritius 29
Mexico 30
Micronesia 30
Moldova 30
Monaco 30
Mongolia 30
Montserrat 30
Morocco 31
Mozambique 31

N
Namibia 31
Nauru 31
Nepal 31
Netherlands 32

Netherlands Antilles 32
New Caledonia 32
New Zealand 32
Nicaragua 32
Niger 33
Nigeria 33
Northern Mariana Is. 33
Norway 33

O
Oman 33

P
Pakistan 34
Palau 34
Panama 34
Papua New Guinea 34
Paraguay 34
Peru 35
Philippines 35
Pitcairn 35
Poland 35
Portugal 36
Puerto Rico 36

Q
Qatar 36

R
Réunion 36
Romania 36
Russia 36
Rwanda 37

S
St Helena 37
St Kitts and Nevis 37
St Lucia 37
St Vincent and the
  Grenadines 37
Samoa 37
San Marino 37
São Tomé and Príncipe 37
Saudi Arabia 37
Senegal 38
Serbia and Montenegro 38
Seychelles 38
Sierra Leone 38
Singapore 39
Slovak Republic 39
Slovenia 39
Solomon Islands 40
Somalia 40
South Africa 40
Spain 40
Sri Lanka 41

Sudan 41
Suriname 41
Swaziland 41
Sweden 42
Switzerland 42
Syria 42

T
Taiwan 42
Tajikistan 43
Tanzania 43
Thailand 43
Togo 43
Tonga 44
Trinidad and Tobago 44
Tunisia 44
Turkey 44
Turkmenistan 44
Turks and Caicos
  Islands 45
Tuvalu 45

U
Uganda 45
Ukraine 45
United Arab
  Emirates 45
United Kingdom 45
United States
  of America 46
Uruguay 46
Uzbekistan 47

V
Vanuatu 47
Vatican City 47
Venezuela 47
Vietnam 47
Virgin Islands, British 48
Virgin Islands, US 48

W
Wallis and Futuna
  Islands 48

Y
Yemen 48

Z
Zambia 48
Zimbabwe 48

Notes

The countries are arranged alphabetically, with Afghanistan as the first entry and Zimbabwe as the last. Information is given for all countries and territories, except for some of the smallest and near uninhabited islands. The form of names for all the countries follows the conventions used in all Philip's world atlases.

The statistical data is the latest available, usually for 2002. In the statistics boxes, country area includes inland water and land areas covered in ice, as in Greenland and Canada, for example. City populations are usually those of the 'urban agglomerations' rather than within the legal city boundaries.

AFGHANISTAN

GEOGRAPHY The Republic of Afghanistan is a landlocked, mountainous country in southern Asia. The central highlands reach a height of more than 7,000 m [22,966 ft] in the east and make up nearly three-quarters of Afghanistan. The main range is the Hindu Kush, which is cut by deep, fertile valleys.

In winter, northerly winds bring cold, snowy weather to the mountains, but summers are hot and dry.

POLITICS & ECONOMY The modern history of Afghanistan began in 1747, when the various tribes in the area united for the first time. In the 19th century, Russia and Britain struggled for control of the country. Following Britain's withdrawal in 1919, Afghanistan became fully independent. Soviet troops invaded Afghanistan in 1979 to support a socialist regime in Kabul, but they withdrew in 1989. By the early 21st century, a group called the Taliban ('Islamic students') controlled 90% of the country. In 2001, following the refusal of the Taliban government to hand over the terrorist leader Osama bin Laden, an international force overthrew the Taliban regime and a coalition government was set up.

Afghanistan is one of the world's poorest countries. About 60% of the people live by farming. Many people are semi-nomadic herders. Natural gas is produced, together with some coal, copper, gold, precious stones and salt.

AREA 652,090 sq km [251,772 sq mi]
POPULATION 27,756,000
CAPITAL (POPULATION) Kabul (1,565,000)
GOVERNMENT Islamic state
ETHNIC GROUPS Pashtun ('Pathan') 38%, Tajik 25%, Hazara 19%, Uzbek 6%, others 12%
LANGUAGES Pashtu, Dari/Persian (both official), Uzbek
RELIGIONS Islam (Sunni Muslim 84%, Shiite Muslim 15%)
CURRENCY Afghani = 100 puls

ALBANIA

GEOGRAPHY The Republic of Albania lies in the Balkan peninsula, facing the Adriatic Sea. About 70% of the land is mountainous, but most Albanians live on the coastal lowlands. Albania's coastal areas have a typical Mediterranean climate, with fairly dry, sunny summers and cool, moist winters. The mountains have a severe climate, with heavy snowfalls in winter.

POLITICS & ECONOMY Albania is one of Europe's poorest nations. A former Communist country, Albania adopted a multiparty system in the early 1990s. The change proved difficult. But after elections in 1997, a socialist government committed to a market system took office. In 2001, the stability of the region was threatened when Albanian-speaking Kosovars and Macedonians, many of whom favoured the creation of a Greater Macedonia, fought with government forces in north-western Macedonia.

In the early 1990s, agriculture employed 56% of the people. The land was divided into large collective and state farms, but private ownership has been encouraged since 1991. Albania has some minerals and chromite, copper and nickel are exported.

AREA 28,750 sq km [11,100 sq mi]
POPULATION 3,545,000
CAPITAL (POPULATION) Tirana (251,000)
GOVERNMENT Multiparty republic
ETHNIC GROUPS Albanian 95%, Greek 3%, Macedonian, Vlachs, Gypsy
LANGUAGES Albanian (official)
RELIGIONS Many people say they are non-believers; of the believers, 65% follow Islam and 33% follow Christianity (Orthodox 20%, Roman Catholic 13%)
CURRENCY Lek = 100 qindars

ALGERIA

 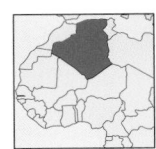

GEOGRAPHY The People's Democratic Republic of Algeria is Africa's second largest country after Sudan. Most Algerians live in the north, on the fertile coastal plains and hill country bordering the Mediterranean Sea. Four-fifths of Algeria is in the Sahara. The coast has a Mediterranean climate, but the arid Sahara is hot by day and cool at night.

POLITICS & ECONOMY France ruled Algeria from 1830 until 1962, when the socialist FLN (National Liberation Front) formed a one-party government. Following the recognition of opposition parties in 1989, a Muslim group, the FIS (Islamic Salvation Front), won an election in 1991. The FLN cancelled the elections and civil conflict broke out. About 100,000 people were killed in the 1990s. In 1999, following the withdrawal of the other candidates who alleged fraud, Abdelaziz Bouteflika, who was assumed to be favoured by the army, was elected president. Bouteflika's peace offensive reduced the violence, but sporadic conflict continued into 2003.

Algeria is a developing country, whose chief resources are oil and natural gas. The natural gas reserves are among the world's largest, and gas and oil account for 90% of Algeria's exports. Cement, iron and steel, textiles and vehicles are manufactured.

AREA 2,381,740 sq km [919,590 sq mi]
POPULATION 32,278,000
CAPITAL (POPULATION) Algiers (1,722,000)
GOVERNMENT Socialist republic
ETHNIC GROUPS Arab-Berber 99%
LANGUAGES Arabic and Berber (official), French
RELIGIONS Sunni Muslim 99%
CURRENCY Algerian dinar = 100 centimes

AMERICAN SAMOA

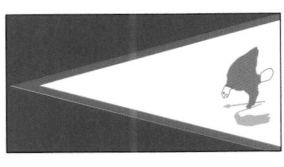 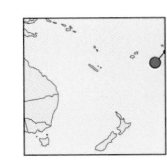

An 'unincorporated territory' of the United States, American Samoa lies in the south-central Pacific Ocean. **AREA** 200 sq km [77 sq mi]; **POPULATION** 69,000; **CAPITAL** Pago Pago.

ANDORRA

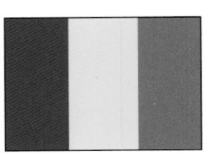 

A mini-state situated in the Pyrenees Mountains, Andorra is a co-principality whose main activity is tourism. Most Andorrans live in the six valleys (the Valls) that drain into the River Valira. **AREA** 453 sq km [175 sq mi]; **POPULATION** 68,000; **CAPITAL** Andorra La Vella.

ANGOLA

 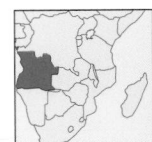

GEOGRAPHY The Republic of Angola is a large country in south-western Africa. Much of the country is part of the plateau that forms most of southern Africa, with a narrow coastal plain in the west.

Angola has a tropical climate, with temperatures of over 20°C [68°F] throughout the year, though the highest areas are cooler. The coastal regions are dry, but the rainfall increases to the north and east.

POLITICS & ECONOMY A former Portuguese colony, Angola gained its independence in 1975, after which rival nationalist forces began a struggle for power. A long-running civil war developed which, despite a cease-fire in the mid-1990s, continued until 2002, when the rebel leader, Jonas Savimbi, was killed in action and his successors negotiated peace.

Angola is a developing country, where 70% of the people are poor farmers. The main food crops are cassava and maize. Coffee is exported. Angola has much economic potential. It has oil reserves near Luanda and in the Cabinda enclave, which is separated from Angola by a strip of land belonging to Congo (Dem. Rep.). Oil is the leading export. Angola also produces diamonds and has reserves of copper, manganese and phosphates.

AREA 1,246,700 sq km [481,351 sq mi]
POPULATION 10,593,000
CAPITAL (POPULATION) Luanda (2,250,000)
GOVERNMENT Multiparty republic
ETHNIC GROUPS Ovimbundu 37%, Kimbundu 25%, Bakongo 13%, others 25%
LANGUAGES Portuguese (official), many others
RELIGIONS Traditional beliefs 47%, Roman Catholic 38%, Protestant 15%
CURRENCY Kwanza = 100 lwei

ANGUILLA

 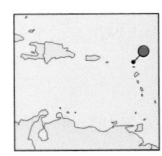

Formerly part of St Kitts and Nevis, Anguilla became a British dependency (now a British overseas territory) in 1980. The main source of revenue is now tourism, although lobster still accounts for half the island's exports. **AREA** 96 sq km [37 sq mi]; **POPULATION** 12,000; **CAPITAL** The Valley.

ANTIGUA AND BARBUDA

 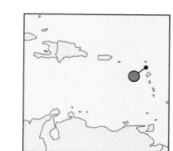

A former British dependency in the Caribbean, Antigua and Barbuda became independent in 1981. Tourism is the main industry. **AREA** 442 sq km [170 sq mi]; **POPULATION** 67,000; **CAPITAL** St John's.

ARGENTINA

GEOGRAPHY The Argentine Republic is South America's second largest and the world's eighth largest country. The Andes range in the west contains Mount Aconcagua, the highest peak in the Americas. In the south, the Andes overlook Patagonia, an arid plateau region. In east-central Argentina lies a fertile, well-watered plain called the *pampas*. Temperatures vary from subtropical to temperate.

POLITICS & ECONOMY Argentina became independent from Spain in the early 19th century, but it later suffered from instability and periods of military rule. In 1982, Argentina invaded the Falkland (Malvinas) Islands, but Britain regained the islands later in the year. Elections were held in 1983 and a new constitution was adopted in 1994.

According to the World Bank, Argentina is an 'upper-middle-income' developing country. Large areas are fertile and the main agricultural products are beef, maize and wheat. But about 87% of the people live in cities and towns. Industries include food processing and the manufacture of cars, electrical equipment and textiles. Oil is the chief natural resource. Major exports include meat, wheat, maize, vegetable oils, hides and skins, and wool. In 1991, Argentina, Brazil, Paraguay and Uruguay set up Mercosur, an alliance aimed to create a common market. However, in late 2001, a severe economic crisis threatened anarchy, but the government struggled to restore confidence in 2002 and 2003.

AREA 2,766,890 sq km [1,068,296 sq mi]
POPULATION 37,813,000
CAPITAL (POPULATION) Buenos Aires (10,990,000)
GOVERNMENT Federal republic
ETHNIC GROUPS European 97%, Mestizo, Amerindian
LANGUAGES Spanish (official)
RELIGIONS Roman Catholic 92%, Protestant 2%, Jewish 2%
CURRENCY Peso = 10,000 australs

ARMENIA

GEOGRAPHY The Republic of Armenia is a landlocked country in south-western Asia. Most of Armenia consists of a rugged plateau, criss-crossed by long faults (cracks). Movements along the faults

cause earthquakes. The highest point is Mount Aragats, at 4,090 m [13,419 ft] above sea level.

The height of the land, which averages 1,500 m [4,920 ft] above sea level gives rise to severe winters and cool summers. The rainfall is generally low.

POLITICS & ECONOMY In 1920, Armenia became a Communist republic and, in 1922, it became, with Azerbaijan and Georgia, part of the Transcaucasian Republic within the Soviet Union. But the three territories became separate Soviet Socialist Republics in 1936. After the break-up of the Soviet Union in 1991, Armenia became an independent republic. Fighting broke out over Nagorno-Karabakh, an area enclosed by Azerbaijan where the majority of the people are Armenians. In 1992, Armenia occupied the territory between it and Nagorno-Karabakh. A cease-fire agreed in 1994 left Armenia in control of about 20% of Azerbaijan's land area. Talks aimed at settling the dispute failed in 2001.

The World Bank classifies Armenia as a 'lower-middle-income' economy. The conflict has badly damaged the economy, but the government has encouraged free enterprise, selling farmland and government-owned businesses.

AREA 29,800 sq km [11,506 sq mi]
POPULATION 3,330,000
CAPITAL (POPULATION) Yerevan (1,256,000)
GOVERNMENT Multiparty republic
ETHNIC GROUPS Armenian 93%, Azerbaijani 3%, Russian, Kurd
LANGUAGES Armenian (official)
RELIGIONS Armenian Orthodox
CURRENCY Dram = 100 couma

ARUBA

 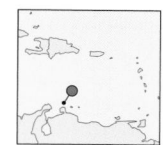

Formerly part of the Netherlands Antilles, Aruba became a separate self-governing Dutch territory in 1986. **AREA** 193 sq km [75 sq mi]; **POPULATION** 70,000; **CAPITAL** Oranjestad.

AUSTRALIA

GEOGRAPHY The Commonwealth of Australia, the world's sixth largest country, is also a continent. Australia is the flattest of the continents and the main highland area is in the east. Here the Great Dividing Range separates the eastern coastal plains from the Central Plains. This range extends from the Cape York Peninsula to Victoria in the far south. The longest rivers, the Murray and Darling, drain the south-eastern part of the Central Plains. The Western Plateau makes up two-thirds of Australia. A few mountain ranges break the monotony of the generally flat landscape.

Only 10% of Australia has an average yearly rainfall of more than 1,000 mm [39 in]. These areas include the tropical north, where Darwin is situated, the north-east coast, and the south-east, where Sydney is located. The interior is dry, and water is quickly evaporated in the heat.

POLITICS & ECONOMY The Aboriginal people of Australia entered the continent from South-east Asia more than 50,000 years ago. The first European explorers were Dutch in the 17th century, but they did not settle. In 1770, the British Captain Cook explored the east coast and, in 1788, the first British settlement was established for convicts on the site of what is now Sydney. Australia has strong ties with the British Isles. But in the last 50 years, people from other parts of Europe and, most recently, from Asia have settled in Australia. Ties with Britain were also weakened by Britain's membership of the European Union. Many Australians believe that they should become more involved with the nations of eastern Asia and the Americas rather than with Europe. In 1999, Australia held a referendum on whether the country should become a republic or remain a constitutional monarchy. By a majority of about 55 to 45, the country retained its status as a monarchy.

Australia is a prosperous country. Crops can be grown on only 6% of the land, but dry pasture covers another 58%. Yet the country remains a major producer and exporter of farm products, particularly cattle, wheat and wool. Grapes grown for wine-making are also important. The country is a major producer of minerals, including bauxite, coal, copper, diamonds, gold, iron ore, manganese, nickel, silver, tin, tungsten and zinc. Australia also produces oil and natural gas. Metals, minerals and farm products account for the bulk of exports. Australia's imports are mostly manufactured products, although the country makes many factory products, especially consumer goods, such as foods and household articles. Major imports include machinery.

AREA 7,686,850 sq km [2,967,893 sq mi]
POPULATION 19,547,000
CAPITAL (POPULATION) Canberra (325,000)
GOVERNMENT Federal constitutional monarchy
ETHNIC GROUPS Caucasian 92%, Asian 7.5%, Aboriginal 1.5%
LANGUAGES English (official)
RELIGIONS Roman Catholic 26%, Anglican 26%, other Christian 24%, non-Christian 24%
CURRENCY Australian dollar = 100 cents

AUSTRIA

GEOGRAPHY Austria is a landlocked country in Europe. Northern Austria contains the valley of the River Danube, which flows from Germany to the Black Sea, and the Vienna basin. Southern Austria contains ranges of the Alps, their highest point at Grossglockner, 3,797 m [12,457 ft] above sea level.

The climate is influenced by westerly and easterly winds. Moist westerly winds bring rain and snow, and moderate temperatures. Dry easterly winds bring cold weather in winter and hot weather in summer.

POLITICS & ECONOMY Formerly part of the monarchy of Austria-Hungary, which collapsed in 1918, Austria was annexed by Germany in 1938. After World War II, the Allies partitioned and occupied the country. In 1955, Austria became a neutral federal republic. It joined the European Union on 1 January 1995, but was a focus of controversy when, in 2000, a coalition government was formed by the right-wing People's Party and the extreme right-wing Freedom Party. The Freedom

AZERBAIJAN

Party lost much of its support in 2002, but it remained part of the ruling coalition.

Austria has a highly developed economy, with plenty of hydroelectric power and some oil, gas and coal reserves. The chief activity is manufacturing metals or metal products. Crops are grown on 18% of the land, and another 24% is pasture. Farming products include dairy and livestock products, barley, potatoes, rye, sugar beet and wheat. Tourism is a major activity.

AREA 83,850 sq km [32,374 sq mi]
POPULATION 8,170,000
CAPITAL (POPULATION) Vienna (1,560,000)
GOVERNMENT Federal republic
ETHNIC GROUPS Austrian 93%, Croatian, Slovene, other
LANGUAGES German (official)
RELIGIONS Roman Catholic 78%, Protestant 5%, Islam and other
CURRENCY Euro = 100 cents

AZERBAIJAN

GEOGRAPHY The Azerbaijani Republic is a country in the south-west of Asia, facing the Caspian Sea to the east. It includes an area called the Naxçivan Autonomous Republic, which is completely cut off from the rest of Azerbaijan by Armenian territory. The Caucasus Mountains border Russia in the north.

Azerbaijan has hot summers and cool winters. The plains are fairly dry, but the mountains are rainy.

POLITICS & ECONOMY After the Russian Revolution of 1917, attempts were made to form a Transcaucasian Federation made up of Armenia, Azerbaijan and Georgia. When this failed, Azerbaijanis set up an independent state. But Russian forces occupied the area in 1920. In 1922, the Communists set up a Transcaucasian Republic consisting of Armenia, Azerbaijan and Georgia under Russian control. In 1936, the three areas became separate Soviet Socialist Republics within the Soviet Union. In 1991, following the break-up of the Soviet Union, Azerbaijan became an independent nation. After independence, the country's economic progress was slow, partly because of the conflict with Armenia over the enclave of Nagorno-Karabakh, a region in Azerbaijan where the majority of people are Armenians. A cease-fire in 1994 left Armenia in control of about 20% of Azerbaijan's area, including Nagorno-Karabakh. Attempts to resolve the problem failed in 2001.

In the mid-1990s, the World Bank classified Azerbaijan as a 'lower-middle-income' economy. Yet by the late 1990s, the enormous oil reserves in the Baku area, on the Caspian Sea and in the sea itself, held out great promise for the future. Oil extraction and manufacturing, including oil refining and the production of chemicals, machinery and textiles, are now the most valuable activities.

AREA 86,600 sq km [33,436 sq mi]
POPULATION 7,798,000
CAPITAL (POPULATION) Baku (1,713,000)
GOVERNMENT Federal multiparty republic
ETHNIC GROUPS Azeri 90%, Dagestani 3%, Russian, Armenian, other
LANGUAGES Azerbaijani (official)
RELIGIONS Islam 93%, Russian Orthodox 2%, Armenian Orthodox 2%
CURRENCY Manat = 100 gopik

BAHAMAS

 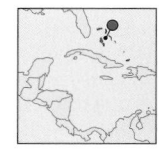

A coral-limestone archipelago off the coast of Florida, the Bahamas became independent from Britain in 1973, and has since developed strong ties with the United States. Tourism and banking are major activities. **AREA** 13,940 sq km [5,380 sq mi]; **POPULATION** 301,000; **CAPITAL** Nassau.

BAHRAIN

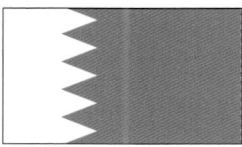 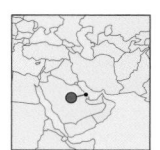

The Kingdom of Bahrain, an island nation in the Gulf, became independent from the UK in 1971. Oil accounts for 80% of the country's exports. **AREA** 678 sq km [262 sq mi]; **POPULATION** 656,000; **CAPITAL** Manama.

BANGLADESH

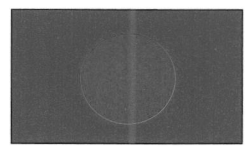 

GEOGRAPHY The People's Republic of Bangladesh is one of the world's most densely populated countries. Apart from hilly regions in the far north-east and south-east, most of the land is flat and covered by fertile alluvium spread over the land by the Ganges, Brahmaputra and Meghna rivers. These rivers overflow when they are swollen by the annual monsoon rains. Floods also occur along the coast, 575 km [357 mi] long, when cyclones (hurricanes) drive sea-water inland.

Bangladesh has a tropical monsoon climate. Dry northerly winds blow in winter, but, in summer, moist winds from the south bring monsoon rains. Heavy monsoon rains cause floods. In 1998, about two-thirds of the entire country was submerged, causing great suffering.

POLITICS & ECONOMY In 1947, British India was partitioned between the mainly Hindu India and the Muslim Pakistan. Pakistan consisted of two parts, West and East Pakistan, which were separated by about 1,600 km [1,000 mi] of Indian territory. Differences developed between West and East Pakistan. In 1971, the East Pakistanis rebelled. After a nine-month civil war, they declared East Pakistan to be a separate nation named Bangladesh.

Bangladesh is one of the world's poorest countries. Its economy depends mainly on agriculture, which employs over half the population. Bangladesh is the world's fourth largest producer of rice.

AREA 144,000 sq km [55,598 sq mi]
POPULATION 133,377,000
CAPITAL (POPULATION) Dhaka (7,832,000)
GOVERNMENT Multiparty republic
ETHNIC GROUPS Bengali 98%, tribal groups
LANGUAGES Bengali, English (both official)
RELIGIONS Islam 83%, Hinduism 16%
CURRENCY Taka = 100 paisas

BARBADOS

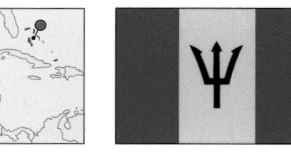 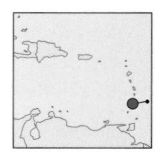

The most easterly Caribbean country, Barbados became independent from the UK in 1960. A densely populated island, Barbados is prosperous by comparison with most Caribbean countries. **AREA** 430 sq km [166 sq mi]; **POPULATION** 277,000; **CAPITAL** Bridgetown.

BELARUS

GEOGRAPHY The Republic of Belarus is a landlocked country in Eastern Europe. The land is low-lying and mostly flat. In the south, much of the land is marshy and this area contains Europe's largest marsh and peat bog, the Pripet Marshes. The climate is affected by both the moderating influence of the Baltic Sea and continental conditions to the east. The winters are cold and the summers warm.

POLITICS & ECONOMY In 1918, Belarus (White Russia) became an independent republic, but Russia invaded the country and, in 1919, a Communist state was set up. In 1922, Belarus became a founder republic of the Soviet Union. In 1991, Belarus again became an independent republic, though Belarus continued to support reunification with Russia. In 1998, Belarus and Russia set up a 'union state', with plans to have a common currency, a customs union, and common foreign and defence policies. But any surrender of sovereignty was not expected. In 2003, the Russian President Vladimir Putin agreed to deepen ties with Belarus, but also stated that he did not wish to create anything like the Soviet Union.

The World Bank classifies Belarus as an 'upper-middle-income' economy. Like other former republics of the Soviet Union, it faces many problems in turning from Communism to a free-market economy.

AREA 207,600 sq km [80,154 sq mi]
POPULATION 10,335,000
CAPITAL (POPULATION) Minsk (1,717,000)
GOVERNMENT Multiparty republic
ETHNIC GROUPS Belarussian 81%, Russian 11%, Polish, Ukrainian
LANGUAGES Belarussian, Russian (both official)
RELIGIONS Eastern Orthodox 80%, other 20%
CURRENCY Belarussian rouble = 100 kopecks

BELGIUM

GEOGRAPHY The Kingdom of Belgium is a densely populated country in western Europe. Behind the coastline on the North Sea, which is 63 km [39 mi] long, lie its coastal plains. Central Belgium consists of low plateaux and the only highland region is the Ardennes in the south-east.

Belgium has a cool, temperate climate. Moist winds from the Atlantic Ocean bring fairly heavy rain, especially in the Ardennes. In January and February much snow falls on the Ardennes.

POLITICS & ECONOMY In 1815, Belgium and the Netherlands united as the 'low countries', but Belgium became independent in 1830. Belgium's economy was weakened by the two World Wars, but, from 1945, the country recovered quickly, first through collaboration with the Netherlands and Luxembourg, which formed a customs union called Benelux, and later through its membership of the European Union.

A central political problem in Belgium has been the tension between the Dutch-speaking Flemings and the French-speaking Walloons. In the 1970s, the government divided the country into three economic regions: Dutch-speaking Flanders, French-speaking Wallonia and bilingual Brussels. In 1993, Belgium adopted a federal constitution, with each region having its own parliament. Elections under this system were held in 1995 and 1999.

Belgium is a major trading nation, with a highly developed economy. Its main products include chemicals, processed food and steel. The textile industry is important. It has existed since medieval times in the Belgian province of Flanders. In 2002, the parliament voted to phase out the use of nuclear energy by 2025.

Agriculture employs only 3% of the people, but Belgian farmers produce most of the food needed by the people. The chief crops are barley and wheat, but the most valuable activities are dairy farming and livestock rearing.

AREA 30,510 sq km [11,780 sq mi]
POPULATION 10,275,000
CAPITAL (POPULATION) Brussels (948,000)
GOVERNMENT Federal constitutional monarchy
ETHNIC GROUPS Belgian 91% (Fleming 58%, Walloon 31%), other 11%
LANGUAGES Dutch, French, German (all official)
RELIGIONS Roman Catholic 75%, other 25%
CURRENCY Euro = 100 cents

BELIZE

GEOGRAPHY Behind the southern coastal plain, the land rises to the Maya Mountains, which reach 1,120 m [3,674 ft] at Victoria Peak. The north is mostly low-lying and swampy. Temperatures are high all year round, while the average annual rainfall ranges from 1,300 mm [51 in] in the north to over 3,800 mm [150 in] in the south. Hurricanes sometimes occur. One in 2001 killed 22 people and left 12,000 homeless.

POLITICS & ECONOMY From 1862, Belize (then called British Honduras) was a British colony. Full independence was achieved in 1981, but Guatemala, which had claimed the area since the early 19th century, opposed Belize's independence and British troops remained to prevent a possible invasion. In 1983, Guatemala reduced its claim to the southern fifth of Belize. Improved relations in the early 1990s led Guatemala to recognize Belize's independence and, in 1992, Britain agreed to withdraw its troops from the country.

The World Bank classifies Belize as a 'lower-middle-income' developing country. Its economy is based on agriculture and sugar cane is the chief commercial crop and export. Other crops include bananas, beans, citrus fruits, maize and rice. Forestry, fishing and tourism are other important activities.

AREA 22,960 sq km [8,865 sq mi]
POPULATION 263,000
CAPITAL (POPULATION) Belmopan (4,000)
GOVERNMENT Constitutional monarchy
ETHNIC GROUPS Mestizo (Spanish-Indian) 44%, Creole (mainly African American) 30%, Mayan Indian 11%, Garifuna (Black-Carib Indian) 7%, other 8%
LANGUAGES English (official), Creole, Spanish
RELIGIONS Roman Catholic 62%, Protestant 30%
CURRENCY Belize dollar = 100 cents

BENIN

 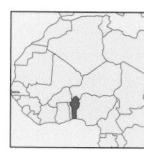

GEOGRAPHY The Republic of Benin is one of Africa's smallest countries. It extends north–south for about 620 km [390 mi]. Lagoons line the short coastline, and the country has no natural harbours.

Benin has a hot, wet climate. The average annual temperature on the coast is about 25°C [77°F], and the average rainfall is about 1,330 mm [52 in]. The inland plains are wetter than the coast.

POLITICS & ECONOMY After slavery was ended in the 19th century, the French began to gain influence in the area. Benin became self-governing in 1958 and fully independent in 1960. After much instability and many changes of government, a military group took over in 1972. The country, renamed Benin in 1975, became a one-party socialist state. Socialism was abandoned in 1989, and multiparty elections were held in 1991, 1996, 1999 and 2001.

Benin is a developing country. About 70% of the people earn their living by farming, though many remain at subsistence level. The chief exports include cotton, petroleum and palm products.

AREA 112,620 sq km [43,483 sq mi]
POPULATION 6,788,000
CAPITAL (POPULATION) Porto-Novo (179,000)
GOVERNMENT Multiparty republic
ETHNIC GROUPS Fon, Adja, Bariba, Yoruba, Fulani
LANGUAGES French (official), Fon, Adja, Yoruba
RELIGIONS Traditional beliefs 50%, Christianity 30%, Islam 20%
CURRENCY CFA franc = 100 centimes

BERMUDA

 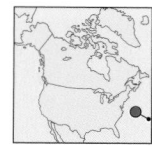

A group of about 150 small islands situated 920 km [570 mi] east of the USA. Bermuda remains Britain's oldest overseas territory, but it has a long tradition of self-government. **AREA** 53 sq km [20 sq mi]; **POPULATION** 64,000; **CAPITAL** Hamilton.

BHUTAN

 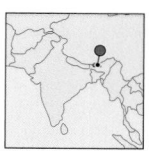

GEOGRAPHY A mountainous, isolated Himalayan country located between India and Tibet. The climate is similar to that of Nepal, being dependent on altitude and affected by monsoonal winds.

POLITICS & ECONOMY The monarch of Bhutan is head of both state and government and this predominantly Buddhist country remains, even in the Asian context, both conservative and poor. Bhutan is the world's most 'rural' country, with about 87% of the population dependent on agriculture and only 7% living in towns.

AREA 47,000 sq km [18,147 sq mi]
POPULATION 2,094,000
CAPITAL (POPULATION) Thimphu (30,000)
GOVERNMENT Constitutional monarchy
ETHNIC GROUPS Bhutanese 50%, Nepali 35%
LANGUAGES Dzongkha (official)
RELIGIONS Buddhism 75%, Hinduism 25%
CURRENCY Ngultrum = 100 chetrum

BOLIVIA

GEOGRAPHY The Republic of Bolivia is a landlocked country which straddles the Andes Mountains in central South America. The Andes rise to a height of 6,542 m [21,464 ft] at Nevado Sajama in the west.

About 40% of Bolivians live on a high plateau called the Altiplano in the Andean region, while the sparsely populated east is essentially a vast lowland plain. The Andean peaks are permanently snow-covered, while the eastern plains are hot and humid.

POLITICS & ECONOMY American Indians have lived in Bolivia for at least 10,000 years. The main groups today are the Aymara and Quechua people.

In the last 50 years, Bolivia, an independent country since 1825, has been ruled by a succession of civilian and military governments, which violated human rights. Constitutional government was restored in 1982. From the 1980s, Bolivia has pursued economic reforms and free-market policies.

Bolivia is one of the poorest countries in South America. It has several natural resources, including tin, silver and natural gas, but the chief activity is agriculture, which employs 47% of the people. Coca, which is used to make cocaine, is exported illegally. In 2002–3, the production of coca plummeted, causing much social unrest and ethnic tensions. The government hoped that oil and gas would soon replace coca as the chief export.

AREA 1,098,580 sq km [424,162 sq mi]
POPULATION 8,445,000
CAPITAL (POPULATION) La Paz (1,126,000)
GOVERNMENT Multiparty republic
ETHNIC GROUPS Mestizo 30%, Quechua 30%, Aymara 25%, White 15%
LANGUAGES Spanish, Aymara, Quechua (all official)
RELIGIONS Roman Catholic 95%
CURRENCY Boliviano = 100 centavos

BOSNIA-HERZEGOVINA

GEOGRAPHY The Republic of Bosnia-Herzegovina is one of the five republics to emerge from the former Federal People's Republic of Yugoslavia. Much of the country is mountainous or hilly, with an arid limestone plateau in the south-west. The River Sava, which forms most of the northern border with Croatia, is a tributary of the River Danube. Because of the country's odd shape, the coastline is limited to a stretch of 20 km [13 mi] on the Adriatic coast.

A Mediterranean climate, with dry, sunny summers and moist, mild winters, prevails only near the coast. Inland, the weather becomes more severe, with hot, dry summers and bitterly cold, snowy winters.

POLITICS & ECONOMY In 1918, Bosnia-Herzegovina became part of the Kingdom of the Serbs, Croats and Slovenes, which was renamed Yugoslavia in 1929. Germany occupied the area during World War II (1939–45). From 1945, Communist governments ruled Yugoslavia as a federation containing six republics, one of which was Bosnia-Herzegovina. In the 1980s, the country faced problems as Communist policies proved unsuccessful and differences arose between ethnic groups.

In 1990, free elections were held in Bosnia-Herzegovina and the non-Communists won a majority. A Muslim, Alija Izetbegovic, was elected president. In 1991, Croatia and Slovenia, other parts of the former Yugoslavia, declared themselves independent. In 1992, Bosnia-Herzegovina held a vote on independence. Most Bosnian Serbs boycotted the vote, while the Muslims and Bosnian Croats voted in favour. Many Bosnian Serbs, opposed to independence, started a war against the non-Serbs. They soon occupied more than two-thirds of the land. The Bosnian Serbs were accused of 'ethnic cleansing' – that is, the killing or expulsion of other ethnic groups from Serb-occupied areas. The war was later extended when Croat forces seized other parts of the country.

In 1995, the warring parties agreed to a solution to the conflict. This involved keeping the present boundaries of Bosnia-Herzegovina, but dividing it into two self-governing provinces, one Bosnian Serb and the other Muslim-Croat, under a central unified government. Elections were held in 1996, 1998 and 2000, and, in the early 21st century, hopes of future stability were high.

The economy of Bosnia-Herzegovina, the least developed of the six republics of the former Yugoslavia apart from Macedonia, was shattered by the war in the early 1990s. Before the war, manufactures were the main exports, including electrical equipment, machinery and transport equipment, and textiles. Farm products include fruits, maize, tobacco, vegetables and wheat, but the country has to import food.

AREA 51,129 sq km [19,745 sq mi]
POPULATION 3,964,000
CAPITAL (POPULATION) Sarajevo (526,000)
GOVERNMENT Federal republic
ETHNIC GROUPS Bosnian 49%, Serb 31%, Croat 17%
LANGUAGES Serbo-Croatian
RELIGIONS Islam 40%, Serbian Orthodox 31%, Roman Catholic 15%, Protestant 4%
CURRENCY Convertible mark = 100 paras

BOTSWANA

 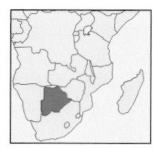

GEOGRAPHY The Republic of Botswana is a landlocked country in southern Africa. The Kalahari, a semi-desert area covered mostly by grasses and thorn scrub, covers much of the country. Most of the south has no permanent streams. But large depressions in the north are inland drainage basins. In one of them, the Okavango River, which rises in Angola, forms a large, swampy delta.

Temperatures are high in the summer months (October to April), but the winter months are much cooler. In winter, night-time temperatures sometimes drop below freezing point. The average annual rainfall ranges from over 400 mm [16 in] in the east to less than 200 mm [8 in] in the south-west.

POLITICS & ECONOMY The earliest inhabitants of the region were the San, who are also called Bushmen. They had a nomadic way of life, hunting wild animals and collecting wild plant foods.

Britain ruled the area as the Bechuanaland Protectorate between 1885 and 1966. When the country became independent, it was renamed Botswana. Since then, the country has been a stable, multiparty democracy. However, a major setback occurred in the early 21st century, when health officials announced that around 25% of the people were infected with HIV/AIDS. In 1966, Botswana was extremely poor, depending on meat and live cattle for its exports. But the discovery of minerals, including coal, cobalt, copper, diamonds and nickel, has boosted the economy. About 22% of the people now depend on agriculture, raising cattle and growing crops. Industries include the processing of farm products.

AREA 581,730 sq km [224,606 sq mi]
POPULATION 1,591,000
CAPITAL (POPULATION) Gaborone (133,000)
GOVERNMENT Multiparty republic
ETHNIC GROUPS Tswana 75%, Shona 12%, San (Bushmen) 3%
LANGUAGES English (official), Setswana
RELIGIONS Traditional beliefs 50%, Christianity 50%
CURRENCY Pula = 100 thebe

BRAZIL

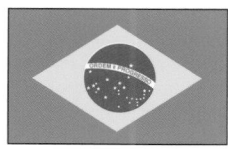 

GEOGRAPHY The Federative Republic of Brazil is the world's fifth largest country. It contains three main regions. The Amazon basin in the north covers more than half of Brazil. The Amazon, the world's second longest river, has a far greater volume than any other river. The second region, the north-east, consists of a coastal plain and the *sertão*, which is the name for the inland plateaux and hill country. The main river in this region is the São Francisco.

The third region is made up of the plateaux in the south-east. This region, which covers about a quarter of the country, is the most developed and densely populated part of Brazil. Its main river is the Paraná, which flows south through Argentina.

Manaus has high temperatures all through the year. The rainfall is heavy, though the period from June to September is drier than the rest of the year. The capital, Brasília, and the city Rio de Janeiro also have tropical climates, with much more marked dry seasons than Manaus. The far south has a temperate climate. The north-eastern interior is the driest region, with an average annual rainfall of only 250 mm [10 in] in places. The rainfall is also unreliable and severe droughts are common in this region.

POLITICS & ECONOMY The Portuguese explorer Pedro Alvarez Cabral claimed Brazil for Portugal in 1500. With Spain occupied in western South America, the Portuguese began to develop their colony, which was more than 90 times as big as Portugal. To do this, they enslaved many local Amerindian people and introduced about 4 million African slaves. Brazil declared itself an independent empire in 1822 and a republic in 1889. From the 1930s, Brazil faced periods of military rule and widespread corruption. Civilian rule was restored in 1985. Brazil adopted a new constitution in 1988.

The United Nations has described Brazil as a 'Rapidly Industrializing Country', or RIC. Its total volume of production is one of the largest in the world. But many people, including poor farmers and residents of the *favelas* (city slums), do not share in the country's fast economic growth. Widespread poverty, together with high inflation and unemployment, led to the election as president of left-winger Luiz Inácio Lula da Silva (popularly known as 'Lula') in 2002.

By the early 1990s, industry was the most valuable activity, employing 25% of the people. Brazil is among the world's top producers of bauxite, chrome, diamonds, gold, iron ore, manganese and tin. It is also a major manufacturing country. Its products include aircraft, cars, chemicals, processed food, including raw sugar, iron and steel, paper and textiles.

Brazil is one of the world's leading farming countries and agriculture employs 22% of the people. Coffee is a major export. Other leading products include bananas, citrus fruits, cocoa, maize, rice, soybeans and sugar cane. Brazil is also the top producer of eggs, meat and milk in South America.

Forestry is a major industry, though many people fear that the exploitation of the rainforests, with 1.5% to 4% of Brazil's forest being destroyed every year, is a disaster for the entire world.

AREA 8,511,970 sq km [3,286,472 sq mi]
POPULATION 176,030,000
CAPITAL (POPULATION) Brasília (2,051,000)
GOVERNMENT Federal republic
ETHNIC GROUPS White 55%, Mulatto 38%, African American 6%, other 1%
LANGUAGES Portuguese (official)
RELIGIONS Roman Catholic 80%
CURRENCY Real = 100 centavos

BRUNEI

 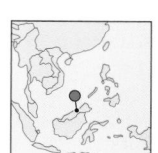

The Islamic Sultanate of Brunei, a British protectorate until 1984, lies on the north coast of Borneo. The climate is tropical and rainforests cover large areas. Brunei is a prosperous country because of its oil and natural gas production, and the Sultan is said to be among the world's richest men. **AREA** 5,770 sq km [2,228 sq mi]; **POPULATION** 351,000; **CAPITAL** Bandar Seri Begawan.

BULGARIA

GEOGRAPHY The Republic of Bulgaria is a country in the Balkan peninsula, facing the Black Sea in the east. The heart of Bulgaria is mountainous. The main ranges are the Balkan Mountains in the centre and the Rhodope (or Rhodopi) Mountains in the south.

Summers are hot and winters are cold, though seldom severe. The rainfall is moderate.

POLITICS & ECONOMY Ottoman Turks ruled Bulgaria from 1396 and ethnic Turks still form a sizeable minority in the country. In 1879, Bulgaria became a monarchy, and in 1908 it became fully independent. Bulgaria was an ally of Germany in World War I (1914–18) and again in World War II (1939–45). In 1944, Soviet troops invaded Bulgaria and, after the war, the monarchy was abolished and the country became a Communist ally of the Soviet Union. In the late 1980s, reforms in the Soviet Union led Bulgaria's government to introduce a multiparty system in 1990. A non-Communist government was elected in 1991, the first free elections in 44 years. Throughout the 1990s, Bulgaria faced many problems. In 2001, a coalition led by the former King Siméon, who had left Bulgaria in 1948, won the elections. Siméon became prime minister.

According to the World Bank, Bulgaria in the 1990s was a 'lower-middle-income' developing country. Bulgaria has some deposits of minerals, including brown coal, manganese and iron ore. But manufacturing is the leading economic activity, though problems arose in the early 1990s, because much industrial technology is outdated. The main products are chemicals, processed foods, metal products, machinery and textiles. Manufactures are the leading exports. Bulgaria trades mainly with countries in Eastern Europe.

AREA 110,910 sq km [42,822 sq mi]
POPULATION 7,621,000
CAPITAL (POPULATION) Sofia (1,139,000)
GOVERNMENT Multiparty republic
ETHNIC GROUPS Bulgarian 83%, Turkish 8%, Gypsy 3%, Macedonian, Armenian, other
LANGUAGES Bulgarian (official), Turkish
RELIGIONS Christianity (Eastern Orthodox 87%), Islam 13%
CURRENCY Lev = 100 stotinki

BURKINA FASO

 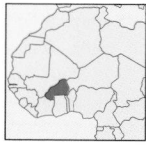

GEOGRAPHY The Democratic People's Republic of Burkina Faso is a landlocked country, a little larger than the United Kingdom, in West Africa. But Burkina Faso has only one-sixth of the population of the UK. The country consists of a plateau, between about 300 m and 700 m [650 ft to 2,300 ft] above sea level. The plateau is cut by several rivers.

The capital city, Ouagadougou, in central Burkina Faso, has high temperatures throughout the year. Most of the rain falls between May and September, but the rainfall is erratic and droughts are common.

POLITICS & ECONOMY The people of Burkina Faso are divided into two main groups. The Voltaic group includes the Mossi, who form the largest single group, and the Bobo. The French conquered the Mossi capital of Ouagadougou in 1897 and they made the area a protectorate. In 1919, the area became a French colony called Upper Volta. After independence in 1960, Upper Volta became a one-party state. But it was unstable – military groups seized power several times and political killings took place. In 1984, the country's name was changed to Burkina Faso. In 1991 and 1998, the former military leader, Captain Blaise Compaoré, was elected president, but the military continued to play an important part in the government.

Burkina Faso is one of the world's 20 poorest countries and has become very dependent on foreign aid. Most of Burkina Faso is dry with thin soils. The country's main food crops are beans, maize, millet, rice and sorghum. Cotton, groundnuts and shea nuts, whose seeds produce a fat used to make cooking oil and soap, are grown for sale abroad. Livestock are also an important export.

The country has few resources and manufacturing is on a small scale. There are some deposits of manganese, zinc, lead and nickel in the north of the country, but there is not yet a good enough transport system there. Many young men seek jobs abroad in Ghana and Ivory Coast. The money they send home to their families is important to the country's economy.

AREA 274,200 sq km [105,869 sq mi]
POPULATION 12,603,000
CAPITAL (POPULATION) Ouagadougou (690,000)
GOVERNMENT Multiparty republic
ETHNIC GROUPS Mossi 48%, Gurunsi, Senufo, Lobi, Bobo, Mande, Fulani
LANGUAGES French (official), Mossi, Fulani
RELIGIONS Islam 50%, traditional beliefs 40%, Christianity 10%
CURRENCY CFA franc = 100 centimes

BURMA (MYANMAR)

 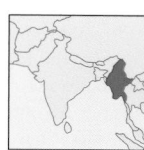

GEOGRAPHY The Union of Burma is now officially known as the Union of Myanmar; its name was changed in 1989. Mountains border the country in the east and west, with the highest mountains in the north. Burma's highest mountain is Hkakabo Razi, which is 5,881 m [19,294 ft] high. Between these ranges is central Burma, which contains the fertile valleys of the Irrawaddy and Sittang rivers. The Irrawaddy delta on the Bay of Bengal is one of the world's leading rice-growing areas. Burma also includes the long Tenasserim coast in the south-east.

Burma has a tropical monsoon climate. There are three seasons. The rainy season runs from late May to mid-October. A cool, dry season follows, between late October and the middle part of February. The hot season lasts from late February to mid-May, though temperatures remain high during the humid rainy season.

POLITICS & ECONOMY Many groups settled in Burma in ancient times. Some, called the hill peoples, live in remote mountain areas where they have retained their own cultures. The ancestors of the country's main ethnic group today, the Burmese, arrived in the 9th century AD.

Britain conquered Burma in the 19th century and made it a province of British India. But, in 1937, the British granted Burma limited self-government. Japan conquered Burma in 1942, but the Japanese were driven out in 1945. Burma became a fully independent country in 1948.

Revolts by Communists and various hill people led to instability in the 1950s. In 1962, Burma became a military dictatorship and, in 1974, a one-party state. Attempts to control minority liberation movements and the opium trade led to repressive rule. The National League for Democracy led by Aung San Suu Kyi won the elections in 1990, but the military continued their repressive rule throughout the 1990s, earning Burma the reputation for having one of the world's worst human rights records. Its admission to ASEAN (Association of South-east Asian Nations) in 1997 may have implied regional recognition of the regime. However, the European Union continued to voice its concerns over human rights abuses, even after the release of the opposition leader Aung San Suu Kyi in 2002.

Agriculture is the main activity, employing 64% of the people. The chief crop is rice. Maize, pulses, oilseeds and sugar cane are other major products. Forestry is important. Teak and rice together make up about two-thirds of the total value of the exports. Burma has many mineral resources, though they are mostly undeveloped, but the country is famous for its precious stones, especially rubies. Manufacturing is mostly on a small scale.

AREA 676,577 sq km [261,228 sq mi]
POPULATION 42,238,000
CAPITAL (POPULATION) Rangoon (2,513,000)
GOVERNMENT Military regime
ETHNIC GROUPS Burman 69%, Shan 9%, Karen 6%, Rakhine 5%, Mon 2%, Kachin 1%
LANGUAGES Burmese (official), Shan, Karen, Rakhine, Mon, Kachin, English, Chin
RELIGIONS Buddhism 89%, Christianity, Islam
CURRENCY Kyat = 100 pyas

BURUNDI

 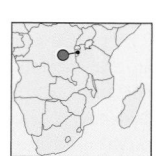

GEOGRAPHY The Republic of Burundi is the fifth smallest country in mainland Africa. It is also the second most densely populated after its northern neighbour, Rwanda. Part of the Great African Rift Valley, which runs throughout eastern Africa into south-western Asia, lies in western Burundi. It includes part of Lake Tanganyika.

Bujumbura, the capital city, lies on the shore of Lake Tanganyika. It has a warm climate. A dry season occurs from June to September, but the other months are fairly rainy. The mountains and plateaux to the east are cooler and wetter, but the rainfall generally decreases to the east.

POLITICS & ECONOMY The Twa, a pygmy people, were the first known inhabitants of Burundi. About 1,000 years ago, the Hutu, a people who speak a Bantu language, gradually began to settle the area, pushing the Twa into remote areas.

From the 15th century, the Tutsi, a cattle-owning people from the north-east, gradually took over the country. The Hutu, although greatly outnumbering the Tutsi, were forced to serve the Tutsi overlords.

Germany conquered the area that is now Burundi and Rwanda in the late 1890s. The area, called

CAMBODIA

Ruanda-Urundi, was taken by Belgium during World War I (1914–18). In 1961, the people of Urundi voted to become a monarchy, while the people of Ruanda voted to become a republic. The two territories became fully independent as Burundi and Rwanda in 1962. After 1962, the rivalries between the Hutu and Tutsi led to periodic outbreaks of fighting. The Tutsi monarchy was ended in 1966 and Burundi became a republic. Instability continued with frequent coups and massacres of thousands of people as Tutsis and Hutus fought for power. In 2001, leaders signed a power-sharing agreement, but conflict continued despite efforts to implement it.

Burundi is one of the world's ten poorest countries. About 93% of the people are farmers who live mostly at subsistence level. The main food crops are beans, cassava, maize and sweet potatoes. Cattle, goats and sheep are raised and fishing is also important. However, Burundi has to import food.

> **AREA** 27,830 sq km [10,745 sq mi]
> **POPULATION** 6,373,000
> **CAPITAL (POPULATION)** Bujumbura (300,000)
> **GOVERNMENT** Republic
> **ETHNIC GROUPS** Hutu 85%, Tutsi 14%, Twa (pygmy) 1%
> **LANGUAGES** French and Kirundi (both official)
> **RELIGIONS** Roman Catholic 62%, traditional beliefs 23%, Islam 10%, Protestant 5%
> **CURRENCY** Burundi franc = 100 centimes

CAMBODIA

GEOGRAPHY The Kingdom of Cambodia is a country in South-east Asia. Low mountains border the country except in the south-east. But most of Cambodia consists of plains drained by the River Mekong, which enters Cambodia from Laos in the north and exits through Vietnam in the south-east. The north-west contains Tonlé Sap (or Great Lake). In the dry season, this lake drains into the River Mekong. But in the wet season, the level of the Mekong rises and water flows in the opposite direction from the river into Tonlé Sap – the lake then becomes the largest freshwater lake in Asia.

Cambodia has a tropical monsoon climate, with high temperatures all through the year. The dry season, when winds blow from the north or north-east, runs from November to April. During the rainy season, from May to October, moist winds blow from the south or south-east. The high humidity and heat often make conditions unpleasant. The rainfall is heaviest near the coast, and rather lower inland.

POLITICS & ECONOMY From 802 to 1432, the Khmer people ruled a great empire, which reached its peak in the 12th century. The Khmer capital was at Angkor. The Hindu stone temples built there and at nearby Angkor Wat form the world's largest group of religious buildings. France ruled the country between 1863 and 1954, when the country became an independent monarchy. But the monarchy was abolished in 1970 and Cambodia became a republic.

In 1970, US and South Vietnamese troops entered Cambodia but left after destroying North Vietnamese Communist camps in the east. The country became involved in the Vietnamese War, and then in a civil war as Cambodian Communists of the Khmer Rouge organization fought for power. The Khmer Rouge took over Cambodia in 1975 and launched a reign of terror in which between 1 million and 2.5 million people were killed. In 1979, Vietnamese and Cambodian troops overthrew the Khmer Rouge government. But fighting continued between several factions. Vietnam withdrew in 1989, and in 1991 Prince Sihanouk was recognized as head of state. Elections were held in May 1993, and in September 1993 the monarchy was restored. Sihanouk again became king. In 1997, the prime minister, Prince Norodom Ranariddh, was deposed, so ending four years of democratic rule. Further elections were held in 1998 and, in 2001, the government set up courts to try leaders of the Khmer Rouge.

Cambodia is a poor country whose economy has been wrecked by war. Until the 1970s, the country's farmers produced most of the food needed by the people. But by 1986, it was only able to supply 80% of its needs. Farming is the main activity and rice, rubber and maize are major products. Manufacturing is almost non-existent, apart from rubber processing and a few factories producing items for sale in Cambodia.

> **AREA** 181,040 sq km [69,900 sq mi]
> **POPULATION** 12,775,000
> **CAPITAL (POPULATION)** Phnom Penh (570,000)
> **GOVERNMENT** Constitutional monarchy
> **ETHNIC GROUPS** Khmer 90%, Vietnamese 5%, Chinese 1%, other 5%
> **LANGUAGES** Khmer (official)
> **RELIGIONS** Buddhism 95%, other 5%
> **CURRENCY** Riel = 100 sen

CAMEROON

GEOGRAPHY The Republic of Cameroon in West Africa got its name from the Portuguese word *camarões*, or prawns. This name was used by Portuguese explorers who fished for prawns along the coast. Behind the narrow coastal plains on the Gulf of Guinea, the land rises to a series of plateaux, with a mountainous region in the south-west where the volcano Mount Cameroon is situated. In the north, the land slopes down towards the Lake Chad basin.

The rainfall is heavy, especially in the highlands. The rainiest months near the coast are June to September. The rainfall decreases to the north and the far north has a hot, dry climate. Temperatures are high on the coast, whereas the inland plateaux are cooler.

POLITICS & ECONOMY Germany lost Cameroon during World War I (1914–18). The country was then divided into two parts, one ruled by Britain and the other by France. In 1960, French Cameroon became the independent Cameroon Republic. In 1961, after a vote in British Cameroon, part of the territory joined the Cameroon Republic to become the Federal Republic of Cameroon. The other part joined Nigeria. In 1972, Cameroon became a unitary state called the United Republic of Cameroon. It adopted the name Republic of Cameroon in 1984, but the country had two official languages. In 1995, partly to placate English-speaking people, Cameroon became the 52nd member of the Commonwealth.

Like most countries in tropical Africa, Cameroon's economy is based on agriculture, which employs 73% of the people. The chief food crops include cassava, maize, millet, sweet potatoes and yams. The country also has plantations to produce such crops as cocoa and coffee for export.

Cameroon is fortunate in having some oil, the country's chief export, and bauxite. Although it has few manufacturing and processing industries, its mineral exports and self-sufficiency in food production make it one of the better-off countries in tropical Africa.

> **AREA** 475,440 sq km [183,567 sq mi]
> **POPULATION** 16,185,000
> **CAPITAL (POPULATION)** Yaoundé (800,000)
> **GOVERNMENT** Multiparty republic
> **ETHNIC GROUPS** Fang 20%, Bamileke and Bamum 19%, Duala, Luanda and Basa 15%, Fulani 10%
> **LANGUAGES** French and English (both official), many others
> **RELIGIONS** Christianity 40%, traditional beliefs 40%, Islam 20%
> **CURRENCY** CFA franc = 100 centimes

CANADA

 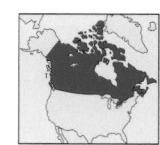

GEOGRAPHY Canada is the world's second largest country after Russia. It is thinly populated, however, with much of the land too cold or too mountainous for human settlement. Most Canadians live within 300 km [186 mi] of the southern border.

Western Canada is rugged. It includes the Pacific ranges and the mighty Rocky Mountains. East of the Rockies are the interior plains. In the north lie the bleak Arctic islands, while to the south lie the densely populated lowlands around lakes Erie and Ontario and in the St Lawrence River valley.

Canada has a cold climate. In winter, temperatures fall below freezing point throughout most of Canada. But the south-western coast has a relatively mild climate. Along the Arctic Circle, mean temperatures are below freezing for seven months a year.

Western and south-eastern Canada experience high rainfall, but the prairies are dry with 250 mm to 500 mm [10 in to 20 in] of rain every year.

POLITICS & ECONOMY Canada's first people, the ancestors of the Native Americans, or Indians, arrived in North America from Asia around 40,000 years ago. Later arrivals were the Inuit (Eskimos), who also came from Asia. Europeans reached the Canadian coast in 1497 and a race began between Britain and France for control of the territory.

France gained an initial advantage, and the French founded Québec in 1608. But the British later occupied eastern Canada. In 1867, Britain passed the British North America Act, which set up the Dominion of Canada, which was made up of Québec, Ontario, Nova Scotia and New Brunswick. Other areas were added, the last being Newfoundland in 1949. Canada fought alongside Britain in both World Wars and many Canadians feel close ties with Britain. Canada is a constitutional monarchy, and the British monarch is Canada's head of state.

Rivalries between French- and English-speaking Canadians continue. In 1995, Québeckers voted against a move to make Québec a sovereign state. The majority was less than 1% and this issue seems unlikely to disappear. Another problem concerns the rights of the Aboriginal minorities, who would like to have more say in the running of their own affairs. To this end, in 1999, Canada created a new territory called Nunavut for the Inuit population in the north. Nunavut covers approximately 64% of what was formerly the eastern part of Northwest Territories.

Canada is a highly developed and prosperous country. Although farmland covers only 8% of the country, Canadian farms are highly productive. Canada is one of the world's leading producers of barley, wheat, meat and milk. Forestry and fishing are other important industries. It is rich in natural resources, especially oil and natural gas, and is a major exporter of minerals. The country also produces copper, gold, iron ore, uranium and zinc. Manufacturing is highly developed, especially in the cities where 78% of the people live. Canada has many factories that process farm and mineral products. It also produces cars, chemicals, electronic goods, machinery, paper and timber products.

AREA 9,976,140 sq km [3,851,788 sq mi]
POPULATION 31,902,000
CAPITAL (POPULATION) Ottawa (1,107,000)
GOVERNMENT Federal multiparty constitutional monarchy
ETHNIC GROUPS British 28%, French 23%, other European 15%, Native American (Amerindian/Inuit) 2%, other 32%
LANGUAGES English and French (both official)
RELIGIONS Roman Catholic 42%, Protestant 40%, Judaism, Islam, Hinduism
CURRENCY Canadian dollar = 100 cents

CAPE VERDE

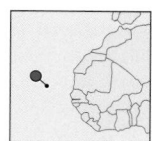

Cape Verde consists of ten large and five small islands, and is situated 560 km [350 mi] west of Dakar in Senegal. The islands have a tropical climate, with high temperatures all year round. Cape Verde became independent from Portugal in 1975 and is rated as a 'low-income' developing country by the World Bank. **AREA** 4,030 sq km [1,556 sq mi]; **POPULATION** 409,000; **CAPITAL** Praia.

CAYMAN ISLANDS

The Cayman Islands are an overseas territory of the UK, consisting of three low-lying islands. Financial services are the main economic activity and the islands offer a secret tax haven to many companies and banks. **AREA** 259 sq km [100 sq mi]; **POPULATION** 36,000; **CAPITAL** George Town.

CENTRAL AFRICAN REPUBLIC

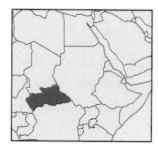

GEOGRAPHY The Central African Republic is a remote, landlocked country in the heart of Africa. It consists mostly of a plateau lying between 600 m and 800 m [1,970 ft to 2,620 ft] above sea level. The Ubangi drains the south, while the Chari (or Shari) River flows from the north to the Lake Chad basin.

The climate is warm throughout the year, while the annual average rainfall in the capital Bangui totals 1,574 mm [62 in]. The north is drier, with an average annual rainfall of about 800 mm [31 in].

POLITICS & ECONOMY France set up an outpost at Bangui in 1899 and ruled the country as a colony from 1894. Known as Ubangi-Shari, the country was ruled by France as part of French Equatorial Africa until it gained independence in 1960.

Central African Republic became a one-party state in 1962, but army officers seized power in 1966. The head of the army, Jean-Bedel Bokassa, made himself emperor in 1976. The country was renamed the Central African Empire, but after a brutal reign, the tyrannical Bokassa was overthrown in a military coup in 1979. The country again became a republic.

The country adopted a new, multiparty constitution in 1991. Multiparty elections were held in 1993 and 1998. However, an army uprising began in 2002, culminating in the overthrow by a military coup of the elected President Patassé in 2003. He was succeeded by General François Bezize.

The World Bank classifies Central African Republic as a 'low-income' developing country. Over 80% of the people are farmers, and most of them produce little more than they need to feed their families. The main crops are bananas, maize, manioc, millet and yams. Coffee, cotton, timber and tobacco are produced for export, mainly on commercial plantations. The country's development has been impeded by its remote position, its poor transport system and its untrained workforce. The country depends heavily on aid, especially from France.

AREA 622,980 sq km [240,533 sq mi]
POPULATION 3,643,000
CAPITAL (POPULATION) Bangui (553,000)
GOVERNMENT Multiparty republic
ETHNIC GROUPS Baya 34%, Banda 27%, Mandjia 21%, Sara 10%, Mbaka 4%, Mboum 4%
LANGUAGES French (official), Sangho
RELIGIONS Traditional beliefs 57%, Christianity 35%, Islam 8%
CURRENCY CFA franc = 100 centimes

CHAD

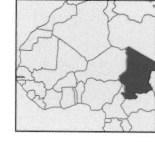

GEOGRAPHY The Republic of Chad is a landlocked country in north-central Africa. It is Africa's fifth largest country and is over twice the size of France, the country which once ruled it as a colony.

Ndjamena in central Chad has a hot, tropical climate, with a dry season from November to April. The south of the country is wetter, with an average yearly rainfall of around 1,000 mm [39 in]. The hot desert in the north has an average yearly rainfall of less than 130 mm [5 in].

POLITICS & ECONOMY Chad straddles two worlds. The north is populated by Muslim Arab and Berber peoples, while black Africans, who follow traditional beliefs or who have converted to Christianity, live in the south.

French explorers were active in the area in the late 19th century. France finally made Chad a colony in 1902. Since becoming independent in 1960, Chad has been hit by ethnic conflict. The 1970s were marked by civil war and coups. Chad and Libya agreed a truce in 1987 and, in 1994, the International Court of Justice ruled against Libya's claim on the Aozou Strip. Chad enjoyed more stability in the 1990s. A new constitution was adopted in 1997.

Hit by drought and civil war, Chad is one of the world's poorest countries. Farming, fishing and livestock raising employ 83% of the people. Groundnuts, millet, rice and sorghum are major food crops in the south, but the chief export crop is cotton. Chad has few manufacturing industries, but its oil reserves hold out hope for development in the 21st century.

AREA 1,284,000 sq km [495,752 sq mi]
POPULATION 8,997,000
CAPITAL (POPULATION) Ndjamena (530,000)
GOVERNMENT Multiparty republic
ETHNIC GROUPS Bagirmi, Kreish and Sara 31%, Sudanic Arab 26%, Teda 7%, Mbum 6%
LANGUAGES French and Arabic (both official), many others
RELIGIONS Islam 50%, Christianity 25%, traditional beliefs 25%
CURRENCY CFA franc = 100 centimes

CHILE

GEOGRAPHY The Republic of Chile stretches about 4,260 km [2,650 mi] from north to south, although the maximum east–west distance is only about 430 km [267 mi]. The high Andes Mountains form Chile's eastern borders with Argentina and Bolivia. To the west are basins and valleys, with coastal uplands overlooking the shore. Most people live in the central valley, where Santiago is situated.

Santiago has a Mediterranean climate, with hot, dry summers and mild, moist winters. The Atacama Desert in the north is one of the world's driest places, while southern Chile is cold and stormy.

POLITICS & ECONOMY Amerindian people reached the southern tip of South America 8,000 years ago. In 1520, Portuguese navigator Ferdinand Magellan was the first European to sight Chile. The country became a Spanish colony in the 1540s. Chile became independent in 1818. During a war (1879–83), it gained mineral-rich areas from Peru and Bolivia.

In 1970, Salvador Allende became the first Communist leader to be elected democratically. He was overthrown in 1973 by army officers, who were supported by the CIA. General Augusto Pinochet then ruled as a dictator. A new constitution was introduced in 1981 and elections were held in 1989. In 2000, a socialist, Ricardo Lagos, was elected president. Pinochet, who had been charged with presiding over acts of torture, was found to be too ill to stand trial in 2001.

The World Bank classifies Chile as a 'lower-middle-income' developing country. Mining is important, especially copper production. Minerals dominate exports. The most valuable activity is manufacturing; products include processed foods, metals, iron and steel, transport equipment and textiles.

AREA 756,950 sq km [292,258 sq mi]
POPULATION 15,499,000
CAPITAL (POPULATION) Santiago (4,691,000)
GOVERNMENT Multiparty republic
ETHNIC GROUPS Mestizo 95%, Amerindian 3%
LANGUAGES Spanish (official)
RELIGIONS Roman Catholic 89%, Protestant 11%
CURRENCY Peso = 100 centavos

CHINA

 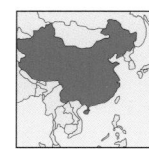

GEOGRAPHY The People's Republic of China is the world's third largest country. Most people live in the east – on the coastal plains or in the fertile valleys of the Huang He (Hwang Ho or Yellow River), the Chang Jiang (Yangtze Kiang), which is Asia's longest river at 6,380 km [3,960 mi], and the Xi Jiang (Si Kiang).

Western China is thinly populated. It includes the bleak Tibetan plateau which is bounded by the Himalaya, the world's highest mountain range. Other ranges include the Kunlun Shan, the Altun Shan and the Tian Shan. Deserts include the Gobi Desert along the Mongolian border and the Taklimakan Desert in the far west.

Beijing in north-eastern China has cold winters and warm summers, with a moderate rainfall. Shanghai, in the east-central region of China, has milder winters and more rain. The south-east has a wet, subtropical climate. In the west, the climate is severe. Lhasa has very cold winters and a low rainfall.

POLITICS & ECONOMY China is one of the world's oldest civilizations, going back 3,500 years. Under the Han dynasty (202 BC to AD 220), the Chinese empire was as large as the Roman empire. Mongols conquered China in the 13th century, but Chinese rule was restored in 1368. The Manchu people of Mongolia ruled the country from 1644 to 1912, when the country became a republic.

War with Japan (1937–45) was followed by civil war between the nationalists and the Communists. The Communists triumphed in 1949, setting up the People's Republic of China. In the 1980s, following the death of the revolutionary leader Mao Zedong (Mao Tse-tung) in 1976, China encouraged formerly forbidden policies, namely private enterprise and foreign investment. But the Communist leaders have not permitted political freedom. Opponents are still harshly treated, while attempts to negotiate some degree of autonomy for Tibet have been rejected.

China's economy has expanded greatly since the 1970s, with many Communist policies being abandoned. Foreign investors have helped to set up many new industries in the east. Between 1989 and 2002, the economy grew by an average of 9.3% per year. With its cheap labour, trained managers and engineers, China has overtaken Japan to become the fourth largest exporter to the United States. It has benefited from the return of Hong Kong in 1997 and its admission to the World Trade Organization (WTO) in 2001. China would also like to regain the prosperous island of Taiwan, also a member of the WTO, but this seems unlikely in the near future.

Despite its recent success, China remains a poor country. In the late 1990s, agriculture still employed nearly half of the people, although only 10% of the land is farmed. Products include rice, sweet potatoes, tea and wheat, and many fruits and vegetables. Livestock farming is important. Pork is popular. China has more than a third of the world's pigs.

Resources include coal, iron ore and other metals. Leading manufactures include cement, chemicals, fertilizers, machinery, telecommunications and recording equipment, and textiles. In recent years, China has also become one of the world's leading producers of consumer goods. It now produces more than half of the world's cameras, 30% of its air conditioners and TV sets, 23% of its washing machines, 20% of its refrigerators, 37% of its hard disk drives and 10% of its computer monitors.

> **AREA** 9,596,960 sq km [3,705,386 sq mi]
> **POPULATION** 1,284,304,000
> **CAPITAL (POPULATION)** Beijing (12,362,000)
> **GOVERNMENT** Single-party Communist republic
> **ETHNIC GROUPS** Han Chinese 92%, 55 minority groups
> **LANGUAGES** Mandarin Chinese (official)
> **RELIGIONS** Atheist (official)
> **CURRENCY** Renminbi yuan = 10 jiao = 100 fen

COLOMBIA

GEOGRAPHY The Republic of Colombia, in north-eastern South America, is the only country in the continent to have coastlines on both the Pacific and the Caribbean Sea. Colombia also contains the northernmost ranges of the Andes Mountains.

There is a tropical climate in the lowlands. But the altitude greatly affects the climate of the Andes. The capital, Bogotá, which stands on a plateau in the eastern Andes at about 2,800 m [9,200 ft] above sea level, has mild temperatures throughout the year. The rainfall is heavy, especially on the Pacific coast.

POLITICS & ECONOMY Amerindian people have lived in Colombia for thousands of years. But today, only a small proportion of the people are of unmixed Amerindian ancestry. Mestizos (people of mixed white and Amerindian ancestry) form the largest group, followed by whites and mulattos (people of mixed European and African ancestry).

Spaniards opened up the area in the early 16th century. They set up a territory known as the Vice-royalty of the New Kingdom of Granada, including Colombia, Ecuador, Panama and Venezuela. In 1819, the area became independent, but Ecuador and Venezuela soon split away, followed by Panama in 1903. Instability has marked its recent history. Political rivalries led to civil wars in 1899–1902 and 1949–57, when a coalition government was formed. The coalition ended in 1986 when the Liberal Party was elected. Colombia faces economic and security problems, notably combating left-wing guerrillas and right-wing paramilitaries, while controlling a large illicit drug industry. In the early 2000s, the US provided aid to help Colombia fight drug-trafficking. Colombia exports oil, coffee and chemicals.

> **AREA** 1,138,910 sq km [439,733 sq mi]
> **POPULATION** 41,008,000
> **CAPITAL (POPULATION)** Bogotá (6,005,000)
> **GOVERNMENT** Multiparty republic
> **ETHNIC GROUPS** Mestizo 58%, White 20%, Mulatto 14%, Black 4%
> **LANGUAGES** Spanish (official)
> **RELIGIONS** Roman Catholic 90%
> **CURRENCY** Peso = 100 centavos

COMOROS

 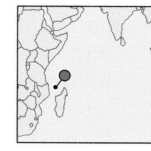

The Federal Islamic Republic of the Comoros consists of three large islands and some smaller ones, lying at the north end of the Mozambique Channel in the Indian Ocean. The country became independent from France in 1974, but the people on a fourth island, Mayotte, voted to remain French. In 1997, secessionists on the island of Anjouan, who favoured a return to French rule, defeated forces from Grand Comore and, in 1998, they voted overwhelmingly to break away from the Comoros. Most people are subsistence farmers, although cash crops such as coconuts, coffee, cocoa and spices are also produced. The main exports are cloves, perfume oils and vanilla. **AREA** 2,230 sq km [861 sq mi]; **POPULATION** 614,000; **CAPITAL** Moroni.

CONGO

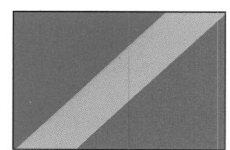 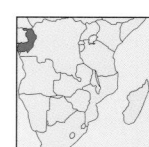

GEOGRAPHY The Republic of Congo is a country on the River Congo in west-central Africa. The Equator runs through the centre of the country. Congo has a narrow coastal plain on which its main port, Pointe Noire, stands. Behind the plain are uplands through which the River Niari has carved a fertile valley. Central Congo consists of high plains. The north contains large swampy areas in the valleys of the tributaries of the River Congo.

Congo has a hot, wet equatorial climate. Brazzaville has a dry season between June and September. The coast is drier and cooler than the rest of Congo, because of the cold offshore Benguela ocean current.

POLITICS & ECONOMY Part of the huge Kongo kingdom between the 15th and 18th centuries, the coast of the Congo later became a centre of the European slave trade. The area came under French protection in 1880. It was later governed as part of a larger region called French Equatorial Africa. The country remained under French control until 1960.

Congo became a one-party state in 1964 and a military group took over the government in 1968. In 1970, Congo declared itself a Communist country, though it continued to seek aid from Western countries. The government officially abandoned its Communist policies in 1990. Multiparty elections were held in 1992, but the elected president, Pascal Lissouba, was overthrown in 1997 by former president Denis Sassou-Nguesso. Civil war again occurred in January 1999, but peace was restored. In 2002, Sassou-Nguesso was elected president.

The World Bank classifies Congo as a 'lower-middle-income' developing country. Agriculture is the most important activity, employing more than 60% of the people. But many farmers produce little more than they need to feed their families. Major food crops include bananas, cassava, maize and rice, while the leading cash crops are coffee and cocoa. Congo's main exports are oil (which makes up 70% of the total) and timber. Manufacturing is relatively unimportant at the moment, still hampered by poor transport links, but it is gradually being developed.

> **AREA** 342,000 sq km [132,046 sq mi]
> **POPULATION** 2,958,000
> **CAPITAL (POPULATION)** Brazzaville (938,000)
> **GOVERNMENT** Military regime
> **ETHNIC GROUPS** Kongo 48%, Sangha 20%, Teke 17%, M'bochi 12%
> **LANGUAGES** French (official), many others
> **RELIGIONS** Christianity 50%, Animist 48%, Islam 2%
> **CURRENCY** CFA franc = 100 centimes

CONGO (DEM. REP. OF THE)

GEOGRAPHY The Democratic Republic of the Congo, formerly known as Zaïre, is the world's 12th largest country. Much of the country lies within the drainage basin of the huge River Congo. The river reaches the sea along the country's coastline, which is 40 km [25 mi] long. Mountains rise in the east, where the country's borders run through lakes Tanganyika, Kivu, Edward and Albert.

The equatorial region has high temperatures and heavy rainfall throughout the year.

POLITICS & ECONOMY Pygmies were the first inhabitants of the region, with Portuguese navigators not reaching the coast until 1482, but the interior was not explored until the late 19th century. In 1885, the country, called Congo Free State, became the personal property of King Léopold II of Belgium. In 1908, the country became a Belgian colony.

The Belgian Congo became independent in 1960 and was renamed Zaïre in 1971. Ethnic rivalries caused instability until 1965, when the country became a one-party state, ruled by President Mobutu. The government allowed the formation of political parties in 1990, but elections were repeatedly postponed. In 1996, fighting broke out in eastern Zaïre, as the Tutsi–Hutu conflict in Burundi and Rwanda spilled over. The rebel leader Laurent Kabila took power in 1997, ousting Mobutu and renaming the country. A rebellion against Kabila broke out in 1998. Rwanda and Uganda supported the rebels, while Angola, Chad, Namibia and Zimbabwe assisted Kabila. A peace treaty was signed in 1999, but fighting continued. Kabila was assassinated in 2001. His son, Major-General Joseph Kabila, who became president, worked to end a war which, by early 2003, had claimed over 2 million lives.

The World Bank classifies the Democratic Republic of the Congo as a 'low-income' developing country, despite its reserves of copper, the main export, and other minerals. Agriculture, mainly at subsistence level, employs 65% of the people.

AREA 2,344,885 sq km [905,365 sq mi]
POPULATION 55,225,000
CAPITAL (POPULATION) Kinshasa (2,664,000)
GOVERNMENT Single-party republic
ETHNIC GROUPS Over 200; the largest are Mongo, Luba, Kongo, Mangbetu-Azande
LANGUAGES French (official), tribal languages
RELIGIONS Roman Catholic 50%, Protestant 20%, Islam 10%, others 20%
CURRENCY Congolese franc

COSTA RICA

GEOGRAPHY The Republic of Costa Rica in Central America has coastlines on both the Pacific Ocean and also on the Caribbean Sea. Central Costa Rica consists of mountain ranges and plateaux with many volcanoes.

The coolest months are December and January. The north-east trade winds bring heavy rain to the Caribbean coast. There is less rainfall in the highlands and on the Pacific coastlands.

POLITICS & ECONOMY Christopher Columbus reached the Caribbean coast in 1502 and rumours of treasure soon attracted many Spaniards to settle in the country. Spain ruled the country until 1821, when Spain's Central American colonies broke away to join Mexico in 1822. In 1823, the Central American states broke with Mexico and set up the Central American Federation. Later, this large union broke up and Costa Rica became fully independent in 1838. From the late 19th century, Costa Rica experienced a number of revolutions, with periods of dictatorship and periods of democracy. In 1948, following a revolt, the armed forces were abolished. Since 1948, Costa Rica has enjoyed a long period of stable democracy, which many in Latin America admire and envy.

Costa Rica is classified by the World Bank as a 'lower-middle-income' developing country and one of the most prosperous countries in Central America. There are high educational standards and a high life expectancy (to an average of 73.5 years). Agriculture employs 20% of the people.

The country's resources include its forests, but it lacks minerals apart from some bauxite and manganese. Manufacturing is increasing. The United States is Costa Rica's chief trading partner. Tourism is a growing industry.

AREA 51,100 sq km [19,730 sq mi]
POPULATION 3,835,000
CAPITAL (POPULATION) San José (1,220,000)
GOVERNMENT Multiparty republic
ETHNIC GROUPS White 85%, Mestizo 8%, Black and Mulatto 3%, East Asian (mostly Chinese) 1%
LANGUAGES Spanish (official)
RELIGIONS Roman Catholic 76%, Evangelical 14%
CURRENCY Colón = 100 céntimos

CROATIA

 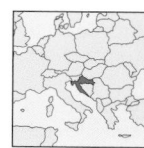

GEOGRAPHY The Republic of Croatia was one of the six republics that made up the former Communist country of Yugoslavia until it became independent in 1991. The region bordering the Adriatic Sea is called Dalmatia. It includes the coastal ranges, which contain large areas of bare limestone. Most of the rest of the country consists of the fertile Pannonian plains.

The coastal area has a typical Mediterranean climate, with hot, dry summers and mild, moist winters. Inland, the climate becomes more continental. Winters are cold, while temperatures often soar to 38°C [100°F] in the summer months.

POLITICS & ECONOMY Slav people settled in the area around 1,400 years ago. In 803, Croatia became part of the Holy Roman empire and the Croats soon adopted Christianity. Croatia was an independent kingdom in the 10th and 11th centuries. In 1102, the king of Hungary also became king of Croatia, creating a union that lasted 800 years. In 1526, part of Croatia came under the Turkish Ottoman empire, while the rest came under the Austrian Habsburgs.

After Austria–Hungary was defeated in World War I (1914–18), Croatia became part of the new Kingdom of the Serbs, Croats and Slovenes. This kingdom was renamed Yugoslavia in 1929. Germany occupied

Yugoslavia during World War II (1939–45). Croatia was proclaimed independent, but it was really ruled by the invaders.

After the war, Communists took power with Josip Broz Tito as the country's leader. Despite ethnic differences between the people, Tito held Yugoslavia together until his death in 1980. In the 1980s, economic and ethnic problems, including a deterioration in relations with Serbia, threatened stability. In the 1990s, Yugoslavia split into five nations, one of which was Croatia, which declared itself independent in 1991.

After Serbia supplied arms to Serbs living in Croatia, war broke out between the two republics, causing great damage. Croatia lost more than 30% of its territory. But in 1992, the United Nations sent a peacekeeping force to Croatia, which effectively ended the war with Serbia.

In 1992, when war broke out in Bosnia-Herzegovina, Bosnian Croats occupied parts of the country. But in 1994, Croatia helped to end Croat–Muslim conflict in Bosnia-Herzegovina and, in 1995, after retaking some areas occupied by Serbs, it helped to draw up the Dayton Peace Accord which ended the civil war there.

The wars of the early 1990s disrupted Croatia's economy, but following the election of a pro-democratic coalition government in 2000, stability, which is so vital for the valuable tourist industry, appeared to be increasing. Croatia has many manufacturing industries. Manufactures are the chief exports.

AREA 56,538 sq km [21,824 sq mi]
POPULATION 4,391,000
CAPITAL (POPULATION) Zagreb (868,000)
GOVERNMENT Multiparty republic
ETHNIC GROUPS Croat 78%, Serb 12%
LANGUAGES Serbo-Croatian
RELIGIONS Roman Catholic 77%, Eastern Orthodox 11%, Islam 1%
CURRENCY Kuna = 100 lipas

CUBA

GEOGRAPHY The Republic of Cuba is the largest island country in the Caribbean Sea. It consists of one large island, Cuba, the Isle of Youth (Isla de la Juventud) and about 1,600 small islets. Mountains and hills cover about a quarter of Cuba. The highest mountain range, the Sierra Maestra in the south-east, reaches 2,000 m [6,562 ft] above sea level. The rest of the land consists of gently rolling country or coastal plains, crossed by fertile valleys carved by the short, mostly shallow and narrow rivers.

Cuba lies in the tropics. But sea breezes moderate the temperature, warming the land in winter and cooling it in summer.

POLITICS & ECONOMY Christopher Columbus discovered the island in 1492 and Spaniards began to settle there from 1511. Spanish rule ended in 1898, when the United States defeated Spain in the Spanish–American War. American influence in Cuba remained strong until 1959, when revolutionary forces under Fidel Castro overthrew the dictatorial government of Fulgencio Batista.

The United States opposed Castro's policies, when he turned to the Soviet Union for assistance. In 1961, Cuban exiles attempting an invasion were defeated. In 1962, the US learned that nuclear missile bases

armed by the Soviet Union had been established in Cuba. The US ordered the Soviet Union to remove the missiles and bases and, after a few days, when many people feared that a world war might break out, the Soviet Union agreed to the American demands.

Cuba's relations with the Soviet Union remained strong until 1991, when the Soviet Union was broken up. The loss of Soviet aid greatly damaged Cuba's economy, but Castro maintained his left-wing policies. In 2000, the United States lifted its food embargo on Cuba, but Cuba again came under fire in 2003 following the arrests of 78 opponents of the regime.

The government runs Cuba's economy and owns 70% of the farmland. Agriculture is important and sugar is the chief export, followed by refined nickel ore. Other exports include cigars, citrus fruits, fish, medical products and rum.

Before 1959, US companies owned most of Cuba's manufacturing industries. But under Fidel Castro, they became government property. After the collapse of Communist governments in the Soviet Union and its allies, Cuba worked to increase its trade with Latin America and China.

AREA 110,860 sq km [42,803 sq mi]
POPULATION 11,224,000
CAPITAL (POPULATION) Havana (2,204,000)
GOVERNMENT Socialist republic
ETHNIC GROUPS Mulatto 51%, White 37%, Black 11%
LANGUAGES Spanish (official)
RELIGIONS Roman Catholic 40%, Protestant 3%
CURRENCY Cuban peso = 100 centavos

CYPRUS

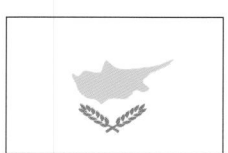 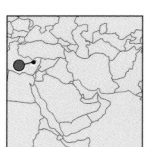

GEOGRAPHY The Republic of Cyprus is an island nation in the north-eastern Mediterranean Sea. Geographers regard it as part of Asia, but it resembles southern Europe in many ways.

Cyprus has scenic mountain ranges, including the Kyrenia range in the north and the Troodos Mountains in the south, which rise to 1,951 m [6,401 ft] at Mount Olympus. The island also contains several fertile lowlands, including the broad Mesaoria plain between the Kyrenia and Troodos mountains.

Cyprus has a Mediterranean climate, with hot, dry summers and mild, moist winters. But the summers are hotter than in the western Mediterranean lands; this is because Cyprus lies close to the hot mainland of south-western Asia.

POLITICS & ECONOMY Greeks settled on Cyprus around 3,200 years ago. From AD 330, the island was part of the Byzantine empire. In the 1570s, Cyprus became part of the Turkish Ottoman empire. Turkish rule continued until 1878 when Cyprus was leased to Britain. Britain annexed the island in 1914 and proclaimed it a colony in 1925.

In the 1950s, Greek Cypriots, who made up four-fifths of the population, began a campaign for enosis (union) with Greece. Their leader was the Greek Orthodox Archbishop Makarios. A secret guerrilla force called EOKA attacked the British, who exiled Makarios. Cyprus became an independent country in 1960, although Britain retained two military bases. Independent Cyprus had a constitution which provided for power-sharing between the Greek and Turkish Cypriots. But the constitution proved unworkable and fighting broke out. In 1964,

the United Nations sent in a peacekeeping force, but communal clashes recurred in 1967.

In 1974, Cypriot forces led by Greek officers overthrew Makarios. This led Turkey to invade northern Cyprus, a territory occupying about 40% of the island. Many Greek Cypriots fled from the north which, in 1979, was proclaimed an independent state called the Turkish Republic of Northern Cyprus. But the United Nations still regarded Cyprus as a single nation under the Greek-Cypriot government in the south. In 2002, the European Union invited Cyprus to become a member in 2004. However, attempts to reunify the island in 2003 ended in failure.

Cyprus got its name from the Greek word *kypros*, meaning copper. But little copper remains and the chief minerals today are asbestos and chromium. However, the most valuable activity in Cyprus is tourism. In the early 1990s, the United Nations reclassified Cyprus as a developed rather than a developing country. But the economy of the Turkish-Cypriot north lags behind that of the more prosperous Greek-Cypriot south.

AREA 9,250 sq km [3,571 sq mi]
POPULATION 767,000
CAPITAL (POPULATION) Nicosia (189,000)
GOVERNMENT Multiparty republic
ETHNIC GROUPS Greek Cypriot 78%, Turkish Cypriot 18%
LANGUAGES Greek and Turkish (both official), English
RELIGIONS Greek Orthodox 78%, Islam 18%
CURRENCY Cyprus pound = 100 cents

CZECH REPUBLIC

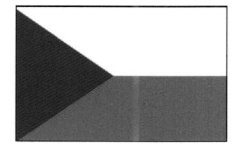 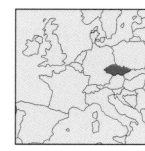

GEOGRAPHY The Czech Republic is the western three-fifths of the former country of Czechoslovakia. It contains two regions: Bohemia in the west and Moravia in the east. Mountains border much of the country in the west. The Bohemian basin in the north-centre is a fertile lowland region, with Prague, the capital city, as its main centre. Highlands cover much of the centre of the country, with lowlands in the south-east.

The climate is influenced by its landlocked position in east-central Europe. Prague has warm, sunny summers and cold winters. The average rainfall is moderate, with 500 mm to 750 mm [20 in to 30 in] every year in lowland areas.

POLITICS & ECONOMY After World War I (1914–18), Czechoslovakia was created. Germany seized the country in World War II (1939–45). In 1948, Communist leaders took power and Czechoslovakia was allied to the Soviet Union. When democratic reforms were introduced in the Soviet Union in the late 1980s, the Czechs also demanded reforms. Free elections were held in 1990, but differences between the Czechs and Slovaks led to the partitioning of the country on 1 January 1993. The Czech Republic became a member of NATO in 1999 and, in 2002, the European Union invited the country to become a member in May 2004.

Under Communist rule the Czech Republic became one of the most industrialized parts of Eastern Europe. The country has deposits of coal, uranium, iron ore, magnesite, tin and zinc. Manufacturing employs about 40% of the Czech Republic's entire

workforce. Farming is also important. Under Communism, the government owned the land, but private ownership is now being restored. The country was admitted into the OECD in 1995.

AREA 78,864 sq km [30,449 sq mi]
POPULATION 10,257,000
CAPITAL (POPULATION) Prague (1,203,000)
GOVERNMENT Multiparty republic
ETHNIC GROUPS Czech 81%, Moravian 13%, Slovak 3%, Polish, German, Silesian, Gypsy, Hungarian, Ukrainian
LANGUAGES Czech (official)
RELIGIONS Atheist 40%, Roman Catholic 39%, Protestant 4%
CURRENCY Czech koruna = 100 haler

DENMARK

GEOGRAPHY The Kingdom of Denmark is the smallest country in Scandinavia. It consists of a peninsula, called Jutland (or Jylland), which is joined to Germany, and more than 400 islands, 89 of which are inhabited.

The land is flat and mostly covered by rocks dropped there by huge ice-sheets during the last Ice Age. The highest point in Denmark is on Jutland. It is only 173 m [568 ft] above sea level.

Denmark has a cool but pleasant climate, except during cold spells in the winter when The Sound between Sjælland and Sweden may freeze over. Summers are warm. Rainfall occurs all through the year.

POLITICS & ECONOMY Danish Vikings terrorized much of Western Europe for about 300 years after AD 800. Danish kings ruled England in the 11th century. In the late 14th century, Denmark formed a union with Norway and Sweden (which included Finland). Sweden broke away in 1523, while Denmark lost Norway to Sweden in 1814.

After 1945, Denmark played an important part in European affairs, becoming a member of the North Atlantic Treaty Organization (NATO). In 1973, Denmark joined the European Union, although it rejected the adoption of the euro in 2000. The Danes now enjoy some of the world's highest living standards, although the extensive social welfare provisions exert a considerable cost.

Denmark has few natural resources apart from some oil and gas from wells deep under the North Sea. But the economy is highly developed. Manufacturing industries, which employ about 17% of all workers, produce a wide variety of products, including furniture, processed food, machinery, television sets and textiles. Farms cover about three-quarters of the land. Farming employs only 4% of the workers, but it is highly scientific and productive. Meat and dairy farming are the chief activities.

AREA 43,070 sq km [16,629 sq mi]
POPULATION 5,369,000
CAPITAL (POPULATION) Copenhagen (1,362,000)
GOVERNMENT Parliamentary monarchy
ETHNIC GROUPS Danish 97%
LANGUAGES Danish (official)
RELIGIONS Lutheran 95%, Roman Catholic 1%
CURRENCY Krone = 100 øre

DJIBOUTI

 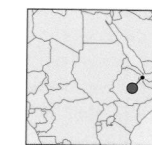

GEOGRAPHY The Republic of Djibouti in eastern Africa occupies a strategic position where the Red Sea meets the Gulf of Aden. Djibouti has one of the world's hottest and driest climates.

POLITICS & ECONOMY France set up a territory called French Somaliland in 1888. Its capital, Djibouti, became important when a railway was built to Addis Ababa and Djibouti became the main outlet for Ethiopian trade.

In 1967, France renamed the dependency the French Territory of the Afars and Issas, but it was renamed Djibouti when it became independent in 1977. Djibouti became a one-party state in 1981, but a new constitution (1992) permitted four parties which had to maintain a balance between the country's ethnic groups. Conflict flared up between the Afars and Issas in 1992 and 1993, but a peace agreement was signed in 1994. Djibouti is a poor country. Its economy is based largely on the revenue it gets from its port and the railway to Addis Ababa.

AREA 23,200 sq km [8,958 sq mi]
POPULATION 473,000
CAPITAL (POPULATION) Djibouti (383,000)
GOVERNMENT Multiparty republic
ETHNIC GROUPS Somali 60%, Afar 35%
LANGUAGES Arabic and French (both official)
RELIGIONS Islam 94%, Christianity 6%
CURRENCY Djibouti franc = 100 centimes

DOMINICA

The Commonwealth of Dominica, a former British colony, became independent in 1978. The island has a mountainous spine and less than 10% of the land is cultivated. Yet agriculture employs more than 60% of the people. Manufacturing, mining and tourism are other minor activities. **AREA** 751 sq km [290 sq mi]; **POPULATION** 70,000; **CAPITAL** Roseau.

DOMINICAN REPUBLIC

GEOGRAPHY Second largest of the Caribbean nations in both area and population, the Dominican Republic shares the island of Hispaniola with Haiti. The country is mountainous, and the generally hot and humid climate eases with altitude.

POLITICS & ECONOMY The Dominican Republic has chaotic origins, having been held by Spain, France, Haiti and the United States at various times. Civil war broke out in 1966 but the conflict soon ended after US intervention. Since 1966, a young democracy has survived violent elections under the watchful eye of the USA.

AREA 48,730 sq km [18,815 sq mi]
POPULATION 8,722,000
CAPITAL (POPULATION) Santo Domingo (2,135,000)
GOVERNMENT Multiparty republic
ETHNIC GROUPS Mulatto 73%, White 16%, Black 11%
LANGUAGES Spanish (official)
RELIGIONS Roman Catholic 95%
CURRENCY Peso = 100 centavos

EAST TIMOR

The Republic of East Timor became fully independent and the world's newest country on 20 May 2002. The land is mainly rugged. Temperatures are generally high and the rainfall is moderate. Portugal ruled the area from the late 19th century, when it was called Portuguese Timor. Portugal withdrew in 1975 and Indonesia seized the area. Guerrilla activity mounted under Indonesian rule and, in 1999, the people voted for independence. Agriculture is the main activity. East Timor is heavily dependent on foreign aid, but its offshore deposits of oil and natural gas are due to come on line in 2004. **AREA** 14,870 sq km [5,731 sq mi]; **POPULATION** 953,000; **CAPITAL** Dili.

ECUADOR

GEOGRAPHY The Republic of Ecuador straddles the Equator on the west coast of South America. Three ranges of the high Andes Mountains form the backbone of the country. Between the towering, snow-capped peaks of the mountains, some of which are volcanoes, lie a series of high plateaux, or basins. Nearly half of Ecuador's population lives on these plateaux.

The climate in Ecuador depends on the height above sea level. Though the coastline is cooled by the cold Peruvian Current, temperatures are between 23°C and 25°C [73°F to 77°F] all through the year. In Quito, at 2,500 m [8,200 ft] above sea level, temperatures are 14°C to 15°C [57°F to 59°F], though the city is just south of the Equator.

POLITICS & ECONOMY The Inca people of Peru conquered much of what is now Ecuador in the late 15th century. They introduced their language, Quechua, which is widely spoken today. Spanish forces defeated the Incas in 1533 and took control of Ecuador. The country became independent in 1822, following the defeat of a Spanish force in a battle near Quito. In the 19th and 20th centuries, Ecuador suffered from political instability, while successive governments failed to tackle the country's social and economic problems. A war with Peru in 1941 led to a loss of territory. Disputes continued until 1995, but a border agreement was signed in January 1998. Economic crises in the early 21st century led the government to abolish the sucre, its official currency, and replace it with the US dollar.

The World Bank classifies Ecuador as a 'lower-middle-income' developing country. Agriculture employs 30% of the people and bananas, cocoa and coffee are all important crops. Fishing, forestry, mining and manufacturing are other activities.

AREA 283,560 sq km [109,483 sq mi]
POPULATION 13,447,000
CAPITAL (POPULATION) Quito (1,574,000)
GOVERNMENT Multiparty republic
ETHNIC GROUPS Mestizo (mixed White and Amerindian) 40%, Amerindian 40%, White 15%, Black 5%
LANGUAGES Spanish (official), Quechua
RELIGIONS Christianity (Roman Catholic 92%)
CURRENCY US dollar = 100 cents

EGYPT

 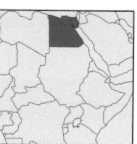

GEOGRAPHY The Arab Republic of Egypt is Africa's second largest country by population after Nigeria, though it ranks 13th in area. Most of Egypt is desert. Almost all the people live either in the Nile Valley and its fertile delta or along the Suez Canal, the artificial waterway between the Mediterranean and Red seas. This canal shortens the sea journey between the United Kingdom and India by 9,700 km [6,027 mi]. Recent attempts have been made to irrigate parts of the western desert and thus redistribute the rapidly growing Egyptian population into previously uninhabited regions.

Apart from the Nile Valley, Egypt has three other main regions. The Western and Eastern deserts are parts of the Sahara. The Sinai peninsula (Es Sina), to the east of the Suez Canal, is a mountainous desert region, geographically within Asia. It contains Egypt's highest peak, Gebel Katherina (2,637 m [8,650 ft]); few people live in this area.

Egypt is a dry country. The low rainfall occurs, if at all, in winter and the country is one of the sunniest places on Earth.

POLITICS & ECONOMY Ancient Egypt, which was founded about 5,000 years ago, was one of the great early civilizations. Throughout the country, pyramids, temples and richly decorated tombs are memorials to its great achievements.

After Ancient Egypt declined, the country came under successive foreign rulers. Arabs occupied Egypt in AD 639–42. They introduced the Arabic language and Islam. Their influence was so great that most Egyptians now regard themselves as Arabs.

Egypt came under British rule in 1882, but it gained partial independence in 1922, becoming a monarchy. The monarchy was abolished in 1952, when Egypt became a republic. The creation of Israel in 1948 led Egypt into a series of wars in 1948–9, 1956, 1967 and 1973. Since the late 1970s, Egypt has sought for peace. In 1979, Egypt signed a peace treaty with Israel and regained the Sinai region which it had lost in a war in 1967. Extremists opposed contacts with Israel and, in 1981, President Sadat, who had signed the treaty, was assassinated.

While Egypt plays a major part in Arab affairs, most of its people are poor. Some Islamic fundamentalists, who dislike Western influences on their way of life, have resorted to violence. In the 1990s, attacks on foreign visitors caused a decline in the valuable tourist industry. In 1999, Hosni Mubarak, president since 1981, was himself attacked by extremists, but he was re-elected to a fourth term in office.

Egypt is Africa's second most industrialized country after South Africa, but it remains a developing country and income levels remain low for the vast majority of Egyptian people. Oil and textiles are the chief exports.

EL SALVADOR

AREA 1,001,450 sq km [386,660 sq mi]
POPULATION 70,712,000
CAPITAL (POPULATION) Cairo (6,800,000)
GOVERNMENT Republic
ETHNIC GROUPS Egyptian 99%
LANGUAGES Arabic (official), French, English
RELIGIONS Islam (Sunni Muslim 94%),
Christianity (mainly Coptic Christian 6%)
CURRENCY Pound = 100 piastres

EL SALVADOR

 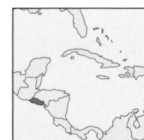

GEOGRAPHY The Republic of El Salvador is the only country in Central America which does not have a coast on the Caribbean Sea. El Salvador has a narrow coastal plain along the Pacific Ocean. Behind the coastal plain, the coastal range is a zone of rugged mountains, including volcanoes, which overlooks a densely populated inland plateau. Beyond the plateau, the land rises to the sparsely populated interior highlands.

The coast has a hot, tropical climate. Inland, the climate is moderated by the altitude. Rain falls on practically every afternoon between May and October.

POLITICS & ECONOMY Amerindians have lived in El Salvador for thousands of years. The ruins of Mayan pyramids built between AD 100 and 1000 are still found in the western part of the country. Spanish soldiers conquered the area in 1524 and 1525, and Spain ruled until 1821. In 1823, all the Central American countries, except for Panama, set up a Central American Federation. But El Salvador withdrew in 1840 and declared its independence in 1841. El Salvador suffered from instability throughout the 19th century. The 20th century saw a more stable government, but from 1931 military dictatorships alternated with elected governments and the country remained poor.

In the 1970s, El Salvador was plagued by conflict as protesters demanded that the government introduce reforms to help the poor. Kidnappings and murders committed by left- and right-wing groups caused instability. A civil war broke out in 1979 between the US-backed, right-wing government forces and left-wing guerrillas in the FMLN (Farabundo Marti National Liberation Front). In 12 years, more than 750,000 people died and hundreds of thousands were made homeless. A cease-fire was agreed on 1 February 1992, and elections were held in 1993 and 1999. By 2003, the economy had shown signs of recovery, but the World Bank still classifies El Salvador as a lower-middle-income economy.

About three-quarters of the country is farmed. Coffee, grown in the highlands, is the main export, followed by sugar and cotton, which grow on the coastal lowlands. Fishing for lobsters and shrimps is important, but manufacturing is on a small scale.

AREA 21,040 sq km [8,124 sq mi]
POPULATION 6,354,000
CAPITAL (POPULATION) San Salvador (1,522,000)
GOVERNMENT Republic
ETHNIC GROUPS Mestizo (mixed White and Amerindian) 89%, White 10%, Amerindian 1%
LANGUAGES Spanish (official)
RELIGIONS Roman Catholic 86%
CURRENCY US dollar; Colón = 100 centavos

EQUATORIAL GUINEA

GEOGRAPHY The Republic of Equatorial Guinea is a small republic in west-central Africa. It consists of a mainland territory which makes up 90% of the land area, called Rio Muni, between Cameroon and Gabon, and five offshore islands in the Bight of Bonny, the largest of which is Bioko. The island of Annobon lies 560 km [350 mi] south-west of Rio Muni. Rio Muni consists mainly of hills and plateaux behind the coastal plains.

The climate is hot and humid. Bioko is mountainous, with the land rising to 3,008 m [9,869 ft], and hence it is particularly rainy. However, there is a marked dry season between the months of December and February. Mainland Rio Muni has a similar climate, though the rainfall diminishes inland.

POLITICS & ECONOMY Portuguese navigators reached the area in 1471. In 1778, Portugal granted Bioko, together with rights over Rio Muni, to Spain.

In 1959, Spain made Bioko and Rio Muni provinces of overseas Spain and, in 1963, it gave the provinces a degree of self-government. Equatorial Guinea became independent in 1968.

The first president of Equatorial Guinea, Francisco Macias Nguema, proved to be a tyrant. He was overthrown in 1979 and a group of officers, led by Lt.-Col. Teodoro Obiang Nguema Mbasogo, set up a Supreme Military Council to rule the country. In 1991, the people voted to set up a multiparty democracy. Elections were held in the 1990s, but accusations of human rights abuses continued.

Equatorial Guinea is a poor country. Agriculture employs over half of the people. The most valuable crop is coffee. Oil has been produced since 1966, but oil revenue has done little to ease poverty.

AREA 28,050 sq km [10,830 sq mi]
POPULATION 498,000
CAPITAL (POPULATION) Malabo (35,000)
GOVERNMENT Multiparty republic (transitional)
ETHNIC GROUPS Fang 83%, Bubi 10%, Ndowe 4%
LANGUAGES Spanish and French (both official)
RELIGIONS Roman Catholic 89%
CURRENCY CFA franc = 100 centimes

ERITREA

 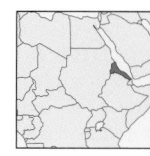

GEOGRAPHY The State of Eritrea consists of a hot, dry coastal plain facing the Red Sea, with a fairly mountainous area in the centre. Most people live in the cooler highland area.

POLITICS & ECONOMY Eritrea, which was an Italian colony from the 1880s, was part of Ethiopia from 1952 until 1993, when it became a fully independent nation. National reconstruction was hampered by conflict with Yemen over three islands in the Red Sea, while in 1998–9, border clashes with Ethiopia caused loss of life. However, a peace agreement was signed in 2000. Farming and livestock-rearing are the main activities in this war-ravaged territory. Eritrea has few manufacturing industries, based mainly in Asmara.

AREA 94,000 sq km [36,293 sq mi]
POPULATION 4,466,000
CAPITAL (POPULATION) Asmara (367,500)
GOVERNMENT Transitional government
ETHNIC GROUPS Tigrinya 49%, Tigre 32%, Afar 4%, Beja 3%, Saho 3%, Kunama 3%, Nara 2%
LANGUAGES Afar, Amharic, Arabic, Tigrinya
RELIGIONS Coptic Christian 50%, Islam 50%
CURRENCY Nakfa

ESTONIA

GEOGRAPHY The Republic of Estonia is the smallest of the three states on the Baltic Sea, which were formerly part of the Soviet Union, but which became independent in the early 1990s. Estonia consists of a generally flat plain which was covered by ice-sheets during the Ice Age. The land is strewn with moraine (rocks deposited by the ice).

The country is dotted with more than 1,500 small lakes, and water, including the large Lake Peipus (Chudskoye Ozero) and the River Narva makes up much of Estonia's eastern border with Russia. Estonia has more than 800 islands, which together make up about a tenth of the country. The largest island is Saaremaa (Sarema).

Despite its northerly position, Estonia has a fairly mild climate because of its nearness to the sea. This is because sea winds tend to warm the land in winter and cool it in summer.

POLITICS & ECONOMY The ancestors of the Estonians, who are related to the Finns, settled in the area several thousand years ago. German crusaders, known as the Teutonic Knights, introduced Christianity in the early 13th century. By the 16th century, German noblemen owned much of the land in Estonia. In 1561, Sweden took the northern part of the country and Poland the south. From 1625, Sweden controlled the entire country until Sweden handed it over to Russia in 1721.

Estonian nationalists campaigned for their independence from around the mid-19th century. Finally, Estonia was proclaimed independent in 1918. In 1919, the government began to break up the large estates and distribute land among the peasants.

In 1939, Germany and the Soviet Union agreed to take over parts of Eastern Europe. In 1940, Soviet forces occupied Estonia, but they were driven out by the Germans in 1941. Soviet troops returned in 1944 and Estonia became one of the 15 Soviet Socialist Republics of the Soviet Union. The Estonians strongly opposed Soviet rule. Many of them were deported to Siberia.

Political changes in the Soviet Union in the late 1980s led to renewed demands for freedom. In 1990, the Estonian government declared the country independent and, finally, the Soviet Union recognized this act in September 1991, shortly before the Soviet Union was dissolved. Estonia adopted a new constitution in 1992, when multiparty elections were held for a new national assembly. In 1993, Estonia negotiated an agreement with Russia to withdraw its troops.

Under Soviet rule, Estonia was the most prosperous of the three Baltic states. Since 1988, Estonia has begun to change its government-dominated economy to one based on private enterprise and, in 2002, the European Union invited Estonia to become a member in May 2004. Estonia's resources include

oil shale and its forests. Industries produce fertilizers, machinery, petrochemical products, processed food, wood products and textiles. Agriculture and fishing are other important activities.

AREA 44,700 sq km [17,300 sq mi]
POPULATION 1,416,000
CAPITAL (POPULATION) Tallinn (435,000)
GOVERNMENT Multiparty republic
ETHNIC GROUPS Estonian 65%, Russian 28%, Ukrainian 3%, Belarussian 2%, Finnish 1%
LANGUAGES Estonian (official), Russian
RELIGIONS Lutheran, Russian and Estonian Orthodox, Methodist, Baptist, Roman Catholic
CURRENCY Kroon = 100 sents

ETHIOPIA

 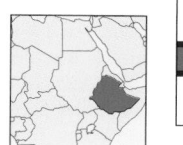

GEOGRAPHY Ethiopia is a landlocked country in north-eastern Africa. The land is mainly mountainous, though there are extensive plains in the east, bordering southern Eritrea, and in the south, bordering Somalia. The highlands are divided into two blocks by an arm of the Great Rift Valley which runs throughout eastern Africa. North of the Rift Valley, the land is especially rugged, rising to 4,620 m [15,157 ft] at Ras Dashen. South-east of Ras Dashen is Lake Tana, source of the River Abay (Blue Nile).

The climate in Ethiopia is greatly affected by the altitude. Addis Ababa, at 2,450 m [8,000 ft], has an average yearly temperature of 20°C [68°F]. The rainfall is generally more than 1,000 mm [39 in]. But the lowlands bordering the Eritrean coast are hot.

POLITICS & ECONOMY Ethiopia was the home of an ancient monarchy, which became Christian in the 4th century. In the 7th century, Muslims gained control of the lowlands, but Christianity survived in the highlands. Ethiopia resisted attempts to colonize it, but Italy invaded the country in 1935. The Italians were driven out in 1941 during World War II.

In 1952, Eritrea, on the Red Sea coast, was federated with Ethiopia. But in 1961, Eritrean nationalists demanded their freedom and began a struggle that ended in their independence in 1993. Clashes along the border with Eritrea occurred in 1998 and 1999, but a peace agreement was signed in 2000, though a disagreement arose in 2003 about the status of Badme, the village where the conflict began. Some Ethiopian minorities would like self-government and, in 1995, the country was divided into nine provinces, each with its own regional assembly.

Ethiopia is one of the world's poorest countries, particularly in the 1970s and 1980s when it was plagued by civil war and famine caused partly by long droughts. Many richer countries have sent aid (money and food) to help the Ethiopian people. Agriculture remains the leading activity.

AREA 1,128,000 sq km [435,521 sq mi]
POPULATION 67,673,000
CAPITAL (POPULATION) Addis Ababa (2,316,000)
GOVERNMENT Federation of nine provinces
ETHNIC GROUPS Oromo 40%, Amharic 32%, Sidamo 9%, Shankella 6%, Somali 6%
LANGUAGES Amharic (official), 280 others
RELIGIONS Islam 47%, Ethiopian Orthodox 40%, traditional beliefs 11%
CURRENCY Birr = 100 cents

FALKLAND ISLANDS

 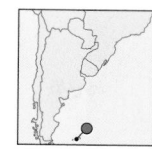

Comprising two main islands and over 200 small islands, the Falkland Islands lie 480 km [300 mi] from South America. Sheep farming is the main activity, though the search for oil and diamonds holds out hope for the future of this harsh and virtually treeless environment. **AREA** 12,170 sq km [4,699 sq mi]; **POPULATION** 3,000; **CAPITAL** Stanley.

FAROE ISLANDS

The Faroe Islands are a group of 18 volcanic islands and some reefs in the North Atlantic Ocean. The islands have been Danish since the 1380s, but they became largely self-governing in 1948. In 1998, the government of the Faroes announced its intention to become independent of Denmark. **AREA** 1,400 sq km [541 sq mi]; **POPULATION** 46,000; **CAPITAL** Torshávn.

FIJI

 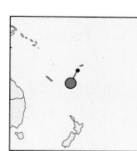

The Republic of Fiji comprises more than 800 Melanesian islands, the biggest being Viti Levu and Vanua Levu. The climate is tropical, with south-east trade winds blowing throughout the year. A former British colony, Fiji became independent in 1970. Its recent history has been marred by efforts by ethnic Fijians to impose their rule, stopping members of the ethnic Indian community from holding senior cabinet posts. Their actions have provoked international criticism. **AREA** 18,270 sq km [7,054 sq mi]; **POPULATION** 856,000; **CAPITAL** Suva.

FINLAND

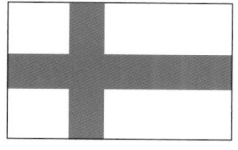 

GEOGRAPHY The Republic of Finland is a beautiful country in northern Europe. In the south, behind the coastal lowlands where most Finns live, lies a region of sparkling lakes worn out by ice-sheets in the Ice Age. The thinly populated northern uplands cover about two-fifths of the country.

Helsinki, the capital city, has warm summers, but the average temperatures between the months of December and March are below freezing point. Snow covers the land in winter. The north has less precipitation than the south, but it is much colder.

POLITICS & ECONOMY Between 1150 and 1809, Finland was under Swedish rule. The close links between the countries continue today. Swedish

remains an official language in Finland and many towns have Swedish as well as Finnish names.

In 1809, Finland became a grand duchy of the Russian empire. It finally declared itself independent in 1917, after the Russian Revolution and the collapse of the Russian empire. But during World War II (1939–45), the Soviet Union declared war on Finland and took part of Finland's territory. Finland allied itself with Germany, but it lost more land to the Soviet Union at the end of the war.

After World War II, Finland became a neutral country and negotiated peace treaties with the Soviet Union. Finland also strengthened its relations with other northern European countries and became an associate member of the European Free Trade Association (EFTA) in 1961. Finland became a full member of EFTA in 1986, but in 1992, along with most of its fellow EFTA members, it applied for membership of the European Union, which it finally achieved on 1 January 1995. On 1 January 2002, the euro became Finland's sole official unit of currency.

Forests are Finland's most valuable resource, and forestry accounts for about 35% of the country's exports. The chief manufactures are wood products, pulp and paper. Since World War II, Finland has set up many other industries, producing such things as machinery and transport equipment. Its economy has expanded rapidly, but there has been a large increase in the number of unemployed people.

AREA 338,130 sq km [130,552 sq mi]
POPULATION 5,184,000
CAPITAL (POPULATION) Helsinki (532,000)
GOVERNMENT Multiparty republic
ETHNIC GROUPS Finnish 93%, Swedish 6%
LANGUAGES Finnish and Swedish (both official)
RELIGIONS Evangelical Lutheran 88%
CURRENCY Euro = 100 cents

FRANCE

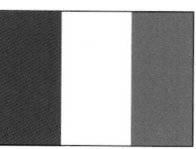 

GEOGRAPHY The Republic of France is the largest country in Western Europe. The scenery is extremely varied. The Vosges Mountains overlook the Rhine valley in the north-east, the Jura Mountains and the Alps form the borders with Switzerland and Italy in the south-east, while the Pyrenees straddle France's border with Spain. The only large highland area entirely within France is the Massif Central in southern France.

Brittany (Bretagne) and Normandy (Normande) form a scenic hill region. Fertile lowlands cover most of northern France, including the densely populated Paris basin. Another major lowland area, the Aquitanian basin, is in the south-west, while the Rhône-Saône valley and the Mediterranean lowlands are in the south-east.

The climate of France varies from west to east and from north to south. The west comes under the moderating influence of the Atlantic Ocean, giving generally mild weather. To the east, summers are warmer and winters colder. The climate also becomes warmer as one travels from north to south. The Mediterranean Sea coast has hot, dry summers and mild, moist winters. The Alps, Jura and Pyrenees mountains have snowy winters. Winter sports centres are found in all three areas. Large glaciers occupy high valleys in the Alps.

FRANCE

POLITICS & ECONOMY The Romans conquered France (then called Gaul) in the 50s BC. Roman rule began to decline in the fifth century AD and, in 486, the Frankish realm (as France was called) became independent under a Christian king, Clovis. In 800, Charlemagne, who had been king since 768, became emperor of the Romans. He extended France's boundaries, but, in 843, his empire was divided into three parts and the area of France contracted. After the Norman invasion of England in 1066, large areas of France came under English rule, but this was finally ended in 1453.

France later became a powerful monarchy. But the French Revolution (1789–99) ended absolute rule by French kings. In 1799, Napoleon Bonaparte took power and fought a series of brilliant military campaigns before his final defeat in 1815. The monarchy was restored until 1848, when the Second Republic was founded. In 1852, Napoleon's nephew became Napoleon III, but the Third Republic was established in 1875. France was the scene of much fighting during World War I (1914–18) and World War II (1939–45), causing great loss of life and much damage to the economy.

In 1946, France adopted a new constitution, establishing the Fourth Republic. But political instability and costly colonial wars slowed France's post-war recovery. In 1958, Charles de Gaulle was elected president and he introduced a new constitution, giving the president extra powers and inaugurating the Fifth Republic.

Since the 1960s, France has made rapid economic progress, becoming one of the most prosperous nations in the European Union. But France's government faced a number of problems, including unemployment, pollution and the growing number of elderly people, who find it difficult to live when inflation rates are high. One social problem concerns the presence in France of large numbers of immigrants from Africa and southern Europe, many of whom live in poor areas.

A socialist government under Lionel Jospin was elected in June 1997. Under Jospin, France adopted the euro, the single European currency, and shortened the working week. The French system of high social security seems likely to continue. France has a long record of independence in foreign affairs and, in 2003, it angered the United States and some of its EU allies by opposing the invasion of Iraq.

France is one of the world's most developed countries. Its natural resources include its fertile soil, together with deposits of bauxite, coal, iron ore, oil and natural gas, and potash. France is also one of the world's top manufacturing nations, and it has often innovated in bold and imaginative ways. The TGV, Concorde and hypermarkets are all typical examples. Paris is a world centre of fashion industries, but France has many other industrial towns and cities. Major manufactures include aircraft, cars, chemicals, electronic products, machinery, metal products, processed food, steel and textiles.

Agriculture employs about 4% of the people, but France is the largest producer of farm products in Western Europe, producing most of the food it needs. Wheat is the leading crop and livestock farming is of major importance. Fishing and forestry are leading industries, while tourism is a major activity.

AREA 551,500 sq km [212,934 sq mi]
POPULATION 59,766,000
CAPITAL (POPULATION) Paris (11,175,000)
GOVERNMENT Multiparty republic
ETHNIC GROUPS Celtic, Latin, Arab, Teutonic, Slavic
LANGUAGES French (official), Breton, Occitan
RELIGIONS Roman Catholic 90%, Islam 3%
CURRENCY Euro = 100 cents

FRENCH GUIANA

GEOGRAPHY French Guiana is the smallest country in mainland South America. The coastal plain is swampy in places, but some dry areas are cultivated. Inland lies a plateau, with the low Tumachumac Mountains in the south. Most of the rivers run north towards the Atlantic Ocean.

French Guiana has a hot, equatorial climate, with high temperatures throughout the year. The rainfall is heavy, especially between December and June, but it is dry between August and October. The north-east trade winds blow constantly across the country.

POLITICS & ECONOMY The first people to live in what is now French Guiana were Amerindians. Today, only a few of them survive in the interior. The first Europeans to explore the coast arrived in 1500, and they were followed by adventurers seeking El Dorado, the mythical city of gold. Cayenne was founded in 1637 by a group of French merchants. The area became a French colony in the late 17th century.

France used the colony as a penal settlement for political prisoners from the times of the French Revolution in the 1790s. From the 1850s to 1945, the country became notorious as a place where prisoners were harshly treated. Many of them died, unable to survive in the tropical conditions.

In 1946, French Guiana became an overseas department of France, and in 1974 it also became an administrative region. An independence movement developed in the 1980s, but most people want to retain their links with France and continue to obtain financial aid to develop their territory.

Although it has rich forest and mineral resources, such as bauxite (aluminium ore), French Guiana is a developing country. It depends greatly on France for money to run its services and the government is the country's biggest employer. Since 1968, Kourou in French Guiana, the European Space Agency's rocket-launching site, has earned money for France by sending communications satellites into space.

AREA 90,000 sq km [34,749 sq mi]
POPULATION 182,000
CAPITAL (POPULATION) Cayenne (42,000)
GOVERNMENT Overseas department of France
ETHNIC GROUPS Mulatto 66%, Chinese and Amerindian 12%, White 10%
LANGUAGES French (official)
RELIGIONS Christianity (Roman Catholic 80%, Protestant 4%)
CURRENCY Euro = 100 cents

FRENCH POLYNESIA

 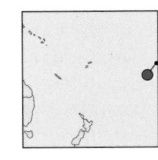

French Polynesia consists of 130 islands, scattered over 4 million sq km [1.5 million sq mi] of the Pacific Ocean. Tribal chiefs in the area agreed to a French protectorate in 1843. They gained increased autonomy in 1984, but the links with France ensure a high standard of living. **AREA** 3,941 sq km [1,520 sq mi]; **POPULATION** 258,000; **CAPITAL** Papeete.

GABON

GEOGRAPHY The Gabonese Republic lies on the Equator in west-central Africa. In area, it is a little larger than the United Kingdom, with a coastline 800 km [500 mi] long. Behind the narrow, partly lagoon-lined coastal plain, the land rises to hills, plateaux and mountains divided by deep valleys carved by the River Ogooué and its tributaries.

Most of Gabon has an equatorial climate, with high temperatures and humidity throughout the year. The rainfall is heavy and the skies are often cloudy.

POLITICS & ECONOMY Gabon became a French colony in the 1880s, but it achieved full independence in 1960. In 1964, an attempted coup was put down when French troops intervened and crushed the revolt. In 1967, Bernard-Albert Bongo, who later renamed himself El Hadj Omar Bongo, became president. He declared Gabon a one-party state in 1968. Opposition parties were legalized in 1991, but Bongo was re-elected president in 1993 and 1998.

Gabon's abundant natural resources include its forests, oil and gas deposits near Port Gentil, together with manganese and uranium. These mineral deposits make Gabon one of Africa's better-off countries. But agriculture still employs about 41% of the population and many farmers produce little more than they need to support their families.

AREA 267,670 sq km [103,347 sq mi]
POPULATION 1,233,000
CAPITAL (POPULATION) Libreville (418,000)
GOVERNMENT Multiparty republic
ETHNIC GROUPS Four major Bantu tribes: Fang, Eshira, Bapounou and Bateke
LANGUAGES French (official), Bantu languages
RELIGIONS Roman Catholic 65%, Protestant 19%, African churches 12%, traditional beliefs 3%, Islam 2%
CURRENCY CFA franc = 100 centimes

GAMBIA, THE

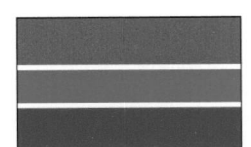 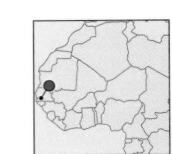

GEOGRAPHY The Republic of The Gambia is the smallest country in mainland Africa. It consists of a narrow strip of land bordering the River Gambia. The Gambia is almost entirely enclosed by Senegal, except along the short Atlantic coastline.

The Gambia has hot and humid summers, but the winter temperatures (November to May) drop to around 16°C [61°F]. In the summer, moist south-westerlies bring rain, which is heaviest on the coast.

POLITICS & ECONOMY English traders bought rights to trade on the River Gambia in 1588, and in 1664 the English established a settlement on an island in the river estuary. In 1765, the British founded a colony called Senegambia, which included parts of The Gambia and Senegal. In 1783, Britain handed this colony over to France.

In the 1860s and 1870s, Britain and France discussed the exchange of The Gambia for some other French territory. But no agreement was reached and Britain made The Gambia a British

colony in 1888. It remained under British rule until it achieved full independence in 1965. In 1970, The Gambia became a republic. Relations between the English-speaking Gambians and the French-speaking Senegalese form a major political issue. In 1981, an attempted coup in The Gambia was put down with the help of Senegalese troops. In 1982, The Gambia and Senegal set up a defence alliance, called the Confederation of Senegambia. But this alliance was dissolved in 1989. In July 1994, a military group overthrew the president, Sir Dawda Jawara, who fled into exile. Captain Yahya Jammeh, who took power, was elected president in 1996 and re-elected in 2001.

Agriculture employs more than 80% of the people. The main food crops include cassava, millet and sorghum, but groundnuts and groundnut products are the chief exports. Tourism is a growing industry.

AREA 11,300 sq km [4,363 sq mi]
POPULATION 1,456,000
CAPITAL (POPULATION) Banjul (171,000)
GOVERNMENT Military regime
ETHNIC GROUPS Mandinka 42%, Fula 18%, Wolof 16%, Jola 10%, Serahuli 9%
LANGUAGES English (official), Mandinka, Wolof, Fula
RELIGIONS Islam 90%, Christianity 9%, traditional beliefs 1%
CURRENCY Dalasi = 100 butut

GEORGIA

GEOGRAPHY Georgia is a country on the borders of Europe and Asia, facing the Black Sea. The land is rugged with the Caucasus Mountains forming its northern border. The highest mountain in this range, Mount Elbrus (5,633 m [18,481 ft]), lies over the border with Russia.

The Black Sea plains have hot summers and mild winters, when temperatures seldom drop below freezing point. The rainfall is heavy, but inland areas are much drier.

POLITICS & ECONOMY The first Georgian state was set up nearly 2,500 years ago. But for much of its history, the area was ruled by various conquerors. Christianity was introduced in AD 330. Georgia freed itself of foreign rule in the 11th and 12th centuries, but Mongol armies attacked in the 13th century. From the 16th to the 18th centuries, Iran and the Turkish Ottoman empire struggled for control of the area, and in the late 18th century Georgia sought the protection of Russia and, by the early 19th century, Georgia was part of the Russian empire. After the Russian Revolution of 1917, Georgia declared its independence, but Russia invaded, making the country part of the Soviet regime. Georgia declared itself independent in 1991. It became a separate country when the Soviet Union was dissolved in December 1991.

Georgia contains three regions containing minority peoples: Abkhazia in the north-west, South Ossetia in north-central Georgia, and Adjaria (also spelled Adzharia) in the south-west. Civil war broke out in South Ossetia in the early 1990s, while fierce fighting continued in Abkhazia until the late 1990s. In 2000, Georgia agreed to recognize Adjaria's autonomy in the country's constitution. In 2002, Russian and Georgian troops attacked Chechen rebels in Pankisi Gorge in north-eastern Georgia. The USA also alleged that terrorists from Afghanistan and elsewhere were hiding in the area.

Georgia is a developing country. Agriculture is important. Major products include barley, citrus fruits, grapes for wine-making, vegetables, maize, tobacco and tea. Food processing and silk and perfume-making are other important activities. Sheep and cattle are reared.

AREA 69,700 sq km [26,910 sq mi]
POPULATION 4,961,000
CAPITAL (POPULATION) Tbilisi (1,253,000)
GOVERNMENT Multiparty republic
ETHNIC GROUPS Georgian 70%, Armenian 8%, Russian 6%, Azeri 6%, Ossetian 3%, Greek 2%, Abkhaz 2%, others 3%
LANGUAGES Georgian (official), Russian
RELIGIONS Georgian Orthodox 65%, Islam 11%, Russian Orthodox 10%, Armenian Apostolic 8%
CURRENCY Lari = 100 tetri

GERMANY

GEOGRAPHY The Federal Republic of Germany is the fourth largest country in Western Europe, after France, Spain and Sweden. The North German plain borders the North Sea in the north-west and the Baltic Sea in the north-east. Major rivers draining the plain include the Weser, Elbe and Oder.

The central highlands contain plateaux and highlands, including the Harz Mountains, the Thuringian Forest (Thüringer Wald), the Ore Mountains (Erzgebirge), and the Bohemian Forest (Böhmerwald) on the Czech border. South Germany is largely hilly, but the land rises in the south to the Bavarian Alps, which contain Germany's highest peak, Zugspitze, at 2,963 m [9,721 ft] above sea level. The scenic Black Forest (Scharzwald) overlooks the River Rhine, which flows through a rift valley in the south-west. The Black Forest contains the source of the River Danube.

North-western Germany has a mild climate, but the Baltic coastlands are cooler. To the south, the climate becomes more continental, especially in the highlands. The precipitation is greatest on the uplands, many of which are snow-capped in winter.

POLITICS & ECONOMY Germany and its allies were defeated in World War I (1914–18) and the country became a republic. Adolf Hitler came to power in 1933 and ruled as a dictator. His order to invade Poland led to the start of World War II (1939–45), which ended with Germany in ruins.

In 1945, Germany was divided into four military zones. In 1949, the American, British and French zones were amalgamated to form the Federal Republic of Germany (West Germany), while the Soviet zone became the German Democratic Republic (East Germany), a Communist state. Berlin, which had also been partitioned, became a divided city. West Berlin was part of West Germany, while East Berlin became the capital of East Germany. Bonn was the capital of West Germany.

Tension between East and West mounted during the Cold War, but West Germany rebuilt its economy quickly. In East Germany, the recovery was less rapid. In the late 1980s, reforms in the Soviet Union led to unrest in East Germany. Free elections were held in East Germany in 1990 and, on 3 October 1990, Germany was reunited.

The united Germany adopted West Germany's official name, the Federal Republic of Germany. Elections in December 1990 returned Helmut Kohl, West Germany's Chancellor (head of government) since 1982, to power. His government faced many problems, especially the restructuring of the economy of the former East Germany. Kohl was defeated in elections in 1998 and was succeeded as Chancellor by Social Democrat Gerhard Schröder. In 1999, Germany's parliament moved from Bonn to the reconstructed Reichstag building in Berlin.

West Germany's 'economic miracle' after the destruction of World War II was greatly helped by foreign aid. Today, despite all the problems caused by reunification, Germany is one of the world's greatest economic and trading nations.

Manufacturing is the most valuable part of Germany's economy and manufactured goods make up the bulk of the country's exports. Cars and other vehicles, cement, chemicals, computers, electrical equipment, processed food, machinery, scientific instruments, ships, steel, textiles and tools are among the leading manufactures. Germany has some coal, lignite, potash and rock salt deposits. But it imports many of the raw materials needed by its industries.

Germany also imports food. Major agricultural products include fruits, grapes for wine-making, potatoes, sugar beet and vegetables. Beef and dairy cattle are raised, together with many other livestock.

AREA 356,910 sq km [137,803 sq mi]
POPULATION 83,252,000
CAPITAL (POPULATION) Berlin (3,426,000)
GOVERNMENT Federal multiparty republic
ETHNIC GROUPS German 93%, Turkish 2%, Serbo-Croat 1%, Italian 1%, Greek, Polish, Spanish
LANGUAGES German (official)
RELIGIONS Protestant (mainly Lutheran) 38%, Roman Catholic 34%, Islam 2%
CURRENCY Euro = 100 cents

GHANA

GEOGRAPHY The Republic of Ghana faces the Gulf of Guinea in West Africa. This hot country, just north of the Equator, was formerly called the Gold Coast. Behind the thickly populated southern coastal plains, which are lined with lagoons, lies a plateau region in the south-west.

Accra has a hot, tropical climate. Rain occurs all through the year, though Accra is drier than areas inland.

POLITICS & ECONOMY Portuguese explorers reached the area in 1471 and named it the Gold Coast. The area became a centre of the slave trade in the 17th century. The slave trade was ended in the 1860s and, gradually, the British took control of the area. After independence in 1957, attempts were made to develop the economy by creating large state-owned manufacturing industries. But debt and corruption, together with falls in the price of cocoa, the chief export, caused economic problems. This led to instability and frequent coups. In 1981, power was invested in a Provisional National Defence Council, led by Flight-Lieutenant Jerry Rawlings.

The government steadied the economy and introduced several new policies, including the relaxation of government controls. In 1992, the

GIBRALTAR

government introduced a new constitution, which allowed for multiparty elections. Rawlings was elected president in 1992 and 1996, but he retired in 2002. The World Bank classifies Ghana as a 'low-income' developing country. Most people are poor and farming employs 59% of the population.

AREA 238,540 sq km [92,100 sq mi]
POPULATION 20,244,000
CAPITAL (POPULATION) Accra (1,781,000)
GOVERNMENT Republic
ETHNIC GROUPS Akan 44%, Moshi-Dagomba 16%, Ewe 13%, Ga 8%, Gurma 3%, Yoruba 1%
LANGUAGES English (official), Akan, Moshi-Dagomba, Ewe, Ga
RELIGIONS Christianity 63%, traditional beliefs 21%, Islam 16%
CURRENCY Cedi = 100 pesewas

GIBRALTAR

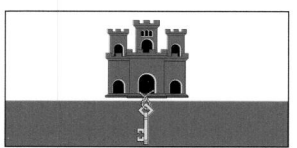 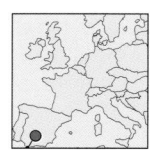

Gibraltar occupies a strategic position on the south coast of Spain where the Mediterranean meets the Atlantic. It was recognized as a British possession in 1713 and, despite Spanish claims, its population has consistently voted to retain its contacts with Britain. **AREA** 6.5 sq km [2.5 sq mi]; **POPULATION** 28,000; **CAPITAL** Gibraltar Town.

GREECE

GEOGRAPHY The Hellenic Republic, as Greece is officially called, is a rugged country situated at the southern end of the Balkan peninsula. Olympus, at 2,917 m [9,570 ft], is the highest peak. Islands make up about a fifth of the land.

Low-lying areas in Greece have mild, moist winters and hot, dry summers. The east coast has more than 2,700 hours of sunshine a year and only about half of the rainfall of the west. The mountains have a more severe climate, with snow on the higher slopes in winter.
POLITICS & ECONOMY After World War II (1939–45), when Germany had occupied Greece, a civil war broke out between Communist and nationalist forces. This war ended in 1949. A military dictatorship took power in 1967. The monarchy was abolished in 1973 and democratic government was restored in 1974. Greece joined the European Community (now the EU) in 1981. Despite efforts to develop the economy, Greece remains one of the EU's poorest nations. On 1 January 2002, the euro became Greece's sole official unit of currency.

Manufacturing is important. Products include processed food, cement, chemicals, metal products, textiles and tobacco. Greece also mines lignite (brown coal), bauxite and chromite.

Farmland covers about a third of the country, and grazing land another 40%. Major crops include barley, grapes for wine-making, dried fruits, olives, potatoes, sugar beet and wheat. Poultry, sheep, goats, pigs and cattle are raised. Greece's beaches and ancient ruins make it a major tourist destination.

AREA 131,990 sq km [50,961 sq mi]
POPULATION 10,645,000
CAPITAL (POPULATION) Athens (3,097,000)
GOVERNMENT Multiparty republic
ETHNIC GROUPS Greek 98%
LANGUAGES Greek (official)
RELIGIONS Greek Orthodox 98%
CURRENCY Euro = 100 cents

GREENLAND

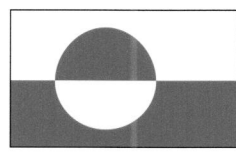 

Greenland is the world's largest island. Settlements are confined to the coast, because an ice-sheet covers four-fifths of the land. Greenland became a Danish possession in 1380. Full internal self-government was granted in 1981 and, in 1997, Danish place names were superseded by Inuit name forms. However, Greenland remains heavily dependent on Danish subsidies. **AREA** 2,175,600 sq km [838,999 sq mi]; **POPULATION** 56,000; **CAPITAL** Nuuk (Godthaab).

GRENADA

 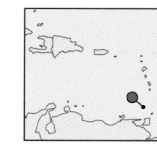

The most southerly of the Windward Islands in the Caribbean Sea, Grenada became independent from the UK in 1974. A military group seized power in 1983, when the prime minister was killed. US troops intervened and restored order and constitutional government. **AREA** 340 sq km [131 sq mi]; **POPULATION** 89,000; **CAPITAL** St George's.

GUADELOUPE

 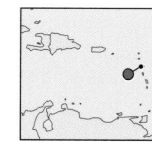

Guadeloupe is a French overseas department which includes seven Caribbean islands, the largest of which is Basse-Terre. French aid has helped to mantain a reasonable standard of living for the people. **AREA** 1,706 sq km [658 sq mi]; **POPULATION** 436,000; **CAPITAL** Basse-Terre.

GUAM

 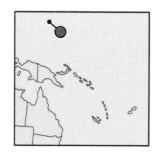

Guam, a strategically important 'unincorporated territory' of the USA, is the largest of the Mariana Islands in the Pacific Ocean. It is composed of a coralline limestone plateau. **AREA** 549 sq km [212 sq mi]; **POPULATION** 161,000; **CAPITAL** Agana.

GUATEMALA

 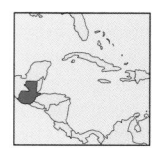

GEOGRAPHY The Republic of Guatemala in Central America contains a thickly populated mountain region, with fertile soils. The mountains, which run in an east–west direction, contain many volcanoes, some of which are active. Volcanic eruptions and earthquakes are common in the highlands. South of the mountains lie the thinly populated Pacific coastlands, while a large inland plain occupies the north.

Guatemala lies in the tropics. The lowlands are hot and rainy. But the central mountain region is cooler and drier. Guatemala City, at about 1,500 m [5,000 ft] above sea level, has a pleasant, warm climate, with a marked dry season between November and April.
POLITICS & ECONOMY In 1823, Guatemala joined the Central American Federation. But it became fully independent in 1839. Since independence, Guatemala has been plagued by instability and periodic violence.

Guatemala has a long-standing claim over Belize, but this was reduced in 1983 to the southern fifth of the country. Violence became widespread in Guatemala from the early 1960s, because of the conflict between left-wing groups, including many Amerindians, and government forces. A peace accord was signed in 1996, ending a war that had lasted 36 years and claimed perhaps 200,000 lives.

The World Bank classifies Guatemala as a 'lower-middle-income' developing country. Agriculture employs nearly half of the population and coffee, sugar, bananas and beef are the leading exports. Other important crops include the spice cardamom and cotton, while maize is the chief food crop. But Guatemala still has to import food to feed the people.

AREA 108,890 sq km [42,042 sq mi]
POPULATION 13,314,000
CAPITAL (POPULATION) Guatemala City (1,167,000)
GOVERNMENT Republic
ETHNIC GROUPS Ladino (mixed Hispanic and Amerindian) 55%, Amerindian 43%, other 2%
LANGUAGES Spanish (official), Amerindian languages
RELIGIONS Roman Catholic 75%, Protestant 25%
CURRENCY US dollar; Quetzal = 100 centavos

GUINEA

 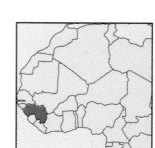

GEOGRAPHY The Republic of Guinea faces the Atlantic Ocean in West Africa. A flat, swampy plain borders the coast. Behind this plain, the land rises to a plateau region called Fouta Djalon. The Upper Niger plains, named after one of Africa's longest rivers, the Niger, which rises there, are in the north-east.

Guinea has a tropical climate and Conakry, on the coast, has heavy rains between May and November. This is also the coolest period in the year. During the dry season, hot, dry harmattan winds blow south-westwards from the Sahara Desert.

POLITICS & ECONOMY Guinea became independent in 1958. Its president, Sékou Touré, pursued socialist policies, though he had to resort to repressive policies to hold on to power. After his death in 1984, a military government, under President Lansana Conté, introduced free enterprise policies. In the late 1990s and early 2000s, Guinea was drawn into the civil conflicts which were taking place in neighbouring Liberia and Sierra Leone.

The World Bank classifies Guinea as a 'low-income' developing country. It has several natural resources, including bauxite (aluminium ore), diamonds, gold, iron ore and uranium. Bauxite and alumina (processed bauxite) account for 90% of the value of the exports. Agriculture, however, employs 78% of the people, many of whom produce little more than they need for their own families. Guinea has some manufacturing industries. Products include alumina, processed food and textiles.

AREA 245,860 sq km [94,927 sq mi]
POPULATION 7,775,000
CAPITAL (POPULATION) Conakry (1,508,000)
GOVERNMENT Multiparty republic
ETHNIC GROUPS Peuml 40%, Malinke 30%, Soussou 20%, other 10%
LANGUAGES French (official)
RELIGIONS Islam 85%, Christianity 8%, traditional beliefs 7%
CURRENCY Guinean franc = 100 cauris

GUINEA-BISSAU

GEOGRAPHY The Republic of Guinea-Bissau, formerly known as Portuguese Guinea, is a small country in West Africa. The land is mostly low-lying, with a broad, swampy coastal plain and many flat offshore islands, including the Bijagós Archipelago.

The country has a tropical climate, with one dry season (December to May) and a rainy season from June to November.
POLITICS & ECONOMY Portugal appointed a governor to administer Guinea-Bissau and the Cape Verde Islands in 1836, but in 1879 the two territories were separated and Guinea-Bissau became a colony, then called Portuguese Guinea. But development was slow, partly because the territory did not attract settlers on the same scale as Portugal's much healthier African colonies of Angola and Mozambique.

In 1956, African nationalists in Portuguese Guinea and Cape Verde founded the African Party for the Independence of Guinea and Cape Verde (PAIGC). Because Portugal seemed determined to hang on to its overseas territories, the PAIGC began a guerrilla war in 1963. By 1968, it held two-thirds of the country. In 1972, a rebel National Assembly, elected by the people in the PAIGC-controlled area, voted to make the country independent as Guinea-Bissau.

In 1974, newly independent Guinea-Bissau faced many problems arising from its under-developed economy and its lack of trained people to work in the administration. One objective of the leaders of Guinea-Bissau was to unite their country with Cape Verde. But, in 1980, army leaders overthrew Guinea-Bissau's government. The Revolutionary Council, which took over, opposed unification with Cape Verde. Guinea-Bissau ceased to be a one-party state in 1991 and multiparty elections were held in 1994. Civil war broke out in 1998 and a military

coup occurred in May 1999. In elections in 1999 and 2000, Kumba Ialá was elected president.

Guinea-Bissau is a poor country. Agriculture employs more than 80% of the people, but most farming is at subsistence level. Major crops include beans, coconuts, groundnuts, maize and rice.

AREA 36,120 sq km [13,946 sq mi]
POPULATION 1,345,000
CAPITAL (POPULATION) Bissau (145,000)
GOVERNMENT 'Interim' government
ETHNIC GROUPS Balanta 30%, Fula 20%, Manjaca 14%, Mandinga 13%, Papel 7%
LANGUAGES Portuguese (official), Crioulo
RELIGIONS Traditional beliefs 50%, Islam 45%, Christianity 5%
CURRENCY CFA franc = 100 centimes

GUYANA

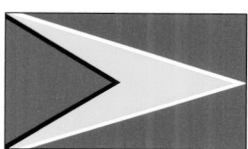

GEOGRAPHY The Co-operative Republic of Guyana is a country facing the Atlantic Ocean in north-eastern South America. The coastal plain is flat and much of it is below sea level.

The climate is hot and humid, though the interior highlands are cooler than the coast. The rainfall is heavy, occurring on more than 200 days a year.
POLITICS & ECONOMY British Guiana became independent in 1966. A black lawyer, Forbes Burnham, became the first prime minister. Under a new constitution adopted in 1980, the president's powers were increased. Burnham became president until his death in 1985. He was succeeded by Hugh Desmond Hoyte. Hoyte was defeated in elections in 1993 by an ethnic Indian, Cheddi Jagan. Jagan died in 1997 and was succeeded by his wife, Janet. In 1999, Bharrat Jagdeo was elected president.

Guyana is a poor country. Its resources include gold, bauxite (aluminium ore) and other minerals, forests and fertile soils. Sugar cane and rice are leading crops. Electric power is in short supply, although the country has great potential for producing hydroelectricity from its many rivers.

AREA 214,970 sq km [83,000 sq mi]
POPULATION 698,000
CAPITAL (POPULATION) Georgetown (200,000)
GOVERNMENT Multiparty republic
ETHNIC GROUPS East Indian 49%, Black 32%, Mixed 12%, Amerindian 6%, Portuguese, Chinese
LANGUAGES English (official), Creole, Hindi, Urdu
RELIGIONS Protestant 34%, Roman Catholic 18%, Hinduism 34%, Islam 9%
CURRENCY Guyana dollar = 100 cents

HAITI

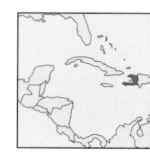

GEOGRAPHY The Republic of Haiti occupies the western third of Hispaniola in the Caribbean. The land is mainly mountainous. The climate is hot and humid, though the northern highlands,

with about 200 mm [79 in], have more than twice as much rainfall as the southern coast.
POLITICS & ECONOMY Visited by Christopher Columbus in 1492, Haiti was later developed by the French. The African slaves revolted in 1791 and the country became independent in 1804. Since independence, Haiti has suffered from instability, violence and dictatorial rule. Elections in 1990 returned Jean-Bertrand Aristide as president, but he was overthrown in 1991. Following US intervention, he returned in 1994. In 1995, René Préval was elected president, but Aristide was again elected president in 2000 amid accusations of vote-rigging.

AREA 27,750 sq km [10,714 sq mi]
POPULATION 7,064,000
CAPITAL (POPULATION) Port-au-Prince (885,000)
GOVERNMENT Multiparty republic
ETHNIC GROUPS Black 95%, Mulatto 5%
LANGUAGES French and Creole (both official)
RELIGIONS Roman Catholic 80%, Voodoo
CURRENCY Gourde = 100 centimes

HONDURAS

GEOGRAPHY The Republic of Honduras is the second largest country in Central America. The northern coast on the Caribbean Sea extends more than 600 km [373 mi], but the Pacific coast in the south-east is only about 80 km [50 mi] long.

Honduras has a tropical climate, but the highlands, where the capital Tegucigalpa is situated, have a cooler climate than the hot coastal plains. The months between May and November are the rainiest. Hurricanes often strike the coast. In 1998, Hurricane Mitch caused great destruction.
POLITICS & ECONOMY In the 1890s, American companies developed plantations in Honduras to grow bananas, which soon became the country's chief source of income. The companies exerted great political influence in Honduras and the country became known as a 'banana republic', a name that was later applied to several other Latin American nations. Instability has continued to mar the country's progress. In 1969, Honduras fought the short 'Soccer War' with El Salvador. The war was sparked off by the treatment of fans during a World Cup soccer series. The real reason was that Honduras had forced Salvadoreans in Honduras to give up land. Since 1980, civilian governments have ruled Honduras, though the military remain influential.

Honduras is a developing country – one of the poorest in the Americas and the least industrialized in Central America. It has few resources besides some silver, lead and zinc, and agriculture dominates the economy. Bananas and coffee are the leading exports, and maize is the main food crop. Manufactures include processed food, textiles, and a variety of wood products.

AREA 112,090 sq km [43,278 sq mi]
POPULATION 6,561,000
CAPITAL (POPULATION) Tegucigalpa (814,000)
GOVERNMENT Republic
ETHNIC GROUPS Mestizo 90%, Amerindian 7%, Black (including Black Carib) 2%, White 1%
LANGUAGES Spanish (official)
RELIGIONS Roman Catholic 85%
CURRENCY Honduran lempira = 100 centavos

HUNGARY

HUNGARY

GEOGRAPHY The Hungarian Republic is a land-locked country in central Europe. The land is mostly low-lying and drained by the Danube (Duna) and its tributary, the Tisza. Most of the land east of the Danube belongs to a region called the Great Plain (Nagyalföld), which covers about half of Hungary.

Hungary lies far from the moderating influence of the sea. As a result, summers are warmer and sunnier, and the winters colder than in Western Europe.

POLITICS & ECONOMY Hungary entered World War II (1939–45) in 1941, as an ally of Germany, but the Germans occupied the country in 1944. The Soviet Union invaded Hungary in 1944 and, in 1946, the country became a republic. The Communists gradually took over the government, taking complete control in 1949. From 1949, Hungary was an ally of the Soviet Union. In 1956, Soviet troops crushed an anti-Communist revolt. But in the 1980s, reforms in the Soviet Union led to the growth of anti-Communist groups in Hungary. In 1989, Hungary adopted a new constitution making it a multiparty state. Elections held in 1990 led to a victory for the non-Communist Democratic Forum. In 2002, the Hungarian Socialist Party, in alliance with the liberal Free Democrats, won a majority in parliament. In 2003, a majority of Hungarians voted in favour of joining the European Union in May 2004.

Before World War II, Hungary's economy was based mainly on agriculture. But the Communists set up many manufacturing industries. The new factories were owned by the government, as also was most of the land. However, from the late 1980s, the government has worked to increase private ownership. This change of policy caused many problems, including inflation and high rates of unemployment. Manufacturing is the chief activity. Major products include aluminium, chemicals, and electrical and electronic goods.

AREA 93,030 sq km [35,919 sq mi]
POPULATION 10,075,000
CAPITAL (POPULATION) Budapest (1,885,000)
GOVERNMENT Multiparty republic
ETHNIC GROUPS Magyar 90%, Gypsy, German, Croat, Romanian, Slovak
LANGUAGES Hungarian (official)
RELIGIONS Roman Catholic 64%, Protestant 23%, Orthodox 1%, Judaism 1%
CURRENCY Forint = 100 fillér

ICELAND

GEOGRAPHY The Republic of Iceland, in the North Atlantic Ocean, is closer to Greenland than Scotland. Iceland sits astride the Mid-Atlantic Ridge. It is slowly getting wider as the ocean is being stretched apart by continental drift.

Iceland has around 200 volcanoes, and eruptions are frequent. An eruption under the Vatnajökull ice-cap in 1996 created a subglacial lake which subsequently burst, causing severe flooding. Geysers and hot springs are other common volcanic features. Ice-caps and glaciers cover about an eighth of the land. The only habitable regions are the coastal lowlands.

Although it lies far to the north, Iceland's climate is moderated by the warm waters of the Gulf Stream. The port of Reykjavik is ice-free all the year round.

POLITICS & ECONOMY Norwegian Vikings colonized Iceland in AD 874, and in 930 the settlers founded the world's oldest parliament, the Althing.

Iceland united with Norway in 1262. But when Norway united with Denmark in 1380, Iceland came under Danish rule. Iceland became a self-governing kingdom, united with Denmark, in 1918. It became a fully independent republic in 1944, following a referendum in which 97% of the people voted to break their country's ties with Denmark.

Iceland has played an important part in European affairs and is a member of the North Atlantic Treaty Organization. Conflict with Britain over fishing rights have occurred since Iceland extended its territorial waters in the 1970s. Other fishing disputes with Norway, Russia and others continued in the 1990s.

Iceland has few resources besides the fishing grounds which surround it. Fishing and fish processing are major industries which dominate Iceland's overseas trade. Barely 1% of the land is used to grow crops, mainly root vegetables and fodder for livestock. But 23% of the country is used for grazing sheep and cattle.

AREA 103,000 sq km [39,768 sq mi]
POPULATION 279,000
CAPITAL (POPULATION) Reykjavik (103,000)
GOVERNMENT Multiparty republic
ETHNIC GROUPS Icelandic 97%, Danish 1%
LANGUAGES Icelandic (official)
RELIGIONS Evangelical Lutheran 92%, other Lutheran 3%, Roman Catholic 1%
CURRENCY Króna = 100 aurar

INDIA

GEOGRAPHY The Republic of India is the world's seventh largest country. In population, it ranks second only to China. The north is mountainous, with mountains and foothills of the Himalayan range. Rivers, such as the Brahmaputra and Ganges (Ganga), rise in the Himalaya and flow across the fertile northern plains. Southern India consists of a large plateau, called the Deccan. The Deccan is bordered by two mountain ranges, the Western Ghats and the Eastern Ghats.

India has three main seasons. The cool season runs from October to February. The hot season runs from March to June. The rainy monsoon season starts in the middle of June and continues into September. Delhi has a moderate rainfall, with about 640 mm [25 in] a year. The south-western coast and the north-east have far more rain. Darjeeling in the north-east has an average annual rainfall of 3,040 mm [120 in]. But parts of the Thar Desert in the north-west have only 50 mm [2 in] of rain per year.

POLITICS & ECONOMY In southern India, most of the people are descendants of the dark-skinned Dravidians, who were among India's earliest people. Most northerners are descendants of lighter-skinned Aryans who arrived around 3,500 years ago.

India was the birthplace of several major religions, including Hinduism, Buddhism and Sikhism. Islam was introduced from about AD 1000. The Muslim Mughal empire was founded in 1526. From the 17th century, Britain began to gain influence. From 1858 to 1947, India was ruled as part of the British empire. An independence movement began after the Sepoy Rebellion (1857–9) and, in 1885, the Indian National Congress was formed. In 1920, Mohandas K. Gandhi became its leader and it soon became a mass movement. When independence was finally achieved in 1947, British India was divided into modern India and Muslim Pakistan. Partition was marred by mass slaughter as Hindus and Sikhs fled from Pakistan, and Indian Muslims poured into Pakistan. In the ensuing disputes, some 1 million people were killed.

Although India has 15 major languages and hundreds of minor ones, together with many religions, the country remains the world's largest democracy. It has faced many problems, especially with Pakistan, over the disputed territory of Jammu and Kashmir. Two wars in 1965 and 1972 failed to alter greatly the 1948 cease-fire lines. In the late 1980s, Kashmiri nationalists in the Indian-controlled area waged a campaign, demanding either integration into Pakistan or independence. India sent in troops and accused Pakistan of intervention. In the 1990s, Pakistani-backed guerrillas fought to break India's hold on the Srinigar valley, Kashmir's most populous region. The tense situation was further aggravated by the testing of nuclear devices by both India and Pakistan in 1998. Between 2000 and 2002, attempts were made to achieve a lasting cease-fire in the region, but the negotiations were unsuccessful.

Economic development has been a major problem and, according to the World Bank, India is a 'low-income' developing country. After socialist policies failed to raise the living standards of the poor, the government introduced private enterprise. Farming employs 64% of the people. The main crops are rice, wheat, millet, sorghum, peas and beans. India has more cattle than any other country. Milk is produced but Hindus do not eat beef. India has reserves of coal, iron ore and oil, and manufacturing has expanded greatly since 1947. Iron and steel, machinery, refined petroleum, textiles, jewellery and transport equipment are major products.

AREA 3,287,590 sq km [1,269,338 sq mi]
POPULATION 1,045,845,000
CAPITAL (POPULATION) New Delhi (7,207,000)
GOVERNMENT Multiparty federal republic
ETHNIC GROUPS Indo-Aryan (Caucasoid) 72%, Dravidian (Aboriginal) 25%, other (mainly Mongoloid) 3%
LANGUAGES Hindi, English, Telugu, Bengali, Marati, Urdu, Gujarati, Malayalam, Kannada, Oriya, Punjabi, Assamese, Kashmiri, Sindhi and Sanskrit are all official languages
RELIGIONS Hinduism 83%, Islam (Sunni Muslim) 11%, Christianity 2%, Sikhism 2%, Buddhism 1%
CURRENCY Rupee = 100 paisa

INDONESIA

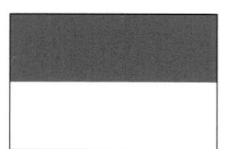 

GEOGRAPHY The Republic of Indonesia is an island nation in South-east Asia. In all, Indonesia contains about 13,600 islands, less than 6,000 of which are inhabited. Three-quarters of the country is made up of five main areas: the islands of Sumatra, Java and Sulawesi (Celebes), together with

Kalimantan (southern Borneo) and Irian Jaya (western New Guinea). The islands are generally mountainous and volcanic. The larger islands have extensive coastal lowlands. The climate is hot and humid, with a high rainfall. Only Java and the Sunda Islands have relatively dry seasons.

POLITICS & ECONOMY Indonesia is the world's most populous Muslim nation, though Islam was introduced as recently as the 15th century. The Dutch became active in the area in the early 17th century and Indonesia became a Dutch colony in 1799. After a long struggle, the Netherlands recognized Indonesia's independence in 1949. The economy has expanded, but ethnic and religious conflict have slowed down economic progress. In the early 21st century, Indonesia was facing many problems, arising from widespread corruption in the government and the army. Separatists were operating in Aceh province in northern Sumatra and in West Papua (formerly Irian Jaya), Christian-Muslim clashes led to loss of life in the Moluccas, and East (formerly Portuguese) Timor became an independent country in May 2002. In October 2002, terrorists bombed a night club in Bali, killing more than 180 people, most of them tourists.

Indonesia is a developing country. Its resources include oil, natural gas, tin and other minerals, its fertile volcanic soils and its forests. Oil and gas are major exports. Timber, textiles, rubber, coffee and tea are also exported. The principal food crop is rice. Manufacturing is increasing, particularly on Java.

> **AREA** 1,889,700 sq km [729,613 sq mi]
> **POPULATION** 231,328,000
> **CAPITAL (POPULATION)** Jakarta (11,500,000)
> **GOVERNMENT** Multiparty republic
> **ETHNIC GROUPS** Javanese 45%, Sundanese 14%, Madurese 7%, Coastal Malays 7%, more than 300 others
> **LANGUAGES** Bahasa Indonesian (official), others
> **RELIGIONS** Islam 88%, Roman Catholic 3%, Hinduism 2%, Buddhism 1%
> **CURRENCY** Indonesian rupiah = 100 sen

IRAN

 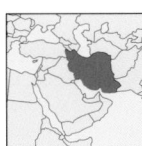

GEOGRAPHY The Republic of Iran contains a barren central plateau which covers about half of the country. It includes the Dasht-e-Kavir (Great Salt Desert) and the Dasht-e-Lut (Great Sand Desert). The Elburz Mountains north of the plateau contain Iran's highest peak, Damavand, while narrow lowlands lie between the mountains and the Caspian Sea. West of the plateau are the Zagros Mountains, beyond which the land descends to the plains bordering the Gulf.

Much of Iran has a severe, dry climate, with hot summers and cold winters. In Tehran, rain falls on only about 30 days in the year and the annual temperature range is more than 25°C [45°F]. The climate in the lowlands, however, is generally milder.

POLITICS & ECONOMY Iran was called Persia until 1935. The empire of Ancient Persia flourished between 550 and 350 BC, when it fell to Alexander the Great. Islam was introduced in AD 641.

Britain and Russia competed for influence in the area in the 19th century, and in the early 20th century the British began to develop the country's oil resources. In 1925, the Pahlavi family took power.

Reza Khan became shah (king) and worked to modernize the country. The Pahlavi dynasty was ended in 1979 when a religious leader, Ayatollah Ruhollah Khomeini, made Iran an Islamic republic. In 1980–8, Iran and Iraq fought a war over disputed borders. Khomeini died in 1989, but his fundamentalist views and anti-Western attitudes continued to dominate politics. In 1997, Mohammad Khatami, a liberal, was elected president. His reform policies won support in elections in 2000, but the conservative clerics made actual reform difficult.

Iran's prosperity is based on its oil production and oil accounts for 95% of the country's exports. However, the economy was severely damaged by the Iran–Iraq war in the 1980s. Oil revenues have been used to develop a growing manufacturing sector. Agriculture is important even though farms cover only a tenth of the land. The main crops are wheat and barley. Livestock farming and fishing are other important activities, although Iran has to import much of the food it needs.

> **AREA** 1,648,000 sq km [636,293 sq mi]
> **POPULATION** 66,623,000
> **CAPITAL (POPULATION)** Tehran (6,759,000)
> **GOVERNMENT** Islamic republic
> **ETHNIC GROUPS** Persian 51%, Azeri 24%, Gilaki and Mazandarani 8%, Kurd 7%, Arab 3%, Lur 2%, Baluchi 2%, Turkmen 2%
> **LANGUAGES** Persian 58%, Turkic 26%, Kurdish
> **RELIGIONS** Islam 99%
> **CURRENCY** Rial = 100 dinars

IRAQ

 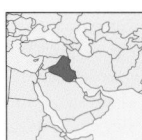

GEOGRAPHY The Republic of Iraq is a south-west Asian country at the head of the Gulf. Rolling deserts cover western and south-western Iraq, with mountains in the north-east. The northern plains, across which flow the rivers Euphrates (Nahr al Furat) and Tigris (Nahr Dijlah), are dry. But the southern plains, including Mesopotamia, and the delta of the Shatt al Arab, the river formed south of Al Qurnah by the combined Euphrates and Tigris, contain irrigated farmland, together with marshes. The climate of Iraq ranges from temperate in the north to subtropical in the south.

POLITICS & ECONOMY Mesopotamia was the home of several great civilizations, including Sumer, Babylon and Assyria. It later became part of the Persian empire. Islam was introduced in AD 637 and Baghdad became the brilliant capital of the powerful Arab empire. But Mesopotamia declined after the Mongols invaded it in 1258. From 1534, Mesopotamia became part of the Turkish Ottoman empire. Britain invaded the area in 1916. In 1921, Britain renamed the country Iraq and set up an Arab monarchy. Iraq finally became independent in 1932.

By the 1950s, oil dominated Iraq's economy. In 1952, Iraq agreed to take 50% of the profits of the foreign oil companies. This revenue enabled the government to pay for welfare services and development projects. But many Iraqis felt that they should benefit more from their oil.

Since 1958, when army officers killed the king and made Iraq a republic, the country has undergone turbulent times. In the 1960s, the Kurds, who live in northern Iraq and also in Iran, Turkey, Syria and Armenia, asked for self-rule. The government rejected their demands and war broke out. A peace treaty was signed in 1975, but conflict has continued.

In 1979, Saddam Hussein became Iraq's president. Under his leadership, Iraq invaded Iran in 1980, starting an eight-year war. Iraqi Kurds supported Iran and the Iraqi government attacked Kurdish villages with poison gas. In 1990, Iraqi troops occupied Kuwait, but an international force drove them out in 1991. Since 1991, Iraqi troops have attacked Shiite Marsh Arabs and Kurds. In 1998, Iraq's failure to permit UN inspectors, charged with disposing of Iraq's deadliest weapons, access to suspect sites led to the Western bombardment of Iraqi military sites. Another major offensive occurred in February 2001. In 2002 and 2003, pressure mounted on Iraq to dispose of its alleged weapons of mass destruction. Its failure to do so led to a coalition force, headed by the United States and the UK, to invade Iraq and overthrow the Saddam regime in March–April 2003.

Civil war, war damage in 1991 and 2003, UN sanctions and mismanagement have all contributed to economic chaos. Oil remains Iraq's main resource, but a UN trade embargo in 1990 halted oil exports. Farmland, including pasture, covers about a fifth of the land. Products include barley, cotton, dates, fruit, livestock, wheat and wool, but Iraq still has to import food. Industries include oil refining and the manufacture of petrochemicals and consumer goods.

> **AREA** 438,320 sq km [169,235 sq mi]
> **POPULATION** 24,002,000
> **CAPITAL (POPULATION)** Baghdad (3,841,000)
> **GOVERNMENT** Republic
> **ETHNIC GROUPS** Arab 77%, Kurdish 19%, Turkmen, Persian, Assyrian
> **LANGUAGES** Arabic (official), Kurdish (official in Kurdish areas)
> **RELIGIONS** Islam 96%, Christianity 4%
> **CURRENCY** Iraqi dinar = 20 dirhams = 1,000 fils

IRELAND

GEOGRAPHY The Republic of Ireland occupies five-sixths of the island of Ireland. The country consists of a large lowland region surrounded by a broken rim of low mountains. The uplands include the Mountains of Kerry where Carrauntoohill, Ireland's highest peak at 1,041 m [3,415 ft], is situated. The River Shannon is the longest in the British Isles. It flows through three large lakes, loughs Allen, Ree and Derg.

Ireland has a mild, damp climate greatly influenced by the warm Gulf Stream current that washes its shores. The effects of the Gulf Stream are greatest in the west. Dublin in the east is cooler than places on the west coast. Rain occurs throughout the year.

POLITICS & ECONOMY In 1801, the Act of Union created the United Kingdom of Great Britain and Ireland. But Irish discontent intensified in the 1840s when a potato blight caused a famine in which a million people died and nearly a million emigrated. Britain was blamed for not having done enough to help. In 1916, an uprising in Dublin was crushed, but between 1919 and 1922 civil war occurred. In 1922, the Irish Free State was created as a Dominion in the British Commonwealth. But Northern Ireland remained part of the UK.

Ireland became a republic in 1949. Since then, Irish governments have sought to develop the economy,

and it was for this reason that Ireland joined the European Community in 1973. In 1998, Ireland took part in the negotiations to produce a constitutional settlement in Northern Ireland. As part of the agreement, Ireland agreed to give up its constitutional claim on Northern Ireland.

Major farm products in Ireland include barley, cattle and dairy products, pigs, potatoes, poultry, sheep, sugar beet and wheat, while fishing provides another valuable source of food. Farming is now profitable, aided by European Union grants, but manufacturing is the leading economic sector. Many factories produce food and beverages. Chemicals and pharmaceuticals, electronic equipment, machinery, paper and textiles are also important.

AREA 70,280 sq km [27,135 sq mi]
POPULATION 3,883,000
CAPITAL (POPULATION) Dublin (1,024,000)
GOVERNMENT Multiparty republic
ETHNIC GROUPS Irish 94%
LANGUAGES Irish and English (both official)
RELIGIONS Roman Catholic 93%, Protestant 3%
CURRENCY Euro = 100 cents

ISRAEL

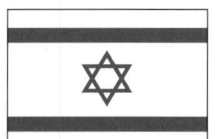 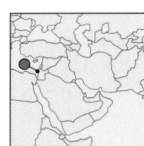

GEOGRAPHY The State of Israel is a small country in the eastern Mediterranean. It includes a fertile coastal plain, where Israel's main industrial cities, Haifa (Hefa) and Tel Aviv-Jaffa are situated. Inland lie the Judaeo-Galilean highlands, which run from northern Israel to the northern tip of the Negev Desert. To the east lies part of the Great Rift Valley which contains the River Jordan, the Sea of Galilee and the Dead Sea.

Summers are hot and dry. Winters on the coast are mild and moist, but the rainfall decreases from west to east and from north to south.

POLITICS & ECONOMY Israel is part of a region called Palestine. Some Jews have always lived in the area, though most modern Israelis are descendants of immigrants who began to settle there from the 1880s. Britain ruled Palestine from 1917. Large numbers of Jews escaping Nazi persecution arrived in the 1930s, provoking an Arab uprising against British rule. In 1947, the UN agreed to partition Palestine into an Arab and a Jewish state. Fighting broke out after Arabs rejected the plan. The State of Israel came into being in May 1948, but fighting continued into 1949. Other Arab–Israeli wars in 1956, 1967 and 1973 led to land gains for Israel.

In 1978, Israel signed a treaty with Egypt which led to the return of the occupied Sinai peninsula to Egypt in 1979. But conflict continued between Israel and the PLO (Palestine Liberation Organization). In 1993, the PLO and Israel agreed to establish Palestinian self-rule in two areas: the occupied Gaza Strip, and in the town of Jericho in the occupied West Bank. The agreement was extended in 1995 to include more than 30% of the West Bank. Israel's prime minister, Yitzhak Rabin, was assassinated in 1995. In 1996, his successor, Simon Peres, was defeated by the right-wing Benjamin Netanyahu, under whom the peace process stalled. In 1999, the left-wing Ehud Barak defeated Netanyahu and revived the peace process. But, following violence between the Palestinians and Israeli forces, Barak resigned. In 2001, Barak was defeated by the right-

wing Ariel Sharon, who adopted a hardline policy against the Palestinians. In 2003, after Sharon won re-election, the United States exerted pressure on him to agree to the setting up of a Palestinian state.

Israel's most valuable activity is manufacturing and the country's products include chemicals, electronic equipment, fertilizers, military equipment, plastics, processed food, scientific instruments and textiles. Fruits and vegetables are leading exports.

AREA 20,600 sq km [7,960 sq mi]
POPULATION 6,030,000
CAPITAL (POPULATION) Jerusalem (591,000)
GOVERNMENT Multiparty republic
ETHNIC GROUPS Jewish 82%, Arab and others 18%
LANGUAGES Hebrew and Arabic (both official)
RELIGIONS Judaism 80%, Islam (mostly Sunni) 14%, Christianity 2%, Druze and others 2%
CURRENCY New Israeli sheqel = 100 agorat

ITALY

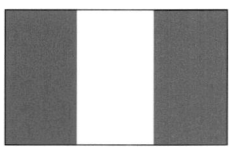 

GEOGRAPHY The Republic of Italy is famous for its history and traditions, its art and culture, and its beautiful scenery. Northern Italy is bordered in the north by the high Alps, with their many climbing and skiing resorts. The Alps overlook the northern plains – Italy's most fertile and densely populated region – drained by the River Po. The rugged Apennines form the backbone of southern Italy. Bordering the range are scenic hilly areas and coastal plains. Southern Italy contains a string of volcanoes, stretching from Vesuvius, through the Lipari Islands, to Etna on Sicily, the largest Mediterranean island.

Northern Italy has cold, often snowy, winters, but the summer months are warm and sunny, with brief summer thunderstorms. Rainfall is abundant. The south has mild, moist winters and warm, dry summers.

POLITICS & ECONOMY Magnificent ruins throughout Italy testify to the glories of the ancient Roman Empire, which was founded, according to legend, in 753 BC. It reached its peak in the AD 100s. It finally collapsed in the 400s, although the Eastern Roman empire, also called the Byzantine empire, survived for another 1,000 years.

In the Middle Ages, Italy was split into many tiny states. These states made a great contribution to the revival of art and learning, called the Renaissance, in the 14th to 16th centuries. Beautiful cities, such as Florence (Firenze) and Venice (Venézia), testify to the artistic achievements of this period.

Italy finally became a united kingdom in 1861, although the Papal Territories (a large area ruled by the Roman Catholic Church) was not added until 1870. The Pope and his successors disputed the take-over of the Papal Territories. The dispute was finally resolved in 1929, when the Vatican City was set up in Rome as a fully independent state.

Italy fought in World War I (1914–18) alongside the Allies – Britain, France and Russia. In 1922, the dictator Benito Mussolini, leader of the Fascist party, took power. Under Mussolini, Italy conquered Ethiopia. During World War II (1939–45), Italy at first fought on Germany's side against the Allies. But in late 1943, Italy declared war on Germany. Italy became a republic in 1946. It has played an important part in European affairs. It was a founder member of the North Atlantic Treaty Organization

(NATO) in 1949 and also of what has now become the European Union in 1958.

After the setting up of the European Union, Italy's economy developed quickly. But the country faced many problems. For example, much of the economic development was in the north. This forced many people to leave the poor south to find jobs in the north or abroad. Social problems, corruption at high levels of society, and a succession of weak coalition governments all contributed to instability. Elections in 1996 were won by the left-wing Olive Tree alliance led by Romano Prodi, who was replaced in 1998 by an ex-Communist, Massimo d'Alema, who tried but failed to introduce a two-party system. In 2001, a centre-right coalition won a substantial majority in parliament and its leader, media tycoon Silvio Berlusconi, became prime minister.

Only 50 years ago, Italy was a mainly agricultural society – today it is a leading industrial power. It lacks mineral resources, and imports most of the raw materials used in industry. Manufactures include textiles, processed food, machinery, cars and chemicals. The chief industrial region is in the north-west.

Farmland covers around 42% of the land, pasture 17%, and forest and woodland 22%. Major crops include citrus fruits, grapes which are used to make wine, olive oil, sugar beet and vegetables. Livestock farming is important, though meat is imported.

AREA 301,270 sq km [116,320 sq mi]
POPULATION 57,716,000
CAPITAL (POPULATION) Rome (2,654,000)
GOVERNMENT Multiparty republic
ETHNIC GROUPS Italian 94%, German, French, Albanian, Ladino, Slovene, Greek
LANGUAGES Italian 94% (official), German, French, Slovene
RELIGIONS Roman Catholic 83%
CURRENCY Euro = 100 cents

IVORY COAST

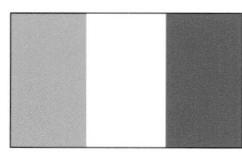 

GEOGRAPHY The Republic of the Ivory Coast, in West Africa, is officially known as Côte d'Ivoire. The south-east coast is bordered by sand bars that enclose lagoons. The south-west coast is lined by rocky cliffs.

Ivory Coast has a hot and humid tropical climate, with high temperatures all year. The south has two rainy seasons: between May and July, and from October to November. Inland, the rainfall decreases and the north has one dry and one rainy season.

POLITICS & ECONOMY From 1895, Ivory Coast was governed as part of French West Africa, a massive union which also included what are now Benin, Burkina Faso, Guinea, Mali, Mauritania, Niger and Senegal. In 1946, Ivory Coast became a territory in the French Union.

Ivory Coast became fully independent in 1960. Its first president, Félix Houphouët-Boigny, became the longest serving head of state in Africa with an uninterrupted period in office which ended with his death in 1993. Houphouët-Boigny, a pro-Western leader, made Ivory Coast a one-party state. In 1983, the National Assembly voted to make Yamoussoukro, the president's birthplace, the new capital. In 1999, a military coup occurred, but civilian rule was restored in 2000, when Laurent Gbagbo was elected president. An army rebellion began in September 2002. It continued into 2003 when a power-sharing coalition was set up, including members from rebel groups.

Agriculture employs about two-thirds of the people, and farm products make up nearly half the value of the exports. Manufacturing has grown in importance since 1960; products include fertilizers, processed food, refined oil, textiles and timber.

AREA 322,460 sq km [124,502 sq mi]
POPULATION 16,805,000
CAPITAL (POPULATION) Yamoussoukro (120,000)
GOVERNMENT Multiparty republic
ETHNIC GROUPS Akan 42%, Voltaic 18%, Northern Mande 16%, Kru 11%, Southern Mande 10%
LANGUAGES French (official), Akan, Voltaic
RELIGIONS Christianity 34%, Islam 27%, traditional beliefs 17%
CURRENCY CFA franc = 100 centimes

JAMAICA

 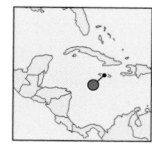

GEOGRAPHY Third largest of the Caribbean islands, half of Jamaica lies above 300 m [1,000 ft] and moist south-east trade winds bring rain to the central mountain range.

The 'cockpit country' in the north-west of the island is an inaccessible limestone area of steep broken ridges and isolated basins.
POLITICS & ECONOMY Britain took Jamaica from Spain in the 17th century, and the island did not gain its independence until 1962. Some economic progress was made by the socialist government in the 1980s, but migration and unemployment remain high. Farming is the leading activity and sugar cane is the main crop, though bauxite production provides much of the country's income. Jamaica has some industries and tourism is a major industry.

AREA 10,990 sq km [4,243 sq mi]
POPULATION 2,680,000
CAPITAL (POPULATION) Kingston (644,000)
GOVERNMENT Constitutional monarchy
ETHNIC GROUPS Black 91%, Mixed 7%, East Indian 1%
LANGUAGES English (official), Creole
RELIGIONS Protestant 61%, Roman Catholic 4%
CURRENCY Dollar = 100 cents

JAPAN

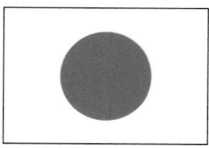 

GEOGRAPHY Japan's four largest islands – Honshu, Hokkaido, Kyushu and Shikoku – make up 98% of the country. But Japan contains thousands of small islands. The four largest islands are mainly mountainous, while many of the small islands are the tips of volcanoes. Japan has more than 150 volcanoes, about 60 of which are active. Volcanic eruptions, earthquakes and tsunamis (destructive sea waves triggered by underwater earthquakes and eruptions) are common because the islands lie in an unstable part of our planet, where continental plates are always on the move. One powerful recent earthquake

killed more than 5,000 people in Kobe in 1995.

The climate of Japan varies greatly from north to south. Hokkaido in the north has cold, snowy winters. At Sapporo, temperatures below –20°C [4°F] have been recorded between December and March. But summers are warm, with temperatures sometimes exceeding 30°C [86°F]. Rain falls throughout the year, though Hokkaido is one of the driest parts of Japan. Tokyo has higher rainfall and temperatures, while the southern islands of Shikoku and Kyushu have warm temperate climates. Summers are long and hot. Winters are cold.
POLITICS & ECONOMY In the late 19th century, Japan began a programme of modernization. Under its new imperial leaders, it began to look for lands to conquer. In 1894–5, it fought a war with China and, in 1904–5, it defeated Russia. Soon its overseas empire included Korea and Taiwan. In 1930, Japan invaded Manchuria (north-east China) and, in 1937, it began a war against China. In 1941, Japan launched an attack on the US base at Pearl Harbor in Hawaii. This drew both Japan and the United States into World War II.

Japan surrendered in 1945 when the Americans dropped atomic bombs on two cities, Hiroshima and Nagasaki. The United States occupied Japan until 1952. During this period, Japan adopted a democratic constitution. The emperor, who had previously been regarded as a god, became a constitutional monarch. Power was vested in the prime minister and cabinet, who are chosen from the Diet (elected parliament).

From the 1960s, Japan experienced many changes as the country rapidly built up new industries. By the early 1990s, Japan had become the world's second richest economic power after the US. But economic success has brought problems. For example, the rapid growth of cities has led to housing shortages and pollution. Another problem is that the proportion of people over 65 years of age is steadily increasing.

Japan has the world's second highest gross domestic product (GDP) after the United States. [The GDP is the total value of all goods and services produced in a country in one year.] The most important sector of the economy is industry. Yet Japan has to import most of the raw materials and fuels it needs for its industries. Its success is based on its use of the latest technology, its skilled and hard-working labour force, its vigorous export policies and its comparatively small government spending on defence. Manufactures dominate its exports, which include machinery, electrical and electronic equipment, vehicles and transport equipment, iron and steel, chemicals, textiles and ships. However, from the late 1990s, Japan experienced an economic slowdown, which merged in a recession in the early 21st century.

Japan is one of the world's top fishing nations and fish is an important source of protein. Because the land is so rugged, only 15% of the country can be farmed. Yet Japan produces about 70% of the food it needs. Rice is the chief crop, taking up about half of the total farmland. Other major products include fruits, sugar beet, tea and vegetables. Livestock farming has increased since the 1950s.

AREA 377,800 sq km [145,869 sq mi]
POPULATION 126,975,000
CAPITAL (POPULATION) Tokyo (17,950,000)
GOVERNMENT Constitutional monarchy
ETHNIC GROUPS Japanese 99%, Chinese, Korean, Ainu
LANGUAGES Japanese (official)
RELIGIONS Shintoism and Buddhism 84% (most Japanese consider themselves to be both Shinto and Buddhist)
CURRENCY Yen = 100 sen

JORDAN

GEOGRAPHY The Hashemite Kingdom of Jordan is an Arab country in south-western Asia. The Great Rift Valley in the west contains the River Jordan and the Dead Sea, which Jordan shares with Israel. East of the Rift Valley is the Transjordan plateau, where most Jordanians live. To the east and south lie vast areas of desert.

Amman has a much lower rainfall and longer dry season than the Mediterranean lands to the west. The Transjordan plateau, on which Amman stands, is a transition zone between the Mediterranean climate zone to the west and the desert climate to the east.
POLITICS & ECONOMY In 1921, Britain created a territory called Transjordan east of the River Jordan. In 1923, Transjordan became self-governing, but Britain retained control of its defences, finances and foreign affairs. This territory became fully independent as Jordan in 1946.

Jordan has suffered from instability arising from the Arab–Israeli conflict since the creation of the State of Israel in 1948. After the first Arab–Israeli War in 1948–9, Jordan acquired East Jerusalem and a fertile area called the West Bank. In 1967, Israel occupied this area. In Jordan, the presence of Palestinian refugees led to civil war in 1970–1.

In 1974, Arab leaders declared that the PLO (Palestine Liberation Organization) was the sole representative of the Palestinian people. In 1988, King Hussein of Jordan renounced Jordan's claims to the West Bank and passed responsibility for it to the PLO. Opposition parties were legalized in 1991 and elections were held in 1993. In October 1994, Jordan and Israel signed a peace treaty, ending a state of war that had lasted more than 40 years. Jordan's King Hussein commanded respect for his role in Middle Eastern affairs until his death in 1999. He was succeeded by his eldest son who became Abdullah II.

Jordan lacks natural resources, apart from phosphates and potash, and the economy depends substantially on aid. The World Bank classifies Jordan as a 'lower-middle-income' developing country. Less than 6% of the land is farmed or used as pasture. Jordan has an oil refinery and manufactures include cement, pharmaceuticals, processed food, fertilizers and textiles.

AREA 89,210 sq km [34,444 sq mi]
POPULATION 5,307,000
CAPITAL (POPULATION) Amman (1,752,000)
GOVERNMENT Constitutional monarchy
ETHNIC GROUPS Arab 99%, of which Palestinians make up roughly half
LANGUAGES Arabic (official)
RELIGIONS Islam (mostly Sunni) 93%, Christianity (mostly Greek Orthodox) 5%
CURRENCY Jordan dinar = 1,000 fils

KAZAKHSTAN

GEOGRAPHY Kazakhstan is a large country in west-central Asia. In the west, the Caspian Sea lowlands include the Karagiye depression, which

reaches 132 m [433 ft] below sea level. The lowlands extend eastwards through the Aral Sea area. The north contains high plains, but the highest land is along the eastern and southern borders. These areas include parts of the Altai and Tian Shan mountain ranges.

Eastern Kazakhstan contains several freshwater lakes, the largest of which is Lake Balkhash. The water in the rivers has been used for irrigation, causing ecological problems. For example, the Aral Sea, deprived of water, shrank from 66,900 sq km [25,830 sq mi] in 1960 to 33,642 sq km [12,989 sq mi] in 1993. Large areas are now barren desert.

Kazakhstan lies far from the moderating influence of the oceans and it has an extreme climate. Winters are cold and snow covers the land for about 100 days at Almaty. The rainfall is generally low.

POLITICS & ECONOMY After the Russian Revolution of 1917, many Kazakhs wanted to make their country independent. But the Communists prevailed and in 1936 Kazakhstan became a republic of the Soviet Union, called the Kazakh Soviet Socialist Republic. During World War II and also after the war, the Soviet government moved many people from the west into Kazakhstan. From the 1950s, people were encouraged to work on a 'Virgin Lands' project, which involved bringing large areas of grassland under cultivation.

Reforms in the Soviet Union in the 1980s led to the break-up of the country in December 1991. Kazakhstan maintained contacts with Russia through the Commonwealth of Independent States (CIS). In 1997, the government moved its capital from Almaty to Aqmola (later renamed Astana), a town in the Russian-dominated north. It hoped that this would bring some Kazakh identity to the area. In the early 21st century, Kazakhstan's economy was in better shape than any other of the Central Asian ex-Soviet republics. However, its President Nursultan Nazarbaev was criticized for cracking down on political dissent and independent newspapers.

The World Bank classifies Kazakhstan as a 'lower-middle-income' developing country. Livestock farming, especially sheep and cattle, is an important activity, and major crops include barley, cotton, rice and wheat. The country is rich in mineral resources, including coal and oil reserves, together with bauxite, copper, lead, tungsten and zinc. Manufactures include chemicals, food products, machinery and textiles. Oil is exported via a pipeline through Russia, though, to reduce dependence on Russia, Kazakhstan signed an agreement in 1997 to build a new pipeline to China. Other exports include metals, chemicals, grain, wool and meat.

AREA 2,717,300 sq km [1,049,150 sq mi]
POPULATION 16,742,000
CAPITAL (POPULATION) Astana (280,000)
GOVERNMENT Multiparty republic
ETHNIC GROUPS Kazakh 53%, Russian 30%, Ukrainian 4%, German 2%, Uzbek 2%
LANGUAGES Kazakh (official); Russian, the former official language, is widely spoken
RELIGIONS Islam 47%, Russian Orthodox 44%
CURRENCY Tenge = 100 tiyn

KENYA

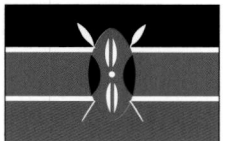

GEOGRAPHY The Republic of Kenya is a country in East Africa which straddles the Equator. It is slightly larger in area than France. Behind the narrow coastal plain on the Indian Ocean, the land rises to high plains and highlands, broken by volcanic mountains, including Mount Kenya, the country's highest peak at 5,199 m [17,057 ft]. Crossing the country is an arm of the Great Rift Valley, on the floor of which are several lakes, including Baringo, Magadi, Naivasha, Nakuru and, on the northern frontier, Lake Turkana (formerly Lake Rudolf).

Mombasa on the coast is hot and humid. But inland, the climate is moderated by the height of the land. As a result, Nairobi, in the thickly populated south-western highlands, has summer temperatures which are 10°C [18°F] lower than Mombasa. Nights can be cool, but temperatures do not fall below freezing. Nairobi's main rainy season is from April to May, with 'little rains' in November and December. However, only about 15% of the country has a reliable rainfall of 800 mm [31 in].

POLITICS & ECONOMY The Kenyan coast has been a trading centre for more than 2,000 years. Britain took over the coast in 1895 and soon extended its influence inland. In the 1950s, a secret movement, called Mau Mau, launched an armed struggle against British rule. Although Mau Mau was eventually defeated, Kenya became independent in 1963.

Many Kenyans felt that Kenya should have a strong central government, and Kenya was a one-party state for much of the time since 1963. But democracy was restored in the early 1990s and elections were held in 1992, 1997 and 2002. In 1999, Kenya, with Tanzania and Uganda, set up an East African Community, which aimed to create a customs union, a common market, a monetary union, and, ultimately, a political union.

According to the United Nations, Kenya is a 'low-income' developing country. Agriculture employs about 80% of the people, but many Kenyans are subsistence farmers, growing little more than they need to support their families. The chief food crop is maize. The main cash crops and leading exports are coffee and tea. Manufactures include chemicals, leather and footwear, processed food, petroleum products and textiles.

AREA 580,370 sq km [224,081 sq mi]
POPULATION 31,139,000
CAPITAL (POPULATION) Nairobi (2,000,000)
GOVERNMENT Multiparty republic
ETHNIC GROUPS Kikuyu 21%, Luhya 14%, Luo 13%, Kalenjin 12%, Kamba 11%
LANGUAGES Kiswahili and English (both official)
RELIGIONS Protestant 45%, Roman Catholic 33%, traditional beliefs 10%, Islam 10%
CURRENCY Kenya shilling = 100 cents

KIRIBATI

The Republic of Kiribati comprises three groups of corall atolls scattered over about 5 million sq km [2 million sq mi]. Kiribati straddles the equator and temperatures are high and the rainfall is abundant.

Formerly part of the British Gilbert and Ellice Islands, Kiribati became independent in 1979. The main export is copra and the country depends heavily on foreign aid. **AREA** 728 sq km [281 sq mi]; **POPULATION** 96,000; **CAPITAL** Tarawa.

KOREA, NORTH

GEOGRAPHY The Democratic People's Republic of Korea occupies the northern part of the Korean peninsula which extends south from north-eastern China. Mountains form the heart of the country, with the highest peak, Paektu-san, reaching 2,744 m [9,003 ft] on the northern border.

North Korea has a fairly severe climate, with bitterly cold winters when winds blow from across central Asia, bringing snow and freezing conditions. In summer, moist winds from the oceans bring rain.

POLITICS & ECONOMY North Korea was created in 1945, when the peninsula, a Japanese colony since 1910, was divided into two parts. Soviet forces occupied the north, with US forces in the south. Soviet occupation led to a Communist government being established in 1948 under the leadership of Kim Il Sung. He initiated a Stalinist regime in which he assumed the role of dictator, and a personality cult developed around him. He was to become the world's most durable Communist leader.

The Korean War began in June 1950 when North Korean troops invaded the south. North Korea, aided by China and the Soviet Union, fought with South Korea, which was supported by troops from the United States and other UN members. The war ended in July 1953. An armistice was signed but no permanent peace treaty was agreed. After the war, North Korea adopted a hostile policy towards South Korea in pursuit of its policy of reunification.

The ending of the Cold War in the late 1980s eased the situation and both North and South Korea joined the United Nations in 1991. The two countries made several agreements, including one in which they agreed not to use force against each other. However, North Korea remained as isolated as ever.

In 1993, North Korea began a new international crisis by announcing that it was withdrawing from the Nuclear Non-Proliferation Treaty. This led to suspicions that North Korea, which had signed the Treaty in 1985, was developing its own nuclear weapons. Kim Il Sung, who had ruled as a virtual dictator from 1948 until his death in 1994, was succeeded by his son, Kim Jong Il.

In the early 2000s, attempts were made to reconcile the two Koreas, though the prospect of reunification seemed remote. In 2003, North Korea's relations with the United States deteriorated sharply when the US accused North Korea of developing nuclear weapons.

North Korea has considerable resources, including coal, copper, iron ore, lead, tin, tungsten and zinc. Under Communism, North Korea has concentrated on developing heavy, state-owned industries. Manufactures include chemicals, iron and steel, machinery, processed food and textiles. Agriculture employs about a third of the people of North Korea and rice is the leading crop. Economic decline and mismanagement, aggravated by three successive crop failures caused by floods in 1995 and 1996 and a drought in 1997, led to famine on a large scale.

AREA 120,540 sq km [46,540 sq mi]
POPULATION 22,224,000
CAPITAL (POPULATION) Pyŏngyang (2,741,000)
GOVERNMENT Single-party people's republic
ETHNIC GROUPS Korean 99%
LANGUAGES Korean (official)
RELIGIONS Buddhism and Confucianism
CURRENCY North Korean won = 100 chon

KOREA, SOUTH

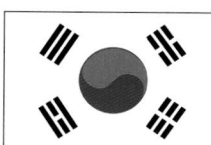 

GEOGRAPHY The Republic of Korea, as South Korea is officially known, occupies the southern part of the Korean peninsula. Mountains cover much of the country. The southern and western coasts are major farming regions. Many islands are found along the west and south coasts. The largest is Cheju-do, which contains South Korea's highest peak, which rises to 1,950 m [6,398 ft].

Like North Korea, South Korea is chilled in winter by cold, dry winds blowing from central Asia. Snow often covers the mountains in the east. The summers are hot and wet, especially in July and August.

POLITICS & ECONOMY After Japan's defeat in World War II (1939–45), North Korea was occupied by troops from the Soviet Union, while South Korea was occupied by United States forces. Attempts to reunify Korea failed and, in 1948, a National Assembly was elected in South Korea. This Assembly created the Republic of Korea, while North Korea became a Communist state. North Korean troops invaded the South in June 1950, sparking off the Korean War (1950–3).

In the 1950s, South Korea had a weak economy, which had been further damaged by the destruction caused by the Korean War. From the 1960s to the 1980s, South Korean governments worked to industrialize the economy. The governments were dominated by military leaders, who often used authoritarian methods and flouted human rights. In 1987, a new constitution was approved, enabling presidential elections to be held every five years. In 1991, South and North Korea became members of the United Nations and they signed agreements, including one in which they agreed not to use force against each other. Tensions continued, though hopes were raised when negotiations between the two countries took place in the early 21st century.

The World Bank classifies South Korea as an 'upper-middle-income' developing country. It is also one of the world's fastest growing industrial economies. The country's resources include coal and tungsten, and its main manufactures are processed food and textiles. Since partition, heavy industries have been built up, making chemicals, fertilizers, iron and steel, and ships. South Korea has also developed the production of such things as computers, cars and television sets. In late 1997, however, the dramatic expansion of the economy was halted by a market crash which affected many of the booming economies of Asia. However, South Korea recovered faster than any other country in the region, and huge inflows of foreign investment and strict financial measures, including the restructuring of its short-term debt, led to the restoration of confidence and economic growth.

Farming remains important in South Korea. Rice is the chief crop, together with fruit, grains and vegetables, while fishing provides a major source of protein.

AREA 99,020 sq km [38,232 sq mi]
POPULATION 48,324,000
CAPITAL (POPULATION) Seoul (10,231,000)
GOVERNMENT Multiparty republic
ETHNIC GROUPS Korean 99%
LANGUAGES Korean (official)
RELIGIONS Christianity 49%, Buddhism 47%, Confucianism 3%
CURRENCY South Korean won = 100 chon

KUWAIT

 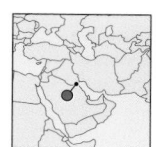

The State of Kuwait at the north end of the Gulf is largely made up of desert. Temperatures are high and the rainfall low. Kuwait became independent from Britain in 1961 and revenues from its oil wells have made it highly prosperous. Iraq invaded Kuwait in 1990 and much damage was inflicted in the ensuing conflict in 1991 when Kuwait was liberated. **AREA** 17,820 sq km [6,880 sq mi]; **POPULATION** 2,112,000; **CAPITAL** Kuwait City.

KYRGYZSTAN

 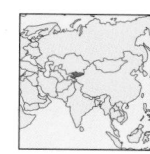

GEOGRAPHY The Republic of Kyrgyzstan is a landlocked country between China, Tajikistan, Uzbekistan and Kazakhstan. The country is mountainous, with spectacular scenery. The highest mountain, Pik Pobedy in the Tian Shan range, reaches 7,439 m [24,406 ft] in the east. The lowlands have warm summers and cold winters. But January temperatures in the mountains plummet to −28°C [−18°F]. Kyrgyzstan has a low annual rainfall.

POLITICS & ECONOMY In 1876, Kyrgyzstan became a province of Russia and Russian settlement in the area began. In 1916, Russia crushed a rebellion among the Kyrgyz, and many subsequently fled to China. In 1922, the area became an autonomous *oblast* (self-governing region) of the newly formed Soviet Union but, in 1936, it became one of the Soviet Socialist Republics. Under Communist rule, local customs and religious worship were suppressed, but education and health services were greatly improved.

In 1991, Kyrgyzstan became an independent country following the break-up of the Soviet Union. The Communist party was dissolved, but the country maintained ties with Russia through an organization called the Commonwealth of Independent States. Kyrgyzstan adopted a new constitution in 1994 and parliamentary elections were held in 1995. In the early 21st century, many people were alarmed when Islamic guerrillas sought to set up an Islamic state in the Fergana valley, where Kyrgyzstan borders Tajikistan and Uzbekistan.

In the early 1990s, when Kyrgyzstan was working to reform its economy, the World Bank classified it as a 'lower-middle-income' developing country. Agriculture, especially livestock rearing, is the chief activity. The chief products include cotton, eggs, fruits, grain, tobacco, vegetables and wool. But food must be imported. Industries are mainly concentrated around the capital Bishkek.

AREA 198,500 sq km [76,640 sq mi]
POPULATION 4,822,000
CAPITAL (POPULATION) Bishkek (589,000)
GOVERNMENT Multiparty republic
ETHNIC GROUPS Kyrgyz 52%, Russian 18%, Uzbek 13%, Ukrainian 3%, German, Tatar
LANGUAGES Kyrgyz and Russian (both official), Uzbek
RELIGIONS Islam
CURRENCY Som = 100 tyiyn

LAOS

GEOGRAPHY The Lao People's Democratic Republic is a landlocked country in South-east Asia. Mountains and plateaux cover much of the country.

Most people live on the plains bordering the River Mekong and its tributaries. This river, one of Asia's longest, forms much of the country's north-western and south-western borders.

Laos has a tropical monsoon climate. Winters are dry and sunny, with winds blowing in from the northeast. The temperatures rise until April, when the wind directions are reversed and moist south-westerly winds reach Laos, heralding the start of the wet monsoon season.

POLITICS & ECONOMY France made Laos a protectorate in the late 19th century and ruled it as part of French Indo-China, a region which also included Cambodia and Vietnam. Laos became a member of the French Union in 1948 and an independent kingdom in 1954.

After independence, Laos suffered from instability caused by a long power struggle between royalist government forces and a pro-Communist group called the Pathet Lao. A civil war broke out in 1960 and continued into the 1970s. The Pathet Lao took control in 1975 and the king abdicated. Laos then came under the influence of Communist Vietnam, which had used Laos as a supply base during the Vietnam War (1957–75). From the early 1980s, the economy deteriorated and opposition appeared when bombings occurred in Vientiane in 2000. They were attributed to rebels in the minority Hmong tribe or to politicians who wanted faster economic reforms.

Laos is one of the world's poorest countries. Agriculture employs about 76% of the people, as compared with 7% in industry and 17% in services. Rice is the main crop, and timber and coffee are both exported. But the most valuable export is electricity, which is produced at hydroelectric power stations on the River Mekong and is exported to Thailand. Laos also produces opium.

AREA 236,800 sq km [91,428 sq mi]
POPULATION 5,777,000
CAPITAL (POPULATION) Vientiane (532,000)
GOVERNMENT Single-party republic
ETHNIC GROUPS Lao Loum 68%, Lao Theung 22%, Lao Soung 9%
LANGUAGES Lao (official), Khmer, Tai, Miao
RELIGIONS Buddhism 58%, traditional beliefs 34%, Christianity 2%, Islam 1%
CURRENCY Kip = 100 at

LATVIA

GEOGRAPHY The Republic of Latvia is one of three states on the south-eastern corner of the Baltic Sea which were ruled as parts of the Soviet Union between 1940 and 1991. Latvia consists mainly of flat plains separated by low hills.

Riga has warm summers, but temperatures between December and March are subzero. Moderate rainfall

occurs throughout the year, with light snow in winter.

POLITICS & ECONOMY In 1800, Russia was in control of Latvia, but Latvians declared their independence after World War I. In 1940, under a German-Soviet pact, Soviet troops occupied Latvia, but they were driven out by the Germans in 1941. Soviet troops returned in 1944 and Latvia became part of the Soviet Union. Under Soviet rule, many Russian immigrants settled in Latvia and many Latvians feared that the Russians would become the dominant ethnic group.

In the late 1980s, when reforms were being introduced in the Soviet Union, Latvia's government ended absolute Communist rule and made Latvian the official language. In 1990, it declared the country to be independent, an act which was finally recognized by the Soviet Union in September 1991.

Latvia held its first free elections to its parliament (the Saeima) in 1993. Voting was limited only to citizens of Latvia on 17 June 1940 and their descendants. This meant that about 34% of Latvian residents were unable to vote. In 1994, Latvia restricted the naturalization of non-Latvians, including many Russian settlers, who were not allowed to vote or own land. However, in 1998, the government agreed that all children born since independence should have automatic citizenship. Since 1990, Latvia has cultivated closer ties with the West and, in 2002, it was invited to become a member of the European Union in May 2004.

The World Bank classifies Latvia as a 'lower-middle-income' country and, in the 1990s, it faced many problems in turning its economy into a free-market system. Products include electronic goods, farm machinery, fertilizers, processed food, plastics, radios and vehicles. Latvia produces only about a tenth of the electricity it needs. It imports the rest from Belarus, Russia and Ukraine.

AREA 64,589 sq km [24,938 sq mi]
POPULATION 2,367,000
CAPITAL (POPULATION) Riga (811,000)
GOVERNMENT Multiparty republic
ETHNIC GROUPS Latvian 56%, Russian 30%, Belarussian 4%, Ukrainian 3%, Polish 2%, Lithuanian, Jewish
LANGUAGES Latvian (official), Russian
RELIGIONS Lutheran, Russian Orthodox and Roman Catholic
CURRENCY Lats = 10 santimi

LEBANON

 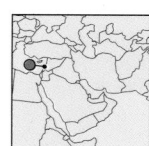

GEOGRAPHY The Republic of Lebanon is a country on the eastern shores of the Mediterranean Sea. Behind the coastal plain are the rugged Lebanon Mountains (Jabal Lubnan), which rise to 3,088 m [10,131 ft]. Another range, the Anti-Lebanon Mountains (Al Jabal Ash Sharqi), form the eastern border with Syria. Between the two ranges is the Bekaa (Beqaa) Valley, a fertile farming region.

The Lebanese coast has the hot, dry summers and mild, wet winters that are typical of many Mediterranean lands. Inland, onshore winds bring heavy rain to the western slopes of the mountains in the winter months, with snow at the higher altitudes.

POLITICS & ECONOMY Lebanon was ruled by Turkey from 1516 until World War I. France ruled

the country from 1923, but Lebanon became independent in 1946. After independence, the Muslims and Christians agreed to share power, and Lebanon made rapid economic progress. But from the late 1950s, development was slowed by periodic conflict between Sunni and Shia Muslims, Druze and Christians. The situation was further complicated by the presence of Palestinian refugees who used bases in Lebanon to attack Israel.

In 1975, civil war broke out as private armies representing the many factions struggled for power. This led to intervention by Israel in the south and Syria in the north. UN peacekeeping forces arrived in 1978, but bombings, assassinations and kidnappings became almost everyday events in the 1980s. From 1991, Lebanon enjoyed an uneasy peace. But, Israel continued to occupy an area in the south. In the 1990s, Israel launched several attacks on pro-Iranian Hezbollah guerrillas in Lebanon, but all Israeli troops were withdrawn in May 2000.

Lebanon's civil war almost destroyed valuable trade and financial services that had been Lebanon's chief source of income, together with tourism. Manufacturing, which had formerly been a major activity, was badly hit.

AREA 10,400 sq km [4,015 sq mi]
POPULATION 3,678,000
CAPITAL (POPULATION) Beirut (1,500,000)
GOVERNMENT Multiparty republic
ETHNIC GROUPS Lebanese 80%, Palestinian 12%, Armenian 5%, Syrian, Kurdish
LANGUAGES Arabic (official)
RELIGIONS Islam 70%, Christianity 30%
CURRENCY Lebanese pound = 100 piastres

LESOTHO

 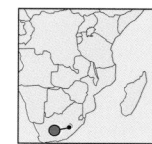

GEOGRAPHY The Kingdom of Lesotho is a landlocked country, completely enclosed by South Africa. The land is mountainous, rising to 3,482 m [11,424 ft] on the north-eastern border. The Drakensberg range covers most of the country.

The climate of Lesotho is greatly affected by the altitude, because most of the country lies above 1,500 m [4,921 ft]. Maseru has warm summers, but the temperatures fall below freezing in the winter. The mountains are colder. The rainfall varies, averaging around 700 mm [28 in].

POLITICS & ECONOMY The Basotho nation was founded in the 1820s by King Moshoeshoe I, who united various groups fleeing from tribal wars in southern Africa. Britain made the area a protectorate in 1868 and, in 1971, placed it under the British Cape Colony in South Africa. But in 1884, Basutoland, as the area was called, was reconstituted as a British protectorate, where whites were not allowed to own land.

The country finally became independent in 1966 as the Kingdom of Lesotho, with Moshoeshoe II, great-grandson of Moshoeshoe I, as its king. Since independence, Lesotho has suffered instability. The military seized power in 1986 and stripped Moshoeshoe II of his powers in 1990, installing his son, Letsie III, as monarch. After elections in 1993, Moshoeshoe II was restored to office in 1995. But after his death in a car crash in 1996, Letsie III again became king. In 1998, an army revolt, following an election in which the ruling party won 79 out of the

80 seats, caused much damage to the economy, despite the intervention of a South African force intended to maintain order.

Lesotho is a 'low-income' developing country. It lacks natural resources. Agriculture, mainly at subsistence level, light manufacturing and money sent home by Basotho working abroad are the main sources of income.

AREA 30,350 sq km [11,718 sq mi]
POPULATION 2,208,000
CAPITAL (POPULATION) Maseru (130,000)
GOVERNMENT Constitutional monarchy
ETHNIC GROUPS Sotho 99%
LANGUAGES Sesotho and English (both official)
RELIGIONS Christianity 80%, traditional beliefs 20%
CURRENCY Loti = 100 lisente

LIBERIA

 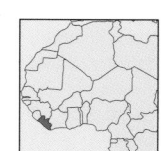

GEOGRAPHY The Republic of Liberia is a country in West Africa. Behind the coastline, 500 km [311 mi] long, lies a narrow coastal plain. Beyond, the land rises to a plateau region, with the highest land along the border with Guinea.

Liberia has a tropical climate with high temperatures and high humidity all through the year. The rainfall is abundant all year round, but there is a particularly wet period from June to November. The rainfall generally increases from east to west.

POLITICS & ECONOMY In the late 18th century, some white Americans in the United States wanted to help freed black slaves to return to Africa. In 1816, they set up the American Colonization Society, which bought land in what is now Liberia.

In 1822, the Society landed former slaves at a settlement on the coast which they named Monrovia. In 1847, Liberia became a fully independent republic with a constitution much like that of the United States. For many years, the Americo-Liberians controlled the country's government. US influence remained strong and the American Firestone Company, which ran Liberia's rubber plantations, was especially influential. Foreign companies were also involved in exploiting Liberia's mineral resources, including its huge iron-ore deposits.

In 1980, a military group composed of people from the local population killed the Americo-Liberian president, William R. Tolbert. An army sergeant, Samuel K. Doe, was made president of Liberia. Elections held in 1985 resulted in victory for Doe.

From 1989, the country was plunged into civil war between various ethnic groups. Doe was assassinated in 1990 and the struggle with rebel groups continued. West African peacekeeping forces arrived in Liberia and, in 1995, a cease-fire was agreed. A council of state, composed of former warlords, was set up and, in 1997, one of the warlords, Charles Taylor, was elected president. A cease-fire in 1998 led to the withdrawal of the peacekeeping forces. But unrest continued and, in 2002, a state of emergency was declared.

Liberia's civil war devastated its economy. Three out of every four people depend on agriculture, though many of them grow little more than they need to feed their families. Major food crops include cassava, rice and sugar cane, while rubber, cocoa and coffee are exported. But the most valuable export is iron ore. Liberia also obtains revenue from its 'flag of

convenience', which is used by about one-sixth of the world's commercial shipping, exploiting low taxes.

> **AREA** 111,370 sq km [43,000 sq mi]
> **POPULATION** 3,288,000
> **CAPITAL (POPULATION)** Monrovia (962,000)
> **GOVERNMENT** Multiparty republic
> **ETHNIC GROUPS** Kpelle 19%, Bassa 14%, Grebo 9%, Gio 8%, Kru 7%, Mano 7%
> **LANGUAGES** English (official), Mande, Mel, Kwa
> **RELIGIONS** Christianity 40%, Islam 20%, traditional beliefs and others 40%
> **CURRENCY** Liberian dollar = 100 cents

LIBYA

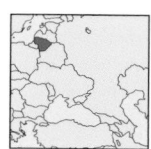

GEOGRAPHY The Socialist People's Libyan Arab Jamahiriya, as Libya is officially called, is a large country in North Africa. Most people live on the coastal plains in the north-east and north-west. The Sahara, which occupies 95% of Libya, reaches the Mediterranean coast along the Gulf of Sidra (Khalij Surt).

The north-eastern and north-western coastal plains have Mediterranean climates, with hot, dry summers and mild, moist winters. Inland, the average annual rainfall drops to 100 mm [4 in] or less.

POLITICS & ECONOMY Italy took over Libya in 1911, but lost it during World War II. Britain and France then jointly ruled Libya until 1951, when the country became an independent kingdom.

In 1969, a military group headed by Colonel Muammar Gaddafi deposed the king and set up a military government. Under Gaddafi, the government took control of the economy and used money from oil exports to finance welfare services and development projects. Gaddafi was criticized for supporting terrorist groups around the world, and Libya became isolated from the mid-1980s. In 1998, he tried to restore Libya's reputation by surrendering for trial two Libyans suspected of planting a bomb on a PanAm plane which exploded over the Scottish town of Lockerbie in 1988. In 2001, one of the Libyans was found guilty and the other acquitted of the bombing. Gaddafi also compensated the family of a British policewoman killed in 1984 in London. However, in 2002, Libya remained on the US blacklist for its alleged support for international terrorism.

The discovery of oil and natural gas in 1959 led to the transformation of Libya's economy. Once one of the world's poorest countries, it has become Africa's richest in terms of its per capita income. It remains a developing country because of its dependence on oil, which accounts for nearly all of its export revenues.

Agriculture is important, although Libya has to import food. Crops include barley, citrus fruits, dates, olives, potatoes and wheat. Cattle, sheep and poultry are raised. Libya has oil refineries and petrochemical plants. Other manufactures include cement and steel.

> **AREA** 1,759,540 sq km [679,358 sq mi]
> **POPULATION** 5,369,000
> **CAPITAL (POPULATION)** Tripoli (960,000)
> **GOVERNMENT** Single-party socialist state
> **ETHNIC GROUPS** Libyan Arab and Berber 97%
> **LANGUAGES** Arabic (official), Berber
> **RELIGIONS** Islam (Sunni)
> **CURRENCY** Libyan dinar = 1,000 dirhams

LIECHTENSTEIN

The tiny Principality of Liechtenstein is sandwiched between Switzerland and Austria. The River Rhine flows along its western border, while Alpine peaks rise in the east and south. The climate is relatively mild. Since 1924, Liechtenstein has been in a customs union with Switzerland. Taxation is low and the country is a haven for foreign companies. In 2003, the people voted to give their head of state, Prince Hans Adam II, sovereign powers. **AREA** 157 sq km [61 sq mi]; **POPULATION** 33,000; **CAPITAL** Vaduz.

LITHUANIA

GEOGRAPHY The Republic of Lithuania is the southernmost of the three Baltic states which were ruled as part of the Soviet Union between 1940 and 1991. Much of the land is flat or gently rolling, with the highest land in the south-east.

Winters are cold. January's temperatures average –3°C [27°F] in the west and –6°C [21°F] in the east. Summers are warm, with average temperatures in July of 17°C [63°F]. The average rainfall in the west is about 630 mm [25 in]. Inland areas are drier.

POLITICS & ECONOMY The Lithuanian people were united into a single nation in the 12th century, and later joined a union with Poland. In 1795, Lithuania came under Russian rule. After World War I (1914–18), Lithuania declared itself independent, and in 1920 it signed a peace treaty with the Russians, though Poland held Vilnius until 1939. In 1940, the Soviet Union occupied Lithuania, but the Germans invaded in 1941. Soviet forces returned in 1944, and Lithuania was integrated into the Soviet Union. In 1988, when the Soviet Union was introducing reforms, the Lithuanians demanded independence. Their language is one of the oldest in the world, and the country was always the most homogenous of the Baltic states, staunchly Catholic and resistant of attempts to suppress their culture. Pro-independence groups won the national elections in 1990 and, in 1991, the Soviet Union recognized Lithuania's independence.

Since 1991, Lithuania has sought to reform its economy and introduce a private enterprise system. Lithuania has also drawn closer to the West and, in 2002, the European Union invited it to become a member in 2004.

The World Bank classifies Lithuania as a 'lower-middle-income' developing country. Lithuania lacks natural resources, but manufacturing, based on imported materials, is the most valuable activity.

> **AREA** 65,200 sq km [25,200 sq mi]
> **POPULATION** 3,601,000
> **CAPITAL (POPULATION)** Vilnius (580,000)
> **GOVERNMENT** Multiparty republic
> **ETHNIC GROUPS** Lithuanian 80%, Russian 9%, Polish 7%, Belarussian 2%
> **LANGUAGES** Lithuanian (official), Russian, Polish
> **RELIGIONS** Mainly Roman Catholic
> **CURRENCY** Litas = 100 centai

LUXEMBOURG

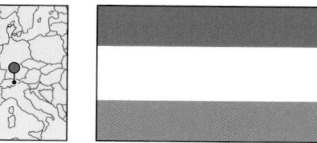
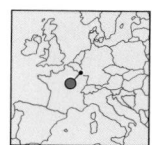

GEOGRAPHY The Grand Duchy of Luxembourg is one of the smallest and oldest countries in Europe. The north belongs to an upland region which includes the Ardenne in Belgium and Luxembourg, and the Eifel highlands in Germany.

Luxembourg has a temperate climate. The south has warm summers and autumns, when grapes ripen in sheltered south-eastern valleys. Winters are sometimes severe, especially in upland areas.

POLITICS & ECONOMY Germany occupied Luxembourg in World Wars I and II. In 1944–5, northern Luxembourg was the scene of the famous Battle of the Bulge. In 1948, Luxembourg joined Belgium and the Netherlands in a union called Benelux and, in the 1950s, it was one of the six founders of what is now the European Union. Luxembourg has played a major role in Europe. Its capital contains the headquarters of several international agencies, including the European Coal and Steel Community and the European Court of Justice. The city is also a major financial centre.

Luxembourg has iron-ore reserves and is a major steel producer. It also has many high-technology industries, producing electronic goods and computers. Steel and other manufactures, including chemicals, rubber products, glass and aluminium, dominate the country's exports. Other major activities include tourism and financial services.

> **AREA** 2,590 sq km [1,000 sq mi]
> **POPULATION** 449,000
> **CAPITAL (POPULATION)** Luxembourg (76,000)
> **GOVERNMENT** Constitutional monarchy (Grand Duchy)
> **ETHNIC GROUPS** Luxembourger 71%, Portuguese 10%, Italian 5%, French 3%, Belgian 3%
> **LANGUAGES** Luxembourgish (official), French, German
> **RELIGIONS** Roman Catholic 95%
> **CURRENCY** Euro = 100 cents

MACEDONIA (FYROM)

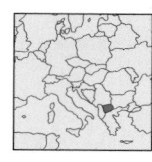

GEOGRAPHY The Republic of Macedonia is a country in south-eastern Europe, which was once one of the six republics that made up the former Federal People's Republic of Yugoslavia. This landlocked country is largely mountainous or hilly.

Macedonia has hot summers, though highland areas are cooler. Winters are cold and snowfalls are often heavy. The climate is fairly continental in character and rain occurs throughout the year.

POLITICS & ECONOMY Until the 20th century, Macedonia's history was closely tied to a larger area, also called Macedonia, which included parts of northern Greece and south-western Bulgaria. This region reached its peak in power at the time of Philip II (382–336 BC) and his son Alexander the Great (336–323 BC). After Alexander's death, his empire was split up and it gradually declined. The area became a Roman province in the 140s BC and part of

the Byzantine Empire from AD 395. In the 6th century, Slavs from eastern Europe settled in the area, followed by the Bulgars from central Asia in the 9th century. The Byzantine Empire regained control in 1018, but Serbia took Macedonia in the early 14th century. In 1371, the Ottoman Turks conquered the area and ruled it for more than 500 years. The Ottoman Empire began to collapse in the late 19th century. In 1913, at the end of the Balkan Wars, the area was divided between Serbia, Bulgaria and Greece. At the end of World War I, Serbian Macedonia became part of the Kingdom of the Serbs. Croats and Slovenes, which was renamed Yugoslavia in 1929. After World War II, Yugoslavia became a Communist country under ex-partisan leader Josip Broz Tito.

Tito died in 1980 and, in the early 1990s, the country broke up into five separate republics. Macedonia declared its independence in September 1991. Greece objected to this territory using the name Macedonia, which it considered to be a Greek name. It also objected to a symbol on Macedonia's flag and a reference in the constitution to the desire to reunite the three parts of the old Macedonia.

Macedonia adopted a new clause in its constitution rejecting any Macedonian claims on Greek territory and, in 1993, the United Nations accepted the new republic as a member under the name of The Former Yugoslav Republic of Macedonia (FYROM).

By the end of 1993, all the countries of the EU, except Greece, were establishing diplomatic relations with the FYROM. In 1995, Greece lifted its trade ban, when Macedonia agreed to redesign its flag and remove territorial claims from its constitution. In 2001, fighting along the Kosovo border spilled over into north-western Macedonia. It was attributed to nationalists who wanted to create a Great Albania, including part of Macedonia. The uprising ended when the Macedonian government gave its Albanian-speakers increased rights.

The World Bank describes Macedonia as a 'lower-middle-income' developing country. Manufactures dominate the country's exports. Macedonia mines coal, but imports all its oil and natural gas. The country is self-sufficient in its basic food needs.

AREA 25,710 sq km [9,927 sq mi]
POPULATION 2,055,000
CAPITAL (POPULATION) Skopje (541,000)
GOVERNMENT Multiparty republic
ETHNIC GROUPS Macedonian 67%, Albanian 23%, Turkish 4%, Romanian 2%, Serb 2%
LANGUAGES Macedonian and Albanian (official)
RELIGIONS Macedonian Orthodox, Islam
CURRENCY Dinar = 100 paras

MADAGASCAR

GEOGRAPHY The Democratic Republic of Madagascar, in south-eastern Africa, is an island nation, which has a larger area than France. Behind the narrow coastal plains in the east lies a highland zone, mostly between 610 m and 1,220 m [2,000 ft to 4,000 ft] above sea level. Broad plains border the Mozambique Channel in the west.

Temperatures in the highlands are moderated by the altitude. The winters (from April to September) are dry, but heavy rains occur in summer. The eastern coastlands are warm and humid. The west is drier and the south and south-west are hot and dry.

POLITICS & ECONOMY People from South-east Asia began to settle on Madagascar around 2,000 years ago. Subsequent influxes from Africa and Arabia added to the island's diverse heritage, culture and language.

French troops defeated a Malagasy army in 1895 and Madagascar became a French colony. In 1960, it achieved full independence as the Malagasy Republic. In 1972, army officers seized control and, in 1975, under the leadership of Lt-Commander Didier Ratsiraka, the country was renamed Madagascar. Parliamentary elections were held in 1977, but Ratsiraka remained president of a one-party socialist state. In 2002, the country came close to civil war when Ratsiraka and his opponent, Marc Ravalomanana, both claimed victory in presidential elections. Ravalomanana was eventually recognized as president and Ratsiraka went into exile.

Madagascar is one of the world's poorest countries. The land has been badly eroded because of the cutting down of the forests and overgrazing of the grasslands. Farming, fishing and forestry employ about 80% of the people. The country's food crops include bananas, cassava, rice and sweet potatoes. Coffee is the leading export.

AREA 587,040 sq km [226,656 sq mi]
POPULATION 16,473,000
CAPITAL (POPULATION) Antananarivo (1,053,000)
GOVERNMENT Republic
ETHNIC GROUPS Merina 27%, Betsimisaraka 15%, Betsileo 11%, Tsimihety 7%, Sakalava 6%
LANGUAGES Malagasy and French (both official)
RELIGIONS Traditional beliefs 52%, Christianity 41%, Islam 7%
CURRENCY Malagasy franc = 100 centimes

MALAWI

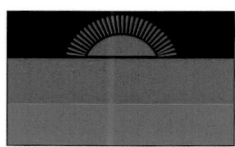 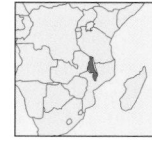

GEOGRAPHY The Republic of Malawi includes part of Lake Malawi, which is drained by the River Shire, a tributary of the River Zambezi. The land is mostly mountainous. The highest peak, Mulanje, reaches 3,000 m [9,843 ft] in the south-east.

While the low-lying areas of Malawi are hot and humid all year round, the uplands have a pleasant climate. Lilongwe, at about 1,100 m [3,609 ft] above sea level, has a warm and sunny climate. Frosts sometimes occur in July and August, in the middle of the long dry season.

POLITICS & ECONOMY Malawi, then called Nyasaland, became a British protectorate in 1891. In 1953, Britain established the Federation of Rhodesia and Nyasaland, which also included what are now Zambia and Zimbabwe. Black African opposition, led in Nyasaland by Dr Hastings Kamuzu Banda, led to the dissolution of the federation in 1963. In 1964, Nyasaland became independent as Malawi, with Banda as prime minister. Banda became president when the country became a republic in 1966 and, in 1971, he was made president for life. Banda ruled autocratically through the only party, the Malawi Congress Party. A multiparty system was restored in 1993. Banda and his party were defeated in elections in 1993. Bakili Muluzi became president and was re-elected in 1999. Banda died in 1997.

Malawi is one of the world's poorest countries. More than 80% of the people are farmers, but many grow little more than they need to feed their families.

AREA 118,480 sq km [45,745 sq mi]
POPULATION 10,702,000
CAPITAL (POPULATION) Lilongwe (395,000)
GOVERNMENT Multiparty republic
ETHNIC GROUPS Maravi (Chewa, Nyanja, Tonga, Tumbuka) 58%, Lomwe 18%, Yao 13%, Ngoni 7%
LANGUAGES Chichewa and English (both official)
RELIGIONS Protestant 55%, Roman Catholic 20%, Islam 20%
CURRENCY Kwacha = 100 tambala

MALAYSIA

GEOGRAPHY The Federation of Malaysia consists of two main parts. Peninsular Malaysia, which is joined to mainland Asia, contains about 80% of the population. The other main regions, Sabah and Sarawak, are in northern Borneo, an island which Malaysia shares with Indonesia. Much of the land is mountainous, with coastal lowlands bordering the rugged interior. The highest peak, Kinabalu, reaches 4,101 m [13,455 ft] in Sabah.

Malaysia has a hot equatorial climate. The temperatures are high all through the year, though the mountains are much cooler than the lowland areas. The rainfall is heavy throughout the year.

POLITICS & ECONOMY Japan occupied what is now Malaysia during World War II, but British rule was re-established in 1945. In the 1940s and 1950s, British troops fought a war against Communist guerrillas, but Peninsular Malaysia (then called Malaya) became independent in 1957. Malaysia was created in 1963, when Malaya, Singapore, Sabah and Sarawak agreed to unite, but Singapore withdrew in 1965.

From the 1970s, Malaysia achieved rapid economic progress and, by the mid-1990s, it was playing a major part in regional affairs, especially through its membership of ASEAN (Association of South-east Asian Nations). However, together with several other countries in eastern Asia, Malaysia was hit by economic recession in 1997, including a major fall in stock market values. In response to the crisis, the government ordered the repatriation of many temporary foreign workers and initiated a series of austerity measures aimed at restoring confidence and avoiding the chronic debt problems affecting some other Asian countries.

The World Bank classifies Malaysia as an 'upper-middle-income' developing country. Malaysia is a leading producer of palm oil, rubber and tin.

Manufacturing now plays a major part in the economy. Manufactures are diverse, including cars, chemicals, a wide range of electronic goods, plastics, textiles, rubber and wood products.

AREA 329,750 sq km [127,316 sq mi]
POPULATION 22,662,000
CAPITAL (POPULATION) Kuala Lumpur (1,145,000)
GOVERNMENT Federal constitutional monarchy
ETHNIC GROUPS Malay and other indigenous groups 58%, Chinese 27%, Indian 8%
LANGUAGES Malay (official), Chinese, English
RELIGIONS Islam 53%, Buddhism 17%, Chinese folk religionist 12%, Hinduism 7%, Christianity 6%
CURRENCY Ringgit (Malaysian dollar) = 100 cents

MALDIVES

 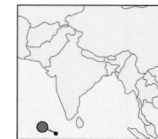

The Republic of the Maldives consists of about 1,200 low-lying coral islands, south of India. The highest point is 24 m [79 ft], but most of the land is only 1.8 m [6 ft] above sea level. The islands became a British territory in 1887 and independence was achieved in 1965. Tourism and fishing are the main industries. **AREA** 298 sq km [115 sq mi]; **POPULATION** 320,000; **CAPITAL** Malé.

MALI

GEOGRAPHY The Republic of Mali is a landlocked country in northern Africa. The land is generally flat, with the highest land in the Adrar des Iforhas on the border with Algeria.

Northern Mali is part of the Sahara, with a hot, practically rainless climate. But the south has enough rain for farming.

POLITICS & ECONOMY France ruled the area, then known as French Sudan, from 1893 until the country became independent as Mali in 1960.

The first socialist government was overthrown in 1968 by an army group led by Moussa Traoré, but he was ousted in 1991. Multiparty democracy was restored in 1992 and Alpha Oumar Konaré was elected president. Konaré stood down in 2002 and Ahmadou Toure, who had restored democracy in 1992, was elected president.

Mali is one of the world's poorest countries and 70% of the land is desert or semi-desert. Only about 2% of the land is used for growing crops, while 25% is used for grazing animals. Despite this, agriculture employs more than 80% of the people, many of whom still subsist by nomadic livestock rearing.

AREA 1,240,190 sq km [478,837 sq mi]
POPULATION 11,340,000
CAPITAL (POPULATION) Bamako (810,000)
GOVERNMENT Multiparty republic
ETHNIC GROUPS Bambara 32%, Fulani
(or Peul) 14%, Senufo 12%, Soninke 9%,
Tuareg 7%, Songhai 7%, Malinke (Mandingo
or Mandinke) 7%
LANGUAGES French (official), Voltaic languages
RELIGIONS Islam 90%, traditional beliefs 9%,
Christianity 1%
CURRENCY CFA franc = 100 centimes

MALTA

 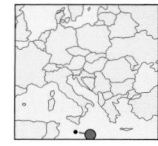

GEOGRAPHY The Republic of Malta consists of two main islands, Malta and Gozo, a third, much smaller island called Comino lying between the two large islands, and two tiny islets.

Malta's climate is typically Mediterranean, with hot and dry summers and mild and wet winters. The sirocco, a hot wind from North Africa, may raise temperatures considerably during the spring.

POLITICS & ECONOMY During World War I (1914–18) Malta was an important naval base. In World War II (1939–45), Italian and German aircraft bombed the islands. In recognition of the bravery of the Maltese, the British King George VI awarded the George Cross to Malta in 1942. In 1953, Malta became a base for NATO (North Atlantic Treaty Organization). Malta became independent in 1964, and in 1974 it became a republic. In 1979, Britain's military agreement with Malta expired, and Malta ceased to be a military base when all the British forces withdrew. In the 1980s, the people declared Malta a neutral country. In the 1990s, Malta applied to join the European Union. The application was scrapped when the Labour Party won the elections in 1996. However, after the Labour Party was defeated in 1998, the European Union in 2002 invited Malta to become a member in 2004. The Maltese people voted in favour of this move in 2003.

The World Bank classifies Malta as an 'upper-middle-income' developing country. It lacks natural resources, and most people work in the former naval dockyards, which are now used for commercial shipbuilding and repairs, in manufacturing, and in tourism. Manufactures include chemicals, processed food and chemicals. Farming is difficult, because of the rocky soils. Crops include barley, fruits, potatoes and wheat. Fishing is also important.

AREA 316 sq km [122 sq mi]
POPULATION 397,000
CAPITAL (POPULATION) Valletta (102,000)
GOVERNMENT Multiparty republic
ETHNIC GROUPS Maltese 96%, British 2%
LANGUAGES Maltese and English (both official)
RELIGIONS Roman Catholic 91%
CURRENCY Maltese lira = 100 cents

MARSHALL ISLANDS

 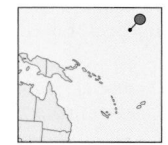

The Republic of the Marshall Islands, a former US territory, became fully independent in 1991. This island nation, lying north of Kiribati in a region known as Micronesia, is heavily dependent on US aid. The main activities are agriculture and tourism. **AREA** 181 sq km [70 sq mi]; **POPULATION** 74,000; **CAPITAL** Dalap-Uliga-Darrit, on Majuro island.

MARTINIQUE

Martinique, a volcanic island nation in the Caribbean, was colonized by France in 1635. It became a French overseas department in 1946. Tourism and agriculture are major activities. About 70% of Martinique's gross domestic product is provided by the French government, allowing for a good standard of living. **AREA** 1,100 sq km [425 sq mi]; **POPULATION** 422,000; **CAPITAL** Fort-de-France.

MAURITANIA

GEOGRAPHY The Islamic Republic of Mauritania in north-western Africa is nearly twice the size of France. But France has more than 28 times as many people. Part of the world's largest desert, the Sahara, covers northern Mauritania and most Mauritanians live in the south-west.

The amount of rainfall and the length of the rainy season increase from north to south. Much of the land is desert, with dry north-east and easterly winds throughout the year. But south-westerly winds bring summer rain to the south.

POLITICS & ECONOMY Originally part of the great African empires of Ghana and Mali, France set up a protectorate in Mauritania in 1903, attempting to exploit the trade in gum arabic. The country became a territory of French West Africa and a French colony in 1920. French West Africa was a huge territory, which included present-day Benin, Burkina Faso, Guinea, Ivory Coast, Mali, Niger and Senegal, as well as Mauritania. In 1958, Mauritania became a self-governing territory in the French Union and it became fully independent in 1960.

In 1976, Spain withdrew from Spanish (now Western) Sahara, a territory bordering Mauritania to the north. Morocco occupied the northern two-thirds of this territory, while Mauritania took the rest. But Saharan guerrillas belonging to POLISARIO (the Popular Front for the Liberation of Saharan Territories) began an armed struggle for independence. In 1979, Mauritania withdrew from the southern part of Western Sahara, which was then occupied by Morocco. In 1991, the country adopted a new constitution when the people voted to create a multiparty government. Multiparty elections were held in 1992 and 1996–7.

The World Bank classifies Mauritania as a 'low-income' developing country. Agriculture employs 40% of the people. Some are herders who move around with herds of cattle and sheep, though recent droughts forced many farmers to seek aid in the cities.

AREA 1,030,700 sq km [397,953 sq mi]
POPULATION 2,829,000
CAPITAL (POPULATION) Nouakchott (735,000)
GOVERNMENT Multiparty Islamic republic
ETHNIC GROUPS Moor (Arab-Berber) 70%,
Wolof 7%, Tukulor 5%, Soninke 3%, Fulani 1%
LANGUAGES Arabic and Wolof (both official),
French
RELIGIONS Islam 99%
CURRENCY Ouguiya = 5 khoums

MAURITIUS

 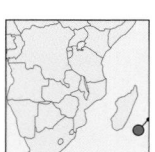

The Republic of Mauritius, an Indian Ocean nation lying east of Madagascar, was previously ruled by France and Britain until it achieved independence in 1968. It became a republic in 1992. Sugar production is in decline but tourism is vital to the economy. **AREA** 1,860 sq km [718 sq mi]; **POPULATION** 1,200,000; **CAPITAL** Port Louis.

MEXICO

GEOGRAPHY The United Mexican States, as Mexico is officially named, is the world's most populous Spanish-speaking country. Much of the land is mountainous, although most people live on the central plateau. Mexico contains two large peninsulas, Lower (or Baja) California in the north-west and the flat Yucatán peninsula in the south-east.

The climate varies according to the altitude. The resort of Acapulco on the south-west coast has a dry and sunny climate. Mexico City, at about 2,300 m [7,546 ft] above sea level, is much cooler. Most rain occurs between June and September. The rainfall decreases north of Mexico City and northern Mexico is mainly arid.

POLITICS & ECONOMY In the mid-19th century, Mexico lost land to the United States, and between 1910 and 1921 violent revolutions created chaos.

Reforms were introduced in the 1920s and, in 1929, the Institutional Revolutionary Party (PRI) was formed. The PRI ruled Mexico effectively as a one-party state until it was finally defeated in 2001. The new president, Vicente Fox, faced many problems, including unemployment and rapid urbanization especially around Mexico City, demands for indigenous rights by Amerindian groups, and illegal emigration to the United States.

The World Bank classifies Mexico as an 'upper-middle-income' developing country. Agriculture is important. Food crops include beans, maize, rice and wheat, while cash crops include coffee, cotton, fruits and vegetables. Beef cattle, dairy cattle and other livestock are raised and fishing is also important.

But oil and oil products are the chief exports, while manufacturing is the most valuable activity. Many factories near the northern border assemble goods, such as car parts and electrical products, for US companies. These factories are called *maquiladoras*. Hope for the future lies in increasing economic co-operation with the USA and Canada through NAFTA (North American Free Trade Association), which came into being on 1 January 1994.

> **AREA** 1,958,200 sq km [756,061 sq mi]
> **POPULATION** 103,400,000
> **CAPITAL (POPULATION)** Mexico City (15,643,000)
> **GOVERNMENT** Federal republic
> **ETHNIC GROUPS** Mestizo 60%, Amerindian 30%, White 9%
> **LANGUAGES** Spanish (official)
> **RELIGIONS** Roman Catholic 90%, Protestant 5%
> **CURRENCY** New peso = 100 centavos

MICRONESIA

 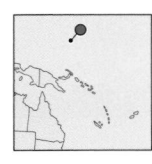

The Federated States of Micronesia, a former US territory covering a vast area in the western Pacific Ocean, became fully independent in 1991. The main export is copra. Fishing and tourism are also important. **AREA** 705 sq km [272 sq mi]; **POPULATION** 136,000; **CAPITAL** Palikir.

MOLDOVA

GEOGRAPHY The Republic of Moldova is a small country sandwiched between Ukraine and Romania. It was formerly one of the 15 republics that made up the Soviet Union. Much of the land is hilly and the highest areas are near the centre of the country.

Moldova has a moderately continental climate, with warm summers and fairly cold winters. Most of the rain comes in the warmer months.

POLITICS & ECONOMY In the 14th century, the Moldavians formed a state called Moldavia. It included part of Romania and Bessarabia (now the modern country of Moldova). The Ottoman Turks took the area in the 16th century, but in 1812 Russia took over Bessarabia. In 1861, Moldavia and Walachia united to form Romania. Russia retook southern Bessarabia in 1878.

After World War I (1914–18), all of Bessarabia was returned to Romania, but the Soviet Union did not recognize this act. From 1944, the Moldovan Soviet Socialist Republic was part of the Soviet Union.

In 1989, the Moldovans asserted their independence and ethnicity by making Romanian the official language and, at the end of 1991, Moldova became an independent country. In 1992, fighting occurred between Moldovans and Russians in Trans-Dniester, a mainly Russian-speaking area east of the River Dniester. The first multiparty elections were held in 1994, when a proposal to unite with Romania was rejected. Economic problems made the government unpopular and, in 2001, Moldova became the first former Soviet state to return the Communist party to power in a general election.

In terms of its GNP per capita, Moldova is Europe's poorest country. Agriculture is the leading activity and products include fruits, maize, tobacco and wine. Moldova has few natural resources and it imports materials and fuels for its industries. Light industries, such as food processing and factories making household appliances, are increasing.

> **AREA** 33,700 sq km [13,010 sq mi]
> **POPULATION** 4,435,000
> **CAPITAL (POPULATION)** Chişinău (658,000)
> **GOVERNMENT** Multiparty republic
> **ETHNIC GROUPS** Moldovan 65%, Ukrainian 14%, Russian 13%, Gagauz 4%, Jewish 2%, Bulgarian
> **LANGUAGES** Moldovan/Romanian (official)
> **RELIGIONS** Eastern Orthodox
> **CURRENCY** Leu = 100 bani

MONACO

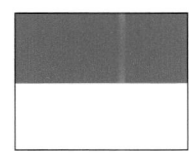 

The tiny Principality of Monaco consists of a narrow strip of coastline and a rocky peninsula on the French Riviera. Its considerable wealth is derived largely from banking, finance, gambling and tourism. Monaco's citizens do not pay any state tax. Its attractions include the Monte Carlo casino and such sporting events as the Monte Carlo Rally and the Monaco Grand Prix. **AREA** 1.5 sq km [0.6 sq mi]; **POPULATION** 32,000; **CAPITAL** Monaco.

MONGOLIA

GEOGRAPHY The State of Mongolia is the world's largest landlocked country. It consists mainly of high plateaux, with the Gobi Desert in the south-east.

Ulan Bator lies on the northern edge of a desert plateau. It has bitterly cold winters. Summer temperatures are moderated by the altitude.

POLITICS & ECONOMY In the 13th century, Genghis Khan united the Mongolian peoples and built up a great empire. Under his grandson, Kublai Khan, the Mongol empire extended from Korea and China to eastern Europe and present-day Iraq.

The Mongol empire broke up in the late 14th century. In the early 17th century, Inner Mongolia came under Chinese control, and by the late 17th century Outer Mongolia had become a Chinese province. In 1911, the Mongolians drove the Chinese out of Outer Mongolia and made the area a Buddhist kingdom. But in 1924, under Russian influence, the Communist Mongolian People's Republic was set up. From the 1950s, Mongolia supported the Soviet Union in its disputes with China. In 1990, the people demonstrated for more freedom, and free elections in June 1990 resulted in victory for the Mongolian People's Revolutionary Party, which was composed of Communists. Communist rule ended in 1996, when the Democratic Union coalition won power. But the Communists regained power in 2000, though they were expected to continue free-market policies.

The World Bank classifies Mongolia as a 'lower-middle-income' developing country. Most people were once nomads, who moved around with their herds of sheep, cattle, goats and horses. Under Communist rule, most people were moved into permanent homes on government-owned farms. But livestock and animal products remain leading exports. The Communists also developed industry, especially the mining of coal, copper, gold, molybdenum, tin and tungsten, and manufacturing. Minerals and fuels now account for around half of Mongolia's exports.

> **AREA** 1,566,500 sq km [604,826 sq mi]
> **POPULATION** 2,694,000
> **CAPITAL (POPULATION)** Ulan Bator (673,000)
> **GOVERNMENT** Multiparty republic
> **ETHNIC GROUPS** Khalkha Mongol 85%, Kazakh 6%
> **LANGUAGES** Khalkha Mongolian (official), Turkic, Russian
> **RELIGIONS** Tibetan Buddhist (Lamaist)
> **CURRENCY** Tugrik = 100 möngös

MONTSERRAT

 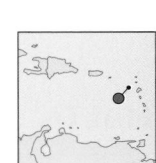

Monserrat is a British overseas territory in the Caribbean Sea. The climate is tropical and hurricanes often cause much damage. Intermittent eruptions of the Soufrière Hills volcano between 1995 and 1998 led to the emigration of many of the inhabitants and the virtual destruction of Plymouth, the capital, in the southern part of the island. **AREA** 102 sq km [39 sq mi]; **POPULATION** 8,000 (prior to the volcanic activity); **CAPITAL** Plymouth.

MOROCCO

GEOGRAPHY The Kingdom of Morocco lies in north-western Africa. Its name comes from the Arabic Maghreb-el-Aksa, meaning 'the farthest west'. Behind the western coastal plain the land rises to a broad plateau and ranges of the Atlas Mountains. The High (Haut) Atlas contains the highest peak, Djebel Toubkal, at 4,165 m [13,665 ft]. East of the mountains, the land descends to the arid Sahara.

The Atlantic coast of Morocco is cooled by the Canaries Current. Inland, summers are hot and dry. The winters are mild. In winter, between October and April, south-westerly winds from the Atlantic Ocean bring moderate rainfall, and snow often falls on the High Atlas Mountains.

POLITICS & ECONOMY The original people of Morocco were the Berbers. But in the 680s, Arab invaders introduced Islam and the Arabic language. By the early 20th century, France and Spain controlled Morocco, which became an independent kingdom in 1956. Although Morocco is a constitutional monarchy, King Hassan II ruled the country in a generally authoritarian way since his accession to the throne in 1961 to his death in 1999. His son and successor Mohamed VI faced several problems, including the future of Western Sahara which Hassan II had vigorously claimed for Morocco.

Morocco is classified as a 'lower-middle-income' developing country. It is the world's third largest producer of phosphate rock, which is used to make fertilizer. One of the reasons why Morocco wants to keep Western Sahara is that it, too, has large phosphate reserves. Farming employs 34% of Moroccans. Crops include barley, beans, citrus fruits, maize and wheat. Tourism is also important.

AREA 446,550 sq km [172,413 sq mi]
POPULATION 31,168,000
CAPITAL (POPULATION) Rabat (1,220,000)
GOVERNMENT Constitutional monarchy
ETHNIC GROUPS Arab 70%, Berber 30%
LANGUAGES Arabic (official), Berber, French
RELIGIONS Islam 99%, Christianity 1%
CURRENCY Moroccan dirham = 100 centimes

MOZAMBIQUE

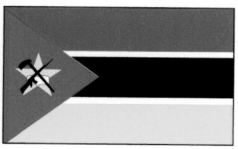 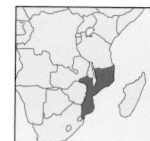

GEOGRAPHY The Republic of Mozambique borders the Indian Ocean in south-eastern Africa. The coastal plains are narrow in the north but broaden in the south. Inland lie plateaux and hills, which make up another two-fifths of Mozambique.

Mozambique has a mostly tropical climate. The capital Maputo, which lies outside the tropics, has hot and humid summers, though the winters are mild and fairly dry.

POLITICS & ECONOMY In 1885, when the European powers divided Africa, Mozambique was recognized as a Portuguese colony. But black African opposition to European rule gradually increased. In 1961, the Front for the Liberation of Mozambique (FRELIMO) was founded to oppose Portuguese rule.

In 1964, FRELIMO launched a guerrilla war, which continued for ten years. Mozambique became independent in 1975.

After independence, Mozambique became a one-party state. Its government aided African nationalists in Rhodesia (now Zimbabwe) and South Africa. But the white governments of these countries helped an opposition group, the Mozambique National Resistance Movement (RENAMO) to lead an armed struggle against Mozambique's government. Civil war, combined with droughts, caused much suffering in the 1980s. In 1989, FRELIMO declared that it had dropped its Communist policies and ended one-party rule. The war ended in 1992 and multiparty elections in 1994 heralded more stable conditions. In 1995 Mozambique became the 53rd member of the Commonwealth.

In the early 1990s, the UN rated Mozambique as one of the world's poorest countries. The second half of the 1990s saw a surge in economic growth, but huge floods in 2000 and 2001 proved to be a major setback. About 80% of the people are poor and agriculture is the main activity. Crops include cassava, cotton, maize, rice and tea.

AREA 801,590 sq km [309,494 sq mi]
POPULATION 19,608,000
CAPITAL (POPULATION) Maputo (2,000,000)
GOVERNMENT Multiparty republic
ETHNIC GROUPS Indigenous tribal groups (Shangaan, Chokwe, Manyika, Sena, Makua, others) 99%
LANGUAGES Portuguese (official), many others
RELIGIONS Traditional beliefs 48%, Roman Catholic 31%, Islam 20%
CURRENCY Metical = 100 centavos

NAMIBIA

GEOGRAPHY The Republic of Namibia was formerly ruled by South Africa, which called it South West Africa. The country became independent in 1990. The coastal region contains the arid Namib Desert, which is virtually uninhabited. Inland is a central plateau, bordered by a rugged spine of mountains stretching north–south. Eastern Namibia contains part of the Kalahari Desert.

Namibia is a warm and arid country. Lying at 1,700 m [5,500 ft] above sea level, Windhoek has an average annual rainfall of about 370 mm [15 in], often occurring during thunderstorms in the hot summer months.

POLITICS & ECONOMY During World War I, South African troops defeated the Germans who ruled what is now Namibia. After World War II, many people challenged South Africa's right to govern the territory and a civil war began in the 1960s between African guerrillas and South African troops. A cease-fire was agreed in 1989 and Namibia became independent in 1990. In the 1990s, the government pursued a policy of 'national reconciliation'. An enclave on the coast, called Walvis Bay (Walvisbaai), remained part of South Africa until 1994, when it was transferred to Namibia. In 1999, a secessionist group staged an unsuccessful uprising in the Caprivi Strip.

Namibia is rich in mineral reserves, including diamonds, uranium, zinc and copper. Minerals make up 90% of the exports. But farming employs about two out of every five Namibians. Sea fishing is also important, though overfishing has reduced the yields of the country's fishing fleet. The country has few industries, but tourism is increasing.

AREA 825,414 sq km [318,434 sq mi]
POPULATION 1,821,000
CAPITAL (POPULATION) Windhoek (126,000)
GOVERNMENT Multiparty republic
ETHNIC GROUPS Ovambo 50%, Kavango 9%, Herero 7%, Damara 7%, White 6%, Nama 5%
LANGUAGES English (official), Ovambo, Afrikaans, German
RELIGIONS Christianity 90% (Lutheran 51%)
CURRENCY Namibian dollar = 100 cents

NAURU

 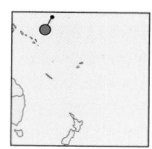

Nauru is the world's smallest republic, located in the western Pacific Ocean, close to the equator. Independent since 1968, Nauru's prosperity is based on phosphate mining, but the reserves are running out. **AREA** 21 sq km [8 sq mi]; **POPULATION** 12,000; **CAPITAL** Yaren.

NEPAL

 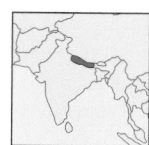

GEOGRAPHY Over three-quarters of Nepal lies in the Himalayan region, culminating in the world's highest peak (Mount Everest, or Chomolongma in Nepali) at 8,850 m [29,035 ft]. As a result, climatic conditions vary widely according to the altitude.

POLITICS & ECONOMY Nepal was united in the late 18th century, although its complex topography has ensured that it remains a diverse patchwork of peoples. From the mid-19th century to 1951, power was held by the royal Rana family. Attempts to introduce a democratic system in the 1950s failed. The first democratic elections in 32 years were held in 1991, but, by the early 21st century, Nepal faced many problems, including the activities of Maoist guerrillas. However, in 2003, a cease-fire was agreed with the Maoist rebels. In 2001, King Birendra and other members of the royal family were shot dead by Crown Prince Dipendra in a family dispute.

Agriculture remains the chief activity in this overwhelmingly rural country and the government is heavily dependent on aid. Tourism, centred around the high Himalaya, grows in importance each year, although Nepal was closed to foreigners until 1951. There are also plans to exploit the hydroelectric potential offered by the Himalayan rivers.

AREA 140,800 sq km [54,363 sq mi]
POPULATION 25,874,000
CAPITAL (POPULATION) Katmandu (535,000)
GOVERNMENT Constitutional monarchy
ETHNIC GROUPS Nepalese 53%, Bihari 18%, Tharu 5%, Tamang 5%, Newar 3%
LANGUAGES Nepali (official), local languages
RELIGIONS Hinduism 86%, Buddhism 8%, Islam 4%
CURRENCY Nepalese rupee = 100 paisa

NETHERLANDS

GEOGRAPHY The Netherlands lies at the western end of the North European Plain, which extends to the Ural Mountains in Russia. Except for the far south-eastern corner, the Netherlands is flat and about 40% lies below sea level at high tide. To prevent flooding, the Dutch have built dykes (sea walls) to hold back the waves. Large areas which were once under the sea, but which have been reclaimed, are called polders. Because of its position on the North Sea, the Netherlands has a temperate climate, with mild, rainy winters.

POLITICS & ECONOMY Before the 16th century, the area that is now the Netherlands was under a succession of foreign rulers, including the Romans, the Germanic Franks, the French and the Spanish. The Dutch declared their independence from Spain in 1581 and their status was finally recognized by Spain in 1648. In the 17th century, the Dutch built up a great overseas empire, especially in South-east Asia. But in the early 18th century, the Dutch lost control of the seas to England.

France controlled the Netherlands from 1795 to 1813. In 1815, the Netherlands, then containing Belgium and Luxembourg, became an independent kingdom. Belgium broke away in 1830 and Luxembourg followed in 1890.

The Netherlands was neutral in World War I (1914–18), but was occupied by Germany in World War II (1939–45). After the war, the Netherlands Indies became independent as Indonesia. The Netherlands became active in West European affairs. With Belgium and Luxembourg, it formed a customs union called Benelux in 1948. In 1949, it joined NATO (the North Atlantic Treaty Organization), and the European Coal and Steel Community (ECSC) in 1953. In 1957, it became a founder member of the European Economic Community (now the European Union) and, in 2002, it adopted the euro as its sole unit of currency. In 2002, an anti-immigration group made sweeping gains in national elections. It joined a coalition government, which collapsed later that year. The group's vote collapsed in new elections in 2003.

The Netherlands is a highly industrialized country and industry and commerce are the most valuable activities. Its resources include natural gas, some oil, salt and china clay. But the Netherlands imports many of the materials needed by its industries and it is, therefore, a major trading country. Industrial products are wide-ranging, including aircraft, chemicals, electronic equipment, machinery, textiles and vehicles. Agriculture employs only 5% of the people, but scientific methods are used and yields are high. Dairy farming is the leading farming activity. Major products include barley, flowers and bulbs, potatoes, sugar beet and wheat.

AREA 41,526 sq km [16,033 sq mi]
POPULATION 16,068,000
CAPITAL (POPULATION) Amsterdam (1,115,000);
The Hague (seat of government, 700,000)
GOVERNMENT Constitutional monarchy
ETHNIC GROUPS Dutch 95%, Indonesian,
Turkish, Moroccan
LANGUAGES Dutch (official), Frisian
RELIGIONS Roman Catholic 34%,
Protestant 21%, Islam 4%
CURRENCY Euro = 100 cents

NETHERLANDS ANTILLES

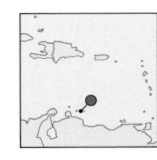

The Netherlands Antilles consists of two different island groups; one off the coast of Venezuela, and the other at the northern end of the Leeward Islands, some 800 km [500 mi] away. They remain a self-governing Dutch territory. The island of Aruba was once part of the territory, but it broke away in 1986. Oil refining and tourism are important activities.
AREA 993 sq km [383 sq mi]; **POPULATION** 214,000;
CAPITAL Willemstad.

NEW CALEDONIA

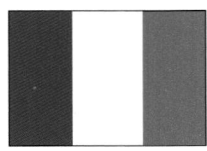

New Caledonia is the most southerly of the Melanesian countries in the Pacific. A French possession since 1853 and an Overseas Territory since 1958. In 1998, France announced an agreement with local Melanesians that a vote on independence would be postponed until 2014. The country is rich in mineral resources, especially nickel.
AREA 18,580 sq km [7,174 sq mi]; **POPULATION** 208,000; **CAPITAL** Nouméa.

NEW ZEALAND

GEOGRAPHY New Zealand lies about 1,600 km [994 mi] south-east of Australia. It consists of two main islands and several other small ones. Much of North Island is volcanic. Active volcanoes include Ngauruhoe and Ruapehu. Hot springs and geysers are common, and steam from the ground is used to produce electricity. The Southern Alps, which contain the country's highest peak Mount Cook (Aoraki), at 3,753 m [12,313 ft] form the backbone of South Island. The island also has some large, fertile plains.

Auckland in the north has a warm, humid climate throughout the year. Wellington has cooler summers, while in Dunedin, in the south-east, temperatures sometimes dip below freezing in winter. The rainfall is heaviest on the western highlands.

POLITICS & ECONOMY Evidence suggests that early Maori settlers arrived in New Zealand more than 1,000 years ago. The Dutch navigator Abel Tasman reached New Zealand in 1642, but his discovery was not followed up. In 1769, the British Captain James Cook rediscovered the islands. In the early 19th century, British settlers arrived and, in 1840, under the Treaty of Waitangi, Britain took possession of the islands. Clashes occurred with the Maoris in the 1860s but, from the 1870s, the Maoris were gradually integrated into society.

In 1907, New Zealand became a self-governing dominion in the British Commonwealth. The country's economy developed quickly and the people became increasingly prosperous. However, after Britain joined the European Economic Community in 1973, New Zealand's exports to Britain shrank and the country had to reassess its economic and defence strategies and seek new markets. The world recession led the government to cut back on welfare spending in the 1990s. The preservation of Maori culture and Maori rights are other major issues.

New Zealand's economy has traditionally depended on agriculture, but manufacturing now employs twice as many people as agriculture. Meat and dairy products are the most valuable items produced on farms. Sheep numbered less than 22 million in 2002. Their importance has greatly declined as the area under cattle, deer and vineyards has increased.

AREA 268,680 sq km [103,737 sq mi]
POPULATION 3,908,000
CAPITAL (POPULATION) Wellington (329,000)
GOVERNMENT Constitutional monarchy
ETHNIC GROUPS New Zealand European 74%,
New Zealand Maori 10%, Polynesian 4%
LANGUAGES English and Maori (both official)
RELIGIONS Anglican 24%, Presbyterian 18%,
Roman Catholic 15%
CURRENCY New Zealand dollar = 100 cents

NICARAGUA

GEOGRAPHY The Republic of Nicaragua is a large country in Central America. In the east is a broad plain bordering the Caribbean Sea. The plain is drained by rivers that flow from the Central Highlands. The fertile western Pacific region contains about 40 volcanoes, many of which are active, and earthquakes are common.

Nicaragua has a tropical climate. Managua is hot throughout the year and there is a marked rainy season from May to October. The Central Highlands and Caribbean region are cooler and wetter. The wettest region is the humid Caribbean plain.

POLITICS & ECONOMY In 1502, Christopher Columbus claimed the area for Spain, which ruled Nicaragua until 1821. By the early 20th century, the United States had considerable influence in the country and, in 1912, US forces entered Nicaragua to protect US interests. From 1927 to 1933, rebels under General Augusto César Sandino, tried to drive US forces out of the country. In 1933, US marines set up a Nicaraguan army, the National Guard, to help to defeat the rebels. Its leader, Anastasio Somoza Garcia, had Sandino murdered in 1934 and, from 1937, Somoza ruled as a dictator.

In the mid-1970s, many people began to protest against Somoza's rule. Many joined a guerrilla force, called the Sandinista National Liberation Front, named after General Sandino. The rebels defeated the Somoza regime in 1979. In the 1980s, the US-supported forces, called the 'Contras', launched a campaign against the Sandinista government. The US government opposed the Sandinista regime, under Daniel José Ortega Saavedra, claiming that it was a Communist dictatorship. A coalition, the National Opposition Union, defeated the Sandinistas in elections in 1990. In 1996 and again in 2001, the Sandinista candidate Daniel Ortega was defeated in presidential elections.

In the early 1990s, Nicaragua faced many problems in rebuilding its shattered economy. Agriculture is the main activity, employing nearly half of the people.

Coffee, cotton, sugar and bananas are grown for export, while rice is the main food crop.

Coffee, cotton, sugar and bananas are grown for export, while rice is the main food crop.

AREA 130,000 sq km [50,193 sq mi]
POPULATION 5,024,000
CAPITAL (POPULATION) Managua (864,000)
GOVERNMENT Multiparty republic
ETHNIC GROUPS Mestizo 69%, White 17%, Black 9%, Amerindian 5%
LANGUAGES Spanish (official), Misumalpan
RELIGIONS Roman Catholic 85%
CURRENCY Córdoba oro (gold córdoba) = 100 centavos

NIGER

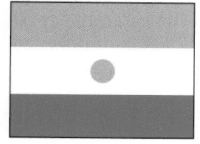 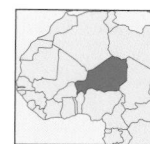

GEOGRAPHY The Republic of Niger is a landlocked nation in north-central Africa. The northern plateaux lie in the Sahara Desert, while Central Niger contains the rugged Aïr Mountains. The most fertile, densely populated region is the Niger valley in the south-west.

Niger has a tropical climate and the south has a rainy season between June and September. The north is practically rainless.

POLITICS & ECONOMY Since independence in 1960, Niger, a French territory from 1900, has suffered severe droughts. Food shortages and the collapse of the traditional nomadic way of life of some of Niger's people have caused political instability. After a period of military rule, a multiparty constitution was adopted in 1992, but the military again seized power in 1996. Later that year, the coup leader, Col. Ibrahim Barre Mainassara, was elected president. He was assassinated in 1999, but parliamentary rule was rapidly restored and Tandja Mamadou was elected president in November.

Niger's chief resource is uranium and it is the fourth largest producer in the world. Some tin and tungsten are also mined, although other mineral resources are largely untouched.

Despite its resources, Niger is one of the world's poorest countries. Farming employs 76% of the population, but only 3% of the land can be used for crops and 8% for grazing.

AREA 1,267,000 sq km [489,189 sq mi]
POPULATION 10,640,000
CAPITAL (POPULATION) Niamey (398,000)
GOVERNMENT Multiparty republic
ETHNIC GROUPS Hausa 56%, Djerma 22%, Tuareg 8%, Fula 8%
LANGUAGES French (official), Hausa, Djerma
RELIGIONS Islam 98%
CURRENCY CFA franc = 100 centimes

NIGERIA

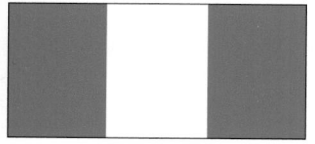 

GEOGRAPHY The Federal Republic of Nigeria is the most populous nation in Africa. The country's main rivers are the Niger and Benue, which meet in central Nigeria. North of the two river valleys are high plains and plateaux. The Lake Chad basin is in the north-east, with the Sokoto plains in the north-west. The south contains hilly uplands and coastal plains.

The south has high temperatures and rain throughout the year. The north is drier and often hotter than the south.

POLITICS & ECONOMY Nigeria has a long artistic tradition. Major cultures include the Nok (500 BC to AD 200), Ife, which developed about 1,000 years ago, and Benin, which flourished between the 15th and 17th centuries. Britain gradually extended its influence over the area in the second half of the 19th century. Nigeria became independent in 1960 and a federal republic in 1963. A federal constitution dividing the country into regions was necessary because Nigeria contains more than 250 ethnic and linguistic groups, as well as several religious ones. Local rivalries have long been a threat to national unity, and six new states were created in 1996 in an attempt to overcome this. Civil war occurred between 1967 and 1970, when the people of the south-east attempted unsuccessfully to secede during the Biafran War. Between 1960 and 1998, Nigeria had only nine years of civilian government. In 1998-9, civilian rule was restored. A former general, Olusegun Obasanjo, was elected president and he was re-elected in 2003. His government faced many problems, including religious clashes in the north, where several states adopted *sharia* (Islamic law).

Nigeria is a developing country with great potential. Its chief natural resource is oil, which accounts for most of its exports. Agriculture employs 43% of the people and the country is a major producer of cocoa, palm oil and palm kernels, groundnuts and rubber.

AREA 923,770 sq km [356,668 sq mi]
POPULATION 129,935,000
CAPITAL (POPULATION) Abuja (339,000)
GOVERNMENT Federal multiparty republic
ETHNIC GROUPS Hausa and Fulani 29%, Yoruba 21%, Ibo (or Igbo) 18%, Ijaw 10%, Kanuri 4%
LANGUAGES English (official), Hausa, Yoruba, Ibo
RELIGIONS Islam 50%, Christianity 40%, traditional beliefs 10%
CURRENCY Naira = 100 kobo

NORTHERN MARIANA ISLANDS

The Commonwealth of the Northern Mariana Islands contains 16 mountainous islands north of Guam in the western Pacific Ocean. In a 1975 plebiscite, the islanders voted for Commonwealth status in union with the USA and, in 1986, they were granted US citizenship. **AREA** 477 sq km [184 sq mi]; **POPULATION** 77,000; **CAPITAL** Saipan.

NORWAY

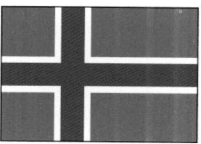 

GEOGRAPHY The Kingdom of Norway forms the western part of the rugged Scandinavian peninsula. The deep inlets along the highly indented coastline were worn out by glaciers during the Ice Age.

The warm North Atlantic Drift off the coast of Norway moderates the climate, with mild winters and cool summers. Nearly all the ports are ice-free throughout the year. Inland, winters are colder and snow cover lasts for at least three months a year.

POLITICS & ECONOMY Under a treaty in 1814, Denmark handed Norway over to Sweden, but it kept Norway's colonies – Greenland, Iceland and the Faroe Islands. Norway briefly became independent, but Swedish forces defeated the Norwegians and Norway had to accept Sweden's king as its ruler.

The union between Norway and Sweden ended in 1903. During World War II (1939–45), Germany occupied Norway. Norway's economy developed quickly after the war and the country now enjoys one of the world's highest standards of living. In 1960, Norway, together with six other countries, formed the European Free Trade Association (EFTA). In 1994, the Norwegians voted against joining the EU.

Norway's chief resources and exports are oil and natural gas which come from wells under the North Sea. Farmland covers only 3% of the land. Dairy farming and meat production are important, but Norway has to import food. Norway has many industries powered by cheap hydroelectricity.

AREA 323,900 sq km [125,050 sq mi]
POPULATION 4,525,000
CAPITAL (POPULATION) Oslo (502,000)
GOVERNMENT Constitutional monarchy
ETHNIC GROUPS Norwegian 97%
LANGUAGES Norwegian (official)
RELIGIONS Lutheran 88%
CURRENCY Krone = 100 ore

OMAN

 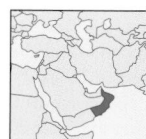

GEOGRAPHY The Sultanate of Oman in the south-eastern Arabian peninsula also includes the tip of the Musandam peninsula. Oman has a hot tropical climate. In Muscat, temperatures may reach 47°C [117°F] in summer.

POLITICS & ECONOMY British influence in Oman dates back to the end of the 18th century, but the country became fully independent in 1971. Since then, using revenue from oil, which was discovered in 1964, the absolute ruler, Qaboos ibn Said, and his government have sought to modernize the country. In 2000, Oman held its first direct elections to its consultative parliament. Unusually for the Gulf region, two women were returned.

The World Bank classifies Oman as an 'upper-middle-income' country. Oil accounts for the bulk of the exports, but agriculture remains important. Major crops include alfalfa, bananas, coconuts, dates, limes, tobacco, vegetables and wheat. Some cattle are raised and fishing, especially for sardines, is important. But Oman still has to import food.

AREA 212,460 sq km [82,031 sq mi]
POPULATION 2,713,000
CAPITAL (POPULATION) Muscat (350,000)
GOVERNMENT Monarchy with consultative council
ETHNIC GROUPS Omani Arab 74%, Pakistani 21%
LANGUAGES Arabic (official), Baluchi, English
RELIGIONS Islam (Ibadiyah), Hinduism
CURRENCY Omani rial = 100 baizas

PAKISTAN

 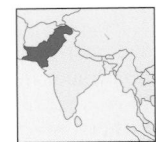

GEOGRAPHY The Islamic Republic of Pakistan contains high mountains, fertile plains and rocky deserts. The Karakoram range, which contains K2, the world's second highest peak, lies in the northern part of Jammu and Kashmir, which is occupied by Pakistan but claimed by India. Other mountains rise in the west. Plains, drained by the River Indus and its tributaries, occupy much of eastern Pakistan. Arid areas include the Thar Desert and the Baluchistan plateau. Most of Pakistan has hot summers and mild winters. The rainfall is sparse.

POLITICS & ECONOMY Pakistan was the site of the Indus Valley civilization which developed about 4,500 years ago. But Pakistan's modern history dates from 1947, when British India was divided into India and Pakistan. Muslim Pakistan was divided into two parts: East and West Pakistan, but East Pakistan broke away in 1971 to become Bangladesh. In 1948–9, 1965 and 1971, Pakistan and India clashed over the disputed territory of Kashmir. In 1998, Pakistan responded in kind to a series of Indian nuclear weapon tests, provoking global controversy.

Pakistan has been subject to several periods of military rule, but elections in 1988 led to Benazir Bhutto becoming prime minister. She was removed from office in 1990, but she returned as prime minister between 1993 and 1996. In 1997, Narwaz Sharif was elected prime minister, but a military coup in 1999 brought General Pervez Musharraf to power. In 2001, Pakistan supported the Western assault on Taliban forces in Afghanistan. In 2002, voters agreed to extend Musharraf's term in office by five years. He made constitutional changes to increase his own powers, but he received a setback at national elections when Islamic parties received substantial support.

According to the World Bank, Pakistan is a 'low-income' developing country. The economy is based on farming or rearing goats and sheep. Agriculture employs nearly half the people. Major crops include cotton, fruits, rice, sugar cane and wheat.

AREA 796,100 sq km [307,374 sq mi]
POPULATION 147,663,000
CAPITAL (POPULATION) Islamabad (525,000)
GOVERNMENT Military regime
ETHNIC GROUPS Punjabi 60%, Sindhi 12%, Pashtun 13%, Baluch, Muhajir
LANGUAGES Urdu (official), many others
RELIGIONS Islam 97%, Christianity, Hinduism
CURRENCY Pakistan rupee = 100 paisa

PALAU

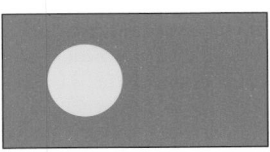 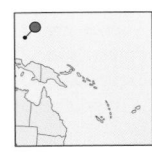

The Republic of Palau became fully independent in 1994, after the USA refused to accede to a 1979 referendum that declared this island nation a nuclear-free zone. The economy relies on US aid, tourism, fishing and subsistence agriculture. The main crops include cassava, coconuts and copra.
AREA 458 sq km [177 sq mi]; **POPULATION** 19,000;
CAPITAL Koror.

PANAMA

GEOGRAPHY The Republic of Panama forms an isthmus linking Central America to South America. The Panama Canal, which is 81.6 km [50.7 mi] long, cuts across the isthmus. It has made the country a major transport centre.

Panama has a tropical climate. Temperatures are high, though the mountains are much cooler than the coastal plains. The main rainy season is between May and December.

POLITICS & ECONOMY Christopher Columbus landed in Panama in 1502 and Spain soon took control of the area. In 1821, Panama became independent from Spain and a province of Colombia.

In 1903, Colombia refused a request by the United States to build a canal. Panama then revolted against Colombia, and became independent. The United States then began to build the canal, which was opened in 1914. The United States administered the Panama Canal Zone, a strip of land along the canal. But many Panamanians resented US influence and, in 1979, the Canal Zone was returned to Panama. Control of the canal itself was handed over by the USA to Panama on 31 December 1999.

Panama's government has changed many times since independence, and there have been periods of military dictatorships. In 1983, General Manuel Antonio Noriega became Panama's leader. In 1988, two US grand juries in Florida indicted Noriega on charges of drug trafficking. In 1989, Noriega was apparently defeated in a presidential election, but the government declared the election invalid. After the killing of a US marine, US troops entered Panama and arrested Noriega, who was convicted by a Miami court of drug offences in 1992. However, Panama held national elections in 1994. In 1999, Mireya Moscoso became Panama's first woman president.

The World Bank classifies Panama as a 'lower-middle-income' developing country. The Panama Canal is an important source of revenue and it generates many jobs in commerce, trade, manufacturing and transport. Away from the Canal, the main activity is agriculture, which employs 16% of the people.

AREA 77,080 sq km [29,761 sq mi]
POPULATION 2,882,000
CAPITAL (POPULATION) Panama City (452,000)
GOVERNMENT Multiparty republic
ETHNIC GROUPS Mestizo 70%, Black and Mulatto 14%, White 10%, Amerindian 6%
LANGUAGES Spanish (official)
RELIGIONS Roman Catholic 84%, Protestant 5%
CURRENCY US dollar; Balboa = 100 centésimos

PAPUA NEW GUINEA

GEOGRAPHY Papua New Guinea is an independent country in the Pacific Ocean, north of Australia. It is part of a Pacific island region called Melanesia. Papua New Guinea includes the eastern part of New Guinea, the Bismarck Archipelago, the northern Solomon Islands, the D'Entrecasteaux Islands and the Louisiade Archipelago. The land is largely mountainous.

Papua New Guinea has a tropical climate, with high temperatures throughout the year. Most of the rain occurs during the monsoon season (from December to April), when the north-westerly winds blow. Winds blow from the south-east during the dry season.

POLITICS & ECONOMY The Dutch took western New Guinea (now part of Indonesia) in 1828, but it was not until 1884 that Germany took north-eastern New Guinea and Britain took the south-east. In 1906, Britain handed the south-east over to Australia. It then became known as the Territory of Papua. When World War I broke out in 1914, Australia took German New Guinea and, in 1921, the League of Nations gave Australia a mandate to rule the area, which was named the Territory of New Guinea.

Japan invaded New Guinea in 1942, but the Allies reconquered the area in 1944. In 1949, Papua and New Guinea were combined into the Territory of Papua and New Guinea. Papua New Guinea became fully independent in 1975.

Since independence, the government has worked to develop its mineral reserves. One of the most valuable mines was on Bougainville, in the northern Solomon Islands. But the people of Bougainville demanded a larger share in the profits of the mine. Conflict broke out, the mine was closed and the Bougainville Revolutionary Army proclaimed the island independent. But their attempted secession was not recognized internationally. An agreement to end the conflict was signed in 1998 and the island was granted local autonomy in 2000.

The World Bank classifies Papua New Guinea as a 'lower-middle-income' developing country. Agriculture employs three out of every four people, many of whom produce little more than they need to feed their families. Minerals, notably copper and gold, are the most valuable exports.

AREA 462,840 sq km [178,703 sq mi]
POPULATION 5,172,000
CAPITAL (POPULATION) Port Moresby (174,000)
GOVERNMENT Constitutional monarchy
ETHNIC GROUPS Papuan, Melanesian
LANGUAGES English (official), Pidgin English, about 800 others
RELIGIONS Traditional beliefs 34%, Roman Catholic 22%, Lutheran 16%
CURRENCY Kina = 100 toea

PARAGUAY

GEOGRAPHY The Republic of Paraguay is a land-locked country and rivers, notably the Paraná, Pilcomayo (Brazo Sur) and Paraguay, form most of its borders. A flat region called the Gran Chaco lies in the north-west, while the south-east contains plains, hills and plateaux.

Northern Paraguay lies in the tropics, while the south is subtropical. Most of the country has a warm, humid climate.

POLITICS & ECONOMY In 1776, Paraguay became part of a large colony called the Vice-royalty of La Plata, with Buenos Aires as the capital. Paraguayans opposed this move and the country declared its independence in 1811.

For many years, Paraguay was torn by internal strife and conflict with its neighbours. A war against Brazil, Argentina and Uruguay (1865–70) led to the deaths of more than half of Paraguay's population, and a great loss of territory.

General Alfredo Stroessner took power in 1954 and ruled as a dictator. His government imprisoned many opponents. Stroessner was overthrown in 1989. Free multiparty elections were held in 1993 and 1998. However, the return of democracy frequently seemed precarious because of rivalries between politicians and army leaders, together with economic problems which arose partly from the problems experienced in neighbouring Argentina and Brazil. The World Bank classifies Paraguay as a 'lower-middle-income' developing country. Farming and forestry are the most important activities. Paraguay produces abundant hydroelectricity and exports power to its neighbours.

AREA 406,750 sq km [157,046 sq mi]
POPULATION 5,884,000
CAPITAL (POPULATION) Asunción (945,000)
GOVERNMENT Multiparty republic
ETHNIC GROUPS Mestizo 90%, Amerindian 3%
LANGUAGES Spanish and Guaraní (both official)
RELIGIONS Roman Catholic 96%, Protestant 2%
CURRENCY Guaraní = 100 céntimos

PERU

GEOGRAPHY The Republic of Peru lies in the tropics in western South America. A narrow coastal plain borders the Pacific Ocean in the west. Inland are ranges of the Andes Mountains, which rise to 6,768 m [22,205 ft] at Mount Huascarán, an extinct volcano. East of the Andes lies the Amazon basin.

Lima, on the coastal plain, has an arid climate. The coastal region is chilled by the cold, offshore Humboldt Current. The rainfall increases inland and many mountains in the high Andes are snow-capped.
POLITICS & ECONOMY Spanish conquistadors conquered Peru in the 1530s. In 1820, an Argentinian, José de San Martín, led an army into Peru and declared it independent. But Spain still held large areas. In 1823, the Venezuelan Simón Bolívar led another army into Peru and, in 1824, one of his generals defeated the Spaniards at Ayacucho. The Spaniards surrendered in 1826. Peru suffered much instability throughout the 19th century.

Instability continued in the 20th century. In 1980, when civilian rule was restored, a left-wing group called the Sendero Luminoso, or the 'Shining Path', began guerrilla warfare against the government. In 1990, Alberto Fujimori, son of Japanese immigrants, became president. In 1992, he suspended the constitution and dismissed the legislature. The guerrilla leader, Abimael Guzmán, was arrested in 1992, but instability continued. Following his victory in disputed presidential elections in 2000, Fujimori resigned and sought sanctuary in Japan. In 2001, Alejandro Toledo became the first Peruvian of Amerindian descent to be elected president.

The World Bank classifies Peru as a 'lower-middle-income' developing country. Agriculture employs 35% of the people and major food crops include beans, maize, potatoes and rice. Fish products are exported, but the most valuable export is copper. Peru also produces lead, silver, zinc and iron ore.

AREA 1,285,220 sq km [496,223 sq mi]
POPULATION 27,950,000
CAPITAL (POPULATION) Lima (Lima-Callao, 6,601,000)
GOVERNMENT Transitional republic
ETHNIC GROUPS Quechua 45%, Mestizo 37%, White 15%
LANGUAGES Spanish and Quechua (both official), Aymara
RELIGIONS Roman Catholic 90%
CURRENCY New sol = 100 centavos

PHILIPPINES

GEOGRAPHY The Republic of the Philippines is an island country in south-eastern Asia. It includes about 7,100 islands, of which 2,770 are named and about 1,000 are inhabited. Luzon and Mindanao, the two largest islands, make up more than two-thirds of the country. The land is mainly mountainous.

The country has a hot tropical climate. The dry season runs from December to April. The rest of the year is wet. Much of the rainfall comes from the typhoons which periodically strike the east coast.
POLITICS & ECONOMY The first European to reach the Philippines was the Portuguese navigator Ferdinand Magellan in 1521. Spanish explorers claimed the region in 1565 when they established a settlement on Cebu. The Spaniards ruled the country until 1898, when the United States took over at the end of the Spanish–American War. Japan invaded the Philippines in 1941, but US forces returned in 1944. The country became fully independent as the Republic of the Philippines in 1946.

Since independence, the country's problems have included armed uprisings by left-wing guerrillas demanding land reform, and Muslim separatist groups, crime, corruption and unemployment. The dominant figure in recent times was Ferdinand Marcos, who ruled in a dictatorial manner from 1965 to 1986. His successors were Corazon Aquino (1986–92), Fidel Ramos (1992–8), and Joseph Estrada, who resigned after massive public protests against his alleged corruption in 2001. He was succeeded by Vice-President Gloria Arroyo. She faced continuing problems in trying, with American help, to defeat the Muslim terrorist groups in the south.

The Philippines is a developing country which has a 'lower-middle-income' economy. Agriculture employs 45% of the people. The main foods are rice and maize, while such crops as bananas, cocoa, coconuts, coffee, sugar cane and tobacco are all grown commercially. Manufacturing now plays an increasingly important role in the economy.

AREA 300,000 sq km [115,300 sq mi]
POPULATION 84,526,000
CAPITAL (POPULATION) Manila (8,594,000)
GOVERNMENT Multiparty republic
ETHNIC GROUPS Tagalog 30%, Cebuano 24%, Ilocano 10%, Hiligaynon Ilongo 9%, Bicol 6%
LANGUAGES Pilipino (Tagalog) and English (both official), Spanish, many others
RELIGIONS Roman Catholic 83%, Protestant 9%, Islam 5%
CURRENCY Philippine peso = 100 centavos

PITCAIRN

 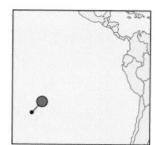

Pitcairn Island is a British overseas territory in the Pacific Ocean. Its inhabitants are descendants of the original settlers – nine mutineers from HMS *Bounty* and 18 Tahitians who arrived in 1790. **AREA** 48 sq km [19 sq mi]; **POPULATION** 50; **CAPITAL** Adamstown.

POLAND

GEOGRAPHY The Republic of Poland faces the Baltic Sea and, behind its lagoon-fringed coast, lies a broad plain. A plateau lies in the south-east, while the Sudeten Highlands straddle part of the border with the Czech Republic. Part of the Carpathian Range (the Tatra) lies in the south-east.

Poland's climate is influenced by its position in Europe. Warm, moist air masses come from the west, while cold air masses come from the north and east. Summers are warm, but winters are cold and snowy.
POLITICS & ECONOMY Poland's boundaries have changed several times in the last 200 years, partly as a result of its geographical location between the powers of Germany and Russia. It disappeared from the map in the late 18th century, when a Polish state called the Grand Duchy of Warsaw was set up. But in 1815, the country was partitioned, between Austria, Prussia and Russia. Poland became independent in 1918, but in 1939 it was divided between Germany and the Soviet Union. The country again became independent in 1945, when it lost land to Russia but gained some from Germany. Communists took power in 1948, but opposition mounted and eventually became focused through an organization called Solidarity.

Solidarity was led by a trade unionist, Lech Walesa. A coalition government was formed between Solidarity and the Communists in 1989. In 1990, the Communist party was dissolved and Walesa became president. But Walesa faced many problems in turning Poland towards a market economy. In presidential elections in 1995, Walesa was defeated by ex-Communist Aleksander Kwasniewski. However, Kwasniewski continued to follow westward-looking policies and he was re-elected president in 2000. Poland joined NATO in 1999 and, in 2002, it was invited to become a member of the European Union in May 2004.

Poland has large reserves of coal and deposits of various minerals which are used in its factories. Manufactures include chemicals, processed food, machinery, ships, steel and textiles.

AREA 312,680 sq km [120,726 sq mi]
POPULATION 38,625,000
CAPITAL (POPULATION) Warsaw (1,626,000)
GOVERNMENT Multiparty republic
ETHNIC GROUPS Polish 98%, Ukrainian 1%, German 1%
LANGUAGES Polish (official)
RELIGIONS Roman Catholic 94%, Orthodox 2%
CURRENCY Zloty = 100 groszy

PORTUGAL

GEOGRAPHY The Republic of Portugal is the most westerly of Europe's mainland countries. The land rises from the coastal plains on the Atlantic Ocean to the western edge of the huge plateau, or Meseta, which occupies most of the Iberian peninsula. Portugal also contains two autonomous regions, the Azores and Madeira island groups.

The climate is moderated by winds blowing from the Atlantic Ocean. Summers are cooler and winters are milder than in other Mediterranean lands.

POLITICS & ECONOMY Portugal became a separate country, independent of Spain, in 1143. In the 15th century, Portugal led the 'Age of European Exploration'. This led to the growth of a large Portuguese empire, with colonies in Africa, Asia and, most valuable of all, Brazil in South America. Portuguese power began to decline in the 16th century and, between 1580 and 1640, Portugal was ruled by Spain. Portugal lost Brazil in 1822 and, in 1910, Portugal became a republic. Instability hampered progress and army officers seized power in 1926. In 1928, they chose Antonio de Salazar to be minister of finance. He became prime minister in 1932 and ruled as a dictator from 1933.

Salazar ruled until 1968, but his successor, Marcello Caetano, was overthrown in 1974 by a group of army officers. The new government made most of Portugal's remaining colonies independent. Free elections were held in 1978. Portugal joined the European Community (now the European Union) in 1986 and, on 1 January 2002, the euro replaced the escudo as Portugal's sole official unit of currency.

Agriculture and fishing were the mainstays of the economy until the mid-20th century. However, manufacturing is now the most valuable sector.

AREA 92,390 sq km [35,670 sq mi]
POPULATION 9,609,000
CAPITAL (POPULATION) Lisbon (2,561,000)
GOVERNMENT Multiparty republic
ETHNIC GROUPS Portuguese 99%
LANGUAGES Portuguese (official)
RELIGIONS Roman Catholic 95%, other Christians 2%
CURRENCY Euro = 100 cents

PUERTO RICO

 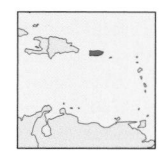

The Commonwealth of Puerto Rico, a mainly mountainous island, is the easternmost of the Greater Antilles chain. The climate is hot and wet. Puerto Rico is a dependent territory of the USA and the people are US citizens. In 1998, 50.2% of the population voted in a referendum on possible statehood to maintain the status quo. Puerto Rico is the most industrialized country in the Caribbean. Tax exemptions attract US companies to the island and manufacturing is expanding. **AREA** 8,900 sq km [3,436 sq mi]; **POPULATION** 3,958,000; **CAPITAL** San Juan.

QATAR

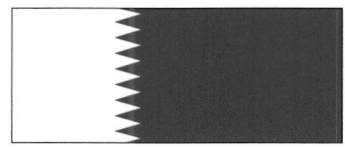 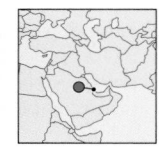

The State of Qatar occupies a low, barren peninsula that extends northwards from the Arabian peninsula into the Gulf. The climate is hot and dry. Qatar became a British protectorate in 1916, but it became fully independent in 1971. Oil, first discovered in 1939, is the mainstay of the economy of this prosperous nation. **AREA** 11,000 sq km [4,247 sq mi]; **POPULATION** 793,000; **CAPITAL** Doha.

RÉUNION

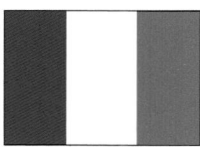 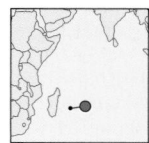

Réunion is a French overseas department in the Indian Ocean. The land is mainly mountainous, though the lowlands are intensely cultivated. Sugar and sugar products are the main exports, but French aid, given to the island in return for its use as a military base, is important to the economy. **AREA** 2,510 sq km [969 sq mi]; **POPULATION** 744,000; **CAPITAL** St-Denis.

ROMANIA

 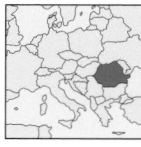

GEOGRAPHY Romania is a country on the Black Sea in eastern Europe. Eastern and southern Romania form part of the Danube river basin. The delta region, near the mouths of the Danube, where the river flows into the Black Sea, is one of Europe's finest wetlands. The southern part of the coast contains several resorts. The heart of the country is called Transylvania. It is ringed in the east, south and west by scenic mountains which are part of the Carpathian mountain system.

Romania has hot summers and cold winters. The rainfall is heaviest in spring and early summer, when thundery showers are common.

POLITICS & ECONOMY From the late 18th century, the Turkish empire began to break up. The modern history of Romania began in 1861 when Walachia and Moldavia united. After World War I (1914–18), Romania, which had fought on the side of the victorious Allies, obtained large areas, including Transylvania, where most people were Romanians. This almost doubled the country's size and population. In 1939, Romania lost territory to Bulgaria, Hungary and the Soviet Union. Romania fought alongside Germany in World War II, and Soviet troops occupied the country in 1944. Hungary returned northern Transylvania to Romania in 1945, but Bulgaria and the Soviet Union kept former Romanian territory. In 1947, Romania officially became a Communist country.

In 1990, Romania held its first free elections since the end of World War II. The National Salvation Front, led by Ion Iliescu and containing many former Communist leaders, won a large majority. A new

constitution, approved in 1991, made the country a democratic republic. Elections held under this constitution in 1992 again resulted in victory for Ion Iliescu, whose party was renamed the Party of Social Democracy (PDSR) in 1993. But the government faced many problems. In 1996, the centre-right Democratic Convention defeated the PDSR, led by Emil Constantinescu, who became president. But Iliescu was re-elected president in 2000.

According to the World Bank, Romania is a 'lower-middle-income' economy. Under Communist rule, industry, including mining and manufacturing, became more important than agriculture.

AREA 237,500 sq km [91,699 sq mi]
POPULATION 22,318,000
CAPITAL (POPULATION) Bucharest (2,028,000)
GOVERNMENT Multiparty republic
ETHNIC GROUPS Romanian 89%, Hungarian 7%, Roma 2%
LANGUAGES Romanian (official), Hungarian, German
RELIGIONS Romanian Orthodox 70%, Protestant 6%, Roman Catholic 3%
CURRENCY Romanian leu = 100 bani

RUSSIA

 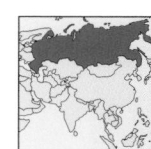

GEOGRAPHY Russia is the world's largest country. About 25% lies west of the Ural Mountains in European Russia, where 80% of the population lives. It is mostly flat or undulating, but the land rises to the Caucasus Mountains in the south, where Russia's highest peak, Elbrus, at 5,633 m [18,481 ft], is found. Asian Russia, or Siberia, contains vast plains and plateaux, with mountains in the east and south. The Kamchatka peninsula in the far east has many active volcanoes. Russia contains many of the world's longest rivers, including the Yenisey-Angara and the Ob-Irtysh. It also includes part of the world's largest inland body of water, the Caspian Sea, and Lake Baikal, the world's deepest lake.

Moscow has a continental climate with cold and snowy winters and warm summers. Krasnoyarsk in south-central Siberia has a harsher, drier climate, but it is not as severe as parts of northern Siberia.

POLITICS & ECONOMY In the 9th century AD, a state called Kievan Rus was formed by a group of people called the East Slavs. Kiev, now capital of Ukraine, became a major trading centre, but, in 1237, Mongol armies conquered Russia and destroyed Kiev. Russia was part of the Mongol empire until the late 15th century. Under Mongol rule, Moscow became the leading Russian city.

In the 16th century, Moscow's grand prince was retitled 'tsar'. The first tsar, Ivan the Terrible, expanded Russian territory. In 1613, after a period of civil war, Michael Romanov became tsar, founding a dynasty which ruled until 1917. In the early 18th century, Tsar Peter the Great began to westernize Russia and, by 1812, when Napoleon failed to conquer the country, Russia was a major European power. But during the 19th century, many Russians demanded reforms and discontent was widespread.

In World War I (1914–18), the Russian people suffered great hardships and, in 1917, Tsar Nicholas II was forced to abdicate. In November 1917, the Bolsheviks seized power under Vladimir Lenin. In 1922, the Bolsheviks set up a new nation, the Union

of Soviet Socialist Republics (also called the USSR or the Soviet Union).

From 1924, Joseph Stalin introduced a socialist economic programme, suppressing all opposition. In 1939, the Soviet Union and Germany signed a non-aggression pact, but Germany invaded the Soviet Union in 1941. Soviet forces pushed the Germans back, occupying eastern Europe. They reached Berlin in May 1945. From the late 1940s, tension between the Soviet Union and its allies and Western nations developed into a 'Cold War'. This continued until 1991, when the Soviet Union was dissolved.

The Soviet Union collapsed because of the failure of its economic policies. From 1991, President Boris Yeltsin introduced democratic and economic reforms. Yeltsin retired in 1999 and, in 2000, was succeeded by Vladimir Putin. Putin has sought to develop increasing contacts with the West, though Russia opposed the invasion of Iraq in 2003. However, the secessionist conflict in Chechenia, which claimed the lives of more than 4,500 Russian troops in 1999–2002, reveals that Russia's sheer size and ethnic diversity make national unity hard to achieve.

Russia's economy was thrown into disarray after the collapse of the Soviet Union, and in the early 1990s the World Bank described Russia as a 'lower-middle-income' economy. Russia was admitted to the Council of Europe in 1997, essentially to discourage instability in the Caucasus. More significantly still, Boris Yeltsin was invited to attend the G7 summit in Denver in 1997. The summit became known as 'the Summit of the Eight' and it appeared that Russia will now be included in future meetings of the world's most powerful economies. Industry is the most valuable activity, though, under Communist rule, manufacturing was less efficient than in the West, and the emphasis was on heavy industry. Today, light industries producing consumer goods are becoming important. Russia's abundant resources include oil and natural gas, coal, timber, metal ores and hydroelectric power.

Most farmland is still government-owned or run as collectives. Russia is a major producer of farm products, though it imports grains. Major crops include barley, flax, fruits, oats, rye, potatoes, sugar beet, sunflower seeds, vegetables and wheat.

AREA 17,075,000 sq km [6,592,800 sq mi]
POPULATION 144,979,000
CAPITAL (POPULATION) Moscow (8,405,000)
GOVERNMENT Federal multiparty republic
ETHNIC GROUPS Russian 82%, Tatar 4%, Ukrainian 3%, Chuvash 1%, more than 100 others
LANGUAGES Russian (official), many others
RELIGIONS Mainly Russian Orthodox, Islam, Judaism
CURRENCY Russian rouble = 100 kopeks

RWANDA

 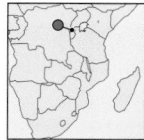

GEOGRAPHY The Republic of Rwanda is a small, landlocked country in east-central Africa. Lake Kivu and the River Ruzizi in the Great African Rift Valley form the country's western border.

Kigali stands on the central plateau of Rwanda. Here, temperatures are moderated by the altitude. The rainfall is abundant, but much heavier rain falls on the western mountains.
POLITICS & ECONOMY Germany conquered the

area, called Ruanda-Urundi, in the 1890s. However, Belgium occupied the region during World War I (1914–18) and ruled it until 1961, when the people of Ruanda voted for their country to become a republic, called Rwanda. This decision followed a rebellion by the majority Hutu people against the Tutsi monarchy. About 150,000 deaths resulted from this conflict. Many Tutsis fled to Uganda, where they formed a rebel army. Burundi became independent as a monarchy, though it became a republic in 1966. Relations between Hutus and Tutsis continued to cause friction. Civil war broke out in 1994 and in 1996 the conflict spilled over into Congo (then Zaïre), where Zaïrean Tutsis staged a rebellion. This led to political instability.

According to the World Bank, Rwanda is a 'low-income' developing country. Most people are poor farmers. Food crops include bananas, beans, cassava and sorghum. Some cattle are raised.

AREA 26,340 sq km [10,170 sq mi]
POPULATION 7,398,000
CAPITAL (POPULATION) Kigali (235,000)
GOVERNMENT Republic
ETHNIC GROUPS Hutu 84%, Tutsi 15%, Twa 1%
LANGUAGES French, English and Kinyarwanda (all official)
RELIGIONS Roman Catholic 53%, Protestant 24%, Adventist 10%
CURRENCY Rwanda franc = 100 centimes

ST HELENA

 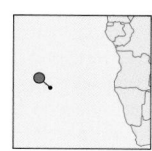

St Helena, which became a British colony in 1834, is an isolated volcanic island in the south Atlantic Ocean. Now a British overseas territory, it is also the administrative centre of Ascension and Tristan da Cunha. **AREA** 122 sq km [47 sq mi]; **POPULATION** 7,000; **CAPITAL** Jamestown.

ST KITTS AND NEVIS

 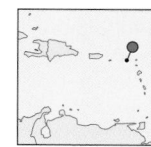

The Federation of St Kitts and Nevis became independent from Britain in 1983. In 1998, a vote for the secession of Nevis fell short of the two-thirds required. **AREA** 360 sq km [139 sq mi]; **POPULATION** 39,000; **CAPITAL** Basseterre.

ST LUCIA

 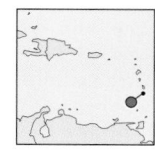

St Lucia, which became independent from Britain in 1979, is a mountainous, forested island of extinct volcanoes. It exports bananas and coconuts, and now attracts many tourists. **AREA** 610 sq km [236 sq mi]; **POPULATION** 160,000; **CAPITAL** Castries.

ST VINCENT AND THE GRENADINES

 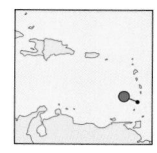

St Vincent and the Grenadines achieved its independence from Britain in 1979. Tourism is growing, but the territory is less prosperous than its neighbours. **AREA** 388 sq km [150 sq mi]; **POPULATION** 116,000; **CAPITAL** Kingstown.

SAMOA

 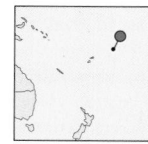

The Independent State of Samoa (formerly Western Samoa) comprises two islands in the South Pacific Ocean. Governed by New Zealand from 1920, the territory became independent in 1962. Exports include coconut cream and beer. **AREA** 2,840 sq km [1,097 sq mi]; **POPULATION** 179,000; **CAPITAL** Apia.

SAN MARINO

San Marino in northern Italy has been independent since 1885 and a republic since the 14th century. It is the world's oldest republic. **AREA** 61 sq km [24 sq mi]; **POPULATION** 28,000; **CAPITAL** San Marino

SÃO TOMÉ AND PRÍNCIPE

 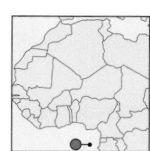

The Democratic Republic of São Tomé and Príncipe, a mountainous island territory west of Gabon, became a Portuguese colony in 1522. Following independence in 1975, the islands became a one-party Marxist state, but multiparty elections were held in 1991. **AREA** 964 sq km [372 sq mi]; **POPULATION** 170,000; **CAPITAL** São Tomé.

SAUDI ARABIA

 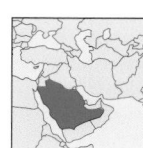

GEOGRAPHY The Kingdom of Saudi Arabia occupies about three-quarters of the Arabian peninsula in south-west Asia. Deserts cover most of the land. Mountains border the Red Sea plains in the west. In the north is the sandy Nafud Desert (An Nafud). In the south is the Rub' al Khali (the 'Empty Quarter'), one of the world's bleakest deserts.

SENEGAL

Saudi Arabia has a hot, dry climate. In the summer months, the temperatures in Riyadh often exceed 40°C [104°F], though the nights are cool.

POLITICS & ECONOMY Saudi Arabia contains the two holiest places in Islam – Mecca (or Makka), the birthplace of the Prophet Muhammad in AD 570, and Medina (Al Madinah) where Muhammad went in 622. These places are visited by many pilgrims.

Saudi Arabia was poor until the oil industry began to operate on the eastern plains in 1933. Oil revenues have been used to develop the country and Saudi Arabia has given aid to poorer Arab nations. The monarch has supreme authority and Saudi Arabia has no formal constitution. In the first Gulf War (1980–8), Saudi Arabia supported Iraq against Iran. But when Iraq invaded Kuwait in 1990, it joined the international alliance to drive Iraq's forces out of Kuwait in 1991. In 2001, relations with the US became strained after the terrorist attacks on 11 September 2001, partly because many alleged terrorists were Saudi nationals. However, Saudi Arabia denounced the attacks.

Saudi Arabia has about 25% of the world's known oil reserves, and oil and oil products make up 85% of its exports. But agriculture still employs 48% of the people. Irrigation and desalination schemes have increased crop production, while the government continues to diversify the country's economy.

AREA 2,149,690 sq km [829,995 sq mi]
POPULATION 23,513,000
CAPITAL (POPULATION) Riyadh (1,800,000)
GOVERNMENT Absolute monarchy with consultative assembly
ETHNIC GROUPS Arab 90%, Afro-Asian 10%
LANGUAGES Arabic (official)
RELIGIONS Islam 100%
CURRENCY Saudi riyal = 100 halalas

SENEGAL

GEOGRAPHY The Republic of Senegal is on the north-west coast of Africa. The volcanic Cape Verde (Cap Vert), on which Dakar stands, is the most westerly point in Africa. Plains cover most of Senegal, though the land rises gently in the south-east.

Dakar has a tropical climate, with a short rainy season between July and October.

POLITICS & ECONOMY In 1882, Senegal became a French colony, and from 1895 it was ruled as part of French West Africa, the capital of which, Dakar, developed as a major port and city.

In 1959, Senegal joined French Sudan (now Mali) to form the Federation of Mali. But Senegal withdrew in 1960 and became the separate Republic of Senegal. Its first president, Léopold Sédar Senghor, served until 1981, when he was succeeded by Abdou Diouf, who was later made 'president for life'. However, in 2000, Diouf was defeated in presidential elections by Abdoulaye Wade.

Senegal and The Gambia have always enjoyed close relations despite their differing French and British traditions. In 1981, Senegalese troops put down an attempted coup in The Gambia and, in 1982, the two countries set up a defence alliance, called the Confederation of Senegambia. But this confederation was dissolved in 1989.

According to the World Bank, Senegal is a 'lower-

middle-income' developing country. It was badly hit in the 1960s and 1970s by droughts, which caused starvation. Agriculture still employs 81% of the population though many farmers produce little more than they need to feed their families. Food crops include groundnuts, millet and rice. Phosphates are the country's chief resource, but Senegal also refines oil which it imports from Gabon and Nigeria. Dakar is a busy port and has many industries.

AREA 196,720 sq km [75,954 sq mi]
POPULATION 10,590,000
CAPITAL (POPULATION) Dakar (1,905,000)
GOVERNMENT Multiparty republic
ETHNIC GROUPS Wolof 44%, Pular 24%, Serer 15%
LANGUAGES French (official), tribal languages
RELIGIONS Islam 92%, traditional beliefs and others 6%, Christianity (mainly Roman Catholic) 2%
CURRENCY CFA franc = 100 centimes

SERBIA AND MONTENEGRO

GEOGRAPHY Serbia and Montenegro are two of the six republics which made up the country of Yugoslavia until it broke up in the early 1990s. From the early 1990s, Serbia and Montenegro were known as the Federal Republic of Yugoslavia. But, in 2003, the two republics became semi-independent and adopted the name of the Union of Serbia and Montenegro.

Behind the coastline on the Adriatic Sea lies an upland region, including the Dinaric Alps and part of the Balkan Mountains. The Pannonian plains, which are drained by the River Danube, are in the north. The coast has a Mediterranean climate. The interior highlands have bitterly cold winters and cool summers. The wettest season is the summer.

POLITICS & ECONOMY People who became known as the South Slavs began to move into the region around 1,500 years ago. Each group, including the Serbs and Croats, founded its own state. But, by the 15th century, foreign countries controlled the region. Serbia and Montenegro were under the Turkish Ottoman empire.

In the 19th century, many Slavs worked for independence and Slavic unity. In 1914, Austria-Hungary declared war on Serbia, blaming it for the assassination of Archduke Francis Ferdinand of Austria–Hungary. This led to World War I and the defeat of Austria–Hungary. In 1918, the South Slavs united in the Kingdom of the Serbs, Croats and Slovenes, which consisted of Bosnia-Herzegovina, Croatia, Dalmatia, Montenegro, Serbia and Slovenia. The country was renamed Yugoslavia in 1929. Germany occupied Yugoslavia during World War II, but partisans, including a Communist force led by Josip Broz Tito, fought the invaders.

From 1945, the Communists controlled the country, which was called the Federal People's Republic of Yugoslavia. But after Tito's death in 1980, the country faced many problems. In 1990, non-Communist parties were permitted and non-Communists won majorities in elections in all but Serbia and Montenegro, where Socialists (former Communists) won control. Yugoslavia split apart in 1991–2 with Bosnia-Herzegovina, Croatia, Macedonia and Slovenia proclaiming their

independence. The two remaining republics of Serbia and Montenegro became the new Yugoslavia.

Fighting broke out in Croatia and Bosnia-Herzegovina as rival groups struggled for power. In 1992, the United Nations withdrew recognition of Yugoslavia because of its failure to halt atrocities committed by Serbs living in Croatia and Bosnia. In 1995, Yugoslavia was involved in the talks that led to the Dayton Peace Accord, which brought peace to Bosnia-Herzegovina. But the issue of Yugoslav repression of minorities flared up again in 1998 in Kosovo, a province where the majority are ethnic Albanians. In response to Serb ethnic cleansing, NATO forces began an offensive against Yugoslavia. A Serb withdrawal was agreed in June 1999. Many Montenegrins wanted to secede and set up their own nation separate from Serbia. In 2002, Serbia and Montenegro agreed to set up a loose union, giving both republics semi-independence. Montenegro agreed that they would not secede from this union, which came into being in 2003, for at least three years.

Under Communist rule, manufacturing became increasingly important in Yugoslavia. But in the early 1990s, the World Bank described what is now Serbia and Montenegro as a 'lower-middle-income' economy. Resources include bauxite, coal, copper and other metals, oil and natural gas. Manufactures, which form the main exports, include aluminium, machinery, plastics, steel, textiles and vehicles. Farming remains important. Crops include fruits, maize, potatoes, tobacco and wheat. Cattle, pigs and sheep are raised.

AREA 102,170 sq km [39,449 sq mi]
POPULATION 10,657,000
CAPITAL (POPULATION) Belgrade (1,598,000)
GOVERNMENT Federal republic
ETHNIC GROUPS Serb 62%, Albanian 17%, Montenegrin 5%, Hungarian, Muslim, Croat
LANGUAGES Serbo-Croat (official), Albanian
RELIGIONS Christianity (mainly Serbian Orthodox), Islam
CURRENCY New dinar = 100 paras

SEYCHELLES

 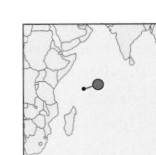

The Republic of Seychelles in the western Indian Ocean achieved independence from Britain in 1976. Coconuts are the main cash crop and fishing and tourism are important. **AREA** 455 sq km [176 sq mi]; **POPULATION** 80,000; **CAPITAL** Victoria.

SIERRA LEONE

GEOGRAPHY The Republic of Sierra Leone in West Africa is about the same size as the Republic of Ireland. The coast contains several deep estuaries in the north, with lagoons in the south. The most prominent feature is the mountainous Freetown (or Sierra Leone) peninsula. Sierra Leone has a tropical climate, with heavy rainfall between April and November.

POLITICS & ECONOMY A former British territory, Sierra Leone became independent in 1961 and a republic in 1971. It became a one-party state in 1978, but, in 1991, the people voted for the restoration of democracy. The military seized power in 1992 and a civil war caused much destruction in 1994–5. Elections in 1996 were followed by another military coup. In 1998, the West African Peace Force restored the deposed President Ahmed Tejan Kabbah. In 1999, a peace agreement followed further conflict. As part of this agreement, Foday Sankoh, one of the rebel leaders, became vice-president. However, he was arrested in 2000 and charged with war crimes. Conflict resumed, but another cease-fire was agreed. Disarmament continued through 2001 and, in 2002, the war seemed to be over.

The World Bank classifies Sierra Leone among the 'low-income' economies. Agriculture provides a living for 70% of the people, though farming is mainly at subsistence level. The most valuable exports are minerals, including diamonds, bauxite and rutile (titanium ore). The country has few manufacturing industries.

> **AREA** 71,740 sq km [27,699 sq mi]
> **POPULATION** 5,615,000
> **CAPITAL (POPULATION)** Freetown (505,000)
> **GOVERNMENT** Single-party republic
> **ETHNIC GROUPS** Mende 35%, Temne 30%, Creole
> **LANGUAGES** English (official), Mende, Temne, Krio
> **RELIGIONS** Islam 60%, traditional beliefs 30%, Christianity 10%
> **CURRENCY** Leone = 100 cents

SINGAPORE

 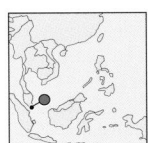

GEOGRAPHY The Republic of Singapore is an island country at the southern tip of the Malay peninsula. It consists of the large Singapore Island and 58 small islands, 20 of which are inhabited.

Singapore has a hot, humid climate. Temperatures are high and rainfall is heavy throughout the year.
POLITICS & ECONOMY In 1819, Sir Thomas Stamford Raffles (1781–1826), agent of the British East India Company, made a treaty with the Sultan of Johor allowing the British to build a settlement on Singapore Island. Singapore soon became the leading British trading centre in South-east Asia and it later became a naval base. Japanese forces seized the island in 1942, but British rule was restored in 1945.

In 1963, Singapore became part of the Federation of Malaysia, which also included Malaya and the territories of Sabah and Sarawak on Borneo. In 1965, Singapore broke away and became independent.

The People's Action Party (PAP) has ruled Singapore since 1959. Its leader, Lee Kuan Yew, served as prime minister from 1959 until 1990, when he resigned and was succeeded by Goh Chok Tong. Under the PAP, the economy has expanded rapidly though some consider its rule rather dictatorial.

The World Bank classifies Singapore as a 'high-income' economy. A skilled workforce has created a fast-growing economy, but the recession in 1997–8 was a setback. Trade and finance are leading activities. Manufactures include electronic products, machinery, scientific instruments, textiles and ships. Singapore has a large oil refinery. Petroleum products and manufactures are the main exports.

> **AREA** 618 sq km [239 sq mi]
> **POPULATION** 4,453,000
> **CAPITAL (POPULATION)** Singapore City (3,866,000)
> **GOVERNMENT** Multiparty republic
> **ETHNIC GROUPS** Chinese 77%, Malay 14%, Indian 8%
> **LANGUAGES** Chinese, Malay, Tamil and English (all official)
> **RELIGIONS** Buddhism, Islam, Christianity, Hinduism
> **CURRENCY** Singapore dollar = 100 cents

SLOVAK REPUBLIC

GEOGRAPHY The Slovak Republic is a predominantly mountainous country, consisting of part of the Carpathian range. The highest peak is Gerlachovka in the Tatra Mountains, which reaches 2,655 m [8,711 ft]. The south is a fertile lowland.

The Slovak Republic has cold winters and warm summers. Kosice, in the east, has average temperatures ranging from –3°C [27°F] in January to 20°C [68°F] in July. The highland areas are much colder. Snow or rain falls throughout the year. Kosice has an average annual rainfall of 600 mm [24 in], the wettest months being July and August.
POLITICS & ECONOMY Slavic peoples settled in the region in the 5th century AD. They were subsequently conquered by Hungary, beginning a millennium of Hungarian rule and suppression of Slovak culture.

In 1867, Hungary and Austria united to form Austria–Hungary, of which the present-day Slovak Republic was a part. Austria–Hungary collapsed at the end of World War I (1914–18). The Czech and Slovak people then united to form a new nation, Czechoslovakia. But Czech domination led to resentment by many Slovaks. In 1939, the Slovak Republic declared itself independent, but Germany occupied the country. At the end of World War II, the Slovak Republic again became part of Czechoslovakia.

The Communist party took control in 1948. In the 1960s, many people sought reform, but they were crushed by the Russians. In the late 1980s, demands for democracy mounted and a non-Communist government took office in 1990. Elections in 1992 led to victory for the Movement for a Democratic Slovakia headed by a former Communist and nationalist, Vladimir Meciar, and the independent Slovak Republic came into existence on 1 January 1993.

Independence raised national aspirations among Slovakia's Magyar-speaking community, but relations with Hungary deteriorated when the Magyars felt that administrative changes under-represented them politically. The government also made Slovak the only official language. The government's autocratic rule and human rights record provoked international criticism. In 1998, Meciar's party was defeated and Mikulas Dzurinda replaced Meciar as prime minister. In 2002, the European Union and the North Atlantic Treaty Organization invited the Slovak Republic to become a member of both organizations in 2004.

Before 1948, the Slovak Republic's economy was based on farming, but Communist governments developed manufacturing industries, producing such things as chemicals, machinery, steel and weapons. Since the late 1980s, many state-run businesses have been handed over to private owners.

> **AREA** 49,035 sq km [18,932 sq mi]
> **POPULATION** 5,422,000
> **CAPITAL (POPULATION)** Bratislava (451,000)
> **GOVERNMENT** Multiparty republic
> **ETHNIC GROUPS** Slovak 86%, Hungarian 11%
> **LANGUAGES** Slovak (official), Hungarian
> **RELIGIONS** Roman Catholic 60%, Protestant 8%, Orthodox 4%
> **CURRENCY** Koruna = 100 halierov

SLOVENIA

GEOGRAPHY The Republic of Slovenia was one of the six republics which made up the former Yugoslavia. Much of the land is mountainous, rising to 2,863 m [9,393 ft] at Mount Triglav in the Julian Alps (Julijske Alpe) in the north-west. Central Slovenia contains the limestone Karst region. The Postojna caves near Ljubljana are among the largest in Europe. The coast has a mild Mediterranean climate, but inland the climate is more continental. The mountains are snow-capped in winter.
POLITICS & ECONOMY In the last 2,000 years, the Slovene people have been independent as a nation for less than 50 years. The Austrian Habsburgs ruled over the region from the 13th century until World War I. Slovenia became part of the Kingdom of the Serbs, Croats and Slovenes (later called Yugoslavia) in 1918. During World War II, Slovenia was invaded and partitioned between Italy, Germany and Hungary, but, after the war, Slovenia again became part of Yugoslavia.

From the late 1960s, some Slovenes demanded independence, but the central government opposed the break-up of the country. In 1990, when Communist governments had collapsed throughout Eastern Europe, elections were held and a non-Communist coalition government was set up. Slovenia then declared itself independent. This led to fighting between Slovenes and the federal army, but Slovenia did not become a battlefield like other parts of the former Yugoslavia. The European Community recognized Slovenia's independence in 1992. The electors returned a coalition led by the Liberal Democrats in 1992, 1996 and 2000. In 2002, the European Union and the North Atlantic Treaty Organization invited Slovenia to become a member of both organizations in 2004.

The reform of the formerly state-run economy caused problems for Slovenia. However, it has enjoyed considerable economic progress, with one of Europe's fastest growing economies. In 1992, the World Bank classified Slovenia's economy as 'upper-middle-income'. Manufacturing is the leading activity and manufactures are the main exports. Manufactures include chemicals, machinery and transport equipment, metal goods and textiles. Agriculture and forestry employ 10% of the people. Fruits, maize, potatoes and wheat are the main crops.

> **AREA** 20,251 sq km [7,817 sq mi]
> **POPULATION** 1,933,000
> **CAPITAL (POPULATION)** Ljubljana (280,000)
> **GOVERNMENT** Multiparty republic
> **ETHNIC GROUPS** Slovene 88%, Croat 3%, Serb 2%, Bosnian 1%
> **LANGUAGES** Slovene (official), Serbo-Croat
> **RELIGIONS** Mainly Roman Catholic
> **CURRENCY** Tolar = 100 stotin

SOLOMON ISLANDS

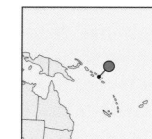

The Solomon Islands, a chain of mainly volcanic islands in the Pacific Ocean, were a British territory between 1893 and 1978. The chain extends for some 2,250 km [1,400 mi]. They were the scene of fierce fighting during World War II.

Most people are Melanesians, and the islands have a young population profile, with half the people aged under 20 years. Fish, coconuts and cocoa are leading products, though development is hampered by mountainous, forested terrain. **AREA** 28,370 sq km [10,954 sq mi]; **POPULATION** 495,000; **CAPITAL** Honiara.

SOMALIA

GEOGRAPHY The Somali Democratic Republic, or Somalia, is in a region known as the 'Horn of Africa'. It is more than twice the size of Italy, the country which once ruled the southern part of Somalia. The most mountainous part of the country is in the north, behind the narrow coastal plains that border the Gulf of Aden.

Rainfall is light throughout Somalia. The wettest regions are the south and the northern mountains, but droughts often occur. Temperatures are high on the low plateaux and plains.

POLITICS & ECONOMY European powers became interested in the Horn of Africa in the 19th century. In 1884, Britain made the northern part of what is now Somalia a protectorate, while Italy took the south in 1905. The new boundaries divided the Somalis into five areas: the two Somalilands, Djibouti (which was taken by France in the 1880s), Ethiopia and Kenya. Since then, many Somalis have longed for reunification in a Greater Somalia.

Italy entered World War II in 1940 and invaded British Somaliland. But British forces conquered the region in 1941 and ruled both Somalilands until 1950, when the United Nations asked Italy to take over the former Italian Somaliland for ten years. In 1960, both Somalilands became independent and united to become Somalia.

Somalia has faced many problems since independence. Economic problems led a military group to seize power in 1969. In the 1970s, Somalia supported an uprising of Somali-speaking people in the Ogaden region of Ethiopia. But Ethiopian forces prevailed and, in 1988, Somalia signed a peace treaty with Ethiopia. The cost of the fighting weakened Somalia's economy. In the 1990s, Somalia gradually broke apart. In 1991, the people in what was formerly British Somaliland set up the 'Somaliland Republic', although it never received international recognition. The north-east, which was called Puntland, also seceded from Somalia, while civil war, based on clan rivalry, raged in the south. US troops sent into the south by the UN in 1993 were forced to withdraw in 1994 and the clan warfare continued. However, hopes of reunification were raised in 2000, when a three-year transitional Assembly was set up in the south, following a peace conference held in Djibouti.

Somalia is a developing country, whose economy has been shattered by drought and war. Catastrophic flooding in late 1997 displaced tens of thousands of people, further damaging the country's infrastructure and destroying hopes of economic recovery.

Many Somalis are nomads who raise livestock. Live animals, meat and hides and skins are major exports, followed by bananas grown in the wetter south. Other crops include citrus fruits, cotton, maize and sugar cane. Mining and manufacturing remain relatively unimportant in the economy.

AREA 637,660 sq km [246,201 sq mi]
POPULATION 7,753,000
CAPITAL (POPULATION) Mogadishu (997,000)
GOVERNMENT Single-party republic, military dominated
ETHNIC GROUPS Somali 85%, Arab 1%
LANGUAGES Somali and Arabic (both official), English, Italian
RELIGIONS Islam (mainly Sunni) 99%
CURRENCY Somali shilling = 100 cents

SOUTH AFRICA

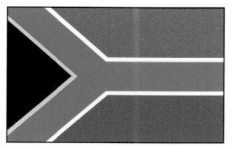

GEOGRAPHY The Republic of South Africa is made up largely of the southern part of the huge plateau which makes up most of southern Africa. The highest peaks are in the Drakensberg range, which is formed by the uplifted rim of the plateau. The coastal plains include part of the Namib Desert in the north-west.

Most of South Africa has a mild, sunny climate. Much of the coastal strip, including the city of Cape Town, has warm, dry summers and mild, rainy winters. Inland, large areas are arid.

POLITICS & ECONOMY Early inhabitants in South Africa were the Khoisan. In the last 2,000 years, Bantu-speaking people moved into the area. Their descendants include the Zulu, Xhosa, Sotho and Tswana. The Dutch founded a settlement at the Cape in 1652, but Britain took over in the early 19th century, making the area a colony. The Dutch, called Boers or Afrikaners, resented British rule and moved inland. Rivalry between the groups led to Anglo-Boer Wars in 1880–1 and 1899–1902.

In 1910, the country was united as the Union of South Africa. In 1948, the National Party won power and introduced a policy known as apartheid, under which non-whites had no votes and their human rights were strictly limited. In 1990, Nelson Mandela, leader of the African National Congress (ANC), was released from prison. Multiracial elections were held in 1994 and Mandela became president. After Mandela's retirement in 1999, his successor, Thabo Mbeki, led the ANC to an emphatic victory in the elections. Mbeki faces many problems, including a health crisis arising from a government estimate in 2002 that 11.4% of the total population was infected with the HIV virus.

South Africa is Africa's most developed country. However, most of the black people are poor, with low standards of living. Natural resources include diamonds, gold and many other metals. Mining and manufacturing are the most valuable activities. Products include chemicals, iron and steel, metal goods, processed food, and vehicles. Major crops include fruits, maize, potatoes, sugar cane, tobacco and wheat. Livestock products are also important.

AREA 1,219,916 sq km [470,566 sq mi]
POPULATION 43,648,000
CAPITAL (POPULATION) Cape Town (legislative, 2,350,000); Pretoria (administrative, 1,080,000); Bloemfontein (judiciary, 300,000)
GOVERNMENT Multiparty republic
ETHNIC GROUPS Black 76%, White 13%, Coloured 9%, Asian 2%
LANGUAGES Afrikaans, English, Ndebele, North Sotho, South Sotho, Swazi, Tsonga, Tswana, Venda, Xhosa and Zulu (all official)
RELIGIONS Christianity 68%, Islam 2%, Hinduism 1%
CURRENCY Rand = 100 cents

SPAIN

GEOGRAPHY The Kingdom of Spain is the second largest country in Western Europe after France. It shares the Iberian peninsula with Portugal. A large plateau, called the Meseta, covers most of Spain. Much of the Meseta is flat, but it is crossed by several mountain ranges, called sierras.

The northern highlands include the Cantabrian Mountains (Cordillera Cantabrica) and the high Pyrenees, which form Spain's border with France. But Mulhacén, the highest peak on the Spanish mainland, is in the Sierra Nevada in the south-east. Spain also contains fertile coastal plains. Other major lowlands are the Ebro river basin in the north-east and the Guadalquivir river basin in the south-west. Spain also includes the Balearic Islands in the Mediterranean Sea and the Canary Islands off the north-west coast of Africa.

The Meseta has a continental climate, with hot summers and cold winters, when temperatures often fall below freezing point. Snow frequently covers the mountain ranges on the Meseta. The Mediterranean coasts have hot, dry summers and mild winters.

POLITICS & ECONOMY In the 16th century, Spain became a world power. At its peak, it controlled much of Central and South America, parts of Africa and the Philippines in Asia. Spain began to decline in the late 16th century. Its sea power was destroyed by a British fleet in the Battle of Trafalgar (1805). By the 20th century, it was a poor country.

Spain became a republic in 1931, but the republicans were defeated in the Spanish Civil War (1936–9). General Francisco Franco (1892–1975) became the country's dictator, though, technically, it was a monarchy. When Franco died, the monarchy was restored. Prince Juan Carlos became king.

Spain has several groups with their own languages and cultures. Some of these people want to run their own regional affairs. In the northern Basque region, some nationalists have waged a terrorist campaign. A truce in 1998 was ended in 1999 when talks failed to produce results. In 2003, Spain's Supreme Court voted to ban Batasuna, the Basque separatist party.

Since the late 1970s, a regional parliament with a considerable degree of autonomy has been set up in the Basque Country (called Euskadi in the indigenous tongue and Pais Vasco in Spanish). Similar parliaments have been initiated in Catalonia in the north-east and Galicia in the north-west. All these regions have their own languages.

The revival of Spain's economy, which was shattered by the Civil War, began in the 1950s and

1960s, especially through the growth of tourism and manufacturing. Since the 1950s, Spain has changed from a poor country, dependent on agriculture, to a fairly prosperous industrial nation.

By the early 1990s, agriculture employed 10% of the people, as compared with industry 35% and services, including tourism, 55%. Farmland, including pasture, makes up about two-thirds of the land, with forest making up most of the rest. Major crops include barley, citrus fruits, grapes for wine-making, olives, potatoes and wheat.

Spain has some high-grade iron ore in the north, though otherwise it lacks natural resources. But it has many manufacturing industries. Manufactures include cars, chemicals, clothing, electronics, processed food, metal goods, steel and textiles. The leading manu-facturing centres are Barcelona, Bilbao and Madrid.

AREA 504,780 sq km [194,896 sq mi]
POPULATION 38,383,000
CAPITAL (POPULATION) Madrid (3,030,000)
GOVERNMENT Constitutional monarchy
ETHNIC GROUPS Castilian Spanish 72%, Catalan 16%, Galician 8%, Basque 2%
LANGUAGES Castilian Spanish (official) 74%, Catalan 17%, Galician 7%, Basque 2%
RELIGIONS Roman Catholic 99%
CURRENCY Euro = 100 cents

SRI LANKA

 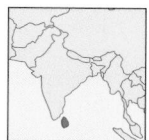

GEOGRAPHY The Democratic Socialist Republic of Sri Lanka is an island nation, separated from the south-east coast of India by the Palk Strait. The land is mostly low-lying, surrounding mountains in the south-centre. Western Sri Lanka has a wet equatorial climate. Temperatures are high and the rainfall is heavy. The east is drier than the west.
POLITICS & ECONOMY From the early 16th century, Ceylon (as Sri Lanka was then known) was ruled successively by the Portuguese, Dutch and British. Independence was achieved in 1948 and the country was renamed Sri Lanka in 1972.

After independence, rivalries between the two main ethnic groups, the Sinhalese and Tamils, marred progress. In the 1950s, the government made Sinhala the official language. Following protests, the prime minister made provisions for Tamil to be used in some areas. In 1959, the prime minister was assassinated by a Sinhalese extremist and he was succeeded by Sirimavo Bandanaraike, who became the world's first woman prime minister.

Conflict between Tamils and Sinhalese continued in the 1970s and 1980s. In 1987, India helped to engineer a cease-fire. Indian troops arrived to enforce the agreement, but withdrew in 1990 after failing to subdue the main guerrilla group, the Tamil Tigers, who wanted to set up an independent Tamil home-land in northern Sri Lanka. In 1993, the country's president was assassinated by a suspected Tamil separatist. Offensives against the Tamil Tigers con-tinued until hopes of peace were raised in 2002, with the signing of a long-term cease-fire.

The World Bank classifies Sri Lanka as a 'low-income' developing country. Agriculture employs half of the workforce, and coconuts, rubber and tea are exported. Rice is the chief food crop. Textiles and clothing, petroleum products and jewellery are also exported.

AREA 65,610 sq km [25,332 sq mi]
POPULATION 19,577,000
CAPITAL (POPULATION) Colombo (1,863,000)
GOVERNMENT Multiparty republic
ETHNIC GROUPS Sinhalese 74%, Tamil 18%
LANGUAGES Sinhala and Tamil (both official)
RELIGIONS Buddhism 69%, Hinduism 16%, Christianity 8%, Islam 7%
CURRENCY Sri Lankan rupee = 100 cents

SUDAN

 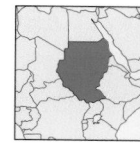

GEOGRAPHY The Republic of Sudan is the largest country in Africa. From north to south, it spans a vast area extending from the arid Sahara in the north to the wet equatorial region in the south. The land is mostly flat, with the highest mountains in the far south. The climate of Khartoum represents a transition between the virtually rainless northern deserts and the equatorial lands in the south.
POLITICS & ECONOMY In the 19th century, Egypt gradually took over Sudan. In 1881, a Muslim religious teacher, the Mahdi ('divinely appointed guide'), led an uprising. Britain and Egypt put the rebellion down in 1898. In 1899, they agreed to rule Sudan jointly as a condominium.

After independence in 1952, the black Africans in the south, who were either Christians or followers of traditional beliefs, feared domination by the Muslim northerners. For example, they objected to the government declaring that Arabic was the only official language. In 1964, civil war broke out and continued until 1972, when the south was given regional self-government, though executive power was still vested in the military government in Khartoum.

In 1983, the government established Islamic law throughout the country. This sparked off further conflict when the Sudan People's Liberation Army (SPLA) in the south launched attacks on government installations. The fighting continued into the 21st century. In 1998, the government announced that it accepted the idea of a referendum on the secession of the south, though definitions of the 'south' varied. In 2002–3, the government signed memoranda of understanding with the SPLA, holding out hope of a total end to the hostilities.

AREA 2,505,810 sq km [967,493 sq mi]
POPULATION 37,090,000
CAPITAL (POPULATION) Khartoum (925,000)
GOVERNMENT Military regime
ETHNIC GROUPS Sudanese Arab 49%, Dinka 12%, Nuba 8%, Beja 6%, Nuer 5%, Azande 3%
LANGUAGES Arabic (official), Nubian, Dinka
RELIGIONS Islam 70%, traditional beliefs 25%
CURRENCY Dinar = 10 Sudanese pounds

SURINAME

GEOGRAPHY The Republic of Suriname is sand-wiched between French Guiana and Guyana in north-eastern South America. The narrow coastal plain was once swampy, but it has been drained and now consists mainly of farmland. Inland lie hills and low mountains, which rise to 1,280 m [4,199 ft].

Suriname has a hot, wet and humid climate. Temperatures are high throughout the year.
POLITICS & ECONOMY In 1667, the British handed Suriname to the Dutch in return for New Amsterdam, an area that is now the state of New York. Slave revolts and Dutch neglect hampered development. In the early 19th century, Britain and the Netherlands disputed the ownership of the area. The British gave up their claims in 1813. Slavery was abolished in 1863 and, soon afterwards, Indian and Indonesian labourers were introduced to work on the plantations. Suriname became fully independent in 1975, but the economy was weakened when thousands of skilled people emigrated from Suriname to the Netherlands. Following a coup in 1980, Suriname was ruled by a military dictator, Dési Bouterse. The adoption of a new constitution led to the restoration of democracy in 1988, though another military coup occurred in 1990. Elections were held in 1996, but instability, deteriorating relations with the Netherlands and economic problems continued. In 1999, Bouterse was convicted in absentia in the Netherlands of having led a cocaine-trafficking ring during and after his tenure in office.

The World Bank classifies Suriname as an 'upper-middle-income' developing country. Its economy is based on mining and metal processing. Suriname is a leading producer of bauxite, from which the metal aluminium is made.

AREA 163,270 sq km [63,039 sq mi]
POPULATION 436,000
CAPITAL (POPULATION) Paramaribo (201,000)
GOVERNMENT Multiparty republic
ETHNIC GROUPS Asian Indian 37%, Creole (mixed White and Black) 31%, Indonesian 14%, Black 9%, Amerindian 3%, Chinese 3%, Dutch 1%
LANGUAGES Dutch (official), Sranantonga
RELIGIONS Hinduism 27%, Roman Catholic 23%, Islam 20%, Protestant 19%
CURRENCY Suriname guilder = 100 cents

SWAZILAND

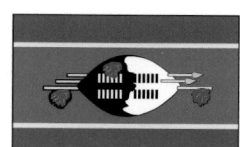 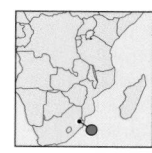

GEOGRAPHY The Kingdom of Swaziland is a small, landlocked country in southern Africa. The country has four regions which run north–south. In the west, the Highveld, with an average height of 1,200 m [3,937 ft], makes up 30% of Swaziland. The Middleveld, between 350 m and 1,000 m [1,148 ft to 3,281 ft], covers 28% of the country. The Lowveld, with an average height of 270 m [886 ft], covers another 33%. Finally, the Lebombo Mountains reach 800 m [2,600 ft] in the east. The Lowveld is almost tropical, with an average annual temperature of 22°C [72°F] and low rainfall. The altitude moderates the climate in the west.
POLITICS & ECONOMY In 1894, Britain and the Boers of South Africa agreed to put Swaziland under the control of the South African Republic (the Transvaal). But at the end of the Anglo–Boer War (1899–1902), Britain took control of the country. In 1968, when Swaziland became fully independent as a constitutional monarchy, the head of state was King Sobhuza II. Sobhuza died in 1982 and was succeeded

by one of his sons, Prince Makhosetive, who, in 1986, was installed as King Mswati III. Elections in 1993 and 1998, in which political parties were banned, failed to satisfy protesters who opposed the absolute monarchy. But Mswati continued to rule by decree. In 2003, he announced that democracy was not suitable for the Swazi people.

The World Bank classifies Swaziland as a 'lower-middle-income' developing country. Agriculture employs 74% of the people, and farm products and processed foods, including soft drink concentrates, sugar, wood pulp, citrus fruits and canned fruit, are the leading exports. Many farmers live at subsistence level, producing little more than they need to feed their own families. Swaziland is heavily dependent on South Africa and the two countries are linked through a customs union.

AREA 17,360 sq km [6,703 sq mi]
POPULATION 1,124,000
CAPITAL (POPULATION) Mbabane (42,000)
GOVERNMENT Monarchy
ETHNIC GROUPS Swazi 84%, Zulu 10%, Tsonga
LANGUAGES Siswati and English (both official)
RELIGIONS Protestant 55%, Islam 10%, Roman Catholic 5%
CURRENCY Lilangeni = 100 cents

SWEDEN

GEOGRAPHY The Kingdom of Sweden is the largest of the countries of Scandinavia in both area and population. It shares the Scandinavian peninsula with Norway. The western part of the country, along the border with Norway, is mountainous. The highest point is Kebnekaise, which reaches 2,117 m [6,946 ft] in the north-west. The climate of Sweden becomes more severe from south to north. Stockholm has cold winters and cool summers. The far south is much milder.
POLITICS & ECONOMY Swedish Vikings plundered areas to the south and east between the 9th and 11th centuries. Sweden, Denmark and Norway were united in 1397, but Sweden regained its independence in 1523. In 1809, Sweden lost Finland to Russia, but, in 1814, it gained Norway from Denmark. The union between Sweden and Norway was dissolved in 1905. Sweden was neutral in World Wars I and II. Since 1945, Sweden has become a prosperous country. In 1995, it joined the European Union. However, many people were sceptical about the advantages of EU membership and Sweden did not adopt the euro, the single EU currency, in 1999.

Sweden has wide-ranging welfare services. But many people are concerned about the high cost of these services and the high taxes they must pay. In 1991, the Social Democrats, who had built up the welfare state, were defeated. They were re-elected in 1994, 1998 and 2002, but they tried to control public spending and expand the economy.

Sweden is a highly developed industrial country. Major products include steel and steel goods. Steel is used in the engineering industry to manufacture aircraft, cars, machinery and ships. Sweden has some of the world's richest iron ore deposits. They are located near Kiruna in the far north. But most of this ore is exported, and Sweden imports most of the materials needed by its industries. In 1996, a decision was taken to decommission all of Sweden's nuclear power stations. This is said to be one of the boldest and most expensive environmental pledges ever made by a government.

AREA 449,960 sq km [173,730 sq mi]
POPULATION 8,877,000
CAPITAL (POPULATION) Stockholm (727,000)
GOVERNMENT Constitutional monarchy
ETHNIC GROUPS Swedish 91%, Finnish 3%
LANGUAGES Swedish (official), Finnish
RELIGIONS Lutheran 89%, Roman Catholic 2%
CURRENCY Swedish krona = 100 öre

SWITZERLAND

GEOGRAPHY The Swiss Confederation is a landlocked country in Western Europe. Much of the land is mountainous. The Jura Mountains lie along Switzerland's western border with France, while the Swiss Alps make up about 60% of the country in the south and east. Four-fifths of the people of Switzerland live on the fertile Swiss plateau, which contains most of Switzerland's large cities.

The climate varies according to the height of the land. The plateau region has warm summers and cold, snowy winters. Rain occurs throughout the year.
POLITICS & ECONOMY In 1291, three small cantons (states) united to defend their freedom against the Habsburg rulers of the Holy Roman Empire. They were Schwyz, Uri and Unterwalden, and they called the confederation they formed 'Switzerland'. Switzerland expanded and, in the 14th century, defeated Austria in three wars of independence. After a defeat by the French in 1515, the Swiss adopted a policy of neutrality, which they still follow. In 1815, the Congress of Vienna expanded Switzerland to 22 cantons and guaranteed its neutrality. Switzerland's 23rd canton, Jura, was created in 1979 from part of Bern. Neutrality combined with the vigour and independence of its people have made Switzerland prosperous. In 1993 and again in 2001, the Swiss people voted against starting negotiations to join the European Union. However, in 2002, the Swiss voted by a narrow majority to join the United Nations.

Although lacking in natural resources, Switzerland is a wealthy, industrialized country. Many workers are highly skilled. Major products include chemicals, electrical equipment, machinery and machine tools, precision instruments, processed food, watches and textiles. Farmers produce about three-fifths of the country's food – the rest is imported. Livestock raising, especially dairy farming, is the chief agricultural activity. Crops include fruits, potatoes and wheat. Tourism and banking are also important. Swiss banks attract investors from all over the world.

AREA 41,290 sq km [15,942 sq mi]
POPULATION 7,302,000
CAPITAL (POPULATION) Bern (942,000)
GOVERNMENT Federal republic
ETHNIC GROUPS German 64%, French 19%, Italian 10%, Serb 3%, Spanish 2%, Romansch 1%
LANGUAGES French, German, Italian and Romansch (all official)
RELIGIONS Roman Catholic 46%, Protestant 40%
CURRENCY Swiss franc = 100 centimes

SYRIA

GEOGRAPHY The Syrian Arab Republic is a country in south-western Asia. The narrow coastal plain is overlooked by a low mountain range which runs north–south. Another range, the Jabal ash Sharqi, runs along the border with Lebanon. South of this range is the Golan Heights, which Israel has occupied since 1967.

The coast has a Mediterranean climate, with dry, warm summers and wet, mild winters. The low mountains cut off Damascus from the sea. It has less rainfall than the coastal areas. To the east, the land becomes drier.
POLITICS & ECONOMY After the collapse of the Turkish Ottoman empire in World War I, Syria was ruled by France. Since independence in 1946, Syria has been involved in the Arab–Israeli wars and, in 1967, it lost a strategic border area, the Golan Heights, to Israel. In 1970, Lieutenant-General Hafez al-Assad took power, establishing a stable but repressive regime. In 1999, Syria had talks with Israel concerning the future of the Golan Heights. These talks formed part of an attempt to establish a peace settlement for the entire east Mediterranean region. Following the death of Assad in 2000, his son, Bashar Assad, succeeded him.

The World Bank classifies Syria as a 'lower-middle-income' developing country. But it has great potential for development. Its main resources are oil, hydro-electricity from the dam at Lake Assad, and fertile land. Oil is the main export; farm products, textiles and phosphates are also important. Agriculture employs about 26% of the workforce.

AREA 185,180 sq km [71,498 sq mi]
POPULATION 17,156,000
CAPITAL (POPULATION) Damascus (1,394,000)
GOVERNMENT Multiparty republic
ETHNIC GROUPS Arab 90%, Kurdish, Armenian, others
LANGUAGES Arabic (official)
RELIGIONS Islam 90%, Christianity 9%
CURRENCY Syrian pound = 100 piastres

TAIWAN

GEOGRAPHY High mountain ranges run down the length of the island, with dense forest in many areas. The climate is warm, moist and suitable for agriculture.
POLITICS & ECONOMY Chinese settlers occupied Taiwan from the 7th century. In 1895, Japan seized the territory from the Portuguese, who had named it Isla Formosa, or 'beautiful island'. China regained the island after World War II. In 1949, it became the refuge of the Nationalists who had been driven out of China by the Communists. They set up the Republic of China, which, with US help, launched an ambitious programme of economic development. Today, it produces a wide range of manufactured goods. Mainland China regards Taiwan as one of its provinces, though reunification seems unlikely in the foreseeable future.

AREA 36,000 sq km [13,900 sq mi]
POPULATION 22,548,000
CAPITAL (POPULATION) Taipei (2,596,000)
GOVERNMENT Unitary multiparty republic
ETHNIC GROUPS Taiwanese (Han Chinese) 84%
LANGUAGES Mandarin (official), Min, Hakka
RELIGIONS Buddhism 43%, Taoism, Confucianism
CURRENCY New Taiwan dollar = 100 cents

TAJIKISTAN

 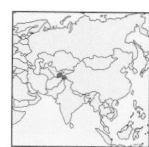

GEOGRAPHY The Republic of Tajikistan is one of the five central Asian republics that formed part of the former Soviet Union. Only 7% of the land is below 1,000 m [3,280 ft], while almost all of eastern Tajikistan is above 3,000 m [9,840 ft]. Summers are hot and dry in the lower valleys, and winters are long and bitterly cold in the mountains.

POLITICS & ECONOMY Russia conquered parts of Tajikistan in the late 19th century and, by 1920, Russia took complete control. In 1924, Tajikistan became part of the Uzbek Soviet Socialist Republic, but, in 1929, it was expanded, taking in some areas populated by Uzbeks, becoming the Tajik Soviet Socialist Republic.

While the Soviet Union began to introduce reforms during the 1980s, many Tajiks demanded freedom. In 1989, the Tajik government made Tajik the official language instead of Russian and, in 1990, it stated that its local laws overruled Soviet laws. Tajikistan became fully independent in 1991, following the break-up of the Soviet Union. As the poorest of the ex-Soviet republics, Tajikistan faced many problems in trying to introduce a free-market system.

In 1992, civil war broke out between the government, which was run by former Communists, and an alliance of democrats and Islamic forces. A cease-fire was agreed in 1996, and in 1997 representatives of the opposition were brought into the government. Presidential elections were held in 1999, followed by parliamentary elections in 2000.

The World Bank classifies Tajikistan as a 'low-income' developing country. Agriculture, mainly on irrigated land, is the main activity and cotton is the chief product. Other crops include fruits, grains and vegetables. The country has large hydroelectric power resources and it produces aluminium.

AREA 143,100 sq km [55,520 sq mi]
POPULATION 6,720,000
CAPITAL (POPULATION) Dushanbe (524,000)
GOVERNMENT Transitional democracy
ETHNIC GROUPS Tajik 65%, Uzbek 25%, Russian
LANGUAGES Tajik (official), Uzbek, Russian
RELIGIONS Islam (mainly Sunni) 80%
CURRENCY Somoni = 100 dirams

TANZANIA

 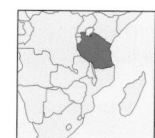

GEOGRAPHY The United Republic of Tanzania consists of the former mainland country of Tanganyika and the island nation of Zanzibar, which also includes the island of Pemba. Behind a narrow coastal plain, most of Tanzania is a plateau, which is broken by arms of the Great African Rift Valley. In the west, this valley contains lakes Nyasa and Tanganyika. The highest peak is Kilimanjaro, Africa's tallest mountain.

The coast has a hot and humid climate, with the greatest rainfall in April and May. The inland plateaux and mountains are cooler and less humid.

POLITICS & ECONOMY Mainland Tanganyika became a German territory in the 1880s, while Zanzibar and Pemba became a British protectorate in 1890. Following Germany's defeat in World War I, Britain took over Tanganyika, which remained a British territory until its independence in 1961. In 1964, Tanganyika and Zanzibar united to form the United Republic of Tanzania. The country's president, Julius Nyerere, pursued socialist policies of self-help (*ujamaa*) and egalitarianism. Many of its social reforms were successful, though the country failed to make economic progress. Nyerere resigned as president in 1985, although he retained much influence until his death in 1999. His successors, Ali Hassan Mwinyi and, from 1995, Benjamin Mkapa, introduced more liberal economic policies.

Tanzania is one of the world's poorest countries. Crops are grown on only 4.2% of the land, yet agriculture employs 80% of the people. Food crops include bananas, cassava, maize, millet and rice.

AREA 945,090 sq km [364,899 sq mi]
POPULATION 37,188,000
CAPITAL (POPULATION) Dodoma (204,000)
GOVERNMENT Multiparty republic
ETHNIC GROUPS Nyamwezi and Sukuma 21%, Swahili 9%, Hehet, Bena, Makonde, Haya
LANGUAGES Swahili and English (both official)
RELIGIONS Christianity 45%, Islam 35% (99% in Zanzibar), traditional beliefs and others 20%
CURRENCY Tanzanian shilling = 100 cents

THAILAND

 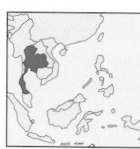

GEOGRAPHY The Kingdom of Thailand is one of the ten countries in South-east Asia. The highest land is in the north, where Doi Inthanon, the highest peak, reaches 2,595 m [8,514 ft]. The Khorat plateau, in the north-east, makes up about 30% of the country and is the most heavily populated part of Thailand. In the south, Thailand shares the finger-like Malay peninsula with Burma and Malaysia.

Thailand has a tropical climate. Monsoon winds from the south-west bring heavy rains between the months of May and October.

POLITICS & ECONOMY The first Thai state was set up in the 13th century. By 1350, it included most of what is now Thailand. European contact began in the early 16th century. But, in the late 17th century, the Thais, fearing interference in their affairs, forced all Europeans to leave. This policy continued for 150 years. In 1782, a Thai General, Chao Phraya Chakkri, became king, founding a dynasty which continues today. The country became known as Siam, and Bangkok became its capital. From the mid-19th century, contacts with the West were restored.

In World War I, Siam supported the Allies against Germany and Austria-Hungary. But in 1941, the country was conquered by Japan and became its ally.

However, after the end of World War II, it became an ally of the United States.

Since 1967, when Thailand became a member of ASEAN (the Association of South-east Asian Nations), its economy has grown, especially its manufacturing and service industries. However, in 1997, it suffered recession along with other fast-developing countries in eastern Asia, and its economic policies had to be modified. The economy still depends on agriculture, which employs more than two-fifths of the people. Rice is the chief crop. Cassava, cotton, maize, rubber, sugar cane and tobacco are also grown. Thailand also mines tin and other minerals. However, the chief exports are manufactures, including food products, machinery, timber products and textiles. Tourism is another major source of income.

AREA 513,120 sq km [198,116 sq mi]
POPULATION 62,354,000
CAPITAL (POPULATION) Bangkok (7,507,000)
GOVERNMENT Constitutional monarchy
ETHNIC GROUPS Thai 75%, Chinese 14%, Malay 4%, Khmer 3%
LANGUAGES Thai (official), Chinese, Malay, English
RELIGIONS Buddhism 94%, Islam, Christianity
CURRENCY Thai baht = 100 satang

TOGO

GEOGRAPHY The Republic of Togo is a long, narrow country in West Africa. From north to south, it extends about 500 km [311 mi]. Its coastline on the Gulf of Guinea is only 64 km [40 mi] long and it is only 145 km [90 mi] at its widest point.

Togo has high temperatures all through the year. The main wet season is from March to July, with a minor wet season in October and November.

POLITICS & ECONOMY Togo became a German protectorate in 1884 but, in 1919, Britain took over the western third of the territory, while France took over the eastern two-thirds. In 1956, the people of British Togoland voted to join Ghana, while French Togoland became an independent republic in 1960.

A military regime took power in 1963. In 1967, General Gnassingbe Eyadema became head of state and suspended the constitution. Under a new constitution adopted in 1992, multiparty elections were held in 1994. However, in 1998, paramilitary policies stopped the count in the presidential elections when it became clear that Eyadema had been defeated. As a result, the leading opposition parties boycotted the elections in 1999 and 2002.

Togo is a poor, developing country. Farming employs 67% of the people and major food crops include cassava, maize, millet and yams. The leading export is phosphate rock, which is used to make fertilizers.

AREA 56,790 sq km [21,927 sq mi]
POPULATION 5,286,000
CAPITAL (POPULATION) Lomé (590,000)
GOVERNMENT Multiparty republic
ETHNIC GROUPS Ewe-Adja 43%, Tem-Kabre 26%, Gurma 16%
LANGUAGES French (official), Ewe, Kabiye
RELIGIONS Traditional beliefs 50%, Christianity 35%, Islam 15%
CURRENCY CFA franc = 100 centimes

TONGA

 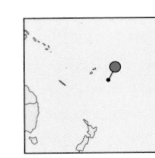

The Kingdom of Tonga, a former British protectorate, became independent in 1970. Situated in the South Pacific Ocean, it contains more than 170 islands, 36 of which are inhabited. Agriculture is the main activity; coconuts, copra, fruits and fish are leading products. **AREA** 750 sq km [290 sq mi]; **POPULATION** 106,000; **CAPITAL** Nuku'alofa.

TRINIDAD AND TOBAGO

The Republic of Trinidad and Tobago became independent from Britain in 1962. These tropical islands, populated by people of African, Asian (mainly Indian) and European origin, are hilly and forested, though there are some fertile plains. Oil production is the main sector of the economy. **AREA** 5,130 sq km [1,981 sq mi]; **POPULATION** 1,164,000; **CAPITAL** Port-of-Spain.

TUNISIA

GEOGRAPHY The Republic of Tunisia is the smallest country in North Africa. The mountains in the north are an eastwards and comparatively low extension of the Atlas Mountains. To the north and east of the mountains lie fertile plains, especially between Sfax, Tunis and Bizerte. In the south, low-lying regions contain a vast salt pan, called the Chott Djerid, and part of the Sahara Desert.

Northern Tunisia has a Mediterranean climate, with dry, sunny summers, and mild winters with a moderate rainfall. The average yearly rainfall decreases towards the south.

POLITICS & ECONOMY In 1881, France established a protectorate over Tunisia and ruled the country until 1956. The new parliament abolished the monarchy and declared Tunisia to be a republic in 1957, with the nationalist leader, Habib Bourguiba, as president. His government introduced many reforms, including votes for women, but various problems arose, including unemployment among the middle class and fears that Western values introduced by tourists might undermine Muslim values. In 1987, the prime minister Zine el Abidine Ben Ali removed Bourguiba from office and succeeded him as president. He was elected in 1989 and re-elected in 1994 and 1999.

The World Bank classifies Tunisia as a 'middle-income' developing country. The main resources and chief exports are phosphates and oil. Most industries are concerned with food processing. Agriculture employs 22% of the people; major crops being barley, dates, grapes, olives and wheat. Fishing is important, as is the tourist industry. About 4.8 million tourists visited Tunisia in 1999.

AREA 163,610 sq km [63,170 sq mi]
POPULATION 9,816,000
CAPITAL (POPULATION) Tunis (1,827,000)
GOVERNMENT Multiparty republic
ETHNIC GROUPS Arab 98%, Berber 1%, French
LANGUAGES Arabic (official), French
RELIGIONS Islam 99%
CURRENCY Dinar = 1,000 millimes

TURKEY

 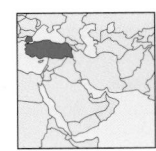 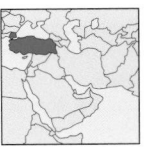

GEOGRAPHY The Republic of Turkey lies in two continents. European Turkey, also called Thrace, lies west of a waterway linking the Mediterranean and Black seas. Most of Asian Turkey consists of plateaux and mountains, which rise to 5,165 m [16,945 ft] at Mount Ararat (Agri Dagi) near the border with Armenia. Earthquakes are common.

Central Turkey has a dry climate, with hot, sunny summers and cold winters. The driest part of the central plateau lies south of the city of Ankara, around Lake Tuz. The west has a Mediterranean climate, but the Black Sea coast has cooler summers.

POLITICS & ECONOMY In AD 330, the Roman empire moved its capital to Byzantium, which it renamed Constantinople. Constantinople became capital of the East Roman (or Byzantine) empire in 395. Muslim Seljuk Turks from central Asia invaded Anatolia in the 11th century. In the 14th century, another group of Turks, the Ottomans, conquered the area. In 1453, the Ottoman Turks took Constantinople, which they called Istanbul.

The Ottoman Turks built up a large empire which finally collapsed during World War I (1914–18). In 1923, Turkey became a republic. Its leader Mustafa Kemal, or Atatürk ('father of the Turks'), launched policies to modernize and secularize the country.

Since the 1940s, Turkey has sought to strengthen its ties with Western powers. It joined NATO (North Atlantic Treaty Organization) in 1951 and it applied to join the European Economic Community in 1987. But Turkey's conflict with Greece, together with its invasion of northern Cyprus in 1974, have led many Europeans to treat Turkey's aspirations with caution. Political instability, military coups, conflict with Kurdish nationalists in eastern Turkey, and Turkey's human rights record are other problems.

Turkey has enjoyed democracy since 1983, though, in 1998, the government banned the Islamist Welfare Party, which it accused of violating secular principles. In 1999, the Muslim Virtue Party (successor to Islamist Welfare Party) lost ground. The largest numbers of parliamentary seats were won by the ruling Democratic Left Party and the far-right National Action Party. However, in the elections in 2002, the moderate Islamic Justice and Development Party (AKP) won 362 of the 500 seats in parliament, while none of the parties in the former ruling coalition won 10% of the vote. In 2003, Turkey opened its airspace to American aircraft during the Iraq war.

The World Bank classifies Turkey as a 'lower-middle-income' developing country. Agriculture employs 37% of the people, and barley, cotton, fruits, maize, tobacco and wheat are major crops. Livestock farming is important and wool is a leading product.

Turkey produces chromium, but manufacturing is the chief activity. Manufactures include processed farm products and textiles, cars, fertilizers, iron and steel, machinery, metal products and paper products.

AREA 779,450 sq km [300,946 sq mi]
POPULATION 67,309,000
CAPITAL (POPULATION) Ankara (3,294,000)
GOVERNMENT Multiparty republic
ETHNIC GROUPS Turkish 80%, Kurdish 20%
LANGUAGES Turkish (official), Kurdish
RELIGIONS Islam 99%
CURRENCY Turkish lira = 100 kurus

TURKMENISTAN

GEOGRAPHY The Republic of Turkmenistan is one of the five central Asian republics which once formed part of the former Soviet Union. Most of the land is low-lying, with mountains lying on the southern and south-western borders. In the west lies the salty Caspian Sea. Most of Turkmenistan is arid and the Garagum, Asia's largest sand desert, covers about 80% of the country. Turkmenistan has a continental climate, with average annual rainfall varying from 80 mm [3 in] in the desert to 300 mm [12 in] in the mountains. Summer months are hot but winter temperatures drop well below freezing point.

POLITICS & ECONOMY Just over 1,000 years ago, Turkic people settled in the lands east of the Caspian Sea and the name 'Turkmen' comes from this time. Mongol armies conquered the area in the 13th century and Islam was introduced in the 14th century. Russia took over the area in the 1870s and 1880s. After the Russian Revolution of 1917, the area came under Communist rule and, in 1924, it became the Turkmen Soviet Socialist Republic. The Communists strictly controlled all aspects of life and discouraged religion. But they improved such services as education, health, housing and transport.

In the 1980s, when the Soviet Union began to introduce reforms, the Turkmen began to demand more freedom. In 1990, the Turkmen government stated that its laws overruled Soviet laws. In 1991, Turkmenistan became fully independent after the break-up of the Soviet Union. But the country kept ties with Russia through the Commonwealth of Independent States (CIS).

In 1992, Turkmenistan adopted a new constitution, allowing for the setting up of political parties, providing that they were not ethnic or religious in character. But, effectively, Turkmenistan remained a one-party state and, in 1992, Saparmurad Niyazov, the former Communist and now Democratic Party leader, was the only candidate. In 1994, a referendum prolonged Niyazov's term of office to 2002, while, in 1999, the parliament declared him president for life. In 2002, Niyazov survived an attempt on his life.

Faced with many economic problems, Turkmenistan began to look south rather than to the CIS for support. As part of this policy, it joined the Economic Co-operation Organization which had been set up in 1985 by Iran, Pakistan and Turkey. In 1996, the completion of a rail link from Turkmenistan to the Iranian coast was seen as a highly significant step for the future economic development of Central Asia.

Turkmenistan's chief resources are oil and natural gas, but the main activity is agriculture, with cotton, grown on irrigated land, as the main crop. Grain and vegetables are also important. Manufactures include cement, glass, petrochemicals and textiles.

AREA 488,100 sq km [188,450 sq mi]
POPULATION 4,689,000
CAPITAL (POPULATION) Ashkhabad (536,000)
GOVERNMENT Single-party republic
ETHNIC GROUPS Turkmen 77%, Russian 17%,
Uzbek 9%, Kazakh 2%, Tatar
LANGUAGES Turkmen (official), Russian, Uzbek,
Kazakh
RELIGIONS Islam
CURRENCY Manat = 100 tenesi

TURKS AND CAICOS ISLANDS

 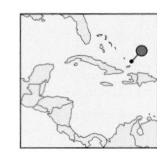

The Turks and Caicos Islands, a British territory in
the Caribbean since 1776, are a group of about 30
islands. Fishing and tourism are major activities.
AREA 430 sq km [166 sq mi]; POPULATION 19,000;
CAPITAL Cockburn Town.

TUVALU

 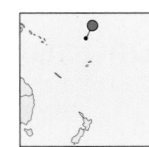

Tuvalu, formerly called the Ellice Islands, was a
British territory from the 1890s until it became
independent in 1978. It consists of nine low-lying
coral atolls in the southern Pacific Ocean. Copra is
the chief export. AREA 24 sq km [9 sq mi];
POPULATION 11,000; CAPITAL Fongafale.

UGANDA

 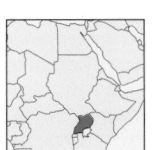

GEOGRAPHY The Republic of Uganda is a landlocked country on the East African plateau. It
contains part of Lake Victoria, Africa's largest lake
and a source of the River Nile, which occupies a
shallow depression in the plateau.

The equator runs through Uganda and the country
is warm throughout the year, though the high altitude
moderates the temperature. The wettest regions
are the lands to the north of Lake Victoria, where
Kampala is situated, and the western mountains,
especially the high Ruwenzori range.

POLITICS & ECONOMY Little is known of the
early history of Uganda. When Europeans first
reached the area in the 19th century, many of the
people were organized in kingdoms, the most
powerful of which was Buganda, the home of the
Baganda people. Britain took over the country
between 1894 and 1914, and ruled it until 1962.

In 1967, Uganda became a republic and Buganda's
Kabaka (king), Sir Edward Mutesa II, was made
president. But tensions between the Kabaka and the
prime minister, Apollo Milton Obote, led to the dis-
missal of the Kabaka in 1966. Obote also abolished
the traditional kingdoms, including Buganda. Obote
was overthrown in 1971 by an army group led by

General Idi Amin Dada. Amin ruled as a dictator.
He forced most Ugandan Asians to leave the country
and had many of his opponents killed.

In 1978, a border dispute between Uganda and
Tanzania led Tanzanian troops to enter Uganda.
With help from Ugandan opponents of Amin, they
overthrew Amin's government. In 1980, Obote led
his party to victory in national elections. But after
charges of fraud, Obote's opponents began guerrilla
warfare. A military group overthrew Obote in 1985,
though strife continued until 1986, when Yoweri
Museveni's National Resistance Movement seized
power. In 1993, Museveni restored the traditional
kingdoms, including Buganda where a new Kabaka
was crowned. Museveni held elections in 1994 but
political parties were not allowed. Museveni was
elected president in 1996 and 2001. In 2003, the
president announced that multiparty democracy would
be restored, but he gave no date for the change.

The strife since the 1960s has greatly damaged the
economy, but the economy grew during a period of
stability in the 1990s. The situation worsened when
Uganda intervened militarily in Congo (then Zaïre) in
1998. Agriculture dominates the economy, employing 80% of the people. The chief export is coffee.

AREA 235,880 sq km [91,073 sq mi]
POPULATION 24,699,000
CAPITAL (POPULATION) Kampala (954,000)
GOVERNMENT Republic in transition
ETHNIC GROUPS Baganda 17%, Karamojong 12%,
Basogo 8%, Iteso 8%, Langi 6%, Rwanda 6%,
Bagisu 5%, Acholi 4%, Lugbara 4%
LANGUAGES English and Swahili (both official),
Ganda
RELIGIONS Roman Catholic 33%, Protestant 33%,
traditional beliefs 18%, Islam 16%
CURRENCY Uganda shilling = 100 cents

UKRAINE

 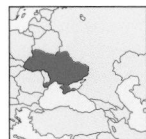

GEOGRAPHY Ukraine is the second largest country
in Europe after Russia. It was formerly part of the
Soviet Union, which split apart in 1991. This mostly
flat country faces the Black Sea in the south. The
Crimean peninsula includes a highland region
overlooking Yalta. Summers are warm, but winters
are cold, becoming more severe from west to east. In
summer, eastern Ukraine is often warmer than the
west. The heaviest rainfall occurs in the summer.

POLITICS & ECONOMY Kiev was the original capital
of the early Slavic civilization known as Kievan Rus.
In the 17th and 18th centuries, parts of Ukraine came
under Polish and Russian rule. But Russia gained
most of Ukraine in the late 18th century. In 1918,
Ukraine became independent, but in 1922 it became
part of the Soviet Union. Millions of people died in
the 1930s as a result of Soviet policies, while millions
more died during the Nazi occupation (1941–4).

In the 1980s, Ukrainian people demanded more say
over their affairs. The country became independent in
1991. Leonid Kuchma, who became president in
1994, came under fire in the early 2000s for
maladministration and for his alleged involvement in
the murder of a journalist. Conflict between the
president and the parliament led to the sacking of
prime minister Victor Yushchenko in 2001 and of his
successor, Anatoly Kinakh, in 2002.

The World Bank classifies Ukraine as a 'lower-

middle-income' economy. Agriculture is important.
Crops include wheat and sugar beet, which are the
major exports, together with barley, maize, potatoes,
sunflowers and tobacco. Livestock rearing and fishing
are also important industries.

Manufacturing is the chief economic activity. Major
manufactures include iron and steel, machinery and
vehicles. Ukraine has large coalfields. The country
imports oil and natural gas, but it has hydroelectric
and nuclear power stations. In 1986, an accident
at the Chernobyl (Chornobyl) nuclear power plant
caused widespread nuclear radiation. The plant was
finally closed in 2001.

AREA 603,700 sq km [233,100 sq mi]
POPULATION 48,396,000
CAPITAL (POPULATION) Kiev (2,621,000)
GOVERNMENT Multiparty republic
ETHNIC GROUPS Ukrainian 73%, Russian 22%,
Jewish 1%, Belarussian 1%, Moldovan,
Bulgarian, Polish
LANGUAGES Ukrainian (official), Russian
RELIGIONS Mostly Ukrainian Orthodox
CURRENCY Hryvnia = 100 kopiykas

UNITED ARAB EMIRATES

 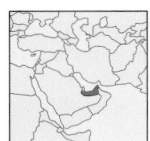

The United Arab Emirates were formed in 1971
when the seven Trucial States of the Gulf (Abu
Dhabi, Dubai, Sharjah, Ajman, Umm al Qawayn,
Ra's al Khaymah and Al Fujayrah) opted to join
together and form an independent country. The
economy of this hot and dry country depends on oil
production, and oil revenues give the United Arab
Emirates one of the highest per capita GNPs in Asia.
AREA 83,600 sq km [32,278 sq mi]; POPULATION
2,446,000; CAPITAL Abu Dhabi.

UNITED KINGDOM

GEOGRAPHY The United Kingdom (or UK) is a
union of four countries. Three of them – England,
Scotland and Wales – make up Great Britain. The
fourth country is Northern Ireland. The Isle of Man
and the Channel Islands, including Jersey and
Guernsey, are not part of the UK. They are self-
governing British dependencies.

The land is highly varied. Much of Scotland and
Wales is mountainous, and the highest peak is
Scotland's Ben Nevis at 1,343 m [4,406 ft]. England
has some highland areas, including the Cumbrian
Mountains (or Lake District) and the Pennine range
in the north. But England also has large areas of
fertile lowland. Northern Ireland is also a mixture of
lowlands and uplands. It contains the UK's largest
lake, Lough Neagh.

The UK has a mild climate, influenced by the
warm Gulf Stream which flows across the Atlantic
from the Gulf of Mexico, then past the British Isles.
Moist winds from the south-west bring rain, but the
rainfall decreases from west to east. Winds from the
east and north bring cold weather in winter.

UNITED STATES OF AMERICA

POLITICS & ECONOMY In ancient times, Britain was invaded by many peoples, including Iberians, Celts, Romans, Angles, Saxons, Jutes, Norsemen, Danes, and Normans, who arrived in 1066. The evolution of the United Kingdom spanned hundreds of years. The Normans finally overcame Welsh resistance in 1282, when King Edward I annexed Wales and united it with England. Union with Scotland was achieved by the Act of Union of 1707. This created a country known as the United Kingdom of Great Britain.

Ireland came under Norman rule in the 11th century, and much of its later history was concerned with a struggle against English domination. In 1801, Ireland became part of the United Kingdom of Great Britain and Ireland. But in 1921, southern Ireland broke away to become the Irish Free State. Most of the people in the Irish Free State were Roman Catholics. In Northern Ireland, where the majority of the people were Protestants, most people wanted to remain citizens of the United Kingdom. As a result, the country's official name changed to the United Kingdom of Great Britain and Northern Ireland.

The modern history of the UK began in the 18th century when the British empire began to develop, despite the loss in 1783 of its 13 North American colonies which became the core of the modern United States. The other major event occurred in the late 18th century, when the UK became the first country to industrialize its economy.

The British empire broke up after World War II (1939–45), though the UK still administers many small, mainly island, territories around the world. The empire was transformed into the Commonwealth of Nations, a free association of independent countries which numbered 54 in 2001.

The UK has retained an important world role. For example, in 2001, it played a prominent role in creating a broad alliance to counter international terrorism following the attacks on the United States. It was also a prominent member of the coalition force which invaded Iraq in 2003. However, the UK has recognized that its economic future lies within Europe. It became a member of the European Economic Community (now the European Union) in 1973. In the early 21st century, most people accepted the importance of the EU to the UK's economic future. But some feared a loss of British identity should the EU ever evolve into a political federation.

The UK is a major industrial and trading nation. It lacks natural resources apart from coal, iron ore, oil and natural gas, and has to import most of the materials it needs for its industries. The UK also has to import food, because it produces only about two-thirds of the food it needs. In the first half of the 20th century, Britain was a major exporter of cars, ships, steel and textiles. But many industries have suffered from competition from other countries, with lower labour costs. Today, industries have to use high-technology in order to compete on the world market.

The UK is one of the world's most urbanized countries, and agriculture employs only 1% of the people. Production is high because of the use of scientific methods and modern machinery. However, in the early 21st century, especially following the outbreak of foot-and-mouth disease in 2001, questions were raised about the future of rural industries. Major crops include barley, potatoes, sugar beet and wheat. Sheep are the leading livestock, but beef and dairy cattle, pigs and poultry are also important. Fishing is another major activity.

Service industries play a major part in the UK's economy. Financial and insurance services bring in much-needed foreign exchange, while tourism has become a major earner.

AREA 243,368 sq km [94,202 sq mi]
POPULATION 59,778,000
CAPITAL (POPULATION) London (8,089,000)
GOVERNMENT Constitutional monarchy
ETHNIC GROUPS White 94%, Asian Indian 1%, Pakistani 1%, West Indian 1%
LANGUAGES English (official), Welsh, Gaelic
RELIGIONS Anglican 57%, Roman Catholic 13%, Presbyterian 7%, Methodist 4%, Baptist 1%, Islam 1%, Judaism, Hinduism, Sikhism
CURRENCY Pound sterling = 100 pence

UNITED STATES OF AMERICA

GEOGRAPHY The United States of America is the world's fourth largest country in area and the third largest in population. It contains 50 states, 48 of which lie between Canada and Mexico, plus Alaska in north-western North America, and Hawaii, a group of volcanic islands in the North Pacific Ocean. Densely populated coastal plains lie to the east and south of the Appalachian Mountains. The central lowlands drained by the Mississippi–Missouri rivers stretch from the Appalachians to the Rocky Mountains in the west. The Pacific region contains fertile valleys, separated by mountain ranges.

The climate varies greatly, ranging from the Arctic cold of Alaska to the intense heat of Death Valley, California. Of the 48 states between Canada and Mexico, winters are cold and snowy in the north, but mild in the south.

POLITICS & ECONOMY The first people in North America, the ancestors of the Native Americans (or American Indians) arrived perhaps 40,000 years ago from Asia. Although Vikings probably reached North America 1,000 years ago, European exploration proper did not begin until the late 15th century.

The first Europeans to settle in large numbers were the British, who founded settlements on the eastern coast in the early 17th century. British rule ended in the War of Independence (1775–83). The country expanded in 1803 when a vast territory in the south and west was acquired through the Louisiana Purchase, while the border with Mexico was fixed in the mid-19th century. The Civil War (1861–5) ended slavery and the serious threat that the nation might split into two parts. In the late 19th century, the West was opened up, while immigrants flooded in from Europe and elsewhere.

During the late 19th and early 20th centuries, industrialization led to the United States becoming the world's leading economic superpower and a pioneer in science and technology. It took on the mantle of the champion of Western democracy and, following the break-up of the former Soviet Union, it became the world's only superpower. But the attacks on the country on 11 September 2001 revealed its vulnerability to terrorists and rogue states. The response was vigorous. In 2001, it attacked the Taliban government in Afghanistan, which was protecting al Qaida terrorists, and, in 2003, it led a coalition force to overthrow the regime in Iraq and remove its weapons of mass destruction.

The United States has the world's largest economy in terms of the total value of its production. Although agriculture employs only about 2% of the people, farming is highly mechanized and scientific, and the United States leads the world in farm production.

Major products include beef and dairy cattle, together with such crops as cotton, fruits, groundnuts, maize, potatoes, soybeans, tobacco and wheat.

The country's natural resources include oil, natural gas and coal. There are also a wide range of metal ores which are used in manufacturing industries, together with timber, especially from the forests of the Pacific north-west. Manufacturing is the single most important activity, employing about 14% of the population. Major products include vehicles, food products, chemicals, machinery, printed goods, metal products and scientific instruments. California is now the leading manufacturing state. Many southern states, petroleum rich and climatically favoured, have also become highly prosperous in recent years.

AREA 9,372,610 sq km [3,618,765 sq mi]
POPULATION 280,562,000
CAPITAL (POPULATION) Washington, D.C. (4,466,000)
GOVERNMENT Federal republic
ETHNIC GROUPS White 70%, Hispanic 13%, African American 12.7%, Asian 4%
LANGUAGES English (official), Spanish, more than 30 others
RELIGIONS Protestant 56%, Roman Catholic 28%, Islam 2%, Judaism 2%
CURRENCY US dollar = 100 cents

URUGUAY

GEOGRAPHY Uruguay is South America's second smallest independent country after Suriname. The land consists mainly of flat plains and hills. The River Uruguay, which forms the country's western border, flows into the Rio de la Plata, a large estuary which leads into the South Atlantic Ocean.

Uruguay has a mild climate, with rain in every month, though droughts sometimes occur. Summers are pleasantly warm, especially near the coast. The weather remains relatively mild throughout the winter.

POLITICS & ECONOMY In 1726, Spanish settlers founded Montevideo in order to halt the Portuguese gaining influence in the area. By the late 18th century, Spaniards had settled in most of the country. Uruguay became part of a colony called the Viceroyalty of La Plata, which also included Argentina, Paraguay, and parts of Bolivia, Brazil and Chile. In 1820 Brazil annexed Uruguay, ending Spanish rule. In 1825, Uruguayans, supported by Argentina, began a struggle for independence. Finally, in 1828, Brazil and Argentina recognized Uruguay as an independent republic. Social and economic developments were slow in the 19th century, but, from 1903, Uruguay became stable and democratic.

From the 1950s, economic problems caused unrest. Terrorist groups, notably the Tupumaros, carried out murders and kidnappings. The army crushed the Tupumaros in 1972, but the army took over the government in 1973. Military rule continued until 1984 when elections were held. In the early 21st century, Uruguay faced many economic problems, many of which were the result of the economic crisis in its neighbour, Argentina, and its imposition of banking controls.

The World Bank classifies Uruguay as an 'upper-middle-income' developing country. Agriculture employs only 4% of the people, but farm products,

notably hides and leather goods, beef and wool, are the leading exports, while the leading manufacturing industries process farm products. The main crops include maize, potatoes, wheat and sugar beet.

AREA 177,410 sq km [68,498 sq mi]
POPULATION 3,387,000
CAPITAL (POPULATION) Montevideo (1,379,000)
GOVERNMENT Multiparty republic
ETHNIC GROUPS White 88%, Mestizo 8%, Mulatto or Black 4%
LANGUAGES Spanish (official)
RELIGIONS Roman Catholic 66%, Protestant 2%, Judaism 1%
CURRENCY Uruguay peso = 100 centésimos

UZBEKISTAN

GEOGRAPHY The Republic of Uzbekistan is one of the five republics in Central Asia which were once part of the Soviet Union. Plains cover most of western Uzbekistan, with highlands in the east. The main rivers, the Amu (or Amu Darya) and Syr (or Syr Darya), drain into the Aral Sea. So much water has been taken from these rivers to irrigate the land that the Aral Sea shrank from 66,900 sq km [25,830 sq mi] in 1960 to 33,642 sq km [12,989 sq mi] in 1993. The dried-up lake area has become desert. The climate is continental, with warm summers and cold winters. The west is extremely arid, with an average annual rainfall of about 200 mm [8 in].

POLITICS & ECONOMY Russia took the area in the 19th century. After the Russian Revolution of 1917, the Communists took over and, in 1924, they set up the Uzbek Soviet Socialist Republic. Under Communism, all aspects of Uzbek life were controlled and religious worship was discouraged. But education, health, housing and transport were improved. In the late 1980s, the people demanded more freedom and, in 1990, the government stated that its laws overruled those of the Soviet Union. Uzbekistan became independent in 1991 when the Soviet Union broke up, but it retained links with Russia through the Commonwealth of Independent States. Islam Karimov, leader of the People's Democratic Party (formerly the Communist Party), was elected president in December 1991. In 1992–3, many opposition leaders were arrested because the government said that they threatened national stability. In 1994–5, the PDP was victorious in national elections and, in 1995, a referendum extended Karimov's term in office until 2000, when he was again re-elected. In 2001, Karimov declared his support for the United States in its campaign against terrorist bases in Afghanistan.

The World Bank classifies Uzbekistan as a 'lower-middle-income' developing country and the government still controls most economic activity. The country produces coal, copper, gold, oil and natural gas.

AREA 447,400 sq km [172,740 sq mi]
POPULATION 25,563,000
CAPITAL (POPULATION) Tashkent (2,118,000)
GOVERNMENT Socialist republic
ETHNIC GROUPS Uzbek 80%, Russian 5%, Tajik 5%, Kazakh 3%, Tatar 2%, Kara-Kalpak 2%
LANGUAGES Uzbek (official), Russian
RELIGIONS Islam 88%, Eastern Orthodox 9%
CURRENCY Som = 100 tyiyn

VANUATU

 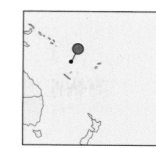

The Republic of Vanuatu, formerly the Anglo-French Condominium of the New Hebrides, became independent in 1980. It consists of a chain of 80 islands in the South Pacific Ocean. Its economy is based on agriculture and it exports copra, beef and veal, timber and cocoa. **AREA** 12,190 sq km [4,707 sq mi]; **POPULATION** 196,000; **CAPITAL** Port-Vila.

VATICAN CITY

 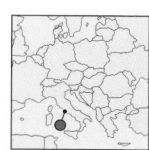

Vatican City State, the world's smallest independent nation, is an enclave on the west bank of the River Tiber in Rome. It forms an independent base for the Holy See, the governing body of the Roman Catholic Church. **AREA** 0.44 sq km [0.17 sq mi]; **POPULATION** 1,000.

VENEZUELA

GEOGRAPHY The Bolivarian Republic of Venezuela, in northern South America, contains the Maracaibo lowlands around the oil-rich Lake Maracaibo in the west. Andean ranges enclose the lowlands and extend across most of northern Venezuela. The Orinoco river basin, containing tropical grasslands called *llanos*, lies between the northern highlands and the Guiana Highlands in the south-east.

Venezuela has a tropical climate. Temperatures are high throughout the year on the lowlands, though the mountains are much cooler. Rainfall is heaviest in the mountains, but much of the country has a marked dry season between December and April.

POLITICS & ECONOMY In the early 19th century, Venezuelans, such as Simón Bolívar and Francisco de Miranda, began a struggle against Spanish rule. Venezuela declared its independence in 1811. But it only became truly independent in 1821, when the Spanish were defeated in a battle near Valencia.

The development of Venezuela in the 19th and the first half of the 20th centuries was marred by instability, violence and periods of harsh dictatorial rule. But Venezuela has had elected governments since 1958. The country has greatly benefited from its oil resources which were first exploited in 1917. In 1960, Venezuela helped to form OPEC (the Organization of Petroleum Exporting Countries) and, in 1976, the government of Venezuela took control of the entire oil industry. In 1999, Hugo Chavez, who had staged an unsuccessful coup in 1992, was elected president. Chavez survived an attempted coup in April 2002 and a crippling general strike staged by his opponents between December 2002 and February 2003.

The World Bank classifies Venezuela as an 'upper-middle-income' developing country. Oil accounts for 80% of the exports. Other exports include bauxite

and aluminium, iron ore and farm products. Agriculture employs 13% of people and cattle ranching is important. The chief industry is petroleum refining. Other manufactures include cement, steel and textiles.

AREA 912,050 sq km [352,143 sq mi]
POPULATION 24,288,000
CAPITAL (POPULATION) Caracas (1,975,000)
GOVERNMENT Federal republic
ETHNIC GROUPS Mestizo 67%, White 21%, Black 10%, Amerindian 2%
LANGUAGES Spanish (official), Goajiro
RELIGIONS Roman Catholic 96%
CURRENCY Bolívar = 100 céntimos

VIETNAM

GEOGRAPHY The Socialist Republic of Vietnam occupies an S-shaped strip of land facing the South China Sea in South-east Asia. The coastal plains include two densely populated, fertile delta regions: the Red (Hong) delta facing the Gulf of Tonkin in the north, and the Mekong delta in the south.

Vietnam has a tropical climate, though the driest months of January to March are a little cooler than the wet, hot summer months, when monsoon winds blow from the south-west. Typhoons (cyclones) sometimes hit the coast, causing much damage.

POLITICS & ECONOMY China dominated Vietnam for a thousand years before AD 939, when a Vietnamese state was founded. The French took over the area between the 1850s and 1880s. They ruled Vietnam as part of French Indo-China, which also included Cambodia and Laos.

Japan conquered Vietnam during World War II (1939–45). In 1946, war broke out between a nationalist group, called the Vietminh, and the French colonial government. France withdrew in 1954 and Vietnam was divided into a Communist North Vietnam, led by the Vietminh leader, Ho Chi Minh, and a non-Communist South.

A force called the Viet Cong rebelled against South Vietnam's government in 1957 and a war began, which gradually increased in intensity. The United States aided the South, but after it withdrew in 1975, South Vietnam surrendered. In 1976, the united Vietnam became a Socialist Republic.

Vietnamese troops intervened in Cambodia in 1978 to defeat the Communist Khmer Rouge government, but it withdrew its troops in 1989. In the 1990s, Vietnam began to introduce reforms. In 1995, the United States opened an embassy in Hanoi and, in 2000, a major trade pact was agreed by the countries.

The World Bank classifies Vietnam as a 'low-income' developing country and agriculture employs 67% of the population. The main food crop is rice. The country also produces chromium, oil (located off the south coast), phosphates and tin.

AREA 331,689 sq km [128,065 sq mi]
POPULATION 81,098,000
CAPITAL (POPULATION) Hanoi (3,056,000)
GOVERNMENT Socialist republic
ETHNIC GROUPS Vietnamese 87%, Tho (Tay), Chinese (Hoa), Tai, Khmer, Muong, Nung
LANGUAGES Vietnamese (official), Chinese
RELIGIONS Buddhism 55%, Roman Catholic 7%
CURRENCY Dong = 10 hao = 100 xu

VIRGIN ISLANDS, BRITISH

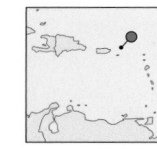

The British Virgin Islands, the most northerly of the Lesser Antilles, comprise four low-lying islands and 36 islets and cays. The islands were 'discovered' by Christopher Columbus in 1493. Dutch from 1648 but British since 1666, they are now a British overseas territory, with a substantial measure of self-government. Tourism is the chief source of income. **AREA** 153 sq km [59 sq mi]; **POPULATION** 21,000; **CAPITAL** Road Town.

VIRGIN ISLANDS, US

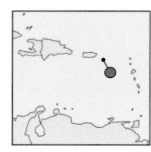

The Virgin Islands of the United States, a group of three islands and 65 small islets, are a self-governing US territory. Purchased from Denmark in 1917, its residents are US citizens and they elect a non-voting delegate to the US House of Representatives. **AREA** 340 sq km [130 sq mi]; **POPULATION** 123,000; **CAPITAL** Charlotte Amalie.

WALLIS AND FUTUNA

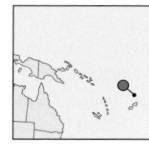

Wallis and Futuna, in the South Pacific Ocean, is the smallest and the poorest of France's overseas territories. **AREA** 200 sq km [77 sq mi]; **POPULATION** 16,000; **CAPITAL** Mata-Utu.

YEMEN

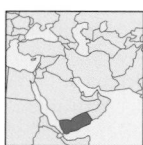

GEOGRAPHY The Republic of Yemen faces the Red Sea and the Gulf of Aden in the south-western corner of the Arabian peninsula. Behind the narrow coastal plain along the Red Sea, the land rises to a mountain region called High Yemen.

The climate ranges from hot and often humid conditions on the coast to the cooler highlands. Most of the country is arid.

POLITICS & ECONOMY After World War I, northern Yemen, which had been ruled by Turkey, began to evolve into a separate state from the south, where Britain was in control. Britain withdrew in 1967 and a left-wing government took power in the south. North Yemen became a republic in 1962, when the monarchy was abolished.

Clashes occurred between the traditionalist Yemen Arab Republic in the north and the formerly British Marxist People's Democratic Republic of Yemen but, in 1990, the two Yemens merged to form a single country. Further conflict occurred in 1994, when southern secessionist forces were defeated. In 1998 and 1999, militants in the Aden-Abyan Islamic army sought to destabilize the country. In 2000, suicide bombers, thought to be part of the al Qaida network, steered a craft into a US destroyer in Aden harbour, killing 17 sailors, while, in 2002, three American missionaries were shot in a hospital in the south.

The World Bank classifies Yemen as a 'low-income' developing country. Agriculture employs up to 63% of the people. Herders raise sheep and other animals, while farmers grow such crops as barley, fruits, wheat and vegetables in highland valleys and around oases. Cash crops include coffee and cotton.

Imported oil is refined at Aden and petroleum extraction began in the north-west in the 1980s. Handicrafts, leather goods and textiles are manufactured. Remittances from Yemenis abroad are a major source of revenue.

AREA 527,970 sq km [203,849 sq mi]
POPULATION 18,701,000
CAPITAL (POPULATION) Sana' (972,000)
GOVERNMENT Multiparty republic
ETHNIC GROUPS Arab 96%, Somali 1%
LANGUAGES Arabic (official)
RELIGIONS Islam
CURRENCY Rial = 100 fils

ZAMBIA

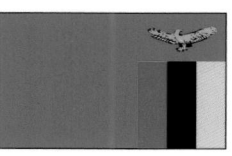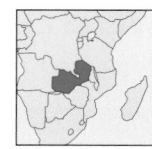

GEOGRAPHY The Republic of Zambia is a landlocked country in southern Africa. Zambia lies on the plateau that makes up most of southern Africa. Much of the land is between 900 m and 1,500 m [2,950 ft to 4,920 ft] above sea level. The Muchinga Mountains in the north-east rise above this flat land.

Lakes include Bangweulu, which is entirely within Zambia, together with parts of lakes Mweru and Tanganyika in the north.

Zambia lies in the tropics, but temperatures are moderated by the altitude. The rainy season runs from November to March.

POLITICS & ECONOMY European contact with Zambia began in the 19th century, when the explorer David Livingstone crossed the River Zambezi. In the 1890s, the British South Africa Company, set up by Cecil Rhodes (1853–1902), the British financier and statesman, made treaties with local chiefs and gradually took over the area. In 1911, the Company named the area Northern Rhodesia. In 1924, Britain took over the government of the country.

In 1953, Britain formed a federation of Northern Rhodesia, Southern Rhodesia (now Zimbabwe) and Nyasaland (now Malawi). Because of African opposition, the federation was dissolved in 1963 and Northern Rhodesia became independent as Zambia in 1964. Kenneth Kaunda became president and one-party rule was introduced in 1972. However, a new constitution was adopted in 1990 and, in 1991, Kaunda's party was defeated and Frederick Chiluba became president. Chiluba was re-elected in 1996, but stood down in 2001, and his party's candidate, Levy Mwanawasa, was elected president.

Copper is the main resource, accounting for 80% of Zambia's exports in 1997. Zambia also produces cobalt, lead, zinc and gemstones. Agriculture employs 69% of workers, as compared with 4% in industry and mining. Maize is the chief crop.

AREA 752,614 sq km [290,586 sq mi]
POPULATION 9,959,000
CAPITAL (POPULATION) Lusaka (982,000)
GOVERNMENT Multiparty republic
ETHNIC GROUPS Bemba 36%, Maravi (Nyanja) 18%, Tonga 15%
LANGUAGES English (official), Bemba, Nyanja, and about 70 others
RELIGIONS Christianity 68%, Islam, Hinduism
CURRENCY Kwacha = 100 ngwee

ZIMBABWE

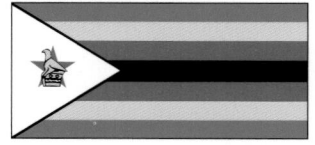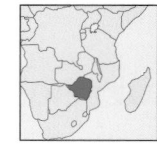

GEOGRAPHY The Republic of Zimbabwe is a landlocked country in southern Africa. Most of the country lies on a high plateau between the Zambezi and Limpopo rivers between 900 m to 1,500 m [2,950 ft to 4,920 ft] above sea level. From October to March, the weather is hot and wet. But daily temperatures may vary greatly in the winter.

POLITICS & ECONOMY The Shona people became dominant in the region about 1,000 years ago. The British South Africa Company, under the statesman Cecil Rhodes (1853–1902), occupied the area in the 1890s, after obtaining mineral rights from local chiefs. The area was named Rhodesia and later Southern Rhodesia. It became a self-governing British colony in 1923. Between 1953 and 1963, Southern and Northern Rhodesia (now Zambia) were joined to Nyasaland (Malawi) in the Central African Federation.

In 1965, the European government of Southern Rhodesia (then called Rhodesia) declared their country independent but Britain refused to accept this. Finally, after a civil war, the country became legally independent in 1980, though rivalries between the Shona and Ndebele people threatened stability. Order was restored when the Shona prime minister, Robert Mugabe, brought his Ndebele rivals into his government. In 1987, Mugabe became the country's executive president and, in 1991, the government renounced its Marxist ideology. Mugabe was re-elected president in 1990 and 1996. During the late 1990s, Mugabe threatened to seize white-owned farms without paying compensation to the owners. Despite international pressure, landless 'war veterans' began to occupy white farms. The situation worsened in the early 2000s, resulting in violence and murder. In 2002, Mugabe was re-elected president amid accusations of electoral irregularities. The Commonwealth suspended Zimbabwe's membership for 12 months. However, in 2003, violence against Mugabe's opponents appeared to be increasing.

The World Bank classifies Zimbabwe as a 'low-income' developing country. The country has valuable mineral resources and mining accounts for a fifth of the country's exports. Agriculture employs 27% of working people. Maize is the chief food crop.

AREA 390,579 sq km [150,873 sq mi]
POPULATION 11,377,000
CAPITAL (POPULATION) Harare (1,189,000)
GOVERNMENT Multiparty republic
ETHNIC GROUPS Shona 71%, Ndebele 16%, other Bantu-speaking Africans 11%, White 1%, Asian 1%
LANGUAGES English (official), Shona, Ndebele
RELIGIONS Christianity 45%, traditional beliefs 40%
CURRENCY Zimbabwe dollar = 100 cents

THE WORLD IN FOCUS

Planet Earth

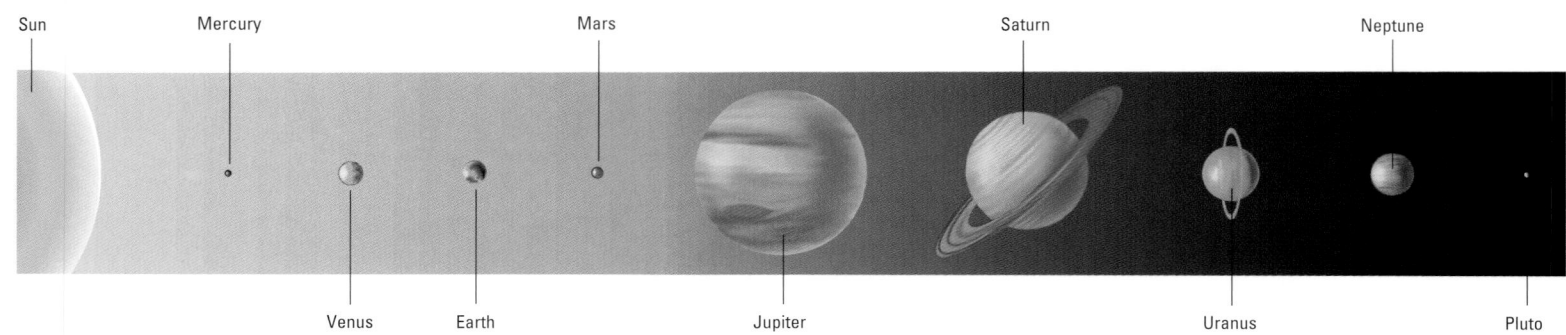

Sun | Mercury | Mars | Saturn | Neptune
Venus | Earth | Jupiter | Uranus | Pluto

The Solar System

A minute part of one of the billions of galaxies (collections of stars) that comprises the Universe, the Solar System lies some 27,000 light-years from the centre of our own galaxy, the 'Milky Way'. Thought to be about 4,600 million years old, it consists of a central sun with nine planets and their moons revolving around it, attracted by its gravitational pull. The planets orbit the Sun in the same direction – anti-clockwise when viewed from the Northern Heavens – and almost in the same plane. Their orbital paths, however, vary enormously.

The Sun's diameter is 109 times that of Earth, and the temperature at its core – caused by continuous thermonuclear fusions of hydrogen into helium – is estimated to be 15 million degrees Celsius. It is the Solar System's only source of light and heat.

Profile of the Planets

	Mean distance from Sun (million km)	Mass (Earth = 1)	Period of orbit (Earth days/years)	Period of rotation (Earth days)	Equatorial diameter (km)	Number of known satellites
Mercury	57.9	0.055	87.97 days	58.67	4,878	0
Venus	108.2	0.815	224.7 days	243.00	12,104	0
Earth	149.6	1.0	365.3 days	1.00	12,756	1
Mars	227.9	0.11	687.0 days	1.028	6,794	2
Jupiter	778	317.9	11.86 years	0.411	143,884	60
Saturn	1,427	95.2	29.46 years	0.427	120,536	31
Uranus	2,870	14.6	84.01 years	0.748	51,118	21
Neptune	4,497	17.2	164.8 years	0.710	50,538	11
Pluto	5,900	0.002	247.7 years	6.39	2,324	1

All planetary orbits are elliptical in form, but only Pluto and Mercury follow paths that deviate noticeably from a circular one. Near perihelion – its closest approach to the Sun – Pluto actually passes inside the orbit of Neptune, an event that last occurred in 1983. Pluto did not regain its station as outermost planet until February 1999.

The Seasons

Seasons occur because the Earth's axis is tilted at an angle of approximately 23½°. When the northern hemisphere is tilted to a maximum extent towards the Sun, on 21 June, the Sun is overhead at the Tropic of Cancer (latitude 23½° North). This is midsummer, or the summer solstice, in the northern hemisphere.

On 22 or 23 September, the Sun is overhead at the Equator, and day and night are of equal length throughout the world. This is the autumn equinox in the northern hemisphere. On 21 or 22 December, the Sun is overhead at the Tropic of Capricorn (23½° South), the winter solstice in the northern hemisphere. The overhead Sun then tracks north until, on 21 March, it is overhead at the Equator. This is the spring (vernal) equinox in the northern hemisphere.

In the southern hemisphere, the seasons are the reverse of those in the north.

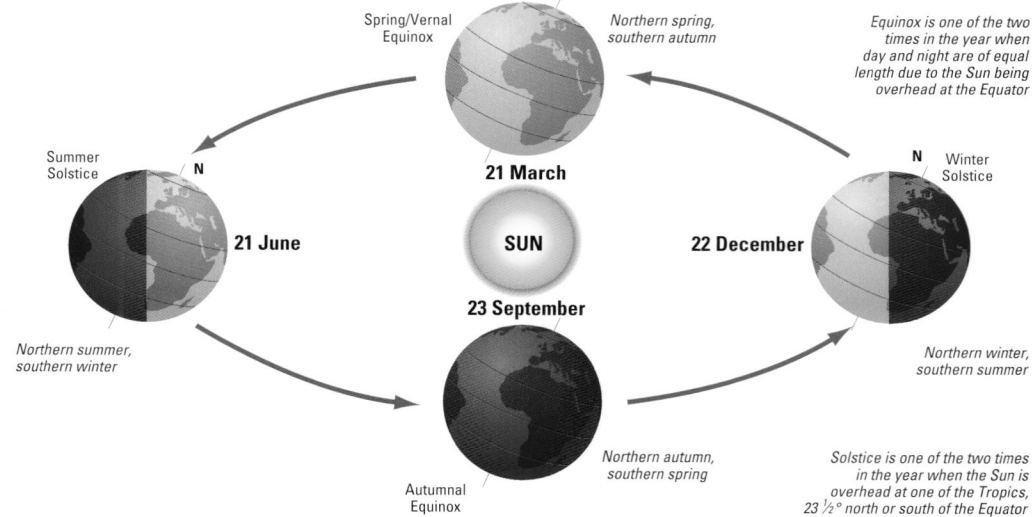

Day and Night

The Sun appears to rise in the east, reach its highest point at noon, and then set in the west, to be followed by night. In reality, it is not the Sun that is moving but the Earth rotating from west to east. The moment when the Sun's upper limb first appears above the horizon is termed sunrise; the moment when the Sun's upper limb disappears below the horizon is sunset.

At the summer solstice in the northern hemisphere (21 June), the Arctic has total daylight and the Antarctic total darkness. The opposite occurs at the winter solstice (21 or 22 December). At the Equator, the length of day and night are almost equal all year.

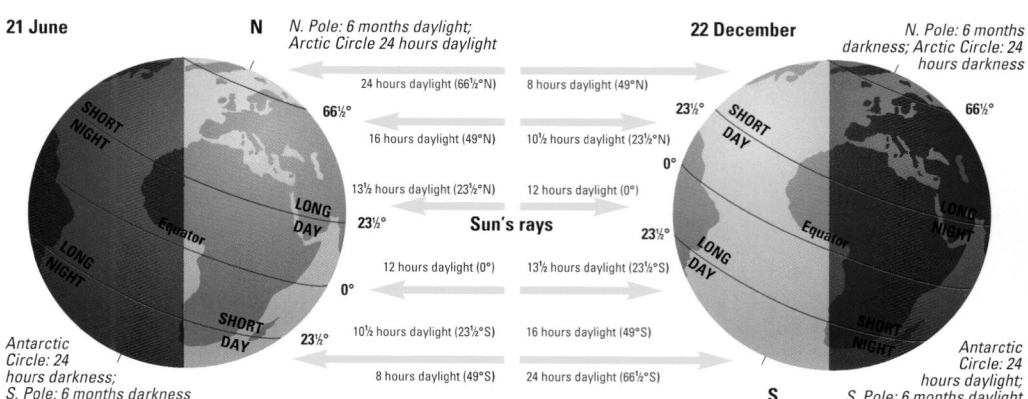

Time

Year: The time taken by the Earth to revolve around the Sun, or 365.24 days.

Leap Year: A calendar year of 366 days, 29 February being the additional day. It offsets the difference between the calendar and the solar year.

Month: The approximate time taken by the Moon to revolve around the Earth. The 12 months of the year in fact vary from 28 (29 in a Leap Year) to 31 days.

Week: An artificial period of 7 days, not based on astronomical time.

Day: The time taken by the Earth to complete one rotation on its axis.

Hour: 24 hours make one day. Usually the day is divided into hours AM (ante meridiem or before noon) and PM (post meridiem or after noon), although most timetables now use the 24-hour system, from midnight to midnight.

Sunrise

Sunset

The Moon

The Moon rotates more slowly than the Earth, making one complete turn on its axis in just over 27 days. Since this corresponds to its period of revolution around the Earth, the Moon always presents the same

Phases of the Moon

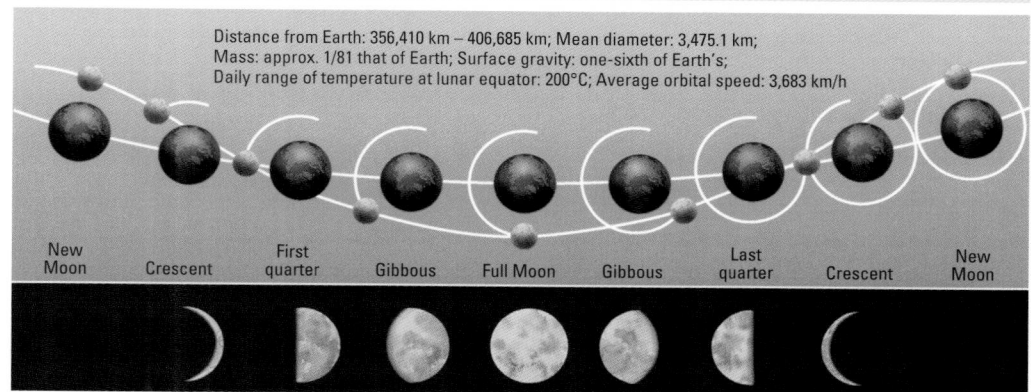

Distance from Earth: 356,410 km – 406,685 km; Mean diameter: 3,475.1 km; Mass: approx. 1/81 that of Earth; Surface gravity: one-sixth of Earth's; Daily range of temperature at lunar equator: 200°C; Average orbital speed: 3,683 km/h

New Moon · Crescent · First quarter · Gibbous · Full Moon · Gibbous · Last quarter · Crescent · New Moon

hemisphere or face to us, and we never see 'the dark side'. The interval between one full Moon and the next (and between new Moons) is about 29½ days – a lunar month. The apparent changes in the shape of the Moon are caused by its changing position in relation to the Earth; like the planets, it produces no light of its own and shines only by reflecting the rays of the Sun.

Eclipses

When the Moon passes between the Sun and the Earth it causes a partial eclipse of the Sun (1) if the Earth passes through the Moon's outer shadow (P), or a total eclipse (2) if the inner cone shadow crosses the Earth's surface. In a lunar eclipse, the Earth's shadow crosses the Moon and, again, provides either a partial or total eclipse.

Eclipses of the Sun and the Moon do not occur every month because of the 5° difference between the plane of the Moon's orbit and the plane in which the Earth moves. In the 1990s only 14 lunar eclipses were possible, for example, seven partial and seven total; each was visible only from certain, and variable, parts of the world. The same period witnessed 13 solar eclipses – six partial (or annular) and seven total.

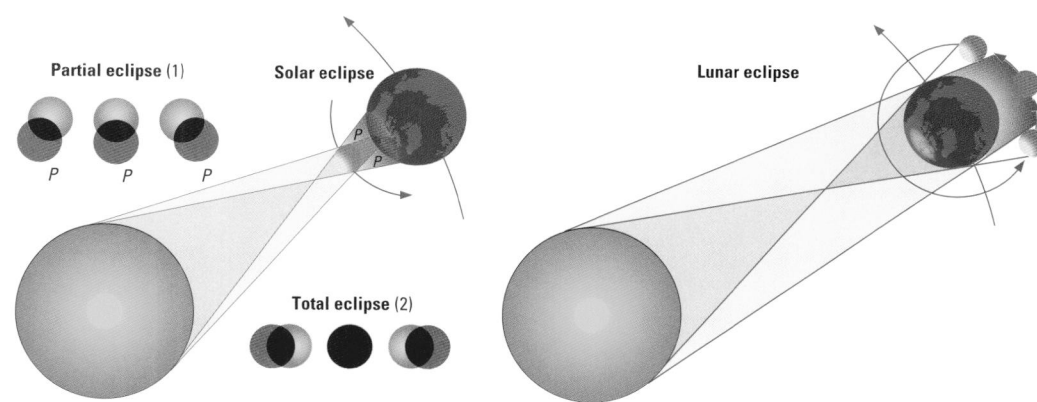

Partial eclipse (1) · Solar eclipse · Lunar eclipse · Total eclipse (2)

Tides

The daily rise and fall of the ocean's tides are the result of the gravitational pull of the Moon and that of the Sun, though the effect of the latter is only 46.6% as strong as that of the Moon. This effect is greatest on the hemisphere facing the Moon and causes a tidal 'bulge'. When the Sun, Earth and Moon are in line, tide-raising forces are at a maximum and Spring tides occur: high tide reaches the highest values, and low tide falls to low levels. When lunar and solar forces are least coincidental with the Sun and Moon at an angle (near the Moon's first and third quarters), Neap tides occur, which have a small tidal range.

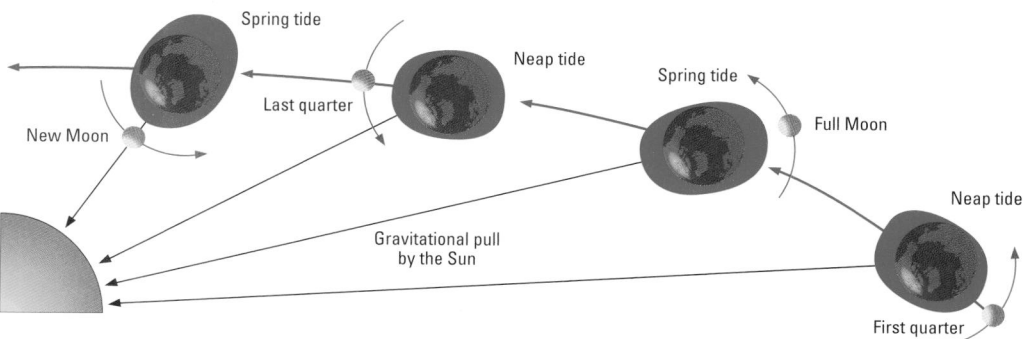

Spring tide · Neap tide · Spring tide · Last quarter · New Moon · Full Moon · Neap tide · Gravitational pull by the Sun · First quarter

Restless Earth

The Earth's Structure

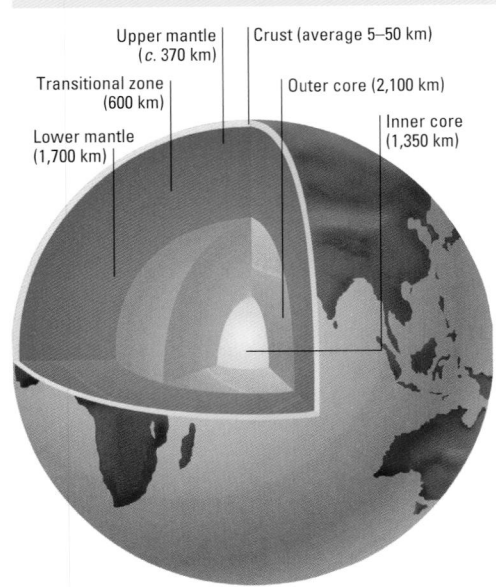

Upper mantle (c. 370 km)
Crust (average 5–50 km)
Transitional zone (600 km)
Outer core (2,100 km)
Lower mantle (1,700 km)
Inner core (1,350 km)

Continental Drift

About 200 million years ago the original Pangaea landmass began to split into two continental groups, which further separated over time to produce the present-day configuration.

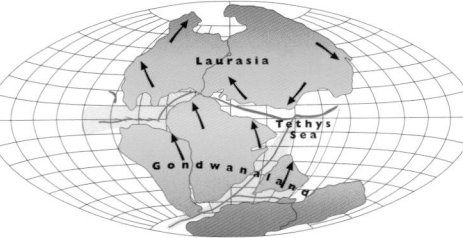

180 million years ago

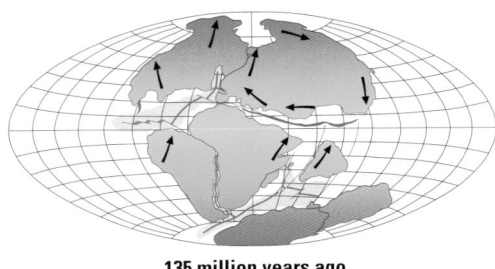

135 million years ago

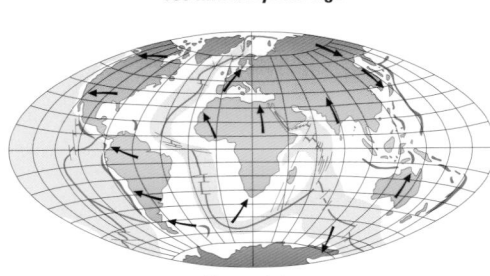

Present day

- Trench
- Rift
- New ocean floor
- Zones of slippage

Notable Earthquakes Since 1900

Year	Location	Richter Scale	Deaths
1906	San Francisco, USA	8.3	503
1906	Valparaiso, Chile	8.6	22,000
1906	San Francisco, USA	7.7	3,000
1906	Valparaiso, Chile	8.6	22,000
1908	Messina, Italy	7.5	83,000
1915	Avezzano, Italy	7.5	30,000
1920	Gansu (Kansu), China	8.6	180,000
1923	Yokohama, Japan	8.3	143,000
1927	Nan Shan, China	8.3	200,000
1932	Gansu (Kansu), China	7.6	70,000
1933	Sanriku, Japan	8.9	2,990
1934	Bihar, India/Nepal	8.4	10,700
1935	Quetta, India (now Pakistan)	7.5	60,000
1939	Chillan, Chile	8.3	28,000
1939	Erzincan, Turkey	7.9	30,000
1960	S. W. Chile	9.5	2,200
1960	Agadir, Morocco	5.8	12,000
1962	Khorasan, Iran	7.1	12,230
1964	Anchorage, USA	9.2	125
1968	N. E. Iran	7.4	12,000
1970	N. Peru	7.7	66,794
1972	Managua, Nicaragua	6.2	5,000
1974	N. Pakistan	6.3	5,200
1976	Guatemala	7.5	22,778
1976	Tangshan, China	8.2	255,000
1978	Tabas, Iran	7.7	25,000
1980	El Asnam, Algeria	7.3	20,000
1980	S. Italy	7.2	4,800
1985	Mexico City, Mexico	8.1	4,200
1988	N.W. Armenia	6.8	55,000
1990	N. Iran	7.7	36,000
1992	Flores, Indonesia	6.8	1,895
1993	Maharashtra, India	6.4	30,000
1994	Los Angeles, USA	6.6	51
1995	Kobe, Japan	7.2	5,000
1995	Sakhalin Is., Russia	7.5	2,000
1996	Yunnan, China	7.0	240
1997	N. E. Iran	7.1	2,400
1998	Takhar, Afghanistan	6.1	4,200
1998	Rostaq, Afghanistan	7.0	5,000
1999	Izmit, Turkey	7.4	15,000
1999	Taipei, Taiwan	7.6	1,700
2001	Gujarat, India	7.7	14,000
2002	Afyon, Turkey	6.5	44
2002	Baghlan, Afghanistan	6.1	1,000
2003	Boumerdes, Algeria	6.8	2,200

Structure and Earthquakes

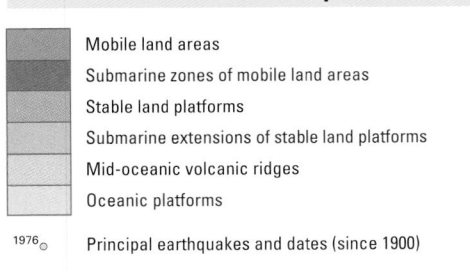

- Mobile land areas
- Submarine zones of mobile land areas
- Stable land platforms
- Submarine extensions of stable land platforms
- Mid-oceanic volcanic ridges
- Oceanic platforms

1976 ○ Principal earthquakes and dates (since 1900)

Earthquakes are a series of rapid vibrations originating from the slipping or faulting of parts of the Earth's crust when stresses within build up to breaking point. They usually happen at depths varying from 8 km to 30 km. Severe earthquakes cause extensive damage when they take place in populated areas, destroying structures and severing communications. Most initial loss of life occurs due to secondary causes such as falling masonry, fires and flooding.

Earthquakes

Earthquake magnitude is usually rated according to either the Richter or the Modified Mercalli scale, both devised by seismologists in the 1930s. The Richter scale measures absolute earthquake power with mathematical precision: each step upwards represents a tenfold increase in shockwave amplitude. Theoretically, there is no upper limit, but the largest earthquakes measured have been rated at between 8.8 and 8.9. The 12–point Mercalli scale, based on observed effects, is often more meaningful, ranging from I (earthquakes noticed only by seismographs) to XII (total destruction); intermediate points include V (people awakened at night; unstable objects overturned), VII (collapse of ordinary buildings; chimneys and monuments fall) and IX (conspicuous cracks in ground; serious damage to reservoirs).

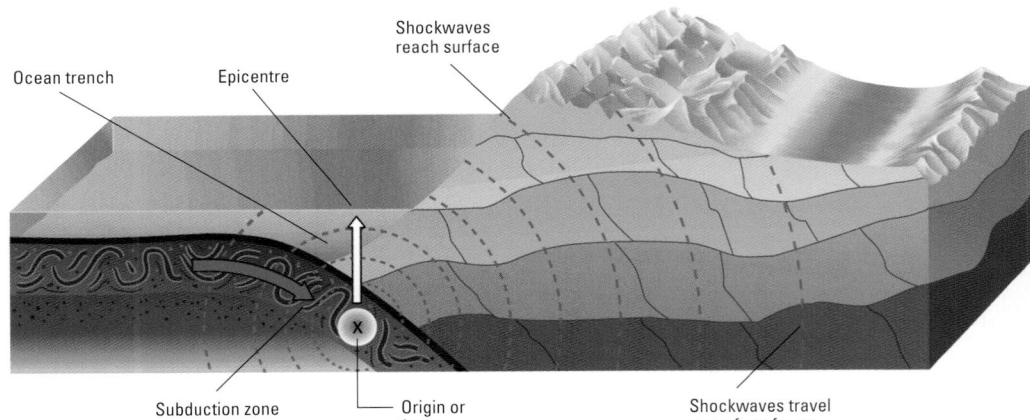

Ocean trench
Epicentre
Shockwaves reach surface
Subduction zone
Origin or focus
Shockwaves travel away from focus

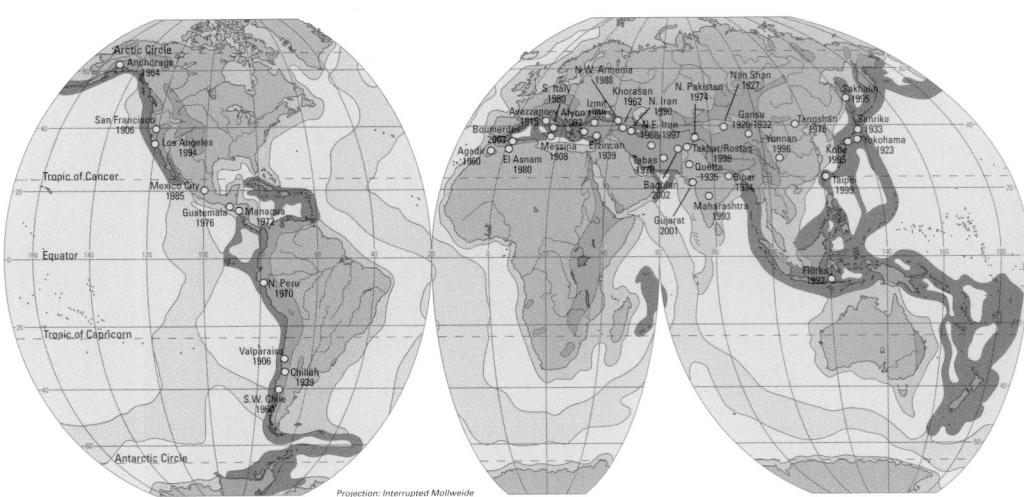

Projection: Interrupted Mollweide

4

Plate Tectonics

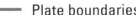 Plate boundaries   PACIFIC Major plates

→ Direction of plate movements and rate of movement (cm/year)

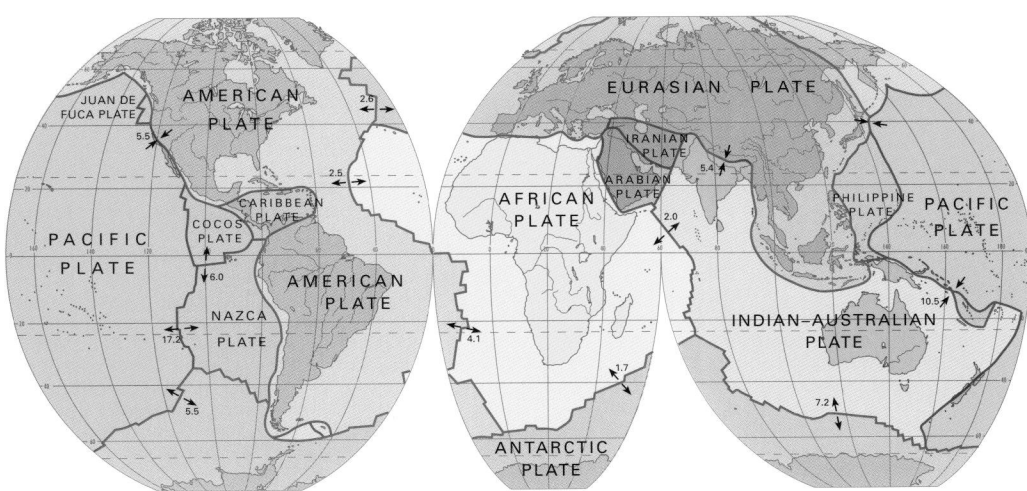

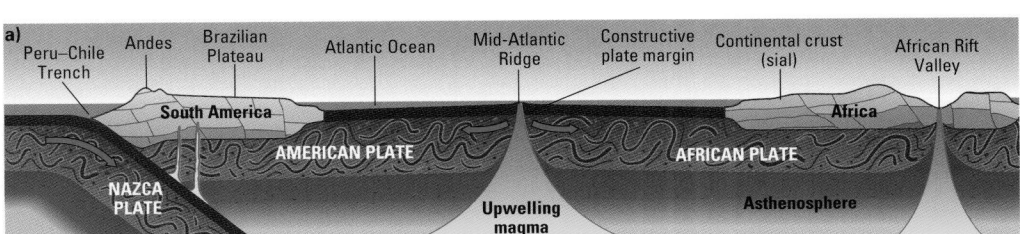

The drifting of the continents is a feature that is unique to Planet Earth. The complementary, almost jigsaw-puzzle fit of the coastlines on each side of the Atlantic Ocean inspired Alfred Wegener's theory of continental drift in 1915. The theory suggested that the ancient super-continent, which Wegener named Pangaea, incorporated all of the Earth's landmasses and gradually split up to form today's continents.

The original debate about continental drift was a prelude to a more radical idea: plate tectonics. The basic theory is that the Earth's crust is made up of a series of rigid plates which float on a soft layer of the mantle and are moved about by continental convection currents within the Earth's interior. These plates diverge and converge along margins marked by seismic activity. Plates diverge from mid-ocean ridges where molten lava pushes upwards and forces the plates apart at rates of up to 40 mm [1.6 in] a year.

The three diagrams, left, give some examples of plate boundaries from around the world. Diagram (a) shows sea-floor spreading at the Mid-Atlantic Ridge as the American and African plates slowly diverge. The same thing is happening in (b) where sea-floor spreading at the Mid-Indian Ocean Ridge is forcing the Indian–Australian plate to collide into the Eurasian plate. In (c) oceanic crust (sima) is being subducted beneath lighter continental crust (sial).

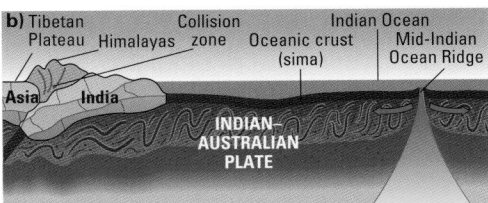

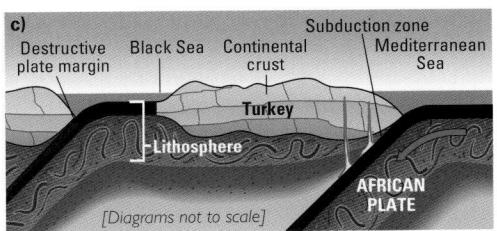

Volcanoes

Volcanoes occur when hot liquefied rock beneath the Earth's crust is pushed up by pressure to the surface as molten lava. Some volcanoes erupt in an explosive way, throwing out rocks and ash, whilst others are effusive and lava flows out of the vent. There are volcanoes which are both, such as Mount Fuji. An accumulation of lava and cinders creates cones of variable size and shape. As a result of many eruptions over centuries, Mount Etna in Sicily has a circumference of more than 120 km [75 miles].

Climatologists believe that volcanic ash, if ejected high into the atmosphere, can influence temperature and weather for several years afterwards. The 1991 eruption of Mount Pinatubo in the Philippines ejected more than 20 million tonnes of dust and ash 32 km [20 miles] into the atmosphere and is believed to have accelerated ozone depletion over a large part of the globe.

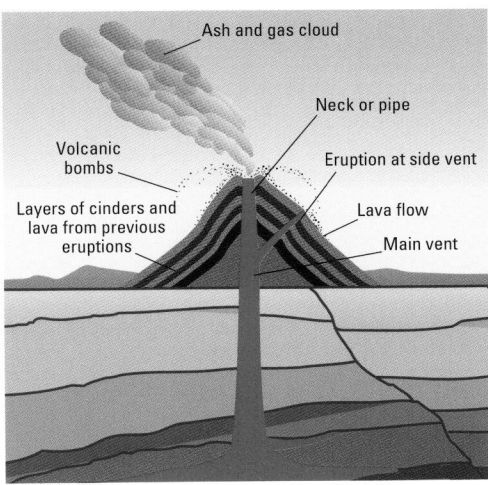

Distribution of Volcanoes

Volcanoes today may be the subject of considerable scientific study but they remain both dramatic and unpredictable: in 1991 Mount Pinatubo, 100 km [62 miles] north of the Philippines capital Manila, suddenly burst into life after lying dormant for more than six centuries. Most of the world's active volcanoes occur in a belt around the Pacific Ocean, on the edge of the Pacific plate, called the 'ring of fire'. Indonesia has the greatest concentration with 90 volcanoes, 12 of which are active. The most famous, Krakatoa, erupted in 1883 with such force that the resulting tidal wave killed 36,000 people and tremors were felt as far away as Australia.

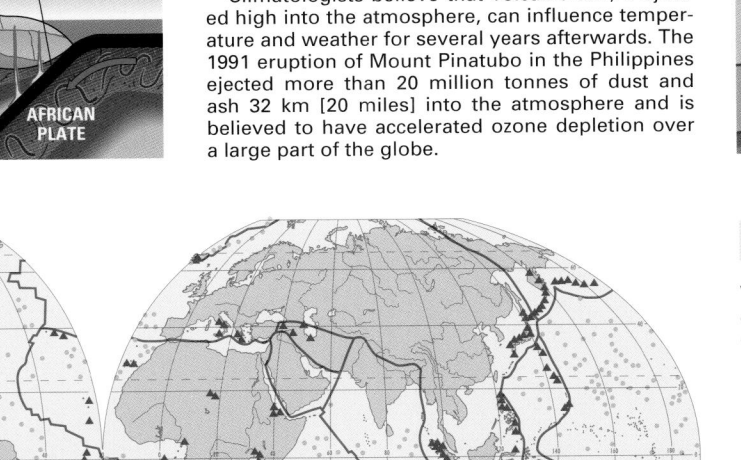

⚬ Submarine volcanoes

▲ Land volcanoes active since 1700

— Boundaries of tectonic plates

Landforms

The Rock Cycle

James Hutton first proposed the rock cycle in the late 1700s after he observed the slow but steady effects of erosion.

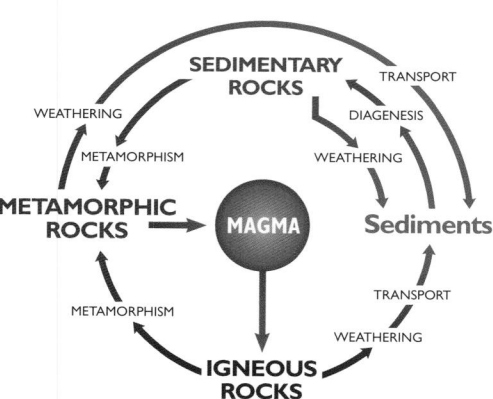

Above and below the surface of the oceans, the features of the Earth's crust are constantly changing. The phenomenal forces generated by convection currents in the molten core of our planet carry the vast segments or 'plates' of the crust across the globe in an endless cycle of creation and destruction. A continent may travel little more than 25 mm [1 in] per year, yet in the vast span of geological time this process throws up giant mountain ranges and creates new land.

Destruction of the landscape, however, begins as soon as it is formed. Wind, water, ice and sea, the main agents of erosion, mount a constant assault that even the most resistant rocks cannot withstand. Mountain peaks may dwindle by as little as a few millimetres each year, but if they are not uplifted by further movements of the crust they will eventually be reduced to rubble and transported away.

Water is the most powerful agent of erosion – it has been estimated that 100 billion tonnes of sediment are washed into the oceans every year. Three Asian rivers account for 20% of this total, the Huang He, in China, and the Brahmaputra and Ganges in Bangladesh.

Rivers and glaciers, like the sea itself, generate much of their effect through abrasion – pounding the land with the debris they carry with them. But as well as destroying they also create new landforms, many of them spectacular: vast deltas like those of the Mississippi and the Nile, or the deep fjords cut by glaciers in British Columbia, Norway and New Zealand.

Geologists once considered that landscapes evolved from 'young', newly uplifted mountainous areas, through a 'mature' hilly stage, to an 'old age' stage when the land was reduced to an almost flat plain, or peneplain. This theory, called the 'cycle of erosion', fell into disuse when it became evident that so many factors, including the effects of plate tectonics and climatic change, constantly interrupt the cycle, which takes no account of the highly complex interactions that shape the surface of our planet.

Mountain Building

Mountains are formed when pressures on the Earth's crust caused by continental drift become so intense that the surface buckles or cracks. This happens where oceanic crust is subducted by continental crust or, more dramatically, where two tectonic plates collide: the Rockies, Andes, Alps, Urals and Himalayas resulted from such impacts. These are all known as fold mountains because they were formed by the compression of the rocks, forcing the surface to bend and fold like a crumpled rug. The Himalayas are formed from the folded former sediments of the Tethys Sea which was trapped in the collision zone between the Indian and Eurasian plates.

The other main mountain-building process occurs when the crust fractures to create faults, allowing rock to be forced upwards in large blocks; or when the pressure of magma within the crust forces the surface to bulge into a dome, or erupts to form a volcano. Large mountain ranges may reveal a combination of those features; the Alps, for example, have been compressed so violently that the folds are fragmented by numerous faults and intrusions of molten igneous rock.

Over millions of years, even the greatest mountain ranges can be reduced by the agents of erosion (most notably rivers) to a low rugged landscape known as a peneplain.

Types of faults: Faults occur where the crust is being stretched or compressed so violently that the rock strata break in a horizontal or vertical movement. They are classified by the direction in which the blocks of rock have moved. A normal fault results when a vertical movement causes the surface to break apart; compression causes a reverse fault. Horizontal movement causes shearing, known as a strike-slip fault. When the rock breaks in two places, the central block may be pushed up in a horst fault, or sink (creating a rift valley) in a graben fault.

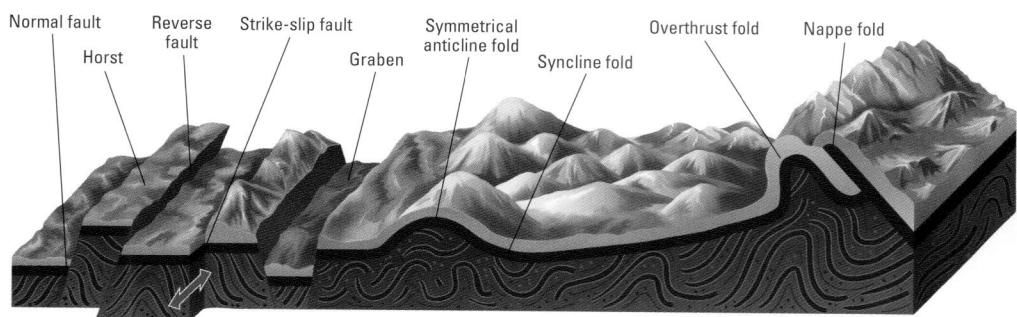

Types of fold: Folds occur when rock strata are squeezed and compressed. They are common therefore at destructive plate margins and where plates have collided, forcing the rocks to buckle into mountain ranges. Geographers give different names to the degrees of fold that result from continuing pressure on the rock. A simple fold may be symmetric, with even slopes on either side, but as the pressure builds up, one slope becomes steeper and the fold becomes asymmetric. Later, the ridge or 'anticline' at the top of the fold may slide over the lower ground or 'syncline' to form a recumbent fold. Eventually, the rock strata may break under the pressure to form an overthrust and finally a nappe fold.

Continental Glaciation

Ice sheets were at their greatest extent about 200,000 years ago. The maximum advance of the last Ice Age was about 18,000 years ago, when ice covered virtually all of Canada and reached as far south as the Bristol Channel in Britain.

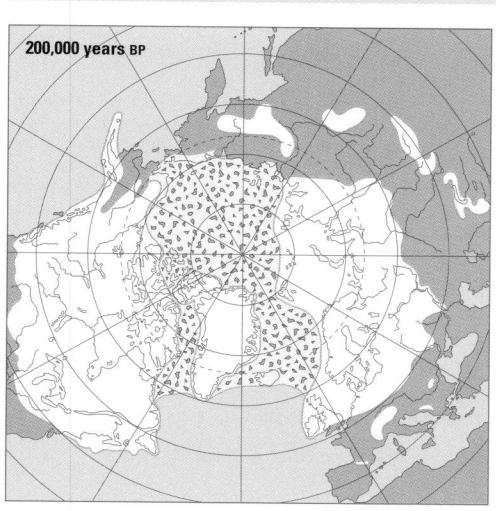

200,000 years BP

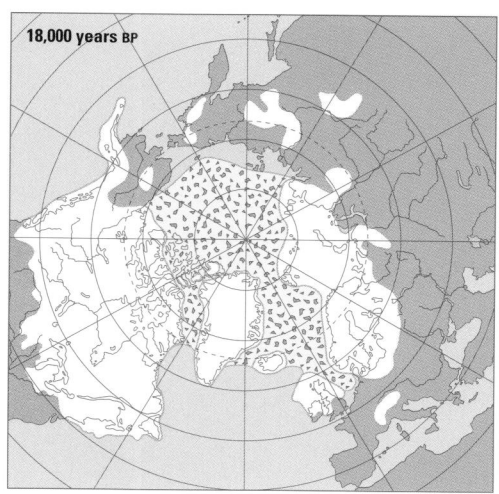

18,000 years BP

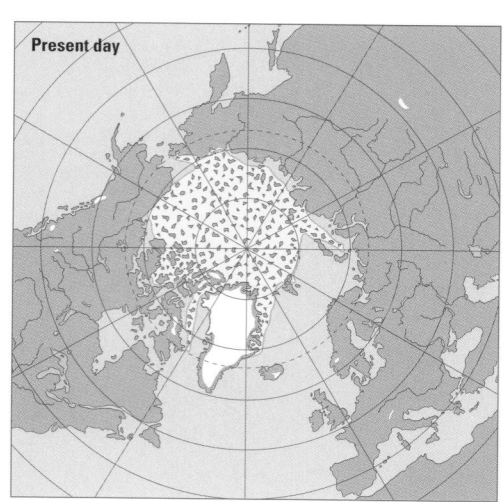

Present day

Natural Landforms

A stylized diagram to show a selection of landforms found in the mid-latitudes.

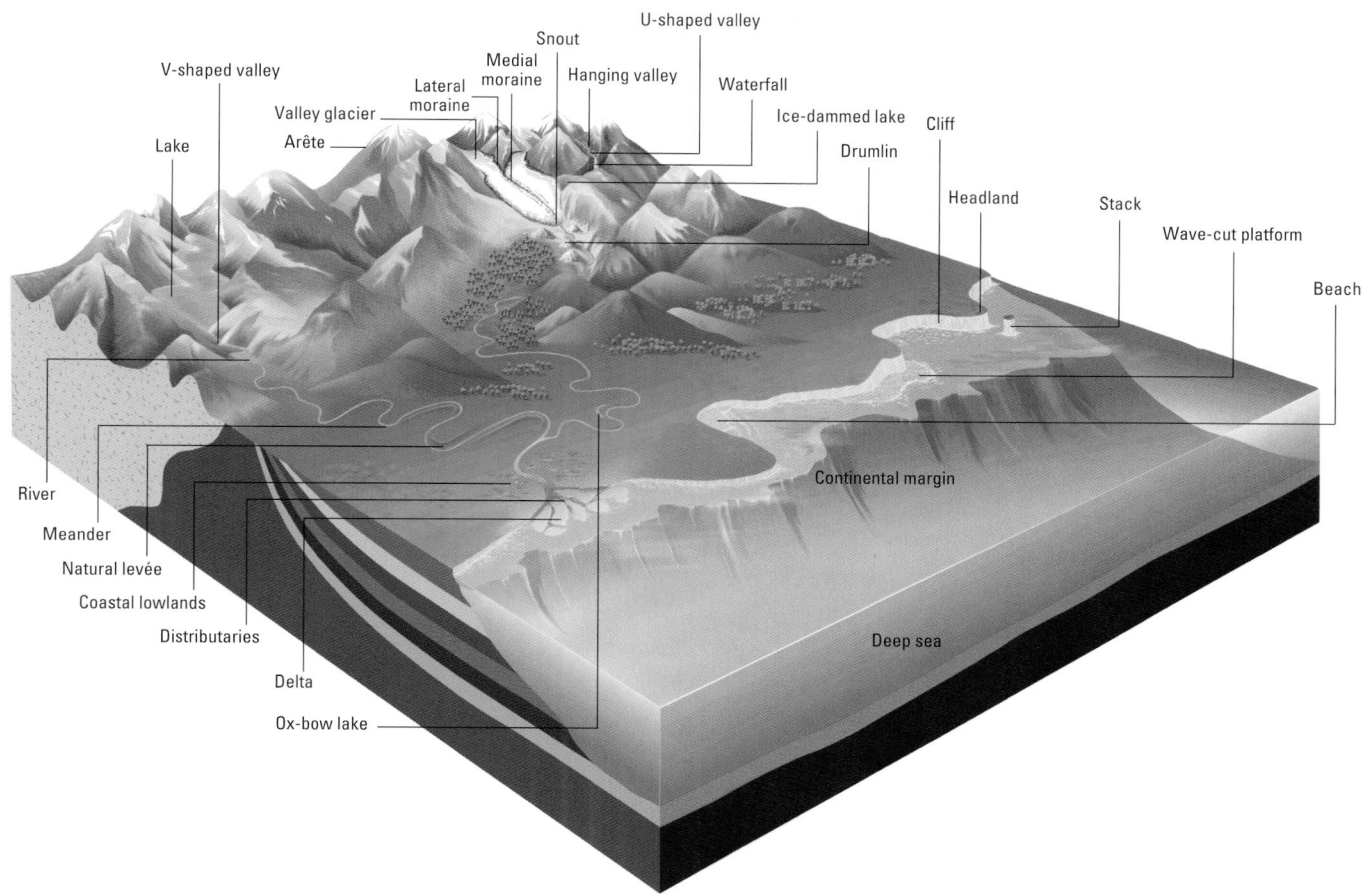

Desert Landscapes

The popular image that deserts are all huge expanses of sand is wrong. Despite harsh conditions, deserts contain some of the most varied and interesting landscapes in the world. They are also one of the most extensive environments – the hot and cold deserts together cover almost 40% of the Earth's surface.

The three types of hot desert are known by their Arabic names: sand desert, called *erg*, covers only about one-fifth of the world's desert; the rest is divided between *hammada* (areas of bare rock) and *reg* (broad plains covered by loose gravel or pebbles).

In areas of *erg*, such as the Namib Desert, the shape of the dunes reflects the character of local winds. Where winds are constant in direction, crescent-shaped *barchan* dunes form. In areas of bare rock, wind-blown sand is a major agent of erosion. The erosion is mainly confined to within 2 m [6.5 ft] of the surface, producing characteristic, mushroom-shaped rocks.

Erg

Hammada

Reg

Surface Processes

Catastrophic changes to natural landforms are periodically caused by such phenomena as avalanches, landslides and volcanic eruptions, but most of the processes that shape the Earth's surface operate extremely slowly in human terms. One estimate, based on a study in the United States, suggested that 1 m [3 ft] of land was removed from the entire surface of the country, on average, every 29,500 years. However, the time-scale varies from 1,300 years to 154,200 years depending on the terrain and climate.

In hot, dry climates, mechanical weathering, a result of rapid temperature changes, causes the outer layers of rock to peel away, while in cold mountainous regions, boulders are prised apart when water freezes in cracks in rocks. Chemical weathering, at its greatest in warm, humid regions, is responsible for hollowing out limestone caves and decomposing granites.

The erosion of soil and rock is greatest on sloping land and the steeper the slope, the greater the tendency for mass wasting – the movement of soil and rock downhill under the influence of gravity. The mechanisms of mass wasting (ranging from very slow to very rapid) vary with the type of material, but the presence of water as a lubricant is usually an important factor.

Running water is the world's leading agent of erosion and transportation. The energy of a river depends on several factors, including its velocity and volume, and its erosive power is at its peak when it is in full flood. Sea waves also exert tremendous erosive power during storms when they hurl pebbles against the shore, undercutting cliffs and hollowing out caves.

Glacier ice forms in mountain hollows and spills out to form valley glaciers, which transport rocks shattered by frost action. As glaciers move, rocks embedded into the ice erode steep-sided, U-shaped valleys. Evidence of glaciation in mountain regions includes cirques, knife-edged ridges, or arêtes, and pyramidal peaks.

Oceans

The Great Oceans

Relative sizes of the world's oceans

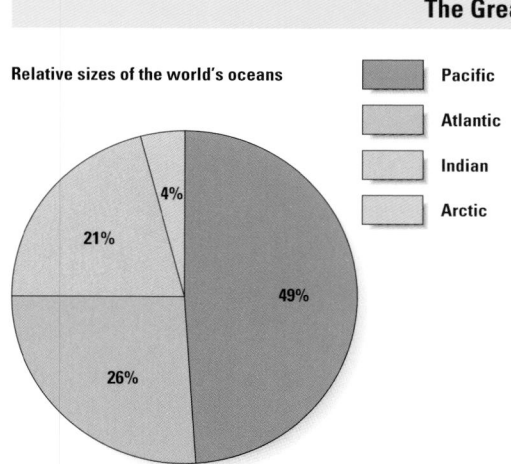

- Pacific
- Atlantic
- Indian
- Arctic

In a strict geographical sense there are only four true oceans – the Atlantic, Indian, Pacific and Arctic. The International Hydrographic Bureau does not recognize the Antarctic Ocean (even less the 'Southern Ocean') as a separate entity. From ancient times to about the 15th century, the legendary 'Seven Seas' comprised the Red Sea, Mediterranean Sea, Persian Gulf, Black Sea, Adriatic Sea, Caspian Sea and Indian Sea.

The Earth is a watery planet: more than 70% of its surface – over 360,000,000 sq km [140,000,000 sq miles] – is covered by the oceans and seas. The mighty Pacific alone accounts for nearly 36% of the total, and 49% of the sea area. Gravity holds in around 1,400 million cu. km [320 million cu. miles] of water, of which over 97% is saline.

The vast underwater world starts in the shallows of the seaside and plunges to depths of more than 11,000 m [36,000 ft]. The continental shelf, part of the landmass, drops gently to around 200 m [650 ft]; here the seabed falls away suddenly at an angle of 3° to 6° – the continental slope. The third stage, called the continental rise, is more gradual with gradients varying from 1 in 100 to 1 in 700. At an average depth of 5,000 m [16,500 ft] there begins the aptly-named abyssal plain – massive submarine depths where sunlight fails to penetrate and few creatures can survive.

From these plains rise volcanoes which, taken from base to top, rival and even surpass the tallest continental mountains in height. Mauna Kea, on Hawaii, reaches a total of 10,203 m [33,400 ft], some 1,355 m [4,500 ft] more than Mount Everest, though scarcely 40% is visible above sea level.

In addition, there are underwater mountain chains up to 1,000 km [600 miles] across, whose peaks sometimes appear above sea level as islands such as Iceland and Tristan da Cunha.

The Ocean Depths

Average and maximum depths of the world's great oceans, in metres

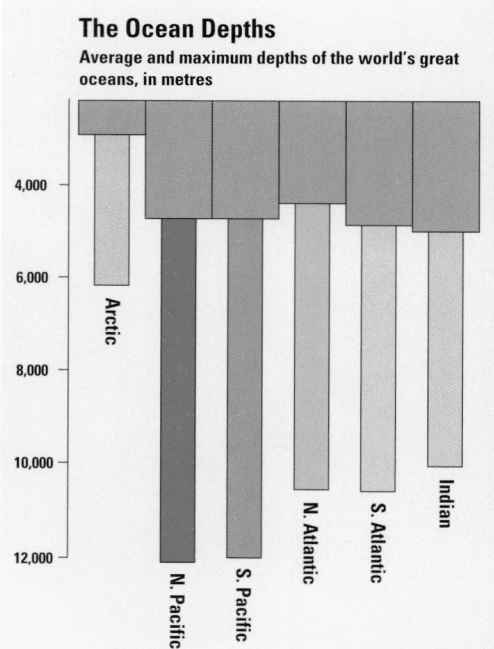

Ocean Currents

January ocean currents

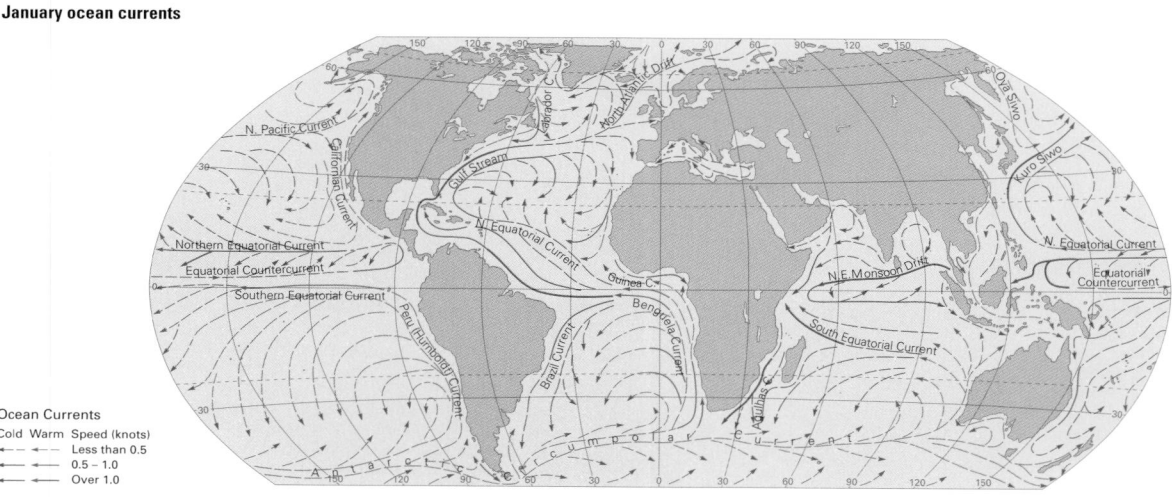

Ocean Currents
Cold Warm Speed (knots)
- Less than 0.5
- 0.5 – 1.0
- Over 1.0

July ocean currents

Ocean Currents
Cold Warm Speed (knots)
- Less than 0.5
- 0.5 – 1.0
- Over 1.0

Moving immense quantities of energy as well as billions of tonnes of water every hour, the ocean currents are a vital part of the great heat engine that drives the Earth's climate. They themselves are produced by a twofold mechanism. At the surface, winds push huge masses of water before them; in the deep ocean, below an abrupt temperature gradient that separates the churning surface waters from the still depths, density variations cause slow vertical movements.

The pattern of circulation of the great surface currents is determined by the displacement known as the Coriolis effect. As the Earth turns beneath a moving object – whether it is a tennis ball or a vast mass of water – it appears to be deflected to one side. The deflection is most obvious near the Equator, where the Earth's surface is spinning eastwards at 1,700 km/h [1,050 mph]; currents moving polewards are curved clockwise in the northern hemisphere and anti-clockwise in the southern.

The result is a system of spinning circles known as gyres. The Coriolis effect piles up water on the left of each gyre, creating a narrow, fast-moving stream that is matched by a slower, broader returning current on the right. North and south of the Equator, the fastest currents are located in the west and in the east respectively. In each case, warm water moves from the Equator and cold water returns to it. Cold currents often bring an upwelling of nutrients with them, supporting the world's most economically important fisheries.

Depending on the prevailing winds, some currents on or near the Equator may reverse their direction in the course of the year – a seasonal variation on which Asian monsoon rains depend, and whose occasional failure can bring disaster to millions.

World Fishing Areas

Main commercial fishing areas (numbered FAO regions)

Catch by top marine fishing areas, thousand tonnes (2000)

1.	Pacific, NW	[61]	23,141	24.4%
2.	Pacific, SE	[87]	15,822	16.7%
3.	Atlantic, NE	[27]	10,920	11.5%
4.	Pacific, WC	[71]	9,899	10.4%
5.	Indian, E	[57]	4,708	5.0%
6.	Indian, W	[51]	3,902	4.1%
7.	Atlantic, EC	[34]	3,523	3.7%
8.	Pacific, NE	[67]	2,518	2.7%
9.	Atlantic, NW	[21]	2,063	2.2%
10.	Atlantic, WC	[31]	1,831	1.9%

Principal fishing areas

Leading fishing nations

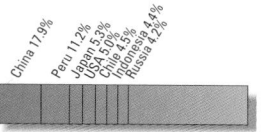

China 17.9%
Peru 11.2%
Japan 5.3%
USA 5.0%
Chile 4.5%
Indonesia 4.4%
Russia 4.2%

World total (2000): 94,849,000 tonnes
(Marine catch 90.7% Inland catch 9.3%)

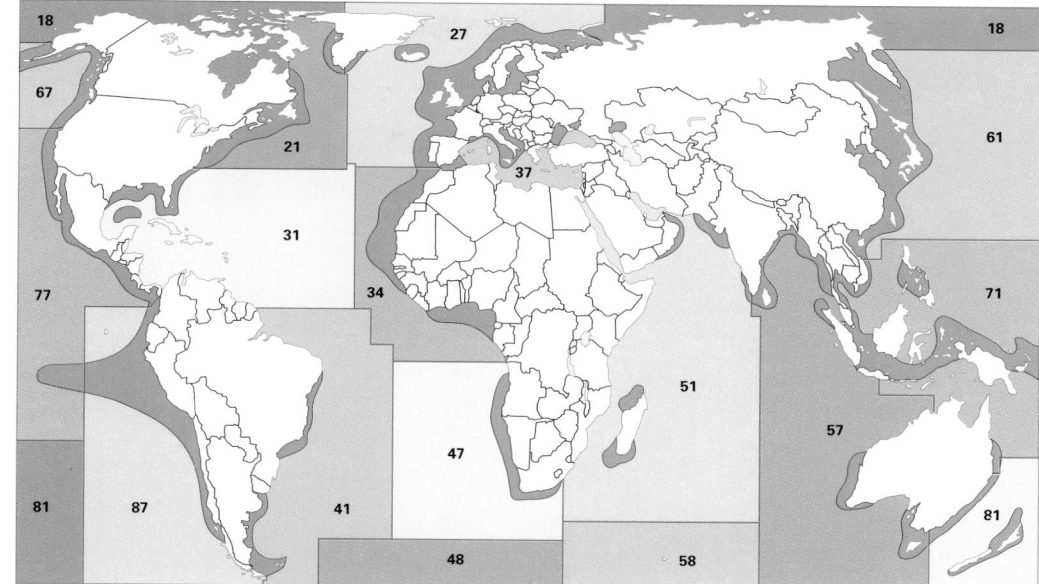

Marine Pollution

Sources of marine oil pollution (latest available year)

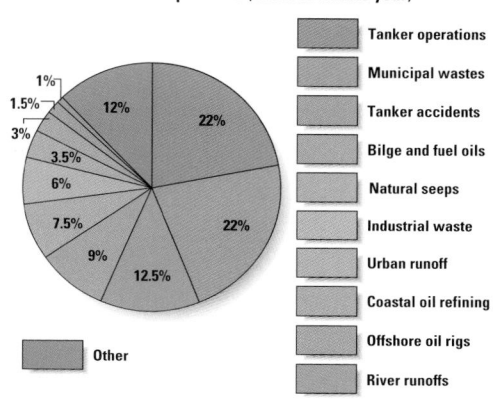

Tanker operations

Municipal wastes

Tanker accidents

Bilge and fuel oils

Natural seeps

Industrial waste

Urban runoff

Coastal oil refining

Offshore oil rigs

River runoffs

Other

Oil Spills

Major oil spills from tankers and combined carriers

Year	Vessel	Location	Spill (barrels)**	Cause
1979	Atlantic Empress	West Indies	1,890,000	collision
1983	Castillo De Bellver	South Africa	1,760,000	fire
1978	Amoco Cadiz	France	1,628,000	grounding
1991	Haven	Italy	1,029,000	explosion
1988	Odyssey	Canada	1,000,000	fire
1967	Torrey Canyon	UK	909,000	grounding
1972	Sea Star	Gulf of Oman	902,250	collision
1977	Hawaiian Patriot	Hawaiian Is.	742,500	fire
1979	Independenta	Turkey	696,350	collision
1993	Braer	UK	625,000	grounding
1996	Sea Empress	UK	515,000	grounding

Other sources of major oil spills

1983	Nowruz oilfield	The Gulf	4,250,000[†]	war
1979	Ixtoc 1 oilwell	Gulf of Mexico	4,200,000	blow-out
1991	Kuwait	The Gulf	2,500,000[†]	war

** 1 barrel = 0.136 tonnes/159 lit./35 Imperial gal./42 US gal. [†] estimated

River Pollution

Sources of river pollution, USA (latest available year)

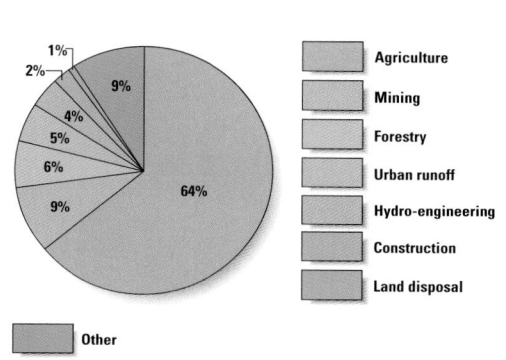

Agriculture

Mining

Forestry

Urban runoff

Hydro-engineering

Construction

Land disposal

Other

Water Pollution

Severely polluted
sea areas and lakes

Polluted sea
areas and lakes

Areas of frequent oil pollution
by shipping

▶ Major oil tanker spills

▲ Major oil rig blow-outs

▼ Offshore dumpsites for industrial
and municipal waste

—— Severely polluted
rivers and estuaries

The most notorious tanker spillage of the
1980s occurred when the *Exxon Valdez* ran
aground in Prince William Sound, Alaska,
in 1989, spilling 267,000 barrels of crude oil
close to shore in a sensitive ecological area.
This rates as the world's 28th worst spill in
terms of volume.

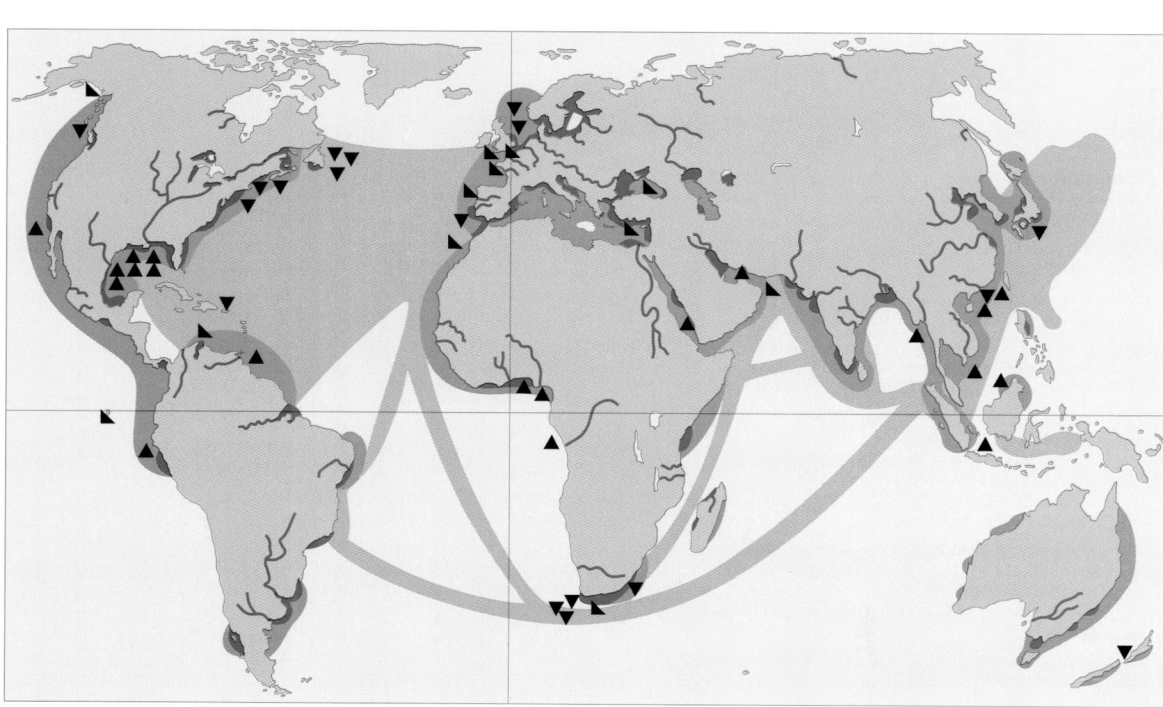

Climate

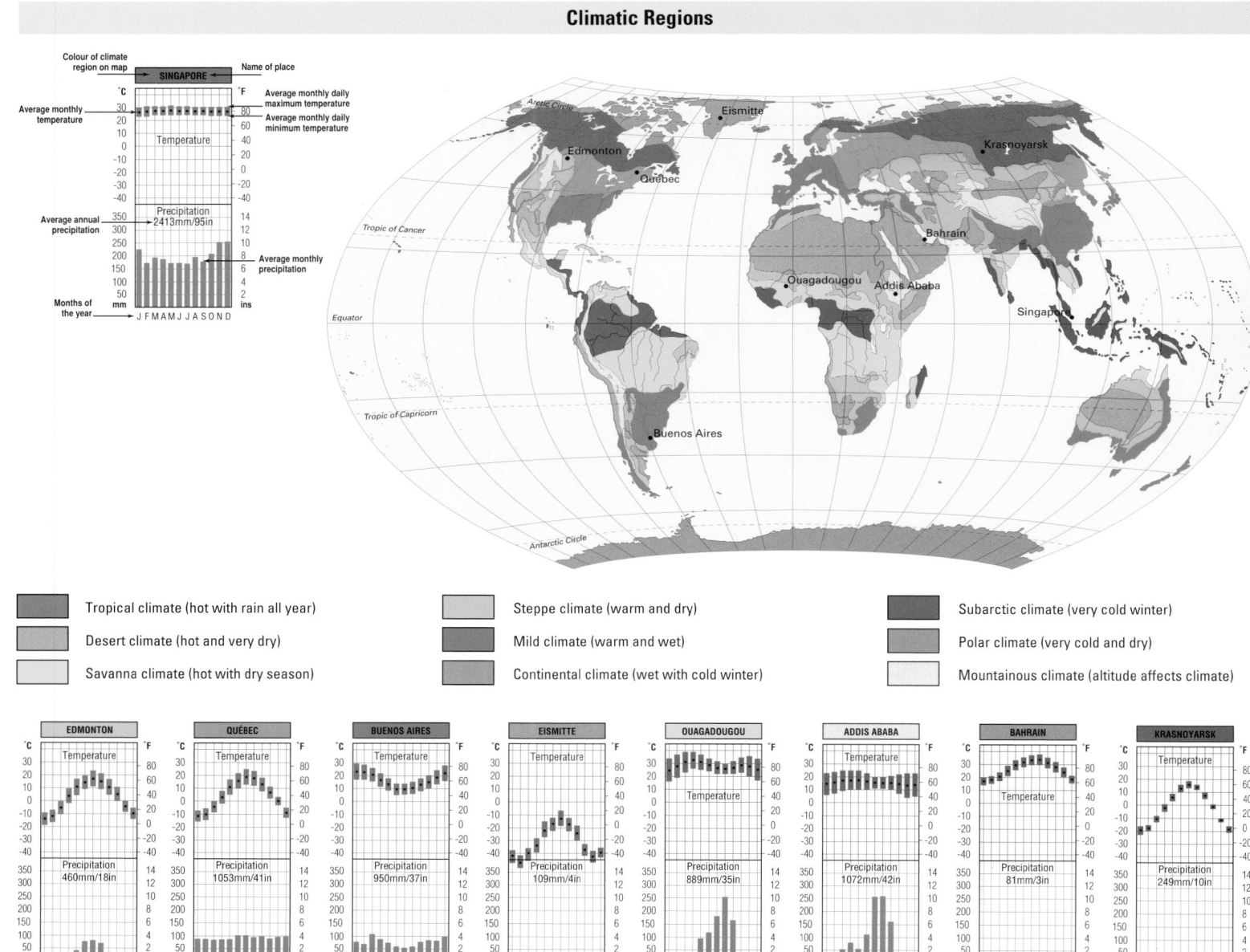

Tropical climate (hot with rain all year)

Desert climate (hot and very dry)

Savanna climate (hot with dry season)

Steppe climate (warm and dry)

Mild climate (warm and wet)

Continental climate (wet with cold winter)

Subarctic climate (very cold winter)

Polar climate (very cold and dry)

Mountainous climate (altitude affects climate)

Climate Records

Temperature

Highest recorded shade temperature: Al Aziziyah, Libya, 58°C [136.4°F], 13 September 1922.

Highest mean annual temperature: Dallol, Ethiopia, 34.4°C [94°F], 1960–66.

Longest heatwave: Marble Bar, W. Australia, 162 days over 38°C [100°F], 23 October 1923 to 7 April 1924.

Lowest recorded temperature (outside poles): Verkhoyansk, Siberia, –68°C [–90°F], 6 February 1933.

Lowest mean annual temperature: Plateau Station, Antarctica, –56.6°C [–72.0°F].

Precipitation

Longest drought: Calama, N. Chile, no recorded rainfall in 400 years to 1971.

Wettest place (12 months): Cherrapunji, Meghalaya, N. E. India, 26,470 mm [1,040 in], August 1860 to August 1861. Cherrapunji also holds the record for the most rainfall in one month: 2,930 mm [115 in], July 1861.

Wettest place (average): Mawsynram, India, mean annual rainfall 11,873 mm [467.4 in].

Wettest place (24 hours): Cilaos, Réunion, Indian Ocean, 1,870 mm [73.6 in], 15–16 March 1952.

Heaviest hailstones: Gopalganj, Bangladesh, up to 1.02 kg [2.25 lb], 14 April 1986 (killed 92 people).

Heaviest snowfall (continuous): Bessans, Savoie, France, 1,730 mm [68 in] in 19 hours, 5–6 April 1969.

Heaviest snowfall (season/year): Paradise Ranger Station, Mt Rainier, Washington, USA, 31,102 mm [1,224.5 in], 19 February 1971 to 18 February 1972.

Pressure and winds

Highest barometric pressure: Agata, Siberia (at 262 m [862 ft] altitude), 1,083.8 mb, 31 December 1968.

Lowest barometric pressure: Typhoon Tip, Guam, Pacific Ocean, 870 mb, 12 October 1979.

Highest recorded wind speed: Mt Washington, New Hampshire, USA, 371 km/h [231 mph], 12 April 1934. This is three times as strong as hurricane force on the Beaufort Scale.

Windiest place: Commonwealth Bay, Antarctica, where gales frequently reach over 320 km/h [200 mph].

Climate

Climate is weather in the long term: the seasonal pattern of hot and cold, wet and dry, averaged over time (usually 30 years). At the simplest level, it is caused by the uneven heating of the Earth. Surplus heat at the Equator passes towards the poles, levelling out the energy differential. Its passage is marked by a ceaseless churning of the atmosphere and the oceans, further agitated by the Earth's diurnal spin and the motion it imparts to moving air and water. The heat's means of transport – by winds and ocean currents, by the continual evaporation and recondensation of water molecules – is the weather itself. There are four basic types of climate, each of which can be further subdivided: tropical, desert (dry), temperate and polar.

Composition of Dry Air

Nitrogen	78.09%	Sulphur dioxide	trace
Oxygen	20.95%	Nitrogen oxide	trace
Argon	0.93%	Methane	trace
Water vapour	0.2–4.0%	Dust	trace
Carbon dioxide	0.03%	Helium	trace
Ozone	0.00006%	Neon	trace

El Niño

In a normal year, south-easterly trade winds drive surface waters westwards off the coast of South America, drawing cold, nutrient-rich water up from below. In an El Niño year (which occurs every 2–7 years), warm water from the west Pacific suppresses up-welling in the east, depriving the region of nutrients. The water is warmed by as much as 7°C [12°F], disturbing the tropical atmospheric circulation. During an intense El Niño, the south-east trade winds change direction and become equatorial westerlies, resulting in climatic extremes in many regions of the world, such as drought in parts of Australia and India, and heavy rainfall in south-eastern USA. An intense El Niño occurred in 1997–8, with resultant freak weather conditions across the entire Pacific region.

Normal year

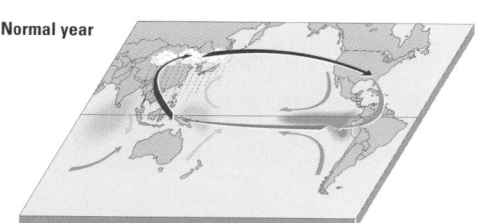

El Niño event

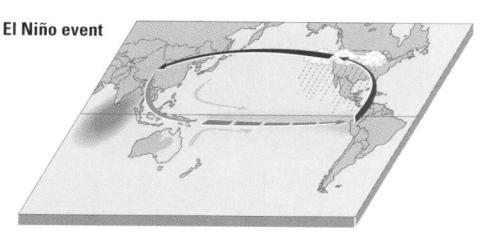

Beaufort Wind Scale

Named after the 19th-century British naval officer who devised it, the Beaufort Scale assesses wind speed according to its effects. It was originally designed as an aid for sailors, but has since been adapted for use on the land.

Scale	Wind speed km/h	mph	Effect
0	0–1	0–1	**Calm** Smoke rises vertically
1	1–5	1–3	**Light air** Wind direction shown only by smoke drift
2	6–11	4–7	**Light breeze** Wind felt on face; leaves rustle; vanes moved by wind
3	12–19	8–12	**Gentle breeze** Leaves and small twigs in constant motion; wind extends small flag
4	20–28	13–18	**Moderate** Raises dust and loose paper; small branches move
5	29–38	19–24	**Fresh** Small trees in leaf sway; wavelets on inland waters
6	39–49	25–31	**Strong** Large branches move; difficult to use umbrellas
7	50–61	32–38	**Near gale** Whole trees in motion; difficult to walk against wind
8	62–74	39–46	**Gale** Twigs break from trees; walking very difficult
9	75–88	47–54	**Strong gale** Slight structural damage
10	89–102	55–63	**Storm** Trees uprooted; serious structural damage
11	103–117	64–72	**Violent storm** Widespread damage
12	118+	73+	**Hurricane**

Conversions

°C = (°F − 32) × 5/9; °F = (°C × 9/5) + 32; 0°C = 32°F
1 in = 25.4 mm; 1 mm = 0.0394 in; 100 mm = 3.94 in

Temperature

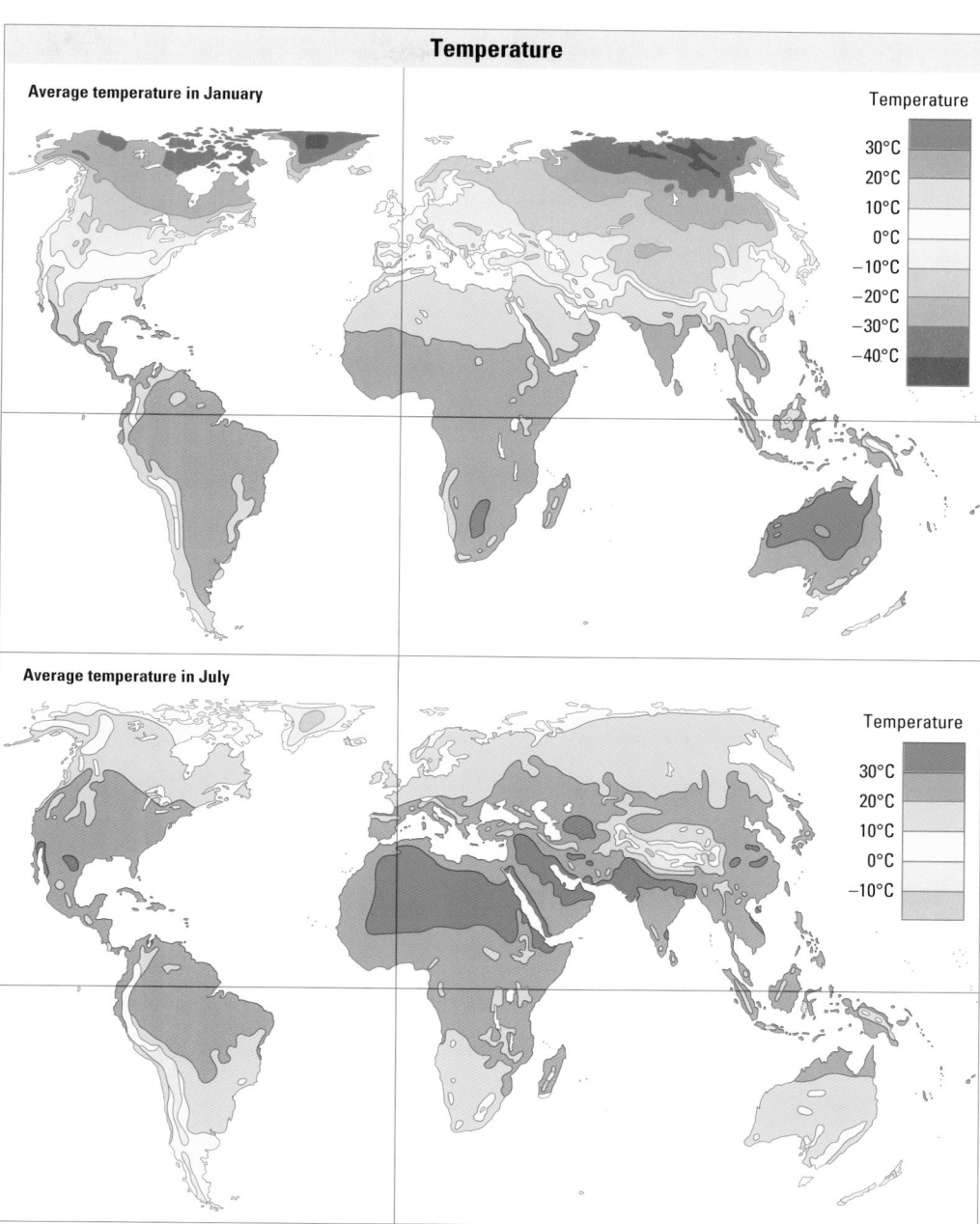

Average temperature in January

Temperature
- 30°C
- 20°C
- 10°C
- 0°C
- −10°C
- −20°C
- −30°C
- −40°C

Average temperature in July

Temperature
- 30°C
- 20°C
- 10°C
- 0°C
- −10°C

Precipitation

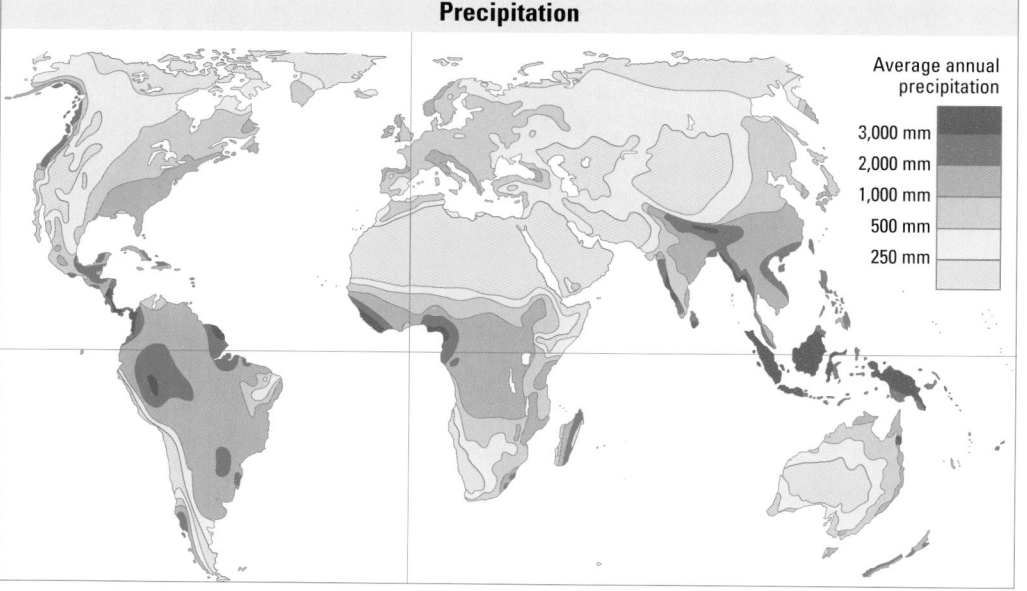

Average annual precipitation
- 3,000 mm
- 2,000 mm
- 1,000 mm
- 500 mm
- 250 mm

Water and Vegetation

The Hydrological Cycle

The world's water balance is regulated by the constant recycling of water between the oceans, atmosphere and land. The movement of water between these three reservoirs is known as the hydrological cycle. The oceans play a vital role in the hydrological cycle: 74% of the total precipitation falls over the oceans and 84% of the total evaporation comes from the oceans.

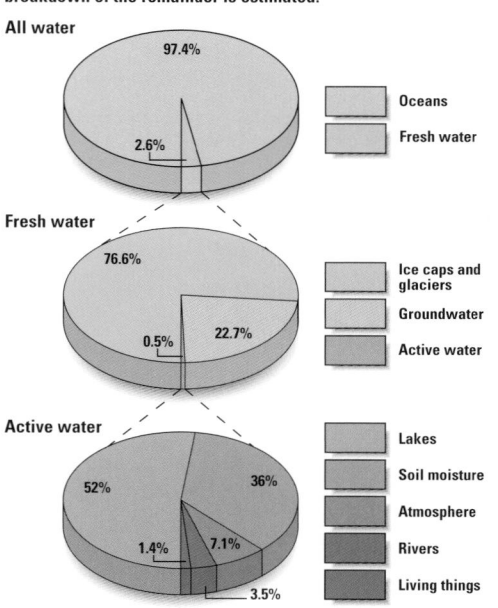

Water Distribution

The distribution of planetary water, by percentage. Oceans and ice caps together account for more than 99% of the total; the breakdown of the remainder is estimated.

All water
- 97.4% Oceans
- 2.6% Fresh water

Fresh water
- 76.6% Ice caps and glaciers
- 0.5% Groundwater
- 22.7% Active water

Active water
- 52% Lakes
- 36% Soil moisture
- 1.4% Atmosphere
- 7.1% Rivers
- 3.5% Living things

Water Utilization

The percentage breakdown of water usage by sector, selected countries (latest available year)

Legend: Domestic | Industrial | Agriculture

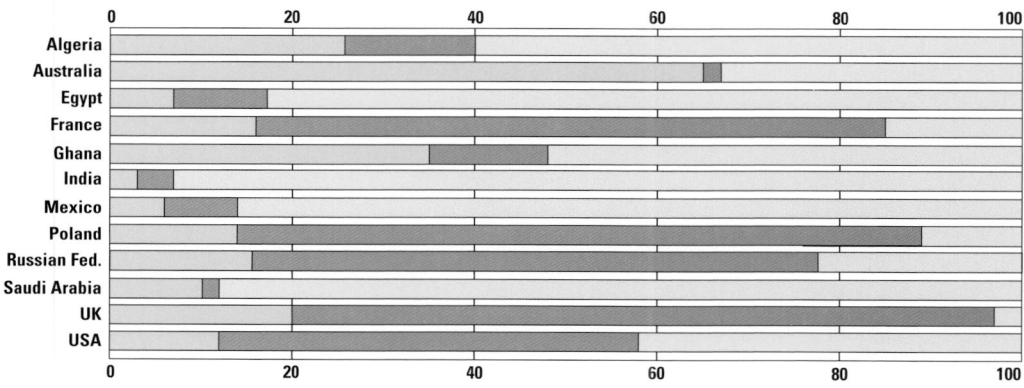

Algeria
Australia
Egypt
France
Ghana
India
Mexico
Poland
Russian Fed.
Saudi Arabia
UK
USA

Water Usage

Almost all the world's water is 3,000 million years old, and all of it cycles endlessly through the hydrosphere, though at different rates. Water vapour circulates over days, even hours, deep ocean water circulates over millennia, and ice-cap water remains solid for millions of years.

Fresh water is essential to all terrestrial life. Humans cannot survive more than a few days without it, and even the hardiest desert plants and animals could not exist without some water. Agriculture requires huge quantities of fresh water: without large-scale irrigation most of the world's people would starve. In the USA, agriculture uses 42% and industry 45% of all water withdrawals.

The United States is one of the heaviest users of water in the world. According to the latest figures the average American uses 380 litres a day and the average household uses 415,000 litres a year. This is two to four times more than in Western Europe.

Water Supply

Percentage of total population with access to safe drinking water (2000)

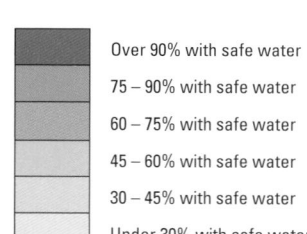

- Over 90% with safe water
- 75 – 90% with safe water
- 60 – 75% with safe water
- 45 – 60% with safe water
- 30 – 45% with safe water
- Under 30% with safe water

△ Under 80 litres per person per day domestic water consumption

▲ Over 320 litres per person per day domestic water consumption

NB: 80 litres of water a day is considered necessary for a reasonable quality of life.

Least well-provided countries

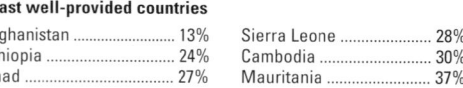

Afghanistan	13%	Sierra Leone	28%
Ethiopia	24%	Cambodia	30%
Chad	27%	Mauritania	37%

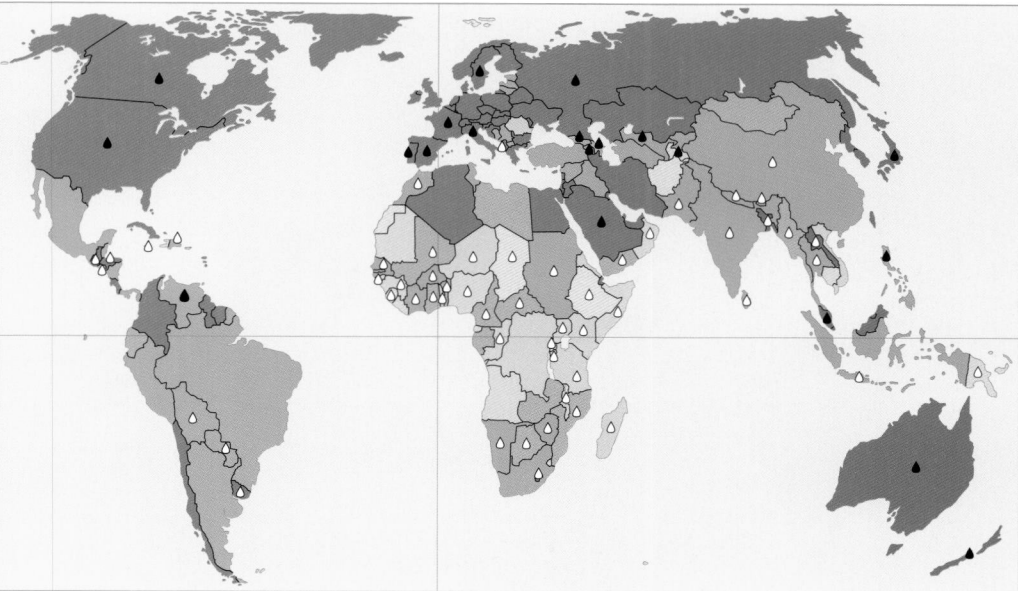

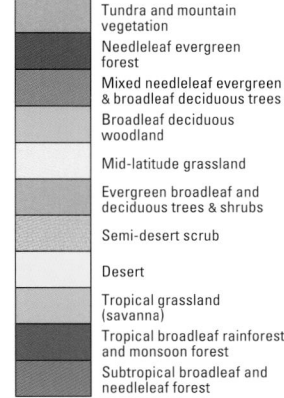

Natural Vegetation

Regional variation in vegetation

- Tundra and mountain vegetation
- Needleleaf evergreen forest
- Mixed needleleaf evergreen & broadleaf deciduous trees
- Broadleaf deciduous woodland
- Mid-latitude grassland
- Evergreen broadleaf and deciduous trees & shrubs
- Semi-desert scrub
- Desert
- Tropical grassland (savanna)
- Tropical broadleaf rainforest and monsoon forest
- Subtropical broadleaf and needleleaf forest

The map shows the natural 'climax vegetation' of regions, as dictated by climate and topography. In most cases, however, agricultural activity has drastically altered the vegetation pattern. Western Europe, for example, lost most of its broadleaf forest many centuries ago, while irrigation has turned some natural semi-desert into productive land.

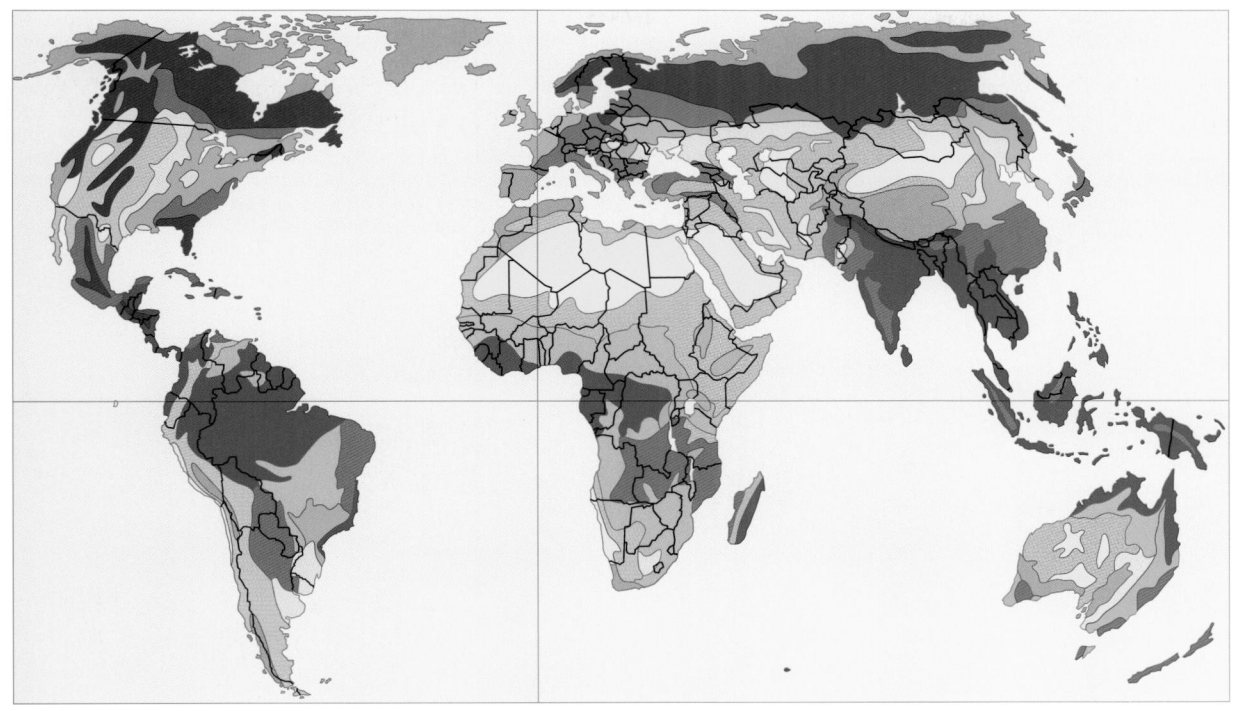

Land Use by Continent

- Forest
- Permanent pasture
- Permanent crops
- Arable
- Other

North America
- 25.7%
- 17.2%
- 0.4%
- 12.1%
- 44.7%

Europe
- 46.0%
- 8.0%
- 0.7%
- 12.8%
- 32.5%

Asia
- 17.8%
- 35.8%
- 1.9%
- 15.7%
- 28.8%

South America
- 50.5%
- 28.7%
- 1.1%
- 5.5%
- 14.2%

Africa
- 21.8%
- 30.2%
- 0.9%
- 6.1%
- 41.0%

Oceania
- 23.3%
- 49.3%
- 0.4%
- 6.2%
- 18.8%

Forestry: Production

	Forest and woodland (million hectares)	Annual production (2001, million cubic metres)	
		Fuelwood	Industrial roundwood*
World	*3,869.5*	*1,784.3*	*1,543.3*
Europe	1,039.3	98.1	462.5
S. America	885.6	189.2	151.1
Africa	649.9	534.5	68.1
N. & C. America	549.3	154.5	596.6
Asia	547.8	795.5	216.0
Oceania	197.6	12.6	48.9

Paper and Board

Top producers (2001)**		Top exporters (2001)**	
USA	81,529	Canada	14,540
China	35,529	Finland	10,875
Japan	31,794	Germany	8,830
Canada	19,865	Sweden	8,733
Germany	17,879	USA	8,355

* roundwood is timber as it is felled
** in thousand tonnes

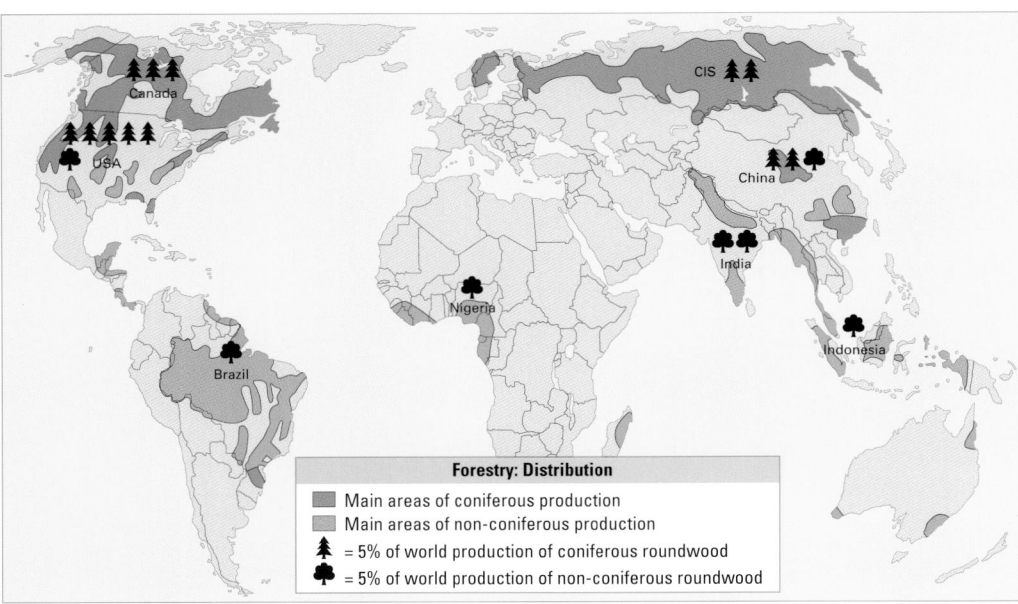

Forestry: Distribution

- Main areas of coniferous production
- Main areas of non-coniferous production
- 🌲 = 5% of world production of coniferous roundwood
- 🌳 = 5% of world production of non-coniferous roundwood

Environment

Humans have always had a dramatic effect on their environment, at least since the development of agriculture almost 10,000 years ago. Generally, the Earth has accepted human interference without obvious ill effects: the complex systems that regulate the global environment have been able to absorb substantial damage while maintaining a stable and comfortable home for the planet's trillions of lifeforms. But advancing human technology and the rapidly-expanding populations it supports are now threatening to overwhelm the Earth's ability to compensate.

Industrial wastes, acid rainfall, desertification and large-scale deforestation all combine to create environmental change at a rate far faster than the great slow cycles of planetary evolution can accommodate. As a result of overcultivation, overgrazing and overcutting of groundcover for firewood, desertification is affecting as much as 60% of the world's croplands. In addition, with fire and chain-saws, humans are destroying more forest in a day than their ancestors could have done in a century, upsetting the balance between plant and animal, carbon dioxide and oxygen, on which all life ultimately depends.

The fossil fuels that power industrial civilization have pumped enough carbon dioxide and other so-called greenhouse gases into the atmosphere to make climatic change a near-certainty. As a result of the combination of these factors, the Earth's average temperature has risen by approximately 0.5°C [1°F] since the beginning of the 20th century, and it is still rising.

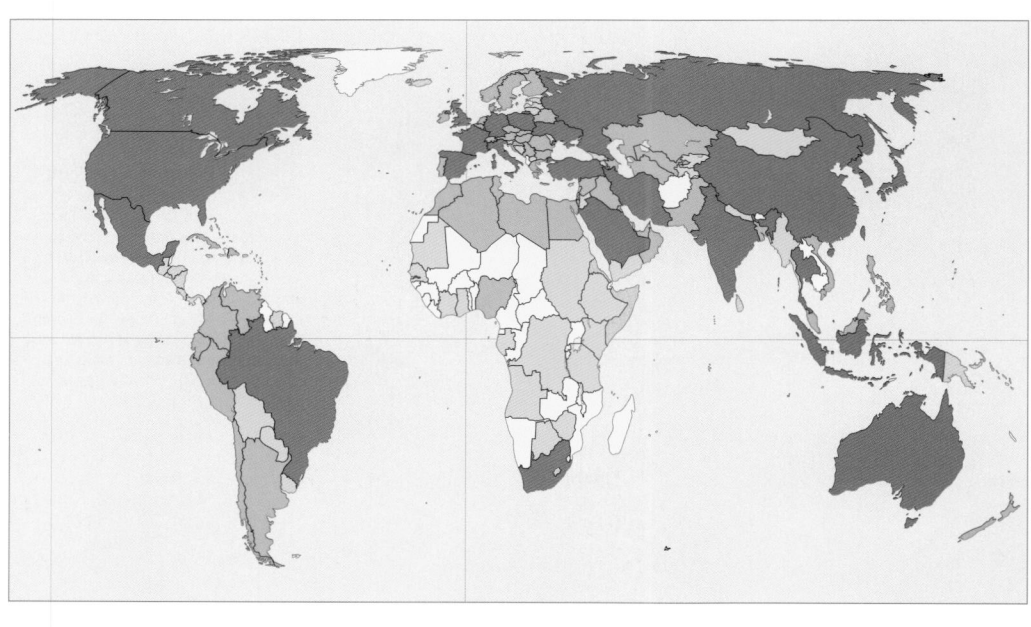
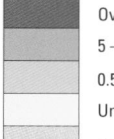

Global Warming

Carbon dioxide emissions in tonnes (1998)

- Over 50 million
- 5 – 50 million
- 0.5 – 5 million
- Under 0.5 million
- No data available

High atmospheric concentrations of heat-absorbing gases appear to be causing a rise in average temperatures worldwide – up to 1.5°C [3°F] by the year 2020, according to some estimates. Global warming is likely to bring about a rise in sea levels that may flood some of the world's densely populated coastal areas.

Greenhouse Power

Relative contributions to the Greenhouse Effect by the major heat-absorbing gases in the atmosphere.

The chart combines greenhouse potency and volume. Carbon dioxide has a greenhouse potential of only 1, but its concentration of 350 parts per million makes it predominant. CFC 12, with 25,000 times the absorption capacity of CO_2, is present only as 0.00044 ppm.

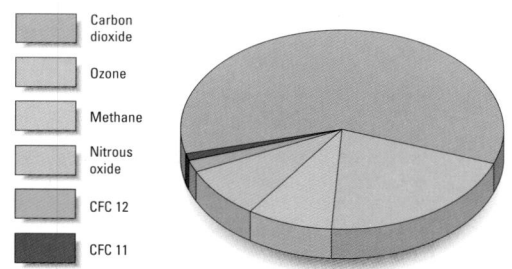

- Carbon dioxide
- Ozone
- Methane
- Nitrous oxide
- CFC 12
- CFC 11

Ozone Layer

The ozone 'hole' over the northern hemisphere in March 2000.

The colours represent Dobson Units (DU). The ozone 'hole' is seen as the dark blue and purple patch in the centre, where ozone values are around 120 DU or lower. Normal levels are around 280 DU. The ozone 'hole' over Antarctica is much larger.

Carbon Dioxide

Estimated percentage share of total world CO_2 emissions (2000)

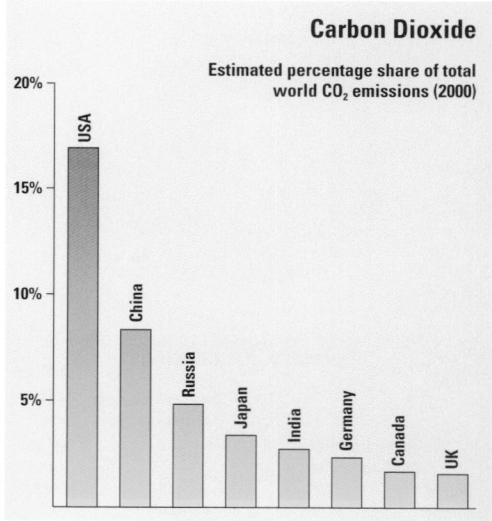

USA, China, Russia, Japan, India, Germany, Canada, UK

The Greenhouse Effect

Carbon dioxide is increased by burning fossil fuels and cutting forests

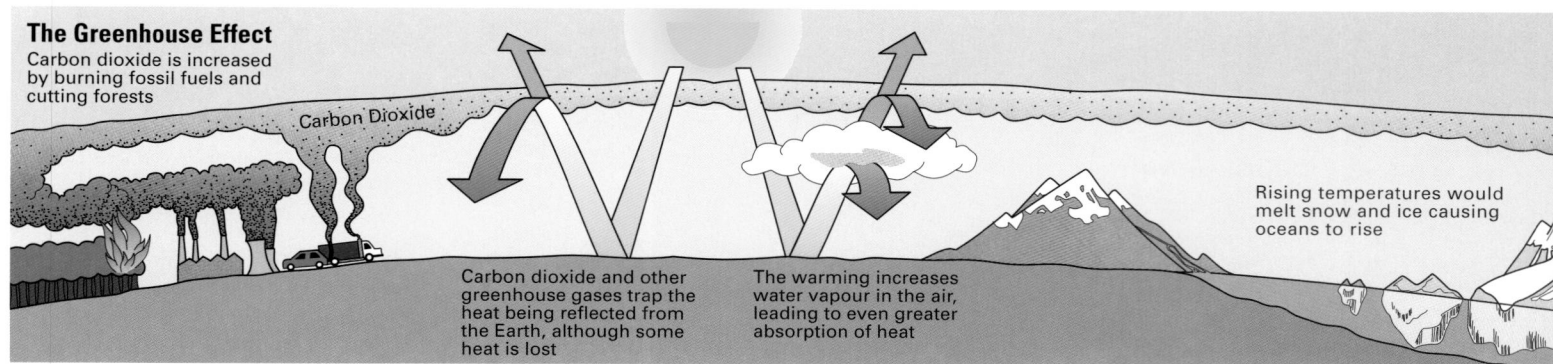

Carbon Dioxide

Carbon dioxide and other greenhouse gases trap the heat being reflected from the Earth, although some heat is lost

The warming increases water vapour in the air, leading to even greater absorption of heat

Rising temperatures would melt snow and ice causing oceans to rise

Desertification

- Existing deserts
- Areas with a high risk of desertification
- Areas with a moderate risk of desertification
- Former areas of rainforest
- Existing rainforest

Forest Clearance

Thousands of hectares of forest cleared annually, tropical countries surveyed 1981–85, 1987–90 and 1990–5. Loss as a percentage of remaining stocks is shown in figures on each column.

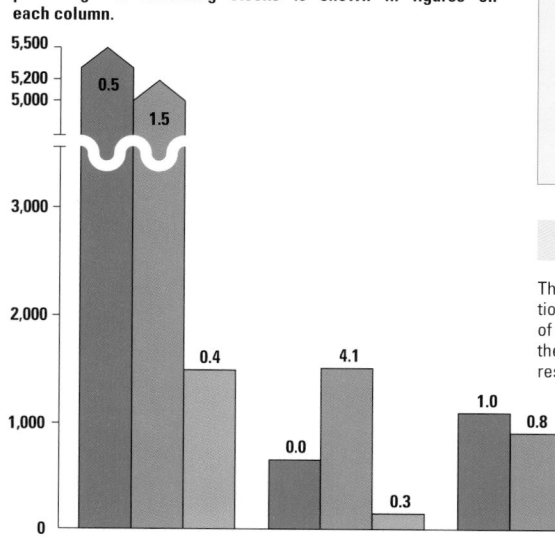

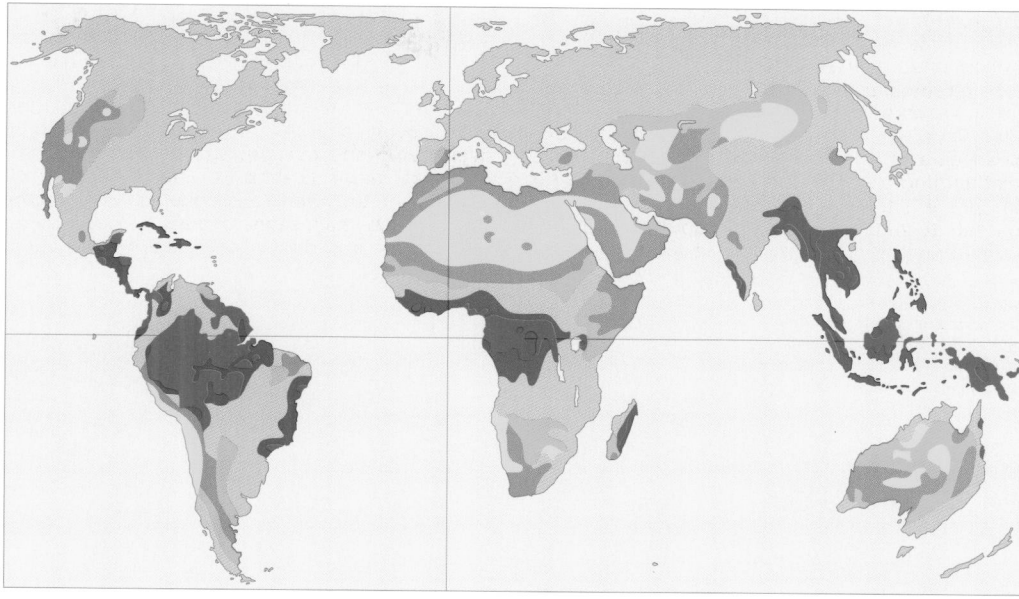

Deforestation

The Earth's remaining forests are under attack from three directions: expanding agriculture, logging, and growing consumption of fuelwood, often in combination. Sometimes deforestation is the direct result of government policy, as in the efforts made to resettle the urban poor in some parts of Brazil; just as often, it comes about despite state attempts at conservation. Loggers, licensed or unlicensed, blaze a trail into virgin forest, often destroying twice as many trees as they harvest. Landless farmers follow, burning away most of what remains to plant their crops, completing the destruction.

Legend: 1990–95 | 1987–90 | 1981–85

Chart data (Loss as percentage on each column):
- **Brazil**: 0.5, 1.5, 0.4
- **India**: 0.0, 4.1, 0.3
- **Indonesia**: 1.0, 0.8, 0.5
- **Burma**: 1.4, 2.1, 0.3
- **Thailand**: 2.6, 2.5, 2.4
- **Vietnam**: 1.4, 2.0, 0.7
- **Philippines**: 3.5, 1.5, 1.0
- **Costa Rica**: 3.0, 7.6, 4.0

Ozone Depletion

The ozone layer, 25–30 km [15–18 miles] above sea level, acts as a barrier to most of the Sun's harmful ultra-violet radiation, protecting us from the ionizing radiation that can cause skin cancer and cataracts. In recent years, however, two holes in the ozone layer have been observed during winter: one over the Arctic and the other, the size of the USA, over Antarctica. By 1996, ozone had been reduced to around a half of its 1970 amount. The ozone (O_3) is broken down by chlorine released into the atmosphere as CFCs (chlorofluorocarbons) – chemicals used in refrigerators, packaging and aerosols.

Air Pollution

Sulphur dioxide is the main pollutant associated with industrial cities. According to the World Health Organization, at least 600 million people live in urban areas where sulphur dioxide concentrations regularly reach damaging levels. One of the world's most dangerously polluted urban areas is Mexico City, due to a combination of its enclosed valley location, 3 million cars and 60,000 factories. In May 1998, this lethal cocktail was added to by nearby forest fires and the resultant air pollution led to over 20% of the population (3 million people) complaining of respiratory problems.

Acid Rain

Killing trees, poisoning lakes and rivers and eating away buildings, acid rain is mostly produced by sulphur dioxide emissions from industry and volcanic eruptions. By the mid 1990s, acid rain had sterilized 4,000 or more of Sweden's lakes and left 45% of Switzerland's alpine conifers dead or dying, while the monuments of Greece were dissolving in Athens' smog. Prevailing wind patterns mean that the acids often fall many hundred kilometres from where the original pollutants were discharged. In parts of Europe acid deposition has slightly decreased, following reductions in emissions, but not by enough.

World Pollution

Acid rain and sources of acidic emissions (latest available year)

Acid rain is caused by high levels of sulphur and nitrogen in the atmosphere. They combine with water vapour and oxygen to form acids (H_2SO_4 and HNO_3) which fall as precipitation.

 Regions where sulphur and nitrogen oxides are released in high concentrations, mainly from fossil fuel combustion

● Major cities with high levels of air pollution (including nitrogen and sulphur emissions)

Areas of heavy acid deposition

pH numbers indicate acidity, decreasing from a neutral 7. Normal rain, slightly acid from dissolved carbon dioxide, never exceeds a pH of 5.6.

- pH less than 4.0 (most acidic)
- pH 4.0 to 4.5
- pH 4.5 to 5.0
- Areas where acid rain is a potential problem

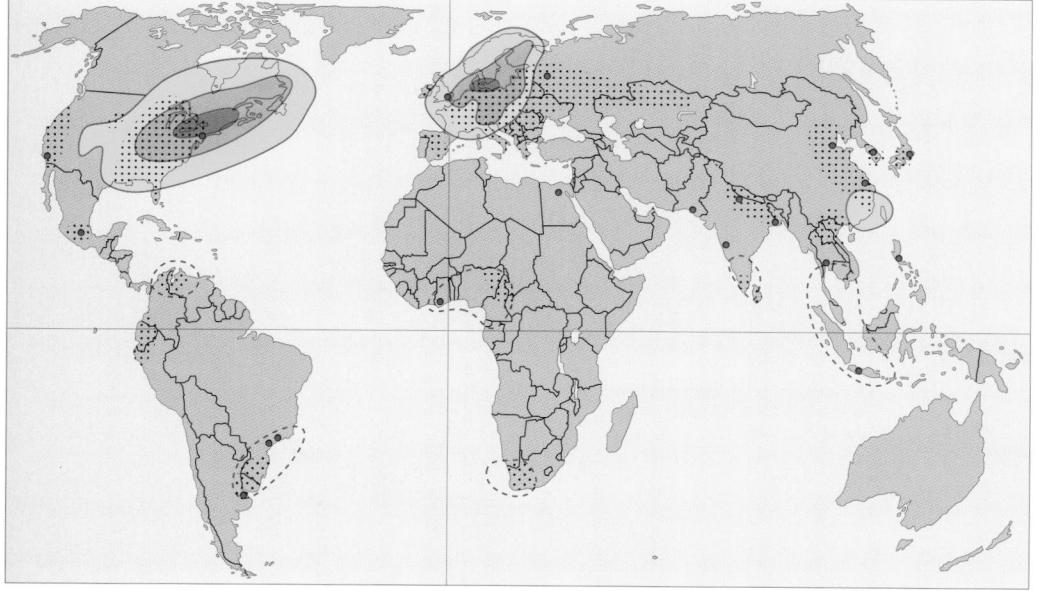

Population

Demographic Profiles

Developed nations such as the UK have populations evenly spread across the age groups and, usually, a growing proportion of elderly people. The great majority of the people in developing nations, however, are in the younger age groups, about to enter their most fertile years. In time, these population profiles should resemble the world profile (even Nigeria has made recent progress with reducing its birth rate), but the transition will come about only after a few more generations of rapid population growth.

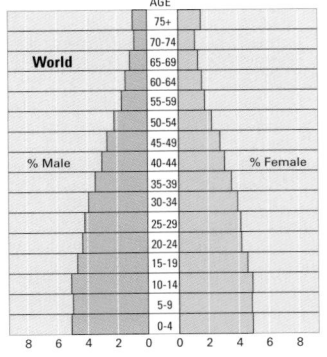

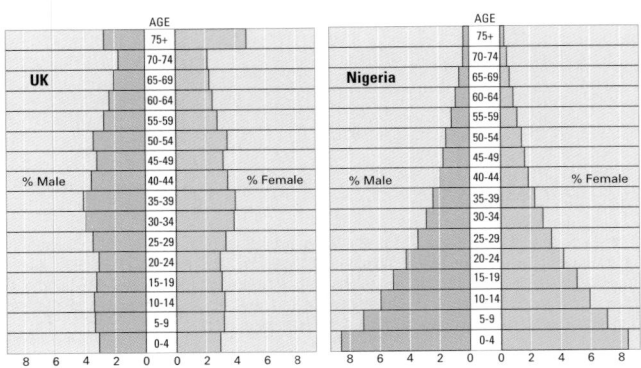

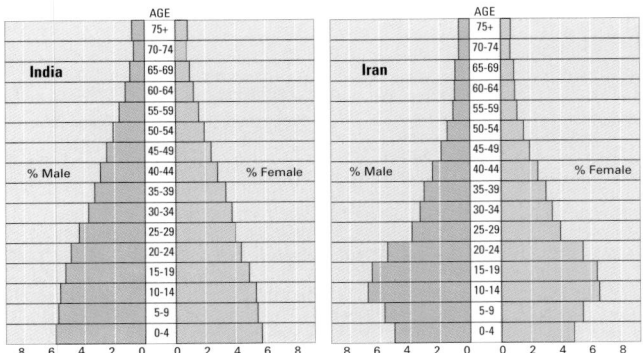

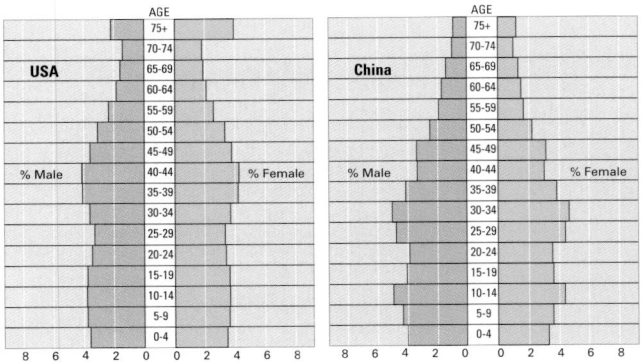

Most Populous Nations [in millions (2002 estimates)]

1.	China	1,284	9.	Nigeria	130	17. Turkey	67
2.	India	1,046	10.	Japan	127	18. Iran	67
3.	USA	281	11.	Mexico	103	19. Thailand	62
4.	Indonesia	231	12.	Philippines	85	20. UK	60
5.	Brazil	176	13.	Germany	83	21. France	60
6.	Pakistan	148	14.	Vietnam	81	22. Italy	58
7.	Russia	145	15.	Egypt	71	23. Congo (Dem. Rep.) 55
8.	Bangladesh	133	16.	Ethiopia	68	24. Ukraine	48

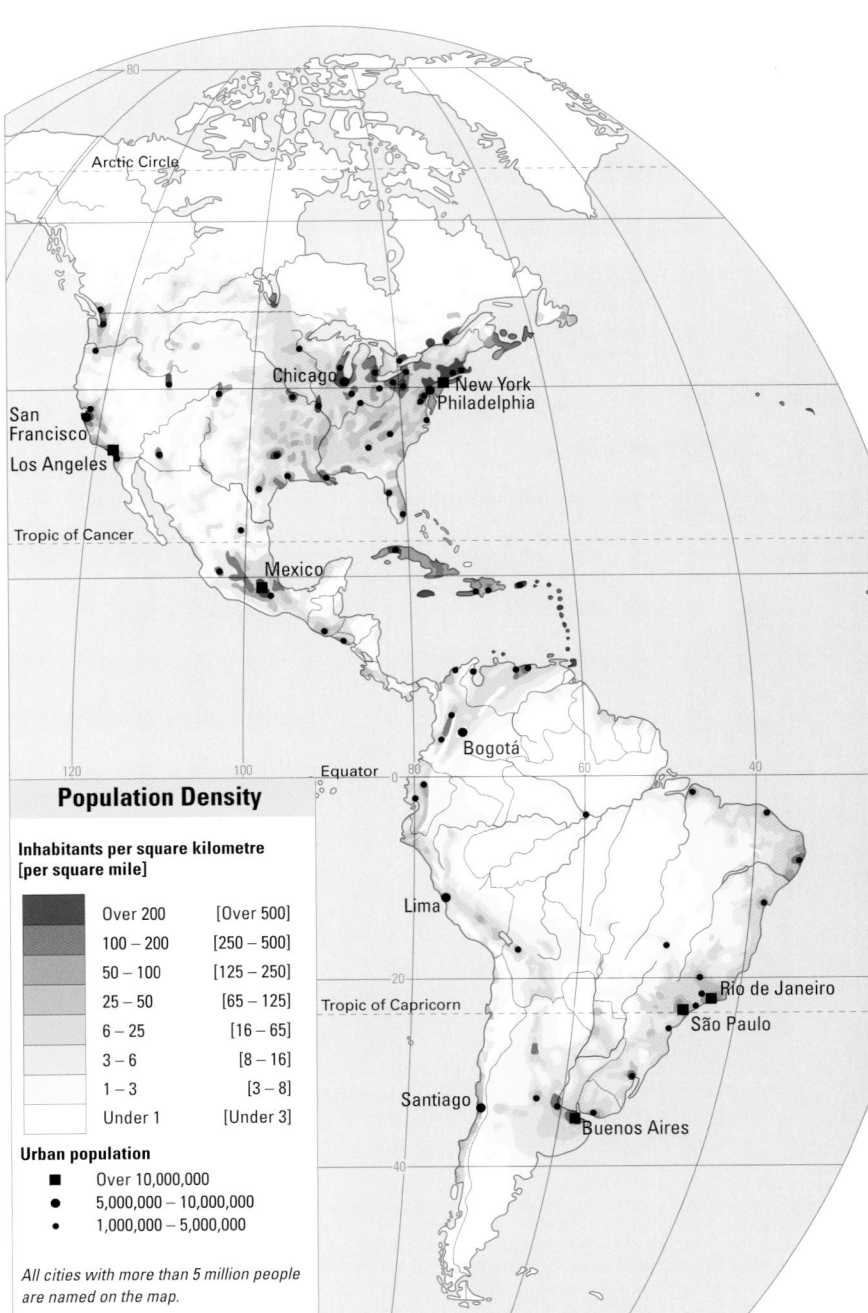

Population Density

Inhabitants per square kilometre [per square mile]

	Over 200	[Over 500]
	100 – 200	[250 – 500]
	50 – 100	[125 – 250]
	25 – 50	[65 – 125]
	6 – 25	[16 – 65]
	3 – 6	[8 – 16]
	1 – 3	[3 – 8]
	Under 1	[Under 3]

Urban population

■ Over 10,000,000
● 5,000,000 – 10,000,000
• 1,000,000 – 5,000,000

All cities with more than 5 million people are named on the map.

Continental Comparisons

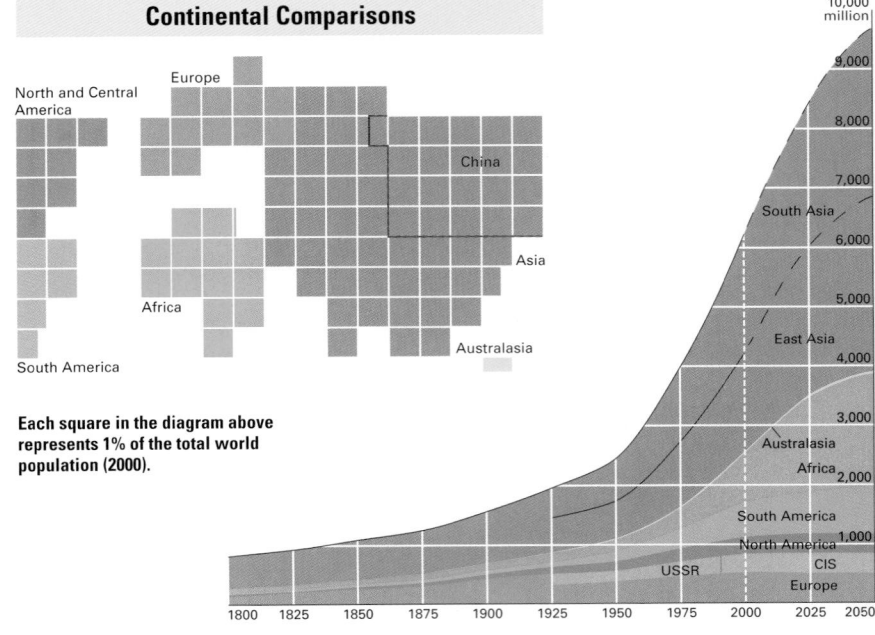

Each square in the diagram above represents 1% of the total world population (2000).

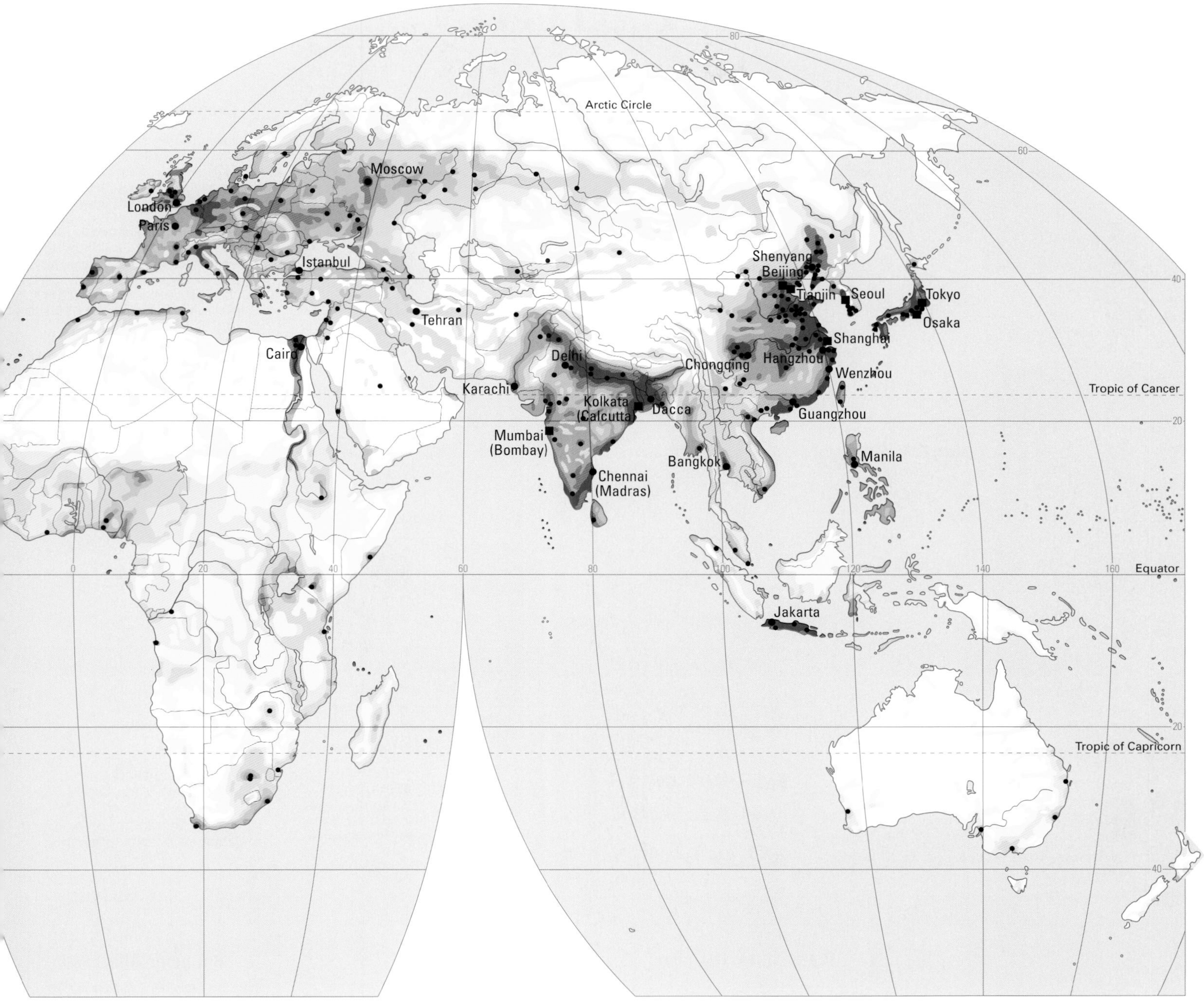

Arctic Circle

80

60

London
Paris

Moscow

40

Istanbul

Tehran

Shenyang
Beijing
Tianjin   Seoul   Tokyo
                   Osaka

Cairo

Delhi

Shanghai

Chongqing

Hangzhou

Karachi

Wenzhou

Tropic of Cancer

Kolkata
(Calcutta)

Dacca

Guangzhou

20

Mumbai
(Bombay)

Chennai
(Madras)

Bangkok

Manila

Jakarta

Equator

Tropic of Capricorn

40

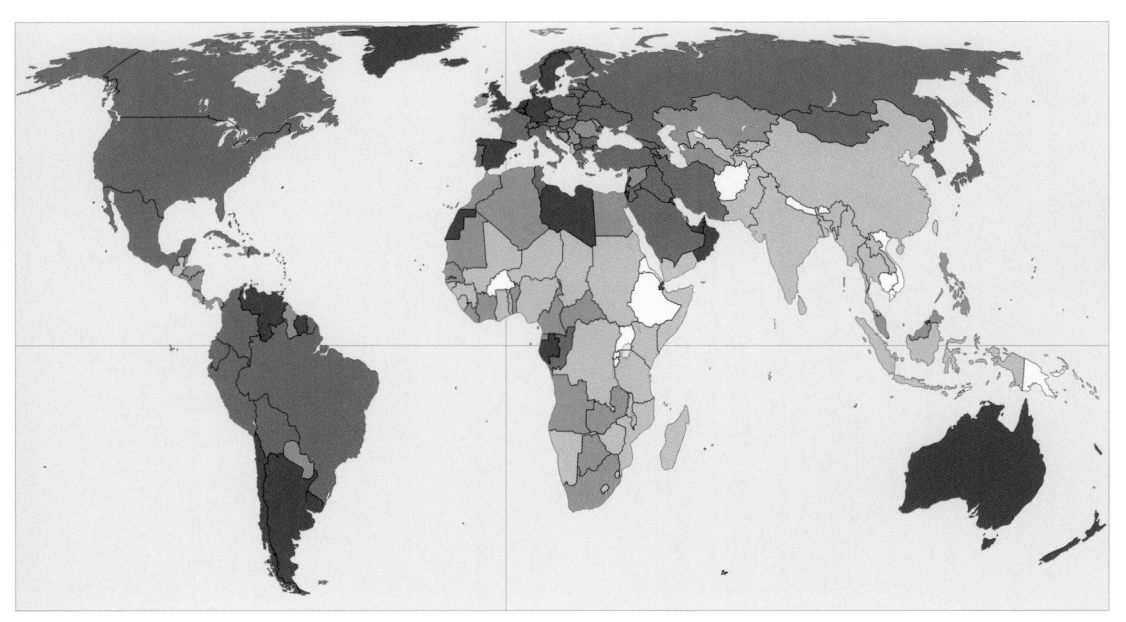

Urban Population

Percentage of total population living in towns and cities (2000)

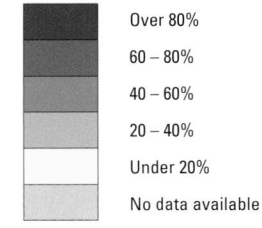

Over 80%

60 – 80%

40 – 60%

20 – 40%

Under 20%

No data available

Most urbanized		Least urbanized	
Singapore	100%	Rwanda	6.4%
Nauru	100%	Bhutan	7.3%
Monaco	100%	East Timor	7.4%
Vatican City	100%	Burundi	9.2%
Belgium	97.3%	Nepal	10.8%

The Human Family

Predominant Languages

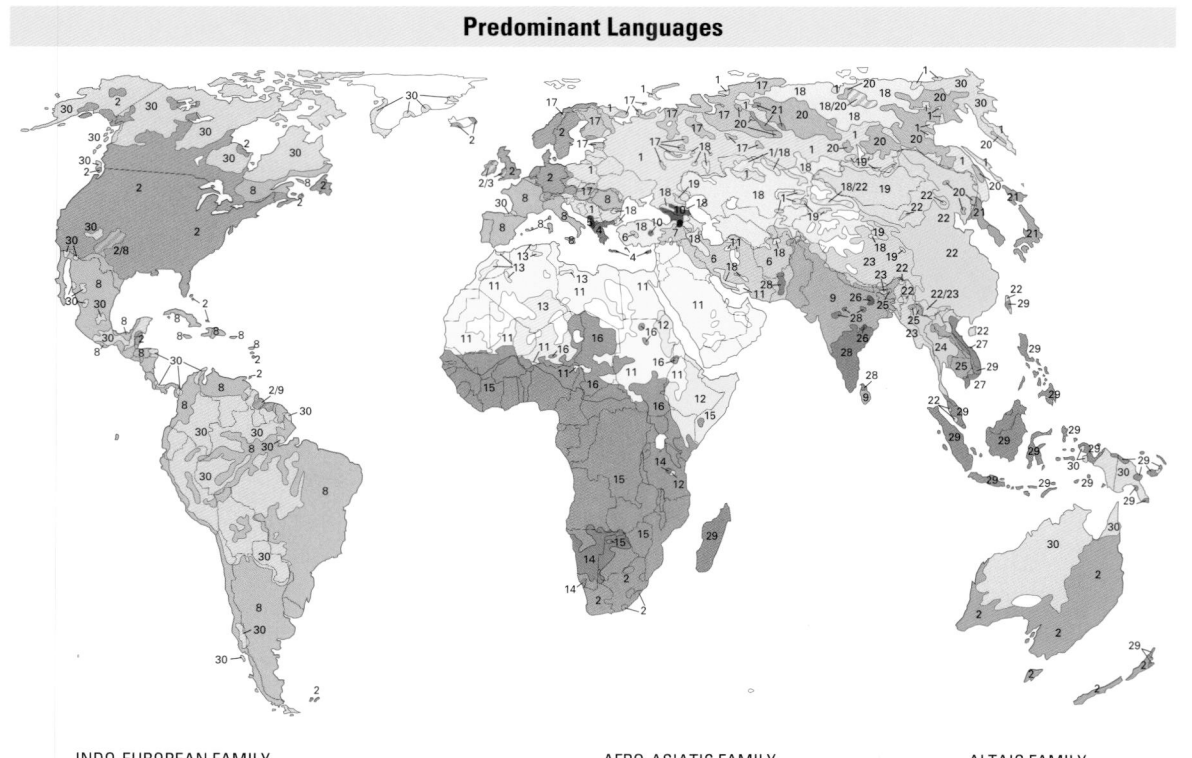

Languages of the World

Language can be classified by ancestry and structure. For example, the Romance and Germanic groups are both derived from an Indo-European language believed to have been spoken 5,000 years ago.

First-language speakers, 1999 (in millions)
Mandarin Chinese 885, Spanish 332, English 322, Bengali 189, Hindi 182, Portuguese 170, Russian 170, Japanese 125, German 98, Wu Chinese 77, Javanese 76, Korean 75, French 72, Vietnamese 68, Yue Chinese 66, Marathi 65, Tamil 63, Turkish 59, Urdu 58.

Official languages (% of total population)
English 27%, Chinese 19%, Hindi 13.5%, Spanish 5.4%, Russian 5.2%, French 4.2%, Arabic 3.3%, Portuguese 3%, Malay 3%, Bengali 2.9%, Japanese 2.3%.

INDO-EUROPEAN FAMILY

1. Balto-Slavic group (incl. Russian, Ukrainian)
2. Germanic group (incl. English, German)
3. Celtic group
4. Greek
5. Albanian
6. Iranian group
7. Armenian
8. Romance group (incl. Spanish, Portuguese, French, Italian)
9. Indo-Aryan group (incl. Hindi, Bengali, Urdu, Punjabi, Marathi)
10. CAUCASIAN FAMILY

AFRO-ASIATIC FAMILY

11. Semitic group (incl. Arabic)
12. Kushitic group
13. Berber group

14. KHOISAN FAMILY
15. NIGER-CONGO FAMILY
16. NILO-SAHARAN FAMILY
17. URALIC FAMILY

ALTAIC FAMILY

18. Turkic group (incl. Turkish)
19. Mongolian group
20. Tungus-Manchu group
21. Japanese and Korean

SINO-TIBETAN FAMILY

22. Sinitic (Chinese) languages (incl. Mandarin, Wu, Yue)
23. Tibetic-Burmic languages

24. TAI FAMILY

AUSTRO-ASIATIC FAMILY

25. Mon-Khmer group
26. Munda group
27. Vietnamese

28. DRAVIDIAN FAMILY (incl. Telugu, Tamil)

29. AUSTRONESIAN FAMILY (incl. Malay-Indonesian, Javanese)

30. OTHER LANGUAGES

Predominant Religions

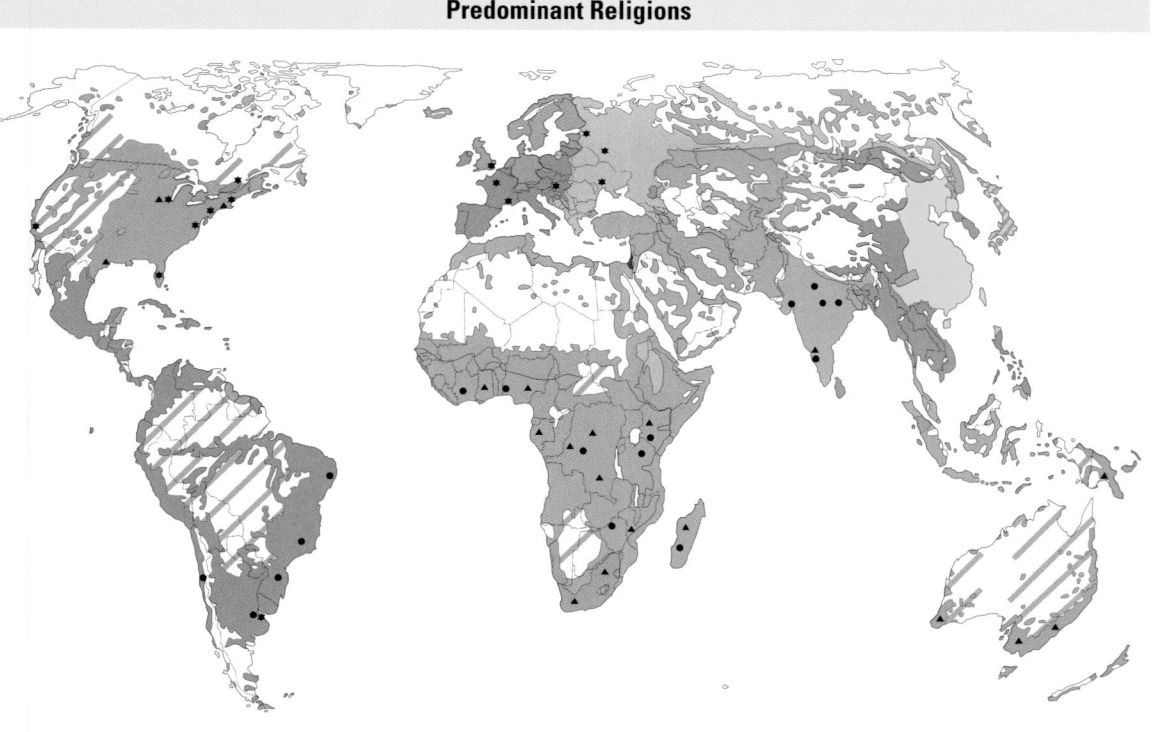

Religious Adherents

Religious adherents in millions (2001)

Christianity	2 019	Hindu	820
Roman Catholic	*1 067*	Chinese folk	387
Protestant	*346*	Buddhism	362
Orthodox	*216*	Ethnic religions	242
Anglican	*80*	New religions	103
Independent	*392*	Sikhism	24
Others	*139*	Judaism	14
Islam	1 207	Spiritism	12
Sunni	*1 002*	Baha'i	7
Shiite	*193*	Confucianism	6
Others	*12*	Jainism	4
Non-religious/		Shintoism	3
Agnostic/Atheist	921		

- Roman Catholicism
- Orthodox and other Eastern Churches
- Protestantism
- Sunni Islam
- Shiite Islam
- Buddhism
- Hinduism
- Confucianism
- Judaism
- Shintoism
- Tribal Religions

United Nations

Created in 1945 to promote peace and co-operation and based in New York, the United Nations is the world's largest international organization, with 191 members and an annual budget of US $1.3 billion (2002). Each member of the General Assembly has one vote, while the five permanent members of the 15-nation Security Council – China, France, Russia, UK and USA – hold a veto. The Secretariat is the UN's principal administrative arm. The 54 members of the Economic and Social Council are responsible for economic, social, cultural, educational, health and related matters. The UN has 16 specialized agencies – based in Canada, France, Switzerland and Italy, as well as the USA – which help members in fields such as education (UNESCO), agriculture (FAO), medicine (WHO) and finance (IFC). By the end of 1994, all the original 11 trust territories of the Trusteeship Council had become independent.

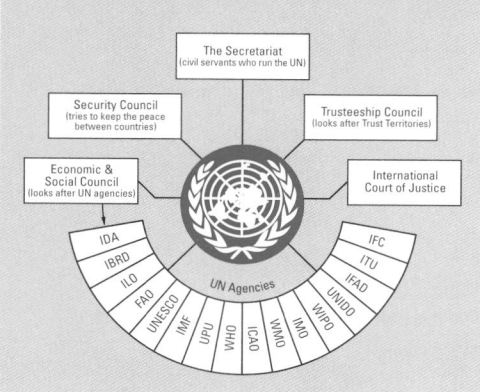

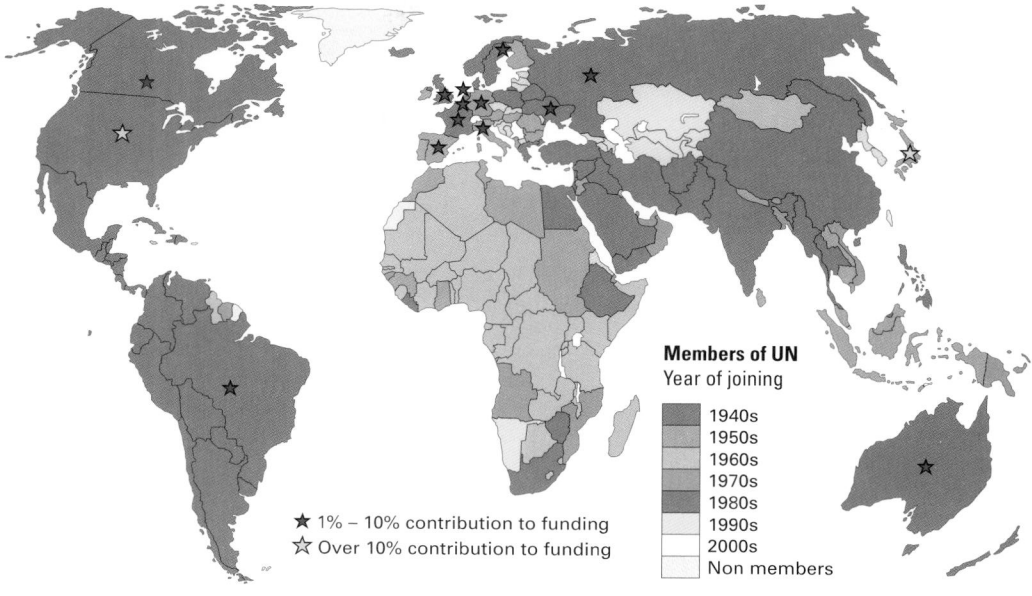

Members of UN
Year of joining

- 1940s
- 1950s
- 1960s
- 1970s
- 1980s
- 1990s
- 2000s
- Non members

★ 1% – 10% contribution to funding
☆ Over 10% contribution to funding

MEMBERSHIP OF THE UN In 1945 there were 51 members; by the end of 2002 membership had increased to 191 following the admission of East Timor and Switzerland. There are 2 independent states which are not members of the UN – Taiwan and the Vatican City. All the successor states of the former USSR had joined by the end of 1992. The official languages of the UN are Chinese, English, French, Russian, Spanish and Arabic.

FUNDING The UN regular budget for 2002 was US $1.3 billion. Contributions are assessed by the members' ability to pay, with the maximum 22% of the total (USA's share), the minimum 0.01%. The 15-country European Union pays over 37% of the budget.

PEACEKEEPING The UN has been involved in 54 peacekeeping operations worldwide since 1948.

International Organizations

ACP African-Caribbean-Pacific (formed in 1963). Members have economic ties with the EU.
ARAB LEAGUE (formed in 1945). The League's aim is to promote economic, social, political and military co-operation. There are 21 member nations.
ASEAN Association of South-east Asian Nations (formed in 1967). Cambodia joined in 1999.
AU The African Union replaced the Organization of African Unity (formed in 1963) in 2002. Its 53 members represent over 94% of Africa's population. Arabic, French, Portuguese and English are recognized as working languages.
CIS The Commonwealth of Independent States (formed in 1991) comprises the countries of the former Soviet Union except for Estonia, Latvia and Lithuania.
COLOMBO PLAN (formed in 1951). Its 25 members aim to promote economic and social development in Asia and the Pacific.
COMMONWEALTH The Commonwealth of Nations evolved from the British Empire; it comprises 16 Queen's realms, 32 republics and 5 indigenous monarchies, giving a total of 53. Nigeria was suspended in 1995, but reinstated in 1999.
EFTA European Free Trade Association (formed in 1960). Portugal left the original 'Seven' in 1989 to join what was then the EC, followed by Austria, Finland and Sweden in 1995. Only 4 members remain: Norway, Iceland, Switzerland and Liechtenstein.
EU European Union (evolved from the European Community in 1993). The 15 members – Austria, Belgium, Denmark, Finland, France, Germany, Greece, Ireland, Italy, Luxembourg, Netherlands, Portugal, Spain, Sweden and the UK – aim to integrate economies, co-ordinate social developments and bring about political union. These members, of what is now the world's biggest market, share agricultural and industrial policies and tariffs on trade. The original body, the European Coal and Steel Community (ECSC), was created in 1951 following the signing of the Treaty of Paris.
LAIA Latin American Integration Association (1980). Its aim is to promote freer regional trade.
NATO North Atlantic Treaty Organization (formed in 1949). It continues after 1991 despite the winding up of the Warsaw Pact. The Czech Republic, Hungary and Poland were the latest members to join in 1999.
OAS Organization of American States (formed in 1948). It aims to promote social and economic co-operation between developed countries of North America and developing nations of Latin America.

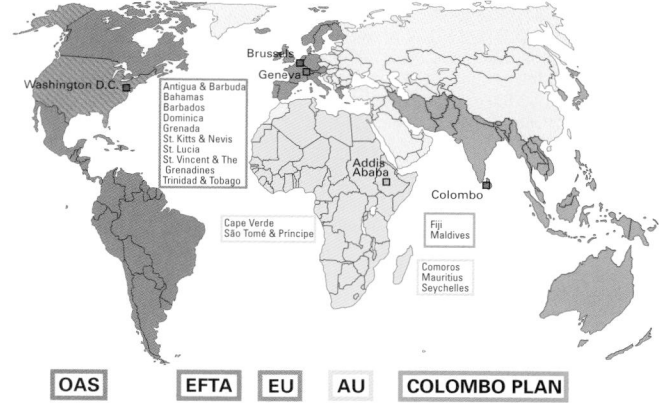

OAS   EFTA   EU   AU   COLOMBO PLAN

OECD Organization for Economic Co-operation and Development (formed in 1961). It comprises 30 major free-market economies. Poland, Hungary and South Korea joined in 1996. 'G8' is its 'inner group' of leading industrial nations, comprising Canada, France, Germany, Italy, Japan, Russia, UK and USA.
OPEC Organization of Petroleum Exporting Countries (formed in 1960). It controls about three-quarters of the world's oil supply. Gabon left the organization in 1996.

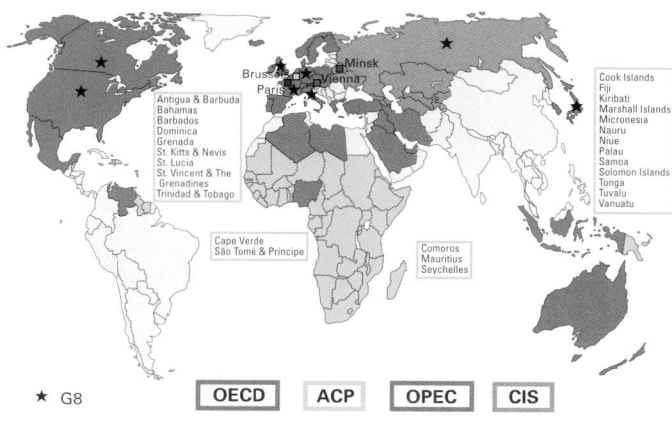

★ G8   OECD   ACP   OPEC   CIS

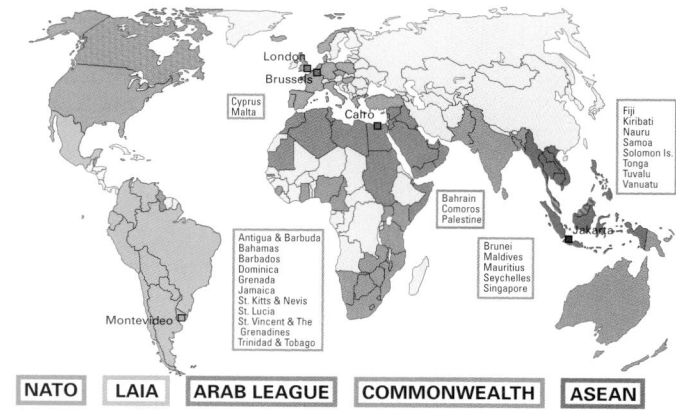

NATO   LAIA   ARAB LEAGUE   COMMONWEALTH   ASEAN

Wealth

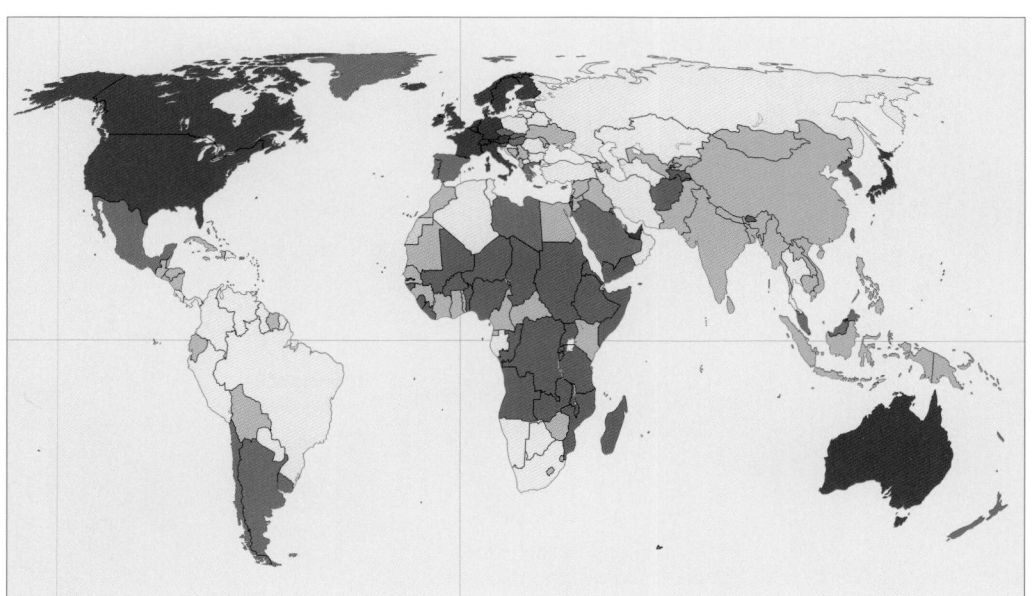

Highest GDP (US $)		Lowest GDP (US $)	
Luxembourg	$36,400	Sierra Leone	$510
USA	$36,200	Congo (Dem. Rep.)	$600
San Marino	$32,000	Ethiopia	$600
Switzerland	$28,600	Somalia	$600
Norway	$27,700	Eritrea	$710

Wealth Creation

The Gross Domestic Product (GDP) of the world's largest economies, US $ million (2001)

1.	USA	10,082,000	23.	Taiwan	386,000
2.	China	5,560,000	24.	Poland	340,000
3.	Japan	3,450,000	25.	Philippines	335,000
4.	India	2,500,000	26.	Pakistan	299,000
5.	Germany	2,174,000	27.	Belgium	268,000
6.	France	1,510,000	28.	Egypt	258,000
7.	UK	1,470,000	29.	Colombia	255,000
8.	Italy	1,402,000	30.	Saudi Arabia	241,000
9.	Brazil	1,340,000	31.	Bangladesh	230,000
10.	Russia	1,200,000	32.	Switzerland	226,000
11.	Mexico	920,000	33.	Austria	220,000
12.	Canada	875,000	34.	Sweden	219,000
13.	South Korea	865,000	35.	Ukraine	205,000
14.	Spain	757,000	36.	Malaysia	200,000
15.	Indonesia	687,000	37.	Greece	190,000
16.	Australia	466,000	38.	Hong Kong	180,000
17.	Argentina	453,000	39.	Algeria	177,000
18.	Turkey	443,000	40.	Portugal	174,000
19.	Iran	426,000	41.	Vietnam	168,000
20.	Netherlands	413,000	42.	Chile	153,000
21.	South Africa	412,000	43.	Romania	153,000
22.	Thailand	410,000	44.	Denmark	150,000

The Wealth Gap

The world's richest and poorest countries, by Gross Domestic Product per capita in US $ (2001)

1.	Luxembourg	43,400	1.	Sierra Leone	500
2.	USA	36,300	2.	East Timor	500
3.	San Marino	34,600	3.	Somalia	550
4.	Norway	31,800	4.	Congo (D. Rep.)	590
5.	Switzerland	31,100	5.	Burundi	600
6.	Denmark	29,000	6.	Tanzania	610
7.	Canada	27,700	7.	Malawi	660
8.	Ireland	27,300	8.	Ethiopia	700
9.	Japan	27,200	9.	Comoros	710
10.	Austria	27,000	10.	Eritrea	740
11.	Monaco	27,000	11.	Afghanistan	800
12.	Finland	26,200	12.	Yemen	820
13.	Germany	26,200	13.	Niger	820
14.	Belgium	26,100	14.	Nigeria	840
15.	Netherlands	25,800	15.	Mali	840
16.	France	25,700	16.	Kiribati	840
17.	Sweden	25,400	17.	Zambia	870
18.	Hong Kong (China)	25,000	18.	Madagascar	870
19.	Iceland	24,800	19.	Mozambique	900
20.	Singapore	24,700	20.	Guinea-Bissau	900

GDP per capita is calculated by dividing a country's Gross Domestic Product by its total population.

Continental Shares

Shares of population and of wealth (GNP) by continent

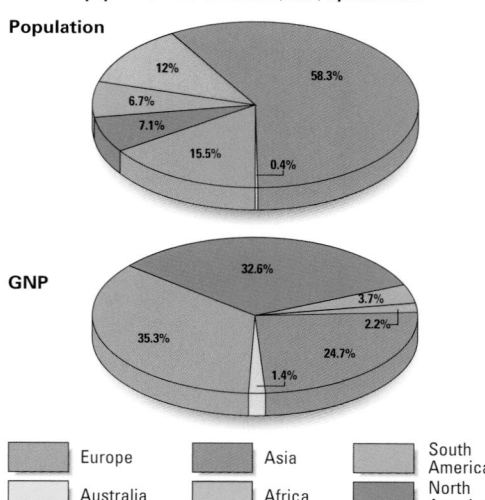

Population

GNP

- Europe
- Australia
- Asia
- Africa
- South America
- North America

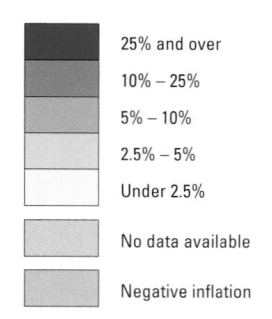
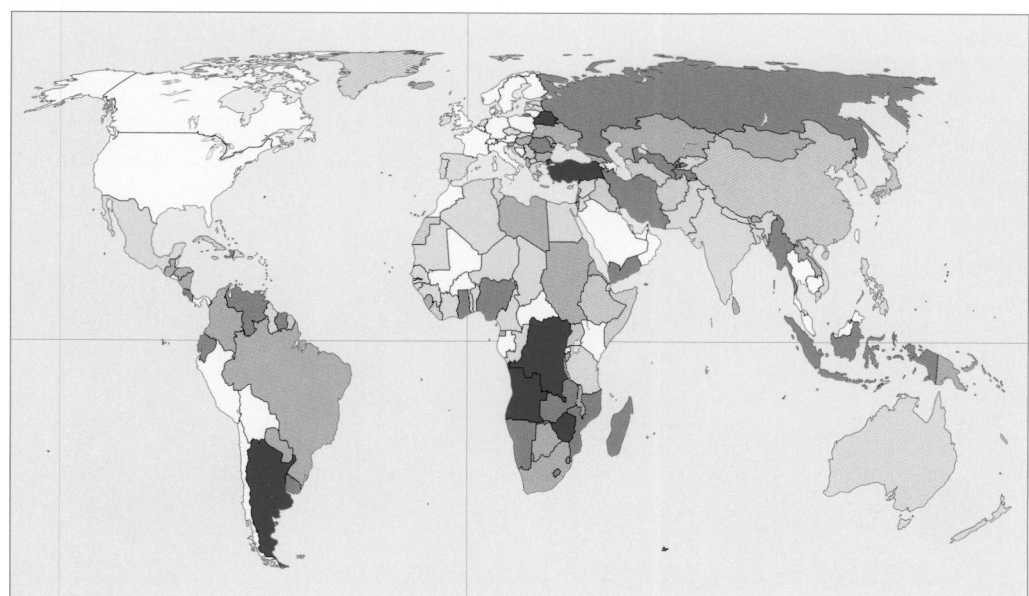

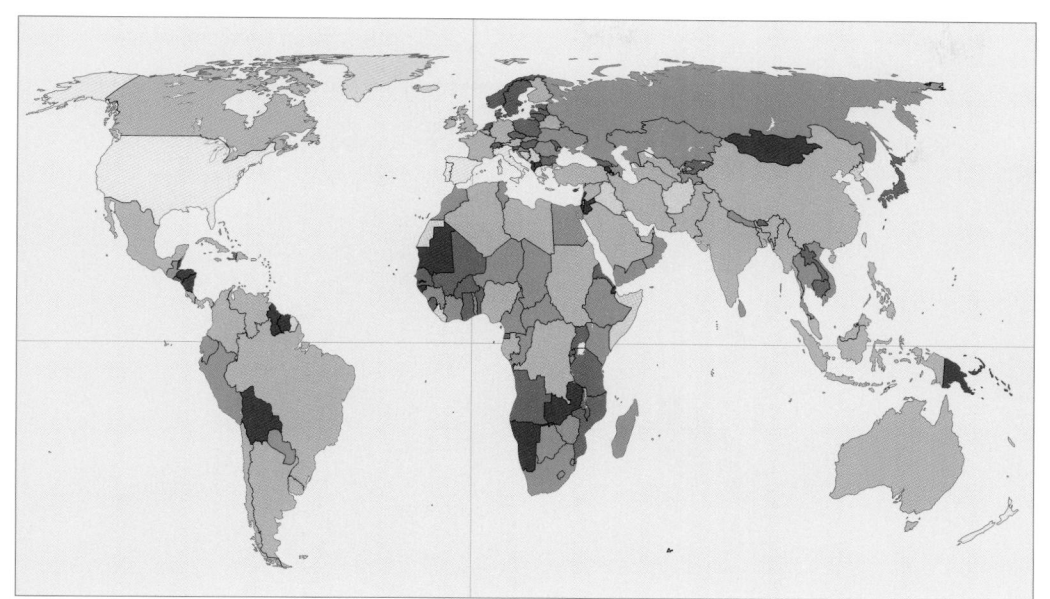

Official Development Assistance (ODA) provided and received, per capita (2002)

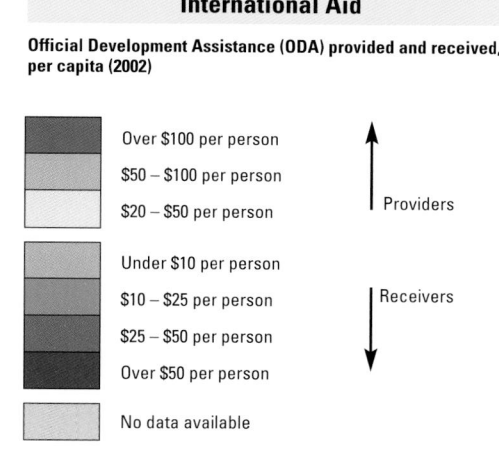

- Over $100 per person
- $50 – $100 per person
- $20 – $50 per person

Providers

- Under $10 per person
- $10 – $25 per person
- $25 – $50 per person
- Over $50 per person

Receivers

- No data available

Debt and Aid

International debtors and the aid they receive

Although aid grants make a vital contribution to many of the world's poorer countries, they are usually dwarfed by the burden of debt that the developing economies are expected to repay. It is estimated that the total debt burden of developing countries is US $410 billion, while the cost of servicing that debt amounts to US $25 billion a year.

Debt, US $ per capita (2000)

Aid, US $ per capita (2000)

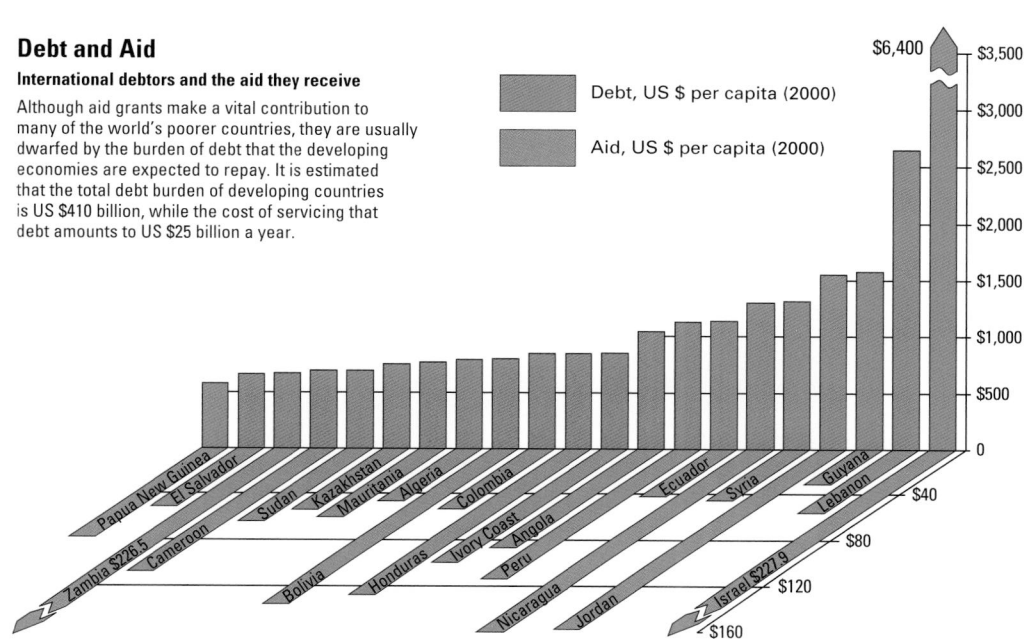

Distribution of Spending

Percentage share of household spending, selected countries

- Food
- Clothing
- Energy & Housing
- Medicine & Education
- Transport
- Other

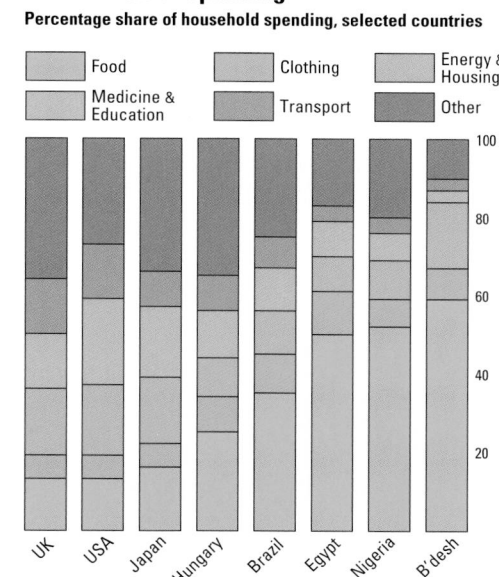

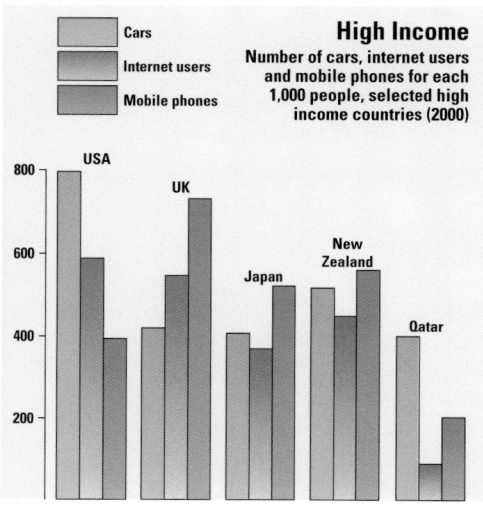

High Income

Number of cars, internet users and mobile phones for each 1,000 people, selected high income countries (2000)

- Cars
- Internet users
- Mobile phones

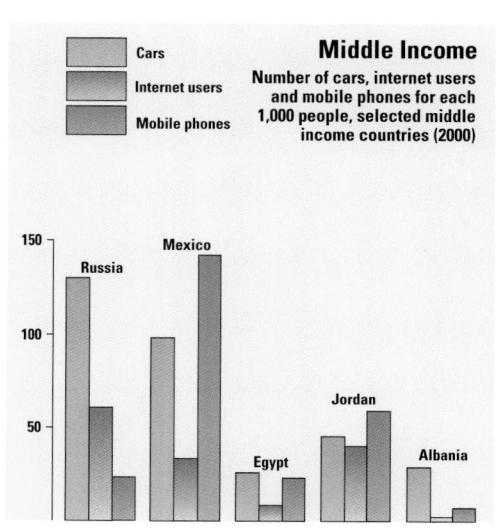

Middle Income

Number of cars, internet users and mobile phones for each 1,000 people, selected middle income countries (2000)

- Cars
- Internet users
- Mobile phones

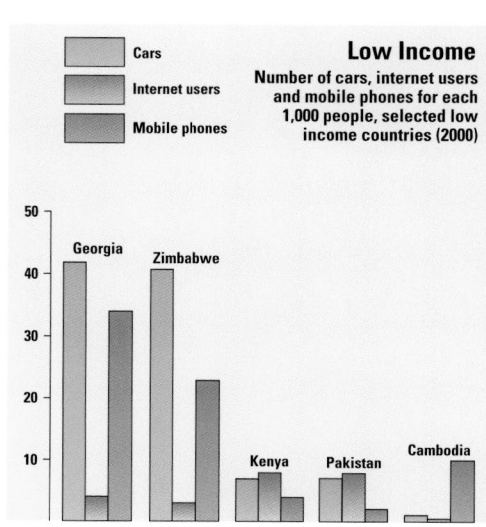

Low Income

Number of cars, internet users and mobile phones for each 1,000 people, selected low income countries (2000)

- Cars
- Internet users
- Mobile phones

Quality of Life

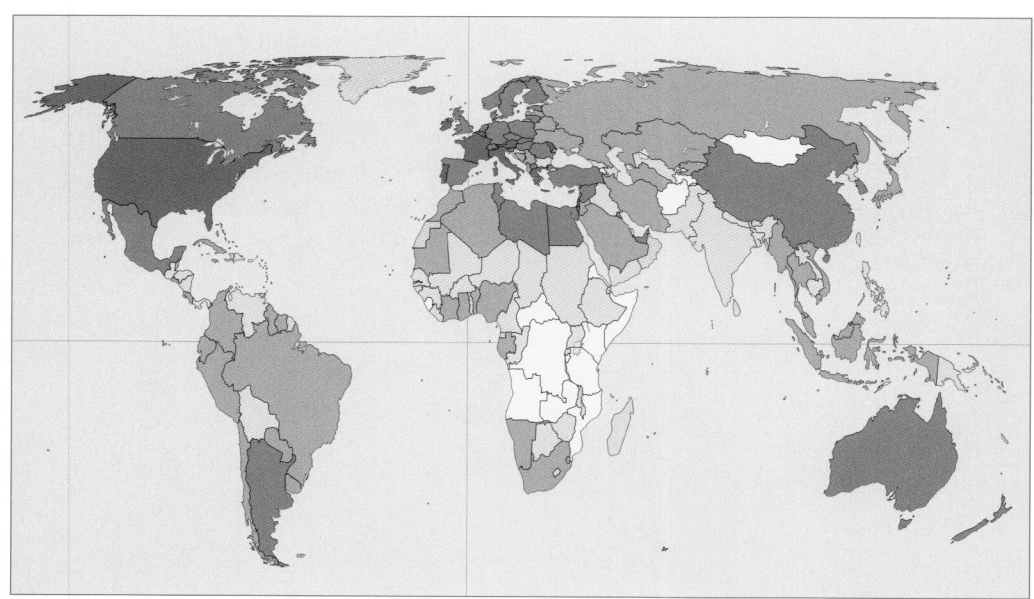

Hospital Capacity

Hospital beds available for each 1,000 people (latest available year)

Highest capacity		Lowest capacity	
Switzerland	20.8	Benin	0.2
Japan	16.2	Nepal	0.2
Tajikistan	16.0	Afghanistan	0.3
Norway	13.5	Bangladesh	0.3
Belarus	12.4	Ethiopia	0.3
Kazakhstan	12.2	Mali	0.4
Moldova	12.2	Burkina Faso	0.5
Ukraine	12.2	Niger	0.5
Latvia	11.9	Guinea	0.6
Russia	11.8	India	0.6

[UK 4.9] [USA 4.2]

Although the ratio of people to hospital beds gives a good approximation of a country's health provision, it is not an absolute indicator. Raw numbers may mask inefficiency and other weaknesses: the high availability of beds in Kazakhstan, for example, has not prevented infant mortality rates over three times as high as in the United Kingdom and the United States.

Life Expectancy

Years of life expectancy at birth, selected countries (2001)

The chart shows combined data for both sexes. On average, women live longer than men worldwide, even in developing countries with high maternal mortality rates. Overall, life expectancy is steadily rising, though the difference between rich and poor nations remains dramatic.

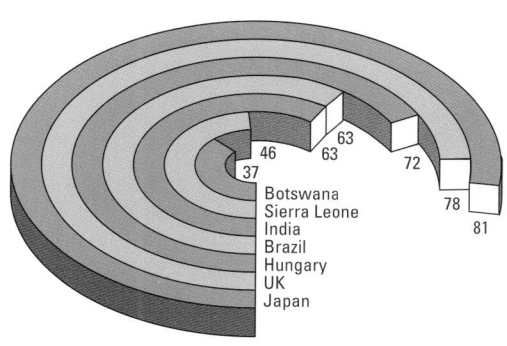

37 — Botswana
46 — Sierra Leone
63 — India
63 — Brazil
72 — Hungary
78 — UK
81 — Japan

Causes of Death

Causes of death for selected countries by percentage

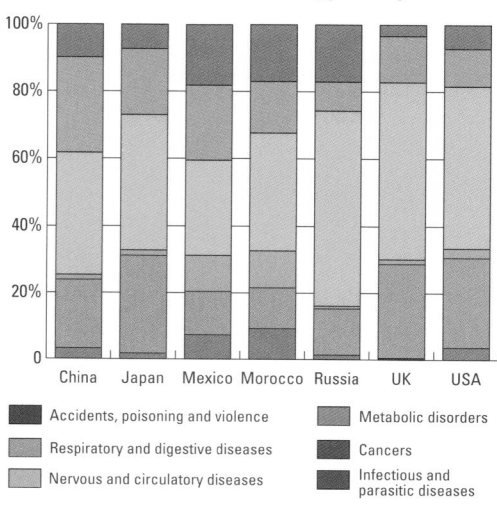

China, Japan, Mexico, Morocco, Russia, UK, USA

- Accidents, poisoning and violence
- Respiratory and digestive diseases
- Nervous and circulatory diseases
- Metabolic disorders
- Cancers
- Infectious and parasitic diseases

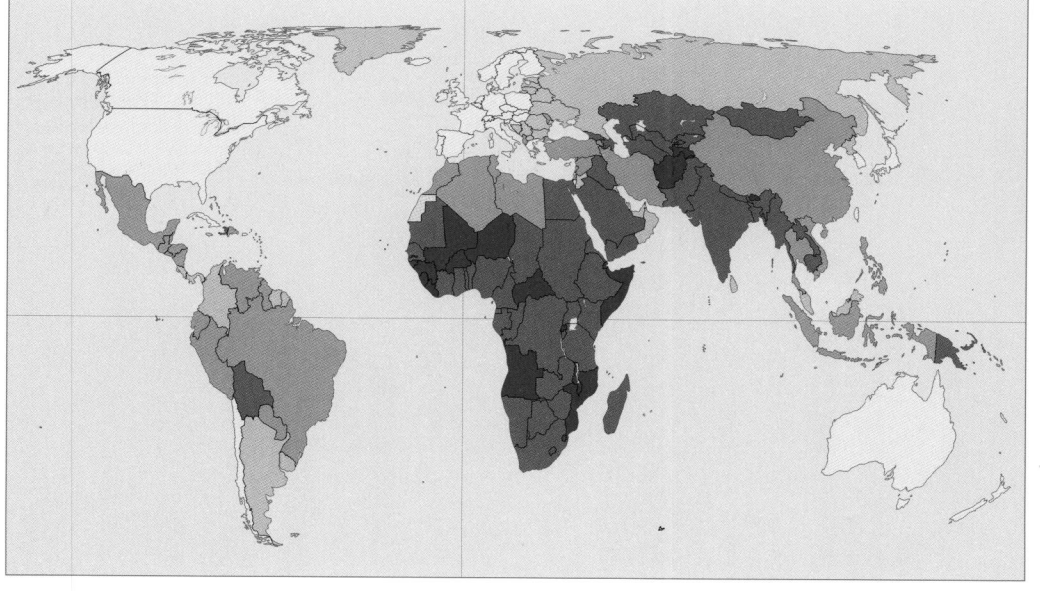

Infant Mortality

Number of babies who died under the age of one, per 1,000 live births (2001)

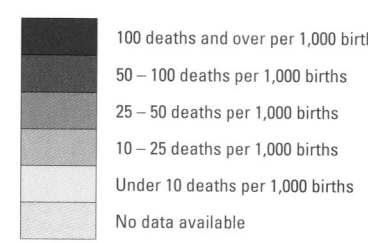

- 100 deaths and over per 1,000 births
- 50 – 100 deaths per 1,000 births
- 25 – 50 deaths per 1,000 births
- 10 – 25 deaths per 1,000 births
- Under 10 deaths per 1,000 births
- No data available

Highest infant mortality		Lowest infant mortality	
Angola	194 deaths	Sweden	3 deaths
Afghanistan	147 deaths	Iceland	4 deaths
Sierra Leone	147 deaths	Singapore	4 deaths
Mozambique	139 deaths	Finland	4 deaths
Liberia	132 deaths	Japan	4 deaths

[UK 6 deaths]

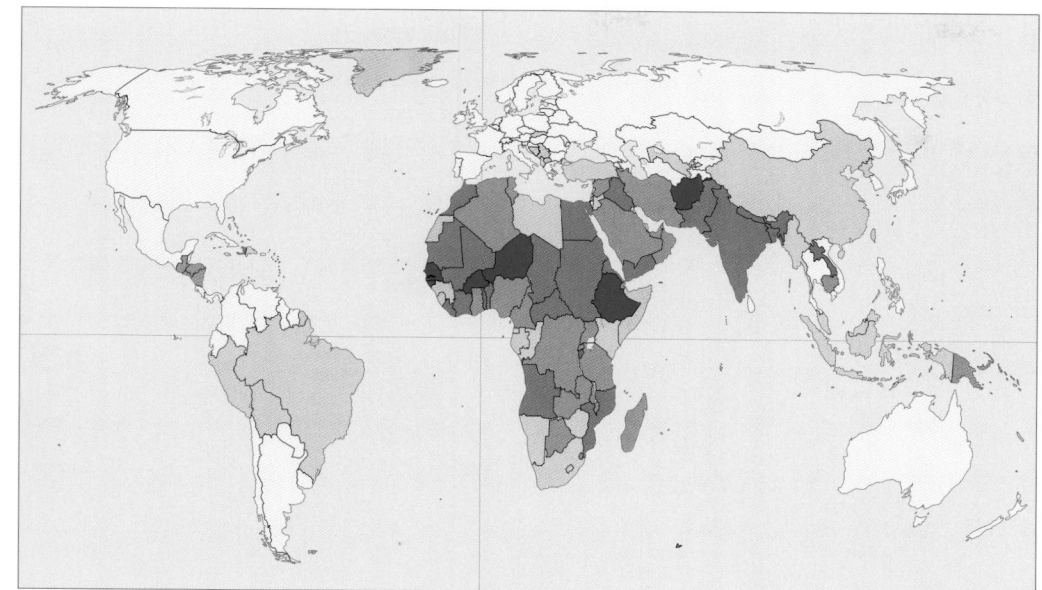

Illiteracy

Percentage of the total adult population unable to read or write (2000)

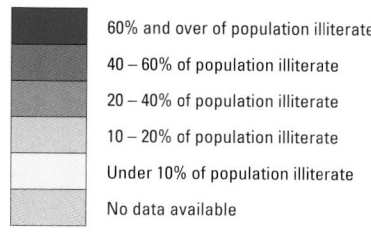

- 60% and over of population illiterate
- 40 – 60% of population illiterate
- 20 – 40% of population illiterate
- 10 – 20% of population illiterate
- Under 10% of population illiterate
- No data available

Countries with the highest and lowest illiteracy rates

Highest		Lowest	
Niger	84	Australia	0
Burkina Faso	76	Denmark	0
Gambia	63	Estonia	0
Afghanistan	63	Finland	0
Senegal	63	Luxembourg	0

[UK 1%]

Fertility and Education

Fertility rates compared with female education, selected countries (1995–2000)

Percentage of females aged 12–17 in secondary education

Fertility rate: average number of children borne per woman

UK, Canada, Greece, Lebanon, USA, Chile, Botswana, Poland, Kuwait, Oman, Thailand, China, Ecuador, Namibia, Yemen, Cambodia, Uganda, Niger

Living Standards

At first sight, most international contrasts in living standards are swamped by differences in wealth. The rich not only have more money, they have more of everything, including years of life. Those with only a little money are obliged to spend most of it on food and clothing, the basic maintenance costs of their existence; air travel and tourism are unlikely to feature on their expenditure lists. However, poverty and wealth are both relative: slum dwellers living on social security payments in an affluent industrial country have far more resources at their disposal than an average African peasant, but feel their own poverty nonetheless. A middle-class Indian lawyer cannot command a fraction of the earnings of a counterpart living in New York, London or Rome; nevertheless, he rightly sees himself as prosperous.

The rich not only live longer, on average, than the poor, they also die from different causes. Infectious and parasitic diseases, all but eliminated in the developed world, remain a scourge in the developing nations. On the other hand, more than two-thirds of the populations of OECD nations eventually succumb to cancer or circulatory disease.

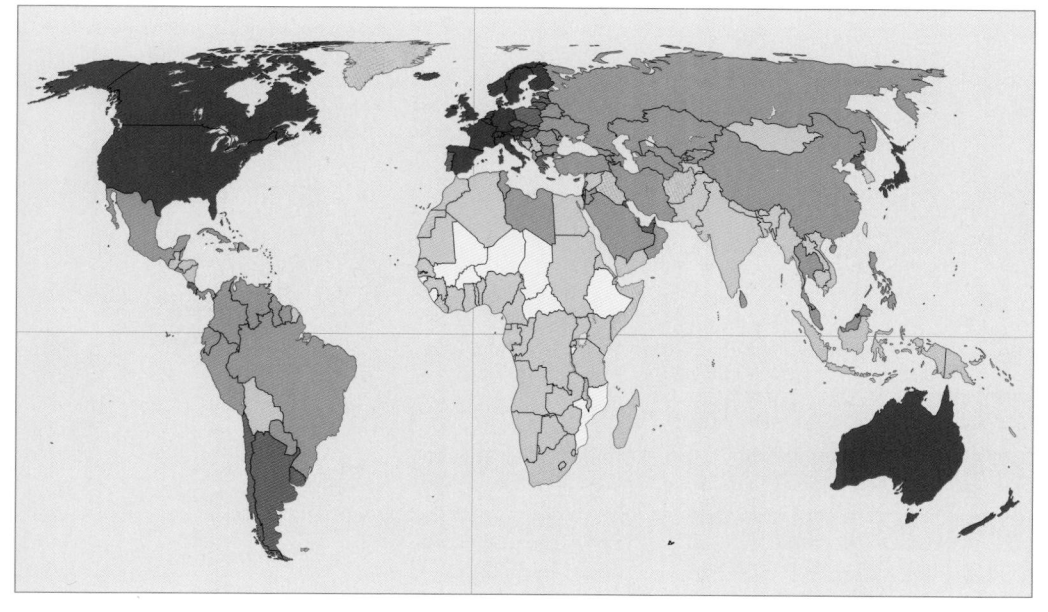

Human Development Index

The Human Development Index (HDI), calculated by the UN Development Programme, gives a value to countries using indicators of life expectancy, education and standards of living in 2000. Higher values show more developed countries.

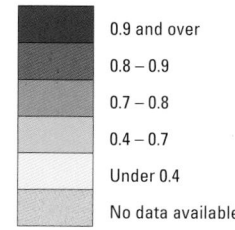

- 0.9 and over
- 0.8 – 0.9
- 0.7 – 0.8
- 0.4 – 0.7
- Under 0.4
- No data available

Highest values		Lowest values	
Norway	0.942	Sierra Leone	0.275
Sweden	0.941	Niger	0.277
Canada	0.940	Burundi	0.313
USA	0.939	Mozambique	0.322
Belgium	0.939	Burkina Faso	0.325

[UK 0.928]

Energy

Production

Each square represents 1% of world energy production (2000)

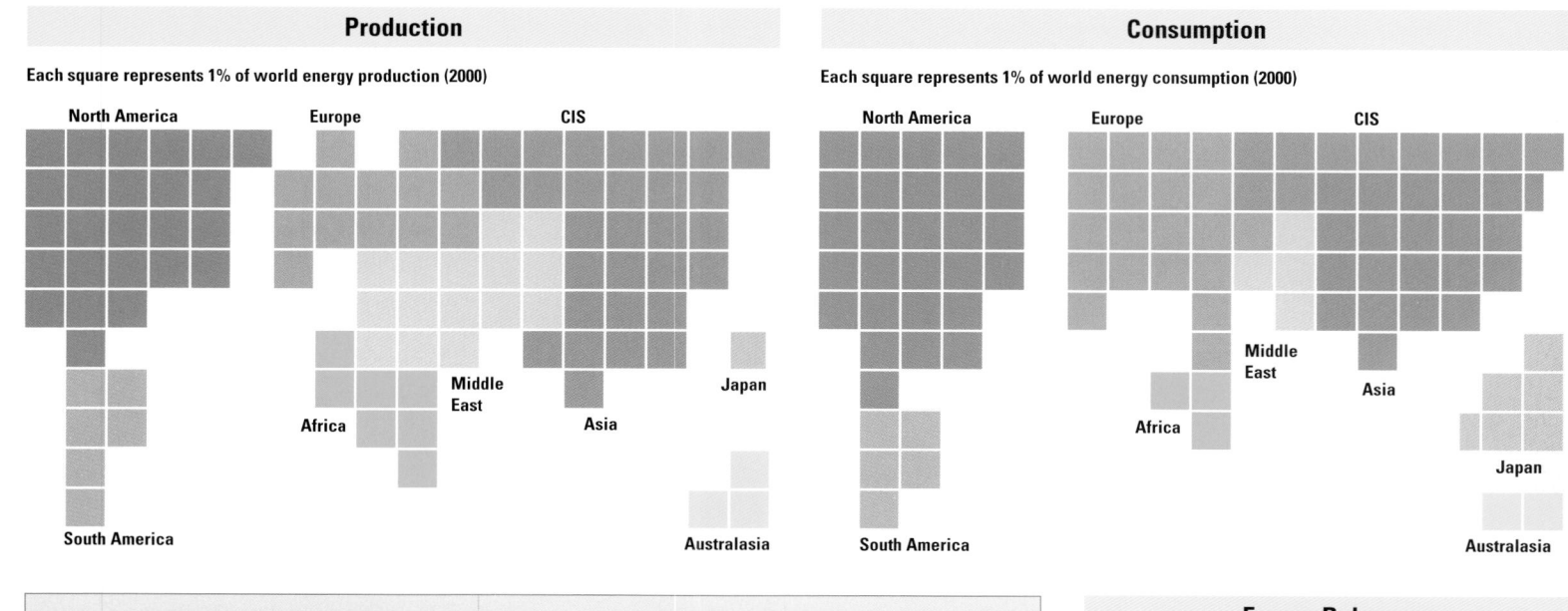

North America   Europe   CIS

Middle East   Japan

Africa   Asia

South America   Australasia

Consumption

Each square represents 1% of world energy consumption (2000)

North America   Europe   CIS

Middle East   Asia

Africa

Japan

South America   Australasia

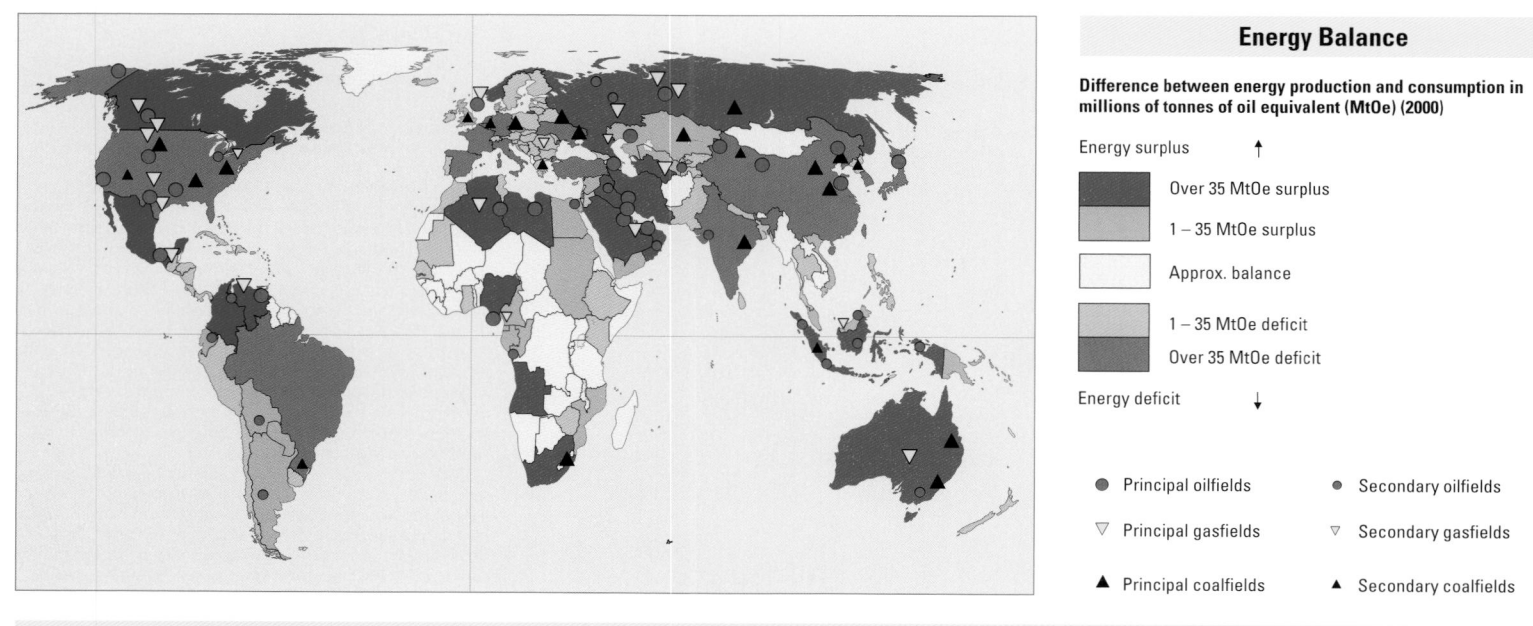

Energy Balance

Difference between energy production and consumption in millions of tonnes of oil equivalent (MtOe) (2000)

Energy surplus ↑

- Over 35 MtOe surplus
- 1 – 35 MtOe surplus
- Approx. balance
- 1 – 35 MtOe deficit
- Over 35 MtOe deficit

Energy deficit ↓

- ● Principal oilfields
- ● Secondary oilfields
- ▽ Principal gasfields
- ▽ Secondary gasfields
- ▲ Principal coalfields
- ▲ Secondary coalfields

World Energy Consumption

Energy consumed by world regions, measured in million tonnes of oil equivalent in 2001. Total world consumption was 9,125 MtOe. Only energy from oil, gas, coal, nuclear and hydroelectric sources are included. Excluded are fuels such as wood, peat, animal waste, wind, solar and geothermal which, though important in some countries, are unreliably documented in terms of consumption statistics.

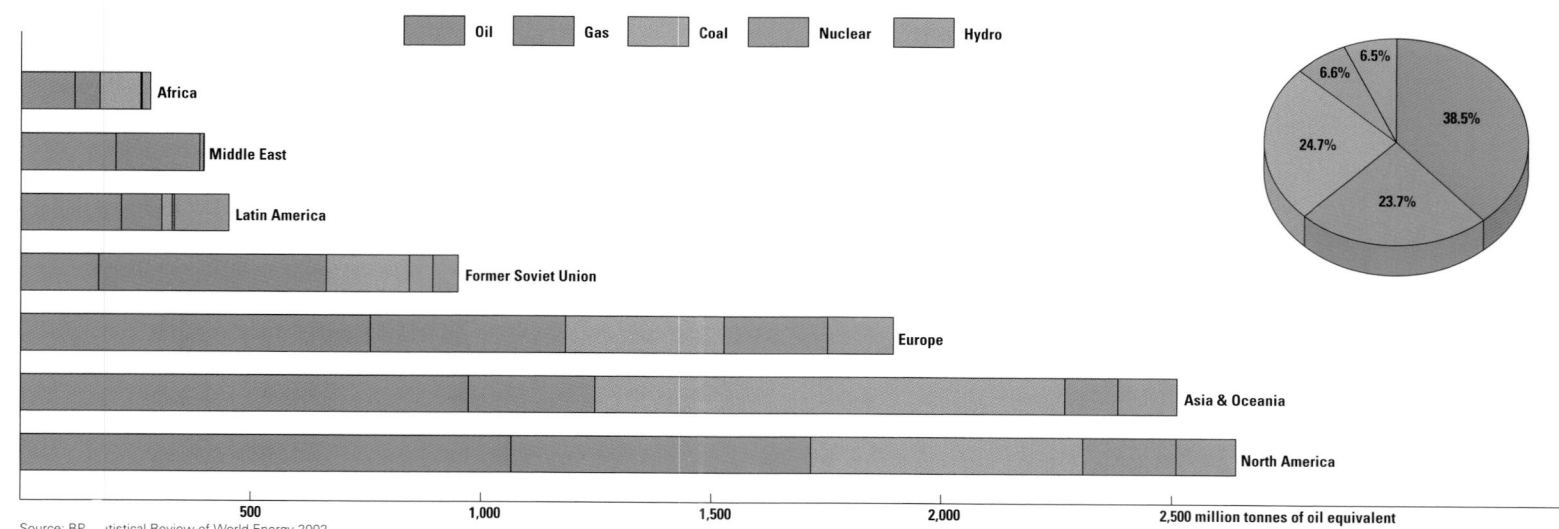

Oil   Gas   Coal   Nuclear   Hydro

Africa

Middle East

Latin America

Former Soviet Union

Europe

Asia & Oceania

North America

6.5%
6.6%
24.7%
38.5%
23.7%

500   1,000   1,500   2,000   2,500 million tonnes of oil equivalent

Source: BP Statistical Review of World Energy 2002

Energy

Energy is used to keep us warm or cool, fuel our industries and our transport systems, and even feed us; high-intensity agriculture, with its use of fertilizers, pesticides and machinery, is heavily energy-dependent. Although we live in a high-energy society, there are vast discrepancies between rich and poor; for example, a North American consumes 13 times as much energy as a Chinese person. But even developing nations have more power at their disposal than was imaginable a century ago.

The distribution of energy supplies, most importantly fossil fuels (coal, oil and natural gas), is very uneven. In addition, the diagrams and map opposite show that the largest producers of energy are not necessarily the largest consumers. The movement of energy supplies around the world is therefore an important component of international trade. In 1999, total world movements in oil amounted to 2,025 million tonnes.

As the finite reserves of fossil fuels are depleted, renewable energy sources, such as solar, hydro-thermal, wind, tidal and biomass, will become increasingly important around the world.

Nuclear Power

Major producers by percentage of world total (2000) and by percentage of domestic electricity generation (1999)

Country	% of world total production	Country	% of nuclear as proportion of domestic electricity
1. USA	30.5%	1. Lithuania	76.1%
2. France	15.7%	2. France	75.1%
3. Japan	12.6%	3. Belgium	58.2%
4. Germany	6.7%	4. Slovak Rep.	47.5%
5. Russia	4.6%	5. Sweden	44.2%
6. South Korea	4.1%	6. Ukraine	41.6%
7. UK	3.8%	7. Bulgaria	41.4%
8. Canada	2.9%	8. South Korea	39.1%
9. Ukraine	2.8%	9. Hungary	38.1%
= Sweden	2.8%	10. Slovenia	35.9%

Although the 1980s were a bad time for the nuclear power industry (major projects ran over budget and fears of long-term environmental damage were heavily reinforced by the 1986 disaster at Chernobyl), the industry picked up in the early 1990s. Whilst the number of reactors is still increasing, however, orders for new plants have shrunk. In 1997, the Swedish government began to decommission the country's 12 nuclear power plants.

Hydroelectricity

Major producers by percentage of world total (2000) and by percentage of domestic electricity generation (1999)

Country	% of world total production	Country	% of hydroelectric as proportion of domestic electricity
1. Canada	13.1%	1. Bhutan	99.9%
2. USA	12.0%	2. Paraguay	99.8%
3. Brazil	11.1%	= Zambia	99.8%
4. China	8.5%	4. Norway	99.1%
5. Russia	6.1%	5. Ethiopia	98.1%
6. Norway	4.6%	6. Congo (Rep. Dem.)	97.9%
7. Japan	3.3%	7. Tajikistan	97.8%
8. India	3.1%	8. Cameroon	97.3%
9. France	2.8%	9. Albania	97.2%
10. Sweden	2.7%	= Laos	97.2%

Countries heavily reliant on hydroelectricity are usually small and non-industrial: a high proportion of hydroelectric power more often reflects a modest energy budget than vast hydroelectric resources. The USA, for instance, produces only 8.5% of its power requirements from hydroelectricity; yet that 8.5% amounts to more than three times the hydropower generated by most of Africa.

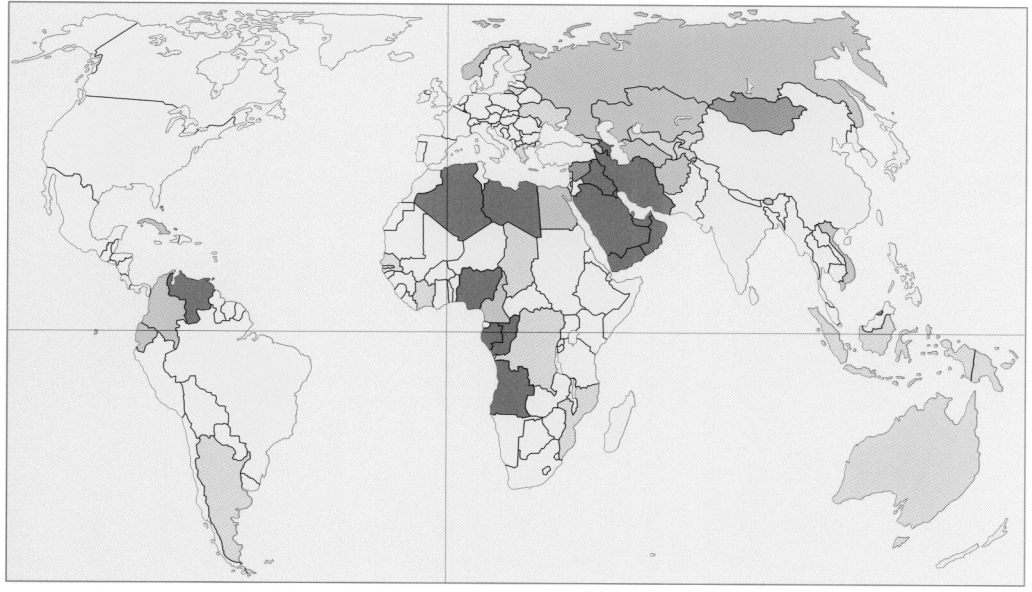

Fuel Exports

Fuels as a percentage of total value of exports (1999)

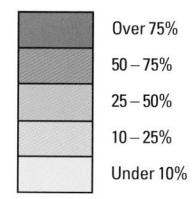

- Over 75%
- 50 – 75%
- 25 – 50%
- 10 – 25%
- Under 10%

In the 1970s, oil exports became a political issue when OPEC sought to increase the influence of developing countries in world affairs by raising oil prices and restricting production. But its power was short-lived, following a fall in demand for oil in the 1980s, due to an increase in energy efficiency and development of alternative resources.

Conversion Rates

1 barrel = 0.136 tonnes or 159 litres or 35 Imperial gallons or 42 US gallons

1 tonne = 7.33 barrels or 1,185 litres or 256 Imperial gallons or 261 US gallons

1 tonne oil = 1.5 tonnes hard coal or 3.0 tonnes lignite or 12,000 kWh

1 Imperial gallon = 1.201 US gallons or 4.546 litres or 277.4 cubic inches

Measurements
For historical reasons, oil is traded in 'barrels'. The weight and volume equivalents (shown right) are all based on average-density 'Arabian light' crude oil.

The energy equivalents given for a tonne of oil are also somewhat imprecise: oil and coal of different qualities will have varying energy contents, a fact usually reflected in their price on world markets.

World Coal Reserves

World coal reserves (including lignite) by region and country, thousand million tonnes (2001)

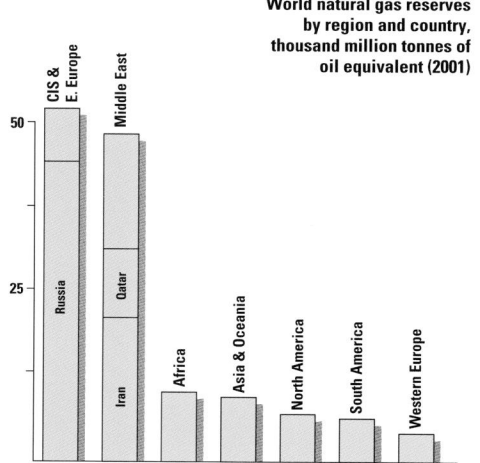

World Gas Reserves

World natural gas reserves by region and country, thousand million tonnes of oil equivalent (2001)

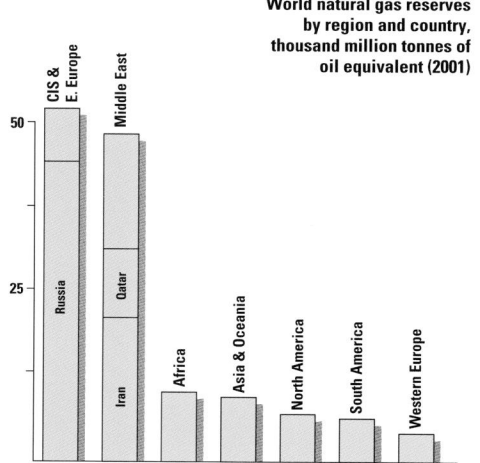

World Oil Reserves

World oil reserves by region and country, thousand million tonnes (2001)

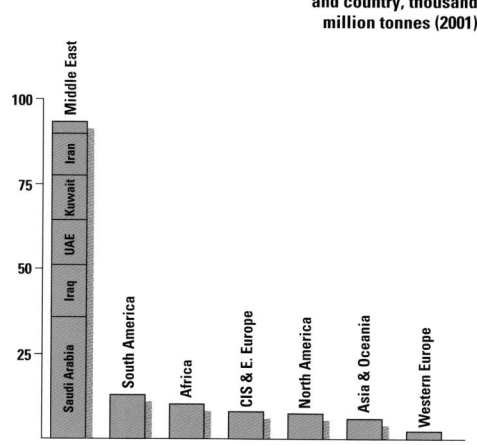

Production

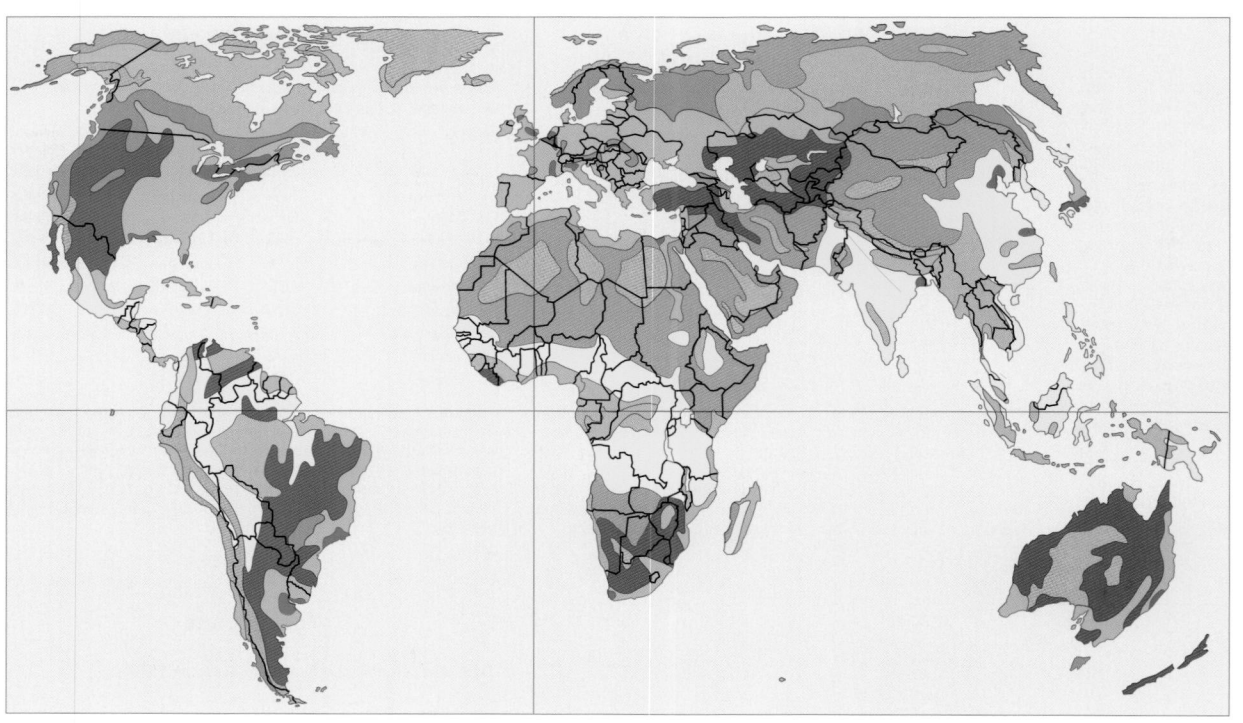

Agriculture

Predominant type of farming or land use.

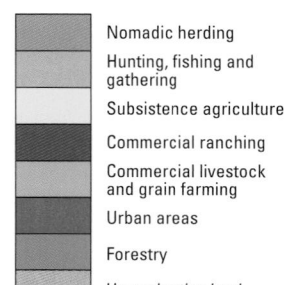

- Nomadic herding
- Hunting, fishing and gathering
- Subsistence agriculture
- Commercial ranching
- Commercial livestock and grain farming
- Urban areas
- Forestry
- Unproductive land

The development of agriculture has transformed human existence more than any other. The whole business of farming is constantly developing: due mainly to the new varieties of rice and wheat, world grain production has increased by over 70% since 1965. New machinery and modern agricultural techniques enable relatively few farmers to produce enough food for the world's 6 billion or so people.

Staple Crops

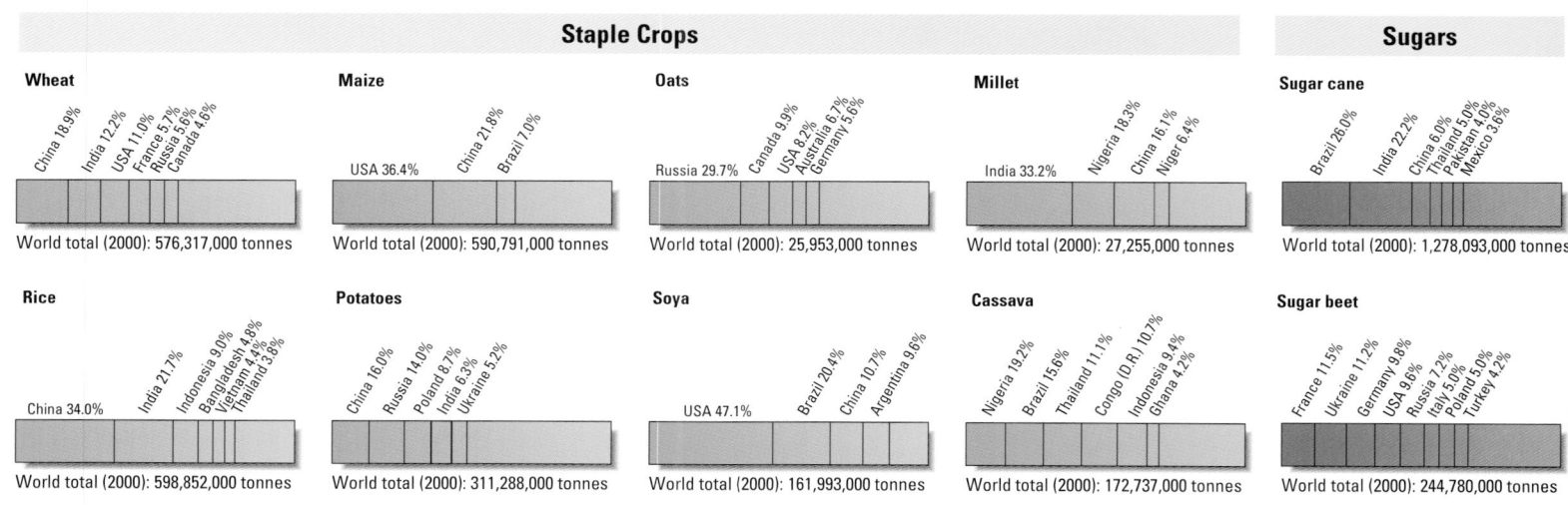

Wheat

China 18.9% | India 12.2% | USA 11.0% | France 5.7% | Russia 5.6% | Canada 4.6%

World total (2000): 576,317,000 tonnes

Maize

USA 36.4% | China 21.6% | Brazil 7.0%

World total (2000): 590,791,000 tonnes

Oats

Russia 29.7% | Canada 9.9% | USA 8.2% | Australia 6.7% | Germany 5.6%

World total (2000): 25,953,000 tonnes

Millet

India 33.2% | Nigeria 18.3% | China 16.1% | Niger 6.4%

World total (2000): 27,255,000 tonnes

Rice

China 34.0% | India 21.7% | Indonesia 9.0% | Bangladesh 4.8% | Vietnam 4.4% | Thailand 3.8%

World total (2000): 598,852,000 tonnes

Potatoes

China 16.0% | Russia 14.0% | Poland 8.7% | India 6.3% | Ukraine 5.2%

World total (2000): 311,288,000 tonnes

Soya

USA 47.1% | Brazil 20.4% | China 10.7% | Argentina 9.6%

World total (2000): 161,993,000 tonnes

Cassava

Nigeria 19.2% | Brazil 15.6% | Thailand 11.1% | Congo (D.R.) 10.7% | Indonesia 9.4% | Ghana 4.2%

World total (2000): 172,737,000 tonnes

Sugars

Sugar cane

Brazil 26.0% | India 22.2% | China 6.0% | Thailand 5.0% | Pakistan 4.0% | Mexico 3.6%

World total (2000): 1,278,093,000 tonnes

Sugar beet

France 11.5% | Ukraine 11.2% | Germany 9.8% | USA 9.6% | Russia 7.2% | Italy 5.0% | Poland 5.0% | Turkey 4.2%

World total (2000): 244,780,000 tonnes

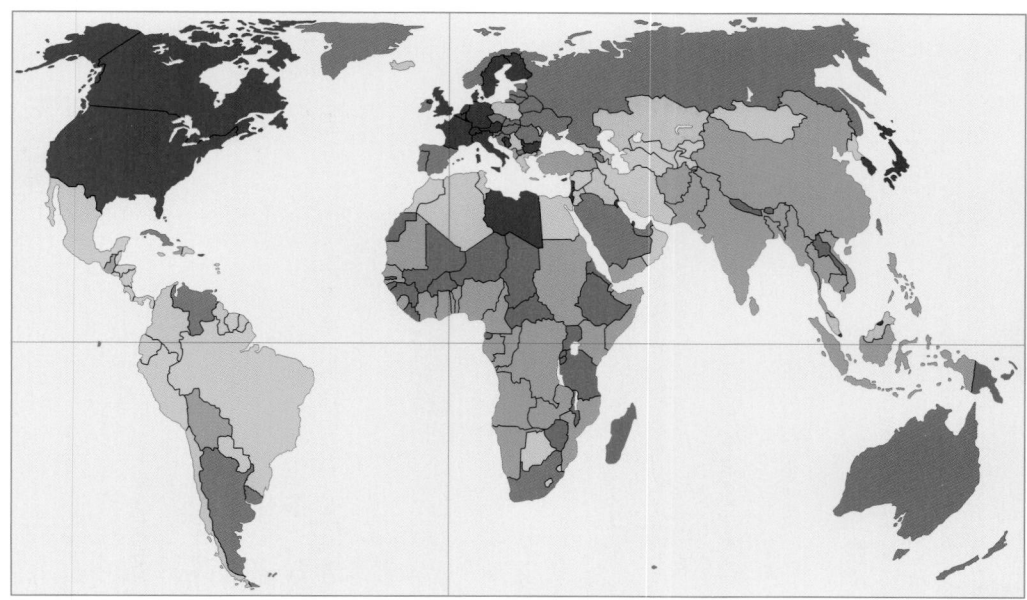

Employment

The number of workers employed in manufacturing for every 100 workers engaged in agriculture (latest available year)

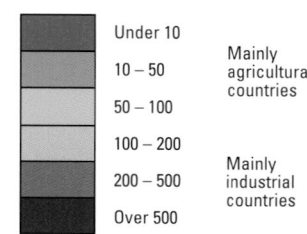

- Under 10 — Mainly agricultural countries
- 10 – 50
- 50 – 100
- 100 – 200
- 200 – 500 — Mainly industrial countries
- Over 500

Selected countries (latest available year)

Singapore	8,860	Germany	800
Hong Kong	3,532	Kuwait	767
UK	1,270	Bahrain	660
Belgium	820	USA	657
Former Yugoslavia	809	Israel	633

Mineral Production

*Figures for aluminium are for refined metal; all other figures refer to ore production.

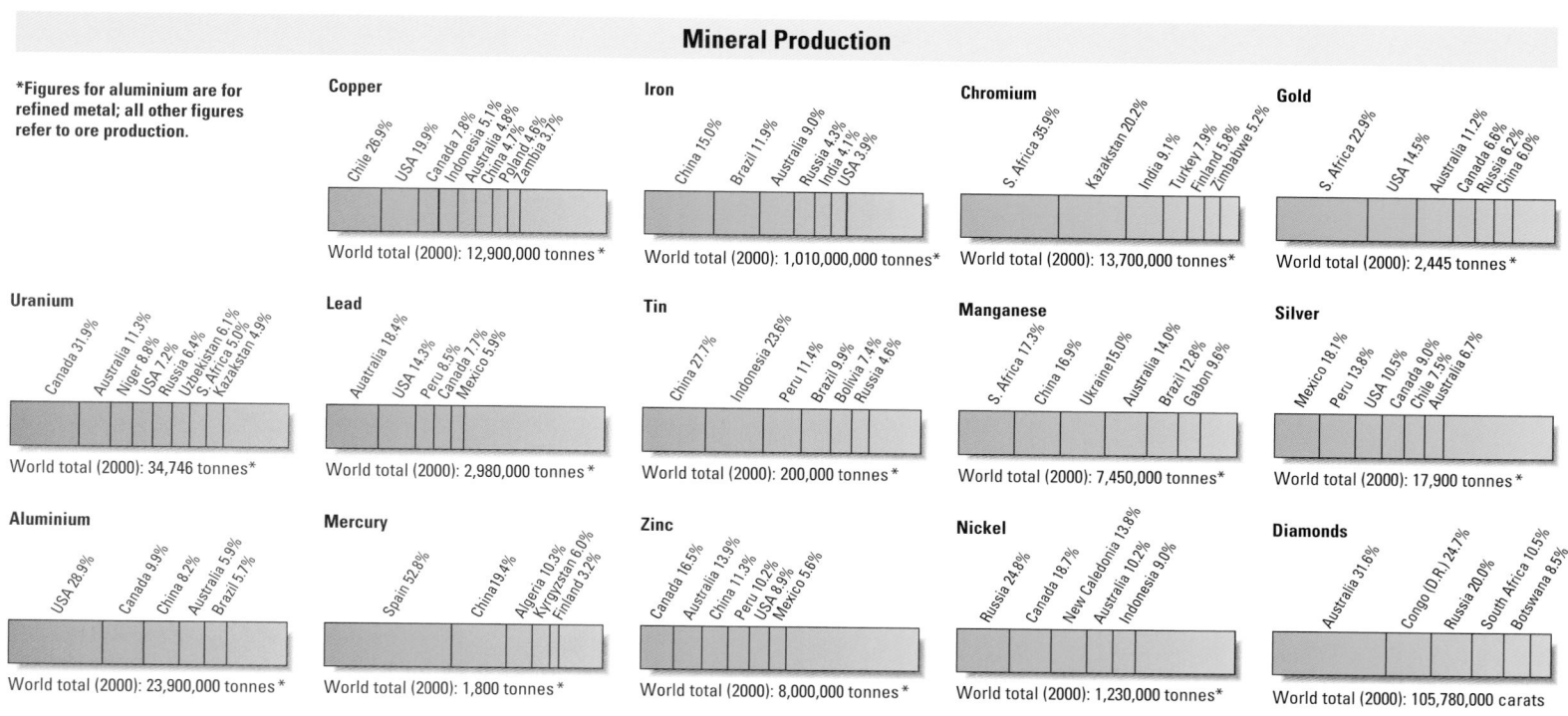

Copper
Chile 26.9% | USA 19.9% | Canada 7.8% | Indonesia 5.1% | Australia 4.8% | China 4.7% | Poland 4.6% | Zambia 3.7%
World total (2000): 12,900,000 tonnes*

Iron
China 15.0% | Brazil 11.9% | Australia 9.0% | Russia 4.2% | India 4.1% | USA 3.9%
World total (2000): 1,010,000,000 tonnes*

Chromium
S. Africa 35.9% | Kazakstan 20.2% | India 9.1% | Turkey 7.9% | Finland 5.8% | Zimbabwe 5.2%
World total (2000): 13,700,000 tonnes*

Gold
S. Africa 22.9% | USA 14.5% | Australia 11.2% | Canada 6.6% | Russia 6.2% | China 6.0%
World total (2000): 2,445 tonnes*

Uranium
Canada 31.9% | Australia 11.3% | Niger 8.8% | USA 7.2% | Russia 6.4% | Uzbekistan 6.1% | S. Africa 5.0% | Kazakstan 4.9%
World total (2000): 34,746 tonnes*

Lead
Australia 18.4% | USA 14.3% | Peru 8.5% | Canada 7.7% | Mexico 5.9%
World total (2000): 2,980,000 tonnes*

Tin
China 27.7% | Indonesia 23.6% | Peru 11.4% | Brazil 9.9% | Bolivia 7.4% | Russia 4.6%
World total (2000): 200,000 tonnes*

Manganese
S. Africa 17.3% | China 16.9% | Ukraine 15.0% | Australia 14.0% | Brazil 12.8% | Gabon 9.6%
World total (2000): 7,450,000 tonnes*

Silver
Mexico 18.1% | Peru 13.8% | USA 10.5% | Canada 9.0% | Chile 7.5% | Australia 6.7%
World total (2000): 17,900 tonnes*

Aluminium
USA 20.9% | Canada 9.9% | China 8.2% | Australia 5.9% | Brazil 5.7%
World total (2000): 23,900,000 tonnes*

Mercury
Spain 52.8% | China 19.4% | Algeria 10.3% | Kyrgyzstan 6.0% | Finland 3.2%
World total (2000): 1,800 tonnes*

Zinc
Canada 16.5% | Australia 13.9% | China 11.3% | Peru 10.2% | USA 8.9% | Mexico 5.6%
World total (2000): 8,000,000 tonnes*

Nickel
Russia 24.8% | Canada 18.7% | New Caledonia 13.8% | Australia 10.2% | Indonesia 9.0%
World total (2000): 1,230,000 tonnes*

Diamonds
Australia 31.6% | Congo (D.R.) 24.7% | Russia 20.0% | South Africa 10.5% | Botswana 8.5%
World total (2000): 105,780,000 carats

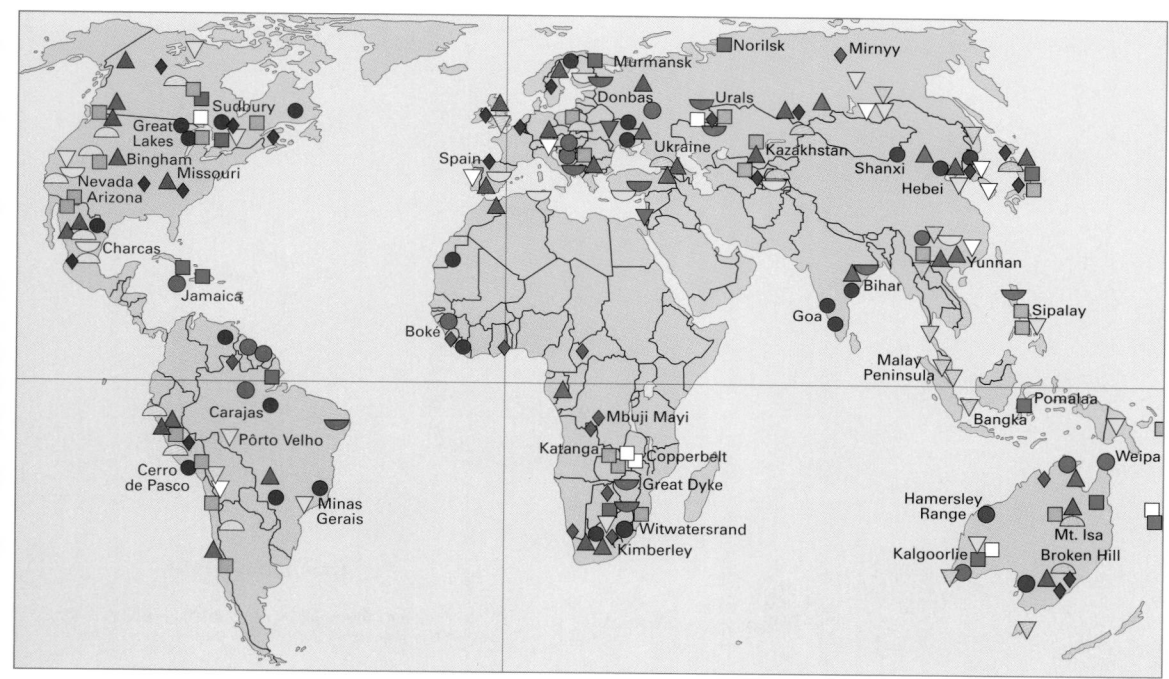

Mineral Distribution

The map shows the richest sources of the most important minerals. Major mineral locations are named.

▽ Gold
◖ Silver
◆ Diamonds
▽ Tungsten
● Iron Ore
■ Nickel
◗ Chrome
▲ Manganese
□ Cobalt
▲ Molybdenum
■ Copper
▲ Lead
● Bauxite
▽ Tin
◆ Zinc
◡ Mercury

The map does not show undersea deposits, most of which are considered inaccessible.

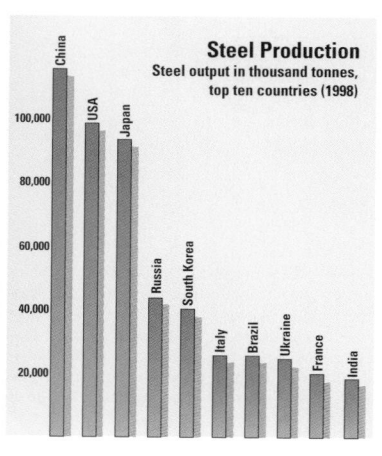

Steel Production
Steel output in thousand tonnes, top ten countries (1998)

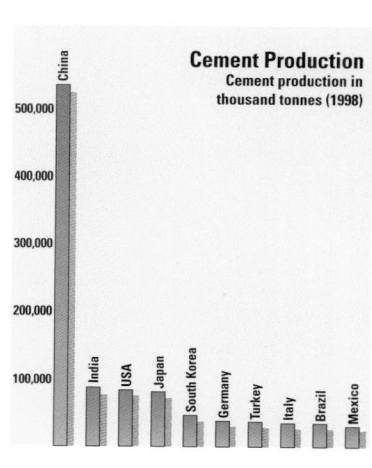

Cement Production
Cement production in thousand tonnes (1998)

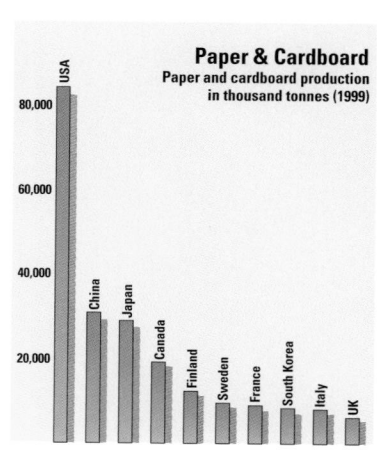

Paper & Cardboard
Paper and cardboard production in thousand tonnes (1999)

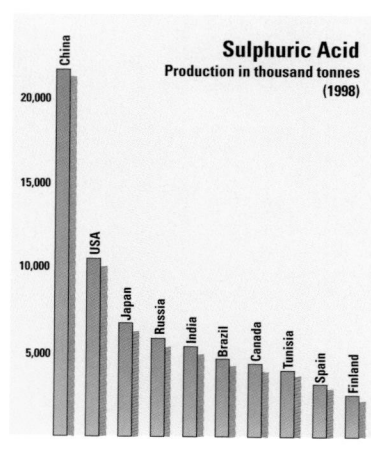

Sulphuric Acid
Production in thousand tonnes (1998)

Trade

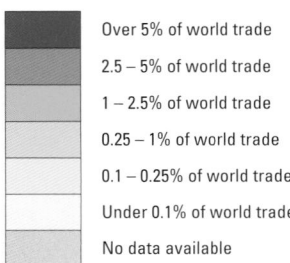

Share of World Trade

Percentage share of total world exports by value (2000)

- Over 5% of world trade
- 2.5 – 5% of world trade
- 1 – 2.5% of world trade
- 0.25 – 1% of world trade
- 0.1 – 0.25% of world trade
- Under 0.1% of world trade
- No data available

International trade is dominated by a handful of powerful maritime nations. The members of 'G8', the inner circle of OECD (see page 19), and the top seven countries listed in the diagram below, account for more than half the total. The majority of nations – including all but four in Africa – contribute less than one quarter of 1% to the worldwide total of exports; the EU countries account for 35%, the Pacific Rim nations over 50%.

The Main Trading Nations

The imports and exports of the top ten trading nations as a percentage of world trade (2001). Each country's trade in manufactured goods is shown in dark blue.

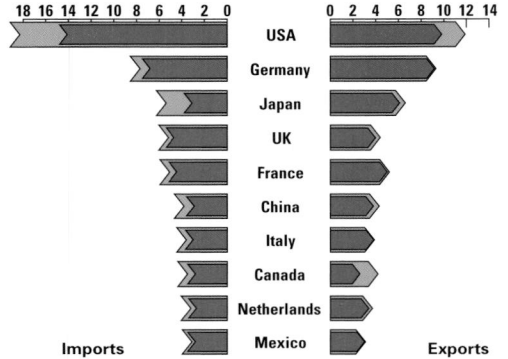

Imports — Exports

USA
Germany
Japan
UK
France
China
Italy
Canada
Netherlands
Mexico

Major exports

Leading manufactured items and their exporters (2000)

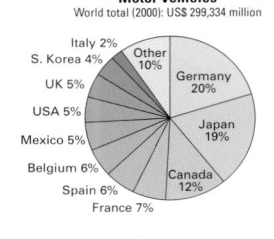

Motor Vehicles
World total (2000): US$ 299,334 million

Italy 2%, S. Korea 4%, Other 10%, UK 5%, Germany 20%, USA 5%, Mexico 5%, Japan 19%, Belgium 6%, Spain 6%, Canada 12%, France 7%

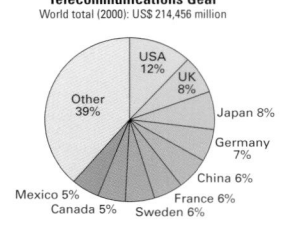

Telecommunications Gear
World total (2000): US$ 214,456 million

USA 12%, UK 8%, Other 39%, Japan 8%, Germany 7%, China 6%, Mexico 5%, France 6%, Canada 5%, Sweden 6%

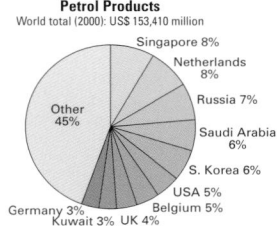

Petrol Products
World total (2000): US$ 153,410 million

Singapore 8%, Netherlands 8%, Russia 7%, Other 45%, Saudi Arabia 6%, S. Korea 6%, USA 5%, Germany 3%, Belgium 5%, Kuwait 3%, UK 4%

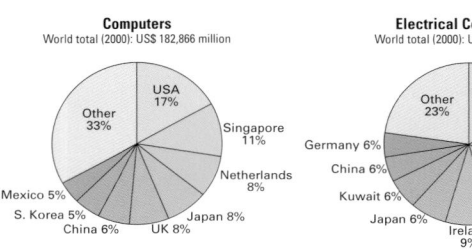

Computers
World total (2000): US$ 182,866 million

USA 17%, Other 33%, Singapore 11%, Netherlands 8%, Mexico 5%, S. Korea 5%, Japan 8%, China 6%, UK 8%

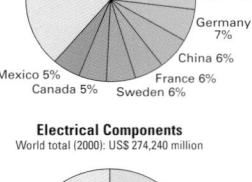

Electrical Components
World total (2000): US$ 274,240 million

Other 23%, Thailand 17%, Germany 6%, Hungary 16%, China 6%, Kuwait 6%, Portugal 13%, Japan 6%, Ireland 9%

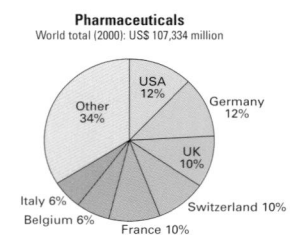

Pharmaceuticals
World total (2000): US$ 107,334 million

USA 12%, Other 34%, Germany 12%, UK 10%, Italy 6%, Switzerland 10%, Belgium 6%, France 10%

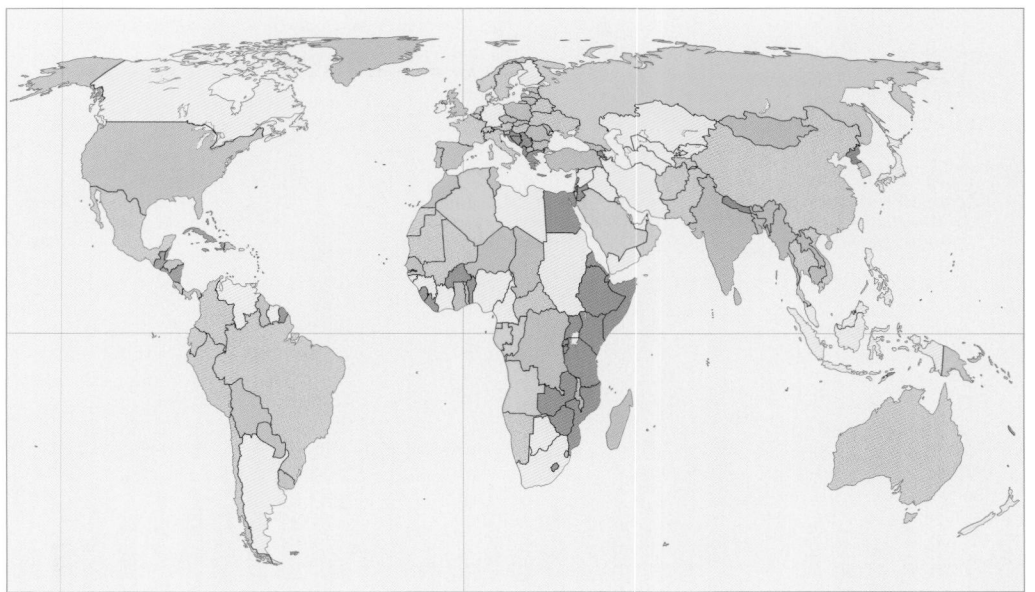

Balance of Trade

Value of exports in proportion to the value of imports (2000)

- More than 40% — Imports exceed exports by:
- 10 – 40%
- 10% either side
- 10 – 40%
- More than 40%% — Exports exceed imports by:
- No data available

The total world trade balance should amount to zero, since exports must equal imports on a global scale. In practice, at least $100 billion in exports go unrecorded, leaving the world with an apparent deficit and many countries in a better position than public accounting reveals. However, a favourable trade balance is not necessarily a sign of prosperity: many poorer countries must maintain a high surplus in order to service debts, and do so by restricting imports below the levels needed to sustain successful economies.

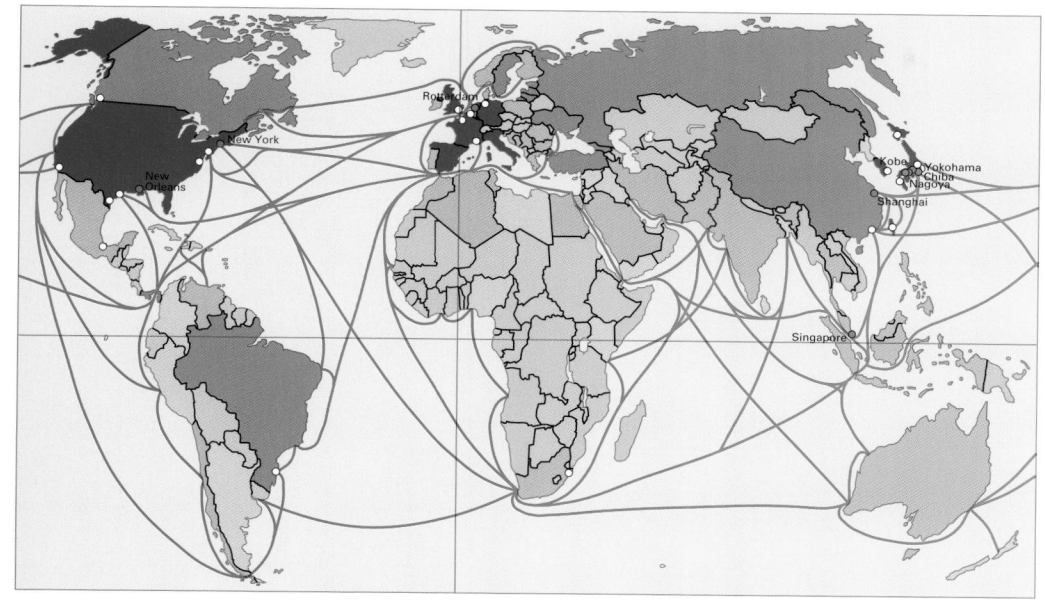

Seaborne Freight

Freight unloaded in millions of tonnes (latest available year)

- Over 100
- 50 – 100
- 10 – 50
- 5 – 10
- Under 5
- Landlocked countries

Major seaports

- ⊙ Over 100 million tonnes per year
- ○ 50–100 million tonnes per year
- ── Major shipping routes

Cargoes

Type of seaborne freight

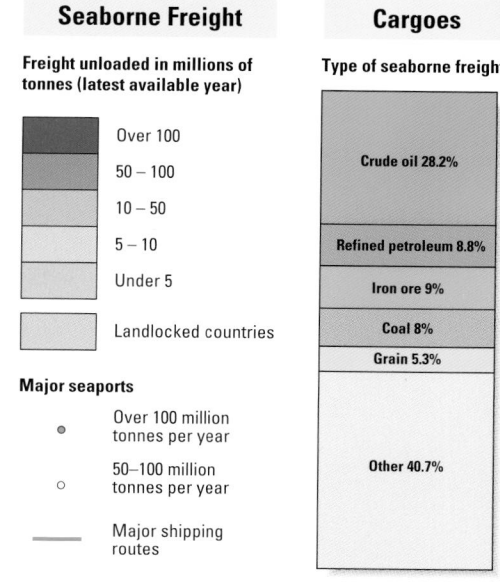

- Crude oil 28.2%
- Refined petroleum 8.8%
- Iron ore 9%
- Coal 8%
- Grain 5.3%
- Other 40.7%

Merchant Fleets

Merchant fleets in thousand gross registered tonnage (2000). Although a large number of vessels are registered in Liberia and Panama, they are not part of the national fleet.

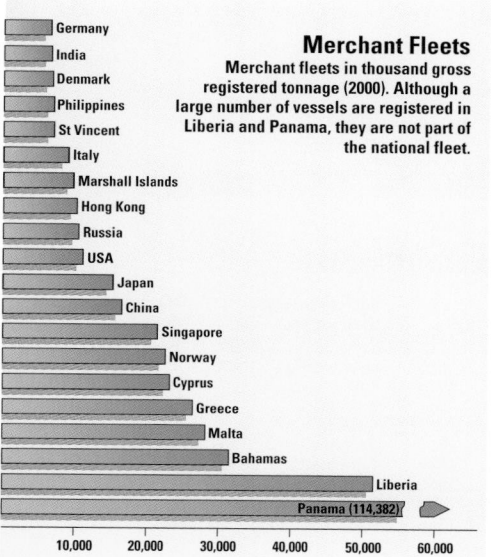

Germany, India, Denmark, Philippines, St Vincent, Italy, Marshall Islands, Hong Kong, Russia, USA, Japan, China, Singapore, Norway, Cyprus, Greece, Malta, Bahamas, Liberia, Panama (114,382)

10,000 20,000 30,000 40,000 50,000 60,000

The Great Ports

Total cargo traffic, in million tonnes (latest available year)

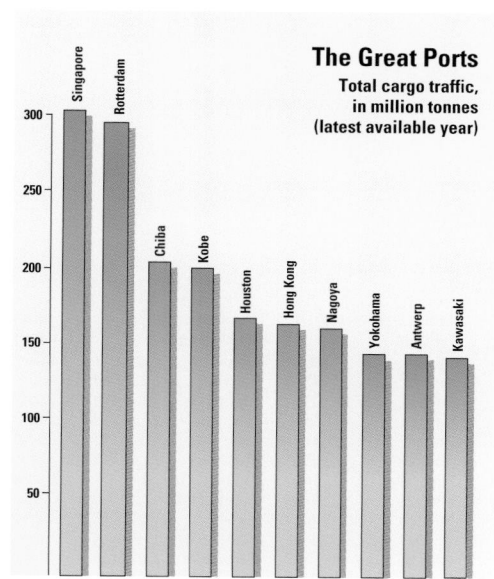

Singapore, Rotterdam, Chiba, Kobe, Houston, Hong Kong, Nagoya, Yokohama, Antwerp, Kawasaki

World Shipping

World merchant fleet by type of vessel and deadweight tonnage (2000)

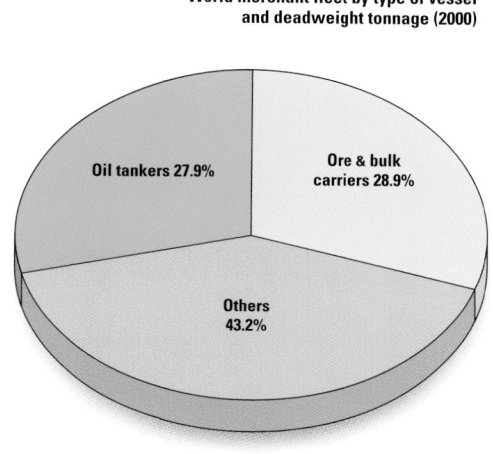

- Oil tankers 27.9%
- Ore & bulk carriers 28.9%
- Others 43.2%

Exports Per Capita

Value of exports in US $, divided by total population (2000)

- Over 10,000
- 5,000 – 10,000
- 1,000 – 5,000
- 500 – 1,000
- 100 – 500
- Under 100

[UK 4,728] [USA 2,791]

Highest per capita

Kuwait	113,614
Liechtenstein	78,848
Singapore	31,860
Aruba (Neths)	31,429
Hong Kong (China)	28,290
Ireland	19,136

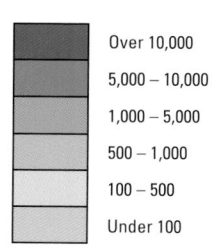

Travel and Tourism

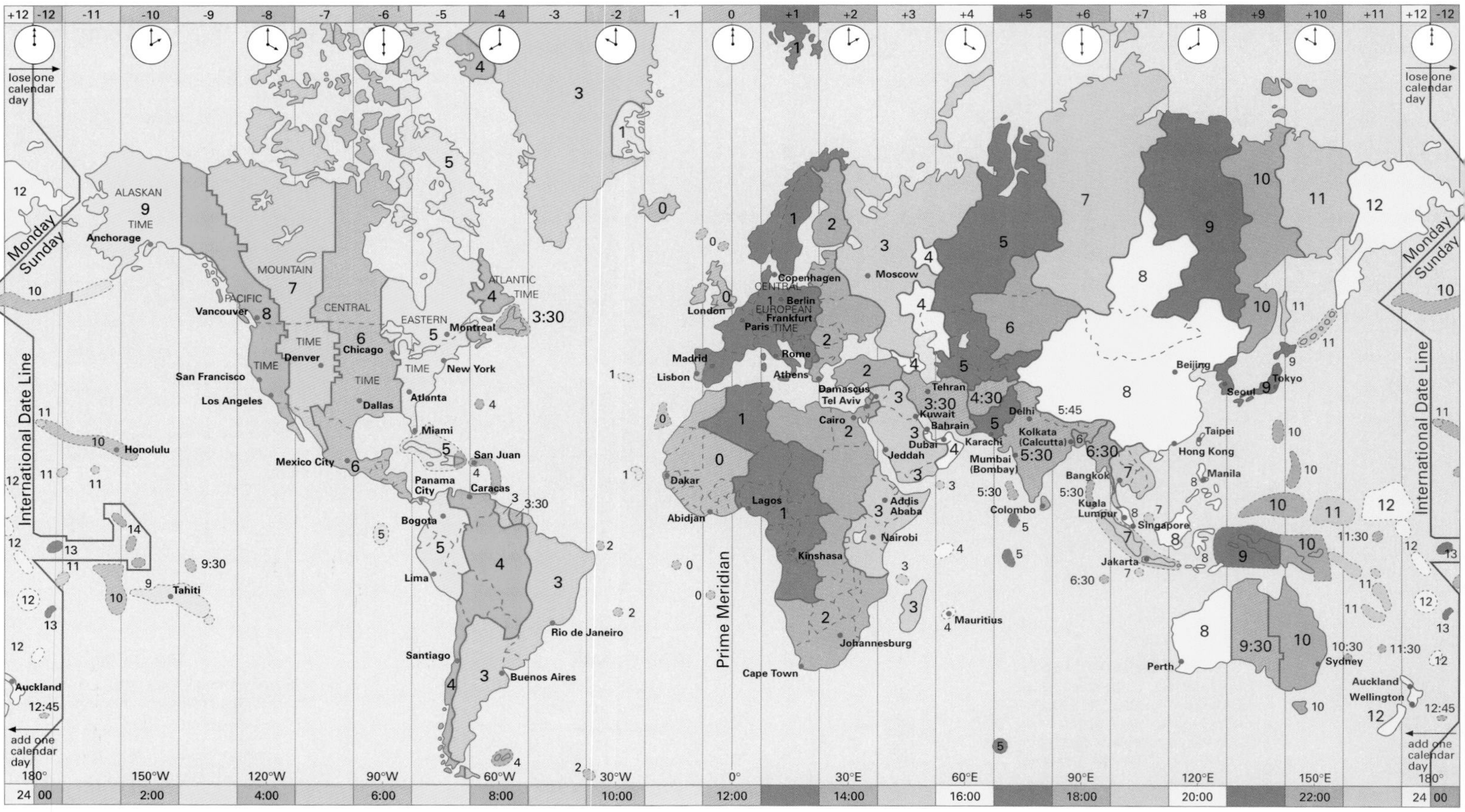

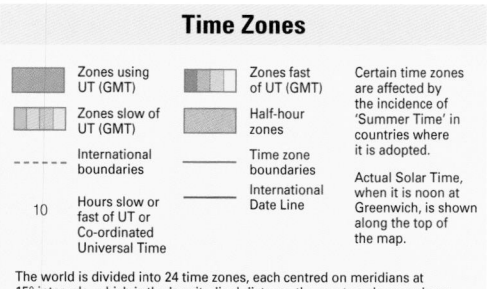

Projection: Mercator

Time Zones

Zones using UT (GMT)		Zones fast of UT (GMT)		Certain time zones are affected by the incidence of 'Summer Time' in countries where it is adopted.
Zones slow of UT (GMT)		Half-hour zones		
----- International boundaries		—— Time zone boundaries		Actual Solar Time, when it is noon at Greenwich, is shown along the top of the map.
10 Hours slow or fast of UT or Co-ordinated Universal Time		—— International Date Line		

The world is divided into 24 time zones, each centred on meridians at 15° intervals, which is the longitudinal distance the sun travels every hour. The meridian running through Greenwich, London, passes through the middle of the first zone.

Rail and Road: The Leading Nations

Total rail network ('000 km)		Passenger km per head per year		Total road network ('000 km)		Vehicle km per head per year		Number of vehicles per km of roads	
1. USA	235.7	Japan	2,017	USA	6,277.9	USA	12,505	Hong Kong	284
2. Russia	87.4	Belarus	1,880	India	2,962.5	Luxembourg	7,989	Taiwan	211
3. India	62.7	Russia	1,826	Brazil	1,824.4	Kuwait	7,251	Singapore	152
4. China	54.6	Switzerland	1,769	Japan	1,130.9	France	7,142	Kuwait	140
5. Germany	41.7	Ukraine	1,456	China	1,041.1	Sweden	6,991	Brunei	96
6. Australia	35.8	Austria	1,168	Russia	884.0	Germany	6,806	Italy	91
7. Argentina	34.2	France	1,011	Canada	849.4	Denmark	6,764	Israel	87
8. France	31.9	Netherlands	994	France	811.6	Austria	6,518	Thailand	73
9. Mexico	26.5	Latvia	918	Australia	810.3	Netherlands	5,984	Ukraine	73
10. South Africa	26.3	Denmark	884	Germany	636.3	UK	5,738	UK	67
11. Poland	24.9	Slovak Rep.	862	Romania	461.9	Canada	5,493	Netherlands	66
12. Ukraine	22.6	Romania	851	Turkey	388.1	Italy	4,852	Germany	62

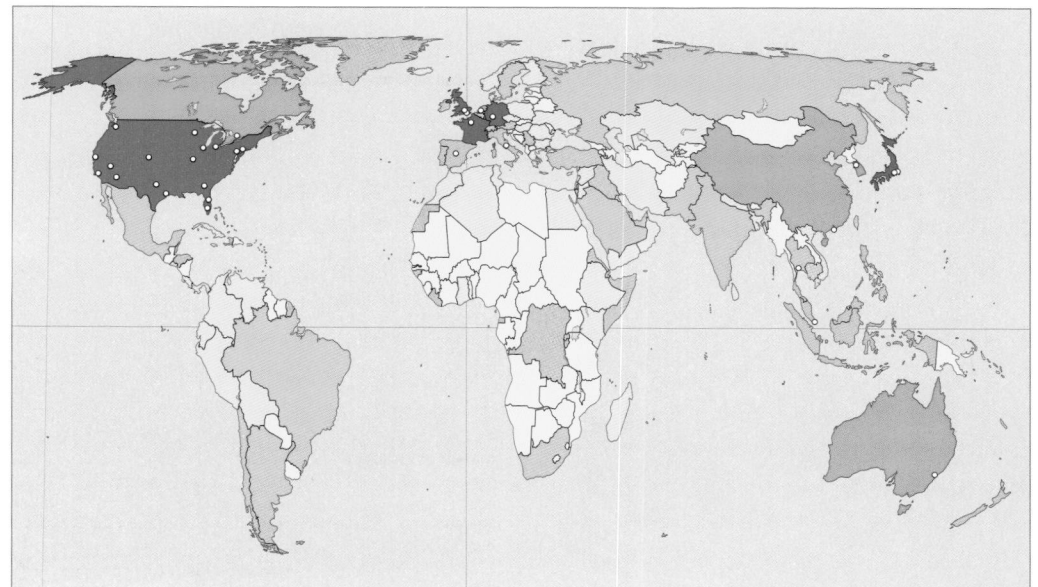

Air Travel

Passenger kilometres flown on scheduled flights (the number of passengers in thousands – international and domestic – multiplied by the distance flown from the airport of origin) (1999)

	Over 100,000 million
	50,000 – 100,000 million
	10,000 – 50,000 million
	1,000 – 10,000 million
	Under 1,000 million
	No data available
o	Major airports (handling over 25 million passengers in 2001)

World's busiest airports (total passengers)		World's busiest airports (international passengers)	
1. Atlanta	(Hartsfield)	1. London	(Heathrow)
2. Chicago	(O'Hare)	2. Paris	(Charles de Gaulle)
3. Los Angeles	(International)	3. Frankfurt	(International)
4. London	(Heathrow)	4. Amsterdam	(Schipol)
5. Tokyo	(Haneda)	5. Hong Kong	(International)

Destinations

- Cultural and historical centres
- Coastal resorts
- Ski resorts
- Centres of entertainment
- Places of pilgrimage
- Places of great natural beauty
- Popular holiday cruise routes

Visitors to the USA

Overseas arrivals to the USA, in thousands (2000)

1. Canada 14,594
2. Mexico 10,322
3. Japan 5,061
4. UK 4,703
5. Germany 1,786
6. France 1,087
7. Brazil .737
8. South Korea 662
9. Venezuela 577
10. Australia 540

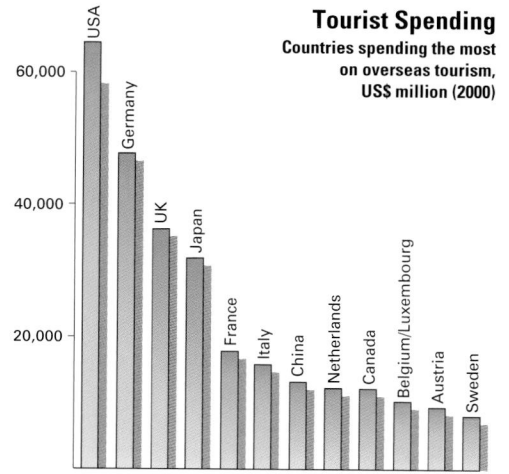

Tourist Spending
Countries spending the most on overseas tourism, US$ million (2000)

Importance of Tourism

		Arrivals from abroad (2001)	% of world total (2001)
1.	France	.76,500,000	.11.0%
2.	Spain	.49,500,000	.7.1%
3.	USA	.45,500,000	.6.6%
4.	Italy	.39,000,000	.5.6%
5.	China	.33,200,000	.4.8%
6.	UK	.23,400,000	.3.4%
7.	Russia	.21,200,000	.3.0%
8.	Mexico	.19,800,000	.2.9%
9.	Canada	.19,700,000	.2.8%
10.	Austria	.18,200,000	.2.6%
11.	Germany	.17,900,000	.2.6%
12.	Hungary	.15,300,000	.2.2%

In 2001, there was a 0.6% drop in the number of tourist arrivals compared to the previous year, to 693 million. This was partly due to the impact of the terrorist attacks in New York City on 11 September 2001, but was also a result of the weakening economies of tourism-generating markets worldwide.

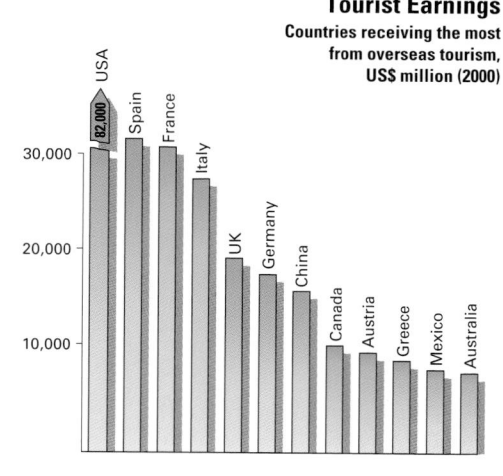

Tourist Earnings
Countries receiving the most from overseas tourism, US$ million (2000)

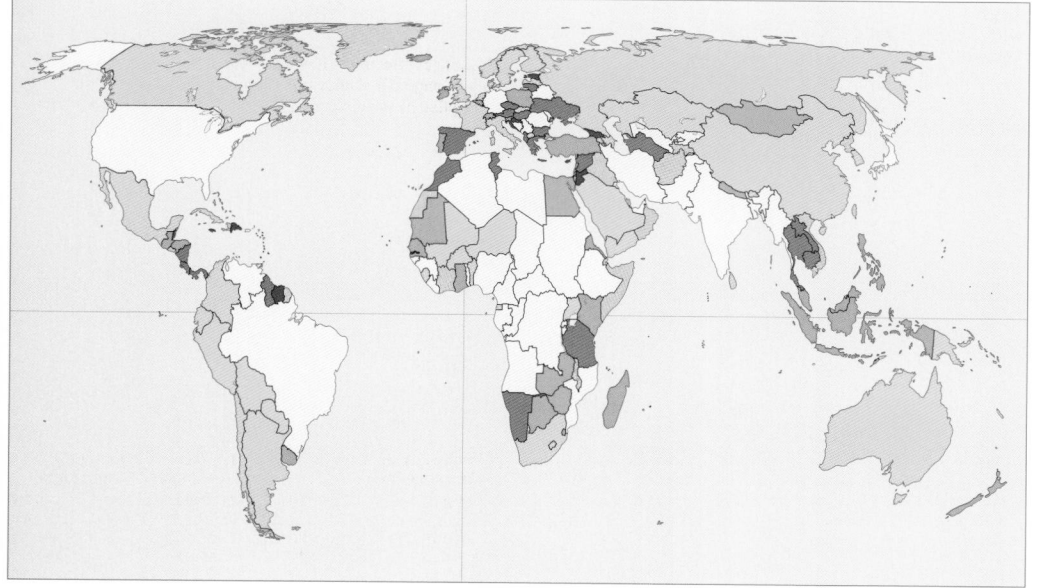

Tourism

Tourism receipts as a percentage of Gross National Income (1999)

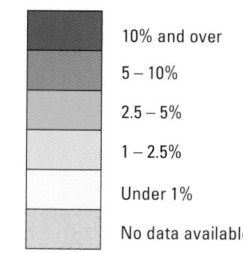

- 10% and over
- 5 – 10%
- 2.5 – 5%
- 1 – 2.5%
- Under 1%
- No data available

Percentage change in tourist arrivals from 2000 to 2001 (top six countries in total number of arrivals)

China	. . . .+6.2%	(increase)
Spain	. . . .+3.4%	
France	. . . .+1.2%	
Italy	. . . .–5.3%	
UK	. . . .–7.4%	
USA	. . . .–10.6%	(decrease)

CARTOGRAPHY BY PHILIP'S. COPYRIGHT PHILIP'S.

The World In Focus: Index

A
Acid rain   15
Agriculture   26
Aid   21
Airports   30
Air travel   30

B
Beaufort Wind Scale   11

C
Carbon dioxide   10, 14
Cement production   27
Climate regions   10
Coal   25
Continental drift   4
Crops   26
Crust   4–5
Currents   8

D
Day and night   2
Debt   21
Deforestation   15
Desertification   15

E
Earth's structure   4
Earthquakes   4
Eclipses   3
Education   23
El Niño   11
Employment   26
Energy balance   24
Epicentre   4
Equinox   2–3

E (cont.)
Erosion   7
European Union   19
Exports   28

F
Faults   6
Female employment   23
Fertility   23
Fishing   9
Folds   6
Food consumption   22
Forestry   13
Fuel exports   25

G
Geothermal energy   25
Glaciers   7
Global warming   14
Greenhouse effect   14
Gross Domestic Product   29
Gross National Product   20

H
Holiday destinations   31
Hospital beds   22
Household spending   21
Human Development Index   23
Hydroelectricity   25
Hydrological cycle   12

I
Illiteracy   23
Imports   28
Infant mortality   22
Infectious diseases   22
Inflation   20

International organizations   19

L
Land use   13
Language   18
Life expectancy   22

M
Mantle   4–5
Mercalli Scale   4
Merchant fleets   29
Metals   27
Mid-ocean ridge   5
Minerals   27
Moon   3
Mountain building   6

N
Nuclear power   25

O
OECD   19, 28
Oil   24–25
Ozone   14–15

P
Paper and cardboard   27
Planets   2
Plate tectonics   5
Pollution   9
Population density   16–17
Ports   29
Precipitation   10–12

R
Railways   30

Rainforest   13, 15
Richter Scale   4
Religions   18
Rivers   7
Roads   30

S
Sea-floor spreading   5
Seasons   2
Shipping   29
Solar System   2
Subduction zone   6
Sulphuric acid   27

T
Telecommunications gear   28
Temperature   11
Tides   3
Time zones   30
Tourism   31
Trading nations   28
Transport networks   30

U
United Nations   19
Urban population   17

V
Vegetation   13
Vehicles   28, 30
Volcanoes   5

W
Water   12
Wealth gap   20
Wind power   25

WORLD CITIES

AMSTERDAM	2	EDINBURGH	11	MOSCOW	19	TEHRAN	30
ATHENS	2	HELSINKI	12	MUMBAI	20	TIANJIN	30
ATLANTA	3	HONG KONG	12	MUNICH	20	TORONTO	30
BAGHDAD	3	ISTANBUL	12	NEW YORK	21	VIENNA	31
BANGKOK	3	JAKARTA	13	OSAKA	22	WARSAW	31
BARCELONA	4	JERUSALEM	13	OSLO	22	WASHINGTON	32
BEIJING	4	JOHANNESBURG	13	PARIS	23	WELLINGTON	32
BERLIN	5	KARACHI	14	PRAGUE	24	INDEX	33–39
BOSTON	6	LAGOS	14	RIO DE JANEIRO	24		
BRUSSELS	6	LISBON	14	ROME	25	WORLD CITIES	
BUDAPEST	7	LONDON	15	SAN FRANCISCO	25	SATELLITE IMAGES	
BUENOS AIRES	7	LOS ANGELES	16	ST PETERSBURG	26	CAPE TOWN	40
CAIRO	7	LIMA	16	SANTIAGO	26	CHICAGO	41
CALCUTTA	8	MADRID	17	SÃO PAULO	26	KARACHI	42
CANTON	8	MANILA	17	SEOUL	26	LONDON	43
CAPE TOWN	8	MELBOURNE	17	SHANGHAI	27	NEW YORK	44
CHICAGO	9	MEXICO CITY	18	SINGAPORE	27	SAN FRANCISCO	45
COPENHAGEN	10	MIAMI	18	STOCKHOLM	28	SANTIAGO	46
DELHI	10	MILAN	18	SYDNEY	28	SYDNEY	47
DUBLIN	11	MONTREAL	19	TOKYO	29	TOKYO	48

CITY MAPS

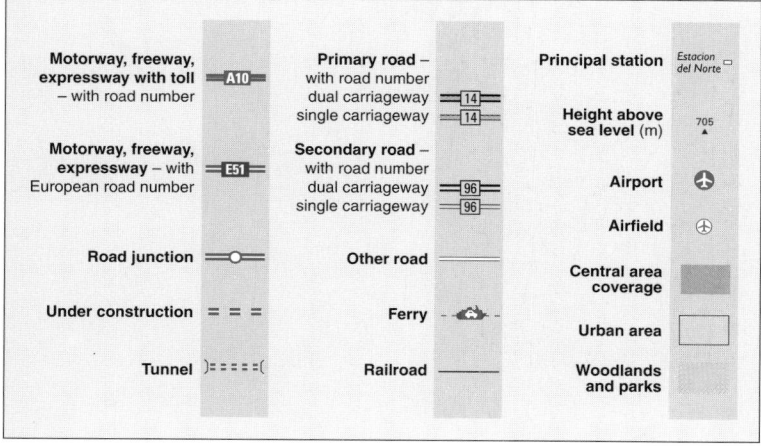

CENTRAL AREA MAPS

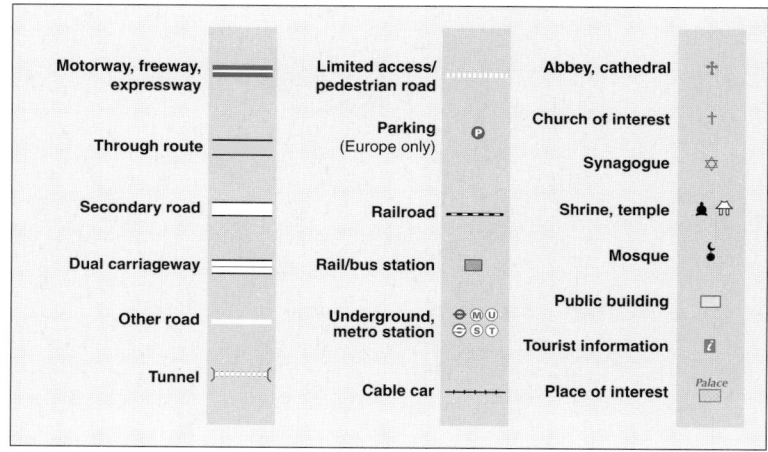

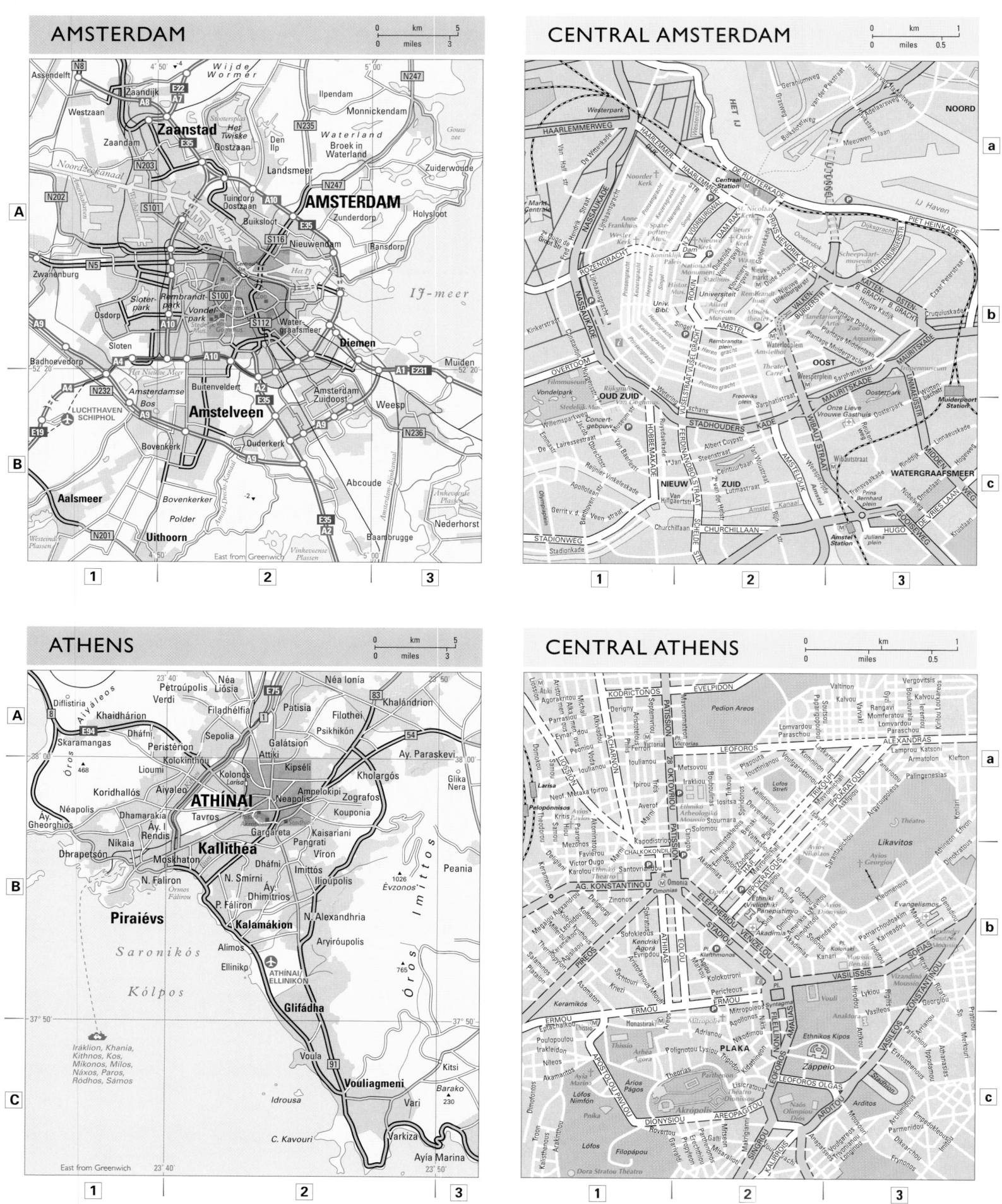

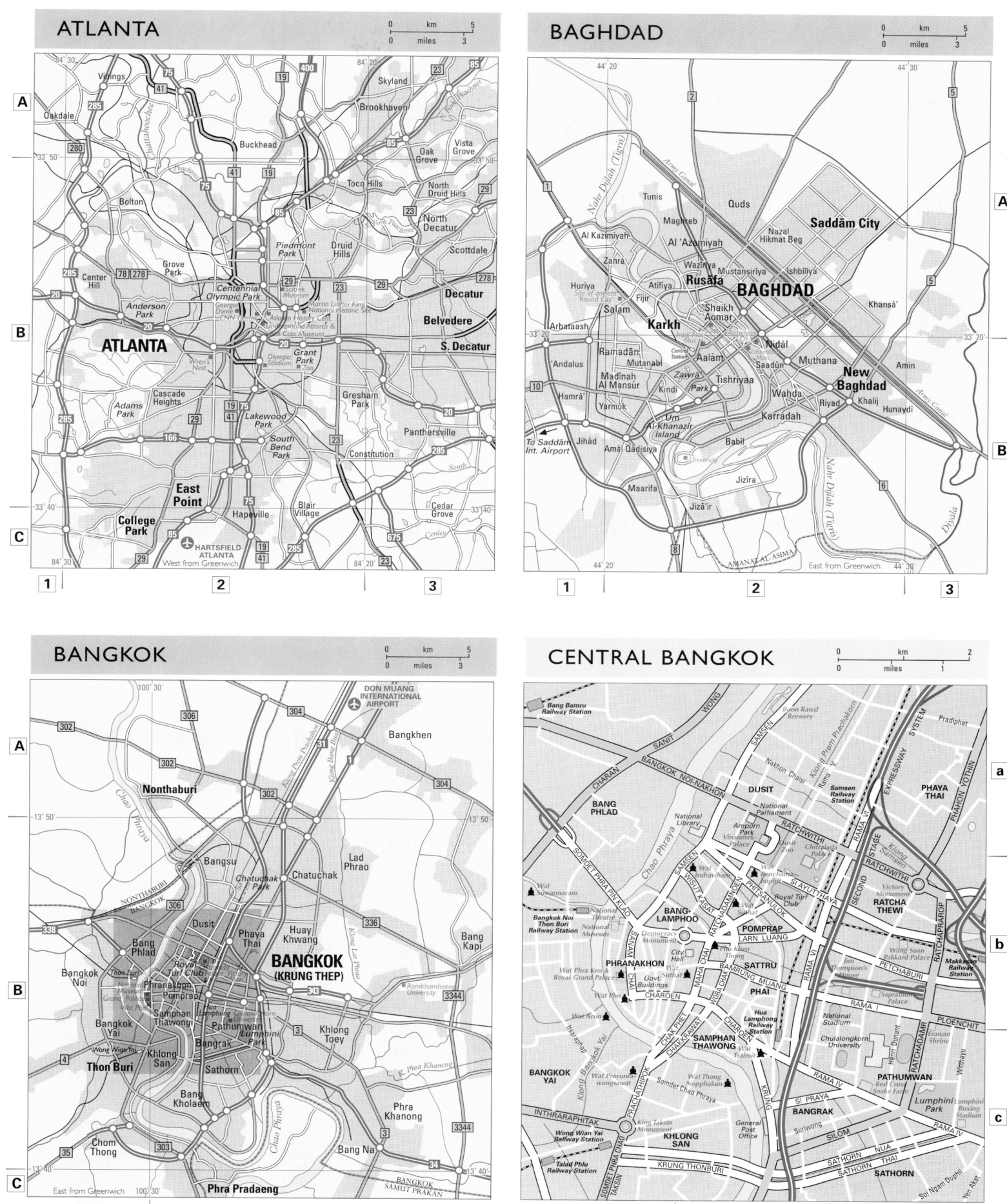

ATLANTA

BANGKOK

BAGHDAD

CENTRAL BANGKOK

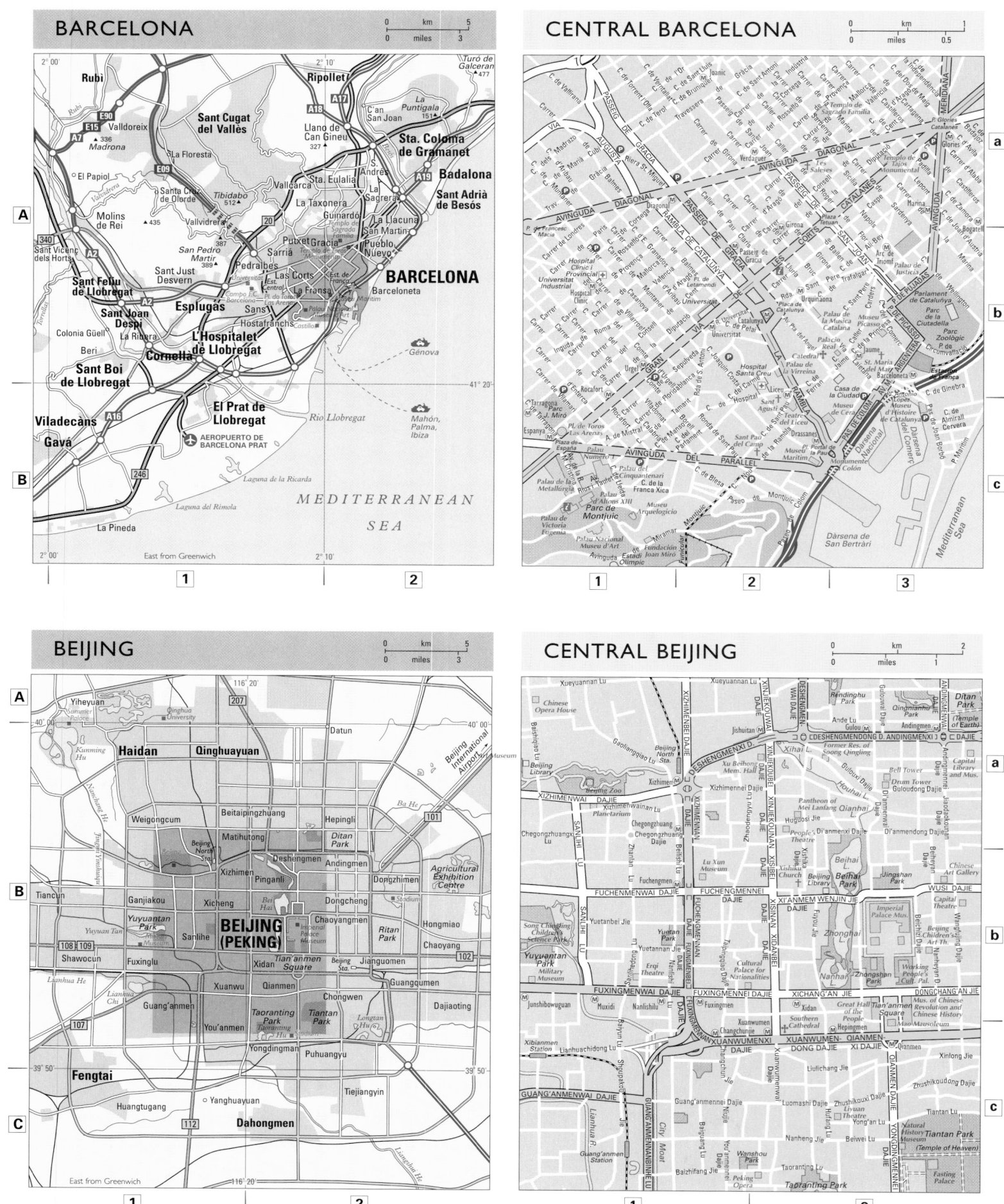

BARCELONA

CENTRAL BARCELONA

BEIJING

CENTRAL BEIJING

BERLIN

0 km 5
0 miles 3

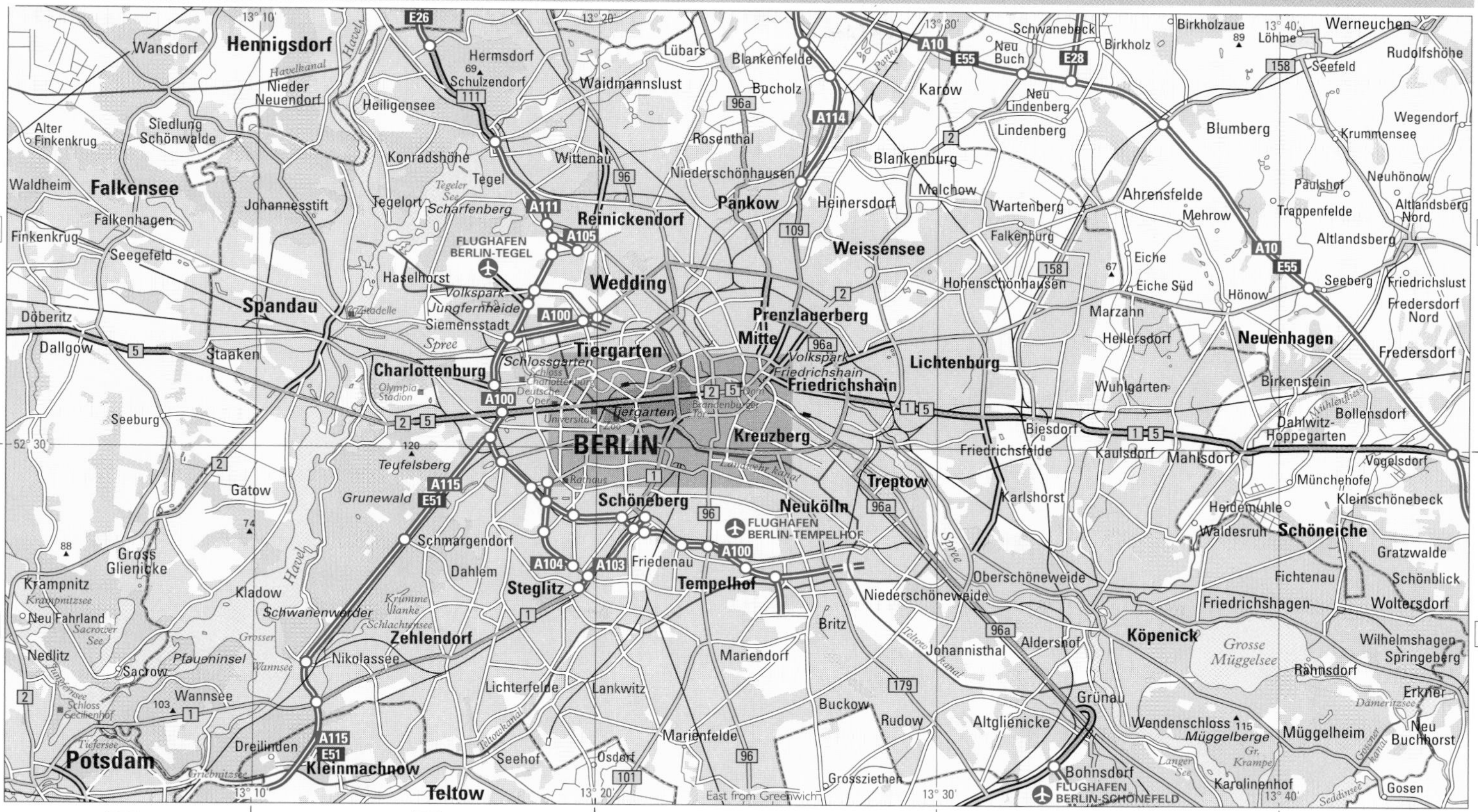

Wansdorf | Hennigsdorf | Hermsdorf | Lübars | Blankenfelde | Schwanebeck | Neu Buch | Birkholzaue | Birkholz | Löhme | Werneuchen
Alter Finkenkrug | Nieder Neuendorf | Siedlung Schönwalde | Schulzendorf | Waidmannslust | Bucholz | Karow | Neu Lindenberg | Rudolfshöhe | Seefeld
Waldheim | **Falkensee** | Falkenhagen | Heiligensee | Konradshöhe | Tegel | Rosenthal | Niederschönhausen | Lindenberg | Blumberg | Krummensee | Wegendorf
Döberitz | Seegefeld | Johannesstift | Tegelort | Scharfenberg | **Reinickendorf** | **Pankow** | Heinersdorf | Wartenberg | Ahrensfelde | Trappenfeld | Neuhönow
Dallgow | Spandau | Haselhorst | **Wedding** | **Weissensee** | Hohenschönhausen | Falkenberg | Mehrow | Altlandsberg Nord
Staaken | Siemensstadt | **Tiergarten** | **Prenzlauerberg** | **Mitte** | Marzahn | Hönow | Seeberg | Friedrichslust
Seeburg | **Charlottenburg** | Schlossgarten | **Friedrichshain** | **Lichtenburg** | Wuhlgarten | Biesdorf | Neuenhagen | Fredersdorf Nord
Gatow | Grunewald | **BERLIN** | **Kreuzberg** | Friedrichsfelde | Kaulsdorf | Mahlsdorf | Bollensdorf
Gross Glienicke | Teufelsberg | Schöneberg | **Neukölln** | **Treptow** | Karlshorst | Münchehofe | Kleinschönebeck
Krampnitz | Schmargendorf | Dahlem | Friedenau | **Tempelhof** | Oberschöneweide | Heidemühle | Schöneiche
Neu Fahrland | Zehlendorf | Lichterfelde | Britz | Niederschöneweide | Aldershof | **Köpenick** | Wilhelmshagen Springeberg
Nedlitz | Nikolassee | Lankwitz | Mariendorf | Johannisthal | Grosse Müggelsee | Rahnsdorf | Erkner
Sacrow | Wannsee | Seehof | Buckow | Rudow | Altglienicke | Grünau | Wendenschloss Müggelberge | Müggelheim
Potsdam | Dreilinden | **Kleinmachnow** | Osdorf | Marienfelde | Grossziethen | Bohnsdorf FLUGHAFEN BERLIN-SCHÖNEFELD | Neu Buchhorst | Gosen
Teltow | Karolinenhof

CENTRAL BERLIN

0 km 1
0 miles 0.5

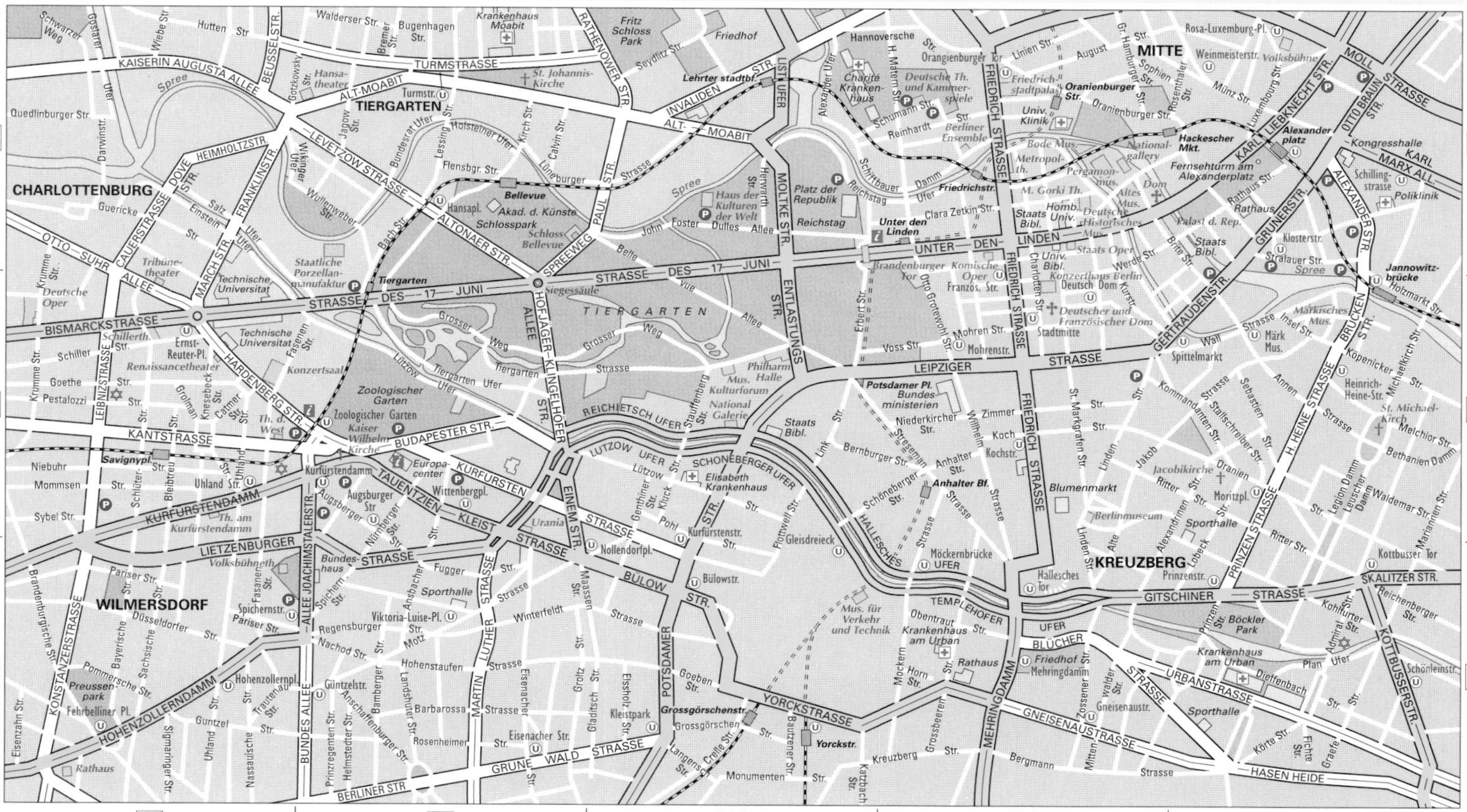

CHARLOTTENBURG | TIERGARTEN | MITTE | KREUZBERG | WILMERSDORF

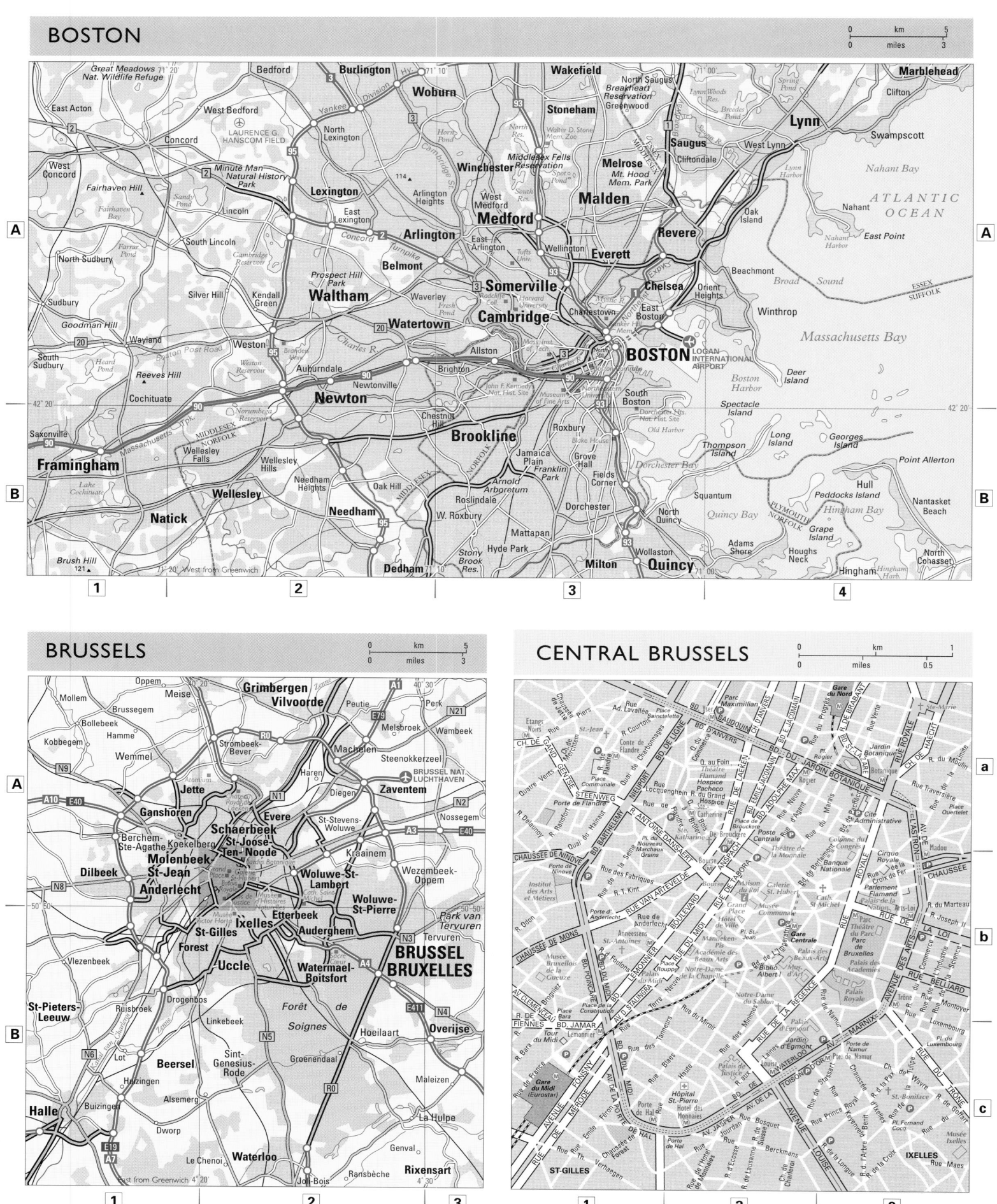

BOSTON

km 5
miles 3

BRUSSELS

km 5
miles 3

CENTRAL BRUSSELS

km 1
miles 0.5

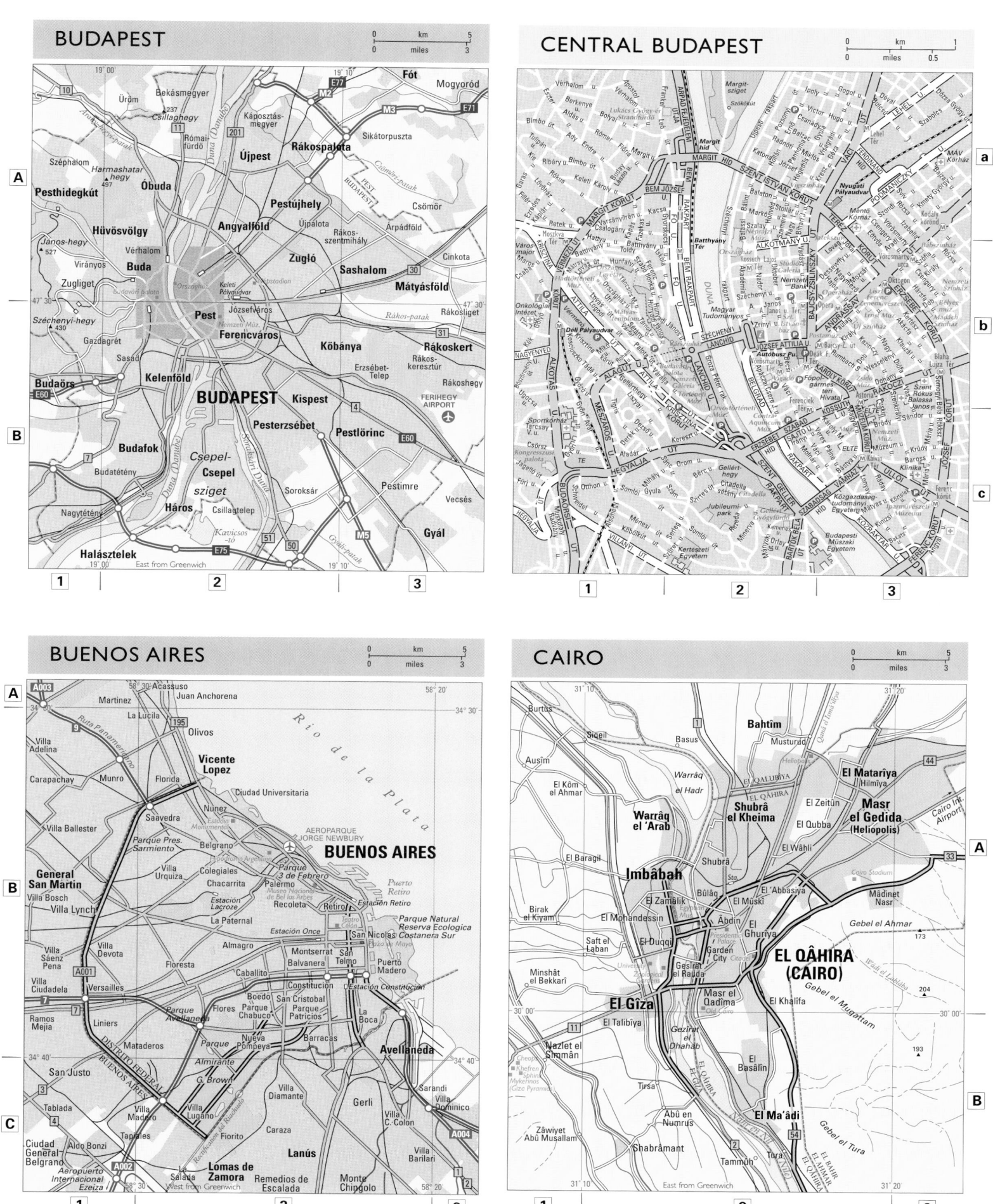

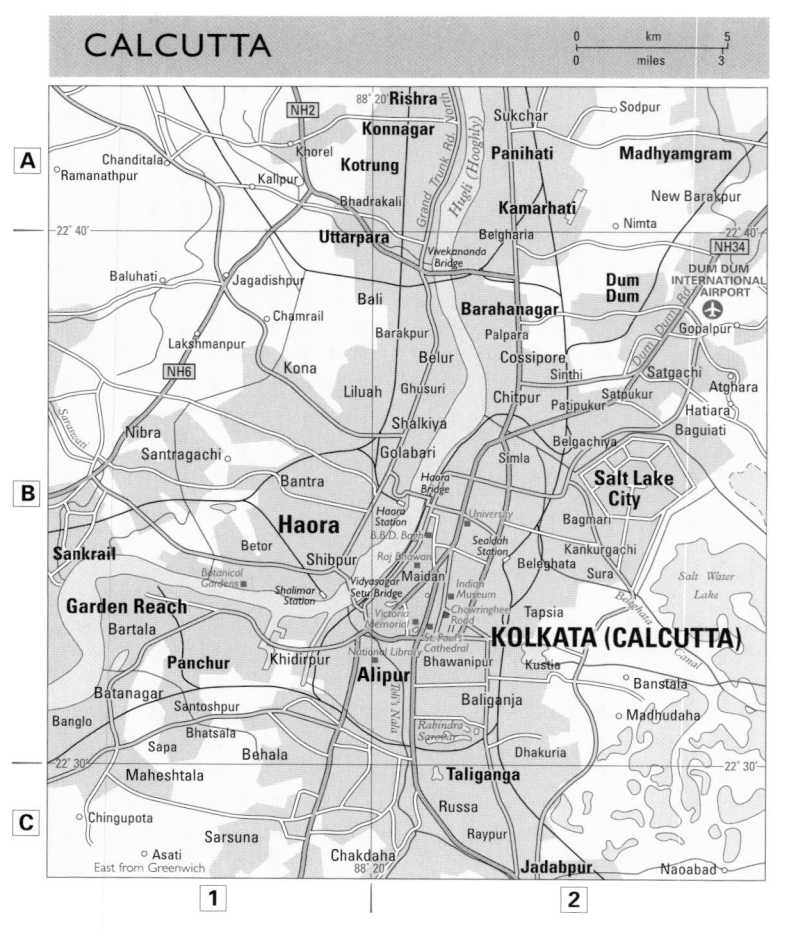

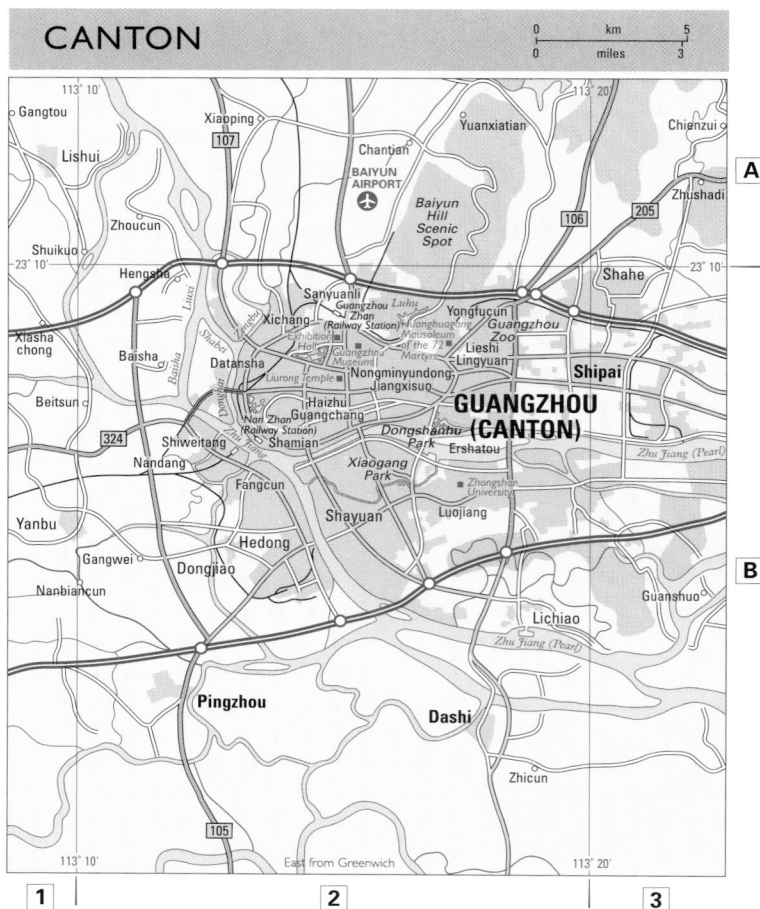

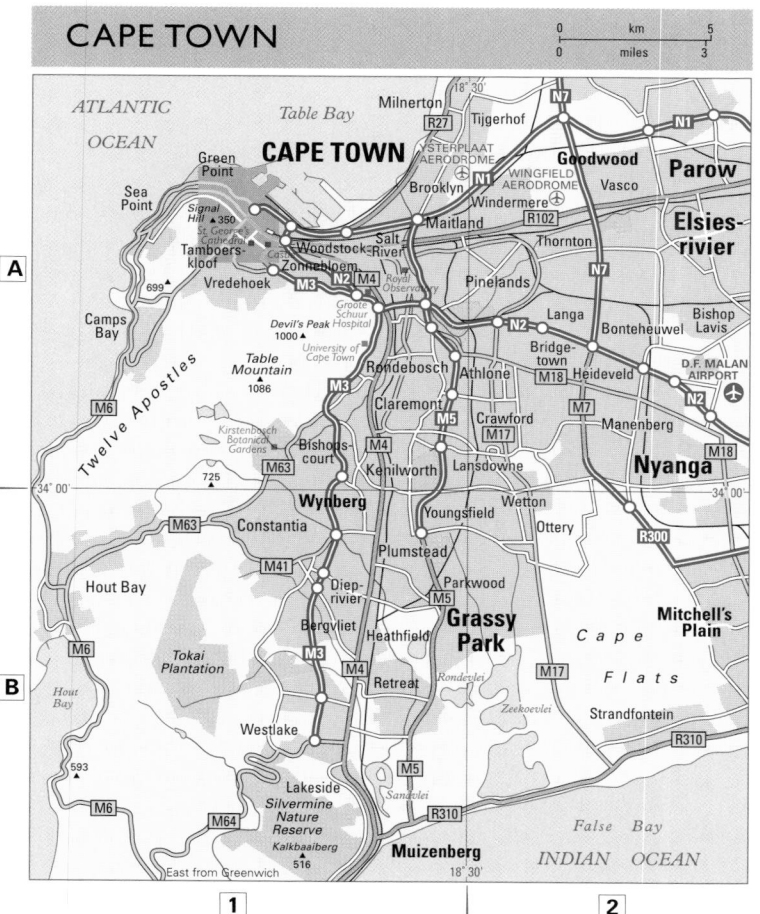

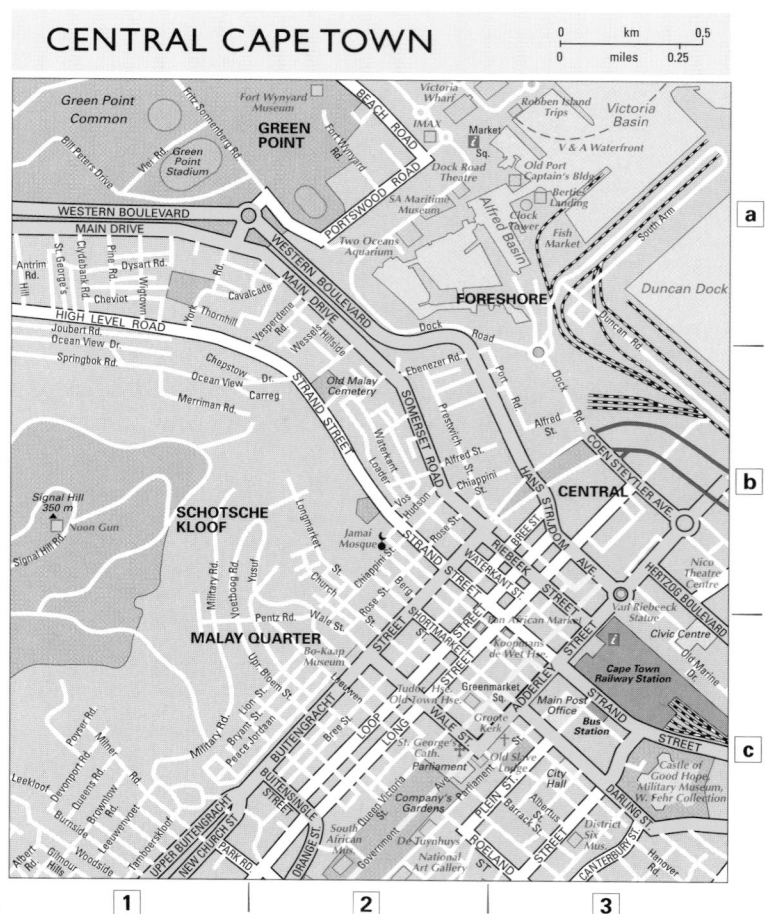

CHICAGO

km 0 — 5
miles 0 — 3

LAKE MICHIGAN

Wilmette
Evanston
Northwestern University
Baha'i Temple
Skokie
Glenview
Morton Grove
Niles
Glenview Countryside
Des Plaines
Park Ridge
Edison Park
Rosemont
CHICAGO O'HARE INTERNATIONAL AIRPORT
Schiller Park
Schiller Woods
Franklin Park
Northlake
Melrose Park
Bellwood
Maywood
Stone Park
Westchester
La Grange Park
La Grange
Brookfield
Riverside
North Riverside
Berwyn
Oak Park
Elmwood Park
River Forest
River Grove
Harwood Heights
Norridge
Dunning
Belmont Cragin
Portage Park
Irving Park
Lincolnwood
Rogers Park
Loyola University
Uptown
Lakeview
Wrigley Field
Avondale
Logan Square
Humboldt Park
West Town
Garfield Park
Lincoln Park
Lincoln Park Zoo
Old Town
Near North
Gold Coast
Navy Pier
Hancock Center
The Loop
CHICAGO
Grant Park
Chinatown
Univ. of Illinois at Chicago
Illinois Inst. of Tech.
Bridgeport
Lawndale
Cicero
Austin
Douglas Park
Stickney
Forest View
Summit
Lyons
McCook
Hodgkins
Indian Head Park
Countryside
Willow Springs
Justice
Bridgeview
Bedford Park
Burbank
Chicago Ridge
Hickory Hills
Palos Hills
Palos Park
Palos Heights
Worth
Oak Lawn
Evergreen Park
Mount Greenwood
Merrionette Park
Hometown
Ashburn
Chicago Lawn
Marquette Park
Gage Park
Brighton Park
McKinley Park
Sherman Park
Ogden Park
Englewood
Washington Park
Hyde Park
Museum of Science & Industry
South Shore
Chatham
Beverly
Morgan Park
Calumet Park
Blue Island
Robbins
Alsip
Roseland
South Deering
Burnham Park
Dan Ryan Expwy.
A.E. Stevenson Expwy.
Dwight D. Eisenhower Expwy.
J.F. Kennedy Expwy.
Edens Expwy.
Chicago Skyway
Bishop Ford Mem. Expwy.
Tri-State Tollway
Argonne Forest
Palos Hills Forest
Adler Planetarium
Field Museum
Burnham Harbor

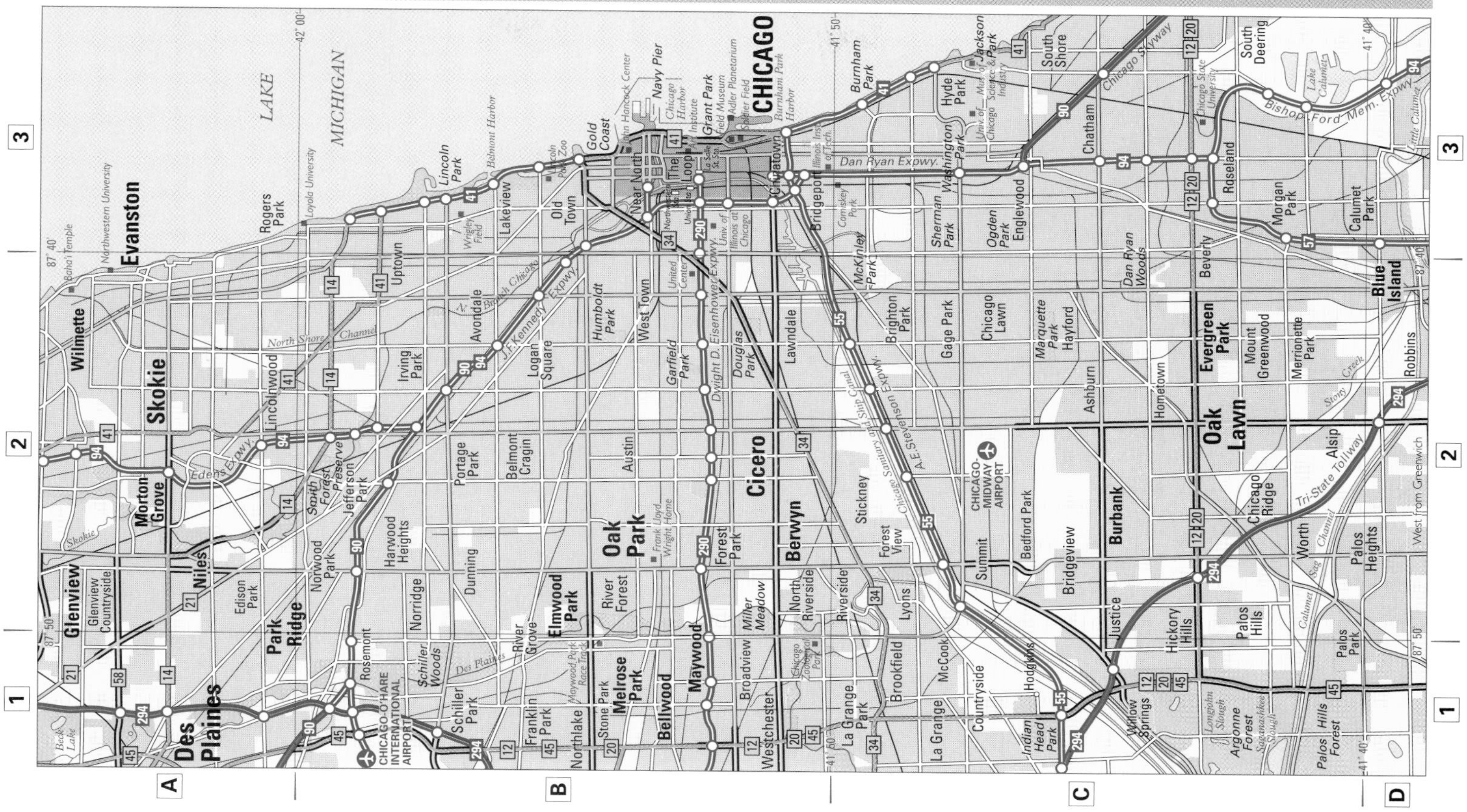

CENTRAL CHICAGO

km 0 — 1
miles 0 — 0.5

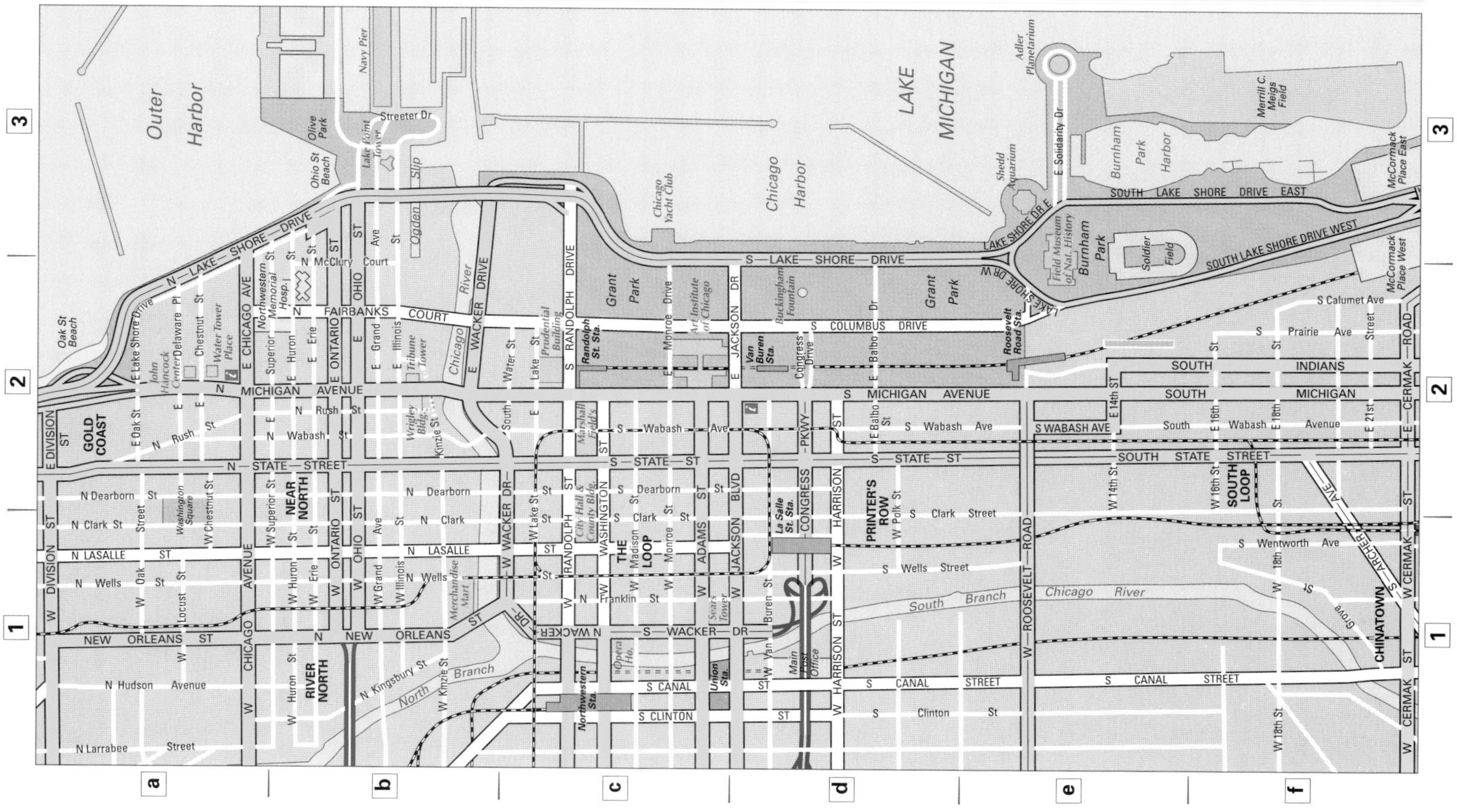

LAKE MICHIGAN
Outer Harbor
Navy Pier
Olive Park
Ohio St Beach
Oak St Beach
Lake Point Tower
Streeter Dr
GOLD COAST
NEAR NORTH
RIVER NORTH
John Hancock Center
Water Tower Place
Northwestern Memorial Hosp.
Tribune Tower
Wrigley Bldg
Merchandise Mart
THE LOOP
Marshall Field's
City Hall & County Bldg
Sears Tower
Prudential Building
Art Institute of Chicago
Grant Park
Buckingham Fountain
Chicago Yacht Club
Chicago Harbor
Roosevelt Road Sta.
Shedd Aquarium
Field Museum of Nat. History
Adler Planetarium
Burnham Park
Soldier Field
Merrill C. Meigs Field
McCormick Place East
McCormick Place West
Burnham Park Harbor
Randolph St Sta.
Van Buren St Sta.
Union Sta.
Northwestern Sta.
Post Office
Opera House
PRINTER'S ROW
SOUTH LOOP
CHINATOWN
South Branch
Chicago River
North Branch
LAKE SHORE DRIVE
SOUTH LAKE SHORE DRIVE EAST
SOUTH LAKE SHORE DRIVE WEST
MICHIGAN AVENUE
STATE STREET
WACKER DR
COLUMBUS DRIVE
ROOSEVELT ROAD
CERMAK RD
ARCHER AVE

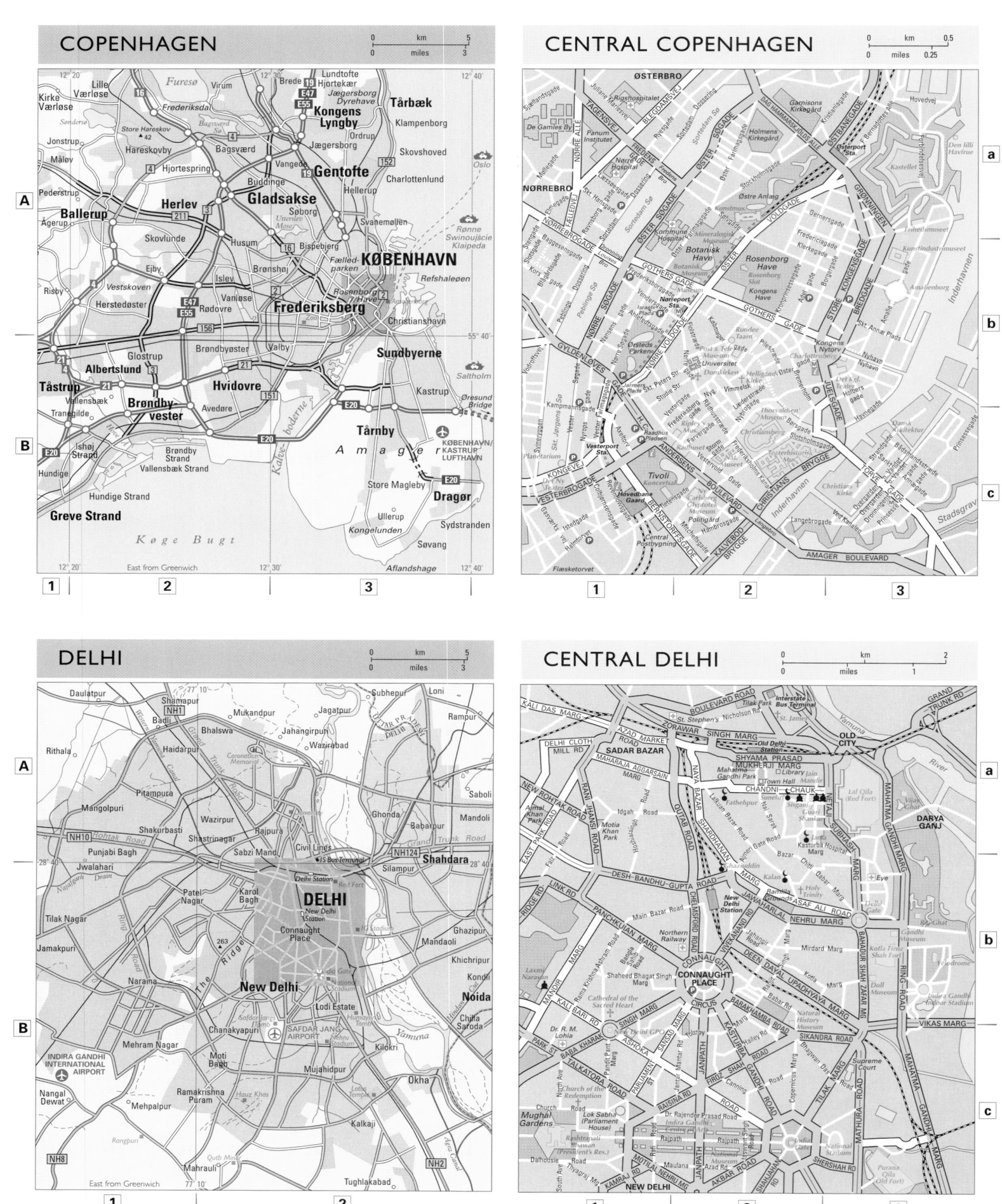

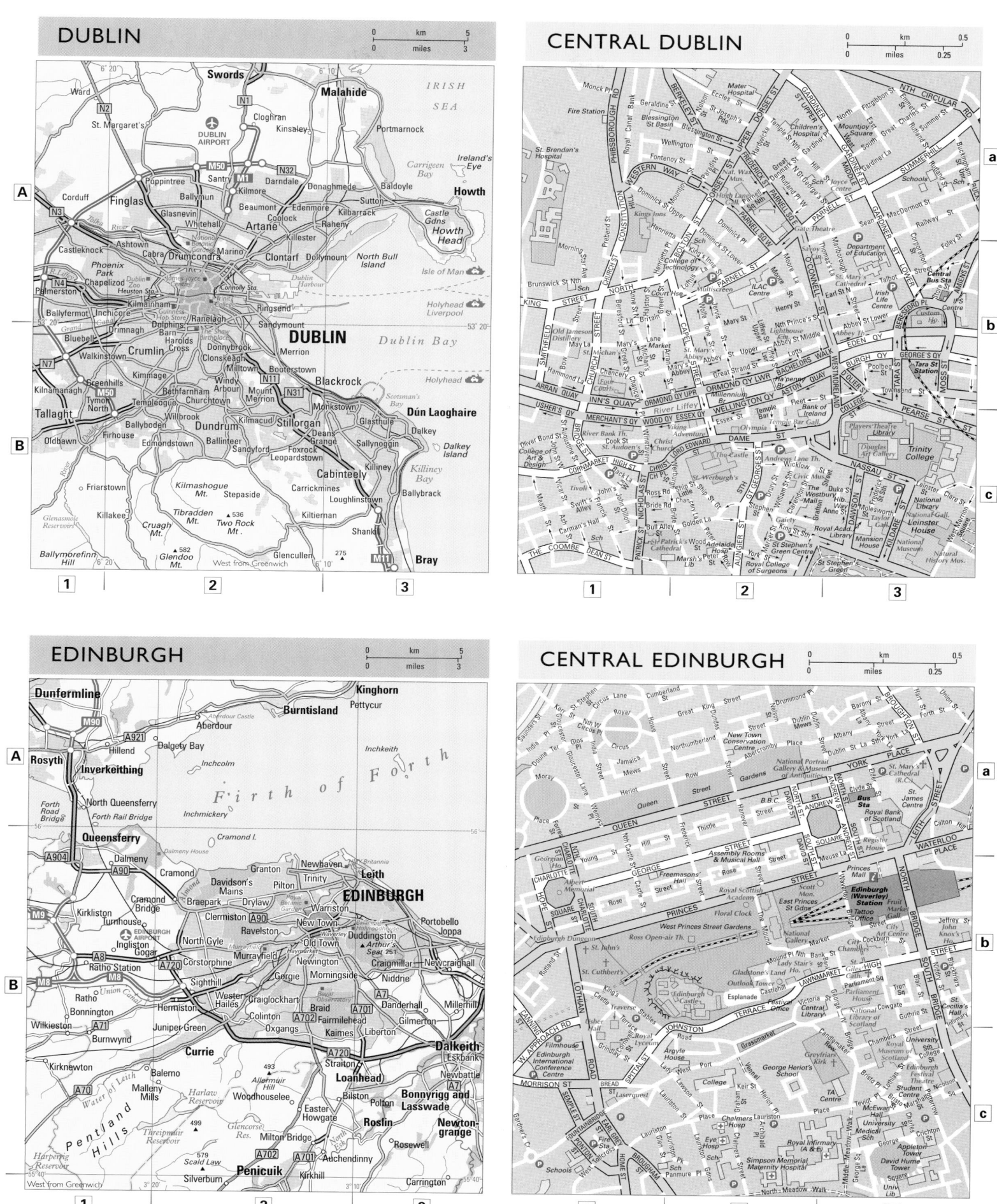

HELSINKI

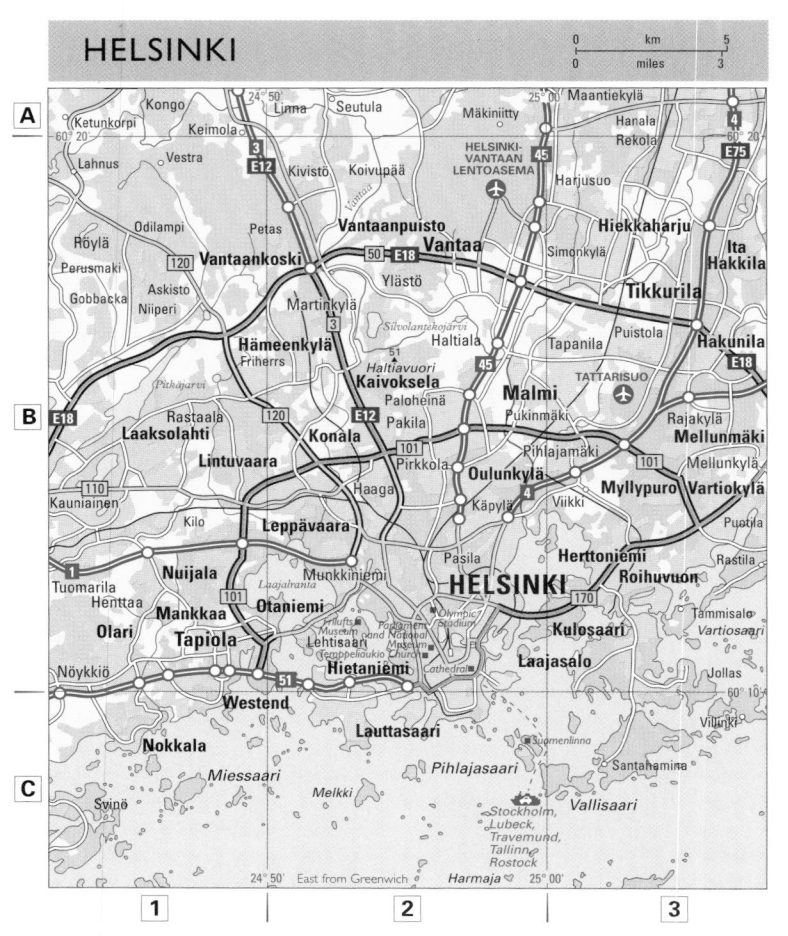

ISTANBUL

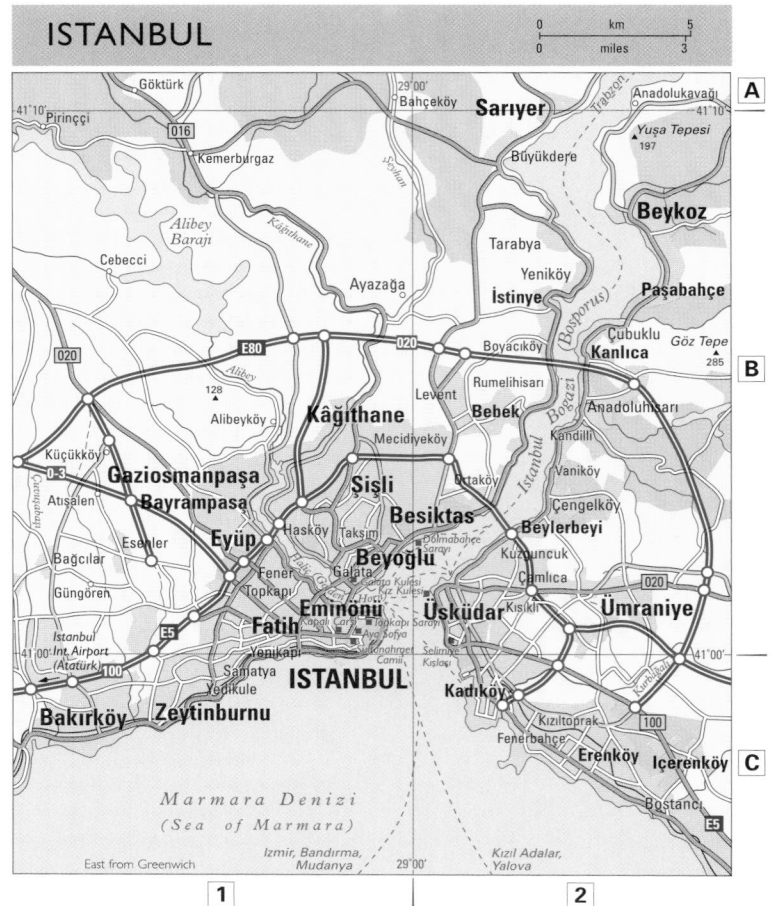

HONG KONG

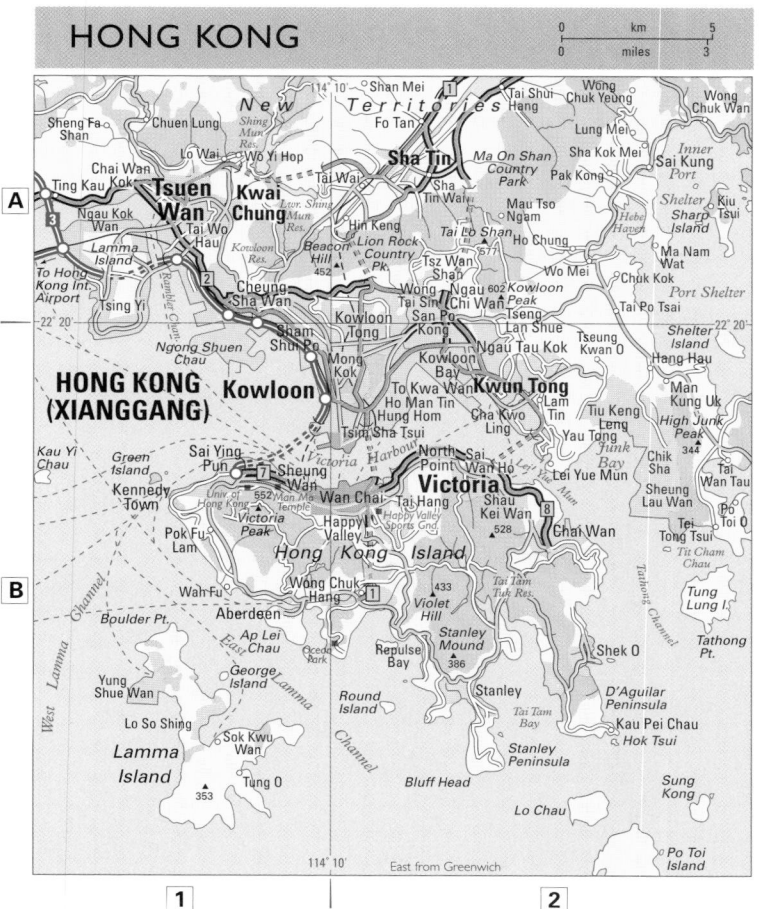

CENTRAL HONG KONG

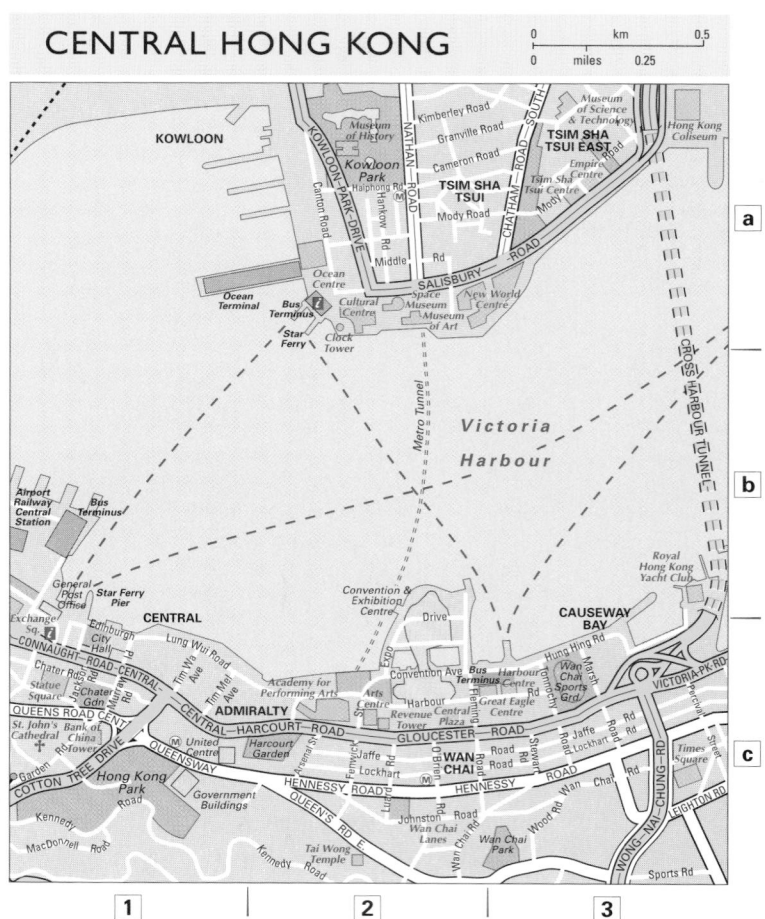

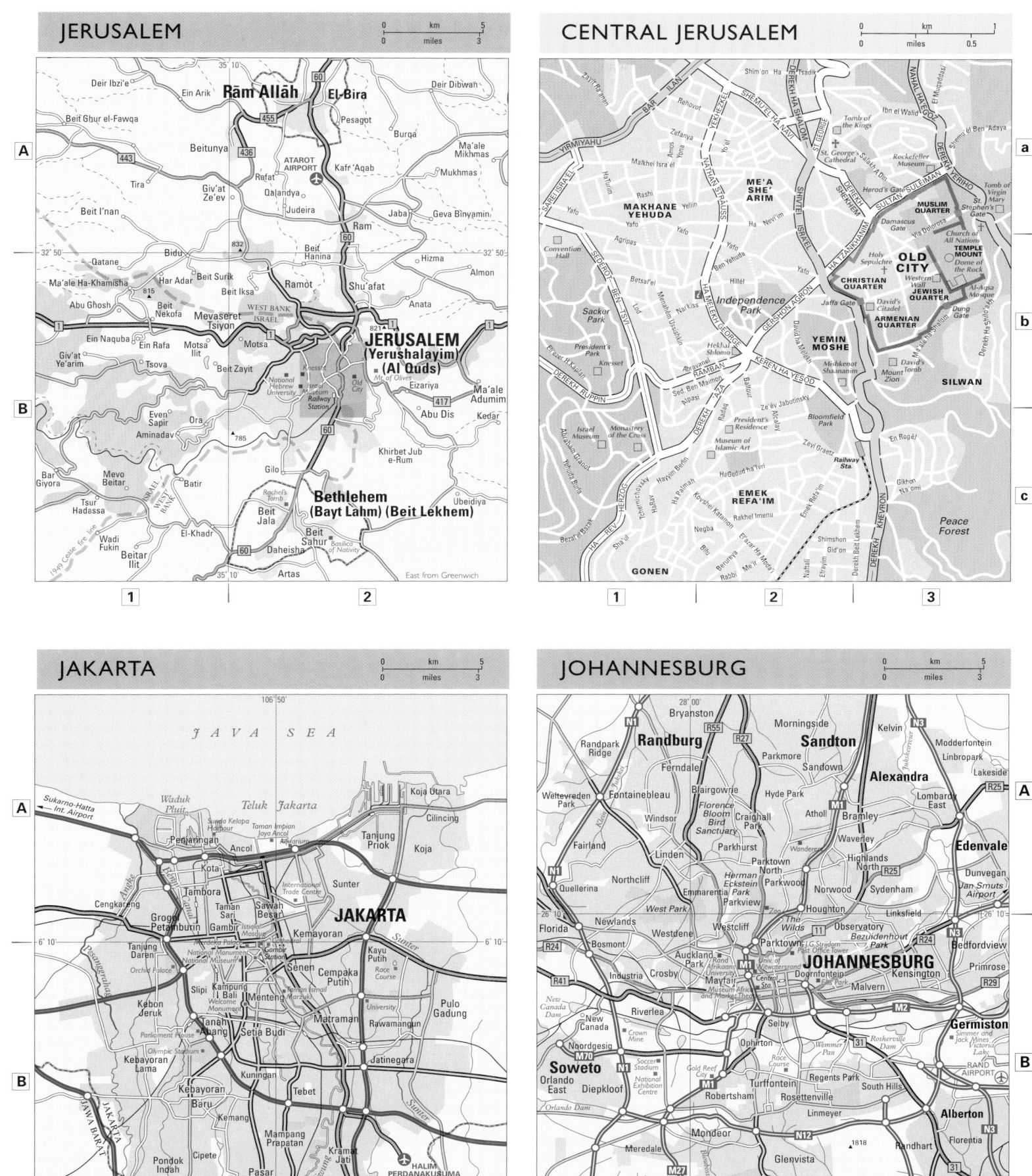

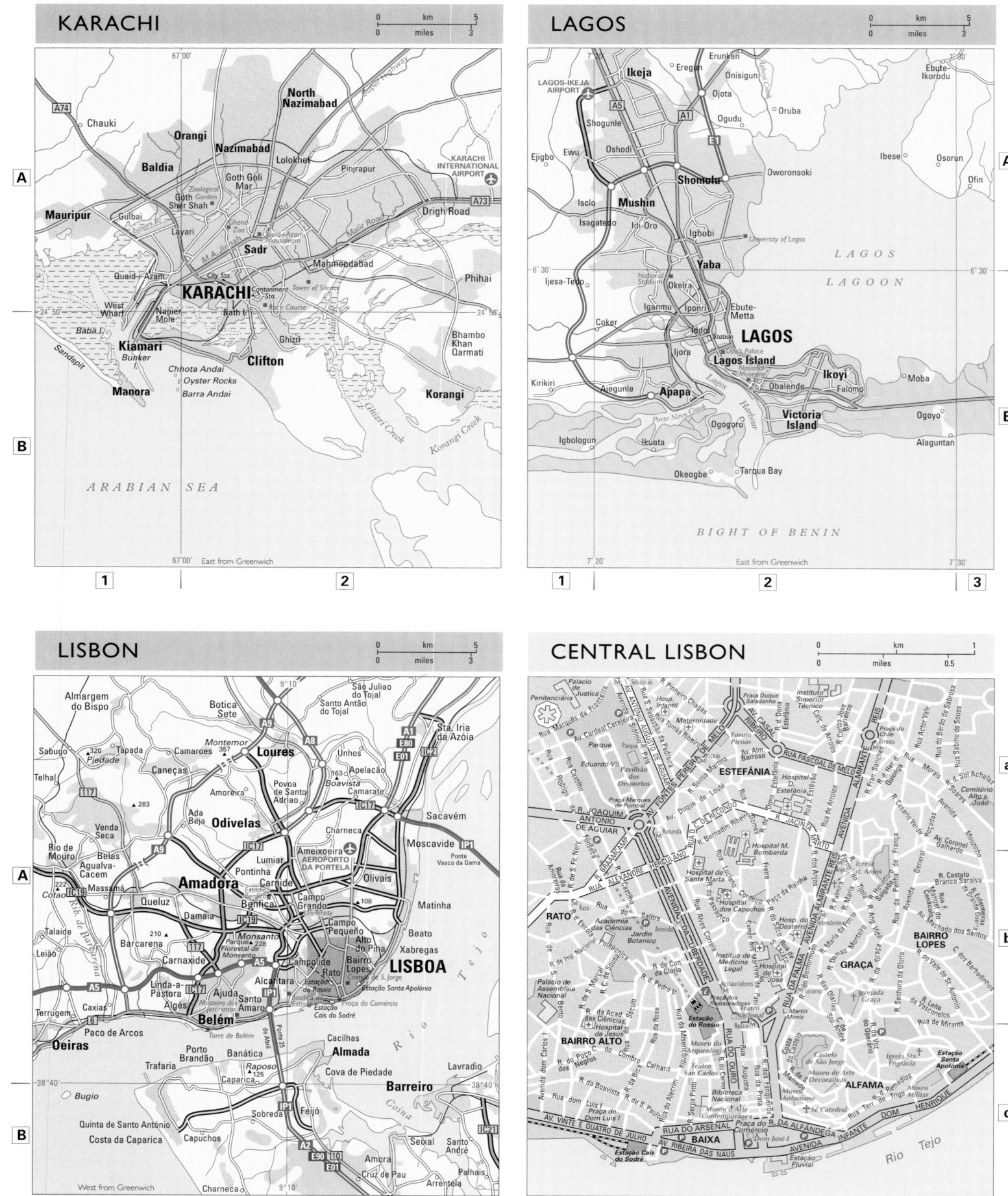

KARACHI

km 0—5
miles 0—3

67°00'

A74 · Chauki
North Nazimabad
Orangi
Nazimabad
Baldia
Lolokhet
Pinjrapur
KARACHI INTERNATIONAL AIRPORT
A73
Zoological Garden
Goth Góli Mar
Goth Sher Shah
Mauripur
Gulbai
Layari
Quaid-i-Azam Mausoleum
Ghand Zoo
Sadr
Mahmoodabad
Drigh Road
Malir Road
City Sta.
Cantonment Sta.
Tower of Silence
Phihai
KARACHI
Race Course
24° 50'
Quaid-i-Azam
West Wharf
Napier Mole
Bath I.
24° 50'
Baba I.
Sandspit
Kiamari
Bunker
Ghizri
Bhambo Khan Qarmati
Chhota Andai
Oyster Rocks
Barra Andai
Clifton
Manora
Ghizri Creek
Korangi
Korangi Creek

ARABIAN SEA

67°00'   East from Greenwich

A   B

1   2

LAGOS

km 0—5
miles 0—3

7°20'   7°30'
Erunkan
LAGOS-IKEJA AIRPORT
Ikeja
Eregun
Onisigun
Oruba
Ebute-Ikorodu
Shogunle
A5
Ojota
A1
Ogudu
E1
Ejigbo
Ewu
Oshodi
Ibese
Osorun
Ofin
Isolo
Mushin
Igi-Oro
Igbobi
Oworonsoki
Isagatedo
University of Lagos
LAGOS LAGOON
6° 30'
Ijesa-Tedo
Yaba
Okeira
6° 30'
Iganmu
Iponri
Ebute-Metta
Coker
Iddo
Station
LAGOS
Ijora
National Museum
Lagos Island
Ikoyi
Moba
Kirikiri
Aiegunle
Obalende
Falomo
Apapa
Lagos Harbour
Porto Novo Creek
Victoria Island
Ogoyo
Igbologun
Ikuata
Ogogoro
Alaguntan
Okeogbe
Tarqua Bay

BIGHT OF BENIN

7°20'   East from Greenwich   7°30'

A   B

1   2   3

LISBON

km 0—5
miles 0—3

9°10'
Almargem do Bispo
Botica Sete
São Julião do Tojal
Santo Antão do Tojal
A9
Montemor 357
Camaroes
Loures
Sabugo
▲320
Tapada da Piedade
A8
Sta. Iria da Azóia
Telhal
Caneças
Unhos
A1 E80 E01 IC2
117
Amoreira
Póvoa de Santo Adriao
Apelação
Boavista
Camarate
IC17
Odivelas
Venda Seca
▲283
A9
Ameixoeira
Charneca
Sacavém
Rio de Mouro
Belas
IC17
Lumiar
Moscavide
IP1
Aagualva-Cacem
Pontinha
Carnide
Ponte Vasco da Gama
Cotao
222
IC19
Massamá
Amadora
Campo Grande
Olivais
Queluz
Benfica
IC19
University
Matinha
Damaia
▲210
Campo Pequeno
▲108
Barcarena
117
Monsanto
Parque Florestal de Monsanto
Alto do Piha
Beato
Carnaxide
228
Campolide
Bairro Lopes
Xabregas
Linda-a-Pastora
A5
Alcántara
Rato
LISBOA
Talaide
Leião
IC17
Ajuda
Santo Amaro
Estação Santa Apolónia
Terrugem
Caxias
Algés
Castelo de S. Jorge
Basílica da Estrela
Praça do Comércio
Estação Cais do Sodré
Rio Tejo
Oeiras
Belém
Torre de Belém
Ponte 25 de Abril
Paco de Arcos
Porto Brandão
Banática
Cacilhas
Trafaria
Raposo ▲125
Almada
Lavradio
38° 40'
Bugio
Caparica
Cova de Piedade
38° 40'
Quinta de Santo António
IP1
Sobreda
Feijó
Barreiro
Costa da Caparica
Capuchos
A2 E90 10 E01
Amora
Seixal
Santo André
IC21
Charneca
9°10'
Cruz de Pau
Palhais
Arrentela

West from Greenwich

A   B

1   2

CENTRAL LISBON

km 0—1
miles 0—0.5

Palacio de Justiça
R. Pinheiro Chagas
Praça Duque Saldanha
Instituto Superior Técnico
Penitenciária
Hosp. Infantil
Forum Picoas
Rua Marquês da Fronteira
AV. ANTONIO AUGUSTO DE AGUIAR
Maternidade
AV. Alm. Barroso
RUA PASCOAL DE MELO
RIBEIRO
Parque Eduardo VII
Pavilhão dos Desportos
ESTEFÁNIA
Hospital D. Estefânia
ALMIRANTE REIS
Cemitério Alto s. João
R. JOAQUIM ANTONIO DE AGUIAR
Praça Marquês de Pombal
Rotunda
AV. FONTES PEREIRA DE MELO
a
Jardim Botânico
RATO
Academia das Ciências
BRAAMCAMP
RUA ALEXANDRE HERCULANO
AVENIDA DA LIBERDADE
Hospital de Santa Marta
Hospital dos Capuchos
Hosp. de S. José
Igreja d. Anjos
BAIRRO LOPES
b
AVENIDA ALMIRANTE REIS
GRAÇA
Palacio da Assembleia Nacional
Instituto de Medicina Legal
RUA DA PALMA
Igreja da Graça
Restauradores
Estação do Rossio
Praça dos Restauradores
Igreja Sta. Engracia
BAIRRO ALTO
Museu do Arqueologia
RUA DO OURO
Teatro San Carlos
Museu de Arte Decorativa
Castelo de São Jorge
ALFAMA
Museu Antoniano
DOM HENRIQUE
Estação Santa Apolónia
Biblioteca Nacional
Sé Catedral
Museu de Arte Contemporanea
Praça do Comércio
INFANTE
AV. VINTE E QUATRO DE JULHO
RUA DO ARSENAL
R. DA ALFANDEGA
AVENIDA
BAIXA
Dom José I
Estação Fluvial
AV. RIBEIRA DAS NAUS
Estação Cais do Sodré
Rio Tejo

a   b   c

1   2   3

LONDON

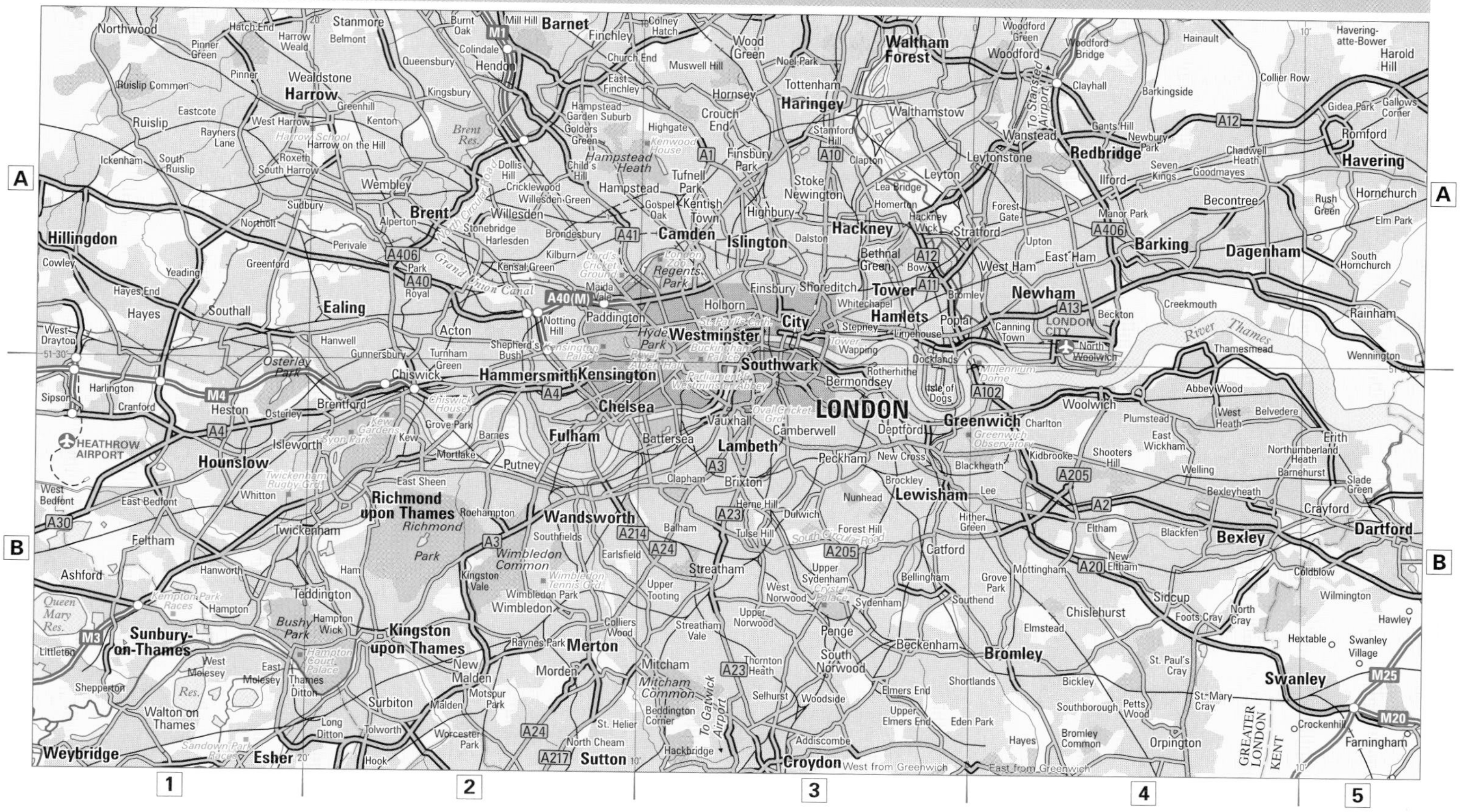

km 5
miles 3

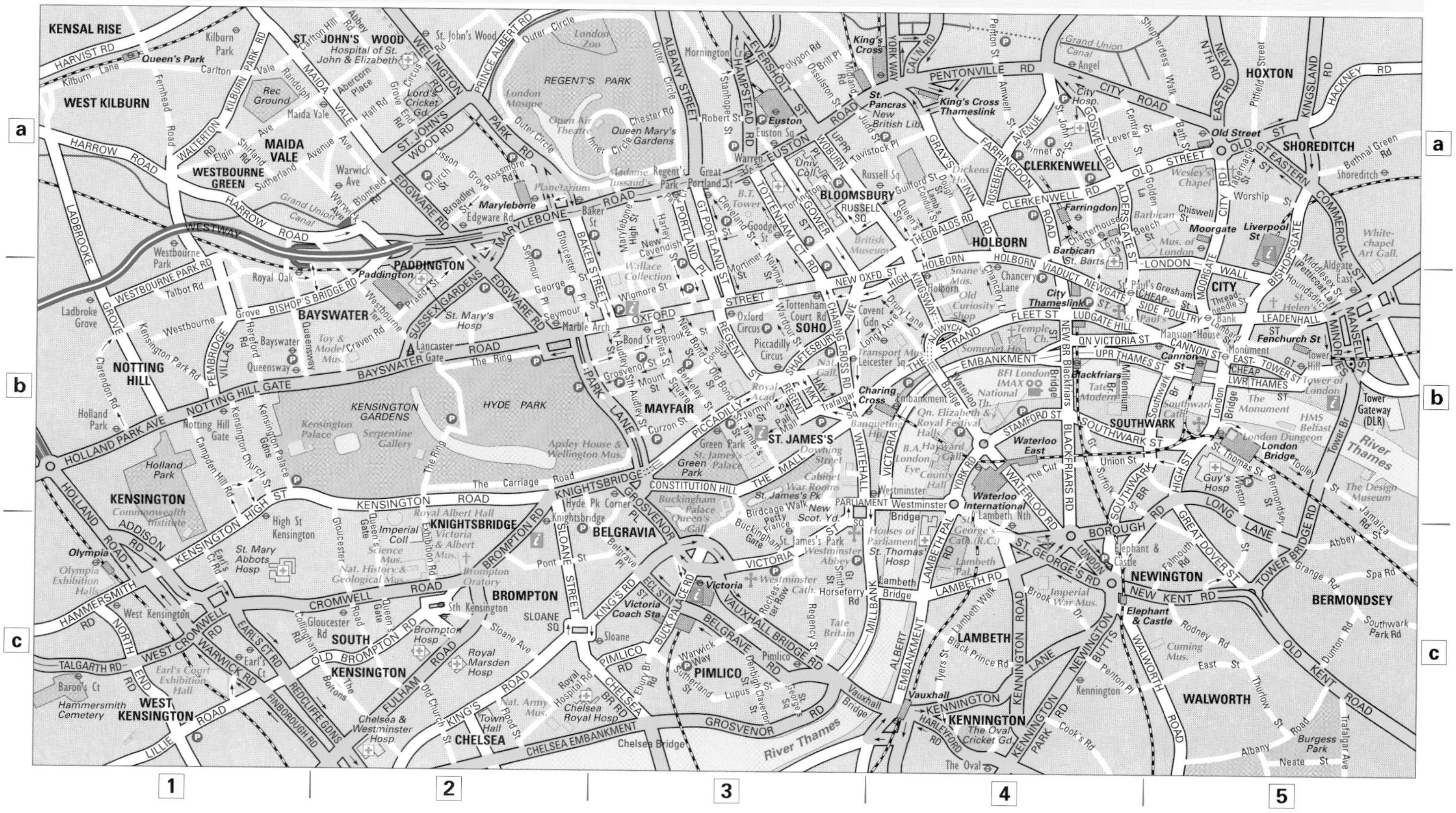

COPYRIGHT GEORGE PHILIP LTD

Northwood Stanmore Mill Hill Barnet Finchley Colney Hatch Wood Green Woodford Waltham Forest Woodford Bridge Hainault Havering-atte-Bower Harold Hill Collier Row Gidea Park Gallows Corner

Ruislip Common Pinner Green Hatch End Harrow Weald Burnt Oak Colindale Hendon Church End East Finchley Muswell Hill Hornsey Tottenham Walthamstow Wanstead Leytonstone Redbridge Ilford Seven Kings Chadwell Heath Goodmayes Romford Havering Hornchurch

HARROW Greenhill Kingsbury Brent Res. Hampstead Garden Suburb Highgate Crouch End HARINGEY Stamford Hill Clapton Leyton Forest Gate Manor Park Becontree Elm Park

Ickenham Ruislip South Ruislip Eastcote Rayners Lane West Harrow Roxeth Harrow on the Hill Wembley Alperton Sudbury Dollis Hill Cricklewood Golders Green Hampstead Tufnell Park Kentish Town Highbury Homerton Hackney Wick West Ham East Ham Upton A406 BARKING DAGENHAM

HILLINGDON Cowley Yeading Northolt Perivale Greenford BRENT Stonebridge Harlesden Willesden Brondesbury Kilburn Kensal Green Gospel Oak CAMDEN ISLINGTON Dalston Bethnal Green Bow Poplar Canning Town LONDON CITY Beckton Creekmouth Rainham

West Drayton EALING Hanwell Acton Shepherd's Bush Notting Hill Paddington HOLBORN CITY Whitechapel Stepney Limehouse North Woolwich Thamesmead

Harlington Cranford HESTON Osterley Park Brentford Chiswick HAMMERSMITH KENSINGTON Hyde Park WESTMINSTER Southwark Bermondsey Rotherhithe Isle of Dogs Docklands Millennium Dome River Thames

HEATHROW AIRPORT Hounslow Isleworth Kew CHELSEA FULHAM Battersea LONDON Camberwell Deptford GREENWICH Charlton Woolwich Plumstead East Wickham Abbey Wood West Heath Belvedere Erith Northumberland Heath

West Bedfont East Bedfont Twickenham Richmond upon Thames Richmond Park Barnes Mortlake Putney LAMBETH Brixton Peckham New Cross Lewisham Brockley Kidbrooke Shooters Hill Welling Bexleyheath Slade Green Crayford

Ashford Feltham Hanworth Teddington Ham Roehampton Southfields WANDSWORTH Clapham Herne Hill Dulwich Forest Hill Hither Green Eltham Blackfen BEXLEY Dartford

Queen Mary Res. Sunbury-on-Thames Hampton Bushy Park Kingston Vale Wimbledon Common Wimbledon Tennis Cl. Balham Tooting Streatham Upper Sydenham Sydenham Catford Grove Park Mottingham Sidcup Foots Cray North Cray Wilmington Hawley

Littleton West Molesey East Molesey Thames Ditton Hampton Wick Kingston upon Thames New Malden Motspur Park Merton Mitcham Streatham Vale Upper Norwood Penge Beckenham Bromley Chislehurst Swanley Village Swanley

Shepperton Walton on Thames Sunbury Esher Surbiton Tolworth Malden Worcester Park North Cheam Sutton St. Helier Mitcham Common Thornton Heath Selhurst Woodside South Norwood Elmers End Eden Park Shortlands Bromley Common Petts Wood St. Mary Cray St. Paul's Cray Crockenhill Farningham

Weybridge Esher Hook Chessington Long Ditton Morden Hackbridge Beddington Corner To Gatwick Airport Croydon Addiscombe Upper Elmers End Hayes Bromley Common Orpington GREATER LONDON KENT M25 M20

West from Greenwich East from Greenwich

CENTRAL LONDON

km 2
miles 1

KENSAL RISE WEST KILBURN ST. JOHN'S WOOD St. John's Wood REGENT'S PARK KING'S CROSS HOXTON SHOREDITCH

MAIDA VALE WESTBOURNE GREEN PADDINGTON MARYLEBONE BLOOMSBURY HOLBORN CLERKENWELL MOORGATE CITY Liverpool St.

NOTTING HILL BAYSWATER Notting Hill Gate HYDE PARK KENSINGTON GARDENS Kensington Palace MAYFAIR SOHO Charing Cross STRAND FLEET ST. Bank

HOLLAND PARK KENSINGTON Olympia Kensington Palace Serpentine Gallery KNIGHTSBRIDGE St. James's Park ST. JAMES'S WHITEHALL EMBANKMENT Waterloo SOUTHWARK London Bridge

WEST KENSINGTON EARL'S COURT BROMPTON SOUTH KENSINGTON BELGRAVIA Buckingham Palace Houses of Parliament Westminster LAMBETH BOROUGH BERMONDSEY

Hammersmith Cemetery WEST KENSINGTON CHELSEA PIMLICO VICTORIA River Thames VAUXHALL KENNINGTON WALWORTH OLD KENT ROAD

River Thames The Oval Chelsea Bridge NEWINGTON Elephant & Castle

COPYRIGHT GEORGE PHILIP LTD

LOS ANGELES

km 5
miles 3

Tarzana · Van Nuys · Burbank · Verdugo Mts. · Altadena · San Gabriel Mts.
101 · Sepulveda Flood Control Basin · San Rafael Hills · Flint Peak 575 · Rose Bowl · 210 · Pasadena · Sierra Madre · Colorado Fwy.
Encino · San Fernando Valley · 170 · North Hollywood · 5 · Disney Studios · 134 · Glendale · 134 · California Inst. of Tech. · 210 · Monrovia
216 · Sherman Oaks · 405 · Studio City · 101 · Warner Bros. Studios · Golden State Fwy. · Glendale Galleria · Eagle Rock · 2 · Arcadia
Encino Reservoir · Universal Studios · Cahuenga Peak 555 · Zoo · Griffith Park · Highland Park · 110 · South Pasadena · San Marino · 19 · Temple City
Santa Monica Mts. · Stone Canyon Reservoir · Hollywood Lake · Hollywood Bowl · Garvanza · El Sereno · Pasadena Fwy. · Southwest Museum · San Gabriel
459 · Beverly Glen · Franklin Reservoir · Hollywood · Silver Lake Reservoir · 5 · California State Univ. · Alhambra · Rosemead
Bel Air · Mann's Chinese Theatre · Sunset Blvd. · Santa Monica Blvd. · Dodger Stadium · Lincoln Heights · San Bernardino Fwy. · 60 · El Monte
Beverly Hills · West Hollywood · Paramount Studios · 110 · Civic Center · Monterey Park · South San Gabriel · South El Monte
University of California Los Angeles · Westwood Village · L.A. County Art Museum · LOS ANGELES · Union Sta. · 10 · Whittier Narrows · Flood Control Basin
Will Rogers State Historical Park · Brentwood Park · 2 · Convention Center · Boyle Heights · 710 · Bicentennial Park · 605
Pacific Palisades · Santa Monica Fwy. · 10 · University of Southern California · East Los Angeles · Montebello · Puente Hills
Santa Monica · 10 · San Diego Fwy. · Culver City · Baldwin Hills Reservoir · Memorial Coliseum Exposition Park · Vernon · 5 · Commerce · Santa Ana Fwy. · Rio Hondo · 19 · Pico Rivera · Rio Pico State Historic Park · Whittier
SANTA MONICA MUNICIPAL AIRPORT · View Park · Maywood · Los Nietos
Venice · 405 · Windsor Hills · Huntington Park · Bell · Bell Gardens · 5 · Santa Fe Springs
PACIFIC OCEAN · Marina del Ray · Westchester · Ladera Heights · Florence · Cudahy · 605
Los Angeles International Airport · University of West Los Angeles · Great Western Forum · 42 · South Gate · 710 · Downey · 19
Lennox · Inglewood · 110 · 42

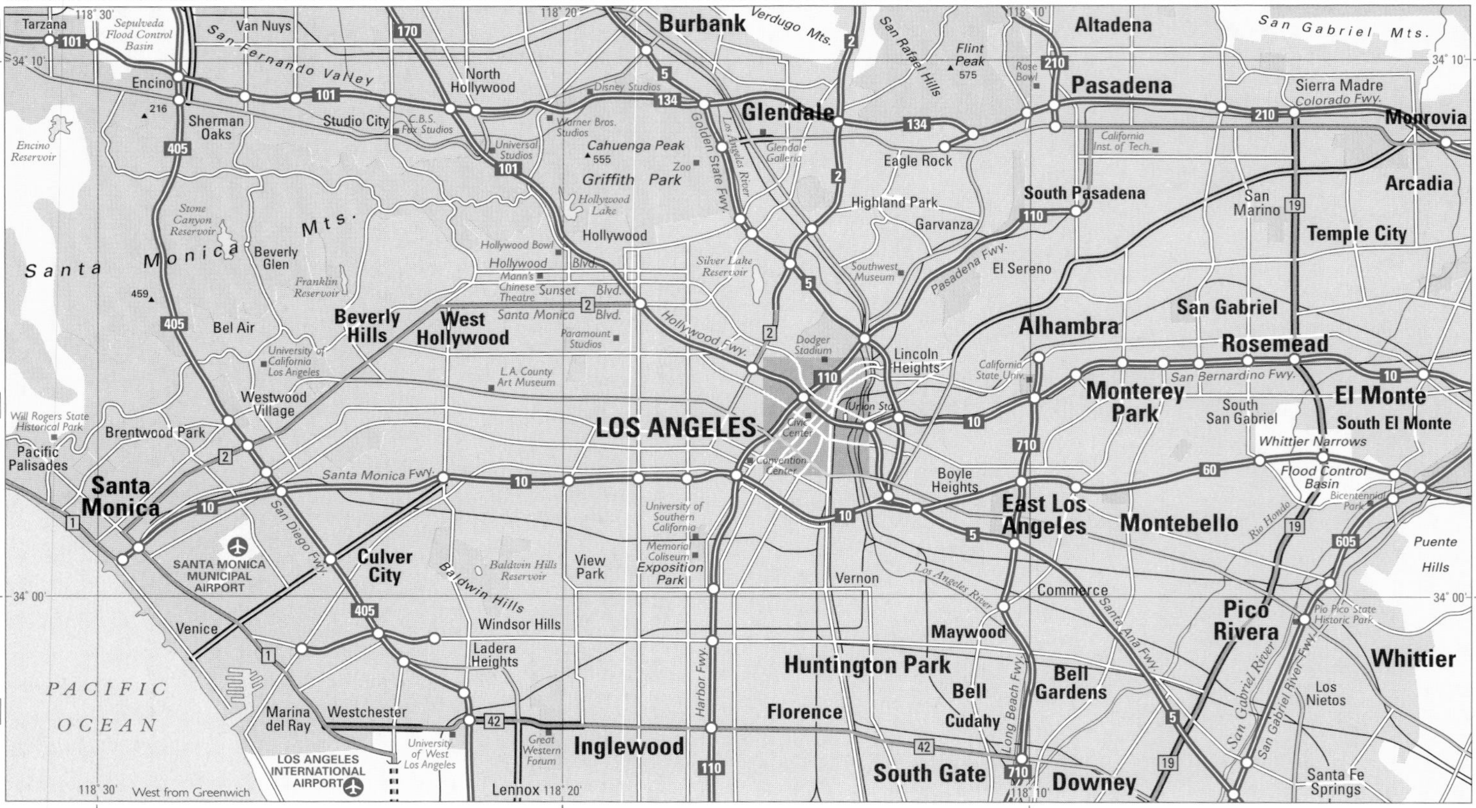

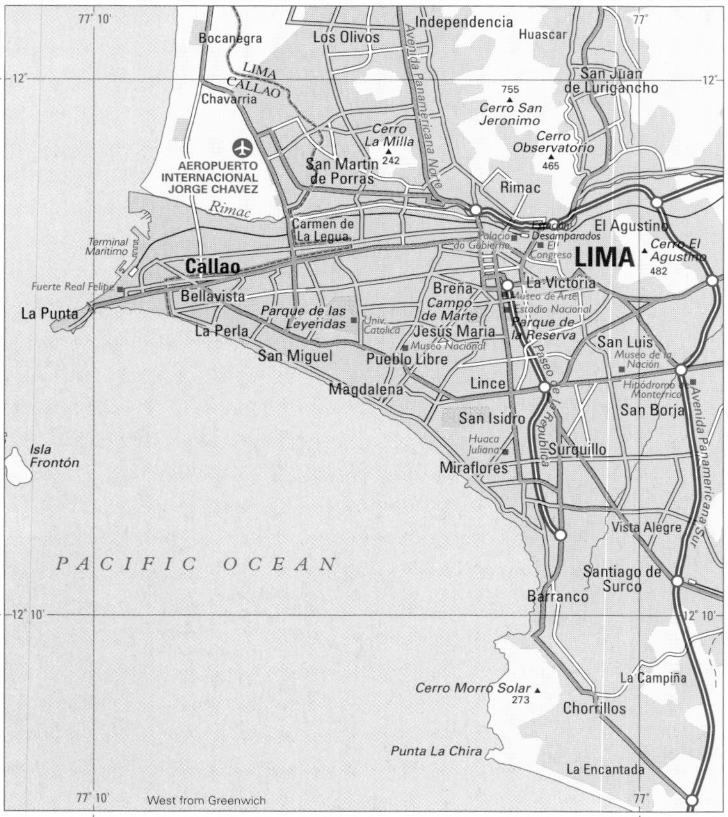

West from Greenwich

A B C · 1 2 3 4

LIMA

km 5
miles 3

Bocanegra · Los Olivos · Independencia · Huascar · 77°10'
Lima Callao · Chavarria · San Juan de Lurigancho
Cerro San Jeronimo 755 · Cerro Observatorio 465
Aeropuerto Internacional Jorge Chavez · San Martin de Porras · Cerro La Milla 242 · Rimac
Rimac · Callao · Carmen de la Legua · Palacio do Gobierno · El Agustino · Cerro El Agustino 482
Terminal Maritimo · Fuerte Real Felipe · Desamparados · LIMA
La Punta · Bellavista · Breña · La Victoria
Parque de las Leyendas · Campo de Marte · Estadio Nacional
La Perla · Jesus Maria · Museo Nacional · San Luis · Museo de la Nacion
San Miguel · Pueblo Libre · Lince · San Borja
Magdalena · Huaca Juliana · San Isidro · Hipodromo Montefrio
Surquillo
Miraflores
Isla Frontón
PACIFIC OCEAN · Vista Alegre
Santiago de Surco
Barranco
Cerro Morro Solar 273 · La Campiña · Chorrillos
Punta La Chira · La Encantada
West from Greenwich

A B C · 1 2 3

CENTRAL LOS ANGELES

km 1
miles 0.5

Echo Park · Elysian Park Ave · Dodger Stadium · Elysian Park
Echo Park · Sunset Boulevard · Broadway · Spring Street
Glendale Blvd · China Town · North Main Street
Civic Center · El Pueblo de Los Angeles Hist. Park · Union Sta. · County Jail
World Trade Center · Board of Education · Terminal Annex Post Office
Arco Plaza · Wells Fargo Center · Central Library · Little Tokyo · Los Angeles River
Pershing Square · Bradbury Bldg. · Parker Center
Olympic Blvd · Greyhound Bus Depot · Broadway · Main Street

a b c · 1 2 3

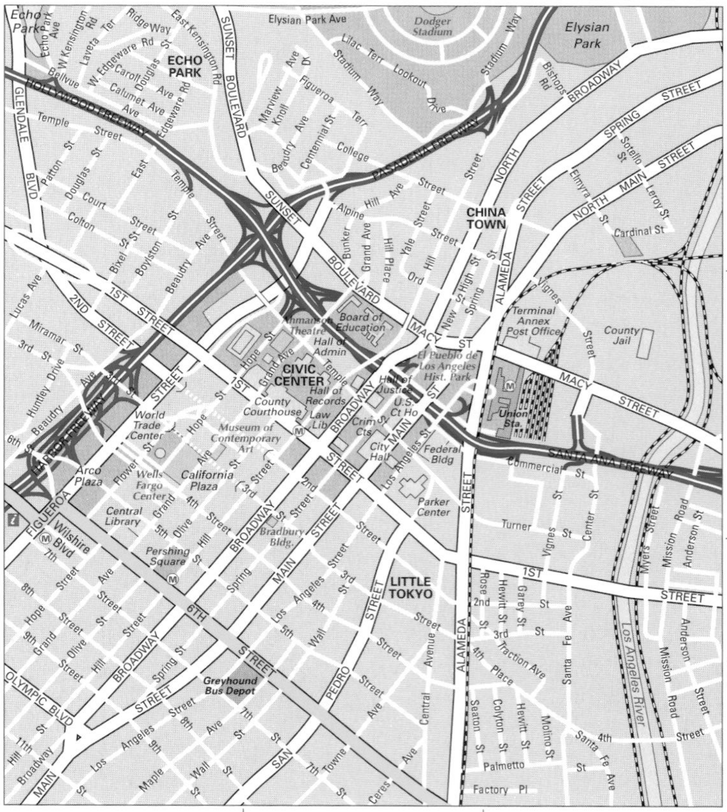

COPYRIGHT GEORGE PHILIP LTD

MADRID

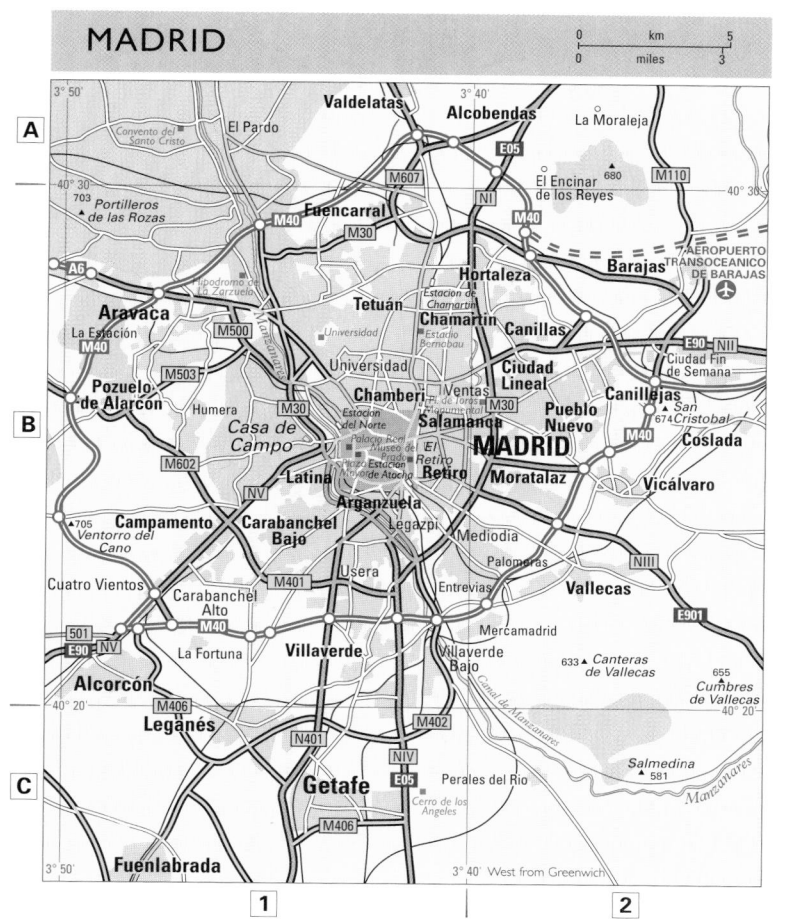

CENTRAL MADRID

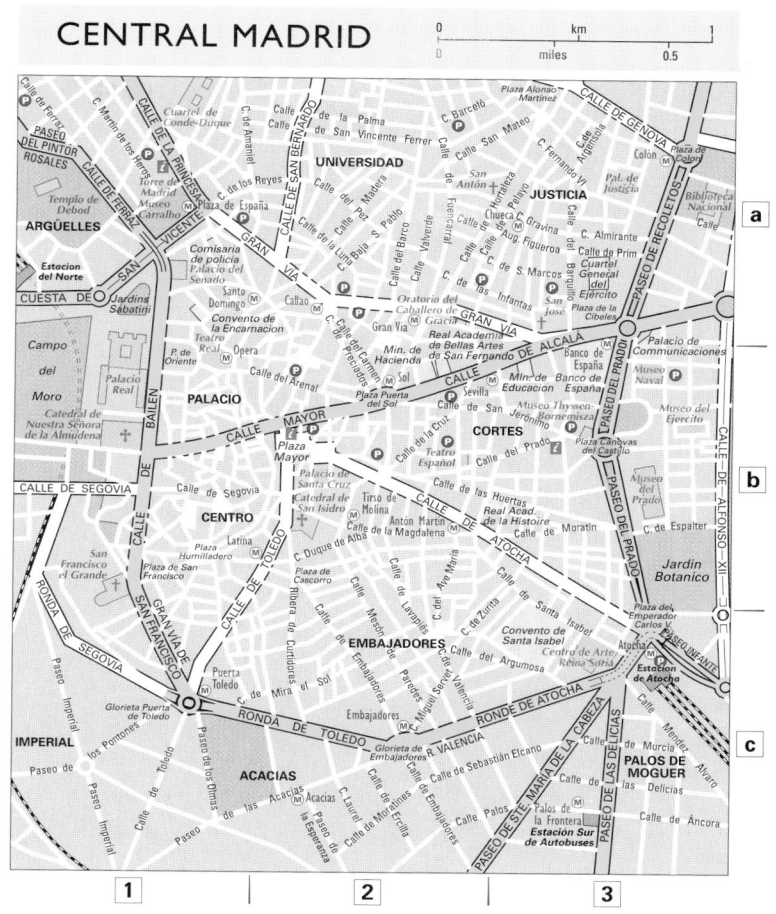

MANILA

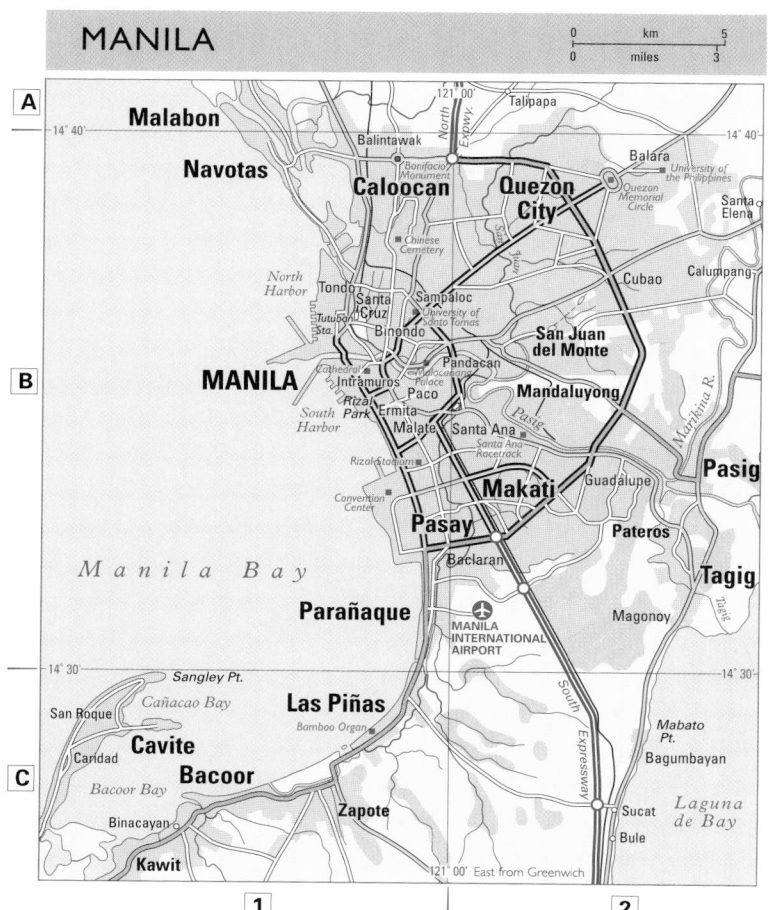

MELBOURNE

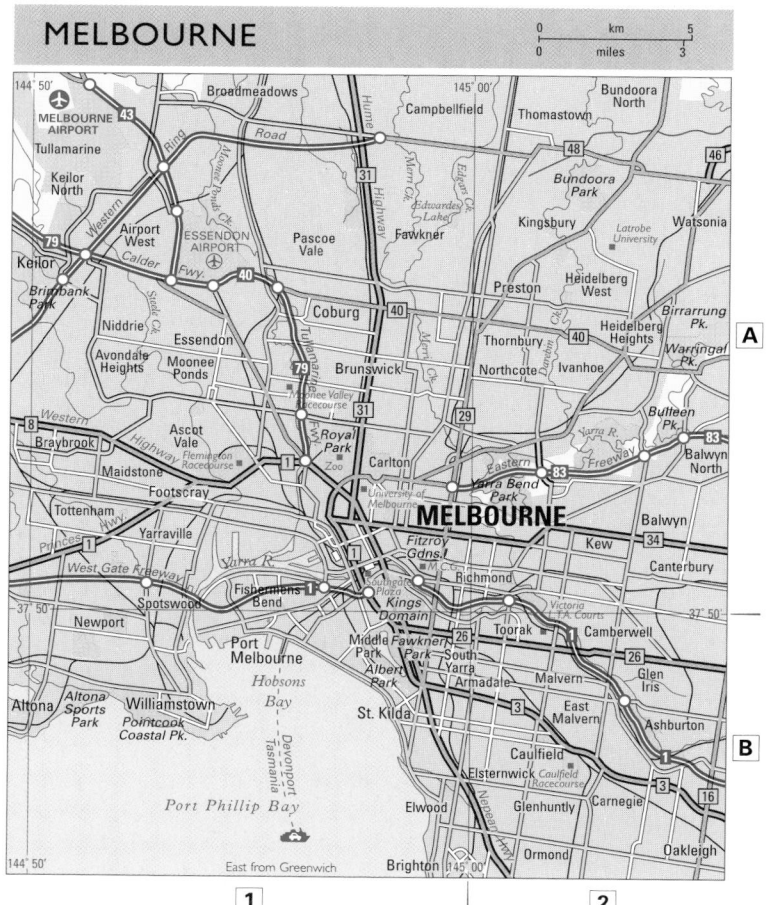

MEXICO CITY

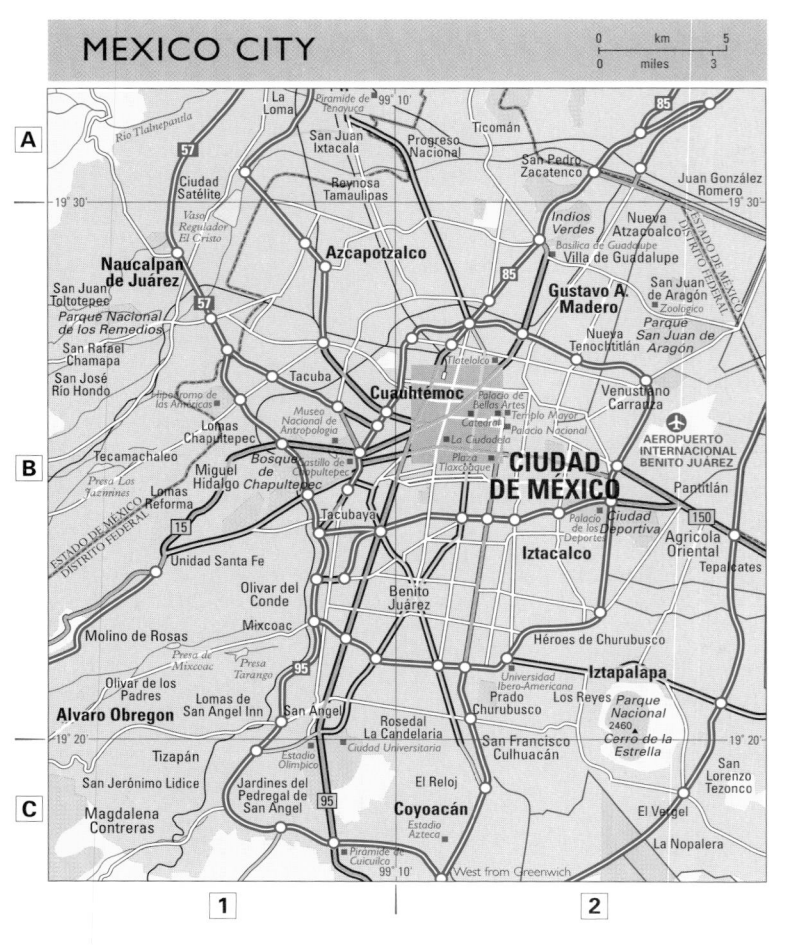

CENTRAL MEXICO CITY

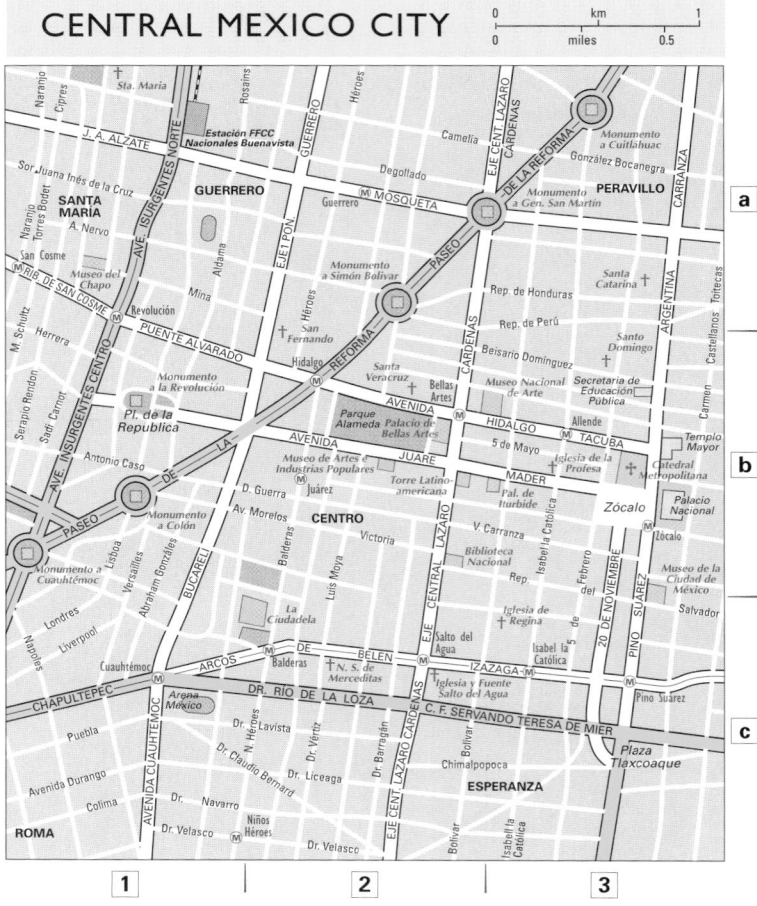

MIAMI

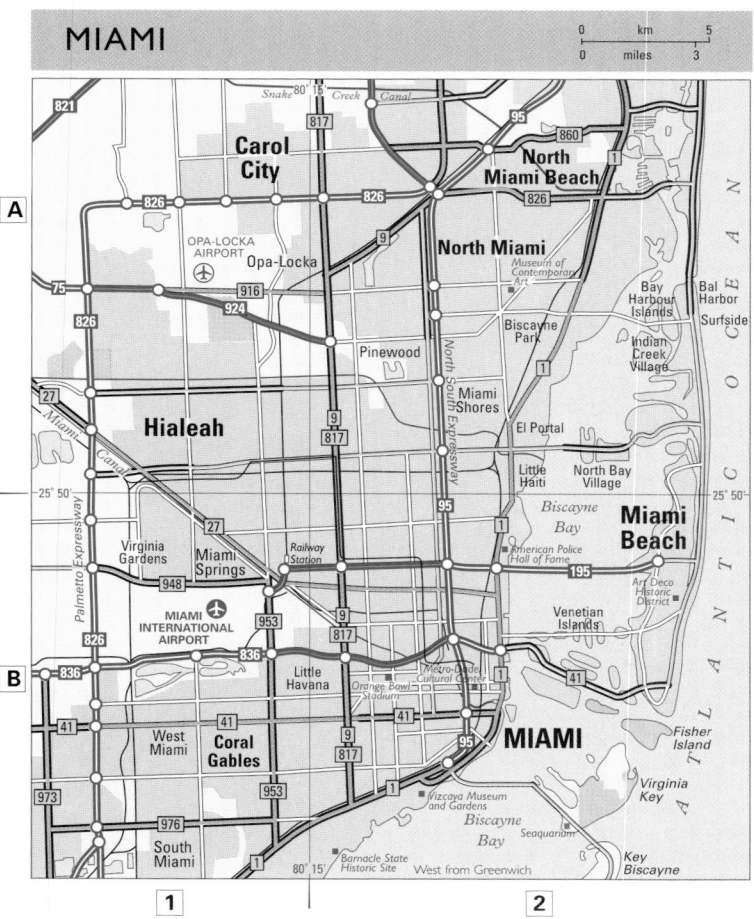

MILAN

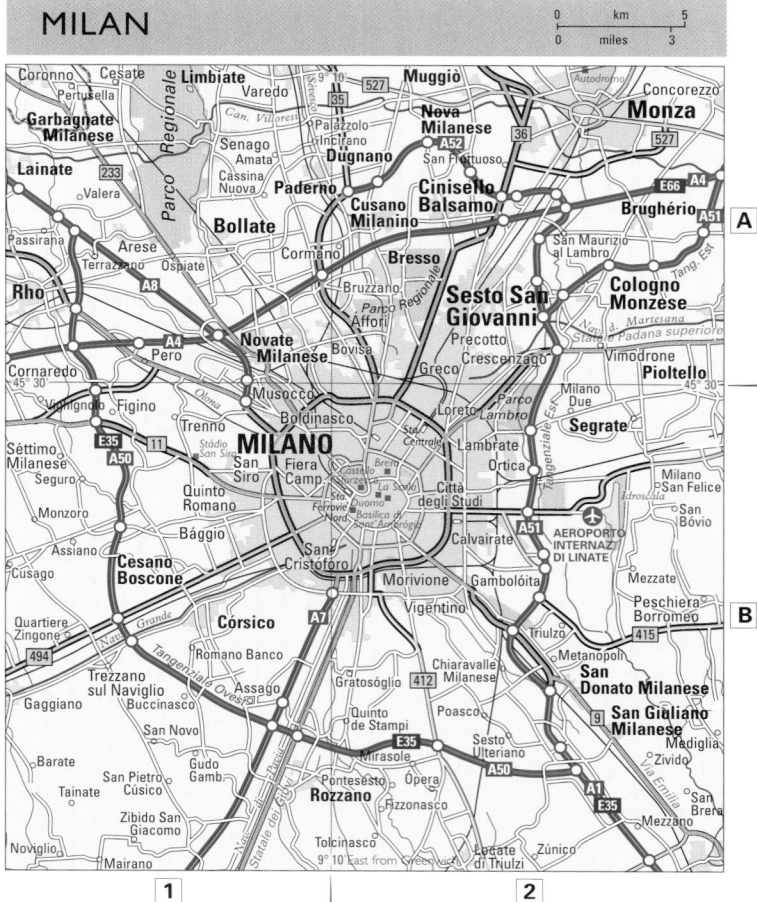

MOSCOW

km 5
miles 3

A

| | |
Novonikolyskoye Putilkovo Bratsevo Sheremetyevo Airport Dëgunino Vladykino Babushkin Medvezhiy Ozyora Medvezhiy Ozyora

Mitino Khimki-Khovrino Gorod Moskva 157▲ 38° Almazova

Chernyovo M10 Nikolskiy Moskva Oblast Pekhra-Pokrovskoye

Krasnogorsk Penyagino Tushino 37°30' Petrovsko-Razumovskoye Dzerzhinskiy Park M8 37°50' Abramtsevo 55°50'

Golyevo Pavshino Strogino Timiryazev Park Ostankino Bogorodskoye Galyanovo Vostochnyy 140▲ Balashikha

M9 Myakinino Troitse-Lykovo Pokrovsko-Sresnevo Petrovskiy Park Sokolniki Park Sokolniki Izmaylovo Gorenki Novaya M7

Arkhangelskoye Khorosovo Frunze Dzerzhinskiy Izmayloskiy Park Vishnyaki Nikolyskoye Pekhra-Yakovievskaya

Zakharkovo Rublovo Tatarovo Mnevniki Sverdlov Leningrad Station Kazan Station 150▲ Leportovo Saltykovka Kutsino

Razdory Cherepkovo MOSKVA Krasno-Presnenskaya Bolshoy Theatre Bauman Kursk Station Reutov Serebryanka Zheleznodorozhnyy

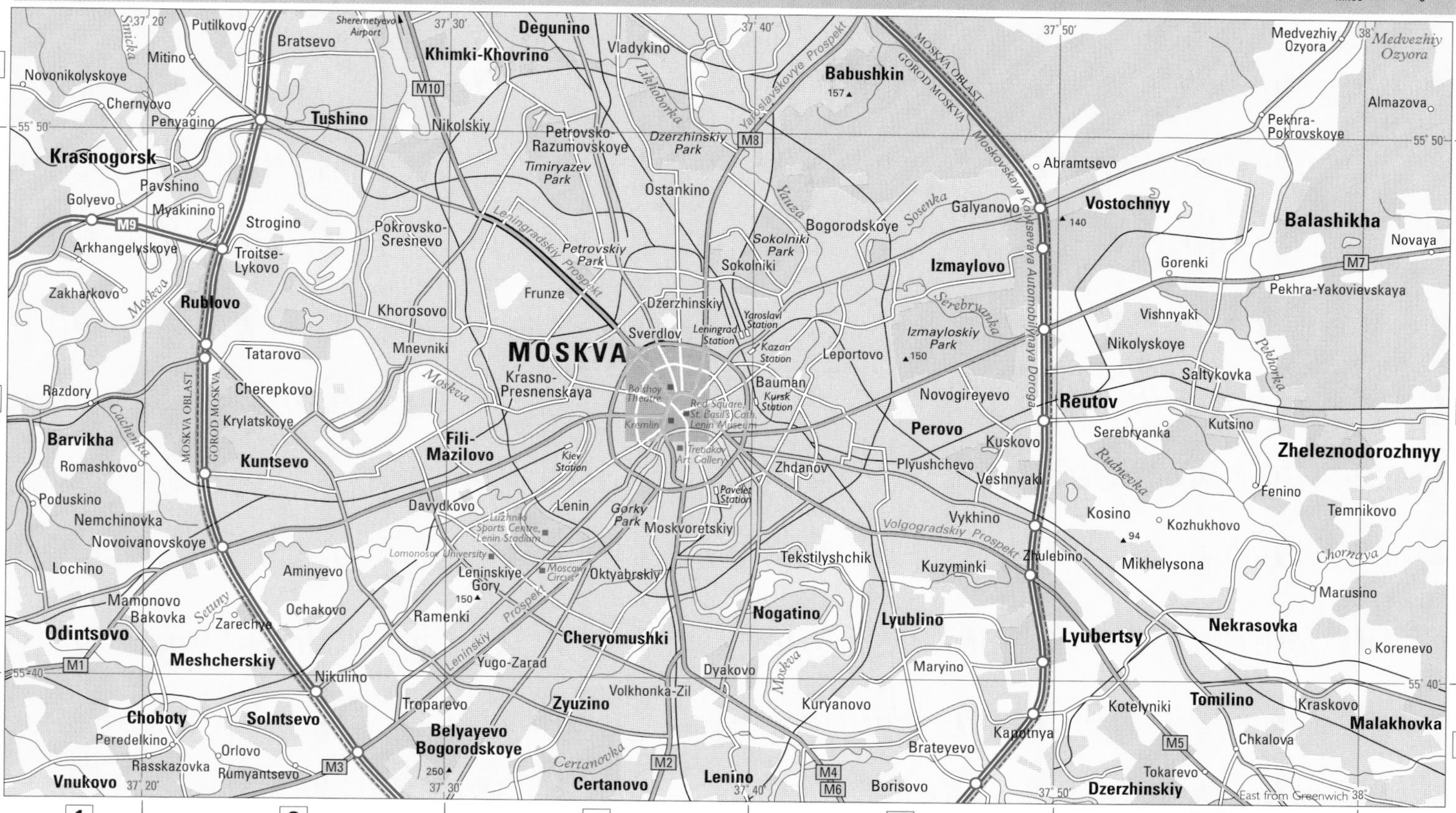

Barvikha Krylatskoye Red Square St Basil's Cath. Lenin Museum Novogireyevo Perovo Kuskovo Fenino

Romashkovo Kuntsevo Fili-Mazilovo Kremlin Kiev Station Zhdanov Plyushchevo Veshnyaki Temnikovo

Poduskino Davydkovo Tretakov Art Gallery Lenin Vykhino Kosino Kozhukhovo Mikhelysona 94▲

Nemchinovka Gorky Park Moskvoretskiy Pavlet Station Tekstilyshchik Zhulebino Marusino

Novoivanovskoye Aminyevo Ramenki Kuzyminki Koreneva

Lochino Lomonosov University Leninskiye Gory Moscow Circus Oktyabrskiy Nogatino Lyublino Lyubertsy Nekrasovka

Mamonovo Bakovka Ochakovo 150▲ Cheryomushki Maryino Kraskovo

Odintsovo Zarechye Nikulino Yugo-Zarad Zyuzino Dyakovo Kuryanovo Kotelniki Tomilino Malakhovka

Meshcherskiy M1 Troparevo Volkhonka-Zil Kapotnya Chkalova

Choboty Solntsevo Belyayevo Bogorodskoye Lenino Brateyevo M5 Dzerzhinskiy

Peredelkino Orlovo 250▲ M2 M4 Tokarevo

Rasskazovka M3 Rumyantsevo Certanovo Lenino M6 Borisovo

Vnukovo 37°20' 37°30' 37°40' 37°50' East from Greenwich 38°

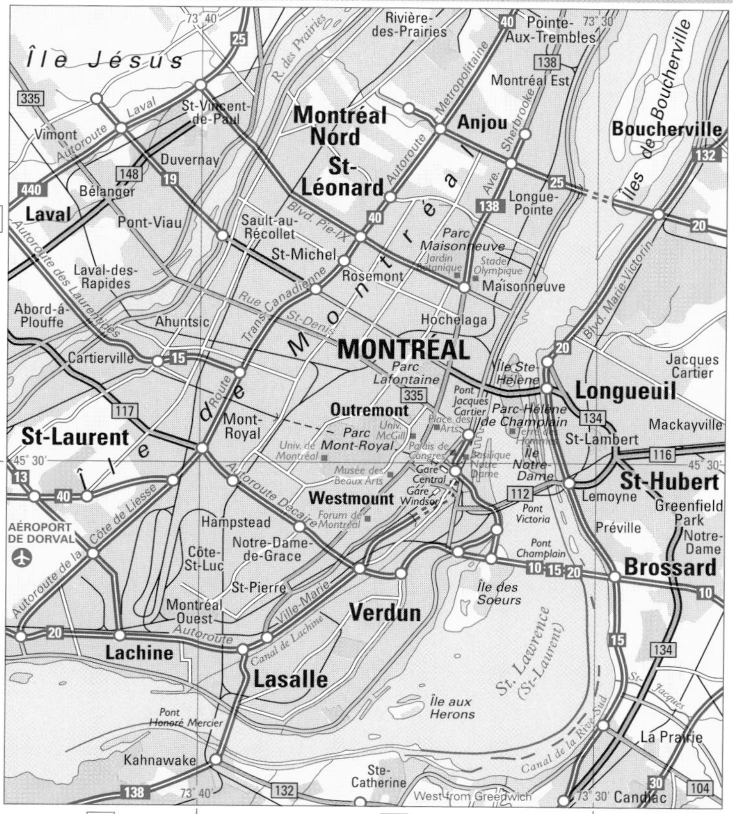

1 2 3 4 5 6

MONTRÉAL

km 5
miles 3

Île Jésus Rivière-des-Prairies Pointe-Aux-Trembles 73°30'

Vimont Laval St-Vincent-de-Paul Montréal Est Boucherville

335 St-Léonard Montréal Nórd Anjou 132 Boucherville

148 Belanger Duvernay Longue-Pointe 138

440 19 Pont-Viau Sault-au-Récollet St-Michel Jardin Botanique 25

Laval Laval-des-Rapides Rosemont Stade Olympique Maisonneuve

Abord-à-Plouffe Ahuntsic Hochelaga Jacques Cartier

Cartierville 15 MONTRÉAL Île Ste-Hélène 20

117 Parc Lafontaine Parc Hélène de Champlain 134 Longueuil

St-Laurent Outremont Univ. McGill St-Lambert Mackayville

13 Mont-Royal Parc Mont-Royal Musée des Beaux-Arts Gare Central 116 112 St-Hubert 45°30'

40 Côte-de-Liesse Westmount Lemoyne Préville Greenfield Park

AÉROPORT DE DORVAL Hampstead Notre-Dame-de-Grace Notre-Dame 10 15 20 Brossard

Côte-St-Luc St-Pierre Île des Soeurs 10

Montréal Ouest 20 Verdun St. Lawrence (St-Laurent) 15 134

Lachine Lasalle Île aux Herons La Prairie

Kahnawake 138 132 West from Greenwich 73°30' Candiac 104 30

1 2 3

CENTRAL MOSCOW

km 1
miles 0.5

SAD.-SAMOTECHNAYA SAD.-SUHAREVSKAYA SAD.-SPASSKAYA

Svetnoy BOULEVARD Old Moscow Circus Suharevskaya Sergievskiy Per.

Mayakovskovo Ploshchad Tchaikovsky Concert Hall Russian Cinema ROZHDESTVENSKY BOULEVARD

Youth Theatre Pushkinskaya Convent of the Nativity of the Virgin Turgenevskaya Turgenev-skaya Pl. Chisty Prudy

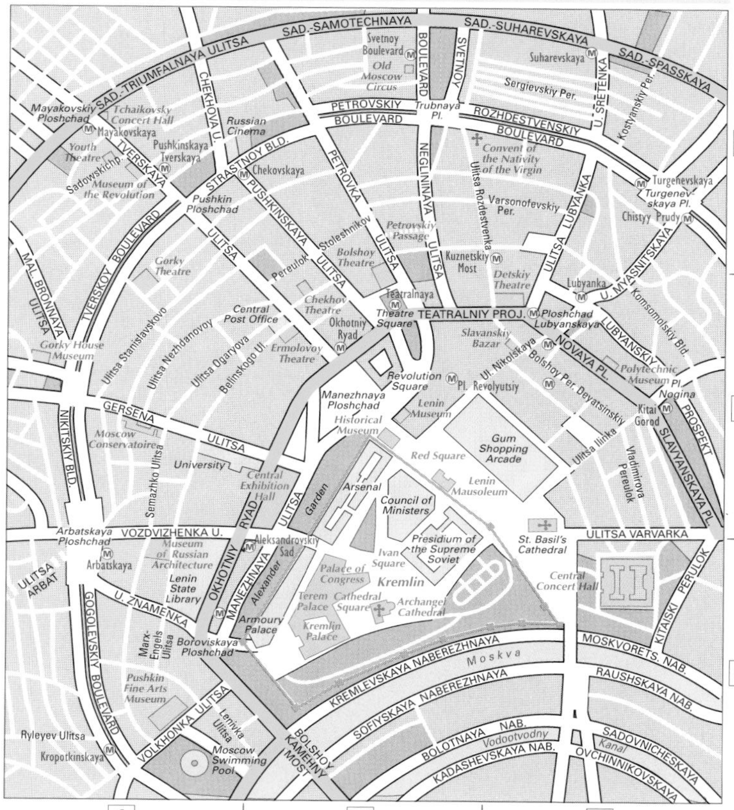

Museum of the Revolution Pushkin Ploshchad Petrovsky Passage Varsonofievsky Per.

Gorky Theatre Stoleshnikov Kuznetskiy Most Detskiy Theatre Lubyanka

Moscow Conservatoire Chekhov Theatre Teatralnaya Teatralniy Proj. PL. Lubyanskaya

University Okhotny Ryad Teatralny Square Slavanskiy Bazar

Gorky House Museum Revolution Square PL. Nikolskaya Bolshoy Per. Devyatinskiy

Arbatskaya Ploshchad Manezhnaya Ploshchad Historical Museum Lenin Museum Gum Shopping Arcade

Central Exhibition Hall Red Square Kitai Gorod

Arbatskaya Museum of Russian Architecture Arsenal Lenin Mausoleum

ULITSA ARBAT Aleksandrovskiy Sad Council of Ministers St. Basil's Cathedral ULITSA VARVARKA

Palace of Congress Ivan the Great Presidium of the Supreme Soviet Central Concert Hall

Lenin State Library Terem Cathedral Kremlin Archangel Cathedral

Armoury Palace Kremlin Palace Cathedral Square

Marx-Engels Muzei Borovitskaya Ploshchad KREMLEVSKAYA NABEREZHNAYA Moskva

Pushkin Fine Arts Museum SOFIYSKAYA NAB. RAUSHSKAYA NAB.

Ryleyev Ulitsa VOLKHONKA ULITSA BOLSHOI KAMENIY MOST Vodootvodny Kanal SADOVNICHESKAYA NAB.

Kropotkinskaya Moscow Swimming Pool BOLOTNAYA NAB. KADASHEVSKAYA NAB. OVCHINNIKOVSKAYA

a b c

1 2 3

MUMBAI

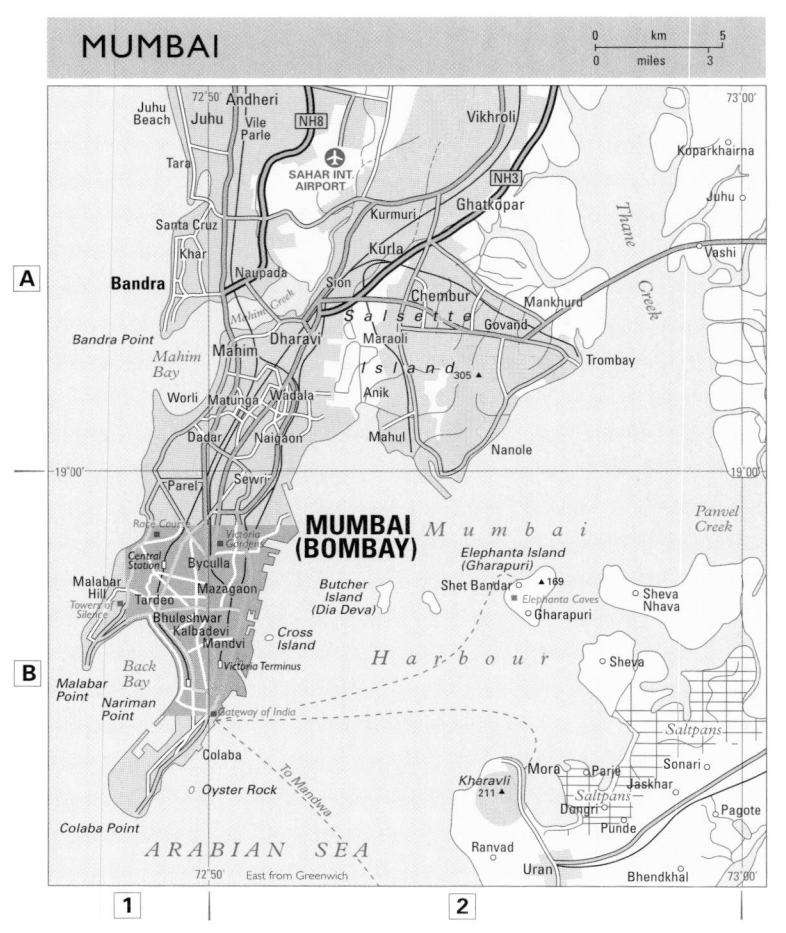

CENTRAL MUMBAI

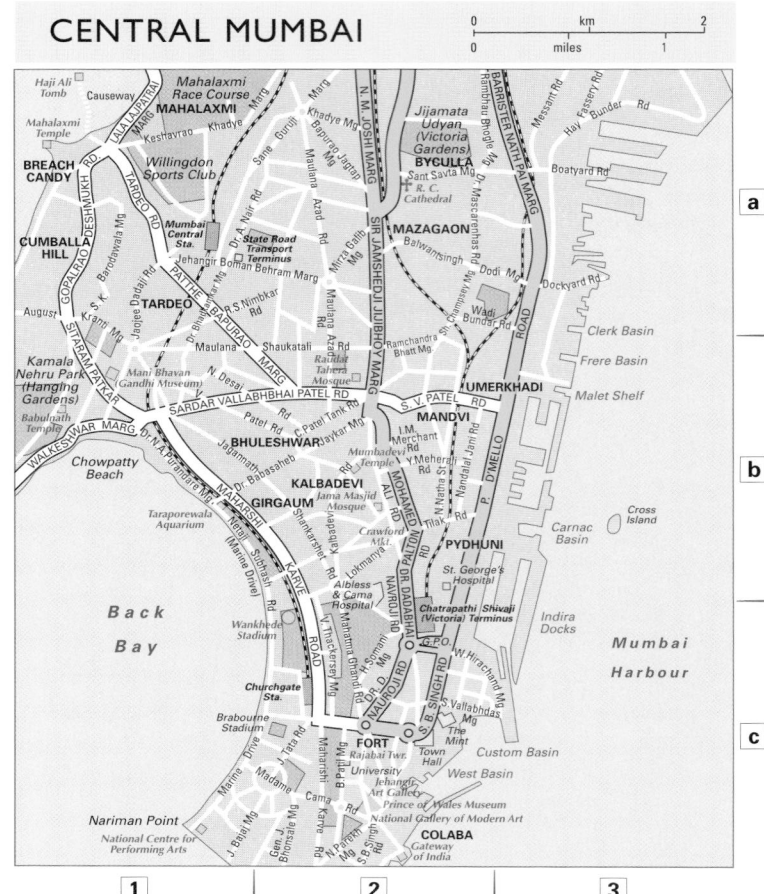

MUNICH

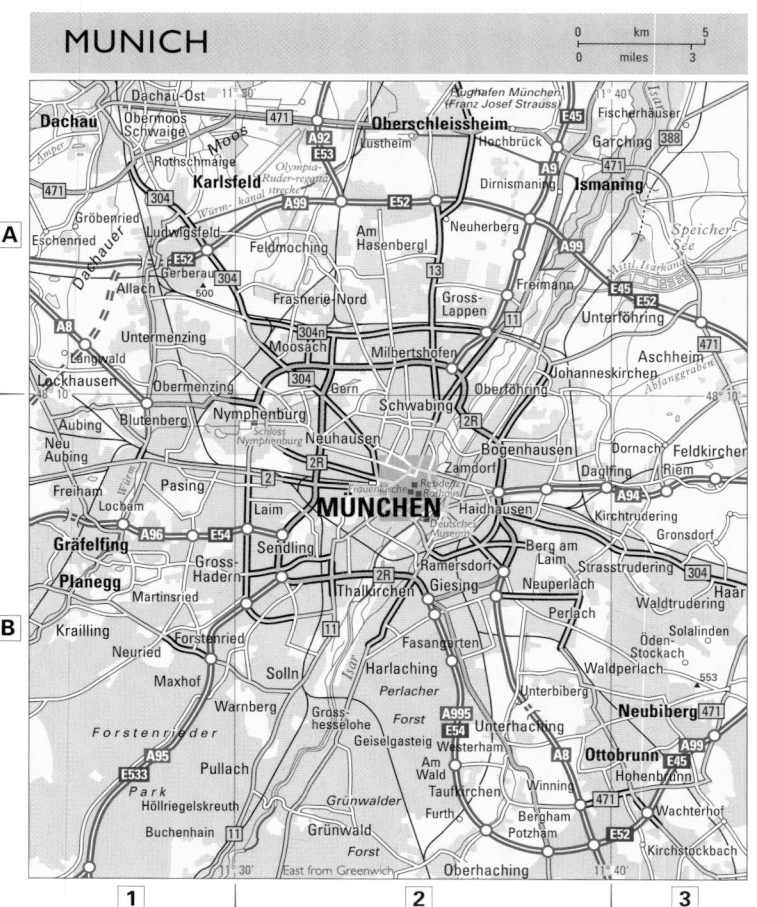

CENTRAL MUNICH

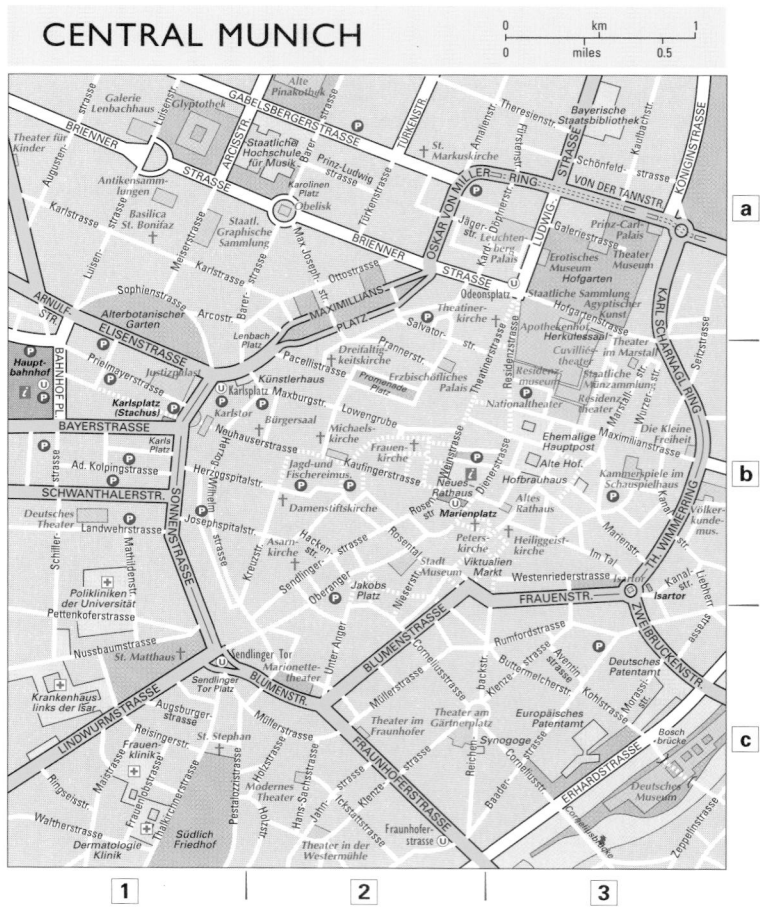

NEW YORK

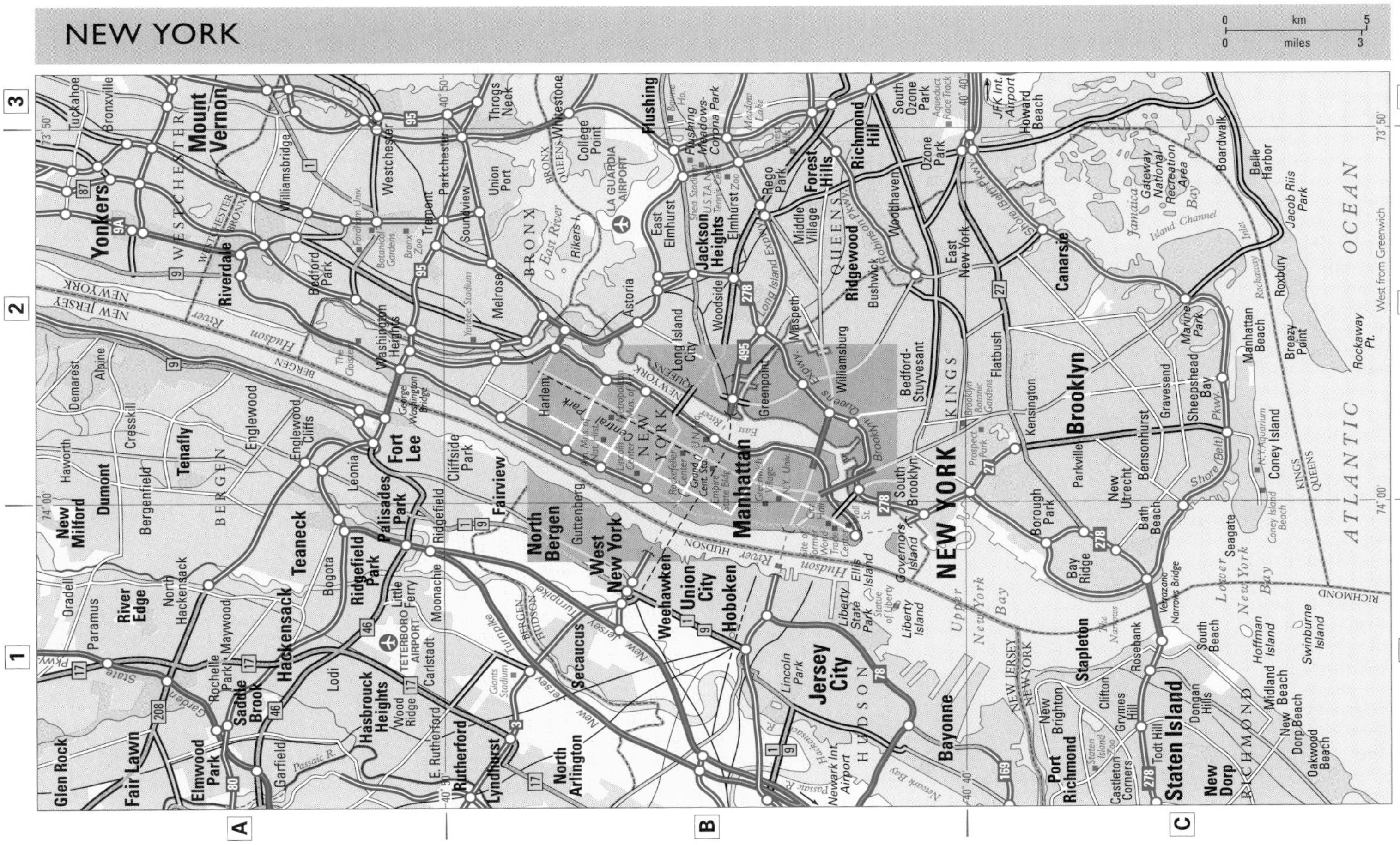

0 km 5
0 miles 3

Yonkers · Mount Vernon · Bronxville · Tuckahoe · WESTCHESTER · Williamsbridge · Westchester · Throgs Neck · Whitestone · College Point · Flushing · Flushing Meadows-Corona Park · South Ozone Park · Richmond Hill · Ozone Park · JFK Int. Airport · Howard Beach · Boardwalk

Riverdale · Bedford Park · Tappan · Union Port · Southview · BRONX · QUEENS · Rikers I. · LA GUARDIA AIRPORT · Astoria · East Elmhurst · Jackson Heights · Elmhurst · Rego Park · Forest Hills · Woodhaven · Belle Harbor · Jacob Riis Park

WESTCHESTER · NEW JERSEY · NEW YORK · BERGEN · Englewood · Englewood Cliffs · Fort Lee · Cliffside Park · Leonia · Fairview · Washington Heights · Harlem · Long Island City · Greenpoint · Woodside · Middle Village · Ridgewood · Bushwick · East New York · Canarsie · ATLANTIC OCEAN

New Milford · Teaneck · Hackensack · Bogota · Ridgefield Park · Palisades Park · Ridgefield · North Bergen · Guttenberg · West New York · Weehawken · Union City · Hoboken · Manhattan · Williamsburg · Bedford-Stuyvesant · KINGS · Flatbush · Kensington · Brooklyn · Gravesend · Sheepshead Bay · Marine Park · Manhattan Beach · Breezy Point · Rockaway Pt.

Oradell · River Edge · North Hackensack · Maywood · Lodi · Little Ferry · Moonachie · Secaucus · NEW YORK · Governors Island · Ellis Island · Liberty State Park · Statue of Liberty · South Brooklyn · Borough Park · New Utrecht · Bath Beach · Bensonhurst · Bay Ridge · Coney Island · Coney Island Beach

Paramus · Rochelle Park · Saddle Brook · Garfield · Hasbrouck Heights · Wood Ridge · Carlstadt · E. Rutherford · Rutherford · Lyndhurst · North Arlington · TETERBORO AIRPORT · Giants Stadium · Jersey City · Lincoln Park · Bayonne · Port Richmond · New Brighton · Stapleton · Clifton · Grymes Hill · Dongan Hills · Staten Island · New Dorp

Glen Rock · Fair Lawn · Elmwood Park · Fairview · New Jersey · Newark Int. Airport · RICHMOND · Castleton Corners · Todt Hill · Oakwood Beach · Dorp Beach

A   B   C

CENTRAL NEW YORK

0 km 2
0 miles 1

HARLEM · UPPER EAST SIDE · UPPER WEST SIDE · Jacqueline Kennedy Onassis Res · Central Park · Metropolitan Museum of Art · American Museum of Natural History · The Lake · Frick Collection · Central Park Zoo · Lincoln Center · Columbus Circle · WEST 57TH ST · EAST 57TH ST · St Patrick's Cathedral · Rockefeller Center · Grand Central Sta. · Chrysler Building · United Nations Headquarters · Queens-Midtown Tunnel

GREENPOINT · McGuinness Boulevard · WILLIAMSBURG · BROOKLYN · East River · WILLIAMSBURG BRIDGE · LOWER EAST SIDE · EAST VILLAGE · GREENWICH VILLAGE · LITTLE ITALY · CHINA TOWN · SOHO · CHELSEA · MANHATTAN · Empire State Building · Madison Square · Pennsylvania Sta. · Port Authority Bus Terminal · Times Square · G.P.O. · Jacob K. Javits Convention Center

WEST NEW YORK · GUTTENBERG · UNION CITY · WEEHAWKEN · HOBOKEN · Hudson River · Holland Tunnel · Lincoln Tunnel · Intrepid Air & Space Museum · Passenger Ship Terminal · ELEVENTH AVE · TWELFTH AVE · WEST STREET

LOWER MANHATTAN · BROOKLYN BRIDGE · MANHATTAN BRIDGE · BROOKLYN HEIGHTS · FLATBUSH AVE · ADAMS ST · US Naval Reserve Center · Wallabout Bay · Fulton Fish Market · City Hall · World Trade Center · Battery Park · Ellis I. & Statue of Liberty · Governors Island · Brooklyn-Battery Tunnel · Staten Island Ferry

a   b   c   d   e   f

OSAKA

km 0 — 5
miles 0 — 3

135° 10' 135° 20' 135° 30'

Hirakata
Funasaka
509
Karato
Takarazuka
Arima
722
Rokkō-Zan
932
462
Itami
Yamada
Kori
Senriyama
OSAKA INTERNATIONAL AIRPORT
171
Toyonaka
Settsu
Neyagawa
1
598
Tanigami
Yamada
Kwansei Gakuin University
Suita
Kadoma
Iwazono
Rokkō Tunnel
173
Higashiyodogawa
Moriguchi
Shijonawate
A — Obu-tōge
365
Nishinomiya
Hirota
Asahi
1
170
A
Maya-Zan
699
Kōbe University
Okamoto
Ashiaya
43 Naruo
Amagasaki
2
Jūsō
Oyodo
Miyakojima
Jōtō
Daitō
Nada
Higashinada
Umeda
Kita
Kōnoike
403
Fukiai
Kanzaki
Fukushima
Higashi
Osaka Castle
Higashinari
Ikuta
Yodo
Nishiyodogawa
Aji
Minami
Ishikiri
KŌBE
Rokkō Island
Konohana
Nishi
Ikuno
308
34° 40'
Nagata
2
Kōbe Harbour
Port Island
Minato
Naniwa
ŌSAKA
Higashiōsaka
34° 40'
Suma
Osaka Shinkansen Suntory Museum
Tennōji
Zoo
Abeno
Kizuri
B
Osaka Harbour
Liberty Osaka Museum
Yao
B
Taishō
Kyūhōji
Yamamoto
Nishinari
Onchi
Kise
Higashisumiyoshi
25
Osaka Bay
Sakai Harbour
Sumiyoshi Shrine
Sumiyoshi
Tainaka
Onchi
Ikeuchi
YAO AIRPORT
26
Kashiwara
Matsubara
135° 10' 135° 20' East from Greenwich 135° 30' Sakai Fujidera

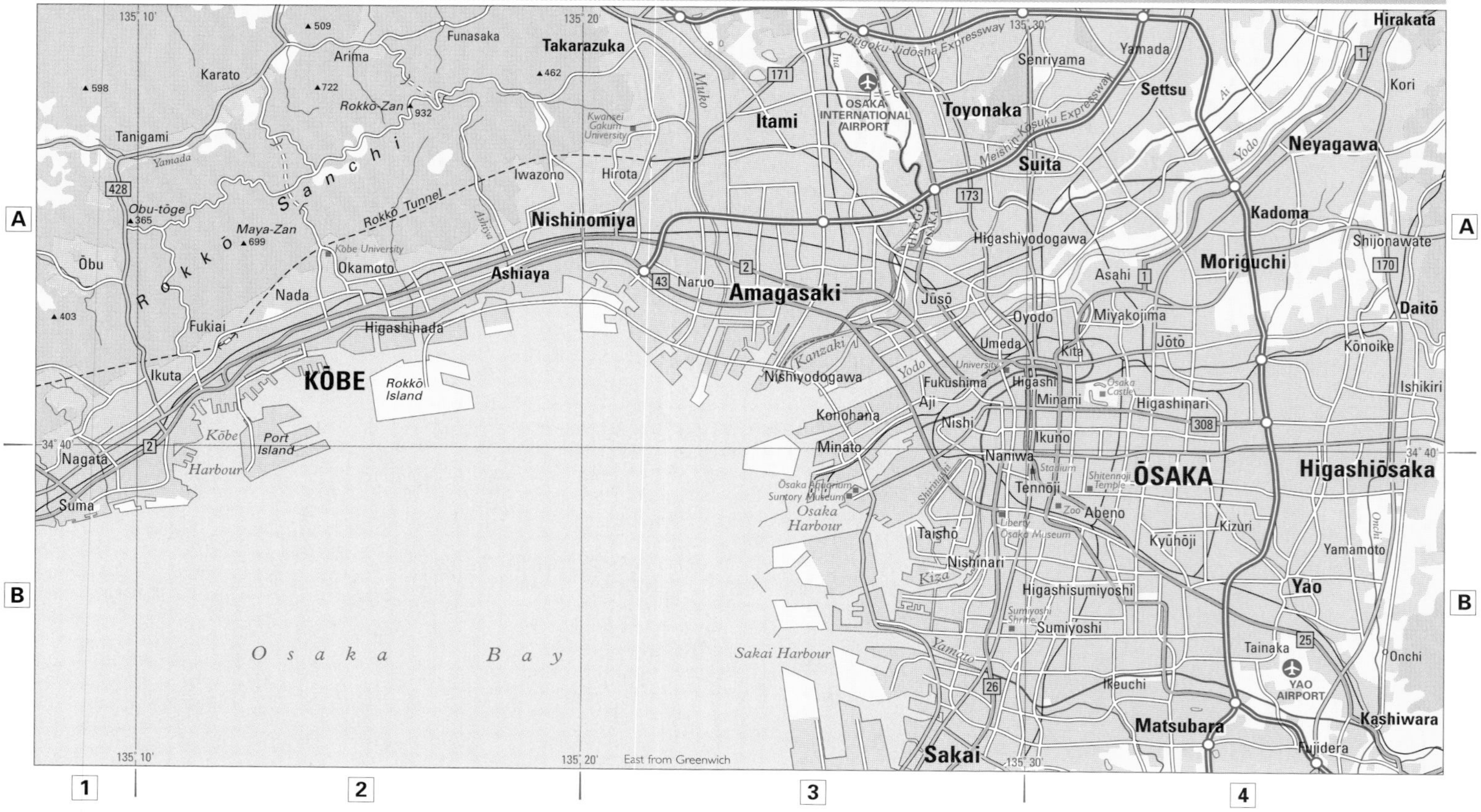

1   2   3   4

OSLO

km 0 — 5
miles 0 — 3

10° 30' 10° 40' 10° 50'

60° 00'
OSLO AKERSHUS
Tryvannshøgda
531
Måridalen
Maridalsvannet
Byre
Bogstadvann
418
60° 00'
Burudvatn
Holmenkollen
Alnsjøen
Sognsvann
Kjelsås
Gorud
Bærums Verk
Ila
Røa
Ris
RING 3
Ullevål
Rødtvet
Lijordet
168
OSLO
Sinsen
4
163
A
Bryn
168
379
Haslum
Ullern
RING 2
Skøyen
Alna
A
Kolsås
E16
160
Stabekk
Lysaker
Universitetet Vestbane sto.
4
Tøyen
Bryn
Bærum
164
166
Norsk Folke Museum
Akershus Slott Sentrum
Ryen
Oppsal
Tanum
Høvik
E18
Bygdøy
Hovedøya
Bøler
Sjøpenden
Snarøya
Fornebu
Lindøya
E18
Bekkelaget
E6
Sandvika
Nesøya
Østøya
Ormøya
Lambertseter
Østmark-kapellet
Hvalstad
165
Brønnøya
Nesoddtangen
Malmøya
Nordstrand
Asker
E18
Frederikshavn Helsingborg København Hirtshals, Kiel
Oksval
Flaskebekk
Skøklefall
Ljabru
Hauketo
59° 50'
Konglungen
155
Blakstad
157
215
Torvvik
Ingierstrand
Klemetsrud
167
Vollen
Nesodden
E6
Slemstad
Fjellstrand
Kolbotn
Svestad
Hasle
156
B
Næsnes
Garder
Oppegård
Blylaget
152 Myrvoll
E18
10° 30' 10° 40' East from Greenwich 10° 50' 134 Oppegård

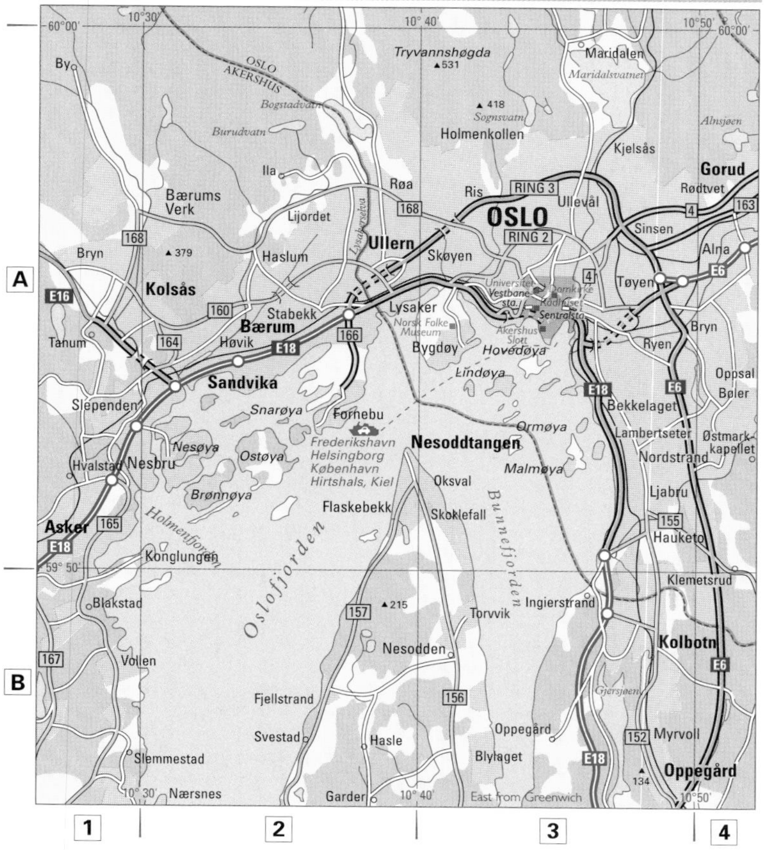

1   2   3   4

CENTRAL OSLO

km 0 — 0.5
miles 0 — 0.25

Stensberg gate
Rikshospitalet
Vår Frelsers Gravlund
Westye Egebergs gate
Nordre gate
Korsgata
Torvald Meyers gate
Welhavens gate
Wessels gate
PILESTREDET
Vor Frue hospital
Damstredet
Brennerveien
PARKVEIEN
Hegdehaugsveien
Ullevålsveien
Dops gt.
Rostedsgate
a
Slotts parken
Nordahl
Kunstindustri mus.
St. Olavs kirke
Akerselva
ST. OLAVS GATE
Deichmanske bibliotek
Det Kongelige Slottet
Historisk museum
St. Olavs gate
Keysers gate
HAMMERSBORG TUNNELEN
Dronningparken
FREDERIKS GATE
Nasjonal galleriet
Universitetet
Carl Johans August gate
KRISTIAN IV GATE
DRAMMENSVEIEN
GRENSEN
Storgata
A
Ibsen-museet
National theatret
Det Norske teater
MØLLERGATA
Brugata
Operaen
Oslo Spektrum
b
MUNKEDAMSVEIEN
Konserthuset
Fridtjof Nansens plass
Stortinget
STENERSGATA
Vestbane stasjonen
Rådhuset
Karl Johans gate
Jernbane-torget
SCHWEIGAARDS
Sentralstasjon
Buss-terminalen
NYLANDSVEIEN
Christiania torv
Hovedpost kontor
Havnegata
Børsen
c
Pipervika
OSLO TUNNELEN
Teater-museet
Museet for samtidskunst
Akershus Slott og festning
Astrup Fearnley museet
BISPEGATA
Bjørvika
Bispevika
Forsvars-museet
Frederikshavn, Helsingborg, København

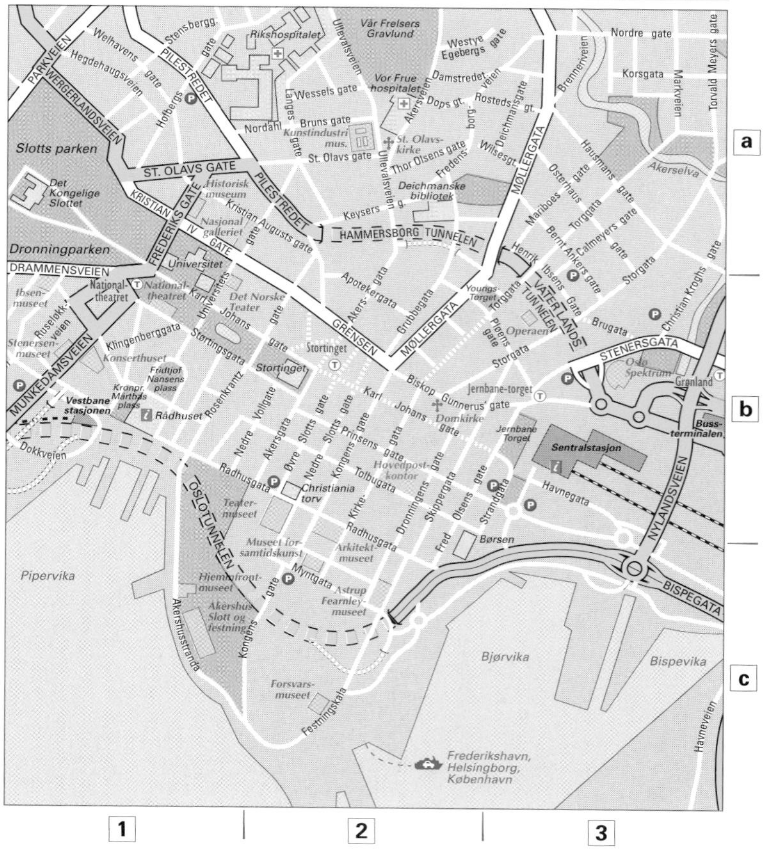

1   2   3

PARIS

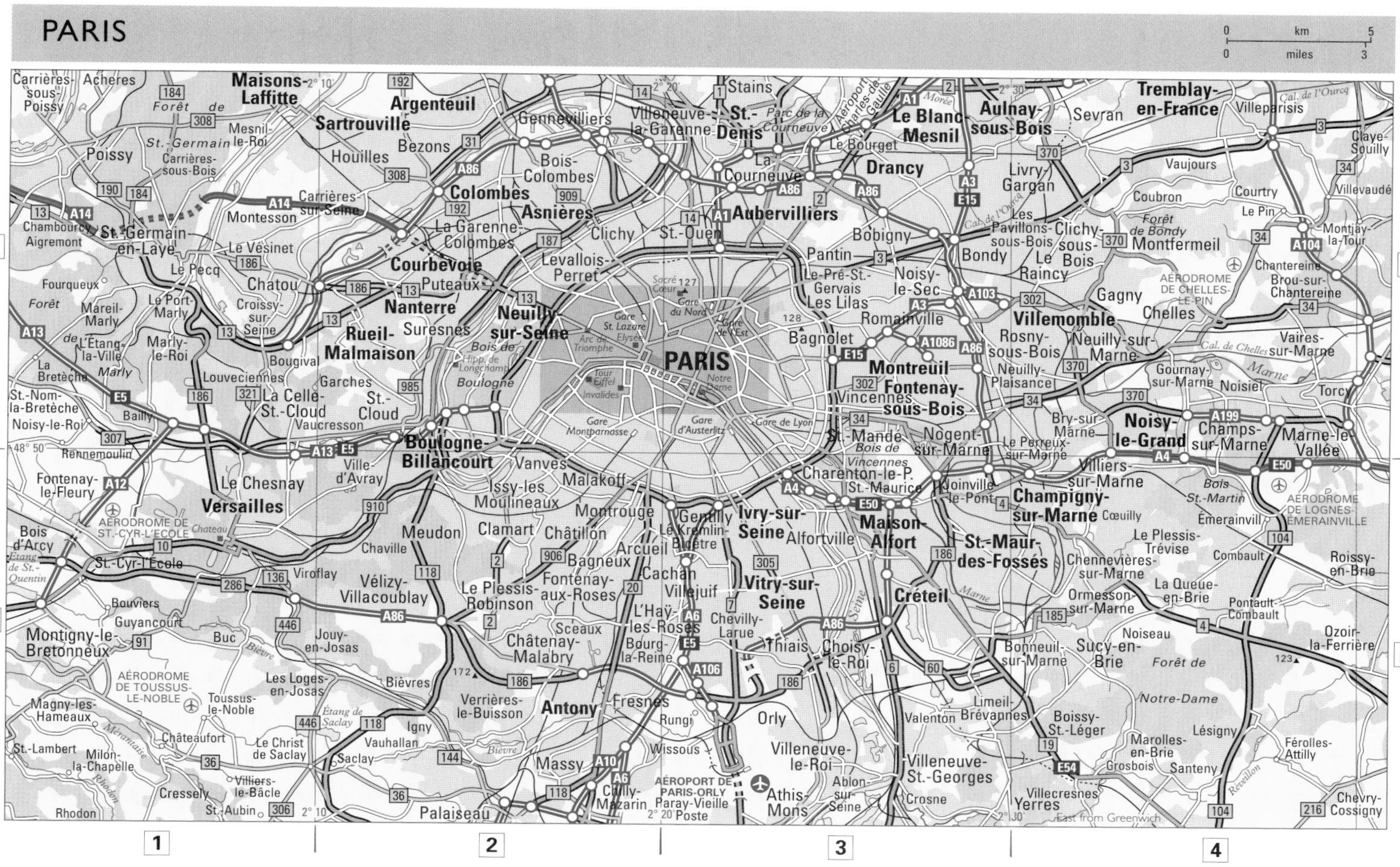
km 0 5
miles 0 3
Maisons-Laffitte
Sartrouville
Argenteuil
Gennevilliers
St.-Denis
Le Blanc-Mesnil
Aulnay-sous-Bois
Sevran
Tremblay-en-France
Villeparisis
Colombes
Asnières
Aubervilliers
Drancy
Le Bourget
Livry-Gargan
Courbevoie
Nanterre
Neuilly-sur-Seine
Rueil-Malmaison
St.-Germain-en-Laye
Bondy
Villemomble
Chelles
Montfermeil
PARIS
Montreuil
Fontenay-sous-Bois
Noisy-le-Grand
Champs-sur-Marne
Marne-la-Vallée
Boulogne-Billancourt
Versailles
Champigny-sur-Marne
Maison-Alfort
St.-Maur-des-Fossés
Ivry-sur-Seine
Vitry-sur-Seine
Créteil
Antony
Orly
AEROPORT DE PARIS-ORLY
AERODROME DE CHELLES-LE-PIN
AERODROME DE LOGNES-EMERAINVILLE
AERODROME DE TOUSSUS-LE-NOBLE
AERODROME DE ST.-CYR-L'ECOLE
A
B
1
2
3
4
East from Greenwich

CENTRAL PARIS

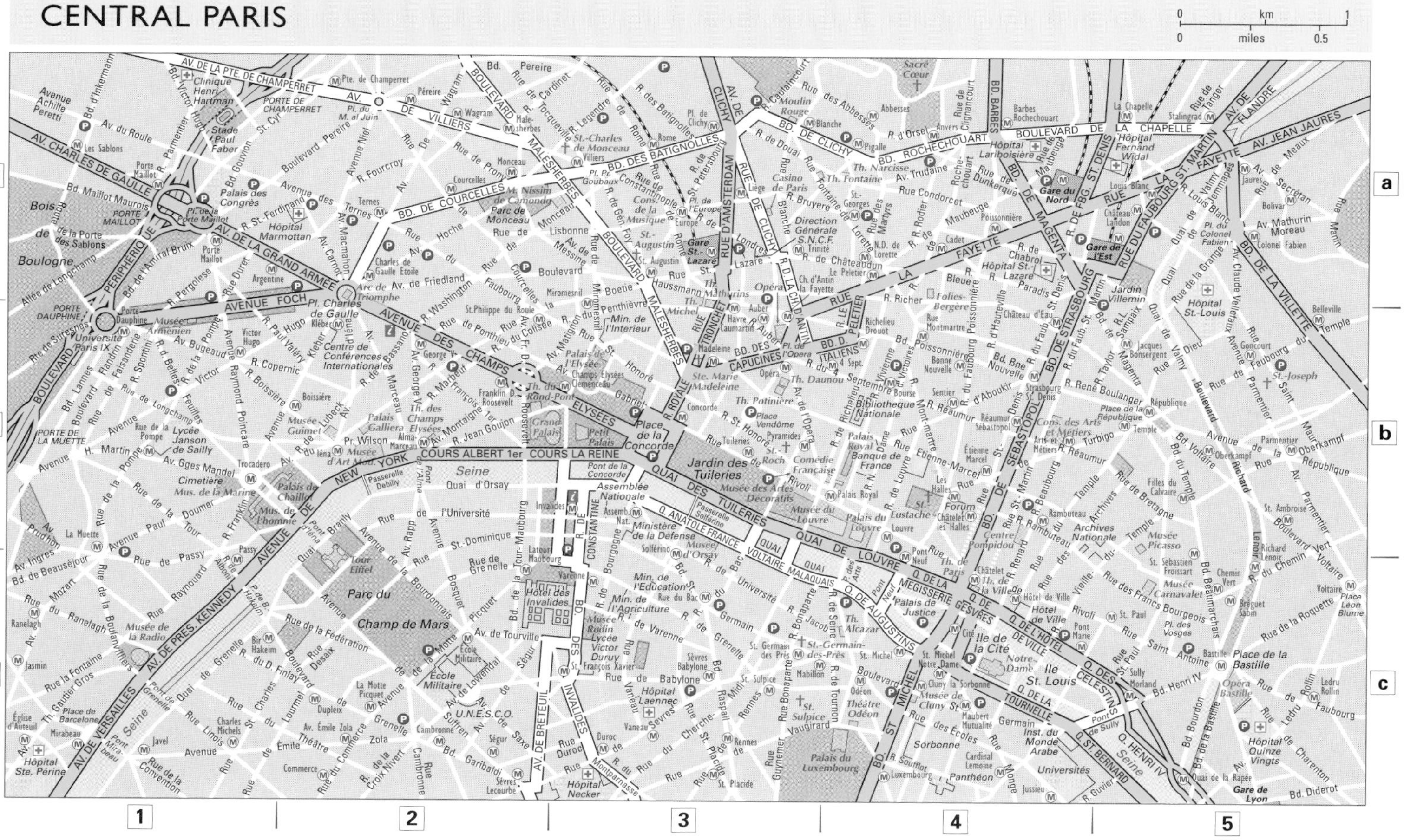
km 0 1
miles 0 0.5
Bois de Boulogne
AVENUE FOCH
AV. CHARLES DE GAULLE
AV. DE LA GRANDE ARMÉE
Arc de Triomphe
Pl. Charles de Gaulle
AVENUE DES CHAMPS ÉLYSÉES
Grand Palais
Petit Palais
Place de la Concorde
Jardin des Tuileries
Musée du Louvre
Palais Royal
Seine
Tour Eiffel
Parc du Champ de Mars
Hôtel des Invalides
Ecole Militaire
U.N.E.S.C.O.
Palais de Chaillot
Assemblée Nationale
Musée d'Orsay
Ile de la Cité
Notre-Dame
Ile St. Louis
Sorbonne
Panthéon
Palais du Luxembourg
Centre Pompidou
Forum des Halles
Place de la Bastille
Gare de Lyon
Gare du Nord
Gare de l'Est
Gare St.-Lazare
Sacré Cœur
Moulin Rouge
Opéra
Madeleine
a
b
c
1
2
3
4
5

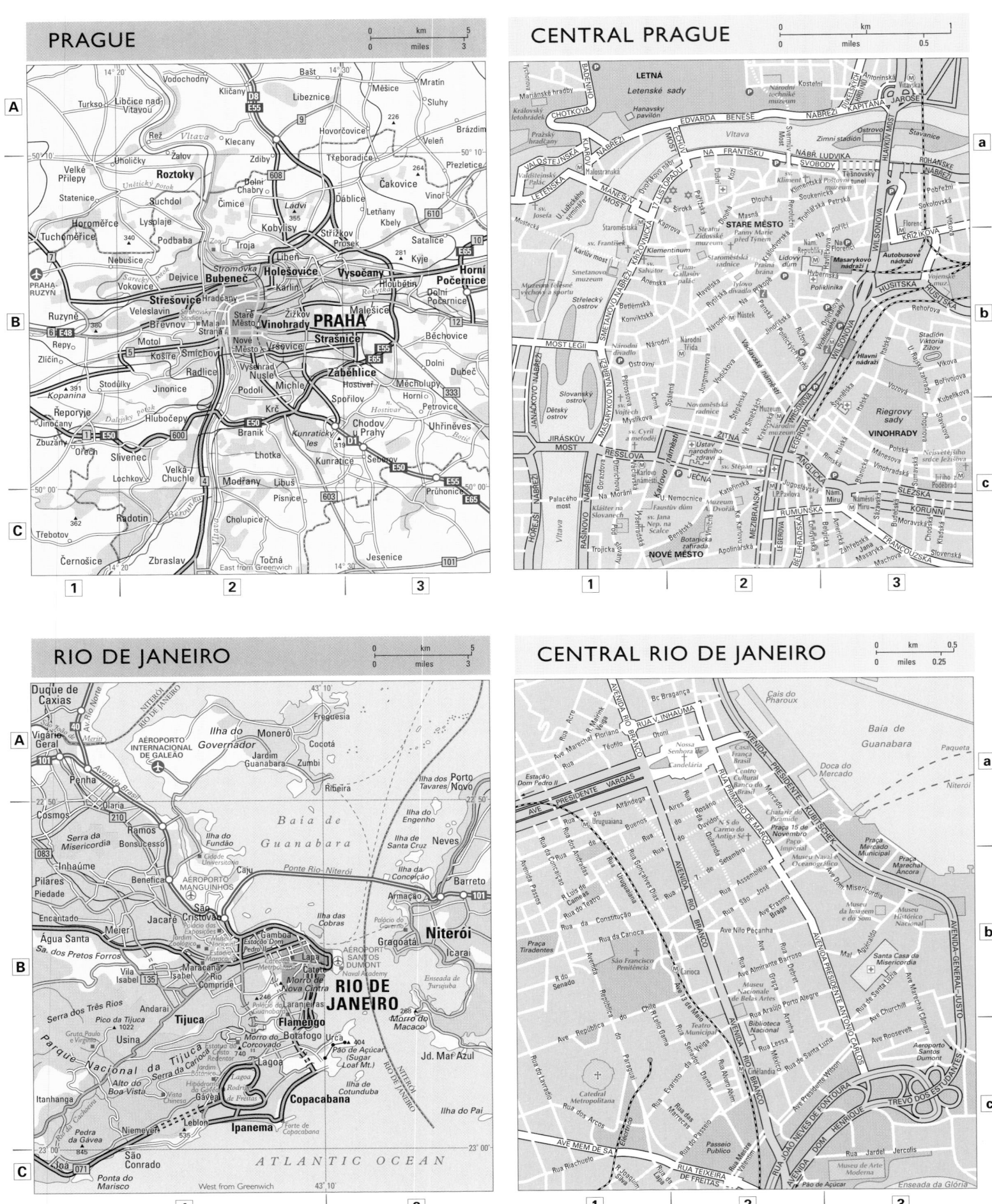

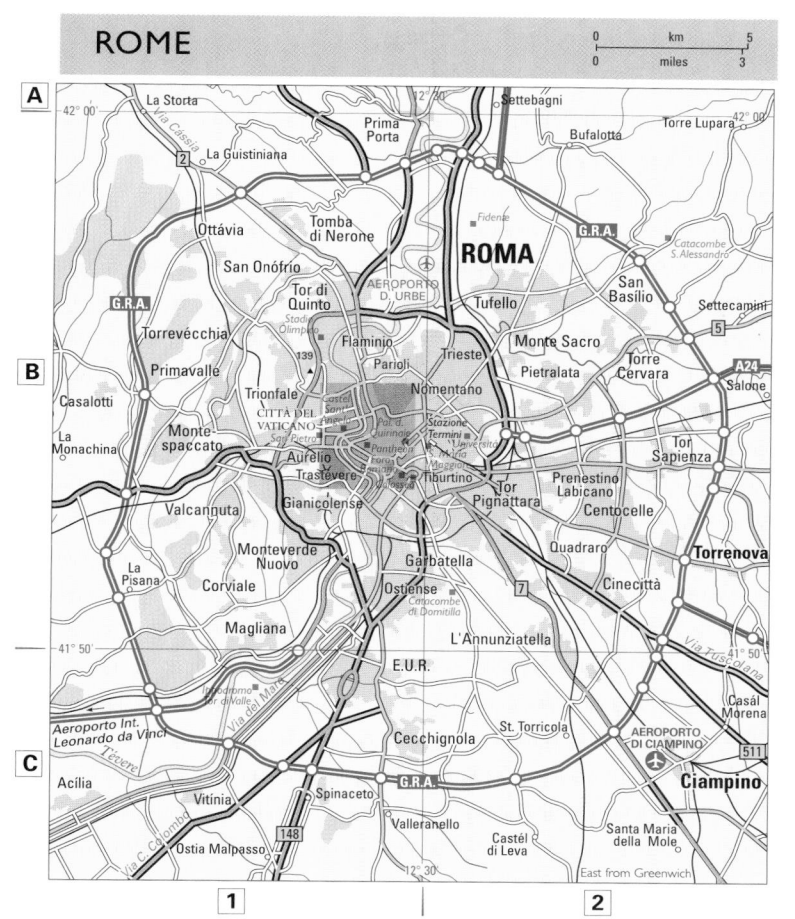

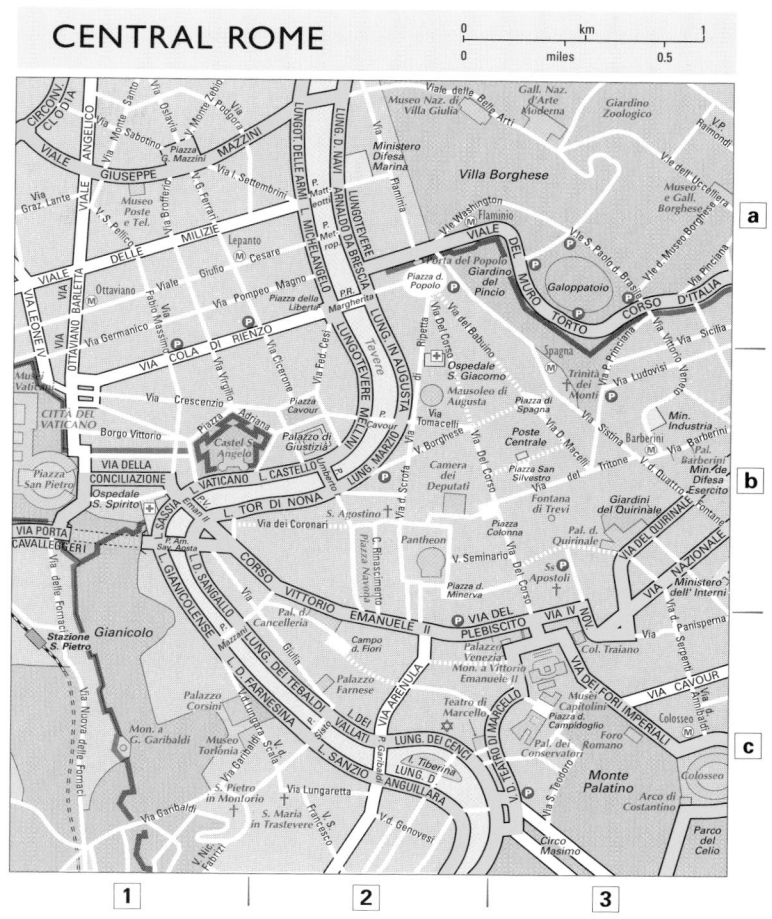

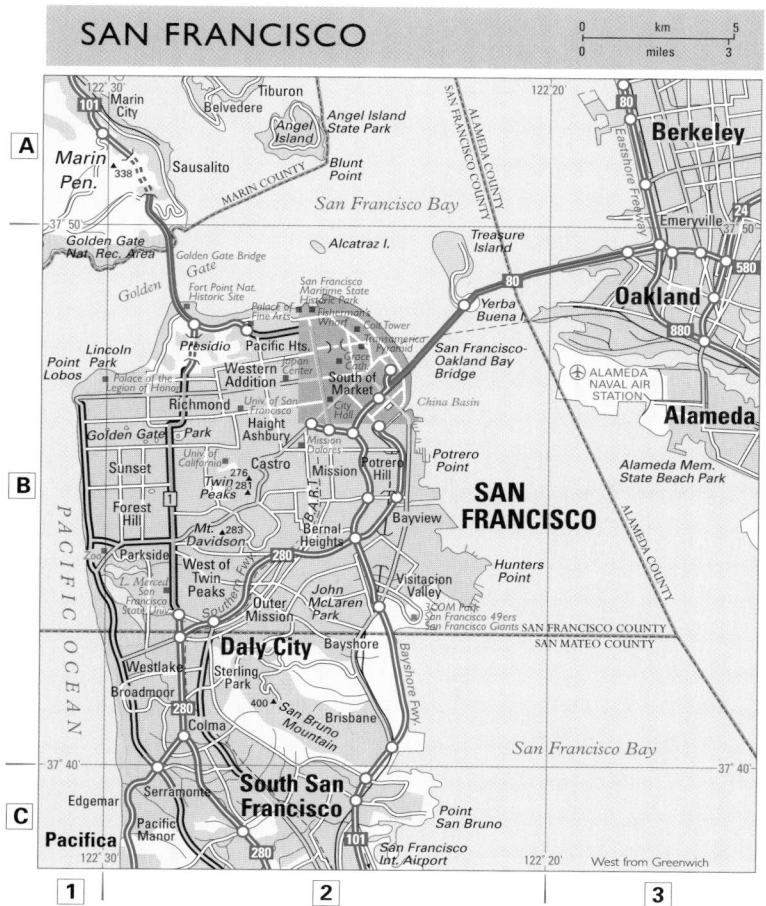

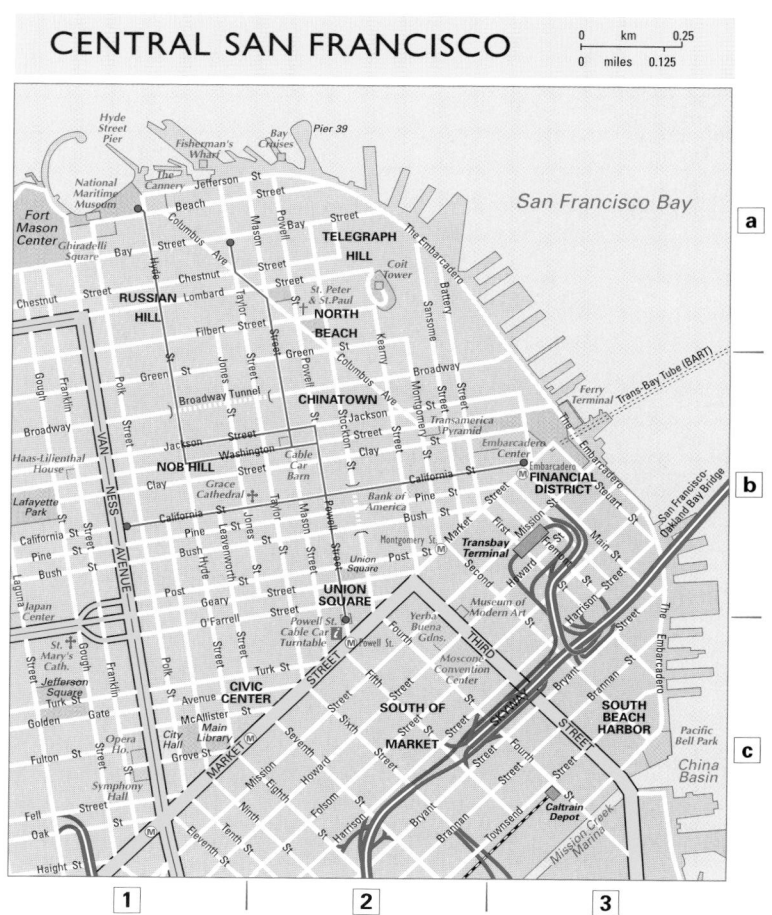

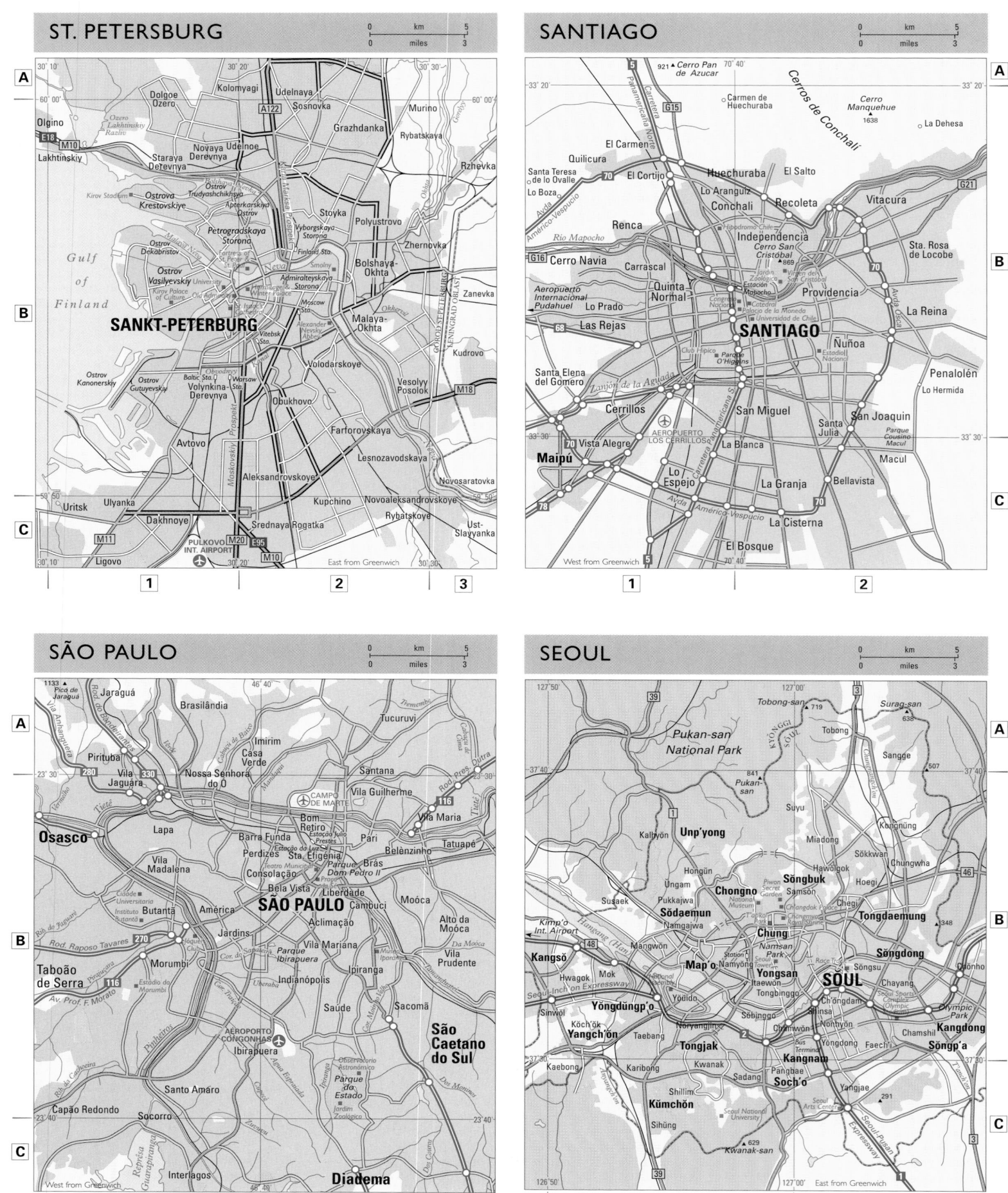

SHANGHAI

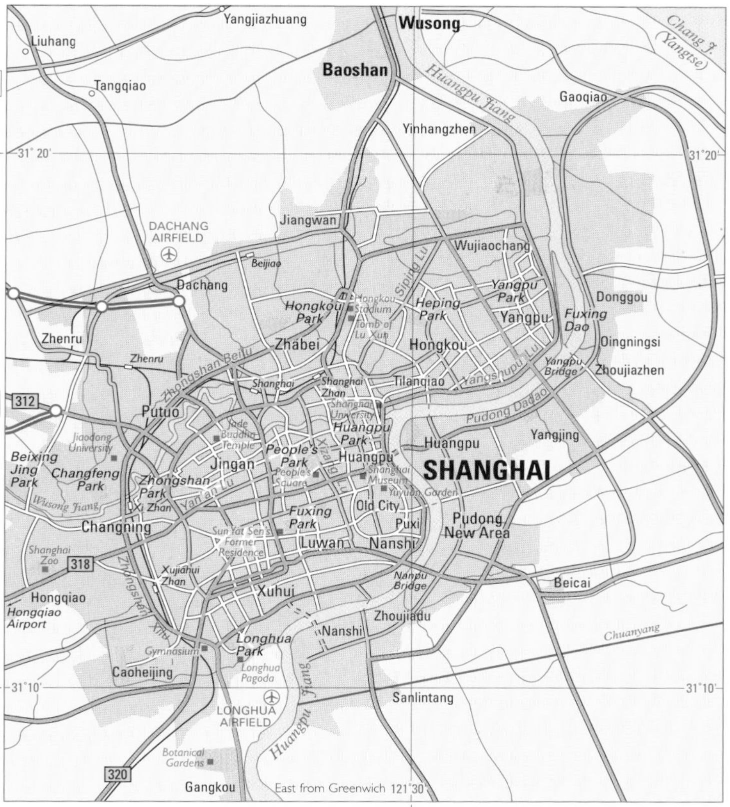

km 0 — 5
miles 0 — 3

A

Liuhang
Yangjiazhuang
Wusong
Tangqiao
Baoshan
Yinhangzhen
Gaoqiao
Huangpu Kiang
Chang J. (Yangtse)

31°20'

Dachang Airfield
Jiangwan
Donggou

B

312
Zhenru
Beijiao
Wujiaochang
Yangpu Park
Fuxing Dao
Dachang
Hongkou Park
Heping Park
Yangpu
Qingningsi
Zhenru
Zhabei
Hongkou
Yangpu Bridge
Zhoujiazhen
Jiaodong University
Shanghai Stadium
Jade Buddha Temple
Shanghai Zhan
Tilanqiao
Yangjing
Beixing Jing Park
Putuo
Huangpu Park
Huangpu
Yangjing
Changfeng Park
Jingan
People's Park
Huangpu
Pudong Daqiao
Zhongshan Park
Xi Zhan
People's Square
Old City
Fuxing Park
Pudong New Area
Changning
Shanghai Zoo
Sun Yat Sen Former Residence
Luwan
Puxi
Nanshi
Xujiahui Zhan
Xuhui
Nanpu Bridge
Beicai
Hongqiao Airport
Gymnasium
Longhua Park
Nanshi
Zhoujiadu
Chuanyang

C

318
Caoheijing
Longhua Airfield
Longhua Pagoda
Sanlintang

31°10'

320
Botanical Gardens
Gangkou
Huangpu Jiang
East from Greenwich 121°30'

1   2

CENTRAL SINGAPORE

km 0 — 1
miles 0 — 0.5

a

CAIRNHILL RD
CLEMENCEAU AVE
CAVENAGH ROAD
Istana (President's Residence)
Kandang Kerbau Hospital
BUKIT-TIMAH-ROAD
Temple
Cuff Rd.
Upper Weld Rd.
Jalan Besar
BIDEFORD RD
Central Park
Sophia Road
MacKenzie
Edinburgh
Mount Emily Park
Wilkie Road
SERANGOON ROAD
SHORT STREET
Dunlop St.
Abdul Gaffoor Mosque
ROCHOR CANAL RD
Bus Station
ORCHARD ROAD
Thong Sia Bldg.
Cuppage Centre
Emerald Hill Rd
Sri Temasek
Sophia Road
Sim Lim Square
Blanco Court
Faber House
Centre-point
Cuppage Road
Orchard Plaza
Orchard Point
El Bukit
N2 Somerset
PENANG ROAD
Handy Road
BENCOOLEN
MIDDLE ROAD
VICTORIA STREET
Bencoolen Mosque
St. Joseph's Church
Raffles Hotel
ORCHARD ROAD
KILLINEY
Lloyd Rd.
Chesed-El synagogue
BOULEVARD
Dhoby Ghaut
BRAS BASAH
Waterloo St.
COLONIAL DISTRICT
Westin Plaza
OXLEY
RIVER VALLEY ROAD
Sacred Heart Church
Singapore Hist. Mus.
CLEMENCEAU
TANK ROAD
Fort Canning Park
Battle Box
STAMFORD
Singapore Art Museum
Shah St.
Sri Thandayuthapani Temple
CITY CENTRE
Canning Rise
HILL STREET
Asian Civ. Mus.
C2 City Hall
War Memorial Park
Hong San See Temple
Van Kleef Aquarium
Singapore Philatelic Mus.
Funan Centre
St. Andrew's Cathedral
NORTH
CONNAUGHT DR.
Esplanade Park
River Valley Road
North Boat Quay
South Boat Quay
Supreme Court
City Hall
Parliament Hse.
Singapore Cricket Club
Victoria Concert Hall & Theatre
HAVELOCK ROAD
MERCHANT ROAD
Clarke Quay
Raffles Landing Site
Empress Place Museum
Merlion Park
Marina Bay
Singapore River
Melaka Mosque
N CANAL RD
Boat Quay
PICKERING STREET
Raffles Place
Pearl's Hill City Park
UPPER CROSS ROAD
SOUTH BRIDGE
CHULIA
OUB Centre
Clifford Pier
SENTOSA
Pearl's Hill Reservoir
NEW BRIDGE ROAD
People's Park Complex
Pagoda St.
Wak Hai Cheng Bio Temple
RAFFLES QUAY
C1 Raffles Place
Jamae Mosque
CHINATOWN
Fak Tak Ch'i Temple
Sri Mariamman Temple
Oriental Theatre

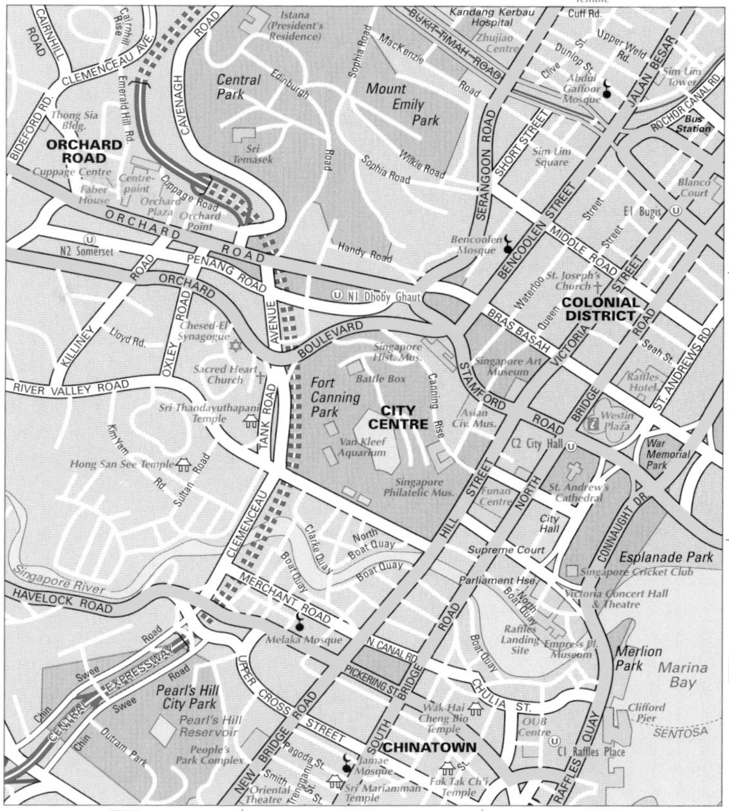

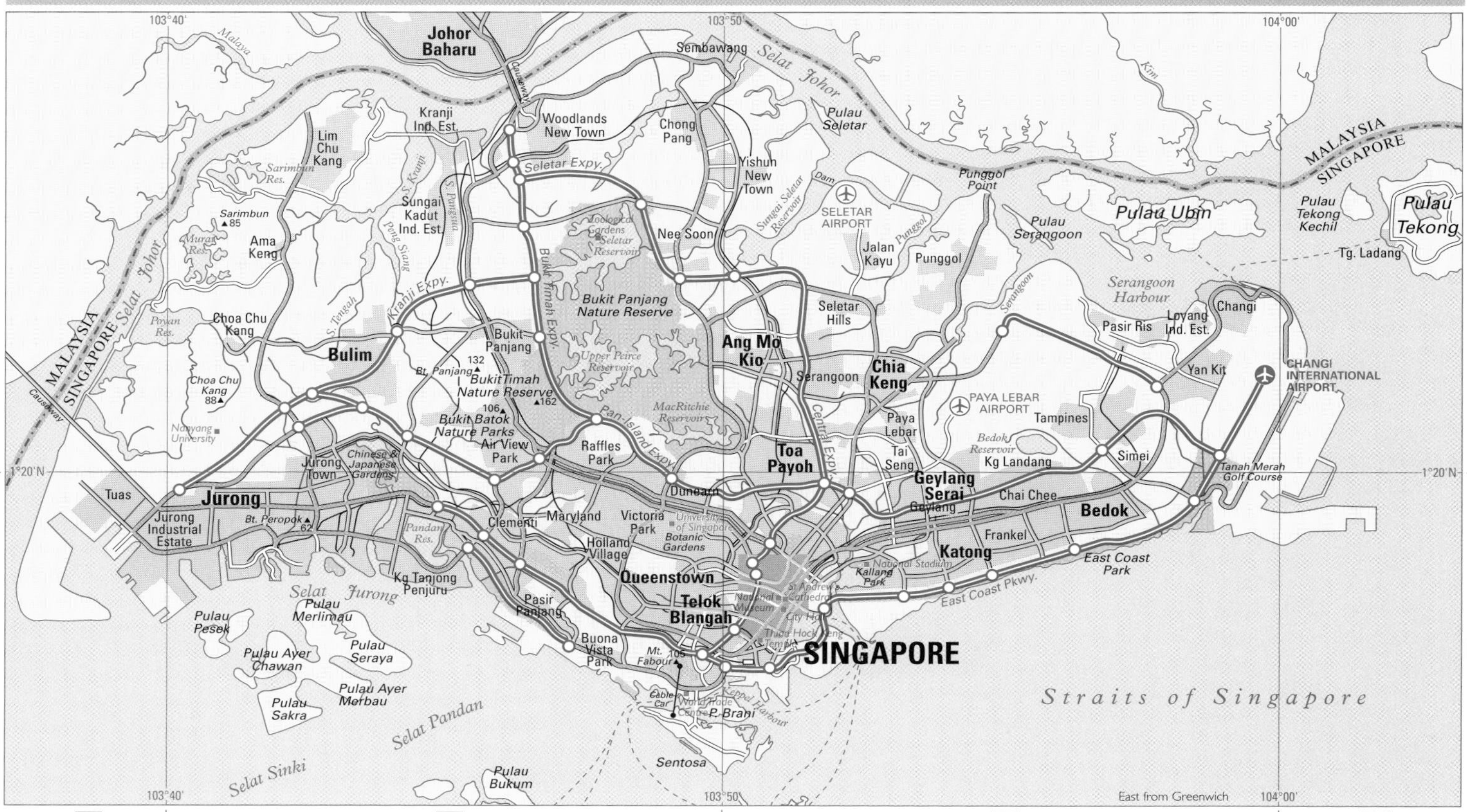

1   2   3

SINGAPORE

km 0 — 10
miles 0 — 6

A

103°40'
Malaysia
Selat Johor
Johor Baharu
Sembawang
Selat Johor
103°50'
Pulau Seletar
104°00'
MALAYSIA
SINGAPORE
MALAYSIA SINGAPORE
Causeway
Kranji Ind. Est.
Woodlands New Town
Chong Pang
Yishun New Town
Punggol Point
Pulau Tekong Kechil
Pulau Tekong
Lim Chu Kang
Seletar Expy.
Dam
SELETAR AIRPORT
Pulau Ubin
Pulau Serangoon
Tg. Ladang
Sarimbun Res.
Sarimbun ▲85
Ama Keng
Sungai Kadut Ind. Est.
Jurong Gardens
Seletar Reservoir
Nee Soon
Jalan Kayu
Punggol
Serangoon Harbour
Choa Chu Kang
Krabi Expy.
S. Punggol
Seletar Hills
Pasir Ris
Loyang Ind. Est.
Changi
Poyan Res.
Choa Chu Kang ▲88
Bukit Panjang
Bt. Panjang 132
Bukit Panjang Nature Reserve
Upper Pierce Reservoir
Ang Mo Kio
Chia Keng
PAYA LEBAR AIRPORT
Yan Kit
CHANGI INTERNATIONAL AIRPORT
Bulim
Bukit Timah Nature Reserve
Bukit Timah Expy.
106▲
▲162
MacRitchie Reservoir
Serangoon
Paya Lebar
Tampines
Simei
Nanyang University
Bukit Batok Nature Parks
Air View Park
Raffles Park
Toa Payoh
Tai Seng
Bedok Reservoir
Kg Landang
Jurong Town
Chinese & Japanese Gardens
Pan Island Expy.
Dunearn
Geylang Serai
Tuas
Jurong
Bt. Peropok ▲62
Clementi
Maryland
Victoria Park
University Botanic Gardens
Chai Chee
Bedok
1°20'N
Jurong Industrial Estate
Pandan Res.
Holland Village
Geylang
Frankel
East Coast Park
Pasir Panjang
Queenstown
National Stadium
Katong
Kg Tanjong Penjuru
Telok Blangah
Kallang
East Coast Pkwy.
Pulau Pesek
Selat Jurong
Pulau Merlimau
Buona Vista Park
Mt. Faber
SINGAPORE
Straits of Singapore
Pulau Ayer Chawan
Pulau Seraya
Cable Car
P. Brani
Pulau Ayer Merbau
Selat Pandan
Pulau Sakra
Selat Sinki
Pulau Bukum
Sentosa
103°40'
103°50'
East from Greenwich
104°00'

B

1   2   3   4

STOCKHOLM

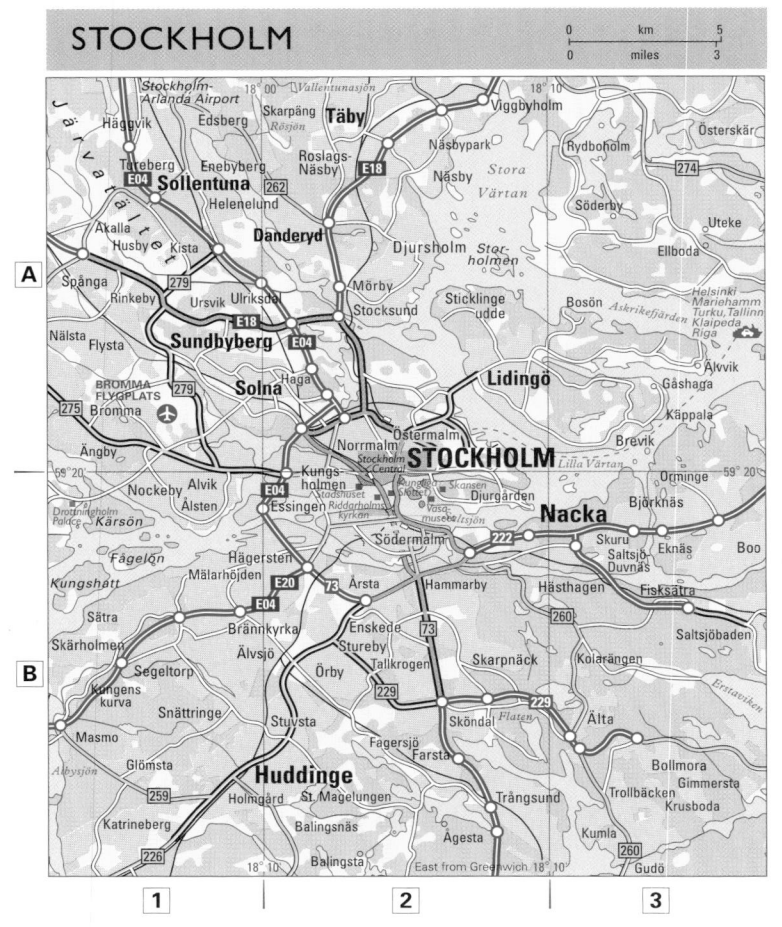

CENTRAL STOCKHOLM

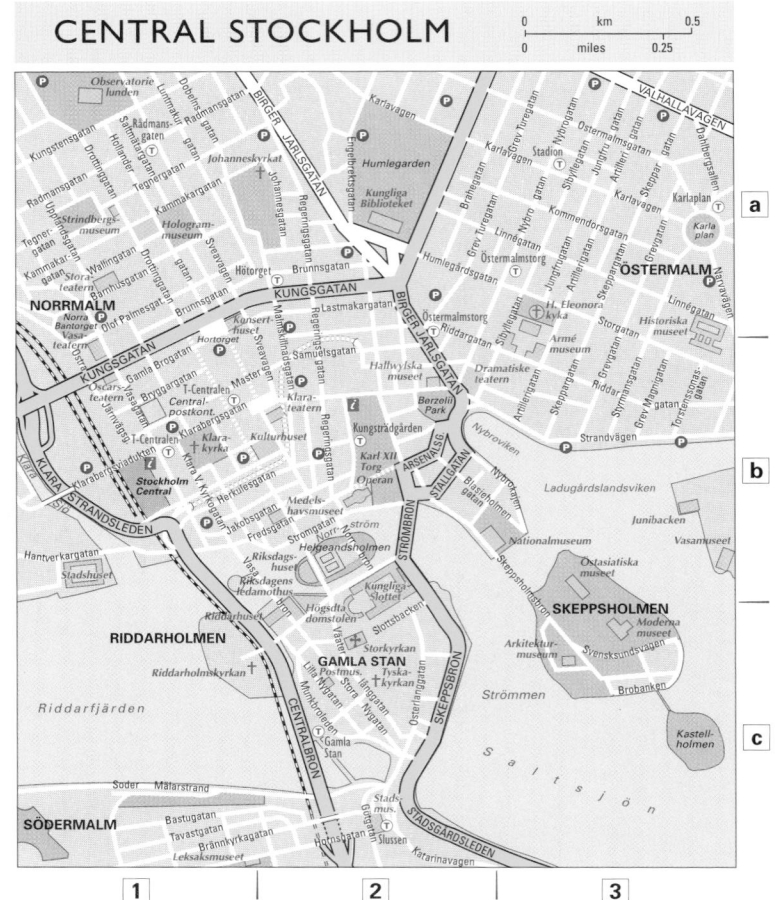

SYDNEY

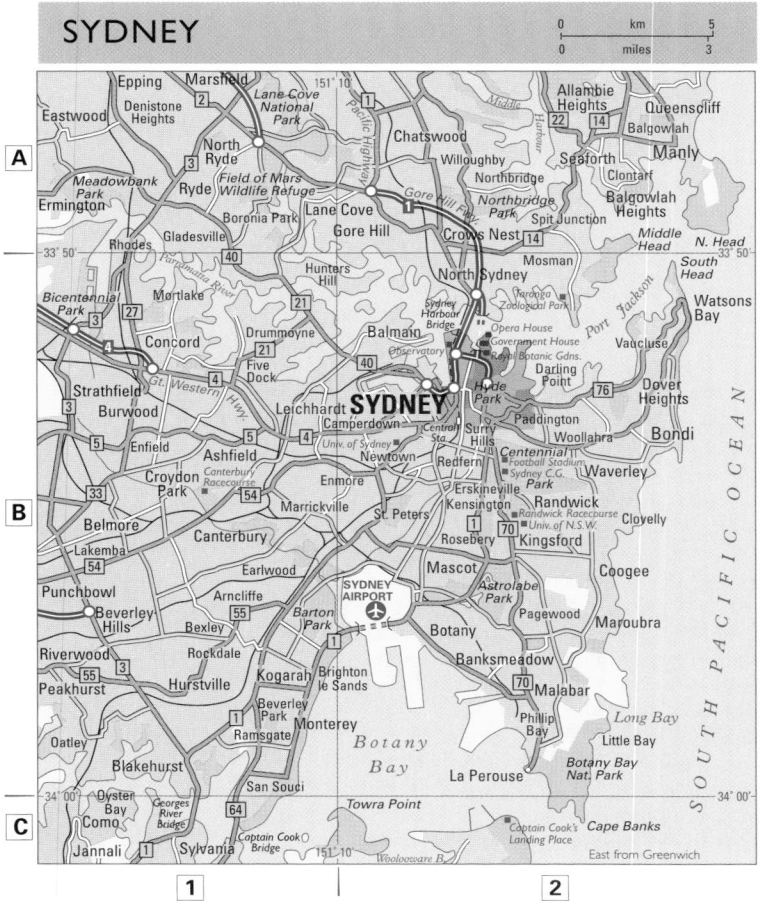

CENTRAL SYDNEY

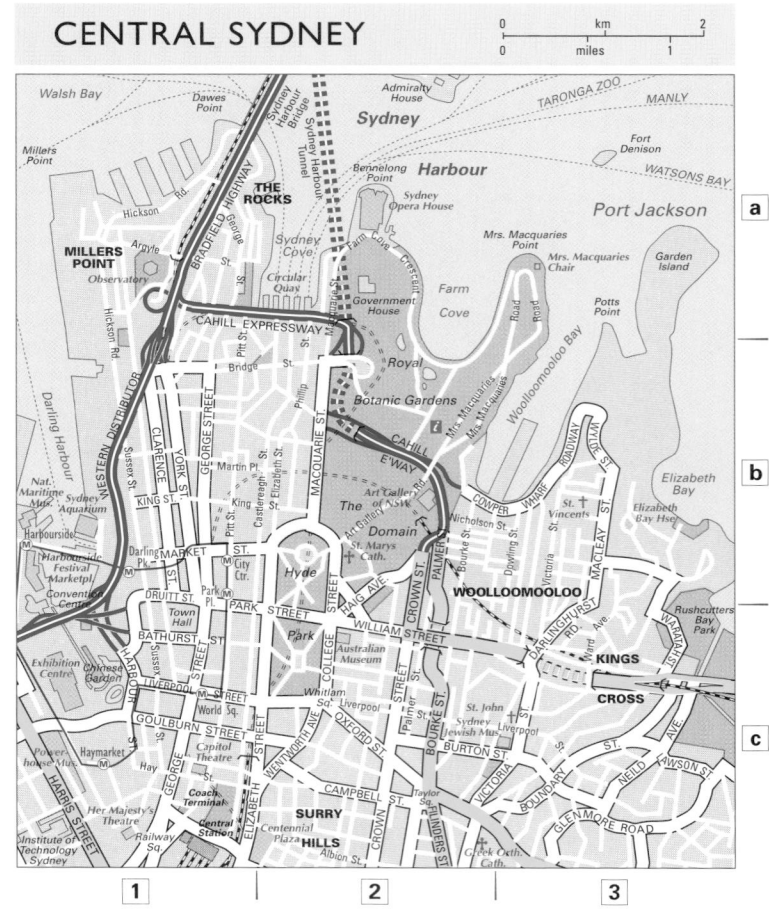

TOKYO

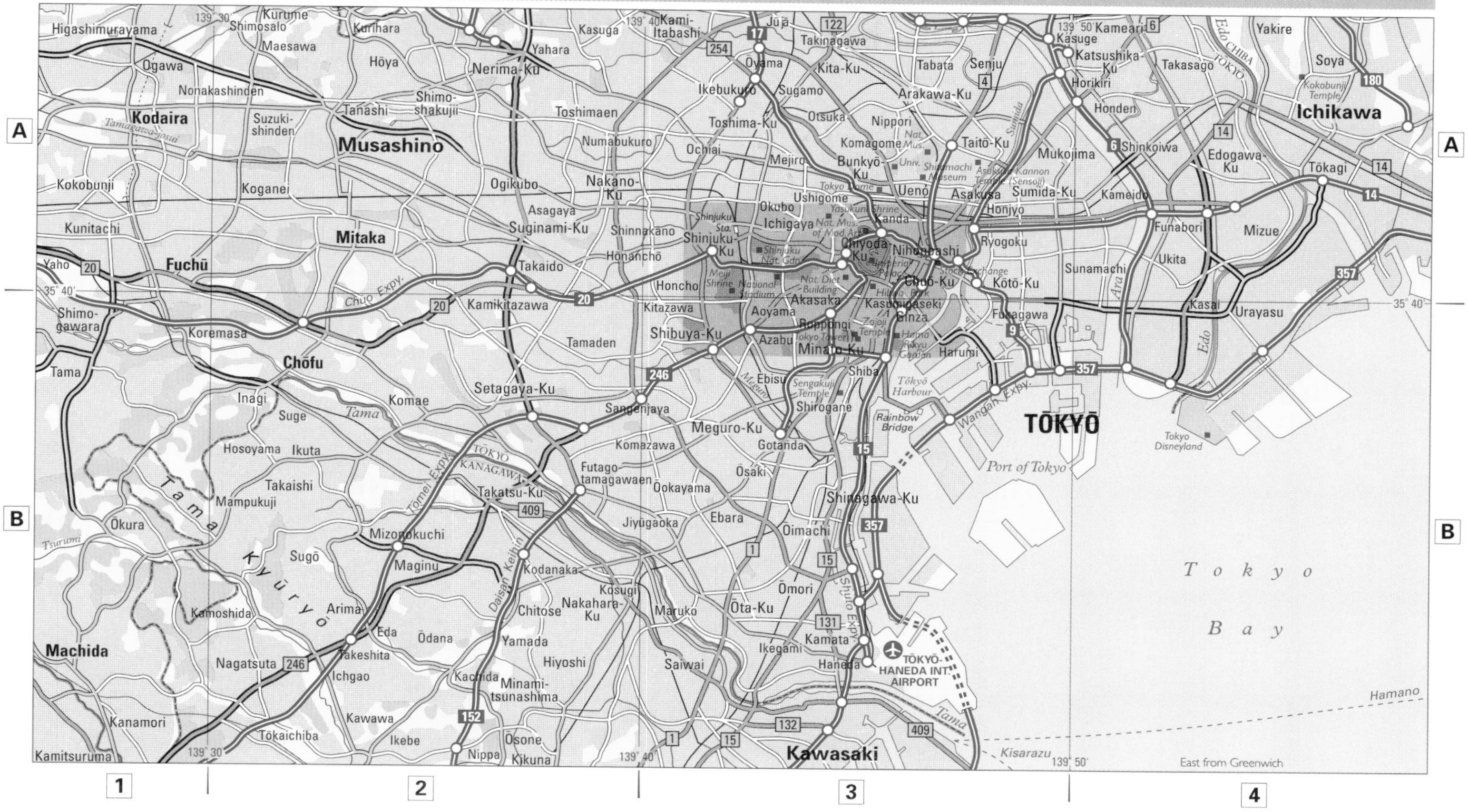

0 km 5
0 miles 3

139°30 Shimosato
Higashimurayama Kurume
Maesawa Kurihara Kasuga Kami-
Ogawa Itabashi 122
Nonakashinden Yahara Oyama Juo 17 Takinagawa Kameari 6 Yakire
Kodaira Hōya Shimo- Nerima-Ku Kita-Ku 254 Kasuge Katsushika- Soya
shakujii Ikebukuro Sugamo Arakawa-Ku Senju Ku Takasago
Kokubunji Tanashi Toshimaen Numabukuro Otsuka Nippori 4 Horikiri Kokunbi
Musashino Ogikubo Toshima-Ku Nat. Mus. Taitō-Ku Shinkoiwa Temple 180
Koganei Asagaya Nakano- Mejiro Bunkyō-Ku Ueno Asakusa Sumida-Ku Kameido Ichikawa
Mitaka Suginami-Ku Ku Shinnakano Shinjuku Tokyo Univ. Honjo Mukojima 14
Kunitachi Koenji Okubo Chiyoda- Nihonbashi Ryogoku Funabori Tōkagi
Fuchū Takaido Honchō Ku Chūo-Ku Koto-Ku Mizue 14
Yaho 20 Chuo Expy. Kamikitazawa Akasaka Ginza Sunamachi Kasai 357
Shimo- 20 Kitazawa Roppongi Harumi Urayasu
gawara Tamaden Aoyama Minato-Ku Shiba Fukagawa
Chōfu Setagaya-Ku Shibuya-Ku Azabu 9
Koremasa Ebisu Shirogane Tōkyō
Tama Sangenjaya Meguro-Ku Sengakuji Harbour TOKYO
Inagi Suge Komazawa Temple Rainbow Port of Tokyo Tokyo
Hosoyama Ikuta Futago- Gotanda Bridge Disneyland
Takaishi tamagawaen Ōsaki 15
Mampukuji Mizonokuchi Jiyugaoka Shinagawa-Ku
Okura Sugō Ebara Tokyo
Takatsu-Ku 409 Kodanaka Oimachi 357 Bay
Maginu Nakahara- Kosugi 1
Machida Arima Chitose Ku Ōmori
Kamoshida Takeshita Yamada Maruko Ōta-Ku 15
Nagatsuta 246 Ichgao Kosugi Kamata 131
Eda Ōdana Minami- Saiwai Haneda TOKYO-HANEDA INT
Kanamori Kachida tsunashima Hiyoshi AIRPORT
Kawawa 152 Hamano
Kamitsuruma Ōsone 132 409 Kisarazu 139°50
Tōkaichiba Nippa Kikuna KAWASAKI East from Greenwich

CENTRAL TOKYO

0 km 1
0 miles 0.5

OTAKIBASHI-DORI OKUBO-DORI OKUBO-DORI AKIHABARA ASAKUSABASHI
SHINJUKU-KU ŌKUBO KUDANKITA Akihabara
SHOKUAN-DORI Station
OME-KAIDO Hanazono-jinja Nicolai
Shrine Yasukuni-jinja Shin-ochanomizu Church
Sumitomo ICHIGAYA Shrine Kudanshita JIMBOCHO KANDA KODENMACHO
Bldg Budokan
Shinjuku Tokyo YASUKUNI-DORI Science Awajicho
Central Park City Hall Shinjuku- Technology Iwamotocho
sanchome Kitano maru Mus.
KOEN-DORI Akebonobashi Park
Shinjuku Sta. Ichigaya Craft Nat. Mus. of
YOTSUYA Mus. Modern Art
Minami-shinjuku Shinjukugyoemmae SANBANCHO Kojimachi East
Station Shinjuku Yotsuya Garden MARUNOUCHI
Yoyogi Sta. Yotsuyasanchome Hanzomon Otemachi Stock
KOSHU-DORI Shinanomachi Fukiage CHIYODA-KU Exchange
Sendagaya Sta. Imperial Tokyo Kitte
YAMATE-DORI Sta. Yotsuya Sta. Garden Sta. NIHONBASHI
Sword St. Ignatius Imperial CHŪO-KU
Museum Palace Tokyo
Sangūbashi Meiji Shrine National Station
Sta. Treasurehouse Jingū Suntory Theatre Nayabashi-mae Outer
Meiji Shrine Inner Art Museum Garden Bridgestone
Inner Garden Garden Nagatacho Sakuradamon Mus. of Art
National Akasaka Sakuradamon International Forum
Stadium Palace Government National Hibiya Ginza-
Meiji Shrine Jingū Buildings Diet Kasumigaseki itchome
Togu Baseball Outer Akasakamitsuke Building Government Hibiya
Memorial Hall Stadium Garden Buildings Park Nissei GINZA
Yoyogi Park Gaienmae Akasaka KASUMIGASEKI Hibiya Theatre Kabuki-za
Yoyogi-hachiman Meiji-jingū-mae AOYAMA-DORI Toranomon Sony Theatre
Sta. Harajuku Sta. AKASAKA TORANOMON Centre
Oriental Nogi-jinja Reinanzaka SHIMBASHI Shintomicho
INOKASHIRA-DORI Bazaar Shrine Church Shimbashi TSUKUDA-
Kanze No OMOTESANDO Nogizaka SHI
Play Theatre Omotesando Aoyama Kamiyacho Atago- Daimon St. Luke's TSUKIJI
SHIBUYA- Cemetery Tokyo cho Int. Hospital
KU Nezu Art Roppongi Tower Tsukiji Hongan-ji
Shibuya Museum Shiba Temple
DOGEN-ZAKA Shibuya Sta. ROPPONGI Park Hama Rikyu Central
Kanze No MINATO-KU Garden Wholesale
KOTTO-DORI Daimon Market
YAMATE-DORI AZABU SHIBA Zojoji Hamamatsucho Sumida-Gawa
Temple Station
MEIJI-DORI Shibakoen Haneda HARUMI
Airport

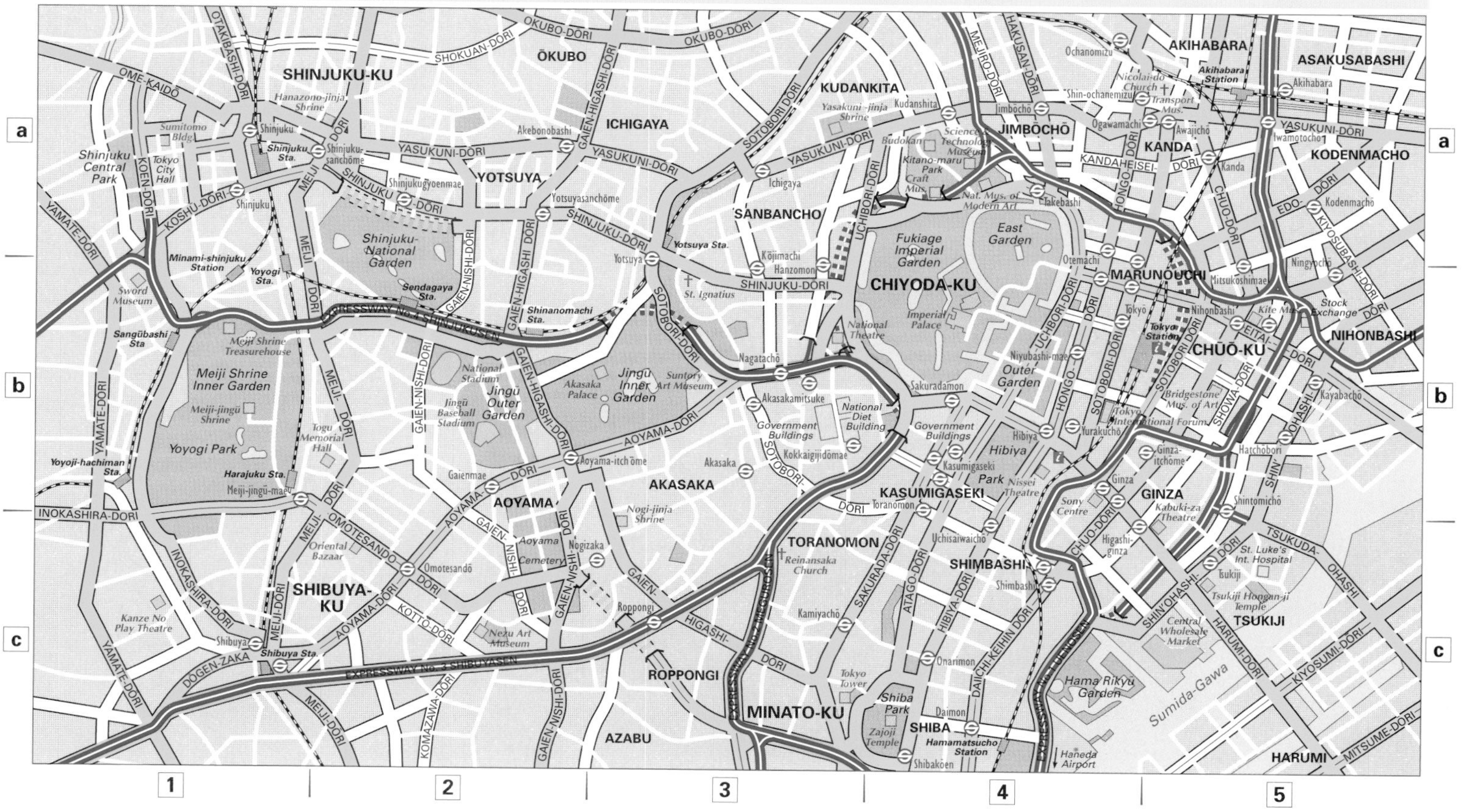

COPYRIGHT GEORGE PHILIP LTD

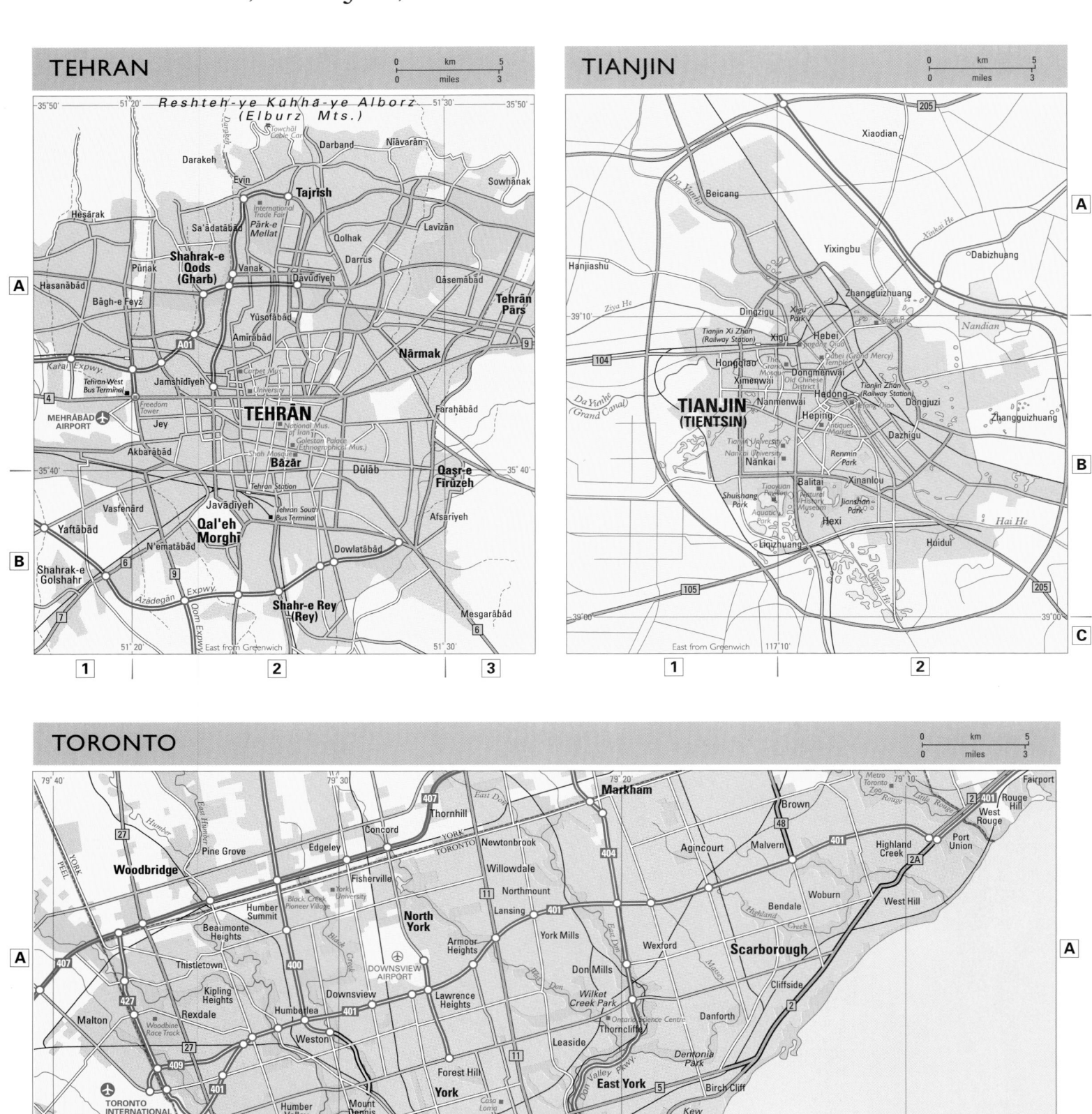

TEHRAN

Reshteh-ye Kūhhā-ye Alborz (Elburz Mts.)

Darakeh, Darband, Nīāvarān, Sowhānak, Darrūs, Lavīzān, Qolhak, Davūdīyeh, Qāsemābād, Tajrīsh, Saʿādatābād, Pārk-e Mellat, International Trade Fair, Evīn, Heşārak, Hasanābād, Bāgh-e Feyż, Pūnak, Shahrak-e Qods (Gharb), Vanak, Yūsofābād, Amīrābād, Tehrān Pārs, Nārmak, Kahak Expwy, Tehran West Bus Terminal, MEHRĀBĀD AIRPORT, Jamshīdīyeh, Freedom Tower, Carpet Mus., University, National Mus. of Iran, Golestan Palace (Ethnographical Mus.), Jey, TEHRĀN, Akbarābād, Farahābād, Soh Mosque, Bāzār, Dūlāb, Qaşr-e Fīrūzeh, Tehran Station, Vasfenārd, Javādīyeh, Tehran South Bus Terminal, Qalʿeh Morghī, Afsarīyeh, Yaftābād, Nʿematābād, Dowlatābād, Shahrak-e Golshahr, Āzādegān Expwy, Qom Expwy, Shahr-e Rey (Rey), Mesgarābād, East from Greenwich

TIANJIN (TIENTSIN)

Xiaodian, Beicang, Dabizhuang, Yixingbu, Da Yunhe, Hanjiashu, Zhangguizhuang, Xinkai He, Nandian, Ziya He, Dingzigu, Xigu Park, Stadium, Tianjin Xi Zhan (Railway Station), Xigu, Hebei, 104, Hongqiao, The Grand Mosque, Dabei (Grand Mercy) Temple, Old Chinese District, Dongmenwai, Ximenwai, Hadong, Da Yunhe (Grand Canal), Nanmenwai, Tianjin Zhan (Railway Station), Dongjuzi, Zhangguizhuang, Heping, Tianjin University, Antiques Market, Dazhigu, TIANJIN (TIENTSIN), Nankai University, Renmin Park, Nankai, Xinanlou, Tiaoyuan, Natural History Museum, Balitai, Jianshan Park, Shuishang Park, Aquatic, Hexi, Hai He, Liqizhuang, Huidui, East from Greenwich

TORONTO

Markham, Fairport, 407, Thornhill, East Don, Brown, West Rouge, Rouge Hill, Port Union, Concord, Edgeley, Newtonbrook, Agincourt, Malvern, Highland Creek, 2A, Pine Grove, Fisherville, Willowdale, Woodbridge, 27, Northmount, Woburn, West Hill, Black Creek Pioneer Village, York University, Lansing, 401, Wexford, Bendale, Humber Summit, Beaumonte Heights, North York, Armour Heights, York Mills, Scarborough, Thistletown, DOWNSVIEW AIRPORT, Don Mills, Cliffside, Kipling Heights, Downsview, Lawrence Heights, Wilket Creek Park, Danforth, Rexdale, Humberlea, 401, Ontario Science Centre, Thorncliffe, Malton, Woodbine Race Track, Weston, Leaside, Dentonia Park, 409, Forest Hill, East York, Birch Cliff, TORONTO INTERNATIONAL AIRPORT (LESTER B. PEARSON), Mount Dennis, York, Casa Loma, Don Valley Pkwy, Kew Gardens, Hanlon, Humber Valley Village, University of Toronto, Riverdale Park, Etobicoke, Lambton Mills, Swansea, City Hall, Parliament Buildings, Islington, Kingsway, High Park, Parkdale, CN Tower & SkyDome, Union Sta., Old Fort York, TORONTO, Markland Wood, 427, Exhibition Place, TORONTO CITY CENTRE AIRPORT, Gardiner Expwy, Burnhamthorpe, Summerville, Humber Bay, Ontario Place, Toronto Harbour, LAKE ONTARIO, Elizabeth Way, Mimico, Toronto Islands, Island Park, Gibraltar Point, Cooksville, Mississauga, New Toronto, Long Branch, West from Greenwich

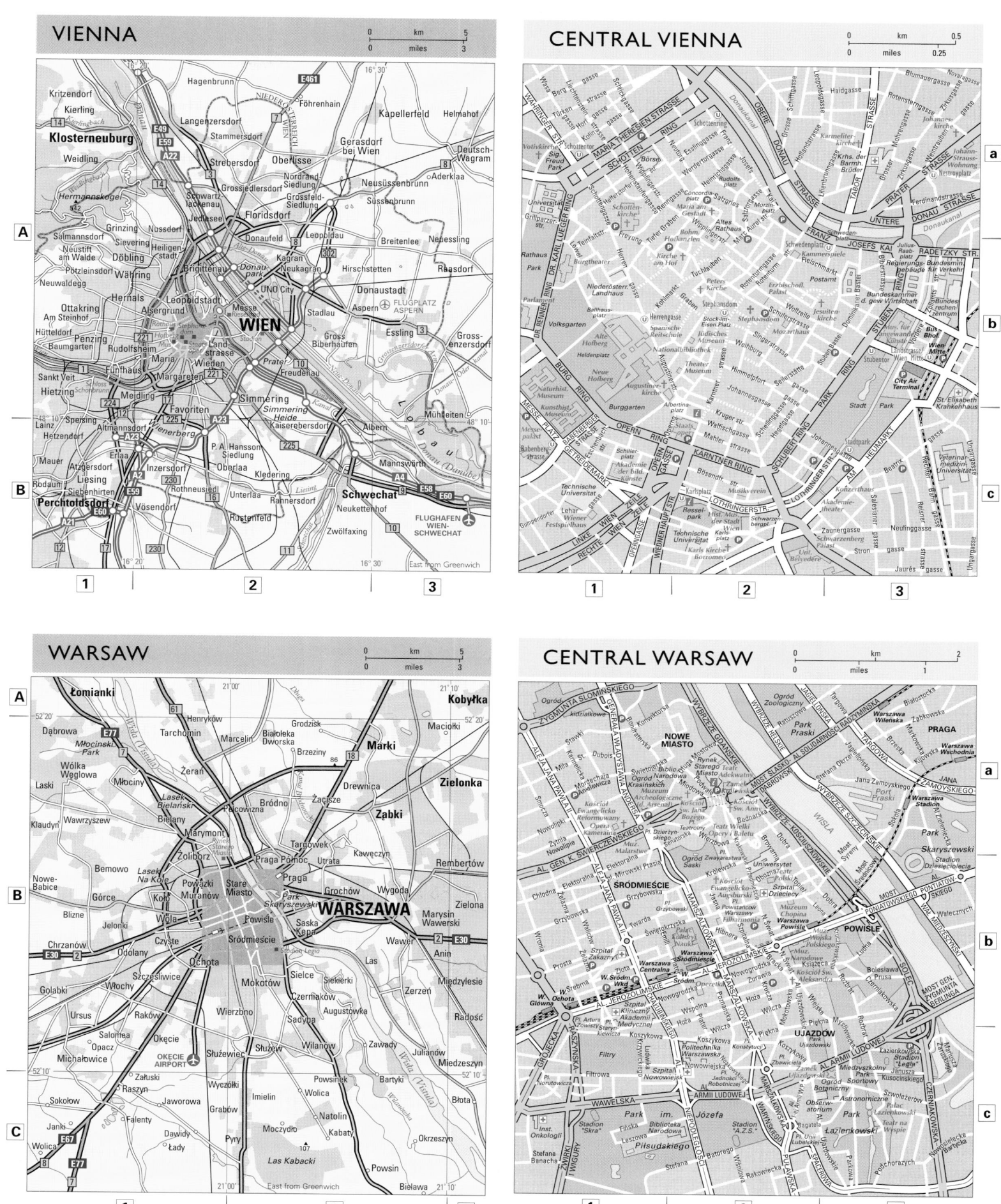

WASHINGTON

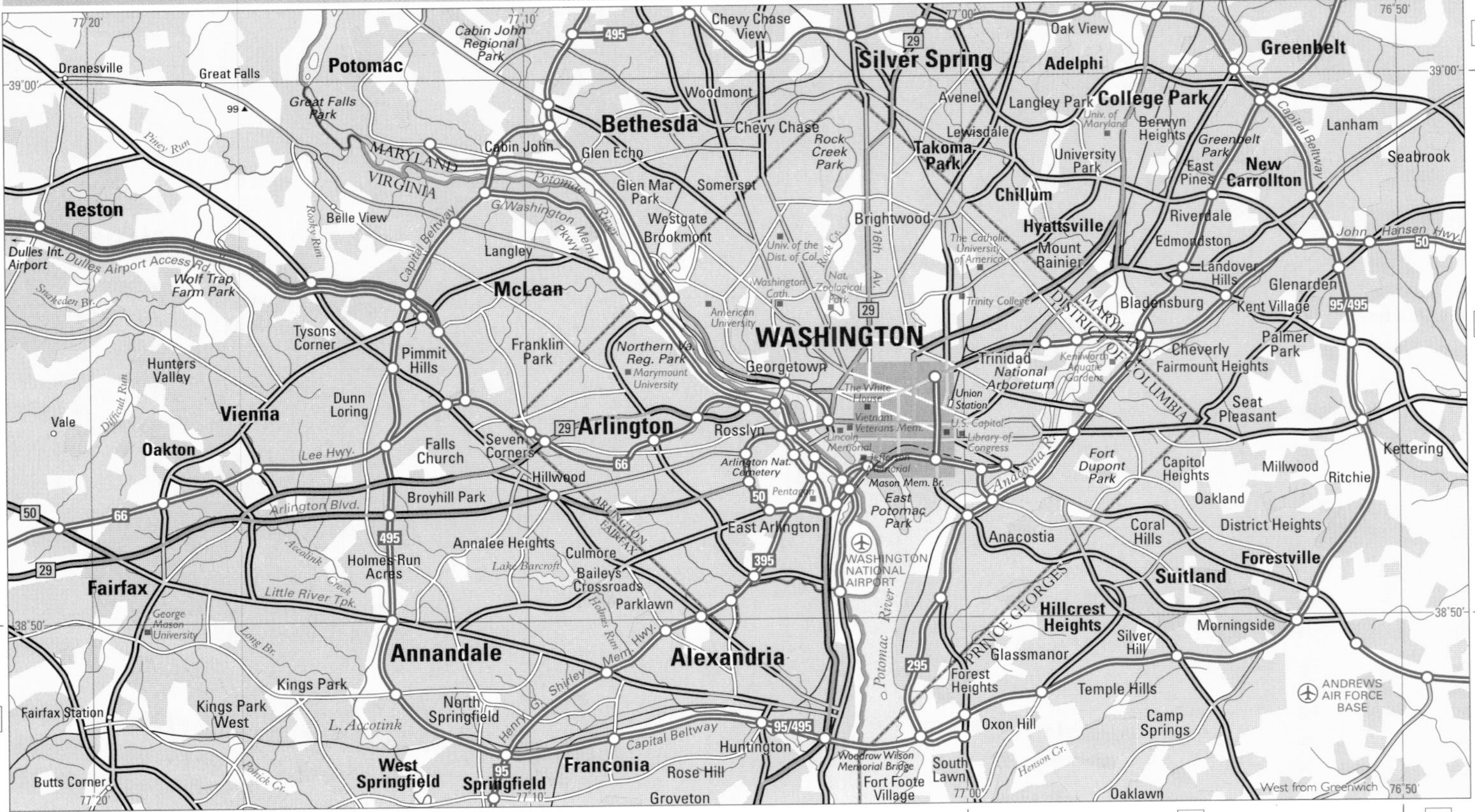

CENTRAL WASHINGTON

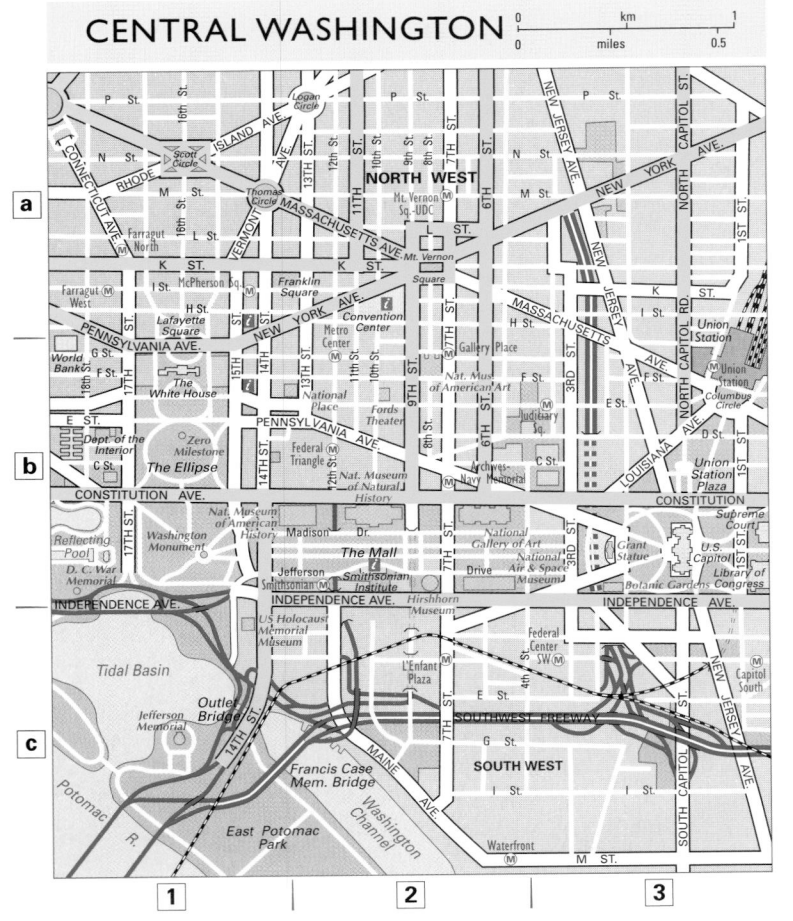

WELLINGTON

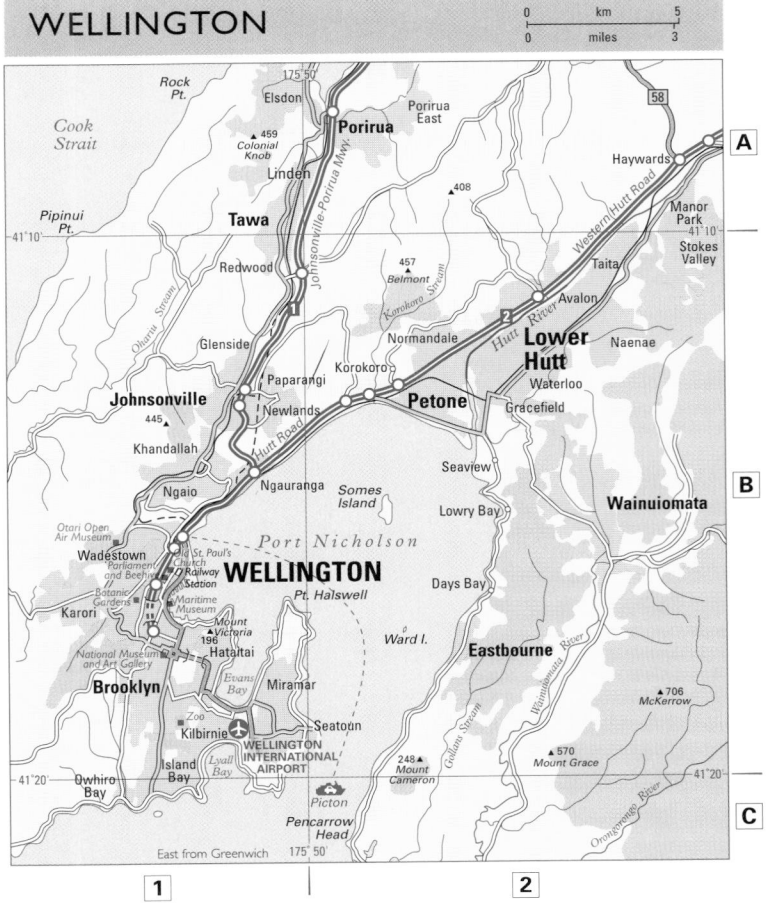

INDEX TO CITY MAPS

The index contains the names of all the principal places and features shown on the City Maps. Each name is followed by an additional entry in italics giving the name of the City Map within which it is located.

The number in bold type which follows each name refers to the number of the City Map page where that feature or place will be found.

The letter and figure which are immediately after the page number give the grid square on the map within which the feature or place is situated. The letter represents the latitude and the figure the longitude. Upper case letters refer to the City Maps, lower case letters to the Central Area Maps. The full geographic reference is provided in the border of the City Maps.

The location given is the centre of the city, suburb or feature and is not necessarily the name. Rivers, canals and roads are indexed to their name. Rivers carry the symbol ➤ after their name.

An explanation of the alphabetical order rules and a list of the abbreviations used are to be found at the beginning of the World Map Index.

A

Aalâm, *Baghdad* **3** B2
Aalsmeer, *Amsterdam* **2** B1
Abbey Wood, *London* **15** B4
Abcoude, *Amsterdam* **2** B2
Âbdin, *Cairo* **7** A2
Abeno, *Osaka* **22** B4
Aberdeen, *Hong Kong* **12** B2
Aberdour, *Edinburgh* **11** A2
Aberdour Castle, *Edinburgh* **11** A2
Abfanggraben ➤, *Munich* **20** B3
Ablon-sur-Seine, *Paris* **23** B3
Abramtsevo, *Moscow* **19** A1
Abramtsevo, *Moscow* **19** B4
Abu Dis, *Jerusalem* **13** B2
Abū en Numrus, *Cairo* **7** B2
Abu Ghosh, *Jerusalem* **13** B1
Acacias, *Madrid* **17** c2
Acassuso, *Buenos Aires* **7** A1
Accotink Cr. ➤, *Washington* **32** B2
Acheres, *Paris* **23** A1
Acília, *Rome* **25** C1
Aclimação, *São Paulo* **26** B2
Açúcar, Pão de, *Rio de Janeiro* **24** B2
Ada Beja, *Lisbon* **14** A1
Adams Park, *Atlanta* **3** B2
Adams Shore, *Boston* **6** B4
Addiscombe, *London* **15** B3
Adelphi, *Washington* **32** A4
Aderklaa, *Vienna* **31** A3
Admiralteyskaya Storona, *St. Petersburg* **26** B2
Áfiori, *Milan* **18** A2
Aflandshage, *Copenhagen* **10** B3
Afsariyeh, *Tehran* **30** B2
Agboyi Cr. ➤, *Lagos* **14** A2
Ågerup, *Copenhagen* **10** A1
Ågesta, *Stockholm* **28** B2
Agincourt, *Toronto* **30** A3
Agora, Arhéa, *Athens* **2** c1
Agra Canal, *Delhi* **10** B2
Agricola Oriental, *Mexico City* **18** B2
Agua Espraiada ➤, *São Paulo* **26** B2
Agualva-Cacem, *Lisbon* **14** A1
Agustino, Cerro El, *Lima* **16** B2
Ahrensfelde, *Berlin* **5** A4
Ahuntsic, *Montreal* **19** A1
Ai ➤, *Osaka* **22** A4
Aigremont, *Paris* **23** A1
Air View Park, *Singapore* **27** A2
Airport West, *Melbourne* **17** A1
Aiyáleo, *Athens* **2** B1
Aiyáleos, Óros, *Athens* **2** B1
Ajegunle, *Lagos* **14** B2
Aji, *Osaka* **22** A3
Ajuda, *Lisbon* **14** A1
Akalla, *Stockholm* **28** A1
Akasaka, *Tokyo* **29** b3
Akbarābād, *Tehran* **30** A2
Akershus Slott, *Oslo* **22** A3
Akihabara, *Tokyo* **29** a5
Akrópolis, *Athens* **2** c2
Al 'Azamiyah, *Baghdad* **3** A2
Al Quds = Jerusalem, *Jerusalem* **13** B2
Alaguntan, *Lagos* **14** B2
Alameda, *San Francisco* **25** B3
Alameda, Parque, *Mexico City* **18** b2
Alameda Memorial State Beach Park, *San Francisco* **25** A2
Albern, *Vienna* **31** B2
Albert Park, *Melbourne* **17** B1
Alberton, *Johannesburg* **13** B2
Albertslund, *Copenhagen* **10** B2
Albysjön, *Stockholm* **28** B1
Alcantara, *Lisbon* **14** A1
Alcatraz I., *San Francisco* **25** B2
Alcobendas, *Madrid* **17** A2
Alcorcón, *Madrid* **17** B1
Aldershof, *Berlin* **5** B4
Aldo Bonzi, *Buenos Aires* **7** C1
Aleksandrovskoye, *St. Petersburg* **26** B2
Alexander Nevsky Abbey, *St. Petersburg* **26** B2
Alexander Soutzos Mouseio, *Athens* **2** b3
Alexandra, *Johannesburg* **13** A2
Alexandra, *Singapore* **27** B2
Alexandra, *Washington* **32** C3
Alfama, *Lisbon* **14** c3
Alfortville, *Paris* **23** B3
Algés, *Lisbon* **14** A1
Alhambra, *Los Angeles* **16** B4
Alibey ➤, *Istanbul* **12** B1
Alibey Baraji, *Istanbul* **12** B1
Alibeyköy, *Istanbul* **12** B1
Alimos, *Athens* **2** B2
Alipur, *Calcutta* **8** B1
Allach, *Munich* **20** A1
Allambie Heights, *Sydney* **28** A1
Allard Pierson Museum, *Amsterdam* **2** b2
Allermuir Hill, *Edinburgh* **11** B2
Allerton, Pt., *Boston* **6** B4
Alston, *Boston* **6** A3

Almada, *Lisbon* **14** A2
Almagro, *Buenos Aires* **7** B2
Almargem do Bispo, *Lisbon* **14** A1
Almazovo, *Moscow* **19** A6
Almirante G. Brown, Parque, *Buenos Aires* **7** C2
Almon, *Jerusalem* **13** B2
Almond ➤, *Edinburgh* **11** B2
Alnabru, *Oslo* **22** A4
Alnsjøen, *Oslo* **22** A4
Alperton, *London* **15** A2
Alpine, *New York* **21** A2
Alrode, *Johannesburg* **13** B2
Alsemerg, *Brussels* **6** B1
Alsergrund, *Vienna* **31** A2
Alsip, *Chicago* **9** C2
Ålsten, *Stockholm* **28** B1
Ålta, *Stockholm* **28** B3
Altadena, *Los Angeles* **16** A4
Alte do Pina, *Lisbon* **14** A2
Alter Finkenkrug, *Berlin* **5** A1
Altes Rathaus, *Munich* **20** b3
Altglienicke, *Berlin* **5** B4
Altlandsberg, *Berlin* **5** A5
Altlandsberg Nord, *Berlin* **5** A5
Altmannsdorf, *Vienna* **31** B1
Alto da Mooca, *São Paulo* **26** B2
Alto de Pina, *Lisbon* **14** A2
Altona, *Melbourne* **17** B1
Álvaro Obregón, *Mexico City* **18** B1
Alvik, *Stockholm* **28** B1
Älvsjo, *Stockholm* **28** B2
Älvvik, *Stockholm* **28** A3
Am Hasenbergl, *Munich* **20** A2
Am Steinhof, *Vienna* **31** A1
Am Wald, *Munich* **20** B2
Ama Keng, *Singapore* **27** A2
Amadora, *Lisbon* **14** A1
Amagasaki, *Osaka* **22** A3
Amager, *Copenhagen* **10** B3
Amål Qådisiya, *Baghdad* **3** B2
Amalienborg, *Copenhagen* **10** b3
Amata, *Milan* **18** A1
Ameixoeira, *Lisbon* **14** A2
América, *São Paulo* **26** B1
Amin, *Baghdad* **3** B2
Aminadov, *Jerusalem* **13** B1
Aminyevo, *Moscow* **19** B2
Amirâbâd, *Tehran* **30** A2
Amora, *Lisbon* **14** B2
Amoreira, *Lisbon* **14** A1
Ampelokipi, *Athens* **2** B2
Amper ➤, *Munich* **20** A1
Amstel, *Amsterdam* **2** b2
Amstel ➤, *Amsterdam* **2** c2
Amstel-Drecht-Kanaal, *Amsterdam* **2** B2
Amstel Station, *Amsterdam* **2** c3
Amstelhof, *Amsterdam* **2** b3
Amstelveen, *Amsterdam* **2** B2
Amsterdam, *Amsterdam* **2** A2
Amsterdam-Rijnkanaal, *Amsterdam* **2** B3
Amsterdam Zoo, *Amsterdam* **2** b3
Amsterdam Zuidoost, *Amsterdam* **2** B2
Amsterdamse Bos, *Amsterdam* **2** B1
Anacostia, *Washington* **32** B4
Anadoluhisari, *Istanbul* **12** B2
Anadolukavağı, *Istanbul* **12** A2
Anata, *Jerusalem* **13** B2
Ancol, *Jakarta* **13** A1
'Andalus, *Baghdad* **3** B1
Andarai, *Rio de Janeiro* **24** B1
Anderlecht, *Brussels* **6** A1
Anderson Park, *Atlanta* **3** B2
Andingmen, *Beijing* **4** B2
Andrews Air Force Base, *Washington* **32** C4
Ang Mo Kio, *Singapore* **27** A2
Angby, *Stockholm* **28** A1
Angel I., *San Francisco* **25** A2
Angel Island State Park, *San Francisco* **25** A2
Angke, Kali ➤, *Jakarta* **13** A1
Angyalföld, *Budapest* **7** A2
Anik, *Mumbai* **20** A2
Anin, *Warsaw* **31** B2
Anjou, *Montreal* **19** A2
Annalee Heights, *Washington* **32** B2
Annandale, *Washington* **32** C2
Anne Frankhuis, *Amsterdam* **2** a1
Antony, *Paris* **23** B2
Anyangch'on, *Seoul* **27** C1
Aoyama, *Tokyo* **29** b2
Ap Lei Chau, *Hong Kong* **12** B1
Apapa, *Lagos* **14** B2
Apelacão, *Lisbon* **14** A2
Apterkarskiy Ostrov, *St. Petersburg* **26** B2
Ar Kazimiyah, *Baghdad* **3** B1
Ara ➤, *Tokyo* **29** B3
Arakawa-Ku, *Tokyo* **29** A3

Arany-hegyi-patak ➤, *Budapest* **7** A2
Aravaca, *Madrid* **17** B1
Arbataash, *Baghdad* **3** B2
Arc de Triomphe, *Paris* **23** a2
Arcadia, *Los Angeles* **16** B4
Arceuil, *Paris* **23** B2
Arco Plaza, *Los Angeles* **16** b1
Arese, *Milan* **18** A1

Arganzuela, *Madrid* **17** B1
Argenteuil, *Paris* **23** A2
Argonne Forest, *Chicago* **9** C1
Argüelles, *Madrid* **17** a1
Arima, *Osaka* **22** A1
Arima, *Tokyo* **29** B2
Ários Págos, *Athens* **2** c1
Arkhangelskoye, *Moscow* **19** B1
Arlington, *Boston* **6** A2
Arlington, *Washington* **32** B3
Arlington Heights, *Boston* **6** A2
Arlington Nat. Cemetery, *Washington* **32** B3
Armação, *Rio de Janeiro* **24** B2
Armadale, *Melbourne* **17** B2
Armenian Quarter, *Jerusalem* **13** b3
Armour Heights, *Toronto* **30** A2
Arncliffe, *Sydney* **28** B1
Arnold Arboretum, *Boston* **6** B3
Arpádföld, *Budapest* **7** A3
Arrentela, *Lisbon* **14** B2
Ársta, *Stockholm* **28** B2
Art Institute, *Chicago* **9** C2
Artane, *Dublin* **11** A2
Artas, *Jerusalem* **13** B2
Arthur's Seat, *Edinburgh* **11** B3
Aryiroúpolis, *Athens* **2** B2
Asagaya, *Tokyo* **29** A2
Asahi, *Osaka* **22** A4
Asakusa, *Tokyo* **29** A3
Asakusabashi, *Tokyo* **29** a5
Asati, *Calcutta* **8** C1
Aschheim, *Munich* **20** A3
Ascot Vale, *Melbourne* **17** A1
Ashburn, *Chicago* **9** C2
Ashburton, *Melbourne* **17** B2
Ashfield, *Sydney* **28** B1
Ashford, *London* **15** B1
Ashiya, *Osaka* **22** A2
Ashtown, *Dublin* **11** A2
Askisto, *Helsinki* **12** B1
Askrikefjärden, *Stockholm* **28** A3
Asnières, *Paris* **23** A2
Aspern, *Vienna* **31** A2
Aspern, Flugplatz, *Vienna* **31** A3
Assago, *Milan* **18** B1
Assemblée Nationale, *Paris* **23** b3
Assendelft, *Amsterdam* **2** A1
Assiano, *Milan* **18** B1
Astoria, *New York* **21** B2
Astrolabe Park, *Sydney* **28** B2
Atatürk Airport, *Jerusalem* **13** A2
Atghara, *Calcutta* **8** B2
Athens = Athínai, *Athens* **2** B2
Athínai, *Athens* **2** B2
Athínai-Ellinikón Airport, *Athens* **2** B2
Athis-Mons, *Paris* **23** B3
Athlone, *Cape Town* **8** A2
Atholl, *Johannesburg* **13** A2
Atífiya, *Baghdad* **3** A2
Atişalen, *Istanbul* **12** B1
Atlanta, *Atlanta* **3** B2
Atlanta History Center, *Atlanta* **3** B2
Atomium, *Brussels* **6** A2
Attiki, *Athens* **2** A2
Atzgersdorf, *Vienna* **31** B1
Aubervilliers, *Paris* **23** A3
Aubing, *Munich* **20** B1
Auburndale, *Boston* **6** A2
Auchenhinny, *Edinburgh* **11** B2
Auckland Park, *Johannesburg* **13** B2
Auderghem, *Brussels* **6** B2
Augusta, Mausoleo di, *Rome* **25** b2
Augustówka, *Warsaw* **31** B2
Aulnay-sous-Bois, *Paris* **23** A3
Aurelio, *Rome* **25** B1
Ausím, *Cairo* **7** A1
Austerlitz, Gare d', *Paris* **23** A3
Austin, *Chicago* **9** B2
Avalon, *Wellington* **32** B2
Avedøre, *Copenhagen* **10** B2
Avellaneda, *Buenos Aires* **7** C2
Avenel, *Washington* **32** B4
Avondale, *Chicago* **9** B2
Avondale Heights, *Melbourne* **17** A1
Avtovo, *St. Petersburg* **26** B1
Ayazağa, *Istanbul* **12** B1
Ayer Chawan, P., *Singapore* **27** B2
Ayer Merbau, P., *Singapore* **27** B2
Ayía Marína, *Athens* **2** A2
Ayía Paraskevi, *Athens* **2** A2
Ayía Sophía, *Rome* **25** b3
Áyios Dhimítrios, *Athens* **2** B2
Áyios Ioánnis Rendís, *Athens* **2** B1
Azabu, *Tokyo* **29** c3
Azcapotzalco, *Mexico City* **18** B1
Azteca, Estadia, *Mexico City* **18** C2
Azucar, Cerro Pan de, *Santiago* **26** A1

B

Baambrugge, *Amsterdam* **2** B2
Baba I., *Karachi* **14** B1
Babarpur, *Delhi* **10** A2
Babushkin, *Moscow* **19** A4
Back B., *Mumbai* **20** B1
Baclaran, *Manila* **17** B1
Bacoor, *Manila* **17** C1

Bacoor B., *Manila* **17** C1
Badalona, *Barcelona* **4** A2
Badhoevedorp, *Amsterdam* **2** A1
Badli, *Delhi* **10** A1
Bærum, *Oslo* **22** A2
Bağcılar, *Istanbul* **12** B1
Bâggio, *Milan* **18** B1
Bâgh-e-Feyz, *Tehran* **30** A1
Baghdad, *Baghdad* **3** A2
Bagmari, *Calcutta* **8** B2
Bagneux, *Paris* **23** B2
Bagnolet, *Paris* **23** A3
Bagsværd, *Copenhagen* **10** A2
Bagsværd Sø, *Copenhagen* **10** A2
Baguiati, *Calcutta* **8** B2
Bagumbayan, *Manila* **17** C2
Bahçeköy, *Istanbul* **12** A1
Bahtim, *Cairo* **7** A2
Baileys Crossroads, *Washington* **32** B3
Bailly, *Paris* **23** A1
Bairro Alto, *Lisbon* **14** c1
Bairro Lopes, *Lisbon* **14** b3
Baisha = Canton **8** B2
Baisha ➤, *Canton* **8** B2
Baixa, *Lisbon* **14** c2
Baiyun Airport, *Canton* **8** A2
Baiyun Hill Scenic Spot, *Canton* **8** B2
Bakırköy, *Istanbul* **12** C1
Bakovka, *Moscow* **19** B2
Bal Harbor, *Miami* **18** A2
Balara, *Manila* **17** B2
Balashikha, *Moscow* **19** B5
Baldia, *Karachi* **14** A1
Baldoyle, *Dublin* **11** A2
Baldwin Hills, *Los Angeles* **16** B2
Baldwin Hills Res., *Los Angeles* **16** B2
Balgowlah, *Sydney* **28** A2
Balgowlah Heights, *Sydney* **28** A2
Bali, *Calcutta* **8** B1
Baliganja, *Calcutta* **8** B2
Balingsnäs, *Stockholm* **28** B2
Balingsta, *Stockholm* **28** B2
Balintawak, *Manila* **17** B1
Balitai, *Tianjin* **30** B2
Ballerup, *Copenhagen* **10** A2
Ballinteer, *Dublin* **11** B2
Ballyboden, *Dublin* **11** B2
Ballyback, *Dublin* **11** A1
Ballyfermot, *Dublin* **11** A1
Ballymorefinn Hill, *Dublin* **11** B1
Ballymun, *Dublin* **11** A2
Balmain, *Sydney* **28** B2
Baluhati, *Calcutta* **8** B1
Balvanera, *Buenos Aires* **7** B2
Balwyn, *Melbourne* **17** A2
Balwyn North, *Melbourne* **17** A2
Banática, *Lisbon* **14** A1
Banco do Brasil, Centro Cultural, *Rio de Janeiro* **24** a2
Bandra, *Mumbai* **20** A1
Bandra Pt., *Mumbai* **20** A1
Bang Kapi, *Bangkok* **3** B2
Bang Kholaem, *Bangkok* **3** B2
Bang Na, *Bangkok* **3** B2
Bang Phlad, *Bangkok* **3** a1
Bangken, *Bangkok* **3** A2
Bangkok = Krung Thep, *Bangkok* **3** B2
Bangkok Noi, *Bangkok* **3** B1
Bangkok Yai, *Bangkok* **3** B1
Bangphongphun, *Bangkok* **3** b2
Banglo, *Calcutta* **8** B1
Bangrak, *Bangkok* **3** B2
Bangsu, *Bangkok* **3** A2
Bank, *London* **15** b5
Bank of America, *San Francisco* **25** b2
Bank of China Tower, *Hong Kong* **12** c1
Banks, *Calcutta* **9** C2
Banksmeadow, *Sydney* **28** B2
Bantra, *Calcutta* **8** B1
Baoshan, *Shanghai* **27** A1
Bar Giyora, *Jerusalem* **13** B1
Barahanagar, *Calcutta* **8** B2
Barajas, *Madrid* **17** B2
Barajas, Aeropuerto Transoceanico de, *Madrid* **17** B2
Barakpur, *Calcutta* **8** A2
Barberini, Palazzo, *Rome* **25** b3
Barbican, *London* **15** a4
Barcarena, *Lisbon* **14** A1
Barcarena, Rib. de ➤, *Lisbon* **14** A1
Barcelona, *Barcelona* **4** A1
Barcelona-Prat, Aeropuerta de, *Barcelona* **4** B1
Barceloneta, *Barcelona* **4** b5
Barking, *London* **15** A4
Barkingside, *London* **15** A4
Barnes, *London* **15** B2
Barnet, *London* **15** A2
Barra Andai, *Karachi* **14** B2
Barra Funda, *São Paulo* **26** B2
Barracas, *Buenos Aires* **7** B2
Barranco, *Lima* **16** B2
Barreiro, *Lisbon* **14** B2
Barreto, *Rio de Janeiro* **24** B2
Bartala, *Calcutta* **8** B1
Barton Park, *Sydney* **28** B1

Bartyki, *Warsaw* **31** C2
Barvikha, *Moscow* **19** B1
Bastille, Place de la, *Paris* **23** c5
Basus, *Cairo* **7** A2
Batamagar, *Calcutta* **8** B1
Bath Beach, *New York* **21** C1
Bath I., *Karachi* **14** B2
Batir, *Jerusalem* **13** B1
Batok, Bukit, *Singapore* **27** A2
Battersea, *London* **15** B3
Battery Park, *New York* **21** e1
Bauman, *Moscow* **19** B4
Baumgarten, *Vienna* **31** A1
Bay Harbour Islands, *Miami* **18** A2
Bay Ridge, *New York* **21** C1
Bayonne, *New York* **21** B1
Bayshore, *San Francisco* **25** B3
Bayswater, *London* **15** b2
Bayt Lahm = Bethlehem, *Jerusalem* **13** B2
Bayview, *San Francisco* **25** B2
Bāzár, *Tehran* **30** A2
Beachmont, *Boston* **6** A4
Beacon Hill, *Hong Kong* **12** A2
Beato, *Lisbon* **14** A2
Beaumont, *Dublin* **11** A2
Beaumonte Heights, *Toronto* **30** A1
Bebek, *Istanbul* **12** B2
Béchovice, *Prague* **24** B3
Beck L., *Chicago* **9** A1
Beckenham, *London* **15** B3
Beckton, *London* **15** A4
Becontree, *London* **15** A4
Beddington Corner, *London* **15** B3
Bedford, *Boston* **6** A2
Bedford Park, *Chicago* **9** C2
Bedford Park, *New York* **21** A2
Bedford Stuyvesant, *New York* **21** B2
Bedford View, *Johannesburg* **13** B2
Bedok, *Singapore* **27** B3
Bedok, Res., *Singapore* **27** A3
Beersel, *Brussels* **6** B1
Behala, *Calcutta* **8** B1
Bei Hai, *Beijing* **4** B2
Beicai, *Shanghai* **27** B2
Beicang, *Tianjin* **30** A1
Beihai Park, *Beijing* **4** b2
Beijing, *Beijing* **4** B1
Beit Ghur el-Fawqa, *Jerusalem* **13** A1
Beit Hanina, *Jerusalem* **13** B2
Beit Iksa, *Jerusalem* **13** B2
Beit I'nan, *Jerusalem* **13** A1
Beit Jala, *Jerusalem* **13** B2
Beit Lekhem = Bethlehem, *Jerusalem* **13** B2
Beit Nekofa, *Jerusalem* **13** B1
Beit Sahur, *Jerusalem* **13** B2
Beit Surik, *Jerusalem* **13** B1
Beit Zayit, *Jerusalem* **13** B1
Beitaipingzhuang, *Beijing* **4** B1
Beitar Ilit, *Jerusalem* **13** B1
Beitsun, *Canton* **8** B2
Beitunya, *Jerusalem* **13** A2
Beixing Jing Park, *Shanghai* **27** B1
Bčkásmegyer, *Budapest* **7** A2
Bekkelaget, *Oslo* **22** A3
Bel Air, *Los Angeles* **16** B2
Bela Vista, *São Paulo* **26** B2
Bélanger, *Montreal* **19** A1
Belas, *Lisbon* **14** A1
Belas Artes, Museu Nacionale de, *Rio de Janeiro* **24** b2
Beleghata, *Calcutta* **8** B2
Belém, *Lisbon* **14** A1
Belém, Torre de, *Lisbon* **14** A1
Belenzinho, *São Paulo* **26** B2
Belgachia, *Calcutta* **8** B2
Belgharia, *Calcutta* **8** B2
Belgrano, *Buenos Aires* **7** B2
Belgravia, *London* **15** c3
Bell, *Los Angeles* **16** C4
Bell Gardens, *Los Angeles* **16** C4
Bell Tower, *Beijing* **4** a2
Bellavista, *Lima* **16** B2
Bellavista, *Santiago* **26** B2
Belle Harbor, *New York* **21** C2
Belle View, *Washington* **32** C3
Bellevue, Schloss, *Berlin* **5** a2
Bellingham, *London* **15** B3
Bellwood, *Chicago* **9** B1
Belmont, *Boston* **6** A2
Belmont, *London* **15** A2
Belmont, *Wellington* **32** A2
Belmont Harbor, *Chicago* **9** B3
Belmore, *Sydney* **28** B1
Belur, *Calcutta* **8** B1
Belvedere, *Atlanta* **3** B3
Belvedere, *San Francisco* **25** B2
Bemowo, *Warsaw* **31** B1
Benaki, Moussío, *Athens* **2** b3
Bendale, *Toronto* **30** A3
Bendkhal, *Mumbai* **20** B2
Benfica, *Rio de Janeiro* **24** B1
Benfica, *Lisbon* **14** A1
Benito Juárez, *Mexico City* **18** B2
Benito Juárez, Aeropuerto Int., *Mexico City* **18** B2
Bensonhurst, *New York* **21** C2
Berchem-Sainte-Agathe, *Brussels* **6** A1

Berg am Laim, *Munich* **20** B2
Bergenfield, *New York* **21** A2
Bergham, *Munich* **20** B2
Bergvliet, *Cape Town* **8** B1
Beri, *Barcelona* **4** A1
Berkeley, *San Francisco* **25** A3
Berlin, *Berlin* **5** A3
Bermondsey, *London* **15** B3
Bernabeu, Estadio, *Madrid* **17** B1
Bernal Heights, *San Francisco* **25** B2
Berwyn, *Chicago* **9** B2
Berwyn Heights, *Washington* **32** B4
Besiktas, *Istanbul* **12** B2
Bethlehem, *Jerusalem* **13** B2
Bethnal Green, *London* **15** A3
Betor, *Calcutta* **8** B1
Beurs, *Amsterdam* **2** b2
Beverley Hills, *Sydney* **28** B1
Beverley Park, *Sydney* **28** B1
Beverly, *Chicago* **9** C3
Beverly Glen, *Los Angeles* **16** B2
Beverly Hills, *Los Angeles* **16** B2
Bexley, *London* **15** B4
Bexley, *London* **15** B4
Bexleyheath, *London* **15** B4
Beykoz, *Istanbul* **12** B2
Beylerbeyi, *Istanbul* **12** B2
Beyoğlu, *Istanbul* **12** B1
Bezons, *Paris* **23** A2
Bezuidenhout Park, *Johannesburg* **13** B2
Bhadrakali, *Calcutta* **8** A2
Bhalswa, *Delhi* **10** A2
Bhambo Khan Qarmati, *Karachi* **14** B2
Bhatsala, *Calcutta* **8** B1
Bhawanipur, *Calcutta* **8** B2
Bhuleshwar, *Mumbai* **20** B2
Białołeka Dworska, *Warsaw* **31** B2
Biblioteca Nacional, *Rio de Janeiro* **24** c2
Bicentennial Park, *Sydney* **28** B1
Bickley, *London* **15** B4
Bidu, *Jerusalem* **13** B1
Bielany, *Warsaw* **31** B1
Bielawa, *Warsaw* **31** C2
Biesdorf, *Berlin* **5** A4
Bièvre ➤, *Paris* **23** B2
Bièvres, *Paris* **23** B2
Bilston, *Edinburgh* **11** B2
Binacayan, *Manila* **17** C1
Binondo, *Manila* **17** B1
Biran, P., *Singapore* **27** A1
Birch Cliff, *Toronto* **30** A3
Birannyrka, *Stockholm* **28** B2
Birkholz, *Berlin* **5** A4
Birkholzaue, *Berlin* **5** A4
Birrarrung Park, *Melbourne* **17** A2
Biscayne Bay, *Miami* **18** B2
Biscayne Park, *Miami* **18** A2
Bishop Lavis, *Cape Town* **8** A2
Bishopscourt, *Cape Town* **8** A1
Bispebjerg, *Copenhagen* **10** A3
Biwon Secret Garden, *Seoul* **27** B1
Björkhagen, *Stockholm* **28** B3
Björknäs, *Stockholm* **28** A3
Black Cr. ➤, *Toronto* **30** A2
Blackfen, *London* **15** B4
Blackheath, *London* **15** B4
Blackrock, *Dublin* **11** B2
Bladensburg, *Washington* **32** B4
Blair Village, *Atlanta* **3** C2
Blairgowrie, *Johannesburg* **13** A2
Blakehurst, *Sydney* **28** B1
Blakstad, *Oslo* **22** A1
Blankenburg, *Berlin* **5** A4
Blankenfelde, *Berlin* **5** A3
Blizne, *Warsaw* **31** B1
Bloomsbury, *London* **15** a3
Błota, *Warsaw* **31** C3
Blue Island, *Chicago* **9** C2
Bluebell, *Dublin* **11** B1
Bluff Hd., *Hong Kong* **12** B2
Blumberg, *Berlin* **5** A4
Blunt Pt., *San Francisco* **25** B2
Blutenberg, *Munich* **20** B1
Blylaget, *Oslo* **22** B3
Bo-Kaap Museum, *Cape Town* **8** c2
Boa Vista, *Rio de Janeiro* **24** B1
Boardwalk, *New York* **21** C2
Boavista, *Lisbon* **14** A2
Bobigny, *Paris* **23** A3
Bocanegra, *Lima* **16** A2
Boedo, *Buenos Aires* **7** B2
Bogenhausen, *Munich* **20** B2
Bogorodskoye, *Moscow* **19** B4
Bogota, *New York* **21** A1
Bohnsdorf, *Berlin* **5** B4
Bois-Colombes, *Paris* **23** A2
Bois-d'Arcy, *Paris* **23** B1
Boissy-St.-Léger, *Paris* **23** B4
Boldinasca, *Milan* **18** A1
Bøler, *Oslo* **22** A4
Bollate, *Milan* **18** A1
Bollebeek, *Brussels* **6** A1
Bollmora, *Stockholm* **28** B3
Bolshaya-Okhta, *St. Petersburg* **26** B2
Bolton, *Atlanta* **3** B2

Bom Retiro, *São Paulo* **26** B2
Bombay = Mumbai, *Mumbai* **20** B2
Bondi, *Sydney* **28** B2
Bondy, *Paris* **23** A3
Bondy, Forêt de, *Paris* **23** A4
Bonifacio Monument, *Manila* **17** B1
Bonneuil-sur-Marne, *Paris* **23** B4
Bonnington, *Edinburgh* **11** B1
Bonnyrig and Lasswade, *Edinburgh* **11** B3
Bonsuccesso, *Rio de Janeiro* **24** B1
Bontehuewel, *Cape Town* **8** A2
Boo, *Stockholm* **28** A3
Booterstown, *Dublin* **11** B2
Borisovo, *Moscow* **19** C4
Borle, *Mumbai* **20** A2
Boronia Park, *Sydney* **28** A1
Borough Park, *New York* **21** C2
Bosmont, *Johannesburg* **13** B1
Bosön, *Stockholm* **28** A3
Bosporus = Istanbul Boğazi, *Istanbul* **12** B2
Bostancı, *Istanbul* **12** C2
Boston Harbor, *Boston* **6** A4
Botafogo, *Rio de Janeiro* **24** B1
Botanik Have, *Copenhagen* **10** b2
Botany, *Sydney* **28** B2
Botany B., *Sydney* **28** B2
Botany Bay Nat. Park, *Sydney* **28** B2
Botič ➤, *Prague* **24** B3
Botica Sete, *Lisbon* **14** A1
Boucherville, *Montreal* **19** A3
Boucherville, Îs. de, *Montreal* **19** A3
Bougival, *Paris* **23** A1
Boulder Pt., *Hong Kong* **12** B1
Boulogne, Bois de, *Paris* **23** A2
Boulogne-Billancourt, *Paris* **23** A2
Bourg-la-Reine, *Paris* **23** B2
Bouviers, *Paris* **23** B1
Bovenkerk, *Amsterdam* **2** B2
Bovenkerker Polder, *Amsterdam* **2** B2
Bovisa, *Milan* **18** A2
Bow, *London* **15** A3
Bowery, *New York* **21** e2
Boyce Heights, *Los Angeles* **16** B3
Boyacıköy, *Istanbul* **12** B2
Bradbury Building, *Los Angeles* **16** b2
Braepark, *Edinburgh* **11** B2
Braid, *Edinburgh* **11** B2
Bramley, *Johannesburg* **13** A2
Brandenburger Tor, *Berlin* **5** A3
Brani, P., *Singapore* **27** A1
Brás, *São Paulo* **26** B2
Brasília, *Prague* **24** B2
Brasilândia, *São Paulo* **26** A1
Brateyevo, *Moscow* **19** C4
Bratsevo, *Moscow* **19** A2
Bray, *Dublin* **11** B3
Braybrook, *Melbourne* **17** A1
Brázdim, *Prague* **24** A3
Breach Candy, *Mumbai* **20** a1
Breakheart Reservation, *Boston* **6** A3
Brede, *Copenhagen* **10** A3
Breeds Pond, *Boston* **6** A4
Breezy Point, *New York* **21** C2
Breitenlee, *Vienna* **31** A3
Breña, *Lima* **16** B2
Brent, *London* **15** A2
Brent Res., *London* **15** A2
Brentford, *London* **15** B2
Brentwood Park, *Los Angeles* **16** B2
Brera, *Milan* **18** B2
Bresso, *Milan* **18** A2
Brevik, *Stockholm* **28** A3
Brevnov, *Prague* **24** B2
Bridgeport, *Chicago* **9** B3
Bridgetown, *Cape Town* **8** A2
Bridgeview, *Chicago* **9** C2
Brighton, *Boston* **6** A3
Brighton, *Melbourne* **17** B1
Brighton le Sands, *Sydney* **28** B1
Brighton Park, *Chicago* **9** C2
Brightwood, *Washington* **32** B3
Brigittenau, *Vienna* **31** A2
Brimbank Park, *Melbourne* **17** A1
Brisbane, *San Francisco* **25** B2
British Museum, *London* **15** a3
Britz, *Berlin* **5** B3
Brixton, *London* **15** B3
Broad Sd., *Boston* **6** A4
Broadmeadows, *Melbourne* **17** A1
Broadmoor, *San Francisco* **25** B2
Broadview, *Chicago* **9** B1
Broadway, *New York* **21** e1
Brockley, *London* **15** B3
Bródno, *Warsaw* **31** B2
Bródnowski, Kanal ➤, *Warsaw* **31** B2
Broek in Waterland, *Amsterdam* **2** A2
Bromley, *London* **15** B4
Bromley Common, *London* **15** B4
Bromma, *Stockholm* **28** A1
Bromma flygplats, *Stockholm* **28** A1
Brompton, *London* **15** c2
Brøndby Strand, *Copenhagen* **10** B2
Brøndbyøster, *Copenhagen* **10** B2
Brøndbyvester, *Copenhagen* **10** B2
Brønnøya, *Oslo* **22** A2
Brønshøj, *Copenhagen* **10** A2

Bronxville, *New York* 21 A3
Brookfield, *Chicago* 9 C1
Brookhaven, *Atlanta* 3 A2
Brookline, *Boston* 6 B3
Brooklyn, *Cape Town* 8 A1
Brooklyn, *New York* 21 C2
Brooklyn, *Wellington* 32 B1
Brooklyn Bridge, *New York* .. 21 f2
Brookmont, *Washington* 32 B3
Brossard, *Montreal* 19 B3
Brou-sur-Chantereine, *Paris* . 23 A4
Brown, *Toronto* 30 A3
Broyhill Park, *Washington* ... 32 B2
Brughério, *Milan* 18 A2
Brunswick, *Melbourne* 17 A1
Brush Hill, *Boston* 6 B1
Brussegem, *Brussels* 6 A1
Brussel Nat. Luchthaven,
  Brussels 6 A2
Brussels = Bruxelles, *Brussels* 6 A2
Bruxelles, *Brussels* 6 A2
Bruzzano, *Milan* 18 A2
Bry-sur-Marne, *Paris* 23 A4
Bryanston, *Johannesburg* 13 A1
Bryn, *Oslo* 22 A1
Brzeziny, *Warsaw* 31 B2
Bubeneč, *Prague* 24 B2
Buc, *Paris* 23 B1
Buchenhain, *Munich* 20 B1
Buchholz, *Berlin* 5 A3
Buckhead, *Atlanta* 3 B2
Buckingham Palace, *London* .. 15 b3
Buckow, *Berlin* 5 B2
Buda, *Budapest* 7 A2
Budafok, *Budapest* 7 B2
Budaörs, *Budapest* 7 B1
Budapest, *Budapest* 7 B2
Budatétény, *Budapest* 7 b2
Budavaripalota, *Budapest* 7 b2
Budinge, *Copenhagen* 10 A2
Budokan, *Tokyo* 29 a4
Buena Vista, *San Francisco* .. 25 B2
Buenos Aires, *Buenos Aires* .. 7 B2
Bufalotta, *Rome* 25 B2
Bugio, *Lisbon* 14 B1
Buiksloot, *Amsterdam* 2 A2
Buitenveldert, *Amsterdam* ... 2 B2
Buizingen, *Brussels* 6 B1
Bukit Panjang Nature
  Reserve, *Singapore* 27 A2
Bukit Timah Nature Reserve,
  Singapore 27 A2
Bukum, P., *Singapore* 7 B2
Bûlâq, *Cairo* 7 A2
Bule, *Manila* 17 C2
Bulim, *Singapore* 27 A2
Bullen Park, *Melbourne* 17 A2
Bundoora North, *Melbourne* .. 17 A2
Bundoora Park, *Melbourne* ... 17 A1
Bunker I., *Karachi* 14 A1
Bunkyo-Ku, *Tokyo* 29 A3
Bunnefjorden, *Oslo* 22 A3
Buona Vista Park, *Singapore* . 27 B2
Burbank, *Chicago* 9 C2
Burbank, *Los Angeles* 16 A3
Burlington, *Boston* 6 A2
Burnham Park, *Chicago* 9 c2
Burnham Park Harbor,
  Chicago 9 C2
Burnhamthorpe, *Toronto* 30 B1
Burnt Oak, *London* 15 A2
Burntisland, *Edinburgh* 11 A2
Burnwynd, *Edinburgh* 11 B1
Burqa, *Jerusalem* 13 A2
Burtus, *Cairo* 7 A1
Burudvatn, *Oslo* 22 A2
Burwood, *Sydney* 28 B1
Bushwick, *New York* 21 C2
Bushy Park, *London* 15 B1
Butantã, *São Paulo* 26 B1
Butcher I., *Mumbai* 20 B2
Butts Corner, *Washington* ... 32 C2
Büyükdere, *Istanbul* 12 B1
Byculla, *Mumbai* 20 b2
Bygdøy, *Oslo* 22 A3

C

C.N. Tower, *Toronto* 30 B2
Cabaçu de Cima ➡,
  São Paulo 26 A2
Caballito, *Buenos Aires* 7 B2
Cabin John, *Washington* 32 B2
Cabin John Regional Park,
  Washington 32 B2
Cabinteely, *Dublin* 11 B3
Cabra, *Dublin* 11 A2
Cabuçu de Baixo ➡,
  São Paulo 26 A2
Cachan, *Paris* 23 B2
Cachenka ➡, *Moscow* 19 B1
Cachoeira, Rib. da ➡,
  São Paulo 26 B1
Cacilhas, *Lisbon* 14 A2
Cahuenga Pk., *Los Angeles* .. 16 B3
Caju = El Qâhira, *Cairo* 7 A2
Caju, *Rio de Janeiro* 24 B1
Cakovice, *Prague* 24 A3
Calcutta = Kolkata, *Calcutta* . 8 B2
California Inst. of Tech.,
  Los Angeles 16 B4
California Plaza, *Los Angeles* 16 b1
California State Univ.,
  Los Angeles 16 B2
Callao, *Lima* 16 B2
Caloocan, *Manila* 17 B1
Calumet Park, *Chicago* 9 C3
Calumet Sag Channel ➡,
  Chicago 9 C2
Calumpang, *Manila* 17 B2
Calvairate, *Milan* 18 B2
Camarate, *Lisbon* 14 A2
Camaroes, *Lisbon* 14 A1
Camberwell, *London* 15 A3
Camberwell, *Melbourne* 17 B2
Cambridge, *Boston* 6 A3
Cambridge Res., *Boston* 6 A2
Cambuci, *São Paulo* 26 B2
Camden, *London* 15 A3
Cameron, Mt., *Wellington* ... 32 B2
Çamlıca, *Istanbul* 12 B2
Camp Springs, *Washington* .. 32 C4
Campamento, *Madrid* 17 B1
Campbellfield, *Melbourne* ... 17 A1
Camperdown, *Sydney* 28 B2
Campidoglio, *Rome* 25 c2
Campo, Casa de, *Madrid* 17 B1
Campo F.C. Barcelona,
  Barcelona 4 b1
Campo Grande, *Lisbon* 14 A2
Campo Pequeño, *Lisbon* 14 A2
Campolide, *Lisbon* 14 A2
Camps Bay, *Cape Town* 8 A1
C'an San Joan, *Barcelona* 4 A2
Cañacao B., *Manila* 17 C1

Canarsie, *New York* 21 C2
Cancelleria, Palazzo dei,
  Rome 25 c2
Candiac, *Montreal* 19 B3
Caneças, *Lisbon* 14 A1
Canillas, *Madrid* 17 B2
Canillejas, *Madrid* 17 B2
Canning Town, *London* 15 A4
Canteras de Vallecas, *Madrid* 17 B2
Canterbury, *Melbourne* 17 A2
Canterbury, *Sydney* 28 B1
Canton = Guangzhou, *Canton* 4 B2
Caoheijing, *Shanghai* 27 B1
Capão Redondo, *São Paulo* .. 26 B1
Caparica, *Lisbon* 14 A2
Caparica, Costa da, *Lisbon* .. 14 B1
Cape Flats, *Cape Town* 8 B2
Cape Town, *Cape Town* 8 A1
Capital Heights, *Washington* . 32 B4
Capitol Hill, *Washington* 32 B4
Capitolini, Musei, *Rome* 25 c3
Captain Cook Bridge, *Sydney* 28 C1
Captain Cook Landing Place
  Park, *Sydney* 28 C2
Capuchos, *Lisbon* 14 B1
Carabanchel Alto, *Madrid* ... 17 B1
Carabanchel Bajo, *Madrid* ... 17 B1
Caराça, *Buenos Aires* 7 C2
Caridad, *Manila* 17 C1
Carioca, Sa. da, *Rio de Janeiro* 24 B1
Carlstadt, *New York* 21 A1
Carlton, *Melbourne* 17 A1
Carmen de Huechuraba,
  Santiago 26 B1
Carmen de la Legua, *Lima* ... 16 B2
Carnaxide, *Lisbon* 14 A1
Carnegie, *Melbourne* 17 B2
Carnegie Hall, *New York* 21 c2
Carnide, *Lisbon* 14 A1
Carol City, *Miami* 18 A1
Carrascal, *Santiago* 26 B1
Carrickmines, *Dublin* 11 B3
Carrières-sous-Bois, *Paris* ... 23 A1
Carrières-sous-Poissy, *Paris* . 23 A1
Carrières-sur-Seine, *Paris* ... 23 A2
Carrigeen Bay, *Dublin* 11 A3
Cartierville, *Montreal* 19 A1
Carze Verde, *São Paulo* 26 A1
Casal Morena, *Rome* 25 C2
Casalotti, *Rome* 25 B1
Cascade Heights, *Atlanta* ... 3 B2
Castél di Leva, *Rome* 25 C2
Castle, *Dublin* 11 c2
Castle, *Edinburgh* 11 b2
Castle of Good Hope,
  Cape Town 8 a3
Castleknock, *Dublin* 11 A1
Castleton Corners, *New York* 21 C1
Catedral Metropolitana,
  Mexico City 18 b3
Catedral Metropolitana,
  Rio de Janeiro 24 c1
Catete, *Rio de Janeiro* 24 B1
Catford, *London* 15 B3
Caulfield, *Melbourne* 17 B2
Causeway Bay, *Hong Kong* .. 12 c3
Cavite, *Manila* 17 C1
Caxias, *Lisbon* 14 A1
Cebecci, *Istanbul* 12 B1
Cecchignola, *Rome* 25 C2
Cecilienhof, Schloss, *Berlin* .. 5 B1
Cedar Grove, *Atlanta* 3 C3
Cempaka Putih, *Jakarta* 13 B2
Çengelköy, *Istanbul* 12 B2
Cengkareng, *Jakarta* 13 A1
Centennial Park, *Sydney* 28 B2
Center Hill, *Atlanta* 3 B2
Centocelle, *Rome* 25 B2
Centraal Station, *Amsterdam* . 2 a2
Central Park, *New York* 21 B2
Cerillos, *Santiago* 26 B1
Cerro de la Estrella,
  Mexico City 18 B2
Cerro de los Angeles, *Madrid* 17 C1
Cerro Navia, *Santiago* 26 B1
Certanovka ➡, *Moscow* 19 C3
Certanovo, *Moscow* 19 C3
Cesano Boscone, *Milan* 18 B1
Cesate, *Milan* 18 A1
Cha Kwo Ling, *Hong Kong* .. 12 B2
Chacarrita, *Buenos Aires* 7 B2
Chadwell Heath, *London* 15 A4
Chai Chee, *Singapore* 27 B3
Chai Wan, *Hong Kong* 12 B2
Chai Wan Kok, *Hong Kong* .. 12 A1
Chaillot, Palais de, *Paris* 23 b2
Chakdaha, *Calcutta* 8 C1
Chamartin, *Madrid* 17 B1
Chamberi, *Madrid* 17 B1
Chambourcy, *Paris* 23 A1
Champ de Mars, Parc du,
  Paris 23 c2
Champigny-sur-Marne, *Paris* . 23 B4
Champlain, Pont, *Montreal* .. 19 B2
Champs Elysées, Avenue des,
  Paris 23 b2
Champs-sur-Marne, *Paris* 23 A4
Chamrail, *Calcutta* 8 B1
Chamshil, *Seoul* 26 B2
Chamwŏn, *Seoul* 26 B2
Chanakyapuri, *Delhi* 10 B2
Chanditala, *Calcutta* 8 A1
Changfeng Park, *Shanghai* .. 27 B1
Changi, *Singapore* 27 A3
Changi Int. Airport,
  Singapore 27 A3
Changning, *Shanghai* 27 B1
Chanteroine, *Paris* 23 A4
Chantian, *Canton* 4 A2
Chao Phraya ➡, *Bangkok* ... 3 B1
Chaoyang, *Beijing* 4 B2
Chaoyangmen, *Beijing* 4 B2
Chapelizod, *Dublin* 11 A1
Chapultepec, Bosque de,
  Mexico City 18 B1
Chapultepec, Castillo de,
  Mexico City 18 B1
Charenton-le-Pont, *Paris* 23 B3
Charing Cross, *London* 15 b4
Charleroi, Kanal de ➡,
  Brussels 6 B1
Charles Bridge, *Prague* 24 b1
Charles Square, *Prague* 24 c2
Charlestown, *Boston* 6 A3
Charlottenburg, *Berlin* 5 A2
Charlottenburg, Schloss,
  Berlin 5 A2
Charlottenlund, *Copenhagen* . 10 A3
Charneca, *Lisbon* 14 B1
Charneca, *Lisbon* 14 A2
Châteaufort, *Paris* 23 B1
Châtenay-Malabry, *Paris* 23 B2
Chatham, *Chicago* 9 C3
Châtillon, *Paris* 23 B2
Chatou, *Paris* 23 A1

Chatpur, *Calcutta* 8 B2
Chatswood, *Sydney* 28 A2
Chatuchak, *Bangkok* 3 B2
Chatuchak Park, *Bangkok* .. 3 B2
Chauki, *Karachi* 14 B2
Chavarria, *Lima* 16 B2
Chaville, *Paris* 23 B2
Chayang, *Seoul* 26 B2
Chegi, *Seoul* 26 B2
Chelles, *Paris* 23 A4
Chelles, Canal de, *Paris* 23 A4
Chells-le-Pin, Aérodrome,
  Paris 23 A4
Chelsea, *Boston* 6 A3
Chelsea, *London* 15 A2
Chelsea, *New York* 21 c1
Chelsea, *Paris* 23 B2
Chembur, *Mumbai* 20 A2
Chemnevières-sur-Marne,
  Paris 23 B4
Cheops, *Cairo* 7 B1
Cherepkovo, *Moscow* 19 B2
Chernyovo, *Moscow* 19 A1
Cheryomushki, *Moscow* 19 B3
Chestnut Hill, *Boston* 6 B2
Cheung Sha Wan, *Hong Kong* 12 A1
Cheverly, *Washington* 32 B4
Chevilly-Larue, *Paris* 23 B3
Chevy-Cossigny, *Paris* 23 B4
Chevy Chase, *Washington* ... 32 B3
Chevy Chase View,
  Washington 32 A3
Chia Keng, *Singapore* 27 A3
Chiaravalle Milanese, *Milan* . 18 B2
Chicago, *Chicago* 9 B3
Chicago Harbor, *Chicago* ... 9 B3
Chicago Lawn, *Chicago* 9 C2
Chicago-Midway Airport,
  Chicago 9 C2
Chicago-O'Hare Int. Airport,
  Chicago 9 B1
Chicago Ridge, *Chicago* 9 C2
Chicago Sanitary and Ship
  Canal, *Chicago* 9 C2
Chienzui, *Canton* 8 A3
Chik Sha, *Hong Kong* 12 B2
Child's Hill, *London* 15 A2
Chilla Saroda, *Delhi* 10 B2
Chillum, *Washington* 32 B4
Chilly-Mazarin, *Paris* 23 B2
Chinatown, *Los Angeles* 16 a3
Chinatown, *New York* 21 e2
Chinatown, *San Francisco* ... 25 b2
Chinatown, *Singapore* 27 c2
Chingupota, *Calcutta* 8 C1
Chislehurst, *London* 15 B4
Chiswick, *London* 15 B2
Chiswick House, *London* 15 b2
Chitose, *Tokyo* 29 B2
Chitralda Palace, *Bangkok* .. 3 B2
Chiyoda-Ku, *Tokyo* 29 b4
Chkalova, *Moscow* 19 C5
Choa Chu Kang, *Singapore* . 27 A2
Choboty, *Moscow* 19 C2
Chodov u Prahy, *Prague* 24 B3
Chōfu, *Tokyo* 29 B2
Choisy-le-Roi, *Paris* 23 B3
Cholupice, *Prague* 24 C2
Chom Thong, *Bangkok* 3 B1
Chong Pang, *Singapore* 27 A2
Ch'ŏngdam, *Seoul* 26 B2
Chongmyo Royal Shrine,
  Seoul 26 B1
Chongno, *Seoul* 26 B1
Chongwen, *Beijing* 4 B2
Chŏnho, *Seoul* 26 B2
Chopin, Muzeum, *Warsaw* .. 31 B6
Chornaya ➡, *Moscow* 19 B6
Chorrillos, *Lima* 16 C2
Chowpatty Beach, *Mumbai* . 20 b1
Christian Quarter, *Jerusalem* 13 b3
Christiansborg, *Copenhagen* . 10 c2
Christianshavn, *Copenhagen* 10 A3
Chrysler Building, *New York* . 21 c2
Chrzanów, *Warsaw* 31 B1
Chuen Lung, *Hong Kong* ... 12 A1
Chuk Kok, *Hong Kong* 12 A2
Chulalongkorn Univ.,
  Bangkok 3 B2
Chung, *Seoul* 26 B1
Chunghwa, *Seoul* 26 B2
Chungnangch'on ➡, *Seoul* .. 26 B2
Chūō-Ku, *Tokyo* 29 b5
Church End, *London* 15 A2
Churchtown, *Dublin* 11 B2
Ciampino, *Rome* 25 C2
Ciampino, Aeroporto di,
  Rome 25 C2
Cicero, *Chicago* 9 B2
Cilandak, *Jakarta* 13 B1
Cilincing, *Jakarta* 13 A2
Ciliwung ➡, *Jakarta* 13 B2
Čimice, *Prague* 24 A2
Cinecittà, *Rome* 25 B2
Ciniselло Bálsamo, *Milan* ... 18 A2
Cinkota, *Budapest* 7 A3
Cipete, *Jakarta* 13 B1
Citadella, *Budapest* 7 c2
Citta degli Studi, *Milan* 18 B2
Città del Vaticano, *Rome* ... 25 B1
City, *London* 15 A3
City Hall, *New York* 21 e1
Ciudad Deportiva,
  Mexico City 18 B2
Ciudad Fin de Semana,
  Madrid 17 B2
Ciudad General Belgrano,
  Buenos Aires 7 C1
Ciudad Lineál, *Madrid* 17 B1
Ciudad Satélite, *Mexico City* . 18 A1
Ciudad Universitaria,
  Buenos Aires 7 B2
Ciudad Universitaria,
  Mexico City 18 C1
Ciutadella, Parc de la,
  Barcelona 4 b3
Civic Center, *Los Angeles* ... 16 b2
Clamart, *Paris* 23 B2
Clapham, *London* 15 B3
Clapton, *London* 15 A3
Claremont, *Cape Town* 8 A1
Clayhall, *London* 15 A4
Clerkenwell, *London* 15 a4
Clermiston, *Edinburgh* 11 B2
Clichy, *Paris* 23 A2
Clichy-sous-Bois, *Paris* 23 A4
Cliffside, *Toronto* 30 A3
Cliffside Park, *New York* 21 B1
Clifton, *Boston* 6 A3
Clifton, *Karachi* 14 B2
Clifton, *New York* 21 C1
Cliftondale, *Boston* 6 A3
Cloghran, *Dublin* 11 A2
Clondalkin, *Dublin* 11 B1
Clonee, *Dublin* 11 A1
Clonskeagh, *Dublin* 11 B2
Clontarf, *Dublin* 11 A2
Clontarf, *Sydney* 28 A2
Clovelly, *Sydney* 28 B2
Cobras, I. das, *Rio de Janeiro* 24 B2
Coburg, *Melbourne* 17 A1

Cochituate, *Boston* 6 A1
Cochituate, L., *Boston* 6 B1
Cocotá, *Rio de Janeiro* 24 A1
Cœuilly, *Paris* 23 B4
Coina, *Lisbon* 14 B2
Coit Tower, *San Francisco* ... 25 a2
Coker, *Lagos* 14 B2
Colaba, *Mumbai* 20 B2
Colaba Pt., *Mumbai* 20 B2
Colegiales, *Buenos Aires* 7 B2
Colindale, *London* 15 A2
Colinton, *Edinburgh* 11 B2
College Park, *Atlanta* 3 C2
College Park, *Washington* ... 32 B4
College Point, *New York* 21 B2
Collégien, *Paris* 23 A4
Collier Row, *London* 15 A4
Colliers Wood, *London* 15 B2
Colma, *San Francisco* 25 B2
Colney Hatch, *London* 15 A3
Cologno Monzese, *Milan* ... 18 A2
Colombes, *Paris* 23 A2
Colón, Monumente,
  Barcelona 4 c3
Colon, Plaza de, *Madrid* 17 A3
Colonia Güell, *Barcelona* ... 4 A1
Colonial Knob, *Wellington* .. 32 A1
Colosseo, *Rome* 25 c3
Columbus Circus, *New York* . 21 b2
Combault, *Paris* 23 B4
Comércio, Praça do, *Lisbon* . 14 A2
Commerce, *Los Angeles* 16 B4
Como, *Sydney* 28 C1
Company's Gardens,
  Cape Town 8 c2
Conceição, I. da,
  Rio de Janeiro 24 B2
Concertgebouw, *Amsterdam* . 2 c1
Conchali, *Santiago* 26 B2
Concord, *Boston* 6 A1
Concord, *Sydney* 28 B1
Concord, *Toronto* 30 A2
Concorde, Place de la, *Paris* . 23 b3
Concorezzo, *Milan* 18 A2
Coney Island, *New York* 21 C2
Congonhas, Aéroporto,
  São Paulo 26 B2
Connaught Place, *Delhi* 10 B2
Conservatori, Palazzo dei,
  Rome 25 c3
Consolação, *São Paulo* 26 B2
Constantia, *Cape Town* 8 B1
Constitución, *Buenos Aires* .. 7 B2
Constitution, *Atlanta* 3 B2
Convention and Exhibition
  Centre, *Hong Kong* 12 b2
Coogee, *Sydney* 28 B2
Cook Str., *Wellington* 32 A1
Cooksville, *Toronto* 30 B1
Coolock, *Dublin* 11 A2
Copacabana, *Rio de Janeiro* . 24 B2
Copenhagen = København,
  Copenhagen 10 A2
Coral Gables, *Miami* 18 B2
Coral Hills, *Washington* 32 B4
Corcovado, Morro do,
  Rio de Janeiro 24 B1
Corduff, *Dublin* 11 A1
Cormano, *Milan* 18 A2
Cormaredo, *Milan* 18 A1
Córsico, *Milan* 18 B1
Corsini, Palazzo, *Rome* 25 c1
Corviale, *Rome* 25 B1
Coslada, *Madrid* 17 B2
Cossigny, *Paris* 23 B4
Cossipore, *Calcutta* 8 B2
Costantino, Arco di, *Rome* .. 25 c3
Costorphine, *Edinburgh* 11 B2
Cotao, *Lisbon* 14 A1
Côte St.-Luc, *Montreal* 19 B2
Cotunduba, I. de,
  Rio de Janeiro 24 B2
Coubron, *Paris* 23 A4
Countryside, *Chicago* 9 C1
Courbevoie, *Paris* 23 A2
Courtry, *Paris* 23 A4
Covent Garden, *London* 15 b4
Cowgate, *Edinburgh* 11 b3
Cowley, *London* 15 A1
Coyoacán, *Mexico City* 18 B2
Cragin, *Chicago* 9 B2
Craighall Park, *Johannesburg* 13 A2
Craiglockhart, *Edinburgh* ... 11 B2
Craigmillar, *Edinburgh* 11 B3
Cramond, *Edinburgh* 11 B1
Cramond Bridge, *Edinburgh* 11 B1
Cramond I., *Edinburgh* 11 B2
Cranford, *London* 15 B1
Crawford, *Cape Town* 8 A2
Crayford, *London* 15 B5
Creekmouth, *London* 15 A4
Crescenzago, *Milan* 18 A2
Cresley, *Paris* 23 B1
Cresskill, *New York* 21 A2
Cricklewood, *London* 15 A2
Cristo Redentor, Estatua do,
  Rio de Janeiro 24 B1
Crockenhill, *London* 15 B4
Croissy-Beaubourg, *Paris* ... 23 B4
Croissy-sur-Seine, *Paris* 23 B1
Crosby, *Johannesburg* 13 B1
Crosne, *Paris* 23 B3
Cross I., *Mumbai* 20 B2
Crouch End, *London* 15 A3
Crown Mine, *Johannesburg* . 13 B1
Crows Nest, *Sydney* 28 A2
Croydon, *London* 15 B3
Croydon Park, *Sydney* 28 B1
Cruagh Mt., *Dublin* 11 B2
Crumlin, *Dublin* 11 B2
Cruz de Pau, *Lisbon* 14 B2
Crystal Palace, *London* 15 B3
Csepel, *Budapest* 7 B2
Csepelsziget, *Budapest* 7 B2
Csillaghegy, *Budapest* 7 A2
Csillagtelep, *Budapest* 7 B2
Csömör, *Budapest* 7 A3
Csömöri-patak ➡, *Budapest* . 7 A3
Cuatro Vientos, *Madrid* 17 B1
Cuauhtémoc, *Mexico City* .. 18 B2
Cubao, *Manila* 17 B2
Çubuklu, *Istanbul* 12 B2
Cudahy, *Los Angeles* 16 C3
Cuicuilco, Pirámide de,
  Mexico City 18 C1
Culver City, *Los Angeles* ... 16 B2
Cumballa Hill, *Mumbai* 20 a1
Cumbres de Vallecas, *Madrid* 17 B2
Cupecé, *São Paulo* 26 B1
Currie, *Edinburgh* 11 B2
Cusago, *Milan* 18 B1
Cusano Milanino, *Milan* 18 A2
Custom House, *Dublin* 11 b3
Çuvuşabaşı ➡, *Istanbul* 12 B1
Czerników, *Warsaw* 31 B2
Czyste, *Warsaw* 31 B1

D

D.F. Malan Airport,
  Cape Town 8 A2
Da Mooca ➡, *São Paulo* 26 B2
Da Yunhe ➡, *Tianjin* 30 A1
Dabizhuang, *Tianjin* 30 A2
Dąbrowa, *Warsaw* 31 B1
Dachang, *Shanghai* 27 B1
Dachang Airfield, *Shanghai* . 27 B1
Dachau-Ost, *Munich* 20 A1
Dadar, *Mumbai* 20 A1
Dagenham, *London* 15 A4
Dagliing, *Munich* 20 B2
Daheisha, *Jerusalem* 13 B2
Dahlem, *Berlin* 5 B2
Dahlwitz-Hoppegarten, *Berlin* 5 A5
Dahongmen, *Beijing* 4 C2
Daitō, *Osaka* 22 A4
Dajiaoting, *Beijing* 4 B2
Dakhnoye, St. Petersburg ... 26 C3
Dalejský potok ➡, *Prague* .. 24 B2
Dalgety Bay, *Edinburgh* 11 A1
Dalkeith, *Edinburgh* 11 B3
Dalkey, *Dublin* 11 B3
Dalkey Island, *Dublin* 11 B3
Dallgow, *Berlin* 5 A1
Dalmeny, *Edinburgh* 11 B1
Dalston, *London* 15 A3
Daly City, *San Francisco* 25 B2
Dam, *Amsterdam* 2 b2
Dam Rak, *Amsterdam* 2 a2
Damaia, *Lisbon* 14 A1
Dämeritzsee, *Berlin* 5 B5
Dan Ryan Woods, *Chicago* .. 9 C2
Danderhall, *Edinburgh* 11 B3
Danderyd, *Stockholm* 28 A1
Danforth, *Toronto* 30 A3
Darakeh, *Tehran* 30 A2
Darband, *Tehran* 30 A2
Darling Harbour, *Sydney* ... 28 B1
Darling Point, *Sydney* 28 B2
Darndale, *Dublin* 11 A2
Darrūs, *Tehran* 30 A2
Dartford, *London* 15 B5
Darya Ganj, *Delhi* 1 a3
Dashi, *Canton* 4 B2
Datansha, *Canton* 4 B1
Datun, *Beijing* 4 B2
Daulatpur, *Delhi* 10 A1
David's Citadel, *Jerusalem* .. 13 b3
David's Tomb, *Jerusalem* ... 13 b3
Davidson, Mt., *San Francisco* 25 B2
Davidson's Mains, *Edinburgh* 11 B2
Dāvūdiyeh, *Tehran* 30 A2
Davydkovo, *Moscow* 19 B2
Dawidy, *Warsaw* 31 C1
Days Bay, *Wellington* 32 B2
Dazhigu, *Tianjin* 30 B2
De Waag, *Amsterdam* 2 b2
Decatur, *Atlanta* 3 B3
Dedham, *Boston* 6 B2
Deer I., *Boston* 6 A4
Degunino, *Moscow* 19 A3
Deir Dibwan, *Jerusalem* 13 A2
Deir Ibzi'e, *Jerusalem* 13 A1
Dejvice, *Prague* 24 B2
Dekabristov, Ostrov,
  St. Petersburg 26 B1
Delhi, *Delhi* 10 B2
Delhi Gate, *Delhi* 1 b3
Demarest, *New York* 21 A2
Den Ilp, *Amsterdam* 2 A2
Denistone Heights, *Sydney* .. 28 A1
Dentonia Park, *Toronto* 30 A3
Deptford, *London* 15 B3
Deputati, Camera dei, *Rome* 25 b2
Des Plaines ➡, *Chicago* 9 B1
Des Plaines ➡, *Chicago* 9 B1
Deschapelles, *Beijing* 4 B2
Deutsch-Wagram, *Vienna* .. 31 A3
Deutsche Oper, *Berlin* 5 A2
Deutscher Museum, *Munich* 20 B2
Devil's Peak, *Cape Town* ... 8 A1
Dháfni, *Athens* 2 B2
Dhakuria, *Calcutta* 8 B2
Dhamarakia, *Athens* 2 A2
Dharavi, *Mumbai* 20 A2
Dhrapersbóri, *Athens* 2 B1
Diadema, *São Paulo* 26 C2
Diegen, *Brussels* 6 A2
Diemen, *Amsterdam* 2 A3
Diepkloof, *Johannesburg* ... 13 B1
Diepriver, *Cape Town* 8 B1
Difficult Run ➡, *Washington* 32 B2
Dilbeek, *Brussels* 6 A1
Dinzigu, *Tianjin* 30 A1
Dirnismaning, *Munich* 20 A2
District Heights, *Washington* 32 B4
Ditan Park, *Beijing* 4 a2
Diyālá ➡, *Jerusalem* 13 B2
Djursholm, *Stockholm* 28 A2
Döbeln, *Vienna* 31 A1
Döbling, *Vienna* 31 A2
Docklands, *London* 15 A3
Dodder, R. ➡, *Dublin* 11 B1
Dodger Stadium, *Los Angeles* 16 B3
Dolgoe Ozero, St. Petersburg 26 B1
Doll Museum, *Delhi* 1 b3
Dollis Hill, *London* 15 A2
Dollymount, *Dublin* 11 A2
Dolni, *Prague* 24 B3
Dolni Chabry, *Prague* 24 A2
Dolni Počernice, *Prague* 24 B3
Dolphins Barn, *Dublin* 11 B2
Dom Pedro II, Parque,
  São Paulo 26 B2
Domain, The, *Sydney* 28 b2
Dome of the Rock, *Jerusalem* 13 b3
Don Mills, *Toronto* 30 A2
Don Muang Int. Airport,
  Bangkok 3 A2
Donaghmede, *Dublin* 11 A2
Donau-Oder Kanal, *Vienna* . 31 A3
Donaufeld, *Vienna* 31 A2
Donaupark, *Vienna* 31 A2
Donaustadt, *Vienna* 31 A3
Dongan Hills, *New York* 21 C1
Donggou, *Shanghai* 27 B2
Dongjiao, *Canton* 4 B2
Dongmenwai, *Tianjin* 30 B2
Dongqi, *Mumbai* 20 A1
Dongri, *Mumbai* 20 B2
Dongshanhu Park, *Canton* .. 4 B2
Dongxinng, *Beijing* 4 B2
Dongzhi Men, *Beijing* 4 A2
Donnybrook, *Dublin* 11 B2
Doornfontein, *Johannesburg* 13 B2
Dorchester, *Boston* 6 B3
Dordrecht, B., *Boston* 6 B3
Dornach, *Munich* 20 B3
Dos Couros ➡, *São Paulo* .. 26 C2

Dos Moninos ➡, *São Paulo* . 26 C2
Douglas Park, *Chicago* 9 B2
Dover Heights, *Sydney* 28 B2
Dowlatābād, *Tehran* 30 B2
Downey, *Los Angeles* 16 C4
Downsview, *Toronto* 30 A1
Dragør, *Copenhagen* 10 B3
Drancy, *Paris* 23 A3
Dranesville, *Washington* 32 A1
Dreilinden, *Berlin* 5 B2
Drewnica, *Warsaw* 31 B2
Drigh Road, *Karachi* 14 A2
Drimnagh, *Dublin* 11 B2
Drogenbos, *Brussels* 6 B1
Druid Hills, *Atlanta* 3 B2
Drum Towwer, *Beijing* 4 a2
Drumcondra, *Dublin* 11 A2
Drummoyne, *Sydney* 28 B2
Drylaw, *Edinburgh* 11 B2
Dubeč, *Prague* 24 B3
Dublin, *Dublin* 11 B2
Dublin Bay, *Dublin* 11 B3
Dublin Harbour, *Dublin* 11 A2
Duddingston, *Edinburgh* 11 B3
Dugnano, *Milan* 18 A2
Dūlāb, *Tehran* 30 B2
Dulwich, *London* 15 B3
Dum Dum, *Calcutta* 8 B2
Dum Dum Int. Airport,
  Calcutta 8 B2
Dumont, *New York* 21 A2
Dún Laoghaire, *Dublin* 11 B3
Duna ➡, *Budapest* 7 A2
Duncan Dock, *Cape Town* .. 8 a3
Dundrum, *Dublin* 11 B2
Dunearn, *Singapore* 27 B2
Dunfermline, *Edinburgh* 11 A1
Dunn Loring, *Washington* ... 32 B2
Dunning, *Chicago* 9 B2
Dunvegan, *Johannesburg* ... 13 A2
Duomo, *Milan* 18 A2
Duque de Caxias,
  Rio de Janeiro 24 A1
Dusit, *Bangkok* 3 B2
Dusit Zoo, *Bangkok* 3 a2
Dusseldorf, *Düsseldorf* 4 B2
Duvernay, *Montreal* 19 A1
Dworp, *Brussels* 6 B1
Dyakovo, *Moscow* 19 B3
Dzerzhinskiy, *Moscow* 19 C5
Dzerzhinsky, *Moscow* 19 B3
Dzerzhinskiy Park, *Moscow* . 19 B3

E

Eagle Rock, *Los Angeles* 16 B3
Ealing, *London* 15 A2
Earl's Court, *London* 15 c1
Earlsfield, *London* 15 B2
Earlwood, *Sydney* 28 B1
East Acton, *London* 6 A1
East Arlington, *Boston* 6 A3
East Arlington, *Washington* . 32 B3
East Bedfont, *London* 15 B1
East Boston, *Boston* 6 A3
East Don ➡, *Toronto* 30 A2
East Elmhurst, *New York* ... 21 B2
East Finchley, *London* 15 A2
East Ham, *London* 15 A4
East Humber ➡, *Toronto* .. 30 A1
East Lamma Channel,
  Hong Kong 12 B1
East Lexington, *Boston* 6 A2
East Molesey, *London* 15 B1
East New York, *New York* .. 21 B2
East Pines, *Washington* 32 B4
East Potomac Park,
  Washington 32 B3
East Pt., *Boston* 6 A4
East River ➡, *New York* ... 21 B2
East Rutherford, *New York* . 21 A1
East Sheen, *London* 15 B2
East Village, *New York* 21 e2
East Wickham, *London* 15 B4
East York, *Toronto* 30 A2
Eastbourne, *Wellington* 32 B2
Eastcote, *London* 15 A1
Easter Howgate, *Edinburgh* . 11 B2
Eastwood, *Sydney* 28 A1
Ebara, *Tokyo* 29 B3
Ebisu, *Tokyo* 29 B3
Ebute-Ikorodu, *Lagos* 14 A2
Ebute-Metta, *Lagos* 14 B2
Echo Park, *Los Angeles* 16 B3
Eda, *Tokyo* 29 B2
Edaké, *Athens* 2 a1
Edendale, *Johannesburg* ... 13 A2
Edenmore, *Dublin* 11 A2
Edgars Cr. ➡, *Melbourne* .. 17 A1
Edgeley, *Toronto* 30 A1
Edgemar, *San Francisco* 25 C2
Edgware, *London* 15 A2
Edinburgh, *Edinburgh* 11 B2
Edison Park, *Chicago* 9 B2
Edmondston, *Washington* ... 32 B4
Edmondstown, *Dublin* 11 B2
Edo ➡, *Tokyo* 29 A4
Edogawa-Ku, *Tokyo* 29 A4
Edsberg, *Stockholm* 28 A1
Edwards L., *Melbourne* 17 A1
Eiche, *Berlin* 5 A5
Eiche Sud, *Berlin* 5 A4
Eichenau, *Munich* 20 B1
Eiffel, Tour, *Paris* 23 b2
Ein Arik, *Jerusalem* 13 A1
Ein Naquba, *Jerusalem* 13 B1
Ein Rafa, *Jerusalem* 13 B1
Eizariya, *Jerusalem* 13 B2
Ejby, *Copenhagen* 10 A2
Ejigbo, *Lagos* 14 A1
Ekeberg, *Oslo* 22 A3
Eknäs, *Stockholm* 28 B3
El 'Abbasiya, *Cairo* 7 A2
El Agustino, *Lima* 16 B2
El Baragil, *Cairo* 7 A1
El Basâtin, *Cairo* 7 B2
El-Bira, *Jerusalem* 13 A2
El Bosque, *Santiago* 26 C2
El Carmen, *Santiago* 26 B1
El Cortijo, *Santiago* 26 B1
El Duqqi, *Cairo* 7 A2
El Encinar de los Reyes,
  Madrid 17 A2
El Ghurîya, *Cairo* 7 A2
El Gîza, *Cairo* 7 A2
El-Khadr, *Jerusalem* 13 B1
El Khalîfa, *Cairo* 7 B2
El Ma'âdi, *Cairo* 7 B2
El Matarya, *Cairo* 7 A2
El Mohandesin, *Cairo* 7 A2
El Monte, *Los Angeles* 16 B4
El Mûski, *Cairo* 7 A2
El Pardo, *Madrid* 17 A1

El Portal, *Miami* 18 A2
El Prat de Llobregat,
  Barcelona 4 B1
El Pueblo de L.A. Historic
  Park, *Los Angeles* 16 b2
El Qâhira, *Cairo* 7 A2
El Qubba, *Cairo* 7 A2
El Reloj, *Mexico City* 18 C2
El Retiro, *Madrid* 17 B1
El Salto, *Santiago* 26 B2
El Sereno, *Los Angeles* 16 B3
El Talibîya, *Cairo* 7 B1
El Vergel, *Mexico City* 18 C2
El Wâhli, *Cairo* 7 A2
El Zamâlik, *Cairo* 7 A2
El Zeitûn, *Cairo* 7 A2
Elephanta Caves, *Mumbai* .. 20 B2
Elephanta I., *Mumbai* 20 B2
Ellboda, *Stockholm* 28 A3
Ellinikón, *Athens* 2 B2
Ellis I., *New York* 21 H1
Elm Park, *London* 15 A5
Elmers End, *London* 15 B3
Elmhurst, *New York* 21 B2
Elmstead, *London* 15 B4
Elmwood Park, *Chicago* 9 B2
Elmwood Park, *New York* .. 21 A1
Elsdon, *Wellington* 32 A1
Elsiesrivier, *Cape Town* 8 A2
Elsternwick, *Melbourne* 17 B2
Eltham, *London* 15 B4
Elwood, *Melbourne* 17 B2
Elysée, *Paris* 23 A2
Elysian Park, *Los Angeles* .. 16 B3
Embajadores, *Madrid* 17 c2
Embarcadero Center,
  San Francisco 25 b3
Emek Refa'im, *Jerusalem* ... 13 c2
Émerainville, *Paris* 23 B4
Emeryville, *San Francisco* .. 25 A3
Eminönü, *Istanbul* 12 B1
Emmarentia, *Johannesburg* . 13 A2
Empire State Building,
  New York 21 c2
Encantado, *Rio de Janeiro* .. 24 B1
Encino, *Los Angeles* 16 B2
Encino Res., *Los Angeles* ... 16 B1
Enebyberg, *Stockholm* 28 A1
Enfield, *Sydney* 28 B1
Engenho, I. do, *Rio de Janeiro* 24 B2
Englewood, *Chicago* 9 C3
Englewood, *New York* 21 A2
Englewood Cliffs, *New York* . 21 A2
Enmore, *Sydney* 28 B2
Enskede, *Stockholm* 28 B2
Entrevias, *Madrid* 17 B1
Epping, *Sydney* 28 A1
Erawan Shrine, *Bangkok* ... 3 c3
Eregun, *Lagos* 14 A2
Erenköy, *Istanbul* 12 C2
Erith, *London* 15 B5
Erlaa, *Vienna* 31 B1
Ermington, *Sydney* 28 A1
Ermita, *Manila* 17 B1
Ershatou, *Canton* 4 B2
Erskineville, *Sydney* 28 B2
Erunkan, *Lagos* 14 A2
Erzsébet-Telep, *Budapest* ... 7 B3
Eschenried, *Munich* 20 A1
Esenler, *Istanbul* 12 B1
Esher, *London* 15 B1
Eskbank, *Edinburgh* 11 B3
Esperanza, *Mexico City* 18 c3
Esplanade Park, *Singapore* .. 27 c3
Esplugas, *Barcelona* 4 A1
Esposizione Univ. di Roma
  (E.U.R.), *Rome* 25 C1
Essendon, *Melbourne* 17 A1
Essendon Airport, *Melbourne* 17 A1
Essingen, *Stockholm* 28 B1
Essling, *Vienna* 31 A3
Est, Gare de l', *Paris* 23 a5
Estadio Maracanã,
  Rio de Janeiro 24 B1
Estado, Parque do, *São Paulo* 26 B2
Estefânia, *Lisbon* 14 a2
Estrela, Basilica da, *Lisbon* . 14 A2
Ethnikó Arheologiko
  Moussío, *Athens* 2 a2
Etobicoke, *Toronto* 30 B1
Etobicoke Cr. ➡, *Toronto* .. 30 B1
Etterbeek, *Brussels* 6 B2
Euston, *London* 15 a4
Evanston, *Chicago* 9 A2
Even Sapir, *Jerusalem* 13 B1
Evere, *Brussels* 6 A2
Everett, *Boston* 6 A3
Evergreen Park, *Chicago* ... 9 C2
Evin, *Tehran* 30 A2
Evzonos, *Athens* 2 A1
Ewu, *Lagos* 14 A1
Exchange Square, *Hong Kong* 12 c1
Exposições, Palácio das,
  Rio de Janeiro 24 B1
Eyüp, *Istanbul* 12 B1

F

Fabour, Mt., *Singapore* 27 B2
Faechi, *Seoul* 26 B2
Felledparken, *Copenhagen* .. 10 A3
Fågelön, *Stockholm* 28 B1
Fagersjö, *Stockholm* 28 B2
Fair Lawn, *New York* 21 A1
Fairfax, *Washington* 32 C2
Fairfax Station, *Washington* . 32 C2
Fairhaven Bay, *Boston* 6 A1
Fairhaven Hill, *Boston* 6 A1
Fairland, *Johannesburg* 13 A1
Fairmilehead, *Edinburgh* ... 11 B2
Fairmount Heights,
  Washington 32 B4
Fairport, *Toronto* 30 A4
Fairview, *New York* 21 B1
Falenty, *Warsaw* 31 C1
Fálirou, Órmos, *Athens* 2 B2
Falkenberg, *Berlin* 5 A4
Falkenhagen, *Berlin* 5 A1
Falls Church, *Washington* ... 32 B2
Falomo, *Lagos* 14 B2
False Bay, *Cape Town* 8 B2
Fangcun, *Canton* 4 B2
Farahābād, *Tehran* 30 A2
Farforovskaya, St. Petersburg 26 B2
Farningham, *London* 15 B5
Farrar Pond, *Boston* 6 A1
Farsta, *Stockholm* 28 B2
Fasanerie-Nord, *Munich* ... 20 A2
Fasangarten, *Munich* 20 B2
Fasting Palace, *Beijing* 4 B1
Fatih, *Istanbul* 12 B1
Favoriten, *Vienna* 31 B2
Fawkner, *Melbourne* 17 A1

Fawkner Park, *Melbourne* .. **17 B1**
Feijó, *Lisbon* **14 B2**
Feldkirchen, *Munich* **20 B3**
Feldmoching, *Munich* **20 A2**
Feltham, *London* **15 B1**
Fener, *Istanbul* **12 B1**
Fenerbahçe, *Istanbul* **12 C2**
Fengtai, *Beijing* **4 C1**
Fenino, *Moscow* **19 B5**
Ferencváros, *Budapest* ... **7 B2**
Ferihegyi Airport, *Budapest* **7 B3**
Ferndale, *Johannesburg* .. **13 A2**
Férolles-Attilly, *Paris* **23 B4**
Fichtenau, *Berlin* **5 B5**
Fields Corner, *Boston* **6 B3**
Fiera Camp, *Milan* **18 B1**
Fifth Avenue, *New York* ... **21 b3**
Figino, *Milan* **18 B1**
Fijir, *Baghdad* **3 A2**
Filadhélfia, *Athens* **2 A2**
Fili-Mazilovo, *Moscow* ... **19 B2**
Filothei, *Athens* **2 A2**
Finchley, *London* **15 A2**
Finglas, *Dublin* **11 A2**
Finsbury, *London* **15 A3**
Finsbury Park, *London* ... **15 A3**
Fiorito, *Buenos Aires* **7 C2**
Firhouse, *Dublin* **11 B2**
Fischerhäuser, *Munich* ... **20 A3**
Fisher Island, *Miami* **18 B2**
Fishermans Bend, *Melbourne* **17 A1**
Fisherman's Wharf,
  San Francisco **25 a1**
Fisherville, *Toronto* **30 A2**
Fisksätra, *Stockholm* **28 B3**
Fitzroy Gardens, *Melbourne* **17 A1**
Five Dock, *Sydney* **28 B1**
Fjellstrand, *Oslo* **22 B3**
Flamengo, *Rio de Janeiro* . **24 B1**
Flaminio, *Rome* **25 B1**
Flaskebekk, *Oslo* **22 A2**
Flatbush, *New York* **21 C2**
Flaten, *Stockholm* **28 B2**
Flemington Racecourse,
  Melbourne **17 A1**
Flint Pk., *Los Angeles* **16 B3**
Florence, *Los Angeles* **16 C3**
Florence Bloom Bird
  Sanctuary, *Johannesburg* **13 A2**
Florentia, *Johannesburg* .. **13 B2**
Flores, *Buenos Aires* **7 B2**
Flores, *Buenos Aires* **7 B2**
Florida, *Buenos Aires* **7 B2**
Florida, *Johannesburg* ... **13 A2**
Floridsdorf, *Vienna* **31 A2**
Flushing, *New York* **21 B3**
Flushing Meadows Corona
  Park, *New York* **21 B2**
Flysta, *Stockholm* **28 A1**
Fo Tan, *Hong Kong* **12 A2**
Föhrenhain, *Vienna* **31 A2**
Fontainebleau, *Munich* ... **20 A1**
Fontenay-aux-Roses, *Paris* **23 B2**
Fontenay-le-Fleury, *Paris* . **23 B1**
Fontenay-sous-Bois, *Paris* **23 B3**
Foots Cray, *London* **15 B4**
Footscray, *Melbourne* **17 A1**
Foreshore, *Cape Town* **8 a3**
Forest, *Brussels* **6 B1**
Forest Gate, *London* **15 A4**
Forest Heights, *Washington* **32 C3**
Forest Hill, *London* **15 B3**
Forest Hill, *Toronto* **30 A2**
Forest Hills, *New York* ... **21 B2**
Forest Park, *Chicago* **9 B2**
Forest View, *Chicago* **9 C2**
Forestville, *Washington* ... **32 B4**
Fornebu, *Oslo* **22 A2**
Fornebu Airport, *Oslo* **22 A2**
Foro Romano, *Rome* **25 c3**
Forstenried, *Munich* **20 B1**
Forstenrieder Park, *Munich* **20 B1**
Fort, *Mumbai* **20 c2**
Fort Canning Park, *Singapore* **27 b2**
Fort Dupont Park,
  Washington **32 B4**
Fort Foote Village,
  Washington **32 C3**
Fort Lee, *New York* **21 A2**
Fort Mason Center,
  San Francisco **25 a1**
Forth, Firth of, *Edinburgh* **11 A2**
Forth Rail Bridge, *Edinburgh* **11 A1**
Forth Road Bridge,
  Edinburgh **11 A1**
Fót, *Budapest* **7 A3**
Fourqueux, *Paris* **23 A1**
Foxrock, *Dublin* **11 B2**
Framingham, *Boston* **6 B1**
Franconia, *Washington* ... **32 C3**
Frankel, *Singapore* **27 B3**
Franklin Park, *Boston* **6 B3**
Franklin Park, *Chicago* ... **9 B1**
Franklin Park, *Washington* **32 B3**
Franklin Res., *Los Angeles* **16 B2**
Frauenkirche, *Munich* **20 b2**
Frederiksberg, *Copenhagen* **10 A3**
Frederiksdal, *Copenhagen* **10 A2**
Fredersdorf, *Berlin* **5 A5**
Freguesia, *Rio de Janeiro* . **24 A1**
Freidrichshain, Volkspark,
  Berlin **5 A3**
Freiham, *Munich* **20 B1**
Freimann, *Munich* **20 A2**
Fresh Pond, *Boston* **6 A3**
Fresnes, *Paris* **23 B2**
Freudenau, *Vienna* **31 A2**
Friarstown, *Dublin* **11 B1**
Frick Collection, *New York* **21 b2**
Friedenau, *Berlin* **5 B3**
Friedrichsfelde, *Berlin* **5 B4**
Friedrichshagen, *Berlin* ... **5 B4**
Friedrichshain, *Berlin* **5 A3**
Friedrichslust, *Berlin* **5 A5**
Friherrs, *Helsinki* **12 B1**
Frontón, 1., *Lima* **16 B1**
Frunze, *Moscow* **19 B3**
Fuchú, *Tokyo* **29 A1**
Fuencarral, *Madrid* **17 B1**
Fuenlabrada, *Madrid* **17 C1**
Fujidera, *Osaka* **22 B4**
Fukagawa, *Tokyo* **29 B3**
Fukiage Imperial Garden,
  Tokyo **29 a4**
Fukiai, *Osaka* **22 A2**
Fukushima, *Osaka* **22 A3**
Fulham, *London* **15 B2**
Funabori, *Tokyo* **29 A4**
Funasaka, *Osaka* **22 A3**
Fundão, 1. do, *Rio de Janeiro* **24 B1**
Fünfhaus, *Vienna* **31 A2**
Furesø, *Copenhagen* **10 A2**
Furth, *Munich* **20 B1**
Futago-tamagawaen, *Tokyo* **29 B2**
Fuxing Dao, *Shanghai* **27 B2**
Fuxing Park, *Shanghai* ... **27 B1**
Fuxinglu, *Beijing* **4 B1**

G

Gage Park, *Chicago* **9 C2**
Gagny, *Paris* **23 A4**
Galata, *Istanbul* **12 B1**
Galátsion, *Athens* **2 A2**
Galeão, Aéroporto Int. de,
  Rio de Janeiro **24 A1**
Galyanovo, *Moscow* **19 B4**
Gambir, *Jakarta* **13 A1**
Gamboa, *Rio de Janeiro* .. **24 B1**
Gamboláita, *Milan* **18 B2**
Gamla Stan, *Stockholm* ... **28 c2**
Gamlebyen, *Oslo* **22 A3**
Gangtou, *Canton* **8 A1**
Gangwei, *Canton* **8 B2**
Ganjiakou, *Beijing* **4 B1**
Ganshoren, *Brussels* **6 A1**
Gants Hill, *London* **15 A4**
Gaoqiao, *Shanghai* **27 A2**
Garbagnate Milanese, *Milan* **18 B2**
Garbatella, *Rome* **25 B2**
Garches, *Paris* **23 A2**
Garching, *Munich* **20 A3**
Garden City, *Cairo* **7 A2**
Garden Reach, *Calcutta* .. **8 B1**
Garder, *Oslo* **22 B2**
Garfield, *New York* **21 A1**
Garfield Park, *Chicago* ... **9 B2**
Gargareta, *Athens* **2 B2**
Garvanza, *Los Angeles* ... **16 B3**
Gåshaga, *Stockholm* **28 A3**
Gateway National Recreation
  Area, *New York* **21 C2**
Gateway of India, *Mumbai* **20 B2**
Gatow, *Berlin* **5 B1**
Gávea, *Rio de Janeiro* **24 B1**
Gávea, Pedra da,
  Rio de Janeiro **24 B1**
Gazdagrét, *Budapest* **7 B1**
Gebel el Ahmar, *Cairo* ... **7 A2**
Gebel el Muqattam, *Cairo* **7 A2**
Gebel el Tura, *Cairo* **7 B2**
Geiselgasteig, *Munich* **20 B2**
General San Martin,
  Buenos Aires **7 B1**
Gennevilliers, *Paris* **23 A2**
Gentilly, *Paris* **23 B3**
Gentofte, *Copenhagen* ... **10 A3**
Genval, *Brussels* **6 B2**
George I., *Hong Kong* **12 B1**
George I., *Boston* **6 A4**
Georges River Bridge, *Sydney* **28 C1**
Georgetown, *Washington* . **32 B3**
Georgia Dome, *Atlanta* ... **3 B2**
Gerasdorf bei Wien, *Vienna* **31 A2**
Gerberau, *Munich* **20 A1**
Gerli, *Buenos Aires* **7 C2**
Germiston, *Johannesburg* . **13 B2**
Gern, *Munich* **20 B2**
Gestrat el Rauda, *Cairo* .. **7 A2**
Getafe, *Madrid* **17 C1**
Geva Binyamin, *Jerusalem* **13 A2**
Geylang Serai, *Singapore* . **27 B3**
Gezirat el Dhahab, *Cairo* . **7 B2**
Gharapuri, *Mumbai* **20 B2**
Ghatkopar, *Mumbai* **20 A2**
Ghazipur, *Delhi* **10 B2**
Ghizri, *Karachi* **14 B2**
Ghizri Cr. ➤, *Karachi* **14 B2**
Ghonda, *Delhi* **10 A2**
Ghusuri, *Calcutta* **8 B2**
Gianicolense, *Rome* **25 B1**
Gianicolo, *Rome* **25 c1**
Gibraltar Pt., *Toronto* **30 B2**
Gidea Park, *London* **15 A5**
Giesing, *Munich* **20 B2**
Gilmerton, *Edinburgh* **11 B3**
Gióia, *Jerusalem* **13 B2**
Gimmersta, *Stockholm* ... **28 B3**
Ginza, *Tokyo* **29 b5**
Girgaum, *Mumbai* **20 B2**
Giv'at Ye'arim, *Jerusalem* **13 B1**
Giv'at Ze'ev, *Jerusalem* .. **13 A2**
Giza Pyramids = Pyramids,
  Cairo **7 B1**
Gjerspen, *Oslo* **22 B3**
Gladesville, *Sydney* **28 B1**
Gladsakse, *Copenhagen* .. **10 A2**
Glasnevin, *Dublin* **11 A2**
Glasthule, *Dublin* **11 B3**
Glen Iris, *Melbourne* **17 B2**
Glen Mar Park, *Washington* **32 B3**
Glen Rock, *New York* **21 A1**
Glenanna, *Washington* ... **32 B4**
Glenasmole Reservoirs,
  Dublin **11 B1**
Glencorse Res., *Edinburgh* **11 B2**
Glencullen, *Dublin* **11 B2**
Glendale, *Los Angeles* **16 B3**
Glendoo Mt., *Dublin* **11 B2**
Glenhuntly, *Melbourne* ... **17 B2**
Glenside, *Wellington* **32 B1**
Glenview, *Chicago* **9 A2**
Glenview Countryside,
  Chicago **9 A2**
Glenvista, *Johannesburg* . **13 B2**
Glifádha, *Athens* **2 B2**
Glömsta, *Stockholm* **28 B1**
Glostrup, *Copenhagen* ... **10 B2**
Gogar, *Edinburgh* **11 B2**
Göktürk, *Istanbul* **12 A1**
Golabari, *Calcutta* **8 B2**
Golabki, *Warsaw* **31 B1**
Gold Coast, *Chicago* **9 a2**
Golden Gate, *San Francisco* **25 B2**
Golden Gate Bridge,
  San Francisco **25 B2**
Golden Gate Park,
  San Francisco **25 B2**
Golden Horn, *Istanbul* ... **12 B1**
Golders Green, *London* ... **15 A2**
Gollans Stream ➤,
  Wellington **32 B2**
Golyevo, *Moscow* **19 B1**
Goodman Hill, *Boston* ... **6 A1**
Goodmayes, *London* **15 A4**
Goodwood, *Cape Town* .. **8 A2**
Gopalpur, *Calcutta* **8 B2**
Górce, *Warsaw* **31 B1**
Gore Hill, *Sydney* **28 A2**
Gorelovo ➤, *St. Petersburg* **26 A3**
Gorenki, *Moscow* **19 B5**
Gorgie, *Edinburgh* **11 B2**
Gorky Park, *Moscow* **19 B3**
Gosen, *Berlin* **5 B5**
Gosener kanal, *Berlin* **5 B5**
Gospel Oak, *London* **15 A3**
Gotanda, *Tokyo* **29 B3**
Goth Goli Mar, *Karachi* .. **14 A2**
Goth Sher Shah, *Karachi* . **14 A1**
Gournay-sur-Marne, *Paris* **23 A4**
Governador, I. do,
  Rio de Janeiro **24 A1**
Governor's I., *New York* .. **21 B1**

H

Haaga, *Helsinki* **12 B2**
Haar, *Munich* **20 B3**
Hackbridge, *London* **15 B3**
Hackensack, *New York* ... **21 A1**
Hackensack ➤, *New York* . **21 B1**
Hackney, *London* **15 A3**
Hackney Wick, *London* ... **15 A3**
Haga, *Stockholm* **28 A2**
Hagenbrunn, *Vienna* **31 A2**
Hägersten, *Stockholm* **28 B1**
Häggvik, *Stockholm* **28 A1**
Hai He ➤, *Tianjin* **30 B2**
Haidan, *Beijing* **4 B1**
Haidhausen, *Munich* **20 B2**
Haight-Ashbury,
  San Francisco **25 B2**
Hainault, *London* **15 A4**
Haizhu Guangchang, *Canton* **8 B2**
Hakunila, *Helsinki* **12 B3**
Halásztelek, *Budapest* **7 B1**
Haliç = Golden Horn,
  Istanbul **12 B1**
Halim Perdanakusuma
  International Airport,
  Jakarta **13 B2**
Graben, *Vienna* **31 b2**
Grabów, *Warsaw* **31 C1**
Graça, *Lisbon* **14 A2**
Grace, Mt., *Wellington* ... **32 B2**
Grace Cathedral,
  San Francisco **25 b1**
Gracefield, *Wellington* ... **32 B2**
Gracia, *Barcelona* **4 A2**
Gräfelfing, *Munich* **20 B1**
Gragoatá, *Rio de Janeiro* . **24 B2**
Grand Central Station,
  New York **21 c2**
Grand Union Canal, *London* **15 A2**
Grande Place, *Brussels* ... **6 b2**
Grant Park, *Atlanta* **3 B2**
Grant Park, *Chicago* **9 c2**
Granton, *Edinburgh* **11 B2**
Grape I., *Boston* **6 B4**
Grassy Park, *Cape Town* .. **8 B2**
Gratosóglio, *Milan* **18 B2**
Gratzwalde, *Berlin* **5 B5**
Gravesend, *New York* **21 C2**
Grazhdanka, *St. Petersburg* **26 B2**
Great Falls, *Washington* .. **32 B2**
Great Falls Park, *Washington* **32 B2**
Great Hall of the People,
  Beijing **4 b2**
Great Meadows National
  Wildlife Refuge, *Boston* . **6 A1**
Greco, *Milan* **18 A2**
Green I., *Hong Kong* **12 B1**
Green Point, *Cape Town* .. **8 A1**
Greenbelt, *Washington* ... **32 A4**
Greenbelt Park, *Washington* **32 B4**
Greenfield Park, *Montreal* **19 B3**
Greenford, *London* **15 A1**
Greenhill, *London* **15 A1**
Greenhills, *Dublin* **11 B1**
Greenmarket Square,
  Cape Town **8 c2**
Greenpoint, *New York* ... **21 B2**
Greenwich, *London* **15 B3**
Greenwich Observatory,
  London **15 B3**
Greenwich Village, *New York* **21 B2**
Greenwood, *Boston* **6 A3**
Grefsen, *Oslo* **22 A3**
Gresham Park, *Atlanta* ... **3 B2**
Greve Strand, *Copenhagen* **10 B1**
Greyfriars Kirk, *Edinburgh* **11 c2**
Griebnitzsee, *Berlin* **5 B1**
Grifhberg, *Los Angeles* ... **16 B3**
Grimbergen, *Brussels* **6 A2**
Grinzing, *Vienna* **31 A2**
Gröbenried, *Munich* **20 A1**
Grochów, *Warsaw* **31 B2**
Grodzisk, *Warsaw* **31 B1**
Groenendaal, *Brussels* **6 B2**
Grogol Petamburin, *Jakarta* **13 A1**
Gronsdorf, *Munich* **20 B3**
Grorud, *Oslo* **22 A4**
Grosse Glienicke, *Berlin* .. **5 A1**
Gross-Hadern, *Munich* ... **20 B1**
Gross-Lappen, *Munich* ... **20 A2**
Grosse Krampe, *Berlin* ... **5 B5**
Grosse Müggelsee, *Berlin* . **5 B4**
Grossenzersdorf, *Vienna* .. **31 A3**
Grossenzersdorfer Arm ➤,
  Vienna **31 A3**
Grosser Biberhaufen, *Vienna* **31 A3**
Grosser Wannsee, *Berlin* . **5 B2**
Grossfeld-Siedlung, *Vienna* **31 A2**
Grosshesselohe, *Munich* .. **20 B2**
Grossjedlersdorf, *Vienna* .. **31 A2**
Grossziethen, *Berlin* **5 B3**
Grove Hall, *Boston* **6 B3**
Grove Park, *Atlanta* **3 B2**
Grove Park, *London* **15 B2**
Grove Park, *London* **15 B4**
Groveton, *Washington* ... **32 C3**
Grünau, *Berlin* **5 B4**
Grunewald, *Berlin* **5 B2**
Grünwald, *Munich* **20 B2**
Grünwalder Forst, *Munich* **20 B2**
Grymes Hill, *New York* ... **21 C1**
Guadalupe, *Manila* **17 B2**
Guadalupe, Basílica de,
  Mexico City **18 B2**
Guanabara, B. de,
  Rio de Janeiro **24 B1**
Guanabara, Jardim,
  Rio de Janeiro **24 A1**
Guanabara, Palácio da,
  Rio de Janeiro **24 B1**
Guang'anmen, *Beijing* **4 B1**
Guangqumen, *Beijing* **4 B2**
Guangzhou, *Canton* **8 B2**
Guanshuo, *Canton* **8 B2**
Gudö, *Stockholm* **28 B3**
Güell, Parque de, *Barcelona* **4 A2**
Guerrero, *Mexico City* ... **18 a1**
Guggenheim Museum,
  New York **21 b3**
Guinardó, *Barcelona* **4 A2**
Gulbai, *Karachi* **14 A1**
Güngören, *Istanbul* **12 B1**
Gunnersbury, *London* **15 B2**
Gustavo A. Madero,
  Mexico City **18 B2**
Guttenberg, *New York* ... **21 B1**
Gutuyevskiy, Ostrov,
  St. Petersburg **26 B1**
Guyancourt, *Paris* **23 B1**
Gyál, *Budapest* **7 B3**
Gyáli-patak ➤, *Budapest* . **7 B2**

Halle, *Brussels* **6 B1**
Haltiala, *Helsinki* **12 B2**
Haltiavuori, *Helsinki* **12 B2**
Ham, *London* **15 B2**
Hämeenkylä, *Helsinki* **12 B1**
Hammarby, *Stockholm* ... **28 B2**
Hamme, *Brussels* **6 A1**
Hammersmith, *London* ... **15 B2**
Hampstead, *London* **15 A2**
Hampstead, *Montreal* **19 B2**
Hampstead Garden Suburb,
  London **15 A2**
Hampstead Heath, *London* **15 A2**
Hampton, *London* **15 B1**
Hampton Court Palace,
  London **15 B1**
Hampton Wick, *London* .. **15 B2**
Hamrā', *Baghdad* **3 B2**
Hanala, *Helsinki* **12 A3**
Hanaoka Gardens, *Mumbai* **20 b1**
Hanjiashu, *Tianjin* **30 A1**
Hanlon, *Toronto* **30 A1**
Hanwell, *London* **15 A1**
Hanworth, *London* **15 B1**
Haora, *Calcutta* **8 B2**
Hapeville, *Atlanta* **3 C2**
Happy Valley, *Hong Kong* **12 B2**
Har Adar, *Jerusalem* **13 B1**
Haren, *Brussels* **6 A2**
Hareskovby, *Copenhagen* **10 A2**
Haringey, *London* **15 A3**
Harjusuo, *Helsinki* **12 B3**
Harlaching, *Munich* **20 B2**
Harlaw Res., *Edinburgh* .. **11 B2**
Harlem, *New York* **21 B2**
Harlesden, *London* **15 A2**
Harlington, *London* **15 B1**
Harmaja, *Helsinki* **12 C2**
Harmashatar hegy, *Budapest* **7 A2**
Harolds Cross, *Dublin* ... **11 B2**
Háros, *Budapest* **7 B2**
Harperrig Reservoir,
  Edinburgh **11 B1**
Harrow, *London* **15 A1**
Harrow on the Hill, *London* **15 A1**
Harrow School, *London* .. **15 A1**
Harrow Weald, *London* .. **15 A1**
Hartsfield-Atlanta
  International Airport,
  Atlanta **3 C2**
Harumi, *Tokyo* **29 c5**
Harvard Univ., *Boston* ... **6 A3**
Harwood Heights, *Chicago* **9 B2**
Hasanäbäd, *Tehran* **30 A1**
Hasbrouck Heights,
  New York **21 A1**
Haselhorst, *Berlin* **5 A2**
Hasköy, *Istanbul* **12 B1**
Hasle, *Oslo* **22 B3**
Haslum, *Oslo* **22 A2**
Hästhagen, *Stockholm* ... **28 B2**
Hataitai, *Wellington* **32 B1**
Hatch End, *London* **15 A1**
Hatiara, *Calcutta* **8 B2**
Hauketo, *Oslo* **22 A3**
Havel ➤, *Berlin* **5 A2**
Havelkanal, *Berlin* **5 A1**
Havering, *London* **15 A5**
Havering-atte-Bower,
  London **15 A5**
Hawŏlgok, *Seoul* **26 B2**
Haworth, *New York* **21 A2**
Hayes, *London* **15 A1**
Hayes, *London* **15 B2**
Hayes End, *London* **15 A1**
Hayford, *Chicago* **9 C2**
Haywards, *Wellington* ... **32 A2**
Heard Pond, *Boston* **6 A2**
Heathfield, *Cape Town* ... **8 B1**
Heathrow Airport, *London* **15 B1**
Hebe Haven, *Hong Kong* . **12 A2**
Hebei, *Tianjin* **30 B2**
Hedong, *Canton* **8 B2**
Hedong, *Tianjin* **30 B2**
Heidelberg Heights,
  Melbourne **17 A2**
Heidelberg West, *Melbourne* **17 A2**
Heidemühle, *Berlin* **5 B5**
Heideveld, *Cape Town* ... **8 A2**
Heiligensee, *Berlin* **5 A2**
Heiligenstadt, *Vienna* **31 A2**
Heinersdorf, *Berlin* **5 A3**
Heldenplatz, *Vienna* **31 b1**
Hélène Champlain, Parc,
  Montreal **19 A2**
Helenelund, *Stockholm* .. **28 A1**
Heliopolis = Masr el Gedida,
  Cairo **7 A2**
Hellersdorf, *Berlin* **5 A4**
Hellerup, *Copenhagen* ... **10 A3**
Helmahof, *Vienna* **31 A3**
Helsingfors = Helsinki,
  Helsinki **12 B2**
Helsinki, *Helsinki* **12 B2**
Helsinki Airport, *Helsinki* **12 B2**
Hendon, *London* **15 A2**
Hengsha, *Canton* **8 B2**
Henley Beach, *London* **15 A2**
Henningsdorf, *Berlin* **5 A2**
Hernyków, *Warsaw* **31 B1**
Henson Cr. ➤, *Washington* **32 C4**
Henttaa, *Helsinki* **12 B1**
Heping, *Tianjin* **30 B2**
Heping Park, *Shanghai* ... **27 B2**
Hepingli, *Beijing* **4 B2**
Herlev, *Copenhagen* **10 A2**
Herman Eckstein Park,
  Johannesburg **13 A2**
Hermannskogel, *Vienna* .. **31 A1**
Hermiston, *Edinburgh* ... **11 B2**
Hermitage and Winter Palace,
  St. Petersburg **26 B1**
Hermsdorf, *Berlin* **5 A3**
Hernals, *Vienna* **31 A2**
Herne Hill, *London* **15 B3**
Heron, *Toronto* **30 A1**
Herons, 1. aux, *Montreal* . **19 B2**
Herstedøster, *Copenhagen* **10 A2**
Herttoniemi, *Helsinki* **12 B3**
Hesãrak, *Tehran* **30 A1**
Heston, *London* **15 B1**
Hetzendorf, *Vienna* **31 A2**
Hexi, *Tianjin* **30 B2**
Hextable, *London* **15 B5**
Hialeah, *Miami* **18 A1**
Hickory Hills, *Chicago* ... **9 C2**
Hiekkaharju, *Helsinki* **12 B3**
Hietaniemi, *Helsinki* **12 B2**
Higashi, *Osaka* **22 A4**
Higashimurayama, *Tokyo* **29 A1**
Higashinada, *Osaka* **22 A1**
Higashiōsaka, *Osaka* **22 A4**
Higashisumiyoshi, *Osaka* **22 B4**
Higashiyodogawa, *Osaka* **22 A3**
High Park, *Toronto* **30 B2**
Highbury, *London* **15 A3**
Highgate, *London* **15 A3**
Highland Cr. ➤, *Toronto* .. **30 A3**
Highland Creek, *Toronto* . **30 A3**
Highland Park, *Los Angeles* **16 B3**
Highlands North,
  Johannesburg **13 A2**
Hillcrest Heights, *Washington* **32 C4**
Hillend, *Edinburgh* **11 A1**
Hillingdon, *London* **15 A1**
Hillwood, *Washington* ... **32 B3**
Hilmiya, *Cairo* **7 A2**
Hin Keng, *Hong Kong* **12 A2**
Hingham, *Boston* **6 B4**
Hingham B., *Boston* **6 B4**
Hingham Harbor, *Boston* . **6 B4**
Hirakata, *Osaka* **22 A4**
Haneda, *Tokyo* **29 B3**
Hirota, *Osaka* **22 A3**
Hirschstetten, *Vienna* **31 A2**
Histórico Nacional, Museu,
  Rio de Janeiro **24 b3**
Hither Green, *London* **15 B3**
Hiyoshi, *Tokyo* **29 B2**
Hizma, *Jerusalem* **13 B2**
Hjortekær, *Copenhagen* .. **10 A3**
Hjortespring, *Copenhagen* **10 A2**
Hlubočepy, *Prague* **24 B2**
Ho Chung, *Hong Kong* ... **12 A2**
Ho Man Tin, *Hong Kong* . **12 B2**
Hobokken, *New York* **21 B1**
Hobsons B., *Melbourne* ... **17 B1**
Hochbrück, *Munich* **20 A2**
Hochelaga, *Montreal* **19 A2**
Hodgkins, *Chicago* **9 C1**
Hoegi, *Seoul* **26 B2**
Hoeilaart, *Brussels* **6 B2**
Hofberg, *Vienna* **31 b1**
Hoffman I., *New York* **21 C1**
Hofgarten, *Munich* **20 a3**
Hogsdtadomstolen,
  Stockholm **28 c2**
Hohenbrunn, *Munich* **20 B3**
Hohenschönhausen, *Berlin* **5 A4**
Holborn, *London* **15 a4**
Holešovice, *Prague* **24 B2**
Holland Village, *Singapore* **27 B2**
Höllriegelskreuth, *Munich* **20 B1**
Hollywood, *Los Angeles* .. **16 B3**
Holmenkollen, *Oslo* **22 A3**
Holmes Run Acres,
  Washington **32 B2**
Holmgård, *Stockholm* **28 B1**
Holysloot, *Amsterdam* ... **2 A3**
Homerton, *London* **15 A3**
Hometown, *Chicago* **9 C2**
Hōnanchō, *Tokyo* **29 A2**
Honden, *Tokyo* **29 A4**
Hondo, Rio ➤, *Los Angeles* **16 B4**
Hong Kong, *Hong Kong* .. **12 B1**
Hong Kong, Univ. of,
  Hong Kong **12 B1**
Hong Kong I., *Hong Kong* **12 B2**
Hong Kong Park, *Hong Kong* **12 c1**
Hongkou, *Shanghai* **27 B1**
Hongkou Park, *Shanghai* . **27 B1**
Hongmiao, *Beijing* **4 B2**
Hongqiao, *Shanghai* **27 B1**
Hongqiao, *Tianjin* **30 B1**
Hongqiao Airport, *Shanghai* **27 B1**
Hongŭn, *Seoul* **26 B1**
Honjyo, *Tokyo* **29 A3**
Honoré Mercier, Pont,
  Montreal **19 B1**
Hōnow, *Berlin* **5 A4**
Hooghly = Hugli ➤, *Calcutta* **8 A2**
Hook, *London* **15 B1**
Horikiri, *Tokyo* **29 A4**
Horn Pond, *Boston* **6 A2**
Hornchurch, *London* **15 A5**
Horni, *Prague* **24 B3**
Horni Počernice, *Prague* . **24 B3**
Hornsey, *London* **15 A3**
Horomêtice, *Prague* **24 A2**
Hortaleza, *Madrid* **17 B2**
Hosoyama, *Tokyo* **29 B2**
Hostafranchs, *Barcelona* . **4 A1**
Hostivař, *Prague* **24 B3**
Hôtel des Invalides, *Paris* . **23 B2**
Houbětin, *Prague* **24 B3**
Houghs Neck, *Boston* **6 B4**
Houghton, *Johannesburg* **13 A2**
Houilles, *Paris* **23 A2**
Hounslow, *London* **15 B1**
Houses of Parliament,
  London **15 c3**
Hout Bay, *Cape Town* **8 B1**
Hove Å ➤, *Copenhagen* .. **10 A1**
Hovedøya, *Oslo* **22 A3**
Høvik, *Oslo* **22 A2**
Hovorčovice, *Prague* **24 A3**
Howard Beach, *New York* . **21 C2**
Howth, *Dublin* **11 A3**
Howth Head, *Dublin* **11 A3**
Hoxton, *London* **15 a5**
Hōya, *Tokyo* **29 A2**
Hradčany, *Prague* **24 B2**
Huanghuagang Mausoleum of
  the 72 Martyrs, *Canton* . **8 B2**
Huangpu, *Shanghai* **27 B2**
Huangpu Jiang ➤, *Shanghai* **27 B1**
Huangpu Park, *Shanghai* . **27 B1**
Huangtugang, *Beijing* **4 C1**
Huascar, *Lima* **16 A2**
Huay Khwang, *Bangkok* .. **3 B2**
Huddinge, *Stockholm* **28 B2**
Hudson ➤, *New York* **21 A2**
Huechuraba, *Santiago* ... **26 B1**
Huertas de San Beltran,
  Barcelona **4 A1**
Hugli ➤, *Calcutta* **8 A2**
Huidui, *Tianjin* **30 B2**
Huizingen, *Brussels* **6 B1**
Hull, *Boston* **6 B4**
Humber ➤, *Toronto* **30 A1**
Humber B., *Toronto* **30 B2**
Humber Bay, *Toronto* **30 B2**
Humber Summit, *Toronto* **30 A1**
Humber Valley Village,
  Toronto **30 A1**
Humberlea, *Toronto* **30 A1**
Humboldt Park, *Chicago* . **9 B2**
Humera, *Madrid* **17 B1**
Hunayd, *Baghdad* **3 B2**
Hundige Strand, *Copenhagen* **10 B2**
Hung Hom, *Hong Kong* .. **12 B2**
Hunters Hill, *Sydney* **28 B1**
Hunters Pt., *San Francisco* **25 B2**
Hunters Valley, *Washington* **32 C2**
Huntington, *Washington* . **32 C3**
Huntington Park, *Los Angeles* **16 C3**
Hurlya, *Baghdad* **3 A1**
Hurstville, *Sydney* **28 B1**
Husby, *Stockholm* **28 A1**
Hushusein, Copenhagen* .. **10 A2**
Husum, *Copenhagen* **10 A2**

Hutt R. ➤, *Wellington* **32 B2**
Hütteldorf, *Vienna* **31 A1**
Hūvösvölgy, *Budapest* ... **7 A2**
Hvalstad, *Oslo* **22 A2**
Hvalstrand, *Oslo* **22 A2**
Hvidovre, *Copenhagen* ... **10 B2**
Hwagok, *Seoul* **26 B1**
Hyattsville, *Washington* .. **32 B4**
Hyde Park, *Boston* **6 B3**
Hyde Park, *Chicago* **9 C3**
Hyde Park, *Johannesburg* **13 A2**
Hyde Park, *London* **15 A2**
Hyde Park, *Sydney* **28 B2**

I

Ibese, *Lagos* **14 A2**
Ibirapuera, *São Paulo* **26 B1**
Ibirapuera, Parque, *São Paulo* **26 B2**
Icaraí, *Rio de Janeiro* **24 B2**
Içerenköy, *Istanbul* **12 C2**
Ichgao, *Tokyo* **29 B2**
Ichigaya, *Tokyo* **29 a3**
Ichikawa, *Tokyo* **29 A4**
Ickenham, *London* **15 A1**
Iddo, *Lagos* **14 A2**
Idi-Oro, *Lagos* **14 A2**
Iganmu, *Lagos* **14 A2**
Igbobi, *Lagos* **14 A2**
Igbologun, *Lagos* **14 B1**
Igny, *Paris* **23 B2**
Ijebu-Tedo, *Lagos* **14 B1**
Ijora, *Lagos* **14 B2**
IJtunnel, *Amsterdam* **2 a3**
Ikebe, *Tokyo* **29 B2**
Ikebukuro, *Tokyo* **29 A3**
Ikegami, *Tokyo* **29 B3**
Ikeja, *Lagos* **14 A2**
Ikeuchi, *Osaka* **22 B4**
Ikoyi, *Lagos* **14 B2**
Ikuta, *Osaka* **22 A2**
Ikuno, *Osaka* **22 A4**
Ikuta, *Osaka* **22 A2**
Ila, *Oslo* **22 A2**
Ilford, *London* **15 A4**
Ilioúpolis, *Athens* **2 B2**
Ilpendam, *Amsterdam* ... **2 A2**
Ilsös ➤, *Athens* **2 B2**
Imagem e do Som, Museu da,
  Rio de Janeiro **24 b3**
Imbâbah, *Cairo* **7 A2**
Imielin, *Warsaw* **31 C2**
Imirim, *São Paulo* **26 A2**
Imittós, *Athens* **2 B2**
Imittós, Óros, *Athens* **2 B2**
Imperial Palace Museum,
  Beijing **4 b2**
Inagi, *Tokyo* **29 B1**
Incheolm, *Edinburgh* **11 A2**
Inchicore, *Dublin* **11 A1**
Inchkeith, *Edinburgh* **11 A2**
Inchmickery, *Edinburgh* . **11 A2**
Incirano, *Milan* **18 A1**
Independencia, *Lima* **16 A2**
Independencia, *Santiago* . **26 B2**
India Gate, *Delhi* **1 c2**
Indian Creek Village, *Miami* **18 A2**
Indian Head Park, *Chicago* **9 C1**
Indianópolis, *São Paulo* .. **26 B2**
Indios Verdes, *Mexico City* **18 B2**
Indira Ghandi International
  Airport, *Delhi* **10 B1**
Industria, *Johannesburg* . **13 B1**
Ingierstrand, *Oslo* **22 B3**
Inglewood, *Los Angeles* .. **16 C3**
Ingleston, *Edinburgh* **11 B2**
Inhaúme, *Rio de Janeiro* . **24 B1**
Inner Port Shelter,
  Hong Kong **12 A2**
Interlagos, *São Paulo* **26 C1**
Intramuros, *Manila* **17 B1**
Invalides, *Paris* **23 b2**
Inverkeithing, *Edinburgh* . **11 A2**
Inzersdorf, *Vienna* **31 B2**
Ipanema, *Rio de Janeiro* . **24 B1**
Ipiranga, *São Paulo* **26 B2**
Ipiranga ➤, *São Paulo* ... **26 B2**
Iponri, *Lagos* **14 B2**
Ireland's Eye, *Dublin* **11 A3**
Irving Park, *Chicago* **9 B2**
Isabel, *Rio de Janeiro* **24 B1**
Isagatedo, *Lagos* **14 A2**
Isar ➤, *Munich* **20 A3**
Ishbîliya, *Baghdad* **3 A2**
Ishikiri, *Osaka* **22 A4**
Ishøj Strand, *Copenhagen* **10 B2**
Island Bay, *Wellington* ... **32 C1**
Island Park, *Toronto* **30 B2**
Isle of Dogs, *London* **15 B3**
Isle of Dogs, *London* **15 B3**
Islev, *Copenhagen* **10 A2**
Isleworth, *London* **15 B2**
Islington, *London* **15 A3**
Islington, *Toronto* **30 B2**
Ismaning, *Munich* **20 A3**
Ismaylovo, *Moscow* **19 B4**
Isolo, *Lagos* **14 A1**
Issy-les-Moulineaux, *Paris* **23 B2**
Istanbul, *Istanbul* **12 C1**
Istanbul Boğazı ➤, *Istanbul* **12 B1**
Istinye, *Istanbul* **12 B2**
Itä Hakkila, *Helsinki* **12 B3**
Itaewŏn, *Seoul* **26 B1**
Itahanga, *Rio de Janeiro* . **24 B1**
Itami, *Osaka* **22 A3**
Ivanhoe, *Melbourne* **17 A2**
Ivry-sur-Seine, *Paris* **23 B3**
Iwazono, *Osaka* **22 A3**
Ixelles, *Brussels* **6 B2**
Izmaylovo, *Moscow* **19 B4**
Iztacalco, *Mexico City* ... **18 B2**
Iztapalapa, *Mexico City* .. **18 B2**

J

Jaba, *Jerusalem* **13 A2**
Jababpur, *Calcutta* **8 C2**
Jacaré, *Rio de Janeiro* **24 B1**
Jackson Heights, *New York* **21 B2**
Jackson Park, *Chicago* **9 C3**
Jacques Cartier, *Montreal* **19 A3**
Jacques Cartier, Pont,
  Montreal **19 A2**
Jade Buddha Temple,
  Shanghai **27 B1**
Jægersborg, *Copenhagen* **10 A3**
Jægersborg Dyrehave,
  Copenhagen **10 A3**
Jagadishpur, *Calcutta* **8 B1**
Jagatpur, *Delhi* **10 A2**

Jaguaré, Rib. do ➤,
  São Paulo **26 B1**
Jahangirpur, *Delhi* **10 A2**
Jakarta, *Jakarta* **13 A1**
Jakarta, Teluk, *Jakarta* .. **13 A1**
Jalan Kayu, *Singapore* ... **27 A3**
Jamaica B., *New York* **21 C3**
Jamaica Plain, *Boston* ... **6 B3**
Jamakpuri, *Delhi* **10 B1**
Jamshidiyeh, *Tehran* **30 A2**
Janki, *Warsaw* **31 C1**
Jannali, *Sydney* **28 C1**
Japan Center, *San Francisco* **25 c1**
Jaraguá, *São Paulo* **26 A1**
Jaraguá, Pico de, *São Paulo* **26 A1**
Jardim Paulista, *São Paulo* **26 B1**
Jardim Botânico, *Brussels* **6 a3**
Järvafältet, *Stockholm* ... **28 A1**
Jaskhar, *Mumbai* **20 B2**
Jatinegara, *Jakarta* **13 B2**
Jävädiyeh, *Tehran* **30 B2**
Jaworowa, *Warsaw* **31 C1**
Jedlesee, *Vienna* **31 A2**
Jefferson Memorial,
  Washington **32 c1**
Jefferson Park, *Chicago* .. **9 B2**
Jelonki, *Warsaw* **31 B1**
Jerónimos, Mosteiro dos,
  Lisbon **14 A1**
Jersey City, *New York* **21 B1**
Jerusalem, *Jerusalem* **13 B2**
Jésus, I., *Montreal* **19 A1**
Jesús Maria, *Lima* **16 B2**
Jette, *Brussels* **6 A1**
Jewish Quarter, *Jerusalem* **13 b3**
Jey, *Isfahan* **30 B2**
Jianguomen, *Beijing* **4 B2**
Jiangwan, *Shanghai* **27 B1**
Jianshan Park, *Tianjin* ... **30 B2**
Jihád, *Baghdad* **3 B2**
Jim Thompson's House,
  Bangkok **3 b3**
Jimbōchō, *Tokyo* **29 a4**
Jingan, *Shanghai* **27 B1**
Jingú Outer Garden, *Tokyo* **29 b2**
Jinočany, *Prague* **24 B1**
Jinonice, *Prague* **24 B2**
Jiyūgaoka, *Tokyo* **29 B3**
Jizã'ir, *Baghdad* **3 B2**
Jizira, *Baghdad* **3 B2**
Johannesburg, *Johannesburg* **13 B2**
Johanneskirchen, *Munich* **20 A2**
Johannesstift, *Berlin* **5 A2**
Johannisthal, *Berlin* **5 B4**
John Hancock Center,
  Chicago **9 a2**
John McLaren Park,
  San Francisco **25 B2**
Johnsonville, *Wellington* . **32 B1**
Joinville-le-Pont, *Paris* ... **23 B3**
Joli-Bois, *Brussels* **6 B3**
Jollas, *Helsinki* **12 B3**
Jonstrup, *Copenhagen* ... **10 A2**
Joppa, *Edinburgh* **11 B3**
Jorge Chavez, Aeropuerto
  Int., *Lima* **16 B2**
Jorge Newbury, Aeroparque,
  Buenos Aires **7 B2**
Jósefa Piłsudskiego Park,
  Warsaw **31 B1**
Jōtō, *Osaka* **22 A4**
Jouy-en-Josas, *Paris* **23 B2**
Juan Anchorena,
  Buenos Aires **7 A2**
Juan González Romero,
  Mexico City **18 A2**
Judeira, *Jerusalem* **13 A2**
Juhu, *Mumbai* **20 A2**
Jūjā, *Tokyo* **29 A3**
Jukskeirivier ➤,
  Johannesburg **13 A2**
Julianów, *Warsaw* **31 B2**
Jungfernheide, Volkspark,
  Berlin **5 A2**
Jungfernsee, *Berlin* **5 B1**
Juniper Green, *Edinburgh* **11 B2**
Junk B., *Hong Kong* **12 B2**
Jurong, *Singapore* **27 B2**
Jurong, Selat, *Singapore* . **27 B2**
Jurong Industrial Estate,
  Singapore **27 B1**
Jurujuba, Enseada de,
  Rio de Janeiro **24 B2**
Jūsō, *Osaka* **22 A3**
Justice, *Chicago* **9 C2**
Justicia, *Madrid* **17 a3**
Jwalahari, *Delhi* **10 B1**

K

Kabaty, *Warsaw* **31 C2**
Kadıköy, *Istanbul* **12 C2**
Kadoma, *Osaka* **22 A4**
Kaebong, *Seoul* **26 C1**
Kafr 'Aqab, *Jerusalem* ... **13 A2**
Kâğıthane ➤, *Istanbul* ... **12 B1**
Kâğıthane, *Istanbul* **12 B1**
Kagran, *Vienna* **31 A2**
Kahnawake, *Montreal* **19 B1**
Kaimes, *Edinburgh* **11 B2**
Kaisariani, *Athens* **2 B2**
Kaiser Wilhelm Kirche, *Berlin* **5 b2**
Kaiserebersdorf, *Vienna* .. **31 A2**
Kaivoksela, *Helsinki* **12 B2**
Kalamákion, *Athens* **2 B2**
Kalbadevi, *Mumbai* **20 b2**
Kalhyŏn, *Seoul* **26 B1**
Kalipur, *Calcutta* **8 A1**
Kalkaji, *Delhi* **10 B2**
Kallithéa, *Athens* **2 B2**
Kalveboderne, *Copenhagen* **10 B3**
Kamarhati, *Calcutta* **8 A2**
Kamata, *Tokyo* **29 B3**
Kamez, *Tokyo* **29 A4**
Kameari, *Tokyo* **29 A4**
Kami-Itabashi, *Tokyo* **29 A3**
Kamikitazawa, *Tokyo* **29 B2**
Kamishakujii, *Tokyo* **29 A2**
Kamoshida, *Tokyo* **29 B2**
Kampong Landang, *Singapore* **27 A3**
Kampong Tanjong Penjuru,
  Singapore **27 B2**
Kampung Bali, *Jakarta* ... **13 B1**
Kanamori, *Tokyo* **29 B1**
Kanda, *Tokyo* **29 a5**
Kandilli, *Istanbul* **12 B2**
Kangdong, *Seoul* **26 B2**
Kangnam, *Seoul* **26 B2**
Kangsŏ, *Seoul* **26 B1**
Kankurgachi, *Calcutta* ... **8 B2**
Kanlıca, *Istanbul* **12 B2**
Kanonerskiy, Ostrov,
  St. Petersburg **26 B1**
Kanzaki ➤, *Osaka* **22 A3**
Kapellerfeld, *Vienna* **31 A2**

Káposztásmegyer, Budapest . 7 A2
Kapotnya, Moscow . 19 C4
Käppala, Stockholm . 28 A3
Käpylä, Helsinki . 12 B2
Karachi, Karachi . 14 A2
Karachi Int. Airport, Karachi 14 A2
Karato, Osaka . 22 A2
Karibong, Seoul . 26 C1
Karkh, Baghdad . 3 A2
Karlin, Prague . 24 B2
Karlsfeld, Munich . 20 A1
Karlshorst, Berlin . 5 B4
Karlsplatz, Munich . 20 b1
Karntner Strasse, Vienna . 31 b2
Karol Bagh, Delhi . 10 B2
Karolinenhof, Berlin . 5 B4
Karori, Wellington . 32 B1
Karow, Berlin . 5 A3
Karrādah, Baghdad . 3 B2
Kärsön, Stockholm . 28 B1
Kasai, Tokyo . 29 B4
Kashiwara, Osaka . 22 B4
Kastellet, Copenhagen . 10 a3
Kastrup, Copenhagen . 10 B3
Kastrup Lufthavn, Copenhagen . 10 B3
Kasuga, Tokyo . 29 A2
Kasuge, Tokyo . 29 A3
Kasumigaseki, Tokyo . 29 b3
Katong, Singapore . 27 B3
Katrineberg, Stockholm . 28 A2
Katsushika-Ku, Tokyo . 29 A4
Kau Pei Chau, Hong Kong 12 B2
Kau Yi Chau, Hong Kong . 12 B1
Kaulsdorf, Berlin . 5 B4
Kauniainen, Helsinki . 12 B1
Kawasaki, Tokyo . 29 B3
Kawawa, Tokyo . 29 B2
Kawęczyn, Warsaw . 31 B2
Kayu Putih, Jakarta . 13 B2
Kbely, Prague . 24 B3
Kebayoran Baru, Jakarta . 13 B1
Kebayoran Lama, Jakarta . 13 B1
Kebon Jeruk, Jakarta . 13 A1
Kedar, Jerusalem . 13 B2
Keilor, Melbourne . 17 A1
Keilor North, Melbourne . 17 A1
Keimola, Helsinki . 12 A1
Kelenföld, Budapest . 7 B2
Kelvin, Johannesburg . 13 A2
Kemang, Jakarta . 13 B2
Kemayoran, Jakarta . 13 B2
Kemerburgaz, Istanbul . 12 B1
Kempton Park Races, London . 15 B1
Kendall Green, Boston . 6 A2
Kenilworth, Cape Town . 8 A1
Kennedy Town, Hong Kong 12 B1
Kennington, London . 15 c4
Kensal Green, London . 15 a1
Kensal Rise, London . 15 a1
Kensington, Johannesburg 13 B2
Kensington, London . 15 B2
Kensington, New York . 21 C2
Kensington, Sydney . 28 B2
Kensington Palace, London 15 A2
Kent Village, Washington 32 B4
Kentish Town, London . 15 A3
Kenton, London . 15 A2
Kenwood House, London . 15 A3
Kepa, Warsaw . 31 B2
Keppel Harbour, Singapore 27 B2
Keramíkos, Athens . 2 b1
Kettering, Washington . 32 B4
Kew, London . 15 B2
Kew, Melbourne . 17 A2
Kew Gardens, London . 15 B2
Kew Gardens, Toronto . 30 B2
Key Biscayne, Miami . 18 B2
Khaidhárion, Athens . 2 A1
Khalándrion, Athens . 2 A2
Khalīj, Baghdad . 3 B2
Khandallah, Wellington . 32 B1
Khansā', Baghdad . 3 A2
Kharavli, Mumbai . 20 B2
Khefren, Cairo . 7 B1
Khichripur, Delhi . 10 B2
Khidirpur, Calcutta . 8 B1
Khimki-Khovrino, Moscow 19 A3
Khirbet Jub e-Rum, Jerusalem 13 B2
Khlong San, Bangkok . 3 B2
Khlong Toey, Bangkok . 3 B2
Kholargós, Athens . 2 A2
Khorel, Calcutta . 8 A1
Khorosovo, Moscow . 19 B2
Kiamari, Karachi . 14 A1
Kierling, Vienna . 31 A1
Kierlingbach →, Vienna . 31 A1
Kifisós →, Athens . 2 B2
Kikuna, Tokyo . 29 B2
Kilbarrack, Dublin . 11 A3
Kilbirnie, Wellington . 32 B1
Kilburn, London . 15 A2
Kilcakee, Dublin . 11 B2
Kilcuster, Dublin . 11 A2
Killiney, Dublin . 11 B3
Killiney Bay, Dublin . 11 B3
Kilmacud, Dublin . 11 B2
Kilmainham, Dublin . 11 A2
Kilmashogue Mt., Dublin 11 B2
Kilmore, Dublin . 11 A2
Kilnamanagh, Dublin . 11 B1
Kilo, Helsinki . 12 B2
Kilokri, Delhi . 10 B2
Kiltiernan, Dublin . 11 B2
Kimmage, Dublin . 11 B2
Kindi, Baghdad . 3 B2
Kinghorn, Edinburgh . 11 A2
King's Cross, London . 15 a4
Kings Cross, Sydney . 28 c3
Kings Domain, Melbourne 17 A1
Kings Park, Washington 32 C2
Kings Park West, Washington 32 C2
Kingsbury, London . 15 A2
Kingsbury, Melbourne . 17 A2
Kingsford, Sydney . 28 B2
Kingston upon Thames, London . 15 B2
Kingston Vale, London . 15 B2
Kingsway, Toronto . 30 B1
Kinsaley, Dublin . 11 A2
Kipling Heights, Toronto 30 A1
Kipséli, Athens . 2 B2
Kirchstockbach, Munich . 20 B3
Kirchtrudering, Munich . 20 B3
Kirikiri, Lagos . 14 B1
Kirke Værlose, Copenhagen 10 A1
Kirkhill, Edinburgh . 11 B1
Kirknewton, Edinburgh . 11 B1
Kirov Palace of Culture, St. Petersburg . 26 B1
Kısıkh, Istanbul . 12 B2
Kispest, Budapest . 7 B2
Kista, Stockholm . 28 A1
Kita, Osaka . 22 A3
Kita-Ku, Tokyo . 29 A3
Kitazawa, Tokyo . 29 B3

Kiu Tsiu, Hong Kong . 12 A2
Kivistö, Helsinki . 12 B2
Kızıltoprak, Istanbul . 12 C2
Kizu →, Osaka . 22 B4
Kizuri, Osaka . 22 B4
Kjelsås, Oslo . 22 A3
Kladow, Berlin . 5 B2
Klampenborg, Copenhagen 10 A3
Klaudyń, Warsaw . 31 B1
Klecany, Prague . 24 A2
Kledering, Vienna . 31 B2
Klein Jukskei →, Johannesburg . 13 A1
Kleinmachnow, Berlin . 5 B2
Kleinschönebeck, Berlin . 5 B5
Klemetsrud, Oslo . 22 A4
Kličany, Prague . 24 A2
Klipriviersberg Nature Reserve, Johannesburg 13 B2
Klosterneuburg, Vienna . 31 A1
Knesset, Jerusalem . 13 b1
Knightsbridge, London . 15 c2
Kőbánya, Budapest . 7 B2
Kobbegem, Brussels . 6 A1
Kobe, Osaka . 22 B2
Kobe Harbour, Osaka . 22 B2
København, Copenhagen 10 A2
Kobylisy, Prague . 24 B2
Kobylka, Warsaw . 31 A3
Kōch'ŏk, Seoul . 26 B1
Kodaira, Tokyo . 29 A1
Kodanaka, Tokyo . 29 B2
Kodenmacho, Tokyo . 29 a5
Koekelberg, Brussels . 6 A1
Koganei, Tokyo . 29 A2
Kogarah, Sydney . 28 B1
Køge Bugt, Copenhagen . 10 B2
Koivupää, Helsinki . 12 B2
Koja, Jakarta . 13 A2
Koja Utara, Jakarta . 13 A2
Kokobunji, Tokyo . 29 A1
Kokobunji-Temple, Tokyo 29 A1
Kolarängen, Stockholm . 28 B3
Kolbotn, Oslo . 22 B3
Kolkata, Calcutta . 8 B2
Kolk, Warsaw . 31 B1
Kolokinthou, Athens . 2 B1
Kolomyagi, St. Petersburg 26 A1
Kolónos, Athens . 2 B1
Kolsås, Oslo . 22 A2
Komae, Tokyo . 29 B2
Komagome, Tokyo . 29 A3
Komazawa, Tokyo . 29 B3
Kona, Calcutta . 8 B1
Kondli, Delhi . 10 B2
Kongelige Slottet, Oslo . 22 a1
Kongelunden, Copenhagen 10 B3
Kongens Lyngby, Copenhagen 10 A3
Kongnúng, Seoul . 26 B2
Kongo, Helsinki . 12 A1
Koninklijk Paleis, Amsterdam 2 b2
Konnagar, Calcutta . 8 A2
Konohana, Osaka . 22 A3
Kōnoike, Osaka . 22 A4
Korashōche, Berlin . 5 A2
Kopanina, Prague . 24 B1
Koparkhairna, Mumbai . 20 A2
Köpenick, Berlin . 5 B4
Korangi, Karachi . 14 B2
Koremasa, Tokyo . 29 B1
Korenevo, Moscow . 19 B6
Kori, Osaka . 22 A4
Koridhallós, Athens . 2 B1
Korokoro, Wellington . 32 B2
Korokoro Stream →, Wellington . 32 B2
Kosino, Moscow . 19 B5
Kosugi, Tokyo . 29 B2
Kota, Calcutta . 8 B2
Kotelniki, Moscow . 19 C5
Kōtō-Ku, Tokyo . 29 A3
Kotrung, Calcutta . 8 A2
Kouponia, Athens . 2 B1
Kowloon, Hong Kong . 12 A2
Kowloon Park, Hong Kong 12 a2
Kowloon Peak, Hong Kong 12 A2
Kowloon Res., Hong Kong 12 A1
Kowloon Tong, Hong Kong 12 A2
Kozhukhovo, Moscow . 19 B5
Kraainem, Brussels . 6 A2
Krailling, Munich . 20 B1
Krampnitz, Berlin . 5 B1
Krampnitzsee, Berlin . 5 B1
Kranji, Sungei →, Singapore 27 A2
Kranji Industrial Estate, Singapore . 27 A2
Kraskovo, Moscow . 19 C5
Krasno-Presnenskaya, Moscow . 19 B3
Krasnogorsk, Moscow . 19 B1
Krč, Prague . 24 B2
Krestovskiye, Ostrov, St. Petersburg . 26 B1
Kreuzberg, Berlin . 5 A3
Kritzendorf, Vienna . 31 A1
Krumme Lanke, Berlin . 5 B2
Krummensee, Berlin . 5 A5
Krung Thep, Bangkok . 3 B2
Krusboda, Stockholm . 28 B3
Krylatskoye, Moscow . 19 B2
Küçükköy, Istanbul . 12 B1
Kudankita, Tokyo . 29 a3
Kudrovo, St. Petersburg 26 B3
Kulosaari, Helsinki . 12 B3
Kulturforum, Berlin . 5 b3
Kultury i Nauki, Palac, Warsaw . 31 b2
Kümch'ŏn, Seoul . 26 C1
Kumla, Stockholm . 28 B3
Kungens kurva, Stockholm 28 B1
Kungliga Slottet, Stockholm 28 b2
Kungsängen, Stockholm . 28 A1
Kungsholmen, Stockholm 28 B1
Kuningan, Jakarta . 13 B1
Kunitachi, Tokyo . 29 A1
Kunming Hu, Beijing . 4 B1
Kunratice, Prague . 24 B2
Kunsthistorischesmuseum, Vienna . 31 b1
Kuntsevo, Moscow . 19 B2
Kupchino, St. Petersburg 26 B2
Kurbağalı →, Istanbul . 12 C2
Kurihara, Tokyo . 29 A2
Kurla, Mumbai . 20 A2
Kurmuri, Mumbai . 20 A2
Kuryanovo, Moscow . 19 C4
Kuskovo, Moscow . 19 B4
Kustia, Calcutta . 8 B2
Kutsino, Tokyo . 29 B5
Kuzguncuk, Istanbul . 12 B2
Kuzyminki, Moscow . 19 B4
Kwai Chung, Hong Kong 12 A1
Kwanak, Seoul . 26 C1
Kwanak-san, Seoul . 26 C1
Kyje, Prague . 24 B3
Kyūhōji, Osaka . 22 B4

L

La Blanca, Santiago . 26 C2
La Boca, Buenos Aires . 7 B2
La Bretèche, Paris . 23 A1
La Campiña, Lima . 16 C2
La Celle-St-Cloud, Paris . 23 A1
La Ciudadela, Mexico City 18 c2
La Courneuve, Paris . 23 A3
La Dehesa, Santiago . 26 B1
La Encantada, Lima . 16 C2
La Estación, Madrid . 17 B1
La Floresta, Barcelona . 4 A1
La Fortuna, Madrid . 17 B1
La Fransa, Barcelona . 4 A1
La Garenne-Colombes, Paris 23 A2
La Giustiniana, Rome . 25 B1
La Grange, Chicago . 9 C1
La Grange Park, Chicago 9 C1
La Granja, Santiago . 26 C2
La Guardia Airport, New York . 21 B2
La Hulpe, Brussels . 6 B2
La Llacuna, Barcelona . 4 A2
La Loma, Mexico City . 18 A1
La Lucila, Buenos Aires . 7 B2
La Maladrerie, Paris . 23 A1
La Milla, Cerro, Lima . 16 B2
La Monachina, Rome . 25 B1
La Moraleja, Madrid . 17 A2
La Nopalera, Mexico City 18 C2
La Paternal, Buenos Aires 7 B2
La Perla, Lima . 16 B2
La Perouse, Sydney . 28 B2
La Pineda, Barcelona . 4 B1
La Pisana, Rome . 25 B1
La Prairie, Montreal . 19 B3
La Punta, Lima . 16 B2
La Puntigala, Barcelona . 4 A2
La Queue-en-Brie, Paris 23 B4
La Reina, Santiago . 26 B2
La Ribera, Barcelona . 4 A1
La Sagrera, Barcelona . 4 A2
La Salada, Buenos Aires 7 C2
La Scala, Milan . 18 B2
La Storta, Rome . 25 A1
La Taxonera, Barcelona . 4 A2
La Victoria, Lima . 16 B2
Laajalahti, Helsinki . 12 B2
Laajasalo, Helsinki . 12 B3
Laaksolahti, Helsinki . 12 B1
Lablāba, W. el →, Cairo . 7 A2
Lac Cisterna, Santiago . 26 C2
Lachine, Montreal . 19 B1
Lad Phrao, Bangkok . 3 B2
Ladera Heights, Los Angeles 16 C2
Ladvi, Prague . 24 B2
Łady, Warsaw . 31 C1
Lafontaine, Parc, Montreal 19 A2
Lagoa, Rio de Janeiro . 24 B1
Lagos, Lagos . 14 B2
Lagos Harbour, Lagos . 14 B2
Lagos-Ikeja Airport, Lagos 14 A1
Lagos Island, Lagos . 14 B2
Lagos Lagoon, Lagos . 14 B2
Laguna de B., Manila . 17 C2
Laim, Munich . 20 B2
Lainate, Milan . 18 A1
Lakemba, Sydney . 28 B1
Lakeside, Cape Town . 8 B1
Lakeside, Johannesburg . 13 A2
Lakeview, Chicago . 9 B3
Lakewood Park, Atlanta . 3 B2
Lakhtinskiy, St. Petersburg 26 B1
Lakhtinskiy Razliv, Oz., St. Petersburg . 26 B1
Lakshmanpur, Calcutta . 8 B1
Lal Qila, Delhi . 10 a3
Lam Tin, Hong Kong . 12 B2
Lambert, Oslo . 22 A3
Lambeth, London . 15 B3
Lambrate, Milan . 18 B2
Lambro, Parco, Milan . 18 B2
Lambton Mills, Toronto . 30 B1
Lamma I., Hong Kong . 12 B1
Lammas Park, Washington 32 B4
Landsmeer, Amsterdam . 2 A2
Landstrasse, Vienna . 31 A2
Landwehr kanal, Berlin . 5 B3
Lane Cove, Sydney . 28 A1
Lane Cove National Park, Sydney . 28 A1
Langenzersdorf, Vienna . 31 A2
Langer See, Berlin . 5 B4
Langley, Washington . 32 B2
Langley Park, Washington 32 B4
Langwald, Munich . 20 B3
Lanham, Washington . 32 B4
Lankwitz, Berlin . 5 B3
L'Annunziatella, Rome . 25 C2
Lansdowne, Cape Town . 8 A2
Lansing, Toronto . 30 A2
Lanús, Buenos Aires . 7 C2
Lapa, Rio de Janeiro . 24 B1
Laranjeiras, Rio de Janeiro 24 B1
Larísa Sta., Athens . 2 a1
Las, Warsaw . 31 B2
Las Corts, Barcelona . 4 A1
Las Kanaki, Warsaw . 31 B2
Las Piñas, Manila . 17 C1
Las Rejas, Santiago . 26 B1
Lasalle, Montreal . 19 B2
Lasek Bielański, Warsaw 31 B1
Lasek Na Kole, Warsaw . 31 B1
Laski, Warsaw . 31 B1
Latina, Madrid . 17 B1
Laurence G. Hanscom Field, Boston . 6 A2
Lauttasaari, Helsinki . 12 C2
Laval, Montreal . 19 A1
Laval-des-Rapides, Montreal 19 A2
Lavižān, Tehran . 30 A2
Lavradio, Lisbon . 14 A2
Lawndale, Chicago . 9 B2
Lawrence Heights, Toronto 30 A2
Layari, Karachi . 14 A2
Lazare, Gare St., Paris . 23 a3
Łazienkowski, Warsaw . 31 B2
Łazienkowski Park, Warsaw 31 B2
Le Blanc-Mesnil, Paris . 23 A3
Le Bourget, Paris . 23 A3
Le Chenoi, Brussels . 6 B2
Le Chesnay, Paris . 23 A1
Le Christ de Saclay, Paris 23 B1
Le Kremlin-Bicêtre, Paris 23 A3
Le Mesnil-le-Roi, Paris . 23 A1
Le Pecq, Paris . 23 A1
Le Perreux, Paris . 23 A4
Le Pin, Paris . 23 A4
Le Plessis-Robinson, Paris 23 B2
Le Plessis-Trévise, Paris 23 B4
Le Port-Marly, Paris . 23 A1
Le Pré-St-Gervais, Paris 23 A3

Le Raincy, Paris . 23 A4
Le Vésinet, Paris . 23 A1
Lea Bridge, London . 15 A3
Leaside, Toronto . 30 B2
Leblon, Rio de Janeiro . 24 B1
Lee, London . 15 B4
Leganés, Madrid . 17 C1
Legazpi, Madrid . 17 B1
Lehtisaari, Helsinki . 12 B2
Lei Yue Mun, Hong Kong 12 B2
Leião, Lisbon . 14 A1
Leicester Square, London 15 b4
Leichhardt, Sydney . 28 B1
Leith, Edinburgh . 11 B3
Lemoyne, Montreal . 19 B3
Lenin, Moscow . 19 B3
Lenino, Moscow . 19 C3
Leninskiye Gory, Moscow 19 B3
Lennox, Los Angeles . 16 C2
Leonia, New York . 21 A2
Leopardstown, Dublin . 11 B2
Leopoldau, Vienna . 31 A2
Leopoldstadt, Vienna . 31 A2
Leporovo, Moscow . 19 B4
Leppävaara, Helsinki . 12 B1
Les Lilas, Paris . 23 A3
Les Loges-en-Josas, Paris 23 B1
Les Pavillons-sous-Bois, Paris 23 A4
Lésigny, Paris . 23 B4
Lesnozavodskaya, St. Petersburg . 26 B2
L'Étang-la-Ville, Paris . 23 A1
Letná, Prague . 24 a1
Letňany, Prague . 24 B2
Levallois-Perret, Paris . 23 A2
Levent, Istanbul . 12 B1
Lewisdale, Washington . 32 B4
Lewisham, London . 15 B3
Lexington, Boston . 6 A2
Leyton, London . 15 A4
Leytonstone, London . 15 A4
L'Hay-les-Roses, Paris . 23 B3
L'Hospitalet de Llobregat, Barcelona . 4 A1
Lhotka, Prague . 24 B2
Liangshui He →, Beijing . 4 C2
Lianhua Chi, Beijing . 4 B1
Lianhua He →, Beijing . 4 B1
Libčice nad Vltavou, Prague 24 A1
Liběn, Prague . 24 B2
Liberdade, São Paulo . 26 B2
Liberdade, Ave da, Lisbon 14 b1
Liberton, Edinburgh . 11 B3
Liberty I., New York . 21 B1
Liberty State Park, New York 21 B1
Libeznice, Prague . 24 A2
Library of Congress, Washington . 32 c3
Libuš, Prague . 24 B2
Lichiao, Canton . 4 B2
Lichtenburg, Berlin . 5 A4
Lichterfelde, Berlin . 5 B3
Lidingö, Stockholm . 28 A2
Lieshi Lingyuan, Canton 4 B2
Liesing, Vienna . 31 B1
Liesing →, Vienna . 31 B1
Liffey, R. →, Dublin . 11 A1
Ligovo, St. Petersburg . 26 C1
Lijordet, Oslo . 22 A2
Likavitos, Athens . 2 b3
Likhoborka →, Moscow . 19 A3
Lilla Värtan, Stockholm . 28 A3
Lilla Essingen, Copenhagen 10 A2
Liluah, Calcutta . 8 B1
Lim Chu Kang, Singapore 27 A2
Lima, Lima . 16 B2
Limbiate, Milan . 18 A1
Limehouse, London . 15 A3
Limeil-Brévannes, Paris 23 B3
Linate, Aeroporto Internazionale di, Milan 18 B2
Linbropark, Johannesburg 13 A2
Lincoln, Boston . 6 A2
Lincoln Center, New York 21 b2
Lincoln Heights, Los Angeles 16 B3
Lincoln Park, Chicago . 9 B3
Lincoln Park, New York . 21 B1
Lincoln Park, San Francisco 25 B1
Lincolnwood, Chicago . 9 A2
Linda-a-Pastora, Lisbon 14 A1
Linden, Johannesburg . 13 A1
Linden, Wellington . 32 A1
Lindenberg, Berlin . 5 A4
Lindöya, Oslo . 22 A3
Liniers, Buenos Aires . 7 B1
Linkebeek, Brussels . 6 B2
Linksfield, Johannesburg 13 A2
Linmeyer, Johannesburg 13 B2
Linna, Helsinki . 12 B2
Lintuvaara, Helsinki . 12 B1
Lion Rock Country Park, Hong Kong . 12 A2
Liouimi, Athens . 2 B2
Liqizhuang, Tianjin . 30 B2
Lisboa, Lisbon . 14 A2
Lisbon = Lisboa, Lisbon 14 A2
Lishui, Canton . 4 B1
Little B., Sydney . 28 B2
Little Calumet →, Chicago 9 D3
Little Ferry, New York . 21 A1
Little Italy, New York . 21 e2
Little Mermaid, Copenhagen 10 a4
Little Rouge →, Toronto 30 A4
Little Tokyo, Los Angeles 16 c2
Liuhang, Shanghai . 27 A1
Liurong Temple, Canton . 4 B2
Liuxi, Canton . 4 B2
Liverpool Street, London 15 a5
Livry-Gargan, Paris . 23 A4
Ljan, Oslo . 22 A3
Llano de Can Gineu, Barcelona . 4 A1
Llobregat →, Barcelona . 4 A1
Lo Aranguiz, Santiago . 26 B2
Lo Boza, Santiago . 26 B1
Lo Chau, Hong Kong . 12 B2
Lo Espejo, Santiago . 26 C1
Lo Hermida, Santiago . 26 B2
Lo Prado, Santiago . 26 B1
Lo So Shing, Hong Kong 12 B1
Lo Wai, Hong Kong . 12 A2
Loanhead, Edinburgh . 11 B3
Lobau, Vienna . 31 A2
Lobos, Pt., San Francisco 25 B1
Locham, Munich . 20 B1
Lochino, Prague . 24 B1
Lochkov, Prague . 24 B1
Lochnausen, Munich . 20 A3
Lodi, New York . 21 A1
Lodi Estate, Delhi . 10 B2
Logan Int. Airport, Boston 6 A4
Logan Square, Chicago . 9 B2
Lognes-Émerainville, Aérodrome de, Paris . 23 B4
Lôhme, Berlin . 5 A5
Lokolbet, Karachi . 14 A2
Lomas Chapultepec, Mexico City . 18 B1

Lomas de San Angel Inn, Mexico City . 18 B1
Lomas de Zamora, Buenos Aires . 7 C2
Lombardy East, Johannesburg 13 A2
Lomus Reforma, Mexico City 18 B1
London, London . 15 A3
London Bridge, London . 15 b5
London City Airport, London 15 A4
London Zoo, London . 15 A3
Long B., Sydney . 28 B2
Long Branch, Toronto . 30 B1
Long Brook →, Washington 32 C2
Long Ditton, London . 15 B2
Long I., Boston . 6 A4
Long Island City, New York 21 B2
Long Street, Cape Town 8 c2
Longchamp, Hippodrôme de, Paris . 23 A2
Longhua Pagoda, Shanghai 27 B1
Longhua Park, Shanghai 27 B1
Longjingcun Slough, Chicago 9 C1
Longtan Hu →, Beijing . 4 B2
Longue-Pointe, Montreal 19 A3
Longueuil, Montreal . 19 A3
Loni, Delhi . 10 A2
Loop, The, Chicago . 9 c1
Lord's Cricket Ground, London . 15 A2
Loreto, Milan . 18 B2
Los Angeles Int. Airport, Los Angeles . 16 C2
Los Cerrillos, Aeropuerto, Santiago . 26 B1
Los Nietos, Los Angeles . 16 C4
Los Olivos, Lima . 16 A2
Los Reyes, Mexico City . 18 B2
Lot, Brussels . 6 B1
Loughlinstown, Dublin . 11 B3
Loures, Lisbon . 14 A1
Louveciennes, Paris . 23 A1
Louvre, Musée du, Paris 23 b4
Louvre, Palais du, Paris . 23 b4
Lower East Side, New York 21 e2
Lower Hutt, Wellington . 32 B2
Lower Manhattan, New York 21 e1
Lower New York B., New York . 21 C1
Lower Shing Mun Res., Hong Kong . 12 A2
Lowry Bay, Wellington . 32 B2
Lu Xun Museum, Beijing 4 b1
Lubars, Berlin . 5 A3
Ludgvetela, Munich . 20 A1
Ludu, Canton . 4 B2
Lumiar, Lisbon . 14 A2
Lumphini Park, Bangkok 3 B2
Lundtofte, Copenhagen . 10 A3
Lung Mei, Hong Kong . 12 A2
Luojiang, Canton . 4 B2
Lusthein, Munich . 20 A3
Luwan, Shanghai . 27 B1
Luxembourg, Palais du, Paris 23 c4
Luzhniki Sports Centre, Moscow . 19 B3
Lyndhurst, New York . 21 B1
Lynn, Boston . 6 A4
Lynn Harbor, Boston . 6 A4
Lynn Woods Res., Boston 6 A3
Lyon, Gare de, Paris . 23 c5
Lyons, Chicago . 9 C2
Lysaker, Oslo . 22 A2
Lysakerselva →, Oslo . 22 A2
Lysolaje, Prague . 24 B2
Lyubertsy, Moscow . 19 B4
Lyublino, Moscow . 19 B4

M

Ma Nam Wat, Hong Kong 12 A2
Ma On Shan Country Park, Hong Kong . 12 A2
Ma'ale Adumim, Jerusalem 13 B2
Ma'ale Ha Khamisha, Jerusalem . 13 B1
Ma'ale Mikhmas, Jerusalem 13 B2
Maantiekylä, Helsinki . 12 A3
Maarifa, Baghdad . 3 B2
Mabato Pt., Manila . 17 C2
Macaco, Morro do, Rio de Janeiro . 24 B2
McCook, Chicago . 9 C2
Machelen, Brussels . 6 A2
Machida, Tokyo . 29 B1
Maciołki, Warsaw . 31 B2
Mackayville, Montreal . 19 A3
McKerrow, Wellington . 32 B2
McKinley Park, Chicago 9 C2
Mclean, Washington . 32 B2
Macopocho, R. →, Santiago 26 B1
Macquette Park, Chicago 9 C2
Macul, Santiago . 26 B2
Madame Tussaud's, London 15 a3
Madhudaha, Calcutta . 8 B2
Madhyamgram, Calcutta 8 A2
Mádinet Nasr, Cairo . 7 A2
Madison Avenue, New York 21 c2
Madison Square, New York 21 d2
Madrid, Madrid . 17 B1
Madrona, Barcelona . 4 A1
Maesawa, Tokyo . 29 A2
Magdalena, Lima . 16 B2
Magdalena Contreras, Mexico City . 18 C1
Maghreb, Baghdad . 3 A2
Maginu, Tokyo . 29 B2
Magliana, Rome . 25 B1
Magny-les-Hameaux, Paris 23 B1
Magonoy, Manila . 17 A2
Mahalaxmi, Mumbai . 20 a1
Maheshtala, Calcutta . 8 C1
Mahim, Mumbai . 20 A2
Mahim B., Mumbai . 20 A2
Mahlsdorf, Berlin . 5 A4
Mahmoodabad, Karachi 14 B2
Mahrauli, Delhi . 10 B1
Mahul, Mumbai . 20 A2
Maida Vale, London . 15 A2
Maidstone, Cape Town . 8 A2
Maipú, Santiago . 26 C1
Maisonneuve, Parc, Montreal 19 A2
Maisons-Alfort, Paris . 23 B3
Maisons-Laffitte, Paris . 23 A1
Maissoneuve, Montreal . 19 A2
Maitland, Cape Town . 8 A1
Makati, Manila . 17 B2
Mākiniitty, Helsinki . 12 A2
Mala Strana, Prague . 24 b1
Malabar, Mumbai . 20 B1
Malabar Hill, Mumbai . 20 B1
Malabar Pt., Mumbai . 20 B1

Malabon, Manila . 17 B1
Malacañang Palace, Manila 17 B1
Malahide, Dublin . 11 A3
Malakhovka, Moscow . 19 C6
Malakoff, Paris . 23 B2
Mälarhöjden, Stockholm 28 B1
Malate, Manila . 17 B1
Malay Quarter, Cape Town 8 c2
Malaya Neva, St. Petersburg 26 B1
Malaya-Okhta, St. Petersburg 26 B2
Malchow, Berlin . 5 A3
Malden, London . 15 B2
Malden, London . 15 B2
Maleizen, Brussels . 6 B2
Malešice, Prague . 24 B2
Malir →, Karachi . 14 B2
Mall, The, Washington . 32 b2
Malleny Mills, Edinburgh 11 B2
Malmi, Helsinki . 12 B2
Malmøya, Oslo . 22 A3
Målov, Copenhagen . 10 A2
Malpasso, Ost., Rome . 25 C1
Malton, Toronto . 30 A1
Malvern, Johannesburg 13 B2
Malvern, Melbourne . 17 B2
Malvern, Toronto . 30 A3
Mamonovo, Moscow . 19 B2
Mampang Prapatan, Jakarta 13 B1
Mampukuji, Tokyo . 29 B2
Man Budrukh, Mumbai . 20 A2
Man Khurd, Mumbai . 20 A2
Mandaluyong, Manila . 17 B2
Mandaoli, Delhi . 10 A2
Mandaqui →, São Paulo . 26 A2
Mandoli, Delhi . 10 A2
Mandvi, Mumbai . 20 B1
Manenberg, Cape Town . 8 A2
Mang Kung Uk, Hong Kong 12 B2
Mangolpuri, Delhi . 10 A1
Manguinhos, Aéroporto, Rio de Janeiro . 24 B1
Mangwon, Seoul . 26 B1
Manhattan, New York . 21 C2
Manhattan Beach, New York 21 C2
Manila, Manila . 17 B1
Manila B., Manila . 17 B1
Mankhaa, Helsinki . 12 B2
Manly, Sydney . 28 A2
Mannswörth, Vienna . 31 B3
Manor Park, London . 15 A4
Manor Park, Wellington 32 A2
Manora, Karachi . 14 B1
Manquehue, Cerro, Santiago 26 B2
Mansfield, London . 15 B2
Manzanares, Canal de, Madrid . 17 C2
Mao Mausoleum, Beijing 4 c2
Map'o, Seoul . 26 B1
Maracanã, Rio de Janeiro 24 B1
Maraoli, Mumbai . 20 A2
Marblehead, Boston . 6 A4
Marcelin, Warsaw . 31 B1
Mareil-Marly, Paris . 23 A1
Margareten, Vienna . 31 A2
Marghera, Venice . 31 A2
Maridalen, Oslo . 22 A3
Maridalsvatnet, Oslo . 22 A3
Mariendorf, Berlin . 5 B3
Marienplatz, Munich . 20 b2
Marikina →, Manila . 17 B2
Marin City, San Francisco 25 A1
Marin Headlands State Park, San Francisco . 25 A2
Marin Pen., San Francisco 25 A2
Marina del Rey, Los Angeles 16 C2
Marine Drive, Mumbai . 20 b1
Maritim, Museu, Barcelona 4 c2
Markham, Toronto . 30 A2
Marki, Warsaw . 31 B2
Markland Wood, Toronto 30 B1
Marly, Forêt de, Paris . 23 A1
Marly-le-Roi, Paris . 23 A1
Marne →, Paris . 23 B4
Marne-la-Vallée, Paris . 23 A4
Marolles-en-Brie, Paris . 23 B4
Maroubra, Sydney . 28 B2
Marquette Park, Chicago 9 C2
Marrickville, Sydney . 28 B1
Marsfield, Sydney . 28 A1
Marshall Field's, Chicago 9 c2
Marte, Campo de, São Paulo 26 B2
Martesana, Navíglio della, Milan . 18 A2
Martin Luther King National Historic Site, Atlanta . 3 B2
Martinez, Buenos Aires . 7 A1
Martinkylä, Helsinki . 12 A2
Martinsried, Munich . 20 B1
Maruko, Tokyo . 29 B3
Marunouchi, Tokyo . 29 b4
Marusino, Moscow . 19 B5
Maryino, Moscow . 19 B4
Maryland, Singapore . 27 B2
Marylebone, London . 15 A2
Marymont, Warsaw . 31 B1
Marysin Wawerski, Warsaw 31 B2
Marzahn, Berlin . 5 A4
Mascot, Sydney . 28 B2
Masmo, Stockholm . 28 B1
Maspeth, New York . 21 B2
Masr el Gedida, Cairo . 7 A2
Masr el Qadima, Cairo . 7 A2
Massachusett's Inst. of Tech., Boston . 6 A3
Massamá, Lisbon . 14 A1
Massy, Toronto . 30 A3
Massy →, Toronto . 30 A3
Massy, Paris . 23 B2
Matinha, Lisbon . 14 A2
Matramann, Jakarta . 13 B2
Matsubara, Osaka . 22 B3
Mattapan, Boston . 6 B3
Mátyásföld, Budapest . 7 A3
Mátyástemplom, Budapest 7 b1
Mau Tso Ngam, Hong Kong 12 A2
Mauer, Vienna . 31 B1
Mauripur, Karachi . 14 A1
Maxhof, Munich . 20 B1
Maybury, Johannesburg 13 A2
Mayfair, London . 15 b3
Mayfair, Johannesburg . 13 B1
Mayor, Plaza, Madrid . 17 b2
Maywood, Chicago . 9 B1
Maywood, New Jersey . 21 A1
Maywood, New York . 21 A1
Mazagaon, Mumbai . 20 B2
Me'a She' Arim, Jerusalem 13 a2
Meadowbank Park, Sydney 28 A1
Medford, Boston . 6 A3
Mediodia, Madrid . 17 B2
Medvezhiy Ozyora, Moscow 19 A5

Meguro →, Tokyo . 29 B3
Meguro-Ku, Tokyo . 29 B3
Mehplapur, Delhi . 10 B1
Mehrābād Airport, Tehran 30 A1
Mehram Nagar, Delhi . 10 B1
Mehrow, Berlin . 5 A4
Mei Lanfang, Beijing . 4 a2
Meidling, Vienna . 31 A2
Méier, Rio de Janeiro . 24 B1
Meiji Shrine, Tokyo . 29 b1
Meise, Brussels . 6 A1
Mejiro, Tokyo . 29 A3
Melbourne, Melbourne . 17 A1
Melbourne, Melbourne . 17 A1
Melkki, Helsinki . 12 C2
Mellunkylä, Helsinki . 12 B3
Mellunmäki, Helsinki . 12 B3
Melrose, Boston . 6 A3
Melrose, New York . 21 B1
Melrose Park, Chicago . 9 B1
Melsbroek, Brussels . 6 A2
Menteng, Jakarta . 13 B1
Méranitsae →, Paris . 23 B1
Mercamadrid, Madrid . 17 B2
Merced, L., San Francisco 25 B2
Meredale, Johannesburg 13 B1
Merlimau, P., Singapore 27 B2
Merri Cr. →, Melbourne . 17 A2
Merrion, Dublin . 11 B2
Merrionette Park, Chicago 9 C2
Merton, London . 15 B2
Mesgarābad, Tehran . 30 B3
Meshcherskiy, Moscow . 19 B2
Messe, Vienna . 31 A2
Messe-palast, Vienna . 31 c1
Metanópoli, Milan . 18 B2
Metropolitan Museum of Art, New York . 21 b3
Meudon, Paris . 23 B2
Mevaseret Tsiyon, Jerusalem 13 B1
Mevo Beitar, Jerusalem . 13 B1
Mexico, Ciudad de, Mexico City . 18 B1
Meyersdal, Johannesburg 13 B2
Mezzano, Milan . 18 A2
Mezzate, Milan . 18 B2
Miadong, Seoul . 26 B2
Miami, Miami . 18 B2
Miami Beach, Miami . 18 B2
Miami Canal →, Miami . 18 A1
Miami Shores, Miami . 18 B2
Miami Springs, Miami . 18 B1
Miasto, Warsaw . 31 B2
Michałowice, Warsaw . 31 B1
Michigan Avenue, Chicago 9 b2
Michle, Prague . 24 B2
Middle Harbour, Sydney 28 A2
Middle Hd., Sydney . 28 A2
Middle Park, Melbourne 17 B1
Middle Village, New York 21 B2
Middlesex Fells Reservation, Boston . 6 A3
Midi, Gare du, Brussels . 6 c1
Midland Beach, New York 21 C1
Miedzeszyn, Warsaw . 31 B2
Międzylesie, Warsaw . 31 B2
Miessaari, Helsinki . 12 C1
Miguel Hidalgo, Mexico City 18 B1
Mikhelysona, Moscow . 19 B5
Milano, Milan . 18 B2
Milano Due, Milan . 18 B2
Milano San Felice, Milan 18 B2
Milbertshofen, Munich . 20 A2
Mill Hill, London . 15 A2
Millennium Dome, London 15 A4
Miller Meadow, Chicago 9 B2
Millerhill, Edinburgh . 11 B3
Millers Point, Sydney . 28 a1
Milltown, Dublin . 11 B2
Millwood, Washington . 32 B4
Milnerton, Cape Town . 8 A1
Milon-la-Chapelle, Paris 23 B1
Milton, Boston . 6 B3
Milton Bridge, Edinburgh 11 B2
Mimico, Toronto . 30 B2
Mimico →, Toronto . 30 A1
Minami, Osaka . 22 A4
Minamitsunashima, Tokyo 29 B2
Minato, Osaka . 22 B3
Minato-Ku, Tokyo . 29 B3
Minshât el Bekkari, Cairo 7 A1
Minute Man Nat. Hist. Park, Boston . 6 A2
Miraflores, Lima . 16 B2
Miramar, Wellington . 32 B1
Misericordia, Sa. da, Rio de Janeiro . 24 B1
Mission, San Francisco . 25 B2
Mississauga, Toronto . 30 B1
Mitaka, Tokyo . 29 A2
Mitcham, London . 15 B3
Mitcham Common, London 15 B3
Mitchell's Plain, Cape Town 8 B2
Mitino, Moscow . 19 A2
Mitte, Berlin . 5 A3
Mittel Isarkanal →, Munich 20 A3
Mixcoac, Mexico City . 18 B1
Mixcoac, Presa de, Mexico City . 18 B1
Miyakojima, Osaka . 22 A4
Mizonokuchi, Tokyo . 29 B2
Mizue, Tokyo . 29 A4
Mlocinski Park, Warsaw 31 B1
Młociny, Warsaw . 31 B1
Mnevniki, Moscow . 19 B2
Moba, Lagos . 14 B2
Moczydło, Warsaw . 31 B1
Modderfontein, Johannesburg 13 A2
Modfany, Prague . 24 B2
Mogyoród, Budapest . 7 A3
Moinho Velho, Cor. →, São Paulo . 26 B2
Mok, Seoul . 26 B1
Mokotów, Warsaw . 31 B2
Molenbeek-Saint-Jean, Brussels . 6 A1
Molino de Rosas, Mexico City 18 B1
Mollem, Brussels . 6 A1
Mollins de Rey, Barcelona 4 A1
Mondeor, Johannesburg 13 B2
Moneda, Palacio de la, Santiago . 26 B2
Monestò, Rio de Janeiro 24 B1
Mong Kok, Hong Kong . 12 B2
Monkstown, Dublin . 11 B3
Monnickendam, Amsterdam 2 A3
Monrovia, Los Angeles . 16 B4
Monsanto, Parque Florestal de, Lisbon . 14 A1
Mont Royal, Montreal . 19 A2
Mont-Royal, Parc, Montreal 19 A2
Montana de Montjuich, Barcelona . 4 A1
Monte Chingolo, Buenos Aires . 7 C2

Monte Palatino, *Rome* — 25 c3
Montebello, *Los Angeles* — 16 B4
Montemor, *Lisbon* — 14 A1
Monterey Park, *Los Angeles* — 16 B4
Montespaccato, *Rome* — 25 B1
Montessori, *Paris* — 23 A1
Monteverde Nuovo, *Rome* — 25 B1
Montfermeil, *Paris* — 23 A4
Montigny-le-Bretonneux, *Paris* — 23 B1
Montjay-la-Tour, *Paris* — 23 A4
Montjuïc, Parc de, *Barcelona* — 4 c1
Montparnasse, Gare, *Paris* — 23 A2
Montréal, *Montreal* — 19 A2
Montréal, Î. de, *Montreal* — 19 A2
Montréal, Univ. de, *Montreal* — 19 A2
Montréal Est, *Montreal* — 19 A2
Montréal Nord, *Montreal* — 19 A1
Montréal Ouest, *Montreal* — 19 B1
Montreuil, *Paris* — 23 A3
Montrouge, *Paris* — 23 B2
Montserrat, *Buenos Aires* — 7 B2
Monza, *Milan* — 18 A2
Monzoro, *Milan* — 18 B1
Móoca, *São Paulo* — 26 B2
Moonachie, *New York* — 21 B1
Moonee Ponds, *Melbourne* — 17 A1
Moonee Valley Racecourse, *Melbourne* — 17 A1
Moosach, *Munich* — 20 A1
Mora, *Mumbai* — 20 B2
Moratalaz, *Madrid* — 17 B2
Mörby, *Stockholm* — 28 A2
Morden, *London* — 15 B2
Morée →, *Paris* — 23 A3
Morgan Park, *Chicago* — 9 C3
Moriguchi, *Osaka* — 22 A4
Morivione, *Milan* — 18 B2
Morningside, *Edinburgh* — 11 B2
Morningside, *Johannesburg* — 13 A2
Morningside, *Washington* — 32 C4
Morro Solar, Cerro, *Lima* — 16 C2
Mortlake, *Lisbon* — 15 B2
Mortlake, *Sydney* — 28 B1
Morton Grove, *Chicago* — 9 A2
Morumbi, *São Paulo* — 26 B1
Moscavide, *Lisbon* — 14 A2
Moscow = Moskva, *Moscow* — 19 B3
Moskhaton, *Athens* — 2 B2
Moskva, *Moscow* — 19 B3
Moskva →, *Moscow* — 19 B2
Moskvoretsky, *Moscow* — 19 B3
Mosman, *Sydney* — 28 A2
Móstoles, *Madrid* — 17 C1
Moti Bagh, *Delhi* — 10 B2
Motol, *Prague* — 24 B1
Motsa, *Jerusalem* — 13 B2
Motsa Ilit, *Jerusalem* — 13 B1
Motspur Park, *London* — 15 B2
Mottingham, *London* — 15 B4
Moulin Rouge, *Paris* — 23 a3
Mount Dennis, *Toronto* — 30 A2
Mount Greenwood, *Chicago* — 9 C2
Mount Hood Memorial Park, *Boston* — 6 A3
Mount Merrion, *Dublin* — 11 B2
Mount Rainier, *Washington* — 32 B4
Mount Vernon, *New York* — 21 A3
Mount Vernon Square, *Washington* — 32 a2
Mount Zion, *Jerusalem* — 13 b3
Mozarthaus, *Vienna* — 31 b2
Müggelberge, *Berlin* — 5 B4
Müggelheim, *Berlin* — 5 B5
Muggiò, *Milan* — 18 A2
Mughal Gardens, *Delhi* — 1 c1
Mühleiten, *Vienna* — 31 A3
Mühlenfliess →, *Berlin* — 5 A5
Muiden, *Amsterdam* — 2 A3
Muiderpoort Station, *Amsterdam* — 2 b3
Muizenberg, *Cape Town* — 8 B1
Mujahidpur, *Delhi* — 10 B2
Mukandpur, *Delhi* — 10 A2
Mukhmas, *Jerusalem* — 13 A2
Muko →, *Osaka* — 22 A3
Mukojima, *Tokyo* — 29 A3
Mulbarton, *Johannesburg* — 13 B2
Mumbai, *Mumbai* — 20 B2
Mumbai Harbour, *Mumbai* — 20 B2
Münchehofe, *Berlin* — 5 B5
München, *Munich* — 20 B2
Munich = München, *Munich* — 20 B2
Munkkiniemi, *Helsinki* — 12 B2
Munro, *Buenos Aires* — 7 B1
Murai Res., *Singapore* — 27 A2
Muranów, *Warsaw* — 31 B1
Murino, *St. Petersburg* — 26 B2
Murrayfield, *Edinburgh* — 11 B2
Musashino, *Tokyo* — 29 A2
Museu Nacional, *Rio de Janeiro* — 24 B1
Mushin, *Lagos* — 14 A2
Musiktheater, *Amsterdam* — 2 b2
Muslim Quarter, *Jerusalem* — 13 a3
Musocco, *Milan* — 18 B1
Mustansiriya, *Baghdad* — 3 A2
Musturud, *Cairo* — 7 A2
Muswell Hill, *London* — 15 A2
Mutanabi, *Baghdad* — 3 B2
Muthana, *Baghdad* — 3 B2
Myakinino, *Moscow* — 19 B2
Mykerinos, *Cairo* — 7 B1
Myllypuro, *Helsinki* — 12 B3

N

Nacka, *Stockholm* — 28 B3
Nada, *Osaka* — 22 A2
Naenae, *Wellington* — 32 B2
Nærsnes, *Oslo* — 22 B1
Nagata, *Osaka* — 22 B1
Nagatsuta, *Tokyo* — 29 B2
Nagytétény, *Budapest* — 7 B1
Nahant, *Boston* — 6 A4
Nahant B., *Boston* — 6 A4
Nahant Harbor, *Boston* — 6 A4
Nahr Dijlah →, *Baghdad* — 3 B2
Najafgarh Drain →, *Delhi* — 10 B1
Nakahara-Ku, *Tokyo* — 29 B3
Nakano-Ku, *Tokyo* — 29 A2
Namgjawa, *Seoul* — 26 B1
Namsan Park, *Seoul* — 26 B1
Namyŏng, *Seoul* — 26 B1
Nanbiancun, *Canton* — 8 B1
Nanchang He →, *Beijing* — 4 B1
Nandang, *Canton* — 8 B2
Nandian, *Tianjin* — 30 B2
Nangal Dewat, *Delhi* — 10 B1
Nanwa, *Osaka* — 22 B3
Nanmenwai, *Tianjin* — 30 B1
Nanole, *Mumbai* — 20 A2
Nanpu Bridge, *Shanghai* — 27 B2

Nanshi, *Shanghai* — 27 B1
Nantasket Beach, *Boston* — 6 B4
Nanterre, *Paris* — 23 A2
Naoabad, *Calcutta* — 8 C2
Napier Mole, *Karachi* — 14 B1
Naraina, *Delhi* — 10 B1
Nariman Point, *Mumbai* — 20 c1
Nariman Pt., *Mumbai* — 20 B1
Nǎrua, *Tehran* — 30 A2
Naruo, *Osaka* — 22 A3
Näsby, *Stockholm* — 28 A2
Näsbypark, *Stockholm* — 28 A2
Nathan Road, *Hong Kong* — 12 a2
National Maritime Museum, *San Francisco* — 25 a1
National Museum, *Bangkok* — 3 b1
Nationalmuseum, *Stockholm* — 28 b2
Natolin, *Warsaw* — 31 C2
Naturhistorischesmuseum, *Vienna* — 31 b1
Naucalpan de Juárez, *Mexico City* — 18 B1
Naupada, *Mumbai* — 20 A2
Navíglio di Pavia, *Milan* — 18 B1
Navíglio Grande, *Milan* — 18 B1
Navona, Piazza, *Rome* — 25 b2
Navotas, *Manila* — 17 B1
Navy Pier, *Chicago* — 9 b3
Nazal Hikmat Beg, *Baghdad* — 3 A2
Nazimabad, *Karachi* — 14 A2
Nazlet el Simmân, *Cairo* — 7 B1
Néa Alexandria, *Athens* — 2 B2
Néa Faliron, *Athens* — 2 A2
Néa Ionía, *Athens* — 2 A2
Néa Liósia, *Athens* — 2 A2
Néa Smírni, *Athens* — 2 B2
Neapolis, *Athens* — 2 b2
Near North, *Chicago* — 9 b2
Nebušice, *Prague* — 24 B1
Nederhorst, *Amsterdam* — 2 B3
Nedlitz, *Berlin* — 5 B1
Nee Soon, *Singapore* — 27 A3
Needham Heights, *Boston* — 6 B2
Nekrasovka, *Moscow* — 19 B5
Nemchinovka, *Moscow* — 19 B1
Nemzeti Muz, *Budapest* — 7 c3
Neponset, *New York* — 21 C2
Nerima-Ku, *Tokyo* — 29 A3
Nesodden, *Oslo* — 22 B3
Nesoddtangen, *Oslo* — 22 A3
Nesøya, *Oslo* — 22 A2
Neu Aubing, *Munich* — 20 B1
Neu Buch, *Berlin* — 5 A4
Neu Fahrland, *Berlin* — 5 B1
Neu Lindenberg, *Berlin* — 5 A4
Neubiberg, *Munich* — 20 B3
Neue Hofburg, *Vienna* — 31 b1
Neuenhagen, *Berlin* — 5 A5
Neuessling, *Vienna* — 31 A3
Neuhausen, *Munich* — 20 B2
Neuherberg, *Munich* — 20 A2
Neuhönow, *Berlin* — 5 A5
Neuilly-Plaisance, *Paris* — 23 A4
Neuilly-sur-Marne, *Paris* — 23 A4
Neuilly-sur-Seine, *Paris* — 23 A2
Neukagran, *Vienna* — 31 A2
Neukettenhof, *Vienna* — 31 B2
Neukölln, *Berlin* — 5 B3
Neuperlach, *Munich* — 20 B2
Neuried, *Munich* — 20 B1
Neustift am Walde, *Vienna* — 31 A1
Neussisentrunn, *Vienna* — 31 A1
Neuwaldegg, *Vienna* — 31 A1
Neva →, *St. Petersburg* — 26 B2
Nevės, *Rio de Janeiro* — 24 B2
New Baghdād, *Baghdad* — 3 B2
New Barakpur, *Calcutta* — 8 A2
New Brighton, *New York* — 21 C1
New Canada, *Johannesburg* — 13 B1
New Canada Dam, *Johannesburg* — 13 B1
New Carrollton, *Washington* — 32 B4
New Cross, *London* — 15 B3
New Delhi, *Delhi* — 10 B2
New Dorp, *New York* — 21 C1
New Dorp Beach, *New York* — 21 C1
New Malden, *London* — 15 B2
New Milford, *New York* — 21 A1
New Territories, *Hong Kong* — 12 A1
New Toronto, *Toronto* — 30 B1
New Town, *Edinburgh* — 11 B2
New Utrecht, *New York* — 21 C2
Newark B., *New York* — 21 B1
Newbattle, *Edinburgh* — 11 B3
Newbury Park, *London* — 15 A4
Newcraighall, *Edinburgh* — 11 B3
Newham, *London* — 15 A4
Newhaven, *Edinburgh* — 11 B2
Newington, *London* — 15 c5
Newlands, *Johannesburg* — 13 B1
Newlands, *Wellington* — 32 B1
Newport, *Melbourne* — 17 B1
Newton, *Boston* — 6 A3
Newtonbrook, *Toronto* — 30 A2
Newtongrange, *Edinburgh* — 11 B3
Newtonville, *Boston* — 6 A2
Newtown, *Sydney* — 28 B2
Neyagawa, *Osaka* — 22 A4
Ngaio, *Wellington* — 32 B1
Ngau Chi Wan, *Hong Kong* — 12 A2
Ngau Tau Kok, *Hong Kong* — 12 B2
Ngauranga, *Wellington* — 32 B1
Ngong Shuen Chau, *Hong Kong* — 12 B1
Ngua Kok Wan, *Hong Kong* — 12 A1
Nhǎvǎrǎn, *Tehran* — 30 A2
Nibra, *Calcutta* — 8 B1
Nidal, *Baghdad* — 3 B2
Niddrie, *Edinburgh* — 11 B3
Niddrie, *Melbourne* — 17 A1
Nieder Neuendorf, *Berlin* — 5 A2
Niederschöneweide, *Berlin* — 5 B3
Niederschönhausen, *Berlin* — 5 A3
Niemeyer, *Rio de Janeiro* — 24 B1
Nieuw Zuid, *Amsterdam* — 2 c2
Nieuwe Kerk, *Amsterdam* — 2 a1
Nieuwendam, *Amsterdam* — 2 A2
Nihonbashi, *Tokyo* — 29 b5
Niipperi, *Helsinki* — 12 B1
Nikaia, *Athens* — 2 B1
Nikolassee, *Berlin* — 5 B2
Nikolskiy, *Moscow* — 19 B2
Nikolyskoye, *Moscow* — 19 B5
Nikulino, *Moscow* — 19 B2
Nil, Nahr en →, *Cairo* — 7 A2
Nile = Nil, Nahr en →, *Cairo* — 7 B2
Niles, *Chicago* — 9 A2
Nimta, *Calcutta* — 8 A2
Ningyuan, *Tianjin* — 30 B2
Nippa, *Tokyo* — 29 B2
Nippori, *Tokyo* — 29 A3
Nishi, *Osaka* — 22 B3
Nishinari-Ku, *Osaka* — 22 B3

Nishiyodogawa, *Osaka* — 22 A3
Niterói, *Rio de Janeiro* — 24 B2
Nob Hill, *San Francisco* — 25 b2
Nockeby, *Stockholm* — 28 B1
Noel Park, *London* — 15 A3
Nogatino, *Moscow* — 19 B4
Nogent-sur-Marne, *Paris* — 23 A3
Noida, *Delhi* — 10 B2
Noiseau, *Paris* — 23 B4
Noisiel, *Paris* — 23 A4
Noisy-le-Grand, *Paris* — 23 A4
Noisy-le-Roi, *Paris* — 23 A1
Noisy-le-Sec, *Paris* — 23 A3
Nokkala, *Helsinki* — 12 C1
Nomentana, *Rome* — 25 B2
Nonakashinden, *Tokyo* — 29 A2
Nongminyundong Jiangxiuso, *Canton* — 8 B2
Nonhyŏn, *Seoul* — 26 B2
Nonthaburi, *Bangkok* — 3 A1
Noon Gun, *Cape Town* — 8 c1
Noorder Kerk, *Amsterdam* — 2 a1
Noordgesig, *Johannesburg* — 13 B1
Noordzeekanaal, *Amsterdam* — 2 A1
Nord, Gare du, *Paris* — 23 a4
Nordrand-Siedlung, *Vienna* — 31 A2
Nordstrand, *Oslo* — 22 A3
Normandale, *Wellington* — 32 B2
Nørrebro, *Copenhagen* — 10 a1
Norridge, *Chicago* — 9 B2
Norrmalm, *Stockholm* — 28 a1
North Arlington, *New York* — 21 B1
North Bay Village, *Miami* — 18 A2
North Bergen, *New York* — 21 B1
North Branch Chicago River →, *Chicago* — 9 B2
North Bull Island, *Dublin* — 11 A3
North Cambridge, *Boston* — 6 A3
North Cheam, *London* — 15 B2
North Cohasset, *Boston* — 6 B4
North Cray, *London* — 15 B4
North Decatur, *Atlanta* — 3 B3
North Druid Hills, *Atlanta* — 3 B3
North Esk →, *Edinburgh* — 11 B2
North Gyle, *Edinburgh* — 11 B2
North Hackensack, *New York* — 21 A1
North Harbor, *Manila* — 17 B1
North Hd., *Sydney* — 28 A2
North Hollywood, *Los Angeles* — 16 B2
North Lexington, *Boston* — 6 A2
North Miami, *Miami* — 18 A2
North Miami Beach, *Miami* — 18 A2
North Nazimabad, *Karachi* — 14 A2
North Pt., *Hong Kong* — 12 B2
North Queensferry, *Edinburgh* — 11 A1
North Quincy, *Boston* — 6 B3
North Res., *Boston* — 6 A3
North Riverside, *Chicago* — 9 B2
North Saugus, *Boston* — 6 A3
North Shore Channel →, *Chicago* — 9 B2
North Springfield, *Washington* — 32 C2
North Sudbury, *Boston* — 6 A1
North Sydney, *Sydney* — 28 B2
North Woolwich, *London* — 15 A4
North York, *Toronto* — 30 A2
Northbridge, *Sydney* — 28 A2
Northbridge Park, *Sydney* — 28 A2
Northcliff, *Johannesburg* — 13 A1
Northcote, *Melbourne* — 17 A2
Northlake, *Chicago* — 9 B1
Northmount, *Toronto* — 30 A2
Northolt, *London* — 15 A1
Northumberland Heath, *London* — 15 B5
Northwood, *London* — 15 A1
Norumbega Res., *Boston* — 6 A2
Norwood, *Johannesburg* — 13 A2
Norwood Park, *Chicago* — 9 B2
Noryangjin, *Seoul* — 26 B1
Nossa Senhora de Candelária, *Rio de Janeiro* — 24 a2
Nossa Senhora do Ó, *São Paulo* — 26 B1
Nossegem, *Brussels* — 6 A1
Notre-Dame, *Montreal* — 19 B3
Notre-Dame, *Paris* — 23 c4
Notre-Dame, Bois, *Paris* — 23 A4
Notre-Dame-de-Grace, *Montreal* — 19 A2
Notting Hill, *London* — 15 b1
Nova Milanese, *Milan* — 18 A2
Novate Milanese, *Milan* — 18 A1
Novaya Derevnya, *St. Petersburg* — 26 A1
Nové Město, *Prague* — 24 B2
Novoaleksandrovskoye, *St. Petersburg* — 26 A1
Novogireyevo, *Moscow* — 19 B4
Novoivanovskoye, *Moscow* — 19 B1
Novonikolyskoye, *Moscow* — 19 B1
Novosaratovka, *St. Petersburg* — 26 B3
Nowe-Babice, *Warsaw* — 31 B1
Nöykkiö, *Helsinki* — 12 B1
Nueva Atzacoalco, *Mexico City* — 18 B2
Nueva Pompeya, *Buenos Aires* — 7 C2
Nueva Tenochtitlán, *Mexico City* — 18 B2
Nuijala, *Helsinki* — 12 B1
Numabukuro, *Tokyo* — 29 A2
Nunez, *Buenos Aires* — 7 B2
Nunhead, *London* — 15 B3
Nuñoa, *Santiago* — 26 B2
Nusle, *Prague* — 24 B2
Nussdorf, *Vienna* — 31 A2
Nyanga, *Cape Town* — 8 A2
Nymphenburg, *Munich* — 20 B2
Nymphenburg, Schloss, *Munich* — 20 B2

O

Oak Grove, *Atlanta* — 3 A3
Oak Island, *Boston* — 6 A4
Oak Lawn, *Chicago* — 9 C2
Oak Park, *Chicago* — 9 B2
Oak View, *Washington* — 32 A4
Oakdale, *Atlanta* — 3 A2
Oakland, *San Francisco* — 25 B3
Oakland, *Washington* — 32 C4
Oaklawn, *Washington* — 32 C4
Oakleigh, *Melbourne* — 17 B2
Oakton, *Washington* — 32 B2
Oakwood Beach, *New York* — 21 C1
Oatley, *Sydney* — 28 B1
Obalende, *Lagos* — 14 B2
Oba's Palace, *Lagos* — 14 B2
Oberföhring, *Munich* — 20 B2
Oberhaching, *Munich* — 20 B2
Oberlaa, *Vienna* — 31 B2

Oberlisse, *Vienna* — 31 A2
Obermenzing, *Munich* — 20 A1
Obermoos Schwaige, *Munich* — 20 A1
Oberschleissheim, *Munich* — 20 A2
Oberschöneweide, *Berlin* — 5 B4
Observatory, *Johannesburg* — 13 B2
Observatory, *Sydney* — 28 a1
Obu, *Osaka* — 22 A1
Obu-tōge, *Osaka* — 22 A1
Óbuda, *Budapest* — 7 A2
Obukhovo, *St. Petersburg* — 26 B2
Obvodnyy Kanal, *St. Petersburg* — 26 B1
Ocean Park, *Hong Kong* — 12 B2
Ochakovo, *Moscow* — 19 B2
Ochota, *Warsaw* — 31 B1
O'Connell Street, *Dublin* — 11 b2
Ōdana, *Tokyo* — 29 B2
Öden-Stockach, *Munich* — 20 B3
Odilampi, *Helsinki* — 12 B1
Odintsovo, *Moscow* — 19 B1
Odolany, *Warsaw* — 31 B1
Oeiras, *Lisbon* — 14 A1
Ofin, *Lagos* — 14 A1
Ogawa, *Tokyo* — 29 A1
Ogden Park, *Chicago* — 9 C2
Ogikubo, *Tokyo* — 29 A2
Ogogoro, *Lagos* — 14 B2
Ogoyo, *Lagos* — 14 B2
Ogudu, *Lagos* — 14 A2
Ohariu Stream →, *Wellington* — 32 B1
O'Higgins, Parque, *Santiago* — 26 B2
Ōimachi, *Tokyo* — 29 B3
Ojota, *Lagos* — 14 A2
Okamoto, *Osaka* — 22 A2
Okęcie, *Warsaw* — 31 B1
Okęcie Airport, *Warsaw* — 31 B1
Okelra, *Lagos* — 14 B2
Okeogbe, *Lagos* — 14 B2
Okha, *Delhi* — 10 B2
Okhta →, *St. Petersburg* — 26 B2
Okkervil →, *St. Petersburg* — 26 B2
Oksval, *Oslo* — 22 A3
Oktyabrskiy, *Moscow* — 19 B3
Ōkubo, *Tokyo* — 29 a1
Ōkura, *Tokyo* — 29 B1
Olari, *Helsinki* — 12 B1
Olaria, *Rio de Janeiro* — 24 B1
Old Admiralty, *St. Petersburg* — 26 b1
Old City, *Delhi* — 1 a3
Old City, *Shanghai* — 27 B1
Old Fort = Purana Qila, *Delhi* — 1 c3
Old Harbor, *Boston* — 6 B3
Old Town, *Chicago* — 9 b3
Old Town, *Edinburgh* — 11 b2
Oldbawn, *Dublin* — 11 B1
Olgino, *St. Petersburg* — 26 A1
Olímpico, Estadio, *Mexico City* — 18 C1
Olivais, *Lisbon* — 14 A2
Olivar de los Padres, *Mexico City* — 18 B1
Olivar del Conde, *Mexico City* — 18 B1
Olivos, *Buenos Aires* — 7 B2
Olona →, *Milan* — 18 B1
Olympia, *London* — 15 c1
Olympic Stadium, *Helsinki* — 12 B2
Olympique, Stade, *Montreal* — 19 A2
Omonias, Pl., *Athens* — 2 b1
Ōmori, *Tokyo* — 29 B3
Onchi, *Osaka* — 22 B4
Onchi →, *Osaka* — 22 A4
Onisigun, *Lagos* — 14 A2
Ōokayama, *Tokyo* — 29 B3
Oosterpark, *Amsterdam* — 2 b3
Oostzaan, *Amsterdam* — 2 A2
Opa-Locka, *Miami* — 18 A1
Opa-Locka Airport, *Miami* — 18 A1
Opacz, *Warsaw* — 31 B1
Opera House, *Sydney* — 28 a2
Ophirton, *Johannesburg* — 13 B2
Oppegård, *Oslo* — 22 B3
Oppem, *Brussels* — 6 A1
Oppsal, *Oslo* — 22 A3
Ora, *Jerusalem* — 13 B1
Oradell, *New York* — 21 A1
Orange Bowl Stadium, *Miami* — 18 B2
Orangi, *Karachi* — 14 A1
Orchard Road, *Singapore* — 27 A1
Ordrup, *Copenhagen* — 10 A3
Orech, *Prague* — 24 B1
Øresund, *Copenhagen* — 10 A3
Orient Heights, *Boston* — 6 A4
Orlando Dam, *Johannesburg* — 13 B1
Orlando East, *Johannesburg* — 13 B1
Orlovo, *Moscow* — 19 C2
Orly, *Paris* — 23 B3
Ormesson-sur-Marne, *Paris* — 23 B4
Ormond, *Melbourne* — 17 B2
Ormøya, *Oslo* — 22 A3
Orpington, *London* — 15 B4
Orsay, Musée d', *Paris* — 23 b3
Országház, *Budapest* — 7 b1
Országos Levéltár, *Budapest* — 7 b1
Ortaköy, *Istanbul* — 12 B2
Ortica, *Milan* — 18 B2
Oruba, *Lagos* — 14 A2
Orvostörteneti Múz., *Budapest* — 7 c2
Osaka, *Osaka* — 22 B4
Osaka B., *Osaka* — 22 B4
Osaka Castle, *Osaka* — 22 A3
Osaka Harbour, *Osaka* — 22 B3
Osaka International Airport, *Osaka* — 22 A3
Ōsaki, *Tokyo* — 29 B3
Osasco, *São Paulo* — 26 B1
Osdorp, *Amsterdam* — 2 A1
Oshodi, *Lagos* — 14 A2
Oslo, *Oslo* — 22 A3
Oslofjorden, *Oslo* — 22 B2
Osorun, *Lagos* — 14 A2
Ostankino, *Moscow* — 19 B3
Ostasiatiskamuséet, *Stockholm* — 28 b3
Osteralm, *Stockholm* — 28 a3
Osterbro, *Copenhagen* — 10 a2
Osterley, *London* — 15 B1
Osterley Park, *London* — 15 B1
Östermalm, *Stockholm* — 28 a3
Östermskär, *Stockholm* — 28 A3
Ostiense, *Rome* — 25 B1
Østmarkspollet, *Oslo* — 22 A3
Østøya, *Oslo* — 22 A2
Ōta-Ku, *Tokyo* — 29 B3
Ota Open Air Museum, *Wellington* — 32 B1
Otsuka, *Tokyo* — 29 A3
Ottakring, *Vienna* — 31 A1

Ottávia, *Rome* — 25 B1
Ottery, *Cape Town* — 8 A2
Ottobrunn, *Munich* — 20 B3
Oud Zuid, *Amsterdam* — 2 b1
Oude Kerk, *Amsterdam* — 2 b2
Ouderkerk, *Amsterdam* — 2 B2
Oulunkylä, *Helsinki* — 12 B2
Ourcq, Canal de l', *Paris* — 23 A3
Outer Mission, *San Francisco* — 25 B2
Outremont, *Montreal* — 19 A2
Overijse, *Brussels* — 6 B3
Owhiro Bay, *Wellington* — 32 C1
Oworonski, *Lagos* — 14 B2
Oxford Street, *London* — 15 b3
Oxgangs, *Edinburgh* — 11 B2
Oxon Hill, *Washington* — 32 C4
Oyodo, *Osaka* — 22 A3
Oyster B., *Sydney* — 28 C1
Oyster Rock, *Mumbai* — 20 B1
Oyster Rocks, *Karachi* — 14 B2
Ozoir-la-Ferrière, *Paris* — 23 B4
Ozone Park, *New York* — 21 B2

P

Pacific Heights, *San Francisco* — 25 B2
Pacific Manor, *San Francisco* — 25 C2
Pacific Palisades, *Los Angeles* — 16 B1
Pacifica, *San Francisco* — 25 C2
Paço, *Manila* — 17 B1
Paco de Arcos, *Lisbon* — 14 A1
Paço Imperial, *Rio de Janeiro* — 24 a2
Paddington, *London* — 15 b2
Paddington, *Sydney* — 28 B2
Paderno, *Milan* — 18 A1
Pagewood, *Sydney* — 28 B2
Pagote, *Mumbai* — 20 B2
Pai, I. do, *Rio de Janeiro* — 24 B2
Pak Kong, *Hong Kong* — 12 A2
Pakila, *Helsinki* — 12 B2
Palacio de Bellas Artes, *Mexico City* — 18 b2
Palacio de Communicaciones, *Madrid* — 17 a3
Palacio Nacional, *Mexico City* — 18 b3
Palacio Real, *Barcelona* — 4 b3
Palacio Real, *Madrid* — 17 b1
Paláion Fáliron, *Athens* — 2 B2
Palais de Justice, *Brussels* — 6 c2
Palais Royal, *Paris* — 23 b4
Palais Royale, *Brussels* — 6 b3
Palaiseau, *Paris* — 23 B2
Palau Nacional Museu d'Art, *Barcelona* — 4 c1
Palazzolo, *Milan* — 18 A1
Palermo, *Buenos Aires* — 7 B2
Palhais, *Lisbon* — 14 B2
Palisades Park, *New York* — 21 A1
Palmer Park, *Washington* — 32 B4
Palmerston, *Dublin* — 11 A1
Paloheinä, *Helsinki* — 12 B2
Palomeras, *Madrid* — 17 B2
Palos Heights, *Chicago* — 9 D2
Palos Hills, *Chicago* — 9 C2
Palos Hills Forest, *Chicago* — 9 C1
Palpara, *Calcutta* — 8 B2
Panchur, *Calcutta* — 8 B1
Pandacan, *Manila* — 17 B2
Pandan, Selat, *Singapore* — 27 B2
Pandan Res., *Singapore* — 27 B2
Panepistimio, *Athens* — 2 b2
Pangbae, *Seoul* — 26 C1
Pangrati, *Athens* — 2 B2
Pangsua, Sungei →, *Singapore* — 27 A2
Panihati, *Calcutta* — 8 A2
Panjang, Bukit, *Singapore* — 27 A2
Panje, *Mumbai* — 20 B2
Panke →, *Berlin* — 5 A3
Pankow, *Berlin* — 5 A3
Panthéon, *Paris* — 23 c4
Pantheon, *Rome* — 25 b2
Pantin, *Paris* — 23 A3
Pantitlan, *Mexico City* — 18 B2
Panvel Cr. →, *Mumbai* — 20 B2
Paparangi, *Wellington* — 32 B1
Papiol, *Barcelona* — 4 A1
Paramus, *New York* — 21 A1
Parañaque, *Manila* — 17 B1
Paray-Vieille-Poste, *Paris* — 23 B3
Parco Regionale, *Milan* — 18 A1
Parel, *Mumbai* — 20 B1
Pari, *São Paulo* — 26 B2
Parioli, *Rome* — 25 B1
Paris, *Paris* — 23 A3
Paris-Orly, Aéroport de, *Paris* — 23 B3
Pärk-e Mellat, *Tehran* — 30 A2
Park Ridge, *Chicago* — 9 A1
Park Royal, *London* — 15 A2
Parkchester, *New York* — 21 B2
Parkdale, *Toronto* — 30 B2
Parkhurst, *Johannesburg* — 13 A2
Parklawn, *Washington* — 32 B3
Parkmore, *Johannesburg* — 13 A2
Parkside, *San Francisco* — 25 B2
Parktown, *Johannesburg* — 13 B2
Parktown North, *Johannesburg* — 13 A2
Parkview, *Johannesburg* — 13 A2
Parkville, *New York* — 21 C2
Parkwood, *Cape Town* — 8 B1
Parkwood, *Johannesburg* — 13 A2
Parow, *Cape Town* — 8 A2
Parque Chabuco, *Buenos Aires* — 7 B2
Parque Patricios, *Buenos Aires* — 7 B2
Parramatta →, *Sydney* — 28 A1
Parthenon, *Athens* — 2 c2
Paşabahçe, *Istanbul* — 12 B2
Pasadena, *Los Angeles* — 16 B4
Pasar Minggu, *Jakarta* — 13 B1
Pasay, *Manila* — 17 B1
Pascoe Vale, *Melbourne* — 17 A1
Paseo de la Reforma, *Mexico City* — 18 b2
Pasig, *Manila* — 17 B2
Pasig →, *Manila* — 17 B2
Pasila, *Helsinki* — 12 B2
Pasing, *Munich* — 20 B1
Pasir Panjang, *Singapore* — 27 B2
Pasir Ris, *Singapore* — 27 A3
Passaic →, *New York* — 21 B1
Passirana, *Milan* — 18 A1
Patel Nagar, *Delhi* — 10 B1
Pateros, *Manila* — 17 B2
Pathersville, *Atlanta* — 3 B3
Pathumwan, *Bangkok* — 3 B2
Patipukur, *Calcutta* — 8 B2
Patisia, *Athens* — 2 A2
Pató E. Virginia, Gruta, *Rio de Janeiro* — 24 B1
Paulshof, *Berlin* — 5 A5

Pavshino, *Moscow* — 19 B1
Paya Lebar, *Singapore* — 27 A3
Peachtree →, *Atlanta* — 3 B2
Peakhurst, *Sydney* — 28 B1
Peania, *Athens* — 2 B2
Peckham, *London* — 15 B3
Peddocks I., *Boston* — 6 B4
Pederstrup, *Copenhagen* — 10 A2
Pedralbes, *Barcelona* — 4 A1
Pedregal de San Angel, Jardines del, *Mexico City* — 18 C1
Pekhorka →, *Moscow* — 19 C6
Pekhra-Pokrovskoye, *Moscow* — 19 A5
Pekhra-Yakovievskaya, *Moscow* — 19 B5
Peking = Beijing, *Beijing* — 4 B1
Pelcowizna, *Warsaw* — 31 B2
Pelopónnisos Sta., *Athens* — 2 a1
Penalolén, *Santiago* — 26 B2
Peñacarrow Hd., *Wellington* — 32 C2
Peravillo, *Mexico City* — 18 a3
Perchtoldsdorf, *Vienna* — 31 B1
Perdizes, *São Paulo* — 26 B2
Peredelkino, *Moscow* — 19 B2
Pergamon Museum, *Berlin* — 5 a4
Peristérion, *Athens* — 2 A2
Perivale, *London* — 15 A2
Perk, *Brussels* — 6 A2
Perlach, *Munich* — 20 B3
Perlacher Forst, *Munich* — 20 B2
Pero, *Milan* — 18 A1
Pershing Square, *Los Angeles* — 16 c1
Pertusella, *Milan* — 18 A1
Pesagot, *Jerusalem* — 13 A2
Pesanggrahan, Kali →, *Jakarta* — 13 B1
Peschiera Borromeo, *Milan* — 18 B2
Pesek, P., *Singapore* — 27 B2
Pest, *Budapest* — 7 B2
Pesterzsébet, *Budapest* — 7 B2
Pesthidegkút, *Budapest* — 7 A1
Pestimre, *Budapest* — 7 B3
Pestlörinc, *Budapest* — 7 B2
Pestújhely, *Budapest* — 7 A2
Petas, *Helsinki* — 12 B2
Petone, *Wellington* — 32 B2
Petrogradskaya Storona, *St. Petersburg* — 26 B2
Petroúpolis, *Athens* — 2 A2
Petrovice, *Prague* — 24 B3
Petrovsky Park, *Moscow* — 19 B3
Petrovsko-Razumovskoye, *Moscow* — 19 B3
Pettycur, *Edinburgh* — 11 A2
Peutie, *Brussels* — 6 A2
Pfaueninsel, *Berlin* — 5 B1
Phaya Thai, *Bangkok* — 3 B2
Phihai, *Karachi* — 14 A2
Phillip B., *Sydney* — 28 B2
Phoenix Park, *Dublin* — 11 A2
Phra Khanong, *Bangkok* — 3 B2
Phra Pradaeng, *Bangkok* — 3 C2
Phranakhon, *Bangkok* — 3 B1
Picasso, Museu, *Barcelona* — 4 b3
Piccadilly, *London* — 15 b3
Pico Rivera, *Los Angeles* — 16 C4
Piedade, *Lisbon* — 14 A1
Piedade, *Rio de Janeiro* — 24 B1
Piedade, Cova da, *Lisbon* — 14 A2
Piedmont Park, *Atlanta* — 3 B2
Pietralata, *Rome* — 25 B2
Pihlajamäki, *Helsinki* — 12 B3
Pihlajasaari, *Helsinki* — 12 C2
Pilares, *Rio de Janeiro* — 24 B1
Pilton, *Edinburgh* — 11 B2
Pimlico, *London* — 15 c3
Pimmit Hills, *Washington* — 32 B2
Pine Grove, *Toronto* — 30 A1
Pinewood, *Miami* — 18 A2
Piney Run →, *Washington* — 32 B2
Pinganli, *Beijing* — 4 B2
Pingzhou, *Canton* — 8 B2
Pinjrapur, *Karachi* — 14 A2
Pinner, *London* — 15 A1
Pinner Green, *London* — 15 A1
Pioltello, *Milan* — 18 A2
Pipinui Pt., *Wellington* — 32 A1
Piraévs, *Athens* — 2 B1
Pirajuçara →, *São Paulo* — 26 B1
Pirinçci, *Istanbul* — 12 B1
Pirituba, *São Paulo* — 26 B1
Pirkkola, *Helsinki* — 12 B2
Pisnice, *Prague* — 24 B2
Pitampura, *Delhi* — 10 A1
Pitkäjärvi, *Helsinki* — 12 B1
Planegg, *Munich* — 20 B1
Plumstead, *Cape Town* — 8 B1
Plumstead, *London* — 15 B4
Plyushchevo, *Moscow* — 19 B4
Pňika, *Athens* — 2 c1
Po Toi I., *Hong Kong* — 12 B2
Po Toi O, *Hong Kong* — 12 B2
Poasco, *Milan* — 18 B2
Podbaba, *Prague* — 24 B2
Podoli, *Prague* — 24 B2
Poduskino, *Moscow* — 19 B1
Pointe-aux-Trembles, *Montreal* — 19 A2
Poissy, *Paris* — 23 A1
Pok Fu Lam, *Hong Kong* — 12 B1
Pokrovsko-Sresnevo, *Moscow* — 19 B3
Polton, *Edinburgh* — 11 B3
Polyustrovo, *St. Petersburg* — 26 B2
Pompidou, Centre, *Paris* — 23 b4
Pomprap, *Bangkok* — 3 B2
Pondok Indah, *Jakarta* — 13 B1
Ponta da Marisco, *Rio de Janeiro* — 24 C1
Pontault-Combault, *Paris* — 23 B4
Pontinha, *Lisbon* — 14 A1
Poplar, *London* — 15 A3
Popolo, Porta del, *Rome* — 25 a2
Poppintree, *Dublin* — 11 A2
Porirua, *Wellington* — 32 B2
Porirua East, *Wellington* — 32 B2
Port I., *Osaka* — 22 B2
Port Melbourne, *Melbourne* — 17 B1
Port Nicholson, *Wellington* — 32 B2
Port Philip Bay, *Melbourne* — 17 B1

Port Richmond, *New York* — 21 C1
Port Shelter, *Hong Kong* — 12 A2
Port Union, *Toronto* — 30 A4
Portage Park, *Chicago* — 9 B2
Portal de la Pau, Pl., *Barcelona* — 4 c2
Portela, Aeroporto da, *Lisbon* — 14 A2
Portmarnock, *Dublin* — 11 A3
Porto Brandão, *Lisbon* — 14 A1
Porto Novo, *Rio de Janeiro* — 24 A2
Porto Novo Cr. →, *Lagos* — 14 B2
Portobello, *Edinburgh* — 11 B3
Portrero, *San Francisco* — 25 B2
Potomac, *Washington* — 32 A2
Potomac →, *Washington* — 32 A2
Potrero Pt., *San Francisco* — 25 B2
Potsdam, *Berlin* — 5 B1
Potsdamer Platz, *Berlin* — 5 b3
Potzham, *Munich* — 20 B2
Pötzleinsdorf, *Vienna* — 31 A1
Povoa de Santo Adriao, *Lisbon* — 14 A2
Powązki, *Warsaw* — 31 B1
Powisle, *Warsaw* — 31 B2
Powsin, *Warsaw* — 31 C2
Powsinek, *Warsaw* — 31 C2
Poyan Res., *Singapore* — 27 A2
Pozuelo de Alarcon, *Madrid* — 17 B1
Prado, Museo del, *Madrid* — 17 b3
Praga, *Warsaw* — 31 B2
Prague = Praha, *Prague* — 24 B2
Praha, *Prague* — 24 B2
Praha-Ruzyně Airport, *Prague* — 24 B1
Praires, R. des →, *Montreal* — 19 A2
Prater, *Vienna* — 31 A2
Precotto, *Milan* — 18 A2
Prenestino Labicano, *Rome* — 25 B2
Prenzlauerberg, *Berlin* — 5 A3
Preston, *Melbourne* — 17 A1
Pretos Forros, Sa. dos, *Rio de Janeiro* — 24 B1
Préville, *Montreal* — 19 B3
Přezletice, *Prague* — 24 A3
Prima Porta, *Rome* — 25 B1
Primavalle, *Rome* — 25 B1
Primrose, *Johannesburg* — 13 B2
Princes Street, *Edinburgh* — 11 b2
Printer's Row, *Chicago* — 9 d2
Progreso Nacional, *Mexico City* — 18 A2
Prosek, *Prague* — 24 B3
Prospect Hill Park, *Boston* — 6 A2
Providencia, *Santiago* — 26 B2
Prudential Building, *Chicago* — 9 c2
Průhonice, *Prague* — 24 C3
Psikhikón, *Athens* — 2 A2
Pudong New Area, *Shanghai* — 27 B2
Pueblo Libre, *Lima* — 16 B2
Pueblo Nuevo, *Barcelona* — 4 A2
Pueblo Nuevo, *Madrid* — 17 B2
Puerta del Sol, Plaza, *Madrid* — 17 b2
Puerto Madero, *Buenos Aires* — 7 B2
Puerto Retiro, *Buenos Aires* — 7 B2
Puhuangyu, *Beijing* — 4 B2
Puistola, *Helsinki* — 12 B3
Pukan-san, *Seoul* — 26 B1
Pukinmäki, *Helsinki* — 12 B3
Pukkajwa, *Seoul* — 26 B1
Pulkovo Int. Airport, *St. Petersburg* — 26 C1
Pullach, *Munich* — 20 B1
Pulo Gadung, *Jakarta* — 13 B2
Punak, *Tehran* — 30 A2
Punchbowl, *Sydney* — 28 B1
Punde, *Mumbai* — 20 B2
Punggol, *Singapore* — 27 A3
Punggol, Sungei →, *Singapore* — 27 A3
Punggol Pt., *Singapore* — 27 A3
Punjabi Bagh, *Delhi* — 10 A1
Puotila, *Helsinki* — 12 B3
Purana Qila, *Delhi* — 1 c3
Puteaux, *Paris* — 23 A2
Putilkovo, *Moscow* — 19 B2
Putney, *London* — 15 B2
Putuo, *Shanghai* — 27 B1
Putxet, *Barcelona* — 4 A1
Puxi, *Shanghai* — 27 B1
Pydhuni, *Mumbai* — 20 b2
Pyramids, *Cairo* — 7 B1
Pyry, *Warsaw* — 31 C1

Q

Qalandya, *Jerusalem* — 13 A2
Qal'eh Morghi, *Tehran* — 30 B2
Qanâ el Ismâ'ilîya, *Cairo* — 7 A2
Qāsemābād, *Tehran* — 30 A3
Qasr-e Fīrūzeh, *Tehran* — 30 B3
Qatane, *Jerusalem* — 13 B1
Qianmen, *Beijing* — 4 B2
Qinghuayuan, *Beijing* — 4 B1
Qingningsi, *Shanghai* — 27 B1
Qolhak, *Tehran* — 30 A2
Quadraro, *Rome* — 25 B2
Quaid-i-Azam, *Karachi* — 14 A1
Quartiere Zingone, *Milan* — 18 B1
Quds, *Baghdad* — 3 A2
Queen Mary Res., *London* — 15 B1
Queen Street, *Edinburgh* — 11 a1
Queensbury, *London* — 15 A2
Queenscliffe, *Sydney* — 28 A2
Queensferry, *Edinburgh* — 11 A1
Queenstown, *Singapore* — 27 B2
Quellerina, *Johannesburg* — 13 A1
Queluz, *Lisbon* — 14 A1
Quezon City, *Manila* — 17 B2
Quezon Memorial Circle, *Manila* — 17 B2
Quilicura, *Santiago* — 26 B1
Quincy, *Boston* — 6 B3
Quincy B., *Boston* — 6 B4
Quinta Normal, *Santiago* — 26 B1
Quinto de Stampi, *Milan* — 18 B2
Quinto Romano, *Milan* — 18 B1
Quirinale, Palazzo del, *Rome* — 25 b3

R

Raasdorf, *Vienna* — 31 A3
Rådhuset, *Oslo* — 22 A3
Radlice, *Prague* — 24 B2
Radość, *Warsaw* — 31 B3
Radotín, *Prague* — 24 C2
Rafat, *Jerusalem* — 13 A2
Raffles Hotel, *Singapore* — 27 b3
Raffles Park, *Singapore* — 27 B2

RAHENY

Raheny, *Dublin* 11 A3
Rahnsdorf, *Berlin* 5 B5
Rainham, *London* 15 A5
Raj Ghat, *Delhi* 1 b3
Rajakylä, *Helsinki* 12 B3
Rajpath, *Delhi* 1 c2
Rajpura, *Delhi* 10 A2
Rákos-patak ✈, *Budapest* 7 B3
Rákoshegy, *Budapest* 7 B3
Rákoskeresztúr, *Budapest* 7 B3
Rákoskert, *Budapest* 7 B3
Rákosliget, *Budapest* 7 B3
Rákospalota, *Budapest* 7 A2
Rákosszentmihály, *Budapest* 7 A2
Raków, *Warsaw* 31 B1
Ram, *Jerusalem* 13 A2
Rām Allāh, *Jerusalem* 13 A2
Ramadān, *Baghdad* 3 B2
Ramakrishna Puram, *Delhi* 10 B1
Ramanathpur, *Calcutta* 8 A1
Rambla, La, *Barcelona* 4 b2
Rambler Channel, *Hong Kong* 12 A1
Ramenki, *Moscow* 19 B2
Ramersdorf, *Munich* 20 B2
Ramos, *Rio de Janeiro* 24 B1
Ramos Mejia, *Buenos Aires* 7 B1
Ramot, *Jerusalem* 13 B2
Rampur, *Delhi* 10 A2
Ramsgate, *Sydney* 28 B1
Rand Afrikaans Univ., *Johannesburg* 13 B2
Rand Airport, *Johannesburg* 13 B2
Randburg, *Johannesburg* 13 A1
Randhart, *Johannesburg* 13 B2
Randpark Ridge, *Johannesburg* 13 A1
Randwick, *Sydney* 28 B2
Ranelagh, *Dublin* 11 A2
Rannersdorf, *Vienna* 31 B2
Ransbèche, *Brussels* 6 B2
Ransdorp, *Amsterdam* 2 A2
Ranvad, *Mumbai* 20 B2
Raposo, *Lisbon* 14 A1
Rashtrapati Bhawan, *Delhi* 1 c1
Rasskazovka, *Moscow* 19 C2
Rastaala, *Helsinki* 12 B1
Rastila, *Helsinki* 12 B3
Raszyn, *Warsaw* 31 C1
Ratcha Thewi, *Bangkok* 3 b3
Rathfarnham, *Dublin* 11 B2
Ratho, *Edinburgh* 11 B1
Ratho Station, *Edinburgh* 11 B1
Rato, *Lisbon* 14 A2
Ravelston, *Edinburgh* 11 B2
Rawamangun, *Jakarta* 13 B2
Rayners Lane, *London* 15 A1
Raynes Park, *London* 15 B2
Raypur, *Calcutta* 8 C2
Razdory, *Moscow* 19 B1
Real Felipe, Fuerte, *Lima* 16 B2
Recoleta, *Buenos Aires* 7 B2
Recoleta, *Santiago* 26 B2
Red Fort = Lal Qila, *Delhi* 1 a3
Redbridge, *London* 15 A4
Redfern, *Sydney* 28 B2
Redwood, *Wellington* 32 B1
Reeves Hill, *Boston* 6 A1
Refshaleøen, *Copenhagen* 10 A3
Regents Park, *Johannesburg* 13 B2
Regent's Park, *London* 15 a2
Rego Park, *New York* 21 B2
Reichstag, *Berlin* 5 a3
Reina Sofia, Centro de Arte, *Madrid* 17 c3
Reinickendorf, *Berlin* 5 A3
Rekola, *Helsinki* 12 B3
Rembertów, *Warsaw* 31 B2
Rembrandthuis, *Amsterdam* 2 b2
Rembrandtpark, *Amsterdam* 2 A2
Rembrandtsplein, *Amsterdam* 2 b2
Remedios, Parque Nacional de los, *Mexico City* 18 B1
Remedios de Escalada, *Buenos Aires* 7 C2
Rémola, Laguna del, *Barcelona* 4 B1
Renca, *Santiago* 26 B1
Renmin Park, *Tianjin* 30 B2
Rennemoulin, *Paris* 23 A1
Řeporyje, *Prague* 24 B1
Republica, Plaza de la, *Mexico City* 18 b1
République, Place de la, *Paris* 23 b5
Repulse Bay, *Hong Kong* 12 B2
Repy, *Prague* 24 B1
Residenz, *Munich* 20 B2
Residenzmuseum, *Munich* 20 b3
Reston, *Washington* 32 B2
Retiro, *Buenos Aires* 7 B2
Retiro, *Madrid* 17 B1
Retreat, *Cape Town* 8 B1
Reutov, *Moscow* 19 B5
Réveillon ✈, *Paris* 23 B4
Revere, *Boston* 6 A3
Rexdale, *Toronto* 30 A1
Reynosa Tamaulipas, *Mexico City* 18 A1
Rho, *Milan* 18 A1
Rhodes, *Sydney* 28 A1
Rhodon, *Paris* 23 B1
Rhodon ✈, *Paris* 23 B1
Ribeira, *Rio de Janeiro* 24 A1
Ricarda, Laguna de la, *Barcelona* 4 B1
Richmond, *Melbourne* 17 A2
Richmond, *San Francisco* 25 B2
Richmond Hill, *New York* 21 B2
Richmond Park, *London* 15 B2
Richmond upon Thames, *London* 15 B2
Riddarholmen, *Stockholm* 28 c1
Riddarhuset, *Stockholm* 28 c2
Ridgefield, *New York* 21 B1
Ridgefield Park, *New York* 21 A1
Ridgewood, *New York* 21 B2
Riem, *Munich* 20 B3
Rijksmuseum, *Amsterdam* 2 b1
Rikers I., *New York* 21 B2
Riksdagensledamothus, *Stockholm* 28 b2
Riksdagshuset, *Stockholm* 28 b2
Rimac, *Lima* 16 B2
Ringsend, *Dublin* 11 A2
Rinkeby, *Stockholm* 28 A1
Rio Compride, *Rio de Janeiro* 24 B1
Rio de Janeiro, *Rio de Janeiro* 24 B1
Rio de la Plata, *Buenos Aires* 7 B2
Rio de Mouro, *Lisbon* 14 A1
Ripollet, *Barcelona* 4 A1
Ris, *Oslo* 22 A3
Risby, *Copenhagen* 10 A1
Rishra, *Calcutta* 8 A2
Ritchie, *Washington* 32 B4
Rithala, *Delhi* 10 A1
Rive Sud, Canal de la, *Montreal* 19 B2
River Edge, *New York* 21 A1
River Forest, *Chicago* 9 B2
River Grove, *Chicago* 9 B1
Riverdale, *New York* 21 A2
Riverdale, *Washington* 32 B4
Riverdale Park, *Toronto* 30 A2
Riverlea, *Johannesburg* 13 B1
Riverside, *Chicago* 9 C2
Riverwood, *Sydney* 28 B1
Rivière-des-Praires, *Montreal* 19 A2
Rixensart, *Brussels* 6 B3
Riyad, *Baghdad* 3 B2
Rizal Park, *Manila* 17 B1
Rizal Stadium, *Manila* 17 B1
Røa, *Oslo* 22 A2
Robbins, *Chicago* 9 D2
Robertsham, *Johannesburg* 13 B2
Rochelle Park, *New York* 21 A1
Rock Cr. ✈, *Washington* 32 B3
Rock Creek Park, *Washington* 32 B3
Rock Pt., *Wellington* 32 A1
Rockaway Pt., *New York* 21 C2
Rockdale, *Sydney* 28 B1
Rockefeller Center, *New York* 21 c2
Rodaon, *Vienna* 31 B1
Rødovre, *Copenhagen* 10 A2
Rodrigo de Freitas, L., *Rio de Janeiro* 24 B1
Roehampton, *London* 15 B2
Rogers Park, *Chicago* 9 A2
Roihuvuori, *Helsinki* 12 B3
Roissy-en-Brie, *Paris* 23 B4
Rokin, *Amsterdam* 2 b2
Rokkō I., *Osaka* 22 A2
Rokkō Sanchi, *Osaka* 22 A2
Rokkō-Zan, *Osaka* 22 A2
Rokytka ✈, *Prague* 24 B3
Roma, *Rome* 25 B1
Római-Fürdö, *Budapest* 7 A2
Romainville, *Paris* 23 A3
Romano Banco, *Milan* 18 B1
Romashkovo, *Moscow* 19 B1
Rome = Roma, *Rome* 25 B1
Romford, *London* 15 A5
Rondebosch, *Cape Town* 8 A1
Roppongi, *Tokyo* 29 c3
Rose Hill, *Washington* 32 C3
Rosebank, *New York* 21 C1
Rosebery, *Sydney* 28 B2
Rosedal La Candelaria, *Mexico City* 18 B2
Roseland, *Chicago* 9 C3
Rosemead, *Los Angeles* 16 B4
Rosemont, *Montreal* 19 A2
Rosenborg Have, *Copenhagen* 10 A3
Rosenthal, *Berlin* 5 A3
Rosettenville, *Johannesburg* 13 B2
Rosewell, *Edinburgh* 11 B3
Rosherville Dam, *Johannesburg* 13 B2
Rösjön, *Stockholm* 28 A2
Roslags-Näsby, *Stockholm* 28 A2
Roslin, *Edinburgh* 11 B3
Roslindale, *Boston* 6 B3
Rosny-sous-Bois, *Paris* 23 A4
Rosslyn, *Washington* 32 B3
Rosyth, *Edinburgh* 11 A1
Rotherhithe, *London* 15 B3
Rothneusiedl, *Vienna* 31 B2
Rothschmaige, *Munich* 20 A1
Rouge Hill, *Toronto* 30 A4
Round I., *Hong Kong* 12 B2
Roxbury, *Boston* 6 B3
Roxeth, *London* 15 A1
Royal Botanic Garden, *Edinburgh* 11 B2
Royal Botanic Gardens, *Sydney* 28 b2
Royal Grand Palace, *Bangkok* 3 b1
Royal Observatory, *Edinburgh* 11 B2
Royal Park, *Melbourne* 17 A1
Royal Turf Club, *Bangkok* 3 b2
Röylä, *Helsinki* 12 B1
Rozas, Portilleros de las, *Madrid* 17 B1
Roztoky, *Prague* 24 B2
Rozzano, *Milan* 18 B1
Rubi ✈, *Barcelona* 4 A1
Rublovo, *Moscow* 19 B2
Rudnevka ✈, *Moscow* 19 B5
Rudolfsheim, *Vienna* 31 A2
Rudolfshöhe, *Berlin* 5 A5
Rudow, *Berlin* 5 B3
Rueil-Malmaison, *Paris* 23 A2
Ruisbroek, *Brussels* 6 B1
Ruislip, *London* 15 A1
Rumelihisarı, *Istanbul* 12 B2
Rumyantsevo, *Moscow* 19 C2
Rungis, *Paris* 23 B3
Rusāfa, *Baghdad* 3 A2
Rush Green, *London* 15 A5
Russa, *Calcutta* 8 C2
Russian Hill, *San Francisco* 25 a1
Rustenfeld, *Vienna* 31 B2
Rutherford, *New York* 21 B1
Ruzyně, *Prague* 24 B1
Rybatskaya, *St. Petersburg* 26 B2
Rydboholm, *Stockholm* 28 A3
Ryde, *Sydney* 28 A1
Rynek, *Warsaw* 31 a2
Ryogoku, *Tokyo* 29 A3
Rzhevka, *St. Petersburg* 26 B3

S

Sa'ādatābād, *Tehran* 30 A2
Saadūn, *Baghdad* 3 B2
Saavedra, *Buenos Aires* 7 B2
Saboli, *Delhi* 10 A2
Sabugo, *Lisbon* 14 A1
Sabzi Mand, *Delhi* 10 A2
Sacavém, *Lisbon* 14 A2
Saclay, *Paris* 23 B2
Saclay, Étang de, *Paris* 23 B1
Sacomã, *São Paulo* 26 B2
Sacré Cœur, *Paris* 23 a4
Sacrow, *Berlin* 5 B1
Sacrower See, *Berlin* 5 B1
Sadang, *Seoul* 26 C1
Sadar Bazar, *Delhi* 1 a1
Saddām City, *Baghdad* 3 A2
Saddle Brook, *New York* 21 A1
Sadr, *Karachi* 14 A2
Sadyba, *Warsaw* 31 B2
Saft el Laban, *Cairo* 7 A2
Saganashkee Slough, *Chicago* 9 C1
Sagene, *Oslo* 22 A3
Sagrada Família, Templo de, *Barcelona* 4 A2
Sagrado Familia, Templo de, *Barcelona* 4 a2
Sahar Int. Airport, *Mumbai* 20 A2
Sai Kung, *Hong Kong* 12 A2
Sai Wan Ho, *Hong Kong* 12 B2
Sai Ying Pun, *Hong Kong* 12 B1
St.-Aubin, *Paris* 23 B1
St.-Cloud, *Paris* 23 A2
St.-Cyr-l'École, *Paris* 23 B1
St.-Cyr-l'École, Aérodrome de, *Paris* 23 B1
St.-Denis, *Paris* 23 A3
St.-Germain, Forêt de, *Paris* 23 A1
St.-Germain-en-Laye, *Paris* 23 A1
St. Giles Cathedral, *Edinburgh* 11 b2
St. Helier, *London* 15 B2
St.-Hubert, *Montreal* 19 B3
St. Hubert, Galerie, *Brussels* 6 b2
St. Isaac's Cathedral, *St. Petersburg* 26 B1
St. Jacques ✈, *Montreal* 19 B3
St. James's, *London* 15 b3
St. John's Cathedral, *Hong Kong* 12 c1
St. Kilda, *Melbourne* 17 B1
St. Lambert, *Montreal* 19 A3
St.-Lambert, *Paris* 23 B1
St.-Laurent, *Montreal* 19 A1
St. Lawrence ✈, *Montreal* 19 B2
St.-Lazare, Gare, *Paris* 23 A2
St.-Léonard, *Montreal* 19 A2
St. Magelungen, *Stockholm* 28 B2
St.-Mandé, *Paris* 23 A3
St. Margaret's, *Dublin* 11 A2
St.-Martin, Bois, *Paris* 23 B4
St. Mary Cray, *London* 15 B4
St.-Maur-des-Fossés, *Paris* 23 B3
St.-Maurice, *Paris* 23 B3
St.-Michel, *Montreal* 19 A2
St. Nikolaus-Kirken, *Prague* 24 B2
St.-Ouen, *Paris* 23 A3
St. Patrick's Cathedral, *Dublin* 11 c1
St. Patrick's Cathedral, *New York* 21 c2
St. Paul's Cathedral, *London* 15 b4
St. Paul's Cray, *London* 15 B4
St. Peters, *Sydney* 28 B2
St. Petersburg = Sankt Peterburg, *St. Petersburg* 26 B1
St.-Pierre, *Montreal* 19 B2
St.-Quentin, Étang de, *Paris* 23 B1
St. Stephen's Green, *Dublin* 11 c3
St.-Vincent-de-Paul, *Montreal* 19 A2
Ste.-Catherine, *Montreal* 19 B2
Ste.-Hélène, Î., *Montreal* 19 A2
Saiwai, *Tokyo* 29 B3
Sakai, *Osaka* 22 B3
Sakai Harbour, *Osaka* 22 B3
Sakra, P., *Singapore* 27 B2
Salam, *Baghdad* 3 A2
Salamanca, *Madrid* 17 B1
Sâllynoggin, *Dublin* 11 B3
Salmannsdorf, *Vienna* 31 A1
Salmedina, *Madrid* 17 C2
Salomea, *Warsaw* 31 B1
Salsette I., *Mumbai* 20 A2
Salt Lake City, *Calcutta* 8 B2
Salt River, *Cape Town* 8 A1
Salt Water L., *Calcutta* 8 B2
Saltsjö-Duvnäs, *Stockholm* 28 B3
Saltykovka, *Moscow* 19 B5
Samatya, *Istanbul* 12 C1
Sampaloc, *Manila* 17 B1
Samphan Thawong, *Bangkok* 3 B2
Samsŏn, *Seoul* 26 B2
San Andrés, *Barcelona* 4 A2
San Angel, *Mexico City* 18 B1
San Angelo, Castel, *Rome* 25 b1
San Basilio, *Rome* 25 B2
San Borja, *Lima* 16 B3
San Bóvio, *Milan* 18 B2
San Bruno, Pt., *San Francisco* 25 C2
San Bruno Mt., *San Francisco* 25 B2
San Cristobal, *Buenos Aires* 7 B2
San Cristobal, *Madrid* 17 B2
San Cristóbal, Cerro, *Santiago* 26 B2
San Cristoforo, *Milan* 18 B1
San Donato Milanese, *Milan* 18 B2
San Francisco, *San Francisco* 25 B2
San Francisco B., *San Francisco* 25 B3
San Francisco Culhuacán, *Mexico City* 18 C2
San Fruttuoso, *Milan* 18 A2
San Gabriel, *Los Angeles* 16 B4
San Giuliano Milanese, *Milan* 18 B2
San Isidro, *Lima* 16 B2
San Jerónimo Lidice, *Mexico City* 18 C1
San Joaquin, *Santiago* 26 B2
San José Rio Hondo, *Mexico City* 18 B1
San Juan ✈, *Manila* 17 B2
San Juan de Aragón, *Mexico City* 18 B2
San Juan de Aragón, Parque, *Mexico City* 18 B2
San Juan de Lurigancho, *Lima* 16 A2
San Juan del Monte, *Manila* 17 B2
San Juan Ixtacala, *Mexico City* 18 A1
San Juan Toltotepec, *Mexico City* 18 B1
San Just Desvern, *Barcelona* 4 A1
San Justo, *Buenos Aires* 7 C1
San Lorenzo Tezonco, *Mexico City* 18 C2
San Luis, *Lima* 16 B2
San Marino, *Los Angeles* 16 B4
San Martin, *Barcelona* 4 A2
San Martin de Porras, *Lima* 16 B2
San Miguel, *Lima* 16 B2
San Miguel, *Santiago* 26 B2
San Nicolas, *Buenos Aires* 7 B2
San Onófrio, *Rome* 25 B1
San Pedro Martir, *Barcelona* 4 A1
San Pedro Zacatenco, *Mexico City* 18 A2
San Pietro, Piazza, *Rome* 25 b1
San Po Kong, *Hong Kong* 12 A2
San Rafael Chamapa, *Mexico City* 18 B1
San Rafael Hills, *Los Angeles* 16 A3
San Roque, *Manila* 17 B2
San Siro, *Milan* 18 B1
San Souci, *Sydney* 28 B1
San Telmo, *Buenos Aires* 7 B2
San Vicenc dels Horts, *Barcelona* 4 A1
Sanbancho, *Tokyo* 29 a3
Sandown, *Johannesburg* 13 A2
Sandown Park Races, *London* 15 B1
Sandton, *Johannesburg* 13 A2
Sandvika, *Oslo* 22 A2
Sandy Pond, *Boston* 6 A2
Sandyford, *Dublin* 11 B2
Sandymount, *Dublin* 11 B2
Sangenjaya, *Tokyo* 29 B2
Sangge, *Seoul* 26 B2
Sangley Pt., *Manila* 17 C1
Sankrail, *Calcutta* 8 B1
Sankt Peterburg, *St. Petersburg* 26 B1
Sankt Veit, *Vienna* 31 A1
Sanlihe, *Beijing* 4 B1
Sanlintang, *Shanghai* 27 C1
Sans, *Barcelona* 4 A1
Sant Agusti, *Barcelona* 4 c2
Sant Ambrogio, Basilica di, *Milan* 18 B2
Sant Boi de Llobregat, *Barcelona* 4 A1
Sant Cugat, *Barcelona* 4 A1
Sant Feliu de Llobregat, *Barcelona* 4 A1
Sant Joan Despi, *Barcelona* 4 A1
Sant Maria del Mar, *Barcelona* 4 b3
Sant Pau del Camp, *Barcelona* 4 c2
Santa Ana, *Manila* 17 B2
Santa Coloma de Gramanet, *Barcelona* 4 A2
Santa Cruz, *Manila* 17 B1
Santa Cruz, *Mumbai* 20 A1
Santa Cruz, I. de, *Rio de Janeiro* 24 B2
Santa Cruz de Olorde, *Barcelona* 4 A1
Santa Efigénia, *São Paulo* 26 B2
Santa Elena, *Manila* 17 B2
Santa Elena del Gomero, *Santiago* 26 B1
Santa Eulalia, *Barcelona* 4 A2
Santa Fe Springs, *Los Angeles* 16 C4
Santa Iria da Azóia, *Lisbon* 14 A2
Santa Julia, *Santiago* 26 C2
Santa Maria, *Mexico City* 18 a1
Santa Monica, *Los Angeles* 16 B2
Santa Monica Mts., *Los Angeles* 16 B2
Santa Rosa De Locobe, *Santiago* 26 B2
Santa Teresa de la Ovalle, *Santiago* 26 B1
Santahamina, *Helsinki* 12 C3
Santana, *São Paulo* 26 A2
Santeny, *Paris* 23 B4
Santiago, *Santiago* 26 B2
Santiago de Surco, *Lima* 16 B2
Santo Amaro, *Lisbon* 14 A1
Santo Amaro, *São Paulo* 26 B1
Santo Andre, *Lisbon* 14 B2
Santo Antão do Tojal, *Lisbon* 14 A2
Santo António, Qta. de, *Lisbon* 14 B1
Santo Tomas, Univ. of, *Manila* 17 B1
Santos Dumont, Aéroport, *Rio de Janeiro* 24 B2
Santoshpur, *Calcutta* 8 B1
Santragachi, *Calcutta* 8 B1
Santry, *Dublin* 11 A2
Sanyuanli, *Canton* 8 B2
São Caetano do Sul, *São Paulo* 26 B2
São Conrado, *Rio de Janeiro* 24 C1
São Cristovão, *Rio de Janeiro* 24 B1
São Francisco Penitência, *Rio de Janeiro* 24 b1
São Jorge, Castelo de, *Lisbon* 14 A2
São Juliao do Tojal, *Lisbon* 14 A2
São Paulo, *São Paulo* 26 B2
Sapa, *Calcutta* 8 B1
Sapateiro, Cor. do ✈, *São Paulo* 26 B1
Sarandi, *Buenos Aires* 7 C2
Saraswati ✈, *Calcutta* 8 A1
Sarecky potok ✈, *Prague* 24 B2
Sarimbun, *Singapore* 27 A2
Sarimbun Res., *Singapore* 27 A2
Sarıyer, *Istanbul* 12 A2
Saronikós Kólpos, *Athens* 2 B1
Sarriá, *Barcelona* 4 A1
Sarsuna, *Calcutta* 8 C1
Sartrouville, *Paris* 23 A2
Sasad, *Budapest* 7 B2
Sashalom, *Budapest* 7 A3
Saska, *Warsaw* 31 B2
Satalice, *Prague* 24 B3
Satgachi, *Calcutta* 8 B2
Sathorn, *Bangkok* 3 B2
Satpukur, *Calcutta* 8 B2
Sätra, *Stockholm* 28 B1
Sattru Pha, *Bangkok* 3 b2
Saúde, *São Paulo* 26 B2
Saugus, *Boston* 6 A3
Saugus ✈, *Boston* 6 A3
Sault-au-Récollet, *Montreal* 19 A2
Sausalito, *San Francisco* 25 A2
Sawah Besar, *Jakarta* 13 A1
Saxonville, *Boston* 6 B1
Scald Law, *Edinburgh* 11 B2
Scarborough, *Toronto* 30 A3
Sceaux, *Paris* 23 B2
Schaerbeek, *Brussels* 6 A2
Scharfenberg, *Berlin* 5 A2
Scheepvartmuseum, *Amsterdam* 2 b3
Schiller Park, *Chicago* 9 B1
Schiller Woods, *Chicago* 9 B1
Schiphol, Luchthaven, *Amsterdam* 2 B1
Schlachtensee, *Berlin* 5 B2
Schlossgarten, *Berlin* 5 A2
Schmargendorf, *Berlin* 5 B2
Schönblick, *Berlin* 5 B5
Schönbrunn, Schloss, *Vienna* 31 A1
Schöneberg, *Berlin* 5 B3
Schöneiche, *Berlin* 5 B5
Schönwalde, *Berlin* 5 A1
Schotschekloof, *Cape Town* 8 b1
Schulzendorf, *Berlin* 5 A2
Schwabing, *Munich* 20 B2
Schwanebeck, *Berlin* 5 A4
Schwanenwerder, *Berlin* 5 B2
Schwarzlackenau, *Vienna* 31 A2
Schwechat, *Vienna* 31 B2
Scitrek Museum, *Atlanta* 3 B2
Scott Monument, *Edinburgh* 11 b2
Scottdale, *Atlanta* 3 B3
Sea Point, *Cape Town* 8 A1
Seabrook, *Washington* 32 B5
Seacliff, *San Francisco* 25 B2
Seaforth, *Sydney* 28 A2
Seagate, *New York* 21 C1
Sears Tower, *Chicago* 9 c1
Seat Pleasant, *Washington* 32 B4
Seaview, *Wellington* 32 B2
Šeberov, *Prague* 24 B3
Secaucus, *New York* 21 B1
Seddinsee, *Berlin* 5 B5
Seeberg, *Berlin* 5 A5
Seeburg, *Berlin* 5 A1
Seefeld, *Berlin* 5 A5
Seegefeld, *Berlin* 5 A1
Seehof, *Berlin* 5 B2
Segeltorp, *Stockholm* 28 B1
Segrate, *Milan* 18 B2
Seguro, *Milan* 18 B1
Seine ✈, *Paris* 23 B3
Seixal, *Lisbon* 14 B2
Selby, *Johannesburg* 13 B2
Seletar, P., *Singapore* 27 A3
Seletar Hills, *Singapore* 27 A3
Seletar Res., *Singapore* 27 A2
Selhurst, *London* 15 B3
Sembawang, *Singapore* 27 A2
Senago, *Milan* 18 A1
Sendinger Tor Platz, *Munich* 20 c1
Sendling, *Munich* 20 B2
Senju, *Tokyo* 29 A3
Senriyama, *Osaka* 22 A4
Sentosa, P., *Singapore* 27 B2
Seoul = Sŏul, *Seoul* 26 B2
Seoul National Univ., *Seoul* 26 C1
Seoul Tower, *Seoul* 26 B1
Sepolia, *Athens* 2 A2
Sepulveda Flood Control Basin, *Los Angeles* 16 A2
Serangoon, *Singapore* 27 A3
Serangoon, P., *Singapore* 27 A3
Serangoon, Sungei ✈, *Singapore* 27 A3
Serangoon Harbour, *Singapore* 27 A3
Seraya, P., *Singapore* 27 B2
Serebryanka, *Moscow* 19 B5
Serebryanka ✈, *Moscow* 19 B4
Serramonte, *San Francisco* 25 C2
Sesto San Giovanni, *Milan* 18 A2
Sesto Ulteriano, *Milan* 18 B2
Setagaya-Ku, *Tokyo* 29 B2
Seter, *Oslo* 22 A3
Setia Budi, *Jakarta* 13 B1
Settebagni, *Rome* 25 A2
Settecamini, *Rome* 25 B2
Séttimo Milanese, *Milan* 18 B1
Settsu, *Osaka* 22 A4
Setuny ✈, *Moscow* 19 B2
Seutula, *Helsinki* 12 A2
Seven Corners, *Washington* 32 B3
Seven Kings, *London* 15 A4
Sévesco ✈, *Milan* 18 A1
Sevran, *Paris* 23 A4
Sewri, *Mumbai* 20 B2
Sforzesso, Castello, *Milan* 18 B2
Sha Kok Mei, *Hong Kong* 12 A2
Sha Tin, *Hong Kong* 12 A2
Sha Tin Wai, *Hong Kong* 12 A2
Shabrâmant, *Cairo* 7 B2
Shahdara, *Delhi* 10 A2
Shahe, *Canton* 8 B2
Shahr-e Rey, *Tehran* 30 B2
Shahrak-e Golshahr, *Tehran* 30 B1
Shahrak-e Qods, *Tehran* 30 A2
Shaikh Aomar, *Baghdad* 3 A2
Shakurbasti, *Delhi* 10 A1
Shalkiya, *Calcutta* 8 B2
Sham Shui Po, *Hong Kong* 12 B1
Shamapur, *Delhi* 10 A1
Shamian, *Canton* 8 B2
Shan Mei, *Hong Kong* 12 A2
Shanghai, *Shanghai* 27 B2
Shankill, *Dublin* 11 B3
Sharp I., *Hong Kong* 12 A2
Shastrinagar, *Delhi* 10 A2
Shau Kei Wan, *Hong Kong* 12 B2
Shawocun, *Beijing* 4 B1
Shayuan, *Canton* 8 B2
Sheepshead Bay, *New York* 21 C2
Shek O, *Hong Kong* 12 B2
Shelter I., *Hong Kong* 12 B2
Sheng Fa Shan, *Hong Kong* 12 A1
Shepherds Bush, *London* 15 A2
Shepperton, *London* 15 B1
Sherman Oaks, *Los Angeles* 16 B2
Sherman Park, *Chicago* 9 C2
Shet Bandar, *Mumbai* 20 B2
Sheung Lau Wan, *Hong Kong* 12 B2
Sheung Wan, *Hong Kong* 12 B1
Sheva, *Mumbai* 20 B2
Sheva Nhava, *Mumbai* 20 B2
Shiba, *Tokyo* 29 c4
Shibpur, *Calcutta* 8 B1
Shibuya-Ku, *Tokyo* 29 c1
Shijōnawate, *Osaka* 22 A4
Shillim, *Seoul* 26 C1
Shimogawara, *Tokyo* 29 B1
Shimosalo, *Tokyo* 29 A2
Shimoshakujii, *Tokyo* 29 A2
Shinagawa-Ku, *Tokyo* 29 B3
Shing Mun Res., *Hong Kong* 12 A1
Shinjuku-Ku, *Tokyo* 29 a1
Shinjuku National Garden, *Tokyo* 29 a2
Shinkoiwa, *Tokyo* 29 A4
Shinnakano, *Tokyo* 29 A3
Shinsa, *Seoul* 26 B2
Shipai, *Canton* 8 B3
Shirinashi ✈, *Osaka* 22 B3
Shirogane, *Tokyo* 29 B3
Shiweitang, *Canton* 8 B2
Shogunle, *Lagos* 14 A2
Shomolu, *Lagos* 14 A2
Shooters Hill, *London* 15 B4
Shoreditch, *London* 15 a5
Shortlands, *London* 15 B4
Shu' afat, *Jerusalem* 13 B2
Shubrâ, *Cairo* 7 A2
Shubrâ el Kheima, *Cairo* 7 A2
Shuikuo, *Canton* 8 A2
Shuishang Park, *Tianjin* 30 B1
Sidcup, *London* 15 B4
Siebenhirten, *Vienna* 31 B1
Siedlung, *Berlin* 5 A1
Siekierki, *Warsaw* 31 B2
Sielce, *Warsaw* 31 B2
Siemensstadt, *Berlin* 5 A2
Sierra Madre, *Los Angeles* 16 B4
Sievering, *Vienna* 31 A2
Sighthill, *Edinburgh* 11 B2
Signal Hill, *Cape Town* 8 A1
Sihŭng, *Seoul* 26 C1
Sikátorpuszta, *Budapest* 7 A3
Silampur, *Delhi* 10 B2
Silver Hill, *Boston* 6 A2
Silver Hill, *Washington* 32 C4
Silver Spring, *Washington* 32 A3
Silvermine Nature Reserve, *Cape Town* 8 B1
Silvolantekojärvi, *Helsinki* 12 B2
Simei, *Singapore* 27 A3
Simla, *Calcutta* 8 B2
Simmering, *Vienna* 31 A2
Simmering Heide, *Vienna* 31 A2
Simonkylä, *Helsinki* 12 B3
Singapore, *Singapore* 27 B3
Singapore, Univ. of, *Singapore* 27 B2
Sinicka ✈, *Moscow* 19 A1
Sinki, Selat, *Singapore* 27 B2
Sint-Genesius-Rode, *Brussels* 6 B2
Sinwŏl, *Seoul* 26 B1
Sion, *Mumbai* 20 A2
Sipson, *London* 15 B1
Siqeil, *Cairo* 7 A1
Şişli, *Istanbul* 12 B1
Skansen, *Stockholm* 28 B2
Skärholmen, *Stockholm* 28 B1
Skarpäng, *Stockholm* 28 A2
Skarpnäck, *Stockholm* 28 B2
Skaryszewski Park, *Warsaw* 31 B2
Skeppsholmen, *Stockholm* 28 c3
Skokie, *Chicago* 9 A2
Skokie ✈, *Chicago* 9 A2
Skoklefall, *Oslo* 22 A3
Sköndal, *Stockholm* 28 B2
Skovlunde, *Copenhagen* 10 A2
Skovshoved, *Copenhagen* 10 A3
Skuru, *Stockholm* 28 B3
Skyland, *Atlanta* 3 A3
Slade Green, *London* 15 B5
Slemmestad, *Oslo* 22 B1
Slependen, *Oslo* 22 A2
Slipi, *Jakarta* 13 B1
Slivenec, *Prague* 24 B2
Sloten, *Amsterdam* 2 A1
Sloterpark, *Amsterdam* 2 A1
Sluhy, *Prague* 24 A3
Służew, *Warsaw* 31 B2
Służewiec, *Warsaw* 31 B2
Smíchov, *Prague* 24 B2
Smith Forest Preserve, *Chicago* 9 B2
Smithsonian Institute, *Washington* 32 b2
Smolny, *St. Petersburg* 26 B2
Snake Creek Canal ✈, *Miami* 18 A2
Snarøya, *Oslo* 22 A2
Snättringe, *Stockholm* 28 B1
Sŏbinggo, *Seoul* 26 B1
Søborg, *Copenhagen* 10 A2
Sobreda, *Lisbon* 14 B1
Soch'o, *Seoul* 26 C1
Sŏdaemun, *Seoul* 26 B1
Söderby, *Stockholm* 28 A3
Södermalm, *Stockholm* 28 B2
Sodpur, *Calcutta* 8 A2
Soeurs, Î. des, *Montreal* 19 B2
Sognsvatn, *Oslo* 22 A3
Soho, *London* 15 b3
Soho, *New York* 21 e1
Soignes, Forêt de, *Brussels* 6 B2
Sok Kwu Wan, *Hong Kong* 12 B1
Sŏkkwan, *Seoul* 26 B2
Sokolniki, *Moscow* 19 B4
Sokolniki Park, *Moscow* 19 B4
Sokołów, *Warsaw* 31 C1
Solalinden, *Munich* 20 B3
Soldier Field, *Chicago* 9 e3
Sollentuna, *Stockholm* 28 A1
Solln, *Munich* 20 B2
Solna, *Stockholm* 28 A1
Solntsevo, *Moscow* 19 C2
Somerset, *Washington* 32 B3
Somerville, *Boston* 6 A3
Somes Is., *Wellington* 32 B2
Sonari, *Mumbai* 20 B2
Søndersø, *Copenhagen* 10 A2
Sŏngbuk, *Seoul* 26 B2
Sŏngdong, *Seoul* 26 B2
Sŏngp'a, *Seoul* 26 B2
Sŏngsu, *Seoul* 26 B2
Soong Qingling, Former Res. of, *Beijing* 4 a2
Soroksár, *Budapest* 7 B2
Soroksari Duna ✈, *Budapest* 7 B2
Sosenka ✈, *Moscow* 19 B4
Sosnovka, *St. Petersburg* 26 B2
Sŏul, *Seoul* 26 B2
Soundview, *New York* 21 B2
South Beach, *New York* 21 C1
South Beach Harbor, *San Francisco* 25 c3
South Bend Park, *Atlanta* 3 B2
South Boston, *Boston* 6 A3
South Brooklyn, *New York* 21 B2
South Decatur, *Atlanta* 3 B3
South Deering, *Chicago* 9 C3
South El Monte, *Los Angeles* 16 B4
South Gate, *Los Angeles* 16 C3
South Harbor, *Manila* 17 B1
South Harrow, *London* 15 A1
South Hd., *Sydney* 28 B2
South Hills, *Johannesburg* 13 B2
South Hornchurch, *London* 15 A5
South Kensington, *London* 15 c2
South Lawn, *Washington* 32 C3
South Lincoln, *Boston* 6 A2
South Miami, *Miami* 18 B1
South Norwood, *London* 15 B3
South of Market, *San Francisco* 25 B2
South Ozone Park, *New York* 21 B3
South Pasadena, *Los Angeles* 16 B4
South Res., *Boston* 6 A3
South Ruislip, *London* 15 A1
South San Francisco, *San Francisco* 25 C2
South San Gabriel, *Los Angeles* 16 B4
South Shore, *Chicago* 9 C3
South Sudbury, *Boston* 6 A1
Southall, *London* 15 A1
Southborough, *London* 15 B4
Southend, *London* 15 B3
Southfields, *London* 15 B2
Southwark, *London* 15 B3
Søvang, *Copenhagen* 10 B3
Soweto, *Johannesburg* 13 B1
Sowhānak, *Tehran* 30 A3
Soya, *Tokyo* 29 A4
Spandau, *Berlin* 5 A1
Spånga, *Stockholm* 28 A1
Spanische Reitschule, *Vienna* 31 b1
Spectacle I., *Boston* 6 A4
Speicher-See, *Munich* 20 A3
Speising, *Vienna* 31 B1
Sphinx, *Cairo* 7 B1
Spinaceto, *Rome* 25 C1
Spit Junction, *Sydney* 28 A2
Spořilov, *Prague* 24 B3
Spot Pond, *Boston* 6 A3
Spotswood, *Melbourne* 17 B1
Spree ✈, *Berlin* 5 A2
Spring Pond, *Boston* 6 A4
Springeberg, *Berlin* 5 B5
Springfield, *Washington* 32 C2
Squantum, *Boston* 6 B3
Srednaya Rogatka, *St. Petersburg* 26 C2
Sródmieście, *Warsaw* 31 B2
Saint-Gilles, *Brussels* 6 B2
Saint-Joose-Ten-Noode, *Brussels* 6 A2
Saint-Pieters-Leeuw, *Brussels* 6 B1
Saint-Stevens-Woluwe, *Brussels* 6 A2
Staaken, *Berlin* 5 A1
Stabekk, *Oslo* 22 A2
Stadhion, *Athens* 2 c3
Stadhuis, *Amsterdam* 2 b2
Stadlau, *Vienna* 31 A2
Stadshuset, *Stockholm* 28 b1
Stains, *Paris* 23 A3
Stamford Hill, *London* 15 A3
Stammersdorf, *Vienna* 31 A2
Stanley, *Hong Kong* 12 B2
Stanley Mound, *Hong Kong* 12 B2
Stanley Pen., *Hong Kong* 12 B2
Stanmore, *London* 15 A2
Stapleton, *New York* 21 C1
Star Ferry, *Hong Kong* 12 a2
Staraya Derevnya, *St. Petersburg* 26 B1
Stare, *Warsaw* 31 B2
Staré Město, *Prague* 24 B2
Starego Miasto, *Warsaw* 31 a2
Staten Island Zoo, *New York* 21 C1
Statenice, *Prague* 24 B1
Statue Square, *Hong Kong* 12 c1
Stedelijk Museum, *Amsterdam* 2 c1
Steele Creek, *Melbourne* 17 A1
Steenokkerzeel, *Brussels* 6 A2
Steglitz, *Berlin* 5 B2
Stepaside, *Dublin* 11 B2
Stephansdom, *Vienna* 31 b2
Stepney, *London* 15 A3
Sterling Park, *San Francisco* 25 B2
Sticklinge udde, *Stockholm* 28 A2
Stickney, *Chicago* 9 C2
Stillorgan, *Dublin* 11 B2
Stockholm, *Stockholm* 28 B2
Stocksund, *Stockholm* 28 A2
Stodůlky, *Prague* 24 B1
Stoke Newington, *London* 15 A3
Stokes Valley, *Wellington* 32 B2
Stone Canyon Res., *Los Angeles* 16 B2
Stone Park, *Chicago* 9 B1
Stonebridge, *London* 15 A2
Stoneham, *Boston* 6 A3
Stony Brook Res., *Boston* 6 B3
Stora Värtan, *Stockholm* 28 A2
Store Hareskov, *Copenhagen* 10 A2
Store Magleby, *Copenhagen* 10 B3
Storholmen, *Stockholm* 28 A2
Stoyka, *St. Petersburg* 26 B2
Straiton, *Edinburgh* 11 B3
Strand, *London* 15 b4
Strandfontein, *Cape Town* 8 B2
Strašnice, *Prague* 24 B2
Strasstrudering, *Munich* 20 B3
Stratford, *London* 15 A4
Strathfield, *Sydney* 28 B1
Streatham, *London* 15 B3
Streatham Vale, *London* 15 B3
Strebersdorf, *Vienna* 31 A2
Střešovice, *Prague* 24 B2
Střížkov, *Prague* 24 B2
Strogino, *Moscow* 19 B2
Strombeek-Bever, *Brussels* 6 A2
Stromovka, *Prague* 24 B2
Studio City, *Los Angeles* 16 B2
Stureby, *Stockholm* 28 B2
Stuvsta, *Stockholm* 28 B2
Subhepur, *Delhi* 10 A2
Sucat, *Manila* 17 C2
Suchdol, *Prague* 24 B2
Sucy-en-Brie, *Paris* 23 B4
Sudbury, *Boston* 6 A1
Sugamo, *Tokyo* 29 A3
Sugar Loaf Mt. = Açúcar, Pão de, *Rio de Janeiro* 24 B2
Suge, *Tokyo* 29 B2
Suginami-Ku, *Tokyo* 29 A2
Sugō, *Tokyo* 29 B2
Suita, *Osaka* 22 A4
Suitland, *Washington* 32 B4
Sukchar, *Calcutta* 8 A2
Suma, *Osaka* 22 B1
Sumida ✈, *Tokyo* 29 A3
Sumida-Ku, *Tokyo* 29 A3
Sumiyoshi, *Osaka* 22 B4
Summerville, *Toronto* 30 B1
Summit, *Chicago* 9 C2
Sunamachi, *Tokyo* 29 A4
Sunbury-on-Thames, *London* 15 B1
Sundbyberg, *Stockholm* 28 A1
Sundbyerne, *Copenhagen* 10 B3
Sung Kong, *Hong Kong* 12 B2
Sungei Kadut Industrial Estate, *Singapore* 27 A2
Sungei Selatar Res., *Singapore* 27 A3
Sunter, *Jakarta* 13 A2
Sunter, Kali ✈, *Jakarta* 13 B2
Suomenlinna, *Helsinki* 12 C2
Supreme Court, *Washington* 32 b3
Sura, *Calcutta* 8 B2
Surag-san, *Seoul* 26 A2
Surbiton, *London* 15 B2
Suresnes, *Paris* 23 A2
Surfside, *Miami* 18 A2
Surquillo, *Lima* 16 B2
Surrey Hills, *Sydney* 28 B2
Susaek, *Seoul* 26 B1
Süssenbrunn, *Vienna* 31 A2
Sutton, *Dublin* 11 A3
Sutton, *London* 15 B2
Suyu, *Seoul* 26 B2
Suzukishinden, *Tokyo* 29 A2
Svanemøllen, *Copenhagen* 10 A3
Sverdlov, *Moscow* 19 B3
Svestad, *Oslo* 22 B2
Svinö, *Helsinki* 12 C1
Swampscott, *Boston* 6 A4
Swanley, *London* 15 B4
Swansea, *Toronto* 30 B2
Swinburne I., *New York* 21 C1
Swords, *Dublin* 11 A2
Sydenham, *Johannesburg* 13 A2
Sydney, *Sydney* 28 B2
Sydney, Univ. of, *Sydney* 28 B2
Sydney Airport, *Sydney* 28 B2
Sydney Harbour Bridge, *Sydney* 28 B2
Sydstranden, *Copenhagen* 10 B3
Sylvania, *Sydney* 28 C1
Syntagma, Pl., *Athens* 2 b3
Syon Park, *London* 15 B2
Szczęśliwice, *Warsaw* 31 B1
Széchnenyi-hegy, *Budapest* 7 B1
Szent Istvánbaz, *Budapest* 7 b2
Széphalom, *Budapest* 7 A1

T

Tabata, *Tokyo* 29 A3
Tablada, *Buenos Aires* 7 C1
Table Bay, *Cape Town* 8 A1
Table Mountain, *Cape Town* 8 A1
Taboão da Serra, *São Paulo* 26 B1
Täby, *Stockholm* 28 A2

Tacuba, *Mexico City* 18 B1
Tacubaya, *Mexico City* 18 B1
Taebang, *Seoul* 26 B1
Tagig, *Manila* 17 B2
Tagig →, *Manila* 17 B2
Tai Hang, *Hong Kong* 12 B2
Tai Lo Shan, *Hong Kong* .. 12 A2
Tai Po Tsai, *Hong Kong* ... 12 A3
Tai Seng, *Singapore* 27 A3
Tai Shui Hang, *Hong Kong* . 12 A2
Tai Tam B., *Hong Kong* ... 12 B2
Tai Tam Tuk Res.,
      Hong Kong 12 B2
Tai Wai, *Hong Kong* 12 A1
Tai Wo Hau, *Hong Kong* ... 12 A1
Tainaka, *Osaka* 22 B4
Taishō, *Osaka* 22 B3
Taita, *Wellington* 32 A1
Tajrīsh, *Tehran* 30 A2
Takaido, *Tokyo* 29 A2
Takaishi, *Tokyo* 29 B2
Takarazuka, *Osaka* 22 A2
Takatsu-Ku, *Tokyo* 29 B2
Takeshita, *Tokyo* 29 B2
Takinegawa, *Tokyo* 29 A3
Takoma Park, *Washington* .. 32 B3
Taksim, *Istanbul* 12 B1
Talaide, *Lisbon* 14 A1
Talpapa, *Calcutta* 8 B2
Talipapa, *Manila* 17 A2
Tallaght, *Dublin* 11 B1
Tallkrogen, *Stockholm* 28 B3
Tama, *Tokyo* 29 B1
Tama →, *Tokyo* 29 B2
Tama Kyūryō, *Tokyo* 29 B2
Tamaden, *Tokyo* 29 A3
Tamagawa-josui →, *Tokyo* . 29 A1
Taman Sari, *Jakarta* 13 A1
Tamandutaí →, *São Paulo* . 26 B2
Tamborskikrof, *Cape Town* . 8 A1
Tambora, *Jakarta* 13 A1
Tammisalo, *Helsinki* 12 B3
Tammūh, *Cairo* 7 A2
Tampines, *Singapore* 27 A3
Tanah Abang, *Jakarta* 13 B1
Tanigami, *Osaka* 22 A2
Tanjung Duren, *Jakarta* ... 13 B1
Tanjung Priok, *Jakarta* 13 A2
Tantallon, *Oslo* 2 B3
Taorantíng Park, *Beijing* 4 c2
Tapada, *Lisbon* 14 A1
Tapanila, *Helsinki* 12 B3
Tapiales, *Buenos Aires* 7 C1
Tapiola, *Helsinki* 12 A1
Tapsia, *Calcutta* 8 B2
Tara, *Mumbai* 20 A1
Tarabya, *Istanbul* 12 B2
Tarango, Presa, *Mexico City* 18 B1
Tårbæk, *Copenhagen* 10 A3
Tarchomin, *Warsaw* 31 B1
Tardeo, *Mumbai* 20 B1
Targówek, *Warsaw* 31 B2
Tárnby, *Copenhagen* 10 B3
Tarqua Bay, *Lagos* 14 B2
Tåstrup, *Copenhagen* 10 A1
Tatarovo, *Moscow* 19 B2
Tathong Channel, *Hong Kong* 12 B2
Tathong Pt., *Hong Kong* .. 12 B2
Tatuapé, *São Paulo* 26 B2
Taufkirchen, *Munich* 20 B2
Tavares, I. dos, *Rio de Janeiro* 24 A2
Távros, *Athens* 2 B2
Tawa, *Wellington* 32 A1
Teaneck, *New York* 21 A1
Teatro Municipal,
      Rio de Janeiro 24 c2
Tebet, *Jakarta* 13 B2
Tecamachaleo, *Mexico City* . 18 B1
Teddington, *London* 15 B1
Tegel, *Berlin* 5 A2
Tegel, Flughafen, *Berlin* ... 5 A2
Tegeler See, *Berlin* 5 A2
Tegelort, *Berlin* 5 A2
Tehrān, *Tehran* 30 A2
Tehrān Pārs, *Tehran* 30 A3
Tei Tong Tsui, *Hong Kong* . 12 B2
Tejo, Rio →, *Lisbon* 14 A2
Tekstilyshchik, *Moscow* 19 B4
Telegraph hill, *San Francisco* 25 a1
Telhal, *Lisbon* 14 A1
Telok Blangah, *Singapore* .. 27 B2
Teltow, *Berlin* 5 B2
Teltow kanal, *Berlin* 5 B3
Temnikovo, *Moscow* 19 B6
Tempelhof, *Berlin* 5 B3
Tempelhof, Flughafen, *Berlin* 5 B3
Temple City, *Los Angeles* .. 16 B4
Temple Hills Park,
      Washington 32 C4
Temple Mount, *Jerusalem* . 13 b3
Templeogue, *Dublin* 11 B2
Templo Mayor, *Mexico City* 18 b3
Tenafly, *New York* 21 A2
Tenayuca, Piramide de,
      Mexico City 18 A1
Tengah →, *Singapore* 27 A2
Tennoji, *Osaka* 22 B4
Tepalcates, *Mexico City* ... 18 B2
Terrazzano, *Milan* 18 A1
Terrugem, *Lisbon* 14 A1
Tervuren, *Brussels* 6 B3
Tervuren, Park van, *Brussels* 6 B3
Tetuán, *Madrid* 17 B1
Teufelsberg, *Berlin* 5 A2
Tévere →, *Rome* 25 B1
Thalkirchen, *Munich* 20 B2
Thames →, *London* 15 A4
Thames Ditton, *London* ... 15 B1
Thamesmead, *London* 15 A4
Thana Cr. →, *Mumbai* ... 20 A2
The Loop, *Chicago* 9 B3
The Ridge, *Delhi* 10 B2
The Wilds, *Johannesburg* .. 13 B2
Theater Carré, *Amsterdam* . 2 b2
Théatro Dionissou, *Athens* . 2 c2
Thiais, *Paris* 23 B3
Thissío, *Athens* 2 c1
Thistletown, *Toronto* 30 A1
Thomastown, *Melbourne* .. 17 A2
Thompson I., *Boston* 6 B4
Thon Buri, *Bangkok* 3 B1
Thornbury, *Melbourne* 17 A2
Thorncliffe, *Toronto* 30 A2
Thornhill, *Toronto* 30 A2
Thornton, *Cape Town* 8 A2
Thornton Heath, *London* .. 15 B3
Threipmuir Res., *Edinburgh* 11 B2
Throgs Neck, *New York* .. 21 B3
Thyssen Bornemisza, Museo,
      Madrid 17 b3
Tian'anmen Square, *Beijing* . 4 c2
Tiancun, *Beijing* 4 B1
Tianjin, *Tianjin* 30 B1
Tiantan Park, *Beijing* 4 c2
Tibidabo, *Barcelona* 4 A1

Tibradden Mt., *Dublin* 11 B2
Tiburon, *San Francisco* 25 A2
Tiburtino, *Rome* 25 B2
Ticomán, *Mexico City* 18 A2
Tiefersee, *Berlin* 5 B1
Tiejiangyin, *Beijing* 4 C2
Tientsin = Tianjin, *Tianjin* . 30 B1
Tiergarten, *Berlin* 5 A3
Tigerhof, *Cape Town* 8 A2
Tigris = Nahr Dijlah →,
      Baghdad 3 B2
Tijuca, *Rio de Janeiro* 24 B1
Tijuca, Parque Nacional da,
      Rio de Janeiro 24 B1
Tijuca, Pico da, *Rio de Janeiro* 24 B1
Tikkurila, *Helsinki* 12 B3
Tilak Nagar, *Delhi* 10 B1
Tilanqiao, *Shanghai* 27 B1
Timírdsh, *Tehran* 30 A2
Timiryazev Park, *Moscow* .. 19 B3
Ting Kau, *Hong Kong* 12 A1
Tira, *Jerusalem* 13 A1
Tirsa, *Oslo* 7 B2
Tishrīyaa, *Baghdad* 3 B2
Tiu Keng Leng, *Hong Kong* 12 B2
Tivoli, *Copenhagen* 10 a3
Tizapán, *Mexico City* 18 C1
Tlalnepantla →, *Mexico City* 18 A1
To Kwai Wan, *Hong Kong* . 12 B2
Toa Payoh, *Singapore* 27 A2
Tobong, *Seoul* 26 B2
Tobong-san, *Seoul* 26 A2
Točná, *Prague* 24 C2
Toco Hills, *Atlanta* 3 B2
Todt Hill, *New York* 21 C1
Tōkagi, *Tokyo* 29 B2
Tokai Plantation, *Cape Town* 8 B1
Tōkaichiba, *Tokyo* 29 B2
Tokarevo, *Moscow* 19 C5
Tōkyō, *Tokyo* 29 B3
Tokyo B., *Tokyo* 29 B4
Tokyo-Haneda Int. Airport,
      Tokyo 29 B3
Tokyo Harbour, *Tokyo* ... 29 B3
Tolka R. →, *Dublin* 11 A1
Tolworth, *London* 15 B2
Tomb of Lu Xun, *Shanghai* . 27 B1
Tomb di Nerone, *Rome* ... 25 B1
Tomba di Nerone, *Rome* .. 25 B1
Tomlino, *Moscow* 19 C5
Tondo, *Manila* 17 B1
Tongbinggo, *Seoul* 26 B1
Tongjak, *Seoul* 26 B1
Tongmaemung, *Seoul* 26 B1
Tongqiao, *Shanghai* 27 A1
Toorak, *Melbourne* 17 B2
Topkapı, *Istanbul* 12 B1
Tor di Quinto, *Rome* 25 B1
Tor Pignattara, *Rome* 25 B2
Tor Sapienza, *Rome* 25 B2
Tōraomon, *Tokyo* 29 b3
Torcy, *Paris* 23 A4
Toronto, *Toronto* 30 B2
Toronto, Univ. of, *Toronto* 30 B2
Toronto Harbour, *Toronto* . 30 B2
Toronto I., *Toronto* 30 B2
Toros Las Arenas, Pl. de,
      Barcelona 4 c1
Toros Monumental, Templo
      de, *Barcelona* 4 a3
Torre Latino-americana,
      Mexico City 18 b2
Torrellas →, *Barcelona* ... 4 A1
Torre Nova, *Rome* 25 B2
Torrevécchia, *Rome* 25 B1
Toshima-Ku, *Tokyo* 29 A3
Toshimaen, *Tokyo* 29 A2
Toussus-le-Noble, *Paris* 23 B1
Toussus-le-Noble, Aérodrome
      de, *Paris* 23 B1
Tower Bridge, *London* 15 b5
Tower Hamlets, *London* ... 15 A3
Tower of London, *London* . 15 A3
Towra Pt., *Sydney* 28 C2
Tøyen, *Oslo* 2 C1
Toyonaka, *Osaka* 22 A3
Trafalgar Square, *London* .. 15 b3
Trafaria, *Lisbon* 14 A1
Traição, Cor. →, *São Paulo* 26 B2
Tranegilde, *Copenhagen* ... 10 B2
Trångsund, *Stockholm* 28 B2
Transamerica Pyramid,
      San Francisco 25 b2
Transbay Terminal,
      San Francisco 25 b2
Trappenfelde, *Berlin* 5 A4
Tr, *Rio de Janeiro* 24 B1
Trebotov, *Prague* 24 C1
Tremblay-en-France, *Paris* . 23 A3
Tremembe →, *São Paulo* . 26 A2
Tremont, *New York* 21 A2
Trenno, *Milan* 18 B1
Treptow, *Berlin* 5 B3
Trés Rios, Sa. dos,
      Rio de Janeiro 24 B1
Trevi, Fontana di, *Rome* ... 25 b3
Trezzano sul Navíglio, *Milan* 18 B1
Tribune Tower, *Chicago* ... 9 b2
Trieste, *Rome* 25 B2
Trinidad, *Washington* 32 B4
Trinity, *Edinburgh* 11 B3
Trinity College, *Dublin* 11 c3
Trionfale, *Rome* 25 B1
Triulzo, *Milan* 18 B2
Trocadero, *Paris* 23 b1
Troitse-Lykovo, *Moscow* .. 19 B2
Troja, *Prague* 24 B2
Trollbäcken, *Stockholm* ... 28 B3
Tropareyo, *Moscow* 19 C2
Tropenmuseum, *Amsterdam* 2 b3
Trudyashchikhsya, Ostrov,
      St. Petersburg 26 B1
Tryvasshøgda, *Oslo* 2 B3
Tseng Lan Shue, *Hong Kong* 12 A2
Tsim Sha Tsui, *Hong Kong* . 12 a2
Tsing Yi, *Hong Kong* 12 A1
Tsova, *Oslo* 2 A2
Tsuen Wan, *Hong Kong* ... 12 A1
Tsukiji, *Tokyo* 29 c3
Tsur Hadassa, *Jerusalem* ... 13 B1
Tsurumi →, *Tokyo* 29 B3
Tsz War Shan, *Hong Kong* . 12 A2
Tuas, *Singapore* 27 B1
Tuchoměřice, *Prague* 24 B1
Tuckahoe, *New York* 21 A3
Tucuruví, *São Paulo* 26 A2
Tufello, *Rome* 25 B2

Tufnell Park, *London* 15 A3
Tughlakabad, *Delhi* 10 B2
Tuileries, Jardin des, *Paris* .. 23 b3
Tuindorp Oostzaan,
      Amsterdam 2 A2
Tullamarine, *Melbourne* ... 17 A1
Tulse Hill, *London* 15 B3
Tung Lung I., *Hong Kong* . 12 B2
Tung O, *Hong Kong* 12 B1
Tunis, *Baghdad* 3 A2
Tuomaria, *Helsinki* 12 B2
Tureberg, *Stockholm* 28 A1
Turffontein, *Johannesburg* . 13 B2
Turkso, *Prague* 24 A1
Turnham Green, *London* .. 15 B2
Turnhouse, *Edinburgh* 11 B1
Tuscolana, Via, *Rome* 25 B2
Tushino, *Moscow* 19 B3
Twelve Apostles, *Cape Town* 8 A1
Twickenham, *London* 15 B1
Twickenham Rugby Ground,
      London 15 B1
Twin Peaks, *San Francisco* . 25 B2
Two Rock Mt., *Dublin* 11 B2
Tymon North, *Dublin* 11 B1
Tysons Corner, *Washington* . 32 B2

U

U.S. Capitol, *Washington* ... 32 b3
Ubeidiya, *Jerusalem* 13 B2
Uberaba →, *São Paulo* ... 26 B2
Ubin, P., *Singapore* 27 A3
Uccle, *Brussels* 6 B2
Udelnaya, *St. Petersburg* ... 26 A2
Udelnoe, *St. Petersburg* ... 26 B1
Udding, *Munich* 20 A1
Ueno, *Tokyo* 29 A3
Uholicky, *Prague* 24 B1
Uhříněves, *Prague* 24 C2
Uithoorn, *Amsterdam* 2 B1
Újpalota, *Budapest* 7 A2
Újpest, *Budapest* 7 A2
Ukita, *Tokyo* 29 A4
Ullerup, *Copenhagen* 10 B3
Ullevål, *Oslo* 2 A3
Ulriksdal, *Stockholm* 28 A1
Ulyanka, St. Petersburg* ... 26 B1
Um Al-Khanazir Island,
      Baghdad 3 B2
Umeda, *Osaka* 22 A3
Umerkhadi, *Mumbai* 20 b2
Ümraniye, *Istanbul* 12 B2
Underground Atlanta, *Atlanta* 3 b2
Unětický potok →, *Prague* 24 B1
Üngam, *Seoul* 26 B1
Unhos, *Lisbon* 14 A2
Unidad Santa Fe, *Mexico City* 18 B1
Union City, *New York* 21 B1
Union Port, *New York* 21 B2
Union Square, *New York* .. 21 d2
Union Square, San Francisco* 25 b2
Union Station, *Washington* . 32 b3
United Nations H.Q.,
      New York 21 c3
Universidad, *Madrid* 17 B1
Universidad de Chile,
      Santiago 26 B2
University Park, *Washington* 32 B4
Unji'yong, *Seoul* 26 B1
Unter den Linden, *Berlin* .. 5 a4
Unterbiberg, *Munich* 20 B2
Unterföhring, *Munich* 20 A3
Unterhaching, *Munich* 20 B2
Unterlaa, *Vienna* 31 B2
Untermenzing, *Munich* 20 A1
Upper East Side, *New York* 21 c3
Upper Elmers End, *London* 15 B3
Upper New York B.,
      New York 21 C1
Upper Norwood, *London* .. 15 B3
Upper Peirce Res., *Singapore* 27 A2
Upper Sydenham, *London* .. 15 B3
Upper Tooting, *London* ... 15 B2
Upper West Side, *New York* 21 a2
Upton, *London* 15 A4
Uptown, *Chicago* 9 B2
Uran, *Mumbai* 20 B2
Urayasu, *Tokyo* 29 A4
Urbe, Aeroporto d', *Rome* . 25 B1
Urca, *Rio de Janeiro* 24 B2
Uritsk, *St. Petersburg* 26 C1
Üröm, *Budapest* 7 A2
Ursus, *Warsaw* 31 B1
Ursvik, *Stockholm* 28 A1
Usera, *Madrid* 17 B1
Ushigome, *Tokyo* 29 A3
Üsküdar, *Istanbul* 12 B2
Ust-Slavyanka, *St. Petersburg* 26 C3
Uteke, *Stockholm* 28 A1
Utrata, *Warsaw* 31 B2
Uttarpara, *Calcutta* 8 B1
Uttersleν Mose, *Copenhagen* 10 A2

V

Vadaul, *Mumbai* 20 A2
Vaires-sur-Marne, *Paris* 23 A4
Valby, *Copenhagen* 10 A3
Valcannuta, *Rome* 25 B1
Valdelatas, *Madrid* 17 A1
Valdemarsvik →, *Berlin* ... 5 B1
Valentoͮn, *Paris* 23 B3
Valera, *Milan* 18 A1
Vallcarca, *Barcelona* 4 A1
Valldoreix, *Barcelona* 4 A1
Vallecas, *Madrid* 17 B2
Vallensbæk, *Copenhagen* ... 10 B2
Vallensbæk Strand,
      Copenhagen 10 B2
Vallentunasjön, *Stockholm* . 28 A2
Valleranello, *Rome* 25 C1
Vallidrera, *Barcelona* 4 A1
Vallvidrera →, *Barcelona* .. 4 A1
Van Goghmuseum,
      Amsterdam 2 c1
Vanak, *Tehran* 30 A2
Vangede, *Copenhagen* 10 A3
Vanikøy, *Istanbul* 12 B2
Vanløse, *Copenhagen* 10 A2
Vantaa, *Helsinki* 12 B2
Vantaankoski, *Helsinki* 12 B2
Vantaanpuisto, *Helsinki* ... 12 B2
Vanves, *Paris* 23 B2
Varedo, *Milan* 18 A1
Várfok, *Budapest* 7 b2
Variza, *Athens* 2 C2
Vartiokylä, *Helsinki* 12 B3

Vartiosaari, *Helsinki* 12 B3
Vasamuseet, *Stockholm* ... 28 b3
Vasco, *Cape Town* 8 A2
Vasfanārd, *Tehran* 30 B2
Vashi, *Mumbai* 20 A2
Vasilyevskiy, Ostrov,
      St. Petersburg 26 B1
Vaso Regulador El Cristo,
      Mexico City 18 B2
Vaucluse, *Sydney* 28 B2
Vaucresson, *Paris* 23 A1
Vauhallan, *Paris* 23 B2
Vaujours, *Paris* 23 A4
Vauxhall, *London* 15 c4
Vecsés, *Budapest* 7 B3
Velen, *Budapest* 7 A3
Veleslavín, *Prague* 24 B2
Vélizy-Villacoublay, *Paris* .. 23 B2
Velka-Chuchle, *Prague* 24 B2
Velké Přílepy, *Prague* 24 A1
Venda Seca, *Lisbon* 14 A1
Venetian Islands, *Miami* ... 18 B2
Venezia, Palazzo, *Rome* ... 25 c2
Venice, *Los Angeles* 16 C2
Ventas, *Madrid* 17 B1
Ventorro del Cano, *Madrid* . 17 B1
Venustiano Carranza,
      Mexico City 18 B2
Verde →, *São Paulo* 26 A2
Verdi, *Athens* 2 A2
Verdun, *Montreal* 19 B2
Vérhalom, *Budapest* 7 A2
Vermelho →, *São Paulo* .. 26 A2
Vernon, *Los Angeles* 16 B3
Verrières-le-Buisson, *Paris* .. 23 B2
Versailles, *Buenos Aires* ... 7 B1
Versailles, *Paris* 23 B1
Veshnyaki, *Moscow* 19 B4
Vesolyy Posëlok,
      St. Petersburg 26 B2
Vestra, *Helsinki* 12 B1
Vestskoven, *Copenhagen* .. 10 A2
Vicálvaro, *Madrid* 17 B2
Vicente Lopez, *Buenos Aires* 7 B2
Victoria, *Hong Kong* 12 B2
Victoria, *London* 15 c3
Victoria, Mt., *Wellington* .. 32 B2
Victoria, Pont, *Montreal* .. 19 B2
Victoria and Albert
      Waterfront, *Cape Town* 8 a1
Victoria Gardens, *Mumbai* . 20 B2
Victoria Harbour, *Hong Kong* 12 B1
Victoria I., *Lagos* 14 B2
Victoria L., *Johannesburg* .. 13 B2
Victoria Lawn Tennis Courts,
      Melbourne 17 B2
Victoria Park, *Singapore* ... 27 A3
Victoria Peak, *Hong Kong* . 12 B1
Victoria Wharf, *Cape Town* . 8 a2
Vienna = Wien, *Vienna* ... 31 A2
Vienna, *Washington* 32 B2
View Park, *Los Angeles* ... 16 C2
Vigário Geral, *Rio de Janeiro* 24 A1
Vigel Village, *Buenos Aires* . 7 B1
Viggbyholm, *Stockholm* ... 28 A2
Vighignolo, *Milan* 18 B1
Viikki, *Helsinki* 12 B2
Vikhroli, *Mumbai* 20 A2
Vila Guilherme, *São Paulo* . 26 B2
Vila Isabel, *Rio de Janeiro* . 24 B1
Vila Jaguára, *São Paulo* ... 26 B1
Vila Madalena, *São Paulo* .. 26 B1
Vila Mariana, *São Paulo* ... 26 B2
Vila Prudente, *São Paulo* .. 26 B2
Viladecans, *Barcelona* 4 B1
Vile Parle, *Mumbai* 20 A2
Villa Adelina, *Buenos Aires* . 7 B1
Villa Ballester, *Buenos Aires* 7 B1
Villa Barilari, *Buenos Aires* . 7 C2
Villa Borghese, *Rome* 25 a3
Villa Bosch, *Buenos Aires* .. 7 B1
Villa C. Colon, *Buenos Aires* 7 C2
Villa de Guadalupe,
      Mexico City 18 B2
Villa Devoto, *Buenos Aires* . 7 B1
Villa Diamante, *Buenos Aires* 7 C2
Villa Dominico, *Buenos Aires* 7 C2
Villa Lugano, *Buenos Aires* . 7 C1
Villa Lynch, *Buenos Aires* .. 7 B1
Villa Madero, *Buenos Aires* . 7 C1
Villa Sáenz Pena,
      Buenos Aires 7 B1
Vila Urquiza, *Buenos Aires* . 7 B2
Villaverde, *Madrid* 17 B1
Villaverde Bajo, *Madrid* ... 17 B1
Ville-d'Avray, *Paris* 23 B2
Villecresnes, *Paris* 23 B4
Villejuif, *Paris* 23 B3
Villemomble, *Paris* 23 A4
Villeneuve-la-Garenne, *Paris* 23 A2
Villeneuve-le-Roi, *Paris* 23 B3
Villeneuve-St.-Georges, *Paris* 23 B3
Villevaudé, *Paris* 23 A4
Villiers-le-Bâcle, *Paris* 23 B1
Villiers-sur-Marne, *Paris* ... 23 B4
Villinki, *Helsinki* 12 B3
Villoresi, Canale, *Milan* ... 18 A1
Vilvoorde, *Brussels* 6 A2
Vimodrone, *Milan* 18 A2
Vimont, *Montreal* 19 A1
Vinanmek Palace, *Bangkok* . 3 a2
Vincennes, *Paris* 23 A3
Vincennes, Bois de, *Paris* .. 23 B3
Vinings, *Atlanta* 3 A2
Vinohrady, *Prague* 24 B2
Vinoͮ, *Prague* 24 B3
Violet Hill, *Hong Kong* ... 12 B2
Virányos, *Budapest* 7 A1
Virgen del San Cristóbal,
      Santiago 26 B2
Virginia Gardens, *Miami* ... 18 B1
Virginia Key, *Miami* 18 B2
Viroflay, *Paris* 23 B2
Víron, *Athens* 2 B2
Virum, *Copenhagen* 10 A3
Vishnyaki, *Moscow* 19 B5
Visitacion Valley,
      San Francisco 25 C2
Vista Alegre, *Lima* 16 B3
Vista Alegre, *Santiago* 26 B2
Vista Grove, *Atlanta* 3 A3
Vitacura, *Santiago* 26 B2
Vitinia, *Rome* 25 C1
Vitry-sur-Seine, *Paris* 23 B3
Vizandinó, Moussío, *Athens* . 2 b3
Vladykino, *Moscow* 19 A3
Vlezenbeek, *Brussels* 6 B1
Vltava →, *Prague* 24 B2
Vnukovo, *Moscow* 19 C1
Vokovice, *Prague* 24 B1
Volgelsdorf, *Berlin* 5 B5
Volhonka-Zil, *Moscow* 19 C3
Volkonovo, *Moscow* 19 C5
Vollen, *Oslo* 2 B1
Volodarskoye, *St. Petersburg* 26 B1

Volynkina-Derevnya,
      St. Petersburg 26 B1
Vondelpark, *Amsterdam* ... 2 c1
Vösendorf, *Vienna* 31 B2
Vostochnyy, *Moscow* 19 B5
Vostochnyy, *Moscow* 19 B5
Voula, *Athens* 2 C2
Vouliagmeni, *Athens* 2 C2
Vredehoek, *Cape Town* ... 8 A1
Vršovice, *Prague* 24 B2
Vyborgskaya Storona,
      St. Petersburg 26 B2
Vykhino, *Moscow* 19 B4
Vyšehrad, *Prague* 24 B2

W

Wachterhof, *Munich* 20 B3
Wadala, *Mumbai* 20 A2
Wadestown, *Wellington* ... 32 B1
Wadi Fukin, *Jerusalem* 13 B1
Wah Fu, *Hong Kong* 12 B1
Wahda, *Baghdad* 3 B2
Währing, *Vienna* 31 A2
Waidmannslust, *Berlin* 5 A3
Wainuiomata, *Wellington* .. 32 B2
Wainuiomata R. →,
      Wellington 32 B2
Wakefield, *Boston* 6 A3
Waldesruh, *Berlin* 5 B4
Waldperlach, *Munich* 20 B3
Waldtrudering, *Munich* 20 B3
Walkinstown, *Dublin* 11 B1
Wall Street, *New York* ... 21 f1
Waltham, *Boston* 6 A2
Waltham Forest, *London* .. 15 A3
Walthamstow, *London* 15 A3
Walton on Thames, *London* 15 B1
Wambeek, *Brussels* 6 A1
Wan Chai, *Hong Kong* 12 c2
Wan Chai Lanes, *Hong Kong* 12 c2
Wandsworth, *London* 15 B2
Wankhede Stadium, *Mumbai* 20 c2
Wannsee, *Berlin* 5 B1
Wansdorf, *Berlin* 5 A2
Wanstead, *London* 15 A4
Wapping, *London* 15 A3
Ward, *Dublin* 11 A1
Ward L., *Wellington* 32 B2
Warnberg, *Munich* 20 B2
Warrâgi el 'Arab, *Cairo* ... 7 A2
Warrâq el Hadr, *Cairo* 7 A2
Warringen Park, *Melbourne* 17 A2
Warriston, *Edinburgh* 11 B3
Warsaw = Warszawa, *Warsaw* 31 B2
Warszawa, *Warsaw* 31 B2
Wartenberg, *Berlin* 5 A4
Warton, *Boston* 6 A3
Washington, *Washington* .. 32 B3
Washington Heights,
      New York 21 A2
Washington Monument,
      Washington 32 b1
Washington Nat. Airport,
      Washington 32 B3
Washington Park, *Chicago* . 9 C3
Wat Arun, *Bangkok* 3 b1
Wat Pho, *Bangkok* 3 b1
Wat Phra Keo, *Bangkok* .. 3 b1
Water of Leith, *Edinburgh* . 11 B1
Water Tower Place, *Chicago* 9 a2
Watergraafsmeer, *Amsterdam* 2 A2
Waterland, *Amsterdam* ... 2 A2
Waterloo, *Brussels* 6 B2
Waterloo, *Wellington* 32 B2
Waterloo International,
      London 15 b4
Watermael-Boitsfort, *Brussels* 6 B2
Watertown, *Boston* 6 A3
Watsonia, *Melbourne* 17 A2
Waverley, *Boston* 6 A3
Waverley, *Johannesburg* ... 13 A2
Waverley, *Sydney* 28 B2
Waverley, *Wellington* 32 B2
Wawer, *Warsaw* 31 B2
Wawrzyszew, *Warsaw* 31 B1
Wayland, *Boston* 6 A1
Wazirabad, *Delhi* 10 A2
Wazirīya, *Baghdad* 3 A2
Wazirpur, *Delhi* 10 A2
Wealdstone, *London* 15 A2
Wedding, *Berlin* 5 A3
Weehawken, *New York* ... 21 B1
Weesp, *Amsterdam* 2 A3
Weidling, *Vienna* 31 A1
Weidlingbach, *Vienna* 31 A1
Weigongcun, *Beijing* 4 B1
Weijin He →, *Tianjin* 30 B2
Weissensee, *Berlin* 5 A3
Wellesley, *Boston* 6 A2
Wellesley Falls, *Boston* 6 A2
Wellesley Hills, *Boston* 6 A2
Welling, *London* 15 B4
Wellington, *Boston* 6 A3
Wellington, *Wellington* ... 32 B1
Wells Fargo Center,
      Los Angeles 16 b1
Weltevreden Park,
      Johannesburg 13 A1
Wembley, *London* 15 A2
Wemmel, *Brussels* 6 A1
Wemmer Pan, *Johannesburg* 13 B2
Wenceslas Square, *Prague* .. 24 c2
Wendenschloss, *Berlin* 5 B4
Wenhuagong, *Tianjin* 30 B2
Wennington, *London* 15 A5
Wentworth, *Sydney* 28 B1
West Bedford, *Boston* 6 A1
West Concord, *Boston* 6 A1
West Don →, *Toronto* ... 30 A2
West Drayton, *London* 15 A1
West Ham, *London* 15 A4
West Harrow, *London* 15 A2
West Heath, *London* 15 B4
West Hill, *Toronto* 30 A3
West Hollywood, *Los Angeles* 16 B2
West Kensington, *London* .. 15 c1
West Lamma Channel,
      Hong Kong 12 B1
West Lynn, *Boston* 6 A3
West Medford, *Boston* 6 A3
West Miami, *Miami* 18 B1
West Molesey, *London* 15 B1
West New York, *New York* 21 B1
West of Twin Peaks,
      San Francisco 25 B2
West Park, *Johannesburg* .. 13 A1
West Rouge, *Toronto* 30 A4
West Roxbury, *Boston* 6 B3
West Springfield, *Washington* 32 C2
West Town, *Chicago* 9 B2
West Wharf, *Karachi* 14 B1
Westbourne Green, *London* . 15 a1
Westchester, *Boston* 6 B3

Westchester, *Los Angeles* .. 16 C2
Westchester, *New York* ... 21 A2
Westcliff, *Johannesburg* ... 13 B2
Westdene, *Johannesburg* ... 13 B1
Westend, *Helsinki* 12 C1
Wester Hailes, *Edinburgh* .. 11 B2
Westerham, *Munich* 20 B3
Western Addition,
      San Francisco 25 B2
Western Wall, *Jerusalem* .. 13 b3
Westgate, *Washington* 32 B3
Westlake, *Cape Town* 8 B1
Westlake, San Francisco* ... 25 B2
Westminster, *London* 15 c3
Westmount, *Montreal* 19 B2
Weston, *Boston* 6 A2
Weston, *Toronto* 30 A1
Weston Res., *Boston* 6 A2
Westwood Village,
      Los Angeles 16 B2
Westzaan, *Amsterdam* 2 A1
Wetton, *Cape Town* 8 B2
Wexford, *Toronto* 30 A3
Weybridge, *London* 15 B1
Wezembeek-Oppem, *Brussels* 6 A2
White House, The,
      Washington 32 b1
Whitechapel, *London* 15 A3
Whitehall, *Dublin* 11 A2
Whitehall, *London* 15 b3
Whittier, *Los Angeles* 16 C4
Whitton, *London* 15 B1
Wichelen, *Vienna* 31 A2
Wien, *Vienna* 31 A2
Wien-Schwechat, Flughafen,
      Vienna 31 B3
Wienerberg, *Vienna* 31 B2
Wierzbno, *Warsaw* 31 B2
Wijde Wormer, *Amsterdam* 2 A2
Wilanów, *Warsaw* 31 C2
Wilanówka →, *Warsaw* ... 31 C2
Wilhelmshagen, *Berlin* 5 B5
Wilket Creek Park, *Toronto* 30 A2
Wilkieston, *Edinburgh* 11 B1
Willbrook, *Dublin* 11 B2
Willesden, *London* 15 A2
Willesden Green, *London* .. 15 A2
Williamsburg, *New York* .. 21 A2
Williamstown, *Melbourne* .. 17 B1
Willoughby, *Sydney* 28 A2
Willow Springs, *Chicago* .. 9 C1
Willowdale, *Toronto* 30 A2
Wilmersdorf, *Berlin* 5 B3
Wilmette, *Chicago* 9 A2
Wilmington, *London* 15 B5
Wilshire Boulevard,
      Los Angeles 16 c1
Wimbledon, *London* 15 B2
Wimbledon Common,
      London 15 B2
Wimbledon Park, *London* .. 15 B2
Wimbledon Tennis Ground,
      London 15 B2
Winchester, *Boston* 6 A3
Windermere, *Cape Town* .. 8 A2
Windsor, *Johannesburg* ... 13 A1
Windsor Hills, *Los Angeles* . 16 C2
Windy Arbour, *Dublin* 11 B2
Winning, *Munich* 20 B2
Winthrop, *Boston* 6 A4
Wissous, *Paris* 23 B2
Wittenau, *Berlin* 5 A3
Witwatersrand, Univ. of,
      Johannesburg 13 B2
Wlochy, *Warsaw* 31 B1
Wo Mei, *Hong Kong* 12 A2
Wo Yi Hop, *Hong Kong* .. 12 A1
Woburn, *Boston* 6 A3
Woburn, *Toronto* 30 A3
Wola, *Warsaw* 31 B1
Wolf Trap Farm Park,
      Washington 32 B2
Wolica, *Warsaw* 31 C2
Wolica Węglowa, *Warsaw* . 31 C1
Wollaston, *Boston* 6 B3
Wolloomooloo, *Sydney* ... 28 b2
Wollstonecraft, *Sydney* 28 C1
Woltersdorf, *Berlin* 5 B5
Woluwe-Saint-Lambert,
      Brussels 6 A2
Woluwe-Saint-Pierre, *Brussels* 6 A2
Wong Chuk Hang,
      Hong Kong 12 B2
Wong Chuk Wan, *Hong Kong* 12 A2
Wong Chuk Yeung,
      Hong Kong 12 A2
Wong Tai Sin, *Hong Kong* . 12 A2
Wood Green, *London* 15 A3
Wood Ridge, *New York* ... 21 A1
Woodbridge, *Toronto* 30 A1
Woodford, *London* 15 A3
Woodford Bridge, *London* . 15 A4
Woodford Green, *London* .. 15 A4
Woodhaven, *New York* ... 21 B2
Woodhouselee, *Edinburgh* . 11 B2
Woodlands New Town,
      Singapore 27 A2
Woodmont, *Washington* ... 32 B3
Woodside, *London* 15 B3
Woodside, *New York* 21 B2
Woodstock, *Cape Town* ... 8 A1
Woollahra, *Sydney* 28 B2
Worth, *Chicago* 9 C2
Wren's Nest, *Atlanta* 3 B2
Wrigley Building, *Chicago* .. 9 b2
Wuhlgarten, *Berlin* 5 A4
Wujiaochang, *Shanghai* ... 27 B1
Würm →, *Munich* 20 B1
Würm-kanal, *Munich* 20 A1
Wusong, *Shanghai* 27 A1
Wyczółki, *Warsaw* 31 C1
Wygoda, *Warsaw* 31 B2
Wynberg, *Cape Town* 8 B1

X

Xabregas, *Lisbon* 14 A2
Xianggang = Hong Kong,
      Hong Kong 12 B2
Xiaodian, *Tianjin* 30 A2
Xiaojing Park, *Canton* 4 B2
Xiasha chong, *Canton* 4 B1
Xichang, *Canton* 4 B2
Xicheng, *Beijing* 4 B1

Xidan, *Beijing* 4 B2
Xigu Park, *Tianjin* 30 A2
Xigucun, *Tianjin* 30 A1
Ximenwai, *Tianjin* 30 B1
Xinanlou, *Tianjin* 30 B2
Xinkai He →, *Tianjin* 30 A2
Xizhimen, *Beijing* 4 B1
Xu Beihong Mem. Hall,
      Beijing 4 a1
Xuanwu, *Beijing* 4 B1
Xuhui, *Shanghai* 27 B1

Y

Yaba, *Lagos* 14 A2
Yaftābād, *Tehran* 30 B1
Yahara, *Tokyo* 29 A1
Yaho, *Tokyo* 29 A1
Yakire, *Tokyo* 29 A4
Yamada, *Osaka* 22 A4
Yamada, *Tokyo* 29 B2
Yamamoto, *Osaka* 22 B3
Yamato →, *Osaka* 22 B3
Yamuna →, *Delhi* 10 B2
Yan Kit, *Singapore* 27 A3
Yanbu, *Canton* 4 B2
Yangch'ŏn, *Seoul* 26 B1
Yanghuayuan, *Beijing* 4 C1
Yangjae, *Seoul* 26 C2
Yangjiazhuang, *Canton* 4 B1
Yangpu, *Shanghai* 27 B2
Yangpu Park, *Shanghai* ... 27 B2
Yao, *Osaka* 22 B4
Yao Airport, *Osaka* 22 B4
Yarmūk, *Baghdad* 3 B1
Yarra →, *Melbourne* 17 A1
Yarra Bend Park, *Melbourne* 17 A2
Yarraville, *Melbourne* 17 A1
Yau Tong, *Hong Kong* 12 A2
Yau Yat Chuen, *Hong Kong* 12 A1
Ycading, *London* 15 A1
Yedikule, *Istanbul* 12 C1
Yemin Moshe, *Jerusalem* .. 13 b2
Yenikapı, *Istanbul* 12 B2
Yenikōy, *Istanbul* 12 B2
Yerba Buena Gardens,
      San Francisco 25 c2
Yerba Buena I., *San Francisco* 25 B2
Yerres, *Paris* 23 B4
Yerushalayim = Jerusalem,
      Jerusalem 13 B2
Yiheyuan, *Beijing* 4 A1
Yinhangzhen, *Shanghai* ... 27 A2
Yishun New Town, *Singapore* 27 A3
Yixingbu, *Tianjin* 30 A2
Ylästö, *Helsinki* 12 B2
Yodo, *Osaka* 22 A4
Yongdingman, *Beijing* 4 B2
Yŏngdŭng'o, *Seoul* 26 B1
Yongfucun, *Canton* 4 B1
Yongjing, *Shanghai* 27 B2
Yongsan, *Seoul* 26 B1
Yonkers, *New York* 21 A2
York, *Toronto* 30 A2
York Mills, *Toronto* 30 A2
Yotsuya, *Tokyo* 29 a2
You'anmen, *Beijing* 4 B1
Yŏŭido, *Seoul* 26 B1
Youndefield, *Cape Town* ... 8 B1
Yuanxiatian, *Canton* 4 B2
Yugo-Zarad, *Moscow* 19 B3
Yung Shue Wan, *Hong Kong* 12 B1
Yūsofābād, *Tehran* 30 A2
Yuyuantan Park, *Beijing* ... 4 B1

Z

Zaandam, *Amsterdam* 2 A1
Zaandijk, *Amsterdam* 2 A1
Zaanstad, *Amsterdam* 2 A1
Záběhlice, *Prague* 24 B2
Zabki, *Warsaw* 31 B2
Zacisze, *Warsaw* 31 B2
Zahrā, *Baghdad* 3 B1
Zakharkovo, *Moscow* 19 A1
Zalov, *Prague* 24 A2
Zaluski, *Warsaw* 31 C1
Zamdorf, *Munich* 20 A3
Zamek Królewski, *Warsaw* . 31 b2
Zamek Ujazdowski, *Warsaw* 31 c3
Zanevka, *St. Petersburg* ... 26 B2
Zapote, *Manila* 17 C1
Záppeio, *Athens* 2 c2
Zarechye, *Moscow* 19 B2
Zaventem, *Brussels* 6 A2
Zawady, *Warsaw* 31 C2
Zâwiyet Abû Musallam, *Cairo* 7 B1
Zawrā' Park, *Baghdad* 3 A2
Zbraslav, *Prague* 24 C2
Zbuzany, *Prague* 24 B1
Zdiby, *Prague* 24 A2
Zeekoevlei, *Cape Town* ... 8 B2
Zehlendorf, *Berlin* 5 B2
Zenne →, *Brussels* 6 A2
Zeran, *Warsaw* 31 B1
Zerzeň, *Warsaw* 31 B2
Zeytinburnu, *Istanbul* 12 C1
Zhabei, *Shanghai* 27 B1
Zhangguizhuang, *Tianjin* .. 30 A3
Zhdanov, *Moscow* 19 B4
Zheleznodorozhnyy, *Moscow* 19 B6
Zhenru, *Shanghai* 27 B1
Zhernovka, *St. Petersburg* . 26 B2
Zhicun, *Shanghai* 27 B1
Zhongshan Park, *Shanghai* . 27 B1
Zhoucun, *Canton* 4 B1
Zhoujiadu, *Shanghai* 27 B1
Zhoujiazhen, *Shanghai* 27 A1
Zhu Jiang →, *Canton* 4 B2
Zhulebino, *Moscow* 19 B5
Zhushadi, *Canton* 4 B1
Zielona, *Warsaw* 31 B3
Ziya He →, *Tianjin* 30 A1
Žižkov, *Prague* 24 B2
Zócalo, *Mexico City* 18 b3
Zografos, *Athens* 2 B2
Zoliborz, *Warsaw* 31 B1
Zonnebloem, *Cape Town* .. 8 a1
Zoo, *Beijing* 4 a1
Zugló, *Budapest* 7 A2
Zuidplas →, *Amsterdam* .. 2 A2
Zumbi, *Rio de Janeiro* 24 A1
Zundercdorp, *Amsterdam* . 2 A2
Zuuvuvu →, *São Paulo* ... 26 C1
Zwanenburg, *Amsterdam* .. 2 A1
Zwölfaxing, *Vienna* 31 B2
Zyuzino, *Moscow* 19 C3

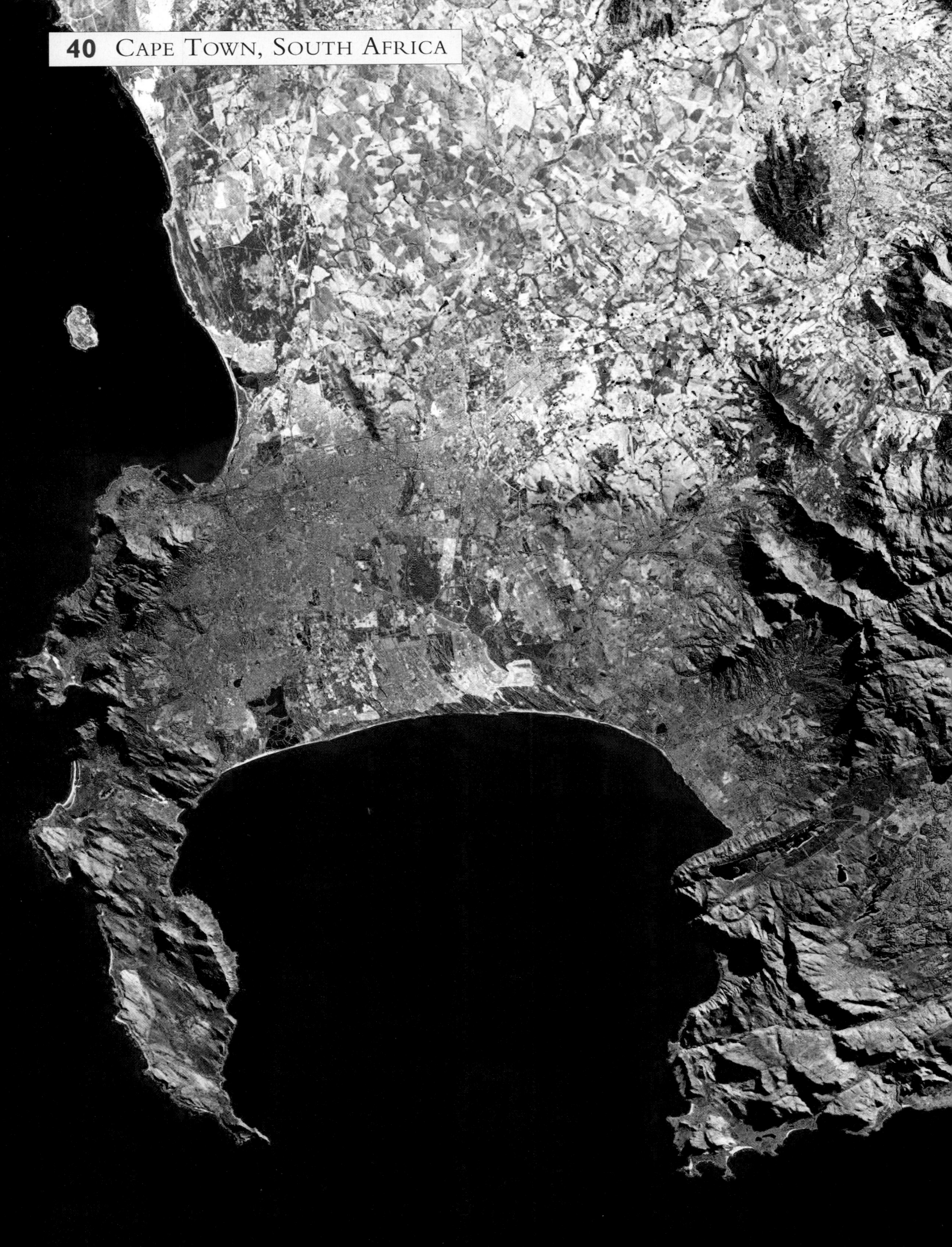

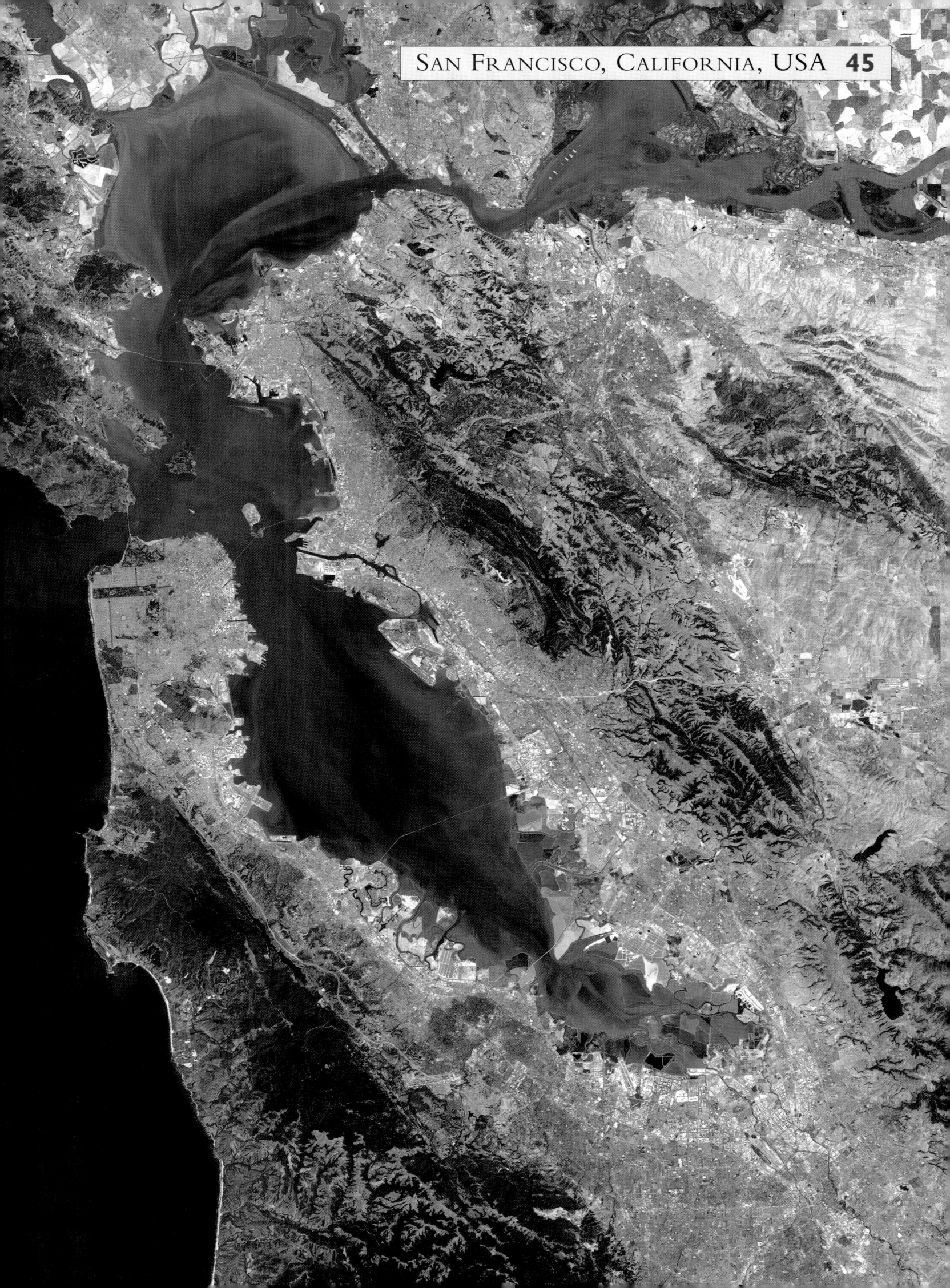

WORLD MAPS

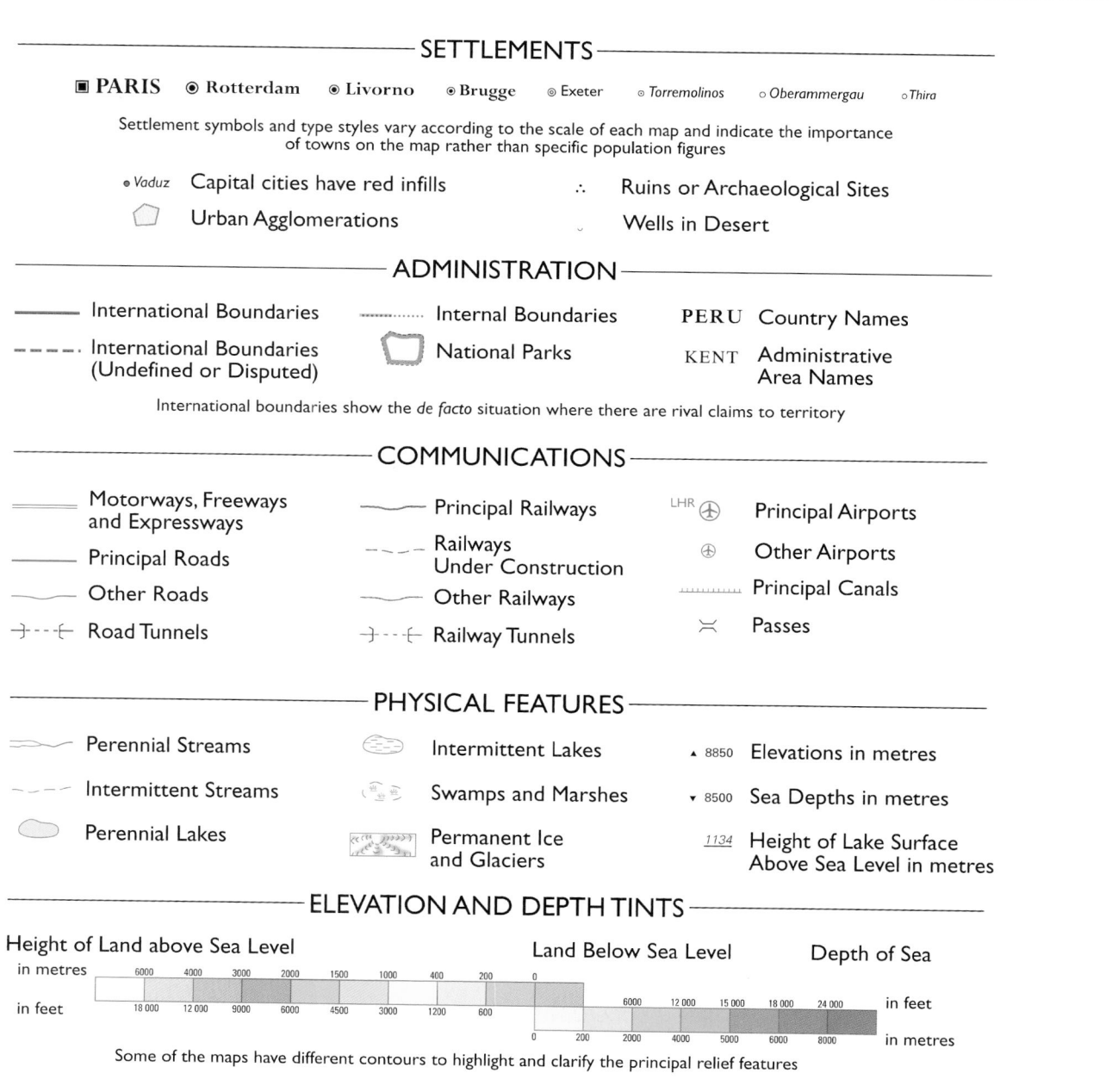

SETTLEMENTS

■ **PARIS**   ◉ Rotterdam   ◉ Livorno   ◉ Brugge   ◎ Exeter   ○ Torremolinos   ○ Oberammergau   ○ Thira

Settlement symbols and type styles vary according to the scale of each map and indicate the importance
of towns on the map rather than specific population figures

• Vaduz   Capital cities have red infills   ∴   Ruins or Archaeological Sites

Urban Agglomerations   Wells in Desert

ADMINISTRATION

——— International Boundaries   ·········· Internal Boundaries   **PERU**   Country Names

– – – · International Boundaries   National Parks   KENT   Administrative
(Undefined or Disputed)   Area Names

International boundaries show the *de facto* situation where there are rival claims to territory

COMMUNICATIONS

——— Motorways, Freeways   ——— Principal Railways   LHR ✈   Principal Airports
and Expressways

——— Principal Roads   – – – Railways   ⊕   Other Airports
Under Construction

——— Other Roads   ——— Other Railways   ·········· Principal Canals

⊣–·–⊢ Road Tunnels   ⊣–·–⊢ Railway Tunnels   ⤬   Passes

PHYSICAL FEATURES

∿ Perennial Streams   Intermittent Lakes   ▲ 8850   Elevations in metres

– – – Intermittent Streams   Swamps and Marshes   ▼ 8500   Sea Depths in metres

Perennial Lakes   Permanent Ice   *1134*   Height of Lake Surface
and Glaciers   Above Sea Level in metres

ELEVATION AND DEPTH TINTS

Height of Land above Sea Level   Land Below Sea Level   Depth of Sea

in metres   6000   4000   3000   2000   1500   1000   400   200   0

in feet   18 000   12 000   9000   6000   4500   3000   1200   600
                                                                  6000   12 000   15 000   18 000   24 000   in feet

                                                                  0   200   2000   4000   5000   6000   8000   in metres

Some of the maps have different contours to highlight and clarify the principal relief features

Hanoi ◉ Capital Cities

COPYRIGHT PHILIP'S

100 0   200 400 600 800 1000 1200 1400 km

1:35 000 000

100 0   200 400 600 800 1000 miles

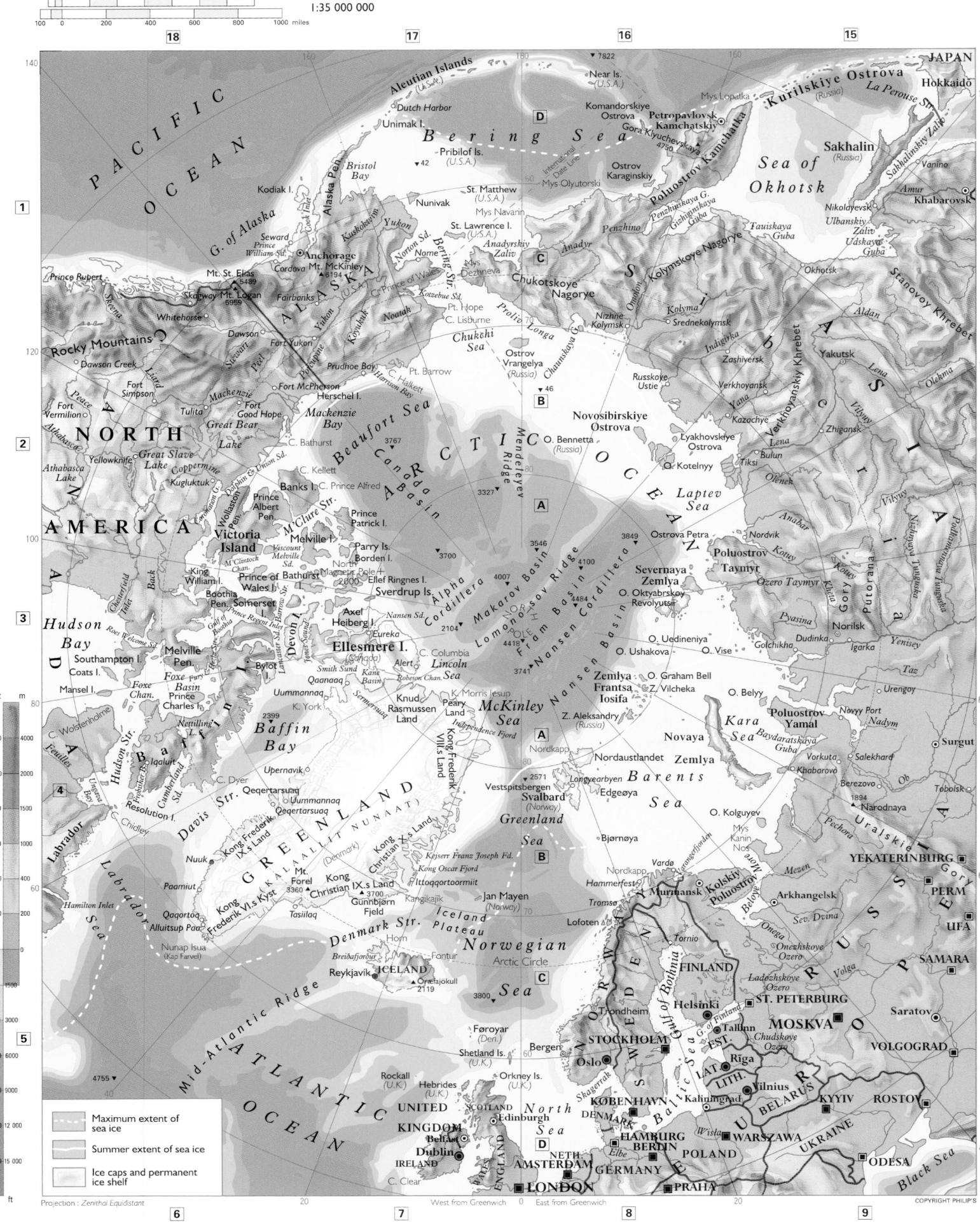

Projection : Zenithal Equidistant

West from Greenwich   East from Greenwich

Maximum extent of sea ice

Summer extent of sea ice

Ice caps and permanent ice shelf

COPYRIGHT PHILIP'S

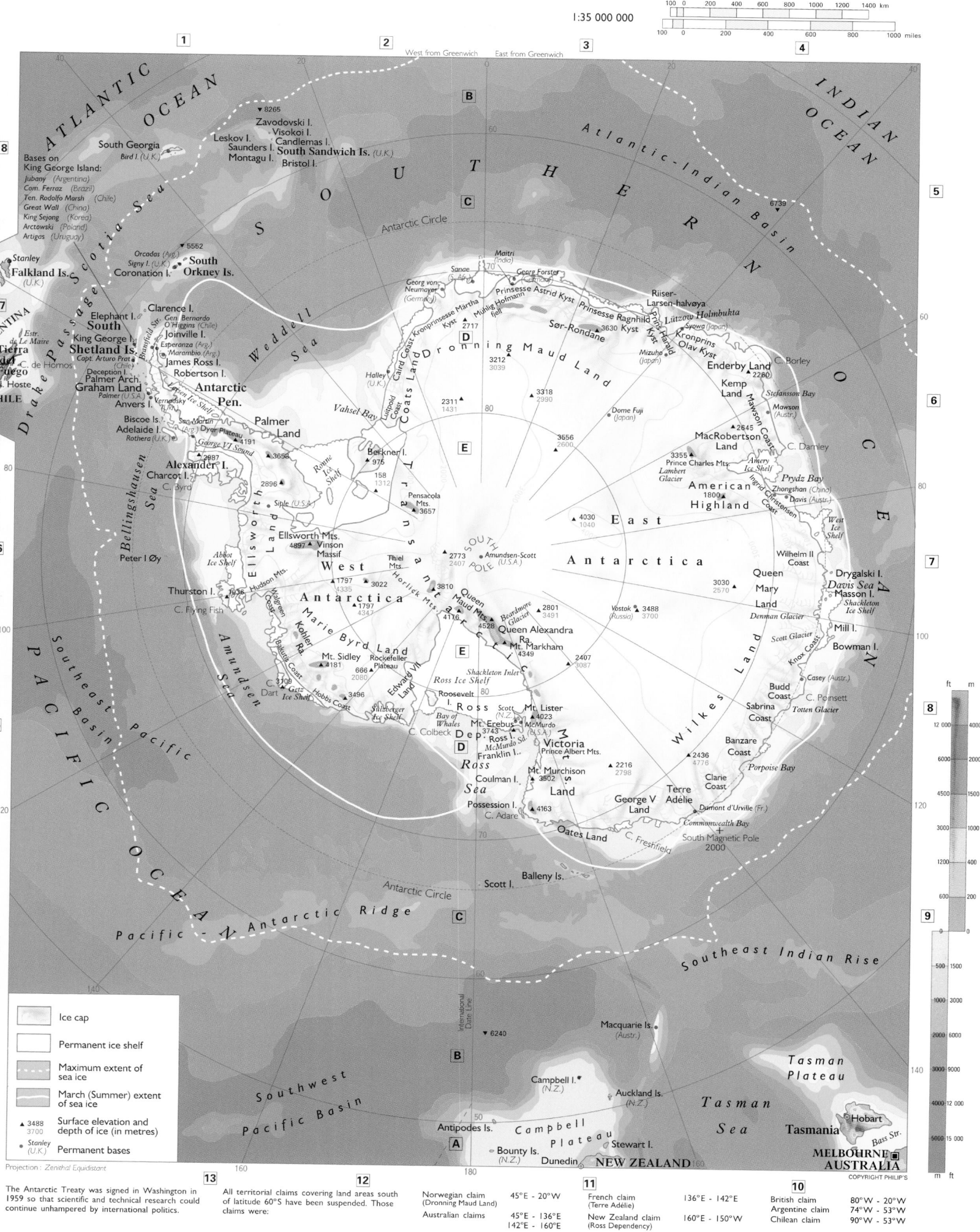

1:35 000 000

ATLANTIC OCEAN

INDIAN OCEAN

SOUTHERN OCEAN

Atlantic-Indian Basin

South Georgia
Bird I. (U.K.)

Zavodovski I.
Leskov I.   Visokoi I.
Saunders I.   Candlemas I.
Montagu I.   South Sandwich Is. (U.K.)
        Bristol I.

Bases on King George Island:
Jubany (Argentina)
Com. Ferraz (Brazil)
Ten. Rodolfo Marsh (Chile)
Great Wall (China)
King Sejong (Korea)
Arctowski (Poland)
Artigas (Uruguay)

Stanley
Falkland Is.
(U.K.)

Scotia Sea

Antarctic Circle

Orcadas (Arg.) ▲5552
Signy I. (U.K.)   **South Orkney Is.**
Coronation I.

Maitri (India)
Sanae
Georg von Neumayer (Germany)   Georg Forster (Ger.)
Prinsesse Astrid Kyst   Prinsesse Ragnhild Kyst
Prinsesse Martha Kyst   Prins Harald Kyst
Muhlig Hofmann fjell   Sør-Rondane   ▲3630
Riiser-Larsen-halvøya
Syowa (Japan)   Lützow Holmbukta
Kronprins Olav Kyst   Mizuho (Japan)

6739 ▲

▲ 2280   **Enderby Land**   C. Borley

ÁNTINA
Estr. de Le Maire
Tierra del Fuego
I. Hoste   C. de Hornos
CHILE

Elephant I.
Clarence I.
Gen. Bernardo O'Higgins (Chile)
Joinville I.
Esperanza (Arg.)
Marambio (Arg.)
South Shetland Is.
King George I.
Capt. Arturo Prat (Chile)
Deception I.
James Ross I.
Robertson I.
Palmer Arch.
Graham Land
Palmer (U.S.A.)
Vernadsky (Ukr.)
Anvers I.   San Martin (Arg.)
Biscoe Is.   Dyer Plateau
Adelaide I.
Rothera (U.K.)

Antarctic Pen.

Palmer Land

Drake Passage
Bellingshausen Sea

Weddell Sea

Halley (U.K.)
Vahsel Bay
Lützow
Filchner Ice Shelf

Dronning Maud Land

2717 ▲

3212 ▲   3039

3318 ▲   2990

2311 ▲   1431

Dome Fuji (Japan)

3556 ▲   2600

Kemp Land

Stefansson Bay
Mawson (Austr.)

MacRobertson Land

American Highland

3355 ▲   Prince Charles Mts   C. Darnley
Lambert Glacier   Amery Ice Shelf
Prydz Bay   Zhongshan (China)
1800   Davis (Austr.)
Ingrid Christensen Coast

Alexander I.   ▲2987
Charcot I.   C. Byrd
Peter I Øy

Berkner I.   975
158   1312

Ronne Ice Shelf

2896 ▲

Siple (U.S.A.)

Pensacola Mts.   3657 ▲

4030 ▲   1040

East Antarctica

Wilhelm II Coast

Davis Sea   Drygalski I.
Masson I.
Shackleton Ice Shelf

SOUTH POLE

Amundsen-Scott (U.S.A.)
2407 ▲   2773

Queen Mary Land

3030 ▲   2570

Mill I.
Bowman I.

Ellsworth Mts.
4897 ▲ Vinson Massif

West Antarctica

Thiel Mts.

1797   3022   4335

3810 ▲

2407 ▲   3087

2801 ▲   3491

Vostok (Russia)   3488 ▲   3700

Scott Glacier
Knox Coast
Casey (Austr.)
C. Poinsett

Wilkes Land

Bellingshausen Sea
Thurston I.   1936
C. Flying Fish

Hudson Mts.

Walgreen Coast

Kohler Ra.

Marie Byrd Land

1797   4347

Mt. Sidley ▲   4181

Rockefeller Plateau   2080
666

Amundsen Sea

Bakutis Coast
C. Dart   3190
Getz Ice Shelf   Hobbs Coast   3496
Siple Coast

Sulzberger Ice Shelf

Edward VII Land

Queen Maud Mts.
Beardmore Glacier
4176 ▲   4528

Queen Alexandra Ra.
Mt. Markham ▲   4349

Horlick Mts.

Trans-Antarctic Mts.

Shackleton Inlet

Ross Ice Shelf

Roosevelt I.
Bay of Whales
C. Colbeck

Ross I.   Scott (N.Z.)
Mt. Erebus   3743
McMurdo Sd.   McMurdo (U.S.A.)
Ross (N.Z.)   Mt. Lister ▲ 4023
Franklin I.

Ross Dep.

Victoria Land
Prince Albert Mts.

Denman Glacier
Scott Glacier
Totten Glacier

Budd Coast
Sabrina Coast

Banzare Coast

2436 ▲   4776

Clarie Coast

Porpoise Bay

SOUTHEAST PACIFIC BASIN

PACIFIC OCEAN

Southeast Pacific Basin

Pacific-Antarctic Ridge

Ross Sea

Coulman I.
Mt. Murchison ▲   3502
Possession I.
C. Adare   ▲4163

2216 ▲   2798

George V Land   **Terre Adélie**
Dumont d'Urville (Fr.)

Oates Land   C. Freshfield
Commonwealth Bay
South Magnetic Pole 2000

Antarctic Circle

Scott I.

Balleny Is.

Southeast Indian Rise

International Date Line

6240 ▲

Macquarie Is. (Austr.)

Tasman Plateau

Southwest Pacific Basin

Campbell I. (N.Z.)   Auckland Is. (N.Z.)

Tasman Sea

Tasmania
Hobart

Antipodes Is.
Campbell Plateau
Bounty Is. (N.Z.)   Stewart I.
Dunedin   **NEW ZEALAND**

MELBOURNE AUSTRALIA
COPYRIGHT PHILIP'S

Legend:

Ice cap

Permanent ice shelf

Maximum extent of sea ice

March (Summer) extent of sea ice

▲ 3488 / 3700   Surface elevation and depth of ice (in metres)

• Stanley (U.K.)   Permanent bases

Projection: Zenithal Equidistant

The Antarctic Treaty was signed in Washington in 1959 so that scientific and technical research could continue unhampered by international politics.

All territorial claims covering land areas south of latitude 60°S have been suspended. Those claims were:

Norwegian claim (Dronning Maud Land)	45°E - 20°W
Australian claims	45°E - 136°E
	142°E - 160°E

| French claim (Terre Adélie) | 136°E - 142°E |
| New Zealand claim (Ross Dependency) | 160°E - 150°W |

British claim	80°W - 20°W
Argentine claim	74°W - 53°W
Chilean claim	90°W - 53°W

Elevation scale:

ft	m
12 000	4000
6000	2000
4500	1500
3000	1000
1200	400
600	200
0	0
500	1500
1000	3000
2000	6000
3000	9000
4000	12 000
5000	15 000
m	ft

1:20 000 000

100 0 100 200 300 400 500 600 700 800 km
100 0 100 200 300 400 500 miles

COPYRIGHT PHILIP'S

Ural Mountains

Ob

Pechora

Ural

Caspian Sea

Caucasus

Elbrus 5642

Armenia

Kurdistan

Tigris

Mesopotamia

Euphrates

Caspian Depression

Ob_shchi Syrt

Volga

Kama

Volga Hts.

Pontine Mts.

Black Sea

Central Russian Uplands

Don

Donets Basin

Donets

Sea of Azov

Crimea

Bosporus

Str. of Kerch

Ukraine

Dniepr

Bug

Danube

Prut

Dniester

Pripet

Anatolia

(Asia Minor)

Taurus Mts.

L. Van

Erciyas Dağ 3916

Rhodes

Cyprus

White Sea

Kola Pen.

Onega

L. Onega

Ladoga

L. Chudskoye

W. Dvina

Niemen

North Sea

Carpathians

Tatra 2655

Plain of Hungary

Tissa

Wallachia

Balkans

Rhodope

Aegean Sea

Crete

Morea

Ionian Is.

Pindus

Str. of Otranto

Ionian Sea

C. Matapan

Finland

Karelia

G. of Finland

Åland

Gotland

Öland

Bornholm

Baltic Sea

Oder

Sudeten

Moravian Hts.

Bohemian Forest

Ergebirge

Dinaric Alps

Adriatic Sea

Gran Sasso d'Italia 2914

Apennines

Vesuvius 1277

Str. of Messina

Etna 3340

Sicily

Tyrrhenian Sea

Malta

Pantelleria

Lapland

Torne

Ume

Indals

Vänern

Vättern

Scandinavia

North Cape

Vesterålen

Lofoten

G. of Bothnia

Jura

Harz

Elbe

Jutland

Kattegat

Skagerrak

Lindesnes

German Bight

Helgoland

Weser

Black Forest

Vosges

Rhine

Hunsrück

Ardennes

Jura

Alps

Mont Blanc 4807

Po

Ligurian Sea

Corsica

Sardinia

Str. of Bonifacio

C. Bon

Mediterranean Sea

Norwegian Sea

Galdhøpiggen 2469

Iceland

Hekla 1491

Snæfell 2119

Arctic Circle

Faroe Is.

Shetland Is.

Orkney Is.

Fair Isle

Hebrides

Great Britain

Ben Nevis 1343

Snowdon 1085

Irish Sea

Ireland

British Isles

Rockall

Shannon

Celtic Sea

English Channel

Channel Is.

Ushant

Brittany

Seine

Loire

Bay of Biscay

Gironde

Garonne

Massif Central

Cévennes

Pyrenees

G. of Lions

Rhône

Puy de Sancy 1886

Ebro

Balearic Is.

Minorca

Majorca

Ibiza

Cantabrian Mts.

Old Castile

New Castile

Iberian Peninsula

Sierra Morena

Sierra Nevada

Mulhacén 3478

Andalusia

Guadalquivir

Guadiana

Tagus

Duero

C. Finisterre

C. St. Vincent

C. Trafalgar

Str. of Gibraltar

Africa

Plateau of the Shotts

Pico de Aneto 3404

ATLANTIC OCEAN

0° East from Greenwich

East from Greenwich

m ft

5000 15 000
4000 12 000
2000 6000
1000 3000
400 1200
200 600
0

200 600
2000 6000
4000 12 000

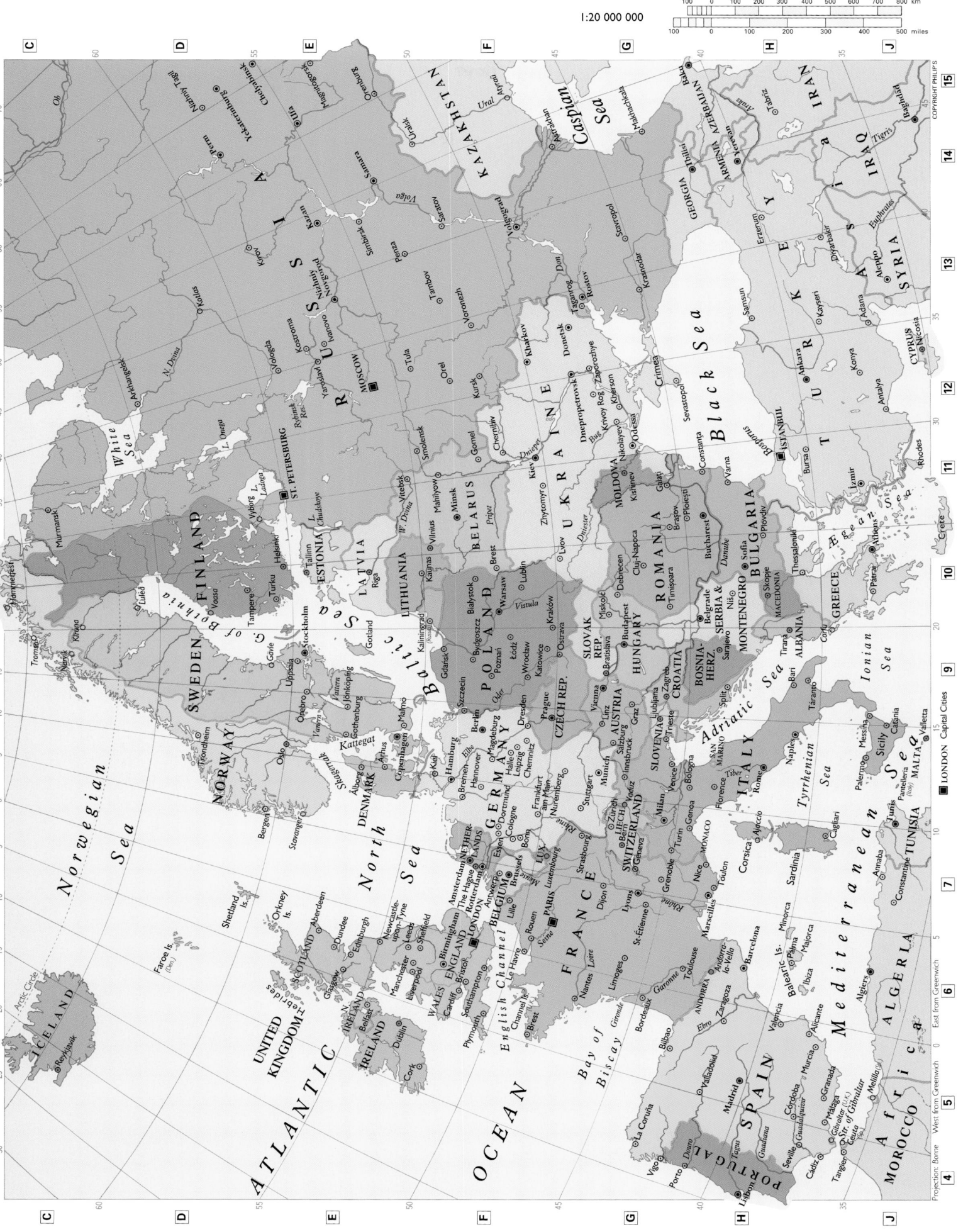

1:20 000 000

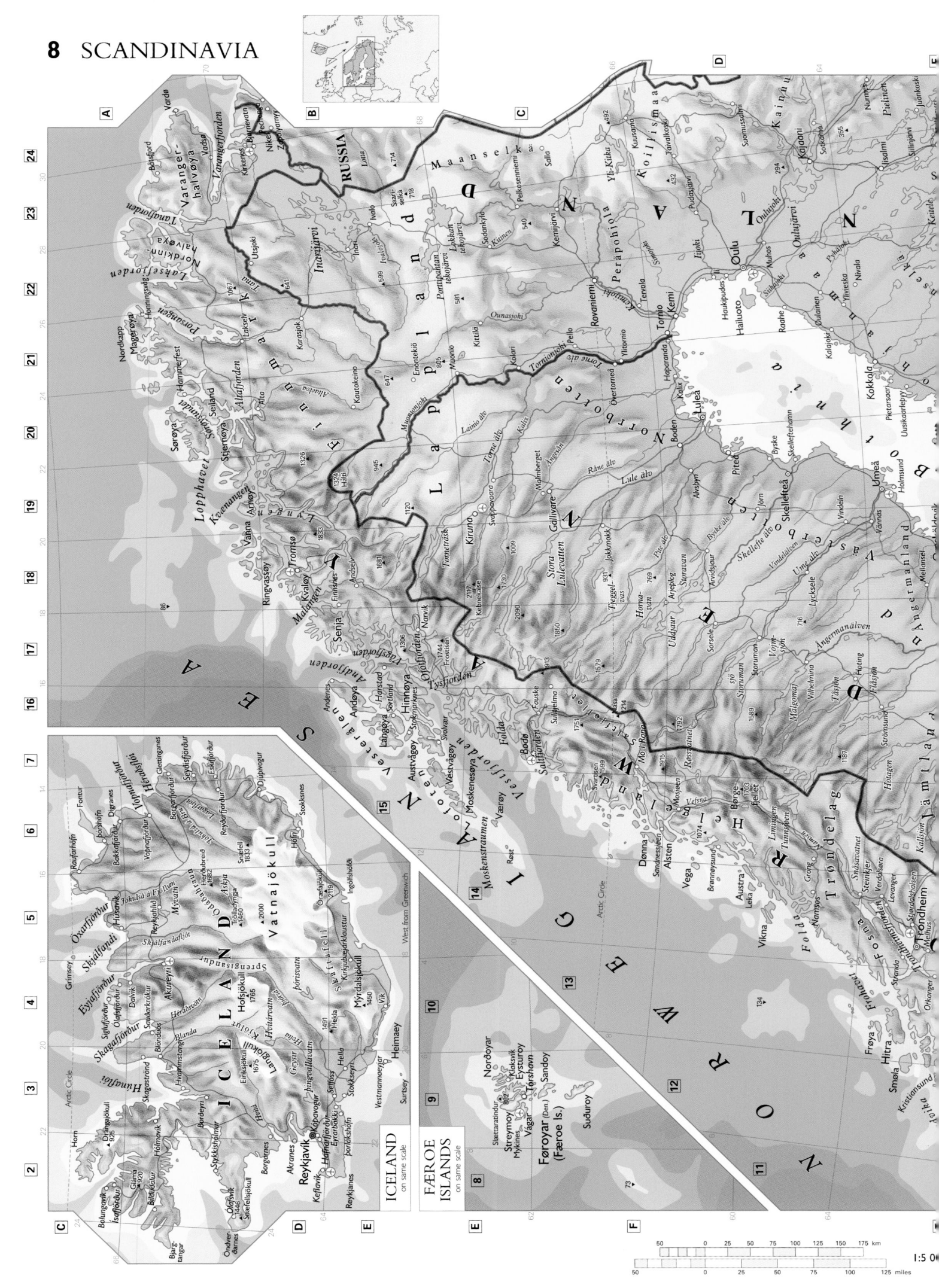

RUSSIA

Maanselkä

Lappland

Norrbotten

Norrland

Jämtland

Trøndelag

NORWEGIAN   SEA

ICELAND
on same scale

FÆROE ISLANDS
on same scale

Vatnajökull

Reykjavík

Foroyar (Den)
(Færoe Is.)

Tórshavn

Arctic Circle

West from Greenwich

50   0   25   50   75   100   125   150   175 km

50   25   0   25   50   75   100   125 miles

1:5 000

Projection: Conical with two standard parallels

East from Greenwich

1:2 000 000

10 0 10 20 30 40 50 60 70 80 km
10 0 10 20 30 40 50 miles

SCOTLAND

IRELAND

NORTHERN IRELAND

Ulster

Connacht

Leinster

Munster

A T L A N T I C   O C E A N

CELTIC SEA

IRISH SEA

North Channel

St. George's Channel

WALES

Counties and places:

DONEGAL, Londonderry, LONDONDERRY, ANTRIM, TYRONE, Belfast, DOWN, ARMAGH, FERMANAGH, MONAGHAN, SLIGO, LEITRIM, CAVAN, MAYO, ROSCOMMON, LONGFORD, MEATH, WESTMEATH, GALWAY, OFFALY, KILDARE, DUBLIN, WICKLOW, LAOIS, CLARE, TIPPERARY, KILKENNY, CARLOW, WEXFORD, LIMERICK, KERRY, CORK, WATERFORD, LOUTH

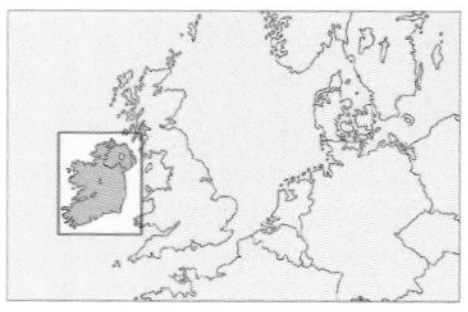

Dublin, Dun Laoghaire, Bray, Greystones, Cork, Limerick, Galway, Waterford, Wexford, Tralee, Killarney, Ennis, Sligo, Letterkenny, Drogheda, Dundalk, Newry, Dungannon, Omagh, Enniskillen, Coleraine, Larne, Carrickfergus, Bangor, Newtownards, Downpatrick, Armagh, Lurgan, Craigavon, Portadown, Banbridge

Physical features:

Malin Hd., Horn Hd., Bloody Foreland, Erris Hd., Mullet Pen., Achill I., Clew Bay, Slyne Hd., Aran Is., Galway Bay, Cliffs of Moher, Loop Hd., Kerry Hd., Dingle Bay, Dunmore Hd., Valencia I., Great Skellig, Bantry Bay, Mizen Hd., C. Clear, Fastnet Rock, Old Head of Kinsale, Cork Harbour, Youghal B., Carnsore Pt., Rosslare, Wexford Harbour, Wicklow Hd., Howth Hd., Lambay I.

Lough Neagh, Lough Erne, Lower L. Erne, Upper L. Erne, Lough Conn, Lough Mask, Lough Corrib, Lough Ree, Lough Derg, Lough Allen, L. Sheelin, L. Gowna, L. Arrow, L. Gara, Poulaphouca Res.

Shannon, Boyne, Liffey, Barrow, Nore, Suir, Blackwater, Bann, Foyle, Erne, Moy

Macgillycuddy's Reeks, Carrauntohill, Galty Mts., Knockmealdown Mts., Comeragh Mts., Wicklow Mts., Lugnaquillia 926, Mts. of Antrim, Sperrin Mts., Mourne Mts., Slieve Donard, Slieve Bloom, Boggeragh Mts., Caha Mts., Slieve Mish, Brandon Mt. 953, Nephin 806, Croagh Patrick 765, Mweelrea 819, Errigal 752, Slieve League, Slieve Gamph, Slieve Aughty, Keeper Hill 694

Projection: Lambert's Conformal Conic

West from Greenwich

COPYRIGHT PHILIP'S

National Parks

1:2 000 000

ORKNEY IS.
on same scale

SHETLAND IS.
on same scale

Forest Parks in Scotland

Key to Scottish unitary
authorities on map

1 CITY OF ABERDEEN
2 DUNDEE CITY
3 WEST DUNBARTONSHIRE
4 EAST DUNBARTONSHIRE
5 CITY OF GLASGOW
6 INVERCLYDE
7 RENFREWSHIRE
8 EAST RENFREWSHIRE
9 NORTH LANARKSHIRE
10 FALKIRK
11 CLACKMANNANSHIRE
12 WEST LOTHIAN
13 CITY OF EDINBURGH
14 MIDLOTHIAN

Projection : Lambert's Conformal Conic

West from Greenwich

COPYRIGHT PHILIP'S

1:2 000 000

10 0 10 20 30 40 50 60 70 80 km
10 0 10 20 30 40 50 miles

Key to English unitary authorities on map

25 HARTLEPOOL
26 DARLINGTON
27 STOCKTON-ON-TEES
28 MIDDLESBROUGH
29 REDCAR AND CLEVELAND
30 BLACKPOOL
31 BLACKBURN WITH DARWEN
32 HALTON
33 WARRINGTON
34 KINGSTON UPON HULL
35 NORTH EAST LINCOLNSHIRE
36 STOKE-ON-TRENT
37 TELFORD AND WREKIN
38 DERBY CITY
39 CITY OF NOTTINGHAM
40 LEICESTER CITY
41 RUTLAND
42 PETERBOROUGH
43 MILTON KEYNES
44 LUTON
45 NORTH SOMERSET
46 CITY OF BRISTOL
47 BATH AND NORTH EAST SOMERSET
48 SWINDON
49 READING
50 WOKINGHAM
51 WINDSOR AND MAIDENHEAD
52 SLOUGH
53 BRACKNELL FOREST
54 THURROCK
55 SOUTHEND-ON-SEA
56 MEDWAY
57 PLYMOUTH
58 TORBAY
59 POOLE
60 BOURNEMOUTH
61 SOUTHAMPTON
62 PORTSMOUTH
63 BRIGHTON AND HOVE

Key to Welsh unitary authorities on map

15 SWANSEA
16 NEATH PORT TALBOT
17 BRIDGEND
18 RHONDDA CYNON TAFF
19 MERTHYR TYDFIL
20 CAERPHILLY
21 BLAENAU GWENT
22 TORFAEN
23 CARDIFF
24 NEWPORT

N O R T H   S E A

I R I S H   S E A

North Channel

NORTHERN IRELAND

SCOTLAND

ENGLAND

WALES

ISLE OF MAN

Edinburgh
Glasgow
Newcastle-upon-Tyne
Sunderland
Middlesbrough
Leeds
Bradford
Sheffield
Manchester
Liverpool
York
Kingston upon Hull
Lincoln
Nottingham
Derby
Stoke-on-Trent
Blackpool
Preston
Chester
Belfast

The Wash

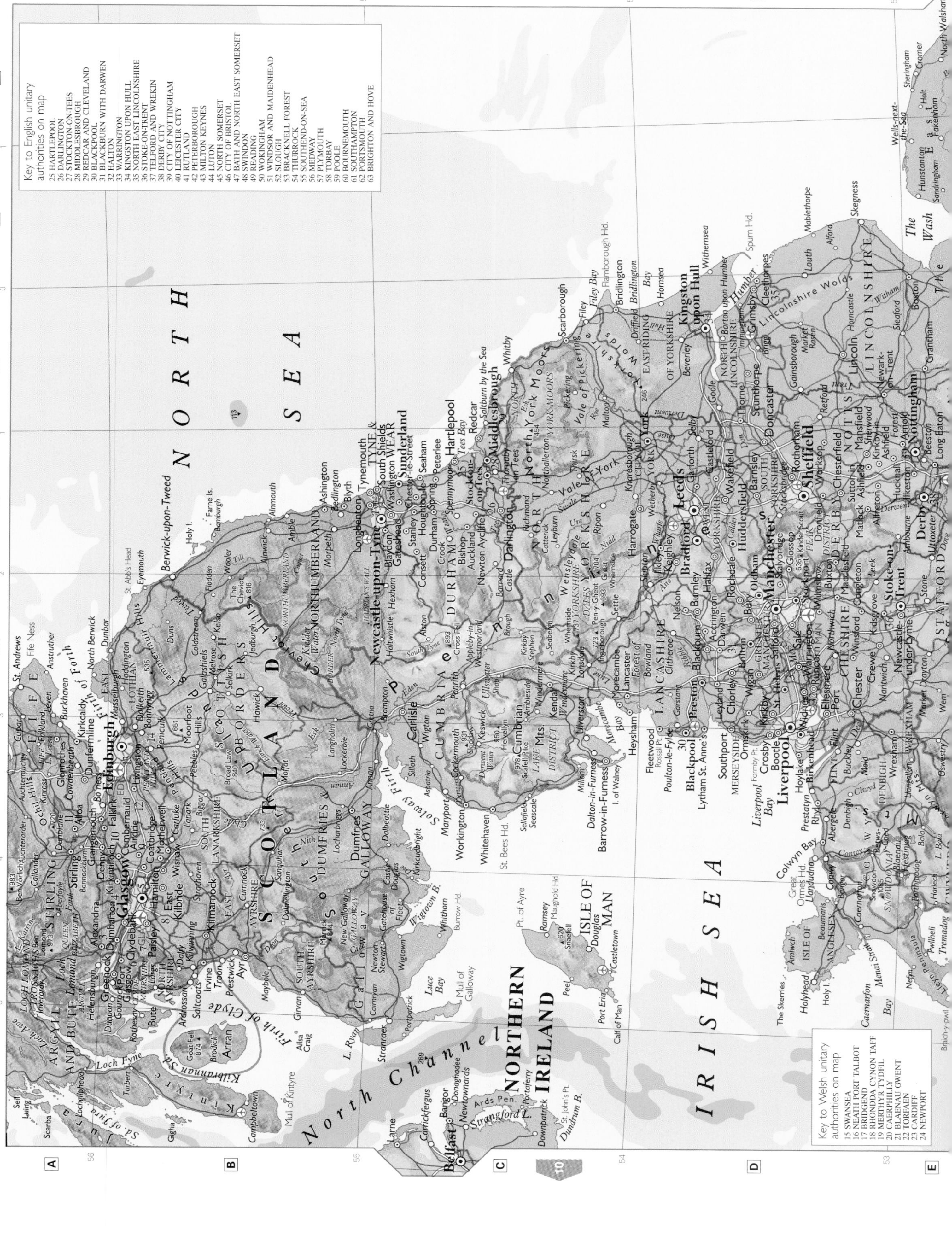

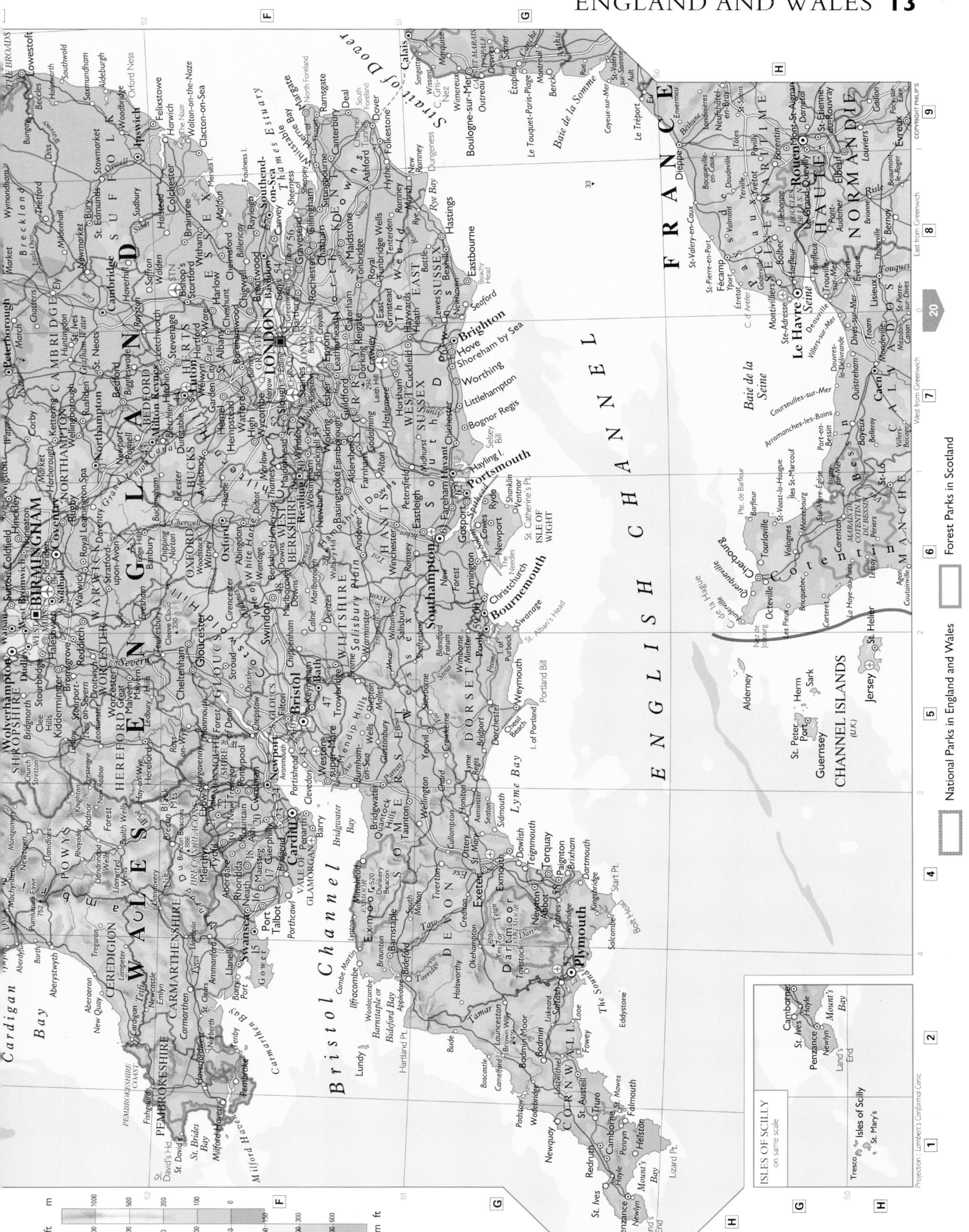

1:5 000 000

50 0 25 50 75 100 125 150 175 km
50 0 25 50 75 100 125 miles

Projection: Conical with two standard parallels

East from Greenwich   COPYRIGHT PHILIP'S

West from Greenwich

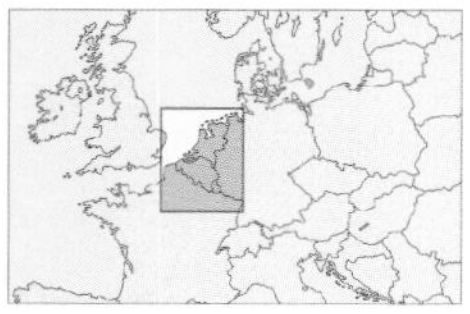

1:2 500 000

10 0 10 20 30 40 50 60 70 80 90 km
10 0 10 20 30 40 50 60 miles

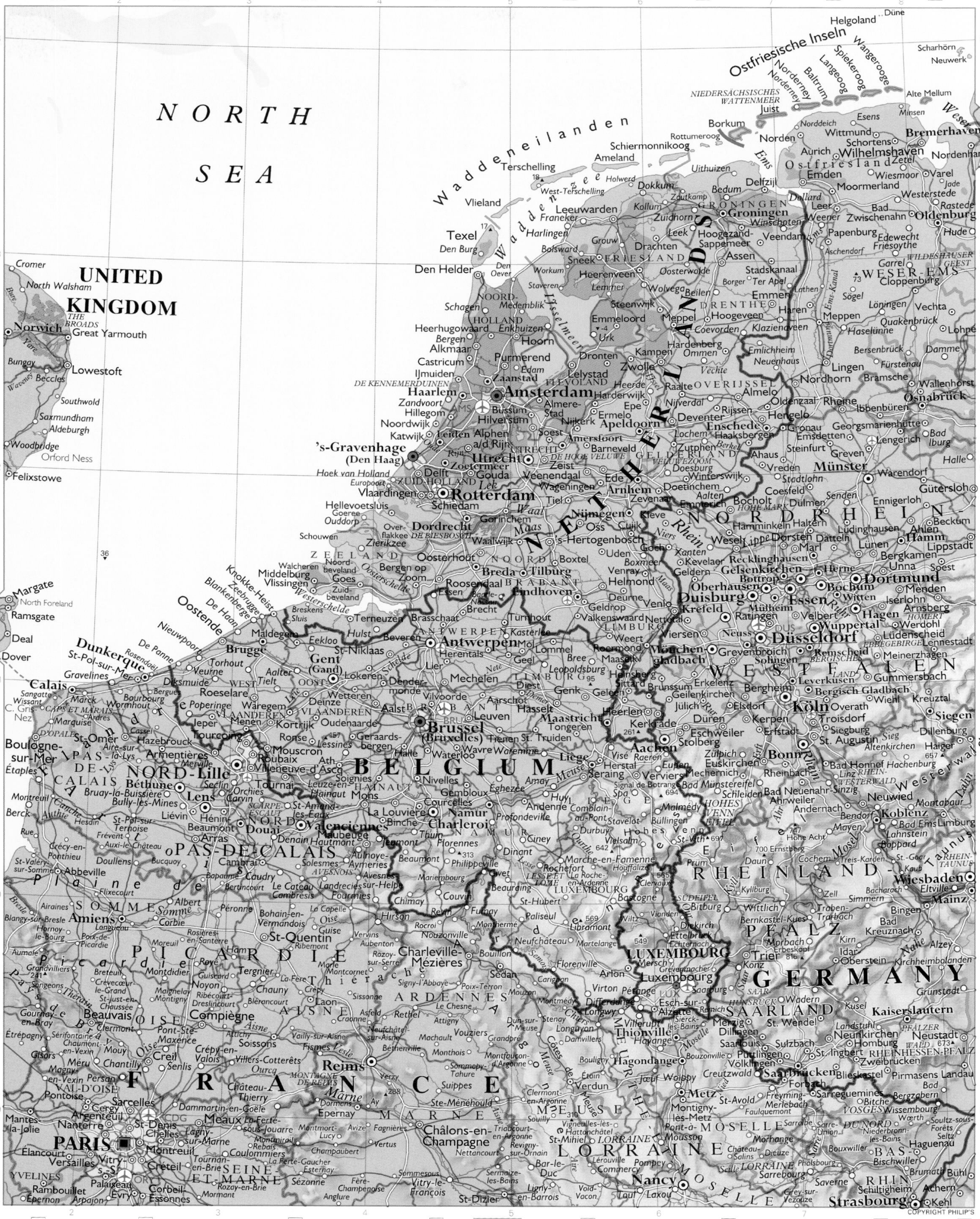

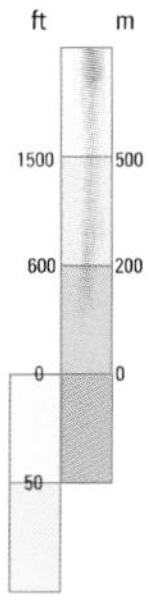

NORTH SEA

UNITED KINGDOM

NETHERLANDS

BELGIUM

GERMANY

FRANCE

LUXEMBOURG

National Parks

Underlined towns give their name to the
administrative area in which they stand.

COPYRIGHT PHILIP'S

ft m

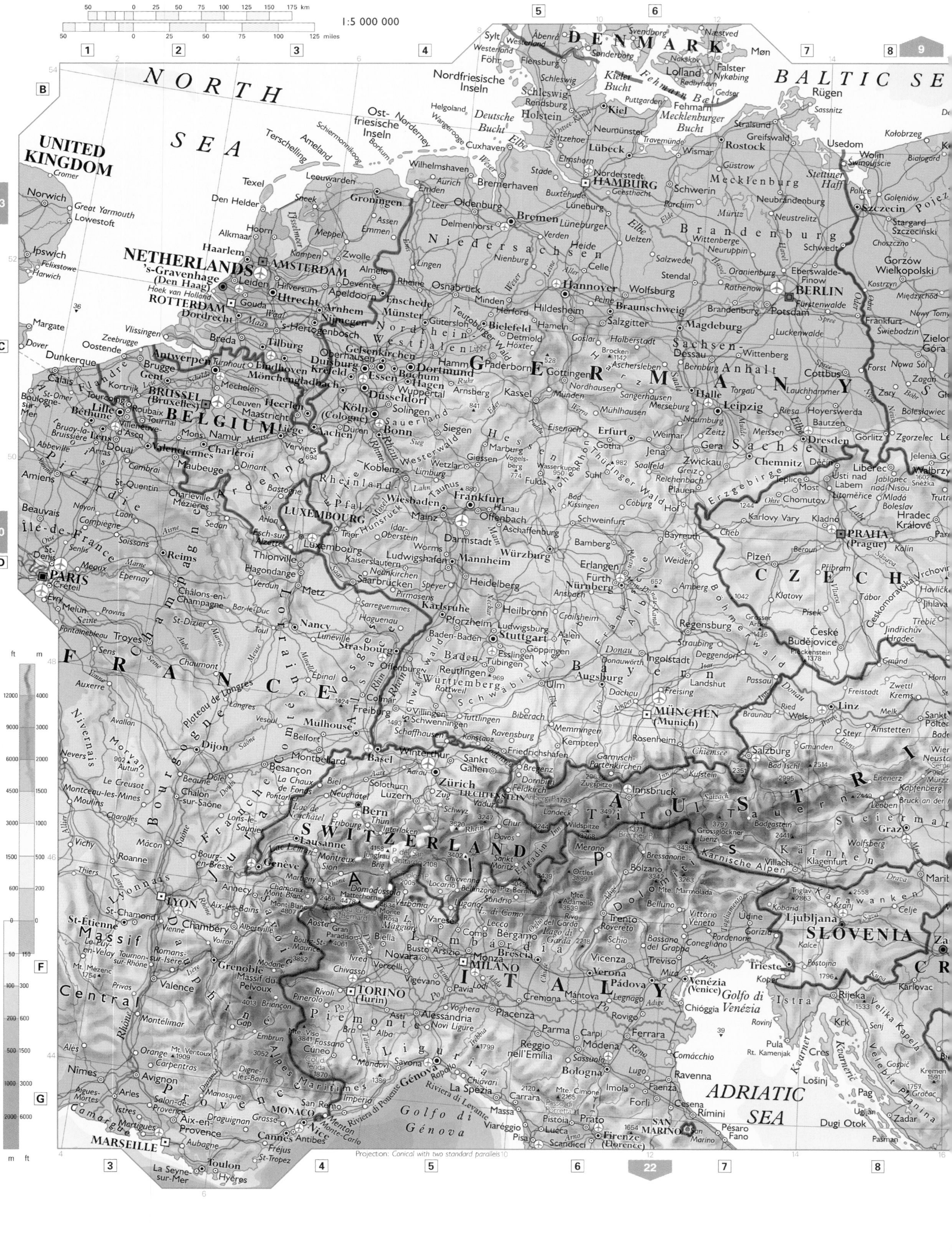

1:5 000 000

50 0 25 50 75 100 125 150 175 km
50 0 25 50 75 100 125 miles

NORTH SEA

BALTIC SEA

DENMARK

UNITED KINGDOM

NETHERLANDS

BELGIUM

LUXEMBOURG

GERMANY

FRANCE

SWITZERLAND

AUSTRIA

CZECH

ITALY

SLOVENIA

ADRIATIC SEA

MONACO

LIECHTENSTEIN

HAMBURG

BERLIN

BREMEN

Hannover

Magdeburg

Leipzig

Dresden

PRAHA (Prague)

Frankfurt

Stuttgart

MÜNCHEN (Munich)

Nürnberg

Köln (Cologne)

Düsseldorf

Essen

Dortmund

Bonn

AMSTERDAM

ROTTERDAM

's-Gravenhage (Den Haag)

Utrecht

BRUSSEL (Bruxelles)

Antwerpen

Gent

LUXEMBOURG

PARIS

LYON

MARSEILLE

TORINO (Turin)

MILANO

Venézia (Venice)

Trieste

Ljubljana

Bern

Zürich

Genève

Projection: Conical with two standard parallels

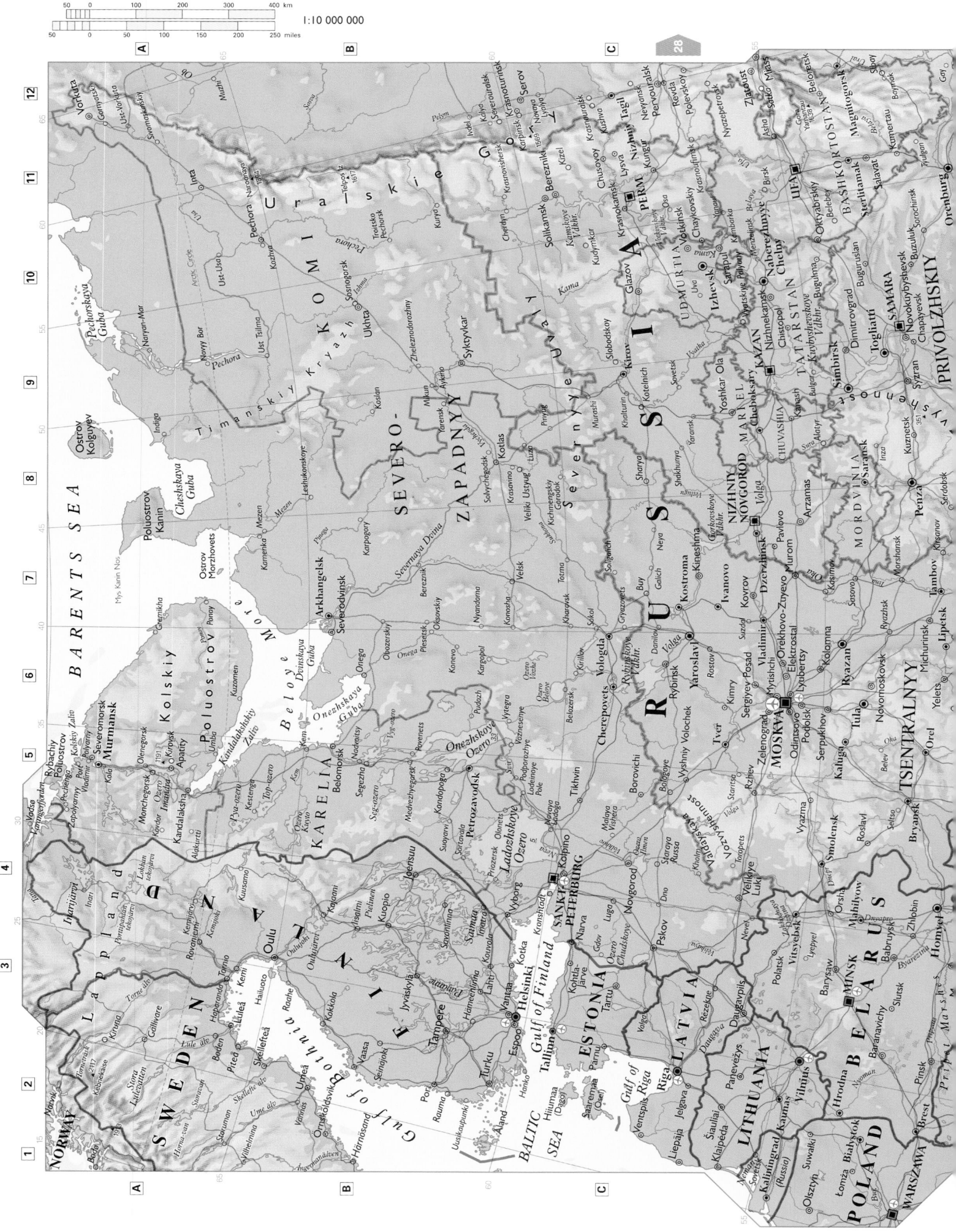

1:10 000 000

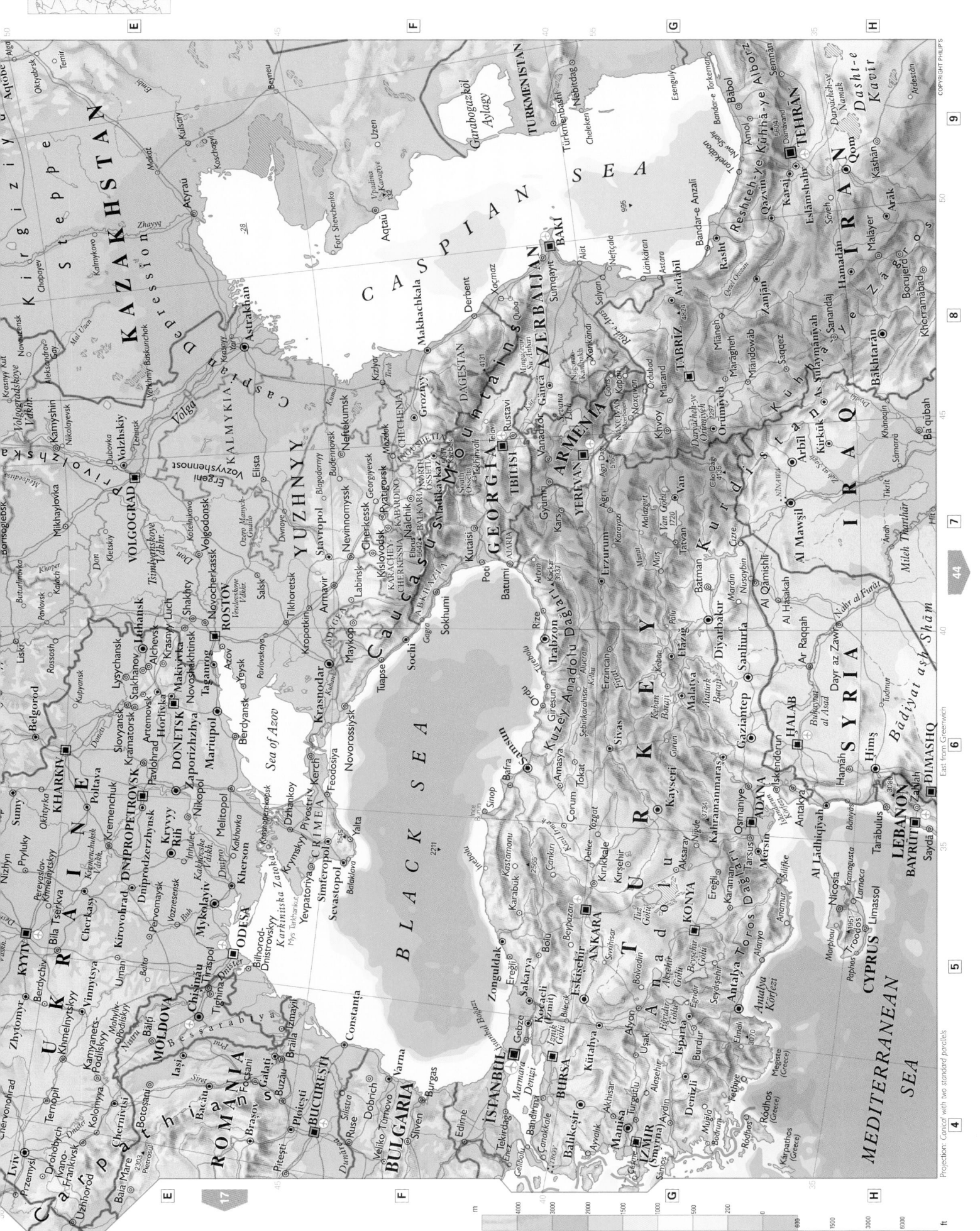

Projection: Conical with two standard parallels

East from Greenwich

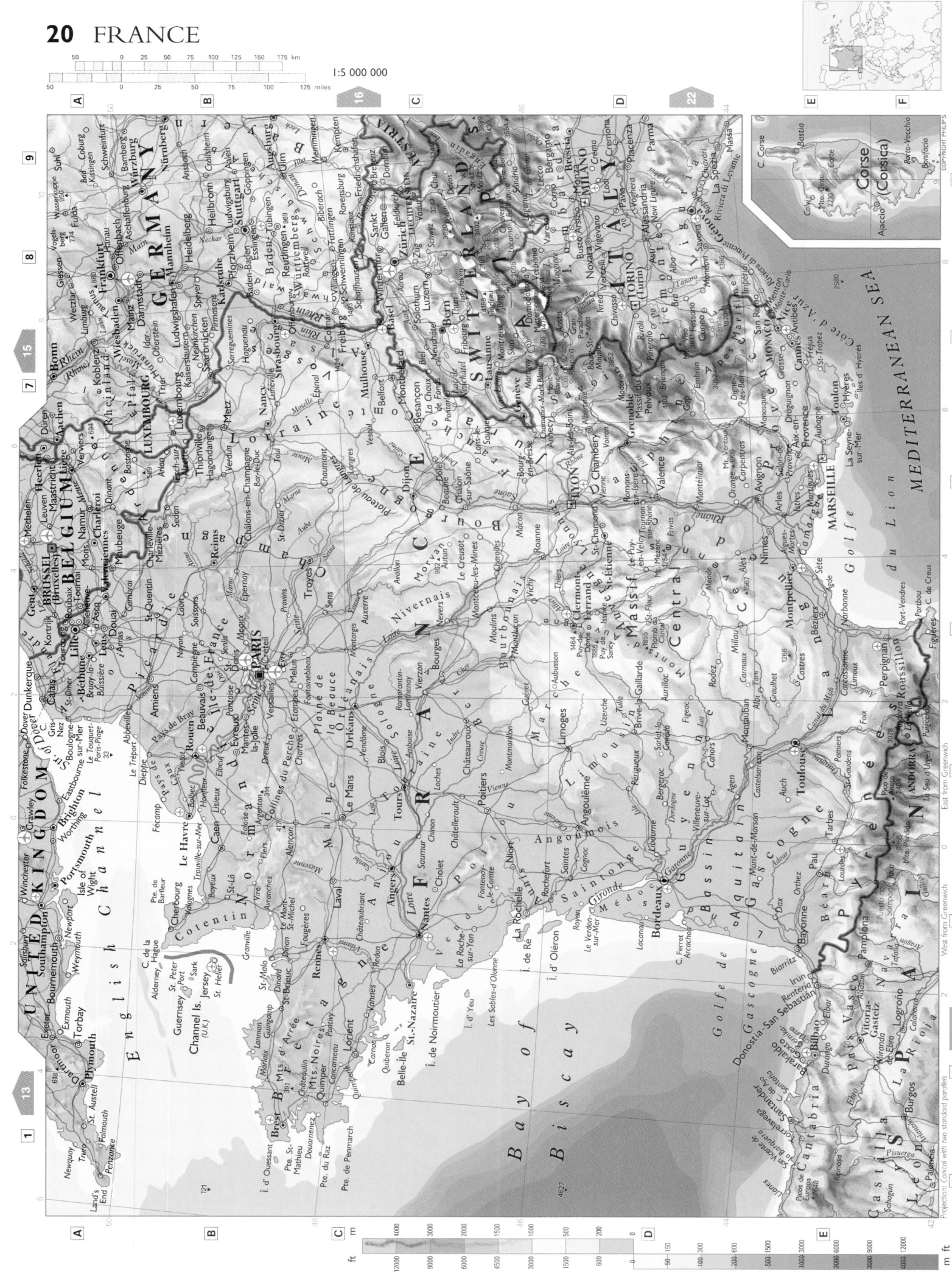

Corse
(Corsica)

MEDITERRANEAN SEA

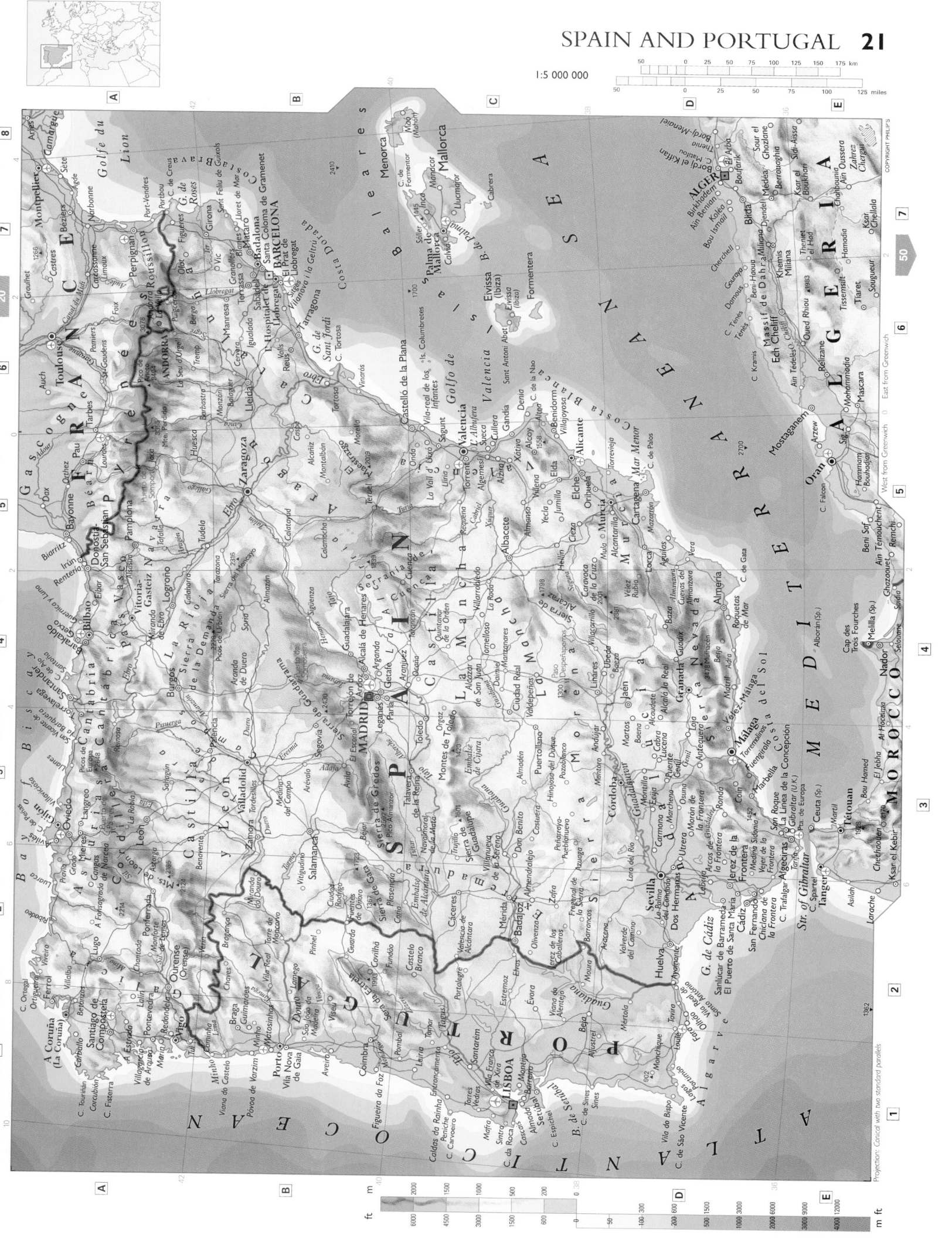

COPYRIGHT PHILIP'S

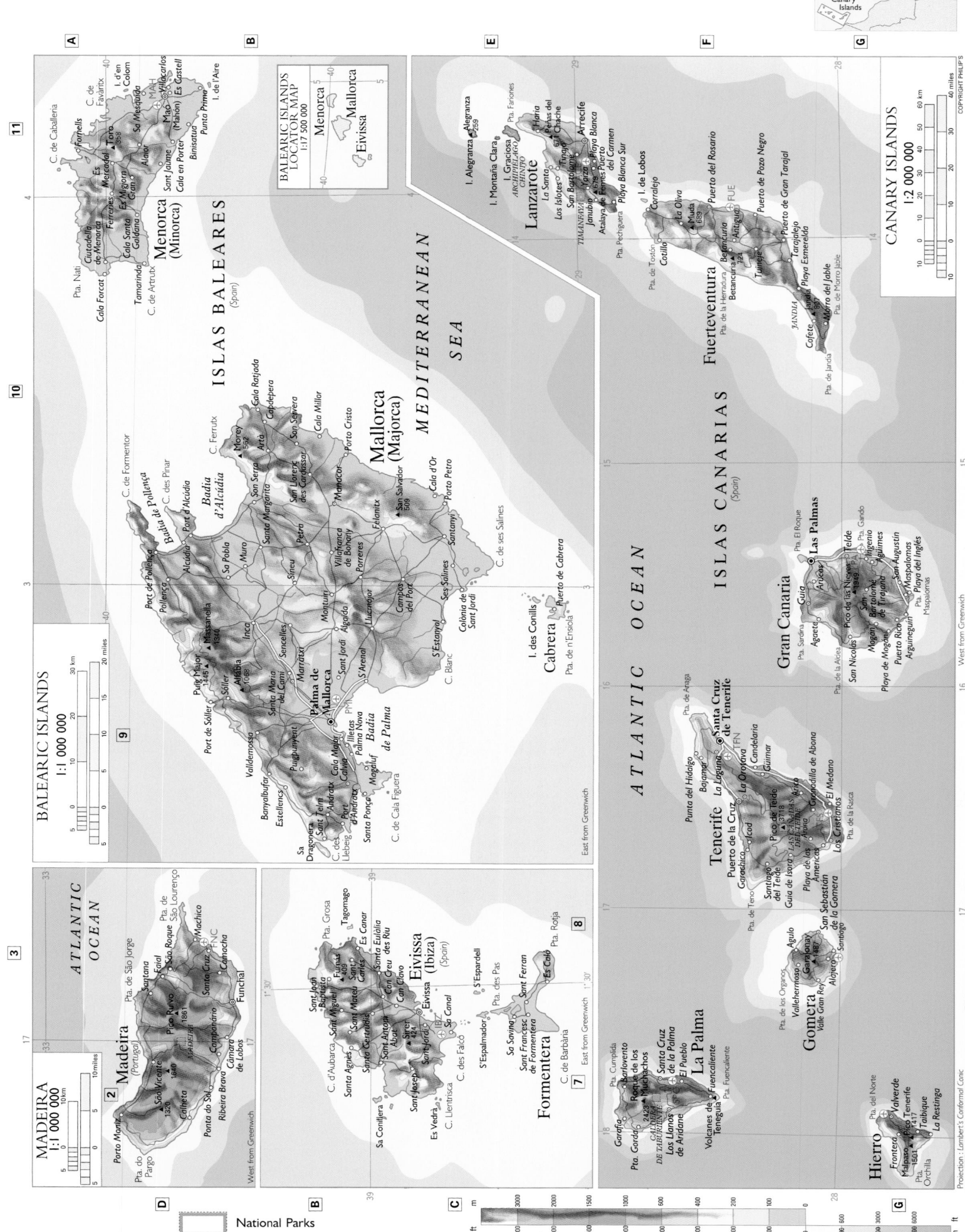

National Parks

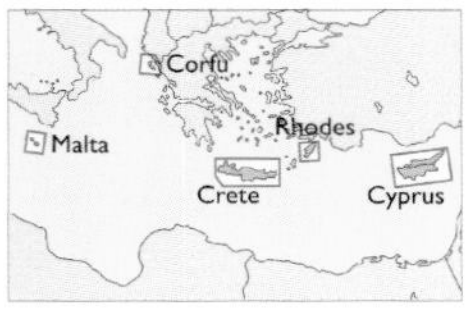

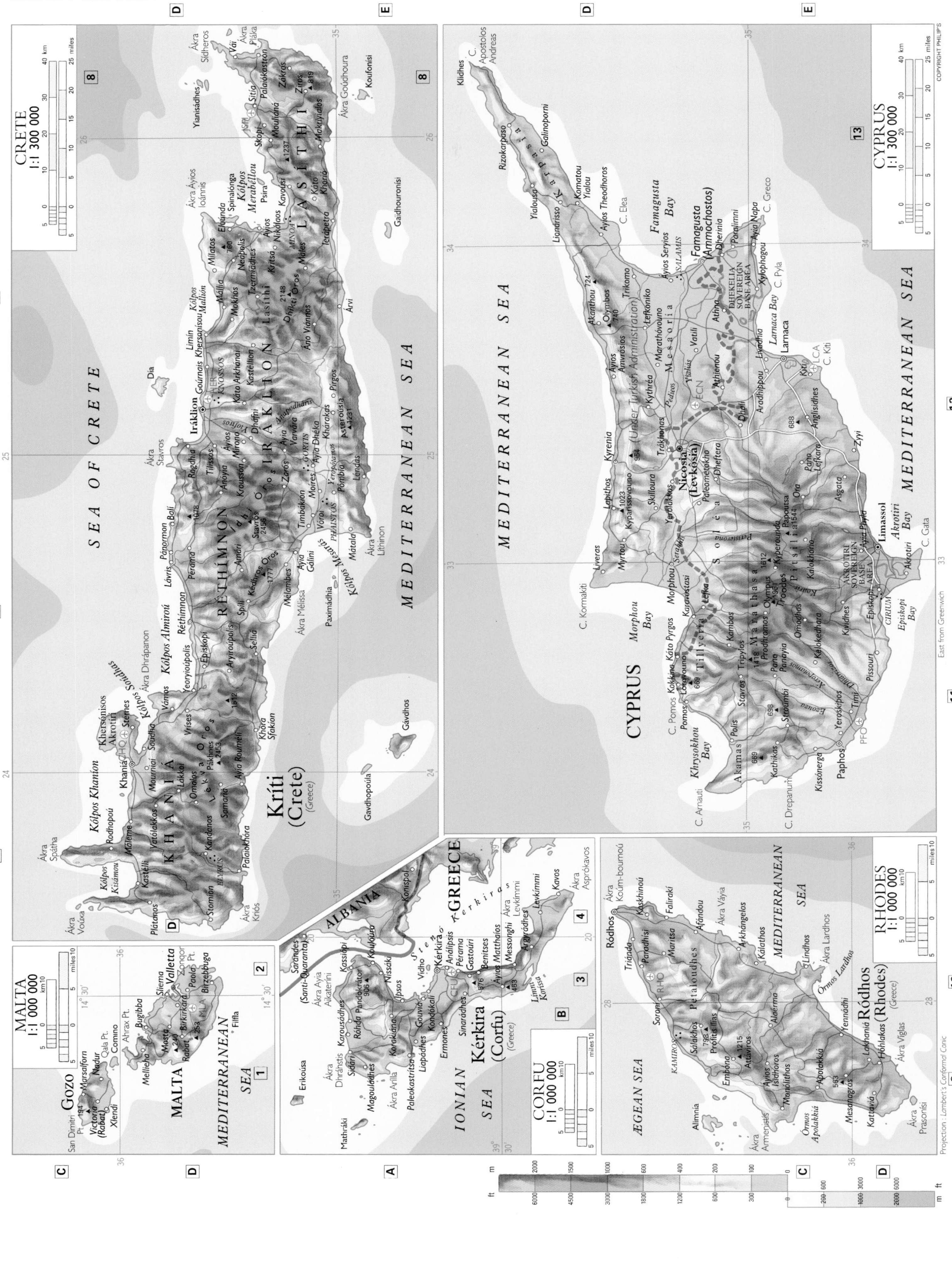

1:50 000 000

Projection: Bonne 30

COPYRIGHT PHILIP'S

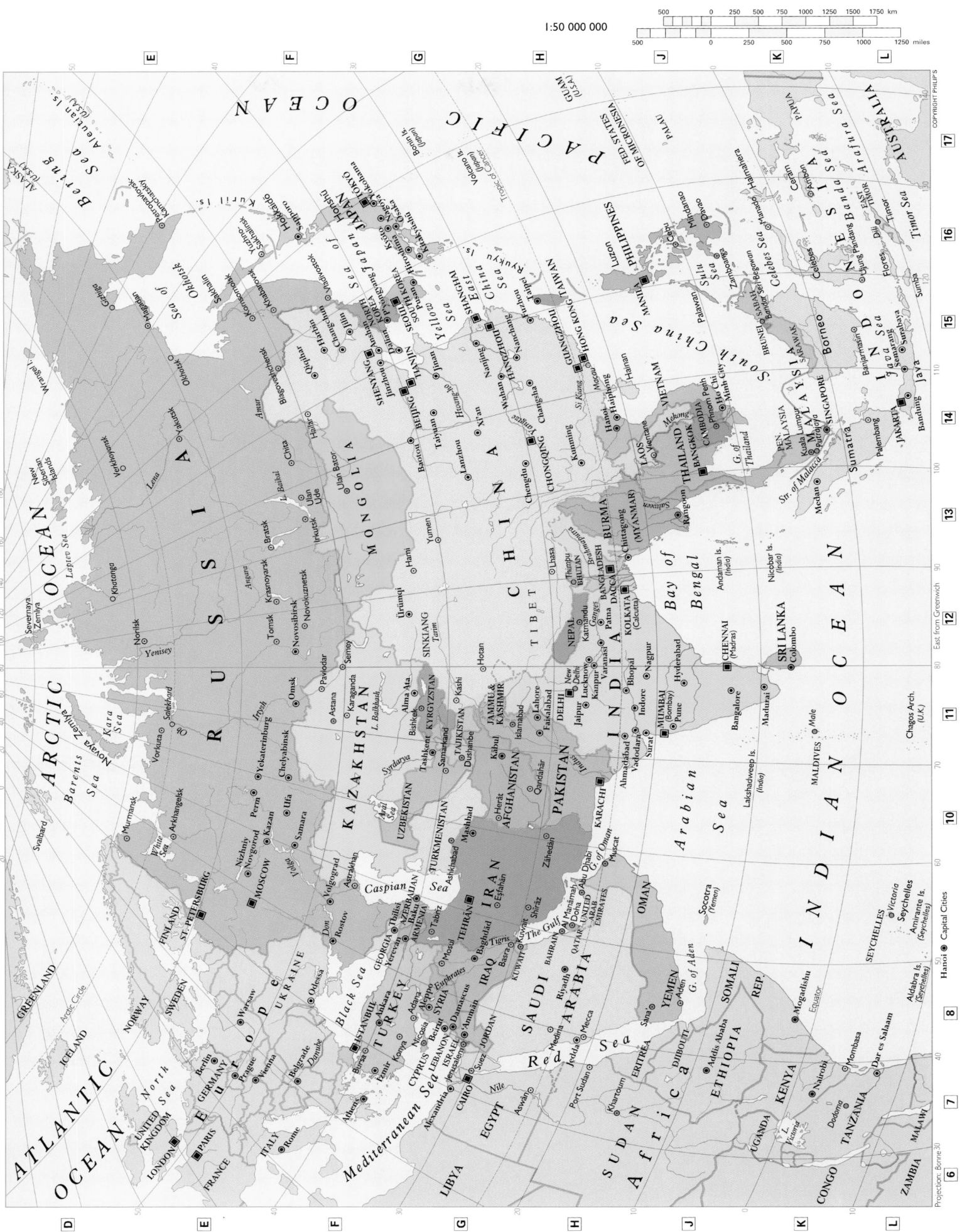

1:50 000 000

500   0   250   500   750   1000   1250   1500   1750 km
500   0   250   500   750   1000   1250 miles

Hanoi ● Capital Cities

COPYRIGHT PHILIP'S

East from Greenwich

Projection: Bonne

1:20 000 000

	RUSSIA
1	Adygea
2	Karachey-Cherkessia
3	Kabardino-Balkaria
4	North Ossetia
5	Ingushetia
6	Chechenia
7	Dagestan
8	Mordvinia
9	Chuvashia
10	Mari El
11	Tatarstan
12	Udmurtia
13	Khakassia
	AZERBAIJAN
14	Naxçivan
	GEORGIA
15	Ajaria
16	Abkhazia
	UKRAINE
17	Crimea

Projection: Conical Orthomorphic with two standard parallels

East from Greenwich

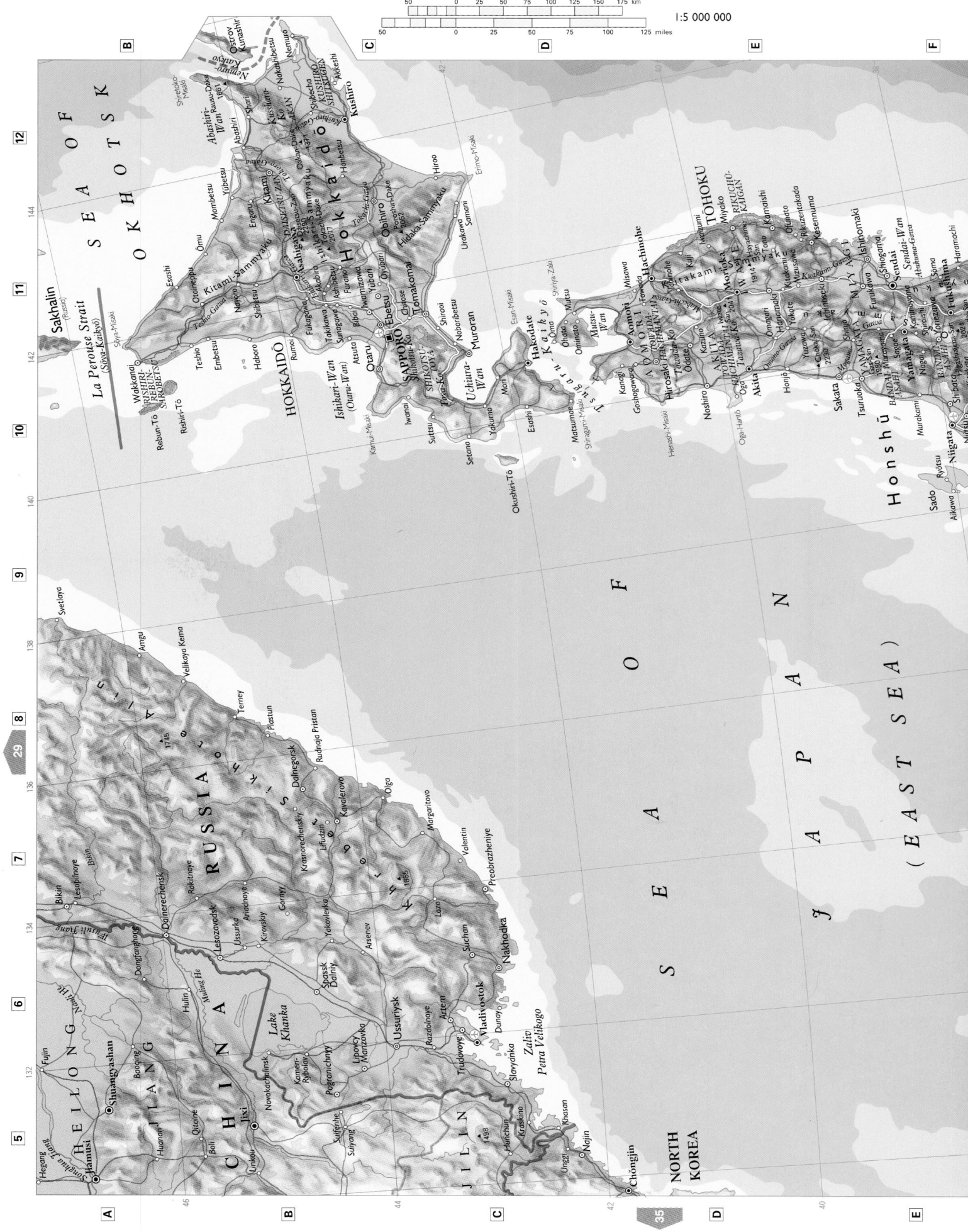

1:5 000 000

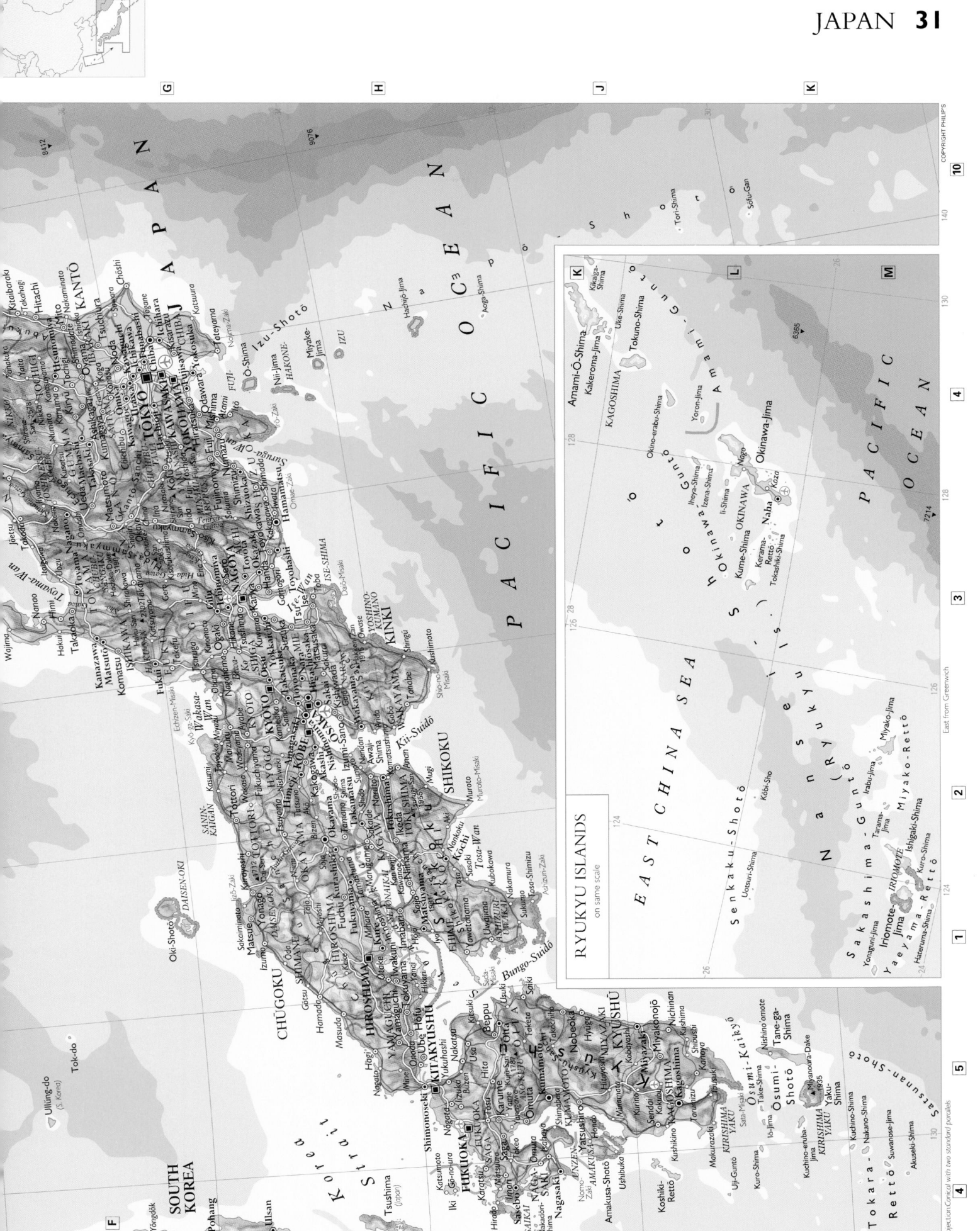

RYUKYU ISLANDS
on same scale

1:15 000 000

100 0 100 200 300 400 500 600 km
100 0 100 200 300 400 miles

Projection: Bonne

East from Greenwich

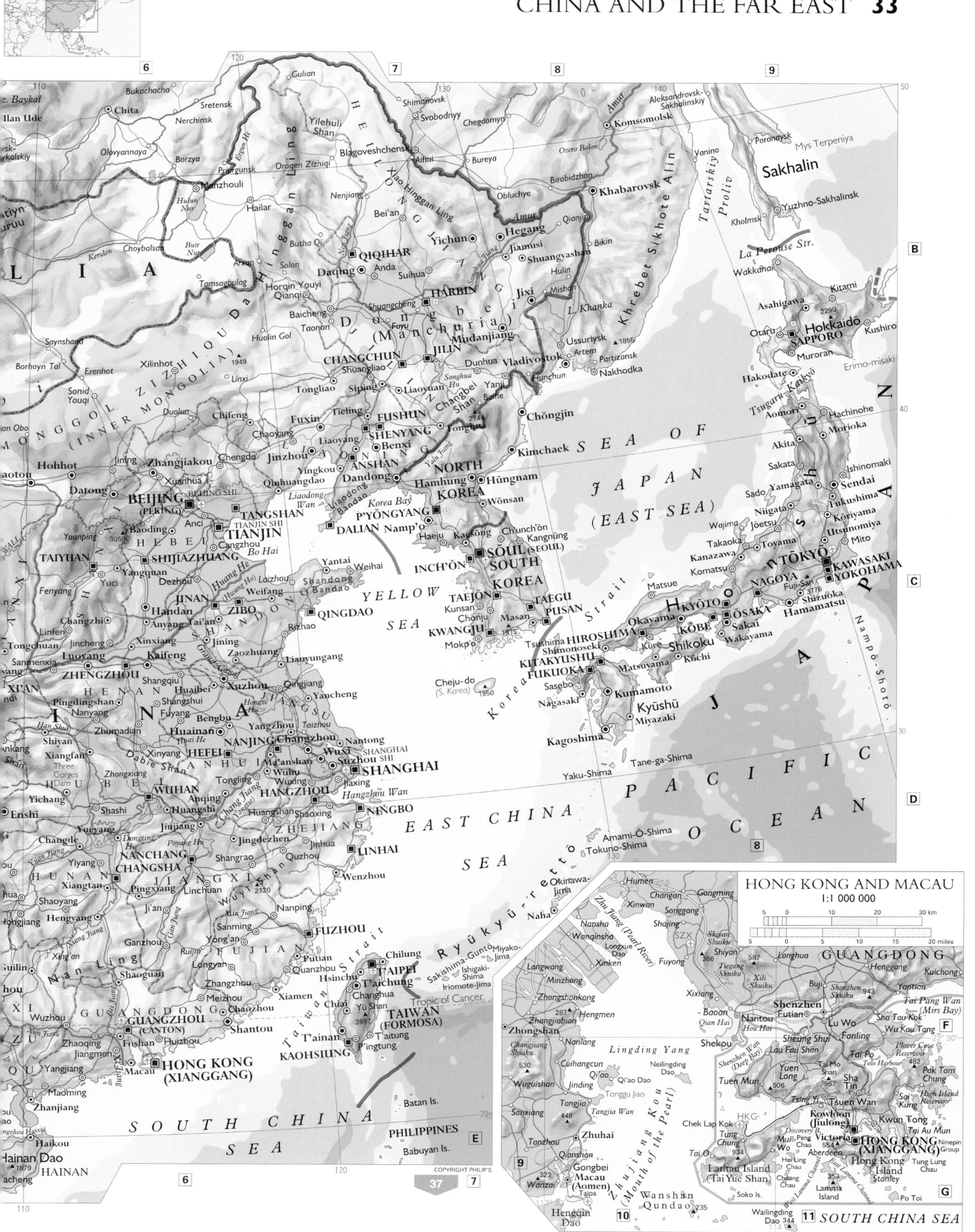

HONG KONG AND MACAU
1:1 000 000

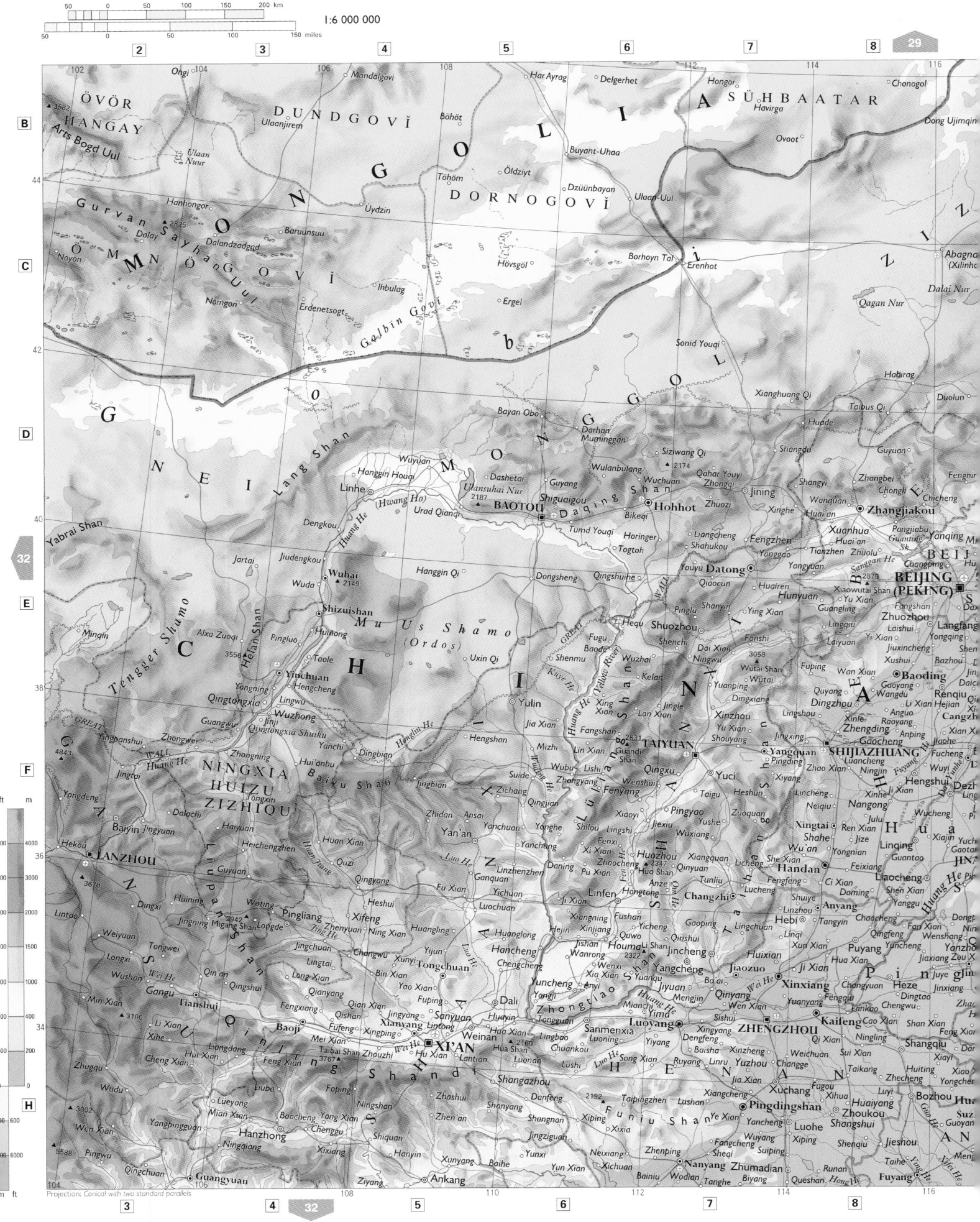

1:6 000 000

Projection: Conical with two standard parallels

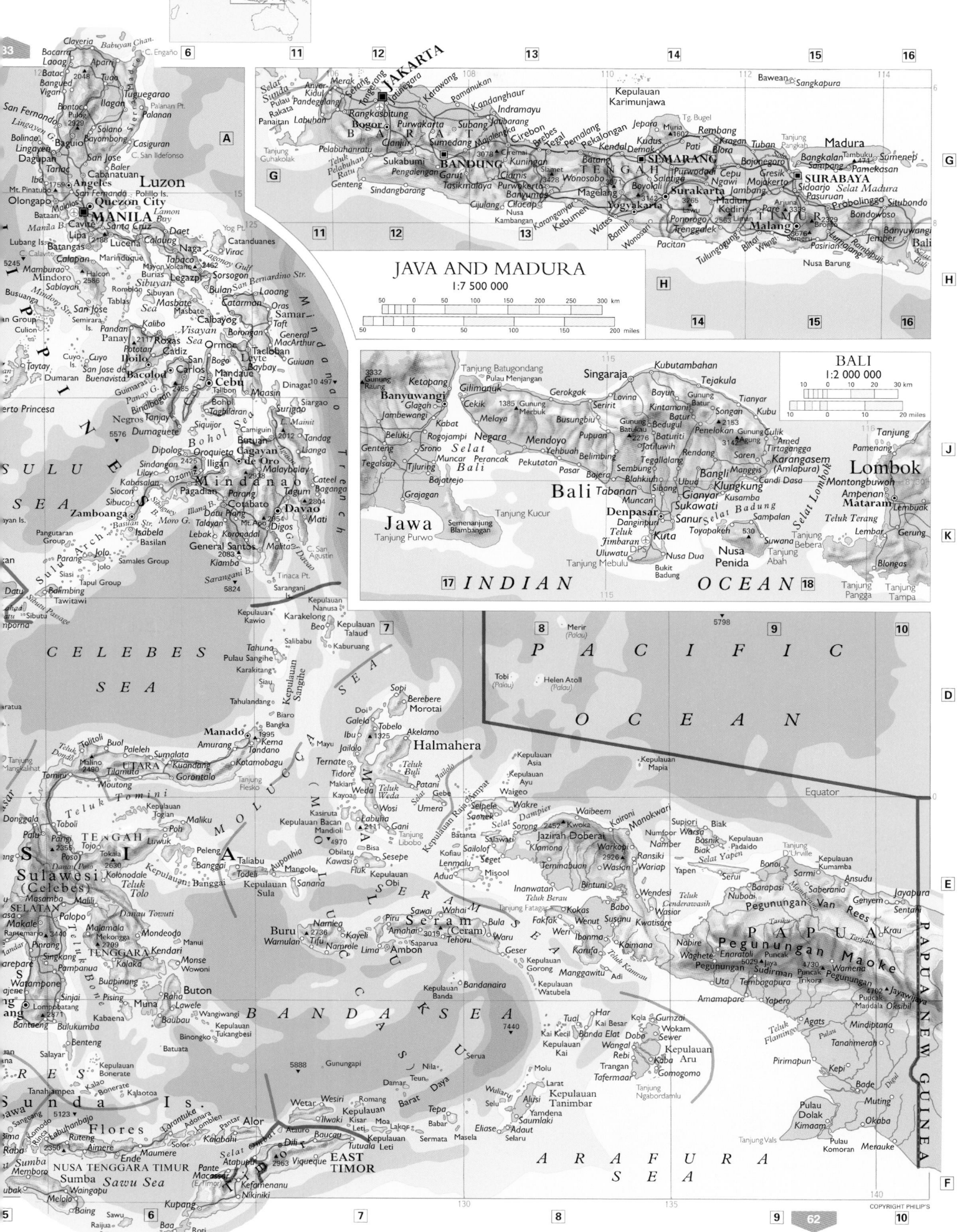

JAVA AND MADURA
1:7 500 000

50   0   50   100   150   200   250   300 km

50   0   50   100   150   200 miles

BALI
1:2 000 000

10   0   10   20   30 km

10   0   10   20 miles

1:6 000 000

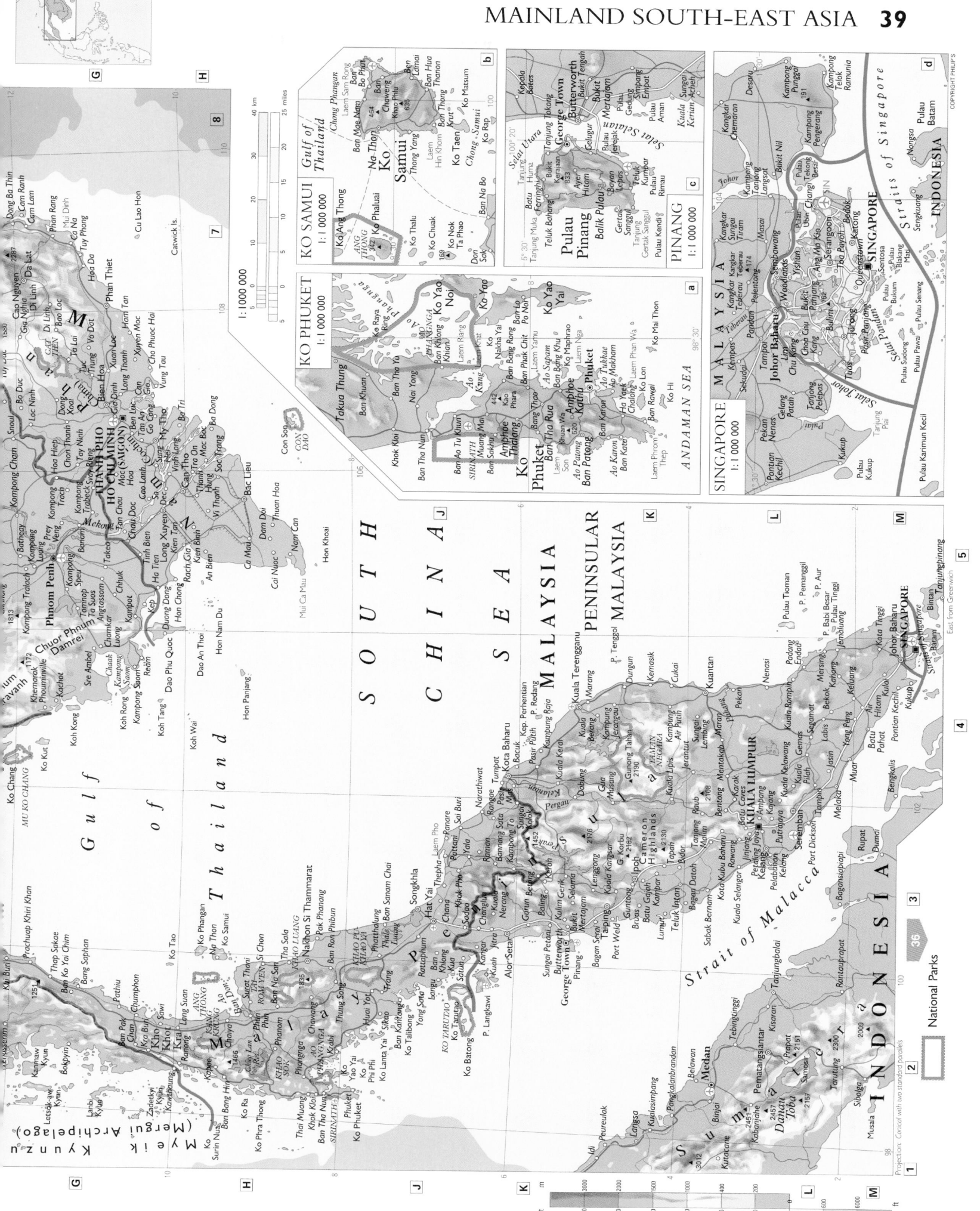

COPYRIGHT PHILIP'S

Gulf of Thailand

KO SAMUI
1:1 000 000

Ko Samui

PINANG
1:1 000 000

Pulau Pinang

George Town
Butterworth

Straits of Singapore

SINGAPORE
MALAYSIA

Singapore

INDONESIA

Johor Baharu

KO PHUKET
1:1 000 000

Phangnga

Ko Yao Yai
Ko Yao Noi

Andaman Sea

Phuket

Ko Phuket

SINGAPORE
1:1 000 000

1:1 000 000

40 km
25 miles

THANH PHO
HO CHI MINH (SAIGON)

Mekong

Phnom Penh

Chuor Phnum Damrei

Gulf

of

Thailand

SOUTH

CHINA

SEA

Con Dao

MU KO CHANG

Ko Chang

Strait of Malacca

MALAYSIA

PENINSULAR
MALAYSIA

KUALA LUMPUR

Kota Baharu

TAMAN NEGARA

Cameron Highlands

Ipoh

George Town
Butterworth
Pinang

Singapore
Johor Baharu

INDONESIA

Sumatera

Medan

Danau Toba

Kyunzu
Myeik
(Mergui Archipelago)

ANG THONG

Nakhon Si Thammarat

Phuket
Ko Phuket

SIRINATH

KHAO LUANG

KHAO SOK

P. Langkawi

Ko Tarutao

National Parks

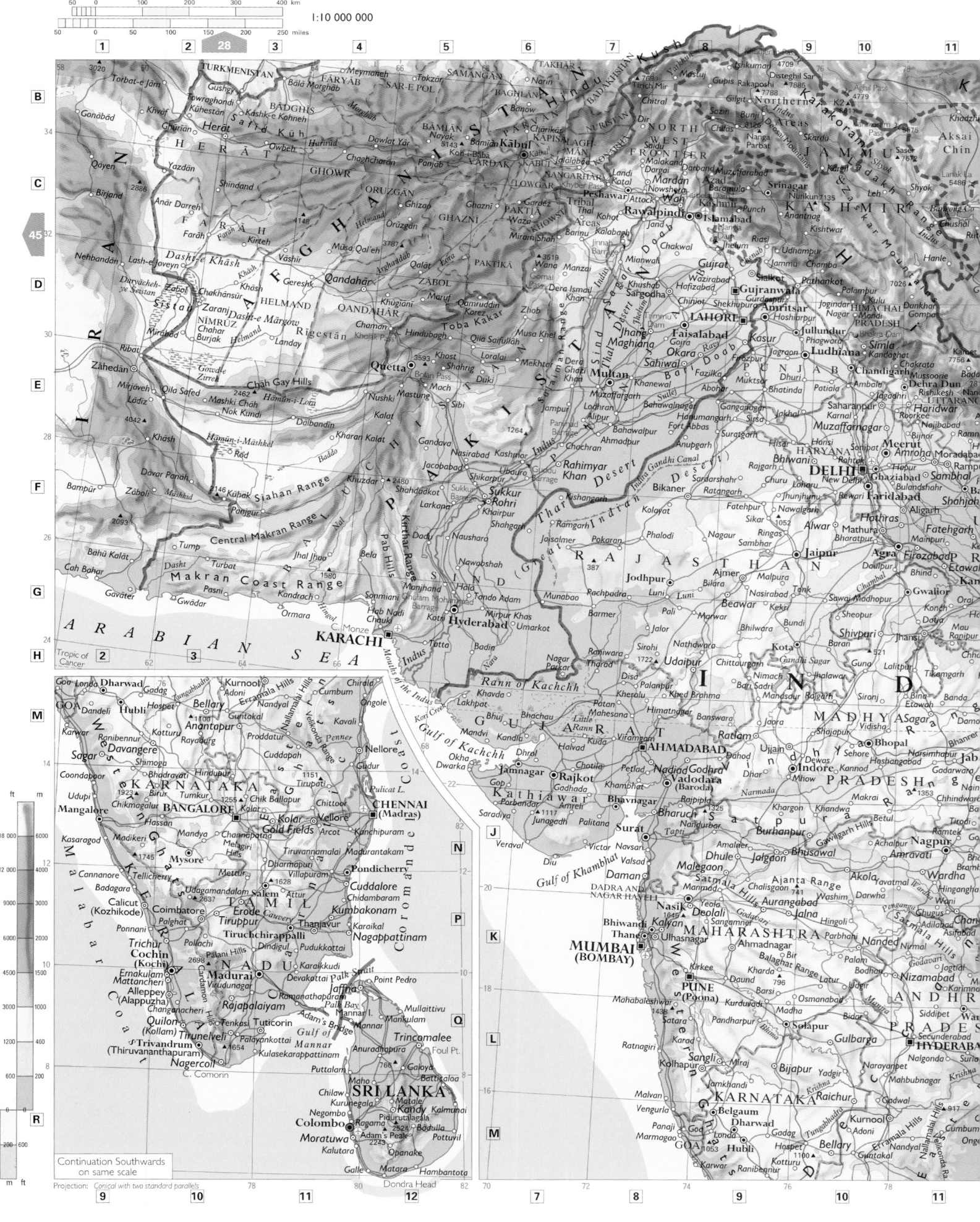

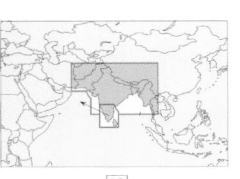

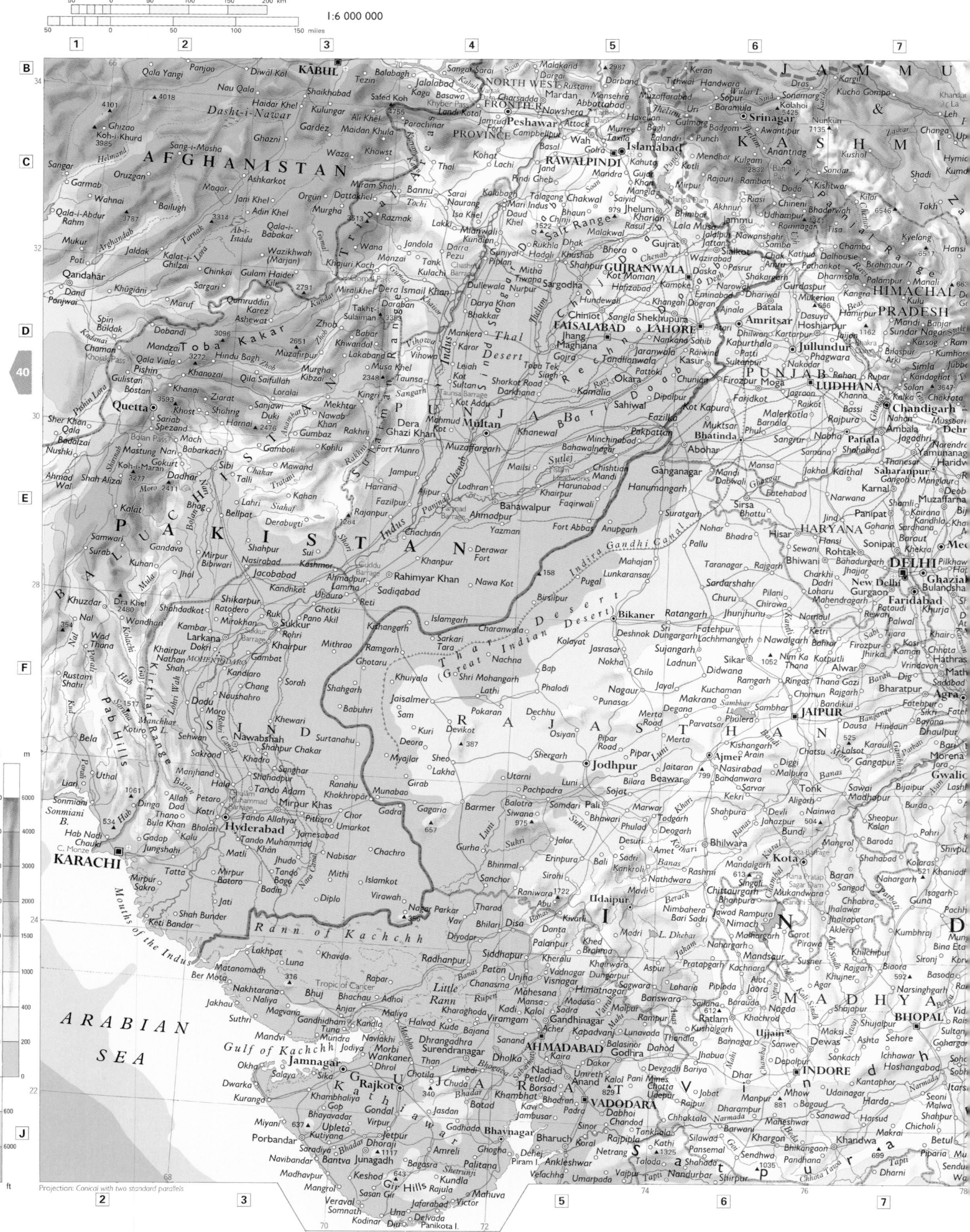

1:6 000 000

Projection: Conical with two standard parallels

JAMMU AND KASHMIR
on same scale

1:7 000 000

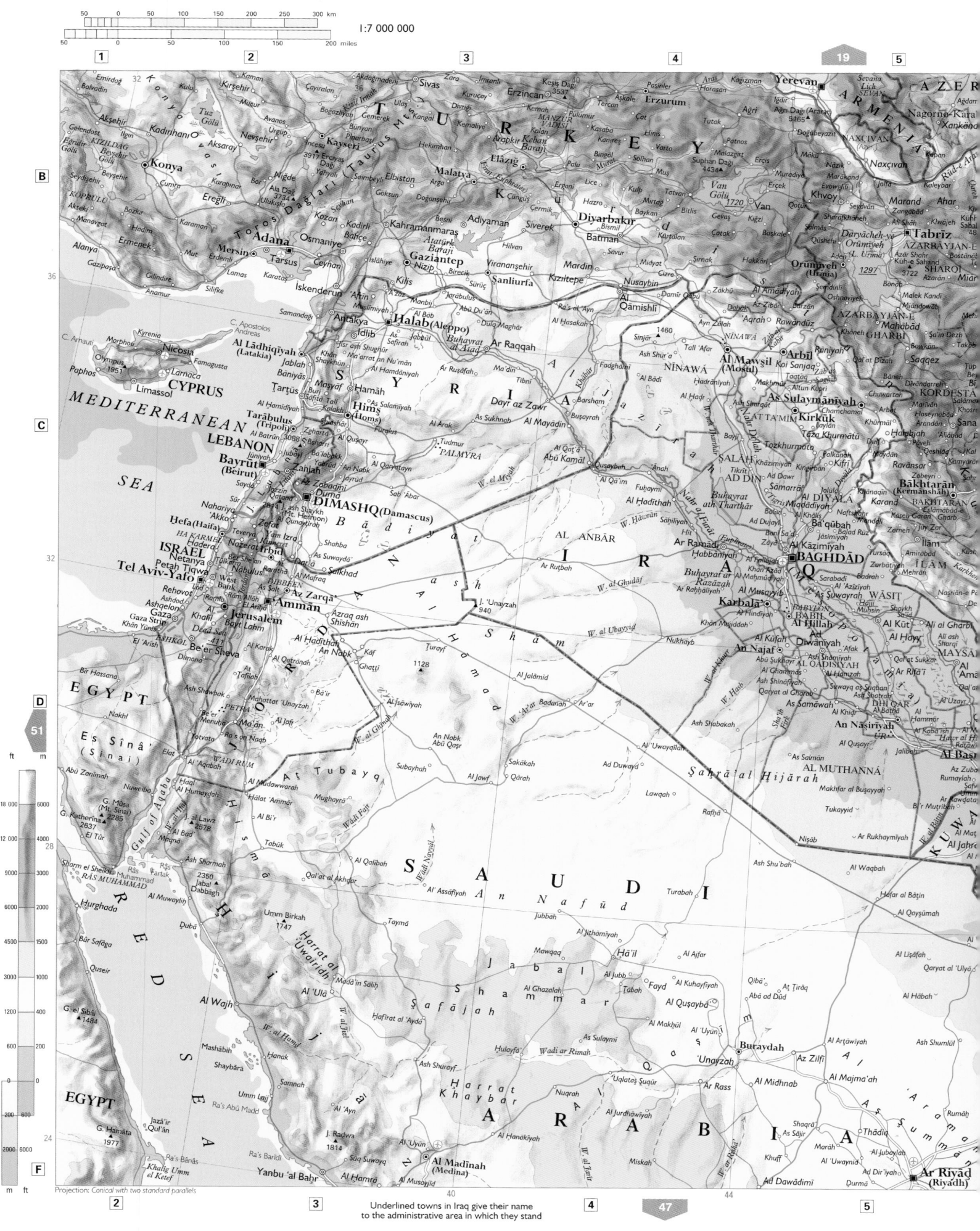

Projection: Conical with two standard parallels

Underlined towns in Iraq give their name
to the administrative area in which they stand

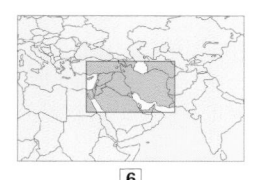

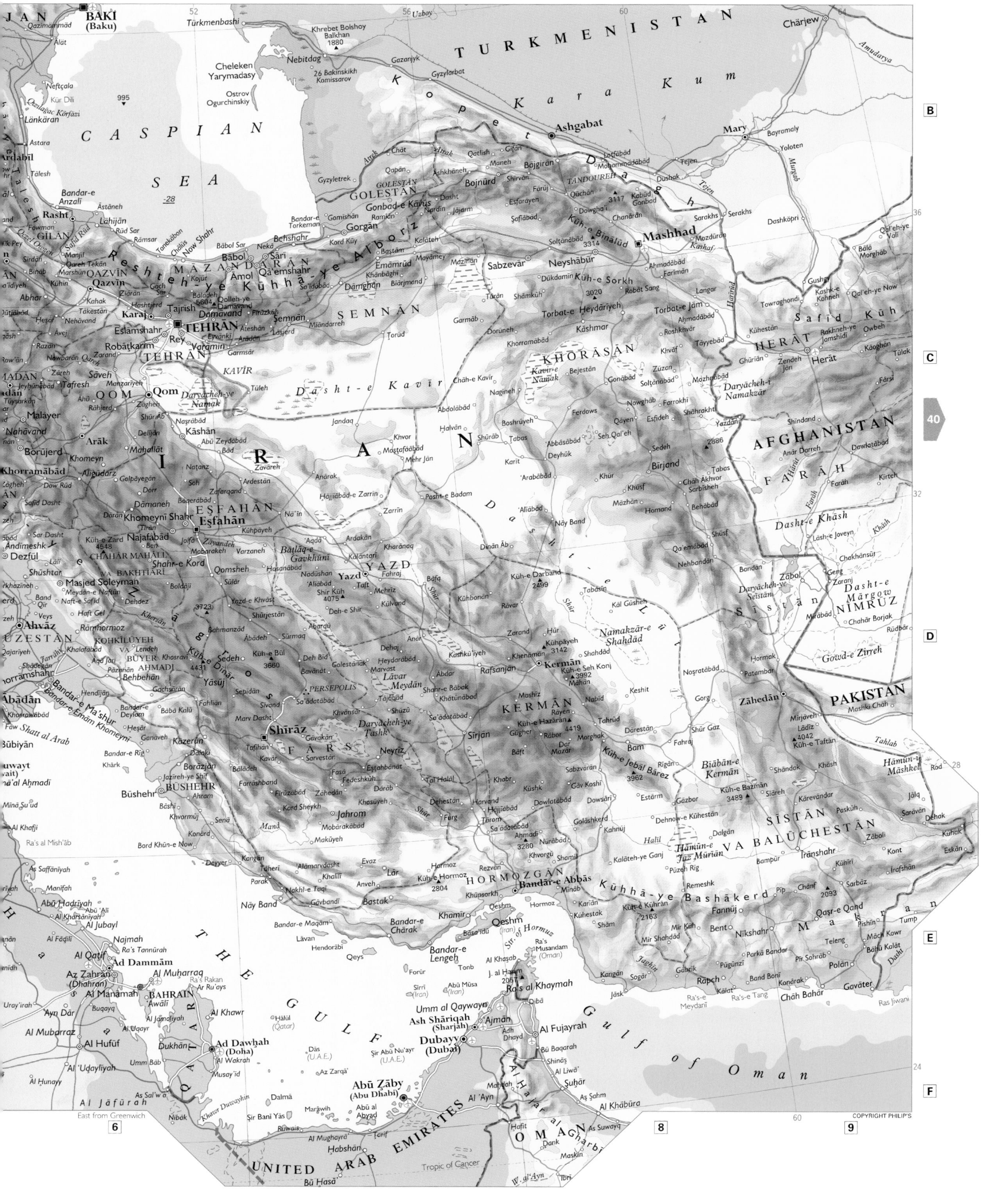

1:2 500 000

10 0 10 20 30 40 50 60 70 80 100 km
10 0 10 20 30 40 50 60 miles

CYPRUS

Paphos
Episkopi
Episkopi Bay
Limassol
Akrotiri Bay
C. Gata

M E D I T E R R A N E A N

S E A

Al Ḥamīdīya
Hims (Homs)
Shinshār
Furqlus
HIMS
Al Mīnā'
Tarābulus (Tripoli)
ASH SHAMĀL
Zgharta
Qurnat as Sawdā 3088
Al Ḥirmil
Al Quṣayr
Al Qaryatayn
Al Batrūn
Bsharri
Al Labwah 2464
Al Burayj
Bi'r Ghadir
Jubayl
Qartaba
Ibrāhīm
An Nabk
2616
Al Biqā'
Ba'labakk
Jūniyah
Bikfayyā
2628
J. Sannīn
Zahlah
Sirghāyā
An Nabk
Khān Abū Shāmat
BAYRŪT (Beirut)
'Alayh
Ash Shuwayfāt
Ad Dāmūr
JABAL LUBNĀN
Hawsh Mūssā
Az Zabadānī
Dumayr
SYRIA
Qurtabā
Saydā (Sidon)
Jazzīn
1942 J. al Bārūk
Ash Shaykh (Mt. Hermon) 2814
Az Zabadānī
Darayyā
DIMASHQ (Damascus)
An Nabaṭīyah at Tahta
AL JANŪB
Marj 'Uyūn
Al Khiyām
Mas'ada
Qaṭanā
Al Kiswah
Al Hājānah
Sūr (Tyre)
Qiryat Shemona
Golan Heights
1197
Al Qunayṭirah
As Sanamayn
Burāq
Nahariyya
Me'ona
Ar Rafid
DAR'Ā
Izra
Shahbā
JABAL AS SUWAYDĀ
'Akko (Acre)
Hagalil
Zefat
Fiq
Shaykh Miskin
Dar'ā
As Suwaydā 1800
Sālah
Mifraz Hefa
Qiryat Yam HAZAFON
Karmi'el
Yam 210
Teverya (Tiberias)
Saham al Jawlān
Hefa (Haifa)
Qiryat Ata
Kinneret
Yarmūk
IRBID
Ar Ramthā
Busrā ash Shām
Dāliyat el Karmel
HA KARMEL
Nazerat (Nazareth)
Afula
Tayiba
Irbid
Salkhad
Malah
TEL MEGIDDO
CAESAREA
Umm el Fahm
Bet She'an
Jordan
AJLŪN
Ajlūn
Al Mafraq
Hadera
Jenin
Shomron
Tūbās
J. Umm ad Darai 1247
Jarash
Umm al Qittayn
Pardes Hanna-Karkur
SAMARIA
JEBEL
JARASH
AL MAFRAQ
ISRAEL
Netanya
Tulkarm
Nābulus
N. az Zarqā
Herzliyya
Benē Beraq
Kefar Sava
Petah Tiqwa
SHILO
AL BALQĀ
As Salt
Az Zarqā
'AMMĀN
Tel Aviv-Yafo
Ramat Gan
West Bank
Wadi as Sīr
Bat Yam
Lōd
Rishon le Ziyyon
Ramla
Rām Allāh
Karama
AMM
Az ZARQĀ
Yavne
Rehovot
El Arīḥā (Jericho)
Na'ūr
Ashdod
Jerusalem (Yerushalayim) (Al Quds)
Ma'daba
At Tunayb
Qiryat Mal'akhi
Bet Shemesh
Bayt Lahm (Bethlehem)
MA'DABA
'AMMAN
Ashqelon
Qiryat Gat
Har Yehuda
Al Khalīl (Hebron)
W. al Ḥaydān
TEL LAKHISH
Az Zāhirīya
Dhibān
Gaza
N. Shiqma
Sederot
Midbar Yehuda
411
Al Haditah
Gaza Strip
Khān Yūnis
Rafah
ESHKOL
Arad
Sedom
Al Karak
AL KARAK
Al Mazar
Bûr Sa'îd (Port Said)
Bûr Fu'ad
Rās Burūn
El Daheir
Be'er Sheva (Beersheba)
Bor Mashash
Dimona
HADAROM
333
W. al Ḥasā
W. Bā'ir
Khalîg el Tîna
Sabkhet el Bardawil
El 'Arîsh
Bir el Garārât
Qezi'ot
Birein
Sedé Boqér
At Ṭafīlah
JORDAN
Râmâni
Bir el 'Abd
Bir el Garārāt
Bir Lahfān
AT TAFĪLAH
Bā'ir
El Qantara
Bir el Jafar
Bir el Duweidar
Wāḥid
Bir Madkûr
SHAMĀL SÎNÎ
Bir Kaseiba
W. el 'Arîsh
Muweilih
892
El Quseima
Nijil
Mahattat 'Unayzah
J. ash Shawmari 1072
Ismâ'ilîya
Talâta
Khamsa
Bir el Mâlhi
Bir Hasana
G. Yi 'Allaq 1094
Mizpe Ramon
Rujm Talāt al Jamā'ah 1736
Al Jafr
Qa'el Jafr
ISMA'ĪLIYA
El Buheirat el Murrat el Kubra (Bitter Lakes)
Bir Gebeil Hisn
W. Qraiya
El 'Agrûd
Ha Negev
PETRA
Wādi Mūsa
Ma'ān
MA'ĀN
Gineifa
W. el Brûk
Bir el Thamâda
N. Paran
N. Hiyyon
Bi'r al Mārī
EGYPT
Mamarr Mitlâ
Es Sinâ' (Sinai)
948 G. el Kabrit
W. Mahashem
Bir Abu Muhammad
'En 'Avrona
Bi'r al Butayyihāt
Ra's an Naqb
Mahattat ash Shidîyah
El Suweis (Suez)
Adabiya
Uyûn Mûsa
Aïn Sudr
Nakhl
W. el Aqaba
El Kuntilla
Yotvata
AL 'AQABA
Ra's an Naqb 1435
Ghubbet el Bûs
Gebel el Tîh
El Thamad
W. Girâfi
1592 1754
WADI RUM
Batn al Ghūl
Rās Matarma
El Wabeira
Bir el Biarât
Elat
Rum
SAUDI
1272
EL SUWEIS
JANŪB SÎNÎ
W. Abu Ga'da
Bir et Taba
Al 'Aqaba
At Tubayq
ARABIA
Abu Sandûq
W. Abu Gifân
Bir el Heisi
1165
Gulf of Aqaba
W. an Nutayqi
Haql
Al Mudawwarah

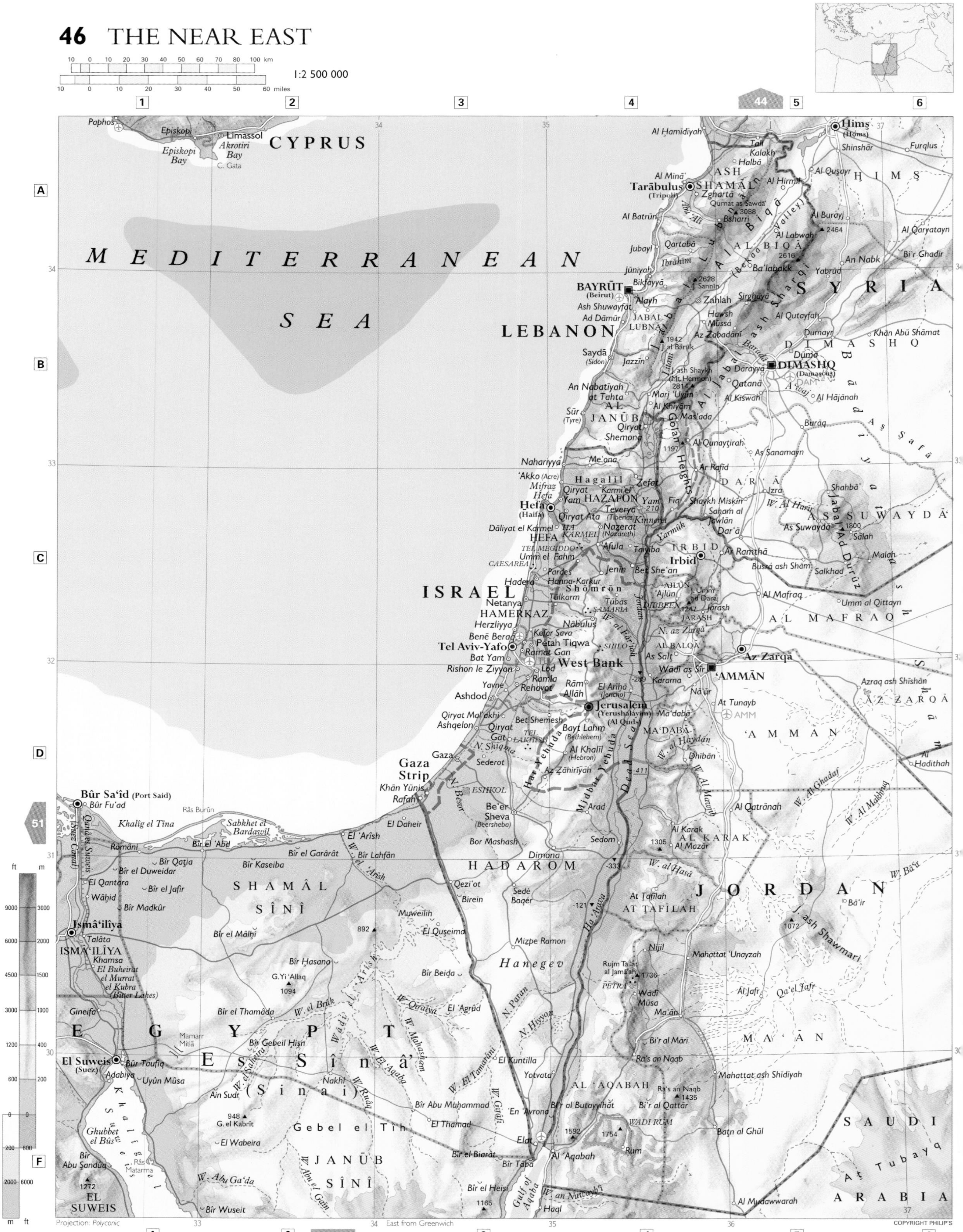

Projection: Polyconic   East from Greenwich   COPYRIGHT PHILIP'S

ft m
9000 3000
6000 2000
4500 1500
3000 1000
1200 600
600 200
0 0
200 600
2000 6000
m ft

= = = 1974 Cease Fire Lines   National Parks

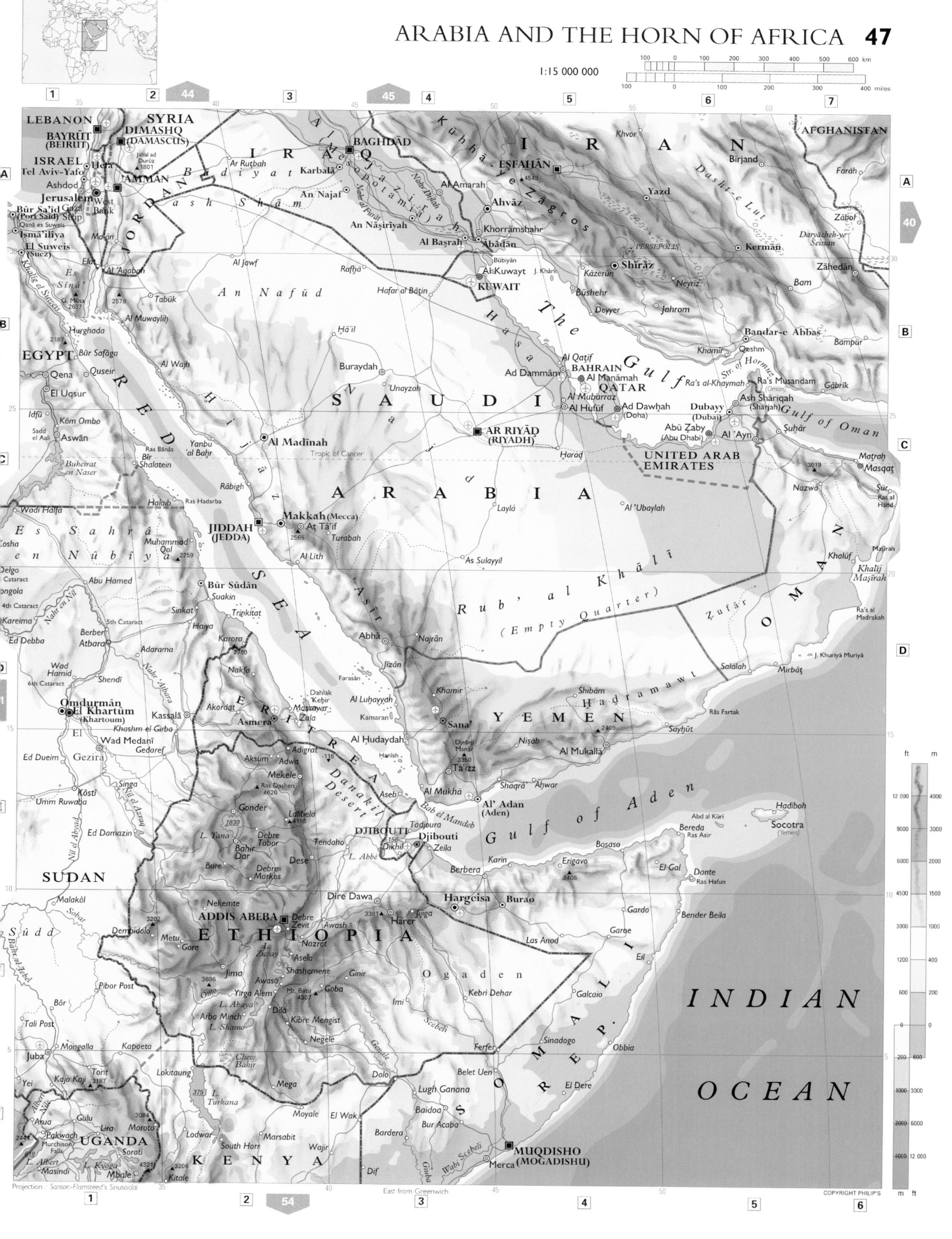

1:42 000 000

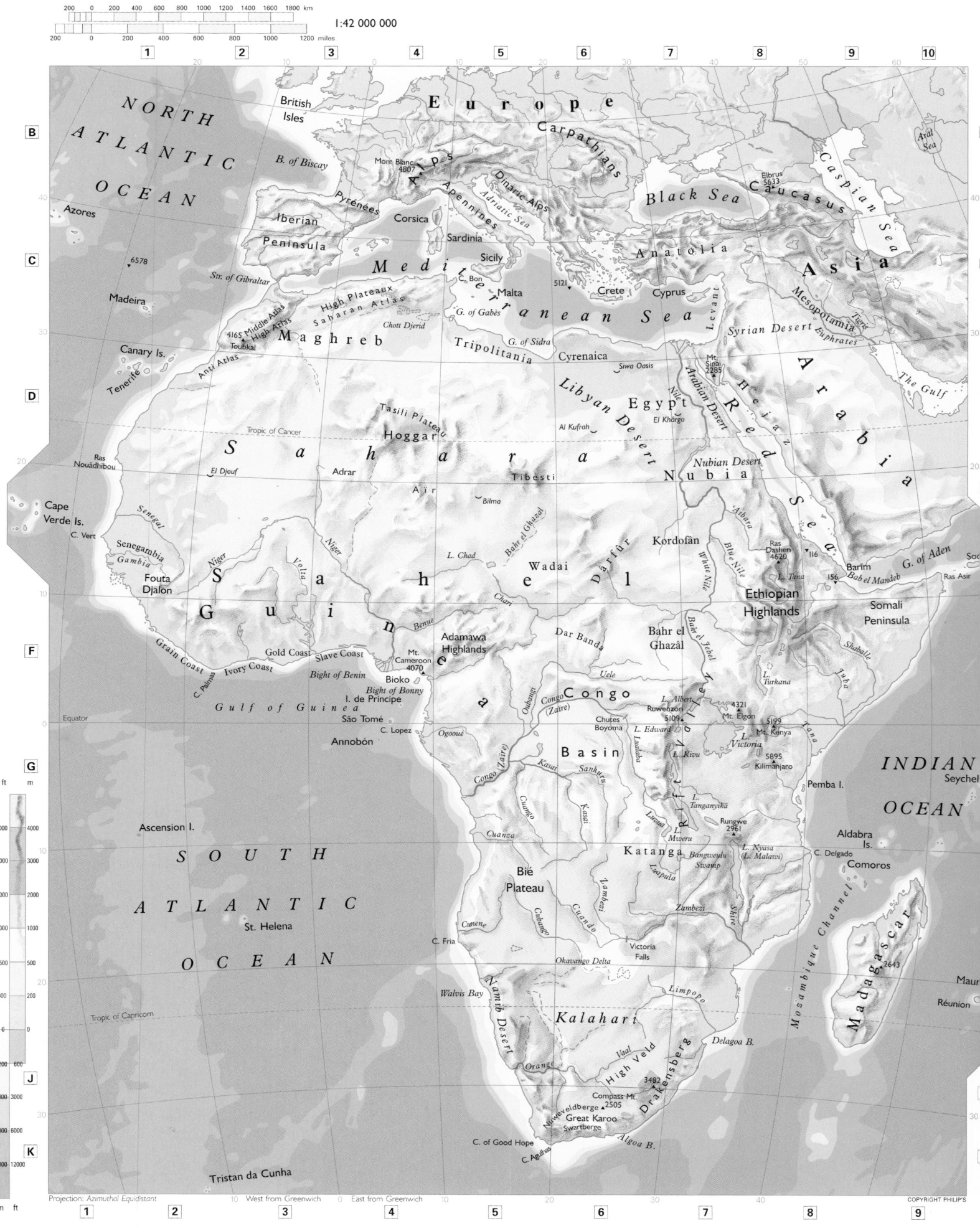

200 0 200 400 600 800 1000 1200 1400 1600 1800 km
200 0 200 400 600 800 1000 1200 miles

NORTH
ATLANTIC
OCEAN

Europe

British
Isles

B. of Biscay

Mont Blanc
4807

Carpathians

ALPS

Dinaric Alps
Apennines
Adriatic Sea

Elbrus
5633

Caucasus

Black Sea

Caspian Sea

Aral
Sea

Pyrénées
Corsica

Azores

Iberian
Peninsula

Sardinia

Sicily

Anatolia

Asia

Madeira

6578

Str. of Gibraltar

Crete

Cyprus

Mesopotamia

Syrian Desert

Euphrates

Tigris

Canary Is.

Tenerife

Middle Atlas
4165
High Atlas
Toubkal

High Plateaux
Saharan Atlas

Maghreb

Chott Djerid

Mediterranean Sea

5121

C. Bon

G. of Gabès

Malta

G. of Sidra

Tripolitania

Cyrenaica

Siwa Oasis

Mt.
Sinai
2285

Levant

Arabian Desert

Hejaz

Arabia

The Gulf

Anti Atlas

Tropic of Cancer

Ras
Nouâdhibou

El Djouf

Tasili Plateau

Hoggar

Adrar

Saha

Aïr

Air

ra

Tibesti

Bilma

Libyan Desert

Egypt

Al Kufrah

El Khârga

Nubian Desert

Nubia

Red Sea

Cape
Verde Is.

Senegal

C. Vert

Senegambia

Gambia

Fouta
Djalon

Niger

Volta

Niger

Benue

S a h e l

L. Chad

Bahr el Ghazal

Wadai

Darfûr

Kordofân

Ras
Dashen
4620

116

White Nile

Blue Nile

Atbara

L. Tana

156

Barim

G. of Aden

Bab el Mandeb

Ras Asir

Soc

Guinea

Grain Coast

C. Palmas

Ivory Coast

Gold Coast

Slave Coast

Bight of Benin

Mt.
Cameroon
4070

Bioko

Bight of Bonny

Adamawa
Highlands

Dar Banda

Bahr el
Ghazâl

Ethiopian
Highlands

Somali
Peninsula

Shabelle

Juba

I. de Principe

São Tomé

C. Lopez

Annobón

Equator

Gulf of Guinea

Ogooué

Oubangui

Uele

Congo
(Zaire)

Congo

Basin

Chutes
Boyoma

L. Albert

Ruwenzori
5109

L. Edward

L. Kivu

L. Lualaba

Mt. Elgon
5199

L.
Victoria

4321

Mt. Kenya
5895

Tana

INDIAN

Seychel

OCEAN

Kasai

Sankuru

Kilimanjaro

Ascension I.

SOUTH

Cuango

Kasai

Congo (Zaire)

Cuanza

L.
Tanganyika

Lualaba

L.
Mweru

Rungwe
2961

Pemba I.

Aldabra
Is.

C. Delgado

Comoros

ATLANTIC

St. Helena

Katanga

Bangweulu
Swamp

Luapula

L. Nyasa
(L. Malawi)

Bié
Plateau

Cunene

Zambezi

Cuando

Zambezi

Shire

Mozambique Channel

Madagascar

2643

OCEAN

C. Fria

Victoria
Falls

Okavango Delta

Walvis Bay

Namib Desert

Kalahari

Limpopo

Maur

Réunion

Tropic of Capricorn

Vaal

High veld

Delagoa B.

Drakensberg

Orange

3482

Compass Mt.
2505

Nuweveldberge

Great Karoo

Swartberge

Algoa B.

C. of Good Hope

C. Agulhas

Tristan da Cunha

ft   m

12000   4000

9000   3000

6000   2000

3000   1000

1500   500

600   200

0   0

200   600

1000   3000

2000   6000

4000   12000

m   ft

1:42 000 000

● Dakar Capital Cities

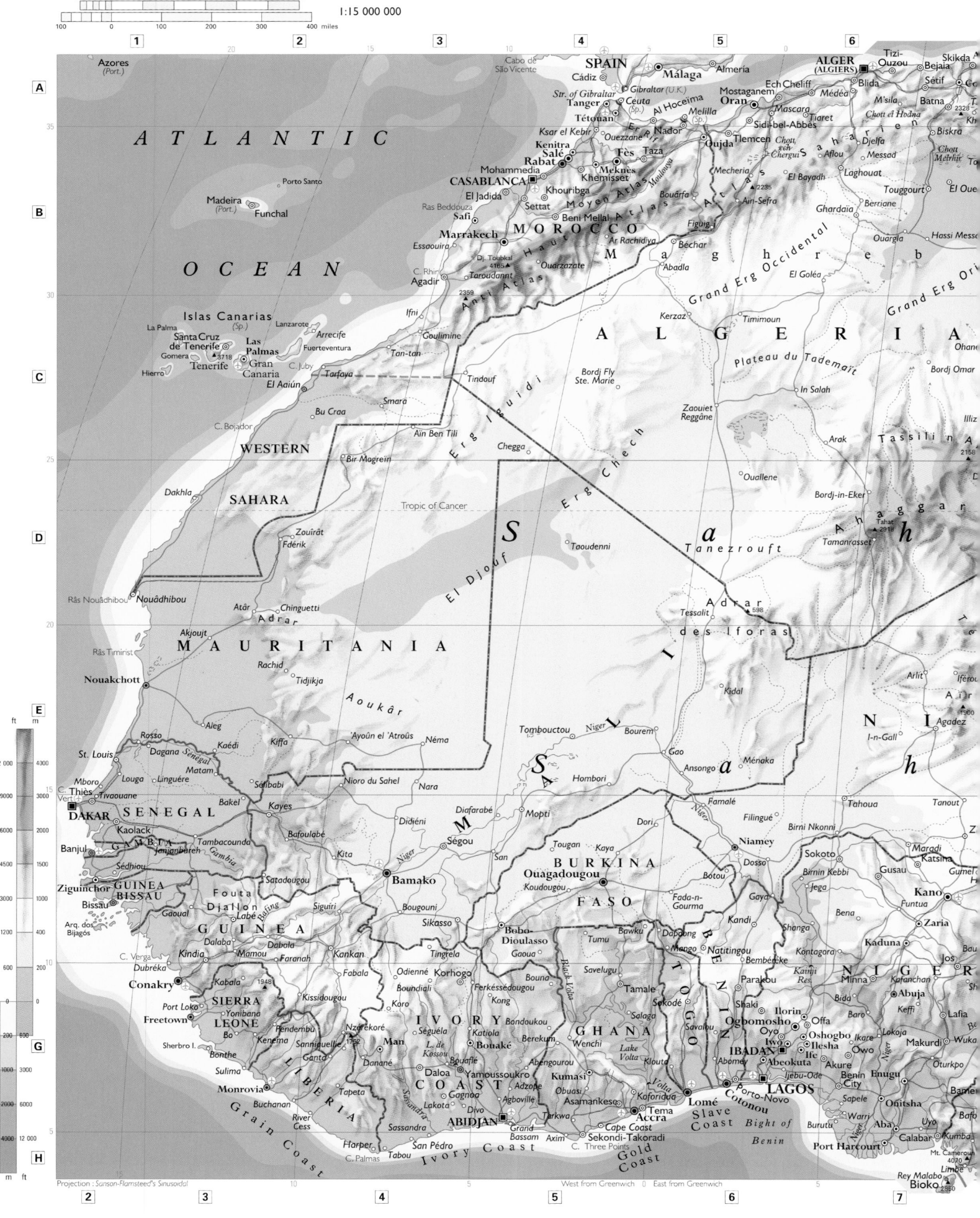

100   0   100   200   300   400   500   600 km
100   0   100   200   300   400 miles

1:15 000 000

Projection : Sanson-Flamsteed's Sinusoidal

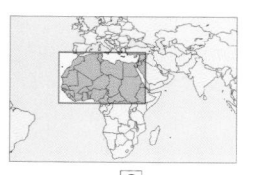

A

B

47

C

D

E

F

G

H

MEDITERRANEAN SEA

GREECE

TURKEY

CYPRUS

SYRIA

IRAQ

LEBANON

ISRAEL

JORDAN

SAUDI ARABIA

Hijaz

RED SEA

LIBYA

Tripolitania

Cyrenaica

Fezzan

Sahrâ' Lîbîya

EGYPT

Es Sahrâ Esh Sharqiya

Es Sinâ'

Sahrâ' Rebiana

Aozou Strip

Tibesti

CHAD

Borkou

Ennedi

Zagaoua

Erg du Djourab

Grand Erg du Bilma

Es Sahrâ en Nûbiya

SUDAN

Dârfûr

Kordofân

ERITREA

ETHIOPIA

Sîdd

Bahr el Ghazâl

CENTRAL AFRICAN REPUBLIC

TUNIS

MALTA

Valletta

Sicilia

Tarābulus (Tripoli)

Al Khums

Misrātah

Banghāzī

Al Marj

Darnah

Tubruq

EL ISKANDARIYA (ALEXANDRIA)

El Mahalla el Kubra

Damanhûr

Dumyât

Bûr Sa'îd

Tanta

El Mansûra

Zagazig

Ismâ'îliya

El Gîza

EL QÂHIRA (CAIRO)

Helwân

El Faiyûm

Beni Suef

El Khartûm (Khartoum)

Omdurmân

Ndjamena

Maiduguri

Banguí

Yaoundé

1:15 000 000

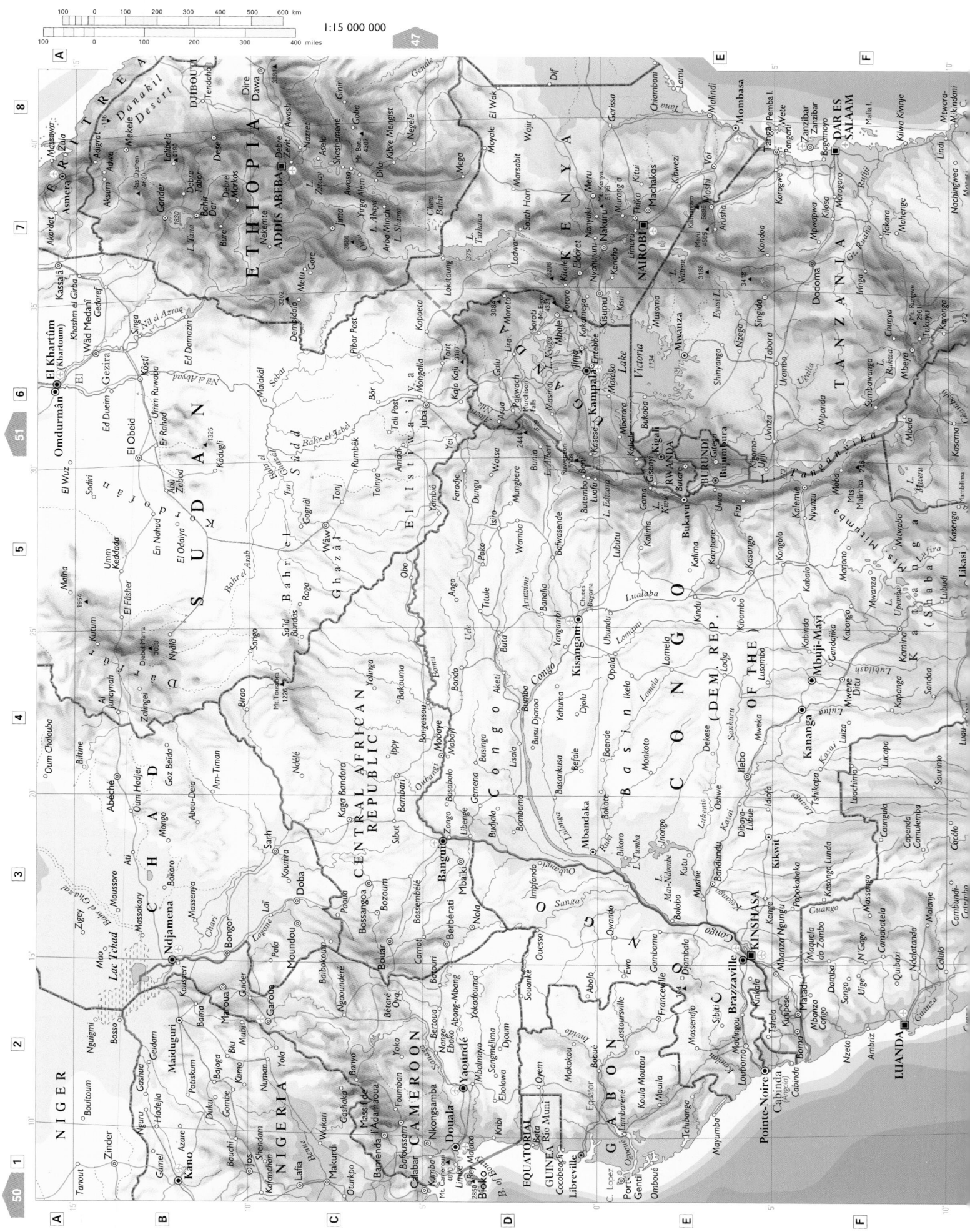

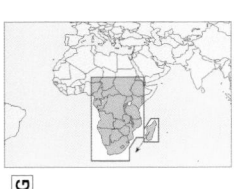

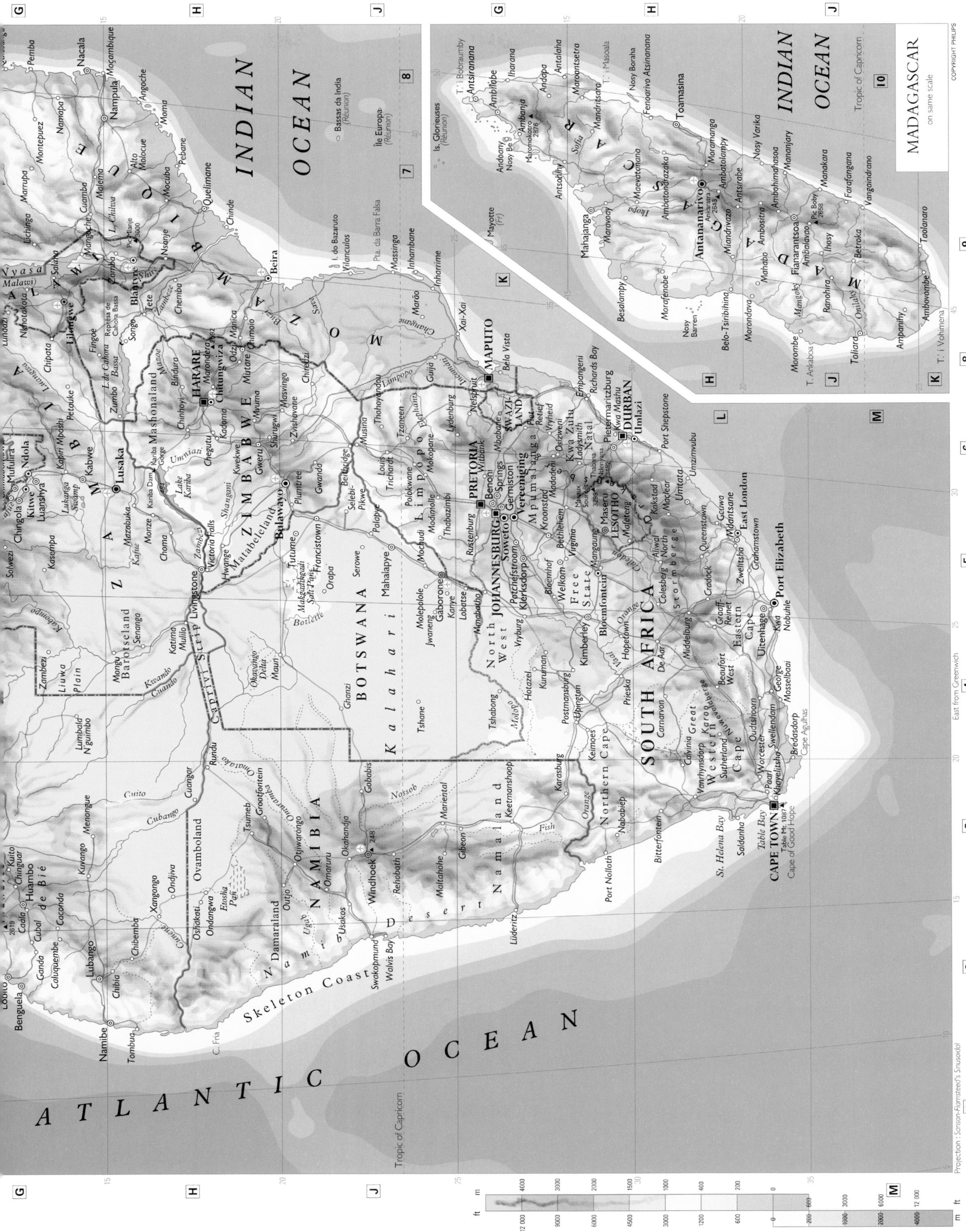

1:8 000 000

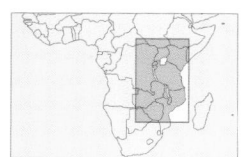

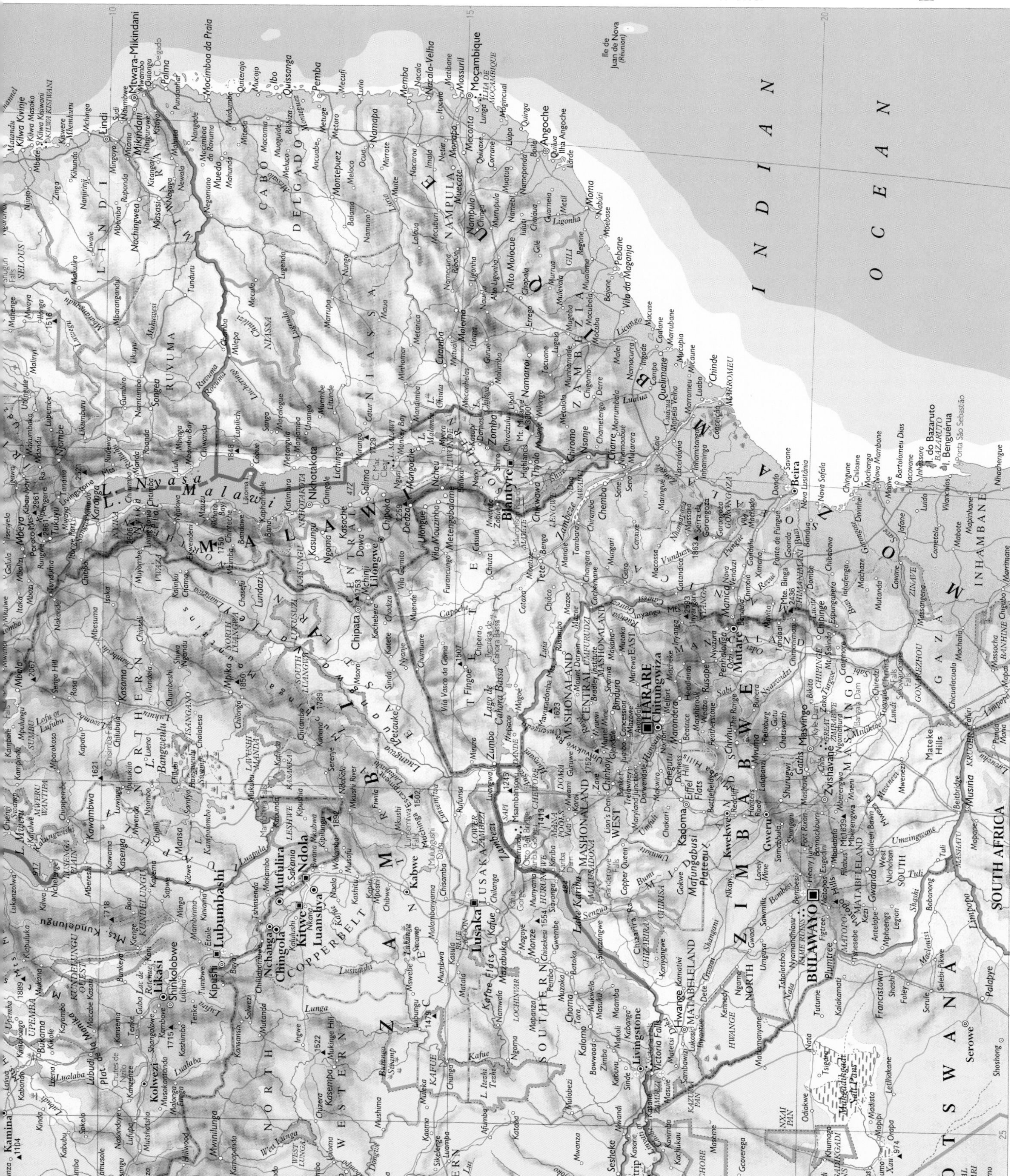

∴ UNESCO World Heritage Sites

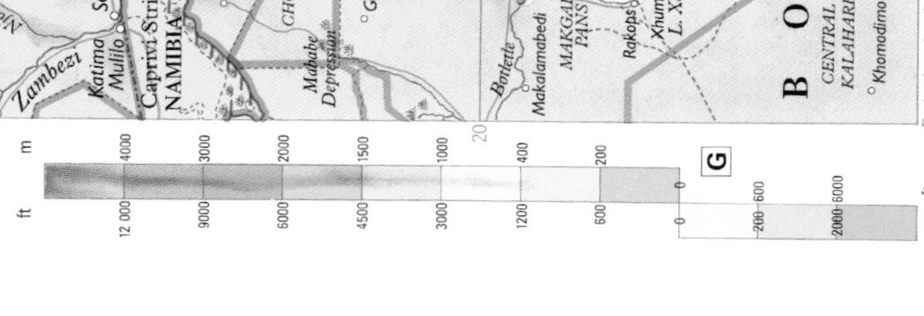

National Parks

Nature Reserves and Game Reserves

Projection: Lambert's Equivalent Azimuthal

COPYRIGHT PHILIP'S

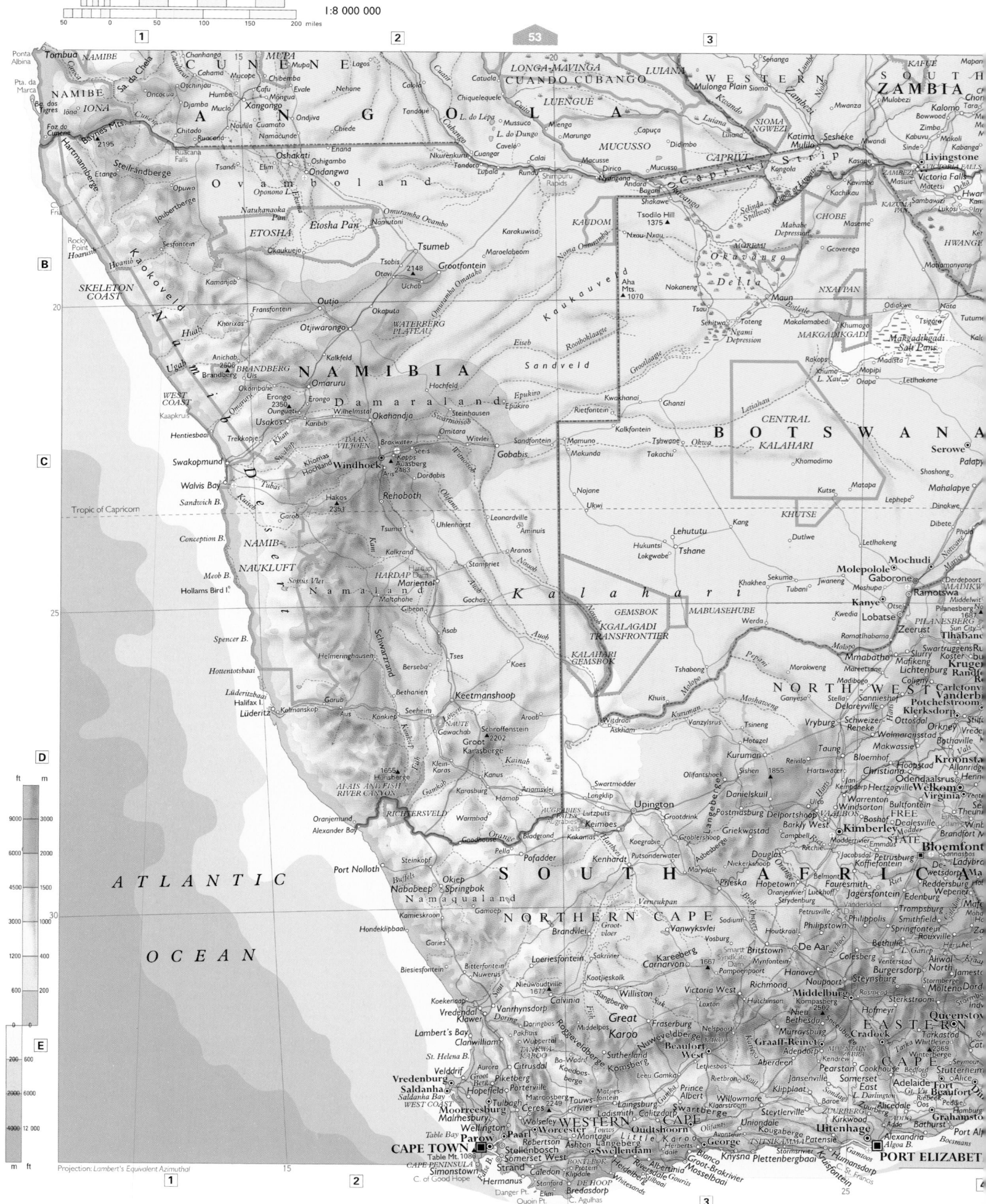

ATLANTIC

OCEAN

Projection: Lambert's Equivalent Azimuthal

MADAGASCAR
on same scale

National Parks

Nature Reserves and
Game Reserves

∴ UNESCO World Heritage Sites

East from Greenwich

COPYRIGHT PHILIP'S

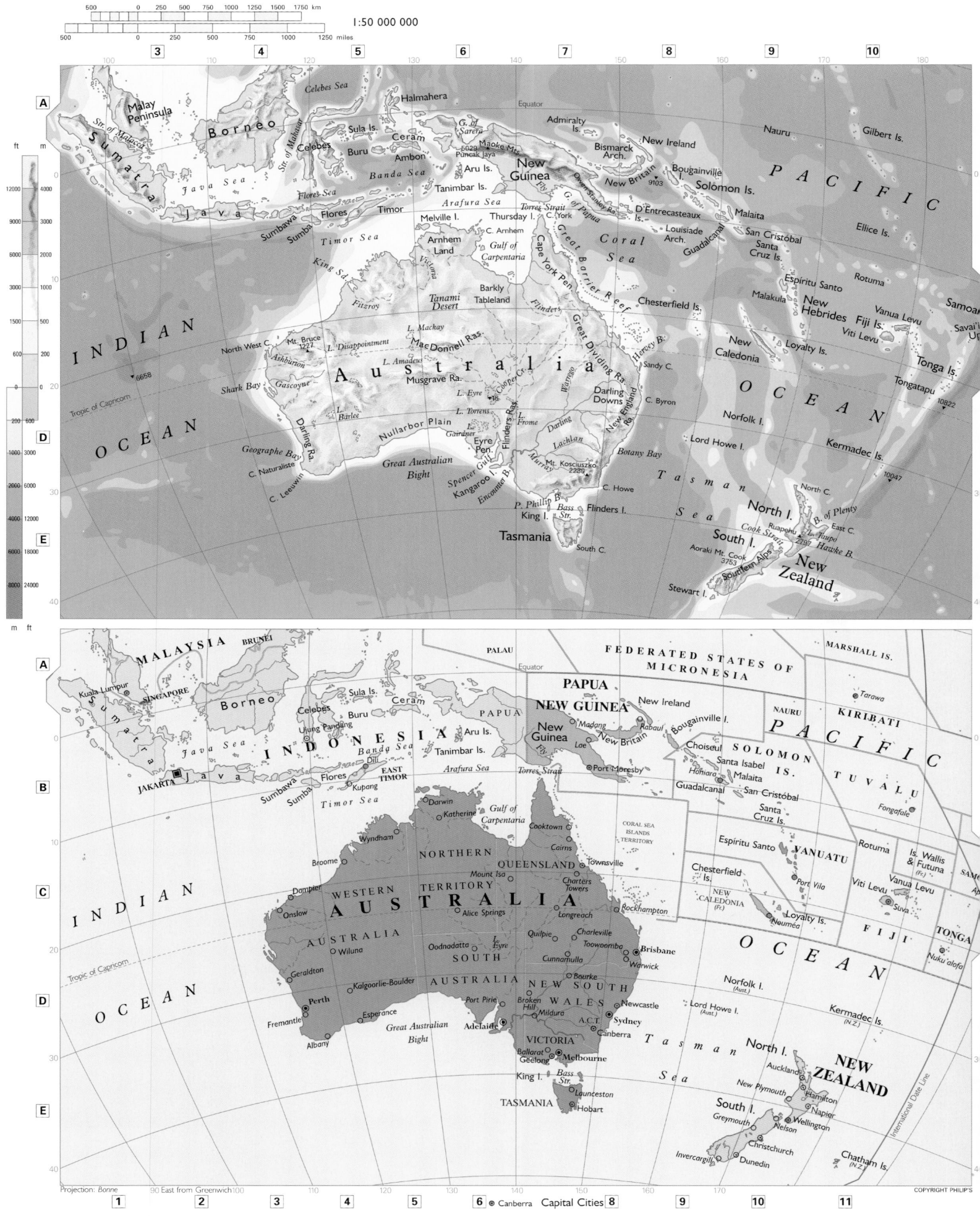

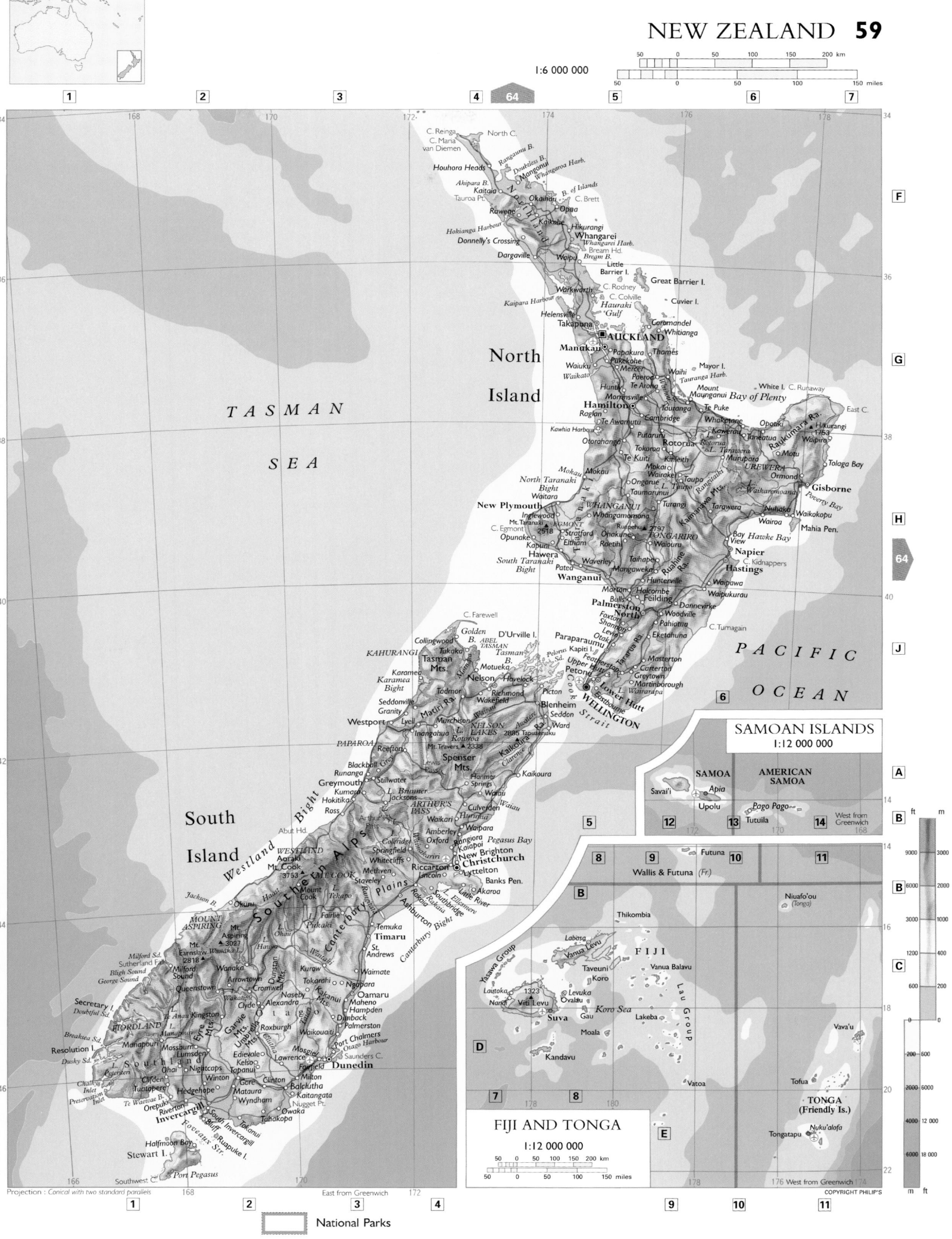

1:6 000 000

50   0   50   100   150   200 km
50   0   50   100   150 miles

F

G

North

Island

TASMAN

SEA

64

H

J

C. Farewell

KAHURANGI

PAPAROA

South

Island

Westland Bight

Jackson B.

ARTHUR'S PASS

PACIFIC

OCEAN

SAMOAN ISLANDS
1:12 000 000

SAMOA   AMERICAN
                        SAMOA
Savai'i   Apia
        Upolu   Pago Pago
                              Tutuila   West from
                                         Greenwich

A

B

12   13   14

B

8   9   Futuna 10   11

Wallis & Futuna (Fr.)

B

Niuafo'ou
(Tonga)

Thikombia

Labasa   Vanua Levu
      Yasawa Group
            Taveuni
            Koro   Vanua Balavu
Lautoka 1323
  Nandi Viti Levu   Levuka   Lau
            Ovalau   Group
  Suva   Gau   Koro Sea   Lakeba
Moala

Kandavu

Vatoa

FIJI

Vava'u

Tofua

C

D

TONGA
(Friendly Is.)

Tongatapu Nuku'alofa

E

7   8

FIJI AND TONGA
1:12 000 000

50   0   50   100   150   200 km
50   0   50   100   150 miles

9   10   11

ft   m

9000   3000

6000   2000
        1000
3000   600
1200   400
600   200
        0
200   600
2000   6000
4000   12 000
6000   18 000

m   ft

B

A

B

C

D

E

Projection : Conical with two standard parallels

East from Greenwich

National Parks

TONGA

Suva

South

Island

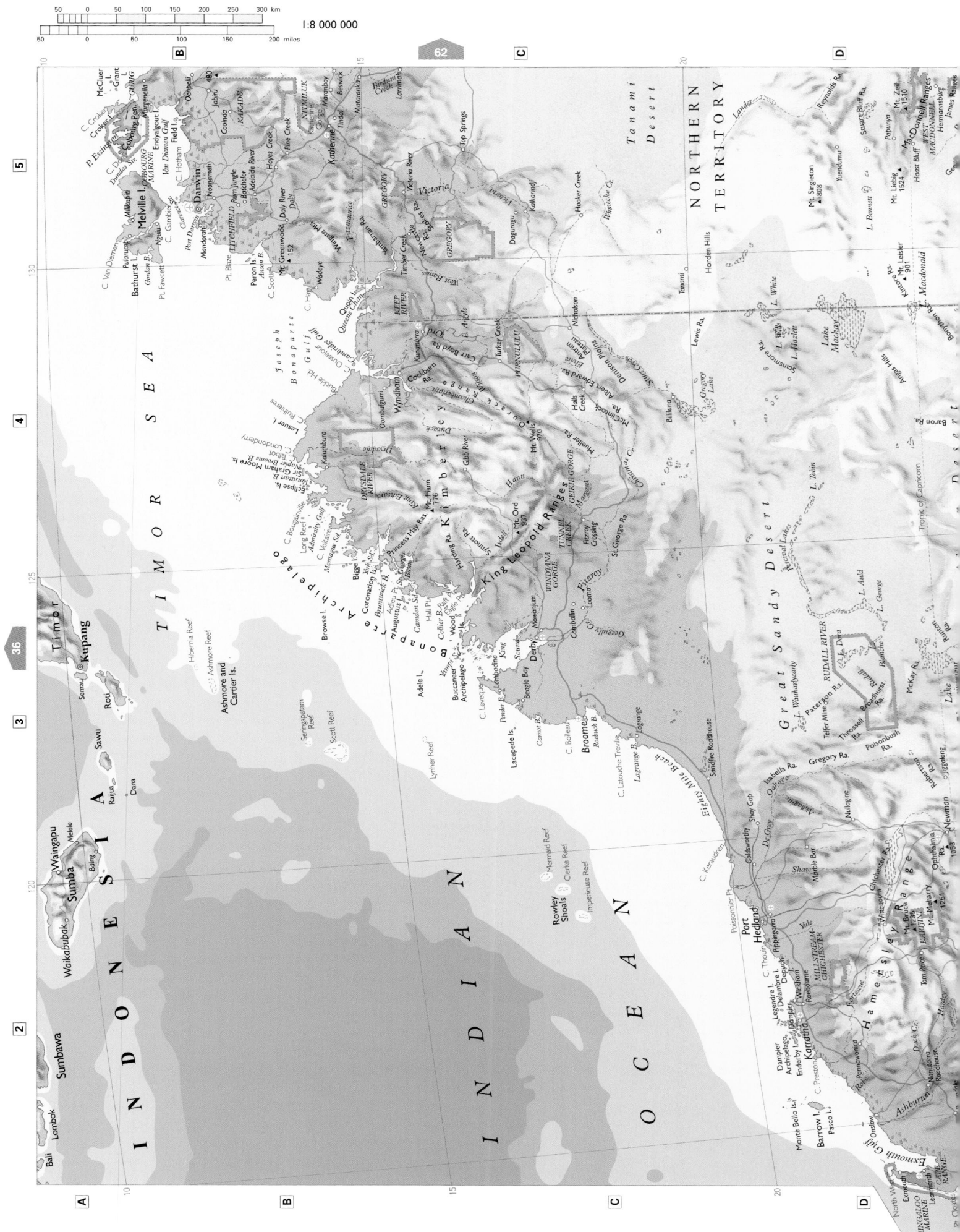

1:8 000 000

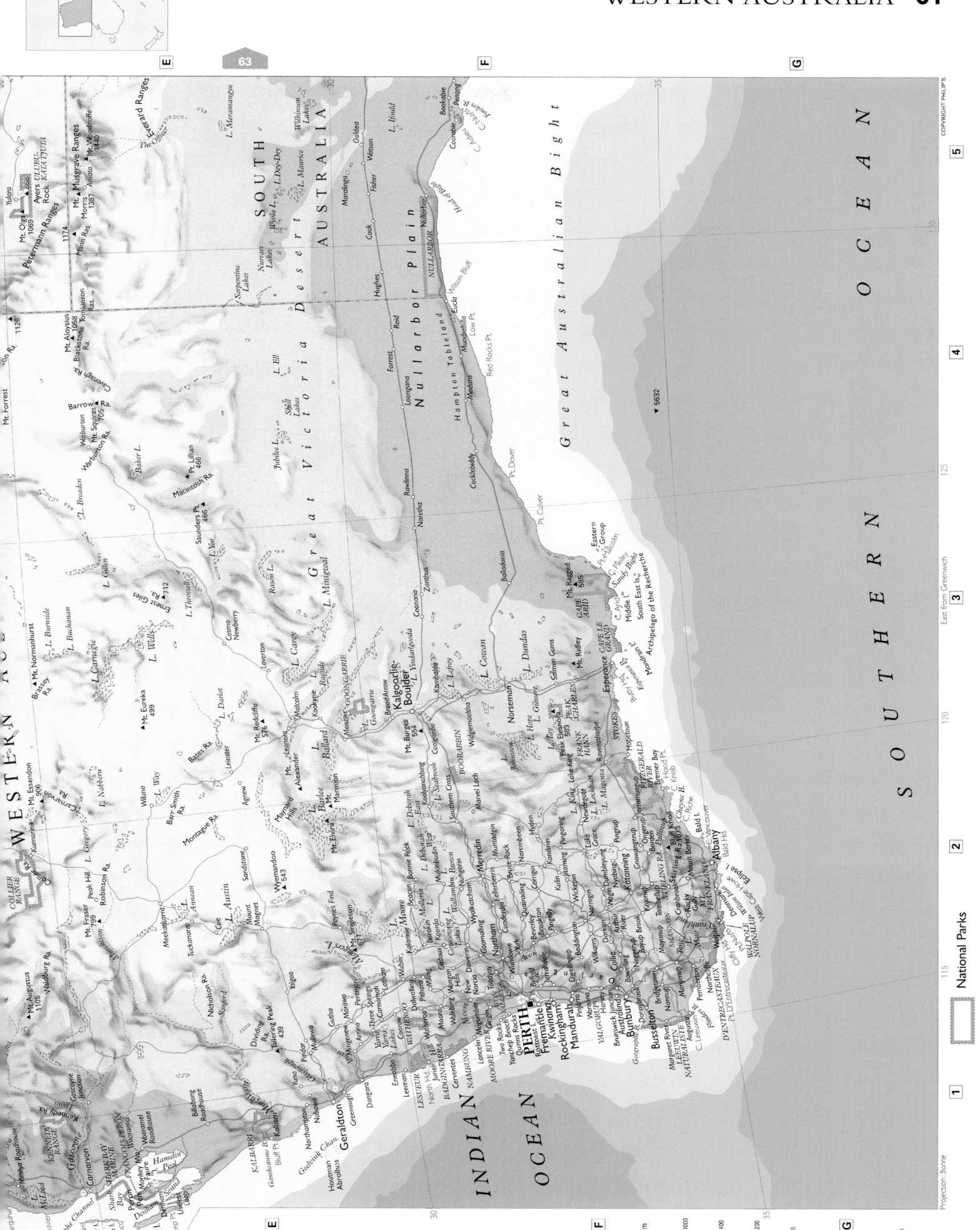

National Parks

Projection Bonne

East from Greenwich

COPYRIGHT PHILIP'S

WESTERN AUSTRALIA

SOUTH AUSTRALIA

INDIAN OCEAN

SOUTHERN OCEAN

Great Australian Bight

Nullarbor Plain

Great Victoria Desert

Hampton Tableland

PERTH
Fremantle
Kwinana
Rockingham
Mandurah
Bunbury
Busselton
Albany
Geraldton
Kalgoorlie-Boulder
Esperance
Carnarvon

Ayers Rock
ULURU-KATA TJUTA
Mt. Musgrave Ranges
Mt. Woodroffe 1440
Amata
Morris 1387
Mann Ra.
Petermann Ranges
Mt. Olga 1069

m ft
4000 12 000
2000 6000
1200 4000
600 2000
200 600
0

m
3000 1000
1200 400
600 200
0

1:8 000 000

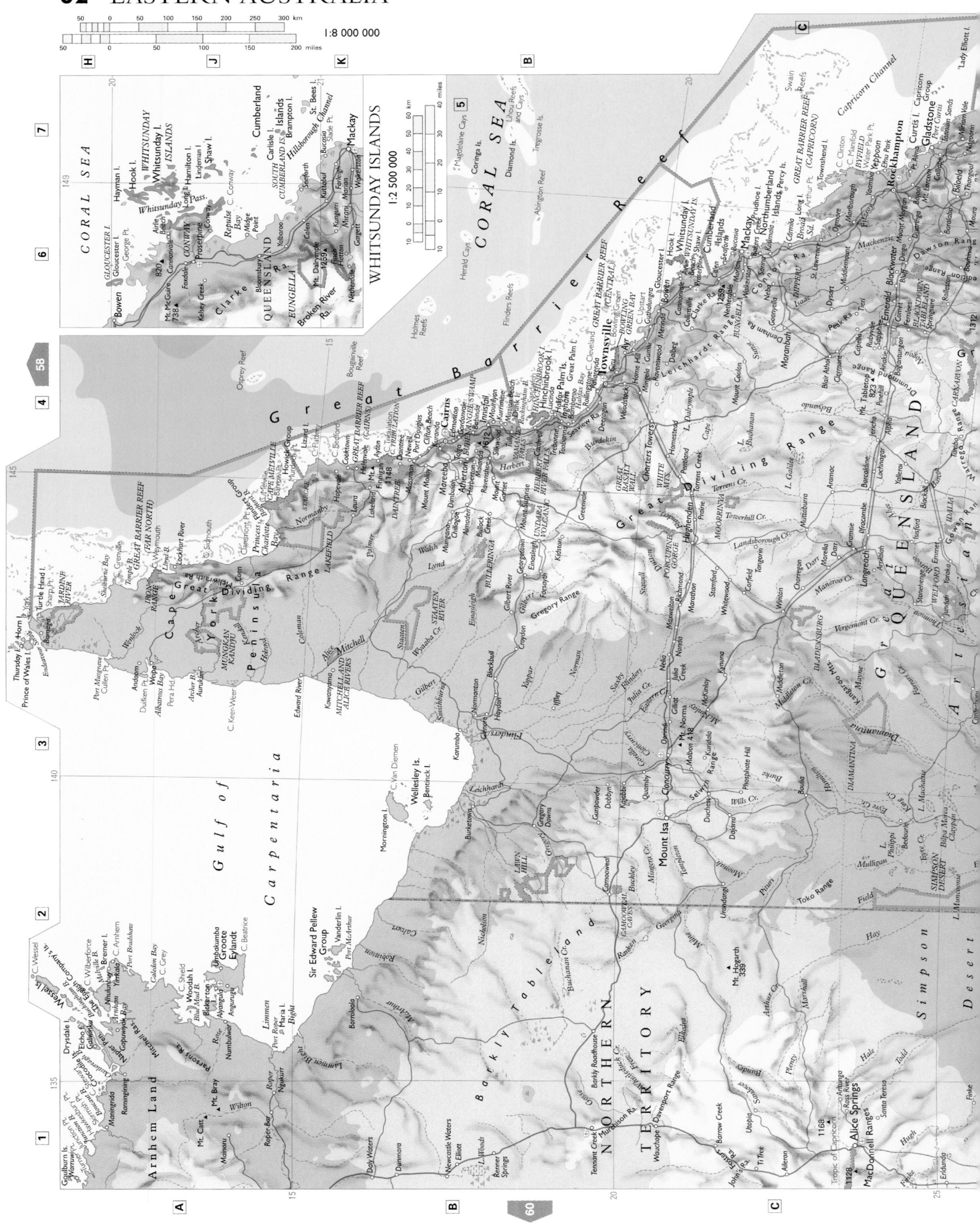

WHITSUNDAY ISLANDS
1:2 500 000

SOUTH AUSTRALIA
NEW SOUTH WALES
TASMAN SEA
Bass Strait
BRISBANE
SYDNEY
CANBERRA
MELBOURNE
ADELAIDE
TASMANIA
Hobart
Kangaroo I.
King Island
Flinders Island
Lake Eyre
Lake Torrens
Lake Gairdner
Great Dividing Range
National Parks
on same scale
East from Greenwich
Projection: Bonne
COPYRIGHT PHILIP'S
61

RUSSIA

MOSKVA
Volga
Yekaterinburg
Tomsk
Novosibirsk
Astana (Aqmola)
Semey
Irkutsk
Chita
Oz. Baykal
Ulaanbaatar
Okhotsk
Sea of Okhotsk
Komandorskiye Ostrova (Russia)
Near Is. (U.S.)
Poluostrov Kamchatka
Petropavlovsk-Kamchatskiy
Aleutian Trench

KAZAKHSTAN
Aral Sea
Balqash Köl
Altai
MONGOLIA
Blagoveshchensk
Khabarovsk
Sakhalin
Kurilskiye Ostrova
Kuril Trench
10,542
Emperor Seamount Chain

Almaty
Ürümqi
Changchun
Harbin
La Pérouse Str.
Sapporo
Vladivostok
Hakodate
Sea of Japan

Toshkent
KYRGYZSTAN
SHENYANG
NORTH KOREA
TAJIKISTAN
BEIJING
TIANJIN
Taiyuan
Dalian
SOUTH KOREA
SOUL
Nagoya
Fuji-San 3776
TOKYO
Sendai

AFGHANISTAN
Kabul
Srinagar
CHINA
Lanzhou
Xi'an
Nanjing
Wuhan
Qingdao
Yellow Sea
Kyoto
Osaka
Shikoku
Kitakyushu
Kyushu
JAPAN
Yokohama
Japan Trench 10,554

PAKISTAN
Lahore
DELHI
Kunlun Shan
XIZANG
Lhasa
Chengdu
CHONGQING
Changsha
HANGZHOU
SHANGHAI
East China Sea
South Honshu Ridge
Ogasawara Gunto (Japan)
Midway Is. (U.S.A.)

Kanpur
Himalaya
Mt. Everest 8848
Brahmaputra
Kunming
Fuzhou
Taipei
Ryukyu-retto (Japan)
Minami-Tori-Shima (Japan)
Lisianski I. (U.S.A.)

Ganga
Kathmandu
BANGLADESH
KOLKATA (Calcutta)
DHAKA
Mandalay
GUANGZHOU
HONG KONG
Macau
TAIWAN
Kazan-Retto (Japan)
Marcus Ridge
Wake I. (U.S.A.)
Necker Ridge

INDIA
Hyderabad
Bay of Bengal
Rangoon
BURMA
LAOS
Hanoi
Hainan
C. Engano
Luzon
Paracel Is.
MANILA
NORTHERN MARIANAS (U.S.A.)
Saipan
MARSHALL IS.
P

CHENNAI (Madras)
Andaman Is. (India)
THAILAND
BANGKOK
CAMBODIA
VIETNAM
Mindoro
PHILIPPINES
Samar
GUAM (U.S.A.) 11,022
Mariana Trench
Micronesia
Enewetak Atoll
Bikini Atoll

Phnom Penh
G. of Thailand
Thanh Pho Ho Chi Minh
South China Sea
Palawan
Mindoro 10,497
Yap
Caroline Is.
Truk
Pohnpei
Palikir
Jaluit
Dalap-Uliga-Darrit

SRI LANKA
Nicobar Is. (India)
MALAYSIA
PEN. MALAYSIA
Sulu Sea
Mindanao
Mindanao Trench
Koror
PALAU
FEDERATED STATES OF MICRONESIA
Butaritari

Colombo
Kuala Lumpur
SINGAPORE
Borneo
BRUNEI
SABAH
SARAWAK
Celebes Sea
Halmahera
4101
Tarawa
Gilbert Is.
Howland
Baker

INDIAN
Sumatera
INDONESIA
Palembang
Ujung Pandang
Sulawesi
Buru
Seram
Maluku
Melanesia
PAPUA NEW GUINEA
Admiralty Is.
New Ireland
Bismarck Arch.
NAURU
Banaba
Phoenix Is.
Abariringa
Enderbury

OCEAN
Selat Sunda
JAKARTA
Jawa
Surabaya
Bali
Java Sea
Flores Sea
Banda Sea
Flores
Puncak Jaya 5029
PAPUA
New Guinea
Lae
New Britain
Rabaul
Bougainville
SOLOMON IS.
TUVALU
Fongafale

Christmas I. (Austral.)
Cocos Is. (Austral.)
Sunda Islands
Sumbawa
Sumba
Timor
EAST TIMOR
7440
Arafura Sea
Torres Strait
C. York
Port Moresby
Honiara
Guadalcanal
Santa Cruz Is. 9165
Rotuma
Is. Wallis & Futuna (Fr.)
SAMOA

C. Arnhem
Gulf of Carpentaria
Darwin
Louisiade Arch.
Coral Sea
Espiritu Santo
Port Vila
VANUATU
Vanua Levu
Viti Levu
Suva
FIJI
Nuku'alofa
TONGA

Broome
North West C.
Cairns
Townsville
Is. Chesterfield
NEW CALEDONIA (Fr.)
Nouméa
Is. Loyauté
7570
10,822

Mount Isa
AUSTRALIA
Alice Springs
Great Barrier Reef
Rockhampton
Great Dividing Ra.
Brisbane
Norfolk I. (Austral.)
Kermadec Trench 10,047

Geraldton
L. Eyre
Darling
Lord Howe I. (Austral.)
Lord Howe Rise

Perth
Great Australian Bight
Adelaide
Murray
Sydney
Canberra
Mt. Kosciuszko 2237
Tasman Sea
NEW ZEALAND
Auckland

Albany
Melbourne
Bass Str.
Tasmania
Hobart
Wellington
Cook Strait
Christchurch

Nouvelle Amsterdam (Fr.)
I. St. Paul (Fr.)
Mid-Indian Ridge
Aoraki Mt. Cook 3753
Dunedin
Invercargill
Bounty Is. (N.Z.)

Is. Crozet (Fr.)
Kerguelen (Fr.)
Auckland Is. (N.Z.)
Antipodes Is. (N.Z.)
Campbell I. (N.Z.)
Macquarie I. (Austral.)

Heard I. (Austral.)

ft | m
12 000 | 4000
9000 | 3000
6000 | 2000
3000 | 1000
1500 | 500
600 | 200
0 | 0
600 | 200
3000 | 1000
6000 | 2000
12 000 | 4000
18 000 | 6000
24 000 | 8000
m | ft

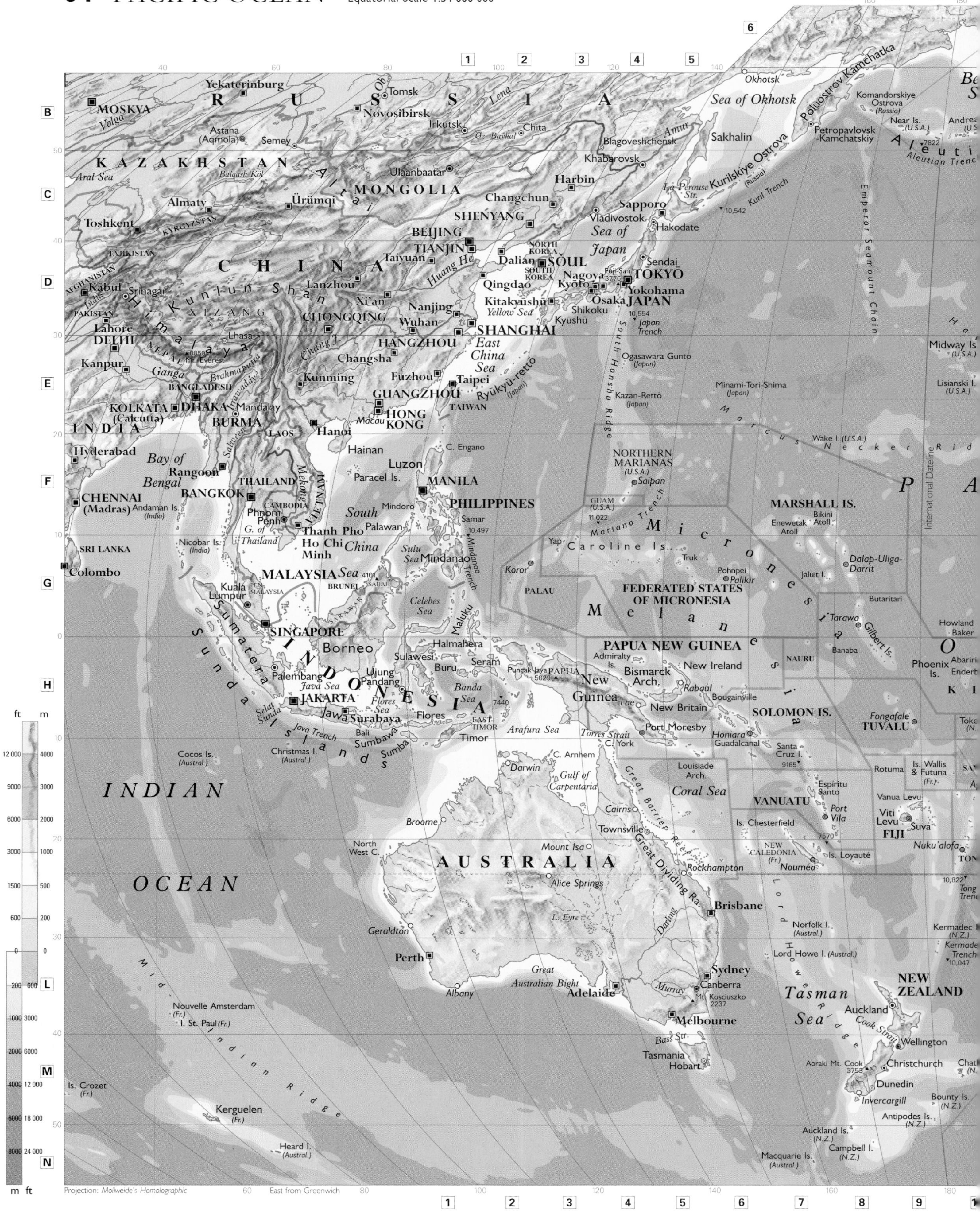

Projection: Mollweide's Homolographic   East from Greenwich

Arctic Circle

ALASKA
(U.S.A.)
Anchorage
5959
Juneau
Gulf of Alaska
Bristol Bay

Prince of Wales I.
(U.S.A.) Prince Rupert
Queen Charlotte Is.
(Canada)

CANADA

Edmonton
Calgary
Regina
Winnipeg
L. Winnipeg

Newfoundland

NORTH

St. Lawrence
Québec
Montréal
Ottawa
St. John's

Vancouver
Vancouver I.
Victoria
Seattle
Portland
Boise
Snake

Minneapolis
Toronto
Detroit
Buffalo
Boston

L. Superior
L. Michigan
L. Huron
L. Ontario
L. Erie

ATLANTIC

C. Mendocino
Sacramento
6741
SAN FRANCISCO
4418

Salt Lake City
Denver
Kansas City
St. Louis
CHICAGO
Pittsburgh
Cincinnati
Washington D.C.

NEW YORK CITY
PHILADELPHIA
Baltimore

UNITED STATES

Appalachian Mts.

OCEAN

LOS ANGELES
San Diego
Guadalupe (Mex.)

Phoenix
Ciudad Juárez
Dallas
Houston
San Antonio
New Orleans

Oklahoma City
Memphis
Atlanta
C. Hatteras
Jacksonville

Bermuda (U.K.)

Tropic of Cancer

Colorado
Gulf of California
Baja California
C. San Lucas

Gulf of Mexico
Monterrey
Miami

Sargasso Sea

BAHAMAS

Honolulu
Oahu
4205
HAWAIIAN IS. (U.S.A.)
Hawaii

C. San Lucas
Is. Revilla Gigedo (Mex.)

Guadalajara
MEXICO
Puebla
Acapulco

La Habana
CUBA
Mérida
Canal de Yucatán
7680
JAMAICA
Kingston

HAITI
9200
DOMINICAN REP.
PUERTO RICO (U.S.A.)

West Indies

Leeward Is.

PACIFIC

GUATEMALA
Guatemala
San Salvador
EL SALVADOR
HONDURAS
BELIZE
NICARAGUA
Managua
San José

BARBADOS
Windward Is.

I. Clipperton (Fr.)

Barranquilla
Maracaibo
Caracas
Orinoco
VENEZUELA

COSTA RICA
PANAMA
Colón
Panamá
I. del Coco (Costa Rica)
I. de Malpelo (Colombia)

Medellín
Cali
Bogotá
COLOMBIA

OCEAN

Palmyra Is. (U.S.A.)
Teraina
Tabuaeran
Kiritimati

Galápagos (Ecuador)

Quito
ECUADOR
Guayaquil
C. Palinas
Iquitos

Amazonas

BRAZIL

Equator

KIRIBATI
Jarvis I. (U.S.A.)
Malden I.
Starbuck I.

Trujillo

6369
PERU
Cuzco
LIMA
L. Titicaca
Nevada Ancohuma
6550

Tongareva
Pukapuka
Manihiki
Vostok I.
Caroline I. (Millennium I.)
Flint I.
Is. Marquises

Suwarrow Is.
Is. de la Société
Papeete
Tahiti
Is. Tuamotu
Mururoa

Arequipa
6866
Peru-Chile
Arica

Cook Is. (N.Z.)
FRENCH POLYNESIA
Australs/Seamount Chain
Rarotonga
Is. Tubuai
Rapa

Iquique
Chile

La Paz
BOLIVIA

Antofagasta

PARAGUAY
Asunción

Tropic of Capricorn

Ducie I.
Pitcairn I. (U.K.)

San Félix (Chile)
San Ambrosio (Chile)
8050
Trench

San Miguel de Tucumán

Sala-y-Gómez (Chile)
I. de Pascua (Chile)

Córdoba
Aconcagua
6960
Valparaíso
Rosario
SANTIAGO
BUENOS AIRES
Concepción

Pôrto Alegre
URUGUAY
Montevideo
Río de la Plata

Arch. de Juan Fernández (Chile)

ARGENTINA

SOUTH

East Pacific Ridge

Chile Rise

ATLANTIC

Pacific-Antarctic Ridge

6212
OCEAN

Punta Arenas
Est. de Magallanes
Tierra del Fuego
C. de Hornos

Falkland Is. (U.K.)

South Georgia (U.K.)

West from Greenwich

COPYRIGHT PHILIP'S

1:35 000 000

ARCTIC OCEAN

Greenland

Asia

Bering Sea

PACIFIC OCEAN

Alaska Range

Rocky Mountains

Great Plains

Great Basin

Western Sierra Madre

Eastern Sierra Madre

Mexican Plateau

Gulf of Mexico

NORTH ATLANTIC OCEAN

Sargasso Sea

Bahamas

Cuba

Greater Antilles

Caribbean Sea

Central America

Andes

Projection: Bonne

West from Greenwich

COPYRIGHT PHILIP'S

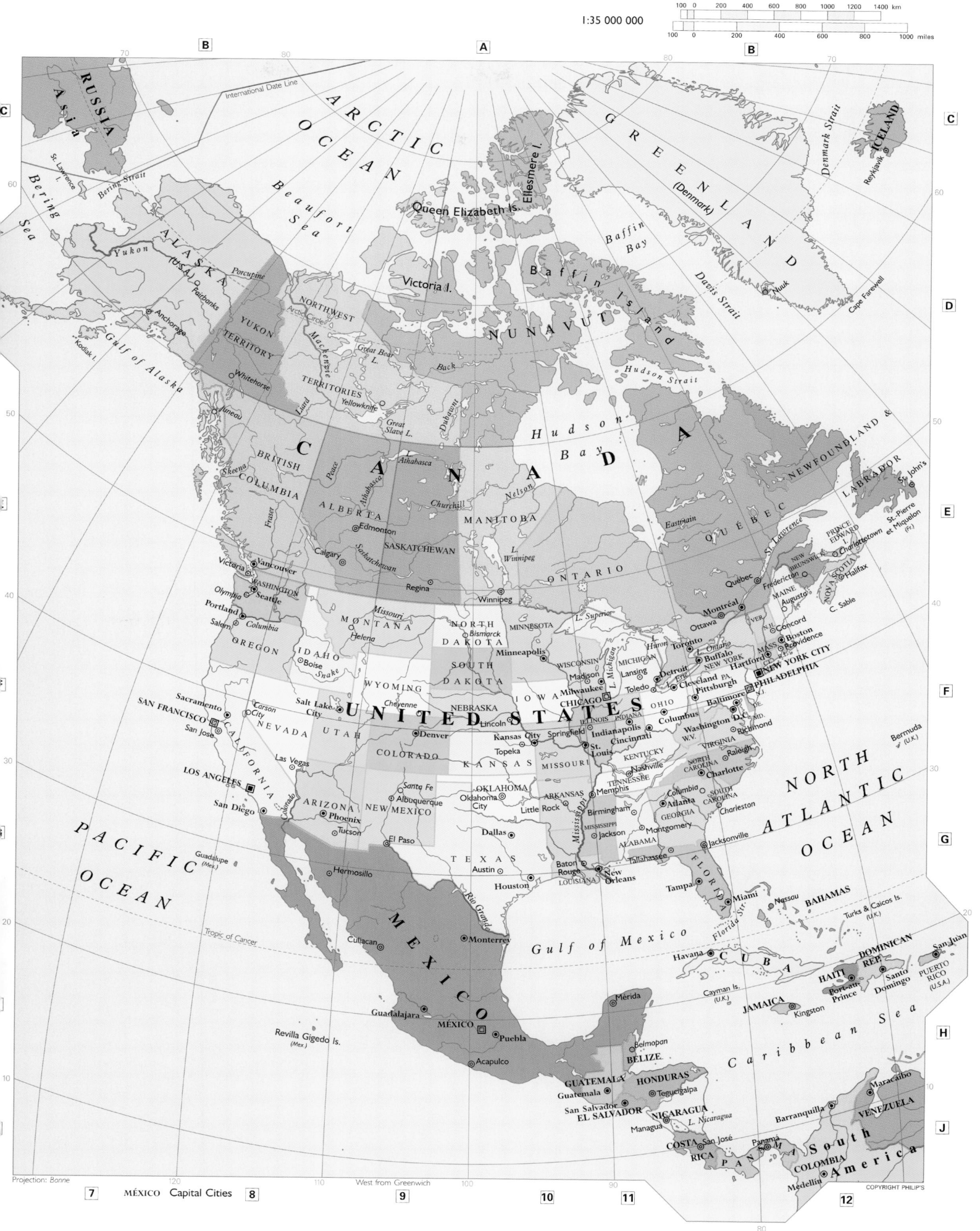

1:35 000 000

100 0 200 400 600 800 1000 1200 1400 km
100 0 200 400 600 800 1000 miles

B   A   B

RUSSIA
Asia

ARCTIC OCEAN

GREENLAND
(Denmark)

ICELAND
Reykjavík

Bering Sea

St. Lawrence

Bering Strait

Beaufort Sea

Queen Elizabeth Is.
Ellesmere I.

Baffin Bay

Denmark Strait

International Date Line

Yukon
ALASKA (USA)
Porcupine
Fairbanks
Anchorage
Kodiak I.
Gulf of Alaska
Juneau

NORTHWEST
Arctic Circle
YUKON TERRITORY
Whitehorse
Liard
Mackenzie
TERRITORIES
Yellowknife
Great Bear L.
Great Slave L.
Back
Dubawnt

Victoria I.

NUNAVUT

Baffin Island

Hudson Strait

Davis Strait

Nuuk

Cape Farewell

BRITISH COLUMBIA
Skeena
Fraser
Peace
Athabasca
ALBERTA
Edmonton
Calgary
Athabasca
Saskatchewan
SASKATCHEWAN
Regina

CANADA

Nelson
Churchill
MANITOBA
L. Winnipeg

Hudson Bay

Eastmain

QUÉBEC

ONTARIO

St. Lawrence
Québec
Montréal
Ottawa

NEWFOUNDLAND & LABRADOR

St. John's

PRINCE EDWARD I.
St. Pierre et Miquelon (Fr)
Charlottetown
NEW BRUNSWICK
Fredericton
NOVA SCOTIA
Halifax
MAINE
Augusta
C. Sable

Victoria
Vancouver
Olympia
WASHINGTON
Seattle
Portland
OREGON
Salem
Columbia

MONTANA
Helena
IDAHO
Boise
Snake

Missouri

NORTH DAKOTA
Bismarck
SOUTH DAKOTA
Minneapolis

MINNESOTA
L. Superior

WISCONSIN
Madison
Milwaukee
MICHIGAN
Lansing

L. Michigan
L. Huron
Toronto
L. Ontario
Detroit
Cleveland
Buffalo
NEW YORK

VER.
N.H.
Concord
MASS. Boston
R.I. Providence
Hartford
CONN.
NEW YORK CITY
PHILADELPHIA

Sacramento
SAN FRANCISCO
Carson City
San Jose
CALIFORNIA
NEVADA
Las Vegas
Salt Lake City
UTAH
WYOMING
Cheyenne

UNITED STATES

NEBRASKA
Lincoln
Denver
COLORADO

IOWA
CHICAGO
ILLINOIS
INDIANA
Springfield
Indianapolis

Toledo
OHIO
Columbus
Cincinnati
PITTSBURGH
PA.
N.J.
Baltimore
Washington D.C.
MD.
Richmond
VIRGINIA
W.V.

LOS ANGELES
San Diego
Colorado

ARIZONA
Phoenix
Tucson

Santa Fe
NEW MEXICO
Albuquerque

Kansas City
Topeka
St. Louis
KANSAS

MISSOURI
KENTUCKY
Nashville
TENNESSEE
Memphis

NORTH CAROLINA
Raleigh
Charlotte
Columbia
SOUTH CAROLINA
Charleston

Bermuda (U.K.)

NORTH ATLANTIC OCEAN

El Paso
OKLAHOMA
Oklahoma City
ARKANSAS
Little Rock
MISSISSIPPI
Jackson
ALABAMA
Birmingham
Montgomery
GEORGIA
Atlanta

Jacksonville
FLORIDA

PACIFIC OCEAN

Guadalupe (Mex.)

Hermosillo

TEXAS
Dallas
Austin
Houston

LOUISIANA
Baton Rouge
New Orleans

Tallahassee

Tampa
Miami
Nassau
BAHAMAS
Turks & Caicos Is. (U.K.)

Tropic of Cancer

MEXICO

Culiacán
Monterrey

Rio Grande

Gulf of Mexico

Havana
CUBA
Florida Str.

Cayman Is. (U.K.)
JAMAICA
Kingston

HAITI
Port-au-Prince
DOMINICAN REP.
Santo Domingo
PUERTO RICO (U.S.A.)
San Juan

Caribbean Sea

Revilla Gigedo Is. (Mex)

Guadalajara
MÉXICO
Puebla
Acapulco
Mérida

BELIZE
Belmopan
GUATEMALA
Guatemala
HONDURAS
Tegucigalpa
San Salvador
EL SALVADOR
NICARAGUA
Managua
L. Nicaragua
COSTA RICA
San José
PANAMA
Panamá

Maracaibo
Barranquilla
VENEZUELA
Medellín
COLOMBIA
SOUTH America

Projection: Bonne

7   MÉXICO Capital Cities   8   9   10   11   12

West from Greenwich

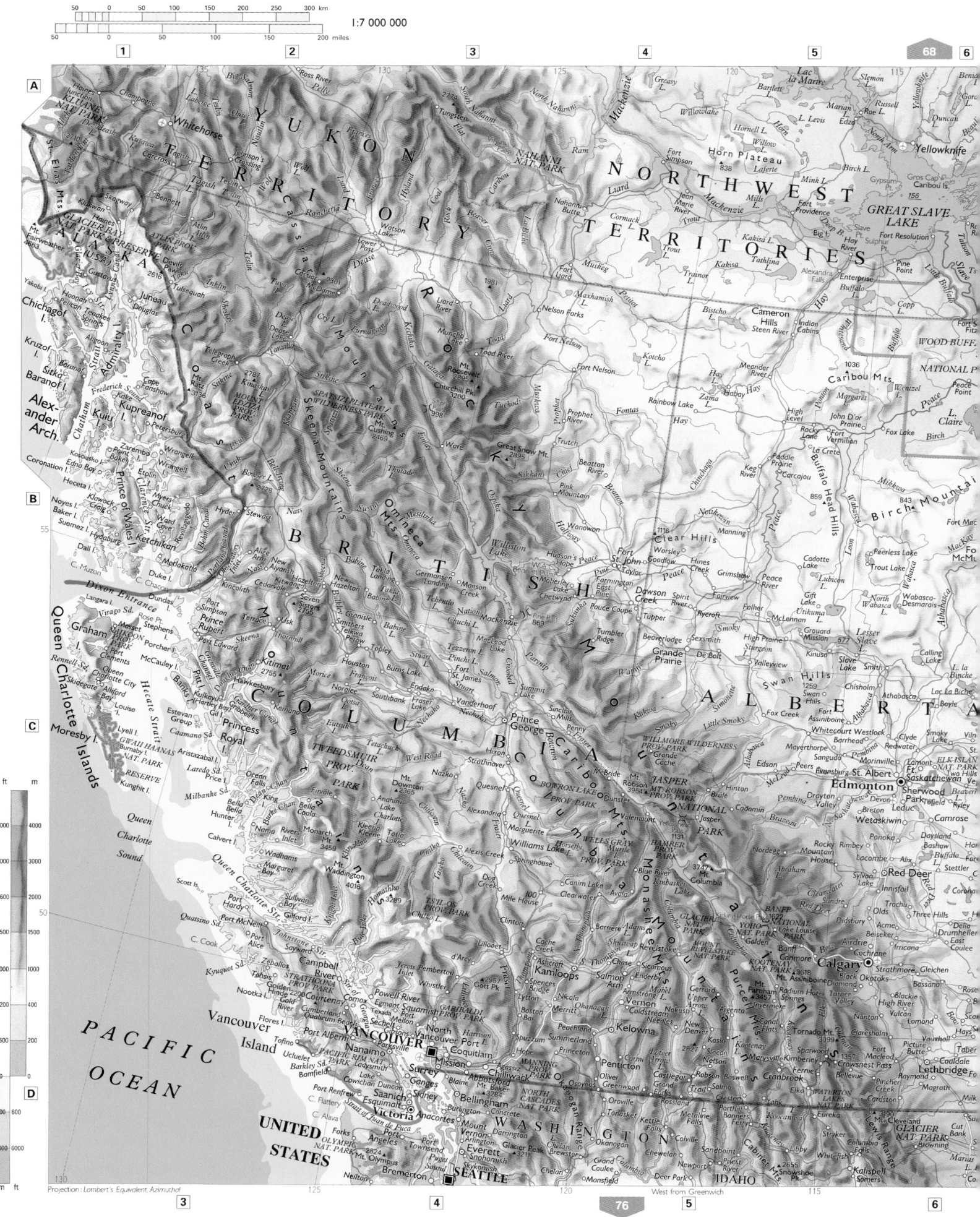

National Parks

1:7 000 000

National Parks

Projection: Lambert's Equivalent Azimuthal

1:12 00 000

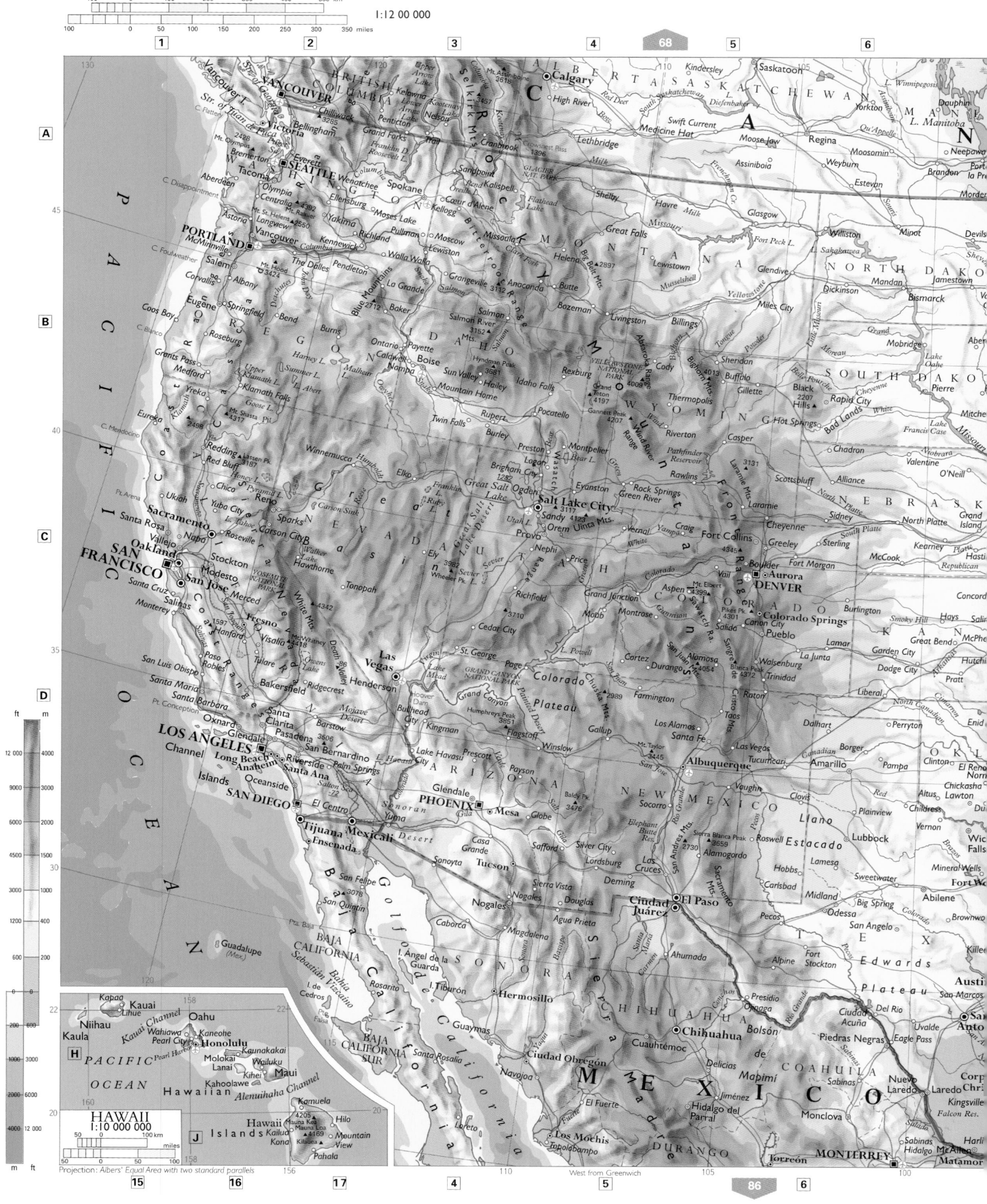

Projection: Albers' Equal Area with two standard parallels

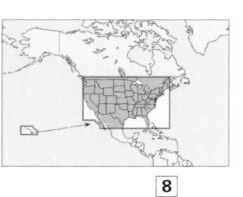

50 0 50 100 150 200 km

50 0 50 100 150 miles

1:6 000 000

80

70

SASKATCHEWAN

ALBERTA

BRITISH COLUMBIA

MONTANA

WYOMING

IDAHO

WASHINGTON

OREGON

NEVADA

UTAH

CALIFORNIA

Vancouver

Seattle

Portland

Salt Lake City

Sacramento

Spokane

Helena

Billings

Bighorn Mountains

Absaroka Range

Wind River Range

Medicine Bow Mts

Bitterroot Mountains

Salmon River Mountains

Sawtooth Range

Columbia Plateau

Blue Mountains

Wallowa Mts

Great Salt Lake

Uinta Mountains

Snake River

Columbia River

Cascade Range

Coast Range

Olympic Mts

Puget Sound

Strait of Juan de Fuca

Reno

Pacific Rim Nat. Park

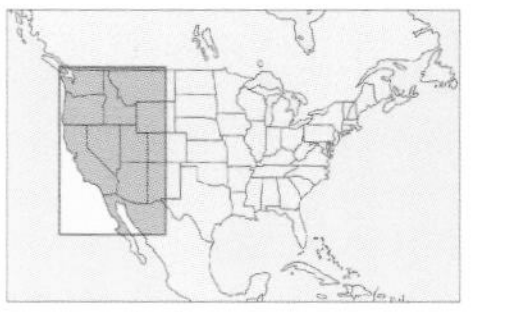

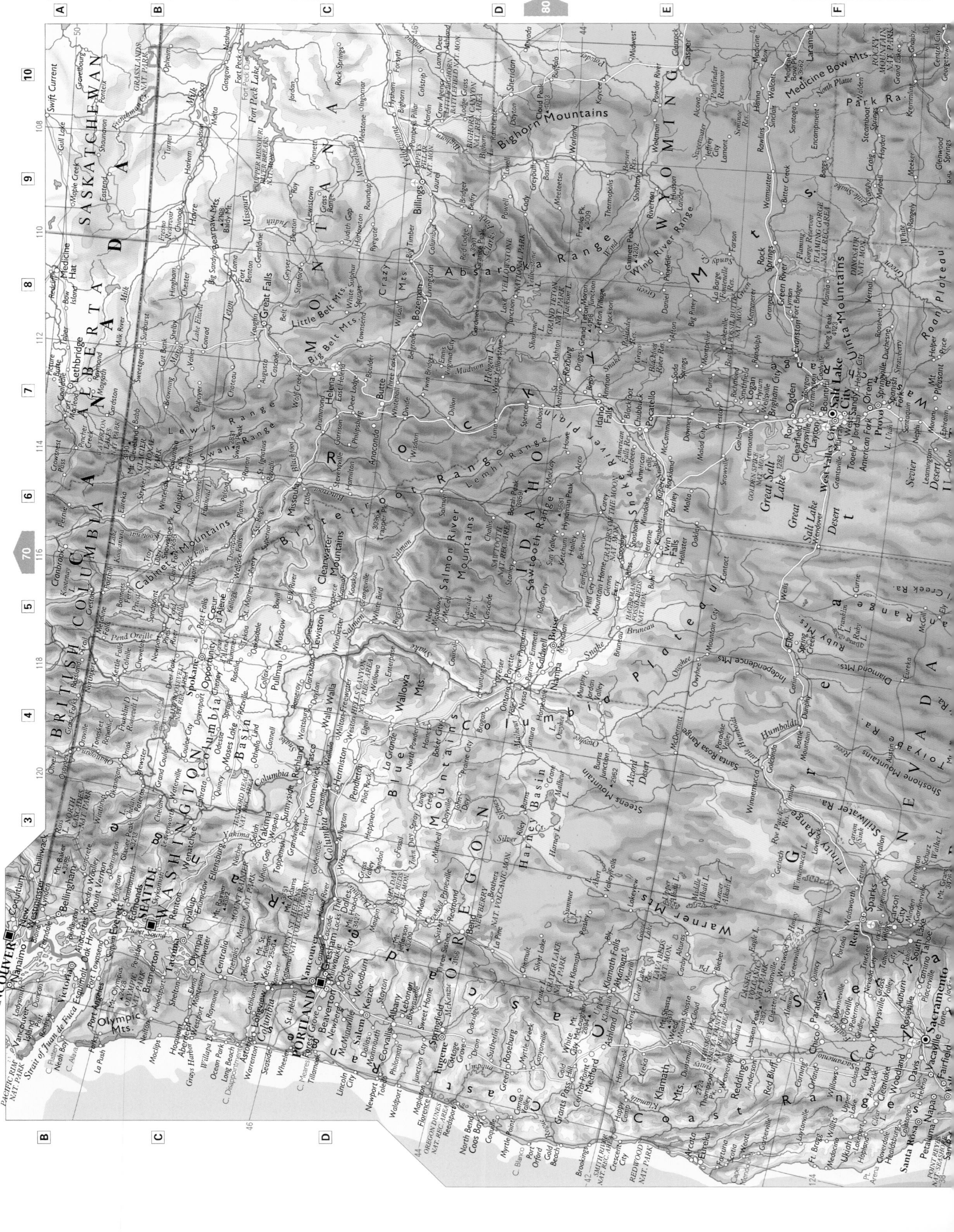

National Parks

Projection: Albers' Equal Area with two standard parallels

10 0 10 20 30 40 50 60 70 80 90 km

10   0   10   20   30   40   50   60 miles

1:2 500 000

WESTERN WASHINGTON
REGION
on same scale

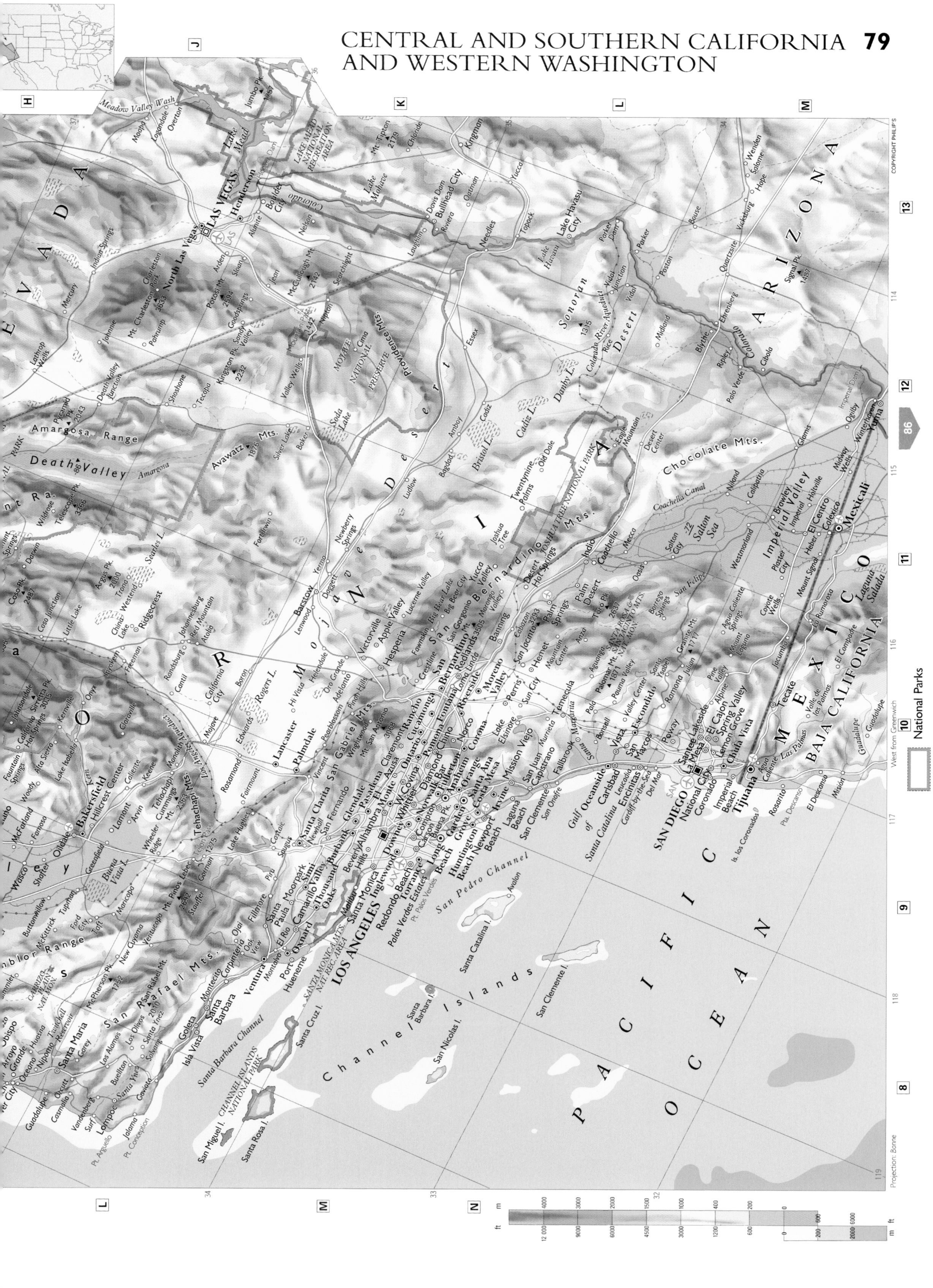

COPYRIGHT PHILIP'S

National Parks

West from Greenwich

Projection: Bonne

PACIFIC OCEAN

NEVADA

ARIZONA

MEXICO

BAJA CALIFORNIA

CALIFORNIA

MOJAVE

Sonoran Desert

Death Valley

Amargosa Range

LOS ANGELES AREA

SAN DIEGO

Las Vegas
North Las Vegas
Henderson
Boulder City
Bakersfield
Lancaster
Palmdale
Barstow
Victorville
Hesperia
San Bernardino
Riverside
Redlands
Ontario
Pomona
Pasadena
Glendale
Burbank
Santa Monica
Long Beach
Anaheim
Santa Ana
Irvine
Oceanside
Carlsbad
Escondido
Chula Vista
Tijuana
Mexicali
Calexico
El Centro
Brawley
Santa Barbara
Ventura
Oxnard
Thousand Oaks
Simi Valley
Palm Springs
Palm Desert
Indio
Coachella
Needles
Bullhead City
Lake Havasu City
Kingman
Parker
Blythe
Yuma

Channel Islands
San Miguel I.
Santa Rosa I.
Santa Cruz I.
Santa Catalina I.
San Clemente I.
San Nicolas I.
San Pedro Channel
Santa Barbara Channel
Santa Monica Bay

CHANNEL ISLANDS NATIONAL PARK
JOSHUA TREE NATIONAL PARK
MOJAVE NATIONAL PRESERVE
LAKE MEAD NATIONAL RECREATION AREA
SANTA MONICA MTS. NAT. REC. AREA

Salton Sea
Imperial Valley
Colorado River Aqueduct
Coachella Canal
Chocolate Mts.
San Bernardino Mts.
San Gabriel Mts.
Tehachapi Mts.
San Rafael Mts.
Argus Range
Telescope Pk.

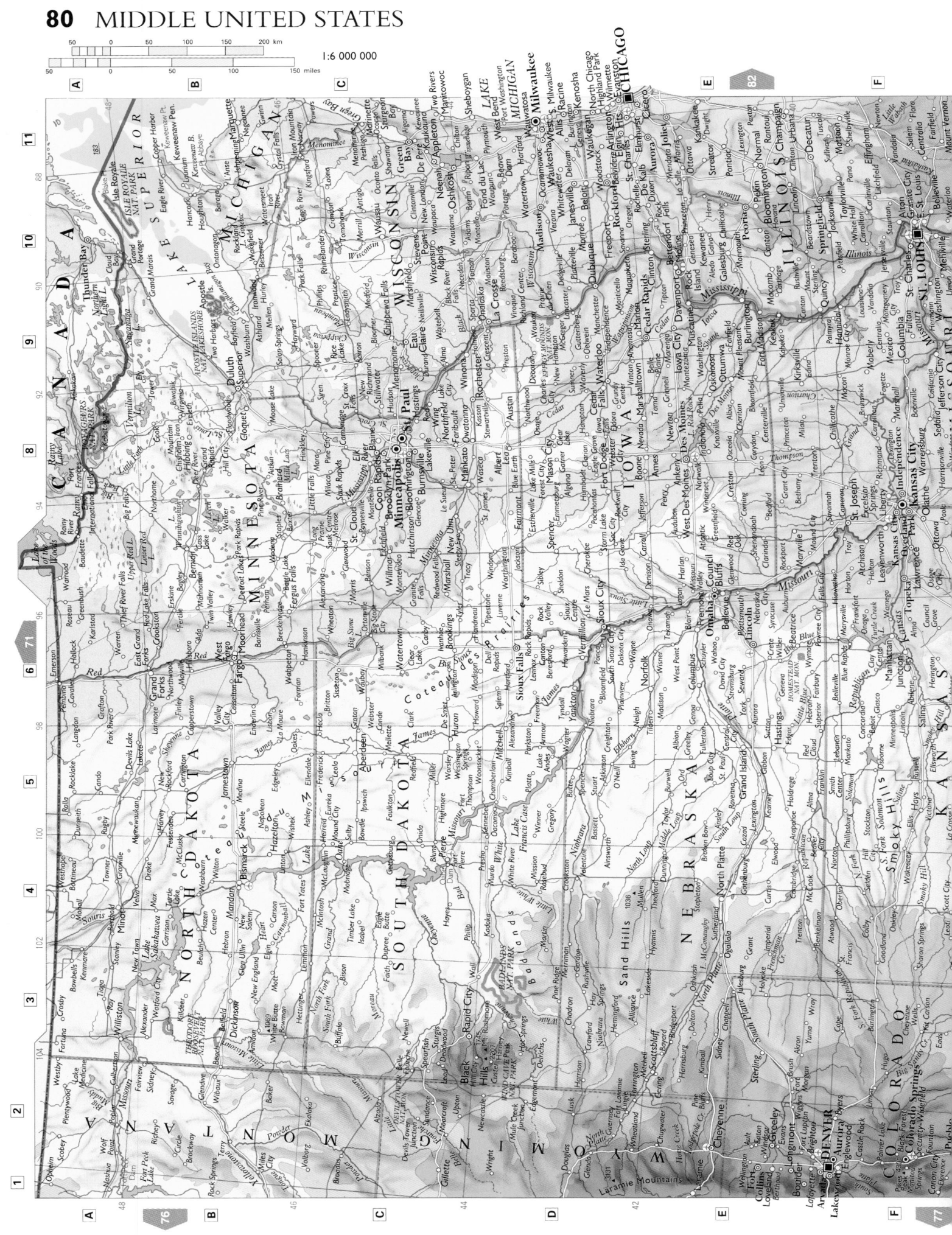

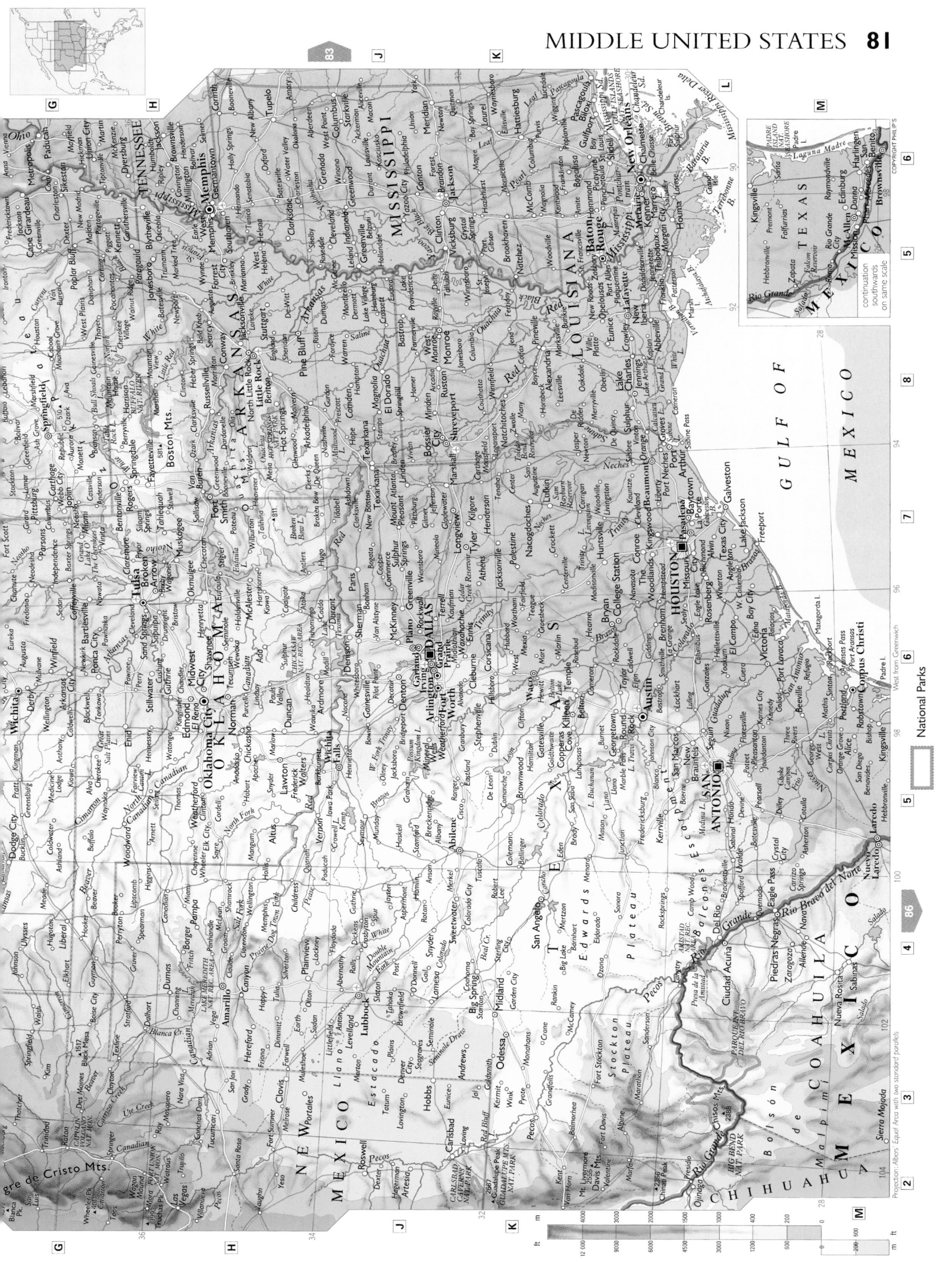

National Parks

continuation southwards on same scale

Projection: Albers Equal Area with two standard parallels

COPYRIGHT PHILIP'S

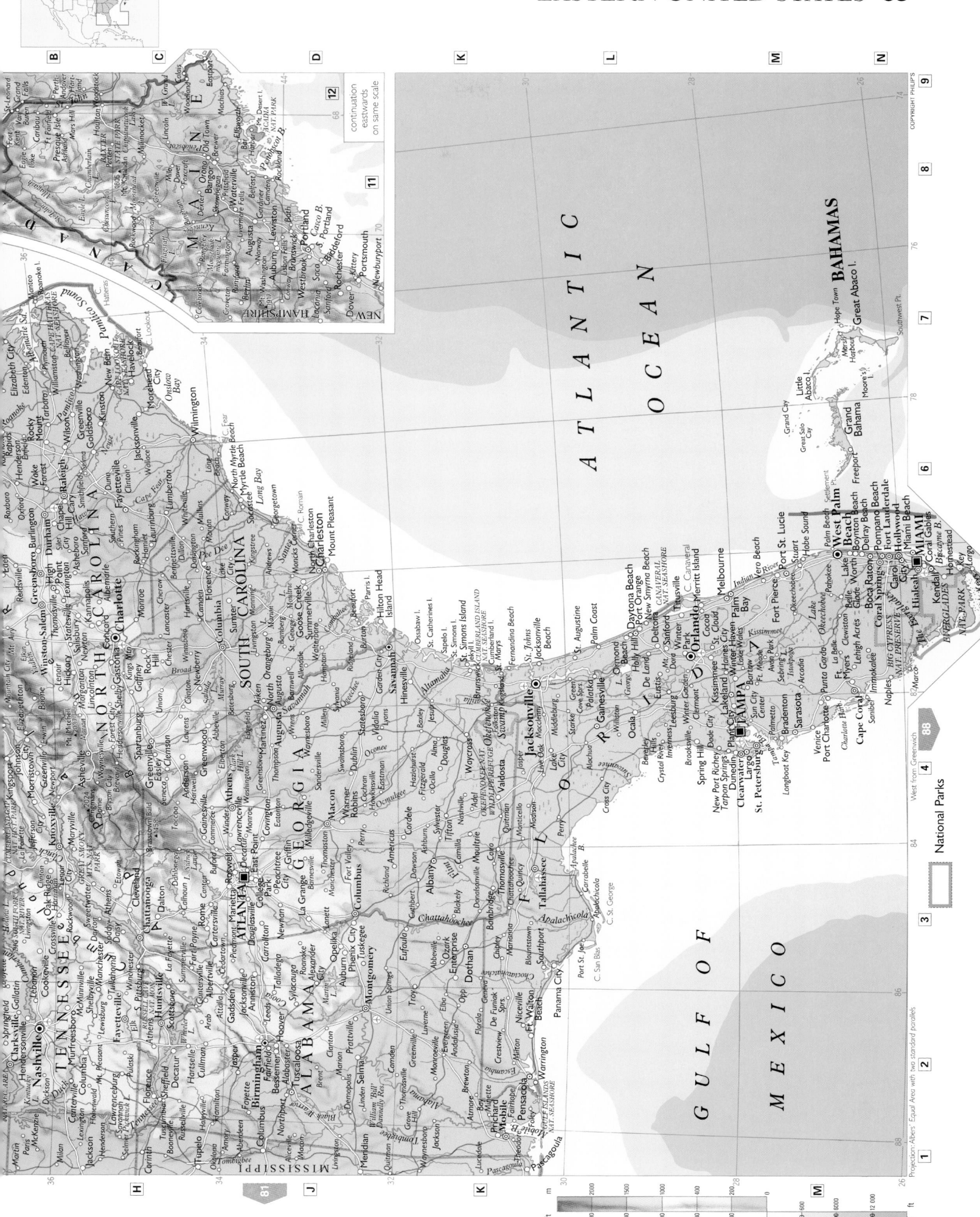

ATLANTIC OCEAN

GULF OF MEXICO

BAHAMAS

FLORIDA

GEORGIA

ALABAMA

MISSISSIPPI

TENNESSEE

NORTH CAROLINA

SOUTH CAROLINA

MAINE

NEW HAMPSHIRE

CANADA

National Parks

continuation eastwards on same scale

1:2 500 000

National Parks

Projection: Bonne

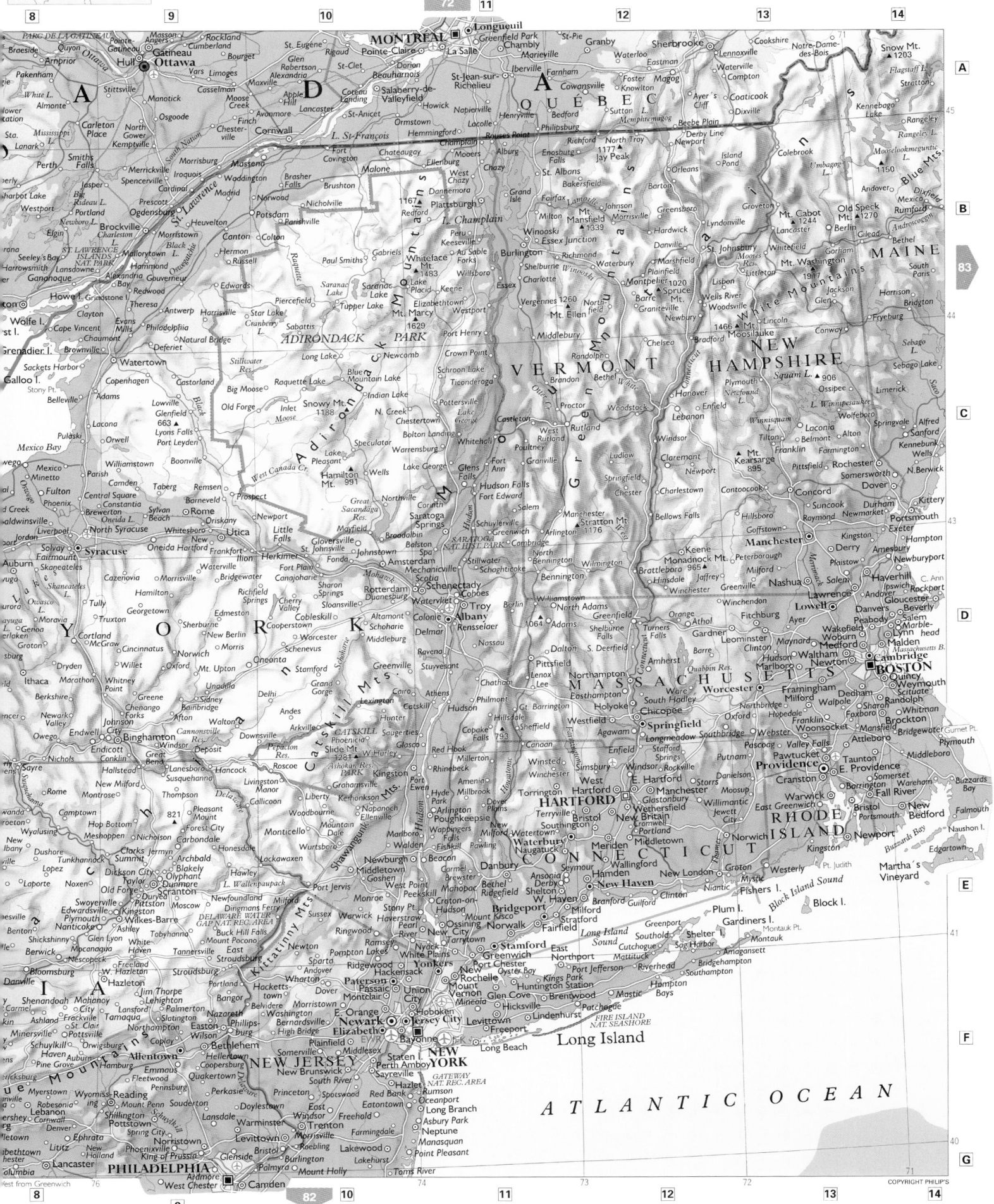

50 0   50 100 150 200 250 300 km
1:8 000 000
50 0   50 100 150 200 miles

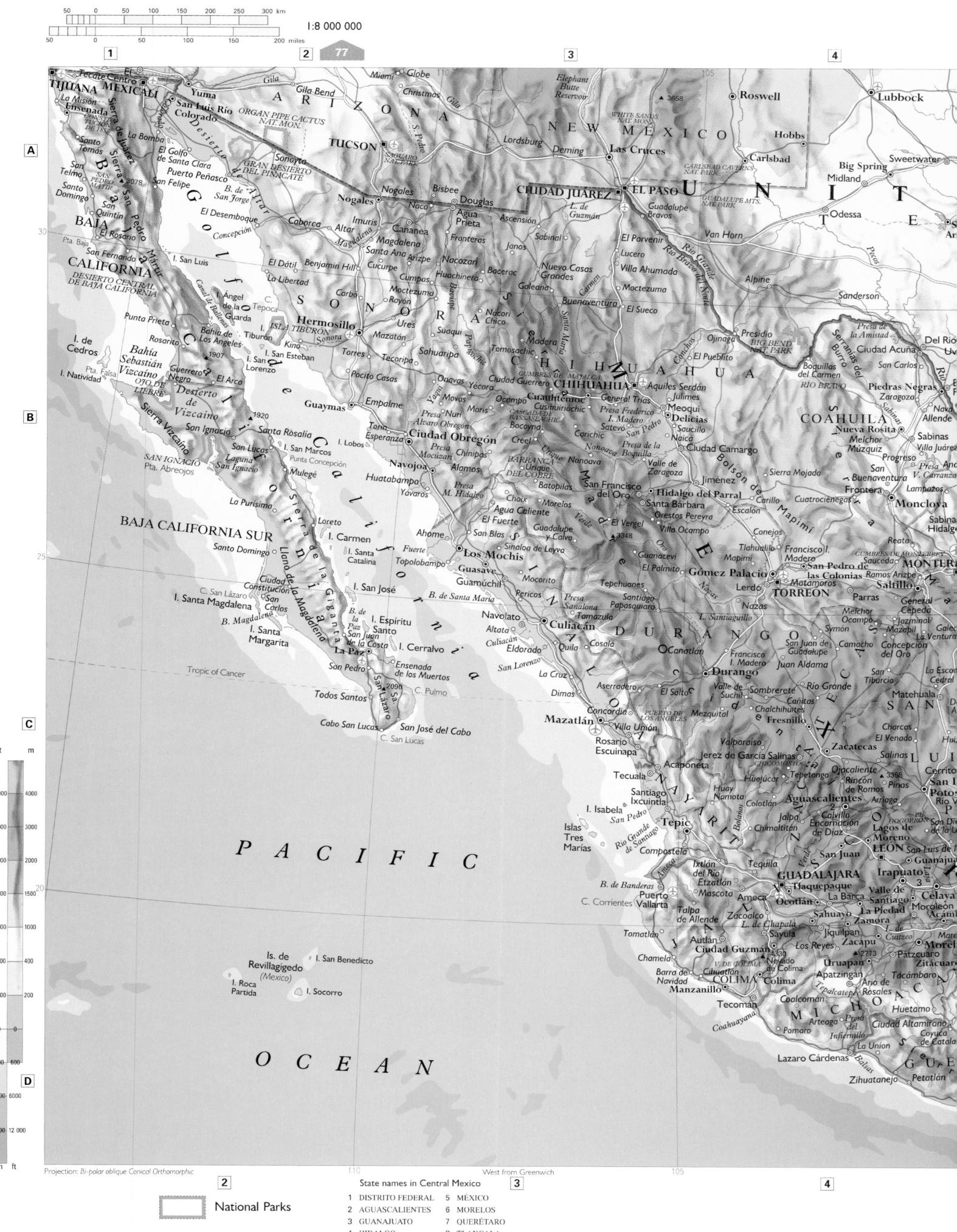

National Parks

State names in Central Mexico

1 DISTRITO FEDERAL   5 MÉXICO
2 AGUASCALIENTES   6 MORELOS
3 GUANAJUATO   7 QUERÉTARO
4 HIDALGO   8 TLAXCALA

Projection: Bi-polar oblique Conical Orthomorphic

West from Greenwich

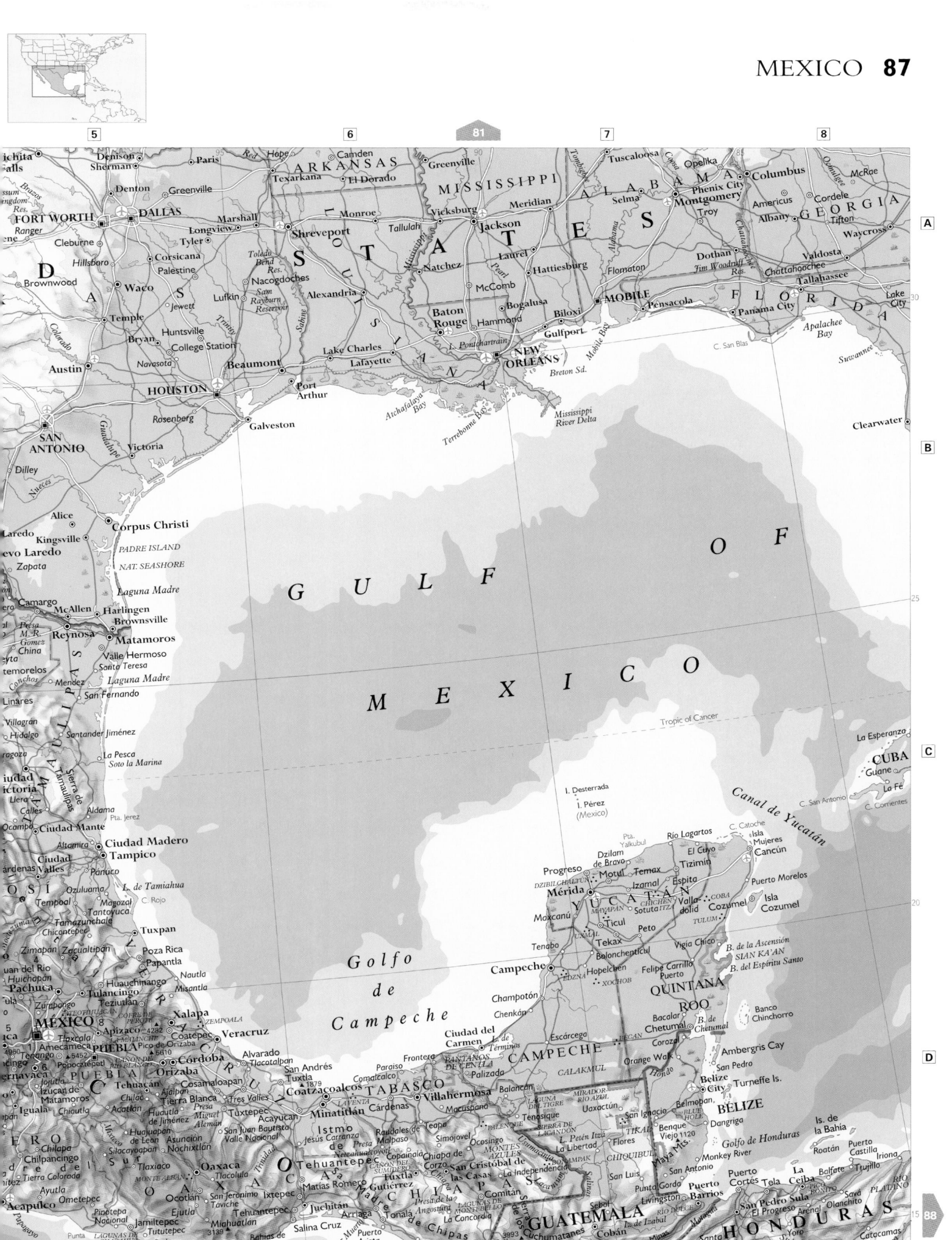

GULF OF MEXICO

G U L F O F

M E X I C O

Golfo de Campeche

Tropic of Cancer

ARKANSAS

MISSISSIPPI ALABAMA GEORGIA

LOUISIANA

FLORIDA

TEXAS

FORT WORTH DALLAS

HOUSTON

SAN ANTONIO

AUSTIN

Corpus Christi

PADRE ISLAND NAT. SEASHORE

Laguna Madre

McAllen Harlingen Brownsville

Reynosa Matamoros

Laguna Madre

MEXICO PUEBLA

Veracruz

Xalapa

Tampico

Mérida YUCATÁN

Cancún

Isla Cozumel

QUINTANA ROO

Campeche

CAMPECHE

TABASCO

Villahermosa

Coatzacoalcos

OAXACA

CHIAPAS

GUATEMALA HONDURAS

BELIZE

CUBA

Canal de Yucatán

JAMAICA
1:3 000 000

GUADELOUPE AND MARTINIQUE
1:2 000 000

Projection: Bi-polar oblique Conical Orthomorphic

ATLANTIC OCEAN

PUERTO RICO
1:3 000 000
10   0   10   20   30   40   50 km
10   0   10   20   30 miles

PUERTO RICO (U.S.A.)

Pta. Aguijereada
Aguadilla   Isabela   Barceloneta
Arecibo   Manati   Vega   Rio Grande
Utuado   Baja   Bayamón   SAN JUAN   Carolina
San Sebastián   Cordillera Central   Caguas   Fajardo   Dewey
Mayagüez   Adjuntas   Cerro   Liquillo   Culebra
Uroyan Mts.   1338 de Punta   Cayey   Humacoa   Naguabo   Vieques
San German   Yauco   Coamo   Yabucoa   Esperanza
Ponce   Guayama
Pta. Aguila   Guanica   I. Caja de Muertos

VIRGIN ISLANDS
1:2 000 000
10   0   10   20   30 km
10   0   10   20 miles

Rufling Pt.   The Settlement
Virgin Islands (U.K.)   Anegada   East Pt.
Jost Van   Great Camanoe
Virgin Is.   Dyke I.   Guana I.   Virgin Gorda
(U.S.A.)   Hans   521   Beef   Spanish Town
Lollik I.   Cruz   Tortola   Road Town   Peter I.
Charlotte   Bay   St.   St. John I.
Amalie   Thomas I.

ST. LUCIA
1:2 000 000
5   0   5   10 km
5   0   5   10 miles

Cap Point
Gros Islet   Pte. Hardy   Esperance Bay
Castries   Marquis   Babonneau
L'Anse la Raye   Dennery
Canaries   Millet   Trou Gras Pt.
Soufrière   Mt. Gimie 960   Micoud
Soufrière   750   Petit Piton   Vierge Pt.
Bay   Gros Piton Pt.   796   Gros Piton
Choiseul   **ST. LUCIA**
Laborie   Vieux Fort
C. Moule à Chique

ATLANTIC OCEAN
Crabhill   North Point
Fustic   Spring Hall
Portland   Boscobelle
Speightstown   245   Belleplaine
Westmoreland   Bathsheba   **BARBADOS**
Alleynes Bay   340   Hillcrest
Holetown   Mt. Hillaby   Martin's Bay
Black Rock   Jackson   Massiah
Ellerton   Street   Ragged Pt.
Bridgetown   Ivy   Edey   Six Cross Roads
Carlisle Bay   Oistins   The Crane
Worthing   St. Martins
Oistins   Chancery Lane
Bay   South Point

BARBADOS
1:2 000 000
5   0   5   10 km
5   0   5   10 miles

ATLANTIC OCEAN

MAS
Arthur's Town
The Bight
Cat I.
San Salvador I.
Conception I.
Rum Cay   Tropic of Cancer
Long I.   Samana Cay
Clarence Town
Crooked I.
Plana Cays
Albert Town   Mayaguana I.
Snug
Acklins I.   Corner
Mira por vos Cay
Cay Verde   Turks & Caicos
Hogsty Reef   Caicos Is. (U.K.)
Little Inagua I.   Grand
Turks Island
INAGUA   Cockburn Town
Lake Rose   Turks Is.
Great
Matthew   Inagua I.
Town

Baracoa
Maisi   Pta. de   Monte
Maisi   Cristi   LA ISABELA
GUANTANAMO   Cap-   Puerto   Santiago de los Cabelleros   Milwaukee
BAY (U.S.A.)   Haïtien   Plata   Deep 9200   Puerto Rico Trench
Jean Rabel   Port-de-   Cora   La Vega   San Francisco de Macorís   Samana
Paix   Central   Nagua
Paso de los Vientos   Gonaïves   3175   Sánchez   Sabana de la Mar
(Windward Passage)   Fort Liberté   Pico Duarte   Hato Mayor   C. Engaño
St-Marc   Hinche   ARMANDO   Higüey   Arecibo   SAN JUAN   Anegada   Virgin Is.   Sombrero (U.K.)
Jérémie   Î. de la Gonâve   BERMUDEZ   Bayamón   Virgin Gorda   Anguilla (U.K.)
Dame   **HAITI   DOMINICAN**   San Pedro   Carolina   Tortola   St.-Martin (Fr.)
Marie   PORT-   **REP.**   San Juan   de Macorís   Aguadilla   Fajardo   Road Town   St.-Barthélemy (Fr.)
C. Carcasse   AU-PRINCE   SANTO   B. de   Ponce   Charlotte Amalie
Les Cayes   Aquin   Goâve   Jacmel   San Cristobal   DOMINGO   Yuma   Mayagüez   Virgin Is.   St. Maarten   Barbuda
Aquin   2280   SIERRA DE   I. Saona   (U.S.A.)   (Neth.)   Saba (Neth.)
Î. à Vache   Barahona   Compostela   Isla   Guayama   Christiansted   Barbuda
Pointe-à-Gravois   BAHORUCO   Mona   **PUERTO**   Frederiksted   St. Croix   St. Eustatius   ANTIGUA
I. Beata   C. Beata   (U.S.A.)   **RICO**   (U.S.A.)   (Neth.)   **& BARBUDA**
Pedernales   (U.S.A.)   Basseterre   **ST. KITTS**   St. John's
Hispaniola   Nevis   **& NEVIS**   Antigua
Redonda
Antilles   Montserrat
(U.K.)

ATLANTIC OCEAN

Ste.-Rose   Moule
GUADELOUPE   La Désirade
Guadeloupe Passage   (Fr.)   1467   Pointe-à-Pitre
Basse-Terre   Marie-Galante (Fr.)
I. des Saintes   Grand-Bourg
(Fr.)   Dominica Passage
Portsmouth   **DOMINICA**
I. de Aves   Roseau   1447   MORNE
(Venezuela)   TROIS PITONS
Martinique Passage
BEAN   SEA   Mt. Pelée   Ste.-Marie
1397   Le François
Fort-de-   Rivière-Pilote
France   **MARTINIQUE**
St. Lucia Channel   (Fr.)
Castries
Soufrière   **ST. LUCIA**
St. Vincent Passage
Soufrière 1234   St. Vincent
Kingstown   Speightstown
Lesser   Antilles   Bridgetown   **BARBADOS**
Hillsborough   **ST. VINCENT**
Grenadines   **& THE**
St. George's   **GRENADINES**
GRENADA

Aruba   Curaçao
Oranjestad   (Neth.)   Bonaire   I. Blanquilla (Ven.)
Pta. Gallinas   C. San Román   Willemstad   **NETH.**   Tobago
MACUIRA   Paraguaná   **ANTILLES**   I. Orchila   I. Los Hermanos   Port of
Pen. de la   Pta.   Punto Fijo   Is. Las Aves   (Ven.)   NUEVA   Is. Los Testigos   Spain   Scarborough
COLOMBIA   Guajira   Espada   (Ven.)   Is. Los Roques   ESPARTA   (Ven.)   Galera
Ríohacha   Uribia   GUAJIRA   Golfo de   MEDANOS DE CORO   (Ven.)   I. La Tortuga   I. de Margarita   Dragon's Mouth   Point
Santa   Venezuela   Coro   La Vela de Coro   (Ven.)   CERRO EL COPEY   Trinidad
Marta   S. NEVADA DE   San   Punta   CUEVA DE LA   Maiquetia   Porlamar   Arima
Cienaga   STA. MARTA   Rafael   Cardón   QUEBRADA   La Guaira   LAGUNA DE   Río Claro
ISLA DE   Sierra Nevada de   Altagracia   DEL TORO   HENRI   CARACAS   LA RESTINGA   Carúpano   Güira
SALAMANCA   Santa Marta   5800   Coro   S.A. DE SAN LUIS   PITTIER   VARGAS   Cumaná   TRINIDAD
Fundación   Valledupar   Villa del   Mene de Mauroa   **FALCÓN**   Puerto   Maracay   Guatire   Caribe   San   **& TOBAGO**
Agustín   Rosario   Cabimas   Baragua   Cabello   MIRANDA   Puerto   Fernando
MAGDALENA   Codazzi   Ciudad   Barquisimeto   CERRO   Valencia   Los Teques   La Cruz   Barcelona   Caicara
Plato   CESAR   Ojeda   LARA   SAROCHIJ   Villa   San Juan   Aragua de   Caripito
Calamar   Machiques   **BARQUISIMETO**   Carora   CARABOBO   de Cura   de los Morros   Barcelona   SUCRE   Maturín
El Banco   ZULIA   Lago de   Mene Grande   YARACUY   Maracaibo   Yaritagua de   El Tocuyo   San Carlos   MONAGAS   **DELTA**
Mompós   Maracaibo   Trujillo   TEREPAIMA   los Morros   de Orituco   Anaco   Cantaura   **AMACURO**
Magangué   PERIJA   La Concepción   San Felipe   COJEDES   El Sombrero   Valle de   Tucupita
Plato   CIENAGAS DEL   TRUJILLO   PORTUGUESA   Acarigua   la Pascua   El Tigre
El Banco   CATATUMBO   Betijoque   Trujillo   GUARICO   Santa María
Zambrano   Valera   GUA-   Guanare   Portuguesa   de Ipire   El Callao
NORTE   SANTANDER   San Carlos   RICO   Calabozo   Santa   Pariaguán   ANZOÁTEGUI   Ciudad Guayana
DE   del Zulia   **BARINAS**   Barinas   ANZOÁTEGUI   María   Soledad   Sierra Imataca
OCAÑA   MÉRIDA   Libertad   San Fernando   Ciudad   Tumeremo
BOLÍVAR   CORD. DE MÉRIDA   Ciudad   de Apure   Bolívar
SANTANDER   Santo   Bolivia   **VENEZUEL A**   Ciudad   Upata
Caucasia   TACHIRA   Barbara   Bruzual   Puerto de Nutrias   Guasipati
San   Achaguas   Orinoco   Mapire
San Fernando   Apure   Caicara   Embalse de Gurí

West from Greenwich

4000 3000 2000 1500 1000 400 200 0
12 000 9000 6000 4500 3000 1200 600 0
600 6000 12 000 18 000 24 000 ft
200 2000 4000 6000 8000 m

National Parks

COPYRIGHT PHILIP'S

1:35 000 000

Projection: Lambert's Azimuthal Equal Area

COPYRIGHT PHILIP'S

1:35 000 000

■ LIMA Capital Cities

Projection: Lambert's Azimuthal Equal Area

COPYRIGHT PHILIP'S

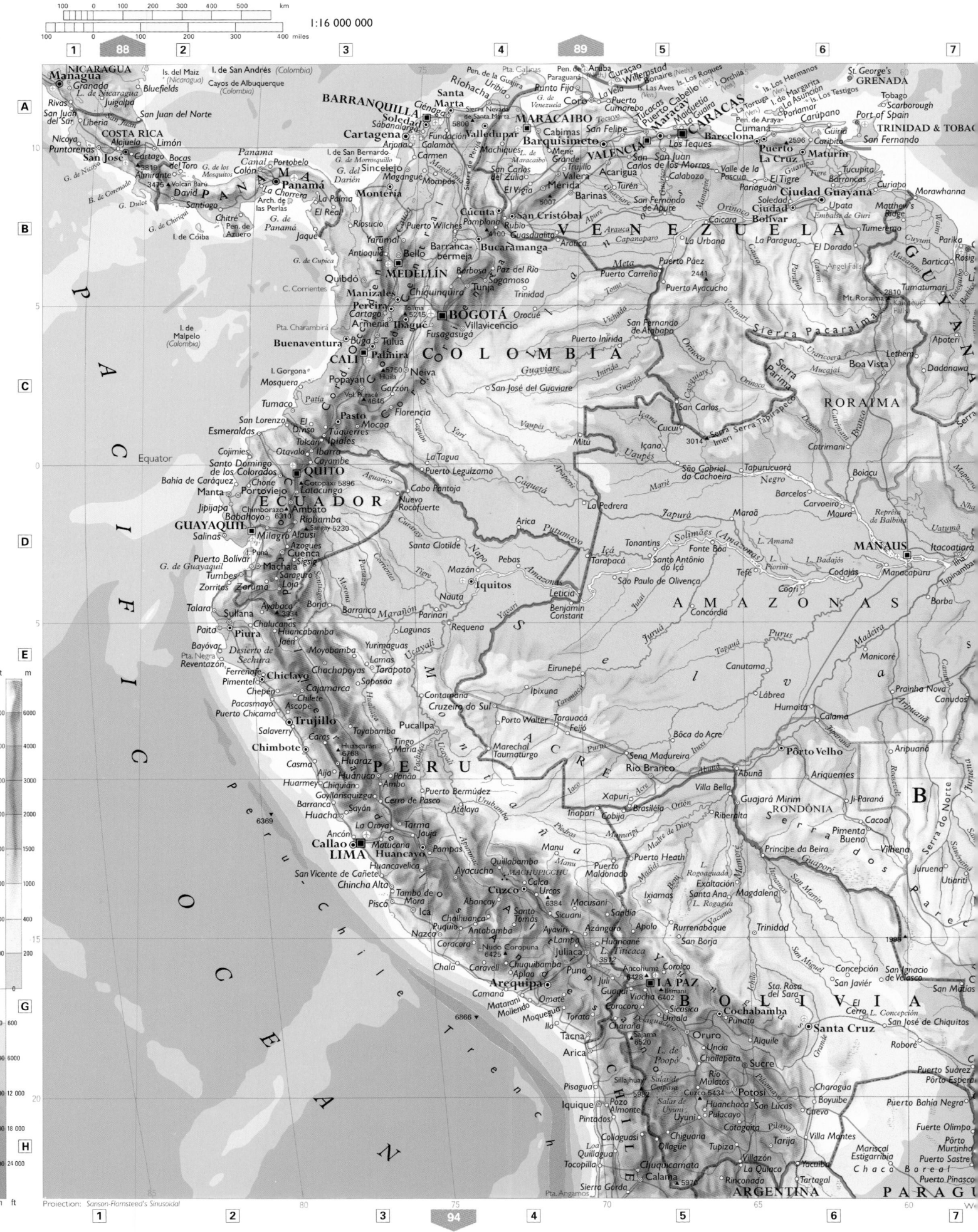

1:16 000 000

Projection: Sanson-Flamsteed's Sinusoidal

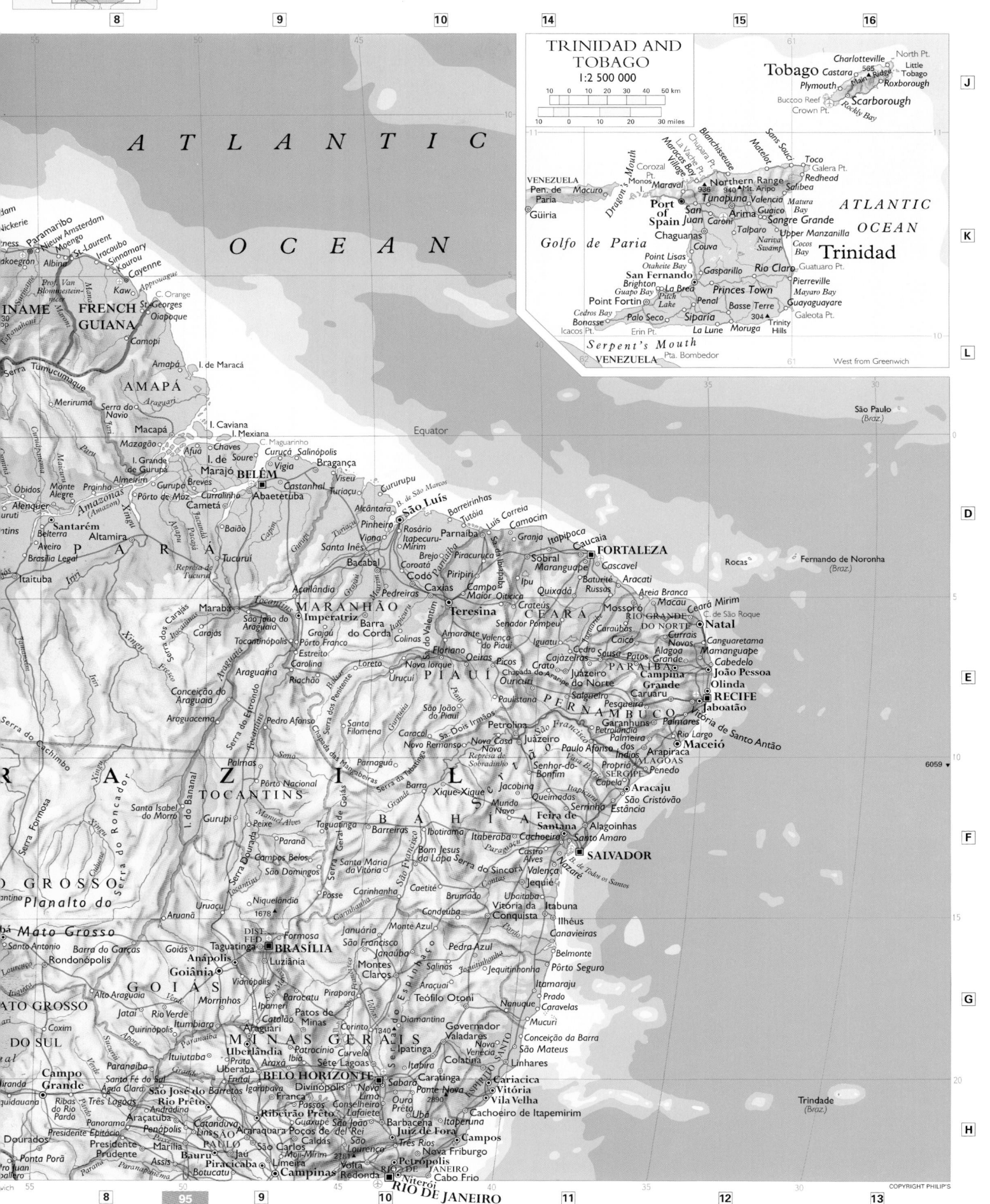

TRINIDAD AND TOBAGO
1:2 500 000

ATLANTIC OCEAN

Tobago
Charlotteville
North Pt.
Castara
Main Ridge 565
Little Tobago
Plymouth
Roxborough
Buccoo Reef
Crown Pt.
Rockly Bay
Scarborough

VENEZUELA
Pen. de Paria
Macuro
Dragon's Mouth
Corozal Pt.
Monos I.
Maraval
La Vache Pt.
Marcas Bay Village
Blanchisseuse
Matelot
Sans Souci
Toco
Redhead
Galera Pt.
936
Northern Range 940 Mt. Aripo
Salibea
Tunapuna Valencia
Güiria
Port of Spain
San Juan
Arima
Guaico
Sangre Grande
Matura Bay
Caroni
Talparo
Upper Manzanilla
ATLANTIC OCEAN
Golfo de Paria
Chaguanas
Couva
Narival Swamp
Cocos Bay
Point Lisas
Otaheite Bay
Gasparillo
Rio Claro
Guatuaro Pt.
San Fernando
Brighton
La Brea
Princes Town
Pierreville
Guapo Bay
Pitch Lake
Penal
Basse Terre
Mayaro Bay
Guayaguayare
Point Fortin
Cedros Bay
Bonasse
Palo Seco
Siparia
304
Galeota Pt.
Icacos Pt.
Erin Pt.
La Lune
Moruga
Trinity Hills
Trinidad

Serpent's Mouth
Pta. Bombedor
West from Greenwich
VENEZUELA

50 0 50 100 150 200 250 300 km
1:8 000 000

50 0 50 100 150 200 miles

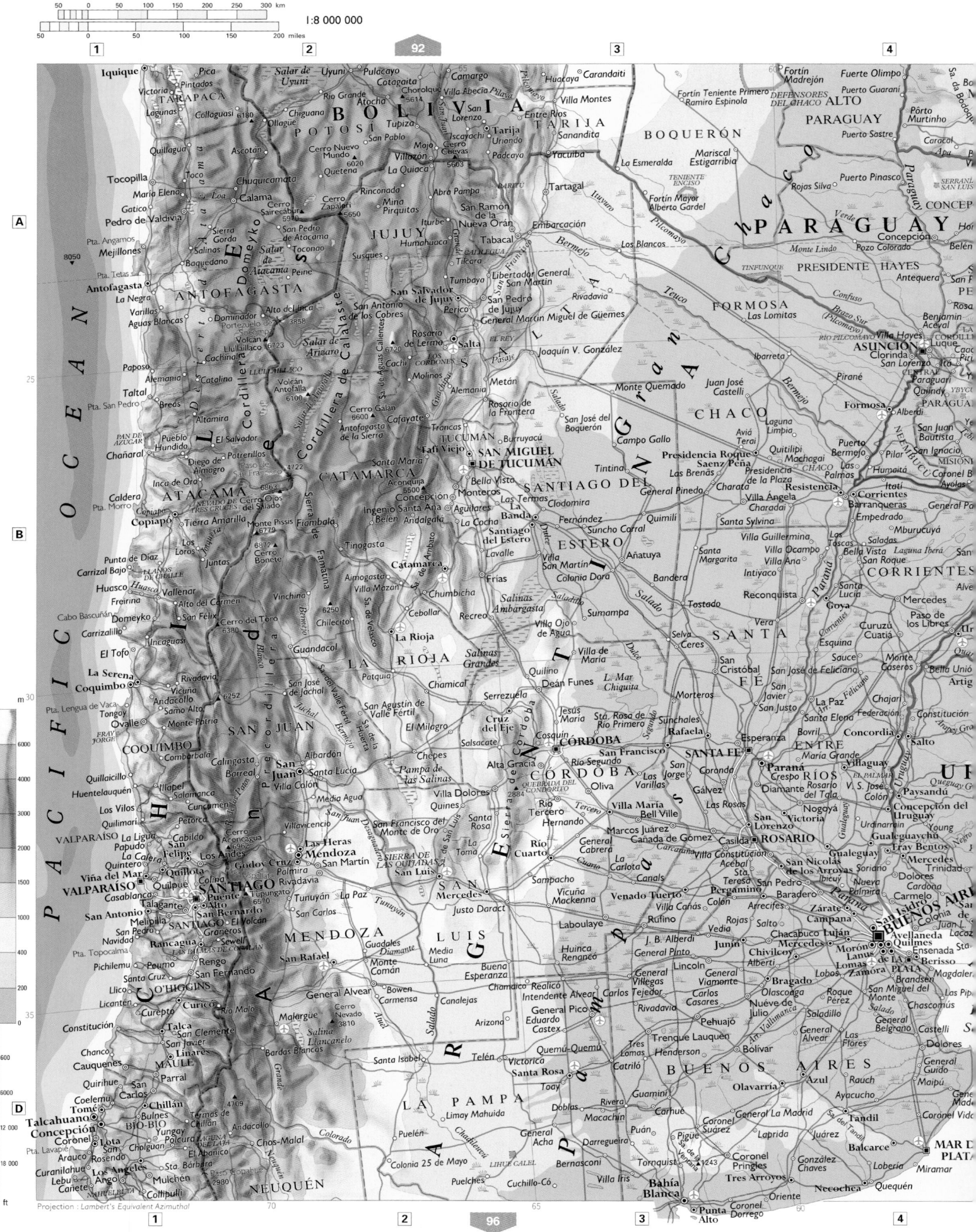

Projection : Lambert's Equivalent Azimuthal

National Parks

COPYRIGHT PHILIP'S

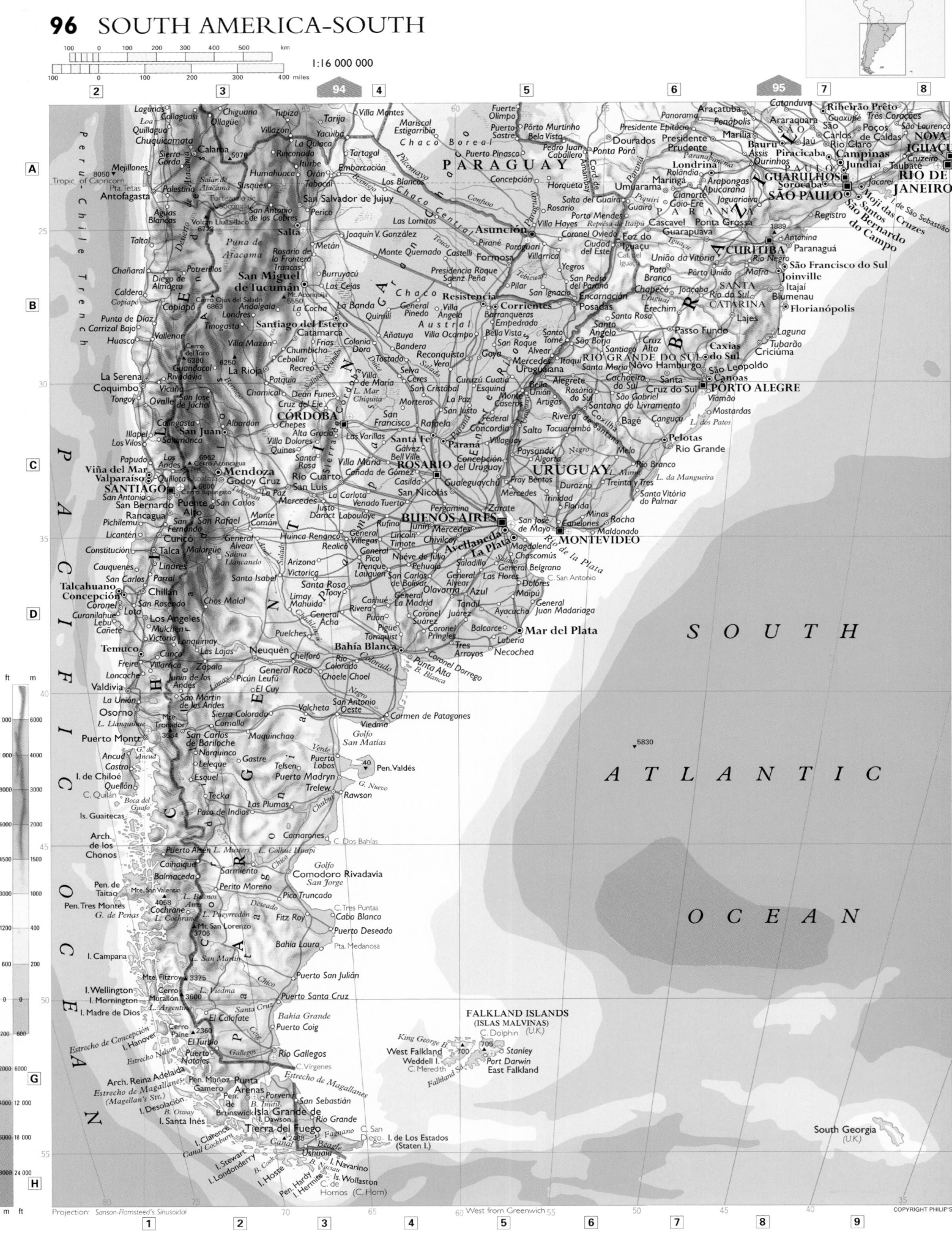

1:16 000 000

INDEX TO WORLD MAPS

The index contains the names of all the principal places and features shown on the World Maps. Each name is followed by an additional entry in italics giving the country or region within which it is located. The alphabetical order of names composed of two or more words is governed primarily by the first word and then by the second. This is an example of the rule:

Mīr Kūh, *Iran*	**45 E8**	26 22N	58 55 E
Mīr Shahdād, *Iran*	**45 E8**	26 15N	58 29 E
Mira, *Italy*	**22 B5**	45 26N	12 8 E
Mira por vos Cay, *Bahamas*	**89 B5**	22 9N	74 30W
Mirador-Río Azul △, *Guatemala*	**88 C2**	17 45N	89 50W
Miraj, *India*	**40 L9**	16 50N	74 45 E

Physical features composed of a proper name (Erie) and a description (Lake) are positioned alphabetically by the proper name. The description is positioned after the proper name and is usually abbreviated:

Erie, L., *N. Amer.* **84 D4** 42 15N 81 0W

Where a description forms part of a settlement or administrative name however, it is always written in full and put in its true alphabetic position:

Mount Morris, *U.S.A.* **84 D7** 42 44N 77 52W

Names beginning with M' and Mc are indexed as if they were spelled Mac. Names beginning St. are alphabetized under Saint, but Sankt, Sint, Sant', Santa and San are all spelt in full and are alphabetized accordingly. If the same place name occurs two or more times in the index and all are in the same country, each is followed by the name of the administrative subdivision in which it is located.

The number in bold type which follows each name in the index refers to the number of the map page where that feature or place will be found. This is usually the largest scale at which the place or feature appears.

The letter and figure which are in bold type immediately after the page number give the grid square on the map page, within which the feature is situated. The letter represents the latitude and the figure the longitude. A lower case letter immediately after the page number refers to an inset map on that page.

In some cases the feature itself may fall within the specified square, while the name is outside. This is usually the case only with features which are larger than a grid square.

The geographical co-ordinates which follow the letter-figure references give the latitude and longitude of each place. The first co-ordinate indicates latitude – the distance north of the Equator. The second co-ordinate indicates longitude – the distance east or west of the Greenwich Meridian. Both latitude and longitude are measured in degrees and minutes (there are 60 minutes in a degree).

The latitude is followed by N(orth) or S(outh) and the longitude by E(ast) or W(est).

Rivers are indexed to their mouths or confluences, and carry the symbol ➔ after their names. The following symbols are also used in the index: ■ country, ☑ overseas territory or dependency, ☐ first order administrative area, △ national park, ◠ other park (provincial park, nature reserve or game reserve), ✈ (LHR) principal airport (and location identifier).

Abbreviations used in the index

A.C.T. – Australian Capital Territory
A.R. – Autonomous Region
Afghan. – Afghanistan
Afr. – Africa
Ala. – Alabama
Alta. – Alberta
Amer. – America(n)
Arch. – Archipelago
Ariz. – Arizona
Ark. – Arkansas
Atl. Oc. – Atlantic Ocean
B. – Baie, Bahía, Bay, Bucht, Bugt
B.C. – British Columbia
Bangla. – Bangladesh
Barr. – Barrage
Bos.-H. – Bosnia-Herzegovina
C. – Cabo, Cap, Cape, Coast
C.A.R. – Central African Republic
C. Prov. – Cape Province
Calif. – California
Cat. – Catarata
Cent. – Central
Chan. – Channel
Colo. – Colorado
Conn. – Connecticut
Cord. – Cordillera
Cr. – Creek
Czech. – Czech Republic
D.C. – District of Columbia
Del. – Delaware
Dem. – Democratic
Dep. – Dependency
Des. – Desert
Dét. – Détroit
Dist. – District
Dj. – Djebel
Domin. – Dominica
Dom. Rep. – Dominican Republic

E. – East
E. Salv. – El Salvador
Eq. Guin. – Equatorial Guinea
Est. – Estrecho
Falk. Is. – Falkland Is.
Fd. – Fjord
Fla. – Florida
Fr. – French
G. – Golfe, Golfo, Gulf, Guba, Gebel
Ga. – Georgia
Gt. – Great, Greater
Guinea-Biss. – Guinea-Bissau
H.K. – Hong Kong
H.P. – Himachal Pradesh
Hants. – Hampshire
Harb. – Harbor, Harbour
Hd. – Head
Hts. – Heights
I.(s). – Île, Ilha, Insel, Isla, Island, Isle
Ill. – Illinois
Ind. – Indiana
Ind. Oc. – Indian Ocean
Ivory C. – Ivory Coast
J. – Jabal, Jebel
Jaz. – Jazīrah
Junc. – Junction
K. – Kap, Kapp
Kans. – Kansas
Kep. – Kepulauan
Ky. – Kentucky
L. – Lac, Lacul, Lago, Lagoa, Lake, Limni, Loch, Lough
La. – Louisiana
Ld. – Land
Liech. – Liechtenstein
Lux. – Luxembourg
Mad. P. – Madhya Pradesh
Madag. – Madagascar
Man. – Manitoba
Mass. – Massachusetts

Md. – Maryland
Me. – Maine
Medit. S. – Mediterranean Sea
Mich. – Michigan
Minn. – Minnesota
Miss. – Mississippi
Mo. – Missouri
Mont. – Montana
Mozam. – Mozambique
Mt.(s) – Mont, Montaña, Mountain
Mte. – Monte
Mti. – Monti
N. – Nord, Norte, North, Northern, Nouveau
N.B. – New Brunswick
N.C. – North Carolina
N. Cal. – New Caledonia
N. Dak. – North Dakota
N.H. – New Hampshire
N.I. – North Island
N.J. – New Jersey
N. Mex. – New Mexico
N.S. – Nova Scotia
N.S.W. – New South Wales
N.W.T. – North West Territory
N.Y. – New York
N.Z. – New Zealand
Nac. – Nacional
Nat. – National
Nebr. – Nebraska
Neths. – Netherlands
Nev. – Nevada
Nfld. – Newfoundland
Nic. – Nicaragua
O. – Oued, Ouadi
Occ. – Occidentale
Okla. – Oklahoma
Ont. – Ontario
Or. – Orientale
Oreg. – Oregon

Os. – Ostrov
Oz. – Ozero
P. – Pass, Passo, Pasul, Pulau
P.E.I. – Prince Edward Island
Pa. – Pennsylvania
Pac. Oc. – Pacific Ocean
Papua N.G. – Papua New Guinea
Pass. – Passage
Peg. – Pegunungan
Pen. – Peninsula, Péninsule
Phil. – Philippines
Pk. – Peak
Plat. – Plateau
Prov. – Province, Provincial
Pt. – Point
Pta. – Ponta, Punta
Pte. – Pointe
Qué. – Québec
Queens. – Queensland
R. – Rio, River
R.I. – Rhode Island
Ra. – Range
Raj. – Rajasthan
Recr. – Recreational, Récréatif
Reg. – Region
Rep. – Republic
Res. – Reserve, Reservoir
Rhld-Pfz. – Rheinland-Pfalz
S. – South, Southern, Sur
Si. Arabia – Saudi Arabia
S.C. – South Carolina
S. Dak. – South Dakota
S.I. – South Island
S. Leone – Sierra Leone
Sa. – Serra, Sierra
Sask. – Saskatchewan
Scot. – Scotland
Sd. – Sound
Sev. – Severnaya
Sib. – Siberia
Sprs. – Springs

St. – Saint
Sta. – Santa
Ste. – Sainte
Sto. – Santo
Str. – Strait, Stretto
Switz. – Switzerland
Tas. – Tasmania
Tenn. – Tennessee
Terr. – Territory, Territoire
Tex. – Texas
Tg. – Tanjung
Trin. & Tob. – Trinidad & Tobago
U.A.E. – United Arab Emirates
U.K. – United Kingdom
U.S.A. – United States of America
Ut. P. – Uttar Pradesh
Va. – Virginia
Vdkhr. – Vodokhranilishche
Vdskh. – Vodoskhovyshche
Vf. – Vírful
Vic. – Victoria
Vol. – Volcano
Vt. – Vermont
W. – Wadi, West
W. Va. – West Virginia
Wall. & F. Is. – Wallis and Futuna Is.
Wash. – Washington
Wis. – Wisconsin
Wlkp. – Wielkopolski
Wyo. – Wyoming
Yorks. – Yorkshire

A

A Coruña, Spain 21 A1 43 20N 8 25W
A Estrada, Spain 21 A1 42 43N 8 27W
A Fonsagrada, Spain 21 A2 43 8N 7 4W
Aachen, Germany .... 16 C4 50 45N 6 6 E
Aalborg = Ålborg, Denmark ... 9 H13 57 2N 9 54 E
Aalen, Germany .... 16 D6 48 51N 10 6 E
Aalst, Belgium .... 15 D4 50 56N 4 2 E
Aalten, Neths. .... 15 C6 51 56N 6 35 E
Aalter, Belgium .... 15 C3 51 5N 3 28 E
Äänekoski, Finland .... 9 E21 62 36N 25 44 E
Aarau, Switz. .... 20 C8 47 23N 8 4 E
Aare →, Switz. .... 20 C8 47 33N 8 14 E
Aarhus = Århus, Denmark ..... 9 H14 56 8N 10 11 E
Aarschot, Belgium .... 15 D4 50 59N 4 49 E
Aba, Dem. Rep. of the Congo .. 54 B3 3 58N 30 17 E
Aba, Nigeria .... 50 G7 5 10N 7 19 E
Ābādān, Iran .... 45 D6 30 22N 48 20 E
Ābādeh, Iran .... 45 D7 31 8N 52 40 E
Abadla, Algeria 50 B5 31 2N 2 45W
Abaetetuba, Brazil 93 D9 1 40S 48 50W
Abagnar Qi, China .... 34 C9 43 52N 116 2 E
Abah, Tanjung, Indonesia ..... 37 K18 8 46S 115 38 E
Abai, Paraguay 95 B4 25 58S 55 54W
Abak, Russia .... 29 D10 53 40N 91 10 E
Abancay, Peru 92 F4 13 35S 72 55W
Abariringa, Kiribati 64 H10 2 50S 171 40W
Abarqū, Iran .... 45 D7 31 10N 53 20 E
Abashiri, Japan .... 30 B12 44 0N 144 15 E
Abashiri-Wan, Japan .... 30 C12 44 0N 144 30 E
Ābay = Nîl el Azraq →, Sudan . 51 E12 15 38N 32 31 E
Abay, Kazakhstan .... 28 E8 49 38N 72 53 E
Abaya, L., Ethiopia .... 47 F2 6 30N 37 50 E
Abaza, Russia .... 28 D9 52 39N 90 6 E
'Abbāsābād, Iran .... 45 C8 33 34N 58 23 E
Abbay = Nîl el Azraq →, Sudan 51 E12 15 38N 32 31 E
Abbaye, Pt., U.S.A. 82 B1 46 58N 88 8W
Abbé, L., Ethiopia .... 47 E3 11 8N 41 47 E
Abbeville, France .... 20 A4 50 6N 1 49 E
Abbeville, Ala., U.S.A. 83 K3 31 34N 85 15W
Abbeville, La., U.S.A. 81 L8 29 58N 92 8W
Abbeville, S.C., U.S.A. 83 H4 34 11N 82 23W
Abbot Ice Shelf, Antarctica ... 5 D16 73 0S 92 0W
Abbottabad, Pakistan .... 42 B5 34 10N 73 15 E
Abd al Kūrī, Yemen .... 47 E5 12 5N 52 20 E
Ābdar, Iran .... 45 D7 30 16N 55 19 E
'Abdolābād, Iran .... 45 C8 34 12N 56 30 E
Abdulpur, Bangla. .... 43 G13 24 15N 88 59 E
Abéché, Chad .... 51 F10 13 50N 20 35 E
Abel Tasman △, N.Z. .... 59 J4 40 59S 173 3 E
Abengourou, Ivory C. 50 G5 6 42N 3 27W
Ābenrå, Denmark .... 9 J13 55 3N 9 25 E
Abeokuta, Nigeria .... 50 G6 7 3N 3 19 E
Aber, Uganda .... 54 B3 2 12N 32 25 E
Aberaeron, U.K. 13 E3 52 15N 4 15W
Aberayron = Aberaeron, U.K. .. 13 E3 52 15N 4 15W
Aberchirder, U.K. 11 D6 57 34N 2 37W
Abercorn, Australia .... 63 D5 25 12S 151 5 E
Aberdare, U.K. 13 F4 51 43N 3 27W
Aberdare →, Kenya .... 54 C4 0 22S 36 44 E
Aberdare Ra., Kenya .... 54 C4 0 15S 36 50 E
Aberdeen, Australia .... 63 E5 32 9S 150 56 E
Aberdeen, Canada 71 C7 52 20N 106 8W
Aberdeen, China .... 33 G11 22 15N 114 9 E
Aberdeen, S. Africa .... 56 E3 32 28S 24 2 E
Aberdeen, U.K. 11 D6 57 9N 2 5W
Aberdeen, Ala., U.S.A. 83 J1 33 49N 88 33W
Aberdeen, Idaho, U.S.A. 76 E7 42 57N 112 50W
Aberdeen, Md., U.S.A. 82 F7 39 31N 76 10W
Aberdeen, S. Dak., U.S.A. 80 C5 45 28N 98 29W
Aberdeen, Wash., U.S.A. 78 D3 46 59N 123 50W
Aberdeen, City of □, U.K. 11 D6 57 10N 2 10W
Aberdeenshire □, U.K. 11 D6 57 17N 2 36W
Aberdovey = Aberdyfi, U.K. ... 13 E3 52 33N 4 3W
Aberdyfi, U.K. 13 E3 52 33N 4 3W
Aberfeldy, U.K. 11 E5 56 37N 3 51W
Aberfoyle, U.K. 11 E4 56 11N 4 23W
Abergavenny, U.K. 13 F4 51 49N 3 1W
Abergele, U.K. 12 D4 53 17N 3 35W
Abernathy, U.S.A. 81 J4 33 50N 101 51W
Abert, L., U.S.A. 76 E3 42 38N 120 14W
Aberystwyth, U.K. 13 E3 52 25N 4 5W
Abhā, Si. Arabia .... 47 D3 18 0N 42 34 E
Abhar, Iran .... 45 B6 36 9N 49 13 E
Abhayapuri, India .... 43 F14 26 24N 90 38 E
Abidjan, Ivory C. 50 G5 5 26N 3 58W
Abilene, Kans., U.S.A. 80 F6 38 55N 97 13W
Abilene, Tex., U.S.A. 81 J5 32 28N 99 43W
Abingdon, U.K. 13 F6 51 40N 1 17W
Abingdon, U.S.A. 83 G5 36 43N 81 59W
Abington Reef, Australia ..... 62 B4 18 0S 149 35 E
Abitibi →, Canada 71 B7 59 53N 109 3W
Abitibi, L., Canada 72 C4 48 40N 79 40W
Abkhaz Republic = Abkhazia □,
  Georgia .... 19 F7 43 12N 41 5 E
Abkhazia □, Georgia .... 19 F7 43 12N 41 5 E
Abminga, Australia .... 63 D1 26 8S 134 51 E
Åbo = Turku, Finland .... 9 F20 60 30N 22 19 E
Abohar, India .... 42 D6 30 10N 74 10 E
Abomey, Benin .... 50 G6 7 10N 2 5 E
Abong-Mbang, Cameroon ...... 52 D2 4 0N 13 8 E
Abou-Deïa, Chad .... 51 F9 11 20N 19 20 E
Aboyne, U.K. 11 D6 57 4N 2 47W
Abra Pampa, Argentina 94 A2 22 43S 65 42W
Abraham L., Canada 70 C5 52 15N 116 35W
Abreojos, Pta., Mexico 86 B2 26 50N 113 40W
Abrud, Romania .... 17 E12 46 19N 23 5 E
Absaroka Range, U.S.A. 76 D9 44 45N 109 50W
Abu, India .... 42 G5 24 41N 72 50 E
Abū al Abyad, U.A.E. .... 45 E7 24 11N 53 50 E
Abū al Khaṣīb, Iraq .... 45 D6 30 25N 48 0 E
Abū 'Alī, Si. Arabia .... 45 E6 27 20N 49 27 E
Abū 'Alī →, Lebanon .... 46 A4 34 25N 35 50 E
Abu Dhabi = Abū Ẓāby, U.A.E. . 45 E7 24 28N 54 22 E
Abū Du'ān, Syria .... 44 B3 36 25N 38 15 E
Abu el Gairi, W. →, Egypt .... 46 F2 29 35N 33 30 E
Abu Ga'da, W. →, Egypt ...... 46 F1 29 15N 32 53 E
Abū Ḥadrīyah, Si. Arabia .... 45 E6 27 20N 48 58 E
Abu Hamed, Sudan .... 51 E12 19 32N 33 13 E
Abū Kamāl, Syria .... 44 C4 34 30N 41 0 E
Abū Madd, Ra's, Si. Arabia ... 44 E3 24 50N 37 7 E
Abū Mūsā, U.A.E. .... 45 E7 25 52N 55 3 E
Abu Qaşr, Si. Arabia .... 44 D3 30 21N 38 34 E
Abu Simbel, Egypt .... 51 D12 22 18N 31 40 E
Abū Şukhayr, Iraq .... 44 D5 31 54N 44 30 E

Abu Zabad, Sudan .... 51 F11 12 25N 29 10 E
Abū Ẓāby, U.A.E. .... 45 E7 24 28N 54 22 E
Abū Zeydābād, Iran .... 45 C6 33 54N 51 45 E
Abuja, Nigeria .... 50 G7 9 5N 7 32 E
Abukuma-Gawa →, Japan ..... 30 E10 38 6N 140 52 E
Abukuma-Sammyaku, Japan ... 30 F10 37 30N 140 45 E
Abunã, Brazil 92 E5 9 40S 65 20W
Abunã →, Brazil 92 E5 9 41S 65 20W
Aburo, Dem. Rep. of the Congo 54 B3 2 4N 30 53 E
Abut Hd., N.Z. .... 59 K3 43 7S 170 15 E
Acadia □, U.S.A. 83 C11 44 20N 68 13W
Açailândia, Brazil 93 D9 4 57S 47 0W
Acajutla, El Salv. 88 D2 13 36N 89 50W
Acámbaro, Mexico 86 D4 20 0N 100 40W
Acaponeta, Mexico 86 C3 22 30N 105 20W
Acapulco, Mexico 87 D5 16 51N 99 56W
Acarai, Serra, Brazil 92 C7 1 50N 57 50W
Acarigua, Venezuela 92 B5 9 33N 69 12W
Acatlán, Mexico 87 D5 18 10N 98 3W
Acayucan, Mexico 87 D6 17 59N 94 58W
Accomac, U.S.A. 82 G8 37 43N 75 40W
Accra, Ghana 50 G5 5 35N 0 6W
Accrington, U.K. 12 D5 53 45N 2 22W
Acebal, Argentina 94 C3 33 20S 60 50W
Aceh □, Indonesia .... 36 D1 4 15N 97 30 E
Achalpur, India .... 40 J10 21 22N 77 32 E
Acheng, China .... 35 B14 45 30N 126 58 E
Acher, India .... 42 H5 23 10N 72 32 E
Achill Hd., Ireland 10 C1 53 58N 10 15W
Achill I., Ireland 10 C1 53 58N 10 1W
Achinsk, Russia .... 29 D10 56 20N 90 20 E
Acireale, Italy .... 22 F6 37 37N 15 10 E
Ackerman, U.S.A. 81 J10 33 19N 89 11W
Acklins I., Bahamas 89 B5 22 30N 74 0W
Acme, Canada 70 C6 51 33N 113 30W
Acme, U.S.A. 84 F5 40 8N 79 26W
Aconcagua, Cerro, Argentina .. 94 C2 32 39S 70 0W
Aconquija, Mt., Argentina 94 B2 27 0S 66 0W
Açores, Is. dos, Atl. Oc. 50 A1 38 0N 27 0W
Acornhoek, S. Africa .... 57 C5 24 37S 31 2 E
Acre = 'Akko, Israel .... 46 C4 32 55N 35 4 E
Acre □, Brazil 92 E4 9 1S 71 0W
Acre →, Brazil 92 E5 8 45S 67 22W
Acton, Canada 84 C4 43 38N 80 3W
Acuña, Mexico 86 B4 29 18N 100 55W
Ad Dammām, Si. Arabia ...... 45 E6 26 20N 50 5 E
Ad Dāmūr, Lebanon .... 46 B4 33 44N 35 27 E
Ad Dawādimī, Si. Arabia ..... 44 E5 24 35N 44 15 E
Ad Dawḩah, Qatar .... 45 E6 25 15N 51 35 E
Ad Dawr, Iraq .... 44 C4 34 27N 43 47 E
Ad Dir'īyah, Si. Arabia ...... 44 E5 24 44N 46 35 E
Ad Dīwānīyah, Iraq .... 44 D5 32 0N 45 0 E
Ad Dujayl, Iraq .... 44 C5 33 51N 44 14 E
Ad Duwayd, Si. Arabia .... 44 D4 30 15N 42 17 E
Ada, Minn., U.S.A. 80 B6 47 18N 96 31W
Ada, Okla., U.S.A. 81 H6 34 46N 96 41W
Adabiya, Egypt .... 46 F1 29 53N 32 28 E
Adair, C., Canada 69 A12 71 30N 71 34W
Adaja →, Spain 21 B3 41 32N 4 52W
Adak I., U.S.A. 68 C2 51 45N 176 45W
Adamaoua, Massif de l',
  Cameroon .... 51 G7 7 20N 12 20 E
Adamawa Highlands =
  Adamaoua, Massif de l',
  Cameroon .... 51 G7 7 20N 12 20 E
Adamello, Mte., Italy .... 20 C9 46 9N 10 30 E
Adaminaby, Australia .... 63 F4 36 0S 148 45 E
Adams, Mass., U.S.A. 85 D11 42 38N 73 7W
Adams, N.Y., U.S.A. 85 C8 43 49N 76 1W
Adams, Wis., U.S.A. 80 D10 43 57N 89 49W
Adams, Mt., U.S.A. 78 D5 46 12N 121 30W
Adam's Bridge, Sri Lanka .... 40 Q11 9 15N 79 40 E
Adams L., Canada 70 C5 51 10N 119 40W
Adam's Peak, Sri Lanka ...... 40 R12 6 48N 80 30 E
Adana, Turkey .... 19 G6 37 0N 35 16 E
Adapazarı = Sakarya, Turkey .. 19 F5 40 48N 30 25 E
Adarama, Sudan .... 51 E12 17 10N 34 52 E
Adare, C., Antarctica .... 5 D11 71 0S 171 0 E
Adaut, Indonesia .... 37 F8 8 8S 131 7 E
Adavale, Australia .... 63 D3 25 52S 144 32 E
Adda →, Italy .... 20 D8 45 8N 9 53 E
Addis Ababa = Addis Abeba,
  Ethiopia .... 47 F2 9 2N 38 42 E
Addis Abeba, Ethiopia .... 47 F2 9 2N 38 42 E
Addison, U.S.A. 84 D7 42 1N 77 14W
Addo, S. Africa .... 56 E4 33 32S 25 45 E
Addo △, S. Africa .... 56 E4 33 30S 25 50 E
Ādeh, Iran .... 44 B5 37 42N 45 11 E
Adel, U.S.A. 83 K4 31 8N 83 25W
Adelaide, Australia .... 63 E2 34 52S 138 30 E
Adelaide, Bahamas 88 A4 25 4N 77 31W
Adelaide, S. Africa .... 56 E4 32 42S 26 20 E
Adelaide I., Antarctica 5 C17 67 15S 68 30W
Adelaide Pen., Canada 68 B10 68 15N 97 30W
Adelaide River, Australia .... 60 B5 13 15S 131 7 E
Adelanto, U.S.A. 79 L9 34 35N 117 22W
Adele I., Australia .... 60 C3 15 32S 123 9 E
Adélie, Terre, Antarctica ..... 5 C10 68 0S 140 0 E
Adélie Land = Adélie, Terre,
  Antarctica .... 5 C10 68 0S 140 0 E
Aden = Al 'Adan, Yemen ...... 47 E4 12 45N 45 0 E
Aden, G. of, Asia .... 47 E4 12 30N 47 30 E
Adendorp, S. Africa .... 56 E3 32 15S 24 30 E
Adh Dhayd, U.A.E. .... 45 E7 25 17N 55 53 E
Adhoi, India .... 42 H4 23 26N 70 32 E
Adi, Indonesia .... 37 E8 4 15S 133 30 E
Adieu, C., Australia .... 61 F5 32 0S 132 10 E
Adieu Pt., Australia .... 60 C3 15 14S 124 35 E
Adige →, Italy .... 22 B5 45 9N 12 20 E
Adigrat, Ethiopia .... 47 E2 14 20N 39 26 E
Adilabad, India .... 40 K11 19 33N 78 20 E
Adirondack △, U.S.A. 85 C10 44 0N 74 20W
Adirondack Mts., U.S.A. 85 C10 44 0N 74 20W
Adjumani, Uganda .... 54 B3 3 20N 31 50 E
Adjuntas, Puerto Rico .... 89 d 18 10N 66 43W
Adlavik Is., Canada 73 B8 55 0N 58 40W
Admiralty G., Australia ...... 60 B4 14 20S 125 55 E
Admiralty I., U.S.A. 68 C6 57 30N 134 30W
Admiralty Is., Papua N. G. ... 64 H6 2 0S 147 0 E
Adonara, Indonesia .... 37 F6 8 15S 123 5 E
Adoni, India .... 40 M10 15 33N 77 18 E
Adour →, France 20 E3 43 32N 1 32W
Adra, India .... 43 H12 23 30N 86 42 E
Adra, Spain 21 D4 36 43N 3 3W
Adrano, Italy .... 22 F6 37 40N 14 50 E
Adrar, Mauritania .... 50 D3 20 30N 7 30 E
Adrar des Iforas, Algeria ..... 50 C5 27 51N 0 11 E

Adrian, Mich., U.S.A. 82 E3 41 54N 84 2W
Adrian, Tex., U.S.A. 81 H3 35 16N 102 40W
Adriatic Sea, Medit. S. .... 22 C6 43 0N 16 0 E
Adua, Indonesia .... 37 E7 1 45S 129 50 E
Adwa, Ethiopia .... 47 E2 14 15N 38 52 E
Adygea □, Russia .... 19 F7 45 0N 40 0 E
Adzhar Republic = Ajaria □,
  Georgia .... 19 F7 41 30N 42 0 E
Adzopé, Ivory C. 50 G5 6 7N 3 49W
Ægean Sea, Medit. S. .... 23 E11 38 30N 25 0 E
Aerhtai Shan, Mongolia ...... 32 B4 46 40N 92 45 E
'Afak, Iraq .... 44 C5 32 4N 45 15 E
Afándou, Greece .... 25 C10 36 18N 28 12 E
Afghanistan ■, Asia .... 40 C4 33 0N 65 0 E
Aflou, Algeria .... 50 B6 34 7N 2 3 E
Africa .... 48 E6 10 0N 20 0 E
'Afrin, Syria .... 44 B3 36 32N 36 50 E
Afton, N.Y., U.S.A. 85 D9 42 14N 75 32W
Afton, Wyo., U.S.A. 76 E8 42 44N 110 56W
Afuá, Brazil 93 D8 0 15S 50 20W
'Afula, Israel .... 46 C4 32 37N 35 17 E
Afyon, Turkey .... 19 G5 38 45N 30 33 E
Afyonkarahisar = Afyon, Turkey 19 G5 38 45N 30 33 E
Agadès = Agadez, Niger ...... 50 E7 16 58N 7 59 E
Agadez, Niger .... 50 E7 16 58N 7 59 E
Agadir, Morocco 50 B4 30 28N 9 55W
Agaete, Canary Is. 24 F4 28 6N 15 43W
Agar, India .... 42 H7 23 40N 76 2 E
Agartala, India .... 41 H17 23 50N 91 23 E
Agassiz, Canada 70 D4 49 14N 121 46W
Agats, Indonesia .... 37 F9 5 33S 138 0 E
Agawam, U.S.A. 85 D12 42 5N 72 37W
Agboville, Ivory C. 50 G5 5 55N 4 15W
Ağdam, Azerbaijan .... 44 B5 40 0N 46 58 E
Agde, France .... 20 E5 43 19N 3 28 E
Agen, France .... 20 D4 44 12N 0 38 E
Āgh Kand, Iran .... 45 B6 37 15N 48 4 E
Aginskoye, Russia .... 29 D12 51 6N 114 32 E
Agnew, Australia .... 61 E3 28 1S 120 31 E
Agori, India .... 43 G10 24 33N 82 57 E
Agra, India .... 42 F7 27 17N 77 58 E
Ağri, Turkey .... 19 G7 39 44N 43 3 E
Agri →, Italy .... 22 D7 40 13N 16 44 E
Ağrı Dağı, Turkey .... 19 G7 39 50N 44 15 E
Ağrı Karaköse = Ağri, Turkey . 19 G7 39 44N 43 3 E
Agrigento, Italy .... 22 F5 37 19N 13 34 E
Agrinion, Greece .... 23 E9 38 37N 21 5 E
Agua Caliente, Baja Calif.,
  Mexico 79 N10 32 29N 116 59W
Agua Caliente, Sinaloa, Mexico 86 B3 26 30N 108 20W
Agua Caliente Springs, U.S.A. . 79 N10 32 56N 116 19W
Água Clara, Brazil 93 H8 20 25S 52 45W
Agua Fria △, U.S.A. 77 J8 34 14N 112 0W
Agua Hechicero, Mexico 79 N10 32 26N 116 14W
Agua Prieta, Mexico 86 A3 31 20N 109 32W
Aguadilla, Puerto Rico .... 89 d 18 26N 67 10W
Aguadulce, Panama 88 E3 8 15N 80 32W
Aguanga, U.S.A. 79 M10 33 27N 116 51W
Aguanish, Canada 73 B7 50 14N 62 2W
Aguanus →, Canada 73 B7 50 13N 62 5W
Aguapey →, Argentina 94 B4 29 7S 56 36W
Aguaray Guazú →, Paraguay .. 94 A4 24 47S 57 19W
Aguarico →, Ecuador 92 D3 0 59S 75 11W
Aguaro-Guariquito △, Venezuela 89 E6 8 20N 66 35W
Aguas Blancas, Chile 94 A2 24 15S 69 55W
Aguas Calientes, Sierra de,
  Argentina 94 B2 25 26S 66 40W
Aguascalientes, Mexico 86 C4 21 53N 102 12W
Aguascalientes □, Mexico 86 C4 22 0N 102 20W
Aguila, Punta, Puerto Rico ... 89 d 17 57N 67 13W
Aguilares, Argentina 94 B2 27 26S 65 35W
Aguilas, Spain 21 D5 37 23N 1 35W
Agüimes, Canary Is. 24 G4 27 58N 15 27W
Aguja, C. de la, Colombia 90 B3 11 18N 74 12W
Agujereada, Pta., Puerto Rico . 89 d 18 30N 67 8W
Agulhas, C., S. Africa .... 56 E3 34 52S 20 0 E
Agulo, Canary Is. 24 F2 28 11N 17 12W
Agung, Gunung, Indonesia ... 36 F5 8 20S 115 28 E
Agur, Uganda .... 54 B3 2 28N 32 55 E
Agusan →, Phil. .... 37 C7 9 0N 125 30 E
Aha Mts., Botswana .... 56 B3 19 45S 21 0 E
Ahaggar, Algeria .... 50 D7 23 0N 6 30 E
Ahar, Iran .... 44 B5 38 35N 47 0 E
Ahipara B., N.Z. .... 59 F4 35 5S 173 5 E
Ahiri, India .... 40 K12 19 30N 80 0 E
Ahmad Wal, Pakistan .... 42 E1 29 18N 65 58 E
Ahmadabad, India .... 42 H5 23 0N 72 40 E
Aḥmadābād, Khorāsān, Iran .. 45 C9 35 3N 60 50 E
Aḥmadābād, Khorāsān, Iran .. 45 C8 35 49N 59 42 E
Aḥmadī, Iran .... 45 E8 27 56N 56 42 E
Ahmadnagar, India .... 40 K9 19 7N 74 46 E
Ahmadpur, Pakistan .... 42 E4 29 12N 71 10 E
Ahmadpur Lamma, Pakistan .. 42 E4 28 19N 70 3 E
Ahmedabad = Ahmadabad, India 42 H5 23 0N 72 40 E
Ahmednagar = Ahmadnagar,
  India .... 40 K9 19 7N 74 46 E
Ahome, Mexico 86 B3 25 55N 109 11W
Ahoskie, U.S.A. 83 G7 36 17N 76 59W
Ahram, Iran .... 45 D6 28 52N 51 16 E
Ahrax Pt., Malta .... 25 D1 36 0N 14 22 E
Āhū, Iran .... 45 C6 34 33N 50 2 E
Ahuachapán, El Salv. 88 D2 13 54N 89 52W
Ahvāz, Iran .... 45 D6 31 20N 48 40 E
Ahvenanmaa = Åland, Finland . 9 F19 60 15N 20 0 E
Aḩwar, Yemen .... 47 E4 13 30N 46 40 E
Ai →, India .... 43 F14 26 26N 90 44 E
Ai-Ais, Namibia .... 56 D2 27 54S 17 59 E
Ai-Ais and Fish River Canyon △,
  Namibia .... 56 C2 24 45S 17 15 E
Aichi □, Japan .... 31 G8 35 0N 137 15 E
Aigua, Uruguay 95 C5 34 13S 54 46W
Aigues-Mortes, France .... 20 E6 43 35N 4 12 E
Aihui, China .... 33 A7 50 10N 127 30 E
Aikawa, Japan .... 30 E9 38 2N 138 15 E
Aiken, U.S.A. 83 J5 33 34N 81 43W
Aileron, Australia .... 62 C1 22 39S 133 20 E
Ailik, Canada 73 A8 55 11N 59 18W
Ailsa Craig, U.K. 11 F3 55 15N 5 6W
Aim, Russia .... 29 D14 59 0N 133 55 E
Aimere, Indonesia .... 37 F6 8 45S 121 3 E
Aimogasta, Argentina 94 B2 28 33S 66 50W
Aïn Ben Tili, Mauritania 50 C4 25 59N 9 27W
Aïn Sefra, Algeria 50 B5 32 47N 0 37W
Ainaži, Latvia .... 9 H21 57 50N 24 24 E
Ainsworth, U.S.A. 80 D5 42 33N 99 52W
Aiquile, Bolivia 92 G5 18 10S 65 10W

Aïr, Niger .... 50 E7 18 30N 8 0 E
Air Force I., Canada 69 B12 67 58N 74 5W
Air Hitam, Malaysia .... 39 M4 1 55N 103 11 E
Airdrie, Canada 70 C6 51 18N 114 2W
Airdrie, U.K. 11 F5 55 52N 3 57W
Aire →, U.K. 12 D7 53 43N 0 55W
Aire, I. de l', Spain .... 24 B11 39 48N 4 16 E
Airlie Beach, Australia .... 62 J6 20 16S 148 43 E
Aisne →, France .... 20 B5 49 26N 2 50 E
Ait, India .... 43 G8 25 54N 79 14 E
Aitkin, U.S.A. 80 B8 46 32N 93 42W
Aiud, Romania .... 17 E12 46 19N 23 44 E
Aix-en-Provence, France ...... 20 E6 43 32N 5 27 E
Aix-la-Chapelle = Aachen,
  Germany .... 16 C4 50 45N 6 6 E
Aix-les-Bains, France .... 20 D6 45 41N 5 53 E
Aíyion, Greece .... 23 E10 38 15N 22 5 E
Aizawl, India .... 41 H18 23 40N 92 44 E
Aizkraukle, Latvia .... 9 H21 56 36N 25 11 E
Aizpute, Latvia .... 9 H19 56 43N 21 40 E
Aizuwakamatsu, Japan .... 30 F9 37 30N 139 56 E
Ajaccio, France .... 20 F8 41 55N 8 40 E
Ajai →, Uganda .... 54 B3 2 52N 31 16 E
Ajaigarh, India .... 43 G9 24 52N 80 16 E
Ajalpan, Mexico 87 D5 18 22N 97 15W
Ajanta Ra., India .... 40 J9 20 28N 75 50 E
Ajari Rep. = Ajaria □, Georgia . 19 F7 41 30N 42 0 E
Ajaria □, Georgia .... 19 F7 41 30N 42 0 E
Ajax, Canada 84 C5 43 50N 79 1W
Ajdābiyā, Libya .... 51 B10 30 54N 20 4 E
Ajka, Hungary .... 17 E9 47 4N 17 31 E
'Ajlūn, Jordan .... 46 C4 32 18N 35 47 E
'Ajlūn □, Jordan .... 46 C4 32 18N 35 47 E
'Ajmān, U.A.E. .... 45 E7 25 25N 55 30 E
Ajmer, India .... 42 F6 26 28N 74 37 E
Ajnala, India .... 42 D6 31 50N 74 48 E
Ajo, U.S.A. 77 K7 32 22N 112 52W
Ajo, C. de, Spain 21 A4 43 31N 3 35W
Akabira, Japan .... 30 C11 43 33N 142 5 E
Akagera △, Rwanda .... 54 C3 1 31S 30 33 E
Akamas, Cyprus .... 25 D11 35 3N 32 18 E
Akan △, Japan .... 30 C12 43 20N 144 20 E
Akanthou, Cyprus .... 25 D12 35 22N 33 45 E
Akaroa, N.Z. .... 59 K4 43 49S 172 59 E
Akashi, Japan .... 31 G7 34 45N 134 58 E
Akbarpur, Bihar, India ...... 43 G10 24 39N 83 58 E
Akbarpur, Ut. P., India .... 43 F10 26 25N 82 32 E
Akelamo, Indonesia .... 37 D7 1 35N 129 40 E
Aketi, Dem. Rep. of the Congo . 52 D4 2 38N 23 47 E
Akharnaí, Greece .... 23 E10 38 5N 23 44 E
Akhelóös →, Greece .... 23 E9 38 19N 21 7 E
Akhisar, Turkey .... 23 E12 38 56N 27 48 E
Akhnur, India .... 43 C6 32 52N 74 45 E
Akhtyrka = Okhtyrka, Ukraine . 19 D5 50 25N 35 0 E
Aki, Japan .... 31 H6 33 30N 133 54 E
Akimiski I., Canada 72 B3 52 50N 81 30W
Akita, Japan .... 30 E10 39 45N 140 7 E
Akita □, Japan .... 30 E10 39 40N 140 30 E
Akjoujt, Mauritania 50 E3 19 45N 14 15W
Akkeshi, Japan .... 30 C12 43 2N 144 51 E
'Akko, Israel .... 46 C4 32 55N 35 4 E
Aklavik, Canada 68 B6 68 12N 135 0W
Aklera, India .... 42 G7 24 26N 76 32 E
Akō, Japan .... 31 G7 34 45N 134 24 E
Akola, India .... 40 J10 20 42N 77 2 E
Akordat, Eritrea .... 47 D2 15 30N 37 40 E
Akpatok I., Canada 69 B13 60 25N 68 8W
Ákrahamn, Norway .... 9 G11 59 15N 5 10 E
Akranes, Iceland 8 D2 64 19N 22 5W
Akron, Colo., U.S.A. 80 E3 40 10N 103 13W
Akron, Ohio, U.S.A. 84 E3 41 5N 81 31W
Akrotiri, Cyprus .... 25 E11 34 36N 32 57 E
Akrotiri Bay, Cyprus .... 25 E12 34 35N 33 10 E
Aksai Chin, China .... 43 B8 35 15N 79 55 E
Aksaray, Turkey .... 19 G5 38 25N 34 2 E
Aksay, Kazakhstan .... 19 D9 51 11N 53 0 E
Akşehir, Turkey .... 44 B1 38 18N 31 30 E
Akşehir Gölü, Turkey .... 19 G5 38 30N 31 25 E
Aksu, China .... 32 B3 41 5N 80 10 E
Aksum, Ethiopia .... 47 E2 14 5N 38 40 E
Aktogay, Kazakhstan .... 28 E8 46 57N 79 40 E
Aktsyabrski, Belarus .... 17 B15 52 38N 28 53 E
Aktyubinsk = Aqtöbe, Kazakhstan 19 D10 50 17N 57 10 E
Akure, Nigeria .... 50 G7 7 15N 5 5 E
Akureyri, Iceland 8 D4 65 40N 18 6W
Akuseki-Shima, Japan .... 31 K4 29 27N 129 37 E
Akyab = Sittwe, Burma ...... 41 J18 20 18N 92 45 E
Al 'Adan, Yemen .... 47 E4 12 45N 45 0 E
Al Ahsā = Hasa □, Si. Arabia . 45 E6 25 50N 49 0 E
Al Amādīyah, Iraq .... 44 B4 37 5N 43 30 E
Al 'Amārah, Iraq .... 44 D5 31 55N 47 15 E
Al 'Aqabah, Jordan .... 46 F4 29 31N 35 0 E
Al 'Aqabah □, Jordan .... 46 F4 29 40N 35 5 E
Al Arak, Syria .... 44 C3 34 38N 38 35 E
Al 'Aramah, Si. Arabia .... 44 E5 25 30N 46 0 E
Al Arṭāwīyah, Si. Arabia ..... 44 E5 26 31N 45 20 E
Al 'Āşimah = 'Ammān □, Jordan 46 D5 31 40N 36 30 E
Al 'Assāfīyah, Si. Arabia ..... 44 D3 28 17N 38 59 E
Al 'Ayn, Si. Arabia .... 44 E3 25 4N 38 6 E
Al 'Ayn, U.A.E. .... 45 E7 24 15N 55 45 E
Al 'Azīzīyah, Iraq .... 44 C5 32 54N 45 4 E
Al Bāb, Syria .... 44 B3 36 23N 37 29 E
Al Bad', Si. Arabia .... 44 D2 28 28N 35 1 E
Al Bādī, Iraq .... 44 C4 35 56N 41 32 E
Al Baḩrah, Kuwait .... 44 D5 29 40N 47 52 E
Al Baḩral Mayyit = Dead Sea,
  Asia .... 46 D4 31 30N 35 30 E
Al Balqā □, Jordan .... 46 C4 32 5N 35 45 E
Al Bārūk, J., Lebanon .... 46 B4 33 39N 35 40 E
Al Başrah, Iraq .... 44 D5 30 30N 47 50 E
Al Baṭḩā, Iraq .... 44 D5 31 6N 45 53 E
Al Batrūn, Lebanon .... 46 A4 34 15N 35 40 E
Al Bayḍā, Lebanon .... 46 B10 32 30N 21 40 E
Al Bi'r, Si. Arabia .... 44 D3 28 51N 36 16 E
Al Burayj, Syria .... 46 A5 34 15N 36 46 E
Al Faḑilī, Si. Arabia .... 45 E6 26 58N 49 10 E
Al Fallūjah, Iraq .... 44 C4 33 20N 43 55 E
Al Fāw, Iraq .... 45 D6 30 0N 48 30 E
Al Fujayrah, U.A.E. .... 45 E8 25 7N 56 18 E
Al Ghadaf, W. →, Jordan .... 46 D5 31 26N 36 43 E
Al Ghammās, Iraq .... 44 D5 31 45N 44 37 E
Al Ghazālah, Si. Arabia ...... 44 E4 26 48N 41 19 E
Al Haḑr, Iraq .... 44 C4 35 35N 42 44 E
Al Hājanah, Syria .... 46 B5 33 20N 36 33 E

Al Ḩajar al Gharbī, Oman ..... 45 E8 24 10N 56 15 E
Al Ḩāmad, Si. Arabia ..... 44 D3 31 30N 39 30 E
Al Ḩamdānīyah, Syria ..... 44 C3 35 25N 36 50 E
Al Ḩamīdīyah, Syria ..... 46 A4 34 42N 35 57 E
Al Ḩammār, Iraq ..... 44 D5 30 57N 46 51 E
Al Ḩamrā', Si. Arabia ..... 44 E3 24 2N 38 55 E
Al Ḩamzah, Iraq ..... 44 D5 31 43N 44 58 E
Al Ḩarīr, W. →, Syria ..... 46 C4 32 44N 35 59 E
Al Ḩasā, W. →, Jordan ..... 46 D4 31 4N 35 29 E
Al Ḩasakah, Syria ..... 44 B4 36 35N 40 45 E
Al Ḩawy, W. →, Jordan ..... 46 D4 31 29N 35 34 E
Al Ḩayy, Iraq ..... 44 C5 32 5N 46 5 E
Al Ḩijarah, Asia ..... 44 D4 30 0N 44 0 E
Al Ḩillah, Iraq ..... 44 C5 32 30N 44 25 E
Al Ḩillah, Si. Arabia ..... 47 B4 23 35N 46 50 E
Al Ḩindīyah, Iraq ..... 44 C5 32 30N 44 10 E
Al Ḩirmil, Lebanon ..... 46 A5 34 26N 36 24 E
Al Hoceïma, Morocco 50 A5 35 8N 3 58W
Al Ḩudaydah, Yemen ..... 47 E3 14 50N 43 0 E
Al Ḩufūf, Si. Arabia ..... 45 E6 25 25N 49 45 E
Al Ḩumaydah, Si. Arabia ..... 44 D2 29 14N 34 56 E
Al Ḩunayy, Si. Arabia ..... 45 E6 25 58N 48 45 E
Al Isāwīyah, Si. Arabia ..... 44 D3 30 43N 37 59 E
Al Jafr, Jordan ..... 46 E5 30 18N 36 14 E
Al Jāfūrah, Si. Arabia ..... 45 E7 25 0N 50 15 E
Al Jaghbūb, Libya ..... 51 C10 29 42N 24 38 E
Al Jahrah, Kuwait ..... 44 D5 29 25N 47 40 E
Al Jalāmīd, Si. Arabia ..... 44 D3 31 20N 40 6 E
Al Jamalīyah, Qatar ..... 45 E6 25 37N 51 5 E
Al Janūb □, Lebanon ..... 46 B4 33 20N 35 20 E
Al Jawf, Libya ..... 51 D10 24 10N 23 24 E
Al Jawf, Si. Arabia ..... 44 D3 29 55N 39 40 E
Al Jazirah, Iraq ..... 44 C5 33 30N 44 0 E
Al Jithāmīyah, Si. Arabia ..... 44 E4 27 41N 41 43 E
Al Jubayl, Si. Arabia ..... 45 E6 27 0N 49 50 E
Al Jubaylah, Si. Arabia ..... 44 E5 24 55N 46 25 E
Al Jubb, Si. Arabia ..... 44 E4 27 11N 42 17 E
Al Junaynah, Sudan ..... 51 F10 13 27N 22 45 E
Al Kabā'ish, Iraq ..... 44 D5 30 58N 47 0 E
Al Karak, Jordan ..... 46 D4 31 11N 35 42 E
Al Karak □, Jordan ..... 46 E5 31 0N 36 0 E
Al Kāẓimīyah, Iraq ..... 44 C5 33 22N 44 18 E
Al Khābūra, Oman ..... 45 F8 23 57N 57 5 E
Al Khafjī, Si. Arabia ..... 45 E6 28 24N 48 29 E
Al Khalīl, West Bank ..... 46 D4 31 32N 35 6 E
Al Khāliṣ, Iraq ..... 44 C5 33 49N 44 32 E
Al Kharsānīyah, Si. Arabia ..... 45 E6 27 13N 49 18 E
Al Khaṣab, Oman ..... 45 E8 26 14N 56 15 E
Al Khawr, Qatar ..... 45 E6 25 41N 51 30 E
Al Khiḍr, Iraq ..... 44 D5 31 12N 45 33 E
Al Khiyām, Lebanon ..... 46 B4 33 20N 35 36 E
Al Khums, Libya ..... 51 B8 32 40N 14 17 E
Al Kiswah, Syria ..... 46 B5 33 23N 36 14 E
Al Kūfah, Iraq ..... 44 C5 32 2N 44 24 E
Al Kufrah, Libya ..... 51 D10 24 17N 23 15 E
Al Kuhayfīyah, Si. Arabia ..... 44 E4 27 12N 43 3 E
Al Kūt, Iraq ..... 44 C5 32 30N 46 0 E
Al Kuwayt, Kuwait ..... 44 D5 29 30N 48 0 E
Al Labwah, Lebanon ..... 46 A5 34 11N 36 20 E
Al Lādhiqīyah, Syria ..... 44 C2 35 30N 35 45 E
Al Līth, Si. Arabia ..... 47 C3 20 9N 40 15 E
Al Liwā', Oman ..... 45 E8 24 31N 56 36 E
Al Luḩayyah, Yemen ..... 47 D3 15 45N 42 40 E
Al Madīnah, Iraq ..... 44 D5 30 57N 47 16 E
Al Madīnah, Si. Arabia ..... 44 E3 24 35N 39 52 E
Al Mafraq, Jordan ..... 46 C5 32 17N 36 14 E
Al Mafraq □, Jordan ..... 46 C5 32 17N 36 15 E
Al Maḩmūdīyah, Iraq ..... 44 C5 33 3N 44 21 E
Al Majma'ah, Si. Arabia ..... 44 E5 25 57N 45 22 E
Al Makhruq, W. →, Jordan ..... 46 D6 31 28N 37 0 E
Al Makhūl, Si. Arabia ..... 44 E4 26 37N 42 39 E
Al Manāmah, Bahrain ..... 45 E6 26 10N 50 30 E
Al Maqwa', Kuwait ..... 44 D5 29 10N 47 59 E
Al Marj, Libya ..... 51 B10 32 25N 20 30 E
Al Maṭlā, Kuwait ..... 44 D5 29 24N 47 40 E
Al Mawjib, W. →, Jordan ..... 46 D4 31 28N 35 36 E
Al Mawṣil, Iraq ..... 44 B4 36 15N 43 5 E
Al Mayādin, Syria ..... 44 C4 35 1N 40 27 E
Al Mazar, Jordan ..... 46 D4 31 4N 35 41 E
Al Midhnab, Si. Arabia ..... 44 E5 25 50N 44 18 E
Al Minā', Lebanon ..... 46 A4 34 24N 35 49 E
Al Miqdādīyah, Iraq ..... 44 C5 34 0N 45 0 E
Al Mubarraz, Si. Arabia ..... 45 E6 25 30N 49 40 E
Al Mudawwarah, Jordan ..... 46 F5 29 19N 36 0 E
Al Mughayrā', U.A.E. ..... 45 E7 24 5N 53 32 E
Al Muḩarraq, Bahrain ..... 45 E6 26 15N 50 40 E
Al Mukallā, Yemen ..... 47 E4 14 33N 49 2 E
Al Mukhā, Yemen ..... 47 E3 13 18N 43 15 E
Al Musayjīd, Si. Arabia ..... 44 E3 24 5N 39 5 E
Al Musayyib, Iraq ..... 44 C5 32 49N 44 20 E
Al Muthanná □, Iraq ..... 44 D5 30 30N 45 15 E
Al Muwaylih, Si. Arabia ..... 44 E2 27 40N 35 30 E
Al Qādisīyah □, Iraq ..... 44 D5 32 0N 45 0 E
Al Qā'im, Iraq ..... 44 C4 34 21N 41 7 E
Al Qalībah, Si. Arabia ..... 44 D3 28 24N 37 42 E
Al Qāmishlī, Syria ..... 44 B4 37 2N 41 14 E
Al Qaryatayn, Syria ..... 46 A6 34 12N 37 13 E
Al Qaṣim, Si. Arabia ..... 44 E4 26 0N 43 0 E
Al Qaṭ'ā, Syria ..... 44 C4 34 40N 40 48 E
Al Qaṭīf, Si. Arabia ..... 45 E6 26 35N 50 0 E
Al Qaṭrānah, Jordan ..... 46 D5 31 12N 36 6 E
Al Qaṭrūn, Libya ..... 51 D9 24 56N 15 3 E
Al Qayṣūmah, Si. Arabia ..... 44 D5 28 20N 46 7 E
Al Quds = Jerusalem, Israel ..... 46 D4 31 47N 35 10 E
Al Qunayṭirah, Syria ..... 46 C4 32 55N 35 45 E
Al Qurnah, Iraq ..... 44 D5 31 1N 47 25 E
Al Quṣayr, Iraq ..... 44 D5 30 39N 45 50 E
Al Quṣayr, Syria ..... 46 A5 34 31N 36 34 E
Al Quṭayfah, Syria ..... 46 B5 33 44N 36 36 E
Al 'Ubaylah, Si. Arabia ..... 47 C5 21 59N 50 57 E
Al 'Udaylīyah, Si. Arabia ..... 45 E6 25 8N 49 18 E
Al 'Ulā, Si. Arabia ..... 44 E3 26 35N 38 0 E
Al 'Uwaynid, Si. Arabia ..... 44 E5 24 50N 46 0 E
Al 'Uwayqīlah, Si. Arabia ..... 44 D4 30 30N 42 10 E
Al 'Uyūn, Ḩijāz, Si. Arabia ..... 44 E3 24 33N 39 35 E
Al 'Uyūn, Najd, Si. Arabia ..... 44 E4 26 30N 43 50 E
Al 'Uzayr, Iraq ..... 44 D5 31 19N 47 25 E
Al Wakrah, Qatar ..... 45 E6 25 10N 51 40 E
Al Waqbah, Si. Arabia ..... 44 D5 28 48N 45 33 E
Al Wari'ah, Si. Arabia ..... 44 E5 27 51N 47 25 E
Ala Dağ, Turkey ..... 44 B2 37 44N 35 9 E
Ala Tau Shankou = Dzungarian Gates, Asia ..... 32 B3 45 0N 82 0 E
Alabama □, U.S.A. 83 J2 33 0N 87 0W
Alabama →, U.S.A. 83 K2 31 8N 87 57W

Alabaster, U.S.A. 83 J2 33 15N 86 49W
Alaçam Dağları, Turkey ..... 23 E13 39 18N 28 49 E
Alacant = Alicante, Spain 21 C5 38 23N 0 30W
Alachua, U.S.A. 83 L4 29 47N 82 30W
Alaérma, Greece ..... 25 C9 36 9N 27 57 E
Alagoa Grande, Brazil 93 E11 7 3S 35 35W
Alagoas □, Brazil 93 E11 9 0S 36 0W
Alagoinhas, Brazil 93 F11 12 7S 38 20W
Alaior, Spain ..... 24 B11 39 57N 4 8 E
Alajero, Canary Is. 24 F2 28 3N 17 13W
Alajuela, Costa Rica 88 D3 10 2N 84 8W
Alakamisy, Madag. ..... 57 C8 21 19S 47 14 E
Alaknanda →, India ..... 43 D8 30 8N 78 36 E
Alakurtti, Russia ..... 18 A5 67 0N 30 30 E
Alamarvdasht, Iran ..... 45 E7 27 37N 52 59 E
Alameda, Calif., U.S.A. 78 H4 37 46N 122 15W
Alameda, N. Mex., U.S.A. 77 J10 35 11N 106 37W
Alamo, U.S.A. 79 J11 37 22N 115 10W
Alamo Crossing, U.S.A. 79 L13 34 16N 113 33W
Alamogordo, U.S.A. 77 K11 32 54N 105 57W
Alamos, Mexico 86 B3 27 0N 109 0W
Alamosa, U.S.A. 77 H11 37 28N 105 52W
Åland, Finland ..... 9 F19 60 15N 20 0 E
Ålands hav, Sweden ..... 9 F18 60 0N 19 30 E
Alania = North Ossetia □, Russia ..... 19 F7 43 30N 44 30 E
Alanya, Turkey ..... 19 G5 36 38N 32 0 E
Alaotra, Farihin', Madag. ..... 57 B8 17 30S 48 30 E
Alapayevsk, Russia ..... 28 D7 57 52N 61 42 E
Alappuzha = Alleppey, India ..... 40 Q10 9 30N 76 28 E
Alarobia-Vohiposa, Madag. ..... 57 C8 20 59S 47 9 E
Alaşehir, Turkey ..... 23 E13 38 23N 28 30 E
Alaska □, U.S.A. 68 B5 64 0N 154 0W
Alaska, G. of, Pac. Oc. 68 C5 58 0N 145 0W
Alaska Peninsula, U.S.A. 68 C4 56 0N 159 0W
Alaska Range, U.S.A. 68 B4 62 50N 151 0W
Älät, Azerbaijan ..... 19 G8 39 58N 49 25 E
Alatyr, Russia ..... 18 D8 54 55N 46 35 E
Alausi, Ecuador 92 D3 2 0S 78 50W
Alava, C., U.S.A. 76 B1 48 10N 124 44W
Alavus, Finland ..... 9 E20 62 35N 23 36 E
Alawoona, Australia ..... 63 E3 34 45S 140 30 E
'Alayh, Lebanon ..... 46 B4 33 46N 35 33 E
Alba, Italy ..... 20 D8 44 42N 8 2 E
Alba-Iulia, Romania ..... 17 E12 46 8N 23 39 E
Albacete, Spain 21 C5 39 0N 1 50W
Albacutya, L., Australia ..... 63 F3 35 45S 141 58 E
Albanel, L., Canada 72 B5 50 55N 73 12W
Albania ■, Europe ..... 23 D9 41 0N 20 0 E
Albany, Australia ..... 61 G2 35 1S 117 58 E
Albany, Ga., U.S.A. 83 K3 31 35N 84 10W
Albany, N.Y., U.S.A. 85 D11 42 39N 73 45W
Albany, Oreg., U.S.A. 76 D2 44 38N 123 6W
Albany, Tex., U.S.A. 81 J5 32 44N 99 18W
Albany →, Canada 72 B3 52 17N 81 31W
Albardón, Argentina 94 C2 31 20S 68 30W
Albatross B., Australia ..... 62 A3 12 45S 141 30 E
Albemarle, U.S.A. 83 H5 35 21N 80 11W
Albemarle Sd., U.S.A. 83 H7 36 5N 76 0W
Alberche →, Spain 21 C3 39 58N 4 46W
Alberdi, Paraguay 94 B4 26 14S 58 20W
Albert, L., Africa ..... 54 B3 1 30N 31 0 E
Albert, L., Australia ..... 63 F2 35 30S 139 10 E
Albert Edward Ra., Australia ..... 60 C4 18 17S 127 57 E
Albert Lea, U.S.A. 80 D8 43 39N 93 22W
Albert Nile →, Uganda ..... 54 B3 3 36N 32 2 E
Albert Town, Bahamas 89 B5 22 37N 74 33W
Alberta □, Canada 70 C6 54 40N 115 0W
Alberti, Argentina 94 D3 35 1S 60 16W
Albertinia, S. Africa ..... 56 E3 34 11S 21 34 E
Alberton, Canada 73 C7 46 50N 64 0W
Albertville, France ..... 20 D7 45 40N 6 22 E
Albertville, U.S.A. 83 H2 34 16N 86 13W
Albi, France ..... 20 E5 43 56N 2 9 E
Albia, U.S.A. 80 E8 41 2N 92 48W
Albina, Suriname 93 B8 5 37N 54 15W
Albina, Ponta, Angola ..... 56 B1 15 52S 11 44 E
Albion, Mich., U.S.A. 82 D3 42 15N 84 45W
Albion, Nebr., U.S.A. 80 E6 41 42N 98 0W
Albion, Pa., U.S.A. 84 E4 41 53N 80 22W
Alborán, Medit. S. 21 E4 35 57N 3 0W
Ålborg, Denmark ..... 9 H13 57 2N 9 54 E
Alborz, Reshteh-ye Kūhhā-ye, Iran ..... 45 C7 36 0N 52 0 E
Albuquerque, U.S.A. 77 J10 35 5N 106 39W
Albuquerque, Cayos de, Caribbean 88 D3 12 10N 81 50W
Alburg, U.S.A. 85 B11 44 59N 73 18W
Albury = Albury-Wodonga, Australia ..... 63 F4 36 3S 146 56 E
Albury-Wodonga, Australia ..... 63 F4 36 3S 146 56 E
Alcalá de Henares, Spain 21 B4 40 28N 3 22W
Alcalá la Real, Spain 21 D4 37 27N 3 57W
Álcamo, Italy ..... 22 F5 37 59N 12 55 E
Alcañiz, Spain 21 B5 41 2N 0 8W
Alcântara, Brazil 93 D10 2 20S 44 30W
Alcántara, Embalse de, Spain 21 C2 39 44N 6 50W
Alcantarilla, Spain 21 D5 37 59N 1 12W
Alcaraz, Sierra de, Spain 21 C4 38 40N 2 20W
Alcaudete, Spain 21 D3 37 35N 4 5W
Alcázar de San Juan, Spain 21 C4 39 24N 3 12W
Alchevsk, Ukraine ..... 19 E6 48 30N 38 45 E
Alcira = Alzira, Spain 21 C5 39 9N 0 30W
Alcova, U.S.A. 76 E10 42 34N 106 43W
Alcoy, Spain 21 C5 38 43N 0 30W
Alcúdia, Spain ..... 24 B10 39 51N 3 7 E
Alcúdia, B. d', Spain ..... 24 B10 39 47N 3 15 E
Aldabra Is., Seychelles ..... 49 G8 9 22S 46 28 E
Aldama, Mexico 87 C5 23 0N 98 4W
Aldan, Russia ..... 29 D13 58 40N 125 30 E
Aldan →, Russia ..... 29 C13 63 28N 129 35 E
Aldea, Pta. de la, Canary Is. 24 G4 28 0N 15 50W
Aldeburgh, U.K. ..... 13 E9 52 10N 1 37 E
Alder Pk., U.S.A. 78 K5 35 53N 121 22W
Aldershot, U.K. 13 F7 51 15N 0 44W
Aledo, U.S.A. 80 E9 41 12N 90 45W
Aleg, Mauritania 50 E3 17 3N 13 55W
Alegranza, Canary Is. 24 E6 29 23N 13 32W
Alegranza, I., Canary Is. 24 E6 29 23N 13 32W
Alegre, Brazil 95 A7 20 50S 41 30W
Alegrete, Brazil 95 B4 29 40S 56 0W
Aleisk, Russia ..... 28 D9 52 40N 83 0 E
Aleksandriya = Oleksandriya, Ukraine ..... 17 C14 50 37N 26 19 E
Aleksandrov Gay, Russia ..... 19 D8 50 9N 48 34 E
Aleksandrovsk-Sakhalinskiy, Russia ..... 29 D15 50 50N 142 20 E
Aleksandry, Z., Russia ..... 4 A10 80 25N 48 0 E

Além Paraíba, Brazil 95 A7 21 52S 42 41W
Alemania, Argentina 94 B2 25 40S 65 30W
Alemania, Chile 94 B2 25 10S 69 55W
Alençon, France ..... 20 B4 48 27N 0 4 E
Alenquer, Brazil 93 D8 1 56S 54 46W
Alenuihaha Channel, U.S.A. 74 H17 20 30N 156 0W
Aleppo = Ḩalab, Syria ..... 44 B3 36 10N 37 15 E
Alert, Canada 4 A4 83 2N 60 0W
Alès, France ..... 20 D6 44 9N 4 5 E
Alessándria, Italy ..... 20 D8 44 54N 8 37 E
Ålesund, Norway ..... 9 E12 62 28N 6 12 E
Aleutian Is., Pac. Oc. 68 C2 52 0N 175 0W
Aleutian Trench, Pac. Oc. ..... 64 C10 48 0N 180 0 E
Alexander, U.S.A. 80 B3 47 51N 103 39W
Alexander, Mt., Australia ..... 61 E3 28 58S 120 16 E
Alexander Arch., U.S.A. 68 C6 56 0N 136 0W
Alexander Bay, S. Africa ..... 56 D2 28 40S 16 30 E
Alexander City, U.S.A. 83 J3 32 56N 85 58W
Alexander I., Antarctica 5 C17 69 0N 70 0W
Alexandra, Australia ..... 63 F4 37 8S 145 40 E
Alexandra, N.Z. ..... 59 L2 45 14S 169 25 E
Alexandra Falls, Canada 70 A5 60 29N 116 18W
Alexandria = El Iskandarîya, Egypt ..... 51 B11 31 13N 29 58 E
Alexandria, B.C., Canada 70 C4 52 35N 122 27W
Alexandria, Ont., Canada 85 A10 45 19N 74 38W
Alexandria, Romania ..... 17 G13 43 57N 25 24 E
Alexandria, S. Africa ..... 56 E4 33 38S 26 28 E
Alexandria, U.K. 11 F4 55 59N 4 35W
Alexandria, La., U.S.A. 81 K8 31 18N 92 27W
Alexandria, Minn., U.S.A. 80 C7 45 53N 95 22W
Alexandria, S. Dak., U.S.A. 80 D6 43 39N 97 47W
Alexandria, Va., U.S.A. 82 F7 38 48N 77 3W
Alexandria Bay, U.S.A. 85 B9 44 20N 75 55W
Alexandrina, L., Australia ..... 63 F2 35 25S 139 10 E
Alexandroúpolis, Greece ..... 23 D11 40 50N 25 54 E
Alexis →, Canada 73 B8 52 33N 56 8W
Alexis Creek, Canada 70 C4 52 10N 123 20W
Alfabia, Spain ..... 24 B9 39 44N 2 44 E
Alfenas, Brazil 95 A6 21 20S 46 10W
Alford, Aberds., U.K. 11 D6 57 14N 2 41W
Alford, Lincs., U.K. ..... 12 D8 53 15N 0 10 E
Alfred, Maine, U.S.A. 85 C14 43 29N 70 43W
Alfred, N.Y., U.S.A. 84 D7 42 16N 77 48W
Alfreton, U.K. 12 D6 53 6N 1 24W
Alga, Kazakhstan ..... 19 E10 49 53N 57 20 E
Algaida, Spain ..... 24 B9 39 33N 2 53 E
Ålgård, Norway ..... 9 G11 58 46N 5 53 E
Algarve, Portugal 21 D1 36 58N 8 20W
Algeciras, Spain 21 D3 36 9N 5 28W
Algemesí, Spain 21 C5 39 11N 0 27W
Alger, Algeria ..... 50 A6 36 42N 3 8 E
Algeria ■, Africa ..... 50 C6 28 30N 2 0 E
Alghero, Italy ..... 22 D3 40 33N 8 19 E
Algiers = Alger, Algeria ..... 50 A6 36 42N 3 8 E
Algoa B., S. Africa ..... 56 E4 33 50S 25 45 E
Algoma, U.S.A. 82 C2 44 36N 87 26W
Algona, U.S.A. 80 D7 43 4N 94 14W
Algonac, U.S.A. 84 D2 42 37N 82 32W
Algonquin ⌒, Canada 72 C4 45 50N 78 30W
Algorta, Uruguay 96 C5 32 25S 57 23W
Alhambra, U.S.A. 79 L8 34 8N 118 6W
Alhucemas = Al Hoceïma, Morocco 50 A5 35 8N 3 58W
'Alī al Gharbī, Iraq ..... 44 C5 32 30N 46 45 E
'Alī ash Sharqī, Iraq ..... 44 C5 32 7N 46 44 E
'Alī Khēl, Afghan. ..... 42 C3 33 57N 69 43 E
Alī Shāh, Iran ..... 44 B5 38 9N 45 50 E
'Alīābād, Khorāsān, Iran ..... 45 C8 32 30N 57 30 E
'Alīābād, Kordestān, Iran ..... 44 C5 35 4N 46 58 E
'Alīābād, Yazd, Iran ..... 45 D7 31 41N 53 49 E
Aliağa, Turkey ..... 23 E12 38 47N 26 59 E
Aliákmon →, Greece ..... 23 D10 40 30N 22 36 E
Alicante, Spain 21 C5 38 23N 0 30W
Alice, S. Africa ..... 56 E4 32 48S 26 55 E
Alice, U.S.A. 81 M5 27 45N 98 5W
Alice →, Queens., Australia ..... 62 C3 24 2S 144 50 E
Alice →, Queens., Australia ..... 62 B3 15 35S 142 20 E
Alice Arm, Canada 70 B3 55 29N 129 31W
Alice Springs, Australia ..... 62 C1 23 40S 133 50 E
Alicedale, S. Africa ..... 56 E4 33 15S 26 4 E
Aliceville, U.S.A. 83 J1 33 8N 88 9W
Aliganj, India ..... 43 F8 27 30N 79 10 E
Aligarh, Raj., India ..... 42 G7 25 55N 76 15 E
Aligarh, Ut. P., India ..... 42 F8 27 55N 78 10 E
Alīgūdarz, Iran ..... 45 C6 33 25N 49 45 E
Alimnía, Greece ..... 25 C9 36 16N 27 43 E
Alingsås, Sweden ..... 9 H15 57 56N 12 31 E
Alipur, Pakistan ..... 42 E4 29 25N 70 55 E
Alipur Duar, India ..... 41 F16 26 30N 89 35 E
Aliquippa, U.S.A. 84 F4 40 37N 80 15W
Alitus = Alytus, Lithuania ..... 9 J21 54 24N 24 3 E
Aliwal North, S. Africa ..... 56 E4 30 45S 26 45 E
Alix, Canada 70 C6 52 24N 113 11W
Aljustrel, Portugal 21 D1 37 55N 8 10W
Alkmaar, Neths. ..... 15 B4 52 37N 4 45 E
All American Canal, U.S.A. 77 K6 32 45N 115 15W
Allagash →, U.S.A. 83 B11 47 6N 69 3W
Allah Dad, Pakistan ..... 42 G2 25 38N 67 34 E
Allahabad, India ..... 43 G9 25 25N 81 58 E
Allan, Canada 71 C7 51 53N 106 4W
Allanridge, S. Africa ..... 56 D4 27 45S 26 40 E
Allegany, U.S.A. 84 D6 42 6N 78 30W
Allegheny →, U.S.A. 84 F5 40 27N 80 1W
Allegheny Mts., U.S.A. 82 G8 38 15N 80 10W
Allegheny Reservoir, U.S.A. 84 E6 41 50N 79 0W
Allègre, Pte., Guadeloupe ..... 88 b 16 22N 61 46W
Allen, Bog of, Ireland 10 C5 53 15N 7 0W
Allen, L., Ireland 10 B3 54 8N 8 4W
Allendale, U.S.A. 83 J5 33 1N 81 18W
Allende, Mexico 86 B4 28 20N 100 50W
Allentown, U.S.A. 85 F9 40 37N 75 29W
Alleppey, India ..... 40 Q10 9 30N 76 28 E
Aller →, Germany ..... 16 B5 52 56N 9 12 E
Alleynes B., Barbados ..... 89 g 13 13N 59 39W
Alliance, Nebr., U.S.A. 80 D3 42 6N 102 52W
Alliance, Ohio, U.S.A. 84 F3 40 55N 81 6W
Allier →, France ..... 20 C5 46 57N 3 4 E
Alliford Bay, Canada 70 C2 53 12N 131 58W
Alligator Pond, Jamaica ..... 88 a 17 52N 77 34W
Alliston = New Tecumseth, Canada 84 B5 44 9N 79 52W
Alloa, U.K. 11 E5 56 7N 3 47W
Allora, Australia ..... 63 D5 28 2S 152 0 E
Alluitsup Paa, Greenland 4 C5 60 30N 45 35W
Alma, Canada 73 C5 48 35N 71 40W
Alma, Ga., U.S.A. 83 K4 31 33N 82 28W
Alma, Kans., U.S.A. 80 F6 39 1N 96 17W

Alma, Mich., U.S.A. 82 D3 43 23N 84 39W
Alma, Nebr., U.S.A. 80 E5 40 6N 99 22W
Alma Ata = Almaty, Kazakhstan ..... 28 E8 43 15N 76 57 E
Almada, Portugal 21 C1 38 40N 9 9W
Almaden, Australia ..... 62 B3 17 22S 144 40 E
Almadén, Spain 21 C3 38 49N 4 52W
Almanor, L., U.S.A. 76 F3 40 14N 121 9W
Almansa, Spain 21 C5 38 51N 1 5W
Almanzor, Pico, Spain 21 B3 40 15N 5 18W
Almanzora →, Spain 21 D5 37 14N 1 46W
Almaty, Kazakhstan ..... 28 E8 43 15N 76 57 E
Almazán, Spain 21 B4 41 30N 2 30W
Almeirim, Brazil 93 D8 1 30S 52 34W
Almelo, Neths. ..... 15 B6 52 22N 6 42 E
Almendralejo, Spain 21 C2 38 41N 6 26W
Almere-Stad, Neths. ..... 15 B5 52 20N 5 15 E
Almería, Spain 21 D4 36 52N 2 27W
Almirante, Panama 88 E3 9 10N 82 30W
Almirou, Kólpos, Greece ..... 25 D6 35 23N 24 20 E
Almond, U.S.A. 84 D7 42 19N 77 44W
Almont, U.S.A. 84 D1 42 55N 83 3W
Almonte, Canada 85 A8 45 14N 76 12W
Almora, India ..... 43 E8 29 38N 79 40 E
Alness, U.K. 11 D4 57 41N 4 16W
Alnmouth, U.K. 12 B6 55 24N 1 37W
Alnwick, U.K. 12 B6 55 24N 1 42W
Aloi, Uganda ..... 54 B3 2 16N 33 10 E
Alon, Burma ..... 41 H19 22 12N 95 5 E
Alor, Indonesia ..... 37 F6 8 15S 124 30 E
Alor Setar, Malaysia ..... 39 J3 6 7N 100 22 E
Alot, India ..... 42 H6 23 56N 75 40 E
Aloysius, Mt., Australia ..... 61 E4 26 0S 128 38 E
Alpaugh, U.S.A. 78 K7 35 53N 119 29W
Alpena, U.S.A. 82 C4 45 4N 83 27W
Alpha, Australia ..... 62 C4 23 39S 146 37 E
Alpha Cordillera, Arctic 4 A2 84 0N 118 0W
Alphen aan den Rijn, Neths. ..... 15 B4 52 7N 4 40 E
Alpine, Ariz., U.S.A. 77 K9 33 51N 109 9W
Alpine, Calif., U.S.A. 79 N10 32 50N 116 46W
Alpine, Tex., U.S.A. 81 K3 30 22N 103 40W
Alps, Europe ..... 20 C8 46 30N 9 30 E
Alsace □, France ..... 20 B7 48 15N 7 25 E
Alsask, Canada 71 C7 51 21N 109 59W
Alsasua, Spain 21 A4 42 54N 2 10W
Alsek →, U.S.A. 70 B1 59 10N 138 12W
Alsten, Norway ..... 8 D15 65 58N 12 40 E
Alston, U.K. 12 C5 54 49N 2 25W
Alta, Norway ..... 8 B20 69 57N 23 10 E
Alta Gracia, Argentina 94 C3 31 40S 64 30W
Alta Sierra, U.S.A. 79 K8 35 42N 118 33W
Altaelva →, Norway ..... 8 B20 69 54N 23 17 E
Altafjorden, Norway ..... 8 A20 70 5N 23 5 E
Altai = Aerhtai Shan, Mongolia ..... 32 B4 46 40N 92 45 E
Altamaha →, U.S.A. 83 K5 31 20N 81 20W
Altamira, Brazil 93 D8 3 12S 52 10W
Altamira, Chile 94 B2 25 47S 69 51W
Altamira, Mexico 87 C5 22 24N 97 55W
Altamont, U.S.A. 85 D10 42 43N 74 3W
Altamura, Italy ..... 22 D7 40 49N 16 33 E
Altanbulag, Mongolia ..... 32 A5 50 16N 106 30 E
Altar, Mexico 86 A2 30 40N 111 50W
Altar, Desierto de, Mexico 86 B2 30 10N 112 0W
Altata, Mexico 86 C3 24 30N 108 0W
Altavista, U.S.A. 82 G6 37 6N 79 17W
Altay, China ..... 32 B3 47 48N 88 10 E
Altea, Spain ..... 21 C5 38 38N 0 2 E
Altiplano, Bolivia 90 E4 17 0S 68 0W
Alto Araguaia, Brazil 93 G8 17 15S 53 20W
Alto Cuchumatanes = Cuchumatanes, Sierra de los, Guatemala 88 C1 15 35N 91 25W
Alto del Carmen, Chile 94 B1 28 46S 70 30W
Alto del Inca, Chile 94 A2 24 10S 68 10W
Alto Ligonha, Mozam. ..... 55 F4 15 30S 38 11 E
Alto Molocue, Mozam. ..... 55 F4 15 50S 37 35 E
Alto Paraguay □, Paraguay 94 A4 21 0S 58 30W
Alto Paraná □, Paraguay 95 B5 25 30S 54 50W
Alton, Canada 84 C4 43 54N 80 5W
Alton, U.K. 13 F7 51 9N 0 59W
Alton, Ill., U.S.A. 80 F9 38 53N 90 11W
Alton, N.H., U.S.A. 85 C13 43 27N 71 13W
Altona, Canada 71 D9 49 6N 97 33W
Altoona, U.S.A. 84 F6 40 31N 78 24W
Altun Kupri, Iraq ..... 44 C5 35 45N 44 9 E
Altun Shan, China ..... 32 C3 38 30N 88 0 E
Alturas, U.S.A. 76 F3 41 29N 120 32W
Altus, U.S.A. 81 H5 34 38N 99 20W
Alucra, Turkey ..... 19 F6 40 22N 38 47 E
Alūksne, Latvia ..... 9 H22 57 24N 27 3 E
Alunite, U.S.A. 79 K12 35 59N 114 55W
Alusi, Indonesia ..... 37 F8 7 35S 131 40 E
Alva, U.S.A. 81 G5 36 48N 98 40W
Alvarado, Mexico 87 D5 18 40N 95 50W
Alvarado, U.S.A. 81 J6 32 24N 97 13W
Alvaro Obregón, Presa, Mexico 86 B3 27 55N 109 52W
Alvear, Argentina 94 B4 29 5S 56 30W
Alvesta, Sweden ..... 9 H16 56 54N 14 35 E
Alvin, U.S.A. 81 L7 29 26N 95 15W
Alvinston, Canada 84 D3 42 49N 81 52W
Älvkarleby, Sweden ..... 9 F17 60 34N 17 26 E
Alvord Desert, U.S.A. 76 E4 42 30N 118 25W
Älvsbyn, Sweden ..... 8 D19 65 40N 21 0 E
Alwar, India ..... 42 F7 27 38N 76 34 E
Alxa Zuoqi, China ..... 34 E3 38 50N 105 40 E
Alyangula, Australia ..... 62 A2 13 55S 136 30 E
Alyata = Älät, Azerbaijan ..... 19 G8 39 58N 49 25 E
Alyth, U.K. 11 E5 56 38N 3 13W
Alytus, Lithuania ..... 9 J21 54 24N 24 3 E
Alzada, U.S.A. 80 C2 45 2N 104 25W
Alzira, Spain 21 C5 39 9N 0 30W
Am Timan, Chad ..... 51 F10 11 0N 20 10 E
Amadeus, L., Australia ..... 61 D5 24 54S 131 0 E
Amadi, Dem. Rep. of the Congo ..... 54 B2 3 40N 26 40 E
Amâdi, Sudan ..... 51 G12 5 29N 30 25 E
Amadjuak L., Canada 69 B12 65 0N 71 8W
Amagansett, U.S.A. 85 F12 40 59N 72 9W
Amagasaki, Japan ..... 31 G7 34 42N 135 20 E
Amahai, Indonesia ..... 37 E7 3 20S 128 55 E
Åmål, Sweden ..... 9 G15 59 3N 12 42 E
Amaliás, Greece ..... 23 F9 37 47N 21 22 E
Amalner, India ..... 40 J9 21 5N 75 5 E
Amambaí, Brazil 95 A4 23 5S 55 13W
Amambaí →, Brazil 95 A5 23 22S 53 56W
Amambay □, Paraguay 95 A4 23 0S 56 0W
Amambay, Cordillera de, S. Amer. 95 A4 23 0S 55 45W

Amami-Guntō, Japan .... 31 L4 27 16N 129 21 E
Amami-Ō-Shima, Japan ...... 31 L4 28 0N 129 0 E
Aman, Pulau, Malaysia ...... 39 c 5 16N 100 24 E
Amaná, L., Brazil 92 D6 2 35S 64 40W
Amanat →, India .... 43 G11 24 7N 84 4 E
Amanda Park, U.S.A. 78 C3 47 28N 123 55W
Amangeldy, Kazakhstan ..... 28 D7 50 10N 65 10 E
Amapá, Brazil 93 C8 2 5N 50 50W
Amapá □, Brazil 93 C8 1 40N 52 0W
Amarante, Brazil 93 E10 6 14S 42 50W
Amaranth, Canada 71 C9 50 36N 98 43W
Amargosa →, U.S.A. 79 J10 36 14N 116 51W
Amargosa Range, U.S.A. 79 J10 36 20N 116 45W
Amári, Greece .... 25 D6 35 13N 24 40 E
Amarillo, U.S.A. 81 H4 35 13N 101 50W
Amarkantak, India .... 43 H9 22 40N 81 45 E
Amaro, Mte., Italy .... 22 C6 42 5N 14 5 E
Amarpur, India .... 43 G12 25 5N 87 0 E
Amarwara, India .... 43 H8 22 18N 79 10 E
Amasya, Turkey .... 19 F6 40 40N 35 50 E
Amata, Australia .... 61 E5 26 9S 131 9 E
Amatikulu, S. Africa ...... 57 D5 29 3S 31 33 E
Amatitlán, Guatemala 88 D1 14 29N 90 38W
Amay, Belgium .... 15 D5 50 33N 5 19 E
Amazon = Amazonas →,
  S. Amer. 93 D9 0 5S 50 0W
Amazonas □, Brazil 92 E6 5 0S 65 0W
Amazonas →, S. Amer. 93 D9 0 5S 50 0W
Ambah, India .... 42 F8 26 43N 78 13 E
Ambahakily, Madag. ...... 57 C7 21 36S 43 41 E
Ambahita, Madag. .... 57 C8 24 1S 45 16 E
Ambala, India .... 42 D7 30 23N 76 56 E
Ambalavao, Madag. .... 57 C8 21 50S 46 56 E
Ambanja, Madag. .... 57 A8 13 40S 48 27 E
Ambararata, Madag. ...... 57 B8 15 3S 48 33 E
Ambarchik, Russia ...... 29 C17 69 40N 162 20 E
Ambarijeby, Madag. ...... 57 A8 14 56S 47 41 E
Ambaro, Helodranon', Madag. . 57 A8 13 23S 48 38 E
Ambato, Ecuador 92 D3 1 5S 78 42W
Ambato, Madag. .... 57 A8 13 24S 48 29 E
Ambato, Sierra de, Argentina . 94 B2 28 25S 66 10W
Ambato Boeny, Madag. ...... 57 B8 16 28S 46 43 E
Ambatofinandrahana, Madag. . 57 C8 20 33S 46 48 E
Ambatolampy, Madag. ...... 57 B8 19 20S 47 35 E
Ambatomainty, Madag. ...... 57 B8 17 41S 45 40 E
Ambatomanoina, Madag. .... 57 B8 18 18S 47 37 E
Ambatondrazaka, Madag. .... 57 B8 17 55S 48 28 E
Ambatosoratra, Madag. ...... 57 B8 17 37S 48 31 E
Ambenja, Madag. .... 57 B8 15 17S 46 58 E
Amberg, Germany .... 16 D6 49 26N 11 52 E
Ambergris Cay, Belize 87 D7 18 0N 88 0W
Amberley, N.Z. .... 59 K4 43 9S 172 44 E
Ambikapur, India .... 43 H10 23 15N 83 15 E
Ambilobé, Madag. .... 57 A8 13 10S 49 3 E
Ambinanindrano, Madag. .... 57 C8 20 5S 48 23 E
Ambinanitelo, Madag. ...... 57 B8 15 21S 49 35 E
Ambinda, Madag. .... 57 B8 16 25S 45 52 E
Amble, U.K. 12 B6 55 20N 1 36W
Ambleside, U.K. 12 C5 54 26N 2 58W
Ambo, Peru 92 F3 10 5S 76 10W
Amboahangy, Madag. ...... 57 C8 24 15S 46 22 E
Ambodifototra, Madag. ...... 57 B8 16 59S 49 52 E
Ambodilazana, Madag. ...... 57 B8 18 6S 49 10 E
Ambodiriana, Madag. ...... 57 B8 17 55S 49 18 E
Ambohidratrimo, Madag. .... 57 B8 18 50S 47 26 E
Ambohidray, Madag. ...... 57 B8 18 36S 48 18 E
Ambohimahamasina, Madag. . 57 C8 21 56S 47 11 E
Ambohimahasoa, Madag. .... 57 C8 21 7S 47 13 E
Ambohimanga, Madag. ...... 57 C8 20 52S 47 36 E
Ambohimitombo, Madag. .... 57 C8 20 43S 47 27 E
Ambohitra, Madag. .... 57 A8 12 30S 49 10 E
Amboise, France .... 20 C4 47 24N 1 2 E
Ambon, Indonesia .... 37 E7 3 43S 128 12 E
Ambondro, Madag. .... 57 D8 25 13S 45 44 E
Amboseli △, Kenya .... 54 C4 2 37S 37 13 E
Amboseli, L., Kenya ...... 54 C4 2 40S 37 10 E
Ambositra, Madag. .... 57 C8 20 31S 47 25 E
Ambovombe, Madag. ...... 57 D8 25 11S 46 5 E
Amboy, U.S.A. 79 L11 34 33N 115 45W
Amboyna Cay, S. China Sea . 36 C4 7 50N 112 50 E
Ambridge, U.S.A. 84 F4 40 36N 80 14W
Ambriz, Angola .... 52 F2 7 48S 13 8 E
Amchitka I., U.S.A. .... 68 C1 51 32N 179 0 E
Amderma, Russia .... 28 C7 69 45N 61 30 E
Amdhi, India .... 43 H9 23 51N 81 27 E
Ameca, Mexico 86 C4 20 30N 104 0W
Ameca →, Mexico 86 C3 20 40N 105 15W
Amecameca, Mexico 87 D5 19 7N 98 46W
Ameland, Neths. .... 15 A5 53 27N 5 45 E
Amenia, U.S.A. 85 E11 41 51N 73 33W
American Falls, U.S.A. 76 E7 42 47N 112 51W
American Falls Reservoir, U.S.A. 76 E7 42 47N 112 52W
American Fork, U.S.A. 76 F8 40 23N 111 48W
American Highland, Antarctica . 5 D6 73 0S 75 0 E
American Samoa ☑, Pac. Oc. . 59 B13 14 20S 170 40W
Americana, Brazil 95 A6 22 45S 47 20W
Americus, U.S.A. 83 K3 32 4N 84 14W
Amersfoort, Neths. .... 15 B5 52 9N 5 23 E
Amersfoort, S. Africa ...... 57 D4 26 59S 29 53 E
Amery Ice Shelf, Antarctica .... 5 C6 69 30S 72 0 E
Ames, U.S.A. 80 E8 42 2N 93 37W
Amesbury, U.S.A. 85 D14 42 51N 70 56W
Amet, India .... 42 G5 25 18N 73 56 E
Amga, Russia .... 29 C14 60 50N 132 0 E
Amga →, Russia .... 29 C14 62 38N 134 32 E
Amgu, Russia .... 29 E14 45 45N 137 15 E
Amgun →, Russia .... 29 D14 52 56N 139 38 E
Amherst, Canada 73 C7 45 48N 64 8W
Amherst, Mass., U.S.A. 85 D12 42 23N 72 31W
Amherst, N.Y., U.S.A. 84 D6 42 59N 78 48W
Amherst, Ohio, U.S.A. 84 E2 41 24N 82 14W
Amherst I., Canada 85 B8 44 8N 76 43W
Amherstburg, Canada 72 D3 42 6N 83 6W
Amiata, Mte., Italy .... 22 C4 42 53N 11 37 E
Amidon, U.S.A. 80 B3 46 29N 103 19W
Amiens, France .... 20 B5 49 54N 2 16 E
Aminuis, Namibia .... 56 C2 23 43S 19 21 E
Amīrābād, Iran .... 44 C5 33 20N 46 16 E
Amirante Is., Seychelles ...... 26 K9 6 0S 53 0 E
Amisk ⌒, Canada 71 B9 56 43N 98 0W
Amisk L., Canada .... 71 C8 54 35N 102 15 E
Amistad ⌒, U.S.A. 81 L4 29 32N 101 12W
Amistad, Presa de la, Mexico . 86 B4 29 24N 101 0W
Amite, U.S.A. 81 K9 30 44N 90 30W
Amla, India .... 42 J8 21 56N 78 7 E
Amlapura = Karangasem,
  Indonesia .... 37 J18 8 27S 115 37 E
Amlia I., U.S.A. 68 C2 52 4N 173 30W

Amlwch, U.K. 12 D3 53 24N 4 20W
'Ammān, Jordan .... 46 D4 31 57N 35 52 E
'Ammān □, Jordan .... 46 D5 31 40N 36 30 E
'Ammān ✈ (AMM), Jordan .... 46 D5 31 45N 36 2 E
Ammanford, U.K. 13 F4 51 48N 3 59W
Ammassalik = Tasiilaq,
  Greenland 4 C6 65 40N 37 20W
Ammochostos = Famagusta,
  Cyprus .... 25 D12 35 8N 33 55 E
Ammon, U.S.A. 76 E8 43 28N 111 58W
Amnat Charoen, Thailand .... 38 E5 15 51N 104 38 E
Amnura, Bangla. .... 43 G13 24 37N 88 25 E
Åmol, Iran .... 45 B7 36 23N 52 20 E
Amorgós, Greece .... 23 F11 36 50N 25 57 E
Amory, U.S.A. 83 J1 33 59N 88 29W
Amos, Canada 72 C4 48 35N 78 5W
Åmot, Norway .... 9 G13 59 57N 9 54 E
Amoy = Xiamen, China ...... 33 D6 24 25N 118 4 E
Ampanavoana, Madag. ...... 57 B9 15 41S 50 22 E
Ampang, Malaysia .... 39 L3 3 8N 101 45 E
Ampangalana, Lakandranon',
  Madag. .... 57 C8 22 48S 47 50 E
Ampanihy, Madag. .... 57 C7 24 40S 44 45 E
Amparafaravola, Madag. .... 57 B8 17 35S 48 13 E
Ampasimanambo, Madag. .... 57 C8 20 31S 48 0 E
Ampasindava, Helodranon',
  Madag. .... 57 A8 13 40S 48 15 E
Ampasindava, Saikanosy,
  Madag. .... 57 A8 13 42S 47 55 E
Ampenan, Indonesia ...... 36 F5 8 34S 116 4 E
Amper →, Germany .... 16 D6 48 29N 11 55 E
Amphoe Kathu, Thailand ...... 39 a 7 55N 98 21 E
Amphoe Thalang, Thailand .... 39 a 8 1N 98 20 E
Ampitsikinana, Réunion ...... 57 A8 12 57S 49 49 E
Ampombiantambo, Madag. .... 57 A8 12 42S 48 57 E
Ampotaka, Madag. .... 57 D7 25 3S 44 41 E
Ampoza, Madag. .... 57 C7 22 20S 44 44 E
Amqui, Canada 73 C6 48 28N 67 27W
Amravati, India .... 40 J10 20 55N 77 45 E
Amreli, India .... 42 J4 21 35N 71 17 E
Amritsar, India .... 42 D6 31 35N 74 57 E
Amroha, India .... 43 E8 28 53N 78 30 E
Amsterdam, Neths. .... 15 B4 52 23N 4 54 E
Amsterdam, U.S.A. 85 D10 42 56N 74 11W
Amsterdam ✈ (AMS), Neths. .. 15 B4 52 18N 4 45 E
Amsterdam, I. = Nouvelle-
  Amsterdam, Î., Ind. Oc. ...... 3 F13 38 30S 77 30 E
Amstetten, Austria .... 16 D8 48 7N 14 51 E
Amudarya →, Uzbekistan .... 28 E6 43 58N 59 34 E
Amundsen Gulf, Canada 68 A7 71 0N 124 0W
Amundsen Sea, Antarctica 5 D15 72 0S 115 0W
Amuntai, Indonesia .... 36 E5 2 28S 115 25 E
Amur →, Russia .... 29 D15 52 56N 141 10 E
Amurang, Indonesia ...... 37 D6 1 5N 124 40 E
Amursk, Russia .... 29 D14 50 14N 136 54 E
Amyderya = Amudarya →,
  Uzbekistan .... 28 E6 43 58N 59 34 E
An Bang, Iraq .... 44 C4 33 25N 42 0 E
An Biên, Vietnam .... 39 H5 9 45N 105 0 E
An Hoa, Vietnam .... 38 E7 15 40N 108 5 E
An Nabatīyah at Tahta, Lebanon 46 B4 33 23N 35 27 E
An Nabk, Si. Arabia .... 44 D3 31 20N 37 20 E
An Nabk, Syria .... 46 A5 34 2N 36 44 E
An Nafūd, Si. Arabia .... 44 D4 28 15N 41 0 E
An Najaf, Iraq .... 44 C5 32 3N 44 15 E
An Nāşirīyah, Iraq .... 44 D5 31 0N 46 15 E
An Nhon, Vietnam .... 38 F7 13 55N 109 7 E
An Nu'ayrīyah, Si. Arabia .... 45 E6 27 30N 48 30 E
An Nuwayb'ī, W. →, Si. Arabia 46 F3 29 18N 34 57 E
An Thoi, Dao, Vietnam ...... 39 H4 9 58N 104 0 E
An Uaimh, Ireland 10 C5 53 39N 6 41W
Anabar →, Russia .... 29 B12 73 8N 113 36 E
'Anabtā, West Bank .... 46 C4 32 19N 35 7 E
Anaconda, U.S.A. 76 C7 46 8N 112 57W
Anacortes, U.S.A. 78 B4 48 30N 122 37W
Anadarko, U.S.A. 81 H5 35 4N 98 15W
Anadolu, Turkey .... 19 G5 39 0N 30 0 E
Anadyr, Russia .... 29 C18 64 35N 177 20 E
Anadyr →, Russia .... 29 C18 64 55N 176 5 E
Anadyrskiy Zaliv, Russia ...... 29 C19 64 0N 180 0 E
Anaga, Pta. de, Canary Is. 24 F3 28 34N 16 9W
'Ānah, Iraq .... 44 C4 34 25N 42 0 E
Anaheim, U.S.A. 79 M9 33 50N 117 55W
Anahim Lake, Canada 70 C3 52 28N 125 18W
Anáhuac, Mexico 86 B4 27 14N 100 9W
Anakapalle, India .... 41 L13 17 42N 83 6 E
Anakie, Australia .... 62 C4 23 32S 147 45 E
Analalava, Madag. .... 57 A8 14 35S 48 0 E
Analavoka, Madag. .... 57 C8 22 23S 46 30 E
Análipsis, Greece .... 25 A3 39 36N 19 55 E
Anambar →, Pakistan ...... 42 D3 30 15N 68 50 E
Anambas, Kepulauan, Indonesia 36 D3 3 20N 106 30 E
Anambas Is. = Anambas,
  Kepulauan, Indonesia ...... 36 D3 3 20N 106 30 E
Anamosa, U.S.A. 80 D9 42 7N 91 17W
Anamur, Turkey .... 19 G5 36 8N 32 58 E
Anan, Japan .... 31 H7 33 54N 134 40 E
Anand, India .... 42 H5 22 32N 72 59 E
Anantapur, India .... 40 M10 14 39N 77 42 E
Anantnag, India .... 43 C6 33 45N 75 10 E
Ananyiv, Ukraine .... 17 E15 47 44N 29 58 E
Anápolis, Brazil 93 G9 16 15S 48 50W
Anapu →, Brazil 93 D8 1 53S 50 53W
Anār, Iran .... 45 D7 30 55N 55 13 E
Anārak, Iran .... 45 C7 33 25N 53 40 E
Anas →, Pakistan .... 45 D5 23 26N 74 0 E
Anatolia = Anadolu, Turkey .... 19 G5 39 0N 30 0 E
Anatsogno, Madag. .... 57 C7 23 33S 43 46 E
Añatuya, Argentina 94 B3 28 20S 62 50W
Anaunethad L., Canada 71 A8 60 55N 104 25W
Anbyŏn, N. Korea .... 35 E14 39 1N 127 35 E
Ancaster, Canada 84 C5 43 13N 79 59W
Anchor Bay, U.S.A. 78 G3 38 48N 123 34W
Anchorage, U.S.A. 68 B5 61 13N 149 54W
Anci, China .... 34 E9 39 20N 116 40 E
Ancohuma, Nevado, Bolivia 92 G5 16 0S 68 50W
Ancón, Peru 92 F3 11 50S 77 10W
Ancona, Italy .... 22 C5 43 38N 13 30 E
Ancud, Chile 96 E2 42 0S 73 50W
Ancud, G. de, Chile 96 E2 42 0S 73 0W
Anda, China .... 33 B7 46 24N 125 19 E
Andacollo, Argentina 94 D1 37 10S 70 42W
Andacollo, Chile 94 C1 30 14S 71 6W
Andaingo, Madag. .... 57 B8 18 12S 48 17 E
Andalgalá, Argentina 94 B2 27 40S 66 30W
Åndalsnes, Norway .... 9 E12 62 35N 7 43 E

Andalucía □, Spain 21 D3 37 35N 5 0W
Andalusia = Andalucía □, Spain 21 D3 37 35N 5 0W
Andalusia, U.S.A. 83 K2 31 18N 86 29W
Andaman Is., Ind. Oc. ...... 27 H13 12 30N 92 45 E
Andaman Sea, Ind. Oc. ...... 36 B1 13 0N 96 0 E
Andamooka Opal Fields,
  Australia .... 63 E2 30 27S 137 9 E
Andapa, Madag. .... 57 A8 14 39S 49 39 E
Andara, Namibia .... 56 B3 18 2S 21 9 E
Andenes, Norway .... 8 B17 69 19N 16 18 E
Andenne, Belgium .... 15 D5 50 28N 5 5 E
Anderson, Alaska, U.S.A. 68 B5 64 25N 149 15W
Anderson, Calif., U.S.A. 76 F2 40 27N 122 18W
Anderson, Ind., U.S.A. 82 E3 40 10N 85 41W
Anderson, Mo., U.S.A. 81 G7 36 39N 94 27W
Anderson, S.C., U.S.A. 83 H4 34 31N 82 39W
Anderson →, Canada 68 B7 69 42N 129 0W
Andes, U.S.A. 85 D10 42 12N 74 47W
Andes, Cord. de los, S. Amer. . 92 H5 20 0S 68 0W
Andfjorden, Norway .... 8 B17 69 10N 16 20 E
Andhra Pradesh □, India ...... 40 L11 18 0N 79 0 E
Andijon, Uzbekistan .... 28 E8 41 10N 72 15 E
Andikíthira, Greece .... 23 G10 35 52N 23 15 E
Andilamena, Madag. .... 57 B8 17 1S 48 35 E
Andímeshk, Iran .... 45 C6 32 27N 48 21 E
Andizhan = Andijon, Uzbekistan 28 E8 41 10N 72 15 E
Andoany, Madag. .... 57 A8 13 25S 48 16 E
Andohahela △, Madag. ...... 57 C8 24 4S 46 44 E
Andoharanofotsy, Madag. .... 57 B8 18 56S 47 35 E
Andong, S. Korea .... 35 F15 36 40N 128 43 E
Andongwei, China .... 35 G10 35 6N 119 20 E
Andoom, Australia .... 62 A3 12 25S 141 53 E
Andorra ■, Europe .... 20 E4 42 30N 1 30 E
Andorra La Vella, Andorra .... 20 E4 42 31N 1 32 E
Andover, U.K. 13 F6 51 12N 1 29W
Andover, Maine, U.S.A. 85 B14 44 38N 70 45W
Andover, Mass., U.S.A. 85 D13 42 40N 71 8W
Andover, N.J., U.S.A. 85 F10 40 59N 74 45W
Andover, N.Y., U.S.A. 84 D7 42 10N 77 48W
Andover, Ohio, U.S.A. 84 E4 41 36N 80 34W
Andøya, Norway .... 8 B16 69 10N 15 50 E
Andradina, Brazil 93 H8 20 54S 51 23W
Andrahary, Mt., Madag. ...... 57 A8 13 37S 49 17 E
Andramasina, Madag. ...... 57 B8 19 11S 47 35 E
Andranopasy, Madag. ...... 57 C7 21 17S 43 44 E
Andranovory, Madag. ...... 57 C7 23 8S 44 10 E
Andratx, Spain .... 24 B9 39 39N 2 25 E
Andreanof Is., U.S.A. 68 C2 51 30N 176 0W
Andrews, S.C., U.S.A. 83 J6 33 27N 79 34W
Andrews, Tex., U.S.A. 81 J3 32 19N 102 33W
Ándria, Italy .... 22 D7 41 13N 16 17 E
Andriamena, Madag. ...... 57 B8 17 26S 47 30 E
Andriandampy, Madag. ...... 57 C8 22 45S 45 41 E
Andriba, Madag. .... 57 B8 17 30S 46 58 E
Andringitra △, Madag. ...... 57 C8 22 13S 46 5 E
Androka, Madag. .... 57 C7 24 58S 44 2 E
Ándros, Greece .... 23 F11 37 50N 24 57 E
Andros I., Bahamas 88 B4 24 30N 78 0W
Andros Town, Bahamas 88 B4 24 43N 77 47W
Androscoggin →, U.S.A. 85 C14 43 58N 70 0W
Andselv, Norway .... 8 B18 69 4N 18 34 E
Andújar, Spain 21 C3 38 3N 4 5W
Andulo, Angola .... 52 G3 11 25S 16 45 E
Anegada I., Br. Virgin Is. ...... 89 e 18 45N 64 20W
Anegada Passage, W. Indies .. 89 C7 18 15N 63 45W
Aneto, Pico de, Spain ...... 21 A6 42 37N 0 40 E
Ang Mo Kio, Singapore ...... 39 d 1 23N 103 50 E
Ang Thong, Thailand .... 38 E3 14 35N 100 31 E
Ang Thong, △, Thailand ...... 39 H2 9 40N 99 43 E
Ang Thong, Ko, Thailand .... 39 b 9 37N 99 41 E
Angamos, Punta, Chile 94 A1 23 1S 70 32W
Angara →, Russia .... 29 D10 58 5N 94 20 E
Angarsk, Russia .... 29 D11 52 30N 104 0 E
Angas Hills, Australia ...... 60 D4 23 0S 127 50 E
Angaston, Australia .... 63 E2 34 30S 139 8 E
Ånge, Sweden .... 9 E16 62 31N 15 35 E
Ángel, Salto = Angel Falls,
  Venezuela 92 B6 5 57N 62 30W
Ángel de la Guarda, I., Mexico . 86 B2 29 30N 113 30W
Angel Falls, Venezuela 92 B6 5 57N 62 30W
Angeles, Phil. .... 37 A6 15 9N 120 33 E
Ängelholm, Sweden .... 9 H15 56 15N 12 58 E
Angels Camp, U.S.A. 78 G6 38 4N 120 32W
Ångermanälven →, Sweden .. 8 E17 62 40N 18 0 E
Ångermanland, Sweden ...... 8 E18 63 36N 17 45 E
Angers, Canada 85 A9 45 31N 75 29W
Angers, France 20 C3 47 30N 0 35W
Ängesån →, Sweden .... 8 C20 66 16N 22 47 E
Angikuni L., Canada 71 A9 62 12N 99 59W
Angkor, Cambodia .... 38 F4 13 22N 103 50 E
Anglesey, Isle of □, U.K. 12 D3 53 16N 4 18W
Angleton, U.S.A. 81 L7 29 10N 95 26W
Anglisidhes, Cyprus .... 25 E12 34 51N 33 27 E
Angmagssalik = Tasiilaq,
  Greenland 4 C6 65 40N 37 20W
Ango, Dem. Rep. of the Congo . 54 B2 4 10N 26 5 E
Angoche, Mozam. .... 55 F4 16 8S 39 55 E
Angoche, I., Mozam. ...... 55 F4 16 20S 39 50 E
Angol, Chile 94 D1 37 56S 72 45W
Angola, Ind., U.S.A. 82 E3 41 38N 85 0W
Angola, N.Y., U.S.A. 84 D5 42 38N 79 2W
Angola ■, Africa .... 53 G3 12 0S 18 0 E
Angoulême, France .... 20 D4 45 39N 0 10 E
Angoumois, France .... 20 D3 45 50N 0 25 E
Angra dos Reis, Brazil 95 A7 23 0S 44 10W
Angren, Uzbekistan .... 28 E8 41 1N 70 12 E
Angtassom, Cambodia ...... 39 G5 11 1N 104 41 E
Angu, Dem. Rep. of the Congo . 54 B1 3 23N 24 10 E
Anguang, China .... 35 B12 45 15N 123 45 E
Anguilla ☑, W. Indies 89 C7 18 14N 63 5W
Anguo, China .... 34 E8 38 28N 115 15 E
Angurugu, Australia .... 62 A2 14 0S 136 25 E
Angus □, U.K. 11 E6 56 46N 2 56W
Angwa →, Zimbabwe ...... 57 B5 16 0S 30 23 E
Anhandui →, Brazil 95 A5 21 46S 52 9W
Anholt, Denmark .... 9 H14 56 42N 11 33 E
Anhui □, China .... 33 C6 32 0N 117 0 E
Anhwei = Anhui □, China .... 33 C6 32 0N 117 0 E
Anichab, Namibia .... 56 C1 21 0S 14 46 E
Animas →, U.S.A. 77 H9 36 43N 108 13W
Anivorano, Madag. .... 57 B8 18 44S 48 58 E
Anjalankoski, Finland ...... 9 F22 60 45N 26 51 E
Anjar, India .... 42 H4 23 6N 70 10 E
Anjou, France 20 C3 47 20N 0 15W
Anjozorobe, Madag. .... 57 B8 18 22S 47 52 E
Anju, N. Korea .... 35 E13 39 36N 125 40 E
Ankaboa, Tanjona, Madag. .... 57 C7 21 58S 43 20 E
Ankang, China .... 34 H5 32 40N 109 1 E
Ankara, Turkey .... 19 G5 39 57N 32 54 E

Ankarafantsika △, Madag. .... 57 B8 16 8S 47 5 E
Ankaramena, Madag. ...... 57 C8 21 57S 46 39 E
Ankaratra, Madag. .... 53 H9 19 25S 47 12 E
Ankasakasa, Madag. .... 57 B7 16 21S 44 52 E
Ankavandra, Madag. ...... 57 B8 18 46S 45 18 E
Ankazoabo, Madag. .... 57 C7 22 18S 44 31 E
Ankazobe, Madag. .... 57 B8 18 20S 47 10 E
Ankeny, U.S.A. 80 E8 41 44N 93 36W
Ankilimalinika, Madag. ...... 57 C7 22 58S 43 45 E
Ankilizato, Madag. .... 57 C8 20 25S 45 1 E
Ankisabe, Madag. .... 57 B8 19 17S 46 58 E
Ankoro, Dem. Rep. of the Congo 54 D2 6 45S 26 55 E
Ankororoka, Madag. .... 57 D8 25 30S 45 11 E
Anmyŏn-do, S. Korea ...... 35 F14 36 25N 126 25 E
Ann, C., U.S.A. 85 D14 42 38N 70 35W
Ann Arbor, U.S.A. 82 D4 42 17N 83 45W
Anna, U.S.A. 81 G10 37 28N 89 15W
Annaba, Algeria .... 50 A7 36 50N 7 46 E
Annalee →, Ireland 10 B4 54 2N 7 24W
Annam, Vietnam .... 38 E7 16 0N 108 0 E
Annamitique, Chaîne, Asia .... 38 D6 17 0N 106 0 E
Annan, U.K. 11 G5 54 59N 3 16W
Annan →, U.K. 11 G5 54 58N 3 16W
Annapolis, U.S.A. 82 F7 38 59N 76 30W
Annapolis Royal, Canada 73 D6 44 44N 65 32W
Annapurna, Nepal .... 43 E10 28 34N 83 50 E
Annean, L., Australia .... 61 E2 26 54S 118 14 E
Annecy, France .... 20 D7 45 55N 6 8 E
Anning, China .... 32 D5 24 55N 102 26 E
Anniston, U.S.A. 83 J3 33 39N 85 50W
Annobón, Atl. Oc. .... 49 G4 1 25S 5 36 E
Annotto Bay, Jamaica ...... 88 a 18 17N 76 45W
Annville, U.S.A. 85 F8 40 20N 76 31W
Áno Viánnos, Greece ...... 25 D7 35 2N 25 21 E
Anorotsangana, Madag. ...... 57 A8 13 56S 47 55 E
Anosibe, Madag. .... 57 B8 19 26S 48 13 E
Anóyia, Greece .... 25 D6 35 16N 24 52 E
Anping, Hebei, China ...... 34 E8 38 15N 115 30 E
Anping, Liaoning, China ...... 35 D12 41 5N 123 30 E
Anqing, China .... 33 C6 30 30N 117 3 E
Anqiu, China .... 35 F10 36 25N 119 10 E
Ansai, China .... 34 F5 36 50N 109 20 E
Ansbach, Germany .... 16 D6 49 28N 10 34 E
Anshan, China .... 35 D12 41 5N 122 58 E
Anshun, China .... 32 D5 26 18N 105 57 E
Ansley, U.S.A. 80 E5 41 18N 99 23W
Anson, U.S.A. 81 J5 32 45N 99 54W
Anson B., Australia .... 60 B5 13 20S 130 6 E
Ansongo, Mali .... 50 E6 15 25N 0 35 E
Ansonia, U.S.A. 85 E11 41 21N 73 5W
Anstruther, U.K. 11 E6 56 14N 2 41W
Ansudu, Indonesia .... 37 E9 2 11S 139 22 E
Antabamba, Peru 92 F4 14 40S 73 0W
Antakya, Turkey .... 19 G6 36 14N 36 10 E
Antalaha, Madag. .... 57 A9 14 57S 50 20 E
Antalya, Turkey .... 19 G5 36 52N 30 45 E
Antalya Körfezi, Turkey ...... 19 G5 36 15N 31 30 E
Antambohobe, Madag. ...... 57 C8 22 20S 46 47 E
Antanambao-Manampotsy,
  Madag. .... 57 B8 19 29S 48 34 E
Antanambe, Madag. .... 57 B8 16 26S 49 52 E
Antananarivo, Madag. ...... 57 B8 18 55S 47 31 E
Antananarivo □, Madag. .... 57 B8 19 0S 47 0 E
Antanifotsy, Madag. .... 57 B8 19 39S 47 19 E
Antanimbaribe, Madag. ...... 57 C7 21 30S 44 48 E
Antanimora, Madag. .... 57 C8 24 49S 45 40 E
Antarctic Pen., Antarctica 5 C18 67 0S 60 0W
Antarctica 5 E3 90 0S 0 0W
Antelope, Zimbabwe .... 55 G2 21 2S 28 31 E
Antequera, Paraguay 94 A4 24 8S 57 7W
Antequera, Spain 21 D3 37 5N 4 33W
Antero, Mt., U.S.A. 77 G10 38 41N 106 15W
Antevamena, Madag. ...... 57 C7 21 2S 44 8 E
Anthony, Kans., U.S.A. 81 G5 37 9N 98 2W
Anthony, N. Mex., U.S.A. 77 K10 32 0N 106 36W
Anti Atlas, Morocco 50 C4 30 0N 8 30W
Anti-Lebanon = Ash Sharqi, Al
  Jabal, Lebanon .... 46 B5 33 40N 36 10 E
Antibes, France .... 20 E7 43 34N 7 6 E
Anticosti, Î. d', Canada 73 C7 49 30N 63 0W
Antigo, U.S.A. 80 C10 45 9N 89 9W
Antigonish, Canada 73 C7 45 38N 61 58W
Antigua, Canary Is. 24 F5 28 24N 14 1W
Antigua, Guatemala 88 D1 14 34N 90 41W
Antigua, W. Indies 89 C7 17 0N 61 50W
Antigua & Barbuda ■, W. Indies 89 C7 17 20N 61 48W
Antilla, Cuba 88 B4 20 40N 75 50W
Antilles = West Indies,
  Cent. Amer. 89 D7 15 0N 65 0W
Antioch, U.S.A. 78 G5 38 1N 121 48W
Antioquia, Colombia 92 B3 6 40N 75 55W
Antipodes Is., Pac. Oc. ...... 64 M9 49 45S 178 40 E
Antlers, U.S.A. 81 H7 34 14N 95 37W
Antoetra, Madag. .... 57 C8 20 46S 47 20 E
Antofagasta, Chile 94 A1 23 50S 70 30W
Antofagasta □, Chile 94 A2 24 0S 69 0W
Antofagasta de la Sierra,
  Argentina 94 B2 26 5S 67 20W
Antofalla, Argentina 94 B2 25 30S 68 5W
Antofalla, Salar de, Argentina . 94 B2 25 40S 67 45W
Anton, U.S.A. 81 J3 33 49N 102 10W
Antongila, Helodrano, Madag. . 57 B8 15 7S 49 20 E
Antonibé, Madag. .... 57 B8 15 7S 47 24 E
Antonibé, Presqu'île d', Madag. 57 A8 14 55S 47 20 E
Antonina, Brazil 95 B6 25 26S 48 42W
Antrim, U.K. 10 B5 54 43N 6 14W
Antrim, U.S.A. 84 F3 40 7N 81 21W
Antrim □, U.K. 10 B5 54 56N 6 25W
Antrim, Mts. of, U.K. 10 A5 55 3N 6 14W
Antrim Plateau, Australia .... 60 C4 18 8S 128 20 E
Antsakabary, Madag. ...... 57 B8 15 3S 48 56 E
Antsalova, Madag. .... 57 B7 18 40S 44 37 E
Antsenavolo, Madag. ...... 57 C8 21 24S 48 3 E
Antsiafabositra, Madag. ...... 57 B8 17 18S 46 57 E
Antsirabe, Antananarivo, Madag. 57 B8 19 55S 47 2 E
Antsirabe, Antsiranana, Madag. 57 A8 12 7S 49 8 E
Antsirabe, Mahajanga, Madag. . 57 B8 15 57S 48 58 E
Antsiranana, Madag. .... 57 A8 12 25S 49 20 E
Antsiranana □, Madag. ...... 57 A8 13 30S 48 58 E
Antsohihy, Madag. .... 57 A8 14 50S 47 59 E
Antsohimbondrona Seranana,
  Madag. .... 57 A8 13 7S 48 48 E
Antu, China .... 35 C15 42 30N 128 20 E
Antwerp = Antwerpen, Belgium 15 C4 51 13N 4 25 E
Antwerp, U.S.A. 85 B9 44 12N 75 37W
Antwerpen, Belgium .... 15 C4 51 13N 4 25 E
Antwerpen □, Belgium ...... 15 C4 51 15N 4 40 E
Anupgarh, India .... 42 E5 29 10N 73 10 E

Anuppur, *India* .... 43 H9   23 6N 81 41 E
Anuradhapura, *Sri Lanka* ..... 40 Q12   8 22N 80 28 E
Anveh, *Iran* .... 45 E7   27 23N 54 11 E
Anvers = Antwerpen, *Belgium* . 15 C4   51 13N   4 25 E
Anvers I., *Antarctica* 5 C17 64 30S 63 40W
Anxi, *China* .... 32 B4   40 30N 95 43 E
Anxious B., *Australia* .... 63 E1   33 24S 134 45 E
Anyang, *China* .... 34 F8   36 5N 114 21 E
Anyer-Kidul, *Indonesia* ...... 37 G11   6 4S 105 53 E
Anyi, *China* .... 34 G6   35 2N 111 2 E
Anza, *U.S.A.* 79 M10 33 35N 116 39W
Anze, *China* .... 34 F7   36 10N 112 12 E
Anzhero-Sudzhensk, *Russia* ... 28 D9   56 10N 86 0 E
Ánzio, *Italy* .... 22 D5   41 27N 12 37 E
Ao Makham, *Thailand* .... 39 a   7 50N 98 24 E
Ao Phangnga △, *Thailand* ..... 39 a   8 10N 98 32 E
Aoga-Shima, *Japan* .... 31 H9   32 28N 139 46 E
Aomen = Macau, *China* .... 33 G10 22 12N 113 33 E
Aomori, *Japan* .... 30 D10 40 45N 140 45 E
Aomori □, *Japan* .... 30 D10 40 45N 140 40 E
Aonla, *India* .... 43 E8   28 16N 79 11 E
Aoraki Mount Cook, *N.Z.* ..... 59 K3   43 36S 170 9 E
Aosta, *Italy* .... 20 D7   45 45N   7 20 E
Aotearoa = New Zealand ■,
  Oceania .... 59 J6   40 0S 176 0 E
Aoukâr, *Mauritania* 50 E4   17 40N 10 0W
Aozou Strip, *Chad* .... 51 D9   22 0N 19 0 E
Apa ➝, *S. Amer.* 94 A4   22 6S 58 2W
Apache, *U.S.A.* 81 H5   34 54N 98 22W
Apache Junction, *U.S.A.* 77 K8   33 25N 111 33W
Apalachee B., *U.S.A.* 83 L4   30 0N 84 0W
Apalachicola, *U.S.A.* 83 L3   29 43N 84 59W
Apalachicola ➝, *U.S.A.* 83 L3   29 43N 84 58W
Apaporis ➝, *Colombia* 92 D5   1 23S 69 25W
Aparados da Serra △, *Brazil* . 95 B5   29 10S 50 8W
Aparri, *Phil.* .... 37 A6   18 22N 121 38 E
Apatity, *Russia* .... 18 A5   67 34N 33 22 E
Apatzingán, *Mexico* 86 D4   19 0N 102 20W
Apeldoorn, *Neths.* .... 15 B5   52 13N   5 57 E
Apennines = Appennini, *Italy* . 22 B4 44 30N 10 0 E
Apia, *Samoa* 59 A13 13 50S 171 50W
Apiacás, Serra dos, *Brazil* .. 92 E7   9 50S 57 0W
Apies ➝, *S. Africa* .... 57 D4   25 15S 28 8 E
Apizaco, *Mexico* 87 D5   19 26N 98 9W
Aplao, *Peru* 92 G4   16 0S 72 40W
Apo, Mt., *Phil.* .... 37 C7   6 53N 125 14 E
Apolakkiá, *Greece* .... 25 C9   36 5N 27 48 E
Apolakkiá, Órmos, *Greece* .... 25 C9   36 5N 27 45 E
Apolo, *Bolivia* 92 F5   14 30S 68 30W
Aporé ➝, *Brazil* 93 G8   19 27S 50 57W
Apostle Is., *U.S.A.* 80 B9   47 0N 90 40W
Apostle Islands △, *U.S.A.* ... 80 B9   46 57N 90 53W
Apóstoles, *Argentina* 95 B4   28 0S 56 0W
Apostolos Andreas, C., *Cyprus* . 25 D13 35 42N 34 35 E
Apoteri, *Guyana* 92 C7   4 2N 58 32W
Appalachian Mts., *U.S.A.* 82 G6   38 0N 80 0W
Appennini, *Italy* .... 22 B4   44 30N 10 0 E
Apple Hill, *Canada* 85 A10 45 13N 74 46W
Apple Valley, *U.S.A.* 79 L9   34 32N 117 14W
Appleby-in-Westmorland, *U.K.* . 12 C5 54 35N   2 29W
Appledore, *U.K.* 13 F3   51 3N   4 13W
Appleton, *U.S.A.* 82 C1   44 16N 88 25W
Approuague ➝, *Fr. Guiana* 93 C8   4 30N 51 57W
Aprília, *Italy* .... 22 D5   41 36N 12 39 E
Apsley, *Canada* 84 B6   44 45N 78 6W
Apucarana, *Brazil* 95 A5   23 55S 51 33W
Apure ➝, *Venezuela* 92 B5   7 37N 66 25W
Apurímac ➝, *Peru* 92 F4   12 17S 73 56W
Aqâ Jari, *Iran* .... 45 D6   30 42N 49 50 E
Aqaba = Al 'Aqabah, *Jordan* .. 46 F4   29 31N 35 0 E
Aqaba, G. of, *Red Sea* .... 44 D2   28 15N 33 20 E
'Aqaba, Khalīj al = Aqaba, G. of,
  Red Sea .... 44 D2   28 15N 33 20 E
'Aqdá, *Iran* .... 45 C7   32 26N 53 37 E
'Aqrah, *Iraq* .... 44 B4   36 46N 43 45 E
Aqtaū, *Kazakhstan* .... 28 E6   43 39N 51 12 E
Aqtöbe, *Kazakhstan* .... 19 D10 50 17N 57 10 E
Aquidauana, *Brazil* 93 H7   20 30S 55 50W
Aquiles Serdán, *Mexico* 86 B3   28 37N 105 54W
Aquin, *Haiti* 89 C5   18 16N 73 24W
Aquitain, Bassin, *France* 20 D3   44 0N   0 30W
Ar Rachidiya = Er Rachidia,
  Morocco 50 B5   31 58N   4 20W
Ar Rafid, *Syria* .... 46 C4   32 57N 35 52 E
Ar Raḩḩāliyah, *Iraq* .... 44 C4   32 44N 43 23 E
Ar Ramādī, *Iraq* .... 44 C4   33 25N 43 20 E
Ar Ramthā, *Jordan* .... 46 C5   32 34N 36 0 E
Ar Raqqah, *Syria* .... 44 C3   35 59N 39 8 E
Ar Rass, *Si. Arabia* .... 44 E4   25 50N 43 40 E
Ar Rifā'ī, *Iraq* .... 44 D5   31 50N 46 10 E
Ar Riyāḍ, *Si. Arabia* .... 44 E5   24 41N 46 42 E
Ar Ru'ays, *Qatar* .... 45 E6   26 8N 51 12 E
Ar Rukhaymīyah, *Iraq* .... 44 D5   29 22N 45 38 E
Ar Ruṣāfah, *Syria* .... 44 C3   35 45N 38 49 E
Ar Ruṭbah, *Iraq* .... 44 C4   33 0N 40 15 E
Ara, *India* .... 43 G11 25 35N 84 32 E
Arab, *U.S.A.* 83 H2   34 19N 86 30W
'Arab, Bahr el ➝, *Sudan* ..... 51 G11   9 0N 29 30 E
Arab, Shatt al ➝, *Asia* ...... 45 D6   30 0N 48 31 E
'Arabābād, *Iran* .... 45 C8   33 2N 57 41 E
Arabia, *Asia* .... 26 G8   25 0N 45 0 E
Arabian Desert = Es Sahrâ' Esh
  Sharqîya, *Egypt* .... 51 C12 27 30N 32 30 E
Arabian Gulf = Gulf, The, *Asia* . 45 E6 27 0N 50 0 E
Arabian Sea, *Ind. Oc.* .... 27 H10 16 0N 65 0 E
Aracaju, *Brazil* 93 F11 10 55S 37 4W
Aracati, *Brazil* 93 D11   4 30S 37 44W
Araçatuba, *Brazil* 95 A5   21 10S 50 30W
Aracena, *Spain* 21 D2   37 53N   6 38W
Araçuaí, *Brazil* 93 G10 16 52S 42 4W
'Arad, *Israel* .... 46 D4   31 15N 35 12 E
Arad, *Romania* .... 17 E11 46 10N 21 20 E
Arādān, *Iran* .... 45 C7   35 21N 52 30 E
Araduppou, *Greece* .... 25 E12 34 57N 33 36 E
Arafura Sea, *E. Indies* ...... 26 K17   9 0S 135 0 E
Aragón □, *Spain* 21 B5   41 25N   0 40W
Aragón ➝, *Spain* 21 A5   42 13N   1 44W
Araguacema, *Brazil* 93 E9   7 12S 49 15W
Araguaia ➝, *Brazil* 93 E9   5 21S 48 41W
Araguaína, *Brazil* 93 E9   7 12S 48 12W
Araguari, *Brazil* 93 G9   18 38S 48 11W
Araguari ➝, *Brazil* 93 C9   1 15N 49 55W
Arain, *India* .... 42 F6   26 27N 75 2 E
Arak, *Algeria* .... 50 C6   25 20N   3 45 E
Arāk, *Iran* .... 45 C6   34 0N 49 40 E
Arakan Coast, *Burma* .... 41 K19 19 0N 94 0 E
Arakan Yoma, *Burma* .... 41 K19 20 0N 94 40 E
Araks = Aras, Rūd-e ➝, *Asia* ... 44 B5 40 5N 48 29 E

Aral, *Kazakhstan* .... 28 E7   46 41N 61 45 E
Aral Sea, *Asia* .... 28 E7   44 30N 60 0 E
Aral Tengizi = Aral Sea, *Asia* . 28 E7 44 30N 60 0 E
Aralsk = Aral, *Kazakhstan* ... 28 E7   46 41N 61 45 E
Aralskoye More = Aral Sea, *Asia* 28 E7 44 30N 60 0 E
Aramac, *Australia* .... 62 C4   22 58S 145 14 E
Aran I., *Ireland* 10 A3   55 0N   8 30W
Aran Is., *Ireland* 10 C2   53 6N   9 38W
Aranda de Duero, *Spain* 21 B4   41 39N   3 42W
Arandān, *Iran* .... 44 C5   35 23N 46 55 E
Aranjuez, *Spain* 21 B4   40 1N   3 40W
Aranos, *Namibia* .... 56 C2   24 9S 19 7 E
Aransas Pass, *U.S.A.* 81 M6   27 55N 97 9W
Aranyaprathet, *Thailand* ..... 38 F4   13 41N 102 30 E
Arapahoe, *U.S.A.* 80 E5   40 18N 99 54W
Arapey Grande ➝, *Uruguay* 94 C4   30 55S 57 49W
Arapgir, *Turkey* .... 44 B3   39 5N 38 30 E
Arapiraca, *Brazil* 93 E11   9 45S 36 39W
Arapongas, *Brazil* .... 95 A5   23 29S 51 28 E
Ar'ar, *Si. Arabia* .... 44 D4   30 59N 41 2 E
Araranguá, *Brazil* 95 B6   29 0S 49 30W
Araraquara, *Brazil* 93 H9   21 50S 48 0W
Ararás, Serra das, *Brazil* ... 95 B5   25 0S 53 10W
Ararat, *Australia* .... 63 F3   37 16S 143 0 E
Ararat, Mt. = Ağrı Dağı, *Turkey* . 19 G7 39 50N 44 15 E
Araria, *India* .... 43 F12 26 9N 87 33 E
Araripe, Chapada do, *Brazil* . 93 E11   7 20S 40 0W
Araruama, L. de, *Brazil* 95 A7   22 53S 42 12W
Aras, Rūd-e ➝, *Asia* .... 44 B5   40 5N 48 29 E
Arauca, *Colombia* 92 B4   7 0N 70 40W
Arauca ➝, *Venezuela* 92 B5   7 24N 66 35W
Arauco, *Chile* 94 D1   37 16S 73 25W
Arawale ➝, *Kenya* .... 54 C5   1 24S 40 9 E
Araxá, *Brazil* 93 G9   19 35S 46 55W
Araya, Pen. de, *Venezuela* ... 92 A6   10 40N 64 0W
Arba Minch, *Ethiopia* .... 47 F2   6 0N 37 30 E
Arbat, *Iraq* .... 44 C5   35 25N 45 35 E
Árbatax, *Italy* .... 22 E3   39 56N   9 42 E
Arbīl, *Iraq* .... 44 B5   36 15N 44 5 E
Arborfield, *Canada* 71 C8   53 6N 103 39W
Arborg, *Canada* 71 C9   50 54N 97 13W
Arbroath, *U.K.* 11 E6   56 34N   2 35W
Arbuckle, *U.S.A.* 78 F4   39 1N 122 3W
Arcachon, *France* 20 D3   44 40N   1 10W
Arcade, Calif., *U.S.A.* 79 L8   34 2N 118 15W
Arcade, N.Y., *U.S.A.* 84 D6   42 32N 78 25W
Arcadia, Fla., *U.S.A.* 83 M5   27 13N 81 52W
Arcadia, La., *U.S.A.* 81 J8   32 33N 92 55W
Arcadia, Pa., *U.S.A.* 84 F6   40 47N 78 51W
Arcata, *U.S.A.* 76 F1   40 52N 124 5W
Archangel = Arkhangelsk, *Russia* 18 B7 64 38N 40 36 E
Archbald, *U.S.A.* 85 E9   41 30N 75 32W
Archer ➝, *Australia* .... 62 A3   13 28S 141 41 E
Archer B., *Australia* .... 62 A3   13 20S 141 30 E
Archer Bend = Mungkan
  Kandju △, *Australia* .... 62 A3   13 35S 142 52 E
Archers Post, *Kenya* .... 54 B4   0 35N 37 35 E
Arches △, *U.S.A.* 77 G9   38 45N 109 25W
Archipel-de-Mingan △, *Canada* . 73 B7 50 13N 63 10W
Archipiélago Chinijo △,
  Canary Is. 24 E6   29 20N 13 30W
Archipiélago Los Roques △,
  Venezuela 89 D6   11 50N 66 44W
Arckaringa Cr. ➝, *Australia* . 63 D2   28 10S 135 22 E
Arco, *U.S.A.* 76 E7   43 38N 113 18W
Arcos de la Frontera, *Spain* . 21 D3   36 45N   5 49W
Arcot, *India* .... 40 N11 12 53N 79 20 E
Arctic Bay, *Canada* 69 A11 73 1N 85 7W
Arctic Ocean, *Arctic* 4 B18   78 0N 160 0W
Arctic Red River = Tsiigehtchic,
  Canada ....
Arctowski, *Antarctica* 5 C18   62 30S 58 0W
Arda ➝, *Bulgaria* .... 23 D12 41 40N 26 30 E
Ardabīl, *Iran* .... 45 B6   38 15N 48 18 E
Ardabīl □, *Iran* .... 45 B6   38 15N 48 20 E
Ardakān = Sepīdān, *Iran* ..... 45 D7   30 20N 52 5 E
Ardakān, *Iran* .... 45 C7   32 19N 53 59 E
Ardee, *Ireland* 10 C5   53 52N   6 33W
Arden, *Canada* 84 B8   44 43N 76 56W
Arden, Calif., *U.S.A.* 78 G5   38 36N 121 33W
Arden, Nev., *U.S.A.* 79 J11 36 1N 115 14W
Ardennes, *Belgium* .... 15 E5   49 50N   5 5 E
Ardennes = Ardenne, *Belgium* . 15 E5 49 50N   5 5 E
Arderin, *Ireland* 10 C4   53 2N   7 39W
Ardestān, *Iran* .... 45 C7   33 20N 52 25 E
Ardivachar, Pt., *U.K.* 11 D1   57 23N   7 26W
Ardlethan, *Australia* .... 63 E4   34 22S 146 53 E
Ardmore, Okla., *U.S.A.* 81 H6   34 10N 97 8W
Ardmore, Pa., *U.S.A.* 85 G9   39 58N 75 18W
Ardnamurchan, Pt. of, *U.K.* .. 11 E2   56 43N   6 14W
Ardnave Pt., *U.K.* 11 F2   55 53N   6 20W
Ardrossan, *Australia* .... 63 E2   34 26S 137 53 E
Ardrossan, *U.K.* 11 F4   55 39N   4 49W
Ards Pen., *U.K.* 10 B6   54 33N   5 34W
Arecibo, *Puerto Rico* .... 89 d   18 29N 66 43W
Areia Branca, *Brazil* 93 E11   5 0S 37 0W
Arena, Pt., *U.S.A.* 78 G3   38 57N 123 44W
Arenal, *Honduras* 88 C2   15 21N 86 50W
Arendal, *Norway* .... 9 G13   58 28N   8 46 E
Arequipa, *Peru* 92 G4   16 20S 71 30W
Arévalo, *Spain* 21 B3   41 3N   4 43W
Arezzo, *Italy* .... 22 C4   43 25N 11 53 E
Arga, *Turkey* .... 44 B3   38 37N 38 0 E
Arganda, *Spain* 21 B4   40 19N   3 26W
Argenta, *Canada* 70 C5   50 11N 116 56W
Argentan, *France* 20 B3   48 45N   0 1W
Argentário, Mte., *Italy* ..... 22 C4   42 24N 11 9 E
Argentia, *Canada* 73 C9   47 18N 53 58W
Argentina ■, *S. Amer.* 96 D3   35 0S 66 0W
Argentino, L., *Argentina* 96 G2   50 10S 73 0W
Argeş ➝, *Romania* .... 17 F14 44 5N 26 38 E
Arghandab ➝, *Afghan.* .... 42 D1   31 30N 64 15 E
Argolikós Kólpos, *Greece* .... 23 F10 37 20N 22 52 E
Árgos, *Greece* .... 23 F10 37 40N 22 43 E
Argostólion, *Greece* .... 23 E9   38 11N 20 29 E
Arguello, Pt., *U.S.A.* 79 L6   34 35N 120 39W
Arguineguín, *Canary Is.* 24 G4   27 46N 15 41W
Argun ➝, *Russia* .... 29 D13 53 20N 121 28 E
Argus Pk., *U.S.A.* 79 K9   35 52N 117 26W
Argyle, *U.S.A.* 80 A6   48 20N 96 49W
Argyle, L., *Australia* .... 60 C4   16 20S 128 40 E
Argyll □, *U.K.* 11 E4   56 6N   5 10W
Argyll & Bute □, *U.K.* 11 E3   56 13N   5 28W
Århus, *Denmark* .... 9 H14   56 8N 10 11 E
Ariadnoye, *Russia* .... 30 B7   45 8N 134 25 E
Ariamsvlei, *Namibia* .... 56 D2   28 9S 19 51 E
Arica, *Chile* 92 G4   18 32S 70 20W
Arica, *Colombia* 92 D4   2 0S 71 50W
Arico, *Canary Is.* 24 F3   28 9N 16 29W

Arid, C., *Australia* .... 61 F3   34 1S 123 10 E
Arida, *Japan* .... 31 G7   34 5N 135 8 E
Arilla, Ákra, *Greece* .... 25 A3   39 43N 19 39 E
Arima, *Trin. & Tob.* 89 D7   10 38N 61 17W
Arinos ➝, *Brazil* 92 F7   10 25S 58 20W
Ario de Rosales, *Mexico* 86 D4   19 12N 102 0W
Aripo, Mt., *Trin. & Tob.* 93 K15 10 45N 61 15W
Aripuanã, *Brazil* 92 E6   9 25S 60 30W
Aripuanã ➝, *Brazil* 92 E6   5 7S 60 25W
Ariquemes, *Brazil* 92 E6   9 55S 63 6W
Arisaig, *U.K.* 11 E3   56 55N   5 51W
Aristazabal I., *Canada* 70 C3   52 40N 129 10W
Arivonimamo, *Madag.* .... 57 B8   19 1S 47 11 E
Arizaro, Salar de, *Argentina* . 94 A2 24 40S 67 50W
Arizona, *Argentina* 94 D2   35 45S 65 25W
Arizona □, *U.S.A.* 77 J8   34 0N 112 0W
Arizpe, *Mexico* 86 A2   30 20N 110 11W
Arjeplog, *Sweden* .... 8 D18   66 3N 18 2 E
Arjona, *Colombia* 92 A3   10 14N 75 22W
Arjuna, *Indonesia* .... 37 G15   7 49S 112 34 E
Arka, *Russia* .... 29 C15 60 15N 142 0 E
Arkadelphia, *U.S.A.* 81 H8   34 7N 93 4W
Arkaig, L., *U.K.* 11 E3   56 59N   5 10W
Arkalyk = Arqalyk, *Kazakhstan* . 28 D7 50 13N 66 50 E
Arkansas □, *U.S.A.* 81 H8   35 0N 92 30W
Arkansas ➝, *U.S.A.* 81 J9   33 47N 91 4W
Arkansas City, *U.S.A.* 81 G6   37 4N 97 2W
Arkaroola, *Australia* .... 63 E2   30 20S 139 22 E
Arkhángelos, *Greece* .... 25 C10 36 13N 28 7 E
Arkhangelsk, *Russia* .... 18 B7   64 38N 40 36 E
Arki, *India* .... 42 D7   31 9N 76 58 E
Arklow, *Ireland* 10 D5   52 48N   6 10W
Arkport, *U.S.A.* 84 D7   42 24N 77 42W
Arkticheskiy, Mys, *Russia* ... 29 A10 81 10N 95 0 E
Arkville, *U.S.A.* 85 D10 42 9N 74 37W
Arlanzón ➝, *Spain* 21 A3   42 3N   4 17W
Arlbergpass, *Austria* .... 16 E6   47 9N 10 12 E
Arles, *France* .... 20 E6   43 41N   4 40 E
Arlington, S. Africa .... 57 D4   28 1S 27 53 E
Arlington, N.Y., *U.S.A.* 85 E11 41 42N 73 54W
Arlington, Oreg., *U.S.A.* 76 D3   45 43N 120 12W
Arlington, S. Dak., *U.S.A.* .. 80 C6   44 22N 97 8W
Arlington, Tex., *U.S.A.* 81 J6   32 44N 97 7W
Arlington, Va., *U.S.A.* 82 F7   38 53N 77 7W
Arlington, Vt., *U.S.A.* 85 C11 43 5N 73 9W
Arlington, Wash., *U.S.A.* 78 B4   48 12N 122 8W
Arlington Heights, *U.S.A.* ... 82 D2   42 5N 87 59W
Arlit, *Niger* .... 50 E7   19 0N   7 38 E
Arlon, *Belgium* .... 15 E5   49 42N   5 49 E
Arltunga, *Australia* .... 62 C1   23 26S 134 41 E
Armagh, *U.K.* 10 B5   54 21N   6 39W
Armagh □, *U.K.* 10 B5   54 18N   6 37W
Armando Bermudez △,
  Dom. Rep. 89 C5   19 3N 71 0W
Armavir, *Russia* .... 19 E7   45 2N 41 7 E
Armenia, *Colombia* 92 C3   4 35N 75 45W
Armenia ■, *Asia* .... 19 F7   40 20N 45 0 E
Armenistís, Ákra, *Greece* .... 25 C9   36 8N 27 42 E
Armidale, *Australia* .... 63 E5   30 30S 151 40 E
Armour, *U.S.A.* 80 D5   43 19N 98 21W
Armstrong, B.C., *Canada* 70 C5   50 25N 119 10W
Armstrong, Ont., *Canada* 72 B2   50 18N 89 4W
Arnarfjörður, *Iceland* 8 D2   65 48N 23 40W
Arnaud ➝, *Canada* 69 B12 59 59N 69 46W
Arnauti, C., *Cyprus* .... 25 D11 35 6N 32 17 E
Arnett, *U.S.A.* 81 G5   36 8N 99 46W
Arnhem, *Neths.* .... 15 C5   51 58N   5 55 E
Arnhem, C., *Australia* .... 62 A2   12 20S 137 30 E
Arnhem B., *Australia* .... 62 A2   12 20S 136 10 E
Arnhem Land, *Australia* ...... 62 A1   13 10S 134 30 E
Arno ➝, *Italy* .... 22 C4   43 41N 10 17 E
Arno Bay, *Australia* .... 63 E2   33 54S 136 34 E
Arnold, *U.K.* 12 D6   53 1N   1 7W
Arnold, *U.S.A.* 78 G6   38 15N 120 20W
Arnot, *Canada* 71 B9   55 56N 96 41W
Arnøy, *Norway* .... 8 A19   70 9N 20 40 E
Arnprior, *Canada* 85 A8   45 26N 76 21W
Arnsberg, *Germany* .... 16 C5   51 24N   8 5 E
Aroab, *Namibia* .... 56 D2   26 41S 19 39 E
Aron, *India* .... 42 G6   25 57N 77 56 E
Arona, *Canary Is.* 24 F3   28 5N 16 40W
Arqalyk, *Kazakhstan* .... 28 D7   50 13N 66 50 E
Arrah = Ara, *India* .... 43 G11 25 35N 84 32 E
Arran, *U.K.* 11 F3   55 34N   5 12W
Arras, *France* .... 20 A5   50 17N   2 46 E
Arrecife, *Canary Is.* 24 F6   28 57N 13 37W
Arrecifes, *Argentina* 94 C3   34 6S 60 9W
Arrée, Mts. d', *France* 20 B2   48 26N   3 55W
Arriaga, Chiapas, *Mexico* 87 D6   16 15N 93 52W
Arriaga, San Luis Potosí, *Mexico* 86 C3 23 43S 143 54 E
Arrilalah, *Australia* .... 62 C3   23 43S 143 54 E
Arrino, *Australia* .... 61 E2   29 30S 115 40 E
Arrow, L., *Ireland* 10 B3   54 3N   8 19W
Arrowhead, L., *U.S.A.* 79 L9   34 16N 117 10W
Arrowtown, *N.Z.* .... 59 L2   44 57S 168 50 E
Arroyo Grande, *U.S.A.* 79 K6   35 7N 120 35W
Ars, *Iran* .... 44 B5   37 9N 47 46 E
Arsenault L., *Canada* 71 B7   55 6N 108 32W
Arseniev, *Russia* .... 30 B6   44 10N 133 15 E
Árta, *Greece* .... 23 E9   39 8N 21 2 E
Artà, *Spain* .... 24 B10 39 41N   3 21 E
Arteaga, *Mexico* 86 D4   18 50N 102 20W
Artem, *Russia* .... 30 C6   43 22N 132 13 E
Artemovsk, *Russia* .... 29 D10 54 45N 93 35 E
Artemovsk, *Ukraine* .... 19 E6   48 35N 38 0 E
Artesia = Mosomane, *Botswana* . 56 C4 24 2S 26 19 E
Artesia, *U.S.A.* 81 J2   32 51N 104 24W
Arthur, *Canada* 84 C4   43 50N 80 32W
Arthur ➝, *Australia* .... 63 G3   41 2S 144 40 E
Arthur Cr. ➝, *Australia* ..... 62 C2   22 30S 136 25 E
Arthur Pt., *Australia* .... 62 C5   22 7S 150 3 E
Arthur River, *Australia* ..... 61 F2   33 20S 117 2 E
Arthur's Pass, *N.Z.* .... 59 K3   42 54S 171 35 E
Arthur's Pass △, *N.Z.* .... 59 K3   42 56S 171 33 E
Arthur's Town, *Bahamas* 89 B4   24 38N 75 42W
Artigas, *Antarctica* 5 C18   62 30S 58 0W
Artigas, *Uruguay* 94 C4   30 20S 56 30W
Artillery L., *Canada* 71 A7   63 9N 107 52W
Artois, *France* .... 20 A5   50 20N   2 30 E
Artrutx, C. de, *Spain* .... 24 B10 39 55N   3 49 E
Artsyz, *Ukraine* .... 17 E15 46 4N 29 26 E
Artvin, *Turkey* .... 19 F7   41 14N 41 44 E
Aru, Kepulauan, *Indonesia* ... 37 F8   6 0S 134 30 E
Aru Is. = Aru, Kepulauan,
  Indonesia .... 37 F8   6 0S 134 30 E
Arua, *Uganda* .... 54 B3   3 1N 30 58 E
Aruanã, *Brazil* 93 F8   14 54S 51 10W
Aruba ☑, *W. Indies* 89 D6   12 30N 70 0W

Arucas, *Canary Is.* 24 F4   28 7N 15 32W
Arun ➝, *Nepal* .... 43 F12 26 55N 87 10 E
Arun ➝, *U.K.* 13 G7   50 49N   0 33W
Arunachal Pradesh □, *India* .. 41 F19 28 0N 95 0 E
Arusha, *Tanzania* .... 54 C4   3 20S 36 40 E
Arusha □, *Tanzania* .... 54 C4   4 0S 36 30 E
Arusha Chini, *Tanzania* ...... 54 C4   3 32S 37 20 E
Aruwimi ➝, *Dem. Rep. of
  the Congo* .... 54 B1   1 13N 23 36 E
Arvada, Colo., *U.S.A.* 80 F2   39 48N 105 5W
Arvada, Wyo., *U.S.A.* 76 D10 44 39N 106 8W
Árvi, *Greece* .... 25 E7   34 59N 25 28 E
Arviat, *Canada* 71 A10 61 6N 93 59W
Arvidsjaur, *Sweden* .... 8 D18   65 35N 19 10 E
Arvika, *Sweden* .... 9 G15   59 40N 12 36 E
Arvin, *U.S.A.* 79 K8   35 12N 118 50W
Arwal, *India* .... 43 G11 25 15N 84 41 E
Arxan, *China* .... 33 B6   47 11N 119 57 E
Aryirádhes, *Greece* .... 25 B3   39 27N 19 58 E
Aryiroúpolis, *Greece* .... 25 D6   35 17N 24 20 E
Arys, *Kazakhstan* .... 28 E7   42 26N 68 48 E
Arzamas, *Russia* .... 18 C7   55 27N 43 55 E
Aş Şafā, *Syria* .... 46 B6   33 10N 37 0 E
Aş Saffānīyah, *Si. Arabia* ... 45 E6   27 55N 48 50 E
Aş Safirah, *Syria* .... 44 B3   36 5N 37 21 E
Aş Şahm, *Oman* .... 45 E8   24 10N 56 53 E
Aş Sājir, *Si. Arabia* .... 44 E5   25 11N 44 36 E
Aş Salamīyah, *Syria* .... 44 C3   35 1N 37 2 E
Aş Salmān, *Iraq* .... 44 D5   30 30N 44 32 E
Aş Salṭ, *Jordan* .... 46 C4   32 2N 35 43 E
Aş Sal'w'a, *Qatar* .... 45 E6   24 23N 50 50 E
Aş Samāwah, *Iraq* .... 44 D5   31 15N 45 15 E
Aş Sanamayn, *Syria* .... 46 B5   33 3N 36 10 E
Aş Sohar = Şuhār, *Oman* ...... 45 E8   24 20N 56 40 E
Aş Sukhnah, *Syria* .... 44 C3   34 52N 38 52 E
Aş Sulaymānīyah, *Iraq* .... 44 C5   35 35N 45 29 E
Aş Sulaymī, *Si. Arabia* ...... 44 E4   26 17N 41 21 E
Aş Sulayyil, *Si. Arabia* ..... 47 C4   20 27N 45 34 E
Aş Summān, *Si. Arabia* .... 44 E5   25 0N 47 0 E
Aş Suwaydā', *Syria* .... 46 C5   32 40N 36 30 E
Aş Suwaydā' □, *Syria* .... 46 C5   32 45N 36 45 E
Aş Suwayq, *Oman* .... 45 F8   23 51N 57 26 E
Aş Şuwayrah, *Iraq* .... 44 C5   32 55N 45 0 E
Asab, *Namibia* .... 56 D2   25 30S 18 0 E
Asad, Buḩayrat al, *Syria* .... 44 C3   36 0N 38 15 E
Asahi-Gawa ➝, *Japan* .... 31 G6   34 36N 133 58 E
Asahigawa, *Japan* .... 30 C11 43 46N 142 22 E
Asamankese, *Ghana* 50 G5   5 50N   0 40W
Asan ➝, *India* .... 43 F8   26 37N 78 24 E
Asansol, *India* .... 43 H12 23 40N 87 1 E
Asbesberg, *S. Africa* .... 56 D3   29 0S 23 0 E
Asbestos, *Canada* 73 C5   45 47N 71 58W
Asbury Park, *U.S.A.* 85 F10 40 13N 74 1W
Ascensión, *Mexico* 86 A3   31 6N 107 59W
Ascensión, B. de la, *Mexico* . 87 D7   19 50N 87 20W
Ascension I., *Atl. Oc.* 49 G2   7 57S 14 23W
Aschaffenburg, *Germany* ...... 16 D5   49 58N   9 6 E
Aschersleben, *Germany* .... 16 C6   51 45N 11 29 E
Áscoli Piceno, *Italy* .... 22 C5   42 51N 13 34 E
Ascope, *Peru* 92 E3   7 46S 79 8W
Ascotán, *Chile* 94 A2   21 45S 68 17W
Aseb, *Eritrea* .... 47 E3   13 0N 42 40 E
Asela, *Ethiopia* .... 47 F2   8 0N 39 0 E
Asenovgrad, *Bulgaria* .... 23 C11 42 1N 24 51 E
Aserradero, *Mexico* 86 C3   23 40N 105 43W
Asgata, *Cyprus* .... 25 E12 34 46N 33 15 E
Ash Grove, *U.S.A.* 81 G8   37 19N 93 35W
Ash Shabakah, *Iraq* .... 44 D4   30 49N 43 39 E
Ash Shamāl □, *Lebanon* .... 46 A5   34 25N 36 0 E
Ash Shāmīyah, *Iraq* .... 44 D5   31 55N 44 35 E
Ash Shāriqah, *U.A.E.* .... 45 E7   25 23N 55 26 E
Ash Sharmah, *Si. Arabia* ..... 44 D2   28 1N 35 16 E
Ash Sharqāt, *Iraq* .... 44 C4   35 27N 43 16 E
Ash Sharqi, Al Jabal, *Lebanon* . 46 B5 33 40N 36 10 E
Ash Shaṭrah, *Iraq* .... 44 D5   31 30N 46 10 E
Ash Shawbak, *Jordan* .... 44 D2   30 32N 35 34 E
Ash Shawmari, J., *Jordan* .... 46 E5   30 35N 36 35 E
Ash Shināfīyah, *Iraq* .... 44 D5   31 35N 44 39 E
Ash Shu'bah, *Si. Arabia* ..... 44 D5   28 54N 44 44 E
Ash Shumlūl, *Si. Arabia* ..... 44 E5   26 31N 47 20 E
Ash Shūr'a, *Iraq* .... 44 C4   35 58N 43 13 E
Ash Shurayf, *Si. Arabia* ..... 44 E3   25 43N 39 14 E
Ash Shuwayfāt, *Lebanon* ...... 46 B4   33 45N 35 30 E
Asha, *Russia* .... 18 D10 55 0N 57 16 E
Ashau, *Vietnam* .... 38 D6   16 6N 107 22 E
Ashbourne, *U.K.* 12 D6   53 2N   1 43W
Ashburn, *U.S.A.* 83 K4   31 43N 83 39W
Ashburton, *N.Z.* .... 59 K3   43 53S 171 48 E
Ashburton ➝, *Australia* ...... 60 D1   21 40S 114 56 E
Ashcroft, *Canada* 70 C4   50 40N 121 20W
Ashdod, *Israel* .... 46 D3   31 49N 34 35 E
Ashdown, *U.S.A.* 81 J7   33 40N 94 8W
Asheboro, *U.S.A.* 83 H6   35 43N 79 49W
Ashern, *Canada* 71 C9   51 11N 98 21W
Asherton, *U.S.A.* 81 L5   28 27N 99 46W
Asheville, *U.S.A.* 83 H4   35 36N 82 33W
Ashewat, *Pakistan* .... 42 D3   31 22N 68 32 E
Asheweig ➝, *Canada* 72 B2   54 17N 87 12W
Ashford, *Australia* .... 63 D5   29 15S 151 3 E
Ashford, *U.K.* .... 13 F8   51 8N   0 53 E
Ashgabat, *Turkmenistan* ...... 28 F6   38 0N 57 50 E
Ashibetsu, *Japan* .... 30 C11 43 31N 142 11 E
Ashikaga, *Japan* .... 31 F9   36 28N 139 29 E
Ashington, *U.K.* 12 B6   55 11N   1 33W
Ashizuri-Uwakai △, *Japan* .... 31 H6   32 56N 132 32 E
Ashizuri-Zaki, *Japan* .... 31 H6   32 44N 133 0 E
Ashkarkot, *Afghan.* .... 42 C2   33 3N 67 58 E
Ashkhabad = Ashgabat,
  Turkmenistan .... 28 F6   38 0N 57 50 E
Áshkhāneh, *Iran* .... 45 B8   37 26N 56 55 E
Ashland, Kans., *U.S.A.* 81 G5   37 11N 99 46W
Ashland, Ky., *U.S.A.* 82 F4   38 28N 82 38W
Ashland, Mont., *U.S.A.* 76 D10 45 36N 106 16W
Ashland, Ohio, *U.S.A.* 84 F2   40 52N 82 19W
Ashland, Oreg., *U.S.A.* 76 E2   42 12N 122 43W
Ashland, Pa., *U.S.A.* 85 F8   40 45N 76 22W
Ashland, Va., *U.S.A.* 82 G7   37 46N 77 29W
Ashland, Wis., *U.S.A.* 80 B9   46 35N 90 53W
Ashley, N. Dak., *U.S.A.* 80 B5   46 2N 99 22W
Ashley, Pa., *U.S.A.* 85 E9   41 12N 75 55W
Ashmore and Cartier Is., *Ind. Oc.* 60 B3 12 14S 123 5 E
Ashmore Reef, *Australia* ..... 60 B3   12 14S 123 5 E
Ashmyany, *Belarus* .... 9 J21   54 26N 25 52 E
Ashokan Reservoir, *U.S.A.* ... 85 E10 41 56N 74 13W
Ashqelon, *Israel* .... 46 D3   31 42N 34 35 E

Ashta, India ... 42 H7 23 1N 76 43 E
Ashtabula, U.S.A. ... 84 E4 41 52N 80 47W
Ashton, S. Africa ... 56 E3 33 50S 20 5 E
Ashton, U.S.A. ... 76 D8 44 4N 111 27W
Ashuanipi, L., Canada ... 73 B6 52 45N 66 15W
Ashuapmushuan →, Canada ... 72 C5 48 37N 72 20W
Ashville, U.S.A. ... 84 F6 40 34N 78 33W
Asia ... 26 E11 45 0N 75 0 E
Asia, Kepulauan, Indonesia ... 37 D8 1 0N 131 13 E
Asifabad, India ... 40 K11 19 20N 79 24 E
Asinara, Italy ... 22 D3 41 4N 8 16 E
Asinara, G. dell', Italy ... 22 D3 41 0N 8 30 E
Asino, Russia ... 28 D9 57 0N 86 0 E
Asipovichy, Belarus ... 17 B15 53 19N 28 33 E
'Asir □, Si. Arabia ... 47 D3 18 40N 42 30 E
Asir, Ras, Somali Rep. ... 47 E5 11 55N 51 10 E
Askersund, Sweden ... 9 G16 58 53N 14 55 E
Askham, S. Africa ... 56 D3 26 59S 20 47 E
Askim, Norway ... 9 G14 59 35N 11 10 E
Askja, Iceland ... 8 D5 65 3N 16 48W
Askøy, Norway ... 9 F11 60 29N 5 10 E
Asmara = Asmera, Eritrea ... 47 D2 15 19N 38 55 E
Asmera, Eritrea ... 47 D2 15 19N 38 55 E
Åsnen, Sweden ... 9 H16 56 37N 14 45 E
Aso Kuju △, Japan ... 31 H5 32 53N 131 6 E
Aspatria, U.K. ... 12 C4 54 47N 3 19W
Aspen, U.S.A. ... 77 G10 39 11N 106 49W
Aspermont, U.S.A. ... 81 J4 33 8N 100 14W
Aspiring, Mt., N.Z. ... 59 L2 44 23S 168 46 E
Asprókavos, Ákra, Greece ... 25 B4 39 21N 20 6 E
Aspur, India ... 42 H6 23 58N 74 7 E
Asquith, Canada ... 71 C7 52 8N 107 13W
Assab = Aseb, Eritrea ... 47 E3 13 0N 42 40 E
Assam □, India ... 41 G18 26 0N 93 0 E
Assateague Island △, U.S.A. ... 82 F8 38 15N 75 10W
Asse, Belgium ... 15 D4 50 24N 4 10 E
Assen, Neths. ... 15 A6 53 0N 6 35 E
Assiniboia, Canada ... 71 D7 49 40N 105 59W
Assiniboine →, Canada ... 71 D9 49 53N 97 8W
Assiniboine, Mt., Canada ... 70 C5 50 52N 115 39W
Assis, Brazil ... 95 A5 22 40S 50 20W
Assisi, Italy ... 22 C5 43 4N 12 37 E
Assynt, L., U.K. ... 11 C3 58 10N 5 3W
Astana, Kazakhstan ... 28 D8 51 10N 71 30 E
Āstāneh, Iran ... 45 B6 37 17N 49 59 E
Astara, Azerbaijan ... 19 G8 38 30N 48 50 E
Asteroúsia, Greece ... 25 E7 34 59N 25 3 E
Asti, Italy ... 20 D8 44 54N 8 12 E
Astipálaia, Greece ... 23 F12 36 32N 26 22 E
Astorga, Spain ... 21 A2 42 29N 6 8W
Astoria, U.S.A. ... 78 D3 46 11N 123 50W
Astrakhan, Russia ... 19 E8 46 25N 48 5 E
Asturias □, Spain ... 21 A3 43 15N 6 0W
Asunción, Paraguay ... 94 B4 25 10S 57 30W
Asunción Nochixtlán, Mexico ... 87 D5 17 28N 97 14W
Aswa →, Uganda ... 54 B3 3 43N 31 55 E
Aswa-Lolim △, Uganda ... 54 B3 2 43N 31 35 E
Aswân, Egypt ... 51 D12 24 4N 32 57 E
Aswan Dam = Sadd el Aali, Egypt ... 51 D12 23 54N 32 54 E
Asyût, Egypt ... 51 C12 27 11N 31 4 E
At Ţafilah, Jordan ... 46 E4 30 45N 35 30 E
At Ţafilah □, Jordan ... 46 E4 30 45N 35 30 E
Aţ Ţa'if, Si. Arabia ... 47 C3 21 5N 40 27 E
At Ta'mim □, Iraq ... 44 C5 35 30N 44 20 E
Aţ Ţirāq, Si. Arabia ... 44 E5 27 19N 44 33 E
Aţ Ţubayq, Si. Arabia ... 44 D3 29 30N 37 0 E
Atacama □, Chile ... 94 B2 27 30S 70 0W
Atacama, Desierto de, Chile ... 94 A2 24 0S 69 20W
Atacama, Salar de, Chile ... 94 A2 23 30S 68 20W
Atalaya, Peru ... 92 F4 10 45S 73 50W
Atalaya de Femes, Canary Is. ... 24 F6 28 56N 13 47W
Atami, Japan ... 31 G9 35 5N 139 4 E
Atapupu, E. Timor ... 37 F6 9 0S 124 51 E
Atâr, Mauritania ... 50 D3 20 30N 13 5W
Atari, Pakistan ... 42 D6 30 56N 74 2 E
Atascadero, U.S.A. ... 78 K6 35 29N 120 40W
Atasu, Kazakhstan ... 28 E8 48 30N 71 0 E
Atatürk Baraji, Turkey ... 19 G6 37 28N 38 30 E
Atauro, E. Timor ... 37 F7 8 10S 125 30 E
'Atbara, Sudan ... 51 E12 17 42N 33 59 E
'Atbara, Nahr →, Sudan ... 51 E12 17 40N 33 56 E
Atbasar, Kazakhstan ... 28 D7 51 48N 68 20 E
Atchafalaya B., U.S.A. ... 81 L9 29 25N 91 25W
Atchison, U.S.A. ... 80 F7 39 34N 95 7W
Āteshān, Iran ... 45 C7 35 35N 52 37 E
Ath, Belgium ... 15 D3 50 38N 3 47 E
Athabasca, Canada ... 70 C6 54 45N 113 20W
Athabasca →, Canada ... 71 B6 58 40N 110 50W
Athabasca, L., Canada ... 71 B7 59 15N 109 15W
Athabasca Sand Dunes △, Canada ... 71 B7 59 4N 108 43W
Athboy, Ireland ... 10 C5 53 37N 6 56W
Athenry, Ireland ... 10 C3 53 18N 8 44W
Athens = Athínai, Greece ... 23 F10 37 58N 23 46 E
Athens, Ala., U.S.A. ... 83 H2 34 48N 86 58W
Athens, Ga., U.S.A. ... 83 J4 33 57N 83 23W
Athens, N.Y., U.S.A. ... 85 D11 42 16N 73 49W
Athens, Ohio, U.S.A. ... 82 F4 39 20N 82 6W
Athens, Pa., U.S.A. ... 85 E8 41 57N 76 31W
Athens, Tenn., U.S.A. ... 83 H3 35 27N 84 36W
Athens, Tex., U.S.A. ... 81 J7 32 12N 95 51W
Atherley, Canada ... 84 B5 44 37N 79 20W
Atherton, Australia ... 62 B4 17 17S 145 30 E
Athienou, Cyprus ... 25 D12 35 3N 33 32 E
Athínai, Greece ... 23 F10 37 58N 23 46 E
Athlone, Ireland ... 10 C4 53 25N 7 56W
Athna, Cyprus ... 25 D12 35 3N 33 47 E
Athol, U.S.A. ... 85 D12 42 36N 72 14W
Atholl, Forest of, U.K. ... 11 E5 56 51N 3 50W
Atholville, Canada ... 73 C6 47 59N 66 43W
Áthos, Greece ... 23 D11 40 9N 24 22 E
Athy, Ireland ... 10 C5 53 0N 7 0W
Ati, Chad ... 51 F9 13 13N 18 20 E
Atiak, Uganda ... 54 B3 3 12N 32 2 E
Atik L., Canada ... 71 B9 55 15N 96 0W
Atikaki △, Canada ... 71 C9 51 30N 95 31W
Atikameg →, Canada ... 72 B3 52 30N 82 46W
Atikokan, Canada ... 72 C1 48 45N 91 37W
Atikonak L., Canada ... 73 B7 52 40N 64 32W
Atitlán △, Cent. Amer. ... 87 E6 14 38N 91 10W
Atka, Russia ... 29 C16 60 50N 151 48 E
Atka I., U.S.A. ... 68 C2 52 7N 174 30W
Atkinson, U.S.A. ... 80 D5 42 32N 98 59W
Atlanta, Ga., U.S.A. ... 83 J3 33 45N 84 23W
Atlanta, Tex., U.S.A. ... 81 J7 33 7N 94 10W
Atlantic, U.S.A. ... 80 E7 41 24N 95 1W
Atlantic City, U.S.A. ... 82 F8 39 21N 74 27W
Atlantic Ocean ... 2 E9 0 0 20 0W
Atlantic-Indian Basin, Antarctica ... 5 B4 60 0S 30 0 E

Atlas Mts. = Haut Atlas, Morocco ... 50 B4 32 30N 5 0W
Atlin, Canada ... 70 B2 59 31N 133 41W
Atlin, □, Canada ... 70 B2 59 10N 134 30W
Atlin, L., Canada ... 70 B2 59 26N 133 45W
Atmore, U.S.A. ... 83 K2 31 2N 87 29W
Atoka, U.S.A. ... 81 H6 34 23N 96 8W
Atolia, U.S.A. ... 79 K9 35 19N 117 37W
Atrai →, Bangla. ... 43 G13 24 7N 89 22 E
Atrak = Atrek →, Turkmenistan ... 45 B8 37 35N 53 58 E
Atrauli, India ... 42 E8 28 2N 78 20 E
Atrek →, Turkmenistan ... 45 B8 37 35N 53 58 E
Atsuta, Japan ... 30 C10 43 24N 141 26 E
Attalla, U.S.A. ... 83 H2 34 1N 86 6W
Attapu, Laos ... 38 E6 14 48N 106 50 E
Attáviros, Greece ... 25 C9 36 12N 27 50 E
Attawapiskat, Canada ... 72 B3 52 56N 82 24W
Attawapiskat →, Canada ... 72 B3 52 57N 82 18W
Attawapiskat L., Canada ... 72 B2 52 18N 87 54W
Attica, Ind., U.S.A. ... 82 E2 40 18N 87 15W
Attica, Ohio, U.S.A. ... 84 E2 41 4N 82 53W
Attikamagen L., Canada ... 73 B6 55 0N 66 30W
Attleboro, U.S.A. ... 85 E13 41 57N 71 17W
Attock, Pakistan ... 42 C5 33 52N 72 20 E
Attopeu = Attapu, Laos ... 38 E6 14 48N 106 50 E
Attur, India ... 40 P11 11 35N 78 30 E
Atuel →, Argentina ... 94 D2 36 17S 66 50W
Åtvidaberg, Sweden ... 9 G17 58 12N 16 0 E
Atwater, U.S.A. ... 78 H6 37 21N 120 37W
Atwood, Canada ... 84 C3 43 40N 81 1W
Atwood, U.S.A. ... 80 F4 39 48N 101 3W
Atyraū, Kazakhstan ... 19 E9 47 5N 52 0 E
Au Sable, U.S.A. ... 84 B1 44 25N 83 20W
Au Sable →, U.S.A. ... 82 C4 44 25N 83 20W
Au Sable Forks, U.S.A. ... 85 B11 44 27N 73 41W
Au Sable Pt., U.S.A. ... 84 B1 44 20N 83 20W
Aubagne, France ... 20 E6 43 17N 5 37 E
Aubarca, C. d', Spain ... 24 B7 39 4N 1 22 E
Aube →, France ... 20 B5 48 34N 3 43 E
Auberry, U.S.A. ... 78 H7 37 7N 119 29W
Auburn, Ala., U.S.A. ... 83 J3 32 36N 85 29W
Auburn, Calif., U.S.A. ... 78 G5 38 54N 121 4W
Auburn, Ind., U.S.A. ... 82 E3 41 22N 85 4W
Auburn, Maine, U.S.A. ... 83 C10 44 6N 70 14W
Auburn, N.Y., U.S.A. ... 85 D8 42 56N 76 34W
Auburn, Nebr., U.S.A. ... 80 E7 40 23N 95 51W
Auburn, Pa., U.S.A. ... 85 F8 40 36N 76 6W
Auburn, Wash., U.S.A. ... 78 C4 47 18N 122 13W
Auburn Ra., Australia ... 63 D5 25 15S 150 30 E
Auburndale, U.S.A. ... 83 L5 28 4N 81 48W
Aubusson, France ... 20 D5 45 57N 2 11 E
Auch, France ... 20 E4 43 39N 0 36 E
Auchterarder, U.K. ... 11 E5 56 18N 3 41W
Auchtermuchty, U.K. ... 11 E5 56 18N 3 13W
Auckland, N.Z. ... 59 G5 36 52S 174 46 E
Auckland Is., Pac. Oc. ... 64 N8 50 40S 166 5 E
Aude →, France ... 20 E5 43 13N 3 14 E
Auden, Canada ... 72 B2 50 14N 87 53W
Audubon, U.S.A. ... 80 E7 41 43N 94 56W
Augathella, Australia ... 63 D4 25 48S 146 35 E
Aughnacloy, U.K. ... 10 B5 54 25N 6 59W
Augrabies Falls, S. Africa ... 56 D3 28 35S 20 20 E
Augrabies Falls △, S. Africa ... 56 D3 28 40S 20 22 E
Augsburg, Germany ... 16 D6 48 25N 10 52 E
Augusta, Australia ... 61 F2 34 19S 115 9 E
Augusta, Italy ... 22 F6 37 13N 15 13 E
Augusta, Ark., U.S.A. ... 81 H9 35 17N 91 22W
Augusta, Ga., U.S.A. ... 83 J5 33 28N 81 58W
Augusta, Kans., U.S.A. ... 81 G6 37 41N 96 59W
Augusta, Maine, U.S.A. ... 69 D13 44 19N 69 47W
Augusta, Mont., U.S.A. ... 76 C7 47 30N 112 24W
Augustów, Poland ... 17 B12 53 51N 23 0 E
Augustus, Mt., Australia ... 61 D2 24 20S 116 50 E
Augustus I., Australia ... 60 C3 15 20S 124 30 E
Aukum, U.S.A. ... 78 G6 38 34N 120 43W
Auld, L., Australia ... 60 D3 22 25S 123 50 E
Ault, U.S.A. ... 80 E2 40 35N 104 44W
Aunis, France ... 20 C3 46 5N 0 50W
Auponhia, Indonesia ... 37 E7 1 58S 125 27 E
Aur, Pulau, Malaysia ... 39 L5 2 35N 104 10 E
Auraiya, India ... 43 F8 26 28N 79 33 E
Aurangabad, Bihar, India ... 43 G11 24 45N 84 18 E
Aurangabad, Maharashtra, India ... 40 K9 19 50N 75 23 E
Aurich, Germany ... 16 B4 53 28N 7 28 E
Aurillac, France ... 20 D5 44 55N 2 26 E
Aurora, Canada ... 84 C5 44 0N 79 28W
Aurora, S. Africa ... 56 E2 32 40S 18 29 E
Aurora, Colo., U.S.A. ... 80 F2 39 44N 104 52W
Aurora, Ill., U.S.A. ... 82 E1 41 45N 88 19W
Aurora, Mo., U.S.A. ... 81 G8 36 58N 93 43W
Aurora, N.Y., U.S.A. ... 85 D8 42 45N 76 42W
Aurora, Nebr., U.S.A. ... 80 E6 40 52N 98 0W
Aurora, Ohio, U.S.A. ... 84 E3 41 21N 81 20W
Aurukun, Australia ... 62 A3 13 20S 141 45 E
Aus, Namibia ... 56 D2 26 35S 16 12 E
Ausable →, Canada ... 84 C3 43 19N 81 46W
Auschwitz = Oświęcim, Poland ... 17 C10 50 2N 19 11 E
Austin, Minn., U.S.A. ... 80 D8 43 40N 92 58W
Austin, Nev., U.S.A. ... 76 G5 39 30N 117 4W
Austin, Pa., U.S.A. ... 84 E6 41 38N 78 6W
Austin, Tex., U.S.A. ... 81 K6 30 17N 97 45W
Austin, L., Australia ... 61 E2 27 40S 118 0 E
Austin I., Canada ... 71 A10 61 10N 94 0W
Austra, Norway ... 8 D14 65 8N 11 55 E
Austral Is. = Tubuai Is., French Polynesia ... 65 K13 25 0S 150 0W
Austral Seamount Chain, Pac. Oc. ... 65 K13 24 0S 150 0W
Australia ■, Oceania ... 64 K5 23 0S 135 0 E
Australian Capital Territory □, Australia ... 63 F4 35 30S 149 0 E
Australind, Australia ... 61 F2 33 17S 115 42 E
Austria ■, Europe ... 16 E8 47 0N 14 0 E
Austvågøy, Norway ... 8 B16 68 20N 14 40 E
Autlán, Mexico ... 86 D4 19 40N 104 30W
Autun, France ... 20 C6 46 58N 4 17 E
Auvergne □, France ... 20 D5 45 20N 3 15 E
Auvergne ⋈, France ... 20 D5 45 20N 3 15 E
Auxerre, France ... 20 C5 47 48N 3 32 E
Ava, U.S.A. ... 81 G8 36 57N 92 40W
Avallon, France ... 20 C5 47 30N 3 53 E
Avalon, U.S.A. ... 79 M8 33 21N 118 20W
Avalon Pen., Canada ... 73 C9 47 30N 53 20W
Avanos, Turkey ... 44 B2 38 43N 34 51 E
Avaré, Brazil ... 95 A6 23 4S 48 58W
Avawatz Mts., U.S.A. ... 79 K10 35 40N 116 30W
Aveiro, Brazil ... 93 D7 3 10S 55 5W

Aveiro, Portugal ... 21 B1 40 37N 8 38W
Āvej, Iran ... 45 C6 35 40N 49 15 E
Avellaneda, Argentina ... 94 C4 34 50S 58 10W
Avellino, Italy ... 22 D6 40 54N 14 47 E
Avenal, U.S.A. ... 78 K6 36 0N 120 8W
Aversa, Italy ... 22 D6 40 58N 14 12 E
Avery, U.S.A. ... 76 C6 47 15N 115 49W
Aves, Is. las, Venezuela ... 89 D6 12 0N 67 30W
Avesta, Sweden ... 9 F17 60 9N 16 10 E
Avezzano, Italy ... 22 C5 42 2N 13 25 E
Aviá Terai, Argentina ... 94 B3 26 45S 60 50W
Aviemore, U.K. ... 11 D5 57 12N 3 50W
Avignon, France ... 20 E6 43 57N 4 50 E
Ávila, Spain ... 21 B3 40 39N 4 43W
Avila Beach, U.S.A. ... 79 K6 35 11N 120 44W
Avilés, Spain ... 21 A3 43 35N 5 57W
Avis, U.S.A. ... 84 E7 41 11N 77 19W
Avoca, Australia ... 63 F3 35 40S 143 43 E
Avoca →, Ireland ... 10 D5 52 48N 6 10W
Avola, Canada ... 70 C5 51 45N 119 19W
Avola, Italy ... 22 F6 36 56N 15 7 E
Avon, U.S.A. ... 84 D7 42 55N 77 45W
Avon →, Australia ... 61 F2 31 40S 116 7 E
Avon →, Bristol, U.K. ... 13 F5 51 29N 2 41W
Avon →, Dorset, U.K. ... 13 G6 50 44N 1 46W
Avon →, Warks., U.K. ... 13 E5 52 0N 2 8W
Avon Park, U.S.A. ... 83 M5 27 36N 81 31W
Avondale, Zimbabwe ... 55 F3 17 43S 30 58 E
Avonlea, Canada ... 71 D8 50 0N 105 0W
Avonmore, Canada ... 85 A10 45 10N 74 58W
Avonmouth, U.K. ... 13 F5 51 30N 2 42W
Avranches, France ... 20 B3 48 40N 1 20W
A'waj →, Syria ... 46 B5 33 23N 36 20 E
Awaji-Shima, Japan ... 31 G7 34 30N 134 50 E
'Awālī, Bahrain ... 45 E6 26 0N 50 30 E
Awantipur, India ... 43 C6 33 55N 75 3 E
Awasa, Ethiopia ... 47 F2 7 2N 38 28 E
Awash, Ethiopia ... 47 F3 9 1N 40 10 E
Awatere →, N.Z. ... 59 J5 41 37S 174 10 E
Awbārī, Libya ... 51 C8 26 46N 12 57 E
Awbārī, Idehan, Libya ... 51 C8 27 36N 11 30 E
Awe, L., U.K. ... 11 E3 56 17N 5 16W
Awjilah, Libya ... 51 C10 29 8N 21 7 E
Axe →, U.K. ... 13 F5 50 42N 3 4W
Axel Heiberg I., Canada ... 4 B3 80 0N 90 0W
Axim, Ghana ... 50 H5 4 51N 2 15W
Axiós →, Greece ... 23 D10 40 57N 22 35 E
Axminster, U.K. ... 13 G4 50 46N 3 0W
Ayabaca, Peru ... 92 D3 4 40S 79 53W
Ayabe, Japan ... 31 G7 35 20N 135 20 E
Ayacucho, Argentina ... 94 D4 37 5S 58 20W
Ayacucho, Peru ... 92 F4 13 0S 74 0W
Ayaguz, Kazakhstan ... 28 E9 48 10N 80 10 E
Ayamonte, Spain ... 21 D2 37 12N 7 24W
Ayan, Russia ... 29 D14 56 30N 138 16 E
Ayaviri, Peru ... 92 F4 14 50S 70 35W
Aydın, Turkey ... 23 F12 37 51N 27 51 E
Ayer, U.S.A. ... 85 D13 42 34N 71 35W
Ayer Hitam, Malaysia ... 39 c 1 54N 100 16 E
Ayer's Cliff, Canada ... 85 A12 45 10N 72 3W
Ayers Rock, Australia ... 61 E5 25 23S 131 5 E
Ayia Aikaterini, Ákra, Greece ... 25 A3 39 50N 19 50 E
Ayia Dhéka, Greece ... 25 D6 35 3N 24 58 E
Ayia Gálini, Greece ... 25 D6 35 6N 24 41 E
Ayia Napa, Cyprus ... 25 E13 34 59N 34 0 E
Ayia Phyla, Cyprus ... 25 E12 34 43N 33 1 E
Ayia Varvára, Greece ... 25 D7 35 8N 25 1 E
Áyios Amvrósios, Cyprus ... 25 D12 35 20N 33 35 E
Áyios Evstrátios, Greece ... 23 E11 39 34N 24 58 E
Áyios Ioánnis, Ákra, Greece ... 25 D7 35 20N 25 40 E
Áyios Isídhoros, Greece ... 25 C9 36 9N 27 51 E
Áyios Matthaíos, Greece ... 25 B3 39 30N 19 47 E
Áyios Nikólaos, Greece ... 25 D7 35 11N 25 41 E
Áyios Seryios, Cyprus ... 25 D12 35 12N 33 53 E
Áyios Theodhoros, Cyprus ... 25 D13 35 22N 34 1 E
Aykino, Russia ... 18 B8 62 15N 49 56 E
Aylesbury, U.K. ... 13 F7 51 49N 0 49W
Aylmer, Canada ... 84 D4 42 46N 80 59W
Aylmer, L., Canada ... 68 B8 64 0N 110 8W
'Ayn, Wādī al, Oman ... 45 F7 22 15N 55 28 E
Ayn Dār, Si. Arabia ... 45 E7 25 55N 49 10 E
Ayn Zālah, Iraq ... 44 B4 36 45N 42 35 E
Ayolas, Paraguay ... 94 B4 27 10S 56 59W
Ayon, Ostrov, Russia ... 29 C17 69 50N 169 0 E
'Ayoûn el 'Atroûs, Mauritania ... 50 E4 16 38N 9 37W
Ayr →, Australia ... 62 B4 19 35S 147 25 E
Ayr, Canada ... 84 C4 43 17N 80 27W
Ayr, U.K. ... 11 F4 55 28N 4 38W
Ayr →, U.K. ... 11 F4 55 28N 4 38W
Ayre, Pt. of, U.K. ... 12 C3 54 25N 4 21W
Ayton, Australia ... 62 B4 15 56S 145 22 E
Aytos, Bulgaria ... 23 C12 42 42N 27 16 E
Ayu, Kepulauan, Indonesia ... 37 D8 0 35N 131 5 E
Ayutla, Guatemala ... 88 D1 14 40N 92 10W
Ayutla, Mexico ... 87 D5 16 58N 99 17W
Ayvacık, Turkey ... 23 E12 39 36N 26 24 E
Ayvalık, Turkey ... 23 E12 39 20N 26 46 E
Az Zabadānī, Syria ... 46 B5 33 43N 36 5 E
Az Zāhiriyah, West Bank ... 46 D3 31 25N 34 58 E
Az Zahrān, Si. Arabia ... 45 E6 26 10N 50 7 E
Az Zarqā, Jordan ... 46 C5 32 5N 36 4 E
Az Zarqā', U.A.E. ... 45 E7 24 53N 53 4 E
Az Zarqā □, Jordan ... 46 C5 32 5N 36 4 E
Az Zāwiyah, Libya ... 51 B8 32 52N 12 56 E
Az Zibār, Iraq ... 44 B5 36 52N 44 4 E
Az Zilfī, Si. Arabia ... 44 E5 26 12N 44 52 E
Az Zubayr, Iraq ... 44 D5 30 26N 47 40 E
Azad Kashmir □, Pakistan ... 43 C5 33 50N 73 50 E
Azamgarh, India ... 43 F10 26 5N 83 13 E
Azángaro, Peru ... 92 F4 14 55S 70 13W
Āzar Shahr, Iran ... 44 B5 37 45N 45 59 E
Āzārbāyjān = Azerbaijan ■, Asia ... 19 F8 40 20N 48 0 E
Āzārbāyjān-e Gharbī □, Iran ... 44 B5 37 0N 44 30 E
Āzārbāyjān-e Sharqī □, Iran ... 44 B5 37 20N 47 0 E
A'zāz, Syria ... 44 B3 36 36N 37 4 E
Azbine = Aïr, Niger ... 50 E7 18 30N 8 0 E
Azerbaijan ■, Asia ... 19 F8 40 20N 48 0 E
Azerbaijchan = Azerbaijan ■, Asia ... 19 F8 40 20N 48 0 E
Azimganj, India ... 43 G13 24 14N 88 16 E
Azogues, Ecuador ... 92 D3 2 35S 78 0W
Azores = Açores, Is. dos, Atl. Oc. ... 50 A1 38 0N 27 0W
Azov, Russia ... 19 E6 47 3N 39 25 E
Azov, Sea of, Europe ... 19 E6 46 0N 36 30 E

Azovskoye More = Azov, Sea of, Europe ... 19 E6 46 0N 36 30 E
Azraq ash Shīshān, Jordan ... 46 D5 31 50N 36 49 E
Aztec, U.S.A. ... 77 H10 36 49N 107 59W
Azúa de Compostela, Dom. Rep. ... 89 C5 18 25N 70 44W
Azuaga, Spain ... 21 C3 38 16N 5 39W
Azuero, Pen. de, Panama ... 88 E3 7 30N 80 30W
Azul, Argentina ... 94 D4 36 42S 59 43W
Azusa, U.S.A. ... 79 L9 34 8N 117 52W

B

Ba Be △, Vietnam ... 38 A5 22 25N 105 37 E
Ba Don, Vietnam ... 38 D6 17 45N 106 26 E
Ba Dong, Vietnam ... 39 H6 9 40N 106 33 E
Ba Ngoi = Cam Lam, Vietnam ... 39 G7 11 54N 109 10 E
Ba Tri, Vietnam ... 39 G6 10 2N 106 36 E
Ba Vì △, Vietnam ... 38 B5 21 1N 105 22 E
Ba Xian = Bazhou, China ... 34 E9 39 8N 116 22 E
Baa, Indonesia ... 37 F6 10 50S 123 0 E
Baardeere = Bardera, Somali Rep. ... 47 G3 2 20N 42 27 E
Baarle-Nassau, Belgium ... 15 C4 51 27N 4 56 E
Bab el Mandeb, Red Sea ... 47 E3 12 35N 43 25 E
Bābā, Koh-i-, Afghan. ... 40 B5 34 30N 67 0 E
Baba Burnu, Turkey ... 23 E12 39 29N 26 2 E
Bābā Kalū, Iran ... 45 D6 30 7N 50 49 E
Babadag, Romania ... 17 F15 44 53N 28 44 E
Babaeski, Turkey ... 23 D12 41 26N 27 6 E
Babahoyo, Ecuador ... 92 D3 1 40S 79 30W
Babai = Sarju →, India ... 43 F9 27 21N 81 23 E
Babar, Indonesia ... 37 F7 8 0S 129 30 E
Babar, Pakistan ... 42 D3 31 7N 69 32 E
Babarkach, Pakistan ... 42 E3 29 45N 68 0 E
Babb, U.S.A. ... 76 B7 48 51N 113 27W
Baberu, India ... 43 G9 25 33N 80 43 E
Babi Besar, Pulau, Malaysia ... 39 L4 2 25N 103 59 E
Babīl □, Iraq ... 44 C5 32 30N 44 30 E
Babinda, Australia ... 62 B4 17 20S 145 56 E
Babine, Canada ... 70 B3 55 22N 126 37W
Babine →, Canada ... 70 B3 55 45N 127 44W
Babine L., Canada ... 70 C3 54 48N 126 0W
Babo, Indonesia ... 37 E8 2 30S 133 30 E
Bābol, Iran ... 45 B7 36 40N 52 50 E
Bābol Sar, Iran ... 45 B7 36 45N 52 45 E
Babruysk, Belarus ... 17 B15 53 10N 29 15 E
Babuhri, India ... 42 F3 26 49N 69 43 E
Babusar Pass, Pakistan ... 43 B5 35 12N 73 59 E
Babuyan Chan., Phil. ... 37 A6 18 40N 121 30 E
Babylon, Iraq ... 44 C5 32 34N 44 22 E
Bac Can, Vietnam ... 38 A5 22 8N 105 49 E
Bac Giang, Vietnam ... 38 B6 21 16N 106 11 E
Bac Lieu, Vietnam ... 39 H5 9 17N 105 43 E
Bac Ninh, Vietnam ... 38 B6 21 13N 106 4 E
Bac Phan, Vietnam ... 38 B5 22 0N 105 0 E
Bac Quang, Vietnam ... 38 A5 22 30N 104 48 E
Bacabal, Brazil ... 93 D10 4 15S 44 45W
Bacalar, Mexico ... 87 D7 18 50N 87 27W
Bacan, Kepulauan, Indonesia ... 37 E7 0 35S 127 30 E
Bacarra, Phil. ... 37 A6 18 15N 120 37 E
Bacău, Romania ... 17 E14 46 35N 26 55 E
Bacerac, Mexico ... 86 A3 30 18N 108 50W
Bach Long Vi, Dao, Vietnam ... 38 B6 20 10N 107 40 E
Bach Ma △, Vietnam ... 38 D6 16 11N 107 49 E
Bachhwara, India ... 43 G11 25 35N 85 54 E
Back →, Canada ... 68 B9 65 10N 104 0W
Bacolod, Phil. ... 37 B6 10 40N 122 57 E
Bacuk, Malaysia ... 39 J4 6 4N 102 25 E
Bād, Iran ... 45 C7 33 41N 52 1 E
Bad →, U.S.A. ... 80 C4 44 21N 100 22W
Bad Axe, U.S.A. ... 84 C2 43 48N 83 0W
Bad Ischl, Austria ... 16 E7 47 44N 13 38 E
Bad Kissingen, Germany ... 16 C6 50 11N 10 4 E
Bad Lands, U.S.A. ... 80 D3 43 40N 102 10W
Bada Barabil, India ... 43 H11 22 7N 85 24 E
Badagara, India ... 40 P9 11 35N 75 40 E
Badajós, L., Brazil ... 92 D6 3 15S 62 50W
Badajoz, Spain ... 21 C2 38 50N 6 59W
Badakhshān □, Afghan. ... 40 A7 36 30N 71 0 E
Badalona, Spain ... 21 B7 41 26N 2 15 E
Badalzai, Afghan. ... 42 E1 29 50N 65 35 E
Badampahar, India ... 41 H15 22 10N 86 10 E
Badanah, Si. Arabia ... 44 D4 30 58N 41 30 E
Badarinath, India ... 43 D8 30 45N 79 30 E
Badas, Kepulauan, Indonesia ... 36 D3 0 45N 107 5 E
Baddo →, Pakistan ... 40 F4 28 0N 64 20 E
Bade, Indonesia ... 37 F9 7 10S 139 35 E
Baden, Austria ... 16 D9 48 1N 16 13 E
Baden, U.S.A. ... 84 F4 40 38N 80 14W
Baden-Baden, Germany ... 16 D5 48 44N 8 13 E
Baden-Württemberg □, Germany ... 16 D5 48 20N 8 40 E
Badgastein, Austria ... 16 E7 47 7N 13 9 E
Badger, Canada ... 73 C8 49 0N 56 4W
Badger, U.S.A. ... 78 J7 36 38N 119 1W
Bādghīs □, Afghan. ... 40 B3 35 0N 63 0 E
Badgingarra △, Australia ... 61 F2 30 23S 115 22 E
Badgom, India ... 43 B6 34 1N 74 45 E
Badin, Pakistan ... 42 G3 24 38N 68 54 E
Badlands △, U.S.A. ... 80 D3 43 38N 102 56W
Badrah, Iraq ... 44 C5 33 6N 45 58 E
Badrinath, India ... 43 D8 30 44N 79 29 E
Badulla, Sri Lanka ... 40 R12 7 1N 81 7 E
Badung, Selat, Indonesia ... 37 K18 8 40S 115 22 E
Baena, Spain ... 21 D3 37 37N 4 20W
Baeza, Spain ... 21 D4 37 57N 3 25W
Baffin B., Canada ... 69 A13 72 0N 64 0W
Baffin I., Canada ... 69 B12 68 0N 75 0W
Bafing →, Mali ... 50 F3 13 49N 10 50W
Bafliyūn, Syria ... 44 B3 36 37N 36 59 E
Bafoulabé, Mali ... 50 F3 13 50N 10 55W
Bafoussam, Cameroon ... 52 C2 5 28N 10 25 E
Bāfq, Iran ... 45 D7 31 40N 55 25 E
Bafra, Turkey ... 19 F6 41 34N 35 54 E
Bāft, Iran ... 45 D8 29 15N 56 38 E
Bafwasende, Dem. Rep. of the Congo ... 54 B2 1 3N 27 5 E
Bagamoyo, Tanzania ... 54 D4 6 28S 38 55 E
Bagan Datoh, Malaysia ... 39 L3 3 59N 100 47 E
Bagan Serai, Malaysia ... 39 K3 5 1N 100 32 E
Baganga, Phil. ... 37 C7 7 34N 126 33 E
Bagani, Namibia ... 56 B3 18 7S 21 41 E
Bagansiapiapi, Indonesia ... 36 D2 2 12N 100 50 E
Bagasra, India ... 42 J4 21 30N 71 0 E
Bagaud, India ... 42 H6 22 19N 75 53 E
Bagdad, U.S.A. ... 79 L11 34 35N 115 53W

Bagdarin, Russia .... 29 D12 54 26N 113 36 E
Bagé, Brazil 95 C5 31 20S 54 15W
Bagenalstown = Muine Bheag,
  Ireland 10 D5 52 42N 6 58W
Baggs, U.S.A. 76 F10 41 2N 107 39W
Bagh, Pakistan .... 43 C5 33 59N 73 45 E
Baghain →, India .... 43 G9 25 32N 81 1 E
Baghdād, Iraq .... 44 C5 33 20N 44 30 E
Bagheria, Italy .... 22 E5 38 5N 13 30 E
Baghlān, Afghan. .... 40 A6 32 12N 68 46 E
Baghlān □, Afghan. .... 40 B6 36 0N 68 30 E
Bagley, U.S.A. 80 B7 47 32N 95 24W
Bago = Pegu, Burma .... 41 L20 17 20N 96 29 E
Bagodar, India .... 43 G11 24 5N 85 52 E
Bagrationovsk, Russia .... 9 J19 54 23N 20 39 E
Baguio, Phil. .... 37 A6 16 26N 120 34 E
Bah, India .... 43 F8 26 53N 78 36 E
Bahadurganj, India .... 43 F12 26 16N 87 49 E
Bahadurgarh, India .... 42 E7 28 40N 76 57 E
Bahama, Canal Viejo de,
  W. Indies 88 B4 22 10N 77 30W
Bahamas ■, N. Amer. 89 B5 24 0N 75 0W
Baharampur, India .... 43 G13 24 2N 88 27 E
Baharu Pandan = Pandan,
  Malaysia .... 39 d 1 32N 103 46 E
Bahawalnagar, Pakistan .... 42 E5 30 0N 73 15 E
Bahawalpur, Pakistan .... 42 E4 29 24N 71 40 E
Baheri, India .... 43 E8 28 45N 79 34 E
Bahgul →, India .... 43 F8 27 45N 79 36 E
Bahi, Tanzania .... 54 D4 5 58S 35 21 E
Bahi Swamp, Tanzania .... 54 D4 6 10S 35 0 E
Bahía = Salvador, Brazil 93 F11 13 0S 38 30W
Bahía □, Brazil 93 F10 12 0S 42 0W
Bahía, Is. de la, Honduras 88 C2 16 45N 86 15W
Bahía Blanca, Argentina 94 D3 38 35S 62 13W
Bahía de Caráquez, Ecuador 92 D2 0 40S 80 27W
Bahía Honda, Cuba 88 B3 22 54N 83 10W
Bahía Laura, Argentina 96 F3 48 10S 66 30W
Bahía Negra, Paraguay 92 H7 20 5S 58 5W
Bahir Dar, Ethiopia .... 47 E2 11 37N 37 10 E
Bahmanzād, Iran .... 45 D6 31 15N 51 47 E
Bahr el Ghazâl □, Sudan .... 51 G11 7 0N 28 0 E
Bahraich, India .... 43 F9 27 38N 81 37 E
Bahrain ■, Asia .... 45 E6 26 0N 50 35 E
Bahror, India .... 42 F7 27 51N 76 20 E
Bāhū Kalāt, Iran .... 45 E9 25 43N 61 25 E
Bai Bung, Mui = Ca Mau, Mui,
  Vietnam .... 39 H5 8 38N 104 44 E
Bai Duc, Vietnam .... 38 C5 18 3N 105 49 E
Bai Thuong, Vietnam .... 38 C5 19 54N 105 23 E
Baia Mare, Romania .... 17 E12 47 40N 23 35 E
Baião, Brazil 93 D9 2 40S 49 40W
Baïbokoum, Chad .... 51 G9 7 46N 15 43 E
Baicheng, China .... 35 B12 45 38N 122 42 E
Baidoa, Somali Rep. .... 47 G3 3 8N 43 30 E
Baie-Comeau, Canada 73 C6 49 12N 68 10W
Baie-St-Paul, Canada 73 C5 47 28N 70 32W
Baie-Trinité, Canada 73 C6 49 25N 67 20W
Baie Verte, Canada 73 C8 49 55N 56 12W
Baihar, India .... 43 H9 22 6N 80 33 E
Baihe, China .... 34 H6 32 50N 110 5 E
Baijnath, India .... 43 E8 29 55N 79 37 E
Baikal, L. = Baykal, Oz., Russia .... 29 D11 53 0N 108 0 E
Baikunthpur, India .... 43 H10 23 15N 82 33 E
Baile Atha Cliath = Dublin,
  Ireland 10 C5 53 21N 6 15W
Băilești, Romania .... 17 F12 44 1N 23 20 E
Bainbridge, Ga., U.S.A. 83 K3 30 55N 84 35W
Bainbridge, N.Y., U.S.A. 85 D9 42 18N 75 29W
Baing, Indonesia .... 37 F6 10 14S 120 34 E
Bainiu, China .... 34 H7 32 50N 112 15 E
Ba'ir, Jordan .... 46 E5 30 45N 36 55 E
Bairiki = Tarawa, Kiribati .... 64 G9 1 30N 173 0 E
Bairin Youqi, China .... 35 C10 43 30N 118 35 E
Bairin Zuoqi, China .... 35 C10 43 58N 119 15 E
Bairnsdale, Australia .... 63 F4 37 48S 147 36 E
Baisha, China .... 34 G7 34 20N 112 32 E
Baitadi, Nepal .... 43 E9 29 35N 80 25 E
Baiyin, China .... 34 F3 36 45N 104 14 E
Baiyu Shan, China .... 34 F4 37 15N 107 30 E
Baj Baj, India .... 43 H13 22 30N 88 5 E
Baja, Hungary .... 17 E10 46 12N 18 59 E
Baja, Pta., Mexico 86 B1 29 50N 116 0W
Baja California, Mexico 86 A1 31 10N 115 12W
Baja California □, Mexico 86 B2 30 0N 115 0W
Baja California Sur □, Mexico 86 B2 25 50N 111 50W
Bajag, India .... 43 H9 22 40N 81 21 E
Bajamar, Canary Is. 24 F3 28 33N 16 20W
Bajana, India .... 42 H4 23 7N 71 49 E
Bajatrejo, Indonesia .... 37 J17 8 29S 114 19 E
Bajera, Indonesia .... 37 J18 8 31S 115 2 E
Bäjgirän, Iran .... 45 B8 37 36N 58 24 E
Bajimba, Mt., Australia .... 63 D5 29 17S 152 6 E
Bajo Nuevo, Caribbean 88 C4 15 40N 78 50W
Bajoga, Nigeria .... 51 F8 10 57N 11 20 E
Bajool, Australia .... 62 C5 23 40S 150 35 E
Bakel, Senegal 50 F3 14 56N 12 20W
Baker, Calif., U.S.A. 79 K10 35 16N 116 4W
Baker, Mont., U.S.A. 80 B2 46 22N 104 17W
Baker, L., Canada 68 B10 64 0N 96 0W
Baker, Nev., U.S.A. 76 B3 40 50N 121 49W
Baker City, U.S.A. 76 D5 44 47N 117 50W
Baker I., Pac. Oc. 64 G10 0 10N 176 35W
Baker I., U.S.A. 70 B2 55 20N 133 40W
Baker L., Australia .... 61 E4 26 54S 126 5 E
Baker Lake, Canada 68 B10 64 20N 96 3W
Bakers Creek, Australia .... 62 C4 21 13S 149 7 E
Bakers Dozen Is., Canada 72 A4 56 45N 78 45W
Bakersfield, Calif., U.S.A. 79 K8 35 23N 119 1W
Bakersfield, Vt., U.S.A. 85 B12 44 45N 72 48W
Bākhtarān, Iran .... 44 C5 34 23N 47 0 E
Bākhtarān □, Iran .... 44 C5 34 0N 46 30 E
Bakı, Azerbaijan .... 19 F8 40 29N 49 56 E
Bakony, Hungary .... 17 E9 47 10N 17 30 E
Bakkafjörður, Iceland 8 C6 66 2N 14 48W
Bakony, Hungary .... 17 E9 47 10N 17 30 E
Bakony Forest = Bakony,
  Hungary .... 17 E9 47 10N 17 30 E
Bakouma, C.A.R. .... 52 C4 5 40N 22 56 E
Bakswaho, India .... 43 G8 24 15N 79 18 E
Baku = Bakı, Azerbaijan .... 19 F8 40 29N 49 56 E
Bakutis Coast, Antarctica 5 D15 74 0S 120 0W
Baky = Bakı, Azerbaijan .... 19 F8 40 29N 49 56 E
Bala, Canada 84 A5 45 1N 79 37W
Bala, U.K. 12 E4 52 54N 3 36W
Bala, L., U.K. 12 E4 52 53N 3 37W
Balabac I., Phil. .... 36 C5 8 0N 117 0 E
Balabac Str., E. Indies .... 36 C5 7 53N 117 5 E
Balabagh, Afghan. .... 42 B4 34 25N 70 12 E

Ba'labakk, Lebanon .... 46 B5 34 0N 36 10 E
Balabalangan, Kepulauan,
  Indonesia .... 36 E5 2 20S 117 30 E
Balad, Iraq .... 44 C5 34 1N 44 9 E
Balad Rūz, Iraq .... 44 C5 33 42N 45 5 E
Bālādeh, Fārs, Iran .... 45 D6 29 17N 51 56 E
Bālādeh, Māzandaran, Iran .... 45 B6 36 12N 51 48 E
Balaghat, India .... 40 J12 21 49N 80 12 E
Balaghat Ra., India .... 40 K10 18 50N 76 30 E
Balaguer, Spain .... 21 B6 41 50N 0 50 E
Balaklava, Ukraine .... 19 F5 44 30N 33 30 E
Balakovo, Russia .... 18 D8 52 4N 47 55 E
Balamau, India .... 43 F9 27 10N 80 21 E
Balancán, Mexico 87 D6 17 48N 91 32W
Balashov, Russia .... 19 D7 51 30N 43 10 E
Balasinor, India .... 42 H5 22 57N 73 23 E
Balasore = Baleshwar, India .... 41 J15 21 35N 87 3 E
Balaton, Hungary .... 17 E9 46 50N 17 40 E
Balbina, Reprêsa de, Brazil 92 D7 2 0S 59 30W
Balboa, Panama 88 E4 9 0N 79 34W
Balbriggan, Ireland 10 C5 53 37N 6 11W
Balcarce, Argentina 94 D4 38 0S 58 10W
Balcarres, Canada 71 C8 50 50N 103 35W
Balchik, Bulgaria .... 23 C13 43 28N 28 11 E
Balclutha, N.Z. .... 59 M2 46 15S 169 45 E
Balcones Escarpment, U.S.A. 81 L5 29 30N 99 15W
Bald Hd., Australia .... 61 G2 35 6S 118 1 E
Bald I., Australia .... 61 F2 34 57S 118 27 E
Bald Knob, U.S.A. 81 H9 35 19N 91 34W
Baldock L., Canada 71 B9 56 33N 97 57W
Baldwin, Mich., U.S.A. 82 D3 43 54N 85 51W
Baldwin, Pa., U.S.A. 84 F5 40 23N 79 59W
Baldwinsville, U.S.A. 85 C8 43 10N 76 20W
Baldy Mt., U.S.A. 76 B9 48 9N 109 39W
Baldy Peak, U.S.A. 77 K9 33 54N 109 34W
Baleares, Is., Spain .... 24 B10 39 30N 3 0 E
Balearic Is. = Baleares, Is., Spain .... 24 B10 39 30N 3 0 E
Baleine = Whale →, Canada 73 A6 58 15N 67 40W
Baleine, Petite R. de la →,
  Canada 72 A4 56 0N 76 45W
Baler, Phil. .... 37 A6 15 46N 121 34 E
Baleshare, U.K. 11 D1 57 31N 7 22W
Baleshwar, India .... 41 J15 21 35N 87 3 E
Balfate, Honduras 88 C2 15 48N 86 25W
Bali, Greece .... 25 D6 35 25N 24 47 E
Bali, India .... 42 G5 25 11N 73 17 E
Bali, Indonesia .... 36 F4 8 20S 115 0 E
Bali □, Indonesia .... 36 F5 8 20S 115 0 E
Bali, Selat, Indonesia .... 37 J17 8 18S 114 25 E
Bali Sea, Indonesia .... 37 J17 8 0S 115 0 E
Baliapal, India .... 43 J12 21 40N 87 17 E
Balik Pulau, Malaysia .... 39 c 5 21N 100 14 E
Balikeşir, Turkey .... 23 E12 39 39N 27 53 E
Balikpapan, Indonesia .... 36 E5 1 10S 116 55 E
Balimbing, Phil. .... 37 C5 5 5N 119 58 E
Baling, Malaysia .... 39 K3 5 41N 100 55 E
Balipara, India .... 41 F18 26 50N 92 45 E
Balkan Mts. = Stara Planina,
  Bulgaria .... 23 C10 43 15N 23 0 E
Balkhash = Balqash, Kazakhstan .... 28 E8 46 50N 74 50 E
Balkhash, Ozero = Balqash Köl,
  Kazakhstan .... 28 E8 46 0N 74 50 E
Balla, Bangla. .... 41 G17 24 10N 91 35 E
Ballachulish, U.K. 11 E3 56 41N 5 8W
Balladonia, Australia .... 61 F3 32 27S 123 51 E
Ballaghaderreen, Ireland 10 C3 53 55N 8 34W
Ballarat, Australia .... 63 F3 37 33S 143 50 E
Ballard, L., Australia .... 61 E3 29 20S 120 40 E
Ballater, U.K. 11 D5 57 3N 3 3W
Ballena Gris = Ojo de Liebre △,
  Mexico 86 B2 27 50N 114 0W
Ballenas, Canal de, Mexico 86 B2 29 10N 113 45W
Balleny Is., Antarctica .... 5 C11 66 30S 163 0 E
Ballia, India .... 43 G11 25 46N 84 12 E
Ballidu, Australia .... 63 D5 28 50S 153 31 E
Ballina, Australia 10 B2 54 7N 9 9W
Ballina, Ireland 10 C3 53 20N 8 13W
Ballinasloe, Ireland 10 C3 53 20N 8 13W
Ballinger, U.S.A. 81 K5 31 45N 99 57W
Ballinrobe, Ireland 10 C2 53 38N 9 13W
Ballinskelligs B., Ireland 10 E1 51 48N 10 13W
Ballston Spa, U.S.A. 85 D11 43 0N 73 51W
Ballybunion, Ireland 10 D2 52 31N 9 40W
Ballycastle, U.K. 10 A5 55 12N 6 15W
Ballyclare, U.K. 10 B5 54 46N 6 0W
Ballyhaunis, Ireland 10 C3 53 46N 8 46W
Ballymena, U.K. 10 B5 54 52N 6 17W
Ballymoney, U.K. 10 A5 55 5N 6 31W
Ballymote, Ireland 10 B3 54 5N 8 31W
Ballynahinch, U.K. 10 B6 54 24N 5 54W
Ballyquintin Pt., U.K. 10 B6 54 20N 5 30W
Ballyshannon, Ireland 10 B3 54 30N 8 11W
Balmaceda, Chile 96 F2 46 0S 71 50W
Balmertown, Canada 71 C10 51 4N 93 41W
Balmoral, Australia .... 63 F3 37 15S 141 48 E
Balmorhea, U.S.A. 81 K3 30 59N 103 45W
Balochistan = Baluchistan □,
  Pakistan .... 40 F4 27 30N 65 0 E
Balonne →, Australia .... 63 D4 28 47S 147 56 E
Balotra, India .... 42 G5 25 50N 72 14 E
Balqash, Kazakhstan .... 28 E8 46 50N 74 50 E
Balqash Köl, Kazakhstan .... 28 E8 46 0N 74 50 E
Balrampur, India .... 43 F10 27 30N 82 20 E
Balranald, Australia .... 63 E3 34 38S 143 33 E
Balsas, Mexico 87 D5 18 0N 99 40W
Balsas →, Brazil 93 E9 7 15S 44 35W
Balsas →, Mexico 86 D4 17 55N 102 10W
Balston Spa, U.S.A. 85 D11 43 0N 73 52W
Balta, Ukraine .... 17 D15 48 2N 29 45 E
Bălți, Moldova .... 17 E14 47 48N 27 58 E
Baltic Sea, Europe .... 9 H18 57 0N 19 0 E
Baltimore, Ireland 10 E2 51 29N 9 22W
Baltimore, Md., U.S.A. 82 F7 39 17N 76 37W
Baltimore, Ohio, U.S.A. 84 G2 39 51N 82 36W
Baltistan, Pakistan .... 43 A6 35 15N 74 40 E
Baltiysk, Russia .... 9 J18 54 41N 19 58 E
Balurghat, India .... 43 G13 25 15N 88 44 E
Balvi, Latvia .... 9 H22 57 8N 27 15 E
Balya, Turkey .... 23 E12 39 44N 27 35 E
Bam, Iran .... 45 D8 29 7N 58 14 E
Bama, Nigeria .... 51 F8 11 33N 13 41 E
Bamaga, Australia .... 62 A3 10 50S 142 25 E
Bamaji L., Canada 72 B1 51 9N 91 25W
Bamako, Mali 50 F4 12 34N 7 55W
Bambari, C.A.R. .... 52 C4 5 40N 20 35 E
Bambaroo, Australia .... 62 B4 18 50S 146 10 E
Bamberg, Germany .... 16 D6 49 54N 10 54 E
Bamberg, U.S.A. 83 J5 33 18N 81 2W

Bambili, Dem. Rep. of the Congo .... 54 B2 3 40N 26 0 E
Bamburgh, U.K. 12 B6 55 37N 1 43W
Bamenda, Cameroon .... 52 C2 5 57N 10 11 E
Bamfield, Canada 70 D3 48 45N 125 10W
Bāmīān □, Afghan. .... 40 B5 35 0N 67 0 E
Bamiancheng, China .... 35 C13 43 15N 124 2 E
Bampūr, Iran .... 45 E9 27 15N 60 21 E
Ban Ao Tu Khun, Thailand .... 39 a 8 9N 98 20 E
Ban Ban, Laos .... 38 C4 19 31N 103 30 E
Ban Bang Hin, Thailand .... 39 H2 9 32N 98 35 E
Ban Bang Khu, Thailand .... 39 a 7 57N 98 23 E
Ban Bang Rong, Thailand .... 39 a 8 3N 98 25 E
Ban Bo Phut, Thailand .... 39 b 9 33N 100 2 E
Ban Chaweng, Thailand .... 39 b 9 32N 100 3 E
Ban Chiang Klang, Thailand .... 38 C3 19 25N 100 55 E
Ban Chik, Laos .... 38 D4 17 15N 102 22 E
Ban Choho, Thailand .... 38 E4 15 2N 102 9 E
Ban Dan Lan Hoi, Thailand .... 38 D2 17 0N 99 35 E
Ban Don = Surat Thani, Thailand .... 39 H2 9 6N 99 20 E
Ban Don, Vietnam .... 38 F6 12 53N 107 48 E
Ban Don, Ao →, Thailand .... 39 H2 9 20N 99 25 E
Ban Dong, Thailand .... 38 C3 19 30N 100 59 E
Ban Hong, Thailand .... 38 C2 18 18N 98 50 E
Ban Hua Thanon, Thailand .... 39 b 9 26N 100 1 E
Ban Kaeng, Thailand .... 38 D3 17 29N 100 7 E
Ban Kantang, Thailand .... 39 J2 7 25N 99 31 E
Ban Karon, Thailand .... 39 a 7 51N 98 18 E
Ban Kata, Thailand .... 39 a 7 50N 98 18 E
Ban Keun, Laos .... 38 C4 18 22N 102 35 E
Ban Khai, Thailand .... 38 F3 12 46N 101 18 E
Ban Kheun, Laos .... 38 B3 20 13N 101 7 E
Ban Khlong Khian, Thailand .... 39 a 8 10N 98 26 E
Ban Khlong Kua, Thailand .... 39 J3 6 57N 100 8 E
Ban Khuan, Thailand .... 39 a 8 20N 98 25 E
Ban Khuan Mao, Thailand .... 39 J2 7 50N 99 37 E
Ban Ko Yai Chim, Thailand .... 39 G2 11 17N 99 26 E
Ban Kok, Thailand .... 38 D4 16 40N 103 40 E
Ban Laem, Thailand .... 38 F2 13 13N 99 59 E
Ban Lamai, Thailand .... 39 b 9 28N 100 3 E
Ban Lao Ngam, Laos .... 38 E6 15 28N 106 10 E
Ban Le Kathe, Thailand .... 38 E2 15 49N 98 53 E
Ban Lo Po Noi, Thailand .... 39 a 9 8N 98 34 E
Ban Mae Chedi, Thailand .... 38 C2 19 11N 99 31 E
Ban Mae Laeng, Thailand .... 38 B2 20 1N 99 17 E
Ban Mae Nam, Thailand .... 39 b 9 34N 100 0 E
Ban Mae Sariang, Thailand .... 38 C1 18 10N 97 56 E
Ban Mê Thuot = Buon Ma Thuot,
  Vietnam .... 38 F7 12 40N 108 3 E
Ban Mi, Thailand .... 38 E3 15 3N 100 32 E
Ban Muong Mo, Laos .... 38 C4 19 4N 103 58 E
Ban Na Bo, Thailand .... 39 b 9 19N 99 41 E
Ban Na Mo, Laos .... 38 D5 17 7N 105 40 E
Ban Na San, Thailand .... 39 H2 8 53N 99 52 E
Ban Na Tong, Laos .... 38 B3 20 56N 101 47 E
Ban Nam Bac, Laos .... 38 B4 20 38N 102 20 E
Ban Nam Ma, Laos .... 38 A3 22 2N 101 37 E
Ban Ngang, Laos .... 38 E6 15 59N 106 11 E
Ban Nong Bok, Laos .... 38 D5 17 5N 104 48 E
Ban Nong Boua, Laos .... 38 E6 15 40N 106 33 E
Ban Nong Pling, Thailand .... 38 E3 15 40N 100 10 E
Ban Pak Chan, Thailand .... 39 G2 10 32N 98 51 E
Ban Patong, Thailand .... 39 a 7 54N 98 18 E
Ban Phai, Thailand .... 38 D4 16 4N 102 44 E
Ban Phak Chit, Thailand .... 39 a 8 0N 98 24 E
Ban Pong, Thailand .... 38 F2 13 50N 99 55 E
Ban Rawai, Thailand .... 39 a 7 47N 98 20 E
Ban Ron Phibun, Thailand .... 39 H2 8 9N 99 51 E
Ban Sakhu, Thailand .... 39 a 8 4N 98 18 E
Ban Sanam Chai, Thailand .... 39 J3 7 33N 100 25 E
Ban Sangkha, Thailand .... 38 E4 14 37N 103 52 E
Ban Tak, Thailand .... 38 D2 17 2N 99 4 E
Ban Tako, Thailand .... 38 E4 14 5N 102 40 E
Ban Tha Dua, Thailand .... 38 D2 17 59N 98 39 E
Ban Tha Li, Thailand .... 38 D3 17 37N 101 25 E
Ban Tha Nun, Thailand .... 39 a 8 12N 98 18 E
Ban Tha Rua, Thailand .... 39 a 7 59N 98 22 E
Ban Tha Yu, Thailand .... 39 a 8 17N 98 22 E
Ban Thahine, Laos .... 38 E5 14 12N 105 33 E
Ban Thong Krut, Thailand .... 39 b 9 25N 99 57 E
Ban Xien Kok, Laos .... 38 B3 20 54N 100 39 E
Ban Yen Nhan, Vietnam .... 38 B6 20 57N 106 2 E
Banaba, Kiribati .... 64 H8 0 45S 169 50 E
Banalia, Dem. Rep. of the Congo .... 54 B2 1 32N 25 5 E
Banam, Cambodia .... 39 G5 11 20N 105 17 E
Bananal, I. do, Brazil 93 F8 11 30S 50 30W
Banaras = Varanasi, India .... 43 G10 25 22N 83 0 E
Banas →, Gujarat, India .... 42 H4 23 45N 71 25 E
Banas →, Mad. P., India .... 43 G9 24 15N 81 30 E
Bânâs, Ras, Egypt .... 51 D13 23 57N 35 59 E
Banbridge, U.K. 10 B5 54 22N 6 16W
Banbury, U.K. 13 E6 52 4N 1 20W
Banchory, U.K. 11 D6 57 3N 2 29W
Bancroft, Canada 84 A7 45 3N 77 51W
Band Bonī, Iran .... 45 E8 25 30N 59 33 E
Band Qir, Iran .... 45 D6 31 39N 48 53 E
Banda, Mad. P., India .... 43 G8 24 3N 78 57 E
Banda, Ut. P., India .... 43 G9 25 30N 80 26 E
Banda, Kepulauan, Indonesia .... 37 E7 4 37S 129 50 E
Banda Aceh, Indonesia .... 36 C1 5 35N 95 20 E
Banda Banda, Mt., Australia .... 63 E5 31 10S 152 28 E
Banda Elat, Indonesia .... 37 F8 5 40S 133 5 E
Banda Is. = Banda, Kepulauan,
  Indonesia .... 37 E7 4 37S 129 50 E
Banda Sea, Indonesia .... 37 F7 6 0S 130 0 E
Bandai-Asahi △, Japan .... 30 F10 37 38N 140 5 E
Bandai-San, Japan .... 30 F10 37 36N 140 4 E
Bandān, Iran .... 45 D9 31 23N 60 44 E
Bandanaira, Indonesia .... 37 E7 4 32S 129 54 E
Bandanwara, India .... 42 F6 26 9N 74 38 E
Bandar = Machilipatnam, India .... 41 L12 16 12N 81 8 E
Bandar-e Abbās, Iran .... 45 E8 27 15N 56 15 E
Bandar-e Anzalī, Iran .... 45 B6 37 30N 49 30 E
Bandar-e Bushehr = Büshehr,
  Iran .... 45 D6 28 55N 50 55 E
Bandar-e Chārak, Iran .... 45 E7 26 45N 54 20 E
Bandar-e Deylam, Iran .... 45 D6 30 5N 50 10 E
Bandar-e Emām Khomeynī, Iran .... 45 D6 30 30N 49 5 E
Bandar-e Lengeh, Iran .... 45 E7 26 35N 54 58 E
Bandar-e Ma'shur, Iran .... 45 D6 30 35N 49 10 E
Bandar-e Rīg, Iran .... 45 D6 29 29N 50 38 E
Bandar-e Torkeman, Iran .... 45 B7 37 0N 54 10 E
Bandar Lampung =
  Tanjungkarang Telukbetung,
  Indonesia .... 36 F3 5 20S 105 10 E
Bandar Maharani = Muar,
  Malaysia .... 39 L4 2 3N 102 34 E

Bandar Penggaram = Batu Pahat,
  Malaysia .... 39 M4 1 50N 102 56 E
Bandar Seri Begawan, Brunei .... 36 C4 4 52N 115 0 E
Bandar Sri Aman, Malaysia .... 36 D4 1 15N 111 32 E
Bandawe, Malawi .... 55 E3 11 58S 34 5 E
Bandeira, Pico da, Brazil 95 A7 20 26S 41 47W
Bandera, Argentina 94 B3 28 55S 62 20W
Banderas, B. de, Mexico 86 C3 20 40N 105 30W
Bandhogarh, India .... 43 H9 23 40N 81 2 E
Bandi →, India .... 42 F6 26 12N 75 47 E
Bandikui, India .... 42 F7 27 3N 76 34 E
Bandırma, Turkey .... 23 D13 40 20N 28 0 E
Bandjarmasin = Banjarmasin,
  Indonesia .... 36 E4 3 20S 114 35 E
Bandon, Ireland 10 E3 51 44N 8 44W
Bandon →, Ireland 10 E3 51 43N 8 37W
Bandula, Mozam. .... 55 F3 19 0S 33 7 E
Bandundu, Dem. Rep. of
  the Congo .... 52 E3 3 15S 17 22 E
Bandung, Indonesia .... 36 F3 6 54S 107 36 E
Bāneh, Iran .... 44 C5 35 59N 45 53 E
Banes, Cuba 89 B4 21 0N 75 42W
Banff, Canada 70 C5 51 10N 115 34W
Banff, U.K. 11 D6 57 40N 2 33W
Banff △, Canada 70 C5 51 30N 116 15W
Bang Fai →, Laos .... 38 D5 16 57N 104 45 E
Bang Hieng →, Laos .... 38 D5 16 10N 105 10 E
Bang Krathum, Thailand .... 38 D3 16 34N 100 18 E
Bang Lamung, Thailand .... 38 F3 13 3N 100 56 E
Bang Mun Nak, Thailand .... 38 D3 16 2N 100 23 E
Bang Pa In, Thailand .... 38 E3 14 14N 100 35 E
Bang Rakam, Thailand .... 38 D3 16 45N 100 7 E
Bang Saphan, Thailand .... 39 G2 11 14N 99 28 E
Bang Thao, Thailand .... 39 a 7 59N 98 18 E
Banga, India .... 43 J13 21 34N 88 52 E
Bangala Dam, Zimbabwe .... 55 G3 21 7S 31 25 E
Bangalore, India .... 40 N10 12 59N 77 40 E
Banganga →, India .... 42 F6 27 6N 77 25 E
Bangaon, India .... 43 H13 23 0N 88 47 E
Bangassou, C.A.R. .... 52 D4 4 55N 23 7 E
Banggai, Indonesia .... 37 E6 1 34S 123 30 E
Banggai, Kepulauan, Indonesia .... 37 E6 1 40S 123 30 E
Banggai Arch. = Banggai,
  Kepulauan, Indonesia .... 37 E6 1 40S 123 30 E
Banggi, Malaysia .... 36 C5 7 17N 117 12 E
Banghāzī, Libya .... 51 B10 32 11N 20 3 E
Bangka, Sulawesi, Indonesia .... 37 D7 1 50N 125 5 E
Bangka, Sumatera, Indonesia .... 36 E3 2 0S 105 50 E
Bangka, Selat, Indonesia .... 37 G15 2 2S 112 46 E
Bangkalan, Indonesia .... 36 D2 0 18N 101 5 E
Bangkinang, Indonesia .... 36 E2 2 5S 102 9 E
Bangko, Indonesia .... 38 F3 13 45N 100 35 E
Bangladesh ■, Asia .... 41 H17 24 0N 90 0 E
Bangli, Indonesia .... 37 J18 8 27S 115 21 E
Bangong Co, India .... 43 B8 35 50N 79 20 E
Bangor, Down, U.K. 10 B6 54 40N 5 40W
Bangor, Gwynedd, U.K. 12 D3 53 14N 4 8W
Bangor, Maine, U.S.A. 69 D13 44 48N 68 46W
Bangor, Pa., U.S.A. 85 F9 40 52N 75 13W
Bangued, Phil. .... 37 A6 17 40N 120 37 E
Bangui, C.A.R. .... 52 D3 4 23N 18 35 E
Banguru, Dem. Rep. of
  the Congo .... 54 B2 0 30N 27 10 E
Bangweulu, L., Zambia .... 55 E3 11 0S 30 0 E
Bangweulu Swamp, Zambia .... 55 E3 11 20S 30 15 E
Banhine, Mozam. .... 57 C5 22 49S 32 55 E
Bani, Dom. Rep. 89 C5 18 16N 70 22W
Banī Sa'd, Iraq .... 44 C5 33 34N 44 32 E
Banihal Pass, India .... 43 C6 33 30N 75 12 E
Bāniyās, Syria .... 44 C3 35 10N 36 0 E
Banja Luka, Bos.-H. .... 22 B7 44 49N 17 11 E
Banjar, India .... 42 D7 31 38N 77 21 E
Banjar →, India .... 43 H9 22 36N 80 22 E
Banjarmasin, Indonesia .... 36 E4 3 20S 114 35 E
Banjul, Gambia 50 F2 13 28N 16 40W
Banka, India .... 43 G12 24 53N 86 55 E
Banket, Zimbabwe .... 55 F3 17 27S 30 19 E
Bankipore, India .... 41 G14 25 35N 85 10 E
Banks I., B.C., Canada 70 C3 53 20N 130 0W
Banks I., N.W.T., Canada 68 A7 73 15N 121 30W
Banks Pen., N.Z. .... 59 K4 43 45S 173 15 E
Banks Str., Australia .... 63 G4 40 40S 148 10 E
Bankura, India .... 43 H12 23 11N 87 18 E
Banmankhi, India .... 43 G12 25 53N 87 11 E
Bann →, Arm., U.K. 10 B5 54 30N 6 31W
Bann →, L'derry., U.K. 10 A5 55 8N 6 41W
Bannang Sata, Thailand .... 39 J3 6 16N 101 16 E
Banning, U.S.A. 79 M10 33 56N 116 53W
Bannockburn, Canada 84 B7 44 39N 77 33W
Bannockburn, U.K. 11 E5 56 5N 3 55W
Bannockburn, Zimbabwe .... 55 G2 20 17S 29 48 E
Bannu, Pakistan .... 40 C7 33 0N 70 18 E
Bano, India .... 43 H11 22 40N 84 55 E
Bansgaon, India .... 43 F10 26 33N 83 21 E
Banská Bystrica, Slovak Rep. .... 17 D10 48 46N 19 14 E
Banswara, India .... 42 H6 23 32N 74 24 E
Bantaeng, Indonesia .... 37 F5 5 32S 119 56 E
Bantry, Ireland 10 E2 51 41N 9 27W
Bantry B., Ireland 10 E2 51 37N 9 44W
Bantul, Indonesia .... 37 G14 7 55S 110 19 E
Bantva, India .... 42 J4 21 29N 70 12 E
Banyak, Kepulauan, Indonesia .... 36 D1 2 10N 97 10 E
Banyalbufar, Spain .... 24 B9 39 42N 2 31 E
Banyo, Cameroon .... 52 C2 6 52N 11 45 E
Banyumas, Indonesia .... 37 G13 7 32S 109 18 E
Banyuwangi, Indonesia .... 37 J17 8 13S 114 21 E
Banzare Coast, Antarctica .... 5 C9 68 0S 125 0 E
Bao Ha, Vietnam .... 38 A5 22 11N 104 21 E
Bao Lac, Vietnam .... 38 A5 22 57N 105 40 E
Bao Loc, Vietnam .... 39 G6 11 32N 107 48 E
Bao'an = Shenzhen, China .... 33 F10 22 32N 114 5 E
Baocheng, China .... 34 H4 33 12N 106 56 E
Baode, China .... 34 E6 39 1N 111 5 E
Baodi, China .... 35 E9 39 38N 117 20 E
Baoding, China .... 34 E8 38 50N 115 28 E
Baoji, China .... 34 G4 34 20N 107 5 E
Baoshan, China .... 34 D6 40 32N 110 2 E
Baoying, China .... 35 H10 33 17N 119 20 E
Bap, India .... 42 F5 27 23N 72 18 E
Bapatla, India .... 41 M12 15 55N 80 30 E
Bāqerābād, Iran .... 45 C6 33 2N 51 58 E
Ba'qūbah, Iraq .... 44 C5 33 45N 44 50 E
Baquedano, Chile 94 A2 23 20S 69 52W
Bar, Serbia & M. .... 23 C8 42 8N 19 6 E
Bar, Ukraine .... 17 D14 49 4N 27 40 E
Bar Bigha, India .... 43 G11 25 21N 85 47 E

Bar Harbor, U.S.A. 83 C11 44 23N 68 13W
Bar-le-Duc, France .... 20 B6 48 47N 5 10 E
Bara, India .... 43 G9 25 16N 81 43 E
Bara Banki, India .... 43 F9 26 55N 81 12 E
Barabai, Indonesia .... 36 E5 2 32S 115 34 E
Baraboo, U.S.A. 80 D10 43 28N 89 45W
Baracoa, Cuba 89 B5 20 20N 74 30W
Baradā →, Syria .... 46 B5 33 33N 36 34 E
Baradero, Argentina 94 C4 33 52S 59 29W
Baraga, U.S.A. 80 B10 46 47N 88 30W
Barah →, India .... 42 F6 27 42N 77 5 E
Barahona, Dom. Rep. 89 C5 18 13N 71 7W
Barail Range, India .... 41 G18 25 15N 93 20 E
Barakaldo, Spain 21 A4 43 18N 2 59W
Barakar →, India .... 43 G12 24 7N 86 14 E
Barakhola, India .... 41 G18 25 0N 92 45 E
Barakot, India .... 43 J11 21 33N 84 59 E
Barakpur, India .... 43 H13 22 44N 88 30 E
Baralaba, Australia .... 62 C4 24 13S 149 50 E
Baralzon L., Canada 71 B9 60 0N 98 3W
Baramula, India .... 43 B6 34 15N 74 20 E
Baran, India .... 42 G7 25 9N 76 40 E
Baran →, Pakistan .... 42 G3 25 13N 68 17 E
Baranavichy, Belarus .... 17 B14 53 10N 26 0 E
Baranof, U.S.A. 70 B2 57 5N 134 50W
Baranof I., U.S.A. 68 C6 57 0N 135 0W
Barapasi, Indonesia .... 37 E9 2 15S 137 5 E
Barasat, India .... 43 H13 22 46N 88 31 E
Barat Daya, Kepulauan,
  Indonesia .... 37 F7 7 30S 128 0 E
Barataria B., U.S.A. 81 L10 29 20N 89 55W
Barauda, India .... 42 H6 23 33N 75 15 E
Baraut, India .... 42 E7 29 13N 77 7 E
Barbacena, Brazil 95 A7 21 15S 43 56W
Barbados ■, W. Indies .... 89 g 13 10N 59 30W
Barbària, C. de, Spain .... 24 C7 38 39N 1 24 E
Barbastro, Spain .... 21 A6 42 2N 0 5 E
Barberton, S. Africa .... 57 D5 25 42S 31 2 E
Barberton, U.S.A. 84 E3 41 0N 81 39W
Barbonneau, St. Lucia .... 89 f 13 59N 60 58W
Barbosa, Colombia 92 B4 5 57N 73 37W
Barbourville, U.S.A. 83 G4 36 52N 83 53W
Barbuda, W. Indies 89 C7 17 30N 61 40W
Barcaldine, Australia .... 62 C4 23 43S 145 6 E
Barcellona Pozzo di Gotto, Italy . 22 E6 38 9N 15 13 E
Barcelona, Spain .... 21 B7 41 21N 2 10 E
Barcelona, Venezuela 92 A6 10 10N 64 40W
Barceloneta, Puerto Rico ..... 89 d 18 27N 66 32W
Barcelos, Brazil 92 D6 1 0S 63 0W
Barcoo →, Australia .... 62 D3 25 30S 142 50 E
Bardaï, Chad .... 51 D9 21 25N 17 0 E
Bardas Blancas, Argentina 94 D2 35 49S 69 45W
Bardawîl, Sabkhet el, Egypt .. 46 D2 31 10N 33 15 E
Barddhaman, India .... 43 H12 23 14N 87 39 E
Bardejov, Slovak Rep. .... 17 D11 49 18N 21 15 E
Bardera, Somali Rep. .... 47 G3 2 20N 42 27 E
Bardīyah, Libya .... 51 B10 31 45N 25 5 E
Bardsey I., U.K. 12 E3 52 45N 4 47W
Bardstown, U.S.A. 82 G3 37 49N 85 28W
Bareilly, India .... 43 E8 28 22N 79 27 E
Barela, India .... 43 H9 23 6N 80 3 E
Barents Sea, Arctic .... 4 B9 73 0N 39 0 E
Barfleur, Pte. de, France 20 B3 49 42N 1 16W
Bargara, Australia .... 62 C5 24 50S 152 25 E
Barguzin, Russia .... 29 D11 53 37N 109 37 E
Barh, India .... 43 G11 25 29N 85 46 E
Barhaj, India .... 43 F10 26 18N 83 44 E
Barharwa, India .... 43 G12 24 52N 87 47 E
Barhi, India .... 43 G11 24 15N 85 25 E
Bari, India .... 42 F7 26 39N 77 39 E
Bari, Italy .... 22 D7 41 8N 16 51 E
Bari Doab, Pakistan .... 42 D5 30 20N 73 0 E
Bari Sadri, India .... 42 G6 24 28N 74 30 E
Barīdī, Ra's, Si. Arabia ...... 44 E3 24 17N 37 31 E
Barim, Yemen .... 48 E8 12 39N 43 25 E
Barinas, Venezuela 92 B4 8 36N 70 15W
Baring, C., Canada 68 B8 70 0N 117 30W
Baringo, L., Kenya .... 54 B4 0 47N 36 16 E
Barisal, Bangla. .... 41 H17 22 45N 90 20 E
Barisal □, Bangla. .... 41 H17 22 40N 90 20 E
Barisan, Bukit, Indonesia .... 36 E2 3 30S 102 15 E
Barito →, Indonesia .... 36 E4 4 0S 114 50 E
Baritú △, Argentina 94 A3 23 43S 64 40W
Bark L., Canada 84 A7 45 27N 77 51W
Barkakana, India .... 43 H11 23 37N 85 29 E
Barker, U.S.A. 84 C6 43 20N 78 33W
Barkley, L., U.S.A. 83 G2 37 1N 88 14W
Barkley Sound, Canada 70 D3 48 50N 125 10W
Barkly East, S. Africa .... 56 E4 30 58S 27 33 E
Barkly Roadhouse, Australia .. 61 B2 19 52S 135 50 E
Barkly Tableland, Australia ... 62 B2 17 50S 136 40 E
Barkly West, S. Africa .... 56 D3 28 5S 24 31 E
Barkol Kazak Zizhixian, China . 32 B4 43 37N 93 2 E
Bârlad, Romania .... 17 E14 46 15N 27 38 E
Bârlad →, Romania .... 17 F14 45 38N 27 32 E
Barlee, L., Australia .... 61 E2 29 15S 119 30 E
Barlee, Mt., Australia .... 61 D4 24 38S 128 13 E
Barletta, Italy .... 22 D7 41 19N 16 17 E
Barlovento, Canary Is. 24 F2 28 48N 17 48W
Barlow L., Canada 71 A8 62 0N 103 0W
Barmedman, Australia .... 63 E4 34 9S 147 21 E
Barmer, India .... 42 G4 25 45N 71 20 E
Barmera, Australia .... 63 E3 34 15S 140 28 E
Barmouth, U.K. 12 E3 52 44N 4 4W
Barna →, India .... 43 G10 25 21N 83 3 E
Barnagar, India .... 42 H6 23 7N 75 19 E
Barnala, India .... 42 D6 30 23N 75 33 E
Barnard Castle, U.K. 12 C6 54 33N 1 55W
Barnaul, Russia .... 28 D9 53 20N 83 40 E
Barnesville, U.S.A. 83 J3 33 3N 84 9W
Barnet □, U.K. 13 F7 51 38N 0 9W
Barneveld, Neths. .... 15 B5 52 7N 5 36 E
Barneveld, U.S.A. 85 C9 43 16N 75 14W
Barnhart, U.S.A. 81 K4 31 8N 101 10W
Barnsley, U.K. 12 D6 53 34N 1 27W
Barnstaple, U.K. 13 F3 51 5N 4 4W
Barnstaple Bay = Bideford Bay,
  U.K. 13 F3 51 5N 4 20W
Barnsville, U.S.A. 80 B6 46 43N 96 28W
Barnwell, U.S.A. 83 J5 33 15N 81 23W
Baro, Nigeria .... 50 G7 8 35N 6 18 E
Baroda = Vadodara, India ... 42 H5 22 20N 73 10 E
Baroda, India .... 42 G7 25 29N 76 35 E
Baroe, S. Africa .... 56 E3 33 13S 24 33 E
Baron Ra., Australia .... 60 D4 23 30S 127 45 E
Barotseland, Zambia .... 53 H4 15 0S 24 0 E
Barpeta, India .... 41 F17 26 20N 91 10 E
Barques, Pt. Aux, U.S.A. 84 B2 44 4N 82 58W

Barquísimeto, Venezuela 92 A5 10 4N 69 19W
Barr Smith Range, Australia .. 61 E3 27 4S 120 20 E
Barra, Brazil 93 F10 11 5S 43 10W
Barra, U.K. 11 E1 57 0N 7 29W
Barra, Sd. of, U.K. 11 D1 57 4N 7 25W
Barra de Navidad, Mexico 86 D4 19 12N 104 41W
Barra do Corda, Brazil 93 E9 5 30S 45 10W
Barra do Piraí, Brazil 95 A7 22 30S 43 50W
Barra Falsa, Pta. da, Mozam. . 57 C6 22 58S 35 37 E
Barra Hd., U.K. 11 E1 56 47N 7 40W
Barra Mansa, Brazil 95 A7 22 35S 44 12W
Barraba, Australia .... 63 E5 30 21S 150 35 E
Barrackpur = Barakpur, India . 43 H13 22 44N 88 30 E
Barradale Roadhouse, Australia 60 D1 22 42S 114 58 E
Barraigh = Barra, U.K. 11 E1 57 0N 7 29W
Barranca, Lima, Peru 92 F3 10 45S 77 50W
Barranca, Loreto, Peru 92 D3 4 50S 76 50W
Barranca del Cobre △, Mexico 86 B3 27 18N 107 40W
Barrancabermeja, Colombia .. 92 B4 7 0N 73 50W
Barrancas, Venezuela 92 B6 8 55N 62 5W
Barrancos, Portugal 21 C2 38 10N 6 58W
Barranqueras, Argentina 94 B4 27 30S 59 0W
Barranquilla, Colombia 92 A4 11 0N 74 50W
Barraute, Canada 72 C4 48 26N 77 38W
Barre, Mass., U.S.A. 85 D12 42 25N 72 6W
Barre, Vt., U.S.A. 85 B12 44 12N 72 30W
Barreal, Argentina 94 C2 31 33S 69 28W
Barreiras, Brazil 93 F10 12 8S 45 0W
Barreirinhas, Brazil 93 D10 2 30S 42 50W
Barreiro, Portugal 21 C1 38 40N 9 6W
Barren, Nosy, Madag. .... 57 B7 18 25S 43 40 E
Barretos, Brazil 93 H9 20 30S 48 35W
Barrhead, Canada 70 C6 54 10N 114 24W
Barrie, Canada 84 B5 44 24N 79 40W
Barrier Ra., Australia .... 63 E3 31 0S 141 30 E
Barrière, Canada 70 C4 51 12N 120 7W
Barrington, U.S.A. 85 E13 41 44N 71 18W
Barrington L., Canada 71 B8 56 55N 100 15W
Barrington Tops, Australia ... 63 E5 32 6S 151 28 E
Barringun, Australia .... 63 D4 29 1S 145 41 E
Barro do Garças, Brazil 93 G8 15 54S 52 16W
Barron, U.S.A. 80 C9 45 24N 91 51W
Barrow, U.S.A. 68 A4 71 18N 156 47W
Barrow →, Ireland 10 D5 52 25S 6 58W
Barrow Creek, Australia ..... 62 C1 21 30S 133 55 E
Barrow I., Australia .... 60 D2 20 45S 115 20 E
Barrow-in-Furness, U.K. 12 C4 54 7N 3 14W
Barrow Pt., Australia .... 62 A3 14 20S 144 40 E
Barrow Pt., U.S.A. 66 B4 71 10N 156 20W
Barrow Ra., Australia .... 61 E4 26 0S 127 40 E
Barrow Str., Canada 4 B3 74 20N 95 0W
Barry, U.K. 13 F4 51 24N 3 16W
Barry's Bay, Canada 84 A7 45 29N 77 41W
Barsat, Pakistan .... 43 A5 36 10N 72 45 E
Barsham, Syria .... 44 C4 35 21N 40 33 E
Barsi, India .... 40 K9 18 10N 75 50 E
Barsoi, India .... 41 G15 25 48N 87 57 E
Barstow, U.S.A. 79 L9 34 54N 117 1W
Barthélemy, Col, Vietnam .... 38 C5 19 26N 104 6 E
Bartica, Guyana 92 B7 6 25N 58 40W
Bartlesville, U.S.A. 81 G7 36 45N 95 59W
Bartlett, U.S.A. 78 J8 36 29N 118 2W
Bartlett, L., Canada 70 A5 63 5N 118 20W
Bartlett, U.S.A. 85 B12 44 45N 72 11W
Barton, U.S.A. 85 B12 44 45N 72 11W
Barton upon Humber, U.K. ... 12 D7 53 41N 0 25W
Bartow, U.S.A. 83 M5 27 54N 81 50W
Barú, Volcan, Panama 88 E3 8 55N 82 35W
Barumba, Dem. Rep. of
  the Congo .... 54 B1 1 3N 23 37 E
Baruunsuu, Mongolia .... 34 C3 43 43N 105 35 E
Barwani, India .... 42 H6 22 2N 74 57 E
Barysaw, Belarus .... 17 A15 54 17N 28 28 E
Barzān, Iraq .... 44 B5 36 55N 44 3 E
Bāsa'idū, Iran .... 45 E7 26 35N 55 20 E
Basal, Pakistan .... 42 C5 33 33N 72 13 E
Basankusa, Dem. Rep. of
  the Congo .... 52 D3 1 5N 19 50 E
Basarabeasca, Moldova ...... 17 E15 46 21N 28 58 E
Basarabia = Bessarabiya,
  Moldova .... 17 E15 47 0N 28 10 E
Basawa, Afghan. .... 42 B4 34 15N 70 50 E
Bascuñán, C., Chile 94 B1 28 52S 71 35W
Basel, Switz. .... 20 C7 47 35N 7 35 E
Bashäkerd, Kühhā-ye, Iran ... 45 E8 26 42N 58 35 E
Bashaw, Canada 70 C6 52 35N 112 58W
Bāshī, Iran .... 45 D6 28 41N 51 4 E
Bashkir Republic =
  Bashkortostan □, Russia ... 18 D10 54 0N 57 0 E
Bashkortostan □, Russia .... 18 D10 54 0N 57 0 E
Basibasy, Madag. .... 57 C7 22 10S 43 40 E
Basilan I., Phil. .... 37 C6 6 35N 122 0 E
Basilan Str., Phil. .... 37 C6 6 50N 122 0 E
Basildon, U.K. .... 13 F8 51 34N 0 28 E
Basim = Washim, India ...... 40 J10 20 3N 77 0 E
Basin, U.S.A. 76 D9 44 23N 108 2W
Basingstoke, U.K. 13 F6 51 15N 1 5W
Baskatong, Rés., Canada 72 C4 46 46N 75 50W
Basle = Basel, Switz. .... 20 C7 47 35N 7 35 E
Basoda, India .... 42 H7 23 52N 77 54 E
Basoko, Dem. Rep. of Congo . 54 B1 1 16N 23 40 E
Basque Provinces = País
  Vasco □, Spain 21 A4 42 50N 2 45W
Basra = Al Başrah, Iraq ...... 44 D5 30 30N 47 50 E
Bass Str., Australia .... 63 F4 39 15S 146 30 E
Bassano, Canada 70 C6 50 48N 112 20W
Bassano del Grappa, Italy ... 22 B4 45 46N 11 44 E
Bassas da India, Ind. Oc. .... 53 J7 22 0S 39 0 E
Basse-Pointe, Martinique .... 88 c 14 52N 61 8W
Basse-Terre, Guadeloupe .... 88 b 16 0N 61 44W
Basse Terre, Trin. & Tob. 93 K15 10 7N 61 19W
Bassein, Burma .... 41 L19 16 45N 94 30 E
Basses, Pte. des, Guadeloupe 88 b 15 52N 61 17W
Basseterre, St. Kitts & Nevis . 89 C7 17 17N 62 43W
Bassett, U.S.A. 80 D5 42 35N 99 32W
Bassi, India .... 42 D7 30 44N 76 21 E
Bastak, Iran .... 45 E7 27 15N 54 25 E
Baştām, Iran .... 45 B7 36 29N 55 4 E
Bastar, India .... 41 K12 19 15N 81 40 E
Basti, India .... 43 F10 26 52N 82 55 E
Bastia, France .... 20 E8 42 40N 9 30 E
Bastogne, Belgium .... 15 D5 50 1N 5 43 E
Bastrop, La., U.S.A. 81 J9 32 47N 91 55W
Bastrop, Tex., U.S.A. 81 K6 30 7N 97 19W
Bat Yam, Israel .... 46 C3 32 2N 34 44 E
Bata, Eq. Guin. .... 52 D1 1 57N 9 50 E
Bataan □, Phil. .... 37 B6 14 40N 120 25 E
Batabanó, Cuba 88 B3 22 40N 82 20W

Batabanó, G. de, Cuba 88 B3 22 30N 82 30W
Batac, Phil. .... 37 A6 18 3N 120 34 E
Batagai, Russia .... 29 C14 67 38N 134 38 E
Batama, Dem. Rep. of the Congo 54 B2 0 58N 26 33 E
Batamay, Russia .... 29 C13 63 30N 129 15 E
Batang, Indonesia .... 37 G13 6 55S 109 45 E
Batangas, Phil. .... 37 B6 13 35N 121 10 E
Batanta, Indonesia .... 37 E8 0 55S 130 40 E
Batatais, Brazil 95 A6 20 54S 47 37W
Batavia, U.S.A. 84 D6 43 0N 78 11W
Batchelor, Australia .... 60 B5 13 4S 131 1 E
Batdambang, Cambodia ..... 38 F4 13 7N 103 12 E
Batemans B., Australia ...... 63 F5 35 40S 150 12 E
Batemans Bay, Australia .... 63 F5 35 44S 150 11 E
Bates Ra., Australia .... 61 E3 27 27S 121 5 E
Batesburg-Leesville, U.S.A. .. 83 J5 33 54N 81 33W
Batesville, Ark., U.S.A. 81 H9 35 46N 91 39W
Batesville, Miss., U.S.A. 81 H10 34 19N 89 57W
Batesville, Tex., U.S.A. 81 L5 28 58N 99 37W
Bath, Canada 85 B8 44 11N 76 47W
Bath, U.K. 13 F5 51 23N 2 22W
Bath, Maine, U.S.A. 83 D11 43 55N 69 49W
Bath, N.Y., U.S.A. 84 D7 42 20N 77 19W
Bath & North East Somerset □,
  U.K. 13 F5 51 21N 2 27W
Batheay, Cambodia .... 39 G5 11 59N 104 57 E
Bathsheba, Barbados .... 89 g 13 13N 59 31W
Bathurst, Australia .... 63 E4 33 25S 149 31 E
Bathurst, Canada 73 C6 47 37N 65 43W
Bathurst, S. Africa .... 56 E4 33 30S 26 50 E
Bathurst, C., Canada 68 A7 70 34N 128 0W
Bathurst B., Australia .... 62 A3 14 16S 144 25 E
Bathurst Harb., Australia .... 63 G4 43 15S 146 10 E
Bathurst I., Australia .... 60 B5 11 30S 130 10 E
Bathurst I., Canada 4 B2 76 0N 100 30W
Bathurst Inlet, Canada 68 B9 66 50N 108 1W
Batlow, Australia .... 63 F4 35 31S 148 9 E
Batman, Turkey .... 19 G7 37 55N 41 5 E
Baţn al Ghūl, Jordan .... 46 F4 29 36N 35 56 E
Batna, Algeria .... 50 A7 35 34N 6 15 E
Batoka, Zambia .... 55 F2 16 45S 27 15 E
Baton Rouge, U.S.A. 81 K9 30 27N 91 11W
Batong, Ko, Thailand .... 39 J2 6 32N 99 12 E
Batopilas, Mexico 86 B3 27 0N 107 45W
Batouri, Cameroon .... 52 D2 4 30N 14 25 E
Båtsfjord, Norway .... 8 A23 70 38N 29 39 E
Battambang = Batdambang,
  Cambodia .... 38 F4 13 7N 103 12 E
Batticaloa, Sri Lanka .... 40 R12 7 43N 81 45 E
Battipáglia, Italy .... 22 D6 40 37N 14 58 E
Battle, U.K. .... 13 G8 50 55N 0 30 E
Battle →, Canada 71 C7 52 43N 108 15W
Battle Creek, U.S.A. 82 D3 42 19N 85 11W
Battle Ground, U.S.A. 78 E4 45 47N 122 32W
Battle Harbour, Canada 73 B8 52 16N 55 35W
Battle Lake, U.S.A. 80 B7 46 17N 95 43W
Battle Mountain, U.S.A. 76 F5 40 38N 116 56W
Battlefields, Zimbabwe ...... 55 F2 18 37S 29 47 E
Battleford, Canada 71 C7 52 45N 108 15W
Batu, Ethiopia .... 47 F2 6 55N 39 45 E
Batu, Kepulauan, Indonesia .. 36 E1 0 30S 98 25 E
Batu Caves, Malaysia .... 39 L3 3 15N 101 40 E
Batu Ferringhi, Malaysia .... 39 c 5 28N 100 15 E
Batu Gajah, Malaysia .... 39 K3 4 28N 101 3 E
Batu Is. = Batu, Kepulauan,
  Indonesia .... 36 E1 0 30S 98 25 E
Batu Pahat, Malaysia .... 39 M4 1 50N 102 56 E
Batuata, Indonesia .... 37 F6 6 12S 122 42 E
Batugondang, Tanjung,
  Indonesia .... 37 J17 8 6S 114 29 E
Batukau, Gunung, Indonesia . 37 J18 8 20S 115 5 E
Batumi, Georgia .... 19 F7 41 39N 41 44 E
Batur, Indonesia .... 37 J18 8 15S 115 20 E
Batur, Gunung, Indonesia ... 37 J18 8 14S 115 23 E
Baturaja, Indonesia .... 36 E2 4 11S 104 15 E
Baturité, Brazil 93 D11 4 28S 38 45W
Baturiti, Indonesia .... 37 J18 8 19S 115 11 E
Bau, Malaysia .... 36 D4 1 25N 110 9 E
Baubau, Indonesia .... 37 F6 5 25S 122 38 E
Baucau, E. Timor .... 37 F7 8 27S 126 27 E
Bauchi, Nigeria .... 50 F7 10 22N 9 48 E
Baudette, U.S.A. 80 A7 48 43N 94 36W
Bauer, C., Australia .... 63 E1 32 44S 134 4 E
Bauhinia, Australia .... 62 C4 24 35S 149 18 E
Baukau = Baucau, E. Timor .. 37 F7 8 27S 126 27 E
Bauld, C., Canada 69 C14 51 38N 55 26W
Bauru, Brazil 95 A6 22 10S 49 0W
Bausi, India .... 43 G12 24 48N 87 1 E
Bauska, Latvia .... 9 H21 56 24N 24 15 E
Bautzen, Germany .... 16 C8 51 10N 14 26 E
Bavānāt, Iran .... 45 D7 30 28N 53 27 E
Bavaria = Bayern □, Germany 16 D6 48 50N 12 0 E
Bavispe →, Mexico 86 B3 29 30N 109 11W
Bawdwin, Burma .... 41 H20 23 5N 97 20 E
Bawean, Indonesia .... 36 F4 5 46S 112 35 E
Bawku, Ghana 50 F5 11 3N 0 19W
Bawlake, Burma .... 41 K20 19 11N 97 21 E
Baxley, U.S.A. 83 K4 31 47N 82 21W
Baxter, U.S.A. 80 B7 46 21N 94 17W
Baxter Springs, U.S.A. 81 G7 37 2N 94 44W
Baxter State △, U.S.A. 83 B11 46 5N 68 57W
Bay City, Mich., U.S.A. 82 D4 43 36N 83 54W
Bay City, Tex., U.S.A. 81 L7 28 59N 95 58W
Bay Minette, U.S.A. 83 K2 30 53N 87 46W
Bay Roberts, Canada 73 C9 47 36N 53 16W
Bay St. Louis, U.S.A. 81 K10 30 19N 89 17W
Bay Springs, U.S.A. 81 K10 31 59N 89 17W
Bay View, N.Z. .... 59 H6 39 25S 176 50 E
Baya, Dem. Rep. of the Congo 55 E2 11 53S 27 25 E
Bayamo, Cuba 88 B4 20 20N 76 40W
Bayamón, Puerto Rico ...... 89 d 18 24N 66 10W
Bayan Har Shan, China ..... 32 C4 34 0N 98 0 E
Bayan Hot = Alxa Zuoqi, China 34 E3 38 50N 105 40 E
Bayan Lepas, Malaysia ...... 39 c 5 17N 100 16 E
Bayan Obo, China .... 34 D5 41 52N 109 59 E
Bayan-Ovoo = Erdenetsogt,
  Mongolia .... 34 C4 42 55N 106 5 E
Bayana, India .... 42 F7 26 55N 77 18 E
Bayanaūyl, Kazakhstan ..... 28 D8 50 45N 75 45 E
Bayandalay, Mongolia ...... 34 C2 43 30N 103 29 E
Bayanhongor, Mongolia ..... 32 B5 46 8N 102 43 E
Bayard, N. Mex., U.S.A. 77 K9 32 46N 108 8W
Bayard, Nebr., U.S.A. 80 E3 41 45N 103 20W
Baybay, Phil. .... 37 B6 10 40N 124 55 E
Baydhabo = Baidoa, Somali Rep. 47 G3 3 8N 43 30 E
Bayern □, Germany .... 16 D6 48 50N 12 0 E
Bayeux, France 20 B3 49 17N 0 42W

Bayfield, Canada 84 C3 43 34N 81 42W
Bayfield, U.S.A. 80 B9 46 49N 90 49W
Bayındır, Turkey .... 23 E12 38 13N 27 39 E
Bayji, Iraq .... 44 C4 35 0N 43 30 E
Baykal, Oz., Russia .... 29 D11 53 0N 108 0 E
Baykan, Turkey .... 44 B4 38 7N 41 44 E
Baykonur = Bayqongyr,
  Kazakhstan .... 28 E7 47 48N 65 50 E
Baymak, Russia .... 18 D10 52 36N 58 19 E
Baynes Mts., Namibia .... 56 B1 17 15S 13 0 E
Bayombong, Phil. .... 37 A6 16 30N 121 10 E
Bayonne, France 20 E3 43 30N 1 28W
Bayonne, U.S.A. 85 F10 40 40N 74 7W
Bayovar, Peru 92 E2 5 50S 81 0W
Bayqongyr, Kazakhstan ..... 28 E7 47 48N 65 50 E
Bayram-Ali = Bayramaly,
  Turkmenistan .... 28 F7 37 37N 62 10 E
Bayramaly, Turkmenistan .... 28 F7 37 37N 62 10 E
Bayramiç, Turkey .... 23 E12 39 48N 26 36 E
Bayreuth, Germany .... 16 D6 49 56N 11 35 E
Bayrūt, Lebanon .... 46 B4 33 53N 35 31 E
Bays, L. of, Canada 84 A5 45 15N 79 4W
Baysville, Canada 84 A5 45 9N 79 7W
Bayt Lahm, West Bank ...... 46 D4 31 43N 35 12 E
Baytown, U.S.A. 81 L7 29 43N 94 59W
Bayun, Indonesia .... 37 J18 8 11S 115 16 E
Baza, Spain 21 D4 37 30N 2 47W
Bazaruto △, Mozam. .... 57 C6 21 42S 35 26 E
Bazaruto, I. do, Mozam. ..... 57 C6 21 40S 35 28 E
Bazhou, China .... 34 E9 39 8N 116 22 E
Bazmān, Kūh-e, Iran .... 45 D9 28 4N 60 1 E
Beach, U.S.A. 80 B3 46 58N 104 0W
Beach City, U.S.A. 84 F3 40 39N 81 35W
Beachport, Australia .... 63 F3 37 29S 140 0 E
Beachy Hd., U.K. .... 13 G8 50 44N 0 15 E
Beacon, Australia .... 61 F2 30 26S 117 52 E
Beacon, U.S.A. 85 E11 41 30N 73 58W
Beaconsfield, Australia ..... 63 G4 41 11S 146 48 E
Beagle, Canal, S. Amer. 96 H3 55 0S 68 30W
Beagle Bay, Australia .... 60 C3 16 58S 122 40 E
Bealanana, Madag. .... 57 A8 14 33S 48 44 E
Beals Cr. →, U.S.A. 81 J4 32 10N 100 51W
Beamsville, Canada 84 C5 43 12N 79 28W
Bear →, Calif., U.S.A. 78 G5 38 56N 121 36W
Bear →, Utah, U.S.A. 74 B4 41 30N 112 8W
Bear I., Ireland 10 E2 51 38N 9 50W
Bear L., Canada 71 B9 55 8N 96 0W
Bear L., U.S.A. 76 F8 41 59N 111 21W
Beardmore, Canada 72 C2 49 36N 87 57W
Beardmore Glacier, Antarctica 5 E11 84 30S 170 0 E
Beardstown, U.S.A. 80 F9 40 1N 90 26W
Bearma →, India .... 43 G8 24 20N 79 51 E
Béarn, France 20 E3 43 20N 0 30W
Bearpaw Mts., U.S.A. 76 B9 48 12N 109 30W
Bearskin Lake, Canada 72 B1 53 58N 91 2W
Beas →, India .... 42 D6 31 10N 74 59 E
Beata, C., Dom. Rep. 89 C5 17 40N 71 30W
Beata, I., Dom. Rep. 89 C5 17 34N 71 31W
Beatrice, U.S.A. 80 E6 40 16N 96 45W
Beatrice, Zimbabwe .... 55 F3 18 15S 30 55 E
Beatrice, C., Australia ...... 62 A2 14 20S 136 55 E
Beatton →, Canada 70 B4 56 15N 120 45W
Beatton River, Canada 70 B4 57 26N 121 20W
Beatty, U.S.A. 78 J10 36 54N 116 46W
Beauce, Plaine de la, France . 20 B4 48 10N 1 45 E
Beauceville, Canada 73 C5 46 13N 70 46W
Beaudesert, Australia .... 63 D5 27 59S 153 0 E
Beaufort, Malaysia .... 36 C5 5 30N 115 40 E
Beaufort, N.C., U.S.A. 83 H7 34 43N 76 40W
Beaufort, S.C., U.S.A. 83 J5 32 26N 80 40W
Beaufort Sea, Arctic 4 B1 72 0N 140 0W
Beaufort West, S. Africa ..... 56 E3 32 18S 22 36 E
Beauharnois, Canada 85 A11 45 20N 73 52W
Beaulieu →, Canada 70 A6 62 3N 113 11W
Beauly, U.K. 11 D4 57 30N 4 28W
Beauly →, U.K. 11 D4 57 29N 4 27W
Beaumaris, U.K. 12 D3 53 16N 4 6W
Beaumont, Belgium .... 15 D4 50 15N 4 14 E
Beaumont, U.S.A. 81 K7 30 5N 94 6W
Beaune, France .... 20 C6 47 2N 4 50 E
Beaupré, Canada 73 C5 47 3N 70 54W
Beauraing, Belgium .... 15 D4 50 7N 4 57 E
Beausejour, Canada 71 C9 50 5N 96 35W
Beauvais, France .... 20 B5 49 25N 2 8 E
Beauval, Canada 71 B7 55 9N 107 37W
Beaver, Okla., U.S.A. 81 G4 36 49N 100 31W
Beaver, Pa., U.S.A. 84 F4 40 42N 80 19W
Beaver, Utah, U.S.A. 77 G7 38 17N 112 38W
Beaver →, B.C., Canada 70 B4 59 52N 124 20W
Beaver →, Ont., Canada 72 A2 55 55N 87 48W
Beaver →, Sask., Canada ... 71 B7 55 26N 107 45W
Beaver →, U.S.A. 81 G5 36 35N 99 30W
Beaver City, U.S.A. 80 E5 40 8N 99 50W
Beaver Creek, Canada 68 B5 63 0N 141 0W
Beaver Dam, U.S.A. 80 D10 43 28N 88 50W
Beaver Falls, U.S.A. 84 F4 40 46N 80 20W
Beaver Hill L., Canada 71 C10 54 5N 94 50W
Beaver I., U.S.A. 82 C3 45 40N 85 33W
Beaverhill L., Canada 70 C6 53 27N 112 32W
Beaverlodge, Canada 70 B5 55 11N 119 29W
Beaverstone →, Canada 72 B2 54 59N 89 25W
Beaverton, Canada 84 B5 44 26N 79 9W
Beaverton, U.S.A. 78 E4 45 29N 122 48W
Beawar, India .... 42 F6 26 3N 74 18 E
Bebedouro, Brazil 95 A6 21 0S 48 25W
Bebera, Tanjung, Indonesia .. 37 K18 8 44S 115 51 E
Beboa, Madag. .... 57 B7 17 22S 44 33 E
Becan, Mexico 87 D7 18 31N 89 28W
Beccles, U.K. .... 13 E9 52 27N 1 35 E
Bečej, Serbia & M. .... 23 B9 45 36N 20 3 E
Béchar, Algeria 50 B5 31 38N 2 18W
Beckley, U.S.A. 82 G5 37 47N 81 11W
Beddouza, Ras, Morocco 50 B4 32 33N 9 9W
Bedford, Canada 85 A12 45 7N 72 59W
Bedford, S. Africa .... 56 E4 32 40S 26 10 E
Bedford, U.K. 13 E7 52 8N 0 28W
Bedford, Ind., U.S.A. 82 F2 38 52N 86 29W
Bedford, Iowa, U.S.A. 80 E7 40 40N 94 44W
Bedford, Ohio, U.S.A. 84 E3 41 23N 81 32W
Bedford, Pa., U.S.A. 84 F6 40 1N 78 30W
Bedford, Va., U.S.A. 82 G6 37 20N 79 31W
Bedford, C., Australia .... 62 B4 15 14S 145 21 E
Bedfordshire □, U.K. 13 E7 52 4N 0 28W
Bedok, Singapore .... 39 d 1 19N 103 56 E
Bedourie, Australia .... 62 C2 24 30S 139 30 E
Bedum, Neths. .... 15 A6 53 18N 6 36 E
Beebe Plain, Canada 85 A12 45 1N 72 9W
Beech Creek, U.S.A. 84 E7 41 5N 77 36W

Beef I., *Br. Virgin Is.* .... **89 e** 18 26N 64 30W
Beenleigh, *Australia* .... **63 D5** 27 43S 153 10 E
Be'er Menuḥa, *Israel* .... **44 D2** 30 19N 35 8 E
Be'er Sheva, *Israel* .... **46 D3** 31 15N 34 48 E
Beersheba = Be'er Sheva, *Israel* **46 D3** 31 15N 34 48 E
Beestekraal, *S. Africa* .... **57 D4** 25 23S 27 38 E
Beeston, *U.K.* **12 E6** 52 56N 1 14W
Beeville, *U.S.A.* **81 L6** 28 24N 97 45W
Befale, *Dem. Rep. of the Congo* **52 D4** 0 25N 20 45 E
Befandriana, *Mahajanga, Madag.* **57 B8** 15 16S 48 32 E
Befandriana, *Toliara, Madag.* **57 C7** 21 55S 44 0 E
Befasy, *Madag.* .... **57 C7** 20 33S 44 39 E
Befotaka, *Antsiranana, Madag.* **57 A8** 13 15S 48 16 E
Befotaka, *Fianarantsoa, Madag.* **57 C8** 23 49S 47 0 E
Bega, *Australia* .... **63 F4** 36 41S 149 51 E
Begusarai, *India* .... **43 G12** 25 24N 86 9 E
Behābād, *Iran* .... **45 C8** 32 24N 59 47 E
Behala, *India* .... **43 H13** 22 30N 88 20 E
Behara, *Madag.* .... **57 C8** 24 55S 46 20 E
Behbehān, *Iran* .... **45 D6** 30 30N 50 15 E
Behm Canal, *U.S.A.* **70 B2** 55 10N 131 0W
Behshahr, *Iran* .... **45 B7** 36 45N 53 35 E
Bei Jiang →, *China* .... **33 D6** 23 2N 112 58 E
Bei'an, *China* .... **33 B7** 48 10N 126 20 E
Beihai, *China* .... **33 D5** 21 28N 109 6 E
Beijing, *China* .... **34 E9** 39 55N 116 20 E
Beijing □, *China* .... **34 E9** 39 55N 116 20 E
Beilen, *Neths.* .... **15 B6** 52 52N 6 27 E
Beilpajah, *Australia* .... **63 E3** 32 54S 143 52 E
Beinn na Faoghla = Benbecula,
U.K. **11 D1** 57 26N 7 21W
Beipiao, *China* .... **35 D11** 41 52N 120 32 E
Beira, *Mozam.* .... **55 F3** 19 50S 34 52 E
Beiseker, *Canada* **70 C6** 51 23N 113 32W
Beitaolaizhao, *China* .... **35 B13** 44 58N 125 58 E
Beitbridge, *Zimbabwe* .... **55 G3** 22 12S 30 0 E
Beizhen = Binzhou, *China* .... **35 F10** 37 20N 118 2 E
Beizhen, *China* .... **35 D11** 41 38N 121 54 E
Beizhengzhen, *China* .... **35 B12** 44 31N 123 30 E
Beja, *Portugal* **21 C2** 38 2N 7 53W
Béja, *Tunisia* .... **51 A7** 36 43N 9 12 E
Bejaïa, *Algeria* .... **50 A7** 36 42N 5 2 E
Béjar, *Spain* **21 B3** 40 23N 5 46W
Bejestān, *Iran* .... **45 C8** 34 30N 58 5 E
Bekaa Valley = Al Biqā, *Lebanon* **46 A5** 34 10N 36 10 E
Békéscsaba, *Hungary* .... **17 E11** 46 40N 21 5 E
Bekily, *Madag.* .... **57 C8** 24 13S 45 19 E
Bekisopa, *Madag.* .... **57 C8** 21 40S 45 54 E
Bekitro, *Madag.* .... **57 C8** 24 33S 45 18 E
Bekodoka, *Madag.* .... **57 B8** 16 58S 45 7 E
Bekok, *Malaysia* .... **39 L4** 2 20N 103 7 E
Bekopaka, *Madag.* .... **57 B7** 19 9S 44 48 E
Bekuli, *Indonesia* .... **37 J17** 8 22S 114 13 E
Bela, *India* .... **43 G10** 25 50N 82 0 E
Bela, *Pakistan* .... **42 F2** 26 12N 66 20 E
Bela Bela, *S. Africa* .... **57 C4** 24 51S 28 19 E
Bela Crkva, *Serbia & M.* .... **23 B9** 44 55N 21 27 E
Bela Vista, *Brazil* **94 A4** 22 12S 56 20W
Bela Vista, *Mozam.* .... **57 D5** 26 10S 32 44 E
Belan →, *India* .... **43 G9** 24 2N 81 45 E
Belarus ■, *Europe* .... **17 B14** 53 30N 27 0 E
Belau = Palau ■, *Pac. Oc.* .... **26 J17** 7 30N 134 30 E
Belavenona, *Madag.* .... **57 C8** 24 50S 47 4 E
Belawan, *Indonesia* .... **36 D1** 3 33N 98 32 E
Belaya →, *Russia* .... **18 C9** 54 40N 56 0 E
Belaya Tserkov = Bila Tserkva,
Ukraine .... **17 D16** 49 45N 30 10 E
Belcher Is., *Canada* **72 A3** 56 15N 78 45W
Belden, *U.S.A.* **78 E5** 40 2N 121 17W
Belebey, *Russia* .... **18 D9** 54 7N 54 7 E
Beled Weyne = Belet Uen,
Somali Rep. .... **47 G4** 4 30N 45 5 E
Belém, *Brazil* **93 D9** 1 20S 48 30W
Belén, *Argentina* **94 B2** 27 40S 67 5W
Belén, *Paraguay* **94 A4** 23 30S 57 6W
Belen, *U.S.A.* **77 J10** 34 40N 106 46W
Belet Uen, *Somali Rep.* .... **47 G4** 4 30N 45 5 E
Belev, *Russia* .... **18 D6** 53 50N 36 5 E
Belfair, *U.S.A.* **78 C4** 47 27N 122 50W
Belfast, *S. Africa* .... **57 D5** 25 42S 30 2 E
Belfast, *U.K.* **10 B6** 54 37N 5 56W
Belfast, *Maine, U.S.A.* **83 C11** 44 26N 69 1W
Belfast, *N.Y., U.S.A.* **84 D6** 42 21N 78 7W
Belfast L., *U.K.* **10 B6** 54 40N 5 50W
Belfield, *U.S.A.* **80 B3** 46 53N 103 12W
Belfort, *France* .... **20 C7** 47 38N 6 50 E
Belfry, *U.S.A.* **76 D9** 45 9N 109 1W
Belgaum, *India* .... **40 M9** 15 55N 74 35 E
Belgium ■, *Europe* .... **15 D4** 50 30N 5 0 E
Belgorod, *Russia* .... **19 D6** 50 35N 36 35 E
Belgorod-Dnestrovskiy =
Bilhorod-Dnistrovskyy, *Ukraine* **19 E5** 46 11N 30 23 E
Belgrade = Beograd, *Serbia & M.* **23 B9** 44 50N 20 37 E
Belgrade, *U.S.A.* **76 D8** 45 47N 111 11W
Belhaven, *U.S.A.* **83 H7** 35 33N 76 37W
Beli Drim →, *Europe* .... **23 C9** 42 6N 20 25 E
Belimbing, *Indonesia* .... **37 J18** 8 24S 115 2 E
Belinyu, *Indonesia* .... **36 E3** 1 35S 105 50 E
Beliton Is. = Belitung, *Indonesia* **36 E3** 3 10S 107 50 E
Belitung, *Indonesia* .... **36 E3** 3 10S 107 50 E
Belize ■, *Cent. Amer.* **87 D7** 17 0N 88 30W
Belize City, *Belize* **87 D7** 17 25N 88 0W
Belkovskiy, Ostrov, *Russia* .... **29 B14** 75 32N 135 44 E
Bell →, *Canada* **72 C4** 49 48N 77 38W
Bell I., *Canada* **73 B8** 50 46N 55 35W
Bell Peninsula, *Canada* **69 B11** 63 50N 82 0W
Bell Ville, *Argentina* **94 C3** 32 40S 62 40W
Bella Bella, *Canada* **70 C3** 52 10N 128 10W
Bella Coola, *Canada* **70 C3** 52 25N 126 40W
Bella Unión, *Uruguay* **94 C4** 30 15S 57 40W
Bella Vista, *Corrientes, Argentina* **94 B4** 28 33S 59 0W
Bella Vista, *Tucuman, Argentina* **94 B2** 27 10S 65 25W
Bellaire, *U.S.A.* **84 F4** 40 1N 80 45W
Bellary, *India* .... **40 M10** 15 10N 76 56 E
Bellata, *Australia* .... **63 D4** 29 53S 149 46 E
Belle-Chasse, *U.S.A.* **81 L10** 29 51N 89 59W
Belle Fourche, *U.S.A.* **80 C3** 44 40N 103 51W
Belle Fourche →, *U.S.A.* **80 C3** 44 26N 102 18W
Belle Glade, *U.S.A.* **83 M5** 26 41N 80 40W
Belle-Île, *France* **20 C2** 47 20N 3 10W
Belle Isle, *Canada* **73 B8** 51 57N 55 25W
Belle Isle, Str. of, *Canada* **73 B8** 51 30N 56 30W
Belle Plaine, *U.S.A.* **80 E8** 41 54N 92 17W
Bellefontaine, *U.S.A.* **82 E4** 40 22N 83 46W
Bellefonte, *U.S.A.* **84 F7** 40 55N 77 47W
Belleoram, *Canada* **73 C8** 47 31N 55 25W

Belleplaine, *Barbados* .... **89 g** 13 15N 59 34W
Belleville, *Canada* **84 B7** 44 10N 77 23W
Belleville, *Ill., U.S.A.* **80 F10** 38 31N 89 59W
Belleville, *Kans., U.S.A.* **80 F6** 39 50N 97 38W
Belleville, *N.Y., U.S.A.* **85 C8** 43 46N 76 10W
Bellevue, *Canada* **70 D6** 49 35N 114 22W
Bellevue, *Idaho, U.S.A.* **76 E6** 43 28N 114 16W
Bellevue, *Nebr., U.S.A.* **80 E7** 41 8N 95 53W
Bellevue, *Ohio, U.S.A.* **84 E2** 41 17N 82 51W
Bellevue, *Wash., U.S.A.* **78 C4** 47 37N 122 12W
Bellin = Kangirsuk, *Canada* **69 B13** 60 0N 70 0W
Bellingen, *Australia* .... **63 E5** 30 25S 152 50 E
Bellingham, *U.S.A.* **68 D7** 48 46N 122 29W
Bellingshausen Sea, *Antarctica* **5 C17** 66 0S 80 0W
Bellinzona, *Switz.* .... **20 C8** 46 11N 9 1 E
Bello, *Colombia* **92 B3** 6 20N 75 33W
Bellows Falls, *U.S.A.* **85 C12** 43 8N 72 27W
Bellpat, *Pakistan* .... **42 E3** 29 0N 68 5 E
Belluno, *Italy* .... **22 A5** 46 9N 12 13 E
Bellwood, *U.S.A.* **84 F6** 40 36N 78 20W
Belmont, *Canada* **84 D3** 42 53N 81 5W
Belmont, *S. Africa* .... **56 D3** 29 28S 24 22 E
Belmont, *U.S.A.* **84 D6** 42 14N 78 2W
Belmonte, *Brazil* **93 G11** 16 0S 39 0W
Belmopan, *Belize* **87 D7** 17 18N 88 30W
Belmullet, *Ireland* **10 B2** 54 14N 9 58W
Belo Horizonte, *Brazil* **93 G10** 19 55S 43 56W
Belo-sur-Mer, *Madag.* .... **57 C7** 20 42S 44 0 E
Belo-Tsiribihina, *Madag.* .... **57 B7** 19 40S 44 30 E
Bologorsk, *Russia* .... **29 D13** 51 0N 128 20 E
Beloha, *Madag.* .... **57 D8** 25 10S 45 3 E
Beloit, *Kans., U.S.A.* **80 F5** 39 28N 98 6W
Beloit, *Wis., U.S.A.* **80 D10** 42 31N 89 2W
Belokorovichi, *Ukraine* .... **17 C15** 51 7N 28 2 E
Belomorsk, *Russia* .... **18 B5** 64 35N 34 54 E
Belonia, *India* .... **41 H17** 23 15N 91 30 E
Beloretsk, *Russia* .... **18 D10** 53 58N 58 24 E
Belorussia = Belarus ■, *Europe* **17 B14** 53 30N 27 0 E
Belovo, *Russia* .... **28 D9** 54 30N 86 0 E
Beloye, *Ozero, Russia* .... **18 B6** 60 10N 37 35 E
Beloye More, *Russia* .... **18 A6** 66 30N 38 0 E
Belozersk, *Russia* .... **18 B6** 60 1N 37 45 E
Belpre, *U.S.A.* **82 F5** 39 17N 81 34W
Beltana, *Australia* .... **63 E2** 30 48S 138 25 E
Belterra, *Brazil* **93 D8** 2 45S 55 0W
Belton, *U.S.A.* **81 K6** 31 3N 97 28W
Belton L., *U.S.A.* **81 K6** 31 8N 97 32W
Beltsy = Bălți, *Moldova* .... **17 E14** 47 48N 27 58 E
Belturbet, *Ireland* **10 B4** 54 6N 7 26W
Belukha, *Russia* .... **28 E9** 49 50N 86 50 E
Beluran, *Malaysia* .... **36 C5** 5 48N 117 35 E
Belvidere, *Ill., U.S.A.* **80 D10** 42 15N 88 50W
Belvidere, *N.J., U.S.A.* **85 F9** 40 50N 75 5W
Belyando →, *Australia* .... **62 C4** 21 38S 146 50 E
Belyy, *Ostrov, Russia* .... **28 B8** 73 30N 71 0 E
Belyy Yar, *Russia* .... **28 D9** 58 26N 84 39 E
Belzoni, *U.S.A.* **81 J9** 33 11N 90 29W
Bemaraha, Lembalemban' i,
Madag. .... **57 B7** 18 40S 44 45 E
Bemarivo, *Madag.* .... **57 C7** 21 45S 44 45 E
Bemarivo →, *Antsiranana,
Madag.* .... **57 A9** 14 9S 50 9 E
Bemarivo →, *Mahajanga,
Madag.* .... **57 B8** 15 27S 47 40 E
Bemavo, *Madag.* .... **57 C8** 21 33S 45 25 E
Bembéréke, *Benin* .... **50 F6** 10 11N 2 43 E
Bembesi, *Zimbabwe* .... **55 G2** 20 0S 28 58 E
Bembesi →, *Zimbabwe* .... **55 F2** 18 57S 27 47 E
Bemetara, *India* .... **43 J9** 21 42N 81 32 E
Bemidji, *U.S.A.* **80 B7** 47 28N 94 53W
Bemolanga, *Madag.* .... **57 B8** 17 44S 45 6 E
Ben, *Iran* .... **45 C6** 32 32N 50 45 E
Ben Cruachan, *U.K.* **11 E3** 56 26N 5 8W
Ben Dearg, *U.K.* **11 D4** 57 47N 4 56W
Ben En △, *Vietnam* .... **38 C5** 19 37N 105 30 E
Ben Hope, *U.K.* **11 C4** 58 25N 4 36W
Ben Lawers, *U.K.* **11 E4** 56 32N 4 14W
Ben Lomond, *N.S.W., Australia* **63 E5** 30 1S 151 43 E
Ben Lomond, *Tas., Australia* .... **63 G4** 41 38S 147 42 E
Ben Lomond, *U.K.* **11 E4** 56 11N 4 38W
Ben Lomond △, *Australia* .... **63 G4** 41 33S 147 39 E
Ben Luc, *Vietnam* .... **39 G6** 10 39N 106 29 E
Ben Macdhui, *U.K.* **11 D5** 57 4N 3 40W
Ben Mhor, *U.K.* **11 D1** 57 15N 7 18W
Ben More, *Arg. & Bute, U.K.* **11 E2** 56 26N 6 1W
Ben More, *Stirl., U.K.* **11 E4** 56 23N 4 32W
Ben More Assynt, *U.K.* **11 C4** 58 8N 4 52W
Ben Nevis, *U.K.* **11 E3** 56 48N 5 1W
Ben Quang, *Vietnam* .... **38 D6** 17 3N 106 55 E
Ben Vorlich, *U.K.* **11 E4** 56 21N 4 14W
Ben Wyvis, *U.K.* **11 D4** 57 40N 4 35W
Bena, *Nigeria* .... **50 F7** 11 20N 5 50 E
Benalla, *Australia* .... **63 F4** 36 30S 146 0 E
Benares = Varanasi, *India* .... **43 G10** 25 22N 83 0 E
Benavente, *Spain* **21 A3** 42 2N 5 43W
Benavides, *U.S.A.* **81 M5** 27 36N 98 25W
Benbecula, *U.K.* **11 D1** 57 26N 7 21W
Benbonyathe, *Australia* .... **63 E2** 30 25S 139 11 E
Bend, *U.S.A.* **76 D3** 44 4N 121 19W
Bender Beila, *Somali Rep.* .... **47 F5** 9 30N 50 48 E
Bendery = Tighina, *Moldova* .... **17 E15** 46 50N 29 30 E
Bendigo, *Australia* .... **63 F3** 36 40S 144 15 E
Benê Beraq, *Israel* .... **46 C3** 32 6N 34 51 E
Benenitra, *Madag.* .... **57 C8** 23 27S 45 5 E
Benevento, *Italy* .... **22 D6** 41 8N 14 45 E
Benga, *Mozam.* .... **55 F3** 16 11S 33 40 E
Bengal, Bay of, *Ind. Oc.* .... **41 M17** 15 0N 90 0 E
Bengalūru = Bangalore, *India* **40 N10** 12 59N 77 40 E
Bengbu, *China* .... **35 H9** 32 58N 117 20 E
Benghazi = Banghāzī, *Libya* .... **51 B10** 32 11N 20 3 E
Bengkalis, *Indonesia* .... **36 D2** 1 30N 102 10 E
Bengkulu, *Indonesia* .... **36 E2** 3 50S 102 12 E
Bengkulu □, *Indonesia* .... **36 E2** 3 48S 102 16 E
Bengough, *Canada* **71 D7** 49 25N 105 10W
Benguela, *Angola* .... **53 G2** 12 37S 13 25 E
Benguérua, I., *Mozam.* .... **57 C6** 21 58S 35 28 E
Beni, *Dem. Rep. of the Congo* **54 B2** 0 30N 29 27 E
Beni →, *Bolivia* **92 F5** 10 23S 65 24W
Beni Mellal, *Morocco* **50 B4** 32 21N 6 21W
Beni Suef, *Egypt* .... **51 C12** 29 5N 31 6 E
Beniah L., *Canada* **70 A6** 63 23N 112 17W
Benicia, *U.S.A.* **78 G4** 38 3N 122 9W
Benidorm, *Spain* **21 C5** 38 33N 0 9W
Benin ■, *Africa* .... **50 G6** 10 0N 2 0 E
Benin, Bight of, *W. Afr.* .... **50 H6** 5 0N 3 0 E
Benin City, *Nigeria* .... **50 G7** 6 20N 5 31 E

Benitses, *Greece* .... **25 A3** 39 32N 19 55 E
Benjamin Aceval, *Paraguay* **94 A4** 24 58S 57 34W
Benjamin Constant, *Brazil* **92 D4** 4 40S 70 15W
Benjamin Hill, *Mexico* **86 A2** 30 10N 111 10W
Benkelman, *U.S.A.* **80 E4** 40 3N 101 32W
Bennett, *Canada* **70 B2** 59 56N 134 53W
Bennetta, Ostrov, *Russia* .... **29 B15** 76 21N 148 56 E
Bennettsville, *U.S.A.* **83 H6** 34 37N 79 41W
Bennington, *N.H., U.S.A.* **85 D11** 43 0N 71 55W
Bennington, *Vt., U.S.A.* **85 D11** 42 53N 73 12W
Benoni, *S. Africa* .... **57 D4** 26 11S 28 18 E
Benque Viejo, *Belize* **87 D7** 17 5N 89 8W
Benson, *Ariz., U.S.A.* **77 L8** 31 58N 110 18W
Benson, *Minn., U.S.A.* **80 C7** 45 19N 95 36W
Bent, *Iran* .... **45 E8** 26 20N 59 31 E
Benteng, *Indonesia* .... **37 F6** 6 10S 120 30 E
Bentinck I., *Australia* .... **62 B2** 17 3S 139 35 E
Bento Gonçalves, *Brazil* **95 B5** 29 10S 51 31W
Benton, *Ark., U.S.A.* **81 H8** 34 34N 92 35W
Benton, *Calif., U.S.A.* **78 H8** 37 48N 118 32W
Benton, *Ill., U.S.A.* **80 G10** 38 0N 88 55W
Benton, *Pa., U.S.A.* **85 E8** 41 12N 76 23W
Benton Harbor, *U.S.A.* **82 D2** 42 6N 86 27W
Bentong, *Malaysia* .... **39 L3** 3 31N 101 55 E
Bentonville, *U.S.A.* **81 G7** 36 22N 94 13W
Benue □, *Nigeria* .... **50 G7** 7 48N 8 46 E
Benxi, *China* .... **35 D12** 41 20N 123 48 E
Beo, *Indonesia* .... **37 D7** 4 25N 126 50 E
Beograd, *Serbia & M.* .... **23 B9** 44 50N 20 37 E
Beppu, *Japan* .... **31 H5** 33 15N 131 30 E
Beqaa Valley = Al Biqā, *Lebanon* **46 A5** 34 10N 36 10 E
Ber Mota, *India* .... **42 H3** 23 27N 68 34 E
Berach →, *India* .... **42 G6** 25 15N 75 2 E
Beraketa, *Madag.* .... **57 C7** 23 7S 44 25 E
Berat, *Albania* .... **23 D8** 40 43N 19 59 E
Berau, Teluk, *Indonesia* .... **37 E8** 2 30S 132 30 E
Beravina, *Madag.* .... **57 B8** 18 10S 45 14 E
Berber, *Sudan* .... **51 E12** 18 0N 34 0 E
Berbera, *Somali Rep.* .... **47 E4** 10 30N 45 2 E
Berbérati, *C.A.R.* .... **52 D3** 4 15N 15 40 E
Berbice →, *Guyana* **92 B7** 6 20N 57 32W
Berdichev = Berdychiv, *Ukraine* **17 D15** 49 57N 28 30 E
Berdsk, *Russia* .... **28 D9** 54 47N 83 2 E
Berdyansk, *Ukraine* .... **19 E6** 46 45N 36 50 E
Berdychiv, *Ukraine* .... **17 D15** 49 57N 28 30 E
Berea, *U.S.A.* **82 G3** 37 34N 84 17W
Berebere, *Indonesia* .... **37 D7** 2 25N 128 45 E
Bereda, *Somali Rep.* .... **47 E5** 11 45N 51 0 E
Berehove, *Ukraine* .... **17 D12** 48 15N 22 35 E
Berekum, *Ghana* **50 G5** 7 29N 2 34W
Berens →, *Canada* **71 C9** 52 25N 97 2W
Berens I., *Canada* **71 C9** 52 18N 97 18W
Berens River, *Canada* **71 C9** 52 25N 97 0W
Beresford, *U.S.A.* **80 D6** 43 5N 96 47W
Berestechko, *Ukraine* .... **17 C13** 50 22N 25 5 E
Berevo, *Mahajanga, Madag.* .... **57 B7** 17 14S 44 17 E
Berevo, *Toliara, Madag.* .... **57 B7** 19 44S 44 58 E
Berezhany, *Ukraine* .... **17 D13** 49 26N 24 58 E
Berezina = Byarezina →, *Belarus* **17 B16** 52 33N 30 14 E
Bereznik, *Russia* .... **18 B7** 62 51N 42 40 E
Berezniki, *Russia* .... **18 C10** 59 24N 56 46 E
Berezovo, *Russia* .... **28 C7** 64 0N 65 0 E
Berga, *Spain* .... **21 A6** 42 6N 1 48 E
Bergama, *Turkey* .... **23 E12** 39 8N 27 11 E
Bérgamo, *Italy* .... **20 D8** 45 41N 9 43 E
Bergen, *Neths.* .... **15 B4** 52 40N 4 43 E
Bergen, *Norway* .... **9 F11** 60 20N 5 20 E
Bergen, *U.S.A.* **84 C7** 43 5N 77 57W
Bergen op Zoom, *Neths.* .... **15 C4** 51 28N 4 18 E
Bergerac, *France* .... **20 D4** 44 51N 0 30 E
Bergholz, *U.S.A.* **84 F4** 40 31N 80 53W
Bergisch Gladbach, *Germany* **15 D7** 50 59N 7 8 E
Berhala, Selat, *Indonesia* .... **36 E2** 1 0S 104 15 E
Berhampore = Baharampur, *India* **43 G13** 24 2N 88 27 E
Berhampur = Brahmapur, *India* **41 K14** 19 15N 84 54 E
Bering Sea, *Pac. Oc.* .... **68 C1** 58 0N 171 0 E
Bering Strait, *Pac. Oc.* **68 B3** 65 30N 169 0W
Beringovskiy, *Russia* .... **29 C18** 63 3N 179 19 E
Berisso, *Argentina* **94 C4** 34 56S 57 50W
Berja, *Spain* **21 D4** 36 50N 2 56W
Berkeley, *U.S.A.* **78 H4** 37 52N 122 16W
Berkner I., *Antarctica* **5 D18** 79 30S 50 0W
Berkshire, *U.S.A.* **85 D8** 42 19N 76 11W
Berkshire Downs, *U.K.* **13 F6** 51 33N 1 29W
Berlin, *Germany* .... **16 B7** 52 30N 13 25 E
Berlin, *Md., U.S.A.* **82 F8** 38 20N 75 13W
Berlin, *N.H., U.S.A.* **85 B13** 44 28N 71 11W
Berlin, *N.Y., U.S.A.* **85 D11** 42 42N 73 23W
Berlin, *Wis., U.S.A.* **82 D1** 43 58N 88 57W
Berlin L., *U.S.A.* **84 E4** 41 3N 81 0W
Bermejo →, *Formosa, Argentina* **94 B4** 26 51S 58 23W
Bermejo →, *San Juan, Argentina* **94 C2** 32 30S 67 30W
Bermen, L., *Canada* **73 B6** 53 35N 68 55W
Bermuda ☒, *Atl. Oc.* **66 F13** 32 45N 65 0W
Bern, *Switz.* .... **20 C7** 46 57N 7 28 E
Bernalillo, *U.S.A.* **77 J10** 35 18N 106 33W
Bernardo de Irigoyen, *Argentina* **95 B5** 26 15S 53 40W
Bernardsville, *U.S.A.* **85 F10** 40 43N 74 34W
Bernasconi, *Argentina* **94 D3** 37 55S 63 44W
Bernburg, *Germany* .... **16 C6** 51 47N 11 44 E
Berne = Bern, *Switz.* .... **20 C7** 46 57N 7 28 E
Berneray, *U.K.* **11 D1** 57 43N 7 11W
Bernier I., *Australia* .... **61 D1** 24 50S 113 12 E
Bernina, Piz, *Switz.* .... **20 C8** 46 20N 9 54 E
Beroroha, *Madag.* .... **57 C8** 21 40S 45 10 E
Beroun, *Czech Rep.* .... **16 D8** 49 57N 14 5 E
Berri, *Australia* .... **63 E3** 34 14S 140 35 E
Berriane, *Algeria* .... **50 B6** 32 50N 3 46 E
Berry, *Australia* .... **63 E5** 34 46S 150 43 E
Berry, *France* .... **20 C5** 46 50N 2 0 E
Berry Is., *Bahamas* **88 A4** 25 40N 77 50W
Berryessa L., *U.S.A.* **78 G4** 38 31N 122 6W
Berryville, *U.S.A.* **81 G8** 36 22N 93 34W
Berseba, *Namibia* .... **56 D2** 26 0S 17 46 E
Bershad, *Ukraine* .... **17 D15** 48 22N 29 31 E
Berthold, *U.S.A.* **80 A4** 48 19N 101 44W
Berthoud, *U.S.A.* **80 E2** 40 19N 105 5W
Bertoua, *Cameroon* .... **52 D2** 4 30N 13 45 E
Bertraghboy B., *Ireland* **10 C2** 53 22N 9 54W
Berwick, *U.S.A.* **85 E8** 41 3N 76 14W
Berwick-upon-Tweed, *U.K.* **12 B6** 55 46N 2 0W
Berwyn Mts., *U.K.* **12 E4** 52 54N 3 26W
Besal, *Pakistan* .... **43 B5** 35 4N 73 56 E
Besalampy, *Madag.* .... **57 B7** 16 43S 44 29 E
Besançon, *France* .... **20 C7** 47 15N 6 2 E

Besar, *Indonesia* .... **36 E5** 2 40S 116 0 E
Besnard L., *Canada* **71 B7** 55 25N 106 0W
Besni, *Turkey* .... **44 B3** 37 41N 37 52 E
Besor, N. →, *Egypt* .... **46 D3** 31 28N 34 22 E
Bessarabiya, *Moldova* .... **17 E15** 47 0N 28 10 E
Bessarabka = Basarabeasca,
Moldova .... **17 E15** 46 21N 28 58 E
Bessemer, *Ala., U.S.A.* **83 J2** 33 24N 86 58W
Bessemer, *Mich., U.S.A.* **80 B9** 46 29N 90 3W
Bessemer, *Pa., U.S.A.* **84 F4** 40 59N 80 30W
Beswick, *Australia* .... **60 B5** 14 34S 132 53 E
Bet She'an, *Israel* .... **46 C4** 32 30N 35 30 E
Bet Shemesh, *Israel* .... **46 D4** 31 44N 35 0 E
Betafo, *Madag.* .... **57 B8** 19 50S 46 51 E
Betancuria, *Canary Is.* **24 F5** 28 25N 14 3W
Betanzos, *Spain* **21 A1** 43 15N 8 12W
Bétaré Oya, *Cameroon* .... **52 C2** 5 40N 14 5 E
Betatao, *Madag.* .... **57 B8** 18 11S 47 52 E
Bethal, *S. Africa* .... **57 D4** 26 27S 29 28 E
Bethanien, *Namibia* .... **56 D2** 26 31S 17 8 E
Bethany, *Canada* **84 B6** 44 11N 78 34W
Bethany, *U.S.A.* **80 E7** 40 16N 94 2W
Bethel, *Alaska, U.S.A.* **68 B3** 60 48N 161 45W
Bethel, *Conn., U.S.A.* **85 E11** 41 22N 73 25W
Bethel, *Maine, U.S.A.* **85 B14** 44 25N 70 47W
Bethel, *Vt., U.S.A.* **85 C12** 43 50N 72 38W
Bethel Park, *U.S.A.* **84 F4** 40 20N 80 1W
Bethlehem = Bayt Laḥm,
West Bank .... **46 D4** 31 43N 35 12 E
Bethlehem, *S. Africa* .... **57 D4** 28 14S 28 18 E
Bethlehem, *U.S.A.* **85 F9** 40 37N 75 23W
Bethulie, *S. Africa* .... **56 E4** 30 30S 25 59 E
Béthune, *France* .... **20 A5** 50 30N 2 38 E
Betioky, *Madag.* .... **57 C7** 23 48S 44 20 E
Betong, *Thailand* .... **39 K3** 5 45N 101 5 E
Betoota, *Australia* .... **62 D3** 25 45S 140 42 E
Betroka, *Madag.* .... **57 C8** 23 16S 46 0 E
Betsiamites, *Canada* **73 C6** 48 56N 68 40W
Betsiamites →, *Canada* **73 C6** 48 56N 68 38W
Betsiboka →, *Madag.* .... **57 B8** 16 3S 46 36 E
Bettendorf, *U.S.A.* **80 E9** 41 32N 90 30W
Bettiah, *India* .... **43 F11** 26 48N 84 33 E
Betul, *India* .... **40 J10** 21 58N 77 59 E
Betung, *Malaysia* .... **36 D4** 1 24N 111 31 E
Betws-y-Coed, *U.K.* **12 D4** 53 5N 3 48W
Beulah, *Mich., U.S.A.* **82 C2** 44 38N 86 6W
Beulah, *N. Dak., U.S.A.* **80 B4** 47 16N 101 47W
Beveren, *Belgium* .... **15 C4** 51 12N 4 16 E
Beverley, *Australia* .... **61 F2** 32 9S 116 56 E
Beverley, *U.K.* **12 D7** 53 51N 0 26W
Beverly Hills, *U.S.A.* **83 L4** 28 56N 82 28W
Beverly, *U.S.A.* **85 D14** 42 33N 70 53W
Beverly Hills, *U.S.A.* **79 L8** 34 4N 118 25W
Bevoalavo, *Madag.* .... **57 D7** 25 13S 45 26 E
Bewas →, *India* .... **43 H8** 23 59N 79 21 E
Bexhill, *U.K.* .... **13 G8** 50 51N 0 29 E
Beyānlū, *Iran* .... **44 C5** 36 0N 47 51 E
Beyneu, *Kazakhstan* .... **19 E10** 45 18N 55 9 E
Beypazarı, *Turkey* .... **19 F5** 40 10N 31 56 E
Beyşehir Gölü, *Turkey* .... **19 G5** 37 41N 31 33 E
Béziers, *France* .... **20 E5** 43 20N 3 12 E
Bezwada = Vijayawada, *India* **41 L12** 16 31N 80 39 E
Bhabua, *India* .... **43 G10** 25 3N 83 37 E
Bhachau, *India* .... **40 H7** 23 20N 70 16 E
Bhadar →, *Gujarat, India* .... **42 H5** 22 17N 72 20 E
Bhadar →, *Gujarat, India* .... **42 J3** 21 27N 69 47 E
Bhadarwah, *India* .... **43 C6** 32 58N 75 46 E
Bhadgaon = Bhaktapur, *Nepal* **43 F11** 27 38N 85 24 E
Bhadohi, *India* .... **43 G10** 25 25N 82 34 E
Bhadra, *India* .... **42 E6** 29 8N 75 14 E
Bhadrak, *India* .... **41 J15** 21 10N 86 30 E
Bhadran, *India* .... **42 H5** 22 19N 72 6 E
Bhadravati, *India* .... **40 N9** 13 49N 75 40 E
Bhag, *Pakistan* .... **42 E2** 29 2N 67 49 E
Bhagalpur, *India* .... **43 G12** 25 10N 87 0 E
Bhagirathi →, *Uttaranchal, India* **43 D8** 30 8N 78 35 E
Bhagirathi →, *W. Bengal, India* **43 H13** 23 25N 88 23 E
Bhakkar, *Pakistan* .... **42 D4** 31 40N 71 5 E
Bhakra Dam, *India* .... **42 D7** 31 30N 76 45 E
Bhaktapur, *Nepal* .... **43 F11** 27 38N 85 24 E
Bhamo, *Burma* .... **41 G20** 24 15N 97 15 E
Bhandara, *India* .... **40 J11** 21 5N 79 42 E
Bhanpura, *India* .... **42 G6** 24 31N 75 44 E
Bhanrer Ra., *India* .... **43 H8** 23 40N 79 45 E
Bhaptiani, *India* .... **43 F12** 26 19N 86 44 E
Bharat = India ■, *Asia* .... **40 K11** 20 0N 78 0 E
Bharatpur, *Chhattisgarh, India* **43 H9** 23 44N 81 46 E
Bharatpur, *Raj., India* .... **42 F7** 27 15N 77 30 E
Bharno, *India* .... **43 H11** 23 14N 84 53 E
Bharuch, *India* .... **40 J8** 21 47N 73 0 E
Bhatinda, *India* .... **42 D6** 30 15N 74 57 E
Bhatpara, *India* .... **43 H13** 22 50N 88 25 E
Bhattu, *India* .... **42 E6** 29 36N 75 19 E
Bhaun, *Pakistan* .... **42 C5** 32 55N 72 40 E
Bhaunagar = Bhavnagar, *India* **40 J8** 21 45N 72 10 E
Bhavnagar, *India* .... **40 J8** 21 45N 72 10 E
Bhawari, *India* .... **42 G5** 25 42N 73 4 E
Bhayavadar, *India* .... **42 J4** 21 51N 70 15 E
Bhera, *Pakistan* .... **42 C5** 32 29N 72 57 E
Bhikangaon, *India* .... **42 J6** 21 52N 75 57 E
Bhilai = Bhilainagar-Durg, *India* **43 J9** 21 13N 81 26 E
Bhilsa = Vidisha, *India* .... **42 H7** 23 28N 77 53 E
Bhilwara, *India* .... **42 G6** 25 25N 74 38 E
Bhima →, *India* .... **40 L10** 16 25N 77 17 E
Bhimbar, *Pakistan* .... **43 C6** 32 59N 74 3 E
Bhind, *India* .... **43 F8** 26 30N 78 46 E
Bhinga, *India* .... **43 F9** 27 43N 81 56 E
Bhinmal, *India* .... **42 G5** 25 0N 72 15 E
Bhiwandi, *India* .... **40 K8** 19 20N 73 0 E
Bhiwani, *India* .... **42 E7** 28 50N 76 9 E
Bhogava →, *India* .... **42 H5** 22 26N 72 20 E
Bhola, *Bangla.* .... **41 H17** 22 45N 90 35 E
Bholari, *Pakistan* .... **42 G3** 25 19N 68 13 E
Bhopal, *India* .... **42 H7** 23 20N 77 30 E
Bhubaneshwar, *India* .... **41 J14** 20 15N 85 50 E
Bhusawal, *India* .... **40 J9** 21 3N 75 46 E
Bhutan ■, *Asia* .... **41 F17** 27 25N 90 30 E
Biafra, B. of = Bonny, Bight of,
Africa .... **52 D1** 3 30N 9 20 E
Biak, *Indonesia* .... **37 E9** 1 10S 136 6 E
Biała Podlaska, *Poland* .... **17 B12** 52 4N 23 6 E
Białogard, *Poland* .... **16 A8** 54 2N 15 58 E
Białystok, *Poland* .... **17 B12** 53 10N 23 10 E
Biaora, *India* .... **42 H7** 23 56N 76 56 E
Biārjmand, *Iran* .... **45 B7** 36 6N 55 53 E
Biaro, *Indonesia* .... **37 D7** 2 5N 125 26 E
Biarritz, *France* **20 E3** 43 29N 1 33W
Bias, *Indonesia* .... **37 J18** 8 24S 115 36 E

Bibai, Japan ... 30 C10 43 19N 141 52 E
Bibby I., Canada ... 71 A10 61 55N 93 0W
Biberach, Germany ... 16 D5 48 5N 9 47 E
Bibungwa, Dem. Rep. of
   the Congo ... 54 C2 2 40S 28 15 E
Bicester, U.K. ... 13 F6 51 54N 1 9W
Bicheno, Australia ... 63 G4 41 52S 148 18 E
Bichia, India ... 43 H9 22 27N 80 42 E
Bickerton I., Australia ... 62 A2 13 45S 136 10 E
Bida, Nigeria ... 50 G7 9 3N 5 58 E
Bidar, India ... 40 L10 17 55N 77 35 E
Biddeford, U.S.A. ... 83 D10 43 30N 70 28W
Bideford, U.K. ... 13 F3 51 1N 4 13W
Bideford Bay, U.K. ... 13 F3 51 5N 4 20W
Bidhuna, India ... 43 F8 26 49N 79 31 E
Bidor, Malaysia ... 39 K3 4 6N 101 15 E
Bié, Planalto de, Angola ... 53 G3 12 0S 16 0 E
Bieber, U.S.A. ... 76 F3 41 7N 121 8W
Biel, Switz. ... 20 C7 47 8N 7 14 E
Bielefeld, Germany ... 16 B5 52 1N 8 33 E
Biella, Italy ... 20 D8 45 34N 8 3 E
Bielsk Podlaski, Poland ... 17 B12 52 47N 23 12 E
Bielsko-Biała, Poland ... 17 D10 49 50N 19 2 E
Bien Hoa, Vietnam ... 39 G6 10 57N 106 49 E
Bienne = Biel, Switz. ... 20 C7 47 8N 7 14 E
Bienville, L., Canada ... 72 A5 55 5N 72 40W
Biesiesfontein, S. Africa ... 56 E2 30 57S 17 58 E
Big →, Canada ... 73 B8 54 50N 58 55W
Big B., Canada ... 73 A7 55 43N 60 35W
Big Bear City, U.S.A. ... 79 L10 34 16N 116 51W
Big Bear Lake, U.S.A. ... 79 L10 34 15N 116 56W
Big Belt Mts., U.S.A. ... 76 C8 46 30N 111 25W
Big Bend, Swaziland ... 57 D5 26 50S 31 58 E
Big Bend △, U.S.A. ... 81 L3 29 20N 103 5W
Big Black →, U.S.A. ... 81 K9 32 3N 91 4W
Big Blue →, U.S.A. ... 80 F6 39 35N 96 34W
Big Creek, U.S.A. ... 78 H7 37 11N 119 14W
Big Cypress △, U.S.A. ... 83 M5 26 0N 81 10W
Big Cypress Swamp, U.S.A. ... 83 M5 26 15N 81 30W
Big Falls, U.S.A. ... 80 A8 48 11N 93 48W
Big Fork →, U.S.A. ... 80 A8 48 31N 93 43W
Big Horn Mts. = Bighorn Mts.,
   U.S.A. ... 76 D10 44 30N 107 30W
Big I., Canada ... 70 A5 61 7N 116 45W
Big Lake, U.S.A. ... 81 K4 31 12N 101 28W
Big Moose, U.S.A. ... 85 C10 43 49N 74 58W
Big Muddy Cr. →, U.S.A. ... 80 A2 48 8N 104 36W
Big Pine, U.S.A. ... 78 H8 37 10N 118 17W
Big Piney, U.S.A. ... 76 E8 42 32N 110 7W
Big Rapids, U.S.A. ... 82 D3 43 42N 85 29W
Big Rideau L., Canada ... 85 B8 44 43N 76 15W
Big River, Canada ... 71 C7 53 50N 107 0W
Big Run, U.S.A. ... 84 F6 40 57N 78 55W
Big Sable Pt., U.S.A. ... 82 C2 44 3N 86 1W
Big Salmon →, Canada ... 70 A2 61 52N 134 55W
Big Sand L., Canada ... 71 B9 57 45N 99 45W
Big Sandy, U.S.A. ... 76 B8 48 11N 110 7W
Big Sandy →, U.S.A. ... 82 F4 38 25N 82 36W
Big Sandy Cr. →, U.S.A. ... 80 F3 38 7N 102 29W
Big Sioux →, U.S.A. ... 80 D6 42 29N 96 27W
Big South Fork △, U.S.A. ... 83 G3 36 27N 84 47W
Big Spring, U.S.A. ... 81 J4 32 15N 101 28W
Big Stone City, U.S.A. ... 80 C6 45 18N 96 28W
Big Stone Gap, U.S.A. ... 83 G4 36 52N 82 47W
Big Stone L., U.S.A. ... 80 C6 45 30N 96 35W
Big Sur, U.S.A. ... 78 J5 36 15N 121 48W
Big Timber, U.S.A. ... 76 D9 45 50N 109 57W
Big Trout L., Canada ... 72 B2 53 40N 90 0W
Big Trout Lake, Canada ... 72 B2 53 45N 90 0W
Biga, Turkey ... 23 D12 40 13N 27 14 E
Bigadiç, Turkey ... 23 E13 39 22N 28 7 E
Biggar, Canada ... 71 C7 52 4N 108 0W
Biggar, U.K. ... 11 F5 55 38N 3 32W
Bigge I., Australia ... 60 B4 14 35S 125 10 E
Biggenden, Australia ... 63 D5 25 31S 152 4 E
Biggleswade, U.K. ... 13 E7 52 5N 0 14W
Biggs, U.S.A. ... 78 F5 39 25N 121 43W
Bighorn, U.S.A. ... 76 C10 46 10N 107 27W
Bighorn →, U.S.A. ... 76 C10 46 10N 107 28W
Bighorn Canyon △, U.S.A. ... 76 D9 45 10N 108 0W
Bighorn L., U.S.A. ... 76 D9 44 55N 108 15W
Bighorn Mts., U.S.A. ... 76 D10 44 30N 107 30W
Bigstone L., Canada ... 71 C9 53 42N 95 44W
Bigwa, Tanzania ... 54 D4 7 10S 39 10 E
Bihać, Bos.-H. ... 16 F8 44 49N 15 57 E
Bihar, India ... 43 G11 25 5N 85 40 E
Bihar □, India ... 43 G12 25 0N 86 0 E
Bihariganj, India ... 43 G12 25 44N 86 59 E
Bihor, Munţii, Romania ... 17 E12 46 29N 22 47 E
Bijagós, Arquipélago dos,
   Guinea-Biss. ... 50 F2 11 15N 16 10W
Bijaipur, India ... 42 F7 26 2N 77 20 E
Bijapur, Chhattisgarh, India ... 41 K12 18 50N 80 50 E
Bijapur, Karnataka, India ... 40 L9 16 50N 75 55 E
Bījār, Iran ... 44 C5 35 52N 47 35 E
Bijawar, India ... 43 G8 24 38N 79 30 E
Bijeljina, Bos.-H. ... 23 B8 44 46N 19 14 E
Bijnor, India ... 42 E8 29 27N 78 11 E
Bikaner, India ... 42 E5 28 2N 73 18 E
Bikapur, India ... 43 F10 26 30N 82 7 E
Bikeqi, China ... 34 D6 40 43N 111 20 E
Bikfayyā, Lebanon ... 46 B4 33 55N 35 41 E
Bikin, Russia ... 29 E14 46 50N 134 20 E
Bikin →, Russia ... 30 A7 46 51N 134 2 E
Bikini Atoll, Marshall Is. ... 64 F8 12 0N 167 30 E
Bikita, Zimbabwe ... 57 C5 20 6S 31 41 E
Bila Tserkva, Ukraine ... 17 D16 49 45N 30 10 E
Bilara, India ... 42 F5 26 14N 73 53 E
Bilaspur, Chhattisgarh, India ... 43 H10 22 2N 82 15 E
Bilaspur, Punjab, India ... 42 D7 31 19N 76 50 E
Bilauk Taungdan, Thailand ... 38 F2 13 0N 99 0 E
Bilbao, Spain ... 21 A4 43 16N 2 56W
Bilbo = Bilbao, Spain ... 21 A4 43 16N 2 56W
Bildudalur, Iceland ... 8 D2 65 41N 23 36W
Bílé Karpaty, Europe ... 17 D9 49 5N 18 0 E
Bilecik, Turkey ... 23 D13 40 5N 30 5 E
Bilgram, India ... 43 F9 27 11N 80 2 E
Bilhaur, India ... 43 F9 26 51N 80 5 E
Bilhorod-Dnistrovskyy, Ukraine ... 19 E5 46 11N 30 23 E
Bilibino, Russia ... 29 C17 68 3N 166 20 E
Bilibiza, Mozam. ... 55 E5 12 30S 40 20 E
Biliran I., Phil. ... 37 B6 11 40N 124 35 E
Billabalong Roadhouse, Australia ... 61 E2 27 25S 115 49 E
Billiluna, Australia ... 60 C4 19 37S 127 41 E
Billings, U.S.A. ... 76 D9 45 47N 108 30W
Billiton Is. = Belitung, Indonesia ... 36 E3 3 10S 107 50 E
Bilma, Niger ... 51 E8 18 50N 13 30 E

Biloela, Australia ... 62 C5 24 24S 150 31 E
Biloxi, U.S.A. ... 81 K10 30 24N 88 53W
Bilpa Morea Claypan, Australia ... 62 D3 25 0S 140 0 E
Biltine, Chad ... 51 F10 14 40N 20 50 E
Bima, Indonesia ... 37 F5 8 22S 118 49 E
Bimini Is., Bahamas ... 88 A4 25 42N 79 25W
Bin Xian, Heilongjiang, China ... 35 B14 45 42N 127 32 E
Bin Xian, Shaanxi, China ... 34 G5 35 2N 108 4 E
Bina-Etawah, India ... 42 G8 24 13N 78 14 E
Bināb, Iran ... 45 B6 36 35N 48 41 E
Binalbagan, Phil. ... 37 B6 10 12N 122 50 E
Binalong, Australia ... 63 E4 34 40S 148 39 E
Binālūd, Kūh-e, Iran ... 45 B8 36 30N 58 30 E
Binatang = Bintangor, Malaysia ... 36 D4 2 10N 111 40 E
Binche, Belgium ... 15 D4 50 26N 4 10 E
Bindki, India ... 43 F9 26 2N 80 36 E
Bindura, Zimbabwe ... 55 F3 17 18S 31 18 E
Bingara, Australia ... 63 D5 29 52S 150 36 E
Bingham, U.S.A. ... 83 C11 45 3N 69 53W
Binghamton, U.S.A. ... 85 D9 42 6N 75 55W
Bingöl, Turkey ... 44 B4 38 53N 40 29 E
Binh Dinh = An Nhon, Vietnam ... 38 F7 13 55N 109 7 E
Binh Khe, Vietnam ... 38 F7 13 57N 108 51 E
Binh Son, Vietnam ... 38 E7 15 20N 108 40 E
Binh China ... 35 G10 34 2N 119 49 E
Binisatua, Spain ... 24 B11 39 50N 4 11 E
Binjai, Indonesia ... 36 D3 3 20N 98 30 E
Binnaway, Australia ... 63 E4 31 28S 149 24 E
Binongko, Indonesia ... 37 F6 5 57S 124 2 E
Binscarth, Canada ... 71 C8 50 37N 101 17W
Bintan, Indonesia ... 36 D2 1 0N 104 0 E
Bintangor, Malaysia ... 36 D4 2 10N 111 40 E
Bintulu, Malaysia ... 36 D4 3 10N 113 0 E
Bintuni, Indonesia ... 37 E8 2 7S 133 32 E
Binzert = Bizerte, Tunisia ... 51 A7 37 15N 9 50 E
Binzhou, China ... 35 F10 37 20N 118 2 E
Bío Bío □, Chile ... 94 D1 37 35S 72 0W
Bioko, Eq. Guin. ... 52 D1 3 30N 8 40 E
Bir, India ... 40 K9 19 4N 75 46 E
Bîr Abu Muḩammad, Egypt ... 46 F3 29 44N 34 14 E
Bi'r ad Dabbāghāt, Jordan ... 46 E4 30 26N 35 32 E
Bi'r al Butayyihāt, Jordan ... 46 F4 29 47N 35 20 E
Bi'r al Māri, Jordan ... 46 E4 30 4N 35 33 E
Bi'r al Qaṭṭār, Jordan ... 46 F4 29 47N 35 32 E
Bîr Atrun, Sudan ... 51 E11 18 15N 26 40 E
Bîr Beida, Egypt ... 46 E3 30 25N 34 29 E
Bîr el 'Abd, Egypt ... 46 D2 31 2N 33 0 E
Bîr el Biarât, Egypt ... 46 F3 29 30N 34 43 E
Bîr el Duweidar, Egypt ... 46 E1 30 56N 32 32 E
Bîr el Garârât, Egypt ... 46 D2 31 3N 33 34 E
Bîr el Heisi, Egypt ... 46 F3 29 22N 34 36 E
Bîr el Jafir, Egypt ... 46 E1 30 50N 32 41 E
Bîr el Mâlḩi, Egypt ... 46 E2 30 38N 33 19 E
Bîr el Thamâda, Egypt ... 46 E2 30 12N 33 27 E
Bîr Gebeil Ḩiṣn, Egypt ... 46 E2 30 2N 33 18 E
Bi'r Ghadir, Syria ... 46 A6 34 6N 37 3 E
Bi'r Ḩasana, Egypt ... 46 E2 30 29N 33 46 E
Bîr Kaseiba, Egypt ... 46 E2 31 0N 33 17 E
Bîr Lahfân, Egypt ... 46 E2 31 0N 33 51 E
Bîr Madkûr, Egypt ... 46 E1 30 44N 32 33 E
Bîr Mogreïn, Mauritania ... 50 C3 25 10N 11 25W
Bi'r Muṭribah, Kuwait ... 44 D5 29 54N 47 17 E
Bîr Qaṭia, Egypt ... 46 E1 30 58N 32 45 E
Bîr Shalatein, Egypt ... 51 D13 23 5N 35 25 E
Biratnagar, Nepal ... 43 F12 26 27N 87 17 E
Birawa, Dem. Rep. of the Congo ... 54 C2 2 20S 28 48 E
Birch →, Canada ... 70 B6 58 28N 112 17W
Birch Hills, Canada ... 71 C7 52 59N 105 25W
Birch I., Canada ... 71 C9 52 26N 99 54W
Birch L., N.W.T., Canada ... 70 A5 62 4N 116 33W
Birch L., Ont., Canada ... 72 B1 51 23N 92 18W
Birch Mts., Canada ... 70 B6 57 30N 113 10W
Birch River, Canada ... 71 C8 52 24N 101 6W
Birchip, Australia ... 63 F3 35 56S 142 55 E
Bird, Canada ... 71 B10 56 30N 94 13W
Bird I. = Las Aves, Is., W. Indies ... 89 C7 15 45N 63 55W
Bird I., Antarctica ... 5 B1 54 0S 38 0W
Birdsville, Australia ... 62 D2 25 51S 139 20 E
Birdum Cr. →, Australia ... 60 C5 15 14S 133 0 E
Birecik, Turkey ... 44 B3 37 2N 38 0 E
Birein, Israel ... 46 E3 30 50N 34 28 E
Bireuen, Indonesia ... 36 C1 5 14N 96 39 E
Birigui, Brazil ... 95 A5 21 18S 50 16W
Birjand, Iran ... 45 C8 32 53N 59 13 E
Birkenhead, U.K. ... 12 D4 53 23N 3 2W
Bîrlad = Bârlad, Romania ... 17 E14 46 15N 27 38 E
Birmingham, U.K. ... 13 E6 52 29N 1 52W
Birmingham, U.S.A. ... 83 J2 33 31N 86 48W
Birmingham International ✈
   (BHX), U.K. ... 13 E6 52 26N 1 45W
Birmitrapur, India ... 41 H14 22 24N 84 46 E
Birni Nkonni, Niger ... 50 F7 13 55N 5 15 E
Birnin Kebbi, Nigeria ... 50 F6 12 32N 4 12 E
Birobidzhan, Russia ... 29 E14 48 50N 132 50 E
Birr, Ireland ... 10 C4 53 6N 7 54W
Birrie →, Australia ... 63 D4 29 43S 146 37 E
Birsilpur, India ... 42 E5 28 11N 72 15 E
Birsk, Russia ... 18 C10 55 25N 55 30 E
Birtle, Canada ... 71 C8 50 30N 101 5W
Birur, India ... 40 N9 13 30N 75 55 E
Biržai, Lithuania ... 9 H21 56 11N 24 45 E
Birzebbugga, Malta ... 25 D2 35 50N 14 32 E
Bisa, Indonesia ... 37 E7 1 15S 127 28 E
Bisalpur, India ... 43 E8 28 14N 79 48 E
Bisbee, U.S.A. ... 77 L9 31 27N 109 55W
Biscay, B. of, Atl. Oc. ... 20 D1 45 0N 2 0W
Biscayne B., U.S.A. ... 83 N5 25 40N 80 12W
Biscoe Is., Antarctica ... 5 C17 66 0S 67 0W
Biscostasing, Canada ... 72 C3 47 18N 82 9W
Bishkek, Kyrgyzstan ... 28 E8 42 54N 74 46 E
Bishnupur, India ... 43 H12 23 8N 87 20 E
Bisho, S. Africa ... 57 E4 32 50S 27 23 E
Bishop, Calif., U.S.A. ... 78 H8 37 22N 118 24W
Bishop, Tex., U.S.A. ... 81 M6 27 35N 97 48W
Bishop Auckland, U.K. ... 12 C6 54 39N 1 40W
Bishop's Falls, Canada ... 73 C8 49 2N 55 30W
Bishop's Stortford, U.K. ... 13 F8 51 52N 0 10 E
Bisina, L., Uganda ... 54 B3 1 38N 33 56 E
Biskra, Algeria ... 50 B7 34 50N 5 44 E
Bismarck, U.S.A. ... 80 B4 46 48N 100 47W
Bismarck Arch., Papua N. G. ... 64 H7 2 30S 150 0 E
Biso, Uganda ... 54 B3 1 44N 31 26 E
Bison, U.S.A. ... 80 C3 45 31N 102 28W
Bisotūn, Iran ... 44 C5 34 23N 47 26 E
Bissagos = Bijagós, Arquipélago
   dos, Guinea-Biss. ... 50 F2 11 15N 16 10W
Bissau, Guinea-Biss. ... 50 F2 11 45N 15 45W
Bistcho L., Canada ... 70 B5 59 45N 118 50W

Bistriţa, Romania ... 17 E13 47 9N 24 35 E
Bistriţa →, Romania ... 17 E14 46 30N 26 57 E
Biswan, India ... 43 F9 27 29N 81 2 E
Bitlis, Turkey ... 44 B4 38 20N 42 3 E
Bitola, Macedonia ... 23 D9 41 1N 21 20 E
Bitolj = Bitola, Macedonia ... 23 D9 41 1N 21 20 E
Bitter Creek, U.S.A. ... 76 F9 41 33N 108 33W
Bitterfontein, S. Africa ... 56 E2 31 1S 18 32 E
Bitterroot →, U.S.A. ... 76 C6 46 52N 114 7W
Bitterroot Range, U.S.A. ... 76 D6 46 0N 114 20W
Bitterwater, U.S.A. ... 78 J6 36 23N 121 0W
Biu, Nigeria ... 51 F8 10 40N 12 3 E
Biwa-Ko, Japan ... 31 G8 35 15N 136 10 E
Biwabik, U.S.A. ... 80 B8 47 32N 92 21W
Bixby, U.S.A. ... 81 H7 35 57N 95 53W
Biyang, China ... 34 H7 32 38N 113 21 E
Biysk, Russia ... 28 D9 52 40N 85 0 E
Bizana, S. Africa ... 57 E4 30 50S 29 52 E
Bizen, Japan ... 31 G7 34 43N 134 8 E
Bizerte, Tunisia ... 51 A7 37 15N 9 50 E
Bjargtangar, Iceland ... 8 D1 65 30N 24 30W
Bjelovar, Croatia ... 22 B7 45 56N 16 49 E
Bjørnevatn, Norway ... 8 B23 69 40N 30 0 E
Bjørnøya, Arctic ... 4 B8 74 30N 19 0 E
Black = Da →, Vietnam ... 38 B5 21 15N 105 20 E
Black →, Canada ... 84 B5 44 42N 79 19W
Black →, Ariz., U.S.A. ... 77 K8 33 44N 110 13W
Black →, Ark., U.S.A. ... 81 H9 35 38N 91 20W
Black →, Mich., U.S.A. ... 84 D2 42 59N 82 27W
Black →, N.Y., U.S.A. ... 85 C8 43 59N 76 4W
Black →, Wis., U.S.A. ... 80 D9 43 57N 91 22W
Black Bay Pen., Canada ... 72 C2 48 38N 88 21W
Black Birch L., Canada ... 71 B7 56 53N 107 45W
Black Canyon of the Gunnison △,
   U.S.A. ... 77 G10 38 40N 107 35W
Black Diamond, Canada ... 70 C6 50 45N 114 14W
Black Duck →, Canada ... 72 A2 56 51N 89 2W
Black Forest = Schwarzwald,
   Germany ... 16 D5 48 30N 8 20 E
Black Forest, U.S.A. ... 80 F2 39 0N 104 43W
Black Hd., Ireland ... 10 C2 53 9N 9 16W
Black Hills, U.S.A. ... 80 D3 44 0N 103 45W
Black I., Canada ... 71 C9 51 12N 96 30W
Black L., Canada ... 71 B7 59 12N 105 15W
Black L., Mich., U.S.A. ... 82 C3 45 28N 84 16W
Black L., N.Y., U.S.A. ... 85 B9 44 31N 75 36W
Black Lake, Canada ... 71 B7 59 11N 105 20W
Black Mesa, U.S.A. ... 81 G3 36 58N 102 58W
Black Mt. = Mynydd Du, U.K. ... 13 F4 51 52N 3 50W
Black Mts., U.K. ... 13 F4 51 55N 3 7W
Black Range, U.S.A. ... 77 K10 33 15N 107 50W
Black River, Jamaica ... 88 a 18 0N 77 50W
Black River Falls, U.S.A. ... 80 C9 44 18N 90 51W
Black Rock, Barbados ... 89 g 13 7N 59 37W
Black Sea, Eurasia ... 19 F6 43 30N 35 0 E
Black Tickle, Canada ... 73 B8 53 28N 55 45W
Black Volta →, Africa ... 50 G5 8 41N 1 33W
Black Warrior →, U.S.A. ... 83 J2 32 32N 87 51W
Blackall, Australia ... 62 C4 24 25S 145 45 E
Blackball, N.Z. ... 59 K3 42 22S 171 26 E
Blackbull, Australia ... 62 B3 17 55S 141 45 E
Blackburn, U.K. ... 12 D5 53 45N 2 29W
Blackburn with Darwen □, U.K. ... 12 D5 53 45N 2 29W
Blackdown Tableland △,
   Australia ... 62 C4 23 52S 149 8 E
Blackfoot, U.S.A. ... 76 E7 43 11N 112 21W
Blackfoot →, U.S.A. ... 76 C7 46 52N 113 53W
Blackfoot River Reservoir, U.S.A. ... 76 E8 43 0N 111 43W
Blackpool, U.K. ... 12 D4 53 49N 3 3W
Blackpool □, U.K. ... 12 D4 53 49N 3 3W
Blackriver, U.S.A. ... 84 B1 44 46N 83 17W
Blacks Harbour, Canada ... 73 C6 45 3N 66 49W
Blacksburg, U.S.A. ... 82 G5 37 14N 80 25W
Blacksod B., Ireland ... 10 B1 54 6N 10 0W
Blackstone, U.S.A. ... 82 G7 37 4N 78 0W
Blackstone Ra., Australia ... 61 E4 26 0S 128 30 E
Blackwater = West Road →,
   Canada ... 70 C4 53 18N 122 53W
Blackwater, Australia ... 62 C4 23 35S 148 53 E
Blackwater →, Meath, Ireland ... 10 C4 53 39N 6 41W
Blackwater →, Waterford, Ireland ... 10 D4 52 4N 7 52W
Blackwater →, U.K. ... 10 B5 54 31N 6 35W
Blackwell, U.S.A. ... 81 G6 36 48N 97 17W
Blackwells Corner, U.S.A. ... 79 K7 35 37N 119 47W
Bladensburg △, Australia ... 62 C3 22 25S 142 59 E
Blaenau Ffestiniog, U.K. ... 12 E4 53 0N 3 56W
Blaenau Gwent □, U.K. ... 13 F4 51 48N 3 12W
Blagodarnoye = Blagodarnyy,
   Russia ... 19 E7 45 7N 43 37 E
Blagodarnyy, Russia ... 19 E7 45 7N 43 37 E
Blagoevgrad, Bulgaria ... 23 C10 42 2N 23 5 E
Blagoveshchensk, Russia ... 29 D13 50 20N 127 30 E
Blahkiuh, Indonesia ... 37 J18 8 31S 115 12 E
Blain, U.S.A. ... 84 F7 40 20N 77 31W
Blaine, Minn., U.S.A. ... 80 C8 45 10N 93 13W
Blaine, Wash., U.S.A. ... 78 B4 48 59N 122 45W
Blaine Lake, Canada ... 71 C7 52 51N 106 52W
Blair, U.S.A. ... 80 E6 41 33N 96 8W
Blair Athol, Australia ... 62 C4 22 42S 147 31 E
Blair Atholl, U.K. ... 11 E5 56 46N 3 50W
Blairgowrie, U.K. ... 11 E5 56 35N 3 21W
Blairsden, U.S.A. ... 78 F6 39 47N 120 37W
Blairsville, U.S.A. ... 84 F5 40 26N 79 16W
Blake Pt., U.S.A. ... 80 A10 48 11N 88 25W
Blakely, Ga., U.S.A. ... 83 K3 31 23N 84 56W
Blakely, Pa., U.S.A. ... 85 E9 41 28N 75 37W
Blanc, Mont, Europe ... 20 D7 45 48N 6 50 E
Blanc-Sablon, Canada ... 73 B8 51 24N 57 12W
Blanca, B., Argentina ... 96 D4 39 10S 61 30W
Blanca Peak, U.S.A. ... 77 H11 37 35N 105 29W
Blanche, C., Australia ... 63 E1 33 1S 134 9 E
Blanche, L., W. Austral., Australia ... 60 D3 22 25S 123 17 E
Blanchisseuse, Trin. & Tob. ... 93 K15 10 48N 61 18W
Blanco, S. Africa ... 56 E3 33 55S 22 23 E
Blanco, U.S.A. ... 81 K5 30 6N 98 25W
Blanco →, Argentina ... 94 C2 30 20S 68 42W
Blanco, C., Costa Rica ... 88 E3 9 34N 85 8W
Blanco, C., U.S.A. ... 76 E1 42 51N 124 34W
Blanda →, Iceland ... 8 D3 65 37N 20 9W
Blandford Forum, U.K. ... 13 G5 50 51N 2 9W
Blanding, U.S.A. ... 77 H9 37 37N 109 29W
Blanes, Spain ... 21 B7 41 40N 2 48 E
Blankenberge, Belgium ... 15 C3 51 20N 3 9 E
Blanquillo, Uruguay ... 95 C4 32 53S 55 37W
Blantyre, Malawi ... 55 F4 15 45S 35 0 E

Blarney, Ireland ... 10 E3 51 56N 8 33W
Blasdell, U.S.A. ... 84 D6 42 48N 78 50W
Blåvands Huk, Denmark ... 9 J13 55 33N 8 4 E
Blaydon, U.K. ... 12 C6 54 58N 1 42W
Blayney, Australia ... 63 E4 33 32S 149 14 E
Blaze, Pt., Australia ... 60 B5 12 56S 130 11 E
Blekinge, Sweden ... 9 H16 56 25N 15 20 E
Blenheim, Canada ... 84 D3 42 20N 82 0W
Blenheim, N.Z. ... 59 J4 41 38S 173 57 E
Bletchley, U.K. ... 13 F7 51 59N 0 44W
Blida, Algeria ... 50 A6 36 30N 2 49 E
Bligh Sound, N.Z. ... 59 L1 44 47S 167 32 E
Blind River, Canada ... 72 C3 46 10N 82 58W
Bliss, Idaho, U.S.A. ... 76 E6 42 56N 114 57W
Bliss, N.Y., U.S.A. ... 84 D6 42 34N 78 15W
Blissfield, U.S.A. ... 84 F3 40 24N 81 58W
Blitar, Indonesia ... 37 H15 8 5S 112 11 E
Block I., U.S.A. ... 85 E13 41 11N 71 35W
Block Island Sd., U.S.A. ... 85 E13 41 15N 71 40W
Bloemfontein, S. Africa ... 56 D4 29 6S 26 7 E
Bloemhof, S. Africa ... 56 D4 27 38S 25 32 E
Blois, France ... 20 C4 47 35N 1 20 E
Blönduós, Iceland ... 8 D3 65 40N 20 12W
Blongas, Indonesia ... 37 K19 8 53S 116 2 E
Bloodvein →, Canada ... 71 C9 51 47N 96 43W
Bloody Foreland, Ireland ... 10 A3 55 10N 8 17W
Bloomer, U.S.A. ... 80 C9 45 6N 91 29W
Bloomfield, Canada ... 84 C7 43 59N 77 14W
Bloomfield, Iowa, U.S.A. ... 80 E8 40 45N 92 25W
Bloomfield, N. Mex., U.S.A. ... 77 H10 36 43N 107 59W
Bloomfield, Nebr., U.S.A. ... 80 D6 42 36N 97 39W
Bloomington, Ill., U.S.A. ... 80 E10 40 28N 89 0W
Bloomington, Ind., U.S.A. ... 82 F2 39 10N 86 32W
Bloomington, Minn., U.S.A. ... 80 C8 44 50N 93 17W
Bloomsburg, U.S.A. ... 85 F8 41 0N 76 27W
Bloomsbury, Australia ... 62 J6 20 48S 148 38 E
Blora, Indonesia ... 37 G14 6 57S 111 25 E
Blossburg, U.S.A. ... 84 E7 41 41N 77 4W
Blouberg, S. Africa ... 57 C4 23 8S 28 59 E
Blountstown, U.S.A. ... 83 K3 30 27N 85 3W
Blue Earth, U.S.A. ... 80 D8 43 38N 94 6W
Blue Hole △, Belize ... 88 C2 17 24N 88 30W
Blue Lagoon △, Zambia ... 55 F2 15 28S 27 26 E
Blue Mesa Reservoir, U.S.A. ... 77 G10 38 28N 107 20W
Blue Mountain Lake, U.S.A. ... 85 C10 43 52N 74 30W
Blue Mountain Pk., Jamaica ... 88 a 18 3N 76 36W
Blue Mts., Maine, U.S.A. ... 85 B14 44 50N 70 35W
Blue Mts., Oreg., U.S.A. ... 76 D4 45 15N 119 0W
Blue Mts., Pa., U.S.A. ... 85 F8 40 30N 76 30W
Blue Mud B., Australia ... 62 A2 13 30S 136 0 E
Blue Nile = Nîl el Azraq →,
   Sudan ... 51 E12 15 38N 32 31 E
Blue Rapids, U.S.A. ... 80 F6 39 41N 96 39W
Blue Ridge Mts., U.S.A. ... 83 G5 36 30N 80 15W
Blue River, Canada ... 70 C5 52 6N 119 18W
Bluefield, U.S.A. ... 82 G5 37 15N 81 17W
Bluefields, Nic. ... 88 D3 12 20N 83 50W
Bluff, Australia ... 62 C4 23 35S 149 4 E
Bluff, N.Z. ... 59 M2 46 37S 168 20 E
Bluff, U.S.A. ... 77 H9 37 17N 109 33W
Bluff Knoll, Australia ... 61 F2 34 24S 118 15 E
Bluff Pt., Australia ... 61 E1 27 50S 114 5 E
Bluffton, U.S.A. ... 82 E3 40 44N 85 11W
Blumenau, Brazil ... 95 B6 27 0S 49 0W
Blunt, U.S.A. ... 80 C4 44 31N 99 59W
Bly, U.S.A. ... 76 E3 42 24N 121 3W
Blyde River Canyon △, S. Africa ... 57 C5 24 37S 31 2 E
Blyth, Canada ... 84 C3 43 44N 81 26W
Blyth, U.K. ... 12 B6 55 8N 1 31W
Blythe, U.S.A. ... 79 M12 33 37N 114 36W
Blytheville, U.S.A. ... 81 H10 35 56N 89 55W
Bo, S. Leone ... 50 G3 7 55N 11 50W
Bo Duc, Vietnam ... 39 G6 11 58N 106 50 E
Bo Hai, China ... 35 E10 39 0N 119 0 E
Bo Xian = Bozhou, China ... 34 H8 33 55N 115 41 E
Boa Vista, Brazil ... 92 C6 2 48N 60 30W
Boaco, Nic. ... 88 D2 12 29N 85 35W
Bo'ai, China ... 34 G7 35 10N 113 3 E
Boalsburg, U.S.A. ... 84 F7 40 46N 77 47W
Boane, Mozam. ... 57 D5 26 6S 32 19 E
Boardman, U.S.A. ... 84 E4 41 2N 80 40W
Bobadah, Australia ... 63 E4 32 19S 146 41 E
Bobbili, India ... 41 K13 18 35N 83 30 E
Bobcaygeon, Canada ... 84 B6 44 33N 78 33W
Bobo-Dioulasso, Burkina Faso ... 50 F5 11 8N 4 13W
Bóbr →, Poland ... 16 B8 52 4N 15 4 E
Bobraomby, Tanjon' i, Madag. ... 57 A8 12 40S 49 10 E
Bobruysk = Babruysk, Belarus ... 17 B15 53 10N 29 15 E
Boby, Pic, Madag. ... 53 J9 22 12S 46 55 E
Boca de Pozo, Venezuela ... 93 K15 11 0N 64 23W
Boca do Acre, Brazil ... 92 E5 8 50S 67 27W
Boca Raton, U.S.A. ... 83 M5 26 21N 80 5W
Bocas del Toro, Panama ... 88 E3 9 15N 82 20W
Bochnia, Poland ... 17 D11 49 58N 20 27 E
Bochum, Germany ... 16 C4 51 28N 7 13 E
Bocoyna, Mexico ... 86 B3 27 52N 107 35W
Bodaybo, Russia ... 29 D12 57 50N 114 0 E
Boddam, U.K. ... 11 B7 59 56N 1 17W
Boddington, Australia ... 61 F2 32 50S 116 30 E
Bodega Bay, U.S.A. ... 78 G3 38 20N 123 3W
Boden, Sweden ... 8 D19 65 50N 21 42 E
Bodensee, Europe ... 20 C8 47 35N 9 25 E
Bodhan, India ... 40 K10 18 40N 77 44 E
Bodmin, U.K. ... 13 G3 50 28N 4 43W
Bodmin Moor, U.K. ... 13 G3 50 33N 4 36W
Bodø, Norway ... 8 C16 67 17N 14 24 E
Bodrog →, Hungary ... 17 D11 48 11N 21 22 E
Bodrum, Turkey ... 23 F12 37 3N 27 30 E
Boende, Dem. Rep. of the Congo ... 52 E4 0 24S 21 12 E
Boerne, U.S.A. ... 81 L5 29 47N 98 44W
Boesmans →, S. Africa ... 56 E4 33 42S 26 39 E
Bogalusa, U.S.A. ... 81 K10 30 47N 89 52W
Bogan →, Australia ... 63 C4 29 59S 146 17 E
Bogan Gate, Australia ... 63 E4 33 7S 147 49 E
Bogantungan, Australia ... 62 C4 23 41S 147 17 E
Bogata, U.S.A. ... 81 J7 33 28N 95 13W
Boggabilla, Australia ... 63 D5 28 36S 150 24 E
Boggabri, Australia ... 63 E5 30 45S 150 5 E
Boggeragh Mts., Ireland ... 10 D3 52 2N 8 55W
Boglan = Solhan, Turkey ... 44 B4 38 57N 41 3 E
Bognor Regis, U.K. ... 13 G7 50 47N 0 40W
Bogo, Phil. ... 37 B6 11 3N 124 0 E
Bogong, Mt., Australia ... 63 F4 36 47S 147 17 E
Bogor, Indonesia ... 36 F3 6 36S 106 48 E
Bogotá, Colombia ... 92 C4 4 34N 74 0W
Bogotol, Russia ... 28 D9 56 15N 89 50 E
Bogra, Bangla. ... 41 G16 24 51N 89 22 E

Boguchany, Russia ... 29 D10 58 40N 97 30 E
Bohemian Forest = Böhmerwald, Germany ... 16 D7 49 8N 13 14 E
Böhmerwald, Germany ... 16 D7 49 8N 13 14 E
Bohol □, Phil. ... 37 C6 9 50N 124 10 E
Bohol Sea, Phil. ... 37 C6 9 0N 124 0 E
Bohuslän, Sweden ... 9 G14 58 25N 12 0 E
Boi, Pta. de, Brazil ... 95 A6 23 55S 45 15W
Boiaçu, Brazil ... 92 D6 0 27S 61 46W
Boileau, C., Australia ... 60 C3 17 40S 122 7 E
Boise, U.S.A. ... 76 E5 43 37N 116 13W
Boise City, U.S.A. ... 81 G3 36 44N 102 31W
Boissevain, Canada ... 71 D8 49 15N 100 5W
Bojador, C., W. Sahara ... 50 C3 26 0N 14 30W
Bojana →, Albania ... 23 D8 41 52N 19 22 E
Bojnūrd, Iran ... 45 B8 37 30N 57 20 E
Bojonegoro, Indonesia ... 37 G14 7 11S 111 54 E
Bokaro, India ... 43 H11 23 46N 85 55 E
Bokhara →, Australia ... 63 D4 29 55S 146 42 E
Boknafjorden, Norway ... 9 G11 59 14N 5 40 E
Bokora △, Uganda ... 54 B3 2 12N 31 32 E
Bokoro, Chad ... 51 F9 12 25N 17 14 E
Bokpyin, Burma ... 39 G2 11 18N 98 42 E
Bolan →, Pakistan ... 42 E2 28 38N 67 42 E
Bolan Pass, Pakistan ... 40 E5 29 50N 67 20 E
Bolaños →, Mexico ... 86 C4 21 14N 104 8W
Bolbec, France ... 20 B4 49 30N 0 30 E
Boldājī, Iran ... 45 D6 31 56N 51 3 E
Bole, China ... 32 B3 45 11N 81 37 E
Bolekhiv, Ukraine ... 17 D12 49 0N 23 57 E
Bolesławiec, Poland ... 16 C8 51 17N 15 37 E
Bolgrad = Bolhrad, Ukraine ... 17 F15 45 40N 28 32 E
Bolhrad, Ukraine ... 17 F15 45 40N 28 32 E
Bolívar, Argentina ... 94 D3 36 15S 60 53W
Bolívar, Mo., U.S.A. ... 81 G8 37 37N 93 25W
Bolívar, N.Y., U.S.A. ... 84 D6 42 4N 78 10W
Bolívar, Tenn., U.S.A. ... 81 H10 35 12N 89 0W
Bolivia ■, S. Amer. ... 92 G6 17 6S 64 0W
Bolivian Plateau = Altiplano, Bolivia ... 90 E4 17 0S 68 0W
Bollnäs, Sweden ... 9 F17 61 21N 16 24 E
Bollon, Australia ... 63 D4 28 2S 147 29 E
Bolmen, Sweden ... 9 H15 56 55N 13 40 E
Bolobo, Dem. Rep. of the Congo ... 52 E3 2 6S 16 20 E
Bologna, Italy ... 22 B4 44 29N 11 20 E
Bologoye, Russia ... 18 C5 57 55N 34 5 E
Bolonchenticul, Mexico ... 87 D7 20 0N 89 49W
Boloven, Cao Nguyen, Laos ... 38 E6 15 10N 106 30 E
Bolpur, India ... 43 H12 23 40N 87 45 E
Bolsena, L. di, Italy ... 22 C4 42 36N 11 56 E
Bolshevik, Ostrov, Russia ... 29 B11 78 30N 102 0 E
Bolshoy Anyuy →, Russia ... 29 C17 68 30N 160 49 E
Bolshoy Begichev, Ostrov, Russia ... 29 B12 74 20N 112 30 E
Bolshoy Kavkas = Caucasus Mountains, Eurasia ... 19 F7 42 50N 44 0 E
Bolshoy Lyakhovskiy, Ostrov, Russia ... 29 B15 73 35N 142 0 E
Bolshoy Tyuters, Ostrov, Russia ... 9 G22 59 51N 27 13 E
Bolsward, Neths. ... 15 A5 53 3N 5 32 E
Bolt Head, U.K. ... 13 G4 50 12N 3 48W
Bolton, Canada ... 84 C5 43 54N 79 45W
Bolton, U.K. ... 12 D5 53 35N 2 26W
Bolton Landing, U.S.A. ... 85 C11 43 32N 73 35W
Bolu, Turkey ... 19 F5 40 45N 31 35 E
Bolungavík, Iceland ... 8 C2 66 9N 23 15W
Boluvadin, Turkey ... 19 G5 38 45N 31 4 E
Bolzano, Italy ... 22 A4 46 31N 11 22 E
Bom Jesus da Lapa, Brazil ... 93 F10 13 15S 43 25W
Boma, Dem. Rep. of the Congo ... 52 F2 5 50S 13 4 E
Bombala, Australia ... 63 F4 36 56S 149 15 E
Bombay = Mumbai, India ... 40 K8 18 55N 72 50 E
Bombedor, Pta., Venezuela ... 93 L15 9 53N 61 37W
Bomboma, Dem. Rep. of the Congo ... 52 D3 2 25N 18 55 E
Bombombwa, Dem. Rep. of the Congo ... 54 B2 1 40N 25 40 E
Bomili, Dem. Rep. of the Congo ... 54 B2 1 45N 27 5 E
Bømlo, Norway ... 9 G11 59 37N 5 13 E
Bomokandi →, Dem. Rep. of the Congo ... 54 B2 3 39N 26 8 E
Bomu →, C.A.R. ... 52 D4 4 40N 22 30 E
Bon, C., Tunisia ... 48 C5 37 1N 11 2 E
Bon Sar Pa, Vietnam ... 38 F6 12 24N 107 35 E
Bonaigarh, India ... 43 J11 21 50N 84 57 E
Bonaire, Neth. Ant. ... 89 D6 12 10N 68 15W
Bonampak, Mexico ... 87 D6 16 44N 91 5W
Bonang, Australia ... 63 F4 37 11S 148 41 E
Bonanza, Nic. ... 88 D3 13 54N 84 35W
Bonaparte Arch., Australia ... 60 B3 14 0S 124 30 E
Bonar Bridge, U.K. ... 11 D4 57 54N 4 20W
Bonasse, Trin. & Tob. ... 93 K15 10 5N 61 54W
Bonaventure, Canada ... 73 C6 48 5N 65 32W
Bonavista, Canada ... 73 C9 48 40N 53 5W
Bonavista, C., Canada ... 73 C9 48 42N 53 5W
Bonavista B., Canada ... 73 C9 48 45N 53 25W
Bondo, Dem. Rep. of the Congo ... 54 B1 3 55N 23 53 E
Bondoukou, Ivory C. ... 50 G5 8 2N 2 47W
Bondowoso, Indonesia ... 37 G15 7 55S 113 49 E
Bone, Teluk, Indonesia ... 37 F6 4 10S 120 50 E
Bonerate, Indonesia ... 37 F6 7 25S 121 5 E
Bonerate, Kepulauan, Indonesia ... 37 F6 6 30S 121 10 E
Bo'ness, U.K. ... 11 E5 56 1N 3 37W
Bonete, Cerro, Argentina ... 94 B2 27 55S 68 40W
Bong Son = Hoai Nhon, Vietnam ... 38 E7 14 28N 109 1 E
Bongor, Chad ... 51 F9 10 35N 15 20 E
Bonham, U.S.A. ... 81 J6 33 35N 96 11W
Boni, Kenya ... 54 C5 1 35S 41 18 E
Bonifacio, France ... 20 F8 41 24N 9 10 E
Bonifacio, Bouches de, Medit. S. ... 22 D3 41 12N 9 15 E
Bonin Is. = Ogasawara Gunto, Pac. Oc. ... 26 G18 27 0N 142 0 E
Bonn, Germany ... 16 C4 50 46N 7 6 E
Bonne Terre, U.S.A. ... 81 G9 37 55N 90 33W
Bonners Ferry, U.S.A. ... 76 B5 48 42N 116 19W
Bonney, L., Australia ... 63 F3 37 50S 140 20 E
Bonnie Rock, Australia ... 61 F2 30 29S 118 22 E
Bonny, Bight of, Africa ... 52 D1 3 30N 9 20 E
Bonnyrigg, U.K. ... 11 F5 55 53N 3 6W
Bonnyville, Canada ... 71 C6 54 20N 110 45W
Bonoi, Indonesia ... 37 E9 1 45S 137 41 E
Bonsall, U.S.A. ... 79 M9 33 16N 117 14W
Bontang, Indonesia ... 36 D5 0 10N 117 30 E
Bontebok △, S. Africa ... 56 E3 34 5S 20 28 E
Bonthe, S. Leone ... 50 G3 7 30N 12 33W
Bontoc, Phil. ... 37 A6 17 7N 120 58 E
Bonython Ra., Australia ... 60 D4 23 40S 128 45 E
Bookabie, Australia ... 61 F5 31 50S 132 41 E

Booker, U.S.A. ... 81 G4 36 27N 100 32W
Booligal, Australia ... 63 E3 33 58S 144 53 E
Boonah, Australia ... 63 D5 27 58S 152 41 E
Boone, Iowa, U.S.A. ... 80 D8 42 4N 93 53W
Boone, N.C., U.S.A. ... 83 G5 36 13N 81 41W
Booneville, Ark., U.S.A. ... 81 H8 35 8N 93 55W
Booneville, Miss., U.S.A. ... 83 H1 34 39N 88 34W
Boonville, Calif., U.S.A. ... 78 F3 39 1N 123 22W
Boonville, Ind., U.S.A. ... 82 F2 38 3N 87 16W
Boonville, Mo., U.S.A. ... 80 F8 38 58N 92 44W
Boonville, N.Y., U.S.A. ... 85 C9 43 29N 75 20W
Boorabbin △, Australia ... 61 F4 31 30S 129 57 E
Boorindal, Australia ... 63 E4 30 22S 146 11 E
Boorowa, Australia ... 63 E4 34 28S 148 44 E
Boosaaso = Bosaso, Somali Rep. ... 47 E4 11 12N 49 18 E
Boothia, Gulf of, Canada ... 69 A11 71 0N 90 0W
Boothia Pen., Canada ... 68 A10 71 0N 94 0W
Bootle, U.K. ... 12 D4 53 28N 3 1W
Booué, Gabon ... 52 E2 0 5S 11 55 E
Boquete, Panama ... 88 E3 8 46N 82 27W
Boquilla, Presa de la, Mexico ... 86 B3 27 40N 105 30W
Boquillas del Carmen, Mexico ... 86 B4 29 17N 102 53W
Bor, Serbia & M. ... 23 B10 44 5N 22 7 E
Bôr, Sudan ... 51 G12 6 10N 31 40 E
Bor Mashash, Israel ... 46 D3 31 7N 34 50 E
Borah Peak, U.S.A. ... 76 D7 44 8N 113 47W
Borås, Sweden ... 9 H15 57 43N 12 56 E
Borāzjān, Iran ... 45 D6 29 22N 51 10 E
Borba, Brazil ... 92 D7 4 12S 59 34W
Borborema, Planalto da, Brazil ... 90 D7 7 0S 37 0W
Bord Khûn-e Now, Iran ... 45 D6 28 3N 51 28 E
Borda, C., Australia ... 63 F2 35 45S 136 34 E
Bordeaux, France ... 20 D3 44 50N 0 36W
Borden, Australia ... 61 F2 34 3S 118 12 E
Borden-Carleton, Canada ... 73 C7 46 18N 63 47W
Borden I., Canada ... 4 B2 78 30N 111 30W
Borden Pen., Canada ... 69 A11 73 0N 83 0W
Border Ranges △, Australia ... 63 D5 28 24S 152 56 E
Borders = Scottish Borders □, U.K. ... 11 F6 55 35N 2 50W
Bordertown, Australia ... 63 F3 36 19S 140 45 E
Borðeyri, Iceland ... 8 D3 65 12N 21 6W
Bordj Fly Ste. Marie, Algeria ... 50 C5 27 19N 2 32W
Bordj-in-Eker, Algeria ... 50 D7 24 9N 5 3 E
Bordj Omar Driss, Algeria ... 50 C7 28 10N 6 40 E
Borehamwood, U.K. ... 13 F7 51 40N 0 15W
Borgå = Porvoo, Finland ... 9 F21 60 24N 25 40 E
Borgarfjörður, Iceland ... 8 D7 65 31N 13 49W
Borgarnes, Iceland ... 8 D3 64 32N 21 55W
Børgefjellet, Norway ... 8 D15 65 20N 13 45 E
Borger, Neths. ... 15 B6 52 54N 6 44 E
Borger, U.S.A. ... 81 H4 35 39N 101 24W
Borgholm, Sweden ... 9 H17 56 52N 16 39 E
Borhoyn Tal, Mongolia ... 34 C6 43 50N 111 58 E
Borikhane, Laos ... 38 C4 18 33N 103 43 E
Borisoglebsk, Russia ... 19 D7 51 27N 42 5 E
Borisov = Barysaw, Belarus ... 17 A15 54 17N 28 28 E
Borja, Peru ... 92 D3 4 20S 77 40W
Borkou, Chad ... 51 E9 18 15N 18 50 E
Borkum, Germany ... 16 B4 53 34N 6 40 E
Borlänge, Sweden ... 9 F16 60 29N 15 26 E
Borley, C., Antarctica ... 5 C5 66 15S 52 30 E
Borneo, E. Indies ... 36 D5 1 0N 115 0 E
Bornholm, Denmark ... 9 J16 55 10N 15 0 E
Borogontsy, Russia ... 29 C14 62 42N 131 8 E
Boron, U.S.A. ... 79 L9 35 0N 117 39W
Borongan, Phil. ... 37 B7 11 37N 125 26 E
Borovichi, Russia ... 18 C5 58 25N 33 55 E
Borrego Springs, U.S.A. ... 79 M10 33 15N 116 23W
Borroloola, Australia ... 62 B2 16 4S 136 17 E
Borşa, Romania ... 17 E13 47 41N 24 50 E
Borsad, India ... 42 H5 22 25N 72 54 E
Borth, U.K. ... 13 E3 52 29N 4 2W
Borūjerd, Iran ... 45 C6 33 55N 48 50 E
Boryslav, Ukraine ... 17 D12 49 18N 23 28 E
Borzya, Russia ... 29 D12 50 24N 116 31 E
Bosa, Italy ... 22 D3 40 18N 8 30 E
Bosanska Gradiška, Bos.-H. ... 22 B7 45 10N 17 15 E
Bosaso, Somali Rep. ... 47 E4 11 12N 49 18 E
Boscastle, U.K. ... 13 G3 50 41N 4 42W
Boscobelle, Barbados ... 89 g 13 16N 59 34W
Boshan, China ... 35 F9 36 28N 117 49 E
Boshof, S. Africa ... 56 D4 28 31S 25 13 E
Boshrūyeh, Iran ... 45 C8 33 50N 57 30 E
Bosna →, Bos.-H. ... 23 B8 45 4N 18 29 E
Bosna i Hercegovina = Bosnia-Herzegovina ■, Europe ... 22 B7 44 0N 18 0 E
Bosnia-Herzegovina ■, Europe ... 22 B7 44 0N 18 0 E
Bosnik, Indonesia ... 37 E9 1 5S 136 10 E
Bosobolo, Dem. Rep. of the Congo ... 52 D3 4 15N 19 50 E
Bosporus = İstanbul Boğazı, Turkey ... 23 D13 41 10N 29 10 E
Bosque Farms, U.S.A. ... 77 J10 34 53N 106 40W
Bossangoa, C.A.R. ... 52 C3 6 35N 17 30 E
Bossier City, U.S.A. ... 81 J8 32 31N 93 44W
Bosso, Niger ... 51 F8 13 43N 13 19 E
Bostan, Pakistan ... 42 D2 30 26N 67 2 E
Bostānābād, Iran ... 44 B5 37 50N 46 50 E
Bosten Hu, China ... 32 B3 41 55N 87 40 E
Boston, U.K. ... 12 E7 52 59N 0 2W
Boston, U.S.A. ... 85 D13 42 22N 71 3W
Boston Bar, Canada ... 70 D4 49 52N 121 30W
Boston Mts., U.S.A. ... 81 H8 35 42N 93 15W
Boswell, Canada ... 70 D5 49 28N 116 45W
Boswell, U.S.A. ... 84 F5 40 10N 79 2W
Botad, India ... 42 H4 22 15N 71 40 E
Botene, Laos ... 38 D3 17 35N 101 12 E
Bothaville, S. Africa ... 56 D4 27 23S 26 34 E
Bothnia, G. of, Europe ... 8 E19 63 0N 20 15 E
Bothwell, Australia ... 63 G4 42 20S 147 1 E
Bothwell, Canada ... 84 D3 42 38N 81 52W
Botletle →, Botswana ... 56 C3 20 10S 23 15 E
Botoşani, Romania ... 17 E14 47 42N 26 41 E
Botou, Burkina Faso ... 50 F6 12 42N 1 59 E
Botswana ■, Africa ... 56 C3 22 0S 24 0 E
Bottineau, U.S.A. ... 80 A4 48 50N 100 27W
Botucatu, Brazil ... 95 A6 22 55S 48 30W
Botwood, Canada ... 73 C8 49 6N 55 23W
Bouaflé, Ivory C. ... 50 G4 7 1N 5 47W
Bouaké, Ivory C. ... 50 G4 7 40N 5 2W
Bouar, C.A.R. ... 52 C3 6 0N 15 40 E
Bouârfa, Morocco ... 50 B5 32 32N 1 58W
Boucaut B., Australia ... 62 A1 11 0S 134 25 E
Bouctouche, Canada ... 73 C7 46 30N 64 45W
Bougainville, C., Australia ... 60 B4 13 57S 126 4 E
Bougainville I., Papua N. G. ... 64 H7 6 0S 155 0 E

Bougainville Reef, Australia ... 62 B4 15 30S 147 5 E
Bougie = Bejaïa, Algeria ... 50 A7 36 42N 5 2 E
Bougouni, Mali ... 50 F4 11 30N 7 20W
Bouillon, Belgium ... 15 E5 49 44N 5 3 E
Boulder, Colo., U.S.A. ... 80 E2 40 1N 105 17W
Boulder, Mont., U.S.A. ... 76 C7 46 14N 112 7W
Boulder City, U.S.A. ... 79 K12 35 59N 114 50W
Boulder Creek, U.S.A. ... 78 H4 37 7N 122 7W
Boulder Dam = Hoover Dam, U.S.A. ... 79 K12 36 1N 114 44W
Boulia, Australia ... 62 C2 22 52S 139 51 E
Boulogne-sur-Mer, France ... 20 A4 50 42N 1 36 E
Boultoum, Niger ... 51 F8 14 45N 10 25 E
Boun Neua, Laos ... 38 B3 21 38N 101 54 E
Boun Tai, Laos ... 38 B3 21 23N 101 58 E
Bouna, Ivory C. ... 50 G5 9 10N 3 0W
Boundary Peak, U.S.A. ... 78 H8 37 51N 118 21W
Boundiali, Ivory C. ... 50 G4 9 30N 6 20W
Bountiful, U.S.A. ... 76 F8 40 53N 111 53W
Bounty Is., Pac. Oc. ... 64 M9 48 0S 178 30 E
Bourbonnais, France ... 20 C5 46 28N 3 0 E
Bourdel L., Canada ... 72 A5 56 43N 74 10W
Bourem, Mali ... 50 E5 17 0N 0 24W
Bourg-en-Bresse, France ... 20 C6 46 13N 5 12 E
Bourg-St-Maurice, France ... 20 D7 45 35N 6 46 E
Bourges, France ... 20 C5 47 9N 2 25 E
Bourget, Canada ... 85 A9 45 26N 75 9W
Bourgogne ⊠, France ... 20 C6 47 0N 4 50 E
Bourke, Australia ... 63 E4 30 8S 145 55 E
Bourne, U.K. ... 12 E7 52 47N 0 22W
Bournemouth, U.K. ... 13 G6 50 43N 1 52W
Bournemouth □, U.K. ... 13 G6 50 43N 1 52W
Bouse, U.S.A. ... 79 M13 33 56N 114 0W
Bouvet I. = Bouvetøya, Antarctica ... 3 G10 54 26S 3 24 E
Bouvetøya, Antarctica ... 3 G10 54 26S 3 24 E
Bovill, U.S.A. ... 76 C5 46 51N 116 24W
Bovril, Argentina ... 94 C4 31 21S 59 26W
Bow →, Canada ... 70 C6 49 57N 111 41W
Bow Island, Canada ... 70 D6 49 50N 111 23W
Bowbells, U.S.A. ... 80 A3 48 48N 102 15W
Bowdle, U.S.A. ... 80 C5 45 27N 99 39W
Bowelling, Australia ... 61 F2 33 25S 116 30 E
Bowen, Argentina ... 94 D2 35 0S 67 31W
Bowen, Australia ... 62 J6 20 0S 148 16 E
Bowen Mts., Australia ... 63 F4 37 0S 147 50 E
Bowie, Ariz., U.S.A. ... 77 K9 32 19N 109 29W
Bowie, Tex., U.S.A. ... 81 J6 33 34N 97 51W
Bowkān, Iran ... 44 B5 36 31N 46 12 E
Bowland, Forest of, U.K. ... 12 D5 54 0N 2 30W
Bowling Green, Ky., U.S.A. ... 82 G2 36 59N 86 27W
Bowling Green, Ohio, U.S.A. ... 82 E4 41 23N 83 39W
Bowling Green, C., Australia ... 62 B4 19 19S 147 25 E
Bowling Green Bay △, Australia ... 80 B3 46 11N 103 24W
Bowman, U.S.A. ... 80 B3 46 11N 103 24W
Bowman, I., Antarctica ... 5 C8 65 0S 104 0 E
Bowmanville = Clarington, Canada ... 84 C6 43 55N 78 41W
Bowmore, U.K. ... 11 F2 55 45N 6 17W
Bowral, Australia ... 63 E5 34 26S 150 27 E
Bowraville, Australia ... 63 E5 30 37S 152 52 E
Bowron →, Canada ... 70 C4 53 10N 121 5W
Bowron Lake △, Canada ... 70 C4 53 10N 121 5W
Bowser L., Canada ... 70 B3 56 30N 129 30W
Bowsman, Canada ... 71 C8 52 14N 101 12W
Bowwood, Zambia ... 55 F2 17 5S 26 20 E
Box Cr. →, Australia ... 63 E3 34 10S 143 50 E
Boxmeer, Neths. ... 15 C5 51 36N 5 58 E
Boxtel, Neths. ... 15 C5 51 36N 5 20 E
Boyce, U.S.A. ... 81 K8 31 23N 92 40W
Boyd L., Canada ... 72 B4 52 46N 76 42W
Boyle, Canada ... 70 C6 54 35N 112 49W
Boyle, Ireland ... 10 C3 53 59N 8 18W
Boyne →, Ireland ... 10 C5 53 43N 6 15W
Boyne City, U.S.A. ... 82 C3 45 13N 85 1W
Boynton Beach, U.S.A. ... 83 M5 26 32N 80 4W
Boyolali, Indonesia ... 37 G14 7 32S 110 35 E
Boyoma, Chutes, Dem. Rep. of the Congo ... 54 B2 0 35S 25 23 E
Boysen Reservoir, U.S.A. ... 76 E9 43 25N 108 11W
Boyuibe, Bolivia ... 92 G6 20 25S 63 17W
Boyup Brook, Australia ... 61 F2 33 50S 116 23 E
Boz Dağları, Turkey ... 23 E13 38 20N 28 0 E
Bozburun, Turkey ... 23 F13 36 43N 28 4 E
Bozcaada, Turkey ... 23 E12 39 49N 26 3 E
Bozdoğan, Turkey ... 23 F13 37 40N 28 17 E
Bozeman, U.S.A. ... 76 D8 45 41N 111 2W
Bozen = Bolzano, Italy ... 22 A4 46 31N 11 22 E
Bozhou, China ... 34 H8 33 55N 115 41 E
Bozoum, C.A.R. ... 52 C3 6 25N 16 35 E
Bra, Italy ... 20 D7 44 42N 7 51 E
Brabant □, Belgium ... 15 D4 50 46N 4 30 E
Brabant L., Canada ... 71 B8 55 58N 103 43W
Brač, Croatia ... 22 C7 43 20N 16 40 E
Bracadale, L., U.K. ... 11 D2 57 20N 6 30W
Bracciano, L. di, Italy ... 22 C5 42 7N 12 14 E
Bracebridge, Canada ... 84 A5 45 2N 79 19W
Brach, Libya ... 51 C8 27 31N 14 20 E
Bräcke, Sweden ... 9 E16 62 45N 15 26 E
Brackettville, U.S.A. ... 81 L4 29 19N 100 25W
Bracknell, U.K. ... 13 F7 51 25N 0 43W
Bracknell Forest □, U.K. ... 13 F7 51 25N 0 44W
Brad, Romania ... 17 E12 46 10N 22 50 E
Bradenton, U.S.A. ... 83 M4 27 30N 82 34W
Bradford, Canada ... 84 B5 44 7N 79 34W
Bradford, U.K. ... 12 D6 53 47N 1 45W
Bradford, Pa., U.S.A. ... 84 E6 41 58N 78 38W
Bradford, Vt., U.S.A. ... 85 C12 43 59N 72 9W
Bradley, Ark., U.S.A. ... 81 J8 33 6N 93 39W
Bradley, Calif., U.S.A. ... 78 K6 35 52N 120 48W
Bradley Institute, Zimbabwe ... 55 F3 17 7S 31 25 E
Brady, U.S.A. ... 81 K5 31 9N 99 20W
Braeside, Canada ... 85 A8 45 28N 76 24W
Braga, Portugal ... 21 B1 41 35N 8 25W
Bragado, Argentina ... 94 D3 35 2S 60 27W
Bragança, Brazil ... 93 D9 1 0S 47 2W
Bragança, Portugal ... 21 B2 41 48N 6 50W
Bragança Paulista, Brazil ... 95 A6 22 55S 46 32W
Brahmanbaria, Bangla. ... 41 H17 23 58N 91 15 E
Brahmani →, India ... 41 J15 20 39N 86 46 E
Brahmapur, India ... 41 K14 19 15N 84 54 E
Brahmaputra →, Asia ... 32 D3 23 40N 90 35 E
Braich-y-pwll, U.K. ... 12 E3 52 47N 4 46W
Braidwood, Australia ... 63 F4 35 27S 149 49 E
Brăila, Romania ... 17 F14 45 19N 27 59 E
Brainerd, U.S.A. ... 80 B7 46 22N 94 12W
Braintree, U.K. ... 13 F8 51 53N 0 34 E
Braintree, U.S.A. ... 85 D14 42 13N 71 0W
Brak →, S. Africa ... 56 D3 29 35S 22 55 E

Brakwater, Namibia ... 56 C2 22 28S 17 3 E
Brampton, Canada ... 84 C5 43 45N 79 45W
Brampton, U.K. ... 12 C5 54 57N 2 44W
Bramton I., Australia ... 62 J7 20 50S 149 17 E
Branco →, Brazil ... 92 D6 1 20S 61 50W
Brandberg, Namibia ... 56 C1 21 10S 14 33 E
Brandberg △, Namibia ... 56 C1 21 10S 14 30 E
Brandenburg = Neubrandenburg, Germany ... 16 B7 53 33N 13 15 E
Brandenburg, Germany ... 16 B7 52 25N 12 33 E
Brandenburg □, Germany ... 16 B6 52 50N 13 0 E
Brandfort, S. Africa ... 56 D4 28 40S 26 30 E
Brandon, Canada ... 71 D9 49 50N 99 57W
Brandon, U.S.A. ... 85 C11 43 48N 73 6W
Brandon B., Ireland ... 10 D1 52 17N 10 8W
Brandon Mt., Ireland ... 10 D1 52 15N 10 15W
Brandsen, Argentina ... 94 D4 35 10S 58 15 E
Brandvlei, S. Africa ... 56 E3 30 25S 20 30 E
Branford, U.S.A. ... 85 E12 41 17N 72 49W
Braniewo, Poland ... 17 A10 54 25N 19 50 E
Bransfield Str., Antarctica ... 5 C18 63 0S 59 0W
Branson, U.S.A. ... 81 G8 36 39N 93 13W
Brantford, Canada ... 84 C4 43 10N 80 15W
Bras d'Or L., Canada ... 73 C7 45 50N 60 50W
Brasher Falls, U.S.A. ... 85 B10 44 49N 74 47W
Brasil, Planalto, Brazil ... 90 E6 18 0S 46 30W
Brasília, Brazil ... 93 G9 15 47S 47 55W
Brasília Legal, Brazil ... 93 D7 3 49S 55 36W
Braslaw, Belarus ... 9 J22 55 38N 27 0 E
Braşov, Romania ... 17 F13 45 38N 25 35 E
Brasschaat, Belgium ... 15 C4 51 19N 4 27 E
Brassey, Banjaran, Malaysia ... 36 D5 5 0N 117 15 E
Brassey Ra., Australia ... 61 E3 25 8S 122 15 E
Brasstown Bald, U.S.A. ... 83 H4 34 53N 83 49W
Brastad, Sweden ... 9 G14 58 23N 11 30 E
Bratislava, Slovak Rep. ... 17 D9 48 10N 17 7 E
Bratsk, Russia ... 29 D11 56 10N 101 30 E
Brattleboro, U.S.A. ... 85 D12 42 51N 72 34W
Braunau, Austria ... 16 D7 48 15N 13 3 E
Braunschweig, Germany ... 16 B6 52 15N 10 31 E
Braunton, U.K. ... 13 F3 51 7N 4 10W
Bravo del Norte, Rio = Grande, Rio →, U.S.A. ... 81 N6 25 58N 97 9W
Brawley, U.S.A. ... 79 N11 32 59N 115 31W
Bray, Ireland ... 10 C5 53 13N 6 7W
Bray, Mt., Australia ... 62 A1 14 0S 134 30 E
Bray, Pays de, France ... 20 B4 49 46N 1 26 E
Brazeau →, Canada ... 70 C5 52 55N 115 14W
Brazil, U.S.A. ... 82 F2 39 32N 87 8W
Brazil ■, S. Amer. ... 93 F9 12 0S 50 0W
Brazilian Highlands = Brasil, Planalto, Brazil ... 90 E6 18 0S 46 30W
Brazo Sur →, S. Amer. ... 94 B4 25 21S 57 42W
Brazos →, U.S.A. ... 81 L7 28 53N 95 23W
Brazzaville, Congo ... 52 E3 4 9S 15 12 E
Brčko, Bos.-H. ... 23 B8 44 54N 18 46 E
Breaden, L., Australia ... 61 E4 25 51S 125 28 E
Breaksea Sd., N.Z. ... 59 L1 45 35S 166 35 E
Bream B., N.Z. ... 59 F5 35 56S 174 28 E
Bream Hd., N.Z. ... 59 F5 35 51S 174 36 E
Breas, Chile ... 94 B1 25 29S 70 24W
Brebes, Indonesia ... 37 G13 6 52S 109 3 E
Brechin, Canada ... 84 B5 44 32N 79 10W
Brechin, U.K. ... 11 E6 56 44N 2 39W
Brecht, Belgium ... 15 C4 51 21N 4 38 E
Breckenridge, Colo., U.S.A. ... 76 G10 39 29N 106 3W
Breckenridge, Minn., U.S.A. ... 80 B6 46 16N 96 35W
Breckenridge, Tex., U.S.A. ... 81 J5 32 45N 98 54W
Breckland, U.K. ... 13 E8 52 30N 0 40 E
Brecon, U.K. ... 13 F4 51 57N 3 23W
Brecon Beacons, U.K. ... 13 F4 51 53N 3 26W
Brecon Beacons △, U.K. ... 13 F4 51 50N 3 30W
Breda, Neths. ... 15 C4 51 35N 4 45 E
Bredasdorp, S. Africa ... 56 E3 34 33S 20 2 E
Bree, Belgium ... 15 C5 51 8N 5 35 E
Bregenz, Austria ... 16 E5 47 30N 9 45 E
Breiðafjörður, Iceland ... 8 D2 65 15N 23 15W
Brejo, Brazil ... 93 D10 3 41S 42 47W
Bremen, Germany ... 16 B5 53 4N 8 47 E
Bremer Bay, Australia ... 61 F2 34 21S 119 20 E
Bremer I., Australia ... 62 A2 12 5S 136 45 E
Bremerhaven, Germany ... 16 B5 53 33N 8 36 E
Bremerton, U.S.A. ... 78 C4 47 34N 122 38W
Brenham, U.S.A. ... 81 K6 30 10N 96 24W
Brennerpass, Austria ... 16 E6 47 2N 11 30 E
Brent, U.S.A. ... 83 J2 32 56N 87 10W
Brentwood, U.K. ... 13 F8 51 37N 0 19 E
Brentwood, Calif., U.S.A. ... 78 H5 37 56N 121 42W
Brentwood, N.Y., U.S.A. ... 85 F11 40 47N 73 15W
Bréscia, Italy ... 20 D9 45 33N 10 15 E
Breskens, Neths. ... 15 C3 51 23N 3 33 E
Breslau = Wrocław, Poland ... 17 C9 51 5N 17 5 E
Bressanone, Italy ... 22 A4 46 43N 11 39 E
Bressay, U.K. ... 11 A7 60 9N 1 6W
Brest, Belarus ... 17 B12 52 10N 23 40 E
Brest, France ... 20 B1 48 24N 4 31W
Brest-Litovsk = Brest, Belarus ... 17 B12 52 10N 23 40 E
Bretagne ⊠, France ... 20 B2 48 10N 3 0W
Breton, Canada ... 70 C6 53 7N 114 28W
Breton Sd., U.S.A. ... 81 L10 29 35N 89 15W
Brett, C., N.Z. ... 59 F5 35 10S 174 20 E
Brevard, U.S.A. ... 83 H4 35 14N 82 44W
Breves, Brazil ... 93 D8 1 40S 50 29W
Brewarrina, Australia ... 63 E4 30 0S 146 51 E
Brewer, U.S.A. ... 83 C11 44 48N 68 46W
Brewer, Mt., U.S.A. ... 78 J8 36 44N 118 28W
Brewster, N.Y., U.S.A. ... 85 E11 41 23N 73 37W
Brewster, Ohio, U.S.A. ... 84 F3 40 43N 81 36W
Brewster, Wash., U.S.A. ... 76 B4 48 6N 119 47W
Brewster, Kap = Kangikajik, Greenland ... 4 B6 70 7N 22 0W
Brewton, U.S.A. ... 83 K2 31 7N 87 4W
Breyten, S. Africa ... 57 D5 26 16S 30 0 E
Briançon, France ... 20 D7 44 54N 6 39 E
Bribie I., Australia ... 63 D5 27 0S 153 10 E
Bribri, Costa Rica ... 88 E3 9 38N 82 50W
Bridgefield, Barbados ... 89 g 13 9N 59 36W
Bridgehampton, U.S.A. ... 85 F12 40 56N 72 19W
Bridgend, U.K. ... 13 F4 51 30N 3 34W
Bridgend □, U.K. ... 13 F4 51 36N 3 36W
Bridgeport, Calif., U.S.A. ... 78 G7 38 15N 119 14W
Bridgeport, Conn., U.S.A. ... 85 E11 41 11N 73 12W
Bridgeport, Nebr., U.S.A. ... 80 E3 41 40N 103 6W
Bridgeport, Tex., U.S.A. ... 81 J6 33 13N 97 45W
Bridger, U.S.A. ... 76 D9 45 18N 108 55W
Bridgeton, U.S.A. ... 82 F8 39 26N 75 14W
Bridgetown, Australia ... 61 F2 33 58S 116 7 E

Name	Ref	Lat	Long
Bridgetown, Barbados	89 g	13 5N	59 30W
Bridgetown, Canada	73 D6	44 55N	65 18W
Bridgewater, Canada	73 D7	44 25N	64 31W
Bridgewater, Mass., U.S.A.	85 E14	41 59N	70 58W
Bridgewater, N.Y., U.S.A.	85 D9	42 53N	75 15W
Bridgewater, C., Australia	63 F3	38 23S	141 23 E
Bridgewater-Gagebrook, Australia	63 G4	42 44S	147 14 E
Bridgnorth, U.K.	13 E5	52 32N	2 25W
Bridgton, U.S.A.	85 B14	44 3N	70 42W
Bridgwater, U.K.	13 F5	51 8N	2 59W
Bridgwater B., U.K.	13 F4	51 15N	3 15W
Bridlington, U.K.	12 C7	54 5N	0 12W
Bridlington B., U.K.	12 C7	54 4N	0 10W
Bridport, Australia	63 G4	40 59S	147 23 E
Bridport, U.K.	13 G5	50 44N	2 45W
Brig, Switz.	20 C7	46 18N	7 59 E
Brigg, U.K.	12 D7	53 34N	0 28W
Brigham City, U.S.A.	76 F7	41 31N	112 1W
Bright, Australia	63 F4	36 42S	146 56 E
Brighton, Australia	63 F2	35 5S	138 30 E
Brighton, Canada	84 B7	44 2N	77 44W
Brighton, Trin. & Tob.	93 K15	10 13N	61 39W
Brighton, U.K.	13 G7	50 49N	0 7W
Brighton, Colo., U.S.A.	80 F2	39 59N	104 49W
Brighton, N.Y., U.S.A.	84 C7	43 8N	77 34W
Brilliant, U.S.A.	84 F4	40 15N	80 39W
Bríndisi, Italy	23 D7	40 39N	17 55 E
Brinkley, U.S.A.	81 H9	34 53N	91 12W
Brinnon, U.S.A.	78 C4	47 41N	122 54W
Brion, Î., Canada	73 C7	47 46N	61 26W
Brisbane, Australia	63 D5	27 25S	153 2 E
Brisbane →, Australia	63 D5	27 24S	153 9 E
Bristol, U.K.	13 F5	51 26N	2 35W
Bristol, Conn., U.S.A.	85 E12	41 40N	72 57W
Bristol, Pa., U.S.A.	85 F10	40 6N	74 51W
Bristol, R.I., U.S.A.	85 E13	41 40N	71 16W
Bristol, Tenn., U.S.A.	83 G4	36 36N	82 11W
Bristol, City of □, U.K.	13 F5	51 27N	2 36W
Bristol B., U.S.A.	68 C4	58 0N	160 0W
Bristol Channel, U.K.	13 F3	51 18N	4 30W
Bristol I., Antarctica	5 B1	58 45S	28 0W
Bristol L., U.S.A.	77 J5	34 23N	116 50W
Bristow, U.S.A.	81 H6	35 50N	96 23W
Britain = Great Britain, Europe	6 E5	54 0N	2 15W
British Columbia □, Canada	70 C3	55 0N	125 15W
British Indian Ocean Terr. = Chagos Arch. ☒, Ind. Oc.	27 K11	6 0S	72 0 E
British Isles, Europe	14 D5	54 0N	4 0W
British Virgin Is. ☒, W. Indies	89 e	18 30N	64 30W
Brits, S. Africa	57 D4	25 37S	27 48 E
Britstown, S. Africa	56 E3	30 37S	23 30 E
Britt, Canada	72 C3	45 46N	80 34W
Brittany = Bretagne ☒, France	20 B2	48 10N	3 0W
Britton, U.S.A.	80 C6	45 48N	97 45W
Brive-la-Gaillarde, France	20 D4	45 10N	1 32 E
Brixen = Bressanone, Italy	22 A4	46 43N	11 39 E
Brixham, U.K.	13 G4	50 23N	3 31W
Brno, Czech Rep.	17 D9	49 10N	16 35 E
Broach = Bharuch, India	40 J8	21 47N	73 0 E
Broad →, U.S.A.	83 J5	34 1N	81 4W
Broad Arrow, Australia	61 F3	30 23S	121 15 E
Broad B., U.K.	11 C2	58 14N	6 18W
Broad Haven, Ireland	10 B2	54 20N	9 55W
Broad Law, U.K.	11 F5	55 30N	3 21W
Broad Sd., Australia	62 C4	22 0S	149 45 E
Broadalbin, U.S.A.	85 C10	43 4N	74 12W
Broadback →, Canada	72 B4	51 21N	78 52W
Broadhurst Ra., Australia	60 D3	22 30S	122 30 E
Broads →, U.K.	13 E9	52 45N	1 30 E
Broads, The, U.K.	12 E9	52 45N	1 30 E
Broadus, U.S.A.	80 C2	45 27N	105 25W
Brochet, Canada	71 B8	57 53N	101 40W
Brochet, L., Canada	71 B8	58 36N	101 35W
Brocken, Germany	16 C6	51 47N	10 37 E
Brockport, U.S.A.	84 C7	43 13N	77 56W
Brockton, U.S.A.	85 D13	42 5N	71 1W
Brockville, Canada	85 B9	44 35N	75 41W
Brockway, Mont., U.S.A.	80 B2	47 18N	105 45W
Brockway, Pa., U.S.A.	84 E6	41 15N	78 47W
Brocton, U.S.A.	84 D5	42 23N	79 26W
Brodeur Pen., Canada	69 A11	72 30N	88 10W
Brodhead, Mt., U.S.A.	84 E7	41 39N	77 47W
Brodick, U.K.	11 F3	55 35N	5 9W
Brodnica, Poland	17 B10	53 15N	19 25 E
Brody, Ukraine	17 C13	50 5N	25 10 E
Brogan, U.S.A.	76 D5	44 15N	117 31W
Broken Arrow, U.S.A.	81 G7	36 3N	95 48W
Broken Bow, Nebr., U.S.A.	80 E5	41 24N	99 38W
Broken Bow, Okla., U.S.A.	81 H7	34 2N	94 44W
Broken Bow Lake, U.S.A.	81 H7	34 9N	94 40W
Broken Hill, Australia	63 E3	31 58S	141 29 E
Broken River Ra., Australia	62 K6	21 0S	148 22 E
Bromley □, U.K.	13 F8	51 24N	0 2 E
Bromo, Indonesia	37 G15	7 55S	112 55 E
Bromsgrove, U.K.	13 E5	52 21N	2 2W
Brønderslev, Denmark	9 H13	57 16N	9 57 E
Bronkhorstspruit, S. Africa	57 D4	25 46S	28 45 E
Brønnøysund, Norway	8 D15	65 28N	12 14 E
Brook Park, U.S.A.	84 E4	41 24N	81 51W
Brookhaven, U.S.A.	81 K9	31 35N	90 26W
Brookings, Oreg., U.S.A.	76 E1	42 3N	124 17W
Brookings, S. Dak., U.S.A.	80 C6	44 19N	96 48W
Brooklin, Canada	84 C6	43 55N	78 55W
Brooklyn Park, U.S.A.	80 C8	45 6N	93 23W
Brooks, Canada	70 C6	50 35N	111 55W
Brooksville, U.S.A.	83 L4	28 33N	82 23W
Brookton, Australia	61 F2	32 22S	117 0 E
Brookville, U.S.A.	84 E5	41 10N	79 5W
Broom, L., U.K.	11 D3	57 55N	5 15W
Broome, Australia	60 C3	18 0S	122 15 E
Brora, U.K.	11 C5	58 0N	3 52W
Brora →, U.K.	11 C5	58 0N	3 51W
Brosna →, Ireland	10 C4	53 14N	7 58W
Brothers, U.S.A.	76 E3	43 49N	120 36W
Brough, U.K.	12 C5	54 32N	2 18W
Brough Hd., U.K.	11 B5	59 8N	3 20W
Broughton Island = Qikiqtarjuaq, Canada	69 B13	67 33N	63 0W
Brown, L., Australia	61 F2	31 5S	118 15 E
Brown, Pt., Australia	63 E1	32 32S	133 50 E
Brown City, U.S.A.	84 C2	43 13N	82 59W
Brown Willy, U.K.	13 G3	50 35N	4 37W
Brownfield, U.S.A.	81 J3	33 11N	102 17W
Browning, U.S.A.	76 B7	48 34N	113 1W
Brownsville, Oreg., U.S.A.	76 D2	44 24N	122 59W
Brownsville, Pa., U.S.A.	84 F5	40 1N	79 53W
Brownsville, Tenn., U.S.A.	81 H10	35 36N	89 16W
Brownsville, Tex., U.S.A.	81 N6	25 54N	97 30W
Brownville, U.S.A.	85 C9	44 0N	75 59W
Brownwood, U.S.A.	81 K5	31 43N	98 59W
Browse I., Australia	60 B3	14 7S	123 33 E
Bruas, Malaysia	39 K3	4 30N	100 47 E
Bruay-la-Buissière, France	20 A5	50 29N	2 33 E
Bruce, Mt., Australia	60 D2	22 37S	118 8 E
Bruce Pen., Canada	84 B3	45 0N	81 30W
Bruce Peninsula △, Canada	84 A3	45 14N	81 36W
Bruce Rock, Australia	61 F2	31 52S	118 8 E
Bruck an der Leitha, Austria	17 D9	48 1N	16 47 E
Bruck an der Mur, Austria	16 E8	47 24N	15 16 E
Brue →, U.K.	13 F5	51 13N	2 59W
Bruges = Brugge, Belgium	15 C3	51 13N	3 13 E
Brugge, Belgium	15 C3	51 13N	3 13 E
Bruin, U.S.A.	84 E5	41 3N	79 43W
Brûlé, Canada	70 C5	53 15N	117 58W
Brumado, Brazil	93 F10	14 14S	41 40W
Brumunddal, Norway	9 F14	60 53N	10 56 E
Bruneau, U.S.A.	76 E6	42 53N	115 48W
Bruneau →, U.S.A.	76 E6	42 56N	115 57W
Brunei = Bandar Seri Begawan, Brunei	36 C4	4 52N	115 0 E
Brunei ■, Asia	36 D4	4 50N	115 0 E
Brunner, L., N.Z.	59 K3	42 37S	171 27 E
Brunssum, Neths.	15 D5	50 57N	5 59 E
Brunswick = Braunschweig, Germany	16 B6	52 15N	10 31 E
Brunswick, Ga., U.S.A.	83 K5	31 10N	81 30W
Brunswick, Maine, U.S.A.	83 D11	43 55N	69 58W
Brunswick, Md., U.S.A.	82 F7	39 19N	77 38W
Brunswick, Mo., U.S.A.	80 F8	39 26N	93 8W
Brunswick, Ohio, U.S.A.	84 E3	41 14N	81 51W
Brunswick, Pen. de, Chile	96 G2	53 30S	71 30W
Brunswick B., Australia	60 C3	15 15S	124 50 E
Brunswick Junction, Australia	61 F2	33 15S	115 50 E
Bruny I., Australia	63 G4	43 20S	147 15 E
Brus Laguna, Honduras	88 C3	15 47N	84 35W
Brush, U.S.A.	80 E3	40 15N	103 37W
Brushton, U.S.A.	85 B10	44 50N	74 31W
Brusque, Brazil	95 B6	27 5S	49 0W
Brussel, Belgium	15 D4	50 51N	4 21 E
Brussels = Brussel, Belgium	15 D4	50 51N	4 21 E
Brussels, Canada	84 C3	43 44N	81 15W
Bruthen, Australia	63 F4	37 42S	147 50 E
Bruxelles = Brussel, Belgium	15 D4	50 51N	4 21 E
Bryan, Ohio, U.S.A.	82 E3	41 28N	84 33W
Bryan, Tex., U.S.A.	81 K6	30 40N	96 22W
Bryan, Mt., Australia	63 E2	33 30S	139 0 E
Bryansk, Russia	18 D4	53 13N	34 25 E
Bryce Canyon △, U.S.A.	77 H7	37 30N	112 10W
Bryne, Norway	9 G11	58 44N	5 38 E
Bryson City, U.S.A.	83 H4	35 26N	83 27W
Bsharri, Lebanon	46 A5	34 15N	36 0 E
Bū Baqarah, U.A.E.	45 E8	25 35N	56 25 E
Bu Craa, W. Sahara	50 C3	26 45N	12 50W
Bū Ḩasā, U.A.E.	45 F7	23 30N	53 20 E
Bua Yai, Thailand	38 E4	15 33N	102 26 E
Buapinang, Indonesia	37 E6	4 40S	121 30 E
Buanza, Burundi	54 C2	3 6S	29 23 E
Būbiyān, Kuwait	45 D6	29 45N	48 15 E
Bucaramanga, Colombia	92 B4	7 0N	73 0W
Bucasia, Australia	62 K7	21 2S	149 10 E
Buccaneer Arch., Australia	60 C3	16 7S	123 20 E
Buccoo Reef, Trin. & Tob.	93 J16	11 10N	60 51W
Buchach, Ukraine	17 D13	49 5N	25 25 E
Buchan, U.K.	11 D6	57 32N	2 21W
Buchan Ness, U.K.	11 D7	57 29N	1 46W
Buchanan, Canada	71 C8	51 40N	102 45W
Buchanan, Liberia	50 G3	5 57N	10 2W
Buchanan, L., Queens., Australia	62 C4	21 35S	145 52 E
Buchanan, L., W. Austral., Australia	61 E3	25 33S	123 2 E
Buchanan, L., U.S.A.	81 K5	30 45N	98 25W
Buchanan Cr. →, Australia	62 B2	19 13S	136 33 E
Buchans, Canada	73 C8	48 50N	56 52W
Bucharest = București, Romania	17 F14	44 27N	26 10 E
Buchon, Pt., U.S.A.	78 K6	35 15N	120 54W
Buck Hill Falls, U.S.A.	85 E9	41 11N	75 16W
Buckeye, U.S.A.	77 K7	33 22N	112 35W
Buckeye Lake, U.S.A.	84 G2	39 55N	82 29W
Buckhannon, U.S.A.	82 F5	39 0N	80 8W
Buckhaven, U.K.	11 E5	56 11N	3 3W
Buckhorn L., Canada	84 B6	44 29N	78 23W
Buckie, U.K.	11 D6	57 41N	2 58W
Buckingham, Canada	72 C4	45 37N	75 24W
Buckingham, U.K.	13 F7	51 59N	0 57W
Buckingham B., Australia	62 A2	12 10S	135 40 E
Buckinghamshire □, U.K.	13 F7	51 53N	0 55W
Buckle Hd., Australia	60 B4	14 26S	127 52 E
Buckleboo, Australia	63 E2	32 54S	136 12 E
Buckley, U.S.A.	12 D4	53 10N	3 5W
Buckley →, Australia	62 C2	20 10S	138 49 E
Bucklin, U.S.A.	81 G5	37 33N	99 38W
Bucks L., U.S.A.	78 F5	39 54N	121 12W
București, Romania	17 F14	44 27N	26 10 E
Bucyrus, U.S.A.	82 E4	40 48N	82 59W
Budalin, Burma	41 H19	22 20N	95 10 E
Budapest, Hungary	17 E10	47 29N	19 5 E
Budaun, India	43 E8	28 5N	79 10 E
Budd Coast, Antarctica	5 C8	68 0S	112 0 E
Bude, U.K.	13 G3	50 49N	4 34W
Budge Budge = Baj Baj, India	43 H13	22 30N	88 5 E
Budgewoi, Australia	63 E5	33 13S	151 34 E
Budjala, Dem. Rep. of the Congo	52 D3	2 50N	19 40 E
Buellton, U.S.A.	79 L6	34 37N	120 12W
Buena Esperanza, Argentina	94 C2	34 45S	65 15W
Buena Park, U.S.A.	79 M9	33 52N	117 59W
Buena Vista, Colo., U.S.A.	77 G10	38 51N	106 8W
Buena Vista, Va., U.S.A.	82 G6	37 44N	79 21W
Buena Vista Lake Bed, U.S.A.	79 K7	35 12N	119 18W
Buenaventura, Colombia	92 C3	3 53N	77 4W
Buenaventura, Mexico	86 B3	29 50N	107 30W
Buenos Aires, Argentina	94 C4	34 30S	58 20W
Buenos Aires, Costa Rica	88 E3	9 10N	83 20W
Buenos Aires □, Argentina	94 D4	36 30S	60 0W
Buenos Aires, L., Chile	96 F2	46 35S	72 30W
Buffalo, Mo., U.S.A.	81 G8	37 39N	93 6W
Buffalo, N.Y., U.S.A.	84 D6	42 53N	78 53W
Buffalo, Okla., U.S.A.	81 G5	36 50N	99 38W
Buffalo, S. Dak., U.S.A.	80 C3	45 35N	103 33W
Buffalo, Wyo., U.S.A.	76 D10	44 21N	106 42W
Buffalo →, Canada	70 A5	60 5N	115 5W
Buffalo →, S. Africa	57 D5	28 43S	30 37 E
Buffalo Head Hills, Canada	70 B5	57 25N	115 55W
Buffalo L., Alta., Canada	70 C6	52 27N	112 54W
Buffalo L., N.W.T., Canada	70 A6	60 12N	115 25W
Buffalo Narrows, Canada	71 B7	55 51N	108 29W
Buffalo Springs, Kenya	54 B4	0 32N	37 35 E
Buffels →, S. Africa	56 D2	29 36S	17 3 E
Buford, U.S.A.	83 H4	34 10N	84 0W
Bug = Buh →, Ukraine	19 E5	46 59N	31 58 E
Bug →, Poland	17 B11	52 31N	21 5 E
Buga, Colombia	92 C3	4 0N	76 15W
Bugala I., Uganda	54 C3	0 40S	32 20 E
Buganda, Uganda	54 C3	0 0	31 30 E
Buganga, Uganda	54 C3	0 3S	32 0 E
Bugel, Tanjung, Indonesia	37 G14	6 26S	111 3 E
Bugibba, Malta	25 D1	35 57N	14 25 E
Bugsuk, Phil.	36 C5	8 15N	117 15 E
Bugulma, Russia	18 D9	54 33N	52 48 E
Bugun Shara, Mongolia	32 B5	49 0N	104 0 E
Bugungu △, Uganda	54 B3	2 17N	31 50 E
Buguruslan, Russia	18 D9	53 39N	52 26 E
Buh →, Ukraine	19 E5	46 59N	31 58 E
Buhera, Zimbabwe	57 B5	19 18S	31 29 E
Buhl, U.S.A.	76 E6	42 36N	114 46W
Builth Wells, U.K.	13 E4	52 9N	3 25W
Buir Nur, Mongolia	33 B6	47 50N	117 42 E
Buji, China	33 F11	22 37N	114 5 E
Bujumbura, Burundi	54 C2	3 16S	29 18 E
Bukachacha, Russia	29 D12	52 55N	116 50 E
Bukama, Dem. Rep. of the Congo	55 D2	9 10S	25 50 E
Bukavu, Dem. Rep. of the Congo	54 C2	2 20S	28 52 E
Bukene, Tanzania	54 C3	4 15S	32 48 E
Bukhara = Bukhoro, Uzbekistan	28 F7	39 48N	64 25 E
Bukhoro, Uzbekistan	28 F7	39 48N	64 25 E
Bukima, Tanzania	54 C3	1 50S	33 25 E
Bukit Badung, Indonesia	37 K18	8 48S	115 10 E
Bukit Kerajaan, Malaysia	39 c	5 25N	100 15 E
Bukit Mertajam, Malaysia	39 c	5 22N	100 28 E
Bukit Ni, Malaysia	39 d	1 22N	104 12 E
Bukit Panjang, Singapore	39 d	1 23N	103 46 E
Bukit Tengah, Malaysia	39 c	5 22N	100 25 E
Bukittinggi, Indonesia	36 E2	0 20S	100 20 E
Bukoba, Tanzania	54 C3	1 20S	31 49 E
Bukum, Pulau, Singapore	39 d	1 14N	103 46 E
Bukuya, Uganda	54 B3	0 40N	31 52 E
Būl, Kuh-e, Iran	45 D7	30 48N	52 45 E
Bula, Indonesia	37 E8	3 6S	130 30 E
Bulahdelah, Australia	63 E5	32 23S	152 13 E
Bulan, Phil.	37 B6	12 40N	123 52 E
Bulandshahr, India	42 E7	28 28N	77 51 E
Bulawayo, Zimbabwe	55 G2	20 7S	28 32 E
Buldan, Turkey	23 E13	38 2N	28 50 E
Buldana, India	40 J10	20 30N	76 18 E
Bulgar, Russia	18 D8	54 57N	49 4 E
Bulgaria ■, Europe	23 C11	42 35N	25 30 E
Buli, Teluk, Indonesia	37 D7	0 48N	128 25 E
Buliluyan, C., Phil.	36 C5	8 20N	117 15 E
Bulim, Singapore	39 d	1 22N	103 43 E
Bulkley →, Canada	70 B3	55 15N	127 40W
Bull Shoals L., U.S.A.	81 G8	36 22N	92 35W
Bulleringa △, Australia	62 B3	17 39S	143 56 E
Bullhead City, U.S.A.	79 K12	35 8N	114 32W
Büllingen, Belgium	15 D6	50 25N	6 16 E
Bullock Creek, Australia	62 B3	17 43S	144 31 E
Bulloo →, Australia	63 D3	28 43S	142 30 E
Bulloo L., Australia	63 D3	28 43S	142 25 E
Bulls, N.Z.	59 J5	40 10S	175 24 E
Bulnes, Chile	94 D1	36 42S	72 19W
Bulsar = Valsad, India	40 J8	20 40N	72 58 E
Bultfontein, S. Africa	56 D4	28 18S	26 10 E
Bulukumba, Indonesia	37 F6	5 33S	120 11 E
Bulun, Russia	29 B13	70 37N	127 30 E
Bumba, Dem. Rep. of the Congo	52 D4	2 13N	22 30 E
Bumbiri I., Tanzania	54 C3	1 40S	31 55 E
Bumhpa Bum, Burma	41 F20	26 51N	97 14 E
Bumi →, Zimbabwe	55 F2	17 0S	28 20 E
Buna, Kenya	54 B4	2 58N	39 30 E
Bunazi, Tanzania	54 C3	1 3S	31 23 E
Bunbury, Australia	61 F2	33 20S	115 35 E
Buncrana, Ireland	10 A4	55 8N	7 27W
Bundaberg, Australia	63 C5	24 54S	152 22 E
Bundey →, Australia	62 C2	21 46S	135 37 E
Bundi, India	42 G6	25 30N	75 35 E
Bundjalung △, Australia	63 D5	29 16S	153 21 E
Bundoran, Ireland	10 B3	54 28N	8 16W
Bung Kan, Thailand	38 C4	18 23N	103 37 E
Bungay, U.K.	13 E9	52 27N	1 28 E
Bungil Cr. →, Australia	62 D4	27 5S	149 5 E
Bungo-Suidō, Japan	31 H6	33 0N	132 15 E
Bungoma, Kenya	54 B3	0 34N	34 34 E
Bungotakada, Japan	31 H5	33 35N	131 25 E
Bunia, Dem. Rep. of the Congo	54 B3	1 35N	30 20 E
Bunji, Pakistan	43 B6	35 45N	74 40 E
Bunkie, U.S.A.	81 K8	30 57N	92 11W
Bunnell, U.S.A.	83 L5	29 28N	81 16W
Buntok, Indonesia	36 E4	1 40S	114 58 E
Bunya Mts. △, Australia	63 D5	26 51S	151 34 E
Bunyu, Indonesia	36 D5	3 35N	117 50 E
Buol, Indonesia	37 D6	1 15N	121 32 E
Buon Brieng, Vietnam	38 F7	13 9N	108 12 E
Buon Ma Thuot, Vietnam	38 F7	12 40N	108 3 E
Buong Long, Cambodia	38 F6	13 44N	106 59 E
Buorkhaya, Mys, Russia	29 B14	71 50N	132 40 E
Buqayq, Si. Arabia	45 E6	26 0N	49 45 E
Būr Acaba, Somali Rep.	47 G3	3 12N	44 20 E
Būr Safāga, Egypt	44 E2	26 43N	33 57 E
Būr Sa'īd, Egypt	51 B12	31 16N	32 18 E
Būr Sûdân, Sudan	51 E13	19 32N	37 9 E
Bura, Kenya	54 C4	1 4S	39 58 E
Burakin, Australia	61 F2	30 31S	117 10 E
Burao, Somali Rep.	47 F4	9 32N	45 32 E
Burāq, Syria	46 B5	33 11N	36 29 E
Buraydah, Si. Arabia	44 E5	26 20N	43 59 E
Burbank, U.S.A.	79 L8	34 11N	118 19W
Burdekin →, Australia	62 B4	19 38S	147 25 E
Burdur, Turkey	19 G5	37 45N	30 17 E
Burdwan = Barddhaman, India	43 H12	23 14N	87 39 E
Bure, Ethiopia	47 E2	10 40N	37 4 E
Bure →, U.K.	12 E9	52 38N	1 43 E
Bureya →, Russia	29 E13	49 27N	129 30 E
Burford, Canada	84 C4	43 7N	80 27W
Burgas, Bulgaria	23 C12	42 33N	27 29 E
Burgeo, Canada	73 C8	47 37N	57 38W
Burgersdorp, S. Africa	56 E4	31 0S	26 20 E
Burges, Mt., Australia	61 F3	30 50S	121 5 E
Burghead, U.K.	11 D5	57 43N	3 30W
Burgos, Spain	21 A4	42 21N	3 41W
Burgsvik, Sweden	9 H18	57 3N	18 19 E
Burgundy = Bourgogne ☒, France	20 C6	47 0N	4 50 E
Burhaniye, Turkey	23 E12	39 30N	26 58 E
Burhanpur, India	40 J10	21 18N	76 14 E
Burhi Gandak →, India	43 G12	25 20N	86 37 E
Burhner →, India	43 H9	22 43N	80 31 E
Burias I., Phil.	37 B6	12 55N	123 5 E
Burica, Pta., Costa Rica	88 E3	8 3N	82 51W
Burien, U.S.A.	78 C4	47 28N	122 21W
Burigi □, Tanzania	54 C3	2 20S	31 6 E
Burigi, L., Tanzania	54 C3	2 2S	31 22 E
Buriram, Thailand	38 E4	15 0N	103 0 E
Burj Sāfiţā, Syria	44 C3	34 48N	36 7 E
Burkburnett, U.S.A.	81 H5	34 6N	98 34W
Burke →, Australia	62 C2	23 12S	139 33 E
Burke Chan., Canada	70 C3	52 10N	127 30W
Burketown, Australia	62 B2	17 45S	139 33 E
Burkina Faso ■, Africa	50 F5	12 0N	1 0W
Burk's Falls, Canada	72 C4	45 37N	79 24W
Burleigh Falls, Canada	84 B6	44 33N	78 12W
Burley, U.S.A.	76 E7	42 32N	113 48W
Burlingame, U.S.A.	78 H4	37 35N	122 21W
Burlington, Canada	84 C5	43 18N	79 45W
Burlington, Colo., U.S.A.	80 F3	39 18N	102 16W
Burlington, Iowa, U.S.A.	80 E9	40 49N	91 14W
Burlington, Kans., U.S.A.	80 F7	38 12N	95 45W
Burlington, N.C., U.S.A.	83 G6	36 6N	79 26W
Burlington, N.J., U.S.A.	85 F10	40 4N	74 51W
Burlington, Vt., U.S.A.	85 B11	44 29N	73 12W
Burlington, Wash., U.S.A.	78 B4	48 28N	122 20W
Burlington, Wis., U.S.A.	82 D1	42 41N	88 17W
Burlyu-Tyube, Kazakhstan	28 E8	46 30N	79 10 E
Burma ■, Asia	41 J20	21 0N	96 30 E
Burnaby I., Canada	70 C2	52 25N	131 19W
Burnet, U.S.A.	81 K5	30 45N	98 14W
Burney, U.S.A.	76 F3	40 53N	121 40W
Burnham, U.S.A.	84 F7	40 38N	77 34W
Burnham-on-Sea, U.K.	13 F5	51 14N	3 0W
Burnie, Australia	63 G4	41 4S	145 56 E
Burnley, U.K.	12 D5	53 47N	2 14W
Burns, U.S.A.	76 E4	43 35N	119 3W
Burns Lake, Canada	70 C3	54 20N	125 45W
Burnside →, Canada	68 B9	66 51N	108 4W
Burnside, L., Australia	61 E3	25 22S	123 0 E
Burnsville, U.S.A.	80 C8	44 47N	93 17W
Burnt, L., Canada	73 B7	53 35N	64 4W
Burnt River, Canada	84 B6	44 41N	78 42W
Burntwood →, Canada	71 B9	56 8N	96 34W
Burntwood L., Canada	71 B8	55 22N	100 26W
Burqān, Kuwait	44 D5	29 0N	47 57 E
Burra, Australia	63 E2	33 40S	138 55 E
Burray, U.K.	11 C6	58 51N	2 54W
Burren →, Ireland	10 C3	53 1N	8 58W
Burren Junction, Australia	63 E4	30 7S	148 59 E
Burrinjuck Res., Australia	63 F4	35 0S	148 36 E
Burro, Serranías del, Mexico	86 B4	29 0N	102 0W
Burrow Hd., U.K.	11 G4	54 41N	4 24W
Burrum Coast △, Australia	63 D5	25 13S	152 36 E
Burruyacú, Argentina	94 B3	26 30S	64 40W
Burry Port, U.K.	13 F3	51 41N	4 15W
Bursa, Turkey	23 D13	40 15N	29 5 E
Burstall, Canada	71 C7	50 39N	109 54W
Burton, Ohio, U.S.A.	84 E3	41 28N	81 8W
Burton, S.C., U.S.A.	83 J5	32 25N	80 45W
Burton, L., Canada	72 B4	54 45N	78 20W
Burton upon Trent, U.K.	12 E6	52 48N	1 38W
Buru, Indonesia	37 E7	3 30S	126 30 E
Burûn, Râs, Egypt	46 D2	31 14N	33 7 E
Burundi ■, Africa	54 C3	3 15S	30 0 E
Bururi, Burundi	54 C2	3 57S	29 37 E
Burutu, Nigeria	50 G7	5 20N	5 29 E
Burwell, U.S.A.	80 E5	41 47N	99 8W
Burwick, U.K.	11 C5	58 45N	2 58W
Bury, U.K.	12 D5	53 35N	2 17W
Bury St. Edmunds, U.K.	13 E8	52 15N	0 43 E
Buryatia □, Russia	29 D11	53 0N	110 0 E
Busan = Pusan, S. Korea	35 G15	35 5N	129 0 E
Busango Swamp, Zambia	55 E2	14 15S	25 45 E
Buşayrah, Syria	44 C4	35 9N	40 26 E
Büshehr, Iran	45 D6	28 55N	50 55 E
Büshehr □, Iran	45 D6	28 20N	51 45 E
Bushell, Canada	71 B7	59 31N	108 45W
Bushenyi, Uganda	54 C3	0 35S	30 10 E
Bushire = Büshehr, Iran	45 D6	28 55N	50 55 E
Businga, Dem. Rep. of the Congo	52 D4	3 16N	20 59 E
Buşra ash Shām, Syria	46 C5	32 30N	36 25 E
Busselton, Australia	61 F2	33 42S	115 15 E
Bussum, Neths.	15 B5	52 16N	5 10 E
Busto Arsízio, Italy	20 D8	45 37N	8 51 E
Busu Djanoa, Dem. Rep. of the Congo	52 D4	1 43N	21 23 E
Busuanga I., Phil.	37 B5	12 10N	120 0 E
Busungbiu, Indonesia	37 J17	8 16S	114 58 E
Buta, Dem. Rep. of the Congo	54 B1	2 50N	24 53 E
Butare, Rwanda	54 C2	2 31S	29 52 E
Butaritari, Kiribati	64 G9	3 30N	174 0 E
Bute, U.K.	11 F3	55 48N	5 2 E
Bute Inlet, Canada	70 C4	50 40N	124 53W
Butemba, Uganda	54 B3	1 9N	31 37 E
Butembo, Dem. Rep. of the Congo	54 B2	0 9N	29 18 E
Butha Qi, China	33 B7	48 0N	122 32 E
Butiaba, Uganda	54 B3	1 50N	31 20 E
Butler, Mo., U.S.A.	80 F7	38 16N	94 20W
Butler, Pa., U.S.A.	84 F5	40 52N	79 54W
Butlers, Indonesia	37 E6	0 5S	122 45 E
Butte, Mont., U.S.A.	76 C7	46 0N	112 32W
Butte, Nebr., U.S.A.	80 D5	42 58N	98 51W
Butte Creek →, U.S.A.	78 F5	39 12N	121 56W
Butterworth = Gcuwa, S. Africa	57 E4	32 20S	28 11 E
Butterworth, Malaysia	39 c	5 24N	100 23 E
Buttevant, Ireland	10 D3	52 14N	8 40W
Buttfield, Mt., Australia	61 D4	24 45S	128 9 E
Button B., Canada	71 B10	58 45N	94 23W
Buttonwillow, U.S.A.	79 K7	35 24N	119 28W
Butty Hd., Australia	61 F3	33 54S	121 39 E
Butuan, Phil.	37 C7	8 57N	125 33 E
Butung = Buton, Indonesia	37 E6	5 0S	122 45 E
Buturlinovka, Russia	19 D7	50 50N	40 35 E
Buxa Duar, India	43 F13	27 45N	89 35 E
Buxar, India	43 G10	25 34N	83 58 E
Buxtehude, Germany	16 B5	53 28N	9 39 E
Buxton, U.K.	12 D6	53 16N	1 54V
Buy, Russia	18 C7	58 28N	41 28 E

üyük Menderes ➔, *Turkey* ... 23 F12 37 28N 27 11 E
üyükçekmece, *Turkey* .... 23 D13 41 2N 28 35 E
uzău, *Romania* .... 17 F14 45 10N 26 50 E
uzău, *Romania* .... 17 F14 45 26N 27 44 E
uzen, *Japan* .... 31 H5 33 35N 131 5 E
uzi ➔, *Mozam.* .... 55 F3 19 50S 34 43 E
uzuluk, *Russia* .... 18 D9 52 48N 52 12 E
uzzards B., *U.S.A.* 85 E14 41 45N 70 37W
uzzards Bay, *U.S.A.* 85 E14 41 44N 70 37W
wana Mkubwe, *Dem. Rep. of
  the Congo* .... 55 E2 13 8S 28 38 E
windi △, *Uganda* .... 54 C2 1 2S 29 42 E
yarezina ➔, *Belarus* .... 17 B16 53 33N 30 14 E
ydgoszcz, *Poland* .... 17 B9 53 10N 18 0 E
yelarus = Belarus ■, *Europe* 17 B14 53 30N 27 0 E
yelorussia = Belarus ■, *Europe* 17 B14 53 30N 27 0 E
yers, *U.S.A.* 80 F2 39 43N 104 14W
yesville, *U.S.A.* 84 G3 39 58N 81 32W
yfield ➔, *Australia* ..... 62 C5 22 52S 150 45 E
ykhaw, *Belarus* .... 17 B16 53 31N 30 14 E
ykhov = Bykhaw, *Belarus* . 17 B16 53 31N 30 14 E
ylas, *U.S.A.* 77 K8 33 8N 110 7W
ylot, *Canada* 71 B10 58 25N 94 8W
ylot I., *Canada* 69 A12 73 13N 78 34W
yrd, C., *Antarctica* 5 C17 69 38S 76 7W
yrock, *Australia* .... 63 E4 30 40S 146 27 E
yron, C., *Australia* ..... 63 D5 28 43S 153 38 E
yron Bay, *Australia* .... 63 D5 28 43S 153 37 E
yrranga, Gory, *Russia* .. 29 B11 75 0N 100 0 E
yrranga Mts. = Byrranga, Gory,
  Russia .... 29 B11 75 0N 100 0 E
yske, *Sweden* .... 8 D19 64 57N 21 11 E
yske älv ➔, *Sweden* .... 8 D19 64 57N 21 13 E
ytom, *Poland* .... 17 C10 50 25N 18 54 E
ytów, *Poland* .... 17 A9 54 10N 17 30 E
yumba, *Rwanda* .... 54 C3 1 35S 30 4 E

C

a ➔, *Vietnam* .... 38 C5 18 45N 105 45 E
a Mau, *Vietnam* .... 39 H5 9 7N 105 8 E
a Mau, Mui, *Vietnam* ... 39 H5 8 38N 104 44 E
a Na, *Vietnam* .... 39 G7 11 20N 108 54 E
aacupé, *Paraguay* 94 B4 25 23S 57 5W
aaguazú △, *Paraguay* .. 95 B4 26 5S 55 31W
aála, *Angola* .... 53 G3 12 46S 15 30 E
aamaño Sd., *Canada* ... 70 C3 52 55N 129 25W
aapzá, *Paraguay* 94 B4 26 8S 56 19W
aazapá □, *Paraguay* 95 B4 26 10S 56 0W
aballería, C. de, *Spain* .. 24 A11 40 5N   4 5 E
abanatuan, *Phil.* .... 37 A6 15 30N 120 58 E
abano, *Canada* 73 C6 47 40N 68 56W
abazon, *U.S.A.* 79 M10 33 55N 116 47W
abedelo, *Brazil* 93 E12 7 0S 34 50W
abildo, *Chile* 94 C1 32 30S 71 5W
abimas, *Venezuela* 92 A4 10 23N 71 25W
abinda, *Angola* .... 52 F2 5 33S 12 11 E
abinda □, *Angola* ...... 52 F2 5 0S 12 30 E
abinet Mts., *U.S.A.* 76 C6 48 0N 115 30W
abo Blanco, *Argentina* .. 96 F3 47 15S 65 47W
abo Frio, *Brazil* 95 A7 22 51S 42 3W
abo Pantoja, *Peru* 92 D3 1 0S 75 10W
abonga, Réservoir, *Canada* 72 C4 47 0N 76 40W
abool, *U.S.A.* 81 G8 37 7N 92 6W
aboolture, *Australia* .... 63 D5 27 5S 152 58 E
abora Bassa Dam = Cahora
  Bassa, Reprêsa de, *Mozam.* 55 F3 15 20S 32 50 E
aborca, *Mexico* 86 A2 30 40N 112 10W
abot, Mt., *U.S.A.* 85 B13 44 30N 71 25W
abot Hd., *Canada* 84 A3 45 14N 81 17W
abot Str., *Canada* 73 C8 47 15N 59 40W
abra, *Spain* 21 D3 37 30N   4 28W
abrera, *Spain* .... 24 B9 39 8N   2 57 E
abri, *Canada* 71 C7 50 35N 108 25W
abriel ➔, *Spain* 21 C5 39 14N   1 3W
açador, *Brazil* 95 B5 26 47S 51 0W
açak, *Serbia & M.* ..... 23 C9 43 54N 20 20 E
açapava do Sul, *Brazil* .. 95 C5 30 30S 53 30W
áceres, *Brazil* 92 G7 16 5S 57 40W
áceres, *Spain* 21 C2 39 26N   6 23W
ache, *Canada* 72 C4 44 26N 78 48W
ache Cr. ➔, *U.S.A.* 78 G5 38 42N 121 42W
ache Creek, *Canada* ... 70 C4 50 48N 121 19W
achi, *Argentina* 94 B2 25 5S 66 10W
achinal de la Sierra, *Chile* 94 A2 24 58S 69 32W
achoeira, *Brazil* 93 F11 12 30S 39 0W
achoeira do Sul, *Brazil* . 95 C5 30 3S 52 53W
achoeira de Itapemirim, *Brazil* 93 H10 20 51S 41 7W
acoal, *Brazil* 92 F6 11 32S 61 18W
acólo, *Angola* .... 52 G3 10 9S 19 21 E
aconda, *Angola* .... 53 G3 13 48S 15 8 E
addo, *U.S.A.* 81 H6 34 7N 96 16W
ader Idris □, *U.K.* 13 E4 52 42N   3 53W
adereyta, *Mexico* 86 B5 25 36N 100 0W
adibarrawirracanna, L.,
  Australia .... 63 D2 28 52S 135 27 E
adillac, *U.S.A.* 82 C3 44 15N 85 24W
adiz, *Phil.* .... 37 B6 10 57N 123 15 E
ádiz, *Spain* 21 D2 36 30N   6 20W
ádiz, Calif., *U.S.A.* 79 L11 34 30N 115 28W
ádiz, G. de, *Spain* 21 D2 36 40N   7 0W
adiz L., *U.S.A.* 77 J6 34 18N 115 24W
adney Park, *Australia* .. 63 D1 27 55S 134 3 E
adomin, *Canada* 70 C5 53 2N 117 20W
adotte Lake, *Canada* ... 70 B5 56 26N 116 23W
adoux, *Australia* .... 63 D2 30 46S 117 7 E
aen, *France* 20 B3 49 10N   0 22W
aernarfon, *U.K.* 12 D3 53 8N   4 16W
aernarfon B., *U.K.* 12 D3 53 4N   4 40W
aernarvon = Caernarfon, *U.K.* 12 D3 53 8N   4 16W
aerphilly, *U.K.* 13 F4 51 35N   3 13W
aerphilly □, *U.K.* 13 F4 51 37N   3 12W
aesarea, *Israel* .... 46 C3 32 30N 34 53 E
aetité, *Brazil* 93 F10 13 50S 42 32W
afayate, *Argentina* 94 B2 26 2S 65 50W
afu, *Angola* .... 56 B2 16 30S 15 8 E
agayan de Oro, *Phil.* .... 37 C6 8 30N 124 40 E
agayan ➔, *Phil.* .... 37 C5 9 40N 121 16 E
agliari, *Italy* .... 22 E3 39 13N   9 7 E
agliari, G. di, *Italy* ..... 22 E3 39 8N   9 11 E
aguán ➔, *Colombia* 92 D4 0 8S 74 18W
aguas, *Puerto Rico* ..... 89 d 18 14N 66 2W

Caha Mts., *Ireland* 10 E2 51 45N   9 40W
Cahama, *Angola* .... 56 B1 16 17S 14 19 E
Caher, *Ireland* 10 D4 52 22N   7 56W
Caherciveen, *Ireland* ... 10 E1 51 56N 10 14W
Cahora Bassa, L. de, *Mozam.* 55 F3 15 35S 32 0 E
Cahora Bassa, Reprêsa de,
  Mozam. .... 55 F3 15 20S 32 50 E
Cahore Pt., *Ireland* 10 D5 52 33N   6 12W
Cahors, *France* .... 20 D4 44 27N   1 27 E
Cahul, *Moldova* .... 17 F15 45 50N 28 15 E
Cai Bau, Dao, *Vietnam* .. 38 B6 21 10N 107 27 E
Cai Nuoc, *Vietnam* ..... 39 H5 8 56N 105 1 E
Caia, *Mozam.* .... 55 F4 17 51S 35 24 E
Caianda, *Angola* .... 55 E1 11 2S 23 31 E
Caibarién, *Cuba* 88 B4 22 30N 79 30W
Caicara, *Venezuela* 92 B5 7 38N 66 10W
Caicó, *Brazil* 93 E11 6 20S 37 44W
Caicos Is., *Turks & Caicos* 89 B5 21 40N 71 40W
Caicos Passage, *W. Indies* 89 B5 22 45N 72 45W
Caird Coast, *Antarctica* . 5 D1 75 0S 25 0W
Cairn Gorm, *U.K.* 11 D5 57 7N   3 39W
Cairngorm Mts., *U.K.* .. 11 D5 57 6N   3 42W
Cairngorms △, *U.K.* ... 11 D5 57 10N   3 50W
Cairnryan, *U.K.* 11 G3 54 59N   5 1W
Cairns, *Australia* .... 62 B4 16 57S 145 45 E
Cairns L., *Canada* 71 C10 51 42N 94 30W
Cairo = El Qâhira, *Egypt* 51 B12 30 1N 31 14 E
Cairo, Ga., *U.S.A.* 83 K3 30 52N 84 13W
Cairo, Ill., *U.S.A.* 81 G10 37 0N 89 11W
Cairo, N.Y., *U.S.A.* 85 D11 42 18N 74 0W
Caithness, *U.K.* 11 C5 58 25N   3 35W
Caithness, Ord of, *U.K.* . 11 C5 58 8N   3 36W
Caja de Muertos, I., *Puerto Rico* 89 d 17 54N 66 32W
Cajamarca, *Peru* 92 E3 7 5S 78 28W
Cajàzeiras, *Brazil* 93 E11 6 52S 38 30W
Cala d'Or, *Spain* .... 24 B10 39 23N   3 4 E
Cala en Porter, *Spain* ... 24 B11 39 52N   4 8 E
Cala Figuera, C. de, *Spain* 24 B9 39 27N   2 31 E
Cala Forcat, *Spain* ..... 24 B10 40 0N   3 47 E
Cala Major, *Spain* ...... 24 B9 39 33N   2 37 E
Cala Mezquida = Sa Mesquida,
  Spain .... 24 B11 39 55N   4 16 E
Cala Millor, *Spain* ...... 24 B10 39 35N   3 22 E
Cala Ratjada, *Spain* .... 24 B10 39 43N   3 27 E
Cala Santa Galdana, *Spain* 24 B10 39 56N   3 58 E
Calabar, *Nigeria* .... 50 H7 4 57N   8 20 E
Calabogie, *Canada* 85 A8 45 18N 76 43W
Calabozo, *Venezuela* ... 92 B5 9 0N 67 28W
Calábria □, *Italy* .... 22 E7 39 0N 16 30 E
Calafate, *Argentina* 96 G2 50 19S 72 15W
Calahorra, *Spain* 21 A5 42 18N   1 59W
Calais, *France* .... 20 A4 50 57N   1 56 E
Calais, *U.S.A.* 83 C12 45 11N 67 17W
Calakmul △, *Mexico* ... 87 D7 18 14N 89 48W
Calalaste, Cord. de, *Argentina* 94 B2 25 0S 67 0W
Calama, *Brazil* 92 E6 8 0S 62 50W
Calama, *Chile* 94 A2 22 30S 68 55W
Calamar, *Colombia* 92 A4 10 15N 74 55W
Calamian Group, *Phil.* .. 37 B5 11 50N 119 55 E
Calamocha, *Spain* 21 B5 40 50N   1 17W
Calang, *Indonesia* ...... 36 D1 4 37N 95 37 E
Calapan, *Phil.* .... 37 B6 13 25N 121 7 E
Cālāraşi, *Romania* ..... 17 F14 44 12N 27 20 E
Calatayud, *Spain* 21 B5 41 20N   1 40W
Calauag, *Phil.* .... 37 B6 13 55N 122 15 E
Calavite, C., *Phil.* ...... 37 B6 13 26N 120 20 E
Calbayog, *Phil.* .... 37 B6 12 4N 124 38 E
Calca, *Peru* 92 F4 13 22S 72 0W
Calcasieu L., *U.S.A.* 81 L8 29 55N 93 18W
Calcutta = Kolkata, *India* 43 H13 22 36N 88 24 E
Calcutta, *U.S.A.* 84 F4 40 40N 80 34W
Caldas da Rainha, *Portugal* 21 C1 39 24N   9 8W
Calder ➔, *U.K.* 12 D6 53 44N   1 22W
Caldera, *Chile* 94 B1 27 5S 70 55W
Caldera de Taburiente △,
  Canary Is. 24 F2 28 43N 17 52W
Caldwell, Idaho, *U.S.A.* . 76 E5 43 40N 116 41W
Caldwell, Kans., *U.S.A.* . 81 G6 37 2N 97 37W
Caldwell, Tex., *U.S.A.* .. 81 K6 30 32N 96 42W
Caledon, *S. Africa* ...... 56 E2 34 14S 19 26 E
Caledon ➔, *S. Africa* .. 56 E4 30 31S 26 5 E
Caledon B., *Australia* ... 62 A2 12 45S 137 0 E
Caledonia, *Canada* 84 C5 43 7N 79 58W
Caledonia, *U.S.A.* 84 D7 42 58N 77 51W
Calemba, *Angola* .... 56 B2 16 0S 15 44 E
Calen, *Australia* .... 62 J6 20 56S 148 48 E
Caletones, *Chile* 94 C1 34 6S 70 27W
Calexico, *U.S.A.* 79 N11 32 40N 115 30W
Calf of Man, *U.K.* 12 C3 54 3N   4 48W
Calgary, *Canada* 70 C6 51 0N 114 10W
Calheta, *Madeira* 24 D2 32 44N 17 11W
Calhoun, *U.S.A.* 83 H3 34 30N 84 57W
Cali, *Colombia* 92 C3 3 25N 76 35W
Calicut, *India* .... 40 P9 11 15N 75 43 E
Caliente, *U.S.A.* 77 H6 37 37N 114 31W
California, *Mo., U.S.A.* .. 80 F8 38 38N 92 34W
California, Pa., *U.S.A.* ... 84 F5 40 4N 79 54W
California □, *U.S.A.* 78 H7 37 30N 119 30W
California, Baja, *Mexico* . 86 A1 32 10N 115 12W
California, Baja, T.S. = Baja
  California □, *Mexico* ... 86 B2 30 0N 115 0W
California, Baja, T.N. = Baja
  California Sur □, *Mexico* 86 B2 25 50N 111 50W
California, G. de, *Mexico* 86 B2 27 0N 111 0W
California City, *U.S.A.* .. 79 K9 35 10N 117 55W
California Hot Springs, *U.S.A.* 79 K8 35 51N 118 41W
Calilegua △, *Argentina* . 94 B3 23 36S 64 50W
Calingasta, *Argentina* ... 94 C2 31 15S 69 30W
Calipatria, *U.S.A.* 79 M11 33 8N 115 31W
Calistoga, *U.S.A.* 78 G4 38 35N 122 35W
Calitzdorp, *S. Africa* .... 56 E3 33 33S 21 42 E
Callabonna, L., *Australia* 63 D3 29 40S 140 5 E
Callan, *Ireland* 10 D4 52 32N   7 24W
Callander, *Canada* 72 C4 46 13N 79 22W
Callander, *U.K.* 11 E4 56 15N   4 13W
Callao, *Peru* 92 F3 12 0S 77 0W
Calles, *Mexico* 87 C5 23 2N 98 42W
Callicoon, *U.S.A.* 85 E9 41 46N 75 3W
Calling Lake, *Canada* ... 70 B6 55 15N 113 12W
Calliope, *Australia* ..... 62 C5 24 0S 151 16 E
Calne, *U.K.* 13 F6 51 26N   2 0W
Calola, *Angola* .... 56 B2 16 25S 17 48 E
Caloundra, *Australia* .... 63 D5 26 45S 153 10 E
Calpella, *U.S.A.* 78 F3 39 14N 123 12W
Calpine, *U.S.A.* 78 F6 39 40N 120 27W
Calstock, *Canada* 72 C3 49 47N 84 9W
Caltagirone, *Italy* ...... 22 F6 37 14N 14 31 E
Caltanissetta, *Italy* ..... 22 F6 37 29N 14 4 E
Calulo, *Angola* .... 52 G2 10 1S 14 56 E

Calvert ➔, *Australia* ... 62 B2 16 17S 137 44 E
Calvert I., *Canada* 70 C3 51 30N 128 0W
Calvert Ra., *Australia* ... 60 D3 24 0S 122 30 E
Calvi, *France* .... 20 E8 42 34N   8 45 E
Calvià, *Spain* .... 21 C7 39 34N   2 31 E
Calvillo, *Mexico* 86 C4 21 51N 102 43W
Calvinia, *S. Africa* ...... 56 E2 31 28S 19 45 E
Calwa, *U.S.A.* 78 J7 36 42N 119 46W
Cam ➔, *U.K.* .... 13 E8 52 21N   0 16 E
Cam Lam, *Vietnam* ..... 39 G7 11 54N 109 10 E
Cam Pha, *Vietnam* ..... 38 B6 21 7N 107 18 E
Cam Ranh, *Vietnam* .... 39 G7 11 54N 109 12 E
Cam Xuyen, *Vietnam* ... 38 C6 18 15N 106 0 E
Camabatela, *Angola* .... 52 F3 8 20S 15 26 E
Camacha, *Madeira* 24 D3 32 41N 16 49W
Camacho, *Mexico* 86 C4 24 25N 102 18W
Camacupa, *Angola* ..... 53 G3 11 58S 17 22 E
Camagüey, *Cuba* 88 B4 21 20N 78 0W
Camaná, *Peru* 92 G4 16 30S 72 50W
Camanche Reservoir, *U.S.A.* 78 G6 38 14N 121 1W
Camaquã, *Brazil* 95 C5 30 51S 51 49W
Camaquã ➔, *Brazil* ... 95 C5 31 17S 51 47W
Câmara de Lobos, *Madeira* 24 D3 32 39N 16 59W
Camargo, *Mexico* 87 B5 26 19N 98 50W
Camarillo, *U.S.A.* 79 L7 34 13N 119 2W
Camarón, C., *Honduras* . 88 C2 16 0N 85 5W
Camarones, *Argentina* .. 96 E3 44 50S 65 40W
Camas, *U.S.A.* 78 E4 45 35N 122 24W
Camas Valley, *U.S.A.* ... 76 E2 43 2N 123 40W
Camballin, *Australia* .... 60 C3 17 59S 124 12 E
Cambará, *Brazil* 95 A5 23 2S 50 5W
Cambay = Khambhat, *India* 42 H5 22 23N 72 33 E
Cambay, G. of = Khambhat, G.
  of, *India* .... 40 J8 20 45N 72 30 E
Cambodia ■, *Asia* ...... 38 F5 12 15N 105 0 E
Camborne, *U.K.* 13 G2 50 12N   5 19W
Cambrai, *France* .... 20 A5 50 11N   3 14 E
Cambria, *U.S.A.* 78 K5 35 34N 121 5W
Cambrian Mts., *U.K.* ... 13 E4 52 3N   3 57W
Cambridge, *Canada* 84 C4 43 23N 80 15W
Cambridge, *Jamaica* ... 88 a 18 18N 77 54W
Cambridge, *N.Z.* .... 59 G5 37 54S 175 29 E
Cambridge, *U.K.* .... 13 E8 52 12N   0 8 E
Cambridge, Mass., *U.S.A.* 85 D13 42 22N 71 6W
Cambridge, Minn., *U.S.A.* 80 C8 45 34N 93 13W
Cambridge, N.Y., *U.S.A.* 85 C11 43 2N 73 22W
Cambridge, Nebr., *U.S.A.* 80 E4 40 17N 100 10W
Cambridge, Ohio, *U.S.A.* 84 F3 40 2N 81 35W
Cambridge Bay = Ikaluktutiak,
  Canada 68 B9 69 10N 105 0W
Cambridge G., *Australia* 60 B4 14 55S 128 15 E
Cambridge Springs, *U.S.A.* 84 E4 41 48N 80 4W
Cambridgeshire □, *U.K.* 13 E7 52 25N   0 7W
Cambuci, *Brazil* 95 A7 21 35S 41 55W
Cambundi-Catembo, *Angola* 52 G3 10 10S 17 35 E
Camden, Ala., *U.S.A.* ... 83 K2 31 59N 87 17W
Camden, Ark., *U.S.A.* .. 81 J8 33 35N 92 50W
Camden, Maine, *U.S.A.* . 83 C11 44 13N 69 4W
Camden, N.J., *U.S.A.* ... 85 G9 39 56N 75 7W
Camden, N.Y., *U.S.A.* .. 85 C9 43 20N 75 45W
Camden, S.C., *U.S.A.* .. 83 H5 34 16N 80 36W
Camden Sd., *Australia* .. 60 C3 15 27S 124 25 E
Camdenton, *U.S.A.* 81 F8 38 1N 92 45W
Camelford, *U.K.* 13 G3 50 37N   4 42W
Cameron, Ariz., *U.S.A.* . 77 J8 35 53N 111 25W
Cameron, La., *U.S.A.* ... 81 L8 29 48N 93 20W
Cameron, Mo., *U.S.A.* .. 80 F7 39 44N 94 14W
Cameron, Tex., *U.S.A.* .. 81 K6 30 51N 96 59W
Cameron Highlands, *Malaysia* 39 K3 4 27N 101 22 E
Cameron Hills, *Canada* . 70 B5 59 48N 118 0W
Cameroon ■, *Africa* .... 51 G7 6 0N 12 30 E
Cameroun, Mt., *Cameroon* 52 D1 4 13N   9 10 E
Cametá, *Brazil* 93 D9 2 12S 49 30W
Camiguin □, *Phil.* ...... 37 C6 18 56N 121 55 E
Camilla, *U.S.A.* 83 K3 31 14N 84 12W
Caminha, *Portugal* 21 B1 41 50N   8 50W
Camino, *U.S.A.* 78 G6 38 44N 120 41W
Camira Creek, *Australia* 63 D5 29 15S 152 58 E
Cammal, *U.S.A.* 84 E7 41 24N 77 28W
Camocim, *Brazil* 93 D10 2 55S 40 50W
Camooweal, *Australia* .. 62 B2 19 56S 138 7 E
Camooweal Caves △, *Australia* 62 C2 20 1S 138 11 E
Camopi, *Fr. Guiana* 93 C8 3 12N 52 17W
Camp Borden, *Canada* . 84 B5 44 18N 79 56W
Camp Hill, *U.S.A.* 84 F8 40 14N 76 55W
Camp Nelson, *U.S.A.* ... 79 J8 36 8N 118 39W
Camp Pendleton, *U.S.A.* 79 M9 33 16N 117 23W
Camp Verde, *U.S.A.* 77 J8 34 34N 111 51W
Camp Wood, *U.S.A.* 81 L5 29 40N 100 1W
Campana, *Argentina* ... 94 C4 34 10S 58 55W
Campana, I., *Chile* 96 F1 48 20S 75 20W
Campanário, *Madeira* .. 24 D2 32 39N 17 2W
Campania □, *Italy* ...... 22 D6 41 0N 14 30 E
Campbell, S. Africa ...... 56 D3 28 48S 23 44 E
Campbell, Calif., *U.S.A.* . 78 H5 37 17N 121 57W
Campbell, Ohio, *U.S.A.* . 84 E4 41 5N 80 37W
Campbell I., *Pac. Oc.* .. 64 N8 52 30S 169 0 E
Campbell L., *Canada* ... 71 A7 63 14N 106 55W
Campbell River, *Canada* 70 C3 50 5N 125 20W
Campbell Town, *Australia* 63 G4 41 52S 147 30 E
Campbellford, *Canada* .. 84 B7 44 18N 77 48W
Campbellpur, *Pakistan* .. 42 C5 33 46N 72 26 E
Campbellsville, *U.S.A.* .. 82 G3 37 21N 85 20W
Campbellton, *Canada* ... 73 C6 47 57N 66 43W
Campbelltown, *Australia* 63 E5 34 4S 150 49 E
Campbeltown, *U.K.* 11 F3 55 26N   5 36W
Campeche, *Mexico* 87 D6 19 50N 90 32W
Campeche □, *Mexico* ... 87 D6 19 50N 90 30W
Campeche, Golfo de, *Mexico* 87 D6 19 30N 93 0W
Camperdown, *Australia* 63 F3 38 14S 143 9 E
Camperville, *Canada* ... 71 C8 51 59N 100 9W
Câmpina, *Romania* ..... 17 F13 45 10N 25 45 E
Campina Grande, *Brazil* 93 E11 7 20S 35 47W
Campinas, *Brazil* 95 A6 22 50S 47 0W
Campo Grande, *Brazil* .. 93 H8 20 25S 54 40W
Campo Maior, *Brazil* ... 93 D10 4 50S 42 12W
Campo Mourão, *Brazil* .. 95 A5 24 3S 52 22W
Campos, *Brazil* 93 H10 21 50S 41 20W
Campos Belos, *Brazil* ... 93 F9 13 10S 47 3W
Campos del Port, *Spain* . 24 B10 39 26N   3 1 E
Campos Novos, *Brazil* .. 95 B5 27 21S 51 50W
Camptonville, *U.S.A.* ... 78 F5 39 27N 121 3W
Camptown, *U.S.A.* 85 E8 41 44N 76 14W
Câmpulung, *Romania* ... 17 F13 45 17N 25 3 E
Camrose, *Canada* 70 C6 53 0N 112 50W
Camsell Portage, *Canada* 71 B7 59 37N 109 15W
Çan, *Turkey* .... 23 D12 40 2N 27 3 E

Can Clavo, *Spain* ...... 24 C7 38 57N   1 27 E
Can Creu, *Spain* .... 24 C7 38 58N   1 28 E
Can Gio, *Vietnam* ...... 39 G6 10 25N 106 58 E
Can Tho, *Vietnam* ...... 39 G5 10 2N 105 46 E
Canaan, *U.S.A.* 85 D11 42 2N 73 20W
Canada ■, *N. Amer.* 68 C10 60 0N 100 0W
Canada Basin, *Arctic* ... 4 B18 80 0N 145 0W
Cañada de Gómez, *Argentina* 94 C3 32 40S 61 30W
Canadian, *U.S.A.* 81 H4 35 55N 100 23W
Canadian ➔, *U.S.A.* ... 81 H7 35 28N 95 3W
Canajoharie, *U.S.A.* 85 D10 42 54N 74 35W
Çanakkale, *Turkey* ..... 23 D12 40 8N 26 24 E
Çanakkale Boğazı, *Turkey* 23 D12 40 17N 26 32 E
Canal Flats, *Canada* 70 C5 50 10N 115 48W
Canalejas, *Argentina* ... 94 D2 35 15S 66 34W
Canals, *Argentina* 94 C3 33 35S 62 53W
Canandaigua, *U.S.A.* ... 84 D7 42 54N 77 17W
Canandaigua L., *U.S.A.* 84 D7 42 47N 77 19W
Cananea, *Mexico* 86 A2 31 0N 110 20W
Canarias, Is., *Atl. Oc.* .. 24 F4 28 30N 16 0W
Canaries, *St. Lucia* ..... 89 f 13 55N 61 4W
Canarreos, Arch. de los, *Cuba* 88 B3 21 35N 81 40W
Canary Is. = Canarias, Is., *Atl. Oc.* 24 F4 28 30N 16 0W
Canaseraga, *U.S.A.* 84 D7 42 27N 77 45W
Canatlán, *Mexico* 86 C4 24 31N 104 47W
Canaveral, C., *U.S.A.* ... 83 L5 28 28N 80 32W
Canaveral, C., *U.S.A.* ... 83 L5 28 27N 80 32W
Canavieiras, *Brazil* 93 G11 15 39S 39 0W
Canberra, *Australia* ..... 63 F4 35 15S 149 8 E
Canby, Calif., *U.S.A.* 76 F3 41 27N 120 52W
Canby, Minn., *U.S.A.* ... 80 C6 44 43N 96 16W
Canby, Oreg., *U.S.A.* ... 78 E4 45 16N 122 42W
Cancún, *Mexico* 87 C7 21 8N 86 44W
Candelaria, *Argentina* .. 95 B4 27 29S 55 44W
Candelaria, *Canary Is.* .. 24 F3 28 22N 16 22W
Candelo, *Australia* ..... 63 F4 36 47S 149 43 E
Candi Dasa, *Indonesia* .. 37 J18 8 30S 115 34 E
Candia = Iráklion, *Greece* 25 D7 35 20N 25 12 E
Candle L., *Canada* 71 C7 53 50N 105 18W
Candlemas I., *Antarctica* 5 B1 57 3S 26 40W
Cando, *U.S.A.* 80 A5 48 32N 99 12W
Canea = Khaniá, *Greece* 25 D6 35 30N   24 4 E
Canelones, *Uruguay* 95 C4 34 32S 56 17W
Cañete, *Chile* 94 D1 37 50S 73 30W
Cañete, *Peru* 92 F3 13 8S 76 30W
Cangas de Narcea, *Spain* 21 A2 43 10N   6 32W
Canguaretama, *Brazil* .. 93 E11 6 20S 35 5W
Canguçu, *Brazil* 95 C5 31 22S 52 43W
Canguçu, Serra do, *Brazil* 95 C5 31 0S 52 20W
Cangzhou, *China* .... 34 E9 38 19N 116 52 E
Caniapiscau ➔, *Canada* 73 A6 56 40N 69 30W
Caniapiscau, L. de, *Canada* 73 B6 54 10N 69 55W
Canicattì, *Italy* .... 22 F5 37 21N 13 51 E
Canim Lake, *Canada* 70 C4 51 47N 120 54W
Canindeyu □, *Paraguay* 95 A4 24 10S 55 0W
Canisteo, *U.S.A.* 84 D7 42 16N 77 36W
Canisteo ➔, *U.S.A.* 84 D7 42 7N 77 8W
Cañitas, *Mexico* 86 C4 23 36N 102 43W
Çankırı, *Turkey* .... 19 F5 40 40N 33 37 E
Cankuzo, *Burundi* ...... 54 C3 3 10S 30 31 E
Canmore, *Canada* 70 C5 51 7N 115 18W
Cann River, *Australia* ... 63 F4 37 35S 149 7 E
Canna, *U.K.* 11 D2 57 3N   6 33W
Cannanore, *India* .... 40 P9 11 53N 75 27 E
Cannes, *France* .... 20 E7 43 32N   7 1 E
Canning Town = Port Canning,
  India .... 43 H13 22 23N 88 40 E
Cannington, *Canada* 84 B5 44 20N 79 2W
Cannock, *U.K.* 13 E5 52 41N   2 1W
Cannon Ball ➔, *U.S.A.* 80 B4 46 20N 100 38W
Cannondale Mt., *Australia* 62 D4 25 13S 148 57 E
Cannonsville Reservoir, *U.S.A.* 85 D9 42 4N 75 22W
Cannonvale, *Australia* .. 62 J6 20 17S 148 43 E
Canoas, *Brazil* 95 B5 29 56S 51 11W
Canoe L., *Canada* 71 B7 55 10N 108 15W
Canon City, *U.S.A.* 80 F2 38 27N 105 14W
Cañon de Rio Blanco △, *Mexico* 87 D5 18 43N 97 15W
Cañón del Sumidero △, *Mexico* 87 D5 19 22N 96 24W
Canora, *Canada* 71 C8 51 40N 102 30W
Canowindra, *Australia* .. 63 E4 33 35S 148 38 E
Canso, *Canada* 73 C7 45 20N 61 0W
Cantabria □, *Spain* 21 A4 43 10N   4 0W
Cantabrian Mts. = Cantábrica,
  Cordillera, *Spain* 21 A3 43 0N   5 10W
Cantábrica, Cordillera, *Spain* 21 A3 43 0N   5 10W
Cantal, Plomb du, *France* 20 D5 45 3N   2 45 E
Canterbury, *Australia* ... 62 D3 25 23S 141 53 E
Canterbury, *U.K.* .... 13 F9 51 16N   1 6 E
Canterbury Bight, *N.Z.* .. 59 L3 44 16S 171 55 E
Canterbury Plains, *N.Z.* . 59 K3 43 55S 171 22 E
Cantil, *U.S.A.* 79 K9 35 18N 117 58W
Canton = Guangzhou, *China* 33 D6 23 5N 113 10 E
Canton, Ga., *U.S.A.* 83 H3 34 14N 84 29W
Canton, Ill., *U.S.A.* 80 E9 40 33N 90 2W
Canton, Miss., *U.S.A.* ... 81 J9 32 37N 90 2W
Canton, Mo., *U.S.A.* 80 E9 40 8N 91 32W
Canton, N.Y., *U.S.A.* ... 85 B9 44 36N 75 10W
Canton, Ohio, *U.S.A.* ... 84 F3 40 48N 81 23W
Canton, Pa., *U.S.A.* 84 E8 41 39N 76 51W
Canton, S. Dak., *U.S.A.* 80 D6 43 18N 96 35W
Canton L., *U.S.A.* 81 G5 36 6N 98 35W
Canudos, *Brazil* 92 E7 7 13S 58 5W
Canumã ➔, *Brazil* 92 D7 3 55S 59 10W
Canutama, *Brazil* 92 E6 6 30S 64 20W
Canutillo, *U.S.A.* 77 L10 31 55N 106 36W
Canvey, *U.K.* .... 13 F8 51 31N   0 37 E
Canyon, *U.S.A.* 81 H4 34 59N 101 55W
Canyon De Chelly △, *U.S.A.* 77 H9 36 5N 109 20W
Canyon of the Ancients △, *U.S.A.* 77 H9 37 30N 108 50W
Canyonlands △, *U.S.A.* 77 G9 38 15N 110 0W
Canyonville, *U.S.A.* 76 E2 42 56N 123 17W
Cao Bang, *Vietnam* ..... 38 A6 22 40N 106 15 E
Cao He ➔, *China* ...... 35 D13 40 10N 124 32 E
Cao Lanh, *Vietnam* ..... 39 G5 10 27N 105 38 E
Cao Xian, *China* .... 34 G8 34 50N 115 35 E
Cap-aux-Meules, *Canada* 73 C7 47 23N 61 52W
Cap-Chat, *Canada* 73 C6 49 6N 66 40W
Cap-de-la-Madeleine, *Canada* 72 C5 46 22N 72 31W
Cap-Haïtien, *Haiti* 89 C5 19 40N 72 20W
Cap Pt., *St. Lucia* .... 89 f 14 7N 60 57W
Capac, *U.S.A.* 84 C2 43 1N 82 56W
Capanaparo ➔, *Venezuela* 92 B5 7 1N 67 7W
Cape ➔, *Australia* ..... 62 C4 20 59S 146 51 E
Cape Arid △, *Australia* . 61 F3 33 58S 123 13 E
Cape Barren I., *Australia* 63 G4 40 25S 148 15 E
Cape Breton Highlands △,
  Canada 73 C7 46 50N 60 40W
Cape Breton I., *Canada* . 73 C7 46 0N 60 30W

Cape Charles, U.S.A. 82 G8 37 16N 76 1W
Cape Coast, Ghana 50 G5 5 5N 1 15W
Cape Cod △, U.S.A. 82 E10 41 56N 70 6W
Cape Coral, U.S.A. 83 M5 26 33N 81 57W
Cape Dorset, Canada 69 B12 64 14N 76 32W
Cape Fear →, U.S.A. 83 H6 33 53N 78 1W
Cape Girardeau, U.S.A. 81 G10 37 19N 89 32W
Cape Hatteras △, U.S.A. 83 H8 35 30N 75 28W
Cape Lee △, Australia .... 61 F3 33 54S 122 26 E
Cape Lookout △, U.S.A. 83 H7 35 45N 76 25W
Cape May, U.S.A. 82 F8 38 56N 74 56W
Cape May Point, U.S.A. 82 F8 38 56N 74 58W
Cape Melville △, Australia .... 62 A3 14 26S 144 28 E
Cape Peninsula △, S. Africa .... 56 E2 34 20S 18 28 E
Cape Range △, Australia .... 60 D1 22 3S 111 0 E
Cape Tormentine, Canada 73 C7 46 8N 63 47W
Cape Town, S. Africa .... 56 E2 33 55S 18 22 E
Cape Tribulation △, Australia .... 62 B4 16 5S 145 25 E
Cape Verde Is. ■, Atl. Oc. 49 E1 16 0N 24 0W
Cape Vincent, U.S.A. 85 B8 44 8N 76 20W
Cape York Peninsula, Australia .... 62 A3 12 0S 142 30 E
Capela, Brazil 93 F11 10 30S 37 0W
Capella, Australia .... 62 C4 23 2S 148 1 E
Capesterre, Guadeloupe .... 88 b 16 4N 61 36W
Capesterre-Belle-Eau,
  Guadeloupe .... 88 b 16 4N 61 36W
Capim →, Brazil 93 D9 1 40S 47 47W
Capitan, U.S.A. 77 K11 33 35N 105 35W
Capitán Arturo Prat, Antarctica 5 C17 63 0S 61 0W
Capitol Reef △, U.S.A. 77 G8 38 15N 111 10W
Capitola, U.S.A. 78 J5 36 59N 121 57W
Capoche →, Mozam. .... 55 F3 15 35S 33 0 E
Capraia, Italy .... 20 E8 43 2N 9 50 E
Capreol, Canada 72 C3 46 43N 80 56W
Capri, Italy .... 22 D6 40 33N 14 14 E
Capricorn Group, Australia .... 62 C5 23 30S 151 55 E
Capricorn Ra., Australia .... 60 D2 23 20S 116 50 E
Caprivi Game △, Namibia .... 56 B3 17 55S 22 37 E
Caprivi Strip, Namibia .... 56 B3 18 0S 23 0 E
Captain's Flat, Australia .... 63 F4 35 35S 149 27 E
Capulin Volcano △, U.S.A. 81 G3 36 47N 103 58W
Caquetá →, Colombia 92 D5 1 15S 69 15W
Caracal, Romania .... 17 F13 44 8N 24 22 E
Caracas, Venezuela 92 A5 10 30N 66 55W
Caracol, Mato Grosso do Sul,
  Brazil 94 A4 22 18S 57 1W
Caracol, Piauí, Brazil 93 E10 9 15S 43 22W
Carajás, Brazil 93 E8 6 5S 50 23W
Carajás, Serra dos, Brazil 93 E8 6 0S 51 30W
Carangola, Brazil 95 A7 20 44S 42 5W
Caransebeş, Romania .... 17 F12 45 28N 22 18 E
Caraquet, Canada 73 C6 47 48N 64 57W
Caras, Peru 92 E3 3 3S 77 47W
Caratasca, L., Honduras 88 C3 15 20N 83 40W
Caratinga, Brazil 93 G10 19 50S 42 10W
Caraúbas, Brazil 93 E11 5 43S 37 33W
Caravaca de la Cruz, Spain 21 C5 38 8N 1 52W
Caravelas, Brazil 93 G11 17 45S 39 15W
Caraveli, Peru 92 G4 15 45S 73 25W
Caravelle, Presqu'île de la,
  Martinique .... 88 c 14 46N 60 48W
Caràzinho, Brazil 95 B5 28 16S 52 46W
Carballo, Spain 21 A1 43 13N 8 41W
Carberry, Canada 71 D9 49 50N 99 25W
Carbó, Mexico 86 B2 29 42N 110 58W
Carbonara, C., Italy .... 22 E3 39 6N 9 31 E
Carbondale, Colo., U.S.A. 76 G10 39 24N 107 13W
Carbondale, Ill., U.S.A. 81 G10 37 44N 89 13W
Carbondale, Pa., U.S.A. 85 E9 41 35N 75 30W
Carbonear, Canada 73 C9 47 42N 53 13W
Carbónia, Italy .... 22 E3 39 10N 8 30 E
Carcajou, Canada 70 B5 57 47N 117 6W
Carcarana →, Argentina 94 C3 32 27S 60 48W
Carcasse, C., Haiti 89 C5 18 30N 74 28W
Carcross, Canada 70 A2 60 13N 134 45W
Cardamon Hills, India .... 40 Q10 9 30N 77 15 E
Cárdenas, Cuba 88 B3 23 0N 81 30W
Cárdenas, San Luis Potosí,
  Mexico 87 C5 22 0N 99 41W
Cárdenas, Tabasco, Mexico 87 D6 17 59N 93 21W
Cardiff, U.K. 13 F4 51 29N 3 10W
Cardiff □, U.K. 13 F4 51 31N 3 12W
Cardiff-by-the-Sea, U.S.A. 79 M9 33 1N 117 17W
Cardigan, U.K. 13 E3 52 5N 4 40W
Cardigan B., U.K. 13 E3 52 30N 4 30W
Cardinal, Canada 85 B9 44 47N 75 23W
Cardona, Uruguay 94 C4 33 53S 57 18W
Cardoso, Ilha do, Brazil 95 B6 25 8S 47 58W
Cardston, Canada 70 D6 49 15N 113 20W
Cardwell, Australia .... 62 B4 18 14S 146 2 E
Careen L., Canada 71 B7 57 0N 108 11W
Carei, Romania .... 17 E12 47 40N 22 29 E
Careme = Ciremay, Indonesia .... 37 G13 6 55S 108 27 E
Carey, U.S.A. 76 E7 43 19N 113 57W
Carey, L., Australia .... 61 E3 29 0S 122 15 E
Carey L., Canada 71 A8 62 12N 102 55W
Carhué, Argentina 94 D3 37 10S 62 50W
Caria, Turkey .... 23 F13 37 20N 28 10 E
Cariacica, Brazil 93 H10 20 16S 40 25W
Caribbean Sea, W. Indies 89 D5 15 0N 75 0W
Cariboo Mts., Canada 70 C4 53 0N 121 0W
Caribou, U.S.A. 83 B12 46 52N 68 1W
Caribou →, Man., Canada 71 B10 59 20N 94 44W
Caribou →, N.W.T., Canada 70 A3 61 27N 125 45W
Caribou I., Canada 72 C2 47 22N 85 49W
Caribou Is., Canada 70 A6 61 55N 113 15W
Caribou L., Man., Canada 71 B9 59 21N 96 10W
Caribou L., Ont., Canada 72 B2 50 25N 89 5W
Caribou Mts., Canada 70 B5 59 12N 115 40W
Caribou River △, Canada 71 B9 59 35N 96 35W
Carichic, Mexico 86 B3 27 56N 107 3W
Carinda, Australia .... 63 E4 30 28S 147 41 E
Carinhanha, Brazil 93 F10 14 15S 44 46W
Carinhanha →, Brazil 93 F10 14 20S 43 47W
Carinthia = Kärnten □, Austria .... 16 E8 46 52N 13 30 E
Caripito, Venezuela 92 A6 10 8N 63 6W
Carleton, U.S.A. 73 C6 47 23N 66 53W
Carleton Place, Canada 85 A8 45 8N 76 9W
Carletonville, S. Africa .... 56 D4 26 23S 27 22 E
Carlin, U.S.A. 76 F5 40 43N 116 7W
Carlingford L., U.K. 10 B5 54 3N 6 9W
Carlinville, U.S.A. 80 F10 39 17N 89 53W
Carlisle, U.K. 12 C5 54 54N 2 56W
Carlisle, U.S.A. 84 F7 40 12N 77 12W
Carlisle B., Barbados .... 89 g 13 5N 59 37W
Carlisle I., Australia .... 62 J7 20 49S 149 18 E

Carlos Casares, Argentina 94 D3 35 32S 61 20W
Carlos Tejedor, Argentina 94 D3 35 25S 62 25W
Carlow, Ireland 10 D5 52 50N 6 56W
Carlow □, Ireland 10 D5 52 43N 6 50W
Carlsbad, Calif., U.S.A. 79 M9 33 10N 117 21W
Carlsbad, N. Mex., U.S.A. 81 J2 32 25N 104 14W
Carlsbad Caverns △, U.S.A. 81 J2 32 10N 104 35W
Carluke, U.K. 11 F5 55 45N 3 50W
Carlyle, Canada 71 D8 49 40N 102 20W
Carmacks, Canada 68 B6 62 5N 136 16W
Carman, Canada 71 D9 49 30N 98 0W
Carmarthen, U.K. 13 F3 51 52N 4 19W
Carmarthen B., U.K. 13 F3 51 40N 4 30W
Carmarthenshire □, U.K. 13 F3 51 55N 4 13W
Carmaux, France .... 20 D5 44 3N 2 10 E
Carmel, U.S.A. 85 E11 41 26N 73 41W
Carmel-by-the-Sea, U.S.A. 78 J5 36 33N 121 55W
Carmel Valley, U.S.A. 78 J5 36 29N 121 43W
Carmelo, Uruguay 94 C4 34 0S 58 20W
Carmen, Colombia 92 B3 9 43N 75 8W
Carmen, Paraguay 95 B4 27 13S 56 12W
Carmen →, Mexico 86 A3 30 42N 106 29W
Carmen, I., Mexico 86 B2 26 0N 111 20W
Carmen de Patagones, Argentina 96 E4 40 50S 63 0W
Carmensa, Argentina 94 D2 35 15S 67 40W
Carmi, Canada 70 D5 49 36N 119 8W
Carmi, U.S.A. 82 F1 38 5N 88 10W
Carmichael, U.S.A. 78 G5 38 38N 121 19W
Carmila, Australia .... 62 C4 21 55S 149 24 E
Carmona, Costa Rica 88 E2 10 0N 85 15W
Carmona, Spain 21 D3 37 28N 5 42W
Carn Ban, U.K. 11 D4 57 7N 4 15W
Carn Eige, U.K. 11 D3 57 17N 5 8W
Carnac, France 20 C2 47 35N 3 6W
Carnamah, Australia .... 61 E2 29 41S 115 53 E
Carnarvon, Australia .... 61 D1 24 51S 113 42 E
Carnarvon, S. Africa .... 56 E3 30 56S 22 8 E
Carnarvon Ra., Queens.,
  Australia .... 62 D4 25 15S 148 30 E
Carnarvon Ra., W. Austral.,
  Australia .... 61 E3 25 20S 120 45 E
Carnation, U.S.A. 78 C5 47 39N 121 55W
Carndonagh, Ireland 10 A4 55 16N 7 15W
Carnduff, Canada 71 D8 49 10N 101 50W
Carnegie, U.S.A. 84 F4 40 24N 80 5W
Carnegie, L., Australia .... 61 E3 26 5S 122 30 E
Carnic Alps = Karnische Alpen,
  Europe .... 16 E7 46 36N 13 0 E
Carniche Alpi = Karnische Alpen,
  Europe .... 16 E7 46 36N 13 0 E
Carnot, C.A.R. .... 52 D3 4 59N 15 56 E
Carnot, C., Australia .... 63 E2 34 57S 135 38 E
Carnot B., Australia .... 60 C3 17 20S 122 15 E
Carnoustie, U.K. 11 E6 56 30N 2 42W
Carnsore Pt., Ireland 10 D5 52 10N 6 22W
Caro, U.S.A. 82 D4 43 29N 83 24W
Carol City, U.S.A. 83 N5 25 56N 80 16W
Carolina, Brazil 93 E9 7 10S 47 30W
Carolina, Puerto Rico .... 89 d 18 23N 65 58W
Carolina, S. Africa .... 57 D5 26 5S 30 6 E
Caroline I., Kiribati 65 H12 9 58S 150 13W
Caroline Is., Micronesia .... 26 J17 8 0N 150 0 E
Caroni, Trin. & Tob. 93 K15 10 34N 61 23W
Caroni →, Venezuela 92 B6 8 21N 62 43W
Caronie = Nébrodi, Monti, Italy .... 22 F6 37 54N 14 35 E
Caroona, Australia .... 63 E5 31 24S 150 26 E
Carpathians, Europe .... 17 D11 49 30N 21 0 E
Carpații Meridionali, Romania .... 17 F13 45 30N 25 0 E
Carpentaria, G. of, Australia .... 62 A2 14 0S 139 0 E
Carpentras, France .... 20 D6 44 3N 5 2 E
Carpi, Italy .... 22 B4 44 47N 10 53 E
Carpinteria, U.S.A. 79 L7 34 24N 119 31W
Carr Boyd Ra., Australia .... 60 C4 16 15S 128 35 E
Carrabelle, U.S.A. 83 L3 29 51N 84 40W
Carranza, Presa V., Mexico 86 B4 27 20N 100 50W
Carrara, Italy .... 20 D9 44 5N 10 6 E
Carrauntoohill, Ireland 10 D2 52 0N 9 45W
Carrick-on-Shannon, Ireland 10 C3 53 57N 8 5W
Carrick-on-Suir, Ireland 10 D4 52 21N 7 24W
Carrickfergus, U.K. 10 B6 54 43N 5 49W
Carrickmacross, Ireland 10 C5 53 59N 6 43W
Carrieton, Australia .... 63 E2 32 25S 138 31 E
Carrington, U.S.A. 80 B5 47 27N 99 8W
Carrizal Bajo, Chile 94 B1 28 5S 71 20W
Carrizalillo, Chile 94 B1 29 5S 71 30W
Carrizo Cr. →, U.S.A. 81 G3 36 55N 103 55W
Carrizo Plain △, U.S.A. 78 K7 35 12N 119 48W
Carrizo Springs, U.S.A. 81 L5 28 31N 99 52W
Carrizozo, U.S.A. 77 K11 33 38N 105 53W
Carroll, U.S.A. 80 D7 42 4N 94 52W
Carrollton, Ga., U.S.A. 83 J3 33 35N 85 5W
Carrollton, Ill., U.S.A. 80 F9 39 18N 90 24W
Carrollton, Ky., U.S.A. 82 F3 38 41N 85 11W
Carrollton, Mo., U.S.A. 80 F8 39 22N 93 30W
Carrollton, Ohio, U.S.A. 84 F3 40 34N 81 5W
Carron →, U.K. 11 D3 57 53N 4 22W
Carron, L., U.K. 11 D3 57 22N 5 35W
Carrot →, Canada 71 C8 53 50N 101 17W
Carrot River, Canada 71 C8 53 17N 103 35W
Carruthers, Canada 71 C7 52 52N 109 16W
Carson, Calif., U.S.A. 79 M8 33 48N 118 17W
Carson, N. Dak., U.S.A. 80 B4 46 25N 101 34W
Carson →, U.S.A. 78 F8 39 45N 118 40W
Carson City, U.S.A. 78 F7 39 10N 119 46W
Carson Sink, U.S.A. 76 G4 39 50N 118 25W
Cartagena, Colombia 92 A3 10 25N 75 33W
Cartagena, Spain 21 D5 37 38N 0 59W
Cartago, Colombia 92 C3 4 45N 75 55W
Cartago, Costa Rica 88 E3 9 50N 83 55W
Cartersville, U.S.A. 83 H3 34 10N 84 48W
Carterton, N.Z. .... 59 J5 41 2S 175 31 E
Carthage, Tunisia .... 51 A8 36 52N 10 20 E
Carthage, Ill., U.S.A. 80 E9 40 25N 91 8W
Carthage, Mo., U.S.A. 81 G7 37 11N 94 19W
Carthage, N.Y., U.S.A. 82 D8 43 59N 75 37W
Carthage, Tex., U.S.A. 81 J7 32 9N 94 20W
Cartier I., Australia .... 60 B3 12 31S 123 29 E
Cartwright, Canada 73 B8 53 41N 56 58W
Caruaru, Brazil 93 E11 8 15S 35 55W
Carúpano, Venezuela 92 A6 10 39N 63 15W
Caruthersville, U.S.A. 81 G10 36 11N 89 39W
Carvoeiro, Brazil 92 D6 1 30S 61 59W
Carvoeiro, C., Portugal 21 C1 39 21N 9 24W
Cary, U.S.A. 83 H6 35 47N 78 46W
Casa Grande, U.S.A. 77 K8 32 53N 111 45W
Casablanca, Chile 94 C1 33 20S 71 25W
Casablanca, Morocco 50 B4 33 36N 7 36W

Cascada de Basaseachic △,
  Mexico 86 B3 28 9N 108 15W
Cascade, Idaho, U.S.A. 76 D5 44 31N 116 2W
Cascade, Mont., U.S.A. 76 C8 47 16N 111 42W
Cascade Locks, U.S.A. 78 E5 45 40N 121 54W
Cascade Ra., U.S.A. 78 D5 47 0N 121 30W
Cascade Reservoir, U.S.A. 76 D5 44 32N 116 3W
Cascais, Portugal 21 C1 38 41N 9 25W
Cascavel, Brazil 95 A5 24 57S 53 28W
Cáscina, Italy .... 22 C4 43 41N 10 33 E
Casco B., U.S.A. 83 D10 43 45N 70 0W
Caserta, Italy .... 22 D6 41 4N 14 20 E
Casey, Antarctica .... 5 C8 66 0S 76 0 E
Caseyr, Raas = Asir, Ras,
  Somali Rep. .... 47 E5 11 55N 51 10 E
Cashel, Ireland 10 D4 52 30N 7 53W
Casiguran, Phil. .... 37 A6 16 22N 122 7 E
Casilda, Argentina 94 C3 33 10S 61 10W
Casino, Australia .... 63 D5 28 52S 153 3 E
Casiquiare →, Venezuela 92 C5 2 1N 67 7W
Casma, Peru 92 E3 9 30S 78 20W
Casmalia, U.S.A. 79 L6 34 50N 120 32W
Caspe, Spain 21 B5 41 14N 0 1W
Casper, U.S.A. 76 E10 42 51N 106 19W
Caspian Depression, Eurasia .... 19 E8 47 0N 48 0 E
Caspian Sea, Eurasia .... 19 F9 43 0N 50 0 E
Cass Lake, U.S.A. 80 B7 47 23N 94 37W
Cassadaga, U.S.A. 84 D5 42 20N 79 19W
Casselman, Canada 85 A9 45 19N 75 5W
Casselton, U.S.A. 80 B6 46 54N 97 13W
Cassiar, Canada 70 B3 59 16N 129 40W
Cassiar Mts., Canada 70 B2 59 30N 130 30W
Cassino, Italy .... 22 D5 41 30N 13 49 E
Cassville, U.S.A. 81 G8 36 41N 93 52W
Castaic, U.S.A. 79 L8 34 30N 118 38W
Castalia, U.S.A. 84 E2 41 24N 82 49W
Castanhal, Brazil 93 D9 1 18S 47 55W
Castara, Trin. & Tob. 93 J16 11 17N 60 42W
Castellammare di Stábia, Italy .... 22 D6 40 42N 14 29 E
Castelli, Argentina 94 D4 36 7S 57 47W
Castelló de la Plana, Spain 21 C5 39 58N 0 3W
Castelo, Brazil 95 A7 20 33S 41 14W
Castelo Branco, Portugal 21 C2 39 50N 7 31W
Castelsarrasin, France .... 20 E4 44 2N 1 7 E
Castelvetrano, Italy .... 22 F5 37 41N 12 47 E
Casterton, Australia .... 63 F3 37 30S 141 30 E
Castile, U.S.A. 84 D6 42 38N 78 3W
Castilla-La Mancha □, Spain 21 C4 39 30N 3 30W
Castilla y Leon □, Spain 21 B3 42 0N 5 0W
Castillos, Uruguay 95 C5 34 12S 53 52W
Castle Dale, U.S.A. 76 G8 39 13N 111 1W
Castle Douglas, U.K. 11 G5 54 56N 3 56W
Castle Rock, Colo., U.S.A. 80 F2 39 22N 104 51W
Castle Rock, Wash., U.S.A. 78 D4 46 17N 122 54W
Castlebar, Ireland 10 C2 53 52N 9 18W
Castlebay, U.K. 11 E1 56 57N 7 31W
Castleblaney, Ireland 10 B5 54 7N 6 44W
Castlederg, U.K. 10 B4 54 42N 7 35W
Castleford, U.K. 12 D6 53 43N 1 21W
Castlegar, Canada 70 D5 49 20N 117 40W
Castlemaine, Australia .... 63 F3 37 2S 144 12 E
Castlepollard, Ireland 10 C4 53 41N 7 19W
Castlerea, Ireland 10 C3 53 46N 8 29W
Castlereagh →, Australia .... 63 E4 30 12S 147 32 E
Castleton, U.S.A. 85 C11 43 37N 73 11W
Castletown, U.K. 12 C3 54 5N 4 38W
Castletown Bearhaven, Ireland 10 E2 51 39N 9 55W
Castor, Canada 70 C6 52 15N 111 50W
Castor →, Canada 85 A9 45 24N 75 20W
Castorland, U.S.A. 85 C9 43 53N 75 31W
Castres, France .... 20 E5 43 37N 2 13 E
Castricum, Neths. .... 15 B4 52 33N 4 40 E
Castries, St. Lucia .... 89 f 14 2N 60 58W
Castro, Brazil 95 A6 24 45S 50 0W
Castro, Chile 96 E2 42 30S 73 50W
Castro Alves, Brazil 93 F11 12 46S 39 33W
Castroville, U.S.A. 78 J5 36 46N 121 45W
Castuera, Spain 21 C3 38 43N 5 37W
Cat △, Vietnam .... 38 B6 20 47N 107 3 E
Cat Ba, Dao, Vietnam .... 38 B6 20 50N 107 0 E
Cat I., Bahamas 89 B4 24 30N 75 30W
Cat L., Canada 72 B1 51 40N 91 50W
Cat Lake, Canada 72 B1 51 40N 91 50W
Cat Tien △, Vietnam .... 39 G6 11 25N 107 17 E
Catacamas, Honduras 88 D2 14 54N 85 56W
Cataguases, Brazil 95 A7 21 23S 42 39W
Catalão, Brazil 93 G9 18 10S 47 57W
Çatalca, Turkey .... 23 D13 41 8N 28 27 E
Catalina, Chile 94 B2 25 13S 69 43W
Catalina, U.S.A. 77 K8 32 30N 110 50W
Catalonia = Cataluña □, Spain .... 21 B6 41 40N 1 15 E
Cataluña □, Spain .... 21 B6 41 40N 1 15 E
Catamarca, Argentina 94 B2 28 30S 65 50W
Catamarca □, Argentina 94 B2 27 0S 65 50W
Catanduanes □, Phil. .... 37 B6 13 50N 124 20 E
Catanduva, Brazil 95 A6 21 5S 48 58W
Catánia, Italy .... 22 F6 37 30N 15 6 E
Catanzaro, Italy .... 22 E7 38 54N 16 35 E
Catarman, Phil. .... 37 B6 12 28N 124 35 E
Catatumbo-Bari △, Colombia 89 E5 9 3N 73 12W
Cateel, Phil. .... 37 C7 7 47N 126 24 E
Catembe, Mozam. .... 57 D5 26 0S 32 33 E
Caterham, U.K. 13 F7 51 15N 0 4W
Cathcart, S. Africa .... 56 E4 32 18S 27 10 E
Cathlamet, U.S.A. 78 D3 46 12N 123 23W
Catlettsburg, U.S.A. 82 F4 38 25N 82 36W
Catoche, C., Mexico 87 C7 21 40N 87 8W
Catriló, Argentina 94 D3 36 26S 63 24W
Catrimani, Brazil 92 C6 0 27N 61 41W
Catrimani →, Brazil 92 C6 0 28N 61 44W
Catskill, U.S.A. 85 D11 42 14N 73 52W
Catskill Mts., U.S.A. 85 D10 42 10N 74 25W
Catt, Mt., Australia .... 62 A1 13 49S 134 23 E
Cattaraugus, U.S.A. 84 D6 42 20N 78 52W
Catterick, U.K. 12 C6 54 23N 1 37W
Catuala, Angola .... 56 B2 16 25S 19 2 E
Catuane, Mozam. .... 57 D5 26 48S 32 18 E
Catur, Mozam. .... 55 E4 13 45S 35 30 E
Catwick Is., Vietnam .... 39 G7 10 0N 109 0 E
Cauca →, Colombia 92 B4 8 54N 74 28W
Caucaia, Brazil 93 D11 3 40S 38 35W
Caucasus Mountains, Eurasia .... 19 F7 42 50N 44 0 E
Caungula, Angola .... 52 F3 8 26S 18 38 E
Cauquenes, Chile 94 D1 36 0S 72 22W
Caura →, Venezuela 92 B6 7 38N 64 53W

Cauresi →, Mozam. .... 55 F3 17 8S 33 0 E
Causapscal, Canada 73 C6 48 19N 67 12W
Cauvery →, India .... 40 P11 11 9N 78 52 E
Caux, Pays de, France .... 20 B4 49 38N 0 35 E
Cavalier, U.S.A. 80 A6 48 48N 97 37W
Cavan, Ireland 10 B4 54 0N 7 22W
Cavan □, Ireland 10 C4 54 1N 7 16W
Cave Creek, U.S.A. 77 K7 33 50N 111 57W
Cavenagh Ra., Australia .... 61 E4 26 12S 127 55 E
Cavendish, Australia .... 63 F3 37 31S 142 2 E
Caviana, I., Brazil 93 C8 0 10N 50 10W
Cavite, Phil. .... 37 B6 14 29N 120 55 E
Cawndilla L., Australia .... 63 E3 32 30S 142 15 E
Cawnpore = Kanpur, India .... 43 F9 26 28N 80 20 E
Caxias, Brazil 93 D10 4 55S 43 20W
Caxias do Sul, Brazil 95 B5 29 10S 51 10W
Cay Sal Bank, Bahamas 88 B4 23 45N 80 0W
Cayambe, Ecuador 92 C3 0 3N 78 8W
Cayenne, Fr. Guiana 93 B8 5 5N 52 18W
Cayey, Puerto Rico .... 89 d 18 7N 66 10W
Cayman Brac, Cayman Is. 88 C4 19 43N 79 49W
Cayman Is. ☑, W. Indies 88 C3 19 40N 80 30W
Cayo Romano, Cuba 88 B4 22 0N 78 0W
Cayuga, Canada 84 D5 42 54N 79 49W
Cayuga L., U.S.A. 85 D8 42 41N 76 41W
Cazenovia, U.S.A. 85 D9 42 56N 75 51W
Cazombo, Angola .... 53 G4 11 54S 22 56 E
Ceanannus Mor, Ireland 10 C5 53 44N 6 53W
Ceará = Fortaleza, Brazil 93 D11 3 45S 38 35W
Ceará □, Brazil 93 E11 5 0S 40 0W
Ceará Mirim, Brazil 93 E11 5 38S 35 25W
Cebaco, I. de, Panama 88 E3 7 33N 81 9W
Cebollar, Argentina 94 B2 29 10S 66 35W
Cebu, Phil. .... 37 B6 10 18N 123 54 E
Cecil Plains, Australia .... 63 D5 27 30S 151 11 E
Cedar →, U.S.A. 80 E9 41 17N 91 21W
Cedar City, U.S.A. 77 H7 37 41N 113 4W
Cedar Creek Reservoir, U.S.A. 81 J6 32 11N 96 4W
Cedar Falls, Iowa, U.S.A. 80 D8 42 32N 92 27W
Cedar Falls, Wash., U.S.A. 78 C5 47 25N 121 45W
Cedar Key, U.S.A. 83 L4 29 8N 83 2W
Cedar L., Canada 71 C9 53 10N 100 0W
Cedar Rapids, U.S.A. 80 E9 41 59N 91 40W
Cedartown, U.S.A. 83 H3 34 1N 85 15W
Cedarvale, Canada 70 B3 55 1N 128 22W
Cedarville, S. Africa .... 57 E4 30 23S 29 3 E
Cedral, Mexico 86 C4 23 50N 100 42W
Cedro, Brazil 93 E11 6 34S 39 3W
Cedros, I. de, Mexico 86 B1 28 10N 115 20W
Cedros B., Trin. & Tob. 93 K15 10 16N 61 54W
Ceduna, Australia .... 63 E1 32 7S 133 46 E
Ceerigaabo = Erigavo,
  Somali Rep. .... 47 E4 10 35N 47 20 E
Cefalù, Italy .... 22 E6 38 2N 14 1 E
Cegléd, Hungary .... 17 E10 47 11N 19 47 E
Cekik, Indonesia .... 37 J17 8 12S 114 27 E
Celaque □, Honduras 88 D2 14 30N 88 43W
Celaya, Mexico 86 C4 20 31N 100 37W
Celebes Sea, Indonesia .... 37 D6 3 0N 123 0 E
Celina, U.S.A. 82 E3 40 33N 84 35W
Celje, Slovenia .... 16 E8 46 16N 15 18 E
Celle, Germany .... 16 B6 52 37N 10 4 E
Celtic Sea, Atl. Oc. 14 F2 50 9N 9 34W
Cenderwasih, Teluk, Indonesia .... 37 E9 3 0S 135 20 E
Center, N. Dak., U.S.A. 80 B4 47 7N 101 18W
Center, Tex., U.S.A. 81 K7 31 48N 94 11W
Centerburg, U.S.A. 84 F2 40 18N 82 42W
Centerville, Calif., U.S.A. 78 J7 36 44N 119 30W
Centerville, Iowa, U.S.A. 80 E8 40 44N 92 52W
Centerville, Pa., U.S.A. 84 F5 40 3N 79 59W
Centerville, Tenn., U.S.A. 83 H2 35 47N 87 28W
Central □, Kenya .... 54 C4 0 30S 37 30 E
Central □, Malawi .... 55 E3 13 30S 33 30 E
Central □, Zambia .... 55 E2 14 25S 28 50 E
Central, Cordillera, Colombia 92 C4 5 0N 75 0W
Central, Cordillera, Costa Rica 88 D3 10 10N 84 5W
Central, Cordillera, Dom. Rep. 89 C5 19 15N 71 0W
Central, Cordillera, Puerto Rico .... 89 d 18 8N 66 35W
Central African Rep. ■, Africa .... 52 C4 7 0N 20 0 E
Central America, America 66 H11 12 0N 85 0W
Central Butte, Canada 71 C7 50 48N 106 31W
Central City, Colo., U.S.A. 76 G11 39 48N 105 31W
Central City, Ky., U.S.A. 82 G2 37 18N 87 7W
Central City, Nebr., U.S.A. 80 E6 41 7N 98 0W
Central I., Kenya .... 54 B4 3 30N 36 0 E
Central Island △, Kenya .... 54 B4 2 33N 36 1 E
Central Kalahari △, Botswana .... 56 C3 22 36S 23 58 E
Central Makran Range, Pakistan .... 40 F4 26 30N 64 15 E
Central Patricia, Canada 72 B1 51 30N 90 9W
Central Point, U.S.A. 76 E2 42 23N 122 55W
Central Russian Uplands, Europe .... 6 E13 54 0N 36 0 E
Central Siberian Plateau, Russia .... 26 C14 65 0N 105 0 E
Central Square, U.S.A. 85 C8 43 17N 76 9W
Centralia, Ill., U.S.A. 80 F10 38 32N 89 8W
Centralia, Mo., U.S.A. 80 F8 39 13N 92 8W
Centralia, Wash., U.S.A. 78 D4 46 43N 122 58W
Cephalonia = Kefalliniá, Greece .... 23 E9 38 15N 20 30 E
Cepu, Indonesia .... 37 G14 7 9S 111 35 E
Ceram = Seram, Indonesia .... 37 E7 3 10S 129 0 E
Ceram Sea = Seram Sea,
  Indonesia .... 37 E7 2 30S 128 30 E
Ceredigion □, U.K. 13 E3 52 16N 4 15W
Ceres, Argentina 94 B3 29 55S 61 55W
Ceres, S. Africa .... 56 E2 33 21S 19 18 E
Ceres, U.S.A. 78 H6 37 35N 120 57W
Cerignola, Italy .... 22 D6 41 17N 15 53 E
Cerigo = Kíthira, Greece .... 23 F10 36 8N 23 0 E
Çerkezköy, Turkey .... 23 D12 41 17N 28 0 E
Cerralvo, I., Mexico 86 C3 24 20N 109 45W
Cerritos, Mexico 86 C4 22 20N 100 20W
Cerro Chato, Uruguay 95 C4 33 6S 55 8W
Cerro Corá, Paraguay 95 A4 22 35S 56 20W
Cerro el Copey △, Venezuela 89 D7 10 59S 63 53W
Cerro Hoya △, Panama 88 E3 7 17N 80 45W
Cerro Saroche △, Venezuela 89 D6 10 10N 69 38W
Cervantes, Australia .... 61 F2 30 31S 115 3 E
Cervera, Spain .... 21 B6 41 40N 1 16 E
Cesena, Italy .... 22 B5 44 8N 12 15 E
Cēsis, Latvia .... 9 H21 57 18N 25 15 E
České Budějovice, Czech Rep. .... 16 D8 48 55N 14 25 E
Českomoravská Vrchovina,
  Czech Rep. .... 16 D8 49 30N 15 40 E
Çeşme, Turkey .... 23 E12 38 20N 26 23 E
Cessnock, Australia .... 63 E5 32 50S 151 21 E
Cetinje, Serbia & M. .... 23 C8 42 23N 18 59 E
Cetraro, Italy .... 22 E6 39 31N 15 55 E

Ceuta, N. Afr. 21 E3 35 52N 5 18W
Cévennes, France ..... 20 D5 44 10N 3 50 E
Ceyhan, Turkey .... 44 B2 37 4N 35 47 E
Ceylon = Sri Lanka ■, Asia 40 R12 7 30N 80 50 E
Cha Pa, Vietnam ...... 38 A4 22 20N 103 47 E
Chacabuco, Argentina 94 C3 34 40S 60 27W
Chachapoyas, Peru 92 E3 6 15S 77 50W
Chachoengsao, Thailand 38 F3 13 42N 101 5 E
Chachran, Pakistan ... 40 E7 28 55N 70 30 E
Chachro, Pakistan .... 42 G4 25 5N 70 15 E
Chaco △, Argentina ... 94 B4 27 0S 59 30W
Chaco □, Argentina ... 94 B3 26 30S 61 0W
Chaco □, Paraguay 94 B4 26 0S 60 0W
Chaco Austral, S. Amer. 96 B4 27 0S 61 30W
Chaco Boreal, S. Amer. 92 H6 22 0S 60 0W
Chaco Central, S. Amer. 96 A4 24 0S 61 0W
Chacon, C., U.S.A. 70 C2 54 42N 132 0W
Chad ■, Africa .... 51 F8 15 0N 17 15 E
Chad, L. = Tchad, L., Chad 51 F8 13 30N 14 30 E
Chadileuvú →, Argentina 94 D2 37 46S 66 0W
Chadiza, Zambia ...... 55 E3 14 45S 32 27 E
Chadron, U.S.A. 80 D3 42 50N 103 0W
Chadyr-Lunga = Ciadâr-Lunga, Moldova 17 E15 46 3N 28 51 E
Chae Hom, Thailand .. 38 C2 18 43N 99 35 E
Chae Son △, Thailand . 38 C2 18 42N 99 20 E
Chaem →, Thailand ... 38 C2 18 11N 98 38 E
Chaeryŏng, N. Korea .. 35 E13 38 24N 125 36 E
Chagai Hills = Châh Gay Hills, Afghan. 40 E3 29 30N 64 0 E
Chagda, Russia .... 29 D14 58 45N 130 38 E
Chaghcharān, Afghan. . 40 B4 34 31N 65 15 E
Chagos Arch. ☑, Ind. Oc. 27 K11 6 0S 72 0 E
Chagres →, Panama ... 88 E4 9 5N 79 37W
Chagrin Falls, U.S.A. . 84 E3 41 26N 81 24W
Chaguanas, Trin. & Tob. 93 K15 10 30N 61 26W
Chāh Akhvor, Iran .... 45 C8 32 41N 59 40 E
Chāh Bahar, Iran ..... 45 E9 25 20N 60 40 E
Chāh-e Kavir, Iran .... 45 C8 34 29N 56 52 E
Chāh Gay Hills, Afghan. 40 E3 29 30N 64 0 E
Chahar Burjak, Afghan. 40 D3 30 15N 62 0 E
Chahār Mahāll va Bakhtīarī □, Iran 45 C6 32 0N 49 0 E
Chai Wan, China ...... 33 G11 22 16N 114 14 E
Chaibasa, India ...... 41 H14 22 42N 85 49 E
Chainat, Thailand .... 38 E3 15 11N 100 8 E
Chaiya, Thailand ..... 39 H2 9 23N 99 14 E
Chaiyaphum, Thailand 38 E4 15 48N 102 2 E
Chaj Doab, Pakistan .. 42 C5 32 15N 73 0 E
Chajari, Argentina ... 94 C4 30 42S 58 0W
Chak Amru, Pakistan . 42 C6 32 22N 75 11 E
Chakar →, Pakistan ... 42 E3 29 29N 68 2 E
Chakari, Zimbabwe ... 57 B4 18 5S 29 51 E
Chake Chake, Tanzania 54 D4 5 15S 39 45 E
Chakhānsūr, Afghan. .. 40 D3 31 10N 62 0 E
Chakonipau, L., Canada 73 A6 56 18N 68 30W
Chakradharpur, India . 43 H11 22 45N 85 40 E
Chakrata, India ...... 42 D7 30 42N 77 51 E
Chakwal, Pakistan .... 42 C5 32 56N 72 53 E
Chala, Peru 92 G4 15 48S 74 20W
Chalchihuites, Mexico 86 C4 23 29N 103 53W
Chalcis = Khalkís, Greece 23 E10 38 27N 23 42 E
Chaleur B., Canada ... 73 C6 47 55N 65 30W
Chalfant, U.S.A. 78 H8 37 32N 118 21W
Chalhuanca, Peru 92 F4 14 15S 73 15W
Chalisgaon, India .... 40 J9 20 30N 75 10 E
Chalk River, Canada .. 72 C4 46 1N 77 27W
Chalky Inlet, N.Z. .... 59 M1 46 3S 166 31 E
Challapata, Bolivia ... 92 G5 18 53S 66 50W
Challis, U.S.A. 76 D6 44 30N 114 14W
Chalmette, U.S.A. 81 L10 29 56N 89 58W
Chalon-sur-Saône, France 20 C6 46 48N 4 50 E
Châlons-en-Champagne, France 20 B6 48 58N 4 20 E
Chālūs, Iran .... 45 B6 36 38N 51 26 E
Cham, Cu Lao, Vietnam 38 E7 15 57N 108 30 E
Chama, U.S.A. 77 H10 36 54N 106 35W
Chamaicó, Argentina .. 94 D3 35 3S 64 58W
Chaman, Pakistan ..... 40 D5 30 58N 66 25 E
Chamba, India .... 42 C7 32 35N 76 10 E
Chamba, Tanzania .... 55 E4 11 37S 37 0 E
Chambal →, India ..... 43 F8 26 29N 79 15 E
Chamberlain, U.S.A. .. 80 D5 43 49N 99 20W
Chamberlain →, Australia 60 C4 15 30S 127 54 E
Chamberlain L., U.S.A. 83 B11 46 14N 69 19W
Chambers, U.S.A. 77 J9 35 11N 109 26W
Chambersburg, U.S.A. 82 F7 39 56N 77 40W
Chambéry, France .... 20 D6 45 34N 5 55 E
Chambeshi →, Zambia . 52 G6 11 53S 29 48 E
Chambly, Canada 85 A11 45 27N 73 17W
Chambord, Canada 73 C5 48 25N 72 6W
Chamchamal, Iraq .... 44 C5 35 32N 44 50 E
Chamela, Mexico 86 D3 19 32N 105 5W
Chamical, Argentina .. 94 C2 30 22S 66 27W
Chamkar Luong, Cambodia 39 G4 11 0N 103 45 E
Chamoli, India .... 43 D8 30 30N 79 21 E
Chamonix-Mont Blanc, France 20 D7 45 55N 6 51 E
Champa, India .... 43 H10 22 2N 82 43 E
Champagne, Canada ... 70 A1 60 49N 136 30W
Champagne, France ... 20 B6 48 40N 4 20 E
Champaign, U.S.A. 82 E1 40 7N 88 15W
Champassak, Laos .... 38 E5 14 53N 105 52 E
Champawat, India .... 43 E9 29 20N 80 6 E
Champdoré, L., Canada 73 A6 55 55N 65 49W
Champion, U.S.A. 84 E4 41 19N 80 51W
Champlain, U.S.A. 85 B11 44 59N 73 27W
Champlain, L., U.S.A. . 85 B11 44 40N 73 20W
Champotón, Mexico ... 87 D6 19 20N 90 50W
Champua, India .... 43 H11 22 5N 85 40 E
Chana, Thailand ...... 39 J3 6 55N 100 44 E
Chañaral, Chile 94 B1 26 23S 70 40W
Chañarán, Iran .... 45 B8 36 39N 59 6 E
Chanasma, India ..... 42 H5 23 44N 72 5 E
Chancery Lane, Barbados 89 g 13 3N 59 30W
Chanco, Chile 94 D1 35 44S 72 32W
Chand, India .... 43 J8 21 57N 79 7 E
Chandan, India .... 43 G12 24 36N 86 40 E
Chandan Chauki, India 43 E9 28 33N 80 47 E
Chandannagar, India . 43 H13 22 52N 88 24 E
Chandausi, India ..... 43 E8 28 27N 78 49 E
Chandeleur Is., U.S.A. 81 L10 29 55N 88 57W
Chandeleur Sd., U.S.A. 81 L10 29 55N 89 0W
Chandigarh, India .... 42 D7 30 43N 76 47 E
Chandil, India .... 43 H12 22 58N 86 3 E
Chandler, Australia ... 63 D1 27 0S 133 19 E

Chandler, Canada 73 C7 48 18N 64 46W
Chandler, Ariz., U.S.A. 77 K8 33 18N 111 50W
Chandler, Okla., U.S.A. 81 H6 35 42N 96 53W
Chandod, India .... 42 J5 21 59N 73 28 E
Chandpur, Bangla. .... 41 H17 23 8N 90 45 E
Chandrapur, India .... 40 K11 19 57N 79 25 E
Chānf, Iran .... 45 E9 26 38N 60 29 E
Chang, Pakistan ...... 42 F3 26 59N 68 30 E
Chang, Ko, Thailand .. 39 F4 12 0N 102 23 E
Ch'ang Chiang = Chang Jiang →, China 33 C7 31 48N 121 10 E
Chang Jiang →, China . 33 C7 31 48N 121 10 E
Changa, India .... 43 C7 33 53N 77 35 E
Changan, China ...... 33 F10 22 48N 113 48 E
Changanacheri, India . 40 Q10 9 25N 76 31 E
Changane →, Mozam. .. 57 C5 24 30S 33 30 E
Changbai, China ..... 35 D15 41 25N 128 5 E
Changbai Shan, China 35 C15 42 20N 129 0 E
Changchiak'ou = Zhangjiakou, China 34 D8 40 48N 114 55 E
Ch'angchou = Changzhou, China 33 C6 31 47N 119 58 E
Changchun, China .... 35 C13 43 57N 125 17 E
Changchunling, China 35 B13 45 18N 125 27 E
Changde, China ...... 33 D6 29 4N 111 35 E
Changdo-ri, N. Korea . 35 E14 38 30N 127 40 E
Changhai = Shanghai, China 33 C7 31 15N 121 26 E
Changhua, Taiwan .... 33 D7 24 2N 120 30 E
Changhǔng, S. Korea . 35 G14 34 41N 126 52 E
Changhǔngni, N. Korea 35 D15 40 24N 128 19 E
Changji, Singapore ... 39 d 1 23N 103 59 E
Changi, Singapore ✈ (SIN), Singapore 39 M4 1 23N 103 59 E
Changjiang, China .... 38 C7 19 20N 108 55 E
Changjiang Shuiku, China 33 G10 22 29N 113 27 E
Changjin, N. Korea ... 35 D14 40 23N 127 15 E
Changjin-chosuji, N. Korea 35 D14 40 30N 127 15 E
Changli, China .... 35 E10 39 40N 119 13 E
Changling, China ..... 35 B12 44 20N 123 58 E
Changlun, Malaysia ... 39 J3 6 25N 100 26 E
Changping, China .... 34 D9 40 14N 116 12 E
Changsha, China ..... 33 D6 28 12N 113 0 E
Changwu, China ...... 34 G4 35 10N 107 45 E
Changyi, China .... 35 F10 36 40N 119 30 E
Changyǒn, N. Korea .. 35 E13 38 15N 125 6 E
Changyuan, China .... 34 G8 35 15N 114 42 E
Changzhi, China ...... 34 F7 36 10N 113 6 E
Changzhou, China .... 33 C6 31 47N 119 58 E
Chanhanga, Angola ... 56 B1 16 0S 14 8 E
Chania = Khaniá, Greece 25 D6 35 30N 24 4 E
Channapatna, India ... 40 N10 12 40N 77 15 E
Channel Is., U.K. 13 H5 49 19N 2 24W
Channel Is., U.S.A. ... 79 M7 33 40N 119 15W
Channel Islands △, U.S.A. 79 L7 34 0N 119 24W
Channel-Port aux Basques, Canada 73 C8 47 30N 59 9W
Channel Tunnel, Europe 13 F9 51 0N 1 30 E
Channing, U.S.A. 81 H3 35 41N 102 20W
Chantada, Spain 21 A2 42 36N 7 46W
Chanthaburi, Thailand 38 F4 12 38N 102 12 E
Chantrey Inlet, Canada 68 B10 67 48N 96 20W
Chanute, U.S.A. 81 G7 37 41N 95 27W
Chao Phraya →, Thailand 38 F3 13 32N 100 36 E
Chao Phraya Lowlands, Thailand 38 E3 15 30N 100 0 E
Chaocheng, China .... 34 F8 36 4N 115 37 E
Chaoyang, China ..... 35 D11 41 35N 120 22 E
Chaozhou, China ..... 33 D6 23 42N 116 32 E
Chapais, Canada 72 C5 49 47N 74 51W
Chapala, Mozam. ..... 55 F4 15 50S 37 35 E
Chapala, L. de, Mexico 86 C4 20 10N 103 20W
Chapayev, Kazakhstan 19 D9 50 25N 51 10 E
Chapayevsk, Russia ... 18 D8 53 0N 49 40 E
Chapecó, Brazil 95 B5 27 14S 52 41W
Chapel Hill, U.S.A. ... 83 H6 35 55N 79 4W
Chapleau, Canada 72 C3 47 50N 83 24W
Chaplin, Canada 71 C7 50 28N 106 40W
Chaplin L., Canada ... 71 C7 50 22N 106 36W
Chappell, U.S.A. 80 E3 41 6N 102 28W
Chapra = Chhapra, India 43 G11 25 48N 84 44 E
Chara, Russia .... 29 D12 56 54N 118 20 E
Charadai, Argentina .. 94 B4 27 35S 59 55W
Charagua, Bolivia 92 G6 19 45S 63 10W
Charambirá, Punta, Colombia 92 C3 4 16N 77 32W
Charaña, Bolivia 92 G5 17 30S 69 25W
Charanwala, India .... 42 F5 27 51N 72 10 E
Charata, Argentina ... 94 B3 27 13S 61 14W
Charcas, Mexico 86 C4 23 10N 101 20W
Charcot I., Antarctica . 5 C17 70 0S 70 0W
Chard, U.K. 13 G5 50 52N 2 58W
Chardon, U.S.A. 84 E3 41 35N 81 12W
Chardzhou = Chärjew, Turkmenistan 28 F7 39 6N 63 34 E
Charente →, France ... 20 D3 45 57N 1 5W
Chari →, Chad .... 51 F8 12 58N 14 31 E
Chārīkār, Afghan. .... 40 B6 35 0N 69 10 E
Chariton →, U.S.A. ... 80 F8 39 19N 92 58W
Chärjew, Turkmenistan 28 F7 39 6N 63 34 E
Charkhari, India ..... 43 G8 25 24N 79 45 E
Charkhi Dadri, India . 42 E7 28 37N 76 17 E
Charleroi, Belgium ... 15 D4 50 24N 4 27 E
Charleroi, U.S.A. 84 F5 40 9N 79 57W
Charles, C., U.S.A. ... 82 G8 37 7N 75 58W
Charles City, U.S.A. .. 80 D8 43 4N 92 41W
Charles L., Canada 71 B6 59 50N 110 33W
Charles Town, U.S.A. . 82 F7 39 17N 77 52W
Charleston, Ill., U.S.A. 82 F1 39 30N 88 10W
Charleston, Miss., U.S.A. 81 H9 34 1N 90 4W
Charleston, Mo., U.S.A. 81 G10 36 55N 89 21W
Charleston, S.C., U.S.A. 83 J6 32 46N 79 56W
Charleston, W. Va., U.S.A. 82 F5 38 21N 81 38W
Charleston L., Canada . 85 B9 44 32N 76 0W
Charleston Peak, U.S.A. 79 J11 36 16N 115 42W
Charlestown, S. Africa 57 D4 27 26S 29 53 E
Charlestown, Ind., U.S.A. 82 F3 38 27N 85 40W
Charlestown, N.H., U.S.A. 85 C12 43 14N 72 25W
Charlestown of Aberlour, U.K. 11 D5 57 28N 3 14W
Charleville = Rath Luirc, Ireland 10 D3 52 21N 8 40W
Charleville, Australia . 63 D4 26 24S 146 15 E
Charleville-Mézières, France 20 B6 49 44N 4 40 E
Charlevoix, U.S.A. 82 C3 45 19N 85 16W
Charlotte, Mich., U.S.A. 82 D3 42 34N 84 50W
Charlotte, N.C., U.S.A. 83 H5 35 13N 80 50W
Charlotte, Vt., U.S.A. . 85 B11 44 19N 73 14W
Charlotte Amalie, U.S. Virgin Is. 89 e 18 21N 64 56W
Charlotte Harbor, U.S.A. 83 M4 26 50N 82 10W
Charlotte L., Canada .. 70 C3 52 12N 125 19W
Charlottesville, U.S.A. 82 F6 38 2N 78 30W

Charlottetown, Nfld. & L., Canada 73 B8 52 46N 56 7W
Charlottetown, P.E.I., Canada 73 C7 46 14N 63 8W
Charlotteville, Trin. & Tob. 93 J16 11 20N 60 33W
Charlton, Australia ... 63 F3 36 16S 143 24 E
Charlton, U.S.A. 80 E8 40 59N 93 20W
Charlton I., Canada ... 72 B4 52 0N 79 20W
Charny, Canada 73 C5 46 43N 71 15W
Charolles, France .... 20 C6 46 27N 4 16 E
Charre, Mozam. ...... 55 F4 17 13S 35 10 E
Charsadda, Pakistan .. 42 B4 34 7N 71 45 E
Charters Towers, Australia 62 C4 20 5S 146 13 E
Chartres, France ..... 20 B4 48 29N 1 30 E
Chascomús, Argentina 94 D4 35 30S 58 0W
Chasefu, Zambia ..... 55 E3 11 55S 33 8 E
Chashma Barrage, Pakistan 42 C4 32 27N 71 20 E
Chāt, Iran .... 45 B7 37 59N 55 16 E
Châteaubriant, France 20 C3 47 43N 1 23W
Chateaugay, U.S.A. ... 85 B10 44 56N 74 5W
Châteauguay, L., Canada 73 A5 56 26N 70 3W
Châteaulin, France ... 20 B1 48 11N 4 8W
Châteauroux, France . 20 C4 46 50N 1 40 E
Châteaux, Pte. des, Guadeloupe 88 b 16 15N 61 10W
Châtellerault, France . 20 C4 46 50N 0 30 E
Chatham = Chatham-Kent, Canada 84 D2 42 24N 82 11W
Chatham = Miramichi, Canada 73 C6 47 2N 65 28W
Chatham, U.K. .... 13 F8 51 22N 0 32 E
Chatham, U.S.A. 85 D11 42 21N 73 36W
Chatham Is., Pac. Oc. . 64 M10 44 0S 176 40W
Chatham-Kent, Canada 84 D2 42 24N 82 11W
Chatmohar, Bangla. .. 43 G13 24 15N 89 15 E
Chatra, India .... 43 G11 24 12N 84 56 E
Chatrapur, India ..... 41 K14 19 22N 85 2 E
Chats, L. des, Canada . 85 A8 45 30N 76 20W
Chatsu, India .... 42 F6 26 36N 75 57 E
Chatsworth, Canada .. 84 B4 44 27N 80 54W
Chatsworth, Zimbabwe 55 F3 19 38S 31 13 E
Chāttagām = Chittagong, Bangla. 41 H17 22 19N 91 48 E
Chattahoochee, U.S.A. 83 K3 30 42N 84 51W
Chattahoochee →, U.S.A. 83 K3 30 54N 84 57W
Chattanooga, U.S.A. .. 83 H3 35 3N 85 19W
Chatteris, U.K. .... 13 E8 52 28N 0 2 E
Chaturat, Thailand ... 38 E3 15 40N 101 51 E
Chau Doc, Vietnam ... 39 G5 10 42N 105 7 E
Chaukan Pass, Burma 41 F20 27 0N 97 15 E
Chaumont, France .... 20 B6 48 7N 5 8 E
Chaumont, U.S.A. 85 B8 44 4N 76 8W
Chaunskaya G., Russia 4 C16 69 0N 169 0 E
Chautauqua L., U.S.A. 84 D5 42 10N 79 24W
Chauvin, Canada 71 C6 52 45N 110 10W
Chaves, Brazil 93 D9 0 15S 49 55W
Chaves, Portugal 21 B2 41 45N 7 32W
Chawang, Thailand ... 39 H2 8 25N 99 30 E
Chaykovskiy, Russia .. 18 C9 56 47N 54 9 E
Chazy, U.S.A. 85 B11 44 53N 73 26W
Cheb, Czech Rep. ..... 16 C7 50 9N 12 28 E
Cheboksary, Russia ... 18 C8 56 8N 47 12 E
Cheboygan, U.S.A. ... 82 C3 45 39N 84 29W
Chech, Erg, Africa 50 D5 25 0N 2 15W
Chechenia □, Russia .. 19 F8 43 30N 45 29 E
Checheno-Ingush Republic = Chechenia □, Russia 19 F8 43 30N 45 29 E
Chechnya = Chechenia □, Russia 19 F8 43 30N 45 29 E
Chech'ǒn, S. Korea ... 35 F15 37 8N 128 12 E
Checotah, U.S.A. 81 H7 35 28N 95 31W
Chedabucto B., Canada 73 C7 45 25N 61 8W
Cheduba I., Burma ... 41 K18 18 45N 93 40 E
Cheepie, Australia ... 63 D4 26 33S 145 1 E
Chegdomyn, Russia .. 29 D14 51 7N 133 1 E
Chegga, Mauritania .. 50 C4 25 27N 5 40W
Chegutu, Zimbabwe .. 55 F3 18 10S 30 14 E
Chehalis, U.S.A. 78 D4 46 40N 122 58W
Chehalis →, U.S.A. ... 78 D3 46 57N 123 50W
Cheju do, S. Korea ... 35 H14 33 29N 126 34 E
Chekiang = Zhejiang □, China 33 D7 29 0N 120 0 E
Chela, Sa. da, Angola . 56 B1 16 20S 13 20 E
Chelan, U.S.A. 76 C4 47 51N 120 1W
Chelan, L., U.S.A. 76 B3 48 11N 120 30W
Cheleken, Turkmenistan 19 G9 39 34N 53 16 E
Cheleken Yarymadasy, Turkmenistan 45 B7 39 30N 53 15 E
Chelforó, Argentina .. 96 D3 39 0S 66 33W
Chelkar = Shalqar, Kazakhstan 28 E6 47 48N 59 39 E
Chelkar Tengiz, Solonchak, Kazakhstan 28 E7 48 5N 63 7 E
Chełm, Poland .... 17 C12 51 8N 23 30 E
Chełmno, Poland ..... 17 B10 53 20N 18 30 E
Chelmsford, U.K. ..... 13 F8 51 44N 0 29 E
Chelsea, U.S.A. 85 C12 43 59N 72 27W
Cheltenham, U.K. 13 F5 51 54N 2 4W
Chelyabinsk, Russia .. 28 D7 55 10N 61 24 E
Chelyuskin, C. = Chelyuskin, Mys, Russia 29 B11 77 30N 103 0 E
Chelyuskin, Mys, Russia 29 B11 77 30N 103 0 E
Chemainus, Canada .. 78 B3 48 55N 123 42W
Chemba, Mozam. ..... 53 H6 17 9S 34 53 E
Chemnitz, Germany .. 16 C7 50 51N 12 54 E
Chemult, U.S.A. 76 E3 43 14N 121 47W
Chen, Gora, Russia ... 29 C15 65 16N 141 50 E
Chenab →, Pakistan .. 42 D4 30 23N 71 2 E
Chenango Forks, U.S.A. 85 D9 42 15N 75 51W
Cheney, U.S.A. 76 C5 47 30N 117 35W
Cheng Xian, China ... 34 H3 33 43N 105 42 E
Chengcheng, China ... 34 G5 35 8N 109 56 E
Chengchou = Zhengzhou, China 34 G7 34 45N 113 34 E
Chengde, China ...... 35 D9 40 59N 117 58 E
Chengdu, China ...... 32 C5 30 38N 104 2 E
Chenggu, China ...... 34 H4 33 10N 107 21 E
Chengjiang, China ... 32 D5 24 39N 103 0 E
Ch'engmai, China .... 38 C7 19 50N 109 58 E
Ch'engtu = Chengdu, China 32 C5 30 38N 104 2 E
Chengyang, China .... 35 F11 36 18N 120 21 E
Chenjiagang, China .. 35 G10 34 23N 119 47 E
Chenkán, Mexico 87 D6 19 8N 90 58W
Chennai, India .... 40 N12 13 8N 80 19 E
Cheo Reo, Vietnam ... 36 B3 13 25N 108 28 E
Cheom Ksan, Cambodia 38 E5 14 13N 104 56 E
Chepén, Peru 92 E3 7 15S 79 23W
Chepes, Argentina ... 94 C2 31 20S 66 35W
Chepo, Panama 88 E4 9 10N 79 6W
Chepstow, U.K. 13 F5 51 38N 2 41W
Chequamegon B., U.S.A. 80 B9 46 40N 90 30W
Cher →, France .... 20 C4 47 21N 0 29 E
Cheraw, U.S.A. 83 H6 34 42N 79 53W
Cherbourg, France ... 20 B3 49 39N 1 40W
Cherdyn, Russia ..... 18 B10 60 24N 56 29 E

Cheremkhovo, Russia . 29 D11 53 8N 103 1 E
Cherepanovo, Russia . 28 D9 54 15N 83 30 E
Cherepovets, Russia .. 18 C6 59 5N 37 55 E
Chergui, Chott ech, Algeria 50 B6 34 21N 0 25 E
Cherikov = Cherykaw, Belarus 17 B16 53 32N 31 20 E
Cherkasy, Ukraine .... 19 E5 49 27N 32 4 E
Cherkessk, Russia .... 19 F7 44 15N 42 10 E
Cherlak, Russia ...... 28 D8 54 15N 74 55 E
Chernaya, Russia ..... 29 B9 70 30N 89 10 E
Chernigov = Chernihiv, Ukraine 18 D5 51 28N 31 20 E
Chernihiv, Ukraine ... 18 D5 51 28N 31 20 E
Chernivtsi, Ukraine ... 17 D13 48 15N 25 52 E
Chernobyl = Chornobyl, Ukraine 17 C16 51 20N 30 15 E
Chernogorsk, Russia . 29 D10 53 49N 91 18 E
Chernovtsy = Chernivtsi, Ukraine 17 D13 48 15N 25 52 E
Chernyakhovsk, Russia 9 J19 54 36N 21 48 E
Chernysheyskiy, Russia 29 C12 63 0N 112 30 E
Cherokee, Iowa, U.S.A. 80 D7 42 45N 95 33W
Cherokee, Okla., U.S.A. 81 G5 36 45N 98 21W
Cherokee Village, U.S.A. 81 G9 36 17N 91 30W
Cherokees, Grand Lake O' The, U.S.A. 81 G7 36 28N 95 2W
Cherrapunji, India ... 41 G17 25 17N 91 47 E
Cherry Valley, Calif., U.S.A. 79 M10 33 59N 116 57W
Cherry Valley, N.Y., U.S.A. 85 D10 42 48N 74 45W
Cherskiy, Russia ..... 29 C17 68 45N 161 18 E
Cherskogo Khrebet, Russia 29 C15 65 0N 143 0 E
Cherven, Belarus ..... 17 B15 53 45N 28 28 E
Chervonohrad, Ukraine 17 C13 50 25N 24 10 E
Cherwell →, U.K. 13 F6 51 44N 1 14W
Cherykaw, Belarus ... 17 B16 53 32N 31 20 E
Chesapeake, U.S.A. .. 82 G7 36 50N 76 17W
Chesapeake B., U.S.A. 82 G7 38 0N 76 10W
Cheshire □, U.K. 12 D5 53 14N 2 30W
Cheshskaya Guba, Russia 18 A8 67 20N 47 0 E
Cheshunt, U.K. 13 F7 51 43N 0 1W
Chesil Beach, U.K. ... 13 G5 50 37N 2 33W
Chesley, Canada 84 B3 44 17N 81 5W
Chester, U.K. 12 D5 53 12N 2 53W
Chester, Calif., U.S.A. 76 F3 40 19N 121 14W
Chester, Ill., U.S.A. .. 81 G10 37 55N 89 49W
Chester, Mont., U.S.A. 76 B8 48 31N 110 58W
Chester, Pa., U.S.A. .. 82 F8 39 51N 75 22W
Chester, S.C., U.S.A. . 83 H5 34 43N 81 12W
Chester, W. Va., U.S.A. 84 F4 40 37N 80 34W
Chester-le-Street, U.K. 12 C6 54 51N 1 34W
Chesterfield, U.K. 12 D6 53 15N 1 25W
Chesterfield, Is., N. Cal. 64 J7 19 52S 158 15 E
Chesterfield Inlet, Canada 68 B10 63 30N 90 45W
Chesterton Ra., Australia 63 D4 25 30S 147 27 E
Chestertown, U.S.A. . 85 C11 43 40N 73 48W
Chesuncook L., U.S.A. 83 C11 46 0N 69 21W
Chéticamp, Canada ... 73 C7 46 37N 60 59W
Chetumal, Mexico 87 D7 18 30N 88 20W
Chetumal, B. de, Mexico 87 D7 18 40N 88 10W
Chetwynd, Canada ... 70 B4 55 45N 121 36W
Cheviot, The, U.K. 12 B5 55 29N 2 9W
Cheviot Hills, U.K. ... 12 B5 55 20N 2 30W
Cheviot Ra., Australia 62 D3 25 20S 143 45 E
Chew Bahir, Ethiopia . 47 G2 4 40N 36 50 E
Chewelah, U.S.A. 76 B5 48 17N 117 43W
Chewore □, Zimbabwe 55 F2 16 0S 29 52 E
Cheyenne, Okla., U.S.A. 81 H5 35 37N 99 40W
Cheyenne, Wyo., U.S.A. 80 E2 41 8N 104 49W
Cheyenne →, U.S.A. .. 80 C4 44 41N 101 18W
Cheyenne Wells, U.S.A. 80 F3 38 49N 102 21W
Cheyne B., Australia . 61 F2 34 35S 118 50 E
Chhabra, India .... 42 G7 24 40N 76 54 E
Chhaktala, India ..... 42 H6 22 6N 74 11 E
Chhapra, India .... 43 G11 25 48N 84 44 E
Chhata, India .... 42 F7 27 42N 77 30 E
Chhatarpur, Jharkhand, India 43 G11 24 23N 84 11 E
Chhatarpur, Mad. P., India 43 G8 24 55N 79 35 E
Chhattisgarh □, India 43 J10 22 0N 82 0 E
Chhep, Cambodia .... 38 F5 13 45N 105 24 E
Chhindwara, Mad. P., India 43 H8 22 2N 78 59 E
Chhindwara, Mad. P., India 43 H8 22 2N 78 59 E
Chhlong, Cambodia .. 39 F5 12 15N 105 58 E
Chhota Tawa →, India 42 H7 22 14N 76 36 E
Chhoti Kali Sindh →, India 42 G6 24 2N 75 31 E
Chhuikhadan, India .. 43 J9 21 32N 80 59 E
Chhuk, Cambodia .... 39 G5 10 46N 104 28 E
Chi →, Thailand ...... 38 E5 15 11N 104 43 E
Chiai, Taiwan .... 33 D7 23 29N 120 25 E
Chiamboni, Somali Rep. 52 E8 1 39S 41 35 E
Chiamussu = Jiamusi, China 33 B8 46 40N 130 26 E
Chiang Dao, Thailand 38 C2 19 22N 98 58 E
Chiang Kham, Thailand 38 C3 19 32N 100 18 E
Chiang Khan, Thailand 38 D3 17 52N 101 36 E
Chiang Khong, Thailand 38 B3 20 17N 100 24 E
Chiang Mai, Thailand 38 C2 18 47N 98 59 E
Chiang Rai, Thailand . 38 B3 19 52N 99 50 E
Chiang Saen, Thailand 38 B3 20 16N 100 5 E
Chiapa →, Mexico 87 D6 16 42N 93 0W
Chiapa de Corzo, Mexico 87 D6 16 42N 93 0W
Chiapas □, Mexico ... 87 D6 17 0N 92 45W
Chiautla, Mexico 87 D5 18 18N 98 34W
Chiávari, Italy .... 20 D8 44 19N 9 19 E
Chiavenna, Italy ..... 20 C8 46 19N 9 24 E
Chiba, Japan .... 31 G10 35 30N 140 7 E
Chiba □, Japan .... 31 G10 35 30N 140 20 E
Chibabava, Mozam. .. 57 C5 20 17S 33 35 E
Chibemba, Cunene, Angola 53 H2 15 48S 14 8 E
Chibemba, Huila, Angola 56 B2 16 20S 15 20 E
Chibi, Zimbabwe ..... 55 G3 20 18S 30 25 E
Chibia, Angola .... 53 H2 15 10S 13 42 E
Chibougamau, Canada 72 C5 49 56N 74 24W
Chibougamau, L., Canada 72 C5 49 50N 74 20W
Chibuto, Mozam. ..... 57 C5 24 40S 33 33 E
Chic-Chocs, Mts., Canada 73 C6 48 55N 66 0W
Chicacole = Srikakulam, India 41 K13 18 14N 83 58 E
Chicago, U.S.A. 82 E2 41 52N 87 38W
Chicago Heights, U.S.A. 82 E2 41 30N 87 38W
Chichagof I., U.S.A. .. 68 C6 57 30N 135 30W
Chichén-Itzá, Mexico . 87 C7 20 40N 88 36W
Chicheng, China ..... 34 D8 40 55N 115 55 E
Chichester, U.K. 13 G7 50 50N 0 47W
Chichester Ra., Australia 60 D2 22 12S 119 15 E
Chichibu, Japan ...... 31 F9 35 59N 139 10 E
Chichibu-Tama △, Japan 31 G9 35 52N 138 42 E
Ch'ich'ihaerh = Qiqihar, China 33 B7 47 26N 124 0 E
Chicholi, India .... 42 H8 22 1N 77 40 E
Chickasha, U.S.A. 81 H6 34 26N 97 0W

Chickasha, U.S.A. 81 H6   35 3N 97 58W
Chiclana de la Frontera, Spain . 21 D2   36 26N   6 9W
Chiclayo, Peru 92 E3   6 42S 79 50W
Chico, U.S.A. 78 F5   39 44N 121 50W
Chico →, Chubut, Argentina . . . 96 E3   44 0S 67 0W
Chico →, Santa Cruz, Argentina . 96 G3   50 0S 68 30W
Chicomo, Mozam. . . . . 57 C5   24 31S 34 6 E
Chicomostoc, Mexico 86 C4   22 28N 102 49W
Chicontepec, Mexico 87 C5   20 58N 98 10W
Chicopee, U.S.A. 85 D12   42 9N 72 37W
Chicoutimi, Canada 73 C5   48 28N 71 5W
Chicualacuala, Mozam. . . . . 57 C5   22 6S 31 42 E
Chidambaram, India . . . . 40 P11   11 20N 79 45 E
Chidenguele, Mozam. . . . . 57 C5   24 55S 34 11 E
Chidley, C., Canada 69 B13   60 23N 64 26W
Chiducuane, Mozam. . . . . 57 C5   24 35S 34 25 E
Chiede, Angola . . . . 56 B2   17 15S 16 22 E
Chiefs Pt., Canada 84 B3   44 41N 81 18W
Chiem Hoa, Vietnam . . . . 38 A5   22 12N 105 17 E
Chiemsee, Germany . . . . 16 E7   47 53N 12 28 E
Chiengi, Zambia . . . . 55 D2   8 45S 29 10 E
Chiengmai = Chiang Mai,
   Thailand . . . . 38 C2   18 47N 98 59 E
Chiese →, Italy . . . . 20 D9   45 8N 10 25 E
Chieti, Italy . . . . 22 C6   42 21N 14 10 E
Chifeng, China . . . . 35 C10   42 18N 118 58 E
Chignecto B., Canada 73 C7   45 30N 64 40W
Chiguana, Bolivia 94 A2   21 0S 67 58W
Chigwell, U.K. . . . . 13 F8   51 37N   0 5 E
Chiha-ri, N. Korea . . . . 35 E14   38 40N 126 30 E
Chihli, G. of = Bo Hai, China . . . 35 E10   39 0N 119 0 E
Chihuahua, Mexico 86 B3   28 40N 106 3W
Chihuahua □, Mexico 86 B3   28 40N 106 3W
Chiili = Shieli, Kazakhstan . . . . 28 E7   44 20N 66 15 E
Chik Bollapur, India . . . . 40 N10   13 25N 77 45 E
Chikmagalur, India . . . . 40 N9   13 15N 75 45 E
Chikwawa, Malawi . . . . 55 F3   16 2S 34 50 E
Chilac, Mexico 87 D5   18 20N 97 24W
Chilam Chavki, Pakistan . . . . . . 43 B6   35 5N 75 5 E
Chilanga, Zambia . . . . 55 F2   15 33S 28 16 E
Chilapa, Mexico 87 D5   17 40N 99 11W
Chilas, Pakistan . . . . 43 B6   35 25N 74 5 E
Chilaw, Sri Lanka . . . . 40 R11   7 30N 79 50 E
Chilcotin →, Canada 70 C4   51 44N 122 23W
Childers, Australia . . . . 63 D5   25 15S 152 17 E
Childress, U.S.A. 81 H4   34 25N 100 13W
Chile ■, S. Amer. 96 D2   35 0S 72 0W
Chile Rise, Pac. Oc. 65 L18   38 0S 92 0W
Chilecito, Argentina 94 B2   29 10S 67 30W
Chilete, Peru 92 E3   7 10S 78 50W
Chililabombwe, Zambia . . . . . . 55 E2   12 18S 27 43 E
Chilin = Jilin, China . . . . 35 C14   43 44N 126 30 E
Chilka L., India . . . . 41 K14   19 40N 85 25 E
Chilko →, Canada 70 C4   52 0N 123 40W
Chilko L., Canada 70 C4   51 20N 124 10W
Chillagoe, Australia . . . . 62 B3   17 7S 144 33 E
Chillán, Chile 94 D1   36 40S 72 10W
Chillicothe, Ill., U.S.A. 80 E10   40 55N 89 29W
Chillicothe, Mo., U.S.A. 80 F8   39 48N 93 33W
Chillicothe, Ohio, U.S.A. 82 F4   39 20N 82 59W
Chilliwack, Canada 70 D4   49 10N 121 54W
Chilo, India . . . . 42 F5   27 25N 73 32 E
Chiloane, I., Mozam. . . . . 57 C5   20 40S 34 55 E
Chiloé, I. de, Chile 96 E2   42 30S 73 50W
Chilpancingo, Mexico 87 D5   17 30N 99 30W
Chiltern Hills, U.K. 13 F7   51 40N   0 53W
Chilton, U.S.A. 82 C1   44 2N 88 10W
Chilubi, Zambia . . . . 55 E2   11 5S 29 58 E
Chilubula, Zambia . . . . 55 E3   10 14S 30 51 E
Chilumba, Malawi . . . . 55 E3   10 28S 34 12 E
Chilung, Taiwan . . . . 33 D7   25 3N 121 45 E
Chilwa, L., Malawi . . . . 55 F4   15 15S 35 40 E
Chimaltitán, Mexico 86 C4   21 46N 103 50W
Chimán, Panama 88 E4   8 45N 78 40W
Chimanimani, Zimbabwe . . . . . . 57 B5   19 48S 32 52 E
Chimanimani △, Zimbabwe . . . . 57 B5   19 48S 33 0 E
Chimay, Belgium . . . . 15 D4   50 3N   4 20 E
Chimayo, U.S.A. 77 H11   36 0N 105 56W
Chimbay, Uzbekistan . . . . 28 E6   42 57N 59 47 E
Chimborazo, Ecuador 92 D3   1 29S 78 55W
Chimbote, Peru 92 E3   9 0S 78 35W
Chimkent = Shymkent,
   Kazakhstan . . . . 28 E7   42 18N 69 36 E
Chimoio, Mozam. . . . . 55 F3   19 4S 33 30 E
Chimpembe, Zambia . . . . 55 D2   9 31S 29 33 E
Chin □, Burma . . . . 41 J18   22 0N 93 0 E
Chin Ling Shan = Qinling Shandi,
   China . . . . 34 H5   33 50N 108 10 E
China, Mexico 87 B5   25 40N 99 20W
China ■, Asia . . . . 33 C6   30 0N 110 0 E
China Lake, U.S.A. 79 K9   35 44N 117 37W
Chinan = Jinan, China . . . . 34 F9   36 38N 117 1 E
Chinandega, Nic. 88 D2   12 35N 87 12W
Chinati Peak, U.S.A. 81 L2   29 57N 104 29W
Chincha Alta, Peru 92 F3   13 25S 76 7W
Chinchaga →, Canada 70 B5   58 53N 118 20W
Chinchilla, Australia . . . . 63 D5   26 45S 150 38 E
Chinchorro, Banco, Mexico 87 D7   18 35N 87 20W
Chinchou = Jinzhou, China . . . . 35 D11   41 5N 121 3 E
Chincoteague, U.S.A. 82 G8   37 56N 75 23W
Chinde, Mozam. . . . . 55 F4   18 35S 36 30 E
Chindo, S. Korea . . . . 35 G14   34 28N 126 15 E
Chindwin →, Burma . . . . 41 J19   21 26N 95 15 E
Chineni, India . . . . 43 C6   33 2N 75 15 E
Chinga, Mozam. . . . . 55 F4   15 13S 38 35 E
Chingola, Zambia . . . . 55 E2   12 31S 27 53 E
Chingole, Malawi . . . . 55 E3   13 4S 34 17 E
Ch'ingtao = Qingdao, China . . . . 35 F11   36 5N 120 20 E
Chinguetti, Mauritania 50 D3   20 25N 12 24W
Chingune, Mozam. . . . . 57 C5   20 33S 34 58 E
Chinhae, S. Korea . . . . 35 G15   35 9N 128 47 E
Chinhanguanine, Mozam. . . . . . 57 D5   25 21S 32 30 E
Chinhoyi, Zimbabwe . . . . 55 F3   17 20S 30 8 E
Chini, India . . . . 42 D8   31 32N 78 15 E
Chiniot, Pakistan . . . . 42 D5   31 45N 73 0 E
Chinipas, Mexico 86 B3   27 22N 108 32W
Chinji, Pakistan . . . . 42 C5   32 42N 72 22 E
Chinju, S. Korea . . . . 35 G15   35 12N 128 2 E
Chinle, U.S.A. 77 H9   36 9N 109 33W
Chinnampo = Namp'o, N. Korea . 35 E13   38 52N 125 10 E
Chino, Japan . . . . 31 G9   35 59N 138 9 E
Chino, U.S.A. 79 L9   34 1N 117 41W
Chino Valley, U.S.A. 77 J7   34 45N 112 27W
Chinon, France . . . . 20 C4   47 10N   0 15 E
Chinook, U.S.A. 76 B9   48 35N 109 14W
Chinsali, Zambia . . . . 55 E3   10 30S 32 2 E
Chióggia, Italy . . . . 22 B5   45 13N 12 17 E
Chíos = Khíos, Greece . . . . . . 23 E12   38 27N 26 9 E

Chipata, Zambia . . . . 55 E3   13 38S 32 28 E
Chipinge, Zimbabwe . . . . 55 G3   20 13S 32 28 E
Chipinge △, Zimbabwe . . . . . . 55 G3   20 14S 33 0 E
Chipley, U.S.A. 83 K3   30 47N 85 32W
Chipman, Canada 73 C6   46 6N 65 53W
Chipoka, Malawi . . . . 55 E3   13 57S 34 28 E
Chippenham, U.K. 13 F5   51 27N   2 6W
Chippewa →, U.S.A. 80 C8   44 25N 92 5W
Chippewa Falls, U.S.A. 80 C9   44 56N 91 24W
Chipping Norton, U.K. 13 F6   51 56N   1 32W
Chiputneticook Lakes, U.S.A. . . . 83 C11   45 35N 67 35W
Chiquián, Peru 92 F3   10 10S 77 0W
Chiquibul △, Belize 88 C2   16 49N 88 52W
Chiquimula, Guatemala 88 D2   14 51N 89 37W
Chiquinquira, Colombia 92 B4   5 37N 73 50W
Chirala, India . . . . 40 M12   15 50N 80 26 E
Chiramba, Mozam. . . . . 55 F3   16 55S 34 39 E
Chirawa, India . . . . 42 E6   28 14N 75 42 E
Chirchiq, Uzbekistan . . . . 28 E7   41 29N 69 35 E
Chiredzi, Zimbabwe . . . . 57 C5   21 0S 31 38 E
Chiricahua →, U.S.A. 77 K9   32 0N 109 20W
Chiricahua Peak, U.S.A. 77 L9   31 51N 109 18W
Chiriquí, G. de, Panama 88 E3   8 0N 82 10W
Chiriquí, L. de, Panama 88 E3   9 10N 82 0W
Chirisa △, Zimbabwe . . . . 55 F2   17 53S 28 15 E
Chirivira Falls, Zimbabwe . . . . . 55 G3   21 10S 32 12 E
Chirmiri, India . . . . 41 H13   23 15N 82 20 E
Chirripó Grande, Cerro,
   Costa Rica 88 E3   9 29N 83 29W
Chirundu, Zimbabwe . . . . 55 F2   16 3S 28 50 E
Chisamba, Zambia . . . . 55 E2   14 55S 28 0 E
Chisapani Garhi, Nepal . . . . . . 41 F14   27 30N 84 2 E
Chisasibi, Canada 72 B4   53 50N 79 0W
Chisholm, Canada 70 C6   54 55N 114 10W
Chisholm, U.S.A. 80 B8   47 29N 92 53W
Chishtian Mandi, Pakistan . . . . . 42 E5   29 50N 72 55 E
Chisimba Falls, Zambia . . . . . . 55 E3   10 12S 30 56 E
Chisimaio, Somali Rep. . . . . . . 49 G8   0 22S 42 32 E
Chişinău, Moldova . . . . 17 E15   47 2N 28 50 E
Chisos Mts., U.S.A. 81 L3   29 5N 103 15W
Chistopol, Russia . . . . 18 C9   55 25N 50 38 E
Chita, Russia . . . . 29 D12   52 0N 113 35 E
Chitose, Japan . . . . 30 C10   42 49N 141 39 E
Chitral, Pakistan . . . . 40 B7   35 50N 71 56 E
Chitré, Panama 88 E3   7 59N 80 27W
Chittagong, Bangla. . . . . 41 H17   22 19N 91 48 E
Chittagong □, Bangla. . . . . 41 G17   24 5N 91 0 E
Chittaurgarh, India . . . . 42 G6   24 52N 74 38 E
Chittoor, India . . . . 40 N11   13 15N 79 5 E
Chitungwiza, Zimbabwe . . . . . . 55 F3   18 0S 31 6 E
Chiusi, Italy . . . . 22 C4   43 1N 11 57 E
Chivasso, Italy . . . . 20 D7   45 11N   7 53 E
Chivhu, Zimbabwe . . . . 55 F3   19 2S 30 52 E
Chivilcoy, Argentina 94 C4   34 55S 60 0W
Chiwanda, Tanzania . . . . 55 E3   11 23S 34 55 E
Chizarira, Zimbabwe . . . . 55 F2   17 36S 27 45 E
Chizarira △, Zimbabwe . . . . . . 55 F2   17 44S 27 52 E
Chizera, Zambia . . . . 55 E2   13 10S 25 0 E
Chkalov = Orenburg, Russia . . . 18 D10   51 45N 55 6 E
Chloride, U.S.A. 79 K12   35 25N 114 12W
Cho Bo, Vietnam . . . . 38 B5   20 46N 105 10 E
Cho-do, N. Korea . . . . 35 E13   38 30N 124 40 E
Cho Phuoc Hai, Vietnam . . . . . . 39 G6   10 26N 107 18 E
Choa Chu Kang, Singapore . . . . 39 d   1 22N 103 41 E
Choba, Kenya . . . . 54 B4   2 30N 38 5 E
Chobe △, Botswana . . . . 56 B4   18 37S 24 23 E
Choch'iwŏn, S. Korea . . . . 35 F14   36 37N 127 18 E
Chocolate Mts., U.S.A. 79 M11   33 15N 115 15W
Choctawhatchee →, U.S.A. 83 K3   30 25N 86 8W
Choele Choel, Argentina 96 D3   39 11S 65 40W
Choiseul, St. Lucia . . . . 89 f   13 47N 61 3W
Choix, Mexico 86 B3   26 40N 108 23W
Chojnice, Poland . . . . 17 B9   53 42N 17 32 E
Chōkai-San, Japan . . . . 30 E10   39 6N 140 3 E
Choke Canyon L., U.S.A. 81 L5   28 30N 98 20W
Chokurdakh, Russia . . . . 29 B15   70 38N 147 55 E
Cholame, U.S.A. 78 K6   35 44N 120 18W
Cholet, France 20 C3   47 4N   0 52W
Choluteca, Honduras 88 D2   13 20N 87 14W
Choluteca →, Honduras 88 D2   13 0N 87 20W
Chom Bung, Thailand . . . . 38 F2   13 37N 99 36 E
Chom Thong, Thailand . . . . 38 C2   18 25N 98 41 E
Choma, Zambia . . . . 55 F2   16 48S 26 59 E
Chomolungma = Everest, Mt.,
   Nepal . . . . 43 E12   28 5N 86 58 E
Chomun, India . . . . 42 F6   27 15N 75 40 E
Chomutov, Czech Rep. . . . . . . 16 C7   50 28N 13 23 E
Chon Buri, Thailand . . . . 38 F3   13 21N 101 1 E
Chon Thanh, Vietnam . . . . 39 G6   11 24N 106 36 E
Ch'onan, S. Korea . . . . 35 F14   36 48N 127 9 E
Chone, Ecuador 92 D3   0 40S 80 0W
Chong Kai, Cambodia . . . . 38 F4   13 57N 103 35 E
Chong Mek, Thailand . . . . 38 E5   15 10N 105 27 E
Chong Phangan, Thailand . . . . . 39 b   9 39N 100 0 E
Chong Samui, Thailand . . . . . . 39 b   9 29N 99 50 E
Chŏngdo, S. Korea . . . . 35 G15   35 38N 128 42 E
Chŏngha, S. Korea . . . . 35 F15   36 12N 129 21 E
Chŏngju, N. Korea . . . . 35 D15   41 47N 129 50 E
Chŏngju, S. Korea . . . . 35 F14   36 39N 127 27 E
Chŏngjin, N. Korea . . . . 35 F14   35 35N 128 2 E
Chongli, China . . . . 34 D8   40 58N 115 15 E
Chongqing, China . . . . 32 D5   29 35N 106 25 E
Chongqing Shi □, China . . . . . . 32 C5   30 0N 108 0 E
Chongoene, Mozam. . . . . 57 C5   25 3S 33 49 E
Chŏngŭp, S. Korea . . . . 35 G14   35 35N 126 50 E
Chonos, Arch. de los, Chile 96 F2   45 0S 75 0W
Chop, Ukraine . . . . 17 D12   48 26N 22 12 E
Chopim →, Brazil 95 B5   25 35S 53 5W
Chor, Pakistan . . . . 42 G3   25 31N 69 46 E
Chorbat La, India . . . . 43 B7   34 42N 76 37 E
Chorley, U.K. 12 D5   53 39N   2 38W
Chornobyl, Ukraine . . . . 17 C16   51 20N 30 15 E
Chorolque, Cerro, Bolivia 94 A2   20 59S 66 5W
Chorregon, Australia . . . . 62 C3   22 40S 143 32 E
Chorro el Indio △, Venezuela . . . 89 E5   7 43N 72 9W
Chortkiv, Ukraine . . . . 17 D13   49 2N 25 46 E
Ch'ŏrwon, S. Korea . . . . 35 E14   38 15N 127 10 E
Chos-Malal, Argentina 94 D1   37 20S 70 15W
Ch'osan, N. Korea . . . . 35 D13   40 50N 125 47 E
Choszczno, Poland . . . . 16 B8   53 7N 15 25 E
Choteau, U.S.A. 76 C7   47 49N 112 11W
Chotila, India . . . . 42 H4   22 23N 71 15 E
Chotta Udepur, India . . . . 42 H6   22 19N 74 1 E
Chowchilla, U.S.A. 78 H6   37 7N 120 16W

Choybalsan, Mongolia . . . . 33 B6   48 4N 114 30 E
Christchurch, N.Z. . . . . 59 K4   43 33S 172 47 E
Christchurch, U.K. 13 G6   50 44N   1 47W
Christian I., Canada 84 B4   44 50N 80 12W
Christiana, S. Africa . . . . 56 D4   27 52S 25 8 E
Christiansted, U.S. Virgin Is. . . . 89 C7   17 45N 64 42W
Christie B., Canada 71 A6   62 32N 111 10W
Christina →, Canada 71 B6   56 40N 111 3W
Christmas Cr. →, Australia . . . . 60 C4   18 29S 125 23 E
Christmas I. = Kiritimati, Kiribati . 65 G12   1 58N 157 27W
Christmas I., Ind. Oc. . . . . 64 J2   10 30S 105 40 E
Christopher L., Australia . . . . . . 61 D4   24 49S 127 42 E
Chtimba, Malawi . . . . 55 E3   10 35S 34 13 E
Chū = Shū, Kazakhstan . . . . . . 28 E8   43 36N 73 42 E
Chū = Shū →, Kazakhstan . . . . 28 E10   45 0N 67 44 E
Chu →, Vietnam . . . . 38 C5   19 53N 105 45 E
Chu Lai, Vietnam . . . . 38 E7   15 28N 108 45 E
Chuak, Ko, Thailand . . . . 39 b   9 28N 99 41 E
Ch'uanchou = Quanzhou, China . 34 G6   34 20N 110 59 E
Chuankou, China . . . . 34 G6   34 20N 110 59 E
Chubbuck, U.S.A. 76 E7   42 55N 112 28W
Chūbu □, Japan . . . . 31 F8   36 45N 137 30 E
Chubu-Sangaku △, Japan . . . . . 31 F8   36 30N 137 40 E
Chubut →, Argentina 96 E3   43 20S 65 5W
Chuchi L., Canada 70 B4   55 12N 124 30W
Chuda, India . . . . 42 H4   22 29N 71 41 E
Chudskoye, Ozero, Russia . . . . 9 G22   58 13N 27 30 E
Chūgoku □, Japan . . . . 31 G6   35 0N 133 0 E
Chūgoku-Sanchi, Japan . . . . . . 31 G6   35 0N 133 0 E
Chugwater, U.S.A. 76 E2   41 46N 104 50W
Chukchi Sea, Russia 29 C19   68 0N 175 0W
Chukotskoye Nagorye, Russia . . 29 C18   68 0N 175 0 E
Chula Vista, U.S.A. 79 N9   32 39N 117 5W
Chulucanas, Peru 92 E2   5 8S 80 10W
Chulym →, Russia . . . . 28 D9   57 43N 83 51 E
Chum Phae, Thailand . . . . 38 D4   16 40N 102 6 E
Chum Saeng, Thailand . . . . . . 38 E3   15 55N 100 15 E
Chumar, India . . . . 43 C8   32 40N 78 35 E
Chumbicha, Argentina 94 B2   29 0S 66 10W
Chumikan, Russia . . . . 29 D14   54 40N 135 10 E
Chumphon, Thailand . . . . 39 G2   10 35N 99 14 E
Chumuare, Mozam. . . . . 55 E3   14 31S 31 50 E
Chumunjin, S. Korea . . . . 35 F15   37 55N 128 54 E
Chuna →, Russia . . . . 29 D10   57 47N 94 37 E
Ch'unch'ŏn, S. Korea . . . . 35 F14   37 58N 127 44 E
Chunchura, India . . . . 43 H13   22 53N 88 27 E
Chunga, Zambia . . . . 55 F2   15 0S 26 2 E
Chunggang-ŭp, N. Korea . . . . . 35 D14   41 48N 126 48 E
Chunghwa, N. Korea . . . . 35 E13   38 52N 125 47 E
Ch'ungju, S. Korea . . . . 35 F14   36 58N 127 58 E
Chungking = Chongqing, China . 32 D5   29 35N 106 25 E
Ch'ungmu, S. Korea . . . . 35 G15   34 50N 128 20 E
Chungt'iaoshan = Zhongtiao
   Shan, China . . . . 34 G6   35 0N 111 10 E
Chunian, Pakistan . . . . 42 D6   30 57N 74 0 E
Chunya, Tanzania . . . . 55 D3   8 30S 33 27 E
Chunyang, China . . . . 35 C15   43 38N 129 23 E
Chupara Pt., Trin. & Tob. 93 K15   10 49N 61 22W
Chuquibamba, Peru 92 G4   15 47S 72 44W
Chuquicamata, Chile 94 A2   22 15S 69 0W
Chur, Switz. . . . . 20 C8   46 52N   9 32 E
Churachandpur, India . . . . 41 G18   24 20N 93 40 E
Church Stretton, U.K. 13 E5   52 32N   2 48W
Churchill, Canada 71 B10   58 47N 94 11W
Churchill →, Man., Canada 71 B10   58 47N 94 12W
Churchill →, Nfld. & L., Canada . 73 B7   53 19N 60 10W
Churchill, C., Canada 71 B10   58 46N 93 12W
Churchill Falls, Canada 73 B7   53 36N 64 19W
Churchill L., Canada 71 B7   55 55N 108 20W
Churchill Pk., Canada 70 B3   58 10N 125 10W
Churki, India . . . . 43 H10   23 50N 83 12 E
Churu, India . . . . 42 E6   28 20N 74 50 E
Churún Merú = Angel Falls,
   Venezuela 92 B6   5 57N 62 30W
Chushal, India . . . . 43 C8   33 40N 78 40 E
Chuska Mts., U.S.A. 77 H9   36 15N 108 50W
Chusovoy, Russia . . . . 18 C10   58 22N 57 50 E
Chute-aux-Outardes, Canada . . . 73 C6   49 7N 68 24W
Chuuronjang, N. Korea . . . . . . 35 D15   41 35N 129 40 E
Chuvash Republic =
   Chuvashia □, Russia . . . . . 18 C8   55 30N 47 0 E
Chuvashia □, Russia . . . . 18 C8   55 30N 47 0 E
Chuwārtah, Iraq . . . . 44 C5   35 43N 45 34 E
Chuy, Uruguay 95 C5   33 41S 53 27W
Ci Xian, China . . . . 34 F8   36 20N 114 25 E
Ciadâr-Lunga, Moldova . . . . . . 17 E15   46 3N 28 51 E
Ciamis, Indonesia . . . . 37 G13   7 20S 108 21 E
Cianjur, Indonesia . . . . 37 G12   6 49S 107 8 E
Cianorte, Brazil 95 A5   23 37S 52 37W
Cibola, U.S.A. 79 M12   33 17N 114 42W
Cicero, U.S.A. 82 E2   41 51N 87 45W
Ciéagas del Cataumbo △,
   Venezuela 89 E5   9 25N 71 54W
Ciechanów, Poland . . . . 17 B11   52 52N 20 38 E
Ciego de Avila, Cuba 88 B4   21 50N 78 50W
Ciénaga, Colombia 92 A4   11 1N 74 15W
Cienfuegos, Cuba 88 B3   22 10N 80 30W
Cieszyn, Poland . . . . 17 D10   49 45N 18 35 E
Cieza, Spain 21 C5   38 17N   1 23W
Cihuatlán, Mexico 86 D4   19 14N 104 35W
Cijara, Embalse de, Spain 21 C3   39 18N   4 52W
Cijulang, Indonesia . . . . 37 G13   7 43S 108 0 E
Cilacap, Indonesia . . . . 37 G13   7 43S 109 0 E
Cill Chainnigh = Kilkenny, Ireland 10 D4   52 39N   7 15W
Cilo Dağı, Turkey . . . . 19 G7   37 28N 43 55 E
Cima, U.S.A. 79 K11   35 14N 115 30W
Cimarron, Kans., U.S.A. 81 G4   37 48N 100 21W
Cimarron, N. Mex., U.S.A. 81 G2   36 31N 104 55W
Cimarron →, U.S.A. 81 G6   36 10N 96 17W
Cimişlia, Moldova . . . . 17 E15   46 34N 28 44 E
Cimone, Mte., Italy . . . . 22 B4   44 12N 10 42 E
Cinca →, Spain . . . . 21 B6   41 26N   0 21 E
Cincar, Bos.-H. . . . . 22 C7   43 55N 17 5 E
Cincinnati, U.S.A. 81 F3   39 6N 84 31W
Cincinnatus, U.S.A. 85 D9   42 33N 75 54W
Çine, Turkey . . . . 23 F13   37 37N 28 2 E
Ciney, Belgium . . . . 15 D5   50 18N   5 5 E
Cinto, Mte., France . . . . 20 E8   42 24N   8 54 E
Circle, Alaska, U.S.A. 68 B5   65 50N 144 4W
Circle, Mont., U.S.A. 80 B2   47 25N 105 35W
Circleville, U.S.A. 82 F4   39 36N 82 57W
Cirebon, Indonesia . . . . 36 F3   6 45S 108 32 E
Ciremay, Indonesia . . . . 37 G13   6 53S 108 24 E
Cirencester, U.K. 13 F6   51 43N   1 57W
Cirium, Cyprus . . . . 25 E11   34 40N 32 53 E
Cisco, U.S.A. 81 J5   32 23N 98 59W
Citlaltépetl = Orizaba, Pico de,
   Mexico 87 D5   19 0N 97 20W

Citrus Heights, U.S.A. 78 G5   38 42N 121 17W
Citrusdal, S. Africa . . . . 56 E2   32 35S 19 0 E
Città di Castello, Italy . . . . 22 C5   43 27N 12 14 E
Ciudad Altamirano, Mexico 86 D4   18 20N 100 40W
Ciudad Bolívar, Venezuela 92 B6   8 5N 63 36W
Ciudad Camargo, Mexico 86 B3   27 41N 105 10W
Ciudad de Valles, Mexico 87 C5   22 0N 99 0W
Ciudad del Carmen, Mexico 87 D6   18 38N 91 50W
Ciudad del Este, Paraguay 95 B5   25 30S 54 50W
Ciudad Delicias = Delicias,
   Mexico 86 B3   28 10N 105 30W
Ciudad Guayana, Venezuela . . . 92 B6   8 0N 62 30W
Ciudad Guerrero, Mexico 86 B3   28 33N 107 28W
Ciudad Guzmán, Mexico 86 D4   19 40N 103 30W
Ciudad Juárez, Mexico 86 A3   31 40N 106 28W
Ciudad Madero, Mexico 87 C5   22 19N 97 50W
Ciudad Mante, Mexico 87 C5   22 50N 99 0W
Ciudad Obregón, Mexico 86 B3   27 28N 109 59W
Ciudad Real, Spain 21 C4   38 59N   3 55W
Ciudad Rodrigo, Spain 21 B2   40 35N   6 32W
Ciudad Victoria, Mexico 87 C5   23 41N 99 9W
Ciudadela, Spain . . . . 24 B10   40 0N   3 50 E
Civitanova Marche, Italy . . . . . . 22 C5   43 18N 13 44 E
Civitavécchia, Italy . . . . 22 C4   42 6N 11 48 E
Cizre, Turkey . . . . 19 G7   37 19N 42 10 E
Clackmannanshire □, U.K. 11 E5   56 10N   3 43W
Clacton-on-Sea, U.K. . . . . 13 F9   51 47N   1 11 E
Claire, L., Canada 70 B6   58 35N 112 5W
Clairton, U.S.A. 84 F5   40 18N 79 53W
Clallam Bay, U.S.A. 78 B2   48 15N 124 16W
Clanton, U.S.A. 83 J2   32 51N 86 38W
Clanwilliam, S. Africa . . . . 56 E2   32 11S 18 52 E
Clara, Ireland 10 C4   53 21N   7 37W
Claraville, U.S.A. 79 K8   35 24N 118 20W
Clare, Australia . . . . 63 E2   33 50S 138 37 E
Clare, U.S.A. 82 D3   43 49N 84 46W
Clare □, Ireland 10 D3   52 45N   9 0W
Clare →, Ireland 10 C2   53 20N   9 2W
Clare I., Ireland 10 C1   53 49N 10 0W
Claremont, Calif., U.S.A. 79 L9   34 6N 117 43W
Claremont, N.H., U.S.A. 85 C12   43 23N 72 20W
Claremont Pt., Australia . . . . . . 62 A3   14 1S 143 41 E
Claremore, U.S.A. 81 G7   36 19N 95 36W
Claremorris, Ireland 10 C3   53 45N   9 0W
Clarence →, Australia . . . . 63 D5   29 25S 153 22 E
Clarence →, N.Z. . . . . 59 K4   42 10S 173 56 E
Clarence, I., Chile 96 G2   54 0S 72 0W
Clarence I., Antarctica 5 C18   61 10S 54 0W
Clarence Str., Australia . . . . . . 60 B5   12 0S 131 0 E
Clarence Town, Bahamas 89 B5   23 6N 74 59W
Clarendon, Pa., U.S.A. 84 E5   41 47N 79 6W
Clarendon, Tex., U.S.A. 81 H4   34 56N 100 53W
Clarenville-Shoal Harbour,
   Canada 73 C9   48 10N 54 1W
Claresholm, Canada 70 D6   50 2N 113 33W
Clarie Coast, Antarctica . . . . . . 5 C9   68 0S 135 0 E
Clarinda, U.S.A. 80 E7   40 44N 95 2W
Clarion, Iowa, U.S.A. 80 D8   42 44N 93 44W
Clarion, Pa., U.S.A. 84 E5   41 13N 79 23W
Clarion →, U.S.A. 84 E5   41 7N 79 41W
Clark, U.S.A. 80 C6   44 53N 97 44W
Clark, Pt., Canada 84 B3   44 4N 81 45W
Clark Fork, U.S.A. 76 B5   48 9N 116 11W
Clark Fork →, U.S.A. 76 B5   48 9N 116 15W
Clarkdale, U.S.A. 77 J7   34 46N 112 3W
Clarke City, Canada 73 B6   50 12N 66 38W
Clarke I., Australia . . . . 63 G4   40 32S 148 10 E
Clarke Ra., Australia . . . . 62 J6   20 40S 148 30 E
Clark's Fork →, U.S.A. 76 D9   45 39N 108 43W
Clark's Harbour, Canada 73 D6   43 25N 65 38W
Clarks Hill L., U.S.A. 83 J4   33 40N 82 12W
Clarks Summit, U.S.A. 85 E9   41 29N 75 42W
Clarksburg, U.S.A. 82 F5   39 17N 80 30W
Clarksdale, U.S.A. 81 H9   34 12N 90 35W
Clarksville, Ark., U.S.A. 81 H8   35 28N 93 28W
Clarksville, Tenn., U.S.A. 83 G2   36 32N 87 21W
Clarksville, Tex., U.S.A. 81 J7   33 37N 95 3W
Clatskanie, U.S.A. 78 D3   46 6N 123 12W
Claude, U.S.A. 81 H4   35 7N 101 22W
Claveria, Phil. . . . . 37 A6   18 37N 121 4 E
Clay, U.S.A. 78 G5   38 17N 121 10W
Clay Center, U.S.A. 80 F6   39 23N 97 8W
Claypool, U.S.A. 77 K8   33 25N 110 51W
Claysburg, U.S.A. 84 F6   40 17N 78 27W
Claysville, U.S.A. 84 F4   40 7N 80 25W
Clayton, N. Mex., U.S.A. 81 G3   36 27N 103 11W
Clayton, N.Y., U.S.A. 85 B8   44 14N 76 5W
Clear, C., Ireland 10 E2   51 25N   9 32W
Clear, L., Canada 84 A7   45 26N 77 12W
Clear Hills, Canada 70 B5   56 40N 119 30W
Clear I., Ireland 78 F4   39 2N 122 47W
Clear Lake, Iowa, U.S.A. 80 D8   43 8N 93 23W
Clear Lake, S. Dak., U.S.A. 80 C6   44 45N 96 41W
Clear Lake Reservoir, U.S.A. . . . 76 F3   41 56N 121 5W
Clearfield, Pa., U.S.A. 84 E6   41 2N 78 27W
Clearfield, Utah, U.S.A. 76 F8   41 7N 112 2W
Clearlake, U.S.A. 76 G2   38 57N 122 38W
Clearlake Highlands, U.S.A. 78 G4   38 57N 122 38W
Clearwater, Canada 70 C4   51 38N 120 2W
Clearwater, U.S.A. 83 M4   27 58N 82 48W
Clearwater →, Alta., Canada . . . 70 C6   52 22N 114 57W
Clearwater →, Alta., Canada . . . 70 B6   56 44N 111 23W
Clearwater L., Canada 71 C9   53 34N 99 49W
Clearwater Lake △, Canada 71 C8   54 0N 101 0W
Clearwater Mts., U.S.A. 76 C6   46 5N 115 20W
Clearwater River △, Canada . . . 71 B7   56 55N 109 10W
Cleburne, U.S.A. 81 J6   32 21N 97 23W
Clee Hills, U.K. 13 E5   52 26N   2 35W
Cleethorpes, U.K. 12 D7   53 33N   0 3W
Cleeve Cloud, U.K. 13 F6   51 56N   2 0W
Clemson, U.S.A. 83 H4   34 41N 82 50W
Clerke Reef, Australia . . . . 60 C2   17 22S 119 20 E
Clermont, Australia . . . . 62 C4   22 49S 147 39 E
Clermont, U.S.A. 83 L5   28 33N 81 46W
Clermont-Ferrand, France . . . . . 20 D5   45 46N   3 4 E
Clervaux, Lux. . . . . 15 D6   50 4N   6 2 E
Cleveland, Miss., U.S.A. 81 J9   33 45N 90 43W
Cleveland, Ohio, U.S.A. 84 E3   41 30N 81 42W
Cleveland, Okla., U.S.A. 81 G6   36 19N 96 28W
Cleveland, Tenn., U.S.A. 83 H3   35 10N 84 53W
Cleveland, Tex., U.S.A. 81 K7   30 21N 95 5W
Cleveland, C., Australia . . . . . . 62 B4   19 11S 147 1 E
Cleveland, Mt., U.S.A. 76 B7   48 56N 113 51W
Cleveland Heights, U.S.A. 84 E3   41 30N 81 34W
Cleve150lândia, Brazil 95 B5   26 24S 52 23W

Clew B., Ireland ... 10 C2 53 50N 9 49W
Clewiston, U.S.A. ... 83 M5 26 45N 80 56W
Clifden, Ireland ... 10 C1 53 29N 10 1W
Clifden, N.Z. ... 59 M1 46 1S 167 42 E
Cliffdell, U.S.A. ... 78 D5 46 56N 121 5W
Cliffy Hd., Australia ... 61 G2 35 1S 116 29 E
Clifton, Australia ... 63 D5 27 59S 151 53 E
Clifton, Ariz., U.S.A. ... 77 K9 33 3N 109 18W
Clifton, Colo., U.S.A. ... 77 G9 39 7N 108 25W
Clifton, Tex., U.S.A. ... 81 K6 31 47N 97 35W
Clifton Beach, Australia ... 62 B4 16 46S 145 39 E
Climax, Canada ... 71 D7 49 10N 108 20W
Clinch →, U.S.A. ... 83 H3 35 53N 84 29W
Clingmans Dome, U.S.A. ... 83 H4 35 34N 83 30W
Clint, U.S.A. ... 77 L10 31 35N 106 14W
Clinton, B.C., Canada ... 70 C4 51 6N 121 35W
Clinton, Ont., Canada ... 84 C3 43 37N 81 32W
Clinton, N.Z. ... 59 M2 46 12S 169 23 E
Clinton, Ark., U.S.A. ... 81 H8 35 36N 92 28W
Clinton, Conn., U.S.A. ... 85 E12 41 17N 72 32W
Clinton, Ill., U.S.A. ... 80 E10 40 9N 88 57W
Clinton, Ind., U.S.A. ... 82 F2 39 40N 87 24W
Clinton, Iowa, U.S.A. ... 80 E9 41 51N 90 12W
Clinton, Mass., U.S.A. ... 85 D13 42 25N 71 41W
Clinton, Miss., U.S.A. ... 81 J9 32 20N 90 20W
Clinton, Mo., U.S.A. ... 80 F8 38 22N 93 46W
Clinton, N.C., U.S.A. ... 83 H6 35 0N 78 22W
Clinton, Okla., U.S.A. ... 81 H5 35 31N 98 58W
Clinton, S.C., U.S.A. ... 83 H5 34 29N 81 53W
Clinton, Tenn., U.S.A. ... 83 G3 36 6N 84 8W
Clinton, Wash., U.S.A. ... 78 C4 47 59N 122 21W
Clinton C., Australia ... 62 C5 22 30S 150 45 E
Clinton Colden L., Canada ... 68 B9 63 58N 107 27W
Clintonville, U.S.A. ... 80 C10 44 37N 88 46W
Clipperton, I., Pac. Oc. ... 65 F17 10 18N 109 13W
Clisham, U.K. ... 11 D2 57 57N 6 49W
Clitheroe, U.K. ... 12 D5 53 53N 2 22W
Clo-oose, Canada ... 78 B2 48 39N 124 49W
Cloates, Pt., Australia ... 60 D1 22 43S 113 40 E
Clocolan, S. Africa ... 57 D4 28 55S 27 34 E
Clodomira, Argentina ... 94 B3 27 35S 64 14W
Clogher Hd., Ireland ... 10 C5 53 48N 6 14W
Clonakilty, Ireland ... 10 E3 51 37N 8 53W
Clonakilty B., Ireland ... 10 E3 51 35N 8 51W
Cloncurry, Australia ... 62 C3 20 40S 140 28 E
Cloncurry →, Australia ... 62 B3 18 37S 140 40 E
Clondalkin, Ireland ... 10 C5 53 19N 6 25W
Clones, Ireland ... 10 B4 54 11N 7 15W
Clonmel, Ireland ... 10 D4 52 21N 7 42W
Cloquet, U.S.A. ... 80 B8 46 43N 92 28W
Clorinda, Argentina ... 94 B4 25 16S 57 45W
Cloud Bay, Canada ... 72 C2 48 5N 89 26W
Cloud Peak, U.S.A. ... 76 D10 44 23N 107 11W
Cloudcroft, U.S.A. ... 77 K11 32 58N 105 45W
Cloverdale, U.S.A. ... 78 G4 38 48N 123 1W
Clovis, Calif., U.S.A. ... 78 J7 36 49N 119 42W
Clovis, N. Mex., U.S.A. ... 81 H3 34 24N 103 12W
Cloyne, Canada ... 84 B7 44 49N 77 11W
Cluj-Napoca, Romania ... 17 E12 46 47N 23 38 E
Clunes, Australia ... 63 F3 37 20S 143 45 E
Clutha →, N.Z. ... 59 M2 46 20S 169 49 E
Clwyd →, U.K. ... 12 D4 53 19N 3 31W
Clyde, Canada ... 70 C6 54 9N 113 39W
Clyde, N.Z. ... 59 L2 45 12S 169 20 E
Clyde, U.S.A. ... 84 C8 43 5N 76 52W
Clyde →, U.K. ... 11 F4 55 55N 4 30W
Clyde, Firth of, U.K. ... 11 F3 55 22N 5 1W
Clyde Muirshiel △, U.K. ... 11 F4 55 50N 4 40W
Clyde River, Canada ... 69 A13 70 30N 68 30W
Clydebank, U.K. ... 11 F4 55 54N 4 23W
Clymer, N.Y., U.S.A. ... 84 D5 42 1N 79 37W
Clymer, Pa., U.S.A. ... 84 D5 40 40N 79 1W
Coachella, U.S.A. ... 79 M10 33 41N 116 10W
Coachella Canal, U.S.A. ... 79 N12 32 43N 114 57W
Coahoma, U.S.A. ... 81 J4 32 18N 101 18W
Coahuayana →, Mexico ... 86 D4 18 41N 103 45W
Coahuila □, Mexico ... 86 B4 27 0N 103 0W
Coal →, Canada ... 70 B3 59 39N 126 57W
Coalane, Mozam. ... 55 F4 17 48S 37 2 E
Coalcomán, Mexico ... 86 D4 18 40N 103 10W
Coaldale, Canada ... 70 D6 49 45N 112 35W
Coalgate, U.S.A. ... 81 H6 34 32N 96 13W
Coalinga, U.S.A. ... 78 J6 36 9N 120 21W
Coalisland, U.K. ... 10 B5 54 33N 6 42W
Coalville, U.K. ... 12 E6 52 44N 1 23W
Coalville, U.S.A. ... 76 F8 40 55N 111 24W
Coamo, Puerto Rico ... 89 d 18 5N 66 22W
Coari, Brazil ... 92 D6 4 8S 63 7W
Coast □, Kenya ... 54 C4 2 40S 39 45 E
Coast Mts., Canada ... 70 C3 55 0N 129 20W
Coast Ranges, U.S.A. ... 78 G4 39 0N 123 0W
Coatbridge, U.K. ... 11 F4 55 52N 4 6W
Coatepec, Mexico ... 87 D5 19 27N 96 58W
Coatepeque, Guatemala ... 88 D1 14 46N 91 55W
Coatesville, U.S.A. ... 82 F8 39 59N 75 50W
Coaticook, Canada ... 85 A13 45 10N 71 46W
Coats I., Canada ... 69 B11 62 30N 83 0W
Coats Land, Antarctica ... 5 D1 77 0S 25 0W
Coatzacoalcos, Mexico ... 87 D6 18 7N 94 25W
Coba, Mexico ... 87 C7 20 31N 87 39W
Cobalt, Canada ... 72 C4 47 25N 79 42W
Cobán, Guatemala ... 88 C1 15 30N 90 21W
Cobar, Australia ... 63 E4 31 27S 145 48 E
Cóbh, Ireland ... 10 E3 51 51N 8 17W
Cobija, Bolivia ... 92 F5 11 0S 68 50W
Cobleskill, U.S.A. ... 85 D10 42 41N 74 29W
Coboconk, Canada ... 84 B6 44 39N 78 48W
Cobourg, Canada ... 84 C6 43 58N 78 10W
Cobourg □, Australia ... 60 B5 11 20S 132 15 E
Cobourg Pen., Australia ... 60 B5 11 20S 132 15 E
Cobram, Australia ... 63 F4 35 54S 145 40 E
Cóbué, Mozam. ... 55 E3 12 0S 34 58 E
Coburg, Germany ... 16 C6 50 15N 10 58 E
Cocanada = Kakinada, India ... 41 L13 16 57N 82 11 E
Cochabamba, Bolivia ... 92 G5 17 26S 66 10W
Cochemane, Mozam. ... 55 F3 17 0S 32 54 E
Cochin, India ... 40 Q10 9 58N 76 20 E
Cochin China = Nam-Phan, Vietnam ... 39 G6 10 30N 106 0 E
Cochran, U.S.A. ... 83 J4 32 23N 83 21W
Cochrane, Alta., Canada ... 70 C6 51 11N 114 30W
Cochrane, Ont., Canada ... 72 C3 49 0N 81 0W
Cochrane, Chile ... 96 F2 47 15S 72 33W
Cochrane →, Canada ... 71 B8 59 0N 103 40W
Cochrane, L., Chile ... 96 F2 47 10S 72 0W
Cochranton, U.S.A. ... 84 E4 41 31N 80 3W
Cockburn, Australia ... 63 E3 32 5S 141 0 E
Cockburn, Canal, Chile ... 96 G2 54 30S 72 0W

Cockburn I., Canada ... 72 C3 45 55N 83 22W
Cockburn Ra., Australia ... 60 C4 15 46S 128 0 E
Cockermouth, U.K. ... 12 C4 54 40N 3 22W
Cocklebiddy, Australia ... 61 F4 32 0S 126 3 E
Cockpit Country, The, Jamaica ... 88 a 18 15N 77 45W
Coco →, Cent. Amer. ... 88 D3 15 0N 83 8W
Coco, I. del, Pac. Oc. ... 65 G19 5 25N 87 55W
Cocoa, U.S.A. ... 83 L5 28 21N 80 44W
Cocobeach, Gabon ... 52 D1 0 59N 9 34 E
Cocos B., Trin. & Tob. ... 93 K15 10 25N 61 2W
Cocos Is., Ind. Oc. ... 64 J1 12 10S 96 55 E
Cod, C., U.S.A. ... 82 D10 42 5N 70 10W
Codajás, Brazil ... 92 D6 3 55S 62 0W
Codó, Brazil ... 93 D10 4 30S 43 55W
Cody, U.S.A. ... 76 D9 44 32N 109 3W
Coe Hill, Canada ... 84 B7 44 52N 77 50W
Coelemu, Chile ... 94 D1 36 30S 72 48W
Coen, Australia ... 62 A3 13 52S 143 12 E
Cœur d'Alene, U.S.A. ... 76 C5 47 45N 116 51W
Cœur d'Alene L., U.S.A. ... 76 C5 47 32N 116 48W
Coevorden, Neths. ... 15 B6 52 40N 6 44 E
Coffeyville, U.S.A. ... 81 G7 37 2N 95 37W
Coffin B., Australia ... 63 E2 34 38S 135 28 E
Coffin Bay, Australia ... 63 E2 34 37S 135 29 E
Coffin Bay △, Australia ... 63 E2 34 34S 135 19 E
Coffin Bay Peninsula, Australia ... 63 E2 34 32S 135 15 E
Coffs Harbour, Australia ... 63 E5 30 16S 153 5 E
Cofre de Perote △, Mexico ... 87 D5 19 29N 97 8W
Cognac, France ... 20 D3 45 41N 0 20W
Cohocton, U.S.A. ... 84 D7 42 30N 77 30W
Cohocton →, U.S.A. ... 84 D7 42 9N 77 6W
Cohoes, U.S.A. ... 85 D11 42 46N 73 42W
Cohuna, Australia ... 63 F3 35 45S 144 15 E
Coiba, I., Panama ... 88 E3 7 30N 81 40W
Coig →, Argentina ... 96 G3 51 0S 69 10W
Coigeach, Rubha, U.K. ... 11 C3 58 6N 5 26W
Coihaique, Chile ... 96 F2 45 30S 71 45W
Coimbatore, India ... 40 P10 11 2N 76 59 E
Coimbra, Brazil ... 92 G7 19 55S 57 48W
Coimbra, Portugal ... 21 B1 40 15N 8 27W
Coín, Spain ... 21 D3 36 40N 4 48W
Coipasa, Salar de, Bolivia ... 92 G5 19 26S 68 9W
Cojimies, Ecuador ... 92 C3 0 20N 80 0W
Cojutepequé, El Salv. ... 88 D2 13 41N 88 54W
Cokeville, U.S.A. ... 76 E8 42 5N 110 57W
Colac, Australia ... 63 F3 38 21S 143 35 E
Colatina, Brazil ... 93 G10 19 32S 40 37W
Colbeck, C., Antarctica ... 5 D13 77 6S 157 48W
Colborne, Canada ... 84 C7 44 0N 77 53W
Colby, U.S.A. ... 80 F4 39 24N 101 3W
Colchester, U.K. ... 13 F8 51 54N 0 55 E
Cold L., Canada ... 71 C7 54 33N 110 5W
Coldstream, Canada ... 70 C5 50 13N 119 11W
Coldstream, U.K. ... 11 F6 55 39N 2 15W
Coldwater, Canada ... 84 B5 44 42N 79 40W
Coldwater, Kans., U.S.A. ... 81 G5 37 16N 99 20W
Coldwater, Mich., U.S.A. ... 82 E3 41 57N 85 0W
Colebrook, U.S.A. ... 85 B13 44 54N 71 30W
Coleman, U.S.A. ... 81 K5 31 50N 99 26W
Coleman →, Australia ... 62 B3 15 6S 141 38 E
Colenso, S. Africa ... 57 D4 28 44S 29 50 E
Coleraine, Australia ... 63 F3 37 36S 141 40 E
Coleraine, U.K. ... 10 A5 55 8N 6 41W
Coleridge, L., N.Z. ... 59 K3 43 17S 171 30 E
Colesberg, S. Africa ... 56 E4 30 45S 25 5 E
Coleville, U.S.A. ... 78 G7 38 34N 119 30W
Colfax, Calif., U.S.A. ... 78 F6 39 6N 120 57W
Colfax, La., U.S.A. ... 81 K8 31 31N 92 42W
Colfax, Wash., U.S.A. ... 76 C5 46 53N 117 22W
Colhué Huapi, L., Argentina ... 96 F3 45 30S 69 0W
Coligny, S. Africa ... 57 D4 26 17S 26 15 E
Colima, Mexico ... 86 D4 19 14N 103 43W
Colima □, Mexico ... 86 D4 19 10N 103 40W
Colima, Nevado de, Mexico ... 86 D4 19 35N 103 45W
Colina, Chile ... 94 C1 33 13S 70 45W
Colinas, Brazil ... 93 E10 6 0S 44 10W
Coll, U.K. ... 11 E2 56 39N 6 34W
Collaguasi, Chile ... 94 A2 21 5S 68 45W
Collarenebri, Australia ... 63 D4 29 33S 148 34 E
Colleen Bawn, Zimbabwe ... 55 G2 21 0S 29 12 E
College Park, U.S.A. ... 83 J3 33 40N 84 27W
College Station, U.S.A. ... 81 K6 30 37N 96 21W
Collie, Australia ... 61 F2 33 22S 116 8 E
Collier B., Australia ... 60 C3 16 10S 124 15 E
Collier Ra., Australia ... 61 D2 24 45S 119 10 E
Collier Range △, Australia ... 61 D2 24 39S 119 7 E
Collina, Passo di, Italy ... 22 B4 44 2N 10 56 E
Collingwood, Canada ... 84 B4 44 29N 80 13W
Collingwood, N.Z. ... 59 J4 40 41S 172 40 E
Collins, Canada ... 72 B2 50 17N 89 27W
Collinsville, Australia ... 62 C4 20 30S 147 56 E
Collipulli, Chile ... 94 D1 37 55S 72 30W
Collooney, Ireland ... 10 B3 54 11N 8 29W
Colmar, France ... 20 B7 48 5N 7 20 E
Colo →, Australia ... 63 E5 33 25S 150 52 E
Cologne = Köln, Germany ... 16 C4 50 56N 6 57 E
Colom, I. d'en, Spain ... 24 B11 39 58N 4 16 E
Coloma, U.S.A. ... 78 G6 38 48N 120 53W
Colomb-Béchar = Béchar, Algeria ... 50 B5 31 38N 2 18W
Colombia ■, S. Amer. ... 92 C4 3 45N 73 0W
Colombian Basin, S. Amer. ... 66 H12 14 0N 76 0W
Colombo, Sri Lanka ... 40 R11 6 56N 79 58 E
Colón, Buenos Aires, Argentina ... 94 C3 33 53S 61 7W
Colón, Entre Ríos, Argentina ... 94 C4 32 12S 58 10W
Colón, Cuba ... 88 B3 22 42N 80 54W
Colón, Panama ... 88 E4 9 20N 79 54W
Colón, Arch. de, Ecuador ... 90 D1 0 0 91 0W
Colònia de Sant Jordi, Spain ... 24 B9 39 19N 2 59 E
Colonia del Sacramento, Uruguay ... 94 C4 34 25S 57 50W
Colonia Dora, Argentina ... 94 B3 28 34S 62 59W
Colonial Beach, U.S.A. ... 82 F7 38 15N 76 58W
Colonie, U.S.A. ... 85 D11 42 43N 73 50W
Colonsay, Canada ... 71 C7 51 59N 105 52W
Colonsay, U.K. ... 11 E2 56 5N 6 12W
Colorado □, U.S.A. ... 77 G10 39 30N 105 30W
Colorado →, Argentina ... 96 D4 39 50S 62 8W
Colorado →, N. Amer. ... 77 L6 31 45N 114 40W
Colorado →, U.S.A. ... 81 L7 28 36N 95 59W
Colorado City, U.S.A. ... 81 J4 32 24N 100 52W
Colorado Plateau, U.S.A. ... 77 H8 37 0N 111 0W
Colorado River Aqueduct, U.S.A. ... 79 L12 34 17N 114 10W
Colorado Springs, U.S.A. ... 80 F2 38 50N 104 49W
Colotlán, Mexico ... 86 C4 22 6N 103 16W
Colstrip, U.S.A. ... 76 D10 45 53N 106 38W
Colton, U.S.A. ... 85 B10 44 33N 74 56W
Columbia, Ky., U.S.A. ... 82 G3 37 6N 85 18W

Columbia, La., U.S.A. ... 81 J8 32 6N 92 5W
Columbia, Miss., U.S.A. ... 81 K10 31 15N 89 50W
Columbia, Mo., U.S.A. ... 80 F8 38 57N 92 20W
Columbia, Pa., U.S.A. ... 85 F8 40 2N 76 30W
Columbia, S.C., U.S.A. ... 83 J5 34 0N 81 2W
Columbia, Tenn., U.S.A. ... 83 H2 35 37N 87 2W
Columbia →, N. Amer. ... 78 D2 46 15N 124 5W
Columbia, C., Canada ... 4 A4 83 6N 69 57W
Columbia, District of □, U.S.A. ... 82 F7 38 55N 77 0W
Columbia, Mt., Canada ... 70 C5 52 8N 117 20W
Columbia Basin, U.S.A. ... 76 C4 46 45N 119 5W
Columbia Falls, U.S.A. ... 76 B6 48 23N 114 11W
Columbia Mts., Canada ... 70 C5 52 0N 119 0W
Columbia Plateau, U.S.A. ... 76 D5 44 0N 117 30W
Columbiana, U.S.A. ... 84 F4 40 53N 80 42W
Columbretes, Is., Spain ... 21 C6 39 50N 0 50 E
Columbus, Ga., U.S.A. ... 83 J3 32 28N 84 59W
Columbus, Ind., U.S.A. ... 82 F3 39 13N 85 55W
Columbus, Kans., U.S.A. ... 81 G7 37 10N 94 50W
Columbus, Miss., U.S.A. ... 83 J1 33 30N 88 25W
Columbus, Mont., U.S.A. ... 76 D9 45 38N 109 15W
Columbus, N. Mex., U.S.A. ... 77 L10 31 50N 107 38W
Columbus, Nebr., U.S.A. ... 80 E6 41 26N 97 22W
Columbus, Ohio, U.S.A. ... 82 F4 39 58N 83 0W
Columbus, Tex., U.S.A. ... 81 L6 29 42N 96 33W
Colusa, U.S.A. ... 78 F4 39 13N 122 1W
Colville, U.S.A. ... 76 B5 48 33N 117 54W
Colville →, U.S.A. ... 68 A4 70 25N 150 30W
Colville, C., N.Z. ... 59 G5 36 29S 175 21 E
Colwood, Canada ... 78 B3 48 26N 123 29W
Colwyn Bay, U.K. ... 12 D4 53 18N 3 44W
Comácchio, Italy ... 22 B5 44 42N 12 11 E
Comalcalco, Mexico ... 87 D6 18 16N 93 13W
Comallo, Argentina ... 96 E2 41 0S 70 5W
Comanche, U.S.A. ... 81 K5 31 54N 98 36W
Comandante Ferraz, Antarctica ... 5 C18 62 30S 58 0W
Comayagua, Honduras ... 88 D2 14 25N 87 37W
Combahee →, U.S.A. ... 83 J5 32 30N 80 31W
Combarbalá, Chile ... 94 C1 31 11S 71 2W
Combe Martin, U.K. ... 13 F3 51 12N 4 3W
Comber, Canada ... 84 D2 42 14N 82 33W
Comber, U.K. ... 10 B6 54 33N 5 45W
Combermere, Canada ... 84 A7 45 22N 77 37W
Comblain-au-Pont, Belgium ... 15 D5 50 29N 5 35 E
Comeragh Mts., Ireland ... 10 D4 52 18N 7 34W
Comet, Australia ... 62 C4 23 36S 148 38 E
Comilla, Bangla. ... 41 H17 23 28N 91 10 E
Comino, Malta ... 25 C1 36 1N 14 20 E
Comino, C., Italy ... 22 D3 40 32N 9 49 E
Comitán, Mexico ... 87 D6 16 18N 92 9W
Commerce, Ga., U.S.A. ... 83 H4 34 12N 83 28W
Commerce, Tex., U.S.A. ... 81 J7 33 15N 95 54W
Committee B., Canada ... 69 B11 68 30N 86 30W
Commonwealth B., Antarctica ... 5 C10 67 0S 144 0 E
Commoron Cr. →, Australia ... 63 D5 28 22S 150 8 E
Communism Pk. = Kommunizma, Pik, Tajikistan ... 28 F8 39 0N 72 2 E
Como, Italy ... 20 D8 45 47N 9 5 E
Como, Lago di, Italy ... 20 D8 46 0N 9 11 E
Comodoro Rivadavia, Argentina ... 96 F3 45 50S 67 40W
Comorin, C., India ... 40 Q10 8 3N 77 40 E
Comoro Is. = Comoros ■, Ind. Oc. ... 49 H8 12 10S 44 15 E
Comoros ■, Ind. Oc. ... 49 H8 12 10S 44 15 E
Comox, Canada ... 70 D4 49 42N 124 55W
Compiègne, France ... 20 B5 49 24N 2 50 E
Compostela, Mexico ... 86 C4 21 15N 104 53W
Comprida, I., Brazil ... 95 A6 24 50S 47 42W
Compton, Canada ... 85 A13 45 14N 71 49W
Compton, U.S.A. ... 79 M8 33 54N 118 13W
Comrat, Moldova ... 17 E15 46 18N 28 40 E
Con Cuong, Vietnam ... 38 C5 19 2N 104 54 E
Con Dao, Vietnam ... 39 H6 8 42N 106 35 E
Con Son, Vietnam ... 39 H6 8 41N 106 37 E
Conakry, Guinea ... 50 G3 9 29N 13 49W
Conara, Australia ... 63 G4 41 50S 147 26 E
Concarneau, France ... 20 C2 47 52N 3 56W
Conceição, Mozam. ... 55 F4 18 47S 36 7 E
Conceição da Barra, Brazil ... 93 G11 18 35S 39 45W
Conceição do Araguaia, Brazil ... 93 E9 8 0S 49 2W
Concepción, Argentina ... 94 B2 27 20S 65 35W
Concepción, Bolivia ... 92 G6 16 15S 62 8W
Concepción, Chile ... 94 D1 36 50S 73 0W
Concepción, Mexico ... 87 D6 18 15N 90 5W
Concepción, Paraguay ... 94 A4 23 22S 57 26W
Concepción □, Chile ... 94 D1 37 0S 72 30W
Concepción →, Mexico ... 86 A2 30 32N 113 2W
Concepción, Est. de, Chile ... 96 G2 50 30S 74 55W
Concepción, L., Bolivia ... 92 G6 17 20S 61 20W
Concepción del Oro, Mexico ... 86 C4 24 40N 101 30W
Concepción del Uruguay, Argentina ... 94 C4 32 35S 58 20W
Conception, Pt., U.S.A. ... 79 L6 34 27N 120 28W
Conception B., Canada ... 73 C9 47 45N 53 0W
Conception B., Namibia ... 56 C1 23 55S 14 22 E
Conception I., Bahamas ... 89 B4 23 52N 75 9W
Concession, Zimbabwe ... 55 F3 17 27S 30 56 E
Conchas Dam, U.S.A. ... 81 H2 35 22N 104 11W
Concho, U.S.A. ... 77 J9 34 28N 109 36W
Concho →, U.S.A. ... 81 K5 31 34N 99 43W
Conchos →, Chihuahua, Mexico ... 86 B4 29 32N 105 0W
Conchos →, Tamaulipas, Mexico ... 87 B5 25 9N 98 35W
Concord, Calif., U.S.A. ... 78 H4 37 59N 122 2W
Concord, N.C., U.S.A. ... 83 H5 35 25N 80 35W
Concord, N.H., U.S.A. ... 85 C13 43 12N 71 32W
Concordia, Argentina ... 94 C4 31 20S 58 2W
Concórdia, Brazil ... 92 D5 4 36S 66 36W
Concordia, Mexico ... 86 C3 23 18N 106 2W
Concordia, U.S.A. ... 80 F6 39 34N 97 40W
Concrete, U.S.A. ... 76 B3 48 32N 121 45W
Condamine, Australia ... 63 D5 26 56S 150 9 E
Conde, U.S.A. ... 80 C5 45 9N 98 6W
Condeúba, Brazil ... 93 E10 14 52S 41 30W
Condobolin, Australia ... 63 E4 33 4S 147 6 E
Condon, U.S.A. ... 76 D3 45 14N 120 11W
Conegliano, Italy ... 22 B5 45 53N 12 18 E
Conejera, I. = Conills, I. des, Spain ... 24 B9 39 11N 2 58 E
Conejos, Mexico ... 86 B4 26 14N 103 53W
Confuso →, Paraguay ... 94 B4 25 9S 57 34W
Congleton, U.K. ... 12 D5 53 10N 2 13W
Congo (Brazzaville) = Congo ■, Africa ... 52 E3 1 0S 16 0 E
Congo (Kinshasa) = Congo, Dem. Rep. of the ■, Africa ... 52 E4 3 0S 23 0 E
Congo ■, Africa ... 52 E3 1 0S 16 0 E
Congo →, Africa ... 52 F2 6 4S 12 24 E

Congo, Dem. Rep. of the ■, Africa ... 52 E4 3 0S 23 0 E
Congo Basin, Africa ... 52 E4 0 10S 24 30 E
Congonhas, Brazil ... 95 A7 20 30S 43 52W
Congress, U.S.A. ... 77 J7 34 9N 112 51W
Conills, I. des, Spain ... 24 B9 39 11N 2 58 E
Coniston, Canada ... 72 C3 46 29N 80 51W
Conjeeveram = Kanchipuram, India ... 40 N11 12 52N 79 45 E
Conklin, Canada ... 71 B6 55 38N 111 5W
Conklin, U.S.A. ... 85 D9 42 2N 75 49W
Conn, L., Ireland ... 10 B2 54 3N 9 15W
Connacht □, Ireland ... 10 C2 53 43N 9 12W
Conneaut, U.S.A. ... 84 E4 41 57N 80 34W
Connecticut □, U.S.A. ... 85 E12 41 30N 72 45W
Connecticut →, U.S.A. ... 85 E12 41 16N 72 20W
Connell, U.S.A. ... 76 C4 46 40N 118 52W
Connellsville, U.S.A. ... 84 F5 40 1N 79 35W
Connemara □, Ireland ... 10 C2 53 29N 9 45W
Connemara △, Ireland ... 10 C2 53 32N 9 52W
Connemaugh →, U.S.A. ... 84 F5 40 28N 79 19W
Connersville, U.S.A. ... 82 F3 39 39N 85 8W
Connors Ra., Australia ... 62 C4 21 40S 149 10 E
Conquest, Canada ... 71 C7 51 32N 107 14W
Conrad, U.S.A. ... 76 B8 48 10N 111 57W
Conran, C., Australia ... 63 F4 37 49S 148 44 E
Conroe, U.S.A. ... 81 K7 30 19N 95 27W
Consecon, Canada ... 84 C7 44 0N 77 31W
Conselheiro Lafaiete, Brazil ... 95 A7 20 40S 43 48W
Consett, U.K. ... 12 C6 54 51N 1 50W
Consort, Canada ... 71 C6 52 1N 110 46W
Constance = Konstanz, Germany ... 16 E5 47 40N 9 10 E
Constance, L. = Bodensee, Europe ... 20 C8 47 35N 9 25 E
Constanţa, Romania ... 17 F15 44 14N 28 38 E
Constantia, U.S.A. ... 85 C8 43 15N 76 1W
Constantine, Algeria ... 50 A7 36 25N 6 42 E
Constitución, Chile ... 94 D1 35 20S 72 30W
Constitución, Uruguay ... 94 C4 31 0S 57 50W
Constitucion de 1857 △, Mexico ... 86 A1 32 4N 115 55W
Consul, Canada ... 71 D7 49 20N 109 30W
Contact, U.S.A. ... 76 F6 41 46N 114 45W
Contai, India ... 43 J12 21 54N 87 46 E
Contamana, Peru ... 92 E4 7 19S 74 55W
Contas →, Brazil ... 93 F11 14 17S 39 1W
Contoocook, U.S.A. ... 85 C13 43 13N 71 45W
Contra Costa, Mozam. ... 57 D5 25 9S 33 30 E
Contwoyto L., Canada ... 68 B8 65 42N 110 50W
Conway = Conwy, U.K. ... 12 D4 53 17N 3 50W
Conway = Conwy →, U.K. ... 12 D4 53 17N 3 50W
Conway, Australia ... 62 J6 20 24S 148 41 E
Conway, Ark., U.S.A. ... 81 H8 35 5N 92 26W
Conway, N.H., U.S.A. ... 85 C13 43 59N 71 7W
Conway, S.C., U.S.A. ... 83 J6 33 51N 79 3W
Conway, C., Australia ... 62 J6 20 34S 148 80 E
Conway, L., Australia ... 63 D2 28 17S 135 35 E
Conwy, U.K. ... 12 D4 53 17N 3 50W
Conwy □, U.K. ... 12 D4 53 10N 3 44W
Conwy →, U.K. ... 12 D4 53 17N 3 50W
Coober Pedy, Australia ... 63 D1 29 1S 134 43 E
Cooch Behar = Koch Bihar, India ... 41 F16 26 22N 89 29 E
Cooinda, Australia ... 60 B5 13 15S 130 5 E
Cook, Australia ... 61 F5 30 37S 130 25 E
Cook, Bahía de, Chile ... 96 H3 55 10S 70 0W
Cook, C., Canada ... 70 C3 50 8N 127 55W
Cook, Mt. = Aoraki Mount Cook, N.Z. ... 59 K3 43 36S 170 9 E
Cook Inlet, U.S.A. ... 68 C4 60 0N 152 0W
Cook Is., Pac. Oc. ... 65 J12 17 0S 160 0W
Cook Strait, N.Z. ... 59 J5 41 15S 174 29 E
Cookeville, U.S.A. ... 83 G3 36 10N 85 30W
Cookhouse, S. Africa ... 56 E4 32 44S 25 47 E
Cookshire, Canada ... 85 A13 45 25N 71 38W
Cookstown, U.K. ... 10 B5 54 39N 6 45W
Cooksville, Canada ... 84 C5 43 36N 79 35W
Cooktown, Australia ... 62 B4 15 30S 145 16 E
Coolabah, Australia ... 63 E4 31 1S 146 43 E
Cooladdi, Australia ... 63 D4 26 37S 145 23 E
Coolah, Australia ... 63 E4 31 48S 149 41 E
Coolamon, Australia ... 63 E4 34 46S 147 8 E
Coolgardie, Australia ... 61 F3 30 55S 121 8 E
Coolidge, U.S.A. ... 77 K8 32 59N 111 31W
Coolidge Dam, U.S.A. ... 77 K8 33 0N 110 20W
Cooloola △, Australia ... 63 D5 26 13S 153 2 E
Cooma, Australia ... 63 F4 36 12S 149 8 E
Coon Rapids, U.S.A. ... 80 C8 45 9N 93 19W
Coonabarabran, Australia ... 63 E4 31 14S 149 18 E
Coonamble, Australia ... 63 E4 30 56S 148 27 E
Coonana, Australia ... 61 F3 31 0S 123 0 E
Coondapoor, India ... 40 N9 13 42N 74 40 E
Cooninie, L., Australia ... 63 D2 26 4S 139 59 E
Cooper, U.S.A. ... 81 J7 33 23N 95 42W
Cooper Cr. →, Australia ... 63 D2 28 29S 137 46 E
Cooperstown, N. Dak., U.S.A. ... 80 B5 47 27N 98 8W
Cooperstown, N.Y., U.S.A. ... 85 D10 42 42N 74 56W
Coorabie, Australia ... 61 F5 31 54S 132 18 E
Coorong, The, Australia ... 63 F2 35 50S 139 20 E
Coorow, Australia ... 61 E2 29 53S 116 2 E
Cooroy, Australia ... 63 D5 26 22S 152 54 E
Coos Bay, U.S.A. ... 76 E1 43 22N 124 13W
Cootamundra, Australia ... 63 E4 34 36S 148 1 E
Cootehill, Ireland ... 10 B4 54 4N 7 5W
Copahue Paso, Argentina ... 94 D1 37 49S 71 8W
Copainalá, Mexico ... 87 D6 17 8N 93 11W
Copake Falls, U.S.A. ... 85 D11 42 7N 73 31W
Copán, Honduras ... 88 D2 14 50N 89 9W
Cope, U.S.A. ... 80 F3 39 40N 102 51W
Copenhagen = København, Denmark ... 9 J15 55 41N 12 34 E
Copenhagen, U.S.A. ... 85 C9 43 54N 75 41W
Copiapó, Chile ... 94 B1 27 30S 70 20W
Copiapó →, Chile ... 94 B1 27 19S 70 56W
Coplay, U.S.A. ... 85 F9 40 44N 75 29W
Copp L., Canada ... 70 A6 60 14N 114 40W
Copper Harbor, U.S.A. ... 82 B2 47 28N 87 53W
Copper Queen, Zimbabwe ... 55 F2 17 29S 29 18 E
Copperas Cove, U.S.A. ... 81 K6 31 8N 97 54W
Copperbelt □, Zambia ... 55 E2 13 15S 27 30 E
Coppermine = Kugluktuk, Canada ... 68 B8 67 49N 115 4W
Coppermine →, Canada ... 68 B8 67 49N 116 4W
Copperopolis, U.S.A. ... 78 H6 37 58N 120 38W
Coquet →, U.K. ... 12 B6 55 20N 1 32W
Coquille, U.S.A. ... 76 E1 43 11N 124 11W
Coquimbo, Chile ... 94 C1 30 0S 71 20W
Coquimbo □, Chile ... 94 C1 31 0S 71 0W

Corabia, Romania .... 17 G13 43 48N   24 30 E
Coracora, Peru 92 G4   15 5S 73 45W
Coraki, Australia .... 63 D5   28 59S 153 17 E
Coral, U.S.A. 84 F5   40 29N 79 10W
Coral Gables, U.S.A. 83 N5   25 45N 80 16W
Coral Harbour, Canada 69 B11 64 8N 83 10W
Coral Sea, Pac. Oc. .... 64 J7   15 0S 150 0 E
Coral Springs, U.S.A. 83 M5   26 16N 80 13W
Coraopolis, U.S.A. 84 F4   40 31N 80 10W
Corato, Italy .... 22 D7   41 9N 16 25 E
Corbin, U.S.A. 82 G3   36 57N 84 6W
Corby, U.K. 13 E7   52 30N   0 41W
Corcaigh = Cork, Ireland 10 E3   51 54N   8 29W
Corcoran, U.S.A. 78 J7   36 6N 119 33W
Corcovado △, Costa Rica 88 E3   8 33N 83 35W
Corcubión, Spain 21 A1   42 56N   9 12W
Cordele, U.S.A. 83 K4   31 58N 83 47W
Cordell, U.S.A. 81 H5   35 17N 98 59W
Córdoba, Argentina 94 C3   31 20S 64 10W
Córdoba, Mexico 87 D5   18 50N 97 0W
Córdoba, Spain 21 D3   37 50N   4 50W
Córdoba □, Argentina 94 C3   31 22S 64 15W
Córdoba, Sierra de, Argentina . 94 C3   31 10S 64 25W
Cordova, U.S.A. 68 B5   60 33N 145 45W
Corella →, Australia .... 62 B3   19 34S 140 47 E
Corfield, Australia .... 62 C3   21 40S 143 21 E
Corfu = Kérkira, Greece ...... 25 A3   39 38N 19 50 E
Corfu, Str. of, Greece .... 25 A4   39 34N 20 0 E
Coria, Spain 21 C2   39 58N   6 33W
Corigliano Cálabro, Italy ...... 22 E7   39 36N 16 31 E
Coringa Is., Australia .... 62 B4   16 58S 149 58 E
Corinth = Kórinthos, Greece .. 23 F10 37 56N 22 55 E
Corinth, Miss., U.S.A. 83 H1   34 56N 88 31W
Corinth, N.Y., U.S.A. 85 C11 43 15N 73 49W
Corinth, G. of = Korinthiakós
   Kólpos, Greece .... 23 E10 38 16N 22 30 E
Corinto, Brazil 93 G10 18 20S 44 30W
Corinto, Nic. 88 D2   12 30N 87 10W
Cork, Ireland 10 E3   51 54N   8 29W
Cork □, Ireland 10 E3   51 57N   8 40W
Cork Harbour, Ireland 10 E3   51 47N   8 16W
Çorlu, Turkey .... 23 D12 41 11N 27 49 E
Cormack L., Canada 70 A4   60 56N 121 37W
Cormorant, Canada 71 C8   54 14N 100 35W
Cormorant L., Canada 71 C8   54 15N 100 50W
Corn Is. = Maíz, Is. del, Nic. .. 88 D3   12 15N 83 4W
Cornélio Procópio, Brazil 95 A5   23 7S 50 40W
Corner Brook, Canada 73 C8   48 57N 57 58W
Corneşti, Moldova .... 17 E15 47 21N 28 1 E
Corning, Ark., U.S.A. 81 G9   36 25N 90 35W
Corning, Calif., U.S.A. 76 G2   39 56N 122 11W
Corning, Iowa, U.S.A. 80 E7   40 59N 94 44W
Corning, N.Y., U.S.A. 84 D7   42 9N 77 3W
Cornwall, Canada 85 A10 45 2N 74 44W
Cornwall, U.S.A. 85 F8   40 17N 76 25W
Cornwall □, U.K. 13 G3   50 26N   4 40W
Corny Pt., Australia .... 63 E2   34 55S 137 0 E
Coro, Venezuela 92 A5   11 25N 69 41W
Coroatá, Brazil 93 D10   4 8S 44 0W
Corocoro, Bolivia 92 G5   17 15S 68 28W
Coroico, Bolivia 92 G5   16 0S 67 50W
Coromandel, N.Z. .... 59 G5   36 45S 175 31 E
Coromandel Coast, India ...... 40 N12 12 30N 81 0 E
Corona, Calif., U.S.A. 79 M9   33 53N 117 34W
Corona, N. Mex., U.S.A. 77 J11 34 15N 105 36W
Coronach, Canada 71 D7   49 7N 105 31W
Coronado, U.S.A. 79 N9   32 41N 117 11W
Coronado, B. de, Costa Rica ... 88 E3   9 0N 83 40W
Coronados, Is. los, U.S.A. 79 N9   32 25N 117 15W
Coronation, Canada 70 C6   52 5N 111 27W
Coronation Gulf, Canada 68 B8   68 25N 110 0W
Coronation I., Antarctica 5 C18   60 45S 46 0W
Coronation Is., Australia ...... 60 B3   14 57S 124 55 E
Coronda, Argentina 94 C3   31 58S 60 56W
Coronel, Chile 94 D1   37 0S 73 10W
Coronel Bogado, Paraguay 94 B4   27 11S 56 18W
Coronel Dorrego, Argentina ... 94 D3   38 40S 61 10W
Coronel Oviedo, Paraguay 94 B4   25 24S 56 30W
Coronel Pringles, Argentina ... 94 D3   38 0S 61 30W
Coronel Suárez, Argentina 94 D3   37 30S 61 52W
Coronel Vidal, Argentina 94 D4   37 28S 57 45W
Coropuna, Nevado, Peru 92 G4   15 30S 72 41W
Corowa, Australia .... 63 F4   35 58S 146 21 E
Corozal, Belize 87 D7   18 23N 88 23W
Corozal Pt., Trin. & Tob. 93 K15 10 44N 61 40W
Corpus, Argentina 95 B4   27 10S 55 30W
Corpus Christi, U.S.A. 81 M6   27 47N 97 24W
Corpus Christi, L., U.S.A. 81 L6   28 2N 97 52W
Corralejo, Canary Is. 24 F6   28 43N 13 53W
Corraun Pen., Ireland 10 C2   53 54N   9 54W
Corrientes, Argentina 94 B4   27 30S 58 45W
Corrientes □, Argentina 94 B4   28 0S 57 0W
Corrientes →, Argentina 94 C4   30 42S 59 38W
Corrientes →, Peru 92 D4   3 43S 74 35W
Corrientes, C., Colombia 92 B3   5 30N 77 34W
Corrientes, C., Cuba 88 B3   21 43N 84 30W
Corrientes, C., Mexico 86 C3   20 25N 105 42W
Corrigan, U.S.A. 81 K7   31 0N 94 52W
Corrigin, Australia .... 61 F2   32 20S 117 53 E
Corry, U.S.A. 84 E5   41 55N 79 39W
Corse, C., France .... 20 E8   43 1N   9 25 E
Corse ⊠, France .... 20 F8   42 0N   9 0 E
Corsica = Corse ⊠, France .... 20 F8   42 0N   9 0 E
Corsicana, U.S.A. 81 J6   32 6N 96 28W
Corte, France .... 20 E8   42 19N   9 11 E
Cortez, U.S.A. 77 H9   37 21N 108 35W
Cortland, N.Y., U.S.A. 85 D8   42 36N 76 11W
Cortland, Ohio, U.S.A. 84 E4   41 20N 80 44W
Çorum, Turkey .... 19 F5   40 30N 34 57 E
Corumbá, Brazil 92 G7   19 0S 57 30W
Corunna = A Coruña, Spain 21 A1   43 20N   8 25W
Corvallis, U.S.A. 76 D2   44 34N 123 16W
Corvette, L. de la, Canada 72 B5   53 25N 74 3W
Corydon, U.S.A. 80 E8   40 46N 93 19W
Cosalá, Mexico 86 C3   24 28N 106 40W
Cosamaloapan, Mexico 87 D5   18 23N 95 50W
Cosenza, Italy .... 22 E7   39 18N 16 15 E
Coshocton, U.S.A. 84 F3   40 16N 81 51W
Cosmo Newberry, Australia .... 61 E3   28 0S 122 54 E
Coso Junction, U.S.A. 79 J9   36 3N 117 57W
Coso Pk., U.S.A. 79 J9   36 13N 117 44W
Cosquín, Argentina 94 C3   31 15S 64 30W
Costa Blanca, Spain 21 C5   38 25N   0 10W
Costa Brava, Spain .... 21 B7   41 30N   3 0 E
Costa del Sol, Spain 21 D3   36 30N   4 30W
Costa Dorada, Spain .... 21 B6   41 12N   1 15 E

Costa Mesa, U.S.A. 79 M9   33 38N 117 55W
Costa Rica ■, Cent. Amer. 88 E3   10 0N 84 0W
Cosumnes →, U.S.A. 78 G5   38 16N 121 26W
Cotabato, Phil. .... 37 C6   7 14N 124 15 E
Cotagaita, Bolivia 94 A2   20 45S 65 40W
Côte-d'Azur, France .... 20 E7   43 25N   7 10 E
Côte-d'Ivoire = Ivory Coast ■,
   Africa 50 G4   7 30N   5 0W
Coteau des Prairies, U.S.A. 80 C6   45 20N 97 50W
Coteau du Missouri, U.S.A. 80 B4   47 0N 100 0W
Cotentin, France 20 B3   49 15N   1 30W
Cotonou, Benin .... 50 G6   6 20N   2 25 E
Cotopaxi, Ecuador 92 D3   0 40S 78 30W
Cotswold Hills, U.K. 13 F5   51 42N   2 10W
Cottage Grove, U.S.A. 76 E2   43 48N 123 3W
Cottbus, Germany .... 16 C8   51 45N 14 20 E
Cottonwood, U.S.A. 77 J7   34 45N 112 1W
Cotulla, U.S.A. 81 L5   28 26N 99 14W
Coudersport, U.S.A. 84 E6   41 46N 78 1W
Couedic, C. du, Australia ...... 63 F2   36 5S 136 40 E
Coulee City, U.S.A. 76 C4   47 37N 119 17W
Coulman I., Antarctica .... 5 D11 73 35S 170 0 E
Coulonge →, Canada 72 C4   45 52N 76 46W
Coulterville, U.S.A. 78 H6   37 43N 120 12W
Council, U.S.A. 76 D5   44 44N 116 26W
Council Bluffs, U.S.A. 80 E7   41 16N 95 52W
Council Grove, U.S.A. 80 F6   38 40N 96 29W
Coupeville, U.S.A. 78 B4   48 13N 122 41W
Courantyne →, S. Amer. 92 B7   5 55N 57 5W
Courcelles, Belgium .... 15 D4   50 28N   4 22 E
Courtenay, Canada 70 D4   49 45N 125 0W
Courtland, U.S.A. 78 G5   38 20N 121 34W
Courtrai = Kortrijk, Belgium .. 15 D3   50 50N   3 17 E
Courtright, Canada 84 D2   42 49N 82 28W
Coushatta, U.S.A. 81 J8   32 1N 93 21W
Coutts Crossing, Australia ..... 63 D5   29 49S 152 55 E
Couva, Trin. & Tob. 93 K15 10 24N 61 30W
Couvin, Belgium .... 15 D4   50 3N   4 29 E
Cove I., Canada 84 A3   45 17N 81 44W
Coventry, U.K. 13 E6   52 25N   1 28W
Covilhã, Portugal 21 B2   40 17N   7 31W
Covington, Ga., U.S.A. 83 J4   33 36N 83 51W
Covington, Ky., U.S.A. 81 G6   39 5N 84 31W
Covington, Okla., U.S.A. 81 G6   36 18N 97 35W
Covington, Tenn., U.S.A. 81 H10 35 34N 89 39W
Covington, Va., U.S.A. 82 G5   37 47N 79 59W
Cowal, L., Australia .... 63 E4   33 40S 147 25 E
Cowan, L., Australia .... 61 F3   31 45S 121 45 E
Cowan L., Canada 71 C7   54 0N 107 15W
Cowangie, Australia .... 63 F3   35 12S 141 26 E
Cowansville, Canada 85 A12 45 14N 72 46W
Coward Springs, Australia ..... 63 D2   29 24S 136 49 E
Cowcowing Lakes, Australia ... 61 F2   30 55S 117 20 E
Cowdenbeath, U.K. 11 E5   56 7N   3 21W
Cowell, Australia .... 63 E2   33 39S 136 56 E
Cowes, U.K. 13 G6   50 45N   1 18W
Cowichan L., Canada 78 B2   48 53N 124 17W
Cowlitz →, U.S.A. 78 D4   46 6N 122 55W
Cowra, Australia .... 63 E4   33 49S 148 42 E
Coxilha Grande, Brazil 95 B5   28 18S 51 30W
Coxim, Brazil 93 G8   18 30S 54 55W
Cox's Bazar, Bangla. .... 41 J17 21 26N 91 59 E
Coyote Wells, U.S.A. 79 N11 32 44N 115 58W
Coyuca de Benítez, Mexico 87 D4   7 1N 100 8W
Coyuca de Catalan, Mexico 86 D4   18 18N 100 41W
Cozad, U.S.A. 80 E5   40 52N 99 59W
Cozumel, Mexico 87 C7   20 31N 86 55W
Cozumel, Isla, Mexico 87 C7   20 30N 86 40W
Crabhill, Barbados .... 89 g   13 19N 59 38W
Cracow, Australia .... 63 D5   25 17S 150 17 E
Cracow = Kraków, Poland ..... 17 C10 50 4N 19 57 E
Cradle Mt.-Lake St Clair △,
   Australia .... 63 G4   41 49S 147 56 E
Cradock, Australia .... 63 E2   32 6S 138 31 E
Cradock, S. Africa .... 56 E4   32 8S 25 36 E
Craig, U.S.A. 76 F10 40 31N 107 33W
Craigavon, U.K. 10 B5   54 27N   6 23W
Craigmore, Zimbabwe .... 55 G3   20 28S 32 50 E
Craik, Canada 71 C7   51 3N 105 49W
Crailsheim, Germany .... 16 D6   49 8N 10 5 E
Craiova, Romania .... 17 F12 44 21N 23 48 E
Cramsie, Australia .... 62 C3   23 20S 144 15 E
Cranberry L., U.S.A. 85 B10 44 11N 74 50W
Cranberry Portage, Canada 71 C8   54 35N 101 23W
Cranbrook, Australia .... 61 F2   34 18S 117 33 E
Cranbrook, Canada 70 D5   49 30N 115 46W
Crandon, U.S.A. 80 C10 45 34N 88 54W
Crane, Oreg., U.S.A. 76 E4   43 25N 118 35W
Crane, Tex., U.S.A. 81 K3   31 24N 102 21W
Cranston, U.S.A. 85 E13 41 47N 71 26W
Crater L., Canada 72 B4   54 20N 76 56W
Crater Lake △, U.S.A. 76 E2   42 55N 122 10W
Craters of the Moon △, U.S.A. .. 76 E7   43 25N 113 30W
Crateús, Brazil 93 E10   5 10S 40 39W
Crato, Brazil 93 E11   7 10S 39 25W
Craven, L., Canada 72 B4   54 20N 76 56W
Crawford, U.S.A. 80 D3   42 41N 103 25W
Crawfordsville, U.S.A. 82 E2   40 2N 86 54W
Crawley, U.K. 13 F7   51 7N   0 11W
Crazy Mts., U.S.A. 76 C8   46 12N 110 20W
Crean L., Canada 71 C7   54 5N 106 9W
Crediton, Canada 84 C3   43 17N 81 33W
Crediton, U.K. 13 G4   50 47N   3 40W
Cree →, Canada 71 B7   58 57N 105 47W
Cree →, U.K. 11 G4   54 55N   4 25W
Cree L., Canada 71 B7   57 30N 106 30W
Creede, U.S.A. 77 H10 37 51N 106 56W
Creekside, U.S.A. 84 F5   40 40N 79 11W
Creel, Mexico 86 B3   27 45N 107 38W
Creemore, Canada 84 B4   44 19N 80 6W
Creighton, Canada 71 C8   54 45N 101 54W
Creighton, U.S.A. 80 D6   42 28N 97 54W
Crema, Italy .... 20 D8   45 22N   9 41 E
Cremona, Italy .... 20 D8   45 7N 10 2 E
Cres, Croatia .... 16 F8   44 58N 14 25 E
Crescent City, U.S.A. 76 F1   41 45N 124 12W
Crespo, Argentina 94 C3   32 2S 60 19W
Cresson, U.S.A. 84 F6   40 28N 78 36W
Crestline, Calif., U.S.A. 79 L9   34 14N 117 18W
Crestline, Ohio, U.S.A. 84 F2   40 47N 82 44W
Creston, Canada 70 D5   49 10N 116 31W
Creston, Calif., U.S.A. 78 K6   35 32N 120 33W
Creston, Iowa, U.S.A. 80 E7   41 4N 94 22W
Crestview, Calif., U.S.A. 78 H8   37 46N 118 58W
Crestview, Fla., U.S.A. 83 K2   30 46N 86 34W
Crete = Kríti, Greece .... 25 D7   35 15N 25 0 E

Crete, U.S.A. 80 E6   40 38N 96 58W
Créteil, France .... 20 B5   48 47N   2 28 E
Creus, C. de, Spain .... 21 A7   42 20N   3 19 E
Creuse →, France .... 20 C4   47 0N   0 34 E
Crewe, U.K. 12 D5   53 6N   2 26W
Crewkerne, U.K. 13 G5   50 53N   2 48W
Crianlarich, U.K. 11 E4   56 24N   4 37W
Criciúma, Brazil 95 B6   28 40S 49 23W
Crieff, U.K. 11 E5   56 22N   3 50W
Crimea □, Ukraine .... 19 E5   45 30N 33 10 E
Crimean Pen. = Krymskyy
   Pivostriv, Ukraine .... 19 F5   45 0N 34 0 E
Crişul Alb →, Romania .... 17 E11 46 42N 21 17 E
Crişul Negru →, Romania ..... 17 E11 46 42N 21 16 E
Crna →, Macedonia .... 23 D9   41 33N 21 59 E
Crna Gora = Montenegro □,
   Serbia & M. .... 23 C8   42 40N 19 20 E
Crna Gora, Macedonia .... 23 C9   42 10N 21 30 E
Crna Reka = Crna →, Macedonia 23 D9   41 33N 21 59 E
Croagh Patrick, Ireland 10 C2   53 46N   9 40W
Croatia ■, Europe .... 16 F9   45 20N 16 0 E
Crocker, Banjaran, Malaysia ... 36 C5   5 40N 116 30 E
Crockett, U.S.A. 81 K7   31 19N 95 27W
Crocodile = Krokodil →, Mozam. 57 D5   25 14S 32 18 E
Crocodile Is., Australia .... 62 A1   12 3S 134 58 E
Crohy Hd., Ireland 10 B3   54 55N   8 26W
Croix, L. La, Canada 72 C1   48 20N 92 15W
Croker, C., Australia .... 60 B5   10 58S 132 35 E
Croker, C., Canada 84 B4   44 58N 80 59W
Croker I., Australia .... 60 B5   11 12S 132 32 E
Cromarty, U.K. 11 D4   57 40N   4 2W
Cromer, U.K. .... 12 E9   52 56N 1 17 E
Cromwell, N.Z. .... 59 L2   3 3S 169 14 E
Cromwell, U.S.A. 85 E12 41 36N 72 39W
Crook, U.K. 12 C6   54 43N   1 45W
Crooked →, Canada 70 C4   54 50N 122 54W
Crooked →, U.S.A. 76 D3   44 32N 121 16W
Crooked I., Bahamas 89 B5   22 50N 74 10W
Crooked Island Passage,
   Bahamas 89 B5   23 0N 74 10W
Crookston, Minn., U.S.A. 80 B6   47 47N 96 37W
Crookston, Nebr., U.S.A. 80 D4   42 56N 100 45W
Crookwell, Australia .... 63 E4   34 28S 149 24 E
Crosby, U.K. 12 D4   53 30N   3 3W
Crosby, N. Dak., U.S.A. 80 A3   48 55N 103 18W
Crosby, Pa., U.S.A. 84 E6   41 45N 78 23W
Crosbyton, U.S.A. 81 J4   33 40N 101 14W
Cross City, U.S.A. 83 L4   29 38N 83 7W
Cross Fell, U.K. 12 C5   54 43N   2 28W
Cross L., Canada 71 C9   54 45N 97 30W
Cross Lake, Canada 71 C9   54 37N 97 47W
Cross Sound, U.S.A. 68 C6   58 0N 135 0W
Crossett, U.S.A. 81 J9   33 8N 91 58W
Crosshaven, Ireland 10 E3   51 47N   8 17W
Crossville, U.S.A. 83 G3   35 57N 85 2W
Croswell, U.S.A. 84 C2   43 16N 82 37W
Croton-on-Hudson, U.S.A. 85 E11 41 12N 73 54W
Crotone, Italy .... 22 E7   39 5N 17 8 E
Crow →, Canada 70 B4   59 41N 124 20W
Crow Agency, U.S.A. 76 D10 45 36N 107 28W
Crow Hd., Ireland 10 E1   51 35N 10 9W
Crowell, U.S.A. 81 J5   33 59N 99 43W
Crowley, U.S.A. 81 K8   30 13N 92 22W
Crowley, L., U.S.A. 78 H8   37 35N 118 42W
Crown Point, Ind., U.S.A. 82 E2   41 25N 87 22W
Crown Point, N.Y., U.S.A. 85 C11 43 57N 73 26W
Crown Pt., Trin. & Tob. 93 J16 11 18N 60 51W
Crownpoint, U.S.A. 77 J9   35 41N 108 9W
Crows Landing, U.S.A. 78 H5   37 23N 121 6W
Crows Nest, Australia .... 63 D5   27 16S 152 4 E
Crowsnest Pass, Canada 70 D6   49 40N 114 40W
Croydon, Australia .... 62 B3   18 13S 142 14 E
Croydon □, U.K. 13 F7   51 22N   0 5W
Crozet, I., Ind. Oc. .... 3 G12 46 27S 52 0 E
Cruz, C., Cuba 88 C4   19 50N 77 50W
Cruz Alta, Brazil 95 B5   28 45S 53 40W
Cruz Bay, U.S. Virgin Is. ...... 89 e   18 20N 64 48W
Cruz del Eje, Argentina 94 C3   30 45S 64 50W
Cruzeiro, Brazil 95 A7   22 33S 45 0W
Cruzeiro do Oeste, Brazil 95 A5   23 46S 53 4W
Cruzeiro do Sul, Brazil 92 E4   7 35S 72 35W
Cry L., Canada 70 B3   58 45N 129 0W
Crystal Bay, U.S.A. 78 F7   39 15N 120 0W
Crystal Brook, Australia ...... 63 E2   33 21S 138 12 E
Crystal City, U.S.A. 81 L5   28 41N 99 50W
Crystal Falls, U.S.A. 82 B1   46 5N 88 20W
Crystal River, U.S.A. 83 L4   28 54N 82 35W
Crystal Springs, U.S.A. 81 K9   31 59N 90 21W
Csongrád, Hungary .... 17 E11 46 43N 20 9 E
Cu Lao Hon, Vietnam .... 39 G7   10 54N 108 18 E
Cua Rao, Vietnam .... 38 C5   19 16N 104 27 E
Cuácua →, Mozam. .... 55 F4   17 54S 37 0 E
Cuamato, Angola .... 56 B2   17 2S 15 7 E
Cuamba, Mozam. .... 55 E4   14 45S 36 22 E
Cuando →, Angola .... 53 H4   17 30S 23 15 E
Cuando Cubango □, Angola ... 56 B3   16 25S 20 0 E
Cuangar, Angola .... 56 B2   17 36S 18 39 E
Cuango = Kwango →, Dem. Rep.
   of the Congo .... 52 E3   3 14S 17 22 E
Cuanza →, Angola .... 52 F2   9 21S 13 9 E
Cuarto →, Argentina 94 C3   33 25S 63 2W
Cuatrociénegas, Mexico 86 B4   26 59N 102 5W
Cuauhtémoc, Mexico 86 B3   28 25N 106 52W
Cuba, N. Mex., U.S.A. 77 J10 36 1N 107 4W
Cuba, N.Y., U.S.A. 84 D6   42 13N 78 17W
Cuba ■, W. Indies 88 B4   22 0N 79 0W
Cubango →, Africa .... 56 B3   18 50S 22 25 E
Cuc Phuong △, Vietnam .... 38 B5   20 17N 105 38 E
Cuchumatanes, Sierra de los,
   Guatemala 88 C1   15 35N 91 25W
Cuckfield, U.K. 13 F7   51 1N   0 8W
Cucui, Brazil 92 C5   1 12N 66 50W
Cucurpe, Mexico 86 A2   30 20N 110 43W
Cúcuta, Colombia 92 B4   7 54N 72 31W
Cuddalore, India .... 40 P11 11 46N 79 45 E
Cuddapah, India .... 40 M11 14 30N 78 47 E
Cuddapan, L., Australia .... 62 D3   25 45S 141 26 E
Cue, Australia .... 61 E2   27 25S 117 54 E
Cuenca, Ecuador 92 D3   2 50S 79 9W
Cuenca, Spain 21 B4   40 5N   2 10W
Cuenca, Serranía de, Spain 21 C5   39 55N   1 50W
Cuernavaca, Mexico 87 D5   18 55N 99 15W
Cuero, U.S.A. 81 L6   29 6N 97 17W
Cueva de la Quebrada del
   Toro △, Venezuela 89 D6   10 46N 69 3W
Cuevas del Almanzora, Spain .. 21 D5   37 18N   1 58W
Cuevo, Bolivia 92 H6   20 15S 63 30W

Cuiabá, Brazil 93 G7   15 30S 56 0W
Cuiabá →, Brazil 93 G7   17 5S 56 36W
Cuihangcun, China .... 33 G10 22 27N 113 32 E
Cuijk, Neths. .... 15 C5   51 44N   5 52 E
Cuilco, Guatemala 88 C1   15 24N 91 58W
Cuillin Hills, U.K. 11 D2   57 13N   6 15W
Cuillin Sd., U.K. 11 D2   57 4N   6 20W
Cuito →, Angola .... 56 B3   18 1S 20 48 E
Cuitzeo, L. de, Mexico 86 D4   19 55N 101 5W
Cukai, Malaysia .... 39 K4   4 13N 103 25 E
Culbertson, U.S.A. 80 A2   48 9N 104 31W
Culcairn, Australia .... 63 F4   35 41S 147 3 E
Culebra, Isla de, Puerto Rico ... 89 d   18 19N 65 18W
Culgoa →, Australia .... 63 D4   29 56S 146 20 E
Culgoa Flood Plain △, Australia 63 D4   28 58S 147 5 E
Culiacán, Mexico 86 C3   24 50N 107 23W
Culiacán →, Mexico 86 C3   24 30N 107 42W
Culik, Indonesia .... 37 J18   8 21S 115 37 E
Culion, Phil. .... 37 B6   11 54N 119 58 E
Cullarin Ra., Australia .... 63 E4   34 30S 149 30 E
Cullen, U.K. 11 D6   57 42N   2 49W
Cullen Pt., Australia .... 62 A3   11 57S 141 54 E
Cullera, Spain 21 C5   39 9N   0 17W
Cullman, U.S.A. 83 H2   34 11N 86 51W
Cullompton, U.K. 13 G4   50 51N   3 24W
Culpeper, U.S.A. 82 F7   38 30N 78 0W
Culuene →, Brazil 93 F8   12 56S 52 51W
Culver, Pt., Australia .... 61 F3   32 54S 124 43 E
Culverden, N.Z. .... 59 K4   42 47S 172 49 E
Cumaná, Venezuela 92 A6   10 30N 64 5W
Cumberland, B.C., Canada 70 D4   49 40N 125 0W
Cumberland, Ont., Canada 85 A9   45 29N 75 24W
Cumberland, U.S.A. 82 F6   39 39N 78 46W
Cumberland →, U.S.A. 83 G2   36 15N 87 0W
Cumberland L., U.S.A. 83 G3   36 57N 84 55W
Cumberland Gap △, U.S.A. 83 G4   36 36N 83 40W
Cumberland Is., Australia ..... 62 J7   20 35S 149 10 E
Cumberland Island ⌒, U.S.A. .. 83 K5   30 12N 81 24W
Cumberland L., Canada 71 C8   54 3N 102 18W
Cumberland Pen., Canada 69 B13 67 0N 64 0W
Cumberland Plateau, U.S.A. ... 83 H3   36 0N 85 0W
Cumberland Sd., Canada 69 B13 65 30N 66 0W
Cumbernauld, U.K. 11 F5   55 57N   3 58W
Cumborah, Australia .... 63 D4   29 40S 147 45 E
Cumbria □, U.K. 12 C5   54 30N   3 0W
Cumbrian Mts., U.K. 12 C5   54 30N   3 0W
Cumbum, India .... 40 M11 15 40N 79 10 E
Cuminá →, Brazil 93 D7   1 30S 56 0W
Cummings Mt., U.S.A. 79 K8   35 2N 118 34W
Cummins, Australia .... 63 E2   34 16S 135 43 E
Cumnock, Australia .... 63 E4   32 59S 148 46 E
Cumnock, U.K. 11 F4   55 28N   4 17W
Cumpas, Mexico 86 B3   30 0N 109 48W
Cumplida, Pta., Canary Is. 24 F2   28 50N 17 48W
Cunco, Chile 96 D2   38 55S 72 2W
Cuncumén, Chile 94 C1   31 53S 70 38W
Cunderdin, Australia .... 61 F2   31 37S 117 12 E
Cunene →, Angola .... 56 B1   17 20S 11 50 E
Cúneo, Italy .... 20 D7   44 23N   7 32 E
Çüngüş, Turkey .... 44 B3   38 13N 39 17 E
Cunillera, I. = Sa Conillera, Spain 24 C7   38 59N   1 13 E
Cunnamulla, Australia .... 63 D4   28 2S 145 38 E
Cupar, Canada 71 C8   50 57N 104 10W
Cupar, U.K. 11 E5   56 19N   3 1W
Cupica, G. de, Colombia 92 B3   6 25N 77 30W
Curaçao, Neth. Ant. 89 D6   12 10N 69 0W
Curanilahue, Chile 94 D1   37 29S 73 28W
Curaray →, Peru 92 D4   2 20S 74 5W
Curepto, Chile 94 D1   35 8S 72 1W
Curiapo, Venezuela 92 B6   8 33N 61 5W
Curicó, Chile 94 C1   34 55S 71 20W
Curitiba, Brazil 95 B6   25 20S 49 10W
Curitibanos, Brazil 95 B5   27 18S 50 36W
Currabubula, Australia .... 63 E5   31 16S 150 44 E
Currais Novos, Brazil 93 E11   6 13S 36 30W
Curralinho, Brazil 93 D9   1 45S 49 46W
Currant, U.S.A. 76 G6   38 51N 115 32W
Currawinya △, Australia ...... 63 D3   28 55S 144 27 E
Current →, U.S.A. 81 G9   36 15N 90 55W
Currie, Australia .... 63 F3   39 56S 143 53 E
Currie, U.S.A. 76 F6   40 16N 114 45W
Curtea de Argeş, Romania .... 17 F13 45 12N 24 42 E
Curtis, U.S.A. 80 E4   40 38N 100 31W
Curtis Group, Australia .... 63 F4   39 30S 146 37 E
Curtis I., Australia .... 62 C5   23 35S 151 10 E
Curuápanema →, Brazil 93 D7   2 25S 55 2W
Curuçá, Brazil 93 D9   0 43S 47 50W
Curuguaty, Paraguay 95 A4   24 31S 55 42W
Curup, Indonesia .... 36 E2   4 26S 102 13 E
Cururupu, Brazil 93 D10   1 50S 44 50W
Curuzú Cuatiá, Argentina 94 B4   29 50S 58 5W
Curvelo, Brazil 93 G10 18 45S 44 27W
Cushing, U.S.A. 81 H6   35 59N 96 46W
Cushing, Mt., Canada 70 B3   57 35N 126 57W
Cusihuiriáchic, Mexico 86 B3   28 10N 106 50W
Custer, U.S.A. 80 D3   43 46N 103 36W
Cut Bank, U.S.A. 76 B7   48 38N 112 20W
Cutchogue, U.S.A. 85 E12 41 1N 72 30W
Cuthbert, U.S.A. 83 K3   31 46N 84 48W
Cutler, U.S.A. 78 J7   36 31N 119 17W
Cuttaburra →, Australia ...... 63 D3   29 43S 144 22 E
Cuttack, India .... 41 J14 20 25N 85 57 E
Cuvier, C., Australia .... 61 D1   23 14S 113 22 E
Cuvier I., N.Z. .... 59 G5   36 27S 175 50 E
Cuxhaven, Germany .... 16 B5   53 51N   8 41 E
Cuyahoga Falls, U.S.A. 84 E3   41 8N 81 29W
Cuyahoga Valley △, U.S.A. .... 37 B6   10 50N 121 5 E
Cuyo, Phil. .... 37 B6   10 50N 121 5 E
Cuyuni →, Guyana 92 B7   6 23N 58 41W
Cuzco, Bolivia 92 H5   20 0S 66 50W
Cuzco, Peru 92 F4   13 32S 72 0W
Cwmbran, U.K. 13 F4   51 39N   3 2W
Cyangugu, Rwanda .... 54 C2   2 29S 28 54 E
Cyclades = Kikládhes, Greece .. 23 F11 37 0N 24 30 E
Cygnet, Australia .... 63 G4   43 8S 147 1 E
Cynthiana, U.S.A. 82 F3   38 23N 84 18W
Cypress Hills, Canada 71 D7   49 40N 109 30W
Cypress Hills △, Canada 71 D7   49 40N 109 30W
Cyprus ■, Asia .... 25 E12 35 0N 33 0 E
Cyrenaica, Libya .... 51 C10 27 0N 23 0 E
Czar, Canada 71 C6   52 27N 110 50W
Czech Rep. ■, Europe .... 16 D8   50 0N 15 0 E
Częstochowa, Poland .... 17 C10 50 49N 19 7 E

D

Da ➤, Vietnam .... **38 B5** 21 15N 105 20 E
Da Hinggan Ling, China ...... **33 B7** 48 0N 121 0 E
Da Lat, Vietnam .... **39 G7** 11 56N 108 25 E
Da Nang, Vietnam .... **38 D7** 16 4N 108 13 E
Da Qaidam, China .... **32 C4** 37 50N 95 15 E
Da Yunhe ➤, China .... **35 G11** 34 25N 120 5 E
Da'an, China .... **35 B13** 45 30N 124 7 E
Daan Viljoen △, Namibia .... **56 C2** 22 2S 16 45 E
Daba Shan, China .... **33 C5** 32 0N 109 0 E
Dabbagh, Jabal, Si. Arabia ... **44 E2** 27 52N 35 45 E
Dabhoi, India .... **42 H5** 22 10N 73 20 E
Dabo = Pasirkuning, Indonesia . **36 E2** 0 30S 104 33 E
Dabola, Guinea **50 F3** 10 50N 11 5W
Dabung, Malaysia .... **39 K4** 5 23N 102 1 E
Dacca = Dhaka, Bangla. ..... **43 H14** 23 43N 90 26 E
Dacca = Dhaka □, Bangla. ... **43 G14** 24 25N 90 25 E
Dachau, Germany .... **16 D6** 48 15N 11 26 E
Dadanawa, Guyana **92 C7** 2 50N 59 30W
Dade City, U.S.A. **83 L4** 28 22N 82 11W
Dadhar, Pakistan .... **42 E2** 29 28N 67 39 E
Dadra & Nagar Haveli □, India . **40 J8** 20 5N 73 0 E
Dadri = Charkhi Dadri, India .. **42 E7** 28 37N 76 17 E
Dadu, Pakistan .... **42 F2** 26 45N 67 45 E
Daet, Phil. .... **37 B6** 14 2N 122 55 E
Dagana, Senegal **50 E2** 16 30N 15 35W
Daggett, U.S.A. **79 L10** 34 52N 116 52W
Daghestan Republic =
  Dagestan □, Russia ...... **19 F8** 42 30N 47 0 E
Dağlıq Qarabağ = Nagorno-
  Karabakh □, Azerbaijan ... **19 F8** 39 55N 46 45 E
Dagö = Hiiumaa, Estonia .... **9 G20** 58 50N 22 45 E
Dagu, China .... **35 E9** 38 59N 117 40 E
Dagupan, Phil. .... **37 A6** 16 3N 120 20 E
Daguragu, Australia .... **60 C5** 17 33S 130 30 E
Dahlak Kebir, Eritrea ...... **47 D3** 15 50N 40 10 E
Dahlonega, U.S.A. **83 H4** 34 32N 83 59W
Dahod, India .... **42 H6** 22 50N 74 15 E
Dahūk, Iraq .... **44 B3** 36 50N 43 1 E
Dai Hao, Vietnam .... **38 C6** 18 1N 106 25 E
Dai-Sen, Japan .... **31 G6** 35 22N 133 32 E
Dai Xian, China .... **34 E7** 39 4N 112 58 E
Daicheng, China .... **34 E9** 38 42N 116 38 E
Daingean, Ireland **10 C4** 53 18N 7 17W
Daintree, Australia .... **62 B4** 16 20S 145 20 E
Daintree △, Australia ...... **62 B4** 16 8S 145 2 E
Daiō-Misaki, Japan .... **31 G8** 34 15N 136 45 E
Daisen-Oki △, Japan .... **31 G6** 35 23N 133 34 E
Daisetsu-Zan, Japan .... **30 C11** 43 30N 142 57 E
Daisetsu-Zan △, Japan ..... **30 C11** 43 30N 142 55 E
Dajarra, Australia .... **62 C2** 21 42S 139 30 E
Dak Dam, Cambodia .... **38 F6** 12 20N 107 21 E
Dak Nhe, Vietnam .... **38 E6** 15 28N 107 48 E
Dak Pek, Vietnam .... **38 E6** 15 4N 107 44 E
Dak Song, Vietnam .... **39 F6** 12 19N 107 35 E
Dak Sui, Vietnam .... **38 E6** 14 55N 107 43 E
Dakar, Senegal **50 F2** 14 34N 17 29W
Dakhla, W. Sahara **50 D2** 23 50N 15 53W
Dakhla, El Wâhât el-, Egypt .. **51 C11** 25 30N 28 50 E
Dakor, India .... **42 H5** 22 45N 73 11 E
Dakota City, U.S.A. **80 D6** 42 25N 96 25W
Đakovica, Serbia & M. ...... **23 C9** 42 22N 20 26 E
Dalachi, China .... **34 F3** 36 48N 105 0 E
Dalai Nur, China .... **34 C9** 43 20N 116 45 E
Dālakī, Iran .... **45 D6** 29 26N 51 17 E
Dalälven ➤, Sweden .... **9 F17** 60 12N 16 43 E
Dalaman ➤, Turkey .... **23 F13** 36 41N 28 43 E
Dalandzadgad, Mongolia .... **34 C3** 43 27N 104 30 E
Dalap-Uliga-Darrit, Marshall Is. . **64 G9** 7 7N 171 24 E
Dalarna, Sweden .... **9 F16** 61 0N 14 0 E
Dālbandīn, Pakistan .... **40 E4** 29 0N 64 23 E
Dalbeattie, U.K. **11 G5** 54 56N 3 50W
Dalbeg, Australia .... **62 C4** 20 16S 147 18 E
Dalby, Australia .... **63 D5** 27 10S 151 17 E
Dale City, U.S.A. **82 F7** 38 38N 77 18W
Dale Hollow L., U.S.A. **83 G3** 36 32N 85 27W
Dalgān, Iran .... **45 E8** 27 31N 59 19 E
Dalhart, U.S.A. **81 G3** 36 4N 102 31W
Dalhousie, Canada **73 C6** 48 5N 66 26W
Dalhousie, India .... **42 C6** 32 38N 75 58 E
Dali, Shaanxi, China ...... **34 G5** 34 48N 109 58 E
Dali, Yunnan, China ...... **32 D5** 25 40N 100 10 E
Dalian, China .... **35 E11** 38 50N 121 40 E
Daliang Shan, China ...... **32 D5** 28 0N 102 45 E
Daling He ➤, China .... **35 D11** 40 55N 121 40 E
Dāliyat el Karmel, Israel .... **46 C4** 32 43N 35 2 E
Dalkeith, U.K. **11 F5** 55 54N 3 4W
Dallas, Oreg., U.S.A. **76 D2** 44 55N 123 19W
Dallas, Tex., U.S.A. **81 J6** 32 47N 96 49W
Dalmā, U.A.E. .... **45 E7** 24 30N 52 20 E
Dalmacija, Croatia .... **22 C7** 43 20N 17 0 E
Dalmas, L., Canada **73 B5** 53 30N 71 50W
Dalmatia = Dalmacija, Croatia . **22 C7** 43 20N 17 0 E
Dalmau, India .... **43 F9** 26 4N 81 2 E
Dalmellington, U.K. **11 F4** 55 19N 4 23W
Dalnegorsk, Russia .... **29 E14** 44 32N 135 33 E
Dalnerechensk, Russia ..... **29 E14** 45 50N 133 40 E
Dalnevostochnyy □, Russia .. **29 C14** 67 0N 140 0 E
Daloa, Ivory C. **50 G4** 7 0N 6 30W
Dalry, U.K. **11 F4** 55 42N 4 43W
Dalrymple, L., Australia .... **62 C4** 20 40S 147 0 E
Dalrymple, Mt., Australia ... **62 K6** 21 1S 148 39 E
Dalsland, Sweden .... **9 G14** 58 50N 12 15 E
Daltenganj, India .... **43 H11** 24 0N 84 4 E
Dalton, Ga., U.S.A. **83 H3** 34 46N 84 58W
Dalton, Mass., U.S.A. **85 D11** 42 28N 73 11W
Dalton, Nebr., U.S.A. **80 E3** 41 25N 102 58W
Dalton-in-Furness, U.K. **12 C4** 54 10N 3 11W
Dalvík, Iceland **8 D4** 65 58N 18 32W
Dalwallinu, Australia ...... **61 F2** 30 17S 116 40 E
Daly ➤, Australia .... **60 B5** 13 35S 130 19 E
Daly City, U.S.A. **78 H4** 37 42N 122 28W
Daly L., Canada **71 B7** 56 32N 105 39W
Daly River, Australia ...... **60 B5** 13 46S 130 42 E
Daly Waters, Australia ..... **62 B1** 16 15S 133 24 E
Dam Doi, Vietnam .... **39 H5** 8 50N 105 12 E
Dam Ha, Vietnam .... **38 B6** 21 21N 107 36 E
Daman, India .... **40 J8** 20 25N 72 57 E
Dāmaneh, Iran .... **45 C6** 33 1N 50 29 E
Damanhûr, Egypt .... **51 B12** 31 0N 30 30 E
Damant L., Canada **71 A7** 61 45N 105 5W
Damanzhuang, China ..... **34 E9** 38 55N 116 30 E
Damar, Indonesia .... **37 F7** 7 7S 128 40 E
Damaraland, Namibia ..... **56 C2** 20 0S 15 0 E
Damascus = Dimashq, Syria .. **46 B5** 33 30N 36 18 E

Damāvand, Iran .... **45 C7** 35 47N 52 0 E
Damāvand, Qolleh-ye, Iran .. **45 C7** 35 56N 52 10 E
Damba, Angola .... **52 F3** 6 44S 15 20 E
Dâmbovița ➤, Romania .... **17 F14** 44 12N 26 26 E
Dame Marie, Haiti **89 C5** 18 36N 74 26W
Dāmghān, Iran .... **45 B7** 36 10N 54 17 E
Damiel, Spain **21 C4** 39 4N 3 37W
Damietta = Dumyât, Egypt .. **51 B12** 31 24N 31 48 E
Daming, China .... **34 F8** 36 15N 115 6 E
Damir Qābū, Syria .... **44 B4** 36 58N 41 51 E
Dammam = Ad Dammām,
  Si. Arabia .... **45 E6** 26 20N 50 5 E
Damodar ➤, India .... **43 H12** 23 17N 87 35 E
Damoh, India .... **43 H8** 23 50N 79 28 E
Dampier, Australia .... **60 D2** 20 41S 116 42 E
Dampier, Selat, Indonesia .. **37 E8** 0 40S 131 0 E
Dampier Arch., Australia ... **60 D2** 20 38S 116 32 E
Damrei, Chuor Phnum,
  Cambodia .... **39 G4** 11 30N 103 0 E
Dan Xian, China .... **38 C7** 19 31N 109 33 E
Dana, Indonesia .... **37 F6** 11 0S 122 52 E
Dana, L., Canada **72 B4** 50 53N 77 20W
Dana, Mt., U.S.A. **78 H7** 37 54N 119 12W
Danakil Desert, Ethiopia ... **47 E3** 12 45N 41 0 E
Danané, Ivory C. **50 G4** 7 16N 8 9W
Danau Poso, Indonesia .... **37 E6** 1 52S 120 35 E
Danbury, U.S.A. **85 E11** 41 24N 73 28W
Danby L., U.S.A. **77 J6** 34 13N 115 5W
Dand, Afghan. .... **42 D1** 31 28N 65 32 E
Dande △, Zimbabwe ...... **55 F3** 15 56S 30 16 E
Dandeldhura, Nepal ...... **43 E9** 29 20N 80 35 E
Dandeli, India .... **40 M9** 15 5N 74 30 E
Dandenong, Australia ..... **63 F4** 38 0S 145 15 E
Dandong, China .... **35 D13** 40 10N 124 20 E
Danfeng, China .... **34 H6** 33 45N 110 25 E
Danger Is. = Pukapuka, Cook Is. . **65 J11** 10 53S 165 49W
Danger Pt., S. Africa ..... **56 E2** 34 40S 19 17 E
Danginpuri, Indonesia .... **37 K18** 8 40S 115 13 E
Dangla Shan = Tanggula Shan,
  China .... **32 C4** 32 40N 92 10 E
Dangrek, Phnom, Thailand .. **38 E5** 14 15N 105 0 E
Dangriga, Belize **87 D7** 17 0N 88 13W
Dangshan, China .... **34 G9** 34 27N 116 22 E
Daniel, U.S.A. **76 E8** 42 52N 110 4W
Daniel's Harbour, Canada .. **73 B8** 50 13N 57 35W
Danielskuil, S. Africa ..... **56 D3** 28 11S 23 33 E
Danielson, U.S.A. **85 E13** 41 48N 71 53W
Danilov, Russia .... **18 C7** 58 16N 40 13 E
Daning, China .... **34 F6** 36 28N 110 45 E
Dank, Oman .... **45 F8** 23 33N 56 16 E
Dankhar Gompa, India .... **40 C11** 32 10N 78 10 E
Danlí, Honduras **88 D2** 14 4N 86 35W
Dannemora, U.S.A. **85 B11** 44 43N 73 44W
Dannevirke, N.Z. .... **59 J6** 40 12S 176 8 E
Dannhauser, S. Africa ..... **57 D5** 28 0S 30 3 E
Dansville, U.S.A. **84 D7** 42 34N 77 42W
Danta, India .... **42 G5** 24 11N 72 46 E
Dantan, India .... **43 J12** 21 57N 87 20 E
Danube = Dunărea ➤, Europe . **17 F15** 45 20N 29 40 E
Danvers, U.S.A. **85 D14** 42 34N 70 56W
Danville, Ill., U.S.A. **82 E2** 40 8N 87 37W
Danville, Ky., U.S.A. **81 G3** 37 39N 84 46W
Danville, Pa., U.S.A. **85 F8** 40 58N 76 37W
Danville, Va., U.S.A. **83 G6** 36 36N 79 23W
Danville, Vt., U.S.A. **85 B12** 44 25N 72 9W
Danzig = Gdańsk, Poland ... **17 A10** 54 22N 18 40 E
Dapaong, Togo .... **50 F6** 10 55N 0 16 E
Daqing Shan, China ...... **34 D6** 40 40N 111 0 E
Dar Banda, Africa .... **48 F6** 8 0N 23 0 E
Dar el Beida = Casablanca,
  Morocco **50 B4** 33 36N 7 36W
Dar es Salaam, Tanzania ... **54 D4** 6 50S 39 12 E
Dar Mazār, Iran .... **45 D8** 29 14N 57 20 E
Dar'ā, Syria .... **46 C5** 32 36N 36 7 E
Dar'ā □, Syria .... **46 C5** 32 55N 36 10 E
Dārāb, Iran .... **45 D7** 28 50N 54 30 E
Daraban, Pakistan .... **42 D4** 31 44N 70 20 E
Daraina, Madag. .... **57 A8** 13 12S 49 40 E
Daraj, Libya .... **51 B8** 30 10N 10 28 E
Dārān, Iran .... **45 C6** 32 59N 50 24 E
Dārayyā, Syria .... **46 B5** 33 28N 36 15 E
Darband, Pakistan .... **42 B5** 34 20N 72 50 E
Darband, Küh-e, Iran ..... **45 D8** 31 34N 57 8 E
Darbhanga, India .... **43 F11** 26 15N 85 55 E
D'Arcy, Canada **70 C4** 50 27N 122 35W
Dardanelle, Ark., U.S.A. ... **81 H8** 35 13N 93 9W
Dardanelle, Calif., U.S.A. .. **78 G7** 38 20N 119 50W
Dardanelles = Çanakkale Boğazı,
  Turkey .... **23 D12** 40 17N 26 32 E
Dārestān, Iran .... **45 D8** 29 9N 58 42 E
Dārfūr, Sudan .... **51 F10** 13 40N 24 0 E
Dargai, Pakistan .... **42 B4** 34 25N 71 55 E
Dargan Ata, Turkmenistan .. **28 E7** 40 29N 62 10 E
Dargaville, N.Z. .... **59 F4** 35 57S 173 52 E
Darhan, Mongolia .... **32 B5** 49 37N 106 21 E
Darhan Muminggan Lianheqi,
  China .... **34 D6** 41 40N 110 28 E
Darıca, Turkey .... **23 D13** 40 45N 29 23 E
Darién △, Panama **88 E4** 7 36N 77 57W
Darién, G. del, Colombia ... **92 B3** 9 0N 77 0W
Dariganga = Ovoot, Mongolia . **34 B7** 45 21N 113 45 E
Darjeeling = Darjiling, India .. **43 F13** 27 3N 88 18 E
Darjiling, India .... **43 F13** 27 3N 88 18 E
Darkan, Australia .... **61 F2** 33 20S 116 43 E
Darkhana, Pakistan ...... **42 D5** 30 39N 72 11 E
Darkhazineh, Iran .... **45 D6** 31 54N 48 39 E
Darkot Pass, Pakistan .... **43 A5** 36 45N 73 26 E
Darling ➤, Australia ..... **63 E3** 34 4S 141 54 E
Darling Downs, Australia ... **63 D5** 27 30S 150 30 E
Darling Ra., Australia .... **61 F2** 32 30S 116 0 E
Darlington, U.K. **12 C6** 54 32N 1 33W
Darlington, U.S.A. **83 H6** 34 18N 79 52W
Darlington □, U.K. **12 C6** 54 32N 1 33W
Darlington, L., S. Africa ... **56 E4** 33 10S 25 9 E
Darłot, L., Australia ..... **61 E3** 27 48S 121 35 E
Darłowo, Poland .... **16 A9** 54 25N 16 25 E
Darmstadt, Germany ..... **16 D5** 49 51N 8 39 E
Darnah, Libya .... **51 B10** 32 45N 22 45 E
Darnall, S. Africa .... **57 D5** 29 23S 31 18 E
Darnley, C., Antarctica ... **5 C6** 68 0S 69 0 E
Darnley B., Canada **68 B7** 69 30N 123 30W
Darr ➤, Australia .... **62 C3** 23 39S 143 50 E
Darra Pezu, Pakistan ..... **42 C4** 32 19N 70 44 E
Darrequeira, Argentina ... **94 D3** 37 42S 63 10W
Darrington, U.S.A. **76 B3** 48 15N 121 36W
Dart ➤, U.K. **13 G4** 50 24N 3 39W
Dart, C., Antarctica **5 D14** 73 6S 126 20W
Dartford, U.K. .... **13 F8** 51 26N 0 13 E

Dartmoor, U.K. **13 G4** 50 38N 3 57W
Dartmoor △, U.K. **13 G4** 50 37N 3 59W
Dartmouth, Canada **73 D7** 44 40N 63 30W
Dartmouth, U.K. **13 G4** 50 21N 3 36W
Dartmouth Res., Australia .. **63 D4** 26 4S 145 18 E
Dartuch, C. = Artrutx, C. de,
  Spain .... **24 B10** 39 55N 3 49 E
Darvaza, Turkmenistan .... **28 E6** 40 11N 58 24 E
Darvel, Teluk = Lahad Datu,
  Teluk, Malaysia .... **37 D5** 4 50N 118 20 E
Darwen, U.K. **12 D5** 53 42N 2 29W
Darwendale, Zimbabwe ... **57 B5** 17 41S 30 33 E
Darwha, India .... **40 J10** 20 15N 77 45 E
Darwin, Australia .... **60 B5** 12 25S 130 51 E
Darwin, U.S.A. **79 J9** 36 15N 117 35W
Darya Khan, Pakistan .... **42 D4** 31 48N 71 6 E
Daryoi Amu = Amudarya ➤,
  Uzbekistan .... **28 E6** 43 58N 59 34 E
Dās, U.A.E. .... **45 E7** 25 20N 53 30 E
Dashen, Ras, Ethiopia .... **47 E2** 13 8N 38 26 E
Dashetai, China .... **34 D5** 41 0N 109 5 E
Dashhowuz, Turkmenistan .. **28 E6** 41 49N 59 58 E
Dashköpri, Turkmenistan .. **45 B9** 36 16N 62 8 E
Dasht, Iran .... **45 B8** 37 17N 56 7 E
Dasht ➤, Pakistan ...... **40 G2** 25 10N 61 40 E
Daska, Pakistan .... **42 C6** 32 20N 74 20 E
Dasuya, India .... **42 D6** 31 49N 75 38 E
Datça, Turkey .... **23 F12** 36 46N 27 40 E
Datia, India .... **43 G8** 25 39N 78 27 E
Datong, China .... **34 D7** 40 6N 113 18 E
Dattakhel, Pakistan ..... **42 C3** 32 54N 69 46 E
Datu, Tanjung, Indonesia .. **36 D3** 2 5N 109 39 E
Datu Piang, Phil. .... **37 C6** 7 2N 124 30 E
Datuk, Tanjong = Datu, Tanjung,
  Indonesia .... **36 D3** 2 5N 109 39 E
Daud Khel, Pakistan ..... **42 C4** 32 53N 71 34 E
Daudnagar, India .... **43 G11** 25 2N 84 24 E
Daugava ➤, Latvia ...... **9 H21** 57 4N 24 3 E
Daugavpils, Latvia ...... **9 J22** 55 53N 26 32 E
Daulpur, India .... **42 F7** 26 45N 77 59 E
Dauphin, Canada **71 C8** 51 9N 100 5W
Dauphin, U.S.A. **84 F8** 40 22N 76 56W
Dauphin L., Canada **71 C9** 51 20N 99 45W
Dauphiné, France .... **20 D6** 45 15N 5 25 E
Dausa, India .... **42 F7** 26 52N 76 20 E
Davao, Phil. .... **37 C7** 7 0N 125 40 E
Davao G., Phil. .... **37 C7** 6 30N 125 48 E
Dāvar Panāh = Sarāvān, Iran . **45 E9** 27 25N 62 15 E
Davenport, Calif., U.S.A. .. **78 H4** 37 1N 122 12W
Davenport, Iowa, U.S.A. .. **80 E9** 41 32N 90 35W
Davenport, Wash., U.S.A. .. **76 C4** 47 39N 118 9W
Davenport Ra., Australia ... **62 C1** 20 28S 134 0 E
Daventry, U.K. **13 E6** 52 16N 1 10W
David, Panama **88 E3** 8 30N 82 30W
David City, U.S.A. **80 E6** 41 15N 97 8W
David Gorodok = Davyd Haradok,
  Belarus .... **17 B14** 52 4N 27 8 E
Davidson, Canada **71 C7** 51 16N 105 59W
Davis, Antarctica ...... **5 C6** 68 34S 77 55 E
Davis, U.S.A. **78 G5** 38 33N 121 44W
Davis Dam, U.S.A. **79 K12** 35 11N 114 34W
Davis Inlet, Canada **73 A7** 55 50N 60 59W
Davis Mts., U.S.A. **81 K2** 30 50N 103 55W
Davis Sea, Antarctica ... **5 C7** 66 0S 92 0 E
Davis Str., N. Amer. **69 B14** 65 0N 58 0W
Davos, Switz. .... **20 C8** 46 48N 9 49 E
Davy L., Canada **71 B7** 58 53N 108 18W
Davyd Haradok, Belarus .. **17 B14** 52 4N 27 8 E
Dawei = Tavoy, Burma ... **38 E2** 14 2N 98 12 E
Dawes Ra., Australia .... **62 C5** 24 40S 150 40 E
Dawlish, U.K. **13 G4** 50 35N 3 28W
Dawna Ra., Burma ...... **38 D2** 16 30N 98 30 E
Dawros Hd., Ireland **10 B3** 54 50N 8 33W
Dawson, Canada **68 B6** 64 10N 139 30W
Dawson, U.S.A. **83 K3** 31 46N 84 27W
Dawson, I., Chile **96 G2** 53 50S 70 50W
Dawson B., Canada **71 C8** 52 53N 100 49W
Dawson Creek, Canada .. **70 B4** 55 45N 120 15W
Dawson Inlet, Canada .. **71 A10** 61 50N 93 25W
Dawson Ra., Australia .. **62 C4** 24 30S 149 48 E
Dax, France **20 E3** 43 44N 1 3W
Daxian, China .... **32 C5** 31 15N 107 23 E
Daxindian, China ...... **35 F11** 37 30N 120 50 E
Daxinggou, China ..... **35 C15** 43 25N 129 40 E
Daxue Shan, China .... **32 C5** 30 30N 101 30 E
Daylesford, Australia ... **63 F3** 37 21S 144 9 E
Dayr az Zawr, Syria ... **44 C4** 35 20N 40 5 E
Daysland, Canada **70 C6** 52 50N 112 20W
Dayton, Nev., U.S.A. .. **78 F7** 39 14N 119 36W
Dayton, Ohio, U.S.A. .. **82 F3** 39 45N 84 12W
Dayton, Pa., U.S.A. ... **84 F5** 40 53N 79 15W
Dayton, Tenn., U.S.A. .. **83 H3** 35 30N 85 1W
Dayton, Wash., U.S.A. .. **76 C4** 46 19N 117 59W
Dayton, Wyo., U.S.A. .. **76 D10** 44 53N 107 16W
Daytona Beach, U.S.A. .. **83 L5** 29 13N 81 1W
Dayville, U.S.A. **76 D4** 44 28N 119 32W
De Aar, S. Africa ..... **56 E3** 30 39S 24 0 E
De Biesbosch △, Neths. .. **15 C4** 51 45N 4 48 E
De Funiak Springs, U.S.A. .. **83 K2** 30 43N 86 7W
De Grey ➤, Australia ... **60 D2** 20 12S 119 13 E
De Haan, Belgium ..... **15 C3** 51 16N 3 2 E
De Hoge Veluwe △, Neths. . **15 B5** 52 5N 5 46 E
De Hoop △, S. Africa .. **56 E3** 34 30S 20 28 E
De Kalb, U.S.A. **80 E10** 41 56N 88 46W
De Kennemerduinen △, Neths. . **15 B4** 52 27N 4 33 E
De Land, U.S.A. **83 L5** 29 2N 81 18W
De Leon, U.S.A. **81 J5** 32 7N 98 32W
De Panne, Belgium .... **15 C2** 51 6N 2 34 E
De Pere, U.S.A. **82 C1** 44 27N 88 4W
De Queen, U.S.A. **81 H7** 34 2N 94 21W
De Quincy, U.S.A. **81 K8** 30 27N 93 26W
De Ridder, U.S.A. **81 K8** 30 51N 93 17W
De Smet, U.S.A. **80 C6** 44 23N 97 33W
De Soto, U.S.A. **80 F9** 38 8N 90 34W
De Tour Village, U.S.A. .. **82 C4** 46 0N 83 56W
De Witt, U.S.A. **81 H9** 34 18N 91 20W
Dead Sea, Asia ...... **46 D4** 31 30N 35 30 E
Deadwood, U.S.A. **80 C3** 44 23N 103 44W
Deadwood L., Canada .. **70 B3** 59 10N 128 30W
Deal, U.K. .... **13 F9** 51 13N 1 25 E
Deal I., Australia ..... **63 F4** 39 30S 147 20 E
Dealesville, S. Africa ... **56 D4** 28 41S 25 44 E
Dean ➤, Canada **70 C3** 52 49N 126 58W
Dean, Forest of, U.K. .. **13 F5** 51 45N 2 33W
Dean Chan., Canada .. **70 C3** 52 30N 127 0W
Deán Funes, Argentina .. **94 C3** 30 20S 64 20W
Dease ➤, Canada **70 B3** 59 56N 128 32W

Dease L., Canada **70 B2** 58 40N 130 5W
Dease Lake, Canada ... **70 B2** 58 25N 130 6W
Death Valley, U.S.A. .. **79 J10** 36 15N 116 50W
Death Valley △, U.S.A. . **79 J10** 36 45N 117 15W
Death Valley Junction, U.S.A. . **79 J10** 36 20N 116 25W
Debar, Macedonia .... **23 D9** 41 31N 20 30 E
Debden, Canada **71 C7** 53 30N 106 50W
Dębica, Poland ...... **17 C11** 50 2N 21 25 E
DeBolt, Canada **70 B5** 55 12N 118 1W
Deborah East, L., Australia . **61 F2** 30 45S 119 0 E
Deborah West, L., Australia . **61 F2** 30 45S 118 50 E
Debre Markos, Ethiopia .. **47 E2** 10 20N 37 40 E
Debre Tabor, Ethiopia .. **47 E2** 11 50N 38 2 E
Debre Zeyit, Ethiopia ... **47 F2** 11 48N 38 30 E
Debrecen, Hungary .... **17 E11** 47 33N 21 42 E
Decatur, Ala., U.S.A. .. **83 H2** 34 36N 86 59W
Decatur, Ga., U.S.A. .. **83 J3** 33 47N 84 18W
Decatur, Ill., U.S.A. ... **80 F10** 39 51N 88 57W
Decatur, Ind., U.S.A. .. **82 E3** 40 50N 84 56W
Decatur, Tex., U.S.A. .. **81 J6** 33 14N 97 35W
Deccan, India .... **40 L11** 18 0N 79 0 E
Deception Bay, Australia . **63 D5** 27 10S 153 5 E
Deception I., Antarctica . **5 C17** 63 0S 60 15W
Deception L., Canada .. **71 B8** 56 33N 104 13W
Dechhu, India .... **42 F5** 26 46N 72 20 E
Děčín, Czech Rep. .... **16 C8** 50 47N 14 12 E
Deckerville, U.S.A. **84 C2** 43 32N 82 44W
Decorah, U.S.A. **80 D9** 43 18N 91 48W
Dedéagach = Alexandroúpolis,
  Greece .... **23 D11** 40 50N 25 54 E
Dedham, U.S.A. **85 D13** 42 15N 71 10W
Dedza, Malawi ...... **55 E3** 14 20S 34 20 E
Dee ➤, Aberds., U.K. .. **11 D6** 57 9N 2 5W
Dee ➤, Dumf. & Gall., U.K. . **11 G4** 54 51N 4 3W
Dee ➤, Wales, U.K. .. **12 D4** 53 22N 3 17W
Deep B. = Shenzhen Wan,
  China .... **33 G10** 22 27N 113 55 E
Deepwater, Australia .. **63 D5** 29 25S 151 51 E
Deer ➤, Canada **71 B10** 58 23N 94 13W
Deer L., Canada **71 C10** 52 40N 94 20W
Deer Lake, Nfld. & L., Canada . **73 C8** 49 11N 57 27W
Deer Lake, Ont., Canada .. **71 C10** 52 36N 94 20W
Deer Lodge, U.S.A. ... **76 C7** 46 24N 112 44W
Deer Park, U.S.A. **76 C5** 47 57N 117 28W
Deer River, U.S.A. ... **80 B8** 47 20N 93 48W
Deeragun, Australia .. **62 B4** 19 16S 146 33 E
Deerdepoort, S. Africa . **56 C4** 24 37S 26 27 E
Deferiet, U.S.A. **85 B9** 44 2N 75 41W
Defiance, U.S.A. **82 E3** 41 17N 84 22W
Degana, India ...... **42 F6** 26 50N 74 20 E
Dégelis, Canada **73 C6** 47 30N 68 35W
Deggendorf, Germany .. **16 D7** 48 50N 12 57 E
Degh ➤, Pakistan .... **42 D5** 31 3N 73 21 E
Deh Bid, Iran ...... **45 D7** 30 39N 53 11 E
Deh-e Shīr, Iran .... **45 D7** 31 29N 53 45 E
Dehaj, Iran .... **45 D7** 30 42N 54 53 E
Dehak, Iran .... **45 E9** 27 11N 62 37 E
Dehdez, Iran ...... **45 D6** 31 43N 50 17 E
Dehej, India ...... **42 J5** 21 44N 72 40 E
Dehestān, Iran .... **45 D7** 28 30N 55 35 E
Dehgolān, Iran .... **44 C5** 35 17N 47 25 E
Dehibat, Tunisia .. **51 B8** 32 0N 10 47 E
Dehlorān, Iran .... **44 C5** 32 41N 47 16 E
Dehnow-e Kühestān, Iran . **45 E8** 27 58N 58 32 E
Dehra Dun, India ... **42 D8** 30 20N 78 4 E
Dehri, India ...... **43 G11** 24 50N 84 15 E
Dehui, China ..... **35 B13** 44 30N 125 40 E
Deinze, Belgium .. **15 D3** 50 59N 3 32 E
Dej, Romania .... **17 E12** 47 10N 23 52 E
Deka ➤, Zimbabwe .. **56 B4** 18 4S 26 42 E
Dekese, Dem. Rep. of the Congo . **52 E4** 3 24S 21 24 E
Del Mar, U.S.A. ... **79 N9** 32 58N 117 16W
Del Norte, U.S.A. .. **77 H10** 37 41N 106 21W
Del Rio, U.S.A. ... **81 L4** 29 22N 100 54W
Delambre I., Australia . **60 D2** 20 26S 117 5 E
Delano, U.S.A. ... **79 K7** 35 46N 119 15W
Delano Peak, U.S.A. . **77 G7** 38 22N 112 22W
Delareyville, S. Africa . **56 D4** 26 41S 25 26 E
Delaronde L., Canada . **71 C7** 54 3N 107 3W
Delavan, U.S.A. .. **80 D10** 42 38N 88 39W
Delaware, U.S.A. .. **82 E4** 40 18N 83 4W
Delaware □, U.S.A. . **82 F8** 39 0N 75 20W
Delaware ➤, U.S.A. . **85 G9** 39 15N 75 20W
Delaware B., U.S.A. . **82 F8** 39 0N 75 10W
Delaware Water Gap △, U.S.A. . **85 E10** 41 10N 74 55W
Delay ➤, Canada .. **73 A5** 56 56N 71 28W
Delegate, Australia . **63 F4** 37 4S 148 56 E
Delevan, U.S.A. .. **84 D6** 42 29N 78 29W
Delft, Neths. .... **15 B4** 52 1N 4 22 E
Delfzijl, Neths. .. **15 A6** 53 20N 6 55 E
Delgado, C., Mozam. . **55 E5** 10 45S 40 40 E
Delgerhet, Mongolia . **34 B6** 45 50N 110 30 E
Delgo, Sudan ... **51 D12** 20 6N 30 40 E
Delhi, Canada ... **84 D4** 42 51N 80 30W
Delhi, India .... **42 E7** 28 38N 77 17 E
Delhi, La., U.S.A. . **81 J9** 32 28N 91 30W
Delhi, N.Y., U.S.A. . **85 D10** 42 17N 74 55W
Delia, Canada .. **70 C6** 51 38N 112 23W
Delice, Turkey .. **19 G5** 39 54N 34 2 E
Delicias, Mexico . **86 B3** 28 13N 105 30W
Délíne, Canada .. **45 C6** 33 59N 56 30 E
Delisle, Canada . **71 C7** 51 55N 107 8W
Dell City, U.S.A. . **77 L11** 31 56N 105 12W
Dell Rapids, U.S.A. . **80 D6** 43 50N 96 43W
Delmar, U.S.A. . **85 D11** 42 37N 73 47W
Delmenhorst, Germany . **16 B5** 53 3N 8 37 E
Delonga, Ostrova, Russia . **29 B15** 76 40S 149 20 E
Deloraine, Australia . **63 G4** 41 30S 146 40 E
Deloraine, Canada . **71 D8** 49 15N 100 29W
Delphi, U.S.A. .. **82 E2** 40 36N 86 41W
Delphos, U.S.A. . **82 E3** 40 51N 84 21W
Delportshoop, S. Africa . **56 D3** 28 22S 24 20 E
Delray Beach, U.S.A. . **83 M5** 26 28N 80 4W
Delta, Colo., U.S.A. . **77 G9** 38 44N 108 4W
Delta, Utah, U.S.A. . **76 G7** 39 21N 112 35W
Delta Junction, U.S.A. . **68 B5** 64 2N 145 44W
Deltona, U.S.A. . **83 L5** 28 54N 81 16W
Delungra, Australia . **63 D5** 29 39S 150 51 E
Delvada, India . **42 J4** 20 46N 71 2 E
Delvinë, Albania . **23 E9** 39 59N 20 6 E
Demak, Indonesia . **37 G14** 6 53S 110 38 E
Demanda, Sierra de la, Spain . **21 A4** 42 15N 3 0W
Demavend = Damāvand, Qolleh-
  ye, Iran .... **45 C7** 35 56N 52 10 E
Dembia, Dem. Rep. of the Congo . **54 B2** 3 33N 25 48 E
Dembidolo, Ethiopia .. **47 F1** 8 34N 34 50 E

Demchok, India 43 C8 32 42N 79 29 E
Demer →, Belgium 15 D4 50 57N 4 42 E
Deming, N. Mex., U.S.A. 77 K10 32 16N 107 46W
Deming, Wash., U.S.A. 78 B4 48 50N 122 13W
Demini →, Brazil 92 D6 0 46S 62 56W
Demirci, Turkey 23 E13 39 2N 28 38 E
Demirköy, Turkey 23 D12 41 49N 27 45 E
Demopolis, U.S.A. 83 J2 32 31N 87 50W
Dempo, Indonesia 36 E2 4 2S 103 15 E
Den Burg, Neths. 15 A4 53 3N 4 47 E
Den Chai, Thailand 38 D3 17 59N 100 4 E
Den Haag = 's-Gravenhage, Neths. 15 B4 52 7N 4 17 E
Den Helder, Neths. 15 B4 52 57N 4 45 E
Den Oever, Neths. 15 B5 52 56N 5 2 E
Denair, U.S.A. 78 H6 37 32N 120 48W
Denau, Uzbekistan 28 F7 38 16N 67 54 E
Denbigh, Canada 84 A7 45 8N 77 15W
Denbigh, U.K. 12 D4 53 12N 3 25W
Denbighshire □, U.K. 12 D4 53 8N 3 22W
Dendang, Indonesia 36 E3 3 7S 107 56 E
Dendermonde, Belgium 15 C4 51 2N 4 5 E
Dengfeng, China 34 G7 34 25N 113 2 E
Dengkou, China 34 D4 40 18N 106 55 E
Denham, Australia 61 E1 25 56S 113 31 E
Denham, Mt., Jamaica 88 a 18 13N 77 32W
Denham Ra., Australia 62 C4 21 55S 147 46 E
Denham Sd., Australia 61 E1 25 45S 113 15 E
Denholm, Canada 71 C7 52 39N 108 1 W
Denia, Spain 21 C6 38 49N 0 8 E
Denial B., Australia 63 E1 32 14S 133 32 E
Deniliquin, Australia 63 F3 35 30S 144 58 E
Denison, Iowa, U.S.A. 80 E7 42 1N 95 21W
Denison, Tex., U.S.A. 81 J6 33 45N 96 33W
Denison Plains, Australia 60 C4 18 35S 128 0 E
Denizli, Turkey 19 G4 37 42N 29 2 E
Denman Glacier, Antarctica 5 C7 66 45S 99 25 E
Denmark, Australia 61 F2 34 59S 117 25 E
Denmark ■, Europe 9 J13 55 45N 10 0 E
Denmark Str., Atl. Oc. 4 C6 66 0N 30 0 W
Dennery, St. Lucia 89 f 13 55N 60 54W
Dennison, U.S.A. 84 F3 40 24N 81 19W
Denny, U.K. 11 E5 56 1N 3 55W
Denpasar, Indonesia 36 F5 8 39S 115 13 E
Denpasar ✕ (DPS), Indonesia 37 K18 8 44S 115 10 E
Denton, Mont., U.S.A. 76 C9 47 19N 109 57W
Denton, Tex., U.S.A. 81 J6 33 13N 97 8W
D'Entrecasteaux △, Australia 61 F2 34 20S 115 33 E
D'Entrecasteaux, Pt., Australia 61 F2 34 50S 115 57 E
Denver, Colo., U.S.A. 80 F2 39 44N 104 59W
Denver, Pa., U.S.A. 85 F8 40 14N 76 8W
Denver City, U.S.A. 81 J3 32 58N 102 50W
Deoband, India 42 E7 29 42N 77 43 E
Deogarh, India 42 G5 25 32N 73 54 E
Deoghar, India 43 G12 24 30N 86 42 E
Deolali, India 40 K8 19 58N 73 50 E
Deoli = Devli, India 42 G6 25 50N 75 20 E
Deora, India 42 F4 26 22N 70 55 E
Deori, India 43 H8 23 24N 79 1 E
Deoria, India 43 F10 26 31N 83 48 E
Deosai Mts., Pakistan 43 B6 35 40N 75 0 E
Deosri, India 43 F14 26 46N 90 29 E
Depalpur, India 42 H6 22 51N 75 33 E
Deping, China 35 F9 37 25N 116 58 E
Deposit, U.S.A. 85 D9 42 4N 75 25W
Depuch I., Australia 60 D2 20 37S 117 44 E
Deputatskiy, Russia 29 C14 69 18N 139 54 E
Dera Ghazi Khan, Pakistan 42 D4 30 5N 70 43 E
Dera Ismail Khan, Pakistan 42 D4 31 50N 70 50 E
Derabugti, Pakistan 42 E3 29 2N 69 9 E
Derawar Fort, Pakistan 42 E4 28 46N 71 20 E
Derbent, Russia 19 F8 42 5N 48 15 E
Derby, Australia 60 C3 17 18S 123 38 E
Derby, U.K. 12 E6 52 56N 1 28W
Derby, Conn., U.S.A. 85 E11 41 19N 73 5W
Derby, Kans., U.S.A. 81 G6 37 33N 97 16W
Derby, N.Y., U.S.A. 84 D6 42 41N 78 58W
Derby City □, U.K. 12 E6 52 56N 1 28W
Derby Line, U.S.A. 85 B12 45 0N 72 6W
Derbyshire □, U.K. 12 D6 53 11N 1 38W
Derdepoort, S. Africa 56 C4 24 38S 26 24 E
Dereham, U.K. 13 E8 52 41N 0 57 E
Derg →, Ukraine 10 B4 54 44N 7 26W
Derg, L., Ireland 10 D3 53 0N 8 20W
Dergaon, India 41 F19 26 45N 94 0 E
Dermott, U.S.A. 81 J9 33 32N 91 26W
Derry = Londonderry, U.K. 10 B4 55 0N 7 20W
Derry = Londonderry □, U.K. 10 B4 55 0N 7 20W
Derry, N.H., U.S.A. 85 D13 42 53N 71 19W
Derry, Pa., U.S.A. 84 F5 40 20N 79 18W
Derryveagh Mts., Ireland 10 B3 54 56N 8 11W
Derwent →, Cumb., U.K. 12 C4 54 39N 3 33W
Derwent →, Derby, U.K. 12 E6 52 57N 1 28W
Derwent →, N. Yorks., U.K. 12 D7 53 45N 0 58W
Derwent Water, U.K. 12 C4 54 35N 3 9W
Des Moines, Iowa, U.S.A. 80 E8 41 35N 93 37W
Des Moines, N. Mex., U.S.A. 81 G3 36 46N 103 50W
Des Moines →, U.S.A. 80 E9 40 23N 91 25W
Desaguadero →, Argentina 94 C2 34 30S 66 46W
Desaguadero →, Bolivia 92 G5 16 35S 69 5W
Desar, Malaysia 39 d 1 31N 104 17 E
Descanso, Pta., Mexico 79 N9 32 21N 117 3W
Deschaillons-sur-St-Laurent, Canada 73 C5 46 32N 72 7W
Deschambault L., Canada 71 C8 54 50N 103 30W
Deschutes →, U.S.A. 76 D3 45 38N 120 55W
Dese, Ethiopia 47 E2 11 5N 39 40 E
Deseado →, Argentina 96 F3 47 45S 65 54W
Desert Center, U.S.A. 79 M11 33 43N 115 24W
Desert Hot Springs, U.S.A. 79 M10 33 58N 116 30W
Deshnok, India 42 F5 27 48N 73 21 E
Desierto Central de Baja California △, Mexico 86 B2 29 40N 114 43W
Desna →, Ukraine 17 C16 50 33N 30 32 E
Desolación, I., Chile 96 G2 53 0S 74 0W
Despeñaperros, Paso, Spain 21 C4 38 24N 3 30W
Dessau, Germany 16 C7 51 51N 12 14 E
Dessye = Dese, Ethiopia 47 E2 11 5N 39 40 E
D'Estrees B., Australia 63 F2 35 55S 137 45 E
Desuri, India 42 G5 25 18N 73 35 E
Det Udom, Thailand 38 E5 14 54N 105 5 E
Dete, Zimbabwe 56 B4 18 38S 26 50 E
Detmold, Germany 16 C5 51 56N 8 52 E
Detour, Pt., U.S.A. 82 C2 45 40N 86 40W
Detroit, U.S.A. 84 D1 42 20N 83 3W
Detroit Lakes, U.S.A. 80 B7 46 49N 95 51W
Deurne, Neths. 15 C5 51 27N 5 49 E
Deutsche Bucht, Germany 16 A5 54 15N 8 0 E

Deva, Romania 17 F12 45 53N 22 55 E
Devakottai, India 40 Q11 9 55N 78 45 E
Devaprayag, India 43 D8 30 13N 78 35 E
Deventer, Neths. 15 B6 52 15N 6 10 E
Deveron →, U.K. 11 D6 57 41N 2 32W
Devgadh Bariya, India 42 H5 22 40N 73 55 E
Devikot, India 42 F4 26 42N 71 12 E
Devils Den, U.S.A. 78 K7 35 46N 119 58W
Devils Lake, U.S.A. 80 A5 48 7N 98 52W
Devils Paw, Canada 70 B2 58 47N 134 0W
Devils Postpile ○, U.S.A. 78 H7 37 37N 119 5W
Devils Tower ○, U.S.A. 80 C2 44 35N 104 43W
Devils Tower Junction, U.S.A. 80 C2 44 31N 104 57W
Devine, U.S.A. 81 L5 29 8N 98 54W
Devizes, U.K. 13 F6 51 22N 1 58W
Devli, India 42 G6 25 50N 75 20 E
Devon, Canada 70 C6 53 24N 113 44W
Devon I., Canada 4 B3 75 10N 85 0W
Devonport, Australia 63 G4 41 10S 146 22 E
Devonport, N.Z. 59 G5 36 49S 174 49 E
Dewas, India 42 H7 22 59N 76 3 E
Dewetsdorp, S. Africa 56 D4 29 33S 26 39 E
Dewey, Puerto Rico 89 d 18 18N 65 18W
Dexter, Maine, U.S.A. 83 C11 45 1N 69 18W
Dexter, Mo., U.S.A. 81 G10 36 48N 89 57W
Dexter, N. Mex., U.S.A. 81 J2 33 12N 104 22W
Dey-Dey, L., Australia 61 E5 29 12S 131 4 E
Deyhūk, Iran 45 C8 33 15N 57 30 E
Deyyer, Iran 45 E6 27 55N 51 55 E
Dezadeash L., Canada 70 A1 60 28N 136 58W
Dezfūl, Iran 45 C6 32 20N 48 30 E
Dezhneva, Mys, Russia 29 C19 66 5N 169 40W
Dezhou, China 34 F9 37 26N 116 18 E
Dhadhar →, India 43 G11 24 56N 85 24 E
Dháfni, Greece 25 D7 35 13N 25 3 E
Dhahiriya = Az Zāhirīyah, West Bank 46 D3 31 25N 34 58 E
Dhahran = Az Zahrān, Si. Arabia 45 E6 26 10N 50 7 E
Dhak, Pakistan 42 C5 32 25N 72 33 E
Dhaka, Bangla. 43 H14 23 43N 90 26 E
Dhaka □, Bangla. 43 G14 24 25N 90 25 E
Dhali, Cyprus 25 D12 35 1N 33 25 E
Dhampur, India 43 E8 29 19N 78 33 E
Dhamtari, India 41 J12 20 42N 81 35 E
Dhanbad, India 43 H12 23 50N 86 30 E
Dhangarhi, Nepal 41 E12 28 55N 80 40 E
Dhankuta, Nepal 43 F12 26 55N 87 40 E
Dhar, India 42 H6 22 35N 75 26 E
Dharampur, India 42 H6 22 13N 75 18 E
Dharamsala = Dharmsala, India 42 C7 32 16N 76 23 E
Dhariwal, India 42 D6 31 57N 75 19 E
Dharla →, Bangla. 43 G13 25 46N 89 42 E
Dharmapuri, India 40 N11 12 10N 78 10 E
Dharmjaygarh, India 43 H10 22 28N 83 13 E
Dharmsala, India 42 C7 32 16N 76 23 E
Dharni, India 42 J7 21 33N 76 53 E
Dharwad, India 40 M9 15 30N 75 4 E
Dhasan →, India 43 G8 25 48N 79 24 E
Dhaulagiri, Nepal 43 E10 28 39N 83 28 E
Dhebar, L., India 42 G6 24 10N 74 0 E
Dheftera, Cyprus 25 D12 35 5N 33 16 E
Dhenkanal, India 41 J14 20 45N 85 35 E
Dherinia, Cyprus 25 D12 35 3N 33 57 E
Dhī Qār □, Iraq 44 D5 31 0N 46 15 E
Dhiarrizos →, Cyprus 25 E11 34 41N 32 34 E
Dhībān, Jordan 46 D4 31 30N 35 46 E
Dhíkti Óros, Greece 25 D7 35 8N 25 30 E
Dhilwan, India 42 D6 31 31N 75 21 E
Dhimarkhera, India 43 H9 23 28N 80 22 E
Dhírfis Óros, Greece 23 E10 38 40N 23 54 E
Dhodhekánisos, Greece 23 F12 36 35N 27 0 E
Dholka, India 42 H5 22 44N 72 29 E
Dhoraji, India 42 J4 21 45N 70 37 E
Dhránios, Ákra, Greece 25 A3 39 48N 19 40 E
Dhrangadhra, India 42 H4 22 59N 71 31 E
Dhrápanon, Ákra, Greece 25 D6 35 28N 24 14 E
Dhrol, India 42 H4 22 33N 70 25 E
Dhuburi, India 41 F16 26 2N 89 59 E
Dhule, India 40 J9 20 58N 74 50 E
Di Linh, Vietnam 39 G7 11 35N 108 4 E
Di Linh, Cao Nguyen, Vietnam 39 G7 11 30N 108 0 E
Día, Greece 25 D7 35 28N 25 14 E
Diablo, Mt., U.S.A. 78 H5 37 53N 121 56W
Diablo Range, U.S.A. 78 J5 37 20N 121 25W
Diafarabé, Mali 50 F5 14 9N 4 57W
Diamante, Argentina 94 C3 32 5S 60 40W
Diamante →, Argentina 94 C2 34 30S 66 46W
Diamantina, Brazil 93 G10 18 17S 43 40W
Diamantina →, Australia 63 D2 26 45S 139 10 E
Diamantino, Brazil 93 F7 14 30S 56 30W
Diamond Bar, U.S.A. 79 L9 34 1N 117 48W
Diamond Harbour, India 43 H13 22 11N 88 14 E
Diamond Is., Australia 62 B5 17 25S 151 5 E
Diamond Mts., U.S.A. 76 G6 39 50N 115 30W
Diamond Springs, U.S.A. 78 G6 38 42N 120 49W
Dībā, Oman 45 E8 25 45N 56 16 E
Dibai, India 42 E8 28 13N 78 15 E
Dibaya-Lubue, Dem. Rep. of the Congo 52 E3 4 12S 19 54 E
Dibbeen △, Jordan 46 C4 32 20N 35 45 E
Dibete, Botswana 56 C4 23 45S 26 32 E
Dibrugarh, India 41 F19 27 29N 94 55 E
Dickens, U.S.A. 81 J4 33 37N 100 50W
Dickinson, U.S.A. 80 B3 46 53N 102 47W
Dickson, U.S.A. 83 G2 36 5N 87 23W
Dickson City, U.S.A. 85 E9 41 29N 75 40W
Didiéni, Mali 50 F4 13 53N 8 6W
Didsbury, Canada 70 C6 51 35N 114 10W
Didwana, India 42 F6 27 23N 74 36 E
Diefenbaker, L., Canada 71 C7 51 0N 106 55W
Diego de Almagro, Chile 94 B1 26 22S 70 3W
Diego Garcia, Ind. Oc. 3 E13 7 50S 72 50 E
Diekirch, Lux. 15 E6 49 52N 6 10 E
Dien Ban, Vietnam 38 E7 15 53N 108 16 E
Dien Bien, Vietnam 38 B4 21 20N 103 0 E
Dien Khanh, Vietnam 39 F7 12 15N 109 6 E
Dieppe, France 20 B4 49 54N 1 4 E
Dierks, U.S.A. 81 H4 34 7N 94 1W
Diest, Belgium 15 D5 50 58N 5 4 E
Dif, Somali Rep. 47 G3 0 59N 40 58 E
Differdange, Lux. 15 E5 49 31N 5 54 E
Dig, India 42 F7 27 28N 77 20 E
Digba, Dem. Rep. of the Congo 54 B2 2 5N 31 E
Digby, Canada 73 D6 44 38N 65 50W
Diggi, India 42 F6 26 22N 75 26 E
Dighinala, Bangla. 41 H18 23 15N 92 5 E

Dighton, U.S.A. 80 F4 38 29N 100 28W
Digne-les-Bains, France 20 D7 44 5N 6 12 E
Digos, Phil. 37 C7 6 45N 125 20 E
Digranes, Iceland 8 C6 66 4N 14 44W
Digul →, Indonesia 37 F9 7 5S 138 42 E
Dihang = Brahmaputra →, Asia 32 D3 23 40N 90 35 E
Dijlah, Nahr →, Asia 44 D5 31 0N 47 25 E
Dijon, France 20 C6 47 20N 5 3 E
Dikhil, Djibouti 47 E3 11 8N 42 20 E
Dikkil = Dikhil, Djibouti 47 E3 11 8N 42 20 E
Diksmuide, Belgium 15 C2 51 2N 2 52 E
Dikson, Russia 28 B9 73 40N 80 5 E
Dila, Ethiopia 47 F2 6 21N 38 22 E
Dili, E. Timor 37 F7 8 39S 125 34 E
Dilley, U.S.A. 81 L5 28 40N 99 10W
Dilli = Delhi, India 42 E7 28 38N 77 17 E
Dillingham, U.S.A. 68 C4 59 3N 158 28W
Dillon, Canada 71 B7 55 56N 108 35W
Dillon, Mont., U.S.A. 76 D7 45 13N 112 38W
Dillon, S.C., U.S.A. 83 H6 34 25N 79 22W
Dillon →, Canada 71 B7 55 56N 108 56W
Dillsburg, U.S.A. 84 F7 40 7N 77 2W
Dilolo, Dem. Rep. of the Congo 52 G4 10 28S 22 18 E
Dimas, Mexico 86 C3 23 43N 106 47W
Dimashq, Syria 46 B5 33 30N 36 18 E
Dimashq □, Syria 46 B5 33 30N 36 30 E
Dimbaza, S. Africa 57 E4 32 50S 27 14 E
Dimboola, Australia 63 F3 36 28S 142 7 E
Dîmbovița = Dâmbovița →, Romania 17 F14 44 12N 26 26 E
Dimbulah, Australia 62 B4 17 8S 145 4 E
Dimitrovgrad, Bulgaria 23 C11 42 5N 25 35 E
Dimitrovgrad, Russia 18 D8 54 14N 49 39 E
Dimitrovo = Pernik, Bulgaria 23 C10 42 35N 23 2 E
Dimmitt, U.S.A. 81 H3 34 33N 102 19W
Dimona, Israel 46 D4 31 2N 35 1 E
Dinagat, Phil. 37 B7 10 10N 125 40 E
Dinajpur, Bangla. 41 G16 25 33N 88 43 E
Dinan, France 20 B2 48 28N 2 2W
Dīnān Āb, Iran 45 C8 32 4N 56 49 E
Dinant, Belgium 15 D4 50 16N 4 55 E
Dinapur, India 43 G11 25 38N 85 5 E
Dinar, Turkey 19 G4 38 5N 30 15 E
Dīnār, Kūh-e, Iran 45 D6 30 42N 51 46 E
Dinard, France 20 B2 48 38N 2 6W
Dinaric Alps = Dinara Planina, Croatia 22 C7 44 0N 16 30 E
Dindigul, India 40 P11 10 25N 78 0 E
Dindori, India 43 H9 22 57N 81 5 E
Ding Xian = Dingzhou, China 34 E8 38 30N 114 59 E
Dinga, Pakistan 42 G2 25 26N 67 10 E
Dingbian, China 34 F4 37 35N 107 32 E
Dingle, Ireland 10 D1 52 9N 10 17W
Dingle B., Ireland 10 D1 52 3N 10 20W
Dingmans Ferry, U.S.A. 85 E10 41 13N 74 55W
Dingo, Australia 62 C4 23 38S 149 19 E
Dingtao, China 34 G8 35 5N 115 35 E
Dingwall, U.K. 11 D4 57 36N 4 26W
Dingxi, China 34 G3 35 30N 104 33 E
Dingxiang, China 34 E7 38 30N 112 58 E
Dingzhou, China 34 E8 38 30N 114 59 E
Dinh, Mui, Vietnam 39 G7 11 22N 109 1 E
Dinh Lap, Vietnam 38 B6 21 33N 107 6 E
Dinira △, Venezuela 89 E6 9 57N 70 6W
Dinokwe, Botswana 56 C4 23 29S 26 37 E
Dinorwic, Canada 71 D10 49 41N 92 30W
Dinosaur ○, Canada 70 C6 50 47N 111 30W
Dinosaur ○, U.S.A. 76 F9 40 30N 108 45W
Dinuba, U.S.A. 78 J7 36 32N 119 23W
Dipalpur, Pakistan 42 D5 30 40N 73 39 E
Diplo, Pakistan 42 G3 24 35N 69 35 E
Dipolog, Phil. 37 C6 8 36N 123 20 E
Dipperu △, Australia 62 C4 21 56S 148 42 E
Dir, Pakistan 40 B7 35 8N 71 59 E
Dire Dawa, Ethiopia 47 F3 9 35N 41 45 E
Diriamba, Nic. 88 D2 11 51N 86 19W
Dirk Hartog I., Australia 61 E1 25 50S 113 5 E
Dirranbandi, Australia 63 D4 28 33S 148 17 E
Disa, India 42 G5 24 18N 72 10 E
Disappointment, C., U.S.A. 76 C2 46 18N 124 5W
Disappointment, L., Australia 60 D3 23 20S 122 40 E
Disaster B., Australia 63 F4 37 15S 149 58 E
Discovery B., Australia 63 F3 38 10S 140 40 E
Discovery B., China 33 G11 22 18N 114 1 E
Disko = Qeqertarsuaq, Greenland 69 B5 69 45N 53 30W
Diss, U.K. 13 E9 52 23N 1 7 E
Disteghil Sar, Pakistan 43 A6 36 20N 75 12 E
Distrito Federal □, Brazil 93 G9 15 45S 47 45W
Distrito Federal □, Mexico 87 D5 19 15N 99 10W
Diu, India 42 J4 20 45N 70 58 E
Dīvāndarreh, Iran 44 C5 35 55N 47 2 E
Divide, U.S.A. 76 D7 45 45N 112 45W
Dividing Ra., Australia 61 E2 27 45S 114 0 E
Divinópolis, Brazil 93 H10 20 10S 44 54W
Divnoye, Russia 19 E7 45 55N 43 21 E
Divo, Ivory C. 50 G4 5 48N 5 15W
Dīwāl Kol, Afghan. 42 B2 34 23N 67 52 E
Dixie Mt., U.S.A. 78 F6 39 55N 120 16W
Dixon, Calif., U.S.A. 78 G5 38 27N 121 49W
Dixon, Ill., U.S.A. 80 E10 41 50N 89 29W
Dixon Entrance, U.S.A. 68 C6 54 30N 132 0W
Dixville, Canada 85 A13 45 4N 71 46W
Diyālá □, Iraq 44 C5 33 45N 44 50 E
Diyālá →, Iraq 44 C5 33 14N 44 31 E
Diyarbakır, Turkey 19 G7 37 55N 40 18 E
Diyodar, India 42 G4 24 8N 71 50 E
Djakarta = Jakarta, Indonesia 36 F3 6 9S 106 49 E
Djamba, Angola 56 B1 16 45S 13 58 E
Djambala, Congo 52 E2 2 32S 14 30 E
Djanet, Algeria 50 D7 24 35N 9 32 E
Djawa = Jawa, Indonesia 36 F3 7 0S 110 0 E
Djelfa, Algeria 50 B6 34 40N 3 15 E
Djema, C.A.R. 54 A2 6 3N 25 15 E
Djerba, I. de, Tunisia 51 B8 33 50N 10 48 E
Djerid, Chott, Tunisia 50 B7 33 42N 8 30 E
Djibouti, Djibouti 47 E3 11 30N 43 5 E
Djibouti ■, Africa 47 E3 12 0N 43 0 E
Djolu, Dem. Rep. of the Congo 52 D4 0 35N 22 5 E
Djoum, Cameroon 52 D2 2 41N 12 35 E
Djourab, Erg du, Chad 51 E9 16 40N 18 50 E
Djugu, Dem. Rep. of the Congo 54 B3 1 55N 30 35 E
Djúpivogur, Iceland 8 D6 64 39N 14 17W
Dmitriya Lapteva, Proliv, Russia 29 B15 73 0N 140 0 E
Dnepr = Dnipro →, Ukraine 19 E5 46 30N 32 18 E
Dneprodzerzhinsk = Dniprodzerzhynsk, Ukraine 19 E5 48 32N 34 37 E
Dnepropetrovsk = Dnipropetrovsk, Ukraine 19 E6 48 30N 35 0 E

Dnestr = Dnister →, Europe 17 E16 46 18N 30 17 E
Dnieper = Dnipro →, Ukraine 19 E5 46 30N 32 18 E
Dniester = Dnister →, Europe 17 E16 46 18N 30 17 E
Dnipro →, Ukraine 19 E5 46 30N 32 18 E
Dniprodzerzhynsk, Ukraine 19 E5 48 32N 34 37 E
Dnipropetrovsk, Ukraine 19 E6 48 30N 35 0 E
Dnister →, Europe 17 E16 46 18N 30 17 E
Dno, Russia 18 C4 57 50N 29 58 E
Dnyapro = Dnipro →, Ukraine 19 E5 46 30N 32 18 E
Doaktown, Canada 73 C6 46 36N 66 8W
Doan Hung, Vietnam 38 B5 21 30N 105 10 E
Doany, Madag. 57 A8 14 21S 49 30 E
Doba, Chad 51 G9 8 40N 16 50 E
Dobandi, Pakistan 42 D2 31 13N 66 50 E
Dobbyn, Australia 62 B3 19 44S 140 2 E
Dobele, Latvia 9 H20 56 37N 23 16 E
Doberai, Jazirah, Indonesia 37 E8 1 25S 133 0 E
Doblas, Argentina 94 D3 37 5S 64 0W
Dobo, Indonesia 37 F8 5 45S 134 15 E
Doboj, Bos.-H. 23 B8 44 46N 18 4 E
Dobrich, Bulgaria 23 C12 43 37N 27 49 E
Dobruja, Europe 17 F15 44 30N 28 15 E
Dobrush, Belarus 17 B16 52 25N 31 10 E
Doc, Mui, Vietnam 38 D6 17 58N 106 30 E
Docker River, Australia 61 D4 24 52S 129 5 E
Doctor Arroyo, Mexico 86 C4 23 40N 100 11W
Doda, India 43 C6 33 10N 75 34 E
Doda, L., Canada 72 C4 49 25N 75 13W
Dodecanese = Dhodhekánisos, Greece 23 F12 36 35N 27 0 E
Dodge City, U.S.A. 81 G5 37 45N 100 1W
Dodge L., Canada 71 B7 59 50N 105 36W
Dodgeville, U.S.A. 80 D9 42 58N 90 8W
Dodoma, Tanzania 54 D4 6 8S 35 45 E
Dodoma □, Tanzania 54 D4 6 0S 36 0 E
Dodori □, Kenya 54 C5 1 55S 41 7 E
Dodsland, Canada 71 C7 51 50N 108 45W
Dodson, U.S.A. 76 B9 48 24N 108 15W
Doesburg, Neths. 15 B6 52 1N 6 9 E
Doetinchem, Neths. 15 C6 51 59N 6 18 E
Dog Creek, Canada 70 C4 51 35N 122 14W
Dog L., Man., Canada 71 C9 51 2N 98 31W
Dog L., Ont., Canada 72 C2 48 48N 89 30W
Dogran, Pakistan 42 D5 31 48N 73 35 E
Doğubayazıt, Turkey 44 B5 39 31N 44 5 E
Doha = Ad Dawḥah, Qatar 45 E6 25 15N 51 35 E
Dohazari, Bangla. 41 H18 22 10N 92 5 E
Dohrighat, India 43 F10 26 16N 83 31 E
Doi, Indonesia 37 D7 2 14N 127 49 E
Doi Inthanon △, Thailand 38 C2 18 33N 98 34 E
Doi Khuntan △, Thailand 38 C2 18 33N 99 14 E
Doi Luang, Thailand 38 C2 18 30N 101 0 E
Doi Luang △, Thailand 38 C2 19 22N 99 35 E
Doi Saket, Thailand 38 C2 18 52N 99 9 E
Doi Suthep △, Thailand 38 C2 18 49N 98 53 E
Dois Irmãos, Sa., Brazil 93 E10 9 0S 42 30W
Dokkum, Neths. 15 A5 53 20N 5 59 E
Dokri, Pakistan 42 F3 27 25N 68 7 E
Dolak, Pulau, Indonesia 37 F9 8 0S 138 30 E
Dolbeau-Mistassini, Canada 73 C5 48 53N 72 14W
Dole, France 20 C6 47 7N 5 31 E
Dolgellau, U.K. 12 E4 52 45N 3 53W
Dolgelley = Dolgellau, U.K. 12 E4 52 45N 3 53W
Dollard, Neths. 15 A7 53 20N 7 10 E
Dolo, Ethiopia 47 G3 4 11N 42 3 E
Dolomites = Dolomiti, Italy 22 A4 46 23N 11 51 E
Dolomiti, Italy 22 A4 46 23N 11 51 E
Dolores, Argentina 94 D4 36 20S 57 40W
Dolores, Uruguay 94 C4 33 34S 58 15W
Dolores, U.S.A. 77 H9 37 28N 108 30W
Dolores →, U.S.A. 77 G9 38 49N 109 17W
Dolphin, C., Falk. Is. 96 G5 51 10S 59 0W
Dolphin and Union Str., Canada 68 B8 69 5N 114 45W
Dom Pedrito, Brazil 95 C5 31 0S 54 40W
Doma ○, Zimbabwe 55 F3 16 28S 30 12 E
Domariaganj →, India 43 F10 26 17N 83 44 E
Domasi, Malawi 55 F4 15 15S 35 22 E
Dombarovskiy, Russia 28 D6 50 46N 59 32 E
Dombås, Norway 9 E13 62 4N 9 8 E
Dom Fuji, Antarctica 5 D7 77 20S 39 45 E
Domel I. = Letsôk-aw Kyun, Burma 39 G2 11 30N 98 25 E
Domeyko, Chile 94 B1 29 0S 71 0W
Domeyko, Cordillera, Chile 94 A2 24 30S 69 0W
Dominador, Chile 94 A2 24 21S 69 20W
Dominica ■, W. Indies 89 C7 15 20N 61 20W
Dominica Passage, W. Indies 89 C7 15 10N 61 20W
Dominican Rep. ■, W. Indies 89 C5 19 0N 70 30W
Domodóssola, Italy 20 C8 46 7N 8 17 E
Domville, Mt., Australia 63 D5 28 1S 151 15 E
Don →, Russia 19 E6 47 4N 39 18 E
Don →, Aberds., U.K. 11 D6 57 11N 2 5W
Don →, S. Yorks., U.K. 12 D7 53 41N 0 52W
Don, C., Australia 60 B5 11 18S 131 46 E
Don Benito, Spain 21 C3 38 53N 5 51W
Don Figuero Mts., Jamaica 88 a 18 5N 77 36W
Don Sak, Thailand 39 b 9 18N 99 41 E
Dona Ana = Nhamaabué, Mozam. 55 F4 17 25S 35 5 E
Donaghadee, U.K. 10 B6 54 39N 5 33W
Donald, Australia 63 F3 36 23S 143 0 E
Donaldsonville, U.S.A. 81 K9 30 6N 90 59W
Donalsonville, U.S.A. 83 K3 31 3N 84 53W
Donau = Dunărea →, Europe 17 F15 45 20N 29 40 E
Donauwörth, Germany 16 D6 48 43N 10 47 E
Doncaster, U.K. 12 D6 53 32N 1 6W
Dondo, Mozam. 55 F3 19 33S 34 46 E
Dondo, Teluk, Indonesia 37 D6 0 50N 120 30 E
Dondra Head, Sri Lanka 40 S12 5 55N 80 40 E
Donegal, Ireland 10 B3 54 39N 8 5W
Donegal □, Ireland 10 B4 54 53N 8 0W
Donegal B., Ireland 10 B3 54 31N 8 49W
Donets →, Russia 19 E7 47 33N 40 55 E
Donets Basin, Ukraine 19 E6 48 0N 37 45 E
Donetsk, Ukraine 19 E6 48 0N 37 45 E
Dong Ba Thin, Vietnam 39 F7 12 8N 109 13 E
Dong Dang, Vietnam 38 B6 21 54N 106 42 E
Dong Giam, Vietnam 38 C5 19 25N 105 31 E
Dong Ha, Vietnam 38 D6 16 55N 107 8 E
Dong Hene, Laos 38 D5 16 40N 105 18 E
Dong Hoi, Vietnam 38 D6 17 29N 106 36 E
Dong Khe, Vietnam 38 A6 22 26N 106 27 E
Dong Ujimqin Qi, China 34 B9 45 32N 116 55 E
Dong Van, Vietnam 38 A5 23 16N 105 22 E
Dong Xoai, Vietnam 39 G6 11 32N 106 55 E
Dongara, Australia 61 E1 29 14S 114 57 E
Dongbei, China 35 D13 45 0N 125 0 E
Dongchuan, China 32 D5 26 8N 103 1 E

Dongfang, China .... 38 C7 18 50N 108 33 E
Dongfeng, China .... 35 C13 42 40N 125 34 E
Donggala, Indonesia .... 37 E5 0 30S 119 40 E
Donggou, China .... 35 E13 39 52N 124 10 E
Dongguang, China .... 34 F9 37 50N 116 30 E
Dongjingcheng, China ... 35 B15 44 5N 129 10 E
Dongning, China .... 35 B16 44 2N 131 5 E
Dongola, Sudan .... 51 E12 19 9N 30 22 E
Dongping, China .... 34 G9 35 55N 116 20 E
Dongsheng, China .... 34 E6 39 50N 110 0 E
Dongtai, China .... 35 H11 32 51N 120 21 E
Dongting Hu, China .... 33 D6 29 18N 112 45 E
Donington, C., Australia ... 63 E2 34 45S 136 0 E
Doniphan, U.S.A. 81 G9 36 37N 90 50W
Dønna, Norway .... 8 C15 66 6N 12 30 E
Donna, U.S.A. 81 M5 26 9N 98 4W
Donnacona, Canada 73 C5 46 41N 71 41W
Donnelly's Crossing, N.Z. ... 59 F4 35 42S 173 38 E
Donnybrook, Australia ..... 61 F2 33 34S 115 48 E
Donnybrook, S. Africa ..... 57 D4 29 59S 29 48 E
Donora, U.S.A. 84 F5 40 11N 79 52W
Donostia = Donostia-San
  Sebastián, Spain 21 A5 43 17N 1 58W
Donostia-San Sebastián, Spain 21 A5 43 17N 1 58W
Doon →, U.K. 11 F4 55 27N 4 39W
Dora, L., Australia .... 60 D3 22 0S 123 0 E
Dora Báltea →, Italy ...... 20 D8 45 11N 8 3 E
Doran L., Canada 71 A7 61 13N 108 6W
Dorchester, U.K. 13 G5 50 42N 2 27W
Dorchester, C., Canada ... 69 B12 65 27N 77 27W
Dordabis, Namibia .... 56 C2 22 52S 17 38 E
Dordogne →, France 20 D3 45 2N 0 36W
Dordrecht, Neths. .... 15 C4 51 48N 4 39 E
Dordrecht, S. Africa ...... 56 E4 31 20S 27 3 E
Doré L., Burkina Faso 71 C7 54 46N 107 17W
Doré Lake, Canada 71 C7 54 38N 107 36W
Dori, Burkina Faso 50 F5 14 3N 0 2W
Doring →, S. Africa .... 56 E2 31 54S 18 39 E
Doringbos, S. Africa ...... 56 E2 31 59S 19 16 E
Dorking, U.K. 13 F7 51 14N 0 19W
Dornbirn, Austria .... 16 E5 47 25N 9 45 E
Dornie, U.K. 11 D3 57 17N 5 31W
Dornoch, U.K. 11 D4 57 53N 4 2W
Dornoch Firth, U.K. 11 D4 57 51N 4 4W
Dornogovĭ □, Mongolia .... 34 C6 44 0N 110 0 E
Dorohoi, Romania .... 17 E14 47 56N 26 23 E
Döröö Nuur, Mongolia .... 32 B4 48 0N 93 0 E
Dorr, U.S.A. .... 45 C6 33 17N 50 38 E
Dorre I., Australia .... 61 E1 25 13S 113 12 E
Dorrigo, Australia .... 63 E5 30 20S 152 44 E
Dorris, U.S.A. 76 F3 41 58N 121 55W
Dorset, Canada 84 A6 45 14N 78 54W
Dorset, U.S.A. 84 E4 41 40N 80 40W
Dorset □, U.K. 13 G5 50 45N 2 26W
Dortmund, Germany .... 16 C4 51 30N 7 28 E
Doruma, Dem. Rep. of the Congo 54 B2 4 42N 27 33 E
Dorüneh, Iran .... 45 C8 35 10N 57 18 E
Dos Bahías, C., Argentina . 96 E3 44 58S 65 32W
Dos Hermanas, Spain 21 D3 37 16N 5 55W
Dos Palos, U.S.A. 78 J6 36 59N 120 37W
Dosso, Niger .... 50 F6 13 0N 3 13 E
Dothan, U.S.A. 83 K3 31 13N 85 24W
Doty, U.S.A. 78 D3 46 38N 123 17W
Douai, France .... 20 A5 50 21N 3 4 E
Douala, Cameroon .... 52 D1 4 0N 9 45 E
Douarnenez, France 20 B1 48 6N 4 21W
Double Island Pt., Australia . 63 D5 25 56S 153 11 E
Double Mountain Fork →, U.S.A. 81 J4 33 16N 100 0W
Doubs □, France .... 20 C6 46 53N 5 1 E
Doubtful Sd., N.Z. .... 59 L1 45 20S 166 49 E
Doubtless B., N.Z. .... 59 F4 34 55S 173 26 E
Douglas, S. Africa .... 56 D3 29 4S 23 46 E
Douglas, U.K. 12 C3 54 10N 4 28W
Douglas, Ariz., U.S.A. 77 L9 31 21N 109 33W
Douglas, Ga., U.S.A. 83 K4 31 31N 82 51W
Douglas, Wyo., U.S.A. 80 D2 42 45N 105 24W
Douglas Apsley △, Australia . 63 G4 41 45S 148 11 E
Douglas Chan., Canada ... 70 C3 53 40N 129 20W
Douglas Pt., Canada 84 B3 44 19N 81 37W
Douglasville, U.S.A. 83 J3 33 45N 84 45W
Dounreay, U.K. 11 C5 58 35N 3 44W
Dourada, Serra, Brazil 93 F9 13 10S 48 45W
Dourados, Brazil 95 A5 22 9S 54 50W
Dourados →, Brazil 95 A5 21 58S 54 18W
Dourados, Serra dos, Brazil . 95 A5 23 30S 53 30W
Douro →, Europe 21 B1 41 8N 8 40W
Dove →, U.K. 12 E6 52 51N 1 36W
Dove Creek, U.S.A. 77 H9 37 46N 108 54W
Dover, Australia .... 63 G4 43 18S 147 2 E
Dover, U.K. .... 13 F9 51 7N 1 19 E
Dover, Del., U.S.A. 82 F8 39 10N 75 32W
Dover, N.H., U.S.A. 85 C14 43 12N 70 56W
Dover, N.J., U.S.A. 85 F10 40 53N 74 34W
Dover, Ohio, U.S.A. 84 F3 40 32N 81 29W
Dover, Pt., Australia ...... 61 F4 32 32S 125 32 E
Dover, Str. of, Europe .... 13 G9 51 0N 1 30 E
Dover-Foxcroft, U.S.A. ... 83 C11 45 11N 69 13W
Dover Plains, U.S.A. 85 E11 41 43N 73 35W
Dovey = Dyfi →, U.K. 13 E3 52 32N 4 3W
Dovrefjell, Norway .... 9 E13 62 15N 9 33 E
Dow Rūd, Iran .... 45 C6 33 28N 49 4 E
Dowa, Malawi .... 55 E13 13 38S 33 58 E
Dowagiac, U.S.A. 82 E2 41 59N 86 6W
Dowerin, Australia .... 61 F2 31 12S 117 2 E
Dowgha'i, Iran .... 45 B8 36 54N 58 32 E
Dowlatābād, Iran .... 45 D8 28 20N 56 40 E
Down □, U.K. 10 B5 54 23N 6 2W
Downey, Calif., U.S.A. ... 79 M8 33 56N 118 7W
Downey, Idaho, U.S.A. ... 76 E7 42 26N 112 7W
Downham Market, U.K. ... 13 E8 52 37N 0 23 E
Downieville, U.S.A. 78 F6 39 34N 120 50W
Downpatrick, U.K. 10 B6 54 20N 5 43W
Downpatrick Hd., Ireland .. 10 B2 54 20N 9 21W
Downton, Mt., Canada ... 70 C4 52 42N 124 52W
Dowsārī, Iran .... 45 D8 28 25N 57 59 E
Doyle, U.S.A. 78 E6 40 2N 120 6W
Doylestown, U.S.A. 85 F9 40 21N 75 10W
Dozois, Rés., Canada 72 C4 47 30N 77 5W
Dra Khel, Pakistan .... 42 F2 27 58N 66 45 E
Drachten, Neths. .... 15 A6 53 7N 6 5 E
Drăgăşani, Romania ..... 17 F13 44 39N 24 17 E
Dragichyn, Belarus ...... 17 B13 52 15N 25 8 E
Dragoman, Prokhod, Bulgaria . 23 C10 42 58N 22 53 E
Dragon's Mouth = Boca de
  Drago, Venezuela 93 K15 11 0N 61 50W
Draguignan, France ...... 20 E7 43 32N 6 27 E
Drain, U.S.A. 76 E2 43 40N 123 19W

Drake, U.S.A. 80 B4 47 55N 100 23W
Drake Passage, S. Ocean .. 5 B17 58 0S 68 0W
Drakensberg, S. Africa ... 57 D4 31 0S 28 0 E
Dráma, Greece .... 23 D11 41 9N 24 10 E
Drammen, Norway .... 9 G14 59 42N 10 12 E
Drangajökull, Iceland 8 C2 66 9N 22 15W
Dras, India .... 43 B6 34 25N 75 48 E
Drau = Drava →, Croatia . 23 B8 45 33N 18 55 E
Drava →, Croatia .... 23 B8 45 33N 18 55 E
Drayton Valley, Canada ... 70 C6 53 12N 114 58W
Drenthe □, Neths. .... 15 B6 52 52N 6 40 E
Drepanum, C., Cyprus ... 25 E11 34 54N 32 19 E
Dresden, Canada 84 D2 42 35N 82 11W
Dresden, Germany .... 16 C7 51 3N 13 44 E
Dreux, France .... 20 B4 48 44N 1 23 E
Driffield, U.K. 12 C7 54 0N 0 26W
Driftwood, U.S.A. 84 E6 41 20N 78 8W
Driggs, U.S.A. 76 E8 43 44N 111 6W
Drin →, Albania .... 23 C8 42 1N 19 38 E
Drina →, Bos.-H. .... 23 B8 44 53N 19 21 E
Drøbak, Norway .... 9 G14 59 39N 10 39 E
Drobeta-Turnu Severin, Romania 17 F12 44 39N 22 41 E
Drochia, Moldova .... 17 D14 48 2N 27 48 E
Drogheda, Ireland 10 C5 53 43N 6 22W
Drogichin = Dragichyn, Belarus . 17 B13 52 15N 25 8 E
Drogobych = Drohobych, Ukraine 17 D12 49 20N 23 30 E
Drohobych, Ukraine ..... 17 D12 49 20N 23 30 E
Droichead Atha = Drogheda,
  Ireland 10 C5 53 43N 6 22W
Droichead Nua, Ireland ... 10 C5 53 11N 6 48W
Droitwich, U.K. 13 E5 52 16N 2 8W
Dromedary, C., Australia .. 63 F5 36 17S 150 10 E
Dromore, U.K. 10 B4 54 31N 7 28W
Dromore West, Ireland ... 10 B3 54 15N 8 52W
Dronfield, U.K. 12 D6 53 19N 1 27W
Dronning Maud Land, Antarctica 5 D3 72 30S 12 0 E
Dronten, Neths. .... 15 B5 52 32N 5 43 E
Drumbo, Canada 84 C4 43 16N 80 35W
Drumheller, Canada 70 C6 51 25N 112 40W
Drummond, U.S.A. 76 C7 46 40N 113 9W
Drummond I., U.S.A. 82 C4 46 1N 83 39W
Drummond Pt., Australia .. 63 E2 34 9S 135 16 E
Drummond Ra., Australia . 62 C4 23 45S 147 10 E
Drummondville, Canada .. 72 C5 45 55N 72 25W
Drumright, U.S.A. 81 H6 35 59N 96 36W
Druskininkai, Lithuania ... 9 J20 54 3N 23 58 E
Drut →, Belarus .... 17 B16 53 8N 30 5 E
Druzhina, Russia .... 29 C15 68 14N 145 18 E
Dry Harbour Mts., Jamaica . 88 a 18 19N 77 24W
Dry Tortugas, U.S.A. 88 B3 24 38N 82 55W
Dryden, Canada 71 D10 49 47N 92 50W
Dryden, U.S.A. 85 D8 42 30N 76 18W
Drygalski I., Antarctica ... 5 C7 66 0S 92 0 E
Drysdale →, Australia ... 60 B4 13 59S 126 51 E
Drysdale I., Australia ..... 62 A2 11 41S 136 0 E
Drysdale River △, Australia . 60 B4 14 56S 127 2 E
Du Bois, U.S.A. 84 E6 41 8N 78 46W
Du Gué →, Canada 72 A5 57 21N 70 45W
Du Quoin, U.S.A. 80 G10 38 1N 89 14W
Duanesburg, U.S.A. 85 D10 42 45N 74 11W
Duaringa, Australia ...... 62 C4 23 42S 149 42 E
Duarte, Pico, Dom. Rep. .. 89 C5 19 2N 70 59W
Qubā, Si. Arabia .... 44 E2 27 10N 35 40 E
Dubai = Dubayy, U.A.E. .. 45 E7 25 18N 55 20 E
Dubāsari, Moldova ..... 17 E15 47 15N 29 10 E
Dubāsari Vdkhr., Moldova . 17 E15 47 30N 29 0 E
Dubawnt →, Canada 71 A8 64 33N 100 6W
Dubawnt L., Canada 71 A8 63 8N 101 28W
Dubayy, U.A.E. .... 45 E7 25 18N 55 20 E
Dubbo, Australia .... 63 E4 32 11S 148 35 E
Dubele, Dem. Rep. of the Congo 54 B2 2 56N 29 35 E
Dublin, Ireland 10 C5 53 21N 6 15W
Dublin, Ga., U.S.A. 83 J4 32 32N 82 54W
Dublin, Tex., U.S.A. 81 J5 32 5N 98 21W
Dublin □, Ireland 10 C5 53 24N 6 20W
Dublin ✈ (DUB), Ireland .. 10 C5 53 26N 6 15W
Dubno, Ukraine .... 17 C13 50 25N 25 45 E
Dubois, U.S.A. 76 D7 44 10N 112 14W
Dubossary = Dubāsari, Moldova 17 E15 47 15N 29 10 E
Dubossary Vdkhr. = Dubāsari
  Vdkhr., Moldova ..... 17 E15 47 30N 29 0 E
Dubovka, Russia .... 19 E7 49 5N 44 50 E
Dubrajpur, India .... 43 H12 23 48N 87 25 E
Dubréka, Guinea 50 G3 9 46N 13 31W
Dubrovitsa = Dubrovytsya,
  Ukraine .... 17 C14 51 31N 26 35 E
Dubrovnik, Croatia ...... 23 C8 42 39N 18 6 E
Dubrovytsya, Ukraine ... 17 C14 51 31N 26 35 E
Dubuque, U.S.A. 80 D9 42 30N 90 41W
Duchesne, U.S.A. 76 F8 40 10N 110 24W
Duchess, Australia ...... 62 C2 21 20S 139 50 E
Ducie I., Pac. Oc. 65 K15 24 40S 124 48W
Duck →, U.S.A. 83 G2 36 2N 87 52W
Duck Cr. →, Australia ... 60 D2 22 37S 116 53 E
Duck Lake, Canada 71 C7 52 50N 106 16W
Duck Mountain △, Canada . 71 C8 51 45N 101 0W
Duckwall, Mt., U.S.A. ... 78 H6 37 58N 120 7W
Dudhi, India .... 41 G13 24 15N 83 10 E
Dudinka, Russia .... 29 C9 69 30N 86 13 E
Dudley, U.K. 13 E5 52 31N 2 5W
Dudwa, India .... 43 E9 28 30N 80 41 E
Duero = Douro →, Europe . 21 B1 41 8N 8 40W
Dufftown, U.K. 11 D5 57 27N 3 8W
Dūghī Kalā, Afghan. ..... 40 C3 32 20N 62 50 E
Dugi Otok, Croatia ...... 16 G8 44 0N 15 3 E
Duifken Pt., Australia .... 62 A3 12 33S 141 38 E
Duisburg, Germany ...... 16 C4 51 26N 6 45 E
Duiwelskloof, S. Africa ... 57 C5 23 42S 30 10 E
Dūkdamin, Iran .... 45 C8 35 59N 57 43 E
Dukelský Průsmyk, Slovak Rep. 17 D11 49 25N 21 42 E
Dukhān, Qatar .... 45 E6 25 25N 50 50 E
Duki, Pakistan .... 40 D6 30 14N 68 25 E
Duku, Nigeria .... 51 F8 10 43N 10 43 E
Dulce, U.S.A. 77 H10 36 56N 107 0W
Dulce →, Argentina 94 C3 30 32S 62 33W
Dulce, G., Costa Rica 88 E3 8 40N 83 20W
Dulf, Iraq .... 44 C5 35 7N 45 51 E
Dulit, Banjaran, Malaysia . 36 D4 3 15N 114 30 E
Duliu, China .... 34 E9 39 2N 116 55 E
Dullewala, Pakistan ..... 42 D4 31 50N 71 25 E
Dullstroom, S. Africa .... 57 D5 25 27S 30 7 E
Dulq Maghār, Syria ..... 44 B3 36 22N 38 39 E
Duluth, U.S.A. 80 B8 46 47N 92 6W
Dum Dum, India .... 43 H13 22 39N 88 33 E
Dum Duma, India ...... 41 F19 27 40N 95 40 E
Dūmā, Syria .... 46 B5 33 34N 36 24 E
Dumaguete, Phil. .... 37 C6 9 17N 123 15 E
Dumai, Indonesia .... 36 D2 1 35N 101 28 E

Dumaran, Phil. .... 37 B5 10 33N 119 50 E
Dumas, Ark., U.S.A. 81 J9 33 53N 91 29W
Dumas, Tex., U.S.A. 81 H4 35 52N 101 58W
Dumayr, Syria .... 46 B5 33 39N 36 42 E
Dumbarton, U.K. 11 F4 55 57N 4 33W
Dumbleyung, Australia ... 61 F2 33 17S 117 42 E
Dumfries, U.K. 11 F5 55 4N 3 37W
Dumfries & Galloway □, U.K. . 11 F5 55 9N 3 58W
Dumka, India .... 43 G12 24 12N 87 15 E
Dumoine →, Canada 72 C4 46 13N 77 51W
Dumoine, L., Canada 72 C4 46 55N 77 55W
Dumont d'Urville, Antarctica . 5 C10 67 0S 110 0 E
Dumraon, India .... 43 G11 25 33N 84 8 E
Dumyât, Egypt .... 51 B12 31 24N 31 48 E
Dún Dealgan = Dundalk, Ireland . 10 B5 54 1N 6 24W
Dún Laoghaire, Ireland ... 10 C5 53 17N 6 8W
Duna = Dunărea →, Europe . 17 F15 45 20N 29 40 E
Dunagiri, India .... 43 D8 30 31N 79 52 E
Dunaj = Dunărea →, Europe . 17 F15 45 20N 29 40 E
Dunakeszi, Hungary .... 17 E10 47 37N 19 8 E
Dunărea →, Europe .... 17 F15 45 20N 29 40 E
Dunaújváros, Hungary ... 17 E10 46 58N 18 57 E
Dunav = Dunărea →, Europe . 17 F15 45 20N 29 40 E
Dunay, Russia .... 30 C6 42 52N 132 22 E
Dunback, N.Z. .... 59 L3 45 23S 170 36 E
Dunbar, U.K. 11 E6 56 0N 2 31W
Dunblane, U.K. 11 E5 56 11N 3 58W
Duncan, Canada 70 D4 48 45N 123 40W
Duncan, Ariz., U.S.A. 77 K9 32 43N 109 6W
Duncan, Okla., U.S.A. ... 81 H6 34 30N 97 57W
Duncan, L., Canada 72 B4 53 29N 77 58W
Duncan L., Canada 70 A6 62 51N 113 58W
Duncan Town, Bahamas .. 88 B4 22 15N 75 45W
Duncansby Head, U.K. ... 11 C5 58 38N 3 1W
Duncansville, U.S.A. 84 F6 40 25N 78 26W
Dundalk, Canada 84 B4 44 10N 80 24W
Dundalk, Ireland 10 B5 54 1N 6 24W
Dundalk, U.S.A. 82 F7 39 16N 76 32W
Dundalk Bay, Ireland 10 C5 53 55N 6 15W
Dundas = Uummannaq,
  Greenland 4 B4 77 0N 69 0W
Dundas = Uummannaq,
  Greenland 4 B5 70 58N 52 0W
Dundas, Canada 84 C5 43 17N 79 59W
Dundas, L., Australia .... 61 F3 32 35S 121 50 E
Dundas I., Canada 70 C2 54 30N 130 50W
Dundas Str., Australia ... 60 B5 11 15S 131 35 E
Dundee, S. Africa .... 57 D5 28 11S 30 15 E
Dundee, U.K. 11 E6 56 28N 2 59W
Dundee, U.S.A. 84 D8 42 32N 76 59W
Dundee City □, U.K. 11 E6 56 30N 2 58W
Dundgovĭ □, Mongolia ... 34 B4 45 10N 106 0 E
Dundrum, U.K. 10 B6 54 16N 5 52W
Dundrum B., U.K. 10 B6 54 13N 5 47W
Dunedin, N.Z. .... 59 L3 45 50S 170 33 E
Dunedin, U.S.A. 83 L4 28 1N 82 47W
Dunfermline, U.K. 11 E5 56 5N 3 27W
Dungannon, Canada 84 C3 43 51N 81 36W
Dungannon, U.K. 10 B5 54 31N 6 46W
Dungarpur, India .... 42 H5 23 52N 73 45 E
Dungarvan, Ireland 10 D4 52 5N 7 37W
Dungarvan Harbour, Ireland . 10 D4 52 4N 7 35W
Dungeness, U.K. .... 13 G8 50 54N 0 59 E
Dungo, L. do, Angola .... 56 B2 17 15S 19 0 E
Dungog, Australia .... 63 E5 32 22S 151 46 E
Dungu, Dem. Rep. of the Congo 54 B2 3 40N 28 32 E
Dungun, Malaysia .... 39 K4 4 45N 103 25 E
Dunhua, China .... 35 C15 43 20N 128 14 E
Dunhuang, China .... 32 B4 40 8N 94 36 E
Dunk I., Australia .... 62 B4 17 59S 146 29 E
Dunkeld, Australia ...... 63 E4 33 25S 149 29 E
Dunkeld, U.K. 11 E5 56 34N 3 35W
Dunkerque, France ...... 20 A5 51 2N 2 20 E
Dunkery Beacon, U.K. ... 13 F4 51 9N 3 36W
Dunkirk = Dunkerque, France . 20 A5 51 2N 2 20 E
Dunkirk, U.S.A. 84 D5 42 29N 79 20W
Dúnleary = Dún Laoghaire,
  Ireland 10 C5 53 17N 6 8W
Dunleer, Ireland 10 C5 53 50N 6 24W
Dunmanus B., Ireland ... 10 E2 51 31N 9 50W
Dunmanway, Ireland 10 E2 51 43N 9 6W
Dunmara, Australia ..... 62 B1 16 42S 133 25 E
Dunmore, U.S.A. 85 E9 41 25N 75 38W
Dunmore Hd., Ireland ... 10 D1 52 10N 10 35W
Dunmore Town, Bahamas . 88 A4 25 30N 76 39W
Dunn, U.S.A. 83 H6 35 19N 78 37W
Dunnellon, U.S.A. 83 L4 29 3N 82 28W
Dunnet Hd., U.K. 11 C5 58 40N 3 21W
Dunning, U.S.A. 80 E4 41 50N 100 6W
Dunnville, Canada 84 D5 42 54N 79 36W
Dunolly, Australia .... 63 F3 36 51S 143 44 E
Dunoon, U.K. 11 F4 55 57N 4 56W
Duns, U.K. 11 F6 55 47N 2 20W
Dunseith, U.S.A. 80 A4 48 50N 100 3W
Dunsmuir, U.S.A. 76 F2 41 13N 122 16W
Dunstable, U.K. 13 F7 51 53N 0 32W
Dunstan Mts., N.Z. ...... 59 L2 44 53S 169 35 E
Dunster, Canada 70 C5 53 8N 119 50W
Dunvegan, U.K. 11 D2 57 27N 6 35W
Dunvegan L., Canada ... 71 A7 60 8N 107 10W
Duolun, China .... 34 C9 42 12N 116 28 E
Duong Dong, Vietnam ... 39 G4 10 13N 103 58 E
Dupree, U.S.A. 80 C4 45 4N 101 35W
Dupuyer, U.S.A. 76 B7 48 13N 112 30W
Duque de Caxias, Brazil .. 95 A7 22 45S 43 19W
Durack →, Australia .... 60 C4 15 33S 127 52 E
Durack Ra., Australia .... 60 C4 16 50S 127 40 E
Durance →, France ..... 20 E6 43 55N 4 45 E
Durand, U.S.A. 80 C9 44 38N 91 58W
Durango, Mexico 86 C4 24 3N 104 39W
Durango, U.S.A. 77 H10 37 16N 107 53W
Durango □, Mexico 86 C4 25 0N 105 0W
Durant, Miss., U.S.A. ... 81 J10 33 4N 89 51W
Durant, Okla., U.S.A. 81 J6 33 59N 96 25W
Durazno, Uruguay 94 C4 33 25S 56 31W
Durazzo = Durrës, Albania . 23 D8 41 19N 19 28 E
Durban, S. Africa .... 57 D5 29 49S 31 1 E
Durbuy, Belgium .... 15 D5 50 21N 5 28 E
Düren, Germany .... 16 C4 50 48N 6 29 E
Durg, India .... 41 J12 21 15N 81 22 E
Durgapur, India .... 43 H12 23 30N 87 20 E
Durham, Canada 84 B4 44 10N 80 49W
Durham, Calif., U.S.A. ... 78 F5 39 39N 121 48W
Durham, N.C., U.S.A. 83 H6 35 59N 78 54W
Durham, N.H., U.S.A. ... 85 C14 43 8N 70 56W

Durham □, U.K. 12 C6 54 42N 1 45W
Qurmā, Si. Arabia ...... 44 E5 24 37N 46 8 E
Durmitor, Serbia & M. .... 23 C8 43 10N 19 0 E
Durness, U.K. 11 C4 58 34N 4 45W
Durrës, Albania .... 23 D8 41 19N 19 28 E
Durrow, Ireland 10 D4 52 51N 7 24W
Dursey I., Ireland 10 E1 51 36N 10 12W
Dursley, U.K. 13 F5 51 40N 2 21W
Dursunbey, Turkey ..... 23 E13 39 35N 28 37 E
Duru, Dem. Rep. of the Congo . 54 B2 4 14N 28 50 E
Durūz, Jabal ad, Jordan .. 46 C5 32 35N 36 40 E
D'Urville, Tanjung, Indonesia . 37 E9 1 28S 137 54 E
D'Urville I., N.Z. .... 59 J4 40 50S 173 55 E
Duryea, U.S.A. 85 E9 41 20N 75 45W
Dushak, Turkmenistan ... 28 F7 37 13N 60 1 E
Dushanbe, Tajikistan .... 28 F7 38 33N 68 48 E
Dushore, U.S.A. 85 E8 41 31N 76 24W
Dusky Sd., N.Z. .... 59 L1 45 47S 166 30 E
Dussejour, C., Australia .. 60 B4 14 45S 128 13 E
Düsseldorf, Germany .... 16 C4 51 14N 6 47 E
Dutch Harbor, U.S.A. 68 C3 53 53N 166 32W
Dutlwe, Botswana ...... 56 C3 23 58S 23 46 E
Dutton, Canada 84 D3 42 39N 81 30W
Dutton →, Australia .... 62 C3 20 44S 143 10 E
Duwayhin, Khawr, U.A.E. . 45 E6 24 20N 51 25 E
Duyun, China .... 32 D5 26 18N 107 29 E
Dvina, Severnaya →, Russia . 18 B7 64 32N 40 30 E
Dvinsk = Daugavpils, Latvia . 9 J22 55 53N 26 32 E
Dvinskaya Guba, Russia .. 18 B6 65 0N 39 0 E
Dwarka, India .... 42 H3 22 18N 69 8 E
Dwellingup, Australia ... 61 F2 32 43S 116 4 E
Dwight, Canada 84 A5 45 20N 79 1W
Dwight, U.S.A. 82 E1 41 5N 88 26W
Dyatlovo = Dzyatlava, Belarus . 17 B13 53 28N 25 28 E
Dyce, U.K. 11 D6 57 13N 2 12W
Dyer, C., Canada 69 B13 66 37N 61 16W
Dyer Bay, Canada 84 A3 45 10N 81 20W
Dyer Plateau, Antarctica .. 5 D17 70 45S 65 30W
Dyersburg, U.S.A. 81 G10 36 3N 89 23W
Dyfi →, U.K. 13 E3 52 32N 4 3W
Dymer, Ukraine .... 17 C16 50 47N 30 18 E
Dysart, Australia .... 62 C4 22 32S 148 23 E
Dzerzhinsk, Russia ..... 18 C7 56 14N 43 30 E
Dzhalinda, Russia ..... 29 D13 53 26N 124 0 E
Dzhambul = Taraz, Kazakhstan . 28 E8 42 54N 71 22 E
Dzhankoy, Ukraine ..... 19 E5 45 40N 34 20 E
Dzhezkazgan = Zhezqazghan,
  Kazakhstan .... 28 E7 47 44N 67 40 E
Dzhizak = Jizzakh, Uzbekistan . 28 E7 40 6N 67 50 E
Dzhugdzur, Khrebet, Russia . 29 D14 57 30N 138 0 E
Dzhungarskiye Vorota =
  Dzungarian Gates, Asia . 32 B3 45 0N 82 0 E
Działdowo, Poland ..... 17 B11 53 15N 20 15 E
Dzibilchaltún, Mexico 87 C7 21 5N 89 36W
Dzibilchaltun, Yucatán, Mexico . 87 C7 21 5N 89 36W
Dzierżoniów, Poland .... 17 C9 50 45N 16 39 E
Dzilam de Bravo, Mexico . 87 C7 21 24N 88 53W
Dzungaria = Junggar Pendi,
  China .... 32 B3 44 30N 86 0 E
Dzungarian Gates, Asia .. 32 B3 45 0N 82 0 E
Dzuumod, Mongolia .... 32 B5 47 45N 106 58 E
Dzyarzhynsk, Belarus ... 17 B14 53 40N 27 1 E
Dzyatlava, Belarus ..... 17 B13 53 28N 25 28 E

E

E.C. Manning △, Canada ... 70 D4 49 5N 120 45W
Eabamet L., Canada 72 B2 51 30N 87 46W
Eads, U.S.A. 80 F3 38 29N 102 47W
Eagar, U.S.A. 77 J9 34 6N 109 17W
Eagle, Alaska, U.S.A. 68 B5 64 47N 141 12W
Eagle, Colo., U.S.A. 76 G10 39 39N 106 50W
Eagle →, Canada 73 B8 53 36N 57 26W
Eagle Butte, U.S.A. 80 C4 45 0N 101 10W
Eagle Grove, U.S.A. 80 D8 42 40N 93 54W
Eagle L., Canada 71 D10 49 42N 93 13W
Eagle L., Calif., U.S.A. ... 76 F3 40 39N 120 45W
Eagle L., Maine, U.S.A. .. 83 B11 46 20N 69 22W
Eagle Lake, Canada 84 A6 45 8N 78 29W
Eagle Lake, Maine, U.S.A. . 83 B11 47 3N 68 36W
Eagle Lake, Tex., U.S.A. .. 81 L6 29 35N 96 20W
Eagle Mountain, U.S.A. .. 79 M11 33 49N 115 27W
Eagle Nest, U.S.A. 77 H11 36 33N 105 16W
Eagle Pass, U.S.A. 81 L4 28 43N 100 30W
Eagle Pk., U.S.A. 78 G7 38 10N 119 25W
Eagle Pt., Australia ..... 60 C3 16 11S 124 23 E
Eagle River, Mich., U.S.A. . 82 B1 47 24N 88 18W
Eagle River, Wis., U.S.A. . 80 C10 45 55N 89 15W
Eaglehawk, Australia .... 63 F3 36 44S 144 15 E
Eagles Mere, U.S.A. 85 E8 41 25N 76 33W
Ealing □, U.K. 13 F7 51 31N 0 20W
Ear Falls, Canada 71 C10 50 38N 93 13W
Earle, U.S.A. 81 H9 35 16N 90 28W
Earlimart, U.S.A. 79 K7 35 53N 119 16W
Earn →, U.K. 11 E5 56 21N 3 18W
Earn, L., U.K. 11 E4 56 23N 4 13W
Earnslaw, Mt., N.Z. ..... 59 L2 44 32S 168 27 E
Earth, U.S.A. 81 H3 34 14N 102 24W
Easley, U.S.A. 83 H4 34 50N 82 36W
East Anglia, U.K. .... 12 E9 52 30N 1 0 E
East Angus, Canada 73 C5 45 30N 71 40W
East Aurora, U.S.A. 84 D6 42 46N 78 37W
East Ayrshire □, U.K. ... 11 F4 55 26N 4 11W
East Bengal, Bangla. .... 41 H17 24 0N 90 0 E
East Beskids = Vychodné
  Beskydy, Europe .... 17 D11 49 20N 22 0 E
East Brady, U.S.A. 84 F5 40 59N 79 36W
East, C., N.Z. .... 59 G7 37 42S 178 35 E
East Chicago, U.S.A. 82 E2 41 38N 87 27W
East China Sea, Asia .... 33 D7 30 0N 126 0 E
East Coulee, Canada 70 C6 51 23N 112 27W
East Dereham = Dereham, U.K. . 13 E8 52 41N 0 57 E
East Dunbartonshire □, U.K. . 11 F4 55 57N 4 13W
East Falkland, Falk. Is. ... 96 G5 51 30S 58 30W
East Grand Forks, U.S.A. . 80 B6 47 56N 97 1W
East Greenwich, U.S.A. . 85 E13 41 40N 71 27W
East Grinstead, U.K. .... 13 F8 51 7N 0 0 E
East Hartford, U.S.A. ... 85 E12 41 46N 72 39W
East Helena, U.S.A. 76 C8 46 35N 111 56W
East Indies, Asia .... 26 K15 0 0 120 0 E
East Kilbride, U.K. 11 F4 55 47N 4 11W
East Lamma Channel, China . 33 G11 22 14N 114 9 E
East Lansing, U.S.A. 82 D3 42 44N 84 29W
East Liverpool, U.S.A. ... 84 F4 40 37N 80 35W

East London, *S. Africa* ... **57 E4** 33 0S 27 55 E
East Lothian □, *U.K.* ... **11 F6** 55 58N 2 44W
East Main = Eastmain, *Canada* ... **72 B4** 52 10N 78 30W
East Northport, *U.S.A.* ... **85 F11** 40 53N 73 20W
East Orange, *U.S.A.* ... **85 F10** 40 46N 74 13W
East Pacific Ridge, *Pac. Oc.* ... **65 J17** 15 0S 110 0W
East Palestine, *U.S.A.* ... **84 F4** 40 50N 80 33W
East Pine, *Canada* ... **70 B4** 55 48N 120 12W
East Point, *U.S.A.* ... **83 J3** 33 41N 84 27W
East Providence, *U.S.A.* ... **85 E13** 41 49N 71 23W
East Pt., *Br. Virgin Is.* ... **89 e** 18 40N 64 18W
East Pt., *Canada* ... **73 C7** 46 27N 61 58W
East Renfrewshire □, *U.K.* ... **11 F4** 55 46N 4 21W
East Retford = Retford, *U.K.* ... **12 D7** 53 19N 0 56W
East Riding of Yorkshire □, *U.K.* **12 D7** 53 55N 0 30W
East Rochester, *U.S.A.* ... **84 C7** 43 7N 77 29W
East St. Louis, *U.S.A.* ... **80 F9** 38 37N 90 9W
East Schelde = Oosterschelde →, *Neths.* ... **15 C4** 51 33N 4 0 E
East Sea = Japan, Sea of, *Asia* ... **30 E7** 40 0N 135 0 E
East Siberian Sea, *Russia* ... **29 B17** 73 0N 160 0 E
East Stroudsburg, *U.S.A.* ... **85 E9** 41 1N 75 11W
East Sussex □, *U.K.* ... **13 G8** 50 56N 0 19 E
East Tawas, *U.S.A.* ... **82 C4** 44 17N 83 29W
East Timor ■, *Asia* ... **37 F7** 8 0S 126 0 E
East Toorale, *Australia* ... **63 E4** 30 27S 145 28 E
East Walker →, *U.S.A.* ... **78 G7** 38 52N 119 10W
East Windsor, *U.S.A.* ... **85 F10** 40 17N 74 34W
Eastbourne, *N.Z.* ... **59 J5** 41 19S 174 55 E
Eastbourne, *U.K.* ... **13 G8** 50 46N 0 18 E
Eastend, *Canada* ... **71 D7** 49 32N 108 50W
Easter I. = Pascua, I. de, *Chile* ... **65 K17** 27 7S 109 23W
Eastern □, *Kenya* ... **54 C4** 0 0 38 30 E
Eastern Cape □, *S. Africa* ... **56 E4** 32 0S 26 0 E
Eastern Cr. →, *Australia* ... **62 C3** 20 40S 141 35 E
Eastern Ghats, *India* ... **40 N11** 14 0N 78 50 E
Eastern Group = Lau Group, *Fiji* **59 C9** 17 0S 178 30W
Eastern Group →, *Australia* ... **61 F3** 33 30S 124 30 E
Eastern Transvaal = Mpumalanga □, *S. Africa* ... **57 D5** 26 0S 30 0 E
Easterville, *Canada* ... **71 C9** 53 8N 99 49W
Easthampton, *U.S.A.* ... **85 D12** 42 16N 72 40W
Eastlake, *U.S.A.* ... **84 E3** 41 40N 81 26W
Eastland, *U.S.A.* ... **81 J5** 32 24N 98 49W
Eastleigh, *U.K.* ... **13 G6** 50 58N 1 21W
Eastmain, *Canada* ... **72 B4** 52 10N 78 30W
Eastmain →, *Canada* ... **72 B4** 52 27N 78 26W
Eastman, *Canada* ... **85 A12** 45 18N 72 19W
Eastman, *U.S.A.* ... **83 J4** 32 12N 83 11W
Easton, *Md., U.S.A.* ... **82 F7** 38 47N 76 5W
Easton, *Pa., U.S.A.* ... **85 F9** 40 41N 75 13W
Easton, *Wash., U.S.A.* ... **78 C5** 47 14N 121 11W
Eastpointe, *U.S.A.* ... **84 D2** 42 27N 82 56W
Eastport, *U.S.A.* ... **83 C12** 44 56N 67 0W
Eastsound, *U.S.A.* ... **78 B4** 48 42N 122 55W
Eaton, *U.S.A.* ... **80 E2** 40 32N 104 42W
Eatonia, *Canada* ... **71 C7** 51 13N 109 25W
Eatonton, *U.S.A.* ... **83 J4** 33 20N 83 23W
Eatontown, *U.S.A.* ... **85 F10** 40 19N 74 4W
Eatonville, *U.S.A.* ... **78 D4** 46 52N 122 16W
Eau Claire, *U.S.A.* ... **80 C9** 44 49N 91 30W
Eau Claire, L. à l', *Canada* ... **72 A5** 56 10N 74 25W
Ebbw Vale, *U.K.* ... **13 F4** 51 46N 3 12W
Ebeltoft, *Denmark* ... **9 H14** 56 12N 10 41 E
Ebensburg, *U.S.A.* ... **84 F6** 40 29N 78 44W
Eberswalde-Finow, *Germany* ... **16 B7** 52 50N 13 49 E
Ebetsu, *Japan* ... **30 C10** 43 7N 141 34 E
Ebey's Landing ○, *U.S.A.* ... **78 B4** 48 13N 122 41W
Ebolowa, *Cameroon* ... **52 D2** 2 55N 11 10 E
Ebro →, *Spain* ... **21 B6** 40 43N 0 54 E
Eceabat, *Turkey* ... **23 D12** 40 11N 26 21 E
Ech Chéliff, *Algeria* ... **50 A6** 36 10N 1 20 E
Echigo-Sammyaku, *Japan* ... **31 F9** 36 50N 139 50 E
Echizen-Misaki, *Japan* ... **31 G7** 35 59N 135 57 E
Echo Bay, *N.W.T., Canada* ... **68 B8** 66 5N 117 55W
Echo Bay, *Ont., Canada* ... **72 C3** 46 29N 84 4W
Echoing →, *Canada* ... **72 B1** 55 51N 92 5W
Echternach, *Lux.* ... **15 E6** 49 49N 6 25 E
Echuca, *Australia* ... **63 F3** 36 10S 144 45 E
Ecija, *Spain* ... **21 D3** 37 30N 5 10W
Eclipse I., *Australia* ... **61 G2** 35 5S 117 58 E
Eclipse Is., *Australia* ... **60 B4** 13 54S 126 19 E
Eclipse Sd., *Canada* ... **69 A11** 72 38N 79 0W
Ecuador ■, *S. Amer.* ... **92 D3** 2 0S 78 0W
Ed Damazin, *Sudan* ... **51 F12** 11 46N 34 21 E
Ed Dar el Beida = Casablanca, *Morocco* ... **50 B4** 33 36N 7 36W
Ed Debba, *Sudan* ... **51 E12** 18 0N 30 51 E
Ed Dueim, *Sudan* ... **51 F12** 14 0N 32 10 E
Edam, *Canada* ... **71 C7** 53 11N 108 46W
Edam, *Neths.* ... **15 B5** 52 31N 5 3 E
Eday, *U.K.* ... **11 B6** 59 11N 2 47W
Eddrachillis B., *U.K.* ... **11 C3** 58 17N 5 14W
Eddystone, *U.K.* ... **13 G3** 50 11N 4 16W
Eddystone Pt., *Australia* ... **63 G4** 40 59S 148 20 E
Ede, *Neths.* ... **15 B5** 52 4N 5 40 E
Edehon L., *Canada* ... **71 A9** 60 25N 97 15W
Eden, *Australia* ... **63 F4** 37 3S 149 55 E
Eden, *N.C., U.S.A.* ... **83 G6** 36 29N 79 53W
Eden, *N.Y., U.S.A.* ... **84 D6** 42 39N 78 55W
Eden, *Tex., U.S.A.* ... **81 K5** 31 13N 99 51W
Eden →, *U.K.* ... **12 C4** 54 57N 3 1W
Edenburg, *S. Africa* ... **56 D4** 29 43S 25 58 E
Edendale, *S. Africa* ... **57 D5** 29 39S 30 18 E
Edenderry, *Ireland* ... **10 C4** 53 21N 7 4W
Edenton, *U.S.A.* ... **83 G7** 36 4N 76 39W
Edenville, *S. Africa* ... **57 D4** 27 37S 27 34 E
Eder →, *Germany* ... **16 C5** 51 12N 9 28 E
Edgar, *U.S.A.* ... **80 E6** 40 22N 97 58W
Edgartown, *U.S.A.* ... **85 E14** 41 23N 70 31W
Edge Hill, *U.K.* ... **13 E6** 52 8N 1 26W
Edgefield, *U.S.A.* ... **83 J5** 33 47N 81 56W
Edgeley, *U.S.A.* ... **80 B5** 46 22N 98 43W
Edgemont, *U.S.A.* ... **80 D3** 43 18N 103 50W
Edgeøya, *Svalbard* ... **4 B9** 77 45N 22 30 E
Édhessa, *Greece* ... **23 D10** 40 48N 22 5 E
Edievale, *N.Z.* ... **59 L2** 45 49S 169 22 E
Edina, *U.S.A.* ... **80 E8** 40 10N 92 11W
Edinboro, *U.S.A.* ... **84 E4** 41 52N 80 8W
Edinburg, *U.S.A.* ... **81 M5** 26 18N 98 10W
Edinburgh, *U.K.* ... **11 F5** 55 57N 3 13W
Edinburgh ✈ (EDI), *U.K.* ... **11 F5** 55 54N 3 22W
Edinburgh, City of □, *U.K.* ... **11 F5** 55 57N 3 17W
Edineţ, *Moldova* ... **17 D14** 48 9N 27 18 E
Edirne, *Turkey* ... **23 D12** 41 40N 26 34 E
Edison, *U.S.A.* ... **78 B4** 48 33N 122 27W
Edithburgh, *Australia* ... **63 F2** 35 5S 137 43 E
Edmeston, *U.S.A.* ... **85 D9** 42 42N 75 15W

Edmond, *U.S.A.* ... **81 H6** 35 39N 97 29W
Edmonds, *U.S.A.* ... **78 C4** 47 49N 122 23W
Edmonton, *Australia* ... **62 B4** 17 2S 145 46 E
Edmonton, *Canada* ... **70 C6** 53 30N 113 30W
Edmund L., *Canada* ... **72 B1** 54 45N 93 17W
Edmundston, *Canada* ... **73 C6** 47 23N 68 20W
Edna, *U.S.A.* ... **81 L6** 28 59N 96 39W
Edremit, *Turkey* ... **23 E12** 39 34N 27 0 E
Edremit Körfezi, *Turkey* ... **23 E12** 39 30N 26 45 E
Edson, *Canada* ... **70 C5** 53 35N 116 28W
Eduardo Castex, *Argentina* ... **94 D3** 35 50S 64 18W
Edward →, *Australia* ... **63 F3** 35 5S 143 30 E
Edward, L., *Africa* ... **54 C2** 0 25S 29 40 E
Edward River, *Australia* ... **62 A3** 14 59S 141 26 E
Edward VII Land, *Antarctica* ... **5 E13** 80 0S 150 0W
Edwards, *Calif., U.S.A.* ... **79 L9** 34 55N 117 51W
Edwards, *N.Y., U.S.A.* ... **85 B9** 44 20N 75 15W
Edwards Air Force Base, *U.S.A.* **79 L9** 34 50N 117 40W
Edwards Plateau, *U.S.A.* ... **81 K4** 30 45N 101 20W
Edwardsville, *U.S.A.* ... **85 E9** 41 15N 75 56W
Edxná, *Mexico* ... **87 D6** 19 35N 90 15W
Edzo, *Canada* ... **70 A5** 62 49N 116 4W
Eeklo, *Belgium* ... **15 C3** 51 11N 3 33 E
Effigy Mounds ○, *U.S.A.* ... **80 D9** 43 5N 91 11W
Effingham, *U.S.A.* ... **82 F1** 39 7N 88 33W
Égadi, Ísole, *Italy* ... **22 F5** 37 55N 12 16 E
Egan Range, *U.S.A.* ... **76 G6** 39 35N 114 55W
Eganville, *Canada* ... **84 A7** 45 32N 77 5W
Eger = Cheb, *Czech Rep.* ... **16 C7** 50 9N 12 28 E
Eger, *Hungary* ... **17 E11** 47 53N 20 27 E
Egersund, *Norway* ... **9 G12** 58 26N 6 1 E
Egg L., *Canada* ... **71 B7** 55 5N 105 30W
Eghezée, *Belgium* ... **15 D4** 50 35N 4 55 E
Egmont, *Canada* ... **70 D4** 49 45N 123 56W
Egmont △, *N.Z.* ... **59 H5** 39 17S 174 4 E
Egmont, C., *N.Z.* ... **59 H5** 39 16S 173 45 E
Egmont, Mt. = Taranaki, Mt., *N.Z.* **59 H5** 39 17S 174 5 E
Egra, *India* ... **43 J12** 21 54N 87 32 E
Eğridir, *Turkey* ... **19 G5** 37 52N 30 51 E
Eğridir Gölü, *Turkey* ... **19 G5** 37 53N 30 50 E
Egvekinot, *Russia* ... **29 C19** 66 19N 179 50W
Egypt ■, *Africa* ... **51 C12** 28 0N 31 0 E
Ehime □, *Japan* ... **31 H6** 33 30N 132 40 E
Ehrenberg, *U.S.A.* ... **79 M12** 33 36N 114 31W
Eibar, *Spain* ... **21 A4** 43 11N 2 28W
Eidsvold, *Australia* ... **63 D5** 25 25S 151 12 E
Eidsvoll, *Norway* ... **9 F14** 60 19N 11 14 E
Eifel, *Germany* ... **16 C4** 50 15N 6 50 E
Eiffel Flats, *Zimbabwe* ... **55 F3** 18 20S 30 0 E
Eigg, *U.K.* ... **11 E2** 56 54N 6 10W
Eighty Mile Beach, *Australia* ... **60 C3** 19 30S 120 40 E
Eil, *Somali Rep.* ... **47 F4** 8 0N 49 50 E
Eil, L., *U.K.* ... **11 E3** 56 51N 5 16W
Eildon, L., *Australia* ... **63 F4** 37 10S 146 0 E
Einasleigh, *Australia* ... **62 B3** 18 32S 144 5 E
Einasleigh →, *Australia* ... **62 B3** 17 30S 142 17 E
Eindhoven, *Neths.* ... **15 C5** 51 26N 5 28 E
Eire ■, *Europe* ... **10 C4** 53 50N 7 52W
Eiríksjökull, *Iceland* ... **8 D3** 64 46N 20 24W
Eirunepé, *Brazil* ... **92 E5** 6 35S 69 53W
Eiseb →, *Namibia* ... **56 C2** 20 33S 20 59 E
Eisenach, *Germany* ... **16 C6** 50 58N 10 19 E
Eisenerz, *Austria* ... **16 E8** 47 32N 14 54 E
Eivissa, *Spain* ... **24 C7** 38 54N 1 26 E
Ejeda, *Madag.* ... **57 C7** 24 25S 44 12 E
Ejutla, *Mexico* ... **87 D5** 16 34N 96 44W
Ekalaka, *U.S.A.* ... **80 C2** 45 53N 104 33W
Eketahuna, *N.Z.* ... **59 J5** 40 38S 175 43 E
Ekibastuz, *Kazakhstan* ... **28 D8** 51 50N 75 10 E
Ekoli, *Dem. Rep. of the Congo* **54 C1** 0 23S 24 13 E
Eksjö, *Sweden* ... **9 H16** 57 40N 14 58 E
Ekuma →, *Namibia* ... **56 B2** 18 40S 16 2 E
Ekwan →, *Canada* ... **72 B3** 53 12N 82 15W
Ekwan Pt., *Canada* ... **72 B3** 53 16N 82 7W
El Aaiún, *W. Sahara* ... **50 C3** 27 9N 13 12W
El Abanico, *Chile* ... **94 D1** 37 20S 71 31W
El 'Agrúd, *Egypt* ... **46 E3** 30 14N 34 24 E
El 'Alamein, *Egypt* ... **51 B11** 30 48N 28 58 E
El 'Aqaba, W. →, *Egypt* ... **46 E2** 30 7N 33 54 E
El Ariha, *West Bank* ... **46 D4** 31 52N 35 27 E
El 'Arish, *Egypt* ... **46 D2** 31 8N 33 50 E
El 'Arish, W. →, *Egypt* ... **46 D2** 31 8N 33 47 E
El Asnam = Ech Chéliff, *Algeria* **50 A6** 36 10N 1 20 E
El Bayadh, *Algeria* ... **50 B6** 33 40N 1 1 E
El Bluff, *Nic.* ... **88 D3** 11 59N 83 40W
El Brûk, W. →, *Egypt* ... **46 E2** 30 15N 33 50 E
El Cajon, *U.S.A.* ... **79 N10** 32 48N 116 58W
El Campo, *U.S.A.* ... **81 L6** 29 12N 96 16W
El Centro, *U.S.A.* ... **79 N11** 32 48N 115 34W
El Cerro, *Bolivia* ... **92 G6** 17 30S 61 40W
El Compadre, *Mexico* ... **79 N10** 32 20N 116 14W
El Cuy, *Argentina* ... **96 D3** 39 55S 68 25W
El Cuyo, *Mexico* ... **87 C7** 21 30N 87 40W
El Daheir, *Egypt* ... **46 D3** 31 13N 34 10 E
El Dátil, *Mexico* ... **86 B2** 30 7N 112 15W
El Dere, *Somali Rep.* ... **47 G4** 3 50N 47 8 E
El Descanso, *Mexico* ... **79 N10** 32 12N 116 58W
El Desemboque, *Mexico* ... **86 A2** 30 30N 112 57W
El Diviso, *Colombia* ... **92 C3** 1 22N 78 14W
El Djouf, *Mauritania* ... **50 D4** 20 0N 9 0W
El Dorado, *Ark., U.S.A.* ... **81 J8** 33 12N 92 40W
El Dorado, *Kans., U.S.A.* ... **81 G6** 37 49N 96 52W
El Dorado, *Venezuela* ... **92 B6** 6 55N 61 37W
El Escorial, *Spain* ... **21 B3** 40 35N 4 7W
El Faiyûm, *Egypt* ... **51 C12** 29 19N 30 50 E
El Fâsher, *Sudan* ... **51 F11** 13 33N 25 26 E
El Ferrol = Ferrol, *Spain* ... **21 A1** 43 29N 8 15W
El Fuerte, *Mexico* ... **86 B3** 26 30N 108 40W
El Gal, *Somali Rep.* ... **47 E5** 10 58N 50 20 E
El Geneina = Al Junaynah, *Sudan* **51 F10** 13 27N 22 45 E
El Gîza, *Egypt* ... **51 C12** 30 0N 31 10 E
El Gogorrón ○, *Mexico* ... **86 C4** 21 50N 100 50W
El Goléa, *Algeria* ... **50 B6** 30 30N 2 50 E
El Guácharo ○, *Venezuela* ... **89 D7** 10 8N 63 14W
El Guache ○, *Venezuela* ... **89 E6** 9 45N 69 30W
El Istiwa'iya, *Sudan* ... **51 G11** 5 0N 28 0 E
El Jadida, *Morocco* ... **50 B4** 33 11N 8 17W
El Jardal, *Honduras* ... **88 D2** 14 54N 88 50W
El Kabrît, G., *Egypt* ... **46 E2** 29 42N 33 16 E
El Khârga, *Egypt* ... **51 C12** 25 30N 30 33 E
El Khartûm, *Sudan* ... **51 E12** 15 31N 32 35 E
El Kuntilla, *Egypt* ... **46 E3** 30 1N 34 45 E
El Maestrazgo, *Spain* ... **21 B5** 40 30N 0 25W
El Mahalla el Kubra, *Egypt* ... **51 B12** 31 0N 31 0 E
El Malpais ○, *U.S.A.* ... **77 J10** 34 53N 108 0W
El Mansûra, *Egypt* ... **51 B12** 31 0N 31 19 E
El Medano, *Canary Is.* ... **24 F3** 28 3N 16 32W

El Milagro, *Argentina* ... **94 C2** 30 59S 65 59W
El Minyâ, *Egypt* ... **51 C12** 28 7N 30 33 E
El Monte, *U.S.A.* ... **79 L8** 34 4N 118 1W
El Obeid, *Sudan* ... **51 F12** 13 8N 30 10 E
El Odaiya, *Sudan* ... **51 F11** 12 8N 28 12 E
El Oro, *Mexico* ... **87 D4** 19 48N 100 8W
El Oued, *Algeria* ... **50 B7** 33 20N 6 58 E
El Palmar △, *Argentina* ... **94 C4** 32 10S 58 31W
El Palmito, Presa, *Mexico* ... **86 B3** 25 40N 105 30W
El Paso, *U.S.A.* ... **77 L10** 31 45N 106 29W
El Paso Robles, *U.S.A.* ... **78 K6** 35 38N 120 41W
El Pinacate y Gran Desierto de Altar = Gran Desierto del Pinacate △, *Mexico* ... **86 A2** 31 51N 113 32W
El Portal, *U.S.A.* ... **78 H7** 37 41N 119 47W
El Porvenir, *Mexico* ... **86 A3** 31 15N 105 51W
El Prat de Llobregat, *Spain* ... **21 B7** 41 18N 2 3 E
El Progreso, *Honduras* ... **88 C2** 15 26N 87 51W
El Pueblito, *Mexico* ... **86 B3** 29 3N 105 4W
El Pueblo, *Canary Is.* ... **24 F2** 28 36N 17 47W
El Puerto de Santa María, *Spain* **21 D2** 36 36N 6 13W
El Qâhira, *Egypt* ... **51 B12** 30 1N 31 14 E
El Qantara, *Egypt* ... **46 E1** 30 51N 32 20 E
El Quseima, *Egypt* ... **46 E3** 30 40N 34 15 E
El Real, *Panama* ... **92 B3** 8 0N 77 40W
El Reno, *U.S.A.* ... **81 H6** 35 32N 97 57W
El Rey △, *Argentina* ... **94 A3** 24 40S 64 34W
El Rio, *U.S.A.* ... **79 L7** 34 14N 119 10W
El Roque, Pta., *Canary Is.* ... **24 F4** 28 10N 15 25W
El Rosarito, *Mexico* ... **86 B2** 28 38N 114 4W
El Saheira, W. →, *Egypt* ... **46 E2** 30 5N 33 25 E
El Salto, *Mexico* ... **86 C3** 23 47N 105 22W
El Salvador ■, *Cent. Amer.* ... **88 D2** 13 50N 89 0W
El Sauce, *Nic.* ... **88 D2** 13 0N 86 40W
El Sueco, *Mexico* ... **86 B3** 29 54N 106 24W
El Suweis, *Egypt* ... **51 C12** 29 58N 32 31 E
El Tamarâni, W. →, *Egypt* ... **46 E3** 30 7N 34 43 E
El Thamad, *Egypt* ... **46 F3** 29 40N 34 28 E
El Tigre, *Venezuela* ... **92 B6** 8 44N 64 15W
El Tîh, Gebal, *Egypt* ... **46 F2** 29 40N 33 50 E
El Tîna, Khalig, *Egypt* ... **46 D1** 31 10N 32 40 E
El Tofo, *Chile* ... **94 B1** 29 22S 71 18W
El Tránsito, *Chile* ... **94 B1** 28 52S 70 17W
El Tûr, *Egypt* ... **44 D2** 28 14N 33 36 E
El Turbio, *Argentina* ... **96 G2** 51 45S 72 5W
El Uqsur, *Egypt* ... **51 C12** 25 41N 32 38 E
El Venado, *Mexico* ... **86 C4** 22 56N 101 10W
El Vergel, *Mexico* ... **86 B3** 26 28N 106 22W
El Vigía, *Venezuela* ... **92 B4** 8 38N 71 39W
El Wabeira, *Egypt* ... **46 F2** 29 34N 33 6 E
El Wak, *Kenya* ... **54 B5** 2 49N 40 56 E
El Wuz, *Sudan* ... **51 E12** 15 5N 30 7 E
Elâzığ, *Turkey* ... **19 G6** 38 37N 39 14 E
Elba, *Italy* ... **22 C4** 42 46N 10 17 E
Elba, *U.S.A.* ... **83 K2** 31 25N 86 4W
Elbasan, *Albania* ... **23 D9** 41 9N 20 9 E
Elbe, *U.S.A.* ... **78 D4** 46 45N 122 10W
Elbe →, *Europe* ... **16 B5** 53 50N 9 0 E
Elbert, Mt., *U.S.A.* ... **77 G10** 39 7N 106 27W
Elberton, *U.S.A.* ... **83 H4** 34 7N 82 52W
Elbeuf, *France* ... **20 B4** 49 17N 1 2 E
Elbidtan, *Turkey* ... **44 B3** 38 13N 37 12 E
Elbing = Elbląg, *Poland* ... **17 A10** 54 10N 19 25 E
Elbląg, *Poland* ... **17 A10** 54 10N 19 25 E
Elbow, *Canada* ... **71 C7** 51 7N 106 35W
Elbrus, *Asia* ... **19 F7** 43 21N 42 30 E
Elburz Mts. = Alborz, Reshteh-ye Kühhä-ye, *Iran* ... **45 C7** 36 0N 52 0 E
Elche, *Spain* ... **21 C5** 38 15N 0 42W
Elcho I., *Australia* ... **62 A2** 11 55S 135 45 E
Elda, *Spain* ... **21 C5** 38 29N 0 47W
Elde →, *Germany* ... **16 B6** 53 7N 11 15 E
Eldon, *Mo., U.S.A.* ... **80 F8** 38 21N 92 35W
Eldon, *Wash., U.S.A.* ... **78 C3** 47 33N 123 3W
Eldora, *U.S.A.* ... **80 D8** 42 22N 93 5W
Eldorado, *Argentina* ... **95 B5** 26 28S 54 43W
Eldorado, *Canada* ... **84 B7** 44 35N 77 31W
Eldorado, *Mexico* ... **86 C3** 24 20N 107 22W
Eldorado, *Ill., U.S.A.* ... **82 G1** 37 49N 88 26W
Eldorado, *Tex., U.S.A.* ... **81 K4** 30 52N 100 36W
Eldorado Springs, *U.S.A.* ... **81 G8** 37 52N 94 1W
Eldoret, *Kenya* ... **54 B4** 0 30N 35 17 E
Eldred, *U.S.A.* ... **84 E6** 41 58N 78 23W
Elea, C., *Cyprus* ... **25 D13** 35 19N 34 4 E
Eleanora, Pk., *Australia* ... **61 F3** 32 57S 121 9 E
Elefantes →, *Africa* ... **57 C5** 24 10S 32 40 E
Elektrostal, *Russia* ... **18 C6** 55 41N 38 32 E
Elephant Butte Reservoir, *U.S.A.* **77 K10** 33 9N 107 11W
Elephant I., *Antarctica* ... **5 C18** 61 0S 55 0W
Eleuthera, *Bahamas* ... **88 B4** 25 0N 76 20W
Elgin, *Canada* ... **85 B8** 44 36N 76 13W
Elgin, *U.K.* ... **11 D5** 57 39N 3 19W
Elgin, *Ill., U.S.A.* ... **82 D1** 42 2N 88 17W
Elgin, *N. Dak., U.S.A.* ... **80 B4** 46 24N 101 51W
Elgin, *Oreg., U.S.A.* ... **76 D5** 45 34N 117 55W
Elgin, *Tex., U.S.A.* ... **81 K6** 30 21N 97 22W
Elgon, Mt., *Africa* ... **54 B3** 1 10N 34 30 E
Eliase, *Indonesia* ... **37 F8** 8 21S 130 48 E
Elim, *Namibia* ... **56 B2** 17 48S 15 31 E
Elim, *S. Africa* ... **56 E2** 34 35S 19 45 E
Elista, *Russia* ... **19 E7** 46 16N 44 14 E
Elizabeth, *Australia* ... **63 E2** 34 42S 138 41 E
Elizabeth, *U.S.A.* ... **85 F10** 40 40N 74 13W
Elizabeth City, *U.S.A.* ... **83 G7** 36 18N 76 14W
Elizabethton, *U.S.A.* ... **83 G4** 36 21N 82 13W
Elizabethtown, *Ky., U.S.A.* ... **82 G3** 37 42N 85 52W
Elizabethtown, *N.Y., U.S.A.* ... **85 B11** 44 13N 73 36W
Elizabethtown, *Pa., U.S.A.* ... **85 F8** 40 9N 76 36W
Elk, *Poland* ... **17 B12** 53 50N 22 21 E
Elk →, *Canada* ... **70 C5** 49 11N 115 14W
Elk →, *U.S.A.* ... **83 H2** 34 46N 87 16W
Elk City, *U.S.A.* ... **81 H5** 35 25N 99 25W
Elk Creek, *U.S.A.* ... **78 G5** 39 36N 122 32W
Elk Grove, *U.S.A.* ... **78 G5** 38 25N 121 22W
Elk Island △, *Canada* ... **70 C6** 53 35N 112 59W
Elk Lake, *Canada* ... **72 C3** 47 40N 80 25W
Elk Point, *Canada* ... **71 C6** 53 54N 110 55W
Elk River, *Idaho, U.S.A.* ... **76 C5** 46 47N 116 11W
Elk River, *Minn., U.S.A.* ... **80 C8** 45 18N 93 35W
Elkedra →, *Australia* ... **62 C2** 21 8S 136 22 E
Elkhart, *Ind., U.S.A.* ... **82 E3** 41 41N 85 58W
Elkhart, *Kans., U.S.A.* ... **81 G4** 37 0N 101 54W
Elkhorn, *Canada* ... **71 D8** 49 59N 101 14W
Elkhorn →, *U.S.A.* ... **80 E6** 41 8N 96 19W
Elkhovo, *Bulgaria* ... **23 C12** 42 10N 26 35 E
Elkin, *U.S.A.* ... **83 G5** 36 15N 80 51W
Elkins, *U.S.A.* ... **82 F6** 38 55N 79 51W

Elkland, *U.S.A.* ... **84 E7** 41 59N 77 19W
Elko, *Canada* ... **70 D5** 49 20N 115 10W
Elko, *U.S.A.* ... **76 F6** 40 50N 115 46W
Elkton, *U.S.A.* ... **84 C1** 43 49N 83 11W
Ell, L., *Australia* ... **61 E4** 29 13S 127 46 E
Ellef Ringnes I., *Canada* ... **4 B2** 78 30N 102 2W
Ellen, Mt., *U.S.A.* ... **85 B12** 44 9N 72 56W
Ellenburg, *U.S.A.* ... **85 B11** 44 54N 73 48W
Ellendale, *U.S.A.* ... **80 B5** 46 0N 98 32W
Ellensburg, *U.S.A.* ... **76 C3** 46 59N 120 34W
Ellenville, *U.S.A.* ... **85 E10** 41 43N 74 24W
Ellerton, *Barbados* ... **89 g** 13 7N 59 33W
Ellery, Mt., *Australia* ... **63 F4** 37 28S 148 47 E
Ellesmere, L., *N.Z.* ... **59 M4** 43 47S 172 28 E
Ellesmere I., *Canada* ... **4 B4** 79 30N 80 0W
Ellesmere Port, *U.K.* ... **12 D5** 53 17N 2 54W
Ellice Is. = Tuvalu ■, *Pac. Oc.* ... **64 H9** 8 0S 178 0 E
Ellicottville, *U.S.A.* ... **84 D6** 42 17N 78 40W
Elliot, *Australia* ... **62 B1** 17 33S 133 32 E
Elliot, *S. Africa* ... **57 E4** 31 22S 27 48 E
Elliot Lake, *Canada* ... **72 C3** 46 25N 82 35W
Elliotdale = Xhora, *S. Africa* ... **57 E4** 31 55S 28 38 E
Ellis, *U.S.A.* ... **80 F5** 38 56N 99 34W
Elliston, *Australia* ... **63 E1** 33 39S 134 53 E
Ellisville, *U.S.A.* ... **81 K10** 31 36N 89 12W
Ellon, *U.K.* ... **11 D6** 57 22N 2 4W
Ellore = Eluru, *India* ... **41 L12** 16 48N 81 8 E
Ellsworth, *Kans., U.S.A.* ... **80 F5** 38 44N 98 14W
Ellsworth, *Maine, U.S.A.* ... **83 C11** 44 33N 68 25W
Ellsworth Land, *Antarctica* ... **5 D16** 76 0S 89 0W
Ellsworth Mts., *Antarctica* ... **5 D16** 78 30S 85 0W
Ellwood City, *U.S.A.* ... **84 F4** 40 52N 80 17W
Elma, *Canada* ... **71 D9** 49 52N 95 55W
Elma, *U.S.A.* ... **78 D3** 47 0N 123 25W
Elmalı, *Turkey* ... **19 G4** 36 44N 29 56 E
Elmhurst, *U.S.A.* ... **82 E2** 41 53N 87 56W
Elmira, *Canada* ... **84 C4** 43 36N 80 33W
Elmira, *U.S.A.* ... **84 D8** 42 6N 76 48W
Elmira Heights, *U.S.A.* ... **84 D8** 42 8N 76 50W
Elmore, *Australia* ... **63 F3** 36 30S 144 37 E
Elmore, *U.S.A.* ... **79 M11** 33 7N 115 49W
Elmshorn, *Germany* ... **16 B5** 53 43N 9 40 E
Elmvale, *Canada* ... **84 B5** 44 35N 79 52W
Elora, *Canada* ... **84 C4** 43 41N 80 26W
Eloúnda, *Greece* ... **25 D7** 35 16N 25 42 E
Eloy, *U.S.A.* ... **77 K8** 32 45N 111 33W
Elrose, *Canada* ... **71 C7** 51 12N 108 0W
Elsie, *U.S.A.* ... **78 E3** 45 52N 123 36W
Elsinore = Helsingør, *Denmark* **9 H15** 56 2N 12 35 E
Eltham, *N.Z.* ... **59 H5** 39 26S 174 19 E
Eluru, *India* ... **41 L12** 16 48N 81 8 E
Elvas, *Portugal* ... **21 C2** 38 50N 7 10W
Elverum, *Norway* ... **9 F14** 60 53N 11 34 E
Elvire →, *Australia* ... **60 C4** 17 51S 128 11 E
Elvire, Mt., *Australia* ... **61 E2** 29 22S 119 36 E
Elwell, L., *U.S.A.* ... **76 B8** 48 22N 111 17W
Elwood, *Ind., U.S.A.* ... **82 E3** 40 17N 85 50W
Elwood, *Nebr., U.S.A.* ... **80 E5** 40 36N 99 52W
Elx = Elche, *Spain* ... **21 C5** 38 15N 0 42W
Ely, *U.K.* ... **13 E8** 52 24N 0 16 E
Ely, *Minn., U.S.A.* ... **80 B9** 47 55N 91 51W
Ely, *Nev., U.S.A.* ... **76 G6** 39 15N 114 54W
Elyria, *U.S.A.* ... **84 E2** 41 22N 82 7W
Emámrüd, *Iran* ... **45 B7** 36 30N 55 0 E
Emba, *Kazakhstan* ... **28 E6** 48 50N 58 8 E
Emba →, *Kazakhstan* ... **19 E9** 46 55N 53 28 E
Embarcación, *Argentina* ... **94 A3** 23 10S 64 0W
Embarras Portage, *Canada* ... **71 B6** 58 27N 111 28W
Embetsu, *Japan* ... **30 B10** 44 44N 141 47 E
Embi = Emba, *Kazakhstan* ... **28 E6** 48 50N 58 8 E
Embi →, Emba →, *Kazakhstan* **19 E9** 46 55N 53 28 E
Embóna, *Greece* ... **25 C9** 36 13N 27 51 E
Embrun, *France* ... **20 D7** 44 34N 6 30 E
Embu, *Kenya* ... **54 C4** 0 32S 37 38 E
Emden, *Germany* ... **16 B4** 53 21N 7 12 E
Emerald, *Australia* ... **62 C4** 23 32S 148 10 E
Emerson, *Canada* ... **71 D9** 49 0N 97 10W
Emet, *Turkey* ... **23 E13** 39 20N 29 15 E
Emi Koussi, *Chad* ... **51 E9** 19 45N 18 55 E
Eminabad, *Pakistan* ... **42 C6** 32 2N 74 8 E
Emine, Nos, *Bulgaria* ... **23 C12** 42 40N 27 56 E
Emissi, Tarso, *Chad* ... **51 D9** 21 27N 18 36 E
Emlenton, *U.S.A.* ... **84 E5** 41 11N 79 43W
Emmaus, *S. Africa* ... **56 D4** 29 2S 25 15 E
Emmaus, *U.S.A.* ... **85 F9** 40 32N 75 30W
Emmeloord, *Neths.* ... **15 B5** 52 44N 5 46 E
Emmen, *Neths.* ... **15 B6** 52 48N 6 57 E
Emmet, *Australia* ... **62 C3** 24 45S 144 30 E
Emmetsburg, *U.S.A.* ... **80 D7** 43 7N 94 41W
Emmett, *Idaho, U.S.A.* ... **76 E5** 43 52N 116 30W
Emmett, *Mich., U.S.A.* ... **84 D2** 42 59N 82 46W
Emmonak, *U.S.A.* ... **68 B3** 62 46N 164 30W
Emo, *Canada* ... **71 D10** 48 38N 93 50W
Empalme, *Mexico* ... **86 B2** 28 1N 110 49W
Empangeni, *S. Africa* ... **57 D5** 28 50S 31 52 E
Empedrado, *Argentina* ... **94 B4** 28 0S 58 46W
Emperor Seamount Chain, *Pac. Oc.* ... **64 D9** 40 0N 170 0 E
Emporia, *Kans., U.S.A.* ... **80 F6** 38 25N 96 11W
Emporia, *Va., U.S.A.* ... **83 G7** 36 42N 77 32W
Emporium, *U.S.A.* ... **84 E6** 41 31N 78 14W
Empress, *Canada* ... **71 C7** 50 57N 110 0W
Empty Quarter = Rub' al Khâlī, *Si. Arabia* ... **47 D4** 19 0N 48 0 E
Ems →, *Germany* ... **16 B4** 53 20N 7 12 E
Emsdale, *Canada* ... **84 A5** 45 32N 79 19W
Emu, *China* ... **35 C15** 43 40N 128 6 E
Emu Park, *Australia* ... **62 C5** 23 13S 150 50 E
'En 'Avrona, *Israel* ... **46 F4** 29 43N 35 0 E
En Nahud, *Sudan* ... **51 F11** 12 45N 28 25 E
Ena, *Japan* ... **31 G8** 35 25N 137 25 E
Enana, *Namibia* ... **56 B2** 17 30S 16 23 E
Enard B., *U.K.* ... **11 C3** 58 5N 5 20W
Enare = Inarijärvi, *Finland* ... **8 B22** 69 0N 28 0 E
Enarotali, *Indonesia* ... **37 E9** 3 55S 136 21 E
Encampment, *U.S.A.* ... **76 F10** 41 12N 106 47W
Encantadas, Serra, *Brazil* ... **95 C5** 30 40S 53 0W
Encarnación, *Paraguay* ... **95 B4** 27 15S 55 50W
Encarnación de Díaz, *Mexico* ... **86 C4** 21 30N 102 13W
Encinitas, *U.S.A.* ... **79 M9** 33 3N 117 17W
Encino, *U.S.A.* ... **77 J11** 34 39N 105 28W
Encounter B., *Australia* ... **63 F2** 35 45S 138 45 E
Endako, *Canada* ... **70 C3** 54 6N 125 2W
Ende, *Indonesia* ... **37 F6** 8 45S 121 40 E
Endeavour Str., *Australia* ... **62 A3** 10 45S 142 0 E
Enderbury I., *Kiribati* ... **64 H10** 3 8S 171 5W
Enderby, *Canada* ... **70 C5** 50 35N 119 10W
Enderby I., *Australia* ... **60 D2** 20 35S 116 30 E

Enderby Land, Antarctica ...... 5 C5 66 0S 53 0 E
Enderlin, U.S.A. 80 B6 46 38N 97 36W
Endicott, U.S.A. 85 D8 42 6N 76 4W
Endwell, U.S.A. 85 D8 42 6N 76 2W
Endyalgout I., Australia ... 60 B5 11 40S 132 35 E
Eneabba, Australia .... 61 E2 29 49S 115 16 E
Enewetak Atoll, Marshall Is. .. 64 F8 11 30N 162 15 E
Enez, Turkey .... 23 D12 40 45N 26 5 E
Enfer, Pte. d', Martinique .. 88 c 14 22N 60 54W
Enfield, Canada 73 D7 44 56N 63 32W
Enfield, Conn., U.S.A. 85 E12 41 58N 72 36W
Enfield, N.H., U.S.A. 85 C12 43 39N 72 9W
Engadin, Switz. .... 20 C9 46 45N 10 10 E
Engaño, C., Dom. Rep. 89 C6 18 30N 68 20W
Engaño, C., Phil. .... 37 A6 18 35N 122 23 E
Engaru, Japan .... 30 B11 44 3N 143 31 E
Engcobo, S. Africa .... 57 E4 31 37S 28 0 E
Engels, Russia .... 19 D8 51 28N 46 6 E
Engemann L., Canada 71 B7 58 0N 106 55W
Enggano, Indonesia .... 36 F2 5 20S 102 40 E
England, U.S.A. 81 H9 34 33N 91 58W
England □, U.K. 13 E5 53 0N 2 0W
Englee, Canada 73 B8 50 45N 56 5W
Englehart, Canada 72 C4 47 49N 79 52W
Englewood, U.S.A. 80 F2 39 39N 104 59W
English ➤, Canada 71 C10 49 12N 91 5W
English Bazar = Ingraj Bazar,
  India .... 43 G13 24 58N 88 10 E
English Channel, Europe ... 13 G6 50 0N 2 0W
English River, Canada 72 C1 49 14N 91 0W
Enid, U.S.A. 81 G6 36 24N 97 53W
Enkhuizen, Neths. .... 15 B5 52 42N 5 17 E
Enna, Italy .... 22 F6 37 34N 14 16 E
Ennadai, Canada 71 A8 61 8N 100 53W
Ennadai L., Canada 71 A8 60 58N 101 20W
Ennedi, Chad .... 51 E10 17 15N 22 0 E
Enngonia, Australia .... 63 D4 29 21S 145 50 E
Ennis, Ireland 10 D3 52 51N 8 59W
Ennis, Mont., U.S.A. 76 D8 45 21N 111 44W
Ennis, Tex., U.S.A. 81 J6 32 20N 96 38W
Enniscorthy, Ireland 10 D5 52 30N 6 34W
Enniskillen, U.K. 10 B4 54 21N 7 39W
Ennistimon, Ireland 10 D2 52 57N 9 17W
Enns ➤, Austria .... 16 D8 48 14N 14 32 E
Enontekiö, Finland .... 8 B20 68 23N 23 37 E
Enosburg Falls, U.S.A. 85 B12 44 55N 72 48W
Enriquillo, L., Dom. Rep. .. 89 C5 18 20N 72 5W
Enschede, Neths. .... 15 B6 52 13N 6 53 E
Ensenada, Argentina 94 C4 34 55S 57 55W
Ensenada, Mexico 86 A1 31 50N 116 50W
Ensenada de los Muertos,
  Mexico 86 C2 23 59N 109 50W
Ensiola, Pta. de n', Spain .. 24 B9 39 7N 2 55 E
Entebbe, Uganda .... 54 B3 0 4N 32 28 E
Enterprise, Canada 70 A5 60 47N 115 45W
Enterprise, Ala., U.S.A. ... 83 K3 31 19N 85 51W
Enterprise, Oreg., U.S.A. ... 76 D5 45 25N 117 17W
Entre Ríos, Bolivia 94 A3 21 30S 64 25W
Entre Ríos □, Argentina ... 94 C4 30 30S 58 30W
Entroncamento, Portugal ... 21 C1 39 28N 8 28W
Enugu, Nigeria .... 50 G7 6 30N 7 30 E
Enumclaw, U.S.A. 78 C5 47 12N 121 59W
Eólie, Ís., Italy .... 22 E6 38 30N 14 57 E
Epe, Neths. .... 15 B5 52 21N 5 59 E
Épernay, France .... 20 B5 49 3N 3 56 E
Ephesus, Turkey .... 23 F12 37 55N 27 22 E
Ephraim, U.S.A. 76 G8 39 22N 111 35W
Ephrata, Pa., U.S.A. 85 F8 40 11N 76 11W
Ephrata, Wash., U.S.A. ... 76 C4 47 19N 119 33W
Épinal, France .... 20 B7 48 10N 6 27 E
Episkopí, Cyprus .... 25 E11 34 40N 32 54 E
Episkopí, Greece .... 25 D6 35 20N 24 20 E
Episkopí Bay, Cyprus ..... 25 E11 34 35N 32 50 E
Epsom, U.K. 13 F7 51 19N 0 16W
Epukiro, Namibia .... 56 C2 21 40S 19 9 E
Equatorial Guinea ■, Africa .. 52 D1 2 0N 8 0 E
Er Rachidia, Morocco 50 B5 31 58N 4 20W
Er Rahad, Sudan .... 51 F12 12 45N 30 32 E
Er Rif, Morocco 50 A5 35 1N 4 1W
Erāwadi Myit = Irrawaddy ➤,
  Burma .... 41 M19 15 50N 95 6 E
Erāwadi Myitwanya = Irrawaddy,
  Mouths of the, Burma .. 41 M19 15 30N 95 0 E
Erbil = Arbīl, Iraq .... 44 B5 36 15N 44 5 E
Erçek, Turkey .... 44 B4 38 39N 43 36 E
Erciyaş Dağı, Turkey ..... 44 B2 38 30N 35 30 E
Érd, Hungary .... 17 E10 47 22N 18 56 E
Erdao Jiang ➤, China ..... 35 C14 43 0N 127 0 E
Erdek, Turkey .... 23 D12 40 23N 27 47 E
Erdene = Ulaan-Uul, Mongolia .. 34 B6 44 13N 111 10 E
Erdenet, Mongolia .... 32 B5 49 2N 104 5 E
Erdenetsogt, Mongolia ..... 34 C4 42 55N 106 5 E
Erebus, Mt., Antarctica ... 5 D11 77 35S 167 0 E
Erechim, Brazil 95 B5 27 35S 52 15W
Ereğli, Konya, Turkey ..... 19 G5 37 31N 34 4 E
Ereğli, Zonguldak, Turkey .. 19 F5 41 15N 31 24 E
Erenhot, China .... 34 C7 43 48N 112 2 E
Eresma ➤, Spain 21 B3 41 26N 4 45W
Erfenisdam, S. Africa ..... 56 D4 28 30S 26 50 E
Erfurt, Germany .... 16 C6 50 58N 11 2 E
Ergani, Turkey .... 44 B3 38 17N 39 49 E
Ergel, Mongolia .... 34 C5 43 8N 109 5 E
Ergeni Vozvyshennost, Russia .. 19 E7 47 0N 44 0 E
Érgli, Latvia .... 9 H21 56 54N 25 38 E
Eriboll, L., U.K. 11 C4 58 30N 4 42W
Érice, Italy .... 22 E5 38 2N 12 35 E
Erie, U.S.A. 84 D4 42 8N 80 5W
Erie, L., N. Amer. 84 D4 42 15N 81 0W
Erie Canal, U.S.A. 84 C7 43 5N 78 43W
Erieau, Canada 84 D3 42 16N 81 57W
Erigavo, Somali Rep. ..... 47 E4 10 35N 47 20 E
Eriksoua, Greece .... 25 A3 39 53N 19 34 E
Eriksdale, Canada 71 C9 50 52N 98 7W
Erimanthos, Greece .... 23 F9 37 57N 21 50 E
Erimo-misaki, Japan .... 30 D11 41 50N 143 15 E
Erin Pt., Trin. & Tob. 93 K15 10 3N 61 40W
Erinpura, India .... 42 G5 25 9N 73 3 E
Eriskay, U.K. 11 D1 57 4N 7 18W
Eritrea ■, Africa .... 47 D2 14 0N 38 30 E
Erlangen, Germany .... 16 D6 49 36N 11 0 E
Erldunda, Australia .... 62 D1 25 14S 133 12 E
Ermelo, Neths. .... 15 B5 52 18N 5 35 E
Ermelo, S. Africa .... 57 D4 26 31S 29 59 E
Ermenek, Turkey .... 44 C5 36 38N 33 0 E
Ermones, Greece .... 25 A3 39 37N 19 46 E
Ernakulam, India .... 40 Q10 9 59N 76 22 E
Erne ➤, Ireland 10 B3 54 30N 8 16W
Erne, Lower L., U.K. 10 B4 54 28N 7 47W

Erne, Upper L., U.K. 10 B4 54 14N 7 32W
Ernest Giles Ra., Australia .. 61 E3 27 0S 123 45 E
Erode, India .... 40 P10 11 24N 77 45 E
Eromanga, Australia .... 63 D3 26 40S 143 11 E
Erongo, Namibia .... 56 C2 21 39S 15 58 E
Erramala Hills, India ..... 40 M11 15 30N 78 15 E
Errigal, Ireland 10 A3 55 2N 8 6W
Erris Hd., Ireland 10 B1 54 19N 10 0W
Erskine, U.S.A. 80 B7 47 40N 96 0W
Ertis = Irtysh ➤, Russia ... 28 C7 61 4N 68 52 E
Erwin, U.S.A. 83 G4 36 9N 82 25W
Erzgebirge, Germany .... 16 C7 50 27N 12 55 E
Erzin, Russia .... 29 D10 50 15N 95 10 E
Erzincan, Turkey .... 19 G6 39 46N 39 30 E
Erzurum, Turkey .... 19 G7 39 57N 41 15 E
Es Caló, Spain .... 24 C8 38 40N 1 30 E
Es Canar, Spain .... 24 B8 39 2N 1 36 E
Es Mercadal, Spain .... 24 B11 39 59N 4 5 E
Es Migjorn Gran, Spain ... 24 B11 39 57N 4 3 E
Es Sahrâ' Esh Sharqîya, Egypt .. 51 C12 27 30N 32 30 E
Es Sînâ', Egypt .... 46 F3 29 0N 34 0 E
Es Vedrà, Spain .... 24 C7 38 52N 1 12 E
Esambo, Dem. Rep. of the Congo 54 C1 3 48S 23 30 E
Esan-Misaki, Japan .... 30 D10 41 40N 141 10 E
Esashi, Hokkaidō, Japan ... 30 B11 44 56N 142 35 E
Esashi, Hokkaidō, Japan ... 30 D10 41 52N 140 7 E
Esbjerg, Denmark .... 9 J13 55 29N 8 29 E
Escalante, U.S.A. 77 H8 37 47N 111 36W
Escalante ➤, U.S.A. 77 H8 37 24N 110 57W
Escalón, Mexico 86 B4 26 46N 104 20W
Escambia ➤, U.S.A. 83 K2 30 32N 87 11W
Escanaba, U.S.A. 82 C2 45 45N 87 4W
Esch-sur-Alzette, Lux. ..... 15 E6 49 32N 5 57 E
Escondido, U.S.A. 79 M9 33 7N 117 5W
Escuinapa, Mexico 86 C3 22 50N 105 50W
Escuintla, Guatemala 88 D1 14 20N 90 48W
Esenguly, Turkmenistan ... 28 F6 37 37N 53 59 E
Eşfahān, Iran .... 45 C6 32 39N 51 43 E
Eşfahān □, Iran .... 45 C6 32 50N 51 50 E
Esfarāyen, Iran .... 45 B8 37 4N 57 30 E
Esfideh, Iran .... 45 C8 33 39N 59 46 E
Esh Sham = Dimashq, Syria .. 46 B5 33 30N 36 18 E
Esher, U.K. 13 F7 51 21N 0 20W
Eshkol △, Israel .... 46 D3 31 20N 34 30 E
Eshowe, S. Africa .... 57 D5 28 50S 31 30 E
Esigodini, Zimbabwe ..... 57 C4 20 18S 28 56 E
Esil = Ishim ➤, Russia ... 28 D8 57 45N 71 10 E
Esira, Madag. .... 57 C8 24 20S 46 42 E
Esk ➤, Cumb., U.K. 11 G5 54 58N 3 2W
Esk ➤, N. Yorks., U.K. ... 12 C7 54 30N 0 37W
Esker, Canada .... 45 E9 26 48N 63 9 E
Esker, Canada 73 B6 53 53N 66 25W
Eskifjörður, Iceland 8 D7 65 3N 13 55W
Eskilstuna, Sweden .... 9 G17 59 22N 16 32 E
Eskimo Point = Arviat, Canada .. 71 A10 61 6N 93 59W
Eskişehir, Turkey .... 19 G5 39 50N 30 30 E
Esla ➤, Spain 21 B2 41 29N 6 3W
Eslāmābād-e Gharb, Iran ... 44 C5 34 10N 46 30 E
Eslāmshahr, Iran .... 45 C6 35 40N 51 10 E
Eşme, Turkey .... 23 E13 38 23N 28 58 E
Esmeraldas, Ecuador 92 C3 1 0N 79 40W
Esnagi L., Canada 72 C3 48 36N 84 33W
Espanola, Canada 72 C3 46 15N 81 46W
Espanola, U.S.A. 77 H10 35 59N 106 5W
Esperance, Australia ..... 61 F3 33 45S 121 55 E
Esperance B., Australia ... 61 F3 33 48S 121 55 E
Esperance B., St. Lucia ... 89 f 14 4N 60 55W
Esperanza, Antarctica 5 C18 65 0S 55 0W
Esperanza, Argentina 94 C3 31 29S 61 3W
Esperanza, Puerto Rico ... 89 d 18 6N 65 28W
Espichel, C., Portugal 21 C1 38 22N 9 16W
Espigão, Serra do, Brazil ... 95 B5 26 35S 50 30W
Espinazo, Sierra del = Espinhaço,
  Serra do, Brazil 93 G10 17 30S 43 30W
Espinhaço, Serra do, Brazil .. 93 G10 17 30S 43 30W
Espinilho, Serra do, Brazil .. 95 B5 28 30S 55 0W
Espírito Santo, Vanuatu ... 64 J8 15 15S 166 50 E
Espírito Santo □, Brazil ... 93 H10 20 0S 40 45W
Espíritu Santo, B. del, Mexico .. 87 D7 19 15N 87 0W
Espíritu Santo, I., Mexico ... 86 C2 24 30N 110 23W
Espita, Mexico 87 C7 21 1N 88 19W
Espoo, Finland .... 9 F21 60 12N 24 40 E
Espungabera, Mozam. ..... 57 C5 20 29S 32 45 E
Esquel, Argentina 96 E2 42 55S 71 20W
Esquimalt, Canada 70 D4 48 26N 123 25W
Esquina, Argentina 94 C4 30 0S 59 30W
Essaouira, Morocco 50 B4 31 32N 9 42W
Essebie, Dem. Rep. of the Congo 54 B3 2 58N 30 40 E
Essen, Belgium .... 15 C4 51 28N 4 28 E
Essen, Germany .... 16 C4 51 28N 7 2 E
Essendon, Mt., Australia ... 61 E3 25 0S 120 29 E
Essequibo ➤, Guyana 92 B7 6 50N 58 30W
Essex, Canada 84 D2 42 10N 82 49W
Essex, Calif., U.S.A. 79 L11 34 44N 115 15W
Essex, N.Y., U.S.A. 85 B11 44 19N 73 21W
Essex □, U.K. .... 13 F8 51 54N 0 27 E
Essex Junction, U.S.A. ... 85 B11 44 29N 73 7W
Esslingen, Germany .... 16 D5 48 44N 9 18 E
Estados, I. de Los, Argentina .. 96 G4 54 40S 64 30W
Eşţahbānāt, Iran .... 45 D7 29 8N 54 4 E
Estância, Brazil 93 F11 11 16S 37 26W
Estancia, U.S.A. 77 J10 34 46N 106 4W
Estārm, Iran .... 45 D8 28 21N 58 21 E
Estcourt, S. Africa .... 57 D4 29 0S 29 53 E
Este, Dom. Rep. 89 C6 18 14N 68 42W
Estelí, Nic. 88 D2 13 9N 86 22W
Estellencs, Spain .... 24 B9 39 39N 2 29 E
Esterhazy, Canada 71 C8 50 37N 102 5W
Estevan, Canada 71 D8 49 10N 102 59W
Estevan Group, Canada ... 70 C3 53 3N 129 38W
Estherville, U.S.A. 80 D7 43 24N 94 50W
Eston, Canada 71 C7 51 8N 108 40W
Estonia ■, Europe .... 9 G21 58 30N 25 30 E
Estrela, Serra da, Portugal .. 21 B2 40 10N 7 45W
Estremoz, Portugal 21 C2 38 51N 7 39W
Estrondo, Serra do, Brazil .. 93 E9 7 20S 48 0W
Esztergom, Hungary .... 17 E10 47 47N 18 44 E
Etah, India .... 43 F8 27 35N 78 40 E
Étampes, France .... 20 B5 48 26N 2 10 E
Etanga, Namibia .... 56 B1 17 55S 13 0 E
Etawah, India .... 43 F8 26 48N 79 6 E
Etawney L., Canada 71 B9 57 50N 96 50W
Ethel, U.S.A. 78 D4 46 32N 122 46W
Ethelbert, Canada 71 C8 51 32N 100 25W
Ethiopia ■, Africa .... 47 F3 8 0N 40 0 E

Ethiopian Highlands, Ethiopia .. 26 J7 10 0N 37 0 E
Etive, L., U.K. 11 E3 56 29N 5 10W
Etna, Italy .... 22 F6 37 50N 14 55 E
Etoile, Dem. Rep. of the Congo 55 E2 11 33S 27 30 E
Etosha △, Namibia .... 56 B2 19 0S 16 0 E
Etosha Pan, Namibia ..... 56 B2 18 40S 16 30 E
Etowah, U.S.A. 83 H3 35 20N 84 32W
Ettelbruck, Lux. .... 15 E6 49 51N 6 5 E
Ettrick Water ➤, U.K. 11 F6 55 31N 2 55W
Etuku, Dem. Rep. of the Congo 54 C2 3 42S 25 45 E
Etzatlán, Mexico 86 C4 20 48N 104 5W
Etzná, Mexico 87 D6 19 35N 90 15W
Etzná-Tixmucuy = Edxná, Mexico 87 D6 19 35N 90 15W
Euboea = Évvoia, Greece ... 23 E11 38 30N 24 0 E
Eucla, Australia .... 61 F4 31 41S 128 52 E
Euclid, U.S.A. 84 E3 41 34N 81 32W
Eucumbene, L., Australia ... 63 F4 36 2S 148 40 E
Eudora, U.S.A. 81 J9 33 7N 91 16W
Eufaula, Ala., U.S.A. 83 K3 31 54N 85 9W
Eufaula, Okla., U.S.A. ... 81 H7 35 17N 95 35W
Eufaula L., U.S.A. 81 H7 35 18N 95 21W
Eugene, U.S.A. 76 E2 44 5N 123 4W
Eugowra, Australia .... 63 E4 33 22S 148 24 E
Eulo, Australia .... 63 D4 28 10S 145 3 E
Eunice, La., U.S.A. 81 K8 30 30N 92 25W
Eunice, N. Mex., U.S.A. ... 81 J3 32 26N 103 10W
Eupen, Belgium .... 15 D6 50 37N 6 3 E
Euphrates = Furāt, Nahr al ➤,
  Asia .... 44 D5 31 0N 47 25 E
Eureka, Canada 4 B3 80 0N 85 56W
Eureka, Calif., U.S.A. 76 F1 40 47N 124 9W
Eureka, Kans., U.S.A. ... 81 G6 37 49N 96 17W
Eureka, Mont., U.S.A. ... 76 B6 48 53N 115 3W
Eureka, Nev., U.S.A. 76 G5 39 31N 115 58W
Eureka, S. Dak., U.S.A. ... 80 C5 45 46N 99 38W
Eureka, Mt., Australia ..... 61 E3 26 35S 121 35 E
Euroa, Australia .... 63 F4 36 44S 145 35 E
Europa, Île, Ind. Oc. ..... 53 J8 22 20S 40 22 E
Europa, Picos de, Spain ... 21 A3 43 10N 4 49W
Europa, Pta. de, Gib. 21 D3 36 3N 5 21W
Europe .... 6 E10 50 0N 20 0 E
Europoort, Neths. .... 15 C4 51 57N 4 10 E
Eustis, U.S.A. 83 L5 28 51N 81 41W
Eutsuk L., Canada 70 C3 53 20N 126 45W
Evale, Angola .... 56 B2 16 33S 15 44 E
Evans, U.S.A. 80 E2 40 23N 104 41W
Evans, L., Canada 72 B4 50 50N 77 0W
Evans Head, Australia ... 63 D5 29 7S 153 27 E
Evans Mills, U.S.A. 85 B9 44 6N 75 48W
Evansburg, Canada 70 C5 53 36N 114 59W
Evanston, Ill., U.S.A. 82 E2 42 3N 87 41W
Evanston, Wyo., U.S.A. ... 76 F8 41 16N 110 58W
Evansville, U.S.A. 82 G2 37 58N 87 35W
Evaz, Iran .... 45 E7 27 46N 53 59 E
Eveleth, U.S.A. 80 B8 47 28N 92 32W
Evensk, Russia .... 29 C16 62 12N 159 30 E
Everard, L., Australia ..... 63 E2 31 30S 135 0 E
Everard Ranges, Australia .. 61 E5 27 5S 132 28 E
Everest, Mt., Nepal ..... 43 E12 28 5N 86 58 E
Everett, Pa., U.S.A. 84 F6 40 1N 78 23W
Everett, Wash., U.S.A. ... 78 C4 47 59N 122 12W
Everglades, U.S.A. 83 N5 25 30N 81 0W
Everglades, The, U.S.A. ... 83 N5 25 50N 81 0W
Everglades City, U.S.A. ... 83 N5 25 52N 81 23W
Evergreen, Ala., U.S.A. ... 83 K2 31 26N 86 57W
Evergreen, Mont., U.S.A. ... 76 B6 48 9N 114 13W
Evesham, U.K. 13 E6 52 6N 1 56W
Evje, Norway .... 9 G12 58 36N 7 51 E
Évora, Portugal 21 C2 38 33N 7 57W
Evowghlī, Iran .... 44 B5 38 43N 45 13 E
Évreux, France .... 20 B4 49 3N 1 8 E
Évros ➤, Greece .... 23 D12 41 40N 26 34 E
Évry, France .... 20 B5 48 38N 2 27 E
Évvoia, Greece .... 23 E11 38 30N 24 0 E
Ewing, U.S.A. 80 D5 42 16N 98 21W
Ewo, Congo .... 52 E2 0 48S 14 45 E
Exaltación, Bolivia 92 F5 13 10S 65 20W
Excelsior Springs, U.S.A. ... 80 F7 39 20N 94 13W
Exe ➤, U.K. 13 G4 50 41N 3 29W
Exeter, Canada 84 C3 43 21N 81 29W
Exeter, U.K. 13 G4 50 43N 3 31W
Exeter, Calif., U.S.A. 78 J7 36 18N 119 9W
Exeter, N.H., U.S.A. 85 D14 42 59N 70 57W
Exmoor, U.K. 13 F4 51 12N 3 45W
Exmoor △, U.K. 13 F4 51 8N 3 42W
Exmouth, Australia .... 60 D1 21 54S 114 10 E
Exmouth, U.K. 13 G4 50 37N 3 25W
Exmouth G., Australia ..... 60 D1 22 15S 114 15 E
Expedition △, Australia ... 62 C4 25 41S 149 7 E
Expedition Ra., Australia ... 62 C4 24 30S 149 12 E
Extremadura □, Spain 21 C2 39 30N 6 5W
Exuma Sound, Bahamas ... 88 B4 24 30N 76 20W
Eyasi, L., Tanzania .... 54 C4 3 30S 35 0 E
Eye Pen., U.K. 11 C2 58 13N 6 10W
Eyemouth, U.K. 11 F6 55 52N 2 5W
Eyjafjörður, Iceland 8 C4 66 15N 18 30W
Eyre (North), L., Australia ... 63 D2 28 30S 137 20 E
Eyre (South), L., Australia ... 63 D2 29 18S 137 25 E
Eyre Mts., N.Z. .... 59 L2 45 25S 168 25 E
Eyre Pen., Australia ..... 63 E2 33 30S 136 17 E
Eysturoy, Færoe Is. 8 E9 62 13N 6 54W
Eyvānki, Iran .... 45 C6 35 24N 51 56 E
Ezine, Turkey .... 23 E12 39 48N 26 20 E
Ezouza ➤, Cyprus .... 25 E11 34 44N 32 27 E

F

F.Y.R.O.M. = Macedonia ■,
  Europe .... 23 D9 41 53N 21 40 E
Fabala, Guinea 50 G4 9 44N 9 5W
Fabens, U.S.A. 77 L10 31 30N 106 10W
Fabriano, Italy .... 22 C5 43 20N 12 54 E
Fachi, Niger .... 51 E8 16 6N 11 34 E
Fada, Chad .... 51 E10 17 13N 21 34 E
Fada-n-Gourma, Burkina Faso .. 50 F6 12 10N 0 30 E
Faddeyevskiy, Ostrov, Russia .. 29 B15 76 0N 144 0 E
Fadghāmī, Syria .... 44 C4 35 53N 40 52 E
Faenza, Italy .... 22 B4 44 17N 11 53 E
Færoe Is. = Føroyar, Atl. Oc. .. 8 F9 62 0N 7 0W
Făgăraş, Romania .... 17 F13 45 48N 24 58 E
Fagersta, Sweden .... 9 F16 60 1N 15 46 E
Fagnano, L., Argentina ... 96 G3 54 30S 68 0W
Fahliān, Iran .... 45 D6 30 11N 51 28 E
Fahraj, Kermān, Iran ..... 45 D8 29 0N 59 0 E
Fahraj, Yazd, Iran .... 45 D7 31 46N 54 36 E
Faial, Madeira 24 D3 32 47N 16 53W
Fair Haven, U.S.A. 82 D9 43 36N 73 16W
Fair Hd., U.K. 10 A5 55 14N 6 9W
Fair Isle, U.K. 14 B6 59 30N 1 40W
Fair Oaks, U.S.A. 78 G5 38 39N 121 16W
Fairbanks, U.S.A. 68 B5 64 51N 147 43W
Fairbury, U.S.A. 80 E6 40 8N 97 11W
Fairfax, U.S.A. 85 B11 44 40N 73 1W
Fairfield, Ala., U.S.A. 83 J2 33 29N 86 55W
Fairfield, Calif., U.S.A. ... 78 G4 38 15N 122 3W
Fairfield, Conn., U.S.A. ... 85 E11 41 9N 73 16W
Fairfield, Idaho, U.S.A. ... 76 E6 43 21N 114 44W
Fairfield, Ill., U.S.A. 82 F1 38 23N 88 22W
Fairfield, Iowa, U.S.A. ... 80 E9 40 56N 91 57W
Fairfield, Tex., U.S.A. ... 81 K7 31 44N 96 10W
Fairford, Canada 71 C9 51 37N 98 38W
Fairhope, U.S.A. 83 K2 30 31N 87 54W
Fairlie, N.Z. .... 59 L3 44 5S 170 49 E
Fairmead, U.S.A. 78 H6 37 5N 120 10W
Fairmont, Minn., U.S.A. ... 80 D7 43 39N 94 28W
Fairmont, W. Va., U.S.A. ... 82 F5 39 29N 80 9W
Fairmount, Calif., U.S.A. ... 79 L8 34 45N 118 26W
Fairmount, N.Y., U.S.A. ... 85 C8 43 5N 76 12W
Fairplay, U.S.A. 77 G11 39 15N 106 2W
Fairport, U.S.A. 84 C7 43 6N 77 27W
Fairport Harbor, U.S.A. ... 84 E3 41 45N 81 17W
Fairview, Canada 70 B5 56 5N 118 25W
Fairview, Mont., U.S.A. ... 80 B2 47 51N 104 3W
Fairview, Okla., U.S.A. ... 81 G5 36 16N 98 29W
Fairweather, Mt., U.S.A. ... 70 B1 58 55N 137 32W
Faisalabad, Pakistan ..... 42 D5 31 30N 73 5 E
Faith, U.S.A. 80 C3 45 2N 102 2W
Faizabad, India .... 43 F10 26 45N 82 10 E
Fajardo, Puerto Rico ..... 89 d 18 20N 65 39W
Fajr, W. ➤, Si. Arabia ... 44 D3 29 10N 38 10 E
Fakenham, U.K. .... 12 E8 52 51N 0 51 E
Fakfak, Indonesia .... 37 E8 2 55S 132 18 E
Faku, China .... 35 C12 42 32N 123 21 E
Falaise, France 20 B3 48 54N 0 12W
Falaise, Mui, Vietnam ..... 38 C5 19 6N 105 45 E
Falam, Burma .... 41 H18 23 0N 93 45 E
Falcó, C. des, Spain ..... 24 C7 38 50N 1 23 E
Falcón, Presa, Mexico ... 87 B5 26 35N 99 10W
Falcon Lake, Canada 71 D9 49 42N 95 15W
Falcon Reservoir, U.S.A. ... 81 M5 26 34N 99 10W
Falconara Maríttima, Italy ... 22 C5 43 37N 13 24 E
Falcone, C. del, Italy ..... 22 D3 40 58N 8 12 E
Falconer, U.S.A. 84 D5 42 7N 79 13W
Faleshty = Fălești, Moldova ... 17 E14 47 32N 27 44 E
Fălești, Moldova .... 17 E14 47 32N 27 44 E
Falfurrias, U.S.A. 81 M5 27 14N 98 9W
Falher, Canada 70 B5 55 44N 117 15W
Faliraki, Greece .... 25 C10 36 22N 28 12 E
Falkenberg, Sweden .... 9 H15 56 54N 12 30 E
Falkirk, U.K. 11 F5 56 0N 3 47W
Falkirk □, U.K. 11 F5 55 58N 3 49W
Falkland, U.K. 11 E5 56 16N 3 12W
Falkland Is. ☑, Atl. Oc. ... 96 G5 51 30S 59 0W
Falkland Sd., Falk. Is. 96 G5 52 0S 60 0W
Falköping, Sweden .... 9 G15 58 12N 13 33 E
Fall River, U.S.A. 85 E13 41 43N 71 10W
Fallbrook, U.S.A. 79 M9 33 23N 117 15W
Fallon, U.S.A. 76 G4 39 28N 118 47W
Falls City, U.S.A. 80 E7 40 3N 95 36W
Falls Creek, U.S.A. 84 E6 41 9N 78 48W
Falmouth, Jamaica .... 88 a 18 30N 77 40W
Falmouth, U.K. 13 G2 50 9N 5 5W
Falmouth, U.S.A. 85 E14 41 33N 70 37W
Falsa, Pta., Mexico 86 B1 27 51N 115 3W
False B., S. Africa .... 56 E2 34 15S 18 40 E
Falso, C., Honduras 88 C3 15 12N 83 21W
Falster, Denmark .... 9 J14 54 45N 11 55 E
Falsterbo, Sweden .... 9 J15 55 23N 12 50 E
Fălticeni, Romania .... 17 E14 47 21N 26 20 E
Falun, Sweden .... 9 F16 60 37N 15 37 E
Famagusta, Cyprus .... 25 D12 35 8N 33 55 E
Famagusta Bay, Cyprus ... 25 D13 35 15N 34 0 E
Famalé, Niger .... 50 F6 14 33N 1 5 E
Famatina, Sierra de, Argentina .. 94 B2 27 30S 68 0W
Family L., Canada 71 C9 51 54N 95 27W
Famoso, U.S.A. 79 K7 35 37N 119 12W
Fan Xian, China .... 34 G8 35 55N 115 38 E
Fanad Hd., Ireland 10 A4 55 17N 7 38W
Fandriana, Madag. .... 57 C8 20 14S 47 21 E
Fang, Thailand .... 38 C2 19 55N 99 13 E
Fangcheng, China .... 34 H7 33 18N 112 59 E
Fangshan, China .... 34 E6 38 3N 111 25 E
Fangzi, China .... 35 F10 36 33N 119 10 E
Fanjakana, Madag. .... 57 C8 21 10S 46 53 E
Fanjiatun, China .... 35 C13 43 40N 125 15 E
Fanling, China .... 33 F11 22 30N 114 8 E
Fannich, L., U.K. 11 D4 57 38N 4 59W
Fannūj, Iran .... 45 E8 26 35N 59 38 E
Fano, Denmark .... 9 J13 55 25N 8 25 E
Fano, Italy .... 22 C5 43 50N 13 1 E
Fanshi, China .... 34 E7 39 12N 113 20 E
Fao = Al Fāw, Iraq .... 45 D6 30 0N 48 30 E
Faqirwali, Pakistan .... 42 E5 29 27N 73 0 E
Far East = Dalnevostochnyy □,
  Russia .... 29 C14 67 0N 140 0 E
Far East, Asia .... 26 E16 40 0N 130 0 E
Faradje, Dem. Rep. of the Congo 54 B2 3 50N 29 45 E
Farafangana, Madag. ..... 57 C8 22 49S 47 50 E
Farāh, Afghan. .... 40 C3 32 20N 62 7 E
Farāh □, Afghan. .... 40 C3 32 25N 62 10 E
Farahalana, Madag. .... 57 A9 14 26S 50 10 E
Faranah, Guinea 50 F3 10 3N 10 45W
Farasān, Jazā'ir, Si. Arabia .. 47 D3 16 45N 41 55 E
Farasān Is. = Farasān, Jazā'ir,
  Si. Arabia .... 47 D3 16 45N 41 55 E
Faratsiho, Madag. .... 57 B8 19 24S 46 57 E
Fareham, U.K. 13 G6 50 51N 1 11W
Farewell, C., N.Z. .... 59 J4 40 29S 172 43 E
Farewell C. = Nunap Isua,
  Greenland 69 C15 59 48N 43 55W
Farghona, Uzbekistan ..... 28 E8 40 23N 71 19 E
Fargo, U.S.A. 80 B6 46 53N 96 48W
Fār'iah, W. al ➤, West Bank .. 46 C4 32 12N 35 27 E
Faribault, U.S.A. 80 C8 44 18N 93 16W
Faridabad, India .... 42 E6 28 26N 77 19 E
Faridkot, India .... 42 D6 30 44N 74 45 E
Faridpur, Bangla. .... 43 H13 23 15N 89 55 E
Faridpur, India .... 43 E8 28 13N 79 33 E
Farīmān, Iran .... 45 C8 35 40N 59 49 E

Farina, Australia · 63 E2 · 30 3S 138 15 E
Fariones, Pta., Canary Is. · 24 E6 · 29 13N 13 28W
Farleigh, Australia · 62 K7 · 21 4S 149 8 E
Farmerville, U.S.A. · 81 J8 · 32 47N 92 24W
Farmingdale, U.S.A. · 85 F10 · 40 12N 74 10W
Farmington, Canada · 70 B4 · 55 54N 120 30W
Farmington, Calif., U.S.A. · 78 H6 · 37 55N 120 59W
Farmington, Maine, U.S.A. · 85 A14 · 44 40N 70 9W
Farmington, Mo., U.S.A. · 81 G9 · 37 47N 90 25W
Farmington, N.H., U.S.A. · 85 C13 · 43 24N 71 4W
Farmington, N. Mex., U.S.A. · 77 H9 · 36 44N 108 12W
Farmington, Utah, U.S.A. · 76 F8 · 41 0N 111 12W
Farmington →, U.S.A. · 85 E12 · 41 51N 72 38W
Farmville, U.S.A. · 82 G6 · 37 18N 78 24W
Farne Is., U.K. · 12 B6 · 55 38N 1 37W
Farnham, Canada · 85 A12 · 45 17N 72 59W
Farnham, Mt., Canada · 70 C5 · 50 29N 116 30W
Faro, Brazil · 93 D7 · 2 10S 56 39W
Faro, Canada · 68 B6 · 62 11N 133 22W
Faro, Portugal · 21 D2 · 37 2N 7 55W
Fårö, Sweden · 9 H18 · 57 55N 19 5 E
Farquhar, C., Australia · 61 D1 · 23 50S 113 36 E
Farrars Cr. →, Australia · 62 D3 · 25 35S 140 43 E
Farrell, U.S.A. · 84 E4 · 41 13N 80 30W
Farrāshband, Iran · 45 D7 · 28 57N 52 5 E
Farrell, U.S.A. · 84 E4 · 41 13N 80 30W
Farrokhī, Iran · 45 C8 · 33 50N 59 31 E
Farruch, C. = Ferrutx, C., Spain · 24 B10 · 39 47N 3 21 E
Fārs □, Iran · 45 D7 · 29 30N 55 0 E
Fársala, Greece · 23 E10 · 39 17N 22 23 E
Farson, U.S.A. · 76 E9 · 42 6N 109 27W
Farsund, Norway · 9 G12 · 58 5N 6 55 E
Fartak, Râs, Si. Arabia · 44 D2 · 28 5N 34 34 E
Fartak, Ra's, Yemen · 47 D5 · 15 38N 52 15 E
Fartura, Serra da, Brazil · 95 B5 · 26 21S 52 52W
Fārūj, Iran · 45 B8 · 37 14N 58 14 E
Farvel, Kap = Nunap Isua, Greenland · 69 C15 · 59 48N 43 55W
Farwell, U.S.A. · 81 H3 · 34 23N 103 2W
Fāryāb □, Afghan. · 40 B4 · 36 0N 65 0 E
Fasã, Iran · 45 D7 · 29 0N 53 39 E
Fasano, Italy · 22 D7 · 40 50N 17 22 E
Fastiv, Ukraine · 17 C15 · 50 7N 29 57 E
Fastnet Rock, Ireland · 10 E2 · 51 22N 9 37W
Fastov = Fastiv, Ukraine · 17 C15 · 50 7N 29 57 E
Fatagar, Tanjung, Indonesia · 37 E8 · 2 46S 131 57 E
Fatehabad, Haryana, India · 42 E6 · 29 31N 75 27 E
Fatehabad, Ut. P., India · 42 F8 · 27 1N 78 19 E
Fatehgarh, India · 43 F8 · 27 25N 79 35 E
Fatehpur, Bihar, India · 43 G11 · 24 38N 85 14 E
Fatehpur, Raj., India · 42 F6 · 28 0N 74 40 E
Fatehpur, Ut. P., India · 43 G9 · 25 56N 81 13 E
Fatehpur, Ut. P., India · 43 F9 · 27 10N 81 13 E
Fatehpur Sikri, India · 42 F6 · 27 6N 77 40 E
Fathom Five △, Canada · 84 A3 · 45 17N 81 40W
Fatima, Canada · 73 C7 · 47 24N 61 53W
Faulkton, U.S.A. · 80 C5 · 45 2N 99 8W
Faure I., Australia · 61 E1 · 25 52S 113 50 E
Fauresmith, S. Africa · 56 D4 · 29 44S 25 17 E
Fauske, Norway · 8 C16 · 67 17N 15 25 E
Favara, Italy · 22 F5 · 37 19N 13 39 E
Favára, C. de, Spain · 24 B11 · 40 0N 4 15 E
Favignana, Italy · 22 F5 · 37 56N 12 20 E
Fawcett, Pt., Australia · 60 B5 · 11 46S 130 2 E
Fawn →, Canada · 72 A2 · 55 20N 87 35W
Fawnskin, U.S.A. · 79 L10 · 34 16N 116 56W
Faxaflói, Iceland · 8 D2 · 64 29N 23 0W
Faya-Largeau, Chad · 51 E9 · 17 58N 19 6 E
Fayd, Si. Arabia · 44 E4 · 27 1N 42 52 E
Fayette, Ala., U.S.A. · 83 J2 · 33 41N 87 50W
Fayette, Mo., U.S.A. · 80 F8 · 39 9N 92 41W
Fayetteville, Ark., U.S.A. · 81 G7 · 36 4N 94 10W
Fayetteville, N.C., U.S.A. · 83 H6 · 35 3N 78 53W
Fayetteville, Tenn., U.S.A. · 83 H2 · 35 9N 86 34W
Fazilka, India · 42 D6 · 30 27N 74 2 E
Fazilpur, Pakistan · 42 E4 · 29 18N 70 29 E
Fdérik, Mauritania · 50 D3 · 22 40N 12 45W
Feale →, Ireland · 10 D2 · 52 27N 9 37W
Fear, C., U.S.A. · 83 J7 · 33 50N 77 58W
Feather →, U.S.A. · 76 G3 · 38 47N 121 36W
Feather Falls, U.S.A. · 78 F5 · 39 36N 121 16W
Featherston, N.Z. · 59 J5 · 41 6S 175 20 E
Featherstone, Zimbabwe · 55 F3 · 18 42S 30 55 E
Fécamp, France · 20 B4 · 49 45N 0 22 E
Fedala = Mohammedia, Morocco · 50 B4 · 33 44N 7 21W
Federación, Argentina · 94 C4 · 31 0S 57 55W
Féderal, Argentina · 96 C5 · 30 57S 58 48W
Federal Way, U.S.A. · 78 C4 · 47 18N 122 19W
Fedeshkūh, Iran · 45 D7 · 28 49N 53 50 E
Fehmarn, Germany · 16 A6 · 54 27N 11 7 E
Fehmarn Bælt, Europe · 9 J14 · 54 35N 11 20 E
Fehmarn Belt = Fehmarn Bælt, Europe · 9 J14 · 54 35N 11 20 E
Fei Xian, China · 35 G9 · 35 18N 117 59 E
Feijó, Brazil · 92 E4 · 8 9S 70 21W
Feilding, N.Z. · 59 J5 · 40 13S 175 35 E
Feira de Santana, Brazil · 93 F11 · 12 15S 38 57W
Feixiang, China · 34 F8 · 36 30N 114 45 E
Felanitx, Spain · 24 B10 · 39 28N 3 9 E
Feldkirch, Austria · 16 E5 · 47 15N 9 37 E
Felipe Carrillo Puerto, Mexico · 87 D7 · 19 38N 88 3W
Felixburg, Zimbabwe · 57 B5 · 19 29S 30 51 E
Felixstowe, U.K. · 13 F9 · 51 58N 1 23 E
Felton, U.S.A. · 78 H4 · 37 3N 122 4W
Femer Bælt = Fehmarn Bælt, Europe · 9 J14 · 54 35N 11 20 E
Femunden, Norway · 9 E14 · 62 10N 11 53 E
Fen He →, China · 34 G6 · 35 36N 110 42 E
Fenelon Falls, Canada · 84 B6 · 44 32N 78 45W
Feng Xian, Jiangsu, China · 34 G9 · 34 43N 116 35 E
Feng Xian, Shaanxi, China · 34 H4 · 33 54N 106 40 E
Fengcheng, China · 35 D13 · 40 28N 124 5 E
Fengfeng, China · 34 F8 · 36 28N 114 8 E
Fengning, China · 34 D9 · 41 10N 116 33 E
Fengqiu, China · 34 G8 · 35 2N 114 25 E
Fengrun, China · 35 E10 · 39 48N 118 8 E
Fengtai, China · 34 E9 · 39 50N 116 18 E
Fengxiang, China · 34 G4 · 34 29N 107 25 E
Fengyang, China · 35 H9 · 32 51N 117 29 E
Fengzhen, China · 34 D7 · 40 25N 113 2 E
Fenoarivo, Fianarantsoa, Madag. · 57 C8 · 21 43S 46 24 E
Fenoarivo, Toamasina, Madag. · 57 B8 · 20 52S 46 53 E
Fenoarivo Afovoany, Madag. · 57 B8 · 18 26S 46 34 E
Fenoarivo Atsinanana, Madag. · 57 B8 · 17 22S 49 25 E
Fens, The, U.K. · 12 E7 · 52 38N 0 2W
Fenton, U.S.A. · 82 D4 · 42 48N 83 42W
Fenxi, China · 34 F6 · 36 40N 111 31 E
Fenyang, China · 34 F6 · 37 18N 111 48 E
Feodosiya, Ukraine · 19 E6 · 45 2N 35 16 E

Ferdows, Iran · 45 C8 · 33 58N 58 2 E
Ferfer, Somali Rep. · 47 F4 · 5 4N 45 9 E
Fergana = Farghona, Uzbekistan · 28 E8 · 40 23N 71 19 E
Fergus, Canada · 84 C4 · 43 43N 80 24W
Fergus Falls, U.S.A. · 80 B6 · 46 17N 96 4W
Ferkéssédougou, Ivory C. · 50 G4 · 9 35N 5 6W
Ferland, Canada · 72 B2 · 50 19N 88 27W
Fermanagh □, U.K. · 10 B4 · 54 21N 7 40W
Fermo, Italy · 22 C5 · 43 9N 13 43 E
Fermont, Canada · 73 B6 · 52 47N 67 5W
Fermoy, Ireland · 10 D3 · 52 9N 8 16W
Fernández, Argentina · 94 B3 · 27 55S 63 50W
Fernandina Beach, U.S.A. · 83 K5 · 30 40N 81 27W
Fernando de Noronha, Brazil · 93 D12 · 4 0S 33 10W
Fernando Póo = Bioko, Eq. Guin. · 52 D1 · 3 30N 8 40 E
Ferndale, U.S.A. · 78 B4 · 48 51N 122 36W
Fernie, Canada · 70 D5 · 49 30N 115 5W
Fernlees, Australia · 62 C4 · 23 51S 148 7 E
Fernley, U.S.A. · 76 G4 · 39 36N 119 15W
Ferozepore = Firozpur, India · 42 D6 · 30 55N 74 40 E
Ferrara, Italy · 22 B4 · 44 50N 11 35 E
Ferreñafe, Peru · 92 E3 · 6 42S 79 50W
Ferrerías, Spain · 24 B11 · 39 59N 4 1 E
Ferret, C., France · 20 D3 · 44 38N 1 15W
Ferriday, U.S.A. · 81 K9 · 31 38N 91 33W
Ferrol, Spain · 21 A1 · 43 29N 8 15W
Ferron, U.S.A. · 77 G8 · 39 5N 111 8W
Ferrutx, C., Spain · 24 B10 · 39 47N 3 21 E
Ferryland, Canada · 73 C9 · 47 2N 52 53W
Fertile, U.S.A. · 80 B6 · 47 32N 96 17W
Fès, Morocco · 50 B5 · 34 0N 5 0W
Fessenden, U.S.A. · 80 B5 · 47 39N 99 38W
Festus, U.S.A. · 80 F9 · 38 13N 90 24W
Feteşti, Romania · 17 F14 · 44 22N 27 51 E
Fethiye, Turkey · 19 G4 · 36 36N 29 6 E
Fetlar, U.K. · 11 A8 · 60 36N 0 52W
Feuilles →, Canada · 69 C12 · 58 47N 70 4W
Fez = Fès, Morocco · 50 B5 · 34 0N 5 0W
Fezzan, Libya · 51 C8 · 27 0N 13 0 E
Fiambalá, Argentina · 94 B2 · 27 45S 67 37W
Fianarantsoa, Madag. · 57 C8 · 21 26S 47 5 E
Fianarantsoa □, Madag. · 57 B8 · 19 30S 47 0 E
Ficksburg, S. Africa · 57 D4 · 28 51S 27 53 E
Field →, Australia · 62 C2 · 23 48S 138 0 E
Field I., Australia · 60 B5 · 12 5S 132 23 E
Fier, Albania · 23 D8 · 40 43N 19 33 E
Fife □, U.K. · 11 E5 · 56 16N 3 1W
Fife Ness, U.K. · 11 E6 · 56 17N 2 35W
Fifth Cataract, Sudan · 51 E12 · 18 22N 33 50 E
Figeac, France · 20 D5 · 44 37N 2 2 E
Figtree, Zimbabwe · 55 G2 · 20 22S 28 20 E
Figueira da Foz, Portugal · 21 B1 · 40 7N 8 54W
Figueres, Spain · 21 A7 · 42 18N 2 58 E
Figuig, Morocco · 50 B5 · 32 5N 1 11W
Fihaonana, Madag. · 57 B8 · 18 36S 47 12 E
Fiherenana, Madag. · 57 B8 · 18 29S 48 24 E
Fiherenana →, Madag. · 57 C7 · 23 19S 43 37 E
Fiji ■, Pac. Oc. · 59 C8 · 17 20S 179 0 E
Filabusi, Zimbabwe · 57 C4 · 20 34S 29 20 E
Filey, U.K. · 12 C7 · 54 12N 0 18W
Filey B., U.K. · 12 C7 · 54 12N 0 15W
Fiffla, Malta · 25 D1 · 35 47N 14 24 E
Filiatrá, Greece · 23 F9 · 37 9N 21 35 E
Filingué, Niger · 50 F6 · 14 21N 3 22 E
Filipstad, Sweden · 9 G16 · 59 43N 14 9 E
Fillmore, Calif., U.S.A. · 79 L8 · 34 24N 118 55W
Fillmore, Utah, U.S.A. · 77 G7 · 38 58N 112 20W
Finch, Canada · 85 A9 · 45 11N 75 7W
Finch Hatton, Australia · 62 K6 · 20 25S 148 39 E
Findhorn →, U.K. · 11 D5 · 57 38N 3 38W
Findlay, U.S.A. · 82 E4 · 41 2N 83 39W
Finger L., Canada · 72 B1 · 53 33N 93 30W
Finger Lakes, U.S.A. · 85 D8 · 42 40N 76 30W
Fingoè, Mozam. · 55 E3 · 14 55S 31 50 E
Finisterre, C. = Fisterra, C., Spain · 21 A1 · 42 50N 9 19W
Finke, Australia · 62 D1 · 25 34S 134 35 E
Finke Gorge △, Australia · 60 D5 · 24 8S 132 49 E
Finland ■, Europe · 8 E22 · 63 0N 27 0 E
Finland, G. of, Europe · 9 G21 · 60 0N 26 0 E
Finlay →, Canada · 70 B3 · 57 0N 125 10W
Finley, Australia · 63 F4 · 35 38S 145 35 E
Finley, U.S.A. · 80 B6 · 47 31N 97 50W
Finn →, Ireland · 10 B4 · 54 51N 7 28W
Finnigan, Mt., Australia · 62 B4 · 15 49S 145 17 E
Finniss, C., Australia · 63 E1 · 33 8S 134 51 E
Finnmark, Norway · 8 B20 · 69 37N 23 57 E
Finnsnes, Norway · 8 B18 · 69 14N 18 0 E
Finspång, Sweden · 9 G16 · 58 43N 15 47 E
Fiora →, Italy · 22 C4 · 42 20N 11 34 E
Fiordland △, N.Z. · 59 L1 · 45 46S 167 0 E
Fiq, Syria · 46 C4 · 32 46N 35 41 E
Firat = Furāt, Nahr al →, Asia · 44 D5 · 31 0N 47 25 E
Fire Island △, U.S.A. · 85 F11 · 40 38N 73 8W
Firebag →, Canada · 71 B6 · 57 45N 111 21W
Firebaugh, U.S.A. · 78 J6 · 36 52N 120 27W
Firedrake L., Canada · 71 A8 · 61 25N 104 30W
Firenze, Italy · 22 C4 · 43 46N 11 15 E
Firk, Sha'ib →, Iraq · 44 D5 · 30 59N 44 34 E
Firozabad, India · 43 F8 · 27 10N 78 25 E
Firozpur, India · 42 D6 · 30 55N 74 40 E
Firozpur-Jhirka, India · 42 F7 · 27 48N 76 57 E
Fīrūzābād, Iran · 45 D7 · 28 52N 52 35 E
Fīrūzkūh, Iran · 45 C7 · 35 50N 52 50 E
Firvale, Canada · 70 C3 · 52 27N 126 13W
Fish →, Namibia · 56 D2 · 28 7S 17 10 E
Fish →, S. Africa · 56 E3 · 31 30S 20 16 E
Fish River Canyon, Namibia · 56 D2 · 27 40S 17 35 E
Fisher, Australia · 61 F5 · 30 30S 131 0 E
Fisher B., Canada · 71 C9 · 51 35N 97 13W
Fishers I., U.S.A. · 85 E13 · 41 15N 72 0W
Fishguard, U.K. · 13 E3 · 52 0N 4 58W
Fishing L., Canada · 71 C9 · 52 10N 95 24W
Fishkill, U.S.A. · 85 E11 · 41 32N 73 54W
Fisterra, C., Spain · 21 A1 · 42 50N 9 19W
Fitchburg, U.S.A. · 85 D13 · 42 35N 71 48W
Fitz Roy, Argentina · 96 F3 · 47 0S 67 0W
Fitzgerald, Canada · 70 B6 · 59 51N 111 36W
Fitzgerald, U.S.A. · 83 K4 · 31 43N 83 15W
Fitzgerald River △, Australia · 61 F3 · 33 53S 120 3 E
Fitzmaurice →, Australia · 60 B5 · 14 45S 130 5 E
Fitzroy →, Queens., Australia · 62 C5 · 23 32S 150 52 E
Fitzroy →, W. Austral., Australia · 60 C3 · 17 31S 123 35 E
Fitzroy, Mte., Argentina · 96 F2 · 49 17S 73 5W
Fitzroy Crossing, Australia · 60 C4 · 18 9S 125 38 E
Fitzwilliam I., Canada · 84 A3 · 45 30N 81 45W
Fiume = Rijeka, Croatia · 16 F8 · 45 20N 14 21 E
Five Points, U.S.A. · 78 J6 · 36 26N 120 6W

Fizi, Dem. Rep. of the Congo · 54 C2 · 4 17S 28 55 E
Flagstaff, U.S.A. · 77 J8 · 35 12N 111 39W
Flagstaff L., U.S.A. · 83 C10 · 45 12N 70 18W
Flaherty I., Canada · 72 A4 · 56 15N 79 15W
Flåm, Norway · 9 F12 · 60 50N 7 7 E
Flambeau →, U.S.A. · 80 C9 · 45 18N 91 14W
Flamborough Hd., U.K. · 12 C7 · 54 7N 0 5W
Flaming Gorge ⌒, U.S.A. · 76 F9 · 41 10N 109 25W
Flaming Gorge Reservoir, U.S.A. · 76 F9 · 41 10N 109 25W
Flanders = Flandre, Europe · 14 F8 · 50 50N 2 30 E
Flandre, Europe · 14 F8 · 50 50N 2 30 E
Flandre-Occidentale = West-Vlaanderen □, Belgium · 15 D2 · 51 0N 3 0 E
Flandre-Orientale = Oost-Vlaanderen □, Belgium · 15 C3 · 51 5N 3 50 E
Flandreau, U.S.A. · 80 C6 · 44 3N 96 36W
Flanigan, U.S.A. · 78 E7 · 40 10N 119 53W
Flannan Is., U.K. · 11 C1 · 58 9N 7 52W
Flåsjön, Sweden · 8 D16 · 64 5N 15 40 E
Flat →, Canada · 68 B4 · 61 33N 125 18W
Flathead L., U.S.A. · 76 C7 · 47 51N 114 8W
Flattery, C., Australia · 62 A4 · 14 58S 145 21 E
Flattery, C., U.S.A. · 78 B2 · 48 23N 124 29W
Flatwoods, U.S.A. · 82 F4 · 38 31N 82 43W
Fleetwood, U.K. · 12 D4 · 53 55N 3 1W
Fleetwood, U.S.A. · 85 F9 · 40 27N 75 49W
Flekkefjord, Norway · 9 G12 · 58 18N 6 39 E
Flemington, U.S.A. · 84 E7 · 41 7N 77 28W
Flensburg, Germany · 16 A5 · 54 47N 9 27 E
Flers, France · 20 B3 · 48 47N 0 33W
Flesherton, Canada · 84 B4 · 44 16N 80 33W
Flesko, Tanjung, Indonesia · 37 D6 · 0 29N 124 30 E
Flevoland □, Neths. · 15 B5 · 52 30N 5 30 E
Flin Flon, Canada · 71 C8 · 54 46N 101 53W
Flinders →, Australia · 62 B3 · 17 36S 140 36 E
Flinders B., Australia · 61 F2 · 34 19S 115 19 E
Flinders Group, Australia · 62 A3 · 14 11S 144 15 E
Flinders I., S. Austral., Australia · 63 E1 · 33 44S 134 41 E
Flinders I., Tas., Australia · 63 G4 · 40 0S 148 0 E
Flinders Ranges, Australia · 63 E2 · 31 30S 138 30 E
Flinders Reefs, Australia · 62 B4 · 17 37S 148 31 E
Flint, U.K. · 12 D4 · 53 15N 3 8W
Flint, U.S.A. · 82 D4 · 43 1N 83 41W
Flint →, U.S.A. · 83 K3 · 30 57N 84 34W
Flint I., Kiribati · 65 J12 · 11 26S 151 48W
Flintshire □, U.K. · 12 D4 · 53 17N 3 17W
Flodden, U.K. · 12 B5 · 55 37N 2 8W
Floodwood, U.S.A. · 80 B8 · 46 55N 92 55W
Flora, U.S.A. · 82 F1 · 38 40N 88 29W
Florala, U.S.A. · 83 K2 · 31 0N 86 20W
Florence = Firenze, Italy · 22 C4 · 43 46N 11 15 E
Florence, Ala., U.S.A. · 83 H2 · 34 48N 87 41W
Florence, Ariz., U.S.A. · 77 K8 · 33 2N 111 23W
Florence, Colo., U.S.A. · 80 F2 · 38 23N 105 8W
Florence, Oreg., U.S.A. · 76 E1 · 43 58N 124 7W
Florence, S.C., U.S.A. · 83 H6 · 34 12N 79 46W
Florence, L., Australia · 63 D2 · 28 53S 138 9 E
Florencia, Colombia · 92 C3 · 1 36N 75 36W
Florennes, Belgium · 15 D4 · 50 15N 4 35 E
Florenville, Belgium · 15 E5 · 49 40N 5 19 E
Flores, Guatemala · 88 C2 · 16 59N 89 50W
Flores, Indonesia · 37 F6 · 8 35S 121 0 E
Flores I., Canada · 70 D3 · 49 20N 126 10W
Flores Sea, Indonesia · 37 F6 · 6 30S 120 0 E
Floreşti, Moldova · 17 E15 · 47 53N 28 17 E
Floresville, U.S.A. · 81 L5 · 29 8N 98 10W
Floriano, Brazil · 93 E10 · 6 50S 43 0W
Florianópolis, Brazil · 95 B6 · 27 30S 48 30W
Florida, Cuba · 88 B4 · 21 32N 78 14W
Florida, Uruguay · 95 C4 · 34 7S 56 10W
Florida □, U.S.A. · 83 L5 · 28 0N 82 0W
Florida, Straits of, U.S.A. · 88 B3 · 25 0N 80 0W
Florida B., U.S.A. · 88 B3 · 25 0N 80 45W
Florida Keys, U.S.A. · 83 N5 · 24 40N 81 0W
Flórina, Greece · 23 D9 · 40 48N 21 26 E
Florø, Norway · 9 F11 · 61 35N 5 1 E
Flower Station, Canada · 85 A8 · 45 10N 76 41W
Flowerpot I., Canada · 84 A3 · 45 18N 81 38W
Floydada, U.S.A. · 81 J4 · 33 59N 101 20W
Fluk, Indonesia · 37 E7 · 1 42S 127 44 E
Flushing = Vlissingen, Neths. · 15 C3 · 51 26N 3 34 E
Flying Fish, C., Antarctica · 5 D15 · 72 6S 102 29W
Foam Lake, Canada · 71 C8 · 51 40N 103 32W
Foça, Turkey · 23 E12 · 38 39N 26 46 E
Fochabers, U.K. · 11 D5 · 57 37N 3 6W
Focşani, Romania · 17 F14 · 45 41N 27 15 E
Fóggia, Italy · 22 D6 · 41 27N 15 34 E
Fogo, Canada · 73 C9 · 49 43N 54 17W
Fogo I., Canada · 73 C9 · 49 40N 54 5W
Föhr, Germany · 16 A5 · 54 43N 8 30 E
Foix, France · 20 F4 · 42 58N 1 38 E
Folda, Nord-Trøndelag, Norway · 8 D14 · 64 32N 10 30 E
Folda, Nordland, Norway · 8 C16 · 67 38N 14 50 E
Foley, Botswana · 56 C4 · 21 34S 27 21 E
Foley, U.S.A. · 83 K2 · 30 24N 87 41W
Foleyet, Canada · 72 C3 · 48 15N 82 25W
Folgefonni, Norway · 9 F12 · 60 3N 6 23 E
Foligno, Italy · 22 C5 · 42 57N 12 42 E
Folkestone, U.K. · 13 F9 · 51 5N 1 12 E
Folkston, U.S.A. · 83 K5 · 30 50N 82 0W
Follansbee, U.S.A. · 84 F4 · 40 19N 80 35W
Folsom, U.S.A. · 78 G5 · 38 42N 121 10W
Fond-du-Lac, Canada · 71 B7 · 59 19N 107 12W
Fond du Lac, U.S.A. · 80 D10 · 43 47N 88 27W
Fond-du-Lac →, Canada · 71 B7 · 59 17N 106 0W
Fonda, U.S.A. · 85 D10 · 42 57N 74 22W
Fondi, Italy · 22 D5 · 41 21N 13 25 E
Fongafale, Tuvalu · 64 H9 · 8 31S 179 13 E
Fonsagrada = A Fonsagrada, Spain · 21 A2 · 43 8N 7 4W
Fonseca, G. de, Cent. Amer. · 88 D2 · 13 10N 87 40W
Fontainebleau, France · 20 B5 · 48 24N 2 40 E
Fontana, U.S.A. · 79 L9 · 34 6N 117 26W
Fontas →, Canada · 70 B4 · 58 14N 121 48W
Fonte Boa, Brazil · 92 D5 · 2 33S 66 0W
Fontenay-le-Comte, France · 20 C3 · 46 28N 0 48W
Fontenelle Reservoir, U.S.A. · 76 E8 · 42 1N 110 4W
Fontur, Iceland · 8 C6 · 66 23N 14 32W
Foochow = Fuzhou, China · 34 H5 · 33 41N 108 0 E
Foping, China · 34 H5 · 33 41N 108 0 E
Forbes, Australia · 63 E4 · 33 22S 148 0 E
Forbesganj, India · 43 F12 · 26 17N 87 18 E
Ford City, Calif., U.S.A. · 79 K7 · 35 9N 119 27W
Ford City, Pa., U.S.A. · 84 F5 · 40 46N 79 32W
Førde, Norway · 9 F11 · 61 27N 5 53 E
Ford's Bridge, Australia · 63 D4 · 29 41S 145 29 E

Fordyce, U.S.A. · 81 J8 · 33 49N 92 25W
Forel, Mt., Greenland · 4 C6 · 66 52N 36 55W
Foremost, Canada · 70 D6 · 49 26N 111 34W
Forest, Canada · 84 C3 · 43 6N 82 0W
Forest, U.S.A. · 81 J10 · 32 22N 89 29W
Forest City, Iowa, U.S.A. · 80 D8 · 43 16N 93 39W
Forest City, N.C., U.S.A. · 83 H5 · 35 20N 81 52W
Forest City, Pa., U.S.A. · 85 E9 · 41 39N 75 28W
Forest Grove, U.S.A. · 78 E3 · 45 31N 123 7W
Forestburg, Canada · 70 C6 · 52 35N 112 1W
Foresthill, U.S.A. · 78 F6 · 39 1N 120 49W
Forestier Pen., Australia · 63 G4 · 43 0S 148 0 E
Forestville, Canada · 73 C6 · 48 48N 69 2W
Forestville, Calif., U.S.A. · 78 G4 · 38 28N 122 54W
Forestville, N.Y., U.S.A. · 84 D5 · 42 28N 79 10W
Forfar, U.K. · 11 E6 · 56 39N 2 53W
Forillon △, Canada · 73 C7 · 48 46N 64 12W
Forks, U.S.A. · 78 C2 · 47 57N 124 23W
Forksville, U.S.A. · 85 E8 · 41 29N 76 35W
Forlì, Italy · 22 B5 · 44 13N 12 3 E
Forman, U.S.A. · 80 B6 · 46 7N 97 38W
Formby Pt., U.K. · 12 D4 · 53 33N 3 6W
Formentera, Spain · 24 C7 · 38 43N 1 27 E
Formentor, C. de, Spain · 24 B10 · 39 58N 3 13 E
Former Yugoslav Republic of Macedonia = Macedonia ■, Europe · 23 D9 · 41 53N 21 40 E
Fórmia, Italy · 22 D5 · 41 15N 13 37 E
Formosa = Taiwan ■, Asia · 33 D7 · 23 30N 121 0 E
Formosa, Argentina · 94 B4 · 26 15S 58 10W
Formosa, Brazil · 93 G9 · 15 32S 47 20W
Formosa □, Argentina · 94 B4 · 25 0S 60 0W
Formosa, Serra, Brazil · 93 F8 · 12 0S 55 0W
Formosa B. = Ungwana B., Kenya · 54 C5 · 2 40S 40 20 E
Fornells, Spain · 24 A11 · 40 3N 4 7 E
Føroyar, Atl. Oc. · 8 F9 · 62 0N 7 0W
Forres, U.K. · 11 D5 · 57 37N 3 37W
Forrest, Australia · 61 F4 · 30 51S 128 6 E
Forrest, Mt., Australia · 61 D4 · 24 48S 127 45 E
Forrest City, U.S.A. · 81 H9 · 35 1N 90 47W
Forsayth, Australia · 62 B3 · 18 33S 143 34 E
Forssa, Finland · 9 F20 · 60 49N 23 38 E
Forst, Germany · 16 C8 · 51 45N 14 37 E
Forsyth, U.S.A. · 76 C10 · 46 16N 106 41W
Fort Abbas, Pakistan · 42 E5 · 29 12N 72 52 E
Fort Albany, Canada · 72 B3 · 52 15N 81 35W
Fort Ann, U.S.A. · 85 C11 · 43 25N 73 30W
Fort Assiniboine, Canada · 70 C6 · 54 20N 114 45W
Fort Augustus, U.K. · 11 D4 · 57 9N 4 42W
Fort Beaufort, S. Africa · 56 E4 · 32 46S 26 40 E
Fort Benton, U.S.A. · 76 C8 · 47 49N 110 40W
Fort Bragg, U.S.A. · 76 G2 · 39 26N 123 48W
Fort Bridger, U.S.A. · 76 F8 · 41 19N 110 23W
Fort Chipewyan, Canada · 71 B6 · 58 42N 111 8W
Fort Clatsop △, U.S.A. · 78 D3 · 46 8N 123 53W
Fort Collins, U.S.A. · 80 E2 · 40 35N 105 5W
Fort-Coulonge, Canada · 72 C4 · 45 50N 76 45W
Fort Covington, U.S.A. · 85 B10 · 44 59N 74 29W
Fort Davis, U.S.A. · 81 K3 · 30 35N 103 54W
Fort-de-France, Martinique · 88 c · 14 36N 61 2W
Fort Defiance, U.S.A. · 77 J9 · 35 45N 109 5W
Fort Dodge, U.S.A. · 80 D7 · 42 30N 94 11W
Fort Edward, U.S.A. · 85 C11 · 43 16N 73 35W
Fort Erie, Canada · 84 D6 · 42 54N 78 56W
Fort Fairfield, U.S.A. · 83 B12 · 46 46N 67 50W
Fort Frances, Canada · 71 D10 · 48 36N 93 24W
Fort Franklin = Déline, Canada · 68 B7 · 65 11N 123 25W
Fort Garland, U.S.A. · 77 H11 · 37 26N 105 26W
Fort George = Chisasibi, Canada · 72 B4 · 53 50N 79 0W
Fort Good Hope, Canada · 68 B7 · 66 14N 128 40W
Fort Hancock, U.S.A. · 77 L11 · 31 18N 105 51W
Fort Hope, Canada · 72 B2 · 51 30N 88 0W
Fort Irwin, U.S.A. · 79 K10 · 35 16N 116 34W
Fort Kent, U.S.A. · 83 B11 · 47 15N 68 36W
Fort Klamath, U.S.A. · 76 E3 · 42 42N 122 0W
Fort Laramie, U.S.A. · 80 D2 · 42 13N 104 31W
Fort Lauderdale, U.S.A. · 83 M5 · 26 7N 80 8W
Fort Liard, Canada · 70 A4 · 60 14N 123 30W
Fort Liberté, Haiti · 89 C5 · 19 42N 71 51W
Fort Lupton, U.S.A. · 80 E2 · 40 5N 104 49W
Fort MacKay, Canada · 70 B6 · 57 12N 111 41W
Fort Macleod, Canada · 70 D6 · 49 45N 113 30W
Fort McMurray, Canada · 70 B6 · 56 44N 111 7W
Fort McPherson, Canada · 68 B6 · 67 30N 134 55W
Fort Madison, U.S.A. · 80 E9 · 40 38N 91 27W
Fort Meade, U.S.A. · 83 M5 · 27 45N 81 48W
Fort Morgan, U.S.A. · 80 E3 · 40 15N 103 48W
Fort Myers, U.S.A. · 83 M5 · 26 39N 81 52W
Fort Nelson, Canada · 70 B4 · 58 50N 122 44W
Fort Nelson →, Canada · 70 B4 · 59 32N 124 0W
Fort Norman = Tulita, Canada · 68 B7 · 64 57N 125 30W
Fort Payne, U.S.A. · 83 H3 · 34 26N 85 43W
Fort Peck, U.S.A. · 76 B10 · 48 1N 106 27W
Fort Peck Dam, U.S.A. · 76 C10 · 48 0N 106 26W
Fort Peck L., U.S.A. · 76 C10 · 48 0N 106 26W
Fort Pierce, U.S.A. · 83 M5 · 27 27N 80 20W
Fort Pierre, U.S.A. · 80 C4 · 44 21N 100 22W
Fort Plain, U.S.A. · 85 D10 · 42 56N 74 37W
Fort Portal, Uganda · 54 B3 · 0 40N 30 20 E
Fort Providence, Canada · 70 A5 · 61 3N 117 40W
Fort Qu'Appelle, Canada · 71 C8 · 50 45N 103 50W
Fort Resolution, Canada · 70 A6 · 61 10N 113 40W
Fort Rixon, Zimbabwe · 55 G2 · 20 2S 29 17 E
Fort Ross, U.S.A. · 78 G3 · 38 32N 123 13W
Fort Rupert = Waskaganish, Canada · 72 B4 · 51 30N 78 40W
Fort St. James, Canada · 70 C4 · 54 30N 124 10W
Fort St. John, Canada · 70 B4 · 56 15N 120 50W
Fort Saskatchewan, Canada · 70 C6 · 53 40N 113 15W
Fort Scott, U.S.A. · 81 G7 · 37 50N 94 42W
Fort Severn, Canada · 72 A2 · 56 0N 87 40W
Fort Shevchenko, Kazakhstan · 19 F9 · 44 35N 50 23 E
Fort Simpson, Canada · 70 A4 · 61 45N 121 15W
Fort Smith, Canada · 70 B6 · 60 0N 111 51W
Fort Smith, U.S.A. · 81 H7 · 35 23N 94 25W
Fort Stockton, U.S.A. · 81 K3 · 30 53N 102 53W
Fort Sumner, U.S.A. · 77 J2 · 34 28N 104 15W
Fort Thompson, U.S.A. · 80 C5 · 44 3N 99 26W
Fort Union △, U.S.A. · 77 J2 · 35 54N 105 1W
Fort Valley, U.S.A. · 83 J4 · 32 33N 83 53W
Fort Vermilion, Canada · 70 B5 · 58 24N 116 0W
Fort Walton Beach, U.S.A. · 83 K2 · 30 25N 86 36W
Fort Wayne, U.S.A. · 82 E3 · 41 4N 85 9W
Fort William, U.K. · 11 E3 · 56 49N 5 7W
Fort Worth, U.S.A. · 81 J6 · 32 45N 97 18W
Fort Yates, U.S.A. · 80 B4 · 46 5N 100 38W
Fort Yukon, U.S.A. · 68 B5 · 66 34N 145 16W
Fortaleza, Brazil · 93 D11 · 3 45S 38 35W

Forteau, *Canada* **73 B8** 51 28N 56 58W
Fortescue →, *Australia* **60 D2** 21 0S 116 4 E
Forth →, *U.K.* **11 E5** 56 9N 3 50W
Forth, Firth of, *U.K.* **11 E6** 56 5N 2 55W
Fortrose, *U.K.* **11 D4** 57 35N 4 9W
Fortuna, *Calif., U.S.A.* **76 F1** 40 36N 124 9W
Fortuna, *N. Dak., U.S.A.* **80 A3** 48 55N 103 47W
Fortune, *Canada* **73 C8** 47 4N 55 50W
Fortune B., *Canada* **73 C8** 47 30N 55 22W
Forūr, *Iran* **45 E7** 26 17N 54 32 E
Foshan, *China* **33 D6** 23 4N 113 5 E
Fosna, *Norway* **8 E14** 63 50N 10 20 E
Fosnavåg, *Norway* **9 E11** 62 22N 5 38 E
Fossano, *Italy* **20 D7** 44 33N 7 43 E
Fossil, *U.S.A.* **76 D3** 45 0N 120 9W
Fossil Butte ⌓, *U.S.A.* **76 F8** 41 50N 110 27W
Foster, *Canada* **85 A12** 45 17N 72 30W
Foster →, *Canada* **71 B7** 55 47N 105 49W
Fosters Ra., *Australia* **62 C1** 21 35S 133 48 E
Fostoria, *U.S.A.* **82 E4** 41 10N 83 25W
Fotadrevo, *Madag.* **57 C8** 24 3S 45 1 E
Fougères, *France* **20 B3** 48 21N 1 14W
Foul Pt., *Sri Lanka* **40 Q12** 8 35N 81 18 E
Foula, *U.K.* **11 A6** 60 10N 2 5W
Foulness I., *U.K.* **13 F8** 51 36N 0 55 E
Foulpointe, *Madag.* **57 B8** 17 41S 49 31 E
Foulweather, C., *U.S.A.* **74 B2** 44 50N 124 5W
Foumban, *Cameroon* **52 C2** 5 45N 10 50 E
Fountain, *U.S.A.* **80 F2** 38 41N 104 42W
Fountain Springs, *U.S.A.* **79 K8** 35 54N 118 51W
Fouriesburg, *S. Africa* **56 D4** 28 38S 28 14 E
Foúrnoi, *Greece* **23 F12** 37 36N 26 32 E
Fourth Cataract, *Sudan* **51 E12** 18 47N 32 3 E
Fouta Djallon, *Guinea* **50 F3** 11 20N 12 10W
Foux, Cap-à-, *Haiti* **89 C5** 19 43N 73 27W
Foveaux Str., *N.Z.* **59 M2** 46 42S 168 10 E
Fowey, *U.K.* **13 G3** 50 20N 4 39W
Fowler, *Calif., U.S.A.* **78 J7** 36 38N 119 41W
Fowler, *Colo., U.S.A.* **80 F3** 38 8N 104 2W
Fowlers B., *Australia* **61 F5** 31 59S 132 34 E
Fowman, *Iran* **45 B6** 37 13N 49 19 E
Fox →, *Canada* **71 B10** 56 3N 93 18W
Fox Creek, *Canada* **70 C5** 54 24N 116 48W
Fox Lake, *Canada* **70 B6** 58 28N 114 31W
Fox Valley, *Canada* **71 C7** 50 30N 109 25W
Foxboro, *U.S.A.* **85 D13** 42 4N 71 16W
Foxdale, *Australia* **62 J6** 20 22S 148 35 E
Foxe Basin, *Canada* **69 B12** 66 0N 77 0W
Foxe Chan., *Canada* **69 B11** 65 0N 80 0W
Foxe Pen., *Canada* **69 B12** 65 0N 76 0W
Foxton, *N.Z.* **59 J5** 40 29S 175 18 E
Foyle, Lough, *U.K.* **10 A4** 55 7N 7 4W
Foynes, *Ireland* **10 D2** 52 37N 9 7W
Foz do Cunene, *Angola* **56 B1** 17 15S 11 48 E
Foz do Iguaçu, *Brazil* **95 B5** 25 30S 54 30W
Frackville, *U.S.A.* **85 F8** 40 47N 76 14W
Fraile Muerto, *Uruguay* **95 C5** 32 31S 54 32W
Fram Basin, *Arctic* **4 A** 87 30N 80 0 E
Framingham, *U.S.A.* **85 D13** 42 17N 71 25W
Franca, *Brazil* **93 H9** 20 33S 47 30W
Francavilla Fontana, *Italy* **23 D7** 40 32N 17 35 E
France ■, *Europe* **20 C5** 47 0N 3 0 E
Frances, *Australia* **63 F3** 36 41S 140 55 E
Frances →, *Canada* **70 A3** 60 16N 129 10W
Frances L., *Canada* **70 A3** 61 23N 129 30W
Franceville, *Gabon* **52 E2** 1 40S 13 32 E
Franche-Comté ⊠, *France* **20 C6** 46 50N 5 55 E
Francis Case, L., *U.S.A.* **80 D5** 43 4N 98 34W
Francisco Beltrão, *Brazil* **95 B5** 26 5S 53 4W
Francisco I. Madero, *Coahuila, Mexico* **86 B4** 25 48N 103 18W
Francisco I. Madero, *Durango, Mexico* **86 C4** 24 32N 104 22W
Francistown, *Botswana* **57 C4** 21 7S 27 33 E
François, *Canada* **73 C8** 47 35N 56 45W
François L., *Canada* **70 C3** 54 0N 125 30W
Francois Peron △, *Australia* **61 E1** 25 42S 113 33 E
Franeker, *Neths.* **15 A5** 53 12N 5 33 E
Frank Hann △, *Australia* **61 F3** 32 52S 120 19 E
Frankford, *Canada* **84 B7** 44 12N 77 36W
Frankfort, *S. Africa* **57 D4** 27 17S 28 30 E
Frankfort, *Ind., U.S.A.* **82 E2** 40 17N 86 31W
Frankfort, *Kans., U.S.A.* **80 F6** 39 42N 96 25W
Frankfort, *Ky., U.S.A.* **82 F3** 38 12N 84 52W
Frankfort, *N.Y., U.S.A.* **85 C9** 43 2N 75 4W
Frankfurt, *Brandenburg, Germany* **16 B8** 52 20N 14 32 E
Frankfurt, *Hessen, Germany* **16 C5** 50 7N 8 41 E
Fränkische Alb, *Germany* **16 D6** 49 10N 11 23 E
Frankland →, *Australia* **61 G2** 35 0S 116 48 E
Franklin, *Ky., U.S.A.* **83 G2** 36 43N 86 35W
Franklin, *La., U.S.A.* **81 L9** 29 48N 91 30W
Franklin, *Mass., U.S.A.* **85 D13** 42 5N 71 24W
Franklin, *N.H., U.S.A.* **85 C13** 43 27N 71 39W
Franklin, *Nebr., U.S.A.* **80 E5** 40 6N 98 57W
Franklin, *Pa., U.S.A.* **84 E5** 41 24N 79 50W
Franklin, *Va., U.S.A.* **83 G7** 36 41N 76 56W
Franklin, *W. Va., U.S.A.* **82 F6** 38 39N 79 20W
Franklin B., *Canada* **68 B7** 69 45N 126 0W
Franklin D. Roosevelt L., *U.S.A.* **76 B4** 48 18N 118 9W
Franklin-Gordon Wild Rivers △, *Australia* **63 G4** 42 19S 145 51 E
Franklin I., *Antarctica* **5 D11** 76 10S 168 30 E
Franklin L., *U.S.A.* **76 F6** 40 25N 115 22W
Franklin Mts., *Canada* **68 B7** 65 0N 125 0W
Franklin Str., *Canada* **68 A10** 72 0N 96 0W
Franklinton, *U.S.A.* **81 K9** 30 51N 90 9W
Franklinville, *U.S.A.* **84 D6** 42 20N 78 27W
Franks Pk., *U.S.A.* **76 E9** 43 58N 109 18W
Frankston, *Australia* **63 F4** 38 8S 145 8 E
Fransfontein, *Namibia* **56 C2** 20 12S 15 1 E
Frantsa Iosifa, Zemlya, *Russia* **28 A6** 82 0N 55 0 E
Franz, *Canada* **72 C3** 48 25N 84 30W
Franz Josef Land = Frantsa Iosifa, Zemlya, *Russia* **28 A6** 82 0N 55 0 E
Fraser, *U.S.A.* **84 D2** 42 32N 82 57W
Fraser →, *B.C., Canada* **70 D4** 49 7N 123 11W
Fraser →, *Nfld. & L., Canada* **73 A7** 56 39N 62 10W
Fraser, Mt., *Australia* **61 E2** 25 35S 118 20 E
Fraser I., *Australia* **63 D5** 25 15S 153 10 E
Fraser Lake, *Canada* **70 C4** 54 0N 124 50W
Fraserburg, *S. Africa* **56 E3** 31 55S 21 30 E
Fraserburgh, *U.K.* **11 D6** 57 42N 2 1W
Fraserdale, *Canada* **72 C3** 49 55N 81 37W
Fray Bentos, *Uruguay* **94 C4** 33 10S 58 15W
Fray Jorge △, *Chile* **94 C1** 30 42S 71 40W
Fredericia, *Denmark* **9 J13** 55 34N 9 45 E
Frederick, *Md., U.S.A.* **82 F7** 39 25N 77 25W
Frederick, *Okla., U.S.A.* **81 H5** 34 23N 99 1W
Frederick, *S. Dak., U.S.A.* **80 C5** 45 50N 98 31W
Fredericksburg, *Pa., U.S.A.* **85 F8** 40 27N 76 26W
Fredericksburg, *Tex., U.S.A.* **81 K5** 30 16N 98 52W
Fredericksburg, *Va., U.S.A.* **82 F7** 38 18N 77 28W
Fredericktown, *Mo., U.S.A.* **81 G9** 37 34N 90 18W
Fredericktown, *Ohio, U.S.A.* **84 F2** 40 29N 82 33W
Frederico I. Madero, Presa, *Mexico* **86 B3** 28 7N 105 40W
Frederico Westphalen, *Brazil* **95 B5** 27 22S 53 24W
Fredericton, *Canada* **73 C6** 45 57N 66 40W
Fredericton Junction, *Canada* **73 C6** 45 41N 66 40W
Frederikshåb = Paamiut, *Greenland* **69 B15** 62 0N 49 43W
Frederikshavn, *Denmark* **9 H14** 57 28N 10 31 E
Frederiksted, *U.S. Virgin Is.* **89 C7** 17 43N 64 53W
Fredonia, *Ariz., U.S.A.* **77 H7** 36 57N 112 32W
Fredonia, *Kans., U.S.A.* **81 G7** 37 32N 95 49W
Fredonia, *N.Y., U.S.A.* **84 D5** 42 26N 79 20W
Fredrikstad, *Norway* **9 G14** 59 13N 10 57 E
Free State □, *S. Africa* **56 D4** 28 30S 27 0 E
Freehold, *U.S.A.* **85 F10** 40 16N 74 17W
Freel Peak, *U.S.A.* **78 G7** 38 52N 119 54W
Freeland, *U.S.A.* **85 E9** 41 1N 75 54W
Freels, C., *Canada* **73 C9** 49 15N 53 30W
Freeman, *Calif., U.S.A.* **79 K9** 35 35N 117 53W
Freeman, *S. Dak., U.S.A.* **80 D6** 43 21N 97 26W
Freeport, *Bahamas* **88 A4** 26 30N 78 47W
Freeport, *Ill., U.S.A.* **80 D10** 42 17N 89 36W
Freeport, *N.Y., U.S.A.* **85 F11** 40 39N 73 35W
Freeport, *Ohio, U.S.A.* **84 F3** 40 12N 81 15W
Freeport, *Pa., U.S.A.* **84 F5** 40 41N 79 41W
Freeport, *Tex., U.S.A.* **81 L7** 28 57N 95 21W
Freetown, *S. Leone* **50 G3** 8 30N 13 17W
Frégate, L. de la, *Canada* **72 B5** 53 15N 74 45W
Fregenal de la Sierra, *Spain* **21 C2** 38 10N 6 39W
Freibourg = Fribourg, *Switz.* **20 C7** 46 49N 7 9 E
Freiburg, *Germany* **16 E4** 47 59N 7 51 E
Freire, *Chile* **96 D2** 38 54S 72 38W
Freirina, *Chile* **94 B1** 28 30S 71 10W
Freising, *Germany* **16 D6** 48 24N 11 45 E
Freistadt, *Austria* **16 D8** 48 30N 14 30 E
Fréjus, *France* **20 E7** 43 25N 6 44 E
Fremantle, *Australia* **61 F2** 32 7S 115 47 E
Fremont, *Calif., U.S.A.* **78 H4** 37 32N 121 57W
Fremont, *Mich., U.S.A.* **82 D3** 43 28N 85 57W
Fremont, *Nebr., U.S.A.* **80 E6** 41 26N 96 30W
Fremont, *Ohio, U.S.A.* **82 E4** 41 21N 83 7W
Fremont →, *U.S.A.* **77 G8** 38 24N 110 42W
French Camp, *U.S.A.* **78 H5** 37 53N 121 16W
French Creek →, *U.S.A.* **84 E5** 41 24N 79 50W
French Guiana ⊠, *S. Amer.* **93 C8** 4 0N 53 0W
French Polynesia ⊠, *Pac. Oc.* **65 K13** 20 0S 145 0W
Frenchman Cr. →, *N. Amer.* **76 B10** 48 31N 107 10W
Frenchman Cr. →, *U.S.A.* **80 E4** 40 14N 100 50W
Fresco →, *Brazil* **93 E8** 7 15S 51 30W
Freshfield, C., *Antarctica* **5 C10** 68 25S 151 10 E
Fresnillo, *Mexico* **86 C4** 23 10N 103 0W
Fresno, *U.S.A.* **78 J7** 36 44N 119 47W
Fresno Reservoir, *U.S.A.* **76 B9** 48 36N 109 57W
Frew →, *Australia* **62 C2** 20 0S 135 38 E
Frewsburg, *U.S.A.* **84 D5** 42 3N 79 10W
Freycinet △, *Australia* **63 G4** 42 11S 148 19 E
Freycinet Pen., *Australia* **63 G4** 42 10S 148 25 E
Fria, C., *Namibia* **56 B1** 18 0S 12 0 E
Friant, *U.S.A.* **78 J7** 36 59N 119 43W
Frías, *Argentina* **94 B2** 28 40S 65 5W
Fribourg, *Switz.* **20 C7** 46 49N 7 9 E
Friday Harbor, *U.S.A.* **78 B3** 48 32N 123 1W
Friedens, *U.S.A.* **84 F6** 40 3N 78 59W
Friedrichshafen, *Germany* **16 E5** 47 39N 9 30 E
Friendly Is. = Tonga ■, *Pac. Oc.* **59 D11** 19 50S 174 30W
Friendship, *U.S.A.* **84 D6** 42 12N 78 8W
Friesland □, *Neths.* **15 A5** 53 5N 5 50 E
Frio →, *U.S.A.* **81 L5** 28 26N 98 11W
Frio, C., *Brazil* **90 F6** 22 50S 41 50W
Friona, *U.S.A.* **81 H3** 34 38N 102 43W
Fritch, *U.S.A.* **81 H4** 35 38N 101 36W
Frobisher B., *Canada* **69 B13** 62 30N 66 0W
Frobisher Bay = Iqaluit, *Canada* **69 B13** 63 44N 68 31W
Frobisher L., *Canada* **71 B7** 56 20N 108 15W
Frohavet, *Norway* **8 E13** 64 0N 9 30 E
Frome, *U.K.* **13 F5** 51 14N 2 19W
Frome →, *U.K.* **13 G5** 50 41N 2 6W
Frome, L., *Australia* **63 E2** 30 45S 139 45 E
Front Range, *U.S.A.* **74 C5** 40 25N 105 45W
Front Royal, *U.S.A.* **82 F6** 38 55N 78 12W
Frontera, *Canary Is.* **24 G2** 27 47N 17 59W
Frontera, *Mexico* **87 D6** 18 30N 92 40W
Fronteras, *Mexico* **86 A3** 30 56N 109 31W
Frosinone, *Italy* **22 D5** 41 38N 13 19 E
Frostburg, *U.S.A.* **82 F6** 39 39N 78 56W
Frostisen, *Norway* **8 B17** 68 14N 17 10 E
Frøya, *Norway* **8 E13** 63 43N 8 40 E
Frunze = Bishkek, *Kyrgyzstan* **28 E8** 42 54N 74 46 E
Frutal, *Brazil* **93 H9** 20 0S 49 0W
Frýdek-Místek, *Czech Rep.* **17 D10** 49 40N 18 20 E
Fryeburg, *U.S.A.* **85 B14** 44 1N 70 59W
Fu Xian = Wafangdian, *China* **35 E11** 39 38N 121 58 E
Fu Xian, *China* **34 G5** 36 0N 109 20 E
Fucheng, *China* **34 F9** 37 50N 116 10 E
Fuchou = Fuzhou, *China* **33 D6** 26 5N 119 16 E
Fuchū, *Japan* **31 G6** 34 34N 133 14 E
Fuencaliente, *Canary Is.* **24 F2** 28 28N 17 50W
Fuencaliente, Pta., *Canary Is.* **24 F2** 28 27N 17 51W
Fuengirola, *Spain* **21 D3** 36 32N 4 41W
Fuentes de Oñoro, *Spain* **21 B2** 40 33N 6 52W
Fuerte →, *Mexico* **86 B3** 25 50N 109 25W
Fuerte Olimpo, *Paraguay* **94 A4** 21 0S 57 51W
Fuerteventura, *Canary Is.* **24 F6** 28 30N 14 0W
Fuerteventura ✕ (FUE), *Canary Is.* **24 F6** 28 24N 13 52W
Fufeng, *China* **34 G5** 34 22N 108 0 E
Fugou, *China* **34 G8** 34 3N 114 25 E
Fugu, *China* **34 E6** 39 2N 111 3 E
Fuhai, *China* **32 B3** 47 2N 87 25 E
Fuḩaymī, *Iraq* **44 C4** 34 16N 42 10 E
Fuji, *Japan* **31 G9** 35 9N 138 39 E
Fuji-Hakone-Izu △, *Japan* **31 G9** 35 15N 138 45 E
Fuji-San, *Japan* **31 G9** 35 22N 138 44 E
Fuji-Yoshida, *Japan* **31 G9** 35 30N 138 46 E
Fujian □, *China* **33 D6** 26 0N 118 0 E
Fujinomiya, *Japan* **31 G9** 35 10N 138 40 E
Fujisawa, *Japan* **31 G9** 35 22N 139 29 E
Fujiyama, Mt. = Fuji-San, *Japan* **31 G9** 35 22N 138 44 E
Fukagawa, *Japan* **30 C11** 43 43N 142 2 E
Fukien = Fujian □, *China* **33 D6** 26 0N 118 0 E
Fukuchiyama, *Japan* **31 G7** 35 19N 135 9 E
Fukue-Shima, *Japan* **31 H4** 32 40N 128 45 E
Fukui, *Japan* **31 F8** 36 5N 136 10 E
Fukui □, *Japan* **31 G8** 36 0N 136 12 E
Fukuoka, *Japan* **31 H5** 33 39N 130 21 E
Fukuoka □, *Japan* **31 H5** 33 30N 131 0 E
Fukushima, *Japan* **30 F10** 37 44N 140 28 E
Fukushima □, *Japan* **30 F10** 37 30N 140 15 E
Fukuyama, *Japan* **31 G6** 34 35N 133 20 E
Fulda, *Germany* **16 C5** 50 32N 9 40 E
Fulda →, *Germany* **16 C5** 51 25N 9 39 E
Fulford Harbour, *Canada* **78 B3** 48 47N 123 27W
Fullerton, *Calif., U.S.A.* **79 M9** 33 53N 117 56W
Fullerton, *Nebr., U.S.A.* **80 E6** 41 22N 97 58W
Fulongquan, *China* **35 B13** 44 20N 124 42 E
Fulton, *Mo., U.S.A.* **80 F9** 38 52N 91 57W
Fulton, *N.Y., U.S.A.* **85 C8** 43 19N 76 25W
Funabashi, *Japan* **31 G10** 35 45N 140 0 E
Funafuti = Fongafale, *Tuvalu* **64 H9** 8 31S 179 13 E
Funchal, *Madeira* **24 D3** 32 38N 16 54W
Funchal ✕ (FNC), *Madeira* **24 D3** 32 42N 16 45W
Fundación, *Colombia* **92 A4** 10 31N 74 11W
Fundão, *Portugal* **21 B2** 40 8N 7 30W
Fundy △, *Canada* **73 C6** 45 35N 65 10W
Fundy, B. of, *Canada* **73 D6** 45 0N 66 0W
Funhalouro, *Mozam.* **57 C5** 23 3S 34 25 E
Funing, *Hebei, China* **35 E10** 39 53N 119 12 E
Funing, *Jiangsu, China* **35 H10** 33 45N 119 50 E
Funiu Shan, *China* **34 H7** 33 30N 112 20 E
Funtua, *Nigeria* **50 F7** 11 30N 7 18 E
Fuping, *Hebei, China* **34 E8** 38 48N 114 12 E
Fuping, *Shaanxi, China* **34 G5** 34 42N 109 10 E
Furano, *Japan* **30 C11** 43 21N 142 23 E
Furāt, Nahr al →, *Asia* **44 D5** 31 0N 47 25 E
Fūrg, *Iran* **45 D7** 28 18N 55 13 E
Furnás, *Spain* **24 B8** 39 3N 1 32 E
Furnas, Reprêsa de, *Brazil* **95 A6** 20 50S 45 30W
Furneaux Group, *Australia* **63 G4** 40 10S 147 50 E
Furqlus, *Syria* **46 A6** 34 36N 37 8 E
Fürstenwalde, *Germany* **16 B8** 52 22N 14 3 E
Fürth, *Germany* **16 D6** 49 28N 10 59 E
Furukawa, *Japan* **30 E10** 38 34N 140 58 E
Fury and Hecla Str., *Canada* **69 B11** 69 56N 84 0W
Fusagasuga, *Colombia* **92 C4** 4 21N 74 22W
Fushan, *Shandong, China* **35 F11** 37 30N 121 15 E
Fushan, *Shanxi, China* **34 G6** 35 58N 111 51 E
Fushun, *China* **35 D12** 41 50N 123 56 E
Fusong, *China* **35 C14** 42 20N 127 15 E
Fustic, *Barbados* **89 g** 13 16N 59 38W
Futian, *China* **33 F11** 22 32N 114 4 E
Futuna, *Wall. & F. Is.* **59 B8** 14 25S 178 20W
Fuxin, *China* **35 C11** 42 5N 121 48 E
Fuyang, *China* **34 H8** 33 0N 115 48 E
Fuyang He →, *China* **34 E9** 38 12N 117 0 E
Fuyong, *China* **33 F10** 22 40N 113 49 E
Fuyu, *China* **35 B13** 45 12N 124 43 E
Fuzhou, *China* **33 D6** 26 5N 119 16 E
Fylde, *U.K.* **12 D5** 53 50N 2 58W
Fyn, *Denmark* **9 J14** 55 20N 10 30 E
Fyne, L., *U.K.* **11 F3** 55 59N 5 23W

G

Gabela, *Angola* **52 G2** 11 0S 14 24 E
Gabès, *Tunisia* **51 B8** 33 53N 10 2 E
Gabès, G. de, *Tunisia* **51 B8** 34 0N 10 30 E
Gabon ■, *Africa* **52 E2** 0 10S 10 0 E
Gaborone, *Botswana* **56 C4** 24 45S 25 57 E
Gabriels, *U.S.A.* **85 B10** 44 26N 74 12W
Gābrīk, *Iran* **45 E8** 25 44N 58 28 E
Gabrovo, *Bulgaria* **23 C11** 42 52N 25 19 E
Gāch Sār, *Iran* **45 B6** 36 7N 51 19 E
Gachsārān, *Iran* **45 D6** 30 15N 50 45 E
Gadag, *India* **40 M9** 15 30N 75 45 E
Gadap, *Pakistan* **42 G2** 25 5N 67 28 E
Gadarwara, *India* **43 H8** 22 50N 78 50 E
Gadhada, *India* **42 J4** 22 0N 71 35 E
Gadra, *Pakistan* **42 G4** 25 40N 70 38 E
Gadsden, *U.S.A.* **83 H3** 34 1N 86 1W
Gadwal, *India* **40 L10** 16 10N 77 50 E
Gaffney, *U.S.A.* **83 H5** 35 5N 81 39W
Gafsa, *Tunisia* **50 B7** 34 24N 8 43 E
Gagaria, *India* **42 G4** 25 43N 70 46 E
Gagnoa, *Ivory C.* **50 G4** 6 56N 5 16W
Gagnon, *Canada* **73 B6** 51 50N 68 5W
Gagnon, L., *Canada* **71 A6** 62 3N 110 27W
Gahini, *Rwanda* **54 C3** 1 50S 30 30 E
Gahmar, *India* **43 G10** 25 27N 83 49 E
Gai Xian = Gaizhou, *China* **35 D12** 40 22N 122 20 E
Gaïdhouronísi, *Greece* **25 E7** 34 53N 25 41 E
Gail, *U.S.A.* **81 J4** 32 46N 101 27W
Gaillimh = Galway, *Ireland* **10 C2** 53 17N 9 3W
Gaines, *U.S.A.* **84 E7** 41 46N 77 35W
Gainesville, *Fla., U.S.A.* **83 L4** 29 40N 82 20W
Gainesville, *Ga., U.S.A.* **83 H4** 34 18N 83 50W
Gainesville, *Mo., U.S.A.* **81 G8** 36 36N 92 26W
Gainesville, *Tex., U.S.A.* **81 J6** 33 38N 97 8W
Gainsborough, *U.K.* **12 D7** 53 24N 0 46W
Gairdner, L., *Australia* **63 E2** 31 30S 136 0 E
Gairloch, *U.K.* **11 D3** 57 43N 5 41W
Gairloch, L., *U.K.* **11 D3** 57 43N 5 45W
Gaizhou, *China* **35 D12** 40 22N 122 20 E
Gaj →, *Pakistan* **42 F2** 26 26N 67 21 E
Gakuch, *Pakistan* **43 A5** 36 7N 73 45 E
Galán, Cerro, *Argentina* **94 B2** 25 55S 66 52W
Galana →, *Kenya* **54 C5** 3 9S 40 8 E
Galápagos = Colón, Arch. de, *Ecuador* **90 D1** 0 0 91 0W
Galashiels, *U.K.* **11 F6** 55 37N 2 49W
Galaţi, *Romania* **17 F15** 45 27N 28 2 E
Galatina, *Italy* **23 D8** 40 10N 18 10 E
Galax, *U.S.A.* **83 G5** 36 40N 80 56W
Galcaio, *Somali Rep.* **47 F4** 6 30N 47 30 E
Galdhøpiggen, *Norway* **9 F12** 61 38N 8 18 E
Galeana, *Chihuahua, Mexico* **86 A3** 30 7N 107 38W
Galeana, *Nuevo León, Mexico* **86 A3** 24 50N 100 4W
Galela, *Indonesia* **37 D7** 1 50N 127 49 E
Galena, *U.S.A.* **68 B4** 64 44N 156 56W
Galeota Pt., *Trin. & Tob.* **93 K16** 10 8N 60 59W
Galera Pt., *Trin. & Tob.* **89 D7** 10 49N 60 54W
Galesburg, *U.S.A.* **80 E9** 40 57N 90 22W
Galeton, *U.S.A.* **84 E7** 41 44N 77 39W
Galich, *Russia* **18 C7** 58 22N 42 24 E
Galicia □, *Spain* **21 A2** 42 43N 7 45W
Galilee = Hagalil, *Israel* **46 C4** 32 53N 35 18 E
Galilee, L., *Australia* **62 C4** 22 20S 145 50 E
Galilee, Sea of = Yam Kinneret, *Israel* **46 C4** 32 45N 35 35 E
Galina Pt., *Jamaica* **88 a** 18 24N 76 58W
Galinoporni, *Cyprus* **25 D13** 35 31N 34 18 E
Galion, *U.S.A.* **84 F2** 40 44N 82 47W
Galiuro Mts., *U.S.A.* **77 K8** 32 30N 110 20W
Galiwinku, *Australia* **62 A2** 12 2S 135 34 E
Gallan Hd., *U.K.* **11 C1** 58 15N 7 2W
Gallatin, *U.S.A.* **83 G2** 36 24N 86 27W
Galle, *Sri Lanka* **40 R12** 6 5N 80 10 E
Gállego →, *Spain* **21 B5** 41 39N 0 51W
Gallegos →, *Argentina* **96 G3** 51 35S 69 0W
Galley Hd., *Ireland* **10 E3** 51 32N 8 55W
Gallinas, Pta., *Colombia* **92 A4** 12 28N 71 40W
Gallipoli = Gelibolu, *Turkey* **23 D12** 40 28N 26 43 E
Gallipoli, *Italy* **23 D8** 40 3N 17 58 E
Gallipolis, *U.S.A.* **82 F4** 38 49N 82 12W
Gällivare, *Sweden* **8 C19** 67 9N 20 40 E
Galloo I., *U.S.A.* **85 C8** 43 55N 76 25W
Galloway, *U.K.* **11 F4** 55 1N 4 29W
Galloway ⌓, *U.K.* **11 F4** 55 3N 4 20W
Galloway, Mull of, *U.K.* **11 G4** 54 39N 4 52W
Gallup, *U.S.A.* **77 J9** 35 32N 108 45W
Galoya, *Sri Lanka* **40 Q12** 8 10N 80 55 E
Galt, *U.S.A.* **78 G5** 38 15N 121 18W
Galty Mts., *Ireland* **10 D3** 52 22N 8 10W
Galtymore, *Ireland* **10 D3** 52 21N 8 11W
Galva, *U.S.A.* **80 E9** 41 10N 90 3W
Galveston, *U.S.A.* **81 L7** 29 18N 94 48W
Galveston B., *U.S.A.* **81 L7** 29 36N 94 50W
Gálvez, *Argentina* **94 C3** 32 0S 61 14W
Galway, *Ireland* **10 C2** 53 17N 9 3W
Galway □, *Ireland* **10 C2** 53 22N 9 1W
Galway B., *Ireland* **10 C2** 53 13N 9 10W
Gam →, *Vietnam* **38 B5** 21 55N 105 12 E
Gamagōri, *Japan* **31 G8** 34 50N 137 14 E
Gambat, *Pakistan* **42 F3** 27 17N 68 26 E
Gambhir →, *India* **42 F6** 26 58N 77 27 E
Gambia ■, *W. Afr.* **50 F2** 13 25N 16 0W
Gambia →, *W. Afr.* **50 F2** 13 28N 16 34W
Gambier, *U.S.A.* **84 F2** 40 22N 82 23W
Gambier, C., *Australia* **60 B5** 11 56S 130 57 E
Gambier Is., *Australia* **63 F2** 35 3S 136 30 E
Gambo, *Canada* **73 C9** 48 47N 54 13W
Gamboli, *Pakistan* **42 E3** 29 53N 68 24 E
Gamboma, *Congo* **52 E3** 1 55S 15 52 E
Gamka →, *S. Africa* **56 E3** 33 18S 21 39 E
Gamkab →, *Namibia* **56 D2** 28 4S 17 54 E
Gamlakarleby = Kokkola, *Finland* **8 E20** 63 50N 23 8 E
Gammon →, *Canada* **71 C9** 51 24N 95 44W
Gammon Ranges △, *Australia* **63 E2** 30 38S 139 8 E
Gamtoos →, *S. Africa* **56 E4** 33 58S 25 1 E
Gan Jiang →, *China* **33 D6** 29 15N 116 0 E
Ganado, *U.S.A.* **77 J9** 35 43N 109 33W
Gananoque, *Canada* **85 B8** 44 20N 76 10W
Ganāveh, *Iran* **45 D6** 29 35N 50 35 E
Gäncä, *Azerbaijan* **19 F8** 40 45N 46 20 E
Gancheng, *China* **38 C7** 18 51N 108 37 E
Gand = Gent, *Belgium* **15 C3** 51 2N 3 42 E
Ganda, *Angola* **53 G2** 13 3S 14 35 E
Gandajika, *Dem. Rep. of the Congo* **52 F4** 6 45S 23 57 E
Gandak →, *India* **43 G11** 25 39N 85 13 E
Gandava, *Pakistan* **42 E2** 28 32N 67 32 E
Gander, *Canada* **73 C9** 48 58N 54 35W
Gander L., *Canada* **73 C9** 48 58N 54 35W
Ganderowe Falls, *Zimbabwe* **55 F2** 17 20S 29 10 E
Gandhi Sagar, *India* **42 G6** 24 40N 75 40 E
Gandhinagar, *India* **42 H5** 23 15N 72 45 E
Gandía, *Spain* **21 C5** 38 58N 0 9W
Gando, Pta., *Canary Is.* **24 G4** 27 55N 15 22W
Ganedidalem = Gani, *Indonesia* **37 E7** 0 48S 128 14 E
Ganga →, *India* **43 H14** 23 20N 90 30 E
Ganga Sagar, *India* **43 J13** 21 38N 88 5 E
Gangan →, *India* **43 E8** 28 38N 78 58 E
Ganganagar, *India* **42 E5** 29 56N 73 56 E
Gangapur, *India* **42 F7** 26 32N 76 49 E
Gangaw, *Burma* **41 H19** 22 5N 94 5 E
Gangdisê Shan, *China* **41 D12** 31 20N 81 0 E
Ganges = Ganga →, *India* **43 H14** 23 20N 90 30 E
Ganges, *Canada* **70 D4** 48 51N 123 31W
Ganges, Mouths of the, *India* **43 J14** 21 30N 90 0 E
Gangoh, *India* **42 E7** 29 46N 77 18 E
Gangotri, *India* **43 D8** 30 50N 79 10 E
Gangtok, *India* **41 F16** 27 20N 88 37 E
Gangu, *China* **34 G3** 34 40N 105 15 E
Gangyao, *China* **35 B14** 44 12N 126 37 E
Gani, *Indonesia* **37 E7** 0 48S 128 14 E
Ganj, *India* **43 F8** 27 45N 78 57 E
Gannett Peak, *U.S.A.* **76 E9** 43 11N 109 39W
Ganquan, *China* **34 F5** 36 20N 109 20 E
Gansu □, *China* **34 G3** 36 0N 104 0 E
Ganta, *Liberia* **50 G4** 7 15N 8 59W
Gantheaume, C., *Australia* **63 F2** 36 4S 137 32 E
Gantheaume B., *Australia* **61 E1** 27 40S 114 10 E
Gantsevichi = Hantsavichy, *Belarus* **17 B14** 52 49N 26 30 E
Ganyem = Genyem, *Indonesia* **37 E10** 2 46S 140 12 E
Ganyu, *China* **35 G10** 34 50N 119 8 E
Ganzhou, *China* **33 D6** 25 51N 114 56 E
Gao, *Mali* **50 E5** 16 15N 0 5W
Gaomi, *China* **35 F10** 36 20N 119 42 E
Gaoping, *China* **34 G7** 35 45N 112 55 E
Gaotang, *China* **34 F9** 36 50N 116 15 E
Gaoua, *Burkina Faso* **50 F5** 10 20N 3 8W
Gaoual, *Guinea* **50 F3** 11 45N 13 25W
Gaoxiong = Kaohsiung, *Taiwan* **33 D7** 22 35N 120 16 E
Gaoyang, *China* **34 E8** 38 40N 115 45 E
Gaoyou Hu, *China* **35 H10** 32 45N 119 20 E
Gaoyuan, *China* **35 F9** 37 8N 117 58 E
Gap, *France* **20 D7** 44 33N 6 5 E
Gapat →, *India* **43 G10** 24 30N 82 28 E
Gapuwiyak, *Australia* **62 A2** 12 25S 135 43 E
Gar, *China* **32 C2** 32 10N 79 58 E
Garabogazköl Aylagy, *Turkmenistan* **19 F9** 41 0N 53 30 E
Garachico, *Canary Is.* **24 F3** 28 22N 16 46W
Garachiné, *Panama* **88 E4** 8 0N 78 12W
Garafia, *Canary Is.* **24 F2** 28 48N 17 57W
Garah, *Australia* **63 D4** 29 5S 149 38 E
Garajonay, *Canary Is.* **24 F2** 28 7N 17 14W
Garamba △, *Dem. Rep. of the Congo* **54 B2** 4 10N 29 40 E
Garanhuns, *Brazil* **93 E11** 8 50S 36 30W
Garautha, *India* **43 G8** 25 34N 79 18 E
Garba Tula, *Kenya* **54 B4** 0 30N 38 32 E
Garberville, *U.S.A.* **76 F2** 40 6N 123 48W
Garbiyang, *India* **43 D9** 30 8N 80 54 E

Garda, L. di, *Italy*	22 B4	45 40N	10 41 E
Garde L., *Canada*	71 A7	62 50N	106 13W
Garden City, Ga., *U.S.A.*	83 J5	32 6N	81 9W
Garden City, Kans., *U.S.A.*	81 G4	37 58N	100 53W
Garden City, Tex., *U.S.A.*	81 K4	31 52N	101 29W
Garden Grove, *U.S.A.*	79 M9	33 47N	117 55W
Gardēz, *Afghan.*	42 C3	33 37N	69 9 E
Gardiner, Maine, *U.S.A.*	83 C11	44 14N	69 47W
Gardiner, Mont., *U.S.A.*	76 D8	45 2N	110 22W
Gardiners I., *U.S.A.*	85 E12	41 6N	72 6W
Gardner, *U.S.A.*	85 D13	42 34N	71 59W
Gardner Canal, *Canada*	70 C3	53 27N	128 8W
Gardnerville, *U.S.A.*	78 G7	38 56N	119 45W
Gardo, *Somali Rep.*	47 F4	9 30N	49 6 E
Garey, *U.S.A.*	79 L6	34 53N	120 19W
Garfield, *U.S.A.*	76 C5	47 1N	117 9W
Garforth, *U.K.*	12 D6	53 47N	1 24W
Gargett, *Australia*	62 K6	21 9S	148 46 E
Garibaldi ○, *Canada*	70 D4	49 50N	122 40W
Garibaldi △, *S. Africa*	56 E2	30 32S	17 59 E
Garigliano →, *Italy*	22 D5	41 13N	13 45 E
Garissa, *Kenya*	54 C4	0 25S	39 40 E
Garland, Tex., *U.S.A.*	81 J6	32 55N	96 38W
Garland, Utah, *U.S.A.*	76 F7	41 47N	112 10W
Garm, *Tajikistan*	28 F8	39 0N	70 20 E
Garmāb, *Iran*	45 C8	35 25N	56 45 E
Garmisch-Partenkirchen, *Germany*	16 E6	47 30N	11 6 E
Garmo, Qullai = Kommunizma, Pik, *Tajikistan*	28 F8	39 0N	72 2 E
Garmsār, *Iran*	45 C7	35 20N	52 25 E
Garner, *U.S.A.*	80 D8	43 6N	93 36W
Garnett, *U.S.A.*	80 F7	38 17N	95 14W
Garo Hills, *India*	43 G14	25 30N	90 30 E
Garoe, *Somali Rep.*	47 F4	8 25N	48 33 E
Garonne →, *France*	20 D3	45 2N	0 36W
Garoowe = Garoe, *Somali Rep.*	47 F4	8 25N	48 33 E
Garot, *India*	42 G6	24 19N	75 41 E
Garoua, *Cameroon*	51 G8	9 19N	13 21 E
Garrauli, *India*	43 G8	25 5N	79 22 E
Garrison, Mont., *U.S.A.*	76 C7	46 31N	112 49W
Garrison, N. Dak., *U.S.A.*	80 B4	47 40N	101 25W
Garrison Res. = Sakakawea, L., *U.S.A.*	80 B4	47 30N	101 25W
Garron Pt., *U.K.*	10 A6	55 3N	5 59W
Garry →, *U.K.*	11 E5	56 44N	3 47W
Garry, L., *Canada*	68 B9	65 58N	100 18W
Garsen, *Kenya*	54 C5	2 20S	40 5 E
Garson L., *Canada*	71 B6	56 19N	110 2W
Garstang, *U.K.*	12 D5	53 55N	2 46W
Garu, *India*	43 H11	23 40N	84 14 E
Garub, *Namibia*	56 D2	26 37S	16 0 E
Garut, *Indonesia*	37 G12	7 14S	107 53 E
Garvie Mts., *N.Z.*	59 L2	45 30S	168 50 E
Garwa = Garoua, *Cameroon*	51 G8	9 19N	13 21 E
Garwa, *India*	43 G10	24 11N	83 47 E
Gary, *U.S.A.*	82 E2	41 36N	87 20W
Garzê, *China*	32 C5	31 38N	100 1 E
Garzón, *Colombia*	92 C3	2 10N	75 40W
Gas-San, *Japan*	30 E10	38 32N	140 1 E
Gasan Kuli = Esenguly, *Turkmenistan*	28 F6	37 37N	53 59 E
Gascogne, *France*	20 E4	43 45N	0 20 E
Gascogne, G. de, *Europe*	20 D2	44 0N	2 0W
Gascony = Gascogne, *France*	20 E4	43 45N	0 20 E
Gascoyne →, *Australia*	61 D1	24 52S	113 37 E
Gascoyne Junction, *Australia*	61 E2	25 2S	115 17 E
Gashaka, *Nigeria*	51 G8	7 20N	11 29 E
Gasherbrum, *Pakistan*	43 B7	35 40N	76 40 E
Gashua, *Nigeria*	51 F8	12 54N	11 0 E
Gasparillo, *Trin. & Tob.*	93 K15	10 18N	61 26W
Gaspé, *Canada*	73 C7	48 52N	64 30W
Gaspé, C. de, *Canada*	73 C7	48 48N	64 7W
Gaspé Pen. = Gaspésie, Pén. de la, *Canada*	73 C6	48 45N	65 40W
Gaspésie ○, *Canada*	73 C6	48 55N	66 10W
Gaspésie, Pén. de la, *Canada*	73 C6	48 45N	65 40W
Gasteiz = Vitoria-Gasteiz, *Spain*	21 A4	42 50N	2 41W
Gastonia, *U.S.A.*	83 H5	35 16N	81 11W
Gastre, *Argentina*	96 E3	42 20S	69 15W
Gata, C., *Cyprus*	25 E12	34 34N	33 2 E
Gata, C. de, *Spain*	21 D4	36 41N	2 13W
Gata, Sierra de, *Spain*	21 B2	40 20N	6 45W
Gataga →, *Canada*	70 B3	58 35N	126 59W
Gatehouse of Fleet, *U.K.*	11 G4	54 53N	4 12W
Gates, *U.S.A.*	84 C7	43 9N	77 42W
Gateshead, *U.K.*	12 C6	54 57N	1 35W
Gatesville, *U.S.A.*	81 K6	31 26N	97 45W
Gateway ○, *U.S.A.*	85 F11	40 26N	73 59W
Gaths, *Zimbabwe*	55 G3	20 2S	30 32 E
Gatico, *Chile*	94 A1	22 29S	70 20W
Gatineau, *Canada*	85 A9	45 29N	75 38W
Gatineau △, *Canada*	72 C4	45 40N	76 0W
Gatineau →, *Canada*	72 C4	45 27N	75 42W
Gatton, *Australia*	63 D5	27 32S	152 17 E
Gatun, L., *Panama*	88 E4	9 7N	79 56W
Gatyana, *S. Africa*	57 E4	32 16S	28 31 E
Gau, *Fiji*	59 D8	18 2S	179 18 E
Gauer L., *Canada*	71 B9	57 0N	97 50W
Gauhati = Guwahati, *India*	41 F17	26 10N	91 45 E
Gauja →, *Latvia*	9 H21	57 10N	24 16 E
Gaula →, *Norway*	8 E14	63 21N	10 14 E
Gauri Phanta, *India*	43 E9	28 41N	80 36 E
Gausta, *Norway*	9 G13	59 48N	8 40 E
Gauteng □, *S. Africa*	57 D4	26 0S	28 0 E
Gāv Koshī, *Iran*	45 D8	28 38N	57 12 E
Gāvakān, *Iran*	45 D7	29 37N	53 10 E
Gavāter, *Iran*	45 E9	25 10N	61 31 E
Gāvbandī, *Iran*	45 E7	27 12N	53 4 E
Gavdhopoúla, *Greece*	25 E6	34 56N	24 0 E
Gávdhos, *Greece*	25 E6	34 50N	24 5 E
Gaviota, *U.S.A.*	79 L6	34 29N	120 13W
Gāvkhūni, Bāţlāq-e, *Iran*	45 C7	32 6N	52 52 E
Gävle, *Sweden*	9 F17	60 40N	17 9 E
Gawachab, *Namibia*	56 D2	27 4S	17 55 E
Gawilgarh Hills, *India*	40 J10	21 15N	76 45 E
Gawler, *Australia*	63 E2	34 30S	138 42 E
Gaxun Nur, *China*	32 B5	42 22N	100 30 E
Gay, *Russia*	18 D10	51 27N	58 27 E
Gaya, *India*	43 G11	24 47N	85 4 E
Gaya, *Niger*	50 F6	11 52N	3 28 E
Gaylord, *U.S.A.*	82 C3	45 2N	84 41W
Gayndah, *Australia*	63 D5	25 35S	151 32 E
Gaysin = Haysyn, *Ukraine*	17 D15	48 57N	29 25 E
Gayvoron = Hayvoron, *Ukraine*	17 D15	48 22N	29 52 E
Gaza, *Gaza Strip*	46 D3	31 30N	34 28 E
Gaza □, *Mozam.*	57 C5	23 10S	32 45 E
Gaza Strip ☑, *Asia*	46 D3	31 29N	34 25 E
Gazanjyk, *Turkmenistan*	45 B7	39 16N	55 32 E
Gāzbor, *Iran*	45 D8	28 5N	58 51 E
Gazi, *Dem. Rep. of the Congo*	54 B1	1 3N	24 30 E
Gaziantep, *Turkey*	19 G6	37 6N	37 23 E
Gazimağosa = Famagusta, *Cyprus*	25 D12	35 8N	33 55 E
Gcoverega, *Botswana*	56 B3	19 8S	24 18 E
Gcuwa, *S. Africa*	57 E4	32 20S	28 11 E
Gdańsk, *Poland*	17 A10	54 22N	18 40 E
Gdańska, Zatoka, *Poland*	17 A10	54 30N	19 20 E
Gdov, *Russia*	9 G22	58 48N	27 55 E
Gdynia, *Poland*	17 A10	54 35N	18 33 E
Gebe, *Indonesia*	37 D7	0 5N	129 25 E
Gebze, *Turkey*	23 D13	40 47N	29 25 E
Gedaref, *Sudan*	51 F13	14 2N	35 28 E
Gediz →, *Turkey*	23 E12	38 35N	26 48 E
Gedser, *Denmark*	9 J14	54 35N	11 55 E
Gedung, Pulau, *Malaysia*	39 c	5 17N	100 23 E
Geegully Cr. →, *Australia*	60 C3	18 32S	123 41 E
Geel, *Belgium*	15 C4	51 10N	4 59 E
Geelong, *Australia*	63 F3	38 10S	144 22 E
Geelvink B. = Cenderwasih, Teluk, *Indonesia*	37 E9	3 0S	135 20 E
Geelvink Chan., *Australia*	61 E1	28 30S	114 0 E
Geesthacht, *Germany*	16 B6	53 26N	10 22 E
Geidam, *Nigeria*	51 F8	12 57N	11 57 E
Geikie →, *Canada*	71 B8	57 45N	103 52W
Geikie Gorge △, *Australia*	60 C4	18 3S	125 41 E
Geistown, *U.S.A.*	84 F6	40 18N	78 52W
Geita, *Tanzania*	54 C3	2 48S	32 12 E
Gejiu, *China*	32 D5	23 20N	103 10 E
Gel, Meydān-e, *Iran*	45 D7	29 4N	54 50 E
Gela, *Italy*	22 F6	37 4N	14 15 E
Gelang Patah, *Malaysia*	39 d	1 27N	103 35 E
Gelderland □, *Neths.*	15 B6	52 5N	6 10 E
Geldrop, *Neths.*	15 C5	51 25N	5 32 E
Geleen, *Neths.*	15 D5	50 57N	5 49 E
Gelibolu, *Turkey*	23 D12	40 28N	26 43 E
Gelsenkirchen, *Germany*	16 C4	51 32N	7 6 E
Gelugur, *Malaysia*	39 c	5 22N	100 18 E
Gemas, *Malaysia*	39 L4	2 37N	102 36 E
Gembloux, *Belgium*	15 D4	50 34N	4 43 E
Gemena, *Dem. Rep. of the Congo*	52 D3	3 13N	19 48 E
Gemerek, *Turkey*	44 B3	39 15N	36 10 E
Gemlik, *Turkey*	23 D13	40 26N	29 9 E
Gemsbok △, *Botswana*	56 D3	25 5S	21 1 E
Genale →, *Ethiopia*	47 F2	6 2N	39 1 E
General Acha, *Argentina*	94 D3	37 20S	64 38W
General Alvear, Buenos Aires, *Argentina*	94 D4	36 0S	60 0W
General Alvear, Mendoza, *Argentina*	94 D2	35 0S	67 40W
General Artigas, *Paraguay*	94 B4	26 52S	56 16W
General Belgrano, *Argentina*	94 D4	36 35S	58 47W
General Bernardo O'Higgins, *Antarctica*	5 C18	63 0S	58 3W
General Cabrera, *Argentina*	94 C3	32 53S	63 52W
General Cepeda, *Mexico*	86 B4	25 23N	101 27W
General Guido, *Argentina*	94 D4	36 40S	57 50W
General Juan Madariaga, *Argentina*	94 D4	37 0S	57 0W
General La Madrid, *Argentina*	94 D3	37 17S	61 20W
General MacArthur, *Phil.*	37 B7	11 18N	125 28 E
General Martin Miguel de Güemes, *Argentina*	94 A3	24 50S	65 0W
General Paz, *Argentina*	94 B4	27 45S	57 36W
General Pico, *Argentina*	94 D3	35 45S	63 50W
General Pinedo, *Argentina*	94 B3	27 15S	61 20W
General Pinto, *Argentina*	94 C3	34 45S	61 50W
General Roca, *Argentina*	96 D3	39 2S	67 35W
General Santos, *Phil.*	37 C7	6 5N	125 14 E
General Trevino, *Mexico*	87 B5	26 14N	99 29W
General Trías, *Mexico*	86 B3	28 21N	106 22W
General Viamonte, *Argentina*	94 D3	35 1S	61 3W
General Villegas, *Argentina*	94 D3	35 5S	63 0W
Genesee, Idaho, *U.S.A.*	76 C5	46 33N	116 56W
Genesee, Pa., *U.S.A.*	84 E7	41 59N	77 54W
Genesee →, *U.S.A.*	84 C7	43 16N	77 36W
Geneseo, Ill., *U.S.A.*	80 E9	41 27N	90 9W
Geneseo, N.Y., *U.S.A.*	84 D7	42 48N	77 49W
Geneva = Genève, *Switz.*	20 C7	46 12N	6 9 E
Geneva, Ala., *U.S.A.*	83 K3	31 2N	85 52W
Geneva, N.Y., *U.S.A.*	84 D8	42 52N	76 59W
Geneva, Nebr., *U.S.A.*	80 E6	40 32N	97 36W
Geneva, Ohio, *U.S.A.*	84 E4	41 48N	80 57W
Geneva, L. = Léman, L., *Europe*	82 D1	42 38N	88 30W
Genève, *Switz.*	20 C7	46 12N	6 9 E
Genil →, *Spain*	21 D3	37 42N	5 19W
Genk, *Belgium*	15 D5	50 58N	5 32 E
Gennargentu, Mti. del, *Italy*	22 D3	40 1N	9 19 E
Genoa = Génova, *Italy*	20 D8	44 25N	8 57 E
Genoa, *Australia*	63 F4	37 29S	149 35 E
Genoa, N.Y., *U.S.A.*	85 D8	42 40N	76 32W
Genoa, Nebr., *U.S.A.*	80 E6	41 27N	97 44W
Genoa, Nev., *U.S.A.*	78 F7	39 2N	119 50W
Génova, *Italy*	20 D8	44 25N	8 57 E
Génova, G. di, *Italy*	22 C3	44 0N	9 0 E
Genriyetty, Ostrov, *Russia*	29 B16	77 6N	156 30 E
Gent, *Belgium*	15 C3	51 2N	3 42 E
Genteng, Bali, *Indonesia*	37 J17	8 22S	114 9 E
Genteng, Jawa, *Indonesia*	37 G12	7 22S	106 24 E
Genyem, *Indonesia*	37 E10	2 46S	140 12 E
Geographe B., *Australia*	61 F2	33 30S	115 15 E
Geographe Chan., *Australia*	61 D1	24 30S	113 0 E
Georg Forster, *Antarctica*	5 D3	71 0S	12 0 E
Georg von Neumayer, *Antarctica*	5 D17	71 0S	8 30W
Georga, Zemlya, *Russia*	28 A5	80 30N	49 0 E
George, *S. Africa*	56 E3	33 58S	22 29 E
George →, *Canada*	73 A6	58 49N	66 10W
George, L., N.S.W., *Australia*	63 F4	35 10S	149 25 E
George, L., S. Austral., *Australia*	63 F3	37 25S	140 0 E
George, L., W. Austral., *Australia*	60 D3	22 45S	123 40 E
George, L., *Uganda*	54 B3	0 5N	30 10 E
George, L., Fla., *U.S.A.*	83 L5	29 17N	81 36W
George, L., N.Y., *U.S.A.*	85 C11	43 37N	73 33W
George Gill Ra., *Australia*	60 D5	24 22S	131 45 E
George Pt., *Australia*	62 J6	20 6S	148 36 E
George River = Kangiqsualujjuaq, *Canada*	69 C13	58 30N	65 59W
George Sound, *N.Z.*	59 L1	44 52S	167 25 E
George Town, *Australia*	63 G4	41 5S	146 49 E
George Town, *Bahamas*	88 B4	23 33N	75 47W
George Town, *Cayman Is.*	88 C3	19 20N	81 24W
George Town, *Malaysia*	39 c	5 25N	100 20 E
George V Land, *Antarctica*	5 C10	69 0S	148 0 E
George VI Sound, *Antarctica*	5 D17	71 0S	68 0W
George West, *U.S.A.*	81 L5	28 20N	98 7W
Georgetown = Janjanbureh, *Gambia*	50 F3	13 30N	14 47W
Georgetown, *Australia*	62 B3	18 17S	143 33 E
Georgetown, Ont., *Canada*	84 C5	43 40N	79 56W
Georgetown, P.E.I., *Canada*	73 C7	46 13N	62 24W
Georgetown, *Guyana*	92 B7	6 50N	58 12W
Georgetown, Calif., *U.S.A.*	78 G6	38 54N	120 50W
Georgetown, Colo., *U.S.A.*	76 G11	39 42N	105 42W
Georgetown, Ky., *U.S.A.*	82 F3	38 13N	84 33W
Georgetown, N.Y., *U.S.A.*	85 D9	42 46N	75 44W
Georgetown, Ohio, *U.S.A.*	82 F4	38 52N	83 54W
Georgetown, S.C., *U.S.A.*	83 J6	33 23N	79 17W
Georgetown, Tex., *U.S.A.*	81 K6	30 38N	97 41W
Georgia □, *U.S.A.*	83 K5	32 50N	83 15W
Georgia ■, *Asia*	19 F7	42 0N	43 0 E
Georgia, Str. of, *Canada*	70 D4	49 25N	124 0W
Georgian B., *Canada*	84 A4	45 15N	81 0W
Georgian Bay Islands △, *Canada*	84 B5	44 53N	79 52W
Georgina →, *Australia*	62 C2	23 30S	139 47 E
Georgina I., *Canada*	84 B5	44 22N	79 17W
Georgiyevsk, *Russia*	19 F7	44 12N	43 28 E
Gera, *Germany*	16 C7	50 53N	12 4 E
Geraardsbergen, *Belgium*	15 D3	50 45N	3 53 E
Geral, Serra, *Brazil*	95 B6	26 25S	50 0W
Geral de Goiás, Serra, *Brazil*	93 F9	12 0S	46 0W
Geraldine, *U.S.A.*	76 C8	47 36N	110 16W
Geraldton, *Australia*	61 E1	28 48S	114 32 E
Geraldton, *Canada*	72 C2	49 44N	86 59W
Gereshk, *Afghan.*	40 D4	31 47N	64 35 E
Gerik, *Malaysia*	39 K3	5 50N	101 15 E
Gering, *U.S.A.*	80 E3	41 50N	103 40W
Gerlach, *U.S.A.*	76 F4	40 39N	119 21W
Germansen Landing, *Canada*	70 B4	55 43N	124 40W
Germantown, *U.S.A.*	81 M10	35 5N	89 49W
Germany ■, *Europe*	16 C6	51 0N	10 0 E
Germī, *Iran*	45 B6	39 1N	48 3 E
Germiston, *S. Africa*	57 D4	26 15S	28 10 E
Gernika-Lumo, *Spain*	21 A4	43 19N	2 40W
Gero, *Japan*	31 G8	35 48N	137 14 E
Gerokgak, *Indonesia*	37 J17	8 1S	114 27 E
Gerona = Girona, *Spain*	21 B7	41 58N	2 46 E
Gerrard, *Canada*	70 C5	50 30N	117 17W
Gertak Sanggul, *Malaysia*	39 c	5 17N	100 12 E
Gertak Sanggul, Tanjung, *Malaysia*	39 c	5 16N	100 11 E
Gerung, *Indonesia*	37 K19	8 43S	116 7 E
Geser, *Indonesia*	37 E8	3 50S	130 54 E
Getafe, *Spain*	21 B4	40 18N	3 44W
Gettysburg, Pa., *U.S.A.*	82 F7	39 50N	77 14W
Gettysburg, S. Dak., *U.S.A.*	80 C5	45 1N	99 57W
Getxo, *Spain*	21 A4	43 21N	2 59W
Getz Ice Shelf, *Antarctica*	5 D14	75 0S	130 0W
Geyser, *U.S.A.*	76 C8	47 16N	110 30W
Geyserville, *U.S.A.*	78 G4	38 42N	122 54W
Ghaggar →, *India*	42 E6	29 30N	74 53 E
Ghaghara →, *India*	43 G11	25 45N	84 40 E
Ghaghat →, *Bangla.*	43 G13	25 19N	89 38 E
Ghagra, *India*	43 H11	23 17N	84 33 E
Ghagra →, *India*	43 F9	27 29N	81 9 E
Ghana ■, *W. Afr.*	50 G5	8 0N	1 0W
Ghansor, *India*	43 H9	22 39N	80 1 E
Ghanzi, *Botswana*	56 C3	21 50S	21 34 E
Ghardaïa, *Algeria*	50 B6	32 20N	3 37 E
Gharyān, *Libya*	51 B8	32 10N	13 0 E
Ghat, *Libya*	51 D8	24 59N	10 11 E
Ghatal, *India*	43 H12	22 40N	87 46 E
Ghatampur, *India*	43 F9	26 8N	80 13 E
Ghats, Eastern, *India*	40 N11	14 0N	78 50 E
Ghats, Western, *India*	40 N9	14 0N	75 0 E
Ghatsila, *India*	43 H12	22 36N	86 29 E
Ghaţţī, *Si. Arabia*	44 D3	31 16N	37 31 E
Ghawdex = Gozo, *Malta*	25 C1	36 3N	14 15 E
Ghazal, Bahr el →, *Chad*	51 F9	13 0N	15 47 E
Ghazâl, Bahr el →, *Sudan*	51 G12	9 31N	30 25 E
Ghaziabad, *India*	42 E7	28 42N	77 26 E
Ghazipur, *India*	43 G10	25 38N	83 35 E
Ghazni, *Afghan.*	42 C6	32 10N	68 20 E
Ghazni □, *Afghan.*	40 C6	32 10N	68 20 E
Ghent = Gent, *Belgium*	15 C3	51 2N	3 42 E
Gheorghe Gheorghiu-Dej = Onești, *Romania*	17 E14	46 17N	26 47 E
Ghīnah, Wādī al →, *Si. Arabia*	44 D3	30 27N	38 14 E
Ghizao, *Afghan.*	42 C1	33 20N	65 44 E
Ghizar →, *Pakistan*	43 A5	36 15N	73 43 E
Ghotaru, *India*	42 F4	27 20N	70 1 E
Ghotki, *Pakistan*	42 E3	28 5N	69 21 E
Ghowr □, *Afghan.*	40 C4	34 0N	64 20 E
Ghudaf, W. al →, *Iraq*	44 C4	32 56N	43 30 E
Ghudāmis, *Libya*	49 C4	30 11N	9 29 E
Ghudāmis □, *Libya*	51 B8	30 11N	10 25 E
Ghughri, *India*	43 H9	22 39N	80 41 E
Ghugus, *India*	40 K11	19 58N	79 12 E
Ghulam Mohammad Barrage, *Pakistan*	42 G3	25 30N	68 20 E
Ghūrīān, *Afghan.*	40 B2	34 17N	61 25 E
Gia Dinh, *Vietnam*	39 G6	10 49N	106 42 E
Gia Lai = Plei Ku, *Vietnam*	38 F7	13 57N	108 0 E
Gia Nghia, *Vietnam*	39 G6	11 58N	107 42 E
Gia Ngoc, *Vietnam*	38 E7	14 50N	108 58 E
Gia Vuc, *Vietnam*	38 E7	14 42N	108 34 E
Giant Forest, *U.S.A.*	78 J8	36 36N	118 43W
Giant Sequoia △, *U.S.A.*	78 K8	36 16N	118 40W
Giants Causeway, *U.K.*	10 A5	55 16N	6 29W
Gianyar, *Indonesia*	37 K18	8 32S	115 20 E
Giarabub = Al Jaghbūb, *Libya*	51 C10	29 42N	24 38 E
Giarre, *Italy*	22 F6	37 43N	15 11 E
Gibara, *Cuba*	88 B4	21 9N	76 11W
Gibb River, *Australia*	60 C4	16 26S	126 26 E
Gibbon, *U.S.A.*	80 E5	40 45N	98 51W
Gibeon, *Namibia*	56 D2	25 9S	17 43 E
Gibraltar ☑, *Europe*	21 D3	36 7N	5 22W
Gibraltar, Str. of, *Medit. S.*	21 E3	35 55N	5 40W
Gibraltar Range △, *Australia*	63 D5	29 37S	152 19 E
Gibson Desert, *Australia*	60 D4	24 0S	126 0 E
Gibsons, *Canada*	70 D4	49 24N	123 32W
Gibsonville, *U.S.A.*	78 F6	39 46N	120 54W
Giddings, *U.S.A.*	81 K6	30 11N	96 56W
Giebnegáisi = Kebnekaise, *Sweden*	8 C18	67 53N	18 33 E
Giessen, *Germany*	16 C5	50 34N	8 41 E
Gīfān, *Iran*	45 B8	37 54N	57 28 E
Gift Lake, *Canada*	70 B5	55 53N	115 49W
Gifu, *Japan*	31 G8	35 30N	136 45 E
Gifu □, *Japan*	31 G8	35 40N	137 0 E
Giganta, Sa. de la, *Mexico*	86 B2	25 30N	111 30W
Gigha, *U.K.*	11 F3	55 42N	5 44W
Giglio, *Italy*	22 C4	42 20N	10 52 E
Gijón, *Spain*	21 A3	43 32N	5 42W
Gil I., *Canada*	70 C3	53 12N	129 15W
Gila →, *U.S.A.*	77 K6	32 43N	114 33W
Gila Bend, *U.S.A.*	77 K7	32 57N	112 43W
Gila Bend Mts., *U.S.A.*	77 K7	33 10N	113 0W
Gila Cliff Dwellings △, *U.S.A.*	77 K9	33 2N	108 16W
Gīlān □, *Iran*	45 B6	37 0N	50 0 E
Gilbert →, *Australia*	62 B3	16 35S	141 15 E
Gilbert Is., *Kiribati*	64 G9	1 0N	172 0 E
Gilbert River, *Australia*	62 B3	18 9S	142 52 E
Gilead, *U.S.A.*	85 B14	44 24N	70 59W
Gilford I., *Canada*	70 C3	50 40N	126 30W
Gilgandra, *Australia*	63 E4	31 43S	148 39 E
Gilgil, *Kenya*	54 C4	0 30S	36 20 E
Gilgit, *India*	43 B6	35 50N	74 15 E
Gilgit →, *Pakistan*	43 B6	35 44N	74 37 E
Gili △, *Mozam.*	55 F4	16 39S	38 27 E
Gilimanuk, *Indonesia*	37 J17	8 10S	114 26 E
Gillam, *Canada*	71 B10	56 20N	94 40W
Gillen, L., *Australia*	61 E3	26 11S	124 38 E
Gilles, L., *Australia*	63 E2	32 50S	136 45 E
Gillette, *U.S.A.*	80 C2	44 18N	105 30W
Gilliat, *Australia*	62 C3	20 40S	141 28 E
Gillingham, *U.K.*	13 F8	51 23N	0 33 E
Gilmer, *U.S.A.*	81 J7	32 44N	94 57W
Gilmore, L., *Australia*	61 F3	32 29S	121 37 E
Gilroy, *U.S.A.*	78 H5	37 1N	121 34W
Gimie, Mt, *St. Lucia*	89 f	13 54N	61 0W
Gimli, *Canada*	71 C9	50 40N	97 0W
Gin Gin, *Australia*	63 D5	25 0S	151 58 E
Gingin, *Australia*	61 F2	31 22S	115 54 E
Gingindlovu, *S. Africa*	57 D5	29 2S	31 30 E
Ginir, *Ethiopia*	47 F3	7 6N	40 40 E
Gióna, Óros, *Greece*	23 E10	38 38N	22 14 E
Gir Hills, *India*	42 J4	21 0N	71 0 E
Girab, *India*	42 F4	26 2N	70 38 E
Girāfi, W. →, *Egypt*	46 F3	29 58N	34 39 E
Girard, Kans., *U.S.A.*	81 G7	37 31N	94 51W
Girard, Ohio, *U.S.A.*	84 E4	41 9N	80 42W
Girard, Pa., *U.S.A.*	84 E4	42 0N	80 19W
Girdle Ness, *U.K.*	11 D6	57 9N	2 3W
Giresun, *Turkey*	19 F6	40 55N	38 30 E
Girga, *Egypt*	51 C12	26 17N	31 55 E
Giri →, *India*	42 D7	30 28N	77 41 E
Giridih, *India*	43 G12	24 10N	86 21 E
Girne = Kyrenia, *Cyprus*	25 D12	35 20N	33 20 E
Girona, *Spain*	21 B7	41 58N	2 46 E
Gironde →, *France*	20 D3	45 32N	1 7W
Girraween △, *Australia*	63 D5	28 46S	151 54 E
Giru, *Australia*	62 B4	19 30S	147 5 E
Girvan, *U.K.*	11 F4	55 14N	4 51W
Gisborne, *N.Z.*	59 H7	38 39S	178 5 E
Gisenyi, *Rwanda*	54 C2	1 41S	29 15 E
Gislaved, *Sweden*	9 H15	57 19N	13 32 E
Gitega, *Burundi*	54 C2	3 26S	29 56 E
Giuba →, *Somali Rep.*	47 G3	1 30N	42 35 E
Giurgiu, *Romania*	17 G13	43 52N	25 57 E
Giza = El Gîza, *Egypt*	51 C12	30 0N	31 10 E
Gizhiga, *Russia*	29 C17	62 3N	160 30 E
Gizhiginskaya Guba, *Russia*	29 C16	61 0N	158 0 E
Giżycko, *Poland*	17 A11	54 2N	21 48 E
Gjirokastër, *Albania*	23 D9	40 7N	20 10 E
Gjoa Haven, *Canada*	68 B10	68 38N	95 53W
Gjøvik, *Norway*	9 F14	60 47N	10 43 E
Glace Bay, *Canada*	73 C8	46 11N	59 58W
Glacier △, *Canada*	70 C5	51 15N	117 30W
Glacier △, *U.S.A.*	76 B7	48 30N	113 18W
Glacier Bay △, *U.S.A.*	70 B1	58 45N	136 30W
Glacier Peak, *U.S.A.*	76 B3	48 7N	121 7W
Gladewater, *U.S.A.*	81 J7	32 33N	94 56W
Gladstone, Queens., *Australia*	62 C5	23 52S	151 16 E
Gladstone, S. Austral., *Australia*	63 E2	33 15S	138 22 E
Gladstone, *Canada*	71 C9	50 13N	98 57W
Gladstone, *U.S.A.*	82 C2	45 51N	87 1W
Gladwin, *U.S.A.*	82 D3	43 59N	84 29W
Glagah, *Indonesia*	37 J17	8 13S	114 18 E
Glåma = Glomma →, *Norway*	9 G14	59 12N	10 57 E
Gláma, *Iceland*	8 D2	65 48N	23 0W
Glamis, *U.K.*	11 E5	56 37N	3 4W
Glamorgan, Vale of □, *U.K.*	13 F4	51 28N	3 25W
Glasco, Kans., *U.S.A.*	80 F6	39 22N	97 50W
Glasco, N.Y., *U.S.A.*	85 D11	42 3N	73 57W
Glasgow, *U.K.*	11 F4	55 51N	4 15W
Glasgow, Ky., *U.S.A.*	82 G3	37 0N	85 55W
Glasgow, Mont., *U.S.A.*	76 B10	48 12N	106 38W
Glasgow, City of □, *U.K.*	11 F4	55 51N	4 12W
Glasgow International ✈ (GLA), *U.K.*	11 F4	55 51N	4 21W
Glaslyn, *Canada*	71 C7	53 22N	108 21W
Glastonbury, *U.K.*	13 F5	51 9N	2 43W
Glastonbury, *U.S.A.*	85 E12	41 43N	72 37W
Glazov, *Russia*	18 C9	58 9N	52 40 E
Gleichen, *Canada*	70 C6	50 52N	113 3W
Gleiwitz = Gliwice, *Poland*	17 C10	50 22N	18 41 E
Glen, *U.S.A.*	85 B13	44 7N	71 11W
Glen Affric, *U.K.*	11 D3	57 17N	5 1W
Glen Canyon, *U.S.A.*	77 H8	37 30N	110 40W
Glen Canyon △, *U.S.A.*	77 H8	37 15N	111 0W
Glen Canyon Dam, *U.S.A.*	77 H8	36 57N	111 29W
Glen Coe, *U.K.*	11 E3	56 40N	5 0W
Glen Cove, *U.S.A.*	85 F11	40 52N	73 38W
Glen Garry, *U.K.*	11 D3	57 3N	5 7W
Glen Innes, *Australia*	63 D5	29 44S	151 44 E
Glen Lyon, *U.S.A.*	85 E8	41 10N	76 5W
Glen Mor, *U.K.*	11 D4	57 9N	4 37W
Glen More △, *U.K.*	11 D5	57 8N	3 40W
Glen Moriston, *U.K.*	11 D4	57 11N	4 52W
Glen Robertson, *Canada*	85 A10	45 22N	74 30W
Glen Spean, *U.K.*	11 E4	56 53N	4 40W
Glen Ullin, *U.S.A.*	80 B4	46 49N	101 50W
Glenariff △, *Ireland*	10 A5	55 2N	6 10W
Glencoe, *Canada*	84 D3	42 45N	81 43W
Glencoe, *S. Africa*	57 D5	28 11S	30 11 E
Glencoe, *U.S.A.*	80 C7	44 46N	94 9W
Glendale, Ariz., *U.S.A.*	77 K7	33 32N	112 11W
Glendale, Calif., *U.S.A.*	79 L8	34 9N	118 15W
Glendale, Zimbabwe	55 F3	17 22S	31 5 E
Glendive, *U.S.A.*	80 B2	47 7N	104 43W
Glendo, *U.S.A.*	80 D2	42 30N	105 2W
Glenelg →, *Australia*	63 F3	38 4S	140 59 E
Glenfield, *U.S.A.*	85 C9	43 43N	75 24W
Glengarriff, *Ireland*	10 E2	51 45N	9 34W
Glenmont, *U.S.A.*	84 F2	40 31N	82 6W
Glenmorgan, *Australia*	63 D4	27 14S	149 42 E
Glenn, *U.S.A.*	78 F4	39 31N	122 1W
Glennallen, *U.S.A.*	68 B5	62 7N	145 33W

lennamaddy, Ireland 10 C3 53 37N 8 33W
lenns Ferry, U.S.A. 76 E6 42 57N 115 18W
lenore, Australia .... 62 B3 17 50S 141 12 E
lenreagh, Australia .... 63 E5 30 2S 153 1 E
lenrock, U.S.A. 76 E11 42 52N 105 52W
lenrothes, U.K. 11 E5 56 12N 3 10W
lens Falls, U.S.A. 85 C11 43 19N 73 39W
lenside, U.S.A. 85 F9 40 6N 75 9W
lenties, Ireland 10 B3 54 49N 8 16W
lenveagh △, Ireland 10 A3 55 3N 8 1W
lenville, U.S.A. 82 F5 38 56N 80 50W
lenwood, Canada 73 C9 49 0N 54 58W
lenwood, Ark., U.S.A. 81 H8 34 20N 93 33W
lenwood, Iowa, U.S.A. 80 E7 41 3N 95 45W
lenwood, Minn., U.S.A. 80 C7 45 39N 95 23W
lenwood, Wash., U.S.A. 78 D5 46 1N 121 17W
lenwood Springs, U.S.A. 76 G10 39 33N 107 19W
lettinganes, Iceland 8 D7 65 30N 13 37W
liwice, Poland .... 17 C10 50 22N 18 41 E
lobe, U.S.A. 77 K8 33 24N 110 47W
logów, Poland .... 16 C9 51 37N 16 5 E
lomma →, Norway .... 9 G14 59 12N 10 57 E
lorieuses, Is., Ind. Oc. .... 57 A8 11 30S 47 20 E
lossop, U.K. 12 D6 53 27N 1 56W
loucester, Australia .... 63 E5 32 0S 151 59 E
loucester, U.K. 13 F5 51 53N 2 15W
loucester, U.S.A. 85 D14 42 37N 70 40W
loucester I., Australia .... 62 J6 20 0S 148 30 E
loucester Island △, Australia .... 62 J6 20 2S 148 30 E
loucester Point, U.S.A. 82 G7 37 15N 76 29W
loucestershire □, U.K. 13 F5 51 46N 2 15W
loversville, U.S.A. 85 C10 43 3N 74 21W
lovertown, Canada 73 C9 48 40N 54 3W
lusk, Belarus .... 17 B15 52 53N 28 41 E
münd, Austria .... 16 D8 48 45N 15 0 E
munden, Austria .... 16 E7 47 55N 13 48 E
niezno, Poland .... 17 B9 52 30N 17 35 E
nowangerup, Australia .... 61 F2 33 58S 117 59 E
o Cong, Vietnam .... 39 G6 10 22N 106 40 E
õ-no-ura, Japan .... 31 H4 33 44N 129 40 E
oa, India .... 40 M8 15 33N 73 59 E
oa □, India .... 40 M8 15 33N 73 59 E
oalen Hd., Australia .... 63 F5 36 33S 150 4 E
oalpara, India .... 41 F17 26 10N 90 40 E
oaltor, India .... 43 H12 22 54N 74 13 E
oalundo Ghat, Bangla. .... 43 H13 23 50N 89 47 E
oat Fell, U.K. 11 F3 55 8N 5 11W
oba, Ethiopia .... 47 F2 7 1N 39 59 E
oba, Mozam. .... 57 D5 26 15S 32 13 E
obabis, Namibia .... 56 C2 22 30S 19 0 E
obi, Asia .... 34 C6 44 0N 110 0 E
obō, Japan .... 31 H7 33 53N 135 10 E
ochas, Namibia .... 56 C2 24 59S 18 55 E
odalming, U.K. 13 F7 51 11N 0 36W
odavari →, India .... 41 L13 16 25N 82 18 E
odavari Pt., India .... 41 L13 17 0N 82 20 E
odbout, Canada 73 C6 49 20N 67 38W
odda, India .... 43 G12 24 50N 87 13 E
oderich, Canada 84 C3 43 45N 81 41W
odfrey Ra., Australia .... 61 D2 24 0S 117 0 E
odhavn = Qeqertarsuaq, Greenland 69 B14 69 15N 53 38W
odhra, India .... 42 H5 22 49N 73 40 E
odoy Cruz, Argentina 94 C2 32 56S 68 52W
ods →, Canada 72 A1 56 22N 92 51W
ods L., Canada 72 B1 54 40N 94 15W
ods River, Canada 71 C10 54 50N 94 5W
odthåb = Nuuk, Greenland 69 B14 64 10N 51 35W
oeie Hoop, Kaap die = Good Hope, C. of, S. Africa .... 56 E2 34 24S 18 30 E
oéland, L. au, Canada 72 C4 49 50N 76 48W
oélands, L. aux, Canada 73 A7 55 27N 64 17W
oeree, Neths. .... 15 C3 51 50N 4 0 E
oes, Neths. .... 15 C3 51 30N 3 55 E
offstown, U.S.A. 85 C13 43 1N 71 36W
ogama, Canada 72 C3 47 35N 81 43W
ogebic, L., U.S.A. 80 B10 46 30N 89 35W
ogra = Ghaghara →, India .... 43 G11 25 45N 84 40 E
ogriål, Sudan .... 51 G11 8 30N 28 8 E
ohana, India .... 42 E7 29 8N 76 42 E
oharganj, India .... 42 H7 23 1N 77 41 E
oi →, India .... 42 H6 22 4N 74 46 E
oiânia, Brazil 93 G9 16 43S 49 20W
oiás, Brazil 93 G8 15 55S 50 10W
oiás □, Brazil 93 F9 12 10S 48 0W
oio-Erê, Brazil 95 A5 24 12S 54 1W
ojô, Japan .... 31 G7 34 21N 135 42 E
ojra, Pakistan .... 42 D5 31 10N 72 40 E
ökçeada, Turkey .... 23 D11 40 10N 25 50 E
ökova Körfezi, Turkey .... 23 F12 36 55N 27 50 E
okteik, Burma .... 41 H20 22 26N 97 0 E
okurt, Pakistan .... 42 E2 29 40N 67 26 E
okwe, Zimbabwe .... 57 B4 18 7S 28 58 E
ola, India .... 43 E9 28 3N 80 32 E
olakganj, India .... 43 F13 26 8N 89 52 E
olan Heights = Hagolan, Syria .... 46 C4 33 0N 35 45 E
oläshkerd, Iran .... 45 E8 27 59N 57 16 E
olchikha, Russia .... 4 B12 71 45N 83 30 E
olconda, U.S.A. 76 F5 40 58N 117 30W
old, U.S.A. 84 E7 41 52N 77 50W
old Beach, U.S.A. 76 E1 42 26N 124 25W
old Coast, W. Afr. 50 H5 4 0N 1 40W
old River, Canada 70 D3 49 46N 126 3W
olden, Canada 70 C5 51 20N 116 59W
olden B., N.Z. .... 59 J4 40 40S 172 50 E
olden Gate Highlands △, S. Africa .... 57 D4 28 40S 28 40 E
olden Hinde, Canada 70 D3 49 40N 125 44W
olden Lake, Canada 84 A7 45 34N 77 21W
olden Spike ○, U.S.A. 76 F7 41 37N 112 33W
olden Vale, Ireland 10 D3 52 33N 8 17W
oldendale, U.S.A. 76 D3 45 49N 120 50W
oldfield, U.S.A. 77 H5 37 42N 117 14W
oldsand L., Canada 71 B8 57 2N 101 8W
oldsboro, U.S.A. 83 H7 35 23N 77 59W
oldsmith, U.S.A. 81 K3 31 59N 102 37W
oldsworthy, Australia .... 60 D2 20 21S 119 30 E
oldthwaite, U.S.A. 81 K5 31 27N 98 34W
oleniów, Poland .... 16 B8 53 35N 14 50 E
olestân □, Iran .... 45 B7 37 20N 55 25 E
olestânak, Iran .... 45 D7 30 36N 54 14 E
oleta, U.S.A. 79 L7 34 27N 119 50W
olfito, Costa Rica 88 E3 8 41N 83 5W
olfo Aranci, Italy .... 22 D3 40 59N 9 38 E
oliad, U.S.A. 81 L6 28 40N 97 23W

Golpāyegān, Iran .... 45 C6 33 27N 50 18 E
Golra, Pakistan .... 42 C5 33 37N 72 56 E
Golspie, U.K. 11 D5 57 58N 3 59W
Goma, Dem. Rep. of the Congo .... 54 C2 1 37S 29 10 E
Gomal Pass, Pakistan .... 42 D3 31 56N 69 20 E
Gomati →, India .... 43 G10 25 32N 83 11 E
Gombari, Dem. Rep. of the Congo .... 54 B2 2 45N 29 3 E
Gombe, Nigeria .... 51 F8 10 19N 11 2 E
Gombe →, Tanzania .... 54 C3 4 38S 31 40 E
Gomel = Homyel, Belarus .... 17 B16 52 28N 31 0 E
Gomera, Canary Is. 24 F2 28 7N 17 14W
Gómez Palacio, Mexico 86 B4 25 40N 104 0W
Gomīshān, Iran .... 45 B7 37 4N 54 6 E
Gomogomo, Indonesia .... 37 F8 6 39S 134 43 E
Gomoh, India .... 41 H15 23 52N 86 10 E
Gompa = Ganta, Liberia 50 G4 7 15N 8 59W
Gonābād, Iran .... 45 C8 34 15N 58 45 E
Gonaïves, Haiti 89 C5 19 20N 72 42W
Gonarezhou △, Zimbabwe .... 55 G3 21 32S 31 55 E
Gonâve, G. de la, Haiti 89 C5 19 29N 72 42W
Gonâve, I. de la, Haiti 89 C5 18 45N 73 0W
Gonbad-e Kāvūs, Iran .... 45 B7 37 20N 55 25 E
Gonda, India .... 43 F9 27 9N 81 58 E
Gondal, India .... 42 J4 21 58N 70 52 E
Gonder, Ethiopia .... 47 E2 12 39N 37 30 E
Gondia, India .... 40 J12 21 23N 80 10 E
Gondola, Mozam. .... 55 F3 19 10S 33 37 E
Gönen, Turkey .... 23 D12 40 6N 27 39 E
Gongbei, China .... 33 G10 22 12N 113 32 E
Gonghe, China .... 32 C5 36 18N 100 32 E
Gongming, China .... 33 F10 22 47N 113 33 E
Gongolgon, Australia .... 63 E4 30 21S 146 54 E
Gongzhuling, China .... 35 C13 43 30N 124 40 E
Gonzales, Calif., U.S.A. 78 J5 36 30N 121 26W
Gonzales, Tex., U.S.A. 81 L6 29 30N 97 27W
González Chaves, Argentina 94 D3 38 2S 60 5W
Good Hope, C. of, S. Africa .... 56 E2 34 24S 18 30 E
Gooderham, Canada 84 B6 44 54N 78 21W
Goodhouse, S. Africa .... 56 D2 28 57S 18 13 E
Gooding, U.S.A. 76 E6 42 56N 114 43W
Goodland, U.S.A. 80 F4 39 21N 101 43W
Goodlow, Canada 70 B4 56 20N 120 8W
Goodooga, Australia .... 63 D4 29 3S 147 28 E
Goodsprings, U.S.A. 79 K11 35 49N 115 27W
Goole, U.K. 12 D7 53 42N 0 53W
Goolgowi, Australia .... 63 E4 33 58S 145 41 E
Goomalling, Australia .... 61 F2 31 15S 116 49 E
Goomeri, Australia .... 63 D5 26 12S 152 6 E
Goonda, Mozam. .... 55 F3 19 48S 33 57 E
Goondiwindi, Australia .... 63 D5 28 30S 150 21 E
Goongarrie △, Australia .... 61 F3 30 3S 121 30 E
Goongarrie, L., Australia .... 61 F3 30 3S 121 9 E
Goonyella, Australia .... 62 C4 21 47S 147 58 E
Goose →, Canada 73 B7 53 20N 60 35W
Goose Creek, U.S.A. 83 J5 32 59N 80 2W
Goose L., U.S.A. 76 F3 41 56N 120 26W
Gop, India .... 40 H6 22 5N 69 50 E
Gopalganj, India .... 43 F11 26 28N 84 30 E
Göppingen, Germany .... 16 D5 48 42N 9 39 E
Gorakhpur, India .... 43 F10 26 47N 83 23 E
Goražde, Bos.-H. .... 23 C8 43 38N 18 58 E
Gorda, U.S.A. 78 K5 35 53N 121 26W
Gorda, Pta., Canary Is. 24 F2 28 45N 18 0W
Gorda, Pta., Nic. 88 D3 14 20N 83 10W
Gordan B., Australia .... 60 B5 11 35S 130 10 E
Gordon, U.S.A. 80 D3 42 48N 102 12W
Gordon →, Australia .... 63 G4 42 27S 145 30 E
Gordon L., Alta., Canada 71 B6 56 30N 110 25W
Gordon L., N.W.T., Canada 70 A6 63 5N 113 11W
Gordonvale, Australia .... 62 B4 17 5S 145 50 E
Gore, Ethiopia .... 47 F2 8 12N 35 32 E
Gore, N.Z. .... 59 M2 46 5S 168 58 E
Gore Bay, Canada 72 C3 45 57N 82 28W
Gorey, Ireland 10 D5 52 41N 6 18W
Gorg, Iran .... 45 D8 29 29N 59 43 E
Gorgān, Iran .... 45 B7 36 50N 54 29 E
Gorgona, I., Colombia 92 C3 3 0N 78 10W
Gorham, U.S.A. 85 B13 44 23N 71 10W
Goriganga →, India .... 43 E9 29 45N 80 23 E
Gorinchem, Neths. .... 15 C4 51 50N 4 59 E
Goris, Armenia .... 19 G8 39 31N 46 22 E
Gorizia, Italy .... 22 B5 45 56N 13 37 E
Gorkiy = Nizhniy Novgorod, Russia .... 18 C7 56 20N 44 0 E
Gorkovskoye Vdkhr., Russia .... 18 C7 57 2N 43 4 E
Gorleston, U.K. .... 13 E9 52 35N 1 44 E
Görlitz, Germany .... 16 C8 51 9N 14 58 E
Gorlovka = Horlivka, Ukraine .... 19 E6 48 19N 38 5 E
Gorman, U.S.A. 79 L8 34 47N 118 51W
Gorna Dzhumayo = Blagoevgrad, Bulgaria .... 23 C10 42 2N 23 5 E
Gorna Oryakhovitsa, Bulgaria .... 23 C11 43 7N 25 40 E
Gorno-Altay □, Russia .... 28 D9 51 0N 86 0 E
Gorno-Altaysk, Russia .... 28 D9 51 50N 86 5 E
Gornyatski, Russia .... 18 A11 67 32N 64 3 E
Gornyy, Russia .... 30 B7 44 57N 133 59 E
Gorodenka = Horodenka, Ukraine .... 17 D13 48 41N 25 29 E
Gorodok = Horodok, Ukraine .... 17 D9 49 46N 23 32 E
Gorokhov = Horokhiv, Ukraine .... 17 C13 50 30N 24 45 E
Goromonzi, Zimbabwe .... 55 F3 17 52S 31 22 E
Gorong, Kepulauan, Indonesia .... 37 E8 3 59S 131 25 E
Gorongose →, Mozam. .... 57 B5 20 30S 34 40 E
Gorongoza, Mozam. .... 55 F3 18 44S 34 2 E
Gorongoza, Sa. da, Mozam. .... 55 F3 18 27S 34 2 E
Gorontalo, Indonesia .... 37 D6 0 35N 123 5 E
Gort, Ireland 10 C3 53 3N 8 49W
Gortis, Greece .... 25 D6 35 4N 24 58 E
Gorzów Wielkopolski, Poland .... 16 B8 52 43N 15 15 E
Gosford, Australia .... 63 E5 33 23S 151 18 E
Goshen, Calif., U.S.A. 78 J7 36 21N 119 25W
Goshen, Ind., U.S.A. 82 E3 41 35N 85 50W
Goshen, N.Y., U.S.A. 85 E10 41 24N 74 20W
Goshogawara, Japan .... 30 D10 40 48N 140 27 E
Gosier, Guadeloupe .... 88 b 16 12N 61 30W
Goslar, Germany .... 16 C6 51 54N 10 25 E
Gospič, Croatia .... 16 F8 44 35N 15 23 E
Gosport, U.K. 13 G6 50 48N 1 9W
Gosse →, Australia .... 62 B1 19 32S 134 37 E
Göta älv →, Sweden .... 9 H14 57 42N 11 54 E
Göta kanal, Sweden .... 9 G16 58 30N 15 58 E
Götaland, Sweden .... 9 G15 57 30N 14 30 E
Göteborg, Sweden .... 9 H14 57 43N 11 59 E
Gotha, Germany .... 16 C6 50 56N 10 42 E
Gothenburg = Göteborg, Sweden .... 9 H14 57 43N 11 59 E
Gothenburg, U.S.A. 80 E4 40 56N 100 10W

Gotland, Sweden .... 9 H18 57 30N 18 33 E
Gotō-Rettō, Japan .... 31 H4 32 55N 129 5 E
Gotska Sandön, Sweden .... 9 G18 58 24N 19 15 E
Gōtsu, Japan .... 31 G6 35 0N 132 14 E
Gott Pk., Canada 70 C4 50 18N 122 16W
Göttingen, Germany .... 16 C5 51 31N 9 55 E
Gottwaldov = Zlín, Czech Rep. .... 17 D9 49 14N 17 40 E
Goubangzi, China .... 35 D11 41 20N 121 52 E
Gouda, Neths. .... 15 B4 52 1N 4 42 E
Goúdhoura, Ákra, Greece .... 25 E8 34 59N 26 6 E
Gough I., Atl. Oc. 2 G9 40 10S 9 45W
Gouin, Rés., Canada 72 C5 48 35N 74 40W
Goulburn, Australia .... 63 E4 34 44S 149 44 E
Goulburn Is., Australia .... 62 A1 11 40S 133 20 E
Goulimine, Morocco 50 C3 28 56N 10 0W
Gourits →, S. Africa .... 56 E3 34 21S 21 52 E
Goúrnais, Greece .... 25 D7 35 19N 25 16 E
Gourock, U.K. 11 F4 55 57N 4 49W
Gouverneur, U.S.A. 85 B9 44 20N 75 28W
Gouviá, Greece .... 25 A3 39 39N 19 50 E
Governador Valadares, Brazil 93 G10 18 15S 41 57W
Governor's Harbour, Bahamas 88 A4 25 10N 76 14W
Govindgarh, India .... 43 G9 24 23N 81 18 E
Gowan Ra., Australia .... 62 D4 25 0S 145 0 E
Gowanda, U.S.A. 84 D6 42 28N 78 56W
Gower, U.K. 13 F3 51 35N 4 10W
Gowna, L., Ireland 10 C4 53 51N 7 34W
Goya, Argentina 94 B4 29 10S 59 10W
Goyder Lagoon, Australia .... 63 D2 27 3S 138 58 E
Goyllarisquisga, Peru 92 F3 10 31S 76 24W
Goz Beïda, Chad .... 51 F10 12 10N 21 20 E
Gozo, Malta .... 25 C1 36 3N 14 15 E
Graaff-Reinet, S. Africa .... 56 E3 32 13S 24 32 E
Gračac, Croatia .... 16 F8 44 18N 15 57 E
Gracias a Dios, C., Honduras 88 D3 15 0N 83 10W
Graciosa, I., Canary Is. 24 E6 29 15N 13 32W
Grado, Spain 21 A2 43 23N 6 4W
Grady, U.S.A. 81 H3 34 49N 103 19W
Grafham Water, U.K. 13 E7 52 19N 0 18W
Grafton, Australia .... 63 D5 29 38S 152 58 E
Grafton, N. Dak., U.S.A. 80 A6 48 25N 97 25W
Grafton, W. Va., U.S.A. 82 F5 39 21N 80 2W
Graham, Canada 72 C1 49 20N 90 30W
Graham, U.S.A. 81 J5 33 6N 98 35W
Graham, Mt., U.S.A. 77 K9 32 42N 109 52W
Graham Bell, Ostrov = Greem-Bell, Ostrov, Russia .... 28 A7 81 0N 62 0 E
Graham I., Canada 70 C2 53 40N 132 30W
Graham Land, Antarctica 5 C17 65 0S 64 0W
Grahamstown, S. Africa .... 56 E4 33 19S 26 31 E
Grahamsville, U.S.A. 85 E10 41 51N 74 33W
Grain Coast, W. Afr. 50 H3 4 20N 10 0W
Grajagan, Indonesia .... 37 K17 8 35S 114 13 E
Grajagan, Teluk, Indonesia .... 37 K17 8 40S 114 18 E
Grajaú, Brazil 93 E9 5 50S 46 4W
Grajaú →, Brazil 93 D10 3 41S 44 48W
Grampian, U.S.A. 84 F6 40 58N 78 37W
Grampian Highlands = Grampian Mts., U.K. 11 E5 56 50N 4 0W
Grampian Mts., U.K. 11 E5 56 50N 4 0W
Grampians, The, Australia .... 63 F3 37 0S 142 20 E
Gran Canaria, Canary Is. 24 G4 27 55N 15 35W
Gran Chaco, S. Amer. 94 B3 25 0S 61 0W
Gran Desierto del Pinacate △, Mexico 86 A2 31 51N 113 32W
Gran Paradiso, Italy .... 20 D7 45 33N 7 17 E
Gran Sasso d'Itália, Italy .... 22 C5 42 27N 13 42 E
Granada, Nic. 88 D2 11 58N 86 0W
Granada, Spain 21 D4 37 10N 3 35W
Granada, U.S.A. 81 F3 38 4N 102 19W
Granadilla de Abona, Canary Is. 24 F3 28 7N 16 33W
Granard, Ireland 10 C4 53 47N 7 30W
Granbury, U.S.A. 81 J6 32 27N 97 47W
Granby, Canada 85 A12 45 25N 72 45W
Granby, U.S.A. 76 F11 40 5N 105 56W
Grand →, Canada 84 D7 42 51N 79 34W
Grand →, Mo., U.S.A. 80 F8 39 23N 93 7W
Grand →, S. Dak., U.S.A. 80 C4 45 40N 100 45W
Grand Bahama, Bahamas 88 A4 26 40N 78 30W
Grand Bank, Canada 73 C8 47 6N 55 48W
Grand Bassam, Ivory C. 50 G5 5 10N 3 49W
Grand-Bourg, Guadeloupe .... 88 b 15 53N 61 19W
Grand Canal = Yun Ho →, China .... 35 E9 39 10N 117 10 E
Grand Canyon, U.S.A. 77 H7 36 3N 112 9W
Grand Canyon △, U.S.A. 77 H7 36 15N 112 30W
Grand Canyon-Parashant △, U.S.A. 77 H7 36 30N 113 20W
Grand Cayman, Cayman Is. 88 C3 19 20N 81 20W
Grand Centre, Canada 71 C6 54 25N 110 13W
Grand Coulee, U.S.A. 76 C4 47 57N 119 0W
Grand Coulee Dam, U.S.A. 76 C4 47 57N 118 59W
Grand Falls, Canada 73 C6 47 3N 67 44W
Grand Falls-Windsor, Canada 73 C8 48 56N 55 40W
Grand Forks, Canada 70 D5 49 0N 118 30W
Grand Forks, U.S.A. 80 B6 47 55N 97 3W
Grand Gorge, U.S.A. 85 D10 42 21N 74 29W
Grand Haven, U.S.A. 82 D2 43 4N 86 13W
Grand I., Mich., U.S.A. 82 B2 46 31N 86 40W
Grand I., N.Y., U.S.A. 84 D6 43 0N 78 58W
Grand Island, U.S.A. 80 E5 40 55N 98 21W
Grand Isle, La., U.S.A. 81 L9 29 14N 90 0W
Grand Isle, Vt., U.S.A. 85 B11 44 43N 73 18W
Grand Junction, U.S.A. 77 G9 39 4N 108 33W
Grand L., N.B., Canada 73 C6 45 57N 66 7W
Grand L., Nfld. & L., Canada 73 B7 53 40N 60 30W
Grand L., Nfld. & L., Canada 73 B8 49 0N 57 30W
Grand L., U.S.A. 76 F11 40 15N 105 49W
Grand Manan I., Canada 73 D6 44 45N 66 52W
Grand Marais, Canada 82 B3 46 40N 85 59W
Grand Marais, U.S.A. 80 B9 47 45N 90 25W
Grand Portage, U.S.A. 80 B10 47 58N 89 41W
Grand Rapids, Canada 71 C9 53 12N 99 19W
Grand Rapids, Mich., U.S.A. 82 D3 42 58N 85 40W
Grand Rapids, Minn., U.S.A. 80 B8 47 14N 93 31W
Grand St-Bernard, Col du, Europe .... 20 D7 45 50N 7 10 E
Grand Staircase-Escalante △, U.S.A. 77 H8 37 5N 112 0W
Grand Teton, U.S.A. 76 E8 43 54N 110 50W
Grand Teton △, U.S.A. 76 D8 43 50N 110 50W
Grand Union Canal, U.K. 13 E7 52 7N 0 53W
Grand-Vigie, Pte. de la, Guadeloupe .... 88 b 16 32N 61 27W
Grande →, Jujuy, Argentina 94 A2 24 20S 65 2W

Grande →, Mendoza, Argentina 94 D2 36 52S 69 45W
Grande →, Bolivia 92 G6 15 51S 64 39W
Grande →, Bahia, Brazil 93 F10 11 30S 44 30W
Grande →, Minas Gerais, Brazil 93 H8 20 6S 51 4W
Grande, B., Argentina 96 G3 50 30S 68 20W
Grande, Rio →, U.S.A. 81 N6 25 58N 97 9W
Grande Baleine, R. de la →, Canada 72 A4 55 16N 77 47W
Grande Cache, Canada 70 C5 53 53N 119 8W
Grande-Entrée, Canada 73 C7 47 30N 61 40W
Grande Prairie, Canada 70 B5 55 10N 118 50W
Grande-Rivière, Canada 73 C7 48 26N 64 30W
Grande-Terre, Guadeloupe .... 88 b 16 20N 61 25W
Grande-Vallée, Canada 73 C6 49 14N 65 8W
Grandfalls, U.S.A. 81 K3 31 20N 102 51W
Grands-Jardins △, Canada 73 C5 47 41N 70 51W
Grandview, Canada 71 C8 51 10N 100 42W
Grandview, U.S.A. 76 C4 46 15N 119 54W
Graneros, Chile 94 C1 34 5S 70 45W
Grangemouth, U.K. 11 E5 56 1N 3 42W
Granger, U.S.A. 76 F9 41 35N 109 58W
Grangeville, U.S.A. 76 D5 45 56N 116 7W
Granisle, Canada 70 C3 54 53N 126 13W
Granite City, U.S.A. 80 F9 38 42N 90 8W
Granite Falls, U.S.A. 80 C7 44 49N 95 33W
Granite L., Canada 73 C8 48 8N 57 5W
Granite Mt., U.S.A. 79 M10 33 5N 116 28W
Granite Pk., U.S.A. 76 D9 45 10N 109 48W
Graniteville, U.S.A. 85 B12 44 8N 72 29W
Granity, N.Z. .... 59 J3 41 39S 171 51 E
Granja, Brazil 93 D10 3 7S 40 50W
Granollers, Spain .... 21 B7 41 39N 2 18 E
Grant, U.S.A. 80 E4 40 53N 101 42W
Grant City, U.S.A. 80 E7 40 29N 94 25W
Grant I., Australia .... 60 B5 11 10S 132 52 E
Grant Range, U.S.A. 77 G6 38 30N 115 25W
Grantham, U.K. 12 E7 52 55N 0 38W
Grantown-on-Spey, U.K. 11 D5 57 20N 3 36W
Grants, U.S.A. 77 J10 35 9N 107 52W
Grants Pass, U.S.A. 76 E2 42 26N 123 19W
Grantsville, U.S.A. 76 F7 40 36N 112 28W
Granville, France 20 B3 48 50N 1 35W
Granville, N. Dak., U.S.A. 80 A4 48 16N 100 47W
Granville, N.Y., U.S.A. 85 C11 43 24N 73 16W
Granville, Ohio, U.S.A. 84 F2 40 4N 82 31W
Granville L., Canada 71 B8 56 18N 100 30W
Graskop, S. Africa .... 57 C5 24 56S 30 49 E
Grass →, Canada 71 B9 56 3N 96 33W
Grass Range, U.S.A. 76 C9 47 0N 109 0W
Grass River △, Canada 71 C8 54 40N 100 50W
Grass Valley, Calif., U.S.A. 78 F6 39 13N 121 4W
Grass Valley, Oreg., U.S.A. 76 D3 45 22N 120 47W
Grasse, France .... 20 E7 43 38N 6 56 E
Grassflat, U.S.A. 84 F6 41 0N 78 6W
Grasslands △, Canada 71 D7 49 11N 107 38W
Grassy, Australia .... 63 G3 40 3S 144 5 E
Graulhet, France .... 20 E4 43 45N 1 59 E
Gravelbourg, Canada 71 D7 49 50N 106 35W
's-Gravenhage, Neths. .... 15 B4 52 7N 4 17 E
Gravenhurst, Canada 84 B5 44 52N 79 20W
Gravesend, Australia .... 63 D5 29 35S 150 20 E
Gravesend, U.K. .... 13 F8 51 26N 0 22 E
Gravois, Pointe-à-, Haiti 89 C5 18 15N 73 56W
Grayling, U.S.A. 82 C3 44 40N 84 43W
Grays, U.K. .... 13 F8 51 28N 0 21 E
Grays Harbor, U.S.A. 76 C1 46 59N 124 1W
Grays L., U.S.A. 76 E8 43 4N 111 26W
Grays River, U.S.A. 78 D3 46 21N 123 37W
Graz, Austria .... 16 E8 47 4N 15 27 E
Greasy L., Canada 70 A4 62 55N 122 12W
Great Abaco I., Bahamas 88 A4 26 25N 77 10W
Great Artesian Basin, Australia .... 62 C3 23 0S 144 0 E
Great Australian Bight, Australia .... 61 F5 33 30S 130 0 E
Great Bahama Bank, Bahamas 88 B4 23 15N 78 0W
Great Barrier I., N.Z. .... 59 G5 36 11S 175 25 E
Great Barrier Reef, Australia .... 62 B4 18 0S 146 50 E
Great Barrier Reef △, Australia .... 62 B4 20 0S 150 0 E
Great Barrington, U.S.A. 85 D11 42 12N 73 22W
Great Basalt Wall △, Australia .... 62 B4 19 52S 145 43 E
Great Basin, U.S.A. 76 G5 40 0N 117 0W
Great Basin △, U.S.A. 76 G6 38 55N 114 14W
Great Bear →, Canada 68 B7 65 0N 124 0W
Great Bear L., Canada 68 B7 65 30N 120 0W
Great Belt = Store Bælt, Denmark .... 9 J14 55 20N 11 0 E
Great Bend, Kans., U.S.A. 80 F5 38 22N 98 46W
Great Bend, Pa., U.S.A. 85 E9 41 58N 75 45W
Great Blasket I., Ireland 10 D1 52 6N 10 32W
Great Britain, Europe 6 E5 54 0N 2 15W
Great Camanoe, Br. Virgin Is. .... 89 e 18 30N 64 35W
Great Codroy, Canada 73 C8 47 51N 59 16W
Great Dividing Ra., Australia .... 62 C4 23 0S 146 0 E
Great Driffield = Driffield, U.K. 12 C7 54 0N 0 26W
Great Exuma I., Bahamas 88 B4 23 30N 75 50W
Great Falls, Canada 76 C8 47 30N 111 17W
Great Fish = Groot Vis →, S. Africa .... 56 E4 33 28S 27 5 E
Great Guana Cay, Bahamas 88 B4 24 0N 76 20W
Great Inagua I., Bahamas 89 B5 21 0N 73 20W
Great Indian Desert = Thar Desert, India .... 42 F5 28 0N 72 0 E
Great Karoo, S. Africa .... 56 E3 31 55S 21 0 E
Great Lake, Australia .... 63 G4 41 50S 146 40 E
Great Lakes, N. Amer. 66 E11 46 0N 84 0W
Great Malvern, U.K. 13 E5 52 7N 2 18W
Great Miami →, U.S.A. 82 F3 39 20N 84 40W
Great Ormes Head, U.K. 12 D4 53 20N 3 52W
Great Ouse →, U.K. .... 12 E8 52 48N 0 21 E
Great Palm I., Australia .... 62 B4 18 45S 146 40 E
Great Pedro Bluff, Jamaica .... 88 a 17 51N 77 44W
Great Plains, N. Amer. 66 E9 47 0N 105 0W
Great Ruaha →, Tanzania .... 54 D4 7 56S 37 52 E
Great Sacandaga Res., U.S.A. 85 C10 43 6N 74 16W
Great Saint Bernard Pass = Grand St-Bernard, Col du, Europe .... 20 D7 45 50N 7 10 E
Great Salt L., U.S.A. 76 F7 41 15N 112 40W
Great Salt Lake Desert, U.S.A. 76 F7 40 50N 113 30W
Great Salt Plains L., U.S.A. 81 G5 36 45N 98 8W
Great Sand Dunes △, U.S.A. 77 H11 37 48N 105 45W
Great Sandy △, Australia .... 63 D5 26 13S 153 2 E
Great Sandy Desert, Australia .... 60 D3 21 0S 124 0 E
Great Sangi = Sangihe, Pulau, Indonesia .... 37 D7 3 35N 125 30 E
Great Skellig, Ireland 10 E1 51 47N 10 33W
Great Slave L., Canada 70 A5 61 23N 115 38W
Great Smoky Mts. △, U.S.A. 83 H4 35 40N 83 40W

Great Snow Mt., Canada	70 B4	57 26N 124 0W
Great Stour = Stour →, U.K.	13 F9	51 18N 1 22 E
Great Victoria Desert, Australia	61 E4	29 30S 126 30 E
Great Wall, Antarctica	5 C18	62 30S 58 0W
Great Wall, China	34 E5	38 30N 109 30 E
Great Whernside, U.K.	12 C6	54 10N 1 58W
Great Yarmouth, U.K.	13 E9	52 37N 1 44 E
Great Zab = Zāb al Kabir →, Iraq	44 C4	36 1N 43 24 E
Great Zimbabwe, Zimbabwe	55 G3	20 16S 30 54 E
Greater Antilles, W. Indies	89 C5	17 40N 74 0W
Greater London □, U.K.	13 F7	51 31N 0 6W
Greater Manchester □, U.K.	12 D5	53 30N 2 15W
Greater St. Lucia Wetlands �, S. Africa	57 D5	28 6S 32 27 E
Greater Sudbury = Sudbury, Canada	72 C3	46 30N 81 0W
Greater Sunda Is., Indonesia	36 F4	7 0S 112 0 E
Greco, C., Cyprus	25 E13	34 57N 34 5 E
Gredos, Sierra de, Spain	21 B3	40 20N 5 0W
Greece, U.S.A.	84 C7	43 13N 77 41W
Greece ■, Europe	23 E9	40 0N 23 0 E
Greeley, Colo., U.S.A.	80 E2	40 25N 104 42W
Greeley, Nebr., U.S.A.	80 E5	41 33N 98 32W
Greem-Bell, Ostrov, Russia	28 A7	81 0N 62 0 E
Green →, U.S.A.	76 E2	43 9N 123 22W
Green →, Ky., U.S.A.	82 G2	37 54N 87 30W
Green →, Utah, U.S.A.	77 G9	38 11N 109 53W
Green B., U.S.A.	82 C2	45 0N 87 30W
Green Bay, U.S.A.	82 C2	44 31N 88 0W
Green C., Australia	63 F5	37 13S 150 1 E
Green Cove Springs, U.S.A.	83 L5	29 59N 81 42W
Green Lake, Canada	71 C7	54 17N 107 47W
Green Mts., U.S.A.	85 C12	43 45N 72 45W
Green River, Utah, U.S.A.	77 G8	38 59N 110 10W
Green River, Wyo., U.S.A.	76 F9	41 32N 109 28W
Green Valley, U.S.A.	77 L8	31 52N 110 56W
Greenbank, U.S.A.	78 B4	48 6N 122 34W
Greenbush, Mich., U.S.A.	84 B1	44 35N 83 19W
Greenbush, Minn., U.S.A.	80 A6	48 42N 96 11W
Greencastle, U.S.A.	82 F2	39 38N 86 52W
Greene, U.S.A.	85 D9	42 20N 75 46W
Greenfield, Calif., U.S.A.	78 J5	36 19N 121 15W
Greenfield, Calif., U.S.A.	79 K8	35 15N 119 0W
Greenfield, Ind., U.S.A.	82 F3	39 47N 85 46W
Greenfield, Iowa, U.S.A.	80 E7	41 18N 94 28W
Greenfield, Mass., U.S.A.	85 D12	42 35N 72 36W
Greenfield, Mo., U.S.A.	81 G8	37 25N 93 51W
Greenfield Park, Canada	85 A11	45 29N 73 29W
Greenland ☑, N. Amer.	4 C5	66 0N 45 0W
Greenland Sea, Arctic	4 B7	73 0N 10 0W
Greenock, U.K.	11 F4	55 57N 4 46W
Greenore, Ireland	10 B5	54 2N 6 8W
Greenore Pt., Ireland	10 D5	52 14N 6 19W
Greenough, Australia	61 E1	28 58S 114 43 E
Greenough →, Australia	61 E1	28 51S 114 38 E
Greenough Pt., Canada	84 B3	44 58N 81 26W
Greenport, U.S.A.	85 E12	41 6N 72 22W
Greensboro, Ga., U.S.A.	83 J4	33 35N 83 11W
Greensboro, N.C., U.S.A.	83 G6	36 4N 79 48W
Greensboro, Vt., U.S.A.	85 B12	44 36N 72 18W
Greensburg, Ind., U.S.A.	82 F3	39 20N 85 29W
Greensburg, Kans., U.S.A.	81 G5	37 36N 99 18W
Greensburg, Pa., U.S.A.	84 F5	40 18N 79 33W
Greenstone Pt., U.K.	11 D3	57 55N 5 37W
Greenvale, Australia	62 B4	18 59S 145 7 E
Greenville, Ala., U.S.A.	83 K2	31 50N 86 38W
Greenville, Calif., U.S.A.	78 E6	40 8N 120 57W
Greenville, Maine, U.S.A.	83 C11	45 28N 69 35W
Greenville, Mich., U.S.A.	82 D3	43 11N 85 15W
Greenville, Miss., U.S.A.	81 J9	33 24N 91 4W
Greenville, Mo., U.S.A.	81 G9	37 8N 90 27W
Greenville, N.C., U.S.A.	83 H7	35 37N 77 23W
Greenville, N.H., U.S.A.	85 D13	42 46N 71 49W
Greenville, N.Y., U.S.A.	85 D10	42 25N 74 1W
Greenville, Ohio, U.S.A.	82 E3	40 6N 84 38W
Greenville, Pa., U.S.A.	84 E4	41 24N 80 23W
Greenville, S.C., U.S.A.	83 H4	34 51N 82 24W
Greenville, Tenn., U.S.A.	83 G4	36 13N 82 51W
Greenville, Tex., U.S.A.	81 J6	33 8N 96 7W
Greenwater Lake �, Canada	71 C8	52 32N 103 30W
Greenwich, Conn., U.S.A.	85 E11	41 2N 73 38W
Greenwich, N.Y., U.S.A.	85 C11	43 5N 73 30W
Greenwich, Ohio, U.S.A.	84 E2	41 2N 82 31W
Greenwich □, U.K.	13 F8	51 29N 0 1 E
Greenwood, Canada	70 D5	49 10N 118 40W
Greenwood, Ark., U.S.A.	81 H7	35 13N 94 16W
Greenwood, Ind., U.S.A.	82 F2	39 37N 86 7W
Greenwood, Miss., U.S.A.	81 J9	33 31N 90 11W
Greenwood, S.C., U.S.A.	83 H4	34 12N 82 10W
Greenwood, Mt., Australia	60 B5	13 48S 130 4 E
Gregory, U.S.A.	80 D5	43 14N 99 20W
Gregory △, Australia	60 C5	15 38S 131 15 E
Gregory →, Australia	62 B2	17 53S 139 17 E
Gregory L., S. Austral., Australia	63 D2	28 55S 139 0 E
Gregory, L., W. Austral., Australia	61 E2	25 38S 119 58 E
Gregory Downs, Australia	62 B2	18 35S 138 45 E
Gregory L., Australia	60 D4	20 0S 127 40 E
Gregory Ra., Queens., Australia	62 B3	19 30S 143 40 E
Gregory Ra., W. Austral., Australia	60 D3	21 20S 121 12 E
Greifswald, Germany	16 A7	54 5N 13 23 E
Greiz, Germany	16 C7	50 39N 12 10 E
Gremikha, Russia	18 A6	67 59N 39 47 E
Grenå, Denmark	9 H14	56 25N 10 53 E
Grenada, U.S.A.	81 J10	33 47N 89 49W
Grenada ■, W. Indies	89 D7	12 10N 61 40W
Grenadier I., U.S.A.	85 B8	44 3N 76 22W
Grenadines, St. Vincent	89 D7	12 40N 61 20W
Grenen, Denmark	9 H14	57 44N 10 40 E
Grenfell, Australia	63 E4	33 52S 148 8 E
Grenfell, Canada	71 C8	50 30N 102 56W
Grenoble, France	20 D6	45 12N 5 42 E
Grenville, C., Australia	62 A3	12 0S 143 13 E
Grenville Chan., Canada	70 C3	53 40N 129 46W
Gresham, U.S.A.	78 E4	45 30N 122 26W
Gresik, Indonesia	37 G15	7 13S 112 38 E
Gretna, U.S.A.	11 F5	55 0N 3 3W
Grevenmacher, Lux.	15 E6	49 41N 6 26 E
Grey →, Canada	73 C8	47 34N 57 6W
Grey →, N.Z.	59 K3	42 27S 171 12 E
Grey, C., Australia	62 A2	13 0S 136 35 E
Grey Ra., Australia	63 D3	27 0S 143 30 E
Greybull, U.S.A.	76 D9	44 30N 108 3W
Greymouth, N.Z.	59 K3	42 29S 171 13 E
Greystones, Ireland	10 C5	53 9N 6 5W
Greytown, N.Z.	59 J5	41 5S 175 29 E
Greytown, S. Africa	57 D5	29 1S 30 36 E
Gribbell I., Canada	70 C3	53 23N 129 0W
Gridley, U.S.A.	78 F5	39 22N 121 42W
Griekwastad, S. Africa	56 D3	28 49S 23 15 E
Griffin, U.S.A.	83 J3	33 15N 84 16W
Griffith, Australia	63 E4	34 18S 146 2 E
Griffith, Canada	84 A7	45 15N 77 10W
Griffith I., Canada	84 B4	44 50N 80 55W
Grimaylov = Hrymayliv, Ukraine	17 D14	49 20N 26 5 E
Grimes, U.S.A.	78 F5	39 4N 121 54W
Grimsay, U.K.	11 D1	57 29N 7 14W
Grimsby, Canada	84 C5	43 12N 79 34W
Grimsby, U.K.	12 D7	53 34N 0 5W
Grímsey, Iceland	8 C5	66 33N 17 58W
Grimshaw, Canada	70 B5	56 10N 117 40W
Grimstad, Norway	9 G13	58 20N 8 35 E
Grindstone I., Canada	85 B8	44 43N 76 14W
Grinnell, U.S.A.	80 E8	41 45N 92 43W
Gris-Nez, C., France	20 A4	50 52N 1 35 E
Groais I., Canada	73 B8	50 55N 55 35W
Groblersdal, S. Africa	57 D4	25 15S 29 25 E
Grodno = Hrodna, Belarus	17 B12	53 42N 23 52 E
Grodzyanka = Hrodzyanka, Belarus	17 B15	53 31N 28 42 E
Groesbeck, U.S.A.	81 K6	31 48N 96 31W
Grójec, Poland	17 C11	51 50N 20 58 E
Grong, Norway	8 D15	64 25N 12 8 E
Groningen, Neths.	15 A6	53 15N 6 35 E
Groningen □, Neths.	15 A6	53 16N 6 40 E
Groom, U.S.A.	81 H4	35 12N 101 6W
Groot →, S. Africa	56 E3	33 45S 24 36 E
Groot Berg →, S. Africa	56 E2	32 47S 18 8 E
Groot-Brakrivier, S. Africa	56 E3	34 2S 22 18 E
Groot Karasberge, Namibia	56 D2	27 20S 18 40 E
Groot-Kei →, S. Africa	57 E4	32 41S 28 22 E
Groot Vis →, S. Africa	56 E4	33 28S 27 5 E
Grootdrink, S. Africa	56 D3	28 33S 21 42 E
Groote Eylandt, Australia	62 A2	14 0S 136 40 E
Grootfontein, Namibia	56 B2	19 31S 18 6 E
Grootlaagte →, Africa	56 C3	20 55S 21 27 E
Grootvloer →, S. Africa	56 E3	30 0S 20 40 E
Gros C., Canada	70 A6	61 59N 113 32W
Gros Islet, St. Lucia	89 f	14 5N 60 58W
Gros Morne △, Canada	73 C8	49 40N 57 50W
Gros Piton, St. Lucia	89 f	13 49N 61 5W
Gros Piton Pt., St. Lucia	89 f	13 49N 61 5W
Grossa, Pta., Spain	24 B8	39 6N 1 36 E
Grosser Arber, Germany	16 D7	49 6N 13 8 E
Grosseto, Italy	22 C4	42 46N 11 8 E
Grossglockner, Austria	16 E7	47 5N 12 40 E
Groswater B., Canada	73 B8	54 20N 57 40W
Groton, Conn., U.S.A.	85 E12	41 21N 72 5W
Groton, N.Y., U.S.A.	85 D8	42 36N 76 22W
Groton, S. Dak., U.S.A.	80 C5	45 27N 98 6W
Grouard Mission, Canada	70 B5	55 33N 116 9W
Groundhog →, Canada	72 C3	48 45N 82 58W
Grouw, Neths.	15 A5	53 5N 5 51 E
Grove City, U.S.A.	84 E4	41 10N 80 5W
Grove Hill, U.S.A.	83 K2	31 42N 87 47W
Groveland, U.S.A.	78 H6	37 50N 120 14W
Grover City, U.S.A.	79 K6	35 7N 120 37W
Groves, U.S.A.	81 L8	29 57N 93 54W
Groveton, U.S.A.	85 B13	44 36N 71 31W
Groznyy, Russia	19 F8	43 20N 45 45 E
Grudziądz, Poland	17 B10	53 30N 18 47 E
Gruinard B., U.K.	11 D3	57 56N 5 35W
Grundy Center, U.S.A.	80 D8	42 22N 92 47W
Gruver, U.S.A.	81 G4	36 16N 101 24W
Gryazi, Russia	18 D6	52 30N 39 58 E
Gryazovets, Russia	18 C7	58 50N 40 10 E
Gua, India	41 H14	22 18N 85 20 E
Gua Musang, Malaysia	39 K3	4 53N 101 58 E
Guacanayabo, G. de, Cuba	88 B4	20 40N 77 20W
Guáchipas →, Argentina	94 B2	25 40S 65 30W
Guadalajara, Mexico	86 C4	20 40N 103 20W
Guadalajara, Spain	21 B4	40 37N 3 12W
Guadalcanal, Solomon Is.	64 H8	9 32S 160 12 E
Guadales, Argentina	94 C2	34 30S 67 55W
Guadalete →, Spain	21 D2	36 35N 6 13W
Guadalquivir →, Spain	21 D2	36 47N 6 22W
Guadalupe = Guadeloupe ☑, W. Indies	88 b	16 20N 61 40W
Guadalupe, Mexico	79 N10	32 4N 116 32W
Guadalupe, U.S.A.	79 L6	34 59N 120 33W
Guadalupe →, Mexico	79 N10	32 6N 116 51W
Guadalupe →, U.S.A.	81 L6	28 27N 96 47W
Guadalupe, Sierra de, Spain	21 C3	39 28N 5 30W
Guadalupe Bravos, Mexico	86 A3	31 20N 106 10W
Guadalupe I., Pac. Oc.	66 G8	29 0N 118 50W
Guadalupe Mts. △, U.S.A.	81 K2	31 40N 104 30W
Guadalupe Peak, U.S.A.	81 K2	31 50N 104 52W
Guadalupe y Calvo, Mexico	86 B3	26 6N 106 58W
Guadarrama, Sierra de, Spain	21 B4	41 0N 4 0W
Guadeloupe ☑, W. Indies	88 b	16 20N 61 40W
Guadeloupe Passage, W. Indies	89 C7	16 50N 62 15W
Guadiana →, Portugal	21 D2	37 14N 7 22W
Guadix, Spain	21 D4	37 18N 3 11W
Guafo, Boca del, Chile	96 E2	43 35S 74 0W
Guaico, Trin. & Tob.	93 K15	10 35N 61 9W
Guainía →, Colombia	92 C5	2 1N 67 7W
Guaíra, Brazil	95 A5	24 5S 54 10W
Guaíra □, Paraguay	94 B4	25 45S 56 30W
Guaitecas, Is., Chile	96 E2	44 0S 74 30W
Guajará-Mirim, Brazil	92 F5	10 50S 65 20W
Guajira, Pen. de la, Colombia	92 A4	12 0N 72 0W
Gualán, Guatemala	88 C2	15 8N 89 22W
Gualeguay, Argentina	94 C4	33 10S 59 14W
Gualeguaychú, Argentina	94 C4	33 3S 59 31W
Gualequay →, Argentina	94 C4	33 19S 59 39W
Guam ☑, Pac. Oc.	64 F6	13 27N 144 45 E
Guamini, Argentina	94 D3	37 1S 62 28W
Guamúchil, Mexico	86 B3	25 25N 108 3W
Guana I., Br. Virgin Is.	89 e	18 30N 64 30W
Guanabacoa, Cuba	88 B3	23 8N 82 18W
Guanacaste, Costa Rica	88 D2	10 40N 85 4W
Guanacaste, Cordillera del, Costa Rica	88 D2	10 40N 85 4W
Guanaceví, Mexico	86 B3	25 40N 106 0W
Guanahani = San Salvador I., Bahamas	89 B5	24 0N 74 40W
Guanajay, Cuba	88 B3	22 56N 82 42W
Guanajuato, Mexico	86 C4	21 0N 101 20W
Guanajuato □, Mexico	86 C4	20 40N 101 20W
Guandacol, Argentina	94 B2	29 30S 68 40W
Guane, Cuba	88 B3	22 10N 84 7W
Guangdong □, China	33 D6	23 0N 113 0 E
Guangling, China	34 E8	39 47N 114 22 E
Guangrao, China	35 F10	37 5N 118 25 E
Guangwu, China	34 F3	37 48N 105 57 E
Guangxi Zhuangzu Zizhiqu □, China	33 D5	24 0N 109 0 E
Guangzhou, China	33 D6	23 5N 113 10 E
Guanica, Puerto Rico	89 d	17 59N 66 55W
Guanipa →, Venezuela	92 B6	9 56N 62 26W
Guannan, China	35 G10	34 8N 119 21 E
Guantánamo, Cuba	89 B4	20 10N 75 14W
Guantánamo B., Cuba	89 C4	19 59N 75 10W
Guantao, China	34 F8	36 42N 115 25 E
Guanyun, China	35 G10	34 20N 119 18 E
Guápiles, Costa Rica	88 D3	10 10N 83 46W
Guapo B., Trin. & Tob.	93 K15	10 12N 61 41W
Guaporé, Brazil	95 B5	28 51S 51 54W
Guaporé →, Brazil	92 F5	11 55S 65 4W
Guaqui, Bolivia	92 G5	16 41S 68 54W
Guaramacal △, Venezuela	89 E5	9 13N 70 12W
Guarapari, Brazil	95 A7	20 40S 40 30W
Guarapuava, Brazil	95 B5	25 20S 51 30W
Guaratinguetá, Brazil	95 A6	22 49S 45 9W
Guaratuba, Brazil	95 B6	25 53S 48 38W
Guarda, Portugal	21 B2	40 32N 7 20W
Guardafui, C. = Asir, Ras, Somali Rep.	47 E5	11 55N 51 10 E
Guárico □, Venezuela	92 B5	8 40N 66 35W
Guarujá, Brazil	95 A6	24 2S 46 25W
Guarulhos, Brazil	95 A6	23 29S 46 33W
Guarus, Brazil	95 A7	21 44S 41 20W
Guasave, Mexico	86 B3	25 34N 108 27W
Guasdualito, Venezuela	92 B4	7 15N 70 44W
Guatemala, Guatemala	88 D1	14 40N 90 22W
Guatemala ■, Cent. Amer.	88 C1	15 40N 90 30W
Guatopo △, Venezuela	89 D6	10 5N 66 30W
Guatuaro Pt., Trin. & Tob.	93 K16	10 19N 60 59W
Guaviare □, Colombia	92 C5	4 3N 67 44W
Guaxupé, Brazil	95 A6	21 10S 47 5W
Guayaguayare, Trin. & Tob.	93 K15	10 12N 61 3W
Guayama, Puerto Rico	89 d	17 59N 66 7W
Guayaquil, Ecuador	92 D3	2 15S 79 52W
Guayaquil, G. de, Ecuador	92 D2	3 10S 81 0W
Guaymas, Mexico	86 B2	27 59N 110 54W
Guba, Dem. Rep. of the Congo	55 E2	10 38S 26 27 E
Gubkin, Russia	19 D6	51 17N 37 32 E
Gudbrandsdalen, Norway	9 F14	61 33N 10 10 E
Guddu Barrage, Pakistan	40 E6	28 30N 69 50 E
Gudur, India	40 M11	14 12N 79 55 E
Guecho = Getxo, Spain	21 A4	43 21N 2 59W
Guelmine = Goulimine, Morocco	50 C3	28 56N 10 0W
Guelph, Canada	84 C4	43 35N 80 20W
Guéret, France	20 C4	46 11N 1 51 E
Guerneville, U.S.A.	78 G4	38 30N 123 0W
Guernica = Gernika-Lumo, Spain	21 A4	43 19N 2 40W
Guernsey, U.K.	13 H5	49 26N 2 35W
Guernsey, U.S.A.	80 D2	42 19N 104 45W
Guerrero □, Mexico	87 D5	17 30N 100 0W
Gügher, Iran	45 D8	29 28N 56 27 E
Guhakolak, Tanjung, Indonesia	37 G11	6 50S 105 14 E
Guia, Canary Is.	24 F4	28 8N 15 38W
Guia de Isora, Canary Is.	24 F3	28 12N 16 46W
Guia Lopes da Laguna, Brazil	95 A4	21 26S 56 7W
Guiana Highlands, S. Amer.	90 C4	5 10N 60 40W
Guidónia-Montecélio, Italy	22 C5	42 1N 12 45 E
Guijá, Mozam.	57 C5	24 27S 33 0 E
Guildford, U.K.	13 F7	51 14N 0 34W
Guilford, U.S.A.	85 E12	41 17N 72 41W
Guilin, China	33 D6	25 18N 110 15 E
Guillaume-Delisle, L., Canada	72 A4	56 15N 76 17W
Güimar, Canary Is.	24 F3	28 18N 16 24W
Guimarães, Portugal	21 B1	41 28N 8 24W
Guimaras □, Phil.	37 B6	10 35N 122 37 E
Guinda, U.S.A.	78 G4	38 50N 122 12W
Guinea, Africa	48 F4	8 0N 8 0 E
Guinea ■, W. Afr.	50 F3	10 20N 11 30W
Guinea, Gulf of, Atl. Oc.	49 F4	3 0N 2 30 E
Guinea-Bissau ■, Africa	50 F3	12 0N 15 0W
Güines, Cuba	88 B3	22 50N 82 0W
Guingamp, France	20 B2	48 34N 3 10W
Güiria, Venezuela	92 A6	10 32N 62 18W
Guiuan, Phil.	37 B7	11 5N 125 55 E
Guiyang, China	32 D5	26 32N 106 40 E
Guizhou □, China	32 D5	27 0N 107 0 E
Gujar Khan, Pakistan	42 C5	33 16N 73 19 E
Gujarat □, India	42 H4	23 20N 71 0 E
Gujranwala, Pakistan	42 C6	32 10N 74 12 E
Gujrat, Pakistan	42 C6	32 40N 74 2 E
Gulbarga, India	40 L10	17 20N 76 50 E
Gulbene, Latvia	9 H22	57 8N 26 52 E
Gulf, The, Asia	45 E6	27 0N 50 0 E
Gulf Islands △, U.S.A.	83 E2	30 10N 87 10W
Gulfport, U.S.A.	81 K10	30 22N 89 6W
Gulgong, Australia	63 E4	32 20S 149 49 E
Gulistan, Pakistan	42 D2	30 30N 66 35 E
Gull Lake, Canada	71 C7	50 10N 108 29W
Güllük, Turkey	23 F12	37 14N 27 35 E
Gulmarg, India	43 B6	34 3N 74 25 E
Gulshad, Kazakhstan	28 E8	46 45N 74 25 E
Gulu, Uganda	54 B3	2 48N 32 17 E
Gulwe, Tanzania	54 D4	6 30S 36 25 E
Gumal →, Pakistan	42 D3	31 40N 71 50 E
Gumbaz, Pakistan	42 D3	30 2N 69 0 E
Gumel, Nigeria	50 F7	12 39N 9 22 E
Gumla, India	43 H11	23 3N 84 33 E
Gumlu, Australia	62 B4	19 53S 147 41 E
Gumma □, Japan	31 F9	36 30N 138 20 E
Gumzai, Indonesia	37 F8	5 28S 134 42 E
Guna, India	42 G7	24 40N 77 19 E
Gunisao →, Canada	71 C9	53 56N 97 53W
Gunisao L., Canada	71 C9	53 33N 96 15W
Gunjyal, Pakistan	42 C4	32 20N 71 55 E
Gunnbjørn Fjeld, Greenland	4 C6	68 55N 29 47W
Gunnedah, Australia	63 E5	30 59S 150 15 E
Gunningbar Cr. →, Australia	63 E4	31 14S 147 6 E
Gunnison, Colo., U.S.A.	77 G10	38 33N 106 56W
Gunnison, Utah, U.S.A.	76 G8	39 9N 111 49W
Gunnison →, U.S.A.	77 G9	39 4N 108 35W
Gunpowder, Australia	62 B2	19 42S 139 22 E
Guntakal, India	40 M10	15 11N 77 27 E
Guntersville, U.S.A.	83 H2	34 21N 86 18W
Guntur, India	41 L12	16 23N 80 30 E
Guoyang, China	34 H9	33 32N 116 12 E
Gupis, Pakistan	43 A5	36 15N 73 20 E
Gurdaspur, India	42 C6	32 5N 75 31 E
Gurdon, U.S.A.	81 J8	33 55N 93 9W
Gurgaon, India	42 E7	28 27N 77 1 E
Gurgueia →, Brazil	93 E10	6 50S 43 24W
Gurha, India	42 G4	25 12N 71 39 E
Guri, Embalse de, Venezuela	92 B6	7 50N 62 52W
Gurig △, Australia	60 B5	11 36S 132 7 E
Gurkha, Nepal	43 E11	28 5N 84 40 E
Gurley, Australia	63 D4	29 45S 149 48 E
Gurnet Point, U.S.A.	85 D14	42 1N 70 34W
Guro, Mozam.	55 F3	17 25S 36 58 E
Gurué, Mozam.	55 F4	15 25S 36 58 E
Gurun, Malaysia	39 K3	5 49N 100 27 E
Gürün, Turkey	19 G6	38 43N 37 15 E
Gurupá, Brazil	93 D8	1 25S 51 35W
Gurupá, I. Grande de, Brazil	93 D8	1 25S 51 45W
Gurupi, Brazil	93 F9	11 43S 49 4W
Gurupi →, Brazil	93 D9	1 13S 46 6W
Guruwe, Zimbabwe	57 B5	16 40S 30 42 E
Guryev = Atyraŭ, Kazakhstan	19 E9	47 5N 52 0 E
Gusau, Nigeria	50 F7	12 12N 6 40 E
Gusev, Russia	9 J20	54 35N 22 10 E
Gushan, China	35 E12	39 50N 123 35 E
Gushgy, Turkmenistan	28 F7	35 20N 62 18 E
Gusinoozersk, Russia	29 D11	51 16N 106 27 E
Gustavus, U.S.A.	70 B1	58 25N 135 44W
Gustine, U.S.A.	78 H6	37 16N 121 0W
Güstrow, Germany	16 B7	53 47N 12 10 E
Gütersloh, Germany	16 C5	51 54N 8 24 E
Gutha, Australia	61 E2	28 58S 115 59 E
Guthalungra, Australia	62 B4	19 52S 147 50 E
Guthrie, Okla., U.S.A.	81 H6	35 53N 97 25W
Guthrie, Tex., U.S.A.	81 J4	33 37N 100 19W
Guttenberg, U.S.A.	80 D9	42 47N 91 6W
Gutu, Zimbabwe	57 B5	19 41S 31 9 E
Guwahati, India	41 F17	26 10N 91 45 E
Guy Fawkes River △, Australia	63 E5	30 0S 152 20 E
Guyana ■, S. Amer.	92 C7	5 0N 59 0W
Guyane française = French Guiana ☑, S. Amer.	93 C8	4 0N 53 0W
Guyang, China	34 D6	41 0N 110 5 E
Guyenne, France	20 D4	44 30N 0 40 E
Guymon, U.S.A.	81 G4	36 41N 101 29W
Guyra, Australia	63 E5	30 15S 151 40 E
Guyuan, Hebei, China	34 D9	41 37N 115 40 E
Guyuan, Ningxia Huizu, China	34 G4	36 0N 106 20 E
Güzelyurt = Morphou, Cyprus	25 D11	35 12N 32 59 E
Guzhen, China	35 H9	33 22N 117 18 E
Guzmán, L. de, Mexico	86 A3	31 25N 107 25 E
Gvardeysk, Russia	9 J19	54 39N 21 5 E
Gwa, Burma	41 L19	17 36N 94 34 E
Gwaai, Zimbabwe	55 F2	19 15S 27 45 E
Gwaai →, Zimbabwe	55 F2	17 59S 26 52 E
Gwabegar, Australia	63 E4	30 31S 149 0 E
Gwādar, Pakistan	40 G3	25 10N 62 18 E
Gwaii Haanas △, Canada	70 C2	52 21N 131 26W
Gwalior, India	42 F8	26 12N 78 10 E
Gwanda, Zimbabwe	55 G2	20 55S 29 0 E
Gwane, Dem. Rep. of the Congo	54 B2	4 45N 25 48 E
Gweebarra B., Ireland	10 B3	54 51N 8 23W
Gweedore, Ireland	10 A3	55 3N 8 13W
Gweru, Zimbabwe	55 F2	19 28S 29 45 E
Gwinn, U.S.A.	82 B2	46 19N 87 27W
Gwydir →, Australia	63 D4	29 27S 149 48 E
Gwynedd □, U.K.	12 E3	52 52N 4 10W
Gyandzhe = Gäncä, Azerbaijan	19 F8	40 45N 46 20 E
Gyaring Hu, China	32 C4	34 50N 97 40 E
Gydanskiy Poluostrov, Russia	28 C8	70 0N 78 0 E
Gympie, Australia	63 D5	26 11S 152 38 E
Gyöngyös, Hungary	17 E10	47 48N 19 56 E
Győr, Hungary	17 E9	47 41N 17 40 E
Gypsum Pt., Canada	70 A6	61 53N 114 35W
Gypsumville, Canada	71 C9	51 45N 98 40W
Gyula, Hungary	17 E11	46 38N 21 17 E
Gyumri, Armenia	19 F7	40 47N 43 50 E
Gyzylarbat, Turkmenistan	28 F6	39 4N 56 23 E
Gyzyletrek, Turkmenistan	45 B7	37 36N 54 46 E

H

Ha 'Arava →, Israel	46 E4	30 50N 35 20 E
Ha Coi, Vietnam	38 B6	21 26N 107 46 E
Ha Dong, Vietnam	38 B5	20 58N 105 46 E
Ha Giang, Vietnam	38 A5	22 50N 104 59 E
Ha Karmel △, Israel	46 C4	32 45N 35 5 E
Ha Tien, Vietnam	39 G5	10 23N 104 29 E
Ha Tinh, Vietnam	38 C5	18 20N 105 54 E
Ha Trung, Vietnam	38 C5	19 58N 105 50 E
Ha Yaek Chalong, Thailand	39 a	7 50N 98 22 E
Haaksbergen, Neths.	15 B6	52 9N 6 45 E
Haapsalu, Estonia	9 G20	58 56N 23 30 E
Haarlem, Neths.	15 B4	52 23N 4 39 E
Haast →, N.Z.	59 K2	43 50S 169 2 E
Haast Bluff, Australia	60 D5	23 22S 132 0 E
Hab →, Pakistan	42 G3	24 53N 66 41 E
Hab Nadi Chauki, Pakistan	42 G2	25 0N 66 50 E
Habaswein, Kenya	54 B4	1 2N 39 30 E
Habay, Canada	70 B5	58 50N 118 44W
Habbānīyah, Iraq	44 C4	33 17N 43 29 E
Haboro, Japan	30 B10	44 22N 141 42 E
Habshān, U.A.E.	45 F7	23 50N 53 37 E
Hachijō-Jima, Japan	31 H9	33 5N 139 45 E
Hachinohe, Japan	30 D10	40 30N 141 29 E
Hachiōji, Japan	31 G9	35 40N 139 20 E
Hachŏn, N. Korea	35 D15	41 29N 129 2 E
Hackensack, U.S.A.	85 F10	40 53N 74 3W
Hackettstown, U.S.A.	85 F10	40 51N 74 50W
Hadali, Pakistan	42 C5	32 16N 72 11 E
Hadarba, Ras, Sudan	51 D13	22 4N 36 51 E
Hadarom □, Israel	46 E4	31 0N 35 0 E
Hadd, Ra's al, Oman	47 C6	22 35N 59 50 E
Haddington, U.K.	11 F6	55 57N 2 47W
Hadejia, Nigeria	50 F7	12 39N 9 2 E
Hadera, Israel	46 C3	32 27N 34 55 E
Hadera, N. →, Israel	46 C3	32 28N 34 52 E
Haderslev, Denmark	9 J13	55 15N 9 30 E
Hadhramaut = Ḥaḍramawt, Yemen	47 D4	15 30N 49 30 E
Hadiboh, Yemen	47 E5	12 35N 54 2 E
Hadong, S. Korea	35 G14	35 5N 127 44 E
Ḥaḍramawt, Yemen	47 D4	15 30N 49 30 E
Ḥadrāniyah, Iraq	44 C4	35 38N 43 14 E

adrian's Wall, U.K. 12 B5 55 0N 2 30W
aeju, N. Korea .... 35 E13 38 3N 125 45 E
aenam, S. Korea .... 35 G14 34 34N 126 35 E
aenertsburg, S. Africa .... 57 C4 24 0S 29 50 E
aerhpin = Harbin, China .... 35 B14 45 48N 126 40 E
afar al Bāṭin, Si. Arabia .... 44 D5 28 32N 45 52 E
afirat al 'Aydā, Si. Arabia .... 44 E3 26 26N 39 12 E
afit, Oman .... 45 F7 23 59N 55 49 E
afizabad, Pakistan .... 42 C5 32 5N 73 40 E
aflong, India .... 41 G18 25 10N 93 5 E
afnarfjörður, Iceland 8 D3 64 4N 21 57W
aft Gel, Iran .... 45 D6 31 30N 49 32 E
afun, Ras, Somali Rep. .... 47 E5 10 29N 51 30 E
agaili, Israel .... 46 C4 32 53N 35 18 E
agen, Germany .... 16 C4 51 21N 7 27 E
agerman, Germany 81 J2 33 7N 104 20W
agerman Fossil Beds ○, U.S.A. 76 E6 42 48N 114 57W
agerstown, U.S.A. 82 F7 39 39N 77 43W
agersville, Canada 84 D4 42 58N 80 3W
agfors, Sweden .... 9 F15 60 3N 13 45 E
agi, Japan .... 31 G5 34 30N 131 22 E
agolan, Syria .... 46 C4 33 0N 35 45 E
agondange, France .... 20 B7 49 16N 6 11 E
ague, C. de la, France 20 B3 49 44N 1 56W
ague Hd., Ireland 10 D2 52 57N 9 28W
ague, The = 's-Gravenhage, Neths. .... 15 B4 52 7N 4 17 E
aguenau, France .... 20 B7 48 49N 7 47 E
ai Duong, Vietnam .... 38 B6 20 56N 106 19 E
aicheng, China .... 35 D12 40 50N 122 45 E
aidar Khel, Afghan. .... 42 C3 33 58N 68 38 E
aidarābād = Hyderabad, India .... 40 L11 17 22N 78 29 E
aidargarh, India .... 43 F9 26 37N 81 22 E
aifa = Hefa, Israel .... 46 C4 32 46N 35 0 E
aikou, China .... 33 D6 20 1N 110 16 E
a'il, Si. Arabia .... 44 E4 27 28N 41 45 E
ailar, China .... 33 B6 49 10N 119 38 E
ailey, U.S.A. 76 E6 43 31N 114 19W
aileybury, Canada 72 C4 47 30N 79 38W
ailin, China .... 35 B15 44 37N 129 30 E
ailong, China .... 35 C13 42 32N 125 40 E
ailuoto, Finland .... 8 D21 65 3N 24 45 E
ainan ○, China .... 33 E5 19 0N 109 30 E
ainaut □, Belgium .... 15 D4 50 30N 4 0 E
aines, Alaska, U.S.A. 70 B1 59 14N 135 26W
aines, Oreg., U.S.A. 76 D5 44 55N 117 56W
aines City, U.S.A. 83 L5 28 7N 81 38W
aines Junction, Canada 70 A1 60 45N 137 30W
aiphong, Vietnam .... 32 D5 20 47N 106 41 E
aiti ■, W. Indies 89 C5 19 0N 72 30W
aiya, Sudan .... 51 E13 18 20N 36 21 E
aiyang, China .... 35 F11 36 47N 121 9 E
aiyuan, China .... 34 F3 36 35N 105 52 E
aizhou, China .... 35 G10 34 37N 119 7 E
aizhou Wan, China .... 35 G10 34 50N 119 20 E
ajdúböszörmény, Hungary .... 17 E11 47 40N 21 30 E
ajipur, India .... 43 G11 25 45N 85 13 E
ajji Muhsin, Iraq .... 44 C5 32 35N 45 29 E
ajjiābād, Iraq .... 45 D7 28 19N 55 55 E
ajjiābād-e Zarrin, Iran .... 45 C7 33 9N 54 51 E
ajnówka, Poland .... 17 B12 52 47N 23 35 E
akansson, Mts., Dem. Rep. of the Congo .... 55 D2 8 40S 25 45 E
akkâri, Turkey .... 44 B4 37 34N 43 44 E
akken-Zan, Japan .... 31 G7 34 10N 135 54 E
akodate, Japan .... 30 D10 41 45N 140 44 E
akos, Namibia .... 56 C2 23 13S 16 21 E
aku-San, Japan .... 31 F8 36 9N 136 46 E
aku-San, Japan .... 31 F8 36 15N 136 45 E
akui, Japan .... 31 F8 36 53N 136 47 E
alab, Pakistan .... 40 G6 25 43N 68 20 E
alab, Syria .... 44 B3 36 10N 37 15 E
alabjah, Iraq .... 44 C5 35 10N 45 58 E
alaib, Sudan .... 51 D13 22 12N 36 30 E
alat 'Ammār, Si. Arabia .... 44 D3 29 10N 36 4 E
albā, Lebanon .... 46 A5 34 34N 36 6 E
alberstadt, Germany .... 16 C6 51 54N 11 3 E
alcombe, N.Z. .... 59 J5 40 8S 175 30 E
alcon, Phil. .... 37 B6 13 0N 121 30 E
alden, Norway .... 9 G14 59 9N 11 23 E
aldia, India .... 41 H16 22 5N 88 3 E
aldimand, Canada 84 D5 42 59N 79 52W
aldwani, India .... 43 E8 29 31N 79 30 E
ale →, Australia .... 62 C2 24 56S 135 53 E
alesowen, U.K. 13 E5 52 27N 2 3W
alesworth, U.K. .... 13 E9 52 20N 1 31 E
aleyville, U.S.A. 83 H2 34 14N 87 37W
alfmoon Bay, N.Z. .... 59 M2 46 50S 168 5 E
alfway →, Canada 70 B4 56 12N 121 32W
alia, India .... 43 G10 24 50N 82 19 E
aliburton, Canada 84 A6 45 3N 78 30W
alifax, Australia .... 62 B4 18 32S 146 22 E
alifax, Canada 73 D7 44 38N 63 35W
alifax, U.K. 12 D6 53 43N 1 52W
alifax, U.S.A. 84 F8 40 25N 76 55W
alifax B., Australia .... 62 B4 18 50S 147 0 E
alifax I., Namibia .... 56 D2 26 38S 15 4 E
alīl →, Iran .... 45 E8 27 40N 58 30 E
alkirk, U.K. 11 C5 58 30N 3 29W
all Beach = Sanirajak, Canada 69 B11 68 46N 81 12W
all Pen., Canada 69 B13 63 30N 66 0W
all Pt., Australia .... 60 C3 15 40S 124 23 E
alland, Sweden .... 9 H15 57 8N 12 47 E
alle, Belgium .... 15 D4 50 44N 4 13 E
alle, Germany .... 16 C6 51 30N 11 56 E
allefors, Sweden .... 9 G16 59 47N 14 31 E
allett, Australia .... 63 E2 33 25S 138 55 E
allettsville, U.S.A. 81 L6 29 27N 96 57W
allim, S. Korea .... 35 H14 33 24N 126 15 E
allingdalselvi →, Norway .... 9 F13 60 23N 9 35 E
allock, U.S.A. 80 A6 48 47N 96 57W
alls Creek, Australia .... 60 C4 18 16S 127 38 E
allsberg, Sweden .... 9 G16 59 5N 15 7 E
almahera, Indonesia .... 37 D7 0 40N 128 0 E
alsingborg = Helsingborg, Sweden .... 9 H15 56 41N 12 52 E
alsingland, Sweden .... 9 F16 61 40N 16 5 E
alstead, U.K. .... 13 F8 51 57N 0 40 E
alti, Finland .... 8 B19 69 17N 21 18 E
alton, U.K. 12 D5 53 22N 2 45W
alūl, Qatar .... 45 E7 25 40N 52 40 E
alvad, India .... 42 H4 23 1N 71 11 E
alvān, Iran .... 45 C8 33 57N 56 15 E
am Tan, Vietnam .... 39 G6 10 40N 107 45 E

Ham Yen, Vietnam .... 38 A5 22 4N 105 3 E
Hamab, Namibia .... 56 D2 28 7S 19 16 E
Hamada, Japan .... 31 G6 34 56N 132 4 E
Hamadān, Iran .... 45 C6 34 52N 48 32 E
Hamadān □, Iran .... 45 C6 35 0N 49 0 E
Hamāh, Syria .... 44 C3 35 5N 36 40 E
Hamamatsu, Japan .... 31 G8 34 45N 137 45 E
Hamar, Norway .... 9 F14 60 48N 11 7 E
Hamâta, Gebel, Egypt .... 44 E2 24 17N 35 0 E
Hambantota, Sri Lanka .... 40 R12 6 10N 81 10 E
Hamber ○, Canada 70 C5 52 20N 118 0W
Hamburg, Germany .... 16 B5 53 33N 9 59 E
Hamburg, Ark., U.S.A. 81 J9 33 14N 91 48W
Hamburg, N.Y., U.S.A. 84 D6 42 43N 78 50W
Hamburg, Pa., U.S.A. 85 F9 40 33N 75 59W
Ḥamd, W. al →, Si. Arabia .... 44 E3 24 55N 36 20 E
Hämeen, Finland .... 9 F20 61 38N 25 10 E
Hämeenlinna, Finland .... 9 F21 61 0N 24 28 E
Hamelin Pool, Australia .... 61 E1 26 22S 114 20 E
Hameln, Germany .... 16 B5 52 6N 9 21 E
Hamerkaz □, Israel .... 46 C3 32 15N 34 55 E
Hamersley Ra., Australia .... 60 D2 22 0S 117 45 E
Hamhung, N. Korea .... 35 E14 39 54N 127 30 E
Hami, China .... 32 B4 42 55N 93 25 E
Hamilton, Australia .... 63 F3 37 45S 142 2 E
Hamilton, Canada 84 C5 43 15N 79 50W
Hamilton, N.Z. .... 59 G5 37 47S 175 19 E
Hamilton, U.K. 11 F4 55 46N 4 2W
Hamilton, Ala., U.S.A. 83 H1 34 9N 87 59W
Hamilton, Mont., U.S.A. 76 C6 46 15N 114 10W
Hamilton, N.Y., U.S.A. 85 D9 42 50N 75 33W
Hamilton, Ohio, U.S.A. 82 F3 39 24N 84 34W
Hamilton, Tex., U.S.A. 81 K5 31 42N 98 7W
Hamilton →, Australia .... 62 C2 23 30S 139 47 E
Hamilton City, U.S.A. 78 F4 39 45N 122 1W
Hamilton I., Australia .... 62 J6 20 21S 148 56 E
Hamilton Inlet, Canada 73 B8 54 0N 57 30W
Hamilton Mt., U.S.A. 85 C10 43 25N 74 22W
Hamina, Finland .... 9 F22 60 34N 27 12 E
Hamirpur, H.P., India .... 42 D7 31 41N 76 31 E
Hamirpur, Ut. P., India .... 43 G9 25 57N 80 9 E
Hamlet, U.S.A. 83 H6 34 53N 79 42W
Hamley Bridge, Australia .... 63 E2 34 17S 138 35 E
Hamlin = Hameln, Germany .... 16 B5 52 6N 9 21 E
Hamlin, N.Y., U.S.A. 84 C7 43 17N 77 55W
Hamlin, Tex., U.S.A. 81 J4 32 53N 100 8W
Hamm, Germany .... 16 C4 51 40N 7 50 E
Ḥammār, Hawr al, Iraq .... 44 D5 30 50N 47 10 E
Hammerfest, Norway .... 8 A20 70 39N 23 41 E
Hammond, Ind., U.S.A. 82 E2 41 38N 87 30W
Hammond, La., U.S.A. 81 K9 30 30N 90 28W
Hammond, N.Y., U.S.A. 85 B9 44 27N 75 42W
Hammondsport, U.S.A. 84 D7 42 25N 77 13W
Hammonton, U.S.A. 82 F8 39 39N 74 48W
Hampden, N.Z. .... 59 L3 45 18S 170 50 E
Hampshire □, U.K. 13 F6 51 7N 1 23W
Hampshire Downs, U.K. 13 F6 51 15N 1 10W
Hampton, N.B., Canada 73 C6 45 30N 65 51W
Hampton, Ont., Canada 84 C6 43 58N 78 45W
Hampton, Ark., U.S.A. 81 J8 33 32N 92 28W
Hampton, Iowa, U.S.A. 80 D8 42 45N 93 13W
Hampton, N.H., U.S.A. 85 D14 42 57N 70 50W
Hampton, S.C., U.S.A. 83 J5 32 52N 81 7W
Hampton, Va., U.S.A. 82 G7 37 2N 76 21W
Hampton Bays, U.S.A. 85 F12 40 53N 72 30W
Hampton Tableland, Australia .... 61 F4 32 0S 127 0 E
Hamyang, S. Korea .... 35 G14 35 32N 127 42 E
Han Pijesak, Bos.-H. .... 23 B8 44 5N 18 57 E
Hanak, Si. Arabia .... 44 E3 25 32N 37 0 E
Hanamaki, Japan .... 30 E10 39 23N 141 7 E
Hanang, Tanzania .... 54 C4 4 30S 35 25 E
Hanau, Germany .... 16 C5 50 7N 8 56 E
Hanbogd = Ihbulag, Mongolia .... 34 C4 43 11N 107 10 E
Hancheng, China .... 34 G6 35 31N 110 25 E
Hancock, Mich., U.S.A. 80 B10 47 8N 88 35W
Hancock, N.Y., U.S.A. 85 E9 41 57N 75 17W
Handa, Japan .... 31 G8 34 53N 136 55 E
Handan, China .... 34 F8 36 35N 114 28 E
Handeni, Tanzania .... 54 D4 5 25S 38 2 E
Handwara, India .... 43 B6 34 21N 74 20 E
Hanegev, Israel .... 46 E4 30 50N 35 0 E
Hanford, U.S.A. 78 J7 36 20N 119 39W
Hanford Reach →, U.S.A. 76 C4 46 40N 119 28W
Hang Chat, Thailand .... 38 C2 18 20N 99 21 E
Hang Dong, Thailand .... 38 C2 18 41N 98 55 E
Hangang →, S. Korea .... 35 F14 37 50N 126 30 E
Hangayn Nuruu, Mongolia .... 32 B4 47 30N 99 0 E
Hangchou = Hangzhou, China .... 33 C7 30 18N 120 11 E
Hanggin Houqi, China .... 34 D4 40 58N 107 4 E
Hanggin Qi, China .... 34 E5 39 52N 108 50 E
Hangu, China .... 35 E9 39 18N 117 53 E
Hangzhou, China .... 33 C7 30 18N 120 11 E
Hangzhou Wan, China .... 33 C7 30 15N 120 45 E
Hanhongor, Mongolia .... 34 C3 43 55N 104 28 E
Ḥanīdh, Si. Arabia .... 45 E6 26 35N 48 38 E
Ḥanīsh, Yemen .... 47 E3 13 45N 42 46 E
Hankinson, U.S.A. 80 B6 46 4N 96 54W
Hanko, Finland .... 9 G20 59 50N 22 57 E
Hanksville, U.S.A. 77 G8 38 22N 110 43W
Hanle, India .... 43 C8 32 42N 79 4 E
Hanmer Springs, N.Z. .... 59 K4 42 32S 172 50 E
Hann →, Australia .... 60 C4 17 26S 126 17 E
Hann, Mt., Australia .... 60 C4 15 45S 126 0 E
Hanna, Canada 70 C6 51 40N 111 54W
Hanna, U.S.A. 76 F10 41 52N 106 34W
Hannah B., Canada 72 B4 51 40N 80 0W
Hannibal, Mo., U.S.A. 80 F9 39 42N 91 22W
Hannibal, N.Y., U.S.A. 85 C8 43 19N 76 35W
Hannover, Germany .... 16 B5 52 22N 9 46 E
Hanoi, Vietnam .... 32 D5 21 5N 105 55 E
Hanover = Hannover, Germany .... 16 B5 52 22N 9 46 E
Hanover, Canada 84 B3 44 9N 81 2W
Hanover, S. Africa .... 56 E3 31 4S 24 29 E
Hanover, N.H., U.S.A. 85 C12 43 42N 72 17W
Hanover, Ohio, U.S.A. 84 F2 40 4N 82 16W
Hanover, Pa., U.S.A. 82 F7 39 48N 76 59W
Hanover, I., Chile 96 G2 51 0S 74 50W
Hans Lollik I., U.S. Virgin Is. .... 89 e 18 24N 64 53W
Hansdiha, India .... 43 G12 24 36N 87 5 E
Hansi, India .... 42 E6 29 10N 75 57 E
Hanson, L., Australia .... 63 E2 31 0S 136 15 E
Hantsavichy, Belarus .... 17 B14 52 49N 26 30 E
Hanumangarh, India .... 42 E6 29 35N 74 19 E
Hanzhong, China .... 34 H4 33 10N 107 1 E
Hanzhuang, China .... 35 G9 34 33N 117 23 E
Haora, India .... 43 H13 22 37N 88 20 E

Haparanda, Sweden .... 8 D21 65 52N 24 8 E
Happy, U.S.A. 81 H4 34 45N 101 52W
Happy Camp, U.S.A. 76 F2 41 48N 123 23W
Happy Valley-Goose Bay, Canada 73 B7 53 15N 60 20W
Hapsu, N. Korea .... 35 D15 41 13N 128 51 E
Hapur, India .... 42 E7 28 45N 77 45 E
Ḥaql, Si. Arabia .... 46 F3 29 10N 34 58 E
Har, Indonesia .... 37 F8 5 16S 133 14 E
Har-Ayrag, Mongolia .... 34 B5 45 47N 109 16 E
Har Hu, China .... 32 C4 38 20N 97 38 E
Har Us Nuur, Mongolia .... 32 B4 48 0N 92 0 E
Har Yehuda, Israel .... 46 D3 31 35N 34 57 E
Ḥaraḍ, Si. Arabia .... 47 C4 24 22N 49 0 E
Haranomachi, Japan .... 30 F10 37 38N 140 58 E
Harbin, China .... 35 B14 45 48N 126 40 E
Harbor Beach, U.S.A. 84 C2 43 51N 82 39W
Harbour Breton, Canada 73 C8 47 29N 55 50W
Harbour Deep, Canada 73 B8 50 25N 56 32W
Harda, India .... 42 H7 22 27N 77 5 E
Hardangerfjorden, Norway .... 9 F12 60 5N 6 0 E
Hardangervidda, Norway .... 9 F12 60 7N 7 20 E
Hardap ○, Namibia .... 56 C2 24 29S 17 45 E
Hardap Dam, Namibia .... 56 C2 24 32S 17 50 E
Hardenberg, Neths. .... 15 B6 52 34N 6 37 E
Harderwijk, Neths. .... 15 B5 52 21N 5 38 E
Hardey →, Australia .... 60 D2 22 45S 116 8 E
Hardin, U.S.A. 76 D10 45 44N 107 37W
Harding, S. Africa .... 57 E4 30 35S 29 55 E
Harding Ra., Australia .... 60 C3 16 17S 124 55 E
Hardisty, Canada 70 C6 52 40N 111 18W
Hardoi, India .... 43 F9 27 26N 80 6 E
Hardwar = Haridwar, India .... 42 E8 29 58N 78 9 E
Hardwick, U.S.A. 85 B12 44 30N 72 22W
Hardy, Pen., Chile 96 H3 55 30S 68 20W
Hare B., Canada 73 B8 51 15N 55 45W
Hareid, Norway .... 9 E12 62 22N 6 1 E
Harer, Ethiopia .... 47 F3 9 20N 42 8 E
Hargeisa, Somali Rep. .... 47 F3 9 30N 44 2 E
Hari →, Indonesia .... 36 E2 1 16S 104 5 E
Haria, Canary Is. 24 E6 29 8N 13 32W
Haridwar, India .... 42 E8 29 58N 78 9 E
Harim, Jabal al, Oman .... 45 E8 25 58N 56 14 E
Haringhata →, Bangla. .... 41 J16 22 0N 89 58 E
Harirūd →, Asia .... 40 A2 37 24N 60 38 E
Härjedalen, Sweden .... 9 E15 62 22N 13 5 E
Harlan, Iowa, U.S.A. 80 E7 41 39N 95 19W
Harlan, Ky., U.S.A. 83 G4 36 51N 83 19W
Harlech, U.K. 12 E3 52 52N 4 6W
Harlem, U.S.A. 76 B9 48 32N 108 47W
Harlingen, Neths. .... 15 A5 53 11N 5 25 E
Harlingen, U.S.A. 81 M6 26 12N 97 42W
Harlow, U.K. .... 13 F8 51 46N 0 8 E
Harlowton, U.S.A. 76 C9 46 26N 109 50W
Harnai, Pakistan .... 42 D2 30 6N 67 56 E
Harney Basin, U.S.A. 76 E4 43 30N 119 0W
Harney L., U.S.A. 76 E4 43 14N 119 8W
Harney Peak, U.S.A. 80 D3 43 52N 103 32W
Härnösand, Sweden .... 9 E17 62 38N 17 55 E
Haroldswick, U.K. 11 A8 60 48N 0 50W
Harp L., Canada 73 A7 55 5N 61 50W
Harper, Liberia 50 H4 4 25N 7 43W
Harrai, India .... 43 H8 22 37N 79 13 E
Harrand, Pakistan .... 42 E4 29 28N 70 3 E
Harricana →, Canada 72 B4 50 56N 79 32W
Harriman, U.S.A. 83 H3 35 56N 84 33W
Harrington Harbour, Canada 73 B8 50 31N 59 30W
Harris, U.K. 11 D2 57 50N 6 55W
Harris, L., Australia .... 63 E2 31 10S 135 10 E
Harris, Sd. of, U.K. 11 D1 57 44N 7 6W
Harris Pt., Canada 84 C2 43 6N 82 9W
Harrisburg, Ill., U.S.A. 81 G10 37 44N 88 32W
Harrisburg, Nebr., U.S.A. 80 E3 41 33N 103 44W
Harrisburg, Pa., U.S.A. 84 F8 40 16N 76 53W
Harrismith, S. Africa .... 57 D4 28 15S 29 8 E
Harrison, Ark., U.S.A. 81 G8 36 14N 93 7W
Harrison, Maine, U.S.A. 85 B14 44 7N 70 39W
Harrison, Nebr., U.S.A. 80 D3 42 41N 103 53W
Harrison, C., Canada 73 B8 54 55N 57 55W
Harrison L., Canada 70 D4 49 33N 121 50W
Harrisonburg, U.S.A. 82 F6 38 27N 78 52W
Harrisonville, U.S.A. 80 F7 38 39N 94 21W
Harriston, Canada 84 C4 43 57N 80 53W
Harrisville, Mich., U.S.A. 84 B1 44 39N 83 17W
Harrisville, N.Y., U.S.A. 85 B9 44 9N 75 19W
Harrisville, Pa., U.S.A. 84 E5 41 8N 80 0W
Harrodsburg, U.S.A. 82 G3 37 46N 84 51W
Harrogate, U.K. 12 C6 54 0N 1 33W
Harrow, U.K. 13 F7 51 35N 0 21W
Harrowsmith, Canada 85 B8 44 24N 76 40W
Harry S. Truman Reservoir, U.S.A. 80 F7 38 16N 93 24W
Harsin, Iran .... 44 C5 34 18N 47 33 E
Harstad, Norway .... 8 B17 68 48N 16 30 E
Harsud, India .... 42 H7 22 6N 76 44 E
Hart, U.S.A. 82 D2 43 42N 86 22W
Hart, L., Australia .... 63 E2 31 10S 136 25 E
Hartbees →, S. Africa .... 56 D3 28 45S 20 32 E
Hartford, Conn., U.S.A. 85 E12 41 46N 72 41W
Hartford, Ky., U.S.A. 82 G2 37 27N 86 55W
Hartford, S. Dak., U.S.A. 80 D6 43 38N 96 57W
Hartford, Wis., U.S.A. 80 D10 43 19N 88 22W
Hartford City, U.S.A. 82 E3 40 27N 85 22W
Hartland, Canada 73 C6 46 20N 67 32W
Hartland Pt., U.K. 13 F3 51 1N 4 32W
Hartlepool, U.K. 12 C6 54 42N 1 13W
Hartlepool □, U.K. 12 C6 54 42N 1 17W
Hartley Bay, Canada 70 C3 53 25N 129 15W
Hartmannberge, Namibia .... 56 B1 17 0S 13 0 E
Hartney, Canada 71 D8 49 30N 100 35W
Harts →, S. Africa .... 56 D3 28 24S 24 17 E
Hartselle, U.S.A. 83 H2 34 27N 86 56W
Hartshorne, U.S.A. 81 H7 34 51N 95 34W
Hartsville, U.S.A. 83 H5 34 23N 80 4W
Hartswater, S. Africa .... 56 D3 27 34S 24 43 E
Hartwell, U.S.A. 83 H4 34 21N 82 56W
Harunabad, Pakistan .... 42 E5 29 35N 73 8 E
Harvand, Iran .... 45 D7 28 25N 55 43 E
Harvey, Australia .... 61 F2 33 5S 115 54 E
Harvey, Ill., U.S.A. 82 E2 41 36N 87 50W
Harvey, N. Dak., U.S.A. 80 B5 47 47N 99 56W
Harwich, U.K. .... 13 F9 51 56N 1 17 E
Haryana □, India .... 42 E7 29 0N 76 10 E
Haryn →, Belarus .... 17 B14 52 7N 27 17 E
Harz, Germany .... 16 C6 51 38N 10 44 E

Hasa □, Si. Arabia .... 45 E6 25 50N 49 0 E
Ḥasanābād, Iran .... 45 C7 32 8N 52 44 E
Ḥasb, W. →, Iraq .... 44 D5 31 45N 44 17 E
Hasdo →, India .... 43 J10 21 44N 82 44 E
Hashimoto, Japan .... 31 G7 34 19N 135 37 E
Hashtjerd, Iran .... 45 C6 35 52N 50 40 E
Haskell, U.S.A. 81 J5 33 10N 99 44W
Haslemere, U.K. 13 F7 51 5N 0 43W
Hasselt, Belgium .... 15 D5 50 56N 5 21 E
Hassi Messaoud, Algeria .... 50 B7 31 51N 6 1 E
Hässleholm, Sweden .... 9 H15 56 10N 13 46 E
Hastings, N.Z. .... 59 H6 39 39S 176 52 E
Hastings, U.K. .... 13 G8 50 51N 0 35 E
Hastings, Mich., U.S.A. 82 D3 42 39N 85 17W
Hastings, Minn., U.S.A. 80 C8 44 44N 92 51W
Hastings, Nebr., U.S.A. 80 E5 40 35N 98 23W
Hastings Ra., Australia .... 63 E5 31 15S 152 14 E
Hat Yai, Thailand .... 39 J3 7 1N 100 27 E
Hatanbulag = Ergel, Mongolia .... 34 C5 43 8N 109 5 E
Hatay = Antalya, Turkey .... 19 G5 36 52N 30 45 E
Hatch, U.S.A. 77 K10 32 40N 107 9W
Hatchet L., Canada 71 B8 58 36N 103 40W
Hateruma-Shima, Japan .... 31 M1 24 3N 123 47 E
Hatfield P.O., Australia .... 63 E3 33 54S 143 49 E
Hatgal, Mongolia .... 32 A5 50 26N 100 9 E
Hathras, India .... 42 F8 27 36N 78 6 E
Hatia, Bangla. .... 41 H17 22 30N 91 5 E
Hato Mayor, Dom. Rep. 89 C6 18 46N 69 15W
Hatta, India .... 43 G8 24 7N 79 36 E
Hattah, Australia .... 63 E3 34 48S 142 17 E
Hatteras, C., U.S.A. 83 H8 35 14N 75 32W
Hattiesburg, U.S.A. 81 K10 31 20N 89 17W
Hatvan, Hungary .... 17 E10 47 40N 19 45 E
Hau Bon = Cheo Reo, Vietnam .... 36 B3 13 25N 108 28 E
Hau Duc, Vietnam .... 38 E7 15 20N 108 13 E
Haugesund, Norway .... 9 G11 59 23N 5 13 E
Haukipudas, Finland .... 8 D21 65 12N 25 20 E
Haultain →, Canada 71 B7 55 51N 106 46W
Hauraki G., N.Z. .... 59 G5 36 35S 175 5 E
Haut Atlas, Morocco 50 B4 32 30N 5 0W
Hautes Fagnes = Hohe Venn, Belgium .... 15 D6 50 30N 6 5 E
Hauts Plateaux, Algeria .... 48 C4 35 0N 1 0 E
Havana = La Habana, Cuba 88 B3 23 8N 82 22W
Havana, U.S.A. 80 E9 40 18N 90 4W
Havant, U.K. 13 G7 50 51N 0 58W
Havasor = Kığzı, Turkey .... 44 B4 38 18N 43 25 E
Havasu, L., U.S.A. 79 L12 34 18N 114 28W
Havel →, Germany .... 16 B7 52 50N 12 3 E
Havelian, Pakistan .... 42 B5 34 2N 73 10 E
Havelock, Canada 84 B7 44 26N 77 53W
Havelock, N.Z. .... 59 J4 41 17S 173 48 E
Havelock, U.S.A. 83 H7 34 53N 76 54W
Haverfordwest, U.K. 13 F3 51 48N 4 58W
Haverhill, U.S.A. 85 D13 42 47N 71 5W
Haverstraw, U.S.A. 85 E11 41 12N 73 58W
Havirga, Mongolia .... 34 B7 45 41N 113 5 E
Havířov, Czech Rep. .... 17 D10 49 46N 18 20 E
Havlíčkův Brod, Czech Rep. .... 16 D8 49 36N 15 33 E
Havre, U.S.A. 76 B9 48 33N 109 41W
Havre-Aubert, Canada 73 C7 47 12N 61 56W
Havre-St.-Pierre, Canada 73 B7 50 18N 63 33W
Haw →, U.S.A. 83 H6 35 36N 79 3W
Hawaii □, U.S.A. 74 H16 19 30N 156 30W
Hawaii I., Pac. Oc. 74 J17 19 30N 155 30W
Hawaiian Is., Pac. Oc. 74 H17 20 30N 156 0W
Hawaiian Ridge, Pac. Oc. 65 E11 24 0N 165 0W
Hawarden, Canada 80 D6 43 0N 96 29W
Hawea, L., N.Z. .... 59 L2 44 28S 169 19 E
Hawera, N.Z. .... 59 H5 39 35S 174 19 E
Hawick, U.K. 11 F6 55 26N 2 47W
Hawk Junction, Canada 72 C3 48 5N 84 38W
Hawke, B., N.Z. .... 59 H6 39 25S 177 20 E
Hawker, Australia .... 63 E2 31 59S 138 22 E
Hawkesbury, Canada 72 C5 45 37N 74 37W
Hawkesbury I., Canada 70 C3 53 37N 129 3W
Hawkesbury Pt., Australia .... 62 A1 11 55S 134 5 E
Hawkinsville, U.S.A. 83 J4 32 17N 83 28W
Hawley, Minn., U.S.A. 80 B6 46 53N 96 19W
Hawley, Pa., U.S.A. 85 E9 41 28N 75 11W
Ḥawrān, W. →, Iraq .... 44 C4 33 58N 42 34 E
Hawsh Mūssá, Lebanon .... 46 B4 33 45N 35 55 E
Hawthorne, U.S.A. 76 G4 38 32N 118 38W
Hay, Australia .... 63 E3 34 30S 144 51 E
Hay →, Australia .... 62 C2 24 50S 138 0 E
Hay, C., Australia .... 60 B4 14 5S 129 29 E
Hay I., Canada 84 B4 44 53N 80 58W
Hay L., Canada 70 B5 58 50N 118 50W
Hay-on-Wye, U.K. 13 E4 52 5N 3 8W
Hay River, Canada 70 A5 60 51N 115 44W
Hay Springs, U.S.A. 80 D3 42 41N 102 41W
Hayachine-San, Japan .... 30 E10 39 34N 141 29 E
Hayden, Australia .... 62 B3 18 0S 141 30 E
Hayes, U.S.A. 80 C4 44 23N 101 1W
Hayes →, Canada 72 A1 57 3N 92 12W
Hayes Creek, Australia .... 60 B5 13 43S 131 22 E
Hayle, U.K. 13 G2 50 11N 5 26W
Hayling I., U.K. 13 G7 50 48N 0 59W
Haymen I., Australia .... 62 J6 20 3S 148 52 E
Hayrabolu, Turkey .... 23 D12 41 12N 27 5 E
Hays, Canada 70 C6 50 6N 111 48W
Hays, U.S.A. 80 F5 38 53N 99 20W
Haysyn, Ukraine .... 17 D15 48 57N 29 25 E
Hayvoron, Ukraine .... 17 D15 48 22N 29 52 E
Hayward, Calif., U.S.A. 78 H4 37 40N 122 5W
Hayward, Wis., U.S.A. 80 B9 46 1N 91 29W
Haywards Heath, U.K. 13 G7 51 0N 0 5W
Hazafon □, Israel .... 46 C4 32 40N 35 20 E
Hazārān, Kūh-e, Iran .... 45 D8 29 35N 57 20 E
Hazard, U.S.A. 82 G4 37 15N 83 12W
Hazaribag, India .... 43 H11 23 58N 85 26 E
Hazaribag Road, India .... 43 G11 24 12N 85 57 E
Hazelton, Canada 70 B3 55 20N 127 42W
Hazen, U.S.A. 80 B4 47 18N 101 38W
Hazlehurst, Ga., U.S.A. 83 K4 31 52N 82 36W
Hazlehurst, Miss., U.S.A. 81 K9 31 52N 90 24W
Hazlet, U.S.A. 85 F10 40 25N 74 12W
Hazleton, U.S.A. 85 F9 40 57N 75 59W
Hazlett, L., Australia .... 60 D4 21 30S 128 48 E
Hazro, Turkey .... 44 B4 38 15N 40 47 E
Head of Bight, Australia .... 61 F5 31 30S 131 25 E
Headlands, Zimbabwe .... 55 F3 18 15S 32 2 E

Healdsburg, U.S.A. 78 G4 38 37N 122 52W
Healdton, U.S.A. 81 H6 34 14N 97 29W
Healesville, Australia .... 63 F4 37 35S 145 30 E
Heany Junction, Zimbabwe .. 57 C4 20 6S 28 54 E
Heard I., Ind. Oc. .... 3 G13 53 0S 74 0 E
Hearne, U.S.A. 81 K6 30 53N 96 36W
Hearst, Canada 72 C3 49 40N 83 41W
Heart →, U.S.A. 80 B4 46 46N 100 50W
Heart's Content, Canada 73 C9 47 54N 53 27W
Heath, Pte., Canada 73 C7 49 8N 61 40W
Heathrow, London ✈ (LHR), U.K. 13 F7 51 28N 0 27W
Heavener, U.S.A. 81 H7 34 53N 94 36W
Hebbronville, U.S.A. 81 M5 27 18N 98 41W
Hebei □, China .... 34 E9 39 0N 116 0 E
Hebel, Australia .... 63 D4 28 58S 147 47 E
Heber, U.S.A. 79 N11 32 44N 115 32W
Heber City, U.S.A. 76 F8 40 31N 111 25W
Heber Springs, U.S.A. 81 H9 35 30N 92 2W
Hebert, Canada 71 C7 50 30N 107 10W
Hebgen L., U.S.A. 76 D8 44 52N 111 20W
Hebi, China .... 34 G8 35 57N 114 7 E
Hebrides, U.K. 6 D4 57 30N 7 0W
Hebrides, Sea of the, U.K. 11 D2 57 5N 7 0W
Hebron = Al Khalīl, West Bank . 46 D4 31 32N 35 6 E
Hebron, Canada 69 C13 58 5N 62 30W
Hebron, N. Dak., U.S.A. 80 B3 46 54N 102 3W
Hebron, Nebr., U.S.A. 80 E6 40 10N 97 35W
Hecate Str., Canada 70 C2 53 10N 130 30W
Heceta I., U.S.A. 70 B2 55 46N 133 40W
Hechi, China .... 32 D5 24 40N 108 2 E
Hechuan, China .... 32 C5 30 2N 106 12 E
Hecla, U.S.A. 80 C5 45 53N 98 9W
Hecla I., Canada 71 C9 51 10N 96 43W
Hede, Sweden .... 9 E15 62 23N 13 30 E
Hedemora, Sweden .... 9 F16 60 18N 15 58 E
Heerde, Neths. .... 15 B6 52 24N 6 2 E
Heerenveen, Neths. .... 15 B5 52 57N 5 55 E
Heerhugowaard, Neths. ...... 15 B4 52 40N 4 51 E
Heerlen, Neths. .... 15 D5 50 55N 5 58 E
Hefa, Israel .... 46 C4 32 46N 35 0 E
Hefa □, Israel .... 46 C4 32 40N 35 0 E
Hefei, China .... 33 C6 31 52N 117 18 E
Hegang, China .... 33 B8 47 20N 130 19 E
Hei Ling Chau, China .... 33 G11 22 15N 114 2 E
Heichengzhen, China .... 34 F4 36 24N 106 3 E
Heidelberg, Germany .... 16 D5 49 24N 8 42 E
Heidelberg, S. Africa .... 56 E3 34 6S 20 59 E
Heilbron, S. Africa .... 57 D4 27 16S 27 59 E
Heilbronn, Germany .... 16 D5 49 9N 9 13 E
Heilongjiang □, China .... 33 B7 48 0N 126 0 E
Heilunkiang = Heilongjiang □,
China .... 33 B7 48 0N 126 0 E
Heimaey, Iceland 8 E3 63 26N 20 17W
Heinola, Finland .... 9 F22 61 13N 26 2 E
Heinze Kyun, Burma .... 38 E1 14 25N 97 45 E
Heishan, China .... 35 D12 41 40N 122 5 E
Heishui, China .... 35 C10 42 8N 119 30 E
Hejaz = Ḥijāz □, Si. Arabia ... 44 E3 24 0N 40 0 E
Hejian, China .... 34 E9 38 25N 116 5 E
Hejin, China .... 34 G6 35 35N 110 42 E
Hekimhan, Turkey .... 44 B3 38 50N 37 55 E
Hekla, Iceland 8 E4 63 56N 19 35W
Hekou, China .... 32 D5 22 30N 103 59 E
Helan Shan, China .... 34 E3 38 30N 105 55 E
Helen Atoll, Pac. Oc. .... 37 D8 2 40N 132 0 E
Helena, Ark., U.S.A. 81 H9 34 32N 90 36W
Helena, Mont., U.S.A. 76 C7 46 36N 112 2W
Helendale, U.S.A. 79 L9 34 44N 117 19W
Helensburgh, U.K. 11 E4 56 1N 4 43W
Helensville, N.Z. .... 59 G5 36 41S 174 29 E
Helenvale, Australia .... 62 B4 15 43S 145 14 E
Helgeland, Norway .... 8 C15 66 7N 13 29 E
Helgoland, Germany .... 16 A4 54 10N 7 53 E
Heligoland = Helgoland,
Germany .... 16 A4 54 10N 7 53 E
Heligoland B. = Deutsche Bucht,
Germany .... 16 A5 54 15N 8 0 E
Hella, Iceland 8 E3 63 50N 20 24W
Hellertown, U.S.A. 85 F9 40 35N 75 21W
Hellespont = Çanakkale Boğazı,
Turkey .... 23 D12 40 17N 26 32 E
Hellevoetsluis, Neths. .... 15 C4 51 50N 4 8 E
Hellhole Gorge △, Australia .. 62 D3 25 31S 144 12 E
Hellín, Spain 21 C5 38 31N 1 40W
Hells Canyon ◠, U.S.A. 76 D5 45 30N 117 45W
Hell's Gate △, Kenya .... 54 C4 0 54S 36 19 E
Helmand □, Afghan. .... 40 D4 31 20N 64 0 E
Helmand →, Afghan. .... 40 D2 31 12N 61 34 E
Helmeringhausen, Namibia .. 56 D2 25 54S 16 57 E
Helmond, Neths. .... 15 C5 51 29N 5 41 E
Helmsdale, U.K. 11 C5 58 7N 3 39W
Helmsdale →, U.K. 11 C5 58 7N 3 40W
Helong, China .... 35 C15 42 40N 129 0 E
Helper, U.S.A. 76 G8 39 41N 110 51W
Helsingborg, Sweden .... 9 H15 56 3N 12 42 E
Helsingfors = Helsinki, Finland 9 F21 60 15N 25 3 E
Helsingør, Denmark .... 9 H15 56 2N 12 35 E
Helsinki, Finland .... 9 F21 60 15N 25 3 E
Helston, U.K. 13 G2 50 6N 5 17W
Helvellyn, U.K. 12 C4 54 32N 3 1W
Helwân, Egypt .... 51 C12 29 50N 31 20 E
Hemel Hempstead, U.K. 13 F7 51 44N 0 28W
Hemet, U.S.A. 79 M10 33 45N 116 58W
Hemingford, U.S.A. 80 D3 42 19N 103 4W
Hemmingford, Canada 85 A11 45 3N 73 35W
Hempstead, U.S.A. 81 K6 30 6N 96 5W
Hemse, Sweden .... 9 H18 57 15N 18 22 E
Henan □, China .... 34 H8 34 0N 114 0 E
Henares →, Spain 21 B4 40 24N 3 30W
Henashi-Misaki, Japan .... 30 D9 40 37N 139 51 E
Henderson, Argentina 94 D3 36 18S 61 43W
Henderson, Ky., U.S.A. 82 G2 37 50N 87 35W
Henderson, N.C., U.S.A. 83 G6 36 20N 78 25W
Henderson, Nev., U.S.A. 79 J12 36 2N 114 59W
Henderson, Tenn., U.S.A. 83 H1 35 26N 88 38W
Henderson, Tex., U.S.A. 81 J7 32 9N 94 48W
Hendersonville, N.C., U.S.A. .. 83 H4 35 19N 82 28W
Hendersonville, Tenn., U.S.A. . 83 G2 36 18N 86 37W
Hendijān, Iran .... 45 D6 30 14N 49 43 E
Hendorābī, Iran .... 45 E7 26 40N 53 37 E
Hengcheng, China .... 34 E4 38 18N 106 28 E
Hengdaohezi, China .... 35 B15 44 52N 129 0 E
Hengelo, Neths. .... 15 B6 52 16N 6 48 E
Henggang, China .... 33 F11 22 39N 114 12 E
Hengmen, China .... 33 F10 22 33N 113 35 E
Hengqin Dao, China .... 33 G10 22 7N 113 34 E
Hengshan, China .... 34 F5 37 58N 109 5 E

Hengshui, China .... 34 F8 37 41N 115 40 E
Hengyang, China .... 33 D6 26 59N 112 22 E
Henley-on-Thames, U.K. 13 F7 51 32N 0 54W
Henlopen, C., U.S.A. 82 F8 38 48N 75 6W
Hennenman, S. Africa .... 56 D4 27 59S 27 1 E
Hennessey, U.S.A. 81 G6 36 6N 97 54W
Henri Pittier △, Venezuela 89 D6 10 26N 67 37W
Henrietta, U.S.A. 81 J5 33 49N 98 12W
Henrietta, Ostrov = Genriyetty,
Ostrov, Russia .... 29 B16 77 6N 156 30 E
Henrietta Maria, C., Canada ... 72 A3 55 9N 82 20W
Henry, U.S.A. 80 E10 41 7N 89 22W
Henryetta, U.S.A. 81 H7 35 27N 95 59W
Henryville, Canada 85 A11 45 8N 73 11W
Hensall, Canada 84 C3 43 26N 81 30W
Hentiesbaai, Namibia .... 56 C1 22 8S 14 18 E
Hentiyn Nuruu, Mongolia .... 33 B5 48 30N 108 30 E
Henty, Australia .... 63 F4 35 30S 147 0 E
Henzada, Burma .... 41 L19 17 38N 95 26 E
Heppner, U.S.A. 76 D4 45 21N 119 33W
Hepworth, Canada 84 B3 44 37N 81 9W
Hequ, China .... 34 E6 39 20N 111 15 E
Héraðsflói, Iceland 8 D6 65 42N 14 12W
Héraðsvötn →, Iceland 8 D4 65 45N 19 25W
Heraklion = Iráklion, Greece .. 25 D7 35 20N 25 12 E
Herald Cays, Australia .... 62 B4 16 58S 149 9 E
Herāt, Afghan. .... 40 B3 34 20N 62 7 E
Herāt □, Afghan. .... 40 B3 35 0N 62 0 E
Herbert →, Australia .... 62 B4 18 31S 146 17 E
Herbert River Falls △, Australia 62 B4 18 15S 145 32 E
Herberton, Australia .... 62 B4 17 20S 145 25 E
Herbertsdale, S. Africa .... 56 E3 34 1S 21 46 E
Herceg-Novi, Serbia & M. ..... 23 C8 42 30N 18 33 E
Herchmer, Canada 71 B10 57 22N 94 10W
Herðubreið, Iceland 8 D5 65 11N 16 21W
Hereford, U.K. 13 E5 52 4N 2 43W
Hereford, U.S.A. 81 H3 34 49N 102 24W
Herefordshire □, U.K. 13 E5 52 8N 2 40W
Herentals, Belgium .... 15 C4 51 12N 4 51 E
Herford, Germany .... 16 B5 52 7N 8 39 E
Herington, U.S.A. 80 F6 38 40N 96 57W
Herkimer, U.S.A. 85 D10 43 0N 74 59W
Herlong, U.S.A. 78 E6 40 8N 120 8W
Herm, U.K. 13 H5 49 30N 2 28W
Hermann, U.S.A. 80 F9 38 42N 91 27W
Hermannsburg, Australia .... 60 D5 23 57S 132 45 E
Hermanus, S. Africa .... 56 E2 34 27S 19 12 E
Hermidale, Australia .... 63 E4 31 30S 146 42 E
Hermiston, U.S.A. 76 D4 45 51N 119 17W
Hermite, I., Chile 96 H3 55 50S 68 0W
Hermon, U.S.A. 85 B9 44 28N 75 14W
Hermon, Mt. = Shaykh, J. ash,
Lebanon .... 46 B4 33 25N 35 50 E
Hermosillo, Mexico 86 B2 29 10N 111 0W
Hernád →, Hungary .... 17 D11 47 56N 21 8 E
Hernandarias, Paraguay 95 B5 25 20S 54 40W
Hernandez, U.S.A. 78 J6 36 24N 120 46W
Hernando, Argentina 94 C3 32 28S 63 40W
Hernando, U.S.A. 81 H10 34 50N 90 0W
Herndon, U.S.A. 84 F8 40 43N 76 51W
Herne, Germany .... 15 C7 51 32N 7 14 E
Herne Bay, U.K. .... 13 F9 51 21N 1 8 E
Herning, Denmark .... 9 H13 56 8N 8 58 E
Heroica = Caborca, Mexico ... 86 A2 30 40N 112 10W
Heroica Nogales = Nogales,
Mexico 86 A2 31 20N 110 56W
Heron Bay, Canada 72 C2 48 40N 86 25W
Herradura, Pta. de la, Canary Is. 24 F5 28 26N 14 8W
Herreid, U.S.A. 80 C4 45 50N 100 4W
Herrin, U.S.A. 81 G10 37 48N 89 2W
Herriot, Canada 71 B8 56 22N 101 16W
Herschel I., Canada 4 C1 69 35N 139 5W
Hershey, U.S.A. 85 F8 40 17N 76 39W
Hersonissos, Greece .... 25 D7 35 18N 25 22 E
Herstal, Belgium .... 15 D5 50 40N 5 38 E
Hertford, U.K. 13 F7 51 48N 0 4W
Hertfordshire □, U.K. 13 F7 51 51N 0 5W
's-Hertogenbosch, Neths. .... 15 C5 51 42N 5 17 E
Hertzogville, S. Africa .... 56 D4 28 9S 25 30 E
Hervey B., Australia .... 62 C5 25 0S 152 52 E
Herzliyya, Israel .... 46 C3 32 10N 34 50 E
Heşār, Fārs, Iran .... 45 D6 29 52N 50 16 E
Heşār, Markazī, Iran .... 45 C6 35 50N 49 12 E
Heshui, China .... 34 G5 35 48N 108 0 E
Heshun, China .... 34 F7 37 22N 113 32 E
Hesperia, U.S.A. 79 L9 34 25N 117 18W
Hesse = Hessen □, Germany .. 16 C5 50 30N 9 0 E
Hessen □, Germany .... 16 C5 50 30N 9 0 E
Hetch Hetchy Aqueduct, U.S.A. 78 H3 37 29N 122 19W
Hettinger, U.S.A. 80 C3 46 0N 102 42W
Heuvelton, U.S.A. 85 B9 44 37N 75 25W
Hexham, U.K. 12 C5 54 58N 2 4W
Hexigten Qi, China .... 35 C9 43 18N 117 30 E
Heydarābād, Iran .... 45 D7 30 33N 55 38 E
Heysham, U.K. 12 C5 54 3N 2 53W
Heywood, Australia .... 63 F3 38 8S 141 37 E
Heze, China .... 34 G8 35 14N 115 20 E
Hi, Ko, Thailand .... 39 a 7 44N 98 22 E
Hi Vista, U.S.A. 79 L9 34 45N 117 46W
Hialeah, U.S.A. 83 N5 25 50N 80 17W
Hiawatha, U.S.A. 80 F7 39 51N 95 32W
Hibbing, U.S.A. 80 B8 47 25N 92 56W
Hibbs B., Australia .... 63 G4 42 35S 145 15 E
Hibernia Reef, Australia ...... 60 B3 12 0S 123 23 E
Hickman, U.S.A. 81 G10 36 34N 89 11W
Hickory, U.S.A. 83 H5 35 44N 81 21W
Hicks, Pt., Australia .... 63 F4 37 49S 149 17 E
Hicks L., Canada 71 A9 61 25N 100 0W
Hicksville, U.S.A. 85 F11 40 46N 73 32W
Hida-Gawa →, Japan .... 31 G8 35 26N 137 3 E
Hida-Sammyaku, Japan ...... 31 F8 36 30N 137 40 E
Hidaka-Sammyaku, Japan .... 30 C11 42 35N 142 45 E
Hidalgo, Mexico 87 C5 24 15N 99 26W
Hidalgo □, Mexico 87 C5 20 30N 99 10W
Hidalgo, Presa M., Mexico 86 B3 26 30N 108 35W
Hidalgo del Parral, Mexico 86 B3 26 56N 105 40W
Hierro, Canary Is. 24 G1 27 44N 18 0W
Higashiajima-San, Japan ..... 30 F10 37 40N 140 10 E
Higashiōsaka, Japan .... 31 G7 34 40N 135 37 E
Higgins, U.S.A. 81 G4 36 7N 100 2W
Higgins Corner, U.S.A. 78 F5 39 2N 121 5W
High Bridge, U.S.A. 85 F10 40 40N 74 54W

High River, Canada 70 C6 50 30N 113 50W
High Tatra = Tatry, Slovak Rep. . 17 D11 49 20N 20 0 E
High Veld, Africa .... 48 J6 27 0S 27 0 E
High Wycombe, U.K. 13 F7 51 37N 0 45W
Highland □, U.K. 11 D4 57 17N 4 21W
Highland Park, U.S.A. 82 D2 42 11N 87 48W
Highmore, U.S.A. 80 C5 44 31N 99 27W
Highrock L., Man., Canada 71 B8 55 45N 100 30W
Highrock L., Sask., Canada 71 B7 57 5N 105 32W
Higüey, Dom. Rep. 89 C6 18 37N 68 42W
Hiiumaa, Estonia .... 9 G20 58 50N 22 45 E
Ḥijāz □, Si. Arabia .... 44 E3 24 0N 40 0 E
Hijo = Tagum, Phil. .... 37 C7 7 33N 125 53 E
Hikari, Japan .... 31 H5 33 58N 131 58 E
Hiko, U.S.A. 78 H11 37 32N 115 14W
Hikone, Japan .... 31 G8 35 15N 136 10 E
Hikurangi, Gisborne, N.Z. ..... 59 H6 37 55S 178 4 E
Hikurangi, Northland, N.Z. .... 59 F5 35 36S 174 17 E
Hildesheim, Germany .... 16 B5 52 9N 9 56 E
Hill →, Australia .... 61 F2 30 23S 115 3 E
Hill City, Idaho, U.S.A. 76 E6 43 18N 115 3W
Hill City, Kans., U.S.A. 80 F5 39 22N 99 51W
Hill City, S. Dak., U.S.A. 80 D3 43 56N 103 35W
Hill Island L., Canada 71 A7 60 30N 109 50W
Hillaby, Mt., Barbados .... 89 g 13 12N 59 35W
Hillcrest, Barbados .... 89 g 13 13N 59 32W
Hillcrest Center, U.S.A. 79 K8 35 23N 118 57W
Hillegom, Neths. .... 15 B4 52 18N 4 35 E
Hillerød, Denmark .... 9 J15 55 56N 12 19 E
Hillsboro, Kans., U.S.A. 80 F6 38 21N 97 12W
Hillsboro, N. Dak., U.S.A. 80 B6 47 26N 97 3W
Hillsboro, N.H., U.S.A. 85 C13 43 7N 71 54W
Hillsboro, Ohio, U.S.A. 82 F4 39 12N 83 37W
Hillsboro, Oreg., U.S.A. 78 E4 45 31N 122 59W
Hillsboro, Tex., U.S.A. 81 J6 32 1N 97 8W
Hillsborough, Grenada 89 D7 12 28N 61 28W
Hillsborough Channel, Australia 62 J7 20 56S 149 15 E
Hillsdale, Mich., U.S.A. 82 E3 41 56N 84 38W
Hillsdale, N.Y., U.S.A. 85 D11 42 11N 73 30W
Hillsport, Canada 72 C2 49 27N 85 34W
Hillston, Australia .... 63 E4 33 30S 145 31 E
Hilo, U.S.A. 74 J17 19 44N 155 5W
Hilton, U.S.A. 84 C7 43 17N 77 48W
Hilton Head Island, U.S.A. 83 J5 32 13N 80 45W
Hilversum, Neths. .... 15 B5 52 14N 5 10 E
Himachal Pradesh □, India ... 42 D7 31 30N 77 0 E
Himalaya, Asia .... 43 E11 29 0N 84 0 E
Himatnagar, India .... 40 H8 23 37N 72 57 E
Himeji, Japan .... 31 G7 34 50N 134 40 E
Himi, Japan .... 31 F8 36 50N 136 55 E
Ḥimṣ, Syria .... 46 A5 34 40N 36 45 E
Ḥimṣ □, Syria .... 46 A6 34 30N 37 0 E
Hinche, Haiti 89 C5 19 9N 72 1W
Hinchinbrook I., Australia .... 62 B4 18 20S 146 15 E
Hinchinbrook Island △, Australia 62 B4 18 14S 146 6 E
Hinckley, U.K. 13 E6 52 33N 1 22W
Hinckley, U.S.A. 80 B8 46 1N 92 56W
Hindaun, India .... 42 F7 26 44N 77 5 E
Hindmarsh, L., Australia ..... 63 F3 36 5S 141 55 E
Hindu Bagh, Pakistan .... 42 D2 30 56N 67 50 E
Hindu Kush, Asia .... 40 B7 36 0N 71 0 E
Hindupur, India .... 40 N10 13 49N 77 32 E
Hines Creek, Canada 70 B5 56 20N 118 40W
Hinesville, U.S.A. 83 K5 31 51N 81 36W
Hinganghat, India .... 40 J11 20 30N 78 52 E
Hingham, U.S.A. 76 B8 48 33N 110 25W
Hingir, India .... 43 J10 21 57N 83 41 E
Hingoli, India .... 40 K10 19 41N 77 15 E
Hinna = Imi, Ethiopia .... 47 F3 6 28N 42 10 E
Hinnøya, Norway .... 8 B16 68 35N 15 50 E
Hinojosa del Duque, Spain ... 21 C3 38 30N 5 9W
Hinsdale, U.S.A. 85 D12 42 47N 72 29W
Hinton, Canada 70 C5 53 26N 117 34W
Hinton, U.S.A. 82 G5 37 40N 80 54W
Hirado, Japan .... 31 H4 33 22N 129 33 E
Hirakud Dam, India .... 41 J13 21 32N 83 45 E
Hiran →, India .... 43 H8 23 6N 79 21 E
Hirapur, India .... 43 G8 24 22N 79 13 E
Hiratsuka, Japan .... 31 G9 35 19N 139 21 E
Hiroo, Japan .... 30 C11 42 17N 143 19 E
Hirosaki, Japan .... 30 D10 40 34N 140 28 E
Hiroshima, Japan .... 31 G6 34 24N 132 30 E
Hiroshima □, Japan .... 31 G6 34 50N 133 0 E
Hisar, India .... 42 E6 29 12N 75 45 E
Hisb, Sha'ib →, Iraq .... 44 D5 31 45N 44 17 E
Ḥismá, Si. Arabia .... 44 D3 28 30N 36 0 E
Hispaniola, W. Indies 89 C5 19 0N 71 0W
Ḥīt, Iraq .... 44 C4 33 38N 42 49 E
Hita, Japan .... 31 H5 33 20N 130 58 E
Hitachi, Japan .... 31 F10 36 36N 140 39 E
Hitchin, U.K. 13 F7 51 58N 0 16W
Hitoyoshi, Japan .... 31 H5 32 13N 130 45 E
Hitra, Norway .... 8 E13 63 30N 8 45 E
Hixon, Canada 70 C4 53 25N 122 35W
Ḥiyyon, N. →, Israel .... 46 E4 30 25N 35 10 E
Hjalmar L., Canada 71 A7 61 33N 109 25W
Hjälmaren, Sweden .... 9 G16 59 18N 15 40 E
Hjørring, Denmark .... 9 H13 57 29N 9 59 E
Hkakabo Razi, Burma .... 41 E20 28 25N 97 23 E
Hlobane, S. Africa .... 57 D5 27 42S 31 0 E
Hluhluwe, S. Africa .... 57 D5 28 1S 32 15 E
Hluhluwe ◠, S. Africa .... 57 D5 28 0S 32 5 E
Hlyboka, Ukraine .... 17 D13 48 5N 25 56 E
Ho Chi Minh City = Thanh Pho
Ho Chi Minh, Vietnam ..... 39 G6 10 58N 106 40 E
Ho Thuong, Vietnam .... 38 C5 19 32N 105 48 E
Hoa Binh, Vietnam .... 38 B5 20 50N 105 20 E
Hoa Da, Vietnam .... 39 G7 11 16N 108 40 E
Hoa Hiep, Vietnam .... 39 G5 11 34N 105 51 E
Hoai Nhon, Vietnam .... 38 E7 14 28N 109 1 E
Hoang Lien Son, Vietnam .... 38 A4 22 0N 104 0 E
Hoanib →, Namibia .... 56 B2 19 27S 12 46 E
Hoare B., Canada 69 B13 65 17N 62 30W
Hobart, Australia .... 63 G4 42 50S 147 21 E
Hobart, U.S.A. 81 H5 35 1N 99 6W
Hobbs, U.S.A. 81 J3 32 42N 103 8W
Hobbs Coast, Antarctica 5 D14 74 50S 131 0W
Hobe Sound, U.S.A. 83 M5 27 4N 80 8W
Hoboken, U.S.A. 85 F10 40 45N 74 4W
Hobro, Denmark .... 9 H13 56 39N 9 46 E
Hoburgen, Sweden .... 9 H18 56 55N 18 7 E
Hochfeld, Namibia .... 56 C2 21 28S 17 58 E
Hodaka-Dake, Japan .... 31 F8 36 17N 137 39 E
Hodeida = Al Ḥudaydah, Yemen 47 E3 14 50N 43 0 E
Hodgeville, Canada 71 C7 50 7N 106 58W
Hodgson, Canada 71 C9 51 13N 97 36W

Hódmezővásárhely, Hungary .. 17 E11 46 28N 20 22 E
Hodna, Chott el, Algeria ...... 50 A6 35 26N 4 43 E
Hodonín, Czech Rep. .... 17 D9 48 50N 17 10 E
Hoeamdong, N. Korea .... 35 C16 42 30N 130 16 E
Hoek van Holland, Neths. .... 15 C4 52 0N 4 7 E
Hoengsŏng, S. Korea .... 35 F14 37 29N 127 59 E
Hoeryong, N. Korea .... 35 C15 42 30N 129 45 E
Hoeyang, N. Korea .... 35 E14 38 43N 127 36 E
Hof, Germany .... 16 C6 50 19N 11 55 E
Hofmeyr, S. Africa .... 56 E4 31 39S 25 50 E
Höfn, Iceland 8 D6 64 15N 15 13W
Hofors, Sweden .... 9 F17 60 31N 16 15 E
Hofsjökull, Iceland 8 D4 64 49N 18 48W
Höfu, Japan .... 31 G5 34 3N 131 34 E
Hogan Group, Australia ...... 63 F4 39 13S 147 1 E
Hogarth, Mt., Australia ...... 62 C2 21 48S 136 58 E
Hoggar = Ahaggar, Algeria ... 50 D7 23 0N 6 30 E
Hogsty Reef, Bahamas 89 B5 21 41N 73 48W
Hoh →, U.S.A. 78 C2 47 45N 124 29W
Hohe Venn, Belgium .... 15 D6 50 30N 6 5 E
Hohenwald, U.S.A. 83 H2 35 33N 87 33W
Hoher Rhön = Rhön, Germany . 16 C5 50 24N 9 58 E
Hohhot, China .... 34 D6 40 52N 111 40 E
Hóhlakas, Greece .... 25 D9 35 57N 27 53 E
Hoi An, Vietnam .... 38 E7 15 30N 108 19 E
Hoi Xuan, Vietnam .... 38 B5 20 25N 105 9 E
Hoisington, U.S.A. 80 F5 38 31N 98 47W
Hōjō, Japan .... 31 H6 33 58N 132 46 E
Hokianga Harbour, N.Z. ...... 59 F4 35 31S 173 22 E
Hokitika, N.Z. .... 59 K3 42 42S 171 0 E
Hokkaidō □, Japan .... 30 C11 43 30N 143 0 E
Holbrook, Australia .... 63 F4 35 42S 147 18 E
Holbrook, U.S.A. 77 J8 34 54N 110 10W
Holden, U.S.A. 76 G7 39 6N 112 16W
Holdenville, U.S.A. 81 H6 35 5N 96 24W
Holdrege, U.S.A. 80 E5 40 26N 99 23W
Holetown, Barbados .... 89 g 13 11N 59 38W
Holguín, Cuba 88 B4 20 50N 76 20W
Hollams Bird I., Namibia ..... 56 C1 24 40S 14 30 E
Holland, Mich., U.S.A. .... 82 D2 42 47N 86 7 W
Holland, N.Y., U.S.A. 84 D6 42 38N 78 32W
Hollandale, U.S.A. 81 J9 33 10N 90 51W
Holley, U.S.A. .... 84 C6 43 14N 78 2 W
Hollidaysburg, U.S.A. 84 F6 40 26N 78 24W
Hollis, U.S.A. 81 H5 34 41N 99 55W
Hollister, Calif., U.S.A. 78 J5 36 51N 121 24W
Hollister, Idaho, U.S.A. 76 E6 42 21N 114 35W
Holly Hill, U.S.A. .... 83 L5 29 16N 81 3 W
Holly Springs, U.S.A. 81 H10 34 46N 89 27W
Hollywood, U.S.A. .... 83 N5 26 1N 80 9 W
Holman, Canada 68 A8 70 44N 117 44W
Hólmavík, Iceland 8 D3 65 42N 21 40W
Holmen, U.S.A. 80 D9 43 58N 91 15W
Holmes Reefs, Australia ...... 62 B4 16 27S 148 0 E
Holmsund, Sweden .... 8 E19 63 41N 20 20 E
Holroyd →, Australia .... 62 A3 14 10S 141 36 E
Holstebro, Denmark .... 9 H13 56 22N 8 37 E
Holsworthy, U.K. 13 G3 50 48N 4 22W
Holton, Canada 73 B8 54 31N 57 12W
Holton, U.S.A. 80 F7 39 28N 95 44W
Holtville, U.S.A. 79 N11 32 49N 115 23W
Holwerd, Neths. .... 15 A5 53 22N 5 54 E
Holy I., Angl., U.K. 12 D3 53 17N 4 37W
Holy I., Northumberland, U.K. . 12 B6 55 40N 1 47W
Holyhead, U.K. 12 D3 53 18N 4 38W
Holyoke, Colo., U.S.A. 80 E3 40 35N 102 18W
Holyoke, Mass., U.S.A. 85 D12 42 12N 72 37W
Holyrood, Canada .... 73 C9 47 27N 53 8 W
Homa Bay, Kenya .... 54 C3 0 36S 34 30 E
Homalin, Burma .... 41 G19 24 55N 95 0 E
Homand, Iran .... 45 C8 32 28N 59 37 E
Homathko →, Canada 70 C4 51 0N 124 56W
Hombori, Mali 50 E5 15 20N 1 38W
Home B., Canada 69 B13 68 40N 67 10W
Home Hill, Australia .... 62 B4 19 43S 147 25 E
Homedale, U.S.A. 76 E5 43 37N 116 56W
Homer, Alaska, U.S.A. 68 C4 59 39N 151 33W
Homer, La., U.S.A. .... 81 J8 32 48N 93 4 W
Homer City, U.S.A. 84 F5 40 32N 79 10W
Homestead, Australia .... 62 C4 20 20S 145 40 E
Homestead, U.S.A. 83 N5 25 28N 80 29W
Homestead ◠, U.S.A. 80 E6 40 35N 96 30W
Homewood, U.S.A. .... 78 F6 39 4N 120 8 E
Homoine, Mozam. .... 57 C6 23 55S 35 8 E
Homs = Ḥimṣ, Syria .... 46 A5 34 40N 36 45 E
Homyel, Belarus .... 17 B16 52 28N 31 0 E
Hon Chong, Vietnam .... 39 G5 10 25N 104 30 E
Hon Me, Vietnam .... 38 C5 19 23N 105 56 E
Honan = Henan □, China ..... 34 H8 34 0N 114 0 E
Honbetsu, Japan .... 30 C11 43 7N 143 37 E
Honcut, U.S.A. 78 F5 39 20N 121 32W
Hondeklipbaai, S. Africa ..... 56 E2 30 19S 17 17 E
Hondo, Japan .... 31 H5 32 27N 130 12 E
Hondo, U.S.A. .... 81 L5 29 21N 99 9 W
Hondo →, Belize 87 D7 18 25N 88 21W
Honduras ■, Cent. Amer. 88 D2 14 40N 86 30W
Honduras, G. de, Caribbean .. 88 C2 16 50N 87 0 W
Hønefoss, Norway .... 9 F14 60 10N 10 18 E
Honesdale, U.S.A. 85 E9 41 34N 75 16W
Honey L., U.S.A. 78 E6 40 15N 120 19W
Honfleur, France .... 20 B4 49 25N 0 13 E
Hong →, Vietnam .... 34 H8 20 57N 105 0 E
Hong Gai, Vietnam .... 38 B6 20 57N 107 5 E
Hong He →, China .... 34 H8 32 25N 115 35 E
Hong Kong □, China .... 33 G11 22 11N 114 14 E
Hong Kong International ✈
(HKG), China .... 33 G10 22 19N 113 57 E
Hongch'ŏn, S. Korea .... 35 F14 37 44N 127 53 E
Hongjiang, China .... 33 D5 27 7N 109 59 E
Hongliu He →, China .... 34 F5 38 0N 109 50 E
Hongor, Mongolia .... 34 B7 45 45N 112 50 E
Hongsa, Laos .... 38 C3 19 43N 101 20 E
Hongshui He →, China ...... 33 D5 23 48N 109 30 E
Hongtong, China .... 34 F6 36 16N 111 40 E
Honguedo, Détroit d', Canada . 73 C7 49 15N 64 0 W
Hongwŏn, N. Korea .... 35 E14 40 0N 127 56 E
Hongze Hu, China .... 35 H10 33 15N 118 35 E
Honiara, Solomon Is. .... 64 H7 9 27S 159 57 E
Honiton, U.K. 13 G4 50 47N 3 11W
Honjō, Japan .... 30 E10 39 23N 140 3 E
Honningsvåg, Norway .... 8 A21 70 59N 25 59 E
Honolulu, U.S.A. 74 H16 21 19N 157 52W
Honshū, Japan .... 33 C8 36 0N 138 0 E
Hood, Mt., U.S.A. 76 D3 45 23N 121 42W
Hood, Pt., Australia .... 61 F2 34 23S 119 34 E

Hood River, U.S.A.	76 D3	45 43N 121 31W
Hoodsport, U.S.A.	78 C3	47 24N 123 9W
Hoogeveen, Neths.	15 B6	52 44N 6 28 E
Hoogezand-Sappemeer, Neths.	15 A6	53 9N 6 45 E
Hooghly = Hugli →, India	43 J13	21 56N 88 4 E
Hooghly-Chinsura = Chunchura, India	43 H13	22 53N 88 27 E
Hook Hd., Ireland	10 D5	52 7N 6 56W
Hook I., Australia	62 J6	20 4S 149 0 E
Hook of Holland = Hoek van Holland, Neths.	15 C4	52 0N 4 7 E
Hooker, U.S.A.	81 G4	36 52N 101 13W
Hooker Creek, Australia	60 C5	18 23S 130 38 E
Hoonah, U.S.A.	70 B1	58 7N 135 27W
Hooper Bay, U.S.A.	68 B3	61 32N 166 6W
Hoopeston, U.S.A.	82 E2	40 28N 87 40W
Hoopstad, S. Africa	56 D4	27 50S 25 55 E
Hoorn, Neths.	15 B5	52 38N 5 4 E
Hoover, U.S.A.	83 J2	33 20N 86 11W
Hoover Dam, U.S.A.	79 K12	36 1N 114 44W
Hooversville, U.S.A.	84 F6	40 9N 78 55W
Hop Bottom, U.S.A.	85 E9	41 42N 75 46W
Hope, Canada	70 D4	49 25N 121 25W
Hope, Ariz., U.S.A.	79 M13	33 43N 113 42W
Hope, Ark., U.S.A.	81 J8	33 40N 93 36W
Hope, L., S. Austral., Australia	63 D2	28 24S 139 18 E
Hope, L., W. Austral., Australia	61 F3	32 35S 120 15 E
Hope, Pt., U.S.A.	4 C17	68 20N 166 50W
Hope I., Canada	84 B4	44 55N 80 11W
Hope Town, Bahamas	88 A4	26 35N 76 57W
Hopedale, Canada	73 A7	55 28N 60 13W
Hopedale, U.S.A.	85 D13	42 8N 71 33W
Hopefield, S. Africa	56 E2	33 3S 18 22 E
Hopei = Hebei □, China	34 E9	39 0N 116 0 E
Hopelchén, Mexico	87 D7	19 46N 89 50W
Hopetoun, Vic., Australia	63 F3	35 42S 142 22 E
Hopetoun, W. Austral., Australia	61 F3	33 57S 120 7 E
Hopetown, S. Africa	56 D3	29 34S 24 3 E
Hopevale, Australia	62 B4	15 16S 145 20 E
Hopewell, U.S.A.	82 G7	37 18N 77 17W
Hopkins, L., Australia	60 D4	24 15S 128 35 E
Hopkinsville, U.S.A.	83 G2	36 52N 87 29W
Hopland, U.S.A.	78 G3	38 58N 123 7W
Hoquiam, U.S.A.	78 D3	46 59N 123 53W
Horden Hills, Australia	60 D5	20 15S 130 0 E
Horinger, China	34 D6	40 28N 111 48 E
Horlick Mts., Antarctica	5 E15	84 0S 102 0W
Horlivka, Ukraine	19 E6	48 19N 38 5 E
Hormak, Iran	45 D9	29 58N 60 51 E
Hormoz, Iran	45 E7	27 35N 55 0 E
Hormoz, Jaz.-ye, Iran	45 E8	27 8N 56 28 E
Hormozgān □, Iran	45 E8	27 30N 56 0 E
Hormuz, Kūh-e, Iran	45 E7	27 27N 55 10 E
Hormuz, Str. of, The Gulf	45 E8	26 30N 56 30 E
Horn, Austria	16 D8	48 39N 15 40 E
Horn →, Canada	70 A5	61 30N 118 1W
Horn, Cape = Hornos, C. de, Chile	96 H3	55 50S 67 30W
Horn Head, Ireland	10 A3	55 14N 8 0W
Horn I., Australia	62 A3	10 37S 142 17 E
Horn Plateau, Canada	70 A5	62 15N 119 15W
Hornavan, Sweden	8 C17	66 15N 17 30 E
Hornbeck, U.S.A.	81 K8	31 20N 93 24W
Hornbrook, U.S.A.	76 F2	41 55N 122 33W
Horncastle, U.K.	12 D7	53 13N 0 7W
Hornell, U.S.A.	84 D7	42 20N 77 40W
Hornell L., Canada	70 A5	62 20N 119 25W
Hornepayne, Canada	72 C3	49 14N 84 48W
Hornings Mills, Canada	84 B4	44 9N 80 12W
Hornitos, U.S.A.	78 H6	37 30N 120 14W
Hornos, C. de, Chile	96 H3	55 50S 67 30W
Hornsea, U.K.	12 D7	53 55N 0 11W
Horobetsu = Noboribetsu, Japan	30 C10	42 24N 141 6 E
Horodenka, Ukraine	17 D13	48 41N 25 29 E
Horodok, Khmelnytskyy, Ukraine	17 D14	49 10N 26 34 E
Horodok, Lviv, Ukraine	17 D12	49 46N 23 32 E
Horokhiv, Ukraine	17 C13	50 30N 24 45 E
Horqin Youyi Qianqi, China	35 A12	46 5N 122 3 E
Horqueta, Paraguay	94 A4	23 15S 56 55W
Horse Creek, U.S.A.	80 E3	41 57N 105 10W
Horse I., Canada	71 C9	53 20N 99 6W
Horse Is., Canada	73 B8	50 15N 55 50W
Horsefly L., Canada	70 C4	52 25N 121 0W
Horseheads, U.S.A.	84 D8	42 10N 76 49W
Horsens, Denmark	9 J13	55 52N 9 51 E
Horsham, Australia	63 F3	36 44S 142 13 E
Horsham, U.K.	13 F7	51 4N 0 20W
Horten, Norway	9 G14	59 25N 10 32 E
Horton, U.S.A.	80 F7	39 40N 95 32W
Horton →, Canada	68 B7	69 56N 126 52W
Horwood L., Canada	72 C3	48 5N 82 20W
Hose, Gunung-Gunung, Malaysia	36 D4	2 5N 114 6 E
Hoseynābād, Khuzestān, Iran	45 C6	32 45N 48 20 E
Hoseynābād, Kordestān, Iran	44 C5	35 33N 47 8 E
Hoshangabad, India	42 H7	22 45N 77 45 E
Hoshiarpur, India	42 D6	31 30N 75 58 E
Hospet, India	40 M10	15 15N 76 20 E
Hoste, I., Chile	96 H3	55 0S 69 0W
Hot, Thailand	38 C2	18 8N 98 29 E
Hot Creek Range, U.S.A.	76 G6	38 40N 116 20W
Hot Springs, Ark., U.S.A.	81 H8	34 31N 93 3W
Hot Springs, S. Dak., U.S.A.	80 D3	43 26N 103 29W
Hot Springs △, U.S.A.	81 H8	34 32N 93 4W
Hotagen, Sweden	8 E16	63 50N 14 30 E
Hotan, China	32 C2	37 25N 79 55 E
Hotazel, S. Africa	56 D3	27 17S 22 58 E
Hotchkiss, U.S.A.	77 G10	38 48N 107 43W
Hotham, C., Australia	60 B5	12 2S 131 18 E
Hotham, Mt., Australia	8 D17	64 8N 16 15 E
Hotte, Massif de la, Haiti	89 C5	18 30N 73 45W
Hottentotsbaai, Namibia	56 D1	26 8S 14 59 E
Hou Hai, China	33 F10	22 32N 113 56 E
Houei Sai, Laos	38 B3	20 18N 100 26 E
Houffalize, Belgium	15 D5	50 8N 5 48 E
Houghton, Mich., U.S.A.	80 B10	47 7N 88 34W
Houghton, N.Y., U.S.A.	84 D6	42 25N 78 9W
Houghton L., U.S.A.	82 C3	44 21N 84 44W
Houghton-le-Spring, U.K.	12 C6	54 51N 1 28W
Houhora Heads, N.Z.	59 F4	34 49S 173 9 E
Houlton, U.S.A.	83 B12	46 8N 67 51W
Houma, U.S.A.	81 L9	29 36N 90 43W
Housatonic →, U.S.A.	85 E11	41 10N 73 7W
Houston, Canada	70 C3	54 25N 126 39W
Houston, Mo., U.S.A.	81 G9	37 22N 91 58W
Houston, Tex., U.S.A.	81 L7	29 46N 95 22W
Hout →, S. Africa	57 C4	23 4S 29 36 E
Houtkraal, S. Africa	56 E3	30 23S 24 5 E
Houtman Abrolhos, Australia	61 E1	28 43S 113 48 E
Hovd, Mongolia	32 B4	48 2N 91 37 E
Hove, U.K.	13 G7	50 50N 0 10W
Hovenweep △, U.S.A.	77 H9	37 20N 109 0W
Hoveyzeh, Iran	45 D6	31 27N 48 4 E
Hövsgöl, Mongolia	34 C5	43 37N 109 39 E
Hövsgöl Nuur, Mongolia	32 A5	51 0N 100 30 E
Howard, Australia	63 D5	25 16S 152 32 E
Howard, Pa., U.S.A.	84 F7	41 1N 77 40W
Howard, S. Dak., U.S.A.	80 C6	44 1N 97 32W
Howe, U.S.A.	76 E7	43 48N 113 0W
Howe, C., Australia	63 F5	37 30S 150 0 E
Howe I., Canada	85 B8	44 16N 76 17W
Howell, U.S.A.	82 D4	42 36N 83 56W
Howick, Canada	85 A11	45 11N 73 51W
Howick, S. Africa	57 D5	29 28S 30 14 E
Howick Group, Australia	62 A4	14 20S 145 30 E
Howitt, L., Australia	63 D2	27 40S 138 40 E
Howland I., Pac. Oc.	64 G10	0 48N 176 38W
Howrah = Haora, India	43 H13	22 37N 88 20 E
Howth Hd., Ireland	10 C5	53 22N 6 3W
Höxter, Germany	16 C5	51 46N 9 22 E
Hoy, U.K.	11 C5	58 50N 3 15W
Høyanger, Norway	9 F12	61 13N 6 4 E
Hoyerswerda, Germany	16 C8	51 26N 14 14 E
Hoylake, U.K.	12 D4	53 24N 3 10W
Hpa-an = Pa-an, Burma	41 L20	16 51N 97 40 E
Hpungan Pass, Burma	41 F20	27 30N 96 55 E
Hradec Králové, Czech Rep.	16 C8	50 15N 15 50 E
Hrodna, Belarus	17 B12	53 42N 23 52 E
Hrodzyanka, Belarus	17 B15	53 31N 28 42 E
Hron →, Slovak Rep.	17 E10	47 49N 18 45 E
Hrvatska = Croatia ■, Europe	16 F9	45 20N 16 0 E
Hrymayliv, Ukraine	17 D14	49 20N 26 5 E
Hsenwi, Burma	41 H20	23 22N 97 55 E
Hsiamen = Xiamen, China	33 D6	24 25N 118 4 E
Hsian = Xi'an, China	34 G5	34 15N 109 0 E
Hsinchu, Taiwan	33 D7	24 48N 120 58 E
Hsinhailien = Lianyungang, China	35 G10	34 40N 119 11 E
Hsüchou = Xuzhou, China	35 G9	34 18N 117 10 E
Hu Xian, China	34 G5	34 8N 108 42 E
Hua Hin, Thailand	38 F2	12 34N 99 58 E
Hua Xian, Henan, China	34 G8	35 30N 114 30 E
Hua Xian, Shaanxi, China	34 G5	34 30N 109 48 E
Huab →, Namibia	56 B2	20 52S 13 25 E
Huachinera, Mexico	86 A3	30 9N 108 55W
Huacho, Peru	92 F3	11 10S 77 35W
Huade, China	34 D7	41 55N 113 59 E
Huadian, China	35 C14	43 0N 126 40 E
Huai Had △, Thailand	38 D5	16 52N 104 17 E
Huai He →, China	33 C6	33 0N 118 30 E
Huai Nam Dang △, Thailand	38 C2	19 30N 98 30 E
Huai Yot, Thailand	39 J2	7 45N 99 37 E
Huai'an, Hebei, China	34 D8	40 30N 114 20 E
Huai'an, Jiangsu, China	35 H10	33 30N 119 10 E
Huaibei, China	34 G9	34 0N 116 48 E
Huaide = Gongzhuling, China	35 C13	43 30N 124 40 E
Huaidezhen, China	35 C13	43 48N 124 50 E
Huainan, China	33 C6	32 38N 116 58 E
Huairen, China	34 E7	39 48N 113 20 E
Huairou, China	34 D9	40 20N 116 35 E
Huaiyang, China	34 H8	33 40N 114 52 E
Huaiyin, China	35 H10	33 30N 119 2 E
Huaiyuan, China	35 H9	32 55N 117 10 E
Huajianzi, China	35 D13	41 23N 125 20 E
Huajuapan de Leon, Mexico	87 D5	17 50N 97 48W
Hualapai Peak, U.S.A.	77 J7	35 5N 113 54W
Huallaga →, Peru	92 E3	5 15S 75 30W
Huambo, Angola	53 G3	12 42S 15 54 E
Huan Jiang →, China	34 G5	34 28N 109 0 E
Huan Xian, China	34 F4	36 33N 107 7 E
Huancabamba, Peru	92 E3	5 10S 79 15W
Huancane, Peru	92 G5	15 10S 69 44W
Huancavelica, Peru	92 F3	12 50S 75 5W
Huancayo, Peru	92 F3	12 5S 75 12W
Huanchaca, Bolivia	92 H5	20 15S 66 40W
Huang Hai = Yellow Sea, China	35 G12	35 0N 123 0 E
Huang He →, China	35 F10	37 55N 118 50 E
Huang Xian, China	35 F11	37 38N 120 30 E
Huangling, China	34 G5	35 34N 109 15 E
Huanglong, China	34 G5	35 30N 109 59 E
Huangshan, China	33 C6	29 42N 118 25 E
Huangshi, China	33 C6	30 10N 115 3 E
Huangsongdian, China	35 C14	43 45N 127 25 E
Huantai, China	35 F9	36 58N 117 56 E
Huánuco, Peru	92 E3	9 55S 76 15W
Huaraz, Peru	92 E3	9 30S 77 32W
Huarmey, Peru	92 F3	10 5S 78 5W
Huascarán, Peru	92 E3	9 8S 77 36W
Huasco, Chile	94 B1	28 30S 71 15W
Huasco →, Chile	94 B1	28 27S 71 13W
Huasna, U.S.A.	79 K6	35 6N 120 24W
Huatabampo, Mexico	86 B3	26 50N 109 50W
Huauchinango, Mexico	87 C5	20 11N 98 3W
Huautla de Jiménez, Mexico	87 D5	18 8N 96 51W
Huay Namota, Mexico	86 C4	21 56N 104 30W
Huayin, China	34 G6	34 35N 110 5 E
Hubbard, Ohio, U.S.A.	84 E4	41 9N 80 34W
Hubbard, Tex., U.S.A.	81 K6	31 51N 96 48W
Hubbart Pt., Canada	71 B10	59 21N 94 41W
Hubei □, China	33 C6	31 0N 112 0 E
Hubli, India	40 M9	15 22N 75 15 E
Huch'ang, N. Korea	35 D14	41 25N 127 2 E
Hucknall, U.K.	12 D6	53 3N 1 13W
Huddersfield, U.K.	12 D6	53 39N 1 47W
Hudiksvall, Sweden	9 F17	61 43N 17 10 E
Hudson, Canada	72 B1	50 6N 92 9W
Hudson, Mass., U.S.A.	85 D13	42 23N 71 34W
Hudson, N.Y., U.S.A.	85 D11	42 15N 73 46W
Hudson, Wis., U.S.A.	80 C8	44 58N 92 45W
Hudson, Wyo., U.S.A.	76 E9	42 54N 108 35W
Hudson →, U.S.A.	85 F10	40 42N 74 2W
Hudson Bay, Nunavut, Canada	69 C11	60 0N 86 0W
Hudson Bay, Sask., Canada	71 C8	52 51N 102 23W
Hudson Falls, U.S.A.	85 C11	43 18N 73 35W
Hudson Mts., Antarctica	5 D16	74 32S 99 20W
Hudson Str., Canada	69 B13	62 0N 70 0W
Hudson's Hope, Canada	70 B4	56 0N 121 54W
Hue, Vietnam	38 D6	16 30N 107 35 E
Huehuetenango, Guatemala	88 C1	15 20N 91 28W
Huejúcar, Mexico	86 C4	22 21N 103 13W
Huelva, Spain	21 D2	37 18N 6 57W
Huentelauquén, Chile	94 C1	31 38S 71 33W
Huerta, Sa. de la, Argentina	94 C2	31 10S 67 30W
Huesca, Spain	21 A5	42 8N 0 25W
Huetamo, Mexico	86 D4	18 36N 100 54W
Hugh →, Australia	62 D1	25 1S 134 1 E
Hughenden, Australia	62 C3	20 52S 144 10 E
Hughes, Australia	61 F4	30 42S 129 31 E
Hughesville, U.S.A.	85 E8	41 14N 76 44W
Hugli →, India	43 J13	21 56N 88 4 E
Hugo, Colo., U.S.A.	80 F3	39 8N 103 28W
Hugo, Okla., U.S.A.	81 H7	34 1N 95 31W
Hugoton, U.S.A.	81 G4	37 11N 101 21W
Hui Xian = Huixian, China	34 G7	35 27N 113 12 E
Hui Xian, China	34 H4	33 50N 106 4 E
Hui'anbu, China	34 F4	37 28N 106 38 E
Huichapán, Mexico	87 C5	20 24N 99 40W
Huifa He →, China	35 C14	43 0N 127 50 E
Huila, Nevado del, Colombia	92 C3	3 0N 76 0W
Huimin, China	35 F9	37 27N 117 28 E
Huinan, China	35 C14	42 40N 126 2 E
Huinca Renancó, Argentina	94 C3	34 51S 64 22W
Huining, China	34 G3	35 38N 105 0 E
Huinong, China	34 E4	39 5N 106 35 E
Huisache, Mexico	86 C4	22 55N 100 25W
Huiting, China	34 G9	34 5N 116 5 E
Huixian, China	34 G7	35 27N 113 12 E
Huixtla, Mexico	87 D6	15 9N 92 28W
Huize, China	32 D5	26 24N 103 15 E
Hukawng Valley, Burma	41 F20	26 30N 96 30 E
Hūksan-chedo, S. Korea	35 G13	34 40N 125 30 E
Hukuntsi, Botswana	56 C3	23 58S 21 45 E
Hulayfā', Si. Arabia	44 E4	25 58N 40 45 E
Hulin He →, China	35 B12	45 0N 122 10 E
Hull = Kingston upon Hull, U.K.	12 D7	53 45N 0 21W
Hull, Canada	85 A9	45 25N 75 44W
Hull →, U.K.	12 D7	53 44N 0 20W
Hulst, Neths.	15 C4	51 17N 4 2 E
Hulun Nur, China	33 B6	49 0N 117 30 E
Huma, Tanjung, Malaysia	39 c	5 29N 100 16 E
Humacao, Puerto Rico	89 d	18 9N 65 50W
Humahuaca, Argentina	94 A2	23 10S 65 25W
Humaitá, Brazil	92 E6	7 35S 63 1W
Humaitá, Paraguay	94 B4	27 2S 58 31W
Humansdorp, S. Africa	56 E3	34 2S 24 46 E
Humbe, Angola	56 B1	16 40S 14 55 E
Humber →, U.K.	12 D7	53 42N 0 27W
Humboldt, Canada	71 C7	52 15N 105 9W
Humboldt, Iowa, U.S.A.	80 D7	42 44N 94 13W
Humboldt, Tenn., U.S.A.	81 H10	35 50N 88 55W
Humboldt →, U.S.A.	76 F4	39 59N 118 36W
Humboldt Gletscher = Sermersuaq, Greenland	4 B4	79 30N 62 0W
Hume, U.S.A.	78 J8	36 48N 118 54W
Hume, L., Australia	63 F4	36 0S 147 5 E
Humen, China	33 F10	22 50N 113 40 E
Humenné, Slovak Rep.	17 D11	48 55N 21 50 E
Humphreys, Mt., U.S.A.	78 H8	37 17N 118 40W
Humphreys Peak, U.S.A.	77 J8	35 21N 111 41W
Humptulips, U.S.A.	78 C3	47 14N 123 57W
Hūn, Libya	51 C9	29 2N 16 0 E
Hun Jiang →, China	35 D13	40 50N 125 38 E
Húnaflói, Iceland	8 D3	65 50N 20 50W
Hunan □, China	33 D6	27 30N 112 0 E
Hunchun, China	35 C16	42 52N 130 28 E
Hundewali, Pakistan	42 D5	31 55N 72 38 E
Hundred Mile House, Canada	70 C4	51 38N 121 18W
Hunedoara, Romania	17 F12	45 40N 22 50 E
Hung Yen, Vietnam	38 B6	20 39N 106 4 E
Hungary ■, Europe	17 E10	47 20N 19 20 E
Hungary, Plain of, Europe	6 F10	47 0N 20 0 E
Hungerford, Australia	63 D3	28 58S 144 24 E
Hŭngnam, N. Korea	35 E14	39 49N 127 45 E
Hunsberge, Namibia	56 D2	27 45S 17 12 E
Hunsrück, Germany	16 D4	49 56N 7 27 E
Hunstanton, U.K.	12 E8	52 56N 0 29 E
Hunter, U.S.A.	85 D10	42 13N 74 13W
Hunter I., Australia	63 G3	40 30S 144 45 E
Hunter I., Canada	70 C3	51 55N 128 0W
Hunter Ra., Australia	63 E5	32 45S 150 15 E
Hunters Road, Zimbabwe	55 F2	19 9S 29 49 E
Hunterville, N.Z.	59 H5	39 56S 175 35 E
Huntingburg, U.S.A.	82 F2	38 18N 86 57W
Huntingdon, Canada	72 C5	45 6N 74 10W
Huntingdon, U.K.	13 E7	52 20N 0 11W
Huntingdon, U.S.A.	84 F6	40 30N 78 1W
Huntington, Ind., U.S.A.	82 E3	40 53N 85 30W
Huntington, Oreg., U.S.A.	76 D5	44 21N 117 16W
Huntington, Utah, U.S.A.	76 G8	39 20N 110 58W
Huntington, W. Va., U.S.A.	82 F4	38 25N 82 27W
Huntington Beach, U.S.A.	79 M9	33 40N 118 5W
Huntington Station, U.S.A.	85 F11	40 52N 73 26W
Huntly, N.Z.	59 G5	37 34S 175 11 E
Huntly, U.K.	11 D6	57 27N 2 47W
Huntsville, Canada	84 A5	45 20N 79 14W
Huntsville, Ala., U.S.A.	83 H2	34 44N 86 35W
Huntsville, Tex., U.S.A.	81 K7	30 43N 95 33W
Hunyani →, Zimbabwe	55 F3	15 57S 30 39 E
Hunyuan, China	34 E7	39 42N 113 42 E
Hunza →, India	43 B6	35 54N 74 20 E
Huo Xian = Huozhou, China	34 F6	36 36N 111 42 E
Huong Khe, Vietnam	38 C5	18 13N 105 41 E
Huonville, Australia	63 G4	43 0S 147 5 E
Huozhou, China	34 F6	36 36N 111 42 E
Hupeh = Hubei □, China	33 C6	31 0N 112 0 E
Hūr, Iran	45 D8	30 50N 57 7 E
Hurd, C., Canada	84 A3	45 13N 81 44W
Hure Qi, China	35 C11	42 45N 121 45 E
Hurghada, Egypt	51 C12	27 15N 33 50 E
Hurley, N. Mex., U.S.A.	77 K9	32 42N 108 8W
Hurley, Wis., U.S.A.	80 B9	46 27N 90 11W
Huron, Calif., U.S.A.	78 J6	36 12N 120 6W
Huron, Ohio, U.S.A.	84 E2	41 24N 82 33W
Huron, S. Dak., U.S.A.	80 C5	44 22N 98 13W
Huron, L., U.S.A.	84 B2	44 30N 82 40W
Huron East, Canada	84 C3	43 37N 81 18W
Hurricane, U.S.A.	77 H7	37 11N 113 17W
Hurungwe △, Zimbabwe	55 F2	16 7S 29 5 E
Hurunui →, N.Z.	59 K4	42 54S 173 18 E
Húsavík, Iceland	8 C5	66 3N 17 21W
Huşi, Romania	17 E15	46 41N 28 7 E
Huskvarna, Sweden	9 H16	57 47N 14 15 E
Hustadvika, Norway	8 E12	63 0N 7 0 E
Hustontown, U.S.A.	84 F6	40 3N 78 2W
Hutchinson, Kans., U.S.A.	81 F6	38 5N 97 56W
Hutchinson, Minn., U.S.A.	80 C7	44 54N 94 22W
Hutte Sauvage, L. de la, Canada	73 A7	56 15N 64 45W
Hutton, Mt., Australia	63 D4	25 51S 148 20 E
Huy, Belgium	15 D5	50 31N 5 15 E
Huzhou, China	33 C7	30 51N 120. 8 E
Hvammstangi, Iceland	8 D3	65 24N 20 57W
Hvar, Croatia	22 C7	43 11N 16 28 E
Hvítá →, Iceland	8 D3	64 30N 21 58W
Hwachŏn-chŏsuji, S. Korea	35 E14	38 5N 127 50 E
Hwang Ho = Huang He →, China	35 F10	37 55N 118 50 E
Hwange, Zimbabwe	55 F2	18 18S 26 30 E
Hwange △, Zimbabwe	56 B4	19 0S 26 30 E
Hyannis, Mass., U.S.A.	82 E10	41 39N 70 17W
Hyannis, Nebr., U.S.A.	80 E4	42 0N 101 46W
Hyargas Nuur, Mongolia	32 B4	49 0N 93 0 E
Hydaburg, U.S.A.	70 B2	55 15N 132 50W
Hyde Park, U.S.A.	85 E11	41 47N 73 56W
Hyden, Australia	61 F2	32 24S 118 53 E
Hyderabad, India	40 L11	17 22N 78 29 E
Hyderabad, Pakistan	42 G3	25 23N 68 24 E
Hyères, France	20 E7	43 8N 6 9 E
Hyères, Îs. d', France	20 E7	43 0N 6 20 E
Hyesan, N. Korea	35 D15	41 20N 128 10 E
Hyland →, Canada	70 B3	59 52N 128 12W
Hymia, India	43 C8	33 40N 78 2 E
Hyndman Peak, U.S.A.	76 E6	43 45N 114 8W
Hyōgo □, Japan	31 G7	35 15N 134 50 E
Hyrum, U.S.A.	76 F8	41 38N 111 51W
Hysham, U.S.A.	76 C10	46 18N 107 14W
Hythe, U.K.	13 F9	51 4N 1 5 E
Hyūga, Japan	31 H5	32 25N 131 35 E
Hyvinge = Hyvinkää, Finland	9 F21	60 38N 24 50 E
Hyvinkää, Finland	9 F21	60 38N 24 50 E

I

I-n-Gall, Niger	50 E7	16 51N 7 1 E
Iaco →, Brazil	92 E5	9 3S 68 34W
Iakora, Madag.	57 C8	23 6S 46 40 E
Ialomiţa →, Romania	17 F14	44 42N 27 51 E
Iaşi, Romania	17 E14	47 10N 27 40 E
Ib →, India	43 J10	21 34N 83 48 E
Iba, Phil.	37 A6	15 22N 120 0 E
Ibadan, Nigeria	50 G6	7 22N 3 58 E
Ibagué, Colombia	92 C3	4 20N 75 20W
Ibar →, Serbia & M.	23 C9	43 43N 20 45 E
Ibaraki □, Japan	31 F10	36 10N 140 10 E
Ibarra, Ecuador	92 C3	0 21N 78 7W
Ibembo, Dem. Rep. of the Congo	54 B1	2 35N 23 35 E
Ibera, L., Argentina	94 B4	28 30S 57 9W
Iberian Peninsula, Europe	6 H5	40 0N 5 0W
Iberville, Canada	85 A11	45 19N 73 17W
Iberville, Lac d', Canada	72 A5	55 55N 73 15W
Ibiá, Brazil	93 G9	19 30S 46 30W
Ibiapaba, Sa. da, Brazil	93 D10	4 0S 41 30W
Ibicuí →, Brazil	95 B4	29 25S 56 47W
Ibicuy, Argentina	94 C4	33 55S 59 10W
Ibiza = Eivissa, Spain	24 C7	38 54N 1 26 E
Ibo, Mozam.	55 E5	12 22S 40 40 E
Ibonma, Indonesia	37 E8	3 29S 133 31 E
Ibotirama, Brazil	93 F10	12 13S 43 12W
Ibrāhīm →, Lebanon	46 A4	34 4N 35 38 E
Ibu, Indonesia	37 D7	1 35N 127 33 E
Ibusuki, Japan	31 J5	31 12N 130 40 E
Ica, Peru	92 F3	14 0S 75 48W
Ica →, Brazil	92 D5	2 55S 67 58W
Icacos Pt., Trin. & Tob.	93 K15	10 3N 61 57W
Içana, Brazil	92 C5	0 21N 67 19W
Içana →, Brazil	92 C5	0 26N 67 19W
İçel = Mersin, Turkey	19 G5	36 51N 34 36 E
Iceland ■, Europe	8 D4	64 45N 19 0W
Iceland Plateau, Arctic	4 C7	64 0N 10 0W
Ich'ang = Yichang, China	33 C6	30 40N 111 20 E
Ichchapuram, India	41 K14	19 10N 84 40 E
Ichhawar, India	42 H7	23 1N 77 1 E
Ichihara, Japan	31 G10	35 28N 140 5 E
Ichikawa, Japan	31 G9	35 44N 139 55 E
Ichilo →, Bolivia	92 G6	15 57S 64 50W
Ichinohe, Japan	30 D10	40 13N 141 17 E
Ichinomiya, Japan	31 G8	35 18N 136 48 E
Ichinoseki, Japan	30 E10	38 55N 141 8 E
Icod, Canary Is.	24 F3	28 22N 16 43W
Ida Grove, U.S.A.	80 D7	42 21N 95 28W
Idabel, U.S.A.	81 J7	33 54N 94 50W
Idaho □, U.S.A.	76 D7	45 0N 115 0W
Idaho City, U.S.A.	76 E6	43 50N 115 50W
Idaho Falls, U.S.A.	76 E7	43 30N 112 2W
Idalia △, Australia	62 C3	24 49S 144 36 E
Idar-Oberstein, Germany	16 D4	49 43N 7 16 E
Idfû, Egypt	51 C12	24 55N 32 49 E
Idhi Óros, Greece	25 D6	35 15N 24 45 E
Idhra, Greece	25 D6	37 20N 23 28 E
Idi, Indonesia	36 C1	5 2N 97 37 E
Idiofa, Dem. Rep. of the Congo	52 E3	4 55S 19 42 E
Idlib, Syria	44 C3	35 55N 36 36 E
Idria, U.S.A.	78 J6	36 25N 120 41W
Idutywa, S. Africa	57 E4	32 8S 28 18 E
Ieper, Belgium	15 D2	50 51N 2 53 E
Ierápetra, Greece	25 E7	35 1N 25 44 E
Iesi, Italy	22 C5	43 31N 13 14 E
Ifakara, Tanzania	52 F7	8 8S 36 41 E
'Ifāl, W. al →, Si. Arabia	44 D2	28 7N 35 3 E
Ifanadiana, Madag.	57 C8	21 19S 47 39 E
Ife, Nigeria	50 G6	7 30N 4 31 E
Iffley, Australia	62 B3	18 53S 141 12 E
Iforas, Adrar des, Africa	50 E6	19 40N 1 40 E
Ifould, L., Australia	61 F5	30 52S 132 6 E
Iganga, Uganda	54 B3	0 37N 33 28 E
Igarapava, Brazil	93 H9	20 3S 47 47W
Igarka, Russia	28 C9	67 30N 86 33 E
Igatimi, Paraguay	95 A4	24 5S 55 40W
Iggesund, Sweden	9 F17	61 39N 17 10 E
Iglésias, Italy	22 E3	39 19N 8 32 E
Igloolik, Canada	69 B11	69 20N 81 49W
Igluligaarjuk = Chesterfield Inlet, Canada	68 B10	63 30N 90 45W
Iglulik = Igloolik, Canada	69 B11	69 20N 81 49W
Ignace, Canada	72 C1	49 30N 91 40W
İğneada Burnu, Turkey	23 D13	41 53N 28 2 E
Igoumenitsa, Greece	23 E9	39 32N 20 18 E
Iguaçu →, Brazil	95 B5	25 36S 54 36W
Iguaçu △, Brazil	95 B5	25 30S 54 0W
Iguaçu, Cat. del, Brazil	95 B5	25 41S 54 26W
Iguaçu Falls = Iguaçu, Cat. del, Brazil	95 B5	25 41S 54 26W
Iguala, Mexico	87 D5	18 21N 99 32W
Igualada, Spain	21 B6	41 37N 1 37 E
Iguassu = Iguaçu →, Brazil	95 B5	25 36S 54 36W
Iguatu, Brazil	93 E11	6 20S 39 18W

Iguazú △, *Argentina* 95 B5   25 42S 54 22W
Iguidi, Erg, *Africa* .... 50 C4   27 0N   7 0 E
Iharana, *Madag.* .... 57 A9   13 25S 50 0 E
Ihbulag, *Mongolia* .... 34 C4   43 11N 107 10 E
Iheya-Shima, *Japan* .... 31 L3   27 4N 127 58 E
Ihosy, *Madag.* .... 57 C8   22 24S 46 8 E
Ihotry, Farihy, *Madag.* ...... 57 C7   21 56S 43 41 E
Ii, *Finland* .... 8 D21 65 19N 25 22 E
Ii-Shima, *Japan* .... 31 L3   26 43N 127 47 E
Iida, *Japan* .... 31 G8   35 35N 137 50 E
Iijoki →, *Finland* .... 8 D21 65 20N 25 20 E
Iisalmi, *Finland* .... 8 E22 63 32N 27 10 E
Iiyama, *Japan* .... 31 F9   36 51N 138 22 E
Iizuka, *Japan* .... 31 H5   33 38N 130 42 E
Ijebu-Ode, *Nigeria* .... 50 G6   6 47N   3 58 E
IJmuiden, *Neths.* .... 15 B4   52 28N   4 35 E
IJssel →, *Neths.* .... 15 B5   52 35N   5 50 E
IJsselmeer, *Neths.* .... 15 B5   52 45N   5 20 E
Ijuí, *Brazil* 95 B5   28 23S 53 55W
Ijuí →, *Brazil* 95 B4   27 58S 55 20W
Ikalamavony, *Madag.* .... 57 C8   21 9S 46 35 E
Ikaluktutiak, *Canada* 68 B9   69 10N 105 0W
Ikare, *Nigeria* .... 50 G7   7 32N   5 40 E
Ikaria, *Greece* .... 23 F12 37 35N 26 10 E
Ikeda, *Japan* .... 31 G6   34 1N 133 48 E
Ikela, *Dem. Rep. of the Congo* . 52 E4   1 6S 23 6 E
Iki, *Japan* .... 31 H4   33 45N 129 42 E
Ikimba L., *Tanzania* .... 54 C3   1 30S 31 20 E
Ikongo, *Madag.* .... 57 C8   21 52S 47 27 E
Ikopa →, *Madag.* .... 57 B8   16 45S 46 40 E
Ikorongo △, *Tanzania* .... 54 C3   1 50S 34 53 E
Ikparjuk = Arctic Bay, *Canada* . 69 A11 73 1N 85 7W
Ikungu, *Tanzania* .... 54 C3   1 33S 33 42 E
Ilagan, *Phil.* .... 37 A6   17 7N 121 53 E
Ilaka, *Madag.* .... 57 B8   19 33S 48 52 E
Ilām, *Iran* .... 44 C5   33 36N 46 36 E
Ilam, *Nepal* .... 43 F12 26 58N 87 58 E
Ilam □, *Iran* .... 44 C5   33 0N 47 0 E
Ilanskiy, *Russia* .... 29 D10 56 14N 96 3 E
Iława, *Poland* .... 17 B10 53 36N 19 34 E
Ile →, *Kazakhstan* .... 28 E8   45 53N 77 10 E
Île-à-la-Crosse, *Canada* 71 B7   55 27N 107 53W
Île-à-la-Crosse, Lac, *Canada* . 71 B7   55 40N 107 45W
Île-de-France □, *France* .... 20 B5   49 0N   2 20 E
Ilebo, *Dem. Rep. of the Congo* . 52 E4   4 17S 20 55 E
Ilek, *Russia* .... 28 D6   51 32N 53 21 E
Ilek →, *Russia* .... 18 D9   51 30N 53 22 E
Ilesha, *Nigeria* .... 50 G6   7 37N   4 40 E
Ilford, *Canada* 71 B9   56 4N 95 35W
Ilfracombe, *Australia* ...... 62 C3   23 30S 144 30 E
Ilfracombe, *U.K.* 13 F3   51 12N   4 8W
Ilha de Moçambique, *Mozam.* . 55 F5   15 4S 40 52 E
Ilhéus, *Brazil* 93 F11 14 49S 39 2W
Ili = Ile →, *Kazakhstan* .... 28 E8   45 53N 77 10 E
Iliamna L., *U.S.A.* 68 C4   59 30N 155 0W
Iligan, *Phil.* .... 37 C6   8 12N 124 13 E
Ilion, *U.S.A.* 85 D9   43 1N 75 2W
Ilkeston, *U.K.* 12 E6   52 58N   1 19W
Ilkley, *U.K.* 12 D6   53 56N   1 48W
Illampu = Ancohuma, Nevado,
  Bolivia 92 G5   16 0S 68 50W
Illana B., *Phil.* .... 37 C6   7 35N 123 45 E
Illapel, *Chile* 94 C1   32 0S 71 10W
Iller →, *Germany* .... 16 D6   48 23N   9 58 E
Illetas, *Spain* .... 24 B9   39 32N   2 35 E
Illimani, Nevado, *Bolivia* ... 92 G5   16 30S 67 50W
Illinois □, *U.S.A.* 80 E10 40 15N 89 30W
Illinois →, *U.S.A.* 80 F9   38 58N 90 28W
Illizi, *Algeria* .... 50 C7   26 31N   8 32 E
Ilmajoki, *Finland* .... 9 E20 62 44N 22 34 E
Ilmen, Ozero, *Russia* .... 18 C5   58 15N 31 10 E
Ilo, *Peru* 92 G4   17 40S 71 20W
Iloilo, *Phil.* .... 37 B6   10 45N 122 33 E
Ilorin, *Nigeria* .... 50 G6   8 30N   4 35 E
Ilwaco, *U.S.A.* 78 D2   46 19N 124 3W
Ilwaki, *Indonesia* .... 37 F7   7 55S 126 30 E
Imabari, *Japan* .... 31 G6   34 4N 133 0 E
Imaloto →, *Madag.* .... 57 C8   23 27S 45 13 E
Imandra, Ozero, *Russia* .... 18 A5   67 30N 33 0 E
Imanombo, *Madag.* .... 57 C8   24 26S 45 49 E
Imari, *Japan* .... 31 H4   33 15N 129 52 E
Imatra, *Finland* .... 18 B4   61 12N 28 48 E
Imbil, *Australia* .... 63 D5   26 22S 152 32 E
imeni 26 Bakinskikh
  Komissarov = Neftçala,
  Azerbaijan .... 19 G8   39 19N 49 12 E
imeni 26 Bakinskikh Komissarov,
  Turkmenistan .... 45 B7   39 22N 54 10 E
Imeri, Serra, *Brazil* 92 C5   0 50N 65 25W
Imerimandroso, *Madag.* ..... 57 B8   17 26S 48 35 E
Imi, *Ethiopia* .... 47 F3   6 28N 42 10 E
Imlay, *U.S.A.* 76 F4   40 40N 118 9W
Imlay City, *U.S.A.* 84 D1   43 2N 83 5W
Immingham, *U.K.* 12 D7   53 37N   0 13W
Immokalee, *U.S.A.* 83 M5   26 25N 81 25W
Ímola, *Italy* .... 22 B4   44 20N 11 42 E
Imperatriz, *Brazil* 93 E9   5 30S 47 29W
Impéria, *Italy* .... 20 E8   43 53N   8 3 E
Imperial, *Canada* 71 C7   51 21N 105 28W
Imperial, Calif., *U.S.A.* 79 N11 32 51N 115 34W
Imperial, Nebr., *U.S.A.* 80 E4   40 31N 101 39W
Imperial Beach, *U.S.A.* 79 N9   32 35N 117 8W
Imperial Dam, *U.S.A.* 79 N12 32 55N 114 25W
Imperial Reservoir, *U.S.A.* .. 79 N12 32 53N 114 28W
Imperial Valley, *U.S.A.* 79 N11 33 0N 115 30W
Imperieuse Reef, *Australia* .. 60 C2   17 36S 118 50 E
Impfondo, *Congo* .... 52 D3   1 40N 18 0 E
Imphal, *India* .... 41 G18 24 48N 93 56 E
İmroz = Gökçeada, *Turkey* ... 23 D11 40 10N 25 50 E
Imuris, *Mexico* 86 A2   30 47N 110 52W
Imuruan B., *Phil.* .... 37 B5   10 40N 119 10 E
In Salah, *Algeria* .... 50 C6   27 10N   2 32 E
Ina, *Japan* .... 31 G8   35 50N 137 55 E
Inagua □, *Bahamas* 89 B5   21 5N 73 24W
Inangahua, *N.Z.* .... 59 J3   41 52S 171 59 E
Inanwatan, *Indonesia* ...... 37 E8   2 8S 132 10 E
Iñapari, *Peru* 92 F5   11 0S 69 40W
Inari, *Finland* .... 8 B22 68 54N 27 5 E
Inarijärvi, *Finland* .... 8 B22 69 0N 28 0 E
Inawashiro-Ko, *Japan* ..... 30 F10 37 29N 140 6 E
Inca, *Spain* .... 24 B9   39 43N   2 54 E
Inca de Oro, *Chile* 94 B2   26 45S 69 54W
Incaguasi, *Chile* 94 B1   29 12S 71 5W
İnce Burun, *Turkey* .... 19 F5   42 7N 34 56 E
İncesu, *Turkey* .... 44 B2   38 38N 35 11 E
Inch'ŏn, *S. Korea* .... 35 F14 37 27N 126 40 E
İncirliova, *Turkey* .... 23 F12 37 50N 27 41 E

Incline Village, *U.S.A.* 76 G4   39 10N 119 58W
Incomáti →, *Mozam.* .... 57 D5   25 46S 32 43 E
Indalsälven →, *Sweden* ...... 9 E17 62 36N 17 30 E
Indaw, *Burma* .... 41 G20 24 15N 96 5 E
Independence, Calif., *U.S.A.* . 78 J8   36 48N 118 12W
Independence, Iowa, *U.S.A.* . 80 D9   42 28N 91 54W
Independence, Kans., *U.S.A.* . 81 G7   37 14N 95 42W
Independence, Ky., *U.S.A.* .. 82 F3   38 57N 84 33W
Independence, Mo., *U.S.A.* .. 80 F7   39 6N 94 25W
Independence Fjord, *Greenland* . 4 A6   82 10N 29 0W
Independence Mts., *U.S.A.* .. 76 F5   41 20N 116 0W
Index, *U.S.A.* 78 C5   47 50N 121 33W
India ■, *Asia* .... 40 K11 20 0N 78 0 E
Indian →, *U.S.A.* 83 M5   27 59N 80 34W
Indian Cabins, *Canada* 70 B5   59 52N 117 40W
Indian Harbour, *Canada* 73 B8   54 27N 57 13W
Indian Head, *Canada* 71 C8   50 30N 103 41W
Indian Lake, *U.S.A.* 85 C10 43 47N 74 16W
Indian Ocean .... 26 K11   5 0S 75 0 E
Indian Springs, *U.S.A.* 79 J11 36 35N 115 40W
Indiana, *U.S.A.* 84 F5   40 37N 79 9W
Indiana □, *U.S.A.* 82 F3   40 0N 86 0W
Indianapolis, *U.S.A.* 82 F2   39 46N 86 9W
Indianola, Iowa, *U.S.A.* 80 E8   41 22N 93 34W
Indianola, Miss., *U.S.A.* 81 J9   33 27N 90 39W
Indiga, *Russia* .... 18 A8   67 38N 49 9 E
Indigirka →, *Russia* .... 29 B15 70 48N 148 54 E
Indio, *U.S.A.* 79 M10 33 43N 116 13W
Indira Gandhi Canal, *India* .. 42 F5   28 0N 72 0 E
Indo-China, *Asia* .... 26 H14 15 0N 102 0 E
Indonesia ■, *Asia* .... 36 F5   5 0S 115 0 E
Indore, *India* .... 42 H6   22 42N 75 53 E
Indramayu, *Indonesia* ...... 37 G13   6 20S 108 19 E
Indravati →, *India* .... 41 K12 19 20N 80 20 E
Indre →, *France* .... 20 C4   47 16N   0 11 E
Indulkana, *Australia* .... 63 D1   26 58S 133 5 E
Indus →, *Pakistan* .... 42 G2   24 20N 67 47 E
Indus, Mouths of the, *Pakistan* . 42 H3   24 0N 68 0 E
İnebolu, *Turkey* .... 19 F5   41 55N 33 40 E
Infiernillo, Presa del, *Mexico* . 86 D4   18 9N 102 0W
Ingenio, Canary Is. 24 G4   27 55N 15 26W
Ingenio Santa Ana, *Argentina* . 94 B2   27 25S 65 40W
Ingersoll, *Canada* 84 C4   43 4N 80 55W
Ingham, *Australia* .... 62 B4   18 43S 146 10 E
Ingleborough, *U.K.* 12 C5   54 10N   2 22W
Inglewood, Queens., *Australia* . 63 D5   28 25S 151 2 E
Inglewood, Vic., *Australia* ... 63 F3   36 29S 143 53 E
Inglewood, N.Z. .... 59 H5   39 9S 174 14 E
Inglewood, *U.S.A.* 79 M8   33 58N 118 21W
Ingólfshöfði, *Iceland* 8 E5   63 48N 16 39W
Ingomar, *U.S.A.* 76 C10 46 35N 107 23W
Ingonish, *Canada* 73 C7   46 42N 60 18W
Ingraj Bazar, *India* .... 43 G13 24 58N 88 10 E
Ingrid Christensen Coast,
  Antarctica .... 5 C6   69 30S 76 0 E
Ingulec = Inhulec, *Ukraine* .. 19 E5   47 42N 33 14 E
Ingushetia □, *Russia* ...... 19 F8   43 20N 44 50 E
Ingwavuma, S. Africa .... 57 D5   27 9S 31 59 E
Inhaca, *Mozam.* .... 57 D5   26 1S 32 57 E
Inhafenga, *Mozam.* .... 57 C5   20 36S 33 53 E
Inhambane, *Mozam.* .... 57 C6   23 54S 35 30 E
Inhambane □, *Mozam.* ..... 57 C5   22 30S 34 20 E
Inhaminga, *Mozam.* .... 55 F4   18 26S 35 0 E
Inharrime, *Mozam.* .... 57 C6   24 30S 35 0 E
Inharrime →, *Mozam.* ...... 57 C6   24 30S 35 0 E
Inhulec, *Ukraine* .... 19 E5   47 42N 33 14 E
Ining = Yining, *China* ...... 28 E9   43 58N 81 10 E
Inírida →, *Colombia* 92 C5   3 55N 67 52W
Inishbofin, *Ireland* 10 C1   53 37N 10 13W
Inisheer, *Ireland* 10 C2   53 3N   9 32W
Inishfree B., *Ireland* 10 A3   55 4N   8 23W
Inishkea North, *Ireland* 10 B1   54 9N 10 11W
Inishkea South, *Ireland* 10 B1   54 7N 10 12W
Inishmaan, *Ireland* 10 C2   53 5N   9 35W
Inishmore, *Ireland* 10 C2   53 8N   9 45W
Inishowen Pen., *Ireland* 10 A4   55 14N   7 15W
Inishshark, *Ireland* 10 C1   53 37N 10 16W
Inishturk, *Ireland* 10 C1   53 42N 10 7W
Inishvickillane, *Ireland* 10 D1   52 3N   10 37W
Injune, *Australia* .... 63 D4   25 53S 148 32 E
Inklin →, *Canada* 70 B2   58 50N 133 10W
Inland Kaikoura Ra., *N.Z.* ... 59 J4   41 59S 173 41 E
Inland Sea = Setonaikai, *Japan* . 31 G6   34 20N 133 30 E
Inle L., *Burma* .... 41 J20 20 30N 96 58 E
Inlet, *U.S.A.* 85 C10 43 45N 74 48W
Inn →, *Austria* .... 16 D7   48 35N 13 28 E
Innamincka, *Australia* ...... 63 D3   27 44S 140 46 E
Inner Hebrides, *U.K.* 11 E2   57 0N   6 30W
Inner Mongolia = Nei Monggol
  Zizhiqu □, *China* .... 34 D7   42 0N 112 0 E
Inner Sound, *U.K.* 11 D3   57 30N   5 55W
Innerkip, *Canada* 84 C4   43 13N 80 42W
Innetalling I., *Canada* 72 A4   56 0N 79 0W
Innisfail, *Australia* .... 62 B4   17 33S 146 5 E
Innisfail, *Canada* 70 C6   52 2N 113 57W
In'noshima, *Japan* .... 31 G6   34 19N 133 10 E
Innsbruck, *Austria* .... 16 E6   47 16N 11 23 E
Inny →, *Ireland* 10 C4   53 30N   7 50W
Inongo, *Dem. Rep. of the Congo* . 52 E3   1 55S 18 30 E
Inoucdjouac = Inukjuak, *Canada* . 69 C12 58 25N 78 15W
Inowrocław, *Poland* .... 17 B10 52 50N 18 12 E
Inpundong, N. Korea .... 35 D14 41 25N 126 34 E
Inscription, C., *Australia* .... 61 E1   25 29S 112 59 E
Insein, *Burma* .... 41 L20 16 50N 96 5 E
Inta, *Russia* .... 18 A11 66 5N 60 8 E
Intendente Alvear, *Argentina* . 94 D3   35 12S 63 32W
Interlaken, *Switz.* .... 20 C7   46 41N   7 50 E
Interlaken, *U.S.A.* 85 D8   42 37N 76 44W
International Falls, *U.S.A.* ... 80 A8   48 36N 93 25W
Intiyaco, *Argentina* 94 B3   28 43S 60 5W
Inukjuak, *Canada* 69 C12 58 25N 78 15W
Inútil, B., *Chile* 96 G2   53 30S 70 15W
Inuvik, *Canada* 68 B6   68 16N 133 40W
Inveraray, *U.K.* 11 E3   56 14N   5 5W
Inverbervie, *U.K.* 11 E6   56 51N   2 17W
Invercargill, *N.Z.* .... 59 M2   46 24S 168 24 E
Inverclyde □, *U.K.* 11 F4   55 55N   4 49W
Inverell, *Australia* .... 63 D5   29 45S 151 8 E
Invergordon, *U.K.* 11 D4   57 41N   4 10W
Inverloch, *Australia* .... 63 F4   38 38S 145 45 E
Invermere, *Canada* 70 C5   50 30N 116 2W
Inverness, *Canada* 73 C7   46 15N 61 19W
Inverness, *U.K.* 11 D4   57 29N   4 13W
Inverness, *U.S.A.* 83 L4   28 50N 82 20W
Inverurie, *U.K.* 11 D6   57 17N   2 23W
Investigator Group, *Australia* . 63 E1   34 45S 134 20 E

Investigator Str., *Australia* ... 63 F2   35 30S 137 0 E
Inya, *Russia* .... 28 D9   50 28N 86 37 E
Inyanga, *Zimbabwe* .... 55 F3   18 12S 32 40 E
Inyangani, *Zimbabwe* ...... 55 F3   18 5S 32 50 E
Inyantue, *Zimbabwe* .... 55 F2   18 33S 26 39 E
Inyo Mts., *U.S.A.* 78 J9   36 40N 118 0W
Inyokern, *U.S.A.* 79 K9   35 39N 117 49W
Inza, *Russia* .... 18 D8   53 55N 46 25 E
Iō-Jima, *Japan* .... 31 J5   30 48N 130 18 E
Ioánnina, *Greece* .... 23 E9   39 42N 20 47 E
Iola, *U.S.A.* 81 G7   37 55N 95 24W
Ione, *U.S.A.* 78 G6   38 21N 120 56W
Ionia, *U.S.A.* 82 D3   42 59N 85 4W
Ionian Is. = Iónioi Nísoi, *Greece* . 23 E9   38 40N 20 0 E
Ionian Sea, Medit. S. .... 23 E7   37 30N 17 30 E
Iónioi Nísoi, *Greece* .... 23 E9   38 40N 20 0 E
Íos, *Greece* .... 23 F11 36 41N 25 20 E
Iowa □, *U.S.A.* 80 D8   42 18N 93 30W
Iowa →, *U.S.A.* 80 E9   41 10N 91 1W
Iowa City, *U.S.A.* 80 E9   41 40N 91 32W
Iowa Falls, *U.S.A.* 80 D8   42 31N 93 16W
Iowa Park, *U.S.A.* 81 J5   33 57N 98 40W
Ipala, *Tanzania* .... 54 C3   4 30S 32 52 E
Ipameri, *Brazil* 93 G9   17 44S 48 9W
Ipatinga, *Brazil* 93 G10 19 32S 42 30W
Ipiales, *Colombia* 92 C3   0 50N 77 37W
Ipin = Yibin, *China* .... 32 D5   28 45N 104 32 E
Ipixuna, *Brazil* 92 E4   7 0S 71 40W
Ipoh, *Malaysia* .... 39 K3   4 35N 101 5 E
Ippy, *C.A.R.* .... 52 C4   6 5N 21 7 E
İpsala, *Turkey* .... 23 D12 40 55N 26 23 E
Ipswich, *Australia* .... 63 D5   27 35S 152 40 E
Ipswich, *U.K.* .... 13 E9   52 4N   1 10 E
Ipswich, Mass., *U.S.A.* 85 D14 42 41N 70 50W
Ipswich, S. Dak., *U.S.A.* ... 80 C5   45 27N 99 2W
Ipu, *Brazil* 93 D10   4 23S 40 44W
Iqaluit, *Canada* 69 B13 63 44N 68 31W
Iquique, *Chile* 92 H4   20 19S 70 5W
Iquitos, *Peru* 92 D4   3 45S 73 10W
Irabu-Jima, *Japan* .... 31 M2   24 50N 125 10 E
Iracoubo, Fr. Guiana 93 B8   5 30N 53 10W
Īrafshān, *Iran* .... 45 E9   26 42N 61 56 E
Iráklion, *Greece* .... 25 D7   35 20N 25 12 E
Iráklion □, *Greece* .... 25 D7   35 10N 25 10 E
Irala, *Paraguay* 95 B5   25 55S 54 35W
Iran ■, *Asia* .... 45 C7   33 0N 53 0 E
Iran, Gunung-Gunung, *Malaysia* . 36 D4   2 20N 114 50 E
Iran, Plateau of, *Asia* ...... 26 F9   32 0N 55 0 E
Iran Ra. = Iran, Gunung-Gunung,
  Malaysia .... 36 D4   2 20N 114 50 E
Īrānshahr, *Iran* .... 45 E9   27 15N 60 40 E
Irapuato, *Mexico* 86 C4   20 40N 101 30W
Iraq ■, *Asia* .... 44 C5   33 0N 44 0 E
Irati, *Brazil* 95 B5   25 25S 50 38W
Irbid, *Jordan* .... 46 C4   32 35N 35 48 E
Irbid □, *Jordan* .... 46 C5   32 15N 36 35 E
Ireland ■, *Europe* 10 C4   53 50N   7 52W
Irhyangdong, N. Korea ..... 35 D15 41 15N 129 30 E
Iri, S. Korea .... 35 G14 35 59N 127 0 E
Irian Jaya = Papua □, *Indonesia* . 37 E9   4 0S 137 0 E
Iringa, *Tanzania* .... 54 D4   7 48S 35 43 E
Iringa □, *Tanzania* .... 54 D4   7 48S 35 43 E
Iriomote △, *Japan* .... 31 M1   24 29N 123 53 E
Iriomote-Jima, *Japan* ...... 31 M1   24 19N 123 48 E
Iriona, *Honduras* 88 C2   15 57N 85 11W
Iriri →, *Brazil* 93 D8   3 52S 52 37W
Irish Republic ■, *Europe* ... 10 C4   53 50N   7 52W
Irish Sea, *U.K.* 12 D3   53 38N   4 48W
Irkutsk, *Russia* .... 29 D11 52 18N 104 20 E
Irma, *Canada* 71 C6   52 55N 111 4W
Irō-Zaki, *Japan* .... 31 G9   34 36N 138 51 E
Iron Baron, *Australia* ...... 63 E2   32 58S 137 11 E
Iron Gate = Portile de Fier,
  Europe .... 17 F12 44 44N 22 30 E
Iron Knob, *Australia* .... 63 E2   32 46S 137 8 E
Iron Mountain, *U.S.A.* 82 C1   45 49N 88 4W
Iron Range △, *Australia* .... 62 A3   12 34S 143 18 E
Iron River, *U.S.A.* 80 B10 46 6N 88 39W
Irondequoit, *U.S.A.* 84 C7   43 13N 77 35W
Ironton, Mo., *U.S.A.* 81 G9   37 36N 90 38W
Ironton, Ohio, *U.S.A.* 82 F4   38 32N 82 41W
Ironwood, *U.S.A.* 80 B9   46 27N 90 9W
Ironwood Forest △, *U.S.A.* .. 77 K8   32 28N 111 36W
Iroquois, *Canada* 85 B9   44 51N 75 19W
Iroquois Falls, *Canada* 72 C3   48 46N 80 41W
Irpin, *Ukraine* .... 17 C16 50 30N 30 15 E
Irrara Cr. →, *Australia* ..... 63 D4   29 35S 145 31 E
Irrawaddy □, *Burma* .... 41 L19 17 0N 95 0 E
Irrawaddy →, *Burma* ...... 41 M19 15 50N 95 6 E
Irrawaddy, Mouths of the, *Burma* . 41 M19 15 30N 95 0 E
Irricana, *Canada* 70 C6   51 19N 113 37W
Irtysh →, *Russia* .... 28 C7   61 4N 68 52 E
Irumu, Dem. Rep. of the Congo . 54 B2   1 32N 29 53 E
Irún, *Spain* 21 A5   43 20N   1 52W
Irunea = Pamplona, *Spain* .. 21 A5   42 48N   1 38W
Irvine, *U.K.* 11 F4   55 37N   4 41W
Irvine, Calif., *U.S.A.* 79 M9   33 41N 117 46W
Irvine, Ky., *U.S.A.* 82 G4   37 42N 83 58W
Irvinestown, *U.K.* 10 B4   54 28N   7 39W
Irvona, *U.S.A.* 84 F6   40 46N 78 33W
Irwin →, *Australia* .... 61 E1   29 15S 114 54 E
Irymple, *Australia* .... 63 E3   34 14S 142 8 E
Isa Khel, *Pakistan* .... 42 C4   32 41N 71 17 E
Isaac →, *Australia* .... 62 C4   22 55S 149 20 E
Isabel, *U.S.A.* 80 C4   45 24N 101 26W
Isabela, Puerto Rico .... 89 d   18 30N 67 2W
Isabela, *Phil.* 86 C3   21 51N 105 55W
Isabela, Cord., Nic. 88 D2   13 30N 85 25W
Isabella, B., *Australia* ..... 60 D3   21 0S 121 4 E
Isafjarðardjúp, *Iceland* 8 C2   66 10N 23 0W
Ísafjörður, *Iceland* 8 C2   66 5N 23 9W
Isagarh, *India* .... 42 G7   24 48N 77 51 E
Isahaya, *Japan* .... 31 H5   32 52N 130 2 E
Isaka, *Tanzania* .... 54 C3   3 56S 32 59 E
Isalo △, *Madag.* .... 57 C8   22 23S 45 16 E
Isana = Içana →, *Brazil* ... 92 C5   0 26N 67 19W
Isangano △, *Zambia* .... 55 E3   11 8S 30 35 E
Isar →, *Germany* .... 16 D7   48 48N 12 57 E
Íschia, *Italy* .... 22 D5   40 44N 13 57 E
Isdell →, *Australia* .... 60 C3   16 27S 124 51 E
Ise, *Japan* .... 31 G8   34 25N 136 45 E
Ise-Shima △, *Japan* .... 31 G8   34 25N 136 48 E
Ise-Wan, *Japan* .... 31 G8   34 43N 136 43 E

Iseramagazi, *Tanzania* 54 C3   4 37S 32 10
Isère →, *France* 20 D6   44 59N   4 51
Isérnia, *Italy* 22 D6   41 36N 14 14
Isfahan = Eşfahān, *Iran* 45 C6   32 39N 51 43
Ishigaki-Shima, *Japan* 31 M2   24 20N 124 10
Ishikari-Gawa →, *Japan* 30 C10 43 15N 141 23
Ishikari-Sammyaku, *Japan* .. 30 C11 43 30N 143 0
Ishikari-Wan, *Japan* 30 C10 43 25N 141 1
Ishikawa □, *Japan* 31 F8   36 30N 136 30
Ishim, *Russia* 28 D7   56 10N 69 30
Ishim →, *Russia* 28 D8   57 45N 71 10
Ishinomaki, *Japan* 30 E10 38 32N 141 20
Ishioka, *Japan* 31 F10 36 11N 140 16
Ishkuman, *Pakistan* 43 A5   36 30N 73 50
Ishpeming, *U.S.A.* 82 B2   46 29N 87 40W
Isil Kul, *Russia* 28 D8   54 55N 71 16
Isiolo, *Kenya* 54 B4   0 24N 37 33
Isiro, Dem. Rep. of the Congo . 54 B2   2 53N 27 40
Isisford, *Australia* 62 C3   24 15S 144 21
Iskenderun, *Turkey* 19 G6   36 32N 36 10
Iskenderun Körfezi, *Turkey* .. 19 G6   36 40N 35 50
Iskŭr →, *Bulgaria* 23 C11 43 45N 24 25
Iskut →, *Canada* 70 B2   56 45N 131 49W
Isla →, *U.K.* 11 E5   56 32N   3 20
Isla Coiba △, *Panama* 88 E3   7 33N 81 36
Isla de Salamanca △, *Colombia* . 89 D5 10 59N 74 40
Isla Gorge △, *Australia* 62 D4   25 10S 149 57
Isla Tiburón y San Esteban △,
  Mexico 86 B2   29 0N 112 27W
Isla Vista, *U.S.A.* 79 L7   34 25N 119 53W
Islam Headworks, *Pakistan* . 42 E5   29 49N 72 33
Islamabad, *Pakistan* 42 C5   33 40N 73 10
Islamgarh, *Pakistan* 42 F4   27 51N 70 48
Islamkot, *Pakistan* 42 G4   24 42N 70 13
Islampur, *India* 43 G11 25 9N 85 12
Island L., *Canada* 71 C10 53 47N 94 25W
Island Lagoon, *Australia* ... 63 E2   31 30S 136 40
Island Pond, *U.S.A.* 85 B13 44 49N 71 53W
Islands, B. of, *Canada* 73 C8   49 11N 58 15W
Islands, B. of, *N.Z.* 59 F5   35 15S 174 6
Islay, *U.K.* 11 F2   55 46N   6 10W
Isle →, *France* 20 D3   44 55N   0 15W
Isle of Wight □, *U.K.* 13 G6   50 41N   1 17W
Isle Royale △, *U.S.A.* 80 A10 48 0N 88 55W
Isleton, *U.S.A.* 78 G5   38 10N 121 37W
Ismail = Izmayil, *Ukraine* ... 17 F15 45 22N 28 46
Ismâ'ilîya, *Egypt* 51 B12 30 37N 32 18
Isoanala, *Madag.* 57 C8   23 50S 45 44
Isogstalo, *India* 43 B8   34 15N 78 46
Isparta, *Turkey* 19 G5   37 47N 30 30
Íspica, *Italy* 22 F6   36 47N 14 55
Israel ■, *Asia* 46 D3   32 0N 34 50
Issoire, *France* 20 D5   45 32N   3 15
Issyk-Kul, Ozero = Ysyk-Köl,
  Kyrgyzstan 28 E8   42 25N 77 15
İstanbul, *Turkey* 23 D13 41 10N 29 0
İstanbul Boğazı, *Turkey* 23 D13 41 10N 29 10
Istiaía, *Greece* 23 E10 38 57N 23 9
Istokpoga, L., *U.S.A.* 83 M5   27 23N 81 17
Istra, *Croatia* 16 F7   45 10N 14 0
Istres, *France* 20 E6   43 31N   4 59
Istria = Istra, *Croatia* 16 F7   45 10N 14 0
Itá, *Paraguay* 94 B4   25 29S 57 21W
Itaberaba, *Brazil* 93 F10 12 32S 40 18W
Itabira, *Brazil* 93 G10 19 37S 43 13W
Itabirito, *Brazil* 95 A7   20 15S 43 48W
Itabuna, *Brazil* 93 F11 14 48S 39 16W
Itacaunas →, *Brazil* 93 E9   5 21S 49 8W
Itacoatiara, *Brazil* 92 D7   3 8S 58 25W
Itaipú, Reprêsa de, *Brazil* .. 95 B5   25 30S 54 30W
Itaituba, *Brazil* 93 D7   4 10S 55 50W
Itajaí, *Brazil* 95 B6   27 50S 48 39W
Itajubá, *Brazil* 95 A6   22 24S 45 30W
Itaka, *Tanzania* 55 D3   8 50S 32 49
Itala △, S. Africa 57 D5   27 30S 31 7
Italy ■, *Europe* 22 C5   42 0N 13 0
Itamaraju, *Brazil* 93 G11 17 5S 39 31W
Itampolo, *Madag.* 57 C7   24 41S 43 57
Itandrano, *Madag.* 57 C8   21 47S 45 17
Itapecuru-Mirim, *Brazil* 93 D10   3 24S 44 20W
Itaperuna, *Brazil* 95 A7   21 10S 41 54W
Itapetininga, *Brazil* 95 A6   23 36S 48 7W
Itapeva, *Brazil* 95 A6   23 59S 48 59W
Itapicuru →, Bahia, *Brazil* .. 93 F11 11 47S 37 32W
Itapicuru →, Maranhão, *Brazil* . 93 D10   2 52S 44 12W
Itapipoca, *Brazil* 93 D11   3 30S 39 35W
Itaquari, *Paraguay* 95 B4   24 30S 54 40W
Itaquari, *Brazil* 95 A7   20 20S 40 25W
Itaqui, *Brazil* 94 B4   29 8S 56 30W
Itararé, *Brazil* 95 A6   24 6S   49 23W
Itarsi, *India* 42 H7   22 36N 77 51
Itatí, *Argentina* 94 B4   27 16S 58 15W
Itatiaia △, *Brazil* 95 A7   22 29S 44 35W
Itchen →, *U.K.* 13 G6   50 55N   1 22
Itezhi Tezhi, L., *Zambia* 55 F2   15 30S 25 30
Íthaca = Itháki, *Greece* 23 E9   38 25N 20 40
Ithaca, *U.S.A.* 85 D8   42 27N 76 30W
Itháki, *Greece* 23 E9   38 25N 20 40
Itiquira →, *Brazil* 93 G7   17 18S 56 44W
Itō, *Japan* 31 G9   34 58N 139 5
Itoigawa, *Japan* 31 F8   37 2N 137 51
Itonamas →, *Bolivia* 92 F6   12 28S 64 24W
Ittoqqortoormiit, *Greenland* .. 4 B6   70 20N 23 0
Itu, *Brazil* 95 A6   23 17S 47 15W
Itu Aba I., S. China Sea 36 B4   10 23N 114 21
Ituiutaba, *Brazil* 93 G9   19 0S 49 25W
Itumbiara, *Brazil* 93 G9   18 20S 49 10W
Ituna, *Canada* 71 C8   51 10N 103 24W
Itunge Port, *Tanzania* 55 D3   9 40S 33 55
Iturbe, *Argentina* 94 A2   23 0S 65 25W
Ituri →, Dem. Rep. of the Congo . 54 B2   1 40N 27 1
Iturup, Ostrov, *Russia* 29 E15 45 0N 148 0
Ituxi →, *Brazil* 92 E6   7 18S 64 51W
Ituyuro →, *Argentina* 94 A3   22 40S 63 50W
Itzehoe, *Germany* 16 B5   53 55N   9 31
Ivahona, *Madag.* 57 C8   23 27S 46 10
Ivaí →, *Brazil* 95 A5   23 18S 53 42W
Ivalo, *Finland* 8 B22 68 38N 27 35
Ivalojoki →, *Finland* 8 B22 68 40N 27 40
Ivanava, *Belarus* 17 B13 52 7N 25 29
Ivanhoe, *Australia* 63 E3   32 56S 144 20
Ivanhoe, Calif., *U.S.A.* 78 J7   36 23N 119 13W
Ivanhoe, Minn., *U.S.A.* 80 C6   44 28N 96 15W
Ivano-Frankivsk, *Ukraine* ... 17 D13 48 40N 24 40
Ivanovo = Ivanava, *Belarus* . 17 B13 52 7N 25 29
Ivanovo, *Russia* 18 C7   57 5N 41 0

Ivato, Madag. .... 57 C8 20 37S 47 10 E
Ivatsevichy, Belarus ...... 17 B13 52 43N 25 21 E
Ivdel, Russia .... 18 B11 60 42N 60 24 E
Ivinheima, Brazil 95 A5 23 14S 53 42W
Ivinhema, Brazil 95 A5 22 10S 53 37W
Ivohibe, Madag. .... 57 C8 22 31S 46 57 E
Ivory Coast, W. Afr. 50 H4   4 20N   5 0W
Ivory Coast ■, Africa 50 G4   7 30N   5 0W
Ivrea, Italy .... 20 D7 45 28N   7 52 E
Ivujivik, Canada 69 B12 62 24N 77 55W
Ivybridge, U.K. 13 G4 50 23N   3 56W
Iwaizumi, Japan .... 30 E10 39 50N 141 45 E
Iwaki, Japan .... 31 F10 37 3N 140 55 E
Iwakuni, Japan .... 31 G6 34 15N 132 8 E
Iwamizawa, Japan .... 30 C10 43 12N 141 46 E
Iwanai, Japan .... 30 C10 42 58N 140 30 E
Iwata, Japan .... 31 G8 34 42N 137 51 E
Iwate □, Japan .... 30 E10 39 30N 141 30 E
Iwate-San, Japan .... 30 E10 39 51N 141 0 E
Iwo, Nigeria .... 50 G6   7 39N   4 9 E
Ixiamas, Bolivia 92 F5 13 50S 68 5W
Ixopo, S. Africa .... 57 E5 30 11S 30 5 E
Ixtepec, Mexico 87 D5 16 32N 95 10W
Ixtlán del Río, Mexico 86 C4 21 5N 104 21W
Iyo, Japan .... 31 H6 33 45N 132 45 E
Izabal, L. de, Guatemala .. 88 C2 15 30N 89 10W
Izamal, Mexico 87 C7 20 56N 89 1W
Izena-Shima, Japan .... 31 L3 26 56N 127 56 E
Izhevsk, Russia .... 18 C9 56 51N 53 14 E
Izhma →, Russia .... 18 A9 65 19N 52 54 E
Izmayil, Ukraine .... 17 F15 45 22N 28 46 E
İzmir, Turkey .... 23 E12 38 25N 27 8 E
İzmit = Kocaeli, Turkey ... 19 F4 40 45N 29 50 E
İznik Gölü, Turkey .... 23 D13 40 27N 29 30 E
Izra, Syria .... 46 C5 32 51N 36 15 E
Izu-Shotō, Japan .... 31 G10 34 30N 140 0 E
Izúcar de Matamoros, Mexico 87 D5 18 36N 98 28W
Izumi, Japan .... 31 G7 34 23N 135 18 E
Izumo, Japan .... 31 G6 35 20N 132 46 E
Izyaslav, Ukraine .... 17 C14 50 5N 26 50 E

J

Jabalpur, India .... 43 H8 23 9N 79 58 E
Jabbūl, Syria .... 44 B3 36 4N 37 30 E
Jabiru, Australia .... 60 B5 12 40S 132 53 E
Jablah, Syria .... 44 C3 35 20N 36 0 E
Jablonec nad Nisou, Czech Rep. 16 C8 50 43N 15 10 E
Jaboatão, Brazil 93 E11 8 7S 35 1W
Jaboticabal, Brazil 95 A6 21 15S 48 17W
Jaca, Spain 21 A5 42 35N   0 33W
Jacareí, Brazil 95 A6 23 20S 46 0W
Jacarèzinho, Brazil 95 A6 23 5S 49 58W
Jackman, U.S.A. 83 C10 45 35N 70 17W
Jacksboro, U.S.A. 81 J5 33 14N 98 15W
Jackson, Barbados .... 89 g   13 7N 59 36W
Jackson, Ala., U.S.A. 83 K2 31 31N 87 53W
Jackson, Calif., U.S.A. ... 78 G6 38 21N 120 46W
Jackson, Ky., U.S.A. 82 G4 37 33N 83 23W
Jackson, Mich., U.S.A. 82 D3 42 15N 84 24W
Jackson, Minn., U.S.A. 80 D7 43 37N 95 1W
Jackson, Miss., U.S.A. 81 J9 32 18N 90 12W
Jackson, Mo., U.S.A. 81 G10 37 23N 89 40W
Jackson, N.H., U.S.A. 85 B13 44 10N 71 11W
Jackson, Ohio, U.S.A. 82 F4 39 3N 82 39W
Jackson, Tenn., U.S.A. 83 H1 35 37N 88 49W
Jackson, Wyo., U.S.A. 76 E8 43 29N 110 46W
Jackson B., N.Z. .... 59 K2 43 58S 168 42 E
Jackson L., U.S.A. 76 E8 43 52N 110 36W
Jacksons, N.Z. .... 59 K3 42 46S 171 32 E
Jackson's Arm, Canada 73 C8 49 52N 56 47W
Jacksonville, Ala., U.S.A. . 83 J3 33 49N 85 46W
Jacksonville, Ark., U.S.A. . 81 H8 34 52N 92 7W
Jacksonville, Calif., U.S.A. 78 H6 37 52N 120 24W
Jacksonville, Fla., U.S.A. . 83 K5 30 20N 81 39W
Jacksonville, Ill., U.S.A. . 80 F9 39 44N 90 14W
Jacksonville, N.C., U.S.A. . 83 H7 34 45N 77 26W
Jacksonville, Tex., U.S.A. . 81 K7 31 58N 95 17W
Jacksonville Beach, U.S.A. . 83 K5 30 17N 81 24W
Jacmel, Haiti 89 C5 18 14N 72 32W
Jacob Lake, U.S.A. 77 H7 36 43N 112 13W
Jacobabad, Pakistan .... 42 E3 28 20N 68 29 E
Jacobina, Brazil 93 F10 11 11S 40 30W
Jacques-Cartier □, Canada . 73 C5 47 15N 71 33W
Jacques-Cartier, Dét. de, Canada 73 C7 50 0N 63 30W
Jacques-Cartier, Mt., Canada 73 C6 48 57N 66 0W
Jacuí →, Brazil 95 C5 30 2S 51 15W
Jacumba, U.S.A. 79 N10 32 37N 116 11W
Jacundá →, Brazil 93 D8   1 57S 50 26W
Jaén, Peru 92 E3   5 25S 78 40W
Jaén, Spain 21 D4 37 44N   3 43W
Jafarabad, India .... 42 J4 20 52N 71 22 E
Jaffa = Tel Aviv-Yafo, Israel 46 C3 32 4N 34 48 E
Jaffa, C., Australia ...... 63 F2 36 58S 139 40 E
Jaffna, Sri Lanka .... 40 Q12 9 45N 80 2 E
Jaffray, Canada 71 D10 49 47N 94 26W
Jaffrey, U.S.A. 85 D12 42 49N 72 2W
Jagadhri, India .... 42 D7 30 10N 77 20 E
Jagadishpur, India .... 43 G11 25 30N 84 21 E
Jagdalpur, India .... 41 K13 19 3N 82 0 E
Jagersfontein, S. Africa .. 56 D4 29 44S 25 27 E
Jaghin →, Iran .... 45 E8 27 17N 57 13 E
Jagodina, Serbia & M. ..... 23 C9 44 5N 21 15 E
Jagraon, India .... 40 D9 30 50N 75 25 E
Jagtial, India .... 40 K11 18 50N 79 0 E
Jaguariaíva, Brazil 95 A6 24 10S 49 50W
Jaguaribe →, Brazil 93 D11 4 25S 37 45W
Jagüey Grande, Cuba 88 B3 22 35N 81 7W
Jahanabad, India .... 43 G11 25 13N 84 59 E
Jahazpur, India .... 42 G6 25 37N 75 17 E
Jahrom, Iran .... 45 D7 28 30N 53 31 E
Jaijon, India .... 42 D7 31 21N 76 9 E
Jailolo, Indonesia .... 37 D7   1 5N 127 30 E
Jailolo, Selat, Indonesia . 37 D7   0 5N 129 5 E
Jaipur, India .... 42 F6 27 0N 75 50 E
Jais, India .... 43 F9 26 15N 81 32 E
Jaisalmer, India .... 42 F4 26 55N 70 54 E
Jaisinghnagar, India ...... 43 H8 23 38N 78 34 E
Jaitaran, India .... 42 G5 26 12N 73 56 E
Jaithari, India .... 43 H8 23 14N 78 37 E
Jajarm, Iran .... 45 B8 36 58N 56 27 E
Jakam →, India .... 42 H6 23 54N 74 13 E
Jakarta, Indonesia .... 36 F3   6 9S 106 49 E
Jakhal, India .... 42 E6 29 48N 75 50 E

Jakhau, India .... 42 H3 23 13N 68 43 E
Jakobstad = Pietarsaari, Finland 8 E20 63 40N 22 43 E
Jal, U.S.A. 81 J3 32 7N 103 12W
Jalālābād, Afghan. .... 42 B4 34 30N 70 29 E
Jalalabad, India .... 43 F8 27 41N 79 42 E
Jalalpur Jattan, Pakistan . 42 C6 32 38N 74 11 E
Jalama, U.S.A. 79 L6 34 29N 120 29W
Jalapa, Guatemala 88 D2 14 39N 89 59W
Jalapa Enríquez = Xalapa,
  Mexico 87 D5 19 32N 96 55W
Jalasjärvi, Finland .... 9 E20 62 29N 22 47 E
Jalaun, India .... 43 F8 26 8N 79 25 E
Jaldhaka →, Bangla. .... 43 F13 26 16N 89 16 E
Jalesar, India .... 42 F8 27 29N 78 19 E
Jaleswar, Nepal .... 43 F11 26 38N 85 48 E
Jalgaon, India .... 40 J9 21 0N 75 42 E
Jalibah, Iraq .... 44 D5 30 35N 46 32 E
Jalisco □, Mexico 86 D4 20 0N 104 0W
Jalkot, Pakistan .... 43 B5 35 14N 73 24 E
Jalna, India .... 40 K9 19 48N 75 38 E
Jalón →, Spain 21 B5 41 47N   1 4W
Jalor, India .... 42 G5 25 21N 72 37 E
Jalpa, Mexico 86 C4 21 38N 102 58W
Jalpaiguri, India .... 41 F16 26 32N 88 46 E
Jaluit I., Marshall Is. ... 64 G8   6 0N 169 30 E
Jalūlā, Iraq .... 44 C5 34 16N 45 10 E
Jamaica ■, W. Indies ...... 88 a 18 10N 77 30W
Jamalpur, Bangla. .... 41 G16 24 52N 89 56 E
Jamalpur, India .... 43 G12 25 18N 86 28 E
Jamalpurganj, India .... 43 H13 23 2N 87 59 E
Jamanxim →, Brazil 93 D7   4 43S 56 18W
Jambewangi, Indonesia ..... 37 J17 8 17S 114 7 E
Jambi, Indonesia .... 36 E2   1 38S 103 30 E
Jambi □, Indonesia .... 36 E2   1 30S 102 30 E
Jambusar, India .... 42 H5 22 3N 72 51 E
James →, S. Dak., U.S.A. .. 80 D6 42 52N 97 18W
James →, Va., U.S.A. 82 G7 36 56N 76 27W
James B., Canada 72 B3 54 0N 80 0W
James Ranges, Australia ... 60 D5 24 10S 132 30 E
James Ross I., Antarctica . 5 C18 63 58S 57 50W
Jamesabad, Pakistan .... 42 G3 25 17N 69 15 E
Jamestown, Australia ...... 63 E2 33 10S 138 32 E
Jamestown, S. Africa ...... 56 E4 31 6S 26 45 E
Jamestown, N. Dak., U.S.A. . 80 B5 46 54N 98 42W
Jamestown, N.Y., U.S.A. ... 84 D5 42 6N 79 14W
Jamestown, Pa., U.S.A. 84 E4 41 29N 80 27W
Jamīlābād, Iran .... 45 C6 34 24N 48 28 E
Jamiltepec, Mexico 87 D5 16 17N 97 49W
Jamira →, India .... 43 J13 21 35N 88 28 E
Jamkhandi, India .... 40 L9 16 30N 75 15 E
Jammu, India .... 42 C6 32 43N 74 54 E
Jammu & Kashmir □, India .. 43 B7 34 25N 77 0 E
Jamnagar, India .... 42 H4 22 30N 70 6 E
Jamni →, India .... 43 G8 25 13N 78 35 E
Jampur, Pakistan .... 42 E4 29 39N 70 40 E
Jamrud, Pakistan .... 42 C4 33 59N 71 24 E
Jämsä, Finland .... 9 F21 61 53N 25 10 E
Jamshedpur, India .... 43 H12 22 44N 86 12 E
Jamtara, India .... 43 H12 23 59N 86 49 E
Jämtland, Sweden .... 8 E15 63 31N 14 0 E
Jan L., Canada 71 C8 54 56N 102 55W
Jan Mayen, Arctic 4 B7 71 0N   9 0W
Janakkala, Finland .... 9 F21 60 54N 24 36 E
Janaúba, Brazil 93 G10 15 48S 43 19W
Jand, Pakistan .... 42 C5 33 30N 72 6 E
Jandaq, Iran .... 45 C7 34 3N 54 22 E
Jandía, Canary Is. 24 F5 28 6N 14 21W
Jandía △, Canary Is. 24 F5 28 4N 14 19W
Jandía, Pta. de, Canary Is. 24 F5 28 3N 14 31W
Jandola, Pakistan .... 42 C4 32 20N 70 9 E
Jandowae, Australia .... 63 D5 26 45S 151 7 E
Janesville, U.S.A. 80 D10 42 41N 89 1W
Jangamo, Mozam. .... 57 C6 24 6S 35 21 E
Janghai, India .... 43 G10 25 33N 82 19 E
Janjanbureh, Gambia 50 F3 13 30N 14 47W
Janjgir, India .... 43 J10 22 1N 82 34 E
Janjina, Madag. .... 57 C8 20 30S 45 50 E
Janos, Mexico 86 A3 30 45N 108 10W
Januária, Brazil 93 G10 15 25S 44 25W
Janūb Sīnī □, Egypt .... 46 F2 29 30N 33 50 E
Janubio, Canary Is. 24 F6 28 56N 13 50W
Jaora, India .... 42 H6 23 40N 75 10 E
Japan ■, Asia .... 31 G8 36 0N 136 0 E
Japan, Sea of, Asia .... 30 E7 40 0N 135 0 E
Japan Trench, Pac. Oc. .... 26 F18 32 0N 142 0 E
Japen = Yapen, Indonesia .. 37 E9   1 50S 136 0 E
Japla, India .... 43 G11 24 33N 84 1 E
Japurá →, Brazil 92 D5   3 8S 65 46W
Jaquarão, Brazil 95 C5 32 34S 53 23W
Jaqué, Panama 88 E4   7 27N 78 8W
Jarābulus, Syria .... 44 B3 36 49N 38 1 E
Jarama →, Spain 21 B4 40 24N   3 32W
Jaranwala, Pakistan .... 42 D5 31 15N 73 26 E
Jarash, Jordan .... 46 C4 32 17N 35 54 E
Jarash □, Jordan .... 46 C4 32 17N 35 54 E
Jardim, Brazil 94 A4 21 28S 56 2W
Jardine River △, Australia 62 A3 11 9S 142 21 E
Jardines de la Reina, Arch. de
  los, Cuba 88 B4 20 50N 78 50W
Jargalang, China .... 35 C12 43 5N 122 55 E
Jari →, Brazil 93 D8   1 9S 51 54W
Jarir, W. al →, Si. Arabia 44 E4 25 38N 42 30 E
Jarosław, Poland .... 17 C12 50 2N 22 42 E
Jarrahdale, Australia ..... 61 F2 32 24S 116 5 E
Jarrahi →, Iran .... 45 D6 30 49N 48 48 E
Jarres, Plaine des, Laos .. 38 C4 19 27N 103 10 E
Jartai, China .... 34 E3 39 45N 105 48 E
Jarud Qi, China .... 35 B11 44 28N 120 50 E
Järvenpää, Finland .... 9 F21 60 29N 25 5 E
Jarvis, Canada 84 D4 42 53N 80 6W
Jarvis I., Pac. Oc. 65 H12 0 15S 160 5W
Jarwa, India .... 43 F10 27 38N 82 30 E
Jasdan, India .... 42 H4 22 2N 71 12 E
Jashpurnagar, India .... 43 H11 22 54N 84 9 E
Jasidih, India .... 43 G12 24 31N 86 39 E
Jāsimīyah, Iraq .... 44 C5 33 45N 44 41 E
Jasin, Malaysia .... 39 L4   2 20N 102 26 E
Jāsk, Iran .... 45 E8 25 38N 57 45 E
Jasło, Poland .... 17 D11 49 45N 21 30 E
Jaso, India .... 43 G9 24 30N 80 29 E
Jasper, Alta., Canada 70 C5 52 55N 118 5W
Jasper, Ont., Canada 85 B9 44 52N 75 57W
Jasper, Ala., U.S.A. 83 J2 33 50N 87 17W
Jasper, Fla., U.S.A. 83 K4 30 31N 82 57W
Jasper, Ind., U.S.A. 82 F2 38 24N 86 56W
Jasper, Tex., U.S.A. 81 K8 30 56N 94 1W
Jasper △, Canada 70 C5 52 50N 118 8W

Jasrasar, India .... 42 F5 27 43N 73 49 E
Jászberény, Hungary .... 17 E10 47 30N 19 55 E
Jataí, Brazil 93 G8 17 58S 51 48W
Jati, Pakistan .... 42 G3 24 20N 68 19 E
Jatibarang, Indonesia ..... 37 G13 6 28S 108 18 E
Jatiluwih, Indonesia ...... 37 J18 8 23S 115 8 E
Jatinegara, Indonesia ..... 37 G12 6 13S 106 52 E
Játiva = Xàtiva, Spain 21 C5 38 59N   0 32W
Jaú, Brazil 95 A6 22 10S 48 30W
Jauja, Peru 92 F3 11 45S 75 15W
Jaunpur, India .... 43 G10 25 46N 82 44 E
Java = Jawa, Indonesia .... 36 F3   7 0S 110 0 E
Java Barat □, Indonesia ... 37 G12 7 0S 107 0 E
Java Sea, Indonesia .... 36 E3   4 35S 107 15 E
Java Tengah □, Indonesia .. 37 G14 7 0S 110 0 E
Java Timur □, Indonesia ... 37 G15 8 0S 113 0 E
Java Trench, Ind. Oc. ..... 36 F3   9 0S 105 0 E
Jawa, Indonesia .... 36 F3   7 0S 110 0 E
Jawad, India .... 42 G6 24 36N 74 51 E
Jaya, Puncak, Indonesia ... 37 E9   3 57S 137 17 E
Jayanti, India .... 41 F16 26 45N 89 40 E
Jayapura, Indonesia .... 37 E10 2 28S 140 38 E
Jayawijaya, Pegunungan,
  Indonesia .... 37 E9   5 0S 139 0 E
Jaynagar, India .... 41 F15 26 43N 86 9 E
Jayrūd, Syria .... 44 C3 33 49N 36 44 E
Jayton, U.S.A. 81 J4 33 15N 100 34W
Jāz Mūriān, Hāmūn-e, Iran . 45 E8 27 20N 58 55 E
Jazireh-ye Shif, Iran ..... 45 D6 29 4N 50 54 E
Jazminal, Mexico 86 C4 24 56N 101 25W
Jazzīn, Lebanon .... 46 B4 33 31N 35 35 E
Jean, U.S.A. 79 K11 35 47N 115 20W
Jean Marie River, Canada .. 70 A4 61 32N 120 38W
Jean Rabel, Haiti 89 C5 19 50N 73 5W
Jeanerette, U.S.A. 81 L9 29 55N 91 40W
Jeanette, Ostrov = Zhannetty,
  Ostrov, Russia .... 29 B16 76 43N 158 0 E
Jeannette, U.S.A. 84 F5 40 20N 79 36W
Jebāl Bārez, Kūh-e, Iran .. 45 D8 28 30N 58 20 E
Jebel, Bahr el →, Sudan ... 51 G12 9 30N 30 25 E
Jedburgh, U.K. 11 F6 55 29N   2 33W
Jedda = Jiddah, Si. Arabia 47 C2 21 29N 39 10 E
Jeddore L., Canada 73 C8 48 3N 55 55W
Jędrzejów, Poland .... 17 C11 50 35N 20 15 E
Jefferson, Iowa, U.S.A. ... 80 D7 42 1N 94 23W
Jefferson, Ohio, U.S.A. ... 84 E4 41 44N 80 46W
Jefferson, Tex., U.S.A. ... 81 J7 32 46N 94 21W
Jefferson, Mt., Nev., U.S.A. 76 G5 38 51N 117 0W
Jefferson, Mt., Oreg., U.S.A. 76 D3 44 41N 121 48W
Jefferson City, Mo., U.S.A. 80 F8 38 34N 92 10W
Jefferson City, Tenn., U.S.A. 83 G4 36 7N 83 30W
Jeffersontown, U.S.A. 82 F3 38 12N 85 35W
Jeffersonville, U.S.A. 82 F3 38 17N 85 44W
Jeffrey City, U.S.A. 76 E10 42 30N 107 49W
Jega, Nigeria .... 50 F6 12 15N   4 23 E
Jeju = Cheju do, S. Korea . 35 H14 33 29N 126 34 E
Jēkabpils, Latvia .... 9 H21 56 29N 25 57 E
Jekyll I., U.S.A. 83 K5 31 4N 81 25W
Jelenia Góra, Poland ...... 16 C8 50 50N 15 45 E
Jelgava, Latvia .... 9 H20 56 41N 23 49 E
Jemaja, Indonesia .... 39 L5   3 5N 105 45 E
Jemaluang, Malaysia .... 39 L4   2 16N 103 52 E
Jember, Indonesia .... 37 H15 8 11S 113 41 E
Jembongan, Malaysia .... 36 C5   6 45N 117 20 E
Jena, Germany .... 16 C6 50 54N 11 35 E
Jenin, West Bank .... 46 C4 32 28N 35 18 E
Jenkins, U.S.A. 82 G4 37 10N 82 38W
Jenner, U.S.A. 78 G3 38 27N 123 7W
Jennings, U.S.A. 81 K8 30 13N 92 40W
Jepara, Indonesia .... 37 G14 7 40S 109 14 E
Jeparit, Australia .... 63 F3 36 8S 142 1 E
Jequié, Brazil 93 F10 13 51S 40 5W
Jequitinhonha, Brazil 93 G10 16 30S 41 0W
Jequitinhonha →, Brazil ... 93 G11 15 51S 38 53W
Jerantut, Malaysia .... 39 L4   3 56N 102 22 E
Jerejak, Pulau, Malaysia .. 39 c   5 19N 100 19 E
Jérémie, Haiti 89 C5 18 40N 74 10W
Jerez, Punta, Mexico 87 C5 22 58N 97 40W
Jerez de García Salinas, Mexico 86 C4 22 39N 103 0W
Jerez de la Frontera, Spain 21 D2 36 41N 6 7W
Jerez de los Caballeros, Spain 21 C2 38 20N 6 45W
Jericho = El Arīḥā, West Bank 46 D4 31 52N 35 27 E
Jericho, Australia .... 62 C4 23 38S 146 6 E
Jerid, Chott el = Djerid, Chott,
  Tunisia .... 50 B7 33 42N   8 30 E
Jerilderie, Australia ..... 63 F4 35 20S 145 41 E
Jermyn, U.S.A. 85 E9 41 31N 75 31W
Jerome, U.S.A. 76 E6 42 44N 114 31W
Jersey, U.K. 13 H5 49 11N   2 7W
Jersey City, U.S.A. 85 F10 40 44N 74 4W
Jersey Shore, U.S.A. 84 E7 41 12N 77 15W
Jerseyville, U.S.A. 80 F9 39 7N 90 20W
Jerusalem, Israel .... 46 D4 31 47N 35 10 E
Jervis B., Australia ...... 63 F5 35 8S 150 46 E
Jervis Inlet, Canada 70 C4 50 0N 123 57W
Jesi = Iesi, Italy .... 22 C5 43 31N 13 14 E
Jessore, Bangla. .... 41 H16 23 10N 89 10 E
Jesup, U.S.A. 83 K5 31 36N 81 53W
Jesús Carranza, Mexico 87 D5 17 28N 95 1W
Jesús María, Argentina 94 C3 30 59S 64 5W
Jetmore, U.S.A. 81 F5 38 4N 99 54W
Jetpur, India .... 42 J4 21 45N 70 10 E
Jevnaker, Norway .... 9 F14 60 15N 10 26 E
Jewett, U.S.A. 84 F3 40 22N 81 2W
Jewett City, U.S.A. 85 E13 41 36N 72 0W
Jeyhūnābād, Iran .... 45 C6 34 58N 48 59 E
Jeypore, India .... 41 K13 18 50N 82 38 E
Jha Jha, India .... 43 G12 24 46N 86 22 E
Jhaarkand = Jharkhand □, India 43 H11 24 0N 85 50 E
Jhajjar, India .... 42 E7 28 37N 76 42 E
Jhal, Pakistan .... 42 E2 28 17N 67 27 E
Jhal Jhao, Pakistan .... 40 F4 26 0N 65 35 E
Jhalawar, India .... 42 G7 24 40N 76 10 E
Jhalida, India .... 43 H11 23 22N 85 58 E
Jhalrapatan, India .... 42 G7 24 33N 76 10 E
Jhang Maghiana, Pakistan .. 42 D5 31 15N 72 22 E
Jhansi, India .... 43 G8 25 30N 78 36 E
Jharia, India .... 43 H12 23 45N 86 26 E
Jharkhand □, India .... 43 H11 24 0N 85 50 E
Jharsuguda, India .... 41 J14 21 56N 84 5 E
Jhelum, Pakistan .... 42 C5 33 0N 73 45 E
Jhelum →, Pakistan .... 42 D5 31 20N 72 10 E

Jhilmilli, India .... 43 H10 23 24N 82 51 E
Jhudo, Pakistan .... 42 G3 24 58N 69 18 E
Jhunjhunu, India .... 42 E6 28 10N 75 30 E
Ji-Paraná, Brazil 92 F6 10 52S 62 57W
Ji Xian, Hebei, China ..... 34 F8 37 35N 115 30 E
Ji Xian, Henan, China ..... 34 G8 35 22N 114 5 E
Ji Xian, Shanxi, China .... 34 F6 36 7N 110 40 E
Jia Xian, Henan, China .... 34 H7 33 59N 113 12 E
Jia Xian, Shaanxi, China .. 34 E6 38 12N 110 28 E
Jiamusi, China .... 33 B8 46 40N 130 26 E
Ji'an, Jiangxi, China ..... 33 D6 27 6N 114 59 E
Ji'an, Jilin, China .... 35 D14 41 5N 126 10 E
Jianchang, China .... 35 D11 40 55N 120 25 E
Jianchangying, China ...... 35 D10 40 10N 118 50 E
Jiangcheng, China .... 32 D5 22 36N 101 52 E
Jiangmen, China .... 33 D6 22 32N 113 0 E
Jiangsu □, China .... 35 H11 33 0N 120 0 E
Jiangxi □, China .... 33 D6 27 30N 116 0 E
Jiao Xian = Jiaozhou, China 35 F11 36 18N 120 1 E
Jiaohe, Hebei, China ...... 34 E9 38 2N 116 20 E
Jiaohe, Jilin, China ...... 35 C14 43 40N 127 22 E
Jiaozhou, China .... 35 F11 36 18N 120 1 E
Jiaozhou Wan, China .... 35 F11 36 5N 120 10 E
Jiaozuo, China .... 34 G7 35 16N 113 12 E
Jiawang, China .... 35 G9 34 28N 117 26 E
Jiaxiang, China .... 34 G9 35 25N 116 20 E
Jiaxing, China .... 33 C7 30 49N 120 45 E
Jiayi = Chiai, Taiwan ..... 33 D7 23 29N 120 25 E
Jibuti = Djibouti ■, Africa 47 E3 12 0N 43 0 E
Jicarón, I., Panama 88 E3   7 10N 81 50W
Jiddah, Si. Arabia .... 47 C2 21 29N 39 10 E
Jido, India .... 41 E19 29 2N 94 58 E
Jieshou, China .... 34 H8 33 18N 115 22 E
Jiexiu, China .... 34 F6 37 2N 111 55 E
Jiggalong, Australia ...... 60 D3 23 21S 120 47 E
Jigni, India .... 43 G8 25 45N 79 25 E
Jihlava, Czech Rep. .... 16 D8 49 28N 15 35 E
Jihlava →, Czech Rep. ..... 17 D9 48 55N 16 36 E
Jijiga, Ethiopia .... 47 F3   9 20N 42 50 E
Jilin, China .... 35 C14 43 44N 126 30 E
Jilin □, China .... 35 C14 44 0N 127 0 E
Jilong = Chilung, Taiwan .. 33 D7 25 3N 121 45 E
Jim Thorpe, U.S.A. 85 F9 40 52N 75 44W
Jima, Ethiopia .... 47 F2   7 40N 36 47 E
Jimbaran, Teluk, Indonesia 37 K18 8 46S 115 9 E
Jiménez, Mexico 86 B4 27 10N 104 54W
Jimo, China .... 35 F11 36 23N 120 30 E
Jin Xian = Jinzhou, China . 34 E8 38 2N 115 2 E
Jin Xian, China .... 35 E11 38 55N 121 42 E
Jinan, China .... 34 F9 36 38N 117 1 E
Jinchang, China .... 32 C5 38 30N 102 10 E
Jincheng, China .... 34 G7 35 29N 112 50 E
Jind, India .... 42 E7 29 19N 76 22 E
Jindabyne, Australia ...... 63 F4 36 25S 148 35 E
Jinding, China .... 33 G10 22 22N 113 33 E
Jindřichův Hradec, Czech Rep. 16 D8 49 10N 15 2 E
Jing He →, China .... 34 G5 34 27N 109 4 E
Jingbian, China .... 34 F5 37 20N 108 30 E
Jingchuan, China .... 34 G4 35 20N 107 20 E
Jingdezhen, China .... 33 D6 29 20N 117 11 E
Jinggu, China .... 32 D5 23 35N 100 41 E
Jinghai, China .... 34 E9 38 55N 116 55 E
Jingle, China .... 34 E6 38 20N 111 55 E
Jingpo, China .... 35 C15 30 30N 105 43 E
Jingpo Hu, China .... 35 C15 43 55N 128 55 E
Jingtai, China .... 34 F3 37 10N 104 6 E
Jingxing, China .... 34 E8 38 2N 114 8 E
Jingyang, China .... 34 G5 34 30N 108 50 E
Jingyu, China .... 35 C14 42 25N 126 45 E
Jingyuan, China .... 34 F3 36 30N 104 40 E
Jingziguan, China .... 34 H6 33 15N 111 0 E
Jinhua, China .... 33 D6 29 8N 119 38 E
Jining, Nei Monggol Zizhiqu,
  China .... 34 D7 41 5N 113 0 E
Jining, Shandong, China ... 34 G9 35 22N 116 34 E
Jinja, Uganda .... 54 B3   0 25N 33 12 E
Jinjang, Malaysia .... 39 L3   3 13N 101 39 E
Jinji, China .... 34 F4 37 58N 106 8 E
Jinnah Barrage, Pakistan .. 40 C7 32 58N 71 33 E
Jinotega, Nic. 88 D2 13 6N 85 59W
Jinotepe, Nic. 88 D2 11 50N 86 10W
Jinsha Jiang →, China ..... 32 D5 28 50N 104 36 E
Jinxi, China .... 35 D11 40 52N 120 50 E
Jinxiang, China .... 34 G9 35 5N 116 22 E
Jinzhou, Hebei, China ..... 34 E8 38 2N 115 2 E
Jinzhou, Liaoning, China .. 35 D11 41 5N 121 3 E
Jiparaná →, Brazil 92 E6   8 3S 62 52W
Jipijapa, Ecuador 92 D2   1 0S 80 40W
Jiquilpan, Mexico 86 D4 19 57N 102 42W
Jishan, China .... 34 G6 35 34N 110 58 E
Jisr ash Shughūr, Syria ... 44 C3 35 49N 36 18 E
Jitarning, Australia ...... 61 F2 32 48S 117 57 E
Jitra, Malaysia .... 39 J3   6 16N 100 25 E
Jiu →, Romania .... 17 F12 43 47N 23 48 E
Jiudengkou, China .... 34 E4 39 56N 106 40 E
Jiujiang, China .... 33 D6 29 42N 115 58 E
Jiulong = Kowloon, China .. 33 G11 22 19N 114 11 E
Jiutai, China .... 35 B13 44 10N 125 50 E
Jiuxincheng, China .... 34 E8 39 17N 115 59 E
Jixi, China .... 35 B16 45 20N 130 50 E
Jiyang, China .... 35 F9 37 0N 117 1 E
Jiyuan, China .... 34 G7 35 7N 112 57 E
Jīzān, Si. Arabia .... 47 D3 17 0N 42 20 E
Jize, China .... 34 F8 36 54N 114 56 E
Jizl, Wādī al →, Si. Arabia 44 E3 25 39N 38 25 E
Jizō-Zaki, Japan .... 31 G6 35 34N 133 20 E
Jizzakh, Uzbekistan .... 28 E7 40 6N 67 50 E
Joaçaba, Brazil 95 B5 27 5S 51 31W
João Pessoa, Brazil 93 E12 7 10S 34 52W
Joaquín V. González, Argentina 94 B3 25 10S 64 0W
Jobat, India .... 42 H6 22 25N 74 34 E
Jodhpur, India .... 42 F5 26 23N 73 8 E
Jodiya, India .... 42 H4 22 42N 70 18 E
Joensuu, Finland .... 8 E23 62 37N 29 49 E
Jōetsu, Japan .... 31 F9 37 12N 138 10 E
Jofane, Mozam. .... 57 C5 21 15S 34 18 E
Jogbani, India .... 43 F12 26 25N 87 15 E
Jõgeva, Estonia .... 9 G22 58 45N 26 24 E
Jogjakarta = Yogyakarta,
  Indonesia .... 37 G14 7 49S 110 22 E
Johannesburg, S. Africa ... 57 D4 26 10S 28 2 E
Johannesburg, U.S.A. 79 K9 35 22N 117 38W
Johilla →, India .... 43 H9 23 37N 81 14 E
John Crow Mts., Jamaica ... 88 a 18 5N 76 25W
John Day, U.S.A. 76 D4 44 25N 118 57W
John Day →, U.S.A. 76 D3 45 44N 120 39W
John Day Fossil Beds △, U.S.A. 76 D4 44 33N 119 38W

John D'Or Prairie, Canada ..... 70 B5　58 30N 115　8W
John F. Kennedy International,
　New York ✖ (JFK), U.S.A. .. 85 F11　40 38N　73 47W
John H. Kerr Reservoir, U.S.A. . 83 G6　36 36N　78 18W
John o' Groats, U.K. .... 11 C5　58 38N　3　4W
Johnnie, U.S.A. .... 79 J10　36 25N 116　5W
John's Ra., Australia .... 62 C1　21 55S 133 23 E
Johnson, Kans., U.S.A. .... 81 G4　37 34N 101 45W
Johnson, Vt., U.S.A. .... 85 B12　44 38N　72 41W
Johnson City, N.Y., U.S.A. .... 85 D9　42　7N　75 58W
Johnson City, Tenn., U.S.A. ... 83 G4　36 19N　82 21W
Johnson City, Tex., U.S.A. .... 81 K5　30 17N　98 25W
Johnsonburg, U.S.A. .... 84 E6　41 29N　78 41W
Johnsondale, U.S.A. .... 79 K8　35 58N 118 32W
Johnsons Crossing, Canada ... 70 A6　60 29N 133 18W
Johnston, L., Australia .... 61 F3　32 25S 120 30 E
Johnston Falls = Mambilima
　Falls, Zambia .... 55 E2　10 31S　28 45 E
Johnston I., Pac. Oc. .... 65 F11　17 10N 169　8W
Johnstone Str., Canada .... 70 C3　50 28N 126　0W
Johnstown, N.Y., U.S.A. ...... 85 C10　43　0N　74 22W
Johnstown, Ohio, U.S.A. ...... 84 F2　40　9N　82 41W
Johnstown, Pa., U.S.A. .... 84 F6　40 20N　78 55W
Johor, Selat, Asia .... 39 d　1 28N 103 47 E
Johor Baharu, Malaysia .... 39 d　1 28N 103 46 E
Jõhvi, Estonia .... 9 G22　59 22N　27 27 E
Joinville, Brazil .... 95 B6　26 15S　48 55W
Joinville I., Antarctica .... 5 C18　65　0S　55 30W
Jojutla, Mexico .... 87 D5　18 37N　99 11W
Jokkmokk, Sweden .... 8 C18　66 35N　19 50 E
Jökulsá á Bru ➤, Iceland ..... 8 D6　65 40N　14 16W
Jökulsá á Fjöllum ➤, Iceland .. 8 C5　66 10N　16 30W
Jolfã, Āzarbājān-e Sharqī, Iran . 44 B5　38 57N　45 38 E
Jolfã, Eşfahan, Iran .... 45 C6　32 58N　51 37 E
Joliet, U.S.A. .... 82 E1　41 32N　88　5W
Joliette, Canada .... 72 C5　46　3N　73 24W
Jolo, Phil. .... 37 C6　6　0N 121　0 E
Jolon, U.S.A. .... 78 K5　35 58N 121　9W
Jombang, Indonesia .... 37 G15　7 33S 112 14 E
Jonava, Lithuania .... 9 J21　55　8N　24 12 E
Jones Sound, Canada .... 4 B3　76　0N　85　0W
Jonesboro, Ark., U.S.A. ...... 81 H9　35 50N　90 42W
Jonesboro, La., U.S.A. .... 81 J8　32 15N　92 43W
Joniškis, Lithuania .... 9 H20　56 13N　23 35 E
Jönköping, Sweden .... 9 H16　57 45N　14　8 E
Jonquière, Canada .... 73 C5　48 27N　71 14W
Joplin, U.S.A. .... 81 G7　37　6N　94 31W
Jora, India .... 42 F6　26 20N　77 49 E
Jordan, Mont., U.S.A. .... 76 C10　47 19N 106 55W
Jordan, N.Y., U.S.A. .... 85 C8　43　4N　76 29W
Jordan ■, Asia .... 46 E5　31　0N　36　0 E
Jordan ➤, Asia .... 46 D4　31 48N　35 32 E
Jordan Valley, U.S.A. .... 76 E5　42 59N 117　3W
Jorhat, India .... 41 F19　26 45N　94 12 E
Jörn, Sweden .... 8 D19　65　4N　20　1 E
Jorong, Indonesia .... 36 E4　3 58S 114 56 E
Jørpeland, Norway .... 9 G11　59　3N　6　1 E
Jorquera ➤, Chile .... 94 B2　28　3S　69 58W
Jos, Nigeria .... 50 G7　9 53N　8 51 E
José Batlle y Ordóñez, Uruguay . 95 C4　33 20S　55 10W
Jose Abad Santos, Phil. 37 C7
Joseph, L., Nfld. & L., Canada .. 73 B6　52 45N　65 18W
Joseph, L., Ont., Canada ...... 84 A5　45 10N　79 44W
Joseph Bonaparte G., Australia . 60 B4　14 35S 128 50 E
Joshinath, India .... 43 D8　30 34N　79 34 E
Joshinetsu-Kōgen △, Japan ... 31 F9　36 42N 138 32 E
Joshua Tree, U.S.A. .... 79 L10　34　8N 116 19W
Joshua Tree △, U.S.A. .... 79 M10　33 55N 116　0W
Jost Van Dyke, Br. Virgin Is. ... 89 e　18 29N　64 47W
Jostedalsbreen, Norway ...... 9 F12　61 40N　6 59 E
Jotunheimen, Norway .... 9 F13　61 35N　8 25 E
Joubertberge, Namibia .... 56 B1　18 30S　14　0 E
Jourdanton, U.S.A. .... 81 L5　28 55N　98 33W
Jovellanos, Cuba .... 88 B3　22 40N　81 10W
Ju Xian, China .... 35 F10　36 35N 118 20 E
Juan Aldama, Mexico .... 86 C4　24 20N 103 23W
Juan Bautista Alberdi, Argentina . 94 C3　34 26S　61 48W
Juan de Fuca Str., Canada ..... 78 B3　48 15N 124　0W
Juan de Nova, Ind. Oc. .... 57 B7　17　3S　43 45 E
Juan Fernández, Arch. de,
　Pac. Oc. .... 90 G2　33 50S　80　0W
Juan José Castelli, Argentina .. 94 B3　25 27S　60 57W
Juan L. Lacaze, Uruguay ...... 94 C4　34 26S　57 25W
Juankoski, Finland .... 8 E23　63　3N　28 19 E
Juárez, Argentina .... 94 D4　37 40S　59 43W
Juárez, Mexico .... 79 N11　32 20N 115 57W
Juárez, Sierra de, Mexico ..... 86 A1　32　0N 116　0W
Juàzeiro, Brazil .... 93 E10　9 30S　40 30W
Juàzeiro do Norte, Brazil ..... 93 E11　7 10S　39 18W
Juba = Giuba ➤, Somali Rep. .. 47 G3　1 30N　42 35 E
Juba, Sudan .... 51 H12　4 50N　31 35 E
Jubany, Antarctica .... 5 C18　62 30S　58　0W
Jubayl, Lebanon .... 46 A4　34　5N　35 39 E
Jubbah, Si. Arabia .... 44 D4　28　2N　40 56 E
Jubbal, India .... 42 D7　31　5N　77 40 E
Jubbulpore = Jabalpur, India .. 43 H8　23　9N　79 58 E
Jubilee L., Australia .... 61 E4　29　0S 126 50 E
Juby, C., Morocco .... 50 C3　28　0N　12 59W
Júcar = Xúquer ➤, Spain ..... 21 C5　39　5N　0 10W
Júcaro, Cuba .... 88 B4　21 37N　78 51W
Juchitán, Mexico .... 87 D5　16 27N　95　5W
Judaea = Har Yehuda, Israel ... 46 D3　31 35N　34 57 E
Judith ➤, U.S.A. .... 76 C9　47 44N 109 39W
Judith, Pt., U.S.A. .... 85 E13　41 21N　71 29W
Judith Gap, U.S.A. .... 76 C9　46 41N 109 45W
Jugoslavia = Serbia &
　Montenegro ■, Europe .... 23 B9　43 20N　20　0 E
Juigalpa, Nic. .... 88 D2　12　6N　85 26W
Juiz de Fora, Brazil .... 95 A7　21 43S　43 19W
Jujuy □, Argentina .... 94 A2　23　0S　65 40W
Julesburg, U.S.A. .... 80 E3　40 59N 102 16W
Juli, Peru .... 92 G5　16 10S　69 25W
Julia Cr. ➤, Australia .... 62 C3　20　0S 141 11 E
Julia Creek, Australia .... 62 C3　20 39S 141 44 E
Juliaca, Peru .... 92 G4　15 25S　70 10W
Julian, U.S.A. .... 79 M10　33　4N 116 38W
Julian, L., Canada .... 72 B4　54 25N　77 57W
Julianatop, Suriname .... 93 C7　3 40N　56 30W
Julianehåb = Qaqortoq,
　Greenland .... 69 B6　60 43N　46　0W
Julimes, Mexico .... 86 B3　28 25N 105 27W
Jullundur, India .... 42 D6　31 20N　75 40 E
Julu, China .... 34 F8　37 15N 115　2 E
Jumbo, Zimbabwe .... 55 F3　17 30S　30 58 E
Jumbo Pk., U.S.A. .... 79 J12　36 12N 114 11W
Jumentos Cays, Bahamas ..... 88 B4　23　0N　75 40W
Jumilla, Spain .... 21 C5　38 28N　1 19W
Jumla, Nepal .... 43 E10　29 15N　82 13 E

Jumna = Yamuna ➤, India .... 43 G9　25 30N　81 53 E
Junagadh, India .... 42 J4　21 30N　70 30 E
Junction, Tex., U.S.A. .... 81 K5　30 29N　99 46W
Junction, Utah, U.S.A. .... 77 G7　38 14N 112 13W
Junction B., Australia .... 62 A1　11 52S 133 55 E
Junction City, Kans., U.S.A. .. 80 F6　39　2N　96 50W
Junction City, Oreg., U.S.A. .. 76 D2　44 13N 123 12W
Junction Pt., Australia .... 62 A1　11 45S 133 50 E
Jundah, Australia .... 62 C3　24 46S 143　2 E
Jundiaí, Brazil .... 95 A6　24 30S　47　0W
Juneau, U.S.A. .... 70 B2　58 18N 134 25W
Junee, Australia .... 63 E4　34 53S 147 35 E
Jungfrau, Switz. .... 20 C7　46 32N　7 58 E
Junggar Pendi, China .... 32 B3　44 30N　86　0 E
Jungshahi, Pakistan .... 42 G2　24 52N　67 44 E
Juniata ➤, U.S.A. .... 84 F7　40 30N　77 40W
Junín, Argentina .... 94 C3　34 33S　60 57W
Junín de los Andes, Argentina . 96 D2　39 45S　71　0W
Jūniyah, Lebanon .... 46 B4　33 59N　35 38 E
Juntas, Chile .... 94 B2　28 24S　69 58W
Juntura, U.S.A. .... 76 E4　43 45N 118　5W
Jur, Nahr el ➤, Sudan .... 51 G11　8 45N　29 15 E
Jura = Jura, Mts. du, Europe .. 20 C7　46 40N　6　5 E
Jura = Schwäbische Alb,
　Germany .... 16 D5　48 20N　9 30 E
Jura, U.K. .... 11 F3　56　0N　5 50W
Jura, Mts. du, Europe .... 20 C7　46 40N　6　5 E
Jura, Sd. of, U.K. .... 11 F3　55 57N　5 45W
Jurbarkas, Lithuania .... 9 J20　55　4N　22 46 E
Jurien, Australia .... 61 F2　30 18S 115　2 E
Jūrmala, Latvia .... 9 H20　56 58N　23 34 E
Jurong, Singapore .... 39 d　1 19N 103 42 E
Juruá ➤, Brazil .... 92 D5　2 37S　65 44W
Juruena, Brazil .... 92 F7　13　0S　58 10W
Juruena ➤, Brazil .... 92 E7　7 20S　58　3W
Juruti, Brazil .... 93 D7　2　9S　56　4W
Justo Daract, Argentina ...... 94 C2　33 52S　65 12W
Jutaí ➤, Brazil .... 92 D5　2 43S　66 57W
Juticalpa, Honduras .... 88 D2　14 40N　86 12W
Jutland = Jylland, Denmark ... 9 H13　56 25N　9 30 E
Juventud, I. de la, Cuba ...... 88 B3　21 40N　82 40W
Jüy Zar, Iran .... 44 C5　33 50N　46 18 E
Juye, China .... 34 G9　35 22N 116　5 E
Jwaneng, Botswana .... 53 J4　24 45S　24 50 E
Jylland, Denmark .... 9 H13　56 25N　9 30 E
Jyväskylä, Finland .... 9 E21　62 14N　25 50 E

K

K2, Pakistan .... 43 B7　35 58N　76 32 E
Kaap Plateau, S. Africa ...... 56 D3　28 30S　24　0 E
Kaapkruis, Namibia .... 56 C1　21 55S　13 57 E
Kaapstad = Cape Town, S. Africa 56 E2　33 55S　18 22 E
Kabaena, Indonesia .... 37 F6　5 15S 122　0 E
Kabala, S. Leone .... 50 G3　9 38N　11 37W
Kabale, Uganda .... 54 C3　1 15S　30　0 E
Kabalo, Dem. Rep. of Congo .. 54 D2　6　0S　27　0 E
Kabambare, Dem. Rep. of
　the Congo .... 54 C2　4 41S　27 39 E
Kabango, Dem. Rep. of
　the Congo .... 55 D2　8 35S　28 30 E
Kabanjahe, Indonesia .... 36 D1　3　6N　98 30 E
Kabardino-Balkar Republic =
　Kabardino-Balkaria □, Russia 19 F7　43 30N　43 30 E
Kabardino-Balkaria □, Russia . 19 F7　43 30N　43 30 E
Kabarega Falls = Murchison
　Falls, Uganda .... 54 B3　2 15N　31 30 E
Kabasalan, Phil. .... 37 C6　7 47N 122 44 E
Kabat, Indonesia .... 37 J17　8 16S 114 19 E
Kabetogama, U.S.A. .... 80 A8　48 28N　92 59W
Kabin Buri, Thailand .... 38 F3　13 57N 101 43 E
Kabinakagami L., Canada ..... 72 C3　48 54N　84 25W
Kabinda, Dem. Rep. of Congo . 52 F4　6 19S　24 20 E
Kabompo, Zambia .... 55 E1　13 36S　24 14 E
Kabompo ➤, Zambia .... 53 G4　14 10S　23 11 E
Kabondo, Dem. Rep. of
　the Congo .... 55 D2　8 58S　25 40 E
Kabongo, Dem. Rep. of
　the Congo .... 54 D2　7 22S　25 33 E
Kabūd Gonbad, Iran .... 45 B8　37　5N　59 45 E
Kābul, Afghan. .... 42 B3　34 28N　69 11 E
Kābul □, Afghan. .... 40 B6　34 30N　69　0 E
Kābul ➤, Pakistan .... 42 C5　33 55N　72 14 E
Kabunga, Dem. Rep. of
　the Congo .... 54 C2　1 38S　28　3 E
Kaburuang, Indonesia .... 37 D7　3 50N 126 30 E
Kabwe, Zambia .... 55 E2　14 30S　28 29 E
Kachchh, Gulf of, India ...... 42 H3　22 50N　69 15 E
Kachchh, Rann of, India ...... 42 H4　24　0N　70　0 E
Kachchhidhana, India .... 43 J8　21 44N　78 46 E
Kachebera, Zambia .... 55 E3　13 50S　32 50 E
Kachikau, Botswana .... 56 B3　18　8S　24 26 E
Kachin □, Burma .... 41 G20　26　0N　97 30 E
Kachira, L., Uganda .... 54 C3　0 40S　31　7 E
Kachiry, Kazakhstan .... 28 D8　53 10N　75 50 E
Kachnara, India .... 42 H6　23 50N　75　6 E
Kachot, Cambodia .... 39 G4　11 30N 103　3 E
Kaçkar, Turkey .... 19 F7　40 45N　41 10 E
Kadan Kyun, Burma .... 38 F2　12 30N　98 20 E
Kadanai ➤, Afghan. .... 42 D1　31 22N　65 45 E
Kadavu, Fiji .... 59 D8　19　0S 178 15 E
Kadhimain = Al Kāẓimīyah, Iraq . 44 C5　33 22N　44 18 E
Kadi, India .... 42 H5　23 18N　72 23 E
Kadina, Australia .... 63 E2　33 55S 137 43 E
Kadipur, India .... 43 F10　26 10N　82　3 E
Kadirli, Turkey .... 44 B3　37 23N　36　5 E
Kadiyevka = Stakhanov, Ukraine 19 E6　48 35N　38 40 E
Kadoka, U.S.A. .... 80 D4　43 50N 101 31W
Kadoma, Zimbabwe .... 55 F2　18 20S　29 52 E
Kâdugli, Sudan .... 51 F11　11　0N　29 45 E
Kaduna, Nigeria .... 50 F7　10 30N　7 21 E
Kaédi, Mauritania .... 50 E3　16　9N　13 28W
Kaeng Khoï, Thailand .... 38 E3　14 35N 101　0 E
Kaeng Kra Chan △, Thailand . 38 F2　12 57N　99 23 E
Kaeng Tana △, Thailand ..... 38 E5　15 25N 105 32 E
Kaesŏng, N. Korea .... 35 F14　37 58N 126 35 E
Kāf, Si. Arabia .... 44 D3　31 25N　37 29 E
Kafan = Kapan, Armenia ..... 19 G8　39 18N　46 27 E
Kafanchan, Nigeria .... 50 G7　9 40N　8 20 E
Kaffrine, Senegal .... 50 F2　14 8N　15 36W
Kafinda, Zambia .... 55 E3　12 32S　30 20 E
Kafirévs, Ákra, Greece .... 23 E11　38　9N　24 38 E
Kafue, Zambia .... 55 F2　15 46S　28　9 E
Kafue △, Zambia .... 55 F2　15 12S　25 38 E
Kafue ➤, Zambia .... 53 H5　15 30S　29　0 E

Kafue Flats, Zambia .... 55 F2　15 40S　27 25 E
Kafulwe, Zambia .... 55 D2　9　0S　29　1 E
Kaga, Afghan. .... 42 B4　34 14N　70 10 E
Kaga Bandoro, C.A.R. .... 52 C3　7　0N　19 10 E
Kagan, Uzbekistan .... 28 F7　39 43N　64 33 E
Kagawa □, Japan .... 31 G7　34 15N 134　0 E
Kagera □, Tanzania .... 54 C3　2　0S　31 30 E
Kagera ➤, Uganda .... 54 C3　0 57S　31 47 E
Kağızman, Turkey .... 44 B4　40　5N　43 10 E
Kagoshima, Japan .... 31 J5　31 35N 130 33 E
Kagoshima □, Japan .... 31 J5　31 30N 130 30 E
Kagul = Cahul, Moldova ...... 17 F15　45 50N　28 15 E
Kahak, Iran .... 45 B6　36　6N　49 46 E
Kahama, Tanzania .... 54 C3　4　8S　32 30 E
Kahan, Pakistan .... 42 E3　29 18N　68 54 E
Kahang, Malaysia .... 39 L4　2 12N 103 32 E
Kahayan ➤, Indonesia .... 36 E4　3 40S 114　0 E
Kahe, Tanzania .... 54 C4　3 30S　37 25 E
Kahnūj, Iran .... 45 E8　27 55N　57 40 E
Kahoka, U.S.A. .... 80 E9　40 25N　91 44W
Kahoolawe, U.S.A. .... 74 H16　20 33N 156 37W
Kahramanmaraş, Turkey ..... 19 G6　37 37N　36 53 E
Kahurangi △, N.Z. .... 59 J4　41 10S 172 32 E
Kahuta, Pakistan .... 42 C5　33 35N　73 24 E
Kahuzi-Biega △, Dem. Rep. of
　the Congo .... 54 C2　1 50S　27 55 E
Kai, Kepulauan, Indonesia .... 37 F8　5 55S 132 45 E
Kai Besar, Indonesia .... 37 F8　5 35S 133　0 E
Kai Is. = Kai, Kepulauan,
　Indonesia .... 37 F8　5 55S 132 45 E
Kai Kecil, Indonesia .... 37 F8　5 45S 132 40 E
Kaiapoi, N.Z. .... 59 K4　43 24S 172 40 E
Kaieteur Falls, Guyana .... 92 B7　5　1N　59 10W
Kaifeng, China .... 34 G8　34 48N 114 21 E
Kaikohe, N.Z. .... 59 F4　35 25S 173 49 E
Kaikoura, N.Z. .... 59 K4　42 25S 173 43 E
Kailash = Kangrinboqe Feng,
　China .... 43 D9　31　0N　81 25 E
Kailu, China .... 35 C11　43 38N 121 18 E
Kailua Kona, U.S.A. .... 74 J17　19 39N 155 59W
Kaimana, Indonesia .... 37 E8　3 39S 133 45 E
Kaimanawa Mts., N.Z. .... 59 H5　39 15S 175 56 E
Kaimganj, India .... 43 F8　27 33N　79 24 E
Kaimur Hills, India .... 43 G10　24 30N　82　0 E
Kainab ➤, Namibia .... 56 D2　28 32S　19 34 E
Kainji Res., Nigeria .... 50 F6　10　1N　4 40 E
Kainuu, Finland .... 8 D23　64 30N　29　7 E
Kaipara Harbour, N.Z. .... 59 G5　36 25S 174 14 E
Kaipokok B., Canada .... 73 B8　54 54N　59 47W
Kaira, India .... 42 H5　22 45N　72 50 E
Kairana, India .... 42 E7　29 24N　77 15 E
Kairiru, Indonesia .... 37 E8　0 47S 133 40 E
Kairouan, Tunisia .... 51 A8　35 45N　10　5 E
Kaiserslautern, Germany ..... 16 D4　49 26N　7 45 E
Kaitaia, N.Z. .... 59 F4　35　8S 173 17 E
Kaitangata, N.Z. .... 59 M2　46 17S 169 51 E
Kaithal, India .... 42 E7　29 48N　76 26 E
Kaitu ➤, Pakistan .... 42 C4　33 10N　70 30 E
Kaiyuan, China .... 35 C13　42 28N 124　1 E
Kajaani, Finland .... 8 D22　64 17N　27 46 E
Kajabbi, Australia .... 62 C3　20　0S 140　1 E
Kajana = Kajaani, Finland .... 8 D22　64 17N　27 46 E
Kajang, Malaysia .... 39 L3　2 59N 101 48 E
Kajiado, Kenya .... 54 C4　1 53S　36 48 E
Kajo Kaji, Sudan .... 51 H12　3 58N　31 40 E
Kakabeka Falls, Canada ...... 72 C2　48 24N　89 37W
Kakadu △, Australia .... 60 B5　12　0S 132　3 E
Kakamas, S. Africa .... 56 D3　28 45S　20 33 E
Kakamega, Kenya .... 54 B3　0 20N　34 46 E
Kakanui Mts., N.Z. .... 59 L3　45 10S 170 30 E
Kakdwip, India .... 43 J13　21 53N　88 11 E
Kake, Japan .... 31 G6　34 36N 132 19 E
Kake, U.S.A. .... 70 B2　56 59N 133 57W
Kakegawa, Japan .... 31 G9　34 45N 138　1 E
Kakeroma-Jima, Japan ...... 31 K4　28 8N 129 14 E
Kakhovka, Ukraine .... 19 E5　46 45N　33 30 E
Kakhovske Vdskh., Ukraine ... 19 E5　47 5N　34　0 E
Kakinada, India .... 41 L13　16 57N　82 11 E
Kakisa ➤, Canada .... 70 A5　61　3N 118 10W
Kakisa L., Canada .... 70 A5　60 56N 117 43W
Kakogawa, Japan .... 31 G7　34 46N 134 51 E
Kakwa ➤, Canada .... 70 C5　54 37N 118 28W
Kāl Gūsheh, Iran .... 45 D8　30 59N　58 12 E
Kal Safid, Iran .... 44 C5　34 52N　47 23 E
Kalaallit Nunaat = Greenland ☒,
　N. Amer. .... 4 C5　66　0N　45　0W
Kalabagh, Pakistan .... 42 C4　33　0N　71 28 E
Kalabahi, Indonesia .... 37 F6　8 13S 124 31 E
Kalach, Russia .... 19 D7　50 22N　41　0 E
Kaladan ➤, Burma .... 41 J18　20 20N　93　5 E
Kaladar, Canada .... 84 B7　44 37N　77　5W
Kalahari, Africa .... 56 C3　24　0S　21 30 E
Kalahari Gemsbok △, S. Africa . 56 D3　25 30S　20 30 E
Kalajoki, Finland .... 8 D20　64 12N　24 10 E
Kalakamati, Botswana .... 57 C4　20 40S　27 25 E
Kalakan, Russia .... 29 D12　55 15N 116 45 E
K'alak'unlun Shank'ou =
　Karakoram Pass, Asia ...... 43 B7　35 33N　77 50 E
Kalam, Pakistan .... 43 B5　35 34N　72 30 E
Kalama, Dem. Rep. of Congo .. 54 C2　2 52S　28 35 E
Kalama, U.S.A. .... 78 E4　46　1N 122 51W
Kalámai, Greece .... 23 F10　37　3N　22 10 E
Kalamata = Kalámai, Greece .. 23 F10　37　3N　22 10 E
Kalamazoo, U.S.A. .... 82 D3　42 17N　85 35W
Kalamazoo ➤, U.S.A. .... 82 D2　42 40N　86 10W
Kalambo Falls, Tanzania ..... 55 D3　8 37S　31 35 E
Kalan, Turkey .... 19 G7　39 7N　39 32 E
Kalannie, Australia .... 61 F2　30 22S 117　5 E
Kalāntarī, Iran .... 45 C7　32 10N　54　8 E
Kalao, Indonesia .... 37 F6　7 21S 121　0 E
Kalaotoa, Indonesia .... 37 F6　7 20S 121 50 E
Kalat, Pakistan .... 40 E5　29　8N　66 31 E
Kalāt, Iran .... 45 E8　25 29N　59 22 E
Kalāteh, Iran .... 45 B7　36 33N　55 41 E
Kalāteh-ye Ganj, Iran .... 45 E8　27 31N　57 55 E
Kalbarri, Australia .... 61 E1　27 40S 114 10 E
Kalbā, Pakistan .... 43 B5　35 53N　72 30 E
Kalce, Slovenia .... 16 F8　45 54N　14 13 E
Kale, Turkey .... 23 F13　37 27N　28 49 E
Kalegauk Kyun, Burma ...... 41 M20　15 33N　97 35 E
Kalehe, Dem. Rep. of Congo .. 54 C2　2 6S　28 50 E
Kalema, Tanzania .... 54 C3　1 12S　31 55 E
Kalemie, Dem. Rep. of Congo . 54 D2　5 55S　29　9 E
Kalewa, Burma .... 41 H19　23 10N　94 15 E
Kaleybar, Iran .... 44 B5　38 47N　47　2 E
Kalgoorlie-Boulder, Australia .. 61 F3　30 40S 121 22 E

Kali ➤, India .... 43 F8　27　6N　79 55 E
Kali Sindh ➤, India .... 42 G6　25 32N　76 17 E
Kaliakra, Nos, Bulgaria .... 23 C13　43 21N　28 30 E
Kalianda, Indonesia .... 36 F3　5 50S 105 45 E
Kalibo, Phil. .... 37 B6　11 43N 122 22 E
Kalima, Dem. Rep. of the Congo 54 C2　2 33S　26 32 E
Kalimantan, Indonesia .... 36 E4　0　0 114　0 E
Kalimantan Barat □, Indonesia . 36 E4　0　0 110 30 E
Kalimantan Selatan □, Indonesia 36 E5　2 30S 115 30 E
Kalimantan Tengah □, Indonesia 36 E4　2　0S 113 30 E
Kalimantan Timur □, Indonesia 36 D5　1 30N 116 30 E
Kálimnos, Greece .... 23 F12　37　0N　27　0 E
Kalimpong, India .... 43 F13　27　4N　88 35 E
Kaliningrad, Russia .... 9 J19　54 42N　20 32 E
Kalinkavichy, Belarus .... 17 B15　52 12N　29 20 E
Kalinkovichi = Kalinkavichy,
　Belarus .... 17 B15　52 12N　29 20 E
Kaliro, Uganda .... 54 B3　0 56N　33 30 E
Kalispell, U.S.A. .... 76 B6　48 12N 114 19W
Kalisz, Poland .... 17 C10　51 45N　18　8 E
Kaliua, Tanzania .... 54 D3　5　5S　31 48 E
Kalix, Sweden .... 8 D20　65 53N　23 12 E
Kalix ➤, Sweden .... 8 D20　65 50N　23 11 E
Kalka, India .... 42 D7　30 46N　76 57 E
Kalkarindji, Australia .... 60 C5　17 30S 130 47 E
Kalkaska, U.S.A. .... 82 C3　44 44N　85 11W
Kalkfeld, Namibia .... 56 C2　20 57S　16 14 E
Kalkfontein, Botswana ...... 56 C3　22　4S　20 57 E
Kalkrand, Namibia .... 56 C2　24　1S　17 35 E
Kallavesi, Finland .... 8 E22　62 58N　27 30 E
Kallsjön, Sweden .... 8 E15　63 38N　13　0 E
Kalmar, Sweden .... 9 H17　56 40N　16 20 E
Kalmyk Republic = Kalmykia □,
　Russia .... 19 E8　46　5N　46　1 E
Kalmykia □, Russia .... 19 E8　46　5N　46　1 E
Kalmykovo, Kazakhstan ...... 19 E9　49　0N　51 47 E
Kalna, India .... 43 H13　23 13N　88 25 E
Kalnai, India .... 43 H10　22 46N　83 30 E
Kalocsa, Hungary .... 17 E10　46 32N　19　0 E
Kalokhorio, Cyprus .... 25 E12　34 51N　33　2 E
Kaloko, Dem. Rep. of the Congo 54 D2　6 47S　25 48 E
Kalol, Gujarat, India .... 42 H5　23 37N　73 31 E
Kalol, Gujarat, India .... 42 H5　23 15N　72 33 E
Kalomo, Zambia .... 55 F2　17　0S　26 30 E
Kalpi, India .... 42 B8　26　8N　79 47 E
Kalu, Pakistan .... 42 G2　25　5N　67 39 E
Kaluga, Russia .... 18 D6　54 35N　36 10 E
Kalulushi, Zambia .... 55 E2　12 50S　28　3 E
Kalundborg, Denmark .... 9 J14　55 41N　11　5 E
Kalush, Ukraine .... 17 D13　49　3N　24 23 E
Kalutara, Sri Lanka .... 40 R12　6 35N　80　0 E
Kalya, Russia .... 18 B10　60 15N　59 59 E
Kalyan, India .... 40 K8　19 15N　73　9 E
Kama, Dem. Rep. of the Congo . 54 C2　3 30S　27　5 E
Kama ➤, Russia .... 18 C9　55 45N　52　0 E
Kamachumu, Tanzania ...... 54 C3　1 37S　31 37 E
Kamaishi, Japan .... 30 E10　39 16N 141 53 E
Kamalia, Pakistan .... 42 D5　30 44N　72 42 E
Kaman, India .... 42 F6　27 39N　77 16 E
Kamanjab, Namibia .... 56 B1　19 35S　14 51 E
Kamapanda, Zambia .... 55 E1　12　5S　24　0 E
Kamarān, Yemen .... 47 D3　15 21N　42 35 E
Kamativi, Zimbabwe .... 56 B4　18 20S　27　6 E
Kambalda, Australia .... 61 F3　31 10S 121 37 E
Kambar, Pakistan .... 42 F3　27 37N　68　1 E
Kambarka, Russia .... 18 C9　56 15N　54 11 E
Kambolé, Zambia .... 55 D3　8 47S　30 48 E
Kambos, Cyprus .... 25 D11　35　2N　32 44 E
Kambove, Dem. Rep. of
　the Congo .... 55 E2　10 51S　26 33 E
Kamchatka, Poluostrov, Russia . 29 D16　57　0N 160　0 E
Kamchatka Pen. = Kamchatka,
　Poluostrov, Russia .... 29 D16　57　0N 160　0 E
Kamchiya ➤, Bulgaria ...... 23 C12　43　4N　27 44 E
Kame Ruins, Zimbabwe ...... 55 G2　20　7S　28 25 E
Kamen, Russia .... 28 D9　53 50N　81 30 E
Kamen-Rybolov, Russia ...... 30 B6　44 46N　132　2 E
Kamenjak, Rt, Croatia .... 16 F7　44 47N　13 55 E
Kamenka, Russia .... 18 A7　65 58N　44 0 E
Kamenka Bugskaya = Kamyanka-
　Buzka, Ukraine .... 17 C13　50　8N　24 16 E
Kamensk Uralskiy, Russia .... 28 D7　56 25N　62　2 E
Kamenskoye, Russia .... 29 C17　62 45N 165 30 E
Kameoka, Japan .... 31 G7　35　0N 135 35 E
Kamiah, U.S.A. .... 76 C5　46 14N 116　2W
Kamieskroon, S. Africa ...... 56 E2　30　9S 17 56 E
Kamilukuak, L., Canada ...... 71 A8　62 22N 101 40W
Kamin-Kashyrskyy, Ukraine .. 17 C13　51 39N　24 56 E
Kamina, Dem. Rep. of the Congo 55 D2　8 45S　25　0 E
Kaminak L., Canada .... 71 A10　62 10N　95　0W
Kaministiquia, Canada ...... 72 C1　48 32N　89 35W
Kaminoyama, Japan .... 30 E10　38　9N 140 17 E
Kamiros, Greece .... 25 C9　36 20N　27 56 E
Kamituga, Dem. Rep. of
　the Congo .... 54 C2　3　2S　28 10 E
Kamla ➤, India .... 43 G12　25 35N　86 36 E
Kamloops, Canada .... 70 C4　50 40N 120 20W
Kamo, Japan .... 30 F9　37 39N 139　3 E
Kamoke, Pakistan .... 42 C6　32　4N　74　4 E
Kampala, Uganda .... 54 B3　0 20N　32 30 E
Kampar, Malaysia .... 39 K3　4 18N 101　9 E
Kampar ➤, Indonesia .... 36 D2　0 30N 103　8 E
Kampen, Neths. .... 15 B5　52 33N　5 53 E
Kampene, Dem. Rep. of
　the Congo .... 54 C2　3 36S　26 40 E
Kamphaeng Phet, Thailand ... 38 D2　16 28N　99 30 E
Kampolombo, L., Zambia .... 55 E2　11 37S　29 42 E
Kampong Chhnang, Cambodia . 38 F5　12 20N 104 35 E
Kampong Pengerang, Malaysia . 39 d　1 22N 104　7 E
Kampong Punggai, Malaysia .. 39 d　1 28N 104　8 E
Kampong Saom, Cambodia ... 39 G4　10 38N 103 30 E
Kampong Saom, Chaak,
　Cambodia .... 39 G4　10 50N 103 32 E
Kampong Tanjong Langsat,
　Malaysia .... 39 d　1 28N 104　1 E
Kampong Telok Ramunia,
　Malaysia .... 39 d　1 22N 104 15 E
Kampot, Cambodia .... 39 G5　10 36N 104 10 E
Kampuchea = Cambodia ■, Asia 38 F5　12 15N 105　0 E
Kampung Air Putih, Malaysia .. 39 K4　4 15N 103 10 E
Kampung Jerangau, Malaysia .. 39 K4　4 50N 103 10 E
Kampung Raja, Malaysia ..... 39 K4　5 45N 102 35 E
Kampungbaru = Tolitoli,
　Indonesia .... 37 D6　1　5N 120 50 E
Kamrau, Teluk, Indonesia .... 37 E8　3 30S 133 36 E
Kamsack, Canada .... 71 C8　51 34N 101 54W

Kamskoye Vdkhr., *Russia* ...... **18 C10** 58 41N 56 7 E
Kamuchawie L., *Canada* **71 B8** 56 18N 101 59W
Kamui-Misaki, *Japan* ...... **30 C10** 43 20N 140 21 E
Kamyanets-Podilskyy, *Ukraine* . **17 D14** 48 45N 26 40 E
Kamyanka-Buzka, *Ukraine* .... **17 C13** 50 8N 24 16 E
Kāmyārān, *Iran* .... **44 C5** 34 47N 46 56 E
Kamyshin, *Russia* .... **19 D8** 50 10N 45 24 E
Kanaaupscow, *Canada* **69 C12** 53 39N 77 9W
Kanaaupscow ➤, *Canada* ... **72 B4** 54 2N 76 30W
Kanab, *U.S.A.* **77 H7** 37 3N 112 32W
Kanab ➤, *U.S.A.* **77 H7** 36 24N 112 38W
Kanagi, *Japan* .... **30 D10** 40 54N 140 27 E
Kanairiktok ➤, *Canada* **73 A7** 55 2N 60 18W
Kananga, *Dem. Rep. of*
  the Congo .... **52 F4** 5 55S 22 18 E
Kanash, *Russia* .... **18 C8** 55 30N 47 32 E
Kanaskat, *U.S.A.* **78 C5** 47 19N 121 54W
Kanastraíon, Ákra = Palioúrion,
  Ákra, Greece .... **23 E10** 39 57N 23 45 E
Kanawha ➤, *U.S.A.* **82 F4** 38 50N 82 9W
Kanazawa, *Japan* .... **31 F8** 36 30N 136 38 E
Kanchanaburi, *Thailand* .... **38 E2** 14 2N 99 31 E
Kanchenjunga, *Nepal* ..... **43 F13** 27 50N 88 10 E
Kanchipuram, *India* .... **40 N11** 12 52N 79 45 E
Kandaghat, *India* .... **42 D7** 30 59N 77 7 E
Kandahar = Qandahār, *Afghan.* . **40 D4** 31 32N 65 43 E
Kandalaksha, *Russia* ...... **18 A5** 67 9N 32 30 E
Kandalakshkiy Zaliv, *Russia* .. **18 A6** 66 0N 35 0 E
Kandangan, *Indonesia* ..... **36 E5** 2 50S 115 20 E
Kandanghaur, *Indonesia* .... **37 G13** 6 21S 108 6 E
Kandanos, *Greece* .... **25 D5** 35 19N 23 44 E
Kandavu = Kadavu, *Fiji* .... **59 D8** 19 0S 178 15 E
Kandhkot, *Pakistan* ...... **42 E3** 28 16N 69 8 E
Kandhla, *India* .... **42 E7** 29 18N 77 19 E
Kandi, *Benin* .... **50 F6** 11 7N 2 55 E
Kandi, *India* .... **43 H13** 23 58N 88 5 E
Kandiaro, *Pakistan* ...... **42 F3** 27 4N 68 13 E
Kandla, *India* .... **42 H4** 23 0N 70 10 E
Kandos, *Australia* .... **63 E4** 32 45S 149 58 E
Kandreho, *Madag.* .... **57 B8** 17 29S 46 6 E
Kandy, *Sri Lanka* .... **40 R12** 7 18N 80 43 E
Kane, *U.S.A.* **84 E6** 41 40N 78 49W
Kane Basin, *Greenland* **4 B4** 79 1N 70 0W
Kaneohe, *U.S.A.* **74 H16** 21 25N 157 48W
Kang, *Botswana* .... **56 C3** 23 41S 22 50 E
Kang Krung △, *Thailand* ... **39 H2** 9 30N 98 50 E
Kangān, *Fārs, Iran* ...... **45 E7** 27 50N 52 3 E
Kangān, *Hormozgān, Iran* ... **45 E8** 25 48N 57 28 E
Kangar, *Malaysia* .... **39 J3** 6 27N 100 12 E
Kangaroo I., *Australia* ..... **63 F2** 35 45S 137 0 E
Kangaroo Mts., *Australia* ... **62 C3** 23 29S 141 51 E
Kangasala, *Finland* ...... **9 F21** 61 28N 24 4 E
Kangāvar, *Iran* .... **45 C6** 34 40N 48 0 E
Kangdong, *N. Korea* ...... **35 E14** 39 9N 126 5 E
Kangean, Kepulauan, *Indonesia* **36 F5** 6 55S 115 23 E
Kangean Is. = Kangean,
  Kepulauan, *Indonesia* .... **36 F5** 6 55S 115 23 E
Kanggye, *N. Korea* .... **35 D14** 41 0N 126 35 E
Kanggyŏng, *S. Korea* ..... **35 F14** 36 10N 127 0 E
Kanghwa, *S. Korea* ...... **35 F14** 37 45N 126 30 E
Kangikajik, *Greenland* **4 B6** 70 7N 22 0W
Kangiqliniq = Rankin Inlet,
  Canada **68 B10** 62 30N 93 0W
Kangiqsualujjuaq, *Canada* .. **69 C13** 58 30N 65 59W
Kangiqsujuaq, *Canada* **69 B12** 61 30N 72 0W
Kangiqtugaapik = Clyde River,
  Canada **69 A13** 70 30N 68 30W
Kangirsuk, *Canada* **69 B13** 60 0N 70 0W
Kangkar Chemaran, *Malaysia* . **39 d** 1 34N 104 12 E
Kangkar Sungai Tiram, *Malaysia* **39 d** 1 35N 103 55 E
Kangkar Teberau, *Malaysia* .. **39 d** 1 32N 103 51 E
Kangnŭng, *S. Korea* ...... **35 F15** 37 45N 128 54 E
Kangping, *China* .... **35 C12** 42 43N 123 18 E
Kangra, *India* .... **42 C7** 32 6N 76 16 E
Kangrinboqe Feng, *China* ... **43 D9** 31 0N 81 25 E
Kangto, *India* .... **41 F18** 27 50N 92 35 E
Kanhar ➤, *India* .... **43 G10** 24 28N 83 8 E
Kaniama, *Dem. Rep. of*
  the Congo .... **54 D1** 7 30S 24 12 E
Kaniapiskau = Caniapiscau ➤,
  Canada **73 A6** 56 40N 69 30W
Kaniapiskau, L. = Caniapiscau, L.
  de, *Canada* **73 B6** 54 10N 69 55W
Kanin, Poluostrov, *Russia* ... **18 A8** 68 0N 45 0 E
Kanin Nos, Mys, *Russia* ... **18 A7** 68 39N 43 32 E
Kanin Pen. = Kanin, Poluostrov,
  Russia .... **18 A8** 68 0N 45 0 E
Kaniva, *Australia* .... **63 F3** 36 22S 141 18 E
Kanjut Sar, *Pakistan* ..... **43 A6** 36 7N 75 25 E
Kankaanpää, *Finland* ..... **9 F20** 61 44N 22 50 E
Kankakee, *U.S.A.* **82 E2** 41 7N 87 52W
Kankakee ➤, *U.S.A.* **82 E1** 41 23N 88 15W
Kankan, *Guinea* **50 F4** 10 23N 9 15W
Kankendy = Xankändi, *Azerbaijan* **19 G8** 39 52N 46 49 E
Kanker, *India* .... **41 J12** 20 10N 81 40 E
Kankroli, *India* .... **42 G5** 25 4N 73 53 E
Kannapolis, *U.S.A.* **83 H5** 35 30N 80 37W
Kannauj, *India* .... **43 F8** 27 3N 79 56 E
Kannod, *India* .... **40 H10** 22 45N 76 40 E
Kano, *Nigeria* .... **50 F7** 12 2N 8 30 E
Kan'onji, *Japan* .... **31 G6** 34 7N 133 39 E
Kanowit, *Malaysia* ...... **36 D4** 2 14N 112 20 E
Kanoya, *Japan* .... **31 J5** 31 25N 130 50 E
Kanpetlet, *Burma* .... **41 J18** 21 10N 93 59 E
Kanpur, *India* .... **43 F9** 26 28N 80 20 E
Kansas □, *U.S.A.* **80 F6** 38 30N 99 0W
Kansas ➤, *U.S.A.* **80 F7** 39 7N 94 37W
Kansas City, *Kans., U.S.A.* .. **80 F7** 39 7N 94 38W
Kansas City, *Mo., U.S.A.* ... **80 F7** 39 6N 94 35W
Kansenia, *Dem. Rep. of*
  the Congo .... **55 E2** 10 20S 26 0 E
Kansk, *Russia* .... **29 D10** 56 20N 95 37 E
Kansŏng, *S. Korea* ...... **35 E15** 38 24N 128 30 E
Kansu = Gansu □, *China* ... **34 G3** 36 0N 104 0 E
Kantaphor, *India* .... **42 H7** 22 35N 76 34 E
Kantharalak, *Thailand* .... **38 E5** 14 39N 104 39 E
Kantli ➤, *India* .... **42 E6** 28 20N 75 30 E
Kantō □, *Japan* .... **31 F9** 36 15N 139 30 E
Kantō-Sanchi, *Japan* ..... **31 G9** 35 59N 138 50 E
Kanturk, *Ireland* **10 D3** 52 11N 8 54W
Kanus, *Russia* .... **31 F9** 36 34N 139 42 E
Kanus, *Namibia* .... **56 D2** 27 50S 18 39 E
Kanye, *Botswana* .... **56 C4** 24 55S 25 28 E
Kanzenze, *Dem. Rep. of*
  the Congo .... **55 E2** 10 30S 25 12 E
Kanzi, Ras, *Tanzania* ..... **54 D4** 7 1S 39 33 E
Kao Phara, *Thailand* ..... **39 a** 8 3N 98 22 E

Kaohsiung, *Taiwan* ...... **33 D7** 22 35N 120 16 E
Kaokoveld, *Namibia* ...... **56 B1** 19 15S 14 30 E
Kaolack, *Senegal* **50 F2** 14 5N 16 8W
Kaoshan, *China* .... **35 B13** 44 38N 124 50 E
Kapaa, *U.S.A.* **74 G15** 22 5N 159 19W
Kapadvanj, *India* .... **42 H5** 23 5N 73 0 E
Kapan, *Armenia* .... **19 G8** 39 18N 46 27 E
Kapanga, *Dem. Rep. of*
  the Congo .... **52 F4** 8 30S 22 40 E
Kapchagai = Qapshaghay,
  Kazakhstan .... **28 E8** 43 51N 77 14 E
Kapela = Velika Kapela, *Croatia* . **16 F8** 45 10N 15 5 E
Kapema, *Dem. Rep. of the Congo* **55 E2** 10 45S 28 22 E
Kapfenberg, *Austria* ...... **16 E8** 47 26N 15 18 E
Kapiri Mposhi, *Zambia* .... **55 E2** 13 59S 28 43 E
Kāpīsā □, *Afghan.* .... **40 B6** 35 0N 69 20 E
Kapiskau ➤, *Canada* **72 B3** 52 47N 81 55W
Kapit, *Malaysia* .... **36 D4** 2 0N 112 55 E
Kapiti I., *N.Z.* .... **59 J5** 40 50S 174 56 E
Kaplan, *U.S.A.* **81 K8** 30 0N 92 17W
Kapoe, *Thailand* .... **39 H2** 9 34N 98 32 E
Kapoeta, *Sudan* .... **51 H12** 4 50N 33 35 E
Kaposvár, *Hungary* ...... **17 E9** 46 25N 17 47 E
Kapowsin, *U.S.A.* **78 D4** 46 59N 122 13W
Kapps, *Namibia* .... **56 C2** 22 32S 17 18 E
Kapsan, *N. Korea* .... **35 D15** 41 4N 128 19 E
Kapsukas = Marijampolė,
  Lithuania .... **9 J20** 54 33N 23 19 E
Kaptai L., *Bangla.* ...... **41 H18** 22 40N 92 20 E
Kapuas ➤, *Indonesia* ..... **36 E3** 0 25S 109 20 E
Kapuas Hulu, Pegunungan,
  Malaysia .... **36 D4** 1 30N 113 30 E
Kapuas Hulu Ra. = Kapuas Hulu,
  Pegunungan, *Malaysia* ... **36 D4** 1 30N 113 30 E
Kapulo, *Dem. Rep. of the Congo* **55 D2** 8 18S 29 15 E
Kapunda, *Australia* ...... **63 E2** 34 20S 138 56 E
Kapuni, *N.Z.* .... **59 H5** 39 29S 174 8 E
Kapurthala, *India* .... **42 D6** 31 23N 75 25 E
Kapuskasing, *Canada* **72 C3** 49 25N 82 30W
Kapuskasing ➤, *Canada* ... **72 C3** 49 49N 82 0W
Kaputar, *Australia* ...... **63 E5** 30 15S 150 10 E
Kaputir, *Kenya* .... **54 B4** 2 5N 35 28 E
Kara, *Russia* .... **28 C7** 69 10N 65 0 E
Kara Bogaz Gol, Zaliv =
  Garabogazköl Aylagy,
  Turkmenistan .... **19 F9** 41 0N 53 30 E
Kara Kalpak Republic =
  Qoraqalpoghistan □,
  Uzbekistan .... **28 E6** 43 0N 58 0 E
Kara Kum, *Turkmenistan* ... **28 F6** 39 30N 60 0 E
Kara Sea, *Russia* .... **28 B7** 75 0N 70 0 E
Karabiğa, *Turkey* .... **23 D12** 40 23N 27 17 E
Karabük, *Turkey* .... **19 F5** 41 12N 32 37 E
Karaburun, *Turkey* ...... **23 E12** 38 41N 26 28 E
Karabutak = Qarabutaq,
  Kazakhstan .... **28 E7** 49 59N 60 14 E
Karacabey, *Turkey* ...... **23 D13** 40 12N 28 21 E
Karacasu, *Turkey* .... **23 F13** 37 43N 28 35 E
Karachey-Cherkessia □, *Russia* . **19 F7** 43 40N 42 0 E
Karachi, *Pakistan* .... **42 G2** 24 53N 67 0 E
Karad, *India* .... **40 L9** 17 15N 74 10 E
Karaganda = Qaraghandy,
  Kazakhstan .... **28 E8** 49 50N 73 10 E
Karagayly, *Kazakhstan* .... **28 E8** 49 26N 76 0 E
Karaginskiy, Ostrov, *Russia* .. **29 D17** 58 45N 164 0 E
Karagiye, Vpadina, *Kazakhstan* . **19 F9** 43 27N 51 45 E
Karagiye Depression = Karagiye,
  Vpadina, *Kazakhstan* .... **19 F9** 43 27N 51 45 E
Karagola Road, *India* ..... **43 G12** 25 29N 87 23 E
Karaikal, *India* .... **40 P11** 10 59N 79 50 E
Karaikkudi, *India* .... **40 P11** 10 5N 78 45 E
Karaj, *Iran* .... **45 C6** 35 48N 51 0 E
Karak, *Malaysia* .... **39 L4** 3 25N 102 2 E
Karakalpakstan =
  Qoraqalpoghistan □,
  Uzbekistan .... **28 E6** 43 0N 58 0 E
Karakelong, *Indonesia* .... **37 D7** 4 35N 126 50 E
Karakitang, *Indonesia* .... **37 D7** 3 14N 125 28 E
Karakol, *Kyrgyzstan* ..... **28 E8** 42 30N 78 20 E
Karakoram Pass, *Asia* .... **43 B7** 35 33N 77 50 E
Karakoram Ra., *Pakistan* ... **43 B7** 35 30N 77 0 E
Karakuwisa, *Namibia* ..... **56 B2** 18 56S 19 40 E
Karalon, *Russia* .... **29 D12** 57 5N 115 50 E
Karama, *Jordan* .... **46 D4** 31 57N 35 35 E
Karaman, *Turkey* .... **19 G5** 37 14N 33 13 E
Karamay, *China* .... **32 B3** 45 30N 84 58 E
Karambu, *Indonesia* ..... **36 E5** 3 53S 116 6 E
Karamea Bight, *N.Z.* ..... **59 J3** 41 22S 171 40 E
Karamnasa ➤, *India* ..... **43 G10** 25 31N 83 52 E
Karand, *Iran* .... **44 C5** 34 16N 46 15 E
Karanganyar, *Indonesia* ... **37 G13** 7 38S 109 37 E
Karangasem, *Indonesia* ... **37 J18** 8 27S 115 37 E
Karanjia, *India* .... **43 J11** 21 47N 85 58 E
Karasburg, *Namibia* ..... **56 D2** 28 0S 18 44 E
Karasino, *Russia* .... **28 C9** 66 50N 86 50 E
Karasjok, *Norway* .... **8 B21** 69 27N 25 30 E
Karasuk, *Russia* .... **28 D8** 53 44N 78 2 E
Karasuyama, *Japan* ...... **31 F10** 36 39N 140 9 E
Karatau, Khrebet = Qarataū,
  Kazakhstan .... **28 E7** 43 30N 69 30 E
Karatsu, *Japan* .... **31 H5** 33 26N 129 58 E
Karaul, *Russia* .... **28 B9** 70 6N 82 15 E
Karauli, *India* .... **42 F7** 26 30N 77 4 E
Karavostasi, *Cyprus* ..... **25 D11** 35 8N 32 50 E
Karawang, *Indonesia* ..... **37 G12** 6 30S 107 15 E
Karawanken, *Europe* ..... **16 E8** 46 30N 14 40 E
Karayazı, *Turkey* .... **19 G7** 39 41N 42 9 E
Karazhal, *Kazakhstan* .... **28 E8** 48 2N 70 49 E
Karbalā', *Iraq* .... **44 C5** 32 36N 44 3 E
Karcag, *Hungary* .... **17 E11** 47 19N 20 57 E
Karcha ➤, *Pakistan* ...... **43 B7** 34 45N 76 10 E
Karchana, *India* .... **43 G9** 25 17N 81 56 E
Kardhítsa, *Greece* ...... **23 E9** 39 23N 21 54 E
Kärdla, *Estonia* .... **9 G20** 58 50N 22 40 E
Kareeberge, *S. Africa* ..... **56 E3** 30 59S 21 50 E
Kareha ➤, *India* .... **43 G12** 25 44N 86 21 E
Kareima, *Sudan* .... **51 E12** 18 30N 31 49 E
Karelia □, *Russia* .... **18 A5** 65 30N 32 30 E
Karelian Republic = Karelia □,
  Russia .... **18 A5** 65 30N 32 30 E
Karera, *India* .... **42 G8** 25 32N 78 9 E
Kārevāndar, *Iran* .... **45 E9** 27 53N 60 44 E
Kargasok, *Russia* .... **28 D9** 59 3N 80 53 E
Kargat, *Russia* .... **28 D9** 55 10N 80 15 E
Kargil, *India* .... **43 B7** 34 32N 76 12 E
Kargopol, *Russia* .... **18 B6** 61 30N 38 58 E
Karhal, *India* .... **43 F8** 27 1N 78 57 E

Kariān, *Iran* .... **45 E8** 26 57N 57 14 E
Karianga, *Madag.* .... **57 C8** 22 25S 47 22 E
Kariba, *Zimbabwe* ...... **55 F2** 16 28S 28 50 E
Kariba, L., *Zimbabwe* .... **55 F2** 16 40S 28 25 E
Kariba Dam, *Zimbabwe* ... **55 F2** 16 30S 28 35 E
Kariba Gorge, *Zambia* .... **55 F2** 16 30S 28 50 E
Karibib, *Namibia* .... **56 C2** 22 0S 15 56 E
Karijini △, *Australia* ..... **60 D2** 23 8S 118 15 E
Karimata, Kepulauan, *Indonesia* **36 E3** 1 25S 109 0 E
Karimata, Selat, *Indonesia* .. **36 E3** 2 0S 108 40 E
Karimata Is. = Karimata,
  Kepulauan, *Indonesia* ... **36 E3** 1 25S 109 0 E
Karimnagar, *India* ...... **40 K11** 18 26N 79 10 E
Karimun Kecil, Pulau, *Indonesia* **39 d** 1 8N 103 22 E
Karimunjawa, Kepulauan,
  Indonesia .... **36 F4** 5 50S 110 30 E
Karin, *Somali Rep.* ...... **47 E4** 10 50N 45 52 E
Karit, *Iran* .... **45 C8** 33 29N 56 55 E
Kariya, *Japan* .... **31 G8** 34 58N 137 1 E
Kariyangwe, *Zimbabwe* ... **57 B4** 18 0S 27 38 E
Karkaralinsk = Qarqaraly,
  Kazakhstan .... **28 E8** 49 26N 75 30 E
Karkheh ➤, *Iran* .... **44 D5** 31 2N 47 29 E
Karkinitska Zatoka, *Ukraine* .. **19 E5** 45 56N 33 0 E
Karkinitskiy Zaliv = Karkinitska
  Zatoka, *Ukraine* ...... **19 E5** 45 56N 33 0 E
Karlovac, *Croatia* ...... **16 F8** 45 31N 15 36 E
Karlovo, *Bulgaria* ...... **23 C11** 42 38N 24 47 E
Karlovy Vary, *Czech Rep.* .. **16 C7** 50 13N 12 51 E
Karlsbad = Karlovy Vary,
  Czech Rep. .... **16 C7** 50 13N 12 51 E
Karlsborg, *Sweden* ...... **9 G16** 58 33N 14 33 E
Karlshamn, *Sweden* ..... **9 H16** 56 10N 14 51 E
Karlskoga, *Sweden* ...... **9 G16** 59 28N 14 33 E
Karlskrona, *Sweden* ..... **9 H16** 56 10N 15 35 E
Karlsruhe, *Germany* ..... **16 D5** 49 0N 8 23 E
Karlstad, *Sweden* .... **9 G15** 59 23N 13 30 E
Karlstad, *U.S.A.* **80 A6** 48 35N 96 31W
Karmi'el, *Israel* .... **46 C4** 32 55N 35 18 E
Karnak, *Egypt* .... **51 C12** 25 43N 32 39 E
Karnal, *India* .... **42 E7** 29 42N 77 2 E
Karnali ➤, *Nepal* .... **43 E9** 28 45N 81 16 E
Karnaphuli Res. = Kaptai L.,
  Bangla. .... **41 H18** 22 40N 92 20 E
Karnaprayag, *India* ...... **43 D8** 30 16N 79 15 E
Karnataka □, *India* ...... **40 N10** 13 15N 77 0 E
Karnes City, *U.S.A.* **81 L6** 28 53N 97 54W
Karnische Alpen, *Europe* ... **16 E7** 46 36N 13 0 E
Kärnten □, *Austria* ...... **16 E8** 46 52N 13 30 E
Karoi, *Zimbabwe* .... **55 F2** 16 48S 29 45 E
Karon, Ao, *Thailand* ..... **39 a** 7 51N 98 17 E
Karonga, *Malawi* .... **55 D3** 9 57S 33 55 E
Karoo △, *S. Africa* ...... **56 E3** 32 18S 22 27 E
Karoonda, *Australia* ..... **63 F2** 35 1S 139 59 E
Karor, *Pakistan* .... **42 D4** 31 15N 70 59 E
Karora, *Sudan* .... **51 E13** 17 44N 38 15 E
Karpasia, *Cyprus* ...... **25 D13** 35 32N 34 15 E
Kárpathos, *Greece* ...... **23 G12** 35 37N 27 10 E
Karpinsk, *Russia* .... **18 C11** 59 45N 60 1 E
Karpogory, *Russia* ...... **18 B7** 64 0N 44 27 E
Karpuz Burnu = Apostolos
  Andreas, C., *Cyprus* .... **25 D13** 35 42N 34 35 E
Kars, *Turkey* .... **19 F7** 40 40N 43 5 E
Karsakpay, *Kazakhstan* ... **28 E7** 47 55N 66 40 E
Karshi = Qarshi, *Uzbekistan* . **28 F7** 38 53N 65 48 E
Karsiyang, *India* .... **43 F13** 26 56N 88 18 E
Karsog, *India* .... **42 D7** 31 23N 77 12 E
Kartaly, *Russia* .... **28 D7** 53 3N 60 40 E
Kartapur, *India* .... **42 D6** 31 27N 75 32 E
Karthaus, *U.S.A.* **84 E6** 41 8N 78 9W
Karufa, *Indonesia* ...... **37 E8** 3 50S 133 20 E
Karuma △, *Uganda* ...... **54 B3** 2 5N 32 15 E
Karumba, *Australia* ..... **62 B3** 17 31S 140 50 E
Karumo, *Tanzania* ...... **54 C3** 2 25S 32 50 E
Karumwa, *Tanzania* ..... **54 C3** 3 12S 32 38 E
Kärün ➤, *Iran* .... **45 D6** 30 26N 48 10 E
Karungu, *Kenya* .... **54 C3** 0 50S 34 10 E
Karviná, *Czech Rep.* ..... **17 D10** 49 53N 18 31 E
Karwan ➤, *India* .... **42 F8** 27 26N 78 4 E
Karwar, *India* .... **40 M9** 14 55N 74 13 E
Karwi, *India* .... **43 G9** 25 12N 80 57 E
Kasache, *Malawi* .... **55 E3** 13 25S 34 20 E
Kasai ➤, *Dem. Rep. of*
  the Congo .... **52 E3** 3 30S 16 10 E
Kasai-Oriental □, *Dem. Rep. of*
  the Congo .... **54 D1** 5 0S 24 30 E
Kasaji, *Dem. Rep. of the Congo* . **55 E1** 10 25S 23 27 E
Kasama, *Zambia* .... **55 E3** 10 16S 31 9 E
Kasan-dong, *N. Korea* .... **35 D14** 41 18N 126 55 E
Kasane, *Namibia* .... **56 B3** 17 34S 24 50 E
Kasanga, *Tanzania* ...... **55 D3** 8 30S 31 10 E
Kasaragod, *India* .... **40 N9** 12 30N 74 58 E
Kasba L., *Canada* **71 A8** 60 20N 102 10W
Kāseh Garān, *Iran* ...... **44 C5** 34 5N 46 2 E
Kasempa, *Zambia* ...... **55 E2** 13 30S 25 44 E
Kasenga, *Dem. Rep. of*
  the Congo .... **55 E2** 10 20S 28 45 E
Kasese, *Uganda* .... **54 B3** 0 13N 30 3 E
Kasewa, *Zambia* .... **55 E2** 14 28S 28 53 E
Kasganj, *India* .... **43 F8** 27 48N 78 42 E
Kashabowie, *Canada* **72 C1** 48 40N 90 26W
Kashaf, *Iran* .... **45 C9** 35 58N 61 7 E
Kāshān, *Iran* .... **45 C6** 34 5N 51 30 E
Kashechewan, *Canada* **72 B3** 52 18N 81 37W
Kashgar = Kashi, *China* ... **32 C2** 39 30N 76 2 E
Kashi, *China* .... **32 C2** 39 30N 76 2 E
Kashimbo, *Dem. Rep. of*
  the Congo .... **55 E2** 11 12S 26 19 E
Kashipur, *India* .... **43 E8** 29 15N 79 0 E
Kashiwazaki, *Japan* ...... **31 F9** 37 22N 138 33 E
Kashk-e Kohneh, *Afghan.* ... **40 B3** 34 55N 62 30 E
Kashkū'īyeh, *Iran* .... **45 D7** 30 31N 55 40 E
Kashmar, *Iran* .... **45 C8** 35 16N 58 26 E
Kashmir, *Asia* .... **43 C7** 34 0N 76 0 E
Kashun Noerh = Gaxun Nur,
  China .... **32 B5** 42 22N 100 30 E
Kasiari, *India* .... **43 H12** 22 8N 87 14 E
Kasimov, *Russia* .... **18 D7** 54 55N 41 20 E
Kasinge, *Dem. Rep. of the Congo* **54 D2** 6 15S 26 58 E
Kasiruta, *Indonesia* ..... **37 E7** 0 25S 127 12 E
Kaskaskia ➤, *U.S.A.* **80 G10** 37 58N 89 57W
Kaskattama ➤, *Canada* **71 B10** 57 3N 90 4W
Kaskinen, *Finland* ...... **9 E19** 62 22N 21 15 E
Kaslo, *Canada* **70 D5** 49 55N 116 55W

Kasmere L., *Canada* **71 B8** 59 34N 101 10W
Kasongo, *Dem. Rep. of*
  the Congo .... **54 C2** 4 30S 26 33 E
Kasongo Lunda, *Dem. Rep. of*
  the Congo .... **52 F3** 6 35S 16 49 E
Kásos, *Greece* .... **23 G12** 35 20N 26 55 E
Kassalâ, *Sudan* .... **51 E13** 15 30N 36 0 E
Kassel, *Germany* .... **16 C5** 51 18N 9 26 E
Kassiópi, *Greece* .... **25 A3** 39 48N 19 53 E
Kasson, *U.S.A.* **80 C8** 44 2N 92 45W
Kastamonu, *Turkey* ..... **19 F5** 41 25N 33 43 E
Kastélli, *Greece* .... **25 D5** 35 29N 23 38 E
Kastéllion, *Greece* ...... **25 D7** 35 12N 25 20 E
Kasterlee, *Belgium* ...... **15 C4** 51 15N 4 59 E
Kastoría, *Greece* .... **23 D9** 40 30N 21 19 E
Kasulu, *Tanzania* .... **54 C3** 4 37S 30 5 E
Kasumi, *Japan* .... **31 G7** 35 38N 134 38 E
Kasungu, *Malawi* .... **55 E3** 13 0S 33 29 E
Kasungu △, *Malawi* ..... **55 E3** 12 53S 33 9 E
Kasur, *Pakistan* .... **42 D6** 31 5N 74 25 E
Kataba, *Zambia* .... **55 F2** 16 5S 25 10 E
Katahdin, Mt., *U.S.A.* **83 C11** 45 54N 68 56W
Katako Kombe, *Dem. Rep. of*
  the Congo .... **54 C1** 3 25S 24 20 E
Katale, *Tanzania* .... **54 C3** 4 52S 31 7 E
Katanda, Katanga, *Dem. Rep. of*
  the Congo .... **54 D1** 7 52S 24 13 E
Katanda, Nord-Kivu, *Dem. Rep.*
  of the Congo .... **54 C2** 0 55S 29 21 E
Katanga □, *Dem. Rep. of*
  the Congo .... **54 D2** 8 0S 25 0 E
Katangi, *India* .... **40 J11** 21 56N 79 50 E
Katanning, *Australia* ..... **61 F2** 33 40S 117 33 E
Katavi △, *Tanzania* ...... **54 D3** 6 51S 31 3 E
Katavi Swamp, *Tanzania* ... **54 D3** 6 50S 31 10 E
Katerini, *Greece* .... **23 D10** 40 18N 22 37 E
Katghora, *India* .... **43 H10** 22 30N 82 33 E
Katha, *Burma* .... **41 G20** 24 10N 96 30 E
Katherîna, Gebel, *Egypt* ... **44 D2** 28 30N 33 57 E
Katherine, *Australia* ..... **60 B5** 14 27S 132 20 E
Katherine Gorge, *Australia* . **60 B5** 14 18S 132 28 E
Kathi, *India* .... **42 J6** 21 47N 74 3 E
Kathiawar, *India* .... **42 H4** 22 20N 71 0 E
Kathikas, *Cyprus* .... **25 E11** 34 55N 32 25 E
Kathmandu = Katmandu, *Nepal* . **43 F11** 27 45N 85 20 E
Kathua, *India* .... **42 C6** 32 23N 75 34 E
Katihar, *India* .... **43 G12** 25 34N 87 36 E
Katima Mulilo, *Zambia* .... **56 B3** 17 28S 24 13 E
Katimbira, *Malawi* ...... **55 E3** 12 40S 34 0 E
Katingan = Mendawai ➤,
  Indonesia .... **36 E4** 3 30S 113 0 E
Katiola, *Ivory C.* **50 G4** 8 10N 5 10W
Katmandu, *Nepal* .... **43 F11** 27 45N 85 20 E
Katni, *India* .... **43 H9** 23 51N 80 24 E
Káto Arkhánai, *Greece* .... **25 D7** 35 15N 25 10 E
Káto Khorió, *Greece* ..... **25 D7** 35 3N 25 47 E
Káto Pyrgos, *Cyprus* ..... **25 D11** 35 11N 32 41 E
Katompe, *Dem. Rep. of*
  the Congo .... **54 D2** 6 2S 26 23 E
Katong, *Singapore* ...... **39 d** 1 18N 103 53 E
Katonga ➤, *Uganda* ..... **54 B3** 0 34N 31 50 E
Katoomba, *Australia* ..... **63 E5** 33 41S 150 19 E
Katowice, *Poland* .... **17 C10** 50 17N 19 5 E
Katrine, L., *U.K.* **11 E4** 56 15N 4 30W
Katrineholm, *Sweden* .... **9 G17** 59 9N 16 12 E
Katsepe, *Madag.* .... **57 B8** 15 45S 46 15 E
Katsina, *Nigeria* .... **50 F7** 13 0N 7 32 E
Katsumoto, *Japan* ...... **31 H4** 33 51N 129 42 E
Katsuura, *Japan* .... **31 G10** 35 10N 140 20 E
Katsuyama, *Japan* ...... **31 F8** 36 3N 136 30 E
Kattaviá, *Greece* .... **25 D9** 35 57N 27 46 E
Kattegat, *Denmark* ...... **9 H14** 56 40N 11 20 E
Katumba, *Dem. Rep. of*
  the Congo .... **54 D2** 7 40S 25 17 E
Katwa, *India* .... **43 H13** 23 30N 88 5 E
Katwijk, *Neths.* .... **15 B4** 52 12N 4 24 E
Kauai, *U.S.A.* **74 H15** 22 3N 159 30W
Kauai Channel, *U.S.A.* **74 H15** 21 45N 158 50W
Kaudom △, *Namibia* ..... **56 B3** 18 45S 20 51 E
Kaufman, *U.S.A.* **81 J6** 32 35N 96 19W
Kauhajoki, *Finland* ...... **9 E20** 62 25N 22 10 E
Kaukauna, *U.S.A.* **82 C1** 44 17N 88 17W
Kaukauveld, *Namibia* .... **56 C3** 20 0S 21 0 E
Kaunakakai, *U.S.A.* **74 H16** 21 6N 157 1W
Kaunas, *Lithuania* ...... **9 J20** 54 54N 23 54 E
Kaunia, *Bangla.* .... **43 G13** 25 46N 89 26 E
Kautokeino, *Norway* ..... **8 B20** 69 0N 23 4 E
Kauwapur, *India* .... **43 F10** 27 31N 82 18 E
Kavacha, *Russia* .... **29 C17** 60 16N 169 51 E
Kavali, *India* .... **40 M12** 14 55N 80 1 E
Kavār, *Iran* .... **45 D7** 29 11N 52 44 E
Kavi, *India* .... **42 H5** 22 12N 72 38 E
Kavimba, *Botswana* ..... **56 B3** 18 2S 24 38 E
Kavīr, Dasht-e, *Iran* ..... **45 C7** 34 30N 55 0 E
Kavos, *Greece* .... **25 B4** 39 23N 20 3 E
Kaw, *Fr. Guiana* **93 C8** 4 30N 52 15W
Kawagama L., *Canada* **84 A6** 45 18N 78 45W
Kawagoe, *Japan* .... **31 G9** 35 55N 139 29 E
Kawaguchi, *Japan* ...... **31 G9** 35 52N 139 45 E
Kawambwa, *Zambia* ..... **55 D2** 9 48S 29 3 E
Kawanoe, *Japan* .... **31 G6** 34 1N 133 34 E
Kawardha, *India* .... **43 J9** 22 0N 81 17 E
Kawasaki, *Japan* .... **31 G9** 35 31N 139 43 E
Kawasi, *Indonesia* ...... **37 E7** 1 38S 127 28 E
Kawerau, *N.Z.* .... **59 H6** 38 7S 176 42 E
Kawhia Harbour, *N.Z.* .... **59 H5** 38 5S 174 51 E
Kawio, Kepulauan, *Indonesia* . **37 D7** 4 30N 125 30 E
Kawnro, *Burma* .... **41 H21** 22 48N 99 8 E
Kawthaung, *Burma* ...... **39 H2** 10 5N 98 36 E
Kawthoolei = Kayin □, *Burma* . **41 L20** 18 0N 97 30 E
Kawthule = Kayin □, *Burma* . **41 L20** 18 0N 97 30 E
Kaya, *Burkina Faso* **50 F5** 13 4N 1 10W
Kayah □, *Burma* .... **41 K20** 19 15N 97 15 E
Kayan ➤, *Indonesia* ..... **36 D5** 2 55N 117 35 E
Kaycee, *U.S.A.* **76 E10** 43 43N 106 38W
Kayeli, *Indonesia* ...... **37 E7** 3 20S 127 10 E
Kayenta, *U.S.A.* **77 H8** 36 44N 110 15W
Kayes, *Mali* **50 F3** 14 25N 11 30W
Kayin □, *Burma* .... **41 L20** 18 0N 97 30 E
Kayomba, *Zambia* ...... **55 E1** 13 11S 24 2 E
Kayseri, *Turkey* .... **19 G6** 38 45N 35 30 E
Kaysville, *U.S.A.* **76 F8** 41 2N 111 56W
Kazachye, *Russia* ...... **29 B14** 70 52N 135 58 E
Kazakhstan ■, *Asia* ..... **28 E7** 50 0N 70 0 E

Kazan, Russia .... 18 C8 55 50N 49 10 E
Kazan ➤, Canada 71 A9 64 2N 95 29W
Kazan-Rettō, Pac. Oc. .... 64 E6 25 0N 141 0 E
Kazanlŭk, Bulgaria ...... 23 C11 42 38N 25 20 E
Kazatin = Kozyatyn, Ukraine ... 17 D15 49 45N 28 50 E
Kāzerūn, Iran .... 45 D6 29 38N 51 40 E
Kazi Magomed = Qazimämmäd,
   Azerbaijan .... 45 A6 40 3N 49 0 E
Kazuma Pan △, Zimbabwe .. 55 F2 18 20S 25 48 E
Kazuno, Japan .... 30 D10 40 10N 140 45 E
Kazym ➤, Russia .... 28 C7 63 54N 65 50 E
Kéa, Greece .... 23 F11 37 35N 24 22 E
Keady, U.K. 10 B5 54 15N 6 42W
Kearney, U.S.A. 80 E5 40 42N 99 5W
Kearny, U.S.A. 77 K8 33 3N 110 55W
Kearsarge, Mt., U.S.A. ... 85 C13 43 22N 71 50W
Keban, Turkey .... 19 G6 38 50N 38 50 E
Keban Baraji, Turkey .... 19 G6 38 41N 38 33 E
Kebnekaise, Sweden ..... 8 C18 67 53N 18 33 E
Kebri Dehar, Ethiopia ... 47 F3 6 45N 44 17 E
Kebumen, Indonesia ..... 37 G13 7 42S 109 40 E
Kechika ➤, Canada 70 B3 59 41N 127 12W
Kecskemét, Hungary ..... 17 E10 46 57N 19 42 E
Kėdainiai, Lithuania .... 9 J21 55 15N 24 2 E
Kedarnath, India .... 43 D8 30 44N 79 4 E
Kedgwick, Canada 73 C6 47 40N 67 20W
Kédhros Óros, Greece ... 25 D6 35 11N 24 37 E
Kediri, Indonesia ...... 36 F4 7 51S 112 1 E
Keeler, U.S.A. 78 J9 36 29N 117 52W
Keeley L., Canada 71 C7 54 54N 108 8W
Keeling Is. = Cocos Is., Ind. Oc. . 64 J1 12 10S 96 55 E
Keelung = Chilung, Taiwan .. 33 D7 25 3N 121 45 E
Keene, Canada 84 B6 44 15N 78 10W
Keene, Calif., U.S.A. 79 K8 35 13N 118 33W
Keene, N.H., U.S.A. 85 D12 42 56N 72 17W
Keene, N.Y., U.S.A. 85 B11 44 16N 73 46W
Keep River △, Australia .. 60 C4 15 49S 129 8 E
Keeper Hill, Ireland ... 10 D3 52 45N 8 16W
Keer-Weer, C., Australia .. 62 A3 14 0S 141 32 E
Keeseville, U.S.A. 85 B11 44 29N 73 30W
Keetmanshoop, Namibia .. 56 D2 26 35S 18 8 E
Keewatin, Canada 71 D10 49 46N 94 34W
Keewatin ➤, Canada 71 B8 56 29N 100 46W
Kefallinía, Greece ..... 23 E9 38 15N 20 30 E
Kefamenanu, Indonesia .. 37 F6 9 28S 124 29 E
Kefar Sava, Israel ...... 46 C3 32 11N 34 54 E
Keffi, Nigeria .... 50 G7 8 55N 7 43 E
Keflavík, Iceland 8 D2 64 2N 22 35W
Keg River, Canada 70 B5 57 54N 117 55W
Kegaska, Canada 73 B7 50 9N 61 18W
Keighley, U.K. 12 D6 53 52N 1 54W
Keila, Estonia .... 9 G21 59 18N 24 25 E
Keimoes, S. Africa ..... 56 D3 28 41S 20 59 E
Keitele, Finland .... 8 E22 63 10N 26 20 E
Keith, Australia .... 63 F3 36 6S 140 20 E
Keith, U.K. 11 D6 57 32N 2 57W
Keizer, U.S.A. 76 D2 44 57N 123 1W
Kejimkujik △, Canada ... 73 D6 44 25N 65 25W
Kejserr Franz Joseph Fd.,
   Greenland 4 B6 73 30N 24 30W
Kekri, India .... 42 G6 26 0N 75 10 E
Kelan, China .... 34 E6 38 43N 111 31 E
Kelang, Malaysia ...... 39 L3 3 2N 101 26 E
Kelantan ➤, Malaysia ... 39 J4 6 13N 102 14 E
Kelberrin, Australia ... 61 F2 31 36S 117 38 E
Kellett, C., Canada 4 B1 72 0N 126 0W
Kelleys I., U.S.A. 84 E2 41 36N 82 42W
Kellogg, U.S.A. 76 C5 47 32N 116 7W
Kells = Ceanannus Mor, Ireland 10 C5 53 44N 6 53W
Kelokedhara, Cyprus ... 25 E11 34 48N 32 39 E
Kelowna, Canada 70 D5 49 50N 119 25W
Kelsey Creek, Australia .. 62 J6 20 26S 148 31 E
Kelseyville, U.S.A. 78 G4 38 59N 122 50W
Kelso, N.Z. .... 59 L2 45 54S 169 15 E
Kelso, U.K. 11 F6 55 36N 2 26W
Kelso, U.S.A. 78 D4 46 9N 122 54W
Keluang, Malaysia ..... 39 L4 2 3N 103 18 E
Kelvington, Canada 71 C8 52 10N 103 30W
Kem, Russia .... 18 B5 65 0N 34 38 E
Kem ➤, Russia .... 18 B5 64 57N 34 41 E
Kema, Indonesia .... 37 D7 1 22N 125 8 E
Kemah, Turkey .... 44 B3 39 32N 39 5 E
Kemaman, Malaysia .... 36 D2 4 12N 103 18 E
Kemano, Canada 70 C3 53 35N 128 0W
Kemasik, Malaysia ..... 39 K4 4 25N 103 27 E
Kemerovo, Russia ..... 28 D9 55 20N 86 5 E
Kemi, Finland .... 8 D21 65 44N 24 34 E
Kemi älv = Kemijoki ➤, Finland 8 D21 65 47N 24 32 E
Kemijärvi, Finland .... 8 C22 66 43N 27 22 E
Kemijoki ➤, Finland ... 8 D21 65 47N 24 32 E
Kemmerer, U.S.A. 76 F8 41 48N 110 32W
Kemmuna = Comino, Malta . 25 C1 36 1N 14 20 E
Kemp, L., U.S.A. 81 J5 33 46N 99 9W
Kemp Land, Antarctica .. 5 C5 69 0S 55 0 E
Kempas, Malaysia ...... 39 d 1 33N 103 42 E
Kempsey, Australia .... 63 E5 31 1S 152 50 E
Kempt, L., Canada 72 C5 47 25N 74 22W
Kempten, Germany ..... 16 E6 47 45N 10 17 E
Kempton, Australia .... 63 G4 42 31S 147 12 E
Kemptville, Canada 85 B9 45 0N 75 38W
Ken ➤, India .... 43 G9 25 13N 80 27 E
Kenai, U.S.A. 68 B4 60 33N 151 16W
Kendal, India .... 43 H10 22 45N 82 37 E
Kendal, Indonesia ..... 37 G14 6 56S 110 14 E
Kendal, U.K. 12 C5 54 20N 2 44W
Kendall, Australia .... 63 E5 31 35S 152 44 E
Kendall, U.S.A. 83 N5 25 41N 80 19W
Kendall ➤, Australia .. 62 A3 14 4S 141 35 E
Kendallville, U.S.A. ... 82 E3 41 27N 85 16W
Kendari, Indonesia .... 37 E6 3 50S 122 30 E
Kendawangan, Indonesia . 36 E4 2 32S 110 17 E
Kendi, Pulau, Malaysia .. 39 c 5 13N 100 11 E
Kendrapara, India ..... 41 J15 20 35N 86 30 E
Kendrew, S. Africa .... 56 E3 32 32S 24 30 E
Kene Thao, Laos .... 38 D3 17 44N 101 10 E
Kenedy, U.S.A. 81 L6 28 49N 97 51W
Kenema, S. Leone 50 G3 7 50N 11 14W
Keng Kok, Laos .... 38 D5 16 26N 105 12 E
Keng Tawng, Burma .... 41 J21 20 45N 98 18 E
Keng Tung, Burma ..... 41 J21 21 0N 99 30 E
Kengeja, Tanzania ..... 54 D4 5 26S 39 45 E
Kenhardt, S. Africa .... 56 D3 29 19S 21 12 E
Kenitra, Morocco 50 B4 34 15N 6 40W
Kenli, China .... 35 F10 37 30N 118 20 E
Kenmare, Ireland 10 E2 51 53N 9 36W
Kenmare, U.S.A. 80 A3 48 41N 102 5W

Kenmare River, Ireland 10 E2 51 48N 9 51W
Kennebago Lake, U.S.A. .. 85 A14 45 4N 70 40W
Kennebec, U.S.A. 80 D5 43 54N 99 52W
Kennebec ➤, U.S.A. 83 D11 43 45N 69 46W
Kennebunk, U.S.A. 85 C14 43 23N 70 33W
Kennedy, Zimbabwe .... 56 B4 18 52S 27 10 E
Kennedy Ra., Australia .. 61 D2 24 45S 115 10 E
Kennedy Range △, Australia 61 D2 24 34S 115 2 E
Kenner, U.S.A. 81 L9 29 59N 90 15W
Kennet ➤, U.K. 13 F7 51 27N 0 57W
Kenneth Ra., Australia .. 61 D2 23 50S 117 8 E
Kennett, U.S.A. 81 G9 36 14N 90 3W
Kennewick, U.S.A. 76 C4 46 12N 119 7W
Kenogami ➤, Canada ... 72 B3 51 6N 84 28W
Kenora, Canada 71 D10 49 47N 94 29W
Kenosha, U.S.A. 82 D2 42 35N 87 49W
Kensington, Canada 73 C7 46 28N 63 34W
Kent, Ohio, U.S.A. 84 E3 41 9N 81 22W
Kent, Tex., U.S.A. 81 K2 31 4N 104 13W
Kent, Wash., U.S.A. 78 C4 47 23N 122 14W
Kent □, U.K. .... 13 F8 51 12N 0 40 E
Kent Group, Australia .. 63 F4 39 30S 147 20 E
Kent Pen., Canada 68 B9 68 30N 107 0W
Kentaū, Kazakhstan .... 28 E7 43 32N 68 36 E
Kentland, U.S.A. 82 E2 40 46N 87 27W
Kenton, U.S.A. 82 E4 40 39N 83 37W
Kentucky □, U.S.A. 82 G3 37 0N 84 0W
Kentucky ➤, U.S.A. 82 F3 38 41N 85 11W
Kentucky L., U.S.A. 83 G2 37 1N 88 16W
Kentville, Canada 73 C7 45 6N 64 29W
Kentwood, U.S.A. 81 K9 30 56N 90 31W
Kenya ■, Africa .... 54 B4 1 0N 38 0 E
Kenya, Mt., Kenya ..... 54 C4 0 10S 37 18 E
Keo Neua, Deo, Vietnam .. 38 C5 18 23N 105 10 E
Keokuk, U.S.A. 80 E9 40 24N 91 24W
Keonjhargarh, India .... 43 J11 21 28N 85 35 E
Kep, Cambodia .... 39 G5 10 29N 104 19 E
Kep, Vietnam .... 38 B6 21 24N 106 16 E
Kepala Batas, Malaysia .. 39 c 5 31N 100 26 E
Kepi, Indonesia .... 37 F9 6 32S 139 19 E
Kerala □, India .... 40 P10 11 0N 76 15 E
Kerama-Rettō, Japan ... 31 L3 26 5N 127 15 E
Keran, Pakistan .... 43 B5 34 35N 73 59 E
Kerang, Australia ..... 63 F3 35 40S 143 55 E
Keraudren, C., Australia . 60 C2 19 58S 119 45 E
Kerava, Finland .... 9 F21 60 25N 25 5 E
Kerch, Ukraine .... 19 E6 45 20N 36 20 E
Kerguelen, Ind. Oc. .... 3 G13 49 15S 69 10 E
Kericho, Kenya .... 54 C4 0 22S 35 15 E
Kerinci, Indonesia ..... 36 E2 1 40S 101 15 E
Kerki, Turkmenistan .... 28 F7 37 50N 65 12 E
Kérkira, Greece .... 25 A3 39 38N 19 50 E
Kerkrade, Neths. ...... 15 D6 50 53N 6 4 E
Kermadec Is., Pac. Oc. .. 64 L10 30 0S 178 15W
Kermadec Trench, Pac. Oc. 64 L10 30 30S 176 0W
Kermān, Iran .... 45 D8 30 15N 57 1 E
Kerman, U.S.A. 78 J6 36 43N 120 4W
Kermān □, Iran .... 45 D8 30 0N 57 0 E
Kermān, Bīābān-e, Iran .. 45 D8 28 45N 59 45 E
Kermānshāh = Bākhtarān, Iran 44 C5 34 23N 47 0 E
Kermit, U.S.A. 81 K3 31 52N 103 6W
Kern ➤, U.S.A. 79 K7 35 16N 119 18W
Kernow = Cornwall □, U.K. . 13 G3 50 26N 4 40W
Kernville, U.S.A. 79 K8 35 45N 118 25W
Keroh, Malaysia .... 39 K3 5 43N 101 1 E
Kerrera, U.K. 11 E3 56 24N 5 33W
Kerrobert, Canada 71 C7 51 56N 109 8W
Kerrville, U.S.A. 81 K5 30 3N 99 8W
Kerry □, Ireland 10 D2 52 7N 9 35W
Kerry Hd., Ireland 10 D2 52 25N 9 56W
Kerulen ➤, Asia .... 33 B6 48 48N 117 0 E
Kerzaz, Algeria 50 C5 29 29N 1 37W
Kesagami ➤, Canada ... 72 B4 51 40N 79 45W
Kesagami L., Canada ... 72 B3 50 23N 80 15W
Keşan, Turkey .... 23 D12 40 49N 26 38 E
Kesennuma, Japan ..... 30 E10 38 54N 141 35 E
Keshit, Iran .... 45 D8 29 43N 58 17 E
Kestell, S. Africa ..... 57 D4 28 17S 28 42 E
Kestenga, Russia ...... 18 A5 65 50N 31 45 E
Keswick, U.K. 12 C4 54 36N 3 8W
Ket ➤, Russia .... 28 D9 58 55N 81 32 E
Ketapang, Bali, Indonesia . 37 J17 8 9S 114 23 E
Ketapang, Kalimantan, Indonesia 36 E4 1 55S 110 0 E
Ketchikan, U.S.A. 70 B2 55 21N 131 39W
Ketchum, U.S.A. 76 E6 43 41N 114 22W
Ketef, Khalîg Umm el, Egypt 44 F2 23 40N 35 35 E
Keti Bandar, Pakistan .. 42 G2 24 8N 67 27 E
Ketri, India .... 42 E6 28 1N 75 50 E
Kętrzyn, Poland .... 17 A11 54 7N 21 22 E
Kettering, U.K. 13 E7 52 24N 0 43W
Kettering, U.S.A. 82 F3 39 41N 84 10W
Kettle ➤, Canada 71 B11 56 40N 89 34W
Kettle Falls, U.S.A. ... 76 B4 48 37N 118 3W
Kettle Pt., Canada 84 C2 43 13N 82 1W
Kettleman City, U.S.A. .. 78 J7 36 1N 119 58W
Keuka L., U.S.A. 84 D7 42 30N 77 9W
Keuruu, Finland ...... 9 E21 62 16N 24 41 E
Kewanee, U.S.A. 80 E10 41 14N 89 56W
Kewaunee, U.S.A. 82 C2 44 27N 87 31W
Keweenaw B., U.S.A. ... 82 B1 47 0N 88 15W
Keweenaw Pen., U.S.A. .. 82 B2 47 30N 88 0W
Keweenaw Pt., U.S.A. .. 82 B2 47 25N 87 43W
Key Largo, U.S.A. 83 N5 25 5N 80 27W
Key West, U.S.A. 75 F10 24 33N 81 48W
Keynsham, U.K. 13 F5 51 24N 2 29W
Keyser, U.S.A. 82 F6 39 26N 78 59W
Kezhma, Russia .... 29 D11 58 59N 101 9 E
Kezi, Zimbabwe .... 57 C4 20 58S 28 32 E
Kgalagadi Transfrontier △, Africa 56 D3 25 10S 21 0 E
Khabarovsk, Russia .... 29 E14 48 30N 135 5 E
Khabr, Iran .... 45 D8 28 51N 56 22 E
Khābūr ➤, Syria ...... 44 C4 35 17N 40 35 E
Khachmas = Xaçmaz, Azerbaijan 19 F8 41 31N 48 42 E
Khachrod, India ...... 42 H6 23 25N 75 20 E
Khadro, Pakistan ..... 42 F3 26 11N 68 50 E
Khadzhilyangar, China . 43 B8 35 45N 79 20 E
Khaga, India .... 43 G9 25 47N 81 7 E
Khagaria, India ...... 43 G12 25 30N 86 32 E
Khaipur, Pakistan .... 42 E5 29 34N 72 17 E
Khair, India .... 42 F7 27 57N 77 46 E
Khairabad, India ..... 43 F9 27 33N 80 47 E
Khairagarh, India .... 43 J9 21 27N 81 2 E
Khairpur, Pakistan ... 42 F3 27 32N 68 49 E
Khairpur Nathan Shah, Pakistan 42 F2 27 6N 67 44 E
Khairwara, India ..... 42 H5 23 58N 73 38 E
Khaisor ➤, Pakistan .. 42 D3 31 17N 68 59 E
Khajuri Kach, Pakistan . 42 C3 32 4N 69 51 E

Khakassia □, Russia ..... 28 D9 53 0N 90 0 E
Khakhea, Botswana ..... 56 C3 24 48S 23 22 E
Khalafābād, Iran .... 45 D6 30 54N 49 24 E
Khalilabad, India ...... 43 F10 26 48N 83 5 E
Khalīlī, Iran .... 45 E7 27 38N 53 17 E
Khalkhāl, Iran .... 45 B6 37 37N 48 32 E
Khalkís, Greece .... 23 E10 38 27N 23 42 E
Khalmer Yu, Russia .... 28 C7 67 58N 65 1 E
Khalturin, Russia ..... 18 C8 58 40N 48 50 E
Khalūf, Oman .... 47 C6 20 30N 58 13 E
Kham Keut, Laos ...... 38 C5 18 15N 104 43 E
Khamaria, India .... 43 H9 23 5N 80 48 E
Khambhaliya, India .... 42 H3 22 14N 69 41 E
Khambhat, India ...... 42 H5 22 23N 72 33 E
Khambhat, G. of, India .. 40 J8 20 45N 72 30 E
Khamir, Iran .... 45 E7 26 57N 55 36 E
Khamir, Yemen .... 47 D3 16 2N 44 0 E
Khamsa, Egypt .... 46 E1 30 27N 32 23 E
Khan ➤, Namibia ...... 56 C2 22 37S 14 56 E
Khān Abū Shāmat, Syria . 46 B5 33 39N 36 53 E
Khān Azād, Iraq .... 44 C5 33 7N 44 22 E
Khān Mujiddah, Iraq ... 44 C4 32 21N 43 48 E
Khān Shaykhūn, Syria .. 44 C3 35 26N 36 38 E
Khān Yūnis, Gaza Strip . 46 D3 31 21N 34 18 E
Khanai, Pakistan ...... 42 D2 30 30N 67 8 E
Khānaqin, Iraq .... 44 C5 34 23N 45 25 E
Khānbāghī, Iran .... 45 B7 36 10N 55 25 E
Khandwa, India .... 40 J10 21 49N 76 22 E
Khandyga, Russia ..... 29 C14 62 42N 135 35 E
Khāneh, Iran .... 44 B5 36 41N 45 8 E
Khanewal, Pakistan ... 42 D4 30 20N 71 55 E
Khangah Dogran, Pakistan 42 D5 31 50N 73 37 E
Khanh Duong, Vietnam . 38 F7 12 44N 108 44 E
Khaniá, Greece .... 25 D6 35 30N 24 4 E
Khaniá □, Greece ..... 25 D6 35 30N 24 0 E
Khaniadhana, India ... 42 G8 25 1N 78 8 E
Khanion, Kólpos, Greece . 25 D5 35 33N 23 55 E
Khanka, L., Asia ...... 29 E14 45 0N 132 24 E
Khankendy = Xankändi,
   Azerbaijan .... 19 G8 39 52N 46 49 E
Khanna, India .... 42 D7 30 42N 76 16 E
Khanozai, Pakistan ... 42 D2 30 37N 67 19 E
Khanpur, Pakistan .... 42 E4 28 42N 70 35 E
Khao Laem △, Thailand . 38 E2 14 58N 98 31 E
Khao Luang △, Thailand . 39 H2 8 34N 99 42 E
Khao Phlu, Thailand ... 39 b 9 29N 99 59 E
Khao Pu-Khao Ya △, Thailand 39 J2 7 26N 99 57 E
Khao Sam Roi Yot △, Thailand 38 F2 12 13N 99 57 E
Khao Sok △, Thailand .. 39 H2 8 55N 98 38 E
Khao Yai △, Thailand .. 38 E3 14 21N 101 29 E
Khaoen Si Nakarin △, Thailand 38 E2 14 47N 99 0 E
Khapalu, Pakistan ..... 43 B7 35 10N 76 20 E
Khapcheranga, Russia .. 29 E12 49 42N 112 24 E
Kharaghoda, India .... 42 H4 23 11N 71 46 E
Kharagpur, India ..... 43 H12 22 20N 87 25 E
Kharan Kalat, Pakistan . 40 E4 28 34N 65 21 E
Kharānaq, Iran .... 45 C7 32 20N 54 45 E
Kharda, India .... 40 K9 18 40N 75 34 E
Khardung La, India ... 43 B7 34 20N 77 43 E
Kharg = Khārk, Jazireh-ye, Iran 45 D6 29 15N 50 28 E
Khârga, El Wâhât-el, Egypt 51 C12 25 10N 30 35 E
Khargon, India .... 40 J9 21 45N 75 40 E
Khari ➤, India .... 42 G6 25 54N 74 31 E
Kharian, Pakistan ..... 42 C5 32 49N 73 52 E
Khārk, Jazireh-ye, Iran . 45 D6 29 15N 50 28 E
Kharkiv, Ukraine ...... 19 E6 49 58N 36 20 E
Kharkov = Kharkiv, Ukraine 19 E6 49 58N 36 20 E
Kharovsk, Russia ...... 18 C7 59 56N 40 13 E
Kharsawangarh, India .. 43 H11 22 48N 85 50 E
Kharta, Turkey .... 23 D13 40 55N 29 7 E
Khartoum = El Khartûm, Sudan 51 E12 15 31N 32 35 E
Khasan, Russia .... 30 C5 42 25N 130 40 E
Khāsh, Iran .... 40 E2 28 15N 61 15 E
Khashm el Girba, Sudan . 51 F13 14 59N 35 58 E
Khaskovo, Bulgaria .... 23 D11 41 56N 25 30 E
Khatanga, Russia ...... 29 B11 72 0N 102 20 E
Khatanga ➤, Russia ... 29 B11 72 55N 106 0 E
Khatauli, India .... 42 E7 29 17N 77 43 E
Khatra, India .... 43 H12 22 59N 86 51 E
Khātūnābād, Iran ..... 45 D7 30 1N 55 25 E
Khatyrka, Russia ...... 29 C18 62 3N 175 15 E
Khavda, India .... 42 H3 23 51N 69 43 E
Khaybar, Harrat, Si. Arabia 44 E4 25 45N 40 0 E
Khayelitsha, S. Africa .. 53 L3 34 5S 18 42 E
Khāzimiyah, Iraq ..... 44 C4 34 46N 43 37 E
Khe Bo, Vietnam ...... 38 C5 19 8N 104 41 E
Khe Long, Vietnam .... 38 B5 21 29N 104 46 E
Khe Sanh, Vietnam .... 38 D6 16 37N 106 45 E
Khed Brahma, India ... 40 G8 24 7N 73 5 E
Khekra, India .... 42 E7 28 52N 77 20 E
Khemarak Phouminville,
   Cambodia .... 39 G4 11 37N 102 59 E
Khemisset, Morocco ... 50 B4 33 50N 6 1W
Khemmarat, Thailand .. 38 D5 16 10N 105 15 E
Khenāmān, Iran .... 45 D8 30 27N 56 29 E
Khenchela, Algeria .... 50 A7 35 28N 7 11 E
Khersān ➤, Iran ...... 45 D6 31 33N 50 22 E
Kherson, Ukraine ..... 19 E5 46 35N 32 35 E
Khersónisos Akrotíri, Greece 25 D6 35 30N 24 10 E
Kheta ➤, Russia ...... 29 B11 71 54N 102 6 E
Khewari, Pakistan ..... 42 F3 26 36N 68 52 E
Khilchipur, India ..... 42 G7 24 2N 76 34 E
Khilok, Russia .... 29 D12 51 30N 110 45 E
Khíos, Greece .... 23 E12 38 27N 26 9 E
Khirsadoh, India ...... 43 H8 22 11N 78 47 E
Khiuma = Hiiumaa, Estonia 9 G20 58 50N 22 45 E
Khiva, Uzbekistan ..... 28 E7 41 30N 60 18 E
Khīyāv, Iran .... 44 B5 38 30N 47 45 E
Khlong Khlung, Thailand 38 D2 16 12N 99 43 E
Khmelnik, Ukraine ..... 17 D14 49 33N 27 58 E
Khmelnitskiy = Khmelnytskyy,
   Ukraine .... 17 D14 49 23N 27 0 E
Khmelnytskyy, Ukraine .. 17 D14 49 23N 27 0 E
Khmer Rep. = Cambodia ■, Asia 38 F5 12 15N 105 0 E
Khoai, Hon, Vietnam ... 39 H5 8 26N 104 50 E
Khodoriv, Ukraine ..... 17 D13 49 24N 24 19 E
Khodzent = Khüjand, Tajikistan 28 E7 40 17N 69 37 E
Khojak Pass, Afghan. ... 39 a 8 17N 98 19 E
Khok Kloi, Thailand ... 39 a 8 17N 98 19 E
Khok Pho, Thailand .... 39 J3 6 43N 101 6 E
Kholm, Russia .... 18 C5 57 10N 31 15 E
Kholmsk, Russia .... 29 E15 47 40N 142 5 E
Kholmas Hochland, Namibia 56 C2 22 40S 16 0 E
Khomeyn, Iran .... 45 C6 33 40N 50 7 E
Khomeynī Shahr, Iran .. 45 C6 32 41N 51 31 E

Khomodino, Botswana ...... 56 C3 22 46S 23 52 E
Khon Kaen, Thailand ..... 38 D4 16 30N 102 47 E
Khong, Cambodia .... 38 F5 13 32N 105 58 E
Khong Sedone, Laos ..... 38 E5 15 34N 105 49 E
Khonuu, Russia .... 29 C15 66 30N 143 12 E
Khoper ➤, Russia .... 19 D6 49 30N 42 20 E
Khóra Sfakíon, Greece ... 25 D6 35 15N 24 9 E
Khorāsān □, Iran .... 45 C8 34 0N 58 0 E
Khorat = Nakhon Ratchasima,
   Thailand .... 38 E4 14 59N 102 12 E
Khorixas, Namibia ...... 56 C1 20 16S 14 59 E
Khorramābād, Khorāsān, Iran 45 C8 35 6N 57 57 E
Khorramābād, Lorestān, Iran 45 C6 33 30N 48 25 E
Khorrāmshahr, Iran ..... 45 D6 30 29N 48 15 E
Khorugh, Tajikistan .... 28 F8 37 30N 71 36 E
Khosravi, Iran .... 45 D6 30 48N 51 28 E
Khosrowābād, Khuzestān, Iran 45 D6 30 10N 48 25 E
Khosrowābād, Kordestān, Iran 44 C5 35 31N 47 38 E
Khost, Pakistan .... 42 D2 30 13N 67 35 E
Khosūyeh, Iran .... 45 D7 28 32N 54 26 E
Khotyn, Ukraine .... 17 D14 48 31N 26 27 E
Khouribga, Morocco 50 B4 32 58N 6 57W
Khowst, Afghan. .... 42 C3 33 22N 69 58 E
Khowst □, Afghan. ...... 40 C6 33 20N 70 0 E
Khoyniki, Belarus ...... 17 C15 51 54N 29 55 E
Khrysokhou B., Cyprus .. 25 D11 35 6N 32 25 E
Khu Khan, Thailand .... 38 E5 14 42N 104 12 E
Khuan Wa, Thailand .... 39 a 7 53N 98 17 E
Khudzhand = Khüjand, Tajikistan 28 E7 40 17N 69 37 E
Khuff, Si. Arabia ...... 44 E5 24 55N 44 53 E
Khūgiāni, Afghan. ...... 42 D2 31 34N 66 32 E
Khuis, Botswana .... 56 D3 26 40S 21 49 E
Khuiyala, India .... 42 F4 27 9N 70 25 E
Khūjand, Tajikistan .... 28 E7 40 17N 69 37 E
Khujner, India .... 42 H7 23 47N 76 36 E
Khulna, Bangla. .... 41 H16 22 45N 89 34 E
Khulna □, Bangla. ..... 41 H16 22 25N 89 35 E
Khumago, Botswana .... 56 C3 20 26S 24 32 E
Khūnsorkh, Iran .... 45 E8 27 9N 56 7 E
Khunti, India .... 43 H11 23 5N 85 17 E
Khūr, Iran .... 45 C8 32 55N 58 18 E
Khurai, India .... 42 G8 24 3N 78 23 E
Khurays, Si. Arabia .... 45 E6 25 6N 48 2 E
Khurīyā Murīyā, Jazā'ir, Oman . 47 D6 17 30N 55 58 E
Khurja, India .... 42 E7 28 15N 77 58 E
Khūrmāl, Iraq .... 44 C5 35 18N 46 2 E
Khurr, Wādī al, Iraq ... 44 C4 32 3N 43 52 E
Khūsf, Iran .... 45 C8 32 46N 58 53 E
Khush, Afghan. .... 40 C3 32 20N 62 10 E
Khushab, Pakistan ..... 42 C5 32 20N 72 20 E
Khust, Ukraine .... 17 D12 48 10N 23 18 E
Khutse △, Botswana ... 56 C3 23 31S 24 12 E
Khuzdar, Pakistan ..... 42 F2 27 52N 66 30 E
Khūzestān □, Iran ..... 45 D6 31 0N 49 0 E
Khvāf, Iran .... 45 C9 34 33N 60 8 E
Khvājeh, Iran .... 44 B5 38 9N 46 35 E
Khvānsār, Iran .... 45 D7 29 56N 54 8 E
Khvor, Iran .... 45 C7 33 45N 55 0 E
Khvorgū, Iran .... 45 E8 27 34N 56 27 E
Khvormūj, Iran .... 45 D6 28 40N 51 30 E
Khvoy, Iran .... 44 B5 38 35N 45 0 E
Khyber Pass, Afghan. ... 42 B4 34 10N 71 8 E
Kiabukwa, Dem. Rep. of
   the Congo .... 55 D1 8 40S 24 48 E
Kiama, Australia ...... 63 E5 34 40S 150 50 E
Kiamba, Phil. .... 37 C6 6 2N 124 46 E
Kiambi, Dem. Rep. of the Congo 54 D2 7 15S 28 0 E
Kiambu, Kenya .... 54 C4 1 8S 36 50 E
Kiangara, Madag. ...... 57 B8 17 58S 47 2 E
Kiangsi = Jiangxi □, China 33 D6 27 30N 116 0 E
Kiangsu = Jiangsu □, China 35 H11 33 0N 120 0 E
Kibale △, Uganda ...... 54 B3 0 16N 30 18 E
Kibanga Port, Uganda .. 54 B3 0 10N 32 58 E
Kibara, Tanzania ...... 54 C3 2 8S 33 30 E
Kibare, Mts., Dem. Rep. of
   the Congo .... 54 D2 8 25S 27 10 E
Kibira △, Burundi ..... 54 C2 3 6S 30 24 E
Kibombo, Dem. Rep. of
   the Congo .... 54 C2 3 57S 25 53 E
Kibondo, Tanzania ..... 54 C3 3 35S 30 45 E
Kibre Mengist, Ethiopia . 47 F2 5 54N 38 59 E
Kibumbu, Burundi ..... 54 C2 3 32S 29 45 E
Kibungo, Rwanda ...... 54 C3 2 10S 30 32 E
Kibuye, Burundi .... 54 C2 3 39S 29 59 E
Kibuye, Rwanda .... 54 C2 2 3S 29 21 E
Kibwesa, Tanzania ..... 54 D2 6 30S 29 58 E
Kibwezi, Kenya .... 54 C4 2 27S 37 57 E
Kichha, India .... 43 E8 28 53N 79 30 E
Kichha ➤, India ...... 43 E8 28 41N 79 18 E
Kichmengskiy Gorodok, Russia 18 B8 59 59N 45 48 E
Kicking Horse Pass, Canada . 70 C5 51 28N 116 16W
Kidal, Mali .... 50 E6 18 26N 1 22 E
Kidderminster, U.K. ... 13 E5 52 24N 2 15W
Kidepo Valley △, Uganda 54 B3 3 52N 33 50 E
Kidete, Tanzania ...... 54 D4 6 25S 36 59 E
Kidnappers, C., N.Z. ... 59 H6 39 38S 177 5 E
Kidsgrove, U.K. 12 D5 53 5N 2 14W
Kidston, Australia .... 62 B3 18 52S 144 8 E
Kidugallo, Tanzania ... 54 D4 6 49S 38 15 E
Kiel, Germany .... 16 A6 54 19N 10 8 E
Kiel Canal = Nord-Ostsee-Kanal,
   Germany .... 16 A5 54 12N 9 32 E
Kielce, Poland .... 17 C11 50 52N 20 42 E
Kielder Water, U.K. 12 B5 55 11N 2 31W
Kieler Bucht, Germany . 16 A6 54 35N 10 25 E
Kien Binh, Vietnam .... 39 H5 9 55N 105 19 E
Kien Tan, Vietnam ..... 39 G5 10 7N 105 17 E
Kienge, Dem. Rep. of the Congo 55 E2 10 30S 27 30 E
Kiev = Kyyiv, Ukraine .. 17 C16 50 30N 30 28 E
Kiffa, Mauritania 50 E3 16 37N 11 24W
Kifrī, Iraq .... 44 C5 34 45N 45 0 E
Kigali, Rwanda .... 54 C3 1 59S 30 4 E
Kigarama, Tanzania ... 54 C3 1 1S 31 50 E
Kigezi □, Uganda ..... 54 C2 0 34S 29 55 E
Kigoma □, Tanzania ... 54 D2 4 55S 29 36 E
Kigoma-Ujiji, Tanzania . 54 C2 4 55S 29 36 E
Kigomasha, Ras, Tanzania 54 C4 4 58S 38 58 E
Kığzı, Turkey .... 44 B4 38 18N 43 25 E
Kihnu, Estonia 74 H16 37 47N 156 28W
Kii-Sanchi, Japan ..... 9 G21 58 9N 24 1 E
Kii-Suidō, Japan ...... 31 G8 34 20N 136 0 E
Kikaiga-Shima, Japan .. 31 H7 33 40N 134 45 E
Kikinda, Serbia & M. .. 31 K4 28 19N 129 59 E
Kikládhes, Greece ..... 23 B9 45 50N 20 30 E
Kikwit, Dem. Rep. of the Congo 23 F11 37 0N 24 30 E
.... 52 E3 5 0S 18 45 E

Kilar, India .... 42 C7   33 6N 76 25 E
Kilauea Crater, U.S.A. 74 J17 19 25N 155 17W
Kilchu, N. Korea .... 35 D15 40 57N 129 25 E
Kilcoy, Australia .... 63 D5   26 59S 152 30 E
Kildare, Ireland 10 C5   53 9N   6 55W
Kildare □, Ireland 10 C5   53 10N   6 50W
Kilfinnane, Ireland 10 D3   52 21N   8 28W
Kilgore, U.S.A. 81 J7   32 23N 94 53W
Kilifi, Kenya .... 54 C4   3 40S 39 48 E
Kilimanjaro, Tanzania .... 54 C4   3 7S 37 20 E
Kilimanjaro □, Tanzania ...... 54 C4   4 0S 38 0 E
Kilindini, Kenya .... 54 C4   4 4S 39 40 E
Kilis, Turkey .... 44 B3   36 42N 37 6 E
Kiliya, Ukraine .... 17 F15 45 28N 29 16 E
Kilkee, Ireland 10 D2   52 41N   9 39W
Kilkeel, U.K. 10 B5   54 4N   6 0W
Kilkenny, Ireland 10 D4   52 39N   7 15W
Kilkenny □, Ireland 10 D4   52 35N   7 15W
Kilkieran B., Ireland 10 C2   53 20N   9 41W
Kilkis, Greece .... 23 D10 40 58N 22 57 E
Killala, Ireland 10 B2   54 13N   9 12W
Killala B., Ireland 10 B2   54 16N   9 8W
Killaloe, Canada 84 A7   45 33N 77 25W
Killaloe, Ireland 10 D3   52 48N   8 28W
Killarney, Australia .... 63 D5   28 20S 152 18 E
Killarney, Canada 71 D9   49 10N 99 40W
Killarney, Ireland 10 D2   52 4N   9 30W
Killarney □, Ireland 10 D2   52 0N   9 33W
Killary Harbour, Ireland 10 C2   53 38N   9 52W
Killdeer, U.S.A. 80 B3   47 26N 102 48W
Killeen, U.S.A. 81 K6   31 7N 97 44W
Killin, U.K. 11 E4   56 28N   4 19W
Killini, Greece .... 23 F10 37 54N 22 25 E
Killorglin, Ireland 10 D2   52 6N   9 47W
Killybegs, Ireland 10 B3   54 38N   8 26W
Kilmarnock, U.K. 11 F4   55 37N   4 29W
Kilmore, Australia .... 63 F3   37 25S 144 53 E
Kilondo, Tanzania .... 55 D3   9 45S 34 20 E
Kilosa, Tanzania .... 54 D4   6 48S 37 0 E
Kilrush, Ireland 10 D2   52 38N   9 29W
Kilwa Kisiwani, Tanzania ..... 55 D4   8 58S 39 32 E
Kilwa Kivinje, Tanzania ...... 55 D4   8 45S 39 25 E
Kilwa Masoko, Tanzania .... 55 D4   8 55S 39 30 E
Kilwinning, U.K. 11 F4   55 39N   4 43W
Kim, U.S.A. 81 G3   37 15N 103 21W
Kimaam, Indonesia .... 37 F9   7 58S 138 53 E
Kimamba, Tanzania .... 54 D4   6 45S 37 10 E
Kimba, Australia .... 63 E2   3 8S 136 23 E
Kimball, Nebr., U.S.A. 80 E3   41 14N 103 40W
Kimball, S. Dak., U.S.A. 80 D5   43 45N 98 57W
Kimberley, Australia .... 60 C4   16 20S 127 0 E
Kimberley, Canada 70 D5   49 40N 115 59W
Kimberley, S. Africa .... 56 D3   28 43S 24 46 E
Kimberly, U.S.A. 76 E6   42 32N 114 22W
Kimch'aek, N. Korea .... 35 D15 40 40N 129 10 E
Kimch'ŏn, S. Korea .... 35 F15 36 11N 128 4 E
Kimje, S. Korea .... 35 G14 35 48N 126 45 E
Kimmirut, Canada 69 B13 62 50N 69 50W
Kimpese, Dem. Rep. of
  the Congo .... 52 F2   5 35S 14 26 E
Kimry, Russia .... 18 C6   56 55N 37 15 E
Kinabalu, Gunong, Malaysia ... 36 C5   6 3N 116 14 E
Kinaskan L., Canada .... 70 B2   57 38N 130 8 E
Kinbasket L., Canada 70 C5   52 0N 118 10W
Kincardine, Canada 84 B3   44 10N 81 40W
Kincolith, Canada 70 C3   55 0N 129 57W
Kinda, Dem. Rep. of the Congo 55 D2   9 18S 25 4 E
Kinde, U.S.A. 84 C2   43 56N 83 0W
Kinder Scout, U.K. 12 D6   53 24N   1 52W
Kindersley, Canada 71 C7   51 30N 109 10W
Kindia, Guinea 50 F3   10 0N 12 52W
Kindu, Dem. Rep. of the Congo 54 C2   2 55S 25 50 E
Kineshma, Russia .... 18 C7   57 30N 42 5 E
Kinesi, Tanzania .... 54 C3   1 25S 33 50 E
King, L., Australia .... 61 F2   33 10S 119 35 E
King, Mt., Australia .... 62 D4   25 10S 147 30 E
King City, U.S.A. 78 J5   36 13N 121 8W
King Cr. ➤, Australia .... 62 C2   24 35S 139 30 E
King Edward ➤, Australia ..... 60 B4   14 14S 126 35 E
King Frederick VI Land = Kong
  Frederik VI Kyst, Greenland 69 B15 63 0N 43 0W
King George B., Falk. Is. 96 G4   51 30S 60 30W
King George I., Antarctica ... 5 C18   60 0S 60 0W
King George Is., Canada 69 C11 57 20N 80 30W
King I. = Kadan Kyun, Burma .. 38 F2   12 30N 98 20 E
King I., Australia .... 63 F3   39 50S 144 0 E
King I., Canada 70 C3   52 10N 127 40W
King Leopold Ranges, Australia 60 C4   17 30S 125 45 E
King of Prussia, U.S.A. 85 F9   40 5N 75 23W
King Sd., Australia .... 60 C3   16 50S 123 20 E
King Sejong, Antarctica 5 C18   62 30S 58 0W
King William I., Canada 68 B10 69 10N 97 25W
King William's Town, S. Africa 56 E4   32 51S 27 22 E
Kingait = Cape Dorset, Canada 69 B12 64 14N 76 32W
Kingaok = Bathurst Inlet, Canada 68 B9 66 50N 108 1W
Kingaroy, Australia .... 63 D5   26 32S 151 51 E
Kingfisher, U.S.A. 81 H6   35 52N 97 56W
Kingirbān, Iraq .... 44 C5   34 40N 44 54 E
Kingisepp = Kuressaare, Estonia 9 G20 58 15N 22 30 E
Kingman, Ariz., U.S.A. 79 K12 35 12N 114 4W
Kingman, Kans., U.S.A. 81 G5   37 39N 98 7W
Kingoonya, Australia .... 63 E2   30 55S 135 19 E
Kingri, Pakistan .... 42 D3   30 27N 69 49 E
Kings ➤, U.S.A. 78 J7   36 3N 119 50W
Kings Canyon △, U.S.A. 78 J8   36 50N 118 40W
King's Lynn, U.K. .... 12 E8   52 45N   0 24 E
Kings Mountain, U.S.A. 83 H5   35 15N 81 20W
Kings Park, U.S.A. 85 F11 40 53N 73 16W
King's Peak, U.S.A. 76 F8   40 46N 110 27W
Kingsbridge, U.K. 13 G4   50 17N   3 47W
Kingsburg, U.S.A. 78 J7   36 31N 119 33W
Kingscote, Australia .... 63 F2   35 40S 137 38 E
Kingscourt, Ireland 10 C5   53 54N   6 48W
Kingsford, U.S.A. 82 C1   45 48N 88 4W
Kingsland, U.S.A. 83 K5   30 48N 81 41W
Kingsport, U.S.A. 80 D7   42 35N 95 58W
Kingston, Canada 85 B8   44 14N 76 30W
Kingston, Jamaica .... 88 a   18 0N 76 50W
Kingston, N.Z. .... 59 L2   45 20S 168 43 E
Kingston, N.H., U.S.A. 85 D13 42 56N 71 3W
Kingston, N.Y., U.S.A. 85 E11 41 56N 73 59W
Kingston, Pa., U.S.A. 85 E9   41 16N 75 54W
Kingston, R.I., U.S.A. 85 E13 41 29N 71 30W
Kingston Pk., U.S.A. 79 K11 35 45N 115 54W
Kingston South East, Australia 63 F2   36 51S 139 55 E

Kingston upon Hull, U.K. 12 D7   53 45N   0 21W
Kingston upon Hull □, U.K. ... 12 D7   53 45N   0 21W
Kingston-upon-Thames □, U.K. . 13 F7   51 24N   0 17W
Kingstown, St. Vincent 89 D7   13 10N 61 10W
Kingstree, U.S.A. 83 J6   33 40N 79 50W
Kingsville, Canada 84 D2   42 2N 82 45W
Kingsville, U.S.A. 81 M6   27 31N 97 52W
Kingussie, U.K. 11 D4   57 6N   4 2W
Kingwood, U.S.A. 81 K7   29 54N 95 18W
Kınık, Turkey .... 23 E12 39 6N 27 24 E
Kinistino, Canada 71 C7   52 57N 105 2W
Kinkala, Congo .... 52 E2   4 18S 14 49 E
Kinki □, Japan .... 31 H8   33 45N 136 0 E
Kinleith, N.Z. .... 59 H5   38 20S 175 56 E
Kinmount, Canada 84 B6   44 48N 78 45W
Kinna, Sweden .... 9 H15   57 32N 12 42 E
Kino, Mexico 86 B2   28 45N 111 59W
Kinoje ➤, Canada 72 B3   52 8N 81 25W
Kinomoto, Japan .... 31 G8   35 30N 136 13 E
Kinoni, Uganda .... 54 C3   0 41S 30 28 E
Kinoosao, Canada 71 B8   57 5N 102 1W
Kinross, U.K. 11 E5   56 13N   3 25W
Kinsale, Ireland 10 E3   51 42N   8 31W
Kinsale, Old Hd. of, Ireland . 10 E3   51 37N   8 33W
Kinsha = Chang Jiang ➤, China 33 C7   31 48N 121 10 E
Kinshasa, Dem. Rep. of
  the Congo .... 52 E3   4 20S 15 15 E
Kinsley, U.S.A. 81 G5   37 55N 99 25W
Kinsman, U.S.A. 84 E4   41 26N 80 35W
Kinston, U.S.A. 83 H7   35 16N 77 35W
Kintamani, Indonesia .... 37 J18   8 14S 115 19 E
Kintore, U.S.A. 11 D6   57 14N   2 20W
Kintore Ra., Australia .... 60 D4   23 15S 128 47 E
Kintyre, U.K. 11 F3   55 30N   5 35W
Kintyre, Mull of, U.K. 11 F3   55 17N   5 47W
Kinushseo ➤, Canada 72 A3   55 15N 83 45W
Kinuso, Canada 70 B5   55 20N 115 25W
Kinyangiri, Tanzania .... 54 C3   4 25S 34 37 E
Kinzua, U.S.A. 84 E6   41 52N 78 58W
Kinzua Dam, U.S.A. 84 E6   41 53N 79 0W
Kiosk, Canada 72 C4   46 6N 78 53W
Kiowa, Kans., U.S.A. 81 G5   37 1N 98 29W
Kiowa, Okla., U.S.A. 81 H7   34 43N 95 54W
Kipahigan L., Canada 71 B8   55 20N 101 55W
Kipanga, Tanzania .... 54 D4   6 15S 35 20 E
Kiparissía, Greece .... 23 F9   37 15N 21 40 E
Kiparissiakós Kólpos, Greece . 23 F9   37 25N 21 25 E
Kipawa, L., Canada 72 C4   46 50N 79 0W
Kipembawe, Tanzania .... 54 D3   7 38S 33 27 E
Kipengere Ra., Tanzania ...... 55 D3   9 12S 34 15 E
Kipili, Tanzania .... 54 D3   7 28S 30 32 E
Kipini, Kenya .... 54 C5   2 30S 40 32 E
Kipling, Canada 71 C8   50 6N 102 38W
Kippure, Ireland 10 C5   53 11N   6 21W
Kipushi, Dem. Rep. of the Congo 55 E2 11 48S 27 12 E
Kiranomena, Madag. .... 57 B8   18 17S 46 2 E
Kirensk, Russia .... 29 D11 57 50N 107 55 E
Kirghizia = Kyrgyzstan ■, Asia 28 E8   42 0N 75 0 E
Kirghizstan = Kyrgyzstan ■, Asia 28 E8 42 0N 75 0 E
Kirgiziya Steppe, Eurasia .... 19 E10 50 0N 55 0 E
Kiribati ■, Pac. Oc. .... 64 H10   5 0S 180 0 E
Kırıkkale, Turkey .... 19 G5   39 51N 33 32 E
Kirillov, Russia .... 18 C6   59 49N 38 24 E
Kirin = Jilin, China .... 35 C14 43 44N 126 30 E
Kirinyaga = Kenya, Mt., Kenya 54 C4   0 10S 37 18 E
Kirishima Yaku △, Japan ...... 31 J5   31 24N 130 50 E
Kiritimati, Kiribati 65 G12   1 58N 157 27W
Kirkby, U.K. 12 D5   53 30N   2 54W
Kirkby-in-Ashfield, U.K. 12 D6   53 6N   1 14W
Kirkby Lonsdale, U.K. 12 C5   54 12N   2 36W
Kirkby Stephen, U.K. 12 C5   54 29N   2 21W
Kirkcaldy, U.K. 11 E5   56 7N   3 9W
Kirkcudbright, U.K. 11 G4   54 50N   4 2W
Kirkee, India .... 40 K8   18 34N 73 56 E
Kirkenes, Norway .... 8 B23   69 40N 30 5 E
Kirkfield, Canada 84 B6   44 34N 78 59W
Kirkintilloch, U.K. 11 F4   55 56N   4 8W
Kirkjubæjarklaustur, Iceland . 8 E4   63 47N 18 4W
Kirkkonummi, Finland .... 9 F21   60 8N 24 26 E
Kirkland Lake, Canada 72 C3   48 9N 80 2W
Kırklareli, Turkey .... 23 D12 41 44N 27 15 E
Kirksville, U.S.A. 80 E8   40 12N 92 35W
Kirkük, Iraq .... 44 C5   35 30N 44 21 E
Kirkwall, U.K. 11 C6   58 59N   2 58W
Kirkwood, S. Africa .... 56 E4   33 22S 25 15 E
Kirov, Russia .... 18 C8   58 35N 49 40 E
Kirovabad = Gäncä, Azerbaijan 19 F8   40 45N 46 20 E
Kirovograd = Kirovohrad,
  Ukraine .... 19 E5   48 35N 32 20 E
Kirovohrad, Ukraine .... 19 E5   48 35N 32 20 E
Kirovsk, Russia .... 18 A5   67 32N 33 41 E
Kirovskiy, Kamchatka, Russia . 29 D16 54 27N 155 42 E
Kirovskiy, Primorsk, Russia .. 30 B6   45 7N 133 30 E
Kirriemuir, U.K. 11 E5   56 41N   3 1W
Kirsanov, Russia .... 18 D7   52 35N 42 40 E
Kırşehir, Turkey .... 19 G5   39 14N 34 5 E
Kirthar Range, Pakistan ...... 42 F2   27 0N 67 0 E
Kirtland, U.S.A. 77 H9   36 44N 108 21W
Kiruna, Sweden .... 8 C19   67 52N 20 15 E
Kirundu, Dem. Rep. of the Congo 54 C2 0 50S 25 35 E
Kiryū, Japan .... 31 F9   36 24N 139 20 E
Kisaga, Tanzania .... 54 C3   4 30S 34 23 E
Kisalaya, Nic. 88 D3   14 40N 84 3W
Kisámou, Kólpos, Greece ...... 25 D5   35 30N 23 38 E
Kisanga, Dem. Rep. of the Congo 54 B2 2 30N 26 35 E
Kisangani, Dem. Rep. of
  the Congo .... 54 B2   0 35N 25 15 E
Kisar, Indonesia .... 37 F7   8 5S 127 10 E
Kisarawe, Tanzania .... 54 D4   6 53S 39 0 E
Kisarazu, Japan .... 31 G9   35 23N 139 55 E
Kishanganga ➤, Pakistan ...... 43 B5   34 18N 73 8 E
Kishanganj, India .... 43 F13 26 3N 88 14 E
Kishangarh, Raj., India ...... 42 F6   26 34N 74 52 E
Kishangarh, Raj., India ...... 42 F4   27 50N 70 30 E
Kishinev = Chişinău, Moldova . 17 E15 47 2N 28 50 E
Kishiwada, Japan .... 31 G7   34 28N 135 22 E
Kishtwar, India .... 43 C6   33 20N 75 48 E
Kisigo ➤, Tanzania .... 54 D3   6 27S 34 17 E
Kisii, Kenya .... 54 C3   0 40S 34 45 E
Kisiju, Tanzania .... 54 D4   7 23S 39 19 E
Kisizi, Uganda .... 54 C3   1 0S 29 58 E
Kiskőrös, Hungary .... 17 E10 46 37N 19 20 E
Kiskunfélegyháza, Hungary .... 17 E10 46 42N 19 53 E
Kiskunhalas, Hungary .... 17 E10 46 28N 19 37 E
Kislovodsk, Russia .... 19 F7   43 50N 42 45 E

Kismayu = Chisimaio,
  Somali Rep. .... 49 G8   0 22S 42 32 E
Kiso-Gawa ➤, Japan .... 31 G8   35 20N 136 45 E
Kiso-Sammyaku, Japan .... 31 G8   35 45N 137 45 E
Kisofukushima, Japan .... 31 G8   35 52N 137 43 E
Kisoro, Uganda .... 54 C2   1 17S 29 48 E
Kissidougou, Guinea 50 G3   9 5N 10 5W
Kissimmee, U.S.A. 83 L5   28 18N 81 24W
Kissimmee ➤, U.S.A. 83 M5   27 9N 80 52W
Kississing L., Canada 71 B8   55 10N 101 20W
Kissónerga, Cyprus .... 25 E11 34 49N 32 24 E
Kisumu, Kenya .... 54 C3   0 3S 34 45 E
Kiswani, Tanzania .... 54 C4   4 5S 37 57 E
Kiswere, Tanzania .... 55 D4   9 27S 39 30 E
Kit Carson, U.S.A. 80 F3   38 46N 102 48W
Kita, Mali 50 F4   13 5N   9 25W
Kitaibaraki, Japan .... 31 F10 36 50N 140 45 E
Kitakami, Japan .... 30 E10 39 20N 141 10 E
Kitakami-Gawa ➤, Japan .... 30 E10 38 25N 141 19 E
Kitakami-Sammyaku, Japan ..... 30 E10 39 30N 141 30 E
Kitakata, Japan .... 30 F9   37 39N 139 52 E
Kitakyūshū, Japan .... 31 H5   33 50N 130 50 E
Kitale, Kenya .... 54 B4   1 0N 35 0 E
Kitami, Japan .... 30 C11 43 48N 143 54 E
Kitami-Sammyaku, Japan .... 30 B11 44 22N 142 43 E
Kitangiri, L., Tanzania ...... 54 C3   4 5S 34 20 E
Kitaya, Tanzania .... 55 E5   10 38S 40 8 E
Kitchener, Canada 84 C4   43 27N 80 29W
Kitega = Gitega, Burundi ..... 54 C2   3 26S 29 56 E
Kitengo, Dem. Rep. of the Congo 54 D1 7 26S 24 8 E
Kitgum, Uganda .... 54 B3   3 17N 32 52 E
Kíthira, Greece .... 23 F10 36 8N 23 0 E
Kíthnos, Greece .... 23 F11 37 26N 24 27 E
Kiti, Cyprus .... 25 E12 34 50N 33 34 E
Kiti, C., Cyprus .... 25 E12 34 48N 33 36 E
Kitimat, Canada 70 C3   54 3N 128 38W
Kitinen ➤, Finland .... 8 C22   67 14N 27 27 E
Kitsuki, Japan .... 31 H5   33 25N 131 37 E
Kittakittaooloo, L., Australia 63 D2   28 3S 138 14 E
Kittanning, U.S.A. 84 F5   40 49N 79 31W
Kittatinny Mts., U.S.A. 85 F10 41 0N 75 0W
Kittery, U.S.A. 83 D10 43 5N 70 45W
Kittilä, Finland .... 8 C21   67 40N 24 51 E
Kitui, Kenya .... 54 C4   1 17S 38 0 E
Kitwanga, Canada 70 B3   55 6N 128 4W
Kitwe, Zambia .... 55 E2   12 54S 28 13 E
Kivarli, India .... 42 G5   24 33N 72 46 E
Kivertsi, Ukraine .... 17 C13 50 50N 25 28 E
Kividhes, Cyprus .... 25 E11 34 46N 32 51 E
Kivu, L., Dem. Rep. of the Congo 54 C2 1 48S 29 0 E
Kiyev = Kyyiv, Ukraine .... 17 C16 50 30N 30 28 E
Kiyevskoye Vdkhr. = Kyyivske
  Vdskh., Ukraine .... 17 C16 51 0N 30 25 E
Kizel, Russia .... 18 C10 59 3N 57 40 E
Kiziguru, Rwanda .... 54 C3   1 46S 30 23 E
Kızıl Irmak ➤, Turkey .... 19 F6   41 44N 35 58 E
Kızıl Jilga, China .... 43 B8   35 26N 78 50 E
Kızıltepe, Turkey .... 44 B4   37 12N 40 35 E
Kizimkazi, Tanzania .... 54 D4   6 28S 39 30 E
Kizlyar, Russia .... 19 F8   43 51N 46 40 E
Kizyl-Arvat = Gyzylarbat,
  Turkmenistan .... 28 F6   39 4N 56 23 E
Kjölur, Iceland 8 D4   64 50N 19 25W
Kladno, Czech Rep. .... 16 C8   50 10N 14 7 E
Klaeng, Thailand .... 38 F3   12 47N 101 39 E
Klagenfurt, Austria .... 16 E8   46 38N 14 20 E
Klaipėda, Lithuania .... 9 J19   55 43N 21 10 E
Klaksvík, Færoe Is. 8 E9   62 14N   6 35W
Klamath ➤, U.S.A. 76 F1   41 33N 124 5W
Klamath Falls, U.S.A. 76 E3   42 13N 121 46W
Klamath Mts., U.S.A. 76 F2   41 20N 123 0W
Klamono, Indonesia .... 37 E8   1 8S 131 30 E
Klappan ➤, Canada 70 B3   58 0N 129 43W
Klarälven ➤, Sweden .... 9 G15   59 23N 13 32 E
Klatovy, Czech Rep. .... 16 D7   49 23N 13 18 E
Klawer, S. Africa .... 56 E2   31 44S 18 36 E
Klazienaveen, Neths. .... 15 B6   52 44N   7 0 E
Kleena Kleene, Canada 70 C4   52 0N 124 59W
Klein-Karas, Namibia .... 56 D2   27 33S 18 7 E
Klerksdorp, S. Africa .... 56 D4   26 53S 26 38 E
Kletsk = Klyetsk, Belarus .... 17 B14 53 5N 26 45 E
Kletskiy, Russia .... 19 E7   49 16N 43 11 E
Klickitat, U.S.A. 76 D3   45 49N 121 9W
Klickitat ➤, U.S.A. 78 E5   45 42N 121 17W
Klidhes, Cyprus .... 25 D13 35 42N 34 36 E
Klinaklini ➤, Canada 70 C3   51 21N 125 40W
Klip ➤, S. Africa .... 57 D4   27 3S 29 3 E
Klipdale, S. Africa .... 56 E2   34 19S 19 57 E
Klipplaat, S. Africa .... 56 E3   33 15S 24 22 E
Kłodzko, Poland .... 17 C9   50 28N 16 38 E
Klong Wang Chao △, Thailand .. 38 D2   16 20N 99 9 E
Klouto, Togo .... 50 G6   6 57N   0 44 E
Kluane △, Canada 70 A1   60 45N 139 30W
Kluane L., Canada 68 B6   61 15N 138 40W
Kluczbork, Poland .... 17 C10 50 58N 18 12 E
Klukwan, U.S.A. 70 B1   59 24N 135 54W
Klungkung, Indonesia .... 37 K18   8 32S 115 24 E
Klyetsk, Belarus .... 17 B14 53 5N 26 45 E
Klyuchevskaya, Gora, Russia .. 29 D17 55 50N 160 30 E
Knaresborough, U.K. 12 C6   54 1N   1 28W
Knee L., Man., Canada 72 A1   55 3N 94 45W
Knee L., Sask., Canada 71 B7   55 51N 107 0W
Knight Inlet, Canada 70 C3   50 45N 125 40W
Knighton, U.K. 13 E4   52 21N   3 3W
Knights Ferry, U.S.A. 78 H6   37 50N 120 40W
Knights Landing, U.S.A. 78 G5   38 48N 121 43W
Knob, C., Australia .... 61 F2   34 32S 119 16 E
Knock, Ireland 10 C3   53 48N   8 55W
Knockmealdown Mts., Ireland .. 10 D4   52 14N   7 56W
Knokke-Heist, Belgium .... 15 C3   51 21N   3 17 E
Knossós, Greece .... 25 D7   35 16N 25 10 E
Knowlton, Canada 85 A12 45 13N 72 31W
Knox, U.S.A. 82 E2   41 18N 86 37W
Knox Coast, Antarctica .... 5 C8   66 30S 108 0 E
Knoxville, Iowa, U.S.A. 80 E8   41 19N 93 6W
Knoxville, Pa., U.S.A. 84 E7   41 57N 77 27W
Knoxville, Tenn., U.S.A. 83 H4   35 58N 83 55W
Knud Rasmussen Land,
  Greenland 4 A5   79 0N 60 0W
Knysna, S. Africa .... 56 E3   34 2S 23 2 E
Ko Kha, Thailand .... 38 C2   18 11N 99 24 E
Ko Tarutao △, Thailand .... 39 J2   6 31N 99 26 E
Ko Yao, Thailand .... 39 a   8 7N 98 35 E
Koartac = Quaqtaq, Canada 69 B13 60 55N 69 40W
Koba, Indonesia .... 37 E8   6 37S 134 37 E
Kobarid, Slovenia .... 16 E7   46 15N 13 30 E
Kobayashi, Japan .... 31 J5   31 56N 130 59 E
Kobe, Japan .... 31 G7   34 45N 135 10 E

København, Denmark .... 9 J15   55 41N 12 34 E
Kōbi-Sho, Japan .... 31 M1   25 56N 123 41 E
Koblenz, Germany .... 16 C4   50 21N   7 36 E
Kobryn, Belarus .... 17 B13 52 15N 24 22 E
Kocaeli, Turkey .... 19 F4   40 45N 29 50 E
Kočani, Macedonia .... 23 D10 41 55N 22 25 E
Koch Bihar, India .... 41 F16 26 22N 89 29 E
Kochang, N. Korea .... 35 G14 35 41N 127 55 E
Kochas, India .... 43 G10 25 15N 83 56 E
Kochi = Cochin, India .... 40 Q10   9 58N 76 20 E
Kōchi, Japan .... 31 H6   33 30N 133 35 E
Kōchi □, Japan .... 31 H6   33 40N 133 30 E
Kochiu = Gejiu, China .... 32 D5   23 20N 103 10 E
Kodarma, India .... 43 G11 24 28N 85 36 E
Kodiak, U.S.A. 68 C4   57 47N 152 24W
Kodiak I., U.S.A. 68 C4   57 30N 152 45W
Kodinar, India .... 42 J4   20 46N 70 46 E
Koedoesberge, S. Africa ...... 56 E3   32 40S 20 11 E
Koes, Namibia .... 56 D2   26 0S 19 15 E
Kofiau, Indonesia .... 37 E7   1 11S 129 50 E
Koforidua, Ghana 50 G5   6 3N   0 17W
Kōfu, Japan .... 31 G9   35 40N 138 30 E
Koga, Japan .... 31 F9   36 11N 139 43 E
Kogaluc ➤, Canada 73 A7   56 12N 61 44W
Køge, Denmark .... 9 J15   55 27N 12 11 E
Koh-i-Khurd, Afghan. .... 42 C1   33 30N 65 59 E
Koh-i-Maran, Pakistan .... 42 E2   29 18N 66 50 E
Kohat, Pakistan .... 42 C4   33 40N 71 29 E
Kohima, India .... 41 G19 25 35N 94 10 E
Kohkılūyeh va Būyer Aḥmadi □,
  Iran .... 45 D6   31 30N 50 30 E
Kohler Ra., Antarctica 5 D15   77 0S 110 0W
Kohlu, Pakistan .... 42 E3   29 54N 69 15 E
Kohtla-Järve, Estonia .... 9 G22   59 20N 27 20 E
Koi Sanjaq, Iraq .... 44 B5   36 5N 44 38 E
Koillismaa, Finland .... 8 D23   65 44N 28 36 E
Koin-dong, N. Korea .... 35 D14 40 28N 126 18 E
Kojō, N. Korea .... 35 E14 38 58N 127 58 E
Kojonup, Australia .... 61 F2   33 48S 117 10 E
Kojūr, Iran .... 45 B6   36 23N 51 43 E
Kokand = Qŭqon, Uzbekistan ... 28 E8   40 30N 70 57 E
Kokas, Indonesia .... 37 E8   2 42S 132 26 E
Kokchetav = Kökshetaū,
  Kazakhstan .... 28 D7   53 20N 69 25 E
Kokemäenjoki ➤, Finland ...... 9 F19   61 32N 21 44 E
Kokkola, Finland .... 8 E20   63 50N 23 8 E
Koko Kyunzu, Burma .... 41 M18 14 10N 93 25 E
Kokomo, U.S.A. 82 E2   40 29N 86 8W
Koksan, N. Korea .... 35 E14 38 46N 126 40 E
Kökshetaū, Kazakhstan .... 28 D7   53 20N 69 25 E
Koksoak ➤, Canada 69 C13 58 30N 68 10W
Kokstad, S. Africa .... 57 E4   30 32S 29 29 E
Kokubu, Japan .... 31 J5   31 44N 130 46 E
Kola, Indonesia .... 37 F8   5 35S 134 30 E
Kola, Russia .... 18 A5   68 45N 33 8 E
Kola Pen. = Kolskiy Poluostrov,
  Russia .... 18 A6   67 30N 38 0 E
Kolachi ➤, Pakistan .... 42 F2   27 8N 67 2 E
Kolahoi, India .... 43 B6   34 12N 75 22 E
Kolaka, Indonesia .... 37 E6   4 3S 121 46 E
Kolar, India .... 40 N11 13 12N 78 15 E
Kolar Gold Fields, India ..... 40 N11 12 58N 78 16 E
Kolaras, India .... 42 G6   25 14N 77 36 E
Kolari, Finland .... 8 C20   67 20N 23 48 E
Kolayat, India .... 40 F8   27 50N 72 50 E
Kolding, Denmark .... 9 J13   55 30N   9 29 E
Kolepom = Dolak, Pulau,
  Indonesia .... 37 F9   8 0S 138 30 E
Kolguyev, Ostrov, Russia ..... 18 A8   69 20N 48 30 E
Kolhapur, India .... 40 L9   16 43N 74 15 E
Kolín, Czech Rep. .... 16 C8   50 2N 15 9 E
Kolkas rags, Latvia .... 9 H20   57 46N 22 37 E
Kolkata, India .... 43 H13 22 36N 88 24 E
Kollam = Quilon, India .... 40 Q10   8 50N 76 38 E
Kollum, Neths. .... 15 A6   53 17N   6 10 E
Kolmanskop, Namibia .... 56 D2   26 45S 15 14 E
Köln, Germany .... 16 C4   50 56N   6 57 E
Koło, Poland .... 17 B10 52 14N 18 40 E
Kołobrzeg, Poland .... 16 A8   54 10N 15 35 E
Kolomna, Russia .... 18 C6   55 8N 38 45 E
Kolomyya, Ukraine .... 17 D13 48 31N 25 2 E
Kolonodale, Indonesia .... 37 E6   2 0S 121 19 E
Kolosib, India .... 41 G18 24 15N 92 45 E
Kolpashevo, Russia .... 28 D9   58 20N 83 5 E
Kolpino, Russia .... 18 C5   59 44N 30 39 E
Kolskiy Poluostrov, Russia ... 18 A6   67 30N 38 0 E
Kolskiy Zaliv, Russia .... 18 A5   69 23N 34 0 E
Kolwezi, Dem. Rep. of the Congo 55 E2 10 40S 25 25 E
Kolyma ➤, Russia .... 29 C17 69 30N 161 0 E
Kolymskoye Nagorye, Russia ... 29 C16 63 0N 157 0 E
Kôm Ombo, Egypt .... 51 D12 24 25N 32 52 E
Komandorskiye Is. =
  Komandorskiye Ostrova,
  Russia .... 29 D17 55 0N 167 0 E
Komandorskiye Ostrova, Russia 29 D17 55 0N 167 0 E
Komárno, Slovak Rep. .... 17 E10 47 49N 18 5 E
Komatipoort, S. Africa .... 57 D5   25 25S 31 55 E
Komatou Yialou, Cyprus .... 25 D13 35 25N 34 8 E
Komatsu, Japan .... 31 F8   36 25N 136 30 E
Komatsushima, Japan .... 31 H7   34 0N 134 35 E
Komi □, Russia .... 18 B10 64 0N 55 0 E
Kommunizma, Pik, Tajikistan .. 37 F5   8 37S 119 20 E
Komodo, Indonesia .... 37 F5   8 37S 119 20 E
Komoran, Pulau, Indonesia .... 37 F9   8 18S 138 45 E
Komoro, Japan .... 31 F9   36 19N 138 26 E
Komotini, Greece .... 23 D11 41 9N 25 26 E
Kompasberg, S. Africa .... 56 E3   31 45S 24 32 E
Kompong Bang, Cambodia .... 39 F5   12 24N 104 40 E
Kompong Cham, Cambodia .... 39 F5   12 0N 105 30 E
Kompong Chhnang = Kompong
  Chhnang, Cambodia .... 39 F5   12 20N 104 35 E
Kompong Chikreng, Cambodia ... 38 F5   13 5N 104 18 E
Kompong Kleang, Cambodia ..... 38 F5   13 6N 104 8 E
Kompong Luong, Cambodia ...... 39 G5   11 49N 104 48 E
Kompong Pranak, Cambodia ..... 38 F5   13 35N 104 55 E
Kompong Som = Kampong
  Saom, Cambodia .... 39 G4   10 38N 103 30 E
Kompong Som, Chhung =
  Kampong Saom, Chaak,
  Cambodia .... 39 G4   10 50N 103 32 E
Kompong Speu, Cambodia .... 39 G5   11 26N 104 32 E
Kompong Sralau, Cambodia ..... 38 E5   14 5N 105 46 E
Kompong Thom, Cambodia .... 38 F5   12 35N 104 51 E
Kompong Trabeck, Cambodia .... 38 F5   13 6N 105 14 E
Kompong Trabeck, Cambodia .... 39 G5   11 25N 105 48 E
Kompong Trach, Cambodia ...... 39 G5   11 25N 105 48 E
Kompong Tralach, Cambodia .... 39 G5   11 54N 104 47 E

Komrat = Comrat, Moldova .... **17 E15** 46 18N 28 40 E
Komsberg, S. Africa .... **56 E3** 32 40S 20 45 E
Komsomolets, Ostrov, Russia .. **29 A10** 80 30N 95 0 E
Komsomolsk, Russia .... **29 D14** 50 30N 137 0 E
Kon Tum, Vietnam .... **38 E7** 14 24N 108 0 E
Kon Tum, Plateau du, Vietnam . **38 E7** 14 30N 108 30 E
Konarhã □, Afghan. .... **40 B7** 34 30N 71 3 E
Konāri, Iran .... **45 D6** 28 13N 51 36 E
Konch, India .... **43 G8** 26 0N 79 10 E
Konde, Tanzania .... **54 C4** 4 57S 39 45 E
Kondinin, Australia .... **61 F2** 32 34S 118 8 E
Kondoa, Tanzania .... **54 C4** 4 55S 35 50 E
Kondókali, Greece .... **25 A3** 39 38N 19 51 E
Kondopaga, Russia .... **18 B5** 62 12N 34 17 E
Kondratyevo, Russia .... **29 D10** 57 22N 98 15 E
Köneürgench, Turkmenistan ... **28 E6** 42 19N 59 10 E
Konevo, Russia .... **18 B6** 62 8N 39 20 E
Kong = Khong ➤, Cambodia .. **38 F5** 13 32N 105 58 E
Kong, Ivory C. **50 G5** 8 54N 4 36W
Kong, Koh, Cambodia .... **39 G4** 11 20N 103 0 E
Kong Christian IX Land,
Greenland **4 C6** 68 0N 36 0W
Kong Christian X Land,
Greenland **4 B6** 74 0N 29 0W
Kong Frederik IX Land,
Greenland **4 C5** 67 0N 52 0W
Kong Frederik VI Kyst, Greenland **69 B15** 63 0N 43 0W
Kong Frederik VIII Land,
Greenland **4 B6** 78 30N 26 0W
Kong Oscar Fjord, Greenland .. **4 B6** 72 20N 24 0W
Kongju, S. Korea .... **35 F14** 36 30N 127 0 E
Konglu, Burma .... **41 F20** 27 13N 97 57 E
Kongola, Namibia .... **56 B3** 17 45S 23 20 E
Kongolo, Kasai-Or., Dem. Rep. of
the Congo .... **54 D1** 5 26S 24 49 E
Kongolo, Katanga, Dem. Rep. of
the Congo .... **54 D2** 5 22S 27 0 E
Kongsberg, Norway .... **9 G13** 59 39N 9 39 E
Kongsvinger, Norway .... **9 F15** 60 12N 12 2 E
Kongwa, Tanzania .... **54 D4** 6 11S 36 26 E
Koni, Dem. Rep. of the Congo . **55 E2** 10 40S 27 11 E
Koni, Mts., Dem. Rep. of
the Congo .... **55 E2** 10 36S 27 10 E
Konin, Poland .... **17 B10** 52 12N 18 15 E
Konjic, Bos.-H. .... **23 C7** 43 42N 17 58 E
Konkiep, Namibia .... **56 D2** 26 49S 17 15 E
Konosha, Russia .... **18 B7** 61 0N 40 5 E
Kōnosu, Japan .... **31 F9** 36 3N 139 31 E
Konotop, Ukraine .... **19 D5** 51 12N 33 7 E
Końskie, Poland .... **17 C11** 51 15N 20 23 E
Konstanz, Germany .... **16 E5** 47 40N 9 10 E
Kont, Iran .... **45 E9** 26 55N 61 50 E
Kontagora, Nigeria .... **50 F7** 10 23N 5 27 E
Konya, Turkey .... **19 G5** 37 52N 32 35 E
Konza, Kenya .... **54 C4** 1 45S 37 7 E
Koocanusa, L., Canada **76 B6** 49 20N 115 15W
Kookynie, Australia .... **61 E3** 29 17S 121 22 E
Koolyanobbing, Australia ...... **61 F2** 30 48S 119 36 E
Koonibba, Australia .... **63 E1** 31 54S 133 25 E
Koorawatha, Australia .... **63 E4** 34 2S 148 33 E
Koorda, Australia .... **61 F2** 30 48S 117 35 E
Kooskia, U.S.A. **76 C6** 46 9N 115 59W
Kootenay ➤, Canada **70 C5** 51 0N 116 0W
Kootenay L., U.S.A. **70 D5** 49 19N 117 39W
Kootenay L., Canada **70 D5** 49 45N 116 50W
Kootjieskolk, S. Africa .... **56 E3** 31 15S 20 21 E
Kopaonik, Serbia & M. ...... **23 C9** 43 10N 20 50 E
Kópavogur, Iceland **8 D3** 64 6N 21 55W
Koper, Slovenia .... **16 F7** 45 31N 13 44 E
Kopervik, Norway .... **9 G11** 59 17N 5 17 E
Kopet Dagh, Asia .... **45 B8** 38 0N 58 0 E
Kopi, Australia .... **63 E2** 33 24S 135 40 E
Köping, Sweden .... **9 G17** 59 31N 16 3 E
Koppeh Dāgh = Kopet Dagh, Asia **45 B8** 38 0N 58 0 E
Koppies, S. Africa .... **57 D4** 27 20S 27 30 E
Koprivnica, Croatia .... **22 A7** 46 12N 16 45 E
Kopychyntsi, Ukraine .... **17 D13** 49 7N 25 58 E
Kora △, Kenya .... **54 C4** 0 14S 38 44 E
Korab, Macedonia .... **23 D9** 41 44N 20 40 E
Korakiána, Greece .... **25 A3** 39 42N 19 45 E
Koral, India .... **42 J5** 21 50N 73 12 E
Korba, India .... **43 H10** 22 20N 82 45 E
Korçë, Albania .... **23 D9** 40 37N 20 50 E
Korčula, Croatia .... **22 C7** 42 56N 16 57 E
Kord Kūy, Iran .... **45 B7** 36 48N 54 7 E
Kord Sheykh, Iran .... **45 D7** 28 31N 52 53 E
Kordestān □, Iran .... **44 C5** 36 0N 47 0 E
Kordofân, Sudan .... **51 F11** 13 0N 29 0 E
Korea, North ■, Asia .... **35 E14** 40 0N 127 0 E
Korea, South ■, Asia .... **35 G15** 36 0N 128 0 E
Korea Bay, Korea .... **35 E13** 39 0N 124 0 E
Korea Strait, Asia .... **35 H15** 34 0N 129 30 E
Korets, Ukraine .... **17 C14** 50 40N 27 5 E
Korhogo, Ivory C. **50 G4** 9 29N 5 28W
Korinthiakós Kólpos, Greece .. **23 E10** 38 16N 22 30 E
Kórinthos, Greece .... **23 F10** 37 56N 22 55 E
Korissa, Limni, Greece ...... **25 B3** 39 27N 19 53 E
Kōriyama, Japan .... **30 F10** 37 24N 140 23 E
Korla, China .... **32 B3** 41 45N 86 4 E
Kormakiti, C., Cyprus .... **25 D11** 35 23N 32 56 E
Korneshty = Cornești, Moldova **17 E15** 47 21N 28 1 E
Koro, Fiji .... **59 C8** 17 19S 179 23 E
Koro, Ivory C. **50 G4** 8 32N 7 30W
Koro Sea, Fiji **59 C9** 17 30S 179 45W
Korogwe, Tanzania .... **54 D4** 5 5S 38 25 E
Koronadal, Phil. .... **37 C6** 6 12N 125 1 E
Koror, Palau .... **64 G5** 7 20N 134 28 E
Körös ➤, Hungary .... **17 E11** 46 43N 20 12 E
Korosten, Ukraine .... **17 C15** 50 54N 28 36 E
Korostyshev, Ukraine .... **17 C15** 50 19N 29 4 E
Korraraika, Helodranon' i,
Madag. .... **57 B7** 17 45S 43 57 E
Korsakov, Russia .... **29 E15** 46 36N 142 42 E
Korshunovo, Russia .... **29 D12** 58 37N 110 10 E
Korsør, Denmark .... **9 J14** 55 20N 11 9 E
Kortrijk, Belgium .... **15 D3** 50 50N 3 17 E
Korwai, India .... **42 G8** 24 7N 78 5 E
Koryakskoye Nagorye, Russia . **29 C18** 61 0N 171 0 E
Koryŏng, S. Korea .... **35 G15** 35 44N 128 15 E
Kos, Greece .... **23 F12** 36 50N 27 15 E
Koschagyl, Kazakhstan ...... **19 E9** 46 40N 54 0 E
Kościan, Poland .... **17 B9** 52 5N 16 40 E
Kosciusko, U.S.A. **81 J10** 33 4N 89 35W
Kosciuszko, Mt., Australia .... **63 F4** 36 27S 148 16 E
Kosha, Sudan .... **51 D12** 20 50N 30 30 E
K'oshih = Kashi, China ...... **32 C2** 39 30N 76 2 E
Koshiki-Rettō, Japan .... **31 J4** 31 45N 129 49 E

Kosi, India .... **42 F7** 27 48N 77 29 E
Kosi ➤, India .... **43 E8** 28 41N 78 57 E
Košice, Slovak Rep. .... **17 D11** 48 42N 21 15 E
Koskinoú, Greece .... **25 C10** 36 23N 28 13 E
Koslan, Russia .... **18 B8** 63 34N 49 14 E
Kosŏng, N. Korea .... **35 E15** 38 40N 128 22 E
Kosovo □, Serbia & M. ...... **23 C9** 42 30N 21 0 E
Kosovska Mitrovica, Serbia & M. **23 C9** 42 54N 20 52 E
Kossou, L. de, Ivory C. **50 G4** 6 59N 5 31W
Koster, S. Africa .... **56 D4** 25 52S 26 54 E
Kôstî, Sudan .... **51 F12** 13 8N 32 43 E
Kostopil, Ukraine .... **17 C14** 50 51N 26 22 E
Kostroma, Russia .... **18 C7** 57 50N 40 58 E
Kostrzyn, Poland .... **16 B8** 52 35N 14 39 E
Koszalin, Poland .... **16 A9** 54 11N 16 8 E
Kot Addu, Pakistan .... **42 D4** 30 30N 71 0 E
Kot Kapura, India .... **42 D6** 30 35N 74 50 E
Kot Moman, Pakistan ...... **42 C5** 32 13N 73 0 E
Kot Sultan, Pakistan .... **42 D4** 30 46N 70 56 E
Kota, India .... **42 G6** 25 14N 75 49 E
Kota Baharu, Malaysia ...... **39 J4** 6 7N 102 14 E
Kota Barrage, India .... **42 G6** 25 6N 75 51 E
Kota Belud, Malaysia .... **36 C5** 6 21N 116 26 E
Kota Kinabalu, Malaysia .... **36 C5** 6 0N 116 4 E
Kota Kubu Baharu, Malaysia . **39 L3** 3 34N 101 39 E
Kota Tinggi, Malaysia ...... **39 M4** 1 44N 103 53 E
Kotaagung, Indonesia ...... **36 F2** 5 38S 104 29 E
Kotabaru, Indonesia .... **36 E5** 3 20S 116 20 E
Kotabumi, Indonesia .... **36 E2** 4 49S 104 54 E
Kotamobagu, Indonesia ...... **37 D6** 0 57N 124 31 E
Kotcho L., Canada **70 B4** 59 7N 121 12W
Kotdwara, India .... **43 E8** 29 45N 78 32 E
Kotelnich, Russia .... **18 C8** 58 22N 48 24 E
Kotelnikovo, Russia .... **19 E7** 47 38N 43 8 E
Kotelnyy, Ostrov, Russia .... **29 B14** 75 10N 139 0 E
Kothari ➤, India .... **42 G6** 25 20N 75 4 E
Kothi, Chhattisgarh, India .... **43 H10** 23 21N 82 3 E
Kothi, Mad. P., India .... **43 G9** 24 45N 80 40 E
Kotiro, Pakistan .... **42 F2** 26 17N 67 13 E
Kotka, Finland .... **9 F22** 60 28N 26 58 E
Kotlas, Russia .... **18 B8** 61 17N 46 43 E
Kotli, Pakistan .... **42 C5** 33 30N 73 55 E
Kotma, India .... **43 H9** 23 12N 81 58 E
Kotmul, Pakistan .... **43 B6** 35 32N 75 10 E
Kotor, Serbia & M. .... **23 C8** 42 25N 18 47 E
Kotovsk, Ukraine .... **17 E15** 47 45N 29 35 E
Kotputli, India .... **42 F7** 27 43N 76 12 E
Kotri, Pakistan .... **42 G3** 25 22N 68 22 E
Kotturu, India .... **40 M10** 14 45N 76 10 E
Kotuy ➤, Russia .... **29 B11** 71 54N 102 6 E
Kotzebue, U.S.A. **68 B3** 66 53N 162 39W
Kouchibouguac △, Canada .. **73 C6** 46 50N 65 0W
Koudougou, Burkina Faso **50 F5** 12 10N 2 20W
Koufonísi, Greece .... **25 E8** 34 56N 26 8 E
Kougaberge, S. Africa ...... **56 E3** 33 48S 23 50 E
Kouilou ➤, Congo .... **52 E2** 4 10S 12 5 E
Koula Moutou, Gabon ...... **52 E2** 1 15S 12 25 E
Koulen = Kulen, Cambodia .. **38 F5** 13 50N 104 40 E
Kouloúra, Greece .... **25 A3** 39 42N 19 54 E
Koúm-bournoú, Ákra, Greece . **25 C10** 36 15N 28 11 E
Koumala, Australia .... **62 C4** 21 38S 149 15 E
Koumra, Chad .... **51 G9** 8 50N 17 35 E
Kounradskiy, Kazakhstan .... **28 E8** 46 59N 75 0 E
Kountze, U.S.A. **81 K7** 30 22N 94 19W
Kouris ➤, Cyprus .... **25 E11** 34 38N 32 54 E
Kourou, Fr. Guiana **93 B8** 5 9N 52 39W
Kousséri, Cameroon .... **51 F8** 12 0N 14 55 E
Kouvola, Finland .... **9 F22** 60 52N 26 43 E
Kovdor, Russia .... **18 A5** 67 34N 30 24 E
Kovel, Ukraine .... **17 C13** 51 11N 24 38 E
Kovrov, Russia .... **18 C7** 56 25N 41 25 E
Kowanyama, Australia ...... **62 B3** 15 29S 141 44 E
Kowloon, China .... **33 G11** 22 19N 114 11 E
Kowŏn, N. Korea .... **35 E14** 39 26N 127 14 E
Koyampattur = Coimbatore, India **40 P10** 11 2N 76 59 E
Köyceğiz, Turkey .... **23 F13** 36 57N 28 40 E
Koza, Japan .... **31 L3** 26 19N 127 46 E
Kozan, Turkey .... **44 B2** 37 26N 35 50 E
Kozáni, Greece .... **23 D9** 40 19N 21 47 E
Kozhikode = Calicut, India .... **40 P9** 11 15N 75 43 E
Kozhva, Russia .... **18 A10** 65 10N 57 0 E
Kozyatyn, Ukraine .... **17 D15** 49 45N 28 50 E
Kra, Isthmus of = Kra, Kho Khot,
Thailand .... **39 G2** 10 15N 99 30 E
Kra, Kho Khot, Thailand .... **39 G2** 10 15N 99 30 E
Kra Buri, Thailand .... **39 G2** 10 22N 98 46 E
Kraai ➤, S. Africa .... **56 E4** 30 40S 26 45 E
Krabi, Thailand .... **39 H2** 8 4N 98 55 E
Kracheh, Cambodia .... **38 F6** 12 32N 106 10 E
Kragan, Indonesia .... **37 G14** 6 43S 111 38 E
Kragerø, Norway .... **9 G13** 58 52N 9 25 E
Kragujevac, Serbia & M. .... **23 B9** 44 2N 20 56 E
Krakatau = Rakata, Pulau,
Indonesia .... **36 F3** 6 10S 105 20 E
Krakatoa = Rakata, Pulau,
Indonesia .... **36 F3** 6 10S 105 20 E
Krakor, Cambodia .... **38 F5** 12 32N 104 12 E
Kraków, Poland .... **17 C10** 50 4N 19 57 E
Kralanh, Cambodia .... **38 F4** 13 35N 103 25 E
Kraljevo, Serbia & M. ...... **23 C9** 43 44N 20 41 E
Kramatorsk, Ukraine .... **19 E6** 48 50N 37 30 E
Kramfors, Sweden .... **9 E17** 62 55N 17 48 E
Kranj, Slovenia .... **16 E8** 46 16N 14 22 E
Krankskop, S. Africa .... **57 D5** 28 0S 30 47 E
Krasavino, Russia .... **18 B8** 60 58N 46 29 E
Kraskino, Russia .... **29 E14** 42 44N 130 48 E
Krásnik, Poland .... **17 C12** 50 55N 22 15 E
Krasnoarmeysk, Russia .... **28 D5** 51 0N 45 42 E
Krasnodar, Russia .... **19 E6** 45 5N 39 0 E
Krasnokamsk, Russia ...... **18 C10** 58 4N 55 48 E
Krasnoperekopsk, Ukraine .. **19 E5** 46 0N 33 54 E
Krasnorechenskiy, Russia .... **30 B7** 44 41N 135 14 E
Krasnoselkup, Russia ...... **28 C9** 65 20N 82 10 E
Krasnoturinsk, Russia ...... **18 C11** 59 46N 60 12 E
Krasnoufimsk, Russia ...... **18 C10** 56 36N 57 38 E
Krasnouralsk, Russia ...... **18 C11** 58 21N 60 3 E
Krasnovishersk, Russia .... **18 B10** 60 23N 57 3 E
Krasnoyarsk, Russia .... **29 D10** 56 8N 93 0 E
Krasnyy Kut, Russia .... **19 D8** 50 50N 47 0 E
Krasnyy Luch, Ukraine ...... **19 E6** 48 13N 39 0 E
Krasnyy Yar, Russia .... **19 E8** 46 43N 48 23 E
Kratie = Kracheh, Cambodia .. **38 F6** 12 32N 106 10 E
Krau, Indonesia .... **37 E10** 3 19S 140 5 E
Kravanh, Chuor Phnum,
Cambodia .... **39 G4** 12 0N 103 32 E
Krefeld, Germany .... **16 C4** 51 20N 6 33 E
Kremen, Croatia .... **16 F8** 44 28N 15 53 E
Kremenchuk, Ukraine ...... **19 E5** 49 5N 33 25 E

Kremenchuksk Vdskh., Ukraine . **19 E5** 49 20N 32 30 E
Kremenets, Ukraine .... **17 C13** 50 8N 25 43 E
Kremmling, U.S.A. **76 F10** 40 4N 106 24W
Krems, Austria .... **16 D8** 48 25N 15 36 E
Kretinga, Lithuania .... **9 J19** 55 53N 21 15 E
Kribi, Cameroon .... **52 D1** 2 57N 9 56 E
Krichev = Krychaw, Belarus .. **17 B16** 53 40N 31 41 E
Kriós, Ákra, Greece .... **25 D5** 35 13N 23 34 E
Krishna ➤, India .... **41 M12** 15 57N 80 59 E
Krishnanagar, India .... **43 H13** 23 24N 88 33 E
Kristiansand, Norway ...... **9 G13** 58 8N 8 1 E
Kristianstad, Sweden ...... **9 H16** 56 2N 14 9 E
Kristiansund, Norway ...... **8 E12** 63 7N 7 45 E
Kristiinankaupunki, Finland .. **9 E19** 62 16N 21 21 E
Kristinehamn, Sweden ...... **9 G16** 59 18N 14 7 E
Kristinestad = Kristiinankaupunki,
Finland .... **9 E19** 62 16N 21 21 E
Kríti, Greece .... **25 D7** 35 15N 25 0 E
Kritsá, Greece .... **25 D7** 35 10N 25 41 E
Krivoy Rog = Kryvyy Rih, Ukraine **19 E5** 47 51N 33 20 E
Krk, Croatia .... **16 F8** 45 8N 14 40 E
Krokodil ➤, Mozam. ...... **57 D5** 25 14S 32 18 E
Krong Kaoh Kong, Cambodia . **36 B2** 11 35N 103 0 E
Kronprins Olav Kyst, Antarctica **5 C5** 69 0S 42 0 E
Kronprinsesse Märtha Kyst,
Antarctica **5 D2** 73 30S 10 0W
Kronshtadt, Russia .... **18 B4** 59 57N 29 51 E
Kroonstad, S. Africa ...... **56 D4** 27 43S 27 19 E
Kropotkin, Russia .... **19 E7** 45 28N 40 28 E
Krosno, Poland .... **17 D11** 49 42N 21 46 E
Krotoszyn, Poland .... **17 C9** 51 42N 17 23 E
Kroussón, Greece .... **25 D6** 35 13N 24 59 E
Kruger △, S. Africa .... **57 C5** 24 50S 26 10 E
Krugersdorp, S. Africa ...... **57 D4** 26 5S 27 46 E
Kruisfontein, S. Africa ...... **56 E3** 33 59S 24 43 E
Krung Thep = Bangkok, Thailand **38 F3** 13 45N 100 35 E
Krupki, Belarus .... **17 A15** 54 19N 29 8 E
Kruševac, Serbia & M. ...... **23 C9** 43 35N 21 28 E
Krychaw, Belarus .... **17 B16** 53 40N 31 41 E
Krymskyy Poluostrov = Krymskyy
Pivostriv, Ukraine .... **19 F5** 45 0N 34 0 E
Krymskyy Pivostriv, Ukraine .. **19 F5** 45 0N 34 0 E
Kryvyy Rih, Ukraine .... **19 E5** 47 51N 33 20 E
Ksar el Kebir, Morocco **50 B4** 35 0N 6 0W
Ksar es Souk = Er Rachidia,
Morocco **50 B5** 31 58N 4 20W
Kuah, Malaysia .... **39 J2** 6 19N 99 51 E
Kuala Belait, Malaysia ...... **36 D4** 4 35N 114 11 E
Kuala Berang, Malaysia .... **39 K4** 5 5N 103 1 E
Kuala Dungun = Dungun,
Malaysia .... **39 K4** 4 45N 103 25 E
Kuala Kangsar, Malaysia .... **39 K3** 4 46N 100 56 E
Kuala Kelawang, Malaysia ... **39 L4** 2 56N 102 5 E
Kuala Kerai, Malaysia ...... **39 K4** 5 30N 102 12 E
Kuala Kerian, Malaysia ...... **39 c** 5 10N 100 25 E
Kuala Lipis, Malaysia ...... **39 K4** 4 10N 102 3 E
Kuala Lumpur, Malaysia .... **39 L3** 3 9N 101 41 E
Kuala Nerang, Malaysia .... **39 J3** 6 16N 100 37 E
Kuala Pilah, Malaysia ...... **39 L4** 2 45N 102 15 E
Kuala Rompin, Malaysia .... **39 L4** 2 49N 103 29 E
Kuala Selangor, Malaysia .... **39 L3** 3 20N 101 15 E
Kuala Sepetang, Malaysia .. **39 K3** 4 49N 100 28 E
Kuala Terengganu, Malaysia . **39 K4** 5 20N 103 8 E
Kualajelai, Indonesia ...... **36 E4** 2 58S 110 46 E
Kualakapuas, Indonesia .... **36 E4** 2 55S 114 20 E
Kualakurun, Indonesia ...... **36 E4** 1 10S 113 50 E
Kualapembuang, Indonesia .. **36 E4** 3 14S 112 38 E
Kualasimpang, Indonesia .... **36 D1** 4 17N 98 3 E
Kuancheng, China .... **35 D10** 40 37N 118 30 E
Kuandang, Indonesia ...... **37 D6** 0 56N 123 1 E
Kuandian, China .... **35 D13** 40 45N 124 45 E
Kuangchou = Guangzhou, China **33 D6** 23 5N 113 10 E
Kuantan, Malaysia .... **39 L4** 3 49N 103 20 E
Kuba = Quba, Azerbaijan .... **19 F8** 41 21N 48 32 E
Kuban ➤, Russia .... **19 E6** 45 20N 37 30 E
Kubokawa, Japan .... **31 H6** 33 12N 133 8 E
Kubu, Indonesia .... **37 J18** 8 16S 115 35 E
Kubutambahan, Indonesia .. **37 J18** 8 5S 115 10 E
Kucar, Tanjung, Indonesia .. **37 K18** 8 39S 114 34 E
Kucha Gompa, India .... **43 B7** 34 25N 76 56 E
Kuchaman, India .... **42 F6** 27 13N 74 47 E
Kuchinda, India .... **43 J11** 21 44N 84 21 E
Kuching, Malaysia .... **36 D4** 1 33N 110 25 E
Kuchino-eruba-Jima, Japan .. **31 J5** 30 28N 130 12 E
Kuchino-Shima, Japan ...... **31 K4** 29 57N 129 55 E
Kuchinotsu, Japan .... **31 H5** 32 36N 130 11 E
Kucing = Kuching, Malaysia .. **36 D4** 1 33N 110 25 E
Kud ➤, Pakistan .... **42 F2** 26 5N 66 20 E
Kuda, India .... **40 H7** 23 10N 71 15 E
Kudat, Malaysia .... **36 C5** 6 55N 116 55 E
Kudus, Indonesia .... **37 G14** 6 48S 110 51 E
Kudymkar, Russia .... **18 C9** 59 1N 54 39 E
Kueiyang = Guiyang, China .. **32 D5** 26 32N 106 40 E
Kufra Oasis = Al Kufrah, Libya **51 D10** 24 17N 23 15 E
Kufstein, Austria .... **16 E7** 47 35N 12 11 E
Kugaaruk = Pelly Bay, Canada **69 B11** 68 38N 89 50W
Kugluktuk, Canada **68 B8** 67 50N 115 5W
Kugong I., Canada **72 A4** 56 18N 79 50W
Kūhak, Iran .... **40 F3** 27 12N 63 10 E
Kuhan, Pakistan .... **42 E2** 28 19N 67 14 E
Kūhbonān, Iran .... **45 D8** 31 23N 56 19 E
Kūhestak, Iran .... **45 E8** 26 47N 57 2 E
Kuhin, Iran .... **45 B6** 36 22N 49 40 E
Kūhīrī, Iran .... **45 E9** 26 55N 61 2 E
Kūhpāyeh, Eşfahan, Iran .... **45 C7** 32 44N 52 20 E
Kūhpāyeh, Kermān, Iran .... **45 D8** 30 35N 57 15 E
Kūhrān, Kūh-e, Iran .... **45 E8** 26 46N 58 12 E
Kui Buri, Thailand .... **39 F2** 12 3N 99 52 E
Kuichong, China .... **33 F11** 22 38N 114 25 E
Kuiseb ➤, Namibia .... **56 C1** 22 59S 14 31 E
Kuito, Angola .... **53 G3** 12 22S 16 55 E
Kuiu I., U.S.A. **70 B2** 57 45N 134 10W
Kujang, N. Korea .... **35 E14** 39 57N 126 1 E
Kuji, Japan .... **30 D10** 40 11N 141 46 E
Kujū-San, Japan .... **31 H5** 33 5N 131 15 E
Kukës, Albania .... **23 C9** 42 5N 20 27 E
Kukup, India .... **42 H6** 23 10N 74 27 E
Kukup, Malaysia .... **39 d** 1 20N 103 27 E
Kukup, Pulau, Malaysia .... **39 d** 1 18N 103 25 E
Kula, Turkey .... **23 E13** 38 32N 28 40 E
Kulachi, Pakistan .... **42 D4** 31 56N 70 27 E
Kulai, Malaysia .... **39 M4** 1 44N 103 35 E
Kulasekarappattinam, India .. **40 Q11** 8 20N 78 5 E
Kuldīga, Latvia .... **9 H19** 56 58N 21 59 E
Kulen, Cambodia .... **38 F5** 13 50N 104 40 E
Kulgam, India .... **43 C6** 33 36N 75 2 E
Kulgera, Australia .... **62 D1** 25 50S 133 18 E
Kulim, Malaysia .... **39 K3** 5 22N 100 34 E
Kulin, Australia .... **61 F2** 32 40S 118 2 E

Kulkayu = Hartley Bay, Canada . **70 C3** 53 25N 129 15W
Kŭlob, Tajikistan .... **28 F7** 37 55N 69 50 E
Kulsary, Kazakhstan .... **19 E9** 46 59N 54 1 E
Kulti, India .... **43 H12** 23 43N 86 50 E
Kulumbura, Australia ...... **60 B4** 13 55N 126 35 E
Kulunda, Russia .... **28 D8** 52 35N 78 57 E
Kulungar, Afghan. .... **42 C3** 34 0N 69 2 E
Kūlvand, Iran .... **45 D7** 31 21N 54 35 E
Kulwin, Australia .... **63 F3** 35 0S 142 42 E
Kulyab = Kŭlob, Tajikistan .. **28 F7** 37 55N 69 50 E
Kuma ➤, Russia .... **19 F8** 44 55N 47 0 E
Kumagaya, Japan .... **31 F9** 36 9N 139 22 E
Kumai, Indonesia .... **36 E4** 2 44S 111 43 E
Kumamba, Kepulauan, Indonesia **37 E9** 1 36S 138 45 E
Kumamoto, Japan .... **31 H5** 32 45N 130 45 E
Kumamoto □, Japan ...... **31 H5** 32 55N 130 55 E
Kumanovo, Macedonia ...... **23 C9** 42 9N 21 42 E
Kumara, N.Z. .... **59 K3** 42 37S 171 12 E
Kumarina, Australia .... **61 D2** 24 41S 119 32 E
Kumasi, Ghana **50 G5** 6 41N 1 38W
Kumba, Cameroon .... **52 D1** 4 36N 9 24 E
Kumbakonam, India .... **40 P11** 10 58N 79 25 E
Kumbarilla, Australia ...... **63 D5** 27 15S 150 55 E
Kumbhraj, India .... **42 G7** 24 22N 77 3 E
Kumbia, Australia .... **63 D5** 26 41S 151 39 E
Kŭmch'ŏn, N. Korea .... **35 E14** 38 10N 126 29 E
Kumdok, India .... **43 C8** 33 32N 78 10 E
Kume-Shima, Japan .... **31 L3** 26 20N 126 47 E
Kumertau, Russia .... **18 D10** 52 45N 55 57 E
Kumharsain, India .... **42 D7** 31 19N 77 27 E
Kŭmhwa, S. Korea .... **35 E14** 38 17N 127 28 E
Kumi, Uganda .... **54 B3** 1 30N 33 58 E
Kumla, Sweden .... **9 G16** 59 8N 15 10 E
Kumo, Nigeria .... **51 F8** 10 1N 11 12 E
Kumon Bum, Burma .... **41 F20** 26 30N 97 15 E
Kunashir, Ostrov, Russia .... **29 E15** 44 0N 146 0 E
Kunda, Estonia .... **9 G22** 59 30N 26 34 E
Kunda, India .... **43 G9** 25 43N 81 31 E
Kundar ➤, Pakistan .... **42 D3** 31 56N 69 19 E
Kundelungu △, Dem. Rep. of
the Congo .... **55 E2** 10 30S 27 40 E
Kundelungu Ouest △, Dem. Rep.
of the Congo .... **55 D2** 9 55S 27 17 E
Kundian, Pakistan .... **42 C4** 32 27N 71 28 E
Kundla, India .... **42 J4** 21 21N 71 25 E
Kung, Ao, Thailand .... **39 a** 8 5N 98 24 E
Kunga ➤, Bangla. .... **43 J13** 21 46N 89 30 E
Kunghit I., Canada **70 C2** 52 6N 131 3W
Kungrad = Qŭnghirot, Uzbekistan **28 E6** 43 6N 58 54 E
Kungsbacka, Sweden ...... **9 H15** 57 30N 12 5 E
Kungur, Russia .... **18 C10** 57 25N 56 57 E
Kungurri, Australia .... **62 K6** 21 4S 148 45 E
Kunhar ➤, Pakistan ...... **43 B5** 34 20N 73 30 E
Kuningan, Indonesia ...... **37 G13** 6 59S 108 29 E
Kunlong, Burma .... **41 H21** 23 20N 98 50 E
Kunlun Shan, Asia .... **32 C3** 36 0N 86 30 E
Kunming, China .... **32 D5** 25 1N 102 41 E
Kunsan, S. Korea .... **35 G14** 35 59N 126 45 E
Kununurra, Australia ...... **60 C4** 15 40S 128 50 E
Kunwari ➤, India .... **43 F8** 26 26N 79 11 E
Kunya-Urgench = Köneürgench,
Turkmenistan .... **28 E6** 42 19N 59 10 E
Kuopio, Finland .... **8 E22** 62 53N 27 35 E
Kupa ➤, Croatia .... **16 F9** 45 28N 16 24 E
Kupang, Indonesia .... **37 F6** 10 19S 123 39 E
Kupreanof I., U.S.A. **70 B2** 56 50N 133 30W
Kupyansk-Uzlovoi, Ukraine .. **19 E6** 49 40N 37 43 E
Kuqa, China .... **32 B3** 41 35N 82 30 E
Kür ➤, Azerbaijan .... **19 G8** 39 29N 49 15 E
Kür Dili, Azerbaijan ...... **45 B6** 39 3N 49 13 E
Kura = Kür ➤, Azerbaijan .. **19 G8** 39 29N 49 15 E
Kuranda, Australia .... **62 B4** 16 48S 145 35 E
Kuranga, India .... **42 H3** 22 4N 69 10 E
Kurashiki, Japan .... **31 G6** 34 40N 133 50 E
Kurayoshi, Japan .... **31 G6** 35 26N 133 50 E
Kürdzhali, Bulgaria .... **23 D11** 41 38N 25 21 E
Kure, Japan .... **31 G6** 34 14N 132 32 E
Kuressaare, Estonia ...... **9 G20** 58 15N 22 30 E
Kurgan, Russia .... **28 D7** 55 26N 65 18 E
Kuri, India .... **42 F4** 26 37N 70 43 E
Kuria Maria Is. = Khuriyā Muriyā,
Jazā'ir, Oman .... **47 D6** 17 30N 55 58 E
Kuridala, Australia .... **62 C3** 21 16S 140 29 E
Kurigram, Bangla. .... **41 G16** 25 49N 89 39 E
Kurikka, Finland .... **9 E20** 62 36N 22 24 E
Kuril Is. = Kurilskiye Ostrova,
Russia .... **29 E15** 45 0N 150 0 E
Kuril Trench, Pac. Oc. ...... **26 E19** 44 0N 153 0 E
Kurilsk, Russia .... **29 E15** 45 14N 147 53 E
Kurilskiye Ostrova, Russia .. **29 E15** 45 0N 150 0 E
Kurino, Japan .... **31 J5** 31 57N 130 43 E
Kurinskaya Kosa = Kür Dili,
Azerbaijan .... **45 B6** 39 3N 49 13 E
Kurnool, India .... **40 M11** 15 45N 78 0 E
Kuro-Shima, Kagoshima, Japan **31 J4** 30 50N 129 57 E
Kuro-Shima, Okinawa, Japan . **31 M2** 24 14N 124 1 E
Kurow, N.Z. .... **59 L3** 44 4S 170 29 E
Kurram ➤, Pakistan ...... **42 C4** 32 36N 71 20 E
Kurri Kurri, Australia ...... **63 E5** 32 50S 151 28 E
Kurrimine, Australia ...... **62 B4** 17 47S 146 6 E
Kurshskiy Zaliv, Russia .... **9 J19** 55 9N 21 6 E
Kursk, Russia .... **18 D6** 51 42N 36 11 E
Kuruçay, Turkey .... **44 B3** 39 39N 38 29 E
Kuruktag, China .... **32 B3** 41 0N 89 0 E
Kuruman, S. Africa .... **56 D3** 27 28S 23 28 E
Kuruman ➤, S. Africa ...... **56 D3** 26 56S 20 39 E
Kurume, Japan .... **31 H5** 33 15N 130 30 E
Kurunegala, Sri Lanka ...... **40 R12** 7 30N 80 23 E
Kurya, Russia .... **18 B10** 61 42N 57 9 E
Kuş Gölü, Turkey .... **23 D12** 40 10N 27 55 E
Kuşadası, Turkey .... **23 F12** 37 52N 27 15 E
Kusadasi, Indonesia ...... **37 K18** 8 34S 115 27 E
Kusatsu, Japan .... **31 F9** 36 37N 138 36 E
Kusawa L., Canada **70 A1** 60 20N 136 13W
Kushalgarh, India .... **42 H6** 23 10N 74 27 E
Kushikino, Japan .... **31 J5** 31 29N 131 14 E
Kushima, Japan .... **31 J5** 31 29N 131 14 E
Kushimoto, Japan .... **31 H7** 33 28N 135 47 E
Kushiro, Japan .... **30 C12** 43 0N 144 25 E
Kushiro-Gawa ➤, Japan .... **30 C12** 42 59N 144 23 E
Kushiro Shitsugen △, Japan . **30 C12** 43 0N 144 26 E
Kushka = Gushgy, Turkmenistan **28 F7** 35 20N 62 18 E
Kūshk, Iran .... **44 C5** 33 31N 47 13 E
Kushol, India .... **43 C7** 33 40N 76 36 E
Kushtia, Bangla. .... **41 H16** 23 55N 89 5 E
Kushva, Russia .... **18 C10** 58 18N 59 45 E

Kuskokwim B., *U.S.A.* **68 C3** 59 45N 162 25W
Kusmi, *India* .... **43 H10** 23 17N 83 55 E
Kussharo-Ko, *Japan* .... **30 C12** 43 38N 144 21 E
Kustanay = Qostanay,
  Kazakhstan .... **28 D7** 53 10N 63 35 E
Kut, Ko, *Thailand* .... **39 G4** 11 40N 102 35 E
Kuta, *Indonesia* .... **37 K18** 8 43S 115 11 E
Kütahya, *Turkey* .... **19 G5** 39 30N 30 2 E
Kutaisi, *Georgia* .... **19 F7** 42 19N 42 40 E
Kutaraja = Banda Aceh,
  Indonesia .... **36 C1** 5 35N 95 20 E
Kutch, Gulf of = Kachchh, Gulf of,
  India .... **42 H3** 22 50N 69 15 E
Kutch, Rann of = Kachchh, Rann
  of, *India* .... **42 H4** 24 0N 70 0 E
Kutiyana, *India* .... **42 J4** 21 36N 70 2 E
Kutno, *Poland* .... **17 B10** 52 15N 19 23 E
Kutse, *Botswana* .... **56 C3** 21 7S 22 16 E
Kuttabul, *Australia* .... **62 K6** 21 1S 148 54 E
Kutu, *Dem. Rep. of the Congo* .... **52 E3** 2 40S 18 11 E
Kutum, *Sudan* .... **51 F10** 14 10N 24 40 E
Kuujjuaq, *Canada* **69 C13** 58 6N 68 15W
Kuujjuarapik, *Canada* **72 A4** 55 20N 77 35W
Kuup-tong, *N. Korea* .... **35 D14** 40 45N 126 1 E
Kuusamo, *Finland* .... **8 D23** 65 57N 29 8 E
Kuusankoski, *Finland* .... **9 F22** 60 55N 26 38 E
Kuwait = Al Kuwayt, *Kuwait* .... **44 D5** 29 30N 48 0 E
Kuwait ■, *Asia* .... **44 D5** 29 30N 47 30 E
Kuwana, *Japan* .... **31 G8** 35 5N 136 43 E
Kuwana →, *India* .... **43 F10** 26 25N 83 15 E
Kuybyshev = Samara, *Russia* .... **18 D9** 53 8N 50 6 E
Kuybyshev, *Russia* .... **28 D8** 55 27N 78 19 E
Kuybyshevskoye Vdkhr., *Russia* .... **18 C8** 55 2N 49 30 E
Kuye He →, *China* .... **34 E6** 38 23N 110 46 E
Küyeh, *Iran* .... **44 B5** 38 45N 47 57 E
Kuyto, Ozero, *Russia* .... **18 B5** 65 6N 31 20 E
Kuyumba, *Russia* .... **29 C10** 60 58N 96 59 E
Kuzey Anadolu Dağları, *Turkey* .... **19 F6** 41 30N 35 0 E
Kuznetsk, *Russia* .... **18 D8** 53 12N 46 40 E
Kuzomen, *Russia* .... **18 A6** 66 22N 36 50 E
Kvænangen, *Norway* .... **8 A19** 70 5N 21 15 E
Kvaløy, *Norway* .... **8 B18** 69 40N 18 30 E
Kvarner, *Croatia* .... **16 F8** 44 50N 14 10 E
Kvarnerič, *Croatia* .... **16 F8** 44 43N 14 37 E
Kwa-Nobuhle, *S. Africa* .... **53 L5** 33 50S 25 22 E
Kwabhaca, *S. Africa* .... **57 E4** 30 51S 29 0 E
Kwakhanai, *Botswana* .... **56 C3** 21 39S 21 16 E
Kwakoegron, *Suriname* **93 B7** 5 12N 55 25W
Kwale, *Kenya* .... **54 C4** 4 15S 39 31 E
KwaMashu, *S. Africa* .... **57 D5** 29 45S 30 58 E
Kwando →, *Africa* .... **56 B3** 18 27S 23 32 E
Kwangchow = Guangzhou, *China* **33 D6** 23 5N 113 10 E
Kwangdaeri, *N. Korea* .... **35 D14** 40 31N 127 32 E
Kwangju, *S. Korea* .... **35 G14** 35 9N 126 54 E
Kwango →, *Dem. Rep. of
  the Congo* .... **52 E3** 3 14S 17 22 E
Kwangsi-Chuang = Guangxi
  Zhuangzu Zizhiqu □, *China* .. **33 D5** 24 0N 109 0 E
Kwangtung = Guangdong □,
  China .... **33 D6** 23 0N 113 0 E
Kwataboahegan →, *Canada* .. **72 B3** 51 9N 80 50W
Kwatisore, *Indonesia* .... **37 E8** 3 18S 134 50 E
KwaZulu Natal □, *S. Africa* .. **57 D5** 29 0S 30 0 E
Kweichow = Guizhou □, *China* .. **32 D5** 27 0N 107 0 E
Kwekwe, *Zimbabwe* .... **55 F2** 18 58S 29 48 E
Kwidzyn, *Poland* .... **17 B10** 53 44N 18 55 E
Kwinana New Town, *Australia* .. **61 F2** 32 15S 115 47 E
Kwoka, *Indonesia* .... **37 E8** 0 31S 132 27 E
Kwun Tong, *China* .... **33 G11** 22 19N 114 13 E
Kyabra Cr. →, *Australia* .. **63 D3** 25 36S 142 55 E
Kyabram, *Australia* .... **63 F4** 36 19S 145 4 E
Kyaikto, *Burma* .... **38 D1** 17 20N 97 3 E
Kyakhta, *Russia* .... **29 D11** 50 30N 106 25 E
Kyambura △, *Uganda* .... **54 C3** 0 7S 30 9 E
Kyancutta, *Australia* .... **63 E2** 33 8S 135 33 E
Kyaukpadaung, *Burma* .... **41 J19** 20 52N 95 8 E
Kyaukpyu, *Burma* .... **41 K18** 19 28N 93 30 E
Kyaukse, *Burma* .... **41 J20** 21 36N 96 10 E
Kyburz, *U.S.A.* **78 G6** 38 47N 120 18W
Kyelang, *India* .... **42 C7** 32 35N 77 2 E
Kyenjojo, *Uganda* .... **54 B3** 0 40N 30 37 E
Kyle, *Canada* **71 C7** 50 50N 108 2W
Kyle Dam, *Zimbabwe* .... **55 G3** 20 15S 31 0 E
Kyle of Lochalsh, *U.K.* **11 D3** 57 17N 5 44W
Kymijoki →, *Finland* .... **9 F22** 60 30N 26 55 E
Kyneton, *Australia* .... **63 F3** 37 10S 144 29 E
Kynuna, *Australia* .... **62 C3** 21 37S 141 55 E
Kyō-ga-Saki, *Japan* .... **31 G7** 35 45N 135 15 E
Kyoga, L., *Uganda* .... **54 B3** 1 35N 33 0 E
Kyogle, *Australia* .... **63 D5** 28 40S 153 0 E
Kyongju, *S. Korea* .... **35 G15** 35 51N 129 14 E
Kyongpyaw, *Burma* .... **41 L19** 17 12N 95 10 E
Kyŏngsŏng, *N. Korea* .... **35 D15** 41 35N 129 36 E
Kyōto, *Japan* .... **31 G7** 35 0N 135 45 E
Kyōto □, *Japan* .... **31 G7** 35 15N 135 45 E
Kyparissovouno, *Cyprus* .... **25 D12** 35 19N 33 10 E
Kyperounda, *Cyprus* .... **25 E11** 34 56N 32 58 E
Kyrenia, *Cyprus* .... **25 D12** 35 20N 33 20 E
Kyrgyzstan ■, *Asia* .... **28 E8** 42 0N 75 0 E
Kyrönjoki →, *Finland* .... **8 E19** 63 14N 21 45 E
Kystatyam, *Russia* .... **29 C13** 67 20N 123 10 E
Kythréa, *Cyprus* .... **25 D12** 35 15N 33 29 E
Kyunhla, *Burma* .... **41 H19** 23 25N 95 15 E
Kyuquot Sound, *Canada* **70 D3** 50 2N 127 22W
Kyūshū, *Japan* .... **31 H5** 33 0N 131 0 E
Kyūshū □, *Japan* .... **31 H5** 33 0N 131 0 E
Kyūshū-Sanchi, *Japan* .... **31 H5** 32 35N 131 17 E
Kyustendil, *Bulgaria* .... **23 C10** 42 16N 22 41 E
Kyusyur, *Russia* .... **29 B13** 70 19N 127 30 E
Kyyiv, *Ukraine* .... **17 C16** 50 30N 30 28 E
Kyyivske Vdskh., *Ukraine* .... **17 C16** 51 0N 30 25 E
Kyzyl, *Russia* .... **29 D10** 51 50N 94 30 E
Kyzyl Kum, *Uzbekistan* .... **28 E7** 42 30N 65 0 E
Kyzyl-Kyya, *Kyrgyzstan* .... **28 E8** 40 16N 72 8 E
Kyzyl-Orda = Qyzylorda,
  Kazakhstan .... **28 E7** 44 48N 65 28 E

L

La Alcarria, *Spain* **21 B4** 40 31N 2 45W
La Amistad △, *Cent. Amer.* .. **88 E3** 9 28N 83 18W
La Asunción, *Venezuela* **92 A6** 11 2N 63 53W
La Baie, *Canada* **73 C5** 48 19N 70 53W
La Banda, *Argentina* **94 B3** 27 45S 64 10W
La Barca, *Mexico* **86 C4** 20 20N 102 40W

La Barge, *U.S.A.* **76 E8** 42 16N 110 12W
La Belle, *U.S.A.* **83 M5** 26 46N 81 26W
La Biche →, *Canada* **70 B4** 59 57N 123 50W
La Biche, L., *Canada* **70 C6** 54 50N 112 5W
La Blanquilla, *Venezuela* **89 D7** 11 51N 64 37W
La Bomba, *Mexico* **86 A1** 31 53N 115 2W
La Brea, *Trin. & Tob.* **93 K15** 10 15N 61 37W
La Calera, *Chile* **94 C1** 32 50S 71 10W
La Campana △, *Chile* **94 C1** 32 58S 71 14W
La Canal = Sa Canal, *Spain* .. **24 C7** 38 51N 1 23 E
La Carlota, *Argentina* **94 C3** 33 30S 63 20W
La Ceiba, *Honduras* **88 C2** 15 40N 86 50W
La Chaux-de-Fonds, *Switz.* .. **20 C7** 47 7N 6 50 E
La Chorrera, *Panama* **88 E4** 8 53N 79 47W
La Cocha, *Argentina* **94 B2** 27 50S 65 40W
La Concepción, *Panama* **88 E3** 8 31N 82 37W
La Concordia, *Mexico* **87 D6** 16 8N 92 38W
La Coruña = A Coruña, *Spain* .. **21 A1** 43 20N 8 25W
La Crescent, *U.S.A.* **80 D9** 43 50N 91 18W
La Crosse, *Kans., U.S.A.* **80 F5** 38 32N 99 18W
La Crosse, *Wis., U.S.A.* **80 D9** 43 48N 91 15W
La Cruz, *Costa Rica* **88 D2** 11 4N 85 39W
La Cruz, *Mexico* **86 C3** 23 55N 106 54W
La Désirade, *Guadeloupe* .... **88 b** 16 18N 61 3W
La Escondida, *Mexico* **86 C5** 24 6N 99 55W
La Esmeralda, *Paraguay* **94 A3** 22 16S 62 33W
La Esperanza, *Cuba* **88 B3** 22 46N 83 44W
La Esperanza, *Honduras* **88 D2** 14 15N 88 10W
La Estrada = A Estrada, *Spain* .. **21 A1** 42 43N 8 27W
La Fayette, *U.S.A.* **83 H3** 34 42N 85 17W
La Fé, *Cuba* **88 B3** 22 2N 84 15W
La Follette, *U.S.A.* **83 G3** 36 23N 84 7W
La Grande, *U.S.A.* **76 D4** 45 20N 118 5W
La Grande →, *Canada* **72 B5** 53 50N 79 0W
La Grande Deux, Rés., *Canada* .. **72 B4** 53 40N 76 55W
La Grande Quatre, Rés., *Canada* **72 B5** 54 0N 73 15W
La Grande Trois, Rés., *Canada* .. **72 B4** 53 40N 75 10W
La Grange, *Calif., U.S.A.* **78 H6** 37 42N 120 27W
La Grange, *Ga., U.S.A.* **83 J3** 33 2N 85 2W
La Grange, *Ky., U.S.A.* **82 F3** 38 25N 85 23W
La Grange, *Tex., U.S.A.* **81 L6** 29 54N 96 52W
La Guaira, *Venezuela* **92 A5** 10 36N 66 56W
La Habana, *Cuba* **88 B3** 23 8N 82 22W
La Independencia, *Mexico* **87 D6** 16 31N 91 47W
La Isabela, *Dom. Rep.* **89 C5** 19 58N 71 2W
La Junta, *U.S.A.* **81 F3** 37 59N 103 33W
La Laguna, *Canary Is.* **24 F3** 28 28N 16 18W
La Libertad, *Guatemala* **88 C1** 16 47N 90 7W
La Libertad, *Mexico* **86 B2** 29 55N 112 41W
La Ligua, *Chile* **94 C1** 32 30S 71 16W
La Línea de la Concepción, *Spain* **21 D3** 36 15N 5 23W
La Loche, *Canada* **71 B7** 56 29N 109 26W
La Louvière, *Belgium* .... **15 D4** 50 27N 4 10 E
La Lune, *Trin. & Tob.* **93 K15** 10 3N 61 22W
La Malbaie, *Canada* **73 C5** 47 40N 70 10W
La Malinche △, *Mexico* **87 D5** 19 15N 98 3W
La Mancha, *Spain* **21 C4** 39 10N 2 54W
La Martre, L., *Canada* **70 A5** 63 15N 117 55W
La Mesa, *U.S.A.* **79 N9** 32 46N 117 3W
La Misión, *Mexico* **86 A1** 32 5N 116 50W
La Moure, *U.S.A.* **80 B5** 46 21N 98 18W
La Negra, *Chile* **94 A1** 23 46S 70 18W
La Oliva, *Canary Is.* **24 F6** 28 36N 13 57W
La Orotava, *Canary Is.* **24 F3** 28 22N 16 31W
La Oroya, *Peru* **92 F3** 11 32S 75 54W
La Palma, *Canary Is.* **24 F2** 28 40N 17 50W
La Palma, *Panama* **88 E4** 8 15N 78 0W
La Palma del Condado, *Spain* .. **21 D2** 37 21N 6 38W
La Paloma, *Chile* **94 C1** 30 35S 71 0W
La Pampa □, *Argentina* **94 D2** 36 50S 66 0W
La Paragua, *Venezuela* **92 B6** 6 50N 63 20W
La Paz, *Entre Ríos, Argentina* .. **94 C4** 30 50S 59 45W
La Paz, *San Luis, Argentina* .. **94 C2** 33 30S 67 20W
La Paz, *Bolivia* **92 G5** 16 20S 68 10W
La Paz, *Honduras* **88 D2** 14 20N 87 47W
La Paz, *Mexico* **86 C2** 24 10N 110 20W
La Paz Centro, *Nic.* **88 D2** 12 20N 86 41W
La Pedrera, *Colombia* **92 D5** 1 18S 69 43W
La Pérade, *Canada* **73 C5** 46 35N 72 12W
La Perouse Str., *Asia* .... **30 B11** 45 40N 142 0 E
La Pesca, *Mexico* **87 C5** 23 46N 97 47W
La Piedad, *Mexico* **86 C4** 20 20N 102 1W
La Pine, *U.S.A.* **76 E3** 43 40N 121 30W
La Plata, *Argentina* **94 D4** 35 0S 57 55W
La Pocatière, *Canada* **73 C5** 47 22N 70 2W
La Porte, *Ind., U.S.A.* **82 E2** 41 36N 86 43W
La Porte, *Tex., U.S.A.* **81 L7** 29 39N 95 1W
La Purísima, *Mexico* **86 B2** 26 10N 112 4W
La Push, *U.S.A.* **78 C2** 47 55N 124 38W
La Quiaca, *Argentina* **94 A2** 22 5S 65 35W
La Restinga, *Canary Is.* **24 G2** 27 38N 17 59W
La Rioja, *Argentina* **94 B2** 29 20S 67 0W
La Rioja □, *Argentina* **94 B2** 29 30S 67 0W
La Rioja □, *Spain* **21 A4** 42 20N 2 20W
La Robla, *Spain* **21 A3** 42 50N 5 41W
La Roche-en-Ardenne, *Belgium* **15 D5** 50 11N 5 35 E
La Roche-sur-Yon, *France* **20 C3** 46 40N 1 25W
La Rochelle, *France* **20 C3** 46 10N 1 9W
La Roda, *Spain* **21 C4** 39 13N 2 15W
La Romana, *Dom. Rep.* **89 C6** 18 27N 68 57W
La Rumorosa, *Mexico* **79 N10** 32 33N 116 4W
La Sabina = Sa Savina, *Spain* .. **24 C7** 38 44N 1 25 E
La Salle, *U.S.A.* **80 E10** 41 20N 89 6W
La Santa, *Canary Is.* **24 E6** 29 5N 13 40W
La Sarre, *Canada* **72 C4** 48 45N 79 15W
La Scie, *Canada* **73 C8** 49 57N 55 36W
La Selva Beach, *U.S.A.* **78 J5** 36 56N 121 51W
La Serena, *Chile* **94 B1** 29 55S 71 10W
La Seu d'Urgell, *Spain* .... **21 A6** 42 22N 1 23 E
La Seyne-sur-Mer, *France* .... **20 E6** 43 7N 5 52 E
La Soufrière, *St. Vincent* **89 D7** 13 20N 61 11W
La Spézia, *Italy* .... **20 D8** 44 7N 9 50 E
La Tagua, *Colombia* **92 C4** 0 3N 74 40W
La Tortuga, *Venezuela* **89 D6** 11 0N 65 22W
La Trinité, *Martinique* .... **88 c** 14 43N 60 58W
La Tuque, *Canada* **72 C5** 47 30N 72 50W
La Unión, *Chile* **96 E2** 40 10S 73 0W
La Unión, *El Salv.* **88 D2** 13 20N 87 50W
La Urbana, *Venezuela* **92 B5** 7 8N 66 56W
La Vache Pt., *Trin. & Tob.* **93 K15** 10 47N 61 37W
La Vall d'Uixó, *Spain* **21 C5** 39 49N 0 15W
La Vega, *Dom. Rep.* **89 C5** 19 20N 70 30W
La Vela de Coro, *Venezuela* .. **92 A5** 11 27N 69 34W
La Venta, *Mexico* **87 D6** 18 8N 94 3W

La Ventura, *Mexico* **86 C4** 24 38N 100 54W
Laas Caanood = Las Anod,
  Somali Rep. .... **47 F4** 8 26N 47 19 E
Labasa, *Fiji* .... **59 C8** 16 30S 179 27 E
Labe = Elbe →, *Europe* .... **16 B5** 53 50N 9 0 E
Labé, *Guinea* **50 F3** 11 24N 12 16W
Laberge, L., *Canada* **70 A1** 61 11N 135 12W
Labinsk, *Russia* .... **19 F7** 44 40N 40 48 E
Labis, *Malaysia* .... **39 L4** 2 22N 103 2 E
Laborie, *St. Lucia* .... **89 f** 13 45N 61 2W
Laboulaye, *Argentina* **94 C3** 34 10S 63 30W
Labrador, *Canada* **73 B7** 53 20N 61 0W
Labrador City, *Canada* **73 B6** 52 57N 66 55W
Labrador Sea, Atl. Oc. **69 C14** 57 0N 54 0W
Lábrea, *Brazil* **92 E6** 7 15S 64 51W
Labuan, *Malaysia* .... **36 C5** 5 20N 115 14 E
Labuan, Pulau, *Malaysia* .... **36 C5** 5 21N 115 13 E
Labuha, *Indonesia* .... **37 E7** 0 30S 127 30 E
Labuhan, *Indonesia* .... **37 G11** 6 22S 105 50 E
Labuhanbajo, *Indonesia* .... **37 F6** 8 28S 119 54 E
Labuk, Telok, *Malaysia* .... **36 C5** 6 10N 117 50 E
Labyrinth, L., *Australia* .... **63 E2** 30 40S 135 11 E
Labytnangi, *Russia* .... **28 C7** 66 39N 66 21 E
Lac-Bouchette, *Canada* **73 C5** 48 16N 72 11W
Lac La Biche, *Canada* **70 C6** 54 45N 111 58W
Lac la Martre = Wha Ti, *Canada* **68 B8** 63 8N 117 16W
Lac La Ronge △, *Canada* **71 B7** 55 9N 104 41W
Lac-Mégantic, *Canada* **73 C5** 45 35N 70 53W
Lac Thien, *Vietnam* .... **38 F7** 12 25N 108 11 E
Lacanau, *France* **20 D3** 44 58N 1 5W
Lacantún →, *Mexico* **87 D6** 16 36N 90 40W
Laccadive Is. = Lakshadweep Is.,
  India .... **27 H11** 10 0N 72 30 E
Lacepede B., *Australia* .... **63 F2** 36 40S 139 40 E
Lacepede Is., *Australia* .... **60 C3** 16 55S 122 0 E
Lacerdónia, *Mozam.* .... **55 F4** 18 3S 35 35 E
Lacey, *U.S.A.* **78 C4** 47 7N 122 49W
Lachhmangarh, *India* .... **42 F6** 27 50N 75 4 E
Lachi, *Pakistan* .... **42 C4** 33 25N 71 20 E
Lachine, *Canada* **72 C5** 45 30N 73 40W
Lachlan →, *Australia* .... **63 E3** 34 22S 143 55 E
Lachute, *Canada* **72 C5** 45 39N 74 21W
Lackawanna, *U.S.A.* **84 D6** 42 50N 78 50W
Lackawaxen, *U.S.A.* **85 E10** 41 29N 74 59W
Lacolle, *Canada* **85 A11** 45 5N 73 22W
Lacombe, *Canada* **70 C6** 52 30N 113 44W
Lacona, *U.S.A.* **85 C8** 43 39N 76 10W
Laconia, *U.S.A.* **85 C13** 43 32N 71 28W
Ladakh Ra., *India* .... **43 C8** 34 0N 78 0 E
Ladismith, *S. Africa* .... **56 E3** 33 28S 21 15 E
Lādīz, *Iran* .... **45 D9** 28 55N 61 15 E
Ladnun, *India* .... **42 F6** 27 38N 74 25 E
Ladoga, L. = Ladozhskoye Ozero,
  Russia .... **18 B5** 61 15N 30 30 E
Ladozhskoye Ozero, *Russia* .. **18 B5** 61 15N 30 30 E
Lady Elliott I., *Australia* .... **62 C5** 24 7S 152 42 E
Lady Grey, *S. Africa* .... **56 E4** 30 43S 27 13 E
Ladybrand, *S. Africa* .... **56 D4** 29 9S 27 29 E
Ladysmith, *Canada* **70 D4** 49 0N 123 49W
Ladysmith, *S. Africa* .... **57 D4** 28 32S 29 46 E
Ladysmith, *U.S.A.* **80 C9** 45 28N 91 12W
Lae, *Papua N. G.* .... **64 H6** 6 40S 147 2 E
Laem Hin Khom, *Thailand* .... **39 b** 9 25N 99 56 E
Laem Khat, *Thailand* .... **39 a** 8 6N 98 26 E
Laem Nga, *Thailand* .... **39 a** 7 55N 98 27 E
Laem Ngop, *Thailand* .... **39 F4** 12 10N 102 26 E
Laem Phan Wa, *Thailand* .... **39 a** 7 40N 98 24 E
Laem Pho, *Thailand* .... **39 J3** 6 55N 101 19 E
Laem Phrom Thep, *Thailand* .. **39 a** 7 45N 98 19 E
Laem Riang, *Thailand* .... **39 a** 8 7N 98 27 E
Laem Sam Rong, *Thailand* .... **39 b** 9 35N 100 4 E
Laem Son, *Thailand* .... **39 a** 7 59N 98 16 E
Laem Yamu, *Thailand* .... **39 a** 7 59N 98 26 E
Læsø, *Denmark* .... **9 H14** 57 15N 11 5 E
Lafayette, *Colo., U.S.A.* **80 F2** 39 58N 105 12W
Lafayette, *Ind., U.S.A.* **82 E2** 40 25N 86 54W
Lafayette, *La., U.S.A.* **81 K9** 30 14N 92 1W
Lafayette, *Tenn., U.S.A.* **83 G2** 36 31N 86 2W
Laferte →, *Canada* **70 A5** 61 53N 117 44W
Lafia, *Nigeria* .... **50 G7** 8 30N 8 34 E
Lafleche, *Canada* **71 D7** 49 45N 106 40W
Lagan →, *U.K.* **10 B6** 54 36N 5 55W
Lagarfljót →, *Iceland* **8 D6** 65 40N 14 18W
Lågen →, *Oppland, Norway* .. **9 F14** 61 8N 10 25 E
Lågen →, *Vestfold, Norway* .. **9 G14** 59 3N 10 3 E
Laghouat, *Algeria* .... **50 B6** 33 50N 2 59 E
Lagoa do Peixe △, *Brazil* **95 C5** 31 12S 50 55W
Lagoa Vermelha, *Brazil* **95 B5** 28 13S 51 32W
Lagonoy G., *Phil.* .... **37 B6** 13 35N 123 50 E
Lagos, *Nigeria* .... **50 G6** 6 25N 3 27 E
Lagos, *Portugal* **21 D1** 37 5N 8 41W
Lagos de Moreno, *Mexico* **86 C4** 21 20N 101 55W
Lagrange, *Australia* .... **60 C3** 18 45S 121 43 E
Lagrange B., *Australia* .... **60 C3** 18 38S 121 42 E
Laguna, *Brazil* **95 B6** 28 30S 48 50W
Laguna, *U.S.A.* **77 J10** 35 2N 107 25W
Laguna Beach, *U.S.A.* **79 M9** 33 33N 117 47W
Laguna de la Restinga △,
  Venezuela **89 D6** 10 58N 64 0W
Laguna del Laja △, *Chile* **94 D1** 37 27S 71 20W
Laguna del Tigre △, *Guatemala* **88 C1** 17 32N 90 56W
Laguna Limpia, *Argentina* **94 B4** 26 32S 59 45W
Lagunas, *Chile* **94 A2** 21 0S 69 45W
Lagunas, *Peru* **92 E3** 5 10S 75 35W
Lagunas de Chacahua △, *Mexico* **87 D5** 16 0N 97 43W
Lagunas de Montebello △,
  Mexico **87 D6** 16 6N 91 30W
Lahad Datu, *Malaysia* .... **37 C5** 5 0N 118 20 E
Lahad Datu, Teluk, *Malaysia* .. **37 D5** 4 50N 118 20 E
Lahan Sai, *Thailand* .... **38 E4** 14 25N 102 52 E
Lahanam, *Laos* .... **38 D5** 16 16N 105 16 E
Lahar, *India* .... **43 F8** 26 12N 78 57 E
Laharpur, *India* .... **43 F9** 27 43N 80 56 E
Lahat, *Indonesia* .... **36 E2** 3 45S 103 30 E
Lāhījān, *Iran* .... **45 B6** 37 10N 50 6 E
Lahn →, *Germany* .... **16 C4** 50 19N 7 37 E
Laholm, *Sweden* .... **9 H15** 56 30N 13 2 E
Lahore, *Pakistan* .... **42 D6** 31 32N 74 22 E
Lahore □, *Pakistan* .... **42 E3** 29 11N 68 13 E
Lahti, *Finland* .... **9 F21** 60 58N 25 40 E
Lahtis = Lahti, *Finland* .... **9 F21** 60 58N 25 40 E
Laï, *Chad* .... **51 G9** 9 25N 16 18 E
Lai Chau, *Vietnam* .... **38 A4** 22 5N 103 3 E
Laila = Layla, *Si. Arabia* .... **47 C4** 22 10N 46 40 E
Laingsburg, *S. Africa* .... **56 E3** 33 9S 20 52 E

Lainio älv →, *Sweden* .... **8 C20** 67 35N 22 40 E
Lairg, *U.K.* **11 C4** 58 2N 4 24W
Laishui, *China* .... **34 E8** 39 23N 115 45 E
Laiwu, *China* .... **35 F9** 36 15N 117 40 E
Laixi, *China* .... **35 F11** 36 50N 120 31 E
Laiyang, *China* .... **35 F11** 36 59N 120 45 E
Laiyuan, *China* .... **34 E8** 39 20N 114 40 E
Laizhou, *China* .... **35 F10** 37 8N 119 57 E
Laizhou Wan, *China* .... **35 F10** 37 30N 119 30 E
Laja →, *Mexico* **86 C4** 20 55N 100 46W
Lajes, *Brazil* **95 B5** 27 48S 50 20W
Lak Sao, *Laos* .... **38 C5** 18 11N 104 59 E
Lakaband, *Pakistan* .... **42 D3** 31 2N 69 15 E
Lake Alpine, *U.S.A.* **78 G7** 38 29N 120 0W
Lake Andes, *U.S.A.* **80 D5** 43 9N 98 32W
Lake Arthur, *U.S.A.* **81 K8** 30 5N 92 41W
Lake Bindegolly △, *Australia* .. **63 D3** 28 0S 144 12 E
Lake Cargelligo, *Australia* .... **63 E4** 33 15S 146 22 E
Lake Charles, *U.S.A.* **81 K8** 30 14N 93 13W
Lake City, *Colo., U.S.A.* **77 G10** 38 2N 107 19W
Lake City, *Fla., U.S.A.* **83 K4** 30 11N 82 38W
Lake City, *Mich., U.S.A.* **82 C3** 44 20N 85 13W
Lake City, *Minn., U.S.A.* **80 C8** 44 27N 92 16W
Lake City, *Pa., U.S.A.* **84 D4** 42 1N 80 21W
Lake City, *S.C., U.S.A.* **83 J6** 33 52N 79 45W
Lake Cowichan, *Canada* **70 D4** 48 49N 124 3W
Lake District △, *U.K.* **12 C4** 54 30N 3 21W
Lake Elsinore, *U.S.A.* **79 M9** 33 38N 117 20W
Lake Eyre △, *Australia* .... **63 D2** 28 40S 137 31 E
Lake Gairdner △, *Australia* .. **63 E2** 31 41S 135 51 E
Lake George, *U.S.A.* **85 C11** 43 26N 73 43W
Lake Grace, *Australia* .... **61 F2** 33 7S 118 28 E
Lake Harbour = Kimmirut,
  Canada **69 B13** 62 50N 69 50W
Lake Havasu City, *U.S.A.* .. **79 L12** 34 27N 114 22W
Lake Hughes, *U.S.A.* **79 L8** 34 41N 118 26W
Lake Isabella, *U.S.A.* **79 K8** 35 38N 118 28W
Lake Jackson, *U.S.A.* **81 L7** 29 3N 95 27W
Lake Junction, *U.S.A.* **76 D8** 44 35N 110 28W
Lake King, *Australia* .... **61 F2** 33 5S 119 45 E
Lake Lenore, *Canada* **71 C8** 52 24N 104 59W
Lake Louise, *Canada* **70 C5** 51 30N 116 10W
Lake Malawi △, *Malawi* .... **55 E3** 14 2S 34 53 E
Lake Mburo △, *Uganda* .... **54 C3** 0 33S 30 56 E
Lake Mead △, *U.S.A.* **79 K12** 36 15N 114 30W
Lake Meredith △, *U.S.A.* **81 H4** 35 50N 101 50W
Lake Mills, *U.S.A.* **80 D8** 43 25N 93 32W
Lake Nakuru △, *Kenya* .... **54 C4** 0 21S 36 8 E
Lake Placid, *U.S.A.* **85 B11** 44 17N 73 59W
Lake Pleasant, *U.S.A.* **85 C10** 43 28N 74 25W
Lake Providence, *U.S.A.* **81 J9** 32 48N 91 10W
Lake Roosevelt △, *U.S.A.* .. **76 C4** 47 57N 118 59W
Lake St. Peter, *Canada* **84 A6** 45 18N 78 2W
Lake Superior △, *Canada* .. **72 C3** 47 45N 84 45W
Lake Torrens △, *Australia* .. **63 E2** 30 55S 137 40 E
Lake Village, *U.S.A.* **81 J9** 33 20N 91 17W
Lake Wales, *U.S.A.* **83 M5** 27 54N 81 35W
Lake Worth, *U.S.A.* **83 M5** 26 37N 80 3W
Lakeba, *Fiji* **59 D9** 18 13S 178 47W
Lakefield, *Canada* **84 B6** 44 25N 78 16W
Lakefield △, *Australia* .... **62 B3** 15 24S 144 26 E
Lakehurst, *U.S.A.* **85 F10** 40 1N 74 19W
Lakeland, *Australia* .... **62 B3** 15 49S 144 57 E
Lakeland, *U.S.A.* **83 M5** 28 3N 81 57W
Lakemba = Lakeba, *Fiji* **59 D9** 18 13S 178 47W
Lakeport, *Calif., U.S.A.* **78 F4** 39 3N 122 55W
Lakeport, *Mich., U.S.A.* **84 C2** 43 7N 82 30W
Lakes Entrance, *Australia* .... **63 F4** 37 50S 148 0 E
Lakeside, *Ariz., U.S.A.* **77 J9** 34 9N 109 58W
Lakeside, *Calif., U.S.A.* **79 N10** 32 52N 116 55W
Lakeside, *Nebr., U.S.A.* **80 D3** 42 3N 102 26W
Lakeside, *Ohio, U.S.A.* **84 E2** 41 32N 82 46W
Lakeview, *U.S.A.* **76 E3** 42 11N 120 21W
Lakeville, *U.S.A.* **80 C8** 44 39N 93 14W
Lakewood, *Colo., U.S.A.* **80 F2** 39 44N 105 5W
Lakewood, *N.J., U.S.A.* **85 F10** 40 6N 74 13W
Lakewood, *N.Y., U.S.A.* **84 D5** 42 6N 79 19W
Lakewood, *Ohio, U.S.A.* **84 E3** 41 29N 81 48W
Lakewood, *Wash., U.S.A.* **78 C4** 47 11N 122 32W
Lakha, *India* .... **42 F4** 26 9N 70 54 E
Lakhaniá, *Greece* .... **25 D9** 35 58N 27 54 E
Lakhimpur, *India* .... **43 F9** 27 57N 80 46 E
Lakhnadon, *India* .... **43 H8** 22 36N 79 36 E
Lakhnau = Lucknow, *India* .. **43 F9** 26 50N 81 0 E
Lakhonpheng, *Laos* .... **38 E5** 15 54N 105 34 E
Lakhpat, *India* .... **42 H3** 23 48N 68 47 E
Lakin, *U.S.A.* **81 G4** 37 57N 101 15W
Lakitusaki →, *Canada* **72 B3** 54 21N 82 25W
Lakki, *Pakistan* .... **42 C4** 32 36N 70 55 E
Lákkoi, *Greece* .... **25 D5** 35 24N 23 57 E
Lakonikós Kólpos, *Greece* .. **23 F10** 36 40N 22 40 E
Lakor, *Indonesia* .... **37 F7** 8 15S 128 17 E
Lakota, *Ivory C.* **50 G4** 5 50N 5 30W
Lakota, *U.S.A.* **80 A5** 48 2N 98 21W
Laksar, *India* .... **42 E8** 29 46N 78 3 E
Laksefjorden, *Norway* .... **8 A22** 70 45N 26 50 E
Lakselv, *Norway* .... **8 A21** 70 2N 25 0 E
Lakshadweep Is., *India* .... **27 H11** 10 0N 72 30 E
Lakshmanpur, *India* .... **43 H10** 22 58N 83 3 E
Lakshmikantapur, *India* .... **43 H13** 22 5N 88 20 E
Lala Musa, *Pakistan* .... **42 C5** 32 40N 73 57 E
Lalaghat, *India* .... **41 G18** 24 30N 92 40 E
Lalago, *Tanzania* .... **54 C3** 3 28S 33 58 E
Lalapanzi, *Zimbabwe* .... **55 F3** 19 20S 30 15 E
L'Albufera, *Spain* **21 C5** 39 20N 0 27W
Lalganj, *India* .... **43 G11** 25 52N 85 13 E
Lalgola, *India* .... **43 G13** 24 25N 88 15 E
Lāli, *Iran* .... **45 C6** 32 21N 49 6 E
Lalibela, *Ethiopia* .... **47 E2** 12 3N 39 0 E
Lalin, *China* .... **35 B14** 45 12N 127 0 E
Lalín, *Spain* **21 A1** 42 40N 8 5W
Lalin He →, *China* .... **35 B13** 45 32N 125 40 E
Lalitapur, *Nepal* .... **43 F11** 27 40N 85 20 E
Lalitpur, *India* .... **43 G8** 24 42N 78 28 E
Lalkua, *India* .... **43 E8** 29 5N 79 31 E
Lalsot, *India* .... **42 F7** 26 34N 76 20 E
Lam, *Vietnam* .... **38 B6** 21 21N 106 31 E
Lam Pao Res., *Thailand* .... **38 D4** 16 50N 103 15 E
Lamaing, *Burma* .... **41 M20** 15 25N 97 53 E
Lamar, *Colo., U.S.A.* **80 F3** 38 5N 102 37W
Lamar, *Mo., U.S.A.* **81 G7** 37 30N 94 16W
Lamas, *Peru* **92 E3** 6 28S 76 31W
Lambaréné, *Gabon* .... **52 E2** 0 41S 10 12 E
Lambasa = Labasa, *Fiji* .... **59 C8** 16 30S 179 27 E
Lambay I., *Ireland* **10 C5** 53 29N 6 1W
Lambert Glacier, *Antarctica* .. **5 D6** 71 0S 70 0 E
Lambert's Bay, *S. Africa* .. **56 E2** 32 5S 18 17 E

Lambeth, *Canada* **84 D3** 42 54N 81 18W
Lambomakondro, *Madag.* .. **57 C7** 22 41S 44 44 E
Lambton Shores, *Canada* .. **84 C3** 43 10N 81 56W
Lame Deer, *U.S.A.* **76 D10** 45 37N 106 40W
Lamego, *Portugal* **21 B2** 41 5N 7 52W
Lamèque, *Canada* **73 C7** 47 45N 64 38W
Lameroo, *Australia* .... **63 F3** 35 19S 140 33 E
Lamesa, *U.S.A.* **81 J4** 32 44N 101 58W
Lamia, *Greece* .... **23 E10** 38 55N 22 26 E
Lamington △, *Australia* .... **63 D5** 28 13S 153 12 E
Lamma I., *China* .... **33 G11** 22 12N 114 8 E
Lammermuir Hills, *U.K.* **11 F6** 55 50N 2 40W
Lamoille ➤, *U.S.A.* **85 B11** 44 38N 73 13W
Lamon B., *Phil.* .... **37 B6** 14 30N 122 20 E
Lamont, *Canada* **70 C6** 53 46N 112 50W
Lamont, *Calif., U.S.A.* **79 K8** 35 15N 118 55W
Lamont, *Wyo., U.S.A.* **76 E10** 42 13N 107 29W
Lampa, *Peru* **92 G4** 15 22S 70 22W
Lampang, *Thailand* .... **38 C2** 18 16N 99 32 E
Lampasas, *U.S.A.* **81 K5** 31 4N 98 11W
Lampazos de Naranjo, *Mexico* . **86 B4** 27 2N 100 32W
Lampedusa, *Medit. S.* ...... **22 G5** 35 36N 12 40 E
Lampeter, *U.K.* **13 E3** 52 7N 4 4W
Lampione, *Medit. S.* .... **22 G5** 35 33N 12 20 E
Lampman, *Canada* **71 D8** 49 25N 102 50W
Lampung □, *Indonesia* ...... **36 F2** 5 30S 104 30 E
Lamta, *India* .... **43 H9** 22 8N 80 7 E
Lamu, *Kenya* .... **54 C5** 2 16S 40 55 E
Lamy, *U.S.A.* **77 J11** 35 29N 105 53W
Lan Xian, *China* .... **34 E6** 38 15N 111 35 E
Lanak La, *China* .... **43 B8** 34 27N 79 32 E
Lanak'o Shank'ou = Lanak La,
  China .... **43 B8** 34 27N 79 32 E
Lanark, *Canada* **85 A8** 45 1N 76 22W
Lanark, *U.K.* **11 F5** 55 40N 3 47W
Lanbi Kyun, *Burma* .... **39 G2** 10 50N 98 20 E
Lancang Jiang ➤, *China* .. **32 D5** 21 40N 101 10 E
Lancashire □, *U.K.* **12 D5** 53 50N 2 48W
Lancaster, *Canada* **85 A10** 45 10N 74 30W
Lancaster, *U.K.* **12 C5** 54 3N 2 48W
Lancaster, *Calif., U.S.A.* .. **79 L8** 34 42N 118 8W
Lancaster, *Ky., U.S.A.* **82 G3** 37 37N 84 35W
Lancaster, *N.H., U.S.A.* .. **85 B13** 44 29N 71 34W
Lancaster, *N.Y., U.S.A.* .. **84 D6** 42 54N 78 40W
Lancaster, *Ohio, U.S.A.* .. **82 F4** 39 43N 82 36W
Lancaster, *Pa., U.S.A.* **85 F8** 40 2N 76 19W
Lancaster, *S.C., U.S.A.* .. **83 H5** 34 43N 80 46W
Lancaster, *Wis., U.S.A.* .. **80 D9** 42 51N 90 43W
Lancaster Sd., *Canada* **69 A11** 74 13N 84 0W
Lancelin, *Australia* .... **61 F2** 31 0S 115 18 E
Lanchow = Lanzhou, *China* . **34 F2** 36 1N 103 52 E
Lanciano, *Italy* .... **22 C6** 42 14N 14 23 E
Lancun, *China* .... **35 F11** 36 25N 120 10 E
Land Between the Lakes △,
  U.S.A. **83 G1** 36 55N 88 7W
Landeck, *Austria* .... **16 E6** 47 9N 10 34 E
Lander, *U.S.A.* **76 E9** 42 50N 108 44W
Lander ➤, *Australia* ...... **60 D5** 22 0S 132 0 E
Landes, *France* **20 D3** 44 0N 1 0W
Landi Kotal, *Pakistan* ...... **42 B4** 34 7N 71 6 E
Landisburg, *U.S.A.* **84 F7** 40 21N 77 19W
Land's End, *U.K.* **13 G2** 50 4N 5 44W
Landsborough Cr. ➤, *Australia* . **62 C3** 22 28S 144 35 E
Landshut, *Germany* .... **16 D7** 48 34N 12 8 E
Landskrona, *Sweden* ...... **9 J15** 55 53N 12 50 E
Lanesboro, *U.S.A.* **85 E9** 41 57N 75 34W
Lanett, *U.S.A.* **83 J3** 32 52N 85 12W
Lang Qua, *Vietnam* .... **38 A5** 22 16N 104 27 E
Lang Shan, *China* .... **34 D4** 41 0N 106 30 E
Lang Son, *Vietnam* .... **38 B6** 21 52N 106 42 E
Lang Suan, *Thailand* ...... **39 H2** 9 57N 99 4 E
La'nga Co, *China* .... **41 D12** 30 45N 81 15 E
Langar, *Iran* .... **45 C9** 35 23N 60 25 E
Langara I., *Canada* **70 C2** 54 14N 133 1W
Langdon, *U.S.A.* **80 A5** 48 45N 98 22W
Langeberg, *S. Africa* ...... **56 E3** 33 55S 21 0 E
Langeberge, *S. Africa* ...... **56 D3** 28 15S 22 33 E
Langeland, *Denmark* ...... **9 J14** 54 56N 10 48 E
Langenburg, *Canada* **71 C8** 50 51N 101 43W
Langholm, *U.K.* **11 F5** 55 9N 3 0W
Langjökull, *Iceland* **8 D3** 64 39N 20 12W
Langkawi, Pulau, *Malaysia* . **39 J2** 6 25N 99 45 E
Langklip, *S. Africa* .... **56 D3** 28 12S 20 20 E
Langkon, *Malaysia* .... **36 C5** 6 30N 116 40 E
Langlade, *St-P. & M.* **73 C8** 46 50N 56 20W
Langley, *Canada* **78 A4** 49 7N 122 39W
Langøya, *Norway* .... **8 B16** 68 45N 14 50 E
Langreo, *Spain* **21 A3** 43 18N 5 40W
Langres, *France* .... **20 C6** 47 52N 5 20 E
Langres, Plateau de, *France* . **20 C6** 47 45N 5 3 E
Langsa, *Indonesia* .... **36 D1** 4 30N 97 57 E
Langtry, *U.S.A.* **81 L4** 29 49N 101 34W
Langu, *Thailand* .... **39 J2** 6 53N 99 47 E
Languedoc, *France* .... **20 E5** 43 58N 3 55 E
Langwang, *China* .... **33 F9** 22 38N 113 27 E
Langxiangzhen, *China* ...... **34 E9** 39 43N 116 8 E
Lanigan, *Canada* **71 C7** 51 51N 105 2W
Lankao, *China* .... **34 G8** 34 48N 114 50 E
Länkäran, *Azerbaijan* ...... **19 G8** 38 48N 48 52 E
Lannion, *France* **20 B2** 48 46N 3 29W
L'Annonciation, *Canada* .. **72 C5** 46 25N 74 55W
Lansdale, *U.S.A.* **85 F9** 40 14N 75 17W
Lansdowne, *Australia* ...... **63 E5** 31 48S 152 30 E
Lansdowne, *Canada* **85 B8** 44 24N 76 1W
Lansdowne, *India* .... **43 E8** 29 50N 78 41 E
Lansdowne House, *Canada* . **72 B2** 52 14N 87 53W
L'Anse, *U.S.A.* **82 B1** 46 45N 88 27W
L'Anse au Loup, *Canada* .. **73 B8** 51 32N 56 50W
L'Anse aux Meadows, *Canada* . **73 B8** 51 36N 55 32W
L'Anse la Raye, *St. Lucia* .. **89 f** 13 55N 61 19W
Lansford, *U.S.A.* **85 F9** 40 50N 75 53W
Lansing, *U.S.A.* **82 D3** 42 44N 84 33W
Lantau, Ko, *Thailand* ...... **39 J2** 7 32N 125 8 E
Lantau I., *China* .... **33 G10** 22 15N 113 56 E
Lantian, *China* .... **34 G5** 34 11N 109 20 E
Lanus, *Argentina* **94 C4** 34 44S 58 27W
Lanusei, *Italy* .... **22 E3** 39 52N 9 34 E
Lanzarote, *Canary Is.* **24 F6** 29 0N 13 40W
Lanzarote ✈ (ACE), *Canary Is.* . **24 F6** 28 57N 13 40W
Lanzhou, *China* .... **34 F2** 36 1N 103 52 E
Lao Bao, *Laos* .... **38 D6** 16 35N 106 30 E
Lao Cai, *Vietnam* .... **38 A4** 22 30N 103 57 E
Laoag, *Phil.* .... **37 A6** 18 7N 120 34 E
Laoang, *Phil.* .... **37 B7** 12 32N 125 8 E
Laoha He ➤, *China* .... **35 C11** 43 25N 120 35 E
Laois □, *Ireland* **10 D4** 52 57N 7 36W
Laon, *France* .... **20 B5** 49 33N 3 35 E

Laona, *U.S.A.* **82 C1** 45 34N 88 40W
Laos ■, *Asia* .... **38 D5** 17 45N 105 0 E
Lapa, *Brazil* **95 B6** 25 46S 49 44W
Lapeer, *U.S.A.* **82 D4** 43 3N 83 19W
Lapithos, *Cyprus* .... **25 D12** 35 21N 33 11 E
Lapland = Lappland, *Europe* . **8 B21** 68 7N 24 0 E
Laporte, *U.S.A.* **85 E8** 41 25N 76 30W
Lappeenranta, *Finland* .... **9 F23** 61 3N 28 12 E
Lappland, *Europe* .... **8 B21** 68 7N 24 0 E
Laprida, *Argentina* **94 D3** 37 34S 60 45W
Lapseki, *Turkey* .... **23 D12** 40 20N 26 41 E
Laptev Sea, *Russia* .... **29 B13** 76 0N 125 0 E
Lapua, *Finland* .... **8 E20** 62 58N 23 0 E
L'Áquila, *Italy* .... **22 C5** 42 22N 13 22 E
Lár, *Ázarbájan-e Sharqí, Iran* . **44 B5** 38 30N 47 52 E
Lár, *Fárs, Iran* .... **45 E7** 27 40N 54 14 E
Laramie, *U.S.A.* **80 E2** 41 19N 105 35W
Laramie ➤, *U.S.A.* **76 F11** 42 13N 104 33W
Laramie Mts., *U.S.A.* **80 E2** 42 0N 105 30W
Laranjeiras do Sul, *Brazil* .. **95 B5** 25 23S 52 23W
Larantuka, *Indonesia* ...... **37 F6** 8 21S 122 55 E
Larat, *Indonesia* .... **37 F8** 7 0S 132 0 E
Larde, *Mozam.* .... **55 F4** 16 28S 39 43 E
Larder Lake, *Canada* **72 C4** 48 5N 79 40W
Lardhós, Ákra = Líndhos, Ákra,
  Greece .... **25 C10** 36 4N 28 10 E
Lardhós, Órmos, *Greece* .. **25 C10** 36 4N 28 2 E
Laredo, *U.S.A.* **81 M5** 27 30N 99 30W
Laredo Sd., *Canada* **70 C3** 52 30N 128 53W
Largo, *U.S.A.* **83 M4** 27 55N 82 47W
Largs, *U.K.* **11 F4** 55 47N 4 52W
Lariang, *Indonesia* .... **37 E5** 1 26S 119 17 E
Larimore, *U.S.A.* **80 B6** 47 54N 97 38W
Lárisa, *Greece* .... **23 E10** 39 36N 22 27 E
Larkana, *Pakistan* .... **42 F3** 27 32N 68 18 E
Larnaca, *Cyprus* .... **25 E12** 34 55N 33 38 E
Larnaca Bay, *Cyprus* ...... **25 E12** 34 53N 33 45 E
Larne, *U.K.* **10 B6** 54 51N 5 51W
Larned, *U.S.A.* **80 F5** 38 11N 99 6W
Larose, *U.S.A.* **81 L9** 29 34N 90 23W
Larrimah, *Australia* .... **60 C5** 15 35S 133 12 E
Larsen Ice Shelf, *Antarctica* . **5 C17** 67 0S 62 0W
Larvik, *Norway* .... **9 G14** 59 4N 10 2 E
Las Animas, *U.S.A.* **80 F3** 38 4N 103 13W
Las Anod, *Somali Rep.* .... **47 F4** 8 26N 47 19 E
Las Aves, Is., *W. Indies* .. **89 C7** 15 45N 63 55W
Las Brenãs, *Argentina* **94 B3** 27 5S 61 7W
Las Cañadas del Teide △,
  Canary Is. **24 F3** 28 15N 16 37W
Las Cejas, *Argentina* **96 B4** 26 53S 64 44W
Las Chimeneas, *Mexico* .. **79 N10** 32 8N 116 5W
Las Cruces, *U.S.A.* **77 K10** 32 19N 106 47W
Las Flores, *Argentina* **94 D4** 36 10S 59 7W
Las Heras, *Argentina* **94 C2** 32 51S 68 49W
Las Lajas, *Argentina* **96 D2** 38 30S 70 25W
Las Lomitas, *Argentina* **94 A3** 24 43S 60 35W
Las Palmas, *Argentina* **94 B4** 27 8S 58 45W
Las Palmas, *Canary Is.* **24 F4** 28 7N 15 26W
Las Palmas ➤, *Mexico* .. **79 N10** 32 26N 116 54W
Las Palmas ✈ (LPA), *Canary Is.* . **24 G4** 27 55N 15 25W
Las Palmas de Cocalán △, *Chile* . **94 C1** 34 18S 71 4W
Las Piedras, *Uruguay* **95 C4** 34 44S 56 14W
Las Pipinas, *Argentina* **94 D4** 35 30S 57 19W
Las Plumas, *Argentina* **96 E3** 43 40S 67 15W
Las Rosas, *Argentina* **94 C3** 32 30S 61 35W
Las Tablas, *Panama* **88 E3** 7 49N 80 14W
Las Termas, *Argentina* **94 B3** 27 29S 64 52W
Las Toscas, *Argentina* **94 B4** 28 21S 59 18W
Las Truchas, *Mexico* **86 D4** 17 57N 102 13W
Las Varillas, *Argentina* **94 C3** 31 50S 62 50W
Las Vegas, *N. Mex., U.S.A.* . **77 J11** 35 36N 105 13W
Las Vegas, *Nev., U.S.A.* .. **79 J11** 36 10N 115 9W
Las Vegas McCarran
  International ✈ (LAS), *U.S.A.* . **79 J11** 36 5N 115 9W
Lascano, *Uruguay* **95 C5** 33 35S 54 12W
Lash-e Joveyn, *Afghan.* .... **40 D2** 31 45N 61 30 E
Lashburn, *Canada* **71 C7** 53 10N 109 40W
Lashio, *Burma* .... **41 H20** 22 56N 97 45 E
Lashkar, *India* .... **42 F8** 26 10N 78 10 E
Lasíthi, *Greece* .... **25 D7** 35 11N 25 31 E
Lasíthi □, *Greece* .... **25 D7** 35 5N 25 50 E
Lásjerd, *Iran* .... **45 C7** 35 24N 53 4 E
Lassen Pk., *U.S.A.* **76 F3** 40 29N 121 31W
Last Mountain L., *Canada* . **71 C7** 51 5N 105 14W
Lastchance Cr. ➤, *U.S.A.* . **78 E5** 40 2N 121 15W
Lastoursville, *Gabon* ...... **52 E2** 0 55S 12 38 E
Lastovo, *Croatia* .... **22 C7** 42 46N 16 55 E
Lat Yao, *Thailand* .... **38 E2** 15 45N 99 48 E
Latacunga, *Ecuador* **92 D3** 0 50S 78 35W
Latakia = Al Lādhiqīyah, *Syria* . **44 C2** 35 30N 35 45 E
Latchford, *Canada* **72 C4** 47 20N 79 50W
Latehar, *India* .... **43 H11** 23 45N 84 30 E
Latham, *Australia* .... **61 E2** 29 44S 116 20 E
Lathi, *India* .... **42 F4** 27 43N 71 23 E
Lathrop Wells, *U.S.A.* **79 J10** 36 39N 116 24W
Latina, *Italy* .... **22 D5** 41 28N 12 52 E
Latium = Lazio □, *Italy* .. **22 C5** 42 10N 12 30 E
Laton, *U.S.A.* **78 J7** 36 26N 119 41W
Latouche Treville, C., *Australia* . **60 C3** 18 27S 121 49 E
Latrobe, *Australia* .... **63 G4** 41 14S 146 30 E
Latrobe, *U.S.A.* **84 F5** 40 19N 79 23W
Latvia ■, *Europe* .... **9 H20** 56 50N 24 0 E
Lau Fau Shan, *China* ...... **33 G10** 22 28N 113 59 E
Lau Group, *Fiji* **59 C9** 17 0S 178 30W
Lauchhammer, *Germany* .. **16 C7** 51 29N 13 47 E
Laughlin, *U.S.A.* **77 J6** 35 8N 114 35W
Laukaa, *Finland* .... **9 E21** 62 24N 25 56 E
Launceston, *Australia* .... **63 G4** 41 24S 147 8 E
Launceston, *U.K.* **13 G3** 50 38N 4 22W
Laune ➤, *Ireland* **10 D2** 52 7N 9 47W
Launglon Bok, *Burma* .... **38 F1** 13 50N 97 54 E
Laura, *Australia* .... **62 B3** 15 32S 144 32 E
Laurel, *Miss., U.S.A.* **81 K10** 31 41N 89 8W
Laurel, *Mont., U.S.A.* **76 D9** 45 40N 108 46W
Laurencekirk, *U.K.* **11 E6** 56 50N 2 28W
Laurens, *U.S.A.* **83 H4** 34 30N 82 1W
Laurentian Plateau, *Canada* . **73 B6** 52 0N 70 0W
Lauria, *Italy* .... **22 E6** 40 2N 15 50 E
Laurie L., *Canada* **71 B8** 56 35N 101 57W
Laurinburg, *U.S.A.* **83 H6** 34 47N 79 28W
Laurium, *U.S.A.* **82 B1** 47 14N 88 27W
Lausanne, *Switz.* .... **20 C7** 46 32N 6 38 E
Laut, *Indonesia* .... **36 D3** 4 45N 108 0 E
Laut, Pulau, *Indonesia* .... **36 E5** 3 40S 116 10 E
Laut Kecil, Kepulauan, *Indonesia* . **36 E5** 4 45S 115 40 E
Lautoka, *Fiji* .... **59 C7** 17 37S 177 27 E

Lava Beds △, *U.S.A.* **76 F3** 41 40N 121 30W
Lavagh More, *Ireland* **10 B3** 54 46N 8 6W
Laval, *France* **20 B3** 48 4N 0 48W
Lavalle, *Argentina* **94 B2** 28 15S 65 15W
Lavant Station, *Canada* .. **85 A8** 45 3N 76 42W
Lāvar Meydān, *Iran* ...... **45 D7** 30 20N 54 30 E
Laverton, *Australia* ...... **61 E3** 28 44S 122 29 E
Lavras, *Brazil* **95 A7** 21 20S 45 0W
Lávrion, *Greece* .... **23 F11** 37 40N 24 4 E
Lávris, *Greece* .... **25 D6** 35 25N 24 40 E
Lavumisa, *Swaziland* ...... **57 D5** 27 20S 31 55 E
Lavushi Manda △, *Zambia* . **55 E3** 12 46S 31 0 E
Lawas, *Malaysia* .... **36 D5** 4 55N 115 25 E
Lawele, *Indonesia* .... **37 F6** 5 13S 122 57 E
Lawn Hill △, *Australia* .... **62 B2** 18 15S 138 6 E
Lawng Pit, *Burma* .... **41 G20** 25 30N 97 25 E
Lawqah, Si. *Arabia* .... **44 D4** 29 49N 42 45 E
Lawrence, *N.Z.* .... **59 L2** 45 55S 169 41 E
Lawrence, *Kans., U.S.A.* .. **80 F7** 38 58N 95 14W
Lawrence, *Mass., U.S.A.* .. **85 D13** 42 43N 71 10W
Lawrenceburg, *Ind., U.S.A.* . **82 F3** 39 6N 84 52W
Lawrenceburg, *Tenn., U.S.A.* . **83 H2** 35 14N 87 20W
Lawrenceville, *Ga., U.S.A.* . **83 J4** 33 57N 83 59W
Lawrenceville, *Pa., U.S.A.* . **84 E7** 41 59N 77 8W
Laws, *U.S.A.* **78 H8** 37 24N 118 20W
Lawton, *U.S.A.* **81 H5** 34 37N 98 25W
Lawu, *Indonesia* .... **37 G14** 7 40S 111 13 E
Laxford, L., *U.K.* **11 C3** 58 24N 5 6W
Layla, Si. *Arabia* .... **47 C4** 22 10N 46 40 E
Laylān, *Iraq* .... **44 C5** 35 18N 44 31 E
Layton, *U.S.A.* **76 F7** 41 4N 111 58W
Laytonville, *U.S.A.* **76 G2** 39 41N 123 29W
Lazarivo, *Madag.* .... **57 C8** 23 54S 44 59 E
Lazio □, *Italy* .... **22 C5** 42 10N 12 30 E
Lazo, *Russia* .... **30 C6** 43 25N 133 55 E
Le Bic, *Canada* **73 C6** 48 20N 68 41W
Le Creusot, *France* ...... **20 C6** 46 48N 4 24 E
Le François, *Martinique* .... **88 c** 14 38N 60 57W
Le Havre, *France* .... **20 B4** 49 30N 0 5 E
Le Lamentin, *Martinique* .. **88 c** 14 35N 61 2W
Le Mans, *France* .... **20 C4** 48 0N 0 10 E
Le Marin, *Martinique* ...... **88 c** 14 27N 60 55W
Le Mars, *U.S.A.* **80 D6** 42 47N 96 10W
Le Mont-St-Michel, *France* . **20 B3** 48 40N 1 30W
Le Prêcheur, *Martinique* .. **88 c** 14 50N 61 12W
Le Puy-en-Velay, *France* .. **20 D5** 45 3N 3 52 E
Le Robert, *Martinique* .... **88 c** 14 40N 60 56W
Le St-Esprit, *Martinique* .. **88 c** 14 34N 60 56W
Le Sueur, *U.S.A.* **80 C8** 44 28N 93 55W
Le Thuy, *Vietnam* .... **38 D6** 17 14N 106 49 E
Le Touquet-Paris-Plage, *France* . **20 A4** 50 30N 1 36 E
Le Tréport, *France* .... **20 A4** 50 3N 1 20 E
Le Verdon-sur-Mer, *France* . **20 C3** 45 33N 1 4W
Lea ➤, *U.K.* .... **13 F8** 51 31N 0 1 E
Leach, *Cambodia* .... **39 F4** 12 21N 103 46 E
Lead, *U.S.A.* **80 C3** 44 21N 103 46W
Leader, *Canada* **71 C7** 50 50N 109 30W
Leadville, *U.S.A.* **77 G10** 39 15N 106 18W
Leaf ➤, *U.S.A.* **81 K10** 30 59N 88 44W
Leaf Rapids, *Canada* **71 B9** 56 30N 99 59W
Leamington, *Canada* **84 D2** 42 3N 82 36W
Leamington, *U.S.A.* **76 G7** 39 32N 112 17W
Leamington Spa = Royal
  Leamington Spa, *U.K.* .. **13 E6** 52 18N 1 31W
Leandro Norte Alem, *Argentina* . **95 B4** 27 34S 55 15W
Leane, L., *Ireland* **10 D2** 52 2N 9 32W
Learmonth, *Australia* ...... **60 D1** 22 13S 114 10 E
Leask, *Canada* **71 C7** 53 5N 106 45W
Leatherhead, *U.K.* **13 F7** 51 18N 0 20W
Leavenworth, *Kans., U.S.A.* . **80 F7** 39 19N 94 55W
Leavenworth, *Wash., U.S.A.* . **76 C3** 47 36N 120 40W
Lebak, *Phil.* .... **37 C6** 6 32N 124 5 E
Lebam, *U.S.A.* **78 D3** 46 34N 123 33W
Lebanon, *Ind., U.S.A.* **82 E2** 40 3N 86 28W
Lebanon, *Kans., U.S.A.* .. **80 F5** 39 49N 98 33W
Lebanon, *Ky., U.S.A.* **82 G3** 37 34N 85 15W
Lebanon, *Mo., U.S.A.* **81 G8** 37 41N 92 40W
Lebanon, *N.H., U.S.A.* .. **85 C12** 43 39N 72 15W
Lebanon, *Oreg., U.S.A.* .. **76 D2** 44 32N 122 55W
Lebanon, *Pa., U.S.A.* **85 F8** 40 20N 76 26W
Lebanon, *Tenn., U.S.A.* .. **83 G2** 36 12N 86 18W
Lebanon ■, *Asia* .... **46 B5** 34 0N 36 0 E
Lebec, *U.S.A.* **79 L8** 34 50N 118 52W
Lebel-sur-Quévillon, *Canada* . **72 C4** 49 3N 76 59W
Lebomboberge, *S. Africa* .. **57 C5** 24 30S 32 0 E
Lębork, *Poland* .... **17 A9** 54 33N 17 46 E
Lebrija, *Spain* **21 D2** 36 53N 6 5W
Lebu, *Chile* **94 D1** 37 40S 73 47W
Lecce, *Italy* .... **23 D8** 40 23N 18 11 E
Lecco, *Italy* .... **20 D8** 45 51N 9 23 E
Lech ➤, *Germany* .... **16 D6** 48 43N 10 56 E
Lecontes Mills, *U.S.A.* **84 E6** 41 5N 78 17W
Ledong, *China* .... **38 C7** 18 41N 109 5 E
Leduc, *Canada* **70 C6** 53 15N 113 30W
Lee, *U.S.A.* **85 D11** 42 19N 73 15W
Lee ➤, *Ireland* **10 E3** 51 53N 8 56W
Lee Vining, *U.S.A.* **78 H7** 37 58N 119 7W
Leech L., *U.S.A.* **80 B7** 47 10N 94 24W
Leechburg, *U.S.A.* **84 F5** 40 37N 79 36W
Leeds, *U.K.* **12 D6** 53 48N 1 33W
Leeds, *U.S.A.* **83 J2** 33 33N 86 33W
Leek, *Neths.* .... **15 A6** 53 10N 6 24 E
Leek, *U.K.* **12 D5** 53 7N 2 1W
Leeman, *Australia* .... **61 E1** 29 57S 114 58 E
Leeper, *U.S.A.* **84 E5** 41 22N 79 18W
Leer, *Germany* .... **16 B4** 53 13N 7 26 E
Leesburg, *U.S.A.* **83 L5** 28 49N 81 53W
Leeston, *N.Z.* .... **59 E4** 43 45S 172 27 E
Leeton, *Australia* .... **63 E4** 34 33S 146 23 E
Leetonia, *U.S.A.* **84 F4** 40 53N 80 45W
Leeu Gamka, *S. Africa* .... **56 E3** 32 47S 21 59 E
Leeuwarden, *Neths.* ...... **15 A5** 53 15N 5 48 E
Leeuwin, C., *Australia* .... **61 F2** 34 20S 115 9 E
Leeuwin Naturaliste △, *Australia* . **61 F2** 34 6S 115 3 E
Leeward Is., *Atl. Oc.* **89 C7** 16 30N 63 30W
Lefka, *Cyprus* .... **25 D11** 35 6N 32 51 E
Lefkoniko, *Cyprus* .... **25 D12** 35 18N 33 44 E
Lefroy, *Canada* **84 B5** 44 16N 79 34W
Lefroy, L., *Australia* ...... **61 F3** 31 21N 121 40 E
Leganés, *Spain* **21 B4** 40 19N 3 45W
Legazpi, *Phil.* .... **37 B6** 13 10N 123 45 E
Legendre I., *Australia* ...... **60 D2** 20 22S 116 55 E
Leghorn = Livorno, *Italy* .. **22 C4** 43 33N 10 19 E
Legionowo, *Poland* ...... **17 B11** 52 25N 20 50 E
Legnago, *Italy* .... **22 B4** 45 11N 11 18 E
Legnica, *Poland* .... **16 C9** 51 12N 16 10 E

Leh, *India* .... **43 B7** 34 9N 77 35 E
Lehigh Acres, *U.S.A.* **83 M5** 26 36N 81 39W
Lehighton, *U.S.A.* **85 F9** 40 50N 75 43W
Lehututu, *Botswana* ...... **56 C3** 23 54S 21 55 E
Leiah, *Pakistan* .... **42 D4** 30 58N 70 58 E
Leicester, *U.K.* **13 E6** 52 38N 1 8W
Leicester City □, *U.K.* **13 E6** 52 38N 1 9W
Leicestershire □, *U.K.* **13 E6** 52 41N 1 17W
Leichhardt ➤, *Australia* .. **62 B2** 17 35S 139 48 E
Leichhardt Ra., *Australia* .. **62 C4** 20 46S 147 40 E
Leiden, *Neths.* .... **15 B4** 52 9N 4 30 E
Leie ➤, *Belgium* .... **15 C3** 51 2N 3 45 E
Leine ➤, *Germany* .... **16 B5** 52 43N 9 36 E
Leinster, *Australia* .... **61 E3** 27 51S 120 36 E
Leinster □, *Ireland* **10 C4** 53 3N 7 8W
Leinster, Mt., *Ireland* **10 D5** 52 37N 6 46W
Leipzig, *Germany* .... **16 C7** 51 18N 12 22 E
Leiria, *Portugal* **21 C1** 39 46N 8 53W
Leirvik, *Norway* .... **9 G11** 59 47N 5 28 E
Leisler, Mt., *Australia* .... **60 D4** 23 23S 129 20 E
Leith, *U.K.* **11 F5** 55 59N 3 11W
Leith Hill, *U.K.* **13 F7** 51 11N 0 22W
Leitrim, *Ireland* **10 B3** 54 0N 8 5W
Leitrim □, *Ireland* **10 B4** 54 8N 8 0W
Leizhou Bandao, *China* .... **33 D6** 21 0N 110 0 E
Lek ➤, *Neths.* .... **15 C4** 51 54N 4 35 E
Leka, *Norway* .... **8 D14** 65 5N 11 35 E
Lékva Óros, *Greece* ...... **25 D6** 35 18N 24 3 E
Leland, *Mich., U.S.A.* **82 C3** 45 1N 85 45W
Leland, *Miss., U.S.A.* **81 J9** 33 24N 90 54W
Leleque, *Argentina* **96 E2** 42 28S 71 0W
Lelystad, *Neths.* .... **15 B5** 52 30N 5 25 E
Léman, L., *Europe* .... **20 C7** 46 26N 6 30 E
Lembar, *Indonesia* ...... **37 K19** 8 45S 116 4 E
Lembuak, *Indonesia* ...... **37 K19** 8 36S 116 11 E
Lemera, *Dem. Rep. of the Congo* . **54 C2** 3 0S 28 55 E
Lemhi Ra., *U.S.A.* **76 D7** 44 30N 113 30W
Lemmer, *Neths.* .... **15 B5** 52 51N 5 43 E
Lemmon, *U.S.A.* **80 C3** 45 57N 102 10W
Lemon Grove, *U.S.A.* **79 N9** 32 45N 117 2W
Lemoore, *U.S.A.* **78 J7** 36 18N 119 46W
Lemvig, *Denmark* .... **9 H13** 56 33N 8 20 E
Lena ➤, *Russia* .... **29 B13** 72 52N 126 40 E
Léndas, *Greece* .... **25 E6** 34 56N 24 56 E
Lendeh, *Iran* .... **45 D6** 30 58N 50 25 E
Lenggong, *Malaysia* ...... **39 K3** 5 6N 100 58 E
Lengua de Vaca, Pta., *Chile* . **94 C1** 30 14S 71 38W
Lengwe △, *Malawi* .... **55 F3** 16 14S 34 45 E
Leninogorsk, *Kazakhstan* .. **28 D9** 50 20N 83 30 E
Leninsk, *Russia* .... **19 E8** 48 40N 45 15 E
Leninsk-Kuznetskiy, *Russia* . **28 D9** 54 44N 86 10 E
Lenkoran = Länkäran, *Azerbaijan* . **19 G8** 38 48N 48 52 E
Lenmalu, *Indonesia* ...... **37 E8** 1 45S 130 15 E
Lennox, *U.S.A.* **80 D6** 43 21N 96 53W
Lennoxville, *Canada* **85 A13** 45 22N 71 51W
Lenoir, *U.S.A.* **83 H5** 35 55N 81 32W
Lenoir City, *U.S.A.* **83 H3** 35 48N 84 16W
Lenore L., *Canada* **71 C8** 52 30N 104 59W
Lenox, *U.S.A.* **85 D11** 42 22N 73 17W
Lens, *France* .... **20 A5** 50 26N 2 50 E
Lensk, *Russia* .... **29 C12** 60 48N 114 55 E
Lentini, *Italy* .... **22 F6** 37 17N 15 0 E
Lenwood, *U.S.A.* **79 L9** 34 53N 117 7W
Lenya, *Burma* .... **36 B1** 11 33N 98 57 E
Leoben, *Austria* .... **16 E8** 47 22N 15 5 E
Leodhas = Lewis, *U.K.* **11 C2** 58 9N 6 40W
Leola, *U.S.A.* **80 C5** 45 43N 98 56W
Leominster, *U.K.* **13 E5** 52 14N 2 43W
Leominster, *U.S.A.* **85 D13** 42 32N 71 46W
León, *Mexico* **86 C4** 21 7N 101 40W
León, *Nic.* **88 D2** 12 20N 86 51W
León, *Spain* **21 A3** 42 38N 5 34W
León □, *Spain* **21 B2** 42 40N 6 0W
León, Montes de, *Spain* .. **21 A2** 42 30N 6 18W
Leonardtown, *U.S.A.* **82 F7** 38 17N 76 38W
Leonardville, *Namibia* .... **56 C2** 23 29S 18 49 E
Leongatha, *Australia* ...... **63 F4** 38 30S 145 58 E
Leonora, *Australia* ...... **61 E3** 28 49S 121 19 E
Leopoldina, *Brazil* **95 A7** 21 28S 42 40W
Leopoldsburg, *Belgium* .. **15 C5** 51 7N 5 13 E
Leoti, *U.S.A.* **80 F4** 38 29N 101 21W
Léova, *Moldova* .... **17 E15** 46 28N 28 15 E
Leoville, *Canada* **71 C7** 53 39N 107 33W
Lepel = Lyepyel, *Belarus* .. **18 D4** 54 50N 28 40 E
Lépo, L. do, *Angola* ...... **56 B2** 17 0S 19 0 E
Leppävirta, *Finland* ...... **9 E22** 62 29N 27 46 E
Lerdo, *Mexico* **86 B4** 25 32N 103 32W
Leribe, *Lesotho* .... **57 D4** 28 51S 28 3 E
Lérida = Lleida, *Spain* .... **21 B6** 41 37N 0 39 E
Lerwick, *U.K.* **11 A7** 60 9N 1 9W
Les Cayes, *Haiti* **89 C5** 18 15N 73 46W
Les Coteaux, *Canada* **85 A10** 45 15N 74 13W
Les Sables-d'Olonne, *France* . **20 C3** 46 30N 1 45W
Lesbos = Lésvos, *Greece* .. **23 E12** 39 10N 26 20 E
Leshan, *China* .... **32 D5** 29 33N 103 41 E
Leshukonskoye, *Russia* .. **18 B8** 64 54N 45 46 E
Leshwe △, *Dem. Rep. of
  the Congo* .... **55 E2** 12 45S 29 30 E
Leskov I., *Antarctica* **5 B1** 56 0S 28 0W
Leskovac, *Serbia & M.* .... **23 C9** 43 0N 21 58 E
Lesopilnoye, *Russia* ...... **30 A7** 46 44N 134 20 E
Lesotho ■, *Africa* .... **57 D4** 29 40S 28 0 E
Lesozavodsk, *Russia* .... **29 E14** 45 30N 133 29 E
Lesse ➤, *Belgium* .... **15 D4** 50 15N 4 54 E
Lesse et Lomme △, *Belgium* . **15 D5** 50 8N 5 9 E
Lesser Antilles, *W. Indies* .. **89 D7** 15 0N 61 0W
Lesser Slave L., *Canada* .. **70 B5** 55 30N 115 25W
Lesser Sunda Is., *Indonesia* . **37 F6** 8 0S 120 0 E
Lessines, *Belgium* ...... **15 D3** 50 42N 3 50 E
Lester, *U.S.A.* **78 C5** 47 12N 121 29W
Lester B. Pearson International,
  Toronto ✈ (YYZ), *Canada* . **84 C5** 43 40N 79 34W
Lestock, *Canada* **71 C8** 51 19N 103 59W
Lesueur, I., *Australia* ...... **60 B4** 13 50S 127 17 E
Lesueur △, *Australia* ...... **61 F2** 30 13N 115 10 E
Lésvos, *Greece* .... **23 E12** 39 10N 26 20 E
Leszno, *Poland* .... **17 C9** 51 50N 16 30 E
Letaba, *S. Africa* .... **57 C5** 23 59S 31 50 E
Letchworth, *U.K.* **13 F7** 51 59N 0 13W
Lethbridge, *Canada* **70 D6** 49 45N 112 45W
Lethem, *Guyana* **92 C7** 3 20N 59 50W
Leti, Kepulauan, *Indonesia* . **37 F7** 8 10S 128 0 E
Leti Is. = Leti, Kepulauan,
  Indonesia .... **37 F7** 8 10S 128 0 E
Letiahau ➤, *Botswana* .... **56 C3** 21 16S 24 0 E
Leticia, *Colombia* **92 D5** 4 9S 70 0W

Leting, China . . . . **35 E10** 39 23N 118 55 E
Letjiesbos, S. Africa . . . . **56 E3** 32 34S 22 16 E
Letlhakane, Botswana . . . . **56 C4** 21 27S 25 30 E
Letlhakeng, Botswana . . . . **56 C3** 24 0S 24 59 E
Letong, Indonesia . . . . **36 D3** 2 58N 105 42 E
Letpadan, Burma . . . . **41 L19** 17 45N 95 45 E
Letpan, Burma . . . . **41 K19** 19 28N 94 10 E
Letsôk-aw Kyun, Burma . . . . . **39 G2** 11 30N 98 25 E
Letterkenny, Ireland **10 B4** 54 57N 7 45W
Leucadia, U.S.A. **79 M9** 33 4N 117 18W
Leuchars, U.K. **11 E6** 56 24N 2 53W
Leuser, G., Indonesia . . . . **36 D1** 3 46N 97 12 E
Leuven, Belgium . . . . **15 D4** 50 52N 4 42 E
Leuze-en-Hainaut, Belgium . . **15 D3** 50 36N 3 37 E
Levádhia, Greece . . . . **23 E10** 38 27N 22 54 E
Levanger, Norway . . . . **8 E14** 63 45N 11 19 E
Levelland, U.S.A. **81 J3** 33 35N 102 23W
Leven, U.K. **11 E6** 56 12N 3 0W
Leven, L., U.K. **11 E5** 56 12N 3 22W
Leven, Toraka, Madag. . . . . **57 A8** 12 30S 47 45 E
Leveque C., Australia . . . . **60 C3** 16 20S 123 0 E
Levice, Slovak Rep. . . . . **17 D10** 48 13N 18 35 E
Levin, N.Z. . . . . **59 J5** 40 37S 175 18 E
Lévis, Canada **73 C5** 46 48N 71 9W
Levis, L., Canada **70 A5** 62 37N 117 58W
Levittown, N.Y., U.S.A. **85 F11** 40 44N 73 31W
Levittown, Pa., U.S.A. **85 F10** 40 9N 74 51W
Levkás, Greece . . . . **23 E9** 38 40N 20 43 E
Levkímmi, Greece . . . . **25 B4** 39 25N 20 3 E
Levkímmi, Ákra, Greece . . . . . **25 B4** 39 29N 20 4 E
Levkôsia = Nicosia, Cyprus . . **25 D12** 35 10N 33 25 E
Levskigrad = Karlovo, Bulgaria **23 C11** 42 38N 24 47 E
Lewes, U.K. . . . . **13 G8** 50 52N 0 1 E
Lewes, U.S.A. **82 F8** 38 46N 75 9W
Lewis, U.K. **11 C2** 58 9N 6 40W
Lewis →, U.S.A. **78 E4** 45 51N 122 48W
Lewis, Butt of, U.K. **11 C2** 58 31N 6 16W
Lewis Range, U.S.A. **76 C7** 48 5N 113 5W
Lewis Run, U.S.A. **84 E6** 41 52N 78 40W
Lewisburg, Pa., U.S.A. **84 F8** 40 58N 76 54W
Lewisburg, Tenn., U.S.A. **83 H2** 35 27N 86 48W
Lewisburg, W. Va., U.S.A. **82 G5** 37 48N 80 27W
Lewisporte, Canada **73 C8** 49 15N 55 3W
Lewiston, Idaho, U.S.A. **76 C5** 46 25N 117 1W
Lewiston, Maine, U.S.A. **83 C11** 44 6N 70 13W
Lewiston, N.Y., U.S.A. **84 C5** 43 11N 79 3W
Lewistown, Mont., U.S.A. **76 C9** 47 4N 109 26W
Lewistown, Pa., U.S.A. **84 F7** 40 36N 77 34W
Lexington, Ill., U.S.A. **80 E10** 40 39N 88 47W
Lexington, Ky., U.S.A. **82 F3** 38 3N 84 30W
Lexington, Mich., U.S.A. **84 C2** 43 16N 82 32W
Lexington, Mo., U.S.A. **80 F8** 39 11N 93 52W
Lexington, N.C., U.S.A. **83 H5** 35 49N 80 15W
Lexington, N.Y., U.S.A. **85 D10** 42 15N 74 22W
Lexington, Nebr., U.S.A. **80 E5** 40 47N 99 45W
Lexington, Ohio, U.S.A. **84 F2** 40 41N 82 35W
Lexington, Tenn., U.S.A. **83 H1** 35 39N 88 24W
Lexington, Va., U.S.A. **82 G6** 37 47N 79 27W
Lexington Park, U.S.A. **82 F7** 38 16N 76 27W
Leyburn, U.K. **12 C6** 54 19N 1 48W
Leyland, U.K. **12 D5** 53 42N 2 43W
Leyte, Phil. . . . . **37 B6** 11 0N 125 0 E
Lezhë, Albania . . . . **23 D8** 41 47N 19 39 E
Lhasa, China . . . . **32 D4** 29 25N 90 58 E
Lhazê, China . . . . **32 D3** 29 5N 87 38 E
Lhokkruet, Indonesia . . . . **36 D1** 4 55N 95 24 E
Lhokseumawe, Indonesia . . . . **36 C1** 5 10N 97 10 E
L'Hospitalet de Llobregat, Spain **21 B7** 41 21N 2 6 E
Li, Thailand . . . . **38 D2** 17 48N 98 57 E
Li Xian, Gansu, China . . . . **34 G3** 34 10N 105 5 E
Li Xian, Hebei, China . . . . **34 E8** 38 30N 115 35 E
Liancourt Rocks = Tok-do, Asia **31 F5** 37 15N 131 52 E
Lianga, Phil. . . . . **37 C7** 8 38N 126 6 E
Liangcheng,
  Nei Monggol Zizhiqu, China . **34 D7** 40 28N 112 25 E
Liangcheng, Shandong, China . **35 G10** 35 32N 119 37 E
Liangdang, China . . . . **34 H4** 33 56N 106 18 E
Liangpran, Indonesia . . . . **36 D4** 1 4N 114 23 E
Lianshanguan, China . . . . **35 D12** 40 53N 123 43 E
Lianshui, China . . . . **35 H10** 33 42N 119 20 E
Lianyungang, China . . . . **35 G10** 34 40N 119 11 E
Liao He →, China . . . . **35 D11** 41 0N 121 50 E
Liaocheng, China . . . . **34 F8** 36 28N 115 58 E
Liaodong Bandao, China . . . . . **35 E12** 40 0N 122 30 E
Liaodong Wan, China . . . . **35 D11** 40 20N 121 10 E
Liaoning □, China . . . . **35 D12** 41 40N 122 30 E
Liaoyang, China . . . . **35 D12** 41 15N 122 58 E
Liaoyuan, China . . . . **35 C13** 42 58N 125 2 E
Liaozhong, China . . . . **35 D12** 41 23N 122 50 E
Liard →, Canada **70 A4** 61 51N 121 18W
Liard River, Canada **70 B3** 59 25N 126 5W
Liari, Pakistan . . . . **42 G2** 25 37N 66 30 E
Libau = Liepāja, Latvia . . . . . . **9 H19** 56 30N 21 0 E
Libby, U.S.A. **76 B6** 48 23N 115 33W
Libenge, Dem. Rep. of the Congo **52 D3** 3 40N 18 55 E
Liberal, U.S.A. **81 G4** 37 3N 100 55W
Liberec, Czech Rep. . . . . **16 C8** 50 47N 15 7 E
Liberia, Costa Rica **88 D2** 10 40N 85 30W
Liberia ■, W. Afr. **50 G4** 6 30N 9 30W
Liberty, Mo., U.S.A. **80 F7** 39 15N 94 25W
Liberty, N.Y., U.S.A. **85 E10** 41 48N 74 45W
Liberty, Pa., U.S.A. **84 E7** 41 34N 77 6W
Liberty, Tex., U.S.A. **81 K7** 30 3N 94 48W
Lîbîya, Sahrâ', Africa . . . . **51 C10** 25 0N 25 0 E
Libobo, Tanjung, Indonesia . . . **37 E7** 0 54S 128 28 E
Libode, S. Africa . . . . **57 E4** 31 33S 29 2 E
Libourne, France **20 D3** 44 55N 0 14W
Libramont, Belgium . . . . **15 E5** 49 55N 5 23 E
Libreville, Gabon . . . . **52 D1** 0 25N 9 26 E
Libya ■, N. Afr. . . . . **51 C9** 27 0N 17 0 E
Libyan Desert = Lîbîya, Sahrâ',
  Africa . . . . **51 C10** 25 0N 25 0 E
Licantén, Chile **94 D1** 35 55S 72 0W
Licata, Italy . . . . **22 F5** 37 6N 13 56 E
Licheng, China . . . . **34 F7** 36 28N 113 20 E
Lichfield, U.K. **13 E6** 52 41N 1 49W
Lichinga, Mozam. . . . . **55 E4** 13 13S 35 11 E
Lichtenburg, S. Africa . . . . **56 D4** 26 8S 26 8 E
Lichtenvoorde, Neths. . . . . **15 C6** 51 59N 6 34 E
Licking →, U.S.A. **82 F3** 39 6N 84 30W
Licungo →, Mozam. . . . . **55 F4** 17 40S 37 15 E
Lida, Belarus . . . . **9 K21** 53 53N 25 15 E
Lidköping, Sweden . . . . **9 G15** 58 31N 13 7 E
Liebig, Mt., Australia . . . . **60 D5** 23 18S 131 22 E
Liechtenstein ■, Europe . . . . . **20 C8** 47 8N 9 35 E
Liège, Belgium . . . . **15 D5** 50 38N 5 35 E
Liège □, Belgium . . . . **15 D5** 50 32N 5 35 E

Liegnitz = Legnica, Poland . . . **16 C9** 51 12N 16 10 E
Lienart, Dem. Rep. of the Congo **54 B2** 3 3N 25 31 E
Lienyünchiangshih =
  Lianyungang, China . . . . **35 G10** 34 40N 119 11 E
Lienz, Austria . . . . **16 E7** 46 50N 12 46 E
Liepāja, Latvia . . . . **9 H19** 56 30N 21 0 E
Lier, Belgium . . . . **15 C4** 51 7N 4 34 E
Lièvre →, Canada **72 C4** 45 31N 75 26W
Liffey →, Ireland **10 C5** 53 21N 6 13W
Lifford, Ireland **10 B4** 54 51N 7 29W
Lifudzin, Russia . . . . **30 B7** 44 21N 134 58 E
Lightning Ridge, Australia . . . . **63 D4** 29 22S 148 0 E
Ligonha →, Mozam. . . . . **55 F4** 16 54S 39 9 E
Ligonier, U.S.A. **84 F5** 40 15N 79 14W
Liguria □, Italy . . . . **20 D8** 44 30N 8 50 E
Ligurian Sea, Medit. S. . . . . . . **22 C3** 43 20N 9 0 E
Lihou Reefs and Cays, Australia **62 B5** 17 25S 151 40 E
Lihue, U.S.A. **74 H15** 21 59N 159 23W
Lihué Calel △, Argentina **94 D2** 38 0S 65 10W
Lijiang, China . . . . **32 D5** 26 55N 100 20 E
Likasi, Dem. Rep. of the Congo **55 E2** 10 55S 26 48 E
Likoma I., Malawi . . . . **55 E3** 12 3S 34 45 E
Likumburu, Tanzania . . . . **55 D4** 9 43S 35 8 E
Lille, France . . . . **20 A5** 50 38N 3 3 E
Lille Bælt, Denmark . . . . **9 J13** 55 20N 9 45 E
Lillehammer, Norway . . . . **9 F14** 61 8N 10 30 E
Lillesand, Norway . . . . **9 G13** 58 15N 8 23 E
Lillian Pt., Australia . . . . **61 E4** 27 40S 126 6 E
Lillooet, Canada **70 C4** 50 44N 121 57W
Lillooet →, Canada **70 D4** 49 15N 121 57W
Lilongwe, Malawi . . . . **55 E3** 14 0S 33 48 E
Liloy, Phil. . . . . **37 C6** 8 4N 122 39 E
Lim →, Bos.-H. . . . . **23 C8** 43 45N 19 15 E
Lim Chu Kang, Singapore . . . . **39 d** 1 26N 103 43 E
Lima, Indonesia . . . . **37 E7** 3 39S 127 58 E
Lima, Peru **92 F3** 12 0S 77 0W
Lima, Mont., U.S.A. **76 D7** 44 38N 112 36W
Lima, Ohio, U.S.A. **82 E3** 40 44N 84 6W
Lima →, Portugal **21 B1** 41 41N 8 50W
Liman, Indonesia . . . . **37 G14** 7 48S 111 45 E
Limassol, Cyprus . . . . **25 E12** 34 42N 33 1 E
Limavady, U.K. **10 A5** 55 3N 6 56W
Limay →, Argentina **96 D3** 39 0S 68 0W
Limay Mahuida, Argentina . . . **94 D2** 37 10S 66 45W
Limbang, Brunei . . . . **36 D5** 4 42N 115 6 E
Limbaži, Latvia . . . . **9 H21** 57 31N 24 42 E
Limbdi, India . . . . **42 H4** 22 34N 71 51 E
Limburg, Germany . . . . **16 C5** 50 22N 8 4 E
Limburg □, Belgium . . . . **15 C5** 51 2N 5 25 E
Limburg □, Neths. . . . . **15 C5** 51 20N 5 55 E
Limeira, Brazil **95 A6** 22 35S 47 28W
Limerick, Ireland **10 D3** 52 40N 8 37W
Limerick, U.S.A. **85 C14** 43 41N 70 48W
Limerick □, Ireland **10 D3** 52 30N 8 50W
Limestone, U.S.A. **84 D6** 42 2N 78 38W
Limestone →, Canada **71 B10** 56 31N 94 7W
Limfjorden, Denmark . . . . **9 H13** 56 55N 9 0 E
Limia = Lima →, Portugal **21 B1** 41 41N 8 50W
Limingen, Norway . . . . **8 D15** 64 48N 13 35 E
Limmen Bight, Australia . . . . . **62 A2** 14 40S 135 35 E
Limmen Bight →, Australia . . . **62 B2** 15 7S 135 44 E
Límnos, Greece . . . . **23 E11** 39 50N 25 5 E
Limoges, Canada **85 A9** 45 20N 75 16W
Limoges, France . . . . **20 D4** 45 50N 1 15 E
Limón, Costa Rica **88 E3** 10 0N 83 2W
Limon, U.S.A. **80 F3** 39 16N 103 41W
Limousin □, France . . . . **20 D4** 45 30N 1 30 E
Limoux, France . . . . **20 E5** 43 4N 2 12 E
Limpopo →, S. Africa . . . . **57 C4** 25 5S 29 0 E
Limpopo →, Africa . . . . **57 D5** 25 5S 33 30 E
Limuru, Kenya . . . . **54 C4** 1 2S 36 35 E
Lin Xian, China . . . . **34 F6** 37 57N 110 58 E
Linares, Chile **94 D1** 35 50S 71 40W
Linares, Mexico **87 C5** 24 50N 99 40W
Linares, Spain **21 C4** 38 10N 3 40W
Lincheng, China . . . . **34 F8** 37 25N 114 30 E
Lincoln = Beamsville, Canada . **84 C5** 43 12N 79 28W
Lincoln, Argentina **94 C3** 34 55S 61 30W
Lincoln, N.Z. . . . . **59 K4** 43 38S 172 30 E
Lincoln, U.K. **12 D7** 53 14N 0 32W
Lincoln, Calif., U.S.A. **78 G5** 38 54N 121 17W
Lincoln, Ill., U.S.A. **80 E10** 40 9N 89 22W
Lincoln, Kans., U.S.A. **80 F5** 39 3N 98 9W
Lincoln, Maine, U.S.A. **83 C11** 45 22N 68 30W
Lincoln, N.H., U.S.A. **85 B13** 44 3N 71 40W
Lincoln, N. Mex., U.S.A. **77 K11** 33 30N 105 23W
Lincoln, Nebr., U.S.A. **80 E6** 40 49N 96 41W
Lincoln City, U.S.A. **76 D1** 44 57N 124 1W
Lincoln Hav = Lincoln Sea, Arctic **4 A5** 84 0N 55 0W
Lincoln Sea, Arctic **4 A5** 84 0N 55 0W
Lincolnshire □, U.K. **12 D7** 53 14N 0 32W
Lincolnshire Wolds, U.K. **12 D7** 53 26N 0 13W
Lincolnton, U.S.A. **83 H5** 35 29N 81 16W
Lind, U.S.A. **76 C4** 46 58N 118 37W
Linda, U.S.A. **78 F5** 39 8N 121 34W
Lindeman I., Australia . . . . **62 J7** 20 27S 149 3 E
Linden, Guyana **92 B7** 6 0N 58 10W
Linden, Ala., U.S.A. **83 J2** 32 18N 87 48W
Linden, Calif., U.S.A. **78 G5** 38 1N 121 5W
Linden, Tex., U.S.A. **81 J7** 33 1N 94 22W
Lindenhurst, U.S.A. **85 F11** 40 41N 73 23W
Lindesnes, Norway . . . . **9 H12** 57 58N 7 3 E
Líndhos, Greece . . . . **25 C10** 36 6N 28 4 E
Líndhos, Ákra, Greece . . . . **25 C10** 36 4N 28 10 E
Lindi, Tanzania . . . . **55 D4** 9 58S 39 38 E
Lindi □, Tanzania . . . . **55 D4** 9 40S 38 30 E
Lindi →, Dem. Rep. of the Congo **54 B2** 0 33N 25 5 E
Lindsay, Canada **84 B6** 44 22N 78 43W
Lindsay, Calif., U.S.A. **78 J7** 36 12N 119 5W
Lindsay, Okla., U.S.A. **81 H6** 34 50N 97 38W
Lindsborg, U.S.A. **80 F6** 38 35N 97 40W
Linesville, U.S.A. **84 E4** 41 39N 80 26W
Linfen, China . . . . **34 F6** 36 3N 111 30 E
Ling Xian, China . . . . **34 F9** 37 22N 116 30 E
Lingao, China . . . . **38 C7** 19 56N 109 42 E
Lingayen, Phil. . . . . **37 A6** 16 1N 120 14 E
Lingayen G., Phil. . . . . **37 A6** 16 10N 120 15 E
Lingbi, China . . . . **35 H9** 33 33N 117 33 E
Lingchuan, China . . . . **34 G7** 35 45N 113 12 E
Lingding Yang, China . . . . **33 G10** 22 25N 113 44 E
Lingen, Germany . . . . **16 B4** 52 31N 7 19 E
Lingga, Indonesia . . . . **36 E2** 0 12S 104 37 E
Lingga, Kepulauan, Indonesia . **36 E2** 0 10S 104 30 E
Lingga Arch. = Lingga,
  Kepulauan, Indonesia . . . . . . **36 E2** 0 10S 104 30 E
Lingle, U.S.A. **80 D2** 42 8N 104 21W

Lingqiu, China . . . . **34 E8** 39 28N 114 22 E
Lingshi, China . . . . **34 F6** 36 48N 111 48 E
Lingshou, China . . . . **34 E8** 38 20N 114 20 E
Lingshui, China . . . . **38 C8** 18 27N 110 0 E
Lingtai, China . . . . **34 G4** 35 0N 107 40 E
Linguère, Senegal **50 E2** 15 25N 15 5W
Lingwu, China . . . . **34 E4** 38 6N 106 20 E
Lingyuan, China . . . . **35 D10** 41 10N 119 15 E
Linhai, China . . . . **33 D7** 28 50N 121 8 E
Linhares, Brazil **93 G10** 19 25S 40 4W
Linhe, China . . . . **34 D4** 40 48N 107 20 E
Linjiang, China . . . . **35 D14** 41 50N 127 0 E
Linköping, Sweden . . . . **9 G16** 58 28N 15 36 E
Linkou, China . . . . **35 B16** 45 15N 130 18 E
Linnhe, L., U.K. **11 E3** 56 36N 5 25W
Linosa, Medit. S. . . . . **22 G5** 35 51N 12 50 E
Linqi, China . . . . **34 G7** 35 45N 113 52 E
Linqing, China . . . . **34 F8** 36 50N 115 42 E
Linqu, China . . . . **35 F10** 36 25N 118 30 E
Linru, China . . . . **34 G7** 34 11N 112 52 E
Lins, Brazil **95 A6** 21 40S 49 44W
Linstead, Jamaica . . . . **88 a** 18 8N 77 2W
Linta →, Madag. . . . . **57 D7** 25 2S 44 5 E
Linton, Ind., U.S.A. **82 F2** 39 2N 87 10W
Linton, N. Dak., U.S.A. **80 B4** 46 16N 100 14W
Lintong, China . . . . **34 G5** 34 20N 109 10 E
Linwood, Canada **84 C4** 43 35N 80 43W
Linxi, China . . . . **35 C10** 43 36N 118 2 E
Linxia, China . . . . **32 C5** 35 36N 103 10 E
Linyanti →, Africa . . . . **56 B4** 17 50S 25 5 E
Linyi, China . . . . **35 G10** 35 5N 118 21 E
Linz, Austria . . . . **16 D8** 48 18N 14 18 E
Linzhenzhen, China . . . . **34 F5** 36 30N 109 59 E
Linzi, China . . . . **35 F10** 36 50N 118 20 E
Lion, G. du, France . . . . **20 E6** 43 10N 4 0 E
Lionárisso, Cyprus . . . . **25 D13** 35 28N 34 8 E
Lions, G. of = Lion, G. du, France **20 E6** 43 10N 4 0 E
Lion's Den, Zimbabwe . . . . **55 F3** 17 15S 30 5 E
Lion's Head, Canada **84 B3** 44 58N 81 15W
Lipa, Phil. . . . . **37 B6** 13 57N 121 10 E
Lipali, Mozam. . . . . **55 E4** 15 50S 35 50 E
Lípari, Italy . . . . **22 E6** 38 26N 14 58 E
Lípari, Is. = Eólie, Ís., Italy . . . **22 E6** 38 30N 14 57 E
Lipcani, Moldova . . . . **17 D14** 48 14N 26 48 E
Lipetsk, Russia . . . . **18 D6** 52 37N 39 35 E
Lipkany = Lipcani, Moldova . . **17 D14** 48 14N 26 48 E
Lipovcy Manzovka, Russia . . . **30 B5** 44 12N 134 10 E
Lipovets, Ukraine . . . . **17 D15** 49 12N 29 1 E
Lippe →, Germany . . . . **16 C4** 51 39N 6 36 E
Lipscomb, U.S.A. **81 G4** 36 14N 100 16W
Liptrap, C., Australia . . . . **63 F4** 38 50S 145 55 E
Liquillo, Sierra de, Puerto Rico **89 d** 18 20N 65 47W
Lira, Uganda . . . . **54 B3** 2 17N 32 57 E
Liria = Lliria, Spain **21 C5** 39 37N 0 35W
Lisala, Dem. Rep. of the Congo **52 D4** 2 12N 21 38 E
Lisboa, Portugal **21 C1** 38 42N 9 10W
Lisbon = Lisboa, Portugal **21 C1** 38 42N 9 10W
Lisbon, N. Dak., U.S.A. **80 B6** 46 27N 97 41W
Lisbon, N.H., U.S.A. **85 B13** 44 13N 71 55W
Lisbon, Ohio, U.S.A. **84 F4** 40 46N 80 46W
Lisbon Falls, U.S.A. **83 D10** 44 0N 70 4W
Lisburn, U.K. **10 B5** 54 31N 6 3W
Lisburne, C., U.S.A. **4 C17** 68 53N 166 13W
Liscannor B., Ireland **10 D2** 52 55N 9 24W
Lishi, China . . . . **34 F6** 37 31N 111 8 E
Lishu, China . . . . **35 C13** 43 20N 124 18 E
Lisianski I., Pac. Oc. **64 E10** 26 2N 174 0W
Lisichansk = Lysychansk, Ukraine **19 E6** 48 55N 38 30 E
Lisieux, France . . . . **20 B4** 49 10N 0 12 E
Liski, Russia . . . . **19 D6** 51 3N 39 30 E
Lismore, Australia . . . . **63 D5** 28 44S 153 21 E
Lismore, Ireland **10 D4** 52 8N 7 55W
Lista, Norway . . . . **9 G12** 58 7N 6 39 E
Lister, Mt., Antarctica . . . . **5 D11** 78 0S 162 0 E
Liston, Australia . . . . **63 D5** 28 39S 152 6 E
Listowel, Canada **84 C4** 43 44N 80 58W
Listowel, Ireland **10 D2** 52 27N 9 29W
Litani →, Lebanon . . . . **46 B4** 33 20N 35 15 E
Litchfield, Calif., U.S.A. **78 E6** 40 24N 120 23W
Litchfield, Conn., U.S.A. **85 E11** 41 45N 73 11W
Litchfield, Ill., U.S.A. **80 F10** 39 11N 89 39W
Litchfield, Minn., U.S.A. **80 C7** 45 8N 94 32W
Litchfield △, Australia . . . . **60 B5** 13 14S 131 1 E
Lithgow, Australia . . . . **63 E5** 33 25S 150 8 E
Líthinon, Ákra, Greece . . . . **25 E6** 34 55N 24 44 E
Lithuania ■, Europe . . . . **9 J20** 55 30N 24 0 E
Lititz, U.S.A. **85 F8** 40 9N 76 18W
Litoměřice, Czech Rep. . . . . . . **16 C8** 50 33N 14 10 E
Little Abaco I., Bahamas **88 A4** 26 50N 77 30W
Little Barrier I., N.Z. . . . . **59 G5** 36 12S 175 8 E
Little Belt Mts., U.S.A. **76 C8** 46 40N 110 45W
Little Bighorn Battlefield △,
  U.S.A. **76 D10** 45 34N 107 26W
Little Blue →, U.S.A. **80 F6** 39 42N 96 41W
Little Buffalo →, Canada **70 A6** 61 0N 113 46W
Little Cayman, Cayman Is. **88 C3** 19 41N 80 3W
Little Churchill →, Canada . . . **71 B9** 57 30N 95 22W
Little Colorado →, U.S.A. **77 H8** 36 12N 111 48W
Little Current, Canada **72 C3** 45 55N 82 0W
Little Current →, Canada **72 B3** 50 57N 84 36W
Little Falls, Minn., U.S.A. **80 C7** 45 59N 94 22W
Little Falls, N.Y., U.S.A. **85 C10** 43 3N 74 51W
Little Fork →, U.S.A. **80 A8** 48 31N 93 35W
Little Grand Rapids, Canada . . **71 C9** 52 0N 95 29W
Little Humboldt →, U.S.A. **76 F5** 41 1N 117 43W
Little Inagua I., Bahamas **89 B5** 21 40N 73 50W
Little Karoo, S. Africa . . . . **56 E3** 33 45S 21 0 E
Little Lake, U.S.A. **79 K9** 35 56N 117 55W
Little Laut Is. = Laut Kecil,
  Kepulauan, Indonesia . . . . . . **36 E5** 4 45S 115 40 E
Little Mecatina = Petit-
  Mécatina →, Canada **73 B8** 50 40N 59 30W
Little Minch, U.K. **11 D2** 57 35N 6 45W
Little Missouri →, U.S.A. **80 B3** 47 36N 102 25W
Little Ouse →, U.K. . . . . **13 E9** 52 22N 1 12 E
Little Rann, India . . . . **42 H4** 23 25N 71 25 E
Little Red →, U.S.A. **81 H9** 35 11N 91 27W
Little River, N.Z. . . . . **59 K4** 43 45S 172 49 E
Little Rock, U.S.A. **81 H8** 34 45N 92 17W
Little Ruaha →, Tanzania . . . . . **54 D4** 7 57S 37 53 E
Little Sable Pt., U.S.A. **82 D2** 43 38N 86 33W
Little Sioux →, U.S.A. **80 E6** 41 48N 96 4W
Little Smoky →, Canada **70 C5** 54 44N 117 11W
Little Snake →, U.S.A. **76 F9** 40 27N 108 26W
Little Tobago, Trin. & Tob. **93 J16** 11 18N 60 30W
Little Valley, U.S.A. **84 D6** 42 15N 78 48W
Little Wabash →, U.S.A. **82 G1** 37 55N 88 5W

Little White →, U.S.A. **80 D4** 43 40N 100 40W
Little Zab = Zāb aş Şaghīr →,
  Iraq . . . . **44 C4** 35 17N 43 29 E
Littlefield, U.S.A. **81 J3** 33 55N 102 20W
Littlehampton, U.K. **13 G7** 50 49N 0 32W
Littleton, U.S.A. **85 B13** 44 18N 71 46W
Liu He →, China . . . . **35 D11** 40 55N 121 35 E
Liuba, China . . . . **34 H4** 33 38N 106 55 E
Liugou, China . . . . **35 D10** 40 57N 118 15 E
Liuhe, China . . . . **35 C13** 42 17N 125 43 E
Liukang Tenggaja = Sabalana,
  Kepulauan, Indonesia . . . . . . **37 F5** 6 45S 118 50 E
Liuli, Tanzania . . . . **55 E3** 11 3S 34 38 E
Liuwa Plain, Zambia . . . . **53 G4** 14 20S 22 30 E
Liuzhou, China . . . . **33 D5** 24 22N 109 22 E
Liuzhuang, China . . . . **35 H11** 33 12N 120 18 E
Livadia, Cyprus . . . . **25 E12** 34 57N 33 38 E
Live Oak, Calif., U.S.A. **78 F5** 39 17N 121 40W
Live Oak, Fla., U.S.A. **83 K4** 30 18N 82 59W
Liveras, Cyprus . . . . **25 D11** 35 23N 32 57 E
Livermore, U.S.A. **78 H5** 37 41N 121 47W
Livermore, Mt., U.S.A. **81 K2** 30 38N 104 11W
Livermore Falls, U.S.A. **83 C11** 44 29N 70 11W
Liverpool, Canada **73 D7** 44 5N 64 41W
Liverpool, U.K. **12 D4** 53 25N 3 0W
Liverpool, U.S.A. **85 C8** 43 6N 76 13W
Liverpool Bay, U.K. **12 D4** 53 30N 3 20W
Liverpool Ra., Australia . . . . . . **63 E5** 31 50S 150 30 E
Livingston, Guatemala **88 C2** 15 50N 88 50W
Livingston, U.K. **11 F5** 55 54N 3 30W
Livingston, Ala., U.S.A. **83 J1** 32 35N 88 11W
Livingston, Calif., U.S.A. **78 H6** 37 23N 120 43W
Livingston, Mont., U.S.A. **76 D8** 45 40N 110 34W
Livingston, S.C., U.S.A. **83 J5** 33 32N 80 53W
Livingston, Tenn., U.S.A. **83 G3** 36 23N 85 19W
Livingston, Tex., U.S.A. **81 K7** 30 43N 94 56W
Livingston, L., U.S.A. **81 K7** 30 50N 95 10W
Livingston Manor, U.S.A. **85 E10** 41 54N 74 50W
Livingstone, Zambia . . . . **55 F2** 17 46S 25 52 E
Livingstone Mts., Tanzania . . . **55 D3** 9 40S 34 20 E
Livingstonia, Malawi . . . . **55 E3** 10 38S 34 5 E
Livny, Russia . . . . **18 D6** 52 30N 37 30 E
Livonia, Mich., U.S.A. **82 D4** 42 23N 83 23W
Livonia, N.Y., U.S.A. **84 D7** 42 49N 77 40W
Livorno, Italy . . . . **22 C4** 43 33N 10 19 E
Livramento, Brazil **95 C4** 30 55S 55 30W
Liwale, Tanzania . . . . **55 D4** 9 48S 37 58 E
Liwonde △, Malawi . . . . **55 E4** 14 48S 35 16 E
Lizard I., Australia . . . . **62 A4** 14 42S 145 30 E
Lizard Pt., U.K. **13 H2** 49 57N 5 13W
Ljubljana, Slovenia . . . . **16 E8** 46 4N 14 33 E
Ljungan →, Sweden . . . . **9 E17** 62 18N 17 23 E
Ljungby, Sweden . . . . **9 H15** 56 49N 13 55 E
Ljusdal, Sweden . . . . **9 F17** 61 46N 16 3 E
Ljusnan →, Sweden . . . . **9 F17** 61 12N 17 8 E
Ljusne, Sweden . . . . **9 F17** 61 13N 17 7 E
Llancanelo, Salina, Argentina . **94 D2** 35 40S 69 8W
Llandeilo, U.K. **13 F4** 51 53S 3 59W
Llandovery, U.K. **13 F4** 51 59N 3 48W
Llandrindod Wells, U.K. **13 E4** 52 14N 3 22W
Llandudno, U.K. **12 D4** 53 19N 3 50W
Llanelli, U.K. **13 F3** 51 41N 4 10W
Llanes, Spain **21 A3** 43 25N 4 50W
Llangollen, U.K. **12 E4** 52 58N 3 11W
Llanidloes, U.K. **13 E4** 52 27N 3 31W
Llano, U.S.A. **81 K5** 30 45N 98 41W
Llano →, U.S.A. **81 K5** 30 39N 98 26W
Llano Estacado, U.S.A. **81 J3** 33 30N 103 0W
Llanos, S. Amer. **92 C4** 5 0N 71 35W
Llanos de Challe △, Chile **94 B1** 28 8S 71 1W
Llanquihue, L., Chile **96 E1** 41 10S 72 50W
Llanwrtyd Wells, U.K. **13 E4** 52 7N 3 38W
Llebeig, C. des, Spain . . . . **24 B9** 39 33N 2 18 E
Lleida, Spain . . . . **21 B6** 41 37N 0 39 E
Llentrisca, C., Spain . . . . **24 C7** 38 52N 1 15 E
Llera, Mexico **87 C5** 23 19N 99 1W
Lleyn Peninsula, U.K. **12 E3** 52 51N 4 36W
Llico, Chile **94 C1** 34 46S 72 5W
Lliria, Spain **21 C5** 39 37N 0 35W
Llobregat →, Spain . . . . **21 B7** 41 19N 2 9 E
Lloret de Mar, Spain . . . . **21 B7** 41 41N 2 53 E
Lloyd B., Australia . . . . **62 A3** 12 45S 143 27 E
Lloyd L., Canada **71 B7** 57 22N 108 57W
Lloydminster, Canada **71 C7** 53 17N 110 0W
Llucmajor, Spain . . . . **24 B9** 39 29N 2 53 E
Llullaillaco △, Chile **94 A2** 24 50S 68 51W
Llullaillaco, Volcán, S. Amer. . . **94 A2** 24 43S 68 30W
Lo →, Vietnam . . . . **38 B5** 21 18N 105 25 E
Loa, U.S.A. **77 G8** 38 24N 111 39W
Loa →, Chile **94 A1** 21 26S 70 41W
Loaita I., S. China Sea . . . . **36 B4** 10 41N 114 25 E
Loange →, Dem. Rep. of
  the Congo . . . . **52 E4** 4 17S 20 2 E
Lobatse, Botswana . . . . **56 D4** 25 12S 25 40 E
Lobería, Argentina **94 D4** 38 10S 58 40W
Lobito, Angola . . . . **53 G2** 12 18S 13 35 E
Lobos, Argentina **94 D4** 35 10S 59 0W
Lobos, I., Mexico **86 B2** 27 15N 110 30W
Lobos, I. de, Canary Is. **24 F6** 28 45N 13 50W
Loc Binh, Vietnam . . . . **38 B6** 21 46N 106 54 E
Loc Ninh, Vietnam . . . . **39 G6** 11 50N 106 34 E
Locarno, Switz. . . . . **20 C8** 46 10N 8 47 E
Loch Baghasdail = Lochboisdale,
  U.K. **11 D1** 57 9N 7 20W
Loch Garman = Wexford, Ireland **10 D5** 52 20N 6 28W
Loch Lomond and the
  Trossachs △, U.K. **11 E4** 56 10N 4 40W
Loch Nam Madadh =
  Lochmaddy, U.K. **11 D1** 57 36N 7 10W
Lochaber, U.K. **11 E3** 56 59N 5 1W
Locharbriggs, U.K. **11 F5** 55 7N 3 35W
Lochboisdale, U.K. **11 D1** 57 9N 7 20W
Loche, L. La, Canada **71 B7** 56 30N 109 30W
Lochem, Neths. . . . . **15 B6** 52 9N 6 26 E
Loches, France . . . . **20 C4** 47 7N 1 0 E
Lochgilphead, U.K. **11 E3** 56 2N 5 26W
Lochinvar △, Zambia . . . . **55 F2** 15 55S 27 15 E
Lochinver, U.K. **11 C3** 58 9N 5 14W
Lochmaddy, U.K. **11 D1** 57 36N 7 10W
Lochnagar, Australia . . . . **62 C4** 23 33S 145 38 E
Lochnagar, U.K. **11 E5** 56 57N 3 15W
Lochy, L., U.K. **11 E4** 57 0N 4 53W
Lock, Australia . . . . **63 E2** 33 34S 135 46 E
Lock Haven, U.S.A. **84 E7** 41 8N 77 28W
Lockeford, U.S.A. **78 G5** 38 10N 121 9W
Lockhart, U.S.A. . . . .
Lockhart, L., Australia . . . .
Lockney, U.S.A. . . . .
Lockport, Canada **73 D6** 43 47N 65 4W
Lockerbie, U.K. **11 F5** 55 7N 3 21W

Lockhart, U.S.A.	81 L6	29 53N	97 40W
Lockhart, L., Australia	61 F2	33 15S	119 3 E
Lockhart River, Australia	62 A3	12 58S	143 30 E
Lockney, U.S.A.	81 H4	34 7N	101 27W
Lockport, U.S.A.	84 C6	43 10N	78 42W
Lod, Israel	46 D3	31 57N	34 54 E
Lodeinoye Pole, Russia	18 B5	60 44N	33 33 E
Lodge Bay, Canada	73 B8	52 14N	55 51W
Lodge Grass, U.S.A.	76 D10	45 19N	107 22W
Lodgepole Cr. →, U.S.A.	80 E2	41 20N	104 30W
Lodhran, Pakistan	42 E4	29 32N	71 30 E
Lodi, Italy	20 D8	45 19N	9 30 E
Lodi, Calif., U.S.A.	78 G5	38 8N	121 16W
Lodi, Ohio, U.S.A.	84 E3	41 2N	82 0W
Lodja, Dem. Rep. of the Congo	54 C1	3 30S	23 23 E
Lodwar, Kenya	54 B4	3 10N	35 40 E
Łódź, Poland	17 C10	51 45N	19 27 E
Loei, Thailand	38 D3	17 29N	101 35 E
Loengo, Dem. Rep. of the Congo	54 C2	4 48S	26 30 E
Loeriesfontein, S. Africa	56 E2	31 0S	19 26 E
Lofoten, Norway	8 B15	68 30N	14 0 E
Logan, Iowa, U.S.A.	80 E7	41 39N	95 47W
Logan, Ohio, U.S.A.	82 F4	39 32N	82 25W
Logan, Utah, U.S.A.	76 F8	41 44N	111 50W
Logan, W. Va., U.S.A.	82 G5	37 51N	81 59W
Logan, Mt., Canada	68 B5	60 34N	140 23W
Logandale, U.S.A.	79 J12	36 36N	114 29W
Logansport, Ind., U.S.A.	82 E2	40 45N	86 22W
Logansport, La., U.S.A.	81 K8	31 58N	94 0W
Logone →, Chad	51 F9	12 6N	15 2 E
Logroño, Spain	21 A4	42 28N	2 27W
Lohardaga, India	43 H11	23 27N	84 45 E
Loharia, India	42 H6	23 45N	74 14 E
Loharu, India	42 E7	28 27N	75 49 E
Lohja, Finland	9 F21	60 12N	24 5 E
Lohri Wah →, Pakistan	42 F2	27 27N	67 37 E
Loi-kaw, Burma	41 K20	19 40N	97 17 E
Loimaa, Finland	9 F20	60 50N	23 5 E
Loir →, France	20 C3	47 33N	0 32W
Loire →, France	20 C2	47 16N	2 10W
Loja, Ecuador	92 D3	3 59S	79 16W
Loja, Spain	21 D3	37 10N	4 10W
Loji = Kawasi, Indonesia	37 E7	1 38S	127 28 E
Lokandu, Dem. Rep. of the Congo	54 C2	2 30S	25 45 E
Lokeren, Belgium	15 C3	51 6N	3 59 E
Lokgwabe, Botswana	56 C3	24 10S	21 50 E
Lokichokio, Kenya	54 B3	4 19N	34 13 E
Lokitaung, Kenya	54 B4	4 12N	35 48 E
Lokkan tekojärvi, Finland	8 C22	67 55N	27 35 E
Lokoja, Nigeria	50 G7	7 47N	6 45 E
Lola, Mt., U.S.A.	78 F6	39 26N	120 22W
Loliondo, Tanzania	54 C4	2 2S	35 39 E
Lolland, Denmark	9 J14	54 45N	11 30 E
Lolo, U.S.A.	76 C6	46 45N	114 5W
Lom, Bulgaria	23 C10	43 48N	23 12 E
Lom Kao, Thailand	38 D3	16 53N	101 14 E
Lom Sak, Thailand	38 D3	16 47N	101 15 E
Loma, U.S.A.	76 C8	47 56N	110 30W
Loma Linda, U.S.A.	79 L9	34 3N	117 16W
Lomami →, Dem. Rep. of the Congo	54 B1	0 46N	24 16 E
Lomas de Zamóra, Argentina	94 C4	34 45S	58 25W
Lombadina, Australia	60 C3	16 31S	122 54 E
Lombárdia □, Italy	20 D8	45 40N	9 30 E
Lombardy = Lombárdia □, Italy	20 D8	45 40N	9 30 E
Lomblen, Indonesia	37 F6	8 30S	123 32 E
Lombok, Indonesia	36 F5	8 45S	116 30 E
Lombok, Selat, Indonesia	37 K18	8 30S	115 50 E
Lomé, Togo	50 G6	6 9N	1 20 E
Lomela, Dem. Rep. of the Congo	54 E4	2 19S	23 15 E
Lomela →, Dem. Rep. of the Congo	52 E4	0 15S	20 40 E
Lommel, Belgium	15 C5	51 14N	5 19 E
Lomond, Canada	70 C6	50 24N	112 36W
Lomond, L., U.K.	11 E4	56 8N	4 38W
Lomonosov Ridge, Arctic	4 A	88 0N	140 0 E
Lomphat, Cambodia	38 F6	13 30N	106 59 E
Lompobatang, Indonesia	37 F5	5 24S	119 56 E
Lompoc, U.S.A.	79 L6	34 38N	120 28W
Łomża, Poland	17 B12	53 10N	22 2 E
Lon, Ko, Thailand	39 a	7 47N	98 23 E
Loncoche, Chile	96 D2	39 20S	72 50W
Londa, India	40 M9	15 30N	74 30 E
Londiani, Kenya	54 C4	0 10S	35 33 E
London, Canada	84 D3	42 59N	81 15W
London, U.K.	13 F7	51 30N	0 3W
London, Ky., U.S.A.	82 G3	37 8N	84 5W
London, Ohio, U.S.A.	82 F4	39 53N	83 27W
London, Greater □, U.K.	13 F7	51 36N	0 5W
London Gatwick ✈ (LGW), U.K.	13 F7	51 10N	0 11W
London Heathrow ✈ (LHR), U.K.	13 F7	51 28N	0 27W
London Stansted ✈ (STN), U.K.	13 F8	51 54N	0 14 E
Londonderry, U.K.	10 B4	55 0N	7 20W
Londonderry □, U.K.	10 B4	55 0N	7 20W
Londonderry, C., Australia	60 B4	13 45S	126 55 E
Londonderry, I., Chile	96 H2	55 0S	71 0W
Londres, Argentina	94 B2	27 43S	67 7W
Londrina, Brazil	95 A5	23 18S	51 10W
Lone Pine, U.S.A.	78 J8	36 36N	118 4W
Lonely Mine, Zimbabwe	57 B4	19 30S	28 49 E
Long B., U.S.A.	83 J6	33 35N	78 45W
Long Beach, Calif., U.S.A.	79 M8	33 47N	118 11W
Long Beach, N.Y., U.S.A.	85 F11	40 35N	73 39W
Long Beach, Wash., U.S.A.	78 D2	46 21N	124 3W
Long Branch, U.S.A.	85 F11	40 18N	74 0W
Long Creek, U.S.A.	76 D4	44 43N	119 6W
Long Eaton, U.K.	12 E6	52 53N	1 15W
Long I., Australia	62 J6	20 22S	148 51 E
Long I., Bahamas	89 B4	23 20N	75 10W
Long I., Canada	72 B4	54 50N	79 20W
Long I., Ireland	10 E2	51 30N	9 34W
Long Island Sd., U.S.A.	85 E12	41 10N	73 0W
Long L., Canada	72 C2	49 30N	86 50W
Long Lake, U.S.A.	85 C10	43 58N	74 25W
Long Point B., Canada	84 D4	42 40N	80 10W
Long Prairie →, U.S.A.	80 C7	46 20N	94 36W
Long Pt., Canada	84 D4	42 35N	80 2W
Long Range Mts., Canada	73 C8	49 30N	57 30W
Long Reef, Australia	60 B4	14 1S	125 48 E
Long Spruce, Canada	71 B10	56 24N	94 21W
Long Str. = Longa, Proliv, Russia	4 C16	70 0N	175 0 E
Long Thanh, Vietnam	39 G6	10 47N	106 57 E
Long Xian, China	34 G4	34 55N	106 55 E
Long Xuyen, Vietnam	39 G5	10 19N	105 28 E
Longa, Proliv, Russia	4 C16	70 0N	175 0 E
Longbenton, U.K.	12 B6	55 1N	1 31W
Longboat Key, U.S.A.	83 M4	27 23N	82 39W
Longde, China	34 G4	35 30N	106 20 E
Longford, Australia	63 G4	41 32S	147 3 E
Longford, Ireland	10 C4	53 43N	7 49W
Longford □, Ireland	10 C4	53 42N	7 45W
Longhua, Guangdong, China	33 F11	22 39N	114 0 E
Longhua, Hebei, China	35 D9	41 18N	117 45 E
Longido, Tanzania	54 C4	2 43S	36 42 E
Longiram, Indonesia	36 E5	0 5S	115 45 E
Longkou, China	35 F11	37 40N	120 18 E
Longlac, Canada	72 C2	49 45N	86 25W
Longmeadow, U.S.A.	85 D12	42 3N	72 34W
Longmont, U.S.A.	80 E2	40 10N	105 6W
Longnawan, Indonesia	36 D4	1 51N	114 55 E
Longreach, Australia	62 C3	23 28S	144 14 E
Longueuil, Canada	85 A11	45 32N	73 28W
Longview, Tex., U.S.A.	81 J7	32 30N	94 44W
Longview, Wash., U.S.A.	78 D4	46 8N	122 57W
Longxi, China	34 G3	34 53N	104 40 E
Longxue Dao, China	33 F10	22 41N	113 38 E
Longyearbyen, Norway	4 B8	78 13N	15 38 E
Lonoke, U.S.A.	81 H9	34 47N	91 54W
Lonquimay, Chile	96 D2	38 26S	71 14W
Lons-le-Saunier, France	20 C6	46 40N	5 31 E
Looe, U.K.	13 G3	50 22N	4 28W
Lookout, C., Canada	72 A3	55 18N	83 56W
Lookout, C., U.S.A.	83 H7	34 35N	76 32W
Loolmalasin, Tanzania	54 C4	3 0S	35 53 E
Loon →, Alta., Canada	70 B5	57 8N	115 3W
Loon →, Man., Canada	71 B8	55 53N	101 59W
Loon Lake, Canada	71 C7	54 2N	109 10W
Loongana, Australia	61 F4	30 52S	127 5 E
Loop Hd., Ireland	10 D2	52 34N	9 56W
Lop Buri, Thailand	38 E3	14 48N	100 37 E
Lop Nor = Lop Nur, China	32 B4	40 20N	90 10 E
Lop Nur, China	32 B4	40 20N	90 10 E
Lopatina, Gora, Russia	29 D15	50 47N	143 10 E
Lopez, U.S.A.	85 E8	41 27N	76 20W
Lopez, C., Gabon	52 E1	0 47S	8 40 E
Lopphavet, Norway	8 A19	70 27N	21 15 E
Lora →, Afghan.	40 D4	31 35N	66 32 E
Lora, Hämün-i-, Pakistan	40 E4	29 38N	64 58 E
Lora Cr. →, Australia	63 D2	28 10S	135 22 E
Lora del Río, Spain	21 D3	37 39N	5 33W
Lorain, U.S.A.	84 E2	41 28N	82 11W
Loralai, Pakistan	42 D3	30 20N	68 41 E
Lorca, Spain	21 D5	37 41N	1 42W
Lord Howe I., Pac. Oc.	64 L7	31 33S	159 6 E
Lord Howe Ridge, Pac. Oc.	64 L8	30 0S	162 30 E
Lordsburg, U.S.A.	77 K9	32 21N	108 43W
Lorestan □, Iran	45 C6	33 30N	48 40 E
Loreto, Brazil	93 E9	7 5S	45 10W
Loreto, Mexico	86 B2	26 1N	111 21W
Lorient, France	20 C2	47 45N	3 23W
Lormi, India	43 H9	22 17N	81 41 E
Lorn, U.K.	11 E3	56 26N	5 10W
Lorn, Firth of, U.K.	11 E3	56 20N	5 40W
Lorne, Australia	63 F3	38 33S	143 59 E
Lorovouno, Cyprus	25 D11	35 8N	32 36 E
Lorraine ⊠, France	20 B7	48 53N	6 0 E
Los Alamos, Calif., U.S.A.	79 L6	34 44N	120 17W
Los Alamos, N. Mex., U.S.A.	77 J10	35 53N	106 19W
Los Altos, U.S.A.	78 H4	37 23N	122 7W
Los Andes, Chile	94 C1	32 50S	70 40W
Los Angeles, Chile	94 D1	37 28S	72 23W
Los Angeles, U.S.A.	79 M8	34 4N	118 15W
Los Angeles, Bahia de, Mexico	86 B2	28 56N	113 34W
Los Angeles Aqueduct, U.S.A.	79 K9	35 22N	118 5W
Los Angeles International ✈ (LAX), U.S.A.	79 M8	33 57N	118 25W
Los Banos, U.S.A.	78 H6	37 4N	120 51W
Los Blancos, Argentina	94 A3	23 40S	62 30W
Los Cardones △, Argentina	94 B2	25 8S	65 55W
Los Chiles, Costa Rica	88 D3	11 2N	84 43W
Los Cristianos, Canary Is.	24 F3	28 3N	16 42W
Los Gatos, U.S.A.	78 H5	37 14N	121 59W
Los Haïtises △, Dom. Rep.	89 C6	19 4N	69 36W
Los Hermanos Is., Venezuela	89 D7	11 45N	64 25W
Los Islotes, Canary Is.	24 E6	29 4N	13 44W
Los Llanos de Aridane, Canary Is.	24 F2	28 38N	17 54W
Los Loros, Chile	94 B1	27 50S	70 6W
Los Lunas, U.S.A.	77 J10	34 48N	106 44W
Los Mochis, Mexico	86 B3	25 45N	108 57W
Los Olivos, U.S.A.	79 L6	34 40N	120 7W
Los Palacios, Cuba	88 B3	22 35N	83 15W
Los Reyes, Mexico	86 D4	19 34N	102 30W
Los Roques Is., Venezuela	89 D6	11 50N	66 45W
Los Teques, Venezuela	92 A5	10 21N	67 2W
Los Testigos, Is., Venezuela	92 A6	11 23N	63 6W
Los Vilos, Chile	94 C1	32 10S	71 30W
Lošinj, Croatia	16 F8	44 30N	14 30 E
Loskop Dam, S. Africa	57 D4	25 23S	29 20 E
Lossiemouth, U.K.	11 D5	57 42N	3 17W
Lostwithiel, U.K.	13 G3	50 24N	4 41W
Lot →, France	20 D4	44 18N	0 20 E
Lota, Chile	94 D1	37 5S	73 10W
Lotfābād, Iran	45 B8	37 32N	59 20 E
Lothair, S. Africa	57 D5	26 22S	30 27 E
Loubomo, Congo	52 E2	4 9S	12 47 E
Loudonville, U.S.A.	84 F2	40 38N	82 14W
Louga, Senegal	50 E2	15 45N	16 5W
Loughborough, U.K.	12 E6	52 47N	1 11W
Loughrea, Ireland	10 C3	53 12N	8 33W
Loughros More B., Ireland	10 B3	54 48N	8 32W
Louis Trichardt, S. Africa	57 C4	23 1S	29 43 E
Louis XIV, Pte., Canada	72 B4	54 37N	79 45W
Louisa, U.S.A.	82 F4	38 7N	82 36W
Louisbourg, Canada	73 C8	45 55N	60 0W
Louise I., Canada	70 C2	52 55N	131 50W
Louiseville, Canada	72 C5	46 20N	72 56W
Louisiade Arch., Papua N. G.	64 J7	11 10S	153 0 E
Louisiana, U.S.A.	80 F9	39 27N	91 3W
Louisiana □, U.S.A.	81 K9	30 50N	92 0W
Louisville, Ky., U.S.A.	82 F3	38 15N	85 46W
Louisville, Miss., U.S.A.	81 J10	33 7N	89 3W
Louisville, Ohio, U.S.A.	84 F3	40 50N	81 16W
Loulé, Portugal	21 D1	37 9N	8 0W
Loup City, U.S.A.	80 E5	41 17N	98 58W
Loups Marins, Lacs des, Canada	72 A5	56 30N	73 45W
Lourdes, France	20 E3	43 6N	0 3W
Louth, Australia	63 E4	30 30S	145 8 E
Louth, Ireland	10 C5	53 58N	6 32W
Louth □, Ireland	10 C5	53 56N	6 34W
Louth, U.K.	12 D7	53 22N	0 1W
Louvain = Leuven, Belgium	15 D4	50 52N	4 42 E
Louwsburg, S. Africa	57 D5	27 37S	31 7 E
Lovech, Bulgaria	23 C11	43 8N	24 42 E
Loveland, U.S.A.	80 E2	40 24N	105 5W
Lovell, U.S.A.	76 D9	44 50N	108 24W
Lovelock, U.S.A.	76 F4	40 11N	118 28W
Loviisa, Finland	9 F22	60 28N	26 12 E
Loving, U.S.A.	81 J2	32 17N	104 6W
Lovington, U.S.A.	81 J3	32 57N	103 21W
Lovisa = Loviisa, Finland	9 F22	60 28N	26 12 E
Low, L., Canada	72 B4	52 29N	76 17W
Low Pt., Australia	61 F4	32 25S	127 25 E
Low Tatra = Nízké Tatry, Slovak Rep.	17 D10	48 55N	19 30 E
Lowa, Dem. Rep. of the Congo	54 C2	1 25S	25 47 E
Lowa →, Dem. Rep. of the Congo	54 C2	1 24S	25 51 E
Lowell, U.S.A.	85 D13	42 38N	71 19W
Lowellville, U.S.A.	84 E4	41 2N	80 32W
Löwen →, Namibia	56 D2	26 51S	18 17 E
Lower Alkali L., U.S.A.	76 F3	41 16N	120 2W
Lower Arrow L., Canada	70 D5	49 40N	118 5W
Lower California = Baja California, Mexico	86 A1	31 10N	115 12W
Lower Hutt, N.Z.	59 J5	41 10S	174 55 E
Lower Lake, U.S.A.	78 G4	38 55N	122 37W
Lower Manitou L., Canada	71 D10	49 15N	93 0W
Lower Post, Canada	70 B3	59 58N	128 30W
Lower Red L., U.S.A.	80 B7	47 58N	95 0W
Lower Saxony = Niedersachsen □, Germany	16 B5	52 50N	9 0 E
Lower Tunguska = Tunguska, Nizhnyaya →, Russia	29 C9	65 48N	88 4 E
Lower Zambezi △, Zambia	55 F2	15 25S	29 40 E
Lowestoft, U.K.	13 E9	52 29N	1 45 E
Lowgar □, Afghan.	40 B6	34 0N	69 0 E
Lowicz, Poland	17 B10	52 6N	19 55 E
Lowville, U.S.A.	85 C9	43 47N	75 29W
Loxton, Australia	63 E3	34 28S	140 31 E
Loxton, S. Africa	56 E3	31 30S	22 22 E
Loyalton, U.S.A.	78 F6	39 41N	120 14W
Loyalty Is. = Loyauté, Îs., N. Cal.	64 K8	20 50S	166 30 E
Loyang = Luoyang, China	34 G7	34 40N	112 26 E
Loyauté, Îs., N. Cal.	64 K8	20 50S	166 30 E
Loyev = Loyew, Belarus	17 C16	51 56N	30 46 E
Loyew, Belarus	17 C16	51 56N	30 46 E
Loyoro, Uganda	54 B3	3 22N	34 14 E
Lu Wo, China	33 F11	22 33N	114 6 E
Luachimo, Angola	52 F4	7 23S	20 48 E
Luajan →, India	43 G11	24 44N	85 1 E
Lualaba →, Dem. Rep. of the Congo	54 B2	0 26N	25 20 E
Luampa, Zambia	55 F1	15 4S	24 20 E
Luan Chau, Vietnam	38 B4	21 38N	103 24 E
Luan He →, China	35 E10	39 20N	119 5 E
Luan Xian, China	35 E10	39 40N	118 40 E
Luanda, Angola	52 F2	8 50S	13 15 E
Luang, Thale, Thailand	39 J3	7 30N	100 15 E
Luang Prabang, Laos	38 C4	19 52N	102 10 E
Luangwa, Zambia	55 F3	15 35S	30 16 E
Luangwa →, Zambia	55 E3	14 25S	30 25 E
Luangwa Valley, Zambia	55 E3	13 30S	31 30 E
Luanne, China	35 D9	40 55N	117 40 E
Luanping, China	35 D9	40 53N	117 23 E
Luanshya, Zambia	55 E2	13 3S	28 28 E
Luapula □, Zambia	55 E2	11 0S	29 0 E
Luapula →, Africa	55 E2	9 26S	28 33 E
Luarca, Spain	21 A2	43 32N	6 32W
Luashi, Dem. Rep. of the Congo	55 E1	10 50S	23 36 E
Luau, Angola	52 G4	10 40S	22 10 E
Lubana, Ozero = Lubānas Ezers, Latvia	9 H22	56 45N	27 0 E
Lubānas Ezers, Latvia	9 H22	56 45N	27 0 E
Lubang Is., Phil.	37 B6	13 50N	120 12 E
Lubango, Angola	53 G2	14 55S	13 30 E
Lubao, Dem. Rep. of the Congo	54 D2	5 17S	25 42 E
Lubbock, U.S.A.	81 J4	33 35N	101 51W
Lübeck, Germany	16 B6	53 52N	10 40 E
Lubefu, Dem. Rep. of the Congo	54 C1	4 47S	24 27 E
Lubefu →, Dem. Rep. of the Congo	54 C1	4 10S	23 0 E
Lubero = Luofu, Dem. Rep. of the Congo	54 C2	0 10S	29 15 E
Lubicon L., Canada	70 B5	56 23N	115 56W
Lubilash →, Dem. Rep. of the Congo	52 F4	6 2S	23 45 E
Lubin, Poland	16 C9	51 24N	16 11 E
Lublin, Poland	17 C12	51 12N	22 38 E
Lubnän, Jabal, Lebanon	46 B4	33 45N	35 40 E
Lubny, Ukraine	28 D4	50 3N	32 58 E
Lubongola, Dem. Rep. of the Congo	54 C2	2 35S	27 50 E
Lubudi, Dem. Rep. of the Congo	52 F5	9 57S	25 58 E
Lubudi →, Dem. Rep. of the Congo	55 D2	9 0S	25 35 E
Lubukllinggau, Indonesia	36 E2	3 15S	102 55 E
Lubuksikaping, Indonesia	36 D2	0 10N	100 15 E
Lubumbashi, Dem. Rep. of the Congo	55 E2	11 40S	27 28 E
Lubunda, Dem. Rep. of the Congo	54 D2	5 12S	26 41 E
Lubungu, Zambia	55 E2	14 35S	26 24 E
Lubutu, Dem. Rep. of the Congo	54 C2	0 45S	26 30 E
Luc An Chau, Vietnam	38 A5	22 6N	104 43 E
Lucan, Canada	84 C3	43 11N	81 24W
Lucania, Mt., Canada	68 B5	61 1N	140 27W
Lucas Channel, Canada	84 A3	45 21N	81 45W
Lucca, Italy	22 C4	43 50N	10 29 E
Luce Bay, U.K.	11 G4	54 45N	4 48W
Lucea, Jamaica	88 a	18 25N	78 10W
Lucedale, U.S.A.	83 K1	30 56N	88 35W
Lucena, Phil.	37 B6	13 56N	121 37 E
Lucena, Spain	21 D3	37 27N	4 31W
Lučenec, Slovak Rep.	17 D10	48 18N	19 42 E
Lucerne = Luzern, Switz.	20 C8	47 3N	8 18 E
Lucerne, U.S.A.	78 F4	39 6N	122 48W
Lucerne Valley, U.S.A.	79 L10	34 27N	116 57W
Lucero, Mexico	86 A3	30 49N	106 30W
Lucheng, China	34 F7	36 20N	113 11 E
Lucheringo →, Mozam.	55 E4	11 43S	36 17 E
Lucia, U.S.A.	78 J5	36 2N	121 33W
Lucinda, Australia	62 B4	18 32S	146 20 E
Luckenwalde, Germany	16 B7	52 5N	13 10 E
Luckhoff, S. Africa	56 D3	29 44S	24 43 E
Lucknow, Canada	84 C3	43 57N	81 31W
Lucknow, India	43 F9	26 50N	81 0 E
Lüda = Dalian, China	35 E11	38 50N	121 40 E
Lüderitz, Namibia	56 D2	26 41S	15 8 E
Lüderitzbaai, Namibia	56 D2	26 36S	15 8 E
Ludhiana, India	42 D6	30 57N	75 56 E
Ludlow, U.K.	13 E5	52 22N	2 42W
Ludlow, Calif., U.S.A.	79 L10	34 43N	116 10W
Ludlow, Pa., U.S.A.	84 E6	41 43N	78 56W
Ludlow, Vt., U.S.A.	85 C12	43 24N	72 42W
Ludvika, Sweden	9 F16	60 8N	15 14 E
Ludwigsburg, Germany	16 D5	48 53N	9 11 E
Ludwigshafen, Germany	16 D5	49 29N	8 26 E
Lueki, Dem. Rep. of the Congo	54 C2	3 20S	25 48 E
Luena, Dem. Rep. of the Congo	55 D2	9 28S	25 43 E
Luena, Zambia	55 E3	10 40S	30 25 E
Luenha = Ruenya →, Africa	55 F3	16 24S	33 48 E
Lüeyang, China	34 H4	33 22N	106 10 E
Lufira →, Dem. Rep. of the Congo	55 D2	9 30S	27 0 E
Lufkin, U.S.A.	81 K7	31 21N	94 44W
Lufupa, Dem. Rep. of the Congo	55 E1	10 37S	24 56 E
Luga, Russia	18 C4	58 40N	29 55 E
Lugano, Switz.	20 C8	46 1N	8 57 E
Lugansk = Luhansk, Ukraine	19 E6	48 38N	39 15 E
Lugard's Falls, Kenya	54 C4	3 6S	38 41 E
Lugela, Mozam.	55 F4	16 25S	36 43 E
Lugenda →, Mozam.	55 E4	11 25S	38 33 E
Lugh Ganana, Somali Rep.	47 G3	3 48N	42 34 E
Lugnaquillia, Ireland	10 D5	52 58N	6 28W
Lugo, Italy	22 B4	44 25N	11 54 E
Lugo, Spain	21 A2	43 2N	7 35W
Lugoj, Romania	17 F11	45 42N	21 57 E
Lugovoy = Qulan, Kazakhstan	28 E8	42 55N	72 43 E
Luhansk, Ukraine	19 E6	48 38N	39 15 E
Luiana, Angola	56 B3	17 25S	22 59 E
Luimneach = Limerick, Ireland	10 D3	52 40N	8 37W
Luing, U.K.	11 E3	56 14N	5 39W
Luís Correia, Brazil	93 D10	3 0S	41 35W
Luitpold Coast, Antarctica	5 D1	78 30S	32 0W
Luiza, Dem. Rep. of the Congo	52 F4	7 40S	22 30 E
Luizi, Dem. Rep. of the Congo	54 D2	6 0S	27 25 E
Luján, Argentina	94 C4	34 45S	59 5W
Lukanga Swamp, Zambia	55 E2	14 30S	27 40 E
Lukenie →, Dem. Rep. of the Congo	52 E3	3 0S	18 50 E
Lukhisaral, India	43 G12	25 11N	86 5 E
Lukolela, Dem. Rep. of the Congo	54 D1	5 23S	24 32 E
Lukosi, Zimbabwe	55 F2	18 30S	26 30 E
Łuków, Poland	17 C12	51 55N	22 23 E
Lukusuzi △, Zambia	55 E3	12 43S	32 36 E
Lule älv →, Sweden	8 D19	65 35N	22 10 E
Luleå, Sweden	8 D20	65 35N	22 10 E
Lüleburgaz, Turkey	23 D12	41 23N	27 22 E
Luling, China	81 L6	29 41N	97 39W
Lulong, China	35 E10	39 53N	118 51 E
Lulonga →, Dem. Rep. of the Congo	52 D3	1 0N	18 10 E
Lulua →, Dem. Rep. of the Congo	52 E4	4 30S	20 30 E
Lumajang, Indonesia	37 H15	8 8S	113 13 E
Lumbala N'guimbo, Angola	53 G4	14 18S	21 18 E
Lumberton, U.S.A.	83 H6	34 37N	79 0W
Lumsden, Canada	71 C8	50 39N	104 52W
Lumsden, N.Z.	59 L2	45 44S	168 27 E
Lumut, Malaysia	39 K3	4 13N	100 37 E
Lumut, Tanjung, Indonesia	36 E3	3 50S	105 58 E
Luna, India	42 H3	23 43N	69 16 E
Lunavada, India	42 H5	23 8N	73 37 E
Lund, Sweden	9 J15	55 44N	13 12 E
Lundazi, Zambia	55 E3	12 20S	33 7 E
Lundi →, Zimbabwe	55 G3	21 43S	32 34 E
Lundu, Malaysia	36 D3	1 40N	109 50 E
Lundy, U.K.	13 F3	51 10N	4 41W
Lune →, U.K.	12 C5	54 0N	2 51W
Lüneburg, Germany	16 B6	53 15N	10 24 E
Lüneburg Heath = Lüneburger Heide, Germany	16 B6	53 10N	10 12 E
Lüneburger Heide, Germany	16 B6	53 10N	10 12 E
Lunenburg, Canada	73 D7	44 22N	64 18W
Lunéville, France	20 B7	48 36N	6 30 E
Lunga →, Zambia	55 E2	14 34S	26 25 E
Lunglei, India	41 H18	22 55N	92 45 E
Luni, India	42 G5	26 0N	73 6 E
Luni →, India	42 G4	24 41N	71 14 E
Luninets = Luninyets, Belarus	17 B14	52 15N	26 50 E
Luning, U.S.A.	76 G4	38 30N	118 11W
Luninyets, Belarus	17 B14	52 15N	26 50 E
Lunkaransar, India	42 E5	28 29S	73 52 E
Lunsemfwa →, Zambia	55 E3	14 54S	30 12 E
Lunsemfwa Falls, Zambia	55 E2	14 30S	29 6 E
Luo He →, China	34 G6	34 35N	110 20 E
Luochuan, China	34 G5	35 45N	109 26 E
Luofu, Dem. Rep. of the Congo	54 C2	0 10S	29 15 E
Luohe, China	34 H8	33 32N	114 2 E
Luonan, China	34 G6	34 5N	110 10 E
Luoning, China	34 G6	34 35N	111 40 E
Luoyang, China	34 G7	34 40N	112 26 E
Luozigou, China	35 C16	43 42N	130 18 E
Lupanshui, China	32 D5	26 38N	104 48 E
Lupilichi, Mozam.	55 E4	11 47S	35 13 E
Luque, Paraguay	94 B4	25 19S	57 25W
Luray, U.S.A.	82 F6	38 40N	78 28W
Lurgan, U.K.	10 B5	54 28N	6 19W
Lusaka, Zambia	55 F2	15 28S	28 16 E
Lusambo, Dem. Rep. of the Congo	54 C1	4 58S	23 28 E
Lusangaye, Dem. Rep. of the Congo	54 C2	4 54S	26 0 E
Luseland, Canada	71 C7	52 5N	109 24W
Lusenga Plain △, Zambia	55 D2	9 22S	29 14 E
Lushan, China	34 H7	33 45N	112 55 E
Lushi, China	34 G6	34 3N	111 3 E
Lushnjë, Albania	23 D8	40 55N	19 41 E
Lushoto, Tanzania	54 C4	4 47S	38 20 E
Lüshun, China	35 E11	38 45N	121 15 E
Lusk, U.S.A.	80 D2	42 46N	104 27W
Lüt, Dasht-e, Iran	45 D8	31 30N	58 0 E
Luta = Dalian, China	35 E11	38 50N	121 40 E
Lutherstadt Wittenberg, Germany	16 C7	51 53N	12 39 E
Luton, U.K.	13 F7	51 53N	0 24W
Luton □, U.K.	13 F7	51 53N	0 24W
Lutselk'e, Canada	71 A6	62 24N	110 44W
Lutsk, Ukraine	17 C13	50 50N	25 15 E
Lützow Holmbukta, Antarctica	5 C4	69 10S	37 30 E
Lutzputs, S. Africa	56 D3	28 3S	20 40 E
Luuq = Lugh Ganana, Somali Rep.	47 G3	3 48N	42 34 E
Luverne, Ala., U.S.A.	83 K2	31 43N	86 16W
Luverne, Minn., U.S.A.	80 D6	43 39N	96 13W
Luvua, Dem. Rep. of the Congo	55 D2	8 48S	25 17 E
Luvua →, Dem. Rep. of the Congo	54 D2	6 50S	27 30 E

uvuvhu ➤, S. Africa	57 C5	22 25S 31 18 E
uwegu ➤, Tanzania	55 D4	8 31S 37 23 E
uwuk, Indonesia	37 E6	0 56S 122 47 E
uxembourg, Lux.	15 E6	49 37N 6 9 E
uxembourg □, Belgium	15 E5	49 58N 5 30 E
uxembourg ■, Europe	20 B7	49 45N 6 0 E
uxembourg ✈ (LUX), Lux.	15 E6	49 37N 6 10 E
uxi, China	32 D4	24 27N 98 36 E
uxor = El Uqsur, Egypt	51 C12	25 41N 32 38 E
uyi, China	34 H8	33 50N 115 35 E
uza, Russia	18 B8	60 39N 47 10 E
uzhou, China	32 D5	28 52N 105 20 E
uziânia, Brazil	93 G9	16 20S 48 0W
uzon, Phil.	37 A6	16 0N 121 0 E
viv, Ukraine	17 D13	49 50N 24 0 E
vov = Lviv, Ukraine	17 D13	49 50N 24 0 E
vakhavichy, Belarus	17 B14	53 2N 26 32 E
vakhovskiye, Ostrova, Russia	29 B15	73 40N 141 0 E
val I., Canada	84 B3	44 57N 81 24W
vbster, U.K.	11 C5	58 18N 3 15W
vcksele, Sweden	8 D18	64 38N 18 40 E
vdda = Lod, Israel	46 D3	31 57N 34 54 E
vdenburg, S. Africa	57 D5	25 10S 30 29 E
vdia, Turkey	23 E13	38 48N 28 19 E
vell, N.Z.	59 J4	41 48S 172 4 E
vell I., Canada	70 C2	52 40N 131 35W
vepyel, Belarus	18 D4	54 50N 28 15 E
vkens, U.S.A.	85 F8	40 34N 76 42W
vman, U.S.A.	76 F8	41 20N 110 18W
vme B., U.K.	13 G4	50 42N 2 53W
vme Regis, U.K.	13 G5	50 43N 2 57W
vmington, U.K.	13 G6	50 45N 1 32W
vna ➤, Poland	9 J19	54 37N 21 14 E
vnchburg, U.S.A.	82 G6	37 25N 79 9W
vnd ➤, Australia	62 B3	16 28S 143 18 E
vnd Ra., Australia	63 D4	25 30S 149 20 E
vnden, Canada	84 C4	43 14N 80 9W
vnden, U.S.A.	78 B4	48 57N 122 27W
vndhurst, Australia	63 E2	30 15S 138 18 E
vndon ➤, Australia	61 D1	23 29S 114 6 E
vndonville, N.Y., U.S.A.	84 C6	43 20N 78 23W
vndonville, Vt., U.S.A.	85 B12	44 31N 72 1W
vngen, Norway	8 B19	69 45N 20 30 E
vnher Reef, Australia	60 C3	15 27S 121 55 E
vnn, U.S.A.	85 D14	42 28N 70 57W
vnn Lake, Canada	71 B8	56 51N 101 3W
vnnwood, U.S.A.	78 C4	47 49N 122 19W
vnton, U.K.	13 F4	51 13N 3 50W
vntupy, Belarus	9 J22	55 4N 26 23 E
vnx L., Canada	71 A7	62 25N 106 15W
von, France	20 D6	45 46N 4 50 E
vonnais, France	20 D6	45 45N 4 15 E
vons = Lyon, France	20 D6	45 46N 4 50 E
vons, U.S.A.	83 J4	32 12N 82 19W
vons, Kans., U.S.A.	80 F5	38 21N 98 12W
vons, N.Y., U.S.A.	84 C8	43 5N 77 0W
vons ➤, Australia	61 E2	25 2S 115 9 E
vons Falls, U.S.A.	85 C9	43 37N 75 22W
vs = Leie ➤, Belgium	15 C3	51 2N 3 45 E
vsva, Russia	18 C10	58 7N 57 49 E
vsychansk, Ukraine	19 E6	48 55N 38 30 E
vtham St. Anne's, U.K.	12 D4	53 45N 3 0W
vttelton, N.Z.	59 K4	43 35S 172 44 E
vtton, Canada	70 C4	50 13N 121 31W
vubertsy, Russia	18 C6	55 39N 37 50 E
vuboml, Ukraine	17 C13	51 11N 24 4 E

1

R. Gomez, Presa, Mexico	87 B5	26 10N 99 0W
a ➤, Vietnam	38 C5	19 47N 105 56 E
a'adaba, Jordan	46 E4	30 43N 35 47 E
aamba, Zambia	56 B4	17 17S 26 28 E
a'ân, Jordan	46 E4	30 12N 35 44 E
a'ân □, Jordan	46 F5	30 0N 36 0 E
aanselkä, Finland	8 C23	63 52N 28 32 E
a'anshan, China	33 C6	31 44N 118 29 E
aarianhamina, Finland	9 F18	60 5N 19 55 E
a'arrat an Nu'mân, Syria	44 C3	35 43N 36 43 E
aas ➤, Neths.	15 C4	51 45N 4 32 E
aaseik, Belgium	15 C5	51 6N 5 45 E
aasin, Phil.	37 B6	10 8N 124 50 E
aastricht, Neths.	15 D5	50 50N 5 40 E
aave, Mozam.	57 C5	21 4S 34 47 E
aave Depression, Botswana	56 B3	18 50S 21 10 E
abalane, Mozam.	57 C5	23 37S 32 31 E
abel L., Canada	70 C5	50 35N 118 43W
abenge, Dem. Rep. of the Congo	54 B1	1 51N 24 12 E
aberly, Canada	85 B8	44 50N 76 32W
ablethorpe, U.K.	12 D8	53 20N 0 15 E
aboma, Dem. Rep. of the Congo	54 B2	2 30N 28 10 E
abuasehube ◯, Botswana	56 D3	25 5S 21 10 E
ac Bac, Vietnam	39 H6	9 46N 106 7 E
acachín, Argentina	94 D3	37 10S 63 43W
acaé, Brazil	95 A7	22 20S 41 43W
acalester, U.S.A.	81 H7	34 56N 95 46W
acallen, U.S.A.	81 M5	26 12N 98 14W
acAlpine L., Canada	68 B9	66 32N 102 45W
acamic, Canada	72 C4	48 45N 79 0W
acao = Macau, China	33 G10	22 12N 113 33 E
acapá, Brazil	93 C8	0 5N 51 4W
acará, Venezuela	89 D6	10 23N 67 7W
acArthur ➤, Australia	62 B2	15 54S 136 40 E
acArthur, Port, Australia	62 B2	16 4S 136 23 E
acau, Brazil	93 E11	5 15S 36 40W
acau, China	33 G10	22 12N 113 33 E
acBride, Canada	70 C4	53 20N 120 19W
acCall, U.S.A.	76 D5	44 55N 116 6W
acCamey, U.S.A.	81 K3	31 8N 102 14W
acCammon, U.S.A.	76 E7	42 39N 112 12W
acCauley I., Canada	70 C2	53 40N 130 15W
acCleary, U.S.A.	78 C3	47 3N 123 16W
acClintock, U.S.A.	83 K4	30 17N 82 7W
acclesfield, U.K.	12 D5	53 15N 2 8W
acClintock Chan., Canada	68 A9	72 0N 102 0W
acClintock Ra., Australia	60 C4	18 44S 127 38 E
acCloud, U.S.A.	76 F2	41 15N 122 8W
acClure I., Australia	60 B5	11 5S 133 0 E
acClure, U.S.A.	84 F7	40 42N 77 19W
acClure Str., Canada	4 B2	75 0N 119 0W
acClusky, U.S.A.	80 B4	47 29N 100 27W

McComb, U.S.A.	81 K9	31 15N 90 27W
McConaughy, L., U.S.A.	80 E4	41 14N 101 40W
McCook, U.S.A.	80 E4	40 12N 100 38W
McCreary, Canada	71 C9	50 47N 99 29W
McCullough Mt., U.S.A.	79 K11	35 35N 115 13W
McCusker ➤, Canada	71 B7	55 32N 108 39W
McDame, Canada	70 B3	59 44N 128 59W
McDermitt, U.S.A.	76 F5	41 59N 117 43W
McDonald, U.S.A.	84 F4	40 22N 80 14W
Macdonald, L., Australia	60 D4	23 30S 129 0 E
McDonald Is., Ind. Oc.	3 G13	53 0S 73 0 E
MacDonnell Ranges, Australia	60 D5	23 40S 133 0 E
MacDowell L., Canada	72 B1	52 15N 92 45W
Macduff, U.K.	11 D6	57 40N 2 31W
Macedonia = Makedhonía □, Greece	23 D10	40 39N 22 0 E
Macedonia, U.S.A.	84 E3	41 19N 81 31W
Macedonia ■, Europe	23 D9	41 53N 21 40 E
Maceió, Brazil	93 E11	9 40S 35 41W
Macerata, Italy	22 C5	43 18N 13 27 E
McFarland, U.S.A.	79 K7	35 41N 119 14W
McFarlane ➤, Canada	71 B7	59 12N 107 58W
Macfarlane, L., Australia	63 E2	32 0S 136 40 E
McGehee, U.S.A.	81 J9	33 38N 91 24W
McGill, U.S.A.	76 G6	39 23N 114 47W
Macgillycuddy's Reeks, Ireland	10 E2	51 58N 9 45W
McGraw, U.S.A.	85 D8	42 36N 76 8W
McGregor, U.S.A.	80 D9	43 1N 91 11W
McGregor Ra., Australia	63 D3	27 0S 142 45 E
McGuire, Mt, Australia	62 J6	20 18S 148 23 E
Mach, Pakistan	40 E5	29 50N 67 20 E
Mäch Kowr, Iran	45 E9	25 48N 61 28 E
Machado = Jiparaná ➤, Brazil	92 E6	8 3S 62 52W
Machagai, Argentina	94 B3	26 56S 60 2W
Machakos, Kenya	54 C4	1 30S 37 15 E
Machala, Ecuador	92 D3	3 20S 79 57W
Machanga, Mozam.	57 C6	20 59S 35 0 E
Machattie, L., Australia	62 C2	24 50S 139 48 E
Machava, Mozam.	57 D5	25 54S 32 28 E
Machece, Mozam.	55 F4	19 15S 35 32 E
Macheke, Zimbabwe	57 B5	18 5S 31 51 E
Machhu ➤, India	42 H4	23 6N 70 46 E
Machias, Maine, U.S.A.	83 C12	44 43N 67 28W
Machias, N.Y., U.S.A.	84 D6	42 25N 78 30W
Machichi ➤, Canada	71 B10	57 3N 92 6W
Machico, Madeira	24 D3	32 43N 16 44W
Machilipatnam, India	41 L12	16 12N 81 8 E
Machiques, Venezuela	92 A4	10 4N 72 34W
Machupicchu, Peru	92 F4	13 8S 72 30W
Machynlleth, U.K.	13 E4	52 35N 3 50W
Macia, Mozam.	57 D5	25 2S 33 8 E
McIlwraith Ra., Australia	62 A3	13 50S 143 20 E
McInnes L., Canada	71 C10	52 13N 93 45W
McIntosh, U.S.A.	80 C4	45 55N 101 21W
McIntosh L., Canada	71 B8	55 45N 105 0W
Macintosh Ra., Australia	61 E4	27 39S 125 32 E
Macintyre ➤, Australia	63 D5	28 37S 150 47 E
Mackay, Australia	62 K7	21 8S 149 11 E
Mackay, U.S.A.	76 E7	43 55N 113 37W
MacKay ➤, Canada	70 B6	57 10N 111 38W
Mackay, L., Australia	60 D4	22 30S 129 0 E
McKay Ra., Australia	60 D3	23 0S 122 30 E
McKeesport, U.S.A.	84 F5	40 21N 79 52W
McKellar, Canada	84 A5	45 30N 79 55W
McKenna, U.S.A.	78 D4	46 56N 122 33W
Mackenzie, Canada	70 B4	55 20N 123 5W
Mackenzie ➤, Australia	62 C4	23 38S 149 46 E
Mackenzie ➤, Canada	68 B6	69 10N 134 20W
McKenzie ➤, U.S.A.	76 D2	44 7N 123 6W
Mackenzie Bay, Canada	4 B1	69 0N 137 30W
Mackenzie City = Linden, Guyana	92 B7	6 0N 58 10W
Mackenzie Mts., Canada	68 B6	64 0N 130 0W
Mackinaw City, U.S.A.	82 C3	45 47N 84 44W
McKinlay, Australia	62 C3	21 16S 141 18 E
McKinlay ➤, Australia	62 C3	20 50S 141 28 E
McKinley, Mt., U.S.A.	68 B4	63 4N 151 0W
McKinley Sea, Arctic	4 A7	82 0N 0 0W
McKinney, U.S.A.	81 J6	33 12N 96 37W
Mackinnon Road, Kenya	54 C4	3 40S 39 1 E
Macklin, Canada	71 C7	52 20N 109 56W
Macksville, Australia	63 E5	30 40S 152 56 E
McLaughlin, U.S.A.	80 C4	45 49N 100 49W
Maclean, Australia	63 D5	29 26S 153 16 E
McLean, U.S.A.	81 H4	35 14N 100 36W
McLeansboro, U.S.A.	80 F10	38 6N 88 32W
Maclear, S. Africa	57 E4	31 2S 28 23 E
Maclear, C., Malawi	55 E3	13 58S 34 49 E
Macleay ➤, Australia	63 E5	30 56S 153 0 E
McLennan, Canada	70 B5	55 42N 116 50W
McLeod ➤, Canada	70 C5	54 9N 115 44W
MacLeod, B., Canada	71 A7	62 53N 110 0W
MacLeod, L., Australia	61 D1	24 9S 113 47 E
MacLeod Lake, Canada	70 C4	54 58N 123 0W
McLoughlin, Mt., U.S.A.	76 E2	42 27N 122 19W
McMechen, U.S.A.	84 G4	39 57N 80 44W
McMinnville, Oreg., U.S.A.	76 D2	45 13N 123 12W
McMinnville, Tenn., U.S.A.	83 H3	35 41N 85 46W
McMurdo Sd., Antarctica	5 D11	77 0S 170 0 E
McMurray = Fort McMurray, Canada	70 B6	56 44N 111 7W
McMurray, U.S.A.	78 B4	48 19N 122 14W
Macodoene, Mozam.	57 C6	23 32S 35 5 E
Macomb, U.S.A.	80 E9	40 27N 90 40W
Mâcon, France	20 C6	46 19N 4 50 E
Macon, Ga., U.S.A.	83 J4	32 51N 83 38W
Macon, Miss., U.S.A.	83 J1	33 7N 88 34W
Macon, Mo., U.S.A.	80 F8	39 44N 92 28W
Macossa, Mozam.	55 F3	17 55S 33 56 E
Macoun L., Canada	71 B8	56 32N 103 40W
Macovane, Mozam.	57 C6	21 30S 35 2 E
McPherson, U.S.A.	80 F6	38 22N 97 40W
McPherson Pk., U.S.A.	79 L7	34 53N 119 53W
McPherson Ra., Australia	63 D5	28 15S 153 15 E
Macquarie ➤, Australia	63 E4	30 7S 147 24 E
Macquarie Harbour, Australia	63 G4	42 15S 145 23 E
Macquarie Is., Pac. Oc.	64 N7	54 36S 158 55 E
MacRobertson Land, Antarctica	5 D6	71 0S 64 0 E
Macroom, Ireland	10 E3	51 54N 8 57W
MacTier, Canada	84 A5	45 9N 79 46W
Macubela, Mozam.	55 F4	16 53S 37 49 E
Macuira ◯, Colombia	89 D5	12 9N 71 21W
Macuiza, Mozam.	55 F3	18 7S 34 29 E
Macuro, Venezuela	93 K15	10 42N 61 55W
Macusani, Peru	92 F4	14 4S 70 29W
Macuse, Mozam.	55 F4	17 45S 37 10 E
Macuspana, Mexico	87 D6	17 46N 92 36W

Macusse, Angola	56 B3	17 48S 20 23 E
Ma'dabā, Jordan	46 D4	31 43N 35 47 E
Madadeni, S. Africa	57 D5	27 43S 30 3 E
Madagascar ■, Africa	57 C8	20 0S 47 0 E
Madā'in Sālih, Si. Arabia	44 E3	26 46N 37 57 E
Madama, Niger	51 D8	22 0N 13 40 E
Madame, I., Canada	73 C7	45 30N 60 58W
Madaripur, Bangla.	41 H17	23 19N 90 15 E
Madauk, Burma	41 L20	17 56N 96 52 E
Madawaska, Canada	84 A7	45 30N 78 0W
Madawaska ➤, Canada	84 A8	45 27N 76 21W
Madaya, Burma	41 H20	22 12N 96 10 E
Maddalena, Italy	22 D3	41 16N 9 23 E
Madeira, Atl. Oc.	24 D3	32 50N 17 0W
Madeira ➤, Brazil	92 D7	3 22S 58 45W
Madeleine, Îs. de la, Canada	73 C7	47 30N 61 40W
Madera, Mexico	86 B3	29 12N 108 7W
Madera, Calif., U.S.A.	78 J6	36 57N 120 3W
Madera, Pa., U.S.A.	84 F6	40 49N 78 26W
Madha, India	40 L9	18 0N 75 30 E
Madhavpur, India	42 J3	21 15N 69 58 E
Madhepura, India	43 F12	26 11N 86 23 E
Madhubani, India	43 F12	26 21N 86 7 E
Madhupur, India	43 G12	24 16N 86 39 E
Madhya Pradesh □, India	42 J8	22 50N 78 0 E
Madidi ➤, Bolivia	92 F5	12 32S 66 52W
Madikeri, India	40 N9	12 30N 75 45 E
Madikwe ◯, S. Africa	57 D5	27 38S 32 15 E
Madill, U.S.A.	81 H6	34 6N 96 46W
Madimba, Dem. Rep. of the Congo	52 E3	4 58S 15 5 E
Ma'din, Syria	44 C3	35 45N 39 36 E
Madingou, Congo	52 E2	4 10S 13 33 E
Madirovalo, Madag.	57 B8	16 26S 46 32 E
Madison, Calif., U.S.A.	78 G5	38 41N 121 59W
Madison, Fla., U.S.A.	83 K4	30 28N 83 25W
Madison, Ind., U.S.A.	82 F3	38 44N 85 23W
Madison, Nebr., U.S.A.	80 E6	41 50N 97 27W
Madison, Ohio, U.S.A.	84 E3	41 46N 81 3W
Madison, S. Dak., U.S.A.	80 D6	44 0N 97 7W
Madison, Wis., U.S.A.	80 D10	43 4N 89 24W
Madison ➤, U.S.A.	76 D8	45 56N 111 31W
Madison Heights, U.S.A.	82 G6	37 25N 79 8W
Madisonville, Ky., U.S.A.	82 G2	37 20N 87 30W
Madisonville, Tex., U.S.A.	81 K7	30 57N 95 55W
Madista, Botswana	56 C4	21 15S 25 6 E
Madiun, Indonesia	36 F4	7 38S 111 32 E
Madoc, Canada	84 B7	44 30N 77 28W
Madona, Latvia	9 H22	56 53N 26 5 E
Madrakah, Ra's al, Oman	47 D6	19 0N 57 50 E
Madras = Chennai, India	40 N12	13 8N 80 19 E
Madras = Tamil Nadu □, India	40 P10	11 0N 77 0 E
Madras, U.S.A.	76 D3	44 38N 121 8W
Madre, Laguna, U.S.A.	81 M6	27 0N 97 30W
Madre, Sierra, Phil.	37 A6	17 0N 122 0 E
Madre de Dios ➤, Bolivia	92 F5	10 59S 66 8W
Madre de Dios, I., Chile	96 G1	50 20S 75 10W
Madre del Sur, Sierra, Mexico	87 D5	17 30N 100 0W
Madre Occidental, Sierra, Mexico	86 B3	27 0N 107 0W
Madre Oriental, Sierra, Mexico	86 C5	25 0N 100 0W
Madri, India	42 G5	24 16N 73 32 E
Madrid, Spain	21 B4	40 25N 3 45W
Madrid, U.S.A.	85 B9	44 45N 75 8W
Madura, Australia	61 F4	31 55S 127 0 E
Madura, Indonesia	37 G15	7 30S 114 0 E
Madura, Selat, Indonesia	37 G15	7 30S 113 20 E
Madurai, India	40 Q11	9 55N 78 10 E
Madurantakam, India	40 N11	12 30N 79 50 E
Mae Chan, Thailand	38 B2	20 9N 99 52 E
Mae Hong Son, Thailand	38 C2	19 16N 97 56 E
Mae Khlong ➤, Thailand	38 F3	13 24N 100 0 E
Mae Phrik, Thailand	38 D2	17 27N 99 7 E
Mae Ramat, Thailand	38 D2	16 58N 98 31 E
Mae Rim, Thailand	38 C2	18 54N 98 57 E
Mae Sot, Thailand	38 D2	16 43N 98 34 E
Mae Suai, Thailand	38 C2	19 39N 99 33 E
Mae Tha, Thailand	38 C2	18 28N 99 8 E
Mae Yom ➤, Thailand	38 C3	18 43N 100 15 E
Maebashi, Japan	31 F9	36 24N 139 4 E
Maesteg, U.K.	13 F4	51 36N 3 40W
Maestra, Sierra, Cuba	88 B4	20 15N 77 0W
Maevatanana, Madag.	57 B8	16 56S 46 49 E
Mafeking = Mafikeng, S. Africa	56 D4	25 50S 25 38 E
Mafeking, Canada	71 C8	52 40N 101 10W
Mafeteng, Lesotho	56 D4	29 51S 27 15 E
Maffra, Australia	63 F4	37 53S 146 58 E
Mafia I., Tanzania	54 D4	7 45S 39 50 E
Mafikeng, S. Africa	56 D4	25 50S 25 38 E
Mafra, Brazil	95 B6	26 10S 49 55W
Mafra, Portugal	21 C1	38 55N 9 20W
Mafungabusi Plateau, Zimbabwe	55 F2	18 30S 29 8 E
Magadan, Russia	29 D16	59 38N 150 50 E
Magadi, Kenya	54 C4	1 54S 36 19 E
Magadi, L., Kenya	54 C4	1 54S 36 19 E
Magaliesburg, S. Africa	57 D4	26 0S 27 32 E
Magallanes, Estrecho de, Chile	96 G2	52 30S 75 0W
Magangué, Colombia	92 B4	9 14N 74 45W
Magdalen Is. = Madeleine, Îs. de la, Canada	73 C7	47 30N 61 40W
Magdalena, Argentina	94 D4	35 5S 57 30W
Magdalena, Bolivia	92 F6	13 13S 63 57W
Magdalena, Mexico	86 A2	30 50N 112 0W
Magdalena ➤, Colombia	92 A4	11 6N 74 51W
Magdalena ➤, Mexico	86 A2	30 40N 112 25W
Magdalena, B., Mexico	86 C2	24 30N 112 10W
Magdalena, Llano de la, Mexico	86 C2	25 0N 111 30W
Magdeburg, Germany	16 B6	52 7N 11 38 E
Magdelaine Cays, Australia	62 B5	16 33S 150 18 E
Magee, U.S.A.	81 K10	31 52N 89 44W
Magelang, Indonesia	36 F4	7 29S 110 13 E
Magellan's Str. = Magallanes, Estrecho de, Chile	96 G2	52 30S 75 0W
Magenta, L., Australia	61 F2	33 30S 119 2 E
Magerøya, Norway	8 A21	71 3N 25 40 E
Maggiore, Lago, Italy	20 D8	45 57N 8 39 E
Maggotty, Jamaica	88 a	18 9N 77 46W
Maghâgha, Egypt	51 C12	28 38N 30 50 E
Magherafelt, U.K.	10 B5	54 45N 6 37W
Maghreb, N. Afr.	50 B5	32 0N 4 0W
Magistralnyy, Russia	29 D11	56 16N 107 36 E
Magnetic Pole (North), Canada	4 A2	88 30N 107 0 E
Magnetic Pole (South), Antarctica	5 C9	64 8S 138 8 E
Magnitogorsk, Russia	18 D10	53 27N 59 4 E
Magnolia, Ark., U.S.A.	81 J8	33 16N 93 14W

Magnolia, Miss., U.S.A.	81 K9	31 9N 90 28W
Magog, Canada	85 A12	45 18N 72 9W
Magoro, Uganda	54 B3	1 45N 34 12 E
Magoša = Famagusta, Cyprus	25 D12	35 8N 33 55 E
Magouládhes, Greece	25 A3	39 45N 19 42 E
Magoye, Zambia	55 F2	16 1S 27 30 E
Magozal, Mexico	87 C5	21 34N 97 59W
Magpie, L., Canada	73 B7	51 0N 64 41W
Magrath, Canada	70 D6	49 25N 112 50W
Maguarinho, C., Brazil	93 D9	0 15S 48 30W
Magude, Mozam.	57 D5	25 2S 32 40 E
Magusa = Famagusta, Cyprus	25 D12	35 8N 33 55 E
Maguse L., Canada	71 A9	61 37N 95 10W
Maguse Pt., Canada	71 A10	61 20N 93 50W
Magvana, India	42 H3	23 13N 69 22 E
Magwe, Burma	41 J19	20 10N 95 0 E
Maha Sarakham, Thailand	38 D4	16 12N 103 16 E
Mahābād, Iran	44 B5	36 50N 45 45 E
Mahabharat Lekh, Nepal	43 E10	28 30N 82 0 E
Mahabo, Madag.	57 C7	20 23S 44 40 E
Mahadeo Hills, India	43 H8	22 20N 78 30 E
Mahaffey, U.S.A.	84 F6	40 53N 78 44W
Mahagi, Dem. Rep. of the Congo	54 B3	2 20N 31 0 E
Mahajamba ➤, Madag.	57 B8	15 33S 47 8 E
Mahajamba, Helodranon' i, Madag.	57 B8	15 24S 47 5 E
Mahajan, India	42 E5	28 48N 73 56 E
Mahajanga, Madag.	57 B8	15 40S 46 25 E
Mahajanga □, Madag.	57 B8	17 0S 47 0 E
Mahajilo ➤, Madag.	57 B8	19 42S 45 22 E
Mahakam ➤, Indonesia	36 E5	0 35S 117 17 E
Mahalapye, Botswana	56 C4	23 1S 26 51 E
Mahale Mts., Tanzania	54 D3	6 20S 30 0 E
Mahale Mts. △, Tanzania	54 D2	6 10S 29 50 E
Mahallāt, Iran	45 C6	33 55N 50 30 E
Māhān, Iran	45 D8	30 5N 57 18 E
Mahan ➤, India	43 H10	23 30N 82 50 E
Mahanadi ➤, India	41 J15	20 20N 86 25 E
Mahananda ➤, India	43 G12	25 12N 87 52 E
Mahanoro, Madag.	57 B8	19 54S 48 48 E
Mahanoy City, U.S.A.	85 F8	40 49N 76 9W
Maharashtra □, India	40 J9	20 30N 75 30 E
Mahasham, W. ➤, Egypt	46 E3	30 15N 34 10 E
Mahasoa, Madag.	57 C8	22 12S 46 6 E
Mahasolo, Madag.	57 B8	19 7S 46 22 E
Mahattat ash Shidīyah, Jordan	46 F4	29 55N 35 55 E
Mahattat 'Unayzah, Jordan	46 E4	30 30N 35 47 E
Mahavavy ➤, Madag.	57 B8	15 57S 45 54 E
Mahaxay, Laos	38 D5	17 22N 105 12 E
Mahbubnagar, India	40 L10	16 45N 77 59 E
Mahdah, Oman	45 E7	24 24N 55 59 E
Mahdia, Tunisia	51 A8	35 28N 11 0 E
Mahe, India	43 C8	33 10N 78 32 E
Mahendragarh, India	42 E7	28 17N 76 14 E
Mahenge, Tanzania	55 D4	8 45S 36 41 E
Maheno, N.Z.	59 L3	45 10S 170 50 E
Mahesana, India	42 H5	23 39N 72 26 E
Maheshwar, India	42 H6	22 11N 75 35 E
Mahgawan, India	43 F8	26 29N 78 37 E
Mahi ➤, India	42 H5	22 15N 72 55 E
Mahia Pen., N.Z.	59 H6	39 9S 177 55 E
Mahilyow, Belarus	17 B16	53 55N 30 18 E
Mahmud Kot, Pakistan	42 D4	30 16N 71 0 E
Mahnomen, U.S.A.	80 B7	47 19N 95 58W
Mahoba, India	43 G8	25 15N 79 55 E
Mahón = Maó, Spain	24 B11	39 53N 4 16 E
Mahone Bay, Canada	73 D7	44 30N 64 20W
Mahopac, U.S.A.	85 E11	41 22N 73 45W
Mahuva, India	42 J4	21 5N 71 48 E
Mai-Ndombe, L., Dem. Rep. of the Congo	52 E3	2 0S 18 20 E
Mai-Sai, Thailand	38 B2	20 20N 99 55 E
Mai Thon, My, Thailand	39 a	7 40N 98 28 E
Maicurú ➤, Brazil	93 D8	2 14S 54 17W
Maidan Khula, Afghan.	42 C3	33 36N 69 50 E
Maidenhead, U.K.	13 F7	51 31N 0 42W
Maidstone, Canada	71 C7	53 5N 109 20W
Maidstone, U.K.	13 F8	51 16N 0 32 E
Maiduguri, Nigeria	51 F8	12 0N 13 20 E
Maihar, India	43 G9	24 16N 80 45 E
Maijdi, Bangla.	41 H17	22 48N 91 10 E
Maikala Ra., India	41 J12	22 0N 81 0 E
Maiko △, Dem. Rep. of the Congo	54 C2	0 30S 27 50 E
Mailani, India	43 E9	28 17N 80 21 E
Mailsi, Pakistan	42 E5	29 48N 72 15 E
Main ➤, Germany	16 C5	50 0N 8 18 E
Main ➤, U.K.	10 B5	54 48N 6 18W
Main Range △, Australia	63 D5	28 11S 152 27 E
Main Ridge, Trin. & Tob.	93 J16	11 16N 60 40W
Maine, France	20 C3	48 20N 0 15W
Maine □, U.S.A.	83 C11	45 20N 69 0W
Maine ➤, Ireland	10 D2	52 9N 9 45W
Maingkwan, Burma	41 F20	26 15N 96 37 E
Mainit, L., Phil.	37 C7	9 31N 125 30 E
Mainland, Orkney, U.K.	11 C5	58 59N 3 8W
Mainland, Shet., U.K.	11 A7	60 15N 1 22W
Mainoru, Australia	62 A1	14 0S 134 6 E
Mainpuri, India	43 F8	27 18N 79 4 E
Maintirano, Madag.	57 B7	18 3S 44 1 E
Mainz, Germany	16 C5	50 1N 8 14 E
Maipú, Argentina	94 D4	36 52S 57 50W
Maiquetía, Venezuela	92 A5	10 36N 66 57W
Mairabari, India	41 F18	26 30N 92 22 E
Maisi, Cuba	89 B5	20 17N 74 9W
Maisí, Pta. de, Cuba	89 B5	20 10N 74 10W
Maitland, N.S.W., Australia	63 E5	32 33S 151 36 E
Maitland, S. Austral., Australia	63 E2	34 23S 137 40 E
Maitland ➤, Canada	84 C3	43 45N 81 43W
Maitri, Antarctica	5 D3	70 0S 3 0W
Maiz, Is. del, Nic.	88 D3	12 15N 83 4W
Maizuru, Japan	31 G7	35 25N 135 22 E
Majalengka, Indonesia	37 G13	6 50S 108 13 E
Majene, Indonesia	37 E5	3 38S 118 57 E
Majete ◯, Malawi	55 F3	15 54S 34 34 E
Majorca = Mallorca, Spain	24 B10	39 30N 3 0 E
Makaha, Zimbabwe	57 B5	17 20S 32 39 E
Makalamabedi, Botswana	56 C3	20 19S 23 51 E
Makale, Indonesia	37 E5	3 6S 119 51 E
Makamba, Burundi	54 C2	4 8S 29 49 E
Makarikari = Makgadikgadi Salt Pans, Botswana	56 C4	20 40S 25 45 E
Makarov Basin, Arctic	4 A	87 0N 150 0W
Makarovo, Russia	29 D11	57 40N 107 45 E
Makasar = Ujung Pandang, Indonesia	37 F5	5 10S 119 20 E
Makasar, Selat, Indonesia	37 E5	1 0S 118 20 E

Makasar, Str. of = Makasar, Selat, Indonesia .... 37 E5 1 0S 118 20 E
Makat, Kazakhstan ...... 19 E9 47 39N 53 19 E
Makedhonía □, Greece .. 23 D10 40 39N 22 0 E
Makedonija = Macedonia ■, Europe .... 23 D9 41 53N 21 40 E
Makeyevka = Makiyivka, Ukraine 19 E6 48 0N 38 0 E
Makgadikgadi △, Botswana 56 C3 20 27S 24 47 E
Makgadikgadi Salt Pans, Botswana .... 56 C4 20 40S 25 45 E
Makhachkala, Russia .... 19 F8 43 0N 47 30 E
Makhfar al Buşayyah, Iraq .. 44 D5 30 0N 46 10 E
Makhmūr, Iraq .... 44 C4 35 46N 43 35 E
Makian, Indonesia ...... 37 D7 0 20N 127 20 E
Makindu, Kenya .... 54 C4 2 18S 37 50 E
Makinsk, Kazakhstan .... 28 D8 52 37N 70 26 E
Makiyivka, Ukraine ..... 19 E6 48 0N 38 0 E
Makkah, Si. Arabia ...... 47 C2 21 30N 39 54 E
Makkovik, Canada 73 A8 55 10N 59 10W
Makó, Hungary .... 17 E11 46 14N 20 33 E
Makokou, Gabon .... 52 D2 0 40N 12 50 E
Makongo, Dem. Rep. of the Congo .... 54 B2 3 25N 26 17 E
Makoro, Dem. Rep. of the Congo 54 B2 3 10N 29 59 E
Makrai, India .... 40 H10 22 2N 77 0 E
Makran Coast Range, Pakistan 40 G4 25 40N 64 0 E
Makrana, India .... 42 F6 27 2N 74 46 E
Makriyialos, Greece ..... 25 D7 35 2N 25 59 E
Mākū, Iran .... 44 B5 39 15N 44 31 E
Makunda, Botswana ..... 56 C3 22 30S 20 7 E
Makurazaki, Japan ...... 31 J5 31 15N 130 20 E
Makurdi, Nigeria .... 50 G7 7 43N 8 35 E
Makūyeh, Iran .... 45 D7 28 7N 53 9 E
Makwassie, S. Africa .... 56 D4 27 17S 26 0 E
Makwiro, Zimbabwe ..... 57 B5 17 58S 30 25 E
Mal B., Ireland 10 D2 52 50N 9 30W
Mala, Pta., Panama 88 E3 7 28N 80 2W
Malabar Coast, India .... 40 P9 11 0N 75 0 E
Malacca, Str. of, Indonesia 39 L3 3 0N 101 0 E
Malad City, U.S.A. 76 E7 42 12N 112 15W
Maladzyechna, Belarus .. 17 A14 54 20N 26 50 E
Málaga, Spain 21 D3 36 43N 4 23W
Malagarasi, Tanzania .... 54 D3 5 5S 30 50 E
Malagarasi →, Tanzania .. 54 D2 5 12S 29 47 E
Malagasy Rep. = Madagascar ■, Africa .... 57 C8 20 0S 47 0 E
Malahide, Ireland 10 C5 53 26N 6 9W
Malaimbandy, Madag. ... 57 C8 20 20S 45 36 E
Malakāl, Sudan .... 51 G12 9 33N 31 40 E
Malakand, Pakistan ..... 42 B4 34 40N 71 55 E
Malakwal, Pakistan ..... 42 C5 32 34N 73 13 E
Malamala, Indonesia .... 37 E6 3 21S 120 55 E
Malanda, Australia ...... 62 B4 17 22S 145 35 E
Malang, Indonesia ...... 36 F4 7 59S 112 45 E
Malangen, Norway ...... 8 B18 69 24N 18 37 E
Malanje, Angola .... 52 F3 9 36S 16 17 E
Mälaren, Sweden .... 9 G17 59 30N 17 10 E
Malargüe, Argentina 94 D2 35 32S 69 30W
Malartic, Canada 72 C4 48 9N 78 9W
Malaryta, Belarus ...... 17 C13 51 50N 24 3 E
Malatya, Turkey .... 19 G6 38 25N 38 20 E
Malawi ■, Africa .... 55 E3 11 55S 34 0 E
Malawi, L. = Nyasa, L., Africa 55 E3 12 30S 34 30 E
Malay Pen., Asia .... 39 J3 7 25N 100 0 E
Malaya Vishera, Russia .. 18 C5 58 55N 32 25 E
Malaybalay, Phil. ...... 37 C7 8 5N 125 7 E
Malāyer, Iran .... 45 C6 34 19N 48 51 E
Malaysia ■, Asia .... 39 K4 5 0N 110 0 E
Malazgirt, Turkey ...... 19 G7 39 10N 42 33 E
Malbon, Australia ...... 62 C3 21 5S 140 17 E
Malbooma, Australia .... 63 E1 30 41S 134 11 E
Malbork, Poland .... 17 B10 54 3N 19 1 E
Malcolm, Australia ..... 61 E3 28 51S 121 25 E
Malcolm, Pt., Australia .. 61 F3 33 48S 123 45 E
Maldah, India .... 43 G13 25 2N 88 9 E
Maldegem, Belgium .... 15 C3 51 14N 3 26 E
Malden, Mass., U.S.A. ... 85 D13 42 26N 71 4W
Malden, Mo., U.S.A. 81 G10 36 34N 89 57W
Malden I., Kiribati 65 H12 4 3S 155 1W
Maldives ■, Ind. Oc. .... 27 J11 5 0N 73 0 E
Maldon, U.K. .... 13 F8 51 44N 0 42 E
Maldonado, Uruguay 95 C5 34 59S 55 0W
Maldonado, Punta, Mexico 87 D5 16 19N 98 35W
Male, Maldives .... 27 J11 4 0N 73 28 E
Malé Karpaty, Slovak Rep. 17 D9 48 30N 17 20 E
Maléa, Ákra, Greece .... 23 F10 36 28N 23 7 E
Malegaon, India .... 40 J9 20 30N 74 38 E
Malei, Mozam. .... 55 F4 17 12S 36 58 E
Malek Kandī, Iran ...... 44 B5 37 9N 46 6 E
Malela, Dem. Rep. of the Congo 54 C2 4 22S 26 8 E
Malema, Mozam. .... 55 E4 14 57S 37 20 E
Máleme, Greece .... 25 D5 35 31N 23 49 E
Maleny, Australia ...... 63 D5 26 45S 152 52 E
Malerkotla, India ...... 42 D6 30 32N 75 58 E
Máles, Greece .... 25 D7 35 6N 25 35 E
Malgomaj, Sweden ..... 8 D17 64 40N 16 30 E
Malha, Sudan .... 51 E11 15 8N 25 10 E
Malhargarh, India ...... 42 G6 24 17N 74 59 E
Malheur →, U.S.A. 76 D5 44 4N 116 59W
Malheur L., U.S.A. 76 E4 43 20N 118 48W
Mali ■, Africa 50 E5 17 0N 3 0W
Mali →, Burma .... 41 G20 25 40N 97 40 E
Mali Kyun, Burma ...... 38 F2 13 0N 98 20 E
Malibu, U.S.A. 79 L8 34 2N 118 41W
Maliku, Indonesia ...... 37 E6 0 39S 123 16 E
Malili, Indonesia .... 37 E6 2 42S 121 6 E
Malimba, Mts., Dem. Rep. of the Congo 54 D2 7 30S 29 30 E
Malin Hd., Ireland 10 A4 55 23N 7 24W
Malin Pen., Ireland 10 A4 55 20N 7 17W
Malindi, Kenya .... 54 C5 3 12S 40 5 E
Malines = Mechelen, Belgium 15 C4 51 2N 4 29 E
Malino, Indonesia ...... 37 D6 1 0N 121 0 E
Malinyi, Tanzania ...... 55 D4 8 56S 36 0 E
Malita, Phil. .... 37 C7 6 19N 125 39 E
Maliwun, Burma .... 36 B1 10 17N 98 40 E
Maliya, India .... 42 H4 23 5N 70 46 E
Malka Mari △, Kenya ... 54 B5 4 11N 40 46 E
Malkara, Turkey .... 23 D12 40 53N 26 53 E
Mallacoota Inlet, Australia 63 F4 37 34S 149 40 E
Mallaig, U.K. 11 D3 57 0N 5 50W
Mallawan, India .... 43 F9 27 4N 80 12 E
Mallawi, Egypt .... 51 C12 27 44N 30 44 E
Mállia, Greece .... 25 D7 35 17N 25 32 E
Mallión, Kólpos, Greece .. 25 D7 35 19N 25 27 E
Mallorca, Spain .... 24 B10 39 30N 3 0 E
Mallorytown, Canada ... 85 B9 44 29N 75 53W
Mallow, Ireland 10 D3 52 8N 8 39W

Malmberget, Sweden ... 8 C19 67 11N 20 40 E
Malmédy, Belgium ..... 15 D6 50 25N 6 2 E
Malmesbury, S. Africa .. 56 E2 33 28S 18 41 E
Malmö, Sweden .... 9 J15 55 36N 12 59 E
Malolos, Phil. .... 37 B6 14 50N 120 49 E
Malolotja △, Swaziland .. 57 D5 26 4S 31 6 E
Malombe L., Malawi .... 55 E4 14 40S 35 15 E
Malone, U.S.A. 85 B10 44 51N 74 18W
Måløy, Norway .... 9 F11 61 57N 5 6 E
Malpaso, Canary Is. 24 G1 27 43N 18 3W
Malpelo, I. de, Colombia .. 92 C2 4 3N 81 35W
Malpur, India .... 42 H5 23 21N 73 27 E
Malpura, India .... 42 F6 26 17N 75 23 E
Malta, Idaho, U.S.A. 76 E7 42 18N 113 22W
Malta, Mont., U.S.A. ... 76 B10 48 21N 107 52W
Malta ■, Europe .... 25 D2 35 55N 14 26 E
Maltahöhe, Namibia .... 56 C2 24 55S 17 0 E
Malton, Canada 84 C5 43 42N 79 38W
Malton, U.K. 12 C7 54 8N 0 49W
Maluku, Indonesia ..... 37 E7 1 0S 127 0 E
Maluku □, Indonesia .... 37 E7 3 0S 128 0 E
Maluku Sea = Molucca Sea, Indonesia 37 E6 0 0 125 0 E
Malvan, India .... 40 L8 16 2N 73 30 E
Malvern, U.S.A. 81 H8 34 22N 92 49W
Malvern Hills, U.K. 13 E5 52 0N 2 19W
Malvinas, Is. = Falkland Is. ☒, Atl. Oc. 96 G5 51 30S 59 0W
Malya, Tanzania .... 54 C3 3 5S 33 38 E
Malyn, Ukraine .... 17 C15 50 46N 29 3 E
Malyy Lyakhovskiy, Ostrov, Russia 29 B15 74 7N 140 36 E
Mama, Russia .... 29 D12 58 18N 112 54 E
Mamanguape, Brazil 93 E11 6 50S 35 4W
Mamarr Mitlā, Egypt .... 46 E1 30 2N 32 54 E
Mamasa, Indonesia ..... 37 E5 2 55S 119 20 E
Mambasa, Dem. Rep. of the Congo 54 B2 1 22N 29 3 E
Mamberamo →, Indonesia 37 E9 2 0S 137 50 E
Mambilima Falls, Zambia .. 55 E2 10 31S 28 45 E
Mambirima, Dem. Rep. of the Congo 55 E2 11 25S 27 33 E
Mambo, Tanzania ...... 54 C4 4 52S 38 22 E
Mambrui, Kenya .... 54 C5 3 5S 40 5 E
Mamburao, Phil. .... 37 B6 13 13N 120 39 E
Mameigwess L., Canada .. 72 B2 52 35N 87 50W
Mammoth, U.S.A. 77 K8 32 43N 110 39W
Mammoth Cave △, U.S.A. .. 82 G3 37 8N 86 13W
Mamoré →, Bolivia 92 F5 10 23S 65 53W
Mamou, Guinea 50 F3 10 15N 12 0W
Mamoudzou, Mayotte ... 49 H8 12 48S 45 14 E
Mampikony, Madag. .... 57 B8 16 6S 47 38 E
Mamuju, Indonesia ..... 37 E5 2 41S 118 50 E
Mamuno, Botswana .... 56 C3 22 16S 20 1 E
Man, Ivory C. 50 G4 7 30N 7 40W
Man, I. of, U.K. 12 C3 54 15N 4 30W
Man-Bazar, India ...... 43 H12 23 4N 86 39 E
Man Na, Burma .... 41 H20 23 27N 97 19 E
Mana →, Fr. Guiana 93 B8 5 45N 53 55W
Mana Pools △, Zimbabwe .. 55 F2 15 56S 29 25 E
Manaar, G. of = Mannar, G. of, Asia 40 Q11 8 30N 79 0 E
Manacapuru, Brazil 92 D6 3 16S 60 37W
Manacor, Spain .... 24 B10 39 34N 3 13 E
Manado, Indonesia ..... 37 D6 1 29N 124 51 E
Managua, Nic. 88 D2 12 6N 86 20W
Managua, L. de, Nic. ... 88 D2 12 20N 86 30W
Manakara, Madag. ..... 57 C8 22 8S 48 1 E
Manali, India .... 42 C7 32 16N 77 10 E
Manama = Al Manāmah, Bahrain 45 E6 26 10N 50 30 E
Manambao →, Madag. ... 57 B7 17 35S 44 0 E
Manambato, Madag. .... 57 A8 13 43S 49 7 E
Manambolo →, Madag. .. 57 B7 19 18S 44 22 E
Manambolosy, Madag. .. 57 B8 16 2S 49 40 E
Mananara, Madag. ..... 57 B8 16 10S 49 46 E
Mananara →, Madag. ... 57 C8 23 21S 47 42 E
Mananara △, Madag. .... 57 B8 16 14S 49 45 E
Mananjary, Madag. ..... 57 C8 21 13S 48 20 E
Manantenina, Madag. .. 57 C8 24 17S 47 19 E
Manaos = Manaus, Brazil .. 92 D7 3 0S 60 0W
Manapire →, Venezuela .. 92 B5 7 42N 66 7W
Manapouri, N.Z. .... 59 L1 45 34S 167 39 E
Manapouri, L., N.Z. .... 59 L1 45 32S 167 32 E
Manār, Jabal, Yemen ... 47 E3 14 2N 44 17 E
Manaravolo, Madag. ... 57 C8 23 59S 45 39 E
Manas, China .... 32 B3 44 17N 85 56 E
Manas →, India .... 41 F17 26 12N 90 40 E
Manaslu, Nepal .... 43 E11 28 33N 84 33 E
Manasquan, U.S.A. 85 F10 40 8N 74 3W
Manassa, U.S.A. 77 H11 37 11N 105 56W
Manatí, Puerto Rico .... 89 d 18 26N 66 29W
Manaung, Burma ...... 41 K18 18 45N 93 40 E
Manaus, Brazil 92 D7 3 0S 60 0W
Manawan L., Canada ... 71 B8 55 24N 103 14W
Manbij, Syria .... 44 B3 36 31N 37 57 E
Manchegorsk, Russia ... 28 C4 67 54N 32 58 E
Manchester, U.K. 12 D5 53 29N 2 12W
Manchester, Calif., U.S.A. 78 G3 38 58N 123 41W
Manchester, Conn., U.S.A. 85 E12 41 47N 72 31W
Manchester, Ga., U.S.A. .. 83 J3 32 51N 84 37W
Manchester, Iowa, U.S.A. 80 D9 42 29N 91 27W
Manchester, Ky., U.S.A. .. 82 G4 37 9N 83 46W
Manchester, N.H., U.S.A. 85 D13 42 59N 71 28W
Manchester, N.Y., U.S.A. 84 D7 42 56N 77 16W
Manchester, Pa., U.S.A. .. 85 F8 40 4N 76 43W
Manchester, Tenn., U.S.A. 83 H2 35 29N 86 5W
Manchester, Vt., U.S.A. .. 85 C11 43 10N 73 5W
Manchester International ✈ (MAN), U.K. 12 D5 53 21N 2 17W
Manchester L., Canada .. 71 A7 61 28N 107 29W
Manchhar L., Pakistan .. 42 F2 26 25N 67 39 E
Manchuria = Dongbei, China 29 E13 45 0N 125 0 E
Manchurian Plain, China .. 26 E16 47 0N 124 0 E
Mand →, India .... 43 J10 21 42N 83 15 E
Mand →, Iran .... 45 D7 28 20N 52 30 E
Manda, Ludewe, Tanzania .. 55 E3 10 30S 34 40 E
Manda, Mbeya, Tanzania .. 54 D3 7 58S 32 29 E
Manda, Mbeya, Tanzania .. 55 D3 8 30S 32 49 E
Mandabé, Madag. ...... 57 C7 21 0S 44 55 E
Mandaguari, Brazil 95 A5 23 32S 51 42W
Mandah = Töhöm, Mongolia 34 B5 44 27N 108 2 E
Mandal, Norway .... 9 G12 58 2N 7 25 E
Mandala, Puncak, Indonesia 37 E10 4 44S 140 20 E
Mandalay, Burma ...... 41 J20 22 0N 96 4 E
Mandale = Mandalay, Burma 41 J20 22 0N 96 4 E
Mandalgarh, India ..... 42 G6 25 12N 75 6 E
Mandalgovi, Mongolia .. 34 B4 45 45N 106 10 E
Mandalī, Iraq .... 44 C5 33 43N 45 28 E

Mandan, U.S.A. 80 B4 46 50N 100 54W
Mandar, Teluk, Indonesia .. 37 E5 3 35S 119 15 E
Mandaue, Phil. .... 37 B6 10 20N 123 56 E
Mandera, Kenya .... 54 B5 3 55N 41 53 E
Mandeville, Jamaica .... 88 a 18 2N 77 31W
Mandi, India .... 42 D7 31 39N 76 58 E
Mandi Dabwali, India ... 42 E6 29 58N 74 42 E
Mandimba, Mozam. .... 55 E4 14 20S 35 40 E
Mandioli, Indonesia .... 37 E7 0 40S 127 20 E
Mandla, India .... 43 H9 22 39N 80 30 E
Mandorah, Australia .... 60 B5 12 32S 130 42 E
Mandoto, Madag. ...... 57 B8 19 34S 46 17 E
Mandra, Pakistan ...... 42 C5 33 23N 73 12 E
Mandrare →, Madag. .... 57 D8 25 10S 46 30 E
Mandritsara, Madag. ... 57 B8 15 50S 48 49 E
Mandronarivo, Madag. .. 57 C8 21 7S 45 38 E
Mandsaur, India .... 42 G6 24 3N 75 8 E
Mandurah, Australia ... 61 F2 32 36S 115 48 E
Mandvi, India .... 42 H3 22 51N 69 22 E
Mandya, India .... 40 N10 12 30N 77 0 E
Mandzai, Pakistan ..... 42 D2 30 55N 67 6 E
Maneh, Iran .... 45 B8 37 39N 57 7 E
Manera, Madag. .... 57 C7 22 55S 44 20 E
Maneroo Cr. →, Australia .. 62 C3 23 21S 143 53 E
Manfalūt, Egypt .... 51 C12 27 20N 30 52 E
Manfredónia, Italy ..... 22 D6 41 38N 15 55 E
Mangabeiras, Chapada das, Brazil 93 F9 10 0S 46 30W
Mangalia, Romania ..... 17 G15 43 50N 28 35 E
Mangalore, India ...... 40 N9 12 55N 74 47 E
Mangan, India .... 43 F13 27 31N 88 32 E
Mangaung, S. Africa ... 53 K5 29 10S 26 25 E
Mangawan, India ...... 43 G9 24 41N 81 33 E
Mangaweka, N.Z. ...... 59 H5 39 48S 175 47 E
Manggar, Indonesia .... 36 E3 2 50S 108 10 E
Manggawitu, Indonesia .. 37 E8 4 8S 133 32 E
Manggis, Indonesia .... 37 J18 8 29S 115 31 E
Mangindrano, Madag. .. 57 A8 14 17S 48 58 E
Mangkalihat, Tanjung, Indonesia 37 D5 1 2N 118 59 E
Mangla, Pakistan ...... 42 C5 33 7N 73 39 E
Mangla Dam, Pakistan .. 43 C5 33 9N 73 44 E
Manglaur, India .... 42 E7 29 44N 77 49 E
Mangnai, China .... 32 C4 37 52N 91 43 E
Mango, Togo .... 50 F6 10 20N 0 30 E
Mangoche, Malawi ..... 55 E4 14 25S 35 16 E
Mangole, Indonesia .... 37 E6 1 50S 125 55 E
Mangombe, Dem. Rep. of the Congo 54 C2 1 20S 26 48 E
Mangonui, N.Z. .... 59 F4 35 1S 173 32 E
Mangoro →, Madag. .... 57 B8 20 0S 48 45 E
Mangrol, Mad. P., India .. 42 J4 21 7N 70 7 E
Mangrol, Raj., India .... 42 G6 25 20N 76 31 E
Mangueira, L. da, Brazil .. 95 C5 33 0S 52 50W
Mangum, U.S.A. 81 H5 34 53N 99 30W
Mangyshlak, Poluostrov, Kazakhstan 28 E6 44 30N 52 30 E
Manhattan, U.S.A. 80 F6 39 11N 96 35W
Manhiça, Mozam. ...... 57 D5 25 23S 32 49 E
Mania →, Madag. ...... 57 B8 19 42S 45 22 E
Manica, Mozam. .... 57 B5 18 58S 32 59 E
Manica □, Mozam. ..... 57 B5 19 10S 33 45 E
Manicaland □, Zimbabwe 55 F3 19 0S 32 30 E
Manicoré, Brazil 92 E6 5 48S 61 16W
Manicouagan →, Canada .. 73 C6 49 30N 68 30W
Manicouagan, Rés., Canada 73 B6 51 5N 68 40W
Maniema □, Dem. Rep. of the Congo 54 C2 3 0S 26 0 E
Manifah, Si. Arabia ..... 45 E6 27 44N 49 0 E
Manifold, C., Australia .. 62 C5 22 41S 150 50 E
Manigotagan, Canada ... 71 C9 51 6N 96 18W
Manigotagan →, Canada .. 71 C9 51 7N 96 20W
Manihari, India .... 43 G12 25 21N 87 38 E
Manihiki, Cook Is. 65 J11 10 24S 161 1W
Manika, Plateau de la, Dem. Rep. of the Congo 55 E2 10 0S 25 5 E
Manikpur, India .... 43 G9 25 4N 81 7 E
Manila, Phil. .... 37 B6 14 40N 121 3 E
Manila, U.S.A. 76 F9 40 59N 109 43W
Manila B., Phil. .... 37 B6 14 40N 120 35 E
Manilla, Australia ..... 63 E5 30 45S 150 43 E
Maningrida, Australia ... 62 A1 12 3S 134 13 E
Manipur □, India ...... 41 G19 25 0N 94 0 E
Manipur →, Burma ..... 41 H19 23 45N 94 20 E
Manisa, Turkey .... 23 E12 38 38N 27 30 E
Manistee, U.S.A. 82 C2 44 15N 86 19W
Manistee →, U.S.A. 82 C2 44 15N 86 21W
Manistique, U.S.A. 82 C2 45 57N 86 15W
Manitoba □, Canada ... 71 B9 53 30N 97 0W
Manitoba, L., Canada ... 71 C9 51 0N 98 45W
Manitou, Canada 71 D9 49 15N 98 32W
Manitou, L., Canada 73 B6 50 55N 65 17W
Manitou Is., U.S.A. 82 C3 45 8N 86 0W
Manitou L., Canada 71 C7 52 43N 109 43W
Manitou Springs, U.S.A. .. 80 F2 38 52N 104 55W
Manitoulin I., Canada ... 72 C3 45 40N 82 30W
Manitouwadge, Canada .. 72 C2 49 8N 85 48W
Manitowoc, U.S.A. 82 C2 44 5N 87 40W
Manizales, Colombia ... 92 B3 5 5N 75 32W
Manja, Madag. .... 57 C7 21 26S 44 20 E
Manjacaze, Mozam. .... 57 C5 24 45S 34 0 E
Manjakandriana, Madag. 57 B8 18 55S 47 47 E
Manjhand, Pakistan .... 42 G3 25 50N 68 10 E
Manjil, Iran .... 45 B6 36 46N 49 30 E
Manjimup, Australia ... 61 F2 34 15S 116 6 E
Manjra →, India .... 40 K10 18 49N 77 52 E
Mankato, Kans., U.S.A. .. 80 F5 39 47N 98 13W
Mankato, Minn., U.S.A. .. 80 C8 44 10N 94 0W
Mankayane, Swaziland .. 57 D5 26 40S 31 4 E
Mankera, Pakistan ..... 42 D4 31 23N 71 26 E
Mankota, Canada 71 D7 49 25N 107 5W
Manlay = Üydzin, Mongolia 34 B4 44 9N 107 0 E
Manmad, India .... 40 J9 20 18N 74 28 E
Mann Ranges, Australia .. 61 E5 26 6S 130 5 E
Manna, Indonesia ...... 36 E2 4 25S 102 55 E
Mannahill, Australia ... 63 E3 32 25S 140 0 E
Mannar, Sri Lanka ..... 40 Q11 9 1N 79 54 E
Mannar, G. of, Asia .... 40 Q11 8 30N 79 0 E
Mannar I., Sri Lanka ... 40 Q11 9 5N 79 45 E
Mannheim, Germany ... 16 D5 49 29N 8 29 E
Manning, Canada 70 B5 56 53N 117 39W
Manning, Oreg., U.S.A. .. 78 E3 45 45N 123 13W
Manning, S.C., U.S.A. .. 83 J5 33 42N 80 13W
Mannum, Australia .... 63 E2 34 50S 139 20 E
Manoharpur, India ..... 43 H11 22 23N 85 12 E
Manokwari, Indonesia .. 37 E8 0 54S 134 0 E
Manombo, Madag. ..... 57 C7 22 57S 43 28 E
Manono, Dem. Rep. of the Congo 54 D2 7 15S 27 25 E

Manosque, France ...... 20 E6 43 49N 5 47 E
Manotick, Canada 85 A9 45 13N 75 41W
Manouane →, Canada ... 73 C5 49 30N 71 10W
Manouane, L., Canada .. 73 B5 50 45N 70 45W
Manp'o, N. Korea ...... 35 D14 41 6N 126 24 E
Manpojin = Manp'o, N. Korea 35 D14 41 6N 126 24 E
Manpur, Chhattisgarh, India 43 H10 23 17N 83 35 E
Manpur, Mad. P., India .. 42 H6 22 26N 75 37 E
Manresa, Spain .... 21 B6 41 48N 1 50 E
Mansa, Gujarat, India ... 42 H5 23 27N 72 45 E
Mansa, Punjab, India ... 42 E6 30 0N 75 27 E
Mansa, Zambia .... 55 E2 11 13S 28 55 E
Mansehra, Pakistan .... 42 B5 34 20N 73 15 E
Mansel I., Canada 69 B11 62 0N 80 0W
Mansfield, Australia ... 63 F4 37 4S 146 6 E
Mansfield, U.K. 12 D6 53 9N 1 11W
Mansfield, La., U.S.A. .. 81 J8 32 2N 93 43W
Mansfield, Mass., U.S.A. 85 D13 42 2N 71 13W
Mansfield, Ohio, U.S.A. .. 84 F2 40 45N 82 31W
Mansfield, Pa., U.S.A. ... 84 E7 41 48N 77 5W
Mansfield, Mt., U.S.A. .. 85 B12 44 33N 72 49W
Manson Creek, Canada .. 70 B4 55 37N 124 32W
Manta, Ecuador 92 D2 1 0S 80 40W
Mantalingajan, Mt., Phil. 36 C5 8 55N 117 45 E
Mantare, Tanzania ..... 54 C3 2 42S 33 13 E
Manteca, U.S.A. 78 H5 37 48N 121 13W
Manteo, U.S.A. 83 H8 35 55N 75 40W
Mantes-la-Jolie, France .. 20 B4 48 58N 1 41 E
Manthani, India .... 40 K11 18 40N 79 35 E
Manti, U.S.A. 76 G8 39 16N 111 38W
Mantiqueira, Serra da, Brazil 95 A7 22 0S 44 0W
Manton, U.S.A. 82 C3 44 25N 85 24W
Mántova, Italy .... 22 B4 45 9N 10 48 E
Mänttä, Finland .... 9 E21 62 0N 24 40 E
Mantua = Mántova, Italy 22 B4 45 9N 10 48 E
Manu, Peru 92 F4 12 10S 70 51W
Manu →, Peru 92 F4 12 16S 70 55W
Manu'a Is., Amer. Samoa 59 B14 14 13S 169 35W
Manuel Alves →, Brazil .. 93 F9 11 19S 48 28W
Manui, Indonesia ...... 37 E6 3 35S 123 5 E
Manukau, N.Z. .... 59 G5 40 43S 175 13 E
Manuripi →, Bolivia 92 F5 11 6S 67 36W
Many, U.S.A. 81 K8 31 34N 93 29W
Manyara, L., Tanzania .. 54 C4 3 40S 35 50 E
Manych-Gudilo, Ozero, Russia 19 E7 46 24N 42 38 E
Manyonga →, Tanzania .. 54 C3 4 10S 34 15 E
Manyoni, Tanzania ..... 54 D3 5 45S 34 55 E
Manzai, Pakistan ...... 42 C4 32 12N 70 15 E
Manzanar ☐, U.S.A. 78 J7 36 44N 118 5W
Manzanares, Spain 21 C4 39 2N 3 22W
Manzanillo, Cuba 88 B4 20 20N 77 31W
Manzanillo, Mexico 86 D4 19 0N 104 20W
Manzanillo, Pta., Panama 88 E4 9 30N 79 40W
Manzano Mts., U.S.A. ... 77 J10 34 40N 106 20W
Manẕarīyeh, Iran ...... 45 C6 34 53N 50 50 E
Manzhouli, China ..... 33 B6 49 35N 117 25 E
Manzini, Swaziland .... 57 D5 26 30S 31 25 E
Mao, Chad .... 51 F9 14 4N 15 19 E
Maó, Spain .... 24 B11 39 53N 4 16 E
Maoke, Pegunungan, Indonesia 37 E9 3 40S 137 30 E
Maolin, China .... 35 C12 43 58N 123 30 E
Maoming, China .... 33 D6 21 50N 110 54 E
Maoxing, China .... 35 B13 45 28N 124 40 E
Mapam Yumco, China .. 32 C3 30 45N 81 28 E
Mapastepec, Mexico 87 D6 15 26N 92 54W
Maphrao, Ko, Thailand .. 39 a 7 56N 98 26 E
Mapia, Kepulauan, Indonesia 37 D8 0 50N 134 20 E
Mapimí, Mexico 86 B4 25 50N 103 50W
Mapimí, Bolsón de, Mexico 86 B4 27 30N 104 15W
Mapinga, Tanzania ..... 54 D4 6 40S 39 12 E
Mapinhane, Mozam. .... 57 C6 22 20S 35 0 E
Maple Creek, Canada ... 71 D7 49 55N 109 29W
Maple Valley, U.S.A. ... 78 C4 47 25N 122 3W
Mapleton, U.S.A. 76 D2 44 2N 123 52W
Mapuera →, Brazil 92 D7 1 5S 57 2W
Mapulanguene, Mozam. 57 C5 24 29S 32 6 E
Maputo, Mozam. .... 57 D5 25 58S 32 32 E
Maputo □, Mozam. ..... 57 D5 26 23S 32 48 E
Maputo →, Mozam. ..... 57 D5 26 0S 32 34 E
Maputo, B. de, Mozam. .. 57 D5 25 50S 32 45 E
Maqiaohe, China ...... 35 B16 44 40N 130 30 E
Maqnā, Si. Arabia ..... 44 D2 28 25N 34 50 E
Maquan He = Brahmaputra →, Asia 32 D3 23 40N 90 35 E
Maquela do Zombo, Angola 52 F3 6 0S 15 15 E
Maquinchao, Argentina .. 96 E3 41 15S 68 50W
Maquoketa, U.S.A. 80 D9 42 4N 90 40W
Mar, Serra do, Brazil ... 95 B6 25 30S 49 0W
Mar Chiquita, L., Argentina 94 C3 30 40S 62 50W
Mar del Plata, Argentina 94 D4 38 0S 57 30W
Mar Menor, Spain 21 D5 37 40N 0 45W
Mara, Tanzania .... 54 C3 1 30S 34 32 E
Mara □, Tanzania ...... 54 C3 1 45S 34 20 E
Maraã, Brazil 92 D5 1 52S 65 25W
Marabá, Brazil 93 E9 5 20S 49 5W
Maracá, I. de, Brazil ... 93 C8 2 10N 50 30W
Maracaibo, Venezuela .. 92 A4 10 40N 71 37W
Maracaibo, L. de, Venezuela 92 B4 9 40N 71 30W
Maracaju, Brazil 95 A4 21 38S 55 9W
Maracas Bay Village, Trin. & Tob. 93 K15 10 46N 61 28W
Maracay, Venezuela 92 A5 10 15N 67 28W
Maradi, Niger .... 50 F7 13 29N 7 20 E
Marāgheh, Iran .... 44 B5 37 30N 46 12 E
Marāh, Si. Arabia ..... 44 E5 25 0N 45 35 E
Marajó, I. de, Brazil 93 D9 1 0S 49 30W
Marākand, Iran .... 44 B5 38 51N 45 16 E
Marakele △, S. Africa ... 57 C4 24 35S 27 32 E
Maralal, Kenya .... 54 B4 1 0N 36 38 E
Maralinga, Australia ... 61 F5 30 13S 131 32 E
Marambio, Antarctica .. 5 C18 64 0S 56 0W
Maran, Malaysia .... 39 L4 3 35N 102 45 E
Marana, U.S.A. 77 K8 32 27N 111 13W
Maranboy, Australia ... 60 B5 14 40S 132 39 E
Marand, Iran .... 44 B5 38 30N 45 45 E
Marang, Malaysia ...... 39 K4 5 12N 103 13 E
Maranguape, Brazil 93 D11 3 55S 38 50W
Maranhão = São Luís, Brazil 93 D10 2 39S 44 15W
Maranhão □, Brazil 93 E9 5 0S 46 0W
Maranoa →, Australia ... 63 D4 27 50S 148 37 E
Marañón →, Peru 92 D4 4 30S 73 35W
Marão, Mozam. .... 57 C5 24 18S 34 2 E
Maraş = Kahramanmaraş, Turkey 19 G6 37 37N 36 53 E
Marathasa, Cyprus ..... 25 E11 34 59N 32 51 E
Marathon, Australia ... 62 C3 20 51S 143 32 E
Marathon, Canada 72 C2 48 44N 86 23W
Marathon, N.Y., U.S.A. .. 85 D8 42 27N 76 2W
Marathon, Tex., U.S.A. .. 81 K3 30 12N 103 15W

arathóvouno, *Cyprus*	**25 D12** 35 13N 33 37 E	Marlow, *U.S.A.*	**81 H6** 34 39N 97 58W
aratua, *Indonesia*	**37 D5** 2 10N 118 35 E	Marmagao, *India*	**40 M8** 15 25N 73 56 E
araval, *Trin. & Tob.*	**93 K15** 10 43N 61 32W	Marmara, *Turkey*	**23 D12** 40 35N 27 34 E
aravatío, *Mexico*	**86 D4** 19 51N 100 25W	Marmara, Sea of = Marmara	
arãwén, *U.A.E.*	**45 E7** 24 18N 53 18 E	Denizi, *Turkey*	**23 D13** 40 45N 28 15 E
arbella, *Spain*	**21 D3** 36 30N 4 57W	Marmara Denizi, *Turkey*	**23 D13** 40 45N 28 15 E
arble Bar, *Australia*	**60 D2** 21 9S 119 44 E	Marmaris, *Turkey*	**23 F13** 36 50N 28 14 E
arble Falls, *U.S.A.*	**81 K5** 30 35N 98 16W	Marmion, Mt., *Australia*	**61 E2** 29 16S 119 50 E
arblehead, *U.S.A.*	**85 D14** 42 30N 70 51W	Marmion L., *Canada*	**72 C1** 48 55N 91 20W
arch, *U.K.*	**13 E8** 52 33N 0 5 E	Marmolada, Mte., *Italy*	**22 A4** 46 26N 11 51 E
arche, *France*	**20 C4** 46 5N 1 20 E	Marmora, *Canada*	**84 B7** 44 28N 77 41W
arche-en-Famenne, *Belgium*	**15 D5** 50 14N 5 19 E	Marne →, *France*	**20 B5** 48 48N 2 24 E
archena, *Spain*	**21 D5** 37 18N 5 23W	Maroala, *Madag.*	**57 B8** 15 23S 47 59 E
arco, *U.S.A.*	**83 N5** 25 58N 81 44W	Maroantsetra, *Madag.*	**57 B8** 15 26S 49 44 E
arcos Juárez, *Argentina*	**94 C3** 32 42S 62 5W	Maroelaboom, *Namibia*	**56 B2** 19 15S 18 53 E
arcus I. = Minami-Tori-Shima,		Marofandilia, *Madag.*	**57 C7** 20 7S 44 34 E
Pac. Oc.	**64 E7** 24 20N 153 58 E	Marojejy △, *Madag.*	**57 A8** 14 26S 49 21 E
arcus Necker Ridge, *Pac. Oc.*	**64 F9** 20 0N 175 0 E	Marolambo, *Madag.*	**57 C8** 20 2S 48 7 E
arcy, Mt., *U.S.A.*	**85 B11** 44 7N 73 56W	Maromandia, *Madag.*	**57 A8** 14 13S 48 5 E
ardan, *Pakistan*	**42 B5** 34 20N 72 0 E	Maromokotro, *Madag.*	**57 A8** 14 0N 48 50 E
ardin, *Turkey*	**19 G7** 37 20N 40 43 E	Marondera, *Zimbabwe*	**55 F3** 18 5S 31 42 E
aree, L., *U.K.*	**11 D3** 57 40N 5 26W	Maroni →, *Fr. Guiana*	**93 B8** 5 30N 54 0W
areeba, *Australia*	**62 B4** 16 59S 145 28 E	Maroochydore, *Australia*	**63 D5** 26 29S 153 5 E
areetsane, *S. Africa*	**56 D4** 26 9S 25 25 E	Maroona, *Australia*	**63 F3** 37 27S 142 54 E
arek = Stanke Dimitrov,		Marosakoa, *Madag.*	**57 B8** 15 26S 46 38 E
Bulgaria	**23 C10** 42 17N 23 9 E	Maroseranana, *Madag.*	**57 B8** 18 32S 48 51 E
arengo, *U.S.A.*	**80 E8** 41 48N 92 4W	Marotandrano, *Madag.*	**57 B8** 16 10S 48 50 E
arerano, *Madag.*	**57 C7** 21 23S 44 52 E	Marotaolano, *Madag.*	**57 A8** 12 47S 49 15 E
arfa, *U.S.A.*	**81 K2** 30 19N 104 1W	Maroua, *Cameroon*	**51 F8** 10 40N 14 20 E
arfa Pt., *Malta*	**25 D1** 35 59N 14 19 E	Marovato, *Madag.*	**57 B8** 15 48S 48 5 E
argaret →, *Australia*	**60 C4** 18 9S 125 41 E	Marovoay, *Madag.*	**57 B8** 16 6S 46 39 E
argaret Bay, *Canada*	**70 C3** 51 20N 127 35W	Marquard, *S. Africa*	**56 D4** 28 40S 27 28 E
argaret L., *Canada*	**70 B5** 58 56N 115 25W	Marquesas Is. = Marquises, Ís.,	
argaret River, *Australia*	**61 F2** 33 57S 115 4 E	*French Polynesia*	**65 H14** 9 30S 140 0W
argarita, I. de, *Venezuela*	**92 A6** 11 0N 64 0W	Marquette, *U.S.A.*	**82 B2** 46 33N 87 24W
argaritovo, *Russia*	**30 C7** 43 25N 134 45 E	Marquis, St. *Lucia*	**89 f** 14 2N 60 54W
argate, *S. Africa*	**57 E5** 30 50S 30 20 E	Marquises, Ís., *French Polynesia*	**65 H14** 9 30S 140 0W
argate, *U.K.*	**13 F9** 51 23N 1 23 E	Marra, Djebel, *Sudan*	**51 F10** 13 10N 24 22 E
argherita Pk., *Uganda*	**54 B3** 0 22N 29 51 E	Marracuene, *Mozam.*	**57 D5** 25 45S 32 35 E
argow, Dasht-e, *Afghan.*	**40 D3** 30 40N 62 30 E	Marrakech, *Morocco*	**50 B4** 31 9N 8 0W
arguerite, *Canada*	**70 C4** 52 30N 122 25W	Marrawah, *Australia*	**63 G3** 40 55S 144 42 E
ari El □, *Russia*	**18 C8** 56 30N 48 0 E	Marree, *Australia*	**63 D2** 29 39S 138 1 E
ari Indus, *Pakistan*	**42 C4** 32 57N 71 34 E	Marrero, *U.S.A.*	**81 L9** 29 54N 90 6W
ari Republic = Mari El □, *Russia*	**18 C8** 56 30N 48 0 E	Marrimane, *Mozam.*	**57 C5** 22 58S 33 34 E
aria Elena, *Chile*	**94 A2** 22 18S 69 40W	Marromeu, *Mozam.*	**57 B6** 18 15S 36 25 E
aria Grande, *Argentina*	**94 C4** 31 45S 59 55W	Marromeu →, *Mozam.*	**57 B6** 19 0S 36 0 E
aria I., N. *Terr., Australia*	**62 A2** 14 52S 135 45 E	Marrowie Cr. →, *Australia*	**63 E4** 33 23S 145 40 E
aria I., *Tas., Australia*	**63 G4** 42 35S 148 0 E	Marrubane, *Mozam.*	**55 F4** 18 0S 37 0 E
aria Island, *Australia*	**63 G4** 42 38S 148 0 E	Marrupa, *Mozam.*	**55 E4** 13 8S 37 30 E
aria van Diemen, C., *N.Z.*	**59 F4** 34 29S 172 40 E	Mars Hill, *U.S.A.*	**83 B12** 46 31N 67 52W
ariakani, *Kenya*	**54 C4** 3 50S 39 27 E	Marsá Matrûh, *Egypt*	**51 B11** 31 19N 27 9 E
ariala △, *Australia*	**63 D4** 25 57S 145 2 E	Marsabit, *Kenya*	**54 B4** 2 18N 38 0 E
arian, *Australia*	**62 K6** 21 9S 148 57 E	Marsabit △, *Kenya*	**54 B4** 2 23N 37 56 E
arian L., *Canada*	**70 A5** 63 0N 116 15W	Marsala, *Italy*	**22 F5** 37 48N 12 26 E
ariana Trench, *Pac. Oc.*	**26 H18** 13 0N 145 0 E	Marsalforn, *Malta*	**25 C1** 36 4N 14 16 E
arianao, *Cuba*	**88 B3** 23 8N 82 24W	Marsden, *Australia*	**63 E4** 33 47S 147 32 E
arianna, *Ark., U.S.A.*	**81 H9** 34 46N 90 46W	Marseille, *France*	**20 E6** 43 18N 5 23 E
arianna, *Fla., U.S.A.*	**83 K3** 30 46N 85 14W	Marseilles = Marseille, *France*	**20 E6** 43 18N 5 23 E
arias →, *U.S.A.*	**76 C8** 47 56N 110 30W	Marsh I., *U.S.A.*	**81 L9** 29 34N 91 53W
ariato, Punta, *Panama*	**88 E3** 7 12N 80 52W	Marshall, *Ark., U.S.A.*	**81 H8** 35 55N 92 38W
aribor, *Slovenia*	**16 E8** 46 36N 15 40 E	Marshall, *Mich., U.S.A.*	**82 D3** 42 16N 84 58W
arico →, *Africa*	**56 C4** 23 35S 26 57 E	Marshall, *Minn., U.S.A.*	**80 C7** 44 25N 95 45W
aricopa, *Ariz., U.S.A.*	**77 K7** 33 4N 112 3W	Marshall, *Mo., U.S.A.*	**80 F8** 39 7N 93 12W
aricopa, *Calif., U.S.A.*	**79 K7** 35 4N 119 24W	Marshall, *Tex., U.S.A.*	**81 J7** 32 33N 94 23W
arié →, *Brazil*	**92 D5** 0 27S 66 26W	Marshall →, *Australia*	**62 C2** 22 59S 136 59 E
arie Byrd Land, *Antarctica*	**5 D14** 79 30S 125 0W	Marshall Is. ■, *Pac. Oc.*	**64 G9** 9 0N 171 0 E
arie-Galante, *Guadeloupe*	**88 b** 15 56N 61 16W	Marshalltown, *U.S.A.*	**80 D8** 42 3N 92 55W
aricourt = Kangiqsujuaq,		Marshbrook, *Zimbabwe*	**57 B5** 18 33S 31 9 E
Canada	**69 B12** 61 30N 72 0W	Marshfield, *Mo., U.S.A.*	**81 G8** 37 15N 92 54W
ariembourg, *Belgium*	**15 D4** 50 6N 4 31 E	Marshfield, *Vt., U.S.A.*	**85 B12** 44 20N 72 20W
ariental, *Namibia*	**56 C2** 24 36S 18 0 E	Marshfield, *Wis., U.S.A.*	**80 C9** 44 40N 90 10W
arienville, *U.S.A.*	**84 E5** 41 28N 79 8W	Marshûn, *Iran*	**45 B6** 36 19N 49 23 E
ariestad, *Sweden*	**9 G15** 58 43N 13 50 E	Märsta, *Sweden*	**9 G17** 59 37N 17 52 E
arietta, *Ga., U.S.A.*	**83 J3** 33 57N 84 33W	Mart, *U.S.A.*	**81 K6** 31 33N 96 50W
arietta, *Ohio, U.S.A.*	**82 F5** 39 25N 81 27W	Martaban, *Burma*	**41 L20** 16 30N 97 35 E
arieville, *Canada*	**85 A11** 45 26N 73 10W	Martaban, G. of, *Burma*	**41 L20** 16 5N 96 30 E
ariinsk, *Russia*	**28 D9** 56 10N 87 20 E	Martapura, *Kalimantan,*	
arijampolė, *Lithuania*	**9 J20** 54 33N 23 19 E	*Indonesia*	**36 E4** 3 22S 114 47 E
arília, *Brazil*	**95 A6** 22 13S 50 0W	Martapura, *Sumatera, Indonesia*	**36 E2** 4 19S 104 22 E
arín, *Spain*	**21 A1** 42 23N 8 42W	Martelange, *Belgium*	**15 E5** 49 49N 5 43 E
arina, *U.S.A.*	**78 J5** 36 41N 121 48W	Martha's Vineyard, *U.S.A.*	**85 E14** 41 25N 70 38W
arinduque, *Phil.*	**37 B6** 13 25N 122 0 E	Martigny, *Switz.*	**20 C7** 46 6N 7 3 E
arine City, *U.S.A.*	**84 D2** 42 43N 82 30W	Martigues, *France*	**20 E6** 43 24N 5 4 E
arinette, *U.S.A.*	**82 C2** 45 6N 87 38W	Martin, *Slovak Rep.*	**17 D10** 49 6N 18 58 E
aringá, *Brazil*	**95 A5** 23 26S 52 2W	Martin, *S. Dak., U.S.A.*	**80 D4** 43 11N 101 44W
arion, *Ala., U.S.A.*	**83 J2** 32 38N 87 19W	Martin, *Tenn., U.S.A.*	**81 G10** 36 21N 88 51W
arion, *Ill., U.S.A.*	**81 G10** 37 44N 88 56W	Martin, L., *U.S.A.*	**83 J3** 32 41N 85 55W
arion, *Ind., U.S.A.*	**82 E3** 40 32N 85 40W	Martina Franca, *Italy*	**22 D7** 40 42N 17 20 E
arion, *Iowa, U.S.A.*	**80 D9** 42 2N 91 36W	Martinborough, *N.Z.*	**59 J5** 41 14S 175 29 E
arion, *Kans., U.S.A.*	**80 F6** 38 21N 97 1W	Martinez, *Calif., U.S.A.*	**78 G4** 38 1N 122 8W
arion, *N.C., U.S.A.*	**83 H5** 35 41N 82 1W	Martinez, *Ga., U.S.A.*	**83 J4** 33 31N 82 4W
arion, *Ohio, U.S.A.*	**82 E4** 40 35N 83 8W	Martinique ☑, *W. Indies*	**88 c** 14 40N 61 0W
arion, *S.C., U.S.A.*	**83 H6** 34 11N 79 24W	Martinique Passage, *W. Indies*	**89 C7** 15 15N 61 0W
arion, *Va., U.S.A.*	**83 G5** 36 50N 81 31W	Martinópolis, *Brazil*	**95 A5** 22 11S 51 12W
arion, L., *U.S.A.*	**83 J5** 33 28N 80 10W	Martin's Bay, *Barbados*	**89 g** 13 12N 59 29W
arion, *U.S.A.*	**78 H7** 37 29N 119 58W	Martins Ferry, *U.S.A.*	**84 F4** 40 6N 80 44W
ariposa, *U.S.A.*	**78 H7** 37 29N 119 58W	Martinsburg, *Pa., U.S.A.*	**84 F6** 40 19N 78 20W
iscal Estigarribia, *Paraguay*	**94 A3** 22 3S 60 40W	Martinsburg, *W. Va., U.S.A.*	**82 F7** 39 27N 77 58W
ritime Alps = Maritimes,		Martinsville, *Ind., U.S.A.*	**82 F2** 39 26N 86 25W
Alpes, Europe	**20 D7** 44 10N 7 10 E	Martinsville, *Va., U.S.A.*	**83 G6** 36 41N 79 52W
ritimes, Alpes, *Europe*	**20 D7** 44 10N 7 10 E	Marton, *N.Z.*	**59 J5** 40 4S 175 23 E
ritsa = Évros →, *Greece*	**23 D12** 41 40N 26 34 E	Martos, *Spain*	**21 D4** 37 44N 3 58W
ritsá, *Greece*	**25 C10** 36 22N 28 8 E	Marudi, *Malaysia*	**36 D4** 4 11N 114 19 E
riupol, *Ukraine*	**19 E6** 47 5N 37 31 E	Maruf, *Afghan.*	**40 D5** 31 30N 67 6 E
riusa △, *Venezuela*	**89 E7** 9 24N 61 27W	Marugame, *Japan*	**31 G6** 34 15N 133 40 E
rīvān, *Iran*	**44 C5** 35 30N 46 25 E	Marungu, Mts., *Dem. Rep. of*	
r 'Uyûn, *Lebanon*	**46 B4** 33 20N 35 35 E	*the Congo*	**54 D3** 7 30S 30 0 E
rkdale, *Canada*	**84 B4** 44 19N 80 39W	Marv Dasht, *Iran*	**45 D7** 29 50N 52 40 E
rked Tree, *U.S.A.*	**81 H9** 35 32N 90 25W	Marvast, *Iran*	**45 D7** 30 30N 54 15 E
rket Drayton, *U.K.*	**12 E5** 52 54N 2 29W	Marvel Loch, *Australia*	**61 F2** 31 28S 119 29 E
rket Harborough, *U.K.*	**13 E7** 52 29N 0 55W	Marwar, *India*	**42 G5** 25 43N 73 45 E
rket Rasen, *U.K.*	**12 D7** 53 24N 0 20W	Mary, *Turkmenistan*	**28 F7** 37 40N 61 50 E
rkham, *Canada*	**84 C5** 43 52N 79 16W	Maryborough = Port Laoise,	
rkham, Mt., *Antarctica*	**5 E11** 83 0S 164 0 E	*Ireland*	**10 C4** 53 2N 7 18W
rkleeville, *U.S.A.*	**78 G7** 38 42N 119 47W	Maryborough, *Queens., Australia*	**63 D5** 25 31S 152 37 E
rkovo, *Russia*	**29 C17** 64 40N 170 24 E	Maryborough, *Vic., Australia*	**63 F3** 37 0S 143 44 E
rksville, *U.S.A.*	**81 K8** 31 8N 92 4W	Maryfield, *Canada*	**71 D8** 49 50N 101 35W
rla, *Australia*	**63 D1** 27 19S 133 33 E	Maryland □, *U.S.A.*	**82 F7** 39 0N 76 30W
rlbank, *Canada*	**84 B7** 44 26N 77 6W	Maryland Junction, *Zimbabwe*	**55 F3** 17 45S 30 31 E
rlboro, *Mass., U.S.A.*	**85 D13** 42 19N 71 33W	Maryport, *U.K.*	**12 C4** 54 44N 3 28W
rlboro, *N.Y., U.S.A.*	**85 E11** 41 36N 73 59W	Mary's Harbour, *Canada*	**73 B8** 52 18N 55 51W
rlborough, *Australia*	**62 C4** 22 46S 149 52 E	Marystown, *Canada*	**73 C8** 47 10N 55 10W
rlborough, *U.K.*	**13 F6** 51 25N 1 43W	Marysville, *Canada*	**70 D5** 49 35N 116 0W
rlborough Downs, *U.K.*	**13 F6** 51 27N 1 53W	Marysville, *Calif., U.S.A.*	**78 F5** 39 9N 121 35W
rlin, *U.S.A.*	**81 K6** 31 18N 96 54W	Marysville, *Kans., U.S.A.*	**80 F6** 39 51N 96 39W
rlow, *U.K.*	**13 F7** 51 34N 0 46W	Marysville, *Mich., U.S.A.*	**84 D2** 42 54N 82 29W
		Marysville, *Ohio, U.S.A.*	**82 E4** 40 14N 83 22W

Marysville, *Wash., U.S.A.*	**78 B4** 48 3N 122 11W	Mathráki, *Greece*	**25 A3** 39 48N 19 31 E
Maryville, *Mo., U.S.A.*	**80 E7** 40 21N 94 52W	Mathura, *India*	**42 F7** 27 30N 77 40 E
Maryville, *Tenn., U.S.A.*	**83 H4** 35 46N 83 58W	Mati, *Phil.*	**37 C7** 6 55N 126 15 E
Marzûq, *Libya*	**51 C8** 25 53N 13 57 E	Matiali, *India*	**43 F13** 26 56N 88 49 E
Masahunga, *Tanzania*	**54 C3** 2 6S 33 18 E	Matías Romero, *Mexico*	**87 D5** 16 53N 95 2W
Masai, *Malaysia*	**39 d** 1 29N 103 53 E	Matibane, *Mozam.*	**55 E5** 14 49S 40 45 E
Masai Mara △, *Kenya*	**54 C4** 1 25S 35 5 E	Matiri Ra., *N.Z.*	**59 J4** 41 38S 172 20 E
Masai Steppe, *Tanzania*	**54 C4** 4 30S 36 30 E	Matjiesfontein, *S. Africa*	**56 E3** 33 14S 20 35 E
Masaka, *Uganda*	**54 C3** 0 21S 31 45 E	Matla →, *India*	**43 J13** 21 40N 88 40 E
Masalembo, Kepulauan,		Matlamanyane, *Botswana*	**56 B4** 19 33S 25 57 E
Indonesia	**36 F4** 5 35S 114 30 E	Matli, *Pakistan*	**42 G3** 25 2N 68 39 E
Masalima, Kepulauan, *Indonesia*	**36 F5** 5 4S 117 5 E	Matlock, *U.K.*	**12 D6** 53 9N 1 33W
Masamba, *Indonesia*	**37 E6** 2 30S 120 15 E	Mato Grosso □, *Brazil*	**93 F8** 14 0S 55 0W
Masan, *S. Korea*	**35 G15** 35 11N 128 32 E	Mato Grosso, Planalto do, *Brazil*	**93 G8** 15 0S 55 0W
Masandam, Ra's, *Oman*	**45 E8** 26 30N 56 30 E	Mato Grosso do Sul □, *Brazil*	**93 G8** 18 0S 55 0W
Masasi, *Tanzania*	**55 E4** 10 45S 38 52 E	Matobo = Matapo △, *Zimbabwe*	**55 G2** 20 30S 29 40 E
Masaya, *Nic.*	**88 D2** 12 0N 86 7W	Matochkin Shar, *Russia*	**28 B6** 73 10N 56 40 E
Masbate, *Phil.*	**37 B6** 12 21N 123 36 E	Matopo Hills, *Zimbabwe*	**55 G2** 20 36S 28 20 E
Mascara, *Algeria*	**50 A6** 35 26N 0 6 E	Matopos, *Zimbabwe*	**55 G2** 20 20S 28 29 E
Mascota, *Mexico*	**86 C4** 20 30N 104 50W	Matosinhos, *Portugal*	**21 B1** 41 11N 8 42W
Masela, *Indonesia*	**37 F7** 8 9S 129 51 E	Matroosberg, *S. Africa*	**56 E2** 33 23S 19 40 E
Maseru, *Lesotho*	**56 D4** 29 18S 27 30 E	Maţruḩ, *Oman*	**47 C6** 23 37N 58 30 E
Mashaba, *Zimbabwe*	**55 G3** 20 2S 30 29 E	Matsue, *Japan*	**31 G6** 35 25N 133 10 E
Mashãbih, *Si. Arabia*	**44 E3** 25 35N 36 30 E	Matsum, Ko, *Thailand*	**39 b** 9 22N 99 59 E
Mashatu △, *Botswana*	**57 C4** 22 5S 29 5 E	Matsumae, *Japan*	**30 D10** 41 26N 140 7 E
Masherbrum, *Pakistan*	**43 B7** 35 38N 76 18 E	Matsumoto, *Japan*	**31 F9** 36 15N 138 0 E
Mashhad, *Iran*	**45 B8** 36 20N 59 35 E	Matsusaka, *Japan*	**31 G8** 34 34N 136 32 E
Mashīz, *Iran*	**45 D8** 29 56N 56 37 E	Matsuura, *Japan*	**31 H4** 33 20N 129 49 E
Mãshkel, Hãmün-i-, *Pakistan*	**40 E3** 28 20N 62 56 E	Matsuyama, *Japan*	**31 H6** 33 45N 132 45 E
Mashki Chãh, *Pakistan*	**40 E3** 29 5N 62 30 E	Mattagami →, *Canada*	**72 B3** 50 43N 81 29W
Mashonaland, *Zimbabwe*	**53 H6** 16 30S 31 0 E	Mattancheri, *India*	**40 Q10** 9 50N 76 15 E
Mashonaland Central □,		Mattawa, *Canada*	**72 C4** 46 20N 78 45W
Zimbabwe	**57 B5** 17 30S 31 0 E	Matterhorn, *Switz.*	**20 D7** 45 58N 7 39 E
Mashonaland East □, *Zimbabwe*	**57 B5** 18 0S 32 0 E	Matthew Town, *Bahamas*	**89 B5** 20 57N 73 40W
Mashonaland West □, *Zimbabwe*	**57 B4** 17 30S 29 30 E	Matthew's Ridge, *Guyana*	**92 B6** 7 37N 60 10W
Mashrakh, *India*	**43 F11** 26 7N 84 48 E	Mattice, *Canada*	**72 C3** 49 40N 83 20W
Masindi, *Uganda*	**54 B3** 1 40N 31 43 E	Mattituck, *U.S.A.*	**85 F12** 40 59N 72 32W
Masindi Port, *Uganda*	**54 B3** 1 43N 32 2 E	Mattō, *Japan*	**31 F8** 36 31N 136 34 E
Maşīrah, *Oman*	**47 C6** 21 0N 58 50 E	Mattoon, *U.S.A.*	**82 F1** 39 29N 88 23W
Maşīrah, Khalīj, *Oman*	**47 C6** 20 10N 58 10 E	Matuba, *Mozam.*	**57 C5** 24 28S 32 49 E
Masisea, *Peru*	**92 E4** 8 35S 74 22W	Matucana, *Peru*	**92 F3** 11 55S 76 25W
Masisi, *Dem. Rep. of the Congo*	**54 C2** 1 23S 28 49 E	Matún = Khowst, *Afghan.*	**42 C3** 33 22N 69 58 E
Masjed Soleyman, *Iran*	**45 D6** 31 55N 49 18 E	Matura B., *Trin. & Tob.*	**93 K15** 10 39N 61 1W
Mask, L., *Ireland*	**10 C2** 53 36N 9 22W	Maturín, *Venezuela*	**92 B6** 9 45N 63 11W
Maskin, *Oman*	**45 F8** 23 30N 56 50 E	Matusadona △, *Zimbabwe*	**55 F2** 16 58S 28 42 E
Masoala △, *Madag.*	**57 B9** 15 30S 50 12 E	Mau, *Mad. P., India*	**43 F8** 26 17N 78 41 E
Masoala, Tanjon' i, *Madag.*	**57 B9** 15 59S 50 13 E	Mau, *Ut. P., India*	**43 G10** 25 56N 83 33 E
Masoarivo, *Madag.*	**57 B7** 19 3S 44 19 E	Mau, *Ut. P., India*	**43 G9** 25 17N 81 23 E
Masohi = Amahai, *Indonesia*	**37 E7** 3 20S 128 55 E	Mau Escarpment, *Kenya*	**54 C4** 0 40S 36 0 E
Masomeloka, *Madag.*	**57 C8** 20 17S 48 37 E	Mau Ranipur, *India*	**43 G8** 25 16N 79 8 E
Mason, *Nev., U.S.A.*	**78 G7** 38 56N 119 8W	Maubeuge, *France*	**20 A6** 50 17N 3 57 E
Mason, *Tex., U.S.A.*	**81 K5** 30 45N 99 14W	Maud, Pt., *Australia*	**60 D1** 23 6S 113 45 E
Mason City, *U.S.A.*	**80 D8** 43 9N 93 12W	Maude, *Australia*	**63 E3** 34 29S 144 18 E
Maspalomas, *Canary Is.*	**24 G4** 27 46N 15 35W	Maudin Sun, *Burma*	**41 M19** 16 0N 94 30 E
Maspalomas, Pta., *Canary Is.*	**24 G4** 27 43N 15 36W	Maués, *Brazil*	**92 D7** 3 20S 57 45W
Masqat, *Oman*	**47 C6** 23 37N 58 36 E	Mauganj, *India*	**41 G12** 24 50N 81 55 E
Massa, *Italy*	**20 D9** 44 1N 10 9 E	Maughold Hd., *U.K.*	**12 C3** 54 18N 4 18W
Massachusetts □, *U.S.A.*	**85 D13** 42 30N 72 0W	Maui, *U.S.A.*	**74 H16** 20 48N 156 20W
Massachusetts B., *U.S.A.*	**85 D14** 42 20N 70 50W	Maulamyaing = Moulmein,	
Massakory, *Chad*	**51 F9** 13 0N 15 49 E	*Burma*	**41 L20** 16 30N 97 40 E
Massanella, *Spain*	**24 B9** 39 48N 2 51 E	Maule □, *Chile*	**94 D1** 36 5S 72 30W
Massangena, *Mozam.*	**57 C5** 21 34S 33 0 E	Maumee, *U.S.A.*	**82 E4** 41 34N 83 39W
Massango, *Angola*	**52 F3** 8 2S 16 21 E	Maumee →, *U.S.A.*	**82 E4** 41 42N 83 28W
Massawa = Mitsiwa, *Eritrea*	**47 D2** 15 35N 39 25 E	Maumere, *Indonesia*	**37 F6** 8 38S 122 13 E
Massena, *U.S.A.*	**85 B10** 44 56N 74 54W	Maun, *Botswana*	**56 C3** 20 0S 23 26 E
Massénya, *Chad*	**51 F9** 11 21N 16 9 E	Mauna Kea, *U.S.A.*	**74 J17** 19 50N 155 28W
Masset, *Canada*	**70 C2** 54 2N 132 10W	Mauna Loa, *U.S.A.*	**74 J17** 19 30N 155 35W
Massiah Street, *Barbados*	**89 g** 13 9N 59 29W	Maungmagan Kyunzu, *Burma*	**38 E1** 14 0N 97 48 E
Massif Central, *France*	**20 D5** 44 55N 3 0 E	Maupin, *U.S.A.*	**76 D3** 45 11N 121 5W
Massillon, *U.S.A.*	**84 F3** 40 48N 81 32W	Maurepas, L., *U.S.A.*	**81 K9** 30 15N 90 30W
Massinga, *Mozam.*	**57 C6** 23 15S 35 22 E	Maurice, L., *Australia*	**61 E5** 29 30S 131 0 E
Massingir, *Mozam.*	**57 C5** 23 51S 32 4 E	Mauricie △, *Canada*	**72 C5** 46 45N 73 0W
Masson-Angers, *Canada*	**85 A9** 45 32N 75 25W	Mauritania ■, *Africa*	**50 E3** 20 50N 10 0W
Masson I., *Antarctica*	**5 C7** 66 10S 93 20 E	Mauritius ■, *Ind. Oc.*	**49 J9** 20 0S 57 0 E
Mastanli = Momchilgrad,		Mauston, *U.S.A.*	**80 D9** 43 48N 90 5W
Bulgaria	**23 D11** 41 33N 25 23 E	Mavli, *India*	**42 G5** 24 45N 73 55 E
Masterton, *N.Z.*	**59 J5** 40 56S 175 39 E	Mavuradonha Mts., *Zimbabwe*	**55 F3** 16 30S 31 30 E
Mastic, *U.S.A.*	**85 F12** 40 47N 72 54W	Mawa, *Dem. Rep. of the Congo*	**54 B2** 2 45N 26 40 E
Mastuj, *Pakistan*	**43 A5** 36 20N 72 36 E	Mawai, *India*	**43 H9** 22 30N 81 4 E
Mastung, *Pakistan*	**40 E5** 29 50N 66 56 E	Mawana, *India*	**42 E7** 29 6N 77 58 E
Masty, *Belarus*	**17 B13** 53 27N 24 38 E	Mawand, *Pakistan*	**42 E3** 29 33N 68 38 E
Masuda, *Japan*	**31 G5** 34 40N 131 51 E	Mawk Mai, *Burma*	**41 J20** 20 14N 97 37 E
Masvingo, *Zimbabwe*	**55 G3** 20 8S 30 49 E	Mawlaik, *Burma*	**41 H19** 23 40N 94 26 E
Masvingo □, *Zimbabwe*	**55 G3** 21 0S 31 30 E	Mawlamyine = Moulmein, *Burma*	**41 L20** 16 30N 97 40 E
Maswa △, *Tanzania*	**54 C3** 2 58S 34 19 E	Mawqaq, *Si. Arabia*	**44 E4** 27 25N 41 8 E
Matabeleland North □,		Mawson Base, *Antarctica*	**5 C6** 67 30S 62 53 E
Zimbabwe	**55 F2** 19 0S 28 0 E	Mawson Coast, *Antarctica*	**5 C6** 68 30S 63 0 E
Matabeleland South □,		Max, *U.S.A.*	**80 B4** 47 49N 101 18W
Zimbabwe	**55 G2** 21 0S 29 0 E	Maxcanú, *Mexico*	**87 C6** 20 40N 92 0W
Matachewan, *Canada*	**72 C3** 47 56N 80 39W	Maxesibeni, *S. Africa*	**57 E4** 30 49S 29 23 E
Matadi, *Dem. Rep. of the Congo*	**52 F2** 5 52S 13 31 E	Maxhamish L., *Canada*	**70 B4** 59 50N 123 17W
Matagalpa, *Nic.*	**88 D2** 13 0N 85 58W	Maxixe, *Mozam.*	**57 C6** 23 54S 35 17 E
Matagami, *Canada*	**72 C4** 49 45N 77 34W	Maxville, *Canada*	**85 A10** 45 17N 74 51W
Matagami, L., *Canada*	**72 C4** 49 50N 77 40W	Maxwell, *U.S.A.*	**78 F4** 39 17N 122 11W
Matagorda B., *U.S.A.*	**81 L6** 28 40N 96 0W	Maxwelton, *Australia*	**62 C3** 20 43S 142 41 E
Matagorda I., *U.S.A.*	**81 L6** 28 15N 96 30W	May, C., *U.S.A.*	**82 F8** 38 56N 74 58W
Matak, *Indonesia*	**36 D3** 3 18N 106 16 E	May Pen, *Jamaica*	**88 a** 17 58N 77 15W
Mátala, *Greece*	**25 E6** 34 59N 24 45 E	Maya →, *Russia*	**29 D14** 60 28N 134 28 E
Matam, *Senegal*	**50 E3** 15 34N 13 17W	Maya Mts., *Belize*	**87 D7** 16 30N 89 0W
Matamoros, *Campeche, Mexico*	**87 D6** 18 50N 71 30W	Mayaguana, *Bahamas*	**89 B5** 22 30N 72 44W
Matamoros, *Coahuila, Mexico*	**86 B4** 25 33N 103 15W	Mayagüez, *Puerto Rico*	**89 d** 18 12N 67 9W
Matamoros, *Tamaulipas, Mexico*	**87 B5** 25 50N 97 30W	Mayãmey, *Iran*	**45 B7** 36 24N 55 42 E
Ma'ṭan as Sarra, *Libya*	**51 D10** 21 45N 22 0 E	Mayanup, *Australia*	**61 F2** 33 57S 116 27 E
Matandu →, *Tanzania*	**55 D3** 8 45S 34 19 E	Mayapan, *Mexico*	**87 C7** 20 38N 89 11W
Matane, *Canada*	**73 C6** 48 50N 67 33W	Mayapán, *Yucatán, Mexico*	**87 C7** 20 30N 89 25W
Matanomadh, *India*	**42 H3** 23 33N 68 57 E	Mayarí, *Cuba*	**89 B4** 20 40N 75 41W
Matanzas, *Cuba*	**88 B3** 23 0N 81 40W	Mayaro B., *Trin. & Tob.*	**93 K16** 10 14N 61 0W
Matapa, *Botswana*	**56 C3** 23 11S 24 39 E	Maybell, *U.S.A.*	**76 F9** 40 31N 108 5W
Matapan, C. = Taínaron, Ákra,		Maybole, *U.K.*	**11 F4** 55 21N 4 42W
Greece	**23 F10** 36 22N 22 27 E	Maydän, *Iraq*	**44 C5** 34 55N 45 37 E
Matapédia, *Canada*	**73 C6** 48 0N 66 59W	Maydena, *Australia*	**63 G4** 42 45S 146 30 E
Matapo △, *Zimbabwe*	**55 G2** 20 30S 29 40 E	Mayenne →, *France*	**20 C3** 47 30N 0 32W
Matara, *Sri Lanka*	**40 S12** 5 58N 80 30 E	Mayer, *U.S.A.*	**77 J7** 34 24N 112 14W
Mataram, *Indonesia*	**36 F5** 8 35S 116 7 E	Mayerthorpe, *Canada*	**70 C5** 53 57N 115 8W
Matarani, *Peru*	**92 G4** 17 0S 72 10W	Mayfield, *Ky., U.S.A.*	**83 G1** 36 44N 88 38W
Mataranka, *Australia*	**60 B5** 14 55S 133 4 E	Mayfield, *N.Y., U.S.A.*	**85 C10** 43 6N 74 16W
Matarma, Râs, *Egypt*	**46 E1** 30 27N 32 44 E	Mayhill, *U.S.A.*	**77 K11** 32 53N 105 29W
Mataró, *Spain*	**21 B7** 41 32N 2 29 E	Maykop, *Russia*	**19 F7** 44 35N 40 10 E
Matatiele, *S. Africa*	**57 E4** 30 20S 28 49 E	Maymyo, *Burma*	**38 A1** 22 2N 96 28 E
Mataura, *N.Z.*	**59 M2** 46 11S 168 51 E	Maynard, *Mass., U.S.A.*	**85 D13** 42 26N 71 27W
Matehuala, *Mexico*	**86 C4** 23 40N 100 40W	Maynard, *Wash., U.S.A.*	**78 C4** 47 59N 122 55W
Mateke Hills, *Zimbabwe*	**55 G3** 21 48S 31 0 E	Maynard Hills, *Australia*	**61 E2** 28 28S 119 49 E
Matelot, *Trin. & Tob.*	**93 K15** 10 50N 61 7W	Mayne →, *Australia*	**62 C3** 23 40S 141 55 E
Matera, *Italy*	**22 D7** 40 40N 16 36 E	Maynooth, *Ireland*	**10 C5** 53 23N 6 34W
Matetsi, *Zimbabwe*	**55 F2** 18 12S 26 0 E	Mayo, *Canada*	**68 B6** 63 38N 135 57W
Mathenikо △, *Uganda*	**54 B3** 2 49N 34 27 E	Mayo □, *Ireland*	**10 C2** 53 53N 9 3W
Mathis, *U.S.A.*	**81 L6** 28 6N 97 50W	Mayon Volcano, *Phil.*	**37 B6** 13 15N 123 41 E
		Mayor I., *N.Z.*	**59 G6** 37 16S 176 17 E

Mayotte ☑, Ind. Oc. .... 53 G9 12 50S 45 10 E
Maysān □, Iraq .... 44 D5 31 55N 47 15 E
Maysville, U.S.A. 82 F4 38 39N 83 46W
Mayu, Indonesia .... 37 D7 1 30N 126 30 E
Mayville, N. Dak., U.S.A. ... 80 B6 47 30N 97 20W
Mayville, N.Y., U.S.A. 84 D5 42 15N 79 30W
Mayya, Russia .... 29 C14 61 44N 130 18 E
Mazabuka, Zambia .... 55 F2 15 52S 27 44 E
Mazagán = El Jadida, Morocco . 50 B4 33 11N 8 17W
Mazagão, Brazil 93 D8 0 7S 51 16W
Mazán, Peru 92 D4 3 30S 73 0W
Māzăndarān □, Iran .... 45 B7 36 30N 52 0 E
Mazapil, Mexico 86 C4 24 38N 101 34W
Mazara del Vallo, Italy ...... 22 F5 37 39N 12 35 E
Mazarrón, Spain 21 D5 37 38N 1 19W
Mazaruni →, Guyana 92 B7 6 25N 58 35W
Mazatán, Mexico 86 B2 29 0N 110 8W
Mazatenango, Guatemala 88 D1 14 35N 91 30W
Mazatlán, Mexico 86 C3 23 13N 106 25W
Mažeikiai, Lithuania .... 9 H20 56 20N 22 20 E
Māzhān, Iran .... 45 C8 32 30N 59 0 E
Mazinān, Iran .... 45 B8 36 19N 56 56 E
Mazoe, Mozam. .... 55 F3 16 42S 33 7 E
Mazoe →, Mozam. .... 55 F3 16 20S 33 30 E
Mazowe, Zimbabwe .... 55 F3 17 28S 30 58 E
Mazurian Lakes = Mazurski,
   Pojezierze, Poland ...... 17 B11 53 50N 21 0 E
Mazurski, Pojezierze, Poland .. 17 B11 53 50N 21 0 E
Mazyr, Belarus .... 17 B15 51 59N 29 15 E
Mbabane, Swaziland .... 57 D5 26 18S 31 6 E
Mbaïki, C.A.R. .... 52 D3 3 53N 18 1 E
Mbala, Zambia .... 55 D3 8 46S 31 24 E
Mbalabala, Zimbabwe ...... 57 C4 20 27S 29 3 E
Mbale, Uganda .... 54 B3 1 8N 34 12 E
Mbalmayo, Cameroon ...... 52 D2 3 33N 11 33 E
Mbamba Bay, Tanzania ...... 55 E3 11 13S 34 49 E
Mbandaka, Dem. Rep. of
   the Congo .... 52 D3 0 1N 18 18 E
Mbanza Congo, Angola ...... 52 F2 6 18S 14 16 E
Mbanza Ngungu, Dem. Rep. of
   the Congo .... 52 F2 5 12S 14 53 E
Mbarangandu, Tanzania ...... 55 D4 10 11S 36 48 E
Mbarara, Uganda .... 54 C3 0 35S 30 40 E
Mbashe →, S. Africa .... 57 E4 32 15S 28 54 E
Mbenkuru →, Tanzania ...... 55 D4 9 25S 39 50 E
Mberengwa, Zimbabwe ...... 55 G2 20 29S 29 57 E
Mberengwa, Mt., Zimbabwe ... 55 G2 20 37S 29 55 E
Mbesuma, Zambia .... 55 E3 10 0S 32 2 E
Mbeya, Tanzania .... 55 D3 8 54S 33 29 E
Mbeya □, Tanzania .... 54 D3 8 15S 33 30 E
Mbinga, Tanzania .... 55 E4 10 50S 35 0 E
Mbini = Río Muni □, Eq. Guin. .. 52 D2 1 30N 10 0 E
Mbour, Senegal 50 F2 14 22N 16 54W
Mbuji-Mayi, Dem. Rep. of
   the Congo .... 54 D1 6 9S 23 40 E
Mbulu, Tanzania .... 54 C4 3 45S 35 30 E
Mburucuyá, Argentina 94 B4 28 1S 58 14W
McCarran International, Las
   Vegas ✕ (LAS), U.S.A. 79 J11 36 5N 115 9W
Mchinja, Tanzania .... 55 D4 9 44S 39 45 E
Mchinji, Malawi .... 55 E3 13 47S 32 58 E
McMurdo, Antarctica ...... 5 D11 77 0S 140 0 E
Mdantsane, S. Africa ...... 53 L5 32 56S 27 46 E
Mead, L., U.S.A. 79 J12 36 1N 114 44W
Meade, U.S.A. 81 G4 37 17N 100 20W
Meadow Lake, Canada 71 C7 54 10N 108 26W
Meadow Lake △, Canada 71 C7 54 27N 109 0W
Meadow Valley Wash →, U.S.A. 79 J12 36 40N 114 34W
Meadville, U.S.A. 84 E4 41 39N 80 9W
Meaford, Canada 84 B4 44 36N 80 35W
Mealy Mts., Canada 73 B8 53 10N 58 0W
Meander River, Canada 70 B5 59 2N 117 42W
Meares, C., U.S.A. 76 D2 45 37N 124 0W
Mearim →, Brazil 93 D10 3 4S 44 35W
Meath □, Ireland 10 C5 53 40N 6 57W
Meath Park, Canada 71 C7 53 27N 105 22W
Meaux, France .... 20 B5 48 58N 2 50 E
Mebechi-Gawa →, Japan ...... 30 D10 40 31N 141 31 E
Mebulu, Tanjung, Indonesia ... 37 K18 8 50S 115 5 E
Mecanhelas, Mozam. ...... 55 F4 15 12S 35 54 E
Mecca = Makkah, Si. Arabia ... 47 C2 21 30N 39 54 E
Mecca, U.S.A. 79 M10 33 34N 116 5W
Mechanicsburg, U.S.A. 84 F8 40 13N 77 1W
Mechanicville, U.S.A. 85 D11 42 54N 73 41W
Mechelen, Belgium .... 15 C4 51 2N 4 29 E
Mecheria, Algeria 50 B5 33 35N 0 18W
Mecklenburg, Germany ...... 16 B6 53 33N 11 40 E
Mecklenburger Bucht, Germany 16 A6 54 20N 11 40 E
Meconta, Mozam. .... 55 E4 14 59S 39 50 E
Medan, Indonesia .... 36 D1 3 40N 98 38 E
Médanos de Coro △, Venezuela 89 D6 11 35N 69 44W
Medanosa, Pta., Argentina ... 96 F3 48 8S 66 0W
Médéa, Algeria .... 50 A6 36 12N 2 50 E
Medellín, Colombia 92 B3 6 15N 75 35W
Medelpad, Sweden .... 9 E17 62 33N 16 30 E
Medemblik, Neths. .... 15 B5 52 46N 5 8 E
Medford, Mass., U.S.A. 85 D13 42 25N 71 7W
Medford, Oreg., U.S.A. 76 E2 42 19N 122 52W
Medford, Wis., U.S.A. 80 C9 45 9N 90 20W
Medgidia, Romania .... 17 F15 44 15N 28 19 E
Media Agua, Argentina 94 C2 31 58S 68 25W
Media Luna, Argentina 94 C2 34 45S 66 44W
Medianeira, Brazil 95 B5 25 17S 54 5W
Mediaş, Romania .... 17 E13 46 9N 24 22 E
Medicine Bow, U.S.A. 76 F10 41 54N 106 12W
Medicine Bow Pk., U.S.A. ... 76 F10 41 21N 106 19W
Medicine Bow Ra., U.S.A. ... 76 F10 41 10N 106 25W
Medicine Hat, Canada 71 D6 50 0N 110 45W
Medicine Lake, U.S.A. 80 A2 48 30N 104 30W
Medicine Lodge, U.S.A. 81 G5 37 17N 98 35W
Medina = Al Madinah, Si. Arabia 44 E3 24 35N 39 52 E
Medina, N. Dak., U.S.A. 80 B5 46 54N 99 18W
Medina, N.Y., U.S.A. 84 C6 43 13N 78 23W
Medina, Ohio, U.S.A. 84 E3 41 8N 81 52W
Medina →, U.S.A. 81 L5 29 16N 98 29W
Medina del Campo, Spain ... 21 B3 41 18N 4 55W
Medina L., U.S.A. 81 L5 29 32N 98 56W
Medina Sidonia, Spain 21 D3 36 28N 5 57W
Medinipur, India .... 43 H12 22 25N 87 21 E
Mediterranean Sea, Europe ... 49 C5 35 0N 15 0 E
Médoc, France 20 D3 45 10N 0 50W
Medveditsa →, Russia ...... 19 E7 49 35N 42 41 E
Medvezhi, Ostrava, Russia ... 29 B17 71 0N 161 0 E
Medvezhyegorsk, Russia ...... 18 B5 63 0N 34 25 E
Medway □, U.K. .... 13 F8 51 25N 0 32 E
Medway →, U.K. .... 13 F8 51 27N 0 46 E
Meekatharra, Australia ...... 61 E2 26 32S 118 29 E
Meeker, U.S.A. 76 F10 40 2N 107 55W

Meelpaeg Res., Canada 73 C8 48 15N 56 33W
Meerut, India .... 42 E7 29 1N 77 42 E
Meeteetse, U.S.A. 76 D9 44 9N 108 52W
Mega, Ethiopia .... 47 G2 3 57N 38 19 E
Mégara, Greece .... 23 F10 37 58N 23 22 E
Megasini, India .... 43 J12 21 38N 86 21 E
Meghalaya □, India .... 41 G17 25 50N 91 0 E
Meghna →, Bangla. .... 41 H17 22 50N 90 50 E
Mégiscane, L., Canada 72 C4 48 35N 75 55W
Meharry, Mt., Australia ...... 60 D2 22 59S 118 35 E
Mehlville, U.S.A. 80 F9 38 30N 90 19W
Mehndawal, India .... 43 F10 26 58N 83 5 E
Mehr Jān, Iran .... 45 C7 33 50N 55 6 E
Mehrābād, Iran .... 44 B5 36 53N 47 55 E
Mehrān, Iran .... 44 C5 33 7N 46 10 E
Mehrīz, Iran .... 45 D7 31 35N 54 28 E
Mei Xian, China .... 34 G4 34 18N 107 55 E
Meiktila, Burma .... 41 J19 20 53N 95 54 E
Meissen, Germany .... 16 C7 51 9N 13 29 E
Meizhou, China .... 33 D6 24 16N 116 6 E
Meja, India .... 43 G10 25 9N 82 7 E
Mejillones, Chile 94 A1 23 10S 70 30W
Mekele, Ethiopia .... 47 E2 13 33N 39 30 E
Mekhtar, Pakistan .... 40 D6 30 30N 69 15 E
Meknès, Morocco 50 B4 33 57N 5 33W
Mekong →, Asia .... 39 H6 9 30N 106 15 E
Mekongga, Indonesia ...... 37 E6 3 39S 121 15 E
Mekvari = Kür →, Azerbaijan .. 19 G8 39 29N 49 15 E
Melagiri Hills, India .... 40 N10 12 20N 77 30 E
Melaka, Malaysia .... 39 L4 2 15N 102 15 E
Melalap, Malaysia .... 36 C5 5 10N 116 5 E
Mélambes, Greece .... 25 D6 35 8N 24 40 E
Melanesia, Pac. Oc. .... 64 H7 4 0S 155 0 E
Melaya, Indonesia .... 37 J17 8 17S 114 30 E
Melbourne, Australia ...... 63 F4 37 50S 145 0 E
Melbourne, U.S.A. 83 L5 28 5N 80 37W
Melchor Múzquiz, Mexico ... 86 B4 27 50N 101 30W
Melchor Ocampo, Mexico ... 86 C4 24 52N 101 40W
Mélèzes →, Canada 72 A5 57 40N 69 29W
Melfort, Canada 71 C8 52 50N 104 37W
Melfort, Zimbabwe .... 55 F3 18 0S 31 25 E
Melhus, Norway .... 8 E14 63 17N 10 18 E
Melilla, N. Afr. 21 E4 35 21N 2 57W
Melipilla, Chile 94 C1 33 42S 71 15W
Melita, Canada 71 D8 49 15N 101 0W
Melitopol, Ukraine .... 19 E6 46 50N 35 22 E
Melk, Austria .... 16 D8 48 13N 15 20 E
Mellansel, Sweden .... 8 E18 63 25N 18 17 E
Mellen, U.S.A. 80 B9 46 20N 90 40W
Mellerud, Sweden .... 9 G15 58 41N 12 28 E
Mellette, U.S.A. 80 C5 45 9N 98 30W
Mellieha, Malta .... 25 D1 35 57N 14 22 E
Melo, Uruguay 95 C5 32 20S 54 10W
Melolo, Indonesia .... 37 F6 9 53S 120 40 E
Melouprey, Cambodia ...... 38 F5 13 48N 105 16 E
Melrose, Australia .... 63 E4 32 42S 146 57 E
Melrose, U.K. 11 F6 55 36N 2 43W
Melrose, Minn., U.S.A. 80 C7 45 40N 94 49W
Melrose, N. Mex., U.S.A. ... 81 H3 34 26N 103 38W
Melstone, U.S.A. 76 C10 46 36N 107 52W
Melton Mowbray, U.K. 12 E7 52 47N 0 54W
Melun, France .... 20 B5 48 32N 2 39 E
Melville, Canada 71 C8 50 55N 102 50W
Melville, C., Australia ...... 62 A3 14 11S 144 30 E
Melville, L., Canada 73 B8 53 30N 60 0W
Melville I., Australia .... 62 A2 12 0S 136 45 E
Melville I., Australia .... 60 B5 11 30S 131 0 E
Melville I., Canada 4 B2 75 30N 112 0W
Melville Pen., Canada 69 B11 68 0N 84 0W
Memba, Mozam. .... 55 E5 14 11S 40 30 E
Memboro, Indonesia .... 37 F5 9 30S 119 30 E
Memel = Klaipėda, Lithuania .. 9 J19 55 43N 21 10 E
Memel, S. Africa .... 57 D4 27 38S 29 36 E
Memmingen, Germany ...... 16 E6 47 58N 10 10 E
Mempawah, Indonesia ...... 36 D3 0 30N 109 5 E
Memphis, Mich., U.S.A. 84 D2 42 54N 82 46W
Memphis, Tenn., U.S.A. 81 H10 35 8N 90 3W
Memphis, Tex., U.S.A. 81 H4 34 44N 100 33W
Memphremagog, L., U.S.A. ... 85 B12 45 0N 72 12W
Mena, U.S.A. 81 H7 34 35N 94 15W
Menai Strait, U.K. 12 D3 53 11N 4 13W
Ménaka, Mali .... 50 E6 15 59N 2 18 E
Menan = Chao Phraya →,
   Thailand .... 38 F3 13 32N 100 36 E
Menarandra →, Madag. ...... 57 D7 25 17S 44 30 E
Menard, U.S.A. 81 K5 30 55N 99 47W
Mendawai →, Indonesia ...... 36 E4 3 30S 113 0 E
Mende, France .... 20 D5 44 31N 3 30 E
Mendeleyev Ridge, Arctic ... 4 B17 80 0N 178 0W
Mendez, Mexico 87 B5 25 7N 98 34W
Mendhar, India .... 43 C6 33 35N 74 10 E
Mendip Hills, U.K. 13 F5 51 17N 2 40W
Mendocino, U.S.A. 76 G2 39 19N 123 48W
Mendocino, C., U.S.A. 76 F1 40 26N 124 25W
Mendota, Calif., U.S.A. 78 J6 36 45N 120 23W
Mendota, Ill., U.S.A. 80 E10 41 33N 89 7W
Mendoyo, Indonesia .... 37 J17 8 23S 114 42 E
Mendoza, Argentina 94 C2 32 50S 68 52W
Mendoza □, Argentina 94 C2 33 0S 69 0W
Mene Grande, Venezuela ... 92 B4 9 49N 70 56W
Menemen, Turkey .... 23 E12 38 34N 27 3 E
Menen, Belgium .... 15 D3 50 47N 3 7 E
Menggala, Indonesia ...... 36 E3 4 30S 105 15 E
Mengjin, China .... 34 G7 34 55N 112 45 E
Mengyin, China .... 35 G9 35 40N 117 58 E
Mengzi, China .... 32 D5 23 20N 103 22 E
Menihek, Canada 73 B6 54 28N 56 36W
Menihek L., Canada 73 B6 54 0N 56 56W
Menin = Menen, Belgium ... 15 D3 50 47N 3 7 E
Menindee, Australia .... 63 E3 32 20S 142 25 E
Menindee L., Australia ...... 63 E3 32 20S 142 25 E
Meningie, Australia .... 63 F2 35 50S 139 18 E
Menjangan, Pulau, Indonesia .. 37 J17 8 7S 114 31 E
Menlo Park, U.S.A. 78 H4 37 27N 122 12W
Menominee, U.S.A. 82 C2 45 6N 87 37W
Menominee →, U.S.A. 82 C2 45 6N 87 36W
Menomonie, U.S.A. 80 C9 44 53N 91 55W
Menongue, Angola .... 53 G3 14 48S 17 52 E
Menorca, Spain .... 24 B11 40 0N 4 0 E
Mentakab, Malaysia .... 39 L4 3 29N 102 21 E
Mentawai, Kepulauan, Indonesia 36 E1 2 0S 99 0 E
Menton, France .... 20 E7 43 50N 7 29 E
Mentor, U.S.A. 84 E3 41 40N 81 21W
Menzelinsk, Russia .... 18 C9 55 47N 53 11 E
Menzies, Australia .... 61 E3 29 40S 121 2 E
Meob B., Namibia .... 56 C1 24 25S 14 34 E
Me'ona, Israel .... 46 B4 33 1N 35 15 E

Meoqui, Mexico 86 B3 28 17N 105 29W
Mepaco, Mozam. .... 55 F3 15 57S 30 48 E
Meppel, Neths. .... 15 B6 52 42N 6 12 E
Merabéllou, Kólpos, Greece ... 25 D7 35 10N 25 50 E
Merak, Indonesia .... 37 F12 6 10N 106 26 E
Meramangye, L., Australia ... 61 E5 28 25S 132 13 E
Meran = Merano, Italy ...... 22 A4 46 40N 11 9 E
Merano, Italy .... 22 A4 46 40N 11 9 E
Merauke, Indonesia .... 37 F10 8 29S 140 24 E
Merbein, Australia .... 63 E3 34 10S 142 2 E
Merbuk, Gunung, Indonesia ... 37 J17 8 13S 114 39 E
Merca, Somali Rep. .... 47 G3 1 48N 44 50 E
Merced, U.S.A. 78 H6 37 18N 120 29W
Merced →, U.S.A. 78 H6 37 21N 120 59W
Merced Pk., U.S.A. 78 H7 37 36N 119 24W
Mercedes, Buenos Aires,
   Argentina 94 C4 34 40S 59 30W
Mercedes, Corrientes, Argentina . 94 B4 29 10S 58 5W
Mercedes, San Luis, Argentina . 94 C2 33 40S 65 21W
Mercedes, Uruguay 94 C4 33 12S 58 0W
Merceditas, Chile 94 B1 28 20S 70 35W
Mercer, N.Z. .... 59 G5 37 16S 175 5 E
Mercer, U.S.A. 84 E4 41 14N 80 15W
Mercer Island, U.S.A. 78 C4 47 35N 122 15W
Mercury, U.S.A. 79 J11 36 40N 115 58W
Mercy, C., Canada 69 B13 65 0N 63 30W
Mere, U.K. 13 F5 51 6N 2 16W
Meredith, C., Falk. Is. 96 G4 52 15S 60 40W
Meredith, L., U.S.A. 81 H4 35 43N 101 33W
Mergui, Burma .... 38 F2 12 26N 98 34 E
Mergui Arch. = Myeik Kyunzu,
   Burma .... 39 G1 11 30N 97 30 E
Mérida, Mexico 87 C7 20 58N 89 37W
Mérida, Spain 21 C2 38 55N 6 25W
Mérida, Venezuela 92 B4 8 24N 71 8W
Mérida, Cord. de, Venezuela .. 92 B4 9 0N 71 0W
Meriden, U.K. 13 E6 52 26N 1 38W
Meriden, U.S.A. 85 E12 41 32N 72 48W
Meridian, Calif., U.S.A. 78 F5 39 9N 121 55W
Meridian, Idaho, U.S.A. 76 E5 43 37N 116 24W
Meridian, Miss., U.S.A. 83 J1 32 22N 88 42W
Merinda, Australia .... 62 C4 20 2S 148 11 E
Merir, Pac. Oc. .... 37 D8 4 10N 132 30 E
Merirumã, Brazil 93 C8 1 15N 54 50W
Merkel, U.S.A. 81 J5 32 28N 100 1W
Merksem, Belgium .... 15 C4 51 16N 4 25 E
Mermaid Reef, Australia ... 60 C2 17 6S 119 36 E
Merredin, Australia .... 61 F2 31 28S 118 18 E
Merrick, U.K. 11 F4 55 8N 4 28W
Merrickville, Canada 85 B9 44 55N 75 50W
Merrill, Oreg., U.S.A. 76 E3 42 1N 121 36W
Merrill, Wis., U.S.A. 80 C10 45 11N 89 41W
Merriman, U.S.A. 80 D4 42 55N 101 42W
Merritt, Canada 70 C4 50 10N 120 45W
Merritt Island, U.S.A. 83 L5 28 21N 80 42W
Merriwa, Australia .... 63 E5 32 6S 150 22 E
Merry I., Canada 72 A4 55 29N 77 31W
Merryville, U.S.A. 81 K8 30 45N 93 33W
Mersch, Lux. .... 15 E6 49 44N 6 7 E
Mersea I., U.K. .... 13 F8 51 47N 0 58 E
Merseburg, Germany ...... 16 C6 51 22N 11 59 E
Mersey →, U.K. 12 D4 53 25N 3 1W
Merseyside □, U.K. 12 D4 53 31N 3 2W
Mersin, Turkey .... 19 G5 36 51N 34 36 E
Mersing, Malaysia .... 39 L4 2 25N 103 50 E
Merta, India .... 42 F6 26 39N 74 4 E
Merta Road, India .... 42 F5 26 43N 73 55 E
Merthyr Tydfil, U.K. 13 F4 51 45N 3 22W
Merthyr Tydfil □, U.K. 13 F4 51 46N 3 21W
Mértola, Portugal 21 D2 37 40N 7 40W
Mertzon, U.S.A. 81 K4 31 16N 100 49W
Meru, Kenya .... 54 B4 0 3N 37 40 E
Meru, Tanzania .... 54 C4 3 15S 36 46 E
Meru △, Kenya .... 54 B4 0 5N 38 10 E
Mesa, U.S.A. 77 K8 33 25N 111 50W
Mesa Verde △, U.S.A. 77 H9 37 11N 108 29W
Mesanagrós, Greece .... 25 C9 36 1N 27 49 E
Mesaoría, Cyprus .... 25 D12 35 12N 33 14 E
Mesarás, Kólpos, Greece ... 25 D6 35 6N 24 47 E
Mesgouez, L., Canada 72 B5 51 20N 75 0W
Meshed = Mashhad, Iran ... 45 B8 36 20N 59 35 E
Meshoppen, U.S.A. 85 E8 41 36N 76 3W
Mesilinka →, Canada 70 B4 56 6N 124 30W
Mesilla, U.S.A. 77 K10 32 16N 106 48W
Mesolóngion, Greece ...... 23 E9 38 21N 21 28 E
Mesopotamia = Al Jazirah, Iraq . 44 C5 33 30N 44 0 E
Mesopotamia, U.S.A. 84 E4 41 27N 80 57W
Mesquite, U.S.A. 77 H6 36 47N 114 6W
Messaad, Algeria .... 50 B6 34 8N 3 30 E
Messalo →, Mozam. ...... 55 E4 12 25S 39 15 E
Messina, Italy .... 22 E6 38 11N 15 34 E
Messina = Musina, S. Africa .. 57 C5 22 20S 30 5 E
Messina, Str. di, Italy ...... 22 F6 38 15N 15 35 E
Messini, Greece .... 23 F10 37 4N 22 1 E
Messiniakós Kólpos, Greece ... 23 F10 36 45N 22 5 E
Messonghi, Greece .... 25 B3 39 29N 19 56 E
Mesta →, Bulgaria .... 23 D11 40 54N 24 49 E
Meta →, S. Amer. 92 B5 6 12N 67 28W
Meta Incognita Pen., Canada .. 69 B13 62 45N 68 30W
Metabetchouan, Canada ... 73 C5 48 26N 71 52W
Metairie, U.S.A. 81 L9 29 58N 90 10W
Metaline Falls, U.S.A. 76 B5 48 52N 117 22W
Metán, Argentina 94 B3 25 30S 65 0W
Metangula, Mozam. ...... 55 E3 12 40S 34 50 E
Metengobalame, Mozam. ... 55 E3 14 49S 34 30 E
Methven, N.Z. .... 59 K3 43 38S 171 40 E
Metil, Mozam. .... 55 F4 16 24S 39 0 E
Metlakatla, U.S.A. 68 C6 55 8N 131 35W
Metropolis, U.S.A. 81 G10 37 9N 88 44W
Metu, Ethiopia .... 47 F2 8 18N 35 35 E
Metz, France .... 20 B7 49 8N . 6 10 E
Meulaboh, Indonesia .... 36 D1 4 11N 96 3 E
Meureudu, Indonesia .... 36 C1 5 19N 96 10 E
Meuse →, Europe .... 15 D5 50 45N 5 41 E
Mexia, U.S.A. 81 K6 31 41N 96 29W
Mexiana, I., Brazil 93 D9 0 0 49 30W
Mexicali, Mexico 79 N11 32 40N 115 30W
Mexican Plateau, Mexico ... 66 G9 25 0N 104 0W
Mexican Water, U.S.A. 77 H9 36 57N 109 32W
México, Mexico 87 D5 19 20N 99 10W
Mexico, Maine, U.S.A. 85 B14 44 34N 70 33W
Mexico, Mo., U.S.A. 80 F9 39 10N 91 53W
México □, Mexico 87 D5 19 20N 99 10W
Mexico ■, Cent. Amer. 86 C4 25 0N 105 0W
Mexico, G. of, Cent. Amer. ... 87 C7 25 0N 90 0W
Mexico B., U.S.A. 85 C8 43 35N 76 20W

Meydān-e Naftūn, Iran ...... 45 D6 31 56N 49 18 E
Meydani, Ra's-e, Iran ...... 45 E8 25 24N 59 6 E
Meymaneh, Afghan. .... 40 B4 35 53N 64 38 E
Mezen, Russia .... 18 A7 65 50N 44 20 E
Mezen →, Russia .... 18 A7 65 44N 44 22 E
Mézenc, Mt., France ...... 20 D6 44 54N 4 11 E
Mezhdurechenskiy, Russia ... 28 D7 59 36N 65 56 E
Mezőkövesd, Hungary ...... 17 E11 47 49N 20 35 E
Mezőtúr, Hungary .... 17 E11 47 1N 20 41 E
Mezquital, Mexico 86 C4 23 29N 104 23W
Mfolozi →, S. Africa ...... 57 D5 28 25S 32 26 E
Mgeta, Tanzania .... 55 D4 8 22S 36 6 E
Mhlaba Hills, Zimbabwe ... 55 F3 18 30S 30 30 E
Mhow, India .... 42 H6 22 33N 75 50 E
Miahuatlán, Mexico 87 D5 16 21N 96 36W
Miami, Fla., U.S.A. 83 N5 25 47N 80 11W
Miami, Okla., U.S.A. 81 G7 36 53N 94 53W
Miami, Tex., U.S.A. 81 H4 35 42N 100 38W
Miami Beach, U.S.A. 83 N5 25 47N 80 8W
Mian Xian, China .... 34 H4 33 10N 106 32 E
Mianchi, China .... 34 G6 34 48N 111 48 E
Miändarreh, Iran .... 45 C7 35 37N 53 39 E
Miändowāb, Iran .... 44 B5 37 0N 46 5 E
Miandrivazo, Madag. ...... 57 B8 19 31S 45 29 E
Miāneh, Iran .... 44 B5 37 30N 47 40 E
Mianwali, Pakistan .... 42 C4 32 38N 71 28 E
Miarinarivo, Antananarivo,
   Madag. .... 57 B8 18 57S 46 55 E
Miarinarivo, Toamasina, Madag. 57 B8 16 38S 48 15 E
Miariravaratra, Madag. ...... 57 C8 20 13S 47 31 E
Miass, Russia .... 18 D11 54 59N 60 6 E
Mica, S. Africa .... 57 C5 24 10S 30 48 E
Michalovce, Slovak Rep. ... 17 D11 48 47N 21 58 E
Michigan □, U.S.A. .... 82 C3 44 0N 85 0 E
Michigan, L., U.S.A. .... 82 D2 44 0N 87 0 E
Michigan City, U.S.A. 82 E2 41 43N 86 54W
Michipicoten I., Canada ... 72 C2 47 40N 85 40W
Michoacan □, Mexico 86 D4 19 0N 102 0W
Michurin, Bulgaria .... 23 C12 42 9N 27 51 E
Michurinsk, Russia .... 18 D7 52 58N 40 27 E
Mico, Pta., Nic. 88 D3 12 0N 83 30W
Micoud, St. Lucia .... 89 f 13 49N 60 54W
Micronesia, Pac. Oc. ...... 64 G7 11 0N 160 0 E
Micronesia, Federated States
   of ■, Pac. Oc. .... 64 G7 9 0N 150 0 E
Midai, Indonesia .... 36 D3 3 0N 107 47 E
Midale, Canada 71 D8 49 25N 103 20W
Middelburg, Neths. .... 15 C3 51 30N 3 36 E
Middelburg, Eastern Cape,
   S. Africa .... 56 E4 31 30S 25 0 E
Middelburg, Mpumalanga,
   S. Africa .... 57 D4 25 49S 29 28 E
Middelpos, S. Africa ...... 56 E3 31 55S 20 13 E
Middelwit, S. Africa .... 56 C4 24 51S 27 3 E
Middle Alkali L., U.S.A. 76 F3 41 27N 120 5W
Middle Bass I., U.S.A. 84 E2 41 41N 82 49W
Middle East, Asia .... 26 F7 38 0N 40 0 E
Middle Fork Feather →, U.S.A. 78 F5 38 33N 121 30W
Middle I., Australia .... 61 F3 34 6S 123 11 E
Middle Loup →, U.S.A. 80 E5 41 17N 98 24W
Middle Sackville, Canada ... 73 D7 44 47N 63 42W
Middleboro, U.S.A. 85 E14 41 54N 70 55W
Middleburg, Fla., U.S.A. ... 83 K5 30 4N 81 52W
Middleburg, N.Y., U.S.A. ... 85 D10 42 36N 74 20W
Middleburg, Pa., U.S.A. ... 84 F7 40 47N 77 3W
Middlebury, U.S.A. 85 B11 44 1N 73 10W
Middlemount, Australia ... 62 C4 22 50S 148 40 E
Middleport, N.Y., U.S.A. ... 84 C6 43 13N 78 29W
Middleport, Ohio, U.S.A. ... 82 F4 39 0N 82 3W
Middlesboro, U.S.A. 83 G4 36 36N 83 43W
Middlesbrough, U.K. 12 C6 54 35N 1 13W
Middlesbrough □, U.K. 12 C6 54 28N 1 13W
Middlesex, Belize 88 C2 17 2N 88 31W
Middlesex, N.J., U.S.A. 85 F10 40 36N 74 30W
Middlesex, N.Y., U.S.A. 84 D7 42 42N 77 16W
Middleton, Australia ...... 62 C3 22 22S 141 32 E
Middleton, Canada 73 D6 44 57N 65 4W
Middleton Cr. →, Australia ... 62 C3 22 35S 141 51 E
Middletown, U.K. 10 B5 54 17N 6 51W
Middletown, Calif., U.S.A. ... 78 G4 38 45N 122 37W
Middletown, Conn., U.S.A. ... 85 E12 41 34N 72 39W
Middletown, N.Y., U.S.A. ... 85 E10 41 27N 74 25W
Middletown, Ohio, U.S.A. ... 82 F3 39 31N 84 24W
Middletown, Pa., U.S.A. ... 84 F8 40 12N 76 44W
Midge Point, Australia ...... 62 J6 20 39S 148 43 E
Midhurst, U.K. 13 G7 50 59N 0 44W
Midi, Canal du →, France ... 20 E4 43 45N 1 21 E
Midland, Canada 84 B5 44 45N 79 50W
Midland, Calif., U.S.A. 79 M12 33 52N 114 48W
Midland, Mich., U.S.A. 82 D3 43 37N 84 14W
Midland, Pa., U.S.A. 84 F4 40 39N 80 27W
Midland, Tex., U.S.A. 81 K3 32 0N 102 3W
Midlands □, Zimbabwe ...... 55 F2 19 40S 29 0 E
Midleton, Ireland 10 E3 51 55N 8 10W
Midlothian, U.S.A. 81 J6 32 30N 97 0W
Midlothian □, U.K. 11 F5 55 51N 3 5W
Midongy, Tangorombohitr' i,
   Madag. .... 57 C8 23 30S 47 0 E
Midongy Atsimo, Madag. ... 57 C8 23 35S 47 1 E
Midway Is., Pac. Oc. 64 E10 28 13N 177 22W
Midway Wells, U.S.A. 79 N11 32 41N 115 7W
Midwest, U.S.A. 75 B9 39 0N 90 0W
Midwest, Wyo., U.S.A. 76 E10 43 25N 106 16W
Midwest City, U.S.A. 81 H6 35 27N 97 24W
Midyat, Turkey .... 44 B4 37 25N 41 23 E
Midzŏr, Bulgaria .... 23 C10 43 24N 22 40 E
Mie □, Japan .... 31 G8 34 30N 136 10 E
Międzychód, Poland ...... 16 B8 52 35N 15 53 E
Międzyrzec Podlaski, Poland .. 17 C12 51 58N 22 45 E
Mielec, Poland .... 17 C11 50 15N 21 25 E
Mienga, Angola .... 56 B2 17 12S 19 48 E
Miercurea-Ciuc, Romania ... 17 E13 46 21N 25 48 E
Mieres, Spain 21 A3 43 18N 5 48W
Mifflintown, U.S.A. 84 F7 40 34N 77 24W
Mifraz Hefa, Israel .... 46 C4 32 52N 35 0 E
Miguel Alemán, Presa, Mexico . 87 D5 18 15N 96 40W
Mihara, Japan .... 31 G6 34 24N 133 5 E
Mikese, Tanzania .... 54 D4 6 48S 37 55 E
Mikhaylovka = Montana,
   Bulgaria .... 23 C10 43 27N 23 16 E
Mikhaylovka, Russia .... 19 D7 50 3N 43 5 E
Mikkeli, Finland .... 9 F22 61 43N 27 15 E
Mikkwa →, Canada 70 B6 58 25N 114 46W
Mikonos, Greece .... 23 F11 37 30N 25 25 E
Mikumi, Tanzania .... 54 D4 7 26S 37 0 E
Mikumi △, Tanzania .... 54 D4 7 35S 37 15 E
Mikun, Russia .... 18 B9 62 20N 50 0 E

Milaca, U.S.A. 80 C8 45 45N 93 39W
Milagro, Ecuador 92 D3 2 11S 79 36W
Milan = Milano, Italy .... 20 D8 45 28N 9 12 E
Milan, Mo., U.S.A. 80 E8 40 12N 93 7W
Milan, Tenn., U.S.A. 83 H1 35 55N 88 46W
Milange, Mozam. .... 55 F4 16 3S 35 45 E
Milano, Italy .... 20 D8 45 28N 9 12 E
Milanoa, Madag. .... 57 A8 13 35S 49 47 E
Milâs, Turkey .... 23 F12 37 20N 27 50 E
Milazzo, Italy .... 22 E6 38 13N 15 15 E
Milbank, U.S.A. 80 C6 45 13N 96 38W
Milbanke Sd., Canada 70 C3 52 15N 128 35W
Milden, Canada 71 C7 51 29N 107 32W
Mildenhall, U.K. .... 13 E8 52 21N 0 32 E
Mildmay, Canada 84 B3 44 3N 81 7W
Mildura, Australia .... 63 E3 34 13S 142 9 E
Miles, Australia .... 63 D5 26 40S 150 9 E
Miles City, U.S.A. 80 B2 46 25N 105 51W
Milestone, Canada 71 D8 49 59N 104 31W
Miletus, Turkey .... 23 F12 37 30N 27 18 E
Milford, Calif., U.S.A. 78 E6 40 10N 120 22W
Milford, Conn., U.S.A. 85 E11 41 14N 73 3W
Milford, Del., U.S.A. 82 F8 38 55N 75 26W
Milford, Mass., U.S.A. 85 D13 42 8N 71 31W
Milford, N.H., U.S.A. 85 D13 42 50N 71 39W
Milford, Pa., U.S.A. 85 E10 41 19N 74 48W
Milford, Utah, U.S.A. 77 G7 38 24N 113 1W
Milford Haven, U.K. 13 F2 51 42N 5 7W
Milford Sd., N.Z. .... 59 L1 44 41S 167 47 E
Milford Sound, N.Z. .... 59 L1 44 41S 167 55 E
Milh, Bahr al = Razāzah, Buhayrat
ar, Iraq .... 44 C4 32 40N 43 35 E
Milikapiti, Australia .... 60 B5 11 26S 130 40 E
Miling, Australia .... 61 F2 30 30S 116 17 E
Milk →, U.S.A. 76 B10 48 4N 106 19W
Milk River, Canada 70 D6 49 10N 112 5W
Mill I., Antarctica .... 5 C8 66 0S 101 30 E
Mill Valley, U.S.A. 78 H4 37 54N 122 32W
Millau, France .... 20 D5 44 8N 3 4 E
Millbridge, Canada 84 B7 44 41N 77 36W
Millbrook, Canada 84 B6 44 10N 78 29W
Millbrook, U.S.A. 85 E11 41 47N 73 42W
Mille Lacs, L. des, Canada 72 C1 48 45N 90 35W
Mille Lacs L., U.S.A. 80 B8 46 15N 93 39W
Milledgeville, U.S.A. 83 J4 33 5N 83 14W
Millen, U.S.A. 83 J5 32 48N 81 57W
Millennium I. = Caroline I.,
Kiribati 65 H12 9 58S 150 13W
Miller, U.S.A. 80 C5 44 31N 98 59W
Millersburg, Ohio, U.S.A. 84 F3 40 33N 81 55W
Millersburg, Pa., U.S.A. 84 F8 40 32N 76 58W
Millerton, U.S.A. 85 E11 41 57N 73 31W
Millerton L., U.S.A. 78 J7 37 1N 119 41W
Millet, St. Lucia .... 89 f 13 55N 60 59W
Millheim, U.S.A. 84 F7 40 54N 77 29W
Millicent, Australia .... 63 F3 37 34S 140 21 E
Millington, U.S.A. 81 H10 35 20N 89 53W
Millinocket, U.S.A. 83 C11 45 39N 68 43W
Millmerran, Australia .... 63 D5 27 53S 151 16 E
Millom, U.K. 12 C4 54 13N 3 16W
Mills L., Canada 70 A5 61 30N 118 20W
Millsboro, U.S.A. 84 G5 40 0N 80 0W
Millstream-Chichester △,
Australia .... 60 D2 21 35S 117 6 E
Milltown Malbay, Ireland 10 D2 52 52N 9 24W
Millville, N.J., U.S.A. 82 F8 39 24N 75 2W
Millville, Pa., U.S.A. 85 E8 41 7N 76 32W
Millwood L., U.S.A. 81 J8 33 42N 93 58W
Milne →, Australia .... 62 C2 21 10S 137 33 E
Milo, Canada 83 C11 45 15N 68 59W
Milos, Greece .... 23 F11 36 44N 24 25 E
Milparinka, Australia .... 63 D3 29 46S 141 57 E
Milton, N.S., Canada 73 D7 44 4N 64 45W
Milton, Ont., Canada 84 C5 43 31N 79 53W
Milton, N.Z. .... 59 M2 46 7S 169 59 E
Milton, Calif., U.S.A. 78 G6 38 3N 120 51W
Milton, Fla., U.S.A. 83 K2 30 38N 87 3W
Milton, Pa., U.S.A. 84 F8 41 1N 76 51W
Milton, Vt., U.S.A. 85 B11 44 38N 73 7W
Milton-Freewater, U.S.A. 76 D4 45 56N 118 23W
Milton Keynes, U.K. 13 E7 52 1N 0 44W
Milton Keynes □, U.K. 13 E7 52 1N 0 44W
Milverton, Canada 84 C4 43 34N 80 55W
Milwaukee, U.S.A. 82 D2 43 2N 87 55W
Milwaukee Deep, Atl. Oc. 89 C6 19 50N 68 0W
Milwaukie, U.S.A. 78 E4 45 27N 122 38W
Min Jiang →, Fujian, China .... 33 D6 26 0N 119 35 E
Min Jiang →, Sichuan, China .... 32 D5 28 45N 104 40 E
Min Xian, China .... 34 G3 34 25N 104 5 E
Mina Pirquitas, Argentina 94 A2 22 40S 66 30W
Mina Su'ud, Si. Arabia .... 45 D6 28 45N 48 28 E
Minā'al Ahmadī, Kuwait .... 45 D6 29 5N 48 10 E
Minago →, Canada 71 C9 54 33N 98 59W
Minaki, Canada 71 D10 49 59N 94 40W
Minamata, Japan .... 31 H5 32 10N 130 30 E
Minami-Arapusa △, Japan .... 31 G9 35 30N 138 9 E
Minami-Tori-Shima, Pac. Oc. .... 64 E7 24 20N 153 58 E
Minas, Uruguay 95 C4 34 20S 55 10W
Minas, Sierra de las, Guatemala 88 C2 15 9N 89 31W
Minas Basin, Canada 73 C7 45 20N 64 12W
Minas Gerais □, Brazil 93 G9 18 50S 46 0W
Minatitlán, Mexico 87 D6 17 59N 94 31W
Minbu, Burma .... 41 J19 20 10N 94 52 E
Minchinabad, Pakistan .... 42 D5 30 10N 73 34 E
Mindanao, Phil. .... 37 C6 8 0N 125 0 E
Mindanao Sea = Bohol Sea, Phil. .... 37 C6 9 0N 124 0 E
Mindanao Trench, Pac. Oc. .... 37 B7 12 0N 126 6 E
Minden, Canada 84 B6 44 55N 78 43W
Minden, Germany .... 16 B5 52 17N 8 55 E
Minden, La., U.S.A. 81 J8 32 37N 93 17W
Minden, Nev., U.S.A. 78 G7 38 57N 119 46W
Mindiptana, Indonesia .... 37 F10 5 55S 140 22 E
Mindoro, Phil. .... 37 B6 13 0N 121 0 E
Mindoro Str., Phil. .... 37 B6 12 30N 120 30 E
Mine, Japan .... 31 G5 34 12N 131 7 E
Minehead, U.K. 13 F4 51 12N 3 29W
Mineola, N.Y., U.S.A. 85 F11 40 45N 73 39W
Mineola, Tex., U.S.A. 81 J7 32 40N 95 29W
Mineral King, U.S.A. 78 J8 36 27N 118 36W
Mineral Wells, U.S.A. 81 J5 32 48N 98 7W
Minersville, U.S.A. 85 F8 40 41N 76 16W
Minerva, U.S.A. 84 F3 40 44N 81 6W
Minetto, U.S.A. 85 C8 43 24N 76 28W
Mingäçevir Su Anbarı,
Azerbaijan .... 19 F8 40 57N 46 50 E
Mingan, Canada 73 B7 50 20N 64 0W

Mingechaurskoye Vdkhr. =
Mingäçevir Su Anbarı,
Azerbaijan .... 19 F8 40 57N 46 50 E
Mingela, Australia .... 62 B4 19 52S 146 38 E
Mingenew, Australia .... 61 E2 29 12S 115 21 E
Mingera Cr. →, Australia .... 62 C2 20 38S 137 45 E
Mingin, Burma .... 41 H19 22 50N 94 30 E
Mingo Junction, U.S.A. 84 F4 40 19N 80 37W
Mingteke Daban = Mintaka Pass,
Pakistan .... 43 A6 37 0N 74 58 E
Mingyuegue, China .... 35 C15 43 2N 128 50 E
Minho = Miño →, Spain 21 A2 41 52N 8 40W
Minho, Portugal 21 B1 41 25N 8 20W
Minidoka, U.S.A. 76 E7 42 45N 113 29W
Minigwal, L., Australia .... 61 E3 29 31S 123 14 E
Minilya →, Australia .... 61 D1 23 45S 114 0 E
Minilya Roadhouse, Australia .... 61 D1 23 55S 114 0 E
Minipi L., Canada 73 B7 52 25N 60 45W
Mink L., Canada 70 A5 61 54N 117 40W
Minna, Nigeria .... 50 G7 9 37N 6 30 E
Minneapolis, Kans., U.S.A. 80 F6 39 8N 97 42W
Minneapolis, Minn., U.S.A. 80 C8 44 59N 93 16W
Minnedosa, Canada 71 C9 50 14N 99 50W
Minnesota □, U.S.A. 80 B8 46 0N 94 15W
Minnesota →, U.S.A. 80 C8 44 54N 93 9W
Minnewaukan, U.S.A. 80 A5 48 4N 99 15W
Minnipa, Australia .... 63 E2 32 51S 135 9 E
Minnitaki L., Canada 72 C1 49 57N 92 10W
Mino, Japan .... 31 G8 35 32N 136 55 E
Miño →, Spain 21 A2 41 52N 8 40W
Minorca = Menorca, Spain .... 24 B11 40 0N 4 0 E
Minot, U.S.A. 80 A4 48 14N 101 18W
Minqin, China .... 34 E2 38 38N 103 20 E
Minsk, Belarus .... 17 B14 53 52N 27 30 E
Mińsk Mazowiecki, Poland .... 17 B11 52 10N 21 33 E
Mintabie, Australia .... 63 D1 27 15S 133 7 E
Mintaka Pass, Pakistan .... 43 A6 37 0N 74 58 E
Minto, Canada 73 C6 46 5N 66 5W
Minto, L., Canada 72 A5 57 13N 75 0W
Minton, Canada 71 D8 49 10N 104 35W
Minturn, U.S.A. 76 G10 39 35N 106 26W
Minusinsk, Russia .... 29 D10 53 43N 91 20 E
Minutang, India .... 41 E20 28 15N 96 30 E
Minzhong, China .... 33 F10 22 37N 113 30 E
Miquelon, Canada 72 C4 49 25N 76 27W
Miquelon, St-P. & M. 73 C8 47 8N 56 22W
Mīr Kūh, Iran .... 45 E8 26 22N 58 55 E
Mīr Shahdād, Iran .... 45 E8 26 15N 58 29 E
Mira, Italy .... 22 B5 45 26N 12 8 E
Mira por vos Cay, Bahamas 89 B5 22 9N 74 30W
Mirador-Río Azul △, Guatemala 88 C2 17 45N 89 50W
Miraj, India .... 40 L9 16 50N 74 45 E
Miram Shah, Pakistan .... 42 C4 33 0N 70 2 E
Miramar, Argentina 94 D4 38 15S 57 50W
Miramar, Mozam. .... 57 C6 23 50S 35 35 E
Miramichi, Canada 73 C6 47 2N 65 28W
Miramichi B., Canada 73 C7 47 15N 65 0W
Miranda, Brazil 93 H7 20 10S 56 15W
Miranda →, Brazil 92 G7 19 25S 57 20W
Miranda de Ebro, Spain 21 A4 42 41N 2 57W
Miranda do Douro, Portugal 21 B2 41 30N 6 16W
Mirandópolis, Brazil 95 A5 21 9S 51 6W
Mirango, Malawi .... 55 E3 13 32S 34 58 E
Mirani, Australia .... 62 K6 21 8S 148 53 E
Mirassol, Brazil 95 A6 20 46S 49 28W
Mirbāt, Oman .... 47 D5 17 0N 54 45 E
Miri, Malaysia .... 36 D4 4 23N 113 59 E
Miriam Vale, Australia .... 62 C5 24 20S 151 33 E
Mirim, L., S. Amer. 95 C5 32 45S 52 50W
Mirnyy, Russia .... 29 C12 62 33N 113 53 E
Mirokhan, Pakistan .... 42 F3 27 46N 68 6 E
Mirond L., Canada 71 B8 55 6N 102 47W
Mirpur, Pakistan .... 43 C5 33 32N 73 56 E
Mirpur Batoro, Pakistan .... 42 G3 24 44N 68 16 E
Mirpur Bibiwari, Pakistan .... 42 E2 28 33N 67 44 E
Mirpur Khas, Pakistan .... 42 G3 25 30N 69 0 E
Mirpur Sakro, Pakistan .... 42 G2 24 33N 67 41 E
Mirs Bay = Tai Pang Wan, H.K. .... 33 F11 22 33N 114 24 E
Mirtağ, Turkey .... 44 B4 38 23N 41 56 E
Miryang, S. Korea .... 35 G15 35 31N 128 44 E
Mirzapur, India .... 43 G10 25 10N 82 34 E
Mirzapur-cum-Vindhyachal =
Mirzapur, India .... 43 G10 25 10N 82 34 E
Misantla, Mexico 87 D5 19 56N 96 50W
Misawa, Japan .... 30 D10 40 41N 141 24 E
Miscou I., Canada 73 C7 47 57N 64 31W
Mish'āb, Ra's al, Si. Arabia .... 45 D6 28 15N 48 43 E
Mishan, China .... 33 B8 45 37N 131 48 E
Mishawaka, U.S.A. 82 E2 41 40N 86 11W
Mishima, Japan .... 31 G9 35 10N 138 52 E
Misión, Mexico 79 N10 32 6N 116 53W
Misiones □, Argentina 95 B5 27 0S 55 0W
Misiones □, Paraguay 94 B4 27 0S 56 0W
Miskah, Si. Arabia .... 44 E4 24 49N 42 56 E
Miskitos, Cayos, Nic. 88 D3 14 26N 82 50W
Miskolc, Hungary .... 17 D11 48 7N 20 50 E
Misoke, Dem. Rep. of the Congo .... 54 C2 0 42S 28 2 E
Misool, Indonesia .... 37 E8 1 52S 130 10 E
Mişrātah, Libya .... 51 B9 32 24N 15 3 E
Missanabie, Canada 72 C3 48 20N 84 6W
Missinaibi →, Canada 72 B3 50 43N 81 29W
Missinaibi L., Canada 72 C3 48 23N 83 40W
Mission, Canada 70 D4 49 10N 122 15W
Mission, S. Dak., U.S.A. 80 D4 43 18N 100 39W
Mission, Tex., U.S.A. 81 M5 26 13N 98 20W
Mission Beach, Australia .... 62 B4 17 53S 146 6 E
Mission Viejo, U.S.A. 79 M9 33 36N 117 40W
Missisa L., Canada 72 B2 52 20N 85 7W
Missisicabi →, Canada 72 B4 51 14N 79 31W
Mississagi →, Canada 72 C3 46 15N 83 9W
Mississauga, Canada 84 C5 43 32N 79 35W
Mississippi □, U.S.A. 81 J10 33 0N 90 0W
Mississippi →, U.S.A. 81 L10 29 9N 89 15W
Mississippi L., Canada 85 A8 45 5N 76 10W
Mississippi River Delta, U.S.A. 81 L9 29 10N 89 15W
Mississippi Sd., U.S.A. 81 K10 30 20N 89 0W
Missoula, U.S.A. 76 C7 46 52N 114 1W
Missouri □, U.S.A. 80 F8 38 25N 92 30W
Missouri →, U.S.A. 80 F9 38 49N 90 7W
Missouri City, U.S.A. 81 L7 29 37N 95 32W
Missouri Valley, U.S.A. 80 E7 41 34N 95 53W
Mist, U.S.A. 78 E3 45 59N 123 15W
Mistassibi →, Canada 73 B5 48 53N 72 13W
Mistassini →, Canada 73 C5 48 42N 72 20W
Mistassini, L., Canada 72 B5 51 0N 73 30W
Mistastin L., Canada 73 A7 55 57N 63 20W
Mistinibi, L., Canada 73 A7 55 56N 64 17W
Mistissini, Canada 73 C5 48 53N 72 12W

Misty L., Canada 71 B8 58 53N 101 40W
Misurata = Mişrātah, Libya .... 51 B9 32 24N 15 3 E
Mitchell, Australia .... 63 D4 26 29S 147 58 E
Mitchell, Canada 84 C3 43 28N 81 12W
Mitchell, Nebr., U.S.A. 80 E3 41 57N 103 49W
Mitchell, Oreg., U.S.A. 76 D3 44 34N 120 9W
Mitchell, S. Dak., U.S.A. 80 D6 43 43N 98 2W
Mitchell →, Australia .... 62 B3 15 12S 141 35 E
Mitchell, Mt., U.S.A. 83 H4 35 46N 82 16W
Mitchell and Alice Rivers △,
Australia .... 62 B3 15 28S 142 5 E
Mitchell Ranges, Australia .... 62 A2 12 49S 135 36 E
Mitchelstown, Ireland 10 D3 52 15N 8 16W
Mitha Tiwana, Pakistan .... 42 C5 32 13N 72 6 E
Mithi, Pakistan .... 42 G3 24 44N 69 48 E
Mithrao, Pakistan .... 42 F3 27 28N 69 40 E
Mitilíni, Greece .... 23 E12 39 6N 26 35 E
Mito, Japan .... 31 F10 36 20N 140 30 E
Mitrovica = Kosovska Mitrovica,
Serbia & M. .... 23 C9 42 54N 20 52 E
Mitsinjo, Madag. .... 57 B8 16 1S 45 52 E
Mitsiwa, Eritrea .... 47 D2 15 35N 39 25 E
Mitsukaidō, Japan .... 31 F9 36 1N 139 59 E
Mittagong, Australia .... 63 E5 34 28S 150 29 E
Mittimatalik = Pond Inlet, Canada 69 A12 72 40N 77 0W
Mitú, Colombia 92 C4 1 15N 70 13W
Mitumba, Tanzania .... 54 D3 7 8S 31 2 E
Mitumba, Mts., Dem. Rep. of
the Congo .... 54 D2 7 0S 27 30 E
Mitwaba, Dem. Rep. of
the Congo .... 55 D2 8 2S 27 17 E
Mityana, Uganda .... 54 B3 0 23N 32 2 E
Mixteco →, Mexico 87 D5 18 11N 98 30W
Miyagi □, Japan .... 30 E10 38 15N 140 45 E
Miyâh, W. el →, Syria .... 44 C3 34 44N 39 57 E
Miyake-Jima, Japan .... 31 G9 34 5N 139 30 E
Miyako, Japan .... 30 E10 39 40N 141 59 E
Miyako-Jima, Japan .... 31 M2 24 45N 125 20 E
Miyako-Rettō, Japan .... 31 M2 24 24N 125 0 E
Miyakonojō, Japan .... 31 J5 31 40N 131 5 E
Miyani, India .... 42 J3 21 50N 69 26 E
Miyanoura-Dake, Japan .... 31 J5 30 20N 130 31 E
Miyazaki, Japan .... 31 J5 31 56N 131 30 E
Miyazaki □, Japan .... 31 H5 32 30N 131 30 E
Miyazu, Japan .... 31 G7 35 35N 135 10 E
Miyet, Bahr el = Dead Sea, Asia .... 46 D4 31 30N 35 30 E
Miyoshi, Japan .... 31 G6 34 48N 132 51 E
Miyun, China .... 34 D9 40 28N 116 50 E
Miyun Shuiku, China .... 35 D9 40 30N 117 0 E
Mizdah, Libya .... 51 B8 31 30N 13 0 E
Mizen Hd., Cork, Ireland 10 E2 51 27N 9 50W
Mizen Hd., Wicklow, Ireland 10 D5 52 51N 6 4W
Mizhi, China .... 34 F6 37 47N 110 12 E
Mizoram □, India .... 41 H18 23 30N 92 40 E
Mizpe Ramon, Israel .... 46 E3 30 34N 34 49 E
Mizuho, Antarctica .... 5 D5 70 30S 41 0 E
Mizusawa, Japan .... 30 E10 39 8N 141 8 E
Mjölby, Sweden .... 9 G16 58 20N 15 10 E
Mjøsa, Norway .... 9 F14 60 40N 11 0 E
Mkata, Tanzania .... 54 D4 5 45S 38 20 E
Mkhaya △, Swaziland .... 57 D5 26 34S 31 45 E
Mkokotoni, Tanzania .... 54 D4 5 55S 39 15 E
Mkomazi, Tanzania .... 54 C4 4 40S 38 7 E
Mkomazi →, S. Africa .... 57 E5 30 12S 30 50 E
Mkulwe, Tanzania .... 55 D3 8 37S 32 20 E
Mkumbi, Ras, Tanzania .... 54 D4 7 38S 39 55 E
Mkushi, Zambia .... 55 E2 14 25S 29 15 E
Mkushi River, Zambia .... 55 E2 13 32S 29 45 E
Mkuze, S. Africa .... 57 D5 27 10S 32 0 E
Mkuze △, S. Africa .... 57 D4 29 27S 29 30 E
Mladá Boleslav, Czech Rep. .... 16 C8 50 27N 14 53 E
Mlala Hills, Tanzania .... 54 D3 6 50S 31 40 E
Mlange = Mulanje, Malawi .... 55 F4 16 2S 35 33 E
Mlanje, Pic, Malawi .... 53 H7 15 57S 35 38 E
Mława, Poland .... 17 B11 53 9N 20 25 E
Mlawula △, Swaziland .... 57 D5 26 12S 32 2 E
Mljet, Croatia .... 22 C7 42 43N 17 30 E
Mmabatho, S. Africa .... 56 D4 25 49S 25 30 E
Mo i Rana, Norway .... 8 C16 66 20N 14 7 E
Moa, Cuba 89 B4 20 40N 74 56W
Moa, Indonesia .... 37 F7 8 0S 128 0 E
Moab, U.S.A. 77 G9 38 35N 109 33W
Moala, Fiji .... 59 D8 18 36S 179 53 E
Moama, Australia .... 63 F3 36 7S 144 46 E
Moamba, Mozam. .... 57 D5 25 36S 32 15 E
Moapa, U.S.A. 79 J12 36 40N 114 37W
Moate, Ireland 10 C4 53 24N 7 44W
Moba, Dem. Rep. of the Congo .... 54 D2 7 0S 29 48 E
Mobārakābād, Iran .... 45 D7 28 24N 53 20 E
Mobaye, C.A.R. .... 52 D4 4 25N 21 5 E
Mobayi, Dem. Rep. of the Congo .... 52 D4 4 15N 21 8 E
Moberley Lake, Canada 70 B4 55 50N 121 44W
Moberly, U.S.A. 80 F8 39 25N 92 26W
Mobile, U.S.A. 83 K1 30 41N 88 3W
Mobile B., U.S.A. 83 K2 30 30N 88 0W
Mobridge, U.S.A. 80 C4 45 32N 100 26W
Moc Chau, Vietnam .... 38 B5 20 50N 104 38 E
Moc Hoa, Vietnam .... 39 G5 10 46N 105 56 E
Mocabe Kasari, Dem. Rep. of
the Congo .... 55 D2 9 58S 26 12 E
Moçambique, Mozam. .... 55 F5 15 3S 40 42 E
Mocanaqua, U.S.A. 85 E8 41 9N 76 8W
Mochima △, Venezuela 89 D7 10 30N 64 5W
Mochudi, Botswana .... 56 C4 24 27S 26 7 E
Mocimboa da Praia, Mozam. .... 55 E5 11 25S 40 20 E
Moclips, U.S.A. 78 C2 47 14N 124 13W
Mocoa, Colombia 92 C3 1 7N 76 35W
Mococa, Brazil 95 A6 21 28S 47 0W
Mocorito, Mexico 86 B3 25 30N 107 53W
Moctezuma, Mexico 86 B3 29 50N 109 0W
Moctezuma →, Mexico 87 C5 21 59N 98 34W
Mocuba, Mozam. .... 55 F4 16 54S 36 57 E
Mocúzari, Presa, Mexico 86 B3 27 10N 109 10W
Modane, France .... 20 D7 45 12N 6 40 E
Modasa, India .... 42 H5 23 30N 73 21 E
Modder →, S. Africa .... 56 D3 29 2S 24 38 E
Modderrivier, S. Africa .... 56 D3 29 2S 24 38 E
Módena, Italy .... 22 B4 44 40N 10 55 E
Modena, U.S.A. 77 H7 37 48N 113 56W
Modesto, U.S.A. 78 H6 37 39N 121 0W
Módica, Italy .... 22 F6 36 52N 14 46 E
Modimolle, S. Africa .... 57 C4 24 42S 28 22 E
Moe, Australia .... 63 F4 38 12S 146 19 E
Moebase, Mozam. .... 55 F4 17 3S 38 41 E
Moengo, Suriname 93 B8 5 45N 54 20W
Moffat, U.K. 11 F5 55 21N 3 27W
Moga, India .... 42 D6 30 48N 75 8 E

Mogadishu = Muqdisho,
Somali Rep. .... 47 G4 2 2N 45 25 E
Mogador = Essaouira, Morocco 50 B4 31 32N 9 42W
Mogalakwena →, S. Africa .... 57 C4 22 38S 28 40 E
Mogami-Gawa →, Japan .... 30 E10 38 45N 140 0 E
Mogán, Canary Is. 24 G4 27 53N 15 43W
Mogaung, Burma .... 41 G20 25 20N 97 0 E
Mogi das Cruzes, Brazil 95 A6 23 31S 46 11W
Mogi-Guaçu →, Brazil 95 A6 20 53S 48 10W
Mogi-Mirim, Brazil 95 A6 22 29S 47 0W
Mogilev = Mahilyow, Belarus .... 17 B16 53 55N 30 18 E
Mogilev-Podolskiy = Mohyliv-
Podilskyy, Ukraine .... 17 D14 48 26N 27 48 E
Mogincual, Mozam. .... 55 F5 15 35S 40 25 E
Mogocha, Russia .... 29 D12 53 40N 119 50 E
Mogok, Burma .... 41 H20 23 0N 96 40 E
Mogollon Rim, U.S.A. 77 J8 34 10N 110 50W
Mogumber, Australia .... 61 F2 31 2S 116 3 E
Mohács, Hungary .... 17 F10 45 58N 18 41 E
Mohales Hoek, Lesotho .... 56 E4 30 7S 27 26 E
Mohall, U.S.A. 80 A4 48 46N 101 31W
Mohammadābād, Iran .... 45 B8 37 52N 59 5 E
Mohammedia, Morocco 50 B4 33 44N 7 21W
Mohana →, India .... 43 G11 24 43N 80 58 E
Mohanlalganj, India .... 43 F9 26 41N 80 58 E
Mohave, L., U.S.A. 79 K12 35 12N 114 34W
Mohawk →, U.S.A. 85 D11 42 47N 73 41W
Mohenjodaro, Pakistan .... 42 F3 27 19N 68 7 E
Moher, Cliffs of, Ireland 10 D2 52 58N 9 27W
Mohicanville Reservoir, U.S.A. 84 F3 40 45N 82 0W
Mohoro, Tanzania .... 54 D4 8 6S 39 8 E
Mohyliv-Podilskyy, Ukraine .... 17 D14 48 26N 27 48 E
Moidart, L., U.K. 11 E3 56 47N 5 52W
Moira →, Canada 84 B7 44 21N 77 24W
Moires, Greece .... 25 D6 35 4N 24 56 E
Moisaküla, Estonia .... 9 G21 58 3N 25 12 E
Moisie, Canada 73 B6 50 12N 66 1W
Moisie →, Canada 73 B6 50 14N 66 5W
Mojave, U.S.A. 79 K8 35 3N 118 10W
Mojave △, U.S.A. 79 K11 35 7N 115 30W
Mojave Desert, U.S.A. 79 L10 35 0N 116 30W
Mojo, Bolivia 94 A2 21 48S 65 33W
Mojokerto, Indonesia .... 37 G15 7 28S 112 26 E
Mokai, N.Z. .... 59 H5 38 32S 175 56 E
Mokambo, Dem. Rep. of
the Congo .... 55 E2 12 25S 28 20 E
Mokameh, India .... 43 G11 25 24N 85 55 E
Mokau, N.Z. .... 59 H5 38 42S 174 39 E
Mokelumne →, U.S.A. 78 G5 38 13N 121 28W
Mokelumne Hill, U.S.A. 78 G6 38 18N 120 43W
Mokhós, Greece .... 25 D7 35 16N 25 27 E
Mokhotlong, Lesotho .... 57 D4 29 22S 29 2 E
Mokokchung, India .... 41 F19 26 15N 94 30 E
Mokolo →, S. Africa .... 57 C4 23 14S 27 43 E
Mokopane, S. Africa .... 57 C4 24 10S 28 55 E
Mokp'o, S. Korea .... 35 G14 34 50N 126 25 E
Mokra Gora, Serbia & M. .... 23 C9 42 50N 20 30 E
Mol, Belgium .... 15 C5 51 11N 5 5 E
Molchanovo, Russia .... 28 D9 57 40N 83 50 E
Mold, U.K. 12 D4 53 9N 3 8W
Moldavia = Moldova ■, Europe .... 17 E15 47 0N 28 0 E
Molde, Norway .... 8 E12 62 45N 7 9 E
Moldova ■, Europe .... 17 E15 47 0N 28 0 E
Moldoveanu, Vf., Romania .... 17 F13 45 36N 24 45 E
Mole →, U.K. 13 F7 51 24N 0 21W
Mole Creek, Australia .... 63 G4 41 34S 146 24 E
Molepolole, Botswana .... 56 C4 24 28S 25 28 E
Molfetta, Italy .... 22 D7 41 12N 16 36 E
Moline, U.S.A. 80 E9 41 30N 90 31W
Molinos, Argentina 94 B2 25 28S 66 15W
Moliro, Dem. Rep. of the Congo .... 54 D3 8 12S 30 30 E
Mollendo, Peru 92 G4 17 0S 72 0W
Mollerin, L., Australia .... 61 F2 30 30S 117 35 E
Molodechno = Maladzyechna,
Belarus .... 17 A14 54 20N 26 50 E
Molokai, U.S.A. 74 H16 21 8N 157 0W
Molong, Australia .... 63 E4 33 5S 148 54 E
Molopo →, Africa .... 56 D3 28 30S 20 12 E
Molson L., Canada 71 C9 54 22N 96 40W
Molteno, S. Africa .... 56 E4 31 22S 26 22 E
Molu, Indonesia .... 37 F8 6 45S 131 40 E
Molucca Sea, Indonesia .... 37 E6 0 0 125 0 E
Moluccas = Maluku, Indonesia .... 37 E7 1 0S 127 0 E
Moma, Dem. Rep. of the Congo .... 54 C1 1 35S 23 52 E
Moma, Mozam. .... 55 F4 16 47S 39 4 E
Mombasa, Kenya .... 54 C4 4 2S 39 43 E
Mombetsu, Japan .... 30 B11 44 21N 143 22 E
Momchilgrad, Bulgaria .... 23 D11 41 33N 25 23 E
Momi, Dem. Rep. of the Congo .... 54 C2 1 42S 27 0 E
Mompós, Colombia 92 B4 9 14N 74 26W
Møn, Denmark .... 9 J15 54 57N 12 20 E
Mon □, Burma .... 41 L20 16 0N 97 30 E
Mona, Canal de la = Mona
Passage, W. Indies 89 C6 18 30N 67 45W
Mona, Isla, Puerto Rico 89 C6 18 5N 67 54W
Mona, Pta., Costa Rica 88 E3 9 37N 82 36W
Mona Passage, W. Indies 89 C6 18 30N 67 45W
Monaca, U.S.A. 84 F4 40 41N 80 17W
Monaco ■, Europe .... 20 E7 43 46N 7 23 E
Monadhliath Mts., U.K. 11 D4 57 10N 4 4W
Monadnock, Mt., U.S.A. 85 D12 42 52N 72 7W
Monaghan, Ireland 10 B5 54 15N 6 57W
Monaghan □, Ireland 10 B5 54 11N 6 56W
Monahans, U.S.A. 81 K3 31 36N 102 54W
Monapo, Mozam. .... 55 E5 14 56S 40 19 E
Monar, L., U.K. 11 D3 57 26N 5 8W
Monarch Mt., Canada 70 C3 51 55N 125 57W
Monashee Mts., Canada 70 C5 51 0N 118 43W
Monasterevin, Ireland 10 C4 53 8N 7 4W
Monastir = Bitola, Macedonia .... 23 D9 41 1N 21 20 E
Moncayo, Sierra del, Spain 21 B5 41 48N 1 50W
Monchegorsk, Russia .... 18 A5 67 54N 32 58 E
Mönchengladbach, Germany .... 16 C4 51 11N 6 27 E
Monchique, Portugal 21 D1 37 19N 8 38W
Moncks Corner, U.S.A. 83 J5 33 12N 80 1W
Monclova, Mexico 86 B4 26 50N 101 30W
Moncton, Canada 73 C7 46 7N 64 51W
Mondego →, Portugal 21 B1 40 9N 8 52W
Mondeodo, Indonesia .... 37 E6 3 34S 122 9 E
Mondoví, Italy .... 20 D7 44 23N 7 49 E
Mondrain I., Australia .... 61 F3 34 9S 122 14 E
Moneague, Jamaica .... 88 a 18 16N 77 7W
Monessen, U.S.A. 84 F5 40 9N 79 54W
Monett, U.S.A. 81 G8 36 55N 93 55W
Moneymore, U.K. 10 B5 54 41N 6 40W
Monforte de Lemos, Spain 21 A2 42 31N 7 33W
Mong Cai, Vietnam .... 38 B6 21 27N 107 54 E
Mong Hsu, Burma .... 41 J21 21 54N 98 30 E

Mong Kung, *Burma* .... 41 J20 21 35N 97 35 E
Mong Nai, *Burma* .... 41 J20 20 32N 97 46 E
Mong Pawk, *Burma* .... 41 H21 22 4N 99 16 E
Mong Ton, *Burma* .... 41 J21 20 17N 98 45 E
Mong Wa, *Burma* .... 41 J22 21 26N 100 27 E
Mong Yai, *Burma* .... 41 H21 22 21N 98 3 E
Mongalla, *Sudan* .... 51 G12 5 8N 31 42 E
Mongers, L., *Australia* ...... 61 E2 29 25S 117 5 E
Monghyr = Munger, *India* ... 43 G12 25 23N 86 30 E
Mongibello = Etna, *Italy* ... 22 F6 37 50N 14 55 E
Mongo, *Chad* .... 51 F9 12 14N 18 43 E
Mongolia ■, *Asia* .... 29 E10 47 0N 103 0 E
Mongu, *Zambia* .... 53 H4 15 16S 23 12 E
Môngua, *Angola* .... 56 B2 16 43S 15 20 E
Monifieth, *U.K.* 11 E6 56 30N 2 48W
Monkey Bay, *Malawi* .... 55 E4 14 7S 35 1 E
Monkey Mia, *Australia* ..... 61 E1 25 48S 113 43 E
Monkey River, *Belize* 87 D7 16 22N 88 29W
Monkoto, *Dem. Rep. of
the Congo* .... 52 E4 1 38S 20 35 E
Monkton, *Canada* 84 C3 43 35N 81 5W
Monmouth, *U.K.* 13 F5 51 48N 2 42W
Monmouth, *Ill., U.S.A.* 80 E9 40 55N 90 39W
Monmouth, *Oreg., U.S.A.* ... 76 D2 44 51N 123 14W
Monmouthshire □, *U.K.* 13 F5 51 48N 2 54W
Mono L., *U.S.A.* 78 H7 38 1N 119 1W
Monolith, *U.S.A.* 79 K8 35 7N 118 22W
Monólithos, *Greece* .... 25 C9 36 7N 27 45 E
Monongahela, *U.S.A.* 84 F5 40 12N 79 56W
Monópoli, *Italy* .... 22 D7 40 57N 17 18 E
Monos I., *Trin. & Tob.* 93 K15 10 42N 61 44W
Monroe, *Ga., U.S.A.* 83 J4 33 47N 83 43W
Monroe, *La., U.S.A.* 81 J8 32 30N 92 7W
Monroe, *Mich., U.S.A.* 82 E4 41 55N 83 24W
Monroe, *N.C., U.S.A.* 83 H5 34 59N 80 33W
Monroe, *N.Y., U.S.A.* 85 E10 41 20N 74 11W
Monroe, *Utah, U.S.A.* 77 G7 38 38N 112 7W
Monroe, *Wash., U.S.A.* 78 C5 47 51N 121 58W
Monroe, *Wis., U.S.A.* 80 D10 42 36N 89 38W
Monroe City, *U.S.A.* 80 F9 39 39N 91 44W
Monroeton, *U.S.A.* 85 E8 41 43N 76 29W
Monroeville, *Ala., U.S.A.* ... 83 K2 31 31N 87 20W
Monroeville, *Pa., U.S.A.* 84 F5 40 26N 79 45W
Monrovia, *Liberia* 50 G3 6 18N 10 47W
Mons, *Belgium* .... 15 D3 50 27N 3 58 E
Monse, *Indonesia* .... 37 E6 4 7S 123 15 E
Mont-de-Marsan, *France* ... 20 E3 43 54N 0 31W
Mont-Joli, *Canada* 73 C6 48 37N 68 10W
Mont-Laurier, *Canada* 72 C4 46 35N 75 30W
Mont-Louis, *Canada* 73 C6 49 15N 65 44W
Mont-St-Michel, Le, *France* . 20 B3 48 40N 1 30W
Mont-Tremblant △, *Canada* . 72 C5 46 30N 74 30W
Montagne d'Ambre △, *Madag.* 57 A8 12 37S 49 8 E
Montagu, *S. Africa* .... 56 E3 33 45S 20 8 E
Montagu I., *Antarctica* 5 B1 58 25S 26 20W
Montague, *Canada* 73 C7 46 10N 62 39W
Montague, I., *Mexico* 86 A2 31 40N 114 56W
Montague Ra., *Australia* .... 61 E2 27 15S 119 30 E
Montague Sd., *Australia* .... 60 B4 14 28S 125 20 E
Montalbán, *Spain* 21 B5 40 50N 0 45W
Montalvo, *Peru* 79 L7 34 15N 119 12W
Montana, *Bulgaria* .... 23 C10 43 27N 23 16 E
Montaña, *Peru* 92 E4 6 0S 73 0W
Montana □, *U.S.A.* 76 C9 47 0N 110 0W
Montaña Clara, I., *Canary Is.* 24 E6 29 17N 13 33W
Montargis, *France* .... 20 C5 47 59N 2 43 E
Montauban, *France* .... 20 D4 44 2N 1 21 E
Montauk, *U.S.A.* 85 E13 41 3N 71 57W
Montauk Pt., *U.S.A.* 85 E13 41 4N 71 52W
Montbéliard, *France* .... 20 C7 47 31N 6 48 E
Montceau-les-Mines, *France* . 20 C6 46 40N 4 23 E
Montclair, *U.S.A.* 85 F10 40 49N 74 13W
Monte Albán, *Mexico* 87 D5 17 3N 96 45W
Monte Alegre, *Brazil* 93 D8 2 0S 54 0W
Monte Azul, *Brazil* 93 G10 15 9S 42 53W
Monte Bello Is., *Australia* ... 60 D2 20 30S 115 45 E
Monte-Carlo, *Monaco* ...... 20 E7 43 44N 7 25 E
Monte Caseros, *Argentina* .. 94 C4 30 10S 57 50W
Monte Comán, *Argentina* ... 94 C2 34 40S 67 53W
Monte Cristi, *Dom. Rep.* 89 C5 19 52N 71 39W
Monte Lindo →, *Paraguay* .. 94 A4 23 56S 57 12W
Monte Patria, *Chile* 94 C1 30 42S 70 58W
Monte Quemado, *Argentina* . 94 B3 25 53S 62 41W
Monte Rio, *U.S.A.* 78 G4 38 28N 123 0W
Monte Santu, C. di, *Italy* ... 22 D3 40 5N 9 44 E
Monte Vista, *U.S.A.* 77 H10 37 35N 106 9W
Monteagudo, *Argentina* 95 B5 27 14S 54 8W
Montebello, *Canada* 72 C5 45 40N 74 55W
Montecito, *U.S.A.* 79 L7 34 26N 119 40W
Montecristo, *Italy* .... 22 C4 42 20N 10 19 E
Montego Bay, *Jamaica* ..... 88 a 18 30N 78 0W
Montélimar, *France* .... 20 D6 44 33N 4 45 E
Montello, *U.S.A.* 80 D10 43 48N 89 20W
Montemorelos, *Mexico* 87 B5 25 11N 99 42W
Montenegro, *Brazil* 95 B5 29 39S 51 29W
Montenegro □, *Serbia & M.* . 23 C8 42 40N 19 20 E
Montepuez, *Mozam.* .... 55 E4 13 8S 38 59 E
Montepuez →, *Mozam.* ..... 55 E5 12 32S 40 27 E
Monterey, *U.S.A.* 78 J5 36 37N 121 55W
Monterey B., *U.S.A.* 78 J5 36 45N 122 0W
Montería, *Colombia* 92 B3 8 46N 75 53W
Monteros, *Argentina* 94 B2 27 11S 65 30W
Monterrey, *Mexico* 86 B4 25 40N 100 30W
Montes Azules △, *Mexico* ... 87 D6 16 21N 91 3W
Montes Claros, *Brazil* 93 G10 16 30S 43 50W
Montesano, *U.S.A.* 78 D3 46 59N 123 36W
Montesilvano, *Italy* .... 22 C6 42 29N 14 8 E
Montevideo, *Uruguay* 95 C4 34 50S 56 11W
Montevideo, *U.S.A.* 80 C7 44 57N 95 43W
Montezuma, *U.S.A.* 80 E8 41 35N 92 32W
Montezuma Castle △, *U.S.A.* 77 J8 34 34N 111 45W
Montgomery, *U.K.* 13 E4 52 34N 3 8W
Montgomery, *Ala., U.S.A.* .. 83 J2 32 23N 86 19W
Montgomery, *Pa., U.S.A.* ... 84 E8 41 10N 76 53W
Montgomery, *W. Va., U.S.A.* 82 F5 38 11N 81 19W
Montgomery City, *U.S.A.* ... 80 F9 38 59N 91 30W
Monticello, *Ark., U.S.A.* 81 J9 33 38N 91 47W
Monticello, *Fla., U.S.A.* 83 K4 30 33N 83 52W
Monticello, *Ind., U.S.A.* 82 E2 40 45N 86 46W
Monticello, *Iowa, U.S.A.* ... 80 D9 42 15N 91 12W
Monticello, *Ky., U.S.A.* 83 G3 36 50N 84 51W
Monticello, *Minn., U.S.A.* .. 80 C8 45 18N 93 48W
Monticello, *Miss., U.S.A.* ... 81 K9 31 33N 90 7W
Monticello, *N.Y., U.S.A.* ... 85 E10 41 39N 74 42W
Monticello, *Utah, U.S.A.* ... 77 H9 37 52N 109 21W
Montijo, *Portugal* 21 C1 38 41N 8 54W
Montilla, *Spain* 21 D3 37 36N 4 40W
Montluçon, *France* .... 20 C5 46 22N 2 36 E

Montmagny, *Canada* 73 C5 46 58N 70 34W
Montmartre, *Canada* 71 C8 50 14N 103 27W
Montmorillon, *France* ...... 20 C4 46 26N 0 50 E
Monto, *Australia* .... 62 C5 24 52S 151 6 E
Montongbuwoh, *Indonesia* .. 37 K19 8 33S 116 4 E
Montoro, *Spain* 21 C3 38 1N 4 27W
Montour Falls, *U.S.A.* 84 D8 42 21N 76 51W
Montoursville, *U.S.A.* 84 E8 41 15N 76 55W
Montpelier, *Idaho, U.S.A.* ... 76 E8 42 19N 111 18W
Montpelier, *Vt., U.S.A.* 85 B12 44 16N 72 35W
Montpellier, *France* .... 20 E5 43 37N 3 52 E
Montréal, *Canada* 72 C3 47 14N 84 39W
Montreal →, *Canada* 71 C7 54 20N 105 45W
Montreal Lake, *Canada* 71 C7 54 3N 105 46W
Montreux, *Switz.* .... 20 C7 46 26N 6 55 E
Montrose, *U.K.* 11 E6 56 44N 2 27W
Montrose, *Colo., U.S.A.* 77 G10 38 29N 107 53W
Montrose, *Pa., U.S.A.* 85 E9 41 50N 75 53W
Monts, Pte. des, *Canada* 73 C6 49 20N 67 12W
Montserrat ☑, *W. Indies* ... 89 C7 16 40N 62 10W
Montuiri, *Spain* .... 24 B9 39 34N 2 58 E
Monywa, *Burma* .... 41 H19 22 7N 95 11 E
Monza, *Italy* .... 20 D8 45 35N 9 16 E
Monze, *Zambia* .... 55 F2 16 17S 27 29 E
Monze, C., *Pakistan* .... 42 G2 24 47N 66 37 E
Monzón, *Spain* .... 21 B6 41 52N 0 10 E
Mooers, *U.S.A.* 85 B11 44 58N 73 35W
Mooi →, *S. Africa* .... 57 D5 28 45S 30 34 E
Mooi River, *S. Africa* ...... 57 D4 29 13S 29 50 E
Moonah →, *Australia* ...... 62 C2 22 3S 138 33 E
Moonda, L., *Australia* ...... 62 D3 25 52S 140 25 E
Moonie, *Australia* .... 63 D5 27 46S 150 20 E
Moonie →, *Australia* .... 63 D4 29 19S 148 43 E
Moonta, *Australia* .... 63 E2 34 6S 137 32 E
Moora, *Australia* .... 61 F2 30 37S 115 58 E
Moorcroft, *U.S.A.* 80 C2 44 16N 104 57W
Moore →, *Australia* .... 61 F2 31 22S 115 30 E
Moore, L., *Australia* .... 61 E2 29 50S 117 35 E
Moore Park, *Australia* ...... 62 C5 24 43S 152 17 E
Moore River △, *Australia* ... 61 F2 31 7S 115 39 E
Moorefield, *U.S.A.* 82 F6 39 5N 78 59W
Moorees Res., *U.S.A.* 85 B13 44 45N 71 50W
Moorfoot Hills, *U.K.* 11 F5 55 44N 3 8W
Moorhead, *U.S.A.* 80 B6 46 53N 96 45W
Moorpark, *U.S.A.* 79 L8 34 17N 118 53W
Moorreesburg, *S. Africa* .... 56 E2 33 6S 18 38 E
Moorrinya △, *Australia* ..... 62 C3 21 42S 144 58 E
Moose →, *Canada* 72 B3 51 20N 80 25W
Moose Creek, *Canada* 85 A10 45 15N 74 58W
Moose Factory, *Canada* 72 B3 51 16N 80 32W
Moose Jaw, *Canada* 71 C7 50 24N 105 30W
Moose Jaw →, *Canada* 71 C7 50 34N 105 18W
Moose Lake, *Canada* 80 B8 46 27N 92 46W
Moose Mountain △, *Canada* . 71 D8 49 48N 102 25W
Moosehead L., *U.S.A.* 83 C11 45 38N 69 40W
Mooselookmeguntic L., *U.S.A.* 83 C10 44 55N 70 49W
Moosilauke, Mt., *U.S.A.* 85 B13 44 3N 71 40W
Moosomin, *Canada* 71 C8 50 9N 101 40W
Moosonee, *Canada* 72 B3 51 17N 80 39W
Moosup, *U.S.A.* 85 E13 41 43N 71 53W
Mopane, *S. Africa* .... 57 C4 22 37S 29 52 E
Mopeia Velha, *Mozam.* ..... 55 F4 17 30S 35 40 E
Mopipi, *Botswana* .... 56 C3 21 6S 24 55 E
Mopoi, *C.A.R.* .... 54 A2 5 6N 26 54 E
Mopti, *Mali* 50 F5 14 30N 4 0W
Moqor, *Afghan.* .... 42 C2 32 50N 67 42 E
Moquegua, *Peru* 92 G4 17 15S 70 46W
Mora, *Sweden* .... 9 F16 61 2N 14 38 E
Mora, *Minn., U.S.A.* 80 C8 45 53N 93 18W
Mora, N. Mex., U.S.A.* 77 J11 35 58N 105 20W
Mora →, *U.S.A.* 81 H2 35 35N 104 25W
Moradabad, *India* .... 43 E8 28 50N 78 50 E
Morafenobe, *Madag.* .... 57 B7 17 50S 44 53 E
Moramanga, *Madag.* .... 57 B8 18 56S 48 12 E
Moran, *Kans., U.S.A.* 81 G7 37 55N 95 10W
Moran, *Wyo., U.S.A.* 76 E8 43 53N 110 37W
Moranbah, *Australia* .... 62 C4 22 1S 148 6 E
Morant Bay, *Jamaica* ...... 88 a 17 53N 76 25W
Morant Cays, *Jamaica* 88 C4 17 22N 76 0W
Morant Pt., *Jamaica* .... 88 a 17 55N 76 12W
Morar, *India* .... 42 F8 26 14N 78 14 E
Moratuwa, *Sri Lanka* ...... 40 R11 6 45N 79 55 E
Morava →, *Serbia & M.* .... 23 B9 44 36N 21 4 E
Morava →, *Slovak Rep.* .... 17 D9 48 10N 16 59 E
Moravia, *U.S.A.* 85 D8 42 43N 76 25W
Moravian Hts. = Českomoravská
Vrchovina, *Czech Rep.* ... 16 D8 49 30N 15 40 E
Morawa, *Australia* .... 61 E2 29 13S 116 0 E
Morawhanna, *Guyana* 92 B7 8 30N 59 40W
Moray □, *U.K.* 11 D5 57 31N 3 18W
Moray Firth, *U.K.* 11 D5 57 40N 3 52W
Morbi, *India* .... 42 H4 22 50N 70 42 E
Morden, *Canada* 71 D9 49 15N 98 10W
Mordovian Republic =
Mordvinia □, *Russia* ..... 18 D7 54 20N 44 30 E
Mordvinia □, *Russia* .... 18 D7 54 20N 44 30 E
Morea, *Greece* .... 6 H10 37 45N 22 10 E
Moreau →, *U.S.A.* 80 C4 45 18N 100 43W
Morecambe, *U.K.* 12 C5 54 5N 2 52W
Morecambe B., *U.K.* 12 C5 54 7N 3 0W
Moree, *Australia* .... 63 D4 29 28S 149 54 E
Morehead, *U.S.A.* 82 F4 38 11N 83 26W
Morehead City, *U.S.A.* 83 H7 34 43N 76 43W
Morel →, *India* .... 42 F7 26 13N 76 36 E
Morelia, *Mexico* 86 D4 19 42N 101 7W
Morella, *Australia* .... 62 C3 23 0S 143 52 E
Morella, *Spain* 21 B5 40 35N 0 5W
Morelos, *Mexico* 86 B3 26 42N 107 40W
Morelos □, *Mexico* 87 D5 18 40N 99 10W
Moremi △, *Botswana* ...... 56 B3 19 18S 23 10 E
Morena, *India* .... 42 F8 26 30N 78 4 E
Morena, Sierra, *Spain* 21 C3 38 20N 4 0W
Moreno Valley, *U.S.A.* 79 M10 33 56N 117 15W
Moresby I., *Canada* 70 C2 52 30N 131 40W
Moreton Island △, *Australia* . 63 D5 27 25S 153 24 E
Morey, *Spain* .... 24 B10 39 44N 3 20 E
Morgan, *Australia* .... 63 E2 34 2S 139 35 E
Morgan, *U.S.A.* 76 F8 41 2N 111 41W
Morgan City, *U.S.A.* 81 L9 29 42N 91 12W
Morgan Hill, *U.S.A.* 78 H5 37 8N 121 39W
Morganfield, *U.S.A.* 82 G2 37 41N 87 55W
Morganton, *U.S.A.* 83 H5 35 45N 81 41W
Morgantown, *U.S.A.* 82 F6 39 38N 79 57W
Morgenzon, *S. Africa* ...... 57 D4 26 45S 29 36 E
Morghak, *Iran* .... 45 D8 29 7N 57 54 E

Morhar →, *India* .... 43 G11 25 29N 85 11 E
Mori, *Japan* .... 30 C10 42 6N 140 35 E
Moriarty, *U.S.A.* 77 J10 34 59N 106 3W
Morice L., *Canada* 70 C3 53 50N 127 40W
Morinville, *Canada* 70 C6 53 49N 113 41W
Morioka, *Japan* .... 30 E10 39 45N 141 8 E
Moris, *Mexico* 86 B3 28 8N 108 32W
Morlaix, *France* 20 B2 48 36N 3 52W
Mornington, *Australia* ..... 63 F4 38 15S 145 5 E
Mornington, I., *Chile* 96 F1 49 50S 75 30W
Mornington I., *Australia* .... 62 B2 16 30S 139 30 E
Moro, *Pakistan* .... 42 F2 26 40N 68 0 E
Moro →, *Pakistan* .... 42 E2 29 42N 67 22 E
Moro G., *Phil.* .... 37 C6 6 30N 123 0 E
Morocco ■, *N. Afr.* 50 B4 32 0N 5 50W
Morogoro, *Tanzania* .... 54 D4 6 50S 37 40 E
Morogoro □, *Tanzania* ..... 54 D4 8 0S 37 0 E
Moroleón, *Mexico* 86 C4 20 8N 101 32W
Morombe, *Madag.* .... 57 C7 21 45S 43 22 E
Morón, *Argentina* 94 C4 34 39S 58 37W
Morón, *Cuba* 88 B4 22 8N 78 39W
Morón de la Frontera, *Spain* . 21 D3 37 6N 5 28W
Morona →, *Peru* 92 D3 4 40S 77 10W
Morondava, *Madag.* .... 57 C7 20 17S 44 17 E
Morongo Valley, *U.S.A.* 79 L10 34 3N 116 37W
Moroni, *Comoros Is.* .... 49 H8 11 40S 43 16 E
Moroni, *U.S.A.* 76 G8 39 32N 111 35W
Morotai, *Indonesia* .... 37 D7 2 10N 128 30 E
Moroto, *Uganda* .... 54 B3 2 28N 34 42 E
Moroto, Mt., *Uganda* ...... 54 B3 2 30N 34 43 E
Morpeth, *U.K.* 12 B6 55 10N 1 41W
Morphou, *Cyprus* .... 25 D11 35 12N 32 59 E
Morphou Bay, *Cyprus* ...... 25 D11 35 15N 32 50 E
Morrilton, *U.S.A.* 81 H8 35 9N 92 44W
Morrinhos, *Brazil* 93 G9 17 45S 49 10W
Morrinsville, *N.Z.* .... 59 G5 37 40S 175 32 E
Morris, *Canada* 71 D9 49 25N 97 22W
Morris, *Ill., U.S.A.* 80 E10 41 22N 88 26W
Morris, *Minn., U.S.A.* 80 C7 45 35N 95 55W
Morris, *N.Y., U.S.A.* 85 D9 42 33N 75 15W
Morris, Mt., *Australia* ...... 61 E5 26 9S 131 4 E
Morris Jesup, Kap, *Greenland* . 4 A5 83 40N 34 0W
Morrisburg, *Canada* 85 B9 44 55N 75 7W
Morristown, *Ariz., U.S.A.* ... 77 K7 33 51N 112 37W
Morristown, *N.J., U.S.A.* 85 F10 40 48N 74 29W
Morristown, *N.Y., U.S.A.* ... 85 B9 44 35N 75 39W
Morristown, *Tenn., U.S.A.* .. 83 G4 36 13N 83 18W
Morrisville, *N.Y., U.S.A.* 85 D9 42 53N 75 35W
Morrisville, *Pa., U.S.A.* 85 F10 40 13N 74 47W
Morrisville, *Vt., U.S.A.* 85 B12 44 34N 72 36W
Morro, Pta., *Chile* 94 B1 27 6S 71 0W
Morro Bay, *U.S.A.* 78 K6 35 22N 120 51W
Morro del Jable, *Canary Is.* .. 24 F5 28 3N 14 23W
Morro Jable, Pta. de, *Canary Is.* 24 F5 28 2N 14 20W
Morrocoy △, *Venezuela* 89 D6 10 48N 68 13W
Morrosquillo, G. de, *Colombia* 88 E4 9 35N 75 40W
Morrumbene, *Mozam.* ...... 57 C6 23 31S 35 16 E
Morshansk, *Russia* .... 18 D7 53 28N 41 50 E
Morteros, *Argentina* 94 C3 30 50S 62 0W
Mortlach, *Canada* 71 C7 50 27N 106 4W
Mortlake, *Australia* .... 63 F3 38 5S 142 50 E
Morton, *Tex., U.S.A.* 81 J3 33 44N 102 46W
Morton, Wash., U.S.A.* 78 D4 46 34N 122 17W
Moruga, *Trin. & Tob.* 93 K15 10 4N 61 16W
Morundah, *Australia* .... 63 E4 34 57S 146 19 E
Moruya, *Australia* .... 63 F5 35 58S 150 3 E
Morvan, *France* .... 20 C6 47 5N 4 3 E
Morven, *Australia* .... 63 D4 26 22S 147 5 E
Morvern, *U.K.* 11 E3 56 38N 5 44W
Morwell, *Australia* .... 63 F4 38 10S 146 22 E
Morzhovets, Ostrov, *Russia* . 18 A7 66 44N 42 35 E
Moscos Is., *Burma* .... 38 E1 14 0N 97 30 E
Moscow = Moskva, *Russia* .. 18 C6 55 45N 37 35 E
Moscow, *Idaho, U.S.A.* 76 C5 46 44N 117 0W
Moscow, *Pa., U.S.A.* 85 E9 41 20N 75 31W
Mosel →, *Europe* .... 20 A7 50 22N 7 36 E
Moselle = Mosel →, *Europe* . 20 A7 50 22N 7 36 E
Moses Lake, *U.S.A.* 76 C4 47 8N 119 17W
Mosgiel, *N.Z.* .... 59 L3 45 53S 170 21 E
Moshaweng →, *S. Africa* ... 56 D3 26 35S 22 50 E
Moshi, *Tanzania* .... 54 C4 3 22S 37 18 E
Moshupa, *Botswana* .... 56 C4 24 46S 25 29 E
Mosjøen, *Norway* .... 8 D15 65 51N 13 12 E
Moskenesøya, *Norway* ..... 8 C15 67 58N 13 0 E
Moskenstraumen, *Norway* .. 8 C15 67 47N 12 45 E
Moskva, *Russia* .... 18 C6 55 45N 37 35 E
Mosomane, *Botswana* ...... 56 C4 24 2S 26 19 E
Mosonmagyaróvár, *Hungary* . 17 E9 47 52N 17 18 E
Mosquera, *Colombia* 92 C3 2 35N 78 24W
Mosquero, *U.S.A.* 81 H3 35 47N 103 58W
Mosquitia, *Honduras* 88 C3 15 20N 84 10W
Mosquito Coast = Mosquitia,
Honduras* 88 C3 15 20N 84 10W
Mosquito Creek L., *U.S.A.* .. 84 E4 41 18N 80 46W
Mosquito L., *Canada* 71 A8 62 35N 103 20W
Mosquitos, G. de los, *Panama* 88 E3 9 15N 81 10W
Moss, *Norway* .... 9 G14 59 27N 10 40 E
Moss Vale, *Australia* ...... 63 E5 34 32S 150 25 E
Mossbank, *Canada* 71 D7 49 56N 105 56W
Mossburn, *N.Z.* .... 59 L2 45 41S 168 15 E
Mosselbaai, *S. Africa* ...... 56 E3 34 11S 22 8 E
Mossendjo, *Congo* .... 52 E2 2 55S 12 42 E
Mossgiel, *Australia* .... 63 E3 33 15S 144 5 E
Mossman, *Australia* .... 62 B4 16 21S 145 15 E
Mossoró, *Brazil* 93 E11 5 10S 37 15W
Mossuril, *Mozam.* .... 55 E5 14 58S 40 42 E
Most, *Czech Rep.* .... 16 C7 50 31N 13 38 E
Mosta, *Malta* .... 25 D1 35 55N 14 26 E
Mostaganem, *Algeria* ...... 50 A6 35 54N 0 5 E
Mostar, Bos.-H.* .... 23 C7 43 22N 17 50 E
Mostardas, *Brazil* 95 C5 31 2S 50 51W
Mostiska = Mostyska, *Ukraine* 17 D12 49 48N 23 4 E
Mosty = Masty, *Belarus* .... 17 B13 53 27N 24 38 E
Mostyska, *Ukraine* .... 17 D12 49 48N 23 4 E
Mosul = Al Mawşil, *Iraq* .... 44 B4 36 15N 43 5 E
Mosúlpo, S. Korea* .... 35 H14 33 20N 126 17 E
Motagua →, *Guatemala* 88 C2 15 44N 88 14W
Motala, *Sweden* .... 9 G16 58 32N 15 1 E
Motaze, *Mozam.* .... 57 C5 24 48S 32 52 E
Moth, *India* .... 43 G8 25 43N 78 57 E
Motihari, *India* .... 43 F11 26 30N 84 55 E
Motozintla de Mendoza, *Mexico* 87 D6 15 21N 92 14W
Motril, *Spain* 21 D4 36 31N 3 37W
Mott, *U.S.A.* 80 B3 46 23N 102 20W
Motueka, *N.Z.* .... 59 J4 41 7S 173 1 E
Motueka →, *N.Z.* .... 59 J4 41 5S 173 1 E

Motul, *Mexico* 87 C7 21 0N 89 20W
Mouchalagane →, *Canada* .. 73 B6 50 56N 68 41W
Moúdhros, *Greece* .... 23 E11 39 50N 25 18 E
Mouila, *Gabon* .... 52 E2 1 50S 11 0 E
Moulamein, *Australia* ...... 63 F3 35 3S 144 1 E
Moule, *Guadeloupe* .... 88 b 16 20N 61 21W
Moule à Chique, C., St. Lucia* 89 f 13 43N 60 57W
Mouliana, *Greece* .... 25 D7 35 10N 25 59 E
Moulins, *France* .... 20 C5 46 35N 3 19 E
Moulmein, *Burma* .... 41 L20 16 30N 97 40 E
Moulouya, O. →, *Morocco* .. 50 B5 35 5N 2 25W
Moultrie, *U.S.A.* 83 K4 31 11N 83 47W
Moultrie, L., *U.S.A.* 83 J5 33 20N 80 5W
Mound City, Mo., U.S.A.* 80 E7 40 7N 95 14W
Mound City, S. Dak., U.S.A.* . 80 C4 45 44N 100 4W
Moundou, *Chad* .... 51 G9 8 40N 16 10 E
Moundsville, *U.S.A.* 84 G4 39 55N 80 44W
Moung, *Cambodia* .... 38 F4 12 46N 103 27 E
Mount Airy, *U.S.A.* 83 G5 36 31N 80 37W
Mount Albert, *Canada* 84 B5 44 8N 79 19W
Mount Aspiring △, *N.Z.* .... 59 L2 44 19S 168 47 E
Mount Barker, S. Austral.,
Australia* .... 63 F2 35 5S 138 52 E
Mount Barker, W. Austral.,
Australia* .... 61 F2 34 38S 117 40 E
Mount Brydges, *Canada* 84 D3 42 54N 81 29W
Mount Burr, *Australia* ..... 63 F3 37 34S 140 26 E
Mount Carmel = Ha Karmel △,
Israel* .... 46 C4 32 45N 35 5 E
Mount Carmel, Ill., U.S.A.* ... 82 F2 38 25N 87 46W
Mount Carmel, Pa., U.S.A.* .. 85 F8 40 47N 76 24W
Mount Charleston, *U.S.A.* .. 79 J11 36 16N 115 37W
Mount Clemens, *U.S.A.* 84 D2 42 35N 82 53W
Mount Coolon, *Australia* ... 62 C4 21 25S 147 25 E
Mount Darwin, *Zimbabwe* .. 55 F3 16 47S 31 38 E
Mount Desert I., *U.S.A.* 83 C11 44 21N 68 20W
Mount Dora, *U.S.A.* 83 L5 28 48N 81 38W
Mount Edziza △, *Canada* ... 70 B2 57 30N 130 45W
Mount Elgon △, E. Afr.* ..... 54 B3 1 4N 34 42 E
Mount Field △, *Australia* ... 63 G4 42 39S 146 35 E
Mount Fletcher, *S. Africa* ... 57 E4 30 40S 28 30 E
Mount Forest, *Canada* 84 C4 43 59N 80 43W
Mount Gambier, *Australia* .. 63 F3 37 50S 140 46 E
Mount Garnet, *Australia* ... 62 B4 17 37S 145 6 E
Mount Holly, *U.S.A.* 85 G10 39 59N 74 47W
Mount Holly Springs, *U.S.A.* 84 F7 40 7N 77 12W
Mount Hope, N.S.W., Australia* 63 E4 32 51S 145 51 E
Mount Hope, S. Austral.,
Australia* .... 63 E2 34 7S 135 23 E
Mount Isa, *Australia* ...... 62 C2 20 42S 139 26 E
Mount Jewett, *U.S.A.* 84 E6 41 44N 78 39W
Mount Kaputar △, *Australia* 63 E5 30 16S 150 10 E
Mount Kenya △, *Kenya* .... 54 C4 0 7S 37 21 E
Mount Kilimanjaro △, *Tanzania* 54 C4 3 2S 37 19 E
Mount Kisco, *U.S.A.* 85 E11 41 12N 73 44W
Mount Laguna, *U.S.A.* 79 N10 32 52N 116 25W
Mount Larcom, *Australia* ... 62 C5 23 48S 150 59 E
Mount Lofty Ra., *Australia* .. 63 E2 34 35S 139 5 E
Mount Magnet, *Australia* ... 61 E2 28 2S 117 47 E
Mount Maunganui, *N.Z.* .... 59 G6 37 40S 176 14 E
Mount Molloy, *Australia* ... 62 B4 16 42S 145 20 E
Mount Morgan, *Australia* ... 62 C5 23 40S 150 25 E
Mount Morris, *U.S.A.* 84 D7 42 44N 77 52W
Mount Pearl, *Canada* 73 C9 47 31N 52 47W
Mount Penn, *U.S.A.* 85 F9 40 20N 75 54W
Mount Perry, *Australia* .... 63 D5 25 13S 151 42 E
Mount Pleasant, Iowa, U.S.A.* 80 E9 40 58N 91 33W
Mount Pleasant, Mich., U.S.A.* 82 D3 43 36N 84 46W
Mount Pleasant, Pa., U.S.A.* . 84 F5 40 9N 79 33W
Mount Pleasant, S.C., U.S.A.* 83 J6 32 47N 79 52W
Mount Pleasant, Tenn., U.S.A.* 83 H2 35 32N 87 12W
Mount Pleasant, Tex., U.S.A.* 81 J7 33 12N 94 58W
Mount Pleasant, Utah, U.S.A.* 76 G8 39 33N 111 27W
Mount Pocono, *U.S.A.* 85 E9 41 7N 75 22W
Mount Rainier △, *U.S.A.* ... 78 D5 46 55N 121 50W
Mount Revelstoke △, *Canada* 70 C5 51 5N 118 30W
Mount Robson △, *Canada* .. 70 C5 53 0N 119 0W
Mount St. Helens △, *U.S.A.* 78 D4 46 14N 122 11W
Mount Selinda, *Zimbabwe* .. 57 C5 20 24S 32 43 E
Mount Shasta, *U.S.A.* 76 F2 41 19N 122 19W
Mount Signal, *U.S.A.* 79 N11 32 39N 115 37W
Mount Sterling, Ill., U.S.A.* .. 80 F9 39 59N 90 45W
Mount Sterling, Ky., U.S.A.* .. 82 F4 38 4N 83 56W
Mount Surprise, *Australia* .. 62 B3 18 10S 144 17 E
Mount Union, *U.S.A.* 84 F7 40 23N 77 53W
Mount Vernon, Ill., U.S.A.* ... 80 F1 38 19N 88 55W
Mount Vernon, Ind., U.S.A.* .. 80 F10 38 17N 88 57W
Mount Vernon, N.Y., U.S.A.* . 85 F11 40 55N 73 50W
Mount Vernon, Ohio, U.S.A.* . 84 F2 40 23N 82 29W
Mount Vernon, Wash., U.S.A.* 78 B4 48 25N 122 20W
Mount William △, *Australia* . 63 G4 40 56S 148 14 E
Mountain Ash, *U.K.* 13 F4 51 40N 3 23W
Mountain Center, *U.S.A.* ... 79 M10 33 42N 116 44W
Mountain City, Nev., U.S.A.* . 76 F6 41 50N 116 0W
Mountain City, Tenn., U.S.A.* 83 G5 36 29N 81 48W
Mountain Dale, *U.S.A.* 85 E10 41 41N 74 32W
Mountain Grove, *U.S.A.* ... 81 G8 37 8N 92 16W
Mountain Home, Ark., U.S.A.* 81 G8 36 20N 92 23W
Mountain Home, Idaho, U.S.A.* 76 E6 43 8N 115 41W
Mountain Iron, *U.S.A.* 80 B8 47 32N 92 37W
Mountain Pass, *U.S.A.* 79 K11 35 29N 115 35W
Mountain View, Ark., U.S.A.* . 81 H8 35 52N 92 7W
Mountain View, Calif., U.S.A.* 78 H4 37 23N 122 5W
Mountain View, Hawaii, U.S.A.* 74 J17 19 33N 155 7W
Mountain Zebra △, S. Africa* . 56 E4 32 14S 25 27 E
Mountainair, *U.S.A.* 77 J10 34 31N 106 15W
Mountlake Terrace, *U.S.A.* . 78 C4 47 47N 122 19W
Mountmellick, *Ireland* 10 C4 53 7N 7 20W
Mountrath, *Ireland* 10 C4 53 0N 7 28W
Moura, *Australia* .... 62 C4 24 35S 149 58 E
Moura, *Brazil* 92 D6 1 32S 61 38W
Moura, *Portugal* 21 C2 38 7N 7 30W
Mourdi, Dépression du, *Chad* 51 E10 18 10N 23 0 E
Mourilyan, *Australia* ...... 62 B4 17 35S 146 3 E
Mourne →, *U.K.* 10 B4 54 52N 7 26W
Mourne Mts., *U.K.* 10 B5 54 10N 6 0W
Mournies, *Greece* .... 25 D6 35 29N 24 1 E
Mournies = Mourniaí, *Greece* 25 D6 35 29N 24 1 E
Mouscron, *Belgium* .... 15 D3 50 45N 3 12 E
Moussoro, *Chad* .... 51 F9 13 41N 16 35 E
Moutong, *Indonesia* .... 37 D6 0 28N 121 13 E
Movas, *Mexico* 86 B3 28 10N 109 25W
Moville, *Ireland* 10 A4 55 11N 7 3W
Mowandjum, *Australia* ..... 60 C3 17 22S 123 40 E
Moy →, *Ireland* 10 B2 54 8N 9 8W
Moyale, *Kenya* .... 54 B4 3 30N 39 0 E
Moyen Atlas, *Morocco* ..... 50 B4 33 0N 5 0 E

Moyne, L. le, *Canada* **73 A6**   56 45N   68 47W
Moyo, *Indonesia* .... **36 F5**   8 10S 117 40 E
Moyobamba, *Peru* **92 E3**   6 0S   77 0W
Moyyero ➜, *Russia* .... **29 C11** 68 44N 103 42 E
Moyynty, *Kazakhstan* .... **28 E8**   47 10N 73 18 E
Mozambique = Moçambique,
   Mozam. .... **55 F5**   15 3S 40 42 E
Mozambique ■, *Africa* .... **55 F4**   19 0S 35 0 E
Mozambique Chan., *Africa* .... **57 B7**   17 30S 42 30 E
Mozdok, *Russia* .... **19 F7**   43 45N 44 48 E
Mozdūrān, *Iran* .... **45 B9**   36 9N 60 35 E
Mozhnābād, *Iran* .... **45 C9**   34 7N 60 6 E
Mozyr = Mazyr, *Belarus* .... **17 B15** 51 59N 29 15 E
Mpanda, *Tanzania* .... **54 D3**   6 23S   31 1 E
Mphoengs, *Zimbabwe* .... **57 C4**   21 10S 27 51 E
Mpika, *Zambia* .... **55 E3**   11 51S 31 25 E
Mpulungu, *Zambia* .... **55 D3**   8 51S 31 5 E
Mpumalanga, *S. Africa* .... **57 D5**   29 50S 30 33 E
Mpumalanga □, *S. Africa* .... **57 D5**   26 0S 30 0 E
Mpwapwa, *Tanzania* .... **54 D4**   6 23S 36 30 E
Mqanduli, *S. Africa* .... **57 E4**   31 49S 28 45 E
Msambansovu, *Zimbabwe* .... **55 F3**   15 50S 30 3 E
M'sila ➜, *Algeria* .... **50 A6**   35 30N   4 29 E
Msoro, *Zambia* .... **55 E3**   13 35S 31 50 E
Mstislavl = Mstsislaw, *Belarus* .. **17 A16** 54 0N 31 50 E
Mstsislaw, *Belarus* .... **17 A16** 54 0N 31 50 E
Mtama, *Tanzania* .... **55 E4**   10 17S 39 21 E
Mtamvuna ➜, *S. Africa* .... **57 E5**   31 6S 30 12 E
Mtilikwe ➜, *Zimbabwe* .... **55 G3**   21 9S 31 30 E
Mtubatuba, *S. Africa* .... **57 D5**   28 30S 32 8 E
Mtwalume, *S. Africa* .... **57 E5**   30 30S 30 38 E
Mtwara-Mikindani, *Tanzania* .. **55 E5**   10 20S 40 20 E
Mu Gia, Deo, *Vietnam* .... **38 D5**   17 40N 105 47 E
Mu Ko Chang △, *Thailand* .... **39 G4**   11 59N 102 22 E
Mu Us Shamo, *China* .... **34 E5**   39 0N 109 0 E
Muang Chiang Rai = Chiang Rai,
   Thailand .... **38 C2**   19 52N 99 50 E
Muang Khong, *Laos* .... **38 E5**   14 7N 105 51 E
Muang Lamphun, *Thailand* .. **38 C2**   18 40N 99 2 E
Muang Mai, *Thailand* .... **39 a**   8 5N 98 21 E
Muang Pak Beng, *Laos* .... **38 C3**   19 54N 101 8 E
Muar, *Malaysia* .... **39 L4**   2 3N 102 34 E
Muarabungo, *Indonesia* .... **36 E2**   1 28S 102 52 E
Muaraenim, *Indonesia* .... **36 E2**   3 40S 103 50 E
Muarajuloi, *Indonesia* .... **36 E4**   0 12S 114 3 E
Muarakaman, *Indonesia* .... **36 E5**   0 2S 116 45 E
Muaratebo, *Indonesia* .... **36 E2**   1 30S 102 26 E
Muaratembesi, *Indonesia* .... **36 E2**   1 42S 103 8 E
Muaratewe, *Indonesia* .... **36 E4**   0 58S 114 52 E
Mubarakpur, *India* .... **43 F10** 26 6N 83 18 E
Mubarraz = Al Mubarraz,
   Si. Arabia .... **45 E6**   25 30N 49 40 E
Mubende, *Uganda* .... **54 B3**   0 33N 31 22 E
Mubi, *Nigeria* .... **51 F8**   10 18N 13 16 E
Mucajaí ➜, *Brazil* **92 C6**   2 25N 60 52W
Muchachos, Roque de los,
   Canary Is. **24 F2**   28 44N 17 52W
Muchinga Mts., *Zambia* .... **55 E3**   11 30S 31 30 E
Muck, *U.K.* **11 E2**   56 50N   6 15W
Muckadilla, *Australia* .... **63 D4**   26 35S 148 23 E
Muckle Flugga, *U.K.* **11 A8**   60 51N   0 54W
Mucuri, *Brazil* **93 G11** 18 0S 39 36W
Mucusso, *Angola* .... **56 B3**   18 1S 21 25 E
Muda, *Canary Is.* **24 F6**   28 34N 13 57W
Mudanjiang, *China* .... **35 B15** 44 38N 129 30 E
Mudanya, *Turkey* .... **23 D13** 40 25N 28 50 E
Muddy Cr. ➜, *U.S.A.* **77 H8**   38 24N 110 42W
Mudgee, *Australia* .... **63 E4**   32 32S 149 31 E
Mudjatik ➜, *Canada* **71 B7**   56 1N 107 36W
Muecate, *Mozam.* .... **55 E4**   14 55S 39 40 E
Mueda, *Mozam.* .... **55 E4**   11 36S 39 28 E
Mueller Ra., *Australia* .... **60 C4**   18 18S 126 46 E
Muende, *Mozam.* .... **55 E3**   14 28S 33 0 E
Muerto, Mar, *Mexico* **87 D6**   16 10N 94 10W
Mufulira, *Zambia* .... **55 E2**   12 32S 28 15 E
Mufumbiro Range, *Africa* .... **54 C2**   1 25S 29 30 E
Mughal Sarai, *India* .... **43 G10** 25 18N 83 7 E
Mughayrā', *Si. Arabia* .... **44 D3**   29 17N 37 41 E
Mugi, *Japan* .... **31 H7**   33 40N 134 25 E
Mugila, Mts., *Dem. Rep. of
   the Congo* .... **54 D2**   7 0S 28 50 E
Muğla, *Turkey* .... **23 F13** 37 15N 28 22 E
Mugu, *Nepal* .... **43 E10** 29 45N 82 30 E
Muhammad, Râs, *Egypt* .... **44 E2**   27 44N 34 16 E
Muhammadabad, *India* .... **43 F10** 26 4N 83 25 E
Muhesi ➜, *Tanzania* .... **54 D4**   7 0S 35 20 E
Mühlhausen, *Germany* .... **16 C6**   51 12N 10 27 E
Mühlig Hofmann fjell, *Antarctica* **5 D3**   72 0S   5 0 E
Muhos, *Finland* .... **8 D22** 64 47N 25 59 E
Muhu, *Estonia* .... **9 G20** 58 36N 23 11 E
Muhutwe, *Tanzania* .... **54 C3**   1 35S 31 45 E
Mui Wo, *China* .... **33 G10** 22 16N 113 59 E
Muine Bheag, *Ireland* **10 D5**   52 42N   6 58W
Muir, L., *Australia* .... **61 F2**   34 30S 116 40 E
Muir of Ord, *U.K.* **11 D4**   57 32N   4 28W
Mujnak = Muynak, *Uzbekistan* .. **28 E6**   43 44N 59 10 E
Muka, Tanjung, *Malaysia* .... **39 c**   5 28N 100 11 E
Mukacheve, *Ukraine* .... **17 D12** 48 27N 22 45 E
Mukachevo = Mukacheve,
   Ukraine .... **17 D12** 48 27N 22 45 E
Mukah, *Malaysia* .... **36 D4**   2 55N 112 5 E
Mukandwara, *India* .... **42 G6**   24 49N 75 59 E
Mukdahan, *Thailand* .... **38 D5**   16 32N 104 43 E
Mukden = Shenyang, *China* .. **35 D12** 41 48N 123 27 E
Mukerian, *India* .... **42 D6**   31 57N 75 37 E
Mukinbudin, *Australia* .... **61 F2**   30 55S 118 5 E
Mukishi, *Dem. Rep. of the Congo* **55 D1**   8 30S 24 44 E
Mukomuko, *Indonesia* .... **36 E2**   2 30S 101 10 E
Mukomwenze, *Dem. Rep. of
   the Congo* .... **54 D2**   6 49S 27 15 E
Muktsar, *India* .... **42 D6**   30 30N 74 30 E
Mukur = Moqor, *Afghan.* .... **42 C2**   32 50N 67 42 E
Mukutawa ➜, *Canada* **71 C9**   53 10N 97 24W
Mukwela, *Zambia* .... **55 F2**   17 0S 26 40 E
Mula, *Spain* **21 C5**   38 3N   1 33W
Mula ➜, *Pakistan* .... **42 F2**   27 57N 67 36 E
Mulange, *Dem. Rep. of
   the Congo* .... **54 C2**   3 40S 27 10 E
Mulanje, *Malawi* .... **55 F4**   16 2S 35 33 E
Mulanje, Mt., *Malawi* .... **55 F4**   16 2S 35 33 E
Mulchén, *Chile* **94 D1**   37 45S 72 20W
Mulde ➜, *Germany* .... **16 C7**   51 53N 12 15 E
Mule Creek Junction, *U.S.A.* .. **80 D2**   43 19N 104 8W
Muleba, *Tanzania* .... **54 C3**   1 50S 31 37 E
Mulejé, *Mexico* **86 B2**   26 53N 112 1W
Muleshoe, *U.S.A.* **81 H3**   34 13N 102 43W
Mulgrave, *Canada* **73 C7**   45 38N 61 31W

Mulhacén, *Spain* **21 D4**   37 4N   3 20W
Mülheim, *Germany* .... **33 C6**   51 25N   6 54 E
Mulhouse, *France* .... **20 C7**   47 40N   7 20 E
Muling, *China* .... **35 B16** 44 35N 130 10 E
Mull, *U.K.* **11 E3**   56 25N   5 56W
Mull, Sound of, *U.K.* **11 E3**   56 30N   5 50W
Mullaittivu, *Sri Lanka* .... **40 Q12** 9 15N 80 49 E
Mullen, *U.S.A.* **80 D4**   42 3N 101 1W
Mullens, *U.S.A.* **82 G5**   37 35N 81 23W
Muller, Pegunungan, *Indonesia* **36 D4**   0 30N 113 30 E
Mullet Pen., *Ireland* **10 B1**   54 13N 10 2W
Mullewa, *Australia* .... **61 E2**   28 29S 115 30 E
Mulligan ➜, *Australia* .... **62 D2**   25 0S 139 0 E
Mullingar, *Ireland* **10 C4**   53 31N   7 21W
Mullins, *U.S.A.* **83 H6**   34 12N 79 15W
Mullumbimby, *Australia* .... **63 D5**   28 30S 153 30 E
Mulobezi, *Zambia* .... **55 F2**   16 45S 25 7 E
Mulroy B., *Ireland* **10 A4**   55 15N   7 46W
Multan, *Pakistan* .... **42 D4**   30 15N 71 36 E
Mulumbe, Mts., *Dem. Rep. of
   the Congo* .... **55 D2**   8 40S 27 30 E
Mulungushi Dam, *Zambia* .. **55 E2**   14 48S 28 48 E
Mulvane, *U.S.A.* **81 G6**   37 29N 97 15W
Mumbai, *India* .... **40 K8**   18 55N 72 50 E
Mumbwa, *Zambia* .... **55 F2**   15 0S 27 0 E
Mun ➜, *Thailand* .... **38 E5**   15 19N 105 30 E
Muna, *Indonesia* .... **37 F6**   5 0S 122 30 E
Munabao, *India* .... **42 G4**   25 45N 70 17 E
Munamagi, *Estonia* .... **9 H22** 57 43N 27 4 E
Muncan, *Indonesia* .... **37 K18** 8 34S 115 11 E
Muncar, *Indonesia* .... **37 J17** 8 26S 114 20 E
München, *Germany* .... **16 D6**   48 8N 11 34 E
München-Gladbach =
   Mönchengladbach, *Germany* **16 C4**   51 11N   6 27 E
Muncho Lake, *Canada* **70 B3**   59 0N 125 50W
Munch'ŏn, *N. Korea* .... **35 E14** 39 14N 127 19 E
Muncie, *U.S.A.* **82 E3**   40 12N 85 23W
Muncoonie, L., *Australia* .... **62 D2**   25 12S 138 40 E
Munday, *U.S.A.* **81 J5**   33 27N 99 38W
Mundiwindi, *Australia* .... **60 D3**   23 47S 120 9 E
Mundo Novo, *Brazil* **93 F10** 11 50S 40 29W
Mundra, *India* .... **42 H3**   22 54N 69 48 E
Mundrabilla, *Australia* .... **61 F4**   31 52S 127 51 E
Mungallala, *Australia* .... **63 D4**   26 28S 147 34 E
Mungallala Cr. ➜, *Australia* .. **63 D4**   28 53S 147 45 E
Mungana, *Australia* .... **62 B3**   17 8S 144 27 E
Mungaoli, *India* .... **42 G8**   24 24N 78 7 E
Mungari, *Mozam.* .... **55 F3**   17 12S 33 30 E
Mungbere, Dem. Rep. of
   the Congo* .... **54 B2**   2 36N 28 28 E
Mungeli, *India* .... **43 H9**   22 4N 81 41 E
Munger, *India* .... **43 G12** 25 23N 86 30 E
Mungkan Kandju △, *Australia* **62 A3**   13 35S 142 52 E
Munich = München, *Germany* **16 D6**   48 8N 11 34 E
Munising, *U.S.A.* **82 B2**   46 25N 86 40W
Munku-Sardyk, *Russia* .... **29 D11** 51 45N 100 20 E
Muñoz Gamero, Pen., *Chile* .. **96 G2**   52 30S 73 5W
Munroe L., *Canada* **71 B9**   59 13N 98 35W
Munsan, *S. Korea* .... **35 F14** 37 51N 126 48 E
Münster, *Germany* .... **16 C4**   51 58N   7 37 E
Munster □, *Ireland* **10 D3**   52 18N   8 44W
Muntadgin, *Australia* .... **61 F2**   31 45S 118 33 E
Muntok, *Indonesia* .... **36 E3**   2 5S 105 10 E
Munyama, *Zambia* .... **55 F2**   16 5S 28 31 E
Muong Beng, *Laos* .... **38 B3**   20 23N 101 46 E
Muong Boum, *Vietnam* .... **38 A4**   22 24N 102 49 E
Muong Et, *Laos* .... **38 B5**   20 49N 104 1 E
Muong Hai, *Laos* .... **38 B3**   21 3N 101 49 E
Muong Hiem, *Laos* .... **38 B4**   20 5N 103 22 E
Muong Houn, *Laos* .... **38 B3**   20 8N 101 23 E
Muong Hung, *Vietnam* .... **38 B4**   20 56N 103 53 E
Muong Kau, *Laos* .... **38 E5**   15 6N 105 47 E
Muong Khao, *Laos* .... **38 C4**   19 38N 103 32 E
Muong Khoua, *Laos* .... **38 B4**   21 5N 102 31 E
Muong Liep, *Laos* .... **38 C3**   18 29N 101 40 E
Muong May, *Laos* .... **38 E6**   14 49N 106 56 E
Muong Ngeun, *Laos* .... **38 B3**   20 36N 101 3 E
Muong Ngoi, *Laos* .... **38 B4**   20 43N 102 41 E
Muong Nhie, *Vietnam* .... **38 A4**   22 12N 102 28 E
Muong Nong, *Laos* .... **38 D6**   16 22N 106 30 E
Muong Ou Tay, *Laos* .... **38 A3**   22 7N 101 48 E
Muong Oua, *Laos* .... **38 C3**   18 18N 101 20 E
Muong Peun, *Laos* .... **38 B4**   20 13N 103 52 E
Muong Phalane, *Laos* .... **38 D5**   16 39N 105 34 E
Muong Phieng, *Laos* .... **38 C3**   19 6N 101 32 E
Muong Phine, *Laos* .... **38 D6**   16 32N 106 2 E
Muong Sai, *Laos* .... **38 B3**   20 42N 101 59 E
Muong Saiapoun, *Laos* .... **38 C3**   18 24N 101 31 E
Muong Sen, *Vietnam* .... **38 C5**   19 24N 104 8 E
Muong Sing, *Laos* .... **38 B3**   21 11N 101 9 E
Muong Son, *Laos* .... **38 B4**   20 27N 103 19 E
Muong Soui, *Laos* .... **38 C4**   19 33N 102 52 E
Muong Va, *Laos* .... **38 B4**   21 53N 102 19 E
Muong Xia, *Vietnam* .... **38 B5**   20 19N 104 50 E
Muonio, *Finland* .... **8 C20** 67 57N 23 40 E
Muonionjoki ➜, *Finland* .... **8 C20** 67 11N 23 34 E
Muping, *China* .... **35 F11** 37 22N 121 36 E
Muqdisho, *Somali Rep.* .... **47 G4**   2 2N 45 25 E
Mur ➜, *Austria* .... **17 E9**   46 18N 16 52 E
Murakami, *Japan* .... **30 E9**   38 14N 139 29 E
Murallón, Cerro, *Chile* **96 F2**   49 48S 73 30W
Muranda, *Rwanda* .... **54 C2**   1 52S 29 20 E
Murang'a, *Kenya* .... **54 C4**   0 45S 37 9 E
Murashi, *Russia* .... **18 C8**   59 30N 49 0 E
Murat, *Turkey* .... **19 G7**   38 46N 40 0 E
Muratlı, *Turkey* .... **23 D12** 41 10N 27 29 E
Murayama, *Japan* .... **30 E10** 38 30N 140 25 E
Murchison ➜, *Australia* .... **61 E1**   27 45S 114 0 E
Murchison, Mt., *Antarctica* .. **5 D11** 73 0S 168 0 E
Murchison Falls, *Uganda* .... **54 B3**   2 15N 31 30 E
Murchison Falls △, *Uganda* .. **54 B3**   2 17N 31 48 E
Murchison Ra., *Australia* .... **62 C1**   20 0S 134 10 E
Murchison Rapids, *Malawi* .. **55 F3**   15 55S 34 35 E
Murcia, *Spain* **21 D5**   38 5N   1 10W
Murcia □, *Spain* **21 D5**   37 50N   1 30W
Murdo, *U.S.A.* **80 D4**   43 53N 100 43W
Murdoch Pt., *Australia* .... **62 A3**   14 37S 144 55 E
Mureş ➜, *Romania* .... **17 E11** 46 15N 20 13 E
Mureşul = Mureş ➜, *Romania* **17 E11** 46 15N 20 13 E
Murewa, *Zimbabwe* .... **57 B5**   17 39S 31 47 E
Murfreesboro, N.C., *U.S.A.* .. **83 G7**   36 27N 77 6W
Murfreesboro, Tenn., *U.S.A.* **83 H2**   35 51N 86 24W
Murgab = Murghob, *Tajikistan* **28 F8**   38 10N 74 2 E
Murgab ➜, *Turkmenistan* .... **45 B9**   38 18N 61 12 E
Murgenella, *Australia* .... **60 B5**   11 34S 132 56 E
Murgha Kibzai, *Pakistan* .... **42 D3**   30 44N 69 25 E

Murghob, *Tajikistan* .... **28 F8**   38 10N 74 2 E
Murgon, *Australia* .... **63 D5**   26 15S 151 54 E
Muri, *India* .... **43 H11** 23 22N 85 52 E
Muria, *Indonesia* .... **37 G14** 6 36S 110 53 E
Muriaé, *Brazil* **95 A7**   21 8S 42 23W
Muriel Mine, *Zimbabwe* .... **55 F3**   17 14S 30 40 E
Murliganj, *India* .... **43 G12** 25 54N 86 59 E
Murmansk, *Russia* .... **18 A5**   68 57N 33 10 E
Muro, *Spain* .... **24 B10** 39 44N   3 3 E
Murom, *Russia* .... **18 C7**   55 35N 42 3 E
Muroran, *Japan* .... **30 C10** 42 25N 141 0 E
Muroto, *Japan* .... **31 H7**   33 18N 134 9 E
Muroto-Misaki, *Japan* .... **31 H7**   33 15N 134 10 E
Murphy, *U.S.A.* **76 E5**   43 13N 116 33W
Murphys, *U.S.A.* **78 G6**   38 8N 120 28W
Murray, Ky., *U.S.A.* **83 G1**   36 37N 88 19W
Murray, Utah, *U.S.A.* **76 F8**   40 40N 111 53W
Murray ➜, *Australia* .... **63 F2**   35 20S 139 22 E
Murray, L., *U.S.A.* **83 H5**   34 3N 81 13W
Murray Bridge, *Australia* .... **63 F2**   35 6S 139 14 E
Murray Harbour, *Canada* **73 C7**   46 0N 62 28W
Murray River △, *Australia* .... **63 E3**   34 23S 140 32 E
Murraysburg, *S. Africa* .... **56 E3**   31 58S 23 47 E
Murree, *Pakistan* .... **42 C5**   33 56N 73 28 E
Murrieta, *U.S.A.* **79 M9**   33 33N 117 13W
Murrumbidgee ➜, *Australia* **63 E3**   34 43S 143 12 E
Murrumburrah, *Australia* .... **63 E4**   34 32S 148 22 E
Murrurundi, *Australia* .... **63 E5**   31 42S 150 51 E
Murshidabad, *India* .... **43 G13** 24 11N 88 19 E
Murtle L., *Canada* **70 C5**   52 8N 119 38W
Murtoa, *Australia* .... **63 F3**   36 35S 142 28 E
Murungu, *Tanzania* .... **54 C3**   4 12S 31 10 E
Mururoa, *French Polynesia* .. **65 K14** 21 52S 138 55W
Murwara, *India* .... **43 H9**   23 46N 80 28 E
Murwillumbah, *Australia* .... **63 D5**   28 18S 153 27 E
Mürzzuschlag, *Austria* .... **16 E8**   47 36N 15 41 E
Muş, *Turkey* .... **19 G7**   38 45N 41 30 E
Mûsa, Gebel, *Egypt* .... **44 D2**   28 33N 33 59 E
Musa Khel, *Pakistan* .... **42 D3**   30 59N 69 52 E
Mûsa Qal'eh, *Afghan.* .... **40 C4**   32 20N 64 50 E
Musafirkhana, *India* .... **43 F9**   26 22N 81 48 E
Musala, *Bulgaria* .... **23 C10** 42 13N 23 37 E
Musala, *Indonesia* .... **36 D1**   1 41N 98 28 E
Musan, *N. Korea* .... **35 C15** 42 12N 129 12 E
Musangu, Dem. Rep. of
   the Congo* .... **55 E1**   10 28S 23 55 E
Musasa, *Tanzania* .... **54 C3**   3 25S 31 30 E
Musay'īd, *Qatar* .... **45 E6**   25 0N 51 33 E
Muscat = Masqaṭ, *Oman* .... **47 C6**   23 37N 58 36 E
Muscatine, *U.S.A.* **80 E9**   41 25N 91 3W
Musengezi = Unsengedsi ➜,
   Zimbabwe .... **55 F3**   15 43S 31 14 E
Musgrave Harbour, *Canada* **73 C9**   49 27N 53 58W
Musgrave Ranges, *Australia* **61 E5**   26 0S 132 0 E
Mushie, Dem. Rep. of the Congo **52 E3**   2 56S 16 55 E
Musi ➜, *Indonesia* .... **36 E2**   2 20S 104 56 E
Musina, *S. Africa* .... **57 C5**   22 20S 30 5 E
Muskeg ➜, *Canada* **70 A4**   60 20N 123 20W
Muskegon, *U.S.A.* **82 D2**   43 14N 86 16W
Muskegon ➜, *U.S.A.* **82 D2**   43 14N 86 21W
Muskegon Heights, *U.S.A.* **82 D2**   43 12N 86 16W
Muskogee, *U.S.A.* **81 H7**   35 45N 95 22W
Muskoka, L., *Canada* **84 B5**   45 0N 79 25W
Muskwa ➜, *Canada* **70 B4**   58 47N 122 48W
Muslimiyah, *Syria* .... **44 B3**   36 19N 37 12 E
Musofu, *Zambia* .... **55 E2**   13 30S 29 0 E
Musoma, *Tanzania* .... **54 C3**   1 30S 33 48 E
Musquaro, L., *Canada* **73 B7**   50 38N 61 5W
Musquodoboit Harbour, *Canada* **73 D7**   44 50N 63 9W
Musselburgh, *U.K.* **11 F5**   55 57N   3 2W
Musselshell ➜, *U.S.A.* **76 C10** 47 21N 107 57W
Mussoorie, *India* .... **42 D8**   30 27N 78 6 E
Mussuco, *Angola* .... **56 B2**   17 2S 19 3 E
Mustafakemalpaşa, *Turkey* .. **23 D13** 40 2N 28 24 E
Mustang, *Nepal* .... **43 E10** 29 10N 83 55 E
Musters, L., *Argentina* **96 F3**   45 20S 69 25W
Musudan, *N. Korea* .... **35 D15** 40 50N 129 43 E
Muswellbrook, *Australia* .... **63 E5**   32 16S 150 56 E
Mût, *Egypt* .... **51 C11** 25 28N 28 58 E
Mut, *Turkey* .... **44 B2**   36 40N 33 28 E
Mutanda, *Mozam.* .... **57 C5**   21 0S 33 34 E
Mutanda, *Zambia* .... **55 E2**   12 24S 26 13 E
Mutare, *Zimbabwe* .... **55 F3**   18 58S 32 38 E
Muting, *Indonesia* .... **37 F10** 7 23S 140 20 E
Mutki = Mirtağ, *Turkey* .... **44 B3**   38 23N 41 56 E
Mutoko, *Zimbabwe* .... **57 B5**   17 24S 32 13 E
Mutoray, *Russia* .... **29 C11** 60 56N 101 0 E
Mutshatsha, Dem. Rep. of
   the Congo* .... **55 E1**   10 35S 24 20 E
Mutsu, *Japan* .... **30 D10** 41 5N 140 55 E
Mutsu-Wan, *Japan* .... **30 D10** 41 5N 140 55 E
Muttaburra, *Australia* .... **62 C3**   22 38S 144 29 E
Mutton I., *Ireland* **10 D2**   52 49N   9 32W
Mutuáli, *Mozam.* .... **55 E4**   14 55S 37 0 E
Muweilih, *Egypt* .... **46 E3**   30 42N 34 19 E
Muy Muy, *Nic.* **88 D2**   12 39N 85 36W
Muyinga, *Burundi* .... **54 C3**   3 14S 30 33 E
Muynak, *Uzbekistan* .... **28 E6**   43 44N 59 10 E
Muzaffarabad, *Pakistan* .... **43 B5**   34 25N 73 30 E
Muzaffargarh, *Pakistan* .... **42 D4**   30 5N 71 14 E
Muzaffarnagar, *India* .... **42 E7**   29 26N 77 40 E
Muzaffarpur, *India* .... **43 F11** 26 7N 85 23 E
Muzhi, *Russia* .... **18 A11** 65 25N 64 40 E
Mvuma, *Zimbabwe* .... **55 F3**   19 16S 30 30 E
Mvurwi, *Zimbabwe* .... **55 F3**   17 0S 30 57 E
Mwabvi △, *Tanzania* .... **54 C3**   1 42S 35 0 E
Mwadui, *Tanzania* .... **54 C3**   3 26S 33 32 E
Mwambo, *Tanzania* .... **55 E5**   10 30S 40 22 E
Mwandi, *Zambia* .... **55 F1**   17 30S 24 51 E
Mwanza, *Dem. Rep. of the Congo* **54 D2**   7 55S 26 43 E
Mwanza, *Tanzania* .... **54 C3**   2 30S 32 58 E
Mwanza, *Zambia* .... **55 F1**   16 58S 24 28 E
Mwanza □, *Tanzania* .... **54 C3**   2 0S 33 0 E
Mwaya, *Tanzania* .... **55 D3**   9 32S 33 55 E
Mweelrea, *Ireland* **10 C2**   53 39N   9 49W
Mweka, *Dem. Rep. of the Congo* **52 E4**   4 50S 21 34 E
Mwenezi, *Zimbabwe* .... **55 G3**   21 15S 30 48 E
Mwenezi ➜, *Mozam.* .... **55 G3**   22 40S 31 50 E
Mwenga, Dem. Rep. of
   the Congo* .... **54 C2**   3 1S 28 28 E
Mweru, L., *Zambia* .... **55 D2**   9 0S 28 40 E
Mweru Wantipa △, *Zambia* **55 D2**   8 39S 29 25 E
Mweza Range, *Zimbabwe* .. **55 G3**   21 0S 30 0 E
Mwilambwe, Dem. Rep. of
   the Congo* .... **54 D2**   8 7S 25 5 E
Mwimbi, *Tanzania* .... **55 D3**   8 38S 31 39 E

Mwinilunga, *Zambia* .... **55 E1**   11 43S 24 25 E
My Tho, *Vietnam* .... **39 G6**   10 29N 106 23 E
Myajlar, *India* .... **42 F4**   26 15N 70 20 E
Myanaung, *Burma* .... **41 K19** 18 18N 95 22 E
Myanmar = Burma ■, *Asia* **41 J20** 21 0N 96 30 E
Myaungmya, *Burma* .... **41 L19** 16 30N 94 40 E
Mycenæ, *Greece* .... **23 F10** 37 39N 22 52 E
Myeik Kyunzu, *Burma* .... **39 G1**   11 30N 97 30 E
Myers Chuck, *U.S.A.* **70 B2**   55 44N 132 11W
Myerstown, *U.S.A.* **85 F8**   40 22N 76 19W
Myingyan, *Burma* .... **41 J19** 21 30N 95 20 E
Myitkyina, *Burma* .... **41 G20** 25 24N 97 26 E
Mykines, *Færoe Is.* **8 E9**   62 7N   7 35W
Mykolayiv, *Ukraine* .... **19 E5**   46 58N 32 0 E
Mymensingh, *Bangla.* .... **41 G17** 24 45N 90 24 E
Mynydd Du, *U.K.* **13 F4**   51 52N   3 50W
Mýrdalsjökull, *Iceland* **8 E4**   63 40N 19 6W
Myrtle Beach, *U.S.A.* **83 J6**   33 42N 78 53W
Myrtle Creek, *U.S.A.* **76 E2**   43 1N 123 17W
Myrtle Point, *U.S.A.* **76 E1**   43 4N 124 8W
Myrtou, *Cyprus* .... **25 D12** 35 18N 33 4 E
Mysia, *Turkey* .... **23 E12** 39 50N 27 0 E
Mysore = Karnataka □, *India* **40 N10** 13 15N 77 0 E
Mysore, *India* .... **40 N10** 12 17N 76 41 E
Mystic, *U.S.A.* **85 E13** 41 21N 71 58W
Myszków, *Poland* .... **17 C10** 50 45N 19 22 E
Mytishchi, *Russia* .... **18 C6**   55 50N 37 50 E
Mývatn, *Iceland* **8 D5**   65 36N 17 0W
Mzimba, *Malawi* .... **55 E3**   11 55S 33 39 E
Mzimkulu ➜, *S. Africa* .... **57 E5**   30 44S 30 28 E
Mzimvubu ➜, *S. Africa* .... **57 E4**   31 38S 29 33 E
Mzuzu, *Malawi* .... **55 E3**   11 30S 33 55 E

N

Na Hearadh = Harris, *U.K.* .. **11 D2**   57 50N   6 55W
Na Noi, *Thailand* .... **38 C3**   18 19N 100 43 E
Na Phao, *Laos* .... **38 D5**   17 35N 105 44 E
Na Sam, *Vietnam* .... **38 A6**   22 3N 106 37 E
Na San, *Vietnam* .... **38 B5**   21 12N 104 2 E
Na Thon, *Thailand* .... **39 b**   9 32N 99 56 E
Naab ➜, *Germany* .... **16 D6**   49 1N 12 2 E
Naantali, *Finland* .... **9 F19** 60 29N 22 2 E
Naas, *Ireland* **10 C5**   53 12N   6 40W
Nababeep, *S. Africa* .... **56 D2**   29 36S 17 46 E
Nabadwip = Navadwip, *India* **43 H13** 23 34N 88 20 E
Nabawa, *Australia* .... **61 E1**   28 30S 114 48 E
Nabberu, L., *Australia* .... **61 E3**   25 50S 120 30 E
Nabeul, *Tunisia* .... **51 A8**   36 30N 10 44 E
Nabha, *India* .... **42 D7**   30 26N 76 14 E
Nabid, *Iran* .... **45 D8**   29 40N 57 38 E
Nabire, *Indonesia* .... **37 E9**   3 15S 135 26 E
Nabisar, *Pakistan* .... **42 G3**   25 8N 69 40 E
Nabisipi ➜, *Canada* **73 B7**   50 14N 62 13W
Nabiswera, *Uganda* .... **54 B3**   1 27N 32 15 E
Nāblus = Nābulus, *West Bank* **46 C4**   32 14N 35 15 E
Naboomspruit, *S. Africa* .... **57 C4**   24 32S 28 40 E
Nābulus, *West Bank* .... **46 C4**   32 14N 35 15 E
Nacala, *Mozam.* .... **55 E5**   14 31S 40 34 E
Nacala-Velha, *Mozam.* .... **55 E5**   14 32S 40 34 E
Nacaome, *Honduras* **88 D2**   13 31N 87 30W
Nacaroa, *Mozam.* .... **55 E4**   14 22S 39 56 E
Naches, *U.S.A.* **76 C3**   46 44N 120 42W
Naches ➜, *U.S.A.* **78 D6**   46 38N 120 31W
Nachicapau, L., *Canada* **73 A6**   56 40N 68 5W
Nachingwea, *Tanzania* .... **55 E4**   10 23S 38 49 E
Nachna, *India* .... **42 F4**   27 34N 71 41 E
Nacimiento, L., *U.S.A.* **78 K6**   35 46N 120 53W
Naco, *Mexico* **86 A3**   31 20N 109 56W
Nacogdoches, *U.S.A.* **81 K7**   31 36N 94 39W
Nácori Chico, *Mexico* **86 B3**   29 39N 109 1W
Nacozari, *Mexico* **86 A3**   30 24N 109 39W
Nadi, *Fiji* .... **59 C7**   17 42S 177 20 E
Nadiad, *India* .... **42 H5**   22 41N 72 56 E
Nador, *Morocco* **50 B5**   35 14N   2 58W
Nadur, *Malta* .... **25 C1**   36 2N 14 18 E
Nadüshan, *Iran* .... **45 C7**   32 2N 53 35 E
Nadvirna, *Ukraine* .... **17 D13** 48 37N 24 30 E
Nadvoitsy, *Russia* .... **18 B5**   63 52N 34 14 E
Nadvornaya = Nadvirna, *Ukraine* **17 D13** 48 37N 24 30 E
Nadym, *Russia* .... **28 C8**   65 35N 72 42 E
Nadym ➜, *Russia* .... **28 C8**   66 12N 72 0 E
Nærbø, *Norway* .... **9 G11** 58 40N   5 39 E
Næstved, *Denmark* .... **9 J14** 55 13N 11 44 E
Naft-e Safīd, *Iran* .... **45 D6**   31 40N 49 17 E
Naftshahr, *Iran* .... **44 C5**   34 0N 45 30 E
Nafud Desert = An Nafüd,
   Si. Arabia .... **44 D4**   28 15N 41 0 E
Naga, *Phil.* .... **37 B6**   13 38N 123 15 E
Nagahama, *Japan* .... **31 G8**   35 23N 136 16 E
Nagai, *Japan* .... **30 E10** 38 6N 140 2 E
Nagaland □, *India* .... **41 G19** 26 0N 94 30 E
Nagano, *Japan* .... **31 F9**   36 40N 138 10 E
Nagano □, *Japan* .... **31 F9**   36 15N 138 0 E
Nagaoka, *Japan* .... **31 F9**   37 27N 138 51 E
Nagappattinam, *India* .... **40 P11** 10 46N 79 51 E
Nagar ➜, *Bangla.* .... **43 G13** 24 27N 89 12 E
Nagar Parkar, *Pakistan* .... **42 G4**   24 28N 70 46 E
Nagasaki, *Japan* .... **31 H4**   32 47N 129 50 E
Nagasaki □, *Japan* .... **31 H4**   32 50N 129 40 E
Nagato, *Japan* .... **31 G5**   34 19N 131 5 E
Nagaur, *India* .... **42 F5**   27 15N 73 45 E
Nagda, *India* .... **42 H6**   23 27N 75 25 E
Nagercoil, *India* .... **40 Q10** 8 12N 77 26 E
Nagina, *India* .... **43 E8**   29 30N 78 30 E
Nagineh, *Iran* .... **45 C8**   34 20N 57 15 E
Nagod, *India* .... **43 A6**   36 12N 74 42 E
Nagod, *India* .... **43 G9**   24 34N 80 36 E
Nagorno-Karabakh □, *Azerbaijan* **19 F8**   39 55N 46 45 E
Nagornyy, *Russia* .... **29 D13** 55 58N 124 57 E
Nagoya, *Japan* .... **31 G8**   35 10N 136 50 E
Nagpur, *India* .... **40 J11** 21 8N 79 10 E
Nagua, *Dom. Rep.* **89 C6**   19 23N 69 50W
Naguabo, *Puerto Rico* .... **89 d**   18 13N 65 44W
Nagykanizsa, *Hungary* .... **17 E9**   46 28N 17 0 E
Nagykőrös, *Hungary* .... **17 E10** 47 5N 19 48 E
Naha, *Japan* .... **31 L3**   26 13N 127 42 E
Nahanni △, *Canada* **70 A4**   61 36N 125 41W
Nahanni Butte, *Canada* **70 A4**   61 2N 123 31W
Nahargarh, Mad. P., *India* .. **42 G6**   24 10N 75 14 E
Nahargarh, Raj., *India* .... **42 G7**   24 55N 76 50 E
Nahariyya, *Israel* .... **44 C2**   33 1N 35 5 E

Nahāvand, Iran ... 45 C6 34 10N 48 22 E
Nahuelbuta △, Chile ... 94 D1 37 44S 72 57W
Nai Yong, Thailand ... 39 a 8 14N 98 22 E
Naicá, Mexico ... 86 B3 27 53N 105 31W
Naicam, Canada ... 71 C8 52 30N 104 30W
Naikoon △, Canada ... 70 C2 53 55N 131 55W
Naimisharanya, India ... 43 F9 27 21N 80 30 E
Nain, Canada ... 73 A7 56 34N 61 40W
Nā'īn, Iran ... 45 C7 32 54N 53 0 E
Naini Tal, India ... 43 E8 29 30N 79 30 E
Nainpur, India ... 40 H12 22 30N 80 10 E
Nainwa, India ... 42 G6 25 46N 75 51 E
Nairn, U.K. ... 11 D5 57 35N 3 53W
Nairobi, Kenya ... 54 C4 1 17S 36 48 E
Nairobi △, Kenya ... 54 C4 1 22S 36 50 E
Naissaar, Estonia ... 9 G21 59 34N 24 29 E
Naivasha, Kenya ... 54 C4 0 40S 36 30 E
Naivasha, L., Kenya ... 54 C4 0 48S 36 20 E
Najaf = An Najaf, Iraq ... 44 C5 32 3N 44 15 E
Najafābād, Iran ... 45 C6 32 40N 51 15 E
Najd, Si. Arabia ... 47 B3 26 30N 42 0 E
Najibabad, India ... 42 E8 29 40N 78 20 E
Najin, N. Korea ... 35 C16 42 12N 130 15 E
Najmah, Si. Arabia ... 45 E6 26 42N 50 6 E
Najrān, Si. Arabia ... 47 D3 17 34N 44 18 E
Naju, S. Korea ... 35 G14 35 3N 126 43 E
Nakadōri-Shima, Japan ... 31 H4 32 57N 129 4 E
Nakalagba, Dem. Rep. of
  the Congo ... 54 B2 2 50N 27 58 E
Nakaminato, Japan ... 31 F10 36 21N 140 36 E
Nakamura, Japan ... 31 H6 32 59N 132 56 E
Nakano, Japan ... 31 F9 36 45N 138 22 E
Nakano-Shima, Japan ... 31 K4 29 51N 129 52 E
Nakashibetsu, Japan ... 30 C12 43 33N 144 59 E
Nakfa, Eritrea ... 47 D2 16 40N 38 32 E
Nakha Yai, Ko, Thailand ... 39 a 8 3N 98 28 E
Nakhichevan = Naxçıvan,
  Azerbaijan ... 19 G8 39 12N 45 15 E
Nakhichevan Rep. = Naxçıvan □,
  Azerbaijan ... 19 G8 39 25N 45 26 E
Nakhl, Egypt ... 46 F2 29 55N 33 43 E
Nakhl-e Taqī, Iran ... 45 E7 27 28N 52 36 E
Nakhodka, Russia ... 29 E14 42 53N 132 54 E
Nakhon Nayok, Thailand ... 38 E3 14 12N 101 13 E
Nakhon Pathom, Thailand ... 38 F3 13 49N 100 3 E
Nakhon Phanom, Thailand ... 38 D5 17 23N 104 43 E
Nakhon Ratchasima, Thailand ... 38 E4 14 59N 102 12 E
Nakhon Sawan, Thailand ... 38 E3 15 35N 100 10 E
Nakhon Si Thammarat, Thailand ... 39 H3 8 29N 100 0 E
Nakhon Thai, Thailand ... 38 D3 17 5N 100 44 E
Nakhtarana, India ... 42 H3 23 20N 69 15 E
Nakina, Canada ... 72 B2 50 10N 86 40W
Nakodar, India ... 42 D6 31 8N 75 31 E
Nakskov, Denmark ... 9 J14 54 50N 11 8 E
Naktong →, S. Korea ... 35 G15 35 7N 128 57 E
Nakuru, Kenya ... 54 C4 0 15S 36 4 E
Nakuru, L., Kenya ... 54 C4 0 23S 36 5 E
Nakusp, Canada ... 70 C5 50 20N 117 45W
Nal, Pakistan ... 42 F2 27 40N 66 12 E
Nal →, Pakistan ... 42 G1 25 20N 65 30 E
Nalázi, Mozam. ... 57 C5 24 3S 33 20 E
Nalchik, Russia ... 19 F7 43 30N 43 33 E
Nalgonda, India ... 40 L11 17 6N 79 15 E
Nalhati, India ... 43 G12 24 17N 87 52 E
Naliya, India ... 42 H3 23 16N 68 50 E
Nallamalai Hills, India ... 40 M11 15 30N 78 50 E
Nam Can, Vietnam ... 39 H5 8 46N 104 59 E
Nam-ch'on, N. Korea ... 35 E14 38 15N 126 26 E
Nam Co, China ... 32 C4 30 30N 90 45 E
Nam Dinh, Vietnam ... 38 B6 20 25N 106 5 E
Nam Du, Hon, Vietnam ... 39 H5 9 41N 104 21 E
Nam Nao △, Thailand ... 38 D3 16 44N 101 32 E
Nam Ngum Dam, Laos ... 38 C4 18 35N 102 34 E
Nam-Phan, Vietnam ... 39 G6 10 30N 106 0 E
Nam Phong, Thailand ... 38 D4 16 42N 102 52 E
Nam Tha, Laos ... 38 B3 20 58N 101 30 E
Nam Tok, Thailand ... 38 E2 14 21N 99 4 E
Namacunde, Angola ... 56 B2 17 18S 15 50 E
Namacurra, Mozam. ... 57 B6 17 30S 36 50 E
Namak, Daryācheh-ye, Iran ... 45 C7 34 30N 52 0 E
Namak, Kavir-e, Iran ... 45 C8 34 30N 57 30 E
Namakzār, Daryācheh-ye, Iran ... 45 C9 34 0N 60 30 E
Namaland, Namibia ... 56 C2 26 0S 17 0 E
Namangan, Uzbekistan ... 28 E8 41 0N 71 40 E
Namapa, Mozam. ... 55 E4 13 43S 39 50 E
Namaqualand, S. Africa ... 56 E2 30 0S 17 25 E
Namasagali, Uganda ... 54 B3 1 2N 33 0 E
Namber, Indonesia ... 37 E8 1 2S 134 49 E
Nambour, Australia ... 63 D5 26 32S 152 58 E
Nambucca Heads, Australia ... 63 E5 30 37S 153 0 E
Nambung △, Australia ... 61 F2 30 30S 115 5 E
Namcha Barwa, China ... 32 D4 29 40N 95 10 E
Namche Bazar, Nepal ... 43 F12 27 51N 86 47 E
Namchonjŏm = Nam-ch'on,
  N. Korea ... 35 E14 38 15N 126 26 E
Namecunda, Mozam. ... 55 E4 14 54S 37 37 E
Nameponda, Mozam. ... 55 E4 15 50S 39 50 E
Nametil, Mozam. ... 55 F4 15 40S 39 21 E
Namew L., Canada ... 71 C8 54 14N 101 56W
Namgia, India ... 43 D8 31 48N 78 40 E
Namib Desert, Namibia ... 56 C2 22 30S 15 0 E
Namib-Naukluft △, Namibia ... 56 C2 24 40S 15 16 E
Namibe, Angola ... 53 H2 15 7S 12 11 E
Namibe □, Angola ... 56 B1 16 35S 12 30 E
Namibia ■, Africa ... 56 C2 22 0S 18 9 E
Namibwoestyn = Namib Desert,
  Namibia ... 56 C2 22 30S 15 0 E
Namlea, Indonesia ... 37 E7 3 18S 127 5 E
Namoi →, Australia ... 63 E4 30 12S 149 30 E
Nampa, U.S.A. ... 76 E5 43 34N 116 34W
Namp'o, N. Korea ... 35 E13 38 52N 125 10 E
Nampō-Shotō, Japan ... 31 J10 32 0N 140 0 E
Nampula, Mozam. ... 55 F4 15 6S 39 15 E
Namrole, Indonesia ... 37 E7 3 46S 126 46 E
Namse Shankou, China ... 41 E13 30 0N 82 25 E
Namsen →, Norway ... 8 D14 64 28N 11 37 E
Namsos, Norway ... 8 D14 64 29N 11 30 E
Namtok Chat Trakan △, Thailand ... 38 D3 17 17N 100 40 E
Namtok Mae Surin △, Thailand ... 38 C2 18 55N 98 2 E
Namtsy, Russia ... 29 C13 62 43N 129 37 E
Namtu, Burma ... 41 H20 23 5N 97 28 E
Namtumbo, Tanzania ... 55 E4 10 30S 36 4 E
Namu, Canada ... 70 C3 51 52N 127 50W
Namur, Belgium ... 15 D4 50 27N 4 52 E
Namur □, Belgium ... 15 D4 50 17N 5 0 E
Namutoni, Namibia ... 56 B2 18 49S 16 55 E
Namwala, Zambia ... 55 F2 15 44S 26 30 E

Namwŏn, S. Korea ... 35 G14 35 23N 127 23 E
Nan, Thailand ... 38 C3 18 48N 100 46 E
Nan →, Thailand ... 38 E3 15 42N 100 9 E
Nan-ch'ang = Nanchang, China ... 33 D6 28 42N 115 55 E
Nanaimo, Canada ... 70 D4 49 10N 124 0W
Nanam, N. Korea ... 35 D15 41 44N 129 40 E
Nanango, Australia ... 63 D5 26 40S 152 0 E
Nanao, Japan ... 31 F8 37 0N 137 0 E
Nanchang, China ... 33 D6 28 42N 115 55 E
Nanching = Nanjing, China ... 33 C6 32 2N 118 47 E
Nanchong, China ... 32 C5 30 43N 106 2 E
Nancy, France ... 20 B7 48 42N 6 12 E
Nanda Devi, India ... 43 D8 30 23N 79 59 E
Nanda Kot, India ... 43 D9 30 17N 80 5 E
Nandan, Japan ... 31 G7 34 10N 134 42 E
Nanded, India ... 40 K10 19 10N 77 20 E
Nandewar Ra., Australia ... 63 E5 30 15S 150 35 E
Nandi = Nadi, Fiji ... 59 C7 17 42S 177 20 E
Nandigram, India ... 43 H12 22 1N 87 58 E
Nandurbar, India ... 40 J9 21 20N 74 15 E
Nandyal, India ... 40 M11 15 30N 78 30 E
Nanga-Eboko, Cameroon ... 52 D2 4 41N 12 22 E
Nanga Parbat, Pakistan ... 43 B6 35 10N 74 35 E
Nangade, Mozam. ... 55 E4 11 5S 39 36 E
Nangapinoh, Indonesia ... 36 E4 0 20S 111 44 E
Nangarhār □, Afghan. ... 40 B7 34 20N 70 0 E
Nangatayap, Indonesia ... 36 E4 1 32S 110 34 E
Nangeya Mts., Uganda ... 54 B3 3 30N 33 30 E
Nangong, China ... 34 F8 37 23N 115 22 E
Nanhuang, China ... 35 F11 36 58N 121 48 E
Nanjeko, Zambia ... 55 F1 15 31S 23 30 E
Nanjing, China ... 33 C6 32 2N 118 47 E
Nanjirinji, Tanzania ... 55 D4 9 41S 39 5 E
Nankana Sahib, Pakistan ... 42 D5 31 27N 73 38 E
Nanking = Nanjing, China ... 33 C6 32 2N 118 47 E
Nankoku, Japan ... 31 H6 33 39N 133 44 E
Nanlang, China ... 35 G10 22 30N 113 32 E
Nanning, China ... 32 D5 22 48N 108 20 E
Nannup, Australia ... 61 F2 33 59S 115 48 E
Nanpara, India ... 43 F9 27 52N 81 33 E
Nanpi, China ... 34 E9 38 2N 116 45 E
Nanping, China ... 33 D6 26 38N 118 10 E
Nanripe, Mozam. ... 55 E4 13 52S 38 52 E
Nansei-Shotō = Ryūkyū-rettō,
  Japan ... 31 M3 26 0N 126 0 E
Nansen Basin, Arctic ... 4 A10 84 0N 50 0 E
Nansen Cordillera, Arctic ... 4 A 87 0N 90 0 E
Nansen Sd., Canada ... 4 A3 81 0N 91 0W
Nansha, China ... 33 F10 22 45N 113 34 E
Nanshan I., S. China Sea ... 36 B5 10 45N 115 49 E
Nansio, Tanzania ... 54 C3 2 3S 33 4 E
Nantes, France ... 20 C3 47 12N 1 33W
Nanticoke, U.S.A. ... 85 E8 41 12N 76 0W
Nanton, Canada ... 70 C6 50 21N 113 46W
Nantong, China ... 33 C7 32 1N 120 52 E
Nantou, China ... 33 F10 22 32N 113 56 E
Nantucket I., U.S.A. ... 82 E10 41 16N 70 5W
Nantwich, U.K. ... 12 D5 53 4N 2 31W
Nanty Glo, U.S.A. ... 84 F6 40 28N 78 50W
Nanuque, Brazil ... 93 G10 17 50S 40 21W
Nanusa, Kepulauan, Indonesia ... 37 D7 4 45N 127 1 E
Nanutarra Roadhouse, Australia ... 60 D2 22 32S 115 30 E
Nanyang, China ... 34 H7 33 11N 112 30 E
Nanyuki, Kenya ... 54 B4 0 2N 37 4 E
Nao, C. de la, Spain ... 21 C6 38 44N 0 14 E
Naococane, L., Canada ... 73 B5 52 50N 70 45W
Napa, U.S.A. ... 78 G4 38 18N 122 17W
Napa →, U.S.A. ... 78 G4 38 10N 122 19W
Napanee, Canada ... 84 B8 44 15N 77 0W
Napanoch, U.S.A. ... 85 E10 41 44N 74 22W
Nape, Laos ... 38 C5 18 18N 105 6 E
Nape Pass = Keo Neua, Deo,
  Vietnam ... 38 C5 18 23N 105 10 E
Napier, N.Z. ... 59 H6 39 30S 176 56 E
Napier Broome B., Australia ... 60 B4 14 2S 126 37 E
Napier Pen., Australia ... 62 A2 12 4S 135 43 E
Napierville, Canada ... 85 A11 45 11N 73 25W
Naples = Nápoli, Italy ... 22 D6 40 50N 14 15 E
Naples, U.S.A. ... 83 M5 26 8N 81 48W
Napo →, Peru ... 92 D4 3 20S 72 40W
Napoleon, N. Dak., U.S.A. ... 80 B5 46 30N 99 46W
Napoleon, Ohio, U.S.A. ... 82 E3 41 23N 84 8W
Nápoli, Italy ... 22 D6 40 50N 14 15 E
Napopo, Dem. Rep. of the Congo ... 54 B2 4 15N 28 0 E
Naqb, Ra's an, Jordan ... 46 F4 30 0N 35 29 E
Naqqāsh, Iran ... 45 C6 35 40N 49 6 E
Nara, Japan ... 31 G7 34 40N 135 49 E
Nara, Mali ... 50 E4 15 10N 7 20W
Nara □, Japan ... 31 G8 34 30N 136 0 E
Nara Canal, Pakistan ... 42 G3 24 30N 69 20 E
Nara Visa, U.S.A. ... 81 H3 35 37N 103 6W
Naracoorte, Australia ... 63 F3 36 58S 140 45 E
Naradhan, Australia ... 63 E4 33 34S 146 17 E
Naraini, India ... 43 G9 25 11N 80 29 E
Narasapur, India ... 41 L12 16 26N 81 40 E
Narathiwat, Thailand ... 39 J3 6 30N 101 48 E
Narayanganj, Bangla. ... 41 H17 23 40N 90 33 E
Narayanpet, India ... 40 L10 16 45N 77 30 E
Narberth, U.K. ... 13 F3 51 47N 4 44W
Narbonne, France ... 20 E5 43 11N 3 0 E
Nardin, Iran ... 45 B7 37 3N 55 59 E
Nardò, Italy ... 23 D8 40 11N 18 2 E
Narembeen, Australia ... 61 F2 32 7S 118 24 E
Narendranagar, India ... 42 D8 30 2N 78 18 E
Nares Str., Arctic ... 66 A13 80 0N 70 0W
Narew →, Poland ... 17 B11 52 26N 20 41 E
Nari →, Pakistan ... 42 F2 28 0N 67 40 E
Narin, Afghan. ... 40 A6 36 5N 69 0 E
Narindra, Helodranon' i, Madag. ... 57 A8 14 55N 47 30 E
Narita, Japan ... 31 G10 35 47N 140 19 E
Nariva Swamp, Trin. & Tob. ... 93 K15 10 26N 61 4W
Narmada →, India ... 42 J5 21 38N 72 36 E
Narmland, Sweden ... 9 F15 60 0N 13 30 E
Narnaul, India ... 42 E7 28 5N 76 11 E
Narodnaya, Russia ... 18 A10 65 5N 59 58 E
Narok, Kenya ... 54 C4 1 55S 35 52 E
Narooma, Australia ... 63 F5 36 14S 150 4 E
Narowal, Pakistan ... 42 C6 32 6N 74 52 E
Narrabri, Australia ... 63 E4 30 19S 149 46 E
Narran →, Australia ... 63 D4 28 37S 148 12 E
Narrandera, Australia ... 63 E4 34 42S 146 31 E
Narrogin, Australia ... 61 F2 32 58S 117 14 E
Narromine, Australia ... 63 E4 32 12S 148 12 E
Narrow Hills △, Canada ... 71 C8 54 0N 104 37W
Narsimhapur, India ... 43 H8 22 54N 79 14 E
Narsinghgarh, India ... 42 H7 23 45N 76 40 E

Naruto, Japan ... 31 G7 34 11N 134 37 E
Narva, Estonia ... 18 C4 59 23N 28 12 E
Narva →, Russia ... 9 G22 59 27N 28 2 E
Narva Bay, Estonia ... 9 G19 59 35N 27 35 E
Narvik, Norway ... 8 B17 68 28N 17 26 E
Narwana, India ... 42 E7 29 39N 76 6 E
Naryan-Mar, Russia ... 18 A9 67 42N 53 12 E
Narym, Russia ... 28 D9 59 0N 81 30 E
Naryn, Kyrgyzstan ... 28 E8 41 26N 75 58 E
Nasa, Norway ... 8 C16 66 29N 15 23 E
Naseby, N.Z. ... 59 L3 45 1S 170 10 E
Naselle, U.S.A. ... 78 D3 46 22N 123 49W
Naser, Buheirat en, Egypt ... 51 D12 23 0N 32 30 E
Nashua, Mont., U.S.A. ... 76 B10 48 8N 106 22W
Nashua, N.H., U.S.A. ... 85 D13 42 45N 71 28W
Nashville, Ark., U.S.A. ... 81 J8 33 57N 93 51W
Nashville, Ga., U.S.A. ... 83 K4 31 12N 83 15W
Nashville, Tenn., U.S.A. ... 83 G2 36 10N 86 47W
Nasik, India ... 40 K8 19 58N 73 50 E
Nasirabad, India ... 42 F6 26 15N 74 45 E
Nasirabad, Pakistan ... 42 E3 28 23N 68 24 E
Nasiriyah = An Nāşiriyah, Iraq ... 44 D5 31 0N 46 15 E
Naşrābād, Iran ... 45 C6 34 8N 51 26 E
Naşrīān-e Pā'īn, Iran ... 44 C5 32 52N 46 52 E
Nass →, Canada ... 70 C3 55 0N 129 40W
Nassau, Bahamas ... 88 A4 25 5N 77 20W
Nassau, U.S.A. ... 85 D11 42 31N 73 37W
Nassau, B., Chile ... 96 H3 55 20S 68 0W
Nasser, L. = Naser, Buheirat en,
  Egypt ... 51 D12 23 0N 32 30 E
Nässjö, Sweden ... 9 H16 57 39N 14 42 E
Nastapoka →, Canada ... 72 A4 56 55N 76 33W
Nastapoka, Is., Canada ... 72 A4 56 55N 76 50W
Nata, Botswana ... 56 C4 20 12S 26 12 E
Nata →, Botswana ... 56 C4 20 14S 26 10 E
Natal, Brazil ... 93 E11 5 47S 35 13W
Natal, Indonesia ... 36 D1 0 35N 99 7 E
Natal, S. Africa ... 53 K6 28 30S 30 30 E
Natal Drakensberg △, S. Africa ... 57 D4 29 27S 29 30 E
Naţanz, Iran ... 45 C6 33 30N 51 55 E
Natashquan, Canada ... 73 B7 50 14N 61 46W
Natashquan →, Canada ... 73 B7 50 7N 61 50W
Natchez, U.S.A. ... 81 K9 31 34N 91 24W
Natchitoches, U.S.A. ... 81 K8 31 46N 93 5W
Nathalia, Australia ... 63 F4 36 1S 145 13 E
Nathdwara, India ... 42 G5 24 55N 73 50 E
Nati, Pta., Spain ... 24 A10 40 3N 3 50 E
Natimuk, Australia ... 63 F3 36 42S 142 0 E
Nation →, Canada ... 70 B4 55 30N 123 32W
National City, U.S.A. ... 79 N9 32 41N 117 6W
Natitingou, Benin ... 50 F6 10 20N 1 26 E
Natividad, I., Mexico ... 86 B1 27 50N 115 10W
Natkyizin, Burma ... 38 E1 14 57N 97 59 E
Natron, L., Tanzania ... 54 C4 2 20S 36 0 E
Natrona Heights, U.S.A. ... 84 F5 40 37N 79 44W
Natukanaoka Pan, Namibia ... 56 B2 18 40S 15 45 E
Natuna Besar, Kepulauan,
  Indonesia ... 36 D3 4 0N 108 15 E
Natuna Is. = Natuna Besar,
  Kepulauan, Indonesia ... 36 D3 4 0N 108 15 E
Natuna Selatan, Kepulauan,
  Indonesia ... 36 D3 2 45N 109 0 E
Natural Bridge, U.S.A. ... 85 B9 44 5N 75 30W
Natural Bridges △, U.S.A. ... 77 H8 37 36N 110 1W
Naturaliste, C., Australia ... 63 G4 40 50S 148 15 E
Nau Qala, Afghan. ... 42 B3 34 5N 68 5 E
Naugatuck, U.S.A. ... 85 E11 41 30N 73 3W
Naujaat = Repulse Bay, Canada ... 69 B11 66 30N 86 30W
Naumburg, Germany ... 16 C6 51 9N 11 47 E
Nā'ūr at Tunayb, Jordan ... 46 D4 31 48N 35 57 E
Nauru ■, Pac. Oc. ... 64 H8 1 0S 166 0 E
Naushahra = Nowshera, Pakistan ... 40 C8 34 0N 72 0 E
Naushahro, Pakistan ... 42 F3 26 50N 68 7 E
Naushon I., U.S.A. ... 85 E14 41 29N 70 45W
Nauta, Peru ... 92 D4 4 31S 73 35W
Nautanwa, India ... 41 F13 27 20N 83 25 E
Nautla, Mexico ... 87 C5 20 13N 96 47W
Nava, Mexico ... 86 B4 28 25N 100 46W
Navadwip, India ... 43 H13 23 34N 88 20 E
Navahrudak, Belarus ... 17 B13 53 40N 25 50 E
Navajo Reservoir, U.S.A. ... 77 H10 36 48N 107 36W
Navalmoral de la Mata, Spain ... 21 C3 39 52N 5 33W
Navan = An Uaimh, Ireland ... 10 C5 53 39N 6 41W
Navarin, Mys, Russia ... 4 C18 62 15N 179 5 E
Navarino, I., Chile ... 96 H3 55 0S 67 40W
Navarra □, Spain ... 21 A5 42 40N 1 40W
Navarre, U.S.A. ... 84 F3 40 43N 81 31W
Navasota, U.S.A. ... 81 K6 30 23N 96 5W
Navassa I., W. Indies ... 89 C5 18 30N 75 0W
Naver →, U.K. ... 11 C4 58 32N 4 14W
Navibandar, India ... 42 J3 21 26N 69 48 E
Navidad, Chile ... 94 C1 33 57S 71 50W
Navirai, Brazil ... 95 A5 23 8S 54 13W
Naviraí, India ... 41 H17 23 40N 90 28 E
Năvodari, Romania ... 17 F15 44 19N 28 36 E
Navoi = Nawoiy, Uzbekistan ... 28 E7 40 9N 65 22 E
Navojoa, Mexico ... 86 B3 27 0N 109 30W
Navolato, Mexico ... 86 C3 24 47N 107 42W
Návpaktos, Greece ... 23 E9 38 24N 21 50 E
Návplion, Greece ... 23 F10 37 33N 22 50 E
Navsari, India ... 40 J8 20 57N 72 59 E
Nawa Kot, Pakistan ... 42 E4 28 21N 71 24 E
Nawab Khan, Pakistan ... 42 D3 30 17N 69 12 E
Nawabganj, Ut. P., India ... 43 F9 26 56N 81 14 E
Nawabganj, Ut. P., India ... 43 E8 28 32N 79 40 E
Nawabshah, Pakistan ... 42 F3 26 15N 68 25 E
Nawada, India ... 43 G11 24 50N 85 33 E
Nawakot, Nepal ... 43 F11 27 55N 85 10 E
Nawalgarh, India ... 42 F6 27 50N 75 15 E
Nawanshahr, India ... 43 C6 32 33N 74 48 E
Nawoiy, Uzbekistan ... 28 E7 40 9N 65 22 E
Naxçıvan, Azerbaijan ... 19 G8 39 25N 45 26 E
Naxçıvan □, Azerbaijan ... 19 G8 39 25N 45 26 E
Náxos, Greece ... 23 F11 37 8N 25 25 E
Nay, Mui, Vietnam ... 38 B3 12 55N 109 23 E
Nay Band, Būshehr, Iran ... 45 E7 27 20N 52 40 E
Nāy Band, Khorāsān, Iran ... 45 C8 32 20N 57 34 E
Nayakhan, Russia ... 29 C16 61 56N 159 0 E
Nayarit □, Mexico ... 86 C4 22 0N 105 0W
Nayoro, Japan ... 30 B11 44 21N 142 28 E
Nayyāl, W. →, Si. Arabia ... 44 D3 28 35N 39 4 E
Nazaré, Brazil ... 93 F11 13 2S 39 0W
Nazareth = Nazerat, Israel ... 46 C4 32 42N 35 17 E

Nazareth, U.S.A. ... 85 F9 40 44N 75 19W
Nazas, Mexico ... 86 B4 25 10N 104 6W
Nazas →, Mexico ... 86 B4 25 35N 103 25W
Nazca, Peru ... 92 F4 14 50S 74 57W
Naze, The, U.K. ... 13 F9 51 53N 1 18 E
Nazerat, Israel ... 46 C4 32 42N 35 17 E
Nāzik, Iran ... 44 B5 39 1N 45 4 E
Nazilli, Turkey ... 23 F13 37 55N 28 15 E
Nazko, Canada ... 70 C4 53 1N 123 37W
Nazko →, Canada ... 70 C4 53 7N 123 34W
Nazret, Ethiopia ... 47 F2 8 32N 39 22 E
Nazwa, Oman ... 47 C6 22 56N 57 32 E
Nchanga, Zambia ... 55 E2 12 30S 27 49 E
Ncheu, Malawi ... 55 E3 14 50S 34 47 E
Ndala, Tanzania ... 54 C3 4 45S 33 15 E
Ndalatando, Angola ... 52 F2 9 12S 14 48 E
Ndareda, Tanzania ... 54 C4 4 12S 35 30 E
Ndélé, C.A.R. ... 52 C4 8 25N 20 36 E
Ndjamena, Chad ... 51 F8 12 10N 14 59 E
Ndola, Zambia ... 55 E2 13 0S 28 34 E
Ndoto Mts., Kenya ... 54 B4 2 0N 37 0 E
Nduguti, Tanzania ... 54 C3 4 18S 34 41 E
Ndumu △, S. Africa ... 57 D5 26 52S 32 15 E
Neagh, Lough, U.K. ... 10 B5 54 37N 6 25W
Neah Bay, U.S.A. ... 78 B2 48 22N 124 37W
Neale, L., Australia ... 60 D5 24 15S 130 0 E
Neápolis, Greece ... 25 D7 35 15N 25 37 E
Near Is., U.S.A. ... 68 C1 52 30N 174 0 E
Neath, U.K. ... 13 F4 51 39N 3 48W
Neath Port Talbot □, U.K. ... 13 F4 51 42N 3 45W
Nebine Cr. →, Australia ... 63 D4 29 27S 146 56 E
Nebitdag, Turkmenistan ... 19 G9 39 30N 54 22 E
Nebo, Australia ... 62 K7 21 42S 148 42 E
Nebraska □, U.S.A. ... 80 E5 41 30N 99 30W
Nebraska City, U.S.A. ... 80 E7 40 41N 95 52W
Nébrodi, Monti, Italy ... 22 F6 37 54N 14 35 E
Necedah, U.S.A. ... 80 C9 44 2N 90 4W
Nechako →, Canada ... 70 C4 53 55N 122 42W
Neches →, U.S.A. ... 81 L8 29 58N 93 51W
Neckar →, Germany ... 16 D5 49 27N 8 29 E
Necochea, Argentina ... 94 D4 38 30S 58 50W
Needles, Canada ... 70 D5 49 53N 118 7W
Needles, U.S.A. ... 79 L12 34 51N 114 37W
Needles, The, U.K. ... 13 G6 50 39N 1 35W
Ñeembucú □, Paraguay ... 94 B4 27 0S 58 0W
Neemuch = Nimach, India ... 42 G6 24 30N 74 56 E
Neenah, U.S.A. ... 82 C1 44 11N 88 28W
Neepawa, Canada ... 71 C9 50 15N 99 30W
Neftçala, Azerbaijan ... 19 G8 39 19N 49 12 E
Neftekumsk, Russia ... 19 F7 44 46N 44 50 E
Nefyn, U.K. ... 12 E3 52 56N 4 31W
Negapatam = Nagappattinam,
  India ... 40 P11 10 46N 79 51 E
Negara, Indonesia ... 37 J17 8 22S 114 37 E
Negaunee, U.S.A. ... 82 B2 46 30N 87 36W
Negele, Ethiopia ... 47 F2 5 20N 39 36 E
Negombo, Sri Lanka ... 40 R11 7 12N 79 50 E
Negotin, Serbia & M. ... 23 B10 44 16N 22 37 E
Negra, Pta., Peru ... 92 E2 6 6S 81 10W
Negrais, C. = Maudin Sun, Burma ... 41 M19 16 0N 94 30 E
Negril, Jamaica ... 88 a 18 22N 78 20W
Negro →, Argentina ... 96 E4 41 2S 62 47W
Negro →, Brazil ... 92 D7 3 0S 60 0W
Negro →, Uruguay ... 95 C4 33 24S 58 22W
Negros, Phil. ... 37 C6 9 30N 122 40 E
Neguac, Canada ... 73 C6 47 15N 65 5W
Nehalem →, U.S.A. ... 78 E3 45 40N 123 56W
Nehāvand, Iran ... 45 C6 35 56N 49 31 E
Nehbandān, Iran ... 45 D9 31 35N 60 5 E
Nei Monggol Zizhiqu □, China ... 34 D7 42 0N 112 0 E
Neijiang, China ... 32 D5 29 35N 104 55 E
Neillsville, U.S.A. ... 80 C9 44 34N 90 36W
Neilton, U.S.A. ... 78 C3 47 25N 123 53W
Neiqiu, China ... 34 F8 37 15N 114 30 E
Neiva, Colombia ... 92 C3 2 56N 75 18W
Neixiang, China ... 34 H6 33 10N 111 52 E
Nejanilini L., Canada ... 71 B9 59 33N 97 48W
Nejd = Najd, Si. Arabia ... 47 B3 26 30N 42 0 E
Nekā, Iran ... 45 B7 36 39N 53 19 E
Nekemte, Ethiopia ... 47 F2 9 4N 36 30 E
Neksø, Denmark ... 9 J16 55 4N 15 8 E
Nelia, Australia ... 62 C3 20 39S 142 12 E
Neligh, U.S.A. ... 80 D5 42 8N 98 2W
Nelkan, Russia ... 29 D14 57 40N 136 4 E
Nellore, India ... 40 M11 14 27N 79 59 E
Nelson, Canada ... 70 D5 49 30N 117 20W
Nelson, N.Z. ... 59 J4 41 18S 173 16 E
Nelson, U.K. ... 12 D5 53 50N 2 13W
Nelson, Ariz., U.S.A. ... 77 J7 35 31N 113 19W
Nelson, Nev., U.S.A. ... 79 K12 35 42N 114 50W
Nelson →, Canada ... 71 C9 54 33N 98 2W
Nelson, C., Australia ... 63 F3 38 26S 141 32 E
Nelson, Estrecho, Chile ... 96 G2 51 30S 75 0W
Nelson Forks, Canada ... 70 B4 59 30N 124 0W
Nelson House, Canada ... 71 B9 55 47N 98 51W
Nelson L., Canada ... 71 B8 55 48N 100 7W
Nelson Lakes △, N.Z. ... 59 J4 41 55S 172 44 E
Nelspoort, S. Africa ... 56 E3 32 7S 23 0 E
Nelspruit, S. Africa ... 57 D5 25 29S 30 59 E
Néma, Mauritania ... 50 E4 16 40N 7 15W
Neman = Nemunas →, Lithuania ... 9 J19 55 25N 21 10 E
Neman, Russia ... 9 J20 55 2N 22 2 E
Nemiscau, Canada ... 72 B4 51 18N 76 54W
Nemiscau, L., Canada ... 72 B4 51 25N 76 40W
Nemunas →, Lithuania ... 9 J19 55 25N 21 10 E
Nemuro, Japan ... 30 C12 43 20N 145 35 E
Nemuro-Kaikyō, China ... 30 C12 43 30N 145 30 E
Nen Jiang →, China ... 35 B13 45 28N 124 30 E
Nenasi, Malaysia ... 39 L4 3 9N 103 23 E
Nene →, U.K. ... 13 E8 52 49N 0 11 E
Nenjiang, China ... 33 B7 49 10N 125 10 E
Neno, Malawi ... 55 F3 15 25S 34 40 E
Neodesha, U.S.A. ... 81 G7 37 25N 95 41W
Neosho, U.S.A. ... 81 G7 36 52N 94 22W
Neosho →, U.S.A. ... 81 H7 36 48N 95 18W
Nepal ■, Asia ... 43 F11 28 0N 84 30 E
Nepalganj, Nepal ... 43 E9 28 5N 81 40 E
Nepalganj Road, India ... 43 E9 28 1N 81 41 E
Nephi, U.S.A. ... 76 G8 39 43N 111 50W
Nephin, Ireland ... 10 B2 54 1N 9 22W
Neptune, U.S.A. ... 85 F10 40 13N 74 2W
Nerang, Australia ... 63 D5 27 58S 153 20 E
Nerchinsk, Russia ... 29 D12 52 0N 116 39 E

Néret, L., *Canada* 73 B5   54 45N   70 44W
Neretva ➤, *Croatia* .... 23 C7   43 1N   17 27 E
Neringa, *Lithuania* .... 9 J19   55 20N   21 5 E
Neris ➤, *Lithuania* .... 9 J21   55 8N   24 16 E
Neryungri, *Russia* .... 29 D13   57 38N 124 28 E
Nescopeck, *U.S.A.* 85 E8   41 3N   76 12W
Ness, L., *U.K.* 11 D4   57 15N   4 32W
Ness City, *U.S.A.* 80 F5   38 27N   99 54W
Nesterov, *Ukraine* .... 17 C12   50 4N   23 58 E
Nesvizh = Nyasvizh, *Belarus* .. 17 B14   53 14N   26 38 E
Netanya, *Israel* .... 46 C3   32 20N   34 51 E
Netarhat, *India* .... 43 H11   23 29N   84 16 E
Nete ➤, *Belgium* .... 15 C4   51 7N   4 14 E
Netherdale, *Australia* .... 62 K6   21 10S 148 33 E
Netherlands ■, *Europe* .... 15 C5   52 0N   5 30 E
Netherlands Antilles ⊘, *W. Indies* 92 A5   12 15N   69 0W
Netrang, *India* .... 42 J5   21 39N   73 21 E
Nettilling L., *Canada* 69 B12   66 30N   71 0W
Netzahualcoyotl, Presa, *Mexico* . 87 D6   17 10N   93 30W
Neubrandenburg, *Germany* .. 16 B7   53 33N   13 15 E
Neuchâtel, *Switz.* .... 20 C7   47 0N   6 55 E
Neuchâtel, Lac de, *Switz.* ... 20 C7   46 53N   6 50 E
Neufchâteau, *Belgium* .... 15 E5   49 50N   5 25 E
Neumünster, *Germany* .... 16 A5   54 4N   9 58 E
Neunkirchen, *Germany* .... 16 D4   49 20N   7 9 E
Neuquén, *Argentina* 96 D3   38 55S   68 0W
Neuquén ⊘, *Argentina* 94 D2   38 0S   69 50W
Neuruppin, *Germany* .... 16 B7   52 55N   12 48 E
Neuse ➤, *U.S.A.* 83 H7   35 6N   76 29W
Neusiedler See, *Austria* .... 17 E9   47 50N   16 47 E
Neustrelitz, *Germany* .... 16 B7   53 21N   13 4 E
Neva ➤, *Russia* .... 18 C5   59 50N   30 30 E
Nevada, Iowa, *U.S.A.* 80 D8   42 1N   93 27W
Nevada, Mo., *U.S.A.* 81 G7   37 51N   94 22W
Nevada ⊘, *U.S.A.* 76 G5   39 0N 117 0W
Nevada City, *U.S.A.* 78 F6   39 16N 121 1W
Nevado, Cerro, *Argentina* .. 94 D2   35 30S   68 32W
Nevado de Colima = Volcán de
  Colima △, *Mexico* 86 D4   19 30N 103 40W
Nevado de Tres Cruces △, *Chile* 94 B2   27 13S   69 5W
Nevel, *Russia* .... 18 C4   56 0N   29 55 E
Nevers, *France* .... 20 C5   47 0N   3 9 E
Nevertire, *Australia* .... 63 E4   31 50S 147 44 E
Neville, *Canada* 71 D7   49 58N 107 39W
Nevinnomyssk, *Russia* .... 19 F7   44 40N   42 0 E
Nevis, *St. Kitts & Nevis* 89 C7   17 0N   62 30W
Nevşehir, *Turkey* .... 44 B2   38 33N   34 40 E
Nevyansk, *Russia* .... 18 C11   57 30N   60 13 E
New ➤, *U.S.A.* 82 F5   38 10N   81 12W
New Aiyansh, *Canada* 70 B3   55 12N 129 4W
New Albany, *Ind., U.S.A.* 82 F3   38 18N   85 49W
New Albany, *Miss., U.S.A.* ... 81 H10   34 29N   89 0W
New Albany, *Pa., U.S.A.* 85 E8   41 36N   76 27W
New Amsterdam, *Guyana* 92 B7   6 15N   57 36W
New Angledool, *Australia* .. 63 D4   29 5S 147 55 E
New Baltimore, *U.S.A.* 84 D2   42 41N   82 44W
New Bedford, *U.S.A.* 85 E14   41 38N   70 56W
New Berlin, *N.Y., U.S.A.* 85 D9   42 37N   75 20W
New Berlin, *Pa., U.S.A.* 84 F8   40 50N   76 57W
New Bern, *U.S.A.* 83 H7   35 7N   77 3W
New Bethlehem, *U.S.A.* 84 F5   41 0N   79 20W
New Bloomfield, *U.S.A.* 84 F7   40 25N   77 11W
New Boston, *U.S.A.* 81 J7   33 28N   94 25W
New Braunfels, *U.S.A.* 81 L5   29 42N   98 8W
New Brighton, *N.Z.* .... 59 K4   43 29S 172 43 E
New Brighton, *U.S.A.* 84 F4   40 42N   80 19W
New Britain, *Papua N. G.* .. 64 H7   5 50S 150 20 E
New Britain, *U.S.A.* 85 E12   41 40N   72 47W
New Brunswick, *U.S.A.* 85 F10   40 30N   74 27W
New Brunswick ⊘, *Canada* .. 73 C6   46 50N   66 30W
New Caledonia ⊘, *Pac. Oc.* .. 64 K8   21 0S 165 0 E
New Castile = Castilla-La
  Mancha ⊘, *Spain* 21 C4   39 30N   3 30W
New Castle, *Ind., U.S.A.* 82 F3   39 55N   85 22W
New Castle, *Pa., U.S.A.* 84 F4   41 0N   80 21W
New City, *U.S.A.* 85 E11   41 9N   73 59W
New Concord, *U.S.A.* 84 G3   39 59N   81 54W
New Cumberland, *U.S.A.* 84 F4   40 30N   80 36W
New Cuyama, *U.S.A.* 79 L7   34 57N 119 38W
New Delhi, *India* .... 42 E7   28 37N   77 13 E
New Denver, *Canada* 70 D5   50 0N 117 25W
New Don Pedro Reservoir, *U.S.A.* 78 H6   37 43N 120 24W
New England, *U.S.A.* 80 B3   46 32N 102 52W
New England Ra., *Australia* .. 63 E5   30 20S 151 45 E
New Forest, *U.K.* 13 G6   50 53N   1 34W
New Galloway, *U.K.* 11 F4   55 5N   4 9W
New Glasgow, *Canada* 73 C7   45 35N   62 36W
New Guinea, *Oceania* .... 26 K17   0 5S 136 0 E
New Hamburg, *Canada* 84 C4   43 23N   80 42W
New Hampshire ⊘, *U.S.A.* .. 85 C13   44 0N   71 30W
New Hampton, *U.S.A.* 80 D8   43 3N   92 19W
New Hanover, *S. Africa* .... 57 D5   29 22S   30 31 E
New Hartford, *U.S.A.* 85 C9   43 4N   75 18W
New Haven, *Conn., U.S.A.* .. 85 E12   41 18N   72 55W
New Haven, *Mich., U.S.A.* .. 84 D2   42 44N   82 48W
New Hazelton, *Canada* 70 B3   55 20N 127 30W
New Hebrides = Vanuatu ■,
  Pac. Oc. .... 64 J8   15 0S 168 0 E
New Holland, *U.S.A.* 85 F8   40 6N   76 5W
New Iberia, *U.S.A.* 81 K9   30 1N   91 49W
New Ireland, *Papua N. G.* .. 64 H7   3 20S 151 50 E
New Jersey ⊘, *U.S.A.* 82 E8   40 0N   74 30W
New Kensington, *U.S.A.* 84 F5   40 34N   79 46W
New Lexington, *U.S.A.* 82 F4   39 43N   82 13W
New Liskeard, *Canada* 72 C4   47 31N   79 41W
New London, *Conn., U.S.A.* .. 85 E12   41 22N   72 6W
New London, *Ohio, U.S.A.* .. 84 E2   41 5N   82 24W
New London, *Wis., U.S.A.* .. 80 C10   44 23N   88 45W
New Madrid, *U.S.A.* 81 G10   36 36N   89 32W
New Martinsville, *U.S.A.* 82 F5   39 39N   80 52W
New Meadows, *U.S.A.* 76 D5   44 58N 116 18W
New Melones L., *U.S.A.* 78 H6   37 57N 120 31W
New Mexico ⊘, *U.S.A.* 77 J10   34 30N 106 0W
New Milford, *Conn., U.S.A.* .. 85 E11   41 35N   73 25W
New Milford, *Pa., U.S.A.* 85 E9   41 52N   75 44W
New Norcia, *Australia* .... 61 F2   30 57S 116 13 E
New Norfolk, *Australia* .... 63 G4   42 46S 147 2 E
New Orleans, *U.S.A.* 81 L9   29 58N   90 4W
New Philadelphia, *U.S.A.* .. 84 F3   40 30N   81 27W
New Plymouth, *N.Z.* .... 59 H5   39 4S 174 5 E
New Plymouth, *U.S.A.* 76 E5   43 58N 116 49W
New Port Richey, *U.S.A.* 83 L4   28 16N   82 43W
New Providence I., *Bahamas* .. 88 A4   25 25N   78 35W
New Quay, *U.K.* 13 E3   52 13N   4 21W
New Radnor, *U.K.* 13 E4   52 15N   3 9W
New Richmond, *Canada* 73 C6   48 15N   65 45W
New Richmond, *U.S.A.* 80 C8   45 7N   92 32W

New River Gorge △, *U.S.A.* .. 82 G5   37 53N   81 5W
New Roads, *U.S.A.* 81 K9   30 42N   91 26W
New Rochelle, *U.S.A.* 85 F11   40 55N   73 47W
New Rockford, *U.S.A.* 80 B5   47 41N   99 8W
New Romney, *U.K.* .... 13 G8   50 59N   0 57 E
New Ross, *Ireland* 10 D5   52 23N   6 57W
New Salem, *U.S.A.* 80 B4   46 51N 101 25W
New Scone = Scone, *U.K.* .. 11 E5   56 25N   3 24W
New Siberian I. = Novaya Sibir,
  Ostrov, *Russia* .... 29 B16   75 10N 150 0 E
New Siberian Is. =
  Novosibirskiye Ostrova, *Russia* 29 B15 75 0N 142 0 E
New Smyrna Beach, *U.S.A.* .. 83 L5   29 1N   80 56W
New South Wales ⊘, *Australia* . 63 E4   33 0S 146 0 E
New Tecumseth, *Canada* 84 B5   44 9N   79 52W
New Town, *U.S.A.* 80 B3   47 59N 102 30W
New Tredegar, *U.K.* 13 F4   51 44N   3 16W
New Ulm, *U.S.A.* 80 C7   44 19N   94 28W
New Waterford, *Canada* 73 C7   46 13N   60 4W
New-Wes-Valley, *Canada* .. 73 C9   49 8N   53 36W
New Westminster, *Canada* .. 78 A4   49 13N 122 55W
New York, *U.S.A.* 85 F11   40 45N   74 0W
New York ⊘, *U.S.A.* 85 D9   43 0N   75 0W
New York J.F. Kennedy
  International ✈ (JFK), *U.S.A.* . 85 F11 40 38N   73 47W
New York Mts., *U.S.A.* 77 J6   35 0N 115 20W
New Zealand ■, *Oceania* .. 59 J6   40 0S 176 0 E
Newaj ➤, *India* .... 42 G7   24 24N   76 49 E
Newala, *Tanzania* .... 55 E4   10 58S   39 18 E
Newark, *Del., U.S.A.* 82 F8   39 41N   75 46W
Newark, *N.J., U.S.A.* 85 F10   40 44N   74 10W
Newark, *N.Y., U.S.A.* 84 C7   43 3N   77 6W
Newark, *Ohio, U.S.A.* 84 F2   40 3N   82 24W
Newark International ✈ (EWR),
  U.S.A. 85 F10   40 42N   74 10W
Newark-on-Trent, *U.K.* 12 D7   53 5N   0 48W
Newark Valley, *U.S.A.* 85 D8   42 14N   76 9W
Newberg, *U.S.A.* 76 D2   45 18N 122 58W
Newberry, *Mich., U.S.A.* .. 82 B3   46 21N   85 30W
Newberry, *S.C., U.S.A.* 83 H5   34 17N   81 37W
Newberry △, *U.S.A.* 76 E2   43 43N 121 15W
Newberry Springs, *U.S.A.* .. 79 L10   34 50N 116 41W
Newboro L., *Canada* 85 B8   44 38N   76 20W
Newbridge = Droichead Nua,
  Ireland 10 C5   53 11N   6 48W
Newburgh, *Canada* 84 B8   44 19N   76 52W
Newburgh, *U.S.A.* 85 E10   41 30N   74 1W
Newbury, *U.K.* 13 F6   51 24N   1 20W
Newbury, *N.H., U.S.A.* 85 B12   43 19N   72 3W
Newbury, *Vt., U.S.A.* 85 B12   44 5N   72 4W
Newburyport, *U.S.A.* 83 D10   42 49N   70 53W
Newcastle, *Australia* .... 63 E5   33 0S 151 46 E
Newcastle, *N.B., Canada* .. 73 C6   47 1N   65 38W
Newcastle, *Ont., Canada* .. 72 D4   43 55N   78 35W
Newcastle, *S. Africa* .... 57 D4   27 45S   29 58 E
Newcastle, *U.K.* 10 B6   54 13N   5 54W
Newcastle, *Calif., U.S.A.* .. 78 G5   38 53N 121 8W
Newcastle, *Wyo., U.S.A.* .. 80 D2   43 50N 104 11W
Newcastle Emlyn, *U.K.* 13 E3   52 2N   4 28W
Newcastle Ra., *Australia* .. 60 C5   15 45S 130 15 E
Newcastle-under-Lyme, *U.K.* . 12 D5   53 1N   2 14W
Newcastle-upon-Tyne, *U.K.* . 12 C6   54 58N   1 36W
Newcastle Waters, *Australia* . 62 B1   17 30S 133 28 E
Newcastle West, *Ireland* .. 10 D2   52 27N   9 3W
Newcomb, *U.S.A.* 85 C10   43 58N   74 10W
Newcomerstown, *U.S.A.* .. 84 F3   40 16N   81 36W
Newdegate, *Australia* .... 61 F2   33 6S 119 0 E
Newell, *Australia* .... 62 B4   16 20S 145 16 E
Newell, *U.S.A.* 80 C3   44 43N 103 25W
Newfane, *U.S.A.* 84 C6   43 17N   78 43W
Newfield, *U.S.A.* 85 D8   42 18N   76 33W
Newfound L., *U.S.A.* 85 C13   43 40N   71 47W
Newfoundland, *Canada* 73 C8   49 0N   55 0W
Newfoundland, *U.S.A.* 85 E9   41 18N   75 19W
Newfoundland & Labrador ⊘,
  Canada 73 B8   53 0N   58 0W
Newhall, *U.S.A.* 79 L8   34 23N 118 32W
Newhaven, *U.K.* .... 13 G8   50 47N   0 3 E
Newkirk, *U.S.A.* 81 G6   36 53N   97 3W
Newlyn, *U.K.* 13 G2   50 6N   5 34W
Newman, *Australia* .... 60 D2   23 18S 119 45 E
Newman, *U.S.A.* 78 H5   37 19N 121 1W
Newmarket, *Canada* 84 B5   44 3N   79 28W
Newmarket, *Ireland* 10 D2   52 13N   9 0W
Newmarket, *U.K.* .... 13 E8   52 15N   0 25 E
Newmarket, *U.S.A.* 85 C14   43 4N   70 56W
Newnan, *U.S.A.* 83 J3   33 23N   84 48W
Newport, *Ireland* 10 C2   53 53N   9 33W
Newport, *I. of W., U.K.* 13 G6   50 42N   1 17W
Newport, *Newp., U.K.* 13 F5   51 35N   3 0W
Newport, *Ark., U.S.A.* 81 H9   35 37N   91 16W
Newport, *Ky., U.S.A.* 82 F3   39 5N   84 30W
Newport, *N.H., U.S.A.* 85 C12   43 22N   72 10W
Newport, *N.Y., U.S.A.* 85 C9   43 11N   75 1W
Newport, *Oreg., U.S.A.* 76 D1   44 39N 124 3W
Newport, *Pa., U.S.A.* 84 F7   40 29N   77 8W
Newport, *R.I., U.S.A.* 85 E13   41 29N   71 19W
Newport, *Tenn., U.S.A.* 83 H4   35 58N   83 11W
Newport, *Vt., U.S.A.* 85 B12   44 56N   72 13W
Newport, *Wash., U.S.A.* 76 B5   48 11N 117 3W
Newport ⊘, *U.K.* 13 F4   51 33N   3 1W
Newport Beach, *U.S.A.* 79 M9   33 37N 117 56W
Newport News, *U.S.A.* 82 G7   36 59N   76 25W
Newport Pagnell, *U.K.* 13 E7   52 5N   0 43W
Newquay, *U.K.* 13 G2   50 25N   5 6W
Newry, *U.K.* 10 B5   54 11N   6 21W
Newton, *U.S.A.* 80 F10   38 59N   88 10W
Newton, *Iowa, U.S.A.* 80 E8   41 42N   93 3W
Newton, *Kans., U.S.A.* 81 F6   38 3N   97 21W
Newton, *Mass., U.S.A.* 85 D13   42 21N   71 12W
Newton, *Miss., U.S.A.* 81 J10   32 19N   89 10W
Newton, *N.C., U.S.A.* 83 H5   35 40N   81 13W
Newton, *N.J., U.S.A.* 85 E10   41 3N   74 45W
Newton, *Tex., U.S.A.* 81 K8   30 51N   93 46W
Newton Abbot, *U.K.* 13 G4   50 32N   3 37W
Newton Aycliffe, *U.K.* 12 C6   54 37N   1 34W
Newton Falls, *U.S.A.* 84 E4   41 11N   80 59W
Newton Stewart, *U.K.* 11 G4   54 57N   4 30W
Newtonmore, *U.K.* 11 D4   57 4N   4 8W
Newtown, *U.K.* 13 E4   52 31N   3 19W
Newtownabbey, *U.K.* 10 B6   54 40N   5 56W
Newtownards, *U.K.* 10 B6   54 36N   5 42W
Newtownbarry = Bunclody,
  Ireland 10 D5   52 39N   6 40W
Newtownstewart, *U.K.* 10 B4   54 43N   7 23W
Newville, *U.S.A.* 84 F7   40 10N   77 24W
Neya, *Russia* .... 18 C7   58 21N   43 49 E

Neyrîz, *Iran* .... 45 D7   29 15N   54 19 E
Neyshābūr, *Iran* .... 45 B8   36 10N   58 50 E
Nezhin = Nizhyn, *Ukraine* .. 19 D5   51 5N   31 55 E
Nezperce, *U.S.A.* 76 C5   46 14N 116 14W
Ngabang, *Indonesia* .... 36 D3   0 23N 109 55 E
Ngabordamlu, Tanjung,
  Indonesia .... 37 F8   6 56S 134 11 E
N'Gage, *Angola* .... 52 F3   7 46S   15 16 E
Ngami Depression, *Botswana* .. 56 C3   20 30S   22 46 E
Ngamo, *Zimbabwe* .... 55 F2   19 3S   27 32 E
Nganglong Kangri, *China* .. 41 C12   33 0N   81 0 E
Ngao, *Thailand* .... 38 C2   18 46N   99 59 E
Ngaoundéré, *Cameroon* .... 52 C2   7 15N   13 35 E
Ngapara, *N.Z.* .... 59 L3   44 57S 170 46 E
Ngara, *Tanzania* .... 54 C3   2 29S   30 40 E
Ngawi, *Indonesia* .... 37 G14   7 24S 111 26 E
Nghia Lo, *Vietnam* .... 38 B5   21 33N 104 28 E
Ngoma, *Malawi* .... 55 E3   13 8S   33 45 E
Ngomahura, *Zimbabwe* .... 55 G3   20 26S   30 43 E
Ngomba, *Tanzania* .... 55 D3   8 20S   32 53 E
Ngoring Hu, *China* .... 32 C4   34 55N   97 5 E
Ngorongoro, *Tanzania* .... 54 C4   3 11S   35 32 E
Ngorongoro △, *Tanzania* .... 54 C4   2 40S   35 30 E
Ngozi, *Burundi* .... 54 C2   2 54S   29 50 E
Ngudu, *Tanzania* .... 54 C3   2 58S   33 25 E
Nguigmi, *Niger* .... 51 F8   14 20N   13 0 E
Nguiu, *Australia* .... 60 B5   11 46S 130 38 E
Ngukurr, *Australia* .... 62 A1   14 44S 134 44 E
Ngunga, *Tanzania* .... 54 C3   3 37S   33 37 E
Nguru, *Nigeria* .... 51 F8   12 56N   10 29 E
Nguru Mts., *Tanzania* .... 54 D4   6 0S   37 30 E
Ngusi, *Malawi* .... 55 E3   14 0S   34 50 E
Nguyen Binh, *Vietnam* .... 38 A5   22 39N 105 56 E
Nha Trang, *Vietnam* .... 39 F7   12 16N 109 10 E
Nhacoongo, *Mozam.* .... 57 C6   24 18S   35 14 E
Nhamaabué, *Mozam.* .... 55 F4   17 25S   35 5 E
Nhamundá ➤, *Brazil* 93 D7   2 12S   56 41W
Nhangulaze, L., *Mozam.* .... 57 C5   24 0S   34 30 E
Nhill, *Australia* .... 63 F3   36 18S 141 40 E
Nho Quan, *Vietnam* .... 38 B5   20 18N 105 45 E
Nhulunbuy, *Australia* .... 62 A2   12 10S 137 20 E
Nia-nia, *Dem. Rep. of the Congo* 54 B2   1 30N   27 40 E
Niagara Falls, *Canada* 84 C5   43 7N   79 5W
Niagara Falls, *U.S.A.* 84 C6   43 5N   79 4W
Niagara-on-the-Lake, *Canada* . 84 C5   43 15N   79 4W
Niah, *Malaysia* .... 36 D4   3 58N 113 46 E
Niamey, *Niger* .... 50 F6   13 27N   2 6 E
Niangara, *Dem. Rep. of
  the Congo* .... 54 B2   3 42N   27 50 E
Niantic, *U.S.A.* 85 E12   41 20N   72 11W
Nias, *Indonesia* .... 36 D1   1 0N   97 30 E
Niassa ⊘, *Mozam.* .... 55 E4   12 4S   36 67 E
Niassa □, *Mozam.* .... 55 E4   13 30S   36 0 E
Nibāk, *Si. Arabia* .... 45 E7   24 25N   50 50 E
Nicaragua ■, *Cent. Amer.* .. 88 D2   11 40N   85 30W
Nicaragua, L. de, *Nic.* 88 D2   12 0N   85 30W
Nicastro, *Italy* .... 22 E7   38 59N   16 19 E
Nice, *France* .... 20 E7   43 42N   7 14 E
Niceville, *U.S.A.* 83 K2   30 31N   86 30W
Nichicun, L., *Canada* 73 B5   53 5N   71 0W
Nichinan, *Japan* .... 31 J5   31 38N 131 23 E
Nicholás, Canal, *W. Indies* .. 88 B3   23 30N   80 5W
Nicholasville, *U.S.A.* 82 G3   37 53N   84 34W
Nichols, *U.S.A.* 85 D8   42 1N   76 22W
Nicholson, *Australia* .... 60 C4   18 2S 128 54 E
Nicholson, *U.S.A.* 85 E9   41 37N   75 47W
Nicholson ➤, *Australia* .... 62 B2   17 31S 139 36 E
Nicholson L., *Canada* 71 A8   62 40N 102 40W
Nicholson Ra., *Australia* .... 61 E2   27 15S 116 45 E
Nicholville, *U.S.A.* 85 B10   44 41N   74 39W
Nicobar Is., *Ind. Oc.* .... 27 J13   8 0N   93 30 E
Nicola, *Canada* 70 C4   50 12N 120 40W
Nicolls Town, *Bahamas* 88 A4   25 8N   78 0W
Nicosia, *Cyprus* .... 25 D12   35 10N   33 25 E
Nicoya, *Costa Rica* 88 D2   10 9N   85 27W
Nicoya, G. de, *Costa Rica* .. 88 E3   10 0N   85 0W
Nicoya, Pen. de, *Costa Rica* . 88 E2   9 45N   85 40W
Nidd ➤, *U.K.* 12 D6   53 59N   1 23W
Niedersachsen □, *Germany* .. 16 B5   52 50N   9 0 E
Niekerkshoop, *S. Africa* .... 56 D3   29 19S   22 51 E
Niemba, *Dem. Rep. of the Congo* 54 D2   5 58S   28 24 E
Niemen = Nemunas ➤,
  Lithuania .... 9 J19   55 25N   21 10 E
Nienburg, *Germany* .... 16 B5   52 39N   9 13 E
Nieu Bethesda, *S. Africa* .. 56 E3   31 51S   24 34 E
Nieuw Amsterdam, *Suriname* . 93 B7   5 53N   55 5W
Nieuw Nickerie, *Suriname* .. 93 B7   6 0N   56 59W
Nieuwoudtville, *S. Africa* .. 56 E2   31 23S   19 7 E
Nieuwpoort, *Belgium* .... 15 C2   51 8N   2 45 E
Nieves, Pico de las, *Canary Is.* 24 G4   27 57N   15 35W
Niğde, *Turkey* .... 19 G5   37 58N   34 40 E
Nigel, *S. Africa* .... 57 D4   26 27S   28 25 E
Niger ■, *W. Afr.* .... 50 E7   17 30N   10 0 E
Niger ➤, *W. Afr.* .... 50 G7   5 33N   6 33 E
Nigeria ■, *W. Afr.* .... 50 G7   8 30N   8 0 E
Nighasin, *India* .... 43 E9   28 14N   80 52 E
Nightcaps, *N.Z.* .... 59 L2   45 57S 168 2 E
Nii-Jima, *Japan* .... 31 G9   34 20N 139 15 E
Niigata, *Japan* .... 30 F9   37 58N 139 0 E
Niigata □, *Japan* .... 31 F9   37 15N 138 45 E
Niihama, *Japan* .... 31 H6   33 55N 133 28 E
Niihau, *U.S.A.* 74 H14   21 54N 160 9W
Niimi, *Japan* .... 31 G6   34 59N 133 28 E
Niitsu, *Japan* .... 30 F9   37 48N 139 7 E
Nijil, *Jordan* .... 46 E4   30 32N   35 33 E
Nijkerk, *Neths.* .... 15 B5   52 13N   5 30 E
Nijmegen, *Neths.* .... 15 C5   51 50N   5 52 E
Nijverdal, *Neths.* .... 15 B6   52 22N   6 28 E
Nik Pey, *Iran* .... 45 B6   36 50N   48 10 E
Nikiniki, *Indonesia* .... 37 F6   9 49S 124 30 E
Nikkō, *Japan* .... 31 F9   36 45N 139 35 E
Nikkō △, *Japan* .... 31 F9   36 53N 139 35 E
Nikolayev = Mykolayiv, *Ukraine* 19 E5   46 58N   32 0 E
Nikolayevsk, *Russia* .... 19 E8   50 0N   45 35 E
Nikolayevsk-na-Amur, *Russia* . 29 D15   53 8N 140 44 E
Nikolskoye, *Russia* .... 29 D17   55 12N 166 0 E
Nikopol, *Ukraine* .... 19 E5   47 35N   34 25 E
Nîkshahr, *Iran* .... 45 E9   26 15N   60 10 E
Nikšić, *Serbia & M.* .... 23 C8   42 50N   18 57 E
Nîl, Nahr en ➤, *Africa* .... 51 B12   30 10N   31 6 E
Nîl el Abyad ➤, *Sudan* .... 51 E12   15 38N   32 31 E
Nîl el Azraq ➤, *Sudan* .... 51 E12   15 38N   32 31 E
Nila, *Indonesia* .... 37 F7   6 44S 129 31 E
Niland, *U.S.A.* 79 M11   33 14N 115 31W
Nile = Nîl, Nahr en ➤, *Africa* . 51 B12   30 10N   31 6 E
Niles, *Mich., U.S.A.* 82 E2   41 50N   86 15W
Niles, *Ohio, U.S.A.* 84 E4   41 11N   80 46W

Nim Ka Thana, *India* .... 42 F6   27 44N   75 48 E
Nimach, *India* .... 42 G6   24 30N   74 56 E
Nimbahera, *India* .... 42 G6   24 37N   74 45 E
Nîmes, *France* .... 20 E6   43 50N   4 23 E
Nimfaíon, Ákra = Pínnes, Ákra,
  Greece .... 23 D11   40 5N   24 20 E
Nimmitabel, *Australia* .... 63 F4   36 29S 149 15 E
Nînawá, *Iraq* .... 44 B4   36 25N   43 10 E
Nînawā □, *Iraq* .... 44 B4   36 15N   43 0 E
Nindigully, *Australia* .... 63 D4   28 21S 148 50 E
Ninepin Group, *China* .... 33 G11   22 16N 114 21 E
Nineveh = Nînawā, *Iraq* .... 44 B4   36 25N   43 10 E
Ning Xian, *China* .... 34 G4   35 30N 107 58 E
Ningaloo △, *Australia* .... 60 D1   22 33S 113 32 E
Ning'an, *China* .... 35 B15   44 22N 129 20 E
Ningbo, *China* .... 33 D7   29 51N 121 28 E
Ningcheng, *China* .... 35 D10   41 32N 119 53 E
Ningjin, *China* .... 34 F8   37 35N 114 57 E
Ningjing Shan, *China* .... 32 D4   30 0N   98 20 E
Ningling, *China* .... 34 G8   34 25N 115 22 E
Ningpo = Ningbo, *China* .... 33 D7   29 51N 121 28 E
Ningqiang, *China* .... 34 H4   32 47N 106 15 E
Ningshan, *China* .... 34 H5   33 21N 108 21 E
Ningsia Hui A.R. = Ningxia Huizu
  Zizhiqu □, *China* .... 34 F4   38 0N 106 0 E
Ningwu, *China* .... 34 E7   39 0N 112 18 E
Ningxia Huizu Zizhiqu □, *China* 34 F4   38 0N 106 0 E
Ningyang, *China* .... 34 G9   35 47N 116 45 E
Ninh Binh, *Vietnam* .... 38 B5   20 15N 105 55 E
Ninh Giang, *Vietnam* .... 38 B6   20 44N 106 24 E
Ninh Hoa, *Vietnam* .... 38 F7   12 30N 109 7 E
Ninh Ma, *Vietnam* .... 38 F7   12 48N 109 21 E
Ninove, *Belgium* .... 15 D4   50 51N   4 2 E
Nioaque, *Brazil* 95 A4   21 5S   55 50W
Niobrara, *U.S.A.* 80 D6   42 45N   98 2W
Niobrara ➤, *U.S.A.* 80 D6   42 46N   98 3W
Nioro du Sahel, *Mali* 50 E4   15 15N   9 30W
Niort, *France* 20 C3   46 19N   0 29W
Nipawin, *Canada* 71 C8   53 20N 104 0W
Nipigon, *Canada* 72 C2   49 0N   88 17W
Nipigon, L., *Canada* 72 C2   49 50N   88 30W
Nipishish L., *Canada* 73 B7   54 12N   60 45W
Nipissing, L., *Canada* 72 C4   46 20N   80 0W
Nipomo, *U.S.A.* 79 K6   35 3N 120 29W
Nipton, *U.S.A.* 79 K11   35 28N 115 16W
Niquelândia, *Brazil* 93 F9   14 33S   48 23W
Nīr, *Iran* .... 44 B5   38 2N   47 59 E
Nirasaki, *Japan* .... 31 G9   35 42N 138 27 E
Nirmal, *India* .... 40 K11   19 3N   78 20 E
Nirmali, *India* .... 43 F12   26 20N   86 35 E
Niš, *Serbia & M.* .... 23 C9   43 19N   21 58 E
Nišāb, *Si. Arabia* .... 44 D5   29 11N   44 43 E
Nişāb, *Yemen* .... 47 E4   14 25N   46 29 E
Nishinomiya, *Japan* .... 31 G7   34 45N 135 20 E
Nishino'omote, *Japan* .... 31 J5   30 43N 130 59 E
Nishiwaki, *Japan* .... 31 G7   34 59N 134 58 E
Niskibi ➤, *Canada* 72 A2   56 29N   88 9W
Nisqually ➤, *U.S.A.* 78 C4   47 6N 122 42W
Nissáki, *Greece* .... 25 A3   39 43N   19 52 E
Nissum Bredning, *Denmark* . 9 H13   56 40N   8 20 E
Nistru = Dnister ➤, *Europe* .. 17 E16   46 18N   30 17 E
Nisutlin ➤, *Canada* 70 A2   60 14N 132 34W
Nitchequon, *Canada* 73 B5   53 10N   70 58W
Niterói, *Brazil* 95 A7   22 52S   43 0W
Nith ➤, *Canada* 84 C4   43 12N   80 23W
Nith ➤, *U.K.* 11 F5   55 14N   3 33W
Nitmiluk △, *Australia* .... 60 B5   14 6S 132 15 E
Nitra, *Slovak Rep.* .... 17 D10   48 19N   18 4 E
Nitra ➤, *Slovak Rep.* .... 17 E10   47 46N   18 10 E
Niuafo'ou, *Tonga* 59 B11   15 30S 175 58W
Niue, *Cook Is.* 65 J11   19 2S 169 54W
Niut, *Indonesia* .... 36 D4   0 55N 110 6 E
Niuzhuang, *China* .... 35 D12   40 58N 122 28 E
Nivala, *Finland* .... 8 E21   63 56N   24 57 E
Nivelles, *Belgium* .... 15 D4   50 35N   4 20 E
Nivernais, *France* .... 20 C5   47 15N   3 30 E
Niwas, *India* .... 43 H9   23 3N   80 26 E
Nixon, *U.S.A.* 81 L6   29 16N   97 46W
Nizamabad, *India* .... 40 K11   18 45N   78 7 E
Nizamghat, *India* .... 41 E19   28 20N   95 45 E
Nizhne Kolymsk, *Russia* .... 29 C17   68 34N 160 55 E
Nizhnegorsk, *Russia* .... 29 D11   55 47N 109 30 E
Nizhnekamsk, *Russia* .... 18 C9   55 38N   51 49 E
Nizhneudinsk, *Russia* .... 29 D10   54 54N   99 3 E
Nizhnevartovsk, *Russia* .... 28 C8   60 56N   76 38 E
Nizhniy Novgorod, *Russia* .. 18 C7   56 20N   44 0 E
Nizhniy Tagil, *Russia* .... 18 C10   57 55N   59 57 E
Nizhyn, *Ukraine* .... 19 D5   51 5N   31 55 E
Nizip, *Turkey* .... 44 B3   37 5N   37 50 E
Nízké Tatry, *Slovak Rep.* .. 17 D10   48 55N   19 30 E
Njakwa, *Malawi* .... 55 E3   11 1S   33 56 E
Njanji, *Zambia* .... 55 E3   14 25S   31 46 E
Njinjo, *Tanzania* .... 55 D4   8 48S   38 54 E
Njombe, *Tanzania* .... 55 D3   9 20S   34 50 E
Njombe ➤, *Tanzania* .... 54 D4   6 56S   35 6 E
Nkana, *Zambia* .... 55 E2   12 50S   28 8 E
Nkandla, *S. Africa* .... 57 D5   28 37S   31 5 E
Nkayi, *Zimbabwe* .... 55 F2   19 41S   29 20 E
Nkhotakota, *Malawi* .... 55 E3   12 56S   34 15 E
Nkhotakota △, *Malawi* .... 55 E3   12 50S   34 0 E
Nkongsamba, *Cameroon* .. 52 D1   4 55N   9 55 E
Nkurenkuru, *Namibia* .... 56 B2   17 42S   18 32 E
Nmai ➤, *Burma* .... 41 G20   25 30N   97 25 E
Noakhali = Maijdi, *Bangla.* .. 41 H17   22 48N   91 10 E
Nobel, *Canada* 84 A4   45 25N   80 6W
Nobeoka, *Japan* .... 31 H5   32 36N 131 41 E
Noblesville, *U.S.A.* 82 E3   40 3N   86 1W
Noboribetsu, *Japan* .... 30 C10   42 24N 141 6 E
Nocera Inferiore, *Italy* .... 22 D6   40 44N   14 38 E
Nocona, *U.S.A.* 81 J6   33 47N   97 44W
Noda, *Japan* .... 31 G9   35 56N 139 52 E
Nogales, *Mexico* 86 A2   31 20N 110 56W
Nogales, *U.S.A.* 77 L8   31 20N 110 56W
Nōgata, *Japan* .... 31 H5   33 48N 130 44 E
Noginsk, *Russia* .... 29 C10   64 30N   90 50 E
Nogoa ➤, *Australia* .... 62 C4   23 40S 147 55 E
Nogoyá, *Argentina* 94 C4   32 24S   59 48W
Nohar, *India* .... 42 E6   29 11N   74 49 E
Nohta, *India* .... 43 H8   23 40N   79 34 E
Noires, Mts., *France* 20 D2   48 11N   3 40W
Noirmoutier, Î. de, *France* .. 20 C2   46 58N   2 10W
Nojane, *Botswana* .... 56 C3   23 15S   20 14 E
Nojima-Zaki, *Japan* .... 31 G9   34 54N 139 53 E
Nok Kundi, *Pakistan* .... 40 E3   28 50N   62 45 E
Nok Ta Phao, Ko, *Thailand* .. 39 b   9 23N   99 40 E
Nokaneng, *Botswana* .... 56 B3   19 40S   22 17 E

Nokia, Finland . . . . 9 F20 61 30N 23 30 E
Nokomis, Canada 71 C8 51 35N 105 0W
Nokomis L., Canada 71 B8 57 0N 103 0W
Nola, C.A.R. . . . . 52 D3 3 35N 16 4 E
Noma Omuramba →, Namibia . 56 B3 18 52S 20 53 E
Nombre de Dios, Panama . . . 88 E4 9 34N 79 28W
Nome, U.S.A. 68 B3 64 30N 165 25W
Nomo-Zaki, Japan . . . . 31 H4 32 35N 129 44 E
Nonacho L., Canada 71 A7 61 42N 109 40W
Nonda, Australia . . . . 62 C3 20 40S 142 28 E
Nong Chang, Thailand . . . . . 38 E2 15 23N 99 51 E
Nong Het, Laos . . . . 38 C4 19 29N 103 59 E
Nong Khai, Thailand . . . . . . 38 D4 17 50N 102 46 E
Nong'an, China . . . . 35 B13 44 25N 125 5 E
Nongoma, S. Africa . . . . 57 D5 27 58S 31 35 E
Nongsa, Indonesia . . . . 39 d 1 11N 104 8 E
Nonoava, Mexico 86 B3 27 28N 106 44W
Nonoava →, Mexico 86 B3 27 29N 106 45W
Nonthaburi, Thailand . . . . . . 38 F3 13 51N 100 34 E
Noonamah, Australia . . . . . . 60 B5 12 40S 131 4 E
Noord Brabant □, Neths. . . . . 15 C5 51 40N 5 0 E
Noord Holland □, Neths. . . . . 15 B4 52 30N 4 45 E
Noordbeveland, Neths. . . . . . 15 C3 51 35N 3 50 E
Noordoostpolder, Neths. . . . . 15 B5 52 45N 5 45 E
Noordwijk, Neths. . . . . 15 B4 52 14N 4 26 E
Nootka I., Canada 70 D3 49 32N 126 42W
Nopiming △, Canada 71 C9 50 30N 95 37W
Noralee, Canada 70 C3 53 59N 126 26W
Noranda = Rouyn-Noranda,
　Canada 72 C4 48 20N 79 0W
Norco, U.S.A. 79 M9 33 56N 117 33W
Nord-Kivu □, Dem. Rep. of
　the Congo . . . . 54 C2 1 0S 29 0 E
Nord-Ostsee-Kanal, Germany . 16 A5 54 12N 9 32 E
Nordaustlandet, Svalbard . . . 4 B9 79 14N 23 0 E
Nordegg, Canada 70 C5 52 29N 116 5W
Norderney, Germany . . . . . . 16 B4 53 42N 7 9 E
Norderstedt, Germany . . . . . 16 B5 53 42N 10 1 E
Nordfjord, Norway . . . . 9 F11 61 55N 5 30 E
Nordfriesische Inseln, Germany 16 A5 54 40N 8 20 E
Nordhausen, Germany . . . . . 16 C6 51 30N 10 47 E
Norðoyar, Færoe Is. 8 E9 62 17N 6 35W
Nordkapp, Norway . . . . 8 A21 71 10N 25 50 E
Nordkapp, Svalbard . . . . 4 A9 80 31N 20 0 E
Nordkinn-halvøya, Norway . . 8 A22 70 55N 27 40 E
Nordrhein-Westfalen □,
　Germany . . . . 16 C4 51 45N 7 30 E
Nordvik, Russia . . . . 29 B12 74 2N 111 32 E
Nore →, Ireland 10 D4 52 25N 6 58W
Norfolk, Canada 84 D4 42 50N 80 23W
Norfolk, Nebr., U.S.A. 80 D6 42 2N 97 25W
Norfolk, Va., U.S.A. 82 G7 36 51N 76 17W
Norfolk □, U.K. . . . . 13 E8 52 39N 0 54 E
Norfolk I., Pac. Oc. . . . . 64 K8 28 58S 168 3 E
Norfork L., U.S.A. 81 G8 36 15N 92 14W
Norilsk, Russia . . . . 29 C9 69 20N 88 6 E
Norma, Mt., Australia . . . . . . 62 C3 20 55S 140 42 E
Normal, U.S.A. 80 E10 40 31N 88 59W
Norman, U.S.A. 81 H6 35 13N 97 26W
Norman →, Australia . . . . . . 62 B3 19 18S 141 51 E
Norman Wells, Canada 68 B7 65 17N 126 51W
Normanby →, Australia . . . . . 62 A3 14 23S 144 10 E
Normandie, France . . . . 20 B4 48 45N 0 10 E
Normandin, Canada 72 C5 48 49N 72 31W
Normandy = Normandie, France 20 B4 48 45N 0 10 E
Normanhurst, Mt., Australia . 61 E3 25 4S 122 30 E
Normanton, Australia . . . . . . 62 B3 17 40S 141 10 E
Normétal, Canada 72 C4 49 0N 79 22W
Norquay, Canada 71 C8 51 53N 102 5W
Norquinco, Argentina 96 E2 41 51S 70 55W
Norrbotten □, Sweden . . . . . . 8 C19 66 30N 22 30 E
Norris Point, Canada 73 C8 49 31N 57 53W
Norristown, U.S.A. 85 F9 40 7N 75 21W
Norrköping, Sweden . . . . 9 G17 58 37N 16 11 E
Norrland, Sweden . . . . 9 E16 62 15N 15 45 E
Norrtälje, Sweden . . . . 9 G18 59 46N 18 42 E
Norseman, Australia . . . . 61 F3 32 8S 121 43 E
Norsk, Russia . . . . 29 D14 52 30N 130 5 E
Norte, Pta. del, Canary Is. . . . 24 G2 27 51N 17 57W
Norte, Serra do, Brazil 92 F7 11 20S 59 0W
North, C., Canada 73 C7 47 2N 60 20W
North Adams, U.S.A. 85 D11 42 42N 73 7W
North America 66 F10 40 0N 100 0W
North Arm, Canada 70 A5 62 0N 114 30W
North Augusta, U.S.A. 83 J5 33 30N 81 59W
North Ayrshire □, U.K. 11 F4 55 45N 4 44W
North Bass I., U.S.A. 84 E2 41 44N 82 53W
North Battleford, Canada . . . 71 C7 52 50N 108 17W
North Bay, Canada 72 C4 46 20N 79 30W
North Belcher Is., Canada . . . 72 A4 56 50N 79 50W
North Bend, Oreg., U.S.A. . . . 76 E1 43 24N 124 14W
North Bend, Pa., U.S.A. 84 E7 41 20N 77 42W
North Bend, Wash., U.S.A. . . . 78 C5 47 30N 121 47W
North Bennington, U.S.A. . . . 85 D11 42 56N 73 15W
North Berwick, U.K. 11 E6 56 4N 2 42W
North Berwick, U.S.A. 85 C14 43 18N 70 44W
North C., Canada 73 C7 47 5N 64 0W
North C., N.Z. . . . . 59 F4 34 23S 173 4 E
North Canadian →, U.S.A. . . . 81 H7 35 16N 95 31W
North Canton, U.S.A. 84 F3 40 53N 81 24W
North Cape = Nordkapp, Norway 8 A21 71 10N 25 50 E
North Cape = Nordkapp,
　Svalbard . . . . 4 A9 80 31N 20 0 E
North Caribou L., Canada . . . 72 B1 52 50N 90 40W
North Carolina □, U.S.A. 83 H6 35 30N 80 0W
North Cascades △, U.S.A. . . . 76 B3 48 45N 121 10W
North Channel, Canada 72 C3 46 0N 83 0W
North Channel, U.K. 11 F3 55 13N 5 52W
North Charleston, U.S.A. 83 J6 32 53N 79 58W
North Chicago, U.S.A. 82 D2 42 19N 87 51W
North Creek, U.S.A. 85 C11 43 41N 73 59W
North Dakota □, U.S.A. 80 B5 47 30N 100 15W
North Downs, U.K. . . . . 13 F8 51 19N 0 21 E
North East, U.S.A. 84 D5 42 13N 79 50W
North East Frontier Agency =
　Arunachal Pradesh □, India . 41 F19 28 0N 95 0 E
North East Lincolnshire □, U.K. 12 D7 53 34N 0 2W
North Eastern □, Kenya . . . . . 54 B5 1 30N 40 0 E
North Esk →, U.K. 11 E6 56 46N 2 24W
North European Plain, Europe . 6 E10 55 0N 25 0 E
North Foreland, U.K. . . . . 13 F9 51 22N 1 28 E
North Fork, U.S.A. 78 H7 37 14N 119 21W
North Fork American →, U.S.A. 78 G5 38 45N 121 8W
North Fork Feather →, U.S.A. . 78 F5 38 33N 121 30W
North Fork Grand →, U.S.A. . . 80 C3 45 47N 102 16W
North Fork Red →, U.S.A. 81 H5 34 24N 99 14W
North Frisian Is. = Nordfriesische
　Inseln, Germany . . . . 16 A5 54 40N 8 20 E

North Gower, Canada 85 A9 45 8N 75 43W
North Hd., Australia . . . . 61 F1 30 14S 114 59 E
North Henik L., Canada 71 A9 61 45N 97 40W
North Highlands, U.S.A. 78 G5 38 40N 121 23W
North Horr, Kenya . . . . 54 B4 4 5N 36 5 E
North I., Kenya . . . . 54 B4 4 5N 36 5 E
North I., N.Z. . . . . 59 H5 38 0S 175 0 E
North Kingsville, U.S.A. 84 E4 41 54N 80 42W
North Kitui △, Kenya . . . . 54 C4 0 15S 38 29 E
North Knife →, Canada 71 B10 58 53N 94 45W
North Koel →, India . . . . 43 G10 24 45N 83 50 E
North Korea ■, Asia . . . . 35 E14 40 0N 127 0 E
North Lakhimpur, India . . . . . 41 F19 27 14N 94 7 E
North Lanarkshire □, U.K. . . . 11 F5 55 52N 3 56W
North Las Vegas, U.S.A. 79 J11 36 12N 115 7W
North Lincolnshire □, U.K. . . . 12 D7 53 36N 0 30W
North Little Rock, U.S.A. 81 H8 34 45N 92 16W
North Loup →, U.S.A. 80 E5 41 17N 98 24W
North Luangwa △, Zambia . . . 55 E3 11 49S 32 9 E
North Magnetic Pole, Canada . 4 A2 88 30N 107 0W
North Minch, U.K. 11 C3 58 5N 5 55W
North Moose L., Canada 71 C8 54 11N 100 6W
North Moose L., Man., Canada . 71 C8 54 4N 100 12W
North Myrtle Beach, U.S.A. . . 83 J6 33 48N 78 42W
North Nahanni →, Canada . . . 70 A4 62 15N 123 20W
North Olmsted, U.S.A. 84 E3 41 25N 81 56W
North Ossetia □, Russia . . . . . 19 F7 43 30N 44 30 E
North Pagai, I. = Pagai Utara,
　Pulau, Indonesia . . . . 36 E2 2 35S 100 0 E
North Palisade, U.S.A. 78 H8 37 6N 118 31W
North Platte, U.S.A. 80 E4 41 8N 100 46W
North Platte →, U.S.A. 80 E4 41 7N 100 42W
North Pole, Arctic . . . . 4 A 90 0N 0 0W
North Portal, Canada 71 D8 49 0N 102 33W
North Powder, U.S.A. 76 D5 45 2N 117 55W
North Pt., Barbados . . . . 89 g 13 20N 59 37W
North Pt., Trin. & Tob. 93 J16 11 21N 60 31W
North Pt., U.S.A. 84 A1 45 2N 83 16W
North Rhine Westphalia =
　Nordrhein-Westfalen □,
　Germany . . . . 16 C4 51 45N 7 30 E
North River, Canada 73 B8 53 49N 57 6W
North Ronaldsay, U.K. 11 B6 59 22N 2 26W
North Saskatchewan →, Canada 71 C7 53 15N 105 5W
North Sea, Europe . . . . 14 C7 56 0N 4 0 E
North Seal →, Canada 71 B9 58 50N 98 7W
North Somerset □, U.K. 13 F5 51 24N 2 45W
North Sporades = Vóriai
　Sporádhes, Greece . . . . 23 E10 39 15N 23 30 E
North Sydney, Canada 73 C7 46 12N 60 15W
North Syracuse, U.S.A. 85 C8 43 8N 76 7W
North Taranaki Bight, N.Z. . . . 59 H5 38 50S 174 15 E
North Thompson →, Canada . . 70 C4 50 40N 120 20W
North Tonawanda, U.S.A. 84 C6 43 2N 78 53W
North Troy, U.S.A. 85 B12 45 0N 72 24W
North Truchas Pk., U.S.A. 77 J11 36 0N 105 30W
North Twin I., Canada 72 B4 53 20N 80 0W
North Tyne →, U.K. 12 B5 55 0N 2 8W
North Uist, U.K. 11 D1 57 40N 7 15W
North Vancouver, Canada . . . 70 D4 49 19N 123 4W
North Vernon, U.S.A. 82 F3 39 0N 85 38W
North Wabasca L., Canada . . . 70 B6 56 0N 113 55W
North Walsham, U.K. . . . . 12 E9 52 50N 1 22 E
North West = Severo-
　Zapadnyy □, Russia . . . . . . 28 C4 65 0N 40 0 E
North-West □, S. Africa . . . . . 56 D4 27 0S 25 0 E
North West C., Australia . . . . 60 D1 21 45S 114 9 E
North West Christmas I. Ridge,
　Pac. Oc. 65 G11 6 30N 165 0W
North West Frontier □, Pakistan 42 C4 34 0N 72 0 E
North West Highlands, U.K. . . 11 D4 57 33N 4 58W
North West River, Canada . . . 73 B7 53 30N 60 10W
North Western □, Zambia . . . . 55 E2 13 30S 25 30 E
North Wildwood, U.S.A. 82 F8 39 0N 74 48W
North York Moors, U.K. 12 C7 54 23N 0 53W
North York Moors △, U.K. . . . 12 C7 54 27N 0 51W
North Yorkshire □, U.K. 12 C6 54 15N 1 25W
Northallerton, U.K. 12 C6 54 20N 1 26W
Northam, Australia . . . . 61 F2 31 35S 116 42 E
Northam, S. Africa . . . . 56 C4 24 56S 27 18 E
Northampton, Australia . . . . . 61 E1 28 27S 114 33 E
Northampton, U.K. 13 E7 52 15N 0 53W
Northampton, Mass., U.S.A. . . 85 D12 42 19N 72 38W
Northampton, Pa., U.S.A. 85 F9 40 41N 75 30W
Northamptonshire □, U.K. . . . 13 E7 52 16N 0 55W
Northbridge, U.S.A. 85 D13 42 9N 71 39W
Northcliffe, Australia . . . . 61 F2 34 39S 116 7 E
Northeast Providence Chan.,
　W. Indies 88 A4 26 0N 76 0W
Northern □, Malawi . . . . 55 E3 11 0S 34 0 E
Northern □, Zambia . . . . 55 E3 10 30S 31 0 E
Northern Areas □, Pakistan . . 43 A5 36 30N 73 0 E
Northern Cape □, S. Africa . . . 56 D3 30 0S 20 0 E
Northern Circars, India . . . . . 41 L13 17 30N 82 30 E
Northern Indian L., Canada . . 71 B9 57 20N 97 20W
Northern Ireland □, U.K. 10 B5 54 45N 7 0W
Northern Light L., Canada . . . 72 C1 48 15N 90 39W
Northern Marianas ☑, Pac. Oc. 64 F6 17 0N 145 0 E
Northern Province □, S. Africa . 57 C4 24 0S 29 0 E
Northern Range, Trin. & Tob. . 93 K15 10 46N 61 15W
Northern Territory □, Australia 60 D5 20 0S 133 0 E
Northfield, Minn., U.S.A. 80 C8 44 27N 93 9W
Northfield, Vt., U.S.A. 85 B12 44 9N 72 40W
Northland □, N.Z. . . . . 59 F4 35 30S 173 30 E
Northome, U.S.A. 80 B7 47 52N 94 17W
Northport, Ala., U.S.A. 83 J2 33 14N 87 35W
Northport, Wash., U.S.A. 76 B5 48 55N 117 48W
Northumberland □, U.K. 12 B6 55 12N 2 0W
Northumberland, C., Australia . 63 F3 38 5S 140 40 E
Northumberland Is., Australia . 62 C4 21 30S 149 50 E
Northumberland Str., Canada . 73 C7 46 20N 64 0W
Northville, U.S.A. 85 C10 43 13N 74 11W
Northwest Providence Channel,
　W. Indies 88 A4 26 0N 78 0W
Northwest Territories □, Canada 68 B9 63 0N 118 0W
Northwich, U.K. 12 D5 53 15N 2 31W
Northwood, Iowa, U.S.A. 80 D8 43 27N 93 13W
Northwood, N. Dak., U.S.A. . . 80 B6 47 44N 97 34W
Norton, U.S.A. 80 F5 39 50N 99 53W
Norton, Zimbabwe . . . . 55 F3 17 52S 30 40 E
Norton Sd., U.S.A. 68 B3 63 50N 164 0W
Norwalk, Calif., U.S.A. 79 M8 33 54N 118 5W
Norwalk, Conn., U.S.A. 85 E11 41 7N 73 22W
Norwalk, Iowa, U.S.A. 80 E8 41 29N 93 41W
Norwalk, Ohio, U.S.A. 84 E2 41 15N 82 37W
Norway, Maine, U.S.A. 83 C10 44 13N 70 32W

Norway, Mich., U.S.A. 82 C2 45 47N 87 55W
Norway ■, Europe . . . . 8 E14 63 0N 11 0 E
Norway House, Canada 71 C9 53 59N 97 50W
Norwegian Sea, Atl. Oc. . . . . . 4 C8 66 0N 1 0 E
Norwich, Canada 84 D4 42 59N 80 36W
Norwich, U.K. . . . . 13 E9 52 38N 1 18 E
Norwich, Conn., U.S.A. 85 E12 41 31N 72 5W
Norwich, N.Y., U.S.A. 85 D9 42 32N 75 32W
Norwood, Canada 84 B7 44 23N 77 59W
Norwood, U.S.A. 85 B10 44 45N 75 0W
Noshiro, Japan . . . . 30 D10 40 12N 140 0 E
Noss Hd., U.K. 11 C5 58 28N 3 3W
Nossob →, S. Africa . . . . 56 D3 26 55S 20 45 E
Nosy Barren, Madag. . . . . . . 53 H8 18 25S 43 40 E
Nosy Be, Madag. . . . . 53 G9 13 25S 48 15 E
Nosy Boraha, Madag. . . . . . . 57 B8 16 50S 49 55 E
Nosy Lava, Madag. . . . . 57 A8 14 33S 47 36 E
Nosy Varika, Madag. . . . . . . 57 C8 20 35S 48 32 E
Noteć →, Poland . . . . 16 B8 52 44N 15 26 E
Notikewin →, Canada 70 B5 57 2N 117 38W
Notodden, Norway . . . . 9 G13 59 35N 9 17 E
Notre Dame B., Canada 73 C8 49 45N 55 30W
Notre-Dame-de-Koartac =
　Quaqtaq, Canada 69 B13 60 55N 69 40W
Notre-Dame-des-Bois, Canada . 85 A13 45 24N 71 4W
Notre-Dame-d'Ivugivic = Ivujivik,
　Canada 69 B12 62 24N 77 55W
Notre-Dame-du-Nord, Canada . 72 C4 47 36N 79 30W
Nottawasaga B., Canada 84 B4 44 35N 80 15W
Nottaway →, Canada 72 B4 51 22N 78 55W
Nottingham, U.K. 12 E6 52 58N 1 10W
Nottingham, City of □, U.K. . . 12 E6 52 58N 1 10W
Nottingham I., Canada 69 B12 63 20N 77 55W
Nottinghamshire □, U.K. 12 D6 53 10N 1 3W
Nottoway →, U.S.A. 82 G7 36 33N 76 55W
Notwane →, Botswana . . . . . 56 C4 23 35S 26 58 E
Nouâdhibou, Mauritania 50 D2 20 54N 17 0W
Nouâdhibou, Ras, Mauritania . 50 D2 20 50N 17 0W
Nouakchott, Mauritania 50 E2 18 9N 15 58W
Nouméa, N. Cal. . . . . 64 K8 22 17S 166 30 E
Noupoort, S. Africa . . . . 56 E3 31 10S 24 57 E
Nouveau Comptoir = Wemindji,
　Canada 72 B4 53 0N 78 49W
Nouvelle-Amsterdam, Î., Ind. Oc. 3 F13 38 30S 77 30 E
Nouvelle-Calédonie = New
　Caledonia ☑, Pac. Oc. . . . . 64 K8 21 0S 165 0 E
Nova Casa Nova, Brazil 93 E10 9 25S 41 5W
Nova Esperança, Brazil 95 A5 23 8S 52 24W
Nova Friburgo, Brazil 95 A7 22 16S 42 30W
Nova Iguaçu, Brazil 95 A7 22 45S 43 28W
Nova Iorque, Brazil 93 E10 7 0S 44 5W
Nova Lima, Brazil 95 A7 19 59S 43 51W
Nova Lusitânia, Mozam. . . . . 55 F3 19 50S 34 34 E
Nova Mambone, Mozam. . . . . 57 C6 21 0S 35 3 E
Nova Scotia □, Canada 73 C7 45 10N 63 0W
Nova Sofala, Mozam. . . . . . . 57 C6 20 7S 34 42 E
Nova Venécia, Brazil 93 G10 18 45S 40 24W
Nova Zagora, Bulgaria . . . . . 23 C11 42 32N 26 1 E
Novar, Canada 84 A5 45 27N 79 15W
Novara, Italy . . . . 20 B3 45 28N 8 38 E
Novato, U.S.A. 78 G4 38 6N 122 35W
Novaya Ladoga, Russia . . . . . 18 B5 60 7N 32 16 E
Novaya Lyalya, Russia . . . . . 18 C11 59 4N 60 45 E
Novaya Sibir, Ostrov, Russia . 29 B16 75 10N 150 0 E
Novaya Zemlya, Russia . . . . . 28 B6 75 0N 56 0 E
Nové Zámky, Slovak Rep. . . . . 17 D10 47 59N 18 8 E
Novgorod, Russia . . . . 18 C5 58 30N 31 25 E
Novgorod-Severskiy =
　Novhorod-Siverskyy, Ukraine . 18 D5 52 2N 33 10 E
Novhorod-Siverskyy, Ukraine . 18 D5 52 2N 33 10 E
Novi Lígure, Italy . . . . 20 D8 44 46N 8 47 E
Novi Pazar, Serbia & M. . . . . 23 C9 43 12N 20 28 E
Novi Sad, Serbia & M. . . . . . . 23 B8 45 18N 19 52 E
Novo Hamburgo, Brazil 95 B5 29 37S 51 7W
Novo Mesto, Slovenia . . . . . . 22 B7 45 47N 15 12 E
Novo Remanso, Brazil 93 E10 9 41S 42 4W
Novoaltaysk, Russia . . . . 28 D9 53 30N 84 0 E
Novocherkassk, Russia . . . . . 19 E7 47 27N 40 15 E
Novogrudok = Navahrudak,
　Belarus . . . . 17 B13 53 40N 25 50 E
Novohrad-Volynskyy, Ukraine . 17 C14 50 34N 27 35 E
Novokachalinsk, Russia . . . . . 30 B6 44 46N 132 0 E
Novokuybyshevsk, Russia . . . 18 D8 53 7N 49 58 E
Novokuznetsk, Russia . . . . . . 28 D9 53 45N 87 10 E
Novomoskovsk, Russia . . . . . 18 D6 54 5N 38 15 E
Novorossiysk, Russia . . . . . . 19 F6 44 43N 37 46 E
Novorybnoye, Russia . . . . . . 29 B11 72 50N 105 50 E
Novoselytsya, Ukraine . . . . . 17 D14 48 14N 26 15 E
Novoshakhtinsk, Russia . . . . 19 E6 47 46N 39 58 E
Novosibirsk, Russia . . . . 28 D9 55 0N 83 5 E
Novosibirskiye Ostrova, Russia 29 B15 75 0N 142 0 E
Novotroitsk, Russia . . . . 18 D10 51 10N 58 15 E
Novouzensk, Russia . . . . 19 D8 50 32N 48 17 E
Novovolynsk, Ukraine . . . . . . 17 C13 50 45N 24 4 E
Novska, Croatia . . . . 22 B7 45 19N 17 0 E
Novvy Urengoy, Russia . . . . . 28 C8 65 48N 76 52 E
Novyy Bor, Russia . . . . 18 A9 66 43N 52 19 E
Novyy Port, Russia . . . . 28 C8 67 40N 72 30 E
Now Shahr, Iran . . . . 45 B6 36 40N 51 30 E
Nowa Sól, Poland . . . . 16 C8 51 48N 15 44 E
Nowata, U.S.A. 81 G7 36 42N 95 38W
Nowbarān, Iran . . . . 45 C6 35 8N 49 42 E
Nowghāb, Iran . . . . 45 C8 33 53N 59 4 E
Nowgong, Assam, India . . . . . 41 F18 26 20N 92 50 E
Nowgong, Mad. P., India . . . . 43 G8 25 4N 79 27 E
Nowra, Australia . . . . 63 E5 34 53S 150 35 E
Nowshera, Pakistan . . . . 40 C8 34 0N 72 0 E
Nowy Sącz, Poland . . . . 17 D11 49 40N 20 41 E
Nowy Targ, Poland . . . . 17 D11 49 29N 20 2 E
Nowy Tomyśl, Poland . . . . . . 16 B9 52 19N 16 10 E
Noxen, U.S.A. 85 E8 41 25N 76 4W
Noxon, U.S.A. 76 C6 48 0N 115 43W
Noyabr'sk, Russia . . . . 28 C8 64 34N 76 21 E
Noyon, France . . . . 20 B5 49 34N 2 59 E
Noyon, Mongolia . . . . 34 C2 43 2N 102 4 E
Nqutu, S. Africa . . . . 57 D5 28 15S 30 40 E
Nsanje, Malawi . . . . 55 F4 16 55S 35 12 E
Nsomba, Zambia . . . . 55 E2 10 45S 29 51 E
Nu Jiang →, China . . . . 32 D4 29 58N 97 25 E
Nu Shan, China . . . . 32 D4 26 0N 99 20 E
Nubia, Africa . . . . 48 D7 21 0N 32 0 E
Nubian Desert = Nûbîya, Es
　Sahrâ en, Sudan . . . . 51 D12 21 30N 33 30 E
Nûbîya, Es Sahrâ en, Sudan . . 51 D12 21 30N 33 30 E
Nuboai, Indonesia . . . . 37 E9 2 10S 136 30 E
Nubra →, India . . . . 43 B7 34 35N 77 35 E
Nueces →, U.S.A. 81 M6 27 51N 97 30W

Nueltin L., Canada 71 A9 60 30N 99 30W
Nueva Gerona, Cuba 88 B3 21 53N 82 49W
Nueva Palmira, Uruguay 94 C4 33 52S 58 20W
Nueva Rosita, Mexico 86 B4 28 0N 101 11W
Nueva San Salvador, El Salv. . 88 D2 13 40N 89 18W
Nuéve de Julio, Argentina . . . 94 D3 35 30S 61 0W
Nuevitas, Cuba 88 B4 21 30N 77 20W
Nuevo, G., Argentina 96 E4 43 0S 64 30W
Nuevo Casas Grandes, Mexico . 86 A3 30 22N 108 0W
Nuevo Guerrero, Mexico 87 B5 26 34N 99 15W
Nuevo Laredo, Mexico 87 B5 27 30N 99 30W
Nuevo León □, Mexico 86 C5 25 0N 100 0W
Nuevo Rocafuerte, Ecuador . . 92 D3 0 55S 75 27W
Nugget Pt., N.Z. . . . . 59 M2 46 27S 169 50 E
Nuhaka, N.Z. . . . . 59 H6 39 3S 177 45 E
Nukey Bluff, Australia . . . . . . 63 E2 32 26S 135 29 E
Nukhayb, Iraq . . . . 44 C4 32 4N 42 3 E
Nuku'alofa, Tonga 59 E12 21 10S 174 0W
Nukus, Uzbekistan . . . . 28 E6 42 27N 59 41 E
Nullagine, Australia . . . . 60 D3 21 53S 120 7 E
Nullagine →, Australia . . . . . 60 D3 21 20S 120 20 E
Nullarbor, Australia . . . . 61 F5 31 28S 130 55 E
Nullarbor △, Australia . . . . . . 61 F2 32 39S 115 37 E
Nullarbor Plain, Australia . . . 61 F4 31 10S 129 0 E
Numalla, L., Australia . . . . . . 63 D3 28 43S 144 20 E
Numan, Nigeria . . . . 51 G8 9 29N 12 3 E
Numata, Japan . . . . 31 F9 36 45N 139 4 E
Numaykoos Lake △, Canada . . 71 B9 57 52N 95 58W
Numazu, Japan . . . . 31 G9 35 7N 138 51 E
Numbulwar, Australia . . . . . . 62 A2 14 15S 135 45 E
Numfoor, Indonesia . . . . 37 E8 1 0S 134 50 E
Numurkah, Australia . . . . 63 F4 36 5S 145 26 E
Nunakaluk I., Canada 73 A7 55 49N 60 20W
Nunap Isua, Greenland 69 C15 59 48N 43 55W
Nunavut □, Canada 69 D8 66 0N 85 0W
Nunda, U.S.A. 84 D7 42 35N 77 56W
Nuneaton, U.K. 13 E6 52 32N 1 27W
Nungarin, Australia . . . . 61 F2 31 12S 118 6 E
Nungo, Mozam. . . . . 55 E4 13 23S 37 43 E
Nungwe, Tanzania . . . . 54 C3 2 48S 32 2 E
Nunivak I., U.S.A. 68 B3 60 10N 166 30W
Nunkun, India . . . . 43 C7 33 57N 76 2 E
Núoro, Italy . . . . 22 D3 40 20N 9 20 E
Nûrābād, Iran . . . . 45 E8 27 47N 57 12 E
Nuremberg = Nürnberg,
　Germany . . . . 16 D6 49 27N 11 3 E
Nuri, Mexico 86 B3 28 2N 109 22W
Nuriootpa, Australia . . . . 63 E2 34 27S 139 0 E
Nuristan □, Afghan. . . . . 40 B7 35 20N 71 0 E
Nurmes, Finland . . . . 8 E23 63 33N 29 10 E
Nürnberg, Germany . . . . 16 D6 49 27N 11 3 E
Nurpur, Pakistan . . . . 42 D4 31 53N 71 54 E
Nurran, L. = Terewah, L.,
　Australia . . . . 63 D4 29 52S 147 35 E
Nurrari Lakes, Australia . . . . 61 E5 29 1S 130 5 E
Nusa Barung, Indonesia . . . . 37 H15 8 30S 113 30 E
Nusa Dua, Indonesia . . . . . . 37 K18 8 48S 115 14 E
Nusa Kambangan, Indonesia . 37 G13 7 40S 108 10 E
Nusa Tenggara Barat □,
　Indonesia . . . . 36 F5 8 50S 117 30 E
Nusa Tenggara Timur □,
　Indonesia . . . . 37 F6 9 30S 122 0 E
Nusaybin, Turkey . . . . 19 G7 37 3N 41 10 E
Nushki, Pakistan . . . . 42 E2 29 35N 66 0 E
Nuuk, Greenland 69 B14 64 10N 51 35W
Nuwakot, Nepal . . . . 43 E10 28 10N 83 55 E
Nuweiba', Egypt . . . . 44 D2 28 59N 34 39 E
Nuwerus, S. Africa . . . . 56 E2 31 8S 18 24 E
Nuweveldberge, S. Africa . . . 56 E3 32 10S 21 45 E
Nuyts, C., Australia . . . . 61 F5 32 2S 132 21 E
Nuyts, Pt., Australia . . . . 61 G2 35 4S 116 38 E
Nuyts Arch., Australia . . . . . . 63 E1 32 35S 133 20 E
Nxai Pan △, Botswana . . . . . 56 B3 19 50S 24 46 E
Nxau-Nxau, Botswana . . . . . 56 B3 18 57S 21 4 E
Nyabing, Australia . . . . 61 F2 33 33S 118 9 E
Nyack, U.S.A. 85 E11 41 5N 73 55W
Nyagan, Russia . . . . 28 C7 62 30N 65 38 E
Nyahanga, Tanzania . . . . 54 C3 2 20S 33 37 E
Nyahua, Tanzania . . . . 54 D3 5 25S 33 23 E
Nyahururu, Kenya . . . . 54 B4 0 2N 36 27 E
Nyainqentanglha Shan, China . 32 D4 30 0N 90 0 E
Nyakanazi, Tanzania . . . . 54 C3 3 2S 31 10 E
Nyâlâ, Sudan . . . . 51 F10 12 2N 24 58 E
Nyamandhlovu, Zimbabwe . . 55 F2 19 55S 28 16 E
Nyambiti, Tanzania . . . . 54 C3 2 48S 33 27 E
Nyamwaga, Tanzania . . . . . . 54 C3 1 27S 34 33 E
Nyandekwa, Tanzania . . . . . . 54 C3 3 57S 32 32 E
Nyandoma, Russia . . . . 18 B7 61 40N 40 12 E
Nyanga △, Zimbabwe . . . . . . 55 F3 18 17S 32 46 E
Nyangana, Namibia . . . . 56 B3 18 0S 20 40 E
Nyanguge, Tanzania . . . . 54 C3 2 30S 33 12 E
Nyanza, Rwanda . . . . 54 C2 2 20S 29 42 E
Nyanza □, Kenya . . . . 54 C3 0 10S 34 15 E
Nyanza-Lac, Burundi . . . . . . 54 C2 4 21S 29 36 E
Nyasa, L., Africa . . . . 55 E3 12 30S 34 30 E
Nyasvizh, Belarus . . . . 17 B14 53 14N 26 38 E
Nyazepetrovsk, Russia . . . . . 18 C10 56 3N 59 36 E
Nyazura, Zimbabwe . . . . 55 F3 18 40S 32 16 E
Nyazwidzi →, Zimbabwe . . . . 55 G3 20 0S 31 17 E
Nybro, Sweden . . . . 9 H16 56 44N 15 55 E
Nyda, Russia . . . . 28 C8 66 40N 72 58 E
Nyeri, Kenya . . . . 54 C4 0 23S 36 56 E
Nyika △, Malawi . . . . 55 E3 10 30S 33 53 E
Nyíregyháza, Hungary . . . . . 17 E11 47 58N 21 47 E
Nykøbing, Storstrøm, Denmark 9 J14 54 56N 11 52 E
Nykøbing, Vestsjælland,
　Denmark . . . . 9 J14 55 55N 11 40 E
Nykøbing, Viborg, Denmark . . 9 H13 56 48N 8 51 E
Nyköping, Sweden . . . . 9 G17 58 45N 17 1 E
Nylstroom = Modimolle, S. Africa 57 C4 24 42S 28 22 E
Nymagee, Australia . . . . 63 E4 32 7S 146 20 E
Nymboida →, Australia . . . . . 63 D5 29 38S 152 26 E
Nynäshamn, Sweden . . . . 9 G17 58 54N 17 57 E
Nyngan, Australia . . . . 63 E4 31 30S 147 8 E
Nyoma Rap, India . . . . 43 C8 33 10N 78 40 E
Nyoman = Nemunas →,
　Lithuania . . . . 9 J19 55 25N 21 10 E
Nysa, Poland . . . . 17 C9 50 30N 17 22 E
Nysa →, Europe . . . . 16 B8 52 4N 14 46 E
Nyssa, U.S.A. 76 E5 43 53N 117 0W
Nyunzu, Dem. Rep. of the Congo 54 D2 5 57S 27 58 E
Nyurba, Russia . . . . 29 C12 63 17N 118 28 E
Nzega, Tanzania . . . . 54 C3 4 10S 33 12 E
Nzérékoré, Guinea 50 G4 7 49N 8 48W
Nzeto, Angola . . . . 52 F2 7 10S 12 52 E
Nzilo, Chutes de, Dem. Rep. of
　the Congo . . . . 55 E2 10 18S 25 27 E
Nzubuka, Tanzania . . . . 54 C3 4 45S 32 50 E

O

Ō-Shima, *Japan* .... **31 G9** 34 44N 139 24 E
Oa, Mull of, *U.K.* **11 F2** 55 35N 6 20W
Oacoma, *U.S.A.* **80 D5** 43 48N 99 24W
Oahe, L., *U.S.A.* **80 C4** 44 27N 100 24W
Oahe Dam, *U.S.A.* **80 C4** 44 27N 100 24W
Oahu, *U.S.A.* **74 H16** 21 28N 157 58W
Oak Harbor, *U.S.A.* **78 B4** 48 18N 122 39W
Oak Hill, *U.S.A.* **82 G5** 37 59N 81 9W
Oak Ridge, *U.S.A.* **83 G3** 36 1N 84 16W
Oak View, *U.S.A.* **79 L7** 34 24N 119 18W
Oakan-Dake, *Japan* .... **30 C12** 43 27N 144 10 E
Oakdale, *Calif., U.S.A.* **78 H6** 37 46N 120 51W
Oakdale, *La., U.S.A.* **81 K8** 30 49N 92 40W
Oakes, *U.S.A.* **80 B5** 46 8N 98 6W
Oakesdale, *U.S.A.* **76 C5** 47 8N 117 15W
Oakey, *Australia* .... **63 D5** 27 25S 151 43 E
Oakfield, *U.S.A.* **84 C6** 43 4N 78 16W
Oakham, *U.K.* **13 E7** 52 40N 0 43W
Oakhurst, *U.S.A.* **78 H7** 37 19N 119 40W
Oakland, *U.S.A.* **78 H4** 37 49N 122 16W
Oakley, *Idaho, U.S.A.* **76 E7** 42 15N 113 53W
Oakley, *Kans., U.S.A.* **80 F4** 39 8N 100 51W
Oakover →, *Australia* ...... **60 D3** 21 0S 120 40 E
Oakridge, *U.S.A.* **76 E2** 43 45N 122 28W
Oakville, *Canada* **84 C5** 43 27N 79 41W
Oakville, *U.S.A.* **78 D3** 46 51N 123 14W
Oamaru, *N.Z.* .... **59 L3** 45 5S 170 59 E
Oasis, *Calif., U.S.A.* **79 M10** 33 28N 116 6W
Oasis, *Nev., U.S.A.* **78 H9** 37 29N 117 55W
Oates Land, *Antarctica* .... **5 C11** 69 0S 160 0 E
Oatlands, *Australia* .... **63 G4** 42 17S 147 21 E
Oatman, *U.S.A.* **79 K12** 35 1N 114 19W
Oaxaca, *Mexico* **87 D5** 17 2N 96 40W
Oaxaca □, *Mexico* **87 D5** 17 0N 97 0W
Ob →, *Russia* .... **28 C7** 66 45N 69 30 E
Oba, *Canada* **72 C3** 49 4N 84 7W
Obama, *Japan* .... **31 G7** 35 30N 135 45 E
Oban, *U.K.* **11 E3** 56 25N 5 29W
Obbia, *Somali Rep.* .... **47 F4** 5 25N 48 30 E
Obera, *Argentina* **95 B4** 27 21S 55 2W
Oberhausen, *Germany* ..... **16 C4** 51 28N 6 51 E
Oberlin, *Kans., U.S.A.* **80 F4** 39 49N 100 32W
Oberlin, *La., U.S.A.* **81 K8** 30 37N 92 46W
Oberlin, *Ohio, U.S.A.* **84 E2** 41 18N 82 13W
Oberon, *Australia* .... **63 E4** 33 45S 149 52 E
Obi, *Indonesia* .... **37 E7** 1 23S 127 45 E
Óbidos, *Brazil* **93 D7** 1 50S 55 30W
Obihiro, *Japan* .... **30 C11** 42 56N 143 12 E
Obilatu, *Indonesia* .... **37 E7** 1 25S 127 20 E
Obluchye, *Russia* .... **29 E14** 49 1N 131 4 E
Obo, *C.A.R.* .... **54 A2** 5 20N 26 32 E
Oboa, Mt., *Uganda* .... **54 B3** 1 45N 34 45 E
Oboyan, *Russia* .... **28 D4** 51 15N 36 21 E
Obozerskaya = Obozerskiy,
   Russia .... **18 B7** 63 34N 40 21 E
Obozerskiy, *Russia* .... **18 B7** 63 34N 40 21 E
Observatory Inlet, *Canada* . **70 B3** 55 10N 129 54W
Obshchi Syrt, *Russia* ..... **6 E16** 52 0N 53 0 E
Obskaya Guba, *Russia* .... **28 C8** 69 0N 73 0 E
Obuasi, *Ghana* **50 G5** 6 17N 1 40W
Ocala, *U.S.A.* **83 L4** 29 11N 82 8W
Ocampo, *Chihuahua, Mexico* **86 B3** 28 9N 108 24W
Ocampo, *Tamaulipas, Mexico* **87 C5** 22 50N 99 20W
Ocaña, *Spain* **21 C4** 39 55N 3 30W
Ocanomowoc, *U.S.A.* **80 D10** 43 7N 88 30W
Occidental, Cordillera, *Colombia* **92 C3** 5 0N 76 0W
Occidental, Grand Erg, *Algeria* **50 B6** 30 20N 1 0 E
Ocean City, *Md., U.S.A.* ... **82 F8** 38 20N 75 5W
Ocean City, *N.J., U.S.A.* ... **82 F8** 39 17N 74 35W
Ocean City, *Wash., U.S.A.* . **78 C2** 47 4N 124 10W
Ocean Falls, *Canada* **70 C3** 52 18N 127 48W
Ocean I. = Banaba, *Kiribati* **64 H8** 0 45S 169 50 E
Ocean Park, *U.S.A.* **78 D2** 46 30N 124 3W
Oceano, *U.S.A.* **79 K6** 35 6N 120 37W
Oceanport, *U.S.A.* **85 F10** 40 19N 74 3W
Oceanside, *U.S.A.* **79 M9** 33 12N 117 23W
Ochil Hills, *U.K.* **11 E5** 56 14N 3 40W
Ocho Rios, *Jamaica* .... **88 a** 18 24N 77 6W
Ocilla, *U.S.A.* **83 K4** 31 36N 83 15W
Ocmulgee →, *U.S.A.* **83 K4** 31 58N 82 33W
Ocniţa, *Moldova* .... **17 D14** 48 25N 27 30 E
Oconee →, *U.S.A.* **83 K4** 31 58N 82 33W
Oconto, *U.S.A.* **82 C2** 44 53N 87 52W
Oconto Falls, *U.S.A.* **82 C1** 44 52N 88 9W
Ocosingo, *Mexico* **87 D6** 17 10N 92 15W
Ocotal, *Nic.* **88 D2** 13 41N 86 31W
Ocotlán, *Mexico* **86 C4** 20 21N 102 42W
Ocotlán de Morelos, *Mexico* **87 D5** 16 48N 96 40W
Oda, *Japan* .... **31 G6** 35 11N 132 30 E
Óðáðahraun, *Iceland* **8 D5** 65 5N 17 0W
Odate, *Japan* .... **30 D10** 40 16N 140 34 E
Odawara, *Japan* .... **31 G9** 35 20N 139 6 E
Odda, *Norway* .... **9 F12** 60 3N 6 35 E
Odei →, *Canada* **71 B9** 56 6N 96 54W
Ödemiş, *Turkey* .... **23 E13** 38 15N 28 0 E
Odendaalsrus, *S. Africa* ... **56 D4** 27 48S 26 45 E
Odense, *Denmark* .... **9 J14** 55 22N 10 23 E
Oder →, *Europe* .... **16 B8** 53 33N 14 38 E
Odesa, *Ukraine* .... **19 E5** 46 30N 30 45 E
Odessa = Odesa, *Ukraine* .. **19 E5** 46 30N 30 45 E
Odessa, *Canada* **85 B8** 44 17N 76 43W
Odessa, *Tex., U.S.A.* **81 K3** 31 52N 102 23W
Odessa, *Wash., U.S.A.* **76 C4** 47 20N 118 41W
Odiakwe, *Botswana* .... **56 C4** 20 12S 25 17 E
Odienné, *Ivory C.* **50 G4** 9 30N 7 34W
Odintsovo, *Russia* .... **18 C6** 55 39N 37 15 E
O'Donnell, *U.S.A.* **81 J4** 32 58N 101 50W
Odorheiu Secuiesc, *Romania* **17 E13** 46 21N 25 21 E
Odra = Oder →, *Europe* .... **16 B8** 53 33N 14 38 E
Odzi, *Zimbabwe* .... **57 B5** 19 0S 32 20 E
Odzi →, *Zimbabwe* .... **57 B5** 19 45S 32 23 E
Oeiras, *Brazil* **93 E10** 7 0S 42 8W
Oelrichs, *U.S.A.* **80 D3** 43 11N 103 14W
Oelwein, *U.S.A.* **80 D9** 42 41N 91 55W
Oenpelli, *Australia* .... **60 B5** 12 20S 133 4 E
Ofanto →, *Italy* .... **22 D7** 41 22N 16 13 E
Offa, *Nigeria* .... **50 G6** 8 13N 4 42 E
Offaly □, *Ireland* **10 C4** 53 15N 7 30W
Offenbach, *Germany* ...... **16 C5** 50 6N 8 44 E
Offenburg, *Germany* ...... **16 D4** 48 28N 7 56 E
Ofotfjorden, *Norway* ...... **8 B17** 68 27N 17 0 E
Ōfunato, *Japan* .... **30 E10** 39 4N 141 43 E
Oga, *Japan* .... **30 E9** 39 55N 139 50 E
Oga-Hantō, *Japan* .... **30 E9** 39 58N 139 47 E

Ōgaki, *Japan* .... **31 G8** 35 21N 136 37 E
Ogallala, *U.S.A.* **80 E4** 41 8N 101 43W
Ogasawara Gunto, *Pac. Oc.* **26 G18** 27 0N 142 0 E
Ogbomosho, *Nigeria* ...... **50 G6** 8 1N 4 11 E
Ogden, *U.S.A.* **76 F7** 41 13N 111 58W
Ogdensburg, *U.S.A.* **85 B9** 44 42N 75 30W
Ogeechee →, *U.S.A.* **83 K5** 31 50N 81 3W
Ogilby, *U.S.A.* **79 N12** 32 49N 114 50W
Oglio →, *Italy* .... **22 B4** 45 2N 10 39 E
Ogmore, *Australia* .... **62 C4** 22 37S 149 35 E
Ogoki, *Canada* **72 B2** 51 38N 85 58W
Ogoki →, *Canada* **72 B2** 51 38N 85 57W
Ogoki L., *Canada* **72 B2** 50 50N 87 10W
Ogoki Res., *Canada* **72 B2** 50 45N 88 15W
Ogooué →, *Gabon* .... **52 E1** 1 0S 9 0 E
Ogowe = Ogooué →, *Gabon* **52 E1** 1 0S 9 0 E
Ogre, *Latvia* .... **9 H21** 56 49N 24 36 E
Ogurchinskiy, Ostrov,
   Turkmenistan .... **45 B7** 38 55N 53 2 E
Ohai, *N.Z.* .... **59 L2** 45 55S 168 0 E
Ohakune, *N.Z.* .... **59 H5** 39 24S 175 24 E
Ohata, *Japan* .... **30 D10** 41 24N 141 10 E
Ohau, L., *N.Z.* .... **59 L2** 44 15S 169 53 E
Ohio □, *U.S.A.* **84 F2** 40 15N 82 45W
Ohio →, *U.S.A.* **82 G1** 36 59N 89 8W
Ohře →, *Czech Rep.* .... **16 C8** 50 30N 14 10 E
Ohrid, *Macedonia* .... **23 D9** 41 8N 20 52 E
Ohridsko Jezero, *Macedonia* **23 D9** 41 8N 20 52 E
Ohrigstad, *S. Africa* ...... **57 C5** 24 39S 30 36 E
Oiapoque, *Brazil* **93** 3 50N 51 50W
Oikou, *China* .... **35 E9** 38 35N 117 42 E
Oil City, *U.S.A.* **84 E5** 41 26N 79 42W
Oil Springs, *Canada* **84 D2** 42 47N 82 7W
Oildale, *U.S.A.* **79 K7** 35 25N 119 1W
Oise →, *France* .... **20 B5** 49 0N 2 4 E
Oistins, *Barbados* .... **89 g** 13 4N 59 33W
Oistins B., *Barbados* ...... **89 g** 13 4N 59 33W
Ōita, *Japan* .... **31 H5** 33 14N 131 36 E
Ōita □, *Japan* .... **31 H5** 33 15N 131 30 E
Oiticica, *Brazil* **93 E10** 5 3S 41 5W
Ojacaliente, *Mexico* **86 C4** 22 34N 102 15W
Ojai, *U.S.A.* **79 L7** 34 27N 119 15W
Ojinaga, *Mexico* **86 B4** 29 34N 104 25W
Ojiya, *Japan* .... **31 F9** 37 18N 138 48 E
Ojo de Liebre △, *Mexico* ... **86 B2** 27 50N 114 0W
Ojos del Salado, Cerro,
   Argentina **94 B2** 27 0S 68 40W
Oka →, *Russia* .... **18 C7** 56 20N 43 59 E
Okaba, *Indonesia* .... **37 F9** 8 6S 139 42 E
Okahandja, *Namibia* ...... **56 C2** 22 0S 16 59 E
Okanagan L., *Canada* **70 D5** 50 0N 119 30W
Okanogan, *U.S.A.* **76 B4** 48 22N 119 35W
Okanogan →, *U.S.A.* **76 B4** 48 6N 119 44W
Okapi △, *Dem. Rep. of the Congo* **54 B2** 2 30N 27 20 E
Okaputa, *Namibia* .... **56 C2** 20 5S 17 0 E
Okara, *Pakistan* .... **42 D5** 30 50N 73 31 E
Okarito, *N.Z.* .... **59 E3** 43 15S 170 9 E
Okavango Delta, *Botswana* . **56 B3** 18 45S 22 45 E
Okavango Swamp = Okavango
   Delta, *Botswana* .... **56 B3** 18 45S 22 45 E
Okaya, *Japan* .... **31 F9** 36 5N 138 10 E
Okayama, *Japan* .... **31 G6** 34 40N 133 54 E
Okayama □, *Japan* .... **31 G6** 35 0N 133 50 E
Okazaki, *Japan* .... **31 G8** 34 57N 137 10 E
Okeechobee, *U.S.A.* **83 M5** 27 15N 80 50W
Okeechobee, L., *U.S.A.* ... **83 M5** 27 0N 80 50W
Okefenokee △, *U.S.A.* **83 K4** 30 44N 82 7W
Okefenokee Swamp, *U.S.A.* **83 K4** 30 40N 82 20W
Okehampton, *U.K.* **13 G4** 50 44N 4 0W
Okha, *India* .... **42 H3** 22 27N 69 4 E
Okha, *Russia* .... **29 D15** 53 40N 143 0 E
Okhotsk, *Russia* .... **29 D15** 59 20N 143 10 E
Okhotsk, Sea of, *Asia* ..... **29 D15** 55 0N 145 0 E
Okhotskiy Perevoz, *Russia* . **29 C14** 61 52N 135 35 E
Okhtyrka, *Ukraine* .... **19 D5** 50 25N 35 0 E
Oki-Shotō, *Japan* .... **31 F6** 36 5N 133 15 E
Okiep, *S. Africa* .... **56 D2** 29 39S 17 53 E
Okinawa, *Japan* .... **31 L4** 26 40N 128 0 E
Okinawa-Guntō, *Japan* .... **31 L4** 26 40N 128 0 E
Okinawa-Jima, *Japan* ..... **31 L4** 26 32N 128 0 E
Okino-erabu-Shima, *Japan* . **31 L4** 27 21N 128 33 E
Oklahoma □, *U.S.A.* **81 H6** 35 20N 97 30W
Oklahoma City, *U.S.A.* **81 H6** 35 30N 97 30W
Okmulgee, *U.S.A.* **81 H7** 35 37N 95 58W
Oknitsa = Ocniţa, *Moldova* . **17 D14** 48 25N 27 30 E
Okolo, *Uganda* .... **54 B3** 2 37N 31 8 E
Okolona, *U.S.A.* **81 J10** 34 0N 88 45W
Okombahe, *Namibia* ...... **56 C2** 21 23S 15 22 E
Okotoks, *Canada* **70 C6** 50 43N 113 58W
Oksibil, *Indonesia* .... **37 E10** 4 59S 140 35 E
Oksovskiy, *Russia* .... **18 B6** 62 33N 39 57 E
Oktabrsk = Oktyabrsk,
   Kazakhstan .... **19 E10** 49 28N 57 25 E
Oktyabrsk, *Kazakhstan* .... **19 E10** 49 28N 57 25 E
Oktyabrskiy = Aktsyabrski,
   Belarus .... **17 B15** 52 38N 28 53 E
Oktyabrskiy, *Russia* ...... **18 D9** 54 28N 53 28 E
Oktyabrskoy Revolyutsii, Ostrov,
   Russia .... **29 B10** 79 30N 97 0 E
Okuru, *N.Z.* .... **59 K2** 43 55S 168 55 E
Okushiri-Tō, *Japan* .... **30 C9** 42 15N 139 30 E
Okwa →, *Botswana* .... **56 C3** 22 30S 23 0 E
Ola, *U.S.A.* **81 H8** 35 2N 93 13W
Ólafsfjörður, *Iceland* **8 C4** 66 4N 18 39W
Ólafsvík, *Iceland* **8 D2** 64 53N 23 43W
Olancha, *U.S.A.* **79 J8** 36 17N 118 1W
Olancha Pk., *U.S.A.* **79 J8** 36 15N 118 7W
Olanchito, *Honduras* **88 C2** 15 30N 86 30W
Öland, *Sweden* .... **9 H17** 56 45N 16 38 E
Olary, *Australia* .... **63 E3** 32 18S 140 19 E
Olascoaga, *Argentina* **94 D3** 35 15S 60 39W
Olathe, *U.S.A.* **80 F7** 38 53N 94 49W
Olavarría, *Argentina* **94 D3** 36 55S 60 20W
Oława, *Poland* .... **17 C9** 50 57N 17 20 E
Ólbia, *Italy* .... **22 D3** 40 55N 9 31 E
Olcott, *U.S.A.* **84 C6** 43 20N 78 42W
Old Bahama Chan. = Bahama,
   Canal Viejo de, *W. Indies* **88 B4** 22 10N 77 30W
Old Baldy Pk. = San Antonio, Mt.,
   U.S.A. **79 L9** 34 17N 117 38W
Old Castile = Castilla y Leon □,
   Spain **21 B3** 42 0N 5 0W
Old Crow, *Canada* **68 B6** 67 30N 139 55W
Old Dale, *U.S.A.* **79 L11** 34 8N 115 47W
Old Forge, *N.Y., U.S.A.* **85 C10** 43 43N 74 58W
Old Forge, *Pa., U.S.A.* **85 E9** 41 22N 75 45W
Old Perlican, *Canada* **73 C9** 48 5N 53 1W
Old Shinyanga, *Tanzania* .. **54 C3** 3 33S 33 27 E

Old Speck Mt., *U.S.A.* **85 B14** 44 34N 70 57W
Old Town, *U.S.A.* **83 C11** 44 56N 68 39W
Old Washington, *U.S.A.* ... **84 F3** 40 2N 81 27W
Old Wives L., *Canada* **71 C7** 50 5N 106 0W
Oldbury, *U.K.* **13 F5** 51 38N 2 33W
Oldcastle, *Ireland* **10 C4** 53 46N 7 10W
Oldeani, *Tanzania* .... **54 C4** 3 22S 35 35 E
Oldenburg, *Germany* ...... **16 B5** 53 9N 8 13 E
Oldenzaal, *Neths.* .... **15 B6** 52 19N 6 53 E
Oldham, *U.K.* **12 D5** 53 33N 2 7W
Oldman →, *Canada* **70 D6** 49 57N 111 42W
Oldmeldrum, *U.K.* **11 D6** 57 20N 2 19W
Olds, *Canada* **70 C6** 51 50N 114 10W
Olduvai Gorge, *Tanzania* .. **54 C4** 2 57S 35 23 E
Oldziyt, *Mongolia* .... **34 B5** 44 40N 109 1 E
Olekma →, *Russia* .... **29 C13** 60 22N 120 42 E
Olekminsk, *Russia* .... **29 C13** 60 25N 120 30 E
Oleksandriya, *Ukraine* .... **17 C14** 50 37N 26 19 E
Olema, *U.S.A.* **78 G4** 38 3N 122 47W
Olenegorsk, *Russia* .... **18 A5** 68 9N 33 18 E
Olenek, *Russia* .... **29 C12** 68 28N 112 18 E
Olenek →, *Russia* .... **29 B13** 73 0N 120 10 E
Oléron, Î. d', *France* **20 D3** 45 55N 1 15W
Oleśnica, *Poland* .... **17 C9** 51 13N 17 22 E
Olevsk, *Ukraine* .... **17 C14** 51 12N 27 39 E
Olga, *Russia* .... **29 E14** 43 50N 135 14 E
Olga, L., *Canada* **72 C4** 49 47N 77 15W
Olga, Mt., *Australia* .... **61 E5** 25 20S 130 50 E
Ölgiy, *Mongolia* .... **32 B3** 48 56N 89 57 E
Olhão, *Portugal* **21 D2** 37 3N 7 48W
Olifants = Elefantes →, *Africa* **57 C5** 24 10S 32 40 E
Olifants →, *Namibia* ...... **56 C2** 25 30S 19 30 E
Olifantshoek, *S. Africa* .... **56 D3** 27 57S 22 42 E
Ólimbos, Óros, *Greece* .... **23 D10** 40 6N 22 23 E
Olimpia, *Brazil* **95 A6** 20 44S 48 54W
Olinda, *Brazil* **93 E12** 8 1S 34 51W
Oliva, *Argentina* **94 C3** 32 0S 63 38W
Olivehurst, *U.S.A.* **78 F5** 39 6N 121 34W
Olivenza, *Spain* **21 C2** 38 41N 7 9W
Oliver, *Canada* **70 D5** 49 13N 119 37W
Oliver L., *Canada* **71 B8** 56 56N 103 22W
Ollagüe, *Chile* **94 A2** 21 15S 68 10W
Olney, Ill., *U.S.A.* **82 F1** 38 44N 88 5W
Olney, *Tex., U.S.A.* **81 J5** 33 22N 98 45W
Olomane →, *Canada* **73 B7** 50 14N 60 37W
Olomouc, *Czech Rep.* ..... **17 D9** 49 38N 17 12 E
Olonets, *Russia* .... **18 B5** 61 0N 32 54 E
Olongapo, *Phil.* .... **37 B6** 14 50N 120 18 E
Olot, *Spain* .... **21 A7** 42 11N 2 30 E
Olovyannaya, *Russia* ...... **29 D12** 50 58N 115 35 E
Oloy →, *Russia* .... **29 C16** 66 29N 159 29 E
Olsztyn, *Poland* .... **17 B11** 53 48N 20 29 E
Olt →, *Romania* .... **17 G13** 43 43N 24 51 E
Olteniţa, *Romania* .... **17 F14** 44 7N 26 42 E
Olton, *U.S.A.* **81 H3** 34 11N 102 8W
Olymbos, *Cyprus* .... **25 D12** 35 21N 33 45 E
Olympia, *Greece* .... **23 F9** 37 39N 21 39 E
Olympia, *U.S.A.* **78 D4** 47 3N 122 53W
Olympic △, *U.S.A.* **78 C3** 47 48N 123 30W
Olympic Dam, *Australia* ... **63 E2** 30 30S 136 55 E
Olympic Mts., *U.S.A.* **78 C3** 47 55N 123 45W
Olympus, *Cyprus* .... **25 E11** 34 56N 32 52 E
Olympus, Mt. = Ólimbos, Óros,
   Greece .... **23 D10** 40 6N 22 23 E
Olympus, Mt. = Uludağ, *Turkey* **23 D13** 40 4N 29 13 E
Olympus, Mt., *U.S.A.* **78 C3** 47 48N 123 43W
Olyphant, *U.S.A.* **85 E9** 41 27N 75 36W
Om →, *Russia* .... **28 D8** 54 59N 73 22 E
Om Koi, *Thailand* .... **38 D2** 17 48N 98 22 E
Ōma, *Japan* .... **30 D10** 41 45N 141 5 E
Ōmachi, *Japan* .... **31 F8** 36 30N 137 50 E
Omae-Zaki, *Japan* .... **31 G9** 34 36N 138 14 E
Ōmagari, *Japan* .... **30 E10** 39 27N 140 29 E
Omagh, *U.K.* **10 B4** 54 36N 7 19W
Omagh □, *U.K.* **10 B4** 54 35N 7 15W
Omaha, *U.S.A.* **80 E7** 41 17N 95 58W
Omak, *U.S.A.* **76 B4** 48 25N 119 31W
Omalos, *Greece* .... **25 D5** 35 19N 23 55 E
Oman ■, *Asia* .... **47 C6** 23 0N 58 0 E
Oman, G. of, *Asia* .... **45 E8** 24 30N 58 30 E
Omaruru, *Namibia* .... **56 C2** 21 26S 16 0 E
Omaruru →, *Namibia* ..... **56 C1** 22 7S 14 15 E
Omate, *Peru* **92 G4** 16 45S 71 0W
Ombai, Selat, *Indonesia* ... **37 F6** 8 30S 124 50 E
Ombouè, *Gabon* .... **52 E1** 1 35S 9 15 E
Ombrone →, *Italy* .... **22 C4** 42 42N 11 5 E
Omdurmân, *Sudan* .... **51 E12** 15 40N 32 28 E
Omemee, *Canada* **84 B6** 44 18N 78 33W
Omeonga, *Dem. Rep. of
   the Congo* .... **54 C1** 3 40S 24 22 E
Ometepe, I. de, *Nic.* **88 D2** 11 32N 85 35W
Ometepec, *Mexico* **87 D5** 16 39N 98 23W
Ominato, *Japan* .... **30 D10** 41 17N 141 10 E
Omineca →, *Canada* **70 B4** 56 3N 124 16W
Omitara, *Namibia* .... **56 C2** 22 16S 18 2 E
Ōmiya, *Japan* .... **31 G9** 35 54N 139 38 E
Ommen, *Neths.* .... **15 B6** 52 31N 6 26 E
Ömnögovi □, *Mongolia* .... **34 C3** 43 15N 104 0 E
Omo →, *Ethiopia* .... **47 F2** 6 25N 36 10 E
Omodhos, *Cyprus* .... **25 E11** 34 51N 32 48 E
Omolon →, *Russia* .... **29 C16** 68 42N 158 36 E
Omono-Gawa →, *Japan* ... **30 E10** 39 46N 140 3 E
Omsk, *Russia* .... **28 D8** 55 0N 73 12 E
Omsukchan, *Russia* ...... **29 C16** 62 32N 155 48 E
Ōmu, *Japan* .... **30 B11** 44 34N 142 58 E
Omul, Vf., *Romania* ...... **17 F13** 45 27N 25 29 E
Ōmura, *Japan* .... **31 H4** 32 56N 129 57 E
Omuramba Omatako →,
   Namibia .... **56 B2** 17 45S 20 25 E
Omuramba Ovambo →, *Namibia* **56 B2** 18 45S 16 59 E
Ōmuta, *Japan* .... **31 H5** 33 5N 130 26 E
Onaga, *U.S.A.* **80 F6** 39 29N 96 10W
Onalaska, *U.S.A.* **80 D9** 43 53N 91 14W
Onamia, *U.S.A.* **80 B7** 46 4N 93 40W
Onancock, *U.S.A.* **82 G8** 37 43N 75 45W
Onang, *Indonesia* .... **37 E5** 3 2S 118 49 E
Onaping L., *Canada* **72 C3** 47 3N 81 30W
Onavas, *Mexico* **86 B3** 28 28N 109 30W
Onawa, *U.S.A.* **80 D6** 42 2N 96 6W
Oncócua, *Angola* .... **56 B1** 16 30S 13 25 E
Onda, *Spain* **21 C5** 39 55N 0 17W
Ondaejin, *N. Korea* .... **35 D15** 41 34N 129 40 E
Ondangwa, *Namibia* ...... **56 B2** 17 57S 16 4 E
Ondjiva, *Angola* .... **56 B2** 16 48S 15 50 E
Öndörshil, *Mongolia* ...... **34 B5** 45 13N 108 5 E
Öndverðarnes, *Iceland* **8 D1** 64 52N 24 0W
One Tree, *Australia* .... **63 E3** 34 11S 144 43 E
Onega, *Russia* .... **18 B6** 64 0N 38 10 E

Onega →, *Russia* .... **18 B6** 63 58N 38 2 E
Onega, G. of = Onezhskaya
   Guba, *Russia* .... **18 B6** 64 24N 36 38 E
Onega, L. = Onezhskoye Ozero,
   Russia .... **18 B6** 61 44N 35 22 E
Oneida, *U.S.A.* **85 C9** 43 6N 75 39W
Oneida L., *U.S.A.* **85 C9** 43 12N 75 54W
O'Neill, *U.S.A.* **80 D5** 42 27N 98 39W
Onekotan, Ostrov, *Russia* . **29 E16** 49 25N 154 45 E
Onema, *Dem. Rep. of the Congo* **54 C1** 4 35S 24 30 E
Oneonta, *U.S.A.* **85 D9** 42 27N 75 4W
Oneşti, *Romania* .... **17 E14** 46 17N 26 47 E
Onezhskaya Guba, *Russia* . **18 B6** 64 24N 36 38 E
Onezhskoye Ozero, *Russia* . **18 B6** 61 44N 35 22 E
Ongarue, *N.Z.* .... **59 H5** 38 42S 175 19 E
Ongers →, *S. Africa* ...... **56 E3** 31 4S 23 13 E
Ongerup, *Australia* .... **61 F2** 33 58S 118 28 E
Ongjin, *N. Korea* .... **35 F13** 37 56N 125 21 E
Ongkharak, *Thailand* ..... **38 E3** 14 8N 101 1 E
Ongniud Qi, *China* .... **35 C10** 43 0N 118 38 E
Ongoka, *Dem. Rep. of the Congo* **54 C2** 1 20S 26 0 E
Ongole, *India* .... **40 M12** 15 33N 80 2 E
Ongon = Havirga, *Mongolia* **34 B7** 45 41N 113 5 E
Onida, *U.S.A.* **80 C4** 44 42N 100 4W
Onilahy →, *Madag.* .... **57 C7** 23 34S 43 45 E
Onoda, *Japan* .... **31 G5** 33 59N 131 11 E
Onpyŏng-ni, *S. Korea* ..... **35 H14** 33 25N 126 55 E
Onslow, *Australia* .... **60 D2** 21 40S 115 12 E
Onslow B., *U.S.A.* **83 H7** 34 20N 77 15W
Ontake-San, *Japan* .... **31 G8** 35 53N 137 29 E
Ontario, *Calif., U.S.A.* **79 L9** 34 4N 117 39W
Ontario, *Oreg., U.S.A.* **76 D5** 44 2N 116 58W
Ontario □, *Canada* **72 B2** 48 0N 83 0W
Ontario, L., *N. Amer.* **84 C7** 43 20N 78 0W
Ontonagon, *U.S.A.* **80 B10** 46 52N 89 19W
Onyx, *U.S.A.* **79 K8** 35 41N 118 14W
Oodnadatta, *Australia* ..... **63 D2** 27 33S 135 30 E
Ooldea, *Australia* .... **61 F5** 30 27S 131 50 E
Oombulgurri, *Australia* .... **60 C4** 15 15S 127 45 E
Oorindi, *Australia* .... **62 C3** 20 40S 141 1 E
Oost-Vlaanderen □, *Belgium* **15 C3** 51 5N 3 50 E
Oostende, *Belgium* .... **15 C2** 51 15N 2 54 E
Oosterhout, *Neths.* .... **15 C4** 51 39N 4 47 E
Oosterschelde →, *Neths.* ... **15 C4** 51 33N 4 0 E
Oosterwolde, *Neths.* ...... **15 B6** 53 0N 6 17 E
Ootacamund = Udagamandalam,
   India .... **40 P10** 11 30N 76 44 E
Ootsa L., *Canada* **70 C3** 53 50N 126 2W
Op Luang △, *Thailand* ..... **38 C2** 18 12N 98 32 E
Opala, *Dem. Rep. of the Congo* **54 C1** 0 40S 24 20 E
Opanake, *Sri Lanka* ...... **40 R12** 6 35N 80 40 E
Opasatika, *Canada* **72 C3** 49 30N 82 50W
Opasquia, *Canada* **72 B1** 53 33N 93 5W
Opava, *Czech Rep.* .... **17 D9** 49 57N 17 58 E
Opelika, *U.S.A.* **83 J3** 32 39N 85 23W
Opelousas, *U.S.A.* **81 K8** 30 32N 92 5W
Opémisca, L., *Canada* **72 C5** 49 56N 74 52W
Opheim, *U.S.A.* **76 B10** 48 51N 106 24W
Ophthalmia Ra., *Australia* . **60 D2** 23 15S 119 30 E
Opinaca →, *Canada* **72 B4** 52 15N 78 2W
Opinaca, Rés., *Canada* **72 B4** 52 39N 76 20W
Opinnagau →, *Canada* **72 B3** 54 12N 82 25W
Opiscotéo, L., *Canada* **73 B6** 53 10N 68 10W
Opole, *Poland* .... **17 C9** 50 42N 17 58 E
Oponono L., *Namibia* ..... **56 B2** 18 8S 15 45 E
Oporto = Porto, *Portugal* .. **21 B1** 41 8N 8 40W
Opotiki, *N.Z.* .... **59 H6** 38 1S 177 19 E
Opp, *U.S.A.* **83 K2** 31 17N 86 16W
Oppdal, *Norway* .... **9 E13** 62 35N 9 41 E
Opportunity, *U.S.A.* **76 C5** 47 39N 117 15W
Opua, *N.Z.* .... **59 F5** 35 19S 174 9 E
Opunake, *N.Z.* .... **59 H4** 39 26S 173 52 E
Opuwo, *Namibia* .... **56 B1** 18 3S 13 45 E
Ora, *Cyprus* .... **25 E12** 34 51N 33 12 E
Oracle, *U.S.A.* **77 K8** 32 37N 110 46W
Oradea, *Romania* .... **17 E11** 47 2N 21 58 E
Öræfajökull, *Iceland* **8 D5** 64 2N 16 39W
Orai, *India* .... **43 G8** 25 58N 79 30 E
Oral = Zhayyq →, *Kazakhstan* **19 E9** 47 0N 51 48 E
Oral, *Kazakhstan* .... **19 D9** 51 20N 51 20 E
Oran, *Algeria* **50 A5** 35 45N 0 39W
Orange, *Australia* .... **63 E4** 33 15S 149 7 E
Orange, *France* .... **20 D6** 44 8N 4 47 E
Orange, *Calif., U.S.A.* **79 M9** 33 47N 117 51W
Orange, *Mass., U.S.A.* **85 D12** 42 35N 72 19W
Orange, *Tex., U.S.A.* **81 K8** 30 6N 93 44W
Orange, *Va., U.S.A.* **82 F6** 38 15N 78 7W
Orange, C., *Brazil* **93 C8** 4 20N 51 30W
Orange Cove, *U.S.A.* **78 J7** 36 38N 119 19W
Orange Free State = Free
   State □, *S. Africa* .... **56 D4** 28 30S 27 0 E
Orange Grove, *U.S.A.* **81 M6** 27 58N 97 56W
Orange Walk, *Belize* **87 D7** 18 6N 88 33W
Orangeburg, *U.S.A.* **83 J5** 33 30N 80 52W
Orangeville, *Canada* **84 C4** 43 55N 80 5W
Oranienburg, *Germany* .... **16 B7** 52 45N 13 14 E
Oranje = Orange →, *S. Africa* **56 D2** 28 41S 16 28 E
Oranjemund, *Namibia* ..... **56 D2** 28 38S 16 29 E
Oranjerivier, *S. Africa* ..... **56 D3** 29 40S 24 12 E
Oranjestad, *Aruba* **89 D5** 12 32N 70 2W
Orapa, *Botswana* .... **53 J5** 21 15S 25 30 E
Oras, *Phil.* .... **37 B7** 12 9N 125 28 E
Orbetello, *Italy* .... **22 C4** 42 27N 11 13 E
Orbisonia, *U.S.A.* **84 F7** 40 15N 77 54W
Orbost, *Australia* .... **63 F4** 37 40S 148 29 E
Orcas I., *Antarctica* **5 C18** 60 44S 44 37W
Orchard City, *U.S.A.* **77 G10** 38 50N 107 58W
Orchila, I., *Venezuela* **89 D6** 11 48N 66 10W
Orchilla, Pta., *Canary Is.* .. **24 G1** 27 42N 18 10W
Orcutt, *U.S.A.* **79 L6** 34 52N 120 27W
Ord →, *Australia* .... **60 C4** 15 33S 128 15 E
Ord, Mt., *Australia* .... **60 C4** 17 20S 125 34 E
Orderville, *U.S.A.* **77 H7** 37 17N 112 38W
Ordos = Mu Us Shamo, *China* **34 E5** 39 0N 109 0 E
Ordu, *Turkey* .... **19 F6** 40 55N 37 53 E
Ordway, *U.S.A.* **80 F3** 38 13N 103 46W
Ore, *Dem. Rep. of the Congo* **54 B2** 3 17N 29 30 E
Ore Mts. = Erzgebirge, *Germany* **16 C7** 50 27N 12 55 E
Örebro, *Sweden* .... **9 G16** 59 20N 15 18 E
Oregon, *U.S.A.* **80 D10** 42 1N 89 20W
Oregon □, *U.S.A.* **76 E3** 44 0N 121 0W
Oregon City, *U.S.A.* **78 E4** 45 21N 122 36W
Oregon Dunes △, *U.S.A.* .. **76 E1** 42 3N 123 26W
Orekhovo–Zuyevo, *Russia* . **18 C6** 55 50N 38 55 E

Orel, Russia . 18 D6 52 57N 36 3 E
Orem, U.S.A. . 76 F8 40 19N 111 42W
Ören, Turkey . 23 F12 37 3N 27 57 E
Orenburg, Russia . 18 D10 51 45N 55 6 E
Orense = Ourense, Spain . 21 A2 42 19N 7 55W
Orepuki, N.Z. . 59 M1 46 19S 167 46 E
Orestiás, Greece . 23 D12 41 30N 26 33 E
Orestos Pereyra, Mexico . 86 B3 26 31N 105 40W
Orford Ness, U.K. . 13 E9 52 5N 1 35 E
Organ Pipe Cactus △, U.S.A. . 77 K7 32 0N 113 10W
Organos, Pta. de los, Canary Is. . 24 F2 28 12N 17 17W
Orgaz, Spain . 21 C4 39 39N 3 53W
Orgeyev = Orhei, Moldova . 17 E15 47 24N 28 50 E
Orhaneli, Turkey . 23 E13 39 54N 28 59 E
Orhangazi, Turkey . 23 D13 40 29N 29 18 E
Orhei, Moldova . 17 E15 47 24N 28 50 E
Orhon Gol →, Mongolia . 32 A5 50 21N 106 0 E
Oriental, Cordillera, Colombia . 92 B4 6 0N 73 0W
Oriental, Grand Erg, Algeria . 50 B7 30 0N 6 30 E
Orientale □, Dem. Rep. of the Congo . 54 B2 2 20N 26 0 E
Oriente, Argentina . 94 D3 38 44S 60 37W
Orihuela, Spain . 21 C5 38 7N 0 55W
Orillia, Canada . 84 B5 44 40N 79 24W
Orinoco →, Venezuela . 92 B6 9 15N 61 30W
Orion, Canada . 71 D6 49 27N 110 49W
Oriskany, U.S.A. . 85 C9 43 10N 75 20W
Orissa □, India . 41 K14 20 0N 84 0 E
Orissaare, Estonia . 9 G20 58 34N 23 5 E
Oristano, Italy . 22 E3 39 54N 8 36 E
Oristano, G. di, Italy . 22 E3 39 50N 8 29 E
Orizaba, Mexico . 87 D5 18 51N 97 6W
Orizaba, Pico de, Mexico . 87 D5 19 0N 97 20W
Orkanger, Norway . 8 E13 63 18N 9 52 E
Orkla →, Norway . 8 E13 63 18N 9 51 E
Orkney, S. Africa . 56 D4 26 58S 26 40 E
Orkney □, U.K. . 11 B5 59 2N 3 13W
Orkney Is., U.K. . 11 B6 59 0N 3 0W
Orland, U.S.A. . 78 F4 39 45N 122 12W
Orlando, U.S.A. . 83 L5 28 33N 81 23W
Orléanais, France . 20 C5 48 0N 2 0 E
Orléans, France . 20 C4 47 54N 1 52 E
Orleans, U.S.A. . 85 B12 44 49N 72 12W
Orléans, Î. d', Canada . 73 C5 46 54N 70 58W
Ormara, Pakistan . 40 G4 25 16N 64 33 E
Ormoc, Phil. . 37 B6 11 0N 124 37 E
Ormond, N.Z. . 59 H6 38 33S 177 56 E
Ormond Beach, U.S.A. . 83 L5 29 17N 81 3W
Ormskirk, U.K. . 12 D5 53 35N 2 54W
Ormstown, Canada . 85 A11 45 8N 74 0W
Örnsköldsvik, Sweden . 8 E18 63 17N 18 40 E
Oro, N. Korea . 35 D14 40 1N 127 27 E
Oro →, Mexico . 86 B3 25 35N 105 2W
Oro Grande, U.S.A. . 79 L9 34 36N 117 20W
Oro Valley, U.S.A. . 77 K8 32 26N 110 58W
Orocué, Colombia . 92 C4 4 48N 71 20W
Orofino, U.S.A. . 76 C5 46 29N 116 15W
Orol Dengizi = Aral Sea, Asia . 28 E7 44 30N 60 0 E
Oromocto, Canada . 73 C6 45 54N 66 29W
Orono, Canada . 84 C6 43 59N 78 37W
Orono, U.S.A. . 83 C11 44 53N 68 40W
Oronsay, U.K. . 11 E2 56 1N 6 15W
Oroqen Zizhiqi, China . 33 A7 50 34N 123 43 E
Oroquieta, Phil. . 37 C6 8 32N 123 44 E
Orosháza, Hungary . 17 E11 46 32N 20 42 E
Orotukan, Russia . 29 C16 62 16N 151 42 E
Oroville, Calif., U.S.A. . 78 F5 39 31N 121 33W
Oroville, Wash., U.S.A. . 76 B4 48 56N 119 26W
Oroville, L., U.S.A. . 78 F5 39 33N 121 29W
Ororoo, Australia . 63 E2 32 43S 138 38 E
Orrville, U.S.A. . 84 F3 40 50N 81 46W
Orsha, Belarus . 18 D5 54 30N 30 25 E
Orsk, Russia . 28 D6 51 12N 58 34 E
Orşova, Romania . 17 F12 44 41N 22 25 E
Ortaca, Turkey . 23 F13 36 49N 28 45 E
Ortegal, C., Spain . 21 A2 43 43N 7 52W
Orthez, France . 20 E3 43 29N 0 48W
Ortigueira, Spain . 21 A2 43 40N 7 50W
Orting, U.S.A. . 78 C4 47 6N 122 12W
Ortles, Italy . 20 C9 46 31N 10 33 E
Ortón →, Bolivia . 92 F5 10 50S 67 0W
Ortonville, U.S.A. . 80 C6 45 19N 96 27W
Orūmīyeh, Iran . 44 B5 37 40N 45 0 E
Orūmīyeh, Daryācheh-ye, Iran . 44 B5 37 50N 45 30 E
Oruro, Bolivia . 92 G5 18 0S 67 9W
Orust, Sweden . 9 G14 58 10N 11 40 E
Oruzgān □, Afghan. . 40 C5 33 30N 66 0 E
Orvieto, Italy . 22 C5 42 43N 12 7 E
Orwell, N.Y., U.S.A. . 85 C9 43 35N 75 50W
Orwell, Ohio, U.S.A. . 84 E4 41 32N 80 52W
Orwell →, U.K. . 13 F9 51 59N 1 18 E
Orwigsburg, U.S.A. . 85 F8 40 38N 76 6W
Oryakhovo, Bulgaria . 23 C10 43 40N 23 57 E
Osa, Russia . 18 C10 57 17N 55 26 E
Osa, Pen. de, Costa Rica . 88 E3 8 0N 84 0W
Osage, U.S.A. . 80 D8 43 17N 92 49W
Osage →, U.S.A. . 80 F9 38 35N 91 57W
Osage City, U.S.A. . 80 F7 38 38N 95 50W
Ōsaka, Japan . 31 G7 34 40N 135 30 E
Osan, S. Korea . 35 F14 37 11N 127 4 E
Osawatomie, U.S.A. . 80 F7 38 31N 94 57W
Osborne, U.S.A. . 80 F5 39 26N 98 42W
Osceola, Ark., U.S.A. . 81 H10 35 42N 89 58W
Osceola, Iowa, U.S.A. . 80 E8 41 2N 93 46W
Oscoda, U.S.A. . 84 B1 44 26N 83 20W
Ösel = Saaremaa, Estonia . 9 G20 58 30N 22 30 E
Osgoode, Canada . 85 A9 45 8N 75 36W
Osh, Kyrgyzstan . 28 E8 40 37N 72 49 E
Oshakati, Namibia . 53 H3 17 45S 15 40 E
Oshawa, Canada . 84 C6 43 50N 78 50W
Oshigambo, Namibia . 56 B2 17 45S 16 5 E
Oshkosh, Nebr., U.S.A. . 80 E3 41 24N 102 21W
Oshkosh, Wis., U.S.A. . 80 C10 44 1N 88 33W
Oshmyany = Ashmyany, Belarus . 9 J21 54 26N 25 52 E
Oshnovīyeh, Iran . 44 B5 37 2N 45 6 E
Oshogbo, Nigeria . 50 G6 7 48N 4 37 E
Oshtorīnān, Iran . 45 C6 34 1N 48 38 E
Oshwe, Dem. Rep. of the Congo . 52 E3 3 25S 19 28 E
Osijek, Croatia . 23 B8 45 34N 18 41 E
Osipovichi = Asipovichy, Belarus . 17 B15 53 19N 28 33 E
Osiyan, India . 42 F5 26 43N 72 55 E
Osizweni, S. Africa . 57 D5 27 49S 30 7 E
Oskaloosa, U.S.A. . 80 E8 41 18N 92 39W
Oskélanéo, Canada . 72 C4 48 5N 75 15W
Öskemen, Kazakhstan . 28 E9 50 0N 82 36 E
Oslo, Norway . 9 G14 59 55N 10 45 E
Oslofjorden, Norway . 9 G14 59 20N 10 35 E

Osmanabad, India . 40 K10 18 5N 76 10 E
Osmaniye, Turkey . 19 G6 37 5N 36 10 E
Osnabrück, Germany . 16 B5 52 17N 8 3 E
Osorio, Brazil . 95 B5 29 53S 50 17W
Osorno, Chile . 96 E2 40 25S 73 0W
Osoyoos, Canada . 70 D5 49 0N 119 30W
Osøyro, Norway . 9 F11 60 9N 5 30 E
Ospika →, Canada . 70 B4 56 20N 124 0W
Osprey Reef, Australia . 62 A4 13 52S 146 36 E
Oss, Neths. . 15 C5 51 46N 5 32 E
Ossa, Mt., Australia . 63 G4 41 52S 146 3 E
Óssa, Óros, Greece . 23 E10 39 47N 22 42 E
Ossabaw I., U.S.A. . 83 K5 31 50N 81 5W
Ossining, U.S.A. . 85 E11 41 10N 73 55W
Ossipee, U.S.A. . 85 C13 43 41N 71 7W
Ossokmanuan L., Canada . 73 B7 53 25N 65 0W
Ossora, Russia . 29 D17 59 20N 163 13 E
Ostend = Oostende, Belgium . 15 C2 51 15N 2 54 E
Oster, Ukraine . 17 C16 50 57N 30 53 E
Osterburg, U.S.A. . 84 F6 40 16N 78 31W
Österdalälven, Sweden . 9 F16 61 30N 13 45 E
Østerdalen, Norway . 9 F14 61 40N 10 50 E
Östersund, Sweden . 8 E16 63 10N 14 38 E
Ostfriesische Inseln, Germany . 16 B4 53 42N 7 0 E
Ostrava, Czech Rep. . 17 D10 49 51N 18 18 E
Ostróda, Poland . 17 B10 53 42N 19 58 E
Ostroh, Ukraine . 17 C14 50 20N 26 30 E
Ostrołęka, Poland . 17 B11 53 4N 21 32 E
Ostrów Mazowiecka, Poland . 17 B11 52 50N 21 51 E
Ostrów Wielkopolski, Poland . 17 C9 51 36N 17 44 E
Ostrowiec-Świętokrzyski, Poland . 17 C11 50 55N 21 22 E
Ostuni, Italy . 23 D7 40 44N 17 35 E
Ōsumi-Kaikyō, Japan . 31 J5 30 55N 131 0 E
Ōsumi-Shotō, Japan . 31 J5 30 30N 130 0 E
Osuna, Spain . 21 D3 37 14N 5 8W
Oswegatchie →, U.S.A. . 85 B9 44 42N 75 30W
Oswego, U.S.A. . 85 C8 43 27N 76 31W
Oswego →, U.S.A. . 85 C8 43 27N 76 30W
Oswestry, U.K. . 12 E4 52 52N 3 3W
Oświęcim, Poland . 17 C10 50 2N 19 11 E
Otago □, N.Z. . 59 L2 45 15S 170 0 E
Otago Harbour, N.Z. . 59 L3 45 47S 170 42 E
Otaheite B., Trin. & Tob. . 93 K15 10 20N 61 30W
Ōtake, Japan . 31 G6 34 12N 132 13 E
Otaki, N.Z. . 59 J5 40 45S 175 10 E
Otaru, Japan . 30 C10 43 10N 141 0 E
Otaru-Wan = Ishikari-Wan, Japan . 30 C10 43 25N 141 1 E
Otavalo, Ecuador . 92 C3 0 13N 78 20W
Otavi, Namibia . 56 B2 19 40S 17 24 E
Otchinjau, Angola . 56 B1 16 30S 13 56 E
Otelnuk, L., Canada . 73 A6 56 9N 68 12W
Othello, U.S.A. . 76 C4 46 50N 119 10W
Otjiwarongo, Namibia . 56 C2 20 30S 16 33 E
Otoineppu, Japan . 30 B11 44 44N 142 16 E
Otorohanga, N.Z. . 59 H5 38 12S 175 14 E
Otoskwin →, Canada . 72 B2 52 13N 88 6W
Otra →, Norway . 9 G13 58 9N 8 1 E
Otranto, Italy . 23 D8 40 9N 18 28 E
Otranto, C. d', Italy . 23 D8 40 7N 18 30 E
Otranto, Str. of, Italy . 23 D8 40 15N 18 40 E
Otse, S. Africa . 56 D4 25 2S 25 45 E
Ōtsu, Japan . 31 G7 35 0N 135 50 E
Ōtsuki, Japan . 31 G9 35 36N 138 57 E
Ottawa = Outaouais →, Canada . 72 C5 45 27N 74 8W
Ottawa, Canada . 85 A9 45 27N 75 42W
Ottawa, Ill., U.S.A. . 80 E10 41 21N 88 51W
Ottawa, Kans., U.S.A. . 80 F7 38 37N 95 16W
Ottawa Is., Canada . 69 C11 59 35N 80 10W
Otter Cr. →, U.S.A. . 85 B11 44 13N 73 17W
Otter L., Canada . 71 B8 55 35N 104 39W
Otterville, Canada . 84 D4 42 55N 80 36W
Ottery St. Mary, U.K. . 13 G4 50 44N 3 17W
Otto Beit Bridge, Zimbabwe . 55 F2 15 59S 28 56 E
Ottosdal, S. Africa . 56 D4 26 46S 25 59 E
Ottumwa, U.S.A. . 80 E8 41 1N 92 25W
Oturkpo, Nigeria . 50 G7 7 16N 8 8 E
Otway, B., Chile . 96 G2 53 30S 74 0W
Otway, C., Australia . 63 F3 38 52S 143 30 E
Otwock, Poland . 17 B11 52 5N 21 20 E
Ou →, Laos . 38 B4 20 4N 102 13 E
Ou Neua, Laos . 38 A3 22 18N 101 48 E
Ou-Sammyaku, Japan . 30 E10 39 20N 140 35 E
Ouachita →, U.S.A. . 81 K9 31 38N 91 49W
Ouachita, L., U.S.A. . 81 H8 34 34N 93 12W
Ouachita Mts., U.S.A. . 81 H7 34 40N 94 25W
Ouagadougou, Burkina Faso . 50 F5 12 25N 1 30W
Ouahran = Oran, Algeria . 50 A5 35 45N 0 39W
Ouallene, Algeria . 50 D6 24 41N 1 11 E
Ouargla, Algeria . 50 B7 31 59N 5 16 E
Ouarzazate, Morocco . 50 B4 30 55N 6 50W
Oubangi →, Dem. Rep. of the Congo . 52 E3 0 30S 17 50 E
Ouddorp, Neths. . 15 C3 51 50N 3 57 E
Oude Rijn →, Neths. . 15 B4 52 12N 4 24 E
Oudenaarde, Belgium . 15 D3 50 50N 3 37 E
Oudtshoorn, S. Africa . 56 E3 33 35S 22 14 E
Ouessant, Î. d', France . 20 B1 48 28N 5 6W
Ouesso, Congo . 52 D3 1 37N 16 5 E
Ouest, Pte. de l', Canada . 73 C7 49 52N 64 40W
Ouezzane, Morocco . 50 B4 34 51N 5 35W
Oughterard, Ireland . 10 C2 53 26N 9 18W
Oujda, Morocco . 50 B5 34 41N 1 55W
Oulainen, Finland . 8 D21 64 17N 24 47 E
Oulu, Finland . 8 D21 65 1N 25 29 E
Oulujärvi, Finland . 8 D22 64 25N 27 15 E
Oulujoki →, Finland . 8 D21 65 1N 25 30 E
Oum Chalouba, Chad . 51 E10 15 48N 20 46 E
Oum Hadjer, Chad . 51 F9 13 18N 19 41 E
Ounasjoki →, Finland . 8 C21 66 31N 25 40 E
Ounguati, Namibia . 56 C2 22 0S 15 46 E
Ounianga Sérir, Chad . 51 E10 18 54N 20 51 E
Our →, Lux. . 15 E6 49 55N 6 5 E
Ouray, U.S.A. . 77 G10 38 1N 107 40W
Ourense, Spain . 21 A2 42 19N 7 55W
Ouricuri, Brazil . 93 E10 7 53S 40 5W
Ourinhos, Brazil . 95 A6 23 0S 49 54W
Ouro Fino, Brazil . 95 A6 22 16S 46 25W
Ouro Prêto, Brazil . 95 A7 20 20S 43 30W
Ourthe →, Belgium . 15 D5 50 29N 5 35 E
Ouse →, E. Susx., U.K. . 13 G8 50 47N 0 4 E
Ouse →, N. Yorks., U.K. . 12 D7 53 44N 0 55W
Outaouais →, Canada . 72 C5 45 27N 74 8W
Outardes →, Canada . 73 C6 49 24N 69 30W
Outer Hebrides, U.K. . 11 D1 57 30N 7 40W
Outjo, Namibia . 56 C2 20 5S 16 7 E
Outlook, Canada . 71 C7 51 30N 107 0W
Outokumpu, Finland . 8 E23 62 43N 29 1 E
Ouyen, Australia . 63 F3 35 1S 142 22 E

Ovalau, Fiji . 59 C8 17 40S 178 48 E
Ovalle, Chile . 94 C1 30 33S 71 18W
Ovamboland, Namibia . 56 B2 18 30S 16 0 E
Overflakkee, Neths. . 15 C4 51 44N 4 10 E
Overijssel □, Neths. . 15 B6 52 25N 6 35 E
Overland Park, U.S.A. . 80 F7 38 55N 94 50W
Overton, U.S.A. . 79 J12 36 33N 114 27W
Övertorneå, Sweden . 8 C20 66 23N 23 38 E
Ovid, U.S.A. . 85 D8 42 41N 76 49W
Oviedo, Spain . 21 A3 43 25N 5 50W
Oviši, Latvia . 9 H19 57 33N 21 44 E
Ovoot, Mongolia . 34 B7 45 21N 113 45 E
Övör Hangay □, Mongolia . 34 B2 45 0N 102 30 E
Ovruch, Ukraine . 17 C15 51 25N 28 45 E
Owaka, N.Z. . 59 M2 46 27S 169 40 E
Owambo = Ovamboland, Namibia . 56 B2 18 30S 16 0 E
Owasco L., U.S.A. . 85 D8 42 50N 76 31W
Owase, Japan . 31 G8 34 7N 136 12 E
Owatonna, U.S.A. . 80 C8 44 5N 93 14W
Owbeh, Afghan. . 40 B3 34 28N 63 10 E
Owego, U.S.A. . 85 D8 42 6N 76 16W
Owen Falls Dam, Uganda . 54 B3 0 30N 33 5 E
Owen Sound, Canada . 84 B4 44 35N 80 55W
Owens →, U.S.A. . 78 J9 36 32N 117 59W
Owens L., U.S.A. . 79 J9 36 26N 117 57W
Owensboro, U.S.A. . 82 G2 37 46N 87 7W
Owl →, Canada . 71 B10 57 51N 92 44W
Owo, Nigeria . 50 G7 7 10N 5 39 E
Owosso, U.S.A. . 82 D3 43 0N 84 10W
Owyhee, U.S.A. . 76 F5 41 57N 116 6W
Owyhee →, U.S.A. . 76 E5 43 49N 117 2W
Owyhee, L., U.S.A. . 76 E5 43 38N 117 14W
Ox Mts. = Slieve Gamph, Ireland . 10 B3 54 6N 9 0W
Öxarfjörður, Iceland . 8 C5 66 15N 16 45W
Oxbow, Canada . 71 D8 49 14N 102 10W
Oxelösund, Sweden . 9 G17 58 43N 17 5 E
Oxford, N.Z. . 59 K4 43 18S 172 11 E
Oxford, U.K. . 13 F6 51 46N 1 15W
Oxford, Mass., U.S.A. . 85 D13 42 7N 71 52W
Oxford, Miss., U.S.A. . 81 H10 34 22N 89 31W
Oxford, N.C., U.S.A. . 83 G6 36 19N 78 35W
Oxford, N.Y., U.S.A. . 85 D9 42 27N 75 36W
Oxford, Ohio, U.S.A. . 82 F3 39 31N 84 45W
Oxford L., Canada . 71 C9 54 51N 95 37W
Oxfordshire □, U.K. . 13 F6 51 48N 1 16W
Oxnard, U.S.A. . 79 L7 34 12N 119 11W
Oxus = Amudarya →, Uzbekistan . 28 E6 43 58N 59 34 E
Oya, Malaysia . 36 D4 2 55N 111 55 E
Oyama, Japan . 31 F9 36 18N 139 48 E
Oyem, Gabon . 52 D2 1 34N 11 31 E
Oyen, Canada . 71 C6 51 22N 110 28W
Oykel →, U.K. . 11 D4 57 56N 4 26W
Oymyakon, Russia . 29 C15 63 25N 142 44 E
Oyo, Nigeria . 50 G6 7 46N 3 56 E
Oyster Bay, U.S.A. . 85 F11 40 52N 73 32W
Ōyūbari, Japan . 30 C11 43 1N 142 5 E
Ozamiz, Phil. . 37 C6 8 15N 123 50 E
Ozark, Ala., U.S.A. . 83 K3 31 28N 85 39W
Ozark, Ark., U.S.A. . 81 H8 35 29N 93 50W
Ozark, Mo., U.S.A. . 81 G8 37 1N 93 12W
Ozark Plateau, U.S.A. . 81 G9 37 20N 91 40W
Ozarks, L. of the, U.S.A. . 80 F8 38 12N 92 38W
Ózd, Hungary . 17 D11 48 14N 20 15 E
Ozette L., U.S.A. . 78 B2 48 6N 124 38W
Ozona, U.S.A. . 81 K4 30 43N 101 12W
Ozuluama, Mexico . 87 C5 21 40N 97 50W

P

Pa-an, Burma . 41 L20 16 51N 97 40 E
Pa Mong Dam, Thailand . 38 D4 18 0N 102 22 E
Pa Sak →, Thailand . 36 B2 15 30N 101 0 E
Paamiut, Greenland . 69 B15 62 0N 49 43W
Paarl, S. Africa . 56 E2 33 45S 18 56 E
Pabbay, U.K. . 11 D1 57 46N 7 14W
Pabianice, Poland . 17 C10 51 40N 19 20 E
Pabna, Bangla. . 41 G16 24 1N 89 18 E
Pabo, Uganda . 54 B3 3 1N 32 10 E
Pacaja →, Brazil . 93 D8 1 56S 50 50W
Pacaraima, Sa., S. Amer. . 92 C6 4 0N 62 30W
Pacasmayo, Peru . 92 E3 7 20S 79 35W
Pachar, India . 42 G7 24 40N 77 42 E
Pachitea →, Peru . 92 E4 8 46S 74 33W
Pachmarhi, India . 43 H8 22 28N 78 26 E
Pachpadra, India . 40 G8 25 58N 72 10 E
Pachuca, Mexico . 87 C5 20 10N 98 40W
Pacific, Canada . 70 C3 54 48N 128 28W
Pacific-Antarctic Ridge, Pac. Oc. . 5 B13 43 0S 115 0W
Pacific Grove, U.S.A. . 78 J5 36 38N 121 56W
Pacific Ocean . 65 G14 10 0N 140 0W
Pacific Rim △, Canada . 70 D4 48 40N 124 45W
Pacifica, U.S.A. . 78 H4 37 36N 122 30W
Pacitan, Indonesia . 37 H14 8 12S 111 7 E
Packwood, U.S.A. . 78 D5 46 36N 121 40W
Padaido, Kepulauan, Indonesia . 37 E9 1 15S 136 30 E
Padang, Indonesia . 36 E2 1 0S 100 20 E
Padang Endau, Malaysia . 39 L4 2 40N 103 38 E
Padangpanjang, Indonesia . 36 E2 0 40S 100 20 E
Padangsidempuan, Indonesia . 36 D1 1 30N 99 15 E
Paddle Prairie, Canada . 70 B5 57 57N 117 29W
Paddockwood, Canada . 71 C7 53 30N 105 30W
Paderborn, Germany . 16 C5 51 42N 8 45 E
Padma, India . 43 G11 24 12N 85 22 E
Pádova, Italy . 22 B4 45 25N 11 53 E
Padra, India . 42 H5 22 15N 73 7 E
Padrauna, India . 43 F10 26 54N 83 59 E
Padre I., U.S.A. . 81 M6 27 10N 97 25W
Padre Island △, U.S.A. . 81 M6 26 36N 97 17W
Padstow, U.K. . 13 G3 50 33N 4 58W
Padua = Pádova, Italy . 22 B4 45 25N 11 53 E
Paducah, Ky., U.S.A. . 82 G1 37 5N 88 37W
Paducah, Tex., U.S.A. . 81 H4 34 1N 100 18W
Paengnyŏng-do, S. Korea . 35 F13 37 57N 124 40 E
Paeroa, N.Z. . 59 G5 37 23S 175 41 E
Pafúri, Mozam. . 57 C5 22 28S 31 17 E
Pag, Croatia . 16 F8 44 25N 15 3 E
Pagadian, Phil. . 37 C6 7 55N 123 30 E
Pagai Selatan, Pulau, Indonesia . 36 E2 3 0S 100 15 E
Pagai Utara, Pulau, Indonesia . 36 E2 2 35S 100 0 E
Pagalu = Annobón, Atl. Oc. . 49 G4 1 25S 5 36 E
Pagara, India . 43 G9 24 22N 80 1 E
Pagastikós Kólpos, Greece . 23 E10 39 15N 23 0 E

Pagatan, Indonesia . 36 E5 3 33S 115 59 E
Page, U.S.A. . 77 H8 36 57N 111 27W
Pago Pago, Amer. Samoa . 59 B13 14 16S 170 43W
Pagosa Springs, U.S.A. . 77 H10 37 16N 107 1W
Pagwa River, Canada . 72 B2 50 2N 85 14W
Pahala, U.S.A. . 74 J17 19 12N 155 29W
Pahang →, Malaysia . 39 L4 3 30N 103 9 E
Pahiatua, N.Z. . 59 J5 40 27S 175 50 E
Pahokee, U.S.A. . 83 M5 26 50N 80 40W
Pahrump, U.S.A. . 79 J11 36 12N 115 59W
Pahute Mesa, U.S.A. . 78 H10 37 20N 116 45W
Pai, Thailand . 38 C2 19 19N 98 27 E
Paicines, U.S.A. . 78 J5 36 44N 121 17W
Paide, Estonia . 9 G21 58 57N 25 31 E
Paignton, U.K. . 13 G4 50 26N 3 35W
Päijänne, Finland . 9 F21 61 30N 25 30 E
Pailani, India . 43 G9 25 45N 80 26 E
Pailin, Cambodia . 38 F4 12 46N 102 36 E
Painan, Indonesia . 36 E2 1 21S 100 34 E
Painesville, U.S.A. . 84 E3 41 43N 81 15W
Paint Hills = Wemindji, Canada . 72 B4 53 0N 78 49W
Paint L., Canada . 71 B9 55 28N 97 57W
Painted Desert, U.S.A. . 77 J8 36 0N 111 0W
Paintsville, U.S.A. . 82 G4 37 49N 82 48W
País Vasco □, Spain . 21 A4 42 50N 2 45W
Paisley, Canada . 84 B3 44 18N 81 16W
Paisley, U.K. . 11 F4 55 50N 4 25W
Paisley, U.S.A. . 76 E3 42 42N 120 32W
Paita, Peru . 92 E2 5 11S 81 9W
Pajares, Puerto de, Spain . 21 A3 42 58N 5 46W
Pak Lay, Laos . 38 C3 18 15N 101 27 E
Pak Phanang, Thailand . 39 H3 8 21N 100 12 E
Pak Sane, Laos . 38 C4 18 22N 103 39 E
Pak Song, Laos . 38 E6 15 11N 106 14 E
Pak Suong, Laos . 38 C4 19 58N 102 15 E
Pak Tam Chung, China . 33 G11 22 24N 114 19 E
Pakenham, Canada . 85 A8 45 18N 76 18W
Pákhnes, Greece . 25 D6 35 16N 24 4 E
Pakhuis, S. Africa . 56 E2 32 9S 19 5 E
Pakistan ■, Asia . 42 E4 30 0N 70 0 E
Pakkading, Laos . 38 C4 18 19N 103 59 E
Pakokku, Burma . 41 J19 21 20N 95 0 E
Pakowki L., Canada . 71 D6 49 20N 111 0W
Pakpattan, Pakistan . 42 D5 30 25N 73 27 E
Paktīā □, Afghan. . 40 C6 33 0N 69 15 E
Paktīkā □, Afghan. . 40 C6 32 30N 69 0 E
Pakwach, Uganda . 54 B3 2 28N 31 27 E
Pakxe, Laos . 38 E5 15 5N 105 52 E
Pal Lahara, India . 43 J11 21 27N 85 11 E
Pala, Chad . 51 G9 9 25N 15 5 E
Pala, Dem. Rep. of the Congo . 54 D2 6 45S 29 30 E
Pala, U.S.A. . 79 M9 33 22N 117 5W
Palabek, Uganda . 54 B3 3 22N 32 33 E
Palacios, U.S.A. . 81 L6 28 42N 96 13W
Palagruža, Croatia . 22 C7 42 24N 16 15 E
Palaiókastron, Greece . 25 D8 35 12N 26 15 E
Palaiokhóra, Greece . 25 D5 35 16N 23 39 E
Palam, India . 40 K10 19 0N 77 0 E
Palampur, India . 42 C7 32 10N 76 30 E
Palana, Australia . 63 F4 39 45S 147 55 E
Palana, Russia . 29 D16 59 10N 159 59 E
Palanan, Phil. . 37 A6 17 8N 122 29 E
Palanan Pt., Phil. . 37 A6 17 17N 122 30 E
Palandri, Pakistan . 43 C5 33 42N 73 40 E
Palanga, Lithuania . 9 J19 55 58N 21 3 E
Palangkaraya, Indonesia . 36 E4 2 16S 113 56 E
Palani Hills, India . 40 P10 10 14N 77 33 E
Palanpur, India . 42 G5 24 10N 72 25 E
Palapye, Botswana . 56 C4 22 30S 27 7 E
Palas, Pakistan . 43 B5 35 4N 73 14 E
Palashi, India . 43 H13 23 47N 88 15 E
Palasponga, India . 43 J11 21 47N 85 34 E
Palatka, Russia . 29 C16 60 6N 150 54 E
Palatka, U.S.A. . 83 L5 29 39N 81 38W
Palau ■, Pac. Oc. . 26 J17 7 30N 134 30 E
Palauk, Burma . 38 F2 13 10N 98 40 E
Palawan, Phil. . 36 C5 9 30N 118 30 E
Palayankottai, India . 40 Q10 8 45N 77 45 E
Paldiski, Estonia . 9 G21 59 23N 24 9 E
Paleleh, Indonesia . 37 D6 1 10N 121 50 E
Palembang, Indonesia . 36 E2 3 0S 104 50 E
Palencia, Spain . 21 A3 42 1N 4 34W
Palenque, Mexico . 87 D6 17 31N 91 58W
Palenque, Ruinas de, Mexico . 87 D6 17 25N 92 1W
Paleokastrítsa, Greece . 25 A3 39 40N 19 41 E
Paleometokho, Cyprus . 25 D12 35 7N 33 11 E
Palermo, Italy . 22 E5 38 7N 13 22 E
Palermo, U.S.A. . 76 G3 39 26N 121 33W
Palestina, Chile . 96 A3 23 50S 69 47W
Palestine, Asia . 46 D4 32 0N 35 0 E
Palestine, U.S.A. . 81 K7 31 46N 95 38W
Paletwa, Burma . 41 J18 21 10N 92 50 E
Palghat, India . 40 P10 10 46N 76 42 E
Pali, India . 42 G5 25 50N 73 20 E
Palikir, Micronesia . 64 G7 6 55N 158 9 E
Palioúrion, Ákra, Greece . 23 E10 39 57N 23 45 E
Palisades Reservoir, U.S.A. . 76 E8 43 20N 111 12W
Paliseul, Belgium . 15 E5 49 54N 5 8 E
Palitana, India . 42 J4 21 32N 71 49 E
Palizada, Mexico . 87 D6 18 18N 92 8W
Palk Bay, Asia . 40 Q11 9 30N 79 15 E
Palk Strait, Asia . 40 Q11 10 0N 79 45 E
Palkānah, Iraq . 44 C5 35 49N 44 26 E
Palkot, India . 43 H11 22 53N 84 39 E
Pallanza = Verbánia, Italy . 20 D8 45 56N 8 33 E
Pallarenda, Australia . 62 B4 19 12S 146 46 E
Pallinup →, Australia . 61 F2 34 27S 118 50 E
Pallisa, Uganda . 54 B3 1 12N 33 43 E
Pallu, India . 42 E6 28 59N 74 14 E
Palm Bay, U.S.A. . 83 L5 28 2N 80 35W
Palm Beach, U.S.A. . 83 M6 26 43N 80 2W
Palm Coast, U.S.A. . 83 L5 29 32N 81 10W
Palm Desert, U.S.A. . 79 M10 33 43N 116 22W
Palm Is., Australia . 62 B4 18 40S 146 35 E
Palm Springs, U.S.A. . 79 M10 33 50N 116 33W
Palma, Mozam. . 55 E5 10 46S 40 29 E
Palma, B. de, Spain . 24 B9 39 30N 2 39 E
Palma Soriano, Cuba . 88 B4 20 15N 76 0W
Palmares, Brazil . 93 E11 8 41S 35 28W
Palmas, Brazil . 95 B5 26 29S 52 0W
Palmas, C., Liberia . 50 H4 4 27N 7 46W
Pálmas, G. di, Italy . 22 E3 39 0N 8 30 E
Palmdale, U.S.A. . 79 L8 34 35N 118 7W
Palmeira das Missões, Brazil . 95 B5 27 55S 53 17W
Palmeira dos Índios, Brazil . 93 E11 9 25S 36 37W

Palmer, Antarctica ... 5 C17 64 35S 60 0W
Palmer, U.S.A. ... 68 B5 61 36N 149 7W
Palmer ➤, Australia ... 62 B3 16 0S 142 26 E
Palmer Lake, U.S.A. ... 80 F2 39 7N 104 55W
Palmer Land, Antarctica ... 5 D18 73 0S 63 0W
Palmerston, Canada ... 84 C4 43 50N 80 51W
Palmerston, N.Z. ... 59 L3 45 29S 170 43 E
Palmerston North, N.Z. ... 59 J5 40 21S 175 39 E
Palmerton, U.S.A. ... 85 F9 40 48N 75 37W
Palmetto, U.S.A. ... 83 M4 27 31N 82 34W
Palmi, Italy ... 22 E6 38 21N 15 51 E
Palmira, Argentina ... 94 C2 32 59S 68 34W
Palmira, Colombia ... 92 C3 3 32N 76 16W
Palmyra = Tudmur, Syria ... 44 C3 34 36N 38 15 E
Palmyra, Mo., U.S.A. ... 80 F9 39 48N 91 32W
Palmyra, N.J., U.S.A. ... 85 F9 40 1N 75 1W
Palmyra, N.Y., U.S.A. ... 84 C7 43 5N 77 18W
Palmyra, Pa., U.S.A. ... 85 F8 40 18N 76 36W
Palmyra Is., Pac. Oc. ... 65 G11 5 52N 162 5W
Palo Alto, U.S.A. ... 78 H4 37 27N 122 10W
Palo Seco, Trin. & Tob. ... 93 K15 10 4N 61 36W
Palo Verde, U.S.A. ... 79 M12 33 26N 114 44W
Palo Verde △, Costa Rica ... 88 D2 10 21N 85 21W
Palomar Mt., U.S.A. ... 79 M10 33 22N 116 50W
Palopo, Indonesia ... 37 E6 3 0S 120 16 E
Palos, C. de, Spain ... 21 D5 37 38N 0 40W
Palos Verdes, U.S.A. ... 79 M8 33 48N 118 23W
Palos Verdes, Pt., U.S.A. ... 79 M8 33 43N 118 26W
Palu, Indonesia ... 37 E5 1 0S 119 52 E
Palu, Turkey ... 19 G7 38 45N 40 0 E
Palwal, India ... 42 E7 28 8N 77 19 E
Pamanukan, Indonesia ... 37 G12 6 16S 107 49 E
Pamekasan, Indonesia ... 37 G15 7 10S 113 28 E
Pamenang, Indonesia ... 37 J19 8 24S 116 6 E
Pamiers, France ... 20 E4 43 7N 1 39 E
Pamir, Tajikistan ... 28 F8 37 40N 73 0 E
Pamlico ➤, U.S.A. ... 83 H7 35 20N 76 28W
Pamlico Sd., U.S.A. ... 83 H8 35 20N 76 0W
Pampa, U.S.A. ... 81 H4 35 32N 100 58W
Pampa de las Salinas, Argentina ... 94 C2 32 1S 66 58W
Pampanua, Indonesia ... 37 E6 4 16S 120 8 E
Pampas, Argentina ... 94 D3 35 0S 63 0W
Pampas, Peru ... 92 F4 12 20S 74 50W
Pamplona, Colombia ... 92 B4 7 23N 72 39W
Pamplona, Spain ... 21 A5 42 48N 1 38W
Pampoenpoort, S. Africa ... 56 E3 31 3S 22 40 E
Pan de Azúcar △, Chile ... 94 B1 26 0S 70 40W
Pana, U.S.A. ... 80 F10 39 23N 89 5W
Panaca, U.S.A. ... 77 H6 37 47N 114 23W
Panaitan, Indonesia ... 37 G11 6 36S 105 12 E
Panaji, India ... 40 M8 15 25N 73 50 E
Panamá, Panama ... 88 E4 8 48N 79 25W
Panama ■, Cent. Amer. ... 88 E4 8 48N 79 55W
Panamá, G. de, Panama ... 88 E4 8 4N 79 20W
Panama Canal, Panama ... 88 E4 9 10N 79 37W
Panama City, U.S.A. ... 83 K3 30 10N 85 40W
Panamint Range, U.S.A. ... 79 J9 36 20N 117 20W
Panamint Springs, U.S.A. ... 79 J9 36 20N 117 28W
Panão, Peru ... 92 E3 9 55S 75 55W
Panare, Thailand ... 39 J3 6 51N 101 30 E
Panay, Phil. ... 37 B6 11 10N 122 30 E
Panay, G., Phil. ... 37 B6 11 0N 122 30 E
Pančevo, Serbia & M. ... 23 B9 44 52N 20 41 E
Panda, Mozam. ... 57 C5 24 2S 34 45 E
Pandan, Malaysia ... 39 d 1 32N 103 46 E
Pandan, Phil. ... 37 B6 11 45N 122 10 E
Pandan, Selat, Singapore ... 39 d 1 15N 103 44 E
Pandan Tampoi = Tampoi, Malaysia ... 39 d 1 30N 103 39 E
Pandegelang, Indonesia ... 37 G12 6 25S 106 5 E
Pandhana, India ... 42 J7 21 42N 76 13 E
Pandharpur, India ... 40 L9 17 41N 75 20 E
Pando, Uruguay ... 95 C4 34 44S 56 0W
Pando, L. = Hope, L., Australia ... 63 D2 28 24S 139 18 E
Pandokrátor, Greece ... 25 A3 39 45N 19 50 E
Pandora, Costa Rica ... 88 E3 9 43N 83 3W
Panevėžys, Lithuania ... 9 J21 55 42N 24 25 E
Panfilov, Kazakhstan ... 28 E8 44 10N 80 0 E
Pang-Long, Burma ... 41 H21 23 11N 98 45 E
Pang Sida △, Thailand ... 38 E4 14 5N 102 17 E
Pang-Yang, Burma ... 41 H21 22 7N 98 48 E
Panga, Dem. Rep. of the Congo ... 54 B2 1 52N 26 18 E
Pangalanes, Canal des = Ampangalana, Lakandranon', Madag. ... 57 C8 22 48S 47 50 E
Pangani, Tanzania ... 54 D4 5 25S 38 58 E
Pangani ➤, Tanzania ... 54 D4 5 26S 38 58 E
Pangfou = Bengbu, China ... 35 H9 32 58N 117 20 E
Pangil, Dem. Rep. of the Congo ... 54 C2 3 10S 26 35 E
Pangkah, Tanjung, Indonesia ... 37 G15 6 51S 112 33 E
Pangkajene, Indonesia ... 37 E5 4 46S 119 34 E
Pangkalanbrandan, Indonesia ... 36 D1 4 1N 98 20 E
Pangkalanbuun, Indonesia ... 36 E4 2 41S 111 37 E
Pangkalpinang, Indonesia ... 36 E3 2 0S 106 0 E
Pangnirtung, Canada ... 69 B13 66 8N 65 43W
Pangong Tso, India ... 42 B8 34 40N 78 40 E
Panguitch, U.S.A. ... 77 H7 37 50N 112 26W
Pangutaran Group, Phil. ... 37 C6 6 18N 120 34 E
Panhandle, U.S.A. ... 81 H4 35 21N 101 23W
Pani Mines, India ... 42 H5 22 29N 73 50 E
Pania-Mutombo, Dem. Rep. of the Congo ... 54 D1 5 11S 23 51 E
Panikota I., India ... 42 J4 20 46N 71 21 E
Panipat, India ... 42 E7 29 25N 77 2 E
Panjal Range = Pir Panjal Range, India ... 42 C7 32 30N 76 50 E
Panjang, Hon, Vietnam ... 39 H4 9 20N 103 28 E
Panjgur, Pakistan ... 40 F4 27 0N 64 5 E
Panjim = Panaji, India ... 40 M8 15 25N 73 50 E
Panjin, China ... 35 D12 41 3N 122 2 E
Panjnad Barrage, Pakistan ... 40 E7 29 22N 71 15 E
Panjnad ➤, Pakistan ... 42 E4 28 57N 70 30 E
Panjwai, Afghan. ... 42 D1 31 26N 65 27 E
Panmunjŏm, N. Korea ... 35 F14 37 59N 126 38 E
Panna, India ... 43 G9 24 40N 80 15 E
Panna Hills, India ... 43 G9 24 40N 81 15 E
Pannawonica, Australia ... 60 D2 21 39S 116 19 E
Pannga, Tanjung, Indonesia ... 37 K19 8 54S 116 2 E
Pannirtuuq = Pangnirtung, Canada ... 69 B13 66 8N 65 43W
Pano Akil, Pakistan ... 42 F3 27 51N 69 7 E
Pano Lefkara, Cyprus ... 25 E12 34 53N 33 20 E
Pano Panayia, Cyprus ... 25 E11 34 55N 32 38 E
Panorama, Brazil ... 95 A5 21 21S 51 51W
Pánormos, Greece ... 25 D6 35 25N 24 41 E
Pansemal, India ... 42 J6 21 39N 74 42 E
Panshan = Panjin, China ... 35 D12 41 3N 122 2 E

Panshi, China ... 35 C14 42 58N 126 5 E
Pantanal, Brazil ... 92 H7 17 30S 57 40W
Pantanos de Centla ◠, Mexico ... 87 D6 18 25N 92 25W
Pantar, Indonesia ... 37 F6 8 28S 124 10 E
Pante Macassar, E. Timor ... 37 F6 9 30S 123 58 E
Pante Makasar = Pante Macassar, E. Timor ... 37 F6 9 30S 123 58 E
Pantelleria, Italy ... 22 F4 36 50N 11 57 E
Pánuco, Mexico ... 87 C5 22 0N 98 15W
Paola, Malta ... 25 D2 35 52N 14 30 E
Paola, U.S.A. ... 80 F7 38 35N 94 53W
Paonia, U.S.A. ... 77 G10 38 52N 107 36W
Paoting = Baoding, China ... 34 E8 38 50N 115 28 E
Paot'ou = Baotou, China ... 34 D6 40 32N 110 2 E
Paoua, C.A.R. ... 52 C3 7 9N 16 20 E
Pápa, Hungary ... 17 E9 47 22N 17 30 E
Papa Stour, U.K. ... 11 A7 60 20N 1 42W
Papa Westray, U.K. ... 11 B6 59 20N 2 55W
Papagayo ➤, Mexico ... 87 D5 16 36N 99 43W
Papagayo, G. de, Costa Rica ... 88 D2 10 30N 85 50W
Papakura, N.Z. ... 59 G5 37 4S 174 59 E
Papantla, Mexico ... 87 C5 20 30N 97 30W
Papar, Malaysia ... 36 C5 5 45N 116 0 E
Paparoa △, N.Z. ... 59 K3 42 7S 171 26 E
Papeete, Tahiti ... 65 J13 17 32S 149 34W
Paphos, Cyprus ... 25 E11 34 46N 32 25 E
Papigochic ➤, Mexico ... 86 B3 29 9N 109 40W
Paposo, Chile ... 94 B1 25 0S 70 30W
Papoutsa, Cyprus ... 25 E12 34 54N 33 4 E
Papua □, Indonesia ... 37 E9 4 0S 137 0 E
Papua New Guinea ■, Oceania ... 64 H6 8 0S 145 0 E
Papudo, Chile ... 94 C1 32 29S 71 27W
Papun, Burma ... 41 K20 18 2N 97 30 E
Papunya, Australia ... 60 D5 23 15S 131 54 E
Pará = Belém, Brazil ... 93 D9 1 20S 48 30W
Pará □, Brazil ... 93 D8 3 20S 52 0W
Paraburdoo, Australia ... 60 D2 23 14S 117 32 E
Paracatu, Brazil ... 93 G9 17 10S 46 50W
Paracel Is., S. China Sea ... 36 A4 15 50N 112 0 E
Parachilna, Australia ... 63 E2 31 10S 138 21 E
Parachinar, Pakistan ... 42 C4 33 55N 70 5 E
Paradhísi, Greece ... 25 C10 36 18N 28 7 E
Paradip, India ... 41 J15 20 15N 86 35 E
Paradise, Calif., U.S.A. ... 78 F5 39 46N 121 37W
Paradise, Nev., U.S.A. ... 79 J11 36 9N 115 10W
Paradise ➤, Canada ... 73 B8 53 27N 57 19W
Paradise Hill, Canada ... 71 C7 53 32N 109 28W
Paradise River, Canada ... 73 B8 53 27N 57 17W
Paradise Valley, U.S.A. ... 76 F5 41 30N 117 32W
Parado, Indonesia ... 37 F5 8 42S 118 30 E
Paragould, U.S.A. ... 81 G9 36 3N 90 29W
Paragua ➤, Venezuela ... 92 B6 6 55N 62 55W
Paraguaçu ➤, Brazil ... 93 F11 12 45S 38 54W
Paraguaçu Paulista, Brazil ... 95 A5 22 22S 50 35W
Paraguaná, Pen. de, Venezuela ... 92 A5 12 0N 70 0W
Paraguarí, Paraguay ... 94 B4 25 36S 57 0W
Paraguarí □, Paraguay ... 94 B4 26 0S 57 10W
Paraguay ■, S. Amer. ... 94 A4 23 0S 57 0W
Paraguay ➤, Paraguay ... 94 B4 27 18S 58 38W
Paraíba = João Pessoa, Brazil ... 93 E12 7 10S 34 52W
Paraíba □, Brazil ... 93 E11 7 0S 36 0W
Paraíba do Sul ➤, Brazil ... 95 A7 21 37S 41 3W
Parainen, Finland ... 9 F20 60 18N 22 18 E
Paraiso, Mexico ... 87 D6 18 24N 93 14W
Parak, Iran ... 45 E7 27 38N 52 25 E
Parakou, Benin ... 50 G6 9 25N 2 40 E
Paralimni, Cyprus ... 25 D12 35 2N 33 58 E
Paramaribo, Suriname ... 93 B7 5 50N 55 10W
Páramos del Batallón y La Negra △, Venezuela ... 89 E5 8 2N 71 55W
Paramushir, Ostrov, Russia ... 29 D16 50 24N 156 0 E
Paran ➤, Israel ... 46 E4 30 20N 35 10 E
Paraná, Argentina ... 94 C3 31 45S 60 30W
Paraná, Brazil ... 93 F9 12 30S 47 48W
Paraná □, Brazil ... 95 A5 24 30S 51 0W
Paraná ➤, Argentina ... 94 C4 33 43S 59 15W
Paranaguá, Brazil ... 95 B6 25 30S 48 30W
Paranaíba, Brazil ... 93 G8 19 40S 51 11W
Paranaíba ➤, Brazil ... 93 H8 20 6S 51 4W
Paranapanema ➤, Brazil ... 95 A5 22 40S 53 9W
Paranapiacaba, Serra do, Brazil ... 95 A6 24 31S 48 35W
Paranavaí, Brazil ... 95 A5 23 4S 52 56W
Parang, Maguindanao, Phil. ... 37 C6 7 23N 124 16 E
Parang, Sulu, Phil. ... 37 C6 5 55N 120 54 E
Parângul Mare, Vf., Romania ... 17 F12 45 20N 23 37 E
Paraparaumu, N.Z. ... 59 J5 40 57S 175 3 E
Parbati ➤, Mad. P., India ... 42 G7 25 50N 76 30 E
Parbati ➤, Raj., India ... 42 F7 26 54N 77 53 E
Parbhani, India ... 40 K10 19 8N 76 52 E
Parchim, Germany ... 16 B6 53 26N 11 52 E
Pardes Hanna-Karkur, Israel ... 46 C3 32 28N 34 57 E
Pardo ➤, Bahia, Brazil ... 93 G11 15 40S 39 0W
Pardo ➤, Mato Grosso, Brazil ... 95 A5 21 46S 52 9W
Pardubice, Czech Rep. ... 16 C8 50 3N 15 45 E
Pare, Indonesia ... 37 G15 7 43S 112 12 E
Pare Mts., Tanzania ... 54 C4 4 0S 37 45 E
Parecis, Serra dos, Brazil ... 92 F7 13 0S 60 0W
Paren, Russia ... 29 C17 62 30N 163 15 E
Parent, Canada ... 72 C5 47 55N 74 35W
Parent, L., Canada ... 72 C4 48 31N 77 1W
Parepare, Indonesia ... 37 E5 4 0S 119 40 E
Párga, Greece ... 23 E9 39 15N 20 29 E
Pargo, Pta. do, Madeira ... 24 D2 32 49N 17 17W
Paria, G. de, Venezuela ... 93 K14 10 20N 62 0W
Pariaguán, Venezuela ... 92 B6 8 51N 64 34W
Paricutín, Cerro, Mexico ... 86 D4 19 28N 102 15W
Parigi, Indonesia ... 37 E6 0 50S 120 5 E
Parika, Guyana ... 92 B7 6 50N 58 20W
Parima, Serra, Brazil ... 92 C6 2 30N 64 0W
Parinari, Peru ... 92 D4 4 35S 74 25W
Pariñas, Pta., S. Amer. ... 90 D2 4 30S 82 0W
Parintins, Brazil ... 93 D7 2 40S 56 50W
Pariparit Kyun, Burma ... 41 M18 14 55N 93 45 E
Paris, Canada ... 84 C4 43 12N 80 25W
Paris, France ... 20 B5 48 50N 2 20 E
Paris, Idaho, U.S.A. ... 76 E8 42 14N 111 24W
Paris, Ky., U.S.A. ... 82 F3 38 13N 84 15W
Paris, Tenn., U.S.A. ... 83 G1 36 18N 88 19W
Paris, Tex., U.S.A. ... 81 J7 33 40N 95 33W
Parish, U.S.A. ... 85 C8 43 25N 76 8W
Parishville, U.S.A. ... 85 B10 44 38N 74 49W
Park, U.S.A. ... 78 B4 48 45N 122 18W
Park City, U.S.A. ... 81 G6 37 48N 97 20W
Park Falls, U.S.A. ... 80 C9 45 56N 90 27W
Park Head, Canada ... 84 B3 44 36N 81 9W
Park Hills, U.S.A. ... 81 G9 37 53N 90 28W
Park Range, U.S.A. ... 76 G10 40 0N 106 30W
Park Rapids, U.S.A. ... 80 B7 46 55N 95 4W

Park River, U.S.A. ... 80 A6 48 24N 97 45W
Park Rynie, S. Africa ... 57 E5 30 25S 30 45 E
Parkā Bandar, Iran ... 45 E8 25 55N 59 35 E
Parkano, Finland ... 9 E20 62 1N 23 0 E
Parker, Ariz., U.S.A. ... 79 L12 34 9N 114 17W
Parker, Pa., U.S.A. ... 84 E5 41 5N 79 41W
Parker Dam, U.S.A. ... 79 L12 34 18N 114 8W
Parkersburg, U.S.A. ... 82 F5 39 16N 81 34W
Parkes, Australia ... 63 E4 33 9S 148 11 E
Parkfield, U.S.A. ... 78 K6 35 54N 120 26W
Parkhill, Canada ... 84 C3 43 15N 81 38W
Parkland, U.S.A. ... 78 C4 47 9N 122 26W
Parkston, U.S.A. ... 80 D6 43 24N 97 59W
Parksville, Canada ... 70 D4 49 20N 124 21W
Parla, Spain ... 21 B4 40 14N 3 46W
Parma, Italy ... 20 D9 44 48N 10 20 E
Parma, Idaho, U.S.A. ... 76 E5 43 47N 116 57W
Parma, Ohio, U.S.A. ... 84 E3 41 23N 81 43W
Parnaguá, Brazil ... 93 F10 10 10S 44 38W
Parnaíba, Brazil ... 93 D10 2 54S 41 47W
Parnaíba ➤, Brazil ... 93 D10 3 0S 41 50W
Parnassós, Greece ... 23 E10 38 35N 22 30 E
Pärnu, Estonia ... 9 G21 58 28N 24 33 E
Paroo ➤, Australia ... 63 E3 31 28S 143 32 E
Páros, Greece ... 23 F11 37 5N 25 12 E
Parowan, U.S.A. ... 77 H7 37 51N 112 50W
Parral, Chile ... 94 D1 36 10S 71 52W
Parras, Mexico ... 86 B4 25 30N 102 20W
Parrett ➤, U.K. ... 13 F4 51 12N 3 1W
Parris I., U.S.A. ... 83 J5 32 20N 80 41W
Parrsboro, Canada ... 73 C7 45 30N 64 25W
Parry I., Canada ... 84 A4 45 18N 80 10W
Parry Is., Canada ... 4 B2 77 0N 110 0W
Parry Sound, Canada ... 84 A5 45 20N 80 0W
Parsnip ➤, Canada ... 70 B4 55 10N 123 2W
Parsons, U.S.A. ... 81 G7 37 20N 95 16W
Parsons Ra., Australia ... 62 A2 13 30S 135 15 E
Partinico, Italy ... 22 E5 38 3N 13 7 E
Partridge I., Canada ... 72 A2 55 59N 87 37W
Paru ➤, Brazil ... 93 D8 1 33S 52 38W
Parvän □, Afghan. ... 40 B6 35 0N 69 0 E
Parvatipuram, India ... 41 K13 18 50N 83 25 E
Parvatsar, India ... 42 F6 26 52N 74 49 E
Parys, S. Africa ... 56 D4 26 52S 27 29 E
Pas, Pta. des, Spain ... 24 C7 38 46N 1 26 E
Pasadena, Canada ... 73 C8 49 1N 57 36W
Pasadena, Calif., U.S.A. ... 79 L8 34 9N 118 9W
Pasadena, Tex., U.S.A. ... 81 L7 29 43N 95 13W
Pasaje ➤, Argentina ... 94 B3 25 39S 63 56W
Pasar, Indonesia ... 37 J17 8 27S 114 54 E
Pascagoula, U.S.A. ... 81 K10 30 21N 88 33W
Pascagoula ➤, U.S.A. ... 81 K10 30 23N 88 37W
Pasco, U.S.A. ... 76 C4 46 14N 119 6W
Pasco, Cerro de, Peru ... 92 F3 10 45S 76 10W
Pasco I., Australia ... 60 D2 20 57S 115 20 E
Pascoag, U.S.A. ... 85 E13 41 57N 71 42W
Pascua, I. de, Chile ... 65 K17 27 7S 109 23W
Pasfield L., Canada ... 71 B7 58 24N 105 20W
Pashmakli = Smolyan, Bulgaria ... 23 D11 41 36N 24 38 E
Pasir Mas, Malaysia ... 39 J4 6 2N 102 8 E
Pasir Panjang, Singapore ... 39 d 1 18N 103 46 E
Pasir Putih, Malaysia ... 39 K4 5 50N 102 24 E
Pasirian, Indonesia ... 37 H15 8 13S 113 8 E
Pasirkuning, Indonesia ... 36 E2 0 30S 104 33 E
Paskūh, Iran ... 45 E9 27 34N 61 39 E
Pasley, C., Australia ... 61 F3 33 52S 123 35 E
Pašman, Croatia ... 16 G8 43 58N 15 20 E
Pasni, Pakistan ... 40 G3 25 15N 63 27 E
Paso Cantinela, Mexico ... 79 N11 32 33N 115 47W
Paso de Indios, Argentina ... 96 E3 43 55S 69 0W
Paso de los Libres, Argentina ... 94 B4 29 44S 57 10W
Paso de los Toros, Uruguay ... 94 C4 32 45S 56 30W
Paso Robles, U.S.A. ... 77 J3 35 38N 120 41W
Paspébiac, Canada ... 73 C6 48 3N 65 17W
Pasrur, Pakistan ... 42 C6 32 16N 74 43 E
Passage West, Ireland ... 10 E3 51 52N 8 21W
Passaic, U.S.A. ... 85 F10 40 51N 74 7W
Passau, Germany ... 16 D7 48 34N 13 28 E
Passero, C., Italy ... 22 F6 36 41N 15 10 E
Passo Fundo, Brazil ... 95 B5 28 10S 52 20W
Passos, Brazil ... 93 H9 20 45S 46 37W
Pastavy, Belarus ... 9 J22 55 4N 26 50 E
Pastaza ➤, Peru ... 92 D3 4 50S 76 52W
Pasto, Colombia ... 92 C3 1 13N 77 17W
Pasuruan, Indonesia ... 37 G15 7 40S 112 44 E
Patagonia, Argentina ... 96 F3 45 0S 69 0W
Patagonia, U.S.A. ... 77 L8 31 33N 110 45W
Patambar, Iran ... 45 D9 29 45N 60 17 E
Patan = Lalitapur, Nepal ... 43 F11 27 40N 85 20 E
Patan, Gujarat, India ... 42 H5 23 54N 72 14 E
Patan, Maharashtra, India ... 42 H5 23 54N 72 14 E
Patani, Indonesia ... 37 D7 0 20N 128 50 E
Pataudi, India ... 42 E7 28 18N 76 48 E
Patchewollock, Australia ... 63 F3 35 22S 142 12 E
Patchogue, U.S.A. ... 85 F11 40 46N 73 1W
Pate, Kenya ... 54 C5 2 10S 41 0 E
Patea, N.Z. ... 59 H5 39 45S 174 30 E
Patensie, S. Africa ... 56 E3 33 46S 24 49 E
Paternò, Italy ... 22 F6 37 34N 14 54 E
Pateros, U.S.A. ... 76 B4 48 3N 119 54W
Paterson, U.S.A. ... 85 F10 40 55N 74 11W
Paterson Ra., Australia ... 60 D3 21 45S 122 10 E
Pathankot, India ... 42 C6 32 18N 75 45 E
Pathein = Bassein, Burma ... 41 L19 16 45N 94 30 E
Pathfinder Reservoir, U.S.A. ... 76 E10 42 28N 106 51W
Pathiu, Thailand ... 39 G2 10 42N 99 1 E
Pathum Thani, Thailand ... 38 E3 14 1N 100 32 E
Pati, Indonesia ... 37 G14 6 45S 111 1 E
Patía ➤, Colombia ... 92 C3 2 13N 78 40W
Patiala, Punjab, India ... 42 D7 30 23N 76 26 E
Patiala, Ut. P., India ... 43 F8 27 43N 79 1 E
Patkai Bum, India ... 41 F19 27 0N 95 30 E
Pátmos, Greece ... 23 F12 37 21N 26 36 E
Patna, India ... 43 G11 25 35N 85 12 E
Pato Branco, Brazil ... 95 B5 26 13S 52 40W
Patong, Ao, Thailand ... 39 a 7 54N 98 17 E
Patonga, Uganda ... 54 B3 2 45N 33 15 E
Patos, Brazil ... 93 E11 6 55S 37 16W
Patos, Río de los ➤, Argentina ... 94 C2 31 18S 69 25W
Patos de Minas, Brazil ... 93 G9 18 35S 46 32W
Patquía, Argentina ... 94 C2 30 2S 66 55W
Patra = Pátrai, Greece ... 23 E9 38 14N 21 47 E
Pátrai, Greece ... 23 E9 38 14N 21 47 E
Patrocínio, Brazil ... 93 G9 18 57S 47 0W
Pattani, Thailand ... 39 J3 6 48N 101 15 E

Pattaya, Thailand ... 36 B2 12 52N 100 55 E
Patten, U.S.A. ... 83 C11 46 0N 68 38W
Patterson, Calif., U.S.A. ... 78 H5 37 28N 121 8W
Patterson, La., U.S.A. ... 81 L9 29 42N 91 18W
Patterson, Mt., U.S.A. ... 78 G7 38 29N 119 20W
Patti, Punjab, India ... 42 D6 31 17N 74 54 E
Patti, Ut. P., India ... 43 G10 25 55N 82 12 E
Pattoki, Pakistan ... 42 D5 31 5N 73 52 E
Patton, U.S.A. ... 84 F6 40 38N 78 39W
Patuakhali, Bangla. ... 41 H17 22 20N 90 25 E
Patuanak, Canada ... 71 B7 55 55N 107 43W
Patuca ➤, Honduras ... 88 D3 15 50N 84 18W
Patuca, Punta, Honduras ... 88 C3 15 50N 84 14W
Pátzcuaro, Mexico ... 86 D4 19 30N 101 40W
Pau, France ... 20 E3 43 19N 0 25W
Pauk, Burma ... 41 J19 21 27N 94 30 E
Paul I., Canada ... 73 A7 56 30N 61 20W
Paul Smiths, U.S.A. ... 85 B10 44 26N 74 15W
Paulatuk, Canada ... 68 B7 69 25N 124 0W
Paulistana, Brazil ... 93 E10 8 9S 41 9W
Paulo Afonso, Brazil ... 93 E11 9 21S 38 15W
Paulpietersburg, S. Africa ... 57 D5 27 23S 30 50 E
Pauls Valley, U.S.A. ... 81 H6 34 44N 97 13W
Pauma Valley, U.S.A. ... 79 M10 33 16N 116 58W
Pauri, India ... 43 D8 30 9N 78 47 E
Pāveh, Iran ... 44 C5 35 3N 46 22 E
Pavia, Italy ... 20 D8 45 7N 9 8 E
Pavilion, U.S.A. ... 84 D6 42 52N 78 1W
Pāvilosta, Latvia ... 9 H19 56 53N 21 14 E
Pavlodar, Kazakhstan ... 28 D8 52 33N 77 0 E
Pavlograd = Pavlohrad, Ukraine ... 19 E6 48 30N 35 52 E
Pavlohrad, Ukraine ... 19 E6 48 30N 35 52 E
Pavlovo, Russia ... 18 C7 55 58N 43 5 E
Pavlovsk, Russia ... 19 D7 50 26N 40 5 E
Pavlovskaya, Russia ... 19 E6 46 17N 39 47 E
Pawai, Pulau, Singapore ... 39 d 1 11N 103 44 E
Pawayan, India ... 43 E9 28 4N 80 6 E
Pawhuska, U.S.A. ... 81 G6 36 40N 96 20W
Pawling, U.S.A. ... 85 E11 41 34N 73 36W
Pawnee, U.S.A. ... 81 G6 36 20N 96 48W
Pawnee City, U.S.A. ... 80 E6 40 7N 96 9W
Pawtucket, U.S.A. ... 85 E13 41 53N 71 23W
Paximádhia, Greece ... 25 E6 35 0N 24 35 E
Paxoí, Greece ... 23 E9 39 14N 20 12 E
Paxton, Ill., U.S.A. ... 82 E1 40 27N 88 6W
Paxton, Nebr., U.S.A. ... 80 E4 41 7N 101 21W
Payakumbuh, Indonesia ... 36 E2 0 20S 100 35 E
Payette, U.S.A. ... 76 D5 44 5N 116 56W
Payne Bay = Kangirsuk, Canada ... 69 B13 60 0N 70 0W
Payne L., Canada ... 69 C12 59 30N 74 30W
Paynes Find, Australia ... 61 E2 29 15S 117 42 E
Paynesville, U.S.A. ... 80 C7 45 23N 94 43W
Paysandú, Uruguay ... 94 C4 32 19S 58 8W
Payson, U.S.A. ... 77 J8 34 14N 111 20W
Paz ➤, Guatemala ... 88 D1 13 44N 90 10W
Paz, B. de la, Mexico ... 86 C2 24 15N 110 25W
Pāzanān, Iran ... 45 D6 30 35N 49 59 E
Pazardzhik, Bulgaria ... 23 C11 42 12N 24 20 E
Pe Ell, U.S.A. ... 78 D3 46 34N 123 18W
Peabody, U.S.A. ... 85 D14 42 31N 70 56W
Peace ➤, Canada ... 70 B6 59 0N 111 25W
Peace Point, Canada ... 70 B6 59 7N 112 27W
Peace River, Canada ... 70 B5 56 15N 117 18W
Peach Springs, U.S.A. ... 77 J7 35 32N 113 25W
Peachland, Canada ... 70 D5 49 47N 119 45W
Peachtree City, U.S.A. ... 83 J3 33 25N 84 35W
Peak, The = Kinder Scout, U.K. ... 12 D6 53 24N 1 52W
Peak Charles △, Australia ... 61 F3 32 42S 121 10 E
Peak District △, U.K. ... 12 D6 53 24N 1 46W
Peak Hill, N.S.W., Australia ... 63 E4 32 47S 148 11 E
Peak Hill, W. Austral., Australia ... 61 E2 25 35S 118 43 E
Peak Ra., Australia ... 62 C4 22 50S 148 20 E
Peake Cr. ➤, Australia ... 63 D2 28 2S 136 7 E
Peale, Mt., U.S.A. ... 77 G9 38 26N 109 14W
Pearblossom, U.S.A. ... 79 L9 34 30N 117 55W
Pearl ➤, U.S.A. ... 81 K10 30 11N 89 32W
Pearl City, U.S.A. ... 74 H16 21 24N 157 59W
Pearl Harbor, U.S.A. ... 74 H16 21 21N 157 57W
Pearl River, U.S.A. ... 85 E10 41 4N 74 2W
Pearsall, U.S.A. ... 81 L5 28 54N 99 6W
Peary Land, Greenland ... 4 A6 82 40N 33 0W
Pease ➤, U.S.A. ... 81 H5 34 12N 99 2W
Peawanuck, Canada ... 69 C11 55 15N 85 0W
Pebane, Mozam. ... 55 F4 17 10S 38 8 E
Pebas, Peru ... 92 D4 3 10S 71 46W
Pebble Beach, U.S.A. ... 78 J5 36 34N 121 57W
Peć, Serbia & M. ... 23 C9 42 40N 20 17 E
Pechenga, Russia ... 18 A5 69 29N 31 4 E
Pechenizhyn, Ukraine ... 17 D13 48 30N 24 48 E
Pechiguera, Pta., Canary Is. ... 24 F6 28 51N 13 53W
Pechora, Russia ... 18 A10 65 10N 57 11 E
Pechora ➤, Russia ... 18 A9 68 13N 54 15 E
Pechorskaya Guba, Russia ... 18 A9 68 40N 54 0 E
Pečory, Russia ... 9 H22 57 48N 27 40 E
Pecos, U.S.A. ... 81 K3 31 26N 103 30W
Pecos ➤, U.S.A. ... 81 L3 29 42N 101 22W
Pécs, Hungary ... 17 E10 46 5N 18 15 E
Pedder, L., Australia ... 63 G4 42 55S 146 10 E
Peddie, S. Africa ... 57 E4 33 14S 27 7 E
Pedernales, Dom. Rep. ... 89 C5 18 2N 71 44W
Pedieos ➤, Cyprus ... 25 D12 35 10N 33 54 E
Pedirka, Australia ... 63 D2 26 40S 135 14 E
Pedra Azul, Brazil ... 93 G10 16 2S 41 17W
Pedreiras, Brazil ... 93 D10 4 32S 44 40W
Pedro Afonso, Brazil ... 93 E9 9 0S 48 10W
Pedro Cays, Jamaica ... 88 C4 17 5N 77 48W
Pedro de Valdivia, Chile ... 94 A2 22 55S 69 38W
Pedro Juan Caballero, Paraguay ... 95 A4 22 30S 55 40W
Pee Dee ➤, U.S.A. ... 83 J6 33 21N 79 16W
Peebinga, Australia ... 63 E3 34 52S 140 57 E
Peebles, U.K. ... 11 F5 55 40N 3 11W
Peekskill, U.S.A. ... 85 E11 41 17N 73 55W
Peel, U.K. ... 12 C3 54 13N 4 40W
Peel ➤, Australia ... 63 E5 30 50S 150 29 E
Peel ➤, Canada ... 68 B6 67 0N 135 0W
Peel Sd., Canada ... 68 A10 73 0N 96 0W
Peera Peera Poolanna L., Australia ... 63 D2 26 30S 138 0 E
Peerless Lake, Canada ... 70 B6 56 37N 114 40W
Peers, Canada ... 70 C5 53 40N 116 0W
Pegasus Bay, N.Z. ... 59 K4 43 20S 173 10 E
Pegu, Burma ... 41 L20 17 20N 96 29 E
Pegu Yoma, Burma ... 41 K20 19 0N 96 0 E
Pehuajó, Argentina ... 94 D3 35 45S 62 0W
Pei Xian = Pizhou, China ... 34 G9 34 44N 116 55 E
Peine, Chile ... 94 A2 23 45S 68 8W
Peine, Germany ... 16 B6 52 19N 10 14 E

Peip'ing = Beijing, China ... **34 E9** 39 55N 116 20 E
Peipus, L. = Chudskoye, Ozero,
  Russia ... **9 G22** 58 13N 27 30 E
Peixe, Brazil ... **93 F9** 12 0S 48 40W
Peixe →, Brazil ... **93 H8** 21 31S 51 58W
Pekalongan, Indonesia ... **36 F3** 6 53S 109 40 E
Pekan, Malaysia ... **39 L4** 3 30N 103 25 E
Pekan Nenas, Malaysia ... **39 d** 1 31N 103 31 E
Pekanbaru, Indonesia ... **36 D2** 0 30N 101 15 E
Pekin, U.S.A. ... **80 E10** 40 35N 89 40W
Peking = Beijing, China ... **34 E9** 39 55N 116 20 E
Pekutatan, Indonesia ... **37 J17** 8 26S 114 49 E
Pelabuhan Kelang, Malaysia ... **39 L3** 3 0N 101 23 E
Pelabuhan Ratu, Teluk, Indonesia **37 G12** 7 5S 106 30 E
Pelabuhanratu, Indonesia ... **37 G12** 7 0S 106 32 E
Pelagie, Is., Italy ... **22 G5** 35 39N 12 33 E
Pelaihari, Indonesia ... **36 E4** 3 55S 114 45 E
Peleaga, Vf., Romania ... **17 F12** 45 22N 22 55 E
Pelée, Mt., Martinique ... **88 c** 14 48N 61 10W
Pelee, Pt., Canada ... **72 D3** 41 54N 82 31W
Pelee I., Canada ... **84 E2** 41 47N 82 40W
Pelekech, Kenya ... **54 B4** 3 52N 35 8 E
Peleng, Indonesia ... **37 E6** 1 20S 123 30 E
Pelentong, Malaysia ... **39 d** 1 32N 103 49 E
Pelican, U.S.A. ... **70 B1** 57 58N 136 14W
Pelican L., Canada ... **71 C8** 52 28N 100 20W
Pelican Narrows, Canada ... **71 B8** 55 10N 102 56W
Pelješac, Croatia ... **22 C7** 42 55N 17 25 E
Pelkosenniemi, Finland ... **8 C22** 67 6N 27 28 E
Pella, S. Africa ... **56 D2** 29 1S 19 6 E
Pella, U.S.A. ... **80 E8** 41 25N 92 55W
Pello, Finland ... **8 C21** 66 47N 23 59 E
Pelly →, Canada ... **68 B6** 62 47N 137 19W
Pelly Bay, Canada ... **69 B11** 68 38N 89 50W
Peloponnese = Pelopónnisos □,
  Greece ... **23 F10** 37 10N 22 0 E
Pelopónnisos □, Greece ... **23 F10** 37 10N 22 0 E
Pelorus Sd., N.Z. ... **59 J4** 40 59S 173 59 E
Pelotas, Brazil ... **95 C5** 31 42S 52 23W
Pelotas →, Brazil ... **95 B5** 27 28S 51 55W
Pelvoux, Massif du, France ... **20 D7** 44 52N 6 20 E
Pemalang, Indonesia ... **37 G13** 6 53S 109 23 E
Pemanggil, Pulau, Malaysia ... **39 L5** 2 37N 104 21 E
Pematangsiantar, Indonesia ... **36 D1** 2 57N 99 5 E
Pemba, Mozam. ... **55 E5** 12 58S 40 30 E
Pemba, Zambia ... **55 F2** 16 30S 27 28 E
Pemba Channel, Tanzania ... **54 D4** 5 0S 39 37 E
Pemba I., Tanzania ... **54 D4** 5 0S 39 45 E
Pemberton, Australia ... **61 F2** 34 30S 116 0 E
Pemberton, Canada ... **70 C4** 50 25N 122 50W
Pembina, U.S.A. ... **80 A6** 48 58N 97 15W
Pembroke, Canada ... **72 C4** 45 50N 77 7W
Pembroke, U.K. ... **13 F3** 51 41N 4 55W
Pembrokeshire □, U.K. ... **13 F3** 51 52N 4 56W
Pembrokeshire Coast △, U.K. ... **13 F2** 51 50N 5 2W
Pen-y-Ghent, U.K. ... **12 C5** 54 10N 2 14W
Penal, Trin. & Tob. ... **93 K15** 10 9N 61 29W
Penang = Pinang, Malaysia ... **39 c** 5 25N 100 15 E
Penápolis, Brazil ... **95 A6** 21 30S 50 0W
Peñarroya-Pueblonuevo, Spain ... **21 C3** 38 19N 5 16W
Penarth, U.K. ... **13 F4** 51 26N 3 11W
Peñas, C. de, Spain ... **21 A3** 43 42N 5 52W
Peñas, G. de, Chile ... **96 F2** 47 0S 75 0W
Peñas del Chache, Canary Is. ... **24 E6** 29 6N 13 33W
Pench'i = Benxi, China ... **35 D12** 41 20N 123 48 E
Pend Oreille →, U.S.A. ... **76 B5** 49 4N 117 37W
Pend Oreille, L., U.S.A. ... **76 C5** 48 10N 116 21W
Pendembu, S. Leone ... **50 G3** 9 7N 11 14W
Pender B., Australia ... **60 C3** 16 45S 122 42 E
Pendleton, U.S.A. ... **76 D4** 45 40N 118 47W
Pendra, India ... **43 H9** 22 46N 81 57 E
Penedo, Brazil ... **93 F11** 10 15S 36 36W
Penelokan, Indonesia ... **37 J18** 8 17S 115 22 E
Penetanguishene, Canada ... **84 B5** 44 50N 79 55W
Penfield, U.S.A. ... **84 E6** 41 13N 78 35W
Peng Chau, China ... **33 G11** 22 17N 114 2 E
Pengalengan, Indonesia ... **37 G12** 7 9S 107 30 E
Penge, Kasai-Or., Dem. Rep. of
  the Congo ... **54 D1** 5 30S 24 33 E
Penge, Sud-Kivu, Dem. Rep. of
  the Congo ... **54 C2** 4 27S 28 25 E
Penglai, China ... **35 F11** 37 48N 120 42 E
Penguin, Australia ... **63 G4** 41 8S 146 6 E
Penhalonga, Zimbabwe ... **55 F3** 18 52S 32 40 E
Peniche, Portugal ... **21 C1** 39 19N 9 22W
Penicuik, U.K. ... **11 F5** 55 50N 3 13W
Penida, Nusa, Indonesia ... **37 K18** 8 45S 115 30 E
Peninsular Malaysia □, Malaysia **39 L4** 4 0N 102 0 E
Penitente, Serra do, Brazil ... **93 E9** 8 45S 46 20W
Penkridge, U.K. ... **12 E5** 52 44N 2 6W
Penmarch, Pte. de, France ... **20 C1** 47 48N 4 22W
Penn Hills, U.S.A. ... **84 F5** 40 28N 79 52W
Penn Yan, U.S.A. ... **84 D7** 42 40N 77 3W
Pennant, Canada ... **71 C7** 50 32N 108 14W
Penner →, India ... **40 M12** 14 35N 80 10 E
Pennines, U.K. ... **12 C5** 54 45N 2 27W
Pennington, U.S.A. ... **78 F5** 39 15N 121 47W
Pennsburg, U.S.A. ... **85 F9** 40 23N 75 29W
Pennsylvania □, U.S.A. ... **82 E7** 40 45N 77 30W
Penny, Canada ... **70 C4** 53 51N 121 20W
Penobscot →, U.S.A. ... **83 C11** 44 30N 68 48W
Penobscot B., U.S.A. ... **83 C11** 44 35N 68 50W
Penola, Australia ... **63 F3** 37 25S 140 48 E
Penong, Australia ... **61 F5** 31 56S 133 1 E
Penonomé, Panama ... **88 E3** 8 31N 80 21W
Penrith, Australia ... **63 E5** 33 43S 150 38 E
Penrith, U.K. ... **12 C5** 54 40N 2 45W
Penryn, U.K. ... **13 G2** 50 9N 5 7W
Pensacola, U.S.A. ... **83 K2** 30 25N 87 13W
Pensacola Mts., Antarctica ... **5 E1** 84 0S 40 0W
Pense, Canada ... **71 C8** 50 25N 104 59W
Penshurst, Australia ... **63 F3** 37 49S 142 20 E
Penticton, Canada ... **70 D5** 49 30N 119 38W
Pentland, Australia ... **62 C4** 20 32S 145 25 E
Pentland Firth, U.K. ... **11 C5** 58 43N 3 10W
Pentland Hills, U.K. ... **11 F5** 55 48N 3 25W
Pentland Hills △, U.K. ... **11 F5** 55 50N 3 20W
Penza, Russia ... **18 D8** 53 15N 45 5 E
Penzance, U.K. ... **13 G2** 50 7N 5 33W
Penzhino, Russia ... **29 C17** 63 30N 167 55 E
Penzhinskaya Guba, Russia ... **29 C17** 61 30N 163 0 E
Peoria, Ariz., U.S.A. ... **77 K7** 33 35N 112 14W
Peoria, Ill., U.S.A. ... **80 E10** 40 42N 89 36W
Pepacton Reservoir, U.S.A. ... **85 D10** 42 5N 74 58W
Pepani →, S. Africa ... **56 D3** 25 49S 22 47 E
Pera Hd., Australia ... **62 A3** 12 55S 141 37 E
Perabumulih, Indonesia ... **36 E2** 3 27S 104 15 E
Perak →, Malaysia ... **39 K3** 4 0N 100 50 E

Pérama, Kérkira, Greece ... **25 A3** 39 34N 19 54 E
Pérama, Kríti, Greece ... **25 D6** 35 20N 24 40 E
Perancak, Indonesia ... **37 J17** 8 24S 114 37 E
Peräpohjola, Finland ... **8 C22** 66 16N 26 10 E
Percé, Canada ... **73 C7** 48 31N 64 13W
Perche, Collines du, France ... **20 B4** 48 30N 0 40 E
Percival Lakes, Australia ... **60 D4** 21 25S 125 0 E
Percy Is., Australia ... **62 C5** 21 39S 150 16 E
Perdido, Mte., Spain ... **21 A6** 42 40N 0 5 E
Perdu, Mt. = Perdido, Mte. Spain **21 A6** 42 40N 0 5 E
Pereira, Colombia ... **92 C3** 4 49N 75 43W
Perenjori, Australia ... **61 E2** 29 26S 116 16 E
Pereyaslav-Khmelnytskyy,
  Ukraine ... **19 D5** 50 3N 31 28 E
Pérez, I., Mexico ... **87 C7** 22 24N 89 42W
Pergamino, Argentina ... **94 C3** 33 52S 60 30W
Pergau →, Malaysia ... **39 K3** 5 23N 102 2 E
Perham, U.S.A. ... **80 B7** 46 36N 95 34W
Perhentian, Kepulauan, Malaysia **39 K4** 5 54N 102 42 E
Péribonka →, Canada ... **73 C5** 48 45N 72 5W
Péribonka, L., Canada ... **73 B5** 50 1N 71 10W
Perico, Argentina ... **94 A2** 24 20S 65 5W
Pericos, Mexico ... **86 B3** 25 3N 107 42W
Périgueux, France ... **20 D4** 45 10N 0 42 E
Perijá △, Venezuela ... **89 E5** 9 30N 72 55W
Perijá, Sierra de, Colombia ... **92 B4** 9 30N 73 3W
Peristerona →, Cyprus ... **25 D12** 35 8N 33 5 E
Perito Moreno, Argentina ... **96 F2** 46 36S 70 56W
Perkasie, U.S.A. ... **85 F9** 40 22N 75 18W
Perlas, Arch. de las, Panama ... **88 E4** 8 41N 79 7W
Perlas, Punta de, Nic. ... **88 D3** 12 30N 83 30W
Perm, Russia ... **18 C10** 58 0N 56 10 E
Pernambuco = Recife, Brazil ... **93 E12** 8 0S 35 0W
Pernambuco □, Brazil ... **93 E11** 8 0S 37 0W
Pernatty Lagoon, Australia ... **63 E2** 31 30S 137 12 E
Pernik, Bulgaria ... **23 C10** 42 35N 23 2 E
Peron Is., Australia ... **60 B5** 13 9S 130 4 E
Peron Pen., Australia ... **61 E1** 26 0S 113 10 E
Perow, Canada ... **70 C3** 54 35N 126 10W
Perpignan, France ... **20 E5** 42 42N 2 53 E
Perris, U.S.A. ... **79 M9** 33 47N 117 14W
Perry, Fla., U.S.A. ... **83 K4** 30 7N 83 35W
Perry, Ga., U.S.A. ... **83 J4** 32 28N 83 44W
Perry, Iowa, U.S.A. ... **80 E7** 41 51N 94 6W
Perry, Okla., U.S.A. ... **81 G6** 36 17N 97 14W
Perryton, U.S.A. ... **81 G4** 36 24N 100 48W
Perryville, U.S.A. ... **81 G10** 37 43N 89 52W
Persepolis, Iran ... **45 D7** 29 55N 52 50 E
Pershotravensk, Ukraine ... **17 C14** 50 13N 27 40 E
Persia = Iran ■, Asia ... **45 C7** 33 0N 53 0 E
Persian Gulf = Gulf, The, Asia ... **45 E6** 27 0N 50 0 E
Perth, Australia ... **61 F2** 31 57S 115 52 E
Perth, Canada ... **85 B8** 44 55N 76 15W
Perth, U.K. ... **11 E5** 56 24N 3 26W
Perth & Kinross □, U.K. ... **11 E5** 56 45N 3 55W
Perth Amboy, U.S.A. ... **85 F10** 40 31N 74 16W
Perth-Andover, Canada ... **73 C6** 46 44N 67 42W
Peru, Ind., U.S.A. ... **82 E2** 40 45N 86 4W
Peru, N.Y., U.S.A. ... **85 B11** 44 35N 73 32W
Peru ■, S. Amer. ... **92 D4** 4 0S 75 0W
Peru Basin, Pac. Oc. ... **65 J18** 20 0S 95 0W
Peru-Chile Trench, Pac. Oc. ... **92 G3** 20 0S 72 0W
Perúgia, Italy ... **22 C5** 43 7N 12 23 E
Pervomaysk, Ukraine ... **19 E5** 48 10N 30 46 E
Pervouralsk, Russia ... **18 C10** 56 59N 59 59 E
Pésaro, Italy ... **22 C5** 43 54N 12 55 E
Pescara, Italy ... **22 C6** 42 28N 14 13 E
Peshawar, Pakistan ... **42 B4** 34 2N 71 37 E
Peshkopi, Albania ... **23 D9** 41 41N 20 25 E
Peshtigo, U.S.A. ... **82 C2** 45 4N 87 46W
Pesqueira, Brazil ... **93 E11** 8 20S 36 42W
Petah Tiqwa, Israel ... **46 C3** 32 6N 34 53 E
Petaling Jaya, Malaysia ... **39 L3** 3 4N 101 42 E
Petaloudhes, Greece ... **25 C10** 36 18N 28 5 E
Petaluma, U.S.A. ... **78 G4** 38 14N 122 39W
Pétange, Lux. ... **15 E5** 49 33N 5 55 E
Petaro, Pakistan ... **42 G3** 25 31N 68 18 E
Petatlán, Mexico ... **86 D4** 17 31N 101 16W
Petauke, Zambia ... **55 E3** 14 14S 31 20 E
Petawawa, Canada ... **72 C4** 45 54N 77 17W
Petén Itzá, L., Guatemala ... **88 C2** 16 58N 89 50W
Peter I., Br. Virgin Is. ... **89 e** 18 22N 64 32W
Peter I. Øy, Antarctica ... **5 C16** 69 0S 91 0W
Peter Pond L., Canada ... **71 B7** 55 55N 108 44W
Peterbell, Canada ... **72 C3** 48 36N 83 21W
Peterborough, Australia ... **63 E2** 32 58S 138 51 E
Peterborough, Canada ... **84 B6** 44 20N 78 20W
Peterborough, U.K. ... **13 E7** 52 35N 0 15W
Peterborough, U.S.A. ... **85 D13** 42 53N 71 57W
Peterborough □, U.K. ... **13 E7** 52 35N 0 15W
Peterculter, U.K. ... **11 D6** 57 6N 2 16W
Peterhead, U.K. ... **11 D7** 57 31N 1 48W
Peterlee, U.K. ... **12 C6** 54 47N 1 20W
Petermann Ranges, Australia ... **60 E5** 26 0S 130 30 E
Petersburg, Alaska, U.S.A. ... **68 C6** 56 48N 132 58W
Petersburg, Pa., U.S.A. ... **84 F6** 40 34N 78 3W
Petersburg, Va., U.S.A. ... **82 G7** 37 14N 77 24W
Petersburg, W. Va., U.S.A. ... **82 F6** 39 1N 79 5W
Petersfield, U.K. ... **13 F7** 51 1N 0 56W
Petit-Canal, Guadeloupe ... **88 b** 16 25N 61 31W
Petit Goâve, Haiti ... **89 C5** 18 27N 72 51W
Petit Jardin, Canada ... **73 C8** 48 28N 59 14W
Petit Lac Manicouagan, Canada **73 B6** 51 25N 67 40W
Petit-Mécatina →, Canada ... **73 B8** 50 40N 59 30W
Petit-Mécatina, Î. du, Canada ... **73 B8** 50 30N 59 25W
Petit Piton, St. Lucia ... **89 f** 13 51N 61 5W
Petit-Saguenay, Canada ... **73 C5** 48 15N 70 4W
Petitcodiac, Canada ... **73 C6** 45 57N 65 11W
Petite Terre, Iles de la,
  Guadeloupe ... **88 b** 16 13N 61 9W
Petitot →, Canada ... **70 A4** 60 14N 123 29W
Petitsikapau L., Canada ... **73 B6** 54 37N 66 25W
Petlad, India ... **42 H5** 22 30N 72 45 E
Peto, Mexico ... **87 C7** 20 10N 88 53W
Petone, N.Z. ... **59 J5** 41 13S 174 53 E
Petorca, Chile ... **94 C1** 32 15S 70 56W
Petoskey, U.S.A. ... **82 C3** 45 22N 84 57W
Petra, Jordan ... **46 E4** 30 20N 35 22 E
Petra, Spain ... **24 B10** 39 37N 3 6 E
Petra, Ostrova, Russia ... **4 B13** 76 15N 118 30 E
Petra Velikogo, Zaliv, Russia ... **30 C6** 42 40N 132 0 E
Petrich, Bulgaria ... **23 D10** 41 24N 23 13 E
Petrified Forest △, U.S.A. ... **77 J9** 35 0N 109 30W
Petrikov = Pyetrikaw, Belarus ... **17 B15** 52 11N 28 29 E
Petrolândia, Brazil ... **93 E11** 9 5S 38 20W
Petrolia, Canada ... **84 D2** 42 54N 82 9W
Petrolina, Brazil ... **93 E10** 9 24S 40 30W
Petropavl, Kazakhstan ... **28 D7** 54 53N 69 13 E

Petropavlovsk = Petropavl,
  Kazakhstan ... **28 D7** 54 53N 69 13 E
Petropavlovsk-Kamchatskiy,
  Russia ... **29 D16** 53 3N 158 43 E
Petrópolis, Brazil ... **95 A7** 22 33S 43 9W
Petroşani, Romania ... **17 F12** 45 28N 23 20 E
Petrovaradin, Serbia & M. ... **23 B8** 45 16N 19 55 E
Petrovsk, Russia ... **18 D8** 52 22N 45 19 E
Petrovsk-Zabaykalskiy, Russia ... **29 D11** 51 20N 108 55 E
Petrozavodsk, Russia ... **18 B5** 61 41N 34 20 E
Petrus Steyn, S. Africa ... **57 D4** 27 38S 28 8 E
Petrusburg, S. Africa ... **56 D4** 29 4S 25 26 E
Peumo, Chile ... **94 C1** 34 21S 71 12W
Peureulak, Indonesia ... **36 D1** 4 48N 97 45 E
Pevek, Russia ... **29 C18** 69 41N 171 19 E
Pforzheim, Germany ... **16 D5** 48 52N 8 41 E
Pha Taem △, Thailand ... **38 E5** 15 32N 105 30 E
Phagwara, India ... **40 D9** 31 10N 75 40 E
Phaistós, Greece ... **25 D6** 35 2N 24 50 E
Phala, Botswana ... **56 C4** 23 45S 26 50 E
Phalera = Phulera, India ... **42 F6** 26 52N 75 16 E
Phalodi, India ... **42 F5** 27 12N 72 24 E
Phaluai, Ko, Thailand ... **39 b** 9 32N 99 41 E
Phan, Thailand ... **38 C2** 19 28N 99 43 E
Phan Rang, Vietnam ... **39 G7** 11 34N 109 0 E
Phan Ri = Hoa Da, Vietnam ... **39 G7** 11 16N 108 40 E
Phan Thiet, Vietnam ... **39 G7** 11 1N 108 9 E
Phanat Nikhom, Thailand ... **38 F3** 13 27N 101 11 E
Phangan, Ko, Thailand ... **39 H3** 9 45N 100 0 E
Phangnga, Thailand ... **39 H2** 8 28N 98 30 E
Phangnga, Ao, Thailand ... **39 a** 8 16N 98 33 E
Phanom Sarakham, Thailand ... **38 F3** 13 45N 101 21 E
Phaphund, India ... **43 F8** 26 36N 79 28 E
Pharenda, India ... **43 F10** 27 5N 83 17 E
Pharr, U.S.A. ... **81 M5** 26 12N 98 11W
Phatthalung, Thailand ... **39 J3** 7 39N 100 6 E
Phayao, Thailand ... **38 C2** 19 11N 99 55 E
Phelps, U.S.A. ... **84 D7** 42 58N 77 3W
Phelps L., Canada ... **71 B8** 59 15N 103 15W
Phenix City, U.S.A. ... **83 J3** 32 28N 85 0W
Phet Buri, Thailand ... **38 F2** 13 1N 99 55 E
Phetchabun, Thailand ... **38 D3** 16 25N 101 8 E
Phetchabun, Thiu Khao, Thailand **38 E3** 16 0N 101 20 E
Phetchaburi = Phet Buri, Thailand **38 F2** 13 1N 99 55 E
Phi Phi, Ko, Thailand ... **39 J2** 7 45N 98 46 E
Phiafay, Laos ... **38 E6** 14 48N 106 0 E
Phibun Mangsahan, Thailand ... **38 E5** 15 14N 105 14 E
Phichai, Thailand ... **38 D3** 17 22N 100 10 E
Phichit, Thailand ... **38 D3** 16 26N 100 22 E
Philadelphia, Miss., U.S.A. ... **81 J10** 32 46N 89 7W
Philadelphia, N.Y., U.S.A. ... **85 B9** 44 9N 75 43W
Philadelphia, Pa., U.S.A. ... **85 G9** 39 57N 75 10W
Philip, U.S.A. ... **80 C4** 44 2N 101 40W
Philippeville, Belgium ... **15 D4** 50 12N 4 33 E
Philippi, U.S.A. ... **82 F5** 39 9N 80 3W
Philippi L., Australia ... **62 C2** 24 20S 138 55 E
Philippine Sea, Pac. Oc. ... **26 H16** 18 0N 125 0 E
Philippines ■, Asia ... **37 B6** 12 0N 123 0 E
Philippolis, S. Africa ... **56 E4** 30 15S 25 16 E
Philippopolis = Plovdiv, Bulgaria **23 C11** 42 8N 24 44 E
Philipsburg, Canada ... **85 A11** 45 2N 73 5W
Philipsburg, Mont., U.S.A. ... **76 C7** 46 20N 113 18W
Philipsburg, Pa., U.S.A. ... **84 F6** 40 54N 78 13W
Philipstown = Daingean, Ireland **10 C4** 53 18N 7 17W
Philipstown, S. Africa ... **56 E3** 30 28S 24 30 E
Phillip I., Australia ... **63 F4** 38 30S 145 12 E
Phillips, U.S.A. ... **80 C9** 45 42N 90 24W
Phillipsburg, Kans., U.S.A. ... **80 F5** 39 45N 99 19W
Phillipsburg, N.J., U.S.A. ... **85 F9** 40 42N 75 12W
Philmont, U.S.A. ... **85 D11** 42 15N 73 39W
Philomath, U.S.A. ... **76 D2** 44 32N 123 22W
Phimai, Thailand ... **38 E4** 15 13N 102 30 E
Phitsanulok, Thailand ... **38 D3** 16 50N 100 12 E
Phnom Dangrek, Thailand ... **36 B2** 14 20N 104 0 E
Phnom Penh, Cambodia ... **39 G5** 11 33N 104 55 E
Phnom Penh = Phnom Penh,
  Cambodia ... **39 G5** 11 33N 104 55 E
Phoenicia, U.S.A. ... **85 D10** 42 5N 74 14W
Phoenix, Ariz., U.S.A. ... **77 K7** 33 27N 112 4W
Phoenix, N.Y., U.S.A. ... **85 C8** 43 14N 76 18W
Phoenix Is., Kiribati ... **64 H10** 3 30S 172 0W
Phoenixville, U.S.A. ... **85 F9** 40 8N 75 31W
Phon, Thailand ... **38 E4** 15 49N 102 36 E
Phon Tiou, Laos ... **38 D5** 17 53N 104 37 E
Phong →, Thailand ... **38 D4** 16 23N 102 56 E
Phong Saly, Laos ... **38 B4** 21 42N 102 9 E
Phong Tho, Vietnam ... **38 A4** 22 32N 103 21 E
Phonhong, Laos ... **38 C4** 18 30N 102 25 E
Phonum, Thailand ... **39 H2** 8 49N 98 48 E
Phosphate Hill, Australia ... **62 C2** 21 53S 139 58 E
Photharam, Thailand ... **38 F2** 13 41N 99 51 E
Phra Nakhon Si Ayutthaya,
  Thailand ... **38 E3** 14 25N 100 30 E
Phra Thong, Ko, Thailand ... **39 H2** 9 5N 98 17 E
Phrae, Thailand ... **38 C3** 18 7N 100 9 E
Phrom Phiram, Thailand ... **38 D3** 17 2N 100 12 E
Phu Chong-Na Yoi △, Thailand . **38 E5** 14 25N 105 30 E
Phu Dien, Vietnam ... **38 C5** 18 58N 105 31 E
Phu Hin Rang Kla △, Thailand ... **38 D3** 17 0N 100 59 E
Phu Kradung △, Thailand ... **38 D3** 17 0N 101 40 E
Phu Loi, Laos ... **38 B4** 20 14N 103 14 E
Phu Luang △, Thailand ... **38 D3** 17 15N 101 29 E
Phu Ly, Vietnam ... **38 B5** 20 35N 105 50 E
Phu Phan △, Thailand ... **38 D4** 17 0N 103 56 E
Phu Quoc, Dao, Vietnam ... **39 G4** 10 20N 104 0 E
Phu Tho, Vietnam ... **38 B5** 21 24N 105 13 E
Phuc Yen, Vietnam ... **38 B5** 21 16N 105 45 E
Phuket, Thailand ... **39 a** 7 53N 98 24 E
Phuket, Ko, Thailand ... **39 a** 8 0N 98 22 E
Phul, India ... **42 D6** 30 19N 75 14 E
Phulad, India ... **42 G5** 25 38N 73 49 E
Phulchari, Bangla. ... **43 G13** 25 11N 89 37 E
Phulera, India ... **42 F6** 26 52N 75 16 E
Phulpur, India ... **43 G10** 25 31N 82 49 E
Phun Phin, Thailand ... **39 H2** 9 7N 99 12 E
Piacenza, Italy ... **20 D8** 45 1N 9 40 E
Pian Cr. →, Australia ... **63 E4** 30 2S 148 12 E
Pian-Upe ☐, Uganda ... **54 B3** 1 44N 34 20 E
Pianosa, Italy ... **22 C4** 42 35N 10 5 E
Piapot, Canada ... **71 D7** 49 59N 109 8W
Piatra Neamţ, Romania ... **17 E14** 46 56N 26 21 E
Piauí □, Brazil ... **93 E10** 7 0S 43 0W
Piauí →, Brazil ... **93 E10** 6 38S 42 42W
Piave →, Italy ... **22 B5** 45 32N 12 44 E
Pibor Post, Sudan ... **51 G12** 6 47N 33 3 E
Picardie □, France ... **20 B5** 49 50N 3 0 E
Picardy = Picardie □, France ... **20 B5** 49 50N 3 0 E

Picayune, U.S.A. ... **81 K10** 30 32N 89 41W
Pichhor, India ... **43 G8** 25 58N 78 20 E
Pichilemu, Chile ... **94 C1** 34 22S 72 0W
Pichor, India ... **42 G8** 25 11N 78 11 E
Pickerel L., Canada ... **72 C1** 48 40N 91 25W
Pickering, U.K. ... **12 C7** 54 15N 0 46W
Pickering, Vale of, U.K. ... **12 C7** 54 14N 0 45W
Pickle Lake, Canada ... **72 B1** 51 30N 90 12W
Pickwick L., U.S.A. ... **83 H1** 35 4N 88 15W
Pico Bonito △, Honduras ... **88 C2** 15 34N 86 46W
Pico Truncado, Argentina ... **96 F3** 46 40S 68 0W
Picos, Brazil ... **93 E10** 7 5S 41 28W
Picton, Australia ... **63 E5** 34 12S 150 34 E
Picton, Canada ... **84 B7** 44 1N 77 9W
Picton, N.Z. ... **59 J5** 41 18S 174 3 E
Pictou, Canada ... **73 C7** 45 41N 62 42W
Picture Butte, Canada ... **70 D6** 49 55N 112 45W
Pictured Rocks ⌂, U.S.A. ... **82 B2** 46 30N 86 30W
Picún Leufú, Argentina ... **96 D3** 39 30S 69 5W
Pidurutalagala, Sri Lanka ... **40 R12** 7 10N 80 50 E
Piedmont = Piemonte □, Italy ... **20 D7** 45 0N 8 0 E
Piedmont, Ala., U.S.A. ... **83 J3** 33 55N 85 37W
Piedmont, S.C., U.S.A. ... **75 D10** 34 0N 81 30W
Piedras Negras, Mexico ... **86 B4** 28 42N 100 31W
Pieksämäki, Finland ... **9 E22** 62 18N 27 10 E
Piemonte □, Italy ... **20 D7** 45 0N 8 0 E
Pienaarsrivier, S. Africa ... **57 D4** 25 15S 28 18 E
Piercefield, U.S.A. ... **85 B10** 44 13N 74 35W
Pierceland, Canada ... **71 C7** 54 20N 109 46W
Pierpont, U.S.A. ... **84 E4** 41 45N 80 34W
Pierre, U.S.A. ... **80 C4** 44 22N 100 21W
Pierreville, Trin. & Tob. ... **93 K16** 10 16N 61 0W
Piet Retief, S. Africa ... **57 D5** 27 1S 30 50 E
Pietarsaari, Finland ... **8 E20** 63 40N 22 43 E
Pietermaritzburg, S. Africa ... **57 D5** 29 35S 30 25 E
Pietersburg = Polokwane,
  S. Africa ... **57 C4** 23 54S 29 25 E
Pietrosul, Vf., Maramureş,
  Romania ... **17 E13** 47 35N 24 43 E
Pietrosul, Vf., Suceava, Romania **17 E13** 47 12N 25 18 E
Pigeon L., Canada ... **84 B6** 44 27N 78 30W
Piggott, U.S.A. ... **81 G9** 36 23N 90 11W
Pigüe, Argentina ... **94 D3** 37 36S 62 25W
Pihani, India ... **43 F9** 27 36N 80 15 E
Pihlajavesi, Finland ... **9 F23** 61 45N 28 45 E
Pijijiapan, Mexico ... **87 D6** 15 42N 93 14W
Pikangikum Berens, Canada ... **71 C10** 51 49N 94 0W
Pikes Peak, U.S.A. ... **80 F2** 38 50N 105 3W
Piketberg, S. Africa ... **56 E2** 32 55S 18 40 E
Pikeville, U.S.A. ... **82 G4** 37 29N 82 31W
Pikou, China ... **35 E12** 39 18N 122 22 E
Pikwitonei, Canada ... **71 B9** 55 35N 97 9W
Piła, Poland ... **17 B9** 53 10N 16 48 E
Pilanesberg △, S. Africa ... **56 D4** 25 15S 27 4 E
Pilani, India ... **42 E6** 28 22N 75 33 E
Pilar, Paraguay ... **94 B4** 26 50S 58 20W
Pilaya →, Bolivia ... **92 H6** 20 55S 64 4W
Pilbara, Australia ... **60 D2** 23 35S 117 25 E
Pilcomayo →, Paraguay ... **94 B4** 25 21S 57 42W
Pilgrim's Rest, S. Africa ... **57 C5** 24 55S 30 44 E
Pilibhit, India ... **43 E8** 28 40N 79 50 E
Pilica →, Poland ... **17 C11** 51 52N 21 17 E
Pilkhawa, India ... **42 E7** 28 43N 77 42 E
Pilliga, Australia ... **63 E4** 30 21S 148 54 E
Pilos, Greece ... **23 F9** 36 55N 21 42 E
Pilot Mound, Canada ... **71 D9** 49 15N 98 54W
Pilot Point, U.S.A. ... **81 J6** 33 24N 96 58W
Pilot Rock, U.S.A. ... **76 D4** 45 29N 118 50W
Pilsen = Plzeň, Czech Rep. ... **16 D7** 49 45N 13 22 E
Pima, U.S.A. ... **77 K9** 32 54N 109 50W
Pimba, Australia ... **63 E2** 31 18S 136 46 E
Pimenta Bueno, Brazil ... **92 F6** 11 35S 61 10W
Pimentel, Peru ... **92 E3** 6 45S 79 55W
Pinang, Malaysia ... **39 c** 5 25N 100 15 E
Pinar, C. des, Spain ... **24 B10** 39 53N 3 12 E
Pinar del Río, Cuba ... **88 B3** 22 26N 83 40W
Pınarhisar, Turkey ... **23 D12** 41 37N 27 30 E
Pinatubo, Mt., Phil. ... **37 A6** 15 8N 120 21 E
Pincher Creek, Canada ... **70 D6** 49 30N 113 57W
Pinchi L., Canada ... **70 C4** 54 38N 124 30W
Pinckneyville, U.S.A. ... **80 F10** 38 5N 89 23W
Pińczów, Poland ... **17 C11** 50 32N 20 32 E
Pindar, Australia ... **61 E2** 28 30S 115 47 E
Pindi Gheb, Pakistan ... **42 C5** 33 14N 72 21 E
Píndos Óros, Greece ... **23 E9** 40 0N 21 0 E
Pindus Mts. = Píndos Óros,
  Greece ... **23 E9** 40 0N 21 0 E
Pine →, B.C., Canada ... **70 B4** 56 8N 120 43W
Pine →, Sask., Canada ... **71 B7** 58 50N 105 38W
Pine, C., Canada ... **73 C9** 46 37N 53 32W
Pine Bluff, U.S.A. ... **81 H9** 34 13N 92 1W
Pine Bluffs, U.S.A. ... **80 E2** 41 11N 104 4W
Pine City, U.S.A. ... **80 C8** 45 50N 92 59W
Pine Cr. →, U.S.A. ... **84 E7** 41 10N 77 16W
Pine Creek, Australia ... **60 B5** 13 50S 131 50 E
Pine Falls, Canada ... **71 C9** 50 34N 96 11W
Pine Flat Res., U.S.A. ... **78 J7** 36 50N 119 20W
Pine Grove, U.S.A. ... **84 F8** 40 33N 76 23W
Pine Pass, Canada ... **70 B4** 55 25N 122 42W
Pine Point, Canada ... **70 A6** 60 50N 114 28W
Pine Ridge, U.S.A. ... **80 D3** 43 2N 102 33W
Pine River, Canada ... **71 C8** 51 45N 100 30W
Pine River, U.S.A. ... **80 B7** 46 43N 94 24W
Pine Valley, U.S.A. ... **79 N10** 32 50N 116 32W
Pinecrest, U.S.A. ... **78 G6** 38 12N 120 1W
Pinedale, Calif., U.S.A. ... **78 J7** 36 50N 119 48W
Pinedale, Wyo., U.S.A. ... **76 E9** 42 52N 109 52W
Pinega →, Russia ... **18 B8** 64 30N 44 19 E
Pinehill, Australia ... **62 C4** 23 38S 146 57 E
Pinehouse L., Canada ... **71 B7** 55 32N 106 35W
Pineimuta →, Canada ... **72 B1** 52 8N 88 33W
Pinerolo, Italy ... **20 D7** 44 53N 7 21 E
Pinetop, U.S.A. ... **77 J9** 34 8N 109 56W
Pinetown, S. Africa ... **57 D5** 29 48S 30 54 E
Pineville, U.S.A. ... **81 K8** 31 19N 92 26W
Ping →, Thailand ... **38 E3** 15 42N 100 9 E
Pingaring, Australia ... **61 F2** 32 40S 118 32 E
Pingding, China ... **34 F7** 37 47N 113 38 E
Pingdingshan, China ... **34 H7** 33 43N 113 27 E
Pingdong, Taiwan ... **33 D7** 22 39N 120 30 E
Pingdu, China ... **35 F10** 36 42N 119 59 E
Pingelly, Australia ... **61 F2** 32 32S 117 5 E
Pingliang, China ... **34 G4** 35 35N 106 31 E
Pinglu, China ... **34 E7** 39 31N 112 30 E
Pingluo, China ... **34 E4** 38 52N 106 30 E
Pingquan, China ... **35 D10** 41 1N 118 37 E
Pingrup, Australia ... **61 F2** 33 32S 118 29 E
P'ingtung, Taiwan ... **33 D7** 22 38N 120 30 E

ingwu, China … 34 H3 32 25N 104 30 E
ingxiang, China … 32 D5 22 6N 106 46 E
ingyao, China … 34 F7 37 12N 112 10 E
ingyi, China … 35 G9 35 30N 117 35 E
ingyin, China … 34 F9 36 20N 116 25 E
ingyuan, China … 34 F9 37 10N 116 22 E
inhal, Brazil … 95 A6 22 10S 46 46W
inheiro, Brazil … 93 D9 2 31S 45 5W
inheiro Machado, Brazil … 95 C5 31 34S 53 23W
inhel, Portugal … 21 B2 40 50N 7 1W
ini, Indonesia … 36 D1 0 10N 98 40 E
iniós →, Greece … 23 E10 39 55N 22 41 E
injarra, Australia … 61 F2 32 37S 115 52 E
ink Mountain, Canada … 70 B4 57 3N 122 52W
innacles, U.S.A. … 78 J5 36 33N 121 19W
innacles △, U.S.A. … 78 J5 36 25N 121 12W
innaroo, Australia … 63 F3 35 17S 140 53 E
innes, Ákra, Greece … 23 D11 40 5N 24 20 E
inon Hills, U.S.A. … 79 L9 34 24N 117 39W
inos, Mexico … 86 C4 22 20N 101 40W
inos, Mt., U.S.A. … 79 L7 34 49N 119 8W
inos Pt., U.S.A. … 77 H3 36 38N 121 57W
inotepa Nacional, Mexico … 87 D5 16 19N 98 3W
inrang, Indonesia … 37 E5 3 46S 119 41 E
ins, Pte. aux, Canada … 84 D3 42 15N 81 51W
insk, Belarus … 17 B14 52 10N 26 1 E
intados, Chile … 92 H5 20 35S 69 40W
inyug, Russia … 18 B8 60 5N 48 0 E
ioche, U.S.A. … 77 H6 37 56N 114 27W
iombino, Italy … 22 C4 42 55N 10 32 E
ioner, Ostrov, Russia … 29 B10 79 50N 92 0 E
iorini, L., Brazil … 92 D6 3 15S 62 35W
iotrków Trybunalski, Poland … 17 C10 51 23N 19 43 E
ip, Iran … 45 E9 26 45N 60 10 E
ipar, India … 42 F5 26 25N 73 31 E
ipar Road, India … 42 F5 26 27N 73 27 E
iparia, Mad. P., India … 42 H8 22 45N 78 23 E
iparia, Mad. P., India … 42 J7 21 49N 77 37 E
ipestone, U.S.A. … 80 D6 44 0N 96 19W
ipestone →, Canada … 72 B2 52 53N 89 23W
ipestone Cr. →, Canada … 71 D8 49 38N 100 15W
iplan, Pakistan … 42 C4 32 17N 71 21 E
iploda, India … 42 H6 23 37N 74 56 E
ippingarra, Australia … 60 D2 20 27S 118 42 E
iqua, U.S.A. … 82 E3 40 9N 84 15W
iquiri →, Brazil … 95 A5 24 3S 54 14W
ir Panjal Range, India … 42 C7 32 30N 76 50 E
ir Sohráb, Iran … 45 E9 25 44N 60 54 E
iracicaba, Brazil … 95 A6 22 45S 47 40W
iracuruca, Brazil … 93 D10 3 50S 41 50W
iræus = Piraiévs, Greece … 23 F10 37 57N 23 42 E
iraiévs, Greece … 23 F10 37 57N 23 42 E
irajuí, Brazil … 95 A6 21 59S 49 29W
iram I., India … 42 J5 21 36N 72 21 E
irané, Argentina … 94 B4 25 42S 59 6W
irapora, Brazil … 93 G10 17 20S 44 56W
irawa, India … 42 G7 24 10N 76 2 E
irgos, Greece … 23 F9 37 40N 21 27 E
iribebuy, Paraguay … 94 B4 25 26S 57 2W
irimapun, Indonesia … 37 F9 6 20S 138 24 E
irin Planina, Bulgaria … 23 D10 41 40N 23 30 E
irineos = Pyrénées, Europe … 20 E4 42 45N 0 18 E
iripiri, Brazil … 93 D10 4 15S 41 46W
irmasens, Germany … 16 D4 49 12N 7 36 E
irot, Serbia & M. … 23 C10 43 9N 22 33 E
iru, Indonesia … 37 E7 3 4S 128 12 E
iru, U.S.A. … 79 L8 34 25N 118 48W
isa, Italy … 22 C4 43 43N 10 23 E
isagua, Chile … 92 G4 19 40S 70 15W
isco, Peru … 92 F3 13 50S 76 12W
isek, Czech Rep. … 16 D8 49 19N 14 10 E
ishan, China … 32 C2 37 30N 78 33 E
ishin, Iran … 45 E9 26 6N 61 47 E
ishin, Pakistan … 42 D2 30 35N 67 0 E
ishin Lora →, Pakistan … 42 E1 29 9N 64 5 E
ishin, Indonesia … 37 F6 5 8S 121 53 E
ismo Beach, U.S.A. … 79 K6 35 9N 120 38W
issis, Cerro, Argentina … 94 B2 27 45S 68 48W
issouri, Cyprus … 25 E11 34 40N 32 42 E
istóia, Italy … 22 C4 43 55N 10 54 E
istol B., Canada … 71 A10 62 25N 92 37W
isuerga →, Spain … 21 B3 41 33N 4 52W
it →, U.S.A. … 76 F2 40 47N 122 6W
itarpunga L., Australia … 63 E3 34 24S 143 30 E
itcairn I., Pac. Oc. … 65 K14 25 5S 130 5W
itch L., Trin. & Tob. … 93 K15 10 12N 61 39W
ite älv →, Sweden … 8 D19 65 20N 21 25 E
iteå, Sweden … 8 D19 65 20N 21 25 E
iteşti, Romania … 17 F13 44 52N 24 54 E
ithapuram, India … 41 L13 17 10N 82 15 E
ithara, Australia … 61 F2 30 20S 116 35 E
ithoragarh, India … 43 E9 29 35N 80 13 E
ithoro, Pakistan … 42 G3 25 31N 69 23 E
itlochry, U.K. … 11 E5 56 42N 3 44W
itsilia, Cyprus … 25 E12 34 55N 33 0 E
ittsburg, Calif., U.S.A. … 78 G5 38 2N 121 53W
ittsburg, Kans., U.S.A. … 81 G7 37 25N 94 42W
ittsburg, Tex., U.S.A. … 81 J7 33 0N 94 59W
ittsburgh, U.S.A. … 84 F5 40 26N 80 1W
ittsfield, Ill., U.S.A. … 80 F9 39 36N 90 49W
ittsfield, Maine, U.S.A. … 83 C11 44 47N 69 23W
ittsfield, Mass., U.S.A. … 85 D11 42 27N 73 15W
ittsfield, N.H., U.S.A. … 85 C13 43 18N 71 20W
ittston, U.S.A. … 85 E9 41 19N 75 47W
ittsworth, Australia … 63 D5 27 41S 151 37 E
ituri →, Australia … 62 C2 22 35S 138 30 E
iura, Peru … 92 E2 5 15S 80 38W
ixley, U.S.A. … 78 K7 35 58N 119 18W
izhou, China … 34 G9 34 44N 116 55 E
iacentia, Canada … 73 C9 47 0N 54 0W
iacentia B., Canada … 73 C9 47 0N 54 40W
iacerville, Cuba … 88 B4 22 15N 79 44W
iainfield, N.J., U.S.A. … 85 F10 40 37N 74 25W
iainfield, Ohio, U.S.A. … 84 F3 40 13N 81 43W
iainfield, Vt., U.S.A. … 85 B12 44 17N 72 26W
iains, Mont., U.S.A. … 76 C6 47 28N 114 53W
iains, Tex., U.S.A. … 81 J3 33 11N 102 50W
iainview, Nebr., U.S.A. … 80 D6 42 21N 97 47W
iainview, Tex., U.S.A. … 81 H4 34 11N 101 43W
iainwell, U.S.A. … 82 D3 42 27N 85 38W
iaistow, U.S.A. … 85 D13 42 50N 71 6W
iáka, Ákra, Greece … 25 D8 35 11N 26 19 E
iana Cays, Bahamas … 89 B5 22 38N 73 30W
ianada, U.S.A. … 78 H6 37 16N 120 19W
iano, U.S.A. … 81 J6 33 1N 96 42W

Plant City, U.S.A. … 83 M4 28 1N 82 7W
Plaquemine, U.S.A. … 81 K9 30 17N 91 14W
Plasencia, Spain … 21 B2 40 3N 6 8W
Plaster City, U.S.A. … 79 N11 32 47N 115 51W
Plaster Rock, Canada … 73 C6 46 53N 67 22W
Plastun, Russia … 30 B8 44 45N 136 19 E
Plata, Río de la, S. Amer. … 94 C4 34 45S 57 30W
Plátani →, Italy … 22 F5 37 23N 13 16 E
Plátanos, Greece … 25 D5 35 28N 23 33 E
Platte, U.S.A. … 80 D5 43 23N 98 51W
Platte →, Mo., U.S.A. … 80 F7 39 16N 94 50W
Platte →, Nebr., U.S.A. … 80 E7 41 4N 95 53W
Platteville, U.S.A. … 80 D9 42 44N 90 29W
Plattsburgh, U.S.A. … 85 B11 44 42N 73 28W
Plattsmouth, U.S.A. … 80 E7 41 1N 95 53W
Plauen, Germany … 16 C7 50 30N 12 8 E
Plavinas, Latvia … 9 H21 56 35N 25 46 E
Playa Blanca, Canary Is. … 24 F6 28 55N 13 37W
Playa Blanca Sur, Canary Is. … 24 F6 28 51N 13 50W
Playa de las Americas, Canary Is. … 24 F3 28 5N 16 43W
Playa de Mogán, Canary Is. … 24 G4 27 48N 15 47W
Playa del Inglés, Canary Is. … 24 G4 27 45N 15 33W
Playa Esmerelda, Canary Is. … 24 F5 28 8N 14 16W
Playgreen L., Canada … 71 C9 54 0N 98 15W
Pleasant Bay, Canada … 73 C7 46 51N 60 48W
Pleasant Hill, U.S.A. … 78 H4 37 57N 122 4W
Pleasant Mount, U.S.A. … 85 E9 41 44N 75 26W
Pleasanton, Calif., U.S.A. … 78 H5 37 39N 121 52W
Pleasanton, Tex., U.S.A. … 81 L5 28 58N 98 29W
Pleasantville, N.J., U.S.A. … 82 F8 39 24N 74 32W
Pleasantville, Pa., U.S.A. … 84 E5 41 35N 79 34W
Plei Ku, Vietnam … 38 F7 13 57N 108 0 E
Plenty →, Australia … 62 C2 23 25S 136 31 E
Plenty, B. of, N.Z. … 59 G6 37 45S 177 0 E
Plentywood, U.S.A. … 80 A2 48 47N 104 34W
Plesetsk, Russia … 18 B7 62 43N 40 20 E
Plessisville, Canada … 73 C5 46 14N 71 47W
Plétipi, L., Canada … 73 B5 51 44N 70 6W
Pleven, Bulgaria … 23 C11 43 26N 24 37 E
Plevlja, Serbia & M. … 23 C8 43 21N 19 21 E
Plevna, Canada … 84 B8 44 58N 76 59W
Płock, Poland … 17 B10 52 32N 19 40 E
Plöckenstein, Germany … 16 D7 48 46N 13 51 E
Ploiești, Romania … 17 F14 44 57N 26 5 E
Plonge, Lac la, Canada … 71 B7 55 8N 107 20W
Plovdiv, Bulgaria … 23 C11 42 8N 24 44 E
Plover Cove Res., China … 33 G11 22 28N 114 15 E
Plum, U.S.A. … 84 F5 40 29N 79 47W
Plum I., U.S.A. … 85 E12 41 11N 72 12W
Plumas, U.S.A. … 78 F7 39 45N 120 4W
Plummer, U.S.A. … 76 C5 47 20N 116 53W
Plumtree, Zimbabwe … 55 G2 20 27S 27 55 E
Plungė, Lithuania … 9 J19 55 53N 21 59 E
Plymouth, Trin. & Tob. … 93 J16 11 14N 60 48W
Plymouth, U.K. … 13 G3 50 22N 4 10W
Plymouth, Calif., U.S.A. … 78 G6 38 29N 120 51W
Plymouth, Ind., U.S.A. … 82 E2 41 21N 86 19W
Plymouth, Mass., U.S.A. … 85 E14 41 57N 70 40W
Plymouth, N.C., U.S.A. … 83 H7 35 52N 76 43W
Plymouth, N.H., U.S.A. … 85 C13 43 46N 71 41W
Plymouth, Pa., U.S.A. … 85 E9 41 14N 75 57W
Plymouth, Wis., U.S.A. … 82 D2 43 45N 87 59W
Plympton-Wyoming, Canada … 84 D2 42 57N 82 7W
Plynlimon = Pumlumon Fawr, U.K. … 13 E4 52 28N 3 46W
Plzeň, Czech Rep. … 16 D7 49 45N 13 22 E
Po →, Italy … 22 B5 44 57N 12 4 E
Po Hai = Bo Hai, China … 35 E10 39 0N 119 0 E
Po Toi, China … 33 G11 22 10N 114 16 E
Pobeda, Russia … 29 C15 65 12N 146 12 E
Pobedy, Pik, Kyrgyzstan … 28 E8 42 0N 79 58 E
Pocahontas, Ark., U.S.A. … 81 G9 36 16N 90 58W
Pocahontas, Iowa, U.S.A. … 80 D7 42 44N 94 40W
Pocatello, U.S.A. … 76 E7 42 52N 112 27W
Pochutla, Mexico … 87 D5 15 50N 96 31W
Pocito Casas, Mexico … 86 B2 28 32N 111 6W
Pocomoke City, U.S.A. … 82 F8 38 5N 75 34W
Poços de Caldas, Brazil … 95 A6 21 50S 46 33W
Podgorica, Serbia & M. … 23 C8 42 30N 19 19 E
Podilska Vysochyna, Ukraine … 17 D14 49 0N 28 0 E
Podolsk, Russia … 18 C6 55 25N 37 30 E
Podporozhye, Russia … 18 B5 60 55N 34 2 E
Pofadder, S. Africa … 56 D2 29 10S 19 22 E
Pogranichnyy, Russia … 30 B5 44 25N 131 24 E
Poh, Indonesia … 37 E6 0 46S 122 51 E
P'ohang, S. Korea … 35 F15 36 1N 129 23 E
Pohjanmaa, Finland … 8 E20 62 58N 22 50 E
Pohnpei, Micronesia … 64 G7 6 55N 158 10 E
Pohri, India … 42 G6 25 32N 77 22 E
Poinsett, C., Antarctica … 5 C8 65 42N 113 18 E
Point Arena, U.S.A. … 78 G3 38 55N 123 41W
Point Baker, U.S.A. … 70 B2 56 21N 133 37W
Point Edward, Canada … 72 D3 43 0N 82 30W
Point Fortin, Trin. & Tob. … 93 K15 10 10N 61 42W
Point Hope, U.S.A. … 68 B3 68 21N 166 47W
Point L., Canada … 68 B8 65 15N 113 4W
Point Lisas, Trin. & Tob. … 93 K15 10 32N 61 30W
Point Pedro, Sri Lanka … 40 Q12 9 50N 80 15 E
Point Pelee △, Canada … 84 E2 41 57N 82 31W
Point Pleasant, N.J., U.S.A. … 85 F10 40 5N 74 4W
Point Pleasant, W. Va., U.S.A. … 82 F4 38 51N 82 8W
Point Reyes △, U.S.A. … 78 G2 38 10N 122 55W
Pointe-à-Pitre, Guadeloupe … 88 b 16 10N 61 32W
Pointe-au-Pic = La Malbaie, Canada … 73 C5 47 40N 70 10W
Pointe-Claire, Canada … 85 A11 45 26N 73 50W
Pointe-Gatineau, Canada … 85 A9 45 28N 75 42W
Pointe-Noire, Congo … 52 E2 4 48S 11 53 E
Pointe Noire, Guadeloupe … 88 b 16 14N 61 47W
Poisonbush Ra., Australia … 60 D3 22 32S 121 30 E
Poissonnier Pt., Australia … 60 C2 19 57S 119 10 E
Poitiers, France … 20 C4 46 35N 0 20 E
Poitou, France … 20 C3 46 40N 0 10W
Pojoaque, U.S.A. … 77 J11 35 54N 106 1W
Pokaran, India … 40 F7 27 0N 71 50 E
Pokataroo, Australia … 63 D4 29 30S 148 36 E
Pokhara, Nepal … 43 E10 28 14N 83 58 E
Poko, Dem. Rep. of the Congo … 54 B2 3 7N 26 52 E
Pokrovsk, Russia … 29 C13 61 29N 129 0 E
Pola = Pula, Croatia … 16 F7 44 54N 13 57 E
Polacca, U.S.A. … 77 J8 35 50N 110 23W
Polan, Iran … 45 E9 25 30N 61 10 E
Poland ■, Europe … 17 C10 52 0N 20 0 E
Polar Bear △, Canada … 72 A2 55 0N 83 45W
Polatsk, Belarus … 18 C4 55 30N 28 50 E
Polcura, Chile … 94 D1 37 17S 71 43W
Polessk, Russia … 9 J19 54 50N 21 8 E

Polesye = Pripet Marshes, Europe … 17 B15 52 10N 28 10 E
Polevskoy, Russia … 18 C11 56 26N 60 11 E
Pŏlgŭ-ri, S. Korea … 35 G14 34 51N 127 21 E
Police, Poland … 16 B8 53 33N 14 33 E
Polillo Is., Phil. … 37 B6 14 56N 122 0 E
Polis, Cyprus … 25 D11 35 2N 32 26 E
Poliyiros, Greece … 23 D10 40 23N 23 25 E
Polk, U.S.A. … 84 E5 41 22N 79 56W
Pollachi, India … 40 P10 10 35N 77 0 E
Pollença, Spain … 24 B10 39 54N 3 1 E
Pollença, B. de, Spain … 24 B10 39 53N 3 8 E
Polnovat, Russia … 28 C7 63 50N 65 54 E
Polokwane, S. Africa … 57 C4 23 54S 29 25 E
Polonne, Ukraine … 17 C14 50 6N 27 30 E
Polonnoye = Polonne, Ukraine … 17 C14 50 6N 27 30 E
Polson, U.S.A. … 76 C6 47 41N 114 9W
Poltava, Ukraine … 19 E5 49 35N 34 35 E
Pŏltsamaa, Estonia … 9 G21 58 41N 25 58 E
Polunochnoye, Russia … 28 C7 60 52N 60 25 E
Pŏlva, Estonia … 9 G22 58 3N 27 3 E
Polyarny, Russia … 18 A5 69 8N 33 20 E
Polynesia, Pac. Oc. … 65 F11 10 0S 162 0W
Polynésie française = French Polynesia ☑, Pac. Oc. … 65 K13 20 0S 145 0W
Pomaro, Mexico … 86 D4 18 20N 103 18W
Pombal, Portugal … 21 C1 39 55N 8 40W
Pómbia, Greece … 25 E6 35 0N 24 51 E
Pomene, Mozam. … 57 C6 22 53S 35 33 E
Pomeroy, Ohio, U.S.A. … 82 F4 39 2N 82 2W
Pomeroy, Wash., U.S.A. … 76 C5 46 28N 117 36W
Pomézia, Italy … 22 D5 41 40N 12 30 E
Pomona, Australia … 63 D5 26 22S 152 52 E
Pomona, U.S.A. … 79 L9 34 4N 117 45W
Pomorskie, Pojezierze, Poland … 17 B9 53 40N 16 37 E
Pomos, Cyprus … 25 D11 35 9N 32 33 E
Pomos, C., Cyprus … 25 D11 35 10N 32 33 E
Pompano Beach, U.S.A. … 83 M5 26 14N 80 8W
Pompeys Pillar, U.S.A. … 76 D10 45 59N 107 57W
Pompeys Pillar △, U.S.A. … 76 D10 46 0N 108 0W
Pompton Lakes, U.S.A. … 85 F10 41 0N 74 17W
Ponape = Pohnpei, Micronesia … 64 G7 6 55N 158 10 E
Ponask L., Canada … 72 B1 54 0N 92 41W
Ponca, U.S.A. … 80 D6 42 34N 96 43W
Ponca City, U.S.A. … 81 G6 36 42N 97 5W
Ponce, Puerto Rico … 89 d 18 1N 66 37W
Ponchatoula, U.S.A. … 81 K9 30 26N 90 26W
Poncheville, L., Canada … 72 B4 50 10N 76 55W
Pond, U.S.A. … 79 K7 35 43N 119 20W
Pond Inlet, Canada … 69 A12 72 40N 77 0W
Pondicherry, India … 40 P11 11 59N 79 50 E
Ponds, I. of, Canada … 73 B8 53 27N 55 52W
Ponferrada, Spain … 21 A2 42 32N 6 35W
Ponnani, India … 40 P9 10 45N 75 59 E
Ponoka, Canada … 70 C6 52 42N 113 40W
Ponorogo, Indonesia … 37 G14 7 52S 111 27 E
Ponoy, Russia … 18 A7 67 0N 41 13 E
Ponoy →, Russia … 18 A7 66 59N 41 17 E
Ponta do Sol, Madeira … 24 D2 32 42N 17 7W
Ponta Grossa, Brazil … 95 B5 25 7S 50 10W
Ponta Pora, Brazil … 95 A4 22 20S 55 35W
Pontarlier, France … 20 C7 46 54N 6 20 E
Pontchartrain L., U.S.A. … 81 K10 30 5N 90 5W
Ponte do Pungué, Mozam. … 55 F3 19 30S 34 33 E
Ponte Nova, Brazil … 95 A7 20 25S 42 54W
Ponteix, Canada … 71 D7 49 46N 107 29W
Pontevedra, Spain … 21 A1 42 26N 8 40W
Pontiac, Ill., U.S.A. … 80 E10 40 53N 88 38W
Pontiac, Mich., U.S.A. … 82 D4 42 38N 83 18W
Pontian Kechil, Malaysia … 39 d 1 29N 103 23 E
Pontianak, Indonesia … 36 E3 0 3S 109 15 E
Pontine Is. = Ponziane, Ísole, Italy … 22 D5 40 55N 12 57 E
Pontine Mts. = Kuzey Anadolu Dağları, Turkey … 19 F6 41 30N 35 0 E
Pontivy, France … 20 B2 48 5N 2 58W
Pontoise, France … 20 B5 49 3N 2 5 E
Ponton →, Canada … 70 B5 58 27N 116 11W
Pontypool, Canada … 84 B6 44 6N 78 38W
Pontypool, U.K. … 13 F4 51 42N 3 2W
Ponziane, Ísole, Italy … 22 D5 40 55N 12 57 E
Poochera, Australia … 63 E1 32 43S 134 51 E
Poole, U.K. … 13 G6 50 43N 1 59W
Poole □, U.K. … 13 G6 50 43N 1 59W
Poona = Pune, India … 40 K8 18 29N 73 57 E
Pooncarie, Australia … 63 E3 33 22S 142 31 E
Poopelloe L., Australia … 63 E3 31 40S 144 0 E
Poopó, L. de, Bolivia … 92 G5 18 30S 67 35W
Popayán, Colombia … 92 C3 2 27N 76 36W
Poperinge, Belgium … 15 D2 50 51N 2 42 E
Popilta L., Australia … 63 E3 33 10S 141 42 E
Popio L., Australia … 63 E3 33 10S 141 52 E
Poplar, U.S.A. … 80 A2 48 7N 105 12W
Poplar →, Canada … 71 C9 53 0N 97 19W
Poplar Bluff, U.S.A. … 81 G9 36 46N 90 24W
Poplarville, U.S.A. … 81 K10 30 51N 89 32W
Popocatépetl, Volcán, Mexico … 87 D5 19 2N 98 38W
Popokabaka, Dem. Rep. of the Congo … 52 F3 5 41S 16 40 E
Poprad, Slovak Rep. … 17 D11 49 3N 20 18 E
Porali →, Pakistan … 42 G2 25 58N 66 26 E
Porbandar, India … 42 J3 21 44N 69 43 E
Porcher I., Canada … 70 C2 53 50N 130 30W
Porcupine →, Canada … 71 B8 59 11N 104 46W
Porcupine →, U.S.A. … 68 B5 66 34N 145 19W
Porcupine Gorge △, Australia … 62 C3 20 22S 144 26 E
Pordenone, Italy … 22 B5 45 57N 12 39 E
Pori, Finland … 9 F19 61 29N 21 48 E
Porlamar, Venezuela … 92 A6 10 57N 63 51W
Poronaysk, Russia … 29 E15 49 13N 143 0 E
Poroshiri-Dake, Japan … 30 C11 42 41N 142 52 E
Poroto Mts., Tanzania … 55 D3 9 0S 33 30 E
Porpoise B., Antarctica … 5 C9 66 0S 127 0 E
Porreres, Spain … 24 B10 39 31N 3 2 E
Porsangen, Norway … 8 A21 70 40N 25 40 E
Porsgrunn, Norway … 9 G13 59 10N 9 40 E
Port Alberni, Canada … 70 D4 49 14N 124 50W
Port Alfred, S. Africa … 56 E4 33 36S 26 55 E
Port Alice, Canada … 70 C3 50 20N 127 25W
Port Allegany, U.S.A. … 84 E6 41 48N 78 17W
Port Allen, U.S.A. … 81 K9 30 27N 91 12W
Port Alma, Australia … 62 C5 23 38S 150 53 E
Port Angeles, U.S.A. … 78 B3 48 7N 123 27W
Port Antonio, Jamaica … 88 a 18 10N 76 30W
Port Aransas, U.S.A. … 81 M6 27 50N 97 4W
Port Arthur, Australia … 63 G4 43 7S 147 50 E
Port Arthur, U.S.A. … 81 L8 29 54N 93 56W
Port au Choix, Canada … 73 B8 50 43N 57 22W
Port au Port B., Canada … 73 C8 48 40N 58 50W

Port-au-Prince, Haiti … 89 C5 18 40N 72 20W
Port Augusta, Australia … 63 E2 32 30S 137 50 E
Port Austin, U.S.A. … 84 B2 44 3N 83 1W
Port Bell, Uganda … 54 B3 0 18N 32 35 E
Port Bergé Vaovao, Madag. … 57 B8 15 33S 47 40 E
Port Blandford, Canada … 73 C9 48 20N 54 10W
Port Bradshaw, Australia … 62 A2 12 30S 137 20 E
Port Broughton, Australia … 63 E2 33 37S 137 56 E
Port Burwell, Canada … 84 D4 42 40N 80 48W
Port Canning, India … 43 H13 22 23N 88 40 E
Port-Cartier, Canada … 73 B6 50 2N 66 50W
Port Chalmers, N.Z. … 59 L3 45 49S 170 30 E
Port Charlotte, U.S.A. … 83 M4 26 59N 82 6W
Port Chester, U.S.A. … 85 F11 41 0N 73 40W
Port Clements, Canada … 70 C2 53 40N 132 10W
Port Clinton, U.S.A. … 82 E4 41 31N 82 56W
Port Colborne, Canada … 84 D5 42 50N 79 10W
Port Coquitlam, Canada … 70 D4 49 15N 122 45W
Port Credit, Canada … 84 C5 43 33N 79 35W
Port Curtis, Australia … 62 C5 23 57S 151 20 E
Port d'Alcúdia, Spain … 24 B10 39 50N 3 7 E
Port Dalhousie, Canada … 84 C5 43 13N 79 16W
Port d'Andratx, Spain … 24 B9 39 32N 2 23 E
Port Darwin, Australia … 60 B5 12 24S 130 45 E
Port Darwin, Falk. Is. … 96 G5 51 50S 59 0W
Port Davey, Australia … 63 G4 43 16S 145 55 E
Port-de-Paix, Haiti … 89 C5 19 50N 72 50W
Port de Pollença, Spain … 24 B10 39 54N 3 4 E
Port de Sóller, Spain … 24 B9 39 48N 2 42 E
Port Dickson, Malaysia … 39 L3 2 30N 101 49 E
Port Douglas, Australia … 62 B4 16 30S 145 30 E
Port Dover, Canada … 84 D4 42 47N 80 12W
Port Edward, Canada … 70 C2 54 12N 130 10W
Port Elgin, Canada … 84 B3 44 25N 81 25W
Port Elizabeth, S. Africa … 56 E4 33 58S 25 40 E
Port Ellen, U.K. … 11 F2 55 38N 6 11W
Port Erin, U.K. … 12 C3 54 5N 4 45W
Port Essington, Australia … 60 B5 11 15S 132 10 E
Port Ewen, U.S.A. … 85 E11 41 54N 73 59W
Port Fairy, Australia … 63 F3 38 22S 142 12 E
Port Gamble, U.S.A. … 78 C4 47 51N 122 35W
Port-Gentil, Gabon … 52 E1 0 40S 8 50 E
Port Germein, Australia … 63 E2 33 1S 138 1 E
Port Gibson, U.S.A. … 81 K9 31 58N 90 59W
Port Glasgow, U.K. … 11 F4 55 56N 4 41W
Port Harcourt, Nigeria … 50 H7 4 40N 7 10 E
Port Hardy, Canada … 70 C3 50 41N 127 30W
Port Harrison = Inukjuak, Canada … 69 C12 58 25N 78 15W
Port Hawkesbury, Canada … 73 C7 45 36N 61 22W
Port Hedland, Australia … 60 D2 20 25S 118 35 E
Port Henry, U.S.A. … 85 B11 44 3N 73 28W
Port Hood, Canada … 73 C7 46 0N 61 32W
Port Hope, Canada … 84 C6 43 57N 78 20W
Port Hope, U.S.A. … 84 C2 43 57N 82 43W
Port Hope Simpson, Canada … 73 B8 52 33N 56 18W
Port Hueneme, U.S.A. … 79 L7 34 7N 119 12W
Port Huron, U.S.A. … 84 D2 42 58N 82 26W
Port Jefferson, U.S.A. … 85 F11 40 57N 73 3W
Port Jervis, U.S.A. … 85 E10 41 22N 74 41W
Port Kelang = Pelabuhan Kelang, Malaysia … 39 L3 3 0N 101 23 E
Port Kenny, Australia … 63 E1 33 10S 134 41 E
Port Laoise, Ireland … 10 C4 53 2N 7 18W
Port Lavaca, U.S.A. … 81 L6 28 37N 96 38W
Port Leyden, U.S.A. … 85 C9 43 35N 75 21W
Port Lincoln, Australia … 63 E2 34 42S 135 52 E
Port Loko, S. Leone … 50 G3 8 48N 12 46W
Port-Louis, Guadeloupe … 88 b 16 28N 61 32W
Port Louis, Mauritius … 49 H9 20 10S 57 30 E
Port MacDonnell, Australia … 63 F3 38 5S 140 48 E
Port McNeill, Canada … 70 C3 50 35N 127 6W
Port Macquarie, Australia … 63 E5 31 25S 152 25 E
Port Maria, Jamaica … 88 a 18 25N 76 55W
Port Matilda, U.S.A. … 84 F6 40 48N 78 3W
Port Mellon, Canada … 70 D4 49 32N 123 31W
Port-Menier, Canada … 73 C7 49 51N 64 15W
Port Moody, Canada … 78 A4 49 17N 122 51W
Port Morant, Jamaica … 88 a 17 54N 76 19W
Port Moresby, Papua N. G. … 64 H6 9 24S 147 8 E
Port Musgrave, Australia … 62 A3 11 55S 141 50 E
Port Neches, U.S.A. … 81 L8 30 0N 93 59W
Port Nolloth, S. Africa … 56 D2 29 17S 16 52 E
Port Nouveau-Québec = Kangiqsualujjuaq, Canada … 69 C13 58 30N 65 59W
Port of Spain, Trin. & Tob. … 89 D7 10 40N 61 31W
Port Orange, U.S.A. … 83 L5 29 9N 80 59W
Port Orchard, U.S.A. … 78 C4 47 32N 122 38W
Port Orford, U.S.A. … 76 E1 42 45N 124 30W
Port Pegasus, N.Z. … 59 M1 47 12S 167 41 E
Port Perry, Canada … 84 B6 44 6N 78 56W
Port Phillip B., Australia … 63 F3 38 10S 144 50 E
Port Pirie, Australia … 63 E2 33 10S 138 1 E
Port Renfrew, Canada … 70 D4 48 30N 124 20W
Port Roper, Australia … 62 A2 14 45S 135 25 E
Port Rowan, Canada … 84 D4 42 40N 80 30W
Port Safaga = Bûr Safâga, Egypt … 44 E2 26 43N 33 57 E
Port Said = Bûr Sa'îd, Egypt … 51 B12 31 16N 32 18 E
Port St. Joe, U.S.A. … 83 L3 29 49N 85 18W
Port St. Johns = Umzimvubu, S. Africa … 57 E4 31 38S 29 33 E
Port St. Lucie, U.S.A. … 83 M5 27 20N 80 20W
Port Sanilac, U.S.A. … 84 C2 43 26N 82 33W
Port Severn, Canada … 84 B5 44 48N 79 43W
Port Shepstone, S. Africa … 57 E5 30 44S 30 28 E
Port Simpson, Canada … 70 C2 54 30N 130 20W
Port Stanley = Stanley, Falk. Is. … 96 G5 51 40S 59 51W
Port Stanley, Canada … 84 D3 42 40N 81 10W
Port Sudan = Bûr Sûdân, Sudan … 51 E13 19 32N 37 9 E
Port Sulphur, U.S.A. … 81 L10 29 29N 89 42W
Port Talbot, U.K. … 13 F4 51 35N 3 47W
Port Townsend, U.S.A. … 78 B4 48 7N 122 45W
Port-Vendres, France … 20 E5 42 32N 3 8 E
Port Vila, Vanuatu … 64 J8 17 45S 168 18 E
Port Vladimir, Russia … 18 A5 69 25N 33 6 E
Port Wakefield, Australia … 63 E2 34 12S 138 10 E
Port Washington, U.S.A. … 82 D2 43 23N 87 53W
Porta Orientalis, Romania … 17 F12 45 6N 22 18 E
Portadown, U.K. … 10 B5 54 25N 6 27W
Portaferry, U.K. … 10 B6 54 23N 5 33W
Portage, Pa., U.S.A. … 84 F6 40 23N 78 41W
Portage, Wis., U.S.A. … 80 D10 43 33N 89 28W
Portage la Prairie, Canada … 71 D9 49 58N 98 18W
Portageville, U.S.A. … 81 G10 36 26N 89 42W
Portalegre, Portugal … 21 C2 39 19N 7 25W
Portales, U.S.A. … 81 H3 34 11N 103 20W
Portarlington, Ireland … 10 C4 53 9N 7 14W
Portbou, Spain … 21 A7 42 25N 3 9 E

Porter L., N.W.T., Canada 71 A7 61 41N 108 5W
Porter L., Sask., Canada 71 B7 56 20N 107 20W
Porterville, S. Africa .... 56 E2 33 0S 19 0 E
Porterville, U.S.A. 78 J8 36 4N 119 1W
Porthcawl, U.K. 13 F4 51 29N 3 42W
Porthill, U.S.A. 76 B5 48 59N 116 30W
Porthmadog, U.K. 12 E3 52 55N 4 8W
Portile de Fier, Europe .... 17 F12 44 44N 22 30 E
Portimão, Portugal 21 D1 37 8N 8 32W
Portishead, U.K. 13 F5 51 29N 2 46W
Portknockie, U.K. 11 D6 57 42N 2 51W
Portland, N.S.W., Australia ... 63 E5 33 20S 150 0 E
Portland, Vic., Australia ..... 63 F3 38 20S 141 35 E
Portland, Canada 85 B8 44 42N 76 12W
Portland, Conn., U.S.A. 85 E12 41 34N 72 38W
Portland, Maine, U.S.A. 69 D12 43 39N 70 16W
Portland, Mich., U.S.A. 82 D3 42 52N 84 54W
Portland, Oreg., U.S.A. 78 E4 45 32N 122 37W
Portland, Pa., U.S.A. 85 F9 40 55N 75 6W
Portland, Tex., U.S.A. 81 M6 27 53N 97 20W
Portland ✈ (PDX), U.S.A. 78 E4 45 35N 122 36W
Portland, I. of, U.K. 13 G5 50 33N 2 26W
Portland B., Australia .... 63 F3 38 15S 141 45 E
Portland Bight, Jamaica .... 88 a 17 52N 77 5W
Portland Bill, U.K. 13 G5 50 31N 2 28W
Portland Canal, U.S.A. 70 B2 55 56N 130 0W
Portland Pt., Jamaica .... 88 a 17 42N 77 11W
Portmadoc = Porthmadog, U.K. .. 12 E3 52 55N 4 8W
Portmore, Jamaica .... 88 a 17 53N 77 33W
Porto, Portugal 21 B1 41 8N 8 40W
Pôrto Alegre, Brazil 95 C5 30 5S 51 10W
Porto Cristo, Spain .... 24 B10 39 33N 3 20 E
Pôrto de Móz, Brazil 93 D8 1 41S 52 13W
Porto Empédocle, Italy .... 22 F5 37 17N 13 32 E
Pôrto Esperança, Brazil 92 G7 19 37S 57 29W
Pôrto Franco, Brazil 93 E9 6 20S 47 24W
Pôrto Mendes, Brazil 95 A5 24 30S 54 15W
Porto Moniz, Madeira 24 D2 32 52N 17 11W
Pôrto Murtinho, Brazil 92 H7 21 45S 57 55W
Pôrto Nacional, Brazil 93 F9 10 40S 48 30W
Porto-Novo, Benin .... 50 G6 6 23N 2 42 E
Porto Petro, Spain .... 24 B10 39 22N 3 13 E
Pôrto Santo, I. de, Madeira ... 50 B2 33 45N 16 25W
Pôrto São José, Brazil 95 A5 22 43S 53 10W
Pôrto Seguro, Brazil 93 G11 16 26S 39 5W
Porto Tórres, Italy .... 22 D3 40 50N 8 24 E
Pôrto União, Brazil 95 B5 26 10S 51 10W
Pôrto Válter, Brazil 92 E4 8 15S 72 40W
Porto-Vecchio, France .... 20 F8 41 35N 9 16 E
Pôrto Velho, Brazil 92 E6 8 46S 63 54W
Portobelo, Panama 88 E4 9 35N 79 42W
Portoferráio, Italy .... 22 C4 42 48N 10 20 E
Portola, U.S.A. 78 F6 39 49N 120 28W
Portoscuso, Italy .... 22 E3 39 12N 8 24 E
Portoviejo, Ecuador 92 D2 1 7S 80 28W
Portpatrick, U.K. 11 G3 54 51N 5 7W
Portree, U.K. 11 D2 57 25N 6 12W
Portrush, U.K. 10 A5 55 12N 6 40W
Portsmouth, Domin. 89 C7 15 34N 61 27W
Portsmouth, U.K. 13 G6 50 48N 1 6W
Portsmouth, N.H., U.S.A. 83 D10 43 5N 70 45W
Portsmouth, Ohio, U.S.A. 82 F4 38 44N 82 57W
Portsmouth, R.I., U.S.A. 85 E13 41 36N 71 15W
Portsmouth, Va., U.S.A. 82 G7 36 50N 76 18W
Portsmouth □, U.K. 13 G6 50 48N 1 6W
Portsoy, U.K. 11 D6 57 41N 2 41W
Portstewart, U.K. 10 A5 55 11N 6 43W
Porttipahtan tekojärvi, Finland . 8 B22 68 5N 26 40 E
Portugal ■, Europe 21 C1 40 0N 8 0W
Portumna, Ireland 10 C3 53 6N 8 14W
Portville, U.S.A. 84 D6 42 3N 78 20W
Porvenir, Chile 96 G2 53 10S 70 16W
Porvoo, Finland .... 9 F21 60 24N 25 40 E
Posadas, Argentina 95 B4 27 30S 55 50W
Poshan = Boshan, China .... 35 F9 36 28N 117 49 E
Posht-e Badam, Iran .... 45 C7 33 2N 55 23 E
Poso, Indonesia .... 37 E6 1 20S 120 55 E
Posong, S. Korea .... 35 G14 34 46N 127 5 E
Posse, Brazil 93 F9 14 4S 46 18W
Possession I., Antarctica ..... 5 D11 72 4S 172 0 E
Possum Kingdom L., U.S.A. 81 J5 32 52N 98 26W
Post, U.S.A. 81 J4 33 12N 101 23W
Post Falls, U.S.A. 76 C5 47 43N 116 57W
Postavy = Pastavy, Belarus .... 9 J22 55 4N 26 50 E
Poste-de-la-Baleine =
  Kuujjuarapik, Canada 72 A4 55 20N 77 35W
Postmasburg, S. Africa .... 56 D3 28 18S 23 5 E
Postojna, Slovenia .... 16 F8 45 46N 14 12 E
Poston, U.S.A. 79 M12 34 0N 114 24W
Postville, Canada 73 B8 54 54N 59 47W
Potchefstroom, S. Africa ...... 56 D4 26 41S 27 7 E
Poteau, U.S.A. 81 H7 35 3N 94 37W
Poteet, U.S.A. 81 L5 29 2N 98 35W
Potenza, Italy .... 22 D6 40 38N 15 48 E
Poteriteri, L., N.Z. .... 59 M1 46 5S 167 10 E
Potgietersrus = Mokopane,
  S. Africa .... 57 C4 24 10S 28 55 E
Poti, Georgia .... 19 F7 42 10N 41 38 E
Potiskum, Nigeria .... 51 F8 11 39N 11 2 E
Potomac →, U.S.A. 82 G7 38 0N 76 23W
Potosí, Bolivia 92 G5 19 38S 65 50W
Potosi Mt., U.S.A. 79 K11 35 57N 115 29W
Pototan, Phil. .... 37 B6 10 54N 122 38 E
Potrerillos, Chile 94 B2 26 30S 69 30W
Potsdam, Germany .... 16 B7 52 25N 13 4 E
Potsdam, U.S.A. 85 B10 44 40N 74 59W
Pottersville, U.S.A. 85 C11 43 43N 73 50W
Pottstown, U.S.A. 85 F9 40 15N 75 39W
Pottsville, U.S.A. 85 F8 40 41N 76 12W
Pottuvil, Sri Lanka .... 40 R12 6 55N 81 50 E
Pouce Coupé, Canada 70 B4 55 40N 120 10W
Poughkeepsie, U.S.A. 85 E11 41 42N 73 56W
Poulaphouca Res., Ireland 10 C5 53 8N 6 30W
Poulsbo, U.S.A. 78 C4 47 44N 122 39W
Poultney, U.S.A. 85 C11 43 31N 73 14W
Poulton-le-Fylde, U.K. 12 D5 53 51N 2 58W
Pouso Alegre, Brazil 95 A6 22 14S 45 57W
Pouthisat, Cambodia .... 38 F4 12 34N 103 50 E
Považská Bystrica, Slovak Rep. . 17 D10 49 8N 18 27 E
Povenets, Russia .... 18 B5 62 50N 34 50 E
Poverty B., N.Z. .... 59 H7 38 43S 178 2 E
Póvoa de Varzim, Portugal 21 B1 41 25N 8 46W
Povungnituk = Puvirnituq,
  Canada 69 B12 60 2N 77 10W
Powassan, Canada 72 C4 46 5N 79 25W
Poway, U.S.A. 79 N9 32 58N 117 2W
Powder →, U.S.A. 80 B2 46 45N 105 26W
Powder River, U.S.A. 76 E10 43 2N 106 59W

Powell, U.S.A. 76 D9 44 45N 108 46W
Powell, L., U.S.A. 77 H8 36 57N 111 29W
Powell River, Canada 70 D4 49 50N 124 35W
Powers, U.S.A. 82 C2 45 41N 87 32W
Powys □, U.K. 13 E4 52 20N 3 20W
Poyang Hu, China .... 33 D6 29 5N 116 20 E
Poyarkovo, Russia .... 29 E13 49 36N 128 41 E
Poza Rica, Mexico 87 C5 20 33N 97 27W
Požarevac, Serbia & M. .... 23 B9 44 35N 21 18 E
Poznań, Poland .... 17 B9 52 25N 16 55 E
Pozo, U.S.A. 79 K6 35 20N 120 24W
Pozo Almonte, Chile 92 H5 20 10S 69 50W
Pozo Colorado, Paraguay 94 A4 23 30S 58 45W
Pozoblanco, Spain 21 C3 38 23N 4 51W
Pozzuoli, Italy .... 22 D6 40 49N 14 7 E
Prachin Buri, Thailand .... 38 E3 14 0N 101 25 E
Prachuap Khiri Khan, Thailand . 39 G2 11 49N 99 48 E
Prado, Brazil 93 G11 17 20S 39 13W
Prague = Praha, Czech Rep. .... 16 C8 50 5N 14 22 E
Praha, Czech Rep. .... 16 C8 50 5N 14 22 E
Praia, C. Verde Is. 49 E1 15 2N 23 34W
Prainha, Amazonas, Brazil 92 E6 7 10S 60 30W
Prainha, Pará, Brazil 93 D8 1 45S 53 30W
Prairie, Australia .... 62 C3 20 50S 144 35 E
Prairie City, U.S.A. 76 D4 44 28N 118 43W
Prairie Dog Town Fork →, U.S.A. 81 H5 34 30N 99 23W
Prairie du Chien, U.S.A. 80 D9 43 3N 91 9W
Prairies, L. of the, Canada ... 71 C8 51 16N 101 32W
Pran Buri, Thailand .... 38 F2 12 23N 99 55 E
Prapat, Indonesia .... 36 D1 2 41N 98 58 E
Prasonísi, Ákra, Greece .... 25 D9 35 42N 27 46 E
Prata, Brazil 93 G9 19 25S 48 54W
Pratabpur, India .... 43 H10 23 28N 83 15 E
Pratapgarh, Raj., India .... 42 G6 24 2N 74 40 E
Pratapgarh, Ut. P., India ..... 43 G9 25 56N 81 59 E
Prato, Italy .... 22 C4 43 53N 11 6 E
Pratt, U.S.A. 81 G5 37 39N 98 44W
Prattville, U.S.A. 83 J2 32 28N 86 29W
Pravia, Spain 21 A2 43 30N 6 12W
Praya, Indonesia .... 36 F5 8 39S 116 17 E
Precipice △, Australia .... 63 D5 25 18S 150 5 E
Precordillera, Argentina 94 C2 30 0S 69 1W
Preeceville, Canada 71 C8 51 57N 102 40W
Preiļi, Latvia .... 9 H22 56 18N 26 43 E
Premont, U.S.A. 81 M5 27 22N 98 7W
Prentice, U.S.A. 80 C9 45 33N 90 17W
Preobrazheniye, Russia .... 30 C6 42 54N 133 54 E
Preparis North Channel, Ind. Oc. 41 M18 15 12N 93 40 E
Preparis South Channel, Ind. Oc. 41 M18 14 36N 93 40 E
Přerov, Czech Rep. .... 17 D9 49 28N 17 27 E
Prescott, Canada 85 B9 44 45N 75 30W
Prescott, Ariz., U.S.A. 77 J7 34 33N 112 28W
Prescott, Ark., U.S.A. 81 J8 33 48N 93 23W
Prescott Valley, U.S.A. 77 J7 34 40N 112 18W
Preservation Inlet, N.Z. ...... 59 M1 46 8S 166 35 E
Presho, U.S.A. 80 D4 43 54N 100 3W
Presidencia de la Plaza,
  Argentina 94 B4 27 0S 59 50W
Presidencia Roque Saenz Peña,
  Argentina 94 B3 26 45S 60 30W
Presidente Epitácio, Brazil ... 93 H8 21 56S 52 6W
Presidente Hayes □, Paraguay .. 94 A4 24 0S 59 0W
Presidente Prudente, Brazil ... 95 A5 22 5S 51 25W
Presidio, Mexico 86 B4 29 29N 104 23W
Presidio, U.S.A. 81 L2 29 34N 104 22W
Prešov, Slovak Rep. .... 17 D11 49 0N 21 15 E
Prespa, L. = Prespansko Jezero,
  Macedonia .... 23 D9 40 55N 21 0 E
Prespansko Jezero, Macedonia .. 23 D9 40 55N 21 0 E
Presque I., U.S.A. 84 D4 42 9N 80 6W
Presque Isle, U.S.A. 83 B12 46 41N 68 1W
Prestatyn, U.K. 12 D4 53 20N 3 24W
Presteigne, U.K. 13 E5 52 17N 3 0W
Preston, Canada 84 C4 43 23N 80 21W
Preston, U.K. 12 D5 53 46N 2 42W
Preston, Idaho, U.S.A. 76 E8 42 6N 111 53W
Preston, Minn., U.S.A. 80 D8 43 40N 92 5W
Preston, C., Australia .... 60 D2 20 51S 116 12 E
Prestonburg, U.S.A. 82 G4 37 39N 82 46W
Prestwick, U.K. 11 F4 55 29N 4 37W
Pretoria, S. Africa .... 57 D4 25 44S 28 12 E
Préveza, Greece .... 23 E9 38 57N 20 45 E
Prey Veng, Cambodia .... 39 G5 11 35N 105 29 E
Pribilof Is., U.S.A. 68 C2 57 0N 170 0W
Příbram, Czech Rep. .... 16 D8 49 41N 14 2 E
Price, U.S.A. 76 G8 39 36N 110 49W
Price I., Canada 70 C3 52 23N 128 41W
Prichard, U.S.A. 83 K1 30 44N 88 5W
Priekule, Latvia .... 9 H19 56 26N 21 35 E
Prienai, Lithuania .... 9 J20 54 38N 23 57 E
Prieska, S. Africa .... 56 D3 29 40S 22 42 E
Priest L., U.S.A. 76 B5 48 35N 116 52W
Priest River, U.S.A. 76 B5 48 10N 116 54W
Priest Valley, U.S.A. 78 J6 36 10N 120 39W
Prievidza, Slovak Rep. .... 17 D10 48 46N 18 36 E
Prikaspiyskaya Nizmennost =
  Caspian Depression, Eurasia . 19 E8 47 0N 48 0 E
Prilep, Macedonia .... 23 D9 41 21N 21 32 E
Priluki = Pryluky, Ukraine .... 19 D5 50 30N 32 24 E
Prime Seal I., Australia ...... 63 G4 40 3S 147 43 E
Primrose L., Canada 71 C7 54 55N 109 45W
Prince Albert, Canada 71 C7 53 15N 105 50W
Prince Albert, S. Africa ...... 56 E3 33 12S 22 2 E
Prince Albert △, Canada 71 C7 54 0N 106 25W
Prince Albert Mts., Antarctica 5 D11 76 0S 161 30 E
Prince Albert Pen., Canada 68 A8 72 30N 116 0W
Prince Albert Sd., Canada 68 A8 70 25N 115 0W
Prince Alfred, C., Canada 4 B1 74 20N 124 40W
Prince Charles I., Canada 69 B12 67 47N 76 12W
Prince Charles Mts., Antarctica 5 D6 72 0S 67 0 E
Prince Edward I. □, Canada 73 C7 46 20N 63 20W
Prince Edward Is., Ind. Oc. ... 3 G11 46 35S 38 0 E
Prince Edward Pt., Canada 84 C8 43 56N 76 52W
Prince George, Canada 70 C4 53 55N 122 50W
Prince of Wales, C., U.S.A. ... 66 C3 65 36N 168 5W
Prince of Wales I., Australia . 62 A3 10 40S 142 10 E
Prince of Wales I., Canada 68 A10 73 0N 99 0W
Prince of Wales I., U.S.A. 68 C6 55 47N 132 50W
Prince Patrick I., Canada 4 B2 77 0N 120 0W
Prince Regent Inlet, Canada ... 4 B3 73 0N 90 0W
Prince Rupert, Canada 70 C2 54 20N 130 20W
Princes Town, Trin. & Tob. 93 K15 10 16N 61 23W
Princess Charlotte B., Australia 62 A3 14 25S 144 0 E
Princess May Ranges, Australia 60 C4 15 30S 125 30 E
Princess Royal I., Canada 70 C3 53 0N 128 40W
Princeton, Canada 70 D4 49 27N 120 30W
Princeton, Calif., U.S.A. 78 F4 39 24N 122 1W
Princeton, Ill., U.S.A. 80 E10 41 23N 89 28W

Princeton, Ind., U.S.A. 82 F2 38 21N 87 34W
Princeton, Ky., U.S.A. 82 G2 37 7N 87 53W
Princeton, Mo., U.S.A. 80 E8 40 24N 93 35W
Princeton, N.J., U.S.A. 85 F10 40 21N 74 39W
Princeton, W. Va., U.S.A. 82 G5 37 22N 81 6W
Principe, I. de, Atl. Oc. ..... 48 F4 1 37N 7 27 E
Principe da Beira, Brazil 92 F6 12 20S 64 30W
Prineville, U.S.A. 76 D3 44 18N 120 51W
Prins Harald Kyst, Antarctica . 5 D4 70 0S 35 1 E
Prinsesse Astrid Kyst, Antarctica 5 D3 70 45S 12 30 E
Prinsesse Ragnhild Kyst,
  Antarctica .... 5 D4 70 15S 27 30 E
Prinzapolca, Nic. 88 D3 13 20N 83 35W
Priozersk, Russia .... 18 B5 61 2N 30 7 E
Pripet = Prypyat →, Europe .... 17 C16 51 20N 30 15 E
Pripet Marshes, Europe .... 17 B15 52 10N 28 10 E
Pripyat Marshes = Pripet
  Marshes, Europe .... 17 B15 52 10N 28 10 E
Pripyats = Prypyat →, Europe .. 17 C16 51 20N 30 15 E
Priština, Serbia & M. .... 23 C9 42 40N 21 13 E
Privas, France .... 20 D6 44 45N 4 37 E
Privolzhskaya Vozvyshennost,
  Russia .... 19 D8 51 0N 46 0 E
Privolzhskiy □, Russia .... 28 D6 56 0N 50 0 E
Prizren, Serbia & M. .... 23 C9 42 13N 20 45 E
Probolinggo, Indonesia .... 37 G15 7 46S 113 13 E
Proctor, U.S.A. 85 C11 43 40N 73 2W
Proddatur, India .... 40 M11 14 45N 78 30 E
Prodhromos, Cyprus .... 25 E11 34 57N 32 50 E
Profítis Ilías, Greece .... 25 C9 36 17N 27 56 E
Profondeville, Belgium .... 15 D4 50 23N 4 52 E
Progreso, Coahuila, Mexico 86 B4 27 28N 101 4W
Progreso, Yucatán, Mexico 87 C7 21 20N 89 40W
Prokopyevsk, Russia .... 28 D9 54 0N 86 45 E
Prokuplje, Serbia & M. .... 23 C9 43 16N 21 36 E
Prome, Burma .... 41 K19 18 49N 95 13 E
Prophet →, Canada 70 B4 58 48N 122 40W
Prophet River, Canada 70 B4 58 6N 122 43W
Propriá, Brazil 93 F11 10 13S 36 51W
Proserpine, Australia .... 62 J6 20 21S 148 36 E
Prosna →, Poland .... 17 B9 52 6N 17 44 E
Prospect, U.S.A. 85 C9 43 18N 75 9W
Prosser, U.S.A. 76 C4 46 12N 119 46W
Prostějov, Czech Rep. .... 17 D9 49 30N 17 9 E
Proston, Australia .... 63 D5 26 8S 151 32 E
Provence, France .... 20 E6 43 40N 5 46 E
Providence, Ky., U.S.A. 82 G2 37 24N 87 46W
Providence, R.I., U.S.A. 85 E13 41 49N 71 24W
Providence Bay, Canada 72 C3 45 41N 82 15W
Providence Mts., U.S.A. 79 K11 35 10N 115 15W
Providencia, I. de, Colombia .. 88 D3 13 25N 81 26W
Provideniya, Russia 29 C19 64 23N 173 18W
Provins, France .... 20 B5 48 33N 3 15 E
Provo, U.S.A. 76 F8 40 14N 111 39W
Provost, Canada 71 C6 52 25N 110 20W
Prudhoe Bay, U.S.A. 68 A5 70 18N 148 22W
Prudhoe I., Australia .... 62 C4 21 19S 149 41 E
Prud'homme, Canada 71 C7 52 20N 105 54W
Pruszków, Poland .... 17 B11 52 9N 20 49 E
Prut →, Romania .... 17 F15 45 28N 28 10 E
Pruzhany, Belarus .... 17 B13 52 33N 24 28 E
Prydz B., Antarctica .... 5 C6 69 0S 74 0 E
Pryluky, Ukraine .... 19 D5 50 30N 32 24 E
Pryor, U.S.A. 81 G7 36 19N 95 19W
Prypyat →, Europe .... 17 C16 51 20N 30 15 E
Przemyśl, Poland .... 17 D12 49 50N 22 45 E
Przhevalsk = Karakol, Kyrgyzstan 28 E8 42 30N 78 20 E
Psará, Greece .... 23 E11 38 37N 25 38 E
Psíra, Greece .... 25 D7 35 12N 25 52 E
Pskov, Russia .... 18 C4 57 50N 28 25 E
Ptich = Ptsich →, Belarus ..... 17 B15 52 9N 28 52 E
Ptolemaís, Greece .... 23 D9 40 30N 21 43 E
Ptsich →, Belarus .... 17 B15 52 9N 28 52 E
Pu Xian, China .... 34 F6 36 24N 111 6 E
Pua, Thailand .... 38 C3 19 11N 100 55 E
Puán, Argentina 94 D3 37 30S 62 45W
Puan, S. Korea .... 35 G14 35 44N 126 44 E
Pucallpa, Peru 92 E4 8 25S 74 30W
Pudasjärvi, Finland .... 8 D22 65 23N 26 53 E
Pudozh, Russia .... 18 B6 61 48N 36 32 E
Puducherry = Pondicherry, India 40 P11 11 59N 79 50 E
Pudukkottai, India .... 40 P11 10 28N 78 47 E
Puebla, Mexico 87 D5 19 3N 98 12W
Puebla □, Mexico 87 D5 18 30N 98 0W
Pueblo, U.S.A. 80 F2 38 16N 104 37W
Pueblo Hundido, Chile 94 B1 26 20S 70 5W
Puelches, Argentina 94 D2 38 5S 65 51W
Puelén, Argentina 94 D2 37 32S 67 38W
Puente Alto, Chile 94 C1 33 32S 70 35W
Puente-Genil, Spain 21 D3 37 22N 4 47W
Puerca, Pta., Puerto Rico ..... 89 d 18 13N 65 36W
Puerco →, U.S.A. 77 J10 34 22N 107 50W
Puerto Aisén, Chile 96 F2 45 27S 73 0W
Puerto Ángel, Mexico 87 D5 15 40N 96 29W
Puerto Arista, Mexico 87 D6 15 56N 93 48W
Puerto Armuelles, Panama 88 E3 8 20N 82 51W
Puerto Ayacucho, Venezuela 92 B5 5 40N 67 35W
Puerto Barrios, Guatemala 88 C2 15 40N 88 32W
Puerto Bermejo, Argentina 94 B4 26 55S 58 34W
Puerto Bermúdez, Peru 92 F4 10 20S 74 58W
Puerto Bolívar, Ecuador 92 D3 3 19S 79 55W
Puerto Cabello, Venezuela 92 A5 10 28N 68 1W
Puerto Cabezas, Nic. 88 D3 14 0N 83 30W
Puerto Cabo Gracias á Dios, Nic. 88 D3 15 0N 83 10W
Puerto Carreño, Colombia 92 B5 6 12N 67 22W
Puerto Castilla, Honduras 88 C2 16 0N 86 0W
Puerto Chicama, Peru 92 E3 7 45S 79 20W
Puerto Coig, Argentina 96 G3 50 54S 69 15W
Puerto Cortés, Costa Rica 88 E3 8 55N 84 0W
Puerto Cortés, Honduras 88 C2 15 51N 88 0W
Puerto Cumarebo, Venezuela 92 A5 11 29N 69 30W
Puerto de Alcudia = Port
  d'Alcúdia, Spain .... 24 B10 39 50N 3 7 E
Puerto de Cabrera, Spain ...... 24 B9 39 8N 2 56 E
Puerto de Gran Tarajal,
  Canary Is. 24 F5 28 13N 14 1W
Puerto de la Cruz, Canary Is. . 24 F3 28 24N 16 32W
Puerto de los Angeles △, Mexico 86 C3 23 30N 105 45W
Puerto de Pozo Negro, Canary Is. 24 F6 28 19N 13 55W
Puerto de Sóller = Port de Sóller,
  Spain .... 24 B9 39 48N 2 42 E
Puerto del Carmen, Spain 24 F6 28 55N 13 38W
Puerto del Rosario, Canary Is. . 24 F6 28 30N 13 52W
Puerto Deseado, Argentina 96 F3 47 55S 66 0W
Puerto Escondido, Mexico 87 D5 15 50N 97 3W
Puerto Heath, Bolivia 92 F5 12 34S 68 39W
Puerto Inírida, Colombia 92 C5 3 53N 67 52W
Puerto Juárez, Mexico 87 C7 21 11N 86 49W

Puerto La Cruz, Venezuela 92 A6 10 13N 64 38
Puerto Leguízamo, Colombia 92 D4 0 12S 74 46
Puerto Limón, Colombia 92 C4 3 23N 73 30
Puerto Lobos, Argentina 96 E3 42 0S 65 3
Puerto Madryn, Argentina 96 E3 42 48S 65 4
Puerto Maldonado, Peru 92 F5 12 30S 69 10
Puerto Manotí, Cuba 88 B4 21 22N 76 50
Puerto Montt, Chile 96 E2 41 28S 73 0
Puerto Morazán, Nic. 88 D2 12 51N 87 11
Puerto Morelos, Mexico 87 C7 20 49N 86 52
Puerto Natales, Chile 96 G2 51 45S 72 15
Puerto Padre, Cuba 88 B4 21 13N 76 35
Puerto Páez, Venezuela 92 B5 6 13N 67 28
Puerto Peñasco, Mexico 86 A2 31 20N 113 33
Puerto Pinasco, Paraguay 94 A4 22 36S 57 50
Puerto Plata, Dom. Rep. 89 C5 19 48N 70 45
Puerto Pollensa = Port de
  Pollença, Spain 24 B10 39 54N 3 4
Puerto Princesa, Phil. 37 C5 9 46N 118 45
Puerto Quepos, Costa Rica 88 E3 9 29N 84 6
Puerto Rico, Canary Is. 24 G4 27 47N 15 42
Puerto Rico ☒, W. Indies ...... 89 d 18 15N 66 45
Puerto Rico Trench, Atl. Oc. .. 89 C6 19 50N 66 0
Puerto San Julián, Argentina .. 96 F3 49 18S 67 43
Puerto Sastre, Paraguay 94 A4 22 2S 57 55
Puerto Suárez, Bolivia 92 G7 18 58S 57 52
Puerto Vallarta, Mexico 86 C3 20 36N 105 15
Puerto Wilches, Colombia 92 B4 7 21N 73 54
Puertollano, Spain 21 C3 38 43N 4 7
Pueyrredón, L., Argentina 96 F2 47 20S 72 0
Puffin I., Ireland 10 E1 51 50N 10 24
Pugachev, Russia 18 D8 52 0N 48 49
Pugal, India 42 E5 28 30N 72 48
Puge, Tanzania 54 C3 4 45S 33 11
Puget Sound, U.S.A. 76 C2 47 50N 122 30
Pugōdong, N. Korea 35 C16 42 5N 130 0
Pugu, Tanzania 54 D4 6 55S 39 4
Pūgūnzī, Iran 45 E8 25 49N 59 10
Puig Major, Spain 24 B9 39 48N 2 47
Puigcerdà, Spain 21 A6 42 24N 1 50
Puigpunyent, Spain 24 B9 39 38N 2 32
Pujon-chōsuji, N. Korea 35 D14 40 35N 127 35
Pukaki, L., N.Z. 59 L3 44 4S 170 1
Pukapuka, Cook Is. 65 J11 10 53S 165 49
Pukaskwa △, Canada 72 C2 48 20N 86 0
Pukatawagan, Canada 71 B8 55 45N 101 20
Pukchin, N. Korea 35 D13 40 12N 125 45
Pukch'ŏng, N. Korea 35 D15 40 14N 128 10
Pukekohe, N.Z. 59 G5 37 12S 174 55
Pukhrayan, India 43 F8 26 14N 79 51
Pula, Croatia 16 F7 44 54N 13 57
Pulacayo, Bolivia 92 H5 20 25S 66 41
Pulai, Malaysia .... 39 d 1 20N 103 31
Pulandian, China 35 E11 39 25N 121 58
Pularumpi, Australia 60 B5 11 24S 130 26
Pulaski, N.Y., U.S.A. 85 C8 43 34N 76 8
Pulaski, Tenn., U.S.A. 83 H2 35 12N 87 2
Pulaski, Va., U.S.A. 82 G5 37 3N 80 47
Pulau →, Indonesia 37 F9 5 50S 138 15
Puławy, Poland 17 C11 51 23N 21 59
Pulga, U.S.A. 78 F5 39 48N 121 29
Pulicat L., India 40 N12 13 40N 80 15
Pullman, U.S.A. 76 C5 46 44N 117 10
Pulog, Mt., Phil. 37 A6 16 40N 120 50
Pułtusk, Poland 17 B11 52 43N 21 6
Pumlumon Fawr, U.K. 13 E4 52 28N 3 46
Puná, I., Ecuador 92 D2 2 55S 80 5
Punakha, Bhutan 41 F16 27 42N 89 52
Punasar, India 42 F5 27 6N 73 6
Punata, Bolivia 92 G5 17 32S 65 50
Punch, India 43 C6 33 48N 74 4
Punch →, Pakistan 42 C5 33 12N 73 40
Punda Maria, S. Africa 57 C5 22 40S 31 5
Pune, India 40 K8 18 29N 73 57
P'ungsan, N. Korea 35 D15 40 50N 128 9
Pungue, Ponte de, Mozam. 55 F3 19 0S 34 0
Punjab □, India 42 D7 31 0N 76 0
Punjab □, Pakistan 42 E6 32 0N 74 30
Puno, Peru 92 G4 15 55S 70 3
Punpun →, India 43 G11 25 31N 85 18
Punta, Cerro de, Puerto Rico .. 89 d 18 10N 66 37
Punta Alta, Argentina 96 D4 38 53S 62 4
Punta Arenas, Chile 96 G2 53 10S 71 0
Punta de Díaz, Chile 94 B1 28 0S 70 45
Punta del Hidalgo, Canary Is. . 24 F3 28 33N 16 19
Punta Gorda, Belize 87 D7 16 10N 88 45
Punta Gorda, U.S.A. 83 M5 26 56N 82 3
Punta Prieta, Mexico 86 B2 28 58N 114 17
Punta Prima, Spain 24 B11 39 48N 4 16
Puntarenas, Costa Rica 88 E3 10 0N 84 50
Punto Fijo, Venezuela 92 A4 11 50N 70 13
Punxsatawney, U.S.A. 84 F6 40 57N 78 59
Pupuan, Indonesia 37 J18 8 19S 115 0
Puquio, Peru 92 F4 14 45S 74 10
Pur →, Russia 28 C8 67 31N 77 55
Purace, Vol., Colombia 92 C3 2 21N 76 23
Puralia = Puruliya, India 43 H12 23 17N 86 24
Puranpur, India 43 E9 28 31N 80 9
Purbeck, Isle of, U.K. 13 G5 50 39N 1 59
Purcell, U.S.A. 81 H6 35 1N 97 22
Purcell Mts., Canada 70 D5 49 55N 116 15
Puri, India 41 K14 19 50N 85 58
Purmerend, Neths. 15 B4 52 32N 4 58
Purnia, India 43 G12 25 45N 87 31
Pursat = Pouthisat, Cambodia .. 38 F4 12 34N 103 50
Purukcahu, Indonesia 36 E4 0 35S 114 35
Puruliya, India 43 H12 23 17N 86 24
Purus →, Brazil 92 D6 3 42S 61 28
Purvis, U.S.A. 81 K10 31 9N 89 25
Purwa, India 43 F9 26 28N 80 47
Purwakarta, Indonesia 37 G12 6 35S 107 29
Purwo, Tanjung, Indonesia 37 K18 8 44S 114 27
Puryŏng, N. Korea 35 C15 42 5N 129 43
Pusa, India 43 G11 25 59N 85 41
Pusan, S. Korea 35 G15 35 5N 129 0
Pushkino, Russia 19 D8 51 16N 47 0
Putahow L., Canada 71 B8 59 54N 100 40
Putao, Burma 41 F20 27 28N 97 30
Putaruru, N.Z. 59 H5 38 2S 175 50
Putignano, Italy 22 D7 40 51N 17 7
Putnam, U.S.A. 85 E13 41 55N 71 55
Putorana, Gory, Russia 29 C10 69 0N 95
Putrajaya, Malaysia 39 L3 2 55N 101 40
Puttalam, Sri Lanka 40 Q11 8 1N 79 55
Puttgarden, Germany 16 A6 54 30N 11 11

utumayo ➤, S. Amer. **92 D5** 3 7S 67 58W
utussibau, Indonesia ..... **36 D4** 0 50N 112 56 E
uvirnituq, Canada **69 B12** 60 2N 77 10W
uy-de-Dôme, France ... **20 D5** 45 46N 2 57 E
uyallup, U.S.A. **78 C4** 47 12N 122 18W
uyang, China .... **34 G8** 35 40N 115 1 E
üzeh Rīg, Iran .... **45 E8** 27 20N 58 40 E
wani □, Tanzania .... **54 D4** 7 0S 39 0 E
weto, Dem. Rep. of the Congo **55 D2** 8 25S 28 51 E
wllheli, U.K. **12 E3** 52 53N 4 25W
ya-ozero, Russia .... **18 A5** 66 5N 30 58 E
yapon, Burma .... **41 L19** 16 20N 95 40 E
yasina ➤, Russia .... **29 B9** 73 30N 87 0 E
yatigorsk, Russia ...... **19 F7** 44 2N 43 6 E
yè = Prome, Burma ...... **41 K19** 18 49N 95 13 E
yhäjoki, Finland .... **8 D21** 64 28N 24 14 E
yinmana, Burma .... **41 K20** 19 45N 96 12 E
yla, C., Cyprus .... **25 E12** 34 56N 32 0 E
ymatuning Reservoir, U.S.A. **84 E4** 41 30N 80 28W
yöktong, N. Korea ...... **35 D13** 40 50N 125 50 E
yŏnggang, N. Korea ..... **35 E14** 38 24N 127 17 E
'yŏngt'aek, S. Korea .... **35 F14** 37 1N 127 4 E
'yŏngyang, N. Korea .... **35 E13** 39 0N 125 30 E
yote, U.S.A. **81 K3** 31 32N 103 8W
yramid L., U.S.A. **76 G4** 40 1N 119 35W
yramid Pk., U.S.A. **79 J10** 36 25N 116 37W
yrénées, Europe .... **20 E4** 42 45N 0 18 E
yu, Burma .... **41 K20** 18 30N 96 28 E

Q

aanaaq, Greenland **4 B4** 77 40N 69 0W
achasnek, S. Africa .... **57 E4** 30 6S 28 42 E
a'el Jafr, Jordan ...... **46 E5** 30 20N 36 25 E
a'emābād, Iran .... **45 D9** 31 44N 60 2 E
ä'emshahr, Iran .... **45 B7** 36 30N 52 53 E
agan Nur, China .... **34 C8** 43 30N 114 55 E
ahar Youyi Zhongqi, China **34 D7** 41 12N 112 40 E
ahremānshahr = Bākhtarān,
  Iran .... **44 C5** 34 23N 47 0 E
aidam Pendi, China .... **32 C4** 37 0N 95 0 E
ajarīyeh, Iran .... **45 D6** 31 1N 48 22 E
ala, Ras il, Malta .... **25 C1** 36 2N 14 20 E
ala-i-Jadid = Spīn Būldak,
  Afghan. .... **42 D2** 31 1N 66 25 E
ala Point = Qala, Ras il, Malta **25 C1** 36 2N 14 20 E
ala Viala, Pakistan ... **42 D2** 30 49N 67 17 E
ala Yangi, Afghan. .... **42 B2** 34 20N 66 30 E
al'at al Akhḍar, Si. Arabia **44 E3** 28 0N 37 10 E
al'at at Dīzah, Iraq ... **44 B5** 36 15N 45 7 E
al'at Ṣāliḥ, Iraq ...... **44 D5** 31 31N 47 16 E
al'at Sukkar, Iraq ..... **44 D5** 31 51N 46 5 E
amani'tuaq = Baker Lake,
  Canada **68 B10** 64 20N 96 3W
amdo, China .... **32 C4** 31 15N 97 6 E
amruddin Karez, Pakistan **42 D3** 31 45N 68 20 E
andahār, Afghan. ...... **40 D4** 31 32N 65 43 E
andahār □, Afghan. .... **40 D4** 31 0N 65 0 E
apān, Iran .... **45 B7** 37 40N 55 47 E
apshaghay, Kazakhstan . **28 E8** 43 51N 77 14 E
aqortoq, Greenland **69 B6** 60 43N 46 0W
ara Qash ➤, China .... **28 B8** 35 0N 78 30 E
arabutaq, Kazakhstan .. **28 E7** 49 59N 60 14 E
araghandy, Kazakhstan . **28 E8** 49 50N 73 10 E
arah, Si. Arabia ...... **44 D4** 29 55N 40 3 E
aratau, Kazakhstan .... **28 E8** 43 10N 70 28 E
arataū, Kazakhstan .... **28 E7** 43 30N 69 30 E
ardho = Gardo, Somali Rep. **47 F4** 9 30N 49 6 E
areh, Iran .... **44 B5** 39 25N 47 22 E
areh Tekān, Iran ...... **45 B6** 36 38N 49 29 E
arqan He ➤, China .... **32 C3** 39 30N 88 30 E
arqaraly, Kazakhstan .. **28 E8** 49 26N 75 30 E
arshi, Uzbekistan ..... **28 F7** 38 53N 65 48 E
artabā, Lebanon .... **46 A4** 34 4N 35 50 E
aryat al Gharab, Iraq . **44 D5** 31 27N 44 48 E
aryat al 'Ulyā, Si. Arabia **44 E5** 27 33N 47 42 E
aşr 'Amra, Jordan ..... **44 D3** 31 48N 36 35 E
aşr-e Qand, Iran ...... **45 E9** 26 15N 60 45 E
aşr Abu Ḥamzah, Egypt . **51 C11** 27 0N 28 1 E
atanā, Syria .... **46 B5** 33 26N 36 4 E
at, Asia .... **45 E6** 25 30N 51 15 E
atlish, Iran .... **45 B8** 37 50N 57 19 E
attāra, Munkhafed el, Egypt **51 C11** 29 30N 27 30 E
attāra Depression = Qattâra,
  Munkhafed el, Egypt ... **51 C11** 29 30N 27 30 E
awām al Ḥamzah = Al Ḥamzah,
  Iraq .... **44 D5** 31 43N 44 58 E
āyen, Iran .... **45 C8** 33 40N 59 10 E
azaqstan = Kazakhstan ■, Asia **28 E7** 50 0N 70 0 E
azīmämmäd, Azerbaijan . **45 A6** 40 3N 49 0 E
azvin, Iran .... **45 B6** 36 15N 50 0 E
azvin □, Iran .... **45 B6** 36 15N 50 0 E
ena, Egypt .... **51 C12** 26 10N 32 43 E
eqertarsuaq, Greenland **69 B5** 69 15N 53 33W
eqertarsuaq, Greenland **69 B14** 69 15N 53 38W
eshläq, Iran .... **44 C5** 34 55N 46 28 E
eshm, Iran .... **45 E8** 26 55N 56 10 E
eys, Iran .... **45 B6** 36 45N 49 22 E
ezi'ot, Israel .... **46 E3** 30 52N 34 26 E
Xian, China .... **34 G8** 34 40N 114 48 E
ian Gorlos, China ..... **35 B13** 45 5N 124 42 E
ian Xian, China .... **33 F10** 22 32N 113 54 E
ian Xian, China .... **34 G5** 34 31N 108 15 E
ianshan, China .... **33 G10** 23 15N 113 31 E
ianyang, China .... **34 G4** 34 40N 107 8 E
i'ao, China .... **33 G10** 22 25N 113 38 E
i'ao Dao, China .... **33 G10** 22 25N 113 38 E
ikiqtarjuaq, Canada ... **69 B13** 67 33N 63 0W
ila Safed, Pakistan ... **40 E2** 29 0N 61 30 E
ila Saifullāh, Pakistan **42 D3** 30 45N 68 17 E
ilian Shan, China ..... **32 C4** 38 30N 96 0 E
in He ➤, China .... **34 H5** 33 50N 108 10 E
in Ling = Qinling Shandi, China **34 H5** 33 50N 108 10 E
in'an, China .... **34 G3** 34 48N 105 40 E
ingcheng, China .... **35 F9** 37 15N 117 40 E
ingfeng, China .... **34 G8** 35 52N 115 8 E
inghai □, China .... **32 C5** 36 0N 98 0 E
inghai Hu, China ...... **32 C5** 36 40N 100 10 E
inghecheng, China ..... **35 D13** 41 28N 124 15 E
inghemen, China .... **35 D11** 41 48N 121 25 E
ingjian, China .... **34 F6** 37 8N 110 8 E

Qingjiang = Huaiyin, China .... **35 H10** 33 30N 119 2 E
Qingshui, China .... **34 G4** 34 48N 106 8 E
Qingshuihe, China ..... **34 E6** 39 55N 111 35 E
Qingtongxia Shuiku, China **34 F3** 37 50N 105 58 E
Qingxu, China .... **34 F7** 37 34N 112 22 E
Qingyang, China .... **34 F4** 36 2N 107 55 E
Qingyuan, China .... **35 C13** 42 10N 124 55 E
Qingyun, China .... **35 F9** 37 45N 117 20 E
Qinhuangdao, China .... **35 E10** 39 56N 119 30 E
Qinling Shandi, China . **34 H5** 33 50N 108 10 E
Qinshui, China .... **34 G7** 35 40N 112 8 E
Qinyang = Jiyuan, China **34 G7** 35 7N 112 57 E
Qinyuan, China .... **34 F7** 36 29N 112 20 E
Qinzhou, China .... **32 D5** 21 58N 108 38 E
Qionghai, China .... **38 C8** 19 15N 110 26 E
Qiongzhou Haixia, China **38 B8** 20 10N 110 15 E
Qiqihar, China .... **29 E13** 47 26N 124 0 E
Qiraïya, W. ➤, Egypt .. **46 E3** 30 27N 34 0 E
Qīryat Ata, Israel .... **46 C4** 32 47N 35 6 E
Qiryat Gat, Israel .... **46 D3** 31 32N 34 46 E
Qiryat Mal'akhi, Israel **46 D3** 31 44N 34 44 E
Qiryat Shemona, Israel **46 B4** 33 13N 35 35 E
Qiryat Yam, Israel .... **46 C4** 32 51N 35 4 E
Qishan, China .... **34 G4** 34 25N 107 38 E
Qixia, China .... **35 F11** 37 17N 120 52 E
Qızılağaç Körfäzi, Azerbaijan **45 B6** 39 9N 49 0 E
Qojūr, Iran .... **44 B5** 36 12N 47 55 E
Qom, Iran .... **45 C6** 34 40N 51 0 E
Qom □, Iran .... **45 C6** 34 40N 51 0 E
Qomolangma Feng = Everest,
  Mt., Nepal .... **43 E12** 28 5N 86 58 E
Qomsheh, Iran .... **45 D6** 32 0N 51 55 E
Qoraqalpoghistan □, Uzbekistan **28 E6** 43 0N 58 0 E
Qostanay, Kazakhstan . **28 D7** 53 10N 63 35 E
Quabbin Reservoir, U.S.A. **85 D12** 42 20N 72 20W
Quairading, Australia . **61 F2** 32 0S 117 21 E
Quakertown, U.S.A. **85 F9** 40 26N 75 21W
Qualicum Beach, Canada **70 D4** 49 22N 124 26W
Quambatook, Australia . **63 F3** 35 49S 143 34 E
Quambone, Australia ... **63 E4** 30 57S 147 53 E
Quamby, Australia ..... **62 C3** 20 22S 140 17 E
Quan Long = Ca Mau, Vietnam . **39 H5** 9 7N 105 8 E
Quanah, U.S.A. **81 H5** 34 18N 99 44W
Quang Ngai, Vietnam ... **38 E7** 15 13N 108 58 E
Quang Tri, Vietnam .... **38 D6** 16 45N 107 13 E
Quang Yen, Vietnam .... **38 B6** 20 56N 106 52 E
Quantock Hills, U.K. .. **13 F4** 51 8N 3 10W
Quanzhou, China .... **33 D6** 24 55N 118 34 E
Qu'Appelle, Canada **71 C8** 50 33N 103 53W
Quaqtaq, Canada **69 B13** 60 55N 69 40W
Quaraí, Brazil **94 C4** 30 15S 56 20W
Quartu Sant'Élena, Italy **22 E3** 39 15N 9 10 E
Quartzsite, U.S.A. **79 M12** 33 40N 114 13W
Quatsino Sd., Canada .. **70 C3** 50 25N 127 58W
Quba, Azerbaijan ...... **19 F8** 41 21N 48 32 E
Qūchān, Iran .... **45 B8** 37 10N 58 27 E
Queanbeyan, Australia . **63 F4** 35 17S 149 14 E
Québec, Canada **73 C5** 46 52N 71 13W
Québec □, Canada **73 C6** 48 0N 74 0W
Quebrada del Condorito △,
  Argentina **94 C3** 31 49S 64 40W
Queen Alexandra Ra., Antarctica **5 E11** 85 0S 170 0 E
Queen Charlotte City, Canada **70 C2** 53 15N 132 2W
Queen Charlotte Is., Canada **70 C2** 53 20N 132 10W
Queen Charlotte Sd., Canada **70 C3** 51 0N 128 0W
Queen Charlotte Strait, Canada **70 C3** 50 45N 127 10W
Queen Elizabeth □, U.K. **11 E4** 56 7N 4 30W
Queen Elizabeth △, Uganda **54 C3** 0 0 30 0 E
Queen Elizabeth Is., Canada **66 B10** 76 0N 95 0W
Queen Mary Land, Antarctica **5 D7** 70 0S 95 0 E
Queen Maud G., Canada **68 B9** 68 15N 102 30W
Queen Maud Land = Dronning
  Maud Land, Antarctica . **5 D3** 72 30S 12 0 E
Queen Maud Mts., Antarctica **5 E13** 86 0S 160 0W
Queens Chan., Australia **60 C4** 15 0S 129 30 E
Queenscliff, Australia **63 F3** 38 16S 144 39 E
Queensland □, Australia **62 C3** 22 0S 142 0 E
Queenstown, Australia . **63 G4** 42 4S 145 35 E
Queenstown, N.Z. ...... **59 L2** 45 1S 168 40 E
Queenstown, Singapore . **39 d** 1 18N 103 48 E
Queenstown, S. Africa . **56 E4** 31 52S 26 52 E
Queets, U.S.A. **78 C2** 47 32N 124 20W
Queguay Grande ➤, Uruguay **94 C4** 32 9S 58 9W
Queimadas, Brazil **93 F11** 11 0S 39 38W
Quelimane, Mozam. ..... **55 F4** 17 53S 36 58 E
Quellón, Chile **96 E2** 43 7S 73 37W
Quelpart = Cheju do, S. Korea **35 H14** 33 29N 126 34 E
Quemado, N. Mex., U.S.A. **77 J9** 34 20N 108 30W
Quemado, Tex., U.S.A. . **81 L4** 28 58N 100 35W
Quemú-Quemú, Argentina **94 D3** 36 3S 63 36W
Quequén, Argentina **94 D4** 38 30S 58 30W
Querétaro, Mexico **86 C4** 20 36N 100 23W
Querétaro □, Mexico ... **86 C5** 20 30N 100 0W
Queshan, China .... **34 H8** 32 55N 114 2 E
Quesnel, Canada **70 C4** 53 0N 122 30W
Quesnel ➤, Canada **70 C4** 52 58N 122 29W
Quesnel L., Canada **70 C4** 52 30N 121 20W
Questa, U.S.A. **77 H11** 36 42N 105 36W
Quetico △, Canada **72 C1** 48 30N 91 45W
Quetta, Pakistan ...... **42 D2** 30 15N 66 55 E
Quezaltenango, Guatemala **88 D1** 14 50N 91 30W
Quezon City, Phil. .... **37 B6** 14 38N 121 0 E
Qufār, Si. Arabia ..... **44 E4** 27 26N 41 37 E
Qui Nhon, Vietnam ..... **38 F7** 13 40N 109 13 E
Quibaxe, Angola .... **52 F2** 8 24S 14 27 E
Quibdo, Colombia **92 B3** 5 42N 76 40W
Quiberon, France **20 C2** 47 29N 3 9W
Quiet L., Canada **70 A2** 61 5N 133 5W
Quiindy, Paraguay **94 B4** 25 58S 57 14W
Quila, Mexico **86 C3** 24 23N 107 13W
Quilán, C., Chile **96 E2** 43 15S 74 30W
Quilimari, Chile **94 C1** 32 5S 71 30W
Quilino, Argentina **94 C3** 30 14S 64 29W
Quill Lakes, Canada ... **71 C8** 51 55N 104 13W
Quillabamba, Peru **92 F4** 12 50S 72 50W
Quillagua, Chile **94 A2** 21 40S 69 40W
Quillaicillo, Chile ... **94 C1** 31 17S 71 40W
Quillota, Chile **94 C1** 32 54S 71 16W
Quilmes, Argentina **94 C4** 34 43S 58 15W
Quilon, India .... **40 Q10** 8 50N 76 38 E
Quilpie, Australia .... **63 D3** 26 35S 144 11 E
Quilpué, Chile **94 C1** 33 5S 71 33W
Quilua, Mozam. .... **55 F4** 16 17S 39 54 E
Quimilí, Argentina **94 B3** 27 40S 62 30W
Quimper, France **20 B1** 48 0N 4 9W
Quimperlé, France **20 C2** 47 53N 3 33W

Quinault ➤, U.S.A. **78 C2** 47 21N 124 18W
Quincy, Calif., U.S.A. **78 F6** 39 56N 120 57W
Quincy, Fla., U.S.A. .. **83 K3** 30 35N 84 34W
Quincy, Ill., U.S.A. .. **80 F9** 39 56N 91 23W
Quincy, Mass., U.S.A. . **85 D14** 42 15N 71 0W
Quincy, Wash., U.S.A. . **76 C4** 47 22N 119 56W
Quines, Argentina **94 C2** 32 13S 65 48W
Quinga, Mozam. .... **55 F5** 15 49S 40 15 E
Quinns Rocks, Australia **61 F2** 31 40S 115 42 E
Quintana Roo □, Mexico **87 D7** 19 0N 88 0W
Quintanar de la Orden, Spain **21 C4** 39 36N 3 5W
Quinte West, Canada ... **84 B7** 44 10N 77 34W
Quintero, Chile **94 C1** 32 45S 71 30W
Quirihue, Chile **94 D1** 36 15S 72 35W
Quirindi, Australia ... **63 E5** 31 28S 150 40 E
Quirinópolis, Brazil .. **93 G8** 18 32S 50 30W
Quissanga, Mozam. ..... **55 E5** 12 24S 40 28 E
Quissico, Mozam. ...... **57 C5** 24 42S 34 44 E
Quitilipi, Argentina .. **94 B3** 26 50S 60 13W
Quitman, U.S.A. **83 K4** 30 47N 83 34W
Quito, Ecuador **92 D3** 0 15S 78 35W
Quixadá, Brazil **93 D11** 4 55S 39 0W
Quixaxe, Mozam. .... **55 F5** 15 17S 40 4 E
Qulan, Kazakhstan ..... **28 E8** 42 55N 72 43 E
Qul'ân, Jazā'ir, Egypt **44 E2** 24 22N 35 31 E
Qumbu, S. Africa ...... **57 E4** 31 10S 28 48 E
Quneitra, Syria .... **46 B4** 33 7N 35 48 E
Qŭnghirot, Uzbekistan . **28 E6** 43 6N 58 54 E
Quoin I., Australia ... **60 B4** 14 54S 129 32 E
Quoin Pt., S. Africa .. **56 E2** 34 46S 19 37 E
Quorn, Australia ...... **63 E2** 32 25S 138 5 E
Qŭqon, Uzbekistan ..... **28 E8** 40 30N 70 57 E
Qurnat as Sawdā', Lebanon **46 A5** 34 18N 36 6 E
Quşaybā', Si. Arabia .. **44 E4** 26 53N 43 35 E
Qusaybah, Iraq .... **44 C4** 34 24N 40 59 E
Quseir, Egypt .... **44 E2** 26 7N 34 16 E
Qūshchī, Iran .... **44 B5** 37 59N 45 3 E
Quthing, Lesotho ...... **57 E4** 30 25S 27 36 E
Qūṭīābād, Iran .... **45 C6** 35 47N 48 30 E
Quwo, China .... **34 G6** 35 38N 111 25 E
Quyang, China .... **34 E8** 38 35N 114 40 E
Quyon, Canada **85 A8** 45 31N 76 14W
Quzhou, China .... **33 D6** 28 57N 118 54 E
Quzi, China .... **34 F4** 36 20N 107 20 E
Qyzylorda, Kazakhstan . **28 E7** 44 48N 65 28 E

R

Ra, Ko, Thailand ...... **39 H2** 9 13N 98 16 E
Raahe, Finland .... **8 D21** 64 40N 24 28 E
Raalte, Neths. .... **15 B6** 52 23N 6 16 E
Raasay, U.K. **11 D2** 57 25N 6 4W
Raasay, Sd. of, U.K. .. **11 D2** 57 30N 6 8W
Raba, Indonesia .... **37 F5** 8 36S 118 55 E
Rába ➤, Hungary .... **17 E9** 47 38N 17 38 E
Rabai, Kenya .... **54 C4** 3 50S 39 31 E
Rabat = Victoria, Malta **25 C1** 36 3N 14 14 E
Rabat, Malta .... **25 D1** 35 53N 14 24 E
Rabat, Morocco **50 B4** 34 2N 6 48W
Rabaul, Papua N. G. ... **64 H7** 4 24S 152 18 E
Rābigh, Si. Arabia .... **47 C2** 22 50N 39 5 E
Râbniţa, Moldova ...... **17 E15** 47 45N 29 0 E
Râbor, Iran .... **45 D8** 29 17N 56 55 E
Race, C., Canada **73 C9** 46 40N 53 5W
Rach Gia, Vietnam ..... **39 G5** 10 5N 105 5 E
Rachid, Mauritania **50 E3** 18 45N 11 35W
Raciborz, Poland ...... **17 C10** 50 7N 18 18 E
Racine, U.S.A. **82 D2** 42 41N 87 51W
Rackerby, U.S.A. **78 F5** 39 26N 121 22W
Radama, Nosy, Madag. . **57 A8** 14 0S 47 47 E
Radama, Saikanosy, Madag. **57 A8** 14 16S 47 53 E
Rădăuţi, Romania ...... **17 E13** 47 50N 25 59 E
Radcliff, U.S.A. **82 G3** 37 51N 85 57W
Radekhiv, Ukraine ..... **17 C13** 50 25N 24 32 E
Radekhov = Radekhiv, Ukraine **17 C13** 50 25N 24 32 E
Radford, U.S.A. **82 G5** 37 8N 80 34W
Radhanpur, India ...... **42 H4** 23 50N 71 38 E
Radhwa, Jabal, Si. Arabia **44 E3** 24 34N 38 18 E
Radisson, Qué., Canada **72 B4** 53 47N 77 37W
Radisson, Sask., Canada **71 C7** 52 30N 107 20W
Radium Hot Springs, Canada **70 C5** 50 35N 116 2W
Radnor Forest, U.K. ... **13 E4** 52 17N 3 10W
Radom, Poland .... **17 C11** 51 23N 21 12 E
Radomsko, Poland ...... **17 C10** 51 5N 19 28 E
Radomyshl, Ukraine .... **17 C15** 50 30N 29 12 E
Radstock, C., Australia **63 E1** 33 12S 134 20 E
Radviliškis, Lithuania **9 J20** 55 49N 23 33 E
Radville, Canada **71 D8** 49 30N 104 15W
Rae, Canada **70 A5** 62 50N 116 3W
Rae Bareli, India ..... **43 F9** 26 18N 81 20 E
Rae Isthmus, Canada ... **69 B11** 66 40N 87 30W
Raeren, Belgium .... **15 D6** 50 41N 6 7 E
Raeside, L., Australia **61 E3** 29 20S 122 0 E
Raetihi, N.Z. .... **59 H5** 39 25S 175 17 E
Rafaela, Argentina **94 C3** 31 10S 61 30W
Rafah, Gaza Strip ..... **46 D3** 31 18N 34 14 E
Rafai, C.A.R. .... **54 B1** 4 59N 23 58 E
Raffâ, Si. Arabia ..... **44 E5** 24 25N 43 35 E
Rafsanjân, Iran .... **45 D8** 30 30N 56 5 E
Raft Pt., Australia ... **60 C3** 16 4S 124 26 E
Râga, Sudan .... **51 G11** 8 28N 25 41 E
Ragachow, Belarus ..... **17 B16** 53 8N 30 5 E
Ragama, Sri Lanka ..... **40 R11** 7 0N 79 50 E
Ragged, Mt., Australia **61 F3** 33 27S 123 25 E
Ragged Pt., Barbados .. **89 g** 13 9N 59 18W
Raghunathpalli, India . **43 H11** 22 14N 84 48 E
Raghunathpur, India ... **43 H12** 23 33N 86 40 E
Raglan, N.Z. .... **59 G5** 37 55S 174 55 E
Ragusa, Italy .... **22 F6** 36 55N 14 44 E
Raha, Indonesia .... **37 E6** 4 55S 123 0 E
Rahaeng = Tak, Thailand **38 D2** 16 52N 99 8 E
Rahatgarh, India ...... **43 H8** 23 47N 78 22 E
Rahimyar Khan, Pakistan **42 E4** 28 30N 70 25 E
Rāhjerd, Iran .... **45 C6** 34 22N 50 22 E
Rahole △, Kenya .... **54 B4** 0 5N 38 57 E
Rahon, India .... **42 D7** 31 3N 76 7 E
Raichur, India .... **40 L10** 16 10N 77 20 E
Raigarh, India .... **41 J13** 21 56N 83 25 E
Raijua, Indonesia ..... **37 F6** 10 37S 121 36 E
Raikot, India .... **42 D6** 30 41N 75 42 E
Railton, Australia .... **63 G4** 41 25S 146 28 E
Rainbow Bridge △, U.S.A. **77 H8** 37 5N 110 58W
Rainbow Lake, Canada . **70 B5** 58 30N 119 23W

Rainier, U.S.A. **78 D4** 46 53N 122 41W
Rainier, Mt., U.S.A. .. **78 D5** 46 52N 121 46W
Rainy L., Canada **71 D10** 48 42N 93 10W
Rainy River, Canada ... **71 D10** 48 43N 94 29W
Raippaluoto, Finland .. **8 E19** 63 13N 21 14 E
Raipur, India .... **41 J12** 21 17N 81 45 E
Raisen, India .... **42 H8** 23 20N 77 48 E
Raisio, Finland .... **9 F20** 60 28N 22 11 E
Raj Nandgaon, India ... **41 J12** 21 5N 81 5 E
Raj Nilgiri, India .... **43 J12** 21 28N 86 46 E
Raja, Ujung, Indonesia **36 D1** 3 40N 96 25 E
Raja Ampat, Kepulauan,
  Indonesia .... **37 E7** 0 30S 130 0 E
Rajahmundry, India .... **41 L12** 17 1N 81 48 E
Rajang ➤, Malaysia .... **36 D4** 2 30N 112 0 E
Rajanpur, Pakistan .... **42 E4** 29 6N 70 19 E
Rajapalaiyam, India ... **40 Q10** 9 25N 77 35 E
Rajasthan □, India .... **42 F5** 26 45N 73 30 E
Rajasthan Canal = Indira Gandhi
  Canal, India .... **42 F5** 28 0N 72 0 E
Rajauri, India .... **43 C6** 33 25N 74 21 E
Rajgarh, Mad. P., India **42 G7** 24 2N 76 45 E
Rajgarh, Raj., India .. **42 F7** 27 14N 76 38 E
Rajgarh, Raj., India .. **42 E6** 28 40N 75 25 E
Rajgir, India .... **43 G11** 25 2N 85 25 E
Rajkot, India .... **42 H4** 22 15N 70 56 E
Rajmahal Hills, India . **43 G12** 24 30N 87 30 E
Rajpipla, India .... **40 J8** 21 50N 73 30 E
Rajpur, India .... **42 H6** 22 18N 74 21 E
Rajpura, India .... **42 D7** 30 25N 76 32 E
Rajshahi, Bangla. ..... **41 G16** 24 22N 88 39 E
Rajshahi □, Bangla. ... **43 G13** 25 0N 89 0 E
Rajula, India .... **42 J4** 21 3N 71 26 E
Rakaia, N.Z. .... **59 K4** 43 45S 172 1 E
Rakaia ➤, N.Z. .... **59 K4** 43 36S 172 15 E
Rakan, Ra's, Qatar .... **45 E6** 26 10N 51 20 E
Rakaposhi, Pakistan ... **43 A6** 36 10N 74 25 E
Rakata, Pulau, Indonesia **36 F3** 6 10S 105 20 E
Rakhiv, Ukraine .... **17 D13** 48 3N 24 12 E
Rakhni, Pakistan ...... **42 D3** 30 4N 69 56 E
Rakhni ➤, Pakistan .... **42 E3** 29 31N 69 36 E
Rakitnoye, Russia ..... **30 B7** 45 36N 134 17 E
Rakops, Botswana ...... **56 C3** 21 1S 24 28 E
Rakvere, Estonia ...... **9 G22** 59 20N 26 25 E
Raleigh, U.S.A. **83 H6** 35 47N 78 39W
Ralls, U.S.A. **81 J4** 33 41N 101 24W
Ralston, U.S.A. **84 E8** 41 30N 76 57W
Ram ➤, Canada **70 A4** 62 1N 123 41W
Râm Allâh, West Bank .. **46 D4** 31 55N 35 10 E
Rama, Nic. **88 D3** 12 9N 84 15W
Ramakona, India .... **43 J8** 21 43N 78 50 E
Ramallah = Râm Allâh,
  West Bank .... **46 D4** 31 55N 35 10 E
Raman, Thailand .... **39 J3** 6 29N 101 18 E
Ramanathapuram, India . **40 Q11** 9 25N 78 55 E
Ramanetaka, B. de, Madag. **57 A8** 14 13S 47 52 E
Ramanujganj, India .... **43 H10** 23 48N 83 42 E
Ramat Gan, Israel ..... **46 C3** 32 4N 34 48 E
Ramatlhabama, S. Africa **56 D4** 25 37S 25 33 E
Ramban, India .... **43 C6** 33 14N 75 12 E
Rambipuji, Indonesia . **37 H15** 8 12S 113 37 E
Rame Hd., Australia ... **63 F4** 37 47S 149 30 E
Ramechhap, Nepal ...... **43 F12** 27 25N 86 10 E
Ramganga ➤, India ..... **43 F8** 27 5N 79 58 E
Ramgarh, Jharkhand, India **43 H11** 23 40N 85 35 E
Ramgarh, Raj., India .. **42 F6** 27 30N 75 14 E
Ramgarh, Raj., India .. **42 F4** 27 30N 70 36 E
Rāmhormoz, Iran .... **45 D6** 31 15N 49 35 E
Ramian, Iran .... **45 B7** 37 3N 55 16 E
Ramingining, Australia **62 A2** 12 19S 135 3 E
Ramla, Israel .... **46 D3** 31 55N 34 52 E
Ramm = Rum, Jordan .... **46 F4** 29 35N 35 24 E
Ramm, Jabal, Jordan ... **46 F4** 29 35N 35 24 E
Ramnad = Ramanathapuram,
  India .... **40 Q11** 9 25N 78 55 E
Ramnagar, Jammu & Kashmir,
  India .... **43 C6** 32 47N 75 18 E
Ramnagar, Uttaranchal, India **43 E8** 29 24N 79 7 E
Râmnicu Sărat, Romania **17 F14** 45 26N 27 3 E
Râmnicu Vâlcea, Romania **17 F13** 45 9N 24 21 E
Ramona, U.S.A. **79 M10** 33 2N 116 52W
Ramore, Canada **72 C3** 48 30N 80 25W
Ramotswa, Botswana .... **56 C4** 24 50S 25 52 E
Rampur, H.P., India ... **42 D7** 31 26N 77 43 E
Rampur, Mad. P., India **42 H5** 23 25N 73 53 E
Rampur, Ut. P., India . **43 E8** 28 50N 79 5 E
Rampur Hat, India ..... **43 G12** 24 10N 87 50 E
Rampura, India .... **42 G6** 24 30N 75 27 E
Ramrama Tola, India ... **43 J8** 21 52N 79 55 E
Ramree I., Burma ...... **41 K19** 19 0N 93 40 E
Râmsar, Iran .... **45 B6** 36 53N 50 41 E
Ramsey, U.K. **12 C3** 54 20N 4 22W
Ramsey L., Canada **72 C3** 47 13N 82 15W
Ramsgate, U.K. .... **13 F9** 51 20N 1 25 E
Ramtek, India .... **40 J11** 21 20N 79 15 E
Rana Pratap Sagar Dam, India . **42 G6** 24 58N 75 38 E
Ranaghat, India .... **43 H13** 23 15N 88 35 E
Ranahu, Pakistan ...... **42 G3** 23 45N 69 45 E
Ranau, Malaysia .... **36 C5** 6 2N 116 40 E
Rancagua, Chile **94 C1** 34 10S 70 50W
Rancheria ➤, Canada ... **70 A3** 60 13N 129 7W
Ranchester, U.S.A. **76 D10** 44 54N 107 10W
Ranchi, India .... **43 H11** 23 19N 85 27 E
Rancho Cucamonga, U.S.A. **79 L9** 34 10N 117 30W
Randalstown, U.K. **10 B5** 54 45N 6 19W
Randers, Denmark ...... **9 H14** 56 29N 10 1 E
Randfontein, S. Africa **57 D4** 26 8S 27 45 E
Randle, U.S.A. **78 D5** 46 32N 121 57W
Randolph, Mass., U.S.A. **85 D13** 42 10N 71 2W
Randolph, N.Y., U.S.A. **84 D6** 42 10N 78 59W
Randolph, Utah, U.S.A. **76 F8** 41 40N 111 11W
Randolph, Vt., U.S.A. . **85 C12** 43 55N 72 40W
Randsburg, U.S.A. **79 K9** 35 22N 117 39W
Råne älv ➤, Sweden .... **8 D20** 65 50N 22 20 E
Rangae, Thailand ...... **39 J3** 6 19N 101 44 E
Rangaunu B., N.Z. ..... **59 F4** 34 51S 173 15 E
Rangeley, U.S.A. **85 B14** 44 58N 70 39W
Rangeley L., U.S.A. ... **85 B14** 44 55N 70 43W
Rangely, U.S.A. **76 F9** 40 5N 108 48W
Ranger, U.S.A. **81 J5** 32 28N 98 41W
Rangia, India .... **41 F17** 26 28N 91 38 E
Rangiora, N.Z. .... **59 K4** 43 19S 172 36 E
Rangitaiki ➤, N.Z. .... **59 G6** 37 54S 176 49 E
Rangitata ➤, N.Z. ..... **59 K3** 43 45S 171 15 E
Rangkasbitung, Indonesia **37 G12** 6 21S 106 15 E
Rangon ➤, Burma .... **41 L20** 16 28N 96 40 E
Rangoon, Burma .... **41 L20** 16 45N 96 20 E

Rangpur, Bangla. 41 G16 25 42N 89 22 E
Rangsit, Thailand 38 F3 13 59N 100 37 E
Ranibennur, India 40 M9 14 35N 75 30 E
Raniganj, Ut. P., India 43 F9 27 3N 82 13 E
Raniganj, W. Bengal, India 41 H15 23 40N 87 5 E
Ranikhet, India 43 E8 29 39N 79 25 E
Raniwara, India 40 G8 24 50N 72 10 E
Rāniyah, Iraq 44 B5 36 15N 44 53 E
Ranka, India 43 H10 23 59N 83 47 E
Ranken →, Australia 62 C2 20 31S 137 36 E
Rankin, U.S.A. 81 K4 31 13N 101 56W
Rankin Inlet, Canada 68 B10 62 30N 93 0W
Rankins Springs, Australia 63 E4 33 49S 146 14 E
Rannoch, L., U.K. 11 E4 56 41N 4 20W
Rannoch Moor, U.K. 11 E4 56 38N 4 48W
Ranobe, Helodranon' i, Madag. 57 C7 23 3S 43 33 E
Ranohira, Madag. 57 C8 22 29S 45 24 E
Ranomafana, Toamasina, Madag. 57 B8 18 57S 48 50 E
Ranomafana, Toliara, Madag. 57 C8 24 34S 47 0 E
Ranomafana △, Madag. 57 C8 21 16S 47 25 E
Ranomena, Madag. 57 C8 23 25S 47 17 E
Ranong, Thailand 39 H2 9 56N 98 40 E
Ranotsara Nord, Madag. 57 C8 22 48S 46 36 E
Ränsa, Iran 45 C6 33 39N 48 18 E
Ransiki, Indonesia 37 E8 1 30S 134 10 E
Rantabe, Madag. 57 B8 15 42S 49 39 E
Rantauprapat, Indonesia 36 D1 2 15N 99 50 E
Rantemario, Indonesia 37 E5 3 15S 119 57 E
Rantoul, U.S.A. 82 E1 40 19N 88 9W
Raoyang, China 34 E8 38 15N 115 45 E
Rap, Ko, Thailand 39 b 9 19N 99 58 E
Rapa, French Polynesia 65 K13 27 35S 144 20W
Rapa Nui = Pascua, I. de, Chile 65 K17 27 7S 109 23W
Rapallo, Italy 20 D8 44 21N 9 14 E
Rapar, India 42 H4 23 34N 70 38 E
Räpch, Iran 45 E8 25 40N 59 15 E
Raper, C., Canada 69 B13 69 44N 67 6W
Rapid City, U.S.A. 80 D3 44 5N 103 14W
Rapid River, U.S.A. 82 C2 45 55N 86 58W
Rapla, Estonia 9 G21 59 1N 24 52 E
Rapti →, India 43 F10 26 18N 83 41 E
Raquette →, U.S.A. 85 B10 45 0N 74 42W
Raquette Lake, U.S.A. 85 C10 43 49N 74 40W
Rarotonga, Cook Is. 65 K12 21 30S 160 0W
Ra's al 'Ayn, Syria 44 B4 36 45N 40 12 E
Ra's al Khaymah, U.A.E. 45 E7 25 50N 55 59 E
Rasca, Pta. de la, Canary Is. 24 G3 27 59N 16 41W
Raseiniai, Lithuania 9 J20 55 25N 23 5 E
Rashmi, India 42 G6 25 4N 74 22 E
Rasht, Iran 45 B6 37 20N 49 40 E
Rasi Salai, Thailand 38 E5 15 20N 104 9 E
Rason L., Australia 61 E3 28 45S 124 25 E
Rasra, India 43 G10 25 50N 83 50 E
Rasul, Pakistan 42 C5 32 42N 73 34 E
Rat Buri, Thailand 38 F2 13 30N 99 54 E
Rat Islands, U.S.A. 68 C1 52 0N 178 0 E
Rat L., Canada 71 B9 56 10N 99 40W
Ratangarh, India 42 E6 28 5N 74 35 E
Raţāwi, Iraq 44 D5 30 38N 47 13 E
Rath, India 43 G8 25 36N 79 37 E
Rath Luirc, Ireland 10 D3 52 21N 8 40W
Rathdrum, Ireland 10 D5 52 56N 6 14W
Rathenow, Germany 16 B7 52 37N 12 19 E
Rathkeale, Ireland 10 D3 52 32N 8 56W
Rathlin I., U.K. 10 A5 55 18N 6 14W
Rathmelton, Ireland 10 A4 55 2N 7 38W
Ratibor = Racibórz, Poland 17 C10 50 7N 18 18 E
Ratlam, India 42 H6 23 20N 75 0 E
Ratnagiri, India 40 L8 16 57N 73 18 E
Ratodero, Pakistan 42 F3 27 48N 68 18 E
Raton, U.S.A. 81 G2 36 54N 104 24W
Rattaphum, Thailand 39 J3 7 8N 100 16 E
Rattray Hd., U.K. 11 D7 57 38N 1 50W
Ratz, Mt., Canada 70 B2 57 23N 132 12W
Raub, Malaysia 39 L3 3 47N 101 52 E
Rauch, Argentina 94 D4 36 45S 59 5W
Raudales de Malpaso, Mexico 87 D6 17 30N 23 30W
Raufarhöfn, Iceland 8 C6 66 27N 15 57W
Raufoss, Norway 9 F14 60 44N 10 37 E
Raukumara Ra., N.Z. 59 H6 38 5S 177 55 E
Rauma, Finland 9 F19 61 10N 21 30 E
Raung, Gunung, Indonesia 37 J17 8 8S 114 3 E
Raurkela, India 43 H11 22 14N 84 50 E
Rausu-Dake, Japan 30 B12 44 4N 145 7 E
Rava-Ruska, Ukraine 17 C12 50 15N 23 42 E
Rava Russkaya = Rava-Ruska, Ukraine 17 C12 50 15N 23 42 E
Ravalli, U.S.A. 76 C6 47 17N 114 11W
Ravānsar, Iran 44 C5 34 43N 46 40 E
Rāvar, Iran 45 D8 31 20N 56 51 E
Ravena, U.S.A. 85 D11 42 28N 73 49W
Ravenna, Italy 22 B5 44 25N 12 12 E
Ravenna, Nebr., U.S.A. 80 E5 41 1N 98 55W
Ravenna, Ohio, U.S.A. 84 E3 41 9N 81 15W
Ravensburg, Germany 16 E5 47 46N 9 36 E
Ravenshoe, Australia 62 B4 17 37S 145 29 E
Ravensthorpe, Australia 61 F3 33 35S 120 2 E
Ravenswood, Australia 62 C4 20 6S 146 54 E
Ravenswood, U.S.A. 82 F5 38 57N 81 46W
Ravi →, Pakistan 42 D4 30 35N 71 49 E
Rawalpindi, Pakistan 42 C5 33 38N 73 8 E
Rawāndūz, Iraq 44 B5 36 40N 44 30 E
Rawang, Malaysia 39 L3 3 20N 101 35 E
Rawene, N.Z. 59 F4 35 25S 173 32 E
Rawlinna, Australia 61 F4 30 58S 125 28 E
Rawlins, U.S.A. 76 F10 41 47N 107 14W
Rawlinson Ra., Australia 61 D4 24 40S 128 30 E
Rawson, Argentina 96 E3 43 15S 65 5W
Raxaul, India 43 F11 26 59N 84 51 E
Ray, U.S.A. 80 A3 48 21N 103 10W
Ray, C., Canada 73 C8 47 33N 59 15W
Raya Ring, Ko, Thailand 39 a 8 18N 98 29 E
Rayadurg, India 40 M10 14 40N 76 50 E
Rayagada, India 41 K13 19 15N 83 20 E
Raychikhinsk, Russia 29 E13 49 46N 129 25 E
Rāyen, Iran 45 D8 29 34N 57 26 E
Rayleigh, U.K. 13 F8 51 36N 0 37 E
Raymond, Canada 70 D6 49 30N 112 35W
Raymond, Calif., U.S.A. 78 H7 37 13N 119 54W
Raymond, N.H., U.S.A. 85 C13 43 2N 71 11W
Raymond, Wash., U.S.A. 78 D3 46 41N 123 44W
Raymondville, U.S.A. 81 M6 26 29N 97 47W
Raymore, Canada 71 C8 51 25N 104 31W
Rayón, Mexico 86 B2 29 43N 110 35W
Rayong, Thailand 38 F3 12 40N 101 20 E
Rayville, U.S.A. 81 J9 32 29N 91 46W
Raz, Pte. du, France 20 C1 48 2N 4 47W

Razan, Iran 45 C6 35 23N 49 2 E
Razāzah, Buḩayrat ar, Iraq 44 C4 32 40N 43 35 E
Razazah, L. = Razāzah, Buḩayrat ar, Iraq 44 C4 32 40N 43 35 E
Razdel'naya = Rozdilna, Ukraine 17 E16 46 50N 30 2 E
Razdolnoye, Russia 30 C5 43 30N 131 52 E
Razeh, Iran 45 C6 32 47N 48 9 E
Razgrad, Bulgaria 23 C12 43 33N 26 34 E
Razim, Lacul, Romania 17 F15 44 50N 29 0 E
Razmak, Pakistan 42 C3 32 45N 69 50 E
Ré, Î. de, France 20 C3 46 12N 1 30W
Reading, U.K. 13 F7 51 27N 0 58W
Reading, U.S.A. 85 F9 40 20N 75 56W
Reading □, U.K. 13 F7 51 27N 0 58W
Realicó, Argentina 94 D3 35 0S 64 15W
Ream, Cambodia 39 G4 10 34N 103 39 E
Reata, Mexico 86 B4 26 8N 101 5W
Reay Forest, U.K. 11 C4 58 22N 4 55W
Rebi, Indonesia 37 F8 6 23S 134 7 E
Rebiana, Libya 51 D10 24 12N 22 10 E
Rebiana, Sahrâ', Libya 51 D10 24 30N 21 0 E
Rebun-Tō, Japan 30 B10 45 23N 141 2 E
Recherche, Arch. of the, Australia 61 F3 34 15S 122 50 E
Rechna Doab, Pakistan 42 D5 31 35N 73 30 E
Rechytsa, Belarus 17 B16 52 21N 30 24 E
Recife, Brazil 93 E12 8 0S 35 0W
Recklinghausen, Germany 15 C7 51 37N 7 12 E
Reconquista, Argentina 94 B4 29 10S 59 45W
Recreo, Argentina 94 B2 29 25S 65 10W
Red →, La., U.S.A. 81 K9 31 1N 91 45W
Red →, N. Dak., U.S.A. 68 C10 49 0N 97 15W
Red Bank, U.S.A. 85 F10 40 21N 74 5W
Red Bay, Canada 73 B8 51 44N 56 25W
Red Bluff, U.S.A. 76 F2 40 11N 122 15W
Red Bluff L., U.S.A. 81 K3 31 54N 103 55W
Red Cliffs, Australia 63 E3 34 19S 142 11 E
Red Cloud, U.S.A. 80 E5 40 5N 98 32W
Red Creek, U.S.A. 85 C8 43 14N 76 45W
Red Deer, Canada 70 C6 52 20N 113 50W
Red Deer →, Alta., Canada 71 C7 50 58N 110 0W
Red Deer →, Man., Canada 71 C8 52 53N 101 1W
Red Deer L., Canada 71 C8 52 55N 101 20W
Red Hook, U.S.A. 85 E11 41 55N 73 53W
Red Indian L., Canada 73 C8 48 35N 57 0W
Red L., Canada 71 C10 51 3N 93 49W
Red Lake, Canada 71 C10 51 3N 93 49W
Red Lake Falls, U.S.A. 80 B6 47 53N 96 16W
Red Lake Road, Canada 71 C10 49 59N 93 25W
Red Lodge, U.S.A. 76 D9 45 11N 109 15W
Red Mountain, U.S.A. 79 K9 35 37N 117 38W
Red Oak, U.S.A. 80 E7 41 1N 95 14W
Red Rock, Canada 72 C2 48 55N 88 15W
Red Rock, L., U.S.A. 80 E8 41 22N 92 59W
Red Rocks Pt., Australia 61 F4 32 13S 127 32 E
Red Sea, Asia 47 C2 25 0N 36 0 E
Red Slate Mt., U.S.A. 78 H8 37 31N 118 52W
Red Sucker L., Canada 72 B1 54 9N 93 40W
Red Tower Pass = Turnu Roşu, P., Romania 17 F13 45 33N 24 17 E
Red Wing, U.S.A. 80 C8 44 34N 92 31W
Redang, Malaysia 39 K4 5 49N 103 2 E
Redange, Lux. 15 E5 49 46N 5 52 E
Redcar, U.K. 12 C6 54 37N 1 4W
Redcar & Cleveland □, U.K. 12 C7 54 29N 1 0W
Redcliff, Canada 71 C6 50 10N 50 50W
Redcliffe, Australia 63 D5 27 12S 153 0 E
Redcliffe, Mt., Australia 61 E3 28 30S 121 30 E
Reddersburg, S. Africa 56 D4 29 41S 26 10 E
Redding, U.S.A. 76 F2 40 35N 122 24W
Redditch, U.K. 13 E6 52 18N 1 55W
Redfield, U.S.A. 80 C5 44 53N 98 31W
Redford, U.S.A. 85 B11 44 38N 73 48W
Redhead, Trin. & Tob. 93 K16 10 44N 60 58W
Redlands, U.S.A. 79 M9 34 4N 117 11W
Redmond, Oreg., U.S.A. 76 D3 44 17N 121 11W
Redmond, Wash., U.S.A. 78 C4 47 41N 122 7W
Redon, France 20 C2 47 40N 2 6W
Redonda, Antigua & B. 89 C7 16 58N 62 19W
Redondela, Spain 21 A1 42 15N 8 38W
Redondo Beach, U.S.A. 79 M8 33 50N 118 23W
Redruth, U.K. 13 G2 50 14N 5 14W
Redvers, Canada 71 D8 49 35N 101 40W
Redwater, Canada 70 C6 53 55N 113 6W
Redwood, U.S.A. 85 B9 44 18N 75 48W
Redwood △, U.S.A. 76 F1 41 40N 124 5W
Redwood City, U.S.A. 78 H4 37 30N 122 15W
Redwood Falls, U.S.A. 80 C7 44 32N 95 7W
Ree, L., Ireland 10 C3 53 35N 8 0W
Reed, L., Canada 71 C8 54 38N 100 30W
Reed City, U.S.A. 82 D3 43 53N 85 31W
Reedley, U.S.A. 78 J7 36 36N 119 27W
Reedsburg, U.S.A. 80 D9 43 32N 90 0W
Reedsport, U.S.A. 76 E1 43 42N 124 6W
Reedsville, U.S.A. 84 F7 40 39N 77 35W
Reefton, N.Z. 59 K3 42 6S 171 51 E
Reese →, U.S.A. 76 F5 40 48N 117 4W
Refugio, U.S.A. 81 L6 28 18N 97 17W
Regensburg, Germany 16 D7 49 1N 12 6 E
Reggâne = Zaouiet Reggâne, Algeria 50 C6 26 32N 0 3 E
Réggio di Calábria, Italy 22 E6 38 6N 15 39 E
Réggio nell'Emília, Italy 22 B4 44 43N 10 36 E
Reghin, Romania 17 E13 46 46N 24 42 E
Regina, Canada 71 C8 50 27N 104 35W
Regina Beach, Canada 71 C8 50 47N 105 0W
Registro, Brazil 95 A6 24 29S 47 49W
Rehar →, India 43 H10 23 55N 82 40 E
Rehli, India 43 H8 23 38N 79 5 E
Rehoboth, Namibia 56 C2 23 15S 17 4 E
Rehovot, Israel 46 D3 31 54N 34 48 E
Reichenbach, Germany 16 C7 50 37N 12 17 E
Reid, Australia 61 F4 30 49S 128 26 E
Reidsville, U.S.A. 83 G6 36 21N 79 40W
Reigate, U.K. 13 F7 51 14N 0 12W
Reims, France 20 B6 49 15N 4 1 E
Reina Adelaida, Arch., Chile 96 G2 52 20S 74 0W
Reina Sofia, Tenerife ✈ (TFS), Canary Is. 24 F3 28 3N 16 33W
Reindeer →, Canada 71 B8 55 36N 103 11W
Reindeer I., Canada 71 C9 52 30N 98 0W
Reindeer L., Canada 71 B8 57 15N 102 15W
Reinga, C., N.Z. 59 F4 34 35S 172 43 E
Reinosa, Spain 21 A3 43 2N 4 15W
Reitz, S. Africa 57 D4 27 48S 28 29 E
Reivilo, S. Africa 56 D3 27 36S 24 8 E
Reliance, Canada 71 A7 63 0N 109 20W
Remarkable, Mt., Australia 63 E2 32 48S 138 10 E
Rembang, Indonesia 37 G14 6 42S 111 21 E

Remedios, Panama 88 E3 8 15N 81 50W
Remeshk, Iran 45 E8 26 55N 58 50 E
Remich, Lux. 15 E6 49 32N 6 22 E
Remscheid, Germany 15 C7 51 11N 7 12 E
Ren Xian, China 34 F8 37 8N 114 40 E
Rendang, Indonesia 37 J18 8 26S 115 25 E
Rendsburg, Germany 16 A5 54 17N 9 39 E
Renfrew, Canada 85 A8 45 30N 76 40W
Renfrew □, U.K. 11 F4 55 49N 4 38W
Renfrewshire □, U.K. 11 F4 55 49N 4 38W
Rengat, Indonesia 36 E2 0 30S 102 45 E
Rengo, Chile 94 C1 34 24S 70 50W
Reni, Ukraine 17 F15 45 28N 28 15 E
Renmark, Australia 63 E3 34 11S 140 43 E
Rennell Sd., Canada 70 C2 53 23N 132 35W
Renner Springs, Australia 62 B1 18 20S 133 47 E
Rennes, France 20 B3 48 7N 1 41W
Rennie L., Canada 71 A7 61 32N 105 35W
Reno, U.S.A. 78 F7 39 31N 119 48W
Reno →, Italy 22 B5 44 38N 12 16 E
Renovo, U.S.A. 84 E7 41 20N 77 45W
Renqiu, China 34 E9 38 43N 116 5 E
Rensselaer, Ind., U.S.A. 82 E2 40 57N 87 9W
Rensselaer, N.Y., U.S.A. 85 D11 42 38N 73 45W
Rentería, Spain 21 A5 43 19N 1 54W
Renton, U.S.A. 78 C4 47 29N 122 12W
Reotipur, India 43 G10 25 33N 83 45 E
Republic, Mo., U.S.A. 81 G8 37 7N 93 29W
Republic, Wash., U.S.A. 76 B4 48 39N 118 44W
Republican →, U.S.A. 80 F6 39 4N 96 48W
Repulse B., Australia 62 J6 20 35S 148 46 E
Repulse Bay, Canada 69 B11 66 30N 86 30W
Requena, Peru 92 E4 5 5S 73 52W
Requena, Spain 21 C5 39 30N 1 4W
Reşadiye = Datça, Turkey 23 F12 36 46N 27 40 E
Reserve, U.S.A. 77 K9 33 43N 108 45W
Resht = Rasht, Iran 45 B6 37 20N 49 40 E
Resistencia, Argentina 94 B4 27 30S 59 0W
Reşiţa, Romania 17 F11 45 18N 21 53 E
Resolution I., Canada 69 B13 61 30N 65 0W
Resolution I., N.Z. 59 L1 45 40S 166 40 E
Ressano Garcia, Mozam. 57 D5 25 25S 32 0 E
Reston, Canada 71 D8 49 33N 101 6W
Retalhuleu, Guatemala 88 D1 14 33N 91 46W
Retenue, L. de, Dem. Rep. of the Congo 55 E2 11 0S 27 0 E
Retford, U.K. 12 D7 53 19N 0 56W
Réthímnon, Greece 25 D6 35 18N 24 30 E
Réthímnon □, Greece 25 D6 35 23N 24 28 E
Reti, Pakistan 42 E3 28 5N 69 48 E
Réunion ■, Ind. Oc. 49 J9 21 0S 56 0 E
Reus, Spain 21 B6 41 10N 1 5 E
Reutlingen, Germany 16 D5 48 29N 9 12 E
Reval = Tallinn, Estonia 9 G21 59 22N 24 48 E
Revda, Russia 18 C10 56 48N 59 57 E
Revelganj, India 43 G11 25 50N 84 40 E
Revelstoke, Canada 70 C5 51 0N 118 10W
Reventazón, Peru 92 E2 6 10S 80 58W
Revillagigedo, Is. de, Pac. Oc. 86 D2 18 40N 112 0W
Revúe →, Mozam. 55 F3 19 50S 34 0 E
Rewa, India 43 G9 24 33N 81 25 E
Rewari, India 42 E7 28 15N 76 40 E
Rexburg, U.S.A. 76 E8 43 49N 111 47W
Rey, Iran 45 C6 35 35N 51 25 E
Rey, I. del, Panama 88 E4 8 20N 78 30W
Rey Malabo, Eq. Guin. 52 D1 3 45N 8 50 E
Reyðarfjörður, Iceland 8 D6 65 2N 14 13W
Reyes, Pt., U.S.A. 78 H3 38 0N 123 0W
Reykjahlíð, Iceland 8 D5 65 40N 16 55W
Reykjanes, Iceland 8 E2 63 48N 22 40W
Reykjavík, Iceland 8 D3 64 10N 21 57W
Reynolds Ra., Australia 60 D5 22 30S 133 0 E
Reynoldsville, U.S.A. 84 E6 41 5N 78 58W
Reynosa, Mexico 87 B5 26 5N 98 18W
Rēzekne, Latvia 9 H22 56 30N 27 17 E
Rezvān, Iran 45 E8 27 34N 56 6 E
Rhayader, U.K. 13 E4 52 18N 3 29W
Rhein →, Europe 15 C6 51 52N 6 2 E
Rhein-Main-Donau-Kanal, Germany 16 D6 49 1N 11 27 E
Rheine, Germany 16 B4 52 17N 7 26 E
Rheinland-Pfalz □, Germany 16 C4 50 0N 7 0 E
Rhin = Rhein →, Europe 15 C6 51 52N 6 2 E
Rhine = Rhein →, Europe 15 C6 51 52N 6 2 E
Rhinebeck, U.S.A. 85 E11 41 56N 73 55W
Rhineland-Palatinate = Rheinland-Pfalz □, Germany 16 C4 50 0N 7 0 E
Rhinelander, U.S.A. 80 C10 45 38N 89 25W
Rhinns Pt., U.K. 11 F2 55 40N 6 29W
Rhino Camp, Uganda 54 B3 3 0N 31 22 E
Rhir, Cap, Morocco 50 B4 30 38N 9 54W
Rhode Island □, U.S.A. 85 E13 41 40N 71 30W
Rhodes = Ródhos, Greece 25 C10 36 15N 28 10 E
Rhodope Mts. = Rhodopi Planina, Bulgaria 23 D11 41 40N 24 20 E
Rhodopi Planina, Bulgaria 23 D11 41 40N 24 20 E
Rhön, Germany 16 C5 50 24N 9 58 E
Rhondda, U.K. 13 F4 51 39N 3 31W
Rhondda Cynon Taff □, U.K. 13 F4 51 42N 3 27W
Rhône □, France 20 E6 45 28N 4 42 E
Rhum, U.K. 11 E2 57 0N 6 20W
Rhyl, U.K. 12 D4 53 20N 3 29W
Riachão, Brazil 93 E9 7 20S 46 37W
Riasi, India 43 C6 33 10N 74 50 E
Riau □, Indonesia 36 D2 0 0 102 35 E
Riau, Kepulauan, Indonesia 36 D2 0 30N 104 20 E
Riau Arch. = Riau, Kepulauan, Indonesia 36 D2 0 30N 104 20 E
Ribadeo, Spain 21 A2 43 35N 7 5W
Ribas do Rio Pardo, Brazil 93 H8 20 27S 53 46W
Ribauè, Mozam. 55 E4 14 57S 38 17 E
Ribble →, U.K. 12 D5 53 52N 2 25W
Ribe, Denmark 9 J13 55 19N 8 44 E
Ribeira Brava, Madeira 24 D2 32 41N 17 4W
Ribeirão Prêto, Brazil 95 A6 21 10S 47 50W
Riberalta, Bolivia 92 F5 11 0S 66 0W
Riccarton, N.Z. 59 K4 43 32S 172 37 E
Rice, U.S.A. 79 L12 34 5N 114 51W
Rice L., U.S.A. 84 B6 44 12N 78 10W
Rice Lake, U.S.A. 80 C9 45 30N 91 44W
Rich, C., Canada 84 B4 44 43N 80 38W
Richards Bay, S. Africa 57 D5 28 48S 32 6 E
Richardson →, Canada 71 B6 58 25N 111 14W
Richardson Lakes, U.S.A. 82 C10 44 46N 70 58W
Richardson Springs, U.S.A. 78 F5 39 51N 121 46W
Riche, C., Australia 61 F2 34 36S 118 47 E
Richey, U.S.A. 80 B2 47 39N 105 4W
Richfield, U.S.A. 77 G8 38 46N 112 5W
Richfield Springs, U.S.A. 85 D10 42 51N 74 59W

Richford, U.S.A. 85 B12 45 0N 72 40W
Richibucto, Canada 73 C7 46 42N 64 54W
Richland, Ga., U.S.A. 83 J3 32 5N 84 40W
Richland, Wash., U.S.A. 76 C4 46 17N 119 18W
Richland Center, U.S.A. 80 D9 43 21N 90 23W
Richlands, U.S.A. 82 G5 37 6N 81 48W
Richmond, Australia 62 C3 20 43S 143 8 E
Richmond, N.Z. 59 J4 41 20S 173 12 E
Richmond, U.K. 12 C6 54 25N 1 43W
Richmond, Calif., U.S.A. 78 H4 37 56N 122 21W
Richmond, Ind., U.S.A. 82 F3 39 50N 84 53W
Richmond, Ky., U.S.A. 82 G3 37 45N 84 18W
Richmond, Mich., U.S.A. 84 D2 42 49N 82 45W
Richmond, Mo., U.S.A. 80 F8 39 17N 93 58W
Richmond, Tex., U.S.A. 81 L7 29 35N 95 46W
Richmond, Utah, U.S.A. 76 F8 41 56N 111 48W
Richmond, Va., U.S.A. 82 G7 37 33N 77 27W
Richmond, Vt., U.S.A. 85 B12 44 24N 72 59W
Richmond Hill, Canada 84 C5 43 52N 79 27W
Richmond Ra., Australia 63 D5 29 0S 152 45 E
Richtersveld △, S. Africa 56 D2 28 15S 17 10 E
Richwood, U.S.A. 82 F5 38 14N 80 32W
Ridder = Leninogorsk, Kazakhstan 28 D9 50 20N 83 30 E
Riddlesburg, U.S.A. 84 F6 40 9N 78 15W
Ridgecrest, U.S.A. 79 K9 35 38N 117 40W
Ridgefield, Conn., U.S.A. 85 E11 41 17N 73 30W
Ridgefield, Wash., U.S.A. 78 E4 45 49N 122 45W
Ridgeland, U.S.A. 83 J5 32 29N 80 59W
Ridgetown, Canada 84 D3 42 26N 81 52W
Ridgewood, U.S.A. 85 F10 40 59N 74 7W
Ridgway, U.S.A. 84 E6 41 25N 78 44W
Riding Mountain △, Canada 71 C9 50 50N 100 0W
Ridley, Mt., Australia 61 F3 33 12S 122 7 E
Riebeek-Oos, S. Africa 56 E4 33 10S 26 10 E
Ried, Austria 16 D7 48 14N 13 30 E
Riesa, Germany 16 C7 51 17N 13 17 E
Rietbron, S. Africa 56 E3 32 54S 23 10 E
Rietfontein, Namibia 56 C3 21 58S 20 58 E
Rieti, Italy 22 C5 42 24N 12 51 E
Rif = Er Rif, Morocco 50 A5 35 1N 4 1W
Riff L., U.S.A. 78 D4 46 32N 122 26W
Rift Valley, Africa 48 G7 7 0N 30 0 E
Rift Valley □, Kenya 54 B4 0 20N 36 0 E
Rīga, Latvia 9 H21 56 53N 24 8 E
Riga, G. of, Latvia 9 H20 57 40N 23 45 E
Rīgān, Iran 45 D8 28 37N 58 58 E
Rīgas Jūras Līcis = Riga, G. of, Latvia 9 H20 57 40N 23 45 E
Rigaud, Canada 85 A10 45 29N 74 18W
Rigby, U.S.A. 76 E8 43 40N 111 55W
Rīgestān, Afghan. 40 D4 30 15N 65 0 E
Riggins, U.S.A. 76 D5 45 25N 116 19W
Rigolet, Canada 73 B8 54 10N 58 23W
Rihand Dam, India 43 G10 24 9N 83 2 E
Riihimäki, Finland 9 F21 60 45N 24 48 E
Riiser-Larsen-halvøya, Antarctica 5 C4 68 0S 35 0 E
Rijeka, Croatia 16 F8 45 20N 14 21 E
Rijssen, Neths. 15 B6 52 19N 6 31 E
Rikuchū-Kaigan △, Japan 30 E11 39 20N 142 0 E
Rikuzentakada, Japan 30 E10 39 0N 141 40 E
Riley, U.S.A. 76 E4 43 32N 119 28W
Rimah, Wadi ar →, Si. Arabia 44 E4 26 5N 41 30 E
Rimau, Pulau, Malaysia 39 c 5 15N 100 16 E
Rimbey, Canada 70 C6 52 35N 114 15W
Rimersburg, U.S.A. 84 E5 41 3N 79 30W
Rímini, Italy 22 B5 44 3N 12 33 E
Rimouski, Canada 73 C6 48 27N 68 30W
Rimrock, U.S.A. 78 D5 46 38N 121 10W
Rinca, Indonesia 37 F5 8 45S 119 35 E
Rincón de Romos, Mexico 86 C4 22 14N 102 18W
Rinconada, Argentina 94 A2 22 26S 66 10W
Rind →, India 43 G9 25 53N 80 33 E
Ringas, India 42 F6 27 21N 75 34 E
Ringkøbing, Denmark 9 H13 56 5N 8 15 E
Ringvassøy, Norway 8 B18 69 56N 19 15 E
Ringwood, U.S.A. 85 E10 41 7N 74 15W
Rinjani, Indonesia 36 F5 8 24S 116 28 E
Rio Branco, Brazil 92 E5 9 58S 67 49W
Río Branco, Uruguay 95 C5 32 40S 53 40W
Río Bravo ↝, N. Amer. 86 B4 29 2N 102 45 E
Rio Bravo del Norte →, Mexico 87 B5 25 57N 97 9W
Rio Brilhante, Brazil 95 A5 21 48S 54 33W
Rio Claro, Brazil 95 A6 22 19S 47 35W
Rio Claro, Trin. & Tob. 89 D7 10 20N 61 25W
Rio Colorado, Argentina 96 D4 39 0S 64 0W
Rio Cuarto, Argentina 94 C3 33 10S 64 25W
Rio das Pedras, Mozam. 57 C6 23 8S 35 28 E
Rio de Janeiro, Brazil 95 A7 23 0S 43 12W
Rio de Janeiro □, Brazil 95 A7 22 50S 43 0W
Rio do Sul, Brazil 95 B6 27 13S 49 37W
Río Dulce △, Guatemala 88 C2 15 43N 88 50W
Río Gallegos, Argentina 96 G3 51 35S 69 15W
Río Grande, Argentina 96 G3 53 50S 67 45W
Río Grande, Brazil 95 C5 32 0S 52 20W
Río Grande, Mexico 86 C4 23 50N 103 2W
Río Grande, Nic. 88 D3 12 54N 83 33W
Río Grande, Puerto Rico 89 d 18 23N 65 50W
Rio Grande City, U.S.A. 81 M5 26 23N 98 49W
Río Grande de Santiago →, Mexico 86 C3 21 36N 105 26 E
Rio Grande do Norte □, Brazil 93 E11 5 40S 36 0W
Rio Grande do Sul □, Brazil 95 C5 30 0S 53 0W
Rio Hato, Panama 88 E3 8 22N 80 10W
Río Lagartos, Mexico 87 C7 21 36N 88 10W
Río Largo, Brazil 93 E11 9 28S 35 50W
Río Mulatos, Bolivia 92 G5 19 40S 66 50W
Río Muni □, Eq. Guin. 52 D2 1 30N 10 0 E
Rio Negro, Brazil 95 B6 26 0S 49 55W
Rio Pardo, Brazil 95 C5 30 0S 52 30W
Río Pilcomayo △, Argentina 94 B4 25 5S 58 5W
Río Platano △, Honduras 88 C3 15 45N 85 0W
Rio Rancho, U.S.A. 77 J10 35 14N 106 38W
Río Segundo, Argentina 94 C3 31 40S 63 59W
Río Tercero, Argentina 94 C3 32 15S 64 8W
Rio Verde, Brazil 93 G8 17 50S 51 0W
Río Verde, Mexico 87 C5 21 56N 99 59W
Rio Vista, U.S.A. 78 G5 38 10N 121 42W
Riobamba, Ecuador 92 D3 1 50S 78 45W
Ríohacha, Colombia 92 A4 11 33N 72 55W
Riosucio, Colombia 92 B3 7 27N 77 7W
Riou L., Canada 71 B7 59 7N 106 25W
Ripley, Canada 84 B3 44 4N 81 35W
Ripley, Calif., U.S.A. 79 M12 33 32N 114 39W
Ripley, N.Y., U.S.A. 84 D5 42 16N 79 43W

ipley, Tenn., U.S.A. 81 H10 35 45N 89 32W
ipley, W. Va., U.S.A. 82 F5 38 49N 81 43W
ipon, U.K. 12 C6 54 9N 1 31W
ipon, Calif., U.S.A. 78 H5 37 44N 121 7W
ipon, Wis., U.S.A. 82 D1 43 51N 88 50W
ishā', W. ar →, Si. Arabia ... 44 E5 25 33N 44 5 E
ishiri-Rebun-Sarobetsu △, Japan ... 30 B10 45 26N 141 30 E
ishiri-Tō, Japan ... 30 B10 45 11N 141 15 E
ishon le Ziyyon, Israel ... 46 D3 31 58N 34 48 E
ison, U.S.A. ... 81 J8 33 58N 92 11W
isør, Norway ... 9 G13 58 43N 9 13 E
ita Blanca Cr →, U.S.A. ... 81 H3 35 40N 102 29W
itter, Mt., U.S.A. ... 78 H7 37 41N 119 12W
ittman, U.S.A. ... 84 F3 40 58N 81 47W
iva del Garda, Italy ... 22 B4 45 53N 10 50 E
ivadavia, Buenos Aires, Argentina ... 94 D3 35 29S 62 59W
ivadavia, Mendoza, Argentina 94 C2 33 13S 68 30W
ivadavia, Salta, Argentina ... 94 A3 24 5S 62 54W
ivadavia, Chile ... 94 B1 29 57S 70 35W
ivas, Nic. ... 88 D2 11 30N 85 50W
iver Cess, Liberia ... 50 G4 5 30N 9 32W
iver Jordan, Canada ... 78 B2 48 26N 124 3W
ivera, Argentina ... 94 D3 37 12S 63 14W
ivera, Uruguay ... 95 C4 31 0S 55 50W
iverbank, U.S.A. ... 78 H6 37 44N 120 56W
iverdale, U.S.A. ... 78 J7 36 26N 119 52W
iverhead, U.S.A. ... 85 F12 40 55N 72 40W
iverhurst, Canada ... 71 C7 50 55N 106 50W
ivers, Canada ... 71 C8 50 2N 100 14W
ivers Inlet, Canada ... 70 C3 51 42N 127 15W
iversdale, S. Africa ... 56 E3 34 7S 21 15 E
iverside, U.S.A. ... 79 M9 33 59N 117 22W
iverton, Australia ... 63 E2 34 10S 138 46 E
iverton, N.Z. ... 59 M2 46 21S 168 0 E
iverton, U.S.A. ... 76 E9 43 2N 108 23W
iverton Heights, U.S.A. ... 78 C4 47 28N 122 17W
iviera, U.S.A. ... 79 K12 35 4N 114 35W
iviera di Levante, Italy ... 20 D8 44 15N 9 30 E
iviera di Ponente, Italy ... 20 D8 44 10N 8 20 E
ivière-au-Renard, Canada ... 73 C7 48 59N 64 23W
ivière-du-Loup, Canada ... 73 C6 47 50N 69 30W
ivière-Pentecôte, Canada ... 73 C6 49 57N 67 1W
ivière-Pilote, Martinique ... 88 c 14 26N 60 53W
ivière St-Paul, Canada ... 73 B8 51 28N 57 45W
ivière-Salée, Martinique ... 88 c 14 31N 61 0W
ivne, Ukraine ... 17 C14 50 40N 26 10 E
ivoli, Italy ... 20 D7 45 3N 7 31 E
ivoli B., Australia ... 63 F3 37 32S 140 3 E
iyadh = Ar Riyāḍ, Si. Arabia ... 44 E5 24 41N 46 42 E
ize, Turkey ... 19 F7 41 0N 40 30 E
izhao, China ... 35 G10 35 25N 119 30 E
izokarpaso, Cyprus ... 25 D13 35 36N 34 23 E
izzuto, C., Italy ... 22 E7 38 53N 17 5 E
iukan, Norway ... 9 G13 59 54N 8 33 E
oad Town, Br. Virgin Is. ... 89 e 18 27N 64 37W
oan Plateau, U.S.A. ... 76 G9 39 20N 109 20W
oanne, France ... 20 C6 46 3N 4 4 E
oanoke, Ala., U.S.A. ... 83 J3 33 9N 85 22W
oanoke, Va., U.S.A. ... 82 G6 37 16N 79 56W
oanoke →, U.S.A. ... 83 H7 35 57N 76 42W
oanoke I., U.S.A. ... 83 H8 35 55N 75 40W
oanoke Rapids, U.S.A. ... 83 G7 36 28N 77 40W
oatán, Honduras ... 88 C2 16 18N 86 35W
obāt Sang, Iran ... 45 C8 35 35N 59 10 E
obat, Iran ... 45 C6 35 35N 50 59 E
obāṭkarim □, Iran ... 45 B6 35 26N 50 59 E
obbins I., Australia ... 63 G4 40 42S 145 0 E
obe →, Australia ... 60 D2 21 42S 116 15 E
obert Lee, U.S.A. ... 81 K4 31 54N 100 29W
obertsdale, U.S.A. ... 84 F6 40 11N 78 6W
obertsganj, India ... 43 G10 24 44N 83 4 E
obertson, S. Africa ... 56 E2 33 46S 19 50 E
obertson I., Antarctica ... 5 C18 65 15S 59 30W
obertson Ra., Australia ... 60 D3 23 15S 121 0 E
obertstown, Australia ... 63 E2 33 58S 139 5 E
oberval, Canada ... 73 C5 48 32N 72 15W
obeson Chan., N. Amer. ... 4 A4 82 0N 61 30W
obesonia, U.S.A. ... 85 F8 40 21N 76 8W
obinson, U.S.A. ... 82 F2 39 0N 87 44W
obinson →, Australia ... 62 B2 16 3S 137 16 E
obinson Ra., Australia ... 61 E2 25 40S 119 0 E
obinvale, Australia ... 63 E3 34 40S 142 45 E
oblin, Canada ... 71 C8 51 14N 101 21W
oboré, Bolivia ... 92 G7 18 10S 59 45W
obson, Canada ... 70 D5 49 20N 117 41W
obson, Mt., Canada ... 70 C5 53 10N 119 10W
obstown, U.S.A. ... 81 M6 27 47N 97 40W
oca, C. da, Portugal ... 21 C1 38 40N 9 31W
oca Partida, I., Mexico ... 86 D2 19 1N 112 2W
ocas, I., Brazil ... 93 D12 4 0S 34 1W
ocha, Uruguay ... 95 C5 34 30S 54 25W
ochdale, U.K. ... 12 D5 53 38N 2 9W
ochefort, Belgium ... 15 D5 50 9N 5 12 E
ochefort, France ... 20 D3 45 56N 0 57W
ochelle, U.S.A. ... 80 E10 41 56N 89 4W
ocher River, Canada ... 70 A6 61 23N 112 44W
ochester, U.K. ... 13 F8 51 23N 0 31 E
ochester, Ind., U.S.A. ... 82 E2 41 4N 86 13W
ochester, Minn., U.S.A. ... 80 C8 44 1N 92 28W
ochester, N.H., U.S.A. ... 85 C14 43 18N 70 59W
ochester, N.Y., U.S.A. ... 84 C7 43 10N 77 37W
ock →, Canada ... 70 A3 60 7N 127 7W
ock Creek, U.S.A. ... 84 E4 41 40N 80 52W
ock Falls, U.S.A. ... 80 E10 41 47N 89 41W
ock Hill, U.S.A. ... 83 H5 34 56N 81 1W
ock Island, U.S.A. ... 80 E9 41 30N 90 34W
ock Rapids, U.S.A. ... 80 D6 43 26N 96 10W
ock Sound, Bahamas ... 88 B4 24 54N 76 12W
ock Springs, Mont., U.S.A. ... 76 C10 46 49N 106 15W
ock Springs, Wyo., U.S.A. ... 76 F9 41 35N 109 13W
ock Valley, U.S.A. ... 80 D6 43 12N 96 18W
ockall, Atl. Oc. ... 6 D3 57 37N 13 42W
ockdale, Tex., U.S.A. ... 81 K6 30 39N 97 0W
ockeby = Mungkan Kandju △, Australia ... 62 A3 13 35S 142 52 E
ockefeller Plateau, Antarctica 5 E14 80 0S 140 0W
ockglen, Canada ... 71 D7 49 11N 105 57W
ockhampton, Australia ... 62 C5 23 22S 150 32 E
ockingham, Australia ... 61 F2 32 15S 115 38 E
ockingham, U.S.A. ... 83 H6 34 57N 79 46W
ockingham B., Australia ... 62 B4 18 5S 146 10 E
ocklake, U.S.A. ... 80 A5 48 47N 99 15W

Rockland, Canada ... 85 A9 45 33N 75 17W
Rockland, Idaho, U.S.A. ... 76 E7 42 34N 112 53W
Rockland, Maine, U.S.A. ... 83 C11 44 6N 69 7W
Rockland, Mich., U.S.A. ... 80 B10 46 44N 89 11W
Rocklin, U.S.A. ... 78 G5 38 48N 121 14W
Rockmart, U.S.A. ... 83 H3 34 0N 85 3W
Rockport, Mass., U.S.A. ... 85 D14 42 39N 70 37W
Rockport, Mo., U.S.A. ... 80 E7 40 25N 95 31W
Rockport, Tex., U.S.A. ... 81 L6 28 2N 97 3W
Rocksprings, U.S.A. ... 81 K4 30 1N 100 13W
Rockville, Conn., U.S.A. ... 85 E12 41 52N 72 28W
Rockville, Md., U.S.A. ... 82 F7 39 5N 77 9W
Rockwall, U.S.A. ... 81 J6 32 56N 96 28W
Rockwell City, U.S.A. ... 80 D7 42 24N 94 38W
Rockwood, Canada ... 84 C4 43 37N 80 8W
Rockwood, Maine, U.S.A. ... 83 C11 45 41N 69 45W
Rockwood, Tenn., U.S.A. ... 83 H3 35 52N 84 41W
Rocky Ford, U.S.A. ... 80 F3 38 3N 103 43W
Rocky Gully, Australia ... 61 F2 34 30S 116 57 E
Rocky Island L., Canada ... 72 C3 46 55N 83 0W
Rocky Lane, Canada ... 70 B5 58 31N 116 22W
Rocky Mount, U.S.A. ... 83 H7 35 57N 77 48W
Rocky Mountain △, U.S.A. ... 76 F11 40 25N 105 45W
Rocky Mountain House, Canada 70 C6 52 22N 114 55W
Rocky Mts., N. Amer. ... 76 G10 49 0N 115 0W
Rocky Point, Namibia ... 56 B2 19 3S 12 30 E
Rod, Pakistan ... 40 E3 28 10N 63 5 E
Rødbyhavn, Denmark ... 9 J14 54 39N 11 22 E
Roddickton, Canada ... 73 B8 50 51N 56 8W
Rodez, France ... 20 D5 44 21N 2 33 E
Rodhopoú, Greece ... 25 D5 35 34N 23 45 E
Ródhos, Greece ... 25 C10 36 15N 28 10 E
Rodney, Canada ... 84 D3 42 34N 81 41W
Rodney, C., N.Z. ... 59 G5 36 17S 174 50 E
Rodriguez, Ind. Oc. ... 3 E13 19 45S 63 20 E
Roe →, U.K. ... 10 A5 55 6N 6 59W
Roebling, U.S.A. ... 85 F10 40 7N 74 47W
Roebourne, Australia ... 60 D2 20 44S 117 9 E
Roebuck B., Australia ... 60 C3 18 5S 122 20 E
Roermond, Neths. ... 15 C6 51 12N 6 0 E
Roes Welcome Sd., Canada ... 69 B11 65 0N 87 0W
Roeselare, Belgium ... 15 D3 50 57N 3 7 E
Rogachev = Ragachow, Belarus 17 B16 53 8N 30 5 E
Rogagua, L., Bolivia ... 92 F5 13 43S 66 50W
Rogatyn, Ukraine ... 17 D13 49 24N 24 36 E
Rogdhia, Greece ... 25 D7 35 22N 25 1 E
Rogers, U.S.A. ... 81 G7 36 20N 94 7W
Rogers City, U.S.A. ... 82 C4 45 25N 83 49W
Rogersville, Canada ... 73 C6 46 44N 65 26W
Roggan →, Canada ... 72 B4 54 24N 79 25W
Roggan L., Canada ... 72 B4 54 8N 77 50W
Roggeveldberge, S. Africa ... 56 E3 32 10S 20 10 E
Rogoaguado, L., Bolivia ... 92 F5 13 0S 65 30W
Rogojampi, Indonesia ... 37 J17 8 19S 114 17 E
Rogue →, U.S.A. ... 76 E1 42 26N 124 26W
Róhda, Greece ... 25 A3 39 48N 19 46 E
Rohnert Park, U.S.A. ... 78 G4 38 16N 122 40W
Rohri, Pakistan ... 42 F3 27 45N 68 51 E
Rohri Canal, Pakistan ... 42 F3 26 15N 68 27 E
Rohtak, India ... 42 E7 28 55N 76 43 E
Roi Et, Thailand ... 38 D4 16 4N 103 40 E
Roja, Latvia ... 9 H20 57 29N 22 43 E
Rojas, Argentina ... 94 C3 34 10S 60 45W
Rojo, C., Mexico ... 87 C5 21 33N 97 20W
Rokan →, Indonesia ... 36 D2 2 0N 100 50 E
Rokiškis, Lithuania ... 9 J21 55 55N 25 35 E
Rolândia, Brazil ... 95 A5 23 18S 51 23W
Rolla, U.S.A. ... 81 G9 37 57N 91 46W
Rolleston, Australia ... 62 C4 24 28S 148 35 E
Rollingstone, Australia ... 62 B4 19 2S 146 24 E
Roma, Australia ... 63 D4 26 32S 148 49 E
Roma, Italy ... 22 D5 41 54N 12 29 E
Roma, Sweden ... 9 H18 57 32N 18 26 E
Romain C., U.S.A. ... 83 J6 33 0N 79 22W
Romaine →, Canada ... 73 B7 50 13N 60 40W
Romaine →, Canada ... 73 B7 50 18N 63 47W
Roman, Romania ... 17 E14 46 57N 26 55 E
Romang, Indonesia ... 37 F7 7 30S 127 20 E
Români, Egypt ... 46 E1 30 59N 32 38 E
Romania ■, Europe ... 17 F12 46 0N 25 0 E
Romano, Cayo, Cuba ... 88 B4 22 0N 77 30W
Romans-sur-Isère, France ... 20 D6 45 3N 5 3 E
Romblon, Phil. ... 37 B6 12 33N 122 17 E
Rome = Roma, Italy ... 22 D5 41 54N 12 29 E
Rome, Ga., U.S.A. ... 83 H3 34 15N 85 10W
Rome, N.Y., U.S.A. ... 85 C9 43 13N 75 27W
Rome, Pa., U.S.A. ... 85 E8 41 51N 76 21W
Romney, U.S.A. ... 82 F6 39 21N 78 45W
Romney Marsh, U.K. ... 13 F8 51 2N 0 54 E
Rømø, Denmark ... 9 J13 55 10N 8 30 E
Romorantin-Lanthenay, France 20 C4 47 21N 1 45 E
Romsdalen, Norway ... 9 E12 62 25N 7 52 E
Romsey, U.K. ... 13 G6 51 0N 1 29W
Ron, Vietnam ... 38 D6 17 53N 106 27 E
Rona, U.K. ... 11 D3 57 34N 5 59W
Ronan, U.S.A. ... 76 C6 47 32N 114 6W
Roncador, Cayos, Colombia ... 88 D3 13 32N 80 4W
Roncador, Serra do, Brazil ... 93 F8 12 30S 52 30W
Ronda, Spain ... 21 D3 36 46N 5 12W
Rondane, Norway ... 9 F13 61 57N 9 50 E
Rondônia □, Brazil ... 92 F6 11 0S 63 0W
Rondonópolis, Brazil ... 93 G8 16 28S 54 38W
Rong, Koh, Cambodia ... 39 G4 10 45N 103 15 E
Ronge, L. la, Canada ... 71 B7 55 6N 105 17W
Rønne, Denmark ... 9 J16 55 6N 14 43 E
Ronne Ice Shelf, Antarctica ... 5 D18 78 0S 60 0W
Ronsard, C., Australia ... 61 D1 24 46S 113 10 E
Ronse, Belgium ... 15 D3 50 45N 3 35 E
Roodepoort, S. Africa ... 57 D4 26 11S 27 54 E
Roof Butte, U.S.A. ... 77 H9 36 28N 109 5W
Rooiboklaagte →, Namibia ... 56 C3 20 50S 21 0 E
Roorkee, India ... 42 E7 29 52N 77 59 E
Roosendaal, Neths. ... 15 C4 51 32N 4 29 E
Roosevelt, U.S.A. ... 76 F8 40 18N 109 59W
Roosevelt →, Brazil ... 92 E6 7 35S 60 20W
Roosevelt, Mt., Canada ... 70 B3 58 26N 125 20W
Roosevelt I., Antarctica ... 5 D12 79 30S 162 0W
Roper →, Australia ... 62 A2 14 43S 135 27 E
Roper Bar, Australia ... 62 A1 14 44S 134 44 E
Roque Pérez, Argentina ... 94 D4 35 25S 59 24W
Roquetas de Mar, Spain ... 21 D4 36 46N 2 36W
Roraima □, Brazil ... 92 C6 2 0N 61 30W
Roraima, Mt., Venezuela ... 92 B6 5 10N 60 40W
Røros, Norway ... 9 E14 62 35N 11 23 E
Rosa, Zambia ... 55 D3 9 33S 31 15 E

Rosa, L., Bahamas ... 89 B5 21 0N 73 30W
Rosa, Monte, Europe ... 20 D7 45 57N 7 53 E
Rosalia, U.S.A. ... 76 C5 47 14N 117 22W
Rosamond, U.S.A. ... 79 L8 34 52N 118 10W
Rosario, Argentina ... 94 C3 33 0S 60 40W
Rosário, Brazil ... 93 D10 3 0S 44 15W
Rosario, Baja Calif., Mexico ... 86 B1 30 0N 115 50W
Rosario, Sinaloa, Mexico ... 86 C3 23 0N 105 52W
Rosario, Paraguay ... 94 A4 24 30S 57 35W
Rosario de la Frontera, Argentina ... 94 B3 25 50S 65 0W
Rosario de Lerma, Argentina ... 94 A2 24 59S 65 35W
Rosario del Tala, Argentina ... 94 C4 32 20S 59 10W
Rosário do Sul, Brazil ... 95 C5 30 15S 54 55W
Rosarito, Mexico ... 79 N9 32 18N 117 4W
Roscoe, U.S.A. ... 85 E10 41 56N 74 55W
Roscommon, Ireland ... 10 C3 53 38N 8 11W
Roscommon □, Ireland ... 10 C3 53 49N 8 23W
Roscrea, Ireland ... 10 D4 52 57N 7 49W
Rose →, Australia ... 62 A2 14 16S 135 45 E
Rose Blanche-Harbour Le Cou, Canada ... 73 C8 47 38N 58 45W
Rose Pt., Canada ... 70 C2 54 11N 131 39W
Rose Valley, Canada ... 71 C8 52 19N 103 49W
Roseau, Domin. ... 89 C7 15 20N 61 24W
Roseau, U.S.A. ... 80 A7 48 51N 95 46W
Rosebery, Australia ... 63 G4 41 46S 145 33 E
Rosebud, S. Dak., U.S.A. ... 80 D4 43 14N 100 51W
Rosebud, Tex., U.S.A. ... 81 K6 31 4N 96 59W
Roseburg, U.S.A. ... 76 E2 43 13N 123 20W
Rosedale, U.S.A. ... 81 J9 33 51N 91 2W
Rosehearty, U.K. ... 11 D6 57 42N 2 7W
Roseland, U.S.A. ... 78 G4 38 25N 122 43W
Rosemary, Canada ... 70 C6 50 46N 112 5W
Rosenberg, U.S.A. ... 81 L7 29 34N 95 49W
Rosenheim, Germany ... 16 E7 47 51N 12 7 E
Roses, G. de, Spain ... 21 A7 42 10N 3 15 E
Rosetown, Canada ... 71 C7 51 35N 107 59W
Roseville, Calif., U.S.A. ... 78 G5 38 45N 121 17W
Roseville, Mich., U.S.A. ... 84 D2 42 30N 82 56W
Rosewood, Australia ... 63 D5 27 38S 152 36 E
Roshkhvār, Iran ... 45 C8 34 58N 59 37 E
Rosignano Maríttimo, Italy ... 22 C4 43 24N 10 28 E
Rosignol, Guyana ... 92 B7 6 15N 57 30W
Roşiori de Vede, Romania ... 17 F13 44 9N 25 0 E
Roskilde, Denmark ... 9 J15 55 38N 12 3 E
Roslavl, Russia ... 18 D5 53 57N 32 55 E
Rosmead, S. Africa ... 56 E4 31 29S 25 8 E
Ross, Australia ... 63 G4 42 2S 147 30 E
Ross, N.Z. ... 59 K3 42 53S 170 49 E
Ross Dependency, Antarctica ... 5 D11 77 30S 168 0 E
Ross I., Antarctica ... 5 D11 77 30S 168 0 E
Ross Ice Shelf, Antarctica ... 5 E12 80 0S 180 0 E
Ross L., U.S.A. ... 76 B3 48 44N 121 4W
Ross-on-Wye, U.K. ... 13 F5 51 54N 2 34W
Ross River, Australia ... 62 C1 23 44S 134 30 E
Ross River, Canada ... 70 A2 62 30N 131 30W
Ross Sea, Antarctica ... 5 D11 74 0S 178 0 E
Rossall Pt., U.K. ... 12 D4 53 55N 3 3W
Rossan Pt., Ireland ... 10 B3 54 42N 8 47W
Rossano, Italy ... 22 E7 39 36N 16 39 E
Rossburn, Canada ... 71 C8 50 40N 100 49W
Rosseau, Canada ... 84 A5 45 16N 79 39W
Rosseau, L., Canada ... 84 A5 45 10N 79 35W
Rosses, The, Ireland ... 10 A3 55 2N 8 20W
Rossignol, L., Canada ... 72 B5 52 43N 73 40W
Rossignol L., Canada ... 73 D6 44 12N 65 10W
Rossland, Canada ... 70 D5 49 6N 117 50W
Rosslare, Ireland ... 10 D5 52 17N 6 24W
Rosslare Harbour, Ireland ... 10 D5 52 15N 6 20W
Rosso, Mauritania ... 50 E2 16 40N 15 45W
Rossosh, Russia ... 19 D6 50 15N 39 28 E
Røssvatnet, Norway ... 8 D16 65 45N 14 5 E
Røst, Norway ... 8 C15 67 32N 12 0 E
Rosthern, Canada ... 71 C7 52 40N 106 20W
Rostock, Germany ... 16 A7 54 5N 12 8 E
Rostov, Don, Russia ... 19 E6 47 15N 39 45 E
Rostov, Yaroslavl, Russia ... 18 C6 57 14N 39 25 E
Roswell, Ga., U.S.A. ... 83 H3 34 2N 84 22W
Roswell, N. Mex., U.S.A. ... 81 J2 33 24N 104 32W
Rotan, U.S.A. ... 81 J4 32 51N 100 28W
Rother →, U.K. ... 13 G8 50 59N 0 45 E
Rothera, Antarctica ... 5 C17 67 20S 63 0W
Rotherham, U.K. ... 12 D6 53 26N 1 20W
Rothes, U.K. ... 11 D5 57 32N 3 13W
Rothesay, Canada ... 73 C6 45 23N 66 0W
Rothesay, U.K. ... 11 F3 55 50N 5 3W
Roti, Indonesia ... 37 F6 10 50S 123 0 E
Roto, Australia ... 63 E4 33 0S 145 30 E
Rotondo, Mte., France ... 20 E8 42 14N 9 8 E
Rotoroa, L., N.Z. ... 59 J4 41 55S 172 39 E
Rotorua, N.Z. ... 59 H6 38 9S 176 16 E
Rotorua, L., N.Z. ... 59 H6 38 5S 176 18 E
Rotterdam, Neths. ... 15 C4 51 55N 4 30 E
Rotterdam, U.S.A. ... 85 D10 42 48N 74 1W
Rottnest I., Australia ... 61 F2 32 0S 115 27 E
Rottumeroog, Neths. ... 15 A6 53 33N 6 34 E
Rottweil, Germany ... 16 D5 48 9N 8 37 E
Rotuma, Fiji ... 64 J9 12 25S 177 5 E
Roubaix, France ... 20 A5 50 40N 3 10 E
Rouen, France ... 20 B4 49 27N 1 4 E
Rouleau, Canada ... 71 C8 50 10N 104 56W
Round Mountain, U.S.A. ... 76 G5 38 43N 117 4W
Round Mt., Australia ... 63 E5 30 26S 152 16 E
Round Rock, U.S.A. ... 81 K6 30 31N 97 41W
Roundup, U.S.A. ... 76 C9 46 27N 108 33W
Rousay, U.K. ... 11 B5 59 10N 3 2W
Rouses Point, U.S.A. ... 85 B11 44 59N 73 22W
Rouseville, U.S.A. ... 84 E5 41 28N 79 42W
Roussillon, France ... 20 E4 42 30N 2 35 E
Rouxville, S. Africa ... 56 E4 30 25S 26 50 E
Rouyn-Noranda, Canada ... 72 C4 48 20N 79 0W
Rovaniemi, Finland ... 8 C21 66 29N 25 41 E
Rovereto, Italy ... 22 B4 45 53N 11 3 E
Rovigo, Italy ... 22 B4 45 4N 11 47 E
Rovinj, Croatia ... 16 F7 45 5N 13 40 E
Rovno = Rivne, Ukraine ... 17 C14 50 40N 26 10 E
Rovuma = Ruvuma →, Tanzania 55 E5 10 29S 40 28 E
Row'ān, Iran ... 45 C6 35 8N 48 51 E
Rowena, Australia ... 63 D4 29 48S 148 55 E
Rowley Shoals, Australia ... 60 C2 17 30S 119 0 E
Roxas, Phil. ... 37 B6 11 36N 122 49 E
Roxboro, U.S.A. ... 83 G6 36 24N 78 59W
Roxborough, Trin. & Tob. ... 93 J16 11 15N 60 35W
Roxburgh, N.Z. ... 59 L2 45 33S 169 19 E
Roy, Mont., U.S.A. ... 76 C9 47 20N 108 58W
Roy, N. Mex., U.S.A. ... 81 H2 35 57N 104 12W
Roy, Utah, U.S.A. ... 76 F7 41 10N 112 2W

Royal Canal, Ireland ... 10 C4 53 30N 7 13W
Royal Leamington Spa, U.K. ... 13 E6 52 18N 1 31W
Royal Natal △, S. Africa ... 57 D4 28 43S 28 51 E
Royal Tunbridge Wells, U.K. ... 13 F8 51 7N 0 16 E
Royale, Isle, U.S.A. ... 80 B10 48 0N 88 54W
Royan, France ... 20 D3 45 37N 1 2W
Royston, U.K. ... 13 E7 52 3N 0 0W
Rozdilna, Ukraine ... 17 E16 46 50N 30 2 E
Rozhyshche, Ukraine ... 17 C13 50 54N 25 15 E
Rtishchevo, Russia ... 18 D7 52 18N 43 46 E
Ruacaná, Namibia ... 56 B1 17 27S 14 21 E
Ruahine Ra., N.Z. ... 59 H6 39 55S 176 2 E
Ruapehu, N.Z. ... 59 H5 39 17S 175 35 E
Ruapuke I., N.Z. ... 59 M2 46 46S 168 31 E
Ruāq, W. →, Egypt ... 46 F2 30 0N 33 49 E
Rub' al Khālī, Si. Arabia ... 47 D4 19 0N 48 0 E
Rubeho Mts., Tanzania ... 54 D4 6 50S 36 25 E
Rubh a' Mhail, U.K. ... 11 F2 55 56N 6 8W
Rubha Hunish, U.K. ... 11 D2 57 42N 6 20W
Rubha Robhanais = Lewis, Butt of, U.K. ... 11 C2 58 31N 6 16W
Rubicon →, U.S.A. ... 78 G5 38 53N 121 4W
Rubio, Venezuela ... 92 B4 7 43N 72 22W
Rubondo △, Tanzania ... 54 C3 2 18S 31 58 E
Rubtsovsk, Russia ... 28 D9 51 30N 81 10 E
Ruby, U.S.A. ... 76 F6 40 30N 115 20W
Ruby Mts., U.S.A. ... 76 F6 40 30N 115 20W
Rubyvale, Australia ... 62 C4 23 25S 147 42 E
Rūd Sar, Iran ... 45 B6 37 8N 50 18 E
Rudall, Australia ... 63 E2 33 43S 136 17 E
Rudall →, Australia ... 60 D3 22 34S 122 13 E
Rudall River △, Australia ... 60 D3 22 38S 122 30 E
Rudewa, Tanzania ... 55 E3 10 7S 34 40 E
Rudnyy, Kazakhstan ... 28 D7 52 57N 63 7 E
Rudolfa, Ostrov, Russia ... 28 A6 81 45N 58 30 E
Rudyard, U.S.A. ... 82 B3 46 14N 84 36W
Ruenya →, Africa ... 55 F3 16 24S 33 48 E
Rufiji □, Tanzania ... 54 D4 7 50S 39 15 E
Rufino, Argentina ... 94 C3 34 20S 62 50W
Rufling Pt., Br. Virgin Is. ... 89 e 18 44N 64 27W
Rufunsa, Zambia ... 55 F2 15 4S 29 34 E
Rugby, U.K. ... 13 E6 52 23N 1 16W
Rugby, U.S.A. ... 80 A5 48 22N 100 0W
Rügen, Germany ... 16 A7 54 22N 13 24 E
Ruhengeri, Rwanda ... 54 C2 1 30S 29 36 E
Ruhnu, Estonia ... 9 H20 57 48N 23 15 E
Ruhr →, Germany ... 16 C4 51 27N 6 43 E
Ruhuhu →, Tanzania ... 55 E3 10 31S 34 34 E
Ruidoso, U.S.A. ... 77 K11 33 20N 105 41W
Ruivo, Pico, Madeira ... 24 D3 32 45N 16 56W
Rujm Tal'at al Jamā'ah, Jordan 46 E4 30 24N 35 30 E
Ruk, Pakistan ... 42 F3 27 50N 68 42 E
Rukhla, Pakistan ... 42 C4 32 27N 71 57 E
Ruki →, Dem. Rep. of the Congo 52 E3 0 5N 18 17 E
Rukwa □, Tanzania ... 54 D3 7 0S 31 30 E
Rukwa, L., Tanzania ... 54 D3 8 0S 32 20 E
Rulhieres, C., Australia ... 60 B4 13 56S 127 22 E
Rum = Rhum, U.K. ... 11 E2 57 0N 6 20W
Rum, Jordan ... 46 F4 29 39N 35 26 E
Rum Cay, Bahamas ... 89 B5 23 40N 74 58W
Rum Jungle, Australia ... 60 B5 13 0S 130 59 E
Ruma □, Kenya ... 54 C3 0 39S 34 18 E
Rumāḥ, Si. Arabia ... 44 E5 25 29N 47 10 E
Rumania = Romania ■, Europe 17 F12 46 0N 25 0 E
Rumaylah, Iraq ... 44 D5 30 47N 47 37 E
Rumbêk, Sudan ... 51 G11 6 54N 29 37 E
Rumford, U.S.A. ... 83 C10 44 33N 70 33W
Rumia, Poland ... 17 A10 54 37N 18 25 E
Rumoi, Japan ... 30 C10 43 56N 141 39 E
Rumonge, Burundi ... 54 C2 3 59S 29 26 E
Rumson, U.S.A. ... 85 F11 40 23N 74 0W
Rumuruti, Kenya ... 54 B4 0 17N 36 32 E
Runan, China ... 34 H8 33 0N 114 30 E
Runanga, N.Z. ... 59 K3 42 25S 171 15 E
Runaway, C., N.Z. ... 59 G6 37 32S 177 59 E
Runaway Bay, Jamaica ... 88 a 18 27N 77 20W
Runcorn, U.K. ... 12 D5 53 21N 2 44W
Rundu, Namibia ... 56 B2 17 52S 19 43 E
Rungwa, Tanzania ... 54 D3 6 55S 33 32 E
Rungwa →, Tanzania ... 54 D3 7 36S 31 50 E
Rungwa □, Tanzania ... 54 D3 7 35S 33 32 E
Rungwe, Mt., Tanzania ... 55 D3 9 8S 33 40 E
Runton Ra., Australia ... 60 D3 23 31S 123 6 E
Ruoqiang, China ... 32 C3 38 55N 88 10 E
Rupa, India ... 41 F18 27 15N 92 21 E
Rupar, India ... 42 D7 30 58N 76 38 E
Rupat, Indonesia ... 36 D2 1 45N 101 40 E
Rupen →, India ... 42 H4 23 28N 71 31 E
Rupert, U.S.A. ... 76 E7 42 37N 113 41W
Rupert →, Canada ... 72 B4 51 29N 78 45W
Rupert B., Canada ... 72 B4 51 35N 79 0W
Rupert House = Waskaganish, Canada ... 72 B4 51 30N 78 40W
Rupsa, India ... 43 J12 21 37N 87 1 E
Rurrenabaque, Bolivia ... 92 F5 14 30S 67 32W
Rusambo, Zimbabwe ... 55 F3 16 30S 32 4 E
Rusape, Zimbabwe ... 55 F3 18 35S 32 8 E
Ruschuk = Ruse, Bulgaria ... 23 C12 43 48N 25 59 E
Ruse, Bulgaria ... 23 C12 43 48N 25 59 E
Rush, Ireland ... 10 C5 53 31N 6 6W
Rushan, China ... 35 F11 36 56N 121 30 E
Rushden, U.K. ... 13 E7 52 18N 0 35W
Rushmore, Mt., U.S.A. ... 80 D3 43 53N 103 28W
Rushville, Ill., U.S.A. ... 80 E9 40 7N 90 34W
Rushville, Ind., U.S.A. ... 82 F3 39 37N 85 27W
Rushville, Nebr., U.S.A. ... 80 D3 42 43N 102 28W
Russas, Brazil ... 93 D11 4 55S 37 50W
Russell, Canada ... 71 C8 50 50N 101 20W
Russell, Kans., U.S.A. ... 80 F5 38 54N 98 52W
Russell, N.Y., U.S.A. ... 85 B9 44 27N 75 9W
Russell, Pa., U.S.A. ... 84 E5 41 56N 79 8W
Russell Cave △, U.S.A. ... 83 H3 34 59N 85 49W
Russell L., Man., Canada ... 71 B8 56 15N 101 30W
Russell L., N.W.T., Canada ... 70 A5 63 5N 115 44W
Russellkonda, India ... 41 K14 19 57N 84 42 E
Russellville, Ala., U.S.A. ... 83 H2 34 30N 87 44W
Russellville, Ark., U.S.A. ... 81 H8 35 17N 93 8W
Russellville, Ky., U.S.A. ... 83 G2 36 51N 86 53W
Russia ■, Eurasia ... 29 C11 62 0N 105 0 E
Russian →, U.S.A. ... 78 G3 38 27N 123 8W
Russkoye Ustie, Russia ... 4 B15 71 0N 149 0 E
Rustam, Pakistan ... 42 B5 34 25N 72 13 E
Rustam Shahr, Pakistan ... 42 F2 26 58N 66 6 E
Rustavi, Georgia ... 19 F8 41 30N 45 0 E
Rustenburg, S. Africa ... 56 D4 25 41S 27 14 E
Ruston, U.S.A. ... 81 J8 32 32N 92 38W

Rutana, Burundi .... 54 C3   3 55S 30 0 E
Ruteng, Indonesia .... 37 F6   8 35S 120 30 E
Ruth, U.S.A. 84 C2 43 42N 82 45W
Rutherford, U.S.A. 78 G4 38 26N 122 24W
Rutland, U.S.A. 85 C12 43 37N 72 58W
Rutland □, U.K. 13 E7 52 38N   0 40W
Rutland Water, U.K. 13 E7 52 39N   0 38W
Rutledge →, Canada 71 A6 61 4N 112 0W
Rutledge L., Canada 71 A6 61 33N 110 47W
Rutshuru, Dem. Rep. of
  the Congo .... 54 C2   1 13S 29 25 E
Ruvu, Tanzania .... 54 D4   6 49S 38 43 E
Ruvu →, Tanzania .... 54 D4   6 23S 38 52 E
Ruvuma □, Burundi .... 54 C2   3 3S 29 33 E
Ruvuma □, Tanzania .... 55 E4 10 20S 36 0 E
Ruvuma →, Tanzania .... 55 E4 10 29S 40 28 E
Ruwais, U.A.E. .... 45 E7 24 5N 52 50 E
Ruwenzori, Africa .... 54 B2   0 30N 29 55 E
Ruwenzori △, Uganda ...... 54 B2   0 20S 30 0 E
Ruya →, Zimbabwe .... 57 B5 16 27S 32 5 E
Ruyigi, Burundi .... 54 C3   3 29S 30 15 E
Ružomberok, Slovak Rep. .. 17 D10 49 3N 19 17 E
Rwanda ■, Africa .... 54 C3   2 0S 30 0 E
Ryan, L., U.K. 11 G3 55 0N   5 2W
Ryazan, Russia .... 18 D6 54 40N 39 40 E
Ryazhsk, Russia .... 18 D7 53 45N 40 3 E
Rybache = Rybachye, Kazakhstan 28 E9 46 40N 81 20 E
Rybachiy Poluostrov, Russia 18 A5 69 43N 32 0 E
Rybachye, Kazakhstan ..... 28 E9 46 40N 81 20 E
Rybinsk, Russia .... 18 C6 58 5N 38 50 E
Rybinskoye Vdkhr., Russia . 18 C6 58 30N 38 25 E
Rybnitsa = Râbniţa, Moldova 17 E15 47 45N 29 0 E
Rycroft, Canada 70 B5 55 45N 118 40W
Ryde, U.K. 13 G6 50 43N   1 9W
Ryderwood, U.S.A. 78 D3 46 23N 123 3W
Rye, U.K. .... 13 G8 50 57N   0 45 E
Rye →, U.K. 12 C7 54 11N   0 44W
Rye Bay, U.K. .... 13 G8 50 52N   0 49 E
Rye Patch Reservoir, U.S.A. 76 F4 40 28N 118 19W
Ryegate, U.S.A. 76 C9 46 18N 109 15W
Ryley, Canada 70 C6 53 17N 112 26W
Rylstone, Australia ...... 63 E4 32 46S 149 58 E
Ryōtsu, Japan .... 30 E9 38 5N 138 26 E
Rypin, Poland .... 17 B10 53 3N 19 25 E
Ryūgasaki, Japan .... 31 G10 35 54N 140 11 E
Ryūkyū Is. = Ryūkyū-rettō, Japan 31 M3 26 0N 126 0 E
Ryūkyū-rettō, Japan ...... 31 M3 26 0N 126 0 E
Rzeszów, Poland .... 17 C11 50 5N 21 58 E
Rzhev, Russia .... 18 C5 56 20N 34 20 E

S

Sa, Thailand .... 38 C3 18 34N 100 45 E
Sa Canal, Spain .... 24 C7 38 51N   1 23 E
Sa Conillera, Spain ...... 24 C7 38 59N   1 13 E
Sa Dec, Vietnam .... 39 G5 10 20N 105 46 E
Sa Dragonera, Spain ...... 24 B9 39 35N   2 19 E
Sa Mesquida, Spain .... 24 B11 39 55N   4 16 E
Sa Savina, Spain .... 24 C7 38 44N   1 25 E
Sa'ādatābād, Fārs, Iran .. 45 D7 30 10N 53 5 E
Sa'ādatābād, Hormozgān, Iran 45 D7 28 3N 55 53 E
Sa'ādatābād, Kermān, Iran . 45 D7 29 40N 55 51 E
Saale →, Germany .... 16 C6 51 56N 11 54 E
Saalfeld, Germany .... 16 C6 50 38N 11 21 E
Saanich, Canada 78 B3 48 29N 123 26W
Saar →, Europe .... 15 E6 49 41N   6 32 E
Saarbrücken, Germany ..... 16 D4 49 14N   6 59 E
Saaremaa, Estonia .... 9 G20 58 30N 22 30 E
Saarijärvi, Finland ...... 9 E21 62 43N 25 16 E
Saariselkä, Finland ...... 8 B23 68 16N 28 15 E
Sab 'Ābar, Syria .... 44 C3 33 46N 37 41 E
Saba, W. Indies 89 C7 17 42N 63 26W
Šabac, Serbia & M. .... 23 B8 44 48N 19 42 E
Sabadell, Spain .... 21 B7 41 28N   2 7 E
Sabah □, Malaysia .... 36 C5   6 0N 117 0 E
Sabak Bernam, Malaysia ... 39 L3   3 46N 100 58 E
Sabalān, Kūhhā-ye, Iran .. 44 B5 38 15N 47 45 E
Sabalana, Kepulauan, Indonesia 37 F5 6 45S 118 50 E
Sábana de la Mar, Dom. Rep. 89 C6 19 7N 69 24W
Sábanalarga, Colombia 92 A4 10 38N 74 55W
Sabang, Indonesia .... 36 C1   5 50N 95 15 E
Sabará, Brazil 93 G10 19 55S 43 46W
Sabarmati →, India .... 42 H5 22 18N 72 22 E
Sabattis, U.S.A. 85 B10 44 6N 74 40W
Saberania, Indonesia ..... 37 E9   2 5S 138 18 E
Sabhah, Libya .... 51 C8 27 9N 14 29 E
Sabi →, India .... 42 E7 28 29N 76 44 E
Sabie, S. Africa .... 57 D5 25 10S 30 48 E
Sabinal, Mexico 86 A3 30 58N 107 25W
Sabinal, U.S.A. 81 L5 29 19N 99 28W
Sabinas, Mexico 86 B4 27 50N 101 10W
Sabinas →, Mexico 86 B4 27 37N 100 42W
Sabinas Hidalgo, Mexico .. 86 B4 26 33N 100 10W
Sabine →, U.S.A. 81 L8 29 59N 93 47W
Sabine L., U.S.A. 81 L8 29 53N 93 51W
Sabine Pass, U.S.A. 81 L8 29 44N 93 54W
Sabinsville, U.S.A. 84 E7 41 52N 77 31W
Sablayan, Phil. .... 37 B6 12 50N 120 50 E
Sable, Canada 73 A6 55 30N 68 21W
Sable, C., Canada 73 D6 43 29N 65 38W
Sable, C., U.S.A. 75 E10 25 9N 81 8W
Sable I., Canada 73 D8 44 0N 60 0W
Sabrina Coast, Antarctica . 5 C9 68 0S 120 0 E
Sabulubbek, Indonesia .... 36 E1   1 36S 98 40 E
Sabzevār, Iran .... 45 B8 36 15N 57 40 E
Sabzvārān, Iran .... 45 D8 28 45N 57 50 E
Sac City, U.S.A. 80 D7 42 25N 95 0W
Săcele, Romania .... 17 F13 45 37N 25 41 E
Sachigo →, Canada 72 A2 55 6N 88 58W
Sachigo, L., Canada 72 B1 53 50N 92 12W
Sachsen □, Germany .... 16 C7 50 55N 13 10 E
Sachsen-Anhalt □, Germany . 16 C7 52 0N 12 0 E
Sackets Harbor, U.S.A. ... 85 C8 43 57N 76 7W
Sackville, Canada 73 C7 45 54N 64 22W
Saco, Maine, U.S.A. 83 D10 43 30N 70 27W
Saco, Mont., U.S.A. 76 B10 48 28N 107 21W
Sacramento, U.S.A. 78 G5 38 35N 121 29W
Sacramento →, U.S.A. 78 G5 38 3N 121 56W
Sacramento Mts., U.S.A. .. 77 K11 32 30N 105 30W
Sacramento Valley, U.S.A. . 78 G5 39 30N 122 0W
Sada-Misaki, Japan .... 31 H6 33 20N 132 1 E
Sadabad, India .... 42 F8 27 27N 78 3 E
Sadani, Tanzania .... 54 D4   5 58S 38 35 E
Sadao, Thailand .... 39 J3   6 38N 100 26 E
Sadd el Aali, Egypt ...... 51 D12 23 54N 32 54 E

Saddle Mt., U.S.A. 78 E3 45 58N 123 41W
Sadimi, Dem. Rep. of the Congo 55 D1 9 25S 23 32 E
Sado, Japan .... 30 F9 38 0N 138 25 E
Sadon, Burma .... 41 G20 25 28N 97 55 E
Sadra, India .... 42 H5 23 21N 72 43 E
Sadri, India .... 42 G5 25 11N 73 26 E
Sæby, Denmark .... 9 H14 57 21N 10 30 E
Saegertown, U.S.A. 84 E4 41 43N 80 9W
Şafājah, Si. Arabia ...... 44 E3 26 25N 39 0 E
Säffle, Sweden .... 9 G15 59 8N 12 55 E
Safford, U.S.A. 77 K9 32 50N 109 43W
Saffron Walden, U.K. ..... 13 E8 52 1N   0 16 E
Safi, Morocco 50 B4 32 18N   9 20W
Şafiābād, Iran .... 45 B8 36 45N 57 58 E
Safid Dasht, Iran .... 45 C6 33 27N 48 11 E
Safid Kūh, Afghan. .... 40 B3 34 45N 63 0 E
Safid Rūd →, Iran .... 45 B6 37 23N 50 11 E
Safipur, India .... 43 F9 26 44N 80 21 E
Şafwān, Iraq .... 44 D5 30 7N 47 43 E
Sag Harbor, U.S.A. 85 F12 41 0N 72 18W
Saga, Japan .... 31 H5 33 15N 130 16 E
Saga □, Japan .... 31 H5 33 15N 130 20 E
Sagae, Japan .... 30 E10 38 22N 140 17 E
Sagamartha = Everest, Mt.,
  Nepal .... 43 E12 28 5N 86 58 E
Sagamore, U.S.A. 84 F5 40 46N 79 14W
Sagar, Karnataka, India .. 40 M9 14 14N 75 6 E
Sagar, Mad. P., India .... 43 H8 23 50N 78 44 E
Sagara, L., Tanzania ..... 54 D3   5 20S 31 0 E
Saginaw, U.S.A. 82 D4 43 26N 83 56W
Saginaw →, U.S.A. 82 D4 43 39N 83 51W
Saginaw B., U.S.A. 82 D4 43 50N 83 40W
Saglouc = Salluit, Canada . 69 B12 62 14N 75 38W
Sagō-ri, S. Korea .... 35 G14 35 25N 126 49 E
Sagua la Grande, Cuba 88 B3 22 50N 80 10W
Saguache, U.S.A. 77 G10 38 5N 106 8W
Saguaro △, U.S.A. 77 K8 32 12N 110 38W
Saguenay →, Canada 73 C5 48 22N 71 0W
Sagunt = Sagunto, Spain .. 21 C5 39 42N   0 18W
Sagunto, Spain 21 C5 39 42N   0 18W
Sagwara, India .... 42 H6 23 41N 74 1 E
Sahagún, Spain 21 A3 42 18N   5 2W
Saham al Jawlān, Syria ... 46 C4 32 45N 35 55 E
Sahamandrevo, Madag. ..... 57 C8 23 15S 45 35 E
Sahand, Kūh-e, Iran ...... 44 B5 37 44N 46 27 E
Sahara, Africa .... 50 D6 23 0N   5 0 E
Saharan Atlas = Saharien, Atlas,
  Algeria .... 50 B6 33 30N   1 0 E
Saharanpur, India .... 42 E7 29 58N 77 33 E
Saharien, Atlas, Algeria . 50 B6 33 30N   1 0 E
Saharsa, India .... 43 G12 25 53N 86 36 E
Sahaswan, India .... 43 E8 28 5N 78 45 E
Sahibganj, India .... 43 G12 25 12N 87 40 E
Sāḥilīyah, Iraq .... 44 C4 33 43N 42 42 E
Sahiwal, Pakistan .... 42 D5 30 45N 73 8 E
Sahrawi, Iran .... 44 C5 34 29N 47 41 E
Sahraoui = Western Sahara ■,
  Africa 50 D3 25 0N 13 0W
Sahuaripa, Mexico 86 B3 29 0N 109 13W
Sahuarita, U.S.A. 77 L8 31 57N 110 58W
Sahuayo, Mexico 86 C4 20 4N 102 43W
Sai →, India .... 43 G10 25 39N 82 47 E
Sai Buri, Thailand .... 39 J3   6 43N 101 45 E
Sai Kung, China .... 33 G11 22 23N 114 16 E
Sa'id Bundas, Sudan ...... 51 G10 8 24N 24 48 E
Sa'īdābād = Sīrjān, Iran . 45 D7 29 30N 55 45 E
Sa'īdābād, Iran .... 45 B7 36 8N 54 11 E
Sa'īdīyeh, Iran .... 45 B6 36 20N 48 55 E
Saidpur, Bangla. .... 41 G16 25 48N 89 0 E
Saidpur, India .... 43 G10 25 33N 83 11 E
Saidu, Pakistan .... 43 B5 34 43N 72 24 E
Saigon = Thanh Pho Ho Chi
  Minh, Vietnam .... 39 G6 10 58N 106 40 E
Saijō, Japan .... 31 H6 33 55N 133 11 E
Saikai △, Japan .... 31 H4 33 12N 129 36 E
Saikanosy Masoala, Madag. . 57 B9 15 45S 50 10 E
Saikhoa Ghat, India ...... 41 F19 27 50N 95 40 E
Saiki, Japan .... 31 H5 32 58N 131 51 E
Sailana, India .... 42 H6 23 28N 74 55 E
Sailolof, Indonesia ...... 37 E8   1 15S 130 46 E
Saimaa, Finland .... 9 F23 61 15N 28 15 E
Şa'in Dezh, Iran .... 44 B5 36 40N 46 25 E
St. Abb's Head, U.K. 11 F6 55 55N   2 8W
St. Alban's, Canada 73 C8 47 51N 55 50W
St. Albans, U.K. 13 F7 51 45N   0 19W
St. Albans, Vt., U.S.A. .. 85 B11 44 49N 73 5W
St. Albans, W. Va., U.S.A. 82 F5 38 23N 81 50W
St. Alban's Head, U.K. ... 13 G5 50 34N   2 4W
St. Albert, Canada 70 C6 53 37N 113 32W
St. Andrew's, Canada 73 C8 47 45N 59 15W
St. Andrews, U.K. 11 E6 56 20N   2 47W
St-Anicet, Canada 85 A10 45 8N 74 22W
St. Ann B., Canada 73 C7 46 22N 60 25W
St. Ann's Bay, Jamaica ... 88 a 18 26N 77 15W
St. Anthony, Canada 73 B8 51 22N 55 35W
St. Anthony, U.S.A. 76 E8 43 58N 111 41W
St-Antoine, Canada 73 C7 46 22N 64 45W
St. Arnaud, Australia .... 63 F3 36 40S 143 16 E
St-Augustin, Canada 73 B8 51 13N 58 38W
St-Augustin →, Canada 73 B8 51 16N 58 40W
St. Augustine, U.S.A. 83 L5 29 54N 81 19W
St. Austell, U.K. 13 G3 50 20N   4 47W
St. Barbe, Canada 73 B8 51 12N 56 46W
St-Barthélemy, W. Indies . 89 C7 17 50N 62 50W
St. Bees Hd., U.K. 12 C4 54 31N   3 38W
St. Bees I., Australia ... 62 J7 20 56S 149 26 E
St. Bride's, Canada 73 C9 46 56N 54 10W
St. Brides B., U.K. 13 F2 51 49N   5 9W
St-Brieuc, France 20 B2 48 30N   2 46W
St. Catharines, Canada ... 84 C5 43 10N 79 15W
St. Catherines I., U.S.A. . 83 K5 31 40N 81 10W
St. Catherine's Pt., U.K. . 13 G6 50 34N   1 18W
St-Chamond, France .... 20 D6 45 28N   4 31 E
St. Charles, Ill., U.S.A. . 82 E1 41 54N 88 19W
St. Charles, Mo., U.S.A. .. 80 F9 38 47N 90 29W
St. Charles, Va., U.S.A. .. 82 F7 36 48N 83 4W
St. Christopher-Nevis = St. Kitts
  & Nevis ■, W. Indies 89 C7 17 20N 62 40W
St. Clair, Mich., U.S.A. .. 84 D2 42 50N 82 30W
St. Clair, Pa., U.S.A. ... 85 F8 40 43N 76 12W
St. Clair →, U.S.A. 84 D2 42 38N 82 31W
St. Clair, L., Canada 72 E3 42 30N 82 45W
St. Clair, L., U.S.A. 84 D2 42 30N 82 45W
St. Clairsville, U.S.A. .. 84 F4 40 5N 80 54W
St. Claude, Canada 71 D9 49 40N 98 20W
St. Clears, U.K. 13 F3 51 49N   4 31W

St-Clet, Canada 85 A10 45 21N 74 13W
St. Cloud, Fla., U.S.A. .. 83 L5 28 15N 81 17W
St. Cloud, Minn., U.S.A. . 80 C7 45 34N 94 10W
St. Cricq, C., Australia . 61 E1 25 17S 113 6 E
St. Croix, U.S. Virgin Is. 89 C7 17 45N 64 45W
St. Croix →, U.S.A. 80 C8 44 45N 92 48W
St. Croix Falls, U.S.A. .. 80 C8 45 24N 92 38W
St. David's, Canada 73 C8 48 12N 58 52W
St. David's, U.K. 13 F2 51 53N   5 16W
St. David's Head, U.K. ... 13 F2 51 54N   5 19W
St-Denis, France .... 20 B5 48 56N   2 22 E
St-Dizier, France .... 20 B6 48 38N   4 56 E
St. Elias, Mt., U.S.A. ... 68 B5 60 18N 140 56W
St. Elias Mts., N. Amer. . 70 A1 60 33N 139 28W
St-Étienne, France .... 20 D6 45 27N   4 22 E
St. Eugène, Canada 85 A10 45 30N 74 28W
St. Eustatius, W. Indies . 89 C7 17 20N 63 0W
St-Félicien, Canada 72 C5 48 40N 72 25W
St-Flour, France .... 20 D5 45 2N   3 6 E
St. Francis, U.S.A. 80 F4 39 47N 101 48W
St. Francis →, U.S.A. 81 H9 34 38N 90 36W
St. Francis, C., S. Africa 56 E3 34 14S 24 49 E
St-François, L., Canada .. 85 A10 45 10N 74 22W
St-Gabriel, Canada 72 C5 46 17N 73 24W
St. Gallen = Sankt Gallen, Switz. 20 C8 47 26N 9 22 E
St-Gaudens, France .... 20 E4 43 6N   0 44 E
St. George, Australia .... 63 D4 28 1S 148 30 E
St. George, Canada 73 C6 45 11N 66 50W
St. George, S.C., U.S.A. . 83 J5 33 11N 80 35W
St. George, Utah, U.S.A. . 77 H7 37 6N 113 35W
St. George, C., Canada ... 73 C8 48 30N 59 16W
St. George, C., U.S.A. ... 83 L3 29 40N 85 5W
St. George Ra., Australia . 60 C4 18 40S 125 0 E
St-Georges, Canada 73 C5 46 8N 70 40W
St. George's, Canada 73 C8 48 26N 58 31W
St. George's, Grenada 89 D7 12 5N 61 43W
St. George's B., Canada .. 73 C8 48 24N 58 53W
St. Georges Basin, N.S.W.,
  Australia .... 63 F5 35 7S 150 36 E
St. Georges Basin, W. Austral.,
  Australia .... 60 C4 15 23S 125 2 E
St. George's Channel, Europe 10 E6 52 0N   6 0W
St. Georges Hd., Australia 63 F5 35 12S 150 42 E
St. Gotthard P. = San Gottardo,
  P. del, Switz. .... 20 C8 46 33N   8 33 E
St. Helena, Atl. Oc. 48 H3 15 58S   5 42W
St. Helena, U.S.A. 76 G2 38 30N 122 28W
St. Helena, Mt., U.S.A. .. 78 G4 38 40N 122 36W
St. Helena B., S. Africa . 56 E2 32 40S 18 10 E
St. Helens, Australia .... 63 G4 41 20S 148 15 E
St. Helens, U.K. 12 D5 53 27N   2 44W
St. Helens, U.S.A. 78 E4 45 52N 122 48W
St. Helens, Mt., U.S.A. .. 78 D4 46 12N 122 12W
St. Helier, U.K. 13 H5 49 10N   2 7W
St-Hubert, Belgium .... 15 D5 50 2N   5 23 E
St-Hyacinthe, Canada 72 C5 45 40N 72 58W
St. Ignace, Canada 82 C3 52 53N 84 44W
St. Ignace I., Canada 72 C2 48 45N 88 0W
St. Ignatius, U.S.A. 76 C6 47 19N 114 6W
St. Ives, Cambs., U.K. ... 13 E7 52 20N   0 4W
St. Ives, Corn., U.K. 13 G2 50 12N   5 30W
St. James, U.S.A. 80 D7 43 59N 94 38W
St-Jean →, Canada 73 B7 50 17N 64 20W
St-Jean, L., Canada 73 C5 48 40N 72 0W
St-Jean-Port-Joli, Canada . 73 C5 47 15N 70 13W
St-Jean-sur-Richelieu, Canada 85 A11 45 20N 73 20W
St-Jérôme, Canada 72 C5 45 47N 74 0W
St. John, Canada 73 C6 45 20N 66 8W
St. John, U.S.A. 81 G5 38 0N 98 46W
St. John →, U.S.A. 83 C12 45 12N 66 5W
St. John, C., Canada 73 C8 50 0N 55 32W
St. John I., U.S. Virgin Is. 89 e 18 20N 64 42W
St. John's, Antigua & B. . 89 C7 17 6N 61 51W
St. John's, Canada 73 C9 47 35N 52 40W
St. Johns, Ariz., U.S.A. . 77 J9 34 30N 109 22W
St. Johns, Mich., U.S.A. . 82 D3 43 0N 84 33W
St. Johns →, U.S.A. 83 K5 30 24N 81 24W
St. John's Pt., Ireland .. 10 B3 54 34N   8 27W
St. Johnsbury, U.S.A. 85 B12 44 25N 72 1W
St. Johnsville, U.S.A. ... 85 D10 43 0N 74 43W
St-Joseph, Martinique .... 88 c 14 39N 61 4W
St. Joseph, La., U.S.A. .. 81 K9 31 55N 91 14W
St. Joseph, Mo., U.S.A. .. 80 F7 39 46N 94 50W
St. Joseph →, U.S.A. 82 D2 42 7N 86 29W
St. Joseph, I., Canada ... 72 C3 46 12N 83 58W
St. Joseph, L., Canada ... 72 B1 51 10N 90 35W
St-Jovite, Canada 72 C5 46 8N 74 38W
St. Kilda, U.K. 14 C2 57 49N   8 34W
St. Kitts & Nevis ■, W. Indies 89 C7 17 20N 62 40W
St. Laurent, Canada 71 C9 50 25N 97 58W
St. Lawrence, Australia .. 62 C4 22 16S 149 31 E
St. Lawrence, Canada 73 C8 46 54N 55 23W
St. Lawrence →, Canada ... 73 C6 49 30N 66 0W
St. Lawrence, Gulf of, Canada 73 C7 48 25N 62 0W
St. Lawrence I., U.S.A. .. 68 B3 63 30N 170 30W
St. Lawrence Islands △, Canada 85 B9 44 27N 75 52W
St. Leonard, Canada 73 C6 47 12N 67 58W
St. Lewis →, Canada 73 B8 52 26N 56 11W
St-Lô, France 20 B3 49 7N   1 5W
St-Louis, Guadeloupe ..... 88 b 15 56N 61 19W
St. Louis, Senegal 50 E2 16 8N 16 27W
St. Louis, U.S.A. 80 F9 38 37N 90 12W
St. Louis →, U.S.A. 80 B8 47 15N 92 45W
St. Lucia ■, W. Indies ... 89 f 14 0N 60 50W
St. Lucia, C., S. Africa . 57 D5 28 5S 32 30 E
St. Lucia Channel, W. Indies 89 D7 14 15N 61 0W
St. Maarten, W. Indies ... 89 C7 18 0N 63 5W
St. Magnus B., U.K. 11 A7 60 25N   1 35W
St-Malo, France 20 B2 48 39N   2 1W
St-Marc, Haiti 89 C5 19 10N 72 41W
St-Martin, W. Indies 89 C7 18 0N 63 0W
St. Martin, L., Canada ... 71 C9 51 40N 98 30W
St-Martin, Martinique .... 88 c 14 52N 61 14W
St. Martins, Barbados .... 89 g 13 5N 59 28W
St. Mary Pk., Australia .. 63 E2 31 32S 138 34 E
St. Marys, Australia ..... 63 G4 41 35S 148 11 E
St. Mary's, Corn., U.K. .. 13 H1 49 55N   6 18W
St. Mary's, Orkney, U.K. . 11 C6 58 54N   2 54W
St. Marys, Canada 84 C3 43 20N 81 10W
St. Marys, Ga., U.S.A. ... 83 K5 30 44N 81 33W
St. Marys, Pa., U.S.A. ... 84 E6 41 26N 78 34W
St. Mary's, C., Canada ... 73 C9 46 50N 54 12W
St. Mary's Bay, Canada ... 73 C9 46 50N 53 50W
St. Marys Bay, Canada 73 D6 44 25N 66 10W
St-Mathieu, Pte., France . 20 B1 48 20N   4 45W
St. Matthew I., U.S.A. ... 68 B2 60 24N 172 42W

St-Maurice →, Canada ..... 72 C5 46 21N 72 1[W]
St. Mawes, U.K. .... 13 G2 50 10N   5 [2W]
St-Nazaire, France .... 20 C2 47 17N   2 1[2W]
St. Neots, U.K. .... 13 E7 52 14N   0 1[6W]
St-Niklaas, Belgium ...... 15 C4 51 10N   4 [8E]
St-Omer, France .... 20 A5 50 45N   2 1[5E]
St-Pamphile, Canada ...... 73 C6 46 58N 69 4[W]
St-Pascal, Canada .... 73 C6 47 32N 69 48[W]
St. Paul, Canada .... 70 C6 54 0N 111 1[W]
St. Paul, Minn., U.S.A. .. 80 C8 44 57N 93 [W]
St. Paul, Nebr., U.S.A. .. 80 E5 41 13N 98 2[W]
St-Paul →, Canada .... 73 B8 51 27N 57 4[W]
St. Paul, I., Ind. Oc. ... 3 F13 38 55S 77 3[E]
St. Paul I., Canada ...... 73 C7 47 12N 60 [W]
St. Peter, U.S.A. .... 80 C7 44 20N 93 5[W]
St. Peter Port, U.K. ..... 13 H5 49 26N   2 [W]
St. Peters, N.S., Canada . 73 C7 45 40N 60 5[W]
St. Peters, P.E.I., Canada 73 C7 46 25N 62 3[W]
St. Petersburg = Sankt-Peterburg,
  Russia .... 18 C5 59 55N 30 2[E]
St. Petersburg, U.S.A. ... 83 M4 27 46N 82 3[W]
St-Pie, Canada .... 85 A12 45 30N 72 5[W]
St-Pierre, Martinique .... 88 c 14 45N 61 1[W]
St-Pierre, St-P. & M. .... 73 C8 46 46N 56 1[W]
St-Pierre, L., Canada .... 72 C5 46 12N 72 5[W]
St-Pierre-et-Miquelon ☑,
  N. Amer. .... 73 C8 46 55N 56 1[W]
St-Quentin, Canada .... 73 C6 47 30N 67 2[W]
St-Quentin, France .... 20 B5 49 50N   3 16[E]
St. Regis, U.S.A. .... 76 C6 47 18N 115 [W]
St. Sebastien, Tanjon' i, Madag. 57 A8 12 26S 48 4[E]
St-Siméon, Canada .... 73 C5 47 51N 69 5[W]
St. Simons I., U.S.A. .... 83 K5 31 12N 81 1[W]
St. Simons Island, U.S.A. . 83 K5 31 9N 81 2[W]
St. Stephen, Canada ...... 73 C6 45 16N 67 1[W]
St. Thomas, Canada .... 84 D3 42 45N 81 1[W]
St. Thomas I., U.S. Virgin Is. 89 e 18 20N 64 5[W]
St-Tite, Canada .... 72 C5 46 45N 72 3[W]
St-Tropez, France .... 20 E7 43 17N   6 3[E]
St-Troud = St. Truiden, Belgium 15 D5 50 48N 5 1[E]
St. Truiden, Belgium ..... 15 D5 50 48N   5 1[E]
St. Vincent, G., Australia 63 F2 35 0S 138 [E]
St. Vincent & the Grenadines ■,
  W. Indies .... 89 D7 13 0N 61 1[W]
St. Vincent Passage, W. Indies 89 D7 13 30N 61 [W]
St-Vith, Belgium .... 15 D6 50 17N   6 [E]
St. Walburg, Canada ...... 71 C7 53 39N 109 1[W]
Ste-Agathe-des-Monts, Canada 72 C5 46 3N 74 1[W]
Ste-Anne, Guadeloupe ..... 88 b 16 13N 61 2[W]
Ste-Anne, L., Canada ..... 73 B6 50 0N 67 4[W]
Ste-Anne-des-Monts-Tourelle,
  Canada .... 73 C6 49 8N 66 3[W]
Ste. Genevieve, U.S.A. ... 80 G9 37 59N 90 [W]
Ste-Marguerite →, Canada . 73 B6 50 9N 66 3[W]
Ste-Marie, Canada .... 73 C5 46 26N 71 [W]
Ste-Marie, Martinique .... 88 c 14 48N 61 [W]
Ste-Rose, Guadeloupe ..... 88 b 16 20N 61 4[W]
Ste. Rose du Lac, Canada . 71 C9 51 4N 99 3[W]
Saintes, France .... 20 D3 45 45N   0 3[W]
Saintes, Îs. des, Guadeloupe 88 b 15 50N 61 3[W]
Saintfield, U.K. .... 10 B6 54 28N   5 4[W]
Saintonge, France .... 20 D3 45 40N   0 5[W]
Saipan, Pac. Oc. .... 64 F6 15 12N 145 4[E]
Sairang, India .... 41 H18 23 50N 92 4[E]
Sairecábur, Cerro, Bolivia 94 A2 22 43S 67 5[W]
Saitama □, Japan .... 31 F9 36 25N 139 3[E]
Saiyid, Pakistan .... 42 C5 33 7N 73 [E]
Sajama, Bolivia .... 92 G5 18 7S 69 [W]
Sajószentpéter, Hungary .. 17 D11 48 12N 20 4[E]
Sajum, India .... 43 C8 33 20N 79 [E]
Sak →, S. Africa .... 56 E3 30 52S 20 2[E]
Sakai, Japan .... 31 G7 34 30N 135 3[E]
Sakaide, Japan .... 31 G6 34 19N 133 5[E]
Sakaiminato, Japan .... 31 G6 35 38N 133 1[E]
Sakākah, Si. Arabia ...... 44 D4 30 0N 40 [E]
Sakakawea, L., U.S.A. .... 80 B4 47 30N 101 2[W]
Sakami →, Canada .... 72 B4 53 40N 76 4[W]
Sakami, L., Canada .... 72 B4 53 15N 77 [W]
Sakania, Dem. Rep. of the Congo 55 E2 12 43S 28 3[E]
Sakaraha, Madag. .... 57 C7 22 55S 44 3[E]
Sakarya, Turkey .... 19 F5 40 48N 30 2[E]
Sakashima-Guntō, Japan ... 31 M2 24 46N 124 [E]
Sakata, Japan .... 30 E9 38 55N 139 5[E]
Sakchu, N. Korea .... 35 D13 40 23N 125 [E]
Sakeny →, Madag. .... 57 C8 20 0S 45 2[E]
Sakha □, Russia .... 29 C13 66 0N 130 [E]
Sakhalin, Russia .... 29 D15 51 0N 143 [E]
Sakhalinskiy Zaliv, Russia 29 D15 54 0N 141 [E]
Šakiai, Lithuania .... 9 J20 54 59N 23 [E]
Sakon Nakhon, Thailand ... 38 D5 17 10N 104 [E]
Sakrand, Pakistan .... 42 F3 26 10N 68 1[E]
Sakri, India .... 43 F12 26 13N 86 [E]
Sakrivier, S. Africa ..... 56 E3 30 54S 20 2[E]
Sakti, India .... 43 H10 22 2N 82 5[E]
Sakuma, Japan .... 31 G8 35 3N 137 4[E]
Sakurai, Japan .... 31 G7 34 30N 135 5[E]
Sala, Sweden .... 9 G17 59 58N 16 3[E]
Sala Consilina, Italy .... 22 D6 40 23N 15 3[E]
Sala-y-Gómez, Pac. Oc. ... 65 K17 26 28S 105 2[W]
Salaberry-de-Valleyfield, Canada 85 A10 45 15N 74 [W]
Salada, L., Mexico .... 77 K6 32 20N 115 4[W]
Saladas, Argentina .... 94 B4 28 15S 58 4[W]
Saladillo, Argentina ..... 94 D4 35 40S 59 5[W]
Salado →, Buenos Aires,
  Argentina .... 94 D4 35 44S 57 2[W]
Salado →, La Pampa, Argentina 96 D3 37 30S 67 [W]
Salado →, Santa Fe, Argentina 94 C3 31 40S 60 4[W]
Salado →, Mexico .... 81 M5 26 52N 99 1[W]
Salaga, Ghana .... 50 G5   8 31N   0 3[W]
Şalakhis, Syria .... 46 C5 32 40N 36 4[E]
Şalāḥ ad Dīn □, Iraq ..... 44 C4 34 35N 43 3[E]
Sálakhos, Greece .... 25 C9 36 17N 27 5[E]
Salālah, Oman .... 47 D5 16 56N 53 5[E]
Salamanca, Chile .... 94 C1 31 46S 70 5[W]
Salamanca, Spain .... 21 B3 40 58N   5 3[W]
Salamanca, U.S.A. .... 84 D6 42 10N 78 4[W]
Salāmatābād, Iran .... 44 C5 35 39N 47 5[E]
Salamis, Cyprus .... 25 D12 35 11N 33 5[E]
Salamís, Greece .... 23 F10 37 56N 23 3[E]
Salar de Atacama, Chile .. 94 A2 23 30S 68 2[W]
Salar de Uyuni, Bolivia .. 92 H5 20 30S 67 4[W]
Salatiga, Indonesia ...... 37 G14 7 19S 110 3[E]
Salavat, Russia .... 18 D10 53 21N 55 5[E]
Salaverry, Peru .... 92 E3   8 15S 79 [W]
Salawati, Indonesia ...... 37 E8   1 7S 130 5[E]
Salaya, India .... 42 H3 22 19N 69 3[E]
Salayar, Indonesia .... 37 F6   6 7S 120 3[E]
Salcombe, U.K. .... 13 G4 50 14N   3 [W]

Idanha, S. Africa .... 56 E2   33 0S 17 58 E
Idanha B., S. Africa .... 56 E2   33 6S 18 0 E
Idus, Latvia .... 9 H20   56 38N 22 30 E
Ie, Australia .... 63 F4   38 6S 147 6 E
Ie, Morocco 50 B4   34 3N   6 48W
Ie, U.K. 12 D5   53 26N   2 19W
Iekhard, Russia .... 28 C7   66 30N 66 35 E
Iem, India .... 40 P11   11 40N 78 11 E
Iem, Ill., U.S.A. 82 F1   38 38N 88 57W
Iem, Ind., U.S.A. 82 F2   38 36N 86 6W
Iem, Mass., U.S.A. 85 D14   42 31N 70 53W
Iem, Mo., U.S.A. 81 G9   39 39N 91 32W
Iem, N.H., U.S.A. 85 D13   42 45N 71 11W
Iem, N.J., U.S.A. 82 F8   39 34N 75 28W
Iem, N.Y., U.S.A. 85 C11   43 10N 73 20W
Iem, Ohio, U.S.A. 84 F4   40 54N 80 52W
Iem, Oreg., U.S.A. 76 D2   44 56N 123 2W
Iem, S. Dak., U.S.A. 80 D6   43 44N 97 23W
Iem, Va., U.S.A. 82 G5   37 18N 80 3W
Ierno, Italy .... 22 D6   40 41N 14 47 E
Iford, U.K. 12 D5   53 30N   2 18W
Igótarján, Hungary .... 17 D10   48 5N 149 47 E
Igueiro, Brazil 93 E11   8 4S 39 6W
Iibabu, Indonesia .... 37 D7   3 51N 126 40 E
Iibea, Trin. & Tob. 93 K15   10 43N 61 2W
Iida, U.S.A. 74 C5   38 32N 106 0W
Iihli, Turkey .... 23 E13   38 28N 28 8 E
Iihorsk, Belarus .... 17 B14   52 51N 27 27 E
Iima, Malawi .... 53 G6   13 47S 34 28 E
Iina, Italy .... 22 E6   38 34N 14 50 E
Iina, Kans., U.S.A. 80 F6   38 50N 97 37W
Iina, Utah, U.S.A. 77 G8   38 58N 111 51W
Iina Cruz, Mexico 87 D5   16 10N 95 10W
Iinas, Brazil 93 G10   16 10S 42 10W
Iinas, Chile 94 A2   23 31S 69 29W
Iinas, Ecuador 92 D2   2 10S 80 58W
Iinas, U.S.A. 78 J5   36 40N 121 39W
Iinas →, Guatemala 87 D6   16 28N 90 31W
Iinas, B. de, Nic. 88 D2   11 4N 85 45W
Iinas, Pampa de las, Argentina 94 C2   31 58S 66 42W
Iinas Ambargasta, Argentina 94 B3   29 0S 66 0W
Iinas de Hidalgo, Mexico .. 86 C4   22 35N 101 40W
Iinas Grandes, Argentina .. 94 C3   30 0S 65 0W
Iinas Pueblo Missions △,
  U.S.A. 77 J10   34 16N 106 5W
Iine →, Ark., U.S.A. 81 J8   33 10N 92 8W
Iine →, Kans., U.S.A. 80 F6   38 52N 97 30W
Iines, C. de ses, Spain .... 24 B10   39 16N   3 4 E
Iinópolis, Brazil 93 D9   0 40S 47 20W
Iisbury, U.K. 13 F6   51 4N   1 47W
Iisbury, Md., U.S.A. 82 F8   38 22N 75 36W
Iisbury, N.C., U.S.A. 83 H5   35 40N 80 29W
Iisbury I., Canada 69 B12   63 30N 77 0W
Iisbury Plain, U.K. 13 F6   51 14N   1 55W
Iikhad, Syria .... 46 C5   32 39N 36 43 E
Iila, Finland .... 8 C23   66 50N 28 49 E
Iiliq = Coral Harbour, Canada 69 B11   64 8N 83 10W
Iilisaw, Canada 81 H7   35 28N 94 47W
Iiluit, Canada 69 B12   62 14N 75 38W
Imäs, Iran .... 44 B5   38 11N 44 47 E
Imo, Canada 70 D5   49 10N 117 20W
Imon, U.S.A. 76 D7   45 11N 113 54W
Imon →, Canada 70 C4   54 3N 122 40W
Imon →, U.S.A. 76 D5   45 51N 116 47W
Imon Arm, Canada 70 C5   50 40N 119 15W
Imon Gums, Australia ..... 61 F3   32 59S 121 38 E
Imon River Mts., U.S.A. ... 76 D6   45 0N 114 30W
Ilo, Finland .... 9 F20   60 22N 23 10 E
Iome, U.S.A. 79 M13   33 47N 113 37W
Ion, India .... 43 F9   26 2N 81 27 E
Ion-de-Provence, France ... 20 E6   43 39N   5 6 E
Ionica = Thessaloníki, Greece 23 D10   40 38N 22 58 E
Ionta, Romania .... 17 E11   46 49N 21 42 E
Ipausselkä, Finland .... 9 F22   61 0N 27 0 E
Isacate, Argentina 94 C2   31 20S 65 5W
Isk, Russia .... 19 E7   46 28N 41 30 E
Iso →, Italy .... 22 F5   37 6N 13 57 E
It →, Canada 70 B6   60 0N 112 25W
It →, U.S.A. 77 K7   33 23N 112 19W
It Lake City, U.S.A. 76 F8   40 45N 111 53W
It Range, Pakistan .... 42 C5   32 30N 72 25 E
Ita, Argentina 94 A2   24 57S 65 25W
Ita □, Argentina 94 A2   24 48S 65 30W
Itash, U.S.A. 13 G3   50 24N   4 14W
Itburn by the Sea, U.K. ... 12 C7   54 35N   0 58W
Itcoats, U.K. 11 F4   55 38N   4 47W
Itee Is., Ireland 10 D5   52 7N   6 37W
Itfjellet, Norway .... 8 C16   66 40N 15 15 E
Itfjorden, Norway .... 8 C16   67 15N 14 10 E
Itillo, Mexico 86 B4   25 25N 101 0W
Ito, Argentina 94 C3   34 20S 60 15W
Ito, Uruguay 94 C4   31 27S 57 50W
Ito →, Italy .... 22 C5   42 26N 12 25 E
Ito del Guaira, Paraguay ... 95 A5   24 3S 54 17W
Iton City, U.S.A. 79 M11   33 29N 115 51W
Iton Sea, U.S.A. 79 M11   33 15N 115 45W
Itsburg, U.S.A. 84 F5   40 9N 79 27W
Iuda →, U.S.A. 83 J5   34 1N 81 4W
Iûm, Egypt .... 51 B11   31 31N 25 7 E
Iur, India .... 41 K13   18 27N 83 18 E
Ivador, Brazil 93 F11   13 0S 38 30W
Ivador, U.S.A. 71 C7   52 10N 109 32W
Ivador, L., U.S.A. 81 L9   29 43N 90 15W
Ivador, El ■, Cent. Amer. .. 88 D2   13 50N 89 0W
Iween →, Burma .... 41 L20   16 31N 97 37 E
Izach, Azerbaijan .... 19 G8   39 33N 48 59 E
Izach, Austria .... 16 D7   48 12N 12 56 E
Izburg, Austria .... 16 E7   47 48N 13 2 E
Izgitter, Germany .... 16 B6   52 9N 10 19 E
Izwedel, Germany .... 16 B6   52 52N 11 10 E
Im, India .... 42 F4   26 50N 70 31 E
Im Neua, Laos .... 38 B5   20 29N 104 5 E
Im Ngao, Thailand .... 38 D2   17 18N 99 0 E
Im Rayburn Reservoir, U.S.A. 81 K7   31 4N 94 5W
Im Son, Vietnam .... 38 C5   19 44N 105 54 E
Im Teu, Laos .... 38 C5   19 59N 104 38 E
Ima de Langreo = Langreo,
  Spain 21 A3   43 18N   5 40W
Imagaltay, Russia .... 29 D10   50 36N 95 3 E
Imales Group, Phil. .... 37 C6   0 0N 122 0 E
Imana, India .... 40 D10   10 10N 76 13 E
Imana Cay, Bahamas 89 B5   23 30N 73 45W
Imanga, U.S.A. .... 55 D4   8 20S 39 13 E
Imangán □, Afghan. ...... 40 B5   36 15N 68 3 E
the Congo .... 54 C1   4 23S 24 10 E
Imani, Japan .... 30 C11   42 7N 142 56 E

Samar, Phil. .... 37 B7   12 0N 125 0 E
Samara, Russia .... 18 D9   53 8N 50 6 E
Samaria = Shōmrōn, West Bank 46 C4   32 15N 35 13 E
Samariá, Greece .... 25 D5   35 17N 23 58 E
Samarinda, Indonesia ...... 36 E5   0 30S 117 9 E
Samarkand = Samarqand,
  Uzbekistan .... 28 F7   39 40N 66 55 E
Samarqand, Uzbekistan .... 28 F7   39 40N 66 55 E
Sāmarrā', Iraq .... 44 C4   34 12N 43 52 E
Samastipur, India .... 43 G11   25 50N 85 50 E
Samba, Dem. Rep. of the Congo 54 C2   4 38S 26 22 E
Samba, India .... 43 C6   32 32N 75 10 E
Sambalpur, India .... 41 J14   21 28N 84 4 E
Sambar, Tanjung, Indonesia . 36 E4   2 59S 110 19 E
Sambas, Indonesia .... 36 D3   1 20N 109 20 E
Sambava, Madag. .... 57 A9   14 16S 50 10 E
Sambawizi, Zimbabwe ..... 55 F2   18 24S 26 13 E
Sambhal, India .... 43 E8   28 35N 78 37 E
Sambhar, India .... 42 F6   26 52N 75 6 E
Sambhar L., India .... 42 F6   26 55N 75 12 E
Sambiase, Italy .... 22 E7   38 58N 16 17 E
Sambir, Ukraine .... 17 D12   49 30N 23 10 E
Sambor, Cambodia .... 38 F6   12 46N 106 0 E
Samborombón, B., Argentina 94 D4   36 5S 57 20W
Samburu △, Kenya .... 54 B4   0 37N 37 31 E
Samch'ŏk, S. Korea .... 35 F15   37 30N 129 10 E
Samch'onp'o, S. Korea .... 35 G15   35 0N 128 6 E
Same, Tanzania .... 54 C4   4 2S 37 38 E
Samfya, Zambia .... 55 E2   11 22S 29 31 E
Samnah, Si. Arabia .... 44 E3   25 10N 37 15 E
Samo Alto, Chile 94 C1   30 22S 71 0W
Samoa ■, Pac. Oc. 59 B13   14 0S 172 0W
Samokov, Bulgaria .... 23 C10   42 18N 23 35 E
Sámos, Greece .... 23 F12   37 45N 26 50 E
Samothráki = Mathráki, Greece 25 A3   39 48N 19 31 E
Samothráki, Greece .... 23 D11   40 28N 25 28 E
Sampacho, Argentina 94 C3   33 20S 64 50W
Sampalan, Indonesia ...... 37 K18   8 41S 115 34 E
Sampang, Indonesia .... 37 G15   7 11S 113 13 E
Sampit, Indonesia .... 36 E4   2 34S 113 0 E
Sampit, Teluk, Indonesia ... 36 E4   3 5S 113 3 E
Samrong, Cambodia .... 38 E4   14 15N 103 30 E
Samrong, Thailand .... 38 E3   15 10N 100 40 E
Samsø, Denmark .... 9 J14   55 50N 10 35 E
Samsun, Turkey .... 19 F6   41 15N 36 22 E
Samui, Ko, Thailand ...... 39 b   9 30N 100 0 E
Samusole, Dem. Rep. of
  the Congo .... 55 E1   10 2S 24 0 E
Samut Prakan, Thailand ... 38 F3   13 32N 100 40 E
Samut Songkhram →, Thailand 36 B1   13 24N 100 1 E
Samwari, Pakistan .... 42 E2   28 30N 66 46 E
San, Mali 50 F5   13 15N   4 57W
San →, Cambodia .... 38 F5   13 32N 105 57 E
San →, Poland .... 17 C11   50 45N 21 51 E
San Agustín, C., Phil. ..... 37 C7   6 20N 126 13 E
San Agustín de Valle Fértil,
  Argentina 94 C2   30 35S 67 30W
San Ambrosio, Pac. Oc. 90 F3   26 28S 79 53W
San Andreas, U.S.A. 78 G6   38 12N 120 41W
San Andrés, I. de, Caribbean . 88 D3   12 42N 81 46W
San Andrés Mts., U.S.A. ... 77 K10   33 0N 106 30W
San Andrés Tuxtla, Mexico . 87 D5   18 30N 95 20W
San Angelo, U.S.A. 81 K4   31 28N 100 26W
San Anselmo, U.S.A. 78 H4   37 59N 122 34W
San Antonio, Belize 87 D7   16 15N 89 2W
San Antonio, Chile 94 C1   33 40S 71 40W
San Antonio, N. Mex., U.S.A. 77 K10   33 55N 106 52W
San Antonio, Tex., U.S.A. .. 81 L5   29 25N 98 30W
San Antonio →, U.S.A. 81 L6   28 30N 96 54W
San Antonio, C., Argentina . 94 D4   36 15S 56 40W
San Antonio, C. de, Cuba ... 88 B3   21 50N 84 57W
San Antonio, Mt., U.S.A. ... 79 L9   34 17N 117 38W
San Antonio de los Baños, Cuba 88 B3   22 54N 82 31W
San Antonio de los Cobres,
  Argentina 94 A2   24 5S 66 17W
San Antonio Oeste, Argentina 96 E4   40 40S 65 0W
San Ardo, U.S.A. 78 J6   36 1N 120 54W
San Agustín, Canary Is. 24 G4   27 47N 15 32W
San Augustine, U.S.A. 81 K7   31 30N 94 7W
San Bartolomé, Canary Is. .. 24 F6   28 59N 13 37W
San Benedetto de Tirajana,
  Canary Is. 24 G4   27 54N 15 34W
San Benedetto del Tronto, Italy 22 C5   42 57N 13 53 E
San Benedicto, I., Mexico .. 86 D2   19 18N 110 49W
San Benito, U.S.A. 81 M6   26 8N 97 38W
San Benito →, U.S.A. 78 J5   36 53N 121 34W
San Benito Mt., U.S.A. 78 J6   36 22N 120 37W
San Bernardino, U.S.A. 79 L9   34 7N 117 19W
San Bernardino Mts., U.S.A. 79 L10   34 10N 116 45W
San Bernardino Str., Phil. .. 37 B6   13 0N 125 0 E
San Bernardo, Chile 94 C1   33 40S 70 50W
San Bernardo, I. de, Colombia 92 B3   9 45N 75 50W
San Blas, Mexico 86 B3   26 4N 108 46W
San Blas, Arch. de, Panama . 88 E4   9 50N 78 31W
San Blas, C., U.S.A. 83 L3   29 40N 85 21W
San Borja, Bolivia 92 F5   14 50S 66 52W
San Buenaventura = Ventura,
  U.S.A. 79 L7   34 17N 119 18W
San Buenaventura, Mexico . 86 B4   27 5N 101 32W
San Carlos = Sant Carles, Spain 24 B8   39 3N   1 34 E
San Carlos, Argentina 94 C2   33 50S 69 0W
San Carlos, Chile 94 D1   36 10S 72 0W
San Carlos, Baja Calif. S., Mexico 86 C2   24 47N 112 6W
San Carlos, Coahuila, Mexico 86 B4   29 0N 100 54W
San Carlos, Nic. 88 D3   11 12N 84 50W
San Carlos, Phil. .... 37 B6   10 29N 123 25 E
San Carlos, Uruguay 95 C5   34 46S 54 58W
San Carlos, U.S.A. 77 K8   33 21N 110 27W
San Carlos, Venezuela 92 B5   9 40N 68 36W
San Carlos de Bariloche,
  Argentina 96 E2   41 10S 71 25W
San Carlos de Bolívar, Argentina 96 D4   36 15S 61 6W
San Carlos del Zulia, Venezuela 92 B4   9 1N 71 55W
San Carlos L., U.S.A. 77 K8   33 11N 110 32W
San Clemente, Chile 94 D1   35 30S 71 29W
San Clemente, U.S.A. 79 M9   33 26N 117 37W
San Clemente I., U.S.A. ... 79 N8   32 53N 118 29W
San Cristóbal = Es Migjorn Gran,
  Spain .... 24 B11   39 57N   4 3 E
San Cristóbal, Argentina ... 94 C3   30 20S 61 10W
San Cristóbal, Dom. Rep. ... 89 C5   18 25N 70 6W
San Cristóbal, Venezuela ... 92 B4   7 46N 72 14W
San Cristóbal de la Casas,
  Mexico 87 D6   16 50N 92 33W
San Diego, Calif., U.S.A. ... 79 N9   32 43N 117 9W
San Diego, Tex., U.S.A. 81 M5   27 46N 98 14W
San Diego, C., Argentina ... 96 G3   54 40S 65 10W
San Diego de la Unión, Mexico 86 C4   21 28N 100 52W

San Diego International ✈ (SAN),
  U.S.A. 79 N9   32 44N 117 11W
San Dimitri, Ras, Malta .... 25 C1   36 4N 14 11 E
San Dimitri Point = San Dimitri,
  Ras, Malta .... 25 C1   36 4N 14 11 E
San Estanislao, Paraguay ... 94 A4   24 39S 56 26W
San Felipe, Chile 94 C1   32 43S 70 42W
San Felipe, Mexico 86 A2   31 0N 114 52W
San Felipe, Venezuela 92 A5   10 20N 68 44W
San Felipe →, U.S.A. 79 M11   33 12N 115 49W
San Félix, Chile 94 B1   28 56S 70 28W
San Félix, Pac. Oc. 90 F2   26 23S 80 0W
San Fernando = Sant Ferran,
  Spain .... 24 C7   38 42N   1 28 E
San Fernando, Baja Calif.,
  Mexico 86 B1   29 55N 115 10W
San Fernando, Tamaulipas,
  Mexico 87 C5   24 51N 98 10W
San Fernando, La Unión, Phil. . 37 A6   16 40N 120 23 E
San Fernando, Pampanga, Phil. 37 A6   15 5N 120 37 E
San Fernando, Spain 21 D2   36 28N   6 17W
San Fernando, Trin. & Tob. . 89 D7   10 20N 61 30W
San Fernando, U.S.A. 79 L8   34 17N 118 26W
San Fernando de Apure,
  Venezuela 92 B5   7 54N 67 15W
San Fernando de Atabapo,
  Venezuela 92 C5   4 3N 67 42W
San Francisco, Argentina ... 94 C3   31 30S 62 5W
San Francisco, U.S.A. 78 H4   37 47N 122 25W
San Francisco →, U.S.A. ... 77 K9   32 59N 109 22W
San Francisco, C. de, Colombia 90 C3   6 18N 77 29W
San Francisco, Paso de, S. Amer. 94 B2   27 0S 68 0W
San Francisco de Macorís,
  Dom. Rep. 89 C5   19 19N 70 15W
San Francisco del Monte de Oro,
  Argentina 94 C2   32 36S 66 8W
San Francisco del Oro, Mexico . 86 B3   26 52N 105 50W
San Francisco International ✈
  (SFO), U.S.A. 78 H4   37 37N 122 22W
San Francisco Javier = Sant
  Francesc de Formentera, Spain 24 C7   38 42N   1 26 E
San Gabriel, Chile 94 C1   33 47S 70 15W
San Gabriel Mts., U.S.A. ... 79 L9   34 20N 118 0W
San German, Puerto Rico ... 89 d   18 4N 67 4W
San Gorgonio Mt., U.S.A. .. 79 L10   34 7N 116 51W
San Gottardo, P. del, Switz. . 20 C8   46 33N   8 33 E
San Gregorio, Uruguay 95 C4   32 37S 55 40W
San Gregorio, U.S.A. 78 H4   37 20N 122 23W
San Ignacio, Belize 87 D7   17 10N 89 0W
San Ignacio, Bolivia 92 G6   16 20S 60 55W
San Ignacio, Mexico 86 B2   27 27N 113 0W
San Ignacio, Paraguay 88 C2   26 52S 57 3W
San Ignacio, L., Mexico 86 B2   26 50N 113 11W
San Ildefonso, C., Phil. .... 37 A6   16 0N 122 1 E
San Isidro, Argentina 94 C4   34 29S 58 31W
San Jacinto, U.S.A. 79 M10   33 47N 116 57W
San Jaime = Sant Jaume, Spain 24 B11   39 54N   4 4 E
San Javier, Misiones, Argentina 95 B4   27 55S 55 5W
San Javier, Santa Fe, Argentina 94 C4   30 40S 59 55W
San Javier, Bolivia 92 G6   16 18S 62 30W
San Javier, Chile 94 D1   35 40S 71 45W
San Jeronimo Taviche, Mexico 87 D5   16 38N 96 32W
San Joaquin, U.S.A. 78 J6   36 36N 120 11W
San Joaquín, Bolivia 92 F6   13 4S 64 49W
San Joaquin →, U.S.A. 78 G5   38 4N 121 51W
San Joaquin Valley, U.S.A. . 78 J6   37 20N 121 0W
San Jon, U.S.A. 81 H3   35 6N 103 20W
San Jordi = Sant Jordi, Spain . 24 B9   39 33N   2 46 E
San Jorge, Argentina 94 C3   31 54S 61 50W
San Jorge, B. de, Mexico ... 86 A2   31 20N 113 20W
San Jorge, G., Argentina ... 96 F3   46 0S 66 0W
San José = Sant Josep, Spain . 24 C7   38 55N   1 18 E
San José, Costa Rica 88 E3   9 55N 84 2W
San José, Guatemala 88 D1   14 0N 90 50W
San José, Mexico 86 C2   25 0N 110 50W
San José, Mind. Occ., Phil. .. 37 B6   12 27N 121 4 E
San Jose, Nueva Ecija, Phil. .. 37 A6   15 45N 120 55 E
San Jose, U.S.A. 78 H5   37 20N 121 53W
San Jose →, U.S.A. 77 J10   34 25N 106 45W
San Jose de Buenavista, Phil. . 37 B6   10 45N 121 56 E
San José de Chiquitos, Bolivia 92 G6   17 53S 60 50W
San José de Feliciano, Argentina 94 C4   30 26S 58 46W
San José de Jáchal, Argentina 94 C2   30 15S 68 46W
San José de Mayo, Uruguay . 94 C4   34 27S 56 40W
San José del Cabo, Mexico .. 86 C3   23 0N 109 40W
San José del Guaviare, Colombia 92 C4   2 35N 72 38W
San Josep, Spain .... 24 C7   38 55N   1 18 E
San Juan, Argentina 94 C2   31 30S 68 30W
San Juan, Mexico 86 C4   21 20N 102 50W
San Juan, Puerto Rico ..... 89 d   18 28N 66 7W
San Juan, Trin. & Tob. 93 K15   10 39N 61 7W
San Juan □, Argentina 94 C2   31 9S 69 0W
San Juan →, Argentina 94 C2   32 20S 67 25W
San Juan →, Nic. 88 D3   10 56N 83 42W
San Juan →, U.S.A. 77 H8   37 16N 110 26W
San Juan Bautista = Sant Joan
  Baptista, Spain .... 24 B8   39 5N   1 31 E
San Juan Bautista, Paraguay . 94 B4   26 37S 57 6W
San Juan Bautista, U.S.A. .. 78 J5   36 51N 121 32W
San Juan Bautista Valle
  Nacional, Mexico 87 D5   17 47N 96 19W
San Juan Capistrano, U.S.A. . 79 M9   33 30N 117 40W
San Juan Cr. →, U.S.A. 78 J5   35 40N 120 22W
San Juan de Guadalupe, Mexico 86 C4   24 38N 102 44W
San Juan de la Costa, Mexico . 86 C2   24 38N 110 45W
San Juan de los Morros,
  Venezuela 92 B5   9 55N 67 21W
San Juan del Norte, Nic. ... 88 D3   10 58N 83 40W
San Juan del Norte, B. de, Nic. 88 D3   11 0N 83 40W
San Juan del Río, Mexico ... 87 C5   20 25N 100 0W
San Juan del Sur, Nic. 88 D2   11 20N 85 51W
San Juan I., U.S.A. 78 B3   48 32N 123 5W
San Juan Island △, U.S.A. .. 78 B4   48 27N 123 10W
San Juan Mts., U.S.A. 77 H10   37 30N 107 0W
San Justo, Argentina 94 C3   30 47S 60 30W
San Kamphaeng, Thailand .. 38 C2   18 45N 99 8 E
San Lázaro, C., Mexico 86 C2   24 50N 112 18W
San Lázaro, Sa., Mexico 86 C3   23 25N 110 0W
San Leandro, U.S.A. 78 H4   37 44N 122 9W
San Lorenzo = Sant Llorenç des
  Cardassar, Spain .... 24 B10   39 37N   3 17 E
San Lorenzo, Argentina ... 94 C3   32 45S 60 45W
San Lorenzo, Ecuador 92 C3   1 15N 78 50W
San Lorenzo, Paraguay 94 B4   25 20S 57 32W
San Lorenzo →, Mexico 86 C3   24 15N 107 24W
San Lorenzo, I., Mexico 86 B2   28 35N 112 50W
San Lorenzo, Mte., Argentina 96 F2   47 40S 72 20W

San Lucas, Bolivia 92 H5   20 5S 65 7W
San Lucas, Baja Calif. S., Mexico 86 C3   22 53N 109 54W
San Lucas, Baja Calif. S., Mexico 86 B2   27 10N 112 14W
San Lucas, U.S.A. 78 J5   36 8N 121 1W
San Lucas, C., Mexico 86 C3   22 50N 110 0W
San Luis, Argentina 94 C2   33 20S 66 20W
San Luis, Cuba 88 B3   22 17N 83 46W
San Luis, Guatemala 88 C2   16 14N 89 27W
San Luis, Ariz., U.S.A. 77 K6   32 29N 114 47W
San Luis, Colo., U.S.A. 77 H11   37 12N 105 25W
San Luis □, Argentina 94 C2   34 0S 66 0W
San Luis, I., Mexico 86 B2   29 58N 114 26W
San Luis, Sierra de, Argentina 94 C2   32 30S 66 10W
San Luis de la Paz, Mexico .. 86 C4   21 19N 100 32W
San Luis Obispo, U.S.A. 79 K6   35 17N 120 40W
San Luis Potosí, Mexico 86 C4   22 9N 100 59W
San Luis Potosí □, Mexico .. 86 C4   22 10N 101 0W
San Luis Reservoir, U.S.A. .. 78 H5   37 4N 121 5W
San Luis Rio Colorado, Mexico . 86 A2   32 29N 114 58W
San Manuel, U.S.A. 77 K8   32 36N 110 38W
San Marcos, Guatemala 88 D1   14 59N 91 52W
San Marcos, Mexico 86 B2   27 13N 112 6W
San Marcos, Calif., U.S.A. .. 79 M9   33 9N 117 10W
San Marcos, Tex., U.S.A. ... 81 L6   29 53N 97 56W
San Marino, San Marino ... 16 G7   43 55N 12 30 E
San Marino ■, Europe ..... 22 C5   43 56N 12 25 E
San Martín, Antarctica 5 C17   68 11S 67 0W
San Martín, Argentina 94 C2   33 5S 68 28W
San Martín →, Bolivia 92 F6   13 8S 63 43W
San Martín, L., Argentina .. 96 F2   48 50S 72 50W
San Martín de los Andes,
  Argentina 96 E2   40 10S 71 20W
San Mateo = Sant Mateu, Spain 24 B7   39 3N   1 23 E
San Mateo, U.S.A. 78 H4   37 34N 122 19W
San Matías, Bolivia 92 G7   16 25S 58 20W
San Matías, G., Argentina .. 96 E4   41 30S 64 0W
San Miguel = Sant Miguel, Spain 24 B7   39 3N   1 26 E
San Miguel, El Salv. 88 D2   13 30N 88 12W
San Miguel, Panama 88 E4   8 27N 78 55W
San Miguel, U.S.A. 78 K6   35 45N 120 42W
San Miguel →, Bolivia 92 F6   13 52S 63 56W
San Miguel de Tucumán,
  Argentina 94 B2   26 50S 65 20W
San Miguel del Monte, Argentina 94 D4   35 23S 58 50W
San Miguel I., U.S.A. 79 L6   34 2N 120 23W
San Nicolás, Canary Is. 24 G4   27 58N 15 47W
San Nicolás de los Arroyas,
  Argentina 94 C3   33 25S 60 10W
San Nicolas I., U.S.A. 79 M7   33 15N 119 30W
San Onofre, U.S.A. 79 M9   33 22N 117 34W
San Pablo, Bolivia 94 A2   21 43S 66 38W
San Pablo, U.S.A. 78 H4   37 58N 122 21W
San Pedro, Buenos Aires,
  Argentina 94 C4   33 40S 59 40W
San Pedro, Misiones, Argentina 95 B5   26 30S 54 10W
San Pedro, Chile 94 C1   33 54S 71 28W
San Pédro, Ivory C. 50 H4   4 50N   6 33W
San Pedro, Mexico 86 C2   23 55N 110 17W
San Pedro □, Paraguay 94 A4   24 0S 57 0W
San Pedro →, Chihuahua,
  Mexico 86 B3   28 20N 106 10W
San Pedro →, Nayarit, Mexico . 86 C3   21 45N 105 30W
San Pedro →, U.S.A. 77 K8   32 59N 110 47W
San Pedro, Pta., Chile 94 B1   25 30S 70 38W
San Pedro Channel, U.S.A. . 79 M8   33 30N 118 25W
San Pedro de Atacama, Chile . 94 A2   22 55S 68 15W
San Pedro de Jujuy, Argentina 94 A3   24 12S 64 55W
San Pedro de las Colonias,
  Mexico 86 B4   25 50N 102 59W
San Pedro de Macorís,
  Dom. Rep. 89 C6   18 30N 69 18W
San Pedro del Norte, Nic. .. 88 D3   13 4N 84 33W
San Pedro del Paraná, Paraguay 94 B4   26 43S 56 13W
San Pedro Mártir △, Mexico . 86 A1   31 0N 115 21W
San Pedro Mártir, Sierra, Mexico 86 A1   31 0N 115 30W
San Pedro Mixtepec, Mexico . 87 D5   16 2N 97 7W
San Pedro Ocampo = Melchor
  Ocampo, Mexico 86 C4   24 52N 101 40W
San Pedro Sula, Honduras .. 88 C2   15 30N 88 0W
San Pietro, Italy .... 22 E3   39 8N   8 17 E
San Quintín, Mexico 86 A1   30 29N 115 57W
San Rafael, Argentina 94 C2   34 40S 68 21W
San Rafael, Calif., U.S.A. ... 78 H4   37 58N 122 32W
San Rafael, N. Mex., U.S.A. . 77 J10   35 7N 107 53W
San Rafael, U.S.A. 79 L7   34 40N 119 50W
San Rafael Mts., U.S.A. 79 L7   34 40N 119 50W
San Ramón de la Nueva Orán,
  Argentina 94 A3   23 10S 64 20W
San Remo, Italy .... 20 E7   43 49N   7 46 E
San Roque, Argentina 94 B4   28 25S 58 45W
San Roque, Spain 21 D3   36 17N   5 21W
San Rosendo, Chile 94 D1   37 16S 72 43W
San Saba, U.S.A. 81 K5   31 12N 98 43W
San Salvador, El Salv. 88 D2   13 40N 89 10W
San Salvador, Spain ...... 24 B10   39 27N   3 11 E
San Salvador de Jujuy,
  Argentina 94 A3   24 10S 64 48W
San Salvador I., Bahamas ... 89 B5   24 0N 74 40W
San Sebastián = Donostia-San
  Sebastián, Spain 21 A5   43 17N   1 58W
San Sebastián, Argentina ... 96 G3   53 10S 68 30W
San Sebastián, Puerto Rico .. 89 d   18 20N 66 59W
San Sebastián de la Gomera,
  Canary Is. 24 F2   28 5N 17 7W
San Serra = Son Serra, Spain . 24 B10   39 43N   3 13 E
San Severo, Italy .... 22 D6   41 41N 15 23 E
San Simeon, U.S.A. 78 K5   35 39N 121 11W
San Simon, U.S.A. 77 K9   32 16N 109 14W
San Telmo = Sant Telm, Spain . 24 B9   39 35N   2 1 E
San Telmo, Mexico 86 A1   30 58N 116 6W
San Tiburcio, Mexico 86 C4   24 8N 101 32W
San Valentin, Mte., Chile ... 96 F2   46 30S 73 30W
San Vicente de la Barquera,
  Spain 21 A3   43 23N   4 29W
San Vito, Costa Rica 88 E3   8 50N 82 58W
Sana', Yemen .... 47 D3   15 27N 44 12 E
Sana →, Bos.-H. .... 16 F9   45 3N 16 23 E
Sanaga →, Cameroon ..... 52 D1   3 35N   9 38 E
Sanaloa, Presa, Mexico 86 C3   24 50N 107 20W
Sanana, Indonesia .... 37 E7   2 5S 125 58 E
Sanand, India .... 42 H5   22 59N 72 25 E
Sanandaj, Iran .... 44 C5   35 18N 47 1 E
Sanandita, Bolivia 94 A3   21 40S 63 45W
Sanawad, India .... 42 H7   22 11N 76 5 E
Sancellas = Sencelles, Spain . 24 B9   39 39N   2 54 E
Sanchahe, China .... 35 B14   44 50N 126 11 E
Sánchez, Dom. Rep. 89 C6   19 15N 69 36W
Sanchor, India .... 42 G4   24 45N 71 55 E

Sancti Spíritus, Cuba 88 B4 21 52N 79 33W
Sancy, Puy de, France .... 20 D5 45 32N 2 50 E
Sand →, S. Africa .... 57 C5 22 25S 30 5 E
Sand Hills, U.S.A. 80 D4 42 10N 101 30W
Sand Lakes ○, Canada 71 B9 57 51N 98 32W
Sand Springs, U.S.A. 81 G6 36 9N 96 7W
Sanda, Japan .... 31 G7 34 53N 135 14 E
Sandakan, Malaysia .... 36 C5 5 53N 118 4 E
Sandan = Sambor, Cambodia .. 38 F6 12 46N 106 0 E
Sandanski, Bulgaria .... 23 D10 41 35N 23 16 E
Sanday, U.K. 11 B6 59 16N 2 31W
Sandefjord, Norway .... 9 G14 59 10N 10 15 E
Sanders, U.S.A. 77 J9 35 13N 109 20W
Sanderson, U.S.A. 81 K3 30 9N 102 24W
Sandersville, U.S.A. 83 J4 32 59N 82 48W
Sandfire Roadhouse, Australia . 60 C3 19 45S 121 15 E
Sandfly L., Canada 71 B7 55 43N 106 6W
Sandfontein, Namibia .... 56 C2 23 48S 29 1 E
Sandía, Peru 92 F5 14 10S 69 30W
Sandila, India .... 43 F9 27 5N 80 31 E
Sandnes, Norway .... 9 G11 58 50N 5 45 E
Sandnessjøen, Norway .... 8 C15 66 2N 12 38 E
Sandoa, Dem. Rep. of the Congo 52 F4 9 41S 23 0 E
Sandomierz, Poland .... 17 C11 50 40N 21 43 E
Sandover →, Australia .... 62 C2 21 43S 136 32 E
Sandoway, Burma .... 41 K19 18 20N 94 30 E
Sandoy, Færoe Is. 8 F9 61 52N 6 46W
Sandpoint, U.S.A. 76 B5 48 17N 116 33W
Sandray, U.K. 11 E1 56 53N 7 31W
Sandringham, U.K. .... 12 E8 52 51N 0 31 E
Sandstone, Australia .... 61 E2 27 59S 119 16 E
Sandusky, Mich., U.S.A. 84 C2 43 25N 82 50W
Sandusky, Ohio, U.S.A. 84 E2 41 27N 82 42W
Sandviken, Sweden .... 9 F17 60 38N 16 46 E
Sandwich, C., Australia .... 62 B4 18 14S 146 18 E
Sandwich B., Canada 73 B8 53 40N 57 15W
Sandwich B., Namibia .... 56 C1 23 25S 14 20 E
Sandy, Oreg., U.S.A. 78 E4 45 24N 122 16W
Sandy, Pa., U.S.A. 84 E6 41 6N 78 46W
Sandy, Utah, U.S.A. 76 F8 40 35N 111 50W
Sandy Bay, Canada 71 B8 55 31N 102 19W
Sandy Bight, Australia .... 61 F3 33 50S 123 20 E
Sandy C., Queens., Australia .. 62 C5 24 42S 153 15 E
Sandy C., Tas., Australia .... 63 G3 41 25S 144 45 E
Sandy Cay, Bahamas 89 B4 23 13N 75 18W
Sandy Cr. →, U.S.A. 76 F9 41 51N 109 47W
Sandy L., Canada 72 B1 53 2N 93 0W
Sandy Lake, Canada 72 B1 53 0N 93 15W
Sandy Valley, U.S.A. 79 K11 35 49N 115 36W
Sanford, Fla., U.S.A. 83 L5 28 48N 81 16W
Sanford, Maine, U.S.A. 83 D10 43 27N 70 47W
Sanford, N.C., U.S.A. 83 H6 35 29N 79 10W
Sanford →, Australia .... 61 E2 27 22S 115 53 E
Sanford, Mt., U.S.A. 68 B5 62 13N 144 8W
Sang-i-Masha, Afghan. .... 42 C2 33 8N 67 27 E
Sanga, Mozam. .... 55 E4 12 22S 35 21 E
Sanga →, Congo .... 52 E3 1 5S 17 0 E
Sangamner, India .... 40 K9 19 37N 74 15 E
Sangar, Afghan. .... 42 C1 32 56N 65 30 E
Sangar, Russia .... 29 C13 64 2N 127 31 E
Sangar Sarai, Afghan. .... 42 B4 34 27N 70 35 E
Sangarh →, Pakistan .... 42 D3 30 43N 70 44 E
Sangay, Ecuador 92 D3 2 0S 78 20W
Sange, Dem. Rep. of the Congo 54 D2 6 58S 28 21 E
Sangeang, Indonesia .... 37 F5 8 12S 119 6 E
Sanger, U.S.A. 78 J7 36 42N 119 33W
Sangerhausen, Germany .... 16 C6 51 28N 11 18 E
Sanggan He →, China .... 34 E9 38 12N 117 15 E
Sanggau, Indonesia .... 36 D4 0 5N 110 30 E
Sanghar, Pakistan .... 42 F3 26 2N 68 57 E
Sangihe, Kepulauan, Indonesia . 37 D7 3 0N 125 30 E
Sangihe, Pulau, Indonesia .... 37 D7 3 35N 125 30 E
Sangju, S. Korea .... 35 F15 36 25N 128 10 E
Sangkapura, Indonesia .... 36 F4 5 52S 112 40 E
Sangkhla, Thailand .... 38 E2 14 57N 98 28 E
Sangkulirang, Indonesia .... 36 D5 0 59N 117 58 E
Sangla, Pakistan .... 42 D5 31 43N 73 23 E
Sangli, India .... 40 L9 16 55N 74 33 E
Sangmélima, Cameroon .... 52 D2 2 57N 12 1 E
Sangod, India .... 42 G7 24 55N 76 17 E
Sangre de Cristo Mts., U.S.A. .. 81 G2 37 30N 105 20W
Sangre Grande, Trin. & Tob. .. 93 K15 10 35N 61 8W
Sangrur, India .... 42 D6 30 14N 75 50 E
Sangudo, Canada 70 C6 53 50N 114 54W
Sangue →, Brazil 92 F7 11 1S 58 39W
Sanibel, U.S.A. 83 M4 26 26N 82 1W
Sanikiluaq, Canada 69 C12 56 32N 79 14W
Sanin-Kaigan △, Japan .... 31 G7 35 39N 134 37 E
Sanirajak, Canada 69 B11 68 46N 81 12W
Sanjawi, Pakistan .... 42 D3 30 17N 68 21 E
Sanje, Uganda .... 54 C3 0 49S 31 30 E
Sanjo, Japan .... 30 F9 37 37N 138 57 E
Sankh →, India .... 43 H11 22 15N 84 48 E
Sankt Gallen, Switz. .... 20 C8 47 26N 9 22 E
Sankt Moritz, Switz. .... 20 C8 46 30N 9 50 E
Sankt-Peterburg, Russia .... 18 C5 59 55N 30 20 E
Sankt Pölten, Austria .... 16 D8 48 12N 15 38 E
Sankuru →, Dem. Rep. of
   the Congo .... 52 E4 4 17S 20 25 E
Sanliurfa, Turkey .... 19 G6 37 12N 38 50 E
Sanlúcar de Barrameda, Spain . 21 D2 36 46N 6 21W
Sanmenxia, China .... 34 G6 34 47N 111 12 E
Sanming, China .... 33 D6 26 15N 117 40 E
Sannaspos, S. Africa .... 56 D4 29 6S 26 34 E
Sannicandro Gargánico, Italy .. 22 D6 41 50N 15 34 E
Sânnicolau Mare, Romania .... 17 E11 46 5N 20 39 E
Sannieshof, S. Africa .... 56 D4 26 30S 25 47 E
Sannin, J., Lebanon .... 46 B4 33 57N 35 52 E
Sanniquellie, Liberia 50 G4 7 19N 8 38W
Sanoe, Antarctica 5 D2 70 20S 9 0W
Sanok, Poland .... 17 D12 49 35N 22 10 E
Sanquhar, U.K. 11 F5 55 22N 3 54W
Sans Souci, Trin. & Tob. 93 K16 10 50N 61 0W
Sant Antoni Abat, Spain .... 24 C7 38 59N 1 19 E
Sant Carles, Spain .... 24 B8 39 3N 1 34 E
Sant Feliu de Guíxols, Spain ... 21 B7 41 45N 3 1 E
Sant Ferran, Spain .... 24 C7 38 42N 1 28 E
Sant Francesc de Formentera,
   Spain .... 24 C7 38 42N 1 26 E
Sant Jaume, Spain .... 24 B11 39 54N 4 4 E
Sant Joan Baptista, Spain .... 24 B8 39 5N 1 31 E
Sant Jordi, Ibiza, Spain .... 24 C7 38 53N 1 24 E
Sant Jordi, Mallorca, Spain .... 24 B9 39 33N 2 46 E
Sant Jordi, G. de, Spain .... 21 B6 40 53N 1 2 E
Sant Llorenç des Cardassar,
   Spain .... 24 B10 39 37N 3 17 E
Sant Mateu, Spain .... 24 B7 39 3N 1 23 E
Sant Miguel, Spain .... 24 B7 39 3N 1 26 E

Sant Telm, Spain .... 24 B9 39 35N 2 21 E
Santa Agnés, Spain .... 24 B7 39 3N 1 21 E
Santa Ana, Bolivia 92 F5 13 50S 65 40W
Santa Ana, El Salv. 88 D2 14 0N 89 31W
Santa Ana, Mexico 86 A2 30 31N 111 8W
Santa Ana, U.S.A. 79 M9 33 46N 117 52W
Sant' Antíoco, Italy .... 22 E3 39 4N 8 27 E
Santa Bárbara, Chile 94 D1 37 40S 72 1W
Santa Bárbara, Honduras 88 D2 14 53N 88 14W
Santa Bárbara, Mexico 86 B3 26 48N 105 50W
Santa Barbara, U.S.A. 79 L7 34 25N 119 42W
Santa Barbara Channel, U.S.A. . 79 L7 34 15N 120 0W
Santa Barbara I., U.S.A. 79 M7 33 29N 119 2W
Santa Catalina, Gulf of, U.S.A. . 79 N9 33 10N 117 50W
Santa Catalina, I., Mexico 86 B2 25 40N 110 50W
Santa Catalina I., U.S.A. 79 M8 33 23N 118 25W
Santa Catarina □, Brazil 95 B6 27 25S 48 30W
Santa Catarina, I. de, Brazil ... 95 B6 27 30S 48 40W
Santa Cecília, Brazil 95 B5 26 56S 50 18W
Santa Clara, Cuba 88 B4 22 20N 80 0W
Santa Clara, Calif., U.S.A. 78 H5 37 21N 121 57W
Santa Clara, Utah, U.S.A. 77 H7 37 8N 113 39W
Santa Clara, El Golfo de, Mexico 86 A2 31 42N 114 30W
Santa Clara de Olimar, Uruguay 95 C5 32 50S 54 54W
Santa Clarita, U.S.A. 79 L8 34 24N 118 30W
Santa Clotilde, Peru 92 D4 2 33S 73 45W
Santa Coloma de Gramenet,
   Spain .... 21 B7 41 27N 2 13 E
Santa Cruz, Argentina 96 G3 50 0S 68 32W
Santa Cruz, Bolivia 92 G6 17 43S 63 10W
Santa Cruz, Chile 94 C1 34 38S 71 27W
Santa Cruz, Costa Rica 88 D2 10 15N 85 35W
Santa Cruz, Madeira 24 D3 32 42N 16 46W
Santa Cruz, Phil. .... 37 B6 14 20N 121 24 E
Santa Cruz →, Argentina 96 G3 50 10S 68 20W
Santa Cruz de la Palma,
   Canary Is. 24 F2 28 41N 17 46W
Santa Cruz de la Palma ✈ (SPC),
   Canary Is. 24 F2 28 40N 17 45W
Santa Cruz de Tenerife,
   Canary Is. 24 F3 28 28N 16 15W
Santa Cruz del Norte, Cuba 88 B3 23 9N 81 55W
Santa Cruz del Sur, Cuba 88 B4 20 44N 78 0W
Santa Cruz do Rio Pardo, Brazil . 95 A6 22 54S 49 37W
Santa Cruz do Sul, Brazil 95 B5 29 42S 52 25W
Santa Cruz I., U.S.A. 79 M7 34 1N 119 43W
Santa Cruz Is., Solomon Is. ... 64 J8 10 30S 166 0 E
Santa Cruz Mts., Jamaica .... 88 a 17 58N 77 43W
Santa Domingo, Cay, Bahamas . 88 B4 21 25N 75 15W
Santa Elena, Argentina 94 C4 30 58S 59 47W
Santa Elena, C., Costa Rica 88 D2 10 54N 85 56W
Santa Eulàlia des Riu, Spain ... 24 C8 38 59N 1 32 E
Santa Fe, Argentina 94 C3 31 35S 60 41W
Santa Fe, U.S.A. 77 J11 35 41N 105 57W
Santa Fé □, Argentina 94 C3 31 50S 60 55W
Santa Fé do Sul, Brazil 93 H8 20 13S 50 56W
Santa Filomena, Brazil 93 E9 9 6S 45 50W
Santa Gertrudis, Spain .... 24 C7 39 0N 1 26 E
Santa Inês, Brazil 93 F11 3 13S 39 48W
Santa Inés, I., Chile 96 G2 54 0S 73 0W
Santa Isabel, Argentina 94 D2 36 10S 66 54W
Santa Isabel do Morro, Brazil . 93 F8 11 34S 50 40W
Santa Lucia, Corrientes,
   Argentina 94 B4 28 58S 59 5W
Santa Lucia, San Juan, Argentina 94 C2 31 30S 68 30W
Santa Lucia, Uruguay 94 C4 34 27S 56 24W
Santa Lucia Range, U.S.A. 78 K5 36 0N 121 20W
Santa Magdalena, I., Mexico ... 86 C2 24 40N 112 15W
Santa Margarita, Argentina 94 D3 38 28S 61 35W
Santa Margarita, Spain .... 24 B10 39 42N 3 6 E
Santa Margarita, U.S.A. 78 K6 35 23N 120 37W
Santa Margarita →, U.S.A. 79 M9 33 13N 117 23W
Santa Margarita, I., Mexico 86 C2 24 30N 111 50W
Santa Maria, Argentina 94 B2 26 40S 66 0W
Santa Maria, Brazil 95 B5 29 40S 53 48W
Santa Maria, U.S.A. 79 L6 34 57N 120 26W
Santa Maria, B. de, Mexico 86 B3 25 10N 108 40W
Santa María →, Mexico 86 A3 31 0N 107 14W
Santa Maria da Vitória, Brazil . 93 F10 13 24S 44 12W
Santa María del Camí, Spain ... 24 B9 39 38N 2 47 E
Santa Maria di Léuca, C., Italy . 23 F8 39 47N 18 22 E
Santa Marta, Colombia 92 A4 11 15N 74 13W
Santa Marta, Sierra Nevada de,
   Colombia 92 A4 10 55N 73 50W
Santa Marta Grande, C., Brazil . 95 B6 28 43S 48 50W
Santa Maura = Levkás, Greece . 23 E9 38 40N 20 43 E
Santa Monica, U.S.A. 79 M8 34 1N 118 29W
Santa Monica Mts. ○, U.S.A. ... 79 L8 34 4N 118 44W
Santa Paula, U.S.A. 79 L7 34 21N 119 4W
Santa Ponça, Spain .... 24 B9 39 30N 2 28 E
Santa Rita, U.S.A. 77 K10 32 48N 108 4W
Santa Rosa, La Pampa, Argentina 94 D3 36 40S 64 17W
Santa Rosa, San Luis, Argentina 94 C2 32 21S 65 10W
Santa Rosa, Brazil 95 B5 27 52S 54 29W
Santa Rosa, Calif., U.S.A. 78 G4 38 26N 122 43W
Santa Rosa, N. Mex., U.S.A. ... 81 H2 34 57N 104 41W
Santa Rosa and San Jacinto
   Mts. ○, U.S.A. 79 M10 33 28N 116 20W
Santa Rosa de Copán, Honduras 88 D2 14 47N 88 46W
Santa Rosa de Río Primero,
   Argentina 94 C3 31 8S 63 20W
Santa Rosa del Sara, Bolivia ... 92 G6 17 7S 63 35W
Santa Rosa I., Calif., U.S.A. ... 79 M6 33 58N 120 6W
Santa Rosa I., Fla., U.S.A. 83 K2 30 20N 86 50W
Santa Rosa Range, U.S.A. 76 F5 41 45N 117 40W
Santa Rosalía, Mexico 86 B2 27 20N 112 20W
Santa Sylvina, Argentina 94 B3 27 50S 61 10W
Santa Tecla = Nueva San
   Salvador, El Salv. 88 D2 13 40N 89 18W
Santa Teresa, Argentina 94 C3 33 25S 60 47W
Santa Teresa, Australia .... 62 C1 24 8S 134 22 E
Santa Teresa, Mexico 87 B5 25 17N 97 51W
Santa Teresa △, Uruguay 95 C5 33 57S 53 52W
Santa Vitória do Palmar, Brazil . 95 C5 33 32S 53 25W
Santa Ynez →, U.S.A. 79 L6 34 37N 120 41W
Santa Ynez Mts., U.S.A. 79 L6 34 30N 120 0W
Santa Ysabel, U.S.A. 79 M10 33 7N 116 40W
Santai, China .... 32 C5 31 5N 104 58 E
Santana, Madeira 24 D3 32 48N 16 52W
Santana, Coxilha de, Brazil 95 C4 30 50S 55 35W
Santana do Livramento, Brazil . 95 C4 30 55S 55 30W
Santander, Spain 21 A4 43 27N 3 51W
Santander Jiménez, Mexico 87 C5 24 11N 98 29W
Santanilla, Is., Honduras 88 C3 17 22N 83 57W
Santany, Spain .... 24 B10 39 20N 3 5 E
Santaquin, U.S.A. 76 G8 39 59N 111 47W
Santarém, Brazil 93 D8 2 25S 54 42W

Santarém, Portugal 21 C1 39 12N 8 42W
Santaren Channel, W. Indies ... 88 B4 24 0N 79 30W
Santee, U.S.A. 79 N10 32 50N 116 58W
Santee →, U.S.A. 83 J6 33 7N 79 17W
Santiago, Brazil 95 B5 29 11S 54 52W
Santiago, Canary Is. 24 F2 28 2N 17 12W
Santiago, Chile 94 C1 33 24S 70 40W
Santiago, Panama 88 E3 8 0N 81 0W
Santiago □, Chile 94 C1 33 30S 70 50W
Santiago →, Mexico 66 G9 25 11N 105 26W
Santiago →, Peru 92 D3 4 27S 77 38W
Santiago de Compostela, Spain . 21 A1 42 52N 8 37W
Santiago de Cuba, Cuba 88 C4 20 0N 75 49W
Santiago de los Cabelleros,
   Dom. Rep. 89 C5 19 30N 70 40W
Santiago del Estero, Argentina . 94 B3 27 50S 64 15W
Santiago del Estero □, Argentina 94 B3 27 40S 63 15W
Santiago del Teide, Canary Is. . 24 F3 28 17N 16 48W
Santiago Ixcuintla, Mexico 86 C3 21 50N 105 11W
Santiago Papasquiaro, Mexico . 86 C3 25 0N 105 20W
Santiaguillo, L. de, Mexico 86 C4 24 50N 104 50W
Santo Amaro, Brazil 93 F11 12 30S 38 43W
Santo Anastácio, Brazil 95 A5 21 58S 51 39W
Santo André, Brazil 95 A6 23 39S 46 29W
Santo Ângelo, Brazil 95 B5 28 15S 54 15W
Santo Antônio do Içá, Brazil ... 92 D5 3 5S 67 57W
Santo Antônio do Leverger,
   Brazil 93 G7 15 52S 56 5W
Santo Domingo, Dom. Rep. 89 C6 18 30N 69 59W
Santo Domingo, Baja Calif.,
   Mexico 86 A1 30 43N 116 2W
Santo Domingo, Baja Calif. S.,
   Mexico 86 B2 25 32N 112 2W
Santo Domingo, Nic. 88 D3 12 14N 84 59W
Santo Domingo de los
   Colorados, Ecuador 92 D3 0 15S 79 9W
Santo Domingo Pueblo, U.S.A. . 77 J10 35 31N 106 22W
Santo Tomás, Mexico 86 A1 31 33N 116 24W
Santo Tomás, Peru 92 F4 14 26S 72 8W
Santo Tomé, Argentina 95 B4 28 40S 56 5W
Santo Tomé de Guayana =
   Ciudad Guayana, Venezuela . 92 B6 8 0N 62 30W
Santoña, Spain 21 A4 43 29N 3 27W
Santorini = Thira, Greece .... 23 F11 36 23N 25 27 E
Santos, Brazil 95 A6 24 0S 46 20W
Santos Dumont, Brazil 95 A7 22 55S 43 10W
Sanur, Indonesia .... 37 K18 8 41S 115 15 E
Sanwer, India .... 42 H6 22 59N 75 50 E
Sanxiang, China .... 33 G9 22 21N 113 25 E
Sanyuan, China .... 34 G5 34 35N 108 58 E
São Bernardo do Campo, Brazil . 95 A6 23 45S 46 34W
São Borja, Brazil 95 B4 28 39S 56 0W
São Carlos, Brazil 95 A6 22 0S 47 50W
São Cristóvão, Brazil 93 F11 11 1S 37 15W
São Domingos, Brazil 93 F9 13 25S 46 19W
São Francisco, Brazil 93 G10 16 0S 44 50W
São Francisco →, Brazil 93 F11 10 30S 36 24W
São Francisco do Sul, Brazil ... 95 B6 26 15S 48 36W
São Gabriel, Brazil 95 C5 30 20S 54 20W
São Gonçalo, Brazil 95 A7 22 48S 43 5W
Sao Hill, Tanzania .... 55 D4 8 20S 35 12 E
São João da Boa Vista, Brazil . 95 A6 22 0S 46 52W
São João da Madeira, Portugal . 21 B1 40 54N 8 30W
São João del Rei, Brazil 95 A7 21 8S 44 15W
São João do Araguaia, Brazil ... 93 E9 5 23S 48 46W
São João do Piauí, Brazil 93 E10 8 21S 42 15W
São Joaquim, Brazil 95 B6 28 18S 49 56W
São Joaquim △, Brazil 95 B6 28 12S 49 37W
São Jorge, Pta. de, Madeira ... 24 D3 32 50N 16 53W
São José, Brazil 95 B6 27 38S 48 39W
São José do Norte, Brazil 95 C5 32 1S 52 3W
São José do Rio Prêto, Brazil ... 95 A6 20 50S 49 20W
São José dos Campos, Brazil ... 95 A6 23 7S 45 52W
São Leopoldo, Brazil 95 B5 29 50S 51 10W
São Lourenço, Brazil 95 A7 22 7S 45 3W
São Lourenço →, Brazil 93 G7 17 53S 57 27W
São Lourenço, Pta. de, Madeira 24 D3 32 44N 16 39W
São Lourenço do Sul, Brazil ... 95 C5 31 22S 51 58W
São Luís, Brazil 93 D10 2 39S 44 15W
São Luís Gonzaga, Brazil 95 B5 28 25S 55 0W
São Marcos →, Brazil 93 G9 18 15S 47 37W
São Marcos, B. de, Brazil 93 D10 2 0S 44 0W
São Mateus, Brazil 93 G11 18 44S 39 50W
São Mateus →, Brazil 95 A8 18 44S 39 50W
São Miguel do Oeste, Brazil ... 95 B5 26 45S 53 34W
São Paulo, Brazil 95 A6 23 32S 46 37W
São Paulo □, Brazil 95 A6 22 0S 49 0W
São Paulo, I., Atl. Oc. 2 D8 0 50N 31 40W
São Paulo de Olivença, Brazil . 92 D5 3 27S 68 48W
São Roque, Madeira 24 D3 32 46N 16 48W
São Roque, C. de, Brazil 93 E11 5 30S 35 16W
São Sebastião, I. de, Brazil 95 A6 23 50S 45 18W
São Sebastião do Paraíso, Brazil 95 A6 20 54S 46 59W
São Tomé, São Tomé & Príncipe 48 F4 0 10N 6 39 E
São Tomé, C. de, Brazil 95 A7 22 0S 40 59W
São Tomé & Príncipe ■, Africa . 49 F4 0 12N 6 39 E
São Vicente, Brazil 95 A6 23 57S 46 23W
São Vicente, Madeira 24 D2 32 48N 17 3W
São Vicente, C. de, Portugal ... 21 D1 37 0N 9 0W
Saona, I., Dom. Rep. 89 C6 18 10N 68 40W
Saône →, France .... 20 D6 45 44N 4 50 E
Saonek, Indonesia .... 37 E8 0 22S 130 55 E
Sapam, Ao, Thailand .... 39 a 8 9N 98 26 E
Saparua, Indonesia .... 37 E7 3 33S 128 40 E
Sapele, Nigeria .... 50 G7 5 50N 5 40 E
Sapelo I., U.S.A. 83 K5 31 25N 81 12W
Sapi △, Zimbabwe .... 55 F2 15 58S 29 59 E
Saposoa, Peru 92 E3 6 55S 76 45W
Sapphire, Australia .... 62 C4 23 28S 147 43 E
Sappho, U.S.A. 78 B2 48 4N 124 16W
Sapporo, Japan .... 30 C10 43 0N 141 21 E
Sapulpa, U.S.A. 81 H6 35 59N 96 5W
Saqqez, Iran .... 44 B5 36 15N 46 20 E
Sar Dasht, Iran .... 45 C6 32 32N 48 52 E
Sar-e Pol □, Afghan. .... 40 B4 36 20N 65 50 E
Sar Gachineh = Yāsūj, Iran .... 45 D6 30 31N 51 31 E
Sar Planina, Macedonia .... 23 C9 42 0N 21 0 E
Sara Buri = Saraburi, Thailand . 38 E3 14 30N 100 55 E
Saráb, Iran .... 44 B5 37 55N 47 40 E
Sarabadi, Iraq .... 44 C5 33 1N 44 48 E
Saraburi, Thailand .... 38 E3 14 30N 100 55 E
Saradiya, India .... 42 J4 21 34N 70 2 E
Saraikela, India .... 43 H11 22 42N 85 56 E
Sarajevo, Bos.-H. .... 23 C8 43 52N 18 26 E
Sarakhs, Turkmenistan .... 45 B9 36 32N 61 13 E

Saran, Gunung, Indonesia .... 36 E4 0 30S 111 25 E
Saranac L., U.S.A. 85 B10 44 20N 74 10W
Saranac Lake, U.S.A. 85 B10 44 20N 74 8W
Saranda, Tanzania .... 54 D3 5 45S 34 59 E
Sarandí del Yi, Uruguay 95 C4 33 18S 55 38W
Sarandí Grande, Uruguay 94 C4 33 44S 56 20W
Sarangani B., Phil. .... 37 C7 6 0N 125 13 E
Sarangani Is., Phil. .... 37 C7 5 25N 125 25 E
Sarangarh, India .... 41 J13 21 30N 83 5 E
Saransk, Russia .... 18 D8 54 10N 45 10 E
Sarapul, Russia .... 18 C9 56 28N 53 48 E
Sarasota, U.S.A. 83 M4 27 20N 82 32W
Saratoga, Calif., U.S.A. 78 H4 37 16N 122 2W
Saratoga, Wyo., U.S.A. 76 F10 41 27N 106 48W
Saratoga △, U.S.A. 85 C11 43 5N 73 47W
Saratoga Springs, U.S.A. 85 C11 43 5N 73 47W
Saratok, Malaysia .... 36 D4 1 55N 111 17 E
Saratov, Russia .... 19 D8 51 30N 46 2 E
Saravane, Laos .... 38 E6 15 43N 106 25 E
Sarawak □, Malaysia .... 36 D4 2 0N 113 0 E
Saray, Turkey .... 23 D12 41 26N 27 55 E
Sarayköy, Turkey .... 23 F13 37 55N 28 54 E
Sarbāz, Iran .... 45 E9 26 38N 61 19 E
Sarbīsheh, Iran .... 45 C8 32 30N 59 40 E
Sarda →, India .... 41 F12 27 21N 81 23 E
Sardarshahr, India .... 42 E6 28 30N 74 29 E
Sardegna □, Italy .... 22 D3 40 0N 9 0 E
Sardhana, India .... 42 E7 29 9N 77 39 E
Sardina, Pta., Canary Is. 24 F4 28 9N 15 42W
Sardinia = Sardegna □, Italy ... 22 D3 40 0N 9 0 E
Sardis, Turkey .... 23 E12 38 28N 28 2 E
Särdūīyeh = Dar Mazār, Iran ... 45 D8 29 14N 57 20 E
Saren, Indonesia .... 37 J18 8 26S 115 30 E
S'Arenal, Spain .... 24 B9 39 30N 2 45 E
Sargasso Sea, Atl. Oc. 66 G13 27 0N 72 0W
Sargodha, Pakistan .... 42 C5 32 10N 72 40 E
Sarh, Chad .... 51 G9 9 5N 18 23 E
Sārī, Iran .... 45 B7 36 30N 53 4 E
Saria, India .... 43 J10 21 38N 83 22 E
Sariab, Pakistan .... 42 D2 30 6N 66 59 E
Sarıgöl, Turkey .... 23 E13 38 14N 28 41 E
Sarikei, Malaysia .... 36 D4 2 8N 111 30 E
Sarila, India .... 43 G8 25 46N 79 41 E
Sarina, Australia .... 62 C4 21 22S 149 13 E
Sarita, U.S.A. 81 M6 27 13N 97 47W
Sariwŏn, N. Korea .... 35 E13 38 31N 125 46 E
Sarju →, India .... 43 F9 27 21N 81 23 E
Sark, U.K. 13 H5 49 25N 2 22W
Sarkari Tala, India .... 42 F4 27 39N 70 52 E
Şarköy, Turkey .... 23 D12 40 36N 27 6 E
Sarlat-la-Canéda, France .... 20 D4 44 54N 1 13 E
Sarmi, Indonesia .... 37 E9 1 49S 138 44 E
Sarmiento, Argentina 96 F3 45 35S 69 5W
Särna, Sweden .... 9 F15 61 41N 13 8 E
Sarnia, Canada 84 D2 42 58N 82 23W
Saroako, Indonesia .... 37 E6 2 19S 121 8 E
Saronikós Kólpos, Greece .... 23 F10 37 45N 23 45 E
Saros Körfezi, Turkey .... 23 D12 40 30N 26 15 E
Sarpsborg, Norway .... 9 G14 59 16N 11 12 E
Sarre = Saar →, Europe .... 15 E6 49 41N 6 32 E
Sarreguemines, France .... 20 B7 49 5N 7 4 E
Sarthe →, France 20 C3 47 33N 0 31W
Saruna →, Pakistan .... 42 F2 26 31N 67 7 E
Sarvar, India .... 42 F6 26 4N 75 0 E
Sarvestān, Iran .... 45 D7 29 20N 53 10 E
Sary-Tash, Kyrgyzstan .... 28 F8 39 44N 73 15 E
Saryshagan, Kazakhstan .... 28 E8 46 12N 73 38 E
Sasan Gir, India .... 42 J4 21 10N 70 36 E
Sasaram, India .... 43 G11 24 57N 84 5 E
Sasebo, Japan .... 31 H4 33 10N 129 43 E
Saser, India .... 43 B7 34 50N 77 50 E
Saskatchewan □, Canada 71 C7 54 40N 106 0W
Saskatchewan →, Canada 71 C8 53 37N 100 40W
Saskatoon, Canada 71 C7 52 10N 106 38W
Saskylakh, Russia .... 29 B12 71 55N 114 1 E
Saslaya △, Nic. 88 D2 13 45N 85 4W
Sasolburg, S. Africa .... 57 D4 26 46S 27 49 E
Sasovo, Russia .... 18 D7 54 25N 41 55 E
Sassandra, Ivory C. 50 H4 4 58S 6 5W
Sassandra →, Ivory C. 50 H4 4 58N 6 5W
Sássari, Italy .... 22 D3 40 43N 8 34 E
Sassnitz, Germany .... 16 A7 54 29N 13 39 E
Sassuolo, Italy .... 22 B4 44 33N 10 47 E
Sasyk, Ozero, Ukraine .... 17 F15 45 45N 29 20 E
Sata-Misaki, Japan .... 31 J5 31 0N 130 40 E
Satadougou, Mali 50 F3 12 25N 11 25W
Satakunta, Finland .... 9 F20 61 45N 23 2 E
Satara, India .... 40 L8 17 44N 73 58 E
Satara, S. Africa .... 57 C5 24 29S 31 47 E
Satarwa, India .... 43 H11 23 6S 84 6 E
Satevó, Mexico 86 B3 27 57N 106 7W
Satilla →, U.S.A. 83 K5 30 59N 81 29W
Satka, Russia .... 18 C10 55 3N 59 1 E
Satmala Hills, India .... 40 J9 20 15N 74 40 E
Satna, India .... 43 G9 24 35N 80 50 E
Sátoraljaújhely, Hungary .... 17 D11 48 25N 21 41 E
Satpura Ra., India .... 40 J10 21 25N 76 10 E
Satsuna-Shotō, Japan .... 31 K5 30 0N 130 0 E
Sattahip, Thailand .... 38 F3 12 41N 100 54 E
Satu Mare, Romania .... 17 E12 47 46N 22 55 E
Satui, Indonesia .... 36 E5 3 50S 115 27 E
Satun, Thailand .... 39 J3 6 43N 100 2 E
Saturnina →, Brazil 92 F7 12 15S 58 10W
Sauce, Argentina 94 C4 30 5S 58 46W
Sauceda, Mexico 86 B4 25 55N 101 19W
Saucillo, Mexico 86 B3 28 1N 105 17W
Sauda, Norway .... 9 G12 59 40N 6 20 E
Sauðárkrókur, Iceland 8 D4 65 45N 19 40W
Saudi Arabia ■, Asia .... 44 B3 26 0N 44 0 E
Sauerland, Germany .... 16 C4 51 12N 7 59 E
Saugeen →, Canada 84 B3 44 30N 81 22W
Saugerties, U.S.A. 85 D11 42 5N 73 57W
Saugus, U.S.A. 79 L8 34 25N 118 32W
Sauk Centre, U.S.A. 80 C7 45 44N 94 57W
Sauk Rapids, U.S.A. 80 C7 45 35N 94 10W
Sault Ste. Marie, Canada 72 C3 46 30N 84 20W
Sault Ste. Marie, U.S.A. 81 B3 46 30N 84 21W
Saumlaki, Indonesia .... 37 F8 7 55S 131 20 E
Saumur, France 20 C3 47 15N 0 5W
Saunders C., N.Z. .... 59 L3 45 53S 170 45 E
Saunders I., Antarctica 5 B1 57 48S 26 28W
Saunders Point, Australia .... 61 E4 27 52S 125 38 E
Saurimo, Angola .... 52 F4 9 40S 20 12 E
Sausalito, U.S.A. 78 H4 37 51N 122 29W
Savá, Honduras 88 C2 15 32N 86 15W
Sava →, Serbia & M. .... 23 B9 44 50N 20 26 E
Savage, U.S.A. 80 B2 47 27N 104 21W

avage I. = Niue, Cook Is. 65 J11 19 2S 169 54W
avage River, Australia ...... 63 G4 41 31S 145 14 E
avai'i, Samoa 59 A12 13 28S 172 24W
avalou, Benin ...... 50 G6 7 57N 1 58 E
avane, Mozam. ...... 55 F4 19 37S 35 8 E
avanna-la-Mar, Jamaica ...... 88 a 18 10N 78 10W
avannah, Ga., U.S.A. 83 J5 32 5N 81 6W
avannah, Mo., U.S.A. 80 F7 39 56N 94 50W
avannah, Tenn., U.S.A. 83 H1 35 14N 88 15W
avannah →, U.S.A. 83 J5 32 2N 80 53W
avannakhet, Laos ...... 38 D5 16 30N 104 49 E
avant Lake, Canada 72 B1 50 16N 90 44W
avant Lake, Canada 72 B1 50 14N 90 40W
avé, Mozam. ...... 57 C5 21 16S 34 0 E
avelugu, Ghana 50 G5 9 38N 0 54W
avo, Finland ...... 8 E22 62 45N 27 30 E
avoie □, France ...... 20 D7 45 26N 6 25 E
avona, Italy ...... 20 D8 44 17N 8 30 E
avona, U.S.A. 84 D7 42 17N 77 13W
avonlinna, Finland ...... 18 B4 61 52N 28 53 E
avoy = Savoie □, France ...... 20 D7 45 26N 6 25 E
avur, Turkey ...... 44 B4 37 34N 40 53 E
awahlunto, Indonesia ...... 36 E2 0 40S 100 52 E
awai, Indonesia ...... 37 E7 3 0S 129 5 E
awai Madhopur, India ...... 42 G7 26 0N 76 25 E
awang Daen Din, Thailand ...... 38 D4 17 28N 103 28 E
awankhalok, Thailand ...... 38 D2 17 19N 99 50 E
awara, Japan ...... 31 G10 35 55N 140 30 E
awatch Range, U.S.A. 77 G10 38 30N 106 30W
awel Mt., U.K. 10 B4 54 50N 7 2W
awi, Thailand ...... 39 G2 10 14N 99 5 E
awmills, Zimbabwe ...... 55 F2 19 30S 28 2 E
awtooth △, U.S.A. 76 D6 44 0N 114 50W
awtooth Range, U.S.A. 76 E6 44 3N 114 58W
awu, Indonesia ...... 37 F6 10 35S 121 50 E
awu Sea, Indonesia ...... 37 F6 9 30S 121 50 E
axby →, Australia ...... 62 B3 18 25S 140 53 E
axmundham, U.K. ...... 13 E9 52 13N 1 30 E
axony = Sachsen □, Germany ...... 16 C7 50 55N 13 10 E
axony, Lower =
Niedersachsen □, Germany .. 16 B5 52 50N 9 0 E
axton, U.S.A. 84 F6 40 13N 78 15W
ayabec, Canada 73 C6 48 35N 67 41W
ayaboury, Laos ...... 38 C3 19 15N 101 45 E
ayán, Peru 92 F3 11 8S 77 12W
ayan, Vostochnyy, Russia ...... 29 D10 54 0N 96 0 E
ayan, Zapadnyy, Russia ...... 29 D10 52 30N 94 0 E
aydā, Lebanon ...... 46 B4 33 35N 35 25 E
ayhandulaan = Oldziyt,
Mongolia ...... 34 B5 44 40N 109 1 E
ayhūt, Yemen ...... 47 D5 15 12N 51 10 E
aylac = Zeila, Somali Rep. ...... 47 E3 11 21N 43 30 E
aynshand, Mongolia ...... 33 B6 44 55N 110 11 E
ayre, Okla., U.S.A. 81 H5 35 18N 99 38W
ayre, Pa., U.S.A. 85 E8 41 59N 76 32W
ayreville, U.S.A. 85 F10 40 28N 74 22W
ayula, Mexico 86 D4 19 50N 103 40W
ayward, Canada 70 C3 50 21N 125 55W
azanit, Albania ...... 23 D8 40 30N 19 20 E
azava →, Czech Rep. ...... 16 D8 49 53N 14 24 E
azin, Pakistan ...... 43 B5 35 35N 73 30 E
afell Pike, U.S.A. 12 C4 54 27N 3 14W
alloway, U.K. 11 A7 60 9N 1 17W
alpay, U.K. 11 D3 57 18N 6 0W
andia, Canada 70 C6 50 20N 112 2W
andicci, Italy ...... 22 C4 43 45N 11 11 E
andinavia, Europe ...... 8 E16 64 0N 12 0 E
apa Flow, U.K. 11 C5 58 53N 3 3W
appoose, U.S.A. 78 E4 45 45N 122 53W
arba, U.K. 11 E3 56 11N 5 43W
arborough, Trin. & Tob. 89 D7 11 11N 60 42W
arborough, U.K. 12 C7 54 17N 0 24W
ariff I., Ireland 10 E1 51 44N 10 15W
arp, U.K. 11 C1 58 1N 7 8W
cebeli, Wabi →, Somali Rep. . 47 G3 2 0N 44 0 E
chaffhausen, Switz. ...... 20 C8 47 42N 8 39 E
chagen, Neths. ...... 15 B4 52 49N 4 48 E
chaghticoke, U.S.A. 85 D11 42 54N 73 35W
chefferville, Canada 73 B6 54 48N 66 50W
chelde →, Belgium ...... 15 C4 51 15N 4 16 E
chell Creek Ra., U.S.A. 76 G6 39 15N 114 30W
chellsburg, U.S.A. 84 F6 40 3N 78 39W
chenectady, U.S.A. 85 D11 42 49N 73 57W
chenevus, U.S.A. 85 D10 42 33N 74 50W
chiedam, Neths. ...... 15 C4 51 55N 4 25 E
chiermonnikoog, Neths. ...... 15 A6 53 30N 6 15 E
chio, Italy ...... 22 B4 45 43N 11 21 E
chiphol, Amsterdam ✈ (AMS),
Neths. ...... 15 B4 52 18N 4 45 E
chleswig, Germany ...... 16 A5 54 31N 9 34 E
chleswig-Holstein □, Germany . 16 A5 54 30N 9 30 E
chœlcher, Martinique ...... 88 c 14 36N 61 7W
choharie, U.S.A. 85 D10 42 40N 74 19W
choharie →, U.S.A. 85 D10 42 57N 74 18W
chouten I., Australia ...... 63 G4 42 20S 148 20 E
chouten Is. = Supiori, Indonesia 37 E9 1 0S 136 0 E
chouwen, Neths. ...... 15 C3 51 43N 3 45 E
chreiber, Canada 72 C2 48 45N 87 20W
chroffenstein, Namibia ...... 56 D2 27 11S 18 42 E
chroon Lake, U.S.A. 85 C11 43 50N 73 46W
chuler, Canada 71 C6 50 20N 110 6W
chumacher, Canada 72 C3 48 30N 81 16W
churz, U.S.A. 76 G4 38 57N 118 49W
chuyler, U.S.A. 80 E6 41 27N 97 4W
chuylerville, U.S.A. 85 C11 43 6N 73 35W
chuylkill →, U.S.A. 85 G9 39 53N 75 12W
chuylkill Haven, U.S.A. 85 F8 40 37N 76 11W
chwäbische Alb, Germany ...... 16 D5 48 20N 9 30 E
chwaner, Pegunungan,
Indonesia ...... 36 E4 1 0S 112 30 E
chwarzrand, Namibia ...... 56 D2 25 37S 16 50 E
chwarzwald, Germany ...... 16 D5 48 30N 8 20 E
chwedt, Germany ...... 16 B8 53 3N 14 16 E
chweinfurt, Germany ...... 16 C6 50 3N 10 14 E
chweizer-Reneke, S. Africa ...... 56 D4 27 11S 25 18 E
chwenningen = Villingen-
Schwenningen, Germany ...... 16 D5 48 3N 8 26 E
chwerin, Germany ...... 16 B6 53 36N 11 22 E
chwyz, Switz. ...... 20 C8 47 2N 8 39 E
ciacca, Italy ...... 22 F5 37 31N 13 3 E
cilla, Italy ...... 22 E6 38 15N 15 43 E
cilly, Isles of, U.K. 13 H1 49 56N 6 22W
cioto →, U.S.A. 82 F4 38 44N 83 1W
cituate, U.S.A. 85 D14 42 12N 70 44W
cobey, U.S.A. 80 A2 48 47N 105 25W

Scone, Australia ...... 63 E5 32 5S 150 52 E
Scone, U.K. 11 E5 56 25N 3 24W
Scoresbysund = Ittoqqortoormiit,
Greenland 4 B6 70 20N 23 0W
Scotia, Calif., U.S.A. 76 F1 40 29N 124 6W
Scotia, N.Y., U.S.A. 85 D11 42 50N 73 58W
Scotia Sea, Antarctica 5 B18 56 5S 56 0W
Scotland, Canada 84 C4 43 1N 80 22W
Scotland □, U.K. 11 E5 57 0N 4 0W
Scott, Antarctica ...... 5 D11 77 0S 165 0 E
Scott, C., Australia ...... 60 B4 13 30S 129 49 E
Scott City, U.S.A. 80 F4 38 29N 100 54W
Scott Glacier, Antarctica ...... 5 C8 66 15S 100 5 E
Scott I., Antarctica ...... 5 C11 67 0S 179 0 E
Scott Is., Canada 70 C3 50 48N 128 40W
Scott L., Canada 71 B7 59 55N 106 18W
Scott Reef, Australia ...... 60 B3 14 0S 121 50 E
Scottburgh, S. Africa ...... 57 E5 30 15S 30 47 E
Scottdale, U.S.A. 84 F5 40 6N 79 35W
Scottsbluff, U.S.A. 80 E3 41 52N 103 40W
Scottsboro, U.S.A. 83 H3 34 40N 86 2W
Scottsburg, U.S.A. 82 F3 38 41N 85 47W
Scottsdale, Australia ...... 63 G4 41 9S 147 31 E
Scottsdale, U.S.A. 77 K7 33 29N 111 56W
Scottsville, Ky., U.S.A. 83 G2 36 45N 86 11W
Scottsville, N.Y., U.S.A. 84 C7 43 2N 77 47W
Scottville, U.S.A. 82 D2 43 58N 86 17W
Scranton, U.S.A. 85 E9 41 25N 75 40W
Scugog, L., Canada 84 B6 44 10N 78 55W
Scunthorpe, U.K. 12 D7 53 36N 0 39W
Scutari = Shkodër, Albania ...... 23 C8 42 4N 19 32 E
Seabrook, L., Australia ...... 61 F2 30 55S 119 40 E
Seaford, U.K. ...... 13 G8 50 47N 0 7 E
Seaford, U.S.A. 82 F8 38 39N 75 37W
Seaforth, Australia ...... 62 J6 20 55S 148 57 E
Seaforth, Canada 84 C3 43 35N 81 25W
Seaforth, L., U.K. 11 D2 57 52N 6 36W
Seagraves, U.S.A. 81 J3 32 57N 102 34W
Seaham, U.K. 12 C6 54 50N 1 20W
Seal →, Canada 71 B10 59 4N 94 48W
Seal L., Canada 73 B7 54 20N 61 30W
Sealy, U.S.A. 81 L6 29 47N 96 9W
Searchlight, U.S.A. 79 K12 35 28N 114 55W
Searcy, U.S.A. 81 H9 35 15N 91 44W
Searles L., U.S.A. 79 K9 35 44N 117 21W
Seascale, U.K. 12 C4 54 24N 3 29W
Seaside, Calif., U.S.A. 78 J5 36 37N 121 50W
Seaside, Oreg., U.S.A. 78 E3 46 0N 123 56W
Seaspray, Australia ...... 63 F4 38 25S 147 15 E
Seattle, U.S.A. 78 C4 47 36N 122 20W
Seattle-Tacoma International ✈
(SEA), U.S.A. 78 C4 47 27N 122 18W
Seaview Ra., Australia ...... 62 B4 18 40S 145 45 E
Sebago L., U.S.A. 85 C14 43 52N 70 34W
Sebago Lake, U.S.A. 85 C14 43 51N 70 34W
Sebastián Vizcaíno, B., Mexico . 86 B2 28 0N 114 30W
Sebastopol = Sevastopol,
Ukraine ...... 19 F5 44 35N 33 30 E
Sebastopol, U.S.A. 78 G4 38 24N 122 49W
Sebewaing, U.S.A. 82 D4 43 44N 83 27W
Sebha = Sabhah, Libya ...... 51 C8 27 9N 14 29 E
Şebinkarahisar, Turkey ...... 19 F6 40 22N 38 28 E
Sebring, Fla., U.S.A. 83 M5 27 30N 81 27W
Sebring, Ohio, U.S.A. 84 F3 40 55N 81 2W
Sebringville, Canada 84 C3 43 24N 81 4W
Sebta = Ceuta, N. Afr. 21 E3 35 52N 5 18W
Sebuku, Indonesia ...... 36 E5 3 30S 116 25 E
Sebuku, Teluk, Malaysia ...... 36 D5 4 0N 118 10 E
Sechelt, Canada 70 D4 49 25N 123 42W
Sechura, Desierto de, Peru 92 E2 6 0S 80 30W
Secretary I., N.Z. ...... 59 L1 45 15S 166 56 E
Secunderabad, India ...... 40 L11 17 28N 78 30 E
Security-Widefield, U.S.A. 80 F2 38 45N 104 45W
Sedalia, U.S.A. 80 F8 38 42N 93 14W
Sedan, France ...... 20 B6 49 43N 4 57 E
Sedan, U.S.A. 81 G6 37 8N 96 11W
Sedbergh, U.K. 12 C5 54 20N 2 31W
Seddon, N.Z. ...... 59 J5 41 40S 174 7 E
Seddonville, N.Z. ...... 59 J4 41 33S 172 1 E
Sedé Boqér, Israel ...... 46 E3 30 52N 34 47 E
Sedeh, Fārs, Iran ...... 45 D7 30 45N 52 11 E
Sedeh, Khorāsān, Iran ...... 45 C8 33 20N 59 14 E
Sederot, Israel ...... 46 D3 31 32N 34 37 E
Sédhiou, Senegal 50 F2 12 44N 15 30W
Sedley, Canada 71 C8 50 10N 104 0W
Sedona, U.S.A. 77 J8 34 52N 111 46W
Sedova, Pik, Russia ...... 28 B6 73 29N 54 58 E
Sedro Woolley, U.S.A. 78 B4 48 30N 122 14W
Seeheim, Namibia ...... 56 D2 26 50S 17 45 E
Seeis, Namibia ...... 56 C2 22 29S 17 39 E
Seekoei →, S. Africa ...... 56 E4 30 18S 25 1 E
Seeley's Bay, Canada 85 B8 44 29N 76 14W
Seferihisar, Turkey ...... 23 E12 38 10N 26 50 E
Seg-ozero, Russia ...... 18 B5 63 20N 33 46 E
Segamat, Malaysia ...... 39 L4 2 30N 102 50 E
Segesta, Italy ...... 22 F5 37 56N 12 50 E
Seget, Indonesia ...... 37 E8 1 24S 130 58 E
Segezha, Russia ...... 18 B5 63 44N 34 19 E
Ségou, Mali 50 F4 13 30N 6 16W
Segovia = Coco →, Cent. Amer. 88 D3 15 0N 83 8W
Segovia, Spain 21 B3 40 57N 4 10W
Segre →, Spain ...... 21 B6 41 40N 0 43 E
Séguéla, Ivory C. 50 G4 7 55N 6 40W
Seguin, U.S.A. 81 L6 29 34N 97 58W
Segundo →, Argentina 94 C3 30 53S 62 44W
Segura →, Spain 21 C5 38 3N 0 44W
Seh Konj, Kūh-e, Iran ...... 45 D8 30 6N 57 30 E
Seh Qal'eh, Iran ...... 45 C8 33 40N 58 24 E
Sehithwa, Botswana ...... 56 C3 20 30S 22 30 E
Sehlabathebe △, Lesotho ...... 57 D4 29 53S 29 7 E
Sehore, India ...... 42 H7 23 10N 77 5 E
Sehwan, Pakistan ...... 42 F2 26 28N 67 53 E
Seil, U.K. 11 E3 56 18N 5 38W
Seiland, Norway ...... 8 A20 70 25N 23 15 E
Seiling, U.S.A. 81 G5 36 9N 98 56W
Seinäjoki, Finland ...... 9 E20 62 40N 22 51 E
Seine →, France ...... 20 B4 49 26N 0 26 E
Seistan = Sīstān, Asia ...... 45 D9 30 50N 61 0 E
Seistan, Daryācheh-ye = Sīstān,
Daryācheh-ye, Iran ...... 45 D9 31 0N 61 0 E
Sekayu, Indonesia ...... 36 E2 2 51S 103 51 E
Seke, Tanzania ...... 54 C3 3 20S 33 31 E
Sekenke, Tanzania ...... 54 C3 4 18S 34 11 E
Sekondi-Takoradi, Ghana 50 H5 4 58N 1 45W
Sekudai, Malaysia ...... 39 d 1 32N 103 39 E
Sekuma, Botswana ...... 56 C3 24 36S 23 50 E
Selah, U.S.A. 76 C3 46 39N 120 32W

Selama, Malaysia ...... 39 K3 5 12N 100 42 E
Selaru, Indonesia ...... 37 F8 8 9S 131 0 E
Selatan, Selat, Malaysia ...... 39 c 5 15N 100 20 E
Selby, U.K. 12 D6 53 47N 1 5W
Selby, U.S.A. 80 C4 45 31N 100 2W
Selçuk, Turkey ...... 23 F12 37 56N 27 22 E
Selden, U.S.A. 80 F4 39 33N 100 34W
Sele →, Italy ...... 22 D6 40 29N 14 56 E
Selebi-Pikwe, Botswana ...... 57 C4 21 58S 27 48 E
Selemdzha →, Russia ...... 29 D13 51 42N 128 53 E
Selenga = Selenge Mörön →,
Asia ...... 32 A5 52 16N 106 16 E
Selenge Mörön →, Asia ...... 32 A5 52 16N 106 16 E
Seletan, Tanjung, Indonesia ...... 36 E4 4 10S 114 40 E
Sélibabi, Mauritania 50 E3 15 10N 12 15W
Seligman, U.S.A. 77 J7 35 20N 112 53W
Selîma, El Wâhât el, Sudan ...... 51 D11 21 22N 29 19 E
Selinda Spillway →, Botswana . 56 B3 18 35S 23 10 E
Selinsgrove, U.S.A. 84 F8 40 48N 76 52W
Selkirk, Canada 71 C9 50 10N 96 55W
Selkirk, U.K. 11 F6 55 33N 2 50W
Selkirk I. = Horse I., Canada 71 C9 53 20N 99 6W
Selkirk Mts., Canada 68 C8 51 15N 117 40W
Sellafield, U.K. 12 C4 54 25N 3 29W
Selliá, Greece ...... 25 D6 35 12N 24 23 E
Sells, U.S.A. 77 L8 31 55N 111 53W
Selma, Ala., U.S.A. 83 J2 32 25N 87 1W
Selma, Calif., U.S.A. 78 J7 36 34N 119 37W
Selma, N.C., U.S.A. 83 H6 35 32N 78 17W
Selmer, U.S.A. 83 H1 35 10N 88 36W
Selous △, Tanzania ...... 55 D4 8 37S 37 42 E
Selowandoma Falls, Zimbabwe . 55 G3 21 15S 31 50 E
Selpele, Indonesia ...... 37 E8 0 1S 130 5 E
Selsey Bill, U.K. 13 G7 50 43N 0 47W
Seltso, Russia ...... 18 D5 53 22N 34 4 E
Selu, Indonesia ...... 37 F8 7 32S 130 55 E
Selva, Argentina 94 B3 29 50S 62 0W
Selva Lancandona = Montes
Azules △, Mexico 87 D6 16 21N 91 3W
Selvas, Brazil 92 E5 6 30S 67 0W
Selwyn L., Canada 71 B8 60 0N 104 30W
Selwyn Mts., Canada 68 B6 63 0N 130 0W
Selwyn Ra., Australia ...... 62 C3 21 10S 140 0 E
Seman →, Albania ...... 23 D8 40 47N 19 30 E
Semarang, Indonesia ...... 36 F4 7 0S 110 26 E
Sembabule, Uganda ...... 54 C3 0 4S 31 25 E
Sembawang, Singapore ...... 39 d 1 27N 103 50 E
Sembung, Indonesia ...... 37 J18 8 28S 115 11 E
Semenanjung Blambangan,
Indonesia ...... 37 K17 8 42S 114 29 E
Semeru, Indonesia ...... 37 H15 8 4S 112 55 E
Semey, Kazakhstan ...... 28 D9 50 30N 80 10 E
Seminoe Reservoir, U.S.A. 76 F10 42 9N 106 55W
Seminole, Okla., U.S.A. 81 H6 35 14N 96 41W
Seminole, Tex., U.S.A. 81 J3 32 43N 102 39W
Seminole Draw →, U.S.A. 81 J3 32 27N 102 20W
Semipalatinsk = Semey,
Kazakhstan ...... 28 D9 50 30N 80 10 E
Semirara Is., Phil. ...... 37 B6 12 0N 121 20 E
Semitau, Indonesia ...... 36 D4 0 29N 111 57 E
Semiyarka, Kazakhstan ...... 28 D8 50 55N 78 23 E
Semiyarskoye = Semiyarka,
Kazakhstan ...... 28 D8 50 55N 78 23 E
Semmering P., Austria ...... 16 E8 47 41N 15 45 E
Semnān, Iran ...... 45 C7 35 40N 53 23 E
Semnān □, Iran ...... 45 C7 36 0N 54 0 E
Semporna, Malaysia ...... 37 D5 4 30N 118 33 E
Semuda, Indonesia ...... 36 E4 2 51S 112 58 E
Sen →, Cambodia ...... 38 F5 13 45N 105 12 E
Senā, Iran ...... 45 D6 28 27N 51 36 E
Sena, Mozam. ...... 55 F4 17 25S 35 0 E
Sena Madureira, Brazil 92 E5 9 5S 68 45W
Senador Pompeu, Brazil 93 E11 5 40S 39 20W
Senang, Pulau, Singapore ...... 39 d 1 10N 103 44 E
Senanga, Zambia ...... 53 H4 16 7S 23 16 E
Senatobia, U.S.A. 81 H10 34 37N 89 58W
Sencelles, Spain ...... 24 B9 39 39N 2 54 E
Sendai, Kagoshima, Japan ...... 31 J5 31 50N 130 20 E
Sendai, Miyagi, Japan ...... 30 E10 38 15N 140 53 E
Sendai-Wan, Japan ...... 30 E10 38 15N 141 0 E
Sendhwa, India ...... 42 J6 21 41N 75 6 E
Seneca, U.S.A. 83 H4 34 41N 82 57W
Seneca Falls, U.S.A. 84 D8 42 55N 76 48W
Seneca L., U.S.A. 84 D8 42 40N 76 54W
Senecaville L., U.S.A. 84 G3 39 55N 81 25W
Senegal ■, W. Afr. 50 F3 14 30N 14 30W
Sénégal →, W. Afr. 50 E2 15 48N 16 32W
Senegambia, Africa 48 E2 12 45N 12 0W
Senekal, S. Africa ...... 57 D4 28 20S 27 36 E
Senga Hill, Zambia ...... 55 E3 9 19S 31 11 E
Senge Khambab = Indus →,
Pakistan ...... 42 G2 24 20N 67 47 E
Sengua →, Zimbabwe ...... 55 F2 17 7S 28 5 E
Senhor-do-Bonfim, Brazil 93 F10 10 30S 40 10W
Senigállia, Italy ...... 22 C5 43 43N 13 13 E
Senj, Croatia ...... 16 F8 45 0N 14 58 E
Senja, Norway ...... 8 B17 69 25N 17 30 E
Senkaku-Shotō, Japan ...... 31 L1 25 45N 124 0 E
Senkuang, Indonesia ...... 39 d 1 11N 104 2 E
Senlis, France ...... 20 B5 49 13N 2 35 E
Senmonorom, Cambodia ...... 38 F6 12 27N 107 12 E
Senneterre, Canada 72 C4 48 25N 77 15W
Seno, Laos ...... 38 D5 16 35N 104 50 E
Sens, France ...... 20 B5 48 11N 3 15 E
Senta, Serbia & M. ...... 23 B9 45 55N 20 3 E
Sentani, Indonesia ...... 37 E10 2 36S 140 37 E
Sentery = Lubao, Dem. Rep. of
the Congo ...... 54 D2 5 17S 25 42 E
Sentinel, U.S.A. 77 K7 32 52N 113 13W
Sentosa, Singapore ...... 39 d 1 15N 103 50 E
Seo de Urgel = La Seu d'Urgell,
Spain ...... 21 A6 42 22N 1 23 E
Seohara, India ...... 43 E8 29 15N 78 33 E
Seonath →, India ...... 43 J10 21 44N 82 28 E
Seondha, India ...... 43 F8 26 9N 78 48 E
Seoni, India ...... 43 H8 22 5N 79 30 E
Seoni Malwa, India ...... 42 H8 22 27N 77 28 E
Seoul = Sŏul, S. Korea ...... 35 F14 37 31N 126 58 E
Sepīdān, Iran ...... 45 D7 30 20N 52 5 E
Sepo-ri, N. Korea ...... 35 E14 38 57N 127 25 E
Sepone, Laos ...... 38 D6 16 45N 106 13 E
Sept-Îles, Canada 73 B6 50 13N 66 22W
Sequim, U.S.A. 78 B3 48 5N 123 6W
Sequoia △, U.S.A. 78 J8 36 30N 118 30W
Seraing, Belgium ...... 15 D5 50 35N 5 32 E
Serakhis →, Cyprus ...... 25 D11 35 13N 32 55 E
Seram, Indonesia ...... 37 E7 3 10S 129 0 E
Seram Sea, Indonesia ...... 37 E7 2 30S 128 30 E

Seranantsara, Madag. ...... 57 B8 18 30S 49 5 E
Serang, Indonesia ...... 37 G12 6 8S 106 10 E
Serangoon, Singapore ...... 39 d 1 23N 103 54 E
Serasan, Indonesia ...... 36 D3 2 29N 109 4 E
Serbia □, Serbia & M. ...... 23 C9 43 30N 21 0 E
Serbia & Montenegro ■, Europe 23 B9 43 20N 20 0 E
Serdobsk, Russia ...... 18 D7 52 28N 44 10 E
Seremban, Malaysia ...... 39 L3 2 43N 101 53 E
Serengeti △, Tanzania ...... 54 C3 2 11S 35 0 E
Serengeti Plain, Tanzania ...... 54 C4 2 40S 35 0 E
Serenje, Zambia ...... 55 E3 13 14S 30 15 E
Sergino, Russia ...... 28 C7 62 25N 65 12 E
Sergipe □, Brazil 93 F11 10 30S 37 30W
Sergiyev Posad, Russia ...... 18 C6 56 20N 38 10 E
Seria, Brunei ...... 36 D4 4 37N 114 23 E
Serian, Malaysia ...... 36 D4 1 10N 110 31 E
Seribu, Kepulauan, Indonesia . 36 F3 5 36S 106 33 E
Sérifos, Greece ...... 23 F11 37 9N 24 30 E
Sérigny →, Canada 73 A6 56 47N 66 0W
Seringapatam Reef, Australia ...... 60 B3 13 38S 122 5 E
Seririt, Indonesia ...... 37 J17 8 12S 114 56 E
Sermata, Indonesia ...... 37 F7 8 15S 128 50 E
Sermersuaq, Greenland 4 B4 79 30N 62 0W
Serov, Russia ...... 18 C11 59 29N 60 35 E
Serowe, Botswana ...... 56 C4 22 25S 26 43 E
Serpentine Lakes, Australia ...... 61 E4 28 30S 129 10 E
Serpent's Mouth = Sierpe, Bocas
de la, Venezuela 93 L15 10 0N 61 30W
Serpukhov, Russia ...... 18 D6 54 55N 37 28 E
Serra do Navio, Brazil 93 C8 0 59N 52 3W
Sérrai, Greece ...... 23 D10 41 5N 23 31 E
Serranía San Luís △, Paraguay . 94 A4 22 25N 57 20W
Serrezuela, Argentina 94 C2 30 40S 65 20W
Serrinha, Brazil 93 F11 11 39S 39 0W
Sertanópolis, Brazil 95 A5 23 4S 51 2W
Serua, Indonesia ...... 37 F8 6 18S 130 1 E
Serui, Indonesia ...... 37 E9 1 53S 136 10 E
Serule, Botswana ...... 56 C4 21 57S 27 20 E
Ses Salines, Spain ...... 24 B10 39 21N 3 3 E
Sese Is., Uganda ...... 54 C3 0 20S 32 20 E
Sesepe, Indonesia ...... 37 E7 1 30S 127 59 E
Sesfontein, Namibia ...... 56 B1 19 7S 13 39 E
S'Espalmador, Spain ...... 24 C7 38 47N 1 26 E
S'Espardell, Spain ...... 24 C7 38 48N 1 29 E
S'Estanyol, Spain ...... 24 B9 39 22N 2 54 E
Setana, Japan ...... 30 C9 42 26N 139 51 E
Sète, France ...... 20 E5 43 25N 3 42 E
Sete Lagôas, Brazil 93 G10 19 27S 44 16W
Sétif, Algeria ...... 50 A7 36 9N 5 26 E
Seto, Japan ...... 31 G8 35 14N 137 6 E
Setonaikai, Japan ...... 31 G6 34 20N 133 30 E
Setonaikai △, Japan ...... 31 G6 34 15N 133 15 E
Settat, Morocco 50 B4 33 0N 7 40W
Setting L., Canada 71 C9 55 0N 98 38W
Settle, U.K. 12 C5 54 5N 2 16W
Settlement Pt., Bahamas 83 M6 26 40N 79 0W
Settlers, S. Africa ...... 57 C4 25 2S 28 30 E
Setúbal, Portugal 21 C1 38 30N 8 58W
Setúbal, B. de, Portugal 21 C1 38 40N 8 56W
Seul, Lac, Canada 72 B1 50 20N 92 30W
Sevan, Ozero = Sevana Lich,
Armenia ...... 19 F8 40 30N 45 20 E
Sevana Lich, Armenia ...... 19 F8 40 30N 45 20 E
Sevastopol, Ukraine ...... 19 F5 44 35N 33 30 E
Seven Sisters, Canada 70 C3 54 56N 128 10W
Severn →, Canada 72 A2 56 2N 87 36W
Severn →, U.K. 13 F5 51 35N 2 40W
Severn L., Canada 72 B1 53 54N 90 48W
Severnaya Zemlya, Russia ...... 29 B10 79 0N 100 0 E
Severnyye Uvaly, Russia ...... 18 C8 60 0N 50 0 E
Severo-Kurilsk, Russia ...... 29 D16 50 40N 156 8 E
Severo-Zapadnyy □, Russia ...... 29 C10 60 0N 93 1 E
Severo-Yeniseyskiy, Russia ...... 29 C10 60 22N 93 1 E
Severodvinsk, Russia ...... 18 B6 64 27N 39 58 E
Severomorsk, Russia ...... 18 A5 69 5S 33 27 E
Severouralsk, Russia ...... 18 B10 60 9N 59 57 E
Sevier, U.S.A. 77 G7 38 39N 112 11W
Sevier →, U.S.A. 76 G7 39 4N 113 6W
Sevier Desert, U.S.A. 76 G7 39 40N 112 45W
Sevier L., U.S.A. 76 G7 38 54N 113 9W
Sevilla, Spain 21 D2 37 23N 5 58W
Seville = Sevilla, Spain 21 D2 37 23N 5 58W
Sevlievo, Bulgaria ...... 23 C11 43 2N 25 6 E
Sewani, India ...... 42 E6 28 58N 75 39 E
Seward, Alaska, U.S.A. 68 B5 60 7N 149 27W
Seward, Nebr., U.S.A. 80 E6 40 55N 97 6W
Seward, Pa., U.S.A. 84 F5 40 25N 79 1W
Seward Peninsula, U.S.A. 68 B3 65 30N 166 0W
Sewell, Chile 94 C1 34 10S 70 23W
Sewer, Indonesia ...... 37 F8 5 53S 134 40 E
Sewickley, U.S.A. 84 F4 40 32N 80 12W
Sexsmith, Canada 70 B5 55 21N 118 47W
Seychelles ■, Ind. Oc. ...... 57 K9 5 0S 56 0 E
Seyðisfjörður, Iceland 8 D6 65 16N 13 57W
Seydişehir, Turkey ...... 19 G5 37 25N 31 51 E
Seydvān, Iran ...... 44 B5 38 34N 45 2 E
Seyhan →, Turkey ...... 44 B2 36 43N 34 53 E
Seym →, Ukraine ...... 19 D5 51 27N 32 34 E
Seymour, Australia ...... 63 F4 37 0S 145 10 E
Seymour, S. Africa ...... 57 E4 32 33S 26 46 E
Seymour, Conn., U.S.A. 85 E11 41 24N 73 4W
Seymour, Ind., U.S.A. 82 F3 38 58N 85 53W
Seymour, Tex., U.S.A. 81 J5 33 35N 99 16W
Sfântu Gheorghe, Romania ...... 17 F13 45 52N 25 48 E
Sfax, Tunisia ...... 51 B8 34 49N 10 48 E
Sha Tau Kok, China ...... 33 F11 22 33N 114 13 E
Sha Tin, China ...... 33 G11 22 23N 114 12 E
Shaanxi □, China ...... 34 G5 35 0N 109 0 E
Shaba = Katanga □, Dem. Rep. of
the Congo ...... 54 D2 8 0S 25 0 E
Shaba □, Kenya ...... 54 B4 0 38N 37 48 E
Shaballe = Scebeli, Wabi →,
Somali Rep. ...... 47 G3 2 0N 44 0 E
Shabogamo L., Canada 73 B6 53 15N 66 30W
Shabunda, Dem. Rep. of
the Congo ...... 54 C2 2 40S 27 16 E
Shache, China ...... 32 C2 38 20N 77 10 E
Shackleton Ice Shelf, Antarctica . 5 C8 66 0S 100 0 E
Shackleton Inlet, Antarctica ...... 5 E11 83 0S 160 0 E
Shādegān, Iran ...... 45 D6 30 40N 48 38 E
Shadi, India ...... 43 C7 33 24N 77 14 E
Shadrinsk, Russia ...... 28 D7 56 5N 63 32 E
Shadyside, U.S.A. 84 G4 39 58N 80 45W
Shafter, U.S.A. 79 K7 35 30N 119 16W
Shaftesbury, U.K. 13 F5 51 0N 2 11W

Shagram, *Pakistan* 43 A5 36 24N 72 20 E
Shah Alizai, *Pakistan* 42 E2 29 25N 66 33 E
Shah Bunder, *Pakistan* 42 G2 24 13N 67 56 E
Shahabad, *Punjab, India* 42 D7 30 10N 76 55 E
Shahabad, *Raj., India* 42 G7 25 15N 77 11 E
Shahabad, *Ut. P., India* 43 F8 27 36N 79 56 E
Shahadpur, *Pakistan* 42 G3 25 55N 68 35 E
Shahba, *Syria* 46 C5 32 52N 36 38 E
Shahdād, *Iran* 45 D8 30 30N 57 40 E
Shahdād, Namakzār-e, *Iran* 45 D8 30 20N 58 20 E
Shahdadkot, *Pakistan* 42 F2 27 50N 67 55 E
Shahdol, *India* 43 H9 23 19N 81 26 E
Shahe, *China* 34 F8 37 0N 114 32 E
Shahganj, *India* 43 F10 26 3N 82 44 E
Shahgarh, *India* 40 F6 27 15N 69 50 E
Shahjahanpur, *India* 43 F8 27 54N 79 57 E
Shahpur, *India* 42 H7 22 12N 77 58 E
Shahpur, *Baluchistan, Pakistan* 42 E3 28 46N 68 27 E
Shahpur, *Punjab, Pakistan* 42 C5 32 17N 72 26 E
Shahpur Chakar, *Pakistan* 42 F3 26 9N 68 39 E
Shahpura, *Mad. P., India* 43 H9 23 10N 80 45 E
Shahpura, *Raj., India* 42 G6 25 38N 74 56 E
Shahr-e Bābak, *Iran* 45 D7 30 7N 55 9 E
Shahr-e Kord, *Iran* 45 C6 32 15N 50 55 E
Shāhrakht, *Iran* 45 C9 33 38N 60 16 E
Shahrig, *Pakistan* 42 D2 30 15N 67 40 E
Shahukou, *China* 34 D7 40 20N 112 18 E
Shajapur, *India* 42 H7 23 27N 76 21 E
Shajing, *China* 33 F10 22 44N 113 48 E
Shakargarh, *Pakistan* 42 C6 32 17N 75 10 E
Shakawe, *Botswana* 56 B3 18 28S 21 49 E
Shaker Heights, *U.S.A.* 84 E3 41 29N 81 32W
Shakhty, *Russia* 19 E7 47 40N 40 16 E
Shakhunya, *Russia* 18 C8 57 40N 46 46 E
Shaki, *Nigeria* 50 G6 8 41N 3 21 E
Shallow Lake, *Canada* 84 B3 44 36N 81 5W
Shalqar, *Kazakhstan* 28 E6 47 48N 59 39 E
Shaluli Shan, *China* 32 C4 30 40N 99 55 E
Shām, *Iran* 45 E8 26 39N 57 21 E
Shām, Bādiyat ash, *Asia* 44 C3 32 0N 40 0 E
Shamāl Sīnī □, *Egypt* 46 E2 30 30N 33 30 E
Shamattawa, *Canada* 72 A1 55 51N 92 5W
Shamattawa →, *Canada* 72 A2 55 1N 85 23W
Shamil, *Iran* 45 E8 27 30N 56 55 E
Shāmkūh, *Iran* 45 C8 35 47N 57 50 E
Shamli, *India* 42 E7 29 32N 77 18 E
Shammar, Jabal, *Si. Arabia* 44 E4 27 40N 41 0 E
Shamo = Gobi, *Asia* 34 C6 44 0N 110 0 E
Shamo, L., *Ethiopia* 47 F2 5 45N 37 30 E
Shamokin, *U.S.A.* 85 F8 40 47N 76 34W
Shamrock, *U.S.A.* 81 H4 35 13N 100 15W
Shamva, *Zimbabwe* 55 F3 17 20S 31 32 E
Shan □, *Burma* 41 J21 21 30N 98 30 E
Shan Xian, *China* 34 G9 34 50N 116 5 E
Shanchengzhen, *China* 35 C13 42 20N 125 20 E
Shāndak, *Iran* 45 D9 28 28N 60 27 E
Shandon, *U.S.A.* 78 K6 35 39N 120 23W
Shandong □, *China* 35 G10 36 0N 118 0 E
Shandong Bandao, *China* 35 F11 37 0N 121 0 E
Shang Xian = Shangzhou, *China* 34 H5 33 50N 109 58 E
Shanga, *Nigeria* 50 F6 11 12N 4 33 E
Shangalowe, *Dem. Rep. of the Congo* 55 E2 10 50S 26 30 E
Shangani, *Zimbabwe* 57 B4 19 41S 29 20 E
Shangani →, *Zimbabwe* 55 F2 18 41S 27 10 E
Shangbancheng, *China* 35 D10 40 50N 118 1 E
Shangdu, *China* 34 D7 41 30N 113 30 E
Shanghai, *China* 33 C7 31 15N 121 26 E
Shanghe, *China* 35 F9 37 20N 117 10 E
Shangnan, *China* 34 H6 33 32N 110 50 E
Shangqiu, *China* 34 G8 34 26N 115 36 E
Shangrao, *China* 33 D6 28 25N 117 59 E
Shangshui, *China* 33 C6 33 42N 114 35 E
Shangzhi, *China* 35 B14 45 22N 127 56 E
Shangzhou, *China* 34 H5 33 50N 109 58 E
Shanhetun, *China* 35 B14 44 33N 127 15 E
Shanklin, *U.K.* 13 G6 50 38N 1 11W
Shannon, *N.Z.* 59 J5 40 33S 175 25 E
Shannon △, *Australia* 61 F2 31 55S 117 51 E
Shannon →, *Ireland* 10 D2 52 35N 9 30W
Shannon, Mouth of the, *Ireland* 10 D2 52 30N 9 55W
Shannon Airport, *Ireland* 10 D3 52 42N 8 57W
Shansi = Shanxi □, *China* 34 F7 37 0N 112 0 E
Shantar, Ostrov Bolshoy, *Russia* 29 D14 55 9N 137 40 E
Shantipur, *India* 43 H13 23 17N 88 25 E
Shantou, *China* 33 D6 23 18N 116 40 E
Shantung = Shandong □, *China* 35 G10 36 0N 118 0 E
Shanxi □, *China* 34 F7 37 0N 112 0 E
Shanyang, *China* 34 H5 33 31N 109 55 E
Shanyin, *China* 34 E7 39 25N 112 56 E
Shaoguan, *China* 33 D6 24 48N 113 35 E
Shaoxing, *China* 33 D7 30 0N 120 35 E
Shaoyang, *China* 33 D6 27 14N 111 25 E
Shap, *U.K.* 12 C5 54 32N 2 40W
Shapinsay, *U.K.* 11 B6 59 3N 2 51W
Shaqra, *Si. Arabia* 44 E5 25 15N 45 16 E
Shaqrā', *Yemen* 47 E4 13 22N 45 44 E
Sharafkhāneh, *Iran* 44 B5 38 11N 45 29 E
Sharbot Lake, *Canada* 85 B8 44 46N 76 41W
Shari, *Japan* 30 C12 43 55N 144 40 E
Sharjah = Ash Shāriqah, *U.A.E.* 45 E7 25 23N 55 26 E
Shark B., *Australia* 61 E1 25 30S 113 32 E
Shark Bay △, *Australia* 61 F2 32 49S 118 49 E
Sharon, *Mass., U.S.A.* 85 D13 42 7N 71 11W
Sharon, *Pa., U.S.A.* 84 E4 41 14N 80 31W
Sharon Springs, *Kans., U.S.A.* 80 F4 38 54N 101 45W
Sharon Springs, *N.Y., U.S.A.* 85 D10 42 48N 74 37W
Sharp Pt., *Australia* 62 A3 10 58S 142 43 E
Sharpe L., *Canada* 72 B1 54 24N 93 40W
Sharpsville, *U.S.A.* 84 E4 41 15N 80 29W
Sharya, *Russia* 18 C8 58 22N 45 20 E
Shashemene, *Ethiopia* 47 F2 7 13N 38 33 E
Shashi, *Botswana* 57 C4 21 15S 27 27 E
Shashi, *China* 33 C6 30 25N 112 14 E
Shashi →, *Africa* 55 G2 21 14S 29 20 E
Shasta, Mt., *U.S.A.* 76 F2 41 25N 122 12W
Shasta L., *U.S.A.* 76 F2 40 43N 122 25W
Shatt al Arab = Arab, Shatt al →, *Asia* 45 D6 30 0N 48 31 E
Shaunavon, *Canada* 71 D7 49 35N 108 25W
Shaver L., *U.S.A.* 78 H7 37 9N 119 18W
Shaw →, *Australia* 60 D2 20 21S 119 17 E
Shaw I., *Australia* 62 J7 20 30S 149 2 E
Shawanaga, *Canada* 84 A4 45 31N 80 17W
Shawangunk Mts., *U.S.A.* 85 E10 41 35N 74 30W

Shawano, *U.S.A.* 82 C1 44 47N 88 36W
Shawinigan, *Canada* 72 C5 46 35N 72 50W
Shawnee, *U.S.A.* 81 H6 35 20N 96 55W
Shay Gap, *Australia* 60 D3 20 30S 120 10 E
Shaybārā, *Si. Arabia* 44 E3 25 26N 36 47 E
Shaykh, J. ash, *Lebanon* 46 B4 33 25N 35 50 E
Shaykh Miskin, *Syria* 46 C5 32 49N 36 9 E
Shaykh Sa'īd, *Iraq* 44 C5 32 34N 46 17 E
Shchuchinsk, *Kazakhstan* 28 D8 52 56N 70 12 E
She Xian, *China* 34 F7 36 30N 113 40 E
Shebele = Scebeli, Wabi →, *Somali Rep.* 47 G3 2 0N 44 0 E
Sheboygan, *U.S.A.* 82 D2 43 46N 87 45W
Shediac, *Canada* 73 C7 46 14N 64 32W
Sheelin, L., *Ireland* 10 C4 53 48N 7 20W
Sheep Haven, *Ireland* 10 A4 55 11N 7 52W
Sheerness, *U.K.* 13 F8 51 26N 0 47 E
Sheet Harbour, *Canada* 73 D7 44 56N 62 31W
Sheffield, *U.K.* 12 D6 53 23N 1 28W
Sheffield, *Ala., U.S.A.* 83 H2 34 46N 87 41W
Sheffield, *Mass., U.S.A.* 85 D11 42 5N 73 21W
Sheffield, *Pa., U.S.A.* 84 E5 41 42N 79 3W
Sheikhpura, *India* 43 G11 25 9N 85 53 E
Shekhupura, *Pakistan* 42 D5 31 42N 73 58 E
Shekou, *China* 33 G10 22 30N 113 55 E
Shelburne, *N.S., Canada* 73 D6 43 47N 65 20W
Shelburne, *Ont., Canada* 84 B4 44 4N 80 15W
Shelburne, *U.S.A.* 85 B11 44 23N 73 14W
Shelburne B., *Australia* 62 A3 11 50S 142 50 E
Shelburne Falls, *U.S.A.* 85 D12 42 36N 72 45W
Shelby, *Mich., U.S.A.* 82 D2 43 37N 86 22W
Shelby, *Miss., U.S.A.* 81 J9 33 57N 90 46W
Shelby, *Mont., U.S.A.* 76 B8 48 30N 111 51W
Shelby, *N.C., U.S.A.* 83 H5 35 17N 81 32W
Shelby, *Ohio, U.S.A.* 84 F2 40 53N 82 40W
Shelbyville, *Ill., U.S.A.* 80 F10 39 24N 88 48W
Shelbyville, *Ind., U.S.A.* 82 F3 39 31N 85 47W
Shelbyville, *Ky., U.S.A.* 82 F3 38 13N 85 14W
Shelbyville, *Tenn., U.S.A.* 83 H2 35 29N 86 28W
Sheldon, *U.S.A.* 80 D7 43 11N 95 51W
Sheldrake, *Canada* 73 B7 50 20N 64 51W
Shelikhova, Zaliv, *Russia* 29 D16 59 30N 157 0 E
Shell Lakes, *Australia* 61 E4 29 20S 127 30 E
Shellbrook, *Canada* 71 C7 53 13N 106 24W
Shellharbour, *Australia* 63 E5 34 31S 150 51 E
Shelter I., *U.S.A.* 85 E12 41 5N 72 21W
Shelton, *Conn., U.S.A.* 85 E11 41 19N 73 5W
Shelton, *Wash., U.S.A.* 78 C3 47 13N 123 6W
Shen Xian, *China* 34 F8 36 15N 115 40 E
Shenandoah, *Iowa, U.S.A.* 80 E7 40 46N 95 22W
Shenandoah, *Pa., U.S.A.* 85 F8 40 49N 76 12W
Shenandoah, *Va., U.S.A.* 82 F6 38 29N 78 37W
Shenandoah →, *U.S.A.* 82 F6 39 19N 77 44W
Shenandoah ∆, *U.S.A.* 82 F7 38 35N 78 37W
Shenchi, *China* 34 E7 39 8N 112 10 E
Shendam, *Nigeria* 50 G7 8 49N 9 30 E
Shendī, *Sudan* 51 E12 16 46N 33 22 E
Shengfang, *China* 34 E9 39 3N 116 42 E
Shenjingzi, *China* 35 B13 44 40N 124 30 E
Shenmu, *China* 34 E6 38 50N 110 29 E
Shenqiu, *China* 34 H8 33 25N 115 5 E
Shensi = Shaanxi □, *China* 34 G5 35 0N 109 0 E
Shenyang, *China* 35 D12 41 48N 123 27 E
Shenzhen, *China* 33 F10 22 32N 114 5 E
Shenzhen ✈ (SZX), *China* 33 F10 22 41N 113 49 E
Shenzhen Shuiku, *China* 33 F11 22 34N 114 8 E
Shenzhen Wan, *China* 33 G10 22 27N 113 55 E
Sheo, *India* 42 F4 26 11N 71 15 E
Sheopur Kalan, *India* 40 G10 25 40N 76 40 E
Shepetivka, *Ukraine* 17 C14 50 10N 27 10 E
Shepetovka = Shepetivka, *Ukraine* 17 C14 50 10N 27 10 E
Shepparton, *Australia* 63 F4 36 23S 145 26 E
Sheppey, I. of, *U.K.* 13 F8 51 25N 0 48 E
Shepton Mallet, *U.K.* 13 F5 51 11N 2 33W
Sheqi, *China* 34 H7 33 12N 112 57 E
Sher Qila, *Pakistan* 43 A6 36 7N 74 2 E
Sherborne, *U.K.* 13 G5 50 57N 2 31W
Sherbro I., *S. Leone* 50 G3 7 30N 12 40W
Sherbrooke, *N.S., Canada* 73 C7 45 8N 61 59W
Sherbrooke, *Qué., Canada* 85 A13 45 28N 71 57W
Sherburne, *U.S.A.* 85 D9 42 41N 75 30W
Shergarh, *India* 42 F5 26 20N 72 18 E
Sherghati, *India* 43 G11 24 34N 84 47 E
Sheridan, *Ark., U.S.A.* 81 H8 34 19N 92 24W
Sheridan, *Wyo., U.S.A.* 76 D10 44 48N 106 58W
Sheringham, *U.K.* 12 E9 52 56N 1 13 E
Sherkin I., *Ireland* 10 E2 51 28N 9 26W
Sherkot, *India* 43 E8 29 22N 78 35 E
Sherman, *U.S.A.* 81 J6 33 40N 96 35W
Sherpur, *India* 43 G10 25 34N 83 47 E
Sherridon, *Canada* 71 B8 55 8N 101 5W
Sherwood Forest, *U.K.* 12 D6 53 6N 1 7W
Sherwood Park, *Canada* 70 C6 53 31N 113 19W
Sheslay →, *Canada* 70 B2 58 48N 132 5W
Shethanei L., *Canada* 71 B9 58 48N 97 50W
Shetland □, *U.K.* 11 A7 60 30N 1 30W
Shetland Is., *U.K.* 11 A7 60 30N 1 30W
Shetrunji →, *India* 42 J5 21 19N 72 7 E
Sheung Shui, *China* 33 F11 22 31N 114 7 E
Sheyenne →, *U.S.A.* 80 B6 47 2N 96 50W
Shibām, *Yemen* 47 D4 15 59N 48 36 E
Shibata, *Japan* 30 F9 37 57N 139 20 E
Shibecha, *Japan* 30 C12 43 17N 144 36 E
Shibetsu, *Japan* 30 B11 44 10N 142 23 E
Shibogama L., *Canada* 72 B2 53 35N 88 15W
Shibushi, *Japan* 31 J5 31 25N 131 8 E
Shickshinny, *U.S.A.* 85 E8 41 9N 76 9W
Shickshock Mts. = Chic-Chocs, Mts., *Canada* 73 C6 48 55N 66 0W
Shidao, *China* 35 F12 36 50N 122 25 E
Shido, *Japan* 31 G7 34 19N 134 10 E
Shiel, L., *U.K.* 11 E3 56 48N 5 34W
Shield, C., *Australia* 62 A2 13 20S 136 20 E
Shieli, *Kazakhstan* 28 E7 44 20N 66 56 E
Shiga □, *Japan* 31 G8 35 20N 136 0 E
Shiguaigou, *China* 34 D6 40 52N 110 15 E
Shihchiachuangi = Shijiazhuang, *China* 34 E8 38 2N 114 28 E
Shihezi, *China* 32 B3 44 15N 86 2 E
Shijiazhuang, *China* 34 E8 38 2N 114 28 E
Shikarpur, *India* 42 E8 28 17N 78 7 E
Shikarpur, *Pakistan* 42 F3 27 57N 68 39 E
Shikohabad, *India* 43 F8 27 6N 78 36 E
Shikoku □, *Japan* 31 H6 33 30N 133 30 E
Shikoku-Sanchi, *Japan* 31 H6 33 30N 133 30 E
Shikotsu-Ko, *Japan* 30 C10 42 45N 141 25 E

Shikotsu-Tōya △, *Japan* 30 C10 44 4N 145 8 E
Shiliguri, *India* 41 F16 26 45N 88 25 E
Shilka, *Russia* 29 D12 52 0N 115 55 E
Shilka →, *Russia* 29 D13 53 20N 121 26 E
Shillelagh, *Ireland* 10 D5 52 45N 6 32W
Shillington, *U.S.A.* 85 F9 40 18N 75 58W
Shillong, *India* 41 G17 25 35N 91 53 E
Shilo, *West Bank* 46 C4 32 4N 35 18 E
Shilou, *China* 34 F6 37 0N 110 48 E
Shimabara, *Japan* 31 H5 32 48N 130 20 E
Shimada, *Japan* 31 G9 34 49N 138 10 E
Shimane □, *Japan* 31 G6 35 0N 132 30 E
Shimanovsk, *Russia* 29 D13 52 15N 127 30 E
Shimba Hills ∆, *Kenya* 54 C4 4 14S 39 25 E
Shimizu, *Japan* 31 G9 35 0N 138 30 E
Shimodate, *Japan* 31 F9 36 20N 139 55 E
Shimoga, *India* 40 N9 13 57N 75 32 E
Shimoni, *Kenya* 54 C4 4 38S 39 20 E
Shimonoseki, *Japan* 31 H5 33 58N 130 55 E
Shimpuru Rapids, *Namibia* 56 B2 17 45S 19 55 E
Shin, L., *U.K.* 11 C4 58 5N 4 30W
Shinano-Gawa →, *Japan* 31 F9 36 50N 138 30 E
Shināṣ, *Oman* 45 E8 24 46N 56 28 E
Shindand, *Afghan.* 40 C3 33 12N 62 8 E
Shinglehouse, *U.S.A.* 84 E6 41 58N 78 12W
Shingū, *Japan* 31 H7 33 40N 135 55 E
Shingwidzi, *S. Africa* 57 C5 23 5S 31 25 E
Shinjō, *Japan* 30 E10 38 46N 140 18 E
Shinshār, *Syria* 46 A5 34 36N 36 43 E
Shinyanga, *Tanzania* 54 C3 3 45S 33 27 E
Shinyanga □, *Tanzania* 54 C3 3 50S 34 0 E
Shio-no-Misaki, *Japan* 31 H7 33 25N 135 45 E
Shiogama, *Japan* 30 E10 38 19N 141 1 E
Shiojiri, *Japan* 31 F8 36 6N 137 58 E
Shipchenski Prokhod, *Bulgaria* 23 C11 42 45N 25 15 E
Shiping, *China* 32 D5 23 45N 102 23 E
Shippagan, *Canada* 73 C7 47 45N 64 45W
Shippensburg, *U.S.A.* 84 F7 40 3N 77 31W
Shippenville, *U.S.A.* 84 E5 41 15N 79 28W
Shiprock, *U.S.A.* 77 H9 36 47N 108 41W
Shiqma, N. →, *Israel* 46 D3 31 37N 34 30 E
Shiquan, *China* 34 H5 33 5N 108 15 E
Shiquan He = Indus →, *Pakistan* 42 G2 24 20N 67 47 E
Shīr Kūh, *Iran* 45 D7 31 39N 54 3 E
Shiragami-Misaki, *Japan* 30 D10 41 24N 140 12 E
Shirakawa, *Fukushima, Japan* 31 F10 37 7N 140 13 E
Shirakawa, *Gifu, Japan* 31 F8 36 17N 136 56 E
Shirane-San, *Gumma, Japan* 31 F9 36 48N 139 22 E
Shirane-San, *Yamanashi, Japan* 31 G9 35 42N 138 9 E
Shiraoi, *Japan* 30 C10 42 33N 141 21 E
Shīrāz, *Iran* 45 D7 29 42N 52 30 E
Shire →, *Africa* 55 F4 17 42S 35 19 E
Shiretoko-Misaki, *Japan* 30 B12 44 21N 145 20 E
Shirinab →, *Pakistan* 42 D2 30 15N 66 28 E
Shiriya-Zaki, *Japan* 30 D10 41 25N 141 30 E
Shiroishi, *Japan* 30 F10 38 0N 140 37 E
Shīrvān, *Iran* 45 B8 37 30N 57 50 E
Shirwa, L. = Chilwa, L., *Malawi* 55 F4 15 15S 35 40 E
Shivpuri, *India* 42 G7 25 26N 77 42 E
Shixian, *China* 35 C15 43 5N 129 50 E
Shiyan, *China* 33 F10 22 42N 113 54 E
Shiyan Shuiku, *China* 33 F10 22 42N 113 54 E
Shizuishan, *China* 34 E4 39 15N 106 50 E
Shizuoka, *Japan* 31 G9 34 57N 138 24 E
Shizuoka □, *Japan* 31 G9 35 15N 138 40 E
Shklov = Shklow, *Belarus* 17 A16 54 16N 30 15 E
Shklow, *Belarus* 17 A16 54 16N 30 15 E
Shkodër, *Albania* 23 C8 42 4N 19 32 E
Shkumbini →, *Albania* 23 D8 41 2N 19 31 E
Shmidta, Ostrov, *Russia* 29 A10 81 0N 91 0 E
Shō-Gawa →, *Japan* 31 F8 36 47N 137 4 E
Shoal L., *Canada* 71 D9 49 33N 95 1W
Shoal Lake, *Canada* 71 C8 50 30N 100 35W
Shōdo-Shima, *Japan* 31 G7 34 30N 134 15 E
Sholapur = Solapur, *India* 40 L9 17 43N 75 56 E
Shōmrōn, *West Bank* 46 C4 32 15N 35 13 E
Shoreham by Sea, *U.K.* 13 G7 50 50N 0 16W
Shori →, *Pakistan* 42 E3 28 29N 69 44 E
Shorkot Road, *Pakistan* 42 D5 30 47N 72 15 E
Shoshone, *Calif., U.S.A.* 79 K10 35 58N 116 16W
Shoshone, *Idaho, U.S.A.* 76 E6 42 56N 114 25W
Shoshone L., *U.S.A.* 76 D8 44 22N 110 43W
Shoshone Mts., *U.S.A.* 76 G5 39 20N 117 25W
Shoshong, *Botswana* 56 C4 22 56S 26 31 E
Shoshoni, *U.S.A.* 76 E9 43 14N 108 7W
Shouguang, *China* 35 F10 37 52N 118 45 E
Shouyang, *China* 34 F7 37 54N 113 8 E
Show Low, *U.S.A.* 77 J9 34 15N 110 2W
Shreveport, *U.S.A.* 81 J8 32 31N 93 45W
Shrewsbury, *U.K.* 13 E5 52 43N 2 45W
Shri Mohangarh, *India* 42 F4 27 17N 71 18 E
Shrirampur, *India* 43 H13 22 44N 88 21 E
Shropshire □, *U.K.* 13 E5 52 36N 2 45W
Shū, *Kazakhstan* 28 E8 43 36N 73 42 E
Shū →, *Kazakhstan* 26 E10 45 0N 67 44 E
Shuangcheng, *China* 35 B14 45 20N 126 15 E
Shuanggou, *China* 35 G9 34 2N 117 30 E
Shuangliao, *China* 35 C12 43 29N 123 30 E
Shuangshanzi, *China* 35 D10 40 20N 119 33 E
Shuangyang, *China* 35 C13 43 28N 125 40 E
Shuangyashan, *China* 33 B8 46 28N 131 5 E
Shuguri Falls, *Tanzania* 55 D4 8 33S 37 22 E
Shuiye, *China* 34 F8 36 7N 114 8 E
Shujalpur, *India* 42 H7 23 18N 76 46 E
Shukpa Kunzang, *India* 43 B8 34 22N 78 22 E
Shulan, *China* 35 B14 44 28N 127 0 E
Shule, *China* 32 C2 39 25N 76 3 E
Shumagin Is., *U.S.A.* 68 C4 55 7N 160 30W
Shumen, *Bulgaria* 23 C12 43 18N 26 55 E
Shumikha, *Russia* 28 D7 55 10N 63 15 E
Shuo Xian = Shuozhou, *China* 34 E7 39 20N 112 33 E
Shuozhou, *China* 34 E7 39 20N 112 33 E
Shūr →, *Fārs, Iran* 45 D7 31 45N 55 15 E
Shūr →, *Kermān, Iran* 45 D8 30 52N 57 37 E
Shūr →, *Yazd, Iran* 45 D7 31 39N 55 1 E
Shūr Āb, *Iran* 45 C6 34 23N 51 11 E
Shūr Gaz, *Iran* 45 D8 29 10N 59 20 E
Shūrāb, *Iran* 45 C8 33 43N 56 29 E
Shūrjestān, *Iran* 45 D7 31 24N 52 25 E
Shurugwi, *Zimbabwe* 55 F3 19 40S 30 0 E
Shūsf, *Iran* 45 D9 31 50N 60 5 E
Shūshtar, *Iran* 45 D6 32 0N 48 50 E
Shuswap L., *Canada* 70 C5 50 55N 119 3W
Shuyang, *China* 35 G10 34 10N 118 42 E
Shūzū, *Iran* 45 D7 29 52N 54 30 E
Shwebo, *Burma* 41 H19 22 30N 95 45 E
Shwegu, *Burma* 41 G20 24 15N 96 26 E

Shweli →, *Burma* 41 H20 23 45N 96 4
Shymkent, *Kazakhstan* 28 E7 42 18N 69 3
Shyok, *India* 43 B8 34 13N 78
Shyok →, *Pakistan* 43 B6 35 13N 75
Si Chon, *Thailand* 39 H2 9 0N 99
Si Kiang = Xi Jiang →, *China* 33 D6 22 5N 113 2
Si Lanna △, *Thailand* 38 C2 19 17N 99
Si-ngan = Xi'an, *China* 34 G5 34 15N 109
Si Prachan, *Thailand* 38 E3 14 37N 100
Si Racha, *Thailand* 38 F3 13 10N 100
Si Xian, *China* 35 H9 33 30N 117
Siachen Glacier, *Asia* 43 B7 35 20N 77
Siahaf →, *Pakistan* 42 E3 29 3N 67
Siahan Range, *Pakistan* 40 F4 27 30N 64
Siaksriindrapura, *Indonesia* 36 D2 0 51N 102
Sialkot, *Pakistan* 42 C6 32 32N 74 3
Siam = Thailand ■, *Asia* 38 E4 16 0N 102
Sian = Xi'an, *China* 34 G5 34 15N 109
Sian Ka'an △, *Mexico* 87 D7 19 35N 87
Siantan, *Indonesia* 36 D3 3 10N 106 1
Siäreh, *Iran* 45 D9 28 5N 60 1
Siargao I., *Phil.* 37 C7 9 52N 126
Siari, *Pakistan* 43 B7 34 55N 76
Siasi, *Phil.* 37 C6 5 34N 120 5
Siau, *Indonesia* 37 D7 2 50N 125 2
Šiauliai, *Lithuania* 9 J20 55 56N 23 1
Sibā'i, Gebel el, *Egypt* 44 E2 25 45N 34 1
Sibang, *Indonesia* 37 K18 8 34S 115 1
Sibay, *Russia* 18 D10 52 42N 58 3
Sibayi, L., *S. Africa* 57 D5 27 20S 32 4
Šibenik, *Croatia* 22 C6 43 48N 15 5
Siberia = Sibirskiy □, *Russia* 29 D10 58 0N 90
Siberia, *Russia* 4 D13 60 0N 100
Siberut, *Indonesia* 36 E1 1 30S 99
Sibi, *Pakistan* 42 E2 29 30N 67 5
Sibil = Oksibil, *Indonesia* 37 E10 4 59S 140 3
Sibiloi △, *Kenya* 54 B4 4 0N 36 2
Sibirskiy □, *Russia* 29 D10 58 0N 90
Sibiti, *Congo* 52 E2 3 38S 13
Sibiu, *Romania* 17 F13 45 45N 24
Sibley, *U.S.A.* 80 D7 43 24N 95 4
Sibolga, *Indonesia* 36 D1 1 42N 98 4
Sibsagar, *India* 41 F19 27 0N 94 3
Sibu, *Malaysia* 36 D4 2 18N 111 4
Sibuco, *Phil.* 37 C6 7 20N 122 1
Sibuguey B., *Phil.* 37 C6 7 50N 122 4
Sibut, *C.A.R.* 52 C3 5 46N 19 1
Sibutu, *Phil.* 37 D5 4 45N 119 3
Sibutu Passage, *E. Indies* 37 D5 4 50N 120
Sibuyan I., *Phil.* 37 B6 12 25N 122 4
Sibuyan Sea, *Phil.* 37 B6 12 30N 122 2
Sicamous, *Canada* 70 C5 50 49N 119
Siccus →, *Australia* 63 E2 31 55S 139 4
Sichuan □, *China* 32 C5 30 30N 103
Sicilia, *Italy* 22 F6 37 30N 14 3
Sicily = Sicilia, *Italy* 22 F6 37 30N 14 3
Sicuani, *Peru* 92 F4 14 21S 71 1
Sidári, *Greece* 25 A3 39 47N 19 4
Siddhapur, *India* 42 H5 23 56N 72 2
Siddipet, *India* 40 K11 18 5N 78 5
Sidhauli, *India* 43 F9 27 17N 80 5
Sidheros, Ákra, *Greece* 25 D8 35 19N 26 1
Sidhi, *India* 43 G9 24 25N 81 5
Sidi-bel-Abbès, *Algeria* 50 A5 35 13N 0 3
Sidi Ifni, *Morocco* 50 C3 29 29N 10 1
Sidlaw Hills, *U.K.* 11 E5 56 32N 3
Sidley, Mt., *Antarctica* 5 D14 77 2S 126
Sidmouth, *U.K.* 13 G4 50 40N 3 1
Sidmouth, C., *Australia* 62 A3 13 25S 143 3
Sidney, *Canada* 70 D4 48 39N 123 2
Sidney, *Mont., U.S.A.* 80 B2 47 43N 104
Sidney, *N.Y., U.S.A.* 85 D9 42 19N 75 2
Sidney, *Nebr., U.S.A.* 80 E3 41 8N 102 5
Sidney, *Ohio, U.S.A.* 82 E3 40 17N 84
Sidney Lanier, L., *U.S.A.* 83 H4 34 10N 84
Sidoarjo, *Indonesia* 37 G15 7 27S 112 4
Sidon = Saydā, *Lebanon* 46 B4 33 35N 35 2
Sidra, G. of = Surt, Khalīj, *Libya* 51 B9 31 40N 18 3
Siedlce, *Poland* 17 B12 52 10N 22 2
Sieg →, *Germany* 16 C4 50 46N 7
Siegen, *Germany* 16 C5 50 51N 8
Siem Pang, *Cambodia* 38 E6 14 7N 106 2
Siem Reap = Siemreab, *Cambodia* 38 F4 13 20N 103 5
Siemreab, *Cambodia* 38 F4 13 20N 103 5
Siena, *Italy* 22 C4 43 19N 11 2
Sieradz, *Poland* 17 C10 51 37N 18 4
Sierpe, Bocas de la, *Venezuela* 93 L15 10 0N 61 3
Sierra Blanca, *U.S.A.* 77 L11 31 11N 105 2
Sierra Blanca Peak, *U.S.A.* 77 K11 33 23N 105 4
Sierra City, *U.S.A.* 78 F6 39 34N 120 3
Sierra Colorada, *Argentina* 96 E3 40 35S 67 5
Sierra de Bahoruco △, *Dom. Rep.* 89 C5 18 10N 71 2
Sierra de La Culata △, *Venezuela* 89 E5 8 45N 71 1
Sierra de Lancandón △, *Guatemala* 88 C1 16 59N 90 2
Sierra de las Quijadas △, *Argentina* 94 C2 32 29S 67
Sierra de San Luis △, *Venezuela* 89 D6 11 20N 69 4
Sierra Gorda, *Chile* 94 A2 22 50S 69 1
Sierra Leone ■, *W. Afr.* 50 G3 9 0N 12
Sierra Madre, *Mexico* 87 D6 16 0N 93
Sierra Mojada, *Mexico* 86 B4 27 19N 103 4
Sierra Nevada, *Spain* 21 D4 37 3N 3
Sierra Nevada, *U.S.A.* 78 H8 39 0N 120 3
Sierra Nevada de Santa Marta △, *Colombia* 89 D5 10 56N 73 3
Sierra Vista, *U.S.A.* 77 L8 31 33N 110 1
Sierraville, *U.S.A.* 78 F6 39 36N 120 2
Sifnos, *Greece* 23 F11 37 0N 24 4
Sifton, *Canada* 71 C8 51 21N 100
Sifton Pass, *Canada* 70 B3 57 52S 126 1
Sighetu-Marmației, *Romania* 17 E12 47 57N 23 5
Sighișoara, *Romania* 17 E13 46 12N 24 5
Sigli, *Indonesia* 36 C1 5 25N 96
Siglufjörður, *Iceland* 8 C4 66 12N 18 5
Signal, *U.S.A.* 79 L13 34 30N 113 3
Signal Pk., *U.S.A.* 79 M12 33 20N 114
Signal de Botrange, *Belgium* 15 D6 50 29N 6
Signy I., *Antarctica* 5 C18 60 45S 45 5
Sigsig, *Ecuador* 92 D3 3 0S 78 5
Sigüenza, *Spain* 21 B4 41 3N 2 4
Siguiri, *Guinea* 50 F4 11 31N 9 2
Sigulda, *Latvia* 9 H21 57 10N 24 5
Sihora, *India* 43 H9 23 29N 80
Siikajoki →, *Finland* 8 D21 64 50N 24 4

Siilinjärvi, *Finland* .... **8 E22** 63 4N 27 39 E
Sijarira Ra. = Chizarira,
　Zimbabwe .... **55 F2** 17 36S 27 45 E
Sika, *India* .... **42 H3** 22 26N 69 47 E
Sikani Chief ➤, *Canada* ... **70 B4** 57 47N 122 15W
Sikao, *Thailand* .... **39 J2** 7 34N 99 21 E
Sikar, *India* .... **42 F6** 27 33N 75 10 E
Sikasso, *Mali* **50 F4** 11 18N 5 35W
Sikeston, *U.S.A.* **81 G10** 36 53N 89 35W
Sikhote Alin, Khrebet, *Russia* **29 E14** 45 0N 136 0 E
Sikhote Alin Ra. = Sikhote Alin,
　Khrebet, *Russia* .... **29 E14** 45 0N 136 0 E
Síkinos, *Greece* .... **23 F11** 36 40N 25 8 E
Sikkim □, *India* .... **41 F16** 27 50N 88 30 E
Sil ➤, *Spain* **21 A2** 42 27N 7 43W
Silacayoapan, *Mexico* **87 D5** 17 30N 98 9W
Silawad, *India* .... **42 J6** 21 54N 74 54 E
Silchar, *India* .... **41 G18** 24 49N 92 48 E
Siler City, *U.S.A.* **83 H6** 35 44N 79 28W
Silesia = Śląsk, *Poland* ...... **16 C9** 51 0N 16 30 E
Silgarhi Doti, *Nepal* .... **43 E9** 29 15N 81 0 E
Silghat, *India* .... **41 F18** 26 35N 93 0 E
Silifke, *Turkey* .... **19 G5** 36 22N 33 58 E
Siliguri = Shiliguri, *India* ... **41 F16** 26 45N 88 25 E
Siling Co, *China* .... **32 C3** 31 50N 89 20 E
Silistra, *Bulgaria* .... **23 B12** 44 6N 27 19 E
Silivri, *Turkey* .... **23 D13** 41 4N 28 14 E
Siljan, *Sweden* .... **9 F16** 60 55N 14 45 E
Silkeborg, *Denmark* .... **9 H13** 56 10N 9 32 E
Silkwood, *Australia* .... **62 B4** 17 45S 146 2 E
Sillajhuay, Cordillera, *Chile* **92 G5** 19 46S 68 40W
Sillamäe, *Estonia* .... **9 G22** 59 24N 27 45 E
Silloth, *U.K.* **12 C4** 54 52N 3 23W
Siloam Springs, *U.S.A.* **81 G7** 36 11N 94 32W
Silsbee, *U.S.A.* **81 K7** 30 21N 94 11W
Šilutė, *Lithuania* .... **9 J19** 55 21N 21 33 E
Silvani, *India* .... **43 H8** 23 18N 78 25 E
Silver City, *U.S.A.* **77 K9** 32 46N 108 17W
Silver Cr. ➤, *U.S.A.* **76 E4** 43 16N 119 13W
Silver Creek, *U.S.A.* **84 D5** 42 33N 79 10W
Silver L., *U.S.A.* **78 G6** 38 39N 120 6W
Silver Lake, *Calif., U.S.A.* ... **79 K10** 35 21N 116 7W
Silver Lake, *Oreg., U.S.A.* ... **76 E3** 43 8N 121 3W
Silverton, *Colo., U.S.A.* **77 H10** 37 49N 107 40W
Silverton, *Tex., U.S.A.* **81 H4** 34 28N 101 19W
Silvies ➤, *U.S.A.* **76 E4** 43 34N 119 2W
Simaltala, *India* .... **43 G12** 24 43N 86 33 E
Simanggang = Bandar Sri Aman,
　Malaysia .... **36 D4** 1 15N 111 32 E
Simard, L., *Canada* **72 C4** 47 40N 78 40W
Simav, *Turkey* .... **23 E13** 39 4N 28 58 E
Simba, *Tanzania* .... **54 C4** 2 10S 37 36 E
Simbirsk, *Russia* .... **18 D8** 54 20N 48 25 E
Simbo, *Tanzania* .... **54 C2** 4 51S 29 41 E
Simcoe, *Canada* **84 D4** 42 50N 80 20W
Simcoe, L., *Canada* **84 B5** 44 25N 79 20W
Simdega, *India* .... **43 H11** 22 37N 84 31 E
Simeria, *Romania* .... **17 F12** 45 51N 23 1 E
Simeulue, *Indonesia* .... **36 D1** 2 45N 95 45 E
Simferopol, *Ukraine* .... **19 F5** 44 55N 34 3 E
Sími, *Greece* .... **23 F12** 36 35N 27 50 E
Simi Valley, *U.S.A.* **79 L8** 34 16N 118 47W
Simikot, *Nepal* .... **43 E9** 30 0N 81 50 E
Simla, *India* .... **42 D7** 31 2N 77 9 E
Simmie, *Canada* **71 D7** 49 56N 108 6W
Simmler, *U.S.A.* **79 K7** 35 21N 119 59W
Simojoki ➤, *Finland* .... **8 D21** 65 35N 25 1 E
Simojovel, *Mexico* **87 D6** 17 12N 92 38W
Simonette ➤, *Canada* **70 B5** 55 9N 118 15W
Simonstown, *S. Africa* ...... **56 E2** 34 14S 18 26 E
Simpang Empat, *Malaysia* ... **39 c** 5 27N 100 29 E
Simplonpass, *Switz.* .... **20 C8** 46 15N 8 3 E
Simpson Desert, *Australia* ... **62 D2** 25 0S 137 0 E
Simpson Desert △, *Australia* **62 C2** 24 59S 138 21 E
Simpson Pen., *Canada* **69 B11** 68 34N 88 45W
Simpungdong, *N. Korea* ..... **35 D15** 40 56N 129 29 E
Simrishamn, *Sweden* .... **9 J16** 55 33N 14 22 E
Simsbury, *U.S.A.* **85 E12** 41 53N 72 48W
Simushir, Ostrov, *Russia* .... **29 E16** 46 50N 152 30 E
Sin Cowe I., *S. China Sea* ... **36 C4** 9 53N 114 19 E
Sinabang, *Indonesia* .... **36 D1** 2 30N 96 24 E
Sinadogo, *Somali Rep.* ...... **47 F4** 5 50N 47 0 E
Sinai = Es Sînâ', *Egypt* ...... **46 F3** 29 0N 34 0 E
Sinai, Mt. = Mûsa, Gebel, *Egypt* **44 D2** 28 33N 33 59 E
Sinai Peninsula, *Egypt* ...... **46 F3** 29 30N 34 0 E
Sinaloa □, *Mexico* **86 C3** 25 0N 107 30W
Sinaloa de Leyva, *Mexico* **86 B3** 25 50N 108 20W
Sinarádhes, *Greece* .... **25 A3** 39 34N 19 51 E
Sincelejo, *Colombia* **92 B3** 9 18N 75 24W
Sinch'ang, *N. Korea* .... **35 D15** 40 7N 128 28 E
Sinchang-ni, *N. Korea* .... **35 E14** 39 24N 126 8 E
Sinclair, *U.S.A.* **76 F10** 41 47N 107 7W
Sinclair Mills, *Canada* **70 C4** 54 5N 121 40W
Sinclair's B., *U.K.* **11 C5** 58 31N 3 5W
Sinclairville, *U.S.A.* **84 D5** 42 16N 79 16W
Sincorá, Serra do, *Brazil* **93 F10** 13 30S 41 0W
Sind, *Pakistan* .... **42 G3** 26 0N 68 30 E
Sind □, *Pakistan* .... **42 G3** 26 0N 69 0 E
Sind ➤, *Jammu & Kashmir,*
　India .... **43 B6** 34 18N 74 45 E
Sind ➤, *Mad. P., India* ...... **43 F8** 26 26N 79 13 E
Sind Sagar Doab, *Pakistan* ... **42 D4** 32 0N 71 30 E
Sindangan, *Phil.* .... **37 C6** 8 10N 123 5 E
Sindangbarang, *Indonesia* ... **37 G12** 7 27S 107 1 E
Sinde, *Zambia* .... **55 F2** 17 28S 25 51 E
Sindh = Sind □, *Pakistan* .... **42 G3** 26 0N 69 0 E
Sindri, *India* .... **43 H12** 23 45N 86 42 E
Sines, *Portugal* **21 D1** 37 56N 8 51W
Sines, C. de, *Portugal* **21 D1** 37 58N 8 53W
Sineu, *Spain* .... **24 B10** 39 38N 3 1 E
Sing Buri, *Thailand* .... **38 E3** 14 53N 100 25 E
Singa, *Sudan* .... **51 F12** 13 10N 33 57 E
Singapore ■, *Asia* .... **39 d** 1 17N 103 51 E
Singapore, Straits of, *Asia* ... **39 d** 1 15N 104 0 E
Singapore Changi ✕ (SIN),
　Singapore .... **39 M4** 1 23N 103 59 E
Singaraja, *Indonesia* .... **36 F5** 8 7S 115 6 E
Singida, *Tanzania* .... **54 C3** 4 49S 34 48 E
Singitikós Kólpos, *Greece* .... **23 D11** 40 6N 24 0 E
Singkaling Hkamti, *Burma* ... **41 G19** 26 0N 95 39 E
Singkang, *Indonesia* .... **37 E6** 4 8S 120 1 E
Singkawang, *Indonesia* ...... **36 D3** 1 0N 108 57 E
Singkep, *Indonesia* .... **36 E2** 0 30S 104 25 E
Singleton, *Australia* .... **63 E5** 32 33S 151 0 E
Singleton, Mt., *N. Terr., Australia* **60 D5** 22 0S 130 46 E
Singleton, Mt., *W. Austral.,*
　Australia .... **61 E2** 29 27S 117 15 E

Singoli, *India* .... **42 G6** 25 0N 75 22 E
Singora = Songkhla, *Thailand* **39 J3** 7 13N 100 37 E
Singosan, *N. Korea* .... **35 E14** 38 52N 127 25 E
Sinhung, *N. Korea* .... **35 D14** 40 11N 127 34 E
Sinjai, *Indonesia* .... **37 F6** 5 7S 120 20 E
Sinjär, *Iraq* .... **44 B4** 36 19N 41 52 E
Sinkat, *Sudan* .... **51 E13** 18 55N 36 49 E
Sinkiang Uighur = Xinjiang
　Uygur Zizhiqu □, *China* .... **32 C3** 42 0N 86 0 E
Sinmak, *N. Korea* .... **35 E14** 38 25N 126 14 E
Sinnamary, *Fr. Guiana* **93 B8** 5 25N 53 0W
Sinni ➤, *Italy* .... **22 D7** 40 8N 16 41 E
Sinop, *Turkey* .... **19 F6** 42 1N 35 11 E
Sinor, *India* .... **42 J5** 21 55N 73 20 E
Sinp'o, *N. Korea* .... **35 E15** 40 0N 128 13 E
Sinsk, *Russia* .... **29 C13** 61 8N 126 48 E
Sintang, *Indonesia* .... **36 D4** 0 5N 111 35 E
Sinton, *U.S.A.* **81 L6** 28 2N 97 31W
Sintra, *Portugal* **21 C1** 38 47N 9 25W
Sinŭiju, *N. Korea* .... **35 D13** 40 5N 124 24 E
Siocon, *Phil.* .... **37 C6** 7 40N 122 10 E
Siófok, *Hungary* .... **17 E10** 46 54N 18 3 E
Sion, *Switz.* .... **20 C7** 46 14N 7 20 E
Sion Mills, *U.K.* **10 B4** 54 48N 7 29W
Sioux City, *U.S.A.* **80 D6** 42 30N 96 24W
Sioux Falls, *U.S.A.* **80 D6** 43 33N 96 44W
Sioux Lookout, *Canada* **72 B1** 50 10N 91 50W
Sioux Narrows, *Canada* **71 D10** 49 25N 94 10W
Siparia, *Trin. & Tob.* **93 K15** 10 8N 61 31W
Siping, *China* .... **35 C13** 43 8N 124 21 E
Sipiwesk L., *Canada* **71 B9** 55 5N 97 35W
Siple, *Antarctica* .... **5 D7** 75 0S 74 0 E
Sipra ➤, *India* .... **42 H6** 23 55N 75 28 E
Sipura, *Indonesia* .... **36 E1** 2 18S 99 40 E
Siquia ➤, *Nic.* **88 D3** 12 10N 84 20W
Siquijor, *Phil.* .... **37 C6** 9 12N 123 35 E
Siquirres, *Costa Rica* **88 D3** 10 6N 83 30W
Şir Abu Nu'ayr, *U.A.E.* .... **45 E7** 25 20N 54 20 E
Şīr Banī Yās, *U.A.E.* .... **45 E7** 24 19N 52 37 E
Sir Edward Pellew Group,
　Australia .... **62 B2** 15 40S 137 10 E
Sir Graham Moore Is., *Australia* **60 B4** 13 53S 126 34 E
Sir James MacBrien, Mt., *Canada* **68 B7** 62 7N 127 41W
Sira ➤, *Norway* .... **9 G12** 58 23N 6 34 E
Siracusa, *Italy* .... **22 F6** 37 4N 15 17 E
Sirajganj, *Bangla.* .... **43 G13** 24 25N 89 47 E
Sirathu, *India* .... **43 G9** 25 39N 81 19 E
Sirdān, *Iran* .... **45 B6** 36 39N 49 12 E
Sirdaryo = Syrdarya ➤,
　Kazakhstan .... **28 E7** 46 3N 61 0 E
Siren, *U.S.A.* **80 C8** 45 47N 92 24W
Sirer, *Spain* .... **24 C7** 38 56N 1 22 E
Siret ➤, *Romania* .... **17 F14** 45 24N 28 1 E
Sirghāyā, *Syria* .... **46 B5** 33 51N 36 8 E
Sīrjān, *Iran* .... **45 D7** 29 30N 55 45 E
Sirmaur, *India* .... **43 G9** 24 51N 81 23 E
Sirohi, *India* .... **42 G5** 24 52N 72 53 E
Sironj, *India* .... **42 G7** 24 5N 77 39 E
Síros, *Greece* .... **23 F11** 37 28N 24 57 E
Sirretta Pk., *U.S.A.* **79 K8** 35 56N 118 19W
Sirrī, *Iran* .... **45 E7** 25 55N 54 32 E
Sirsa, *India* .... **42 E6** 29 33N 75 4 E
Sirsa ➤, *India* .... **43 F8** 26 51N 79 4 E
Sisak, *Croatia* .... **16 F9** 45 30N 16 21 E
Sisaket, *Thailand* .... **38 E5** 15 8N 104 23 E
Sishen, *S. Africa* .... **56 D3** 27 47S 22 59 E
Sishui, *Henan, China* .... **34 G7** 34 48N 113 15 E
Sishui, *Shandong, China* ..... **35 G9** 35 42N 117 18 E
Sisipuk L., *Canada* **71 B8** 55 45N 101 50W
Sisophon, *Cambodia* .... **38 F4** 13 38N 102 59 E
Sisseton, *U.S.A.* **80 C6** 45 40N 97 3W
Sīstān, *Asia* .... **45 D9** 30 50N 61 0 E
Sīstān, Daryācheh-ye, *Iran* ... **45 D9** 31 0N 61 0 E
Sīstān va Balūchestān □, *Iran* **45 E9** 27 0N 62 0 E
Sisters, *Australia* **76 D3** 44 18N 121 33W
Siswa Bazar, *India* .... **43 F10** 27 9N 83 46 E
Sitamarhi, *India* .... **43 F11** 26 37N 85 30 E
Sitampiky, *Madag.* .... **57 B8** 16 41S 46 6 E
Sitapur, *India* .... **43 F9** 27 38N 80 45 E
Siteki, *Swaziland* .... **57 D5** 26 32S 31 58 E
Sitges, *Spain* .... **21 B6** 41 17N 1 47 E
Sitía, *Greece* .... **25 D8** 35 13N 26 6 E
Sitka, *U.S.A.* **70 B1** 57 3N 135 20W
Sitoti, *Botswana* .... **56 C3** 23 15S 23 40 E
Sittang Myit ➤, *Burma* ...... **41 L20** 17 20N 96 45 E
Sittard, *Neths.* .... **15 C5** 51 0N 5 52 E
Sittingbourne, *U.K.* .... **13 F8** 51 21N 0 45 E
Sittoung = Sittang Myit ➤,
　Burma .... **41 L20** 17 20N 96 45 E
Sittwe, *Burma* .... **41 J18** 20 18N 92 45 E
Situbondo, *Indonesia* .... **37 G16** 7 42S 114 0 E
Siuna, *Nic.* **88 D3** 13 37N 84 45W
Siuri, *India* .... **43 H12** 23 50N 87 34 E
Sivand, *Iran* .... **45 D7** 30 5N 52 55 E
Sivas, *Turkey* .... **19 G6** 39 43N 36 58 E
Siverek, *Turkey* .... **44 B3** 37 50N 39 19 E
Sivomaskinskiy, *Russia* ...... **18 A11** 66 40N 62 35 E
Sivrihisar, *Turkey* .... **19 G5** 39 30N 31 35 E
Sîwa, *Egypt* .... **51 C11** 29 11N 25 31 E
Sîwa, El Wâhât es, *Egypt* ..... **48 D6** 29 10N 25 30 E
Siwa Oasis = Sîwa, El Wâhât es,
　Egypt .... **48 D6** 29 10N 25 30 E
Siwalik Range, *Nepal* .... **43 F10** 28 0N 83 0 E
Siwan, *India* .... **43 F11** 26 13N 84 21 E
Siwana, *India* .... **42 G5** 25 38N 72 25 E
Six Cross Roads, *Barbados* ... **89 g** 13 10N 59 28W
Sixmilebridge, *Ireland* **10 D3** 52 44N 8 46W
Sixth Cataract, *Sudan* .... **51 E12** 16 20N 32 42 E
Siziwang Qi, *China* .... **34 D6** 41 25N 111 40 E
Sjælland, *Denmark* .... **9 J14** 55 30N 11 30 E
Sjumen = Shumen, *Bulgaria* .. **23 C12** 43 18N 26 55 E
Skadarsko Jezero, *Serbia & M.* **23 C8** 42 10N 19 20 E
Skaftafell, *Iceland* **8 D5** 64 1N 17 0W
Skagafjörður, *Iceland* **8 D4** 65 54N 19 35W
Skagastølstindane, *Norway* ... **9 F12** 61 28N 7 52 E
Skagaströnd, *Iceland* **8 D3** 65 50N 20 19W
Skagen, *Denmark* .... **9 H14** 57 43N 10 35 E
Skagerrak, *Denmark* .... **9 H13** 57 30N 9 0 E
Skagit ➤, *U.S.A.* **78 B4** 48 23N 122 22W
Skagway, *U.S.A.* **68 C6** 59 28N 135 19W
Skala-Podilska, *Ukraine* ..... **17 D14** 48 50N 26 15 E
Skala Podolskaya = Skala-
　Podilska, *Ukraine* .... **17 D14** 48 50N 26 15 E
Skalat, *Ukraine* .... **17 D13** 49 23N 25 55 E
Skåne, *Sweden* .... **9 J15** 55 59N 13 30 E
Skaneateles, *U.S.A.* **85 D8** 42 57N 76 26W

Skaneateles L., *U.S.A.* **85 D8** 42 51N 76 22W
Skara, *Sweden* .... **9 G15** 58 25N 13 30 E
Skardu, *Pakistan* .... **43 B6** 35 20N 75 44 E
Skarżysko-Kamienna, *Poland* **17 C11** 51 7N 20 52 E
Skeena ➤, *Canada* **70 C2** 54 9N 130 5W
Skeena Mts., *Canada* **70 B3** 56 40N 128 30W
Skegness, *U.K.* .... **12 D8** 53 9N 0 20 E
Skeldon, *Guyana* **92 B7** 5 55N 57 20W
Skeleton Coast △, *Namibia* .. **56 C1** 20 0S 13 20 E
Skellefte älv ➤, *Sweden* ..... **8 D19** 64 45N 21 10 E
Skellefteå, *Sweden* .... **8 D19** 64 45N 20 50 E
Skelleftehamn, *Sweden* ...... **8 D19** 64 40N 21 9 E
Skerries, The, *U.K.* **12 D3** 53 25N 4 36W
Ski, *Norway* .... **9 G14** 59 43N 10 52 E
Skíathos, *Greece* .... **23 E10** 39 12N 23 30 E
Skibbereen, *Ireland* **10 E2** 51 33N 9 16W
Skiddaw, *U.K.* **12 C4** 54 39N 3 9W
Skidegate, *Canada* **70 C2** 53 15N 132 1W
Skien, *Norway* .... **9 G13** 59 12N 9 35 E
Skierniewice, *Poland* .... **17 C11** 51 58N 20 10 E
Skikda, *Algeria* .... **50 A7** 36 50N 6 58 E
Skilloura, *Cyprus* .... **25 D12** 35 14N 33 10 E
Skipton, *U.K.* **12 D5** 53 58N 2 3W
Skírmish Pt., *Australia* .... **62 A1** 11 59S 134 17 E
Skíros, *Greece* .... **23 E11** 38 55N 24 34 E
Skive, *Denmark* .... **9 H13** 56 33N 9 2 E
Skjálfandafljót ➤, *Iceland* ... **8 D5** 65 59N 17 25W
Skjálfandi, *Iceland* **8 C5** 66 5N 17 30W
Skoghall, *Sweden* .... **9 G15** 59 20N 13 30 E
Skole, *Ukraine* .... **17 D12** 49 3N 23 30 E
Skópelos, *Greece* .... **23 E10** 39 9N 23 47 E
Skopi, *Greece* .... **25 D8** 35 11N 26 2 E
Skopje, *Macedonia* .... **23 C9** 42 1N 21 26 E
Skövde, *Sweden* .... **9 G15** 58 24N 13 50 E
Skovorodino, *Russia* .... **29 D13** 54 0N 124 0 E
Skowhegan, *U.S.A.* **83 C11** 44 46N 69 43W
Skull, *Ireland* **10 E2** 51 32N 9 34W
Skunk ➤, *U.S.A.* **80 E9** 40 42N 91 7W
Skuodas, *Lithuania* .... **9 H19** 56 16N 21 33 E
Skvyra, *Ukraine* .... **17 D15** 49 44N 29 40 E
Skye, *U.K.* **11 D2** 57 15N 6 10W
Skykomish, *U.S.A.* **76 C3** 47 42N 121 22W
Skyros = Skíros, *Greece* ...... **23 E11** 38 55N 24 34 E
Slade Pt., *Australia* .... **62 K7** 21 5S 149 13 E
Slættaratindur, *Færoe Is.* **8 E9** 62 18N 7 1W
Slagelse, *Denmark* .... **9 J14** 55 23N 11 19 E
Slamet, *Indonesia* .... **37 G13** 7 16S 109 8 E
Slaney ➤, *Ireland* **10 D5** 52 26N 6 33W
Slangberge, *S. Africa* .... **56 E3** 31 32S 20 48 E
Śląsk, *Poland* .... **16 C9** 51 0N 16 30 E
Slate Is., *Canada* **72 C2** 48 40N 87 0W
Slatina, *Romania* .... **17 F13** 44 28N 24 22 E
Slatington, *U.S.A.* **85 F9** 40 45N 75 37W
Slaton, *U.S.A.* **81 J4** 33 26N 101 39W
Slave ➤, *Canada* **70 A6** 61 18N 113 39W
Slave Coast, *W. Afr.* .... **50 G6** 6 0N 2 30 E
Slave Lake, *Canada* **70 B6** 55 17N 114 43W
Slave Pt., *Canada* **70 A5** 61 11N 115 56W
Slavgorod, *Russia* .... **28 D8** 53 1N 78 37 E
Slavonski Brod, *Croatia* ...... **23 B8** 45 11N 18 1 E
Slavuta, *Ukraine* .... **17 C14** 50 15N 27 2 E
Slavyanka, *Russia* .... **30 C5** 42 53N 131 21 E
Slavyansk = Slovyansk, *Ukraine* **19 E6** 48 55N 37 36 E
Slawharad, *Belarus* .... **17 B16** 53 27N 31 0 E
Sleaford, *U.K.* **12 D7** 53 0N 0 24W
Sleaford B., *Australia* .... **63 E2** 34 55S 135 45 E
Sleat, Sd. of, *U.K.* **11 D3** 57 5N 5 47W
Sleeper Is., *Canada* **69 C11** 58 30N 81 0W
Sleeping Bear Dunes △, *U.S.A.* **82 C2** 44 50N 86 5W
Sleepy Eye, *U.S.A.* **80 C7** 44 18N 94 43W
Slemon L., *Canada* **70 A5** 63 13N 116 4W
Slide Mt., *U.S.A.* **85 E10** 42 0N 74 25W
Slidell, *U.S.A.* **81 K10** 30 17N 89 47W
Sliema, *Malta* .... **25 D2** 35 55N 14 30 E
Slieve Aughty, *Ireland* **10 C3** 53 4N 8 30W
Slieve Bloom, *Ireland* **10 C4** 53 4N 7 40W
Slieve Donard, *U.K.* **10 B6** 54 11N 5 55W
Slieve Gamph, *Ireland* **10 B3** 54 6N 9 0W
Slieve Gullion, *U.K.* **10 B5** 54 7N 6 26W
Slieve League, *Ireland* **10 B3** 54 40N 8 42W
Slieve Mish, *Ireland* **10 D2** 52 12N 9 50W
Slievenamon, *Ireland* **10 D4** 52 25N 7 34W
Sligeach = Sligo, *Ireland* **10 B3** 54 16N 8 28W
Sligo, *Ireland* **10 B3** 54 16N 8 28W
Sligo, *U.S.A.* **84 E5** 41 6N 79 29W
Sligo □, *Ireland* **10 B3** 54 8N 8 42W
Sligo B., *Ireland* **10 B3** 54 18N 8 40W
Slippery Rock, *U.S.A.* **84 E4** 41 3N 80 3W
Slite, *Sweden* .... **9 H18** 57 42N 18 48 E
Sliven, *Bulgaria* .... **23 C12** 42 42N 26 19 E
Sloan, *U.S.A.* **79 K11** 35 57N 115 13W
Sloansville, *U.S.A.* **85 D10** 42 45N 74 22W
Slobodskoy, *Russia* .... **18 C9** 58 40N 50 6 E
Slobozia, *Romania* .... **17 F14** 44 34N 27 23 E
Slocan, *Canada* **70 D5** 49 48N 117 28W
Slonim, *Belarus* .... **17 B13** 53 4N 25 19 E
Slough, *U.K.* **13 F7** 51 30N 0 36W
Slough □, *U.K.* **13 F7** 51 30N 0 36W
Sloughhouse, *U.S.A.* **78 G5** 38 26N 121 12W
Slovak Rep. ■, *Europe* ...... **17 D10** 48 45N 20 0 E
Slovakia = Slovak Rep. ■, *Europe* **17 D10** 48 30N 20 0 E
Slovakian Ore Mts. = Slovenské
　Rudohorie, *Slovak Rep.* .... **17 D10** 48 45N 20 0 E
Slovenia ■, *Europe* .... **16 F8** 45 58N 14 30 E
Slovenija = Slovenia ■, *Europe* **16 F8** 45 58N 14 30 E
Slovenské Rudohorie,
　Slovak Rep. .... **17 D10** 48 45N 20 0 E
Slovyansk, *Ukraine* .... **19 E6** 48 55N 37 36 E
Sluch ➤, *Ukraine* .... **17 C14** 51 37N 26 38 E
Sluis, *Neths.* .... **15 C3** 51 18N 3 23 E
Słupsk, *Poland* .... **17 A9** 54 30N 17 3 E
Slurry, *S. Africa* .... **56 D4** 25 49S 25 42 E
Slutsk, *Belarus* .... **17 B14** 53 2N 27 31 E
Slyne Hd., *Ireland* **10 C1** 53 25N 10 10W
Slyudyanka, *Russia* .... **29 D11** 51 40N 103 40 E
Småland, *Sweden* .... **9 H16** 57 15N 15 25 E
Smalltree L., *Canada* **71 A8** 61 0N 105 0W
Smallwood Res., *Canada* **73 B7** 54 5N 64 30W
Smarhon, *Belarus* .... **17 A14** 54 20N 26 24 E
Smartt Syndicate Dam, *S. Africa* **56 E3** 30 45S 23 10 E
Smartville, *U.S.A.* **78 F5** 39 13N 121 18W
Smeaton, *Canada* **71 C8** 53 30N 104 49W
Smederevo, *Serbia & M.* ..... **23 B9** 44 40N 20 57 E
Smerwick Harbour, *Ireland* ... **10 D1** 52 12N 10 23W
Smethport, *U.S.A.* **84 E6** 41 49N 78 27W
Smidovich, *Russia* .... **29 E14** 48 36N 133 49 E
Smith, *Canada* **70 B6** 55 10N 114 0W

Smith Center, *U.S.A.* **80 F5** 39 47N 98 47W
Smith River, *U.S.A.* **76 F2** 41 55N 124 0W
Smith Sd., *N. Amer.* **4 B4** 78 25N 74 0W
Smithburne ➤, *Australia* .... **62 B3** 17 3S 140 57 E
Smithers, *Canada* **70 C3** 54 45N 127 10W
Smithfield, *S. Africa* .... **57 E4** 30 9S 26 30 E
Smithfield, *N.C., U.S.A.* **83 H6** 35 31N 78 21W
Smithfield, *Utah, U.S.A.* **76 F8** 41 50N 111 50W
Smiths Falls, *Canada* **85 B9** 44 55N 76 0W
Smithton, *Australia* .... **63 G4** 40 53S 145 6 E
Smithville, *Canada* **84 C5** 43 6N 79 33W
Smithville, *U.S.A.* **81 K6** 30 1N 97 10W
Smoky ➤, *Canada* **70 B5** 56 10N 117 21W
Smoky Bay, *Australia* .... **63 E1** 32 22S 134 13 E
Smoky Hill ➤, *U.S.A.* **80 F6** 39 4N 96 48W
Smoky Hills, *U.S.A.* **80 F5** 39 15N 99 30W
Smoky Lake, *Canada* **70 C6** 54 10N 112 30W
Smøla, *Norway* .... **8 E13** 63 23N 8 3 E
Smolensk, *Russia* .... **18 D5** 54 45N 32 5 E
Smolikas, Óros, *Greece* ...... **23 D9** 40 9N 20 58 E
Smolyan, *Bulgaria* .... **23 D11** 41 36N 24 38 E
Smooth Rock Falls, *Canada* .. **72 C3** 49 17N 81 37W
Smoothstone L., *Canada* **71 C7** 54 40N 106 50W
Smorgon = Smarhon, *Belarus* **17 A14** 54 20N 26 24 E
Smyrna = İzmir, *Turkey* ..... **23 E12** 38 25N 27 8 E
Smyrna, *U.S.A.* **82 F8** 39 18N 75 36W
Snæfell, *Iceland* **8 D6** 64 48N 15 34W
Snaefell, *U.K.* **12 C3** 54 16N 4 27W
Snæfellsjökull, *Iceland* **8 D2** 64 49N 23 46W
Snake ➤, *U.S.A.* **76 C4** 46 12N 119 2W
Snake I., *Australia* .... **63 F4** 38 47S 146 33 E
Snake Range, *U.S.A.* **76 G6** 39 0N 114 20W
Snake River Plain, *U.S.A.* **76 E7** 42 50N 114 0W
Snåsavatnet, *Norway* .... **8 D14** 64 12N 12 0 E
Sneek, *Neths.* .... **15 A5** 53 2N 5 40 E
Sneeuberge, *S. Africa* .... **56 E3** 31 46S 24 20 E
Snelling, *U.S.A.* **78 H6** 37 31N 120 26W
Snežka, *Europe* .... **16 C8** 50 41N 15 50 E
Snizort, L., *U.K.* **11 D2** 57 33N 6 28W
Snøhetta, *Norway* .... **9 E13** 62 19N 9 16 E
Snohomish, *U.S.A.* **78 C4** 47 55N 122 6W
Snow Hill, *U.S.A.* **82 F8** 38 11N 75 24W
Snow Lake, *Canada* **71 C8** 54 52N 100 3W
Snow Mt., *Calif., U.S.A.* **78 F4** 39 23N 122 45W
Snow Mt., *Maine, U.S.A.* **85 A14** 45 18N 70 48W
Snow Shoe, *U.S.A.* **84 E7** 41 2N 77 57W
Snowbird L., *Canada* **71 A8** 60 45N 103 0W
Snowdon, *U.K.* **12 D3** 53 4N 4 5W
Snowdonia △, *U.K.* **12 D4** 53 7N 3 59W
Snowdrift = Łutselk'e, *Canada* **71 A6** 62 24N 110 44W
Snowdrift ➤, *Canada* **71 A6** 62 24N 110 44W
Snowflake, *U.S.A.* **77 J8** 34 30N 110 5W
Snowshoe Pk., *U.S.A.* **76 B6** 48 13N 115 41W
Snowtown, *Australia* .... **63 E2** 33 46S 138 14 E
Snowville, *U.S.A.* **76 F7** 41 58N 112 43W
Snowy ➤, *Australia* .... **63 F4** 37 46S 148 30 E
Snowy Mt., *U.S.A.* **85 C10** 43 42N 74 23W
Snowy Mts., *Australia* .... **63 F4** 36 30S 148 20 E
Snug Corner, *Bahamas* **89 B5** 22 33N 73 52W
Snyatyn, *Ukraine* .... **17 D13** 48 27N 25 38 E
Snyder, *Okla., U.S.A.* **81 H5** 34 40N 98 57W
Snyder, *Tex., U.S.A.* **81 J4** 32 44N 100 55W
Soahanina, *Madag.* .... **57 B7** 18 42S 44 13 E
Soalala, *Madag.* .... **57 B8** 16 6S 45 20 E
Soaloka, *Madag.* .... **57 B8** 18 32S 45 15 E
Soamanonga, *Madag.* .... **57 C7** 23 52S 44 47 E
Soan ➤, *Pakistan* .... **42 C5** 33 1N 71 44 E
Soanierana-Ivongo, *Madag.* .. **57 B8** 16 55S 49 35 E
Soanindrariny, *Madag.* ...... **57 B8** 19 54S 47 14 E
Soavina, *Madag.* .... **57 C8** 20 23S 46 56 E
Soavinandriana, *Madag.* ..... **57 B8** 19 9S 46 45 E
Sobat, Nahr ➤, *Sudan* ...... **51 G12** 9 22N 31 33 E
Sobhapur, *India* .... **42 H8** 22 47N 78 17 E
Sobradinho, Represa de, *Brazil* **93 E10** 9 30S 42 0W
Sobral, *Brazil* **93 D10** 3 50S 40 20W
Soc Giang, *Vietnam* .... **38 A6** 22 54N 106 1 E
Soc Trang, *Vietnam* .... **39 H5** 9 37N 105 50 E
Socastee, *U.S.A.* **83 J6** 33 41N 79 1W
Soch'e = Shache, *China* ...... **32 C2** 38 20N 77 10 E
Sochi, *Russia* .... **19 F6** 43 35N 39 40 E
Société, Is. de la,
　French Polynesia **65 J12** 17 0S 151 0W
Society Is. = Société, Is. de la,
　French Polynesia **65 J12** 17 0S 151 0W
Socompa, Portezuelo de, *Chile* **94 A2** 24 27S 68 18W
Socorro, *N. Mex., U.S.A.* **77 J10** 34 4N 106 54W
Socorro, *Tex., U.S.A.* **77 L10** 31 39N 106 18W
Socorro, I., *Mexico* **86 D2** 18 45N 110 58W
Socotra, *Yemen* .... **47 E5** 12 30N 54 0 E
Soda L., *U.S.A.* **77 J5** 35 10N 116 4W
Soda Plains, *India* .... **43 B8** 35 30N 79 0 E
Soda Springs, *U.S.A.* **76 E8** 42 39N 111 36W
Sodankylä, *Finland* .... **8 C22** 67 29N 26 40 E
Soddy-Daisy, *U.S.A.* **83 H3** 35 17N 85 10W
Söderhamn, *Sweden* .... **9 F17** 61 18N 17 10 E
Söderköping, *Sweden* .... **9 G17** 58 31N 16 20 E
Södermanland, *Sweden* ...... **9 G17** 58 56N 16 55 E
Södertälje, *Sweden* .... **9 G17** 59 12N 17 39 E
Sodiri, *Sudan* .... **51 F11** 14 27N 29 0 E
Sodus, *U.S.A.* **84 C7** 43 14N 77 4W
Sodwana Bay △, *S. Africa* ... **57 D5** 27 35S 32 43 E
Soekmekaar, *S. Africa* .... **57 C4** 23 30S 29 55 E
Soest, *Neths.* .... **15 B5** 52 9N 5 19 E
Sofala □, *Mozam.* .... **57 B5** 19 30S 34 30 E
Sofia = Sofiya, *Bulgaria* ...... **23 C10** 42 45N 23 20 E
Sofia ➤, *Madag.* .... **57 B8** 15 27S 47 23 E
Sofiya, *Bulgaria* .... **23 C10** 42 45N 23 20 E
Sōfu-Gan, *Japan* .... **31 K10** 29 49N 140 21 E
Sogamoso, *Colombia* **92 B4** 5 43N 72 56W
Sogār, *Iran* .... **45 E8** 25 53N 58 6 E
Sogndalsfjøra, *Norway* .... **9 F12** 61 14N 7 5 E
Søgne, *Norway* .... **9 G12** 58 5N 7 48 E
Sognefjorden, *Norway* .... **9 F11** 61 10N 5 50 E
Sŏgwipo, *S. Korea* .... **35 H14** 33 13N 126 34 E
Soh, *Iran* .... **45 C6** 33 26N 50 58 E
Sohâg, *Egypt* .... **51 C12** 26 33N 31 43 E
Soignies, *Belgium* .... **15 D4** 50 35N 4 5 E
Soissons, *France* .... **20 B5** 49 25N 3 19 E
Sōja, *Japan* .... **31 G6** 34 40N 133 45 E
Sojat, *India* .... **42 G5** 25 55N 73 45 E
Sokal, *Ukraine* .... **17 C13** 50 31N 24 15 E
Söke, *Turkey* .... **23 F12** 37 48N 27 28 E
Sokelo, *Dem. Rep. of the Congo* **55 D1** 9 55S 24 36 E
Sokhumi, *Georgia* .... **19 F7** 43 0N 41 0 E

Soko Islands, *China*	33 G10	22 10N 113 54 E
Sokodé, *Togo*	50 G6	9 0N 1 11 E
Sokol, *Russia*	18 C7	59 30N 40 5 E
Sokółka, *Poland*	17 B12	53 25N 23 30 E
Sokołów Podlaski, *Poland*	17 B12	52 25N 22 15 E
Sokoto, *Nigeria*	50 F7	13 2N 5 16 E
Sol Iletsk, *Russia*	18 D10	51 10N 55 0 E
Solai, *Kenya*	54 B4	0 2N 36 12 E
Solan, *India*	42 D7	30 55N 77 7 E
Solano, *Phil.*	37 A6	16 31N 121 15 E
Solapur, *India*	40 L9	17 43N 75 56 E
Soldotna, *U.S.A.*	68 B4	60 29N 151 3W
Soléa, *Cyprus*	25 D12	35 5N 33 4 E
Soledad, *Colombia*	92 A4	10 55N 74 46W
Soledad, *U.S.A.*	78 J5	36 26N 121 20W
Soledad, *Venezuela*	92 B6	8 10N 63 34W
Solent, The, *U.K.*	13 G6	50 45N 1 25W
Solfonn, *Norway*	9 F12	60 2N 6 57 E
Solhan, *Turkey*	44 B4	38 57N 41 3 E
Soligalich, *Russia*	18 C7	59 5N 42 10 E
Soligorsk = Salihorsk, *Belarus*	17 B14	52 51N 27 27 E
Solihull, *U.K.*	13 E6	52 26N 1 47W
Solikamsk, *Russia*	18 C10	59 38N 56 50 E
Solila, *Madag.*	57 C8	21 25S 46 37 E
Solimões = Amazonas →, *S. Amer.*	93 D9	0 5S 50 0W
Solingen, *Germany*	16 C4	51 10N 7 5 E
Sollefteå, *Sweden*	8 E17	63 12N 17 20 E
Sóller, *Spain*	24 B9	39 46N 2 43 E
Solo →, *Indonesia*	37 G15	6 47S 112 22 E
Sologne, *France*	20 C4	47 40N 1 45 E
Solok, *Indonesia*	36 E2	0 45S 100 40 E
Sololá, *Guatemala*	88 D1	14 49N 91 10W
Solomon, N. Fork →, *U.S.A.*	80 F5	39 29N 98 26W
Solomon, S. Fork →, *U.S.A.*	80 F5	39 25N 99 12W
Solomon Is. ■, *Pac. Oc.*	64 H7	6 0S 155 0 E
Solon, *China*	33 B7	46 32N 121 10 E
Solon Springs, *U.S.A.*	80 B9	46 22N 91 49W
Solor, *Indonesia*	37 F6	8 27S 123 0 E
Solothurn, *Switz.*	20 C7	47 13N 7 32 E
Šolta, *Croatia*	22 C7	43 24N 16 15 E
Soltānābād, *Khorāsān, Iran*	45 C8	34 13N 59 58 E
Soltānābād, *Khorāsān, Iran*	45 B8	36 29N 58 5 E
Solunska Glava, *Macedonia*	23 D9	41 44N 21 31 E
Solvang, *U.S.A.*	79 L6	34 36N 120 8W
Solvay, *U.S.A.*	85 C8	43 3N 76 13W
Sölvesborg, *Sweden*	9 H16	56 5N 14 35 E
Solvychegodsk, *Russia*	18 B8	61 21N 46 56 E
Solway Firth, *U.K.*	12 C4	54 49N 3 35W
Solwezi, *Zambia*	55 E2	12 11S 26 21 E
Sōma, *Japan*	30 F10	37 40N 140 50 E
Soma, *Turkey*	23 E12	39 10N 27 35 E
Somabhula, *Zimbabwe*	57 B4	19 42S 29 40 E
Somali Pen., *Africa*	48 F8	7 0N 46 0 E
Somali Rep. ■, *Africa*	47 F4	7 0N 47 0 E
Somalia = Somali Rep. ■, *Africa*	47 F4	7 0N 47 0 E
Sombor, *Serbia & M.*	23 B8	45 46N 19 9 E
Sombra, *Canada*	84 D2	42 43N 82 29W
Sombrerete, *Mexico*	86 C4	23 40N 103 40W
Sombrero, *Anguilla*	89 C7	18 37N 63 30W
Somdari, *India*	42 G5	25 47N 72 38 E
Somers, *U.S.A.*	76 B6	48 5N 114 13W
Somerset, *Ky., U.S.A.*	82 G3	37 5N 84 36W
Somerset, *Mass., U.S.A.*	85 E13	41 47N 71 8W
Somerset, *Pa., U.S.A.*	84 F5	40 1N 79 5W
Somerset □, *U.K.*	13 F5	51 9N 3 0W
Somerset East, *S. Africa*	56 E4	32 42S 25 35 E
Somerset I., *Canada*	68 A10	73 30N 93 0W
Somerset West, *S. Africa*	56 E2	34 8S 18 50 E
Somersworth, *U.S.A.*	85 C14	43 16N 70 52W
Somerton, *U.S.A.*	77 K6	32 36N 114 43W
Somerville, *U.S.A.*	85 F10	40 35N 74 38W
Someş →, *Romania*	17 D12	47 49N 22 43 E
Somme →, *France*	20 A4	50 11N 1 38 E
Somnath, *India*	42 J4	20 53N 70 22 E
Somosierra, Puerto de, *Spain*	21 B4	41 4N 3 35W
Somoto, *Nic.*	88 D2	13 28N 86 37W
Somport, Puerto de, *Spain*	20 E3	42 48N 0 31W
Son →, *India*	43 G11	25 42N 84 52 E
Son Ha, *Vietnam*	38 E7	15 3N 108 34 E
Son Hoa, *Vietnam*	38 F7	13 2N 108 58 E
Son La, *Vietnam*	38 B4	21 20N 103 50 E
Son Serra, *Spain*	24 B10	39 43N 3 13 E
Son Tay, *Vietnam*	38 B5	21 8N 105 30 E
Soná, *Panama*	88 E3	8 0N 81 20W
Sonamarg, *India*	43 B6	34 18N 75 21 E
Sonamukhi, *India*	43 H12	23 18N 87 27 E
Sonar →, *India*	43 G8	24 24N 79 56 E
Sŏnch'ŏn, *N. Korea*	35 E13	39 48N 124 55 E
Sondags →, *S. Africa*	56 E4	33 44S 25 51 E
Sondar, *India*	43 C6	33 28N 75 56 E
Sønderborg, *Denmark*	9 J13	54 55N 9 49 E
Sóndrio, *Italy*	20 C8	46 10N 9 52 E
Sone, *Mozam.*	55 F3	17 23S 34 55 E
Sonepur, *India*	41 J13	20 55N 83 50 E
Song, *Thailand*	38 C3	18 28N 100 11 E
Song Cau, *Vietnam*	38 F7	13 27N 109 18 E
Song Xian, *China*	34 G7	34 12N 112 8 E
Songan, *Indonesia*	37 J18	8 13S 115 24 E
Sŏngch'ŏn, *N. Korea*	35 E14	39 12N 126 15 E
Songea, *Tanzania*	55 E4	10 40S 35 40 E
Songgang, *China*	33 F10	22 46N 113 50 E
Songhua Hu, *China*	35 C14	43 35N 126 50 E
Songhua Jiang →, *China*	33 B8	47 45N 132 30 E
Songimvelo △, *S. Africa*	57 D5	25 50S 31 2 E
Songjin, *N. Korea*	35 D15	40 40N 129 10 E
Songjŏng-ni, *S. Korea*	35 G14	35 8N 126 47 E
Songkhla, *Thailand*	39 J3	7 13N 100 37 E
Songnim, *N. Korea*	35 E13	38 45N 125 39 E
Songo, *Mozam.*	53 H6	15 34S 32 38 E
Songo, *Sudan*	51 G10	9 47N 24 21 E
Songpan, *China*	32 A5	32 40N 103 30 E
Songwe, Dem. Rep. of the Congo	54 C2	3 20S 26 16 E
Songwe →, *Africa*	55 D3	9 44S 33 58 E
Sonhat, *India*	43 H10	23 29N 82 31 E
Sonid Youqi, *China*	34 C7	42 45N 112 48 E
Sonipat, *India*	42 E7	29 0N 77 5 E
Sonkach, *India*	42 H7	22 59N 76 21 E
Sonmiani, *Pakistan*	42 G2	25 25N 66 40 E
Sonmiani B., *Pakistan*	42 G2	25 15N 66 30 E
Sono →, *Brazil*	93 E9	9 58S 48 11W
Sonoma, *U.S.A.*	78 G4	38 18N 122 28W
Sonora, *Calif., U.S.A.*	78 H6	37 59N 120 23W
Sonora, *Tex., U.S.A.*	81 K4	30 34N 100 39W
Sonora □, *Mexico*	86 B2	29 0N 111 0W
Sonora →, *Mexico*	86 B2	28 50N 111 33W
Sonoran Desert, *U.S.A.*	79 L12	33 40N 114 15W

Sonoyta, *Mexico*	86 A2	31 51N 112 50W
Sŏnsan, *S. Korea*	35 F15	36 14N 128 17 E
Sonsonate, *El Salv.*	88 D2	13 43N 89 44W
Soochow = Suzhou, *China*	33 C7	31 19N 120 38 E
Sooke, *Canada*	78 B3	48 13N 123 43W
Sop Hao, *Laos*	38 B5	20 33N 104 27 E
Sop Prap, *Thailand*	38 D2	17 53N 99 20 E
Sopi, *Indonesia*	37 D7	2 34N 128 28 E
Sopot, *Poland*	17 A10	54 27N 18 31 E
Sopron, *Hungary*	17 E9	47 45N 16 32 E
Sopur, *India*	43 B6	34 18N 74 27 E
Sør-Rondane, *Antarctica*	5 D4	72 0S 25 0 E
Sorah, *Pakistan*	42 F3	27 13N 68 56 E
Soraon, *India*	43 G9	25 37N 81 51 E
Sorel-Tracy, *Canada*	72 C5	46 0N 73 10W
Sórgono, *Italy*	22 D3	40 1N 9 6 E
Soria, *Spain*	21 B4	41 43N 2 32W
Soriano, *Uruguay*	94 C4	33 24S 58 19W
Sorkh, Kuh-e, *Iran*	45 C8	35 40N 58 30 E
Soroca, *Moldova*	17 D15	48 8N 28 12 E
Sorocaba, *Brazil*	95 A6	23 31S 47 27W
Sorochinsk, *Russia*	18 D9	52 26N 53 10 E
Soroki = Soroca, *Moldova*	17 D15	48 8N 28 12 E
Sorong, *Indonesia*	37 E8	0 55S 131 15 E
Soroní, *Greece*	25 C10	36 21N 28 1 E
Soroti, *Uganda*	54 B3	1 43N 33 35 E
Sørøya, *Norway*	8 A20	70 40N 22 30 E
Sørøysundet, *Norway*	8 A20	70 25N 23 0 E
Sorrell, *Australia*	63 G4	42 47S 147 34 E
Sorsele, *Sweden*	8 D17	65 31N 17 30 E
Sorsogon, *Phil.*	37 B6	13 0N 124 0 E
Sortavala, *Russia*	18 B5	61 42N 30 41 E
Sortland, *Norway*	8 B16	68 42N 15 25 E
Sŏsan, *S. Korea*	35 F14	36 47N 126 27 E
Soscumica, L., *Canada*	72 B4	50 15N 77 27W
Sosnogorsk, *Russia*	18 B9	63 37N 53 51 E
Sosnowiec, *Poland*	17 C10	50 20N 19 10 E
Sossus Vlei, *Namibia*	56 C2	24 40S 15 23 E
Sŏsura, *N. Korea*	35 C16	42 16N 130 36 E
Sot →, *India*	43 F8	27 27N 79 37 E
Sotkamo, *Finland*	8 D23	64 8N 28 23 E
Soto la Marina →, *Mexico*	87 C5	23 40N 97 40W
Sotuta, *Mexico*	87 C7	20 29N 89 43W
Souanké, *Congo*	52 D2	2 10N 14 3 E
Souderton, *U.S.A.*	85 F9	40 19N 75 19W
Soúdha, *Greece*	25 D6	35 29N 24 4 E
Soúdhas, Kólpos, *Greece*	25 D6	35 25N 24 10 E
Soufrière, *Guadeloupe*	88 b	16 5N 61 40W
Soufrière, *St. Lucia*	89 f	13 51N 61 3W
Soufrière Bay, *Domin.*	89 f	13 53N 61 6W
Soukhouma, *Laos*	38 E5	14 38N 105 48 E
Sŏul, *S. Korea*	35 F14	37 31N 126 58 E
Sound, The, *U.K.*	13 G3	50 20N 4 10W
Sources, Mt. aux, *Lesotho*	57 D4	28 45S 28 50 E
Soure, *Brazil*	93 D9	0 35S 48 30W
Souris, *Man., Canada*	71 D8	49 40N 100 20W
Souris, *P.E.I., Canada*	73 C7	46 21N 62 15W
Souris →, *Canada*	80 A5	49 40N 99 34W
Sousa, *Brazil*	93 E11	6 45S 38 10W
Sousse, *Tunisia*	51 A8	35 50N 10 38 E
Sout →, *S. Africa*	56 E2	31 35S 18 24 E
South Africa ■, *Africa*	56 E3	32 0S 23 0 E
South America	90 E5	10 0S 60 0W
South Aulatsivik I., *Canada*	73 A7	56 45N 61 30W
South Australia □, *Australia*	63 E2	32 0S 139 0 E
South Ayrshire □, *U.K.*	11 F4	55 18N 4 41W
South Baldy, *U.S.A.*	77 J10	33 59N 107 11W
South Bass I., *U.S.A.*	84 E2	41 38N 82 53W
South Bend, *Ind., U.S.A.*	82 E2	41 41N 86 15W
South Bend, *Wash., U.S.A.*	78 D3	46 40N 123 48W
South Boston, *U.S.A.*	83 G6	36 42N 78 54W
South Branch, *Canada*	73 C8	47 55N 59 2W
South Brook, *Canada*	73 C8	49 26N 56 5W
South Carolina □, *U.S.A.*	83 J5	34 0N 81 0W
South Charleston, *U.S.A.*	82 F5	38 22N 81 44W
South China Sea, *Asia*	36 C4	10 0N 113 0 E
South Cumberland Is. △, *Australia*	62 J7	20 42S 149 11 E
South Dakota □, *U.S.A.*	80 C5	44 15N 100 0W
South Deerfield, *U.S.A.*	85 D12	42 29N 72 37W
South Downs, *U.K.*	13 G7	50 52N 0 25W
South East □, *Australia*	63 G4	43 40S 146 50 E
South-East Indian Rise, *Ind. Oc.*	5 B10	43 0S 80 0 E
South East Is., *Australia*	61 F3	34 17S 123 30 E
South Esk →, *U.K.*	11 E6	56 43N 2 31W
South Foreland, *U.K.*	13 F9	51 8N 1 24 E
South Fork American →, *U.S.A.*	78 G5	38 45N 121 5W
South Fork Feather →, *U.S.A.*	78 F5	39 17N 121 36W
South Fork Grand →, *U.S.A.*	80 C3	45 43N 102 17W
South Fork Republican →, *U.S.A.*	80 E4	40 3N 101 31W
South Georgia, *Antarctica*	96 G9	54 30S 37 0W
South Gloucestershire □, *U.K.*	13 F5	51 32N 2 28W
South Hadley, *U.S.A.*	85 D12	42 16N 72 35W
South Haven, *U.S.A.*	82 D2	42 24N 86 16W
South Henik L., *Canada*	71 A9	61 30N 97 20W
South Honshu Ridge, *Pac. Oc.*	64 E6	23 0N 143 0 E
South Horr, *Kenya*	54 B4	2 12N 36 56 E
South I., *Kenya*	54 B4	2 35N 36 35 E
South I., *N.Z.*	59 L3	44 0S 170 0 E
South Indian Lake, *Canada*	71 B9	56 47N 98 56W
South Invercargill, *N.Z.*	59 M2	46 26S 168 23 E
South Island △, *Kenya*	54 B4	2 39N 36 35 E
South Kitui △, *Kenya*	54 C4	1 48S 38 46 E
South Knife →, *Canada*	71 B10	58 55N 94 37W
South Koel →, *India*	43 H11	22 32N 85 14 E
South Korea ■, *Asia*	35 G15	36 0N 128 0 E
South Lake Tahoe, *U.S.A.*	78 G6	38 57N 119 59W
South Lanarkshire □, *U.K.*	11 F5	55 37N 3 53W
South Loup →, *U.S.A.*	80 E5	41 4N 98 39W
South Luangwa △, *Zambia*	55 E3	13 0S 31 20 E
South Magnetic Pole, *Antarctica*	5 C9	64 8S 138 8 E
South Milwaukee, *U.S.A.*	82 D2	42 55N 87 52W
South Molton, *U.K.*	13 F4	51 1N 3 51W
South Moose L., *Canada*	71 C8	53 46N 100 8W
South Nahanni →, *Canada*	70 A4	61 3N 123 21W
South Nation →, *Canada*	85 A9	45 34N 75 6W
South Natuna Is. = Natuna Selatan, Kepulauan, *Indonesia*	36 D3	2 45N 109 0 E
South Negril Pt., *Jamaica*	88 a	18 14N 78 30W
South Orkney Is., *Antarctica*	5 C18	63 0S 45 0W
South Ossetia □, *Georgia*	19 F7	42 21N 44 2 E
South Pagai, I. = Pagai Selatan, Pulau, *Indonesia*	36 E2	3 0S 100 15 E
South Paris, *U.S.A.*	85 B14	44 14N 70 31W
South Pittsburg, *U.S.A.*	83 H3	35 1N 85 42W
South Platte →, *U.S.A.*	80 E4	41 7N 100 42W
South Pole, *Antarctica*	5 E	90 0S 0 0W

South Porcupine, *Canada*	72 C3	48 30N 81 12W
South Portland, *U.S.A.*	83 D10	43 38N 70 15W
South Pt., *Barbados*	89 g	13 2N 59 32W
South Pt., *U.S.A.*	84 B1	44 52N 83 19W
South River, *Canada*	72 C4	45 52N 79 23W
South River, *U.S.A.*	85 F10	40 27N 74 23W
South Ronaldsay, *U.K.*	11 C6	58 48N 2 58W
South Sandwich Is., *Antarctica*	5 B1	57 0S 27 0W
South Saskatchewan →, *Canada*	71 C7	53 15N 105 5W
South Seal →, *Canada*	71 B9	58 48N 98 8W
South Shetland Is., *Antarctica*	5 C18	62 0S 59 0W
South Shields, *U.K.*	12 C6	55 0N 1 25W
South Sioux City, *U.S.A.*	80 D6	42 28N 96 24W
South Taranaki Bight, *N.Z.*	59 H5	39 40S 174 5 E
South Thompson →, *Canada*	70 C4	50 40N 120 20W
South Twin I., *Canada*	72 B4	53 7N 79 52W
South Tyne →, *U.K.*	12 C5	54 59N 2 8W
South Uist, *U.K.*	11 D1	57 20N 7 15W
South West Africa = Namibia ■, *Africa*	56 C2	22 0S 18 9 E
South West C., *Australia*	63 G4	43 34S 146 3 E
South Williamsport, *U.S.A.*	84 E8	41 13N 77 0W
South Yorkshire □, *U.K.*	12 D6	53 27N 1 36W
Southampton, *Canada*	84 B3	44 30N 81 25W
Southampton, *U.K.*	13 G6	50 54N 1 23W
Southampton, *U.S.A.*	85 F12	40 53N 72 23W
Southampton □, *U.K.*	13 G6	50 54N 1 23W
Southampton I., *Canada*	69 B11	64 30N 84 0W
Southaven, *U.S.A.*	81 H9	34 59N 90 2W
Southbank, *Canada*	70 C3	54 2N 125 46W
Southbridge, *N.Z.*	59 K4	43 48S 172 16 E
Southbridge, *U.S.A.*	85 D12	42 5N 72 2W
Southeast Pacific Basin, *Pac. Oc.*	5 C15	16 30S 92 0W
Southend, *Canada*	71 B8	56 19N 103 22W
Southend-on-Sea, *U.K.*	13 F8	51 32N 0 44 E
Southend-on-Sea □, *U.K.*	13 F8	51 32N 0 44 E
Southern = Yuzhnyy □, *Russia*	28 E5	44 0N 40 0 E
Southern □, *Malawi*	55 F4	15 0S 35 0 E
Southern □, *Zambia*	55 F2	16 20S 26 20 E
Southern Alps, *N.Z.*	59 K3	43 41S 170 11 E
Southern Cross, *Australia*	61 F2	31 12S 119 15 E
Southern Indian L., *Canada*	71 B9	57 10N 98 30W
Southern Ocean, *Antarctica*	5 C6	62 0S 60 0 E
Southern Pines, *U.S.A.*	83 H6	35 11N 79 24W
Southern Uplands, *U.K.*	11 F5	55 28N 3 52W
Southington, *U.S.A.*	85 E12	41 36N 72 53W
Southland □, *N.Z.*	59 L1	45 30S 168 0 E
Southold, *U.S.A.*	85 E12	41 4N 72 26W
Southport, *Australia*	63 D5	27 58S 153 25 E
Southport, *U.K.*	12 D4	53 39N 3 0W
Southport, *Fla., U.S.A.*	83 K3	30 17N 85 38W
Southport, *N.Y., U.S.A.*	84 D8	42 3N 76 49W
Southwest △, *Australia*	63 G4	43 8S 146 5 E
Southwest, *N.Z.*	59 M1	47 17S 167 28 E
Southwold, *U.K.*	13 E9	52 20N 1 41 E
Southwood △, *Australia*	63 D5	27 48S 150 2 E
Soutpansberg, *S. Africa*	57 C4	23 0S 29 30 E
Sovetsk, *Kaliningrad, Russia*	9 J19	55 6N 21 50 E
Sovetsk, *Kirov, Russia*	18 C8	57 38N 48 53 E
Sovetskaya Gavan = Vanino, *Russia*	29 E15	48 50N 140 5 E
Soweto, *S. Africa*	57 D4	26 14S 27 54 E
Sōya-Kaikyō = La Perouse Str., *Asia*	30 B11	45 40N 142 0 E
Sōya-Misaki, *Japan*	30 B10	45 30N 141 55 E
Sozh →, *Belarus*	17 B16	51 57N 30 48 E
Spa, *Belgium*	15 D5	50 29N 5 53 E
Spain ■, *Europe*	21 B4	39 0N 4 0W
Spalding, *Australia*	63 E2	33 30S 138 37 E
Spalding, *U.K.*	12 E7	52 48N 0 9W
Spangler, *U.S.A.*	84 F6	40 39N 78 48W
Spanish, *Canada*	72 C3	46 12N 82 20W
Spanish Fork, *U.S.A.*	76 F8	40 7N 111 39W
Spanish Town, *Br. Virgin Is.*	89 e	17 43N 64 26W
Spanish Town, *Jamaica*	88 a	18 0N 76 57W
Sparks, *U.S.A.*	78 F7	39 32N 119 45W
Sparta = Spárti, *Greece*	23 F10	37 5N 22 25 E
Sparta, *Mich., U.S.A.*	82 D3	43 10N 85 42W
Sparta, *N.J., U.S.A.*	85 E10	41 2N 74 38W
Sparta, *Wis., U.S.A.*	80 D9	43 56N 90 49W
Spartanburg, *U.S.A.*	83 H5	34 56N 81 57W
Spartansburg, *U.S.A.*	84 E5	41 49N 79 41W
Spárti, *Greece*	23 F10	37 5N 22 25 E
Spartivento, C., *Calábria, Italy*	22 F7	37 55N 16 4 E
Spartivento, C., *Sard., Italy*	22 E3	38 53N 8 50 E
Sparwood, *Canada*	70 D6	49 44N 114 53W
Spassk Dalniy, *Russia*	29 E14	44 40N 132 48 E
Spátha, Ákra, *Greece*	25 D5	35 42N 23 43 E
Spatsizi →, *Canada*	70 B3	57 42N 128 7W
Spatsizi Plateau Wilderness △, *Canada*	70 B3	57 40N 128 0W
Spean →, *U.K.*	11 E4	56 55N 4 59W
Spearfish, *U.S.A.*	80 C3	44 30N 103 52W
Spearman, *U.S.A.*	81 G4	36 12N 101 12W
Speculator, *U.S.A.*	85 C10	43 30N 74 25W
Speightstown, *Barbados*	89 g	13 15N 59 39W
Speke Gulf, *Tanzania*	54 C3	2 20S 32 50 E
Spence Bay = Taloyoak, *Canada*	68 B10	69 32N 93 32W
Spencer, *Idaho, U.S.A.*	76 D7	44 22N 112 11W
Spencer, *Iowa, U.S.A.*	80 D7	43 9N 95 9W
Spencer, *N.Y., U.S.A.*	85 D8	42 13N 76 30W
Spencer, *Nebr., U.S.A.*	80 D5	42 53N 98 42W
Spencer, *W. Va., U.S.A.*	82 F5	38 48N 81 21W
Spencer, C., *Australia*	63 F2	35 20S 136 53 E
Spencer B., *Namibia*	56 D1	25 30S 14 47 E
Spencer G., *Australia*	63 E2	34 0S 137 20 E
Spencerville, *Canada*	85 B9	44 51N 75 33W
Spences Bridge, *Canada*	70 C4	50 25N 121 20W
Spennymoor, *U.K.*	12 C6	54 42N 1 36W
Spenser Mts., *N.Z.*	59 K4	42 15S 172 45 E
Sperrin Mts., *U.K.*	10 B5	54 50N 7 0W
Spey →, *U.K.*	11 D5	57 40N 3 6W
Speyer, *Germany*	16 D5	49 29N 8 25 E
Spezand, *Pakistan*	42 E2	29 59N 67 0 E
Spíli, *Greece*	25 D6	35 13N 24 31 E
Spin Būldak, *Afghan.*	42 D2	31 1N 66 25 E
Spinalónga, *Greece*	25 D7	35 18N 25 44 E
Spirit Lake, *U.S.A.*	78 D4	46 15N 122 9W
Spirit River, *Canada*	70 B5	55 45N 118 50W
Spiritwood, *Canada*	71 C7	53 24N 107 33W
Spithead, *U.K.*	13 G6	50 45N 1 10W
Spitzbergen = Svalbard, *Arctic*	4 B8	78 0N 17 0 E
Spjelkavik, *Norway*	9 E12	62 28N 6 22 E
Split, *Croatia*	22 C7	43 31N 16 26 E
Split L., *Canada*	71 B9	56 8N 96 15W
Split Lake, *Canada*	71 B9	56 8N 96 15W
Spofford, *U.S.A.*	81 L4	29 10N 100 25W
Spokane, *U.S.A.*	76 C5	47 40N 117 24W

Spoleto, *Italy*	22 C5	42 44N 12 44 E
Spooner, *U.S.A.*	80 C9	45 50N 91 53W
Sporyy Navolok, Mys, *Russia*	28 B7	75 50N 68 40 E
Sprague, *U.S.A.*	76 C5	47 18N 117 59W
Spratly I., *S. China Sea*	36 C4	8 38N 111 55 E
Spratly Is., *S. China Sea*	36 C4	8 20N 112 0 E
Spray, *U.S.A.*	76 D4	44 50N 119 48W
Spree →, *Germany*	16 B7	52 32N 13 13 E
Sprengisandur, *Iceland*	8 D5	64 52N 18 7W
Spring City, *U.S.A.*	85 F9	40 11N 75 33W
Spring Creek, *U.S.A.*	76 F6	40 45N 115 38W
Spring Garden, *U.S.A.*	78 F6	39 52N 120 47W
Spring Hall, *Barbados*	89 g	13 18N 59 36W
Spring Hill, *U.S.A.*	83 L4	28 27N 82 41W
Spring Mts., *U.S.A.*	77 H6	36 0N 115 45W
Spring Valley, *U.S.A.*	79 N10	32 45N 117 5W
Springbok, *S. Africa*	56 D2	29 42S 17 54 E
Springboro, *U.S.A.*	84 E4	41 48N 80 22W
Springdale, *Canada*	73 C8	49 30N 56 6W
Springdale, *U.S.A.*	81 G7	36 11N 94 8W
Springer, *U.S.A.*	81 G2	36 22N 104 36W
Springerville, *U.S.A.*	77 J9	34 8N 109 17W
Springfield, *Canada*	84 D4	42 50N 80 56W
Springfield, *N.Z.*	59 K3	43 19S 171 56 E
Springfield, *Colo., U.S.A.*	81 G3	37 24N 102 37W
Springfield, *Ill., U.S.A.*	80 F10	39 48N 89 39W
Springfield, *Mass., U.S.A.*	85 D12	42 6N 72 35W
Springfield, *Mo., U.S.A.*	81 G8	37 13N 93 17W
Springfield, *Ohio, U.S.A.*	82 F4	39 55N 83 49W
Springfield, *Oreg., U.S.A.*	76 D2	44 3N 123 1W
Springfield, *Tenn., U.S.A.*	83 G2	36 31N 86 53W
Springfield, *Vt., U.S.A.*	85 C12	43 18N 72 29W
Springfontein, *S. Africa*	56 E4	30 15S 25 40 E
Springhill, *Canada*	73 C7	45 40N 64 4W
Springhill, *U.S.A.*	81 J8	33 0N 93 28W
Springhouse, *Canada*	70 C4	51 56N 122 7W
Springs, *S. Africa*	57 D4	26 13S 28 25 E
Springsure, *Australia*	62 C4	24 8S 148 6 E
Springvale, *U.S.A.*	85 C14	43 28N 70 48W
Springville, *Calif., U.S.A.*	78 J8	36 8N 118 49W
Springville, *N.Y., U.S.A.*	84 D6	42 31N 78 40W
Springville, *Utah, U.S.A.*	76 F8	40 10N 111 37W
Springwater, *U.S.A.*	84 D7	42 38N 77 35W
Spruce-Creek, *U.S.A.*	84 F6	40 36N 78 9W
Spruce Knob-Seneca Rocks △, *U.S.A.*	82 F6	38 50N 79 30W
Spruce Mt., *U.S.A.*	85 B12	44 12N 72 19W
Spur, *U.S.A.*	81 J4	33 28N 100 52W
Spurn Hd., *U.K.*	12 D8	53 35N 0 8 E
Spuzzum, *Canada*	70 D4	49 37N 121 23W
Squam L., *U.S.A.*	85 C13	43 45N 71 32W
Squamish, *Canada*	70 D4	49 45N 123 10W
Square Islands, *Canada*	73 B8	52 47N 55 47W
Squires, Mt., *Australia*	61 E4	26 14S 127 28 E
Srbija = Serbia □, *Serbia & M.*	23 C9	43 30N 21 0 E
Sre Ambel, *Cambodia*	39 G4	11 8N 103 46 E
Sre Khtum, *Cambodia*	39 F6	12 10N 106 52 E
Sre Umbell = Sre Ambel, *Cambodia*	39 G4	11 8N 103 46 E
Srebrenica, Bos.-H.	23 B8	44 6N 19 18 E
Sredinny Ra. = Sredinnyy Khrebet, *Russia*	29 D16	57 0N 160 0 E
Sredinnyy Khrebet, *Russia*	29 D16	57 0N 160 0 E
Srednekolymsk, *Russia*	29 C16	67 27N 153 40 E
Śrem, *Poland*	17 B9	52 6N 17 2 E
Sremska Mitrovica, *Serbia & M.*	23 B8	44 59N 19 38 E
Srepok →, *Cambodia*	38 F6	13 33N 106 16 E
Sretensk, *Russia*	29 D12	52 10N 117 40 E
Sri Lanka ■, *Asia*	40 R12	7 30N 80 50 E
Srikakulam, *India*	41 K13	18 14N 83 58 E
Srinagar, *India*	43 B6	34 5N 74 50 E
Srono, *Indonesia*	37 J17	8 24S 114 16 E
Staaten →, *Australia*	62 B3	16 24S 141 17 E
Staaten River △, *Australia*	62 B3	16 15S 142 40 E
Stade, *Germany*	16 B5	53 35N 9 29 E
Stadskanaal, *Neths.*	15 A6	53 4N 6 55 E
Staffa, *U.K.*	11 E2	56 27N 6 21W
Stafford, *U.K.*	12 E5	52 49N 2 7W
Stafford, *U.S.A.*	81 G5	37 58N 98 36W
Stafford Springs, *U.S.A.*	85 E12	41 57N 72 18W
Staffordshire □, *U.K.*	12 E5	52 53N 2 10W
Staines, *U.K.*	13 F7	51 26N 0 29W
Stakhanov, *Ukraine*	19 E6	48 35N 38 40 E
Stalis, *Greece*	25 D7	35 17N 25 25 E
Stalowa Wola, *Poland*	17 C12	50 34N 22 3 E
Stalybridge, *U.K.*	12 D5	53 28N 2 3W
Stamford, *Australia*	62 C3	21 15S 143 46 E
Stamford, *U.K.*	13 E7	52 39N 0 29W
Stamford, *Conn., U.S.A.*	85 E11	41 3N 73 32W
Stamford, *N.Y., U.S.A.*	85 D10	42 25N 74 38W
Stamford, *Tex., U.S.A.*	81 J5	32 57N 99 48W
Stampriet, *Namibia*	56 C2	24 20S 18 28 E
Stamps, *U.S.A.*	81 J8	33 22N 93 30W
Standerton, *S. Africa*	57 D4	26 55S 29 7 E
Standish, *U.S.A.*	84 D1	43 59N 83 57W
Stanford, *S. Africa*	56 E2	34 26S 19 29 E
Stanford, *U.S.A.*	76 C8	47 9N 110 13W
Stanger, *S. Africa*	57 D5	29 27S 31 14 E
Stanislaus →, *U.S.A.*	78 H5	37 40N 121 14W
Stanke Dimitrov, *Bulgaria*	23 C10	42 17N 23 9 E
Stanley, *Australia*	63 G4	40 46S 145 19 E
Stanley, *China*	33 G11	22 13N 114 12 E
Stanley, *Falk. Is.*	96 G5	51 40S 59 51W
Stanley, *U.K.*	12 C6	54 53N 1 41W
Stanley, *Idaho, U.S.A.*	76 D6	44 13N 114 56W
Stanley, *N. Dak., U.S.A.*	80 A3	48 19N 102 23W
Stanley, *N.Y., U.S.A.*	84 D7	42 48N 77 6W
Stanley Mission, *Canada*	71 B8	55 25N 104 33W
Stanovoy Khrebet, *Russia*	29 D13	55 0N 130 0 E
Stanovoy Ra. = Stanovoy Khrebet, *Russia*	29 D13	55 0N 130 0 E
Stansmore Ra., *Australia*	60 D4	21 23S 128 33 E
Stansted, London ✈ (STN), *U.K.*	13 F8	51 54N 0 14 E
Stanthorpe, *Australia*	63 D5	28 36S 151 59 E
Stanton, *U.S.A.*	81 J4	32 8N 101 48W
Stanwood, *U.S.A.*	78 B4	48 15N 122 23W
Staples, *U.S.A.*	80 B7	46 21N 94 48W
Star City, *Canada*	71 C8	52 50N 104 20W
Star Lake, *U.S.A.*	85 B9	44 10N 75 2W
Stara Planina, *Bulgaria*	23 C10	43 15N 23 0 E
Stara Zagora, *Bulgaria*	23 C11	42 26N 25 39 E
Starachowice, *Poland*	17 C11	51 3N 21 2 E
Staraya Russa, *Russia*	18 C5	57 58N 31 23 E
Starbuck I., *Kiribati*	65 H12	5 37S 155 55W
Starcke △, *Australia*	62 A4	14 56S 145 2 E
Stargard Szczeciński, *Poland*	16 B8	53 20N 15 0 E
Staritsa, *Russia*	18 C5	56 33N 34 55 E

Starke, *U.S.A.* **83 L4** 29 57N 82 7W
Starogard Gdański, *Poland* .... **17 B10** 53 59N 18 30 E
Starokonstantinov =
   Starokonstyantyniv, *Ukraine* . **17 D14** 49 48N 27 10 E
Starokonstyantyniv, *Ukraine* .. **17 D14** 49 48N 27 10 E
Start Pt., *U.K.* **13 G4** 50 13N 3 39W
Starry Chartoriysk, *Ukraine* .. **17 C13** 51 15N 25 54 E
Staryy Oskol, *Russia* .... **19 D6** 51 19N 37 55 E
State College, *U.S.A.* **84 F7** 40 48N 77 52W
Stateline, *U.S.A.* **78 G7** 38 57N 119 56W
Staten, I. = Estados, I. de Los,
   Argentina **96 G4** 54 40S 64 30W
Staten I., *U.S.A.* **85 F10** 40 35N 74 9W
Statesboro, *U.S.A.* **83 J5** 32 27N 81 47W
Statesville, *U.S.A.* **83 H5** 35 47N 80 53W
Stauffer, *U.S.A.* **79 L7** 34 45N 119 3W
Staunton, *Ill., U.S.A.* **80 F10** 39 1N 89 47W
Staunton, *Va., U.S.A.* **82 F6** 38 9N 79 4W
Stavanger, *Norway* .... **9 G11** 58 57N 5 40 E
Staveley, *N.Z.* .... **59 K3** 43 40S 171 32 E
Stavelot, *Belgium* .... **15 D5** 50 23N 5 55 E
Stavern, *Norway* .... **9 G14** 59 0N 10 1 E
Stavoren, *Neths.* .... **15 B5** 52 53N 5 22 E
Stavropol, *Russia* .... **19 E7** 45 5N 42 0 E
Stavros, *Cyprus* .... **25 D11** 35 1N 32 38 E
Stavrós, *Greece* .... **25 D6** 35 12N 24 45 E
Stavrós, Ákra, *Greece* .... **25 D6** 35 26N 24 58 E
Stawell, *Australia* .... **63 F3** 37 5S 142 47 E
Stawell →, *Australia* .... **62 C3** 20 20S 142 55 E
Stayner, *Canada* **84 B4** 44 25N 80 5W
Stayton, *U.S.A.* **76 D2** 44 48N 122 48W
Steamboat Springs, *U.S.A.* ... **76 F10** 40 29N 106 50W
Steele, *U.S.A.* **80 B5** 46 51N 99 55W
Steelton, *U.S.A.* **84 F8** 40 14N 76 50W
Steen River, *Canada* **70 B5** 59 40N 117 12W
Steens Mt., *U.S.A.* **76 E4** 42 35N 118 40W
Steenwijk, *Neths.* .... **15 B6** 52 47N 6 7 E
Steep Pt., *Australia* .... **61 E1** 26 8S 113 8 E
Steep Rock, *Canada* **71 C9** 51 30N 98 48W
Stefanie L. = Chew Bahir,
   Ethiopia .... **47 G2** 4 40N 36 50 E
Stefansson Bay, *Antarctica* ... **5 C6** 67 20S 59 8 E
Steiermark □, *Austria* .... **16 E8** 47 26N 15 0 E
Steilacoom, *U.S.A.* **78 C4** 47 10N 122 36W
Steilrandberge, *Namibia* ..... **56 B1** 17 45S 13 20 E
Steinbach, *Canada* **71 D9** 49 32N 96 40W
Steinhausen, *Namibia* .... **56 C2** 21 49S 18 20 E
Steinkjer, *Norway* .... **8 D14** 64 1N 11 31 E
Steinkopf, *S. Africa* .... **56 D2** 29 18S 17 43 E
Stellarton, *Canada* **73 C7** 45 32N 62 30W
Stellenbosch, *S. Africa* ...... **56 E2** 33 58S 18 50 E
Stendal, *Germany* .... **16 B6** 52 36N 11 53 E
Steornabhaigh = Stornoway,
   U.K. **11 C2** 58 13N 6 23W
Stepanakert = Xankändi,
   Azerbaijan .... **19 G8** 39 52N 46 49 E
Stephens Creek, *Australia* .... **63 E3** 31 50S 141 30 E
Stephens I., *Canada* **70 C2** 54 10N 130 45W
Stephens L., *Canada* **71 B9** 56 32N 95 0W
Stephenville, *Canada* **73 C8** 48 31N 58 35W
Stephenville, *U.S.A.* **81 J5** 32 13N 98 12W
Steppe, *Asia* .... **26 D9** 50 0N 50 0 E
Sterkstroom, *S. Africa* .... **56 E4** 31 32S 26 32 E
Sterling, *Colo., U.S.A.* **80 E3** 40 37N 103 13W
Sterling, *Ill., U.S.A.* **80 E10** 41 48N 89 42W
Sterling, *Kans., U.S.A.* **80 F5** 38 13N 98 12W
Sterling City, *U.S.A.* **81 K4** 31 51N 101 0W
Sterling Heights, *U.S.A.* **82 D4** 42 35N 83 0W
Sterling Run, *U.S.A.* **84 E6** 41 25N 78 12W
Sterlitamak, *Russia* .... **18 D10** 53 40N 56 0 E
Stérnes, *Greece* .... **25 D6** 35 30N 24 9 E
Stettin = Szczecin, *Poland* ... **16 B8** 53 27N 14 27 E
Stettiner Haff, *Germany* ..... **16 B8** 53 47N 14 15 E
Stettler, *Canada* **70 C6** 52 19N 112 40W
Steubenville, *U.S.A.* **84 F4** 40 22N 80 37W
Stevenage, *U.K.* **13 F7** 51 55N 0 13W
Stevens Point, *U.S.A.* **80 C10** 44 31N 89 34W
Stevenson, *U.S.A.* **78 E5** 45 42N 121 53W
Stevenson L., *Canada* **71 C9** 53 55N 96 0W
Stevensville, *U.S.A.* **76 C6** 46 30N 114 5W
Stewart, *Canada* **70 B3** 55 56N 129 57W
Stewart, *U.S.A.* **78 F7** 39 5N 119 46W
Stewart →, *Canada* **68 B6** 63 19N 139 26W
Stewart, C., *Australia* .... **62 A1** 11 57S 134 56 E
Stewart, I., *Chile* **96 G2** 54 50S 71 15W
Stewart I., *N.Z.* .... **59 M1** 46 58S 167 54 E
Stewarts Point, *U.S.A.* **78 G3** 38 39N 123 24W
Stewartville, *U.S.A.* **80 D8** 43 51N 92 29W
Stewiacke, *Canada* **73 C7** 45 9N 63 22W
Steynsburg, *S. Africa* .... **56 E4** 31 15S 25 49 E
Steyr, *Austria* .... **16 D8** 48 3N 14 25 E
Steytlerville, *S. Africa* .... **56 E3** 33 17S 24 19 E
Stigler, *U.S.A.* **81 H7** 35 15N 95 8W
Stikine →, *Canada* **70 B2** 56 40N 132 30W
Stilfontein, *S. Africa* .... **56 D4** 26 51S 26 50 E
Stillwater, *N.Z.* .... **59 K3** 42 27S 171 20 E
Stillwater, *Minn., U.S.A.* **80 C8** 45 3N 92 49W
Stillwater, *N.Y., U.S.A.* **85 D11** 42 55N 73 41W
Stillwater, *Okla., U.S.A.* **81 G6** 36 7N 97 4W
Stillwater Range, *U.S.A.* **76 G4** 39 50N 118 5W
Stillwater Reservoir, *U.S.A.* .. **85 C9** 43 54N 75 3W
Stilwell, *U.S.A.* **81 H7** 35 49N 94 38W
Stip, *Macedonia* .... **23 D10** 41 42N 22 10 E
Stirling, *Canada* **84 B7** 44 18N 77 33W
Stirling, *U.K.* **11 E5** 56 8N 3 57W
Stirling □, *U.K.* **11 E4** 56 12N 4 18W
Stirling Ra., *Australia* .... **61 F2** 34 23S 118 0 E
Stirling Range △, *Australia* .. **61 F2** 34 26S 118 20 E
Stittsville, *Canada* **85 A9** 45 15N 75 55W
Stjernøya, *Norway* .... **8 A20** 70 20N 22 40 E
Stjørdalshalsen, *Norway* ..... **8 E14** 63 29N 10 51 E
Stockerau, *Austria* .... **16 D9** 48 24N 16 12 E
Stockholm, *Sweden* .... **9 G18** 59 20N 18 3 E
Stockport, *U.K.* **12 D5** 53 25N 2 9W
Stocksbridge, *U.K.* **12 D6** 53 29N 1 35W
Stockton, *U.K.* **78 H5** 53 59N 1 20W
Stockton, *Kans., U.S.A.* **80 F5** 39 26N 99 16W
Stockton, *Mo., U.S.A.* **81 G8** 37 42N 93 48W
Stockton-on-Tees, *U.K.* **12 C6** 54 35N 1 19W
Stockton-on-Tees □, *U.K.* **12 C6** 54 35N 1 19W
Stockton Plateau, *U.S.A.* **81 K3** 30 30N 102 30W
Stoeng Treng, *Cambodia* .... **38 F5** 13 31N 105 58 E
Stoer, Pt. of, *U.K.* **11 C3** 58 16N 5 23W
Stoke-on-Trent, *U.K.* **12 D5** 53 1N 2 11W
Stoke-on-Trent □, *U.K.* **12 D5** 53 1N 2 11W
Stokes △, *Australia* .... **61 E2** 29 55S 115 6 E
Stokes Pt., *Australia* .... **63 G3** 40 10S 143 56 E

Stokes Ra., *Australia* .... **60 C5** 15 50S 130 50 E
Stokksnes, *Iceland* **8 D6** 64 14N 14 58W
Stokmarknes, *Norway* .... **8 B16** 68 34N 14 54 E
Stolac, *Bos.-H.* .... **23 C7** 43 5N 17 59 E
Stolbovoy, Ostrov, *Russia* ... **29 B14** 74 44N 135 14 E
Stolbtsy = Stowbtsy, *Belarus* . **17 B14** 53 30N 26 43 E
Stolin, *Belarus* .... **17 C14** 51 53N 26 50 E
Stómion, *Greece* .... **25 D5** 35 21N 23 32 E
Stone, *U.K.* **12 E5** 52 55N 2 9W
Stoneboro, *U.S.A.* **84 E4** 41 20N 80 7W
Stonehaven, *U.K.* **11 E6** 56 59N 2 12W
Stonehenge, *Australia* .... **62 C3** 24 22S 143 17 E
Stonehenge, *U.K.* **13 F6** 51 9N 1 45W
Stonewall, *Canada* **71 C9** 50 10N 97 19W
Stony L., *Man., Canada* **71 B9** 58 51N 98 40W
Stony L., *Ont., Canada* **84 B6** 44 30N 78 5W
Stony Point, *U.S.A.* **85 E11** 41 14N 73 59W
Stony Pt., *U.S.A.* **85 C8** 43 50N 76 18W
Stony Rapids, *Canada* **71 B7** 59 16N 105 50W
Stony Tunguska = Tunguska,
   Podkamennaya →, *Russia* . **29 C10** 61 50N 90 13 E
Stonyford, *U.S.A.* **78 F4** 39 23N 122 33W
Stora Lulevatten, *Sweden* .... **8 C18** 67 10N 19 30 E
Storavan, *Sweden* .... **8 D18** 65 45N 18 10 E
Stord, *Norway* .... **9 G11** 59 52N 5 23 E
Store Bælt, *Denmark* .... **9 J14** 55 20N 11 0 E
Storm B., *Australia* .... **63 G4** 43 10S 147 30 E
Storm Lake, *U.S.A.* **80 D7** 42 39N 95 13W
Stormberge, *S. Africa* .... **56 E4** 31 16S 26 17 E
Stormsrivier, *S. Africa* .... **56 E3** 33 59S 23 52 E
Stornoway, *U.K.* **11 C2** 58 13N 6 23W
Storozhinets = Storozhynets,
   Ukraine .... **17 D13** 48 14N 25 45 E
Storozhynets, *Ukraine* .... **17 D13** 48 14N 25 45 E
Storrs, *U.S.A.* **85 E12** 41 49N 72 15W
Storsjön, *Sweden* .... **8 E16** 63 9N 14 30 E
Storuman, *Sweden* .... **8 D17** 65 5N 17 10 E
Storuman, sjö, *Sweden* ...... **8 D17** 65 13N 16 50 E
Stouffville, *Canada* **84 C5** 43 58N 79 15W
Stoughton, *Canada* **71 D8** 49 40N 103 0W
Stour →, *Dorset, U.K.* **13 G6** 50 43N 1 47W
Stour →, *Kent, U.K.* .... **13 F9** 51 18N 1 22 E
Stour →, *Suffolk, U.K.* .... **13 F9** 51 57N 1 4 E
Stourbridge, *U.K.* **13 E5** 52 28N 2 8W
Stout L., *Canada* **71 C10** 52 0N 94 40W
Stove Pipe Wells Village, *U.S.A.* **79 J9** 36 35N 117 11W
Stow, *U.S.A.* **84 E3** 41 10N 81 26W
Stowbtsy, *Belarus* .... **17 B14** 53 30N 26 43 E
Stowmarket, *U.K.* .... **13 E9** 52 12N 1 0 E
Strabane, *U.K.* **10 B4** 54 50N 7 27W
Strahan, *Australia* .... **63 G4** 42 9S 145 20 E
Stralsund, *Germany* .... **16 A7** 54 18N 13 4 E
Strand, *S. Africa* .... **56 E2** 34 9S 18 48 E
Stranda, *Møre og Romsdal,*
   Norway .... **9 E12** 62 19N 6 58 E
Stranda, *Nord-Trøndelag,*
   Norway .... **8 E14** 63 33N 10 14 E
Strangford L., *U.K.* **10 B6** 54 30N 5 37W
Stranraer, *U.K.* **11 G3** 54 54N 5 1W
Strasbourg, *Canada* **71 C8** 51 4N 104 55W
Strasbourg, *France* .... **20 B7** 48 35N 7 42 E
Stratford, *Canada* **84 C4** 43 23N 81 0W
Stratford, *N.Z.* .... **59 H5** 39 20S 174 19 E
Stratford, *Calif., U.S.A.* **78 J7** 36 11N 119 49W
Stratford, *Conn., U.S.A.* **85 E11** 41 12N 73 8W
Stratford, *Tex., U.S.A.* **81 G3** 36 20N 102 4W
Stratford-upon-Avon, *U.K.* ... **13 E6** 52 12N 1 42W
Strath Spey, *U.K.* **11 D5** 57 9N 3 49W
Strathalbyn, *Australia* .... **63 F2** 35 13S 138 53 E
Strathaven, *U.K.* **11 F4** 55 40N 4 5W
Strathcona △, *Canada* **70 D3** 49 38N 125 40W
Strathmore, *Canada* **70 C6** 51 5N 113 18W
Strathmore, *U.K.* **11 E5** 56 37N 3 7W
Strathmore, *U.S.A.* **78 J7** 36 9N 119 4W
Strathnaver, *Canada* **70 C4** 53 20N 122 33W
Strathpeffer, *U.K.* **11 D4** 57 35N 4 32W
Strathroy, *Canada* **84 D3** 42 58N 81 38W
Strathy Pt., *U.K.* **11 C4** 58 36N 4 1W
Strattanville, *U.S.A.* **84 E5** 41 12N 79 19W
Stratton, *U.S.A.* **85 A14** 45 8N 70 26W
Stratton Mt., *U.S.A.* **85 C12** 43 4N 72 55W
Straubing, *Germany* .... **16 D7** 48 52N 12 34 E
Straumnes, *Iceland* **8 C2** 66 26N 23 8W
Strawberry →, *U.S.A.* **76 F8** 40 10N 110 24W
Streaky B., *Australia* .... **63 E1** 32 48S 134 13 E
Streaky Bay, *Australia* .... **63 E1** 32 51S 134 18 E
Streator, *U.S.A.* **80 E10** 41 8N 88 50W
Streetsboro, *U.S.A.* **84 E3** 41 14N 81 21W
Streetsville, *Canada* **84 C5** 43 35N 79 42W
Strelka, *Russia* .... **29 D10** 58 5N 93 3 E
Streng →, *Cambodia* .... **38 F4** 13 12N 103 37 E
Streymoy, *Færoe Is.* **8 E9** 62 8N 7 5W
Strezhevoy, *Russia* .... **28 C8** 60 42N 77 34 E
Strímón →, *Greece* .... **23 D11** 40 46N 23 51 E
Strimonikós Kólpos, *Greece* .. **23 D11** 40 33N 24 0 E
Stroma, *U.K.* **11 C5** 58 41N 3 7W
Strómboli, *Italy* .... **22 E6** 38 47N 15 13 E
Stromeferry, *U.K.* **11 D3** 57 21N 5 33W
Stromness, *U.K.* **11 C5** 58 58N 3 17W
Stromsburg, *U.S.A.* **80 E6** 41 7N 97 36W
Strömstad, *Sweden* .... **9 G14** 58 56N 11 10 E
Strömsund, *Sweden* .... **8 E16** 63 51N 15 33 E
Strongsville, *U.S.A.* **84 E3** 41 19N 81 50W
Stronsay, *U.K.* **11 B6** 59 7N 2 35W
Stroud, *U.K.* **13 F5** 51 45N 2 13W
Stroud Road, *Australia* ...... **63 E5** 32 18S 151 57 E
Stroudsburg, *U.S.A.* **85 F9** 40 59N 75 12W
Stroumbi, *Cyprus* .... **25 E11** 34 53N 32 29 E
Struer, *Denmark* .... **9 H13** 56 30N 8 35 E
Strumica, *Macedonia* .... **23 D10** 41 28N 22 41 E
Struthers, *Canada* **84 E4** 41 41N 85 51W
Struthers, *U.S.A.* **84 E4** 41 4N 80 39W
Stryker, *U.S.A.* **76 B6** 48 41N 114 46W
Stryy, *Ukraine* .... **17 D12** 49 16N 23 48 E
Strzelecki Cr. →, *Australia* ... **63 D2** 29 37S 139 59 E
Stuart, *Fla., U.S.A.* **83 M5** 27 12N 80 15W
Stuart, *Nebr., U.S.A.* **80 D5** 42 36N 99 8W
Stuart →, *Canada* **70 C4** 54 0N 123 35W
Stuart Bluff Ra., *Australia* ... **60 D5** 22 50S 131 52 E
Stuart L., *Canada* **70 C4** 54 30N 124 30W
Stuart Ra., *Australia* .... **63 D1** 29 10S 134 56 E
Stull L., *Canada* **72 B1** 54 24N 92 34W

Sturgeon Falls, *Canada* **72 C4** 46 25N 79 57W
Sturgeon L., *Alta., Canada* ... **70 B5** 55 6N 117 32W
Sturgeon L., *Ont., Canada* ... **72 C1** 50 0N 90 45W
Sturgeon L., *Ont., Canada* ... **84 B6** 44 28N 78 43W
Sturgis, *Canada* **71 C8** 51 56N 102 36W
Sturgis, *Mich., U.S.A.* **82 E3** 41 48N 85 25W
Sturgis, *S. Dak., U.S.A.* **80 C3** 44 25N 103 31W
Sturt △, *Australia* .... **63 D3** 27 17S 141 37 E
Sturt Cr. →, *Australia* .... **60 C4** 19 8S 127 50 E
Stutterheim, *S. Africa* .... **56 E4** 32 33S 27 28 E
Stuttgart, *Germany* .... **16 D5** 48 48N 9 11 E
Stuttgart, *U.S.A.* **81 H9** 34 30N 91 33W
Stuyvesant, *U.S.A.* **85 D11** 42 23N 73 45W
Stykkishólmur, *Iceland* **8 D2** 65 2N 22 40W
Styria = Steiermark □, *Austria* **16 E8** 47 26N 15 0 E
Su Xian = Suzhou, *China* .... **34 H9** 33 41N 116 59 E
Suakin, *Sudan* .... **51 E13** 19 8N 37 20 E
Suan, *N. Korea* .... **35 E14** 38 42N 126 22 E
Suaqui, *Mexico* **86 B3** 29 12N 109 41W
Suar, *India* .... **43 E8** 29 2N 79 3 E
Subang, *Indonesia* .... **37 G12** 6 34S 107 45 E
Subansiri →, *India* .... **41 F18** 26 48N 93 50 E
Subarnarekha →, *India* ...... **43 H12** 22 34N 87 24 E
Subayhah, *Si. Arabia* .... **44 D3** 30 2N 38 50 E
Subi, *Indonesia* .... **36 D3** 2 58N 108 50 E
Subotica, *Serbia & M.* .... **23 A8** 46 6N 19 39 E
Suceava, *Romania* .... **17 E14** 47 38N 26 16 E
Suchan, *Russia* .... **30 C6** 43 8N 133 9 E
Suchitoto, *El Salv.* **88 D2** 13 56N 89 0W
Suchou = Suzhou, *China* ..... **33 C7** 31 19N 120 38 E
Süchow = Xuzhou, *China* .... **35 G9** 34 18N 117 10 E
Suck →, *Ireland* **10 C3** 53 17N 8 3W
Sucre, *Bolivia* **92 G5** 19 0S 65 15W
Sucuriú →, *Brazil* **93 H8** 20 47S 51 38W
Sud, Pte. du, *Canada* **73 C7** 49 3N 62 14W
Sud-Kivu □, *Dem. Rep. of*
   the Congo .... **54 C2** 3 0S 28 30 E
Sud-Ouest, Pte., *Canada* **73 C7** 49 23S 63 36W
Sudan, *U.S.A.* **81 H3** 34 4N 102 32W
Sudan ■, *Africa* .... **51 E11** 15 0N 30 0 E
Sudbury, *Canada* **72 C3** 46 30N 81 0W
Sudbury, *U.K.* .... **13 E8** 52 2N 0 45 E
Sûdd, *Sudan* .... **51 G12** 8 20N 30 0 E
Sudeten Mts. = Sudety, *Europe* **17 C9** 50 20N 16 45 E
Sudety, *Europe* .... **17 C9** 50 20N 16 45 E
Suðuroy, *Færoe Is.* **8 F9** 61 32N 6 50W
Sudi, *Tanzania* .... **55 E4** 10 11S 39 57 E
Sudirman, Pegunungan,
   Indonesia .... **37 E9** 4 30S 137 0 E
Sudong, Pulau, *Singapore* .... **39 d** 1 12N 103 43 E
Sueca, *Spain* **21 C5** 39 12N 0 21W
Suemez I., *U.S.A.* **70 B2** 55 15N 133 20W
Suez = El Suweis, *Egypt* ..... **51 C12** 29 58N 32 31 E
Suez, G. of = Suweis, Khalîg el,
   Egypt .... **51 C12** 28 40N 33 0 E
Suez Canal = Suweis, Qanâ es,
   Egypt .... **51 B12** 31 0N 32 20 E
Suffield, *Canada* **70 C6** 50 12N 111 10W
Suffolk, *U.S.A.* **82 G7** 36 44N 76 35W
Suffolk □, *U.K.* .... **13 E9** 52 16N 1 0 E
Sugargrove, *U.S.A.* **84 E5** 41 59N 79 21W
Sugarive →, *India* .... **43 F12** 26 16N 86 24 E
Sugluk = Salluit, *Canada* **69 B12** 62 14N 75 38W
Şuḩār, *Oman* .... **45 E8** 24 20N 56 40 E
Sühbaatar □, *Mongolia* ...... **34 B8** 45 30N 114 0 E
Suhl, *Germany* .... **16 C6** 50 36N 10 42 E
Sui, *Pakistan* .... **42 E3** 28 37N 69 19 E
Sui Xian, *China* .... **34 G8** 34 25N 115 2 E
Suide, *China* .... **34 F6** 37 30N 110 12 E
Suifenhe, *China* .... **35 B16** 44 25N 131 10 E
Suihua, *China* .... **33 B7** 46 32N 126 55 E
Suining, *China* .... **35 H9** 33 56N 117 58 E
Suiping, *China* .... **34 H7** 33 10N 113 59 E
Suir →, *Ireland* **10 D4** 52 16N 7 9W
Suisun City, *U.S.A.* **78 G4** 38 15N 122 2W
Suiyang, *China* .... **35 B16** 44 30N 130 56 E
Suizhong, *China* .... **35 D11** 40 21N 120 20 E
Sujangarh, *India* .... **42 F6** 27 42N 74 31 E
Sukabumi, *Indonesia* .... **37 G12** 6 56S 106 50 E
Sukadana, *Indonesia* .... **36 E3** 1 10S 110 0 E
Sukagawa, *Japan* .... **31 F10** 37 17N 140 23 E
Sukaraja, *Indonesia* .... **36 E4** 2 28S 110 25 E
Sukawati, *Indonesia* .... **37 K18** 8 35S 115 17 E
Sukch'ŏn, *N. Korea* .... **35 E13** 39 22N 125 35 E
Sukhona →, *Russia* .... **18 C6** 61 15N 46 39 E
Sukhothai, *Thailand* .... **38 D2** 17 1N 99 49 E
Sukhumi = Sokhumi, *Georgia* . **19 F7** 43 0N 41 0 E
Sukkur, *Pakistan* .... **42 F3** 27 42N 68 54 E
Sukkur Barrage, *Pakistan* .... **42 F3** 27 40N 68 50 E
Sukri →, *India* .... **42 G4** 25 4N 71 43 E
Sukumo, *Japan* .... **31 H6** 32 56N 132 44 E
Sukunka →, *Canada* **70 B4** 55 45N 121 15W
Sula, Kepulauan, *Indonesia* .. **37 E7** 1 45S 125 0 E
Sulaco →, *Honduras* **88 C2** 15 2N 87 44W
Sulaiman Range, *Pakistan* ... **42 D3** 30 30N 69 50 E
Sūlār, *Iran* .... **45 D6** 31 53N 51 54 E
Sulawesi Sea = Celebes Sea,
   Indonesia .... **37 D6** 3 0N 123 0 E
Sulawesi Selatan □, *Indonesia* **37 E6** 2 30S 120 0 E
Sulawesi Utara □, *Indonesia* . **37 D6** 1 0N 122 30 E
Sulima, *S. Leone* **50 G3** 6 58N 11 32W
Sulina, *Romania* .... **17 F15** 45 10N 29 40 E
Sulitjelma, *Norway* .... **8 C17** 67 9N 16 3 E
Sullana, *Peru* **92 D2** 4 52S 80 39W
Sullivan, *Ill., U.S.A.* **80 F10** 39 36N 88 37W
Sullivan, *Ind., U.S.A.* **82 F2** 39 6N 87 24W
Sullivan, *Mo., U.S.A.* **80 F9** 38 13N 91 10W
Sullivan Bay, *Canada* **70 C3** 50 55N 126 50W
Sullivan I. = Lanbi Kyun, *Burma* **39 G2** 10 50N 98 20 E
Sullom Voe, *U.K.* **11 A7** 60 27N 1 20W
Sulphur, *La., U.S.A.* **81 K8** 30 14N 93 23W
Sulphur, *Okla., U.S.A.* **81 H6** 34 31N 96 58W
Sulphur Pt., *Canada* **70 A6** 60 56N 114 48W
Sulphur Springs, *U.S.A.* **81 J7** 33 8N 95 36W
Sultan, *Canada* **72 C3** 47 36N 82 47W
Sultan, *U.S.A.* **78 C5** 47 36N 121 49W
Sultanpur, *Mad. P., India* .... **42 H8** 23 9N 77 56 E
Sultanpur, *Punjab, India* .... **42 D6** 31 13N 75 11 E
Sultanpur, *Ut. P., India* ..... **43 F10** 26 18N 82 4 E
Sulu Arch., *Phil.* .... **37 C6** 6 0N 121 0 E
Sulu Sea, *E. Indies* .... **37 C6** 8 0N 120 0 E
Suluq, *Libya* .... **51 B10** 31 44N 20 14 E
Sulzberger Ice Shelf, *Antarctica* **5 E13** 78 0S 150 0W
Sumalata, *Indonesia* .... **37 D6** 1 0N 122 31 E
Sumampa, *Argentina* **94 B3** 29 25S 63 29W
Sumatera □, *Indonesia* ...... **36 D2** 0 40N 100 20 E
Sumatera Barat □, *Indonesia* . **36 E2** 1 0S 101 0 E

Sumatera Utara □, *Indonesia* . **36 D1** 2 30N 98 0 E
Sumatra = Sumatera □,
   Indonesia .... **36 D2** 0 40N 100 20 E
Sumba, *Indonesia* .... **37 F5** 9 45S 119 35 E
Sumba, Selat, *Indonesia* ..... **37 F5** 9 0S 118 40 E
Sumbawa, *Indonesia* .... **36 F5** 8 26S 117 30 E
Sumbawa Besar, *Indonesia* .. **36 F5** 8 30S 117 26 E
Sumbawanga □, *Tanzania* ... **52 F6** 8 0S 31 30 E
Sumbe, *Angola* .... **52 G2** 11 10S 13 48 E
Sumbu △, *Zambia* .... **55 D3** 8 43S 30 22 E
Sumburgh Hd., *U.K.* **11 B7** 59 52N 1 17W
Sumdeo, *India* .... **43 D8** 31 26N 78 44 E
Sumdo, *China* .... **43 B8** 35 6N 78 44 E
Sumedang, *Indonesia* .... **37 G12** 6 52S 107 55 E
Šumen = Shumen, *Bulgaria* .. **23 C12** 43 18N 26 55 E
Sumenep, *Indonesia* .... **37 G15** 7 1S 113 52 E
Sumgait = Sumqayıt, *Azerbaijan* **19 F8** 40 34N 49 38 E
Summer L., *U.S.A.* **76 E3** 42 50N 120 45W
Summerland, *Canada* **70 D5** 49 32N 119 41W
Summerside, *Canada* **73 C7** 46 24N 63 47W
Summersville, *U.S.A.* **82 F5** 38 17N 80 51W
Summerville, *Ga., U.S.A.* **83 H3** 34 29N 85 21W
Summerville, *S.C., U.S.A.* **83 J5** 33 1N 80 11W
Summit Lake, *Canada* **70 C4** 54 20N 122 40W
Summit Peak, *U.S.A.* **77 H10** 37 21N 106 42W
Sumner, *Iowa, U.S.A.* **80 D8** 42 51N 92 6W
Sumner, *Wash., U.S.A.* **78 C4** 47 12N 122 14W
Sumoto, *Japan* .... **31 G7** 34 21N 134 54 E
Šumperk, *Czech Rep.* .... **17 D9** 49 59N 16 59 E
Sumqayıt, *Azerbaijan* .... **19 F8** 40 34N 49 38 E
Sumter, *U.S.A.* **83 J5** 33 55N 80 21W
Sumy, *Ukraine* .... **19 D5** 50 57N 34 50 E
Sun City, *S. Africa* .... **56 D4** 25 17S 27 3 E
Sun City, *Ariz., U.S.A.* **77 K7** 33 36N 112 17W
Sun City, *Calif., U.S.A.* **79 M9** 33 42N 117 11W
Sun City Center, *U.S.A.* **83 M4** 27 43N 82 18W
Sun Lakes, *U.S.A.* **77 K8** 33 10N 111 52W
Sun Valley, *U.S.A.* **76 E6** 43 42N 114 21W
Sunagawa, *Japan* .... **30 C10** 43 29N 141 55 E
Sunan, *N. Korea* .... **35 E13** 39 15N 125 40 E
Sunart, L., *U.K.* **11 E3** 56 42N 5 43W
Sunburst, *U.S.A.* **76 B8** 48 53N 111 55W
Sunbury, *Australia* .... **63 F3** 37 35S 144 44 E
Sunbury, *U.S.A.* **85 F8** 40 52N 76 48W
Sunchales, *Argentina* **94 C3** 30 58S 61 35W
Suncho Corral, *Argentina* **94 B3** 27 55S 63 27W
Sunch'ŏn, *S. Korea* .... **35 G14** 34 52N 127 31 E
Suncook, *U.S.A.* **85 C13** 43 8N 71 27W
Sunda, Selat, *Indonesia* ...... **36 F3** 6 20S 105 30 E
Sunda Is., *Indonesia* .... **26 K14** 5 0S 105 0 E
Sunda Str. = Sunda, Selat,
   Indonesia .... **36 F3** 6 20S 105 30 E
Sundance, *Canada* **71 B10** 56 32N 94 4W
Sundance, *U.S.A.* **80 C2** 44 24N 104 23W
Sundar Nagar, *India* .... **42 D7** 31 32N 76 53 E
Sundarbans, *Asia* .... **41 J16** 22 0N 89 0 E
Sundargarh, *India* .... **41 H14** 22 4N 84 5 E
Sundays = Sondags →, *S. Africa* **56 E4** 33 44S 25 51 E
Sunderland, *Canada* **84 B5** 44 16N 79 4W
Sunderland, *U.K.* **12 C6** 54 55N 1 23W
Sundown △, *Australia* .... **63 D5** 28 49S 151 38 E
Sundre, *Canada* **70 C6** 51 49N 114 38W
Sundsvall, *Sweden* .... **9 E17** 62 23N 17 17 E
Sung Hei, *Vietnam* .... **39 G6** 10 20N 106 2 E
Sungai Acheh, *Malaysia* ..... **39 c** 5 8N 100 30 E
Sungai Kolok, *Thailand* ...... **39 J3** 6 2N 101 58 E
Sungai Lembing, *Malaysia* ... **39 L4** 3 55N 103 3 E
Sungai Petani, *Malaysia* ..... **39 K3** 5 37N 100 30 E
Sungaigerong, *Indonesia* ..... **36 E2** 2 59S 104 52 E
Sungailiat, *Indonesia* .... **36 E3** 1 51S 106 8 E
Sungaipenuh, *Indonesia* ..... **36 E2** 2 1S 101 20 E
Sungari = Songhua Jiang →,
   China .... **33 B8** 47 45N 132 30 E
Sunghua Chiang = Songhua
   Jiang →, *China* .... **33 B8** 47 45N 132 30 E
Sunland Park, *U.S.A.* **77 L10** 31 50N 106 40W
Sunndalsøra, *Norway* .... **9 E13** 62 40N 8 33 E
Sunnyside, *U.S.A.* **76 C3** 46 20N 120 0W
Sunnyvale, *U.S.A.* **78 H4** 37 23N 122 2W
Suntar, *Russia* .... **29 C12** 62 15N 117 30 E
Suomenselkä, *Finland* .... **8 E21** 62 52N 24 0 E
Suomussalmi, *Finland* .... **8 D23** 64 54N 29 10 E
Suoyarvi, *Russia* .... **18 B5** 62 3N 32 20 E
Supai, *U.S.A.* **77 H7** 36 15N 112 41W
Supaul, *India* .... **43 F12** 26 10N 86 40 E
Superior, *Ariz., U.S.A.* **77 K8** 33 18N 111 6W
Superior, *Mont., U.S.A.* **76 C6** 47 12N 114 53W
Superior, *Nebr., U.S.A.* **80 E5** 40 1N 98 4W
Superior, *Wis., U.S.A.* **80 B8** 46 44N 92 6W
Superior, L., *N. Amer.* **72 C2** 47 0N 87 0W
Suphan Buri, *Thailand* .... **38 E3** 14 14N 100 10 E
Suphan Dağı, *Turkey* .... **44 B4** 38 54N 42 48 E
Supiori, *Indonesia* .... **37 E9** 1 0S 136 0 E
Supung Shuiku, *China* .... **35 D13** 40 35N 124 50 E
Sūq Suwayq, *Si. Arabia* ..... **44 E3** 24 23N 38 27 E
Suqian, *China* .... **35 H10** 33 54N 118 8 E
Suquṭra = Socotra, *Yemen* ... **47 E5** 12 30N 54 0 E
Sūr, *Lebanon* .... **46 B4** 33 19N 35 16 E
Şūr, *Oman* .... **47 C6** 22 34N 59 32 E
Sur, Pt., *U.S.A.* **78 J5** 36 18N 121 54W
Sura →, *Russia* .... **18 C8** 56 6N 46 0 E
Surab, *Pakistan* .... **42 E2** 28 25N 66 15 E
Surabaja = Surabaya, *Indonesia* **36 F4** 7 17S 112 45 E
Surabaya, *Indonesia* .... **36 F4** 7 17S 112 45 E
Surakarta, *Indonesia* .... **36 F4** 7 35S 110 48 E
Surat, *Australia* .... **63 D4** 27 10S 149 6 E
Surat, *India* .... **40 J8** 21 12N 72 55 E
Surat Thani, *Thailand* .... **39 H2** 9 6N 99 20 E
Suratgarh, *India* .... **42 E5** 29 18N 73 55 E
Surendranagar, *India* .... **42 H4** 22 45N 71 40 E
Surf, *U.S.A.* **79 L6** 34 41N 120 36W
Surgut, *Russia* .... **28 C8** 61 14N 73 20 E
Suri, *India* .... **43 H12** 23 50N 87 34 E
Surianet →, *India* .... **40 L11** 17 10N 79 40 E
Surigao, *Phil.* .... **37 C7** 9 47N 125 29 E
Surin, *Thailand* .... **38 E4** 14 50N 103 34 E
Surin Nua, Ko, *Thailand* ..... **39 H1** 9 30N 97 55 E
Surinam ■, *S. Amer.* **93 C7** 4 0N 56 0W
Suriname □, *S. Amer.* **93 C7** 4 0N 56 0W
Suriname →, *Suriname* **93 B7** 5 50N 55 15W
Surmaq, *Iran* .... **45 D7** 31 3N 52 48 E
Surrey □, *U.K.* **13 F7** 51 15N 0 31W
Sursand, *India* .... **43 F11** 26 39N 85 43 E
Sursar →, *India* .... **43 F12** 26 14N 87 3 E
Surt, *Libya* .... **51 B9** 31 11N 16 39 E
Surt, Khalīj, *Libya* .... **51 B9** 31 40N 18 30 E
Surtanahu, *Pakistan* .... **42 F4** 26 22N 70 0 E

Surtsey, *Iceland* 8 E3   63 20N   20 30W
Suruga-Wan, *Japan* . . . . 31 G9   34 45N 138 30 E
Susaki, *Japan* . . . . 31 H6   33 22N 133 17 E
Süsangerd, *Iran* . . . . 45 D6   31 35N   48 6 E
Susanville, *U.S.A.* 76 F3   40 25N 120 39W
Susner, *India* . . . . 42 H7   23 57N   76 5 E
Susquehanna, *U.S.A.* 85 E9   41 57N   75 36W
Susquehanna →, *U.S.A.* 85 G8   39 33N   76 5W
Susques, *Argentina* 94 A2   23 35S   66 25W
Sussex, *Canada* 73 C6   45 45N   65 37W
Sussex, *U.S.A.* 85 E10 41 13N   74 37W
Sussex, E. □, *U.K.* . . . . 13 G8   51 0N   0 20 E
Sussex, W. □, *U.K.* 13 G7   51 0N   0 30W
Sustut →, *Canada* 70 B3   56 20N 127 30W
Susuman, *Russia* . . . . 29 C15 62 47N 148 10 E
Susunu, *Indonesia* . . . . 37 E8   3 7S 133 39 E
Susurluk, *Turkey* . . . . 23 E13 39 54N   28 8 E
Sutherland, *S. Africa* . . . . . . 56 E3   32 24S   20 40 E
Sutherland, *U.K.* 11 C4   58 12N   4 50W
Sutherland, *U.S.A.* 80 E4   41 10N 101 8W
Sutherland Falls, *N.Z.* . . . . . . 59 L1   44 48S 167 46 E
Sutherlin, *U.S.A.* 76 E2   43 23N 123 19W
Suthri, *India* . . . . 42 H3   23 3N   68 55 E
Sutlej →, *Pakistan* . . . . 42 E4   29 23N   71 3 E
Sutter, *U.S.A.* 78 F5   39 10N 121 45W
Sutter Creek, *U.S.A.* 78 G6   38 24N 120 48W
Sutton, *Canada* 85 A12   45 6N   72 37W
Sutton, *Nebr., U.S.A.* 80 E6   40 36N   97 52W
Sutton, *W. Va., U.S.A.* 82 F5   38 40N   80 43W
Sutton →, *Canada* 72 A3   55 15N   83 45W
Sutton Coldfield, *U.K.* 13 E6   52 35N   1 49W
Sutton in Ashfield, *U.K.* 12 D6   53 8N   1 16W
Sutton L., *Canada* 72 B3   54 15N   84 42W
Suttor →, *Australia* . . . . 62 C4   21 36S 147 2 E
Suttsu, *Japan* . . . . 30 C10 42 48N 140 14 E
Suva, *Fiji* . . . . 59 D8   18 6S 178 30 E
Suva Planina, *Serbia & M.* . . 23 C10 43 10N   22 5 E
Suvorov Is. = Suwarrow Is.,
  Cook Is. 65 J11 15 0S 163 0W
Suwałki, *Poland* . . . . 17 A12 54 8N   22 59 E
Suwana, *Indonesia* . . . . 37 K18   8 44S 115 36 E
Suwannaphum, *Thailand* . . . . 38 E4   15 33N 103 47 E
Suwannee →, *U.S.A.* 83 L4   29 17N   83 10W
Suwanose-Jima, *Japan* . . . . . 31 K4   29 38N 129 43 E
Suwarrow Is., *Cook Is.* 65 J11 15 0S 163 0W
Suwayq aş Şuqban, *Iraq* . . . . 44 D5   31 32N   46 7 E
Suweis, Khalîg el, *Egypt* . . . . 51 C12 28 40N   33 0 E
Suweis, Qanâ es, *Egypt* . . . . 51 B12 31 0N   32 20 E
Suwŏn, *S. Korea* . . . . 35 F14 37 17N 127 1 E
Suzdal, *Russia* . . . . 18 C7   56 29N   40 26 E
Suzhou, *Anhui, China* . . . . . . 34 H9   33 41N 116 59 E
Suzhou, *Jiangsu, China* . . . . 33 C7   31 19N 120 38 E
Suzu, *Japan* . . . . 31 F8   37 25N 137 17 E
Suzu-Misaki, *Japan* . . . . 31 F8   37 31N 137 21 E
Suzuka, *Japan* . . . . 31 G8   34 55N 136 36 E
Svalbard, *Arctic* . . . . 4 B8   78 0N   17 0 E
Svappavaara, *Sweden* . . . . . . 8 C19 67 40N   21 3 E
Svartisen, *Norway* . . . . 8 C15 66 40N   13 50 E
Svay Chek, *Cambodia* . . . . . . 38 F4   13 48N 102 58 E
Svay Rieng, *Cambodia* . . . . . 39 G5   11 9N 105 45 E
Svealand □, *Sweden* . . . . 9 G16 60 20N   15 0 E
Sveg, *Sweden* . . . . 9 E16 62 2N   14 21 E
Svendborg, *Denmark* . . . . 9 J14 55 4N   10 35 E
Sverdrup Is., *Canada* 4 B3   79 0N   97 0W
Svetlaya, *Russia* . . . . 30 A9   46 33N 138 18 E
Svetlogorsk = Svyetlahorsk,
  Belarus . . . . 17 B15 52 38N   29 46 E
Svir →, *Russia* . . . . 18 B5   60 30N   32 48 E
Svishtov, *Bulgaria* . . . . 23 C11 43 36N   25 23 E
Svislach, *Belarus* . . . . 17 B13 53 3N   24 2 E
Svobodnyy, *Russia* . . . . 29 D13 51 20N 128 0 E
Svolvær, *Norway* . . . . 8 B16 68 15N   14 34 E
Svyetlahorsk, *Belarus* . . . . . . 17 B15 52 38N   29 46 E
Swabian Alps = Schwäbische
  Alb, *Germany* . . . . 16 D5   48 20N   9 30 E
Swaffham, *U.K.* . . . . 13 E8   52 39N   0 42 E
Swainsboro, *U.S.A.* 83 J4   32 36N   82 20W
Swakop →, *Namibia* . . . . 56 C2   22 38S   14 36 E
Swakopmund, *Namibia* . . . . . 56 C1   22 37S   14 30 E
Swale →, *U.K.* 12 C6   54 5N   1 20W
Swan →, *Australia* . . . . 61 F2   32 3S 115 45 E
Swan →, *Canada* 71 C8   52 30N 100 45W
Swan Hill, *Australia* . . . . 63 F3   35 20S 143 33 E
Swan Hills, *Canada* 70 C5   54 43N 115 24W
Swan Is. = Santanilla, Is.,
  Honduras 88 C3   17 22N   83 57W
Swan L., *Canada* 71 C8   52 30N 100 40W
Swan Peak, *U.S.A.* 76 C7   47 43N 113 38W
Swan Ra., *U.S.A.* 76 C7   48 0N 113 45W
Swan River, *Canada* 71 C8   52 10N 101 16W
Swanage, *U.K.* 13 G6   50 36N   1 58W
Swansea, *Australia* . . . . 63 G4   42 8S 148 4 E
Swansea, *Canada* 84 C5   43 38N   79 28W
Swansea, *U.K.* 13 F4   51 37N   3 57W
Swansea □, *U.K.* 13 F3   51 38N   3 3W
Swar →, *Pakistan* . . . . 43 B5   34 40N   72 5 E
Swartberge, *S. Africa* . . . . . . 56 E3   33 20S   22 0 E
Swartmodder, *S. Africa* . . . . 56 D3   28 1S   20 32 E
Swartnossob →, *Namibia* . . . 56 C2   23 49S   18 72 E
Swartruggens, *S. Africa* . . . . 56 D4   25 39S   26 42 E
Swastika, *Canada* 72 C3   48 7N   80 6W
Swatow = Shantou, *China* . . . 33 D6   23 18N 116 40 E
Swaziland ■, *Africa* . . . . 57 D5   26 30S   31 30 E
Sweden ■, *Europe* . . . . 9 G16 57 0N   15 0 E
Sweet Home, *U.S.A.* 76 D2   44 24N 122 44W
Sweetgrass, *U.S.A.* 76 B8   48 59N 111 58W
Sweetwater, *Nev., U.S.A.* . . . 78 G7   38 27N 119 9W
Sweetwater, *Tenn., U.S.A.* . . 83 H3   35 36N   84 28W
Sweetwater, *Tex., U.S.A.* . . . 81 J4   32 28N 100 25W
Sweetwater →, *U.S.A.* 76 E10 42 31N 107 2W
Swellendam, *S. Africa* . . . . . 56 E3   34 1S   20 26 E
Świdnica, *Poland* . . . . 17 C9   50 50N   16 30 E
Świdnik, *Poland* . . . . 17 C12 51 13N   22 39 E
Świebodzin, *Poland* . . . . 16 B8   52 15N   15 31 E
Świecie, *Poland* . . . . 17 B10 53 25N   18 30 E
Swift Current, *Canada* 71 C7   50 20N 107 45W
Swift Current →, *Canada* . . . 71 C7   50 38N 107 44W
Swilly, L., *Ireland* 10 A4   55 12N   7 33W
Swindon, *U.K.* 13 F6   51 34N   1 46W
Swindon □, *U.K.* 13 F6   51 34N   1 46W
Swinemünde = Świnoujście,
  Poland . . . . 16 B8   53 54N   14 16 E
Swinford, *Ireland* 10 C3   53 57N   8 58W
Świnoujście, *Poland* . . . . 16 B8   53 54N   14 16 E
Switzerland ■, *Europe* . . . . . 20 C8   46 30N   8 0 E
Swords, *Ireland* 10 C5   53 28N   6 13W
Swoyerville, *U.S.A.* 85 E9   41 18N   75 53W

Sydenham →, *Canada* 84 D2   42 33N   82 25W
Sydney, *Australia* . . . . 63 E5   33 53S 151 10 E
Sydney, *Canada* 73 C7   46 7N   60 7W
Sydney L., *Canada* 71 C10 50 41N   94 25W
Sydney Mines, *Canada* 73 C7   46 18N   60 15W
Sydprøven = Alluitsup Paa,
  Greenland 69 B15 60 30N   45 35W
Sydra, G. of = Surt, Khalîj, *Libya* 51 B9   31 40N   18 30 E
Sykesville, *U.S.A.* 84 E6   41 3N   78 50W
Syktyvkar, *Russia* . . . . 18 B9   61 45N   50 40 E
Sylacauga, *U.S.A.* 83 J2   33 10N   86 15W
Sylarna, *Sweden* . . . . 8 E15 63 2N   12 13 E
Sylhet, *Bangla.* . . . . 41 G17 24 54N   91 52 E
Sylhet □, *Bangla.* . . . . 41 G17 24 50N   91 50 E
Sylt, *Germany* . . . . 16 A5   54 54N   8 22 E
Sylvan Beach, *U.S.A.* 85 C9   43 12N   75 44W
Sylvan Lake, *Canada* 70 C6   52 20N 114 3W
Sylvania, *U.S.A.* 83 J5   32 45N   81 38W
Sylvester, *U.S.A.* 83 K4   31 32N   83 50W
Sym, *Russia* . . . . 28 C9   60 20N   88 18 E
Symón, *Mexico* 86 C4   24 42N 102 35W
Synnott Ra., *Australia* . . . . . . 60 C4   16 30S 125 20 E
Syowa, *Antarctica* . . . . 5 C5   68 50S   1 0 E
Syracuse, *Kans., U.S.A.* 81 G4   37 59N 101 45W
Syracuse, *N.Y., U.S.A.* 85 C8   43 3N   76 9W
Syracuse, *Nebr., U.S.A.* 80 E6   40 39N   96 11W
Syrdarya →, *Kazakhstan* . . . 28 E7   46 3N   61 0 E
Syria ■, *Asia* . . . . 44 C3   35 0N   38 0 E
Syrian Desert = Shâm, Bâdiyat
  ash, *Asia* . . . . 44 C3   32 0N   40 0 E
Syzran, *Russia* . . . . 18 D8   53 12N   48 30 E
Szczecin, *Poland* . . . . 16 B8   53 27N   14 27 E
Szczecinek, *Poland* . . . . 17 B9   53 43N   16 41 E
Szczeciński, Zalew = Stettiner
  Haff, *Germany* . . . . 16 B8   53 47N   14 15 E
Szczytno, *Poland* . . . . 17 B11 53 33N   21 0 E
Szechwan = Sichuan □, *China* 32 C5   30 30N 103 0 E
Szeged, *Hungary* . . . . 17 E11 46 16N   20 10 E
Székesfehérvár, *Hungary* . . . 17 E10 47 15N   18 25 E
Szekszárd, *Hungary* . . . . 17 E10 46 22N   18 42 E
Szentes, *Hungary* . . . . 17 E11 46 39N   20 21 E
Szolnok, *Hungary* . . . . 17 E11 47 10N   20 15 E
Szombathely, *Hungary* . . . . . 17 E9   47 14N   16 38 E

T

Ta Khli Khok, *Thailand* . . . . . . 38 E3   15 18N 100 20 E
Ta Lai, *Vietnam* . . . . 39 G6   11 24N 107 23 E
Tabacal, *Argentina* 94 A3   23 15S   64 15W
Tabaco, *Phil.* . . . . 37 B6   13 22N 123 44 E
Tābah, *Si. Arabia* . . . . 44 E4   26 55N   42 38 E
Tabanan, *Indonesia* . . . . 37 K18   8 32S 115 8 E
Tabas, *Khorāsān, Iran* . . . . . 45 C9   32 48N   60 12 E
Tabas, *Khorāsān, Iran* . . . . . 45 C8   33 35N   56 55 E
Tabasará, Serranía de, *Panama* 88 E3   8 35N   81 40W
Tabasco □, *Mexico* 87 D6   17 45N   93 30W
Tabāsīn, *Iran* . . . . 45 D8   31 12N   57 54 E
Tabatinga, Serra da, *Brazil* . . 93 F10 10 30S   44 0W
Taber, *Canada* 70 D6   49 47N 112 8W
Taberg, *U.S.A.* 85 C9   43 18N   75 37W
Tablas I., *Phil.* . . . . 37 B6   12 25N 122 2 E
Table B., *Canada* 73 B8   53 40N   56 25W
Table Mt., *S. Africa* . . . . 56 E2   33 35S   18 25 E
Table Mt., *S. Africa* . . . . 56 E2   34 0S   18 22 E
Table Rock L., *U.S.A.* 81 G8   36 36N   93 19W
Tabletop, Mt., *Australia* . . . . . 62 C4   23 24S 147 11 E
Tábor, *Czech Rep.* . . . . 16 D8   49 25N   14 39 E
Tabora, *Tanzania* . . . . 54 D3   5 2S   32 50 E
Tabora □, *Tanzania* . . . . 54 D3   5 0S   33 0 E
Tabou, *Ivory C.* 50 H4   4 30N   7 20W
Tabrīz, *Iran* . . . . 44 B5   38 7N   46 20 E
Tabuaeran, *Kiribati* 65 G12   3 51N 159 22W
Tabūk, *Si. Arabia* . . . . 44 D3   28 23N   36 36 E
Tacámbaro de Codallos, *Mexico* 86 D4   19 14N 101 28W
Tacheng, *China* . . . . 32 B3   46 40N   82 58 E
Tach'ing Shan = Daqing Shan,
  China . . . . 34 D6   40 40N 111 0 E
Tacloban, *Phil.* . . . . 37 B6   11 15N 124 58 E
Tacna, *Peru* 92 G4   18 0S   70 20W
Tacoma, *U.S.A.* 78 C4   47 14N 122 26W
Tacuarembó, *Uruguay* 95 C4   31 45S   56 0W
Tademaït, Plateau du, *Algeria* 50 C6   28 30N   2 30 E
Tadjoura, *Djibouti* . . . . 47 E3   11 50N   42 55 E
Tadmor, *N.Z.* . . . . 59 J4   41 27S 172 45 E
Tadoule L., *Canada* 71 B9   58 36N   98 20W
Tadoussac, *Canada* 73 C6   48 11N   69 42W
Tadzhikistan = Tajikistan ■, *Asia* 28 F8   38 30N   70 0 E
Taechŏn-ni, *S. Korea* . . . . 35 F14 36 21N 126 36 E
Taegu, *S. Korea* . . . . 35 G15 35 50N 128 37 E
Taegwan, *N. Korea* . . . . 35 D13 40 13N 125 12 E
Taejŏn, *S. Korea* . . . . 35 F14 36 20N 127 28 E
Taen, Ko, *Thailand* . . . . 39 b   9 22N   99 57 E
Tafalla, *Spain* 21 A5   42 30N   1 41W
Tafelbaai = Table B., *S. Africa* 56 E2   33 35S   18 25 E
Tafermaar, *Indonesia* . . . . . . 37 F8   6 47S 134 10 E
Tafí Viejo, *Argentina* 94 B2   26 43S   65 17W
Tafīhān, *Iran* . . . . 45 D7   29 25N   52 39 E
Tafresh, *Iran* . . . . 45 C6   34 45N   49 57 E
Taft, *Iran* . . . . 45 D7   31 45N   54 14 E
Taft, *Phil.* . . . . 37 B7   11 57N 125 30 E
Taft, *U.S.A.* 79 K7   35 8N 119 28W
Taftān, Kūh-e, *Iran* . . . . 45 D9   28 40N   61 0 E
Taga Dzong, *Bhutan* . . . . 41 F16 27 5N   89 55 E
Taganrog, *Russia* . . . . 19 E6   47 12N   38 50 E
Tagbilaran, *Phil.* . . . . 37 C6   9 39N 123 51 E
Tagish, *Canada* 70 A2   60 19N 134 16W
Tagish L., *Canada* 70 A2   60 10N 134 20W
Tagliamento →, *Italy* . . . . 22 B5   45 38N   13 6 E
Tagomago, *Spain* . . . . 24 B8   39 2N   1 39 E
Taguatinga, *Brazil* 93 F10 12 16S   42 26W
Tagum, *Phil.* . . . . 37 C7   7 33N 125 53 E
Tagus = Tejo →, *Europe* 21 C1   38 40N   9 24W
Tahakopa, *N.Z.* . . . . 59 M2   46 30S 169 23 E
Tahan, Gunong, *Malaysia* . . . 39 K4   4 34N 102 17 E
Tahat, *Algeria* . . . . 50 D7   23 18N   5 33 E
Tāherī, *Iran* . . . . 45 E7   27 43N   52 20 E
Tahiti, *French Polynesia* 65 J13 17 37S 149 27W
Tahlequah, *U.S.A.* 81 H7   35 55N   94 58W
Tahoe, L., *U.S.A.* 78 G6   39 10N 120 9W
Tahoe City, *U.S.A.* 78 F6   39 10N 120 9W
Tahoka, *U.S.A.* 81 J4   33 10N 101 48W
Taholah, *U.S.A.* 78 C2   47 21N 124 17W
Tahoua, *Niger* . . . . 50 F7   14 57N   5 16 E
Tahrūd, *Iran* . . . . 45 D8   29 26N   57 49 E
Tahsis, *Canada* 70 D3   49 55N 126 40W

Tahta, *Egypt* . . . . 51 C12 26 44N   31 32 E
Tahulandang, *Indonesia* . . . . 37 D7   2 27N 125 23 E
Tahuna, *Indonesia* . . . . 37 D7   3 38N 125 30 E
Tai Au Mun, *China* . . . . 33 G11 22 18N 114 17 E
Tai Mo Shan, *China* . . . . 33 G11 22 25N 114 7 E
Tai O, *China* . . . . 33 G10 22 15N 113 52 E
Tai Pang Wan, *H.K.* . . . . 33 F11 22 33N 114 24 E
Tai Po, *China* . . . . 33 G11 22 27N 114 10 E
Tai Rom Yen △, *Thailand* . . . . 39 H2   8 45N   99 30 E
Tai Shan, *China* . . . . 35 F9   36 25N 117 20 E
Tai Yue Shan = Lantau I., *China* 33 G10 22 15N 113 56 E
Tai'an, *China* . . . . 35 F9   36 12N 117 8 E
Taibei = T'aipei, *Taiwan* . . . . 33 D7   25 2N 121 30 E
Taibique, *Canary Is.* 24 G2   27 42N   17 58W
Taibus Qi, *China* . . . . 34 D8   41 54N 115 22 E
T'aichung, *Taiwan* . . . . 33 D7   24 9N 120 37 E
Taïeri →, *N.Z.* . . . . 59 M3   46 3S 170 12 E
Taigu, *China* . . . . 34 F7   37 28N 112 30 E
Taihang Shan, *China* . . . . 34 G7   36 0N 113 30 E
Taihape, *N.Z.* . . . . 59 H5   39 41S 175 48 E
Taihe, *China* . . . . 34 H8   33 20N 115 42 E
Taikang, *China* . . . . 34 G8   34 5N 114 50 E
Tailem Bend, *Australia* . . . . . 63 F2   35 12S 139 29 E
Taimyr Peninsula = Taymyr,
  Poluostrov, *Russia* . . . . 29 B11 75 0N 100 0 E
Tain, *U.K.* 11 D4   57 49N   4 4W
T'ainan, *Taiwan* . . . . 33 D7   23 0N 120 10 E
Taïnaron, Ákra, *Greece* . . . . . 23 F10 36 22N   22 27 E
Taipa, *China* . . . . 33 G10 22 10N 113 35 E
T'aipei, *Taiwan* . . . . 33 D7   25 2N 121 30 E
Taiping, *Malaysia* . . . . 39 K3   4 51N 100 44 E
Taipingzhen, *China* . . . . 34 H6   33 35N 111 42 E
Tairbeart = Tarbert, *U.K.* 11 D2   57 54N   6 49W
Taita Hills, *Kenya* . . . . 54 C4   3 25S   38 15 E
Taitao, Pen. de, *Chile* 96 F2   46 30S   75 0W
T'aitung, *Taiwan* . . . . 33 D7   22 43N 121 4 E
Taivalkoski, *Finland* . . . . 8 D23 65 33N   28 12 E
Taiwan ■, *Asia* . . . . 33 D7   23 30N 121 0 E
Taïyetos Óros, *Greece* . . . . . . 23 F10 37 0N   22 23 E
Taiyiba, *Israel* . . . . 46 C4   32 36N   35 27 E
Taiyuan, *China* . . . . 34 F7   37 52N 112 33 E
Taizhong = T'aichung, *Taiwan* 33 D7   24 9N 120 37 E
Ta'izz, *Yemen* . . . . 47 E3   13 35N   44 2 E
Tājābād, *Iran* . . . . 45 D7   30 2N   54 24 E
Tajikistan ■, *Asia* . . . . 28 F8   38 30N   70 0 E
Tajima, *Japan* . . . . 31 F9   37 12N 139 46 E
Tajo = Tejo →, *Europe* 21 C1   38 40N   9 24W
Tajrīsh, *Iran* . . . . 45 C6   35 48N   51 25 E
Tak, *Thailand* . . . . 38 D2   16 52N   99 8 E
Takāb, *Iran* . . . . 44 B5   36 24N   47 7 E
Takachiho, *Japan* . . . . 31 H5   32 42N 131 18 E
Takachu, *Botswana* . . . . 56 C3   22 37S   21 58 E
Takada, *Japan* . . . . 31 F9   37 7N 138 15 E
Takahagi, *Japan* . . . . 31 F10 36 43N 140 45 E
Takaka, *N.Z.* . . . . 59 J4   40 51S 172 50 E
Takamatsu, *Japan* . . . . 31 G7   34 20N 134 5 E
Takaoka, *Japan* . . . . 31 F8   36 47N 137 0 E
Takapuna, *N.Z.* . . . . 59 G5   36 47S 174 47 E
Takasaki, *Japan* . . . . 31 F9   36 20N 139 0 E
Takatsuki, *Japan* . . . . 31 G7   34 51N 135 37 E
Takaungu, *Kenya* . . . . 54 C4   3 38S   39 52 E
Takayama, *Japan* . . . . 31 F8   36 18N 137 11 E
Take-Shima, *Japan* . . . . 31 J5   30 49N 130 26 E
Takefu, *Japan* . . . . 31 G8   35 50N 136 10 E
Takengon, *Indonesia* . . . . 36 D1   4 45N   96 50 E
Takeo, *Japan* . . . . 31 H5   33 12N 130 1 E
Takeshima = Tok-do, *Asia* . . . 31 F5   37 15N 131 52 E
Tākestān, *Iran* . . . . 45 C6   36 0N   49 40 E
Takev, *Cambodia* . . . . 39 G5   10 59N 104 47 E
Takh, *India* . . . . 43 C7   33 6N   77 32 E
Takht-Sulaiman, *Pakistan* . . . 42 D3   31 40N   69 58 E
Takikawa, *Japan* . . . . 30 C10 43 33N 141 54 E
Takla →, *Canada* 70 B3   55 15N 125 45W
Takla Landing, *Canada* 70 B3   55 30N 125 50W
Takla Makan = Taklamakan
  Shamo, *China* . . . . 32 C3   38 0N   83 0 E
Taklamakan Shamo, *China* . . 32 C3   38 0N   83 0 E
Taku →, *Canada* 70 B2   58 30N 133 50W
Takua Thung, *Thailand* . . . . . 39 a   8 24N   98 27 E
Takum, *Nigeria* . . . . 50 G7   7 18N   9 59 E
Tal Halāl, *Iran* . . . . 45 D7   28 54N   55 1 E
Tala, *Uruguay* 95 C4   34 21S   55 46W
Talagang, *Pakistan* . . . . 42 C5   32 55N   72 25 E
Talagante, *Chile* 94 C1   33 40S   70 50W
Talamanca, Cordillera de,
  Cent. Amer. 88 E3   9 20N   83 20W
Talara, *Peru* 92 D2   4 38S   81 18W
Talas, *Kyrgyzstan* . . . . 28 E8   42 30N   72 13 E
Talâta, *Egypt* . . . . 46 E1   30 36N   32 20 E
Talaud, Kepulauan, *Indonesia* 37 D7   4 30N 126 50 E
Talaud Is. = Talaud, Kepulauan,
  Indonesia . . . . 37 D7   4 30N 126 50 E
Talavera de la Reina, *Spain* . . 21 C3   39 55N   4 46W
Talayan, *Phil.* . . . . 37 C6   6 52N 124 24 E
Talbandh, *India* . . . . 43 H12 22 3N   86 20 E
Talbot, C., *Australia* . . . . 60 B4   13 48S 126 43 E
Talbragar →, *Australia* . . . . . 63 E4   32 12S 148 37 E
Talca, *Chile* 94 D1   35 28S   71 40W
Talcahuano, *Chile* 94 D1   36 40S   73 10W
Talcher, *India* . . . . 41 J14 21 0N   85 18 E
Taldy Kurgan = Taldyqorghan,
  Kazakhstan . . . . 28 E8   45 10N   78 45 E
Taldyqorghan, *Kazakhstan* . . 28 E8   45 10N   78 45 E
Tālesh, *Iran* . . . . 45 B6   37 58N   48 58 E
Tālesh, Kūhhā-ye, *Iran* . . . . . 45 B6   37 42N   48 55 E
Tali Post, *Sudan* . . . . 51 G12 5 55N   30 44 E
Taliabu, *Indonesia* . . . . 37 E6   1 50S 125 0 E
Talibon, *Phil.* . . . . 37 B6   10 9N 124 20 E
Talibong, Ko, *Thailand* . . . . . 39 J2   7 15N   99 23 E
Talihina, *U.S.A.* 81 H7   34 45N   95 3W
Taliwang, *Indonesia* . . . . 36 F5   8 50S 116 55 E
Tall 'Afar, *Iraq* . . . . 44 B4   36 22N   42 27 E
Tall Kalakh, *Syria* . . . . 46 A5   34 41N   36 15 E
Talladega, *U.S.A.* 83 J2   33 26N   86 6W
Tallahassee, *U.S.A.* 83 K3   30 27N   84 17W
Tallangatta, *Australia* . . . . . . 63 F4   36 15S 147 19 E
Tallering Pk., *Australia* . . . . . 61 E2   28 6S 115 37 E
Talli, *Pakistan* . . . . 42 E3   29 32N   68 8 E
Tallinn, *Estonia* . . . . 9 G21 59 22N   24 48 E
Tallmadge, *U.S.A.* 84 E3   41 6N   81 27W
Tallulah, *U.S.A.* 81 J9   32 25N   91 11W
Taloyoak, *Canada* 68 B10 69 32N   93 32W
Talpa de Allende, *Mexico* . . . 86 C4   20 23N 104 51W
Talparo, *Trin. & Tob.* 93 K15 10 30N   61 17W
Talsi, *Latvia* . . . . 9 H20 57 10N   22 30 E
Taltal, *Chile* 94 B1   25 23S   70 33W
Taltson →, *Canada* 70 A6   61 24N 112 46W

Talwood, *Australia* . . . . 63 D4   28 29S 149 29 E
Talyawalka Cr. →, *Australia* . 63 E3   32 28S 142 22 E
Tam Ky, *Vietnam* . . . . 38 E7   15 34N 108 29 E
Tam Quan, *Vietnam* . . . . 38 E7   14 35N 109 3 E
Tama, *U.S.A.* 80 E8   41 58N   92 35W
Tamale, *Ghana* 50 G5   9 22N   0 50W
Taman Negara △, *Malaysia* . . 39 K4   4 38N 102 26 E
Tamano, *Japan* . . . . 31 G6   34 29N 133 59 E
Tamanrasset, *Algeria* . . . . . . 50 D7   22 50N   5 30 E
Tamaqua, *U.S.A.* 85 F9   40 48N   75 58W
Tamar →, *U.K.* 13 G3   50 27N   4 15W
Tamarinda, *Spain* . . . . 24 B10 39 55N   3 9 E
Tamashima, *Japan* . . . . 31 G6   34 32N 133 40 E
Tamaulipas □, *Mexico* 87 C5   24 0N   99 0W
Tamaulipas, Sierra de, *Mexico* 87 C5   23 30N   98 20W
Tamazula, *Mexico* 86 C3   24 55N 106 58W
Tamazunchale, *Mexico* 87 C5   21 16N   98 47W
Tambacounda, *Senegal* 50 F3   13 45N   13 40W
Tambelan, Kepulauan, *Indonesia* 36 D3   1 0N 107 30 E
Tambellup, *Australia* . . . . 61 F2   34 4S 117 37 E
Tambo, *Australia* . . . . 62 C4   24 54S 146 14 E
Tambo de Mora, *Peru* 92 F3   13 30S   76 8W
Tambohorano, *Madag.* . . . . . 57 B7   17 30S   43 58 E
Tambora, *Indonesia* . . . . 36 F5   8 12S 118 5 E
Tambov, *Russia* . . . . 18 D7   52 45N   41 28 E
Tambuku, *Indonesia* . . . . 37 G15 8 5S 113 40 E
Tâmega →, *Portugal* 21 B1   41 5N   8 21W
Tamenglong, *India* . . . . 41 G18 25 0N   93 35 E
Tamiahua, L. de, *Mexico* 87 C5   21 30N   97 30W
Tamil Nadu □, *India* . . . . 40 P10 11 0N   77 0 E
Tamluk, *India* . . . . 43 H12 22 18N   87 58 E
Tammerfors = Tampere, *Finland* 9 F20 61 30N   23 50 E
Tammisaari, *Finland* . . . . 9 F20 60 0N   23 26 E
Tamo Abu, Pegunungan,
  Malaysia . . . . 36 D5   3 10N 115 5 E
Tampa, *U.S.A.* 83 M4   27 57N   82 27W
Tampa, Tanjung, *Indonesia* . . 37 K19 8 55S 116 12 E
Tampa B., *U.S.A.* 83 M4   27 50N   82 30W
Tampere, *Finland* . . . . 9 F20 61 30N   23 50 E
Tampico, *Mexico* 87 C5   22 20N   97 50W
Tampin, *Malaysia* . . . . 39 L4   2 28N 102 13 E
Tampoi, *Malaysia* . . . . 39 d   1 30N 103 39 E
Tamu, *Burma* . . . . 41 G19 24 13N   94 12 E
Tamworth, *Australia* . . . . 63 E5   31 7S 150 58 E
Tamworth, *Canada* 84 B8   44 29N   77 0W
Tamworth, *U.K.* 13 E6   52 39N   1 41W
Tamyang, *S. Korea* . . . . 35 G14 35 19N 126 59 E
Tan An, *Vietnam* . . . . 39 G6   10 32N 106 25 E
Tan Chau, *Vietnam* . . . . 39 G5   10 48N 105 12 E
Tan-Tan, *Morocco* 50 C3   28 29N   11 1W
Tana →, *Kenya* . . . . 54 C5   2 32S   40 31 E
Tana →, *Norway* . . . . 8 A23 70 30N   28 14 E
Tana, L., *Ethiopia* . . . . 47 E2   13 5N   37 30 E
Tana River Primate △, *Kenya* . 54 C5   1 55S   40 7 E
Tanabe, *Japan* . . . . 31 H7   33 44N 135 22 E
Tanafjorden, *Norway* . . . . 8 A23 70 45N   28 25 E
Tanahbala, *Indonesia* . . . . . . 36 E1   0 30S   98 30 E
Tanahgrogot, *Indonesia* . . . . 36 E5   1 55S 116 15 E
Tanahjampea, *Indonesia* . . . . 37 F6   7 10S 120 35 E
Tanahmasa, *Indonesia* . . . . . 36 E1   0 12S   98 39 E
Tanahmerah, *Indonesia* . . . . . 37 F10 6 5S 140 16 E
Tanakpur, *India* . . . . 43 E9   29 5N   80 7 E
Tanakura, *Japan* . . . . 31 F10 37 10N 140 20 E
Tanami, *Australia* . . . . 60 C4   19 59S 129 43 E
Tanami Desert, *Australia* . . . . 60 C5   18 50S 132 0 E
Tanana, *U.S.A.* 68 B4   65 10N 151 58W
Tananarive = Antananarivo,
  Madag. . . . . 57 B8   18 55S   47 31 E
Tánaro →, *Italy* . . . . 20 D8   44 55N   8 40 E
Tancheng, *China* . . . . 35 G10 34 25N 118 20 E
Tanch'ŏn, N. Korea . . . . 35 D15 40 27N 128 54 E
Tanda, Ut. P., *India* . . . . 43 F10 26 33N   82 35 E
Tanda, Ut. P., *India* . . . . 43 E8   28 57N   78 56 E
Tanda, *Ivory C.* 50 G5   7 4N   3 8W
Tandag, *Phil.* . . . . 37 C7   9 4N 126 9 E
Tandaia, *Tanzania* . . . . 55 D3   9 25S   34 15 E
Tandaué, *Angola* . . . . 56 B2   16 58S   18 5 E
Tandil, *Argentina* 94 D4   37 15S   59 6W
Tandil, Sa. del, *Argentina* . . . 94 D4   37 30S   59 15W
Tandlianwala, *Pakistan* . . . . . 42 D5   31 3N   73 9 E
Tando Adam, *Pakistan* . . . . . 42 G3   25 45N   68 40 E
Tando Allahyar, *Pakistan* . . . 42 G3   25 28N   68 43 E
Tando Bago, *Pakistan* . . . . . . 42 G3   24 47N   68 58 E
Tando Mohommed Khan,
  Pakistan . . . . 42 G3   25 8N   68 32 E
Tandou L., *Australia* . . . . 63 E3   32 40S 142 5 E
Tandragee, *U.K.* 10 B5   54 21N   6 24W
Tane-ga-Shima, *Japan* . . . . . 31 J5   30 30N 131 0 E
Taneatua, *N.Z.* . . . . 59 H6   38 4S 177 1 E
Tanen Tong Dan = Dawna Ra.,
  Burma . . . . 38 D2   16 30N   98 30 E
Tanezrouft, *Algeria* . . . . 50 D6   23 9N   0 1 E
Tang, Koh, *Cambodia* . . . . . . 39 G4   10 16N 103 7 E
Tang, Ra's-e, *Iran* . . . . 45 E8   25 21N   59 52 E
Tang Krasang, *Cambodia* . . . 38 F5   12 34N 105 3 E
Tanga, *Tanzania* . . . . 54 D4   5 5S   39 2 E
Tanga □, *Tanzania* . . . . 54 D4   5 20S   38 0 E
Tanganyika, L., *Africa* . . . . . . 54 D3   6 40S   30 0 E
Tanger, *Morocco* 50 A4   35 50N   5 49W
Tangerang, *Indonesia* . . . . . . 37 G12 6 11S 106 37 E
Tanggula Shan, *China* . . . . . . 32 C4   32 40N   92 10 E
Tanghe, *China* . . . . 34 H7   32 47N 112 50 E
Tangier = Tanger, *Morocco* . . 50 A4   35 50N   5 49W
Tangjia, *China* . . . . 33 G10 22 21N 113 36 E
Tangjia Wan, *China* . . . . 33 G10 22 21N 113 36 E
Tangorin, *Australia* . . . . 62 C3   21 47S 144 12 E
Tangorombohitr'i Makay,
  Madag. . . . . 57 C8   21 0S   45 15 E
Tangshan, *China* . . . . 35 E10 39 38N 118 10 E
Tangtou, *China* . . . . 35 G10 35 28N 118 30 E
Tanimbar, Kepulauan, *Indonesia* 37 F8   7 30S 131 30 E
Tanimbar Is. = Tanimbar,
  Kepulauan, *Indonesia* . . . . 37 F8   7 30S 131 30 E
Taninthari = Tenasserim, *Burma* 39 F2   12 6N   99 3 E
Tanjay, *Phil.* . . . . 37 C6   9 30N 123 5 E
Tanjong Malim, *Malaysia* . . . 39 L3   3 42N 101 31 E
Tanjong Pelepas, *Malaysia* . . 39 d   1 21N 103 33 E
Tanjore = Thanjavur, *India* . . 40 P11 10 48N   79 12 E
Tanjung, *India* . . . . 37 J19 8 21S 116 9 E
Tanjung, *Phil.* . . . . 36 E5   2 10S 115 25 E
Tanjung Tokong, *Malaysia* . . 39 c   5 28N 100 18 E
Tanjungbatu, *Indonesia* . . . . 36 D5   2 55N   99 44 E
Tanjungkarang Telukbetung,
  Indonesia . . . . 36 F3   5 20S 105 10 E
Tanjungpandan, *Indonesia* . . 36 E3   2 43S 107 38 E
Tanjungpinang, *Indonesia* . . . 36 D2   2 9N 104 30 E

Tanjungredeb, *Indonesia* ...... **36 D5**   2 9N 117 29 E
Tanjungselor, *Indonesia* ...... **36 D5**   2 55N 117 25 E
Tank, *Pakistan* .... **42 C4** 32 14N 70 25 E
Tankhala, *India* .... **42 J5** 21 58N 73 47 E
Tankwa-Karoo △, *S. Africa* ... **56 E2** 32 14S 19 50 E
Tannersville, *U.S.A.* **85 E9** 41 3N 75 18W
Tannu-Ola, *Russia* .... **29 D10** 51 0N 94 0 E
Tannum Sands, *Australia* ..... **62 C5** 23 57S 151 22 E
Tanout, *Niger* .... **50 F7** 14 50N   8 55 E
Tanta, *Egypt* .... **51 B12** 30 45N 30 57 E
Tantoyuca, *Mexico* **87 C5** 21 21N 98 10W
Tantung = Dandong, *China* ... **35 D13** 40 10N 124 20 E
Tanunda, *Australia* .... **63 E2** 34 30S 139 0 E
Tanzania ■, *Africa* .... **54 D3**   6 0S 34 0 E
Tanzhou, *China* .... **33 G9** 22 16N 113 28 E
Tanzilla →, *Canada* **70 B2** 58 8N 130 43W
Tao, Ko, *Thailand* .... **39 G2** 10 5N 99 52 E
Tao'an = Taonan, *China* ..... **35 B12** 45 22N 122 40 E
Tao'er He →, *China* .... **35 B13** 45 45N 124 5 E
Taolanaro, *Madag.* .... **57 D8** 25 2S 47 0 E
Taole, *China* .... **34 E4** 38 48N 106 40 E
Taonan, *China* .... **35 B12** 45 22N 122 40 E
Taos, *U.S.A.* **77 H11** 36 24N 105 35W
Taoudenni, *Mali* **50 D5** 22 40N   3 55W
Tapa, *Estonia* ....   **9 G21** 59 15N 25 50 E
Tapa Shan = Daba Shan, *China* . **33 C5** 32 0N 109 0 E
Tapachula, *Mexico* **87 E6** 14 54N 92 17W
Tapah, *Malaysia* .... **39 K3**   4 12N 101 15 E
Tapajós →, *Brazil* **93 D8**   2 24S 54 41W
Tapaktuan, *Indonesia* .... **36 D1**   3 15N 97 10 E
Tapanahoni →, *Suriname* **93 C8**   4 20N 54 25W
Tapanui, *N.Z.* .... **59 L2** 45 56S 169 18 E
Tapauá →, *Brazil* **92 E6**   5 40S 64 21W
Tapes, *Brazil* **95 C5** 30 40S 51 23W
Tapeta, *Liberia* **50 G4**   6 29N   8 52W
Taphan Hin, *Thailand* .... **38 D3** 16 13N 100 26 E
Tapi →, *India* .... **40 J8** 21 8N 72 41 E
Tapirapecó, Serra, *Venezuela* . **92 C6**   1 10N 65 0W
Tapo-Capara △, *Venezuela* ... **89 E5**   7 55N 71 15W
Tapuaenuku, *N.Z.* .... **59 K4** 42 0S 173 39 E
Tapul Group, *Phil.* .... **37 C6**   5 35N 120 50 E
Tapurucuará, *Brazil* **92 D5**   0 24S 65 2W
Taqtaq, *Iraq* .... **44 C5** 35 53N 44 35 E
Taquara, *Brazil* **95 B5** 29 36S 50 46W
Taquari →, *Brazil* **92 G7** 19 15S 57 17W
Tara, *Australia* .... **63 D5** 27 17S 150 31 E
Tara, *Canada* **84 B3** 44 28N 81 9W
Tara, *Russia* .... **28 D8** 56 55N 74 24 E
Tara, *Zambia* .... **55 F2** 16 58S 26 45 E
Tara →, *Serbia & M.* ...... **23 C8** 43 21N 18 51 E
Tarābulus, *Lebanon* .... **46 A4** 34 31N 35 50 E
Tarābulus, *Libya* .... **51 B8** 32 49N 13 7 E
Taradehi, *India* .... **43 H8** 23 18N 79 21 E
Tarajalejo, *Canary Is.* **24 F5** 28 12N 14 7W
Tarakan, *Indonesia* .... **36 D5**   3 20N 117 35 E
Tarakit, Mt., *Kenya* .... **54 B4**   2 2N 35 10 E
Tarama-Jima, *Japan* .... **31 M2** 24 39N 124 42 E
Taran, Mys, *Russia* ....   **9 J18** 54 56N 19 59 E
Taranagar, *India* .... **42 E6** 28 43N 74 50 E
Taranaki □, *N.Z.* .... **59 H5** 39 25S 174 30 E
Taranaki, Mt., *N.Z.* .... **59 H5** 39 17S 174 5 E
Tarancón, *Spain* **21 B4** 40 1N   3 0W
Tarangire △, *Tanzania* ..... **54 C4**   4 21S 36 7 E
Taransay, *U.K.* **11 D1** 57 54N   7 0W
Táranto, *Italy* .... **22 D7** 40 28N 17 14 E
Táranto, G. di, *Italy* ...... **22 D7** 40 8N 17 20 E
Tarapacá, *Colombia* **92 D5**   2 56S 69 46W
Tarapacá □, *Chile* **94 A2** 20 45S 69 30W
Tarapoto, *Peru* **92 E3**   6 30S 76 20W
Tararua →, *Brazil* .... **59 J5** 40 45S 175 25 E
Tarashcha, *Ukraine* .... **17 D16** 49 30N 30 31 E
Tarauacá, *Brazil* **92 E4**   8 6S 70 48W
Tarauacá →, *Brazil* **92 E5**   6 42S 69 48W
Tarawa, *Kiribati* .... **64 G9**   1 30N 173 0 E
Tarawera, *N.Z.* .... **59 H6** 39 2S 176 36 E
Tarawera, L., *N.Z.* .... **59 H6** 38 13S 176 27 E
Taraz, *Kazakhstan* .... **28 E8** 42 54N 71 22 E
Tarazona, *Spain* **21 B5** 41 55N   1 43W
Tarbagatay, Khrebet, *Kazakhstan* **28 E9** 48 0N 83 0 E
Tarbat Ness, *U.K.* **11 D5** 57 52N   3 47W
Tarbela Dam, *Pakistan* ..... **42 B5** 34 8N 72 52 E
Tarbert, *Arg. & Bute, U.K.* ... **11 F3** 55 52N   5 25W
Tarbert, *W. Isles, U.K.* **11 D2** 57 54N   6 49W
Tarbes, *France* .... **20 E4** 43 15N   0 3 E
Tarboro, *U.S.A.* **83 H7** 35 54N 77 32W
Tarcoola, *Australia* .... **63 E1** 30 44S 134 36 E
Tarcoon, *Australia* .... **63 E4** 30 15S 146 43 E
Taree, *Australia* .... **63 E5** 31 50S 152 30 E
Tarfaya, *Morocco* **50 C3** 27 55N 12 55W
Târgoviște, *Romania* .... **17 F13** 44 55N 25 27 E
Târgu-Jiu, *Romania* .... **17 F12** 45 5N 23 19 E
Târgu Mureş, *Romania* ..... **17 E13** 46 31N 24 38 E
Tarif, *U.A.E.* .... **45 E7** 24 3N 53 46 E
Tarifa, *Spain* **21 D3** 36 1N   5 36W
Tarija, *Bolivia* **94 A3** 21 30S 64 40W
Tarija □, *Bolivia* **94 A3** 21 30S 63 30W
Tariku →, *Indonesia* ...... **37 E9**   2 55S 138 26 E
Tarim Basin = Tarim Pendi, *China* **32 B3** 40 0N 84 0 E
Tarim He →, *China* .... **32 C3** 39 30N 88 30 E
Tarim Pendi, *China* .... **32 B3** 40 0N 84 0 E
Taritatu →, *Indonesia* ..... **37 E9**   2 54S 138 27 E
Tarka →, *S. Africa* .... **56 E4** 32 10S 26 0 E
Tarkastad, *S. Africa* ...... **56 E4** 32 0S 26 16 E
Tarkhankut, Mys, *Ukraine* ... **19 E5** 45 25N 32 30 E
Tarko Sale, *Russia* .... **28 C8** 64 55N 77 50 E
Tarkwa, *Ghana* **50 G5**   5 20N   2 0W
Tarlac, *Phil.* .... **37 A6** 15 29N 120 35 E
Tarma, *Peru* **92 F3** 11 25S 75 45W
Tarn →, *France* .... **20 E4** 44 5N   1 6 E
Târnăveni, *Romania* .... **17 E13** 46 19N 24 13 E
Tarnobrzeg, *Poland* .... **17 C11** 50 35N 21 41 E
Tarnów, *Poland* .... **17 C11** 50 3N 21 0 E
Tarnowskie Góry, *Poland* ... **17 C10** 50 27N 18 54 E
Tārom, *Iran* .... **45 D7** 28 11N 55 46 E
Taroom, *Australia* .... **63 D4** 25 36S 149 48 E
Taroudannt, *Morocco* **50 B4** 30 30N   8 52W
Tarpon Springs, *U.S.A.* **83 L4** 28 9N 82 45W
Tarragona, *Spain* .... **21 B6** 41 5N   1 17 E
Tarraleah, *Australia* ...... **63 G4** 42 17S 146 26 E
Tarrasa = Terrassa, *Spain* ... **21 B7** 41 34N   2 1 E
Tarrytown, *U.S.A.* **85 E11** 41 4N 73 52W
Tarshiha = Me'ona, *Israel* ... **46 B4** 33 1N 35 15 E
Tarsus, *Turkey* .... **19 G5** 36 58N 34 55 E
Tartagal, *Argentina* **94 A3** 22 30S 63 50W
Tartu, *Estonia* .... **9 G22** 58 20N 26 44 E
Tarţūs, *Syria* .... **44 C2** 34 55N 35 55 E
Tarumizu, *Japan* .... **31 J5** 31 29N 130 42 E

Tarutao = Ko Tarutao △, *Thailand* **39 J2**   6 31N 99 26 E
Tarutao, Ko, *Thailand* ...... **39 J2**   6 33N 99 40 E
Tarutung, *Indonesia* .... **36 D1**   2 0N 98 54 E
Taseko →, *Canada* **70 C4** 52 8N 123 45W
Tash-Kömür, *Kyrgyzstan* .... **28 E8** 41 40N 72 10 E
Tash-Kumyr = Tash-Kömür,
  Kyrgyzstan .... **28 E8** 41 40N 72 10 E
Tashauz = Dashhowuz,
  Turkmenistan .... **28 E6** 41 49N 59 58 E
Tashi Chho Dzong = Thimphu,
  Bhutan .... **41 F16** 27 31N 89 45 E
Tashk, Daryācheh-ye, *Iran* ... **45 D7** 29 45N 53 35 E
Tashkent = Toshkent, *Uzbekistan* **28 E7** 41 20N 69 10 E
Tashtagol, *Russia* .... **28 D9** 52 47N 87 53 E
Tasiilaq, *Greenland* **4 C6** 65 40N 37 20W
Tasikmalaya, *Indonesia* .... **37 G13** 7 18S 108 12 E
Tåsjön, *Sweden* .... **8 D16** 64 15N 15 40 E
Taskan, *Russia* .... **29 C16** 62 59N 150 20 E
Tasman B., *N.Z.* .... **59 J4** 40 59S 173 25 E
Tasman Mts., *N.Z.* .... **59 J4** 41 3S 172 25 E
Tasman Pen., *Australia* ..... **63 G4** 43 10S 148 0 E
Tasman Sea, *Pac. Oc.* ...... **64 L8** 36 0S 160 0 E
Tasmania □, *Australia* ..... **63 G4** 42 0S 146 30 E
Tassili n'Ajjer, *Algeria* ..... **50 C7** 25 47N   8 1 E
Tatabánya, *Hungary* .... **17 E10** 47 32N 18 25 E
Tataouine, *Tunisia* .... **51 B8** 32 56N 10 27 E
Tataouine, *Tunisia* .... **51 B8** 32 57N 10 29 E
Tatar Republic = Tatarstan □,
  Russia .... **18 C9** 55 30N 51 30 E
Tatarbunary, *Ukraine* ...... **17 F15** 45 50N 29 39 E
Tatarsk, *Russia* .... **28 D8** 55 14N 76 0 E
Tatarstan □, *Russia* .... **18 C9** 55 30N 51 30 E
Tateyama, *Japan* .... **31 G9** 35 0N 139 50 E
Tathlina L., *Canada* **70 A5** 60 33N 117 39W
Tathra, *Australia* .... **63 F4** 36 44S 149 59 E
Tatinnai L., *Canada* **71 A9** 60 55N 97 40W
Tatla L., *Canada* **70 C4** 52 0N 124 20W
Tatnam, C., *Canada* **71 B10** 57 16N 91 0W
Tatra = Tatry, *Slovak Rep.* ... **17 D11** 49 20N 20 0 E
Tatry, *Slovak Rep.* .... **17 D11** 49 20N 20 0 E
Tatshenshini →, *Canada* **70 B1** 59 28N 137 45W
Tatsuno, *Japan* .... **31 G7** 34 52N 134 33 E
Tatta, *Pakistan* .... **42 G2** 24 42N 67 55 E
Tatuí, *Brazil* **95 A6** 23 25S 47 53W
Tatum, *U.S.A.* **81 J3** 33 16N 103 19W
Tat'ung = Datong, *China* ... **34 D7** 40 6N 113 18 E
Tatvan, *Turkey* .... **19 G7** 38 31N 42 15 E
Taubaté, *Brazil* **95 A6** 23 0S 45 36W
Tauern, *Austria* .... **16 E7** 47 15N 12 40 E
Taumarunui, *N.Z.* .... **59 H5** 38 53S 175 15 E
Taumaturgo, *Brazil* **92 E4**   8 54S 72 51W
Taung, *S. Africa* .... **56 D3** 27 33S 24 47 E
Taungdwingyi, *Burma* ...... **41 J19** 20 1N 95 40 E
Taunggyi, *Burma* .... **41 J20** 20 50N 97 0 E
Taungup, *Burma* .... **41 K19** 18 51N 94 14 E
Taungup Taunggya, *Burma* ... **41 K18** 18 20N 93 40 E
Taunsa, *Pakistan* .... **42 D4** 30 42N 70 39 E
Taunsa Barrage, *Pakistan* ... **42 D4** 30 42N 70 50 E
Taunton, *U.K.* **13 F4** 51 1N   3 5W
Taunton, *U.S.A.* **85 E13** 41 54N 71 6W
Taunus, *Germany* .... **16 C5** 50 13N   8 34 E
Taupo, *N.Z.* .... **59 H6** 38 41S 176 7 E
Taupo, L., *N.Z.* .... **59 H5** 38 46S 175 55 E
Tauragė, *Lithuania* .... **9 J20** 55 14N 22 16 E
Tauranga, *N.Z.* .... **59 G6** 37 42S 176 11 E
Tauranga Harb., *N.Z.* ...... **59 G6** 37 30S 176 5 E
Taureau, Rés., *Canada* **72 C5** 46 46N 73 50W
Taurianova, *Italy* .... **22 E7** 38 21N 16 1 E
Taurus Mts. = Toros Dağları,
  Turkey .... **19 G5** 37 0N 32 30 E
Tavda, *Russia* .... **28 D7** 58 7N 65 8 E
Tavda →, *Russia* .... **28 D7** 57 47N 67 18 E
Taveta, *Tanzania* .... **54 C4**   3 23S 37 37 E
Taveuni, *Fiji* **59 C9** 16 51S 179 58W
Tavira, *Portugal* **21 D2** 37 8N   7 40W
Tavistock, *Canada* **84 C4** 43 19N 80 50W
Tavistock, *U.K.* **13 G3** 50 33N   4 9W
Tavoy, *Burma* .... **38 E2** 14 2N 98 12 E
Taw →, *U.K.* **13 F3** 51 4N   4 4W
Tawa →, *India* .... **42 H8** 22 48N 77 48 E
Tawas City, *U.S.A.* **82 C4** 44 16N 83 31W
Tawau, *Malaysia* .... **36 D5**   4 20N 117 55 E
Tawitawi, *Phil.* .... **37 B6**   5 10N 120 0 E
Taxco de Alarcón, *Mexico* ... **87 D5** 18 33N 99 36W
Taxila, *Pakistan* .... **42 C5** 33 42N 72 52 E
Tay →, *U.K.* **11 E5** 56 43N   3 59W
Tay →, *U.K.* **11 E5** 56 37N   3 38W
Tay, Firth of, *U.K.* **11 E5** 56 25N   3 8W
Tay, L., *Australia* .... **61 F3** 32 55S 120 48 E
Tay, L., *U.K.* **11 E4** 56 32N   4 8W
Tay Ninh, *Vietnam* .... **39 G6** 11 20N 106 5 E
Tayabamba, *Peru* **92 E3**   8 15S 77 16W
Taylakova, *Russia* .... **28 D8** 59 13N 74 0 E
Taylakovy = Taylakova, *Russia* **28 D8** 59 13N 74 0 E
Taylor, *Canada* **70 B4** 56 13N 120 40W
Taylor, *Nebr., U.S.A.* **80 E5** 41 46N 99 23W
Taylor, *Pa., U.S.A.* **85 E9** 41 23N 75 43W
Taylor, *Tex., U.S.A.* **81 K6** 30 34N 97 25W
Taylor, Mt., *U.S.A.* **77 J10** 35 14N 107 37W
Taylorville, *U.S.A.* **80 F10** 39 33N 89 18W
Taymā, *Si. Arabia* .... **44 E3** 27 35N 38 45 E
Taymyr, Oz., *Russia* .... **29 B11** 74 20N 102 0 E
Taymyr, Poluostrov, *Russia* ... **29 B11** 75 0N 100 0 E
Tayport, *U.K.* **11 E6** 56 27N   2 52W
Tayrona □, *Colombia* **89 D5** 11 20N 74 2W
Tayshet, *Russia* .... **29 D10** 55 58N 98 1 E
Tāyyebād, *Iran* .... **45 C9** 34 45N 60 45 E
Tāyyebād □, *Iran* .... **45 C9** 34 44N 60 44 E
Taz →, *Russia* .... **28 C8** 67 32N 78 40 E
Taza, *Morocco* **50 B5** 34 16N   4 6W
Tāza Khurmātū, *Iraq* ...... **44 C5** 35 18N 44 20 E
Tazawa-Ko, *Japan* .... **30 E10** 39 43N 140 40 E
Tazin →, *Canada* **71 B7** 59 48N 109 55W
Tazin L., *Canada* **71 B7** 59 44N 108 42W
Tazovskiy, *Russia* .... **28 C8** 67 30N 78 44 E
Tbilisi, *Georgia* .... **19 F7** 41 43N 44 50 E
Tchad = Chad ■, *Africa* .... **51 F8** 15 0N 17 15 E
Tchad, L., *Chad* .... **51 F8** 13 30N 14 30 E
Tch'eng-tou = Chengdu, *China* **32 C5** 30 38N 104 2 E
Tchentlo L., *Canada* **70 B4** 55 15N 125 0W
Tchibanga, *Gabon* .... **52 E2**   2 45S 11 0 E
Tch'ong-k'ing = Chongqing,
  China .... **32 D5** 29 35N 106 25 E
Tczew, *Poland* .... **17 A10** 54 8N 18 50 E
Te Anau, L., *N.Z.* .... **59 L1** 45 15S 167 45 E
Te Aroha, *N.Z.* .... **59 G5** 37 32S 175 44 E

Te Awamutu, *N.Z.* .... **59 H5** 38 1S 175 20 E
Te Kuiti, *N.Z.* .... **59 H5** 38 20S 175 11 E
Te Puke, *N.Z.* .... **59 G6** 37 46S 176 22 E
Te Waewae B., *N.Z.* ...... **59 M1** 46 13S 167 33 E
Teague, *U.S.A.* **81 K6** 31 38N 96 17W
Teapa, *Mexico* **87 D6** 18 35N 92 56W
Tebakang, *Malaysia* .... **36 D4**   1 6N 110 30 E
Teberu, *Malaysia* .... **39 d**   1 30N 103 42 E
Tébessa, *Algeria* .... **50 A7** 35 22N   8 8 E
Tebicuary →, *Paraguay* **94 B4** 26 36S 58 16W
Tebingtinggi, *Riau, Indonesia* . **36 E2**   1 0N 102 45 E
Tebingtinggi, *Sumatera Utara,
  Indonesia* .... **36 D1**   3 20N 99 9 E
Tecate, *Mexico* **79 N10** 32 34N 116 38W
Teca, *Argentina* **96 E2** 33 29S 70 48W
Tecomán, *Mexico* **86 D4** 18 55N 103 53W
Tecopa, *U.S.A.* **79 K10** 35 51N 116 13W
Tecuala, *Mexico* **86 C3** 22 23N 105 27W
Tecuci, *Romania* .... **17 F14** 45 51N 27 27 E
Tecumseh, *Canada* **84 D2** 42 19N 82 54W
Tecumseh, *Mich., U.S.A.* ... **82 D4** 42 0N 83 57W
Tecumseh, *Okla., U.S.A.* ... **81 H6** 35 15N 96 56W
Tedzhen = Tejen, *Turkmenistan* **28 F7** 37 23N 60 31 E
Tees →, *U.K.* **12 C6** 54 37N   1 9W
Tees B., *U.K.* **12 C6** 54 40N   1 9W
Teeswater, *Canada* **84 C3** 43 59N 81 17W
Tefé, *Brazil* **92 D6**   3 25S 64 50W
Tegal, *Indonesia* .... **36 F3**   6 52S 109 8 E
Tegallalang, *Indonesia* ..... **37 J18** 8 27S 115 17 E
Tegalsari, *Indonesia* ...... **37 J17** 8 25S 114 8 E
Tegid, L. = Bala, L., *U.K.* ... **12 E4** 52 53N   3 37W
Tegucigalpa, *Honduras* **88 D2** 14 5N 87 14W
Tehachapi, *U.S.A.* **79 K8** 35 8N 118 27W
Tehachapi Mts., *U.S.A.* **79 L8** 35 0N 118 30W
Teheran = Tehrān, *Iran* .... **45 C6** 35 44N 51 30 E
Tehoru, *Indonesia* .... **37 E7**   3 23S 129 30 E
Tehrān, *Iran* .... **45 C6** 35 44N 51 30 E
Tehrān □, *Iran* .... **45 C6** 35 30N 51 30 E
Tehri, *India* .... **43 D8** 30 23N 78 29 E
Tehuacán, *Mexico* **87 D5** 18 30N 97 30W
Tehuantepec, *Mexico* **87 D5** 16 21N 95 13W
Tehuantepec, G. de, *Mexico* . **87 D5** 15 50N 95 12W
Tehuantepec, Istmo de, *Mexico* **87 D6** 17 0N 94 30W
Teide, Pico de, *Canary Is.* ... **24 F3** 28 15N 16 38W
Teifi →, *U.K.* **13 E3** 52 5N   4 41W
Teign →, *U.K.* **13 G4** 50 32N   3 32W
Teignmouth, *U.K.* **13 G4** 50 33N   3 31W
Tejakula, *Indonesia* .... **37 J18** 8 8S 115 20 E
Tejam, *India* .... **43 E9** 29 57N 80 11 E
Tejen, *Turkmenistan* ...... **28 F7** 37 23N 60 31 E
Tejen →, *Turkmenistan* ..... **45 B9** 37 24N 60 38 E
Tejo →, *Europe* **21 C1** 38 40N   9 24W
Tejon Pass, *U.S.A.* **79 L8** 34 49N 118 53W
Tekamah, *U.S.A.* **80 E6** 41 47N 96 13W
Tekapo, L., *N.Z.* .... **59 K3** 43 53S 170 33 E
Tekax, *Mexico* **87 C7** 20 11N 89 18W
Tekeli, *Kazakhstan* .... **28 E8** 44 50N 79 0 E
Tekirdağ, *Turkey* .... **23 D12** 40 58N 27 30 E
Tekkali, *India* .... **41 K14** 18 37N 84 15 E
Tekoa, *U.S.A.* **76 C5** 47 14N 117 4W
Tekong Besar, Pulau, *Singapore* **39 d**   1 25N 104 3 E
Tel Aviv ✈ (TLV), *Israel* ... **46 C3** 32 5N 34 49 E
Tel Aviv-Yafo, *Israel* ...... **46 C3** 32 4N 34 48 E
Tel Lakhish, *Israel* .... **46 D3** 31 34N 34 51 E
Tel Megiddo, *Israel* .... **46 C4** 32 35N 35 11 E
Tela, *Honduras* **88 C2** 15 40N 87 28W
Telanaipura = Jambi, *Indonesia* **36 E2**   1 38S 103 30 E
Telavi, *Georgia* .... **19 F8** 42 0N 45 30 E
Telde, *Canary Is.* **24 G4** 27 59N 15 25W
Telegraph Creek, *Canada* ... **70 B2** 58 0N 131 10W
Telekhany = Tsyelyakhany,
  Belarus .... **17 B13** 52 30N 25 46 E
Telemark, *Norway* .... **9 G12** 59 15N   7 40 E
Telén, *Argentina* **94 D2** 36 15S 65 31W
Teleng, *Iran* .... **45 E9** 25 47N 61 3 E
Teles Pires →, *Brazil* **92 E7**   7 21S 58 3W
Telescope Pk., *U.S.A.* **79 J9** 36 10N 117 5W
Telfer Mine, *Australia* ..... **60 C3** 21 40S 122 12 E
Telford, *U.K.* **13 E5** 52 40N   2 27W
Telford and Wrekin □, *U.K.* . **12 E5** 52 45N   2 27W
Telkwa, *Canada* **70 C3** 54 41N 127 5W
Tell City, *U.S.A.* **82 G2** 37 57N 86 46W
Tellicherry, *India* .... **40 P9** 11 45N 75 30 E
Telluride, *U.S.A.* **77 H10** 37 56N 107 49W
Teloloapán, *Mexico* **87 D5** 18 21N 99 51W
Telpos I, *Russia* .... **18 B10** 63 16N 59 13 E
Telsen, *Argentina* **96 E3** 42 30S 66 50W
Telšiai, *Lithuania* .... **9 H20** 55 59N 22 14 E
Teluk Anson = Teluk Intan,
  Malaysia .... **39 K3**   4 3N 101 0 E
Teluk Bahang, *Malaysia* .... **39 K3**   4 3N 101 0 E
Teluk Betung = Tanjungkarang
  Telukbetung, *Indonesia* ... **36 F3**   5 20S 105 10 E
Teluk Intan, *Malaysia* ..... **39 K3**   4 3N 101 0 E
Teluk Kumbar, *Malaysia* .... **39 c**   5 18N 100 14 E
Telukbutun, *Indonesia* ..... **36 D3**   4 13N 108 12 E
Telukdalem, *Indonesia* ..... **36 D1**   0 33N 97 50 E
Tema, *Ghana* **50 G5**   5 41N   0 0W
Temax, *Mexico* **87 C7** 21 10N 88 50W
Temba, *S. Africa* .... **57 D4** 25 20S 28 17 E
Tembagapura, *Indonesia* ... **37 E9**   4 20S 137 0 E
Tembe, *Dem. Rep. of the Congo* **54 C2**   0 16S 28 14 E
Tembe, *S. Africa* .... **57 D5** 26 51S 32 24 E
Temblor Range, *U.S.A.* **79 K7** 35 20N 119 50W
Teme →, *U.K.* **13 E5** 52 11N   2 13W
Temecula, *U.S.A.* **79 M9** 33 30N 117 9W
Temerloh, *Malaysia* .... **36 D2**   3 27N 102 25 E
Teminabuan, *Indonesia* .... **37 E8**   1 26S 132 1 E
Temir, *Kazakhstan* .... **19 E10** 49 1N 57 14 E
Temirtau, *Kazakhstan* ..... **28 D8** 50 10N 87 30 E
Temirtau, *Russia* .... **28 D9** 53 10N 87 30 E
Témiscamie →, *Canada* **72 C4** 50 59N 73 5W
Témiscaming, *Canada* **72 C4** 46 44N 79 5W
Témiscamingue, L., *Canada* . **72 C4** 47 10N 79 25W
Temosachic, *Mexico* **86 B3** 28 58N 107 50W
Tempe, *U.S.A.* **77 K8** 33 25N 111 56W
Tempiute, *U.S.A.* **78 H11** 37 39N 115 38W
Temple, *U.S.A.* **81 K6** 31 6N 97 21W
Temple B., *Australia* ...... **62 A3** 12 15S 143 3 E
Templemore, *Ireland* **10 D4** 52 47N   7 51W
Templeton, *U.S.A.* **78 K6** 35 33N 120 42W
Templeton →, *Australia* .... **62 C2** 21 0S 138 40 E
Tempoal, *Mexico* **87 C5** 21 31N 98 23W
Temuco, *Chile* **96 D2** 38 45S 72 40W
Temuka, *N.Z.* .... **59 L3** 44 14S 171 17 E

Tenabo, *Mexico* **87 C6** 20 2N 90 12W
Tenaha, *U.S.A.* **81 K7** 31 57N 94 15W
Tenakee Springs, *U.S.A.* ... **70 B1** 57 47N 135 13W
Tenali, *India* .... **41 L12** 16 15N 80 35 E
Tenancingo, *Mexico* **87 D5** 19 0N 99 33W
Tenango, *Mexico* **87 D5** 19 7N 99 33W
Tenasserim, *Burma* .... **39 F2** 12 6N 99 3 E
Tenasserim □, *Burma* ..... **38 F2** 14 0N 98 30 E
Tenby, *U.K.* **13 F3** 51 40N   4 42W
Tenda, Colle di, *France* .... **20 D7** 44 7N   7 36 E
Tendaho, *Ethiopia* .... **47 E3** 11 48N 40 54 E
Tendukhera, *India* .... **43 H8** 23 24N 79 33 E
Teneguía, Volcanes de,
  Canary Is. **24 F2** 28 28N 17 51W
Tenerife, *Canary Is.* **24 F3** 28 15N 16 35W
Tenerife, Pico, *Canary Is.* ... **24 G1** 27 43N 18 1W
Tenerife Norte ✈ (TFN),
  Canary Is. **24 F3** 28 28N 16 17W
Tenerife Sur ✈ (TFS), *Canary Is.* **24 F3** 28 28N 16 33W
Teng Xian, *China* .... **35 G9** 35 5N 117 10 E
Tengah □, *Indonesia* ...... **37 E6**   1 30S 121 0 E
Tengah, Kepulauan, *Indonesia* . **36 F5**   7 5S 118 15 E
Tengchong, *China* .... **32 D4** 25 0N 98 28 E
Tengchowfu = Penglai, *China* . **35 F11** 37 48N 120 42 E
Tenggara □, *Indonesia* ..... **37 E6**   3 50S 122 0 E
Tenggarong, *Indonesia* .... **36 E5**   0 24S 116 58 E
Tenggol, Pulau, *Malaysia* ... **39 K4**   4 48N 103 41 E
Tengiz, Ozero, *Kazakhstan* .. **28 D7** 50 30N 69 0 E
Teniente Enciso △, *Paraguay* . **94 A3** 21 5S 61 8W
Teniente Rodolfo Marsh,
  Antarctica **5 C18** 62 30S 58 0W
Tenino, *U.S.A.* **78 D4** 46 51N 122 51W
Tenkasi, *India* .... **40 Q10** 8 55N 77 20 E
Tenke, Katanga, Dem. Rep. of
  the Congo .... **55 E2** 11 22S 26 40 E
Tenke, Katanga, Dem. Rep. of
  the Congo .... **55 E2** 10 32S 26 7 E
Tennant Creek, *Australia* ... **62 B1** 19 30S 134 15 E
Tennessee □, *U.S.A.* **83 H2** 36 0N 86 30W
Tennessee →, *U.S.A.* **82 G1** 37 4N 88 34W
Teno, Pta. de, *Canary Is.* ... **24 F3** 28 21N 16 55W
Tenom, *Malaysia* .... **36 C5**   5 4N 115 57 E
Tenosique, *Mexico* **87 D6** 17 30N 91 24W
Tenryū-Gawa →, *Japan* .... **31 G8** 35 39N 137 48 E
Tenterden, *U.K.* .... **13 F8** 51 4N   0 42 E
Tenterfield, *Australia* ...... **63 D5** 29 0S 152 0 E
Teófilo Otoni, *Brazil* **93 G10** 17 50S 41 30W
Tepa, *Indonesia* .... **37 F7**   7 52S 129 31 E
Tepalcatepec →, *Mexico* ... **86 D4** 18 35N 101 59W
Tepehuanes, *Mexico* **86 B3** 25 21N 105 44W
Tepetongo, *Mexico* **86 C4** 22 28N 103 9W
Tepic, *Mexico* **86 C4** 21 30N 104 54W
Teplice, *Czech Rep.* .... **16 C7** 50 40N 13 48 E
Tepoca, C., *Mexico* **86 A2** 30 20N 112 25W
Tequila, *Mexico* **86 C4** 20 54N 103 47W
Ter →, *Spain* .... **21 A7** 42 2N   3 12 E
Ter Apel, *Neths.* .... **15 B7** 52 53N   7 5 E
Teraina, *Kiribati* **65 G11** 4 43N 160 25W
Téramo, *Italy* .... **22 C5** 42 39N 13 42 E
Terang, *Australia* .... **63 F3** 38 15S 142 55 E
Terang, Teluk, *Indonesia* ... **37 K19** 8 44S 116 0 E
Tercero →, *Argentina* **94 C3** 32 58S 61 47W
Terebovlya, *Ukraine* ...... **17 D13** 49 18N 25 44 E
Terek →, *Russia* .... **19 F8** 44 0N 47 30 E
Terepaima △, *Venezuela* ... **89 E6**   9 58N 69 17W
Teresina, *Brazil* **93 E10** 5 9S 42 45W
Teridgerie Cr. →, *Australia* . **63 E4** 30 25S 148 50 E
Termez = Termiz, *Uzbekistan* . **28 F7** 37 15N 67 15 E
Términi Imerese, *Italy* ..... **22 F5** 37 59N 13 42 E
Términos, L. de, *Mexico* **87 D6** 18 35N 91 30W
Termiz, *Uzbekistan* .... **28 F7** 37 15N 67 15 E
Térmoli, *Italy* .... **22 C6** 42 0N 15 0 E
Ternate, *Indonesia* .... **37 D7**   0 45N 127 25 E
Terneuzen, *Neths.* .... **15 C3** 51 20N   3 50 E
Terney, *Russia* .... **29 E14** 45 3N 136 37 E
Terni, *Italy* .... **22 C5** 42 34N 12 37 E
Ternopil, *Ukraine* .... **17 D13** 49 30N 25 40 E
Ternopol = Ternopil, *Ukraine* . **17 D13** 49 30N 25 40 E
Terowie, *Australia* .... **63 E2** 33 8S 138 55 E
Terra Bella, *U.S.A.* **79 K7** 35 58N 119 3W
Terra Nova △, *Canada* **73 C9** 48 33N 119 31W
Terrace, *Canada* **70 C3** 54 30N 128 35W
Terrace Bay, *Canada* **72 C2** 48 47N 87 5W
Terracina, *Italy* .... **22 D5** 41 17N 13 15 E
Terralba, *Italy* .... **22 E3** 39 43N   8 39 E
Terranova = Ólbia, *Italy* .... **22 D3** 40 55N   9 31 E
Terrassa, *Spain* .... **21 B7** 41 34N   2 1 E
Terre Haute, *U.S.A.* **82 F2** 39 28N 87 25W
Terrebonne B., *U.S.A.* **81 L9** 29 5N 90 35W
Terrell, *U.S.A.* **81 J6** 32 44N 96 17W
Terrenceville, *Canada* **73 C9** 47 40N 54 44W
Terry, *U.S.A.* **80 B2** 46 47N 105 19W
Terryville, *U.S.A.* **85 E11** 41 41N 73 3W
Terschelling, *Neths.* ...... **15 A5** 53 25N   5 20 E
Teruel, *Spain* **21 B5** 40 22N   1 8W
Tervola, *Finland* .... **8 C21** 66 6N 24 49 E
Teryaweyna L., *Australia* ... **63 E3** 32 18S 143 22 E
Teshio, *Japan* .... **30 B10** 44 53N 141 44 E
Teshio-Gawa →, *Japan* .... **30 B10** 44 53N 141 44 E
Tesiyn Gol →, *Mongolia* **32 A4** 50 40N 132 43W
Teslin, *Canada* **70 A2** 60 10N 132 43W
Teslin →, *Canada* **70 A2** 61 34N 134 35W
Teslin L., *Canada* **70 A2** 60 15N 132 57W
Tessalit, *Mali* .... **50 D6** 20 12N   1 0 E
Test →, *U.K.* **13 G6** 50 56N   1 29W
Testigos, Is. Las, *Venezuela* . **89 D7** 11 23S 63 7W
Tetachuck L., *Canada* **70 C3** 53 18N 125 55W
Tetas, Pta., *Chile* **94 A1** 23 31S 70 38W
Tete, *Mozam.* .... **55 F3** 16 13S 33 33 E
Tete □, *Mozam.* .... **55 F3** 15 15S 32 40 E
Teterev →, *Ukraine* .... **23 C16** 51 1N 30 5 E
Teteven, *Bulgaria* .... **23 C11** 42 58N 24 17 E
Tethul →, *Canada* **70 A6** 60 35N 112 12W
Tetiyev, *Ukraine* .... **17 D15** 49 22N 29 38 E
Teton →, *U.S.A.* **76 C8** 47 56N 110 31W
Tétouan, *Morocco* **50 A4** 35 35N   5 21W
Tetovo, *Macedonia* .... **23 C9** 42 1N 20 59 E
Teuco →, *Argentina* **94 B3** 25 35S 60 11W
Teulon, *Canada* **71 C9** 50 23N 97 16W
Teun, *Indonesia* .... **37 F7**   6 59S 129 8 E
Teutoburger Wald, *Germany* . **16 B5** 52 5N   8 22 E
Tevere →, *Italy* .... **22 D5** 41 44N 12 14 E
Teverya, *Israel* .... **46 C4** 32 47N 35 32 E
Teviot →, *U.K.* **11 F6** 55 29N   2 38W
Tewantin, *Australia* .... **63 D5** 26 27S 153 3 E
Tewkesbury, *U.K.* **13 F5** 51 59N   2 9W

Texada I., Canada .... 70 D4　49 40N 124 25W
Texarkana, Ark., U.S.A. .. 81 J8　33 26N　94　2W
Texarkana, Tex., U.S.A. .. 81 J7　33 26N　94　3W
Texas, Australia .... 63 D5　28 49S 151　9 E
Texas □, U.S.A. .... 81 K5　31 40N　98 30W
Texas City, U.S.A. .... 81 L7　29 24N　94 54W
Texel, Neths. .... 15 A4　53　5N　4 50 E
Texline, U.S.A. .... 81 G3　36 23N 103　2W
Texoma, L., U.S.A. .... 81 J6　33 50N　96 34W
Tezin, Afghan. .... 42 B3　34 24N　69 30 E
Teziutlán, Mexico .... 87 D5　19 50N　97 22W
Tezpur, India .... 41 F18　26 40N　92 45 E
Tezzeron L., Canada ...... 70 C4　54 43N 124 30W
Tha-anne →, Canada ...... 71 A10　60 31N　94 37W
Tha Deua, Laos .... 38 D4　17 57S 102 53 E
Tha Deua, Laos .... 38 C3　19 26N 101 50 E
Tha Pla, Thailand .... 38 D3　17 48N 100 32 E
Tha Rua, Thailand .... 38 E3　14 34N 100 44 E
Tha Sala, Thailand .... 39 H2　8 40N　99 56 E
Tha Song Yang, Thailand .. 38 D1　17 34N　97 55 E
Thaba Putsoa, Lesotho .... 57 D4　29 45S　28　0 E
Thabana Ntlenyana, Lesotho .. 57 D4　29 30S　29 16 E
Thabazimbi, S. Africa ...... 57 C4　24 40S　27 21 E
Thādiq, Si. Arabia .... 44 E5　25 18N　45 52 E
Thai Binh, Vietnam .... 38 B6　20 35N 106　1 E
Thai Muang, Thailand .... 39 H2　8 24N　98 16 E
Thai Nguyen, Vietnam .... 38 B5　21 35N 105 55 E
Thailand ■, Asia .... 38 E4　16　0N 102　0 E
Thailand, G. of, Asia ...... 39 G3　11 30N 101　0 E
Thakhek, Laos .... 38 D5　17 25N 104 45 E
Thal, Pakistan .... 42 C4　33 28N　70 33 E
Thal Desert, Pakistan ...... 42 D4　31 10N　71 30 E
Thala La = Hkakabo Razi, Burma 41 E20　28 25N　97 23 E
Thalabarivat, Cambodia .. 38 F5　13 33N 105 57 E
Thallon, Australia .... 63 D4　28 39S 148 49 E
Thalu, Ko, Thailand ...... 39 b　9 26N　99 54 E
Thames, N.Z. .... 59 G5　37　7S 175 34 E
Thames →, Canada ...... 84 D2　42 20N　82 25W
Thames →, U.K. .... 13 F8　51 29N　0 34 E
Thames →, U.S.A. .... 85 E12　41 18N　72　5W
Thames Estuary, U.K. .... 13 F8　51 29N　0 52 E
Thamesford, Canada ...... 84 C4　43　4N　81　0W
Thamesville, Canada ...... 84 D3　42 33N　81 59W
Than, India .... 42 H4　22 34N　71 11 E
Than Uyen, Vietnam ...... 38 B4　22　0N 103 54 E
Thana Gazi, India .... 42 F7　27 25N　76 19 E
Thandla, India .... 42 H6　23　0N　74 34 E
Thane, India .... 40 K8　19 12N　72 59 E
Thanesar, India .... 42 D7　30　1N　76 52 E
Thanet, I. of, U.K. .... 13 F9　51 21N　1 20 E
Thangool, Australia ...... 62 C5　24 38S 150 42 E
Thanh Hoa, Vietnam ...... 38 C5　19 48N 105 46 E
Thanh Hung, Vietnam .... 39 H5　9 55N 105 43 E
Thanh Pho Ho Chi Minh, Vietnam 39 G6　10 58N 106 40 E
Thanh Thuy, Vietnam .... 38 A5　22 55N 104 51 E
Thanjavur, India .... 40 P11　10 48N　79 12 E
Thano Bula Khan, Pakistan 42 G2　25 22N　67 50 E
Thaolinta L., Canada ...... 71 A9　61 30N　96 25W
Thap Lan △, Thailand .... 38 E4　14 15N 102 16 E
Thap Sakae, Thailand .... 39 G2　11 30N　99 37 E
Thap Than, Thailand ...... 38 E2　15 27N　99 54 E
Thar Desert, India .... 42 F5　28　0N　72　0 E
Tharad, India .... 42 G4　24 30N　71 44 E
Thargomindah, Australia .. 63 D3　27 58S 143 46 E
Tharrawaddy, Burma ...... 41 L19　17 38N　95 48 E
Tharthār, Buḩayrat ath, Iraq 44 C4　34　0N　43 15 E
Tharthar, L. = Tharthār, Buḩayrat ath, Iraq .. 44 C4　34　0N　43 15 E
Tharthār, W. ath →, Iraq .. 44 C4　33 59N　43 12 E
Thásos, Greece .... 23 D11　40 40N　24 40 E
That Khe, Vietnam .... 38 A6　22 16N 106 28 E
Thatcher, Ariz., U.S.A. .... 77 K9　32 51N 109 46W
Thatcher, Colo., U.S.A. .... 81 G2　37 33N 104　7W
Thaton, Burma .... 41 L20　16 55N　97 22 E
Thaungdut, Burma .... 41 G19　24 30N　94 40 E
Thayer, U.S.A. .... 81 G9　36 31N　91 33W
Thayetmyo, Burma .... 41 K19　19 20N　95 10 E
Thazi, Burma .... 41 J20　21　0N　96　5 E
The Alberga →, Australia .. 63 D2　27　6S 135 33 E
The Bight, Bahamas ...... 89 B4　24 19N　75 24W
The Crane, Barbados ...... 89 g　13　6N　59 27W
The Dalles, U.S.A. .... 76 D3　45 36N 121 10W
The English Company's Is., Australia .... 62 A2　11 50S 136 32 E
The Frome →, Australia .. 63 D2　29　8S 137 54 E
The Great Divide = Great Dividing Ra., Australia 62 C4　23　0S 146　0 E
The Hague = 's-Gravenhage, Neths. .... 15 B4　52　7N　4 17 E
The Hamilton →, Australia 63 D2　26 40S 135 19 E
The Macumba →, Australia 63 D2　27 52S 137 12 E
The Neales →, Australia .. 63 D2　28　8S 136 47 E
The Officer →, Australia .. 61 E5　27 46S 132 30 E
The Pas, Canada .... 71 C8　53 45N 101 15W
The Range, Zimbabwe .... 55 F3　19　2S　31　2 E
The Rock, Australia ...... 63 F4　35 15S 147　2 E
The Salt L., Australia ...... 63 E3　30　6S 142　8 E
The Sandheads, India .... 43 J13　21 10N　88 20 E
The Settlement, Br. Virgin Is. 89 e　18 43N　64 22W
The Stevenson →, Australia 63 D2　27　6S 135 33 E
The Warburton →, Australia 63 D2　28　4S 137 28 E
The Woodlands, U.S.A. .. 81 K7　30　9N　95 27W
Thebes = Thívai, Greece .. 23 E10　38 19N　23 19 E
Thebes, Egypt .... 51 C12　25 40N　32 35 E
Thedford, U.S.A. .... 80 E4　41 59N 100 35W
Theebine, Australia ...... 63 D5　25 57S 152 34 E
Thekulthili L., Canada .... 71 A7　61　3N 110　0W
Thelon →, Canada .... 71 A8　64 16N　96　4W
Theodore, Australia ...... 62 C5　24 55S 150　3 E
Theodore, Canada .... 71 C8　51 26N 102 55W
Theodore, U.S.A. .... 83 K1　30 33N　88 10W
Theodore Roosevelt △, U.S.A. 80 B3　47　0N 103 25W
Theodore Roosevelt L., U.S.A. 77 K8　33 40N 111 10W
Thepha, Thailand .... 39 J3　6 52N 100 58 E
Theresa, U.S.A. .... 85 B9　44 13N　75 48W
Thermaïkós Kólpos, Greece 23 D10　40 15N　22 45 E
Thermopolis, U.S.A. ...... 76 E9　43 39N 108 13W
Thermopylae P., Greece .. 23 E10　38 48N　22 35 E
Thessalon, Canada .... 72 C3　46 20N　83 30W
Thessaloníki, Greece ...... 23 D10　40 38N　22 58 E
Thessaloníki, Gulf of = Thermaïkós Kólpos, Greece 23 D10　40 15N　22 45 E
Thetford, U.K. .... 13 E8　52 25N　0 45 E
Thetford Mines, Canada .. 73 C5　46　8N　71 18W
Theun →, Laos .... 38 C5　18 19N 104　0 E
Theunissen, S. Africa .... 56 D4　28 26S　26 43 E
Thevenard, Australia ...... 63 E1　32　9S 133 38 E

Thibodaux, U.S.A. .... 81 L9　29 48N　90 49W
Thicket Portage, Canada .. 71 B9　55 19N　97 42W
Thief River Falls, U.S.A. .. 80 A6　48　7N　96 10W
Thiel Mts., Antarctica .... 5 E16　85 15S　91　0W
Thiers, France .... 20 D5　45 52N　3 33 E
Thiès, Senegal .... 50 F2　14 50N　16 51W
Thika, Kenya .... 54 C4　1　1S　37　5 E
Thikombia, Fiji .... 59 B9　15 44S 179 55W
Thimphu, Bhutan .... 41 F16　27 31N　89 45 E
Pingvallavatn, Iceland .... 8 D3　64 11N　21　9W
Thionville, France .... 20 B7　49 20N　6 10 E
Thíra, Greece .... 23 F11　36 23N　25 27 E
Third Cataract, Sudan .... 51 E12　19 42N　30 20 E
Thirsk, U.K. .... 12 C6　54 14N　1 19W
Thiruvananthapuram = Trivandrum, India ...... 40 Q10　8 41N　77　0 E
Thisted, Denmark .... 9 H13　56 58N　8 40 E
Thistle I., Australia ...... 63 F2　35　0S 136　8 E
Thívai, Greece .... 23 E10　38 19N　23 19 E
Þjórsá →, Iceland .... 8 E3　63 47N　20 48W
Thlewiaza →, Canada .... 71 A10　60 29N　94 40W
Thmar Puok, Cambodia .. 38 F4　13 57N 103　4 E
Tho Vinh, Vietnam ...... 38 C5　19 16N 105 42 E
Thoa →, Canada .... 71 A7　60 31N 109 47W
Thoen, Thailand .... 38 D2　17 43N　99 12 E
Thoeng, Thailand .... 38 C3　19 41N 100 12 E
Thohoyandou, S. Africa .. 53 J6　22 58S　30 29 E
Tholdi, Pakistan .... 43 B7　35　5N　76　6 E
Thomas, U.S.A. .... 81 H5　35 45N　98 45W
Thomas, L., Australia .... 63 D2　26　4S 137 58 E
Thomaston, U.S.A. .... 83 J3　32 53N　84 20W
Thomasville, Ala., U.S.A. .. 83 K2　31 55N　87 44W
Thomasville, Ga., U.S.A. .. 83 K4　30 50N　83 59W
Thomasville, N.C., U.S.A. .. 83 H5　35 53N　80　5W
Thompson, Canada .... 71 B9　55 45N　97 52W
Thompson, U.S.A. .... 85 E9　41 52N　75 31W
Thompson →, Canada .... 70 C4　50 15N 121 24W
Thompson →, U.S.A. ...... 80 F8　39 46N　93 37W
Thompson Falls, U.S.A. .. 76 C6　47 36N 115 21W
Thompson Pk., U.S.A. .... 76 F2　41　0N 123　0W
Thompson Springs, U.S.A. 77 G9　38 58N 109 43W
Thompsontown, U.S.A. .. 84 F7　40 33N　77 14W
Thomson, U.S.A. .... 83 J4　33 28N　82 30W
Thomson →, Australia .. 62 C3　25 11S 142 53 E
Thong Yang, Thailand .... 39 b　9 28N　99 56 E
Þórisvatn, Iceland .... 8 D4　64 20N　18 55W
Thornaby on Tees, U.K. .. 12 C6　54 33N　1 18W
Thornbury, Canada ...... 84 B4　44 34N　80 26W
Thorne, U.K. .... 12 D7　53 37N　0 57W
Thornhill, Canada .... 70 C3　54 31N 128 32W
Thorold, Canada .... 84 C5　43　7N　79 12W
Þórshöfn, Iceland .... 8 C6　66 12N　15 20W
Thouin, C., Australia ...... 60 D2　20 20S 118 10 E
Thousand Oaks, U.S.A. .. 79 L8　34 10N 118 50W
Thrace, Turkey .... 23 D12　41　0N　27　0 E
Three Forks, U.S.A. ...... 76 D8　45 54N 111 33W
Three Hills, Canada ...... 70 C6　51 43N 113 15W
Three Hummock I., Australia 63 G3　40 25S 144 55 E
Three Points, C., Ghana .. 50 H5　4 42N　2　6W
Three Rivers, Calif., U.S.A. 78 J8　36 26N 118 54W
Three Rivers, Tex., U.S.A. 81 L5　28 28N　98 11W
Three Sisters, U.S.A. ...... 76 D3　44　4N 121 51W
Three Springs, Australia .. 61 E2　29 32S 115 45 E
Throssell, L., Australia .... 61 E3　27 33S 124 10 E
Throssell Ra., Australia .. 60 D3　22　3S 121 43 E
Thrushton △, Australia .. 63 D4　27 47S 147 40 E
Thuan Hoa, Vietnam ...... 39 H5　8 58N 105 30 E
Thubun Lakes, Canada .. 71 A6　61 30N 112　0W
Thuin, Belgium .... 15 D4　50 20N　4 17 E
Thule = Qaanaaq, Greenland 4 B4　77 40N　69　0W
Thule Air Base = Uummannaq, Greenland .... 4 B5　70 58N　52　0W
Thun, Switz. .... 20 C7　46 45N　7 38 E
Thunder B., U.S.A. .... 84 B1　45　0N　83 20W
Thunder Bay, Canada .... 72 C2　48 20N　89 15W
Thung Salaeng Luang △, Thailand .... 38 D3　16 43N 100 50 E
Thung Song, Thailand .... 39 H2　8 10N　99 40 E
Thunkar, Bhutan .... 41 F17　27 55N　91　0 E
Thuong Tra, Vietnam ...... 38 D6　16　2N 107 42 E
Thüringer Wald, Germany 16 C6　50 35N　11　0 E
Thurles, Ireland .... 10 D4　52 41N　7 49W
Thurrock □, U.K. .... 13 F8　51 31N　0 23 E
Thursday I., Australia .... 62 A3　10 30S 142　3 E
Thurso, Canada .... 72 C4　45 36N　75 15W
Thurso, U.K. .... 11 C5　58 36N　3 32W
Thurso →, U.K. .... 11 C5　58 36N　3 32W
Thurston I., Antarctica .. 5 D16　72　0S 100　0W
Thutade L., Canada ...... 70 B3　57　0N 126 55W
Thyolo, Malawi .... 55 F4　16　7S　35　5 E
Ti Tree, Australia .... 62 C1　22　5S 133 22 E
Tian Shan, Asia .... 32 B3　40 30N　76　0 E
Tianjin, China .... 35 E9　39　8N 117 10 E
Tianshui, China .... 34 G3　34 32N 105 40 E
Tianyar, Indonesia ...... 37 J18　8 12S 115 30 E
Tianzhen, China .... 34 D8　40 24N 114　5 E
Tianzhuangtai, China .... 35 D12　40 43N 122　5 E
Tiaret, Algeria .... 50 A6　35 20N　1 21 E
Tibagi, Brazil .... 95 A5　24 30S　50 24W
Tibagi →, Brazil .... 95 A5　22 47S　51　1W
Tiber = Tevere →, Italy .. 22 D5　41 44N　12 14 E
Tiberias = Teverya, Israel 46 C4　32 47N　35 32 E
Tiberias, L. = Yam Kinneret, Israel .... 46 C4　32 45N　35 35 E
Tibesti, Chad .... 51 D9　21　0N　17 30 E
Tibet = Xizang Zizhiqu □, China 32 C3　32　0N　88　0 E
Tibet, Plateau of, Asia .. 26 F12　32　0N　86　0 E
Tibni, Syria .... 44 C3　35 36N　39 50 E
Tibooburra, Australia .... 63 D3　29 26S 142　1 E
Tiburón, I., Mexico ...... 86 B2　29　0N 112 30W
Ticino →, Italy .... 20 D8　45　9N　9 14 E
Ticonderoga, U.S.A. ...... 85 C11　43 51N　73 26W
Ticul, Mexico .... 87 C7　20 20N　89 31W
Tidaholm, Sweden ...... 9 G15　58 12N　13 58 E
Tiddim, Burma .... 41 H18　23 28N　93 45 E
Tidioute, U.S.A. .... 84 E5　41 41N　79 24W
Tidjikja, Mauritania ...... 50 E3　18 29N　11 35W
Tidore, Indonesia .... 37 D7　0 40N 127 25 E
Tiegang Shuiku, China .. 33 F10　22 37N 113 53 E
Tiel, Neths. .... 15 C5　51 53N　5 26 E
Tieling, China .... 35 C12　42 20N 123 55 E
Tielt, Belgium .... 15 C3　51　0N　3 20 E
Tien Shan = Tian Shan, Asia 32 B3　40 30N　76　0 E
Tien-tsin = Tianjin, China 35 E9　39　8N 117 10 E
Tien Yen, Vietnam .... 38 B6　21 20N 107 24 E
T'ienching = Tianjin, China 35 E9　39　8N 117 10 E
Tienen, Belgium .... 15 D4　50 48N　4 57 E

Tientsin = Tianjin, China .. 35 E9　39　8N 117 10 E
Tieri, Australia .... 62 C4　23　2S 148 21 E
Tierra Amarilla, Chile .... 94 B1　27 28S　70 18W
Tierra Amarilla, U.S.A. .. 77 H10　36 42N 106 33W
Tierra Colorada, Mexico .. 87 D5　17 10N　99 35W
Tierra de Campos, Spain .. 21 A3　42 10N　4 50W
Tierra del Fuego, I. Gr. de, Argentina .... 96 G3　54　0S　69　0W
Tiétar →, Spain .... 21 C3　39 50N　6　1W
Tietê →, Brazil .... 95 A5　20 40S　51 35W
Tiffin, U.S.A. .... 82 E4　41　7N　83 11W
Tifton, U.S.A. .... 83 K4　31 27N　83 31W
Tifu, Indonesia .... 37 E7　3 39S 126 24 E
Tighina, Moldova .... 17 E15　46 50N　29 30 E
Tigil, Russia .... 29 D16　57 49N 158 40 E
Tignish, Canada .... 73 C7　46 58N　64　2W
Tigre →, Peru .... 92 D4　4 30S　74 10W
Tigre →, Venezuela ...... 92 B6　9 20N　62 30W
Tigris = Dijlah, Nahr →, Asia 44 D5　31　0N　47 25 E
Tigyaing, Burma .... 41 H20　23 45N　96 10 E
Tijara, India .... 42 F7　27 56N　76 31 E
Tijuana, Mexico .... 79 N9　32 30N 117 10W
Tikal, Guatemala .... 88 C2　17 13N　89 24W
Tikal △, Guatemala ...... 88 C2　17 23N　89 34W
Tikamgarh, India .... 43 G8　24 44N　78 50 E
Tikhoretsk, Russia ...... 19 E7　45 56N　40　5 E
Tikhvin, Russia .... 18 C5　59 35N　33 30 E
Tikiraqjuaq = Whale Cove, Canada .... 71 A10　62 10N　92 34W
Tikrīt, Iraq .... 44 C4　34 35N　43 37 E
Tiksi, Russia .... 29 B13　71 40N 128 45 E
Tilamuta, Indonesia ...... 37 D6　0 32N 122 23 E
Tilburg, Neths. .... 15 C5　51 31N　5　6 E
Tilbury, Canada .... 84 D2　42 17N　82 23W
Tilbury, U.K. .... 13 F8　51 27N　0 22 E
Tilcara, Argentina .... 94 A2　23 36S　65 23W
Tilden, U.S.A. .... 81 L5　28 27N　98 33W
Tilhar, India .... 43 F8　28　0N　79 45 E
Tilichiki, Russia .... 29 C17　60 27N 166　5 E
Tilissos, Greece .... 25 D7　35 20N　25　1 E
Till →, U.K. .... 12 B5　55 41N　2 13W
Tillamook, U.S.A. .... 76 D2　45 27N 123 51W
Tillsonburg, Canada ...... 84 D4　42 53N　80 44W
Tillyeria, Cyprus .... 25 D11　35　6N　32 40 E
Tilos, Greece .... 23 F12　36 27N　27 27 E
Tilpa, Australia .... 63 E3　30 57S 144 24 E
Tilt →, U.K. .... 11 E5　56 46N　3 51W
Tilton, U.S.A. .... 85 C13　43 27N　71 36W
Tiltonsville, U.S.A. ...... 84 F4　40 10N　80 41W
Timagami, L., Canada .... 72 C3　47　0N　80 10W
Timanfaya △, Canary Is. 24 F6　29　0N　13 46W
Timanskiy Kryazh, Russia 18 A9　65 58N　52　0 E
Timaru, N.Z. .... 59 L3　44 23S 171 14 E
Timau, Kenya .... 54 B4　0　4N　37 15 E
Timbákion, Greece ...... 25 D6　35　4N　24 45 E
Timber Creek, Australia .. 60 C5　15 40S 130 29 E
Timber Lake, U.S.A. ...... 80 C4　45 26N 101　5W
Timber Mt., U.S.A. ...... 78 H10　37　6N 116 28W
Timbuktu = Tombouctou, Mali 50 E5　16 50N　3　0W
Timi, Cyprus .... 25 E11　34 44N　32 31 E
Timimoun, Algeria ...... 50 C6　29 14N　0 16 E
Timirist, Râs, Mauritania 50 E2　19 21N　16 30W
Timiskaming, L. = Témiscamingue, L., Canada 72 C4　47 10N　79 25W
Timişoara, Romania ...... 17 F11　45 43N　21 15 E
Timmins, Canada .... 72 C3　48 28N　81 25W
Timok →, Serbia & M. .. 23 B10　44 10N　22 40 E
Timor, Asia .... 37 F7　9　0S 125　0 E
Timor Leste = East Timor ■, Asia 37 F7　8 50S 126　0 E
Timor Sea, Ind. Oc. ...... 60 B4　12　0S 127　0 E
Tin Can Bay, Australia .. 63 D5　25 56S 153　0 E
Tin Mt., U.S.A. .... 78 J9　36 50N 117 10W
Tina →, S. Africa .... 57 E4　31 18S　29 13 E
Tinaca Pt., Phil. .... 37 C7　5 30N 125 25 E
Tinajo, Canary Is. .... 24 E6　29　4N　13 42W
Tindal, Australia .... 60 B5　14 31S 132 22 E
Tindouf, Algeria .... 50 C4　27 42N　8 10W
Tinfunque △, Paraguay .. 94 A3　23 55S　60 17W
Tinggi, Pulau, Malaysia .. 39 L5　2 18N 104　7 E
Tingo Maria, Peru .... 92 E3　9 10S　75 54W
Tingrela, Ivory C. .... 50 F4　10 27N　6 25W
Tinh Bien, Vietnam ...... 39 G5　10 36N 104 57 E
Tinnevelly = Tirunelveli, India 40 Q10　8 45N　77 45 E
Tinogasta, Argentina .... 94 B2　28　5S　67 32W
Tinos, Greece .... 23 F11　37 33N　25　8 E
Tinpahar, India .... 43 G12　24 59N　87 44 E
Tintina, Argentina ...... 94 B3　27　2S　62 45W
Tintinara, Australia ...... 63 F3　35 48S 140　2 E
Tioga, N. Dak., U.S.A. .. 80 A3　48 23N 102 56W
Tioga, Pa., U.S.A. .... 84 E7　41 55N　77　8W
Tioman, Pulau, Malaysia 39 L5　2 50N 104 10 E
Tionesta, U.S.A. .... 84 E5　41 30N　79 28W
Tipongpani, India .... 41 F19　27 20N　95 55 E
Tipperary, Ireland ...... 10 D3　52 28N　8 10W
Tipperary □, Ireland .... 10 D4　52 37N　7 55W
Tipton, Calif., U.S.A. .... 78 J7　36　4N 119 19W
Tipton, Iowa, U.S.A. .... 80 E9　41 46N　91　8W
Tiptonville, U.S.A. ...... 81 G10　36 23N　89 29W
Tīrān, Iran .... 45 C6　32 45N　51　8 E
Tiranë, Albania .... 23 D8　41 18N　19 49 E
Tiraspol, Moldova ...... 17 E15　46 55N　29 35 E
Tire, Turkey .... 23 E12　38　5N　27 45 E
Tirebolu, Turkey .... 19 F6　40 58N　38 45 E
Tiree, U.K. .... 11 E2　56 31N　6 55W
Tiree, Passage of, U.K. .. 11 E2　56 30N　6 30W
Tîrgovişte = Târgovişte, Romania 17 F13　44 55N　25 27 E
Tîrgu-Jiu = Târgu-Jiu, Romania 17 F12　45　5N　23 19 E
Tîrgu Mureş = Târgu Mureş, Romania .... 17 E13　46 31N　24 38 E
Tirich Mir, Pakistan ...... 40 A7　36 15N　71 55 E
Tírnavos, Greece .... 23 E10　39 45N　22 18 E
Tirodi, India .... 40 J11　21 40N　79 44 E
Tirol □, Austria .... 16 E6　47　3N　10 43 E
Tirso →, Italy .... 22 E3　39 53N　8 32 E
Tiruchchirappalli, India .. 40 P11　10 45N　78 45 E
Tirunelveli, India .... 40 Q10　8 45N　77 45 E
Tirupati, India .... 40 N11　13 39N　79 25 E
Tiruppur, India .... 40 P10　11　5N　77 22 E
Tiruvannamalai, India .. 40 N11　12 15N　79　5 E
Tisa →, Serbia & M. .... 23 B9　45 15N　20 17 E
Tisa, India .... 43 C6　32 50N　76　9 E
Tisdale, Canada .... 71 C8　52 50N 104　0W
Tishomingo, U.S.A. ...... 81 H6　34 14N　96 41W
Tisza = Tisa →, Serbia & M. 23 B9　45 15N　20 17 E
Tit-Ary, Russia .... 29 B13　71 55N 127　2 E
Tithwal, Pakistan .... 43 B5　34 21N　73 50 E

Titicaca, L., S. Amer. .... 92 G5　15 30S　69 30W
Titule, Dem. Rep. of the Congo 54 B2　3 15N　25 31 E
Titusville, Fla., U.S.A. .. 83 L5　28 37N　80 49W
Titusville, Pa., U.S.A. .. 84 E5　41 38N　79 41W
Tivaouane, Senegal ...... 50 F2　14 56N　16 45W
Tiverton, U.K. .... 13 G4　50 54N　3 29W
Tivoli, Italy .... 22 D5　41 58N　12 45 E
Tizi-Ouzou, Algeria ...... 50 A6　36 42N　4　3 E
Tizimín, Mexico .... 87 C7　21　0N　88　1W
Tjeggelvas, Sweden ...... 8 C17　66 37N　17 45 E
Tjirebon = Cirebon, Indonesia 36 F3　6 45S 108 32 E
Tjluring, Indonesia ...... 37 J17　8 25S 114 13 E
Tjörn, Sweden .... 9 G14　58　0N　11 35 E
Tlacotalpan, Mexico .... 87 D5　18 37N　95 40W
Tlahualilo, Mexico ...... 86 B4　26 20N 103 30W
Tlaquepaque, Mexico .... 86 C4　20 39N 103 19W
Tlaxcala, Mexico .... 87 D5　19 20N　98 14W
Tlaxcala □, Mexico ...... 87 D5　19 30N　98 20W
Tlaxiaco, Mexico .... 87 D5　17 18N　97 40W
Tlemcen, Algeria .... 50 B5　34 52N　1 21W
To Bong, Vietnam .... 38 F7　12 45N 109 16 E
Toa Payoh, Singapore .... 39 d　1 20N 103 51 E
Toad →, Canada .... 70 B4　59 25N 124 57W
Toad River, Canada ...... 70 B3　58 51N 125 14W
Toamasina, Madag. ...... 57 B8　18 10S　49 25 E
Toamasina □, Madag. .. 57 B8　18　0S　49　0 E
Toay, Argentina .... 94 D3　36 43S　64 38W
Toba, Japan .... 31 G8　34 30N 136 51 E
Toba, Danau, Indonesia .. 36 D1　2 30N　97 30 E
Toba Kakar, Pakistan .... 42 D3　31 30N　69　0 E
Toba Tek Singh, Pakistan 42 D5　30 55N　72 25 E
Tobago, Trin. & Tob. .... 89 D7　11 10N　60 30W
Tobelo, Indonesia ...... 37 D7　1 45N 127 56 E
Tobermory, Canada ...... 84 A3　45 12N　81 40W
Tobermory, U.K. .... 11 E2　56 38N　6　5W
Tobi, Pac. Oc. .... 37 D8　2 40N 131 10 E
Tobin, U.S.A. .... 78 F5　39 55N 121 19W
Tobin, L., Australia ...... 60 D4　21 45S 125 49 E
Tobin, L., Canada .... 71 C8　53 35N 103 30W
Toboali, Indonesia ...... 36 E3　3　0S 106 25 E
Tobol →, Russia .... 28 D7　58 10N　68 12 E
Toboli, Indonesia .... 37 E6　0 38S 120　5 E
Tobolsk, Russia .... 28 D7　58 15N　68 10 E
Tobruk = Ţubruq, Libya .. 51 B10　32　7N　23 55 E
Tobyhanna, U.S.A. ...... 85 E9　41 11N　75 25W
Tobyl = Tobol →, Russia 28 D7　58 10N　68 12 E
Tocantinópolis, Brazil .. 93 E9　6 20S　47 25W
Tocantins □, Brazil ...... 93 F9　10　0S　48　0W
Tocantins →, Brazil .... 93 D9　1 45S　49 10W
Toccoa, U.S.A. .... 83 H4　34 35N　83 19W
Tochi →, Pakistan ...... 42 C4　32 49N　70 41 E
Tochigi, Japan .... 31 F9　36 25N 139 45 E
Tochigi □, Japan .... 31 F9　36 45N 139 45 E
Toco, Trin. & Tob. ...... 93 K16　10 50N　60 57W
Toconao, Chile .... 94 A2　23 11S　68　1W
Tocopilla, Chile .... 94 A1　22　5S　70 10W
Tocumwal, Australia .... 63 F4　35 51S 145 31 E
Tocuyo →, Venezuela .. 92 A5　11　3N　68 23W
Todd →, Australia ...... 62 C2　24 52S 135 48 E
Todeli, Indonesia .... 37 E6　1 40S 124 29 E
Todenyang, Kenya ...... 54 B4　4 35N　35 56 E
Todgarh, India .... 42 G5　25 42N　73 58 E
Todos os Santos, B. de, Brazil 93 F11　12 48S　38 38W
Todos Santos, Mexico .. 86 C2　23 27N 110 13W
Toe Hd., U.K. .... 11 D1　57 50N　7　8W
Tofield, Canada .... 70 C6　53 25N 112 40W
Tofino, Canada .... 70 D3　49 11N 125 55W
Tofua, Tonga .... 59 D11　19 45S 175　5W
Tōgane, Japan .... 31 G10　35 33N 140 22 E
Togian, Kepulauan, Indonesia 37 E6　0 20S 121 50 E
Togliatti, Russia .... 18 D8　53 32N　49 24 E
Togo ■, W. Afr. .... 50 G6　8 30N　1 35 E
Togtoh, China .... 34 D6　40 15N 111 10 E
Tōhoku □, Japan .... 30 E10　39 50N 141 45 E
Tōhōm, Mongolia ...... 34 B5　44 27N 108　2 E
Toinya, Sudan .... 51 G11　6 17N　29 46 E
Toiyabe Range, U.S.A. .. 76 G5　39 30N 117　0W
Tojikiston = Tajikistan ■, Asia 28 F8　38 30N　70　0 E
Tojo, Indonesia .... 37 E6　1 20S 121 15 E
Tōjō, Japan .... 31 G6　34 53N 133 16 E
Tok, U.S.A. .... 68 B5　63 20N 142 59W
Tok-do, Asia .... 31 F5　37 15N 131 52 E
Tokachi-Dake, Japan .... 30 C11　43 17N 142　5 E
Tokachi-Gawa →, Japan 30 C11　42 44N 143 42 E
Tokala, Indonesia ...... 37 E6　1 30S 121 40 E
Tōkamachi, Japan ...... 31 F9　37　8N 138 43 E
Tokanui, N.Z. .... 59 M2　46 34S 168 56 E
Tokara-Rettō, Japan .... 31 K4　29 37N 129 43 E
Tokarahi, N.Z. .... 59 L3　44 56S 170 39 E
Tokat, Turkey .... 19 F6　40 22N　36 35 E
Tokashiki-Shima, Japan 31 L3　26 11N 127 21 E
Tōkch'ŏn, N. Korea ...... 35 E14　39 45N 126 18 E
Tokeland, U.S.A. .... 78 D3　46 42N 123 59W
Tokelau Is., Pac. Oc. .... 64 H10　9　0S 171 45W
Tokmak, Kyrgyzstan .... 28 E8　42 49N　75 15 E
Toko Ra., Australia ...... 62 C2　23　5S 138 20 E
Tokoro-Gawa →, Japan 30 B12　44　7N 144　5 E
Tokushima, Japan ...... 31 G7　34　4N 134 34 E
Tokushima □, Japan .... 31 H7　33 55N 134　0 E
Tokuyama, Japan ...... 31 G5　34　3N 131 50 E
Tōkyō, Japan .... 31 G9　35 45N 139 45 E
Tolaga Bay, N.Z. .... 59 H7　38 21S 178 20 E
Tolbukhin = Dobrich, Bulgaria 23 C12　43 37N　27 49 E
Toledo, Brazil .... 95 A5　24 44S　53 45W
Toledo, Spain .... 21 C3　39 50N　4　2W
Toledo, Ohio, U.S.A. .. 82 E4　41 39N　83 33W
Toledo, Oreg., U.S.A. .. 76 D2　44 37N 123 56W
Toledo, Wash., U.S.A. .. 76 C2　46 26N 122 51W
Toledo, Montes de, Spain 21 C3　39 33N　4 20W
Toledo Bend Reservoir, U.S.A. 81 K8　31 11N　93 34W
Toliara, Madag. .... 57 C7　23 21S　43 40 E
Toliara □, Madag. ...... 57 C8　21　0S　45　0 E
Tolima, Colombia ...... 92 C3　4 40N　75 19W
Tolitoli, Indonesia ...... 37 D6　1　5N 120 50 E
Tollhouse, U.S.A. ...... 78 H7　37　1N 119 24W
Tolo, Teluk, Indonesia .. 37 E6　2 20S 122 10 E
Tolo Harbour, China .... 33 F11　22 28N 114 13 E
Toluca, Mexico .... 87 D5　19 20N　99 40W
Tom Burke, S. Africa .... 57 C4　23　5S　28　0 E
Tom Price, Australia .... 60 D2　22 40S 117 48 E
Tomah, U.S.A. .... 80 D9　43 59N　90 30W
Tomahawk, U.S.A. ...... 80 C10　45 28N　89 44W
Tomakomai, Japan ...... 30 C10　42 38N 141 36 E
Tomales, U.S.A. .... 78 G4　38 15N 122 53W
Tomales B., U.S.A. ...... 78 G3　38 15N 123 58W

Tomar, Portugal 21 C1 39 36N 8 25W
Tomaszów Mazowiecki, Poland 17 C10 51 30N 20 2 E
Tomatlán, Mexico 86 D3 19 56N 105 15W
Tombador, Serra do, Brazil 92 F7 12 0S 58 0W
Tombigbee →, U.S.A. 83 K2 31 8N 87 57W
Tombouctou, Mali 50 E5 16 50N 3 0W
Tombstone, U.S.A. 77 L8 31 43N 110 4W
Tombua, Angola 56 B1 15 55S 11 55 E
Tomé, Chile 94 D1 36 36S 72 57W
Tomelloso, Spain 21 C4 39 10N 3 2W
Tomini, Indonesia 37 D6 0 30N 120 30 E
Tomini, Teluk, Indonesia 37 E6 0 10S 121 0 E
Tomkinson Ranges, Australia 61 E4 26 11S 129 5 E
Tommot, Russia 29 D13 59 4N 126 20 E
Tomnop Ta Suos, Cambodia 39 G5 11 20N 104 15 E
Tomo →, Colombia 92 B5 5 20N 67 48W
Toms Place, U.S.A. 78 H8 37 34N 118 41W
Toms River, U.S.A. 85 G10 39 58N 74 12W
Tomsk, Russia 28 D9 56 30N 85 5 E
Tonalá, Mexico 87 D6 16 8N 93 41W
Tonantins, Brazil 92 D5 2 45S 67 45W
Tonasket, U.S.A. 76 B4 48 42N 119 26W
Tonawanda, U.S.A. 84 D6 43 1N 78 53W
Tonb, Iran 45 E7 26 15N 55 15 E
Tonbridge, U.K. 13 F8 51 11N 0 17 E
Tondano, Indonesia 37 D6 1 35N 124 54 E
Tondoro, Namibia 56 B2 17 45S 18 50 E
Tone →, Australia 61 F2 34 25S 116 25 E
Tone-Gawa →, Japan 31 F9 35 44N 140 51 E
Tonekābon, Iran 45 B6 36 45N 51 12 E
Tong Xian, China 34 E9 39 55N 116 35 E
Tonga ■, Pac. Oc. 59 D11 19 50S 174 30W
Tonga Trench, Pac. Oc. 64 J10 18 0S 173 0W
Tongaat, S. Africa 57 D5 29 33S 31 9 E
Tongareva, Cook Is. 65 H12 9 0S 158 0W
Tongario △, N.Z. 59 H5 39 8S 175 33 E
Tongatapu Group, Tonga 59 E12 21 0S 175 0W
Tongchŏn-ni, N. Korea 35 E14 39 50N 127 25 E
Tongchuan, China 34 G5 35 6N 109 3 E
Tongeren, Belgium 15 D5 50 47N 5 28 E
Tonggu Jiao, China 33 G10 22 22N 113 37 E
Tongguan, China 34 G6 34 40N 110 25 E
Tonghae, S. Korea 35 F15 37 29N 129 7 E
Tonghua, China 35 D13 41 42N 125 58 E
Tongjosŏn Man, N. Korea 35 E15 39 30N 128 0 E
Tongking, G. of = Tonkin, G. of, Asia 32 E5 20 0N 108 0 E
Tongliao, China 35 C12 43 38N 122 18 E
Tongling, China 33 C6 30 55N 117 48 E
Tongnae, S. Korea 35 G15 35 12N 129 5 E
Tongobory, Madag. 57 C7 23 32S 44 20 E
Tongoy, Chile 94 C1 30 16S 71 31W
Tongres = Tongeren, Belgium 15 D5 50 47N 5 28 E
Tongsa Dzong, Bhutan 41 F17 27 31N 90 31 E
Tongue →, U.K. 11 C4 58 29N 4 25W
Tongue →, U.S.A. 80 B2 46 25N 105 52W
Tongwei, China 34 G3 35 0N 105 5 E
Tongxin, China 34 F3 36 59N 105 58 E
Tongyang, N. Korea 35 E14 39 9N 126 53 E
Tongyu, China 35 B12 44 45N 123 4 E
Tonj, Sudan 51 G11 7 20N 28 44 E
Tonk, India 42 F6 26 6N 75 54 E
Tonkawa, U.S.A. 81 G6 36 41N 97 18W
Tonkin = Bac Phan, Vietnam 38 B5 22 0N 105 0 E
Tonkin, G. of, Asia 32 E5 20 0N 108 0 E
Tonle Sap, Cambodia 38 F4 13 0N 104 0 E
Tono, Japan 30 E10 39 19N 141 32 E
Tonopah, U.S.A. 77 G5 38 4N 117 14W
Tonosí, Panama 88 E3 7 20N 80 20W
Tøns →, Haryana, India 42 D7 30 30N 77 39 E
Tons →, Ut. P., India 43 F10 26 1N 83 33 E
Tønsberg, Norway 9 G14 59 19N 10 25 E
Tonto △, U.S.A. 77 K8 33 39N 111 7W
Toobanna, Australia 62 B4 18 42S 146 9 E
Toodyay, Australia 61 F2 31 34S 116 28 E
Tooele, U.S.A. 76 F7 40 32N 112 18W
Toompine, Australia 63 D3 27 15S 144 19 E
Toora, Australia 63 F4 38 39S 146 23 E
Toora-Khem, Russia 29 D10 52 28N 96 17 E
Toowoomba, Australia 63 D5 27 32S 151 56 E
Top-ozero, Russia 18 A5 65 35N 32 0 E
Top Springs, Australia 60 C5 16 37S 131 51 E
Topaz, U.S.A. 78 G7 38 41N 119 30W
Topeka, U.S.A. 80 F7 39 3N 95 40W
Topley, Canada 70 C3 54 49N 126 18W
Topocalma, Pta., Chile 94 C1 34 10S 72 2W
Topock, U.S.A. 79 L12 34 46N 114 29W
Topol'čany, Slovak Rep. 17 D10 48 35N 18 12 E
Topolobampo, Mexico 86 B3 25 40N 109 4W
Toppenish, U.S.A. 76 C3 46 23N 120 19W
Toraka Vestale, Madag. 57 B7 16 20S 43 58 E
Torata, Peru 92 G4 17 23S 70 1W
Torbalı, Turkey 23 E12 38 10N 27 21 E
Torbat-e Heydārīyeh, Iran 45 C8 35 15N 59 12 E
Torbat-e Jām, Iran 45 C9 35 16N 60 35 E
Torbay, Canada 73 C9 47 40N 52 42W
Torbay △, U.K. 13 G4 50 26N 3 31W
Tordesillas, Spain 21 B3 41 30N 5 0W
Torfaen □, U.K. 13 F4 51 43N 3 3W
Torgau, Germany 16 C7 51 34N 13 0 E
Torhout, Belgium 15 C3 51 5N 3 7 E
Tori-Shima, Japan 31 J10 30 29N 140 19 E
Torin, Mexico 86 B2 27 33N 110 15W
Torino, Italy 20 D7 45 3N 7 40 E
Torit, Sudan 51 H12 4 27N 32 31 E
Torkamān, Iran 44 B5 37 35N 47 23 E
Tormes →, Spain 21 B2 41 18N 6 29W
Tornado Mt., Canada 70 D6 49 55N 114 40W
Torneå = Tornio, Finland 8 D21 65 50N 24 12 E
Torneälv →, Sweden 8 D21 65 50N 24 12 E
Torneträsk, Sweden 8 B18 68 24N 19 15 E
Tornio, Finland 8 D21 65 50N 24 12 E
Tornionjoki →, Finland 8 D21 65 50N 24 12 E
Tornquist, Argentina 94 D3 38 8S 62 15W
Toro, Spain 24 B11 39 59N 4 8 E
Toro △, Uganda 54 C3 0 5S 30 22 E
Toro, Cerro del, Chile 94 B2 29 10S 69 50W
Toro Pk., U.S.A. 79 M10 33 34N 116 24W
Toroníios Kólpos, Greece 23 D10 40 5N 23 30 E
Toronto, Canada 84 C5 43 39N 79 20W
Toronto, U.S.A. 84 F4 40 28N 80 36W
Toronto Lester B. Pearson International ✈ (YYZ), Canada 84 C5 43 46N 79 34W
Toropets, Russia 18 C5 56 30N 31 40 E
Tororo, Uganda 54 B3 0 45N 34 12 E
Toros Dağları, Turkey 19 G5 37 0N 32 30 E

Torpa, India 43 H11 22 57N 85 6 E
Torquay, U.K. 13 G4 50 27N 3 32W
Torrance, U.S.A. 79 M8 33 50N 118 19W
Torre de Moncorvo, Portugal 21 B2 41 12N 7 8W
Torre del Greco, Italy 22 D6 40 47N 14 22 E
Torrejón de Ardoz, Spain 21 B4 40 27N 3 29W
Torrelavega, Spain 21 A3 43 20N 4 5W
Torremolinos, Spain 21 D3 36 38N 4 30W
Torrens, L., Australia 63 E2 31 0S 137 50 E
Torrens Cr. →, Australia 62 C4 22 23S 145 9 E
Torrens Creek, Australia 62 C4 20 48S 145 3 E
Torrent, Spain 21 C5 39 27N 0 28W
Torreón, Mexico 86 B4 25 33N 103 26W
Torres, Brazil 95 B5 29 21S 49 44W
Torres, Mexico 86 B2 28 46N 110 47W
Torres Strait, Australia 64 H6 9 50S 142 20 E
Torres Vedras, Portugal 21 C1 39 5N 9 15W
Torrevieja, Spain 21 D5 37 59N 0 42W
Torrey, U.S.A. 77 G8 38 18N 111 25W
Torridge →, U.K. 13 G3 51 0N 4 13W
Torridon, L., U.K. 11 D3 57 35N 5 50W
Torrington, Conn., U.S.A. 85 E11 41 48N 73 7W
Torrington, Wyo., U.S.A. 80 D2 42 4N 104 11W
Tórshavn, Færoe Is. 8 E9 62 5N 6 56W
Tortola, Br. Virgin Is. 89 e 18 19N 64 45W
Tortosa, Spain 21 B6 40 49N 0 31 E
Tortosa, C., Spain 21 B6 40 41N 0 52 E
Tortue, I. de la, Haiti 89 B5 20 5N 72 57W
Tortuguero △, Costa Rica 88 D3 10 31N 83 29W
Torūd, Iran 45 C7 35 25N 55 5 E
Toruń, Poland 17 B10 53 2N 18 39 E
Tory I., Ireland 10 A3 55 16N 8 14W
Tosa, Japan 31 H6 33 24N 133 23 E
Tosa-Shimizu, Japan 31 H6 32 52N 132 58 E
Tosa-Wan, Japan 31 H6 33 15N 133 30 E
Toscana □, Italy 22 C4 43 25N 11 0 E
Toshkent, Uzbekistan 28 E7 41 20N 69 10 E
Tostado, Argentina 94 B3 29 15S 61 50W
Tostón, Pta. de, Canary Is. 24 F5 28 42N 14 2W
Tosu, Japan 31 H5 33 22N 130 31 E
Toteng, Botswana 56 C3 20 22S 22 58 E
Totma, Russia 18 C7 60 0N 42 40 E
Totnes, U.K. 13 G4 50 26N 3 42W
Totonicapán, Guatemala 88 D1 14 58N 91 12W
Totten Glacier, Antarctica 5 C8 66 45S 116 10 E
Tottenham, Australia 63 E4 32 14S 147 21 E
Tottenham, Canada 84 B5 44 1N 79 49W
Tottori, Japan 31 G7 35 30N 134 15 E
Tottori □, Japan 31 G7 35 30N 134 12 E
Toubkal, Djebel, Morocco 50 B4 31 0N 8 0W
Tougan, Burkina Faso 50 F5 13 11N 2 58W
Touggourt, Algeria 50 B7 33 6N 6 4 E
Toul, France 20 B6 48 40N 5 53 E
Toulon, France 20 E6 43 10N 5 55 E
Toulouse, France 20 E4 43 37N 1 27 E
Toummo, Niger 51 D8 22 45N 14 8 E
Toungoo, Burma 41 K20 19 0N 96 30 E
Touraine, France 20 C4 47 20N 0 30 E
Tourcoing, France 20 A5 50 42N 3 10 E
Touriñán, C., Spain 21 A1 43 3N 9 18W
Tournai, Belgium 15 D3 50 35N 3 25 E
Tournon-sur-Rhône, France 20 D6 45 4N 4 50 E
Tours, France 20 C4 47 22N 0 40 E
Toussora, Mt., C.A.R. 52 C4 9 7N 23 14 E
Touws →, S. Africa 56 E3 33 45S 21 11 E
Touwsrivier, S. Africa 56 E3 33 20S 20 2 E
Towada, Japan 30 D10 40 37N 141 13 E
Towada-Hachimantai △, Japan 30 D10 40 28N 140 55 E
Towada-Ko, Japan 30 D10 40 28N 140 55 E
Towanda, U.S.A. 85 E8 41 46N 76 27W
Towang, India 41 F17 27 37N 91 50 E
Tower, U.S.A. 80 B8 47 48N 92 17W
Towerhill Cr. →, Australia 62 C3 22 28S 144 35 E
Towner, U.S.A. 80 A4 48 21N 100 25W
Townsend, U.S.A. 76 C8 46 19N 111 31W
Townshend I., Australia 62 C5 22 10S 150 31 E
Townsville, Australia 62 B4 19 15S 146 45 E
Towraghondi, Afghan. 40 B3 35 13N 62 16 E
Towson, U.S.A. 82 F7 39 24N 76 36W
Towuti, Danau, Indonesia 37 E6 2 45S 121 32 E
Toya-Ko, Japan 30 C10 42 35N 140 51 E
Toyama, Japan 31 F8 36 40N 137 15 E
Toyama □, Japan 31 F8 36 45N 137 30 E
Toyama-Wan, Japan 31 F8 37 0N 137 30 E
Toyapakeh, Indonesia 37 K18 8 41S 115 29 E
Toyohashi, Japan 31 G8 34 45N 137 25 E
Toyokawa, Japan 31 G8 34 48N 137 27 E
Toyonaka, Japan 31 G7 34 50N 135 28 E
Toyooka, Japan 31 G7 35 35N 134 48 E
Toyota, Japan 31 G8 35 3N 137 7 E
Tozeur, Tunisia 50 B7 33 56N 8 8 E
Tozkhurmato, Iraq 44 C5 34 56N 44 38 E
Trá Li = Tralee, Ireland 10 D2 52 16N 9 42W
Tra On, Vietnam 39 H5 9 58N 105 55 E
Trabzon, Turkey 19 F6 41 0N 39 45 E
Tracadie-Sheila, Canada 73 C7 47 30N 64 55W
Tracy, Calif., U.S.A. 78 H5 37 44N 121 26W
Tracy, Minn., U.S.A. 80 C7 44 14N 95 37W
Trafalgar, C., Spain 21 D2 36 10N 6 2W
Trail, Canada 70 D5 49 5N 117 40W
Trainor L., Canada 70 A4 60 24N 120 17W
Trákhonas, Cyprus 25 D12 35 12N 33 21 E
Tralee, Ireland 10 D2 52 16N 9 42W
Tralee B., Ireland 10 D2 52 17N 9 55W
Tramore, Ireland 10 D4 52 10N 7 10W
Tramore B., Ireland 10 D4 52 9N 7 10W
Tran Ninh, Cao Nguyen, Laos 38 C4 19 30N 103 10 E
Tranås, Sweden 9 G16 58 3N 14 59 E
Trancas, Argentina 94 B2 26 11S 65 20W
Trang, Thailand 39 J2 7 33N 99 38 E
Trangahy, Madag. 57 B7 19 7S 44 31 E
Trangan, Indonesia 37 F8 6 40S 134 20 E
Trangie, Australia 63 E4 32 4S 148 0 E
Trani, Italy 22 D7 41 17N 16 25 E
Tranoroa, Madag. 57 C8 24 42S 45 4 E
Tranqueras, Uruguay 95 C4 31 13S 55 45W
Transantarctic Mts., Antarctica 5 E12 85 0S 170 0W
Transilvania, Romania 17 E12 46 30N 24 0 E
Transilvanian Alps = Carpații Meridionali, Romania 17 F13 45 30N 25 0 E
Transylvania = Transilvania, Romania 17 E12 46 30N 24 0 E
Trápani, Italy 22 E5 38 1N 12 29 E
Trapper Pk., U.S.A. 76 D6 45 54N 114 18W
Traralgon, Australia 63 F4 38 12S 146 34 E
Trasimeno, L., Italy 22 C5 43 8N 12 6 E
Trat, Thailand 39 F4 12 14N 102 33 E

Tratani →, Pakistan 42 E3 29 19N 68 20 E
Traun, Austria 16 D8 48 14N 14 15 E
Traveller's L., Australia 63 E3 33 20S 142 0 E
Travemünde, Germany 16 B6 53 57N 10 52 E
Travers, Mt., N.Z. 59 K4 42 1S 172 45 E
Traverse City, U.S.A. 82 C3 44 46N 85 38W
Travis, L., U.S.A. 81 K5 30 24N 97 55W
Travnik, Bos.-H. 23 B7 44 17N 17 39 E
Trébbia →, Italy 20 D8 45 4N 9 41 E
Trebíč, Czech Rep. 16 D8 49 14N 15 55 E
Trebinje, Bos.-H. 23 C8 42 44N 18 22 E
Trebonne, Australia 62 B4 18 37S 146 5 E
Tregaron, U.K. 13 E4 52 14N 3 56W
Tregrosse Is., Australia 62 B5 17 41S 150 43 E
Treherne, Canada 71 D9 49 38N 98 42W
Treinta y Tres, Uruguay 95 C5 33 16S 54 17W
Trelawney, Zimbabwe 57 B5 17 30S 30 30 E
Trelew, Argentina 96 E3 43 10S 65 20W
Trelleborg, Sweden 9 J15 55 20N 13 10 E
Tremadog Bay, U.K. 12 E3 52 51N 4 18W
Tremonton, U.S.A. 76 F7 41 43N 112 10W
Tremp, Spain 21 A6 42 10N 0 52 E
Trenche →, Canada 72 C5 47 46N 72 53W
Trenčín, Slovak Rep. 17 D10 48 52N 18 4 E
Trenggalek, Indonesia 37 H14 8 3S 111 43 E
Trent →, Canada 84 B7 44 6N 77 34W
Trent →, U.K. 12 D7 53 41N 0 42W
Trento, Italy 22 A4 46 4N 11 8 E
Trenton = Quinte West, Canada 84 B7 44 10N 77 34W
Trenton, Mo., U.S.A. 80 E8 40 5N 93 37W
Trenton, N.J., U.S.A. 85 F10 40 14N 74 46W
Trenton, Nebr., U.S.A. 80 E4 40 11N 101 1W
Trepassey, Canada 73 C9 46 43N 53 25W
Tres Arroyos, Argentina 94 D3 38 26S 60 20W
Três Corações, Brazil 95 A6 21 44S 45 15W
Três Lagoas, Brazil 93 H8 20 50S 51 43W
Tres Lomas, Argentina 94 D3 36 27S 62 51W
Tres Marías, Islas, Mexico 86 C3 21 25N 106 28W
Tres Montes, C., Chile 96 F1 46 50S 75 30W
Três Pinos, U.S.A. 78 J5 36 48N 121 19W
Três Pontas, Brazil 95 A6 21 23S 45 29W
Tres Puentes, Chile 94 B1 27 50S 70 15W
Tres Puntas, C., Argentina 96 F3 47 0S 66 0W
Três Rios, Brazil 95 A7 22 6S 43 15W
Tres Valles, Mexico 87 D5 18 15N 96 8W
Tresco, U.K. 13 H1 49 57N 6 20W
Treviso, Italy 22 B5 45 40N 12 15 E
Triabunna, Australia 63 G4 42 30S 147 55 E
Triánda, Greece 25 C10 36 25N 28 10 E
Triangle, Zimbabwe 57 C5 21 2S 31 28 E
Tribal Areas □, Pakistan 42 C4 33 0N 70 0 E
Tribulation, C., Australia 62 B4 16 5S 145 29 E
Tribune, U.S.A. 80 F4 38 28N 101 45W
Trichinopoly = Tiruchchirappalli, India 40 P11 10 45N 78 45 E
Trichur, India 40 P10 10 30N 76 18 E
Trida, Australia 63 E4 33 1S 145 1 E
Trier, Germany 16 D4 49 45N 6 38 E
Trieste, Italy 22 B5 45 40N 13 46 E
Triglav, Slovenia 16 E7 46 21N 13 50 E
Tríkkala, Greece 23 E9 39 34N 21 47 E
Trikomo, Cyprus 25 D12 35 17N 33 52 E
Trikora, Puncak, Indonesia 37 E9 4 15S 138 45 E
Trim, Ireland 10 C5 53 33N 6 48W
Trincomalee, Sri Lanka 40 Q12 8 38N 81 15 E
Trindade, Brazil 93 G9 16 40S 49 30W
Trindade, I., Atl. Oc. 2 F8 20 20S 29 50W
Trinidad, Bolivia 92 F6 14 46S 64 50W
Trinidad, Cuba 88 B4 21 48N 80 0W
Trinidad, Trin. & Tob. 89 D7 10 30N 61 15W
Trinidad, Uruguay 94 C4 33 30S 56 50W
Trinidad, U.S.A. 81 G2 37 10N 104 31W
Trinidad →, Mexico 87 D5 17 49N 95 9W
Trinidad & Tobago ■, W. Indies 89 D7 10 30N 61 20W
Trinity, Canada 73 C9 48 59N 53 55W
Trinity →, Calif., U.S.A. 76 F2 41 11N 123 42W
Trinity →, Tex., U.S.A. 81 L7 29 45N 94 43W
Trinity B., Canada 73 C9 48 20N 53 10W
Trinity Hills, Trin. & Tob. 93 K15 10 16N 61 6W
Trinity Is., U.S.A. 68 C4 56 33N 154 25W
Trinity Range, U.S.A. 76 F4 40 15N 118 45W
Trinkitat, Sudan 51 E13 18 45N 37 51 E
Trinway, U.S.A. 84 F2 40 9N 82 1W
Tripoli = Tarābulus, Lebanon 46 A4 34 31N 35 50 E
Tripoli = Tarābulus, Libya 51 B8 32 49N 13 7 E
Trípolis, Greece 23 F10 37 31N 22 25 E
Tripolitania, N. Afr. 51 B8 31 0N 13 0 E
Tripura □, India 41 H18 24 0N 92 0 E
Tripylos, Cyprus 25 E11 34 59N 32 41 E
Tristan da Cunha, Atl. Oc. 49 K2 37 6S 12 20W
Trisul, India 43 D8 30 19N 79 47 E
Trivandrum, India 40 Q10 8 41N 77 0 E
Trnava, Slovak Rep. 17 D9 48 23N 17 35 E
Trochu, Canada 70 C6 51 50N 113 13W
Trodely I., Canada 72 B4 52 15N 79 26W
Troglav, Croatia 22 C7 43 56N 16 36 E
Troilus, L., Canada 72 B5 50 50N 74 35W
Trois-Pistoles, Canada 73 C6 48 5N 69 10W
Trois-Rivières, Canada 72 C5 46 25N 72 34W
Trois-Rivières, Guadeloupe 88 b 15 57N 61 40W
Troitsk, Russia 28 D7 54 10N 61 35 E
Troitsko Pechorsk, Russia 18 B10 62 40N 56 10 E
Trölladyngja, Iceland 8 D5 64 54N 17 16W
Trollhättan, Sweden 9 G15 58 17N 12 20 E
Trollheimen, Norway 8 E13 62 46N 9 1 E
Trombetas →, Brazil 93 D7 1 55S 55 35W
Tromsø, Norway 8 B18 69 40N 18 56 E
Trona, U.S.A. 79 K9 35 46N 117 23W
Tronador, Mte., Argentina 96 E2 41 10S 71 50W
Trøndelag, Norway 8 D14 64 17N 11 50 E
Trondheim, Norway 8 E14 63 36N 10 25 E
Trondheimsfjorden, Norway 8 E14 63 35N 10 30 E
Troodos, Cyprus 25 E11 34 55N 32 52 E
Troon, U.K. 11 F4 55 33N 4 39W
Tropic, U.S.A. 77 H7 37 37N 112 5W
Trostan, U.K. 10 A5 55 3N 6 10W
Trou Gras Pt., St. Lucia 89 f 13 54N 60 53W
Trout →, Canada 70 A5 61 19N 119 51W
Trout L., N.W.T., Canada 70 A4 60 40N 121 14W
Trout L., Ont., Canada 71 C10 51 20N 93 15W
Trout Lake, Canada 70 B6 56 30N 114 32W
Trout Lake, U.S.A. 78 E5 46 0N 121 32W
Trout River, Canada 73 C8 49 29N 58 8W
Trout Run, U.S.A. 84 E7 41 23N 77 3W
Trouville-sur-Mer, France 20 B4 49 21N 0 5 E
Trowbridge, U.K. 13 F5 51 18N 2 12W

Troy, Turkey 23 E12 39 57N 26 12 E
Troy, Ala., U.S.A. 83 K3 31 48N 85 58W
Troy, Kans., U.S.A. 80 F7 39 47N 95 5W
Troy, Mo., U.S.A. 80 F9 38 59N 90 59W
Troy, Mont., U.S.A. 76 B6 48 28N 115 53W
Troy, N.Y., U.S.A. 85 D11 42 44N 73 41W
Troy, Ohio, U.S.A. 82 E3 40 2N 84 12W
Troy, Pa., U.S.A. 85 E8 41 47N 76 47W
Troyes, France 20 B6 48 19N 4 3 E
Truchas Peak, U.S.A. 81 H2 35 58N 105 39W
Trucial States = United Arab Emirates ■, Asia 45 F7 23 50N 54 0 E
Truckee, U.S.A. 78 F6 39 20N 120 11W
Trudovoye, Russia 30 C6 43 17N 132 5 E
Trujillo, Honduras 88 C2 16 0N 86 0W
Trujillo, Peru 92 E3 8 6S 79 0W
Trujillo, Spain 21 C3 39 28N 5 55W
Trujillo, U.S.A. 81 H2 35 32N 104 42W
Trujillo, Venezuela 92 B4 9 22N 70 38W
Truk, Micronesia 64 G7 7 25N 151 46 E
Trumann, U.S.A. 81 H9 35 41N 90 31W
Trumansburg, U.S.A. 85 D8 42 33N 76 40W
Trumbull, Mt., U.S.A. 77 H7 36 25N 113 8W
Trundle, Australia 63 E4 32 53S 147 35 E
Trung-Phan = Annam, Vietnam 38 E7 16 0N 108 0 E
Truro, Canada 73 C7 45 21N 63 14W
Truro, U.K. 13 G2 50 16N 5 4W
Truskavets, Ukraine 17 D12 49 17N 23 30 E
Trutch, Canada 70 B4 57 44N 122 57W
Truth or Consequences, U.S.A. 77 K10 33 8N 107 15W
Trutnov, Czech Rep. 16 C8 50 37N 15 54 E
Truxton, U.S.A. 85 D8 42 45N 76 2W
Tryonville, U.S.A. 84 E5 41 42N 79 48W
Tsandi, Namibia 56 B1 17 42S 14 50 E
Tsangpo = Brahmaputra →, Asia 32 D3 23 40N 90 35 E
Tsaratanana, Madag. 57 B8 16 47S 47 39 E
Tsaratanana, Mt. de = Maromokotro, Madag. 57 A8 14 0S 49 0 E
Tsarevo = Michurin, Bulgaria 23 C12 42 9N 27 51 E
Tsau, Botswana 56 C3 20 8S 22 22 E
Tsavo East △, Kenya 54 C4 2 44S 38 47 E
Tsavo West △, Kenya 54 C4 3 19S 37 57 E
Tsentralnyy □, Russia 28 D4 52 0N 40 0 E
Tses, Namibia 56 D2 25 58S 18 8 E
Tsetserleg, Mongolia 32 B5 47 36N 101 32 E
Tshabong, Botswana 56 D3 26 2S 22 29 E
Tshane, Botswana 56 C3 24 5S 21 54 E
Tshela, Dem. Rep. of the Congo 52 E2 4 57S 13 4 E
Tshesebe, Botswana 57 C4 21 51S 27 32 E
Tshibeke, Dem. Rep. of the Congo 54 C2 2 40S 28 35 E
Tshibinda, Dem. Rep. of the Congo 54 C2 2 23S 28 43 E
Tshikapa, Dem. Rep. of the Congo 52 F4 6 28S 20 48 E
Tshilenge, Dem. Rep. of the Congo 54 D1 6 17S 23 48 E
Tshinsenda, Dem. Rep. of the Congo 55 E2 12 20S 28 0 E
Tshofa, Dem. Rep. of the Congo 54 D2 5 13S 25 16 E
Tshwane, Botswana 56 C3 22 24S 22 1 E
Tsigara, Botswana 56 C4 20 22S 25 54 E
Tsihombe, Madag. 57 D8 25 10S 45 41 E
Tsiigehtchic, Canada 68 B6 67 15N 134 0W
Tsimlyansk Res. = Tsimlyanskoye Vdkhr., Russia 19 E7 48 0N 43 0 E
Tsimlyanskoye Vdkhr., Russia 19 E7 48 0N 43 0 E
Tsinan = Jinan, China 34 F9 36 38N 117 1 E
Tsineng, S. Africa 56 D3 27 5S 23 5 E
Tsing Yi, China 33 G11 22 21N 114 6 E
Tsinghai = Qinghai □, China 32 C4 36 0N 98 0 E
Tsingtao = Qingdao, China 35 F11 36 5N 120 20 E
Tsingy de Bemaraha △, Madag. 57 B8 18 35S 45 25 E
Tsingy de Namoraka △, Madag. 57 B8 16 29S 45 25 E
Tsinjoarivo, Madag. 57 B8 19 37S 47 40 E
Tsinjomitondraka, Madag. 57 B8 15 40S 47 8 E
Tsiroanomandidy, Madag. 57 B8 18 46S 46 2 E
Tsitondroina, Madag. 57 C8 21 19S 46 0 E
Tsitsikamma △, S. Africa 56 E3 34 0S 23 40 E
Tsivory, Madag. 57 C8 24 4S 46 5 E
Tskhinvali, Georgia 19 F7 42 14N 44 1 E
Tsna →, Russia 18 D7 54 55N 41 58 E
Tsodilo Hill, Botswana 56 B3 18 49S 21 43 E
Tsogttsetsiy = Baruunsuu, Mongolia 34 C3 43 43N 105 35 E
Tsolo, S. Africa 57 E4 31 18S 28 37 E
Tsomo, S. Africa 57 E4 32 0S 27 42 E
Tsu, Japan 31 G8 34 45N 136 25 E
Tsu L., Canada 70 A6 60 40N 111 52W
Tsuchiura, Japan 31 F10 36 5N 140 15 E
Tsuen Wan, China 33 G11 22 22N 114 6 E
Tsugaru-Kaikyō, Japan 30 D10 41 35N 141 0 E
Tsumeb, Namibia 56 B2 19 9S 17 44 E
Tsumis, Namibia 56 C2 23 39S 17 29 E
Tsuruga, Japan 31 G8 35 45N 136 2 E
Tsurugi-San, Japan 31 H7 33 51N 134 6 E
Tsuruoka, Japan 30 E9 38 44N 139 50 E
Tsushima, Gifu, Japan 31 G8 35 10N 136 43 E
Tsushima, Nagasaki, Japan 31 G4 34 20N 129 20 E
Tsuyama, Japan 31 G7 35 3N 134 0 E
Tsyelyakhany, Belarus 17 B13 52 30N 25 46 E
Tual, Indonesia 37 F8 5 38S 132 44 E
Tuam, Ireland 10 C3 53 31N 8 51W
Tuamotu Arch. = Tuamotu Is., French Polynesia 65 J13 17 0S 144 0W
Tuamotu Is., French Polynesia 65 J13 17 0S 144 0W
Tuamotu Ridge, Pac. Oc. 65 K14 20 0S 138 0W
Tuao, Phil. 37 A6 17 55N 121 22 E
Tuapse, Russia 19 F6 44 5N 39 10 E
Tuas, Singapore 39 d 1 19N 103 38 E
Tuatapere, N.Z. 59 M1 46 8S 167 41 E
Tuba City, U.S.A. 77 H8 36 8N 111 14W
Tuban, Indonesia 37 G15 6 54S 112 3 E
Tubani, Botswana 56 C3 24 46S 24 18 E
Tubarão, Brazil 95 B6 28 30S 49 0W
Tubas, West Bank 46 C4 32 20N 35 22 E
Tubas →, Namibia 56 C2 24 54S 14 35 E
Tübingen, Germany 16 D5 48 31N 9 4 E
Tubruq, Libya 51 B10 32 7N 23 55 E
Tubuai Is., French Polynesia 65 K13 25 0S 150 0W
Tuc Trung, Vietnam 39 G6 11 1N 107 12 E
Tucacas, Venezuela 92 A5 10 48N 68 19W
Tuchodi →, Canada 70 B4 58 17N 123 42W
Tuckanarra, Australia 61 E2 27 7S 118 5 E
Tucson, U.S.A. 77 K8 32 13N 110 58W

Tucumán □, *Argentina* **94 B2** 26 48S 66 2W
Tucumcari, *U.S.A.* **81 H3** 35 10N 103 44W
Tucupita, *Venezuela* **92 B6**   9 2N 62 3W
Tucuruí, *Brazil* **93 D9**   3 42S 49 44W
Tucuruí, Reprêsa de, *Brazil* ... **93 D9**   4 0S 49 30W
Tudela, *Spain* **21 A5** 42 4N   1 39W
Tudmur, *Syria* .... **44 C3** 34 36N 38 15 E
Tudor, L., *Canada* **73 A6** 55 50N 65 25W
Tuen Mun, *China* .... **33 G10** 22 24N 113 59 E
Tugela →, *S. Africa* .... **57 D5** 29 14S 31 30 E
Tuguegarao, *Phil.* .... **37 A6** 17 35N 121 42 E
Tugur, *Russia* .... **29 D14** 53 44N 136 45 E
Tui, *Spain* **21 A1** 42 3N   8 39W
Tuineje, *Canary Is.* **24 F5** 28 19N 14 3W
Tukangbesi, Kepulauan,
  Indonesia .... **37 F6**   6 0S 124 0 E
Tukarak I., *Canada* **72 A4** 56 15N 78 45W
Tukayyid, *Iraq* .... **44 D5** 29 47N 45 36 E
Tukkae, Ko, *Thailand* .... **39 a**   7 51N 98 25 E
Tuktoyaktuk, *Canada* **68 B6** 69 27N 133 2W
Tukums, *Latvia* .... **9 H20** 56 58N 23 10 E
Tukuyu, *Tanzania* .... **55 D3**   9 17S 33 35 E
Tula, *Hidalgo, Mexico* **87 C5** 20 5N 99 20W
Tula, *Tamaulipas, Mexico* **87 C5** 23 0N 99 40W
Tula, *Russia* .... **18 D6** 54 13N 37 38 E
Tulancingo, *Mexico* **87 C5** 20 5N 99 22W
Tulare, *U.S.A.* **78 J7** 36 13N 119 21W
Tulare Lake Bed, *U.S.A.* **78 K7** 36 0N 119 48W
Tularosa, *U.S.A.* **77 K10** 33 5N 106 1W
Tulbagh, *S. Africa* .... **56 E2** 33 16S 19 6 E
Tulcán, *Ecuador* **92 C3**   0 48N 77 43W
Tulcea, *Romania* .... **17 F15** 45 13N 28 46 E
Tulchyn, *Ukraine* .... **17 D15** 48 41N 28 49 E
Tūleh, *Iran* .... **45 C7** 34 35N 52 33 E
Tulemalu L., *Canada* **71 A9** 62 58N 99 25W
Tuli, *Zimbabwe* .... **55 G2** 21 58S 29 13 E
Tulia, *U.S.A.* **81 H4** 34 32N 101 46W
Tulita, *Canada* **68 B7** 64 57N 125 30W
Tülkarm, *West Bank* .... **46 C4** 32 19N 35 2 E
Tulla, *Ireland* **10 D3** 52 53N   8 46W
Tullahoma, *U.S.A.* **83 H2** 35 22N 86 13W
Tullamore, *Australia* .... **63 E4** 32 39S 147 36 E
Tullamore, *Ireland* **10 C4** 53 16N   7 31W
Tulle, *France* .... **20 D4** 45 16N   1 46 E
Tullow, *Ireland* **10 D5** 52 49N   6 45W
Tully, *Australia* .... **62 B4** 17 56S 145 55 E
Tully, *U.S.A.* **85 D8** 42 48N 76 7W
Tulsa, *U.S.A.* **81 G7** 36 10N 95 55W
Tulsequah, *Canada* **70 B2** 58 39N 133 35W
Tulua, *Colombia* **92 C3**   4 6N 76 11W
Tulun, *Russia* .... **29 D11** 54 32N 100 35 E
Tulungagung, *Indonesia* ...... **37 H14** 8 5S 111 54 E
Tuma →, *Nic.* **88 D3** 13 6N 84 35W
Tumacacori △, *U.S.A.* **77 L8** 31 34N 111 3W
Tumaco, *Colombia* **92 C3**   1 50N 78 45W
Tumatumari, *Guyana* **92 B7**   5 20N 58 55W
Tumba, *Sweden* .... **9 G17** 59 12N 17 48 E
Tumba, L., *Dem. Rep. of*
  the Congo .... **52 E3**   0 50S 18 0 E
Tumbarumba, *Australia* ...... **63 F4** 35 44S 148 0 E
Tumbaya, *Argentina* **94 A2** 23 50S 65 26W
Tumbes, *Peru* **92 D2**   3 37S 80 27W
Tumbwe, *Dem. Rep. of*
  the Congo .... **55 E2** 11 25S 27 15 E
Tumby Bay, *Australia* .... **63 E2** 34 21S 136 8 E
Tumd Youqi, *China* .... **34 D6** 40 30N 110 30 E
Tumen, *China* .... **35 C15** 43 0N 129 50 E
Tumen Jiang →, *China* .... **35 C16** 42 20N 130 35 E
Tumeremo, *Venezuela* **92 B6**   7 18N 61 30W
Tumkur, *India* .... **40 N10** 13 18N 77 6 E
Tump, *Pakistan* .... **40 F3** 26 7N 62 16 E
Tumpat, *Malaysia* .... **39 J4**   6 11N 102 10 E
Tumu, *Ghana* **50 F5** 10 56N   1 56W
Tumucumaque, Serra, *Brazil* .. **93 C8**   2 0N 55 0W
Tumut, *Australia* .... **63 F4** 35 16S 148 13 E
Tumwater, *U.S.A.* **78 C4** 47 1N 122 54W
Tuna, *India* .... **42 H4** 22 59N 70 5 E
Tunapuna, *Trin. & Tob.* **93 K15** 10 38N 61 24W
Tunas de Zaza, *Cuba* **88 B4** 21 39N 79 34W
Tunbridge Wells = Royal
  Tunbridge Wells, *U.K.* .... **13 F8** 51 7N   0 16 E
Tuncurry, *Australia* .... **63 E5** 32 17S 152 29 E
Tundla, *India* .... **42 F8** 27 12N 78 17 E
Tunduru, *Tanzania* .... **55 E4** 11 8S 37 25 E
Tundzha →, *Bulgaria* .... **23 C11** 41 40N 26 35 E
Tung Chung, *China* .... **33 G10** 22 17N 113 57 E
Tung Lung Chau, *China* ...... **33 G11** 22 15N 114 17 E
Tungabhadra →, *India* .... **40 M11** 15 57N 78 15 E
Tungla, *Nic.* **88 D3** 13 24N 84 21W
Tungsten, *Canada* **70 A3** 61 57N 128 16W
Tunguska, Nizhnyaya →, *Russia* **29 C9** 65 48N 88 4 E
Tunguska, Podkamennaya →,
  Russia .... **29 C10** 61 50N 90 13 E
Tunica, *U.S.A.* **81 H9** 34 41N 90 23W
Tunis, *Tunisia* .... **50 A7** 36 50N 10 11 E
Tunisia ■, *Africa* .... **50 B6** 33 30N   9 10 E
Tunja, *Colombia* **92 B4**   5 33N 73 25W
Tunkhannock, *U.S.A.* **85 E9** 41 32N 75 57W
Tunliu, *China* .... **34 F7** 36 13N 112 52 E
Tunnel Creek △, *Australia* .... **60 C4** 17 41S 125 18 E
Tunnsjøen, *Norway* .... **8 D15** 64 45N 13 25 E
Tunungayualok I., *Canada* **73 A7** 56 0N 61 0W
Tunuyán, *Argentina* **94 C2** 33 35S 69 0W
Tunuyán →, *Argentina* **94 C2** 33 33S 67 30W
Tuolumne, *U.S.A.* **78 H6** 37 58N 120 15W
Tuolumne →, *U.S.A.* **78 H5** 37 36N 121 13W
Tūp Āghāj, *Iran* .... **44 B5** 36 3N 47 50 E
Tupā, *Brazil* **95 A5** 21 57S 50 28W
Tupelo, *U.S.A.* **83 H1** 34 16N 88 43W
Tupinambaranas, *Brazil* **92 D7**   3 0S 58 0W
Tupiza, *Bolivia* **94 A2** 21 30S 65 40W
Tupman, *U.S.A.* **79 K7** 35 18N 119 21W
Tupper, *Canada* **70 B4** 55 32N 120 1W
Tupper Lake, *U.S.A.* **85 B10** 44 14N 74 28W
Tupungato, Cerro, *S. Amer.* ... **94 C2** 33 15S 69 50W
Túquerres, *Colombia* **92 C3**   1 5N 77 37W
Tura, *Russia* .... **29 C11** 64 20N 100 17 E
Turabah, *Si. Arabia* .... **44 D4** 28 20N 43 15 E
Tūrān, *Iran* .... **45 C8** 35 39N 56 42 E
Turan, *Russia* .... **29 D10** 51 55N 95 0 E
Ţurayf, *Si. Arabia* .... **44 D3** 31 41N 38 39 E
Turda, *Romania* .... **17 E12** 46 34N 23 47 E
Turek, *Poland* .... **17 B10** 52 3N 18 30 E
Turen, *Venezuela* **92 B5**   9 17N 69 6W
Turfan = Turpan, *China* ...... **32 B3** 43 58N 89 10 E
Turfan Depression = Turpan
  Hami, *China* .... **26 E12** 42 40N 89 25 E

Turgeon →, *Canada* **72 C4** 50 0N 78 56W
Tŭrgovishte, *Bulgaria* .... **23 C12** 43 17N 26 38 E
Turgutlu, *Turkey* .... **23 E12** 38 30N 27 43 E
Turgwe →, *Zimbabwe* .... **57 C5** 21 31S 32 15 E
Turia →, *Spain* **21 C5** 39 27N   0 19W
Turiaçu, *Brazil* **93 D9**   1 40S 45 19W
Turiaçu →, *Brazil* **93 D9**   1 36S 45 19W
Turin = Torino, *Italy* .... **20 D7** 45 3N   7 40 E
Turkana, L., *Africa* .... **54 B4**   3 30N 36 5 E
Turkestan = Türkistan,
  Kazakhstan .... **28 E7** 43 17N 68 16 E
Turkey ■, *Eurasia* .... **19 G6** 39 0N 36 0 E
Turkey Creek, *Australia* ..... **60 C4** 17 2S 128 12 E
Türkistan, *Kazakhstan* .... **28 E7** 43 17N 68 16 E
Türkmenbashi, *Turkmenistan* .. **19 G9** 40 5N 53 5 E
Turkmenistan ■, *Asia* .... **28 F6** 39 0N 59 0 E
Turks & Caicos Is. ☑, *W. Indies* **89 B5** 21 20N 71 20W
Turks Island Passage, *W. Indies* **89 B5** 21 30N 71 30W
Turku, *Finland* .... **9 F20** 60 30N 22 19 E
Turkwel →, *Kenya* .... **54 B4**   3 6N 36 6 E
Turlock, *U.S.A.* **78 H6** 37 30N 120 51W
Turnagain →, *Canada* **70 B3** 59 12N 127 35W
Turnagain, C., *N.Z.* .... **59 J6** 40 28S 176 38 E
Turneffe Is., *Belize* **87 D7** 17 20N 87 50W
Turner, *U.S.A.* **76 B9** 48 51N 108 24W
Turner Pt., *Australia* .... **62 A1** 11 47S 133 32 E
Turner Valley, *Canada* **70 C6** 50 40N 114 17W
Turners Falls, *U.S.A.* **85 D12** 42 36N 72 33W
Turnhout, *Belgium* .... **15 C4** 51 19N   4 57 E
Turnor L., *Canada* **71 B7** 56 35N 108 35W
Tŭrnovo = Veliko Tŭrnovo,
  Bulgaria .... **23 C11** 43 5N 25 41 E
Turnu Măgurele, *Romania* .... **17 G13** 43 46N 24 56 E
Turnu Roşu, P., *Romania* .... **17 F13** 45 33N 24 17 E
Turpan, *China* .... **32 B3** 43 58N 89 10 E
Turpan Hami, *China* .... **26 E12** 42 40N 89 25 E
Turriff, *U.K.* **11 D6** 57 32N   2 27W
Tursāq, *Iraq* .... **44 C5** 33 27N 45 47 E
Turtle Head I., *Australia* ..... **62 A3** 10 56S 142 37 E
Turtle L., *Canada* **71 C7** 53 36N 108 38W
Turtle Lake, *U.S.A.* **80 B4** 47 31N 100 53W
Turtleford, *Canada* **71 C7** 53 23N 108 57W
Turuépano △, *Venezuela* **89 D7** 10 34N 62 43W
Turukhansk, *Russia* .... **29 C9** 65 21N 88 5 E
Tuscaloosa, *U.S.A.* **83 J2** 33 12N 87 34W
Tuscany = Toscana □, *Italy* .. **22 C4** 43 25N 11 0 E
Tuscarawas →, *U.S.A.* **84 F3** 40 24N 81 25W
Tuscarora Mt., *U.S.A.* **84 F7** 40 55N 77 55W
Tuscola, Ill., *U.S.A.* **82 F1** 39 48N 88 17W
Tuscola, Tex., *U.S.A.* **81 J5** 32 12N 99 48W
Tuscumbia, *U.S.A.* **83 H2** 34 44N 87 42W
Tuskegee, *U.S.A.* **83 J3** 32 25N 85 42W
Tustin, *U.S.A.* **79 M9** 33 44N 117 49W
Tuticorin, *India* .... **40 Q11** 8 50N 78 12 E
Tutóia, *Brazil* **93 D10** 2 45S 42 20W
Tutong, *Brunei* .... **36 D4**   4 47N 114 40 E
Tutrakan, *Bulgaria* .... **23 B12** 44 2N 26 40 E
Tuttle Creek L., *U.S.A.* **80 F6** 39 22N 96 40W
Tuttlingen, *Germany* .... **16 E5** 47 58N   8 48 E
Tutuala, *E. Timor* .... **37 F7**   8 25S 127 15 E
Tutuila, *Amer. Samoa* **59 B13** 14 19S 170 50W
Tutume, *Botswana* .... **53 J5** 20 30S 27 5 E
Tututepec, *Mexico* **87 D5** 16 9N 97 38W
Tuva □, *Russia* .... **29 D10** 51 30N 95 0 E
Tuvalu ■, *Pac. Oc.* .... **64 H9**   8 0S 178 0 E
Tuxpan, *Mexico* **87 C5** 20 58N 97 23W
Tuxtla Gutiérrez, *Mexico* **87 D6** 16 50N 93 10W
Tuy = Tui, *Spain* **21 A1** 42 3N   8 39W
Tuy An, *Vietnam* .... **38 F7** 13 17N 109 16 E
Tuy Duc, *Vietnam* .... **39 F6** 12 15N 107 27 E
Tuy Hoa, *Vietnam* .... **38 F7** 13 5N 109 10 E
Tuy Phong, *Vietnam* .... **39 G7** 11 14N 108 43 E
Tuya L., *Canada* **70 B2** 59 7N 130 35W
Tuyen Hoa, *Vietnam* .... **38 D6** 17 50N 106 10 E
Tuyen Quang, *Vietnam* .... **38 B5** 21 50N 105 10 E
Tūysarkān, *Iran* .... **45 C6** 34 33N 48 27 E
Tuz Gölü, *Turkey* .... **19 G5** 38 42N 33 18 E
Ţūz Khurmāţū = Tozkhurmato,
  Iraq .... **44 C5** 34 56N 44 38 E
Tuzigoot △, *U.S.A.* **77 J7** 34 46N 112 2W
Tuzla, *Bos.-H.* .... **23 B8** 44 34N 18 41 E
Tver, *Russia* .... **18 C6** 56 55N 35 55 E
Twain, *U.S.A.* **78 E5** 40 1N 121 3W
Twain Harte, *U.S.A.* **78 G6** 38 2N 120 14W
Tweed, *Canada* **84 B7** 44 29N 77 19W
Tweed →, *U.K.* **11 F6** 55 45N   2 0W
Tweed Heads, *Australia* ...... **63 D5** 28 10S 153 31 E
Tweedsmuir △, *Canada* **70 C3** 53 0N 126 0W
Twentynine Palms, *U.S.A.* **79 L10** 34 8N 116 3W
Twillingate, *Canada* **73 C9** 49 42N 54 45W
Twin Bridges, *U.S.A.* **76 D7** 45 33N 112 20W
Twin Falls, *Canada* **73 B7** 53 30N 64 32W
Twin Falls, *U.S.A.* **76 E6** 42 34N 114 28W
Twin Valley, *U.S.A.* **80 B6** 47 16N 96 16W
Twinsburg, *U.S.A.* **84 E3** 41 18N 81 26W
Twitchell Reservoir, *U.S.A.* ... **79 L6** 34 59N 120 19W
Two Harbors, *U.S.A.* **80 B9** 47 2N 91 40W
Two Hills, *Canada* **70 C6** 53 43N 111 52W
Two Rivers, *U.S.A.* **82 C2** 44 9N 87 34W
Two Rocks, *Australia* .... **61 F2** 31 30S 115 35 E
Twofold B., *Australia* .... **63 F4** 37 8S 149 59 E
Tyachiv, *Ukraine* .... **17 D12** 48 1N 23 35 E
Tychy, *Poland* .... **17 C10** 50 9N 18 59 E
Tyler, Minn., *U.S.A.* **80 C6** 44 18N 96 8W
Tyler, Tex., *U.S.A.* **81 J7** 32 21N 95 18W
Tynda, *Russia* .... **29 D13** 55 10N 124 43 E
Tyndall, *U.S.A.* **80 D6** 43 0N 97 50W
Tyne →, *U.K.* **12 C6** 54 59N   1 32W
Tyne & Wear □, *U.K.* **12 B6** 55 6N   1 17W
Tynemouth, *U.K.* **12 B6** 55 1N   1 26W
Tyre = Sūr, *Lebanon* .... **46 B4** 33 19N 35 16 E
Tyrifjorden, *Norway* .... **9 F14** 60 2N 10 8 E
Tyrol = Tirol □, *Austria* ..... **16 E6** 47 3N 10 43 E
Tyrone, *U.S.A.* **84 F6** 40 40N 78 14W
Tyrone □, *U.K.* **10 B4** 54 38N   7 11W
Tyrrell →, *Australia* .... **63 F3** 35 26S 142 51 E
Tyrrell, L., *Australia* .... **63 F3** 35 20S 142 50 E
Tyrrell L., *Canada* **71 A7** 63 7N 105 27W
Tyrrhenian Sea, *Medit. S.* ... **22 E5** 40 0N 12 30 E
Tysfjorden, *Norway* .... **8 B17** 68 7N 16 25 E
Tyulgan, *Russia* .... **18 D10** 52 22N 56 12 E
Tyumen, *Russia* .... **28 D7** 57 11N 65 29 E
Tywi →, *U.K.* **13 F3** 51 48N   4 21W
Tywyn, *U.K.* **13 E3** 52 35N   4 5W
Tzaneen, *S. Africa* .... **57 C5** 23 47S 30 9 E
Tzermiádhes, *Greece* .... **25 D7** 35 12N 25 29 E
Tzukong = Zigong, *China* ..... **32 D5** 29 15N 104 48 E

U

U Taphao, *Thailand* .... **38 F3** 12 35N 101 0 E
U.S.A. = United States of
  America ■, *N. Amer.* **74 C7** 37 0N 96 0W
U.S. Virgin Is. ☑, *W. Indies* .. **89 e**   18 20N 65 0W
Uatumã →, *Brazil* **92 D7**   2 26S 57 37W
Uaupés, *Brazil* **92 D5**   0 8S 67 5W
Uaupés →, *Brazil* **92 C5**   0 2N 67 16W
Uaxactún, *Guatemala* **88 C2** 17 25N 89 29W
Ubá, *Brazil* **95 A7** 21 8S 43 0W
Ubaitaba, *Brazil* **93 F11** 14 18S 39 20W
Ubangi = Oubangi →, *Dem. Rep.*
  of the Congo .... **52 E3**   0 30S 17 50 E
Ubauro, *Pakistan* .... **42 E3** 28 15N 69 45 E
Ubayyiḍ, W. al →, *Iraq* ...... **44 C4** 32 34N 43 48 E
Ube, *Japan* .... **31 H5** 33 56N 131 15 E
Úbeda, *Spain* **21 C4** 38 3N   3 23W
Uberaba, *Brazil* **93 G9** 19 50S 47 55W
Uberlândia, *Brazil* **93 G9** 19 0S 48 20W
Ubin, Pulau, *Singapore* ...... **39 d**   1 25N 103 56 E
Ubolratna Res., *Thailand* .... **38 D4** 16 45N 102 30 E
Ubombo, *S. Africa* .... **57 D5** 27 31S 32 4 E
Ubon Ratchathani, *Thailand* .. **38 E5** 15 15N 104 50 E
Ubondo, *Dem. Rep. of the Congo* **54 C2**   0 55S 25 42 E
Ubort →, *Belarus* .... **17 B15** 52 6N 28 30 E
Ubud, *Indonesia* .... **37 J18** 8 30S 115 16 E
Ubundu, *Dem. Rep. of the Congo* **54 C2**   0 22S 25 30 E
Ucayali →, *Peru* **92 D4**   4 30S 73 30W
Uchab, *Namibia* .... **56 B2** 19 47S 17 42 E
Uchiura-Wan, *Japan* .... **30 C10** 42 25N 140 40 E
Uchquduq, *Uzbekistan* .... **28 E7** 41 50N 62 50 E
Uchur →, *Russia* .... **29 D14** 58 48N 130 35 E
Ucluelet, *Canada* **70 D3** 48 57N 125 32W
Uda →, *Russia* .... **29 D14** 54 42N 135 14 E
Udagamandalam, *India* .... **40 P10** 11 30N 76 44 E
Udainagar, *India* .... **42 H7** 22 33N 76 13 E
Udaipur, *India* .... **42 G5** 24 36N 73 44 E
Udaipur Garhi, *Nepal* .... **43 F12** 27 0N 86 35 E
Udala, *India* .... **43 J12** 21 35N 86 34 E
Uddevalla, *Sweden* .... **9 G14** 58 21N 11 55 E
Uddjaur, *Sweden* .... **8 D17** 65 56N 17 49 E
Uden, *Neths.* .... **15 C5** 51 40N   5 37 E
Udgir, *India* .... **40 K10** 18 25N 77 5 E
Udhampur, *India* .... **43 C6** 33 0N 75 5 E
Údine, *Italy* .... **22 A5** 46 3N 13 14 E
Udmurtia □, *Russia* .... **18 C9** 57 30N 52 30 E
Udon Thani, *Thailand* .... **38 D4** 17 29N 102 46 E
Udupi, *India* .... **40 N9** 13 25N 74 42 E
Udzungwa △, *Tanzania* ...... **54 D4**   7 52S 36 35 E
Udzungwa Range, *Tanzania* ... **54 D4**   7 50S 36 35 E
Ueda, *Japan* .... **31 F9** 36 24N 138 16 E
Uedineniya, Os., *Russia* ..... **4 B12** 78 0N 85 0 E
Uele →, *Dem. Rep. of the Congo* **54 B1**   3 45N 24 45 E
Uelen, *Russia* **29 C19** 66 10N 170 0W
Uelzen, *Germany* .... **16 B6** 52 57N 10 32 E
Ufa, *Russia* .... **18 D10** 54 45N 55 55 E
Ufa →, *Russia* .... **18 D10** 54 40N 56 0 E
Ugab →, *Namibia* .... **56 C1** 20 55S 13 30 E
Ugalla →, *Tanzania* .... **54 D3**   5 8S 30 42 E
Ugalla River △, *Tanzania* .... **54 D3**   5 50S 31 54 E
Uganda ■, *Africa* .... **54 B3**   2 0N 32 0 E
Ugie, *S. Africa* .... **57 E4** 31 10S 28 13 E
Uglegorsk, *Russia* .... **29 E15** 49 5N 142 2 E
Ugljan, *Croatia* .... **16 F8** 44 12N 15 10 E
Uhlenhorst, *Namibia* .... **56 C2** 23 45S 17 55 E
Uhrichsville, *U.S.A.* **84 F3** 40 24N 81 21W
Uíbhist a Deas = South Uist, *U.K.* **11 D1** 57 20N   7 15W
Uíbhist a Tuath = North Uist, *U.K.* **11 D1** 57 40N   7 15W
Uig, *U.K.* **11 D2** 57 35N   6 21W
Uíge, *Angola* .... **52 F2**   7 30S 14 40 E
Uijõngbu, *S. Korea* .... **35 F14** 37 48N 127 0 E
Ŭiju, *N. Korea* .... **35 D13** 40 15N 124 35 E
Uinta Mts., *U.S.A.* **76 F8** 40 45N 110 30W
Uis, *Namibia* .... **56 C1** 21 8S 14 49 E
Uitenhage, *S. Africa* .... **56 E4** 33 40S 25 28 E
Uithuizen, *Neths.* .... **15 A6** 53 24N   6 41 E
Ujh →, *India* .... **42 C6** 32 10N 75 18 E
Ujhani, *India* .... **43 F8** 28 0N 79 6 E
Uji-guntõ, *Japan* .... **31 J4** 31 15N 129 25 E
Ujjain, *India* .... **42 H6** 23 9N 75 43 E
Ujung Pandang, *Indonesia* ... **37 F5**   5 10S 119 20 E
Uka, *Russia* .... **29 D17** 57 50N 162 0 E
Ukara I., *Tanzania* .... **54 C3**   1 50S 33 0 E
Uke-Shima, *Japan* .... **31 K4** 28 2N 129 14 E
Ukerewe I., *Tanzania* .... **54 C3**   2 0S 33 0 E
Ukhrul, *India* .... **41 G19** 25 10N 94 25 E
Ukhta, *Russia* .... **18 B9** 63 34N 53 41 E
Ukiah, *U.S.A.* **78 F3** 39 9N 123 13W
Ukmergė, *Lithuania* .... **9 J21** 55 15N 24 45 E
Ukraine ■, *Europe* .... **19 E5** 49 0N 32 0 E
Ukwi, *Botswana* .... **56 C3** 23 29S 20 30 E
Ulaan-Uul, *Mongolia* .... **34 B6** 44 13N 111 10 E
Ulaanbaatar, *Mongolia* .... **32 B5** 47 55N 106 53 E
Ulaangom, *Mongolia* .... **32 A4** 50 5N 92 10 E
Ulaanjirem, *Mongolia* .... **34 B3** 45 5N 105 30 E
Ulamba, *Dem. Rep. of the Congo* **55 D1**   9 3S 23 38 E
Ulan Bator = Ulaanbaatar,
  Mongolia .... **32 B5** 47 55N 106 53 E
Ulan Ude, *Russia* .... **29 D11** 51 45N 107 40 E
Ulaya, Morogoro, *Tanzania* ... **54 D4**   7 3S 36 55 E
Ulaya, Tabora, *Tanzania* ..... **54 C3**   4 25S 33 30 E
Ulcinj, *Serbia & M.* .... **23 D8** 41 58N 19 10 E
Ulco, *S. Africa* .... **56 D3** 28 21S 24 15 E
Ulefoss, *Norway* .... **9 G13** 59 17N   9 16 E
Ulhasnagar, *India* .... **40 K8** 19 15N 73 10 E
Uliastay, *Mongolia* .... **32 B4** 47 56N 97 28 E
Ulladulla, *Australia* .... **63 F5** 35 21S 150 29 E
Ullapool, *U.K.* **11 D3** 57 54N   5 9W
Ullswater, *U.K.* **12 C5** 54 34N   2 52W
Ullŭng-do, *S. Korea* .... **35 F16** 37 30N 130 30 E
Ulm, *Germany* .... **16 D5** 48 23N   9 58 E
Ulonguè, *Mozam.* .... **55 E3** 14 37S 34 19 E
Ulricehamn, *Sweden* .... **9 H15** 57 46N 13 26 E
Ulsan, *S. Korea* .... **35 G15** 35 20N 129 15 E
Ulsta, *U.K.* **11 A7** 60 30N   1 9W
Ulster □, *U.K.* **10 B5** 54 35N   6 30W
Ulubat Gölü, *Turkey* .... **23 D13** 40 9N 28 35 E
Uludağ, *Turkey* .... **23 D13** 40 4N 29 13 E
Uluguru Mts., *Tanzania* ...... **54 D4**   7 15S 37 40 E
Ulungur He →, *China* .... **32 B3** 47 1N 87 24 E
Uluru = Ayers Rock, *Australia* **61 E5** 25 23S 131 5 E
Uluru-Kata Tjuta △, *Australia* **61 E5** 25 30S 131 5 E
Ulutau, *Kazakhstan* .... **28 E7** 48 39N 67 1 E
Uluwatu, *Indonesia* .... **37 K18** 8 50S 115 5 E

Ulva, *U.K.* **11 E2** 56 29N   6 13W
Ulverston, *U.K.* **12 C4** 54 13N   3 5W
Ulverstone, *Australia* .... **63 G4** 41 11S 146 11 E
Ulya, *Russia* .... **29 D15** 59 10N 142 0 E
Ulyanovsk = Simbirsk, *Russia* . **18 D8** 54 20N 48 25 E
Ulyasutay = Uliastay, *Mongolia* **32 B4** 47 56N 97 28 E
Ulysses, *U.S.A.* **81 G4** 37 35N 101 22W
Umala, *Bolivia* **92 G5** 17 25S 68 5W
Uman, *Ukraine* .... **17 D16** 48 40N 30 12 E
Umaria, *India* .... **41 H12** 23 35N 80 50 E
Umarkot, *Pakistan* .... **40 G6** 25 15N 69 40 E
Umarpada, *India* .... **42 J5** 21 27N 73 30 E
Umatilla, *U.S.A.* **76 D4** 45 55N 119 21W
Umba, *Russia* .... **18 A5** 66 42N 34 11 E
Umbagog L., *U.S.A.* **85 B13** 44 46N 71 3W
Umbakumba, *Australia* .... **62 A2** 13 47S 136 50 E
Umbrella Mts., *N.Z.* .... **59 L2** 45 35S 169 5 E
Ume älv →, *Sweden* .... **8 E19** 63 45N 20 20 E
Umeå, *Sweden* .... **8 E19** 63 45N 20 20 E
Umera, *Indonesia* .... **37 E7**   0 12S 129 37 E
Umfolozi □, *S. Africa* .... **57 D5** 28 18S 31 50 E
Umfuli →, *Zimbabwe* .... **55 F2** 17 30S 29 23 E
Umfurudzi △, *Zimbabwe* ..... **55 F3** 17 6S 31 40 E
Umgusa, *Zimbabwe* .... **55 F2** 19 29S 27 52 E
Umkomaas, *S. Africa* .... **57 E5** 30 13S 30 48 E
Umlazi, *S. Africa* .... **53 L6** 29 59S 30 54 E
Umm ad Daraj, J., *Jordan* .... **46 C4** 32 18S 35 48 E
Umm al Qaywayn, *U.A.E.* ..... **45 E7** 25 30N 55 35 E
Umm al Qittayn, *Jordan* ...... **46 C5** 32 18N 36 40 E
Umm Bāb, *Qatar* .... **45 E6** 25 12N 50 48 E
Umm Durman = Omdurmân,
  Sudan .... **51 E12** 15 40N 32 28 E
Umm el Fahm, *Israel* .... **46 C4** 32 31N 35 9 E
Umm Keddada, *Sudan* .... **51 F11** 13 33N 26 35 E
Umm Lajj, *Si. Arabia* .... **44 E3** 25 0N 37 23 E
Umm Ruwaba, *Sudan* .... **51 F12** 12 50N 31 20 E
Umnak I., *U.S.A.* **68 C3** 53 15N 168 20W
Umniati →, *Zimbabwe* .... **55 F2** 16 49S 28 45 E
Umpqua →, *U.S.A.* **76 E1** 43 40N 124 12W
Umreth, *India* .... **42 H5** 22 41N 73 4 E
Umtata, *S. Africa* .... **57 E4** 31 36S 28 49 E
Umuarama, *Brazil* **95 A5** 23 45S 53 20W
Umvukwe Ra., *Zimbabwe* ..... **55 F3** 16 45S 30 45 E
Umzimvubu, *S. Africa* .... **57 E4** 31 38S 29 33 E
Umzingwane →, *Zimbabwe* ... **55 G2** 22 12S 29 56 E
Umzinto, *S. Africa* .... **57 E5** 30 15S 30 45 E
Una, *India* .... **42 J4** 20 46N 71 8 E
Una →, *Bos.-H.* .... **16 C7** 45 0N 16 20 E
Unadilla, *U.S.A.* **85 D9** 42 20N 75 19W
Unalakleet, *U.S.A.* **68 B3** 63 52N 160 47W
Unalaska, *U.S.A.* **68 C3** 53 53N 166 32W
Unalaska I., *U.S.A.* **68 C3** 53 35N 166 50W
'Unayzah, Si. Arabia .... **44 E4** 26 6N 43 58 E
'Unayzah, J., Asia .... **44 C3** 32 12N 39 18 E
Uncía, *Bolivia* **92 G5** 18 25S 66 40W
Uncompahgre Peak, *U.S.A.* ... **77 G10** 38 4N 107 28W
Uncompahgre Plateau, *U.S.A.* . **77 G9** 38 16N 108 20W
Undara Volcanic △, *Australia* . **62 B3** 18 14S 144 41 E
Underbool, *Australia* .... **63 F3** 35 10S 141 51 E
Ungarie, *Australia* .... **63 E4** 33 38S 146 56 E
Ungarra, *Australia* .... **63 E2** 34 12S 136 2 E
Ungava, Pén. d', *Canada* **69 C12** 60 0N 74 0W
Ungava B., *Canada* **69 C13** 59 30N 67 30W
Ungeny = Ungheni, *Moldova* .. **17 E14** 47 11N 27 51 E
Unggi, *N. Korea* .... **35 C16** 42 16N 130 28 E
Ungheni, *Moldova* .... **17 E14** 47 11N 27 51 E
Ungwana B., *Kenya* .... **54 C5**   2 40S 40 20 E
União da Vitória, *Brazil* **95 B5** 26 13S 51 5W
Unimak I., *U.S.A.* **68 C3** 54 45N 164 0W
Union, Miss., *U.S.A.* **81 J10** 32 34N 89 7W
Union, Mo., *U.S.A.* **80 F9** 38 27N 91 0W
Union, S.C., *U.S.A.* **83 H5** 34 43N 81 37W
Union City, Calif., *U.S.A.* **78 H4** 37 36N 122 1W
Union City, N.J., *U.S.A.* **85 F10** 40 45N 74 2W
Union City, Pa., *U.S.A.* **84 E5** 41 54N 79 51W
Union City, Tenn., *U.S.A.* **81 G10** 36 26N 89 3W
Union Gap, *U.S.A.* **76 C3** 46 33N 120 28W
Union Springs, *U.S.A.* **83 J3** 32 9N 85 43W
Uniondale, *S. Africa* .... **56 E3** 33 39S 23 7 E
Uniontown, *U.S.A.* **82 F6** 39 54N 79 44W
Unionville, *U.S.A.* **80 E8** 40 29N 93 1W
United Arab Emirates ■, *Asia* . **45 F7** 23 50N 54 0 E
United Kingdom ■, *Europe* ... **14 E6** 53 0N   2 0W
United States of America ■,
  N. Amer. **74 C7** 37 0N 96 0W
Unity, *Canada* **71 C7** 52 30N 109 5W
University Park, *U.S.A.* **77 K10** 32 17N 106 45W
Unjha, *India* .... **42 H5** 23 46N 72 24 E
Unnao, *India* .... **43 F9** 26 35N 80 30 E
Unsengedsi →, *Zimbabwe* .... **55 F3** 15 43S 31 14 E
Unst, *U.K.* **11 A8** 60 44N   0 53W
Unuk →, *Canada* **70 B2** 56 5N 131 3W
Unzen-Amakusa △, *Japan* .... **31 H5** 32 15S 130 10 E
Uozu, *Japan* .... **31 F8** 36 48N 137 24 E
Upata, *Venezuela* **92 B6**   8 1N 62 24W
Upemba △, *Dem. Rep. of*
  the Congo .... **55 D2**   9 0S 26 35 E
Upemba, L., *Dem. Rep. of*
  the Congo .... **55 D2**   8 30S 26 20 E
Upernavik, *Greenland* **4 B5** 72 49N 56 20W
Upington, *S. Africa* .... **56 D3** 28 25S 21 15 E
Upleta, *India* .... **42 J4** 21 46N 70 16 E
'Upolu, *Samoa* **59 A13** 13 58S 172 0W
Upper Alkali L., *U.S.A.* **76 F3** 41 47N 120 38W
Upper Arrow L., *Canada* **70 C5** 50 30N 117 50W
Upper Foster L., *Canada* **71 B7** 56 47N 105 20W
Upper Hutt, *N.Z.* .... **59 J5** 41 8S 175 5 E
Upper Klamath L., *U.S.A.* **76 E3** 42 25N 121 55W
Upper Lake, *U.S.A.* **78 F4** 39 10N 122 54W
Upper Manzanilla, *Trin. & Tob.* **93 K15** 10 31N 61 4W
Upper Missouri River Breaks △,
  U.S.A. **76 C9** 47 50N 108 55W
Upper Musquodoboit, *Canada* . **73 C7** 45 10N 62 58W
Upper Red L., *U.S.A.* **80 A7** 48 8N 94 45W
Upper Sandusky, *U.S.A.* **84 E2** 40 50N 83 17W
Upper Volta = Burkina Faso ■,
  Africa **50 F5** 12 0N   1 0W
Uppland, *Sweden* .... **9 F17** 59 59N 17 48 E
Uppsala, *Sweden* .... **9 G17** 59 53N 17 38 E
Upshi, *India* .... **43 C7** 33 48N 77 52 E
Upstart, C., *Australia* .... **62 B4** 19 41S 147 45 E
Upton, *U.S.A.* **80 C2** 44 6N 104 38W
Uqsuqtuuq = Gjoa Haven,
  Canada **68 B10** 68 38N 95 53W
Ur, *Iraq* .... **44 D5** 30 55N 46 25 E
Urad Qianqi, *China* .... **34 D5** 40 40N 108 30 E
Urakawa, *Japan* .... **30 C11** 42 9N 142 47 E

ral = Uralskiy □, Russia ...... 28 C7 64 0N 70 0 E
ral = Zhayyq ➜, Kazakhstan . 19 E9 47 0N 51 48 E
ral, Australia .... 63 E4 33 21S 146 12 E
ral Mts. = Uralskie Gory,
  Eurasia .... 18 C10 60 0N 59 0 E
ralla, Australia .... 63 E5 30 37S 151 29 E
ralsk = Oral, Kazakhstan ... 19 D9 51 20N 51 20 E
ralskie Gory, Eurasia .... 18 C10 60 0N 59 0 E
ralskiy □, Russia .... 28 C7 64 0N 70 0 E
rambo, Tanzania .... 54 D3 5 4S 32 0 E
randangi, Australia .... 62 C2 21 32S 138 14 E
ranium City, Canada 71 B7 59 34N 108 37W
raricoera ➜, Brazil 92 C6 3 2N 60 30W
rawa, Japan .... 31 G9 35 50N 139 40 E
ray'irah, Si. Arabia .... 45 E6 25 57N 48 53 E
rbana, Ill., U.S.A. 82 E1 40 7N 88 12W
rbana, Ohio, U.S.A. 82 E4 40 7N 83 45W
rbino, Italy .... 22 C5 43 43N 12 38 E
rbión, Picos de, Spain 21 A4 42 1N 2 52W
rcos, Peru 92 F4 13 40S 71 38W
rdinarrain, Argentina 94 C4 32 37S 58 52W
rdzhar, Kazakhstan .... 28 E9 47 5N 81 38 E
re ➜, U.K. 12 C6 54 5N 1 20W
res, Mexico 86 B2 29 30N 110 30W
rewera △, N.Z. .... 59 H6 38 29S 177 7 E
rfa = Sanliurfa, Turkey ..... 19 G6 37 12N 38 50 E
rganch, Uzbekistan .... 28 E7 41 40N 60 41 E
rgench = Urganch, Uzbekistan 28 E7 41 40N 60 41 E
rgüp, Turkey .... 44 B2 38 38N 34 56 E
ri, India .... 43 B6 34 8N 74 2 E
ribia, Colombia 92 A4 11 43N 72 16W
riondo, Bolivia 94 A3 21 41S 64 41W
rique, Mexico 86 B3 27 13N 107 55W
rique ➜, Mexico 86 B3 26 29N 107 58W
rk, Neths. .... 15 B5 52 39N 5 36 E
rmia = Orūmīyeh, Iran ..... 44 B5 37 40N 45 0 E
rmia, L. = Orūmīyeh,
  Daryācheh-ye, Iran ...... 44 B5 37 50N 45 30 E
roševac, Serbia & M. .... 23 C9 42 23N 21 10 E
royan, Montanas de,
  Puerto Rico .... 89 d 18 12N 67 0W
ruaçu, Brazil 93 F9 14 30S 49 10W
ruapan, Mexico 86 D4 19 30N 102 0W
rubamba ➜, Peru 92 F4 10 43S 73 48W
ruçara, Brazil 92 D7 2 32S 57 45W
ruçuí, Brazil 93 E10 7 20S 44 28W
ruguai ➜, Brazil 95 B5 26 0S 53 30W
ruguaiana, Brazil 94 B4 29 50S 57 0W
ruguay ■, S. Amer. 94 C4 32 30S 56 30W
ruguay ➜, S. Amer. 94 C4 34 12S 58 18W
rumchi = Ürümqi, China ... 28 E9 43 45N 87 45 E
rümqi, China .... 28 E9 43 45N 87 45 E
rup, Ostrov, Russia .... 29 E16 46 0N 151 0 E
rus ➜, Russia .... 18 A10 66 16N 59 49 E
ryak, Turkey .... 19 G4 38 43N 29 28 E
sakos, Namibia .... 56 C2 21 54S 15 31 E
sedom, Germany .... 16 B8 53 55N 14 2 E
seless Loop, Australia ...... 61 E1 26 8S 113 23 E
sh-Tobe, Kazakhstan .... 28 E8 45 16N 78 0 E
shakova, Ostrov, Russia .... 4 A12 82 0N 80 0 E
shant = Ouessant, Î. d', France 20 B1 48 28N 5 6W
shashi, Tanzania .... 54 C3 1 59S 33 57 E
shibuka, Japan .... 31 H5 33 11N 130 1 E
shuaia, Argentina 96 G3 54 50S 68 23W
shumun, Russia .... 29 D13 52 47N 126 32 E
sk, Canada 70 C3 54 38N 128 26W
sk ➜, U.K. 13 F5 51 33N 2 58W
ska, India .... 43 F10 27 12N 83 7 E
sman, Russia .... 18 D6 52 5N 39 48 E
soke, Tanzania .... 54 D3 5 8S 32 24 E
solye Sibirskoye, Russia ... 29 D11 52 48N 103 40 E
spallata, P. de, Argentina . 94 C2 32 37S 69 22W
spenskiy, Kazakhstan .... 28 E8 48 41N 72 43 E
ssuri ➜, Asia .... 30 A7 48 27N 135 0 E
ssuriysk, Russia .... 29 E14 43 48N 131 59 E
ssurka, Russia .... 30 B6 45 12N 133 31 E
st-Bolsheretsk, Russia .... 29 D16 52 50N 156 15 E
st-Chaun, Russia .... 29 C18 68 47N 170 30 E
st-Ilimsk, Russia .... 29 D11 58 3N 102 39 E
st-Ishim, Russia .... 28 D8 57 45N 71 10 E
st-Kamchatsk, Russia .... 29 D17 56 10N 162 28 E
st-Kamenogorsk = Öskemen,
  Kazakhstan .... 28 E9 50 0N 82 36 E
st-Khayryuzovo, Russia ..... 29 D16 57 15N 156 45 E
st-Kut, Russia .... 29 D11 56 50N 105 42 E
st-Kuyga, Russia .... 29 B14 70 1N 135 43 E
st-Maya, Russia .... 29 C14 60 30N 134 28 E
st-Mil, Russia .... 29 D14 59 40N 133 11 E
st-Nera, Russia .... 29 C15 64 35N 143 15 E
st-Nyukzha, Russia .... 29 D13 56 34N 121 37 E
st-Olenek, Russia .... 29 B12 73 0N 120 5 E
st-Omchug, Russia .... 29 C15 61 9N 149 38 E
st-Port, Russia .... 28 C9 69 40N 84 26 E
st-Tsilma, Russia .... 18 A9 65 28N 52 11 E
st Urt = Ustyurt Plateau, Asia 28 E6 44 0N 55 0 E
st-Usa, Russia .... 18 A10 66 2N 56 57 E
st-Vorkuta, Russia .... 18 A11 67 24N 64 0 E
stí nad Labem, Czech Rep. . 16 C8 50 41N 14 3 E
stica, Italy .... 22 E5 38 42N 13 11 E
stinov = Izhevsk, Russia .... 18 C9 56 51N 53 14 E
styurt Plateau, Asia .... 28 E6 44 0N 55 0 E
su, China .... 32 B3 44 27N 84 40 E
suki, Japan .... 31 H5 33 8N 131 49 E
sulután, El Salv. 88 D2 13 25N 88 28W
sumacinta ➜, Mexico 87 D6 17 0N 91 0W
sumbura = Bujumbura, Burundi 54 C2 3 16S 29 18 E
sure, Tanzania .... 54 C3 4 40S 34 22 E
sutuo ➜, Mozam. .... 57 D5 26 48S 32 7 E
ta, Indonesia .... 37 E9 4 33S 136 0 E
tah □, U.S.A. 76 G8 39 20N 111 30W
tah L., U.S.A. 76 F8 40 10N 111 58W
tara, Selat, Malaysia .... 39 c 5 28N 100 20 E
tarni, India .... 42 F4 26 5N 71 58 E
tatlan, Guatemala 88 C1 15 2N 91 11W
te Creek ➜, U.S.A. 81 H3 35 21N 103 50W
tena, Lithuania .... 9 J21 55 27N 25 40 E
tete, Tanzania .... 54 D4 8 0S 38 45 E
thai Thani, Thailand .... 38 E3 15 22N 100 3 E
thal, Pakistan .... 42 G2 25 44N 66 40 E
tiariti, Brazil 92 F7 13 0S 58 10W
tica, N.Y., U.S.A. 85 C9 43 6N 75 14W
tica, Ohio, U.S.A. 84 F2 40 14N 82 27W
tikuma, L., Canada 70 B5 55 50N 115 30W
topia, Australia .... 62 C1 22 14S 134 33 E
traula, India .... 43 F10 27 19N 82 25 E

Utrecht, Neths. .... 15 B5 52 5N 5 8 E
Utrecht, S. Africa .... 57 D5 27 38S 30 20 E
Utrecht □, Neths. .... 15 B5 52 6N 5 7 E
Utrera, Spain 21 D3 37 12N 5 48W
Utsjoki, Finland .... 8 B22 69 51N 26 59 E
Utsunomiya, Japan .... 31 F9 36 30N 139 50 E
Uttar Pradesh □, India ..... 43 F9 27 0N 80 0 E
Uttaradit, Thailand .... 38 D3 17 36N 100 5 E
Uttaranchal □, India .... 43 D8 30 0N 79 30 E
Uttoxeter, U.K. 12 E6 52 54N 1 52W
Utuado, Puerto Rico .... 89 d 18 16N 66 42W
Uummannaq, Greenland 4 B4 77 0N 69 0W
Uummannaq, Greenland 4 B5 70 58N 52 0W
Uummannarsuaq = Nunap Isua,
  Greenland 69 C15 59 48N 43 55W
Uusikaarlepyy, Finland ...... 8 E20 63 32N 22 31 E
Uusikaupunki, Finland .... 9 F19 60 47N 21 25 E
Uva, Russia .... 18 C9 56 59N 52 13 E
Uvalde, U.S.A. 81 L5 29 13N 99 47W
Uvat, Russia .... 28 D7 59 5N 68 50 E
Uvinza, Tanzania .... 54 D3 5 5S 30 24 E
Uvira, Dem. Rep. of the Congo 54 C2 3 22S 29 3 E
'Uwairidh, Ḥarrat al, Si. Arabia 44 E3 26 50N 38 0 E
Uwajima, Japan .... 31 H6 33 10N 132 35 E
Uwanda △, Tanzania .... 54 D3 7 46S 32 0 E
Uweinat, Jebel, Sudan .... 51 D10 21 54N 24 58 E
Uxbridge, Canada 84 B5 44 6N 79 7W
Uxin Qi, China .... 34 E5 38 50N 109 5 E
Uxmal, Mexico 87 C7 20 22N 89 46W
Uxmal, Ruinas, Mexico 87 C7 20 22N 89 46W
Üydzin, Mongolia .... 34 B4 44 9N 107 0 E
Uyo, Nigeria .... 50 G7 5 1N 7 53 E
Uyûn Mûsa, Egypt .... 46 F1 29 53N 32 40 E
Uyuni, Bolivia 92 H5 20 28S 66 47W
Uzbekistan ■, Asia .... 28 E7 41 30N 65 0 E
Uzen, Kazakhstan .... 19 F9 43 29N 52 54 E
Uzen, Mal ➜, Kazakhstan .. 19 E8 49 4N 49 44 E
Uzerche, France .... 20 D4 45 25N 1 34 E
Uzh ➜, Ukraine .... 17 C16 51 15N 30 12 E
Uzhgorod = Uzhhorod, Ukraine 17 D12 48 36N 22 18 E
Uzhhorod, Ukraine .... 17 D12 48 36N 22 18 E
Užice, Serbia & M. .... 23 C8 43 55N 19 50 E
Uzunköprü, Turkey .... 23 D12 41 16N 26 43 E

V

Vaal ➜, S. Africa .... 56 D3 29 4S 23 38 E
Vaal Dam, S. Africa .... 57 D4 27 0S 28 14 E
Vaalbos △, S. Africa .... 56 D3 28 22S 24 20 E
Vaalwater, S. Africa .... 57 C4 24 15S 28 8 E
Vaasa, Finland .... 8 E19 63 6N 21 38 E
Vác, Hungary .... 17 E10 47 49N 19 10 E
Vacaria, Brazil 95 B5 28 31S 50 52W
Vacaville, U.S.A. 78 G5 38 21N 121 59W
Vach = Vakh ➜, Russia .... 28 C8 60 45N 76 45 E
Vache, Î. à, Haiti 89 C5 18 2N 73 35W
Vadnagar, India .... 42 H5 23 47N 72 40 E
Vadodara, India .... 42 H5 22 20N 73 10 E
Vadsø, Norway .... 8 A23 70 3N 29 50 E
Vaduz, Liech. .... 20 C8 47 8N 9 31 E
Værøy, Norway .... 8 C15 67 40N 12 40 E
Vágar, Færøe Is. 8 E9 62 5N 7 15W
Vågsfjorden, Norway .... 8 B17 68 50N 16 50 E
Váh ➜, Slovak Rep. .... 17 D9 47 43N 18 7 E
Vahsel B., Antarctica 5 D1 75 0S 35 0W
Vái, Greece .... 25 D8 35 15N 26 18 E
Vaigach, Russia .... 28 B6 70 10N 59 0 E
Vail, U.S.A. 74 C5 39 40N 106 20W
Vaisali ➜, India .... 43 F8 26 28N 78 53 E
Vakh ➜, Russia .... 28 C8 60 45N 76 45 E
Val-d'Or, Canada 72 C4 48 7N 77 47W
Val Marie, Canada 71 D7 49 15N 107 45W
Valahia, Romania .... 17 F13 44 35N 25 0 E
Valandovo, Macedonia ...... 23 D10 41 19N 22 34 E
Valcheta, Argentina 96 E3 40 40S 66 8W
Valdai Hills = Valdayskaya
  Vozvyshennost, Russia .. 18 C5 57 0N 33 30 E
Valdayskaya Vozvyshennost,
  Russia .... 18 C5 57 0N 33 30 E
Valdepeñas, Spain 21 C4 38 43N 3 25W
Valdés, Pen., Argentina 96 E4 42 30S 63 45W
Valdez, U.S.A. 68 B5 61 7N 146 16W
Valdivia, Chile 96 D2 39 50S 73 14W
Valdosta, U.S.A. 83 K4 30 50N 83 17W
Valdres, Norway .... 9 F13 61 5N 9 5 E
Vale, U.S.A. 76 E5 43 59N 117 15W
Vale of Glamorgan □, U.K. . 13 F4 51 28N 3 25W
Valemount, Canada 70 C5 52 50N 119 17W
Valença, Brazil 93 F11 13 20S 39 5W
Valença do Piauí, Brazil 93 E10 6 20S 41 45W
Valence, France .... 20 D6 44 57N 4 54 E
Valencia, Spain 21 C5 39 27N 0 23W
Valencia, Trin. & Tob. 93 K15 10 39N 61 11W
Valencia, U.S.A. 77 J10 34 48N 106 43W
Valencia, Venezuela 92 A5 10 11N 68 0W
Valencia □, Spain 21 C5 39 20N 0 40W
Valencia, G. de, Spain ...... 21 C6 39 30N 0 20 E
Valencia de Alcántara, Spain 21 C2 39 25N 7 14W
Valencia I., Ireland 10 E1 51 54N 10 22W
Valenciennes, France .... 20 A5 50 20N 3 34 E
Valentim, Sa. do, Brazil 93 E10 6 0S 43 30W
Valentin, Russia .... 30 C7 43 8N 134 17 E
Valentine, U.S.A. 81 K2 30 35N 104 30W
Valera, Venezuela 92 B4 9 19N 70 37W
Valga, Estonia .... 9 H22 57 47N 26 2 E
Valier, U.S.A. 76 B7 48 18N 112 16W
Valjevo, Serbia & M. .... 23 B8 44 18N 19 53 E
Valka, Latvia .... 9 H21 57 42N 25 57 E
Valkeakoski, Finland .... 9 F20 61 16N 24 2 E
Valkenswaard, Neths. .... 15 C5 51 21N 5 29 E
Vall de Uxó = La Vall d'Uixó,
  Spain 21 C5 39 49N 0 15W
Valladolid, Mexico 87 C7 20 40N 88 11W
Valladolid, Spain 21 B3 41 38N 4 43W
Valldemossa, Spain .... 24 B9 39 43N 2 37 E
Valle de la Pascua, Venezuela 92 B5 9 13N 66 0W
Valle de las Palmas, Mexico 79 N10 32 20N 116 43W
Valle de Santiago, Mexico .. 86 C4 20 25N 101 15W
Valle de Suchil, Mexico 86 C4 23 38N 103 55W
Valle de Zaragoza, Mexico . 86 B3 27 28N 105 49W
Valle Fértil, Sierra del, Argentina 94 C2 30 20S 68 0W
Valle Gran Rey, Canary Is. . 24 F2 28 5N 17 20W
Valle Hermoso, Mexico 87 B5 25 35N 97 40W
Valledupar, Colombia 92 A4 10 29N 73 15W

Vallehermoso, Canary Is. ... 24 F2 28 10N 17 15W
Vallejo, U.S.A. 78 G4 38 7N 122 14W
Vallenar, Chile 94 B1 28 30S 70 50W
Valletta, Malta .... 25 D2 35 54N 14 31 E
Valley Center, U.S.A. 79 M9 33 13N 117 2W
Valley City, U.S.A. 80 B6 46 55N 98 0W
Valley Falls, Oreg., U.S.A. . 76 E3 42 29N 120 17W
Valley Falls, R.I., U.S.A. 85 E13 41 54N 71 24W
Valley Springs, U.S.A. 78 G6 38 12N 120 50W
Valley View, U.S.A. 85 F8 40 39N 76 33W
Valley Wells, U.S.A. 79 K11 35 27N 115 46W
Valleyview, Canada 70 B5 55 5N 117 17W
Vallimanca, Arroyo, Argentina 94 D4 35 40S 59 10W
Valls, Spain .... 21 B6 41 18N 1 15 E
Valmiera, Latvia .... 9 H21 57 37N 25 29 E
Valognes, France 20 B3 49 30N 1 28W
Valona = Vlorë, Albania ..... 17 A14 54 35N 29 30 E
Valozhyn, Belarus .... 17 A14 54 3N 26 30 E
Valparaíso, Chile 94 C1 33 2S 71 40W
Valparaíso, Mexico 86 C4 22 50N 103 32W
Valparaiso, U.S.A. 82 E2 41 28N 87 4W
Valparaíso □, Chile 94 C1 33 2S 71 40W
Vals ➜, S. Africa .... 56 D4 27 23S 26 30 E
Vals, Tanjung, Indonesia ... 37 F9 8 26S 137 25 E
Valsad, India .... 40 J8 20 40N 72 58 E
Valverde, Canary Is. 24 G2 27 48N 17 55W
Valverde del Camino, Spain 21 D2 37 35N 6 47W
Vammala, Finland .... 9 F20 61 20N 22 54 E
Vámos, Greece .... 25 D6 35 24N 24 13 E
Van, Turkey .... 19 G7 38 30N 43 20 E
Van, L. = Van Gölü, Turkey 19 G7 38 30N 43 0 E
Van Alstyne, U.S.A. 81 J6 33 25N 96 35W
Van Blommestein Meer,
  Suriname 93 C7 4 45N 55 5W
Van Buren, Canada 73 C6 47 10N 67 55W
Van Buren, Ark., U.S.A. 81 H7 35 26N 94 21W
Van Buren, Maine, U.S.A. .. 83 B11 47 10N 67 58W
Van Buren, Mo., U.S.A. 81 G9 37 0N 91 1W
Van Canh, Vietnam .... 38 F7 13 37N 109 0 E
Van Diemen, C., N. Terr.,
  Australia .... 60 B5 11 9S 130 24 E
Van Diemen, C., Queens.,
  Australia .... 62 B2 16 30S 139 46 E
Van Diemen G., Australia ... 60 B5 11 45S 132 0 E
Van Gölü, Turkey .... 19 G7 38 30N 43 0 E
Van Horn, U.S.A. 81 K2 31 3N 104 50W
Van Ninh, Vietnam .... 38 F7 12 42N 109 14 E
Van Rees, Pegunungan,
  Indonesia .... 37 E9 2 35S 138 15 E
Van Wert, U.S.A. 82 E3 40 52N 84 35W
Van Yen, Vietnam .... 38 B5 21 4N 104 42 E
Vanadzor, Armenia .... 19 F7 40 48N 44 30 E
Vanavara, Russia .... 29 C11 60 22N 102 16 E
Vancouver, Canada 70 D4 49 15N 123 10W
Vancouver, U.S.A. 78 E4 45 38N 122 40W
Vancouver, C., Australia .... 61 G2 35 2S 118 11 E
Vancouver I., Canada 70 D3 49 50N 126 0W
Vancouver International ✈ (YVR),
  U.S.A. 78 A3 49 10N 123 10W
Vandalia, Ill., U.S.A. 80 F10 38 58N 89 6W
Vandalia, Mo., U.S.A. 80 F9 39 19N 91 29W
Vandenburg, U.S.A. 79 L6 34 35N 120 33W
Vanderbijlpark, S. Africa .... 57 D4 26 42S 27 54 E
Vanderhoof, Canada 70 C4 54 0N 124 0W
Vanderkloof Dam, S. Africa 56 E3 30 4S 24 40 E
Vanderlin I., Australia .... 62 B2 15 44S 137 2 E
Vänern, Sweden .... 9 G15 58 47N 13 30 E
Vänersborg, Sweden .... 9 G15 58 26N 12 19 E
Vang Vieng, Laos .... 38 C4 18 58N 102 32 E
Vanga, Kenya .... 54 C4 4 35S 39 12 E
Vangaindrano, Madag. ...... 57 C8 23 21S 47 36 E
Vanguard, Canada 71 D7 49 55N 107 20W
Vanino, Russia .... 29 E15 48 50N 140 5 E
Vanna, Norway .... 8 A18 70 6N 19 50 E
Vännäs, Sweden .... 8 E18 63 58N 19 48 E
Vannes, France 20 C2 47 40N 2 47W
Vanrhynsdorp, S. Africa ..... 56 E2 31 36S 18 44 E
Vansbro, Sweden .... 9 F16 60 32N 14 15 E
Vansittart B., Australia .... 60 B4 14 3S 126 17 E
Vantaa, Finland .... 9 F21 60 18N 24 57 E
Vanua Balavu, Fiji 59 C9 17 40S 178 57W
Vanua Levu, Fiji .... 59 C8 16 33S 179 15 E
Vanuatu ■, Pac. Oc. .... 64 J8 15 0S 168 0 E
Vanwyksvlei, S. Africa .... 56 E3 30 18S 21 49 E
Vanzylsrus, S. Africa .... 56 D3 26 52S 22 4 E
Vapnyarka, Ukraine .... 17 D15 48 32N 28 45 E
Varāmīn, Iran .... 45 C6 35 20N 51 39 E
Varāmīn □, Iran .... 45 C6 35 18N 51 35 E
Varanasi, India .... 43 G10 25 22N 83 0 E
Varangerfjorden, Norway ... 8 A23 70 3N 29 25 E
Varangerhalvøya, Norway .. 8 A23 70 25N 29 30 E
Varaždin, Croatia .... 16 E9 46 20N 16 20 E
Varberg, Sweden .... 9 H15 57 6N 12 20 E
Vardak □, Afghan. .... 40 B6 34 0N 68 0 E
Vardar = Axiós ➜, Greece .. 23 D10 40 57N 22 35 E
Varde, Denmark .... 9 J13 55 38N 8 29 E
Vardø, Norway .... 8 A24 70 23N 31 5 E
Varella, Mui, Vietnam .... 38 F7 12 54N 109 26 E
Varêna, Lithuania .... 9 J21 54 12N 24 30 E
Varese, Italy .... 20 B8 45 48N 8 50 E
Varginha, Brazil 95 A6 21 33S 45 25W
Varillas, Chile 94 A1 24 0S 70 10W
Varkaus, Finland .... 9 E22 62 19N 27 50 E
Varna, Bulgaria .... 23 C12 43 13N 27 56 E
Värnamo, Sweden .... 9 H16 57 10N 14 3 E
Vars, Canada 85 A9 45 21N 75 21W
Varysburg, U.S.A. 84 D6 42 46N 78 19W
Varzaneh, Iran .... 45 C7 32 25N 52 40 E
Vasa Barris ➜, Brazil 93 F11 11 10S 37 10W
Vascongadas = País Vasco □,
  Spain 21 A4 42 50N 2 45W
Vasht = Khāsh, Iran .... 40 E2 28 15N 61 15 E
Vasilevichi, Belarus .... 17 B15 52 15N 29 50 E
Vasilkov = Vasylkiv, Ukraine 17 C16 50 7N 30 15 E
Vaslui, Romania .... 17 E14 46 38N 27 42 E
Vassar, Canada 71 D9 49 10N 95 55W
Vassar, U.S.A. 82 D4 43 22N 83 35W
Västerås, Sweden .... 9 G17 59 37N 16 38 E
Västerbotten, Sweden .... 8 D18 64 36N 20 4 E
Västerdalälven ➜, Sweden 9 F16 60 30N 15 7 E
Västervik, Sweden .... 9 H17 57 43N 16 33 E
Västmanland, Sweden .... 9 G16 59 45N 16 20 E
Vasto, Italy .... 22 C6 42 8N 14 40 E
Vasylkiv, Ukraine .... 17 C16 50 7N 30 15 E
Vatersay, U.K. 11 E1 56 55N 7 32W
Vatican City ■, Europe ...... 22 D5 41 54N 12 27 E

Vatili, Cyprus .... 25 D12 35 6N 33 40 E
Vatnajökull, Iceland 8 D5 64 30N 16 48W
Vatoa, Fiji 59 D9 19 50S 178 13W
Vatólakkos, Greece .... 25 D5 35 27N 23 53 E
Vatoloha, Madag. .... 57 B8 17 52S 47 48 E
Vatomandry, Madag. .... 57 B8 19 20S 48 59 E
Vatra-Dornei, Romania ...... 17 E13 47 22N 25 22 E
Vatrak ➜, India .... 42 H5 23 9N 73 2 E
Vättern, Sweden .... 9 G16 58 25N 14 30 E
Vaudreuil-Dorion, Canada .. 85 A10 45 23N 74 3W
Vaughn, Mont., U.S.A. 76 C8 47 33N 111 33W
Vaughn, N. Mex., U.S.A. ... 77 J11 34 36N 105 13W
Vaujours C., Canada 72 A5 55 27N 74 15W
Vaupés = Uaupés ➜, Brazil 92 C5 0 2N 67 16W
Vaupes □, Colombia 92 C4 1 0N 71 0W
Vauxhall, Canada 70 C6 50 5N 112 9W
Vav, India .... 42 G4 24 22N 71 31 E
Vavatenina, Madag. .... 57 B8 17 28S 49 12 E
Vava'u, Tonga 59 D12 18 36S 174 0W
Vawkavysk, Belarus .... 17 B13 53 9N 24 30 E
Växjö, Sweden .... 9 H16 56 52N 14 50 E
Vaygach, Ostrov, Russia .... 28 C6 70 0N 60 0 E
Váyia, Ákra, Greece .... 25 C10 36 15N 28 11 E
Vechte ➜, Neths. .... 15 B6 52 34N 6 6 E
Vedea ➜, Romania .... 17 G13 43 42N 25 41 E
Vedia, Argentina 94 C3 34 30S 61 31W
Veendam, Neths. .... 15 A6 53 5N 6 52 E
Veenendaal, Neths. .... 15 B5 52 2N 5 34 E
Vefsna ➜, Norway .... 8 D15 65 48N 13 10 E
Vega, Norway .... 8 D14 65 40N 11 55 E
Vega, U.S.A. 81 H3 35 15N 102 26W
Vega Baja, Puerto Rico ...... 89 d 18 27N 66 23W
Vegreville, Canada 70 C6 53 30N 112 5W
Vejer de la Frontera, Spain 21 D3 36 15N 5 59W
Vejle, Denmark .... 9 J13 55 43N 9 30 E
Velas, C., Costa Rica 88 D2 10 21N 85 52W
Velasco, Sierra de, Argentina 94 B2 29 20S 67 10W
Velddrif, S. Africa .... 56 E2 32 42S 18 11 E
Velebit Planina, Croatia ..... 16 F8 44 50N 15 20 E
Veles, Macedonia .... 23 D9 41 46N 21 47 E
Vélez-Málaga, Spain 21 D3 36 48N 4 5W
Vélez Rubio, Spain 21 D4 37 41N 2 5W
Velhas ➜, Brazil 93 G10 17 13S 44 49W
Velika Kapela, Croatia .... 16 F8 45 10N 15 5 E
Velika Kema, Russia .... 30 B8 45 30N 137 12 E
Veliki Ustyug, Russia .... 18 B8 60 47N 46 20 E
Velikiye Luki, Russia .... 18 C5 56 25N 30 32 E
Veliko Tǔrnovo, Bulgaria ... 23 C11 43 5N 25 41 E
Velikonda Range, India ...... 40 M11 14 45N 79 10 E
Velletri, Italy .... 22 D5 41 41N 12 47 E
Vellore, India .... 40 N11 12 57N 79 10 E
Velsk, Russia .... 18 B7 61 10N 42 5 E
Veluwezoom △, Neths. ...... 15 B6 52 5N 6 2 E
Velva, U.S.A. 80 A4 48 4N 100 56W
Venado Tuerto, Argentina .. 94 C3 33 50S 62 0W
Vendée □, France 20 C3 46 50N 1 35W
Vendôme, France .... 20 C4 47 47N 1 3 E
Venézia, Italy .... 22 B5 45 27N 12 21 E
Venézia, G. di, Italy .... 22 B5 45 15N 13 0 E
Venezuela ■, S. Amer. 92 B5 8 0N 66 0W
Venezuela, G. de, Venezuela 92 A4 11 30N 71 0W
Vengurla, India .... 40 M8 15 53N 73 45 E
Venice = Venézia, Italy ...... 22 B5 45 27N 12 21 E
Venice, U.S.A. 83 M4 27 6N 82 27W
Venkatapuram, India .... 41 K12 18 20N 80 30 E
Venlo, Neths. .... 15 C6 51 22N 6 11 E
Vennesla, Norway .... 9 G12 58 15N 7 59 E
Venray, Neths. .... 15 C6 51 31N 6 0 E
Ventana, Punta de la, Mexico 86 C3 24 4N 109 48W
Ventana, Sa. de la, Argentina 94 D3 38 0S 62 30W
Ventersburg, S. Africa .... 56 D4 28 7S 27 9 E
Venterstad, S. Africa .... 56 E4 30 47S 25 48 E
Ventnor, U.K. 13 G6 50 36N 1 12W
Ventoténe, Italy .... 22 D5 40 47N 13 25 E
Ventoux, Mt., France .... 20 D6 44 10N 5 17 E
Ventspils, Latvia .... 9 H19 57 25N 21 32 E
Ventuari ➜, Venezuela 92 C5 3 58N 67 2W
Ventucopa, U.S.A. 79 L7 34 50N 119 29W
Ventura, U.S.A. 79 L7 34 17N 119 18W
Venus B., Australia .... 63 F4 38 40S 145 42 E
Vera, Argentina 94 B3 29 30S 60 20W
Vera, Spain 21 D5 37 15N 1 51W
Veracruz, Mexico 87 D5 19 10N 96 10W
Veracruz □, Mexico 87 D5 19 0N 96 15W
Veraval, India .... 42 J4 20 53N 70 27 E
Verbánia, Italy .... 20 B8 45 56N 8 33 E
Vercelli, Italy .... 20 B8 45 19N 8 25 E
Verdalsøra, Norway .... 8 E14 63 48N 11 30 E
Verde ➜, Argentina 96 E3 41 56S 65 5W
Verde ➜, Goiás, Brazil 93 G8 18 1S 50 14W
Verde ➜, Mato Grosso do Sul,
  Brazil 93 H8 21 25S 52 20W
Verde ➜, Chihuahua, Mexico 86 B3 26 29N 107 58W
Verde ➜, Oaxaca, Mexico .. 87 D5 15 59N 97 50W
Verde ➜, Veracruz, Mexico 86 C4 21 10N 102 50W
Verde ➜, Paraguay 94 A4 23 9S 57 37W
Verde, Cay, Bahamas 88 B4 23 0N 75 5W
Verden, Germany .... 16 B5 52 55N 9 14 E
Verdi, U.S.A. 78 F7 39 31N 119 59W
Verdun, France .... 20 B6 49 9N 5 24 E
Vereeniging, S. Africa .... 57 D4 26 38S 27 57 E
Verga, C., Guinea 50 F3 10 30N 14 10W
Vergara, Uruguay 95 C5 32 56S 53 57W
Vergemont Cr. ➜, Australia 62 C3 24 16S 143 16 E
Vergennes, U.S.A. 85 B11 44 10N 73 15W
Verín, Spain 21 B2 41 57N 7 27W
Verkhnevilyuysk, Russia .... 29 C13 63 27N 120 18 E
Verkhniy Baskunchak, Russia 19 E8 48 14N 46 44 E
Verkhoyansk, Russia .... 29 C14 67 35N 133 25 E
Verkhoyanskiy Khrebet, Russia 29 C13 66 0N 129 0 E
Verkhoyanskiy Khrebet, Russia 29 C13 66 0N 129 0 E
Vermilion, Canada 71 C6 53 20N 110 50W
Vermilion, U.S.A. 84 E2 41 25N 82 22W
Vermilion ➜, Canada 71 C6 53 22N 110 51W
Vermilion, B., U.S.A. 81 L9 29 45N 91 55W
Vermilion Bay, Canada 71 D10 49 51N 93 34W
Vermilion L., U.S.A. 80 B8 47 53N 92 26W
Vermillion, U.S.A. 80 D6 42 47N 96 56W
Vermillion ➜, Canada 72 C5 47 38N 72 56W
Vermont □, U.S.A. 85 C12 44 0N 73 0W
Vernal, U.S.A. 76 F9 40 27N 109 32W
Vernalis, U.S.A. 78 H5 37 36N 121 17W
Verner, Canada 72 C3 46 25N 80 8W

Verneukpan, S. Africa . . . . 56 E3 30 0S 21 0 E
Vernon, Canada 70 C5 50 20N 119 15W
Vernon, U.S.A. 81 H5 34 9N 99 17W
Vernonia, U.S.A. 78 E3 45 52N 123 11W
Vero Beach, U.S.A. 83 M5 27 38N 80 24W
Véroia, Greece . . . . 23 D10 40 34N 22 12 E
Verona, Canada 85 B8 44 29N 76 42W
Verona, Italy . . . . 22 B4 45 27N 10 59 E
Verona, U.S.A. . . . . 20 B5 ...
Versailles, France . . . . 20 B5 48 48N 2 8 E
Vert, C., Senegal 50 F2 14 45N 17 30W
Verulam, S. Africa . . . . 57 D5 29 38S 31 2 E
Verviers, Belgium . . . . 15 D5 50 37N 5 52 E
Veselovskoye Vdkhr., Russia . . . 19 E7 46 58N 41 25 E
Vesoul, France . . . . 20 C7 47 40N 6 11 E
Vesterålen, Norway . . . . 8 B16 68 45N 15 0 E
Vestfjorden, Norway . . . . 8 C15 67 55N 14 0 E
Vestmannaeyjar, Iceland 8 E3 63 27N 20 15W
Vestspitsbergen, Svalbard . . . . . 4 B8 78 40N 17 0 E
Vestvågøy, Norway . . . . 8 B15 68 18N 13 50 E
Vesuvio, Italy . . . . 22 D6 40 49N 14 26 E
Vesuvius, Mt. = Vesuvio, Italy . . 22 D6 40 49N 14 26 E
Veszprém, Hungary . . . . 17 E9 47 8N 17 57 E
Vetlanda, Sweden . . . . 9 H16 57 24N 15 3 E
Vetlugu →, Russia . . . . 18 C8 56 36N 46 4 E
Vettore, Mte., Italy . . . . 22 C5 42 49N 13 16 E
Veurne, Belgium . . . . 15 C2 51 5N 2 40 E
Veys, Iran . . . . 45 D6 31 30N 49 0 E
Vezhen, Bulgaria . . . . 23 C11 42 50N 24 20 E
Vi Thanh, Vietnam . . . . 39 H5 9 42N 105 26 E
Viacha, Bolivia 92 G5 16 39S 68 18W
Viamão, Brazil 95 C5 30 5S 51 0W
Viana, Brazil 93 D10 3 13S 44 55W
Viana do Alentejo, Portugal 21 C2 38 17N 7 59W
Viana do Castelo, Portugal 21 B1 41 42N 8 50W
Vianden, Lux. . . . . 15 E6 49 56N 6 12 E
Viangchan = Vientiane, Laos . . . 38 D4 17 58N 102 36 E
Vianópolis, Brazil 93 G9 16 40S 48 35W
Viaréggio, Italy . . . . 22 C4 43 52N 10 14 E
Vibo Valéntia, Italy . . . . 22 E7 38 40N 16 6 E
Viborg, Denmark . . . . 9 H13 56 27N 9 23 E
Vic, Spain . . . . 21 B7 41 58N 2 19 E
Vicenza, Italy . . . . 22 B4 45 33N 11 33 E
Vich = Vic, Spain . . . . 21 B7 41 58N 2 19 E
Vichada →, Colombia 92 C5 4 55N 67 50W
Vichy, France . . . . 20 C5 46 9N 3 26 E
Vicksburg, Ariz., U.S.A. 79 M13 33 45N 113 45W
Vicksburg, Miss., U.S.A. 81 J9 32 21N 90 53W
Victor, India . . . . 42 J4 21 0N 71 30 E
Victor, U.S.A. 84 D7 42 58N 77 24W
Victor Harbor, Australia . . . . . . 63 F2 35 30S 138 37 E
Victoria, Argentina 94 C3 32 40S 60 10W
Victoria, Canada 70 D4 48 30N 123 25W
Victoria, Chile 96 D2 38 13S 72 20W
Victoria, China . . . . 33 G1 22 17N 114 9 E
Victoria, Malta . . . . 25 C1 36 3N 14 14 E
Victoria, Kans., U.S.A. 80 F5 38 52N 99 9W
Victoria, Tex., U.S.A. 81 L6 28 48N 97 0W
Victoria □, Australia . . . . 63 F3 37 0S 144 0 E
Victoria →, Australia . . . . 60 C4 15 10S 129 40 E
Victoria, Grand L., Canada 72 C4 47 31N 77 30W
Victoria, L., Africa . . . . 54 C3 1 0S 33 0 E
Victoria, L., Australia . . . . 63 E3 33 57S 141 15 E
Victoria, Mt., Burma . . . . 41 J18 21 15N 93 55 E
Victoria Beach, Canada 71 C9 50 40N 96 35W
Victoria de Durango = Durango, Mexico 86 C4 24 3N 104 39W
Victoria de las Tunas, Cuba 88 B4 20 58N 76 59W
Victoria Falls, Zimbabwe . . . . . . 55 F2 17 58S 25 52 E
Victoria Harbour, Canada 84 B5 44 45N 79 45W
Victoria I., Canada 68 A8 71 0N 111 0W
Victoria L., Canada 73 C8 48 20N 57 27W
Victoria Ld., Antarctica . . . . . . 5 D11 75 0S 160 0 E
Victoria Nile →, Uganda . . . . . . 54 B3 2 14N 31 26 E
Victoria River, Australia . . . . . . 60 C5 16 25S 131 0 E
Victoria Str., Canada 68 B9 69 31N 100 30W
Victoria West, S. Africa . . . . . . 56 E3 31 25S 23 4 E
Victoriaville, Canada 73 C5 46 4N 71 56W
Victorica, Argentina 94 D2 36 20S 65 30W
Victorville, U.S.A. 79 L9 34 32N 117 18W
Vicuña, Chile 94 C1 30 0S 70 50W
Vicuña Mackenna, Argentina . . . 94 C3 33 53S 64 25W
Vidal, U.S.A. 79 L12 34 7N 114 31W
Vidal Junction, U.S.A. 79 L12 34 11N 114 34W
Vidalia, U.S.A. 83 J4 32 13N 82 25W
Vidho, Greece . . . . 25 A3 39 38N 19 55 E
Vidin, Bulgaria . . . . 23 C10 43 59N 22 50 E
Vidisha, India . . . . 42 H7 23 28N 77 53 E
Vidzy, Belarus . . . . 9 J22 55 23N 26 37 E
Viedma, Argentina 96 E4 40 50S 63 0W
Viedma, L., Argentina 96 F2 49 30S 72 30W
Vielsalm, Belgium . . . . 15 D5 50 17N 5 54 E
Vieng Pou Kha, Laos . . . . 38 B3 20 41N 101 4 E
Vienna = Wien, Austria . . . . . . 16 D9 48 12N 16 22 E
Vienna, Ill., U.S.A. 81 G10 37 25N 88 54W
Vienna, Mo., U.S.A. 80 F9 38 11N 91 57W
Vienne, France . . . . 20 C4 45 31N 4 53 E
Vienne →, France . . . . 20 C4 47 13N 0 5 E
Vientiane, Laos . . . . 38 D4 17 58N 102 36 E
Vientos, Paso de los, Caribbean . 89 C5 20 0N 74 0W
Vieques, Isla de, Puerto Rico . . . 89 d 18 8N 65 25W
Vierge Pt., St. Lucia . . . . 89 f 13 49N 60 53W
Vierzon, France . . . . 20 C5 47 13N 2 5 E
Vietnam ■, Asia . . . . 38 C5 19 0N 106 0 E
Vieux Fort, St. Lucia . . . . 89 f 13 46N 60 58W
Vigan, Phil. . . . . 37 A6 17 35N 120 28 E
Vigévano, Italy . . . . 20 D8 45 19N 8 51 E
Vigia, Brazil 93 D9 0 50S 48 5W
Vigia Chico, Mexico 87 D7 19 46N 87 35W
Víglas, Ákra, Greece . . . . 25 D9 35 54N 27 51 E
Vigo, Spain 21 A1 42 12N 8 41W
Vihowa, Pakistan . . . . 42 D4 31 8N 70 30 E
Vihowa →, Pakistan . . . . 42 D4 31 8N 70 41 E
Vijayawada, India . . . . 41 L12 16 31N 80 39 E
Vijosë →, Albania . . . . 23 D8 40 37N 19 24 E
Vík, Iceland 8 E4 63 25N 19 1W
Vikeke = Viqueque, E. Timor . . . 37 F7 8 52S 126 23 E
Viking, Canada 70 C6 53 7N 111 50W
Vikna, Norway . . . . 8 D14 64 55N 10 58 E
Vila da Maganja, Mozam. . . . . . 55 F4 17 18S 37 30 E
Vila de Bispo, Portugal 21 D1 37 5N 8 53W
Vila Franca de Xira, Portugal . . . 21 C1 38 57N 8 59W
Vila Gamito, Mozam. . . . . 55 E3 14 12S 33 0 E
Vila Gomes da Costa, Mozam. . . . 57 C5 24 20S 33 37 E
Vila Machado, Mozam. . . . . 55 F3 19 15S 34 14 E
Vila Mouzinho, Mozam. . . . . . . 55 E3 14 48S 34 25 E
Vila Nova de Gaia, Portugal 21 B1 41 8N 8 37W

Vila Real, Portugal 21 B2 41 17N 7 48W
Vila-real de los Infantes, Spain . 21 C5 39 55N 0 3W
Vila Real de Santo António, Portugal 21 D2 37 10N 7 28W
Vila Vasco da Gama, Mozam. . . . 55 E3 14 54S 32 14 E
Vila Velha, Brazil 95 A7 20 20S 40 17W
Vilagarcía de Arousa, Spain . . . 21 A1 42 34N 8 46W
Vilaine →, France 20 C2 47 30N 2 27W
Vilanandro, Tanjona, Madag. . . 57 B7 16 11S 44 27 E
Vilanculos, Mozam. . . . . 57 C6 22 1S 35 17 E
Vilanova i la Geltrú, Spain . . . . 21 B6 41 13N 1 40 E
Vilcheka, Z., Russia . . . . 4 A11 80 30N 60 30 E
Vileyka, Belarus . . . . 17 A14 54 30N 26 53 E
Vilhelmina, Sweden . . . . 8 D17 64 35N 16 39 E
Vilhena, Brazil 92 F6 12 40S 60 5W
Viliga, Russia . . . . 29 C16 61 36N 156 56 E
Viliya = Neris →, Lithuania . . . . 9 J21 55 8N 24 16 E
Viljandi, Estonia . . . . 9 G21 58 28N 25 30 E
Vilkitskogo, Proliv, Russia . . . . 29 B11 78 0N 103 0 E
Vilkovo = Vylkove, Ukraine . . . . 17 F15 45 28N 29 32 E
Villa Abecia, Bolivia 94 A2 21 0S 68 18W
Villa Ahumada, Mexico 86 A3 30 38N 106 30W
Villa Ana, Argentina 94 B4 28 28S 59 40W
Villa Ángela, Argentina 94 B3 27 34S 60 45W
Villa Bella, Bolivia 92 F5 10 25S 65 22W
Villa Cañás, Argentina 94 C3 34 0S 61 35W
Villa Colón, Argentina 94 C2 31 38S 68 20W
Villa Constitución, Argentina . . . 94 C3 33 15S 60 20W
Villa de María, Argentina 94 B3 29 55S 63 43W
Villa Dolores, Argentina 94 C2 31 58S 65 15W
Villa Frontera, Mexico 86 B4 26 56N 101 27W
Villa Guillermina, Argentina . . . 94 B4 28 15S 59 29W
Villa Hayes, Paraguay 94 B4 25 5S 57 20W
Villa Iris, Argentina 94 D3 38 12S 63 12W
Villa Juárez, Mexico 86 B4 27 37N 100 44W
Villa María, Argentina 94 C3 32 20S 63 10W
Villa Mazán, Argentina 94 B2 28 40S 66 30W
Villa Montes, Bolivia 94 A3 21 10S 63 30W
Villa Ocampo, Argentina 94 B4 28 30S 59 20W
Villa Ocampo, Mexico 86 B3 26 29N 105 30W
Villa Ojo de Agua, Argentina . . . 94 B3 29 30S 63 44W
Villa San Martín, Argentina 94 C4 32 12S 58 15W
Villa San Martín, Argentina 94 B3 28 15S 64 9W
Villa Unión, Mexico 86 C3 23 12N 106 14W
Villacarlos, Spain . . . . 24 B11 39 53N 4 17 E
Villacarrillo, Spain 21 C4 38 7N 3 3W
Villach, Austria . . . . 16 E7 46 37N 13 51 E
Villafranca de los Caballeros, Spain . . . . 24 B10 39 34N 3 25 E
Villagrán, Mexico 87 C5 24 29N 99 29W
Villaguay, Argentina 94 C4 32 0S 59 0W
Villahermosa, Mexico 87 D6 17 59N 92 55W
Villajoyosa, Spain 21 C5 38 30N 0 12W
Villalba, Spain 21 A2 43 26N 7 40W
Villanueva, U.S.A. 83 H2 35 16N 105 22W
Villanueva de la Serena, Spain . . 21 C3 38 59N 5 50W
Villanueva y Geltrú = Vilanova i la Geltrú, Spain . . . . 21 B6 41 13N 1 40 E
Villarreal = Vila-real de los Infantes, Spain 21 C5 39 55N 0 3W
Villarrica, Chile 96 D2 39 15S 72 15W
Villarrica, Paraguay 94 B4 25 40S 56 30W
Villarrobledo, Spain 21 C4 39 18N 2 36W
Villavicencio, Argentina 94 C2 32 28S 69 0W
Villavicencio, Colombia 92 C4 4 9N 73 37W
Villaviciosa, Spain 21 A3 43 32N 5 27W
Villazón, Bolivia 94 A2 22 0S 65 35W
Ville-Marie, Canada 72 C4 47 20N 79 30W
Ville Platte, U.S.A. 81 K8 30 41N 92 17W
Villena, Spain 21 C5 38 39N 0 52W
Villeneuve-d'Ascq, France . . . . 20 A5 50 38N 3 9 E
Villeneuve-sur-Lot, France . . . . 20 D4 44 24N 0 42 E
Villiers, S. Africa . . . . 57 D4 27 2S 28 36 E
Villingen-Schwenningen, Germany . . . . 16 D5 48 3N 8 26 E
Vilna, Canada 70 C6 54 7N 111 55W
Vilnius, Lithuania . . . . 9 J21 54 38N 25 19 E
Vilvoorde, Belgium . . . . 15 D4 50 56N 4 26 E
Vilyuy →, Russia . . . . 29 C13 64 24N 126 26 E
Vilyuysk, Russia . . . . 29 C13 63 40N 121 35 E
Viña del Mar, Chile 94 C1 33 0S 71 30W
Vinarós, Spain . . . . 21 B6 40 30N 0 27 E
Vincennes, U.S.A. 82 F2 38 41N 87 32W
Vincent, U.S.A. 79 L8 34 33N 118 11W
Vinchina, Argentina 94 B2 28 45S 68 15W
Vindelälven →, Sweden . . . . . . 8 E18 63 55N 19 50 E
Vindeln, Sweden . . . . 8 D18 64 12N 19 43 E
Vindhya Ra., India . . . . 42 H7 22 50N 77 0 E
Vineland, U.S.A. 82 F8 39 29N 75 2W
Vinh, Vietnam . . . . 38 C5 18 45N 105 38 E
Vinh Linh, Vietnam . . . . 38 D6 17 4N 107 2 E
Vinh Long, Vietnam . . . . 39 G5 10 16N 105 57 E
Vinh Yen, Vietnam . . . . 38 B5 21 21N 105 35 E
Vinita, U.S.A. 81 G7 36 39N 95 9W
Vinkovci, Croatia . . . . 23 B8 45 19N 18 48 E
Vinnitsa = Vinnytsya, Ukraine . . 17 D15 49 15N 28 30 E
Vinnytsya, Ukraine . . . . 17 D15 49 15N 28 30 E
Vinson Massif, Antarctica 5 D16 78 35S 85 25W
Vinton, Calif., U.S.A. 78 F6 39 48N 120 10W
Vinton, Iowa, U.S.A. 80 D8 42 10N 92 1W
Vinton, La., U.S.A. 81 K8 30 11N 93 35W
Viqueque, E. Timor . . . . 37 F7 8 52S 126 23 E
Virac, Phil. . . . . 37 B6 13 30N 124 20 E
Virachey, Cambodia . . . . 38 F6 13 59N 106 49 E
Virachey △, Cambodia . . . . 38 E6 14 14N 106 55 E
Virago Sd., Canada 70 C2 54 0N 132 30W
Viramgam, India . . . . 42 H5 23 5N 72 0 E
Viranşehir, Turkey . . . . 44 B3 37 13N 39 45 E
Virawah, Pakistan . . . . 42 G4 24 31N 70 46 E
Virden, Canada 71 D8 49 50N 100 56W
Vire, France 20 B3 48 50N 0 53W
Vírgenes, C., Argentina 96 G3 52 19S 68 21W
Virgin →, U.S.A. 77 H6 36 28N 114 21W
Virgin Gorda, Br. Virgin Is. . . . . 89 e 18 30N 64 26W
Virgin Is. (British) ☑, W. Indies . 89 e 18 30N 64 30W
Virgin Is. (U.S.) ☑, W. Indies . . 89 e 18 20N 65 0W
Virginia, S. Africa . . . . 56 D4 28 8S 26 55 E
Virginia, U.S.A. 80 B8 47 31N 92 32W
Virginia □, U.S.A. 82 G7 37 30N 78 45W
Virginia Beach, U.S.A. 82 G8 36 51N 75 59W
Virginia City, Mont., U.S.A. 76 D8 45 18N 111 56W
Virginia City, Nev., U.S.A. 78 F7 39 19N 119 39W
Virginia Falls, Canada 70 A3 61 38N 125 42W
Virginiatown, Canada 72 C4 48 9N 79 36W
Viroqua, U.S.A. 80 D9 43 34N 90 53W
Virovitica, Croatia . . . . 22 B7 45 51N 17 21 E

Virpur, India . . . . 42 J4 21 51N 70 42 E
Virton, Belgium . . . . 15 E5 49 35N 5 32 E
Virudunagar, India . . . . 40 Q10 9 30N 77 58 E
Virunga △, Dem. Rep. of the Congo . . . . 54 B2 0 5N 29 38 E
Vis, Croatia . . . . 22 C7 43 4N 16 10 E
Visalia, U.S.A. 78 J7 36 20N 119 18W
Visayan Sea, Phil. . . . . 37 B6 11 30N 123 30 E
Visby, Sweden . . . . 9 H18 57 37N 18 18 E
Viscount Melville Sd., Canada . . 4 B2 74 10N 108 0W
Visé, Belgium . . . . 15 D5 50 44N 5 41 E
Višegrad, Bos.-H. . . . . 23 C8 43 47N 19 17 E
Viseu, Brazil 93 D9 1 10S 46 5W
Viseu, Portugal 21 B2 40 40N 7 55W
Vishakhapatnam, India . . . . . . 41 L13 17 45N 83 20 E
Visnagar, India . . . . 42 H5 23 45N 72 32 E
Viso, Mte., Italy . . . . 20 D7 44 38N 7 5 E
Visokoi I., Antarctica 5 B1 56 43S 27 15W
Vista, U.S.A. 79 M9 33 12N 117 14W
Vistula = Wisła →, Poland . . . . 17 A10 54 22N 18 55 E
Vitebsk = Vitsyebsk, Belarus . . . 18 C5 55 10N 30 15 E
Viterbo, Italy . . . . 22 C5 42 25N 12 6 E
Viti Levu, Fiji . . . . 59 C7 17 30S 177 30 E
Vitigudino, Spain 21 B2 41 1N 6 26W
Vitim, Russia . . . . 29 D12 59 28N 112 35 E
Vitim →, Russia . . . . 29 D12 59 26N 112 34 E
Vitória, Brazil 93 H10 20 20S 40 22W
Vitória da Conquista, Brazil 93 F10 14 51S 40 51W
Vitória de São Antão, Brazil 93 E11 8 10S 35 20W
Vitoria-Gasteiz, Spain 21 A4 42 50N 2 41W
Vitsyebsk, Belarus . . . . 18 C5 55 10N 30 15 E
Vittória, Italy . . . . 22 F6 36 57N 14 32 E
Vittório Véneto, Italy . . . . 22 B5 45 59N 12 18 E
Viveiro, Spain 21 A2 43 39N 7 38W
Vivian, U.S.A. 81 J8 32 53N 93 59W
Vizcaíno, Desierto de, Mexico . . 86 B2 27 40N 113 50W
Vizcaíno, Sierra, Mexico 86 B2 27 30N 114 0W
Vize, Turkey . . . . 23 D12 41 34N 27 45 E
Vizianagaram, India . . . . 41 K13 18 6N 83 30 E
Vlaardingen, Neths. . . . . 15 C4 51 55N 4 21 E
Vladikavkaz, Russia . . . . 19 F7 43 0N 44 35 E
Vladimir, Russia . . . . 18 C7 56 15N 40 30 E
Vladimir Volynskiy = Volodymyr-Volynskyy, Ukraine . . . . 17 C13 50 50N 24 18 E
Vladivostok, Russia . . . . 29 E14 43 10N 131 53 E
Vlieland, Neths. . . . . 15 A4 53 16N 4 55 E
Vlissingen, Neths. . . . . 15 C3 51 26N 3 34 E
Vlorë, Albania . . . . 23 D8 40 32N 19 28 E
Vltava →, Czech Rep. . . . . 16 D8 50 21N 14 30 E
Vo Dat, Vietnam . . . . 39 G6 11 9N 107 31 E
Voe, U.K. 11 A7 60 21N 1 16W
Vogelkop = Doberai, Jazirah, Indonesia . . . . 37 E8 1 25S 133 0 E
Vogelsberg, Germany . . . . 16 C5 50 31N 9 12 E
Voghera, Italy . . . . 20 D8 44 59N 9 1 E
Vohibinany, Madag. . . . . 57 B8 18 49S 49 4 E
Vohilava, Madag. . . . . 57 C8 21 4S 48 0 E
Vohimarina = Iharana, Madag. . . 57 A9 13 25S 50 0 E
Vohimena, Tanjon' i, Madag. . . 57 D8 25 36S 45 8 E
Vohipeno, Madag. . . . . 57 C8 22 22S 47 51 E
Voi, Kenya . . . . 54 C4 3 25S 38 32 E
Voiron, France . . . . 20 D6 45 22N 5 35 E
Voisey B., Canada 73 A7 56 15N 61 50W
Vojmsjön, Sweden . . . . 8 D17 64 55N 16 40 E
Vojvodina □, Serbia & M. . . . . 23 B9 45 20N 20 0 E
Volborg, U.S.A. 80 C2 45 51N 105 41W
Volcán de Colima △, Mexico . . . 86 D4 19 30N 103 40W
Volcano Is. = Kazan-Rettō, Pac. Oc. . . . . 64 E6 25 0N 141 0 E
Volcans △, Rwanda . . . . 54 C2 1 30S 29 26 E
Volda, Norway . . . . 9 E12 62 9N 6 5 E
Volga = Privolzhskiy □, Russia . . 19 D8 56 0N 50 0 E
Volga →, Russia . . . . 19 E8 46 0N 48 30 E
Volga Hts. = Privolzhskaya Vozvyshennost, Russia . . . . . 19 D8 51 0N 46 0 E
Volgodonsk, Russia . . . . 19 E7 47 33N 42 5 E
Volgograd, Russia . . . . 19 E7 48 40N 44 25 E
Volgogradskoye Vdkhr., Russia . 19 D8 50 0N 45 20 E
Volkhov →, Russia . . . . 18 B5 60 8N 32 20 E
Volkovysk = Vawkavysk, Belarus 17 B13 53 9N 24 30 E
Volksrust, S. Africa . . . . 57 D4 27 24S 29 53 E
Volochanka, Russia . . . . 29 B10 71 0N 94 28 E
Volodymyr-Volynskyy, Ukraine . . 17 C13 50 50N 24 18 E
Vologda, Russia . . . . 18 C6 59 10N 39 45 E
Vólos, Greece . . . . 23 E10 39 24N 22 59 E
Volovets, Ukraine . . . . 17 D12 48 43N 23 11 E
Volozhin = Valozhyn, Belarus . . 17 A14 54 3N 26 30 E
Volsk, Russia . . . . 18 D8 52 5N 47 22 E
Volta →, Ghana . . . . 48 F4 5 46N 0 41 E
Volta, L., Ghana 50 G6 7 30N 0 0W
Volta Redonda, Brazil 95 A7 22 31S 44 5W
Voltaire, C., Australia . . . . 60 B4 14 16S 125 35 E
Volterra, Italy . . . . 22 C4 43 24N 10 51 E
Volturno →, Italy . . . . 22 D5 41 1N 13 55 E
Volzhskiy, Russia . . . . 19 E7 48 56N 44 46 E
Vondrozo, Madag. . . . . 57 C8 22 49S 47 20 E
Vopnafjörður, Iceland 8 D6 65 45N 14 50W
Vóriai Sporádhes, Greece . . . . . 23 E10 39 15N 23 30 E
Vorkuta, Russia . . . . 18 A11 67 48N 64 20 E
Vormsi, Estonia . . . . 9 G20 59 1N 23 13 E
Voronezh, Russia . . . . 19 D6 51 40N 39 10 E
Võrts Järv, Estonia . . . . 9 G22 58 16N 26 3 E
Võru, Estonia . . . . 9 H22 57 48N 26 54 E
Vosges, France . . . . 20 B7 48 20N 7 10 E
Voss, Norway . . . . 9 F12 60 38N 6 26 E
Vostok, Antarctica . . . . 5 D8 78 30S 106 50 E
Vostok I., Kiribati 65 J12 10 5S 152 23W
Votkinsk, Russia . . . . 18 C9 57 0N 53 55 E
Votkinskoye Vdkhr., Russia . . . . 18 C10 57 22N 55 12 E
Votsuri-Shima, Japan . . . . 31 M1 25 45N 123 29 E
Vouga →, Portugal 21 B1 40 41N 8 40W
Vóuxa, Ákra, Greece . . . . 25 D5 35 37N 23 32 E
Voyageurs △, U.S.A. 80 A8 48 32N 93 0W
Vozhe, Ozero, Russia . . . . 18 B6 60 45N 39 0 E
Voznesensk, Ukraine . . . . 19 E5 47 35N 31 21 E
Voznesenye, Russia . . . . 18 B6 61 0N 35 28 E
Vrangelya, Ostrov, Russia . . . . 29 B19 71 0N 180 0 E
Vranje, Serbia & M. . . . . 23 C9 42 34N 21 54 E
Vratsa, Bulgaria . . . . 23 C10 43 15N 23 30 E
Vrbas →, Bos.-H. . . . . 22 B7 45 8N 17 29 E
Vrede, S. Africa . . . . 57 D4 27 24S 29 6 E
Vredefort, S. Africa . . . . 56 D4 27 0S 27 22 E
Vredenburg, S. Africa . . . . 56 E2 32 56S 18 0 E
Vredendal, S. Africa . . . . 56 E2 31 41S 18 35 E
Vrindavan, India . . . . 42 F7 27 37N 77 40 E
Vríses, Greece . . . . 25 D6 35 23N 24 13 E
Vršac, Serbia & M. . . . . 23 B9 45 8N 21 3 E

Vryburg, S. Africa 56 D3 26 55S 24 45
Vryheid, S. Africa 57 D5 27 45S 30 47
Vu Liet, Vietnam 38 C5 18 43N 105 23
Vukovar, Croatia 23 B8 45 21N 18 59
Vulcan, Canada 70 C6 50 25N 113 15W
Vulcan, Romania 17 F12 45 23N 23 17
Vulcanești, Moldova 17 F15 45 41N 28 18
Vulcano, Italy 22 E6 38 24N 14 58
Vulkaneshty = Vulcanești, Moldova 17 F15 45 41N 28 18
Vunduzi →, Mozam. 55 F3 18 56S 34 1
Vung Tau, Vietnam 39 G6 10 21N 107 4
Vwaza △, Malawi 55 E3 10 58S 33 25
Vyatka = Kirov, Russia 18 C8 58 35N 49 40
Vyatka →, Russia 18 C9 55 37N 51 28
Vyatskiye Polyany, Russia 18 C9 56 14N 51 23
Vyazemskiy, Russia 29 E14 47 32N 134 45
Vyazma, Russia 18 C5 55 10N 34 15
Vyborg, Russia 18 B4 60 43N 28 47
Vychegda →, Russia 18 B8 61 18N 46 36
Vychodné Beskydy, Europe 17 D11 49 20N 22 0
Vyg-ozero, Russia 18 B5 63 47N 34 29
Vylkove, Ukraine 17 F15 45 28N 29 32
Vynohradiv, Ukraine 17 D12 48 9N 23 2
Vyrnwy, L., U.K. 12 E4 52 48N 3 31W
Vyshniy Volochek, Russia 18 C5 57 30N 34 30
Vyshza = imeni 26 Bakinskikh Komissarov, Turkmenistan . . 45 B7 39 22N 54 10
Vyškov, Czech Rep. 17 D9 49 17N 17 0
Vytegra, Russia 18 B6 61 0N 36 27

W

W.A.C. Bennett Dam, Canada . . 70 B4 56 2N 122 6W
Waal →, Neths. 15 C5 51 37N 5 0
Waalwijk, Neths. 15 C5 51 42N 5 4
Wabakimi △, Canada 72 B2 50 43N 89 29W
Wabana, Canada 73 C9 47 40N 53 0W
Wabasca →, Canada 70 B5 58 22N 115 20W
Wabasca-Desmarais, Canada . . 70 B6 55 57N 113 56W
Wabash, U.S.A. 82 E3 40 48N 85 49W
Wabash →, U.S.A. 82 G1 37 48N 88 2W
Wabigoon L., Canada 71 D10 49 44N 92 44W
Wabowden, Canada 71 C9 54 55N 98 38W
Wabuk Pt., Canada 72 A2 55 20N 85 5W
Wabush, Canada 73 B6 52 55N 66 52W
Waco, U.S.A. 81 K6 31 33N 97 9W
Waconichi, L., Canada 72 B5 50 8N 74 0W
Wad Hamid, Sudan 51 E12 16 30N 32 45
Wad Medani, Sudan 51 F12 14 28N 33 30
Wad Thana, Pakistan 42 F2 27 22N 66 23
Wadai, Africa 48 E5 12 0N 19 0
Wadayama, Japan 31 G7 35 19N 134 52
Waddeneilanden, Neths. 15 A5 53 20N 5 10
Waddenzee, Neths. 15 A5 53 6N 5 10
Waddington, U.S.A. 85 B9 44 52N 75 12W
Waddington, Mt., Canada 70 C3 51 23N 125 15W
Waddy Pt., Australia 63 C5 24 58S 153 21
Wadebridge, U.K. 13 G3 50 31N 4 51W
Wadena, Canada 71 C8 51 57N 103 47W
Wadena, U.S.A. 80 B7 46 26N 95 8W
Wadeye, Australia 60 B4 14 28S 129 52
Wadhams, Canada 70 C3 51 30N 127 30W
Wādī as Sīr, Jordan 46 D4 31 56N 35 49
Wadi Halfa, Sudan 51 D12 21 53N 31 19
Wadi Rum △, Jordan 46 F4 29 30N 35 20
Wadsworth, Nev., U.S.A. 76 G4 39 38N 119 17W
Wadsworth, Ohio, U.S.A. 84 E3 41 2N 81 44W
Waegwan, S. Korea 35 G15 35 59N 128 23
Wafangdian, China 35 E11 39 38N 121 58
Wafrah, Si. Arabia 44 D5 28 33N 47 56
Wageningen, Neths. 15 C5 51 58N 5 40
Wager B., Canada 69 B11 65 26N 88 40W
Wagga Wagga, Australia 63 F4 35 7S 147 24
Waghete, Indonesia 37 E9 4 10S 135 50
Wagin, Australia 61 F2 33 17S 117 25
Wagner, U.S.A. 80 D5 43 5N 98 18W
Wagon Mound, U.S.A. 81 G2 36 1N 104 42W
Wagoner, U.S.A. 81 H7 35 58N 95 22W
Wah, Pakistan 42 C5 33 45N 72 40
Wahai, Indonesia 37 E7 2 48S 129 35
Wahiawa, U.S.A. 74 H16 21 30N 158 2W
Wâhid, Egypt 46 E1 30 48N 32 21
Wahnai, Afghan. 42 C1 32 40N 65 50
Wahoo, U.S.A. 80 E6 41 13N 96 37W
Wahpeton, U.S.A. 80 B6 46 16N 96 36W
Waiau →, N.Z. 59 K4 42 47S 173 22
Waibeem, Indonesia 37 E8 0 30S 132 59
Waigeo, Indonesia 37 E8 0 20S 130 40
Waihi, N.Z. 59 G5 37 23S 175 52
Waihou →, N.Z. 59 G5 37 15S 175 40
Waika, Dem. Rep. of the Congo . 54 C2 2 22S 25 42
Waikabubak, Indonesia 37 F5 9 45S 119 25
Waikaremoana, L., N.Z. 59 H6 38 49S 177 9
Waikari, N.Z. 59 K4 42 58S 172 41
Waikato →, N.Z. 59 G5 37 23S 174 43
Waikerie, Australia 63 E3 34 9S 140 0
Waikokopu, N.Z. 59 H6 39 3S 177 52
Waikouaiti, N.Z. 59 L3 45 36S 170 41
Wailingding Dao, China 33 G11 22 6N 114 1
Wailuku, U.S.A. 74 H16 20 53N 156 30W
Waimakariri →, N.Z. 59 K4 43 24S 172 42
Waimate, N.Z. 59 L3 44 45S 171 3
Wainganga →, India 40 K11 18 50N 79 55
Waingapu, Indonesia 37 F6 9 35S 120 11
Waini →, Guyana 92 B7 8 20N 59 50W
Wainwright, Canada 71 C6 52 50N 110 50W
Waiouru, N.Z. 59 H5 39 28S 175 41
Waipara, N.Z. 59 K4 43 3S 172 46
Waipawa, N.Z. 59 H6 39 56S 176 38
Waipiro, N.Z. 59 H7 38 2S 178 22
Waipu, N.Z. 59 F5 35 59S 174 29
Waipukurau, N.Z. 59 J6 40 1S 176 33
Wairakei, N.Z. 59 H6 38 37S 176 6
Wairarapa, L., N.Z. 59 J5 41 14S 175 15
Wairoa, N.Z. 59 H6 39 3S 177 25
Waitaki →, N.Z. 59 L3 44 56S 171 7
Waitara, N.Z. 59 H5 38 59S 174 15
Waitsburg, U.S.A. 76 C4 46 16N 118 9W
Waiuku, N.Z. 59 G5 37 15S 174 45
Wajima, Japan 31 F8 37 30N 137 0
Wajir, Kenya 54 B5 1 42N 40 5
Wakasa, Japan 31 G7 35 20N 134 24
Wakasa-Wan, Japan 31 G7 35 40N 135 30
Wakatipu, L., N.Z. 59 L2 45 5S 168 33

Wakaw, Canada 71 C7 52 39N 105 44W
Wakayama, Japan .... 31 G7 34 15N 135 15 E
Wakayama □, Japan ..... 31 H7 33 50N 135 30 E
Wake I., Pac. Oc. .... 64 F8 19 18N 166 36 E
Wake Forest, U.S.A. 83 H6 35 59N 78 30W
Wakkanai, Japan .... 30 B10 45 28N 141 35 E
Wakkerstroom, S. Africa .. 57 D5 27 24S 30 10 E
Wakool, Australia .... 63 F3 35 28S 144 23 E
Wakool →, Australia ..... 63 F3 35 5S 143 33 E
Wakre, Indonesia .... 37 E8 0 19S 131 5 E
Wakuach, L., Canada 73 A6 55 34N 67 32W
Walamba, Zambia .... 55 E2 13 30S 28 42 E
Wałbrzych, Poland ...... 16 C9 50 45N 16 18 E
Walbury Hill, U.K. 13 F6 51 21N 1 28W
Walcha, Australia .... 63 E5 30 55S 151 31 E
Walcheren, Neths. .... 15 C3 51 30N 3 35 E
Walcott, U.S.A. 76 F10 41 46N 106 51W
Wałcz, Poland .... 16 B9 53 17N 16 27 E
Waldburg Ra., Australia .. 61 D2 24 40S 117 35 E
Walden, Colo., U.S.A. 76 F10 40 44N 106 17W
Walden, N.Y., U.S.A. 85 E10 41 34N 74 11W
Waldport, U.S.A. 76 D1 44 26N 124 4W
Waldron, U.S.A. 81 H7 34 54N 94 5W
Walebing, Australia ..... 61 F2 30 41S 116 13 E
Wales □, U.K. 13 E3 52 19N 4 43W
Walgett, Australia ...... 63 E4 30 0S 148 5 E
Walgreen Coast, Antarctica . 5 D15 75 15S 105 0W
Walker, U.S.A. 80 B7 47 6N 94 35W
Walker, L., Canada 73 B6 50 20N 67 11W
Walker L., Canada 71 C9 54 42N 95 57W
Walker L., U.S.A. 76 G4 38 42N 118 43W
Walkerston, Australia ... 62 K7 21 11S 149 8 E
Walkerton, Canada 84 B3 44 10N 81 10W
Wall, U.S.A. 80 D3 44 0N 102 8W
Walla Walla, U.S.A. 76 C4 46 4N 118 20W
Wallace, Idaho, U.S.A. ... 76 C6 47 28N 115 56W
Wallace, N.C., U.S.A. 83 H7 34 44N 77 59W
Wallaceburg, Canada 84 D2 42 34N 82 23W
Wallachia = Valahia, Romania . 17 F13 44 35N 25 0 E
Wallal, Australia .... 63 D4 26 32S 146 7 E
Wallam Cr. →, Australia .. 63 D4 28 40S 147 20 E
Wallambin, L., Australia .. 61 F2 30 57S 117 35 E
Wallangarra, Australia ... 63 D5 28 56S 151 58 E
Wallaroo, Australia ..... 63 E2 33 56S 137 39 E
Wallenpaupack, L., U.S.A. . 85 E9 41 25N 75 15W
Wallingford, U.S.A. 85 E12 41 27N 72 50W
Wallis & Futuna, Is., Pac. Oc. . 64 J10 13 18S 176 10W
Wallowa, U.S.A. 76 D5 45 34N 117 32W
Wallowa Mts., U.S.A. 76 D5 45 20N 117 30W
Walls, U.K. 11 A7 60 14N 1 33W
Walls of Jerusalem △, Australia . 63 G4 41 56S 146 15 E
Wallula, U.S.A. 76 C4 46 5N 118 54W
Wallumbilla, Australia ... 63 D4 26 33S 149 9 E
Walmsley, L., Canada ... 71 A7 63 25N 108 36W
Walney, I. of, U.K. 12 C4 54 6N 3 15W
Walnut Canyon △, U.S.A. . 77 J8 35 15N 111 20W
Walnut Creek, U.S.A. 78 H4 37 54N 122 4W
Walnut Ridge, U.S.A. 81 G9 36 4N 90 57W
Walpole, Australia ...... 61 F2 34 58S 116 44 E
Walpole, U.S.A. 85 D13 42 9N 71 15W
Walsall, U.K. 13 E6 52 35N 1 58W
Walsenburg, U.S.A. 81 G2 37 38N 104 47W
Walsh, U.S.A. 81 G3 37 23N 102 17W
Walsh →, Australia ...... 62 B3 16 31S 143 42 E
Walterboro, U.S.A. 83 J5 32 55N 80 40W
Walters, U.S.A. 81 H5 34 22N 98 19W
Waltham, U.S.A. 85 D13 42 23N 71 14W
Walton, U.S.A. 76 E10 43 4N 107 12W
Walton, U.S.A. 85 D9 42 10N 75 8W
Walton-on-the-Naze, U.K. . 13 F9 51 51N 1 17 E
Walvis Bay, Namibia .... 56 C1 23 0S 14 28 E
Walvisbaai = Walvis Bay, Namibia . 56 C1 23 0S 14 28 E
Wamba, Dem. Rep. of the Congo 54 B2 2 10N 27 57 E
Wamba, Kenya .... 54 B4 0 58N 37 19 E
Wamego, U.S.A. 80 F6 39 12N 96 18W
Wamena, Indonesia ..... 37 E9 4 4S 138 57 E
Wamsutter, U.S.A. 76 F9 41 40N 107 58W
Wamulan, Indonesia .... 37 E7 3 27S 126 7 E
Wan Xian, China .... 34 E8 38 47N 115 7 E
Wana, Pakistan .... 42 C3 32 20N 69 32 E
Wanaaring, Australia ... 63 D3 29 38S 144 9 E
Wanaka, N.Z. .... 59 L2 44 42S 169 9 E
Wanaka, L., N.Z. .... 59 L2 44 33S 169 7 E
Wanapitei L., Canada ... 72 C3 46 45N 80 40W
Wandel Sea = McKinley Sea, Arctic . 4 A7 82 0N 0 0W
Wanderer, Zimbabwe ... 55 F3 19 36S 30 1 E
Wandhari, Pakistan ..... 42 F2 27 42N 66 48 E
Wandoan, Australia .... 63 D4 26 5S 149 55 E
Wanfu, China .... 35 D12 40 8N 122 38 E
Wang →, Thailand ...... 38 D2 17 8N 99 2 E
Wang Noi, Thailand .... 38 E3 14 13N 100 44 E
Wang Saphung, Thailand . 38 D3 17 18N 101 46 E
Wang Thong, Thailand .. 38 D3 16 50N 100 26 E
Wanga, Dem. Rep. of the Congo 54 B2 2 58N 29 12 E
Wangal, Indonesia ...... 37 F8 6 8S 134 9 E
Wanganella, Australia ... 63 F3 35 6S 144 49 E
Wanganui, N.Z. .... 59 H5 39 56S 175 3 E
Wangaratta, Australia ... 63 F4 36 21S 146 19 E
Wangary, Australia ..... 63 E2 34 35S 135 29 E
Wangdu, China .... 34 E8 38 40N 115 7 E
Wangerooge, Germany .. 16 B4 53 47N 7 54 E
Wangiwangi, Indonesia .. 37 F6 5 22S 123 37 E
Wangqing, China .... 35 C15 43 12N 129 42 E
Wankaner, India .... 42 H4 22 35N 71 0 E
Wanless, Canada 71 C8 54 11N 101 21W
Wanning, China .... 38 C8 18 48N 110 22 E
Wannoo Billabong Roadhouse, Australia . 61 E1 27 38S 114 14 E
Wanon Niwat, Thailand . 38 D4 17 38N 103 46 E
Wanqinsha, China ...... 33 F10 22 43N 113 33 E
Wanquan, China .... 34 D8 40 50N 114 40 E
Wanrong, China .... 34 G6 35 25N 110 50 E
Wanshan Qundao, China . 33 G10 21 57N 113 45 E
Wantage, U.K. 13 F6 51 35N 1 25W
Wanxian, China .... 33 G10 22 12N 113 31 E
Wanzai, China .... 33 D6 28 7N 114 30 E
Wapakoneta, U.S.A. 82 E3 40 34N 84 12W
Wapato, U.S.A. 76 C3 46 27N 120 25W
Wapawekka L., Canada .. 71 C8 54 55N 104 40W
Wapikopa L., Canada ... 72 B2 52 56N 87 53W
Wapiti →, Canada 70 B5 55 5N 118 18W
Wappingers Falls, U.S.A. . 85 E11 41 36N 73 55W

Wapsipinicon →, U.S.A. .. 80 E9 41 44N 90 19W
Wapusk △, Canada 71 B10 57 46N 93 22W
Wapusk Nat. Park △ ..... 71 B10 90 0S 180 0 E
Warangal, India .... 40 L11 17 58N 79 35 E
Waraseoni, India .... 43 J9 21 45N 80 2 E
Waratah, Australia ..... 63 G4 41 30S 145 30 E
Waratah B., Australia ... 63 F4 38 54S 146 5 E
Warburton, Vic., Australia . 63 F4 37 47S 145 42 E
Warburton, W. Austral., Australia 61 E4 26 8S 126 35 E
Warburton →, Australia .. 63 D2 28 4S 137 28 E
Warburton Ra., Australia . 61 E4 25 55S 126 28 E
Ward, N.Z. .... 59 J5 41 49S 174 11 E
Ward →, Australia ...... 63 D4 26 28S 146 6 E
Ward Mt., U.S.A. 78 H8 37 12N 118 54W
Warden, S. Africa ...... 57 D4 27 50S 29 0 E
Wardha, India .... 40 J11 20 45N 78 39 E
Wardha →, India .... 40 K11 19 57N 79 11 E
Ware, Canada 70 B3 57 26N 125 41W
Ware, U.K. 13 F8 51 49N 0 0W
Ware, U.S.A. 85 D12 42 16N 72 14W
Waregem, Belgium ..... 15 D3 50 53N 3 27 E
Wareham, U.S.A. 85 E14 41 46N 70 43W
Waremme, Belgium ..... 15 D5 50 43N 5 15 E
Warialda, Australia .... 63 D5 29 29S 150 33 E
Wariap, Indonesia ...... 37 E8 1 30S 134 5 E
Warin Chamrap, Thailand . 38 E5 15 12N 104 53 E
Warkopi, Indonesia ..... 37 E8 1 12S 134 9 E
Warm Springs, U.S.A. ... 77 G5 38 10N 116 20W
Warman, Canada 71 C7 52 19N 106 30W
Warmbad = Bela Bela, S. Africa 57 C4 24 51S 28 19 E
Warmbad, Namibia ..... 56 D2 28 25S 18 42 E
Warminster, U.K. 13 F5 51 12N 2 10W
Warminster, U.S.A. 85 F9 40 12N 75 6W
Warner Mts., U.S.A. 76 F3 41 40N 120 15W
Warner Robins, U.S.A. .. 83 J4 32 37N 83 36W
Waroona, Australia ..... 61 F2 32 50S 115 58 E
Warracknabeal, Australia . 63 F3 36 9S 142 26 E
Warragul, Australia .... 63 F4 38 10S 145 58 E
Warrego →, Australia .... 63 E4 30 24S 145 21 E
Warrego Ra., Australia .. 62 C4 24 58S 146 0 E
Warren, Australia ...... 63 E4 31 42S 147 51 E
Warren, Ark., U.S.A. 81 J8 33 37N 92 4W
Warren, Mich., U.S.A. ... 82 D4 42 30N 83 0W
Warren, Minn., U.S.A. ... 80 A6 48 12N 96 46W
Warren, Ohio, U.S.A. 84 E4 41 14N 80 49W
Warren, Pa., U.S.A. 84 E5 41 51N 79 9W
Warrenpoint, U.K. 10 B5 54 6N 6 15W
Warrensburg, Mo., U.S.A. . 80 F8 38 46N 93 44W
Warrensburg, N.Y., U.S.A. . 85 C11 43 29N 73 46W
Warrenton, S. Africa .... 56 D3 28 9S 24 47 E
Warrenton, U.S.A. 78 D3 46 10N 123 56W
Warri, Nigeria .... 50 G7 5 30N 5 41 E
Warrina, Australia ...... 63 D2 28 12S 135 50 E
Warrington, U.K. 12 D5 53 24N 2 35W
Warrington, U.S.A. 83 K2 30 23N 87 17W
Warrington □, U.K. 12 D5 53 24N 2 35W
Warrnambool, Australia .. 63 F3 38 25S 142 30 E
Warroad, U.S.A. 80 A7 48 54N 95 19W
Warruwi, Australia ..... 62 A1 11 36S 133 20 E
Warsa, Indonesia .... 37 E9 0 47S 135 55 E
Warsak Dam, Pakistan .. 42 B4 34 11N 71 19 E
Warsaw = Warszawa, Poland . 17 B11 52 13N 21 0 E
Warsaw, Ind., U.S.A. 82 E3 41 14N 85 51W
Warsaw, N.Y., U.S.A. 84 D6 42 45N 78 8W
Warsaw, Ohio, U.S.A. ... 84 F3 40 20N 82 0W
Warszawa, Poland ...... 17 B11 52 13N 21 0 E
Warta →, Poland .... 16 B8 52 35N 14 39 E
Warthe = Warta →, Poland 16 B8 52 35N 14 39 E
Waru, Indonesia .... 37 E8 3 30S 130 36 E
Warwick, Australia ..... 63 D5 28 10S 152 1 E
Warwick, U.K. 13 E6 52 18N 1 35W
Warwick, N.Y., U.S.A. ... 85 E10 41 16N 74 22W
Warwick, R.I., U.S.A. ... 85 E13 41 42N 71 28W
Warwickshire □, U.K. ... 13 E6 52 14N 1 38W
Wasaga Beach, Canada .. 84 B4 44 31N 80 1W
Wasagaming, Canada ... 71 C9 50 39N 99 58W
Wasatch Ra., U.S.A. 76 F8 40 30N 111 15W
Wasbank, S. Africa ..... 57 D5 28 15S 30 9 E
Wasco, Calif., U.S.A. 79 K7 35 36N 119 20W
Wasco, Oreg., U.S.A. 76 D3 45 36N 120 42W
Waseca, U.S.A. 80 C8 44 5N 93 30W
Wasekamio L., Canada .. 71 B7 56 45N 108 45W
Wash, The, U.K. .... 12 E8 52 58N 0 20 E
Washago, Canada 84 B5 44 45N 79 20W
Washburn, N. Dak., U.S.A. . 80 B4 47 17N 101 2W
Washburn, Wis., U.S.A. .. 80 B9 46 40N 90 54W
Washim, India .... 40 J10 20 3N 77 0 E
Washington, U.K. 12 C6 54 55N 1 30W
Washington, D.C., U.S.A. . 82 F7 38 54N 77 2W
Washington, Ga., U.S.A. . 83 J4 33 44N 82 44W
Washington, Ind., U.S.A. . 82 F2 38 40N 87 10W
Washington, Iowa, U.S.A. . 80 E9 41 18N 91 42W
Washington, Mo., U.S.A. . 80 F9 38 33N 91 1W
Washington, N.C., U.S.A. . 83 H7 35 33N 77 3W
Washington, N.J., U.S.A. . 85 F10 40 46N 74 59W
Washington, Pa., U.S.A. .. 84 F4 40 10N 80 15W
Washington, Utah, U.S.A. . 77 H7 37 8N 113 31W
Washington □, U.S.A. ... 76 C3 47 30N 120 30W
Washington, Mt., U.S.A. . 85 B13 44 16N 71 18W
Washington Court House, U.S.A. 82 F4 39 32N 83 26W
Washington I., U.S.A. ... 82 C2 45 23N 86 54W
Washougal, U.S.A. 78 E4 45 35N 122 21W
Washpool △, Australia ... 63 D5 29 22S 152 20 E
Wasian, Indonesia ...... 37 E8 1 47S 133 19 E
Wasilla, U.S.A. 68 B5 61 35N 149 26W
Wasior, Indonesia ...... 37 E8 2 43S 134 30 E
Wāsiṭ, Iraq .... 44 C5 32 30N 46 0 E
Waskaganish, Canada ... 72 B4 51 30N 78 40W
Waskaiowaka, L., Canada . 71 B9 56 33N 96 23W
Waskesiu Lake, Canada .. 71 C7 53 55N 106 5W
Wasserkuppe, Germany .. 16 C5 50 29N 9 55 E
Waswanipi, Canada 72 C4 49 40N 76 29W
Waswanipi, L., Canada .. 72 C4 49 35N 76 40W
Watampone, Indonesia .. 37 E6 4 29S 120 25 E
Watamu, Kenya .... 54 C5 3 23S 40 0 E
Watarrka △, Australia ... 60 D5 24 20S 131 30 E
Water Park Pt., Australia . 62 C5 22 56S 150 47 E
Water Valley, U.S.A. 81 H10 34 10N 89 38W
Waterberg Plateau △, Namibia 56 C2 20 25S 17 18 E
Waterberge, S. Africa .... 57 C4 24 10S 28 0 E
Waterbury, Conn., U.S.A. . 85 E11 41 33N 73 3W
Waterbury, Vt., U.S.A. ... 85 B12 44 20N 72 46W
Waterbury L., Canada ... 71 B8 58 10N 104 22W
Waterdown, Canada 84 C5 43 20N 79 53W
Waterford, Canada 84 D4 42 56N 80 17W
Waterford, Ireland 10 D4 52 15N 7 8W
Waterford, Calif., U.S.A. . 78 H6 37 38N 120 46W
Waterford, Pa., U.S.A. ... 84 E5 41 57N 79 59W

Waterford □, Ireland 10 D4 52 10N 7 40W
Waterford Harbour, Ireland . 10 D5 52 8N 6 58W
Waterhen L., Canada ... 71 C9 52 10N 99 40W
Waterloo, Belgium ..... 15 D4 50 43N 4 25 E
Waterloo, Ont., Canada .. 84 C4 43 30N 80 32W
Waterloo, Qué., Canada .. 85 A12 45 22N 72 32W
Waterloo, Ill., U.S.A. 80 F9 38 20N 90 9W
Waterloo, Iowa, U.S.A. .. 80 D8 42 30N 92 21W
Waterloo, N.Y., U.S.A. ... 84 D8 42 54N 76 52W
Watersmeet, U.S.A. 80 B10 46 16N 89 11W
Waterton Lakes △, Canada . 70 D6 48 45N 115 0W
Watertown, Conn., U.S.A. . 85 E11 41 36N 73 7W
Watertown, N.Y., U.S.A. . 85 C9 43 59N 75 55W
Watertown, S. Dak., U.S.A. . 80 C6 44 54N 97 7W
Watertown, Wis., U.S.A. . 80 D10 43 12N 88 43W
Waterval-Boven, S. Africa . 57 D5 25 40S 30 18 E
Waterville, Canada 85 A13 45 16N 71 54W
Waterville, Maine, U.S.A. . 83 C11 44 33N 69 38W
Waterville, N.Y., U.S.A. .. 85 D9 42 56N 75 23W
Waterville, Pa., U.S.A. ... 84 E7 41 19N 77 21W
Waterville, Wash., U.S.A. . 76 C3 47 39N 120 4W
Watervliet, U.S.A. 85 D11 42 44N 73 42W
Wates, Indonesia ...... 37 G14 7 51S 110 10 E
Watford, Canada 84 D3 42 57N 81 53W
Watford, U.K. 13 F7 51 40N 0 24W
Watford City, U.S.A. 80 B3 47 48N 103 17W
Wathaman →, Canada ... 71 B8 57 16N 102 59W
Wathaman L., Canada ... 71 B8 56 58N 103 44W
Watheroo, Australia .... 61 F2 30 15S 116 0 E
Watheroo △, Australia ... 61 F2 30 19S 115 48 E
Wating, China .... 34 G4 35 40N 106 38 E
Watkins Glen, U.S.A. 84 D8 42 23N 76 52W
Watling I. = San Salvador I., Bahamas . 89 B5 24 0N 74 40W
Watonga, U.S.A. 81 H5 35 51N 98 25W
Watrous, Canada 71 C7 51 40N 105 25W
Watrous, U.S.A. 81 H2 35 48N 104 59W
Watsa, Dem. Rep. of the Congo 54 B2 3 4N 29 30 E
Watseka, U.S.A. 82 E2 40 47N 87 44W
Watson, Australia ...... 61 F5 30 29S 131 31 E
Watson, Canada 71 C8 52 10N 104 30W
Watson Lake, Canada ... 70 A3 60 6N 128 49W
Watsontown, U.S.A. 84 E8 41 5N 76 52W
Watsonville, U.S.A. 78 J5 36 55N 121 45W
Wattiwarriganna Cr. →, Australia . 63 D2 28 57S 136 10 E
Watuata = Batuata, Indonesia . 37 F6 6 12S 122 42 E
Watubela, Kepulauan, Indonesia . 37 E8 4 28S 131 35 E
Watubela Is. = Watubela, Kepulauan, Indonesia . 37 E8 4 28S 131 35 E
Wau = Wâw, Sudan .... 51 G11 7 45N 28 1 E
Waubamik, Canada 84 A4 45 27N 80 1W
Waubay, U.S.A. 80 C6 45 20N 97 18W
Wauchope, N.S.W., Australia . 63 E5 31 28S 152 45 E
Wauchope, N. Terr., Australia . 62 C1 20 36S 134 15 E
Wauchula, U.S.A. 83 M5 27 33N 81 49W
Waukarlycarly, L., Australia . 60 D3 21 18S 121 56 E
Waukegan, U.S.A. 82 D2 42 22N 87 50W
Waukesha, U.S.A. 82 D1 43 1N 88 14W
Waukon, U.S.A. 80 D9 43 16N 91 29W
Waupaca, U.S.A. 80 C10 44 21N 89 5W
Waupun, U.S.A. 80 D10 43 38N 88 44W
Waurika, U.S.A. 81 H6 34 10N 98 0W
Wausau, U.S.A. 80 C10 44 58N 89 38W
Wautoma, U.S.A. 80 C10 44 4N 89 18W
Wauwatosa, U.S.A. 82 D2 43 3N 88 0W
Waveney →, U.K. ...... 13 E9 52 35N 1 39 E
Waverley, N.Z. .... 59 H5 39 46S 174 37 E
Waverly, Iowa, U.S.A. ... 80 D8 42 44N 92 29W
Waverly, N.Y., U.S.A. ... 85 E8 41 7N 76 32W
Wavre, Belgium .... 15 D4 50 43N 4 38 E
Wâw, Sudan .... 51 G11 7 45N 28 1 E
Wāw al Kabīr, Libya .... 51 C9 25 20N 16 43 E
Wawa, Canada 72 C3 47 59N 84 47W
Wawanesa, Canada 71 D9 49 36N 99 40W
Wawona, U.S.A. 78 H7 37 32N 119 39W
Waxahachie, U.S.A. 81 J6 32 24N 96 51W
Way, L., Australia ...... 61 E3 26 45S 120 16 E
Waycross, U.S.A. 83 K4 31 13N 82 21W
Wayland, U.S.A. 84 D7 42 34N 77 35W
Wayne, Nebr., U.S.A. ... 80 D6 42 14N 97 1W
Wayne, W. Va., U.S.A. ... 82 F4 38 13N 82 27W
Waynesboro, Ga., U.S.A. . 83 J4 33 6N 82 1W
Waynesboro, Miss., U.S.A. . 83 K1 31 40N 88 39W
Waynesboro, Pa., U.S.A. . 82 F7 39 45N 77 35W
Waynesboro, Va., U.S.A. . 82 F6 38 4N 78 53W
Waynesville, U.S.A. 83 H4 35 28N 82 58W
Waynoka, U.S.A. 81 G5 36 35N 98 53W
Wazirabad, Pakistan ... 42 C6 32 30N 74 8 E
We, Indonesia .... 36 C1 5 51N 95 18 E
Weald, The, U.K. ...... 13 F8 51 4N 0 20 E
Wear →, U.K. 12 C6 54 55N 1 23W
Weatherford, Okla., U.S.A. . 81 H5 35 32N 98 43W
Weatherford, Tex., U.S.A. . 81 J6 32 46N 97 48W
Weaverville, U.S.A. 76 F2 40 44N 122 56W
Webb City, U.S.A. 81 G7 37 9N 94 28W
Webequie, Canada 72 B2 52 59N 87 21W
Webster, Mass., U.S.A. .. 85 D13 42 3N 71 53W
Webster, N.Y., U.S.A. ... 84 C7 43 13N 77 26W
Webster, S. Dak., U.S.A. . 80 C6 45 20N 97 31W
Webster City, U.S.A. 80 D8 42 28N 93 49W
Webster Springs, U.S.A. . 82 F5 38 29N 80 25W
Weda, Indonesia .... 37 D7 0 21N 127 50 E
Weda, Teluk, Indonesia .. 37 D7 0 20N 128 0 E
Weddell I., Falk. Is. 96 G4 51 50S 61 0W
Weddell Sea, Antarctica .. 5 D1 72 30S 40 0W
Wedderburn, Australia .. 63 F3 36 26S 143 33 E
Wedgeport, Canada 73 D6 43 44N 65 59W
Wedza, Zimbabwe ..... 55 F3 18 40S 31 33 E
Wee Waa, Australia .... 63 E4 30 11S 149 26 E
Weed, U.S.A. 76 F2 41 25N 122 23W
Weed Heights, U.S.A. ... 78 G4 38 59N 119 13W
Weedsport, U.S.A. 85 C8 43 3N 76 35W
Weedville, U.S.A. 84 E6 41 17N 78 30W
Weenen, S. Africa ...... 57 D5 28 48S 30 7 E
Weert, Neths. .... 15 C5 51 15N 5 43 E
Wei He →, Hebei, China . 34 F8 36 10N 115 45 E
Wei He →, Shaanxi, China . 34 G6 34 38N 110 15 E
Weichang, China ...... 35 D9 41 58N 117 49 E
Weichuan, China ...... 34 G7 34 20N 113 59 E
Weiden, Germany ...... 16 D7 49 41N 12 10 E
Weifang, China .... 35 F10 36 44N 119 7 E
Weihai, China .... 35 F12 37 30N 122 6 E
Weimar, Germany ...... 16 C6 50 58N 11 19 E
Weinan, China .... 34 G5 34 31N 109 29 E
Weipa, Australia .... 62 A3 12 40S 141 50 E
Weir →, Australia ...... 63 D4 28 20S 149 50 E

Weir →, Canada 71 B10 56 54N 93 21W
Weir River, Canada 71 B10 56 49N 94 6W
Weirton, U.S.A. 84 F4 40 24N 80 35W
Weiser, U.S.A. 76 D5 44 10N 117 0W
Weishan, China .... 35 G9 34 47N 117 5 E
Weiyuan, China .... 34 G3 35 7N 104 10 E
Wejherowo, Poland .... 17 A10 54 35N 18 12 E
Wekusko L., Canada 71 C9 54 40N 99 50W
Welch, U.S.A. 82 G5 37 26N 81 35W
Welford △, Australia .... 62 D3 25 5S 143 16 E
Welkom, S. Africa ..... 56 D4 28 0S 26 46 E
Welland, Canada 84 D5 43 0N 79 15W
Welland →, U.K. 13 E7 52 51N 0 5W
Wellesley Is., Australia .. 62 B2 16 42S 139 30 E
Wellingborough, U.K. .. 13 E7 52 19N 0 41W
Wellington, Australia ... 63 E4 32 35S 148 59 E
Wellington, Canada 84 C7 43 57N 77 20W
Wellington, N.Z. ...... 59 J5 41 19S 174 46 E
Wellington, S. Africa ... 56 E2 33 38S 19 1 E
Wellington, Telford & Wrekin, U.K. . 13 G4 50 58N 3 13W
Wellington, I., Chile ... 13 E5 52 42N 2 30W
Wellington, Colo., U.S.A. . 80 E2 40 42N 105 0W
Wellington, Kans., U.S.A. . 81 G6 37 16N 97 24W
Wellington, Nev., U.S.A. . 78 G7 38 45N 119 23W
Wellington, Ohio, U.S.A. . 84 E2 41 10N 82 13W
Wellington, Tex., U.S.A. . 81 H4 34 51N 100 13W
Wellington, I., Chile .... 63 F4 38 6S 147 20 E
Wellington, L., Australia . 63 F4 38 6S 147 20 E
Wells, U.K. 13 F5 51 13N 2 39W
Wells, Maine, U.S.A. ... 85 C14 43 20N 70 35W
Wells, N.Y., U.S.A. 85 C10 43 24N 74 17W
Wells, Nev., U.S.A. 76 F6 41 7N 114 58W
Wells, L., Australia ..... 61 E3 26 44S 123 15 E
Wells, Mt., Australia .... 60 C4 17 25S 127 8 E
Wells Gray △, Canada ... 70 C4 52 30N 120 15W
Wells-next-the-Sea, U.K. . 12 E8 52 57N 0 51 E
Wells River, U.S.A. 85 B12 44 9N 72 4W
Wellsboro, U.S.A. 84 E7 41 45N 77 18W
Wellsburg, U.S.A. 84 F4 40 16N 80 37W
Wellsville, N.Y., U.S.A. .. 84 D7 42 7N 77 57W
Wellsville, Ohio, U.S.A. . 84 F4 40 36N 80 39W
Wellsville, Utah, U.S.A. . 76 F8 41 38N 111 56W
Wellton, U.S.A. 77 K6 32 40N 114 8W
Wels, Austria .... 16 D8 48 9N 14 1 E
Welshpool, U.K. 13 E4 52 39N 3 8W
Welwyn Garden City, U.K. . 13 F7 51 48N 0 12W
Wem, U.K. 12 E5 52 52N 2 44W
Wembere →, Tanzania .. 54 C3 4 10S 34 15 E
Wemindji, Canada 72 B4 53 0N 78 49W
Wen Xian, China ...... 34 G7 34 55N 113 5 E
Wenatchee, U.S.A. 76 C3 47 25N 120 19W
Wenchang, China ...... 38 C8 19 38N 110 42 E
Wenchi, Ghana 50 G5 7 46N 2 8W
Wenchow = Wenzhou, China . 33 D7 28 0N 120 38 E
Wenden, U.S.A. 79 M13 33 49N 113 33W
Wendeng, China .... 35 F12 37 15N 122 5 E
Wendesi, Indonesia .... 37 E8 2 30S 134 17 E
Wendover, U.S.A. 76 F6 40 44N 114 2W
Wenlock →, Australia ... 62 A3 12 2S 141 55 E
Wenshan, China .... 32 D5 23 20N 104 18 E
Wenshang, China ...... 34 G9 35 45N 116 30 E
Wenshui, China .... 34 F7 37 26N 112 1 E
Wensleydale, U.K. 12 C6 54 17N 2 0W
Wensu, China .... 32 B3 41 15N 80 10 E
Wensum →, U.K. ...... 12 E8 52 40N 1 15 E
Wentworth, Australia ... 63 E3 34 2S 141 54 E
Wentzel L., Canada 70 B6 59 2N 114 28W
Wenut, Indonesia ...... 37 E8 3 11S 133 19 E
Wenxi, China .... 34 G6 35 20N 111 10 E
Wenxian, China .... 34 H3 32 43N 104 36 E
Wenzhou, China .... 33 D7 28 0N 120 38 E
Weott, U.S.A. 76 F2 40 20N 123 55W
Wepener, S. Africa ..... 56 D4 29 42S 27 3 E
Werda, Botswana ...... 56 D3 25 24S 23 15 E
Weri, Indonesia .... 37 E8 3 10S 132 38 E
Werra →, Germany ..... 16 C5 51 24N 9 39 E
Werrimull, Australia .... 63 E3 34 25S 141 38 E
Werris Creek, Australia .. 63 E5 31 18S 150 38 E
Weser →, Germany ..... 16 B5 53 36N 8 28 E
Wesiri, Indonesia ...... 37 F7 7 30S 126 30 E
Weslemkoon L., Canada . 84 A7 45 2N 77 25W
Wesleyville, Canada 84 D4 42 9N 80 0W
Wessel, C., Australia ... 62 A2 10 59S 136 46 E
Wessel Is., Australia .... 62 A2 11 10S 136 45 E
Wessington Springs, U.S.A. . 80 C5 44 5N 98 34W
West, U.S.A. 81 K6 31 48N 97 6W
West →, U.S.A. 85 D12 42 52N 72 33W
West Antarctica, Antarctica . 5 D15 80 0S 90 0W
West Baines →, Australia . 60 C4 15 38S 129 59 E
West Bank ⊠, Asia ..... 46 C4 32 6N 35 13 E
West Bend, U.S.A. 82 D1 43 25N 88 11W
West Bengal □, India ... 43 H13 23 0N 88 0 E
West Berkshire □, U.K. . 13 F6 51 25N 1 17W
West Beskids = Západné Beskydy, Europe . 17 D10 49 30N 19 0 E
West Branch, U.S.A. 82 C3 44 17N 84 14W
West Branch Susquehanna →, U.S.A. . 85 F8 40 53N 76 48W
West Bromwich, U.K. ... 13 E6 52 32N 1 59W
West Burra, U.K. 11 A7 60 5N 1 21W
West Canada Cr. →, U.S.A. . 85 C10 43 1N 74 58W
West Chazy, U.S.A. 85 B11 44 49N 73 28W
West Chester, U.S.A. ... 85 G9 39 58N 75 36W
West Coast □, Namibia .. 56 C1 21 53S 14 14 E
West Coast △, S. Africa . 56 E2 33 13S 18 0 E
West Columbia, U.S.A. . 81 L7 29 9N 95 39W
West Covina, U.S.A. 79 L9 34 4N 117 54W
West Des Moines, U.S.A. . 80 E8 41 35N 93 43W
West End, Bahamas 88 A4 26 41N 78 58W
West Falkland, Falk. Is. .. 96 G5 51 40S 60 0W
West Fargo, U.S.A. 80 B6 46 52N 96 54W
West Hazleton, U.S.A. .. 84 E4 41 0N 76 0W
West Fjord = Vestfjorden, Norway . 8 C15 67 55N 14 0 E
West Fork Trinity →, U.S.A. . 81 J6 32 48N 96 54W
West Frankfort, U.S.A. .. 80 G10 37 54N 88 55W
West Hartford, U.S.A. ... 85 E12 41 45N 72 44W
West Haven, U.S.A. 85 E12 41 17N 72 57W
West Hazleton, U.S.A. .. 85 F9 40 58N 76 0W
West Helena, U.S.A. 81 H9 34 33N 90 38W
West Hurley, U.S.A. 85 E10 41 59N 74 7W
West Ice Shelf, Antarctica . 5 C7 67 0S 85 0 E
West Indies, Cent. Amer. . 89 D7 15 0N 65 0W
West Jordan, U.S.A. 76 F8 40 36N 111 56W

West Lamma Channel, China .. 33 G11 22 13N 114 4 E
West Lorne, Canada 84 D3 42 36N 81 36W
West Lothian □, U.K. 11 F5 55 54N 3 36W
West Lunga →, Zambia ...... 55 E1 13 6S 24 39 E
West MacDonnell △, Australia . 60 D5 23 38S 132 59 E
West Memphis, U.S.A. 81 H9 35 9N 90 11W
West Midlands □, U.K. 13 E6 52 26N 2 0W
West Mifflin, U.S.A. 84 F5 40 22N 79 52W
West Milton, U.S.A. 84 E8 41 1N 76 50W
West Monroe, U.S.A. 81 J8 32 31N 92 9W
West Newton, U.S.A. 84 F5 40 14N 79 46W
West Nicholson, Zimbabwe .. 55 G2 21 2S 29 20 E
West Palm Beach, U.S.A. 83 M5 26 43N 80 3W
West Plains, U.S.A. 81 G9 36 44N 91 51W
West Point, N.Y., U.S.A. 85 E11 41 24N 73 58W
West Point, Nebr., U.S.A. 80 E6 41 51N 96 43W
West Point, Va., U.S.A. 82 G7 37 32N 76 48W
West Pt. = Ouest, Pte. de l',
   Canada 73 C7 49 52N 64 40W
West Pt., Australia ...... 63 F2 35 1S 135 56 E
West Road →, Canada 70 C4 53 18N 122 53W
West Rutland, U.S.A. 85 C11 43 38N 73 5W
West Schelde =
   Westerschelde →, Neths. .. 15 C3 51 25N 3 25 E
West Seneca, U.S.A. 84 D6 42 51N 78 48W
West Siberian Plain, Russia .... 26 C11 62 0N 75 0 E
West Sussex □, U.K. 13 G7 50 55N 0 30W
West-Terschelling, Neths. .. 15 A5 53 22N 5 13 E
West Valley City, U.S.A. 76 F8 40 42N 111 57W
West Virginia □, U.S.A. 82 F5 38 45N 80 30W
West-Vlaanderen □, Belgium .. 15 D2 51 0N 3 0 E
West Walker →, U.S.A. 78 G7 38 54N 119 9W
West Wyalong, Australia .... 63 E4 33 56S 147 10 E
West Yellowstone, U.S.A. 76 D8 44 40N 111 6W
West Yorkshire □, U.K. 12 D6 53 45N 1 40W
Westall, Pt., Australia ...... 63 E1 32 55S 134 4 E
Westbrook, U.S.A. 83 D10 43 41N 70 22W
Westbury, Australia ...... 63 G4 41 30S 146 51 E
Westby, U.S.A. 80 A2 48 52N 104 3W
Westend, U.S.A. 79 K9 35 42N 117 24W
Westerland, Germany ...... 9 J13 54 54N 8 17 E
Westerly, U.S.A. 85 E13 41 22N 71 50W
Western □, Kenya ...... 54 B3 0 30N 34 30 E
Western □, Zambia ...... 55 F1 15 0S 24 4 E
Western Australia □, Australia . 61 E2 25 0S 118 0 E
Western Cape □, S. Africa .. 56 E3 34 0S 20 0 E
Western Dvina = Daugava →,
   Latvia ...... 9 H21 57 4N 24 3 E
Western Ghats, India ...... 40 N9 14 0N 75 0 E
Western Isles □, U.K. 11 D1 57 30N 7 10W
Western Sahara ■, Africa 50 D3 25 0N 13 0W
Western Samoa = Samoa ■,
   Pac. Oc. 59 B13 14 0S 172 0W
Westernport, U.S.A. 82 F6 39 29N 79 3W
Westerschelde →, Neths. .. 15 C3 51 25N 3 25 E
Westerwald, Germany ...... 16 C4 50 38N 7 56 E
Westfield, Mass., U.S.A. 85 D12 42 7N 72 45W
Westfield, N.Y., U.S.A. 84 D5 42 20N 79 35W
Westfield, Pa., U.S.A. 84 E7 41 55N 77 32W
Westhill, U.K. 11 D6 57 9N 2 19W
Westhope, U.S.A. 80 A4 48 55N 101 1W
Westland △, N.Z. ...... 59 K2 43 16S 170 16 E
Westland Bight, N.Z. ...... 59 K3 42 55S 170 5 E
Westlock, Canada 70 C6 54 9N 113 55W
Westmar, Australia ...... 63 D4 27 55S 149 44 E
Westmeath □, Ireland 10 C4 53 33N 7 34W
Westminster, U.K. 82 F7 39 34N 76 59W
Westmont, U.S.A. 84 F6 40 19N 78 58W
Westmoreland, Barbados .... 89 g 13 13N 59 37W
Westmorland, U.S.A. 79 M11 33 2N 115 37W
Weston, Oreg., U.S.A. 76 D4 45 49N 118 26W
Weston, W. Va., U.S.A. 82 F5 39 2N 80 28W
Weston I., Canada 72 B4 52 33N 79 36W
Weston-super-Mare, U.K. .. 13 F5 51 21N 2 58W
Westover, U.S.A. 84 F6 40 45N 78 40W
Westport, Canada 85 B8 44 40N 76 25W
Westport, Ireland 10 C2 53 48N 9 31W
Westport, N.Z. ...... 59 J3 41 46S 171 37 E
Westport, N.Y., U.S.A. 85 B11 44 11N 73 26W
Westport, Oreg., U.S.A. 78 D3 46 8N 123 23W
Westport, Wash., U.S.A. 78 D2 46 53N 124 6W
Westray, Canada 71 C8 53 36N 101 24W
Westray, U.K. 11 B5 59 18N 3 0W
Westree, Canada 72 C3 47 26N 81 34W
Westville, U.S.A. 78 F6 39 8N 120 42W
Westwood, U.S.A. 76 F3 40 18N 121 0W
Wetar, Indonesia ...... 37 F7 7 48S 126 30 E
Wetaskiwin, Canada 70 C6 52 55N 113 24W
Wete, Tanzania ...... 52 F7 5 4S 39 43 E
Wetherby, U.K. 12 D6 53 56N 1 23W
Wethersfield, U.S.A. 85 E12 41 42N 72 40W
Wetteren, Belgium ...... 15 D3 51 0N 3 53 E
Wetzlar, Germany ...... 16 C5 50 32N 8 31 E
Wewoka, U.S.A. 81 H6 35 9N 96 30W
Wexford, Ireland 10 D5 52 20N 6 28W
Wexford □, Ireland 10 D5 52 20N 6 25W
Wexford Harbour, Ireland .. 10 D5 52 20N 6 25W
Weyburn, Canada 71 D8 49 40N 103 50W
Weymouth, Canada 73 D6 44 30N 66 1W
Weymouth, U.K. 13 G5 50 37N 2 28W
Weymouth, U.S.A. 85 D14 42 13N 70 58W
Weymouth, C., Australia .... 62 A3 12 37S 143 27 E
Wha Ti, Canada 68 B8 63 8N 117 16W
Whakatane, N.Z. ...... 59 G6 37 57S 177 1 E
Whale →, Canada 73 A6 58 15N 67 40W
Whale Cove, Canada 71 A10 62 10N 92 34W
Whales, B. of, Antarctica 5 D12 78 0S 165 0W
Whalsay, U.K. 11 A8 60 22N 0 59W
Whangamomona, N.Z. ...... 59 H5 39 8S 174 44 E
Whanganui, N.Z. ...... 59 H5 39 17S 174 53 E
Whangarei, N.Z. ...... 59 F5 35 43S 174 21 E
Whangarei Harb., N.Z. .... 59 F5 35 45S 174 28 E
Wharfe →, U.K. 12 D6 53 51N 1 9W
Wharfedale, U.K. 12 C5 54 6N 2 1W
Wharton, N.J., U.S.A. 85 F10 40 54N 74 35W
Wharton, Pa., U.S.A. 84 E6 41 31N 78 1W
Wharton, Tex., U.S.A. 81 L6 29 19N 96 6W
Wheatland, Calif., U.S.A. .. 78 F5 39 1N 121 25W
Wheatland, Wyo., U.S.A. .. 80 D2 42 3N 104 58W
Wheatley, Canada 84 D2 42 6N 82 27W
Wheaton, Md., U.S.A. 82 F7 39 3N 77 3W
Wheaton, Minn., U.S.A. .. 80 C6 45 48N 96 30W
Wheelbarrow Pk., U.S.A. .. 78 H10 37 26N 116 5W
Wheeler, Oreg., U.S.A. .. 76 D2 45 41N 123 53W
Wheeler, Tex., U.S.A. .. 81 H4 35 27N 100 16W
Wheeler →, Canada 73 A6 57 2N 67 13W
Wheeler L., U.S.A. 83 H2 34 48N 87 23W

Wheeler Pk., N. Mex., U.S.A. ... 77 H11 36 34N 105 25W
Wheeler Pk., Nev., U.S.A. ... 77 G6 38 57N 114 15W
Wheeler Ridge, U.S.A. 79 L8 35 0N 118 57W
Wheeling, U.S.A. 84 F4 40 4N 80 43W
Whernside, U.K. 12 C5 54 14N 2 24W
Whiskey Jack L., Canada .. 71 B8 58 23N 101 55W
Whiskeytown-Shasta-Trinity △,
   U.S.A. 76 F2 40 45N 122 15W
Whistleduck Cr. →, Australia .. 62 C2 20 15S 135 18 E
Whistler, Canada 70 C4 50 7N 122 58W
Whitby, Canada 84 C6 43 52N 78 56W
Whitby, U.K. 12 C7 54 29N 0 37W
White →, Ark., U.S.A. 81 J9 33 57N 91 5W
White →, Ind., U.S.A. 82 F2 38 25N 87 45W
White →, S. Dak., U.S.A. .. 80 D5 43 42N 99 27W
White →, Tex., U.S.A. 81 J4 33 14N 100 56W
White →, Utah, U.S.A. 76 F9 40 4N 109 41W
White →, Vt., U.S.A. 85 C12 43 37N 72 20W
White →, Wash., U.S.A. .. 78 C4 47 12N 122 15W
White, L., Australia ...... 60 D4 21 9S 128 56 E
White B., Canada 73 C8 50 0N 56 35W
White Bird, U.S.A. 76 D5 45 46N 116 18W
White Butte, U.S.A. 80 B3 46 23N 103 18W
White City, U.S.A. 76 E2 42 26N 122 51W
White Cliffs, Australia .... 63 E3 30 50S 143 10 E
White Hall, U.S.A. 80 F9 39 26N 90 24W
White Haven, U.S.A. 85 E9 41 4N 75 47W
White Horse, Vale of, U.K. .. 13 F6 51 37N 1 30W
White I., N.Z. ...... 59 G6 37 30S 177 13 E
White L., Canada 85 A8 45 18N 76 31W
White L., U.S.A. 81 L8 29 44N 92 30W
White Mountain Peak, U.S.A. .. 77 G4 37 38N 118 15W
White Mts., Calif., U.S.A. .. 78 H8 37 30N 118 15W
White Mts., N.H., U.S.A. .. 85 B13 44 15N 71 15W
White Nile = Nîl el Abyad →,
   Sudan ...... 51 E12 15 38N 32 31 E
White Otter L., Canada 72 C1 49 5N 91 55W
White Pass, U.S.A. 78 D5 46 38N 121 24W
White Plains, U.S.A. 85 E11 41 2N 73 46W
White River, Canada 72 C2 48 35N 85 20W
White River, S. Africa .... 57 D5 25 20S 31 0 E
White River, U.S.A. 80 D4 43 34N 100 45W
White Rock, Canada 78 A4 49 2N 122 48W
White Russia = Belarus ■,
   Europe ...... 17 B14 53 30N 27 0 E
White Sands △, U.S.A. 77 K10 32 46N 106 20W
White Sea = Beloye More, Russia . 18 A6 66 30N 38 0 E
White Sulphur Springs, Mont.,
   U.S.A. 76 C8 46 33N 110 54W
White Sulphur Springs, W. Va.,
   U.S.A. 82 G5 37 48N 80 18W
White Swan, U.S.A. 78 D6 46 23N 120 44W
Whitecliffs, N.Z. ...... 59 K3 43 26S 171 55 E
Whitecourt, Canada 70 C5 54 10N 115 45W
Whiteface Mt., U.S.A. 85 B11 44 22N 73 54W
Whitefield, U.S.A. 85 B13 44 23N 71 37W
Whitefish, U.S.A. 76 B6 48 25N 114 20W
Whitefish L., Canada 71 A7 62 41N 106 48W
Whitefish Point, U.S.A. 82 B3 46 45N 84 59W
Whitegull, L. = Goélands, L. aux,
   Canada 73 A7 55 27N 64 17W
Whitehall, Mich., U.S.A. .. 82 D2 43 24N 86 21W
Whitehall, Mont., U.S.A. .. 76 D7 45 52N 112 6W
Whitehall, N.Y., U.S.A. .. 85 C11 43 33N 73 24W
Whitehall, Wis., U.S.A. .. 80 C9 44 22N 91 19W
Whitehaven, U.K. 12 C4 54 33N 3 35W
Whitehorse, Canada 70 A1 60 43N 135 3W
Whitemark, Australia ...... 63 G4 40 7S 148 3 E
Whiteriver, U.S.A. 77 K9 33 50N 109 58W
Whitesand →, Canada 70 A5 60 9N 115 45W
Whitesands, S. Africa .... 56 E3 34 23S 20 50 E
Whitesboro, N.Y., U.S.A. .. 85 C9 43 7N 75 18W
Whitesboro, Tex., U.S.A. .. 81 J6 33 39N 96 54W
Whiteshell △, Canada 71 D9 50 0N 95 40W
Whitesville, U.S.A. 84 D7 42 2N 77 46W
Whiteville, U.S.A. 83 H6 34 20N 78 42W
Whitewater, U.S.A. 82 D1 42 50N 88 44W
Whitewater Baldy, U.S.A. .. 77 K9 33 20N 108 39W
Whitewater L., Canada 72 B2 50 50N 89 10W
Whitewood, Australia ...... 62 C3 21 28S 143 30 E
Whitewood, Canada 71 C8 50 20N 102 20W
Whithorn, U.K. 11 G4 54 44N 4 26W
Whitianga, N.Z. ...... 59 G5 36 47S 175 41 E
Whitman, U.S.A. 85 D14 42 5N 70 56W
Whitney, Canada 84 A6 45 31N 78 14W
Whitney, Mt., U.S.A. 78 J8 36 35N 118 18W
Whitney Point, U.S.A. 85 D9 42 20N 75 58W
Whitstable, U.K. ...... 13 F9 51 21N 1 3 E
Whitsunday I., Australia .. 62 J7 20 15S 149 4 E
Whitsunday Islands △, Australia . 62 J7 20 15S 149 0 E
Whitsunday Passage, Australia . 62 J6 20 16S 148 51 E
Whittier, U.S.A. 79 M8 33 58N 118 3W
Whittlesea, Australia ...... 63 F4 37 27S 145 9 E
Wholdaia L., Canada 71 A8 60 43N 104 20W
Whyalla, Australia ...... 63 E2 33 2S 137 30 E
Wiang Kosai △, Thailand .. 38 D2 17 54N 99 29 E
Wiarton, Canada 84 B3 44 40N 81 10W
Wiay, U.K. 11 D1 57 24N 7 13W
Wibaux, U.S.A. 80 B2 46 59N 104 11W
Wichian Buri, Thailand .... 38 E3 15 39N 101 7 E
Wichita, U.S.A. 81 G6 37 42N 97 20W
Wichita Falls, U.S.A. 81 J5 33 54N 98 30W
Wick, U.K. 11 C5 58 26N 3 5W
Wicked Pt., Canada 84 C7 43 52N 77 15W
Wickenburg, U.S.A. 77 K7 33 58N 112 44W
Wickepin, Australia ...... 61 F2 32 50S 117 30 E
Wickham, Australia ...... 60 D2 20 42S 117 11 E
Wickham, C., Australia .... 63 F3 39 35S 143 57 E
Wickliffe, U.S.A. 84 E3 41 36N 81 28W
Wicklow, Ireland 10 D5 52 59N 6 3W
Wicklow □, Ireland 10 D5 52 57N 6 25W
Wicklow Hd., Ireland 10 D6 52 58N 6 0W
Wicklow Mts., Ireland 10 C5 53 6N 6 21W
Widgeegoara Cr. →, Australia . 63 D4 28 51S 146 34 E
Widgiemooltha, Australia .. 61 F3 31 30S 121 34 E
Widnes, U.K. 12 D5 53 23N 2 45W
Wieluń, Poland ...... 17 C10 51 15N 18 34 E
Wien, Austria ...... 16 D9 48 12N 16 22 E
Wiener Neustadt, Austria .. 16 E9 47 49N 16 16 E
Wiesbaden, Germany ...... 16 C5 50 4N 8 14 E
Wigan, U.K. 12 D5 53 33N 2 38W
Wiggins, Colo., U.S.A. 80 E2 40 14N 104 4W
Wiggins, Miss., U.S.A. .. 81 K10 30 51N 89 8W
Wight, I. of □, U.K. 13 G6 50 40N 1 20W
Wigston, U.K. 13 E6 52 35N 1 6W
Wigton, U.K. 12 C4 54 50N 3 10W

Wigtown, U.K. 11 G4 54 53N 4 27W
Wigtown B., U.K. 11 G4 54 46N 4 15W
Wilber, U.S.A. 80 E6 40 29N 96 58W
Wilberforce, Canada 84 A6 45 2N 78 13W
Wilberforce, C., Australia .. 62 A2 11 54S 136 35 E
Wilburton, U.S.A. 81 H7 34 55N 95 19W
Wilcannia, Australia ...... 63 E3 31 30S 143 26 E
Wilcox, U.S.A. 84 E6 41 35N 78 41W
Wildrose, U.S.A. 79 J9 36 14N 117 11W
Wildspitze, Austria ...... 16 E6 46 53N 10 53 E
Wilge →, S. Africa ...... 57 D4 27 3S 28 20 E
Wilhelm II Coast, Antarctica . 5 C7 68 0S 90 0 E
Wilhelmshaven, Germany .. 16 B5 53 31N 8 7 E
Wilhelmstal, Namibia ...... 56 C2 21 58S 16 21 E
Wilkes-Barre, U.S.A. 85 E9 41 15N 75 53W
Wilkes Land, Antarctica .. 5 D9 69 0S 120 0 E
Wilkie, Canada 71 C7 52 27N 108 42W
Wilkinsburg, U.S.A. 84 F5 40 26N 79 53W
Wilkinson Lakes, Australia . 61 E5 29 40S 132 39 E
Willandra Creek →, Australia . 63 E4 33 22S 145 52 E
Willapa B., U.S.A. 76 C2 46 40N 124 0W
Willapa Hills, U.S.A. 78 D3 46 35N 123 25W
Willard, N.Y., U.S.A. 84 D8 42 40N 76 50W
Willard, Ohio, U.S.A. 84 E2 41 3N 82 44W
Willcox, U.S.A. 77 K9 32 15N 109 50W
Willemstad, Neth. Ant. 89 D6 12 5N 69 0W
Willet, U.S.A. 85 D9 42 28N 75 55W
William →, Canada 71 B7 59 8N 109 19W
William 'Bill' Dannely Res.,
   U.S.A. 83 J2 32 10N 87 10W
William Creek, Australia .. 63 D2 28 58S 136 22 E
Williams, Australia ...... 61 F2 33 2S 116 52 E
Williams, Ariz., U.S.A. 77 J7 35 15N 112 11W
Williams, Calif., U.S.A. .. 78 F4 39 9N 122 9W
Williams Harbour, Canada . 73 B8 52 33N 55 47W
Williams Lake, Canada 70 C4 52 10N 122 10W
Williamsburg, Ky., U.S.A. .. 83 G3 36 44N 84 10W
Williamsburg, Pa., U.S.A. .. 84 F6 40 28N 78 12W
Williamsburg, Va., U.S.A. .. 82 G7 37 17N 76 44W
Williamson, N.Y., U.S.A. .. 84 C7 43 14N 77 11W
Williamson, W. Va., U.S.A. .. 82 G4 37 41N 82 17W
Williamsport, U.S.A. 84 E7 41 15N 77 0W
Williamston, U.S.A. 83 H7 35 51N 77 4W
Williamstown, Australia .. 63 F3 37 51S 144 52 E
Williamstown, Ky., U.S.A. .. 82 F3 38 38N 84 34W
Williamstown, Mass., U.S.A. . 85 D11 42 41N 73 12W
Williamstown, N.Y., U.S.A. . 85 C9 43 26N 75 53W
Willimantic, U.S.A. 85 E12 41 43N 72 13W
Willingboro, U.S.A. 82 E8 40 3N 74 54W
Williston, S. Africa ...... 56 E3 31 20S 20 53 E
Williston, Fla., U.S.A. 83 L4 29 23N 82 27W
Williston, N. Dak., U.S.A. .. 80 A3 48 9N 103 37W
Williston L., Canada 70 B4 56 0N 124 0W
Willits, U.S.A. 76 G2 39 25N 123 21W
Willmar, U.S.A. 80 C7 45 7N 95 3W
Willmore Wilderness △, Canada . 70 C5 53 45N 119 30W
Willoughby, U.S.A. 84 E3 41 39N 81 24W
Willow Bunch, Canada 71 D7 49 20N 105 35W
Willow L., Canada 70 A5 62 10N 119 8W
Willow Wall, The, China .. 35 C12 42 10N 122 0 E
Willowick, U.S.A. 84 E3 41 38N 81 28W
Willowlake →, Canada 70 A4 62 42N 123 8W
Willowmore, S. Africa .... 56 E3 33 15S 23 30 E
Willows, U.S.A. 78 F4 39 31N 122 12W
Willowvale = Gatyana, S. Africa . 57 E4 32 16S 28 31 E
Wills, L., Australia ...... 60 D4 21 25S 128 51 E
Wills Cr. →, Australia .... 62 C3 22 43S 140 2 E
Willsboro, U.S.A. 85 B11 44 21N 73 24W
Willunga, Australia ...... 63 F2 35 15S 138 30 E
Wilmette, U.S.A. 82 D2 42 5N 87 42W
Wilmington, Australia .... 63 E2 32 39S 138 7 E
Wilmington, Del., U.S.A. .. 82 F8 39 45N 75 33W
Wilmington, N.C., U.S.A. .. 83 H7 34 14N 77 55W
Wilmington, Ohio, U.S.A. .. 82 F4 39 27N 83 50W
Wilmington, Vt., U.S.A. .. 85 D12 42 52N 72 52W
Wilmslow, U.K. 12 D5 53 19N 2 13W
Wilpena Cr. →, Australia .. 63 E2 31 25S 139 29 E
Wilsall, U.S.A. 76 D8 45 59N 110 38W
Wilson, N.C., U.S.A. 83 H7 35 44N 77 55W
Wilson, N.Y., U.S.A. 84 C6 43 19N 78 50W
Wilson, Pa., U.S.A. 85 F9 40 41N 75 15W
Wilson →, Australia ...... 60 C4 16 48S 128 16 E
Wilson Bluff, Australia .... 61 F4 31 41S 129 0 E
Wilson Inlet, Australia .... 61 G2 35 0S 117 22 E
Wilsons Promontory, Australia . 63 F4 38 55S 146 25 E
Wilton, U.S.A. 80 B4 47 10N 100 47W
Wilton →, Australia ...... 62 A1 14 45S 134 33 E
Wiltshire □, U.K. 13 F6 51 18N 1 53W
Wiltz, Lux. ...... 15 E5 49 57N 5 55 E
Wiluna, Australia ...... 61 E3 26 36S 120 14 E
Wimborne Minster, U.K. .. 13 G6 50 48N 1 59W
Wimmera →, Australia .... 63 F3 36 8S 141 56 E
Winam G., Kenya ...... 54 C3 0 20S 34 15 E
Winburg, S. Africa ...... 56 D4 28 30S 27 2 E
Winchendon, U.S.A. 85 D12 42 41N 72 3W
Winchester, U.K. 13 F6 51 4N 1 18W
Winchester, Conn., U.S.A. . 85 E11 41 53N 73 9W
Winchester, Idaho, U.S.A. . 76 C5 46 14N 116 38W
Winchester, Ind., U.S.A. .. 82 E3 40 10N 84 59W
Winchester, Ky., U.S.A. .. 82 G3 38 0N 84 11W
Winchester, N.H., U.S.A. .. 85 D12 42 46N 72 23W
Winchester, Nev., U.S.A. .. 79 J11 36 6N 115 10W
Winchester, Tenn., U.S.A. . 83 H2 35 11N 86 7W
Winchester, Va., U.S.A. .. 82 F6 39 11N 78 10W
Wind →, U.S.A. 76 E9 43 12N 108 12W
Wind Cave △, U.S.A. 80 D3 43 32N 103 17W
Wind River Range, U.S.A. .. 76 E9 43 0N 109 30W
Windau = Ventspils, Latvia . 9 H19 57 25N 21 32 E
Windber, U.S.A. 84 F6 40 14N 78 50W
Winder, U.S.A. 83 J4 34 0N 83 45W
Windermere, U.K. 12 C5 54 23N 2 55W
Windhoek, Namibia ...... 56 C2 22 35S 17 4 E
Windom, U.S.A. 80 D7 43 52N 95 7W
Windorah, Australia ...... 62 D3 25 24S 142 36 E
Window Rock, U.S.A. 77 J9 35 41N 109 3W
Windrush →, U.K. 13 F6 51 43N 1 24W
Windsor, Australia ...... 63 E5 33 37S 150 50 E
Windsor, N.S., Canada 73 D6 44 59N 64 5W
Windsor, Ont., Canada 84 D2 42 18N 83 0W
Windsor, U.K. 13 F7 51 29N 0 36W
Windsor, Colo., U.S.A. 80 E2 40 29N 104 54W
Windsor, Conn., U.S.A. .. 85 E12 41 50N 72 39W
Windsor, Mo., U.S.A. 80 F8 38 32N 93 31W
Windsor, N.Y., U.S.A. 85 D9 42 5N 75 37W
Windsor, Vt., U.S.A. 85 C12 43 29N 72 24W
Windsor & Maidenhead □, U.K. . 13 F7 51 29N 0 40W
Windsorton, S. Africa .... 56 D3 28 16S 24 44 E
Windward Is., W. Indies .. 89 D7 13 0N 61 0W

Windward Passage = Vientos,
   Paso de los, Caribbean 89 C5 20 0N 74 0W
Winefred L., Canada 71 B6 55 30N 110 30W
Winfield, U.S.A. 81 G6 37 15N 96 59W
Wingate Mts., Australia .. 60 B5 14 25S 130 40 E
Wingham, Australia ...... 63 E5 31 48S 152 22 E
Wingham, Canada 84 C3 43 55N 81 20W
Winisk, Canada 72 A2 55 20N 85 15W
Winisk →, Canada 72 A2 55 17N 85 5W
Winisk L., Canada 72 B2 52 55N 87 22W
Wink, U.S.A. 81 K3 31 45N 103 9W
Winkler, Canada 71 D9 49 10N 97 56W
Winlock, U.S.A. 78 D4 46 30N 122 56W
Winnebago, L., U.S.A. 82 D1 44 0N 88 26W
Winnecke Cr. →, Australia . 60 C5 18 35S 131 34 E
Winnemucca, U.S.A. 76 F5 40 58N 117 44W
Winnemucca L., U.S.A. .. 76 F4 40 7N 119 21W
Winnett, U.S.A. 76 C9 47 0N 108 21W
Winnfield, U.S.A. 81 K8 31 56N 92 38W
Winnibigoshish, L., U.S.A. . 80 B7 47 27N 94 13W
Winnipeg, Canada 71 D9 49 54N 97 9W
Winnipeg →, Canada 71 C9 50 38N 96 19W
Winnipeg, L., Canada 71 C9 52 0N 97 0W
Winnipeg Beach, Canada .. 71 C9 50 30N 96 58W
Winnipegosis, Canada 71 C9 51 39N 99 55W
Winnipegosis L., Canada .. 71 C9 52 30N 100 0W
Winnipesaukee, L., U.S.A. . 85 C13 43 38N 71 21W
Winnisquam L., U.S.A. .. 85 C13 43 33N 71 31W
Winnsboro, La., U.S.A. .. 81 J9 32 10N 91 43W
Winnsboro, S.C., U.S.A. .. 83 H5 34 23N 81 5W
Winnsboro, Tex., U.S.A. .. 81 J7 32 58N 95 17W
Winokapau, L., Canada .. 73 B7 53 15N 62 50W
Winona, Minn., U.S.A. .. 80 C9 44 3N 91 39W
Winona, Miss., U.S.A. .. 81 J10 33 29N 89 44W
Winooski, U.S.A. 85 B11 44 29N 73 11W
Winooski →, U.S.A. 85 B11 44 32N 73 17W
Winschoten, Neths. ...... 15 A7 53 9N 7 3 E
Winsford, U.K. 12 D5 53 12N 2 31W
Winslow, Ariz., U.S.A. .. 77 J8 35 2N 110 42W
Winslow, Wash., U.S.A. .. 78 C4 47 38N 122 31W
Winsted, U.S.A. 85 E11 41 55N 73 4W
Winston-Salem, U.S.A. .. 83 G5 36 6N 80 15W
Winter Garden, U.S.A. .. 83 L5 28 34N 81 35W
Winter Haven, U.S.A. .. 83 M5 28 1N 81 44W
Winter Park, U.S.A. .. 83 L5 28 36N 81 20W
Winterhaven, U.S.A. .. 79 N12 32 47N 114 39W
Winters, U.S.A. 78 G5 38 32N 121 58W
Winterswijk, Neths. .. 15 C6 51 58N 6 43 E
Winterthur, Switz. ...... 20 C8 47 30N 8 44 E
Winthrop, U.S.A. 76 B3 48 28N 120 10W
Winton, Australia ...... 62 C3 22 24S 143 3 E
Winton, N.Z. ...... 59 M2 46 8S 168 20 E
Wirrulla, Australia ...... 63 E1 32 24S 134 31 E
Wisbech, U.K. ...... 13 E8 52 41N 0 9 E
Wisconsin □, U.S.A. .. 80 C10 44 45N 89 30W
Wisconsin →, U.S.A. .. 80 D9 43 0N 91 15W
Wisconsin Rapids, U.S.A. .. 80 C10 44 23N 89 49W
Wisdom, U.S.A. 76 D7 45 37N 113 27W
Wishaw, U.K. 11 F5 55 46N 3 54W
Wishek, U.S.A. 80 B5 46 16N 99 33W
Wisła →, Poland ...... 17 A10 54 22N 18 55 E
Wismar, Germany ...... 16 B6 53 54N 11 29 E
Wisner, U.S.A. 80 E6 41 59N 96 55W
Witbank, S. Africa ...... 57 D4 25 51S 29 14 E
Witdraai, S. Africa ...... 56 D3 26 58S 20 48 E
Witham →, U.K. 13 E8 53 3N 0 8W
Witham, U.K. ...... 13 F8 51 48N 0 40 E
Withernsea, U.K. ...... 12 D8 53 44N 0 1 E
Witjira △, Australia ...... 63 D2 26 22S 135 37 E
Witney, U.K. 13 F6 51 48N 1 28W
Witnossob →, Namibia .. 56 D3 23 55S 18 45 E
Wittenberge, Germany .. 16 B6 53 0N 11 45 E
Wittenoom, Australia .. 60 D2 22 15S 118 20 E
Witvlei, Namibia ...... 56 C2 22 23S 18 32 E
Wkra →, Poland ...... 17 B11 52 27N 20 44 E
Wlingi, Indonesia ...... 37 H15 8 5S 112 25 E
Włocławek, Poland ...... 17 B10 52 40N 19 3 E
Włodawa, Poland ...... 17 C12 51 33N 23 31 E
Woburn, U.S.A. 85 D13 42 29N 71 9W
Wodian, China ...... 34 H7 32 50N 112 35 E
Wodonga = Albury-Wodonga,
   Australia ...... 63 F4 36 3S 146 56 E
Wokam, Indonesia ...... 37 F8 5 45S 134 28 E
Woking, U.K. 13 F7 51 19N 0 34W
Wokingham, U.K. 13 F7 51 24N 0 49W
Wokingham □, U.K. 13 F7 51 25N 0 51W
Wolf →, Canada 70 A2 60 17N 132 33W
Wolf Creek, U.S.A. 76 C7 47 0N 112 4W
Wolf L., Canada 70 A2 60 24N 131 40W
Wolf Point, U.S.A. 80 A2 48 5N 105 39W
Wolfe I., Canada 85 B8 44 7N 76 20W
Wolfeboro, U.S.A. 85 C13 43 35N 71 13W
Wolfsberg, Austria ...... 16 E8 46 50N 14 52 E
Wolfsburg, Germany .. 16 B6 52 25N 10 48 E
Wolin, Poland ...... 16 B8 53 50N 14 37 E
Wollaston, Is., Chile 96 H3 55 40S 67 30W
Wollaston L., Canada 71 B8 58 7N 103 10W
Wollaston Lake, Canada .. 71 B8 58 3N 103 33W
Wollaston Pen., Canada .. 68 B8 69 30N 115 0W
Wollongong, Australia .... 63 E5 34 25S 150 54 E
Wolmaransstad, S. Africa . 56 D4 27 12S 25 59 E
Wolseley, S. Africa ...... 56 E2 33 26S 19 7 E
Wolsey, U.S.A. 80 C5 44 24N 98 28W
Wolstenholme, C., Canada . 66 C12 62 35N 77 30W
Wolvega, Neths. ...... 15 B6 52 52N 6 0 E
Wolverhampton, U.K. .. 13 E5 52 35N 2 7W
Wondai, Australia ...... 63 D5 26 20S 151 49 E
Wongalarroo L., Australia . 63 E3 31 32S 144 0 E
Wongan Hills, Australia .. 61 F2 30 51S 116 37 E
Wŏnju, S. Korea ...... 35 F14 37 22N 127 58 E
Wonosari, Indonesia .... 37 G14 7 58S 110 36 E
Wonosobo, Indonesia .... 37 G13 7 22S 109 54 E
Wonowon, Canada 70 B4 56 44N 121 48W
Wŏnsan, N. Korea ...... 35 E14 39 11N 127 27 E
Wonthaggi, Australia .... 63 F4 38 37S 145 37 E
Wood Buffalo △, Canada .. 70 B6 59 0N 113 41W
Wood Is., Australia ...... 60 C3 16 24S 123 19 E
Wood L., Canada 71 B8 55 17N 103 17W
Woodah, I., Australia .... 62 A2 13 27S 136 10 E
Woodbourne, U.S.A. 85 E10 41 46N 74 36W
Woodbridge, Canada 84 C5 43 47N 79 36W
Woodbridge, U.K. ...... 13 E9 52 6N 1 20 E
Woodburn, U.S.A. 76 D2 45 9N 122 51W
Woodenbong, Australia .. 63 D5 28 24S 152 39 E
Woodend, Australia ...... 63 F3 37 20S 144 33 E
Woodford, Australia ...... 63 D5 26 58S 152 47 E
Woodfords, U.S.A. 78 G7 38 47N 119 50W

odlake, U.S.A. 78 J7 36 25N 119 6W
odland, Calif., U.S.A. 78 G5 38 41N 121 46W
odland, Maine, U.S.A. 83 C12 45 9N 67 25W
odland, Pa., U.S.A. 84 F6 40 59N 78 21W
odland, Wash., U.S.A. 78 E4 45 54N 122 45W
odland Caribou △, Canada 71 C10 51 0N 94 45W
odlands, Singapore ...... 39 d 1 27N 103 47 E
odridge, Canada 71 D9 49 20N 96 9W
odroffe, Mt., Australia ...... 61 E5 26 20S 131 45 E
ods, L., Australia ...... 62 B1 17 50S 133 30 E
ods, L. of the, Canada 71 D10 49 15N 94 45W
odstock, Australia ...... 62 B4 19 35S 146 50 E
odstock, N.B., Canada 73 C6 46 11N 67 37W
odstock, Ont., Canada 84 C4 43 10N 80 45W
odstock, U.K. 13 F6 51 51N 1 20W
odstock, Ill., U.S.A. 80 D10 42 19N 88 27W
odstock, Vt., U.S.A. 85 C12 43 37N 72 31W
odsville, N.Z. ...... 59 J5 40 20S 175 53 E
odville, Miss., U.S.A. 81 K9 31 6N 91 18W
odville, Tex., U.S.A. 81 K7 30 47N 94 25W
odward, U.S.A. 81 G5 36 26N 99 24W
ody, U.S.A. 79 K8 35 42N 118 50W
ody →, Canada 71 C8 52 31N 100 51W
olacombe, U.K. 13 F3 51 10N 4 13W
olamai, C., Australia ...... 63 F4 38 30S 145 23 E
oler, U.K. 12 B5 55 33N 2 1W
olgoolga, Australia ...... 63 E5 30 6S 153 11 E
omera, Australia ...... 63 E2 31 5S 136 50 E
onsocket, R.I., U.S.A. 85 E13 42 0N 71 31W
onsocket, S. Dak., U.S.A. 80 C5 44 3N 98 17W
oramel →, Australia ...... 61 E1 25 47S 114 10 E
oramel Roadhouse, Australia 61 E1 25 45S 114 17 E
oster, U.S.A. 84 F3 40 48N 81 56W
rcester, S. Africa ...... 56 E2 33 39S 19 27 E
rcester, U.K. 13 E5 52 11N 2 12W
rcester, Mass., U.S.A. 85 D13 42 16N 71 48W
rcester, N.Y., U.S.A. 85 D10 42 36N 74 45W
rcestershire □, U.K. 13 E5 52 13N 2 10W
rkington, U.K. 12 C4 54 39N 3 33W
rksop, U.K. 12 D6 53 18N 1 7W
rkum, Neths. ...... 15 B5 52 59N 5 26 E
rland, U.S.A. 76 D10 44 1N 107 57W
rms, Germany ...... 16 D5 49 37N 8 21 E
rsley, Canada 70 B5 56 31N 119 8W
rtham, U.S.A. 81 K6 31 47N 96 28W
rthing, Barbados ...... 89 g 13 5N 59 35W
rthing, U.K. 13 G7 50 49N 0 21W
rthington, Minn., U.S.A. 80 D7 43 37N 95 36W
rthington, Pa., U.S.A. 84 F5 40 50N 79 38W
si, Indonesia ...... 37 E7 0 15S 128 0 E
u-han = Wuhan, China ...... 33 C6 30 31N 114 18 E
usi = Wuxi, China ...... 33 C7 31 33N 120 18 E
woni, Indonesia ...... 37 E6 4 5S 123 5 E
angel I. = Vrangelya, Ostrov, Russia ...... 29 B19 71 0N 180 0 E
angell, U.S.A. 70 B2 56 28N 132 23W
angell Mts., U.S.A. 68 B5 61 30N 142 0W
ath, C., Canada 11 C3 58 38N 5 1W
ay, U.S.A. 80 E3 40 5N 102 13W
ekin, The, U.K. 13 E5 52 41N 2 32W
ens, U.S.A. 83 J4 31 32N 82 23W
exham, U.K. 12 D4 53 3N 3 0W
exham □, U.K. 12 D5 53 1N 2 58W
ght, U.S.A. 80 D2 43 47N 105 30W
ght Pt., Canada 84 C3 43 48N 81 44W
ghtson, Mt., U.S.A. 77 L8 31 42N 110 51W
ghtwood, U.S.A. 79 L9 34 21N 117 38W
gley, Canada 68 B7 63 16N 123 37W
ocław, Poland ...... 17 C9 51 5N 17 5 E
eśnia, Poland ...... 17 B9 52 21N 17 36 E
Jiang →, China ...... 32 D5 29 40N 107 20 E
Kau Tang, China ...... 33 F11 22 30N 114 14 E
'an, China ...... 34 F8 36 40N 114 15 E
bu, Australia ...... 61 F2 30 6S 116 37 E
bu, China ...... 34 F6 37 28N 110 42 E
chang, China ...... 35 B14 44 55N 127 5 E
cheng, China ...... 34 F9 37 12N 116 20 E
chuan, China ...... 34 D6 41 5N 111 28 E
di, China ...... 35 F9 37 40N 117 35 E
ding He →, China ...... 34 F6 37 2N 110 23 E
dinna, Australia ...... 63 E2 33 0S 135 22 E
du, China ...... 34 H3 33 22N 104 54 E
guishan, China ...... 33 G9 22 25N 113 25 E
han, China ...... 33 C6 30 31N 114 18 E
he, China ...... 35 H9 33 10N 117 50 E
hsi = Wuxi, China ...... 33 C7 31 33N 120 18 E
hu, China ...... 33 C6 31 22N 118 21 E
kari, Nigeria ...... 50 G7 7 51N 9 42 E
laple, China ...... 35 B14 44 6N 126 33 E
lanbulang, China ...... 34 D6 41 5N 110 55 E
lar L., India ...... 43 B6 34 20N 74 30 E
lian, China ...... 35 G10 35 40N 119 12 E
liaru, Indonesia ...... 37 F8 7 27S 131 0 E
luk'omushih Ling, China ...... 32 C3 36 25N 87 25 E
lumuchi = Ürümqi, China ...... 28 E9 43 45N 87 45 E
ndowie, Australia ...... 61 F2 31 47S 116 23 E
nnummin L., Canada 72 B2 52 55N 89 10W
ntho, Australia ...... 41 H19 23 55N 95 45 E
patki △, U.S.A. 77 J8 35 35N 111 20W
ppertal, Germany ...... 16 C4 51 16N 7 12 E
ppertal, S. Africa ...... 56 E2 32 13S 19 12 E
qing, China ...... 35 E9 39 23N 117 4 E
rtsboro, U.S.A. 85 E10 41 35N 74 29W
rzburg, Germany ...... 16 D5 49 46N 9 55 E
shan, China ...... 34 G3 34 43N 104 53 E
sui Jiang = Ussuri →, Asia 30 A7 48 27N 135 0 E
ting = Huimin, China ...... 35 F9 37 27N 117 28 E
tonghaolai, China ...... 35 C11 42 50N 120 5 E
tongqiao, China ...... 32 D5 29 22N 103 50 E
wei, China ...... 32 C5 37 57N 102 34 E
xi, China ...... 33 C7 31 33N 120 18 E
xiang, China ...... 34 H7 36 49N 112 50 E
yang, China ...... 34 F8 37 46N 112 50 E
yi Shan, China ...... 33 D6 27 0N 117 0 E
zhai, China ...... 34 E6 38 54N 111 48 E
zhi Shan, China ...... 38 C7 18 45N 109 45 E
zhong, China ...... 34 E4 38 2N 106 12 E
zhou, China ...... 33 D6 23 0N 111 15 E
aaba Cr. →, Australia ...... 62 B3 16 27S 141 35 E
alkatchem, Australia ...... 61 F2 31 8S 117 22 E
alusing, U.S.A. 85 E8 41 40N 76 16W
andotte, U.S.A. 82 D4 42 12N 83 9W
andra, Australia ...... 63 D4 27 12S 145 56 E
angala, L., Australia ...... 63 E4 33 54S 149 0 E

Wyara, L., Australia ...... 63 D3 28 42S 144 14 E
Wycheproof, Australia ...... 63 F3 36 5S 143 17 E
Wye →, U.K. 13 F5 51 38N 2 40W
Wyemandoo, Australia ...... 61 E2 28 28S 118 29 E
Wymondham, U.K. ...... 13 E9 52 35N 1 7 E
Wymore, U.S.A. 80 E6 40 7N 96 40W
Wyndham, Australia ...... 60 C4 15 33S 128 3 E
Wyndham, N.Z. ...... 59 M2 46 20S 168 51 E
Wynne, U.S.A. 81 H9 35 14N 90 47W
Wynyard, Australia ...... 63 G4 41 5S 145 44 E
Wynyard, Canada 71 C8 51 45N 104 10W
Wyola L., Australia ...... 61 E5 29 8S 130 17 E
Wyoming = Plympton-Wyoming, Canada 84 D2 42 57N 82 7W
Wyoming □, U.S.A. 76 E10 43 0N 107 30W
Wyomissing, U.S.A. 85 F9 40 20N 75 59W
Wyong, Australia ...... 63 E5 33 14S 151 24 E
Wytheville, U.S.A. 82 G5 36 57N 81 5W

X

Xaafuun, Somali Rep. ...... 47 E5 10 25N 51 16 E
Xaçmaz, Azerbaijan ...... 19 F8 41 31N 48 42 E
Xai-Xai, Mozam. ...... 57 D5 25 6S 33 31 E
Xainza, China ...... 32 C3 30 58N 88 35 E
Xalapa, Mexico 87 D5 19 32N 96 55W
Xangongo, Angola ...... 56 B2 16 45S 15 5 E
Xankändi, Azerbaijan ...... 19 G8 39 52N 46 49 E
Xánthi, Greece ...... 23 D11 41 10N 24 58 E
Xanxerê, Brazil 95 B5 26 53S 52 23W
Xapuri, Brazil 92 F5 10 35S 68 35W
Xar Moron He →, China ...... 35 C11 43 25N 120 35 E
Xátiva, Spain 21 C5 38 59N 0 32W
Xau, L., Botswana ...... 56 C3 21 15S 24 44 E
Xavantina, Brazil 95 A5 21 15S 52 48W
Xenia, U.S.A. 82 F4 39 41N 83 56W
Xeropotamos →, Cyprus ...... 25 E11 34 42N 32 33 E
Xhora, S. Africa ...... 57 E4 31 55S 28 38 E
Xhumo, Botswana ...... 56 C3 21 7S 24 35 E
Xi Jiang →, China ...... 33 D6 22 5N 113 20 E
Xi Xian, China ...... 34 F6 36 41N 110 58 E
Xia Xian, China ...... 34 G6 35 8N 111 12 E
Xiachengzi, China ...... 35 B16 44 40N 130 18 E
Xiaguan, China ...... 32 D5 25 32N 100 16 E
Xiajin, China ...... 34 F9 36 56N 116 0 E
Xiamen, China ...... 33 D6 24 25N 118 4 E
Xi'an, China ...... 34 G5 34 15N 109 0 E
Xian Xian, China ...... 34 E9 38 12N 116 6 E
Xiang →, China ...... 33 D6 28 55N 112 50 E
Xiangcheng, Henan, China ...... 34 H8 33 29N 114 52 E
Xiangcheng, Henan, China ...... 34 H7 33 50N 113 27 E
Xiangfan, China ...... 33 C6 32 2N 112 8 E
Xianggang = Hong Kong □, China ...... 33 G11 22 11N 114 14 E
Xianghuang Qi, China ...... 34 C7 42 2N 113 50 E
Xiangning, China ...... 34 G6 35 58N 110 50 E
Xiangquan, China ...... 34 F7 36 30N 113 1 E
Xiangquan He = Sutlej →, Pakistan ...... 42 E4 29 23N 71 3 E
Xiangshui, China ...... 35 G10 34 12N 119 33 E
Xiangtan, China ...... 33 D6 27 51N 112 54 E
Xianyang, China ...... 34 G5 34 20N 108 40 E
Xiao Hinggan Ling, China ...... 33 B7 49 0N 127 0 E
Xiao Xian, China ...... 34 G9 34 15N 116 55 E
Xiaoyi, China ...... 34 F6 37 8N 111 48 E
Xiawa, China ...... 35 C11 42 35N 120 38 E
Xiayi, China ...... 34 G9 34 15N 116 10 E
Xichang, China ...... 32 D5 27 51N 102 19 E
Xichuan, China ...... 34 H6 33 0N 111 30 E
Xieng Khouang, Laos ...... 38 C4 19 17N 103 25 E
Xifei He →, China ...... 34 H9 32 45N 116 40 E
Xifeng, Gansu, China ...... 34 G4 35 40N 107 40 E
Xifeng, Liaoning, China ...... 35 C13 42 42N 124 45 E
Xifengzhen = Xifeng, China ...... 34 G4 35 40N 107 40 E
Xigazê, China ...... 32 D3 29 5N 88 45 E
Xihe, China ...... 34 G3 34 2N 105 20 E
Xihua, China ...... 34 H8 33 45N 114 30 E
Xili Shuiku, China ...... 33 F10 22 36N 113 57 E
Xiliao He →, China ...... 35 C12 43 32N 123 35 E
Ximana, Mozam. ...... 55 F3 19 24S 33 58 E
Xin Xian = Xinzhou, China ...... 34 E7 38 22N 112 46 E
Xinavane, Mozam. ...... 57 D5 25 2S 32 47 E
Xinbin, China ...... 35 D13 41 40N 125 2 E
Xing Xian, China ...... 34 E6 38 27N 111 7 E
Xing'an, China ...... 33 D6 25 38N 110 40 E
Xingcheng, China ...... 35 D11 40 40N 120 45 E
Xinghe, China ...... 34 D7 40 55N 113 55 E
Xinghua, China ...... 35 H10 32 58N 119 48 E
Xinglong, China ...... 35 D9 40 25N 117 30 E
Xingping, China ...... 34 G5 34 20N 108 28 E
Xingtai, China ...... 34 F8 37 3N 114 32 E
Xingu →, Brazil 93 D8 1 30S 51 53W
Xingyang, China ...... 34 G7 34 45N 112 52 E
Xinhe, China ...... 34 F8 37 30N 115 15 E
Xining, China ...... 32 C5 36 34N 101 40 E
Xinjiang, China ...... 34 G6 35 34N 111 11 E
Xinjiang Uygur Zizhiqu □, China 32 C3 42 0N 86 0 E
Xinjin = Pulandian, China ...... 35 E11 39 25N 121 58 E
Xinkai He →, China ...... 35 C12 43 32N 123 35 E
Xinken, China ...... 33 F10 22 39N 113 36 E
Xinle, China ...... 34 E8 38 25N 114 40 E
Xinlitun, China ...... 35 D12 42 0N 122 8 E
Xinmin, China ...... 35 D12 41 59N 122 50 E
Xintai, China ...... 35 G9 35 55N 117 45 E
Xinwan, China ...... 33 F10 22 47N 113 40 E
Xinxiang, China ...... 34 G7 35 18N 113 50 E
Xinzhan, China ...... 35 C14 43 50N 127 18 E
Xinzheng, China ...... 34 G7 34 20N 113 45 E
Xinzhou, China ...... 34 E7 38 22N 112 46 E
Xiongyuecheng, China ...... 35 D12 40 12N 122 5 E
Xiping, Henan, China ...... 34 H8 33 22N 114 5 E
Xiping, Henan, China ...... 34 H6 33 25N 111 8 E
Xique-Xique, Brazil 93 F10 10 50S 42 40W
Xisha Qundao = Paracel Is., S. China Sea ...... 36 A4 16 30N 112 0 E
Xiuyan, China ...... 35 D12 40 18N 123 11 E
Xixabangma Feng, China ...... 41 E14 28 20N 85 40 E
Xixia, China ...... 34 H6 33 25N 111 29 E
Xixiang, China ...... 34 H4 33 0N 107 44 E
Xiyang, China ...... 34 F7 37 38N 113 38 E
Xizang Zizhiqu □, China ...... 32 C3 32 0N 88 0 E
Xlendi, Malta ...... 25 C1 36 1N 14 12 E
Xochob, Mexico 87 D7 19 28N 89 45W
Xuan Loc, Vietnam ...... 39 G6 10 56N 107 14 E
Xuanhua, China ...... 34 D8 40 40N 115 2 E

Xuchang, China ...... 34 G7 34 2N 113 48 E
Xun Xian, China ...... 34 G8 35 42N 114 33 E
Xunyang, China ...... 34 H5 32 48N 109 22 E
Xunyi, China ...... 34 G5 35 8N 108 20 E
Xúquer →, Spain 21 C5 39 5N 0 10W
Xushui, China ...... 34 E8 39 2N 115 40 E
Xuyen Moc, Vietnam ...... 39 G6 10 34N 107 25 E
Xuzhou, China ...... 35 G9 34 18N 117 10 E
Xylophagou, Cyprus ...... 25 E12 34 54N 33 51 E

Y

Ya Xian, China ...... 38 C7 18 14N 109 29 E
Yaamba, Australia ...... 62 C5 23 8S 150 22 E
Yaapeet, Australia ...... 63 F3 35 45S 142 3 E
Yablonovy Ra. = Yablonovyy Khrebet, Russia ...... 29 D12 53 0N 114 0 E
Yablonovyy Khrebet, Russia ...... 29 D12 53 0N 114 0 E
Yabrai Shan, China ...... 34 E2 39 40N 103 0 E
Yabrūd, Syria ...... 46 B5 33 58N 36 39 E
Yabucoa, Puerto Rico ...... 89 d 18 3N 65 53W
Yacambú △, Venezuela 89 E6 9 42N 69 27W
Yacheng, China ...... 33 E5 18 22N 109 6 E
Yacuiba, Bolivia 94 A3 22 0S 63 43W
Yacuma →, Bolivia 92 F5 13 38S 65 23W
Yadgir, India ...... 40 L10 16 45N 77 5 E
Yadkin →, U.S.A. 83 H5 35 29N 80 9W
Yaeyama-Rettō, Japan ...... 31 M1 24 30N 123 40 E
Yagodnoye, Russia ...... 29 C15 62 33N 149 40 E
Yahila, Dem. Rep. of the Congo 54 B1 0 13N 24 28 E
Yahk, Canada 70 D5 49 6N 116 10W
Yahuma, Dem. Rep. of the Congo 52 D4 1 0N 23 10 E
Yaita, Japan ...... 31 F9 36 48N 139 56 E
Yaiza, Canary Is. 24 F6 28 57N 13 46W
Yakima, U.S.A. 76 C3 46 36N 120 31W
Yakima →, U.S.A. 76 C3 47 0N 120 30W
Yakobi I., U.S.A. 70 B1 58 0N 136 30W
Yakovlevka, Russia ...... 30 B6 44 26N 133 28 E
Yaku-Shima, Japan ...... 31 J5 30 20N 130 30 E
Yakumo, Japan ...... 30 C10 42 15N 140 16 E
Yakutat, U.S.A. 68 C6 59 33N 139 44W
Yakutia = Sakha □, Russia ...... 29 C13 66 0N 130 0 E
Yakutsk, Russia ...... 29 C13 62 5N 129 50 E
Yala, Thailand ...... 39 J3 6 33N 101 18 E
Yalboroo, Australia ...... 62 J6 20 50S 148 40 E
Yale, U.S.A. 84 C2 43 8N 82 48W
Yalgoo, Australia ...... 61 E2 28 16S 116 39 E
Yalgorup △, Australia ...... 61 D2 24 34S 115 2 E
Yalinga, C.A.R. ...... 52 C4 6 33N 23 10 E
Yalleroi, Australia ...... 62 C4 24 3S 145 42 E
Yalobusha →, U.S.A. 81 J9 33 33N 90 10W
Yalong Jiang →, China ...... 32 D5 26 40N 101 55 E
Yalova, Turkey ...... 23 D13 40 41N 29 15 E
Yalta, Ukraine ...... 19 F5 44 30N 34 10 E
Yalu Jiang →, China ...... 35 E13 40 0N 124 22 E
Yam Ha Melah = Dead Sea, Asia 46 D4 31 30N 35 30 E
Yam Kinneret, Israel ...... 46 C4 32 45N 35 35 E
Yamada, Japan ...... 31 H5 33 33N 130 49 E
Yamagata, Japan ...... 30 E10 38 15N 140 15 E
Yamagata □, Japan ...... 30 E10 38 30N 140 0 E
Yamaguchi, Japan ...... 31 G5 34 10N 131 32 E
Yamaguchi □, Japan ...... 31 G5 34 20N 131 40 E
Yamal, Poluostrov, Russia ...... 28 B8 71 0N 70 0 E
Yamal Pen. = Yamal, Poluostrov, Russia ...... 28 B8 71 0N 70 0 E
Yamanashi □, Japan ...... 31 G9 35 40N 138 40 E
Yamanie Falls △, Australia ...... 62 B4 18 29S 146 9 E
Yamantau, Gora, Russia ...... 18 D10 54 15N 58 6 E
Yamba, Australia ...... 63 D5 29 26S 153 23 E
Yambarran Ra., Australia ...... 60 C5 15 10S 130 25 E
Yâmbiô, Sudan ...... 51 H11 4 35N 28 16 E
Yambol, Bulgaria ...... 23 C12 42 30N 26 30 E
Yamdena, Indonesia ...... 37 F8 7 45S 131 20 E
Yame, Japan ...... 31 H5 33 13N 130 35 E
Yamethin, Burma ...... 41 J20 20 29N 96 18 E
Yamma-Yamma, L., Australia ...... 63 D3 26 16S 141 20 E
Yamoussoukro, Ivory C. 50 G4 6 49N 5 17W
Yampa →, U.S.A. 76 F9 40 32N 108 59W
Yampi Sd., Australia ...... 60 C3 16 8S 123 38 E
Yampil, Moldova ...... 17 D15 48 15N 28 15 E
Yampol = Yampil, Moldova ...... 17 D15 48 15N 28 15 E
Yamuna →, India ...... 43 G9 25 30N 81 53 E
Yamunanagar, India ...... 42 D7 30 7N 77 17 E
Yamzho Yumco, China ...... 32 D4 28 48N 90 35 E
Yana →, Russia ...... 29 B14 71 30N 136 0 E
Yanagawa, Japan ...... 31 H5 33 10N 130 24 E
Yanai, Japan ...... 31 H6 33 58N 132 7 E
Yan'an, China ...... 34 F5 36 35N 109 26 E
Yanaul, Russia ...... 18 C10 56 25N 55 0 E
Yanbu 'al Bahr, Si. Arabia ...... 44 F3 24 0N 38 5 E
Yanchang, China ...... 34 F6 36 43N 110 1 E
Yancheng, Henan, China ...... 34 H8 33 35N 114 0 E
Yancheng, Jiangsu, China ...... 35 H11 33 23N 120 8 E
Yanchep Beach, Australia ...... 61 F2 31 33S 115 37 E
Yanchi, China ...... 34 F4 37 48N 107 20 E
Yanchuan, China ...... 34 F6 36 51N 110 10 E
Yanco Cr. →, Australia ...... 63 F4 35 14S 145 35 E
Yandoon, Burma ...... 41 L19 17 0N 95 40 E
Yang Xian, China ...... 34 H4 33 15N 107 30 E
Yangambi, Dem. Rep. of the Congo ...... 54 B1 0 47N 24 24 E
Yangcheng, China ...... 34 G7 35 28N 112 22 E
Yangch'ü = Taiyuan, China ...... 34 F7 37 52N 112 33 E
Yanggao, China ...... 34 D7 40 21N 113 55 E
Yanggu, China ...... 34 F8 36 8N 115 43 E
Yangliuqing, China ...... 35 E9 39 2N 117 5 E
Yangon = Rangoon, Burma ...... 41 L20 16 45N 96 20 E
Yangpingguan, China ...... 34 H4 32 58N 106 5 E
Yangquan, China ...... 34 F7 37 58N 113 31 E
Yangtse = Chang Jiang →, China 33 C7 31 48N 121 10 E
Yangtze Kiang = Chang Jiang →, China ...... 33 C7 31 48N 121 10 E
Yangyang, S. Korea ...... 35 E15 38 4N 128 38 E
Yangzhou, China ...... 33 C6 32 21N 119 26 E
Yanji, China ...... 35 C15 42 59N 129 30 E
Yankton, U.S.A. 80 D6 42 53N 97 23W
Yanonge, Dem. Rep. of the Congo ...... 54 B1 0 35N 24 38 E
Yanqi, China ...... 32 B3 42 5N 86 35 E
Yanqing, China ...... 34 D8 40 30N 115 58 E
Yanshan, China ...... 35 E9 38 4N 117 22 E
Yanshou, China ...... 35 B15 45 28N 128 22 E
Yantabulla, Australia ...... 63 D4 29 21S 145 0 E

Yantai, China ...... 35 F11 37 34N 121 22 E
Yantian, China ...... 33 F11 22 35N 114 16 E
Yanzhou, China ...... 34 G9 35 35N 116 49 E
Yao Noi, Ko, Thailand ...... 39 a 8 7N 98 37 E
Yao Xian, China ...... 34 G5 34 55N 108 59 E
Yao Yai, Ko, Thailand ...... 39 a 8 0N 98 35 E
Yaoundé, Cameroon ...... 52 D2 3 50N 11 35 E
Yaowan, China ...... 35 G10 34 15N 118 3 E
Yap, Pac. Oc. ...... 64 G5 9 30N 138 10 E
Yapen, Indonesia ...... 37 E9 1 50S 136 0 E
Yapen, Selat, Indonesia ...... 37 E9 1 20S 136 10 E
Yapero, Indonesia ...... 37 E9 4 59S 137 11 E
Yappar →, Australia ...... 62 B3 18 22S 141 16 E
Yaqui →, Mexico 86 B2 27 37N 110 39W
Yar-Sale, Russia ...... 28 C8 66 50N 70 50 E
Yaraka, Australia ...... 62 C3 24 53S 144 3 E
Yaransk, Russia ...... 18 C8 57 22N 47 49 E
Yare →, U.K. ...... 13 E9 52 35N 1 38 E
Yaremcha, Ukraine ...... 17 D13 48 27N 24 33 E
Yarensk, Russia ...... 18 B8 62 11N 49 15 E
Yari →, Colombia 92 D4 0 20S 72 20W
Yarkand = Shache, China ...... 32 C2 38 20N 77 10 E
Yarker, Canada 85 B8 44 23N 76 46W
Yarkhun →, Pakistan ...... 43 A5 36 17N 72 30 E
Yarlung Ziangbo Jiang = Brahmaputra →, Asia ...... 32 D3 23 40N 90 35 E
Yarmouth, Canada 73 D6 43 50N 66 7W
Yarmūk →, Syria ...... 46 C4 32 42N 35 40 E
Yaroslavl, Russia ...... 18 C6 57 35N 39 55 E
Yarqa, W. →, Egypt ...... 46 F2 30 0N 33 49 E
Yarra Yarra Lakes, Australia ...... 61 E2 29 40S 115 45 E
Yarram, Australia ...... 63 F4 38 29S 146 39 E
Yarraman, Australia ...... 63 D5 26 50S 152 0 E
Yarras, Australia ...... 63 E5 31 25S 152 20 E
Yartsevo, Russia ...... 29 C10 60 20N 90 0 E
Yarumal, Colombia 92 B3 6 58N 75 24W
Yasawa Group, Fiji ...... 59 C7 17 0S 177 23 E
Yaselda, Belarus ...... 17 B14 52 7N 26 28 E
Yasin, Pakistan ...... 43 A5 36 24N 73 23 E
Yasinski, L., Canada 72 B4 53 16N 77 35W
Yasinya, Ukraine ...... 17 D13 48 16N 24 21 E
Yasothon, Thailand ...... 38 E5 15 50N 104 10 E
Yass, Australia ...... 63 E4 34 49S 148 54 E
Yāsūj, Iran ...... 45 D6 30 31N 51 31 E
Yatağan, Turkey ...... 23 F13 37 20N 28 10 E
Yates Center, U.S.A. 81 G7 37 53N 95 44W
Yathkyed L., Canada 71 A9 62 40N 98 0W
Yatsushiro, Japan ...... 31 H5 32 30N 130 40 E
Yatta Plateau, Kenya ...... 54 C4 2 0S 38 0 E
Yauco, Puerto Rico ...... 89 d 18 2N 66 51W
Yavari →, Peru 92 D4 4 21S 70 2W
Yávaros, Mexico 86 B3 26 42N 109 31W
Yavatmal, India ...... 40 J11 20 20N 78 15 E
Yavne, Israel ...... 46 D3 31 52N 34 45 E
Yavoriv, Ukraine ...... 17 D12 49 55N 23 20 E
Yavorov = Yavoriv, Ukraine ...... 17 D12 49 55N 23 20 E
Yawatahama, Japan ...... 31 H6 33 27N 132 24 E
Yazd, Iran ...... 45 D7 31 55N 54 27 E
Yazd □, Iran ...... 45 D7 32 0N 55 0 E
Yazd-e Khvāst, Iran ...... 45 D7 31 31N 52 7 E
Yazman, Pakistan ...... 42 E4 29 8N 71 45 E
Yazoo →, U.S.A. 81 J9 32 22N 90 54W
Yazoo City, U.S.A. 81 J9 32 51N 90 25W
Ybycuí △, Paraguay 94 B4 26 5S 56 46W
Ybytyruzú △, Paraguay 95 B4 25 51S 56 11W
Yding Skovhøj, Denmark ...... 9 J13 55 59N 9 46 E
Ye Xian, China ...... 34 H7 33 35N 113 25 E
Yebyu, Burma ...... 38 E2 14 15N 98 13 E
Yechŏn, S. Korea ...... 35 F15 36 39N 128 27 E
Yecla, Spain 21 C5 38 35N 1 5W
Yécora, Mexico 86 B3 28 20N 108 58W
Yedintsy = Edineţ, Moldova ...... 17 D14 48 9N 27 18 E
Yegros, Paraguay 94 B4 26 20S 56 25W
Yehbuah, Indonesia ...... 37 J17 8 23S 114 45 E
Yehuda, Midbar, Israel ...... 46 D4 31 35N 35 15 E
Yei, Sudan ...... 51 H12 4 9N 30 40 E
Yekaterinburg, Russia ...... 28 D7 56 50N 60 30 E
Yelarbon, Australia ...... 63 D5 28 33S 150 38 E
Yelets, Russia ...... 18 D6 52 40N 38 30 E
Yelizavetgrad = Kirovohrad, Ukraine ...... 19 E5 48 35N 32 20 E
Yell, U.K. 11 A7 60 35N 1 5W
Yell Sd., U.K. 11 A7 60 33N 1 15W
Yellow Sea, China ...... 35 G12 35 0N 123 0 E
Yellowhead Pass, Canada 70 C5 52 53N 118 25W
Yellowknife, Canada 70 A6 62 27N 114 29W
Yellowknife →, Canada 70 A6 62 31N 114 19W
Yellowstone △, U.S.A. 76 D9 44 40N 110 30W
Yellowstone →, U.S.A. 76 B3 47 59N 103 59W
Yellowstone L., U.S.A. 76 D8 44 27N 110 22W
Yelsk, Belarus ...... 17 C15 51 50N 29 10 E
Yemen ■, Asia ...... 47 E3 15 0N 44 0 E
Yen Bai, Vietnam ...... 38 B5 21 42N 104 52 E
Yenangyaung, Burma ...... 41 J19 20 30N 95 0 E
Yenbo = Yanbu 'al Bahr, Si. Arabia ...... 44 F3 24 0N 38 5 E
Yenda, Australia ...... 63 E4 34 13S 146 14 E
Yenice, Turkey ...... 23 E12 39 55N 27 17 E
Yenisey →, Russia ...... 28 B9 71 50N 82 40 E
Yeniseysk, Russia ...... 29 D10 58 27N 92 13 E
Yeniseyskiy Zaliv, Russia ...... 28 B9 72 20N 81 0 E
Yennádhi, Greece ...... 25 C9 36 2N 27 56 E
Yenyuka, Russia ...... 29 D13 57 57N 121 15 E
Yeo →, U.K. 13 G5 51 2N 2 49W
Yeo, L., Australia ...... 61 E3 28 0S 124 30 E
Yeo I., Canada 84 A3 45 24N 81 48W
Yeola, India ...... 40 J9 20 2N 74 30 E
Yeoryioúpolis, Greece ...... 25 D6 35 20N 24 15 E
Yeovil, U.K. 13 G5 50 57N 2 38W
Yeppoon, Australia ...... 62 C5 23 5S 150 47 E
Yerbent, Turkmenistan ...... 28 F6 39 30N 58 50 E
Yerbogachen, Russia ...... 29 C11 61 16N 108 0 E
Yerevan, Armenia ...... 19 F7 40 10N 44 31 E
Yerington, U.S.A. 76 G4 38 59N 119 10W
Yermak, Kazakhstan ...... 28 D8 52 2N 76 55 E
Yermo, U.S.A. 79 L10 34 54N 116 50W
Yerólakkos, Cyprus ...... 25 D12 35 11N 33 15 E
Yeropol, Russia ...... 29 C17 65 15N 168 40 E
Yeropótamos →, Greece ...... 25 D6 35 3N 24 50 E
Yeroskípou, Cyprus ...... 25 E11 34 46N 32 28 E
Yershov, Russia ...... 19 D8 51 23N 48 27 E
Yerushalayim = Jerusalem, Israel 46 D4 31 47N 35 10 E
Yes Tor, U.K. 13 G4 50 41N 4 0W
Yesan, S. Korea ...... 35 F14 36 41N 126 51 E
Yeso, U.S.A. 81 H2 34 26N 104 37W
Yessey, Russia ...... 29 C11 68 29N 102 10 E
Yetman, Australia ...... 63 D5 28 56S 150 48 E
Yeu, Î. d', France 20 C2 46 42N 2 20W

Yevpatoriya, Ukraine .... 19 E5 45 15N 33 20 E
Yeysk, Russia .... 19 E6 46 40N 38 12 E
Yezd = Yazd, Iran .... 45 D7 31 55N 54 27 E
Yhati, Paraguay 94 B4 25 45S 56 35W
Yhú, Paraguay 95 B4 25 0S 56 0W
Yi →, Uruguay 94 C4 33 7S 57 8W
Yi 'Allaq, G., Egypt .... 46 E2 30 22N 33 32 E
Yi He →, China .... 35 G10 34 10N 118 8 E
Yi Xian, Hebei, China ...... 34 E8 39 20N 115 30 E
Yi Xian, Liaoning, China .... 35 D11 41 30N 121 22 E
Yialiás →, Cyprus .... 25 D12 35 9N 33 44 E
Yialousa, Cyprus .... 25 D13 35 32N 34 10 E
Yianisádhes, Greece ...... 25 D8 35 20N 26 10 E
Yiannitsa, Greece .... 23 D10 40 46N 22 24 E
Yibin, China .... 32 D5 28 45N 104 32 E
Yichang, China .... 33 C6 30 40N 111 20 E
Yicheng, China .... 34 G6 35 42N 111 40 E
Yichuan, China .... 34 F6 36 2N 110 10 E
Yichun, China .... 33 B7 47 44N 128 52 E
Yidu, China .... 35 F10 36 43N 118 28 E
Yijun, China .... 34 G5 35 28N 109 8 E
Yıldız Dağları, Turkey ..... 23 D12 41 48N 27 36 E
Yilehuli Shan, China ...... 33 A7 51 20N 124 20 E
Yimianpo, China .... 35 B15 45 7N 128 2 E
Yinchuan, China .... 34 E4 38 30N 106 15 E
Yindarlgooda, L., Australia .. 61 F3 30 40S 121 52 E
Ying He →, China .... 34 H9 32 30N 116 30 E
Ying Xian, China .... 34 E7 39 32N 113 10 E
Yingkou, China .... 35 D12 40 37N 122 18 E
Yining, China .... 28 E9 43 58N 81 10 E
Yinmabin, Burma .... 41 H19 22 10N 94 55 E
Yiofiros →, Greece .... 25 D7 35 20N 25 6 E
Yirga Alem, Ethiopia ...... 47 F2 6 48N 38 22 E
Yirrkala, Australia .... 62 A2 12 14S 136 56 E
Yishan, China .... 32 D5 24 28N 108 38 E
Yishui, China .... 35 G10 35 47N 118 30 E
Yishun, Singapore .... 39 d 1 26N 103 50 E
Yithion, Greece .... 23 F10 36 46N 22 34 E
Yitong, China .... 35 C13 43 13N 125 20 E
Yiyang, Henan, China ..... 34 G7 34 27N 112 10 E
Yiyang, Hunan, China ..... 33 D6 28 35N 112 18 E
Yli-Kitka, Finland .... 8 C23 66 8N 28 30 E
Ylitornio, Finland .... 8 C20 66 19N 23 39 E
Ylivieska, Finland .... 8 D21 64 4N 24 28 E
Yoakum, U.S.A. 81 L6 29 17N 97 9W
Yog Pt., Phil. .... 37 B6 14 6N 124 12 E
Yogyakarta, Indonesia ..... 36 F4 7 49S 110 22 E
Yoho △, Canada 70 C5 51 25N 116 30W
Yojoa, L. de, Honduras 88 D2 14 53N 88 0W
Yōju, S. Korea .... 35 F14 37 20N 127 35 E
Yok Don △, Vietnam ...... 38 F6 12 50N 107 40 E
Yokadouma, Cameroon .... 52 D2 3 26N 14 55 E
Yokkaichi, Japan .... 31 G8 34 55N 136 38 E
Yoko, Cameroon .... 52 C2 5 32N 12 20 E
Yokohama, Japan .... 31 G9 35 27N 139 28 E
Yokosuka, Japan .... 31 G9 35 20N 139 40 E
Yokote, Japan .... 30 E10 39 20N 140 30 E
Yola, Nigeria .... 51 G8 9 10N 12 29 E
Yolaina, Cordillera de, Nic. .. 88 D3 11 30N 84 0W
Yoloten, Turkmenistan .... 45 B9 37 18N 62 21 E
Yom →, Thailand .... 36 A2 15 35N 100 1 E
Yonago, Japan .... 31 G6 35 25N 133 19 E
Yonaguni-Jima, Japan .... 31 M1 24 27N 123 0 E
Yŏnan, N. Korea .... 35 F14 37 55N 126 11 E
Yonezawa, Japan .... 30 F10 37 57N 140 4 E
Yong Peng, Malaysia ..... 39 L4 2 0N 103 3 E
Yong Sata, Thailand ...... 39 J2 7 8N 99 41 E
Yongamp'o, N. Korea ..... 35 E13 39 56N 124 23 E
Yongcheng, China .... 34 H9 33 55N 116 20 E
Yŏngch'ŏn, S. Korea ..... 35 G15 35 58N 128 56 E
Yongdeng, China .... 34 F2 36 38N 103 25 E
Yŏngdŏk, S. Korea .... 35 F15 36 24N 129 22 E
Yŏngdŭngpo, S. Korea .... 35 F14 37 31N 126 54 E
Yonghe, China .... 34 F6 36 46N 110 38 E
Yŏnghŭng, N. Korea ..... 35 E14 39 31N 127 18 E
Yongji, China .... 34 G6 34 52N 110 28 E
Yŏngju, S. Korea .... 35 F15 36 50N 128 40 E
Yongnian, China .... 34 F8 36 47N 114 29 E
Yongning, China .... 34 E4 38 15N 106 14 E
Yongqing, China .... 34 E9 39 25N 116 28 E
Yŏngwŏl, S. Korea .... 35 F15 37 11N 128 28 E
Yonibana, S. Leone 50 G3 8 30N 12 19W
Yonkers, U.S.A. 85 F11 40 56N 73 54W
Yonne →, France .... 20 B5 48 23N 2 58 E
York, Australia .... 61 F2 31 52S 116 47 E
York, U.K. 12 D6 53 58N 1 6W
York, Ala., U.S.A. 81 J10 32 29N 88 18W
York, Nebr., U.S.A. 80 E6 40 52N 97 36W
York, Pa., U.S.A. 82 F7 39 58N 76 44W
York, C., Australia .... 62 A3 10 42S 142 31 E
York, City of □, U.K. 12 D6 53 58N 1 6W
York, Kap, Greenland 4 B4 75 55N 66 25W
York, Vale of, U.K. 12 C6 54 15N 1 25W
York Haven, U.S.A. 84 F8 40 7N 76 46W
York Sd., Australia ...... 60 C4 15 0S 125 5 E
Yorke Pen., Australia ..... 63 E2 34 50S 137 40 E
Yorkshire Dales △, U.K. .. 12 C5 54 12N 2 10W
Yorkshire Wolds, U.K. 12 C7 54 8N 0 31W
Yorkton, Canada 71 C8 51 11N 102 28W
Yorkville, U.S.A. 78 G3 38 52N 123 13W
Yoro, Honduras 88 C2 15 9N 87 7W
Yoron-Jima, Japan ...... 31 L4 27 2N 128 26 E
Yos Sudarso, Pulau = Dolak,
  Pulau, Indonesia ...... 37 F9 8 0S 138 30 E
Yosemite △, U.S.A. 78 H7 37 45N 119 40W
Yosemite Village, U.S.A. .. 78 H7 37 45N 119 35W
Yoshino-Kumano △, Japan 31 H8 34 12N 135 55 E
Yoshkar Ola, Russia ..... 18 C8 56 38N 47 55 E
Yŏsu, S. Korea .... 35 G14 34 47N 127 45 E
Yotvata, Israel .... 46 F4 29 55N 35 2 E
Youbou, Canada 78 B2 48 53N 124 13W
Youghal, Ireland 10 E4 51 56N 7 52W
Youghal B., Ireland 10 E4 51 55N 7 49W
Young, Australia .... 63 E4 34 19S 148 18 E
Young, Canada 71 C7 51 47N 105 45W
Young, Uruguay 94 C4 32 44S 57 36W
Younghusband, L., Australia 63 E2 30 50S 136 5 E
Younghusband Pen., Australia 63 F2 36 0S 139 25 E
Youngstown, Canada 71 C6 51 35N 111 10W
Youngstown, N.Y., U.S.A. . 84 C5 43 15N 79 3W
Youngstown, Ohio, U.S.A. . 84 E4 41 6N 80 39W
Youngsville, U.S.A. 84 E5 41 51N 79 19W
Youngwood, U.S.A. 84 F5 40 14N 79 34W
Youyu, China .... 34 D7 40 10N 112 20 E
Yozgat, Turkey .... 19 G5 39 51N 34 47 E
Ypacaraí, Paraguay 94 B4 25 18S 57 19W
Ypané →, Paraguay 94 A4 23 29S 57 19W
Ypres = Ieper, Belgium ... 15 D2 50 51N 2 53 E

Yreka, U.S.A. 76 F2 41 44N 122 38W
Ystad, Sweden .... 9 J15 55 26N 13 50 E
Ysyk-Köl, Kyrgyzstan .... 28 E8 42 25N 77 15 E
Ythan →, U.K. 11 D7 57 19N 1 59W
Ytyk-Kyuyel, Russia ..... 29 C14 62 30N 133 45 E
Yu Jiang →, China ...... 33 D6 23 22N 110 3 E
Yu Xian = Yuzhou, China . 34 G7 34 10N 113 28 E
Yu Xian, Hebei, China .... 34 E8 39 50N 114 35 E
Yu Xian, Shanxi, China ... 34 E7 38 5N 113 20 E
Yuan Jiang →, China .... 33 D6 28 55N 111 50 E
Yuanqu, China .... 34 G6 35 18N 111 40 E
Yuanyang, China .... 34 G7 35 3N 113 58 E
Yuba →, U.S.A. 78 F5 39 8N 121 36W
Yuba City, U.S.A. 78 F5 39 8N 121 37W
Yūbari, Japan .... 30 C10 43 4N 141 59 E
Yūbetsu, Japan .... 30 B11 44 13N 143 50 E
Yucatán □, Mexico 87 C7 21 30N 86 30W
Yucatán, Canal de, Caribbean 88 B2 22 0N 86 30W
Yucatán, Península de, Mexico 66 H11 19 30N 89 0W
Yucatan Basin, Cent. Amer. 66 H11 19 0N 86 0W
Yucatan Channel = Yucatán,
  Canal de, Caribbean 88 B2 22 0N 86 30W
Yucca, U.S.A. 79 L12 34 52N 114 9W
Yucca Valley, U.S.A. 79 L10 34 8N 116 27W
Yucheng, China .... 34 F9 36 55N 116 32 E
Yuci, China .... 34 F7 37 42N 112 46 E
Yuen Long, China .... 33 G11 22 26N 114 2 E
Yuendumu, Australia .... 60 D5 22 16S 131 49 E
Yugoslavia = Serbia &
  Montenegro ■, Europe .. 23 B9 43 20N 20 0 E
Yukon →, U.S.A. 68 B3 62 32N 163 54W
Yukon Territory □, Canada 68 B6 63 0N 135 0W
Yukta, Russia .... 29 C11 63 26N 105 42 E
Yukuhashi, Japan .... 31 H5 33 44N 130 59 E
Yulara, Australia .... 61 E5 25 10S 130 55 E
Yule →, Australia .... 60 D2 20 41S 118 17 E
Yuleba, Australia .... 63 D4 26 37S 149 24 E
Yülin, Hainan, China ..... 39 C7 18 10N 109 31 E
Yulin, Shaanxi, China .... 34 E5 38 20N 109 30 E
Yuma, Ariz., U.S.A. 79 N12 32 43N 114 37W
Yuma, Colo., U.S.A. 80 E3 40 8N 102 43W
Yuma, B. de, Dom. Rep. .. 89 C6 18 20N 68 35W
Yumbe, Uganda .... 54 B3 3 28N 31 15 E
Yumbi, Dem. Rep. of the Congo 54 C2 1 12S 26 15 E
Yumen, China .... 32 C4 39 50N 97 30 E
Yun Ho →, China .... 35 E9 39 10N 117 10 E
Yuna, Australia .... 61 E2 28 20S 115 0 E
Yuncheng, Henan, China .. 34 G8 35 36N 115 57 E
Yuncheng, Shanxi, China . 34 G6 35 2N 111 0 E
Yungas, Bolivia 92 G5 17 0S 66 0W
Yungay, Chile 94 D1 37 10S 72 5W
Yunnan □, China .... 32 D5 25 0N 102 0 E
Yunta, Australia .... 63 E2 32 34S 139 36 E
Yunxi, China .... 34 H6 33 0N 110 22 E
Yupyongdong, N. Korea .. 35 D15 41 49N 128 53 E
Yuraygir △, Australia .... 63 D5 29 45S 153 15 E
Yurga, Russia .... 28 D9 55 42N 84 51 E
Yurimaguas, Peru 92 E3 5 55S 76 7W
Yurubí △, Venezuela 89 D6 10 26N 68 42W
Yuscarán, Honduras 88 D2 13 58N 86 45W
Yushe, China .... 34 F7 37 4N 112 58 E
Yushu, Jilin, China ...... 35 B14 44 43N 126 38 E
Yushu, Qinghai, China ... 32 C4 33 5N 96 55 E
Yutai, China .... 34 G9 35 0N 116 45 E
Yutian, China .... 35 E9 39 53N 117 45 E
Yuxari Qarabağ = Nagorno-
  Karabakh □, Azerbaijan . 19 F8 39 55N 46 45 E
Yuxi, China .... 32 D5 24 30N 102 35 E
Yuzawa, Japan .... 30 E10 39 10N 140 30 E
Yuzhno-Sakhalinsk, Russia . 29 E15 46 58N 142 45 E
Yuzhnyy □, Russia ...... 28 E5 44 0N 40 0 E
Yuzhou, China .... 34 G7 34 10N 113 28 E
Yvetot, France .... 20 B4 49 37N 0 44 E

Z
Zaanstad, Neths. .... 15 B4 52 27N 4 50 E
Zāb al Kabīr →, Iraq .... 44 C4 36 1N 43 24 E
Zāb aş Şaghīr →, Iraq ... 44 C4 35 17N 43 29 E
Zabaykalsk, Russia ..... 29 E12 49 40N 117 25 E
Zābol, Iran .... 45 D9 31 0N 61 32 E
Zābol □, Afghan. .... 40 D5 32 0N 67 0 E
Zābolī, Iran .... 45 E9 27 10N 61 35 E
Zabrze, Poland .... 17 C10 50 18N 18 50 E
Zacapa, Guatemala 88 D2 14 59N 89 31W
Zacapu, Mexico 86 D4 19 50N 101 43W
Zacatecas, Mexico 86 C4 22 49N 102 34W
Zacatecas □, Mexico 86 C4 23 30N 103 0W
Zacatecoluca, El Salv. ... 88 D2 13 29N 88 51W
Zachary, U.S.A. 81 K9 30 39N 91 9W
Zacoalco, Mexico 86 C4 20 14N 103 33W
Zacualtipán, Mexico 87 C5 20 39N 98 36W
Zadar, Croatia .... 16 F8 44 8N 15 14 E
Zadetkyi Kyun, Burma ... 39 G1 10 0N 98 25 E
Zafarqand, Iran .... 45 C7 33 11N 52 29 E
Zafra, Spain 21 C2 38 26N 6 30W
Żagań, Poland .... 16 C8 51 39N 15 22 E
Zagaoua, Chad .... 51 E10 15 30N 22 24 E
Zagazig, Egypt .... 51 B12 30 40N 31 30 E
Zāgheh, Iran .... 45 C6 33 30N 48 42 E
Zagreb, Croatia .... 16 F9 45 50N 15 58 E
Zāgros, Kūhhā-ye, Iran .. 45 C6 33 45N 48 5 E
Zagros Mts. = Zāgros, Kūhhā-ye,
  Iran .... 45 C6 33 45N 48 5 E
Zahamena △, Madag. ... 57 B8 17 37S 48 49 E
Zāhedān, Fārs, Iran ..... 45 D7 28 46N 53 52 E
Zāhedān, Sīstān va Balūchestān,
  Iran .... 45 D9 29 30N 60 50 E
Zahlah, Lebanon .... 46 B4 33 52N 35 50 E
Zaïre = Congo →, Africa . 52 F2 6 4S 12 24 E
Zaječar, Serbia & M. .... 23 C10 43 53N 22 18 E
Zaka, Zimbabwe .... 57 C5 20 20S 31 29 E
Zakamensk, Russia ..... 29 D11 50 23N 103 17 E
Zakhodnaya Dzvina =
  Daugava →, Latvia .... 9 H21 57 4N 24 3 E
Zākhū, Iraq .... 44 B4 37 10N 42 50 E
Zákinthos, Greece ...... 23 F9 37 47N 20 54 E
Zakopane, Poland ...... 17 D10 49 18N 19 57 E
Zákros, Greece .... 25 D8 35 6N 26 10 E
Zalaegerszeg, Hungary .. 17 E9 46 53N 16 47 E
Zalău, Romania .... 17 E12 47 12N 23 3 E
Zaleshchiki = Zalishchyky,
  Ukraine .... 17 D13 48 45N 25 45 E
Zalew Wiślany, Poland ... 17 A10 54 20N 19 50 E
Zalingei, Sudan .... 51 F10 12 51N 23 29 E

Zalishchyky, Ukraine .... 17 D13 48 45N 25 45 E
Zama L., Canada 70 B5 58 45N 119 5W
Zambeke, Dem. Rep. of
  the Congo .... 54 B2 2 8N 25 17 E
Zambeze →, Africa ..... 55 F4 18 35S 36 20 E
Zambezi = Zambeze →, Africa 55 F4 18 35S 36 20 E
Zambezi, Zambia .... 53 G4 13 30S 23 15 E
Zambezi △, Zimbabwe ... 55 F2 17 54S 25 41 E
Zambezia □, Mozam. .... 55 F4 16 15S 37 30 E
Zambia ■, Africa .... 55 F2 15 0S 28 0 E
Zamboanga, Phil. .... 37 C6 6 59N 122 3 E
Zamora, Mexico 86 D4 20 0N 102 21W
Zamora, Spain 21 B3 41 30N 5 45W
Zamość, Poland .... 17 C12 50 43N 23 15 E
Zandvoort, Neths. ...... 15 B4 52 22N 4 32 E
Zanesville, U.S.A. 84 G2 39 56N 82 1W
Zangābād, Iran .... 44 B5 38 26N 46 44 E
Zangue →, Mozam. ..... 55 F4 17 50S 35 21 E
Zanjān, Iran .... 45 B6 36 40N 48 35 E
Zanjān □, Iran .... 45 B6 37 20N 49 30 E
Zanjān →, Iran .... 45 B6 37 8N 47 47 E
Zante = Zákinthos, Greece 23 F9 37 47N 20 54 E
Zanthus, Australia ...... 61 F3 31 2S 123 34 E
Zanzibar, Tanzania ..... 54 D4 6 12S 39 12 E
Zaouiet El-Kala = Bordj Omar
  Driss, Algeria .... 50 C7 28 10N 6 40 E
Zaouiet Reggâne, Algeria . 50 C6 26 32N 0 3 E
Zaozhuang, China ...... 35 G9 34 50N 117 35 E
Zap Suyu = Zāb al Kabīr →, Iraq 44 C4 36 1N 43 24 E
Zapadnaya Dvina = Daugava →,
  Latvia .... 9 H21 57 4N 24 3 E
Západné Beskydy, Europe 17 D10 49 30N 19 0 E
Zapala, Argentina 96 D2 39 0S 70 5W
Zapaleri, Cerro, Bolivia .. 94 A2 22 49S 67 11W
Zapata, U.S.A. 81 M5 26 55N 99 16W
Zapolyarnyy, Russia .... 18 A5 69 26N 30 51 E
Zaporizhzhya, Ukraine .. 19 E6 47 50N 35 10 E
Zaporozhye = Zaporizhzhya,
  Ukraine .... 19 E6 47 50N 35 10 E
Zara, Turkey .... 44 B3 39 58N 37 43 E
Zaragoza, Coahuila, Mexico 86 B4 28 30N 101 0W
Zaragoza, Nuevo León, Mexico 87 C5 24 0N 99 46W
Zaragoza, Spain 21 B5 41 39N 0 53W
Zarand, Kermān, Iran ... 45 D8 30 46N 56 34 E
Zarand, Markazī, Iran ... 45 C6 35 18N 50 25 E
Zaranj, Afghan. .... 40 D2 30 55N 61 55 E
Zarasai, Lithuania ...... 9 J22 55 40N 26 20 E
Zárate, Argentina 94 C4 34 7S 59 0W
Zard, Kūh-e, Iran ...... 45 C6 32 22N 50 4 E
Zāreh, Iran .... 45 C6 35 7N 49 9 E
Zaria, Nigeria .... 50 F7 11 0N 7 40 E
Zarneh, Iran .... 44 C5 33 55N 46 10 E
Zarós, Greece .... 25 D6 35 8N 24 54 E
Zarqā', Nahr az →, Jordan 46 C4 32 10N 35 37 E
Zarrīn, Iran .... 45 C7 32 46N 54 37 E
Zaruma, Ecuador 92 D3 3 40S 79 38W
Żary, Poland .... 16 C8 51 37N 15 10 E
Zarzis, Tunisia .... 51 B8 33 31N 11 2 E
Zaskar →, India .... 43 B7 34 13N 77 20 E
Zaskar Mts., India ..... 43 C7 33 15N 77 30 E
Zastron, S. Africa ...... 56 E4 30 18S 27 7 E
Zavāreh, Iran .... 45 C7 33 29N 52 28 E
Zave, Zimbabwe .... 57 B5 17 6S 30 1 E
Zavitinsk, Russia ...... 29 D13 50 10N 129 20 E
Zavodovski, I., Antarctica . 5 B1 56 0S 27 45W
Zawiercie, Poland ...... 17 C10 50 30N 19 24 E
Zāwiyat al Bayḍā = Al Bayḍā,
  Libya .... 51 B10 32 50N 21 44 E
Zāya, Iraq .... 44 C5 33 33N 44 13 E
Zāyandeh →, Iran ...... 45 C7 32 35N 52 0 E
Zaysan, Kazakhstan .... 28 E9 47 28N 84 52 E
Zaysan, Oz., Kazakhstan . 28 E9 48 0N 83 0 E
Zayū, China .... 32 D4 28 48N 97 27 E
Zazafotsy, Madag. ..... 57 C8 21 11S 46 21 E
Zbarazh, Ukraine ...... 17 D13 49 43N 25 44 E
Zdolbuniv, Ukraine ..... 17 C14 50 30N 26 15 E
Zduńska Wola, Poland .. 17 C10 51 37N 18 59 E
Zeballos, Canada 70 D3 49 59N 126 50W
Zebediela, S. Africa .... 57 C4 24 20S 29 17 E
Zeebrugge, Belgium .... 15 C3 51 19N 3 12 E
Zeehan, Australia ...... 63 G4 41 52S 145 25 E
Zeeland □, Neths. ...... 15 C3 51 30N 3 50 E
Zeerust, S. Africa ...... 56 D4 25 31S 26 4 E
Zefat, Israel .... 46 C4 32 58N 35 29 E
Zeil, Mt., Australia ..... 60 D5 23 30S 132 23 E
Zeila, Somali Rep. ..... 47 E3 11 21N 43 30 E
Zeist, Neths. .... 15 B5 52 5N 5 15 E
Zeitz, Germany .... 16 C7 51 2N 12 7 E
Zelenograd, Russia ..... 18 C6 56 1N 37 12 E
Zelenogradsk, Russia ... 9 J19 54 53N 20 29 E
Zelienople, U.S.A. 84 F4 40 48N 80 8W
Zémio, C.A.R. .... 54 A2 5 2N 25 5 E
Zempoala, Mexico 87 D5 19 27N 96 24W
Zemun, Serbia & M. .... 23 B9 44 51N 20 25 E
Zenica, Bos.-H. .... 23 B7 44 10N 17 57 E
Zevenaar, Neths. .... 15 C6 51 56N 6 5 E
Zeya, Russia .... 29 D13 53 48N 127 14 E
Zeya →, Russia .... 29 D13 51 42N 128 53 E
Zêzere →, Portugal 21 C1 39 28N 8 20W
Zghartâ, Lebanon ...... 46 A4 34 21N 35 53 E
Zgorzelec, Poland ...... 16 C8 51 10N 15 0 E
Zhabinka, Belarus ..... 17 B13 52 13N 24 2 E
Zhailma, Kazakhstan ... 28 D7 51 37N 61 33 E
Zhambyl = Taraz, Kazakhstan 28 E8 42 54N 71 22 E
Zhangaqazaly, Kazakhstan 28 E7 45 48N 62 6 E
Zhangbei, China .... 34 D8 41 10N 114 45 E
Zhangguangcai Ling, China 35 B15 45 25N 129 0 E
Zhangjiabian, China .... 33 F9 22 33N 113 28 E
Zhangjiakou, China .... 34 D8 40 48N 114 55 E
Zhangwu, China .... 35 C12 42 43N 123 52 E
Zhangye, China .... 32 C5 38 50N 100 23 E
Zhangzhou, China ..... 33 D6 24 30N 117 35 E
Zhanhua, China .... 35 F10 37 40N 118 8 E
Zhanjiang, China ...... 33 D6 21 15N 110 20 E
Zhannetty, Ostrov, Russia 29 B16 76 43N 158 0 E
Zhanyi, China .... 32 D5 25 38N 103 48 E
Zhanyu, China .... 35 B12 44 30N 122 30 E
Zhao Xian, China ...... 34 F8 37 43N 114 45 E
Zhaocheng, China ..... 34 F6 36 22N 111 38 E
Zhaotong, China ...... 32 D5 27 20N 103 44 E
Zhaoyuan, Heilongjiang, China 35 B13 45 27N 125 0 E
Zhaoyuan, Shandong, China 35 F11 37 20N 120 23 E
Zhashkiv, Ukraine ..... 17 D16 49 15N 30 5 E
Zhashui, China .... 34 H5 33 40N 109 8 E
Zhayyq →, Kazakhstan . 19 E9 47 0N 51 48 E
Zhdanov = Mariupol, Ukraine 19 E6 47 5N 37 31 E
Zhecheng, China ...... 34 G8 34 7N 115 20 E

Zhejiang □, China 33 D7 29 0N 120
Zheleznodorozhnyy, Russia 18 B9 62 35N 50 5
Zheleznogorsk-Ilimskiy, Russia 29 D11 56 34N 104
Zhen'an, China 34 H5 33 27N 109
Zhengding, China 34 E8 38 8N 114 3
Zhengzhou, China 34 G7 34 45N 113 3
Zhenlai, China 35 B12 45 50N 123
Zhenping, China 34 H7 33 10N 112 1
Zhenyuan, China 34 G4 35 35N 107 3
Zhetiqara, Kazakhstan .. 28 D7 52 11N 61 1
Zhezqazghan, Kazakhstan 28 E7 47 44N 67 4
Zhidan, China 34 F5 36 48N 108 4
Zhigansk, Russia 29 C13 66 48N 123
Zhilinda, Russia 29 C12 70 0N 114 2
Zhitomir = Zhytomyr, Ukraine 17 C15 50 20N 28 4
Zhlobin, Belarus 17 B16 52 55N 30
Zhmerinka = Zhmerynka, Ukraine 17 D15 49 2N 28
Zhmerynka, Ukraine ... 17 D15 49 2N 28
Zhob, Pakistan 42 D3 31 20N 69 3
Zhob →, Pakistan 42 C3 32 4N 69 5
Zhodino = Zhodzina, Belarus 17 A15 54 5N 28 1
Zhodzina, Belarus 17 A15 54 5N 28 1
Zhokhova, Ostrov, Russia 29 B16 76 4N 152
Zhongdian, China 32 D4 27 48N 99 4
Zhongning, China 34 F3 37 29N 105
Zhongshan, Antarctica .. 5 C6 69 0S 39
Zhongshan, China 33 G9 22 26N 113
Zhongtiao Shan, China .. 34 G6 35 0N 111 1
Zhongwei, China 34 F3 37 30N 105
Zhongyang, China 34 F6 37 20N 111
Zhoucun, China 35 F9 36 47N 117 4
Zhouzhi, China 34 G5 34 10N 108
Zhuanghe, China 35 E12 39 40N 123
Zhucheng, China 35 G10 36 0N 119 2
Zhugqu, China 34 H3 33 40N 104 3
Zhuhai, China 33 G10 22 17N 113 3
Zhujiang Kou, China ... 33 G10 22 17N 113 3
Zhumadian, China 34 H8 32 59N 114
Zhuo Xian = Zhuozhou, China 34 E8 39 28N 115 1
Zhuolu, China 34 D8 40 20N 115 1
Zhuozhou, China 34 E8 39 28N 115 1
Zhuozi, China 34 D7 41 0N 112 2
Zhytomyr, Ukraine 17 C15 50 20N 28 4
Ziārān, Iran 45 B6 36 7N 50 3
Ziarat, Pakistan 42 D2 30 25N 67 4
Zibo, China 35 F10 36 47N 118
Zichang, China 34 F5 37 18N 109 4
Zidi = Wandhari, Pakistan 42 F2 27 42N 66 4
Zielona Góra, Poland ... 16 C8 51 57N 15 3
Zierikzee, Neths. 15 C3 51 40N 3 5
Zigey, Chad 51 F9 14 43N 15 5
Zigong, China 32 D5 29 15N 104 4
Ziguinchor, Senegal ... 50 F2 12 35N 16 2
Zihuatanejo, Mexico ... 86 D4 17 38N 101 3
Žilina, Slovak Rep. 17 D10 49 12N 18 4
Zillah, Libya 51 C9 28 30N 17 3
Zima, Russia 29 D11 54 0N 102
Zimapán, Mexico 87 C5 20 54N 99
Zimba, Zambia 55 F2 17 20S 26 1
Zimbabwe, Zimbabwe .. 55 G3 20 16S 30 5
Zimbabwe ■, Africa ... 55 F3 19 0S 30
Zimnicea, Romania 17 G13 43 40N 25 2
Zinave △, Mozam. 57 C5 21 35S 33 4
Zinder, Niger 50 F7 13 48N 9
Zinga, Tanzania 55 D4 9 16S 38 4
Zion □, U.S.A. 77 H7 37 15N 113
Ziros, Greece 25 D8 35 5N 26
Zirreh, Gowd-e, Afghan. . 40 E3 29 45N 62
Zitácuaro, Mexico 86 D4 19 28N 100 2
Zitundo, Mozam. 57 D5 26 48S 32 4
Ziwa Magharība = Kagera □,
  Tanzania 54 C3 2 0S 31 3
Ziway, L., Ethiopia 47 F2 8 0N 38 5
Ziyang, China 34 H5 32 32N 108 3
Zlatograd, Bulgaria 23 D11 41 22N 25
Zlatoust, Russia 18 C10 55 10N 59
Zlín, Czech Rep. 17 D9 49 14N 17 4
Zmeinogorsk, Kazakhstan 28 D9 51 10N 82 1
Znojmo, Czech Rep. ... 16 D9 48 50N 16
Zobeyrī, Iran 44 C5 34 10N 46 4
Zobia, Dem. Rep. of the Congo 54 B2 3 0N 25 5
Zoetermeer, Neths. 15 B4 52 3N 4
Zolochev = Zolochiv, Ukraine 17 D13 49 45N 24 5
Zolochiv, Ukraine 17 D13 49 45N 24 5
Zomba, Malawi 55 F4 15 22S 35 1
Zongo, Dem. Rep. of the Congo 52 D3 4 20N 18 3
Zonguldak, Turkey 19 F5 41 28N 31 5
Zongor Pt., Malta 25 C2 35 52N 14 3
Zorritos, Peru 92 D2 3 43S 80 4
Zou Xiang, China 34 G9 35 30N 116 5
Zouar, Chad 51 D9 20 30N 16 3
Zouérate = Zouîrât, Mauritania 50 D3 22 44N 12 2
Zouîrât, Mauritania ... 50 D3 22 44N 12 2
Zoutkamp, Neths. 15 A6 53 20N 6 1
Zrenjanin, Serbia & M. . 23 B9 45 22N 20 2
Zufar, Oman 47 D5 17 40N 54
Žug, Switz. 20 C8 47 10N 8 3
Zugspitze, Germany ... 16 E6 47 25N 10 5
Zuid-Holland □, Neths. . 15 C4 52 0N 4 3
Zuidbeveland, Neths. .. 15 C3 51 30N 3 5
Zuidhorn, Neths. 15 A6 53 15N 6 2
Zula, Eritrea 47 D2 15 17N 39 4
Zumbo, Mozam. 55 F3 15 35S 30 2
Zumpango, Mexico 87 D5 19 48N 99
Zunhua, China 35 D9 40 18N 117 5
Zuni, U.S.A. 77 J9 35 4N 108 5
Zunyi, China 32 D5 27 42N 106 5
Zurbātīyah, Iraq 44 C5 33 9N 46 3
Zürich, Switz. 20 C8 47 22N 8 3
Zutphen, Neths. 15 B6 52 9N 6 1
Zuurberg △, S. Africa .. 56 E4 33 12S 25 3
Zūzan, Iran 45 C8 33 20N 59 3
Zvenigorodka, Russia .. 28 D7 54 26N 64 5
Zvishavane, Zimbabwe . 55 G3 20 17S 30
Zvolen, Slovak Rep. ... 17 D10 48 33N 19 1
Zwelitsha, S. Africa ... 53 L5 32 55N 27
Zwettl, Austria 16 D8 48 35N 15
Zwickau, Germany 16 C7 50 44N 12 3
Zwolle, Neths. 15 B6 52 31N 6
Zyrardów, Poland 17 B11 52 3N 20 2
Zyryan, Kazakhstan ... 28 E9 49 43N 84 2
Zyryanka, Russia 29 C16 65 45N 150 5
Zyryanovsk = Zyryan, Kazakhstan 28 E9 49 43N 84 2
Zywiec, Poland 17 D10 49 42N 19 1
Zyyi, Cyprus 25 E12 34 43N 33 2

World: Regions in the News

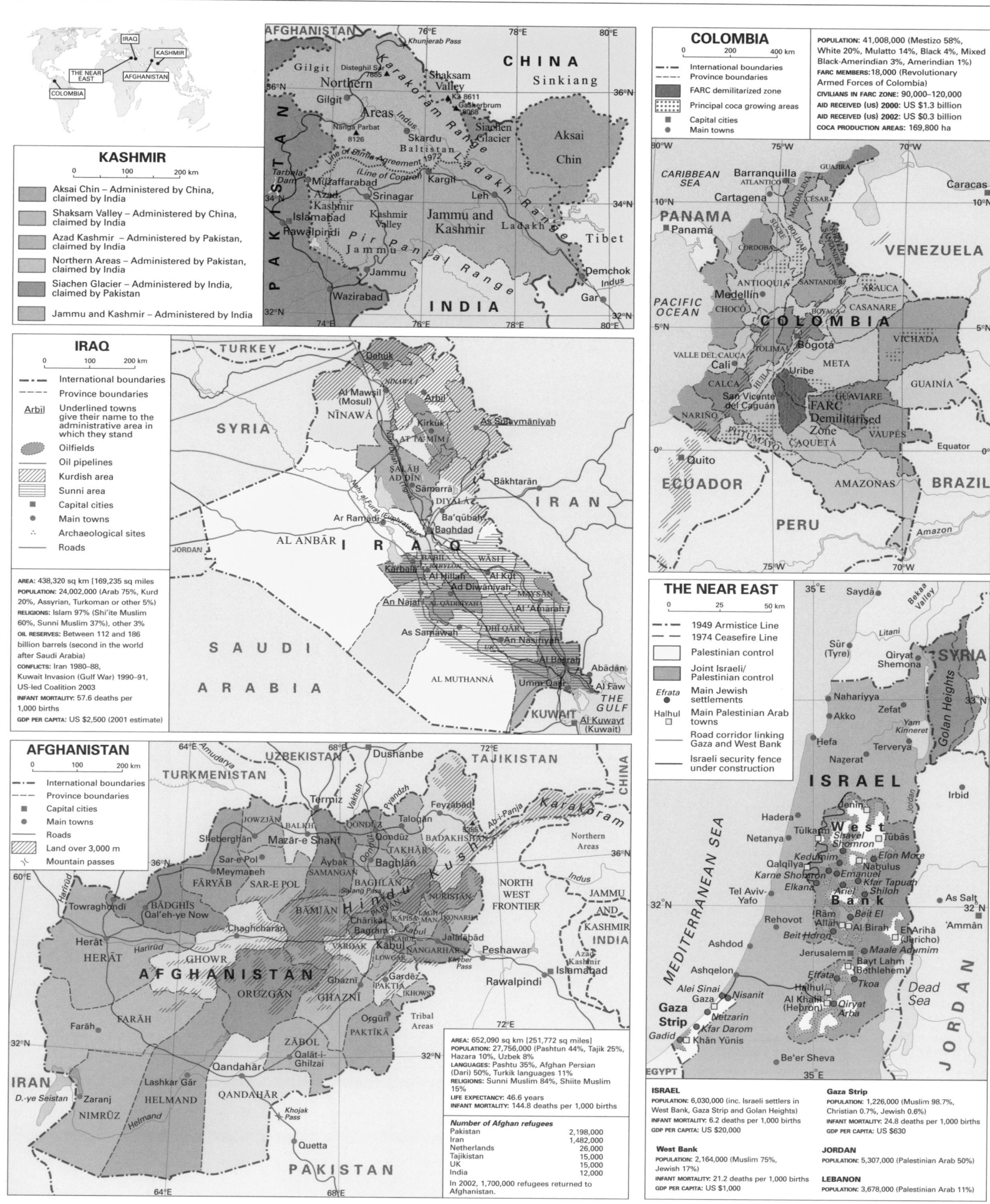

KEY TO EUROPEAN MAP PAGES

 Large scale maps
(>1:2 500 000)

 Medium scale maps
(1:2 800 000 – 1:9 900 000)

 Small scale maps
(<1:10 000 000)

8 ICELAND

Arctic Circle

WORLD COUNTRY INDEX

Afghanistan	40
Albania	23
Algeria	50
Angola	52–53
Argentina	94, 96
Armenia	19
Australia	60–63
Austria	16–17
Azerbaijan	19
Bahamas	88–89
Bahrain	45
Bangladesh	41
Barbados	89
Belarus	17, 18–19
Belgium	15
Belize	88
Benin	50
Bhutan	41
Bolivia	92
Bosnia-Herzegovina	22–23
Botswana	56
Brazil	92–93, 95
Brunei	36
Bulgaria	23
Burkina Faso	50
Burma (Myanmar)	41
Burundi	54
Cambodia	38–39
Canary Is.	24
Cameroon	52
Canada	68–73
Central African Republic	52
Chad	51
Chile	94, 96–97
China	32–35
Colombia	92
Congo	52
Congo, Dem. Rep. of the	52–53, 54–55
Costa Rica	88
Croatia	22–23
Cuba	88–89
Cyprus	25
Czech Republic	16–17
Denmark	9
Djibouti	47
Dominican Republic	89
Ecuador	92
Egypt	51
El Salvador	88
England	12–13
Equatorial Guinea	52
Eritrea	47
Estonia	9
Ethiopia	47, 52
Fiji	59
Finland	8–9
France	20–21
French Guiana	93
Gabon	52
Gambia	50
Georgia	19
Germany	16

Ghana	50
Greece	23
Greenland	4
Guadeloupe	88
Guatemala	88
Guinea	50
Guinea-Bissau	50
Guyana	92
Haiti	89
Honduras	88
Hungary	17
Iceland	8
India	40–43
Indonesia	36–37
Iran	44–45
Iraq	44–45
Irish Republic	10
Israel	46
Italy	22–23
Ivory Coast	50
Jamaica	88
Japan	30–31
Jordan	46
Kazakhstan	28
Kenya	54
Korea, North	35
Korea, South	35
Kuwait	44–45
Kyrgyzstan	28
Laos	38
Latvia	9
Lebanon	46
Lesotho	57
Liberia	50
Libya	51
Lithuania	9
Luxembourg	15
Macedonia	23
Madagascar	57
Malawi	55
Malaysia	36–37, 39
Mali	50
Malta	25
Martinique	88
Mauritania	50
Mexico	86–87
Moldova	17
Mongolia	32
Morocco	50
Mozambique	55, 57
Namibia	56
Nepal	43
Netherlands	15
New Zealand	59
Nicaragua	88
Niger	50–51
Nigeria	50–51
Northern Ireland	10
Norway	8–9
Oman	47

Pakistan	40, 42
Panama	88
Papua New Guinea	64
Paraguay	94–95
Peru	92
Philippines	37
Poland	16–17
Portugal	21
Puerto Rico	89
Qatar	45
Romania	17
Russia	18–19, 28–29
Rwanda	54
St. Lucia	89
Samoa	59
Saudi Arabia	44–45, 47
Scotland	11
Senegal	50
Serbia and Montenegro	23
Sierra Leone	50
Singapore	39
Slovak Republic	17
Slovenia	22
Solomon Is.	64
Somali Republic	47
South Africa	56–57
Spain	21
Sri Lanka	40
Sudan	51
Suriname	92–93
Swaziland	57
Sweden	8–9
Switzerland	16
Syria	44, 46
Taiwan	33
Tajikistan	28
Tanzania	54–55
Thailand	38–39
Togo	50
Tonga	59
Trinidad and Tobago	93
Tunisia	50–51
Turkey	19
Turkmenistan	28
Uganda	54
Ukraine	18–19
United Arab Emirates	47
United Kingdom	10–13
USA	74–85
Uruguay	94–95
Uzbekistan	28
Vanuatu	64
Venezuela	92–93
Vietnam	38–39
Wales	12–13
Yemen	47
Zambia	55, 56–57
Zimbabwe	55

8

14 11

11

12

10 16

UNITED KINGDOM

IRELAND 15

20

FRA

21

ANDORRA

PORTUGAL SPAIN

24

MOROCCO